COMPACT
BIBLE
COMMENTARY

EARL RADMACHER
RON ALLEN & H. WAYNE HOUSE

THOMAS NELSON
Since 1798

NASHVILLE   DALLAS   MEXICO CITY   RIO DE JANEIRO   BEIJING

Published in Nashville, TN, by Thomas Nelson. Thomas Nelson is a trademark of Thomas Nelson, Inc.

Thomas Nelson, Inc., titles may be purchased in bulk for educational, business, fund-raising, or sales promotional use. For information, please email SpecialMarkets@Thomas Nelson.com.

Unless otherwise indicated, Scripture quotations are from the New King James Version (NKJV) of the Bible, © 1979, 1980, 1982, 1990, Thomas Nelson, Inc., Publishers.

Book composition by *A&W Publishing Electronic Services, Inc.,*
Chicago, Illinois

Library of Congress Cataloging-in-Publication data is available upon request.

Nelson's compact™ Bible commentary, 2004 edition

General Editor, Radmacher, Earl; Old Testament Editor, Allen, Ron;
New Testament Editor, House, H. Wayne

ISBN 10: 0-7852-5248-7
ISBN 13: 978-0-7852-5248-1

Printed in the United States of America

08 09 10 11 12 13 — 16 15 14 13 12 11

Table of Contents

Abbreviations

The Old Testament

Genesis	Gen.	Habakkuk	Hab.
Exodus	Ex.	Zephaniah	Zeph.
Leviticus	Lev.	Haggai	Hag.
Numbers	Num.	Zechariah	Zech.
Deuteronomy	Deut.	Malachi	Mal.
Joshua	Josh.		
Judges	Judg.	**The New Testament**	
Ruth	Ruth	Matthew	Matt.
1 Samuel	1 Sam.	Mark	Mark
2 Samuel	2 Sam.	Luke	Luke
1 Kings	1 Kin.	John	John
2 Kings	2 Kin.	Acts	Acts
1 Chronicles	1 Chr.	Romans	Rom.
2 Chronicles	2 Chr.	1 Corinthians	1 Cor.
Ezra	Ezra	2 Corinthians	2 Cor.
Nehemiah	Neh.	Galatians	Gal.
Esther	Esth.	Ephesians	Eph.
Job	Job	Philippians	Phil.
Psalms	Ps.	Colossians	Col.
Proverbs	Prov.	1 Thessalonians	1 Thess.
Ecclesiastes	Eccl.	2 Thessalonians	2 Thess.
Song of Solomon	Song	1 Timothy	1 Tim.
Isaiah	Is.	2 Timothy	2 Tim.
Jeremiah	Jer.	Titus	Titus
Lamentations	Lam.	Philemon	Philem.
Ezekiel	Ezek.	Hebrews	Heb.
Daniel	Dan.	James	James
Hosea	Hos.	1 Peter	1 Pet.
Joel	Joel	2 Peter	2 Pet.
Amos	Amos	1 John	1 John
Obadiah	Obad.	2 John	2 John
Jonah	Jon.	3 John	3 John
Micah	Mic.	Jude	Jude
Nahum	Nah.	Revelation	Rev.

Editors and Contributors

Editors

Earl D. Radmacher, Th.D. – General Editor
Ronald B. Allen, Th.D. – Old Testament Editor
H. Wayne House, Th.D., J.D. – New Testament Editor

Contributors

Ronald B. Allen, Th.D.
Barry J. Beitzel, Ph.D.
Darrell Lane Bock, Ph.D.
James Borland, Th.D.
Robert B. Chisholm Jr., Th.D.
G. Michael Cocoris, D.D.
Ronald Dennis Cole, Th.D.
Joseph Edward Coleson, Ph.D.
W. Robert Cook, Th.D.
Barry C. Davis, Ph.D.
Darryl DelHousaye, D.Min.
Gary Wayne Derickson, Ph.D.
Jospeh C. Dillow, Th.D.
Duane Arthur Dunham, Th.D.
David J. Eckman, Ph.D.
Stanley A. Ellisen, Th.D.
Arthur L. Farstad, Th.D.
H. Wayne House, Th.D., J.D.
David M. Howard Jr., Ph.D.
Thomas Ice, Ph.D.
S. Lewis Johnson Jr., Th.D.
Walter C. Kaiser Jr., Ph.D.
Deborah Jane Kappas, Th.M.

J. Carl Laney, Th.D.
Donald H. Launstein, Th.D.
Asa Boyd Luter Jr., Ph.D.
Walter Creighton Marlowe, Ph.D.
Eugene H. Merrill, Ph.D.
Bruce M. Metzger, Ph.D.
Thomas Kem Oberholtzer, Th.D.
Gregory W. Parsons, Th.D.
Dorothy Kelley Patterson, D.Min., Th.D.
Richard D. Patterson, Ph.D.
Susan Perlman
Earl D. Radmacher, Th.D.
Moishe Rosen
Ray C. Stedman, D.D. (deceased)
Stanley D. Toussaint, Th.D.
Willem VanGemeren, Ph.D.
Bruce K. Waltke, Ph.D., Th.D.
John F. Walvoord, Th.D., D.D., Litt.D.
Ralph Winter, Th.D.
Naomi Taylor Wright

Genesis

Introduction

The Book of Genesis was written and compiled by Moses in the Wilderness of Sinai to encourage the early Israelites while they were preparing to enter the land of Canaan, the Promised Land. The content of Genesis would have been especially significant to them. It explains why their ancestors went to Egypt, why their nation was destined for another Promised Land, and why God had revealed Himself so dramatically to them in the wilderness.

Genesis has two parts. The first part (chs. 1—11) serves as a prologue to the second part (chs. 12–50). This prologue provides keys that unlock the rest of the book and the rest of the Bible. Four key concepts presented in Genesis 1 through 11 are crucial for comprehending the rest of the Bible. First, the God who entered the lives of Abram and Sarai is the same God who created the entire universe. He is the only true and living God—Yahweh, the Creator. Second, humanity inherited a state of sinfulness from Adam and Eve's rebellion in the garden of Eden. Third, God judges and will judge the actions of all people. God cannot let evil reign free in His creation. Fourth, sin continues to plague all of humanity. God has a plan to save humanity from its own evil deeds.

Central to God's plan in Genesis was His covenant with Abraham—the *Abrahamic covenant* (see 12:1–3; 15:1–21). God, the awesome Creator of the universe, freely chose to make everlasting promises to Abraham and his descendants. These promises in the Abrahamic covenant were the foundation for God's subsequent promises and covenants in the Bible. Genesis is not just a beginning; it provides the foundation for the rest of the biblical narrative.

1:1 In the beginning can be paraphrased, "here is the story of God's creation of the heavens and the earth." In ch. 1 the focus is on the creation of the material world—the heavens and the earth. God: This standard Hebrew term for deity, *Elohim,* is in the form called the plural of majesty. In contrast to the ordinary plural (gods), this plural means "the fullness of deity"

or "God—very God." The verb for **created** means "to fashion anew." **The heavens and the earth** mean "all of creation" or "the cosmos."

1:2 The words **without form ... void** express one concept—chaos. **Darkness** is a potent biblical symbol of evil and wrong (Job 3:5; Ps. 143:3; Is. 8:22; John 3:19). The **deep** is a term for the secret places of the waters (see also 7:11). From this portrait of utter ruin, God brought an orderly creation. **The Spirit of God was hovering** like a mother stork might hover over her nest, (the Spirit is described as a dove in Matt. 3:16).

1:3 Let there be light: These words express a principal theme of the Bible: God bringing light into the darkness (see Is. 9:1, 2). God **said** it, and it was done: **there was light.** His command caused reality.

1:4 Having examined the light, God declared it to be **good**—a powerful term of God's blessing.

1:5 Day ... Night: The naming of these elements of creation is a mark of God's sovereignty. In the thinking of the peoples of the ancient Near East, naming something was a mark of power or lordship. For them, names were not just labels, but descriptions with some force to them.

1:6 In biblical usage, the term **firmament** means "heavens." Literally, it means "something stretched out, like hammered metal."

1:7, 8 divided the waters: The notion of upper and lower waters is somewhat mysterious. The language may simply refer to waters gathered in a liquid state and to moisture in the atmosphere.

1:9 The gathering of the waters and the separation of the **dry land** are further actions of God in establishing control over the chaos described in v. 2. Each act of separation and distinction brings order out of disorder, form out of formlessness, cosmos out of chaos.

1:10 The naming of the **earth** in this verse suggests that the term was used in anticipation in v. 2.

1:11–13 The broad words **grass, tree,** and **fruit tree** encompass all plants, shrubs, and trees. The reference to **seed** and **kind** speaks of the fact that the plant kingdom will continue to reproduce.

1:14, 15 The creation of the sun, moon, and stars is described in general terms in these verses; vv. 16–18 spell out the details. **Lights in the firmament** are luminaries (objects that shine). **signs and seasons:** The two words form a pair that may be translated *seasonal signs.*

1:16 lights: The word can either designate the sun, which emits light, or the moon, which reflects light. **He made the stars also:** This is a remarkable statement. In the ancient Near East, other religions worshiped, deified, and mystified the stars. Israel's neighbors revered the stars and looked to them for guidance Such a statement showed great contempt for ancient Babylonian astrology (see Pss. 29; 93).

1:17–19 God set them: The principal issue throughout these verses is that God alone is in control.

1:20, 21 The verb for **created** is the same one used in 1:1. **According to its kind** suggests the capability to reproduce themselves (see v. 12). God gave them the power to propagate and to proliferate, to fill the air and the seas.

1:22, 23 God blessed them: The first use of this important phrasing in the Bible (see 1:28; 2:3; 12:2, 3), and it is used of fish and birds!

1:24 The expression **living creature** contains the word sometimes used for the soul, but the word can also mean "life," "being," "living thing," or "person," depending on the context **cattle and creeping thing and beast of the earth:** Three sweeping categories make the point that God created all living things.

1:25 God saw that it was good: The sixth time that this phrasing is used (see 1:4, 10, 12, 18, 21). Everything that God had made so far was good.

1:26 Let Us make is emphatic, The use of a plural for God allows for the later revelation of the Trinity (see 11:7; Matt. 28:19). Man is made in the image of God.. **in Our image:** What is the image of God in man? The traditional view is that God's image is certain moral, ethical, and intellectual abilities. In ancient times an emperor might command statues of himself to be placed in remote parts of his empire. These symbols would declare that these areas were under his power and reign. So God placed humankind as living symbols of Himself on earth to represent His reign. **according to Our likeness:** Since God is Spirit (John 4:24), there can be no "image" or "likeness" of Him in the normal sense of these words. *We are His images; it is we who are in His likeness.* **have dominion:** Rule as God's regent. That is, people are to rule as God would—wisely and prudently—over all that God has made (fish, birds, cattle, and so on).

1:27 So God created man: The third time the verb for *create* is used in Gen. 1 (see vv. 1, 21); here it is used three times. The language of vv. 26, 28 is elevated prose; this verse is pure poetry. The twelve words of the original Hebrew are arranged in three lines that have their own poetic repetition and cadence. The term for man is likely associated with the term for the red earth. Here the word is generic, including **male and female.** These words are sexual. Some have thought that the "discovery" of human sexuality was the forbidden fruit of ch. 3. However, these words indicate that human sexuality was a part of the original creation (5:2). Although the misuse of human sexuality is soundly condemned in Scripture (Lev. 18), its proper use is celebrated (2:24, 25; Song). Verses 26–28 include the woman no less than the man in the story of creation.

1:28 God blessed them: God delighted in what He had made (Prov. 8:30, 31). The word translated **subdue** means "bring into bondage." This term is used elsewhere of military conquest (Zech. 9:15) and of God subduing our iniquities (Mic. 7:19). Subdue does not mean "destroy" or "ruin." It does mean to "act as managers who have the authority to run everything as God planned."

1:29, 30 Many suggest that Adam and Eve were vegetarians because God gave them **every herb** and **every tree.**

1:31 This is the seventh use of the term **good** in the creation story (1:4, 10, 12, 18, 21, 25).

2:1 While mention is made of the heavens, the focus in the first chapter has been on the earth.

2:2 The verb translated as **rested** is related to the word for Sabbath, which means "rest." Many assume that the basic meaning of the Sabbath is worship, but this is not the case (Ex. 20:9–11; Deut. 5:12–14).

2:3 God blessed the birds and fish (1:22), humans (1:28), and now **the seventh day** (Saturday). He **sanctified** it. Thus, from the beginning of time, God placed special value on a certain day of the week.

2:4 The term translated as **history** is found in ten significant passages in the Book of Genesis (here and 5:1; 6:9; 10:1; 11:10, 27; 25:12, 19; 36:1, 9; 37:2). **In the day** means "when." **The LORD God** is a significant new term for God. The word translated as *God* is the same word as in 1:1. The word translated as LORD is the proper name for God. (see Ex. 3:14, 15). The God of ch. 1 and the LORD God of ch. 2 are the same.

2:5 The order of events in the second creation story is somewhat different from the first account (1:1—2:3). **not caused it to rain** Here was an element of creation that was still in process. **man to till the ground:** The Hebrew term for man sounds similar to the term for ground (1:26; 2:7).

2:6 The precise meaning of the term translated as **mist** is unknown. Obviously it refers to some manner of irrigation before the Lord brought the cycles of rain into being.

2:7 formed is the term for a potter's shaping of pots. God created man by fashioning a body out of mud and clay, and then breathed life into it. This **breath** may be the narrator's way of describing the infusion of the human spirit, with its moral, intellectual, relational, and spiritual capacities. **living being:** This is the same term used of animal life in 1:24, but the breath of life makes humans distinct from all other creatures.

2:8 Eden is not explained except that it is **eastward.** The exact location is not known.

2:9 Eden was an extraordinarily appointed garden, with choice specimens of the finest trees and plants. Two trees of very special importance were also there, **the tree of life** and **the tree of the knowledge of good and evil** (2:17; 3:24).

2:10–14 God provided a grand **river** in order to water the garden. With great care, He prepared the habitation of His people. The names Pishon, Gihon, Hiddekel, and Euphrates relate to later rivers that were known to the first readers of the text.

2:15 The **garden** was man's home and he was **to tend and keep it.** Even the biblical paradise required work (1:26–28)!

2:16 In His great grace, God gave permission before He gave restriction, and the permission was broad (**of every tree**) It appears that man limited his diet to vegetation at first; only after the Flood is there mention of God's gift of meat as well (see 9:3).

2:17 the tree of the knowledge of good and evil: The phrase suggests "full knowledge" by tying together two contrasting words. We know little about this tree. **shall surely die:** These emphatic words are made of two forms of the verb meaning "to die."

2:18 It is not good: The first time a negative assessment appears in Genesis (see 1:31). God did not want Adam to be lonely, so He fashioned a **helper comparable to him.** This phrase indicates that this helper (or partner) would be truly fitting and fully adequate—just right. It does not refer to someone who is secondary or inferior.

2:19 The same verb for **formed** suggests a potter at work casting his pots. But now, the pots are a lion and a raccoon, a raven and a stork. It appears that God presented each animal **to see what he would call them.** In giving each animal its **name,** Adam demonstrated his right as God's regent (see 1:26–28). He was lord over all created order.

2:20 Adam did not find **a helper comparable to him.** He needed a companion just like him, not a servant or an aide (see v. 18); but another like himself.

2:21 This is the first surgery, and God was the Surgeon. In His kindness, God used an unusually **deep sleep** as an anesthetic for the task. God's use of a **rib** was fitting. The identification of Adam with his partner would be ensured.

2:22 The verb **made** means "to build." The expansion of one small part into a complete body makes sense in today's understanding of molecular structure and DNA.

2:23 This is now means "At last!" **bone of my bones:** Adam's wording is poetic and exalted. Here was a mirror of himself, someone just like him, and yet different! **She shall be called Woman:** The name that he gave her matched his own. She was woman, and he was man—perfectly suited for each other.

2:24 In marriage, a man is to **leave** his family, join his wife, and unite with her. The words **be joined** speak of both a physical embrace and more general aspects of marital bonding. **One flesh** suggests both a physical, sexual bonding and a lifelong relationship. In the New Testament, Jesus refers to this text as the foundation of the biblical view of marriage (Matt. 19:5; 1 Cor. 6:16).

2:25 They **were not ashamed** even though **they were both naked.** They were comfortable in their physical bodies, in their sexuality, in their relationship, and in their work. The wording of vv. 24, 25 suggests the couple experienced sexual relations in the garden as a part of their God-intended experience.

3:1 The **serpent** appeared in the garden. The serpent symbolizes something both fascinating and loathsome. The Hebrew word for **cunning** sounds like the Hebrew word for *naked* in 2:25. Adam and Eve were naked in innocence; the serpent was crafty and sneaky. **Has God indeed said:** Note that the serpent did not use the divine name Yahweh.

3:2 We may eat: Eve repeated the positive words of God (see 2:16).

3:3 There was one tree Eve knew to be off limits. This tree was in the middle of the garden. **nor shall you touch it:** The first sin was eating the fruit that God had forbidden. Her words reflected the original command well enough.

3:4 Satan lied: **You will not surely die.** Lying was Satan's craft right from the beginning (John 8:44). The serpent boldly denied the truth of what God had said.

3:5 you will be like God: God's fullness of knowledge was only one of the superiorities that set Him apart from the woman. But the serpent appealed to her pride.

3:6 It was **good for food.** There was nothing in the tree that was poisonous or harmful, and it was **desirable.** The issue was one

of obedience to the Word of God. **She took:** The first step. She **ate:** The final step. Once she disobeyed God, all the world changed. (Note, however, that Rom. 5:12 speaks of the sin of Adam rather than the sin of Eve.) Because she did not die, she **gave** it **to her husband. And he ate:** Adam sinned with his eyes wide open. He knew the fruit was forbidden.

3:7 Their eyes **were opened.** They knew that **they were naked.** They were ashamed and they covered themselves with **fig leaves.**

3:8 The scene is sad. Lord comes for an evening walk but, Adam and Eve avoid being seen by the Creator of the universe. What had been a perfect fellowship has turned into dreadful fear of God. The raw terror of being discovered in sin.

3:9, 10 God, in His mercy, called out to them and interacted with them (see vv. 10–12).

3:11 The Lord carried the interrogation to its sad ending by posing one question after another.

3:12 Adam blamed **the woman,** and then he blamed God for having given her to him.

3:13 the serpent deceived me and I ate: A simple statement of fact.

3:14 to the serpent: The Lord turned first to the serpent and brought His judgment upon him. The word translated as **cursed** in this verse is used only of the curse on the serpent and on the ground (v. 17). The woman and the man were not cursed (God had already blessed them; 1:28).

3:15 enmity between you and the woman: This is not about snakes; it is about the enemy of our souls, Satan. **your seed and her Seed:** The language contains the promise of a child. The term *seed* may be translated *offspring* (as in 15:3) or *descendants* (as in 15:5, 13, 18). The term may refer to an individual (Gal. 3:16) or a group of people. The Seed of the woman is the Promised One, the coming Messiah of Israel. *Seed* continues to be used throughout the Bible as a messianic term (see Num. 24:7; Is. 6:13). The meaning of the phrase **your seed** as it applies to the serpent is uncertain (but see John 8:37–47). The reference is ultimately to Satan. **your head:** This is sometimes called the "first gospel" because these words promise the

Coming One, the Messiah. The Lord was showing mercy even as He judged (see also 4:15). **Bruise His heel** speaks of a serious injury, but it is contrasted with the bruising of the **head**—the defeat—of the serpent's seed. When Jesus went to the Cross, He was bruised in His heel. In His resurrection, He defeated His enemy. From that moment on, Satan has lived on borrowed time. He is already defeated.

3:16 your sorrow and your conception: These two words mean "your sorrowful conception" (see 1:2; 4:12; 9:2; Ps. 9:2). That is, the woman's joy in conceiving and bearing children will be saddened by the pain of it. The word **desire** can also mean "an attempt to usurp or control" as in 4:7. The battle of the sexes has begun. The antidote is in the restoration of mutual respect and dignity through Jesus Christ (see Eph. 5:21–33).

3:17–19 Cursed is the ground: Though the curse was not directed at the man, it is trouble for the man. Now his life will be marked by **toil, thorns and thistles, sweat,** and death. These words imply that before the Fall the ground was not filled with noxious weeds and work was pleasant (2:15). **to dust you shall return:** Death will now come to humankind, whereas there had been the possibility of living forever (see Rom. 5:12–14). The word of God was sure: God had stated that they would certainly die (2:17).

3:20 The name **Eve** is related to the verb meaning "to live." Eve is our common mother, just as Adam is our common father. This is Adam's second name for her.

3:21 This is the first place the Bible mentions the killing of animals for human use—this time for **tunics.**

3:22 become like one of Us: The fruit of the **tree of life** stopped aging. To eat of this tree was **to live forever.** One day this tree will be planted anew and its fruit will be for the healing of the nations (Rev. 22:2).

3:23 The man had been formed by God outside the **garden** (2:5–8, 15) and had been given the task of tending and keeping it. Now he was removed from the garden and sent back to till the soil **from which he was taken** (see 2:5; 3:17–19).

3:24 Even though Eve sinned first, this section (vv. 22–24) focuses on the **man,** Adam. This is the first reference to holy angels or the **cherubim** in the Book of Genesis. The creation of the angels preceded the creation activities described in chs. 1 and 2. A cherub (pl., cherubim) is an angel who takes on a particular form (see Ex. 25:18–22; compare Ezek. 1:5–28). Cherubim, like all angels, are spirit beings, but they can take on physical bodies. Adam and Eve were barred from the garden that God had planted for their enjoyment. **a flaming sword:** There was no way back in. The fact that the **tree of life** remained, even though guarded by angels and a sword, was a ray of hope.

4:1 The verb **knew** is a euphemism for sexual intercourse. It describes an intimate relationship that includes ardor and passion, but also mutuality and oneness. The name **Cain** is related to a word meaning "craftsman" or "metalworker." It also sounds like the Hebrew word translated **I have acquired.**

4:2 We have no explanation of the name **Abel** as we have with Cain (v. 1). Perhaps after Abel was murdered (v. 8), the parents looked back with sadness on the brevity of his life and called him Abel (meaning "vapor") because his life was over so quickly. Keeping **sheep** and tilling the **ground** were equally valid occupations. They reflected different interests of the two brothers, not their character.

4:3 Genesis does not explain how the practice of sacrificial worship began. Some people assume that Cain's sacrifice of **fruit** was deficient because it did not involve the shedding of blood, which God required for forgiveness of sins (see Heb. 9:22). But nothing in ch. 4 indicates that Cain and Abel came to God for forgiveness: their sacrifices were acts of worship. Cain's sacrifice was deficient because Cain did not "do well" (v. 7), not because the sacrifice was the "fruit of the ground."

4:4 Abel's sacrifice was the best that he had to offer—**the firstborn** and **their fat.** There are no similar descriptive words for Cain's sacrifice. God **respected** or looked with favor first upon the person, *then* on his sacrifice (see Ps. 40:6–8). Abel's offering was "more excellent" than Cain's because of Abel's faith in the Lord (Heb. 11:4).

4:5 Instead of repenting, Cain became angry and, we discover, filled with jealousy (v. 8).

4:6, 7 The gracious words of the Lord were that Cain could get it right! He could **do well.** Sin was lying at the **door,** about to pounce on him as a lion.

4:8, 9 The murder was stunning in its lack of precedent, its suddenness, and its finality. Jesus spoke of this ghastly event as a historical fact (Matt. 23:35).

4:10 That **blood** of Abel **cries** out until the blood of One even more innocent than Abel is shed as well (Heb. 12:24).

4:11, 12 Cain was the third to be **cursed** of God; first was the serpent (3:14) and second was the ground (3:17).

4:13 My punishment: Usually rendered "iniquity" (as in Ex. 20:5), here the term speaks of the result of iniquity.

4:14, 15 Sadly, Cain expressed his distress only at the punishment he received, not at the crime he had done. **anyone who finds me:** Most have assumed that the others whom Cain feared were sisters and brothers already born but not mentioned or those yet to be born. This idea is based on the wording of 5:4, "and he (Adam) had sons and daughters." Some have proposed that God created others outside the Garden of Eden, but the Scriptures give no indication of this. It makes sense to conclude that Cain was afraid of his siblings.

4:16 The land of Nod is a word-play on the term for *vagabond* (vv. 12, 14). The point is more theological than geographical; to be apart from the presence of the Lord is to be a vagabond in a "vagabond-land."

4:17 Cain most likely acquired a **wife** from among his siblings (see v. 14). The name **Enoch** means "Dedicated One"—the same name as the godly descendant of Seth who "walked with God" (5:21–24). The fact that Cain built a **city** named after his son speaks of a dramatic, rapid increase in population.

4:18 Six generations from Cain to Lamech are mentioned. The verse indicates a rapidly expanding population, for the listing of each of these sons includes corresponding wives.

4:19–21 Lamech represents skill and strength, as well as arrogance and vengeance. This

Lamech is not the same as Lamech, the son of Methuselah (5:28–31). **two wives:** This act suggests a deliberate attempt by Lamech to subvert the original pattern of God of one man and one woman (2:24; see also the words of Jesus on the subject, Matt. 19:4–6). **Adah ... Zillah:** Only rarely are the names of women mentioned.

4:22 Some suggest that **iron** was not known during the time of **Tubal-Cain,** and this verse means that later metal workers who did work with iron could look back to Tubal-Cain as the "father" of metallurgy in general. **Naamah:** Even more rare than the names of wives in these accounts (v. 19) is the listing of the names of daughters and sisters.

4:23, 24 What follows is a boastful taunt song that captures the violent spirit of **Lamech. I have killed a man:** In this boast, Lamech indicates that he has followed in the worst pattern of his ancestor Cain. In his wicked braggadocio, he taunted God by his words **seventy-sevenfold.** Lamech boasted that by himself he would greatly magnify the vengeance on anyone who attacked him.

4:25 and Adam knew his wife again: With the death of Abel (v. 8) and the expulsion of Cain (vv. 11, 12), Adam and Eve had no son to carry on their line for good and for the promise of the Messiah. Hence the importance of the birth of **Seth.** His name is related to a Hebrew verb meaning "to place" or "to set" for he was **appointed** to take the *place* of the murdered son in the plan of God.

4:26 The birth of **Enosh** meant that the line of Seth would continue; the promise of the Lord (see 3:15) would not be forgotten. **began to call on the name of the LORD:** These words can hardly mean that only now did people begin to pray to God. Rather, the verb *call* means "to make proclamation." That is, this is the beginning of preaching, of witnessing, and testifying *in* the name of the Lord (12:8).

5:1 The word **genealogy** (or "family histories") is found in ten significant passages in the Book of Genesis. **likeness of God:** What God made humankind to be (1:26–28) continues after the Fall (ch. 3; compare also 9:6, after the Flood).

5:2 The original creation of humanity is in two complementary genders, **male and female,** as 1:26–28 clearly states (see 1:27).

5:3 one hundred and thirty years: One suggestion is that these ages were possible because of tremendously different climate and environmental conditions that were in effect before the Flood (chs. 6—9). A second suggestion is that these are hyperbolic figures that use exaggeration to indicate significance in the ancient world.

5:4 sons and daughters: There may have been a very large number of children born from our first parents. We may presume intermarriage among them, of course.

5:5 and he died: This refrain is given at the conclusion of each of the ten names in this chapter except one (Enoch; v. 24). The judgment of God on fallen man was fulfilled in the death of Adam and each of his successors (3:19; 6:3). Death entered the world through this one man, and through him passed to all people (see Rom. 5:12; 1 Cor. 15:22).

5:6–20 The pattern of the genealogies is as follows: (1) name "A" lived "x" years; (2) name "A" begot name "B"; (3) name "A" then lived "y" years; (4) name "A" lived "z" ("x"+ "y") years in all; (5) and he died. See also the pattern in the line of Shem (11:10–26). These lists indicate major figures over an extended period of time. In this case, the point is to tie the line of continuity between Adam and Noah through the line of Seth.

5:21–24 The most fascinating name in this listing is that of **Enoch.** The phrase, **Enoch walked with God** (vv. 22, 24), expresses a life of fellowship with and obedience to the Lord. **he was not:** This phrase does not mean that Enoch ceased to exist, instead it means that he was taken into God's presence, **for God took him.** Enoch's remarkable experience was a testimony of his deep faith in God (see Heb. 11:5, 6) and a reminder that there is life in God's presence for the people of God.

5:25–27 Methuselah lived longer than any other figure mentioned in Genesis—969 years.

5:28–31 Lamech is remembered for his descendant Noah. The name **Noah** means "to rest" and is associated with **comfort.** Noah's name refers to a reversal of the curse.

5:32 These sons of Noah, **Shem, Ham, and Japheth,** figure in the story of the Flood (chs. 6—9).

6:1 The term **daughters** clearly means female children of human parents.

6:2 The sons of God refer to a different group from either the **men** or their **daughters.** The phrase occurs elsewhere in the Bible and clearly means "angels." Job 1:6 presents Satan and his angels coming into the presence of the Lord for an audience with His Majesty. Satan's angels are there called "the sons of God," with the suggestion that these angelic beings were once holy ones who served the Lord, but were now allied with the evil one.

6:3 My Spirit: This is the second reference to the Holy Spirit in Genesis. The first is in anticipation of order and wonder (1:2); this second is in anticipation of destruction. Scholars are not sure what the Hebrew term **strive** means; it is found only here. **Flesh** speaks of the mortality of humankind (see 3:19; 5:5). **his days:** This phrase means that God will extend a "grace period" of 120 years before expending His wrath (in the Flood).

6:4 The Hebrew word for **giants** means "fallen ones." Many ancient cultures have legends of titans and demigods. This verse appears to be explaining this common memory of humankind.

6:5, 6 was sorry: In these words we sense the passion of the Lord. He had desired so much from humanity—and was overwhelmingly disappointed.

6:7 I will destroy: Humanity's ruin extends to all living things that God had made on the earth.

6:8 But Noah: Were there not a man and a family who by God's grace stood out from the wickedness of their day, there would have been a new beginning on the part of God that would have omitted all of us!

6:9 just ... perfect: These words together mean "genuine righteousness." The phrase **walked with God** is also used of Enoch in

5:22, 24. It indicates a continual pattern of life—a marked contrast with the pattern of life of the rest of the people of the world at the time!

6:10 These **three sons** will form the nations following the Flood.

6:11, 12 The verb translated **corrupt** has the idea of being ruined, spoiled, or destroyed.

6:13 The Creator of the universe took one man into His confidence! **end of all flesh:** It would appear that the God's "grace period" of 120 years (v. 3) was now complete.

6:14 The word **ark** means "a box," the same term is used of the box in which the baby Moses was placed in the Nile (Ex. 2:3). The Hebrew word for **gopherwood** is transliterated because that type of wood is not known today. Noah made **rooms** in the ark and used **pitch** to seal the ark against leaks.

6:15 The **cubit** is about 18 inches. Hence, the ark was about 450 feet long, 75 feet wide, and 45 feet high.

6:16 The **window** was an "opening." The need for circulation of air, yet protection from the torrents of water, demanded a good deal of engineering and crafting.

6:17 I Myself: The Hebrew text places significant emphasis on the personal role of God in the ensuing storm.

6:18–21 God in His mercy established His **covenant** with Noah. This is the first time the word *covenant* is used in the Bible; some believe the concept of covenant is found in 3:15. The details of this covenant were given after the Flood (9:9). God promised to preserve Noah's family and **two of every sort** of animal.

6:22 Noah's complete obedience is similar to Abram's (12:4; 22:3).

7:1 The initiative is **the LORD's** (8:15), just as in the call of Abram (12:1).

7:2, 3 The command to take **seven of every clean animal** is a new detail (6:19). The additional clean animals could be used for food and for sacrifice once the waters subsided (8:20–22).

7:4, 5 The number **forty** is a significant number, representing a special fullness of time (see v. 12; Num. 32:13; 1 Kin. 19:8; Matt. 4:2).

7:6 six hundred years old: This is the second

notice of the age of Noah; he was 500 years old when he became a father (5:32).

7:7–9 The time had now come for the family and the animals to enter **the ark.** The events of these few verses summarize an immense labor; yet the gathering of the animals must have been largely the work of the Lord and their management the work of Noah and his sons.

7:10 The number **seven** follows the pattern of symbolic numbers begun in 2:3 (see also 4:24).

7:11, 12 fountains of the great deep ... windows of heaven: The waters of the ocean were raised, and the waters of the heavens fell, both converging in a super-inundation of **rain** for the forty days (v. 4).

7:13–15 The animals seem to have been drawn to the ark and **to Noah** by the compelling force of the Lord.

7:16 shut him in: The Lord who had drawn them now closed the door on them. That shut door was a symbol of closure, safety, and God's deliverance.

7:17, 18 Four times in this passage the phrase **the waters prevailed** is used (vv. 18–20, 24).

7:19, 20 the high hills under the whole heaven were covered: These words suggest a flood that covers the entire earth.

7:21, 22 Death extended to every creature—**all flesh**—whose home was on the land.

7:23, 24 man: People died—only **Noah** and those with him escaped the terrible, universal death of the wicked. Jesus affirmed the historicity of the "days of Noah" (Matt. 24:37, 38; Luke 17:26, 27).

8:1, 2 God, in His great mercy, **remembered** Noah. God faithfully loved the people with whom He had covenanted.

8:3 hundred and fifty days: Note the symmetry of time: it took the same amount of time for the waters to recede as it took for them to rage over the earth (7:24).

8:4, 5 tops of the mountains: The surging of the waters had been so great that the mountains had been submerged (see 7:19, 20).

8:6 The rains came for forty days (7:12); after **forty days the window was opened.**

8:7 The flight of the **raven** was observed

from the ark; this hardy bird kept flying until it located land.

8:8–11 The **dove,** sought land; finding none, it returned to the ark. Later, this bird was sent out again; it returned with an olive leaf, a symbol of peace and restoration.

8:12–14 God had again brought the waters of the earth into their place, and He had **dried** the earth. The Flood began in Noah's year 600, month 2, day 17 (7:11) and ended in Noah's year 601, month 2, day 27 (8:14).

8:15 The fact that **God spoke to Noah** is another mark of God's great grace to Noah and of how much He valued him.

8:16–19 As God called Noah and his family to enter the ark (7:1), so now He tells them to **go out of the ark.**

8:20 an altar: In joyful and magnificent devotion to the Lord, Noah sacrificed animals and birds from all the clean animals and birds he had preserved on the ark (7:2).

8:21 a soothing aroma: The sacrifices were acceptable and pleasing to God (4:3; Lev. 1:9). **I will never again curse the ground:** The awful devastation of the Flood will never be repeated. **the imagination of man's heart is evil from his youth:** This is the same charge against man with which the Flood story began (6:5).

8:22 while the earth remains: The words of this verse are in a poem of powerful effect (12:1–3).

9:1 The blessing of God on the family of Noah provided a new beginning for humankind.

9:2 the fear of you and the dread of you: The two phrases express the same idea. The animals and birds will have an innate fear of humans, and they are placed under human authority.

9:3 From this verse it may be argued that up to this point men and women ate only vegetation (see 2:16).

9:4 blood: Represents the animal's life. It may be used in sacrifice, for all life belongs to the Lord.

9:5 lifeblood: More sacred than the life of an animal is the life of a person.

9:6, 7 The **image of God** (see 1:26, 27; 5:1) is still in man. God values humans more highly than animal life because only humankind has His image.

9:8–10 God promised that He would establish His covenant with Noah, and here He accomplished this (see 15:18; contrast 3:15). This covenant extends to animals. (v. 10).

9:11–17 The **rainbow** is a memorial to God's promise never to flood the earth again and a constant reminder of His oath.

9:18, 19 The sons of Noah mentioned here sets the stage for what happens next. **the father of Canaan:** This identification was particularly important to the first readers of Genesis.

9:20, 21 The **vineyard** was a standard feature in the agricultural setting of ancient Israel. Here it is noted because of Noah's drunkenness (v. 21).

9:22 It is not clear whether seeing his father's **nakedness** was Ham's chief offense.

9:23, 24 Shem and Japheth took great pains to honor their father.

9:25 The three sons had been blessed with their father (see v. 1). Thus Noah **cursed** Ham indirectly by cursing his son **Canaan** (see 10:6).

9:26, 27 Shem is given precedence over his brothers. Eber and Abram were descended from Shem (11:10–30) so Shem's blessing is ultimately a blessing on Israel.

9:28, 29 Noah's death was the end of an era. Only he and his family spanned two worlds, that of the earth before and after the Flood.

10:1 Genealogy the **sons of Noah** were first named in 5:32 (see 6:10; 7:13; 9:18).

10:2–4 The listing of **the sons of Japheth** is more brief than the others. Among the persons and peoples mentioned is **Javan** (vv. 2, 4), an ancient name for the Greek people.

10:5 The migrations of the peoples to different **lands** would come after the events of 11:1–9.

10:6 Ham's family included **Cush, Mizraim, Put,** and **Canaan** Ham's four sons. Cush is the ancient name for Ethiopia; Mizraim is a name for Egypt. The sons of Cush are given in vv. 7–12, the sons of Mizraim in vv. 13, 14, and the sons of Canaan in verses 15–19. This section does not list the sons of Put.

10:7–11 The sons of Cush include the infamous **Nimrod** (vv. 9–12). The description of him as **a mighty hunter before the LORD** suggests great arrogance. His territory was in the lands of the east, the fabled ancient cities of Mesopotamia; these include **Babel, Erech, Accad, and Calneh** (v. 10).

10:12–15 The names associated with **Canaan** (see 9:22) are peoples who settled in the region of greater Canaan. Some of these names were still associated with the land at the time of Abraham. The sites of **Sodom** and its allied cities were later destroyed in the firestorm of Gen. 19.

10:16–20 This summary verse speaks of **families ... languages ... lands ... nations** as in v. 5.

10:21–31 Eber is the name that gives rise to the term *Hebrew,* which is first used of Abraham in 14:13. Such a name is patronymic (a father name). Eber is directly the son of **Salah** (v. 24). Abraham is the father of the Hebrew nation, but Abraham descends from Eber, and Eber from Shem. The other names associated with Shem include **Elam, Asshur,** and **Aram,** major people groups in the Old Testament.

10:32 the families of the sons of Noah: Although not every ancient people group is listed in this "Table of the Nations," its clear teaching is that all the varied peoples of the earth, no matter of what land or language, are descended from Noah.

11:1 one language: This account speaks of a time soon after the Flood, a time before the family had begun to disperse (contrast 10:5, 20, 31, 32).

11:2 The land of Shinar is the region of ancient Babylon in Mesopotamia (see 10:10), part of modern Iraq. This is one region traditionally suggested as the location of the Garden of Eden.

11:3 The use of **bricks** for building a large structure was common in this early period.

11:4 These people wanted to **make a name** for themselves. **lest we be scattered:** They feared that they might be dispersed—by implication, by the Lord—and not achieve the greatness they sought.

11:5 the LORD came down to see: A figurative way of speaking that indicates the omniscience (the all-embracing knowledge) of the Lord (see 18:21).

11:6 nothing that they propose: The potential is that humankind will become as willfully sinful as they were before the Flood. God will not allow this to happen.

11:7 The **Us** in this passage is similar to the language of 1:26–28. Variation in **language,** culture, values, and clans all started at this point. Were it not for human arrogance, this division would not have been necessary.

11:8 the LORD scattered them: There are three great judgments on sinful humanity in the first section of Genesis (chs. 1—11). The first is the expulsion from Eden (ch. 3); the second is the Flood (chs. 6—9), and the third is the scattering of the people from Babel (see Luke 1:51).

11:9 There is a pun in the name **Babel**. The verb for *confuse* sounds similar to the name of the city. The principal city of ancient paganism (Babylon) is just a site of confusion because **there the LORD confused the language.**

11:10–25 Genealogy (or family histories) is found in ten significant passages in the Book of Genesis (see the list at 2:4). The Jewish nation came from **Shem.** Hence, the accounts that follow make much of him and his family. The pattern in this **genealogy** is similar to that in ch. 5; but here only the first three elements are given: (1) name "A" lived "x" years; (2) name "A" begot name "B"; (3) name "A" then lived "y" years. Note also that while the people listed in ch. 11 lived very long lives, they did not live nearly as long as those mentioned in ch. 5. In fact, the people lived progressively *shorter* lives, from the 600 years of Shem (vv. 10, 11) to the 148 years of Nahor (vv. 24, 25).

11:26 Terah: At long last we come to the family of Terah and the births of **Abram, Nahor, and Haran.** Years later, Abram would be renamed Abraham (see 17:5), and would become the father of Isaac (21:1–5).

11:27 Abram, Nahor, and Haran: These three sons of Terah would be expected to carry on his name (but see 11:31). **Haran begot Lot:** Lot is a nephew of Abram; he figures prominently in the upcoming account (see 12:4, 5; 13:1–13).

11:28 The untimely death of Haran leaves his son Lot to carry on his name and to establish his destiny. Scholars have believed **Ur of the Chaldeans** to be the famous Ur located near the ancient delta in the Persian Gulf where the Tigris and Euphrates Rivers flow together.

11:29 Sarai means "Princess," implying a person of noble birth. The name Milcah is related to the verb that would be translated "to reign" and means "Queen."

11:30 The sad fact that **Sarai was barren** marred her life and yet led to an opportunity for God to accomplish a miracle on her behalf (see 21:1–5).

11:31, 32 Abram's epic move to Canaan begins in ch. 12 with Abram receiving a command from the Lord to leave his land to go to a new land. **Terah**, for his own reasons, decided to move from Ur to Canaan. They went to Haran, where **Terah died.** This was the first step of the journey of Abram and Sarai to the land of promise.

12:1 The name Yahweh, translated as **LORD**, is not explained until Ex. 3:14, 15. In a world that believed in many gods, the name of the true and living God was significant. **Abram** means "Exalted Father." Later it will be changed to Abraham, meaning "Father of Many." **country ... family ... father's house:** God's commands to Abram were intensely demanding because they caused him to leave his place, his clan, and his family. The Lord's words to Abram commanded that he was to leave everything and go to a place that God would not even identify until Abram got there.

12:2, 3 This celebrated passage is a prologue to the set of passages that together form the *Abrahamic covenant* (see the list at 15:1–21), the irrevocable promise of God. God commanded Abram to leave his home and family, promising to create **a great nation** through him—the people of God (18:18). God promised to **bless** Abram. The promise of His personal blessing to Abram and Sarai included the benefits of a long and healthy life (see 15:15; especially 24:1), plus wealth and importance (see 13:2). That one's **name** would live on long after one's lifetime was a supreme honor (6:4). **be a blessing:** The phrase is a command. **him who curses:** Whereas God would bless the peoples (plural) who blessed

Abram or his descendants, His curse came upon the individual (singular) who cursed Abram or his descendants. **all the families of the earth:** All men would be blessed through them.

12:4 Abram obeyed (see 17:23; 22:3). **Lot went with him:** Some have imagined that Abram disobeyed God by taking Lot with him. However, the verse suggests that Lot made the decision. **seventy-five years old:** The Bible rarely indicates a person's age when events occur, but it does so several times for Abram.

12:5 This is the first mention in the Bible of **Canaan.** Canaan was populated with peoples involved in gross idolatry (15:16). God promised this land to Abram and Sarai.

12:6 passed through: Here the Hebrew Abram was "passing through" the land, crossing over to his destination. **Shechem:** This ancient site was in the center of the land **tree of Moreh:** A terebinth or ancient oak tree would serve as a lasting marker for future generations to observe (see also 13:18; 18:1; 23:17). The land was already occupied by **the Canaanites** (see 13:7), but by God's promise it would belong to Abraham's descendants.

12:7 the LORD appeared: This was the first time God appeared to Abram in the land of Canaan (see 13:14–17). **To your descendants:** The land of Canaan was a gift to the descendants of Abram. God owned the land (Ps. 24:1); it was His to do with as He pleased. The people of Canaan had lost their right to occupy the land because of their awful depravity (see 15:16).

12:8 Later, in the time of Jacob, the site of **Bethel** would play an important role (see 28:10–22). **Ai** means "Ruin." Abram responded to God's appearance by building **an altar** and worshiping the Lord. **called on the name of the LORD:** Not a private prayer, but a public proclamation. Abram was evangelizing—God had commanded him to be a blessing to the nations (12:2) and he was doing it.

12:9 South: This Hebrew word is often transliterated as the *Negev* (see 13:1; 24:62).

12:10 Sometime after Abram's arrival in Canaan, **famine** forced him to leave. **to Egypt:**

The Scripture does not say whether Abram wanted to go.

12:11 beautiful countenance: Only rarely does the Bible refer to a person's appearance. Sarai's physical beauty was remarkable given her advanced age—she was ten years younger than Abram, or about 65 (12:4; 17:17).

12:12 Abram and his entourage would not be able to slip into Egypt secretly. The Egyptians would **see** them, and Abram knew that Sarai's beauty would be noticed too.

12:13, 14 my sister: Sarai *was* Abram's half sister, the daughter of his father but not of his mother (20:12).

12:15 commended her: A form of praise (much like that in Ps. 113:1). **to Pharaoh's house:** Abram's ploy backfired!

12:16 treated Abram well: Abram was enriched by Pharaoh's actions, but at the possible loss of his wife. To have a camel in this period was like having an expensive limousine.

12:17 the LORD plagued Pharaoh: The first example of the cursing and blessing element of God's promise (see 12:2, 3).

12:18–20 In spite of his indignation, Pharaoh dismissed the couple. The Lord protected Abram and Sarai.

13:1, 2 Abram and Sarai returned from Egypt **to the South** or to the Negev (see 12:9; 24:62), a region where they could live with their considerable wealth in **livestock, silver,** and **gold.** From there they journeyed back to **Bethel,** the site where God had appeared to him.

13:3–7 Lot shared in his uncle Abram's prosperity to some degree. The crowding of range lands led to disputes and **strife** between their herdsmen. **The Canaanites and the Perizzites:** The point of this phrase is that the land was already populated; Abram and Lot had to compete for available land for their rapidly growing herds and flocks.

13:8, 9 we are brethren: Abram acted with kindness, not wanting to fight his nephew's family and herdsmen. Abram gave Lot his choice. In doing this, Abram showed confidence in God's continuing provision for him.

13:10–12 Lot wanted the well-watered region in **the plain of Jordan,** near the Dead Sea. **Sodom and Gomorrah:** In light of the fate of these infamous cities (chs. 18; 19),it is amazing to learn of the abundant water the region had once enjoyed. The "little" town of **Zoar** later figured in Lot's life (19:22).

13:13 Lot's choice of the more favorable land led him into territory that was populated by the worst of the Canaanites, the infamous evil people of **Sodom** (see chs. 18; 19).

13:14 The LORD reaffirmed His promise to Abram after his **separation from Lot.**

13:15–17 all the land: None of the land was outside the promise. **Your descendants** translates the Hebrew word for seed. **as the dust of the earth:** A hyperbole or overstatement (15:5; 22:17). Abram's **walk in the land** is a symbolic act of taking possession. Abraham himself would not take possession of the land (see Heb. 11:13–16); his descendants would (see 12:7; 15:17–21).

13:18 Hebron became one of the principal centers for Abram's stay in the land (23:2). Abram continued to build **altars** to worship the living God (see 12:7, 8; 13:4).

14:1, 2 Most scholars no longer think it is likely that **Amraphel king of Shinar** was the famous Hammurabi of Babylon.

14:3 The Valley of Siddim is likely submerged under the Dead Sea.

14:4 they served: The kings from Mesopotamia forced the kings of the cities in the Valley of Siddim to pay tribute.

14:5–9 The raid took at least a year to organize and must have been formidable, given the list of cities they **attacked** as they made their way to the encounter with the rebellious kings.

14:10 asphalt pits: The Hebrew term for pits is written twice ("pits pits"), meaning that bitumen pits were everywhere.

14:11, 12 all the goods ... Lot: Lot was not only captured, but he was also now living in the city of Sodom, an "exceedingly wicked and sinful" city (see 13:11–13).

14:13 Here is this first use of the word **Hebrew** in the Bible. The word is related to a verb meaning "cross over" or "pass through."

14:14, 15 The fact that Abram could field 318 fighting men from among his own **servants** is an indication of the great wealth and honor that the Lord had given him (see 12:2, 3).

14:16 Abram's raid was a complete success. He regained **all the goods** stolen by the raiding party from Mesopotamia and rescued his nephew Lot.

14:17 When Abram returned from his successful attack on the raiding party from Mesopotamia, he was met by two kings, one from **Sodom** and one from Salem. Abram turns at first to the king of Salem.

14:18 Melchizedek means "My King Is Righteous." **king of Salem:** Salem is an older, shorter name for Jerusalem. The word is based on the root from which we get the word *shalom*, "peace." **the priest of God Most High:** The term for God used here expresses God's power over the nations. Melchizedek appears from nowhere, without mention of parents or background. This mysterious quality of Melchizedek allows the writer of Hebrews to compare him with another priest, the Lord Jesus Christ (see Heb. 5—9; see also Ps. 110:4).

14:19 And he blessed him: Melchizedek blesses Abram; thus he comes under the special provision of God's promise of blessing (see 12:3). **Blessed be Abram:** The words of the blessing are in two lines of poetry. **Possessor** may also mean "Creator" (see Prov. 8:22).

14:20 blessed be God Most High: When we bless God, we acknowledge Him as the source of all our blessings (see Ps. 103:1, 2). Melchizedek declared the true nature of Abram's victory—God **delivered** him. Here is the first mention of the **tithe** in the Bible (see Deut. 14:22). Abram's gift indicates that he considered Melchizedek a true priest of the living God; in giving this gift Abram was giving to the Lord.

14:21 Abram seems to have ignored the **king of Sodom** (see v. 17) until he had worshiped with the king of Salem. This king asked for his people but not for his goods.

14:22 Abram **raised** his **hand** as a symbol of a strong oath. Abram **the** LORD, with the **God Most High.**

14:23 I will take nothing: In these words, Abram strongly rebuked Sodom and its king (see 13:12, 13).

14:24 Aner, Eshcol, and Mamre: Abram's allies (v. 13) were not bound by his resolution.

15:1 the word of the LORD **... in a vision:** The use of a vision is one of the means by which God interacts with His servants. This was the third appearance of the Lord to Abram since his arrival in the land of Canaan (the first at 12:7; the second at 13:14–17).

15:2 Lord GOD translates the Hebrew word for Lord (*Adonai*) and the name Yahweh. Abram and Sarai were **childless** (see 11:29, 30). **heir of my house:** According to long-standing custom, a man who was childless would adopt someone to be his principal heir. If the man later had a child, then the natural child would replace the adopted son as the principal heir. We read of **Eliezer of Damascus** only here, but he had the honor of being Abram's heir because Abram and Sarai had no child of their own.

15:3 Offspring represents a word that is also translated *seed* and *descendants* (see 3:15; 15:5, 13, 18).

15:4 from your own body: God promised that Abram himself would father a child.

15:5 Only God can count the stars; the descendants of Abram would be innumerable (see 22:17; compare 13:16). **Your descendants** translates the Hebrew word for *seed*.

15:6 When God made a promise, Abram **believed in the** LORD. When God commanded Abram, he obeyed (see 12:4; 22:3). **He accounted it to him for righteousness:** Abram was saved by believing in God and so being declared righteous by Him.

15:7 I am the LORD, **who brought you out:** This is the self-authenticating declaration of the Lord.

15:8 how shall I know: Abram was asking the Lord for a commemorative sign of His promise.

15:9, 10 Abram had to prepare the sacrifice and **bring** it to God; the Lord would enact the sign (see v. 17).

15:11 Abram drove the **vultures** away from the animals while waiting for God's sign.

15:12 Abram fell into the same sort of **deep sleep** that God placed on Adam (see 2:21).

Abram was still aware of events around him. **horror ... darkness:** Abram was about to experience the presence of the Almighty. This was a moment of profound dread and holy awe.

15:13 Strangers are those who dwell temporarily in a foreign place. Abram was a *stranger* in the land of Canaan; his descendants would become strangers in another land (Egypt). **four hundred years:** They were the generation who came to fulfill God's promise! (See Ex. 12:40–42.)

15:14 I will judge: God fulfilled this prophecy in the ten plagues (Ex. 7–11). The Israelites of the Exodus acquired **great possessions** when they plundered the Egyptians (see Ex. 12:31–36).

15:15 go **to your fathers:** A way of speaking about death; the phrase may include the promise of life after death as well (see 25:8; 35:29; 49:33; see also 1 Sam. 12:23).

15:16 in the fourth generation: This expression reflects the longer life spans of people in Abram's day (compare 400 years in v. 13). **iniquity of the Amorites:** The command of God to take the land from the Canaanite peoples (see Deut. 20) would come only when their iniquity was **complete.**

15:17 The **sun** went down. Now in heavy darkness, he saw supernatural light. **a smoking oven and a burning torch:** This oven and torch imagery may indicate the impending judgment on Canaan. **between those pieces:** In agreements between equals both parties would pass between the bloody pieces of animals and birds. Here only God passes through.

15:18 The **same day** that Abram believed in the Lord (v. 6) and God counted it to him for righteousness, God made a covenant with him. **covenant:** The first time this very significant word is used of God's promise to Abraham. **Descendants:** The Jews who would descend from Abram would fulfill this promise as the seed (collectively); so also the Christ who is the Seed (singular) would ultimately fulfill this promise (see Gal. 3:16). **This land:** The promise will be fulfilled in its fullness when Jesus Christ returns (see Is. 9:1–7).

15:19 the Kenites ... Jebusites: This list of nations served two purposes: (1) It defined the borders of the land. (2) It impressed. The Israelites who heard these words must have been greatly encouraged.

15:20 Most **Hittites** lived in Asia Minor (modern Turkey), but there were some Hittites in Canaan (see ch. 23). **the Rephaim:** A people of unusually tall stature; they are called giants in 2 Sam. 21:15–22 (see Num. 13:33; Deut. 2:11; 3:11, 13).

15:21 The term **Canaanite** could be used broadly to include all the people groups in Canaan (see 12:6), or more narrowly, as here, to indicate a particular people group (see 10:15–20).

16:1 had borne him no children: When a woman was not able to conceive a child, her husband might divorce her. Sarai's desperate ploy to have a child through **Hagar** was fully in accord with the practices of those days.

16:2 Sarai knew that conception was from the Lord (see 4:1); her words, **the LORD has restrained me,** expressed her grief. Earlier her husband had complained to the Lord that he was childless (see 15:2). **go in to my maid:** In the culture of the ancient Near East this would have been expected. **obtain children by her:** Hagar would become a surrogate mother for Sarai. At the time of birth, the mother would undress herself and stay near the birth mother. As the child was born it might be placed on the wife's body, a ritual indicating that it was born on behalf of the woman.

16:3 Sarai and Abram enlisted Hagar's aid after **ten years** of waiting for God's promise to be fulfilled. At this point, Abram would have been 85 years old and Sarai 75 (12:4; 17:17).

16:4 despised: Sarai paid an emotional price for doing what the culture accepted. Using a surrogate mother may have been expedient and acceptable to the culture, but the hatred and belittling by the arrogant young servant woman was excruciating for Sarai.

16:5 The LORD judge: This is as close as we come to the use of cursing among God's people in the Bible; such words arose out of Sarai's utter desperation.

16:6 Sarai's frustration led her to treat Hagar **harshly.** Neither she nor Abram behaved well during this stressful time.

16:7 the Angel of the LORD: This wonderful phrase is used to speak of God as He relates Himself directly to His people. **by a spring of water in the wilderness:** The detail is appropriate for Hagar's experience.

16:8, 9 and He said: On several occasions this passage states that the Angel of the Lord spoke directly to Hagar (vv. 9, 10, 11).

16:10 God's promise to Hagar to **multiply** her descendants is similar to the one given to Abram and Sarai (see 15:5; 17:20; 22:15–18).

16:11 The name **Ishmael** means "God hears."

16:12 This is something of a mixed blessing. **Wild man** suggests that Ishmael and his descendants would be unsettled, ever on the move. **His hand ... against** suggests that his descendants would often be at war. Still this people would endure. They would **dwell in the presence of all his brethren.** This has indeed been the case, for Ishmael's descendants are the Arab peoples who populate most of the Middle East today.

16:13–16 Though Hagar was Egyptian, she had evidently come to faith in **the LORD** of Abram and Sarai. As a recipient of God's blessing, she gave Him a commemorative name, **You-Are-the-God-Who-Sees.** Her words, **have I also seen him,** suggest amazement at God's grace and humility in His presence.

17:1 ninety-nine years old: Abram was 75 years old when he came to the land of Canaan (12:4). At 86 he became the father of Ishmael (see 16:16). Then 13 more years passed without a son being born to Sarai. For the fourth time, **the LORD** appeared to Abram in the land of Canaan. **I am Almighty God:** God used the name *Shaddai* for Himself for the first time.

17:2–4 a father of many nations: Abram's principal descendants are the Israelites, but Abram is also the father of Ishmael and the Arab peoples (see ch. 16), as well as a number of other people groups descended from Keturah (see 25:1–6).

IN DEPTH   Circumcision

The rite of circumcision (Gen. 17:10) became a powerful, enduring symbol of God's covenant relationship with Abraham and his offspring. Technically speaking, circumcision refers to the surgical removal of a male's foreskin. The procedure was widely practiced in the ancient world, including the Egyptian and Canaanite cultures. But they performed the rite at the beginning of puberty as an initiation into manhood. By contrast, the Hebrews circumcised infant boys as a sign of their responsibility to serve God as His special, holy people in the midst of a pagan world.

God instructed Abraham to circumcise every male child in his household, including servants (17:11) as a visible, physical sign of the covenant between the Lord and His people. Any male not circumcised was to be "cut off from his people" and regarded as a covenant breaker (17:14). The custom was performed on the eighth day after birth (17:12), at which time a name was given to the son (Luke 1:59; 2:21). In the early history of the Hebrews, the rite was performed by the father but eventually was carried out by a specialist.

The Hebrew people came to take great pride in circumcision. In fact, it became a badge of their spiritual and national superiority. This attitude fostered a spirit of exclusivism instead of compassion to reach out to other nations as God intended. Gentiles came to be regarded as the "uncircumcision," a term of disrespect implying that non-Jewish peoples were outside the circle of God's love.

Eventually the terms "circumcised" and "uncircumcised" became charged with emotion, as is plain from the discord the issue brought about centuries later in the early church (Gal. 2:12).

17:5, 6 Abram ... Abraham: This name change is significant. Abram means "Exalted Father." Abraham means "Father of Many."

The Abrahamic **covenant** (see 12:1–3) is the foundation upon which later divine covenants with God's people are based. **Everlasting** means the covenant would last through all time. **to be God to you:** With these remarkable words, God pledged His ongoing relationship with the seed of Abraham.

17:8, 9 The promise clearly included the Israelite people *and* **the land** (Canaan). The two are linked in the language of the covenant in ch. 15.

17:10, 11 Circumcision means "cutting around," a minor operation that removes the foreskin from the male organ.

17:12, 13 An **eight**-day-old boy and his immune system would be strong enough for the operation.

17:14 There is something of a pun in the expression, **cut off.** Any man who did not accept circumcision would be cut off from the community.

17:15 Sarai ... Sarah: Both names mean "Princess."

17:16 bless her: The Lord's blessing was for Sarah as well as Abraham (see 12:1–3). The writer to the Hebrews also celebrated Sarah's faithfulness to the Lord (see Heb. 11:11).

17:17 Fell on his face recalls the words of v. 3. Abraham's laugh is unexpected and shocking—but completely understandable! For 24 years Abraham had heard—and believed—the same promise: one day he would become the father of a son who would found the nation of promise. He had tried to force the birth of a legitimate heir (see chs. 15; 16), but God had assured him that the true heir would not be an adopted slave (15:4) nor the child of a surrogate mother (16:11, 12). Even if Sarah were to conceive now, she would be 90 when the baby was born and he would be 100! And so at last he **laughed.**

17:18 Abraham's plea shows his love for his son.

17:19 Isaac means "Laughter" (see 21:1–6).

17:20 God had **blessed** Ishmael before he was born (see 16:11, 12) and here He renewed and amplified the blessing. Ishmael would have **twelve** sons (25:12–18).

17:21 Isaac whom Sarah shall bear: The promise was plain. The father and mother were named, the child was named, and the time was named.

17:22 God went up: We sometimes read of the Lord coming down from heaven; here we read of Him returning there.

17:23–27 Abraham took Ishmael: On the very day he received the command from God, he did just as the Lord commanded.

18:1 This is the fifth time **the LORD appeared** to Abraham in the land of Canaan. **Mamre** was one of Abram's allies in his battle against the invading kings from Mesopotamia (see 14:13). The place name Mamre was probably associated with a personal name. This region came to be known as Hebron (see 13:18; 23:17).

18:2–8 Verse 1 states that it was the Lord who appeared to Abraham; v. 2 speaks of **three men;** v. 13 suggests that one of these men was the Lord. Abraham's words **My Lord** suggests that he suspected the identity of the visitors.

18:9 Where is Sarah The focus here is on Sarah.

18:10 Sarah your wife shall have: The wording was important because the couple had tried in the past to achieve the fulfillment of God's promise (see chs. 15; 16).

18:11 had passed the age of childbearing: The text uses three phrases to describe the advanced age of Abraham and Sarah, with a special focus on the fact that Sarah had ceased to menstruate.

18:12 therefore Sarah laughed: She acted like Abraham had on an earlier occasion (17:17). She knew the facts of life, but she would soon be greatly surprised by the One who determined them.

18:13 the LORD said: Here the text makes it plain that the Lord Himself was one of the three guests. **Why did Sarah laugh?:** The woman of faith, like her husband, had believed for years in God's promise. But now she found her faith stretched to the limit. God knew she had laughed.

18:14 Is anything too hard for the LORD?:

That is, there is no wonder that God cannot do. You have done wonderful *things* (Is. 25:1).

18:15 Afraid of being found out, Sarah **denied** that she had laughed. In His mercy God did not punish her, but neither did He allow her denial to stand. She *had* laughed.

18:16 looked toward Sodom: This verse begins the account of God's judgment on the sinful cities of Sodom and Gomorrah. **and Abraham went with them:** Abraham's hospitality enabled him to talk further with the living God.

18:17, 18 the LORD said: Two of the guests of Abraham and Sarah were angels and the third was none other than the living God! **Shall I hide:** Abraham had a vested interest in the city of Sodom because Lot lived there (see 14:12; 19:1).

18:19 for I have known him: The language here speaks of the intimate relationship, which motivates the Lord to accomplish His purpose in Abraham (see 22:12).

18:20 The outcry against Sodom and Gomorrah suggests a moral center in the universe; the outrageous sins of these cities are an affront to the righteousness of God (19:4–8).

18:21 I will go down now: There is nothing that God does not know, although we may say that He "comes down" to see "what is going on" in His earth (see also Ps. 113:4–6).

18:22–26 The exchange between Abraham and God serves as a dramatic *theodicy,* a justification of the Lord's ways. Abraham's concern was for his nephew Lot and his family (see 14:12; 19:1).

18:27–33 Abraham was determined to go on bargaining, but he knew that he was arguing with God. So he went one step at a time, pleading the case for the **righteous** in smaller and smaller numbers: from **forty-five** down to **ten.** Perhaps Abraham thought there were at least ten righteous persons in the city; but alas, there were not (as the report of ch. 19 shows).

19:1 Lot's fortunes had gone very well. The **gate** of a city was the place where the town elders met (Ruth 4:1). **bowed himself:** Lot's act of reverence to special guests (compare 18:2). The angels appeared as men (18:2), and Lot greeted them as such.

19:2, 3 My lords is a greeting of respect for special visitors. **your servant's house:** Lot's generous offer of hospitality may have been motivated out of kindness toward them as well as his sense of the dangers his city might hold for them.

19:4 The men of Sodom were aggressive homosexuals, bent on raping innocent travelers.

19:5 The Hebrew verb for **know** is ordinarily used of normal sexual relations between a male and female (4:1). Here it is used to describe the perversion of homosexual sex between men. See Rom. 1:18–32, especially vv. 26, 27. The term sodomite comes from this passage.

19:6–8 Lot's plight was severe; he had invited guests into his home for protection and was now in danger of seeing them abused by an unruly mob. Lot's desperation led him to risk the lives of his own **two daughters** to protect the lives of strangers from the mob.

19:9, 10 Stand back: The crazed crowd was now about to attack Lot.

19:11 Those who were morally blind were now stricken with physical **blindness** by the angelic guests (see a similar angelic blight in 2 Kin. 6:18). Only the confusion and panic of these wicked men spared Lot and his family from vicious assault.

19:12 The angelic guests had completed their search and were about to bring down the judgment of God on the city. There simply were not sufficient righteous persons in the city for it to be spared (v. 13; 18:24–33).

19:13–15 Arise can mean "make haste."

19:16 he lingered: Lot and his family needed to be propelled from their home by physical force. **the LORD being merciful:** This is the whole point of the story. God could have destroyed the city of Sodom with no word to Lot or Abraham (18:17).

19:17–22 Zoar: "Insignificant in Size."

19:23–25 The rain of **brimstone and fire** may be explained in a couple of ways. It is possible that God used a volcanic eruption or some similar kind of natural disaster. It is also possible that the destruction of these cities was an act of judgment outside the normal range of natural occurrences.

19:26 The command was clear, not to look back or linger (v. 17). Lot's wife disobeyed

and looked back. By implication, she was reluctant to leave. **pillar of salt:** Her destruction was sudden. Nothing was left of her but
a mineral heap. "Remember Lot's wife," Jesus warned (Luke 17:32).

19:27, 28 On the very **morning** that the cities were destroyed, Abraham looked on
from a distance and saw the destruction.
When he saw the **smoke,** he must have
known the truth: there were not even ten
righteous in the city (18:32).

19:29 Part of the reason for God's grace to
Lot was that **God remembered Abraham.**
Lot could barely tolerate the wickedness in
the city (see 2 Pet. 2:7, 8). If it were not for
Abraham, Lot would have died with the
other inhabitants.

19:30, 31 Lot had begged the angels to give
him a safe haven in the little city of **Zoar** (vv.
18–22), a request they granted. Lot did not
even feel safe in this city. So he lived in a
cave.

19:32 Lot's daughters now conspired together to make their father drunk so that he
would have sexual relations with them. **the
lineage of our father:** We can hardly approve of their action, yet their desperation
was real. Should they die childless, there
would be no one to carry on their family
name. For the peoples of biblical cultures,
this was an overwhelming loss (see ch. 38).

19:33–35 and he did not know: The narrator
inserts this phrase twice (also in v. 35) to
protect Lot. This was not deliberate incest
on his part; the daughters alone were responsible for what happened.

19:36–38 The shameful act of incest led to the
births of two sons who would later greatly
trouble Israel, **Moab** and **Ben-Ammi.**

20:1 Abraham's deception about Sarah in
the city of **Gerar** was later to be repeated by
his son Isaac (see ch. 26). The present story
is also a replay of Abraham's earlier mistakes
in Egypt (12:10–20).

20:2 Sarah was the half **sister** of Abraham
(v. 12). **Abimelech ... took her:** This action put Sarah in the king's harem, but not in
his bed.

20:3 Presumably, Abimelech was a pagan
king. Yet God warned him of the wrong that
he was about to commit. **a man's wife:** The

Hebrew words speak of Sarah and Abraham
on a level of equality and dignity. Both are
spoken of as a lords or nobles, literally "a noble wife of a noble man."

**20:4, 5 Lord, will You slay a righteous na-
tion also?:** Abimelech had not even touched
Sarah; he did not want to die for a sin he had
not committed. He argued that his actions so
far were innocent. They were based on what
Abraham and Sarah had told him.

20:6 This passage emphasizes the **dream**
state Abimelech was in. The Lord's response
to him was one of grace; God had kept the
king from touching Sarah.

20:7 This is the first use of the term **prohet** in
the Bible. Abraham's relationship to God was
the basis for God's command that Sarah be restored to her husband.

20:8–10 Abimelech's questions of Abraham
are especially touching: **What have you
done to us?** is followed by the reverse **How
have I offended you?**

20:11–13 Abraham gave two reasons for his
actions. The first was based on his assumption that he was in hostile territory. Second,
Sarah was **truly my sister.** The marriages of
the family of Terah were very close.

20:14–16 Abimelech made a significant payment to Abraham in silver in order to compensate **Sarah**'s hardship. His words **your
brother** may have been sarcastic. The Hebrew verb translated as **rebuked** can mean
"vindicated." This verb is used in legal terminology to describe the settlement of a dispute.

20:17 So Abraham prayed to God: However
the situation began, it ended in mercy with
Abraham acting as a priest for Abimelech
before the true and living God. In this way,
the people of Gerar learned about the Lord,
as had happened in Egypt years earlier
(12:10–20).

20:18 the LORD had closed up all the wombs:
Three things are indicated by these words.
First, the stay of Abraham and Sarah had
been prolonged in Gerar before Sarah's identity became known. This means that Sarah
had lived in the harem of the king for several
months. Second, the Lord reached out to
these people in a way they would find difficult to resist; the wish to procreate was

relentless in the ancient world, as these accounts consistently emphasize. Third, God graciously protected Sarah—and Abraham. The chapter ends with irony. Soon the Lord would open Sarah's womb to give her a child, long after she was too old to conceive naturally (21:1, 2).

21:1 And the LORD visited Sarah: The verb *visit* is an extraordinary choice here, because it means that the Lord entered directly into the affairs of His people. This was what He did for Sarah.

21:2 It appears that **Sarah conceived** while she and Abraham were living in Gerar (20:1; 21:22). **bore Abraham a son:** A great fact that the Bible elsewhere celebrates (see 25:19; Heb. 11:11). **in his old age:** The writer of Hebrews says Abraham was "as good as dead" (Heb. 11:12). What a miracle this was! To both Abraham (17:21) and Sarah (18:14), God had emphasized the concept of His **set time.**

21:3 Isaac means "He (God) Is Laughing (Now)." At one time Abraham had laughed at the improbability of having a son in his old age (17:17); Sarah had laughed too (see 18:12). But now, with the birth of the child, laughter took on its happier meaning. Sarah got the joke (vv. 5, 6)!

21:4 circumcised his son: Abraham's pattern of obedience to the Lord continued unchanged (12:4; 17:23; 22:3). The sign of the covenant was most important for the son of promise (17:9–14).

21:5 one hundred years old: Amusingly, Abraham was precisely the age that caused him to laugh aloud (17:17).

21:6 Among the many name jokes in the Bible, few are as wonderful as this one; the words for **laugh** in this verse are related to the name Isaac (see v. 3).

21:7 nurse children: Wondrously, this woman of 90 (17:17) now had breasts filled with milk and her arms full with a child!

21:8 The life of Isaac was to be marked by celebration, **a feast.** As glad parents, Abraham and Sarah rejoiced in each major step of his life.

21:9 The Hebrew verb for **scoffing** is related to the name for Isaac (see 21:3, 5). Here is a bad turn on a wonderful joke. Young Ishmael,

now perhaps 17, was mocking the joy of Sarah and Abraham in their young son.

21:10 In that culture it was reprehensible to send Ishmael away. When a surrogate wife had borne a son to one's husband, that mother and child could not be dismissed even if the first wife subsequently gave birth to a son. This partly explains Abraham's reluctance to do what Sarah demanded (v. 11). What is more, he still loved **his son** Ishmael (16:15; 17:18).

21:11, 12 but God said: This is the sixth time Abraham received a direct word from the Lord in Canaan. **listen to her voice:** Abraham needed to hear God give him permission to send Hagar and Ishmael from his home. **In Isaac** alone would the principal covenant be fulfilled. Ishmael had his own promise (v. 13; compare 16:10–12).

21:13, 14 This scene must have been exceedingly difficult for Abraham. He had no idea that another **morning** in his life would be even worse (see 22:3). **Bread and a skin of water** are meager provisions. The skin refers to a water bag made of animal skin. **sent her away:** Years before, Hagar left the same household while pregnant with Ishmael (16:6).

21:15 water ... used up: It would not take long for the two refugees to use up their meager provisions.

21:16 let me not see: Hagar loved her son. The thought that she was about to lose him to the desert heat was unbearable for her.

21:17 God heard: There is no pain of His people that He does not see or hear about (see Is. 40:27, 28; Heb. 2:10, 18; 4:15). God was near to deliver; the child would not die.

21:18 God renewed his promise to Hagar and Ishmael; Ishmael would become a **great nation** (see 16:10–12).

21:19 Hagar was so overcome with grief that she was unaware of the provision of water right before her. God showed her **a well of water.** Often in the Old Testament, a spring or well of water is a symbol of spiritual salvation as well as physical deliverance (see Is. 12:3; Jer. 2:13).

21:20 God's promise was realized in Ishmael's life. He became **an archer;** that is, he learned to hunt.

21:21 wife: Hagar made sure that Ishmael married an Egyptian, one of her own people, much as Abraham's servant searched for a wife for Isaac from among his parents' people (24:4).

21:22 Abimelech: It appears from this verse that Abraham and Sarah were still living in the region of Gerar (20:15). **Phichol:** This commander of the army is also mentioned in the later encounter with Isaac (see 26:26). **God is with you:** With these words, Abimelech and Phichol introduced their desire to form a treaty with Abraham.

21:23, 24 swear to me by God: This kind of oath was a complete, binding obligation (see 22:16). God would be witness to the act and a witness against anyone who might break it.

21:25, 26 It turned out that there was a dispute between the two about a **well.** For those who tended sheep and goats, water rights and wells mattered a great deal. **Abimelech** agreed to settle the issue promptly.

21:27 This is the first use of the word **covenant** for a parity treaty (15:18). A parity treaty is a binding agreement between two equals, similar to today's business contract.

21:28–31 Abraham presented **seven ewe lambs** to Abimelech. The Hebrew number seven is similar in sound to the verb meaning "to swear" (see v. 24). Thus **Beersheba** would be the well where they swore and the well of the seven ewe lambs.

21:32, 33 The **tamarisk tree** would long mark the spot of this major treaty. **called on the name:** As in 12:8, Abraham made proclamation in the Lord's name, telling everyone about **the LORD, the Everlasting God.**

21:34 Although Abraham had been promised the whole of the land for his posterity (see 12:7; 15:18–21), in his own life he lived under agreements with others in their **land** (Heb. 11:13–16). The name Palestine comes from the word for *Philistine.*

22:1 after these things: A new story is about to begin (15:1). The term **God** includes the definite article ("the God"; see 6:2; 27:28; 31:11; 46:3; 48:15). This is a way of indicating that the "Genuine Deity" or the "True God" is making these demands, not a false god or a demon.

22:2 only son: Abraham had one son by Hagar (ch. 16), and six sons by Keturah (ch. 25). But only Isaac was *uniquely born.* The point is not that Abraham had no other children, but that this was the unique child in whom all the promises of God resided. **Moriah:** "Where the Lord Provides" or "Where the Lord Appears." **burnt offering:** Abraham was commanded to go through the steps of offering a sacrifice that burned an animal or person entirely.

22:3, 4 Nothing is said of Abraham's thoughts; all we read is the account of the father's complete obedience to God (see 12:4; 17:23).

22:5 we will come back: The three verbs all show a strong determination on the part of the speaker (see also 12:2): "We are determined to go, we are determined to worship, we are determined to return." He had heard, many times, God's promise to create a nation through Isaac (12:1–3, 7; 13:14–17; 15:1–21; 17:1–22; 18:1–15). He still believed it. He had concluded that even if he had to destroy his son, God would bring him back from death (see Heb. 11:17–19).

22:6 The **fire** would be live coals in a clay pot of some kind. A special **knife** was used in sacrificial worship.

22:7 My father ... where is the lamb?: Isaac still did not know what Abraham planned to do.

22:8 for Himself: The wording is stronger in this order: "God Himself will provide."

22:9, 10 the place: The site of Moriah is significant (see vv. 2–4, 14). **bound Isaac:** At this point, Isaac knew that he was the sacrificial victim. Like the Savior on an even darker day he was willing to do his father's will.

22:11, 12 the Angel of the LORD: God spoke to **Abraham** from heaven; twice He called out his name. **Do not lay your hand:** The words used demanded an instant response. Abraham was just about to strike his son, then God stopped his hand (see 15:1). **now I know:** Certainly God knew ahead of time how this event would end. But in these words, God stood beside his servant Abraham, experiencing each moment with him and applauding his complete trust (18:19).

22:13 Abraham had not seen the **ram** until he looked for it. His earlier words of God's provision came to pass (v. 8).

22:14, 15 The-LORD-Will-Provide. God provided a ram instead of Abraham's son, so one day He would provide His own Son! Moriah is where Jerusalem and later the temple were built. And it was at Jerusalem that the Savior would die.

22:16 By Myself I have sworn: When a man took an oath, it was considered unchangeable (see 25:33). When God took an oath, His eternity guaranteed the fulfillment of His word.

22:17 blessing I will bless you: The doubling of these verbs and the ones that follow (**multiplying I will multiply**) is a Hebrew idiom that powerfully emphasizes the certainty of the action. **as the stars ... as the sand:** This promise from God's part (15:5; also 13:16) must have overwhelmed Abraham.

22:18 At times the term **seed** refers to a large number of descendants (as in 13:16); at other times it refers to one unique descendant, the Coming One (as here, also Gal. 3:16). Here the seed was Isaac.

22:19 As he had said (v. 5), Abraham **returned** with his son, and they all **went together** (v. 8) back to **Beersheba.**

22:20–24 Milcah: The family of Nahor had first been noted at 11:29. It is touching to observe that there was correspondence between the families; but this genealogical notice also leads to the birth of **Rebekah.**

23:1 Sarah's 127 years allowed her to see her son Isaac reach adulthood.

23:2 Kirjath Arba means the "Village of Four" (see Josh. 14:15). Abraham had lived for a while near **Hebron** at the location of some ancient terebinth trees (13:18; 18:1; 23:17). At this point the name **Canaan** would be particularly bitter to Abraham. He had negotiated for water rights and herding privileges (21:22–34), but the land was not his; it still belonged to the Canaanites (12:6).

23:3 The Hittites had their principal center in Anatolia (modern Turkey). But there were some enclaves of Hittites (**sons of Heth**) in Canaan (see 15:20), and it was with Hittites that Abraham negotiated to buy a burial spot for his beloved wife Sarah.

23:4, 5 I am a foreigner and a visitor: Abraham was a "resident alien" in the land. His words were self-deprecating, to help him establish a bargaining position.

23:6 The sons of Heth (Hittites) responded with complimentary words. The adjective **mighty** is the term for deity (*elohim* as in 1:1). The Hittites let Abraham use one of their places for the **burial** of his dead family members.

23:7–11 Abraham stood up and bowed: Abraham's posture followed the customs of the time (see also v. 12). Abraham was not willing to bury Sarah in a borrowed tomb; he wanted to have a place that would belong to his family long after his death.

23:12, 13 I will give you money: He was not interested in the field, and he offered again to buy the cave. Abraham was offering a generous weight of silver.

23:14, 15 The dialogue of the chapter presents a step-by-step description of the bargaining process. Ephron gave the purchase price, then seemed to dismiss it (**What is that between you and me?**).

23:16 Abraham weighed out the silver: He paid the agreed upon amount there would be no question at a later date.

23:17 Abraham had to purchase not only the **field** and the **cave,** but also the **trees.** All was done in the formal, legal manner of the time.

23:18–20 Abraham buried Sarah. Abraham would be buried in the same cave (25:10).

24:1, 2 Some have thought **the oldest servant** to be Eliezer of 15:2 because of his high position over all that Abraham had.

24:3 swear by the LORD: Such an oath indicated how exceedingly important the matter was to Abraham. **from the daughters of the Canaanites:** This was not an issue of racism, as is sometimes thought—it was theological. The Canaanite peoples worshiped the false gods Baal and Asherah (see 15:16; compare also Deut. 7:3).

24:4–7 Abraham repeated a major theme of God's covenant to him. His **descendants** would inherit the land.

24:8–10 The possession of **camels** in this ancient period was regarded as a mark of extraordinary wealth. **Mesopotamia** means

"Aram of the Two Rivers." The location is northern Syria beyond the Euphrates. The **city of Nahor** is known as Haran (11:31).

24:11, 12 O LORD God of my master Abraham: The Lord had made His covenant with Abraham. The servant was making his appeal on the basis of God's covenant loyalty to Abraham.

24:13–15 Rebekah's name may mean "Ensnaring Beauty." She was of the family circle of Abraham (22:20–23).

24:16–18 Such commentary on a woman's **beautiful** appearance is rare in the Bible. Her chastity is noted: **a virgin; no man had known her.** The word translated *virgin* is not a precise term; hence the clarification, "no man had known her."

24:19 I will draw water for your camels: This gesture went far beyond her social duties. This was precisely the proof that the servant had requested from the Lord.

24:20–25 Whose daughter are you?: After stating her family ties (v. 24; see 22:20–23), Rebekah responded that there was plenty of room for him to lodge with them (v. 25).

24:26 Abraham's servant was overwhelmed by God's grace, so he **worshiped the LORD.**

24:27 Blessed be the LORD: In these and the following words, Abraham's servant gave God true, public praise. **Mercy** and **truth** together mean something like "the Lord's utterly unswerving loyalty."

24:28, 29 Laban from appears to be a gentle servant of God, recognizing Abraham's servant with gracious hospitality (v. 31).

24:30–51 It is surprising that **Bethuel** the father was not more active in these proceedings (vv. 29–31). Laban, Rebekah's brother, seems to be the one making decisions. Brother and father recognized the work of God, and they responded graciously and immediately.

24:52 Before doing anything else, Abraham's servant **worshiped the LORD** by prostrating himself before God and by giving public acknowledgment of His provision (v. 26).

24:53–57 In the manner of the East and with the abundance that belonged to Abraham, the servant gave costly gifts of **jewelry,** first to Rebekah and then to her family.

24:58 Until now nothing had been said about Rebekah's desires, but her words **I will go** showed her willingness.

24:59 It was no easier for this family to **send away** their beloved daughter and sister **Rebekah** than it would be for us. This was an act of courage and faith in the Lord for all concerned.

24:60, 61 they blessed Rebekah: In the customs of the ancient Near East, the family gave a formal blessing on her wedded life (see Ruth 4:11, 12). These words are not mere sentiment nor are they a magical charm, but a prayer for God's blessing on her life. **The mother of thousands of ten thousands:** The term translated *ten thousands* means "myriads," "uncountable." It may be a play on the name Rebekah because in Hebrew the words sound similar.

24:62 Beer Lahai Roi was named in the story of Hagar's first expulsion from Abraham and Sarah's household (16:13, 14).

24:63–65 In the manner of the East, wearing **a veil** would have been appropriate behavior for a young, unmarried woman who was about to come into the company of a man.

24:66 From the earlier recital to Laban (vv. 32–49), we can imagine the enthusiasm of the **servant** speaking to Isaac.

24:67 Isaac brought Rebekah to his mother's **tent,** the preeminent place for a woman in the household. **his wife, and he loved her:** Isaac's sense of grief at the death of his mother was now replaced by joy in the newness of married love.

25:1 The Hebrew phrase **again took** can be interpreted as "had taken." **Keturah:** In Genesis she is call Abraham's wife. In 1 Chr. 1:32 she is called a concubine.

25:2 Midian was the father of the Midianites, some of whom later bought Joseph from his brothers (see 36:35; 37:28, 36).

25:3–5 Isaac received the grand share of his father's fortune; beyond that, he received the blessing of God (v. 11; 26:2–5).

25:6 The sons concubines: Abraham gave appropriate gifts to his lesser sons and sent them away.

25:7 God gave Abraham a long **life** as He had promised (see 12:2; 15:15).

25:8 gathered to his people: A burial. The phrase also indicates an afterlife.

25:9 Abraham purchased **the cave of Machpelah** for the burial of his wife **Sarah** (ch. 23).

25:10, 11 God blessed Isaac because He had already established "an everlasting covenant" with him (see 17:19; Heb. 11:17). Later God renewed the covenant with Isaac (26:2–5).

25:12–16 genealogy of Ishmael: This passage distinguishes Ishmael's line, the line of the natural son (16:10–15), from Isaac's line (starting at v. 19), the line of the son of promise. God fulfilled his promise to Abraham (17:20). The descendants of Ishmael had **twelve princes** to govern them, just as the Israelites were divided into twelve tribes (ch. 49).

25:17, 18 they dwelt: The descendants of Ishmael lived in a large area, including the Arabian peninsula and the desert land between Canaan and Mesopotamia.

25:19 genealogy of Isaac: There are ten significant genealogies in Genesis.

25:20 The story of the marriage of **Rebekah** and Isaac is recorded in ch. 24.

25:21 The Hebrew verb for **pleaded** indicates that Isaac prayed passionately for his wife. Isaac waited twenty years for God to grant his prayer (vv. 20, 26). **barren:** Rebekah experienced a period of infertility just like Sarah, Rachel, and Leah (see 16:1; 29:31; 30:9). After a period of barrenness, the LORD specifically gave each a child in the line of promise.

25:22 struggled: Rebekah's pregnancy was difficult. It seemed as though the two children were competing in her womb.

25:23 The LORD spoke directly to Rebekah (16:8–11). **two nations:** In the ancient Near East, the firstborn would have preeminence. But this time God chose to bless the **younger.**

25:24 The birth of **twins** was regarded as a special blessing.

25:25 The name **Esau** sounds like the Hebrew word that means "hairy."

25:26 The younger brother grasped for his older brother's **heel** from birth. The Hebrew word that means "heel" sounds similar to the name **Jacob.**

25:27 hunter ... mild man: The contrasting temperaments and interests of the two sons.

25:28 Isaac loved Esau: The following story illustrates the folly of parental favoritism.

25:29, 30 The ruddy color of his complexion (v. 25) was tied to his strong desire for the red food and later to the red land he inherited (36:8). Now Esau was known as "Red"—that is, **Edom.**

25:31, 32 Esau, as the firstborn, had a **birthright** to a double portion of the family estate. Moreover he inherited from Isaac the privilege of an everlasting covenant with God (Gen. 12:1–3).

25:33 swear to me: The formal oath, even though unwitnessed, would have been regarded as binding by both parties.

25:34 The Hebrew verb for **despised** implies utter contempt (Num. 15:31; 2 Sam. 12:9; Mal. 1:6). Esau scorned God's promises given to the heirs of Isaac.

26:1 An earlier famine occurred during the **days of Abraham** (12:10–20). The **Philistines** came to the coastland of Canaan following their defeat by the Egyptians around 1200 B.C. They were apparently Greek peoples who migrated eastward (see 1 Sam. 4:1; 2 Sam. 5:17).

26:2 The LORD appeared to Isaac for the first time on record. Interestingly, God had already spoken to Rebekah (see 25:22, 23). Even though Egypt's conditions may have been hospitable, the Lord prohibited Isaac from going **to Egypt** as his father had during the earlier famine (12:10).

26:3 bless you: The Lord established His everlasting covenant with Isaac, just as He had with Abraham.

26:4, 5 God promised to make Isaac's descendants **as the stars** because of Abraham's faithfulness (22:17). God promised to bless **all the nations** through Isaac's descendants.

26:6 Gerar was better for farming than the arid regions of the Negev.

26:7 Rebekah was a close relative, 22:20–23 but not Isaac's **sister.** Isaac was even more deceitful than his father Abraham.

26:8 showing endearment: This Hebrew wordplay on the name Isaac literally means "He Who Laughs was laughing with Rebekah his wife."

26:9, 10 how could you: A sense of moral outrage from the Philistine king.

26:11–13 The **Lord blessed** him so much that he became **very prosperous** and the envy of his neighbors.

26:14, 15 Abraham had made a covenant with Abimelech about the rights to **wells** (see 21:22–34). But enmity had led to acts of sabotage against these old wells.

26:16, 17 Although Isaac moved from **Gerar,** he did not leave the area.

26:18, 19 On the basis of Isaac's rights to the water in the area, his men **dug** new wells, giving these wells the same names as the old ones.

26:20, 21 Sitnah is related to the Hebrew term for "Satan."

26:22, 23 Isaac moved out of Gerar as the famine ended and water became more available. He returned **to Beersheba,** the land of his youth (22:19).

26:24 God of your father Abraham: God was faithful. He promised to the son what He had already promised to the father.

26:25 Isaac made **an altar** and called on **the name of the LORD:** At this altar Isaac not only prayed to the Lord; he also affirmed the reality of the living God in this special land (12:8; 21:33).

26:26 Abimelech came to end the animosity between his people and Isaac's because he recognized God's blessing on Isaac (vv. 28, 29).

26:27, 28 the LORD is with you: God's extraordinary blessing on His people would attract others to Himself (12:2, 3). The **covenant** formally bound both parties.

26:29, 30 ate and drank: This ceremonial meal expressed the new relationship and memorialized the alliance (27:3, 4; 31:46, 54).

26:31 peace: The Hebrew term *shalom* suggests that things were as they ought to be between the two parties.

26:32 Either a brand-new **well** or a redigging of Abraham's well at that location (21:30, 31). The discovery of **water** was regarded as a blessing from God on their actions.

26:33 Shebah: The name is a word-play on the Hebrew words that mean "swear" (v. 31) and "seven." The name **Beersheba** may mean either "Well of the Oath" or "Well of the Seven."

26:34, 35 Esau married Hittite women, who believed in many different gods. His parents wanted him to marry a woman who worshiped the living God (27:46; 28:8; 36:1–8).

27:1–3 Isaac was old: Isaac actually did not die for many years (35:27–29). His actions were precautionary. **his eyes:** Isaac's failed vision allowed Jacob and Rebekah to trick him (vv. 11–29). Ordinarily, a father would give the primary blessing to the firstborn, in this case **Esau** (25:29–34). Yet God worked contrary to cultural expectations and Isaac's favoritism (37:4).

27:4 Isaac wanted to memorialize his blessing on Esau with a ceremonial meal of **savory food** (see 27:30).

27:5–10 obey my voice: Rebekah wanted to circumvent the blessing that her husband planned to give to Esau. Here Rebekah appears to be calculating and devious. Yet God had told her that her younger son would have precedence over the older (25:23).

27:11, 12 Jacob wanted to know how he could pass as his brother. Esau had been **hairy** from birth (25:25). **deceiver:** Jacob feared that he would be discovered, not that he was doing wrong.

27:13–20 I am Esau: Jacob lied, then his lies led him to blasphemy.

27:21–26 come near: Isaac had to **feel** Jacob (vv. 21, 22), hear him (v. 22), question him (v. 24), **kiss** and **smell** him (vv. 26, 27) before he finally believed Jacob's repeated lies.

27:27–29 peoples serve you: Isaac prophesied that Jacob's descendants would obtain supremacy over other peoples. **mother's sons:** Isaac intended that Jacob would bow to Esau. Yet because of Jacob's deception, Isaac blessed Jacob instead. **Cursed ... blessed:** Isaac blessed Jacob with the words originally spoken by the Lord to Abram (12:3). Jacob became the heir to the everlasting covenant between Abraham's descendants and the Lord.

27:30–32 Who are you?: Surely Isaac recognized his older son's voice.

27:33 Isaac, in despair, realized he had been

duped by his own son. **he shall be blessed:** Isaac's words of blessing had power—indeed, they were backed by the power of the Lord (vv. 27–29). They could not be withdrawn.

27:34 He cried. Esau's anguish was unbearable. **Bless me:** Surely Isaac had reserved some blessing for Esau.

27:35 Jacob had stolen the blessing Isaac had intended for Esau. **deceit:** Later, Jacob would be deceived by his uncle Laban (29:25).

27:36–38 rightly named: One meaning of the name Jacob is "He Who Grasps at the Heel (of Another)." The **blessing** was for the firstborn son. Esau, as the firstborn, probably hoped to overcome the loss of his **birthright** (25:29–34) with Isaac's powerful blessing. As it turned out, Jacob achieved both. The blessing was irrevocable (v. 37).

27:39 Behold: The blessing for Esau was much weaker than the blessing for Jacob.

27:40 Esau's descendants would **serve** his **brother.** Yet eventually they would free themselves from domination.

27:41–45 Apparently Esau revealed his evil decision to someone. Again, **Rebekah** intervened. **Laban** was Rebekah's brother and **Haran** was her homeland (ch. 24). **bereaved:** Rebekah would lose both her sons if Esau killed Jacob. Sadly, she died before Jacob returned (31:18; 35:27–29).

27:46 daughters of Heth: Rebekah spoke to Isaac about Jacob's future wife because they had already regretted Esau's marrying Hittite women (26:34, 35).

28:1 Isaac agreed with Rebekah that intermarriage with the pagan women of **Canaan** was dangerous. These women would bring their own false gods into the household.

28:2 Padan Aram is a region of Haran in northern Aram (Syria) near the Euphrates River.

28:3 God Almighty: This Hebrew phrase, *El Shaddai,* is used by or in the hearing of Abraham, Isaac, and Jacob (35:11). God later identified Himself to Moses with this same name (Ex. 6:3).

28:4, 5 Isaac formally passed on to his son Jacob the **blessing** that God had first given to his father Abraham (12:1–3).

28:6–9 Esau attempted to find favor in Isaac's eyes by doing what Isaac wished. By marrying **Mahalath the daughter of Ishmael.** Sadly, Esau could not regain his lost blessing.

28:10–13 I am the Lord: God identified Himself as the God whom both Abraham and Isaac believed. Isaac, in his blessing, predicted Jacob would inherit this **land** (vv. 3, 4). Now God promised it!

28:14 The Lord ratified Isaac's blessing on Jacob's **descendants** (vv. 3, 4). **all the families:** Every time the covenant was renewed, God repeated His promise to show mercy to all people through Abraham's descendants (12:3; 22:18; 26:4).

28:15 I am with you: Jacob was running away from the consequences of his lies. Yet God promised to be with him.

28:16, 17 Afraid indicates a fear of God similar to terror. **Awesome** indicates a fear of God similar to wonder and worship (22:12; Ex. 20:20; Prov. 1:7). **house of God ... gate of heaven:** God and heaven had come down to the very place where Jacob was sleeping!

28:18 stone ... as a pillar: To commemorate the great event, Jacob set a stone on end and **poured oil on top** to consecrate it to God. Later he would refer to the Lord as "The Stone of Israel" (49:24).

28:19 Bethel means "House of God." God had also appeared to Abraham near Bethel (12:7–8).

28:20 vow: Although Jacob made a conditional promise to be faithful to God, he based it on God's promises to him (v. 15).

28:21, 22 Jacob promised to give **a tenth** of his possessions to God.

29:1 The **people of the East** were not Canaanites.

29:2–4 Shepherds would naturally gather at a **well.** Because God allowed a number of significant events to occur at wells, they become a symbol of God's blessing and care (see 16:14; 21:19, 30; 26:32; Is. 12:3; John 4:1–26).

29:5 The term **son** is being used in a loose sense. **Nahor** was actually the grandfather of **Laban** (22:20–23). Laban's father was Bethuel (24:15, 50).

29:6–8 Rachel is a term of endearment, meaning "Ewe Lamb." As the daughter of his mother's brother, Rachel was a cousin of Jacob.

29:9, 10 still speaking: Rachel's arrival at that moment is a mirror of Rebekah's action to Abraham's servant so long ago (24:15–20). Again, God's timing is perfect.

29:11 kissed Rachel: Doubtless Jacob had heard the story of his mother's encounter with the servant of Abraham many times. He knew their meeting was from God.

29:12–16 Leah was Rachel's older sister. Her name may be a term of endearment meaning "Wild Cow."

29:17 Delicate means a special loveliness in her eyes, or perhaps, a weakness. **beautiful of form:** Rachel's description is similar to the descriptions of Sarai (12:11) and of Rebekah (24:16).

29:18, 19 loved Rachel: A rare biblical example of "love at first sight." The **seven years** of service provides a stunning demonstration of the value Jacob placed on Rachel.

29:20, 21 seemed only a few days: A rare statement in the Bible on romantic love.

29:22 The Hebrew term **feast** indicates that there was drinking.

29:23 A public feast in recognition of the union made the marriage between Jacob and Leah official—even though Leah was the wrong woman.

29:24, 25 The Hebrew name **deceived** means "to act treacherously with" or "to betray" (1 Sam. 19:17). Jacob the deceiver had been deceived by Laban (27:35).

29:26 must not be done: The cultural necessity of Laban's actions is doubtful.

29:27 Laban deceived Jacob in order to get **another seven years'** work from him. Jacob loved Rachel so much that he was willing to work another seven years (v. 28).

29:28, 29 As did Zilpah (v. 24), **Bilhah** later served as a surrogate mother when Rachel was barren (30:3–8).

29:30, 31 Unloved actually means "hated." The Lord graciously enabled Leah to conceive a child because she was unloved. Although she was the beloved wife of Jacob, **Rachel** could not conceive. She desired Leah's ability to conceive, and Leah desired the love that Jacob showered on Rachel.

29:32 Leah praised God for giving her a son. Perhaps Leah joyfully shouted "Behold a Son!" at **Reuben**'s birth.

29:33 The name **Simeon** celebrates the fact that the Lord hears. He had heard Leah's prayers.

29:34, 35 Later, God chose the tribe of Levi to become priests and caretakers of the tabernacle. Then, the name **Levi** implied "Attached to the Lord."

30:1, 2 The Hebrew verb for **envied** describes a strong inner feeling of rage.

30:3–5 Rachel's desperation led her to bring her maid **Bilhah** to Jacob as a surrogate wife. This was accepted practice in the ancient Middle East to protect an infertile wife.

30:6 Dan: In giving a name related to the Hebrew word that means "judge," Rachel thanked the Lord for hearing and answering her pleas.

30:7, 8 With the name **Naphtali,** Rachel expressed the vehemence of her struggle with her sister.

30:9, 10 The now infertile Leah used her maid **Zilpah** to acquire more sons.

30:11–13 Leah was **happy** because of her numerous sons, so she named her son **Asher.**

30:14 Mandrakes are a special type of herb that the peoples of the ancient Middle East regarded as an aid to conception. Their aroma was associated with lovemaking (Song 7:13).

30:15–21 The name **Dinah** is related to the word that means "judgment."

30:22 Finally, God enabled Rachel to have a child. The three verbs, **remembered, listened,** and **opened,** emphasize that conception is a gift from God.

30:23 my reproach: In Rachel's culture a married woman without children was scorned.

30:24 By giving Rachel a son, God had removed her shame and brought joy to her life.

30:25 With the birth of **Joseph** by his beloved wife, Jacob was ready to go to his **own place.** God had promised to bring him back to his homeland (28:4, 15).

30:26 Laban had fathered sons who would threaten Jacob's status in the family (31:1). Hence he asked Laban to **let** him **go.**

30:27 God **blessed** Laban through Jacob.

30:28–31 name your wages: These words must have sounded hollow to Jacob, given his earlier experience in striking a deal with Laban (29:15–30; 31:7).

30:32 Presumably, the **speckled and spotted sheep** would be the smaller part of the flock. The deal was to Laban's advantage.

30:33–35 my righteousness: Jacob asserted his trustworthiness.

30:36 three days' journey: Jacob's and Laban's herds were separated so the animals would not mix. Jacob still tended **Laban's flocks.**

30:37–40 rods of green poplar: Jacob placed sticks of various colors in the watering troughs. God blessed Jacob as He had promised (28:13–15). Jacob added all the speckled and spotted animals to his own herd.

30:41–43 With the symbolic multicolored rods, Jacob asked God to bless him with speckled and spotted animals from the **stronger livestock** in Laban's herd. God promised to do that in a dream (31:10), and Jacob became wealthy (v. 43).

31:1 These sons probably were born to **Laban** after Jacob had arrived in Haran (30:26). Concerned about their welfare, the sons accused Jacob of being a thief.

31:2, 3 God repeated the promises He gave Jacob at Bethel. He promised to be with Jacob as he returned to his homeland.

31:4–8 speckled … streaked: Apparently, Laban kept on switching the deal as he watched the births of a variety of colored animals. But with every new deal, God always increased Jacob's herd.

31:9–11 God revealed Himself in Jacob's **dream** (see 28:13–17; 32:22–30). **Jacob:** In the past, Jacob ("He Who Supplants") had achieved what he wanted by deceit and trickery. Now he had achieved great wealth because of God's blessing.

31:12, 13 The Lord identified Himself as the same God who had revealed Himself to Jacob at **Bethel** (see 28:10–19).

31:14 Rachel and Leah agreed that it was proper to leave their father's home (30:26). The births of sons to their father may have displaced their **inheritance.**

31:15 Both daughters resented the way their father had **sold** them (29:15). Furthermore, they argued that whatever God had taken from their father belonged to them anyway.

31:16–19 household idols: In this culture, possession of the household idols was the right of the principal heir. Rachel probably did not steal the idols in order to worship them, but to retain the rights of the principal heir for Jacob.

31:20–24 in a dream: From time to time, God warned others not to harm His people.

31:25, 26 The sudden departure, Laban charges, was similar to a raiding party that took **captives.**

31:27–29 God of your father: Only God's warning in v. 24 stilled Laban's rage.

31:30–32 Jacob explained that he left in secret because of a genuine fear that he would not be permitted to leave with his family. Furthermore, he declared his household innocent of the alleged theft and cursed the thief of the idols with death.

31:33 Laban, certain that Jacob had stolen the idols, began his search in **Jacob's tent.** Last, he entered **Rachel's tent.** The fact that each wife had her own tent indicates that Jacob was rich.

31:34, 35 Rachel hid the idols in her saddle bags and sat on them while she made her excuses. Laban did not ask Rachel to move because of a male taboo respecting a woman who was experiencing her monthly period.

31:36 Jacob, in his anger, recited the woes of working for Laban. **Trespass** means to "overstep a boundary." **Sin** means "to miss a target" (as an archer might do).

31:37 they may judge: Jacob had some leverage. Laban had been humiliated before his own men. His resolve to stop Jacob necessarily had to weaken.

31:38 Jacob had served 14 years for his two wives (29:15–30). After that, he worked another six years for his flocks (see v. 41). **not miscarried:** Here, Jacob affirmed his superior skills in managing the herds and God's blessing.

31:39–41 Jacob never charged Laban for any **loss** so that he could never charge Jacob for mismanagement. Furthermore, Jacob described the seasonal extremes that he suffered.

31:42 The Fear of Isaac: This name for God means that Isaac feared God with a reverential awe (Ps. 119:120).

31:43 Laban considered Jacob's **children** part of his extended family.

31:44 Covenant in this situation refers to a parity covenant—an agreement between equals.

31:45–48 Jacob, for a second time, set up a **stone** as a memorial. On the way to Haran at Bethel, he had already set up a pillar to mark the place where God spoke to him (28:18).

31:49, 50 Mizpah means "Outlook Point" and is related to the Hebrew word that means "to watch." God above had His eyes on both men to make them keep their covenant!

31:51, 52 The **heap** and the **pillar** were a double **witness** between the two men. Neither was to cross these symbols in order to **harm** the other.

31:53 The wording in Laban's oath suggests that Abraham, Nahor, and their father Terah all worshiped the same God, **the God of Abraham.**

31:54, 55 Jacob offered a sacrifice: This is the only time Genesis records Jacob engaging in sacrificial worship (compare 12:7, 8; 22:13).

32:1 the angels of God: In a magnificent display of His care for him, God allowed Jacob to see that he was not traveling alone.

32:2 Jacob discovered that God's armies were encamped around his family's camp.

32:3–5 Jacob sent **messengers** to Esau with a report of his life over the last 20 years and with a request for **favor,** that is, grace.

32:6 Jacob viewed his brother's coming as a threat to his family, particularly when he learned that **four hundred men** were with him!

32:7 Here, the Hebrew term for **afraid** refers to fright or terror (see 31:42). Jacob divided his family into two groups in order to save one from the rage of his brother.

32:8–11 Jacob prayed to God that he might be delivered from Esau's rage. The Hebrew term for **father** indicates either the immediate father or a more remote male ancestor. By mentioning both **Isaac** and Abraham,

Jacob appealed to the God who had spoken to his fathers. Then Jacob confessed his humility before God's mercy in the words **I am not worthy.**

32:12–21 a present for Esau: Jacob had prayed in faith; now he acted in faith. He gave Esau an overabundance of gifts. By giving the gifts at three different times, Jacob hoped to appease Esau gradually.

32:22–24 Some believe that the **Man** who **wrestled** Jacob was the pre-incarnate Jesus Christ. Others believe the Man was the Angel of God (Gen. 21:17; 31:11). In any case, Jacob wrestled with a manifestation of God (vv. 28–30), and because of God's mercy he survived.

32:25, 26 He did not prevail: The Man could not turn Jacob away from the struggle. This Hebrew verb translated **touched** refers to God's special touch. Here, God's touch caused pain (see Josh. 9:19; 2 Sam. 14:10). Yet Jacob would not release the Man until he received a blessing.

32:27, 28 God gave Jacob a new name, **Israel,** meaning "Prince with God," or perhaps it carries the idea of struggling or persisting.

32:29 Jacob asks for the Man's **name** because Jacob had given his name. The Man does not answer. But Jacob might have developed his own name for the Man who had wrestled with him: "The Mighty God of Jacob" (see 49:24).

32:30, 31 Jacob's experience with God physically changed him—he **limped.** The experience also had a spiritual impact on his life.

32:32 to this day: The Jewish rule against eating this muscle continues into modern times.

33:1 For all Jacob knew, **Esau was coming** with 400 men to destroy his family.

33:2 maidservants and their children in front: Jacob aligned his family in a pattern that would protect them. He placed his favorite wife, Rachel, in the rear.

33:3 bowed himself: Jacob expressed his sorrow for the way he had wronged Esau.

33:4–9 Instead of taking his revenge, **Esau** welcomed Jacob with joy. The event turned into a grand family reunion.

33:10 your face as … face of God: Jacob presented his gifts to his brother as if they were gifts to God.

33:11–16 take my blessing: Before, Jacob had done all he could to take Esau's blessing (25:29–34; 27:1–45). Now a wiser man, Jacob wanted to restore the broken relationship with his brother.

33:17 Jacob stopped his journey and built temporary shelters east of the Jordan River.

33:18 Shechem (12:6): Jacob did not live in the city, because it was devoted to pagan gods. Instead, he lived outside the city in a **tent.**

33:19 Jacob bought a **parcel of land.** Even though God promised the entire land to Abraham's family (see 12:7), they had to buy it one little piece at a time.

33:20 Jacob, now named Israel, built an **altar** for the worship of the Lord, just as his grandfather had (see 12:7). The name he gave the altar reflected his mature faith in "God, the God of Israel."

34:1 Apparently **Dinah** was Leah's only daughter (30:21). It was natural for her to seek the companionship of other women.

34:2 Shechem noticed Dinah and forced her to have intercourse. Despite what he did, Shechem **loved** Dinah.

34:3, 4 Shechem's appeal to his father suggests that marriages were commonly arranged by parents.

34:5 When Jacob heard, he must have been enraged. The verb translated **defiled** means "to make unclean."

34:6–17 uncircumcised: Here, Jacob's sons took the symbol of their holy faith (see 17:9–14) and used it as a weapon against their foes.

34:18, 19 Shechem proved his love for Dinah by his willingness to undergo circumcision as an adult.

34:20–29 Most likely, Jacob's other **sons** joined Simeon and Levi in plundering the city.

34:30, 31 Jacob rebuked his sons for their terrible behavior (done in the name of the Lord). Instead of making the family a blessing to other nations (12:3), they were making the family **obnoxious** to its neighbors.

35:1 God, for a fifth time, visited Jacob. After the debacle at Shechem (ch. 34), God told Jacob to continue **to Bethel** (28:10–19). This is the first time in the Bible that God commanded **an altar** to be made for Him.

35:2 Jacob's command included the household idols that Rachel had stolen (31:22–35) as well as any idols among his servants. **purify yourselves, and change your garments:** Jacob's household prepared for an encounter with the living and holy God.

35:3 I will make an altar: Jacob declared his intention to obey God's command (v. 1). **who answered me … has been with me:** Jacob recalled God's constant protection (ch. 32) and His fulfillment of His promises (28:13–15) as a reason to obey and worship God.

35:4 As suggested by the nearby phrase **foreign gods,** these **earrings** probably represented some form of idolatry. Because the **terebinth** tree lived a long time, ancient people often used it to commemorate important events or to mark places of worship (see Hos. 4:13).

35:5 God protected Jacob's family as they traveled. The Hebrew term for **terror** is related to the verb meaning "to be shattered" or "to be dismayed."

35:6 Luz … Bethel: The change of name is explained at 28:19 (see also Josh. 18:13; Judg. 1:23).

35:7 El Bethel: Naming **an altar** added to the solemnity of the worship conducted there (see 22:14).

35:8 Deborah was a nurse of Rebekah (see 24:59). Deborah had already died, but at this point the family commemorated her death and buried her at Bethel.

35:9 God renewed His everlasting covenant with Jacob (see 15:1–21).

35:10 God validated Jacob's change of **name** and reaffirmed His promises to him. Now Jacob would be called Israel (32:28).

35:11, 12 This is the third use of the name, *El Shaddai,* **God Almighty** (see 17:1; 28:3; compare Ex. 6:3). God used His great name to attest His strong relationship with Jacob.

35:13 God went up: The living God had made His will known and now returned to His abode.

35:14 This is the second **pillar** Jacob set up

to commemorate God's revelation at Bethel (28:18). **drink offering:** Jacob consecrated the pillar by pouring wine and **oil** over it.

35:15, 16 Ephrath is an alternative name for the region around Bethlehem (v. 19; 48:7; compare Ruth 1:3; Mic. 5:2).

35:17, 18 fear: Rachel's sorrow and fear that her second son might be stillborn became a symbol for all mothers who fear for their child's life. Jacob's name for his new son **Benjamin** indicates his youngest son's special place in the family—at Jacob's right hand.

35:19 Rachel was the only one of the principal characters in Abraham's family of promise who was not **buried** at the cave of Machpelah (23:19, 20).

35:20 Jacob had set up pillars to mark the Lord's great works in his. Here he erected a **pillar** to mark his sorrow.

35:21 Eder means "flock." This flock tower is mentioned only here and perhaps in Mic. 4:8.

35:22–26 Reuben, Jacob's firstborn son, may have been asserting his right to be the principal heir. By sleeping with his father's concubine, he was asserting that he would succeed his father. Ironically, this very action caused him to lose the blessing he desired (see 49:3, 4).

35:27, 28 After more than twenty years of absence, **Jacob** finally visited his **father.** Sadly, his mother Rebekah was probably dead.

35:29 gathered to his people: Isaac's formerly feuding sons, **Esau and Jacob,** joined together to bury Isaac with his father and mother in the cave at Machpelah (see 49:31).

36:1 . At birth, **Esau** was notably ruddy in color (25:25) and he was called **Edom,** meaning "Red" (v. 8).

36:2, 3 Because Esau took **his wives from the daughters of Canaan,** his family would be no different from other families of Canaan.

36:4–11 Genesis describes the growth of Esau's family and possessions. He moved to **Mount Seir.** Eventually, the region would be named after Esau—Edom, the "Red" land (v. 43).

36:12–19 Timna's son, **Amalek,** founded a people that later would trouble the Israelites (see Num. 14:39–45).

36:20–30 The people of **Seir,** the Horites, had close interrelationships with Esau's family.

36:31–39 This list follows the list of the chiefs of **Edom** (vv. 15–19). The eight names in this list are unrelated, indicating that they were chosen for reasons other than royal descent.

36:40–43 Esau was the father of the Edomites: Although Esau is not the heir of God's everlasting covenant with the family of Abraham, God still blessed his family. They too became a nation.

37:1 The word for **stranger** can also mean "sojourner" or "alien."

37:2 a bad report: Joseph was probably not slandering his brothers, but accurately reporting some negligence on their part. Whatever his intentions, his brothers resented him.

37:3 son of his old age: Jacob's favoritism for his son Joseph may be explained as well by the special love he had for the boy's mother (29:30). **a tunic of many colors:** The robe was distinctive in color or design and was probably costly.

37:4 they hated him: Jacob's discriminatory actions made Joseph unpopular in the family!

37:5, 6 Joseph told his family about his **dream.** Although the dream was prophetic, it alienated his brothers **even more.**

37:7 my sheaf arose: Joseph's dream pictured the prominence that he would eventually have in the family.

37:8 shall you indeed reign: The brothers understood immediately the meaning of Joseph's dream. Of course what they and he could not have known was that this dream would be fulfilled literally.

37:9 Joseph's second dream was even more alarming. According to this dream, even the sun and moon, presumably his father and mother, would bow to Joseph.

37:10, 11 Now, even **his father** was insulted by Joseph's behavior. **kept the matter:** Jacob pondered Joseph's dreams for they were clearly from God.

37:12, 13 The brothers journeyed north from Hebron (see 35:27–29), to find better pastures for their flocks.

37:14–16 bring back word: Because Joseph had earlier brought back a bad report, he would not be welcomed by his brothers.

37:17 Dothan is about ten miles north of Shechem, near Mt. Gilboa.

37:18 saw him a far off: His distinctive tunic allowed the brothers to recognize Joseph at a distance (vv. 3, 23, 31). **to kill him:** His brothers' hatred and envy led them to discuss murder (see vv. 4, 5, 8, 11).

37:19, 20 this dreamer: The Hebrew phrase expresses contempt and literally means "master of dreams." The brothers feared that Joseph's **dreams** may actually come true. By killing him, they could prevent this.

37:21 Reuben, intervened to spare Joseph's life.

37:22–24 shed no blood: Reuben attempted to save Joseph's life by getting his brothers to leave Joseph in a pit. Reuben planned to rescue him in time. Once Reuben convinced his brothers not to kill Joseph, he left (v. 29).

37:25 The **Ishmaelites** were wandering traders. The name **Ishmaelites** (referring to descendants of Ishmael is loosely equivalent to the name Midianite (v. 28).

37:26 What profit: The brothers started discussing how they could make the crime profitable.

37:27, 28 Twenty shekels of silver may have been the going rate for a slave at the time.

37:29, 30 Reuben returned, failed to find Joseph, and tore his clothes to express his grief.

37:31, 32 The brothers used **Joseph's tunic** as a grisly symbol of his supposed death.

37:33 torn to pieces: The fact that only the tunic was found suggested the destruction of Joseph's body.

37:34 Jacob **tore his clothes** just like Reuben did to express his sorrow.

37:35 I shall go down into the grave: Joseph's loss made Jacob love him more and withdraw from the rest of the family.

37:36 Potiphar: An Egyptian name. **captain of the guard:** May mean the palace guard. Potiphar was an important official in the Egyptian royal court.

38:1 Judah departed from his brothers: Judah, the fourth son of Leah, left the family circle and sought Canaanite friends.

38:2 daughter of a certain Canaanite: Judah then took a Canaanite woman, the daughter of **Shua,** as his wife.

38:3–5 Three sons were born to Judah and the daughter of Shua. **Chezib** is probably three miles southwest of Adullam.

38:6 Judah now he found a Canaanite wife, Tamar, for his firstborn son, **Er.** In this way, Judah intermingled his family with the Canaanites.

38:7 The Lord judged Er, the **wicked** firstborn son of Judah.

38:8 to your brother's wife: In order to maintain the family line and the name of the deceased, a brother or another near relative would marry the man's widow and father a child that would carry on the man's family. This is called *levirate* marriage, from a Latin word meaning "husband's brother." The custom became part of the Mosaic Law (Deut. 25:5–10; Ruth 4:1–12).

38:9 emitted on the ground: Because of his own selfishness and wicked attitude toward his deceased brother, Onan would not allow his brother's widow to conceive a child.

38:10 The LORD judged Onan, just as He judged Er (v. 7).

38:11 Remain a widow: Judah blamed the innocent Tamar. He feared that he would lose his last son. So Judah stalled her by insincerely promising to marry her to his last son when he was of age.

38:12 The death of **Judah's wife** means that Judah had only one surviving son. Unless Judah remarried, his posterity was dependant on Shelah.

38:13–16 Tamar's continuing use of a **widow's** clothing shows her desire to marry the surviving brother of her husbands. She wore **a veil** to avoid Judah's detection. Her desperate act was driven by a sense of injustice.

38:17 Judah's promise to give her a goat would ordinarily have been sufficient. However, Tamar insisted on **a pledge.**

38:18 The **signet** seal was an ancient means of identification. The seal was distinctively etched in stone, metal, or ivory and would hang on a person's neck.

38:19 garments of her widowhood: Tamar resumed wearing the clothing of a widow.

38:20 the young goat: By the time Hirah (see vv. 1, 12) came to pay what Judah had promised (see v. 17), Tamar had already left.

38:21 Harlot translates a Hebrew term that literally means "holy woman" and refers to sacred or cultic prostitutes.

38:22–24 played the harlot: After about three months, Tamar's pregnancy was showing. Judah seized the opportunity to get rid of Tamar, demanding that she **be burned.**

38:25, 26 She has been more righteous: Judah confessed his sins.

38:27 The birth of **twins** was a special blessing from the Lord.

38:28 his hand: The midwife used a scarlet thread to make sure everyone knew which baby had been born first.

38:29 breach: The other baby burst forth after his brother's hand had been withdrawn. Perez was the firstborn. He became the one who is in the lineage of David—and ultimately Jesus (Ruth 4:18; Matt. 1:3).

38:30 Both Perez and **Zerah** established families in the house of Judah (1 Chr. 2:3–8); even Shelah established a family (see Num. 26:19–22). Tamar became a member of the family of promise, even though she was a Canaanite. Matthew mentions Tamar in the lineage of the Messiah.

39:1 Joseph had been taken down to Egypt: This verse repeats the sense of 37:36 and resumes the Joseph story that was interrupted by the story of Judah and Tamar (ch. 38). **Potiphar:** Because of God's blessing, Joseph was sold to a rich and important royal official.

39:2 The Lord was with Joseph: God cared for, protected, and blessed Joseph. He occupied a very high station for a slave.

39:3 Potiphar recognized that Joseph was successful because **the Lord was with him.**

39:4 found favor: Joseph exemplified the faithful steward and illustrated that one who is faithful in a little will be given charge over much (Matt. 25:21; 1 Cor. 4:2).

39:5 the Lord blessed the Egyptian's house: Here Joseph brought God's blessing to an Egyptian official's home.

39:6 all that he had: Potiphar's trust in Joseph was so complete that Potiphar had no care except for his menu.

39:7 Potiphar's **wife** began to flirt with Joseph. The Hebrew term translated as *officer* in v. 1 ordinarily means "eunuch." If Potiphar was a eunuch, this might help to explain his wife's actions.

39:8 But he refused: Joseph exemplified the highest standard of personal behavior.

39:9, 10 sin against God: Here Joseph not only stood up for his beliefs, but he also told a woman who probably believed in many gods about the righteousness of the one true God!

39:11 none of the men: The master's wife caught Joseph alone.

39:12, 13 She grabbed Joseph. In the ensuing struggle, she wound up holding **his garment.** Joseph fled.

39:14–18 he has brought: She insulted her husband in front of other slaves. The term **Hebrew** is used here as a racial slur. **to mock:** The verb suggests racial hatred. The charge of attempted rape of a master's wife by a foreign slave would have been an exceptional outrage.

39:19 The **anger** of Potiphar is understandable and expected.

39:20 into the prison: Surprisingly, Potiphar did not kill Joseph outright. Is it possible that Potiphar did not fully believe the story his wife told him? In any case, Joseph wound up in prison for something he had refused to do.

39:21, 22 The Lord continued to be **with Joseph** in prison. **Mercy** can be translated *loyal love* (see Ps. 13:5). Here in a Egyptian prison, Joseph experienced God's loyal love. **the keeper of the prison:** This was the warden who was under the "captain of the guard" (40:3), namely, Potiphar (see 39:1).

39:23 the Lord made it prosper: Because of God's blessing, everything Joseph did prospered.

40:1, 2 The butler and the baker of the king were important offices in the royal court. **Offended** stands for the word ordinarily translated as *sinned.* The nature of their offenses is not explained.

40:3 The reference to **the house** implies a type of house arrest associated with, but not in, the prison itself.

40:4 As a trustee of the prison, Joseph also **served** the high officials who were under house arrest awaiting the disposition of the charges against them.

40:5 Each ... dream had **its own interpretation;** they contained symbols that demanded explanation.

40:6 Joseph came to see the butler and baker because it was part of his duties as the prison trustee.

40:7, 8 Joseph's statement that **interpretations belong to God** was a bold testimony. But Joseph not only announced his faith; he then quickly acted upon it.

40:9–12 Joseph's words to the butler, **lift up your head,** form a grisly pun in the passage. Here they speak of the restoration of the butler to his former honor; in v. 19 they speak of death.

40:13, 14 Joseph asked the butler to **remember me.** Joseph spoke of a binding obligation that his interpretation of the dream had placed upon the butler.

40:15 Presumably the butler would recognize the unfairness of Joseph's condition, since he had been unfairly charged as well.

40:16, 17 Perhaps **the chief baker's** sensed that the time was right to announce his own dream. Both of these men respected Joseph's interpretations as true.

40:18 The interpretation of the baker's dream was bad news indeed: In three days the baker would be executed.

40:19 lift off your head: Literally, "Pharaoh will lift your head ... *from you.*" It is not simply baked goods **the birds** will eat (v. 17), but the flesh of the baker.

40:20–22 Pharaoh brought both of the prisoners. The one he restored (v. 21), and the other he hanged (v. 22). Pharaoh did this in the presence of **all of Pharaoh's servants** in order to both warn and encourage the servant household.

40:23 The butler **did not remember** his promise made to Joseph.

41:1 Pharaoh had an unusual **dream** to which he attached great significance. **The river** is the Nile, the life stream of Egypt.

41:2 In ancient Semitic thought, the number **seven** had special significance, which probably had its roots in the seven days of creation (ch. 1).

41:3, 4 ugly and gaunt: The second group of seven cows contrasts strongly with the first. **ate up:** The scrawny cows devour the healthy ones.

41:5–7 The **second** dream was very much like the first, only this time it presented heads of grain. The numeral **seven** again was prominent.

41:8 magicians: The Hebrew term is related to the word for *stylus,* a writing instrument. Thus, the magicians were associated with writing and knowledge The **wise men** were either functionaries of pagan religions as here, or observers and interpreters of life.

41:9 faults: At last the butler remembered his experience with the young Hebrew prisoner who interpreted his dream (40:9–15).

41:13, 14 out of the dungeon: Joseph was manager of the prison (39:22, 23). Egyptian men not only **shaved** their face, but their entire body.

41:15 you can understand a dream: Pharaoh was desperate. He wanted a correct interpretation of his dream.

41:16 Joseph praised the power of the living God in the pagan court of Pharaoh. **an answer of peace:** His answer suggests that Joseph already knew the dream contained some good news for the Pharaoh.

41:17–24 in my dream: Pharaoh repeated the information he had given earlier to his own magicians and wise men (41:1–8; compare vv. 1–4).

41:25 God has shown Pharaoh: God sent the dreams; God enabled Joseph to understand them; and ultimately God controlled all things.

41:26–28 God has shown Pharaoh: The repetition of this phrase (v. 25) is for emphasis (v. 32).

41:29, 30 the plenty will be forgotten: The famine would be so severe that everyone would forget the years of plenty.

41:31, 32 God, and God: Joseph made it clear that he was speaking about the one God, not the numerous false gods that filled the Egyptian court.

41:33 a discerning and wise man: An exceedingly wise man.

41:34 One-fifth may seem large. However, the large amount would allow for spoilage, for trade, and grain to plant after the famine.

41:35 Pharaoh would view this large tax as an expansion of his own **authority.**

41:36–38 in whom is the Spirit of God: Pharaoh testified to the reality of God's power in Joseph's life.

41:39, 40 You shall be over my house: Joseph was the first choice for administering the collection of grain. **in regard to the throne:** Only Pharaoh was above him.

41:41, 42 With the **signet ring,** Joseph's orders would have the same authority as the word of Pharaoh (Esth. 3:10; 8:2). The ring had the signature of the Pharaoh in Egyptian hieroglyphics (38:18). Joseph would use the ring to mark clay or wax to authenticate royal documents and laws.

41:43, 44 Bow the knee: The Egyptian people bowed as a sign of respect and homage to Joseph's position—not a sign of worship.

41:45 Zaphnath-Paaneah: Pharaoh honors Joseph by giving him an Egyptian name that probably means "The God Speaks and Lives," and refers to the true God of Joseph. **Asenath:** An Egyptian name meaning "Belonging to (the Goddess) Neith." **On** is a city in northern Egypt. Although Joseph married a pagan priest's daughter, he trained his sons to worship the living God.

41:46 thirty years old: Thirteen years had passed since Joseph was sold by his brothers (37:2).

41:47 seven plentiful years: Just as God had revealed, the years of plenty came.

41:48, 49 The task was enormous for there was **much grain.** The skills he learned in Potiphar's household and in the royal prison must have been helpful. But in the end, God made Joseph succeed (v. 52; 39:23).

41:50–53 Asenath's **two sons** carry on the two-son motif in Genesis.

41:54, 55 the seven years of famine: As Joseph had warned (41:30), bad years followed the seven years of plenty.

41:56, 57 all countries: The whole known world came to Egypt to buy grain.

42:1 Jacob said to his sons: Judah had returned to Jacob (see ch. 38).

42:2–4 Benjamin: Jacob still played favorites

(see 37:3). However, there is no mention of jealousy among the other brothers (37:8).

42:5, 6 bowed before him: God fulfilled the dreams He gave to Joseph at the age of 17 (see 37:5–11).

42:7, 8 acted as a stranger: These men standing before Joseph had sold him as a slave 20 years before! Now here they were, bowing before him, just as he had dreamed! What went through Joseph's mind as he recognized his brothers? No doubt shock, confusion, and anger. Joseph may have **spoke roughly** in order to control his emotions.

42:9–12 Joseph **remembered the dreams.** He accused his brothers of something he knew they did not do. In this way, Joseph set out to learn whether his brothers had changed.

42:13 the youngest: At the mention of his younger brother, Benjamin, Joseph must have had great difficulty hiding his feelings. **and one is no more:** Although his brothers supposed he was dead, he was right before their eyes!

42:14, 15 Twice, Joseph accused them of being **spies.** The brothers must have been overcome with fear. They were standing before a man who had absolute, autocratic power. At his word they could be executed.

42:16, 17 Joseph demanded that Benjamin, his full **brother,** be brought to him. At the time, Benjamin was with Jacob (v. 4).

42:18–20 Here, Joseph gave his brothers a clue about who he was. In effect, Joseph told them, "I fear the one **God**" (see 41:32).

42:21 truly guilty: The brothers realized that they were being punished for what they had done to Joseph so many years ago.

42:22 Only **Reuben** had tried to save Joseph on that awful day (37:22). **his blood:** According to Reuben, the brothers would be punished for killing Joseph.

42:23 Joseph had been speaking in Egyptian and an interpreter was translating to the brothers. The brothers did not suspect that this Egyptian official **understood** what they said in their own language.

42:24 wept: At last Joseph's emotions went beyond his control. **he took Simeon:** Joseph took Simeon hostage (35:23–26).

42:25–27 fill their sacks: The returned money would enable the brothers to come another time for another purchase. On the other hand, they might be accused of stealing it.

42:28 The discovery of some of their **money** frightened the brothers (but see v. 35).

42:29–34 The brothers truthfully reported to their father **Jacob** all that had transpired.

42:35 The discovery of the **money** in the sack of one of the brothers (vv. 27, 28) could have been explained as a mistake. But now they learned that each man's money was in his sack!

42:36 You have bereaved me: Jacob's grief increased. One son was dead; another was in prison; and now a third was threatened by an Egyptian official.

42:37 Kill my two sons: Reuben took the lead. He tried to comfort his father, just as he had tried to stop his brothers from hurting Joseph (37:22).

42:38 My son shall not go: Jacob was resolute. He didn't want to risk Benjamin, his favorite.

43:1–7 deal so wrongfully: Jacob blamed his sons for telling the Egyptian there was still another brother. His sons replied that they had simply answered the questions they were asked.

43:8 Send the lad with me: Judah promised that he would keep Benjamin safe. Judah had changed tremendously. Instead of leaving the family, he protected his brother and was concerned about his father's welfare.

43:9–13 Blame is from the Hebrew verb often translated as *sin* (see 40:1; 41:9).

43:14 God is called *El Shaddai* (see 17:1; 28:3; 35:11). **If I am bereaved:** Jacob finally realized there was no other option.

43:15–18 The brothers must have been surprised Joseph invited them into his house to **dine** with him.

43:19–23 The steward did not accuse the brothers of anything; instead, he invited them into the house with a blessing of **peace.**

43:24–26 For the second time (42:6) the brothers of Joseph **bowed** down to him, just as his dreams had predicted (37:5–11).

43:27–29 Benjamin: The relationship between Joseph and his younger brother must have been particularly close, since Joseph was overwhelmed when he saw Benjamin (v. 30).

43:30–32 place by himself: Joseph followed the Egyptian custom of eating at a table separate from the Hebrews. **abomination:** This word can indicate the strongest revulsion, something that might cause physical illness (see 46:34).

43:33, 34 according to his birthright: The brothers might have been surprised that they had been seated according to their ages.

44:1–5 Joseph continued to test the character of his brothers by commanding his servants to place his brothers' **money** in their sacks and a **silver cup** in Benjamin's sack.

44:6–12 Joseph's brothers insisted on their innocence and promised to give up whoever had Joseph's silver cup. After searching all the brothers' sacks, the servant found the cup with Benjamin.

44:13 In genuine despair for Benjamin's predicament, the brothers **tore their clothes.** They could not let Benjamin die!

44:14 Although Reuben was the oldest, **Judah** took the leadership role in this section (46:28).

44:15 Here, **divination** is the practice of consulting the will of the gods by observing the liquid in a special cup. Allegedly Benjamin had stolen not only a silver cup from an Egyptian ruler, but a significant one.

44:16 Judah offered no excuse; what had happened was the will of **God.** He presented himself and all his brothers as slaves to Joseph.

44:17 Joseph demanded that Benjamin become his slave. Joseph's parting words, **go up in peace to your father,** were a test. Would the brothers leave Benjamin as a slave in Egypt?

44:18–34 Judah explained to Joseph the deep despair his father would experience if he lost Benjamin. Judah offered his own life to save Benjamin's.

45:1, 2 Joseph **wept** so loudly that his voice was heard throughout the whole palace (46:29)!

45:3 I am Joseph: Joseph must have said this in Hebrew. Still, the brothers could not believe their ears.

45:4 Joseph told his brothers to **come** closer so they could recognize his face and voice. He identified himself as the brother whom they had **sold.**

45:5–7 God sent me before you to preserve life: God had worked through the brothers' evil actions to preserve not only Jacob's family, but also the lives of many in the ancient world.

45:8 Joseph repeated that **God** had accomplished His good purpose through the evil actions of his brothers.

45:9, 10 Joseph told his brothers that they must live in Egypt during the famine.

45:11 I will provide for you: Joseph could make sure his family had enough during the famine.

45:12, 13 my mouth: Joseph still had to convince his brothers that he was really their brother.

45:14 Benjamin was Joseph's only full brother. Finally they were reunited.

45:15–20 Because Joseph was preserving the nation from destruction, Pharaoh was providing the **best** for Joseph.

45:21 Joseph sent his brothers back to his father with the Pharaoh's blessing and many gifts.

45:22 Benjamin, received the greatest blessing.

45:23–28 before I die: Jacob could see his favorite son, whom he had believed to be dead.

46:1 Jacob's **journey** to Egypt began a 400-year sojourn away from the Promised Land of Canaan. Jacob entered Egypt with his twelve sons, including Joseph; 400 years later Jacob's descendants would leave Egypt as a small nation. At **Beersheba,** Jacob **offered sacrifices** and consecrated his family to the Lord before he left the Promised Land.

46:2 God appeared to **Israel** for the seventh time (35:1, 9).

46:3 Jacob's family numbered 70 (v. 27). Out of this family, God would bring **a great nation** (Ex. 1:1–7). Again, God renewed His promises to Jacob (35:11).

46:4–7 go down with you: God promised to be with His people—even in a foreign land. **Joseph will put:** God promised Jacob that his beloved Joseph would be with him at his deathbed.

46:8 Reuben: Jacob's firstborn lost the right of the firstborn because of his sin with Bilhah (35:22; 49:3, 4).

46:9, 10 Shaul, the son of a Canaanite woman: Only Simeon and Judah married Canaanite women (Joseph's wife is Egyptian).

46:11 The sons of **Levi, Gershon, Kohath, and Merari** became the founders of the Levitical families (Ex. 6:16–19). The sons of Kohath became the founders of the priestly family, from which Aaron and Moses descended (Ex. 6:20–25).

46:12–14 The story of **Judah**'s family, including the untimely deaths of **Er and Onan,** is found in ch. 38.

46:15 Dinah's sad story is reported in ch. 34.

46:16–26 The total is **sixty-six,** and when Jacob, Joseph, and Joseph's two sons are added, the grand total is **seventy.**

46:27, 28 Jacob treated **Judah** as the leader among the brothers

46:29 Joseph went to meet his family in **Goshen,** where they would settle.

46:30 Now let me die: Jacob's reunion with his son Joseph was the crowning event of his long life. Jacob lived for 17 more years (47:28).

46:31–34 These verses show Joseph's leadership ability. **Abomination** is a term referring to the strongest revulsion and distaste.

47:1–6 Joseph's plan worked. Pharaoh let Jacob's family live in **Goshen,** an area in the Nile delta that is well watered The Egyptians detested **shepherds** (see 46:31–34).

47:7–10 The presentation of Joseph's father **before Pharaoh** must have been a grand occasion. **Jacob blessed Pharaoh.** Pharaoh as the host might have pronounced a blessing on Jacob. But instead the visitor blessed the host in the name of the living God! **how old:** Jacob would live to the age of 147 and would die in Egypt (47:28).

47:11 Joseph arranged the perfect place for his family members to live.

47:12 provided ... bread: Joseph made sure that his family was well supplied.

47:13 Now there was no bread: The famine was severe even in Egypt.

47:14 The Egyptians gave up their silver, their cattle, and their property in the process of buying food to keep themselves alive.

47:15–19 When they ran out of **money** (silver), the people brought their **livestock**

(v. 17) to purchase grain. When they no longer had livestock they sold their **land.**

47:20–22 The Pharaoh's ownership of **the land** would eventually lead to gross abuses of power.

47:23–26 The state supplied the seed for planting, but one-fifth of the proceeds became the property of Pharaoh. This became standard practice in Egypt (v. 26).

47:27 Jacob's family did not have to sell their **possessions** in order to acquire food.

47:28 seventeen years: Even though Jacob had been willing to die when he rejoined his son Joseph (see 45:28; 46:30), God gave him a good number of years to enjoy his family.

47:29–31 your hand under my thigh: The action suggests a most solemn and binding promise. **deal kindly and truly with me:** The expression means "demonstrate to me the utmost covenant loyalty. **do not bury me in Egypt:** Jacob demonstrated his faith in God's promises by asking to be buried in the land promised to his descendants.

48:1, 2 two sons: God works in ways different from the expected course of events.

48:3, 4 God Almighty: This is the fifth time the name *El Shaddai* is found in Genesis.

48:5–7 The **two sons** of Joseph were Manasseh and Ephraim (41:50–52). Jacob said that they were as much his sons as **Reuben and Simeon**. But Jacob gave the double share to Joseph (v. 22). Joseph's two sons are then counted with their uncles as founders of the tribes of Israel. **Rachel died beside me:** The aged Jacob remembered the great love of his life, Rachel, who died giving birth to Benjamin.

48:8–11 I had not thought to see: Jacob recalled again his grief at the thought of Joseph's death and his joy at being able to see him again in this life (46:29).

48:12–14 Joseph placed his sons so that his father's right hand would rest on the head of the older son and the left hand on the younger. But Jacob deliberately reversed his hands, putting Ephraim first.

48:15 In his blessing, Jacob reaffirmed his great faith in the living God. Jacob used the definite article with the word **God** to emphasize "the Genuine Deity" (as in 6:2; 22:1; 27:28; 31:11; 46:3).

48:16 my name: Jacob wanted Joseph's two sons to inherit the blessing God gave to Abraham, Isaac, and himself.

48:17 Joseph realized that his father's right hand was on the head of the younger boy, and he attempted to rearrange his father's hands. But in spite of his dimmed eyesight, Jacob knew what he was doing.

48:18–20 as Ephraim and as Manasseh: Jacob recited the names of Joseph's sons with the youngest first. From then on, Joseph's two sons were known in that order.

48:21 Jacob promised Joseph that he would return to the land of Canaan.

48:22 one portion above: By blessing the two sons of Joseph on the same level as his own sons, Jacob gave to Joseph the double share. **from the hand of the Amorite:** This promise would be fulfilled when the Israelites returned to Canaan to possess the land God had given them (see 15:12–21).

49:1 in the last days: Jacob described the future for his descendants.

49:2–4 Jacob began with warm words of praise to **Reuben,** his **firstborn** son (for his birth, see 29:31, 32). But he ended with a rebuke of Reuben's presumptuous actions with Bilhah (35:22). By going to his **father's bed,** Reuben was attempting to solidify his claims as the firstborn son. In fact, he doomed his cause.

49:5–7 Simeon and Levi are linked because of the fierce and cruel revenge they took against Shechem and his people (see ch. 34). Because of what they did, Jacob described them as **instruments of cruelty.** Because of their actions, they would be scattered in Israel.

49:8 Judah ... shall praise: This verse is a word-play on the meaning of Judah's name, "Let God Be Praised." Jacob's praise for Judah was surpassed only by his praise for Joseph (vv. 22–26; see ch. 48). Judah rose to the leadership of the twelve sons as Jacob passed over Reuben, Simeon, and Levi.

49:9 The **lion** is an ancient royal symbol.

49:10 The **scepter** is an ornate staff or rod that is a symbol of royal authority. A **lawgiver** is the one who issues statutes.

49:11, 12 Wine recalls the color of **blood.** The colors of his **eyes** and **teeth** speak of vitality and victory. The language of this passage expresses the mystery and wonder surrounding this Coming One, Shiloh.

49:13 Zebulun is given precedence over his brother Issachar. His blessing will be the northern coastlands bordering Phoenicia (compare Josh. 18:10–16).

49:14 Jacob's words to **Issachar** portend a heavy enslavement following a time of plenty (see Is. 9:1).

49:15, 16 Dan shall judge: Dan's name is related to the word meaning "judge."

49:17, 18 a viper by the path: This possibly means that some of Dan's descendants would abandon their faith in the Lord. Yet the godly can still expect **salvation** from the Lord.

49:19 Gad, a troop shall tramp upon him: Although the tribe of Gad will endure hardship, ultimate victory is promised.

49:20 The brief words to **Asher** were happy and hopeful.

49:21 Naphtali: Again, the brief words promised hope and joy.

49:22 Joseph: Only the promises given to Judah (vv. 8–12) can rival the praise Jacob gave to Joseph.

49:23 The imagery of **archers** who **shot at him** represents Joseph's personal experience at the hands of his brothers and then the Egyptians (chs. 37; 39; 40).

49:24 Not only did Joseph have great strength of character represented by the strong **bow,** he was protected by **the Mighty God of Jacob.**

49:25 Earlier, Jacob had described the Lord as the God of Abraham and Isaac (48:15). Here he expressed his faith in the God who had blessed him.

49:26 Jacob's blessing on Joseph concluded with the most enthusiastic words. **Separate** is the word also used for the Nazirites (Num. 6:1–21).

49:27 Benjamin: The image of a **wolf** is ominous (Judg. 20:21–25).

49:28 the twelve tribes of Israel: Jacob's blessings are prophecies about the destiny of each tribe. Some of the blessings are obscure.

49:29 bury me with my fathers: Jacob

challenged his sons not to bury him in Egypt.

49:30–33 Jacob identified the place as **the cave ... Machpelah,** where Jacob's father, mother, grandfather, and grandmother were buried.

50:1 wept: Joseph expressed his strong, genuine love for his father (see 45:1–3; 46:29).

50:2, 3 embalm: Joseph directed that his father be embalmed.

50:4–9 Joseph made his request to leave Egypt to bury his father's remains in Canaan. The expression **to the household of Pharaoh** indicates that even Joseph did not always have immediate access to the Pharaoh's presence.

50:10–11 At **Atad** in the Transjordan, they mourned another seven days. This is the entrance to the Promised Land.

50:12–15 Joseph's brothers had a new fear. With Jacob dead, would Joseph take revenge?

50:16, 17 trespass ... sin: The evil the brothers had done to Joseph. **Joseph wept:** Joseph accepted the confession in the message as a sincere confession from his brothers.

50:18–21 you meant evil: Joseph spoke clearly about how he viewed the events of his life (45:4–8). **God meant it for good:** God transformed the evil of a group of men into an exceedingly great work.

50:22 one hundred and ten years: God blessed Joseph with a long life.

50:23 children of Machir: The listing of the children of Ephraim before the children of Manasseh is a step in the fulfillment of Jacob's blessing.

50:24 God will surely visit you: On his deathbed, Joseph expressed continuing faith in the promises of God.

50:25 an oath: Joseph had buried his father Jacob in Canaan (50:7–14). Now he had the Israelites swear that they would take his bones to the Promised Land when the entire nation of Israel returned to Canaan. In this oath Joseph expressed his faith that God would keep His promise to give the land of Canaan to the Israelites (Heb. 11:22).

50:26 Joseph was **embalmed,** like Jacob (vv. 1–3).

Exodus

Introduction

The Book of Exodus describes the central historical event for the Israelites—their salvation from slavery in Egypt. God saved them from Egyptian slavery and in the process molded them into a nation, as He promised Abram in Gen. 12:1–3. Throughout this entire drama, God demonstrated His power and holiness through miraculous signs and wonders. Finally, through Moses at Mt. Sinai God taught His people how to become a kingdom of priests and a holy nation dedicated to serving and worshiping Him (19:6).

Traditionally, scholars have agreed that Moses wrote Exodus. Exodus has two principal sections. The first section, written as a story of epic prose (chs. 1—18), portrays God as the Savior and Provider of His people. The second section is a series of detailed laws and instructions (chs. 19—40). However, these laws are no ordinary laws. They reveal the very character of God, showing Him as a Lawgiver and as the Holy One.

Exodus concludes with instructions about the tabernacle—its construction, furnishing, and services. When this worship center was completed, the glory of the Lord came to fill it (40:34). God had saved His people, provided for them, made a treaty with them, and taught them how to live. Finally He lived with them (Ex. 25:8; 29:45). All was ready, it seemed, for the journey to the Land of Promise.

1:1 Israel is also called Jacob. His twelve sons became the founders of the twelve tribes of the nation Israel.

1:2–4 The sons are listed according to their mothers and their ages. **Reuben, Simeon, Levi, Judah, Issachar** and **Zebulun** are all sons of Leah. **Benjamin** is the son of Rachel. **Dan** and **Naphtali** are sons of Bilhah, the maid of Rachel. **Gad** and **Asher** are sons of Zilpah, the maid of Leah.

1:5, 6 seventy persons: See Gen. 46:1–27. **Joseph** was not included among the seventy.

1:7 The extraordinary growth of the family of promise in Egypt is evidence of God's blessing. God **multiplied** a small family of twelve sons and one daughter into a nation.

1:8–10 The **new king** did not remember Joseph. This pharaoh was probably one of the Hyksos kings who descended from foreign invaders. These kings perceived the growing numbers of Hebrews as a challenge to their control over Egypt.

1:11 By God's mercy, the Israelites were left to themselves for most of the four hundred years they were in Egypt. But the time finally came when Pharaoh put **taskmasters,** meaning "chiefs of slave gangs," over them.

1:12 God **multiplied** His people in times of distress. The term **dread** means "to feel a sickening dread" (as in Num. 21:4).

1:13, 14 rigor: With every task the Egyptians gave to the Hebrews, they made things increasingly difficult for them.

1:15 The **king of Egypt** mentioned here is probably not the Hyksos king alluded to in vv. 8–14. This king, perhaps Thutmose I (c. 1539–1514 B.C.), ruled Egypt when Moses was born (2:1–10). **Hebrew midwives:** Probably Hebrews themselves, these two women headed a guild of midwives.

1:16 The custom was to support the mother on a **birthstool** during delivery. **sons:** Pharaoh ordered the midwives to kill the baby boys because he feared the Hebrews as a military threat.

1:17–19 The Hebrew term for **fear** is the word regularly used for piety, obedience, and the true worship of God (see Gen. 22:12; Ex. 20:20). The midwives would not obey the evil commands of a human ruler because they wanted to please the God of heaven.

1:20, 21 God blessed the midwives because they **feared God. He provided households for them:** Ordinarily households were established for men. God established the families of these two midwives (see Gen. 18:19) because they were faithful to Him.

1:22 Pharaoh commanded the Egyptians to kill the Hebrew male babies by drowning them in **the river**—the Nile.

2:1 Both of Moses' parents were from **the house of Levi.** God chose this family to be the priests for Israel.

2:2–4 bore a son: This is not their first child. Moses' older sister was Miriam; Aaron was three years older than this son (see 7:7). The mother hid her baby from the authorities, who wanted to kill him. After **three months,** she found it impossible (see 1:22). The **ark** in which she placed her baby would be the means of saving him. She hoped that someone would find the ark and adopt the boy. She sent his **sister,** Miriam, to see what would happen.

2:5 This **daughter of Pharaoh** was probably one of many daughters. **to bathe:** Bathing in the Nile was a ritual dipping in the waters the Egyptians believed to be sacred.

2:6 The baby was **one of the Hebrews' children.** A Hebrew baby would have been circumcised on the eighth day. The women would have seen the baby's "special mark."

2:7 The daughter of Pharaoh was not prepared to care for the baby. Since it was a Hebrew child, who would be better than a Hebrew woman to **nurse** it?

2:8 the maiden: The Hebrew term means a young woman of marriageable age.

2:9 Not only did God protect the child from death, but through Pharaoh's treasury, he provided **wages** to the mother for caring for her own son!

2:10 The mother brought **her son** to Pharaoh's daughter, who then adopted the boy. Pharaoh's daughter explains the meaning of Moses' name: **"Because I drew him out of water."** In Hebrew, Moses means "He Who Draws Out."

2:11 The training of Moses in the pharaoh's court was the best education in the world at that time. He would have learned three languages: Egyptian, Akkadian, and Hebrew. **his brethren:** At about the age of forty, Moses was confronted with a great personal crisis. He saw the mistreatment of his own people by his adopted people.

2:12–14 Moses realized that there was no legal procedure for him to stop the abuses of the Egyptian taskmasters. Moved by a sense of injustice, he rashly **killed** the taskmaster.

2:15 Pharaoh **sought to kill** Moses because he had committed a capital crime. **The land of Midian** is the region of the Sinai Peninsula and Arabian deserts where the seminomadic Midianites lived.

2:16 the priest of Midian appears to be a foreigner who had come to worship the true and living God. His **daughters** came to the well since typically the women **drew water** (see Gen. 24).

2:17 The shepherds had probably acted disrespectfully toward these women before. **Moses stood up** and came to the aid of the women.

2:18, 19 Reuel is also called Jethro (4:18). His daughters reported to him that they had been delivered by **an Egyptian.** The dress, appearance, and language of Moses would have given this impression.

2:20 Reuel's invitation to **eat bread** was about more than a casual bite to eat. He was recruiting Moses to marry one of his seven daughters.

2:21 Moses was content: For a fugitive from the powerful hand of the Egyptian pharaoh, the offer of a home, protection, and a new life would be appealing. Moses would have become part of Reuel's household in the deal (see 4:18).

2:22 Gershom means "A Stranger There." Moses was doubly removed from his land.

2:23–25 the king of Egypt died: The death of Pharaoh (likely Thutmose III, who died about 1447 B.C.) meant that Moses could return to Egypt. At the death of a pharaoh, Egyptian authorities dropped all pending charges, even in capital cases (see 4:19). Four different Hebrew words—translated **groaned, cried out, cry,** and **groaning**—are used to describe the Israelites' complaint (see 6:5). Corresponding to the four terms for the people's distress, four wonderful verbs are used to describe the Lord's response to His people: **heard, remembered, looked,** and **acknowledged.**

3:1 Horeb, another name for Mt. Sinai, means "Desolate Place." Because of God's appearance on the mountain (here and in chs. 19; 20), it would become holy, **the mountain of God** (see 4:27).

3:2 the Angel of the LORD: An appearance of God. The **flame of fire** was an extraordinary sight, particularly since the bush **was not consumed.**

3:3–5 The ground had become **holy;** it was set apart by the divine presence.

3:6, 7 God identified Himself as **the God of**

your father—the God worshiped by Abraham, Isaac, and Jacob (v. 15). In announcing these names, the Lord was assuring Moses that His covenant with the fathers of Israel was still in effect.

3:8–10 The words **come down** speak of God's gracious intervention on the earth (Ps. 40:1). Not only was God intimately aware of the troubles of His people, but now He would act on their behalf. The **good and large land** of Canaan was God's great pledge to His people (Gen. 12:7; 15:12–21; see also Ex. 6:8).

3:11, 12 God promised to **be with** Moses. God gave Moses **a sign,** a final proof that this experience was a divine manifestation and not a dream.

3:13, 14 I AM WHO I AM: The One who spoke to Moses declared Himself to be the Eternal One—uncaused and independent. Only the Creator of all things can call Himself the **I AM** in the absolute sense; all other creatures are in debt to Him for their existence.

3:15–17 the LORD: This represents the Hebrew name Yahweh. The Hebrew word meaning "I Am" used in v. 14 is very similar. Translations into English often use LORD in small capitals to represent God's name, Yahweh. Here, God does not just declare His absolute existence; He declares His relationship to His people. He is the God who made an eternal covenant with **Abraham, Isaac,** and **Jacob** (see v. 6).

3:18 The fact that Israelites had **to go** somewhere else to **sacrifice to the LORD** may have been an implied slur on the land of Egypt.

3:19 The **mighty hand** is the Lord's hand. God was the One who forced the Pharaoh to free the Israelites (v. 20; see also 6:1).

3:20 The Lord's extended **hand** of mercy to the Israelites and of rage against the Egyptians is a constant theme in Exodus. **My wonders** are the ten plagues of chs. 7—12. The word refers to things only God can do, and which are designed to inspire reverence in His worshipers and fear in His enemies.

3:21, 22 God would so humiliate their leader Pharaoh that the common people of Egypt would become favorably disposed toward Israel. The Israelites, who had been slaves in Egypt, would not leave **empty-handed.** They would **plunder the Egyptians** by asking for precious goods (for the fulfillment of this prophecy, see 11:2; 12:35, 36).

4:1–5 God turned Moses' **rod**—probably a long wooden pole with the familiar shepherd's crook at one end—into a snake to demonstrate the reality of His power and presence.

4:6, 7 Again God demonstrated His power to Moses by making **his hand** leprous and then healing it.

4:8, 9 The third sign would be the transformation of the water from the Nile into **blood.** In fact, this occurred in the first plague (7:14–25).

4:10–12 God reminded Moses that it was He who had made Moses' **mouth.** Then He promised to instruct Moses as to precisely what to **say.**

4:13, 14 At this point, Moses saw a flash of God's **anger**. God was already arranging some assistance for Moses. He was sending **Aaron** to him (for their meeting, see v. 27).

4:15, 16 words in his mouth: As Moses was a prophet of God, so Aaron was to be a prophet of Moses (7:1). Moses would be **as God** to Aaron because he would tell him what to say, just as God would tell Moses what to say.

4:17, 18 Moses needed to gain permission from his father-in-law to leave. Moses had become an official part of Jethro's family (2:16–22; 3:1).

4:19, 20 Moses took **his sons.** Gershom, Moses' firstborn, is mentioned in 2:22. The name of the second son is not given until 18:4, after Israel's deliverance. This is Eliezer, whose name means "My God Is Help." Moses also took **the rod of God,** that is, the rod that God had used to demonstrate His power (vv. 2–5, 17).

4:21 Pharaoh, most likely Amenhotep II (c. 1447–1421 B.C.), is not simply the king of Egypt, but a symbol for all who resist God. **I will harden his heart:** Some interpret these words as meaning that God would confirm what Pharaoh had stubbornly determined to do. In the first five plagues, the hardening is attributed to Pharaoh (see 7:13, 22; 8:15, 19, 32; 9:7). Then for the sixth plague, God hardened a heart that Pharaoh had already hardened (9:12).

4:22, 23 The nation Israel is God's **son** and naturally God is his Father. In the course of time, others—all those who would believe in God's Son—would become God's children (see John 1:12). But the nation Israel is His **firstborn.**

4:24 The **encampment** might have been a primitive inn on Moses' route back to Egypt. **the Lord met him and sought to kill him:** The precise meaning of this passage is unclear. Clearly someone in Moses' family was not circumcised, despite what God had commanded.

4:25, 26 At this time, circumcision was practiced with **stone** knives rather than bronze. Many of Israel's neighboring peoples practiced circumcision, but none except Israel circumcised infants.

4:27, 28 The meeting of these two brothers after forty years must have been a very emotional moment. How fitting that the two would meet **on the mountain of God** (3:1).

4:29–31 When Moses and Aaron arrived in Egypt, they gathered the elders together. The people **believed** and **worshiped** the God who had sent these signs and messengers. God **had visited** them!

5:1 Moses and Aaron approached the powerful tyrant of Egypt with strong, daring words in the name of their God: **"Let My people go."**

5:2 Who is the LORD: Later these arrogant words would haunt Pharaoh (12:31, 32). Meanwhile, Pharaoh believed himself to be a god. Sadly for him, he had never encountered the true and living God, hence his response, **nor will I let Israel go,** just as God had said (3:19; 4:21–23).

5:3 The boldness of Moses and Aaron's first words (v. 1) is replaced with panic. The Israelites had to obey their God.

5:4–9 To punish Moses and Aaron, Pharaoh imposed severe measures on the Hebrew workers, who needed **straw** to strengthen the sun-dried bricks they were making. Until now the Egyptians had provided it for them.

5:10–19 The Hebrew leaders of the work gangs, the **officers** or subordinate officials,

complained about the new work rules. Pharaoh claimed that the people were **idle** (v. 8) and ordered them to continue.

5:20, 21 The Hebrew crew chiefs turned their anger on Moses and Aaron. Their words, **Let the LORD look on you and judge,** are a harsh curse.

5:22 Moses' complaint to God, **Why is it You have sent me?** alludes to his initial reluctance to be the Lord's agent of deliverance (4:10–17).

5:23 speak in Your name: Moses must have expected Pharaoh to cave in as soon as he heard the use of the Lord's name Yahweh. Yet God had warned Moses that Pharaoh would do the opposite.

6:1 The Lord's response, **Now you shall see,** was designed to encourage him.

6:2 By explaining His purpose for Israel, God encouraged Moses after his disheartening experience with Pharaoh (see 5:1–9). The words **I am the LORD** begin and conclude this section (vv. 2, 8).

6:3 The patriarchs had known **God Almighty.** It is not that they had never heard the name Yahweh, but they had not **known** God in an intimate way. The patriarchs had not had the revelation that was granted to Moses and the people of his day.

6:4 My covenant: The Abrahamic covenant celebrated in Genesis. **pilgrimage:** They were **strangers** in Egypt, resident aliens, without citizenship in their own country.

6:5 groaning: This verse recalls the Israelites' cry in 2:23–25. The Lord was now ready to state His plan for Israel (vv. 6–8).

6:6–8 These verses express four aspects of God's plan for Israel: (1) He would deliver them from Egypt; (2) He would make them His people; (3) He would be their God; and (4) He would bring them to Canaan, the Promised Land.

6:9 Despite God's powerful words to Moses, the people were still unwilling to believe. Their cruel suffering overwhelmed them.

6:10, 11 The Lord renewed His command to Moses (4:22, 23).

6:12 Moses complained that his own people would not listen to him. How then would **Pharaoh?** Moses was still convinced that his **uncircumcised lips** would ruin everything (see 4:10).

6:13 The Lord's response was to repeat the initial **command.** This was not something to be negotiated.

6:14–30 The family history of Moses, Aaron, and Miriam briefly interrupts the narrative. But this was not just a matter of public record; it was something to celebrate! All of Israel's priests would eventually come from this line.

7:1, 2 you as God: As Moses was the prophet of the Lord, so Aaron became Moses' **prophet.**

7:3, 4 I will harden Pharaoh's heart: It was in God's plan that Pharaoh would be inflexibly stubborn, thus setting the scene for God to deliver His people by powerful **signs and ... wonders.** These two words paired together mean "irrefutable works."

7:5 God also planned from the beginning that **the Egyptians** would **know** that He and He alone was the living God. In the first nine plagues, God used forces of creation in a supernatural way to bring judgment on the Egyptians. In the tenth plague, the destruction of the firstborn of Egypt, God would **stretch out** His **hand** and bring judgment Himself.

7:6 did so ... so they did: The obedience of Moses and Aaron is a recurring theme in the Pentateuch (see 12:28; Num. 8:20–22).

7:7 eighty ... eighty-three: In a sense, these men had already lived a lifetime (see Ps. 90:10) before their principal life work had begun! Moses was to lead the nation of Israel for another 40 years before he died (see Deut. 29:5; 31:2; 34:5). Aaron died in the same year as his younger brother, at the age of 123 (Num. 20:22–29; 33:38, 39).

7:8 Then the LORD spoke to Moses and Aaron: This is the first time Moses and Aaron are referred to as receiving a message from God together.

7:9 This time they would perform a **miracle,** a special display of God's power.

7:10 The sign that God had done before Moses, turning his rod into **a serpent** (4:1–5), was now repeated before Pharaoh and his courtiers.

7:11 Pharaoh was not about to be outdone. **Wise men** refers to his counselors, men of

learning and insight. **Sorcerers** refers to those who practiced divination. The **magicians** of Egypt were believed to have occult knowledge. But in their encounter with Moses and Aaron, these men were no match for the power of God (8:19; 9:11)!

7:12 his rod ... serpents: The text does not say whether this was a genuine transformation or a trick of Pharaoh's evil sorcerers. In any event, their serpents were no match for Aaron's serpent; his swallowed theirs!

7:13, 14 Pharaoh's heart grew hard, meaning he became insensitive and dull to the demonstration of God's power. This was **as the LORD had said.**

7:15 Some of the plagues were announced **to Pharaoh** beforehand; others came without warning. **to the water ... the river's bank:** Pharaoh's bath in the Nile was a sacred Egyptian rite connected to Pharaoh's claim of divinity. **rod:** This rod is called the rod of God (4:20) and the rod of Aaron (7:9).

7:16 The LORD God of the Hebrews: A similar identification of the Lord was used in the initial encounter of Moses before Pharaoh (see 5:1, 3). The statement **serve Me in the wilderness** conveys the idea of sacred worship.

7:17 The waters of the Nile changed to **blood.**

7:18, 19 The waters of Egypt came from the Nile.

7:20, 21 Moses and Aaron obeyed God's command and invoked the plague with **the rod.**

7:22 magicians ... with their enchantments: Perhaps the tricksters of Pharaoh were able to attempt to duplicate the sign of the Lord in the Nile River (7:11). The heart of Pharaoh **grew hard ... as the LORD had said.**

7:23–25 Pharaoh **turned and went into his house.** He also seemed oblivious to the suffering of his people.

8:1, 2 Frogs, which in moderate numbers were regarded as signs of life, renewal, and happiness, would now become pests.

8:3–5 The **rod** of Aaron (7:19) was a powerful symbol of God's power in the hand of His servant. It is not clear in this passage whether the Hebrews were spared the effects of this plague **on the land of Egypt.**

8:6, 7 the magicians ... with their enchantments: We do not know how or in what quantity the magicians produced frogs.

8:8 Pharaoh **called for Moses and Aaron** to **entreat the LORD** (translated "intercede" in v. 9) on his behalf.

8:9 Accept the honor: Moses invites him to set the time for Moses' prayer for relief from the frogs. In this way, Pharaoh would not be able to say that it was just a coincidence that the frogs began to abate at a certain time.

8:10, 11 The Bible asserts again and again that **there is no one like the LORD our God.** Here the living God is compared with the false gods of Egypt.

8:12 cried out to the Lord: The Hebrew verb translated *cry* places emphasis on the need at hand and suggests God's willingness to stoop down to answer that need (see 22:27; Ps. 40:1).

8:13, 14 There were so many dead frogs **the land stank.**

8:15 During the time of stress, Pharaoh was willing to promise anything. But as soon as the stress ended, he **hardened his heart** and became unwilling to do what he had promised.

8:16, 17 The plague of **lice** was the first not to be announced to Pharaoh beforehand. **All the dust of the land became lice:** Suggests unprecedented trouble with insects in countless numbers.

8:18 The magicians ... with their enchantments (see 7:11) failed this time.

8:19 It is remarkable that Pharaoh's magicians attributed the plague to **the finger of God.**

8:20–22 The pressure on Pharaoh intensified with this plague. For the first time, God vowed to **set apart the land of Goshen** for the protection of His people. Swarms of flies would be everywhere except near the Hebrews.

8:23–28 By using the strong terminology **the abomination of the Egyptians:** The sacrificial animals of Israel would include sheep, something the Egyptians regarded as detestable.

8:29 Moses promised to pray for relief from

the plague of **flies,** but he also warned Pharaoh to keep his promise (see 7:22; 8:15, 19).

8:30–32 As soon as the Lord removed the swarms of flies, Pharaoh reverted to his earlier stubbornness against Moses, Israel, and God—and **hardened his heart.**

9:1, 2 the LORD God of the Hebrews: God forcefully identified Himself as the God of the Hebrews just as He said He would (3:18).

9:3 A very severe pestilence on the livestock of Egypt would destroy much of the economy of Egypt as well as its military preparedness.

9:4 As the Egyptians' animals would fall all about them, the animals of the Hebrews would continue to flourish.

9:5 Just as it had been announced, the plague began at a **set time.** The timing was a significant part of these plagues as was the subsequent relief (see 9:18).

9:6, 7 As with the fourth plague (see 8:24), **the LORD did this thing.** Even though **Pharaoh sent** his agents and confirmed that the animals of the Hebrews had been spared this calamity, **the heart of Pharaoh became hard.**

9:8 ashes: Moses' use of a symbolic act **in the sight of Pharaoh** indicated that the outbreak of disease was not a coincidence. This disease was from the Lord.

9:9, 10 It is not clear from the text whether the Hebrews were spared the plague of **boils,** but it seems reasonable to think so.

9:11 The reference to the hapless **magicians** (7:11) is almost humorous. Not only were they powerless, but they also suffered from the plague.

9:12 hardened the heart of Pharaoh: See 3:19; 4:21; 5:2; 7:3, 13, 14.

9:13, 14 The words **to your very heart** suggest a growing intensity in the plagues. **none like Me:** God is distinct from all the supposed gods of Egypt.

9:15 if I had: The Lord points out that He could have destroyed the stubborn Pharaoh right at the beginning.

9:16 for this ... I have raised you up: God used Pharaoh's stubbornness to demonstrate His **power** and to make known His

name (see 10:2; Rom. 9:17, 18). Pharaoh set himself up as a god who maintained the stability of his kingdom.

9:17 The term **you exalt yourself** has the idea of self-aggrandizement.

9:18 tomorrow: One theme in the plagues is the certainty of their timing (see 7:20; 9:5).

9:19–21 God warned the Egyptians to **gather** their **livestock** so they might be spared the hailstorm. Even some members of Pharaoh's court now took the **word of the LORD** seriously.

9:22–25 We hear from time to time of terrible hailstorms with hail as large as "baseballs." The wording of this text suggests that no hailstorm had ever been as terrible as this.

9:26 The exclusion of **the land of Goshen** from the Lord's plagues was part of the miracle (see 8:22; 11:7).

9:27, 28 For Pharaoh to say **I have sinned** was a stunning admission, as was his confession, **the LORD is righteous.** What a change from his initial arrogance (see 5:2)! But sadly, these words of contrition would not hold.

9:29, 30 I will spread out my hands: This is a gesture of prayer (see Ps. 134:2) tied here to a request (v. 28; see 8:8). Pharaoh finally admitted that **the earth is the LORD's** (see Ps. 24:1).

9:31, 32 As in Canaan, **barley** was the first crop to be harvested in the late spring; **wheat** would be harvested in the summer. From this verse the timing of the year-long series of plagues can be estimated (see 7:19).

9:33–35 It took a miracle to stop the plague as well as to start it. Sadly, Pharaoh's remorse (see v. 27) was short-lived; **he hardened his heart.**

10:1 God commanded Moses to **go in to Pharaoh** (see 7:15). **I have hardened his heart:** Three verbs are used in Exodus to describe God's hardening of Pharaoh's heart. Usually the verb meaning "to make hard" is used (see 4:21). In 7:3, the Hebrew verb meaning "to make stiff" is used. Here the Hebrew verb that means "to make heavy" or "to make insensitive" is used.

10:2 your son and your son's son: The story of God's deliverance of Israel from Egypt

was to be told by one generation to the next. **the mighty things I have done:** This whole phrase translates an unusual Hebrew verb that literally means "to make sport of" or "to toy with." The Lord was saying, "I have just been playing games with Pharaoh."

10:3 refuse to humble yourself: Pharaoh's pride was his undoing.

10:4 The Lord used a part of His own creation, **locusts**—well known as a recurring cause of destruction—to bring unparalleled devastation to Egypt.

10:5–7 The term **snare** can be used to describe a trap for birds (as in Amos 3:5). Here it speaks of Moses as a symbol of destruction. **Egypt is destroyed:** This admission by Pharaoh's counselors fulfilled God's prediction that the Egyptians would acknowledge God's supremacy over Pharaoh.

10:8, 9 Pharaoh's questions implied that he was not serious about releasing the Israelites. **Who are the ones that are going?** was a preposterous question. From the beginning, Moses had demanded the release of the entire population of Hebrews, and he stated this again.

10:10, 11 Pharaoh grudgingly gave permission for the **men** to leave.

10:12–15 Since Pharaoh was still obstinate, the Lord brought on the **locusts** and **they covered the face of the whole earth.** This was an unprecedented disaster in **all the land of Egypt.**

10:16–18 Pharaoh confessed **I have sinned,** and Moses **entreated the LORD** on his behalf. The text is careful to attribute the relief to God and not to Moses.

10:19 a very strong wind: As in the case of the frogs (8:10–14) and the hail (9:33), Pharaoh saw God's power over the forces of nature.

10:20 But the LORD hardened Pharaoh's heart: See 3:19; 4:21; 5:2; 7:3, 13, 14.

10:21–26 A comparison with other passages (see 10:12, 13) suggests that when **Moses stretched out his hand** he was holding the rod of God. **thick darkness:** The Egyptians worshiped many gods, but none so much as the sun. Even a normal solar eclipse would have had an impact, but an enshrouding darkness that lasted **for three days** was a frontal attack on their gods, on their Pharaoh and his supposed control of nature, and on all Pharaoh's counselors who were helpless.

10:27 But the LORD hardened Pharaoh's heart: See 3:19; 4:21; 5:2; 7:3, 13, 14.

10:28, 29 There can be no mistaking the intent of Pharaoh's threat, **you shall die,** or of Moses' reply, **I will never see your face again.**

11:1, 2 one more plague: At this point, the series of plagues had come to its climax. **lets you go ... drive you out:** Pharaoh would be glad to be rid of the Israelites.

11:3 Another remarkable component of the Exodus was the Egyptians' **favor** (or grace) toward the Hebrews and admiration for their leader. The positive feelings for Moses were shared, amazingly enough, even by **Pharaoh's servants.**

11:4 About midnight I will go out: The Lord was the power behind all ten plagues. But in none of the earlier ones did He become personally involved as He did here.

11:5 firstborn of Pharaoh ... of the female servant: The use of these social opposites indicates totality. None would escape this plague.

11:6 Prediction of the **great cry** to come only intensified the tragedy. Pharaoh had been warned of this (see 4:22, 23).

11:7 God served notice that He did recognize **a difference between the Egyptians and Israel** (see 8:22; 9:4). The institution of the Passover (ch. 12) accentuated this great distinction.

11:8 Moses repeated God's prophecy: Pharaoh's **servants** would honor Moses and beg him for mercy.

11:9, 10 Pharaoh would **not heed** God's commands or warnings. Only in the face of Pharaoh's stubbornness might the power of God be displayed.

12:1, 2 This month, called Abib in 13:4, corresponds to April-May and is also called Nisan. **first month:** The Hebrew people began to mark time relative to the month of their departure from Egypt.

12:3 Each family took a lamb on the **tenth of** the **month** but waited until the fourteenth day to kill it (see v. 6), perhaps allowing time

to notice any problems that might make the animal unfit for this holy sacrifice.

12:4 Any household **too small** to eat a lamb in one meal was to join with another.

12:5 Sacrifice was not a way to get rid of unwanted animals. Only the best lambs **without blemish** were suitable. **a male of the first year:** God meant the Passover lamb sacrificed for the Israelites to be a picture (a type or model) of the coming death of the Savior, Jesus Christ (see 1 Cor. 5:7).

12:6, 7 Each family took a lamb on the tenth of the month and waited until the **fourteenth day** to kill it (see v. 3). The **blood** of the Passover lamb on the **doorposts and ... lintel** was the Lord's provision for salvation from physical death, just as the blood of Jesus is the Lord's provision for our salvation from spiritual death.

12:8–10 Verses 15–20 expand on the instructions for **unleavened bread. Bitter herbs** reminded the people of the unpleasantness of slavery.

12:11 The people were to dress for travel, in readiness to march at the Lord's bidding. Ordinarily they would not wear **sandals** (or shoes) in the house. One's **staff** would be propped near the door, but not on this night. They were to **eat in haste,** ready to leave. **It is the LORD's Passover:** The commands for this night readied the people for God's quick and miraculous deliverance.

12:12 Pass through (also in v. 23) refers to linear motion, as in crossing over a stream (Gen. 31:21). Here it is used ominously of the anticipated journey of the Lord to destroy the **firstborn in the land of Egypt.**

12:13 The term **sign** can mean a reminder, memorial, or symbol, or a miracle that points to the power of God (as in 7:3). The verb translated **pass over** means "to spare" or "skip."

12:14 Henceforth the day would be **a memorial. feast to the LORD:** Some of the religious duties require fasting. The Passover was a feast of celebration.

12:15, 16 seven days: Shall be cut off means "shall be executed" (see Gen. 17:14). The term **convocation** means "gathering."

12:17–24 As vv. 17–20 repeat and expand on the ideas of vv. 15, 16, so vv. 21–24 take up the main ideas of the Passover (vv. 1–14) and expand on them.

12:25–28 when your children say: These words are implemented in a significant part of the Passover Haggadah (liturgy): Questions are provided for children to ask, and the answers are prepared as well. **He struck:** The Lord Himself passed over the homes of the faithful in Israel, and the Lord Himself struck the homes of the Egyptians (see v. 29).

12:29 Moses, at the very beginning of his commission, was told about the death of the Egyptians' **firstborn** (4:22, 23). Furthermore, he announced it directly to Pharaoh (see 11:4–8).

12:30 The **great cry in Egypt** gives us only a glimpse of how Pharaoh's people paid for his choices. **Not a house** escaped. Wherever there was a family there was a death.

12:31 called for Moses and Aaron: Pharaoh was grief-stricken at the death of his first-born son.

12:32 your flocks and your herds: At last Pharaoh capitulated (see 10:9, 26). His words **and bless me also** show a softening of his heart. The death of his son—and the deaths of firstborn sons everywhere—must have shattered him to the core of his being.

12:33 The Egyptians urged the people to leave because they feared they might all die if the Israelites did not leave soon.

12:34 The dough before it was leavened: The Israelites did not have enough time to let the leaven (yeast) work in their dough. From that day on, unleavened bread would remind them of the haste of that night of flight from slavery.

12:35 asked from the Egyptians: The slaves were now being paid for their years of servitude.

12:36 plundered the Egyptians: Newly freed slaves do not usually make their escape with their masters pushing the family silver into their hands. But this is what happened when Israel left Egypt.

12:37 The number **six hundred thousand men** indicates a total population of some three million people.

12:38 The **mixed multitude** included Egyptians and perhaps other ethnic groups who had their own reasons for leaving. The movement of this vast population was further complicated by their **flocks and herds,** which they needed for food as well as for sacrifices to the Lord.

12:39 The people baked **unleavened cakes** in obedience to God's command (vv. 1–20).

12:40, 41 four hundred and thirty years: If the Exodus took place around 1446 B.C., Jacob's arrival in Egypt would have been around 1876 B.C.

12:42 The departure of Israel from Egypt was to be **a night of solemn observance.** The Passover has been carefully observed by Jews since that time. Jesus' last supper with his disciples which took place at the time of the Passover.

12:43 no foreigner: The holy feast was designed for those who had come to faith in the living God.

12:44, 45 A **servant** who had faith in God and was circumcised could partake of the holy feast (Gen. 17:12). But persons who did not share in Israel's faith were excluded (v. 45).

12:46 in one house: The first Passover was celebrated in each home (see vv. 1–13), for each house was marked by the blood of the Passover lamb. **nor ... break one of its bones:** Not breaking the bones of the lamb foreshadowed Jesus' death: None of the Savior's bones were broken. (see Ps. 34:20; John 19:33, 36).

12:47 All the congregation of Israel: This demanded participation from all of those who were part of the community.

12:48–50 The term **stranger** is different from that in v. 43. The term in v. 43 sometimes has negative overtones. It would not be a light decision for a male sojourner to come to the Passover meal—he would have to be **circumcised!**

13:1 The LORD spoke to Moses often, but Moses' close relationship with God was special (see 33:11; Num. 12:8).

13:2 The term translated **consecrate** means "to make holy." **it is Mine:** Meaning the consecration of the firstborn males to the Lord.

13:3 Remember this day: See 12:41, 42, 51.

13:4 in the month Abib: This verse defines the month of 12:2.

13:5–8 Even later generations of Israelites who had not been part of the Exodus were to say, "This is what **the LORD did for me.**"

13:9–11 Sign: Jews would fasten a small box containing passages of Scripture to their hand and forehead during prayer to serve as a memorial. God's instructions were to become a rule for one's life.

13:12 Set apart helps explain the meaning of *consecrate* in v. 2. The idea is "to treat as distinct," "to mark out as special."

13:13, 14 The Israelites were to **redeem** their firstborn sons; they were never to kill them in human sacrifice. The Lord had spared their firstborn even as He killed the firstborn of Egypt, human and animal, to buy their freedom.

13:15, 16 A sign was a reminder, memorial, or symbol; see v. 9 (compare Deut. 6:8).

13:17 If the people of Israel had traveled directly to Canaan, it would have been in a northerly direction along the coastal plain. Later this plain would be known as **the land of the Philistines.**

13:18 the way of the wilderness: The traditional route has the people moving in a southerly direction along the western shore of the Sinai Peninsula until they reached Mt. Sinai in the far south-central region of the peninsula. The rendering **the Red Sea** comes from the Septuagint, the Greek translation of the Old Testament. The Hebrew phrase means "Sea of Reeds."

13:19 the bones of Joseph: The story of the last wish of Joseph and his death is found in Gen. 50:22–26.

13:20 We do not know the location of **Succoth, Etham,** and certain other early encampments of Israel.

13:21, 22 God's presence with His people was made dramatically apparent in **a pillar of cloud** and **a pillar of fire** (14:19, 20, 24; 40:38; Num. 9:21).

14:1, 2 The locations of **Pi Hahiroth, Migdol,** and **Baal Zephon** are not known today.

14:3 The Egyptians would note Israel's route of escape, note the change in direction (v. 2), and conclude that **they** were **bewildered.** This was a ruse, of course, orchestrated by God Himself.

14:4, 5 then I will harden Pharaoh's heart: One more blow against Pharaoh was determined. With Pharaoh's final defeat, the name **the LORD** (that is, Yahweh) and its association with the people of Israel would be known and **gain honor** abroad.

14:6, 7 he made ready his chariot: At Pharaoh's command, the commander of the chariots pursued the Israelites. **Six hundred choice chariots** was a formidable force.

14:8 the LORD hardened the heart of Pharaoh: As He promised in 14:4.

14:9–11 We cannot fault the people for being **very afraid;** fear itself is not a sin. But the sarcastic remark to Moses that there were **no graves in Egypt** showed a lack of faith.

14:12 The statement **let us alone** refers to Israel's response to Moses and Aaron after their first, disastrous approach to Pharaoh (5:21).

14:13, 14 Moses did not lash out against the complaining people. Instead he sought to encourage them with a promise that they would see **the salvation of the LORD.**

14:15 The people were to **go forward**—not go back and not give up.

14:16–18 Moses' **rod** is the same celebrated rod of God (see 4:20) that Moses and Aaron had used in bringing forth many of the plagues against the Egyptians. **stretch out your hand:** The power of God would be demonstrated in a formidable manner. The Israelites thought of **the sea** as an uncontrollable enemy. The parting of the Red Sea was an unforgettable demonstration that every force in all creation was completely under God's control.

14:19 Here, the **Angel of God** and the **pillar of cloud** cooperated to protect and lead the Israelites (see 23:20, 23; 33:9–11). The name Angel of God is an alternative expression for the Angel of the LORD.

14:20 The pillar became two different realities—a curse to the pursuing Egyptians and a blessing to the entrapped Israelites. **all that night:** At night, God confused the Egyptians and let the Israelites pass through the sea.

14:21 Moses stretched ... and the LORD caused: God commanded Moses to stretch out the rod of God (see v. 16). One of the forces the Lord used to part the waters was a **strong east wind.**

14:22 It was an act of faith on Israel's part to cross over on this **dry ground.**

14:23 Egyptians pursued: The Egyptians pursued the Israelites even into the Red Sea.

14:24 The Lord caused confusion to fall among the Egyptians **in the morning watch,** while it was still dark.

14:25–27 Without their **wheels,** the chariots were more liability than threat. **the LORD fights for them:** The Lord fought for the Israelites (see vv. 4, 17, 18).

14:28, 29 Of all the Egyptian men, horses, and equipment that entered the dry bed of the sea, **not so much as one** survived. No doubt some Egyptian warriors had not actually entered the water and had survived. It was they who would spread the word about the Lord, the Warrior of Israel.

14:30, 31 The great work literally means "the great hand." That is, God did it; Moses was just the visible executor (see 15:6). When we read **so the people feared the LORD** and the words that follow, we are meant to understand that the community had come to faith.

15:1 Moses and the children of Israel sang in worship together, as a community of believers, not just as a nation. And they sang **to the LORD;** the living God was their main audience. The term **triumphed gloriously** is an emphatic construction, expressing exuberant joy over God's great victory (see also 18:8).

15:2 Because **my strength and my song** is such an unusual pairing of words, some have thought that the word translated *song* must mean "power," "fortress," or something similar. A person of faith may regard the living, omnipotent God as the reason for singing! **my salvation:** With the terrifying sea before them and the pursuing Egyptians behind them, they were trapped. Yet God surprised them with His deliverance!

15:3–5 the LORD is His name: It is difficult to exaggerate the importance of God's name Yahweh in the Bible (3:14, 15). By knowing a god's secret name, a priest supposedly had special access to that god. But the living God has made His name known to all, and salvation is found in His name alone.

15:6 The Exodus narrative has emphasized the extended, powerful **right hand** of God throughout (see vv. 12, 16). God did not deliver Israel "from afar"; He "came down" to act among them (3:8).

15:7, 8 The powerful wind that made the waters pile up on either side of the people (see 14:21) is described in poetry as a **blast of Your nostrils.**

15:9–12 Who is like You: No person, god, or thing can be compared to the one true God.

 IN DEPTH | **Miracles—Not an Everyday Occurrence**

The parting of the Red Sea (Ex. 14:21) is one of the most well-known biblical examples of miracles, which are supernatural interventions by God into the natural order in a way that accomplishes His purposes and brings glory to His name.

One might suppose that every act of God is a miracle, and from the human perspective that may be so. Nevertheless, God usually seems to allow nature to operate according to the principles or laws with which He originally created it. Thus, for example, the normal course for the Red Sea would be for its waters to obey the laws of gravity and remain unparted.

But the Bible reveals certain times when God sovereignly overrules natural laws and causes matter to operate in ways that go beyond the ordinary. These are miracles, also called "signs," "wonders," or "mighty acts." At the Red Sea, God caused the waters to temporarily "disobey" the normal principles of gravity and thus the children of Israel were able to cross on dry ground.

15:13 mercy: Best rendered as "loyal love," God's faithful love for His people (see Ps. 13:5). **Redeemed** is from a word that has to do with protecting family rights. God had protected His family, the Israelites.

15:14, 15 The nations were to be put on alert: God fought for Israel, and Israel was on the march! They struggled to trust in their powerful God.

15:16 fear and dread: A pairing of words to express one thought, "overwhelming dread."

15:17 bring them in: The verse speaks of the hope for the near future, the conquest of the land of Canaan, as well as the hope for the building of the temple.

15:18 the LORD shall reign forever and ever: Ultimately the salvation of Israel from Egypt points to the coming reign of the living God on earth over His redeemed people.

15:19–21 Miriam, Moses' sister, is mentioned here by name for the first time. She is called a **prophetess** (see Deborah, Judg. 4:4; the wife of Isaiah, Is. 8:3; Huldah, 2 Kin. 22:14). This passage also describes the Israelites' first worship service following their deliverance from the Red Sea. Women led this worship **with timbrels and with dances,** something later celebrated in the Psalms (Ps. 68:25).

15:22 The lack of **water** in this area would prove a constant test of Israel's faith in the God who had so miraculously rescued them (see ch. 17).

15:23, 24 The verb **complained** sometimes rendered "to murmur" (16:2, 7; Num. 14:2; 16:11; 17:5). The people's recent deliverance from the Egyptian armies makes this complaint seem fickle and a true test of God's mercy.

15:25 The use of the **tree** made the miracle of cleansing easier to perceive.

15:26 none of the diseases: God promised to preserve His people from illness (see 23:25). The descriptive phrase **I am the LORD who heals you** testifies to the mercy and power of God.

15:27 The **wells** and **palms** of Elim were a welcome relief from the barrenness of the wasteland. Many times the Bible compares wells and springs to salvation and palm trees to blessing (see Ps. 1).

16:1 The term **second month** means one month from the time of their departure from Egypt (compare 12:2, 18, 40).

16:2 the whole congregation: This phrase indicates a general dissent, not that there were no exceptions.

16:3 died by the hand of the LORD: After God's great deliverance of the Israelites from the Egyptians and his provision of water, couldn't they see that providing sufficient food for them would be a small thing for Him?

16:4 The Lord's response to the people's complaint was a promise of **bread from heaven** (manna, see v. 15). God Himself would supply their food. But the Israelites' reception of this wonderful blessing from God was already tarnished by their attitude. **A certain quota** meant a daily amount (see v. 5).

16:5 The gathering of **twice as much** on the sixth day would allow for the Sabbath rest (see v. 25).

16:6–9 you shall know: The people would experience God's power in a new way (see also v. 12). **see the glory:** They would have a renewed sense of God's presence and further evidence of God's mercy.

16:10, 11 Because God is Spirit (John 4:24), He has varied the ways in which He has shown Himself. **The glory of the LORD** is one of the grand *theophanies* (appearances of God) recorded in Exodus. We do not know exactly what the people saw **in the cloud,** but the sight certainly made them aware of God's majestic presence (see Ps. 97:2–5).

16:12 God promised ample provision for His people in **meat** and **bread.**

16:13 God provided meat through a natural event, the migration of **quails** through the region. It still was God's benevolent provision; the quails came at just the right time and in large numbers.

16:14, 15 a small round substance: There have been many attempts to explain manna as a naturally occurring substance. But the description of the manna in these two verses is necessary precisely because it was *not* a naturally occurring substance (see the description in Num. 11:1–15). **the LORD has**

given: The bread was a specific gift from God.

16:16 There would be sufficient manna for **each person.**

16:17–19 The Israelites' daily dependence on manna was an act of faith, hence the instruction **let no one leave any.** There would be more manna on the next day.

16:20 The Hebrew word translated **stank** is the same Hebrew word used by the crew chiefs to describe how the Hebrew people fared when Moses and Aaron first approached Pharaoh (see 5:21).

16:21 it melted: The ungathered manna would disappear during the day.

16:22–26 On the sixth day of the week, the people were to gather a two-day supply of manna for each person. On any other day, manna that was kept from the day before would spoil and fill with worms. But on the Sabbath, the manna from the previous day would be as fresh as when first gathered.

16:27–30 Some of the Israelites went out on the Sabbath to gather manna. **How long:** The Lord's command had been clear, and yet the people ignored it.

16:31 coriander seed ... honey: Apparently the manna was very tasty. It was also quite nutritious, and it was the staple of the Israelites for a full generation!

16:32, 33 The memorial pot of manna kept for later **generations** would serve as a reminder of this miraculous work of the Lord during Israel's wilderness period.

16:34–36 forty years: The completion of the story is anticipated.

17:1 Rephidim may be located at Wadi Refayid in southwest Sinai. **no water:** Adequate water for the people and for their flocks must have been an immense problem.

17:2 There would have been no sin in asking for water. But the Israelites **contended** with Moses. Moses judged this to be a challenge to God's faithful mercy, and evidence of unbelief in His provision.

17:3, 4 Why ... to kill us? Their genuine concern for water led the people to accuse Moses of having an outrageous motivation. Ultimately their attacks pointed at God.

17:5 The participation of **some of the elders** shows that not all the people were making the strong, malicious accusations that are described in verses 2 and 3.

17:6 Moses was to **strike** a **rock** in a dry desert so that water would come from it. The striking of the rock pictured the coming death of the Savior. **Moses did so:** The implication seems to be that the water came rushing out and the people had plenty to drink and to water their flocks.

17:7 Massah ... Meribah: Had the people not behaved so horribly, God would have provided the water in a context of blessing, and the names for the place would have been positive.

17:8 The people of **Amalek** were descendants of Esau, the Edomites (see Gen. 36:1, 12). Their attack on Israel was unprovoked. The Lord regarded this attack as particularly heinous (see vv. 14–16).

17:9 This is the first mention of **Joshua,** the man who would later succeed Moses. He had chosen Joshua to be his close aide (24:13; 32:17; 33:11).

17:10 Joshua led the battle. God had trained Moses for his work; He was now training Joshua to succeed him. **Hur:** The first mention of this close associate of Moses and Aaron (see 24:14).

17:11 Moses **held up his hand** as a visible sign that Israel's victory was in God's hands.

17:12 Moses was not a young man, and even a youth would grow weary sooner or later, so his aides **supported his hands.** Only in this way would Israel prevail; only in the power of God would they win their battle.

17:13 Joshua defeated: The armies of Israel would fight with normal combat techniques. But the victory was assured because of God's power on His people's behalf.

17:14 Write this: It is reasonable to assert that Moses wrote some passages of the first five books at the clear command of God, as this verse indicates, and then the rest later to record the full story of God's dealing with the Israelites during his lifetime (see also 34:27, 28).

17:15 Moses built and named an **altar.** Naming an altar gave it special significance by marking out a characteristic of God that was associated with worship there, **The-LORD-Is-My-Banner.**

17:16 The Hebrew translated as **the LORD has sworn** is somewhat obscure, but appears to mean "Surely there is a hand on the throne of the LORD."

18:1 God wanted the salvation of **Israel out of Egypt** to be **heard** throughout the world (see 15:14, 15). Word of God's deliverance of the Israelites had **Jethro, the priest of Midian**.

18:2 Zipporah: After the shocking story of the circumcision of Zipporah's son, the narrative of Exodus does not mention her again until this verse (see 2:16–21; 4:24–26). Most likely, Zipporah had returned to her father after that traumatic event. Now she visited Moses with her father. She is not mentioned again in the Bible. Later, it appears that Moses married another woman (Num. 12:1).

18:3 Now Zipporah's **two sons** stayed with Moses and became part of the families of Israel.

18:4 Eliezer means "My God Is Help" or perhaps "My God Is Power," it is only at this relatively late point in the second son's life that his name is mentioned.

18:5, 6 Moses had been adopted into the family of **Jethro** when he had been a man adrift; his marriage brought certain lasting obligations. He had asked Jethro's permission to return to his own people in obedience to God's call (4:18). The repetition of the term **father-in-law** in this passage suggests more than a courtesy title. Jethro had true authority over Moses.

18:7, 8 bowed down, and kissed him: The acts of bowing and kissing were not acts of worship, but signs of respect and reminders of obligations between two people.

18:9, 10 When Jethro **rejoiced,** he did more than express personal happiness. His joy came from his acknowledgment of the true and living God.

18:11 Jethro's words **now I know that the LORD is greater** declares full faith in God as the supreme deity.

18:12 The **burnt offering** was totally consumed. However the **other sacrifices** were fellowship offerings. The elders of Israel and the priest of Midian ate their part of the sacrifices together in common faith in the one true God.

18:13 Judge here means "to render decisions."

18:14, 15 The lively interchange between Moses and Jethro shows a very human side of Moses. His activities were far too time-consuming for one man to bear alone.

18:16 Many of the specific laws in the Book of Exodus are the result of this process, the application of general principles to specific cases (see 21:1).

18:17–19 Jethro gave his **counsel** in the context of his new faith in God, but it was rooted in experience and wisdom he had gained throughout his life.

18:20–22 Major matters would still be brought to Moses. Jethro listed only five qualifications for the men who would aid Moses. (1) They were to be **able men** having strength, efficiency, and wealth. (2) They were to **fear God,** showing piety, reverence, godly humility, and ready obedience. (3) They were to be **men of truth,** conforming to God's character. (4) They were to be haters of **covetousness,** so they could not be bribed. (5) They were to be ranked, with **rulers** over them.

18:23 and God so commands: Any arrangement must be in keeping with God's will if it is to be blessed by Him.

18:24–27 heeded: Moses was willing to listen to others and to improve the way he was doing things.

19:1, 2 The arrival of the community of Israel at Mt. Sinai was a momentous event The narrator (Moses) was impressed with the Lord's timing. Likely, **the same day** means exactly two months after the Exodus. When the Lord first confronted Moses, it was **before the mountain.** The Lord had promised that the Israelites would worship God at this place (see 3:12).

19:3 Moses went up to God because God had made His presence known on the mountain, and Moses was the intermediary between the Lord and the people.

19:4 The poetic expression **on eagles' wings** is a lovely way of describing the people's deliverance from Egypt. The Lord had whisked the Israelites away from slavery and brought them to Himself.

19:5–8 For the first time in Exodus, the term **covenant** is used to refer to the Lord's solemn arrangement with the Israelites at Mount Sinai, sometimes called the Mosaic Covenant (see also 24:1–8; 31:12–18; 34:27, 28).

19:9 God was able to reveal only so much of His splendor to the people, hence, He appeared to them **in the thick cloud.**

19:10, 11 The people to **consecrate** themselves, or, go through purifying rites to be ceremonially prepared for the meeting.

19:12 God commanded Moses to **set bounds** for the people. None could come near the mountain.

19:13 not live: The threat of death demonstrated the seriousness of what was about to happen. What must it have been like to anticipate with terror and wonder a close encounter with the living God?

19:14, 15 Sexual relations were also forbidden during the three days, for this would make the people ritually unclean.

19:16, 17 The epiphany of the Lord was a spectacular event of **thunderings and lightnings and a thick cloud.** Amazingly, the **trumpet** sounded from heaven rather than from the camp of Israel (compare Is. 27:13; 1 Cor. 15:52; 1 Thess. 4:16). None of the Israelites had ever heard such a blast! No wonder they **trembled** (20:18, 19).

19:18 the LORD descended: The omnipotent Creator came down to meet the Israelites. His presence evoked an overwhelming sense of awe. The **smoke** and **fire** reminded the Israelites of that great glory.

19:19–25 The **blast of the trumpet** (see v. 16) was not simply a distraction. It was a part of the physical assault on the senses—a sound and sight overload.

20:1 And God spoke: The following words of God are known as the Law of Moses. However, Moses was just a prophet, a mouthpiece for God's words. This law is really the Law of God.

20:2 I am the LORD your God: First, the Great King identified Himself by speaking His name (see 3:14, 15). **who brought you out:** Then, God reminded the Israelites of His gracious actions on their behalf.

20:3 no other gods: He was and is the only living God. He alone was to be worshiped by the Israelites.

20:4 not make ... a carved image: Peoples in the ancient world produced many kinds of idols. Israel was forbidden to do this.

20:5 The phrase **bow down ... nor serve** form a pair of Hebrew words that describes one idea: any form of worship to another god. God is **a jealous God:** In other words, He has a *zeal* for the truth that He alone is God, and He is *jealous* of any rivals.

20:6 The Lord's **mercy** would extend even more to the descendants of righteous people. The contrasting of the phrases "third and fourth" (v. 5) with **thousands** demonstrates that God's mercy is greater than His wrath.

20:7 The third commandment concerns the sanctity of God's name (see 3:14, 15). Use of God's name **in vain** involved: (1) trivializing His name by regarding it as insignificant; (2) trying to use it to advance evil purposes by coaxing God to violate His character and purposes; and even (3) using it in worship thoughtlessly.

20:8–11 The fourth commandment, **remember the Sabbath day,** was the special sign of the covenant with Israel at Mount Sinai (see 31:12–18). The word Sabbath means "Rest." The day was kept **holy** by ceasing all labor on that day. The Sabbath was specifically **the seventh day,** Saturday. It was patterned after the seventh day of rest for God following the six days of creation.

20:12 Honor your father and your mother: The term *honor* means "to treat with significance." It is the opposite of **in vain** (v. 7). Care of one's elderly parents was a basic element of social responsibility and godly piety in Israel. Here it is tied directly to how a person would fare in **the land.** People who were faithless to God in disregarding their parents would not last long in the new Promised Land.

20:13 The sixth to ninth commandments were designed to build a cohesive society in ancient Israel. Each was based on the value that God placed on people. The sixth commandment, **you shall not murder,** did not forbid all taking of life, for the Law itself included provisions for capital punishment (21:15–17, 23) as well as warfare (17:8–16). The deliberate murder of another person (outside the legitimate provisions of capital punishment or war) flagrantly violated the sanctity of life.

20:14 The seventh commandment concerned **adultery.** God regarded the sanctity of marriage as a sacred trust similar to the sanctity of life (v. 13).

20:15 The eighth commandment protected the sanctity of property by prohibiting theft.

20:16 The ninth commandment prohibited bearing **false witness.** This command protected the reputation of people from libel by others. In ancient Israelite law, the judging of a person's guilt or innocence was based on testimony by faithful witnesses (see Deut. 17:6).

20:17 Covet means "to have a strong desire for." Coveting was not just an appreciation of something from a distance, but an uncontrolled, inordinate, selfish desire. This tenth command governed an internal matter: the sin of coveting occurred in the mind.

20:18–20 do not fear: Moses told the people to stop being afraid; God was not going to hurt them. God wanted His people to respect the obvious hazards of wanton sin. Appropriate fear of God in this sense would make them reverent, obedient, and worshipful, so that they might **not sin.**

20:21 God remained in **thick darkness**—a symbol of His elusive presence (see Ps. 97:2). Only Moses could come near.

20:22–24 Israel was forbidden to make any altar more elaborate than **an altar of earth.**

20:25, 26 your nakedness: The worship of the gods of Canaan involved sexually perverse acts. Nothing obscene or unseemly was permitted in the pure worship of the living God.

21:1 The word translated here **the judgments** is one of several Hebrew words that describe the Law (the Torah). This word describes God's response to a specific action, something like an umpire's call. When Moses had to render a decision on an issue that he was not sure about, he would ask the Lord.

21:2 if you buy a Hebrew servant: Moses ruled that the period of enslavement was not to exceed six years, and **in the seventh he shall go free.** Perpetual slavery of Hebrew men and women was prohibited.

21:3–5 Other rulings followed: (1) A slave who was married at the time of his enslavement would keep his wife. (2) If the marriage took place during the period of slavery, the wife and children belonged to the master.

21:6 If the slave being freed did not wish to leave his family behind, he was allowed to make a commitment of lifelong servitude. The slave would be taken before **judges,** where he would be given the opportunity to declare his intentions.

21:7–11 In ancient times, a family might be reduced to such a desperate state that they would **sell** a **daughter** into bondage. If she were not acceptable to her new master, he would **let her be redeemed.** In no case was she to be sold to a **foreign people.** If she were purchased as a bride for a man's son, she was to be treated as one would treat a daughter. If the man took another wife later, **her food, her clothing, and her marriage rights** would continue.

21:12 This verse lays out the basic circumstances for capital punishment. A family who had suffered death or injury believed they had just cause to exact a penalty from the offender. These laws were meant to place limits on the penalties that might be carried out.

21:13 A person who accidentally murdered another could escape punishment by fleeing to a city of refuge (see Num. 35:9–34). **God delivered him:** A phrase indicating that the death was accidental.

21:14, 15 acts with premeditation: The Hebrew word means "to boil up" or "to act with presumption."

21:16, 17 curses: Breaking the fifth commandment (see 20:12) in this harsh manner was also a capital offense.

21:18, 19 This ruling allowed the victim of a fight to be compensated for lost time and treatment of injury.

21:20, 21 These provisions guarded somewhat against the abuse of slaves. They did not endorse the practice of slavery.

21:22–23 No matter how it is translated, this verse contains nothing that would support the modern practice of abortion on demand. **She gives birth prematurely** is one possible translation of the Hebrew. More probably the

Hebrew means that the woman suffers a mis-carriage. **If no harm follows:** If the woman did not die from the blow, then the offender would be fined for the loss of her child. If, however, she were to die, then the penalty was **life for life.**

21:24–25 Here we encounter the best-known statement of *lex talionis* ("law of retaliation"). Many ancient cultures allowed punishments greatly out of proportion to the offense. In Israel, a judgment corresponded to the nature of the injury, **eye for eye,** etc.

21:26, 27 In this instance, the verb **strike** means to cause injury. A master who inflicted harm on his slaves could be compelled to set them free.

21:28–32 An ox that caused human death was to be destroyed; if the ox had a history of injuring others and subsequently killed a free person, the owner could be put to death as well.

21:33–36 An unattended **pit** that caused the death of an animal would require restitution to the animal's owner because animals were the livelihood of their owners.

22:1–4 The stealing of **an ox or a sheep** carried heavy penalties.. **the sun has risen on him:** To strike the thief after the act would be considered inappropriate use of force. The thief who could not offer restitution was to **be sold** into slavery.

22:5–15 In some cases of suspected misman-agement, an **oath of the LORD** would be an acceptable testimony of innocence.

22:16, 17 The violation of a young woman was regarded as a serious affront. The payment of the **bride price** also meant that the one who had enticed her had to marry her.

22:18–21 The Bible does not record any executions of sorcerers or sorceresses, but it does recount the deadly consequences of false worship (see ch. 32; Num. 25).

22:22–27 God also had a special concern for **the poor** in Israel. They were not to be subject to the abusive practices of moneylenders nor have goods they needed for survival taken as collateral.

22:28 revile God nor curse a ruler: Since God is the ultimate sovereign, to curse a lesser ruler might encourage disrespect for God's authority.

22:29, 30 Promptness was commanded both in offering the first fruits of the field and in the presentation of one's sons to the Lord. The sons were to be redeemed (see 13:11–16) **on the eighth day.**

22:31 holy: Israel was to be set apart from other nations (see 19:5, 6). **Meat torn by beasts** was not to be eaten, presumably because the blood had not been drained from it.

23:1, 2 false report: Malicious talk is every-where condemned in Scripture (see James 3:1–12).

23:3 partiality to a poor man: God's support of the poor (see 22:25–27) did not overrule His justice.

23:4, 5 The **enemy** in this context would be another member of the Hebrew commu-nity.

23:6–12 Let it rest and lie fallow: Letting the land rest allowed the poor to glean any pro-duce that might grow during the fallow year. It also gave the land time to rejuvenate for greater productivity in subsequent years.

23:13–16 The Feast of Harvest is also called the Feast of Weeks (34:22). **The Feast of Ingathering** is also called the Feast of Ta-bernacles or Sukkoth (34:22; Lev. 23).

23:17 Lord GOD: Here two names for God, Adonai, translated as *Lord,* and Yahweh, translated as *GOD,* are used together. This expression emphasizes God's sovereignty.

23:18, 19 You shall not boil a young goat in its mother's milk is a command that forbade the Israelites to imitate the cruel sacrifices of their pagan neighbors.

23:20–23 an Angel: In v. 23, this being is de-scribed as "My Angel," an equivalent to the expression "the Angel of the LORD." **To keep you ... to bring you:** The Angel led and protected the Israelites just as the pillar of cloud did. **My name is in Him:** This is perhaps the strongest identification of the Angel with God. **His voice ... I speak:** The interplay of these words also identifies the Angel with God.

23:24, 25 The Canaanite gods, including Baal and his consorts, Anat and Asherah, were to be utterly destroyed. The **sacred pillars,** sym-bols of the overt sexuality of the Canaanite cult, were also to be destroyed.

23:26 miscarriage ... be barren: God's promises to make the Israelites fertile reminded the Israelites that there was no need to turn to the fertility cult that was so pervasive in Canaan.

23:27–31 not drive ... in one year: This is the first description of God's plan for the gradual conquest of Canaan. **your bounds:** These boundaries concur with the original promise given to Abraham (Gen. 15:18–21).

23:32, 33 covenant: Israel was forbidden to make treaties lest they be corrupted by the perverse customs of their neighbors.

24:1, 2 Come up to the Lord speaks of God's grace and His holiness. God could be approached only on His terms.

24:3, 4 Moses wrote: Scripture attests that Moses wrote down everything that he had heard from the Lord (see also 17:14; 34:27, 28; Num. 33:2). **Twelve tribes:** The whole nation was to be represented in worship.

24:5 Burnt offerings were incinerated in their entirety on the altar (see Lev. 1). **Peace offerings** were the prelude to a great, celebratory meal before the Lord (see Lev. 3).

24:6 The sprinkling of **blood** on the altar must have been an awe-inspiring ceremony. The blood of the Old Testament sacrifice anticipated, of course, the death of the Lord Jesus Christ.

24:7 The Book of the Covenant had been recorded by Moses existed in written form, and it was **read** to the people.

24:8 The sprinkling of **blood** on the people brought them into a covenant with the Lord. As their houses had been "under the blood" at the time of the Passover in Egypt (ch. 12), now the people themselves were under **the blood of the covenant** of the Lord.

24:9–11 The people mentioned in v. 1 **saw the God of Israel.** The mention of **His feet** and **His hand** indicates that they saw a manifestation of God. Perhaps this was an appearance of Jesus before His Incarnation (see 23:20). **And they ate and drank:** The festive covenant meal was a grand celebration of the presence of the living God.

24:12 Come up to me: Only Moses could draw near to God at that time. Today, we are all called to draw near to God through Jesus (see Heb. 4:14–16).

24:13, 14 Joshua was first mentioned during Israel's battle with Amalek (17:9–14; see also 32:17; 33:11). **for us:** The plural wording of these verses suggests that Joshua accompanied Moses at least part of the way up Mount Sinai.

24:15, 16 Moses then witnessed the appearance of the Lord in the midst of a **cloud** (see 19:9). **The glory of the LORD** is closely associated with the cloud, as in 33:9. It is possible that the **seventh day** of waiting was also the seventh day of the week, the Sabbath.

24:17, 18 The sight of the glory of the LORD again is not described for us. All that the people could see was something like **a consuming fire.** The significance of the **forty days and forty nights** is not specified in Scripture.

25:1, 2 bring me ... willingly: God does not need the gifts of His people, but He receives their gifts as a part of their true worship of Him. Yet in this passage God asks His people for specific, voluntary gifts.

25:3–7 Bronze was commonly used in this period. The list contains items and materials of significant value. The people gave these valuables to the Lord to express their desire to worship Him in spirit and in truth.

25:8 Sanctuary means "holy place." God, whose true dwelling place is beyond the heavens, desired a structure that would represent His holy presence among His people.

25:9 The pattern suggests that there is a heavenly reality that the earthly tabernacle was designed to resemble (see also v. 40; 26:30; 27:8; Acts 7:44; Heb. 8:5).

25:10 The most important religious symbol associated with the tabernacle was the holy **ark** or box. The highly decorated, beautifully fashioned ark kept the charter of the nation's relationship with God—the two stone tablets of the Ten Commandments—along with other symbols of God's mercy to them. The **cubit** was a measurement taken from the length of a man's arm from elbow to extended middle finger. The commonly accepted estimate for the cubit is eighteen inches. Therefore, the ark was about four feet long and two and one quarter feet wide and high.

25:11–15 The **gold** was used to **overlay** the ark, within and without, a decorative **molding of gold** adorned the box. The **rings of gold** allowed the ark to be carried on poles. It was not to be picked up by hand or carted about (see 2 Sam. 6).

25:16 The Testimony was the two tablets of the Ten Commandments.

25:17 The mercy seat is a familiar English translation of a Hebrew noun derived from the verb meaning "atone for," "to cover over," or "to make propitiation." The noun means "the place of propitiation." The mercy seat was the lid for the ark as well as the base on which the cherubim were to be placed.

25:18–20 two cherubim: The cherub was likely a composite creature with the body of a lion, a human-like face, and the wings of a great bird. The cherubim's **wings** stretched out and faced inward, shading the mercy seat. Their **faces** gazed on the mercy seat itself.

25:21, 22 The LORD promised Moses that He would **meet** with him at the mercy seat. The verb carries a specific meaning, "to meet at an appointed place."

25:23 The **table** was used to display twelve loaves of bread in the presence of the Lord. It was approximately three feet long, eighteen inches wide, and twenty-seven inches high.

25:24, 25 Like the ark, the table was to be overlaid with **gold** and was to have a decorative **molding of gold** (see v. 11). The **frame** was a decorative element that kept objects on the table from being disturbed.

25:26–28 The table was to have **rings** and **poles** so that it could be transported properly.

25:29 pure gold: All of the implements for making bread were also to be costly and wonderfully designed to physically represent their holiness.

25:30 The **showbread** itself is described more fully in Lev. 24:5–9. Twelve loaves representing the twelve tribes were placed in two rows with six loaves in each row. It was called showbread because it was placed symbolically before the "face" of God.

25:31 Perhaps the loveliest ornament in the tabernacle was the golden **lampstand.**

These seven lamps, fashioned with great care and precision, were to be placed on a magnificent lampstand. **of one piece:** All elements of the lampstand were to be hammered out of one solid piece of gold.

25:32 One of the seven lamps was to be placed in the center, flanked by three **branches** on either side. This became the basic design for the menorah of later Judaism.

25:33–36 The **bowls, branches,** and **knobs** were highly decorative. The lamp illuminated the interior of the holy place, but it also was a work of art in its own right, showing God's pleasure in artistry.

25:37 light in front: The wicks would all be on the same side of the lampstand so that the light would be shed principally in one direction. The lights would burn even when no priest was present.

25:38 The implements used in servicing the lamps were also to be made **of gold.**

25:39 A talent weighed about 75 pounds. It is very difficult to estimate the monetary value of the lampstand, since there were no coins or currency at this time. We can assume it was enormously valuable and exquisitely beautiful.

25:40 the pattern: Moses was not only told how to make the implements. He actually "saw" in some manner on Sinai a heavenly pattern for them (see v. 9; see also 26:30; 27:8; Acts 7:44; Heb. 8:5).

26:1 The word **tabernacle** means "dwelling place" or "tent." The **ten curtains** of the tabernacle are described first. These ten curtains were divided into two sets. The inner curtains were made of delicate fabric with brilliant colors and exquisite design.

26:2, 3 Each curtain was about forty-two feet long and six feet wide. The curtains were grouped in ten sections so they could be moved more easily.

26:4–6 Every detail of the curtains was specified, including directions for making the **loops** and **clasps.** With these the curtains were linked together to form the tent.

26:7 curtains of goat's hair: Goat's hair was a rich, black fabric highly prized in the ancient world. **Eleven curtains:** The outer curtains had to be larger than the inner curtains to assure complete coverage (see vv. 1, 2). The extra outer curtain was used over the front of the tent (see v. 9).

26:8–19 Precise directions were given for making of the **boards,** their **tenons** (or tabs), and their **sockets.** Each **board** was about fifteen feet long and two and one-half feet wide. **Twenty boards** were on the north side, twenty on the south, and six on the west. Corner posts stabilized the structure. The **sockets of silver** were costly and beautiful but functional.

26:20–28 The **bars** (or crossbars) of the tabernacle were placed at right angles to the upright **boards** (vv. 15–25) to stabilize the lattice-work structure. **Five bars … the middle bar:** On each of the three paneled sides of the tabernacle (north, south, and west), five bars were added to make the frame strong and rigid.

26:29 The fine acacia wood used to form the **boards** and **bars** also was overlaid with **gold.**

26:30 according to its pattern: Moses was reminded of the pattern he had seen (see 25:9, 40; 27:8; Acts 7:44; Heb. 8:5).

26:31–33 Perhaps the most beautiful and intricate of all the fabrics in the tabernacle, the **veil** was to hang from **pillars** by **clasps,** dividing the chamber into two separate rooms. The larger room would be called **the holy place** and the smaller room **the Most Holy** Place.

26:34–37 The **ark** with its **mercy seat** was the only object that would stay in the **Most Holy** Place of the tabernacle. The **lampstand** and the **table** were to be in the holy place. Each object was purposely placed to reflect the pattern, order, and design given to Moses (v. 30).

27:1 The **altar** was about seven and one-half feet square, with a height of four and one-half feet. The **cubit** was approximately eighteen inches.

27:2 The horns were projections on each corner of the square altar. They could have been used to secure the sacrificial animal to the altar.

27:3–7 Various implements were made of **bronze,** including the **grate,** which was to be suspended above the altar.

27:8 A hollow altar would allow the ashes to fall down through its center.

27:9–18 The courtyard of the tabernacle separated the ceremonies of worship from common areas.

27:19 utensils: These numerous tools and utensils were used only for the tabernacle. The **pegs** made of bronze **were** used for ropes to hold the supporting pillars of the courtyard.

27:20 The fuel for the lamps, **pure oil of pressed olives** (see also Lev. 24:1–4), burned with little smoke.

27:21 shall tend it: The lamp was never to go out. This command was a perpetual **statute** throughout the period of the Aaronic priesthood. The priests were also to burn the sweet incense on the altar of incense (see 30:7, 8).

28:1 Aaron and Aaron's sons: Aaron is first mentioned when he is reunited with his **brother** Moses after Moses' forty-year exile in Midian (4:14, 27–31). **minister to me as priest:** The ministry of the priests was for the sake of the people, but its principal focus was toward the Lord.

28:2 The holy garments were made holy by their consecration to God's service, as the materials of the tabernacle had been. **For glory and for beauty:** It is likely that the magnificent clothing of the priests represented the concept of imputed righteousness before the Lord (see Zech. 3:1–5).

28:3 gifted artisans: This is the first description of the craftsmen who would fashion the items for tabernacle worship. **the spirit of wisdom:** God added to this skill a special endowment of the Spirit to aid their work.

28:4 The garments of the priest are specified: **ephod** (vv. 5–14), **breastplate** (vv. 15–30), **robe** (vv. 31–35), **tunic** (v. 39), **turban** (vv. 36–38), **sash** (v. 39). Other garments were prepared for Aaron's **sons** (vv. 40–43).

28:5–14 The **ephod** has been described as a vest made of fine linen with brilliant colors. Its two main sections covered the chest and back, with seams at the shoulders and a band at the waist. The two **onyx stones,** engraved with the names of the tribes of Israel, were set in **gold.** The priest was to represent the people before the Lord.

28:15 The **breastplate** was decorated with twelve stones, one for each of the tribes of Israel. Within the pouch were the Urim and Thummim (see 28:30). The **breastplate of judgment** was used by the priest in seeking judgment—that is, a decision from the Lord on an issue presented for divine discernment.

28:16 a square: It measured nine inches on each side. The **span** was determined as the length from the tip of the thumb to the tip of the small finger on an outstretched hand.

28:17–28 Four rows of precious and semiprecious **stones** were fastened to the breastplate. These twelve stones bore the names of the **twelve tribes.**

28:29 Over his heart was a touching phrase that reminded the priest of his solemn responsibility. He represented the nation before the living God.

28:30 The **breastplate** held the mysterious stones called **the Urim and the Thummim.** These transliterated Hebrew words mean "Lights" and "Perfections" (both superlative plurals). Together their names may mean "perfect knowledge" or a similar idea. Hence, the expression "to consult with the Urim and the Thummim" might mean presenting a matter before the Lord with Urim and Thummim.

28:31, 32 The **robe** was a long, flowing garment made of **blue.**

28:33–35 The **pomegranates** on the hem were decorative. The **bells** would tinkle as the priest moved about within the sacred places.

28:36–38 The **turban** of the high priest was made of white linen on which was secured a gold **plate** engraved with the words HOLINESS TO THE LORD. The plate rested on the **forehead** of the priest. The meaning of the phrase **bear the iniquity** seems to indicate that the **holy gifts** of the people would be acceptable only when presented through mediations of a holy priest.

28:39 The record of the completion of these items is given in 39:27–29.

28:40, 41 put them on ... anoint ... consecrate ... sanctify: The rites of consecrating the priests for their holy work are detailed more fully in ch. 29, in 40:13–15, and in Lev. 8–10.

28:42 This command to wear **trousers** protected the modesty of the priests.

28:43 that they do not incur iniquity and die: It is difficult for us to grasp the gravity of the priests' responsibility as they ministered before the living God. To fail would invite judgment—even death.

29:1 The Hebrew word translated **hallow** describes actions that would mark the priests as distinct, holy, or set aside for God's purposes—as people who would approach Him in His service. The instruction to present animals **without blemish** reminds us that offering the best animals was an act of faith that expressed thanksgiving and confidence in God's provision.

29:2 unleavened bread: As it was at Passover (12:8), the use of leaven was prohibited in this rite also. Leaven was allowed for everyday baking.

29:3, 4 wash them: The bathing of the priests symbolized the necessity of cleanness before the Lord.

29:5–7 The directions for mixing **the anointing oil** are given in 30:22–33. To **pour it on his head** was a lavish gesture, later celebrated by a psalmist (Ps. 133:2).

29:8, 9 The **sons** were to be dressed after their father was. The verb translated **consecrate** literally means "to fill one's hand."

29:10, 11 The slaying of the **bull** happened only after the priests had **put their hands** on its **head.** This showed that the animal had been designated as their substitute.

29:12 blood: The application of the blood to **the horns of the altar** may have been to make the display of blood more prominent (see 12:7). The rest of the blood was poured **at the base of the altar.**

29:13, 14 sin offering: The burning of the **fat** and the **kidneys** on the altar would have produced an acrid odor. Yet, these sacrifices are described at times as "sweet-smelling" to the Lord (see 29:18). The rest of the animal was burned **outside the camp.**

29:15–18 Burnt offering is a translation of a Hebrew term that can be rendered "that which goes up (in smoke)."

29:19 the other ram: That is, the second of the two rams mentioned in v. 1 (compare the first ram, vv. 15–18).

29:20, 21 The **blood** that was daubed on the priests signified that they were entirely "under the blood" that atoned for sin (see 12:7). It is possible that the anointing of the **ear** represented the hearing of the Word of God, that the anointing of the **thumb** represented the accomplishment of the will of God, and that the anointing of the **toe** represented the walk with God.

29:22–24 A wave offering was to be made of the **fat** of the **ram** and the **unleavened bread** (described first in v. 2). The elements would be held high and then waved back and forth before the altar.

29:25 After this symbolic act (vv. 22–24), the fat and the unleavened breads were burned as a **burnt offering**, or **an offering made by fire.**

29:26 The **breast of the ram** was **waved** as a symbol of giving and receiving, and was then kept by the priests as their portion to eat as a gift from the Lord.

29:27, 28 The word translated **heave offering** means "something held up (before the Lord)."

29:29–34 The priests were to eat the meat of **the ram of the consecration** (see vv. 19–28) in a meal of celebration, along with the **bread** (vv. 2, 23) that had not been burned. **An outsider** was not to eat this food, nor were any leftovers permitted. Anything not eaten as a part of the sacred feast had to be burned.

29:35–39 The rites of consecration lasted **seven days**.

29:40, 41 One tenth of an ephah was about two quarts; **one fourth of a hin** was about one quart.

29:42, 43 The purpose of the **tabernacle** and its **offering** are reiterated. It was here that the Lord would **meet** with His people, **speak** with them, and display His **glory.**

29:44, 45 consecrate: The same idea, to set apart for God's service, is expressed in v. 9 with the Hebrew idiom "to fill the hand."

29:46 I am the LORD their God: Using His personal name, God declared to the Israelites that He was *their* God (see 15:2).

30:1, 2 This smaller **altar** was a stand used for burning the sweet-smelling incense. This altar was made of **acacia wood** (25:10). It

was eighteen inches square and three feet high.

30:3 Like the larger altar, the smaller was overlaid with **gold.** The **horns** were a decorative copy of those on the altar of burnt offering (see 27:2).

30:4, 5 Rings and **poles** were used to carry the altar.

30:6 The altar was situated within the holy place near the **veil** that divided it from the Most Holy Place. The mention of the **ark of the Testimony** reminds us of the most significant furnishing in the tabernacle.

30:7, 8 Aaron was directed to burn **sweet incense** each morning and at twilight, along with his tending of the **lamps** (27:20, 21).

30:9 Strange may mean "foreign" or perhaps "common" **incense.** No other kinds of offerings were to be made on this altar.

30:10, 11 Once a year: This Day of Atonement was later specified in Lev. 16. The "atoning" was a ritual cleansing to make **holy** before the Lord.

30:12, 13 The term **ransom** is related to the words for atonement and propitiation (see v. 10; 29:36, 37). The Israelites had to acknowledge that their lives were from God and governed by Him by giving an offering of money.

30:14–17 Every male was to provide a half-shekel ransom. The sum was not based on the worth or wealth of the person. The collection supported the Levites who cared for the tabernacle.

30:18 laver of bronze ... its base: The shape of the laver is not specified, but it clearly had two parts, the laver itself and its base.

30:19–21 washing their hands and their feet: The constant need for cleansing the priests' hands is understandable. But the feet of the priests would also be readily soiled because they wore sandals.

30:22–25 The priests used the holy oil in rites of anointing (see 29:7). The **perfumer,** like his counterparts who worked with wood, fabric, and metal, was a highly skilled craftsman (v. 35).

30:26–29 Everything connected with divine worship had to be anointed with the special oils. In this way, the creations of the workmen became holy, set aside for special use in the worship of God.

30:30 Anointing initiated the **priests** into the privilege of God's service.

30:31–33 The oil was reserved exclusively for the consecration of the tabernacle and all its furnishings. Any other use would result in divine judgment.

30:34–36 before the testimony: A portion of the fragrant incense was to be taken into the Most Holy Place as a holy symbol for the people before the Lord.

30:37, 38 No **incense** was to be made for personal use nor was it to be used for any other purpose than that which God commanded.

31:1, 2 called by name: The Lord now designated specifically the man who would be the principal artisan for the tabernacle. The name **Bezalel** means "in the shadow of God."

31:3 filled him with the Spirit of God: The first use of this expression indicated God's gifting to enable Bezalel to complete this important work.

31:4–6 The name **Aholiab,** given to the principal assistant to Bezalel, means "Tent of the Father." The **wisdom in the hearts** was a divine gift that allowed these craftsmen to complete their holy work.

31:7–14 My Sabbaths reminds us that keeping the Sabbath is the Lord's idea, not a human invention. **a sign:** The Sabbath was not for casual recreation, but for worshiping God.

31:15–17 Here the **Sabbath** is declared to be **a sign** between the Lord and Israel forever.

31:18 an end of speaking: This dramatic verse reminds the reader that the entire section beginning at 25:1 is a report of the divine encounter Moses experienced on the mountain (see 24:18; 25:1). When he returned to the people, he wrote down what he had seen and heard. The Spirit of God directed him to recall the amazing complex of details, ideas, and concepts of holy worship. **The finger of God** underscores the divine origin of the Law. The Ten Commandments were not the product of man, but the revelation of the Lord.

32:1 The people saw that Moses delayed

coming down from the mountain: The extended absence of Moses (24:18) and the terrifying setting into which he had disappeared (24:9–17) led the people to think that he might never return. **make us gods that shall go before us:** The people were asking not for the true God, but for other gods.

32:2, 3 The golden earrings were part of the treasure from Egypt.

32:4, 5 A molded calf was an ominous worship symbol, the cow and the bull worshiped in Egypt. **This is your god** gave credit for their deliverance to other than God.

32:6 The worship expressed here involved sacrifices combined with possibly sexual acts of profane worship. The words **and rose up to play** suggest the latter idea.

32:7, 8 The Lord alerted Moses to the fact of Israel's sin. **Have corrupted themselves:** The Hebrew means "to pervert," "to ruin."

32:9 a stiff-necked people: This is the first occasion of this phrase, which describes the stubbornness of the people who refused to follow the ways of God (see 33:3, 5; 34:9; Deut. 9:6, 13; 10:16).

32:10 God then threatened to destroy the nation entirely and begin anew with Moses (see Num. 14:11, 12). Moses interceded on behalf of the people for God's mercy (see vv. 11–13).

32:11–13 Moses used three principal arguments in this great prayer to assuage the anger of the Lord. (1) The deliverance of Israel from Egypt was the work of the Lord. How could He abandon them now? (2) The Egyptians would hear of this judgment and would believe that they had triumphed after all. How could He destroy them now? (3) The covenant had been established long before by divine oath. How could He revoke this promise now?

32:14 so the Lord relented: Here is a wonderful example of the interaction of faithful intercessory prayer and the purpose of the Lord. God intended to spare Israel. But He drew Moses into the process by causing him to pray for the right outcome.

32:15, 16 The two tablets of the Testimony are the tablets of the Ten Commandments (see 31:18).

32:17, 18 It appears that **Joshua** had accompanied Moses on at least a part of the journey to Mount Sinai (see 24:13, 14). While Moses was alone with God, Joshua seems to have remained nearby. He was the first to hear the raucous worship of the golden calf and report it to Moses.

32:19, 20 In great rage, Moses destroyed the **tablets.** This gesture suggested that the law had been "broken" by the actions of the people. Then Moses destroyed the **calf,** finally making the people drink its residue mixed with water.

32:21–24 Moses then turned on Aaron, demanding to know how such wickedness had happened. Aaron passed the blame onto the people rather than admit his own complicity in this terrible sin.

32:25 Despite the return of Moses, some of **the people were unrestrained,** perhaps still conducting themselves in the unseemly behavior of worshipers of Baal.

32:26 whoever is on the Lord's side: The first to respond to Moses were men from the tribe of Levi.

32:27, 28 Moses sent the Levites to **kill** the people engaged in evil. It was painful for a Levite to slay **his brother … his companion … his neighbor.** But the wicked had to be destroyed lest the whole camp perish under God's judgment.

32:29 consecrate yourselves: The people needed to turn completely back to the living God in the hope that He would receive them in **blessing** again.

32:30, 31 The terrible sin of the people needed to be removed. Moses hoped to **make atonement** for the people.

32:32, 33 Blot me out of your book: This is the most touching moment in Moses' leadership of the Israelites.

32:34 God promises His **Angel** (23:20–23) will still lead the people, but coupled with that promise is a solemn threat of **punishment.**

32:35 It is not clear whether the Lord plagued **the people** after Moses' prayer or if this passage refers to the judgment God had already sent upon the people (see vv. 26–28).

33:1, 2 depart … go up: The time had come for the march into Canaan.

33:3, 4 God announced that He would **not** go up among his people because they were **stiff-necked. This bad news,** the command to move on without the presence of the Lord, was hardly a message that they wanted to hear.

33:5, 6 I could come suggested that the threat of judgment was still very real (see 32:35). The **ornaments** were associated with the idolatrous worship of the golden calf (32:2, 3). Their removal was a mark of repentance and renewal.

33:7 his tent … the tabernacle of meeting: Moses moved his own tent **outside the camp** to symbolize the Lord's departure from His people. Moses called his tent **the tabernacle of meeting,** for here he met with the living God.

33:8 all the people rose … stood: The people responded reverently to the living God. Only Moses could approach God, but those who were nearby could respond from a distance in awe and worship.

33:9 This **pillar of cloud** is the same one that guided the Israelites out of Egypt (13:21, 22; 24:15, 16).

33:10 saw … worshiped: From a distance, the people saw the pillar and recognized the presence of God, and they worshiped by bowing low to the ground.

33:11 the LORD: The identification of the pillar with the Lord is now unmistakable. **His servant Joshua:** The bold man of God who would become Moses' successor.

33:12 The message the Lord had given to Moses and the people, recorded at the beginning of the chapter (vv. 1–3), troubled Moses. Thus, he pressed the Lord to grant His presence in the adventure of faith that the people were to undertake.

33:13 The words **Your way** refer in this context to the divine Presence among His people. **Your people** was Moses' reminder of God's promise that He would make the Israelites His people (see 6:1–8).

33:14–16 Rest refers to the land of Canaan. Moses even dared to say that the **Presence** of the Lord in the midst of His people was the only acceptable condition for further advance.

33:17 God's **grace** was accompanied by His intimate knowledge of and care for Moses, represented in the expression **I know you by name.**

33:18 The word **glory** conveys the idea of weight, significance, and importance. Moses requested an even greater experience of God's Presence.

33:19 My goodness speaks of the sense of the wonder of God, of His divine attributes, of His essential worth and majesty. **be gracious ... have compassion:** The Lord's sovereignty is paramount in His dealings with people. In His mercy, He responded to Moses' plea.

33:20 cannot see My face: Human language is simply too limited to describe what Moses experienced in this dramatic encounter. God is Spirit (John 4:24).

33:21 The **place** is generally assumed to be a cleft in the rock of Mount Sinai. Moses experienced the Lord who was his Rock (see Deut. 32:4) while standing **on the rock.**

33:22, 23 The use of words such as **hand, back,** and **face** is anthropomorphic, a way of describing God, who is Spirit, in terms familiar to humankind.

34:1, 2 The command to **cut two tablets of stone** is one of the great demonstrations of God's mercy. He was willing to begin again with them.

34:3, 4 As in the preparation of the people in ch. 19, the warning that **no man shall come up with you** was meant to protect the careless or the curious who would die if they trespassed on holy ground.

34:5 As at other times (see 33:9–11) the people saw the **cloud,** which Moses knew as the visible symbol of the living God before him.

34:6 long-suffering: The idea of the Hebrew idiom is that God is very slow to anger. The Hebrew word for **goodness** means "loyal love"; the word for **truth** means "faithfulness," "truth," and "constancy."

34:7, 8 thousands ... the third and the fourth: This phrase resembles the words of 20:5, 6, but the order is changed for emphasis here. The point is that God is more willing to show his **mercy** than His wrath.

34:9 Go among us indicates that Moses was still praying for a reversal of God's judgment announced in 33:1–3. The Lord responded

to these pleasing words by restoring the covenant (see vv. 10–28).

34:10, 11 I make a covenant: Concurrent with the announcement of the covenant is the promise that the people will experience **an awesome thing,** namely the conquest of Canaan. The enormity of Israel's refusal to obey God's command and conquer the land (see Num. 13, 14) is to be seen in the light of this extraordinary promise (see also Deut. 4:32–40).

34:12–14 covenant: Israel was forbidden to make treaties with nearby peoples. Instead, they were to destroy those nations, lest they be ruined by their perverted ideas and false religious affections.

34:15 Unfortunately, the phrase **to play the harlot** was probably not just a figure of speech. **To eat of his sacrifice** alludes to the love feast that preceded the orgy, reminiscent of the episode with the golden calf (see 32:5, 6, 19, 25).

34:16 take of his daughters for your sons: God's prohibition against intermarriage was not a matter of prejudice. Intermarriage would be the quickest route to compromise with false religion and immoral behavior.

34:17, 18 Israel had, in fact, already paid the price for fashioning **molded gods.**

34:19, 20 The law of the **firstborn** is also found in 13:2; 22:29, 30.

34:21 The law of the Sabbath is repeated from 20:8–11; 31:12–18.

34:22–27 The commands of the three annual **feasts** are repeated from 23:14–17.

34:28 The period of **forty days and forty nights** matched Moses' earlier pilgrimage to Sinai (see 24:18). **bread ... water:** No one can go without water for more than three or four days, so, we must view Moses' continued existence as a miracle of the Lord. The Lord then **wrote ... the Ten Commandments:** The Writer was the Lord Himself (see 31:18; 32:15, 16; 34:1, 4).

34:29, 30 The people were **afraid to come near.** With all they had seen and heard, they had reason to be cautious.

34:31, 32 Moses sought to calm their fear and to teach them the **commandments** the Lord had sent him to proclaim.

34:33–35 The **veil** Moses wore concealed the glow of his face.

35:1–3 The principal teaching the **Sabbath** is the fourth commandment (20:8–11), and this teaching is expanded in 31:12–18. To **kindle ... fire** was considered a breach of the command.

35:4–9 This section is based on the instructions of 25:1–8.

35:10–19 gifted artisans: The call now went out for artisans who would create the tabernacle furnishings and the garments for the priests.

35:20–29 The offerings for the tabernacle are perhaps the most impressive offering ever taken from God's people for any endeavor! The key was the stirring of the **heart** and the willingness of the **spirit** of those who gave. At last they had to be told to stop giving (see 36:2–7)!

35:30–33 filled him with the Spirit of God: The Spirit of God in this artisan attested to the importance the Lord attached to the aesthetic beauty of the tabernacle.

35:34, 35 The ability to teach shows the same Spirit was also at work among His people in the Old Testament period.

36:1–8 gifted artisans: The demands of God's design (ch. 26) called for careful, detailed, and artistic work.

36:9–19 Here we read about the fashioning of the outer **curtains** (v. 14).

36:20–30 A discussion of the tabernacle frame. See 26:15–25 for its design.

36:31–34 See 26:26–30 for the earlier instructions for the design of the crossbars for the outer structure of the tabernacle.

36:35, 36 The description of the **veil** that divided the holy place and the Most Holy Place.

36:37, 38 The description of the screen for the **door** of the tabernacle.

37:1–9 This section describes how **Bezalel** (see 31:2) constructed the holy ark, including the mercy seat and the cherubs, following the pattern that the Lord gave to Moses on the mountain (see 25:10–22).

37:10–16 The construction of the table for the showbread corresponds in every detail to the instructions given to Moses by the Lord in 25:23–30.

37:17–29 The creation of the golden **lampstand.** The earlier text contains instruction for lighting the lamps, which Moses did when everything was completed (see 40:4, 25).

38:1–7 The construction of the altar of burnt offering. All was done as the Lord had commanded.

38:8 The crafting of the bronze **laver.** For the corresponding instructions, see 30:17–21.

38:9–23 The building of the **court** of the tabernacle. For the corresponding instructions, see 27:9–19.

38:24 The weight of **all the gold** used in the work may have been about a ton. The **talent** weighed about 70 pounds and equaled 3,000 **shekels.**

38:25 all the silver: The quantity of silver was enormous, about 7,000 pounds.

38:26 A **bekah** (half-shekel) of silver, required of each man over the age of twenty, came from 603,550 people, which corresponds with other estimates of the Exodus community (see Num. 1).

38:27, 28 Enormous amounts of **silver** appeared in the most mundane elements of the tabernacle and its furnishings. It was a glorious dwelling for the presence of the living God in the midst of His people.

38:29–31 The weight of the **bronze** was about 5,000 pounds.

39:1 This verse is a summary statement that confirms the completion of the priests' garments first described in 28:1–4.

39:2–7 This section details the crafting of Aaron's **ephod,** according to the explicit instructions given to Moses in 28:5–14.

39:8–21 Here we read about the **breastplate,** made according to the directions spelled out in 28:15–30.

39:22–26 The fashioning of the **robe** followed the divine commands given to Moses.

39:27–29 The fashioning of the **tunics,** the **turban,** and the **sash** follow the commands given in 28:39. **short trousers:** These were for modesty.

39:30, 31 The fashioning of the **plate** that was attached to the **turban** of the high priest followed precisely the commands that the Lord had given to Moses (28:36–38).

39:32–42 These verses list **all the work** that God had commanded through Moses. It was now completed.

39:43 The words **Moses looked** suggest he conducted a final inspection. Then **Moses blessed them,** a magnanimous gesture of approval for the work accomplished.

40:1, 2 This **first month** was the month Abib, also called Nisan (see 12:2; 13:4). The tabernacle was completed nine months after the arrival of the people at Mount Sinai (see 19:1) and two weeks before the second celebration of the Passover (see v. 17).

40:3–8 Moses directed the placement of furnishings, including the **ark,** the **table** of showbread, the **altar** for the incense, the **altar of the burnt offering,** the **laver,** and the **court** along with appropriate **screens.** The lamps were to be **lit** and **water** was to be placed in the laver. See ch. 25 for a list of the furnishings.

40:9–11 Following the placement of the furnishings, the Lord instructed Moses to **anoint** everything in the tabernacle so that it would be **holy.**

40:12–15 wash them: The priests had to be clean before they were dressed in their **holy garments.** Moses, acting as God's representative, was then to **anoint** them as he had anointed the furnishings. The family of Aaron was to have **an everlasting priesthood.**

40:16–19 Moses scrupulously obeyed every detail of God's commands (see 7:10).

40:20, 21 The Testimony is the stone tablets of the Ten Commandments (see 25:16). **The mercy seat on top of the ark:** See the description in 25:17–22.

40:22, 23 the table … the bread: See the description in 25:23–30.

40:24, 25 the lampstand … lamps: See the description in 25:31–40; 27:20, 21.

40:26, 27 the gold altar: See the description in 30:1–10. **incense:** See the description in 30:34–38.

40:28 the screen: See the description in 26:36, 37.

40:29 the altar of burnt offering: See the description in 27:1–8.

40:30–32 the laver (v. 30): See the description in 30:17–21.

40:33 the court: See the description in 27:9–19.

40:34 cloud … glory: When everything the Lord had commanded had been completed, He came near in an epiphany, that manifested His glory and presence among His people (see 19:20; 34:5). When the Lord came near in the event described at 19:20, the people were terrified. But in His coming near the tabernacle the people were overjoyed. This was not a descent in judgment, but in mercy.

40:35 Although Moses had been intimately involved in preparing the tabernacle, the glory of the Lord was present and that even Moses could not enter it. **The cloud rested** speaks of God living among His people.

40:36, 37 the cloud: The glory of the Lord, which now was among His people, also directed the Israelites' movement (see 13:21, 22; Num. 9:15–23). The appearance of His glory is sometimes called the Shekinah or the Shekinah glory, from the Hebrew for "to dwell."

40:38 the cloud of the Lord: How wonderful that the Book of Exodus concludes with this image of the gracious God, hovering protectively over His people.

Leviticus

Introduction

The name Leviticus is derived from the name of the tribe of Levi, the tribe that supplied the priests for Israel. Leviticus addresses many of the activities of the priests. It gives extensive instructions for the sacrificial system that atoned for both ceremonial and moral impurity. Yet Leviticus is not just a manual for priests. It was intended for the entire Israelite community, with at least two purposes: (1) that people would know and value their privileges and responsibilities before God; and (2) that priests could not gain oppressive power over the people with any monopoly on the knowledge of how to approach God.

Jewish and Christian tradition has regarded Moses as the author of Leviticus. After delivering Israel out of Egypt, God revealed His covenant to Moses at Mount Sinai. Leviticus records a large part of that covenant. If Moses or a scribe acting as his secretary wrote down the revelation as God gave it, Leviticus was composed shortly after 1440 B.C. or shortly after 1290 B.C., depending on the date assigned to the Exodus.

The purpose of Leviticus was to show the Israelites how they could live in ritual and moral purity. When they maintained their purity, God could live among them and they could approach Him in worship. Many of the required sacrifices described in Leviticus were for the atonement of sins. On the other hand, the voluntary sacrifices brought the people to fellowship and feast with God, their family, and others.

The distinctions between clean and unclean and the various laws for holy living promoted the Israelites' own welfare and marked them out as a people separated to God. Israel's witness to God's holiness and their visible well-being as a result of holy living before Him would vividly demonstrate to their neighbors God's power and His care for His people. Ultimately, Leviticus calls God's people of all ages to the great adventure of patterning life after God's holy purposes.

1:1 Now connects Leviticus with Exodus. God was now ready to instruct Moses on *how* the Israelites should approach Him in the earthly dwelling they had built for Him. **The tabernacle of meeting** was the center of Israel's public worship until Solomon's temple was built in Jerusalem centuries later.

1:2 The children of Israel: Now that God had entered into covenant with them, Israel was a people and no longer just a band of refugees (Ex. 6:2–8).

1:3 The **burnt sacrifice** was the only sacrifice that was entirely consumed on the altar. **male without blemish:** A male animal without blemish was of great value to the worshiper. To offer it on the altar was a real sacrifice. **before the LORD:** God was present everywhere, but His presence was felt in an unusual manner at the site of His holy worship.

1:4 Each worshiper brought his or her own offering and then placed his or her own **hand** on the animal's **head.** No one could send another person to offer sacrifices for his or her sins.

1:5 the priests, Aaron's sons: Aaron was Moses' older brother and the one whom God had designated to be high priest of Israel (Ex. 28:1). Aaron's sons were Nadab, Abihu, Eleazar, and Ithamar. **sprinkle the blood:** The lifeblood of the sacrificial animal on the altar substituted for the life of the guilty worshiper.

1:6–9 sweet aroma to the LORD: Never, in this image or elsewhere, does Scripture represent God as eating the offerings brought to Him, as the pagan gods were thought to do.

1:10–13 The procedure for the burnt offering was the same when the animal was a sheep or a goat (Ex. 12:5).

1:14–17 While the richest Israelites offered bulls, most of the people offered sheep or goats. The poorest were allowed to bring **turtledoves or young pigeons.** The different offerings were accepted by God without prejudice or favoritism.

2:1 Anyone translates an inclusive term, emphasizing that male or female, native Israelite or convert, could come to God with an offering (see 1:2). **Fine flour** was from the best grain and was free from impurities. Olive **oil** was a primary part of the diet and a prominent symbol of blessing and prosperity. **Frankincense** was a costly incense from South Arabia and East Africa.

2:2 The handful of the offering burned on the altar included **all the frankincense.** This helped to make the offering **a sweet aroma to the LORD.**

2:3 Aaron's and his sons': A significant portion of the priests' daily food came from this part of the grain offering. **most holy:** Only the consecrated priests were allowed to eat the offerings, and only within the tabernacle (6:16).

2:4–7 These verses list three types of *cooked* grain offerings: (1) bread **baked in the oven;** (2) cakes **baked** or fried **in a pan;** and (3) cakes **baked in a covered pan.** All were made of **fine flour mixed with oil.**

2:8–10 The priests' presentation of these cooked grain offerings on the **altar** was essentially the same as for the uncooked grain offerings.

2:11 Prohibiting **leaven** in grain offerings that were burned on the altar might have been based on the same principle that prohibited eating the blood of animals. As blood is the life force of animals, leaven represents the life force of the vegetable kingdom.

2:12 A separate offering of the **firstfruits** of the harvest is described later (23:9–21).

2:13 The salt of the covenant of your God was to be used in every grain offering, a reminder of the covenant God had made with Israel at Sinai.

2:14–16 This **grain offering** had to be prepared from the first of the year's grain harvest.

3:1 peace offering: The Hebrew word for *peace* means "wholeness, completeness, soundness, health." The peace offerings were times of feasting, drinking, talking, singing, and enjoying salvation as a great gift from God (see 7:11–21).

3:2 As with the burnt sacrifice, the presenter brought the animal, laid **his hand** on its **head,** and killed it. Then the priests sprinkled **the blood all around on the altar.**

3:3, 4 The fat, the **two kidneys,** and the fatty lobe attached to the **liver** (vv. 9, 10, 14, 15) specifically belonged to God. The fat was the most prized portion of the meat. The kidneys were viewed as the seat of the emotions. The liver was the essential organ for telling the future in the pagan cultures surrounding Israel (see Ezek. 21:21); such fortunetelling was strictly forbidden in Israel (Deut. 18:10).

3:5 Upon the burnt sacrifice indicates that the peace offering normally followed the burnt offering, which was entirely consumed on the altar. Being reconciled to God through the burnt offering, the worshiper was in a position to fellowship with God and with his or her family by sharing in the feast of the peace offering.

3:6, 7 before the LORD: Not a redundancy, but a reminder of the Lamb of God and that all offerings are offered before God (1:3).

3:8, 9 the whole fat tail: The tail of the Palestinian broad-tailed sheep is almost entirely fat and can weigh more than 16 pounds.

3:10, 11 The mention of **food** does not mean that God desired, needed, or ate the sacrifice, as the pagan gods were thought to do.

3:12–15 In the regulations for offering a **goat,** the animal's sex is not mentioned as it is in the regulations for cattle and sheep. Otherwise, the regulations are the same as those for the sacrifice of a sheep.

3:16 All the fat is the LORD's is a reminder that our gifts to God must be from the best that we have.

3:17 perpetual ... dwellings: This prohibition of eating fat or blood applied wherever an Israelite might live.

4:1, 2 sins unintentionally: Sin that occurred without the sinner realizing it still offended the holiness of God and polluted His earthly dwelling place. Cleansing was required.

4:3 anointed priest: Since the high priest represented the people before God, his sin brought **guilt on the people.** Until the sin was atoned for, the priest could not come before God, and the people's intermediary with God was set aside.

4:4, 5 Whether it was the **bull** for the **anointed priest** or the **whole congregation,** the male **kid** for the **ruler,** or the female

kid or **lamb** for the **common** person, the worshiper brought the animal, laid a hand on its head, and killed it.

4:6 Seven symbolizes completeness in the Bible. The **veil** was a heavy linen curtain that separated the Most Holy Place from the rest of the tabernacle (Ex. 26:31). Sprinkling the **blood** before, or on, the **veil** purified the Most Holy Place.

4:7 The altar of sweet incense was in the Holy Place (Ex. 30:1–6). Incense was burned on this altar. Still, this part of the tabernacle also needed purification—through the application of blood.

4:8–10 The instructions the **fat** were the same as for the fat of the peace offering.

4:11, 12 Burning **the whole bull** ensured that the priest did not profit from the atonement for his sin. Carrying it **outside the camp** symbolized the seriousness of the pollution of the by the high priest's sin. Even the **ashes** from the altar symbolized the atonement necessary for sin. Therefore, the ground **outside the camp** where they were **poured out** was considered **clean.**

4:13, 14 hidden: A sin committed without anyone being aware that it was sin.

4:15 The elders represented the whole **congregation** as they laid their **hands on the head of the bull.**

4:16–22 ruler: Literally, "one lifted up," a leader or chief of the people.

4:23, 24 A kid of the goats was designated for a ruler of the people.

4:25 The altar of burnt offering stood in the outer court of the tabernacle.

4:26 The priest was not guilty of sin in this case, so he was entitled to the meat from the sacrificial animal brought by the ruler.

4:27–35 common people: Literally, "the people of the land," those who held no office.

5:1 utterance of an oath: Anyone with information about the oath was obligated to come forward and give testimony.

5:2 unclean: The difference between clean and unclean animals is carefully spelled out in ch. 11.

5:3 human uncleanness: Primarily the body fluids that caused a person to become unclean (see ch. 15). Contact with a corpse

would also be included, as would contact with another person's waste.

5:4 thoughtlessly: Rashly, in the grip of strong emotion or without thinking the matter through. **to do evil or to do good:** A rash vow is rash, whether the intention is good or evil.

5:5 in any of these matters: This was a reminder that these sins were to be taken seriously; they required atonement.

5:6 trespass offering: This section still deals with purification offerings for inadvertent guilt.

5:7 two turtledoves: Part of the purification offering was burned on the altar and part was not burned. To accomplish this when offering birds, the worshiper brought two.

5:8–10 The first bird for the sin offering was sacrificed for its blood. The second was burned, like the fat and vital organs of the larger animals.

5:11 Oil and **frankincense** were not added as they were to the grain offering.

5:12, 13 Part of the offering was burned **on the altar,** the rest belonged to the priests.

5:14, 15 commits a trespass: The offering righted the wrong of the offense and cleared the conscience of the sinner. **the holy things of the LORD:** Anything separated from common use and dedicated to the sacred use of the Lord.

5:16 make restitution: A guiding principle of biblical law and ethics is that when a person has caused harm to another the one offending is responsible to make good the loss. **add one-fifth to it:** As a fine, in addition to the ram and the full **restitution.**

5:17 he does not know: Ignorance did not make an offense harmless. The offender was still **guilty** and bore responsibility for his **iniquity.**

5:18 In such a situation, the offering of a ram brought atonement for the unknown offense. **His ignorance in which he erred and did not know it:** This was not a sin of rebellion.

5:19 he has certainly trespassed against the LORD: The emphasis on the worshiper's ignorance of his sin is matched here by the statement that his offering had been accepted.

6:1–3 lying to his neighbor: Saying the property was lost, stolen, or destroyed, when he had kept it for himself. **delivered to him for safekeeping:** People would leave valuables with trusted neighbors or business associates when they went on a long journey. **a pledge:** A security deposit or collateral on a loan. **any one of these things:** A person betrayed his neighbor's trust, taking or keeping property illegally and then lying about it under oath.

6:4 is guilty: Since his oath in court had placed him beyond the reach of punishment, only the offender's guilty conscience could bring him to justice.

6:5, 6 A **one-fifth** fine was evidence of genuine repentance. Then the offender could bring the ram for the trespass offering and be forgiven for the sin of swearing falsely in God's name.

6:7–9 Aaron and his sons, the priests, were responsible for the correct preparation and presentation of all offerings. **shall be kept burning:** The fire on the altar was never to go out.

6:10 linen garment ... linen trousers: The sacred clothing of the priests, worn only in the tabernacle (see 16:4; Ex. 28:40–43).

6:11 The linen **garments** were not worn when carrying the ashes **outside the camp.**

6:12, 13 the fire ... shall not be put out: There are at least three reasons for this: (1) The original fire on the altar came from God (9:24). (2) Perpetual fire symbolized the perpetual worship of God. (3) Perpetual fire symbolized the continual need for atonement which was the purpose of the offerings.

6:14–18 all the males ... Aaron: This included all the priests, as well as descendants of Aaron. **must be holy:** Only those who had been consecrated to God could touch or use the reserved sacrificial portions.

6:19, 20 beginning ... anointed: The high priest personally was to offer this sacrifice twice daily for as long as he was in office. **half of it ... at night:** The idea of a morning and an evening appointment with God is open to every believer through the high priestly work of Christ.

6:21, 22 The priest ... in his place: Aaron's successors as high priest, beginning with his son Eleazar (see Num. 20:25–28). **statute forever:** This grain offering and the burnt offering were sacrificed daily.

6:23 it shall not be eaten: The principle here was that no one should profit from an offering which he himself had given.

6:24–27 The **blood** of the sin offering was for the atonement of the one bringing the offering; as such, the blood was holy.

6:28, 29 The breaking of the **earthen vessel,** a clay cooking pot, is a striking contrast to the scouring of the **bronze pot.** A clay vessel is permeable and the residue of cooking could never be removed completely from it, even by a thorough scrubbing.

6:30 The blood of the sin offering was **brought into the tabernacle of meeting** (4:5–7, 16–18). The priests were forbidden to eat the flesh of these offerings.

7:1, 2 In the place: At the door of the tabernacle of meeting before the Lord (1:3).

7:3, 4 The burning of the **fat** was commanded as it was for the peace offering (3:9–11). The fat was considered the best part of the meat. It was offered to God.

7:5–7 the priest who makes atonement: The priests would take turns officiating and would receive equal proportions of the sacrifices.

7:8 The skin was the only part that was not burned (1:6). The officiating priest received it as part of his wages.

7:9 Each **grain offering** belonged to the priest who offered it.

7:10 By contrast, an offering of unbaked grain belonged to **all the sons of Aaron, to one as much as the other.**

7:11–13 The sacrifice of **thanksgiving** required three kinds of **unleavened cakes** and **leavened bread.**

7:14 The **heave offering** was given to the officiating priest. The offering was waved before the Lord as an acknowledgment that He is the giver of all gifts.

7:15 the same day it is offered: The festive worshiper bringing his peace offering for a family feast at the tabernacle demonstrated trust in God for the next day's provision.

7:16, 17 The **vow** and the **voluntary** peace offering could be eaten on the second day without jeopardizing the purity of the tabernacle.

7:18 it shall not be ... imputed: The sacrifice would lose all its benefit to the worshiper.

7:19 touches any unclean thing: An unclean object pollutes a clean object.

7:20, 21 unclean: Chapters 11—15; 22 detail various kinds of uncleanness in persons and things. **shall be cut off:** This meant either execution, banishment, or denial of citizenship privileges.

7:22, 23 The **fat** belonged to God.

7:24 used in any other way: That is, for softening leather, for fuel, or in any other way but eating it.

7:25–29 The portions of the peace **offering** that belonged to the Lord included the fat, which was burned on the altar (v. 31), and the breast and thigh, which were the priests' portions (vv. 30–34).

7:30 His own hands: A worshiper could not delegate his worship, thanksgiving, or praise. **The breast** was one of the finer portions of the meat that was allowed to be eaten. The breast of the sacrificial animal was brought to the priest as a **wave offering** symbolizing that the entire sacrifice was dedicated to God.

7:31 The **breast** (the elevated offering) was **Aaron's and his sons'**—it belonged to all the priests.

7:32, 33 heave offering: The **right** (front) **thigh** (heave offering) of the sacrificial animal belonged to the officiating priest, and all the priests received a further portion, the breast (wave offering).

7:34–38 A summary listing of the offerings of chs. 1—7, with the reminder that these sacrifices were prescribed by God Himself on Mount Sinai.

8:1, 2 Aaron had presided over Israel's idolatry with the golden calf. Now God gave him a second chance by allowing him to be ordained as God's own high priest.

8:3 the congregation: The ordination of the priests was so important that all the people needed to witness it.

8:4, 5 This is what the LORD commanded, it was important that God's instructions for worship be carried out meticulously.

8:6 Moses brought Aaron: As the prophet of God and the leader of God's people (Deut.

18:15–18; 34:1–12), Moses was the only person qualified to ordain Aaron and his sons as Israel's priests. **washed them with water:** This symbolized moral purity.

8:7 The **ephod** was the outer garment of the high priest, made of gold thread; violet, purple, and scarlet woolen thread; and fine linen thread (Ex. 28:5, 6).

8:8 the Urim and the Thummim: Sacred lots used to determine the will of God. Apparently, the high priest phrased questions so the answers would be "yes" or "no," depending on how the lots came up.

8:9 The golden plate was also known as **the holy crown** of the high priest. On it was engraved HOLINESS TO THE LORD (Ex. 28:36).

8:10, 11 Since **the altar** was sprinkled **seven times** representing the complete consecration of the tabernacle and all its furnishings and utensils to God's service.

8:12 anointed: The high priests, beginning with Aaron, were anointed, as were the kings of Israel (1 Sam. 10:1; 16:13) and at least some of the prophets (1 Kin. 19:16).

8:13 Aaron's sons were set apart or ordained as priests, they too were anointed, (Ex. 40:15).

8:14, 15 Moses' purpose is clear from the statement that he **purified the altar ... and consecrated it.** The priests, the altar, and everything associated with the sacrificial system had to be pure and consecrated to God.

8:16–23 The reason for applying the blood of the sacrifice to Aaron's **ear, thumb,** and **big toe** is unclear.

8:24, 25 The right thigh, in this case, was a consecration offering for all the priests, so it was burned on the altar.

8:26–29 Moses' part: Moses, acting as priest in this first sacrifice, received the breast, which from that time on would go to Aaron and his sons.

8:30–32 Moses' act of consecration here used anointing oil together with blood from the altar.

8:33, 34 seven days: This period of confinement to the tabernacle emphasized the significance of the event. **consecrate you:** Literally, "fill your hand."

8:35 That you may not die was a reminder that it is dangerous to approach God carelessly, without reverence, ignoring His instructions.

8:36 All those involved obeyed all **the LORD had commanded.** Their ordination was complete. God would accept their service and their intercession for the people.

9:1 the eighth day: After the seven days of Aaron and his sons' consecration (8:33–36) were completed.

9:2 A young bull was the prescribed **sin offering** for the high priest (4:3). Before he could offer the sacrifices of others, his own sin needed atonement. The bull of the sin offering and the **ram** of the **burnt offering** (1:4, 10) accomplished this.

9:3 you shall speak: Now that Aaron had been anointed high priest, he would begin to instruct Israel on how to bring sacrifices.

9:4 All four of the regular public offerings—the burnt offering, the sin offering, the **peace** offering, and the **grain offering**—were performed on this first day of Israel's sacrificial worship in the tabernacle. **the LORD will appear to you:** The sacrifices were not an end in themselves; they allowed the worshiper to meet with God without being destroyed.

9:5, 6 So they brought … and … drew near: The immediate and total obedience of the people is emphasized, in contrast to the complaining and rebellion that marked their response to Moses and to God (Ex. 32; Num. 14).

9:7 Aaron could **make atonement** for himself and for the people.

9:8 The high priest had to kill **the calf of the sin offering** himself, since the sacrifice was for him.

9:9–11 Aaron did not sprinkle the **blood** before the veil (4:6). Also, the **altar** here is the altar of burnt offering, not the altar of incense (4:7).

9:12–14 Aaron killed the ram himself (9:2), since it was a burnt offering for him.

9:15–17 The goat as the **sin offering** looked forward to the Day of Atonement (16:5, 9), rather than back to the normal sin offering for all the people, which required a bull (4:14).

9:18–21 The fact that God sent fire to consume these offerings signaled His future acceptance of all the sacrifices He had commanded the Israelites to bring.

9:22 Aaron … blessed them: When God gave the priestly blessing, He said that the priests would put His name on the children of Israel, and He would bless them (Num. 6:27).

9:23 the tabernacle of meeting: Moses and Aaron went into the tent itself where the altar of incense, the table of showbread, and the golden lampstand (the menorah) stood. **glory of the LORD appeared:** as God had promised through Moses (vv. 4, 6).

9:24 fire came out: The sacrifices were consumed, not by fire ignited by Aaron, but by fire **from before the LORD. fell on their faces:** This response to the glory of God's presence was called fear.

10:1 Nadab and Abihu were Aaron's eldest sons. **profane fire:** Nadab and Abihu violated God's holiness. in **Profane** is literally "strange."

10:2 Fire went out from the LORD in punishment against Nadab and Abihu. Their deaths were a result of their rebellious action.

10:3 those who come near Me: God referred to the priests, Aaron and his sons. **Aaron held his peace:** Though he was grieving the sudden loss of his sons, Aaron recognized that their action was rebellion against God.

10:4 carry: Though priests were forbidden to come into contact with the dead, Moses called Aaron's cousins to carry the bodies of Nadab and Abihu **out of the camp** for burial.

10:5 as Moses had said: The pattern of obedience interrupted by Nadab and Abihu's sin was reestablished.

10:6 uncover your heads nor tear your clothes: These were conventional signs of mourning (see Ezek. 24:16–17).

10:7, 8 the LORD spoke to Aaron: This is the only place in Leviticus where God speaks to Aaron alone.

10:9, 10 Holy and unholy had been the subject of the preceding instructions about sacrifices and their first implementation (chs. 1—9). **Unclean and clean** would be the subject of the following instructions about animals, diseases, bodily discharges, and so on (chs. 11—15).

10:11–13 you may teach ... the statutes: The priests were primarily responsible for teaching the people of Israel the Law of God. Parents were to teach their children (Deut. 6:6–9, 20–25).

10:14 a clean place: a place that had been ritually cleansed from the kinds of uncleanness described in chs. 11—15.

10:15 Moses reassured his brother that God would allow him to remain as high priest.

10:16 careful inquiry: Moses was responsible to see that Nadab and Abihu's sin did not cause further punishment to fall on Israel.

10:17, 18 The priests were to eat the flesh of any sin offering whose **blood was not brought inside the holy place**. Eleazar and Ithamar had not done this, but had burned up all the goat of the sin offering.

10:19 Aaron said: Aaron replied, taking responsibility for his family, as was proper in Israel's patriarchal society. **would it have been accepted:** Aaron was arguing that God would prefer the priest to err on the side of caution rather than presumption.

10:20 Moses ... was content: Moses recognized that Aaron's failure was not rebellion, that his argument had merit, and that Aaron could be forgiven.

11:1 the LORD spoke: Aaron, as high priest, was responsible for teaching and administering the law. So God spoke to Moses and Aaron together with further instructions (10:10, 11).

11:2 on the earth: As distinct from the sea and the air.

11:3 chewing the cud: That is, the ruminants, like cows, sheep, goats, deer, and antelope. The ruminants eat only plants, mainly grasses and grains. No meat-eating animal chews the cud.

11:4 The camel would not have been an important source of meat for Israel even if it had been permitted, for it never was numerous in Israel or important to Israel's economy.

11:5 The rock hyrax lives in colonies among the rocks (see Prov. 30:26). Hyraxes appear to chew constantly while sitting outside their dens sunning themselves.

11:6 The hare is not a ruminant nor does it have a hoof.

11:7 The swine is the best known of the unclean animals and continues to be avoided by Jews.

11:8 Eating **unclean** animals' meat or touching their dead carcasses caused an Israelite to be unclean. However, touching a live animal did not make a person unclean, and an Israelite could raise and use a donkey or camel as a beast of burden without becoming unclean.

11:9 A water creature had to have both **fins and scales** in order to be eaten. Oysters, clams, crabs, lobsters, and eels were unclean.

11:10–12 The phrasing is careful, deliberate to remove any possibility of finding any exception. **Abomination** implies not just avoidance, but active, fierce repulsion. Fins and scales are "appropriate" for water creatures.

11:13–19 The hoopoe is a migratory bird that spends its winters in Africa and its summers in Israel. **The bat** is not a bird, but was grouped with birds because it has wings and flies.

11:20 Creep on all fours is an idiom for crawling on the ground. Many insects move about in filth and eat refuse.

11:21 Insects with jointed legs were permitted to be eaten. The joints are the enlarged third legs of locusts and grasshoppers that enable them to leap. Locusts and grasshoppers eat only plants.

11:22–24 Touching unclean carcass caused a person to be **unclean until evening,** when the new day began.

11:25 If a person carried or picked up a **carcass** that person's uncleanness was greater. Therefore, the remedy had to be more thorough.

11:26 The word **carcass** is not in the Hebrew text, but clearly that is what is meant here. A live unclean animal, such as a donkey or camel, could not make a person unclean simply by touch.

11:27, 28 Whatever goes on its paws is **unclean**. To touch a **carcass** was to be **unclean** and to carry a carcass was to be even more unclean.

11:29, 30 that creep on the earth: The group includes small rodents, such as mice, moles, shrews, and hamsters, as well as some kinds of lizard.

11:31 when they are dead: Literally, "in their death" or "in their dying." The Israelite farmer was more likely to kill a small rodent in the course of the day than any other creature named in this chapter. It was important to remember as they killed these pests that they themselves would be **unclean until evening** if they touched them.

11:32 Expensive vessels of wood, fabric, leather, or fiber were to **be put in water** or soaked **until evening**. But at evening, the start of the new Jewish day, they would **be clean**.

11:33 Any earthen vessel ... you shall break: Pottery was plentiful, cheap, and easily replaced. Vessels made of pottery were also used for food preparation and eating.

11:34 The contents of any vessel made **unclean** in this way became unclean also.

11:35 These ovens were made of clay and so had to be **broken** also.

11:36 A spring or a cistern could hardly be emptied. Only the person removing the **carcass** became unclean—probably until evening.

11:37, 38 Dry **planting seed** did not become unclean.

11:39, 40 if any animal ... dies: This refers to animals that died of natural causes, and not those killed for food. The **carcass** caused the person who touched it to be **unclean** because its blood had not been drained.

11:41–43 Crawls on its belly and **has many feet** are new descriptions. They were not mentioned in the previous ban on eating **creeping things.**

 IN DEPTH   **Not Like Others**

People tend to put a lot of effort into being like those around them. But God challenges His people not to be like everybody else. In the OT, God instructed Israel not to pattern itself after the nations around it. Instead, He called the Israelites to consecrate themselves (set themselves apart from others) and be holy, for He, the Lord their God, was holy (Lev. 11:44, 45).

One of the main ways that Israel was to be different was in its worship. Worship in the surrounding cultures included many rituals that Israel was not to follow. These forbidden practices were based on values that were not holy or rooted in a high view of God, people, or creation. Among them were:

- Divination or magic.
- Frenzied, chaotic dances.
- Self-mutilation.
- Ritual prostitution.
- Sensuality and orgiastic fertility rites.
- Human sacrifices.
- Sacrifices for the dead.

By contrast, Israel's worship was measured against God's holiness and defined the nation as God's people. There was no need to compete with other nations, cultures, or religions. The closing song at the end of Leviticus, Israel's manual for ritual and worship, says: "I will walk among you and be your God, and you shall be My people" (Lev. 26:12). This promise became a watchword for Israel (Hos. 1:9, 10; 2:23; Jer. 31:33; Ezek. 36:28). Later, the church also came to define itself as belonging to God first and foremost, with a responsibility for holy worship and living (1 Pet. 1:13–16; 2:9, 10).

11:44 I am the LORD your God: The word for *LORD* is Yahweh, the name by which God had revealed Himself to Moses (Ex. 3:14, 15; 6:2, 3). **You shall be holy; for I am holy:** To be holy means to "be separate." To be separate *to* God is much more important than to be separate *from* other things.

11:45 For emphasis, God reaffirmed His identity. Then He added an astounding commitment to Israel. His purpose in bringing them **up out of the land of Egypt** was **to be** their **God.** Because of God's holy nature, they also had to **be holy.**

11:46, 47 To distinguish reminds the reader that these were instructions for the people as well as the priests.

12:1, 2 The child did not cause the mother to be **unclean.** Rather, it was the blood and other fluids in childbirth that made the mother ritually unclean for a period of time, just as other bodily fluids caused people to be unclean (ch. 15). **Seven days** of uncleanness for a male child was the same length of time as the uncleanness for the woman's menstrual period or **customary impurity** (15:19–24).

12:3 Medical science has concluded that **the eighth day** is the best time for circumcision. Before the eighth day, blood does not clot as well, and after it, sensitivity to pain becomes greater. In Israel circumcision was the outward symbol of God's covenant with Abraham (Gen. 17:9–14).

12:4 The eighth day also marked the end of the mother's uncleanness with regard to everyday objects and activities; she no longer would make them unclean by touching them. But her personal uncleanness would continue for another **thirty-three days. blood of her purification:** Blood is the carrier of life in the body and the agent of purification from sin.

12:5 The birth of **a female child** doubled the period of ritual impurity. No reason for this is given.

12:6 The sacrifices required were the same **for a son or a daughter.** The **burnt offering** (ch. 1) and the **sin offering** (ch. 4) were a woman's responsibility following the birth of a child, though her husband normally would accompany her .

12:7 The phrase **a male or a female** reemphasizes the equal worth of a girl and a boy.

12:8 If she is not able to bring a lamb is, literally, "If she cannot find in her hand enough for a lamb."

13:1, 2 A swelling, a scab, or a bright spot would often be a minor ailment that healed within a few days and caused no further concern. **he shall be brought:** The most serious result of the priest's examination was to be declared unclean and banished from the camp.

13:3 The priest shall examine: The priest made the diagnosis. The subject of the passage is not medical treatment but ritual impurity.

13:4–6 he shall wash his clothes: Personal hygiene was an important factor in identifying and preventing the spread of infectious diseases.

13:7–11 shall not isolate him: Isolation, or quarantine, was for the purpose of protecting the community until a diagnosis was reached.

13:12–17 Some of these diseases were healed, either spontaneously or with treatment. After another examination, **the priest** would then **pronounce** the patient **clean.**

13:18–46 'Unclean! Unclean!': The afflicted person had to warn people away. Others would become unclean by coming into contact with him. **All the days:** Not every disease was incurable. **He shall dwell alone ... outside the camp:** This ensured that the rest of the community and the sanctuary did not become ritually impure.

13:47–49 Leprous plague would include any mold, mildew, or other fungus growths on clothing.

13:50–59 The procedures for diagnosing a problem with clothing were similar to those for diagnosing human skin ailments. A seven-day period of quarantine and a second examination were required. Infected clothes had to be burned. If the **plague** had not spread, a garment could be salvaged.

14:1, 2 He shall be brought to the priest: The priest administered the sacrifices and other rituals that marked and celebrated the return of the person to the community of Israel.

14:3 The priest shall go out of the camp: Even if the person was healed, he still was unclean and could not come into the camp until the proper rituals had been carried out (v. 8). **if the leprosy is healed:** These rites were to confirm and celebrate the healing that already had occurred, to cleanse the patient, and to readmit him into the community and its worship.

14:4 Cedar wood was used perhaps because of its durability and resistance to decay, symbolizing the patient's recovery from the decay that had threatened his life. **Scarlet** was probably a scarlet thread or cord. Scarlet symbolized blood. **Hyssop** was an aromatic herb used for food flavoring, fragrance, and medicine.

14:5 Running water is literally "living water." This is water from a spring or stream, as opposed to water from a cistern, vessel, or pool. Stagnant water symbolized potential death. The blood of the bird ran into the water in the **earthen vessel.**

14:6, 7 It is likely that the sprigs of **hyssop** were tied to the **cedar wood** with the **scarlet** thread. With that in one hand and the **living bird** in the other hand, the priest would **dip** them all in the **blood**-and-water mixture in the pottery bowl and then shake them over the head of the one **to be cleansed.** This procedure was performed **seven times.** After being dipped in the blood of the dead bird, **the living bird** was let **loose in the open field.** It symbolically took away from the camp and the tabernacle the uncleanness of the person who was returning to the camp.

14:8, 9 Two washings of clothes and body and two head shavings, seven days apart, completed the ritual cleansing.

14:10–12 The eighth day was the day of circumcision for a newborn male. The symbolism of starting again, almost of being born again into the community of faith, was continued.

14:13 in the place ... holy place: The place where the lamb was killed is referred to as the *holy place.* Therefore, it must have been inside the door, in the court of the tabernacle.

14:14–18 These rites encompassed the entire body, symbolizing a reversal in the person's status before God, from outside the community to a member of the community once again.

14:19, 20 With these three offerings and the trespass offering (v. 12), the formerly unclean person had brought all the mandatory sacrifices that it was impossible to bring during the time of uncleanness.

14:21–32 God's legislation for Israel showed special concern for the **poor.** In these sacrifices, the poor Israelite still had to bring a lamb for the **trespass offering.** But for the **sin offering** and the **burnt offering,** he was allowed to bring **turtledoves** or **pigeons.**

14:33, 34 The land of Canaan, which I give you refers to the land God had promised Abraham He would give to his descendants (Gen. 15:18–21). **Leprous plague** is the same Hebrew term used in 13:2 to indicate serious skin diseases.

14:35–45 If every effort to save the house failed, it was destroyed and removed.

14:46, 47 Lies down probably means to sleep overnight in the house.

14:48–53 The rite for cleansing a house was the same as for cleansing a person.

14:54–57 The common characteristic of these problems, whether on persons, garments, or the walls of houses, was that they were harmful surface growths. If their uncleanness could not be removed, the thing that carried the uncleanness had to be removed from among God's people.

15:1, 2 Discharge refers to any abnormal flow. **Body** is used here as a euphemism for the sexual organ.

15:3–11 A man with a discharge was unclean, as was anyone who came into contact with him, his spit, or any object that he touched. The other person made unclean was required to wash his clothes and himself and would be unclean **until evening.**

15:12 The vessel of earth ... of wood: Here the purpose was to prevent the spread of the disease through food and food utensils.

15:13 Seven days was enough time to be sure the discharge had ceased.

15:14 Two turtledoves or two young pigeons was the smallest, least expensive sacrifice allowed. The degree of uncleanness caused by genital discharges was less than that caused by skin diseases.

15:15–17 This passage concerns emissions of semen apart from sexual intercourse, which is the subject of v. 18.

15:18 Both the male and the female are involved in sexual intercourse. Both had to wash afterward, and both were ritually **unclean** until evening.

15:19–23 This passage provides regulations a woman's menstrual period. Her ritual uncleanness lasted seven days. Any person or object she touched became **unclean.**

15:24 This regulation did not forbid intercourse during menstruation; see, however, 18:19; 20:18. The man became ritually unclean for seven days, the same length of time as for the woman. No sacrifice was required; menstruation was not regarded as sinful.

15:25–27 If a woman had a flow of blood at any time other than her normal monthly period, her uncleanness continued the whole time and passed to all she touched. Such was the case with the woman who touched Jesus secretly (Luke 8:43–48).

15:28–30 At the end of her abnormal discharge, a woman's obligation was the same as a man's. She was to bring the smallest allowable sacrifice for the atonement of sins she may have committed during the period of her uncleanness, when she was barred from the tabernacle.

15:31–33 The focus of these regulations **uncleanness** was on keeping God's **tabernacle** undefiled so that Israel would have a place to come for the atonement of sin and the privilege of meeting with God.

16:1 The two sons of Aaron died because of how they **offered profane fire,** literally, "drew near," **before the LORD.** Aaron had to know how to do it properly to avoid the fate his sons had suffered.

16:2, 3 God's command **not to come at just any time** limited Aaron's entrance to a specific day. **the Holy Place inside the veil:** The Most Holy Place, the inner sanctuary of the tabernacle, was separated by a veil of fine blue, purple, and scarlet linen.

16:4, 5 Holy garments are the simple linen garments the priests wore when on duty at the altar. On this day, the high priest went in simplicity and humility; he offered atonement for himself first, then for his family, and finally for all of Israel.

16:6–11 After atoning **for himself,** the high priest could offer the sacrifice to atone for the people.

16:12 beaten fine: That is, of the highest quality.

16:13–19 Aaron offered **the goat ... for the people.** The further actions involved in this sacrifice made it clear that the sins of the people had a defiling effect.

16:20 Aaron performed these actions out of the sight of the people.

16:21 Sending the goat into the wilderness was a public ceremony. Everyone could see Aaron symbolically place the sins of the people on the goat's head. **Iniquities ... transgressions ... sins,** all of these offenses were placed on the head of the goat, which took them away from the camp, away from the people, and away from God.

16:22 shall bear on itself all their iniquities: This is the origin of the common expression "scapegoat." This goat was not guilty of the sins he bore.

16:23–25 Aaron burned **the fat of the sin offering** as instructed in 4:8–10.

16:26–28 The bull and goat of the two sin offerings were burned according to the instructions in 4:11, 12.

16:29 afflict your souls: Examine yourselves and seek God's forgiveness.

16:30, 31 A sabbath of solemn rest was more strictly observed than the normal Sabbath.

16:32, 33 In his father's place emphasizes that this day was to be observed throughout Israel's generations.

16:34 And he did as the LORD commanded Moses indicates that Aaron, as high priest, carried out everything God had commanded for this all-important day.

17:1–3 Kills probably indicates a sacrifice, for only the sacrificial animals the **ox, lamb,** and **goat** are listed.

17:4 The guilt of bloodshed usually refers to killing a human being. However, the blood of the sacrifice was the only means of atonement for sin.

17:5 Which they offer means "which they might offer." Sacrifice in an open field was prohibited.

17:6, 7 Demons were thought to inhabit the wilderness. **They have played the harlot** indicates (1) Israel's worship of other gods and (2) God's attitude to this worship.

17:8, 9 This regulation specifically extends the command to **strangers who dwell among you.**

17:10 Eating **blood** was forbidden. **Any blood** means blood in any form, including blood not drained from the animal when it was slaughtered.

17:11, 12 The **life** of animals and of humans **is in the blood. I have given** emphasizes that blood has no *intrinsic* power to atone for sin. God appointed blood to have this power because it represents the life of the creature.

17:13, 14 That may be eaten refers to animals that are clean according to the regulations in ch. 11. **Cover it with dust** is a token of burial.

17:15 The reason for uncleanness in this context was contact with a carcass in which there was still blood that had not been drained. The Law forbade eating any animal that had died a natural death (Deut. 14:21).

17:16 guilt: The mild degree of ritual uncleanness became a serious sin if the required cleansing was not done.

18:1, 2 The LORD here translates the divine name Yahweh. God was basing His claim to the Israelites' devotion on His willingness to reveal Himself to them, to redeem them, and to be their God.

18:3 Israel had lived in **Egypt** for generations and had been dominated by the Egyptians. **Canaan** is the land God would give Israel. The Israelites would be tempted to imitate the Canaanites physically, culturally, and religiously.

18:4, 5 ordinances ... statutes: These are decrees, laws, and acts of a permanent nature. **Judgments** refers to judicial decisions involving situations that might not be addressed in the statutes. Through the ordinances and the judgments of God, Israel would know how to live.

18:6 Anyone who is near of kin covers cases such as incest between father and daughter and between brother and full sister. To **uncover** someone's **nakedness** is to have sexual intercourse with that person.

18:7 The nakedness of your father does not imply a homosexual act. Rather, it emphasizes that to commit incest with the wife of one's father is symbolically to uncover the father's nakedness also, because the two are one flesh through marriage.

18:8 Father's wife may refer to a father's marriage partner after the death or divorce of one's mother, or it may refer to a wife or concubine who is not one's mother.

18:9, 10 Your sister refers to a half sister, since she is defined either as **the daughter of your father** or **the daughter of your mother.** The word **elsewhere** refers to cases in which a father maintained multiple households of wives or concubines.

18:11, 12 Here, **begotten by your father** is a legal term to indicate adoption. Legally she would be a full sister.

18:13–17 a woman and her daughter: This might involve a widow who lived with her daughter and son-in-law.

18:18 as a rival to her sister: An example of the problems this situation can cause is the family life of Jacob, who married the sisters Leah and Rachel.

18:19 Her customary impurity refers to a woman's menstrual period.

18:20, 21 Adultery is forbidden in Ex. 20:14; its penalty is given in Lev. 20:10.

18:22 Homosexuality here is labeled an **abomination,** something detestable to God.

18:23 Bestiality is labeled **perversion,** something out of the natural order.

18:24–30 The land had become so **defiled** by the perverted practices of the Canaanites that it was vomiting it out.

19:1–3 Revere means to respect and to obey. Young children are to obey their parents. Adult children are to respect their parents and concern themselves with their parents' welfare.

19:4, 5 The **peace offering** was a **free will** offering. When we have peace, or wholeness, in God through the peace offering of Christ (see Col. 1:19, 20), we can offer freely everything we are, everything we have, and everything we do.

19:6–10 Providing for **the poor and the stranger** (the alien who could not own land) was a priority in ancient Israelite society. Reserving the **gleanings** of a harvest for the poor was an effective way of providing food for them.

19:11–13 wages ... until morning: A day laborer needed his pay daily to provide food for himself and his family. To withhold it for one's own gain was forbidden (see James 5:4).

19:14, 15 In court, neither **the poor,** nor **the mighty** were to be given any special treatment.

19:16 A **talebearer** is not just a gossip, but a slanderer, actively seeking to destroy another's reputation.

19:17 rebuke your neighbor: Ideally this would involve resolving the issue face to face. However, it also could involve taking the issue to court to settle it legally rather than taking it into one's own hands or allowing it to fester in one's heart.

19:18 Vengeance belongs to God because His vengeance is entirely just. **Bear any grudge** means actively keeping a grudge alive with an eye toward vengeance. **You shall love your neighbor as yourself:** Jesus identified this as one of only two commandments that, if kept, would fulfill all of the Law (Matt. 22:37–40).

19:19 Holiness means purity, in three important areas: (1) animal husbandry, (2) agriculture, and (3) domestic life. This principle also reflects reverence for creation as God made it.

19:20 The concubine, a woman of low social standing and few rights, may not have had the freedom to cry out when approached sexually. Therefore, she remained guiltless.

19:21–25 Young trees need to preserve their strength for growth rather than fruit. The owner probably would have clipped off the blossoms in the first three years. The harvest of the fourth year was a kind of firstfruits (2:14).

19:26 Divination and **soothsaying** reveal a lack of trust in God to bring the best future.

19:27 Beards were standard among Israelite men. Shaving one's hair or beard often was a sign of mourning.

19:28 Cutting one's flesh **for the dead** and tattooing one's body had religious significance among Israel's pagan neighbors. In Israel, such practices were forbidden.

19:29, 30 For a man in debt, facing the loss of his land, hiring out his daughter as a prostitute might have seemed like an alternative.

19:31 Mediums and familiar spirits are different from what is mentioned in v. 26. All contact with such spirits was strictly forbidden. Such practices demonstrated lack of faith in God.

19:32 To **rise** when an elder entered one's presence was another way of showing reverence for God and submission to Him.

19:33, 34 Generous treatment of a **stranger,** or a resident alien, in the land was based on God's generous treatment of the Israelites when they were **strangers in the land of Egypt.** What God had done for them they were to pass along to others.

19:35–37 Injustice in judgment is injustice in legal transactions (vv. 11, 12, 15–18). **Injustice ... in measurement** is one kind of injustice in business transactions.

20:1–5 strangers: All of the people dwelling in the land, whether citizens or not, were required to abstain from religious practices that defiled God's **sanctuary** and profaned His **holy name.** Execution by stoning seems to have been the way God set His face against the offender.

20:6–8 Who sanctifies you means "who sets you apart (to Myself)." The worshiper accepted God's gifts and agreed to forsake all other allegiances.

20:9 One **who curses his father or his mother** was very far from honoring them (see 19:3; Ex. 20:12). **His blood shall be upon him** signifies that capital punishment was deserved.

20:10 The adulterer and the adulteress both entered freely into the affair. Both were punished.

20:11, 12 Perversion literally means "mixing, confusion" of the natural order.

20:13, 14 Marries (literally *takes*) probably means to have as a common-law wife. **burned ... he and they:** Perhaps this was done after the stoning to prevent burial. Not to be buried was thought to make a peaceful afterlife impossible.

20:15–19 her sickness: That is, her menstrual flow (15:19–24; 18:19). **exposed ... her blood:** In menstruation, the mysterious powers of blood and sex are drawn together. Casual disregard shows disrespect for God as the Creator as well as for the human role in procreation.

20:20 They shall die childless may not seem to be a severe penalty, but it was greatly dreaded in the ancient world, where continuation of the family line was extremely important. If this situation were an extramarital affair, as implied by the verb **lies with,** the childlessness would affect two families.

20:21 takes: If a man died childless before his father's death and the division of the family property, his brother was to marry the widow. Their firstborn would be considered the dead brother's heir.

20:22, 23 I am casting out: God took full responsibility for His judgment on the wickedness of the people of Canaan, for which He would use Israel as His instrument.

20:24–27 Flowing with milk and honey conveys the agricultural potential of the land. **Has separated you** emphasizes that the people of Israel were distinct from the people of Canaan.

21:1 defile himself: Contact with a dead body made a person unclean. Since the priests ministered before the altar of the Lord, if unclean they could not perform their priestly duties.

21:2, 3 The only exceptions for the priest were his closest relatives. For them he could attend mourning rites. The wife is probably included in the term **relatives who are nearest to him.** The **virgin sister** still belonged to the priest's father's family. A married sister belonged to her husband's family; the priest could not attend mourning rites for her.

21:4, 5 These were pagan mourning customs. All Israelites were forbidden to observe them (19:27, 28).

21:6 The bread belonged to God because it was sacrificed on His altar. The priests received

portions of it as one part of God's provision for them and their families (6:14—7:36).

21:7 A priest could marry a widow, but other women who had been with a man in any sexual relationship were forbidden to him.

21:8, 9 Prostitution was the opposite of holiness, the ultimate faithfulness. The priest's daughter was to reflect her father's holiness to God.

21:10–12 The high priest was not allowed to become ritually unclean, even at the death of his father or mother. Nor could he display signs of mourning.

21:13–17 The high priest could marry only a **virgin. His posterity** had to be pure.

21:18–19 Most of these physical conditions were permanent; a person afflicted by them could never serve as a priest. But some, like a broken limb or a skin condition, would heal with time. The priest suffering from them was barred from serving as a priest only so long as he was afflicted.

21:20, 21 Neither **eczema** nor **scab** is included in the list of things that made an ordinary Israelite unclean (13:1–46). As with mourning rites and marriage partners, the priests were held to a higher standard because the priests had a more public role in modeling holiness to God.

21:22 He may eat: Physical defect did not imply a moral defect. The person afflicted still had access to the food of the altar by which the priests lived. He was not denied his provision, nor was he forced to leave the sanctuary.

21:23 My sanctuaries probably refers to the two divisions of the tabernacle: (1) the holy place, where the altar of incense stood; and (2) the Most Holy Place, where the ark of the covenant rested. This implies that the person with a physical defect had access to the outer court as long as he did not come too close to the **altar** of burnt offering, which stood in the outer court.

21:24 These instructions were not given secretly to the priests, but publicly. Each Israelite was to know what God expected of him or her, and what God expected of the priests.

22:1, 2 separate ... holy things: When the priests were ritually impure, they were not to come near the offerings the Israelites had brought to the tabernacle for dedication to God.

22:3 Cut off from My presence does not mean executed or banished from the community, but permanently denied the privilege of ministering as a priest.

22:4 leper: Regulations about leprosy are given in 13:1–46; 14:1–32. Regulations about **discharge** are found in 15:1–18.

22:5, 6 creeping thing ... until evening: Clean and unclean animals are listed in ch. 11.

22:7 it is his food: The sacrifices brought by the Israelites were a major part of the daily provisions for the priests.

22:8, 9 Ordinary Israelites could eat this meat (17:15; 16). The priests were held to a higher standard.

22:10 Three groups of persons were denied access to the meat of the offerings: (1) the **outsider** (literally *any stranger*), whether a foreigner or an Israelite not of Aaron's family line; (2) the **one who dwells** as a guest **with the priest;** and (3) **a hired servant,** who was not a member of the priest's household but worked in it on a daily basis.

22:11 Slaves, whether bought or born in the household, were allowed to eat of the priest's share of the consecrated food. They were part of his household.

22:12 A priest's daughter became a member of her husband's family when she married. If her husband was not a priest, she lost her right to eat consecrated food.

22:13–16 Restitution plus one-fifth was the penalty for an ineligible person who ate of the **holy offering.** In 5:14–16, the penalty was the sacrifice of a ram and restitution plus one-fifth.

22:17, 18 strangers: If a resident alien accepted the Israelites' God as his God, he was accepted at the Lord's sanctuary under the same conditions as any Israelite.

22:19–21 without blemish: This standard was addressed later by the prophet Malachi when some in his day were bringing defective animals to sacrifice on God's altar (Mal. 1:7–14).

22:22, 23 An exception was made for a **freewill offering,** since it was not required and was not made in fulfillment of **a vow.**

22:24, 25 cut: Castrated animals were not acceptable for sacrifice. **from a foreigner's hand:** Israel's sacrificial animals were to be raised by Israelites who worshiped God, not by foreigners who worshiped a multitude of pagan gods.

22:26, 27 The eighth day parallels the time of circumcision for the human male baby. The mother was not to be deprived of her newborn in the first days after its birth, when both her maternal instincts and her milk supply were at their highest.

22:28–33 All of these elements had been expressed before, but not all together. God's person, His name, His present action in sanctifying His people, and His past action in rescuing them from slavery in Egypt—all are given as the basis of Israel's worship.

23:1 the LORD spoke to Moses: The instructions about each convocation are marked off in this chapter by the normal introduction for a speech in Leviticus. The instructions for each could be read separately, while still reminding the people that each had been ordained by God.

23:2 The feasts of the LORD literally means "appointed times of the Lord." **Holy convocations** were sacred assemblies of all the people called together at the appointed times by the priests.

23:3, 4 Six days shall work be done: Work is one of the ways humans bear the image of God. The regular **seventh day** of rest and other holidays from work are ordained for our refreshment and the chance to commune more closely with God and His people. **A Sabbath of solemn rest** may be restated as "a Sabbath that is all a Sabbath should be." **In all your dwellings** emphasized the universal nature of the Sabbath. It was to be celebrated in every household.

23:5 fourteenth day of the first month: This would fall between mid-March and mid-April. The **Passover** celebrated Israel's exodus from Egypt (Ex. 12:1–28).

23:6–9 The Feast of Unleavened Bread immediately followed Passover, beginning the **fifteenth day** of Nisan. In practice, the Passover and the Feast of Unleavened Bread were observed together as an eight-day festival. **Customary work** was work that could be left a day or two without problems. Essential or emergency tasks could be done.

23:10 a sheaf of the firstfruits: This bundle of the first harvested barley belonged to God acknowledging God's provision of the harvest.

23:11, 12 To **wave the sheaf** was to elevate the offering before God.

23:13 Two-tenths of an ephah was twice the grain offering for the regular morning and evening burnt offerings and a **drink offering** was to accompany the regular morning and evening offerings. **Wine** was the third major agricultural product of the land, along with grain and oil.

23:14 An Israelite could not eat the grain of a new harvest until he had brought the offering of the firstfruits to the sanctuary. **Parched grain** was a favorite food of those working in the harvest.

23:15–17 Firstfruits refers to the firstfruits of wheat. The Feast of Weeks comes near the end of the wheat harvest in Palestine. Either the grain for baking these firstfruit loaves was set aside at the beginning of the harvest, or the first grain used from the new harvest qualified as its firstfruits.

23:18–20 for the priest: Grain and meat from the sacrificial offerings were a large part of God's provision for the priests and their families (7:1–14, 31–36).

23:21, 22 The Israelites were to be generous when they reaped a plentiful harvest because God gave the harvest to them (19:9, 10).

23:23, 24 Blowing of trumpets marked solemn, joyful, and urgent occasions in ancient Israel.

23:25 an offering made by fire: The animals and amounts of grain for this offering are listed in Num. 29:2–5.

23:26, 27 Day of Atonement: Literally, it is the "Day of Atonements"—that is, the day above all days, when complete atonement was made for all Israel.

23:28 do no work: On the Day of Atonement, the only work was done by the high priest in the Most Holy Place.

23:29, 30 I will destroy: God Himself would see to it that the transgressor of day would be called to account.

23:31, 32 This is the third time in this passage that the Israelites were commanded to **afflict** their **souls,** indicating the importance of this duty for this day.

23:33–36 A sacred assembly indicates the last day of a joyous eight-day celebration.

23:37, 38 Besides ... which you give was a gentle warning not to bring an offering for a special festival day and then attempt to use it again for one of the regular offerings commanded in chs. 1—7.

23:39, 40 the fruit of beautiful trees: In celebrating the Feast of Tabernacles today, people use the citron, a fruit like the lemon, but larger. **Leafy trees** is thought to be the myrtle.

23:41, 42 The **booths** were made of the tree branches.

23:43, 44 Dwelling in booths for seven days reminded the Israelites of God's goodness in preserving them in the wilderness. The Feast of Tabernacles was both a celebration of harvest and a thanksgiving for God's protection of His people.

24:1–4 Pure oil was needed for the lampstand because it stood within the tabernacle. **pressed olives:** Oil for the sacred lampstand was extracted by pounding olives in a mortar by hand, a process that produced the finest, lightest olive oil. **From evening until morning** indicates tending the lamps twice a day, not tending them throughout the night.

24:5–9 twelve cakes: One for each of the tribes of Israel. The **frankincense on each row** was not poured on the loaves because the priests had to eat them. When the loaves were replaced, the frankincense was burned as **an offering** to the Lord. **Every Sabbath,** new loaves replaced the ones that had been there for a week.

24:10–12 Blaspheming **the name of the LORD** was forbidden (Ex. 22:28).

24:13, 14 The offender was taken **outside the camp** so that his death would not defile the camp. **Lay their hands on his head** was a witness that they had heard the words of blasphemy and a sign that his sin was his own responsibility.

24:15 His God Anyone who cursed the Creator bore the responsibility for the **sin** and was executed. Foreigners were not to worship their own gods while living among the people of Israel (17:8, 9).

24:16, 17 To blaspheme **the name of the LORD** was rebellion, which carried the death penalty.

24:18–20 eye for eye: This law is also found in Ex. 21:23–25. Its purpose was to *forbid* the injured party from inflicting *greater* bodily harm.

24:21–23 One reason for these seemingly unrelated laws at this place in Leviticus was to anticipate the question of whether other laws would also apply to non-Israelites. The answer was yes, they would apply to the **stranger.**

25:1 Mount Sinai was where God gave the covenant. Thus the following was part of the covenant and should be observed in order to keep faith with God.

25:2 The land which I give you is a reminder that the land belongs to God. All of the laws of the Sabbath year and of the Jubilee were based on this premise. If Israel would follow God's direction while occupying the land, He would bless them abundantly. **A sabbath to the LORD** is the same phrase used for the weekly Sabbath (23:3). The people rested weekly from their work; the land was to rest every seventh year from its work.

25:3–7 shall not reap: Reaping and gathering for storage and selling were not permitted in the Sabbath year. However, harvesting for daily needs was permitted.

25:8–10 To **proclaim liberty** meant specifically that all debts were canceled, all Israelites who had been forced to sell themselves into slavery were freed, and all land reverted to its original owner.

25:11, 12 The fiftieth or **Jubilee** year was itself a Sabbath year (vv. 2–7). Observing the Jubilee year would have meant two years of rest in a row for the land.

25:13–17 To refrain from oppressing a fellow citizen is one way of showing **fear,** or reverence and respect, for God.

25:18, 19 If those who live in God's land follow His instructions, they will **dwell there in safety,** free from want and external threats.

25:20–22 I will command My blessing on you: If the Israelites would obey God's command to let the land rest, they could be sure that the land would provide for their needs.

25:23–28 The principle governing all of these laws was that the land did not belong to Israel; it belonged to God. **you are strangers and sojourners:** God emphasized that the Israelites would live in a land that was not their own.

25:29, 30 A walled city indicates one of the larger cities of the land. These provided more economic diversity than villages. A person's survival did not depend on owning a city house. Therefore, the time limit to redeem these houses was one year. They were bought and sold without regard to the Jubilee year.

25:31 An unwalled village in ancient Israel was tiny by today's standards. Many had only a handful of families. The basic economic activity was farming the land within a walking radius of the village. For people living in these villages, losing the family home would be nearly as great a disaster as the loss of their farmland. Therefore, village **houses** were included in the laws of redemption and Jubilee.

25:32–34 The Levites' **houses,** too, were protected under the basic law of redemption and Jubilee (vv. 25–28) because their homes were their only substantial assets.

25:35–37 Charging interest on a loan to **your brother** would hinder his financial progress. This law probably did not prohibit interest on commercial loans, which was another level of economic activity, one that did not threaten anyone's survival. Some might have been tempted to refuse to lend money to a poor fellow citizen, preferring to lend to non-Israelites in order to collect interest. This explains the command **then you shall help him, like a stranger or a sojourner.**

25:38 The motivation to be generous to the poor should have come from a person's gratitude to God for His generosity in bringing Israel out of **Egypt,** giving them **the land of Canaan,** and making a covenant to be their God.

25:39–46 Foreign **slaves** could be bought, sold, and inherited like other property. This does not mean God approves of slavery.

25:47–55 Though this order of kinship in redeeming is not mandatory, it was the natural progression from close relative to more distant relative. A brother, if he could, would be the one to **redeem.** If no brother could or if the man had no brother, an uncle would be next, and then a cousin.

26:1 A sacred pillar was a stone or wooden column erected to represent a pagan god or goddess. It was not a likeness, but a symbol. Together, the four terms used in this verse cover all the possibilities for pagan images. **I am the LORD your God** confronts the Israelites with a choice of allegiances. Would they love the living God or idols?

26:2–5 God promised the resources for abundant supplies of food, including rain whenever it would be needed.

26:6–10 God promised security and **peace** in the land. **clear out the old:** Israel would not finish eating the old harvest before the new one was brought in.

26:11–13 God also promised His presence in Israel's midst. He would **set** His **tabernacle among** them. Furthermore, He would actively **walk among** them, looking out for their welfare, helping and protecting them. **I will be your God, and you shall be My people** is the covenant by which God bound Himself to Israel and Israel to Him.

26:14, 15 These two verses state the conditions under which God would bring disaster on His people in an effort to turn their hearts back to Him. **Commandments ... statutes ... judgments ... covenant** cover all of the legislation God had given at Sinai and the agreement Israel had entered into with God.

26:16, 17 Terror, various diseases, and famine caused by military defeat would be God's first attempts to call Israel back to Himself.

26:18–20 This second series of curses would be fulfilled if the first failed to get Israel's attention. **your heavens like iron and your earth like bronze:** Rainfall was essential to the agriculture of ancient Israel. Without rainfall, planting was futile.

26:21, 22 If drought did not bring the Israelites to their senses, God would visit them with **seven times more plagues**—this time **wild beasts.**

26:23–28 If Israel did not repent after the wild beasts, God would multiply their punishment another **seven times** with war, resulting in epidemics and famine. **when you are gathered:** When enemies invaded a land the people living in unwalled villages fled to the walled cities for refuge. If a city then was besieged for a long time, unsanitary conditions led to epidemics and famine.

26:29 Further disobedience would result in cannibalism, (see 2 Kin. 6:28, 29; Lam. 2:20; 4:10).

26:30–32 High places and **incense altars** were dedicated to the worship of pagan gods. To defile them with human **carcasses** would make them permanently unfit for worship.

26:33–35 scatter: This threat was fulfilled in the Babylonian exile of 587–536 B.C.

26:36, 37 those of you who are left: Survivors would not enjoy relief or peace of mind after escaping the disasters. They would still be timid, even when no one pursued them.

26:38, 39 Having been exiled to foreign lands, the people would **waste away,** perhaps wishing they had not escaped the quick death that had overtaken so many others.

26:40–42 God's **covenant** with the patriarchs was the basis for their deliverance and the covenant at Sinai.

26:43–45 Ultimately, God would **remember the covenant** and not **utterly destroy them.**

26:46 This summary statement confirms the authority of Leviticus because its source is **the LORD.**

27:1–7 While people could dedicate themselves or their children (see 1 Sam. 1:11, 22) to God, only the Levites were allowed to serve God as priests. Therefore, those vowed in service to God had to be redeemed. The chief factor in determining value was physical strength. A man brought a higher price than a woman because he could do heavier work.

27:8 A person might dedicate himself as God's possession and go redeem the vow only to have the priest discover he was **too poor to pay** that value. In that case, the priest set a redemption value **according to the ability** to pay.

27:9, 10 Rash vows and afterthoughts about vows were discouraged. If one vowed or brought a clean animal for sacrifice, then regretted the decision, the animal could not be exchanged.

27:11–13 Unclean animals could not be sacrificed. The priest set a value on any unclean animal brought as a gift and the sanctuary would receive the monetary value of the gift.

27:14, 15 The priest also set the value of a house given to fulfill a vow. Obviously, the priests had to be knowledgeable in many kinds of commercial enterprises.

27:16–25 A field could be dedicated to the Lord. If it was part of a family's inheritance, it could be redeemed before the Jubilee. The price for a parcel requiring a **homer of barley seed** to sow it was **fifty shekels.** The price to redeem the parcel was about a shekel a year, the cost of its seed each year.

27:26, 27 Animal firstborns could not be dedicated to God, since they belonged to Him already (see Ex. 13:2). Clean animals could not be redeemed; they would have been sacrificed. Unclean animals could not be sacrificed, and they could be redeemed with money.

27:28, 29 Nothing devoted could be redeemed. Persons devoted (**under the ban**) were to **be put to death.** No private citizen would have had the power to put himself or anyone else under the ban.

27:30, 31 For a person living a distance from the sanctuary, it may have been easier to redeem the tithes of his crops than to bring the crops to the sanctuary.

27:32, 33 Sheep and goats were counted and inspected when they passed **under the rod,** which the shepherd placed across the entrance to the fold. Each year, the newborn animals were counted this way. Every tenth animal was part of the tithe that belonged to God.

27:34 The commandments: The Book of Leviticus has much to teach the follower of Christ. Holy living still should be our goal because we have been redeemed through the blood of Christ. This is infinitely more precious than the blood of any sacrificial animal.

Numbers

Introduction

The Book of Numbers describes the events right before the Israelites entered the Promised Land. Similar to the tension-filled days before a great battle or election day, these events reveal the Israelites' restlessness and impatience, but also the anticipation of what God would do.

The long lists of numbers and names in Numbers must be viewed as the ancient Israelites viewed them. The lists were the final roll call before the battle. They prompted praise to God for His faithfulness to the Israelites. He had protected them and multiplied their numbers even in the middle of a barren wilderness.

The Book of Numbers is the fourth of the first five books of the Old Testament, the Pentateuch. The English name Numbers comes from the title that the translators of the Septuagint (a Greek translation of the Old Testament) gave the book, a name that refers to the two prominent census lists contained within.

Most evangelical writers have insisted on Moses' authorship and compilation of the Pentateuch, including the Book of Numbers. Given the long sojourn of the Israelites in the wilderness, Moses would certainly have had the time to compile the materials and write most of the books. However, he may have overseen some additions to the books, and certain later editors under the leading of the Spirit may have added other materials.

Numbers has two basic sections. Each of them begins with a census. The first census (chs. 1—4) numbered the men of war of the first generation of those who had left Egypt. This census and the triumphal march into the Promised Land quickly turned into disaster. The first generation of Israelites did not trust God and did not thank Him for His provision. Instead, they doubted God, accused Him, and rebelled against His gracious instructions. This demanded discipline: the first generation would not inherit the land because they had been faithless.

After forty years of wandering in the wilderness, the second census (ch. 26) numbered the men of war of the second generation. Finally, they were prepared to do what their parents had failed to do. But underlying the narrative of chapters 26 through 36 is the nagging question: "Will the second generation be successful, or will they repeat the errors of their fathers?" The book ends with a positive expectation. The second generation would succeed; the people of God would inherit the promise of the land of Canaan—at last!

1:1 The phrase **now the LORD spoke to Moses** sets the tone for the book. God's act of revelation to His servant Moses is mentioned over 150 times in Numbers. **Wilderness of Sinai:** The geographical setting of Numbers is the wilderness. The time reference, **on the first day of the second month, in the second year,** is dated from the pivotal event in Israel's history, the deliverance of the people from slavery in Egypt. The second month corresponds roughly to April, a time that would be known later in Canaan as the month of the general harvest between Firstfruits and Pentecost. The events of Numbers cover a period of 38 years, most likely in the second half of the fifteenth century B.C.

1:2, 3 The stated purpose of this **census** was to be a military roster. The census would help Israel to prepare its **armies** for the war of conquest against the peoples of Canaan. Therefore, those who were numbered were able-bodied males over the age of **twenty.**

1:4 A man from every tribe would aid Moses and Aaron in the task of numbering the nation. The participation of one person from each tribe would ensure that the numbering was done fairly and that each tribe was represented accurately.

1:5–16 leaders: The leaders were "lifted up" or "selected" for their positions of leadership.

1:17–19 As the LORD commanded: The tone in chs. 1—10 is one of compliance on the part of Moses and the people to the revealed will of God. When God commanded, Moses and his agents responded.

1:20–43 Now the children of Reuben: Each of the twelve mini-paragraphs in vv. 20–43 follows the same pattern, giving the name of the tribe, the particulars of the family houses, the stipulation that the ones numbered were able-bodied males over the age of twenty, the name of the tribe again, and then the number in that tribe. The only variation is in vv. 32–35, where it is explained that Ephraim and Manasseh are sons of Joseph (as in v. 10). This notice reminds the reader that Joseph received a double share among the tribes of Israel. His two sons had equal shares with their uncles in Israel's posterity.

1:44–46 These are the ones who were numbered: The total number of able-bodied men (who were at least twenty years old) was 603,550. The likely number of women, children, and older or infirm men not counted in this census would indicate a total population of between two and five million.

1:47, 48 The Levites were not to be included among the "lay" tribes. The tribe of Levi was sacred. It belonged to the Lord alone.

1:49, 50 The tabernacle of the Testimony is called "the tabernacle of meeting" in v. 1 and "the tabernacle" in v. 51. The term *tabernacle* by itself points to the portable nature of the tent; it was a movable shrine, specially designed for the worship of God by a people on the march. *Testimony* suggests the covenantal significance of the tent. Within that tent were the symbols of the presence of God among His people.

1:51–53 The outsider refers not to a person of foreign birth, but to a non-Levite (see Ex. 12:43). God's presence was both a blessing and a curse in the camp—a blessing for those who had a proper sense of awe and respect of the nearness of God and a curse for those who had no respect for the Divine Presence.

1:54 So they did sets the tone of obedience for the first part of the Book of Numbers. The later rebellion (ch. 11) surprises the reader after phrases such as this.

2:1, 2 by his own standard: God Himself placed each tribe in a specific place around His **tabernacle.** A person's identity was not only derived from his or her tribe, but also from his or her place in relation to the tabernacle. **some distance:** None dared draw too close to the tabernacle, so that God's holiness might be maintained (see Is. 6:1–5).

2:3–9 The three tribes **on the east side** had pride of place. The west was the place of the setting sun. On the other hand, the east faced the rising sun, a picture of promise and power (see Ps. 19:4–6). In the line of march, **Judah,** with its allied tribes **Issachar** and **Zebulun,** set out first.

2:10–16 Positioned **on the south side** were the tribe of **Reuben** and its allied tribes **Simeon** and **Gad.** They set out second, after the tribes allied with Judah.

2:17 Levites in the middle: Only the consecrated people were allowed to move with the **tabernacle of meeting.** In the line of march, the tabernacle was in the central position—a symbol of the presence of God among His people.

2:18–24 Positioned **on the west side** were the tribe of **Ephraim** and its allied tribes **Manasseh** and **Benjamin.** In the line of march, they were the third group to move out from their encampments.

2:25–31 The tribe of **Dan** and its allied tribes **Asher** and **Naphtali** were positioned **on the north side.** In the line of march, they were the last group to move out of the camp.

2:32–34 These verses summarize this stately chapter. The four sets of triads yielded the same total as the sum of the twelve individual units: 603,550 (see 1:46).

3:1 the records of Aaron: The focus of ch. 3 is on the priests and the families of the tribes of Levi.

3:2–4 the sons of Aaron: Nadab, the firstborn, Aaron's expected heir would prove to be a disappointment. With his brother **Abihu,** Nadab offered **profane fire** before God, an offense that cost them their lives (Lev. 10:1, 2). Two of Aaron's other sons, **Eleazar** and **Ithamar** continued to minister as priests before God.

3:5–10 the tribe of Levi: Here the Levites were given their sphere of work in the care of the tabernacle. The Levites were not priests; only **Aaron and his sons** could be priests. The Levites, who assisted in the care of the holy things, drew near to the Divine Presence. Yet the priests, who ministered in the tabernacle, drew even nearer. But only the high priest, on whose ministry the hope of the community was based, entered the

Most Holy Place where the Divine Presence resided.

3:11–13 I Myself points to God's direct involvement in redemption. When God redeemed and saved His people, it was by His own person. **The firstborn are Mine:** When God passed over the homes of the Hebrew families who had obeyed His commands in the Passover (see Ex. 12:29–51), He declared the surviving firstborn Hebrew children—and also the firstborn of animals—to be His own (Ex. 13:1, 2). Now the firstborn children needed to be redeemed. An exchange was made. God took the entire tribe of Levi as His special possession, instead of the firstborn child of each family (3:40–51).

3:14–21 the children of Levi: The three families of the Levites were **Gershon, Kohath, and Merari.** The Levites were distinguished from the other, non-priestly tribes in several ways: (1) They were numbered separately from those numbered for war; (2) they were appointed as ministers in the worship of God, rather than as soldiers in His army; (3) they were given certain restrictions for the conduct of their life; (4) they represented the gift of the firstborn of each family to the Lord (3:40–51); and (5) they would live in cities among the various tribes instead of living together in a single region (35:1–8).

3:22–26 The family of **Gershon** cared for and handled the elements of the **tabernacle.**

3:27–32 The work of the family of **Kohath** concerned the sacred implements and furnishings within the tabernacle. Aaron's son **Eleazar** supervised their work as the **chief over the leaders,** likely because the holy furnishings could only be carried in certain prescribed ways.

3:33–37 The work of the family of **Merari** concerned the structural elements of the tabernacle along with its utensils.

3:38, 39 The placement of Moses, Aaron, and Aaron's sons **on the east** indicated a most-favored status. Their responsibility was to guard against improper approach to God's holy tabernacle.

3:40–42 Number all the firstborn: The Israelites' firstborn sons were redeemed by the dedication of the Levites to the Lord's service. The phrase **instead of** emphasizes the substitution of the Levites for the firstborn.

3:43–48 The payment of **five shekels** was as much a lesson to the Israelites on the importance of the individual as it was an act of substitution for those involved. Each individual's redemption had to be covered. The payment of the shekels **to Aaron and his sons** was appropriate. Just as the Levites were given to the Lord in order to assist Aaron in his duties at the holy tabernacle, the redemption money was also given to Aaron to further this same holy work.

3:49–51 The weight of the collected **money** (1,365 shekels) indicates the impressive nature of the transaction. The number is 5 times 273, since there was one Levite for each firstborn and five shekels for each firstborn beyond the number of Levites. In this way, each of the firstborn was accounted for in God's plan of redemption.

4:1, 2 The Book of Numbers moves in an orderly, planned manner, following the pattern of Hebrew thought which moves from the general to the specific, from the whole to the parts. Chapter 4 deals with the functions of the Levitical families. This **census** was distinct from the one in ch. 3. This census numbered those between the ages of thirty and fifty, those who were specifically able to work in the service of the Lord in the holy things of worship.

4:3 According to 8:24, the Levites were to be twenty-five years old, which seems to contradict the **thirty years** here. The work of the Levites and that of the priests whom they served was complex and demanding. It is possible that the extra five years of 8:24 includes a period of apprenticeship to prepare these servants of the Lord for the tasks that lay before them.

4:4 The care and preservation of the **most holy things** were given to the Kohathites (3:29–31). The Kohathites were not to touch the holy items nor even look casually on them, lest they die. **Holy things** are items and utensils that have been taken out of common use and given over to the service of the Lord.

4:5, 6 The various materials used in the tabernacle and its furnishings may have had symbolic meanings to the ancients which have not been preserved for us. We do get a sense that the materials were costly and dear.

4:7–13 Colors—including **blue, scarlet,** and **purple**—played a significant role in Israel's worship.

4:14, 15 The means of transporting the holy things of the tabernacle was to **carry them** by poles on foot.

4:16 duty of Eleazar: The priest had functions that were reserved only for him. Any other approach to God would result in death. This was both a gracious gift and a warning. On one hand, God mercifully granted that a priest could serve Him and approach Him. On the other hand, if the priest were faithless, no person could substitute for him. The Israelites had to approach God in the way He prescribed.

4:17–28 The men of **Gershon** were responsible for the **curtains** and for numerous parts of the tabernacle worship system. These men were allowed to touch the holy things they dealt with, but they could not be casual in their work.

4:29–33 The tasks of **Merari** first mentioned in 3:33–37 are reiterated here. The men of Merari cared for tabernacle posts and pegs, boards and sockets, and so on. Each individual son of Merari was given **by name** the items he had to carry.

4:34–49 According to the commandment of the Lord: According to Hebrew prose style, a summary of Moses' compliance with God's commands is given.

5:1–4 defile: God's principal concern was the purity of the heart of an individual (Deut. 10:12–20) and not just skin problems (Lev. 15:2, 25). The central issue in these restrictions was not disease; it was the fact of God's presence in the camp. God was holy, and hence the people had to maintain their purity and holiness.

5:5–8 restitution: As in Lev. 6:1–7, it was not sufficient just to confess a wrongdoing. One had to repay in full and add a penalty of one-fifth of the value to the one wronged (Lev. 22:14; 27:11–13, 31). If the one who was defrauded was no longer alive and had no relative surviving either, then the debt had to be paid to the priest.

5:9–15 Determining impurity in marital relations was difficult. Therefore, the issue had to be resolved by **the priest** in the presence of God.

5:16–18 Bitter water that brings a curse was not a "magic potion," nor was there some hidden ingredient in the water. The addition of dust from the floor of the tabernacle to a vessel of holy water and the scrapings from the bill of indictment were signs of a spiritual reality. Holy water and dust from the holy place symbolized that God was the One who determined the innocence or guilt of the woman who had come before the priest.

5:19–21 Your thigh rot and your belly swell In the biblical world, a woman who was unable to bear children was regarded as being under a curse; in this case it would have been true.

5:22 Amen is the woman's strong agreement to the terms of the ritual. If she were innocent, this ritual was the means of her protection. If she were guilty, she would be bringing judgment upon herself.

5:23–31 her guilt: The gravity of the ritual demonstrates that marital infidelity was regarded as a serious matter in Israel.

6:1, 2 The **Nazirite** was one who made a special vow to the Lord for a time of unusual devotion to God. Ordinarily this public vow was for a limited time (v. 13).

6:3, 4 wine and similar drink Wine is made from fermented fruit, usually grapes; beer is produced from fermented grains. The Nazirite, for the period of the vow, renounced this part of ordinary life as a mark of his or her special devotion to God.

6:5, 6 no razor: The male Nazirite over a period of time would have had unusually long hair, a sign of his special vow of devotion to the Lord (see Judg. 16:17).

6:7 The extent of the prohibition contact with a dead body is profoundly moving when it extends to the unexpected death of a **father, mother, brother, or sister.** In such a case, the Nazirite could not even fulfill the normal obligations that would be expected of a grieving relative. Such was the nature of the Nazirite vow of **separation to God.**

6:8, 9 So important was the concept of separation from contact with a dead body that the law included a provision for unexpected contact with the body of a person who **dies very suddenly** in one's proximity. In this case, the hair of the Nazirite was to be shaved, certain offerings presented, and the provisions of the vow continued, with allowance for the time inadvertently lost.

6:10–13 days of his separation are fulfilled: The focus is on the hair, a visible symbol of the temporary vow. Therefore, in addition to presenting the required sacrifices (vv. 14–17), the man or woman who completed a Nazirite vow had to shave his or her head and burn the hair along with the peace offering (v. 18).

6:14–21 law of the Nazirite: The summary in this verse not only adds detail, but also serves to solemnize the nature of the Nazirite vow. It is likely that John the Baptist, who presumably did practice abstinence, was a Nazirite from birth.

6:22–24 you shall bless: This famous Aaronic benediction is a blessing on all of the people. God freely blessed His people as a mark of His outstanding grace and mercy.

6:25 The idea of the phrase **make His face shine** is that of pleasure in the presence of God. The people as a whole would have some sense of the God's glorious presence in their lives.

6:26 The idea of the phrase **lift up His** countenance is that of sensing God's smile.

6:27 Perhaps the most impressive element of the passage is this conclusion. God intended to place His **name** on the people. They would bear the benediction of His name as a mark of identification that they were a people peculiarly related to God Himself.

7:1 when Moses had finished: Moses **anointed** and **consecrated** the tabernacle, its furnishings, the altar, and its utensils.

7:2–10 Each of the leaders of the twelve tribes brought a special gift from his tribe to the Lord **for the altar.**

7:11–83 The paragraph for each tribe is almost exactly the same as for the other tribes, with the exception of the day of the presentation, the name of the leader, and the name of the tribe. The passage was designed to be read aloud in a slow and stately manner. As each tribal leader and his tribe was mentioned, members of that tribe would take special pleasure.

7:84–88 This was the dedication offering: The totals of the twelve gifts are enumerated, demonstrating again the sense of order and control in the Book of Numbers.

7:89 More stunning than the gifts and their totals is this last verse of the chapter. When all was done, Moses **heard the voice** of God speaking from the innermost sanctuary.

8:1–4 The seven lamps must have been exquisite, the finest work possible by artisans of the day. But the placement of these oil lamps was as important as their craftsmanship.

8:5–9 To **shave** the entire **body** of the Levites was, in a sense, a physical symbol of a return to innocence. In addition to shaving their bodies, the Levites were also sprinkled with the water of purification and their clothing was washed.

8:10–12 lay their hands on: This ancient symbol of dedication (1) specified with a physical gesture the ones being dedicated, (2) expressed identification with the ones on whom the hands were placed, and (3) called for a divine sanction of this public and physical act. Aaron then presented the Levites to the Lord.

8:13–16 The Hebrew words for **wholly given to Me** are an emphatic doubling: "given, given." The story of the Exodus was always just under the surface of the theology of the Old Testament, for this saving event shaped the nation of Israel.

8:17–19 no plague: With their service in the tabernacle, the Levites functioned as a protective hedge between the people and the symbols of the Divine Presence. They both warned others not to draw too close and instructed them on how to approach the living God appropriately.

8:20–26 From twenty-five years old seems to disagree with the lower limit of thirty years given in 4:3. The difference is not easily resolved, but there is the possibility that the five years in dispute may have served as some sort of apprenticeship.

9:1 The first month of the second year indicates that the material of this chapter precedes the command to take a census in 1:1. With the tabernacle completed, the camp ritually purified, the religious functionaries cleansed and in place, the hovering symbols of God being experienced in the camp, and the Passover celebrated anew—all was ready for the triumphal march of God's citizen army to the Promised Land.

9:2–5 When the first **Passover** was celebrated in Egypt, the command was given to commemorate it throughout Israel's generations (see Ex. 12:14). It was time now at the base of Mount Sinai to celebrate the Passover before the people began their march into Canaan.

9:6–10 There were some who **could not keep the Passover** at its appointed time. These people came willingly to ask Moses what they might do. God's intent was that the Passover would be celebrated by all of His people. Reasons of ritual impurity should not prevent a person from enjoying the night. The ritually impure would celebrate the Passover a month later.

9:11 The specification of **bitter herbs** indicates that those who celebrated the Passover a month later would celebrate the exact details of it. They were not to rush through the ceremony, but were to take part in it fully, eating the lamb, the unleavened bread, and the bitter herbs.

9:12 nor break one of its bones: The Passover was not an ordinary meal. The food commemorated the great saving event of God in Israel's history. The meal was to be eaten with extraordinary attention to the lamb itself.

9:13 ceases to keep the Passover: Some people would simply refuse to celebrate the Passover, not for legitimate reasons, but because of ingratitude and insolence. Such persons would be **cut off from among** the people and would bear the responsibility for their sins.

9:14 Those who lived with the Hebrew people could be included in the celebration of Passover, but they first had to be circumcised. This was a rite that applied to the citizen as well as to the alien.

9:15–23 at the command of the LORD: When the cloud rose, the people were to set out.

When the cloud settled, the people were to encamp. There was nothing predictable in the movement or settling of the cloud; all was dependent on God's sovereignty.

10:1, 2 The **two silver trumpets** were different from the curved ram's horn trumpets. The cloud would begin to move, the trumpets would sound, and the people would begin to break camp and move out within their ordered ranks.

10:3, 4 but if they blow only one: The number of trumpets that sounded and the notes they played were signals for various groups within the encampments as well as for the people as a whole.

10:5–8 begin their journey: Even when the trumpets sounded, there was never to be a pell-mell rush of the people. The tone throughout this section is one of discipline and order.

10:9 The trumpets were signals for the movement of the camp in the wilderness; later they functioned as signals for the army in Canaan. The sounding of the trumpets would be a part of Israel's **war** against the inhabitants of the **land.**

10:10 day of your gladness: The trumpets were also played in the context of worship, particularly on days of feasting and the celebrations of the beginning of the month. **I am the LORD your God** indicates that the preceding was a divine revelation of the will of God.

10:11 The time had finally come for the people to set out on the triumphal journey for which God had been preparing them. When **the cloud was taken up** by the Lord Himself, the Israelites packed up their camp and left.

10:12, 13 The Wilderness of Paran is in the northeastern Sinai peninsula, south of the Negev, the desert area below Judah. Paran was a good staging area for the conquest of the land.

10:14–28 This section conveys a sense of pageantry, drama, and ordered design. The section was designed to be read aloud as a narrative of God's faithfulness to all of His people and of their proper response to His guidance.

10:29–32 Reuel (perhaps to be identified with

Jethro) is mentioned in Ex. 2:18–21 as the priest of Midian who befriended Moses and gave his daughter Zipporah to him as his wife. Moses invited **Hobab the son of Reuel** to join Israel on their triumphal journey. At first Hobab declined. But at Moses' insistence, Hobab continued with the Israelites (see Judg. 1:16), serving as the **eyes** of the people in the wilderness.

10:33–36 Rise up, O LORD and **Return, O LORD** are words of a triumphant song. These are affirmations of God's presence among His people and prayers that His presence would have its effect in the lives and destiny of the people.

11:1–3 Now when the people complained Here, after a journey of only three days, they murmured against the Lord for unspecified reasons. The **fire of the LORD** seems to have come both as a warning and as a purifying agent, since it hit only the outskirts of the camps.

11:4 The mixed multitude indicates the presence of others who had escaped from slavery or poverty in Egypt, but were not Israelites (Ex. 12:38). These people were an encouragement to the continual murmuring that characterized the Israelites in the wilderness. Those who did not share Israel's faith in God would make every discomfort an excuse to agitate rebellion against Him and His appointed leadership in Moses.

11:5, 6 The tone of the words **this manna** is one of contempt. The provision of manna was regarded by the Israelites as monotonous, something that caused the inner being to be dried up.

11:7–9 The provision of **manna** is clearly miraculous. God provided manna throughout the forty-year experience in the wilderness. Then it ceased to appear as mysteriously as it had begun (Ex. 16:35).

11:10, 11 In this instance, the fact that **Moses also was displeased** caused him to pray for help in dealing with the complaints of the people and their many needs (vv. 12–15).

11:12–15 Did I conceive all these people? God was the "mother" of the Israelites; Moses was their "wet nurse." Moses asked the Lord to kill him (see 1 Kin. 19:4) rather than force him to continue in this sorry situation.

11:16, 17 Moses' provocation led to the appointment of **seventy men** to assist him in the administration of the camp. They formed a body of administrative assistants for Moses to reduce the burden he felt in attempting to meet the needs of the vast population by himself.

11:18–20 you shall eat meat: The complaint of the people had so angered the Lord that He determined to cause them to have an overabundance of meat. God would give them so much meat that it would become sickening to them.

11:21–24 The idea of such plentiful meat in the wilderness was something at which even Moses balked. God's response to Moses, **has the LORD's arm been shortened?** is a challenge to all people of faith. There is no limiting the power of God.

11:25–30 Eldad and Medad did not join the other elders at the tabernacle of meeting (v. 16). Nonetheless, the Spirit of God came upon them and empowered them in their own camp. Joshua was afraid that their possible influence in the community would detract from the authority of Moses, but Moses responded by wishing that all of God's people were Spirit-empowered.

11:31–33 True to His promise (vv. 18–20), the Lord provided meat in the form of **quail from the sea.** He sent a strong wind that brought vast numbers of quail fluttering about three feet off the ground. The people fell into a frenzy, killing the birds and gathering them all through the night and on into the next day.

11:34 Kibroth Hattaavah ("Graves of Craving") was a vast graveyard of needlessly craving, ungrateful people.

11:35 Hazeroth ("Enclosures") allowed the people a respite from the journey and its judgments.

12:1 The order of the names **Miriam and Aaron** suggests that Miriam was the instigator of the attack against Moses. Note also that the principal punishment falls on Miriam (v. 10). Pointing at the **Ethiopian woman** whom Moses married seems to have been a pretext for attacking Moses. The real issue dividing Miriam and Aaron from their brother was the special relationship Moses had with God.

12:2 only through Moses: The prophetess Miriam (see Ex. 15:20) had very high status in the camp. Nonetheless, neither Miriam nor Aaron had the same proximity to God that Moses had. The verse ends ominously with the words **And the LORD heard it.** God was going to act on what He had heard.

12:3 Some people argue that a **very humble** man would hardly write about his unparalleled humility. Others contend that a humble man who was writing through God's inspiration might speak of his own humility. Another possibility is that the Hebrew word translated as *humble* may mean "miserable" in this context. The events described in ch. 11 may have taken an enormous toll on Moses. This verse may be a description of Moses' utter sense of brokenness as he experienced his brother and sister's betrayal.

12:4, 5 Then the LORD came down: Suddenly God spoke to Moses, Aaron, and Miriam, and then descended dramatically in the midst of the cloud. God came down, stood, and then called Aaron and Miriam forward.

12:6–8 The language conveys that God was in control. He spoke to whomever He wished and in the manner of His choosing. The phrase **face to face** speaks of the most intimate relationship that God had with Moses.

12:9, 10 The singling out of **Miriam** suggests that she was the instigator in this challenge to Moses (v. 1). **Leprous** refers to a serious skin disorder that made her unclean (5:1–4).

12:11 Aaron's words of confession—**we have done foolishly**—on behalf of his sister and himself are touching, and a sure sign of his deference to the leadership of his brother.

12:12–14 Moses' appeal to God on behalf of his sister was met with stern words from God that speak of a public humiliation. We are not told what might provoke a father to **spit** in the **face** of his daughter, but it would have had to be something quite shameful.

12:15 The delay in moving the camp for the seven days of Miriam's isolation indicates the high regard that Moses and the people held for Miriam.

12:16 The Wilderness of Paran had been the destination of the people since they set out from Mount Sinai (10:12). Sadly, the character of the people had changed en route. The people had murmured and rebelled against God and Moses, God's anointed.

13:1–3 According to Deut. 1:21–23, the sending of **men to spy** was the idea of the people. Moses was then instructed by the Lord to proceed with the plan.

13:4–15 The list of **names** of the men from each of the twelve tribes was not a mere duplicate of earlier lists (ch. 1). Presumably, these men were regarded not only as leaders in their tribal units, but also as men who were physically and spiritually capable of great exploits.

13:16 Changing **Hoshea**'s name to **Joshua** probably indicated great esteem on Moses' part. As God often changed the names of people who had a special relationship with Him, so Moses changed the name of the one who would eventually become his spiritual heir.

13:17–20 The spies were to spy out the land, determine what they could about the people and their cities, and observe the produce and forests. Then they were to bring back **some of the fruit of the land.**

13:21–25 Although the spies went all the way north to the region of Syria—**near the entrance of Hamath**—few details are recorded of their journey. Emphasis is given to **Hebron,** where **descendants of Anak** were found (v. 28), and to **the Valley of Eshcol,** where an enormous cluster of grapes was discovered.

13:26 The report of the spies came as a grievous surprise. The spies went to the people at **Kadesh** in the **Wilderness of Paran.**

13:27 The phrase **flows with milk and honey** is a slogan of redemption, a slogan expressing God's goodness in His promise of the land of Canaan. *Milk* probably refers to goats' milk; *honey* refers to bees, which were especially associated with the propagation of fruitful pastures and fields in Canaan. The phrase evoked visions of pleasure and plenty for the Israelites.

13:28 The spies quickly focused on the troubles of the land—the strength of its inhabitants, the fortification of its cities, and the immense size of **the descendants of Anak** in Hebron (v. 22). Apparently, this was a family whose hereditary stature was legendary in the ancient Middle East (v. 33).

13:29 The spies listed **the Amalekites** and the other peoples to support their claim that the land was not empty, that people had settled throughout its borders (see Gen. 15:18–21). God did not promise Israel virgin territory, but a place that was inhabited by those whom God wished to displace because of their iniquity.

13:30 Only **Caleb** spoke out against the flow of negative reports. He urged immediate attack based on his confidence in the armies of Israel, and, we may presume, on his underlying faith in God, who would fight for His people (10:35, 36).

13:31–33 The other spies were steadfast in their **bad report.** They described the land as evil and its inhabitants as giants. Their contentious description was ultimately an attack on God, the giver of the land.

14:1 Following the scandalous report of the spies, **the people wept that night.** They wept not because of the sinful attitude of the spies, but because of their own loss of dream, their own sense that they had made a mistake in leaving Egypt.

14:2–4 Following the night of weeping, the people conspired together in despair. They **complained against Moses and Aaron.** They speculated that they would have been better off dying in Egypt or in the desert. They plotted to select a leader to take them back to Egypt.

14:5–9 The response of Moses, Aaron, Joshua, and Caleb contrasted with the foolish terror of the people. They also wept, but for the sins of the people against the Lord and His mercy. The two faithful spies, Caleb and Joshua, gave a good report of the land in the context of robust faith in God. They knew that the living and faithful God would give it to His people.

14:10 The bold words of the good spies elicited two responses: rejection by the congregation, who attempted to stone them, and the sudden appearance of the glory of God to save the lives of His faithful servants.

14:11, 12 The people rejected God's miraculous **signs.** God's preliminary judgment was to utterly reject the nation. They clearly had rejected Him, dismissing the signs that He had done among them. In response, God again offered to use Moses to begin a new people.

14:13–19 Moses protested that this drastic act of judgment would taint the reputation of God among the nations. Then Moses quoted the Lord His great mercy (v. 18 cites Ex. 34:6, 7) and begged Him to pardon the iniquity of the people.

14:20–25 Moses' dramatic recitation led to God's pardon of the rebels. God scolded the people who had ignored the many evidences of His glory in their midst, and who had put Him to the test **now these ten times.** God's judgment was that the people who rejected Him would not see the land. Everyone was included except Caleb, whom God called **My servant,** and Joshua (v. 38). God then warned the people to bypass the region of the Amalekites. This was no longer a time for war, but for retreating into the wilderness.

14:26–38 This section forms what seems to be God's second response to the prayer of Moses (vv. 13–19). This second response contains some new elements. First, the **little ones** would be the only survivors of the wilderness wanderings. All over the age of twenty would die in the wilderness over the period of **forty years.** The forty days of the spies' journey would correspond to forty years of aimless wandering in the wilderness. Finally, a distinction was made between the cowardly spies and the two faithful ones. Only Joshua and Caleb lived. The evil spies died immediately by a plague from the Lord.

14:39–45 An abortive attempt at an invasion of the land by a still-rebellious people concludes this sad narrative. Heedless of Moses' warning that **the LORD** was **not among** them, the people went into battle. The result was disastrous. The name **Hormah** means "Utter Destruction." At this point, the focus of the Book of Numbers shifts to the younger generation, who would enter the land.

15:1, 2 The words **when you have come into the land** may seem inappropriate following the events of chs. 13; 14. Yet God had not rejected the Israelites entirely. Their children would enter the land that their parents had rejected.

15:3, 4 a grain offering: The use of grain was as important in the sacrificial system of ancient Israel as was the offering of animals. **Fine flour** was luxurious, rather than ordinary. The mixing of certain proportions of fine flour with olive oil indicated that only the very best could be used in the worship of God.

15:5–12 a drink offering: Wine was used in drink offerings (vv. 7, 10) as an accompaniment to the burnt offerings of the goat, lamb, ram, and bull. In the pouring out of this wine on the altar, the worshiper poured out something of great value. This represented the self-deprivation of the worshipers before God.

15:13–16 The words **all who are native-born** seem to point to a time after the wilderness experience—when the Israelites had already entered the land. As in the celebration of the Passover, the presentation of these offerings was to be done in the same way, whether the worshiper was born in the land or **a stranger.**

15:17–21 The **heave offering** is also known as the wave offering. Right at the beginning of the harvest, the harvester had to acknowledge that his produce was a gift from God. By holding up the very first produce from a harvest or of the first cake made from the first grain of the season, the worshiper thanked God as the giver of all good gifts.

15:22–29 If you sin unintentionally: Some sacrifices were offered on behalf of the nation as a whole, for there was always the possibility of an unintentional or unknown sin in the life of the people.

15:30, 31 The Hebrew phrase translated **presumptuously** means "with a high hand," with open disdain for the will and work of God.

15:32–36 It is quite possible that **gathering sticks on the Sabbath day** is a specific example of the kind of thing mentioned in vv. 30, 31. One who flagrantly went out gathering sticks on the Sabbath was clearly in breach of the command to honor the Sabbath day (see

Ex. 20:8–11). This individual was caught and then brought to Moses for judgment.

15:37–40 The wearing of **tassels** on the corners of garments was a beautiful sign of great significance. **Harlotry** of the **heart** is unfaithfulness to God.

15:41 I am the LORD your God: God identified Himself as the One who gave these commands. He declared that He had a relationship with the Israelites. He was their God, and He had saved them from slavery.

16:1 Yet another rebellion against Moses was led by **Korah,** a Kohathite (see 1 Chr. 6:22, 23). Korah and his allies were not satisfied with the role God had given them in the service of the tabernacle, so they decided to press for the priesthood (v. 10).

16:2, 3 Korah and the 250 leaders argued that the entire nation was **holy** to the Lord (see Ex. 6:7) and that Moses and Aaron had presumptuously taken leadership positions. The root of their complaint was that God had not elevated them sufficiently.

16:4–8 Moses' response was complex. First, he submitted to the will of God, as seen in his action of falling **on his face.** Then he issued a challenge based on an expectation of an overt display of the will of God. He instructed each of the dissenters to take a **censer,** a metal holder for incense used in worship, and place incense on it as a sign of approach to God. Then each would await God's decision.

16:9–11 The men were being contemptuous of the place to which God had appointed them. Moses' response was condescending and scathing: **Is it a small thing to you?** The dissenters should have realized how gracious God had been in giving them the life work He had provided.

16:12–17 Dathan and Abiram, two allies of Korah, were so arrogant that they would not even come to stand before Moses. They attacked Moses, claiming he acted like a prince. These two approached absurdity when they charged Moses with leading them away from the land that flows **with milk and honey.**

16:18, 19 The next day, each man lit incense in his censer. Korah brought the people near because he wanted witnesses to the events.

Then the glory of the LORD appeared is a somber reminder of the words of 12:5, a similar setting of impending judgment.

16:20–22 The announcement of judgment begins with God's warning to Moses and Aaron that they should back away so that He might destroy the entire congregation. The very leaders who were under assault intervened for the people, asking God to spare them even if He had to judge the guilty.

16:23–27 God demanded that the people back away from the tents of the rebels, and the people withdrew. Korah, Dathan, and Abiram were isolated at their tents with their families.

16:28–30 Moses called for a sign from God because he did not want anyone to think that what was about to happen was just coincidence.

16:31–35 In answer to Moses' prayer, God's judgment was sudden and dramatic. He caused the earth to swallow the rebels alive. The families of Dathan and Abiram died with those two men. But the family of Korah was spared (26:11). The judgment was so sudden and severe that the people rushed back in fear, thinking that they might suffer the same fate. The 250 would-be priests were destroyed by fire **from the LORD.**

16:36–40 the censers ... are holy: An amazing thing about this chapter is the Lord's concern that the censers be reused. The censers were gathered and hammered together for a covering for the altar.

16:41–45 Israel complained: Unbelievably, the people attacked Moses and Aaron as being the ones who caused the deaths of **the people of the LORD.** In calling them this, the people asserted that they recognized Korah and the rest as spiritual leaders. Their affection for Korah and his associates had caused them to miss the greater reality, the leadership roles God had given to Moses and Aaron and God's judgment on those rebellious men. Again, there was a sudden appearance of the **glory of the LORD**—a symbol of further judgment. Again the Lord threatened to destroy the congregation, and again Moses and Aaron fell on their faces, interceding for the people's wickedness.

16:46–50 Moses' command to Aaron to **take a censer** is a fitting end to this chapter. Aaron and his sons were the divinely appointed priests. Only they could minister at the altar of God. Aaron rushed to the sacred tasks to make **atonement** for the sinning congregation because a **plague** had fallen on them.

17:1–5 The rebellion of Korah and its aftermath (ch. 16) left a level of uncertainty among the people about the divine appointment of Aaron and his sons as the true priests of God. The point of Aaron's rod budding was to eliminate the continuing complaint of the people against Moses and Aaron. One rod was presented from each tribe with the name of the tribal leader inscribed on it. Then the **twelve rods** were placed in the Most Holy Place. God would signal His choice of priestly leadership by causing the rod of one tribe and its leader to **blossom**—life from a dead stick.

17:6, 7 The text focuses on **the rod of Aaron** among the twelve. Aaron was near the end of his life. He and his wife, Elisheba, had four sons. Two, Nadab and Abihu, had died because of their own improper approach to God (3:2–4). Two, Eleazar and Ithamar, lived. On the impending death of Aaron, there had to be no question as to which family was divinely ordered to continue in the priestly office.

17:8, 9 When the rods were examined the next day, not only had the rod of Aaron sprouted; it had even **yielded ripe almonds.** This was a complete vindication of Aaron as the true priest of God.

17:10, 11 as a sign: The rod of Aaron that budded and produced ripe almonds was placed there as well. Aaron's rod was a sign to God of His mercy. He had chosen the Levites to minister before Him.

17:12, 13 Surely we die: Finally, the people realized that God had revealed His will through His miraculous actions among them. None of them except the one whom God had designated could approach God in His Holy Place. Any person who approached without heeding God's clear instructions could only expect death.

18:1 Chapters 18 and 19 deal with the duties of priests and Levites. The expression **bear**

the iniquity speaks of the formidable work that was demanded of the priests of God. The priests stood as the intermediaries between God and man.

18:2–4 The Levites were the servants of the priests, but were limited in what they were able to do.

18:5–7 Only the priests were allowed to attend to the duties of the sanctuary and the altar. The **outsider** was not a foreigner, but a non-authorized Israelite.

18:8–20 Offerings that were not burned on the altars, although made to the Lord, became the food for the priests. **I am your portion:** The priests had no inheritance in the land itself. They lived off the produce of the land as God provided for them through the gifts of His people. God was their inheritance.

18:21–24 all the tithes in Israel: The Levites also were the beneficiaries of the Lord's service. Like the priests, the Levites would not inherit land, but would be provided for in a manner suitable for their service to God.

18:25–32 The Levites who lived from the tithes of the people were themselves under obligation to make offerings to the Lord, **a tenth of the tithe.** Those who lived from the tithes were to give tithes so that they also might thank God for what He had given them.

19:1, 2 The **red heifer** was to be sacrificed in a special ritual outside the camp. Everything about this sacrifice was unusual. Ordinarily, the sacrificial animal was male; this one was female. The mention of the color of the animal is also unusual; in no other animal sacrifice was the color of the animal specified.

19:3 The naming of **Eleazar the priest** was a logical sequel to the test of the true priestly family in ch. 17. Before his father Aaron died, Eleazar had to start functioning in a prominent position before the congregation to ensure a smooth transition to his leadership.

19:4–8 The total burning of the animal was also unusual, particularly since this animal was burned away from the altar. Symbolic items associated with cleansing—**cedar wood and hyssop and scarlet** (see Lev. 14:4)—were then added to the fire. All were burned to ashes. The ritual made both the priest and those who helped him unclean.

19:9, 10 The **ashes of the heifer** were used in sacrificial rituals. The ashes were added to water, and the resultant mixture was used in certain rites of purification.

19:11–13 The ashes and water had particular meaning for a person who had touched a **dead body.** Again, the sprinkling of **the water of purification** was more than a physical cleansing; it signified a submission to spiritual cleansing as well.

19:14–19 Various instances of death and uncleanness are listed in these verses. This passage may have been a response to practical questions posed by the people. For example, if a man died in a tent, the people would certainly want to know what was required of them and how far the uncleanness extended. And what would happen if a person touched the body of a dead man in the field or in a grave?

19:20–22 One who did not **purify himself** rejected God's grace and consequently incurred His wrath. The issues were so serious that the one who applied the waters of purification to another became unclean also. These rituals were not given to make the lives of the people difficult. They were given to instruct the people about the nature of true holiness.

20:1 The expression **the first month** lacks the notice of a year. Most likely, this was the fortieth year, the end of the sojourn in the wilderness.

20:2–7 no water: Having no water was the subject of the first crisis that the Israelites had in their journey out of Egypt (Ex. 17). Here, in the fortieth year since the Exodus, the same problem arose, provoking the same ingratitude and anger from the people.

20:8, 9 Moses was to take his rod, but was only to **speak to the rock.** A generation earlier, God's words were equally specific. At that time, Moses was told to take his rod and "strike the rock" (Ex. 17:6). On the first occasion, Moses did exactly what God had commanded; on the second occasion, he did not.

20:10 Hear now, you rebels!: These words of Moses are the words of one who had crossed the line, whose patience had been tried to the breaking point.

20:11 Moses did not speak to the rock as God had commanded. Instead he raised his rod and **struck the rock twice.** When he disobeyed, Moses violated all that he had stood for over the last forty years! God was not displaying anger, but Moses fell into deliberate, unrighteous anger. And in his anger, Moses lost his own place in the Promised Land. What a huge loss for just a moment of disobedience!

20:12 God's judgment comes in expected severity, given the nature of Moses' offense. Moses is charged with the double sin of not believing in God and not hallowing Him before the people. God saw Moses' action as a lack of respect and awe for His holiness. Aaron also was indicted and sentenced by the Lord. Neither of them would enter Canaan.

20:13 Meribah, or " Contention," is the name given to the place of Moses' sin. This is the same name that was given 40 years earlier to the location of the first water crisis (Ex. 17:7).

20:14–21 Moses used diplomacy in his appeal to **the king of Edom,** testifying to the saving work of the Lord in delivering the people of Israel from Egypt. He also made what appears to be a most reasonable request: **let us pass through your country.** When Edom refused passage, Moses countered with an even more gentle request and reassured the Edomites that the Israelites had not come to conquer. This request was refused with a show of force.

20:22–29 Mount Hor: It was here that the sad news came that Aaron was going to die. **Eleazar** received the duties of Aaron's priesthood. The **thirty days** of mourning for Aaron indicates the high esteem in which he was held by his brother and the people.

21:1–3 The first of Israel's military victories against the Canaanites came as the result of an attack by **the king of Arad.** The Israelites fought valiantly and God fought for them. The Israelites triumphed over the army of Arad and destroyed its cities.

21:4, 5 The long journey **around the land of Edom** was necessary because the king of Edom refused to grant Moses' request for passage through his territory (20:14–21). After the first flush of victory (21:1–3), this circuitous route was particularly unpleasant to the people of Israel. Once again, they started complaining against Moses and God. The people again (see 11:6) protested God's provision of manna, calling it **this worthless bread.**

21:6 God's discipline came upon the people in the form of **fiery serpents.** Snakes with poisonous venom for which there was no antidote caused raging fevers and agonizing deaths.

21:7–9 The pain of the venomous bites drove the people to repent, and they begged Moses to intervene on their behalf. God instructed Moses to make an image of one of the serpents and to **set it on a pole.** Anyone who had been bitten and looked at the image **lived.** Jesus pointed to this stunning image in His dialogue with Nicodemus (see John 3:14, 15) as an analogy to His own execution.

21:10–13 The Israelites went around the region of Edom and entered the territory of Moab, which was just east of Jericho. It became the new staging area for the conquest of the land.

21:14, 15 The Book of the Wars of the LORD refers to an early collection of songs and writings known today only from this citation. The fact that Numbers draws upon other early Hebrew writings shows that the ancient Hebrew peoples had other literature in addition to Scripture.

21:16–20 Beer means "Well." At last the people had come to a place where they could dig a well and find adequate water. God had graciously provided for them.

21:21–26 The defeat of **Sihon king of the Amorites** began with his rejection of a request for safe passage, not unlike a similar rejection from the king of Edom (20:14–21). Sihon not only rejected the request of Israel, but gathered for war against Israel at **Jahaz.** Israel completely defeated Sihon. This was the first of her victories east of the Jordan River.

21:27–32 Those who speak in proverbs refers not to wisdom sayings as in the Book of Proverbs, but to taunt songs. The song begins with a recital of the earlier victory of the Amorites over the people of Moab and their god **Chemosh.** After defeating Sihon and the Amorites, Israel became a formidable threat to Moab (22:3).

21:33–35 The defeat of **Og king of Bashan** immediately followed the defeat of the Amorites. The people of Israel had gained the control of all the land east of the Jordan River and north of the Arnon River. These early victories were part of the holy war of God and were celebrated by Israel as a part of her worship tradition.

22:1 the plains of Moab: With these words we come to the end of the travels of Israel described in the Book of Numbers. Not until the Book of Joshua does the story line of travel and conquest resume. **On the side of the Jordan across from Jericho** refers to the area they had conquered so far, territory that would be settled by two and one-half tribes (ch. 32).

22:2–4 Chapters 22—24 focus on **Balak,** the king of Moab, and **Balaam,** whom Balak hired to destroy Israel by spiritual means. Moab was not yet facing Israel's threatening armies. But Balak knew that his enemy Sihon of Heshbon had been defeated by Israel (21:21–32), and he had reason to fear that he and his kingdom would be next. Balak believed that he could not fight Israel on the field of battle and win. So he decided to fight them on another level—that of spiritual warfare. **The elders of Midian** with whom Balak consulted were the leaders of a mobile people with whom Balak may have had a mutual agreement of protection.

22:5 Balak sought out a prophet named Balaam who might engage Israel in spiritual warfare by causing her "gods," as they thought, to quit protecting them. Only then would Balak and Moab be safe from this formidable foe.

22:6–8 The strong reputation of Balaam is indicated in the phrasing **he whom you bless is blessed, and he whom you curse is cursed.** In v. 8, Balaam speaks of **the LORD** as though he were intimate with Him.

22:9–14 The first encounter of the servants of Moab and Midian with Balaam ended in failure. God mercifully instructed Balaam, in what may have been a night vision, that he was not to go with the men to curse Israel, because they were **blessed.**

22:15–21 The second encounter of the emissaries of Moab and Midian with Balaam seemed to reverse things. The emissaries came with more noble persons and with grander gifts, bribes, and promises. Again, Balaam spoke of God in a familiar manner: **the word of the LORD my God.**

22:22–30 God's anger was aroused against Balaam, apparently because Balaam intended to do what Balak had hired him to do, to curse Israel. God could not have been angry at his going, for He had given Balaam permission (v. 20). But He had also given Balaam orders to speak "only the word which I speak to you" (v. 20). **The donkey saw the Angel of the LORD:** In this situation, the "seer" was blind to the presence of the true God. It was the animal who was the seer, perceiving the true will of God in the angel that blocked the path.

22:31–35 Then the LORD opened Balaam's eyes: The spiritually blind seer finally saw the majesty of the One whom the donkey saw all along. Now the pagan prophet was brought to his knees. In the strongest manner, the Angel of the Lord instructed Balaam to speak only what God spoke to him.

22:36–40 Balaam's statement, **the word that God puts in my mouth, that I must speak,** must have been puzzling to Balak (see 23:11, 25; 24:10, 25). The sacrifices of v. 40 were not to God, of course. These were pagan sacrifices to idols. That which Balak sent **to Balaam** included the livers, which Balaam used in divination (24:1).

22:41 The high places of Baal were selected because of the view they afforded. They were also places of pagan worship.

23:1–6 The use of **seven altars** and the offering of a bull and a ram on each one was a part of Balaam's pagan ritual. Afterward, God in His mercy gave Balaam a true message to speak. The expression **the LORD put a word in Balaam's mouth** is the same type of language used of true prophets (see Jer. 1:9).

23:7–10 The first oracle of Balaam set the pace for the rest. There were seven oracles in all. Each is introduced with the words **he took up his oracle and said** (23:7, 18; 24:3, 15, 20, 21, 23). In the first oracle, Balaam described the purpose for which he was called, to curse Israel. However, he was unable to curse Israel because God would not allow it. From the worship site of pagan idolatry (see 22:41), he viewed Israel from a distance and saw that they were a people distinct from all other nations.

23:11, 12 The response of Balak was one of stunned horror. He had brought Balaam to curse Israel, but Balaam had **blessed them bountifully!**

23:13–17 Balak foolishly thought that going to another place would influence God to allow a curse to be placed on His people. **Then the LORD met Balaam:** Again Balaam's words came from the only living God.

23:18–24 The second oracle was addressed to Balak, an unwilling listener. Balaam confessed a wondrous truth about the God of Israel: He is unable to change; He cannot lie. Because God had blessed Israel, Balaam was powerless to change this to a curse.

23:25–30 Neither curse them at all, nor bless them at all! Balak nearly said, "I will pay you just to be quiet!" But again he thought all that was needed was a better location.

24:1, 2 it pleased the LORD to bless Israel: God was determined to bless His own people. The words **the Spirit of God came upon him** refer to the empowerment that gave Balaam his message and its direction. Dramatically, God controlled Balaam and spoke clearly through a person who was His enemy.

24:3–9 The third **oracle** is marked by a lengthy introduction that speaks of the powerful things that had taken place within Balaam. The heart of the third oracle is a blessing on the tribes of Israel as they were about to enter the land of Canaan. Those who bless Israel will be blessed. Those who curse Israel will be cursed.

24:10–14 In the aftermath of the third oracle,

Balak wanted to dismiss Balaam entirely. But Balaam was not to be stopped.

24:15–19 The fourth oracle has the longest introduction, which builds on the introduction to the third oracle (vv. 3, 4). **I see Him, but not now ... A Star shall come out of Jacob:** This poetic language clearly refers to the Messiah. The pagan Balaam had a vision of the coming of the Hebrew Messiah, the Lord Jesus Christ! He was visible from afar. He was like a Star, radiant and beautiful. He was like a **Scepter,** majestic and powerful. And He is the victor over His enemies, including Moab—the nation that hired Balaam to curse Israel!

24:20 The fifth oracle is brief, coming without a pause. It is a curse on **Amalek,** the first people to fight with Israel in their wilderness experience, and the first to bring defeat upon themselves (see Ex. 17:8–16).

24:21, 22 The Kenites were a Midianite tribe (see 10:29; Judg. 1:16). This oracle makes a word-play between the word *Kenite* and the similar Hebrew word for *nest*. **Asshur** is Assyria.

24:23–25 In this last oracle the identification of the nations is difficult, but the general sense is clear: One nation would rise against another, only to face its doom. The Hebrew word translated **Cyprus** was used later in reference to Rome (Dan. 11:30).

25:1, 2 Acacia Grove is another name for the staging area of Israel in the Transjordan across from Jericho. With these words, the focus of Numbers returns to the camp of Israel. At the end of their long wilderness wanderings, the Israelites had their first encounter with the false religion of Canaan. The phrase **the women of Moab** is the connecting link between this chapter and chs. 22—24. What the men of Moab could not do, the women were able to accomplish. They lead the Israelite men in sexual immorality and false worship. For this God punished them.

25:3 Baal of Peor: Balaam had taken his stance at this high place for pagan worship (23:28) in preparation for his last set of oracles. It is grimly fitting that the near destruction of the people of Israel should be associated with the debased sexual and idolatrous practices of this site.

25:4, 5 God's **anger** flashed yet again toward His errant people. But this was not just another time of trouble; this was the most serious challenge yet. The people had been seduced into joining the worship of Baal. And it was Baal worship that they had been sent to Canaan to eliminate!

25:6–9 Zimri (v. 14), a Hebrew man, became involved with a Midianite woman named Cozbi (v. 15), who may have been a priestess of Baal. Although the nature of the offense isn't made clear in the text, it could be that their sinful actions were performed **at the door of the tabernacle,** in full view of the congregation. **Phinehas the son of Eleazar,** zealous for God's honor, killed both Zimri and Cozbi with a javelin, thus ending the plague that resulted from this offense.

25:10–15 zealous with My zeal: God's response is one of praise for Phinehas. The Hebrew word translated *zealous* can also be translated *jealous*. Phinehas did not want the Israelite camp to be defiled with immorality connected to Baal worship. God honored Phinehas for his zeal.

25:16–18 Harass the Midianites: God commanded Moses to institute a holy war against Midian in retaliation for the unholy and immoral war waged against Israel by that nation.

26:1 after the plague: These words are a turning point in Numbers. The plague was the end of the first generation. Under God's grace, their sons and daughters were ready to begin anew. They would inherit the Promised Land.

26:2–4 The words **take a census** remind us of the beginning of the Book of Numbers (1:2). This is a new beginning and a new census. The numbers compare favorably with the numbers of the first generation. In spite of all the people who had died in the wilderness, the total population was not markedly different. Again, this was a sign of God's blessing on the Israelites.

26:5–50 The children of Reuben: This chapter focuses specifically on the tribal units, with considerable attention paid to the family groupings and the notable persons. It is fitting that this census is considerably more complete than the one in ch. 1. These were the people who would actually enter and inherit the Promised Land.

26:51 who were numbered: The totals of the twelve tribes are very similar in the two census listings. The total decreased slightly, from 603,550 to 601,730.

26:52–56 The land of Canaan was the **inheritance** of the people from the Lord. It was His gift to them, prompted by His love. Two principles were to be used in dividing the land: large tribes were to get large portions, but the determinations were to be made by lot.

26:57–62 The numbering of the **Levites** follows that of the other tribes, just as in the first census. In this case more names and families are given, for this was the list that would be used once the people were in the land.

26:63–65 not a man of those: The persons numbered in the second census did not include any who were numbered in the first census. Of the survivors, only Caleb and Joshua had been over the age of 20 at the time of the debacle at Kadesh (chs. 13; 14).

27:1–5 Five sisters—**the daughters of** Zelophehad—approached Moses and Eleazar to make a claim for their inheritance in the land. Their father had died in the wilderness, as had his entire generation. Since he had no sons, there was no inheritance for him. On the basis of their father's memory, the daughters asked Moses for **a possession among our father's brothers.** In doing this, they were cutting across the social mores of the day. In ancient Israel, women did not inherit land. Moses took the issue to the Lord.

27:6–11 speak what is right: God's decision was that the daughters of Zelophehad had presented a just cause. They would inherit land in the name of their father. The case would become a precedent for other families in which there were no sons, only daughters. If there were no daughters, the inheritance would go to the nearest surviving relative.

27:12–14 The time for the beginning of the conquest was near, which meant that the end of Moses' life was also near. Although

God would not allow Moses to enter the land, He would allow Moses to **see the land** from afar.

27:15–17 set a man over the congregation: Moses' concern was for the well-being of the community, not for himself. Who would lead Israel after his death?

27:18–23 It appears that there were two candidates to succeed Moses: Caleb and Joshua, the two spies who had honored the Lord when the entire nation would not (ch. 14). God's choice was Joshua. The Lord instructed Moses to present Joshua to the congregation so that there would not be a power struggle after his death. Further, Moses began to delegate work to Joshua so that the transition would begin while Moses was still alive.

28:1–6 My offerings made by fire: The Book of Numbers frequently inserts various materials into the flow of the narrative. Among such materials are the sections on sacrifice in chs. 28 and 29. The following chapters focus on the nature of the offerings God required on a seasonal and festival basis.

28:7, 8 In this case, the **drink offering** was beer; usually it was wine. Beer is made from fermented grains; wine is made from fruit, usually grapes. Both were used in the worship of God, to be poured on the altar in required measure.

28:9, 10 The offerings **on the Sabbath day** were in addition to the offerings made every day.

28:11–15 The offerings **at the beginnings of your months** were in addition to daily and weekly offerings.

28:16–25 The celebration of **Passover** (9:1–14) included special sacrifices at the altar. On the first and seventh day of the period, no work was done. The entire period was marked by the eating of unleavened bread.

28:26–31 The **Feast of Weeks** occurred 50 days after Passover and the Feast of Unleavened Bread.

29:1–6 The celebration of the Feast of **Trumpets** involved blowing ram's horns (contrast the silver trumpets in 10:2). Later, this festival became identified with the new year festival.

29:7–11 The Day of Atonement, or Yom Kippur, was regarded as the most holy day of all.

Lev. 16 describes this as a day of fasting rather than feasting, of solemnity rather than rejoicing.

29:12–38 The celebration of the Feast of Tabernacles or Succoth was complex. There was an order to be followed over a period of eight days, and the eighth day had its own distinct ceremony.

29:39, 40 These verses conclude the summary of sacrifices of chs. 28 and 29. The sacrifices and offerings listed in these two chapters are the bare minimum the people had to present to the Lord throughout the year.

30:1, 2 One who makes a vow **shall not break his word.** Vows that are made to the Lord must be carried out (see Deut. 23:21–23; Eccl. 5:1–7).

30:3–5 if a woman makes a vow to the LORD: In Israelite culture, an unmarried young woman was under the protection of her father. If she entered into a vow, that vow might have brought her father into an obligation he did not want to fulfill or could not fulfill. For that reason, the father could overrule the vow.

30:6–8 The preexisting **vows** of a newly married woman could have brought her husband under some obligation. Therefore, the husband had the opportunity to overrule vows his wife may have made before she came under his protection. In such a case, God would release the woman from her vow.

30:9 The **vow of a widow or a divorced woman** would stand, because it did not complicate the obligations of either father or husband.

30:10–16 In the case of a woman who entered into a vow to the Lord after marriage, the husband could overrule the vow. His silence would allow it to remain in force.

31:1, 2 Chapter 31 refers back to ch. 25, the debacle of Israel's sin at Baal Peor and the role that the Midianites played in orchestrating the event.

31:3–6 The preparations for battle included setting apart **a thousand from each tribe,** a way of ensuring the sense of participation of the whole people in the war. **Phinehas,** the heroic figure who stemmed a plague with his bold action (25:7, 8), was commander in the field.

31:7–11 Victory was assured, given the blessing of God on the armies of Israel. The Israelites killed **all the males** and the **kings,** and took the **women** and **their little ones** as captives.

31:12–24 Have you kept all the women alive: These women had caused Israel to sin, as had been counseled by **Balaam.** Balaam had been killed, along with the kings and notables of the people (v. 8). Now the women and their male children needed to be killed as well. Only the young girls who were still virgins were to be kept alive.

31:25–47 The balance of the chapter details the division of the plunder. The numbers are huge, suggesting a great victory. The division among those who had gone to war and those who had not set a standard for future battles. The portion that was to be regarded as the Lord's also became a standard.

31:48–54 not a man of us is missing: None of the Israelite soldiers, not one, was lost in the battle. In praise and gratitude to God, the officers made a special offering, which Moses brought into the tabernacle as a memorial. The officers' gift consisted of over 400 pounds of gold!

32:1–5 The tribes of **Reuben** and **Gad** wanted the land east of the Jordan River which Israel had taken from Sihon and Og (ch. 21). The flocks and herds of Reuben and Gad were large, and the people of these tribes believed that the conquered area east of the Jordan River would be good for them.

32:6–15 Moses was concerned that these tribes were going to shirk their duty to help the other tribes conquer the territory west of the Jordan River. The encounter with these men gave Moses an opportunity to rehearse the story of God's redemption of Israel and Israel's subsequent history and to use that story as a warning for these people.

32:16–19 The men of Reuben and Gad reassured Moses that they were not opting out of the battle. They simply wanted to build some provision for their wives and families while they were gone, and then they would join Israel's army until the entire Promised Land was secured.

32:20–27 Moses and the men of Reuben and Gad negotiated. Plans were made for the fighting men of these tribes to join the armies of Israel for the period of the conquest.

32:28–32 Finally the deal is struck between Moses and the leaders of Reuben and Gad. If the people would fight alongside the others until the conquest was complete, they could certainly live in the land they chose—the land east of the Jordan River. If not, they would lose all choice in the land at all.

32:33–42 It is not until the end of the narrative that we learn that one-half of the tribe of Manasseh had joined Reuben and Gad in their proposal. Moses agreed to their plan and led them in the distribution of the land east of the Jordan River.

33:1 These are the journeys: Chapter 33 records the journey of the people of Israel from Rameses in Egypt (v. 3) to the plains of Moab (v. 49). Most of the places cited are not known today, since they were not cities but encampments in the wilderness of Sinai.

33:2 Moses wrote down: These remarkable words indicate that Moses himself wrote down the following passage.

33:3–5 Rameses is usually identified with Tanis (see Gen. 47:11; Ex. 1:11). There is a certain structural symmetry to the listing of these place names in this chapter. In essence, this list of place names is a song of praise to God's faithfulness. With every step and with every encampment, God led them triumphally to the Promised Land.

33:6–37 Succoth, Etham, and **Pi Hahiroth** were west of the Sea of Reeds. The rest of the sites were in the Sinai Desert.

33:38–49 Mount Hor: With the mention of this place, a quick memorial is given of **Aaron,** the high priest. **fortieth year:** The journey from Rameses to Mt. Hor completed the forty-year cycle. Aaron died on the last year of the Israelites' wanderings in the desert.

33:50–56 if you do not drive out the inhabitants of the land: God's commands to Israel to eradicate the Canaanites from the land were ultimately expressions of His mercy to Israel. If the idolatrous Canaanites were allowed to live among God's people, they would have been a constant source of trouble for the Israelites, like an irritant in the eye. Indeed, if the Canaanites were allowed to remain, Israel would become like them.

34:1–12 the land of Canaan to its boundaries: Chapter 34 serves as a detailed display of the grandeur of the land that God was about to give to His people (33:53).

34:13–15 To the nine tribes and to the half-tribe is a reminder that Reuben, Gad, and the half-tribe of Manasseh would have their settlements east of the Jordan River (32:33). The land of Canaan proper would be inhabited by the remaining nine tribes and the other half-tribe of Manasseh.

34:16–28 The listing of the names of the men serves several purposes: (1) to give authenticity to the record; (2) to memorialize these individuals in the history of Israel; (3) to serve as a legal arrangement so that the

transfer of the land to the tribes would be done in order.

34:29 There is a sense in the words these are the ones that the second generation was now the fully accredited substitute for the rebellious first generation.

35:1–29 give the Levites cities: The Levites were separated from the rest of the population for the holy service of God 1:47–53. They were not to have an allotment of land along with the other tribes (18:24). The decision of the Lord was that they would be distributed throughout the land in 48 cities. In this way, the Levites were distributed among the people as a symbol of the holy service of God (see Josh. 20; 21).

35:30–34 Whoever kills a person: The people were not to confuse accidental manslaughter

---

IN DEPTH   **Cities of Refuge**

In the ancient Middle East, custom dictated that the taking of a life, even by accident, had to be avenged by a member of the victim's family. In response to this ancient practice, God ordered six Levitical cities to be stationed in the land as cities of refuge. A person guilty of unintentional manslaughter could escape blood revenge by fleeing to one of these cities (Josh. 20). No matter where a person lived, there would be a city of refuge within a reasonable distance, because they were strategically spread all over the land—three to the east of the Jordan and three to the west. The Hebrew term translated *refuge* or *asylum* designates a place of escape from the *avenger*, who was the protector of the family's rights, the one who made things right. (The Hebrew word for *avenger* is the same word used for Boaz, translated *relative* in Ruth 2:1.)

Seeking refuge was not a private act, however. Certain regulations governed whether it was applicable to a specific situation, and judgments would be made about each case (Num. 35:22–25). The provisions for seeking refuge in one of the designated cities were spelled out in some detail. (1) The slaying had to have been accidental and not premeditated (Num. 35:16–21). (2) The person had to flee immediately to the city of refuge. The person was safe from the avenger only when he or she was within the city. (3) The person was not safe from vengeance if he or she decided to leave the city. Basically, the unintentional murderer was a virtual prisoner within the city's walls (Num. 35:26–28). (4) The statute of limitations was based on the death of the high priest. When the high priest died, the avenger could no longer pursue the offender. The latter was free to return home (Num. 35:25, 28). (5) The law of asylum pertained to the alien as well as the citizen (Num. 35:15). (6) The manslayer could not pay a ransom instead of fleeing to or staying in a city of refuge. Otherwise a poor person would have been at a great disadvantage (Num. 35:31).

With all these specific regulations, God demonstrated His gracious concern for the innocent. He provided a place for an innocent person to find mercy and safety from the harsh ancient practice of avenging for family deaths.

with premeditated murder. A person who had committed homicide was not permitted to flee to a city of refuge. His crime was to be punished by death.

36:1–4 Chapter 36 presents the interest of the relatives of **Zelophehad,** who were worried about possible complications of the decision to allow Zelophehad's daughters to inherit their father's possession in the land (ch. 27). If the daughters were to marry outside their tribe and family, then the tribal allowances would be hopelessly confused and perhaps even lost.

36:5–13 they may marry only within the family: Moses decided that the family's concern was legitimate. He did not overrule the earlier decision to allow the women to inherit the portion that would have gone to their father, but He regulated their marriage choices to maintain the integrity of the tribal allotments. In this account, we see the way case law worked in ancient Israel. Specific instances that were not covered clearly in the general legislation would be brought to Moses for disposition. He would seek the word of the Lord on that specific issue and then would pronounce the decision.

Deuteronomy

Introduction

With the nation of Israel poised at the entrance of Canaan, Moses seized one last opportunity to prepare the people for their new life in the land of their inheritance. Since Moses would not be entering the land with the people, he wanted to make sure that the nation did not forget its covenant with God. Moses' careful review of the laws of God is recorded in the Book of Deuteronomy.

The name Deuteronomy means "the second law." This name is derived from the Septuagint, the ancient Greek translation of the Old Testament, which interprets the words in 17:18, "a copy of this law," as "the second law." The name is somewhat of a misnomer because Deuteronomy does not contain a second law. However, it does explain God's law revealed at Mount Sinai to a second generation of Israelites.

Throughout the centuries, Jews and Christians have believed that Moses wrote Deuteronomy. Mosaic authorship is supported by the book's consistent covenantal theology, its claims of Mosaic authorship, and the witness of New Testament writers.

Deuteronomy is basically the last will of Moses. In this will, he challenged Israel to remain faithful to the covenant, reminded them of their past history, and pointed to their future of blessings or cursings in the land of Canaan, depending upon their belief and behavior.

Moses' emphasis on the covenant throughout Deuteronomy is remarkable. He testified to its importance by repeatedly calling the new generation of Israelites to follow its provisions (30:11–20). He described the covenant renewal ceremony that would take place between Mount Ebal and Mount Gerizim. He instructed the Levites to recite on the barren mountaintop of Ebal the curses for those who rejected God's Law. On the lush slopes of Gerizim, the rich blessings for those who obeyed God's law would be recited. With these instructions, Moses anticipated the renewal of the covenant on the other side of the Jordan River. There, the people would gather for the grand moment when they would renew the covenant once again, but this time as inhabitants of the Promised Land (11:29, 30; 27:1–8, 12, 13; Josh. 8:30–35).

1:1 words which Moses spoke: Most of Deuteronomy consists of Moses' explanation of God's law and His exhortation to follow it. **This side of the Jordan** is literally "across the Jordan." This is the land east of the Jordan River, or across it from the perspective of the land of Canaan (3:8, 20, 25; 4:41; 11:30).

1:2 eleven days: A journey that might have taken Israel less than two weeks to complete lasted forty years because of unbelief and disobedience (Num. 13; 14). **Horeb** is a name for Mount Sinai (4:10, 15; Ex. 3:1), where the Lord revealed His glory, gave His law, and made a covenant with Israel. **Kadesh Barnea,** an oasis in the Negev, 50 miles southwest of Beersheba, figured prominently in the story of the wilderness wandering (Num. 13, 14).

1:3 fortieth year: In early Israel, dates were given with reference to the Exodus from Egypt. Hence, this is forty years after the Exodus. It had taken Israel about a year to arrive at Kadesh Barnea from Mt. Horeb and another year to reach the place where Moses was addressing them in this passage. The 38 years between had been spent wandering in the desert—God's punishment for their disobedience.

1:4 These victories under Moses' leadership (2:26–37; Num. 21:21–35) opened up the conquest of the land from the east. They were a foretaste of the victories God would give the Israelites under Joshua's leadership.

1:5 The Hebrew word translated **law** basically means "instruction." It is God's gracious teaching to the Israelites on the right way for them to live (see 6:1–3; Ps. 19).

1:6 The LORD our God is an emphatic reference to the divine revelation at Mount Sinai. Moses reminded Israel that God had revealed His glory, made His covenant with them, and assured them of His presence.

1:7, 8 Turn ... and go refers to the departure for the Promised Land. The extent of

God's gift was enormous, even as the people were numerous. Moses emphasized God's faithfulness to His promises. The Promised Land extended from the Negev, **the South** (Gen. 12:9) to **the River Euphrates** (Gen. 15:18–21).

1:9 I alone: Moses felt inadequate to take care of all aspects of leadership himself because the people were so numerous (Ex. 18:13–26).

1:10, 11 multiplied ... stars of heaven Moses' rhetoric celebrates God's faithfulness in fulfilling His word to Abraham (Gen. 15:5; 22:17). **a thousand times:** The Lord had greatly blessed Israel in numbers (Ex. 1:1–7); His blessing in their past was to be a measure of His blessing in their future.

1:12, 13 wise ... knowledgeable: The qualities of the leaders reflect attributes of God. Wisdom refers to the ability to bring harmony even when great differences exist. Understanding refers to the ability to penetrate the realities of life from God's perspective and to deal fairly with all parties in a dispute. Knowledge is the broad experience gained by living life, by watching people, and by making correct choices based on God's word.

1:14–16 heads: A number of men were charged with the administrative, judicial, and military tasks of creating unity among the people. Some of them were also called **judges.**

1:17, 18 not show partiality: God demanded absolute fairness regardless of age or social status.

1:19 Great and terrible wilderness describes the Israelites' journey by using two words for one idea, that of "a truly horrible wilderness."

1:20 The Amorites were one of the groups Israel encountered in their approach to the Promised Land. The term is often a general designation for the Canaanites, particularly those who lived in mountainous regions (Num. 13:29).

1:21 do not fear or be discouraged: Even though the future seemed uncertain, Moses exhorted the Israelites to have faith that God would take care of their needs.

1:22–23 every one of you: The initiative for

sending the spies out came from the people, but it was something the Lord agreed to as well (Num. 13:2).

1:24, 25 The Valley of Eshcol was a region near Hebron (Num. 13:23); it is remembered for the huge clusters of grapes the spies found there.

1:26 you would not go up, but rebelled: The present generation was not directly involved in this rebellion, but as the descendants of the rebellious generation they shared in the guilt of the disobedience of their forebears. On the other hand, they were also the inheritors of God's promises to those who had gone before.

1:27 hates us ... to destroy us: The rebels refused to acknowledge God's clear expressions of saving love to them. They did not trust the God who had saved them from slavery and provided for their needs on numerous occasions.

1:28 The Anakim were an ancient people known for their great size (Num. 13:28).

1:29, 30 goes before you ... fight for you: The Lord would fight for His people and give them victory.

1:31 carried: God cared for His people and loved them as an adoring parent cares for a child (Ex. 19:4). **his son:** The Israelites were God's children by covenant (Is. 63:16; 64:8, 9).

1:32 you did not believe: The people did not walk by faith, despite all that God had done in their lives. The language indicates that God could hardly believe the ingratitude and lack of obedience on the part of those to whom He had demonstrated such lavish love.

1:33 to search out: The Lord had always explored the next step for the Israelites, since He was leading them Himself. **The cloud** over the Most Holy Place symbolized God's presence.

1:34, 35 one ... of this evil generation: Because of their rebellion, God excluded adults age 20 and older at that time from the blessing of the land (Num. 14:29).

1:36 Caleb was faithful (Num. 13:30—14:28). God permitted Him to enter the land and receive the area of Hebron as his family estate (Josh. 15:13).

1:37 also angry with me: Even Moses, the leader of the people, was the object of God's wrath. He could not enter the land because he disobeyed God by striking the rock at Meribah (see Num. 20:10–13).

1:38 God allowed **Joshua** to lead the Israelites into the land because of his trust in God (Num. 13:30–14:28). Before his death, Moses exhorted Joshua, encouraged him, and transferred to him the authority to lead the people into the Promised Land (3:28; 31:1–29; 34:9).

1:39 your little ones and your children: The most outrageous of Israel's complaints against God was that He had wanted their children to die (Num. 14:31). But the Lord demonstrated His love and faithfulness to His people by protecting those younger than 20 so that they could inherit the land.

1:40 The Way of the Red Sea probably means the way toward Elath by the Red Sea (the Gulf of Aqaba).

1:41 In their statement, **we have sinned,** the Israelites showed regret but not true repentance.

1:42, 43 I am not among you: The Lord would not protect them. Therefore, victory was out of the question.

1:44–46 As bees do is an expression that signifies alarming pursuit by a swarm of menacing enemies (Ex. 23:28; Ps. 118:12; Is. 7:18). **Hormah,** a name meaning "Destruction," probably refers to a site south of the Amorite hill country by Kadesh Barnea that came to be called by that name.

2:1–3 the Lord spoke to me: We see regularly in Genesis through Deuteronomy that Moses reported God's very words to him.

2:4 The descendants of Esau are the Edomites (Gen. 36:1–8).

2:5 I have given … to Esau: God had extended His blessing to the Edomites by giving them land, just as He was about to give Israel the Promised Land.

2:6, 7 The Israelites could not take **food** or **water** by force, beg for it, or steal it. God demanded that they pay the expenses of their journey through Edom.

2:8 Away from Elath and Ezion Geber refers to turning away from the way of the Red Sea, on which these cities were located.

2:9–11 The Moabites were related to the Israelites through **Lot** (see Gen. 19:37). **Ar** is a synonym for the region of Moab. The Lord had given land to both Edom and Moab. However, His principal gift of land was to Israel.

2:12, 13 The Valley of the Zered was east of the Dead Sea at the border between Edom and Moab.

2:14–19 When God saved His people, it was by His **hand** (Ex. 15:6). Sadly, it was by His hand that He brought judgment on them as well.

2:20 The **Zamzummin** were a people who lived in the Ammonite territory, possibly the Zuzim (Gen. 14:5).

2:21–23 The Avim lived in villages between the Jordan River and the Mediterranean coast. **Gaza** was a Philistine city on the Mediterranean coast. **Caphtor** is possibly the same as Crete (see Gen. 10:14).

2:24 The River Arnon was the traditional border between Moab and Ammon. **Heshbon** refers both to the city and the territory ruled by Sihon.

2:25 The mighty acts of God through Israel would fill the nations with **dread and fear** (Ex. 15:14–16; Josh. 2:9). The fear of the nations would soften them for the time of conquest. But the dissemination of knowledge about God's works would glorify Him (4:6).

2:26–29 The Wilderness of Kedemoth was a desert within the territory of Sihon, located on its eastern border, east of the Dead Sea.

2:30–32 Jahaz was located north of Kedemoth (Is. 15:4).

2:33 our God delivered … we defeated him: God gave Israel the victory, but the Israelites still had to fight courageously.

2:34, 35 By the law of the ban, every living thing, human and animal, was to be **utterly destroyed**—that is, put to death (7:1, 2; 20:17). The ban included fighting men and civilians, males and females, adults and children. God used the people of Israel to punish the Canaanites for their continual wickedness through the generations.

2:36, 37 Aroer was a city on the northern bank of the River Arnon at the border between Sihon's territory and the Moabite kingdom. **Jabbok** was the river Jacob crossed on his way back to Canaan (Gen. 32:22).

3:1–3 Bashan was the region east of the Sea of Galilee. **Og:** The territory of Og may have extended south of the River Yarmuk into Gilead.

3:4–8 The territory of Sihon and Og extended **from the River Arnon to Mount Hermon** (2:24–3:7). Mount Hermon is the mountain range in the north between Canaan and Lebanon.

3:9–13 The Sidonians were the Phoenicians. **Bedstead** could also be translated "sarcophagus," that is, stone coffin. **Rabbah** was on the site of the capital of modern Jordan, Amman.

3:14 Jair had captured these settlements (Num. 32:41). The **Geshurites** lived east of the Sea of Galilee and south of Mount Hermon. The **Maachathites** were descended from Abraham's brother Nahor (Gen. 22:24) and lived north of the Geshurites.

3:15–17 The northernmost section of **Gilead** was given to **Machir** (Num. 32:39), son of Manasseh (Gen. 50:23). The southern section was given to Reuben and Gad.

3:18, 19 The Lord ... has given: The text regularly emphasizes that the land was God's gift (1:39). **men of valor:** The battle would be fought by armed men under the command of God (Ex. 15:3).

3:20, 21 Joshua, as one of the original spies (Num. 13; 14), had a great advantage. Along with Caleb, he had **seen** the land. Joshua also had witnessed the victories the Lord had given east of the Jordan River.

3:22 your God Himself fights: The Lord is the Divine Warrior who delivers and fights for His faithful people (Ex. 15:3).

3:23 Moses **pleaded** with God. But God refused to answer Moses' prayer, not because Moses lacked faith, but because Moses had disobeyed God and had not treated Him as holy (Num. 20:12).

3:24 O Lord God: The Hebrew has the word for "Lord" or "Master" followed by the personal name of God, Yahweh. This phrase indicates the depth of Moses' relationship with the Lord (9:26).

3:25 let me cross over: The verb is charged with energy expressing Moses' deep emotion.

Moses did not ask that Joshua be removed as leader of the nation. He only requested to **see** the land that God had promised.

3:26–28 Enough: God ordered Moses not to ask Him about it again. But God showed His mercy to Moses by showing him the land from a distance (34:1–3).

3:29 Beth Peor was a pagan site dedicated to Baal of Peor (Num. 25:3, 5) and was the scene of Israel's first disastrous encounter with the sexually-centered worship of Baal (4:3).

4:1 you may live: In contrast, Moses could not enter the land (v. 22). But for the people, God's gift of His law was designed for their good. By obeying the Law, the people could experience a fruitful life (6:1–3).

4:2 not add ... nor take from it: The Israelites had to learn to live by God's word without trying to justify their disobedience or explaining away God's clear commands (Rev. 22:18, 19).

4:3, 4 Baal Peor: See 3:29. Twenty-four thousand were executed there by plague (Num. 25:9). That name reminded the Israelites of the terror of God's judgment.

4:5 Moses was the mediator of God's word, not its originator (compare 2 Pet. 1:20, 21). **my God commanded me:** Throughout Deuteronomy, Moses always deferred to the Lord as the source of his message.

4:6–8 in the sight of the peoples: By living in obedience to God, Israel would become a countercultural force by its manner of life, government, and society (see Rom. 12:2). God's blessings on Israel would cause the nations to seek to learn about Him.

4:9 your eyes have seen: The people had witnessed God's redemption, His revelation, and the giving of His gracious covenant. Now, they had to adhere to the covenantal regulations and **teach** their **children** the story of God's saving acts and His promises to Israel.

4:10 My words are the Ten Commandments (v. 13).

4:11 The appearance of God is often described as accompanied by **darkness** and **fire** (Ex. 19:18). The fire speaks of His holiness, majesty, and transcendence, but also of His judgment against evil (v. 24). The darkness speaks of His unapproachable nature, of our sin, and of the possibility of impending judgment.

4:12 heard ... but saw no form: The Lord revealed His glory to the Israelites, but they saw no visual image other than darkness and fire.

4:13 Obedience to God's commandments was an expression of loyalty to and love for the Lord who had initiated a **covenant** with Israel.

4:14 teach: Moses mediated God's revelation to the people. As their teacher, he applied the Law (Ex. 20:19).

4:15, 16 There was no way of describing or of giving shape with any image to the experience of God's presence at Sinai (Ex. 20:18). Since Israel had not seen the **form** of God, they could not represent Him in any way.

4:17–19 likeness of any animal: Animals were created by God (Gen. 1:20–25). They cannot serve as a medium for spiritual awareness or as a representation for God.

4:20 taken you and brought you: God chose Israel to be His people and to have a covenant with Him. **inheritance:** The people redeemed by the Lord belonged to Him and had a glorious future with Him.

4:21, 22 I must die: How hard these words must have been to Moses!

4:23, 24 God is a **consuming fire.** Israel had witnessed His righteous anger during the wilderness journey as well as in Canaan (Heb. 12:29).

4:25 Children and grandchildren is a reference to a future rebellion, when a generation would disobey the Lord.

4:26 witness against you: Creation would act as God's witness against a rebellious and obstinate people (30:19; Is. 1:2). **utterly perish ... be utterly destroyed:** The curses of the covenant would overtake the Israelites (Ps. 1:6). The Lord would discipline them and exile them from the land.

4:27 Scatter you among the peoples is a prophetic warning of the exiles that would take place in 722 and 586 B.C.

4:28, 29 Moses warned against the folly of idolatry. **Neither see ... nor smell** declares the impotence of idols (see Ps. 115:6; Is. 40:19, 20; 41:7, 22–24). Turning from

the living God to false, nonexistent "gods" was in effect moving from life to death (1 Thess. 1:9, 10).

4:30 The latter days simply means "in the future." But the prophets developed this phrase into a more technical designation for a new era characterized by God's blessings, the age of Messiah.

4:31 The emphasis on God's mercy in this verse is a necessary balance to the emphasis that Moses placed on God's refining wrath (v. 24). **not forsake ... nor forget:** The Lord was free to scatter His people. But after His discipline, He would regather them and show them His favor. God was and is faithful to His promises.

4:32–34 The Creator of all the earth is the same God who spoke to the Israelites at Mount Sinai.

4:35 there is none other besides Him: Moses emphasizes the theme that the living God is the only one there is (see 4:39; 5:7; 6:4; 32:39).

4:36, 37 God's revelation to the Israelites was intended to graciously **instruct,** guide, and discipline the Israelites in the way of righteousness (compare 2 Tim. 3:16, 17).

4:38 nations greater and mightier: God is praised for the miraculous growth of Israel's family during their sojourn in Egypt (Ex. 1:7, 9, 10). On the other hand, the nation of Israel is described as small in number compared to the other nations around her. Hence, God deserves the glory for Israel's victories.

4:39 God in heaven ... there is no other: Since no other God was Creator, Lord of history, Teacher, and the Lover of His people, Israel had to respond to God alone.

4:40 The promise of blessing **in the land** was conditional—it required obedience (5:29; 6:24; 14:23; 19:9; 28:29, 33).

4:41–43 The regulations the cities to which a person guilty of manslaughter could flee are further developed in 19:1–13. The narrative the division of the land (3:12–20) resumes with the appointment of the **three cities** of refuge in the Transjordan (Num. 35:9–28; Josh. 20).

4:44 The law refers to the commandments detailed in chs. 5—26. *Law* basically means "instruction."

4:45 These are ... the judgments: This law is the same as that given to the previous generation at Mount Sinai.

4:46–49 in the land of Sihon ... of Og: Israel had recently acquired this land east of the Jordan River and was now preparing to cross the river and enter Canaan.

5:1–4 Did not make this covenant with our fathers, but with us emphasizes the privileged position of the present generation as they were preparing to enter Canaan.

5:5 I stood between the LORD and you reflects Moses' role as mediator of the covenant (Ex. 20:18–21).

5:6, 7 no other gods: Many ancient Middle Eastern cultures absorbed other gods into their own belief systems, using them for their own purposes. But the Israelites served only one God, who would not allow any rivals.

5:8–10 Even when an **image** functioned as a symbol for deity, it led worshipers away from the true worship of the living God. **to the third and fourth generations:** Even as God would bless generation upon generation for their true worship of Him, He would also punish generation upon generation for faithlessness to Him.

5:11 Take ... in vain refers to the abuse, misuse, blasphemy, cursing, or manipulation of the Lord's name.

5:12–15 These verses contain the positive command to regard the Sabbath as **holy**—separated for God's purposes. **you shall do no work ... rest:** On the Sabbath, the Israelites were to rest from work and celebrate God's good gifts.

5:16 Honor your father and your mother: Respect for parents would build strong families. Strong, godly families, in turn, would teach children the ways of God, and the covenant community dedicated to serving and worshiping God would remain intact.

5:17 Premeditated **murder** was the concern of this law. For commands other forms of homicide, see chs. 19—21. The basis of respect for life lay in God's act of creating humans in His image (Gen. 9:6).

5:18 Adultery was a betrayal not only of a commitment, but of a relationship. Anyone who treated marriage lightly would also treat his or her relationship with God lightly.

5:19 not steal: Stealing could take many forms: illegitimate removal of property, kidnapping, or manipulation of a person and his property to one's advantage.

5:20 not bear false witness: This included any testimony that falsely incriminated someone or negatively affected someone's reputation, such as gossip and slander.

5:21 You shall not covet: Desiring what someone else possessed was self-interestedness. This attitude was the opposite of a concern for the other person's welfare.

5:22 He wrote them on two tablets: The two tablets were two complete copies of the Law. Usually, two copies were made of ancient near Eastern treaties. One was retained by each of the two contracting parties as a witness to the agreement. But with the Ten Commandments, both copies were placed before God. Not only did the Lord covenant with the Israelites; He also witnessed the agreement.

5:23–26 why should we die ... living God: The people needed to realize that the living God was powerful, great, and demanded perfection, so that they as sinners would recognize their need for His mercy.

5:27 we will hear and do it: God's revelation of Himself prompted the people to express their willingness to comply with the Lord's commands.

5:28–31 The people were impressed with what they saw and heard, but their **heart** was unchanged.

5:32, 33 in all the ways ... God has commanded you: Out of all the nations, God had chosen Israel to be instructed in His law. But the real test of the distinctiveness of these people was their response to God's revelation.

6:1 commanded to teach you: Moses was God's instrument in giving His law to Israel (5:22, 23). It was not really "the Law of Moses" but the Law of God.

6:2 The **fear** of the Lord includes awe for His greatness and holiness, love for Him, and submission to His will. Initially, the fear of God may involve fright. Yet it leads to a sense of wonder, a commitment to worship, and delight in knowing God.

6:3 that it may be well with you: God instructed His people so they might live good lives full of meaning and peace. **A land flowing with milk and honey** indicates a fruitful and blessed land (11:9; 26:9, 15; 27:3; 31:20).

6:4 This verse is the celebrated Shema, the basic confession of faith in Judaism (see Matt. 22:37, 38; Mark 12:29, 30; Luke 10:27). The people must listen and obey. **The LORD our God** indicates the people's relationship with the living God. He had saved them from slavery in Egypt, guided them through the wilderness, and given them His instructions. **The LORD is one** means "the Lord alone." There is only one God.

6:5, 6 Moses repeatedly exhorted the Israelites to respond to God's love with devotion. God commanded His people to choose Him with all their being, and in the process to deny all other supposed deities.

6:7 talk of them when you sit: God's revelation should be so central to a godly family that they should naturally talk about Him while they perform their activities.

6:8, 9 a sign ... frontlets: The idea is that God's laws should be close to the mind and hands of His people at all times (compare Ex. 13:9, 16; Prov. 3:3; 6:21). **write them on the doorposts:** Jewish custom is to attach a small vessel called a *mezuzah* to the doorpost. In it is placed a small scroll containing the text of Deut. 6:4–9; 11:13–21 and God's name Shaddai.

6:10–12 Moses warned the people not to forget that their possessions were God's gifts. The Israelites needed continually to praise and thank God for His mercy toward them.

6:13–15 serve: The Lord demanded absolute commitment to Himself. Out of gratitude, the people were to do this willingly. **oaths in His name:** The fact that God had revealed His name assures the people of God's goodness to them. He wanted them to look to Him alone for refuge and sustenance.

6:16–19 God may test His children, but they may never test or **tempt** Him by their rebelliousness or sin (see Matt. 4:7; Luke 4:12). **to cast out all your enemies:** Canaan's false

worship and immorality could not influence the Israelites if the Canaanites were thrown out of the land.

6:20–24 your son asks: Moses commanded the Israelites to teach their children the significance of their rituals and customs.

6:25 Moses did not offer the people a works-righteousness by keeping the law. **Righteousness** is a right relationship with God. God initiates this relationship, and His children respond to it as an expression of love.

7:1 The Hittites came originally from Asia Minor. **The Girgashites** are an unknown people mentioned also in Gen. 10:16 and 1 Chr. 1:14. **The Amorites** were the native population of Canaan that had settled in the mountains. **The Canaanites** were the native population that had settled in the coastlands. **The Perizzites** were the native population that had settled in the hill country. **The Hivites** were the native population settled south of the Lebanon mountains. **The Jebusites** were the native population settled near what later became Jerusalem.

7:2 Covenant refers to any treaty with the Canaanite nations that might undermine God's covenant with Israel.

7:3, 4 Intermarriage with the Canaanite population would have tempted the Israelites to adopt Canaanite culture. This would have threatened Israel's ability to be a countercultural force. They were not to "blend in."

7:5, 6 destroy ... break down: The destruction of idolatrous sites was meant to keep the Israelites from imitating and borrowing false pagan practices (12:2; 16:21, 22).

7:7 The Israelites had no reason for pride, for they were the **least of all peoples.** Whatever privileges or possessions they enjoyed were because of God's grace.

7:8 The biblical authors paint a wonderful picture of God: the powerful God extending His **mighty hand** to save His people.

7:9, 10 faithful God ... for a thousand generations: Throughout all time, God has remained true to His commitment made to Abraham, Isaac, and Jacob. **love Him and keep His commandments:** Loving God always finds expression in doing His will.

7:11–16 bless the fruit … increase: God's blessings extended to the quality of life, with the assurance of children, health, food, drink, and peace. The people's immediate responsibility was to **destroy** the Canaanites' wicked presence and influence in the land (2:34).

7:17–19 you shall remember: The past saving acts of God demonstrated His nature and power. The people were to remember the details of His actions so that they could face the present moment in the light of eternity.

7:20, 21 The hornet (Ex. 23:28; Josh. 24:12) may refer to a dramatic act of God, such as a violent storm or a plague of insects. It may refer to campaigns by other armies that weakened the Canaanites before the Israelites arrived.

7:22–26 little by little: The conquest of the land was in two stages: (1) a rapid, broad conquest under Joshua; (2) a gradual, area-by-area, city-by-city conquest that followed. God's plan was that not all of the Promised Land would fall to Israel at once. Indeed, much of the land remained to be conquered after Joshua (Josh. 13:1–6).

8:1 Live, in this context, has the same meaning as saving one's soul in James 1:21; 5:20.

8:2 remember: Reflecting on the past acts of God encouraged loyalty and devotion to Him.

8:3 God supplied His people with food in the wilderness (see Ex. 16) so that they would learn that **man shall not live by bread alone.** Humans have a spiritual nature that can be satisfied only by the spiritual nutrients of God's Word.

8:4 In addition to providing manna and water, the Lord made the clothing and shoes of the people last for 40 years!

8:5–9 The land had everything necessary to sustain life and develop an economy: water, crops, and metals for industry (11:8–12). The varied forms of plant life were surprising to the people who had wandered in the wilderness.

8:10–16 bless the LORD: The proper response to plenty is thanksgiving and worship. In the absence of proper worship, people would **forget,** become complacent and greedy, and even deny that God provided for them (v. 17).

God who brought … who led you … who brought water … who fed: These four historical allusions recall (1) the redemption from Egypt, (2) the presence of God in the wilderness, (3) the provision of water, and (4) the provision of manna.

8:17 Moses warned the people that prosperity and **wealth** often leads to an exaltation of self and a rejection of God.

8:18 God's **power** is different from human manipulation, power politics, competition, and other ways of getting ahead. God gives grace.

8:19, 20 The threat was that the people would **perish** in the same manner as the nations whom they had come to drive out.

9:1–3 Hear, O Israel: Moses called on the people to see the future occupation of the land as a gift of divine grace, not the result of any righteousness of their own. The future was open to them if only they could learn from the past.

9:4–6 possess their land: The reasons for the conquest of the Promised Land were (1) the immorality of its inhabitants and (2) the promises God made to Abraham, Isaac, and Jacob (Gen. 15:18–21). **stiff-necked people:** Israel's history demonstrated how often the people grumbled, complained, and disobeyed.

9:7, 8 rebellious: The people were characteristically stubborn. They continued to test the Lord (v. 27).

9:9 A person cannot go more than about three days without **water** and survive. God supernaturally preserved Moses during the **forty days.**

9:10–19 the LORD delivered to me … finger of God: God initiated the covenant with His people and gave Moses His laws. With God's approval, Moses taught the Law to the people.

9:20–23 See Num. 11 and 13.

9:24–29 Moses took God's judgment seriously. Nevertheless, he did not resign himself to God's justice, but appealed to God's faithfulness, mercy, and honor.

10:1, 2 I will write: The condescension of the Lord is almost beyond belief. He prepared the tablets a second time, even after the first set was broken.

10:3 The **acacia** tree is still found in the Sinai Peninsula, but in smaller numbers than when the Israelites passed through.

10:4, 5 He wrote ... according to the first writing: The Lord did not add to or take away from the commandments.

10:6–11 Levi: The responsibilities of the Levites included: (1) care for the ark of the covenant (Num. 3); (2) service in offering, worship, teaching, and legal matters (18:1–8); and (3) blessing Israel (Num. 6:22–27).

10:12–15 Heaven and the highest heavens: The sky and the whole universe belong to God.

10:16 circumcise the foreskin of your heart: Circumcision was a *physical* sign of the covenant; faith and repentance were *spiritual* signs. Since the Canaanite worship system involved sexual excess, the distinctive sign on the body of the male Hebrew would be a significant reminder not to participate in the rituals of the Canaanites.

10:17, 18 Moses proclaims that the God of Israel alone is **God,** the sovereign Lord, the just and great King of all. The proper response to this God is awe, love, and service. **fatherless ... stranger:** God uses His power to uphold justice—especially for those have no powerful ally (1:16; 24:17–22).

10:19 God's provision for their needs should have motivated the Israelites to **love the stranger** among them. To love and provide for the disadvantaged was in fact following God's example.

10:20, 21 He is your praise: Reflecting on the Creator-Redeemer—whose love, justice, and power extended beyond the covenant people—leads to worship, love, and obedience.

10:22 stars of heaven: God faithfully fulfilled His promise to Abraham (Gen. 15:5, 6).

11:1–5 Moses traced the mighty acts of God in order to encourage his hearers to respond to God's revelation.

11:6, 7 Dathan and Abiram rebelled against Aaron's priesthood and lost their lives (Num. 16).

11:8–12 land for which the LORD your God cares: God would control the seasons and rains to provide for His people (vv. 14, 15).

11:13–17 The early rain encouraged the sprouting of seed and new growth. **The latter rain** brought the crops to maturity. **Lord's anger:** God is gracious and loving, but also just when provoked by arrogant people.

11:18–25 The opposite of a blessing is a **curse.** As God's blessing brings vitality, so His curse takes it away.

11:26–32 Gerizim ... Ebal: See Josh. 8:30–35.

12:1 giving you to possess: God was about to give the people the land. Yet He demanded their obedience as a condition for its occupation and enjoyment (chs. 28; 29).

12:2 mountains: The Canaanites built their temples on high places, believing that their gods resided in palaces on the mountains. The Canaanites would worship at a **green tree** because they believed this would bring success and prosperity.

12:3, 4 Sacred pillars were monuments dedicated to pagan gods. They represented the power of fertility. **Wooden images** refers to the poles or trees dedicated to the goddess Asherah.

12:5 place where the LORD your God chooses: God blessed His people with His presence in the tabernacle in the wilderness and later at Shiloh, in the temple in Jerusalem, and finally through Jesus Christ (John 2:18–22).

12:6 The **heave** offering was a communal offering, which the priest lifted up to signify that it was a gift to the Lord (Ex. 29:27, 28; Lev. 7:34). The priest took his due (Lev. 7:14, 32, 34), while the worshiper and his family ate the rest of the offering. A **vowed** offering was made in fulfillment of a vow (Lev. 7:16, 17; 22:21; Num. 6:21; 15:3–16; 30:11). A **freewill** offering was voluntary (23:23; Ex. 35:27–29; 36:3; Lev. 7:16; Ezek. 46:12).

12:7 eat ... rejoice: The communal offerings were to be eaten and enjoyed by those who offered them. It was a time of celebration before the Lord. **blessed:** God favored His people by giving them children, flocks, and the crops of the land.

12:8 every man ... own eyes: In the wilderness, the people did not develop a common focus on the Lord and become a body of believers. Moses challenged the new generation to repent and return to the Lord.

12:9, 10 Moses envisioned a future state of **rest** for the people. Rest would mean that God's people would enjoy His blessings and live together in unity, free from fear of assault (Ps. 133; Jer. 31:2; Heb. 4:8–11).

12:11, 12 The Hebrew word for **rejoice** describes a deep enjoyment by the entire community of God's good gifts.

12:13–15 slaughter ... meat: Butchering and eating meat was permitted wherever the Israelites settled.

12:16 The prohibition of eating or drinking **blood** in any form was an important restriction. Since blood represented life, the Israelites were to show respect for the vital fluids of animals (Gen. 9:4; Lev. 17:11).

12:17, 18 within your gates: Aspects of God's worship that were designed for community celebration were not to be done in the privacy of the home. Instead, God would designate the place where He would be worshiped.

12:19 The **Levite** received no tribal inheritance in the land and was dependent on the people for food.

12:20–27 enlarges your border: Moses emphasized the potential greatness of God's blessings on the people. The land might become so large that for many people frequent journeys to the central sanctuary would be impossible. In this case, provisions were made for the enjoyment of meat at home.

12:28 that it may go well: The Lord promised His blessing to all those who responded to His benevolent instructions. **and your children:** God's blessing extended to the succeeding generations (Gen. 1:27, 28; 9:1, 7; 17:19).

12:29, 30 God cuts off: The conquest was God's, but the Israelites were His responsible agents (v. 2).

 IN DEPTH   **A New Culture**

Israel was on the verge of a momentous occasion. Not only were they preparing to enter the Promised Land and conquer its inhabitants, they were also preparing to establish a brand new culture. The primary focus of this new culture would be on the living God. Every part of it would reflect His nature.

God's commandments gave the Israelites a concrete expression of how God wanted the people to live. In short, He wanted a people that loved and worshiped Him alone. By keeping a number of purity laws, the Israelites were to demonstrate their commitment to Him by keeping ritually clean. Ideally, this outward purity would reflect inward purity. Since God was perfect, He wanted His people to resist the immoral practices of the neighboring nations. But He not only wanted them to resist evil, He also wanted them to reflect His loving and compassionate nature by helping strangers, widows, orphans, and the poor. By following God's extensive instructions, the Israelites could establish their society on the just laws of the living God.

Many parts of the Israelite culture were distinctive in the ancient world, such as prohibitions against eating pork. These outward distinctions were a sign that the Israelites were set apart to God's holy purposes. However, the most prominent distinction was Israel's absolute allegiance to one God. Israel's entire society—its legal system, economic structure, family life, and individual and communal ethics—reflected this allegiance. While the nations that surrounded Israel worshiped a variety of gods at numerous shrines located all over the landscape, the Israelites (ideally) worshiped one God in one way at one place, the place He would choose. In the Promised Land, God planned to bless the Israelites abundantly. In turn, He expected the Israelites to live responsibly, in a culture unlike any that had preceded it.

12:31 God hated the Canaanite practices and was concerned that His children would be enticed by them (Lev. 18:21; 20:2–5). **burn ... sons and daughters:** This is an example of one of the worst Canaanite practices, in which the Israelites later joined (2 Kin. 21:1–9; 2 Chr. 28:1–4).

12:32 not add to it nor take away from it: The Word of God is not subject to whim, taste, or passing fancy.

13:1, 2 a prophet or a dreamer: Both prophecy and dreams were legitimate forms of revelation. The fulfillment of a prophecy, **a sign,** or **a wonder** ordinarily validated the entire message of the prophet (18:22). **let us serve them:** Even if a wonder accompanied the message, a prophet who led the people away from the living God was a false prophet.

13:3, 4 The revelation of God through Moses was the test of any sign or message. When the message deviated from God's prior revelation, Israel had to discern the false teaching. **love ... heart and ... soul:** True faith is a commitment of one's whole being to the true God.

13:5 The offense was serious and so was the punishment, **death.** It was better for a false prophet to be executed than for one to escape judgment and mislead the people. **So you shall put away the evil from your midst:** Discipline, punishment, and testing were God's means of keeping His people pure.

13:6–11 your hand shall be first: The relative who brought the charge would lead in the capital punishment of the relative who suggested idolatrous practices.

13:12–14 The term translated **corrupt men** denotes wicked, depraved people who oppose the will and work of God. **inquire ... ask diligently:** Proper investigation before a public trial guaranteed justice for everyone.

13:15, 16 strike the inhabitants: The people of the city, who were responsible for letting evil get out of hand became subject to punishment. They were no better than the immoral Canaanites who were under God's present judgment (7:2; 12:2, 3).

13:17, 18 compassion ... to keep all His commandments: The seemingly harsh judgment

of evil was an act of obedience. God required the harsh punishment of evildoers so that immoral practices would not spread throughout the land.

14:1 cut ... nor shave: Pagan mourning rituals encouraged physical abuse. These practices were a form of magic by which people sought to exercise control over their well-being and over the gods (1 Kin. 18:28).

14:2 As a **holy people,** the Israelites were set apart to the Lord, separated from the nations, and chosen to practice the will of God on earth.

14:3 not eat: The dietary regulations set Israel apart from the nations (Lev. 11). Most likely, God prohibited certain animals from being eaten in order to distinguish the practices of Israel from those of neighboring nations. With this physical sign, God symbolized Israel's holiness.

14:4–11 Animals prohibited for food either did not have cloven hooves or did not chew the cud (Lev. 11).

14:12–18 These unclean birds were mainly birds of prey and scavengers. They were associated with dead flesh and were likely carriers of disease.

14:19 Creeping thing that flies refers to insects that could not be eaten.

14:20 may eat: Some of God's laws prohibit, while others permit.

14:21 not boil ... in its mother's milk: Unlike the Canaanites who boiled young goats alive in the milk of their mothers as a sacrifice to fertility gods, Israel was to practice a more humane method of animal sacrifice.

14:22–27 Money refers to uncoined silver. Coins were not struck until the Persian period.

14:28, 29 Every third year the tithe was given to the Levites and the poor.

15:1 every seven years: God taught His people to think in cycles of holy time: six days of work and the seventh of rest; six years of business and the seventh of giving freedom to the poor; six years of agricultural cultivation and the seventh of rest (Ex. 23:10, 11; Lev. 25:1–7). **Debts** were suspended as described in vv. 2–6.

15:2, 3 creditor ... release it: The debtor could not repay in the seventh year because the fields could not be cultivated (Lev. 25:1–7). If creditors demanded repayment, the poor would sink even further into debt. In this, God showed His care and concern for the poor.

15:4, 5 no poor among you: God promised to bless every individual among His people.

15:6 lend … not borrow: God's blessing would bring a surplus. Israel's wealth and prominence among the nations would grow.

15:7, 8 not harden: The people's attitude toward the poor should have been a reflection of their gratitude for God's gifts to them.

15:9, 10 The creditor might have been wary of lending anything to the poor because the seventh year, the year that all debts were erased, was approaching. Even though the creditor would not benefit from the loan, he was encouraged to lend to those in need.

15:11 The poor will never cease is a realistic statement compared with the ideal expressed in v. 4 (see Matt. 26:11).

15:12, 13 When a poor man lost all his property, he could sell himself for work for **six** years. **let him go free:** The year of release canceled debts and freed the debtor (Ex. 21:2).

15:14 supply him liberally: The debtor-slave had been an instrument by which God had blessed the master. Upon the slave's departure, the slave would receive his or her due. In this way, the master acknowledged both the work of the slave and the sovereignty of the Lord.

15:15–18 remember that you were a slave: God's grace to the Israelites in freeing them from Egyptian slavery was a model for all Israelites to follow in relation to the poor.

15:19 The owners of **firstborn males** could not profit from the firstborn because they belonged to the Lord and were to be presented as an offering to Him once a year (v. 20). The basis for this law was the death of the Egyptians' firstborn and the preservation of the firstborn of the Israelites (Ex. 12:12, 29; 13:2).

15:20–23 if there is a defect in it: God expected the best from the Israelites. To sacrifice one's best to the Lord was a leap of faith. One had to believe that God would bless one's flock despite the absence of its very best.

16:1–5 Passover was observed on the fourteenth day (Ex. 12:18) of **Abib** or Nisan, which corresponds to our March-April.

16:6, 7 The **twilight** sacrifice was in commemoration of the Exodus, which had occurred at that time (Ex. 12:29).

16:8–12 The last day of the Feast of Unleavened Bread was marked by a final **sacred assembly** of God's people.

16:13–15 The Feast of Tabernacles was a harvest festival (Ex. 23:16; 34:22). During this pilgrimage, God's people joined together to celebrate God's goodness and to remember how they had once lived in tents (tabernacles or booths) during the wilderness wanderings. **rejoice:** Sometimes modern people perceive the Israelites' worship as excessively burdened with details, ritual, and regulations, and imagine that the Israelites' worship experience must have been unpleasant. But sincere worshipers rejoiced in God's detailed instructions and enjoyed the symbols and ritual which reminded them of God's characteristics.

16:16, 17 These verses summarize the regulations for the three annual pilgrimages to the central place of worship (Ex. 23:17; 34:23).

16:18 in all your gates: The areas framed by the towers in the gateways of ancient cities were the centers of community life and the places where the judges of the city would sit.

16:19 Justice is the quality of dealing fairly with people. Judges particularly were expected to reflect God's just nature (32:4) by not dealing with the accused on the basis of discrimination, false witness, or hearsay.

16:20 follow: Godliness is to imitate God in a love for what is just and true.

16:21, 22 The Canaanites used certain trees and wooden images as representations of fertility gods. The Hebrew word translated **wooden image** is the Hebrew name for the Canaanite goddess of fertility, Asherah.

17:1 Sacrifice in Israel was never to be regarded as a means of dumping the unwanted or the unneeded. It showed faith that as one gave one's best to the Lord, He would make what remained suitable and plentiful for one's needs.

17:2, 3 The Hebrew verb for **transgressing** is used elsewhere to indicate the crossing of a border or a stream. Here the word is used to indicate "crossing over" the boundaries that God had set for His people.

17:4–6 inquire diligently: An investigation, rather than gossip, determined the truth of any report of idolatry. The guilty was condemned to death only after guilt was established by **two or three witnesses** (compare Matt. 18:16; 2 Cor. 13:1; 1 Tim. 5:19; Heb. 10:28).

17:7 hands … first: The witnesses participated in the stoning of the guilty because they were responsible for the person's condemnation.

17:8 The more complex cases were sent to a higher court. **Degrees of guilt** refers to cases of manslaughter or murder—that is, accidental or intentional homicide.

17:9–11 The descendants of the family of Aaron were the **priests** of Israel. The **Levites** were the other descendants of Levi, who served in the tabernacle.

17:12 The man who acts presumptuously is one who knows, but turns away from priestly instructions.

17:13 To **hear** God is to acknowledge Him, to respond to Him, and to obey Him (6:4). To **fear** God is to reverence Him and to worship Him (6:2).

17:14 The regulations that follow anticipate the request that the Israelites would make for **a king.** With Saul's kingship, God finally granted Israel's request for a national king (1 Sam. 8:4–9).

17:15–17 These regulations limited the power and splendor of the future king. He would not be dependent on military power and riches. He was exhorted to guide the nation into obedience to God's law.

17:18 a copy of this law: The true king of Israel would be bound to God's instructions and would rule in accordance with God's revealed will.

17:19, 20 fear: Only if the king lived in proper reverence of God would the people follow suit. If the king were impious, the people's decline into evil practices would be accelerated.

18:1 A portion of the dedication **offerings** was taken by the priests for their sustenance.

18:2–4 Unlike the other tribes, the Levites did not have a land **inheritance** in Canaan. They were to regard God as their inheritance. They had a special relationship with God that would be better than any grant of property.

18:5 to minister: The priests were God's servants mediating between Him and the people (10:8; 21:5).

18:6 All the desire of his mind indicates wholehearted devotion. The suggestion is that there might have been people from the tribe of Levi who were not worthy to minister before the Lord. Their ancestry alone could not qualify them.

18:7, 8 equal portions: The priests and Levites, who served before the Lord, were honored for that noble work.

18:9–11 Some ancient pagan customs demanded that a **son** or **daughter** be offered as a sacrifice in order to learn about the future or to seek favor from a supposed deity. **calls up the dead:** Apart from His revelation, God prohibited any attempts to know the future.

18:12 The pagan practices were **an abomination to the LORD** because they were based on an attempt to circumvent His revelation.

18:13 Blameless indicates integrity and dependence on the Lord alone.

18:14 Israel was to be distinct among the **nations.** Israel constituted a holy people—not only in what they ate, but in their faith toward God.

18:15–22 All true prophets among the Hebrew people were raised up by **the Lord.** None could become a true prophet by self-will or desire. **does not happen:** The test of a true prophet was the fulfillment of his words.

19:1 Deuteronomy was written in anticipation of the conquest of Canaan, God's gift to His people. The **cities** of the land would become the possession of the people of Israel. The Israelites were not to destroy the cities in conquest, but to destroy the people who lived in them.

19:2 Three cities of refuge would be selected in Canaan, to be added to the three that were east of the Jordan River.

19:3, 4 The cities of refuge were intertribal cities. Anyone from any tribe could flee to the city that was closest to him. **manslayer:** Use of these cities for refuge was restricted to cases of unintentional homicide.

19:5 goes to the woods: An example is given of a situation that might lead to unintentional homicide.

19:6, 7 The avenger of blood was possibly a relative commissioned by the elders of the city to execute justice. This Hebrew word sometimes translated *kinsman redeemer* and here translated *avenger* means "protector of family rights." This was the individual who stood up for the family, either to redeem property and persons or to obtain vengeance.

19:8, 9 enlarges your territory: God placed before the people not only the immediate prospect of the conquest of Canaan, but also the expansion of territory beyond the initial borders (12:20).

19:10 The shedding of **innocent blood** brought the **guilt of bloodshed** on the land. A nation of murderers would come under the judgment of God.

19:11, 12 For a person guilty of premeditated murder, there was no provision for refuge in the cities. He would be delivered over to the **avenger of blood.**

19:13 That it may go well with you indicates that God's concern was for the good of the community.

19:14 Removing a **landmark** was far more than moving a stone. It was changing a property line and in effect cheating some family out of the inheritance of land that God had given them.

19:15 Requiring **two or three witnesses** was a safeguard against the lies of an individual.

19:16, 17 The prospect of **a false witness** was chilling, particularly if it was a matter of one person's word against another's.

19:18–21 life ... for life ... foot for foot: The law of retribution established the principle that the punishment should fit the crime (Ex. 21:23–25; Lev. 24:17–20).

20:1 The Lord's presence is much greater than the enemy's military advantage of **horses and chariots** (Ps. 20:7). God the

Divine Warrior would fight for His people (Ex. 15:3).

20:2–5 The owner of a new house was exempt from battle duty.

20:6 The vinedresser was exempt from battle. It took as many as five years for a **vineyard** to begin to produce. A man who had waited for several years for the first produce from his vines was allowed to oversee the vines until they produced grapes.

20:7 betrothed: Betrothal was a commitment to be married; it was more binding than an engagement today. The betrothed man was exempt from battle. This exemption also applied to the newly married (24:5).

20:8, 9 fearful and fainthearted: The man who was nervous or who did not trust the Lord (v. 3) was exempt from battle. Since the battle was God's, the number of warriors was not nearly as important as the army's belief that God was fighting for them.

20:10, 11 This **offer of peace** specified that the people surrender, open up the city, and accept whatever conditions were laid down.

20:12 not make peace: Some cities would refuse the terms of the treaty and come out in battle, as Sihon did.

20:13, 14 The reprisals for refusal were severe. **strike every male:** The men of war of the city were to be killed, for they posed a threat as long as they were able to bear arms.

20:15, 16 The rules of the spoil (vv. 13, 14) applied only to distant **cities.** Different rules applied to the cities of Canaan (vv. 17, 18). They were to destroy the people of Canaan as part of God's judgment on those immoral peoples.

20:17, 18 utterly destroy: The Hebrew text uses two forms of the same verb to emphasize complete destruction of the Canaanites. This was not just a symbolic war; the entire Canaanite population was to be destroyed. **lest they teach you:** If the Canaanites were cut out of the land, the Israelites could thrive in the land by obeying God. Otherwise, the immoral Canaanite practices might slowly spread throughout the land.

20:19, 20 Trees, a part of God's creation, were useful for food, shade, and building material. In a long siege, the armies of Israel were not to cut down the trees and destroy the land.

21:1, 2 killed: The death may have been due to accidental or intentional homicide. This is a case of unsolved murder.

21:3, 4 heifer: The people of the nearest city were responsible for initiating a rite that established the people's innocence of the murder.

21:5–7 The **elders** of the city bore the responsibility for the murder, even though they were not personally guilty. It was up to them to seek atonement for the murder.

21:8 Breaking the heifer's neck did not **provide atonement.** It was symbolic of the horrendous crime. God Himself graciously forgave.

21:9 Killing an **innocent** person was a serious offense in ancient Israel. Unless the crime was solved or the rite was performed, there would be no real rest for the community.

21:10, 11 Presumably the **enemies** were from distant cities (20:13–15), since the Israelites took **captives.** God had commanded the utter destruction of enemies within the Promised Land.

21:12 shave her head: This ritual was intended to give the woman time to adjust to the new culture and to mourn over the forceful separation from her family.

21:13 Since a foreign woman's distinctive clothes might have associations with the idolatrous practices of her former family, these clothes were taken from her. She was not allowed to keep anything that she might use to tempt the Israelites to worship false gods.

21:14 if you have no delight in her: The man might have experienced rejection in the marriage relationship. Perhaps the woman would not convert to the true worship of the Lord. Perhaps she was unable to conceive a child. In any event, the man was given permission to divorce her or **set her free.**

21:15 two wives: Polygamy was commonly practiced in the cultures of the ancient Middle East and was assumed in the Law of Moses.

21:16 A father was expected to show consideration for the **firstborn** child, regardless of his attitude toward the child's mother.

21:17 Ancient Middle Eastern custom approved preferential treatment of the firstborn son. The **double portion** was a mark of the father's blessing.

21:18 The **stubborn and rebellious son** was not an "ordinary" rebellious youth, but one who had been immoral over a long period of time.

21:19 his father and his mother: The parents were responsible to the community for their children. The **elders** bore the responsibility for the actions of the community as a whole.

21:20 A glutton and a drunkard is an expression for "a good-for-nothing."

21:21 All the men of the community shared in the responsibility for executing the rebellious youth. The community could not allow the rebellious youth to spread his immoral practices.

21:22, 23 hang: The hanging was actually an impaling of the corpse for public viewing after death by stoning. Everyone would know that individual had brought guilt on the community.

22:1 hide yourself from them: Israelites could not ignore problems or misfortunes of their neighbors. Every individual in the community bore a responsibility to uphold justice within that community (compare Gal. 6:2).

22:2–4 it shall remain with you: Community responsibility included taking care of lost property, whether animals or objects.

22:5 Cross-dressing was forbidden by God in ancient Israel. In the ancient Middle East, dressing in the clothing of the opposite sex was a magical practice intended to bring harm to people. For example, a transvestite male would predict that the soldiers of another army would be as weak as females.

22:6, 7 The **eggs** or young of a **nest** could be eaten for food. But the mother had to be freed because she perpetuated the species.

22:8 A **parapet** was a barrier erected on a roof to keep people from falling off. The **roof** of an ancient Israelite house was used like another room, particularly during warm weather.

22:9–12 Most likely, these regulations were based on the same principle as that of dietary restrictions. The Israelites were to be different from their neighbors in all aspects of life to show their separation to the living God.

22:13 Detests indicates a loathing following the consummation of the marriage because the husband found out that his new bride was not a virgin.

22:14 Charges her indicates a public accusation. In ancient times, virginity was highly regarded. The indisputable legitimacy of children was vital to ancient society and inheritance rights.

22:15–17 The **father and mother** would come to defend the girl and protect their name.

22:18, 19 A false accusation would be punished. A man was not permitted to bring a frivolous charge against his wife.

22:20, 21 If the woman was not a virgin, she would be punished for her immorality. **the door of her father's house:** The parents also shared in her punishment. They were publicly disgraced because they did not dissuade her from such actions.

22:22 Both the man and the woman had to **die** (Lev. 18:20; 20:10).

22:23, 24 bring them both out: Both parties were presumed guilty in this instance. In this situation, the woman could have screamed for help since she was in a city.

22:25–27 no sin deserving of death: The woman was presumed innocent by virtue of the isolated place where she could not receive help no matter how much she resisted.

22:28, 29 This law warned young men that they would be made responsible for their actions. A **young woman** was not freely available just because she was not betrothed.

22:30 Uncover his father's bed is a euphemism for sexual relations (Lev. 18:8). This was the sin of Reuben, who slept with the mother of his brothers (Gen. 35:22).

23:1 Emasculated means that all or part of the sexual organs had been removed. This was done to men who were put in charge of harems to prevent intercourse with the women. It was also a pagan religious practice. Genital mutilation was prohibited in Israel.

23:2 Illegitimate birth may refer to the offspring of an illicit cultic union, such as the child of a temple prostitute (vv. 17, 18).

23:3–5 Since the Ammonites and Moabites showed hostility to the Israelites, they were not allowed to become citizens and participate in the worship of the Lord (see Num. 22—24).

23:6, 7 You shall not seek their peace is a prohibition against making any treaty with these nations. Moab and Ammon were persistent enemies of Israel.

23:8 third generation: While the people of Moab and Ammon were excluded from the congregation, the people of Edom and Egypt had an opportunity to join the true worshipers of the living God. The provision for the Egyptians might have been because of their initial kindness to Jacob's family in letting them move to Goshen (Gen. 47). The provision for the Edomites was based on the close ties they had with the Israelites. They were descendants of Jacob's brother, Esau.

23:9–11 Unclean by some occurrence in the night possibly refers to an involuntary emission (Lev. 15:16) or urination. God provided a way for an unclean person to become clean. The person could go outside the camp until the next evening and wash.

23:12, 13 Digging latrines was a part of military life. Such attention to cleanliness not only promoted ritual purity, but also proper hygiene to prevent disease from spreading through the camp.

23:14 your God walks in the midst of your camp: The Holy One was present with Israel's soldiers whenever they went to war. His soldiers should not tolerate unhealthy living conditions in camp.

23:15, 16 The **slave** presumably entered Israel's territory from another country.

23:17 The **ritual harlot** was regarded by the Canaanites as one "set apart" for the worship of gods and goddesses of fertility. In Canaanite religious fertility rites, men lay with cultic prostitutes. The Canaanites believed that this act would bring fertility to their families, fruitful fields, and growth of their herds. This debased system of worship was one of the reasons God brought such strong judgment against the Canaanites.

23:18 Harlot here describes a common prostitute.

23:19, 20 Interest in the ancient Middle East was very high. Borrowing inevitably led to greater debt and sometimes to the enslavement of the debtor (Ex. 22:25–27; Lev. 25:36). **Your brother** refers to a fellow Israelite.

23:21, 22 A **vow** was a commitment to show one's love for the Lord in a particular way. Though a vow was voluntary, one was obligated to fulfill it once it was made. God expected His people to keep their commitments.

23:23–25 A traveler was permitted to eat **grapes** or **grain** while passing a field, but harvesting or storing the food for use at a later time was clearly prohibited.

24:1, 2 uncleanness: The nature of the problem is not specified. It could have been a physical problem, such as the inability to bear children. The **certificate of divorce** was a legal document that provided rights to the divorcee (Lev. 21:7, 14; 22:13; Num. 30:9; Matt. 19:3–9). Such a certificate allowed the woman to remarry.

24:3, 4 defiled: Returning to her first husband after an intervening marriage might have placed the woman in the same position as an unfaithful wife.

24:5, 6 A **millstone** was a stone used for grinding grain into flour. The principle is clear: A family was not to be deprived of the necessities of daily life.

24:7–9 Leprosy refers to a variety of infectious skin diseases. The disease known today as leprosy, Hansen's disease, is different from the diseases referred to here.

24:10–13 A **pledge** was a token that a debt would be repaid. Since this involved the poor within the covenant community, the regulations protected the debtor's privacy (vv. 10, 11) and ability to provide for his family (vv. 12, 13).

24:14–17 The following laws allowed property owners and laborers to receive a due profit from their properties and their labor. At the same time, both the owners and the laborers were to resist any greedy actions that would prevent a reasonable provision for the disadvantaged people in their communities.

24:18–22 The passage exhorts the Israelites

to **remember** their people's own slavery in Egypt (v. 22). Just as God showed compassion on them when they were oppressed (15:15), they were to show compassion on those who were now disadvantaged.

25:1–3 A rod was probably used for the beating (Ex. 21:20). **Forty blows:** Later Jewish law restricted the number to forty minus one (2 Cor. 11:24) to make sure that the authorities remained within the set limits.

25:4 not muzzle an ox: Muzzling kept the animal from eating while it worked. This law encouraged kindness and consideration for animals.

25:5, 6 The ancients greatly feared having no heirs to carry on the family's name. Furthermore, a widow with no children to take care of her would quickly become a beggar. Taking a brother's widow as a second **wife** protected her and preserved the name, memory, and interests of the deceased brother.

25:7–10 he will not perform: Legally, the brother-in-law was bound to keep the family name alive. His refusal was not just a private matter, but also a public issue. For his insistence on his rights over the widow's rights he deserved to be publicly disgraced. The accusation of the widow had to be validated by **the elders** of the city. To **remove** one's **sandal** was a sign of the loss of one's rights in the community; perhaps it was a loss of the right to walk on one's own land (Ruth 4:7). To **spit** in someone's **face** was an act of strong, public contempt. Such a public disgrace discouraged men from shrinking from their duty as a brother-in-law.

25:11–14 A merchant could defraud a customer by using different-sized **weights,** depending on whether he was selling or buying, to tilt the scales to his advantage (see Amos 8:5).

25:15, 16 Perfect and just refers to weights that were exact.

25:17, 18 Israel was to tell the story of what **Amalek** had done and never to forget it (Ex. 17:8–16; Num. 14:39–45).

25:19 blot out the remembrance of Amalek: The Amalekites would in effect come under the ban which God had placed over the people of Canaan (Lev. 27:29; Josh. 6:17, 18).

26:1 into the land: The author of Deuteronomy is always anticipating God's gift of Canaan to the Israelites (19:1).

26:2 By offering the **first** of the produce to the Lord, the people expressed their trust in God's provision and their gratitude for His good gifts.

26:3 In the land that God planned to give the Israelites, crops, orchards, and vineyards would be theirs to enjoy. God had exceedingly blessed them, and they were to express their thanks.

26:4 Even before the temple was built, there was always an **altar** for sacrifices.

26:5, 6 My father was a Syrian (Aramean) is a reference to Jacob, whose parents' ancestral home was in Aram (Gen. 24:1–10). **A nation, great, mighty, and populous** is a reference to the great increase God gave His people while they were in Egypt (Ex. 1:5, 7).

26:7 the LORD heard: God's response to His people was one of the great manifestations of His grace (Ex. 2:23–25). He cared enough to answer their cries.

26:8 mighty hand ... outstretched arm: This phrase celebrates the direct involvement of the Lord in the salvation of the Israelites from slavery.

26:9, 10 I have brought the firstfruits: The worshiper needed to say aloud what he was doing as he did it. This added solemnity and dignity to the offering.

26:11–14 you shall say: As in the case of the firstfruits (vv. 1–11), the spoken word accompanied the act to reinforce the significance and purpose of the offering.

26:15 Your holy habitation: People direct their prayers to heaven, acknowledging at the same time that God is everywhere (Is. 66:1, 2).

26:16 To **observe** or do the will of God was not meant to be the means by which a person would be made righteous before God. Instead it would be part of a loving response to God's gracious covenant.

26:17 The first generation had declared their loyalty to God at Mount Sinai (Ex. 24:7). In this covenant renewal ceremony, the new generation confirmed their commitment to God.

26:18 The Hebrew word for **special people**

speaks of God's great delight and pleasure in His people. They are like a very special jewel, an adornment that He treasures. The word denotes an elect people, set apart by the Lord to Himself.

26:19 in praise ... in honor: The future of God's people was in His hands. He had promised to bestow honor on them. In a similar manner, the Lord has lifted up the people of His church, separating them from the nations and regarding them as a holy people (1 Pet. 2:9).

27:1 The elders of Israel joined Moses at this point. This joint declaration demonstrated the validity of God's revelation through Moses, even after his death.

27:2, 3 The **large stones** were memorial stones on which the law of God was to be written (v. 8).

27:4 Mount Ebal was north of Mount Gerizim (vv. 12, 13). Between the two mountains was the city of Shechem (Gen. 12:6, 7; 33:18–20). Shechem and its two mountains are roughly in the center of the land of Canaan.

27:5, 6 The Lord rejected an impressive altar for a humble altar of **whole stones,** that is, uncut stones. Perhaps an impressive altar would have diverted the worshipers' attention from God (Ex. 20:25).

27:7 Peace offerings were occasions of great joy, celebrations of belonging to God, sensing His presence, and remembering and thanking Him for His good gifts.

27:8 write very plainly: The words of God's law had to be easily read. They were not to be obscured by ornamentation or trivialized by carelessness.

27:9, 10 The authority of the **priests** and **Levites** came from their close association with Moses. They were the guardians and interpreters of the law and stood together with Moses at this solemn moment.

27:11–14 Mount Ebal, because of topographical and climatic conditions, is normally a barren peak while **Mount Gerizim** is usually covered with vegetation. Consequently, Mount Ebal was an ideal place for the curses to be recited, and Mount Gerizim was suitable for the blessings.

27:15, 16 The first curse pertained to idolatry. A **carved or molded image** defied the first or second commandment or both (5:7–9). The second curse pertained to an infraction of the fifth commandment (5:16; 21:18–21).

27:17 The third curse pertained to justice and greed. **landmark:** Moving the stone with the intent of extending the boundary of one's land enhanced one's own personal prosperity at the expense of others (19:14).

27:18 The fourth curse required the humane treatment of disabled people.

27:19 The fifth curse had to do with compassion toward those who were defenseless. The **stranger, the fatherless, and widow** did not have the legal and social resources to defend themselves.

27:20–23 The sixth through the ninth curses covered sexual morality. Sexual relations with animals (bestiality) and incest were strictly prohibited.

27:24, 25 The tenth and eleventh curses addressed justice when a homicide occurred. **bribe ... innocent person:** Both a hired assassin and the person who did the hiring would have been guilty.

27:26 The twelfth curse was on anyone who broke any part of the **law.** The Lord expected not only full submission to the law, but also a love for Him.

28:1–9 if you diligently obey: God demanded diligent obedience from the Israelites in order for them to receive all of God's rich blessings in the land (Is. 48:17–19).

28:10, 11 afraid: The nations would see God's presence and His blessing on His people and would stand in awe of the greatness of the Lord.

28:12 God gave graciously to the Israelites from the **good treasure** that He had stored up for them. The people received God's blessings solely because of His grace. **rain ... season:** The Canaanites believed that Baal was the giver of dew and rain (1 Kin. 17:1). But God assured Israel that He controlled the heavens and would make their lands fruitful (Ps. 104:3, 13).

28:13 The phrase **the head and not the tail** indicates that Israel would rise to a place of honor among the nations.

28:14 not turn ... to the right or the left:

Since the Lord alone was the source of blessing, the Israelites had to follow Him alone in the pursuit of their happiness.

28:15–19 if you do not obey: God's promises of the fullness of His blessing were dependent upon the obedience of His people.

28:20 hand: The curse would affect all human activities so that they would come to nothing (Ps. 112:10). The fruitfulness that came with God's overabundant blessings would disappear.

28:21, 22 Plague refers to devastations from pestilence and contagious diseases.

28:23, 24 Bronze and **iron** represent the harshness of God's wrath in withholding rain from His people (Lev 26:19).

28:25, 26 carcasses: The idea of birds eating the flesh of the dead was particularly repugnant in ancient times. The lack of proper burial was a mark of disregard for the person who had died (1 Sam. 31:11–13).

28:27, 28 boils of Egypt: The disease inflicted on the Egyptians (Ex. 9:10) would now be visited on the people of God for their disobedience. If the people obeyed God's laws, He promised to deliver them from such diseases (Ex. 15:26).

28:29–34 betroth a wife ... build a house ... plant a vineyard: The momentous events of life could not be enjoyed because of disasters and wars.

28:35, 36 Severe boils refers to skin diseases, such as Job experienced (Job 2:7).

28:37–43 The curses on the Israelites for disobedience were the direct opposite of the blessings the Israelites would receive for obedience.

28:44–47 The disasters would be **a sign** that would remind the people of their disobedience. **serve ... with joy ... for the abundance:** The expected response to God's goodness was joy and a heartfelt willingness to do His will. The absence of these responses incurred God's wrath.

28:48 Yoke of iron is an expression of servitude and enslavement.

28:49, 50 The enemy **nation** is compared to a soaring eagle that swoops down on its prey (Jer. 48:40; Hos. 8:1). The enemy would show no compassion on the people whether old or **young.**

28:51–57 besiege you: The horrors of siege, hunger, and deprivation would lead people to behave in ways that they otherwise could never imagine. **she will eat them:** Nothing could compare to the horror of a mother eating her own children.

28:58 The Hebrew words translated **glorious and awesome** together mean "overwhelmingly awesome." The **name** of the Lord inspired awe and fear because He had demonstrated His power in both Egypt and the wilderness.

28:59–68 The following verses are a summary of all the curses that would fall upon disobedient Israel. Many are reversals of the blessing list in vv. 1–14.

29:1 The Hebrew phrase translated as **these are the words of the covenant** can be interpreted as a conclusion to the previous chapters or as an introduction to chs. 29—32. **In the land of Moab** is a reference to the beginning of Deuteronomy (1:1–5).

29:2–5 Great trials … great wonders refers to the miraculous acts of God in Egypt, the wilderness, and the land east of the Jordan River. Moses pointed out that God had supported the Israelites even in less dramatic ways, such as seeing that their **clothes** and **sandals** were **not worn out.**

29:6 Although the people did not eat **bread** in the wilderness, God had supplied them with manna from heaven.

29:7, 8 The winning of the area east of the Jordan River (2:26—3:22) was the glorious beginning of the conquest of the land. But there was still greater glory to come—the winning of the territory west of the river.

29:9–13 the words of this covenant: The members of the covenant community included all adults, children, and strangers who had joined the Israelites, as well as those yet to be born.

29:14–18 Every individual **man** and **woman** was responsible to the community as a whole for his or her relationship to God. Since the entire community was covenanted to God Himself, every individual had to follow Him.

29:19 he blesses himself: The self-absorbed person would consider himself worthy of the blessings of God; the righteous person would live by God's grace and obey His commands.

29:20, 21 For the memory of a person's **name** to be lost was considered a terrible fate in the ancient Middle Eastern culture. For God to record and remember their names was a glorious hope for the ancient Israelites (see Ps. 87).

29:22, 23 God's judgments on a disobedient Israel would be a sign of His holiness for the future **generation** and for other nations. **Brimstone, salt, and burning** are images reminiscent of God's judgment of Sodom and Gomorrah (Gen. 19:24–29).

29:24–27 The lesson of the faithless Israel would become known among the **nations.** The nations were supposed to learn about God's grace from Israel's example; what a shame if they were to learn of His wrath instead!

29:28 This day refers to the day of God's judgment on His people.

29:29 The secret things refers to the future, as well as the way in which the curses would come to pass. The will of God had been **revealed** in the Law. If these revelations were acted upon, the people would receive God's great blessing. To ignore the express commandments of God would be folly.

30:1 When all these things come upon you refers to the blessings and curses detailed in ch. 28, particularly the curses. God allowed Moses to foresee Israel's future apostasy and God's dispersal of the people among the nations.

30:2–6 Not only did Moses foresee the future apostasy and **captivity** of Israel; he also saw Israel's future repentance and **return** to the land. This passage could also await a future fulfillment. **circumcise your heart:** God Himself would work in the hearts of His people so that they would love Him (10:16). **all your heart and … soul:** God's intentions for His people have always been for the whole person to respond to Him.

30:7 God did not abandon His principle of reward and punishment for the nations (and for the individuals) based on their treatment of His covenant people. He would repay Israel's **enemies.**

30:8, 9 The Old Testament tends to focus on the disobedience of God's people to His revelation. But there were periods of national faithfulness to God, and there were always individuals who were faithful.

30:10 This Book of the Law is the Book of Deuteronomy (31:24, 26). God's blessing would come to those who obeyed the law.

30:11–14 not in heaven ... Nor is it beyond the sea: Obedience to the law did not require a superhuman effort, because God had revealed the law to the Israelites (Rom. 10:6–10).

30:15–17 Moses challenged the people to determine what path they would follow. One way led to **life** (Ps. 1:6; John 14:6) because God's blessings rested on it (Ps. 23:6). The other way led to **death and evil** because God's curses rested on it.

30:18 The emphasis on **today** is remarkable in this passage. Moses establishes here the best pattern for the preaching of the Word of God. Responses to God should not be delayed.

30:19 heaven and earth as witnesses: All of creation witnessed Moses' instruction, his challenge to the Israelites to love and obey God, and the people's response (32:1). **choose ... that both you and your descendants may live:** The present generation's choice would determine the direction of future generations.

30:20 If the people loved God they would find true **life,** because God is the source of all life. By rejecting God and His ways, the Israelites would by default choose the way of death.

31:1–3 Again Moses spoke of God's refusal to permit him to enter the Promised Land (1:37, 38; 3:23–29). Yet he encouraged the people that **God Himself** would still protect them and fight for them.

31:4–6 He will not leave you nor forsake you: Moses reminded the people that God had promised to remain with them, to protect them, bless them, and fight for them (Josh. 1:5; 1 Kin. 8:57).

31:7, 8 With encouraging and challenging words, Moses publicly transferred his authority to **Joshua** (1:38; 31:14, 23; 32:44; 34:9).

31:9 Moses wrote this law and delivered it: In accordance with ancient Middle Eastern practices international treaties, Moses made provisions for the future reading of the law and instruction in it.

31:10–14 The words **the days approach** must have brought a renewed heaviness to Moses. He was ready to die, but his heart yearned to see the Promised Land.

31:15 The pillar of cloud was the symbol of the presence of God during the wilderness journey (Ex. 13:21, 22).

31:16 The phrase **rest with your fathers** suggests that the body of the person would be laid to rest in a tomb. After the flesh had decayed, the bones would be placed with the bones of one's ancestors. Thus, the person's remains were "with his fathers."

31:17, 18 I will forsake them: Should the worst occur, the anger of God would be aroused. **to other gods:** The principal reason for God's judgment on His people was their continual idolatry. They abandoned His grace and embraced the evil religious practices of the Canaanites.

31:19–21 This song is the Song of Moses recorded in 31:30–32:43. God commanded Moses and Joshua to **teach** this song to the Israelites.

31:22 Moses wrote ... and taught it: These words create an anticipation of v. 30. Psalm 90 is attributed to Moses as well.

31:23–25 Be strong and of good courage: God encouraged Joshua with the same words that Moses used to encourage the people (v. 6). **I will be with you:** God assured Joshua of His presence during the conquest (Josh. 1:5; Hag. 2:4).

31:26–28 This Book of the Law is the Book of Deuteronomy. This book would be a witness against Israel when they turned from the living God to worship other gods.

31:29, 30 For I know: It is unclear whether Moses' words here were based on his own experience with the people or on a revelation from the Lord. Perhaps both were at work.

32:1 O heavens ... O earth: Isaiah similarly called on heaven and earth to witness (Is. 1:2).

32:2 rain ... dew ... raindrops ... showers: These four similes express the refreshing and invigorating nature of the instruction.

32:3 Ascribe greatness to our God: True

wisdom and obedience always lead to the praise of God (Ps. 145:3; 150:2).

32:4 Unlike the powerless gods of the nations (v. 37), God gives life, stability, and happiness to His people (vv. 15, 18, 30, 31). The joyful life that He gives is based on His **perfect** works. Like a firm **Rock** that stands against the raging waters of a stormy sea, God and His works stand firm against the chaos produced by sinful lives. He is the sure foundation for all **truth** in a world of deception.

32:5 perverse and crooked generation: Compared to the perfect God of truth, the Israelites were corrupt, blemished, and deceptive (v. 20).

32:6 The ancient Israelites knew God was their **Father** (see Is. 63:16; 64:8), but they rarely confessed this great truth. God had chosen them, loved them, and cared for them. He had brought them out of Egypt and had even **established** them as a nation.

32:7 Remember ... they will tell you: Here the song uses the language of wisdom literature to exhort the Israelites to search out God's ways.

32:8, 9 Most High: This designation for God's supremacy is unique to Deuteronomy. He is the sovereign God over all, even the **boundaries** of the nations.

32:10 In a desert land is a poetic reference to Egypt. **He instructed him:** God gave Israel His revelation and His laws in order to lead them in all truth.

32:11 The **eagle** is a bird of prey commonly found in desert regions. The song compares God's actions towards Israel with the care a mother bird showers on her young. God not only protected His children; He provided for them, got them moving, watched over them, and guided them to the Promised Land (Ex. 19:4).

32:12 the LORD alone ... no foreign god: Deuteronomy is an extended argument against idolatry and paganism. The Israelites had no reason to abandon the God of grace and love who had given them all they needed.

32:13, 14 produce ... honey ... oil: The Lord had promised to supply His people with crops, rich food, olive oil, and even dairy products in the Promised Land—all of which the people lacked in the wilderness.

32:15, 16 Jeshurun, a pet name for Israel, means "Uprightness." This part of the song contrasts what Israel should have been and what they became. Since the nation had received God's revelation and His instruction, it should have become upright (v. 4). Instead, the nation would grow fat and rebel.

32:17 Rarely in the Old Testament (Ps. 106:37; see also Amos 2:1) are references made to **demons** and demonic powers. Although the Scriptures make it clear that the false gods do not exist as such, this passage identifies the power behind these gods: demons.

32:18, 19 Fathered literally means "gave birth." This is one of several places where God is portrayed in terms that liken His role to that of a nurturing, life-giving mother (compare Is. 66:13).

32:20, 21 I will see what their end will be: Even though Israel would reject Him, God would be patient with His rebellious children.

32:22–24 hunger ... pestilence ... destruction: Instead of blessing His chosen people, God would send curses on them in order to discipline them.

32:25–27 young man ... virgin: The pairings of opposites in this verse indicate that God's judgment would be comprehensive. It would affect all of society.

32:28 This verse anticipates God's judgment of Israel and Judah in the days of Isaiah (Is. 1:3; 6:9, 10).

32:29, 30 Often the phrase **latter end** is understood as "glorious future"; here it speaks of "ruinous future" for the rebellious Israelites.

32:31–33 The enemy nations were like the people of **Sodom** and **Gomorrah**—cruel, immoral, and oppressive.

32:34–36 Vengeance is Mine ... judge His people: Only the God who is completely just can judge and make right all the wrongs committed. **compassion on His servants:** God would discern one day between the righteous and the wicked (Mal. 3:16). He would deal kindly with the remnant that loved and followed Him.

32:37, 38 Where are their gods: The song mocks those who follow false gods. They abandoned the Rock of truth for a **rock** that was not even a pebble.

32:39 I, even I, am He is a glorious affirmation of the incomparability of God (Ps. 113:4–6). Because God is free to do what He wants, only He can either curse or bless, wound or heal, kill or give life.

32:40–42 I raise My hand to heaven: God made an oath to Himself that He would avenge His people (Gen. 22:16; Heb. 6:13–18). He would make right all wrongs.

32:43–45 Rejoice, O Gentiles, with His people: God in this song invited all nations to join in the worship of the living God, to praise Him for promising to restore justice.

32:46 Law here may signify the Song of Moses or Deuteronomy as a whole (compare 31:26).

32:47 prolong your days: The intention of God's instruction was to show the Israelites the path that leads to fullness of life and rich blessing.

32:48, 49 Mount Nebo is a mountain peak near Heshbon about ten miles east of the northern end of the Dead Sea.

32:50–52 you did not hallow Me: Moses did not completely obey God's instructions at Kadesh. Because of this, Moses could not enter the Promised Land (1:37; 3:23–26; 4:21, 22; 31:2; Num. 20:10–13). Yet God would graciously allow Moses to **see the land** (34:1–8).

33:1 Moses is to be remembered for his faithfulness in spite of his failure (Heb. 3:1–6). Scriptures describe him as a servant of God (Num. 12:6–8), a friend of God (Ex. 33:11), and a **man of God.**

33:2, 3 came from … dawned … shone forth: These verbs reminded the Israelites of the awe-inspiring revelation of God in all of His glory. God came down to Israel and revealed His covenant and law to them at Mt. **Sinai.**

33:4, 5 heritage: What made Israel unique was its reception of the law of God mediated through Moses. God had chosen Israel alone to receive His instructions. The Lord alone was the **King** over His people.

33:6 Let Reuben live … men be few: Moses predicted that the Reubenites would have a

future, but not a glorious one. Settled east of the Dead Sea, the Reubenites would eventually isolate themselves from the other tribes (Judg. 5:15, 16).

33:7 Moses prayed that **the LORD** would be present with **Judah** in its military leadership and would give it success in battle.

33:8, 9 Moses prayed for God's guidance to rest on the Levites, who were responsible for judging cases. The **Urim** and **Thummim** (Ex. 28:30) were God's appointed instruments for deciding innocence or guilt and for guiding His people. **Massah … Meribah:** The Levites passed the test when the other tribes failed to believe in the Lord's ability to provide and care for His people (6:16; 9:22).

33:10, 11 teach: The Levites were charged with the responsibility of instructing the Israelites. They had modeled loyalty (v. 9). Now they had to help Israel understand how to live by God's revelation.

33:12–16 As the beloved son of Jacob, Benjamin was also **the beloved of the LORD** (Gen. 44:20). The Lord would give the tribe of Benjamin peace and **safety.**

33:17 glory … horns: God would give Ephraim and Manasseh prowess in battle and victory in warfare. Like oxen, these two tribes would **push** their enemies away from them.

33:18, 19 The tribe of Zebulun would be located by the **seas.** The seas and their shores were God's appointed place for the tribe's prosperity.

33:20, 21 Moses compared Gad's military role to the power of a ravenous **lion** and predicted that this tribe would join the others in the conquest of Canaan (Josh. 22:1–6).

33:22 Lion's whelp may refer to the small size of the tribe of Dan. Though Dan's land inheritance was close to Judah by the coastal plains, the tribe would not be able keep their inheritance because of the hostility of the Philistines. Therefore, the Danites would one day migrate to the region of **Bashan,** south of Mount Hermon (Judg. 18).

33:23 Moses' **blessing** on Naphtali indicates that this tribe would enjoy God's blessings of abundance. The tribe would inherit the land **west** and **south** of the Sea of Galilee.

33:24, 25 Dip his foot in oil is an image of God's rich blessing to Asher (Ps. 133:2).

33:26, 27 rides the heavens ... the clouds: Like a soldier, the Lord is constantly on the lookout for ways to defend His people from attack. God is a **refuge** or fortress for the people to flee to in times of distress (Ps. 90:1; 91:9). **everlasting arms:** The God who redeemed Israel with His strong arm will always be with His people in love and power.

33:28 Then Israel will dwell in safety: Moses affirmed the truth of the promise God gave through the pagan prophet Balaam (Num. 23:9).

33:29 shield ... sword: These military images point to God, the source of all human protection. **tread down their high places:** God would break down with His own feet the places of idolatrous worship.

34:1 Moab was where Moses had given Israel an explanation of the law (1:5) and had led them in a covenant renewal ceremony (29:1–28). **Jericho** was the first city in Canaan to be conquered. **And the LORD showed him:** Though he was still in Moab, Moses was granted by God a close-up view of the land.

34:2 Judah refers to the highlands west of Jericho and of the Dead Sea. The **Western Sea** is the Mediterranean.

34:3, 4 South refers to the Negev, the dry county south of Judah. **The plain** is the region around the Dead Sea, from the valley of Jericho to **Zoar,** the city in the southern plain where Lot escaped with his daughters (Gen. 19:22).

34:5 Moses remained God's faithful **servant.** A servant of God is a person who has a close and trusted relationship with God.

34:6, 7 no one knows his grave: If Moses' burial place had been known, some people most likely would have made it a shrine and begun to worship there. **not dim ... diminished:** Moses died because it was God's will and not because of normal physical deterioration associated with old age (31:2).

34:8 Thirty days was the customary period of mourning. Though Moses was buried alone, he was not forgotten by his people.

34:9 Joshua was recognized for his **wisdom** as he followed the call of the Lord in his life.

34:10–12 a prophet like Moses: As important as Joshua was, he should not be confused with the One who would fulfill God's promise of a prophet who would have an even greater status than Moses (18:15). **Face to face** describes the unusual intimacy between Moses and the Lord (Ex. 33:11; Num. 12). **Moses performed:** The miraculous works accomplished by Moses were God's works through Moses' hand.

Joshua

Introduction

The Book of Joshua describes the Israelites' conquest of Canaan—from the initial invasion across the Jordan River to the final division of the land. Like most military histories, Joshua focuses on the commander. Yet for this unique war, the commander was God Himself (5:15). The book repeatedly emphasizes that the Israelites' victories were due to God's intervention (chs. 10; 11).

This book is named for the man who figures most prominently in it, Moses' successor and Israel's leader during the conquest of Canaan. Appropriately, Joshua's name in Hebrew means "The Lord Saves" or "May the Lord Save." The Book of Joshua does not state who wrote it. Joshua himself undoubtedly wrote portions of the book, since 24:26 states, "Then Joshua wrote these words in the Book of the Law of God." But it is uncertain how much of the rest of the book he wrote. The events in Joshua occurred within a time span of less than a decade, forty years after the Exodus, probably around 1406 B.C.

The two most prominent themes in Joshua are the possession of the land and the covenant. God had repeatedly promised the land of Canaan to Abraham (Gen. 12:7; 13:14), to Isaac (Gen. 26:3, 4), to Jacob (Gen. 28:4, 13; 35:12), and to the succeeding generations (Gen. 48:4–22; 50:24). The Book of Joshua emphasizes that the conquest of Canaan was a direct fulfillment of that promise. God was fighting for the Israelites and giving them the land in the process. Since God was demonstrating His faithfulness to Israel, He expected Israel to be faithful to His covenant with them.

1:1 Joshua begins where Deuteronomy ends, **after the death of Moses.** Moses is called the **servant of the LORD,** a title that was first given to him at the end of his life (Deut. 34:5). Joshua was **Moses' assistant** (Ex. 24:13; Num. 11:28).

1:2 God's speech encouraging Joshua is a warmhearted, tender speech, assuring Joshua of His care, protection, and presence,

and urging him to obey His law. **the land which I am giving:** The land of Canaan had first been promised to Abraham hundreds of years before.

1:3 You here is plural, referring to all Israel. Sometimes (as in v. 2), the land is pictured as in the process of being given to Israel ("I am giving to them"). In other places, as here, it is pictured as already having been given. This is also the language of Gen. 15:18. **as I said to Moses:** God keeps His promises.

1:4 This description of the land gives its southern and northern extremities, and its western border; the eastern border is not mentioned, probably because it extended to where Joshua was standing on the plains of Moab, east of the Jordan River. The land of Canaan here is designated by one of its prominent ethnic groups, **the Hittites. The Great Sea** is the Mediterranean Sea.

1:5 God's great promise to Moses **I will be with you** (Ex. 3:12) is now given to Joshua (1:9; 3:7). Joshua had been present during the many demonstrations of God's presence in Moses' life and would have known how significant this promise was.

1:6 The command to **be strong and of good courage** was for Joshua's encouragement, and God repeated these words three times (vv. 6, 7, 9). **you shall divide:** This is the first notation of what Joshua's actual duties would be, that of giving the land to Israel on God's behalf.

1:7 very courageous: Joshua's success depended more on his spiritual state and his degree of obedience to God than on any military strategy. **the law which Moses ... commanded you:** Some scholars have questioned whether Moses gave the law to Israel, arguing that the laws found in the Pentateuch come from a much later time. This passage, along with many others (8:31–35; Deut. 31:24–26), states that Moses did indeed give the law to Israel. The term translated **prosper** means much more than mere financial success. It includes spiritual well-being.

1:8, 9 To **meditate** means that one should reflect upon God's Word in a thoughtful way, appropriating its truths personally and applying them to life (Ps. 1:2, 3).

1:10 The **officers** were officials who helped in the organization of Israel's affairs.

1:11 Provisions referred to the food needed for the next several days as the Israelites prepared themselves to cross the Jordan River. **within three days:** During these three days, the Israelites prepared themselves to enter the land. These were the same three days that the spies hid in the hills outside of Jericho (mentioned in 2:16, 22). After the spies returned, the Israelites waited another three days before crossing the Jordan River (3:2).

1:12–15 Joshua reminded the two and one half-tribes that were settling east of the Jordan River that they had promised to fight with the rest of the Israelites for the land across the river. The account in Joshua indicates that they kept their promise. The promise of **rest** echoes Num. 32:20–22; Deut. 3:18–20. This rest was God's gift to Israel. In Joshua, it primarily means rest from conflict with enemies. **Mighty men of valor** were the elite of the military.

1:16–18 The text does not say clearly who **answered Joshua,** the officers of the people (v. 10) or the tribes from east of the Jordan River (v. 12). From vv. 10, 12 it appears that Joshua's words to the officers in v. 11 and to the tribes in vv. 13–15 are part of one event. The response in vv. 16–18 is therefore probably that of all Israel. In this way, the entire nation affirmed Joshua's leadership at the beginning of his duties as leader. **the LORD your God be with you:** The Israelites affirmed Joshua in the same terms that God Himself used in promising to be with him.

2:1 The **Acacia Grove** was the place east of the Jordan River where the Israelites had been encamped for some time (Num. 25:1). **Rahab** was a Canaanite prostitute, and yet her story is one of the most inspiring stories in the Bible. Her actions in caring for the Israelite spies in enemy territory demonstrated a faith in Israel's God. The term translated **harlot** is the word for a common prostitute, not a cultic prostitute.

2:2, 3 it was told: In spite of the secrecy of the spies (v. 1), news of their arrival in Jericho traveled fast. The **king of Jericho** ruled over a small kingdom that included his city and the territory around it. As is often the case in the ancient world, his "kingdom" was actually a city-state.

2:4–6 Rahab lied to the men searching for the Israelite spies, but this does not constitute an endorsement for lying as such. All major cities in Canaan were walled and had a large **gate** for protection. Like most houses, Rahab's had a flat **roof.** She hid the men there where she had laid out **stalks of flax** for drying.

2:7, 8 The River Jordan was nearly a hundred feet wide near Jericho, and from five to twelve feet deep. There were no bridges, and shallow **fords** were used for crossing.

2:9, 10 Rahab's use of God's personal name Yahweh, translated here as **LORD,** indicates that she had come to faith in the living God (v. 11). **the terror of you has fallen on us:** Israel's reputation went before them.

2:11 Rahab made a dramatic statement of her faith in the Lord. **He is God in heaven:** She affirmed God's sovereignty over heaven and earth in language reminiscent of the Psalms (compare Ps. 113:5, 6).

2:12–14 Rahab asked the spies to **swear to her.** Even though to swear in God's name was a serious matter, the spies agreed to Rahab's request (vv. 14, 17, 20).

2:15 The Hebrew phrase translated **her house was on the city wall** suggests that Rahab's house was *in* the city wall rather than *on top of* it. The phrase might be rendered "in the double walls." This refers to a kind of defensive wall found around many cities in biblical times. Rahab's family may have lived in one of these residences.

2:16, 17 Get to the mountain: The only hills near Jericho are to the west. This is the opposite direction from the route the pursuers had taken: they had gone east, down to the Jordan River (v. 7).

2:18–21 The spies gave Rahab a line of **scarlet cord** to hang out the window as a sign of the agreement they had made. The cord's color is undoubtedly significant; it represents the color of the blood of atonement (Ex. 12:7, 13). It also alludes to the story of Tamar, since a scarlet thread was tied to the wrist of her first son (Gen. 38:28, 30). Both of these women were non-Israelite ancestors of Jesus (Matt. 1:3, 5).

2:22, 23 A "day" for the ancient Israelites could mean any portion of a day. Thus **three days** would refer to parts of three days.

2:24 faint-hearted: The spies reported to Joshua exactly what Rahab had said to them (v. 9).

3:1 The location of **Acacia Grove** is unknown today, but it was where Israel had been camped for some time after arriving at the plains of Moab, at the northern end of the Dead Sea (Num. 22:1; 25:1). The day after the spies returned from Jericho, Joshua led the people from this place to the Jordan River.

3:2 After three days, the **officers** went through the camp with instructions about the crossing itself. These instructions (v. 3) were different from the instructions given in 1:11, and this three-day period started on the day after the spies returned from Jericho. The previous three-day period in 1:11 (and 2:22) began when the spies went into Jericho to begin with. After these two three-day periods, the Israelites crossed the Jordan River on the next day, the seventh day after the book's action begins (3:5).

3:3 Chapter 3 emphasizes the significance of **the ark of the covenant,** mentioning it more than 11 times. The ark symbolized God's presence. Everyone had to be careful to keep a healthy distance from it (3:4). The priesthood was restricted to **Levites** in general, and more specifically to Aaron's family (Num. 25:7–13; Deut. 18:1, 5).

3:4 The Hebrew word for **yet** is emphatic and might be translated "be very sure." This emphasizes the importance of the command to keep one's distance from the ark. **Two thousand cubits** was more than half a mile.

3:5, 6 Sanctify yourselves: The Book of Joshua emphasizes the idea of holiness. The basic meaning of holiness is separation from things that are unclean or common. **Wonders** translates the Hebrew word for what today are called miracles.

3:7, 8 With the words **I will begin to exalt you,** God reaffirmed Joshua's place as successor to Moses (1:5, 9). **that they may know:** God performed miracles to reveal Himself to His people.

3:9 Here, Joshua functions as a prophet of God, even though he is never specifically called a prophet, because he stood before the people as spokesman for God.

3:10, 11 The miraculous events that follow not only brought the Israelites across the Jordan River; they also attested to the fact that the living God was with them (4:24). God Himself was working on their behalf. **Canaanites ... Jebusites:** This text mentions seven people groups. *Canaanites* sometimes denoted anyone living in Canaan, regardless of their ethnic identity (Gen. 36:2, 3; Judg. 5:19). Yet the present text distinguishes a specific group as Canaanites. In this case the Canaanites were probably the peoples living near the sea (5:1) who were known later as the Phoenicians. The **Perizzites** appear to have lived in the forested areas of central Palestine (Gen. 13:7). **Amorites** is sometimes a synonym for *Canaanites* in its broader usage (Gen. 15:16; Judg. 1:34, 35). Here the name probably refers to inhabitants of the central hill country. The **Jebusites** lived in Jerusalem (15:8; 18:28).

3:12 twelve men: One man from each tribe was selected. The Hebrew emphasizes that it was to be only one from each tribe.

3:13, 14 The reference to **the ark** here parallels the phrase in v. 11. The reference to **the LORD, the Lord of all the earth** uses both His name and His title.

3:15 The parenthetical statement **for the Jordan overflows** is significant because it makes the point that a great miracle was involved. God did not just slow the Jordan River to a trickle during a time of drought; rather, He stopped the waters when the river was high. **during the whole time of harvest:** This phrase refers to the early summer harvest. At this time, the river was still swollen from the spring melting and rains.

3:16 Adam: A city about 18 miles north of Jericho, near where the Jordan and Jabbok rivers converge. **The Sea of the Arabah** is the Dead Sea, into which the Jordan River flows from the north.

3:17 This crossing of the Jordan River was similar to the crossing of the Red Sea. The miracle was so effective in both cases that the Israelites crossed on dry ground, not mud or shallow water.

4:1–3 The **twelve stones** (one stone per tribe) would mark the spot where God performed His wonderful miracle in stopping the waters of the Jordan River so the Israelites could cross. The stones would remind the people of the great event and serve as conversation starters with their children, who would ask what they symbolized (vv. 6, 21).

4:4–7 The Hebrew term for **sign** can mean "miracle" (Ex. 7:3), but here it means "memorial marker." **when your children ask:** The stones would inevitably stimulate a child's questions. These questions would be opportunities for instruction.

4:8, 9 the children of Israel did so: A standard feature of Hebrew narratives is repetition. This verse repeats almost verbatim the instructions given in v. 5. Such repetitions are a sophisticated literary device. The pattern is for a character in the story to give the instructions and then for the narrator to confirm, using the same words, that the instructions were carried out.

4:10 the people hurried and crossed over: This paragraph represents something of a flashback, since 3:17 and 4:1 have already stated that the crossing was completed. The purpose is to look back and reflect upon the people's obedience.

4:11 The priests who were standing on dry ground in the middle of the river (3:17) were finally able to cross over themselves with the ark.

4:12 The men of the Transjordan tribes acted exactly **as Moses had spoken**—that is, in direct obedience to the instructions Moses gave when Israel was still on the Plains of Moab (Num. 32:20–22; Deut. 3:18–20).

4:13 The number of warriors from Reuben, Gad, and half of Manasseh is **forty thousand,** much smaller than that listed in Num. 26. There the warriors from Reuben alone number 43,730 (Num. 26:7). The number here was most likely a portion of the warriors from the three tribes; the rest probably stayed with the women, children, and elderly to protect them.

4:14, 15 the Lord exalted Joshua: Once again, God affirmed Joshua's place as Moses' successor (1:5, 17; 3:7). In this context, **they feared him** indicates respect, reverence, or awe, not terror. The Israelites obeyed Joshua in the same way they had obeyed Moses.

4:16, 17 The Hebrew word for **Testimony** also means "reminder," and it is used in Ex. 31:18 to refer to the tablets on which the Ten Commandments were written, "the two tablets of the Testimony." The ark is called "the ark of the Testimony" because it contained the two stone tablets on which were written the Ten Commandments (Ex. 40:20; Deut. 10:1–5).

4:18 This verse is a mirror image of 3:15. This neatly concludes the miraculous episode, showing the forces of nature resuming their natural course and reminding us of the marvelous nature of the miracle of God stopping the waters.

4:19 The crossing of the Jordan River was on **the tenth day of the first month,** that is, the month of Nisan (Abib), corresponding to March-April. This was an important day because it coincides with the day that the Passover lamb was selected (Ex. 12:3). It foreshadows the keeping of the Passover in 5:10, on the fourteenth day of the month, when the lamb is actually killed (Ex. 12:6, 18). The location of **Gilgal** is uncertain; it was somewhere east of Jericho in the Jordan valley.

4:20 The stones which the Israelites had brought up out of the Jordan River (v. 8) were now set up permanently at Gilgal.

4:21–24 that all the peoples … may know: The miracle was a sign to all peoples that God was powerful.

5:1 God's drying up the waters of the Jordan River caused the inhabitants of Canaan to fear Israel greatly.

5:2–5 Flint is a rock found in abundance in biblical lands. Only in two places in the Old Testament is the Hebrew word *flint* found, here and in Ex. 4:26, both in connection with circumcision. This they had to do **again the second time** (vv. 4, 5). The males of the generation that left Egypt in the Exodus had all been circumcised. However, that generation died in the wilderness and the practice had been neglected. Thus it was necessary to perform it again, especially before the important celebration of Passover.

5:6–9 Anyone who was not circumcised was to be cut off from enjoying the blessings of God's people (Gen. 17:14). God's promises to Abraham's descendants would be fulfilled to the nation as a whole, but not every individual would automatically participate: faith and obedience were required. God **raised up** another generation to replace the one He had consigned to perish in the wilderness. The land God had promised to Israel was no wilderness, but **a land flowing with milk and honey,** a fertile land ready to supply all the Israelites' needs.

5:10 The Israelites celebrated the Passover on the **fourteenth day of the month,** four days after they crossed the Jordan River (4:19), **at twilight.**

5:11, 12 The celebration of the Passover marked a significant turning point in Israel's life: right after this they began to live from the land they were about to possess. The miraculous provision of **manna** in the wilderness stopped.

5:13, 14 The stranger did not respond to Joshua's question, but instead identified Himself. He was the **Commander of the army of the LORD.** This elicited a response of humble worship from Joshua. Rather than any further questions about this Man's loyalties, Joshua asked how he could serve this One greater than him: **What does my Lord say to His servant?** His question was silenced, and humble worship was evoked.

5:15 The command given to Joshua to **take your sandal off your foot** is virtually identical with the one given to Moses at the burning bush (Ex. 3:5). Joshua was confronted with the living God, just as Moses had been (Ex. 33:9–11).

6:1, 2 The verb **have given** communicates that something has already happened, emphasizing the role of God in Israel's victories (2:24).

6:3 The site of Jericho measured less than half a mile in circumference, only about seven acres, so the **march around the**

city would have been completed quickly. The phrase **men of war** (also found in 5:4, 6; 10:24) is essentially synonymous with "mighty men of valor" (v. 2).

6:4 The number **seven** figures prominently in this passage: seven priests, seven trumpets, seven days, and seven trips around the city. It is a number that signifies completion. Its use here helps to demonstrate that the conquest of Jericho was part of a larger spiritual exercise.Another reminder of the spiritual significance of the event is the presence of **the ark** with the people.

6:5 The terms **ram's horn** and **trumpet** refer to the same kind of instrument. Here it both signaled God's presence and announced Jericho's impending doom.

6:6, 7 Joshua's instructions here repeat God's instructions to him in vv. 2–5. The repetition highlights the importance of the solemn ceremony of marching around the city.

6:8, 9 The term **rear guard** is rare, found only in vv. 9, 13, in Num. 10:25, and figuratively of God in Is. 52:12. The contingent of warriors assigned to the ark is indeed impressive: first the armed men (vv. 7, 9), next the priests blowing horns, then the ark itself carried by priests (v. 8), and finally the rear guard (v. 9).

6:10, 11 he had the ark … circle the city: The narrative continues placing the ark in a prominent position. The people circled the city as well, but the focus is on the ark.

6:12 The phrase **rose early in the morning** indicates a good start to a day.

6:13–16 On the seventh day the Israelites marched around the city **seven times,** symbolizing completion of the task.

6:17, 18 The important Hebrew word translated as **doomed to destruction, accursed,** or **curse** occurs in these two verses five times. This word indicates that the city of Jericho, along with its inhabitants and everything in it, was to be completely destroyed as an offering to the Lord.

6:19 The word translated **consecrated** means "holy." The valuable metal objects were not to be destroyed, but rather to be set apart for the Lord.

6:20 With a great blast of the horns and a great shout from the people, God miraculously delivered Jericho into their hands: **the wall fell down flat** ("under itself"). This first great obstacle to Israel's possession of the land fell at a shout of the people and illustrates God's complete and effortless mastery over all His people's opponents.

6:21–23 The two **spies** who had visited Rahab's house went into her home and rescued her and her entire family. She became a member of the family line of Jesus (Ruth 4:18–22; Matt. 1:5).

6:24, 25 she dwells in Israel to this day: This may indicate that this portion of the Book of Joshua, if not the entire book, was written within the lifetime of Rahab.

6:26 Joshua charged them: Literally "caused them to take an oath." The word **cursed** is one of the common Hebrew words for cursing; it is the opposite of *blessed.* Joshua cursed any attempts at rebuilding Jericho. Joshua's curse found a dramatic fulfillment many centuries later when Hiel of Bethel laid its

---

 IN DEPTH | **Lying**

The Bible clearly condemns lying. Its commands forbid it, prophets condemn it, and godly people avoid doing it (Ex. 20:16; Jer. 9:4–9; Zech. 8:16; Eph. 4:25). Behind all these is God Himself, who cannot lie (Num. 23:19).

But what about Rahab? She lied to protect the spies of Israel who had come to scout out the city of Jericho. The story of her heroics paint her in a very positive light; Joshua praised her efforts, and both testaments of the Bible praise and honor Rahab for doing this (Josh. 6:22–25; Heb. 11:31; James 2:25). Her action made her part of God's people, ultimately placing her in the line of ancestry to David and Jesus. Her lie was also part of the conquest of Canaan, a task that God commissioned and blessed. Does her example mean that lying can sometimes be an acceptable course of action?

In Rahab's case, there are three possibilities. Either her lie was not a sin, or it was a sin but excusable, or it was a sin and inexcusable. Those who say her lie was not a sin will sometimes say they believe that "the loving thing" is all that matters; a "little lie" told in the name of love is no sin. In fact, it is the right thing to do.

Others have said that Rahab's sin was excusable because of a greater value, the lives of the spies. Those who hold this view believe that some sins are worse than others, and sometimes a person has to choose among them. In Rahab's case, the necessity of preserving the lives of the spies had a higher value than the truth. She did the right thing in misdirecting the king's men because it was more important to save their lives than to tell the king's men where they were.

The third possibility is that a lie is a lie, and that even Rahab's action was wrong. In this view, Rahab sinned no matter how noble her intentions. Of course, in her case, her sin is understandable because she lacked a complete knowledge of the living God. That is, what she did was wrong, but she did not know any better. We must be careful to make a distinction between Rahab's faith and the way Rahab expressed it. The Bible praises Rahab because of her faith in God, not because of her lying. That is, her actions would have been more noble had she protected the spies in some other fashion; as it is, she did the best she could.

Further, though the Bible calls Rahab a prostitute, we are not meant to take that as an endorsement for immorality. Rahab, like the rest of us, had a mixed character, but she believed in God and strove to honor Him and His people. That is what draws her praise. We should honor Rahab the way the Bible does. She was a great heroine of the faith, who came from the most surprising place. In time, her name would be honored not only for what she did for Israel, but for what she became: a mother in the line of Jesus (Ruth 4:18–22; Matt. 1:5).

foundation and rebuilt its gates at great personal cost (1 Kin. 16:34).

6:27 As a result of this first dramatic conquest in the land of Canaan, it was apparent that **the LORD was with Joshua,** and news of this spread far and wide.

7:1 The phrase **committed a trespass** means "committed a treacherous violation." The names of **Achan** and his forebears in this verse are found again in 1 Chr. 2:6, 7. Usually whenever the **anger of the LORD burned** against Israel; He raised up an adversary against the nation to threaten and overpower it. Here God used the small army of Ai.

7:2, 3 Ai, which is beside Beth Aven, on the east side of Bethel: Ai was a small city west of Jericho. **spy out:** The Hebrew word for *spies* (see 2:1) and *spying* is related to the word for "feet." The spies investigated the land by going through it on foot.

7:4 Israel's force of **three thousand men** was a very small contingent indeed compared to the totals that they had available.

7:5 Israel suffered **thirty-six** casualties before retreating. Although minor, this was Israel's first defeat in the land and a great surprise. **the descent:** The topography west of Jericho rises sharply up out of the Jordan valley. It appears that the men of Ai chased the Israelites eastward, down the steep hills, toward Jericho, from where they had come. **the hearts of the people melted:** The very words that Rahab used to describe the Jericho's fears in the face of the Israelites (2:11) are now used of the Israelites' fears of the men of Ai.

7:6 tore his clothes, and fell to the earth ... put dust on their heads: The actions of mourning here are much more dramatic than typical mourning customs in the modern world. However, these were common actions in Israel and the ancient Middle East.

7:7, 8 The certainty of the past was often preferable to the difficulties of the present and the uncertainty of the future. Joshua's desire to have remained **on the other** (east) **side of the Jordan** demonstrated his selective memory, since that spot had problems of its own.

7:9, 10 Despite Joshua's shortsightedness in v. 7, here he showed that he was aware of the larger issue at stake: God's **great name**—His reputation.

7:11 Hebrew has several words for sin. **Sinned** means "missing the mark" of a standard set by God; **transgressed** means "crossing a boundary" set by God. This verse highlights the seriousness of Achan's offense, attributed here to the nation Israel, by referring to the sin in various ways: Israel had (1) **sinned,** (2) **transgressed** the Lord's **covenant,** (3) **taken some of the accursed things,** (4) **stolen,** (5) **deceived,** and (6) put the things **among their own stuff.**

7:12 That God would declare the people of Israel **doomed to destruction** because of their sin was a serious statement. It meant God would not be with Israel until the sin was removed from the camp.

7:13, 14 The relationship between obedience and blessing and disobedience and cursing is well illustrated here: Israel would have no further successes until the sin had been uncovered.

7:15, 16 The Hebrew word translated **a disgraceful thing** denotes a blatant and senseless disregard for God's will. God indicated that **the tribe of Judah was taken** and the guilty party found out.

7:17–19 give glory to the LORD ... and make confession ... and tell me: These three actions commanded by Joshua are aspects of one event. By telling Joshua his sin, Achan was confessing to God, and by his confession, he was indeed glorifying God.

7:20, 21 a beautiful Babylonian garment: Literally, "one beautiful garment of Shinar." The land of Shinar is mentioned in Gen. 11:2 as the place where men built the Tower of Babel. **two hundred shekels of silver:** The shekel was the basic unit of weight for silver, and it was slightly more than four-tenths of an ounce. The gold Achan took weighed **fifty shekels,** or about 20 ounces. **coveted:** Achan's actions, besides violating God's instructions, also were a violation of the tenth commandment (Ex. 20:17). Achan had made fruitless attempts to hide his sin from God, from whom nothing can be **hidden** (Ps. 139:7–12).

7:22–26 Achan was brought out to be stoned, not only with each of the items he had stolen, but also with **all that he had** and his entire household. This was a severe punishment, but it illustrated God's firm insistence on holiness. Achan's sin had infected all Israel (7:1), and ridding Israel of the stain of this sin required the annihilation of everything with which Achan had intimate contact.

8:1 The words **Do not be afraid, nor be dismayed** echo the words God used to encourage Joshua in 1:9. The sins of Achan had broken the special relationship God had established with His people, and so God reiterated His encouragement to Joshua. **people of war:** The usual term is "men of war" (5:4, 6). This phrase seems to emphasize the unity of the entire nation in doing battle.

8:2 booty for yourselves: In contrast to the instructions about Jericho (6:17–19), this time the Israelites were allowed to take and keep spoils of war for themselves.

8:3–6 A select group of men was to **lie in ambush ... behind** the city, that is, to the west. The main group of people would then be stationed north of the city (vv. 12, 13).

8:7 the LORD your God will deliver it into your hand: Here as elsewhere in the historical books, military victories are attributed to God.

8:8 commandment: After the disobedience in ch. 7, strict obedience was important here. Joshua urged obedience to God's commands, and the people complied (vv. 2, 8, 27).

8:9–13 The phrase **its rear guard** refers to the ambush forces stationed to the west of the city (vv. 3, 12). The largest contingent of warriors was stationed to the north. It appears that Joshua spent the night with the people, across the valley from Ai (v. 11), but late in the night he got up and went into the valley in preparation for the day's events (v. 13).

8:14, 15 the way of the wilderness: This may indicate only that the men of Ai fled in disarray into the wilderness.

8:16, 17 Bethel is an important city in the

Bible that goes back to patriarchal times, when Abraham offered a sacrifice to God there (Gen. 13:3) and Jacob had a dream from God there (Gen. 28:10–22). The inhabitants of Bethel came out of their city to help the men of Ai. Its king is listed among those conquered by Joshua (12:16).

8:18 God told Joshua to **stretch out the spear** toward the city to begin the attack. Evidently this signal was relayed in some way to those lying in ambush (v. 19).

8:19 set the city on fire: Among all the cities that the Israelites captured, only three are said to have been burned: Jericho (6:24), Ai (8:19), and Hazor (11:11). The people of Israel were to live in and enjoy the cities of the land.

8:20–23 The Israelites were to treat **the king of Ai** exactly as they had the king of Jericho (v. 2). Chapter 6 does not specify what they did to the king of Jericho, but we can infer from 8:29 that they killed him and exposed his body in a humiliating way.

8:24–26 Joshua did not draw back his hand: This verse shows Joshua maintaining his arm outstretched, with his spear in hand, until the defeat of Ai was completed The upraised spear was a symbol of God's presence and help in the battle (v. 1).

8:27 according to the word of the LORD: God had specified that the Israelites could take the city's possessions and livestock, but nothing else (v. 2), and this verse indicates that they carried out His instructions.

8:28 The word **heap** refers to a mound of ruins. Ai was not rebuilt; therefore it remained a heap of ruins.

8:29 As God instructed (v. 27), Joshua executed the king of Ai and exposed his body **on a tree** (see the similar action in 10:26). But he took down the body at sundown in accordance with the injunction in Deuteronomy that a body could not remain exposed overnight (Deut. 21:22–23). In these texts, **hanged** means exposing the dead body on a sharpened stake as a mark of shame and horror, not hanging by the neck.

8:30 Mount Ebal is mentioned only here and in Deut. 11:29; 27:4, 13. It and Mount Gerizim, directly south of it, were the sites to be used for proclaiming blessings and curses when the Israelites came into the land; specifically, Ebal was to be the site of the curses (Deut. 11:29).

8:31 Moses ... had commanded this in Deut. 27:2–10. This is another example of the explicit fulfillment of God's words; the Israelites wanted to make doubly sure they did it right this time. **An altar of whole stones** refers to unfinished stones (Deut. 27:4), which was in accord with God's earlier instructions about making altars (Ex. 20:25).

8:32 Joshua publicly wrote **a copy of the law** on stones.

8:33 This Hebrew word for **stranger** could more precisely be translated "resident alien." It refers to those foreigners who lived as permanent residents within Israel. Resident aliens enjoyed certain rights even though they were not Israelites by birth. They were allowed to take gleanings from the fields (Lev. 19:10; 23:22), and the Israelites were to give special care to them, along with the poor, the widow, and the orphan (Ex. 22:21; 23:9; Deut. 10:17–22).

8:34, 35 This was the first public reading of **the Book of the Law,** the entire body of the Law given by Moses, mentioned after Moses' death.

9:1, 2 Though a coalition of Canaanite kings banded together to oppose Israel, the text does not say whether this coalition ever actually fought Israel. It disappears from the scene after v. 2. Six ethnic groups in Canaan, who often are mentioned together (3:10), are listed here. God told Israel to destroy these nations, and He did not want Israel to become allies with them under any circumstances (Ex. 23:28–33; Deut. 7:1–5; 20:16–18).

9:3 Gibeon was relatively close to Ai and about five miles northwest of Jerusalem.

9:4–6 The Gibeonites went to great lengths to make it look as though they had **come from a far country.. A covenant** was a legal treaty.

9:7, 8 The people of Gibeon are called **Hivites,** and were among the groups slated for destruction (Ex. 34:11; Deut. 20:17). Israel should not have made a treaty with them. This verse shows that the Israelites were initially suspicious of the Gibeonites.

9:9, 10 The fame of the Israelites' victories had preceded them among the Gibeonites, in the same way that it did among the inhabitants of Jericho earlier (2:9, 10).

9:11–14 The Israelites **took some of** the Gibeonites' **provisions** in order to inspect them, to confirm the Gibeonites' words. Significantly, the Israelites **did not ask counsel of the LORD,** contrary to God's explicit instructions to Joshua (Num. 27:21). The mistake on Israel's part was not so much that they were deceived, but that they did not ask for the Lord's counsel.

9:15 Joshua made peace with them: The treaty made in this chapter has much in common with typical ancient Middle Eastern treaties of the times. Its binding nature (v. 18) forms the basis for the actions taken in 10:1–27, where the Gibeonites found themselves threatened by a Canaanite coalition and appealed to the Israelites for help.

9:16–19 Chephirah, Beeroth, and Kirjath Jearim were all towns near Gibeon. The first two were in Benjamite territory (18:25, 26), and the third was on its border (18:14, 15).

9:20–23 the oath which we swore: Because of the sacred, unbreakable nature of an oath, this covenant the Israelites made with the Gibeonites could not be revoked, even though it was obtained under false pretenses.

9:24–26 The report that reached the Gibeonites about the Israelites (v. 3) frightened them so much that they conjured up this deception.

9:27 The phrase **the place which He would choose** indicates that the Gibeonites were to serve only at sanctioned Israelite worship centers and not Canaanite ones. Until the Jerusalem temple was built, these centers included Shiloh (18:1) and Gibeon itself (1 Chr. 16:39).

10:1–4 Political and military calculations led the five Canaanite kings to conclude their only option was to band together and attack (v. 5).

10:5 The name **Amorites** probably refers to the inhabitants of the central mountain region of Palestine, although only **Jerusalem** and **Hebron** are really in the hill country. The king of Jerusalem was leader of a coalition of five kings against Gibeon.

10:6–8 Joshua ascended from Gilgal because Gilgal and Jericho were in the deep Jordan valley; he would have had to go up into the hill country in the central portion of Canaan to help the Gibeonites.

10:9 For Joshua's men to have **marched all night from Gilgal** and then attacked speaks well of their stamina. Their night march covered about 20 miles up steep terrain, with gear, under stress, in the middle of the night, and with a battle still before them.

10:10, 11 the LORD routed them: Despite Joshua's presence with his warriors (v. 7), it was God who gave the victory and God who received the credit. **the road that goes to Beth Horon:** One escape route for the Canaanite kings went northwest, toward the coast. **Azekah** was over the hills to the southwest of Gibeon, some distance away.

10:12 In the sight of Israel, Joshua commanded the **Sun** and the **Moon** to **stand still over Gibeon** until the Israelites completed their task.

10:13 The Book of Jasher (mentioned again in 2 Sam. 1:18) confirms what the Book of Joshua reports here. It is not part of the Bible, and no part of it has survived.

10:14–18 the LORD heeded: The author of Joshua marvels that God listened to the voice of one man and fought on Israel's behalf so grandly.

10:19 delivered them into your hand: Again Joshua gave God credit for the Israelites' victory. **enter their cities:** The fortified cities of Canaan offered some protection to their people. That is why the ambush at Ai was designed to draw the people out of the city (8:17). In v. 20, we see that some people escaped into the fortified cities.

10:20, 21 The slaughter of the Canaanites was great, but some escaped. This explains why there were still people in these towns later (see especially vv. 31–37).

10:22–24 Joshua told the captains to put their **feet on the necks of these kings** as a clear declaration of victory. Ancient sculptural reliefs show Assyrian kings doing this to their vanquished enemies.

10:25 be strong and of good courage: Joshua encouraged the people in the same terms

God had used to encourage him (1:6, 9; 10:8).

10:26, 27 hanged them on five trees ... until evening: Joshua did to these five kings what he had earlier done to the king of Ai (8:29). As before, he took the bodies down before sundown in accordance with Mosaic legislation (8:29).

10:28, 29 The first city mentioned is the one toward which the Canaanite coalition had fled, **Makkedah** (vv. 10, 16). The five kings had fled and hidden themselves in a cave.

10:30–32 We are reminded that **the LORD** was Israel's warrior.

10:33–39 The account of the capture of **Gezer** is mentioned only incidentally to the account of the capture of Lachish.

10:40 Here we see that Joshua was victorious over all who lived in **the mountain country** (the word is the same as "hills" in 9:1) **and the South and the lowland and the wilderness slopes.** This summary statement covers the central and southern portions of the land of Canaan, but it does not include the coastlands (13:2–6).

10:41–43 Neither **Kadesh Barnea** nor **Gaza** has been mentioned previously in Joshua; their inclusion here marks the southernmost limits of the land conquered. Gaza was a Philistine city, unconquered in 13:3. **Goshen, even as far as Gibeon** marks the southern and northern limits of this conquest.

11:1 Hazor was a large and strategic city in northern Israel; it is called "the head of all those kingdoms" in v. 10.

11:2 The geographical description here names areas rather than cities. **Chinneroth** is another name for the Sea of Galilee (see 12:3). **the heights of Dor on the west:** Dor was a seaport on the Mediterranean.

11:3 The inclusion of **the Jebusite,** that is, the inhabitants of Jerusalem, is striking because Jerusalem was south of Jericho. Mount **Hermon in the land of Mizpah** was in the far north, the highest point in northern Palestine.

11:4, 5 Horses at this time were for pulling **chariots.** These vehicles accompanied the infantry and carried a rider with a bow or spears. The Canaanite armies did not use mounted warriors. These armies came well-armed to fight the Israelites, but it did not matter. God still defeated them. Only in the battles of Jericho and Ai did the Israelites initiate the action. God limited the size of the Israelite army so that the Israelites would not trust their military power.

11:6, 7 God promised to deliver Israel's enemies into their hands by **tomorrow about this time.**

11:8 Greater Sidon was a Phoenician city on the Mediterranean coast, and the **Brook Misrephoth** was south of it.

11:9 as the LORD had told him: Joshua was careful to do exactly as instructed (see v. 6).

11:10 Hazor was formerly the head: This is probably why Joshua struck at Hazor first.. Excavation of Hazor has shown several destructions in the Late Bronze Age, one from about 1400 B.C. that could easily be attributed to Joshua.

11:11–13 Jericho and Ai were the only other cities burned. Most of the cities of Canaan were taken without being destroyed. In this way, the cities could be inhabited by Israel without rebuilding.

11:14, 15 The Israelites were allowed to take **all the spoil** for themselves (8:2, 27). Their treatment of the inhabitants was the pattern for all their Canaanite targets: **They left none breathing,** but killed everyone (6:21; 8:22; 10:28, 30, 32, 33, 35, 37, 39, 40; 11:8, 11, 12). God had told Moses why Israel to carry out this destruction in Canaan (Deut. 7:2–11; 20:16–18): the Canaanites were being judged by God for their wickedness.

11:16, 17 These verses summarize both the northern campaign and this entire section of the book (chs. 9—11). Verse 16 mentions many of the same territories as does 10:40, 41. The southern limit of the conquest is given here; **Mount Halak** is near Kadesh Barnea (10:41), and **Seir** is the hill country of Edom, southeast of the Dead Sea. **Baal Gad ... Mount Hermon:** This is the northern limit of the conquest. Baal Gad was in the Lebanon valley, northwest of Mount Hermon.

11:18–20 to harden their hearts: The persons whose hearts God hardened were not good people, but were people already committed to doing evil.

11:21, 22 The destruction of the **Anakim** from the hill country was especially significant. Their fearsome presence had caused the Israelites to rebel against God's command to enter Canaan (Num. 13:22, 28, 32, 33). But as this generation learned, their size did not matter.

11:23 The statement **the land rested from war** draws the first section of the book to a close. The next section before the distribution of Israel's inheritance is the list of defeated Canaanite kings (ch. 12).

12:1–5 The Israelites' earlier conquests are mentioned here, their victories over **Sihon,** king of Heshbon, and **Og,** king of Bashan. The Israelites defeated them under Moses' leadership and took possession of their land at that time (Num. 21:21–35). Verse 6 confirms that this indeed had been given as an inheritance to the two and one-half tribes who settled there.

12:6–24 The language of these verses makes it plain that Joshua succeeded Moses in his various roles, first as conqueror and second as giver of land. The two men are described in the same way: As conquerors, **Joshua and the children of Israel** (v. 7), follow **Moses ... and the children of Israel** (v. 6). As land-giver, **Joshua gave** (v. 7), as **Moses ... had given** (v. 6).

13:1–13 God told Joshua that **there remains very much land yet to be possessed.** The famous five cities of the Philistines are mentioned (Gaza, Ashdod, Ashkelon, Gath, and Ekron). But Joshua was too old to command the remaining struggle for the land. God Himself would drive out the remaining inhabitants; Joshua only had to apportion the land to the nine and one-half tribes west of the Jordan River.

13:14–21 to the tribe of Levi He had given no inheritance: This is an important concept in the Book of Joshua. Here, previous directives about the Levites' inheritance were obeyed (Num. 18:20–24; Deut. 10:8, 9; 18:1–5). The Levites did have cities in the territories of each tribe (21:1–42). Instead of a land inheritance, the sacrifices of God would be their privileged inheritance.

13:22 Balaam was the pagan fortune-teller who had been hired by Balak, king of Moab, to curse the Israelites in the wilderness (Num. 22—24). He found that he could speak only what God told him to, yet he sinned by inciting the Moabite women to seduce the Israelite men (Num. 25:1–9; 31:16). Hence, **the children of Israel also killed ... Balaam.** This record of Balaam's death echoes the notice found at Num. 31:8.

13:23–32 The cities and their villages made up the small city-states typical of Canaan at this time. The villages were permanent settlements without walls, or outlying farming villages.

13:33 Levi ... as He had said to them: This verse reiterates the information about the Levites' landless inheritance (compare v. 14); here, however, the inheritance is said to be God Himself and not the sacrifices.

14:1–5 God had commanded the casting of lots to determine Israel's inheritance (Num. 26:55). Thus, that **their inheritance was by lot** does not mean that it was by chance, but that God Himself determined who got what land.

14:6 Caleb is described here and elsewhere as **the Kenizzite** (14:14; Num. 32:12). The Kenizzites were a non-Israelite group descended from Esau through Kenaz (Gen. 15:19; 36:11, 15, 42). Some of this group had apparently associated themselves with Judah at an early stage (Num. 13:6).

14:7–9 The promise of Caleb's inheritance mentioned in v. 9 refers to God's words in Num. 14:24.

14:10, 11 According to v. 7, Caleb was forty when he was sent in to spy out the land. Now it was forty-five years later. Since forty years were spent in the wilderness, the conquest occupied five years.

14:12 It was **the Anakim** who had frightened ten of the Israelite spies forty-five years before, triggering Israel's rebellion against God (Num. 13). Caleb was no more afraid of them now than he had been then, even though he was now considerably older.

14:13 Joshua blessed him: To bless others in the name of the Lord expresses the desire for them to experience God's best (Gen. 27:27–29; 47:10; 49:1–28; Judg.

5:24; Neh. 11:2). It is more than wishful thinking, because blessing in the name of God taps into the power and resources of God.

14:14 Caleb's wholehearted devotion to God was never in question, even in the wilderness: **He wholly followed the LORD** (v. 8). As a result, he received the land that he requested.

14:15 Kirjath Arba: This was the former name of the city of Hebron (Gen. 23:2); it means "city of Arba." **the land had rest from war:** This comment echoes 11:23, which concludes the account of the southern and northern campaigns.

15:1–12 The boundaries of Judah in southern Canaan are now described in detail. This reinforces the importance of the inheritance and the exact location that each tribe received.

15:13–19 This second passage about Caleb's inheritance (see 14:6–15 for the first one) explains how he also took Debir, another city that originally had been taken by Joshua (10:38–39). This section closely parallels Judg. 1:12–15.

15:20–62 The cities that Judah inherited number more than one hundred and include their surrounding villages. The list has four parts: (1) cities in the south (vv. 21–32); (2) cities in the lowland (vv. 33–47); (3) cities in the mountain country (vv. 48–60); and (4) cities in the wilderness near the Dead Sea (vv. 61, 62).

15:63 The Jebusites stubbornly held on to Jerusalem because the tribe of Judah did not follow through on its obligation to destroy them completely. God did not want Israel to make peace with the inhabitants of the land, but instead to drive them out and utterly destroy them (Num. 33:52–55; Deut. 7:1–5; 20:16–18). The city effectively belonged to the Jebusites until the time of David (2 Sam. 5:5–10).

16:1–4 A single lot determined the inheritance of both of the tribes of Joseph—Ephraim and Manasseh. That these two tribes together received only one lot caused them later to complain (17:14–18).

16:5–9 The separate cities: Some of Ephraim's cities were actually part of Manasseh's inheritance (see also 17:9). The reason for this is not clear, but it may have its basis in the greater blessing extended to Ephraim by Jacob (Gen. 48). Manasseh also inherited towns from the territories of two other tribes, Issachar and Asher (17:11).

16:10 they did not drive out the Canaanites: This previews the many statements about incomplete conquests in Judg. 1. **forced laborers:** The status of the Canaanites in Gezer was somewhat similar to that of the Gibeonites (9:27), except that there was no treaty involved here, so the status of these Canaanites was somewhat lower.

17:1, 2 Manasseh's firstborn child **Machir** (Gen. 50:23; Num. 26:29) had already received a separate portion, Gilead and Bashan—that is, Manasseh's portion east of the Jordan River (13:29–31). The rest of Manasseh's portion was west of the Jordan River (vv. 2–13).

17:3–13 Joshua carried out the commands of God in the matter of the inheritance of Zelophehad. Joshua made sure that the daughters received their inheritance as promised.

17:14–18 The episode here revives the complaint of the two tribes of Joseph that they together had received only one lot. Joshua encouraged them to take land in the hill country despite their fears of the Canaanites there (vv. 15, 17, 18; Num. 13:28–33).

18:1, 2 Up to this point, Israel's central encampment in the land had been at Gilgal, near Jericho. Now they moved to **Shiloh,** about 15 miles northwest of Jericho, where they set up the tent of meeting. **tabernacle of meeting:** The tabernacle was an elaborate tent that served as God's "home" when the Israelites were in the wilderness. In it were the ark of the covenant and other holy items.

18:3, 4 How long will you neglect to go: Joshua's rebuke of the seven tribes shows that it was not enough to defeat the inhabitants of the land; they also had to take possession of it.

18:5–28 wrote the survey in a book: See 18:11—19:51.

19:1–46 Simeon did not get an independent inheritance, but rather inherited scattered

lands within Judah's allotment. Their father Jacob had predicted this (Gen. 49:5–7). Later Simeon and **Judah** acted together (Judg. 1:3).

19:47, 48 The Danites were forced out of their territory in the south (Judg. 1:34) and migrated north (Judg. 18:27–31), where they captured **Leshem** and renamed it **Dan.**

19:49, 50 The section ends, appropriately enough, with **Joshua** receiving his **inheritance** in Ephraim. **According to the word of the LORD:** The promise to Caleb and Joshua in Num. 14:30 guaranteed both an inheritance in the land.

19:51 The involvement of **Eleazar the priest, Joshua, ... and the heads of the ... tribes,** as well as the mention of the tabernacle at **Shiloh,** all lend an air of importance and solemnity. The entire distribution of the land had taken place under God's watchful eye, decently and in order.

20:1–6 The word translated *avenger* in **avenger of blood** is translated *close relative* in Ruth 3:13; 4:1. The basic meaning of the word is "protector of family rights." God's provision of the cities of refuge put a limit on private acts of vengeance.

20:7–9 The cities of refuge were evenly distributed so that none was more than a day's journey from any part of Israel's land. Golan, Ramoth Gilead, and Bezer were on the east side of the Jordan River, and Kedesh, Shechem, and Kirjath Arba (Hebron) were on the west.

21:1–3 The Levites came to Joshua to claim their rightful territory, which included cities throughout the territories. The **common-lands** refers to land that surrounded each city.

21:4–8 Here the Levitical cities are determined by the **lot.** In this case it was a God-directed method of choosing the cities.

21:9–42 The priestly branch of the **Kohathites,** descended through Aaron, received 13 cities from Judah, Simeon, and Benjamin.

21:43–45 This glorious conclusion to these two chapters and to the entire section (chs. 13—21) celebrates the fact that **all came to pass** exactly as God promised. The God of Israel is a promise-keeping God, who gave

Israel the land in accordance with the promises He had made to the patriarchs.

22:1–3 The obedience of the tribes settled east of the Jordan River is commended here.

22:4 rest ... as He promised: This idea of rest as a gift from God is part of the fabric of the Book of Joshua.

22:5 The passionate exhortation to **take careful heed** captures the heart of this chapter. The verbs in this verse give a comprehensive picture of what a proper relationship to God includes: to **love** God, to **walk** in His ways, to **hold fast** (or cling) to Him, and to **serve** Him.

22:6–9 Joshua blessed them: The blessing here involves many riches from the spoils of the land (v. 7).

22:10, 11 have built an altar: The account does not reveal why this altar was built until after the events have developed into a full-blown crisis.

22:12 God had commanded Israel not to offer burnt offerings or sacrifices at any location except the tabernacle. The punishment for violating the law was death, and this is why **Israel gathered ... to go to war** against their brethren.

22:13, 14 First, the nine and one-half tribes west of the Jordan River acted in perfect unity, carefully choosing one representative each, the highest ranking ruler from each tribe. Second, they sent the priest **Phinehas** to head up the delegation, reflecting their concern that true worship be maintained.

22:15, 16 We know how serious Phinehas considered the offense from the term he used for it, **treachery.**

22:17 The iniquity of Peor included the fact that the Israelites worshiped the Moabite gods and committed immoral acts with the women of Moab. The phrase **not cleansed till this day** implies that Israel had never completely rid itself of this sin.

22:18–20 He will be angry with the whole congregation: If the tribes east of the Jordan River were indeed sinning, then the entire nation would feel the effects.

22:21, 22 The repetition of **the LORD God of gods** reveals the deep emotion in the response of the tribes east of the Jordan River. They firmly maintained their innocence and

tried to convince their fellow countrymen of it.

22:23–25 The tribes from east of the Jordan River were afraid that geographical distance would isolate them and the Israelites west of the Jordan River would reject them. Thus they built the **altar** to prevent the existing unity from being lost.

22:26–29 Here is the replica: The word *replica* clearly shows that they never intended this altar to be a substitute for the true altar at the tabernacle. They intended it to serve as a **witness.**

22:30–33 The eastern tribes' impassioned defense quickly defused the crisis, satisfying the people's representatives. The western tribes accepted the words of the Transjordan tribes on this matter, and the altar remained.

22:34 The climax of the chapter asserts that the altar was **a witness ... that the LORD is God.**

23:1–5 He who has fought for you: A reminder that the Lord gave the land to Israel, even to the extent of fighting on their behalf (1:3; 8:7; 10:14, 19, 42).

23:6 be very courageous: Again, Joshua used the same words that God had spoken to him years earlier.

23:7–9 That **no one has been able to stand** against the tribes of Israel was a fulfillment of God's promise in 1:5.

23:10 One man ... shall chase a thousand: The power God's people had over their enemies was miraculous.

23:11 The exhortation to **love the LORD your God** comes from Deut. 6:5.

23:12 The word translated **cling** is the same word translated *hold fast* in v. 8, bringing the different instances of clinging into sharp contrast. God wanted His people to cling to Him. This required that they not **make marriages** with unbelieving foreigners.

23:13, 14 not one thing has failed: A strong affirmation of God's faithfulness.

23:15, 16 you shall perish quickly from the good land: Israel's rebellion began almost immediately, during the period of the judges, when Israel began to do precisely what was warned against here (Judg. 2:16–23; 3:1–6).

24:1 Shechem is a site with an ancient tradition of religious significance. Archaeological excavation has uncovered a series of temples, sanctuaries, and ceremonial standing stones from almost every period of its existence.

24:2–4 Israel's ancestors did not worship the true God at first; until God called them, Abraham and his relatives had **served other gods** (Gen. 31:1–4, 19, 34, 35). The words of this verse are used in the Passover celebration of the Jews all over the world today. Those who celebrate confess that the Lord's choice of their fathers was not because of an innate superiority in Abraham.

24:5–9 Afterward I brought you out: God did not just make Himself known in ages past; He also worked mightily and graciously for the people of Joshua's day.

24:10 I would not listen to Balaam: For the full story on Balaam, see Num. 22—24.

24:11, 12 God's use of **the hornet** to aid Israel fulfilled the promise of Ex. 23:28. The phrase **two kings** refers to Sihon and Og, whom Israel had defeated in the wilderness (Num. 21:21–35).

24:13 A land for which you did not labor: The land was God's gift to His people.

24:14, 15 Joshua's words contain a rare appeal to Israel to choose between God and the many false substitutes. Of course, the appeal is rhetorical; from God's perspective there is only one option. With his words, Joshua clearly took his stand on the side of the living God.

24:16–18 In their response to Joshua's challenge, the people acknowledged their debt to God for all their good fortune. As long as they remembered what God had done for them, they would be inclined to serve Him.

24:19–21 Immediately after Joshua exhorted the Israelites to serve God (v. 14), he stated **you cannot serve the LORD!** This use of exaggeration emphasizes the gravity of the obligation to which the people committed themselves.

24:22–27 Joshua and **the people** sealed their covenant to serve the Lord by writing these words in **the Book of the Law of God** and by the erecting a **large stone** under an oak tree, the same tree that Jacob had encountered when he came to Shechem. The stone under the oak tree functioned as a legal reminder or witness of the covenant just entered into by the people.

24:28 When Joshua dismissed the people, it was **each to his own inheritance,** fittingly closing this section with a reminder of one of the book's major themes.

24:29 This reference to Joshua as the **servant of the LORD** shows clearly how Joshua served the people and the purpose of God.

24:30, 31 Joshua was buried in the city he had asked for and built, Timnath Serah (19:50).

24:32 The burial of Joseph's body in this place is the fulfillment of prophecy given hundreds of years earlier (Gen. 50:24, 25).

24:33 Eleazar the high priest also receives a decent burial in his own land.

Judges

Introduction

The Book of Judges is a historical narrative that contrasts God's faithfulness with Israel's apostasy. In spite of the repeated falling away of His people, God provided deliverers—namely, the judges—time and again. The real hero of Judges is God Himself, who alone remains faithful in spite of the failings of His people.

The author of this collection of historical writings about the judges is never identified. Neither are there any clues elsewhere in Scripture. Late Jewish tradition ascribed its authorship to Samuel. This is certainly possible, but there is no way of knowing for sure.

In contrast to the serene way in which the Book of Joshua ends, with Israel in harmony with God's commands, Judges reveals that Israel began to disobey God even in the time of Joshua, and that this disobedience grew more serious—and more debased—over time. Judges 2:16–23 establishes the cyclical pattern of sin, slavery, and salvation that would dominate the time of the judges. However, the book makes clear that the cycle had a downward spiral. Each new outbreak of disobedience and idolatry took Israel further away from God and deeper into sin and misery. By the end of the book, it is clear that Israel had violated its covenant with God in almost every imaginable way.

1:1 Now after the death of Joshua: Judges begins with reference to the death of the previous leader. Yet no new leader was commissioned to lead Israel after Joshua; rather, the tribe of Judah was designated to lead in the fight against the Canaanites (1:1–4).

1:2, 3 History bound the tribes of **Judah** and **Simeon** together. They were both descended from the same mother (Gen. 29:33, 35), and Simeon had inherited land in Judah's territory (Josh. 19:1, 9). Theirs was a natural alliance.

1:4, 5 The site of the battle of **Bezek** between Israelites and Canaanites is unknown.

1:6, 7 Adoni-Bezek: The name of this minor king means "Lord of Bezek." To **cut off his thumbs and big toes** would prevent Adoni-Bezek from engaging in battle again, since a thumb was needed to hold a sword and the big toes were necessary for running.

1:8, 9 Jerusalem was captured and burned, but not settled. Verse 21 states that Benjamin did not drive out the Jebusites from the city.

1:10 Hebron means "Confederacy." This city's name was formerly **Kirjath Arba** (literally "city of four"). From the names it is conjectured that Hebron was originally a close-knit alliance of four cities.

1:11 Debir was the next city captured by the Israelites. Its former name Kirjath Sepher means "City of the Book"; it may have been an administrative center where records were kept.

1:12–15 As a dowry, Caleb's daughter asked for springs of water in addition to the land he had given her. Land without fresh water was almost worthless, so her request was an astute one.

1:16, 17 References to the **South** (that is, the Negev) in vv. 9; 15 included mention of the descendants of **the Kenite,** Moses' father-in-law, Jethro (Ex. 3:1). **City of Palms** is a reference to Jericho nestled deep in the Jordan valley, northeast of Jerusalem.

1:18 Gaza ... Ashkelon ... Ekron were three of five major cities in the Philistine kingdom (the other two were Ashdod and Gath: see Josh. 13:2, 3). By Samson's day, all three cities were in Philistine hands again (14:19; 16:1).

1:19, 20 they could not drive out the inhabitants of the lowland: This verse must mean that the Israelites had no success beyond the three cities. **Chariots of iron** were effective on the flat coastal plains but not in the hill country of Canaan.

1:21 Benjamin did not drive out the Jebusites: See Josh. 15:63.

1:22 The house of Joseph was Ephraim and Manasseh (Gen. 48:5, 6; Deut. 33:17), who had split the inheritance of their father. **Bethel** means "The House of God." It was a site with an honored history, beginning with Abraham's first sacrifice to God (Gen.

13:3–4) and Jacob's revelation from God there (Gen. 31:13).

1:23–25 Luz means "Deceit" or "Perversion," but Jacob had changed its name to Bethel after his encounter with God there.

1:26 land of the Hittites: Archaeologists have unearthed a great Hittite kingdom in Asia Minor (present-day Turkey), dating from about 1800 to 1200 B.C.

1:27 Manasseh did not drive out: The Israelites failed to uproot the Canaanites (see Josh. 10:28–43). That failure resulted in much grief in the years following. We see in ch. 2—and indeed throughout the rest of the book—the effects this had on Israel's life.

1:28–33 They put the Canaanites under tribute means they forced their captives to work as involuntary, unpaid laborers.

1:34–36 Amorites were Canaanite peoples living in the central hill country, and they blocked Dan's entry into this region. The Danites were forced to migrate northward (18:1; Josh. 19:47).

2:1 The Angel of the LORD appears as God's representative here, speaking authoritatively to the people about their covenant disobedience. **Gilgal** was the site where Israel had first encamped west of the Jordan River (Josh. 4:19). **Bochim** was possibly near Bethel. **I led you up from Egypt:** The reference to **you** is plural, indicating the entire nation.

2:2–5 you shall make no covenant: God's commands to make no covenants with pagan nations and to tear down their altars are found in Ex. 23:32; 34:13; Deut. 12:3. Israel's disobedience meant that these nations would become snares to them, just as God had warned (Ex. 23:33; Num. 33:55; Josh. 23:13).

2:6–9 The author identifies the death of Joshua as a starting point for the trouble to come. The grammatical construction in 1:1 is a common one, and it is clear that the events of ch. 1 are events that *followed* Joshua's death. Most likely the reference to Joshua's death in 1:1 is correctly placed and this subsequent passage has been inserted by the author out of sequence. It is a "flashback" that leads into the second major section of the book (2:6—3:6).

2:10 Another generation arose ... who did not know the LORD: The meaning of *did not know* is that the people deliberately refused to acknowledge God's authority. It is not simply that they were ignorant, but that they were in unbelief.

2:11, 12 The children of Israel did evil in the sight of the LORD is a statement also found in 3:7, 12; 4:1; 6:1; 10:6; 13:1 and in 1 and 2 Kings. Israel would stray frequently from the Lord. Only God's grace and the leadership of a few godly men and women spared the nation from complete corruption.

2:13 Ashtoreths: Ashtoreth (Astarte) was a female fertility goddess and a goddess of love and war, closely associated with Baal (10:6; 1 Sam. 7:4; 12:10). She appears by the name Ishtar in Mesopotamian texts.

2:14, 15 As the LORD had sworn refers to God's promise to deliver Israel into their enemies' hands if they forsook Him (Deut. 28:25; Josh. 23:13).

2:16 The LORD raised up judges: The judges of Israel did not normally hold court, or make legal decisions (except for Deborah, see 4:4, 5). Rather, they were political leaders who delivered Israel from oppression. The Lord alone is the true Judge of His people (11:27), and He hands out blessing and punishment. Six of the judges (Shamgar, Tola, Jair, Ibzan, Elon, and Abdon) are known as "minor" judges because of the few details given about them in the narrative. The "major" judges—Othniel, Ehud, Deborah, Gideon, Jephthah, and Samson—were distinguished by their military prowess or heroic deeds.

2:17 Played the harlot is a powerful and familiar metaphor used to describe Israel's unfaithfulness to God.

2:18 The Hebrew verb translated **moved to pity** is elsewhere translated *relent* (1 Sam. 15:29; Jon. 3:10). God changed His course because of His compassion for their suffering.

2:19 Their fathers refers to those of the preceding generation, whereas in v. 17 *fathers* refers to those of Joshua's day.

2:20 this nation: Usually the word was used for Israel's neighbors, while Israel itself was called *the people.* The choice of the impersonal word *nation* reflects the distance between God and His people.

2:21–23 I also will no longer drive out ... any of the nations: This fulfilled a warning that God gave the Israelites through Joshua (see vv. 15, 23).

3:1, 2 that He might test Israel: The idea of testing implies difficulty and adversity; God was testing Israel to refine it.

3:3 Sidonians: Sidon was a port city northwest of Israel, in what today is Lebanon. Little is known about the **Hivites.** From the geographical description in this verse, it appears that they lived in northern Palestine (Josh. 9:7). **Mount Lebanon** was beyond the northern borders of Israel. Evidently, hostile nations surrounded Israel on every side.

3:4–6 Canaanites: On the various peoples in this verse, see Josh. 3:10.

3:7 the Baals and Asherahs: The plural is used for both gods because each was worshiped in different forms in the different local communities.

3:8 Cushan-Rishathaim was from much farther away than Israel's other enemies. The judge Othniel, who was from Judah, was chosen to lead in this campaign. Cushan-Rishathaim's name means "Cushan of Double Wickedness"; this may not have been his actual name, but instead a name pinned on him by the author of Judges for ridicule.

3:9, 10 Othniel was from Judah and was Caleb's near kinsman and son-in-law. The Spirit of the Lord came upon him, and he prevailed against Cushan-Rishathaim.

3:11 The land had rest for forty years is the first of several references to forty-year or eighty-year periods of peace in the Book of Judges (3:30; 5:31; 8:28).

3:12 Moab was a plateau southeast of the Dead Sea. It sat on either side of the King's Highway, an important north-south trade route. The Bible frequently mentions conflict between the two peoples, except for the Book of Ruth, the events of which occurred during a time of stable relations between Moab and Israel.

3:13–18 The City of Palms was Jericho, the only city on record that Eglon captured, although he ruled the Israelites 18 years (v. 14).

3:19 These **images** were clearly important in this passage—and prominent enough to be landmarks—since they appear again in v. 26, bracketing the account of Ehud's murder of Eglon. **Gilgal** was the Israelites' first encampment in Canaan and an important religious center.

3:20–23 upstairs in his cool private chamber: The coolest place in the house was on the roof.

3:24–26 Seirah is mentioned only here in the Bible, and its location is unknown.

3:27–30 The trumpet described here is the ram's horn, which could sound only a few notes.

3:31 Shamgar is mentioned only here and in 5:6. The next chapter begins with the death of Ehud, the previous judge. Moreover, Shamgar delivered Israel but did not *judge* it. Even the name Shamgar is not Hebrew. Yet he was the **son of Anath**—clearly a Semitic name.

4:1–3 Jabin king of Canaan, who reigned in Hazor: Probably Jabin was a title rather than a proper name, resembling the use of the title Abimelech among the Philistines (Gen. 20:2; 26:1) or Ben-Hadad among the kings of Damascus.

4:4 Deborah is one of five women to be called a prophetess in the Old Testament. The others are Miriam (Ex. 15:20), Huldah (2 Kin. 22:14; 2 Chr. 34:22), Isaiah's wife (Is. 8:3), and Noadiah, a false prophetess (Neh. 6:14).

4:5 Ramah and Bethel were in the southern part of the land, near Judah. Ramah was in the territory of Benjamin (Josh. 18:25), and Bethel was near the border between Benjamin and Ephraim (Josh. 8:17; 18:13).

4:6, 7 Deborah summoned Barak from **Kedesh in Naphtali,** a settlement southwest of the Sea of Galilee. The soldiers were to gather at Mt. Tabor, where the territories of Issachar, Naphtali, and Zebulun met (v. 6). The battle would be fought along **the River Kishon,** which flows northwest into the Mediterranean Sea.

4:8–10 Barak hesitated to lead the Israelites in battle. His lack of nerve forced Deborah to go with him, and subsequently the glory for the victory would go to a woman. Jael, a

Kenite woman, killed the notorious Sisera (vv. 17–22). Both women were heroines. In fact, Deborah is shown in the best light of all the judges in the book. She is called a prophetess and "a mother in Israel."

4:11–16 The centerpiece of Sisera's impressive army was **nine hundred chariots of iron.** However, the chariots seem to have become mired in the waters of the River Kishon (5:19–22).

4:17–24 The details of Sisera's death are told in the slow, suspenseful manner that characterized the story of Eglon's death.

5:1 The verb **sang** here is in a feminine singular form, which supports the point made earlier about Deborah's prominence over Barak (4:8, 9).

5:2, 3 When leaders lead: The phrase literally means "the long-haired ones who let their hair hang loose." The precise meaning of the phrase is obscure, but it may mean that loosed locks or flowing hair were signs of great strength or leadership. **People willingly offer themselves** tells of the glad cooperation of the Israelites.

5:4, 5 A brief historical review now follows the calls to worship in vv. 2, 3.

5:6–9 The phrase **a mother in Israel** occurs twice in the Old Testament, here and 2 Sam. 20:19. The title is given to Deborah as one of honor, respect, and prominence.

5:10–13 This verse calls all classes of society to bear witness to the mighty acts of God, from the ruling classes, those riding on **white donkeys,** to the lowest classes, those **who walk along the road.**

5:14–16 Machir is identified here with western Manasseh, in whose territory the battle took place.

5:17, 18 The reference to Dan remaining **on ships** probably reflects the location of their original inheritance, which was along the south-central coastal plain where they would have had access to the sea.

5:19–23 The victory proper is now described in vivid terms, and a curse is pronounced on Meroz, a site otherwise unknown (v. 23). The **stars** themselves were fighting against Sisera (v. 20). The frantic pounding of the horses' hooves, their **galloping, galloping,** suggests the

chaos caused by the waters of the River Kishon (vv. 21, 22; see 4:7).

5:24–27 The poem speaks of **Sisera** sinking and falling at Jael's feet as she strikes his head, while the prose account tells us he was already lying down when she struck him (4:21). The poem is using graphic, emotive language, which it repeats several times to make the point.

5:28–30 The point of this pathetic story of Sisera's mother is not to elicit sympathy for her. She expected her son to shower his people with plunder; instead, he lay dead at Jael's feet.

5:31 The hymn concludes with praise to the Lord, as many psalms do.

6:1 The Midianites were descendants of Abraham through his wife Keturah (Gen. 25:1, 2), so they were distantly related to the Israelites. Generally speaking, Israel counted Midian among its foes. In this account, the Midianites were menacing Israel, burning, looting, and leaving many near starvation (6:4, 5).

6:2 the dens, the caves: That the Israelites were forced to abandon their homes and live in caves indicates the desperate straits they were in.

6:3, 4 The **Amalekites** were a nomadic people who lived in the Sinai desert and were descendants of Esau (Gen. 36:12) and here joined the Midianites against Israel. **People of the East** were unspecified nomads who also plundered Israel.

6:5–7 as numerous as locusts: Locust plagues were a fairly common occurrence in the Middle East.

6:8–10 the LORD sent a prophet: God sent a prophet to rebuke His people. This prophet reminded the Israelites of God's faithfulness, and how the people had rejected Him (vv. 8–10).

6:11, 12 The Palestinian **terebinth tree** is a large tree with a thick trunk and heavy branches, sometimes confused with the oak. It can grow as high as 25 feet. The exact location of **Ophrah** is unknown, but it was a city somewhere in the territory of Manasseh. A **winepress** was a square or circular pit carved into rock in which grapes were crushed. Wheat was usually separated on open threshing floors so the wind could carry away the chaff. The fact that Gideon was forced to thresh wheat hidden inside a winepress shows again the desperate state the Israelites were in.

6:13, 14 My lord was a polite form of address, but **the LORD** is the personal name of God (Yahweh). The Hebrew word for **miracles** means "wonderful things," and it is translated elsewhere as *wonders*.

6:15 I am the least in my father's house: Gideon's objection is reminiscent of the words spoken by Moses (Ex. 3:11) and Jeremiah (Jer. 1:6).

6:16 I will be with you was God's promise of His presence. This should have greatly encouraged Gideon, but he still expressed doubts (vv. 17, 36–40).

6:17, 18 Gideon's faith needed such bolstering that he asked God for **a sign.** Here as elsewhere, Gideon was slow to respond to God (vv. 39, 40).

6:19–21 An ephah of flour was two-thirds of a bushel, or about 20 pounds of flour.

6:22, 23 Gideon perceived: When the Angel of the Lord vanished, Gideon realized who it was and feared for his life. This reaction of fear appears to have been rooted in the knowledge that anyone who gazed upon God would die. Gideon's fear was a proper response for those who found themselves in the presence of God's Angel. This was also Manoah's reaction when the Angel visited him (13:21, 22).

6:24 To this day: This expression lends authenticity to the account. It is the author's way of declaring to later generations that they could verify the story by going and seeing this altar themselves. **Abiezrites** were descendants of Joseph through his son Manasseh.

6:25 The Hebrew word for **wooden image** here is Asherah, the name of the Canaanite goddess. Wooden poles were erected at places where she was worshiped. **The second bull** is a phrase by which the Lord was specifying more clearly to Gideon which bull should be sacrificed.

6:26, 27 The wood of the image: The proper sacrifice that Gideon was to offer would be burned with the wood of the destroyed idol.

6:28 The phrase **early in the morning** occurs in Judges at 6:28, 38; 7:1; 9:33; 19:5, 8, 9; 21:4.

6:29–31 Would you plead for Baal: Joash refused to put his son to death, arguing that Baal should be able to take care of himself if he were indeed a god.

6:32–34 Gideon's father **called him Jerubbaal** to deride those who would put their trust in Baal. The name means "Let Baal Plead," so Gideon became a living reminder of Baal's impotence.

6:35 Gideon sent messengers through the four northern tribes adjacent to each other: Manasseh, Asher, Zebulun, and Naphtali.

6:36–39 Let me test: The word translated *test* is the same one used when God tested Israel (2:22; 3:1). Gideon himself was aware that he was doing something unwise, since he asked God not to be angry with him.

6:40 God did so that night. That is, He accommodated both of Gideon's requests. Many people have relied on Gideon's example as a way seeking guidance from the Lord, "putting out a fleece" in some way. Gideon already knew God's will for his life.

7:1, 2 lest Israel claim glory for itself: Right from the beginning, God made it clear that the glory for this victory was to be His.

7:3 When Gideon allowed those soldiers who were **fearful** to leave, more than two-thirds departed, leaving only ten thousand.

7:4–9 Gideon thinned his army even more by using a strange distinction—how his men drank water from a brook. The reference to the way **a dog laps** might even be derogatory since dogs were despised creatures in the ancient world.

7:10, 11 Ironically, Gideon himself was afraid, but he had not been dismissed to go home as had the other men (v. 3).

7:12 This verse notes again the strength of Israel's enemies, including their intimidating numbers and their innumerable camels (6:3–5).

7:13 Tumbled in this context literally means "overturned." Here, the loaf "overturned" the Midianite camp.

7:14, 15 The sword of Gideon is the key to the interpretation of the dream. It provided the confirmation that Gideon needed. As a result, **he worshiped** God.

7:16–18 The ram's-horn **trumpet** was used as a signal call.

7:19 middle watch: The nighttime hours were divided into three watches, which put the time of this attack at 10:00 P.M.

7:20–22 The sword of the LORD and of Gideon: A more literal rendering of the Hebrew is "A sword for the Lord and for Gideon!"

7:23 The tribes mentioned in 6:35 now pursued the Midianites, with the exception of Zebulun, which is not mentioned. Ephraim also joined in the pursuit (v. 24).

7:24, 25 The watering places probably refers to small tributaries that flowed into the Jordan River. Seizing them would seal off the enemy's escape routes. **The other side of the Jordan** is the east side of the Jordan River, where the Israelites caught the enemy (Josh. 13:32; 18:7).

8:1–3 The men of Ephraim complained to Gideon that they had been called out late (v. 1). Gideon's flattering response had a calming effect on these men.

8:4–10 Zebah and Zalmunna are unflattering names meaning "Victim" and "Protection Refused."

8:11, 12 Gideon's aggression contrasts sharply with the caution and fear so evident in ch. 6.

8:13, 14 he wrote down for him the leaders: Their writing systems were complex and only a tiny portion of the population could read and write. However, the spread of alphabetic systems vastly simplified the task of reading and writing. Even a youth whom Gideon happened upon wrote down for Gideon the names of 77 men.

8:15–18 The killings to which Gideon refers do not appear anywhere else in the text. The answer from the two kings was flattering: **As you are, so were they.** They compared Gideon to the son of a king.

8:19–21 As a man is, so is his strength was a challenge to Gideon's manhood, and Gideon responded by killing the two kings himself. **Crescent ornaments** are mentioned again only one other time in the Bible (Is. 3:18).

8:22 Immediately Gideon's men asked him to **rule over** them. This request failed to

acknowledge that it was God, not Gideon, who had delivered His people.

8:23 Gideon's answer was theologically correct: **the LORD shall rule over you.** The word order of the Hebrew makes it clear that God's claim was exclusive; it might be paraphrased, "It is the Lord, and no one else, who shall rule over you." When the people of Israel asked Gideon to rule because of his military success, Gideon could only refuse, since their motivation was flawed and short-sighted.

8:24–28 The total weight of the offerings brought for making the ephod—**one thousand seven hundred shekels**—was impressive. Assuming the unit of weight here to be the shekel (it is not specified in the Hebrew text), the total weight was more than 42 pounds of gold (a shekel was about two-fifths of an ounce). The original **ephod** was an ornate ceremonial garment worn by the high priest (Ex. 28; 39).

8:29–32 Although Gideon had seventy sons (v. 30), only **Abimelech** is mentioned by name. The name means "My Father Is King."

8:33–35 Baal-Berith means "Baal of the Covenant," an ironic contrast to the covenant God of Israel whom the Israelites should have been worshiping.

9:1–6 Abimelech killed his own brothers to strengthen his royal claims. **The temple of Baal-Berith** was a pagan sanctuary, a vivid sign of Israel's continuing apostasy (8:33). **worthless and reckless men:** Abimelech's character can certainly be judged by the company that he kept.

9:7–21 Jotham, the only brother of Abimelech who escaped, condemned Abimelech's treachery publicly by telling a fable. In this fable, the noble trees of the forest reject a call to kingship, which is finally conferred on the lowly bramble bush (vv. 8–15). **let fire come:** Jotham issued a warning to the people of Shechem—fire would devour them and Abimelech too if they had not acted properly. The threat was fulfilled when fire devoured a large number of Shechemites and Abimelech was killed by a Shechemite woman (vv. 49, 54).

9:22, 23 A spirit of ill will can be translated literally "an evil spirit." The only other person in

Scripture whose affliction is described with these words is Saul.

9:24–38 Where indeed is your mouth now is Zebul's challenge to Gaal, taunting him to back up the boastful words he had uttered earlier (v. 28).

9:39–43 Interestingly, Abimelech divided his forces into **three companies** to attack Shechem.

9:44, 45 Sowing Shechem **with salt** turned it into a barren, uninhabitable desert.

9:46, 47 the temple of the god Berith: The "god Berith" means El-Berith, the Baal-Berith named in 8:33.

9:48–52 The location of **Mount Zalmon** is uncertain. The snow-covered Mount Zalmon mentioned in Ps. 68:14 appears to be a different place.

9:53 an upper millstone: Mills used for grinding grain were typically made with two large stones. The upper one was moved back and forth or rotated on the lower one, and the grain was ground between them. An upper millstone would have easily crushed Abimelech's skull, as this verse asserts.

9:54, 55 kill me: Being killed by a woman was a disgrace to a warrior.

9:56, 57 God actively intervened against Abimelech, repaying his evil act of murdering his brothers. Note that his sin was murder (v. 56), not declaring himself king.

10:1, 2 Tola was the sixth judge, the second of the minor judges. He arose to **save** Israel after the reign of Abimelech.

10:3–5 Jair was the seventh judge, the third minor judge, and he judged Israel for 22 years. He was rather well off (v. 4), and he lived in Gilead, east of the Jordan River, as would the next judge, Jephthah (11:1).

thirty donkeys ... thirty towns: Literally, the Hebrew has "thirty donkeys ... thirty donkeys." The word used here for *donkeys* is an unusual one that resembles the Hebrew word for *towns*. A later scribe mistakenly repeated the word for donkey.

10:6 The gods of Syria ... Sidon ... Moab ... Ammon ... the Philistines demonstrate the extent of Israel's idolatry. Not only did the people worship the major Canaanite gods (Baal, Asherah, Ashtoreth), but they also absorbed the religions of other groups. Seven gods are mentioned here, a symbolic number that forms a counterpoint to the seven nations mentioned in vv. 11, 12.

10:7–10 The Philistines and the people of Ammon were the Israelites' principal adversaries at this time. The next two major judges—Jephthah and Samson—were God's instruments against these two groups, Jephthah against the Ammonites and Samson against the Philistines.

10:11, 12 In these two verses, we find seven peoples from whom God had already delivered the Israelites. **Egyptians:** God had dramatically saved Israel from Egyptian oppression (Ex. 14; 15). **Amorites:** God had rescued His people from Sihon and Og, kings of the Amorites (Josh. 2:10). **Ammon:** The Ammonites had been part of a coalition under Eglon, whom Ehud defeated (3:13). **Philistines:** Shamgar had already won a victory over the Philistines (3:31). **Sidonians:** There is no record of a previous triumph, but these people were among Israel's oppressors. **Amalekites:** They had already opposed the Israelites in the time of the judges (3:13; 6:3), and their enmity with Israel went back much further (Ex. 17:8–16). The **Maonites** appear later in Israel's history as adversaries (2 Chr. 20:1; 26:7 [Meunites]), but they are not mentioned earlier. Possibly what is meant is the Midianites, a people who had been defeated by Gideon (chs. 7; 8).

10:13, 14 The gods which you have chosen is a response of confrontation. When Israel cried out to God, He reminded them again of their faithless ways. Other examples in Judges of confrontation include the Angel's indictment (2:1–5) and the prophet's message (6:7–10).

10:15–18 Not only is God a God of great justice; He is a God of great mercy, as the phrase **His soul could no longer endure the misery of Israel** reminds us. Despite their constant sinning and backsliding, God still loved the Israelites and shared their misery.

11:1–3 Jephthah was from Gilead. He was a "mighty man of valor," but he was illegitimate, which caused his half brothers to expel him from his father's house. The territory of

Gilead was in northern Transjordan (Josh. 17:1, 3; 5:17). The **Gileadites** were descended from a man named Gilead. In this passage and in Josh. 17:1, 3, the term refers both to a region and a person.

11:4–7 Come and be our commander: Here we see a leader for Israel being commissioned by the people. God is given little place in the proceedings other than to confirm the choice (v. 10), another sign of spiritual deterioration.

11:8, 9 That you may go with us and fight is almost the same phrase that the Israelites used when they asked Samuel for a king in 1 Sam. 8:20.

11:10 The LORD will be a witness: Literally, "The Lord will be listening." God is called to be a witness to the covenant agreement (1 Sam. 20:12).

11:11 The people made Jephthah **head and commander** because he had demanded somewhat opportunistically to be their "head" as the price for helping them as "commander," so in the end he was made both. Jephthah's **words before the LORD** are a strange mixture of faith and foolishness. While Jephthah did acknowledge God here and later (11:21, 23, 27, 30, 31; 12:3), his self-interest and foolishness often overruled his faith.

11:12–22 In this speech, Jephthah's verbal gifts are readily apparent. **Israel took away my land:** The Ammonites claimed that Israel had taken their land. Jephthah responded with a careful rebuttal. He declared that **the LORD God of Israel** Himself had dispossessed these peoples (vv. 21, 23, 24) and that Israel was not an aggressor but just a recipient of the Lord's generosity.

11:23, 24 Whatever Chemosh your god gives you was a derisive jab at the Ammonites' deity. Jephthah's point was that Israel's God had given His people much territory, whereas Chemosh, the god of the Ammonites, had done very little for them.

11:25, 26 Three hundred years may be an approximation, but it still gives us an important clue for determining the date of the Exodus and understanding how long the period of the judges lasted.

11:27, 28 the LORD, the Judge: This is the only place in the Book of Judges where a single individual is specifically called a judge. Significantly, it is a name of God. He ultimately was—and is—the source of all justice. He has the right to judge every man and woman.

11:29–34 Some have interpreted Jephthah's vow **whatever comes out of the doors** as a clear intention to offer a human sacrifice. His surprise then is not that he had to sacrifice a human being, but that the unfortunate person was his daughter. The phrase **to meet me** seems to refer more appropriately to a human than to an animal. Undoubtedly, Jephthah knew that human sacrifice was strictly forbidden in Israel but his foolishness caused him to make a reckless vow.

11:35 I have given my word is literally "I have opened my mouth." But did Jephthah have to follow through on his vow? Ordinarily the answer would be yes. Vows were made only to God, and they were solemn pledges that had to be kept.

11:36–40 The text does not explicitly say that he killed his daughter, only that **he carried out his vow.** When the verse goes on to say that **she knew no man,** some take this to mean that she was "sacrificed" by being dedicated to a life of perpetual virginity. Until the wicked reigns of Ahaz and Manasseh centuries later (2 Kin. 16:3; 21:6), there is no record of human sacrifice in Israel. The great respect that Jephthah had for God surely would have prevented him from making such a perverse offering. And the fact that Jephthah permitted his daughter to bewail her virginity (vv. 37, 38) for two months fits an explanation of perpetual virginity better than human sacrifice. In ancient Israelite society, the father had the power to prohibit a daughter to marry. The conjunction in Jephthah's pivotal statement in v. 31, that whatever or whoever came out of the door "shall be the LORD's, *and* I will offer it up as a burnt offering" could be translated *or.* Thus, if a person came out first, he would dedicate that person to the Lord, or if an animal came out first, he would offer the animal as a burnt sacrifice.

12:1–4 The tribe of Ephraim sulks because they were left out of the battle. **You Gileadites are fugitives of Ephraim:** This is the taunt that triggers the civil war. The insult may have its roots in the division of the nation into eastern and western groups.

12:5 The fords of the Jordan were crossing points of strategic military value.

12:6, 7 Shibboleth … Sibboleth: This test devised by the Gileadites to catch the Ephraimites is the most famous example in the Bible of linguistic differences between the tribes. Today the English word *shibboleth* means an otherwise minor difference that becomes a sticking point because it distinguishes one side from another.

12:8–10 Ibzan was Israel's ninth judge. He allowed his 30 sons and 30 daughters to marry foreigners (v. 9).

12:11, 12 Elon was the tenth judge.

12:13–15 Abdon was the eleventh judge, and like Jair and Ibzan had many children. He also possessed some wealth (vv. 13–15).

13:1, 2 Zorah was in the foothills west of Jerusalem, near Philistine territory, in the lowlands that separated the Philistine plain from the hill country of Judah. Manoah, Samson's father, was from the tribe of Dan, in whose territory Zorah lay (Josh. 19:41). Zorah is also mentioned among the inheritance of Judah (Josh. 15:33), indicating that it was along the border between the two tribes.

13:3 The Angel of the LORD made a supernatural appearance, described here as "very awesome" (v. 6). Manoah's wife recognized him as "a Man of God" (v. 6).

13:4, 5 The Angel declared that the woman's son should be a **Nazirite** from the womb and for the rest of his life. The regulations of the Nazirite vows are found in Num. 6:1–21 and included three provisions: (1) abstinence from wine, strong drink, and the fruit of the vine; (2) not cutting the hair; and

 IN DEPTH The Philistines

The conflict between the Israelites and the Philistines that preceded the birth of Samson (Judg. 13:1) was one of many between the two peoples throughout biblical history. Probably no other group was as much a thorn in the side of the Israelites as their neighbors along the southwestern Mediterranean Coast in the land known as Philistia.

It is hard to say for sure where the Philistines originated. They were descendants of Noah's son Ham through his son Mizraim and grandson Casluhim (Gen. 10:13, 14). The name "Philistines" was used by the Egyptian pharaoh Ramses III to describe one of the peoples," a coalition of invaders that he repelled in a naval battle in about 1188 B.C.

The Bible regularly associates the Philistines with the land of Caphtor, believed to be Crete, and its inhabitants, the Caphtorim (1 Chr. 1:12; Jer. 47:4; Amos 9:7). This is consistent with the view that as the Greeks moved into the Aegean area beginning in about 1500 B.C., the Philistines and other "sea peoples" migrated south and east. Some eventually settled on the southwestern coast of Canaan. Apparently this migration occurred in two waves. An early Philistine king, Abimilech of Gerar, was known to Abraham and Isaac (Gen. 20; 21; 26). By the time of the Exodus, a second wave had arrived and established five principal city-states that made up Philistia: Ekron, Ashdod, Gath, and Ashkelon, and Gaza.

Possessing weapons of iron, which were superior to those of the Israelites, the Philistines hacked away at Israelite territory after the conquest under Joshua. In fact, God used these attacks to discipline His people and to attempt to return them to the covenant (Judg. 3:1–3). But the revivals were usually short-lived. In the days of Eli the judge, the Israelites foolishly carried the ark of the covenant into battle, and the Philistines captured it (1 Sam. 4). The ark was eventually recovered, but the Philistine threat continued for centuries, right up to the fall of Jerusalem in 586 B.C.

(3) no contact with the dead (Num. 6:3–8). The announcement that **he shall begin to deliver Israel** was welcome news.

13:6–13 Man of God was a term used for prophets elsewhere in the Old Testament. At first, Samson's mother may have thought she was talking to a prophet, but His radiant appearance convinced her otherwise. Throughout this entire episode the Man of God **did not tell … His name** (vv. 16–18).

13:14, 15 The requirements for Samson's Nazirite vow were somewhat irregular (v. 5). Samson's mother was also required to observe a strict ritual (v. 4).

13:16–18 it is wonderful: The Angel's name is too wonderful to comprehend, and so He does not reveal it to Samson's parents. Immediately afterward, the Angel did a "wondrous thing" by ascending into the heavens in a flame (vv. 19, 20).

13:19–22 When Manoah discovered that it was **the Angel of the LORD,** he feared for their lives because he and his wife had **seen God.**

13:23, 24 The name **Samson** is related to the Hebrew word for *sun.* The story makes no comment on the meaning of his name

13:25 the Spirit of the LORD began to move upon him: The Hebrew verb translated *move* can also be translated *impel.* The Spirit of the Lord was pushing Samson toward doing the work that God wanted him to do (14:4). The verb here is different from the one in 14:6 that is translated *came mightily.*

14:1 Timnah was a town on the northwest border of Judah (Josh. 15:10) and was counted in the allotment of the tribe of Dan (Josh. 19:43). By Samson's day it was occupied by the Philistines.

14:2, 3 The Philistines were Israel's neighbors but were almost always at war with them. **She pleases me well** is literally "she is right in my eyes." Samson's words revealed his self-centered attitude. Instead of seeking to serve God, he was seeking to please himself.

14:4 The narrator adds that Samson's parents **did not know that it was of the LORD.** God would use Samson's defiant wish as a way of defeating the Philistines and providing relief for His people.

14:5–7 the Spirit of the LORD came mightily upon him: The Old Testament speaks numerous times of God's Spirit coming mightily upon individuals, usually to empower them physically for great feats of strength.

14:8, 9 Touching the dead lion violated Samson's Nazirite vow (13:5).

14:10, 11 The word translated **feast** denotes a banquet with considerable drinking, another violation of Samson's Nazirite vow (13:5).

14:12, 13 In Hebrew the words **let me pose a riddle to you** literally reads "let me riddle you a riddle," using repetition to grab the reader's attention. The Hebrew word for **linen garments** is not the usual word for clothes, but appears only three times in the Bible. In Prov. 31:24; Is. 3:23, it refers to fine linens worn or sold by women. Samson's offer was extravagant given the value of such finery.

14:14 This is the best example of a riddle in the Scriptures.

14:15–17 Samson's wife pleaded with him for **seven days** to tell her the secret of the riddle, knowing the threat she faced from the young men.

14:18 Samson's statement expresses his outrage that the men had not played fairly with him but had consulted his wife.

14:19 Ashkelon was one of the five main cities of the Philistines.

14:20 his companion … his best man: The Hebrew words here are the same, meaning "friend."

15:1–3 The time of wheat harvest was late May or early June. The wheat harvest was associated with the second of the three great festivals in Israel, the Feast of Weeks, also known as Pentecost.

15:4 The **three hundred foxes** were probably jackals, the same Hebrew word is used for both. Foxes are solitary animals, but jackals travel in packs and large numbers of them could be caught more easily.

15:5 the shocks and the standing grain: Shocks are bundles of wheat stacked together in the fields. Samson's jackals burned whole crops of grain, grapes, and olives. This damage outraged the Philistines.

15:6 the Philistines ... burned her: The Philistines held Samson's wife and father-in-law responsible for the deed and killed them both. Samson's wife had earlier escaped such a death by telling Samson's companions the answer to a riddle (14:15).

15:7, 8 The exact meaning of the phrase **he attacked them hip and thigh** is obscure. The following phrase—**with a great slaughter**—perhaps gets us closer to the meaning, suggesting that he not only killed but dismembered them.. **Etam** is otherwise unknown, but Samson obviously found a secure place to hide, perhaps a cave that was accessible only through a narrow fissure in the rocky crags near Zorah.

15:9–13 two new ropes: Ropes were made of leather, hair, or plant fibers; one common fiber was flax (Josh. 2:6). The reference in v. 14 to the ropes becoming like burned flax suggests that this was the fiber. Being new, these ropes were the strongest possible.

15:14, 15 A fresh jawbone would have been tough, resilient, and virtually unbreakable.

15:16–20 Heaps upon heaps is a word-play, since the Hebrew word for *heaps* resembles the word for *donkey.*

16:1 Gaza is one of the five major Philistine cities, three miles inland from the Mediterranean coast. **a harlot:** a common prostitute, such as the one Samson was consorting with.

16:2 At the gate reads literally "in the gate." The Philistines waited in the recesses of the gate, hoping to trap Samson. He evidently slipped through unnoticed while they waited in one of the rooms.

16:3 Given the large size of city gates, Samson's feat was astounding. Samson's trip to the top of a hill that **faces Hebron** would have taken the better part of a day.

16:4 Delilah was the third Philistine woman that Samson entangled himself with (14:1; 16:1).

16:5, 6 Eleven hundred pieces of silver was a large sum of money. This price was multiplied by five (each of the five lords offered the same amount). The total reward probably weighed more than a hundred pounds.

16:7, 8 The first test of Samson's strength was breaking **seven fresh bowstrings** of animal gut. Samson was showing contempt for his adversaries, who wanted to capture him quickly.

16:9–11 In this second test, Samson toyed with the Philistines, suggesting they use the **new ropes** that had proven worthless on an earlier occasion (15:13).

16:12, 13 The third test involving **the web of the loom** got closer to revealing Samson's secret, since his hair was involved. The loom that held Samson's hair was likely an upright one, supported by two posts that were firmly anchored in the ground. This was a more difficult test of strength for Samson, but he passed this one easily as well.

16:14, 15 she wove it tightly Samson was able to free himself in this case, but he eventually would fall victim to a woman's plot.

16:16 Delilah **pestered him,** just as Samson's wife had done earlier (14:17).

16:17, 18 A **razor** in Samson's day would have been like a bronze knife with a handle of wood or bone. **a Nazirite to God:** See 13:5. **he had told her all his heart:** Delilah knew that Samson was finally telling the truth. This reference contrasts with the one in v. 15, where he withheld his heart from Delilah.

16:19–22 the LORD had departed from him: See 14:6. They shackled Samson's hands or feet with a pair of **bronze fetters.** Samson became **a grinder,** forced to grind grain, most likely with a hand mill.

16:23–25 Dagon was the principal Philistine god. Dagon was once commonly thought to be a fish god, but modern excavations have shown that he was a god of grain.

16:26, 27 the pillars which support the temple: Numerous temples from this era with the supporting pillars described here have been excavated. Many were built around a courtyard. The roof, supported by the pillars, was where the spectators gathered.

16:28–30 Samson demonstrated faith in calling upon God and in believing that God would help him..Yet Samson's plea was basically a desire for revenge against the Philistines.

16:31 The story of the judges concludes with final editorial comments. Samson, the last judge, had been empowered by God's Spirit, just as the first had been. Despite the manifold failings of the judges themselves, God had delivered Israel and caused other nations to bow before Him.

17:1–3 Micah, an Ephraimite, had stolen some silver from his mother, which he later returned to her. We learn that she had dedicated this silver to the Lord, but returned it to Micah so that he could make **a carved image and a molded image.**

17:4, 5 a shrine: Literally "a house of God." This was a perversion of the true sanctuary where all worship was to take place. At this time, "the house of God" was at Shiloh (18:31). Micah also made an **ephod** (8:27) and various household idols. Micah further violated the law by appointing his own son as his private priest. Micah sinned because his son had not descended from Aaron nor was he even a Levite.

17:6–8 what was right in his own eyes: This editorial comment is echoed in the last verse of the book (21:25).

17:9 The **Levite from Bethlehem in Judah** had been living there as a resident alien. Levites did not have a permanent land inheritance, but they had been granted 48 cities, scattered throughout the other tribes' territories (Josh. 21). However, Bethlehem was not one of these cities, and this Levite was seeking a place to settle down. He was glad to accept Micah's offer (vv. 10, 11).

17:10–13 be a father and a priest to me: To be called a father was a title of honor. Micah wanted the Levite to be his priest, since his priestly background would lend legitimacy to his service. Micah thought this would bring him God's favor (v. 13).

18:1 The **Danites** were looking for a place to settle because they had been unable to settle effectively in their allotted territory. Compare their allotment in Josh. 19:41–47 and their failure to capture it all in 1:34, 35.

18:2 The Danites decided **to spy out the land.** The Hebrew word for *spy* is related to the word for *foot,* the idea being that spies went quietly on foot, scouting what they could see.

18:3 The Danite spies asked rapid-fire questions. Other places in Judges feature similar quick questioning (see 6:31).

18:4–7 The Danite spies found the city of **Laish** an attractive place to live and decided to seize it (vv. 7–10). The city was later renamed Dan (Josh. 19:47).

18:8–14 Six hundred men was either a small part of the Danite army or a remnant that had survived recent fighting.

18:15–20 The Danites took the gods for themselves. The Danites' offer to Micah's Levite—**be a father and a priest to us**—was the same plea Micah had made earlier (17:10). Yet their offer was more attractive, for it allowed him to be priest over an entire tribe.

18:21–30 King Jeroboam I of Israel would establish idolatrous shrines in Dan and Bethel (1 Kin. 12).

18:31 Micah's image remained while the house of God was at Shiloh. Therefore, these events took place some time before about 1050 B.C. when Shiloh was destroyed (Ps. 78:60; Jer. 7:12, 14; 26:6).

19:1, 2 A concubine was a female servant regarded as part of the family, often chosen to bear children. Several of the patriarchs had children with concubines: Abraham with Hagar (Gen. 16); Jacob with Bilhah and Zilpah (Gen. 30:4–13).

19:3–9 Obliged by custom, the Levite stayed in the home of his concubine's father for five days.

19:10, 11 Jebus (that is, Jerusalem): The city of Jerusalem was at this time in the hands of the Jebusites, and it is called "a city of foreigners" in v. 12.

19:12–14 Gibeah was four miles west of Jerusalem. Because it was in Benjamin, the Levite thought it would be a safer place to spend the night—a fatal misjudgment.

19:15–17 The open square of the city was a public area just inside the city gate. A traveler could expect an invitation to stay the night, but none was forthcoming from any inhabitant of Gibeah. **an old man:** The Levite received kindness from an outsider, an old man who was passing through Gibeah.

19:18–21 The people of Gibeah were cold, even though the Levite had all that he needed with him, and even more than enough. He offered to take care of the old man and his servants, too.

19:22–26 That we may know him means that the men of Gibeah wanted to sodomize the Levite. The same expression is found in Gen. 19:5, where the men of Sodom wanted to force homosexual relations on Lot's guests.

19:27–29 The Levite's indifferent reaction to his concubine's collapse is followed by a gruesome deed. After carrying her away, he cut her body into twelve pieces, sending a piece to each tribe. This gesture was practically a call to arms; Saul did the same with oxen (1 Sam. 11:7).

19:30 The phrase **no such deed has been done** is ambiguous; it is uncertain whether they were horrified by discovering the dismembered body or by learning about the cruel rape and murder.

20:1 From Dan to Beersheba is a common expression for the full extent of the land of Israel from north to south (1 Sam. 3:20; 2 Sam. 24:2; 1 Kin. 4:25).

20:2–8 The assembly usually means the congregation of Israel as assembled for a religious event (Chr. 28:8) or a military campaign (Num. 22:4; 1 Sam. 17:47).

20:9–14 The tribes agreed to send a tenth of their men (v. 10), choosing them **by lot.** God's role is not mentioned here. To their credit, the Israelite tribes were **united together as one man,** a quality notably absent up to this point in the Book of Judges.

20:15 The Benjamite force of **twenty-six thousand men** was considerably smaller than the Israelite army of four hundred thousand (v. 17).

20:16, 17 The Benjamites counted on **seven hundred select men who were left-handed,** an advantage since their shots would come from unaccustomed angles.

20:18–20 Judah first: The book begins and ends with Judah in this prominent position (1:1, 2).

20:21–25 Go up against him: The Lord graciously answered the Israelites twice when they called upon Him (v. 18).

20:26, 27 The Israelites suffered a second major defeat (v. 25). The result drove them to fasting and sacrificing at Bethel, something done very rarely in this period. **The house of God** literally reads "Bethel," and probably the town is meant. Bethel was a Benjamite town that had been religiously prominent since Jacob met God there (Gen. 28:16–19).

20:28–30 Phinehas was the one who had stopped the plague at Peor (Num. 25:6–11). The fact that he was still alive shows that the organization of the Book of Judges is not strictly chronological.

20:31–34 The highways were probably made of stone or gravel. The Hebrew word means "something raised," that is, a roadway elevated above the normal ground level (Is. 49:11).

20:35–37 The LORD defeated Benjamin as punishment for the heinous crimes committed in Gibeah (ch. 19) and for disrupting Israel's unity, which He valued.

20:38–46 The burning of Gibeah and the resulting rout of the Benjamites are almost an exact replay of the ambush of Ai (Josh. 8:17–22).

20:47, 48 Six hundred men of Benjamin survived the rout. They would become the remnant that would carry on the tribe's name (21:12–23).

21:1–4 The details of an **oath at Mizpah** appear for the first time. It was presumably made when the people assembled at Mizpah before attacking Benjamin.

21:5–7 The **great oath** sworn by the Israelites provided the justification for punishing Jabesh Gilead and for providing wives for the Benjamites. Every tribe was expected to heed the Levite's call, since he had sent the concubine's corpse "throughout all the territory of Israel" (19:29).

21:8 Jabesh Gilead was a town east of the Jordan River.

21:9–11 The phrase **utterly destroy** is found numerous times in the Book of Joshua in regard to the conquest of the Canaanites. However, there is no hint that God supported the bloodbath at Jabesh Gilead.

21:12–14 Four hundred young virgins were captured to become wives for the six hundred survivors of Benjamin (20:47). Still, four hundred were not enough, and the Israelites contrived to take more from Shiloh (vv. 19–22).

21:15–19 Some scholars believe that the **yearly feast of the LORD in Shiloh** was the Passover, held in the spring because of the dancing associated with it (vv. 21, 23). They point to the dancing of Miriam and the Israelite women after they had crossed the Red Sea as evidence for this practice (Ex. 15:20). However, the celebration was more likely the Feast of Tabernacles, celebrated in the fall, since vineyards are mentioned (vv. 20, 21). The grape harvest came in the early fall.

21:20–23 The Benjamites were allowed to abduct enough women from Shiloh to supply every man with a wife. No justification is given except for the supposed needs of the Benjamites. To sidestep their oath, Israelites allowed the Benjamites to capture the young women. In this way, they could not be held responsible for giving brides to the six hundred, which they swore at Mizpah they would never do (v. 1).

21:24, 25 every man to his inheritance: The Hebrew words here are the same as those found at the end of the Book of Joshua (24:28). However, the book's final comment (v. 25) indicates that times were far worse than they had been in Joshua's day.

Ruth

Introduction

The Book of Ruth is a beautiful story of love, loyalty, and redemption. It tells the story of the salvation of Ruth, the Moabitess. Through her relationship with her mother-in-law Naomi, Ruth learned about the living God and became His devoted follower. Abandoning her family and homeland, she demonstrated both her love for her widowed mother-in-law and her faith in Israel's God.

Traditionally, Samuel has been identified as the author of Ruth. The story of Ruth takes place during the time of the judges—a period characterized by extreme spiritual and moral decay in Israel (c. 1380–1050 B.C.). The beautiful love story of Ruth contrasts strongly with the pervasive depravity of the period, giving a rare glimmer of hope in an otherwise bleak era.

The Book of Ruth underscores an overarching theme of the Bible: God desires all to believe in Him, even non-Israelites. This was God's plan from the beginning. He had covenanted with Abraham and his descendants in order to bless other nations through the Israelites and draw all nations to Himself (Gen. 12:1–3).

Dying without an heir was considered a tragedy in the ancient Middle East. To rectify this situation, the brother of a deceased man was expected to marry the widow in order to produce a child, who would be considered the heir of the deceased. This was called a levirate marriage. Boaz willingly took on this duty, even though he was not the nearest relative (3:12, 13). He bought the land from Naomi, married Ruth, and carried on the family name through the birth of their son. Through all these actions, Boaz exemplified the compassion and love of a redeemer. His life is an illustration for us of the compassion of Jesus, who is our Redeemer (Gal. 3:13).

1:1 when the judges ruled: The events of Ruth took place before the establishment of the monarchy in Israel. The story of Ruth

---

 IN DEPTH   **Can Anything Good Come from Moab?**

The name "Moab" (Ruth 1:1) recalls two unpleasant incidents: the birth of Moab and the trouble his descendants caused Israel during their wilderness journey to the Promised Land. Moab was born in the aftermath of Sodom and Gomorrah. Lot fled Sodom with his family and, in effect, took the sin from the city with him into the wilderness. His wife disobeyed God's instructions and was turned into a pillar of salt (Gen. 19:26). Lot's daughters plotted to get their father drunk so that he might commit incest with them and father their children. One daughter gave birth to Moab, the other to Ammon (Gen. 19:30–38). In time, their descendants grew into rival nations that have contended with Israel to this day.

One of the most grievous offenses that Moab committed occurred during Israel's wilderness wanderings. The king of Moab attempted to hire Balaam the seer to curse the Israelites, but Balaam eventually blessed them instead (Num. 22—24). However, the seer came up with a plan to seduce God's people into idolatry by sending Moabite women to entice them. The plan worked and 24,000 people died as a result. Thus the Law prohibited a Moabite or Ammonite from ever becoming a member of the Israelite community (Deut. 23:3).

But the question raised by the opening of the Book of Ruth—can anything good come from Moab?—is a resounding yes! From Moab comes Ruth, and from Ruth, Obed; from Obed comes Jesse, then David (Ruth 4:18–22); and through David comes Jesus Christ (Matt. 1:1, 5, 6).

shines as a bright spot during a dark age in Israel's history. **Moab** is located east of the Dead Sea. The Moabites descended from Lot as a result of his incestuous relation with his older daughter (Gen. 19:30–37).

1:2, 3 Because of the famine, **Elimelech,** whose name means "God Is King," journeyed to Moab with his wife and two sons. The names of the two sons **Mahlon** and **Chilion** mean "Sickly" and "Failing." The early deaths of these two sons in Moab showed that their names were appropriate (v. 5). **Ephrathites:** Ephrathah was another name for the region of Bethlehem (Gen. 48:7; Mic. 5:2).

1:4, 5 The Moabite name **Ruth** connotes "Friendship." While the law of Moses did not prohibit Israelite men from marrying Moabite women, it did exclude Moabites from the congregation of Israel for ten generations (Deut. 23:1–4).

1:6, 7 the LORD: God Himself is at the center of the book.

1:8 The Hebrew word translated as **kindly** is often used to describe God, and means "loyal love." Here Naomi expressed the hope that the Lord's covenantal love would extend to her daughters-in-law, who were outside the land of Israel and were not Jewish.

1:9 The concept of **rest** referred to here is the security that is found in marriage.

1:10–13 Naomi's daughters-in-law insisted on returning with her. Naomi pointed out that she could not provide husbands for them and expressed concern for their happiness. **grieves:** Naomi was bitter that she was without husband and sons and attributed her circumstances to God's discipline.

1:14 In this verse, the responses of **Orpah** and **Ruth** are contrasted. Orpah did the expected thing and returned home. Yet Ruth unexpectedly stayed with her impoverished mother-in-law. Ruth's action brought her into the Messiah's family line (4:18–22).

1:15 Naomi tried one last time to convince Ruth to return to Moab. The word for **gods** refers to the deities of Moab.

1:16, 17 In a beautiful, emotionally charged poetic response, Ruth described her determination to remain with Naomi. Her assertion that Naomi's God would be her God is

especially striking. This is an affirmation of faith in the Lord, the God of Israel. Ruth's use of the divine name Yahweh translated as **the LORD** in an oath indicates her commitment to the living God. She was choosing to cling not only to Naomi, her land, and her people, but also to her God.

1:18–20 Naomi wanted her name to reflect her bitterness over her circumstances so she named herself **Mara,** meaning "Bitter."

1:21 The concepts of fullness and emptiness appear here. Naomi left for Moab complete, with a husband and two sons. But now she returned to Bethlehem **empty.**

1:22 Ruth the Moabitess: As the story explains, God extended His protection to Ruth even though she was a foreigner. Ruth and Naomi arrived at **the beginning of barley harvest.** Barley was the first crop to ripen, and this period would be the beginning of the harvest season.

2:1 Boaz was related to Naomi's husband, **Elimelech.** As a relative, Boaz could stand up for the rights of these two women. He was described as **a man of great wealth,** a person of noble character and of high standing in the community. The name Boaz probably means "Swift Strength."

2:2 The law of Moses allowed the poor to **glean** in the farmers' fields (Lev. 23:22).

2:3–6 happened to come: Though Ruth did not intentionally go to the field of Boaz, the Lord providentially directed her steps.

2:7 Ruth was not presumptuous here but in gentleness asked for a favor that she might have claimed as an entitlement.

2:8, 9 Boaz demonstrated extraordinary concern for Ruth's provision and protection. He even thought of Ruth's need for water in the heat of the day.

2:10–12 Boaz explained that he favored Ruth because she had shown "loyal love" to her mother-in-law, Naomi. He then gave her a blessing, asking that God would abundantly **reward** Ruth for her remarkable loyalty.

2:13 Now Ruth called herself the **maidservant** of Boaz. She no longer called herself a foreigner as she had in v. 10.

2:14–16 Boaz repeatedly demonstrated God's compassion toward the Moabite woman. Boaz went beyond the letter of the Law. He not only let Ruth **glean;** he also amply supplied her with food.

2:17–19 The amount of **barley** that Ruth gleaned was more than half a bushel, more than would normally be expected for a day's work. The generosity of Boaz and the labor of Ruth produced this substantial supply.

2:20–23 Naomi praised the Lord for His **kindness,** His "loyal love." God had not abandoned Ruth and Naomi. Instead, He had faithfully provided for their needs.

3:1 Once again, Naomi returned to the subject of **security** or rest, which she addressed in 1:9. In the first instance, she had asked God to provide her daughters-in-law the "rest" of marriage. Now she was determined to seek this rest for Ruth.

3:2 The **threshing floor** was located in a public place. Boaz had to stay the night to guard his grain from thieves.

3:3 best garment: This probably referred to an outer garment that Ruth wore to keep warm in the night. **eating and drinking:** Festivity accompanied the end of the harvest.

3:4–6 uncover his feet: Ruth would remove the edge of Boaz's outer garment from his feet and lie down by his uncovered feet. Touching and holding his feet was an act of submission. This action would call for a decision on his part to be her protector—and, likely, her husband.

3:7, 8 Ruth came **softly,** that is, secretly, so that no one would see her. That she came at night was also a means of protecting Boaz from embarrassment in case he decided not to exercise his duty as a close relative.

3:9 your wing: Ruth used the same word that Boaz used in reference to God in 2:12. The final phrase, **for you are a close relative,** shows that she was seeking his refuge in the sense of requesting him as her marriage partner. Since her husband had died without giving her a child, it was the responsibility of a close relative to marry her in order to provide an heir for her deceased husband.

3:10, 11 Boaz understood that Ruth was making a marriage proposal and praised her for not seeking younger men to marry. He knew that Ruth's initiative was in keeping with the Law. A levirate marriage would provide her deceased husband with an heir (Deut. 25:5–10).

3:12 The suspense in the narrative increases when Boaz announces that there is a **relative closer than** he. The nearest relative would have the opportunity to carry out that responsibility first.

3:13 Boaz wanted to take immediate responsibility for Ruth and Naomi, so he asked her to **stay** with him so she would not be exposed to any danger by returning to her home in the middle of the night. The statement **as the LORD lives** reinforces the resolve of Boaz to take responsibility for Ruth.

3:14 before one could recognize another: Ruth left at early dawn, in order to avoid anyone who might recognize her. Boaz probably did not want anyone to misconstrue what had taken place.

3:15 Again Boaz demonstrated loyal love or kindness by his gift of barley grain to Ruth and Naomi.

3:16 Is that you: These words are possibly a comment on the radiance of the woman whose life was about to change so radically.

3:17 empty-handed: The theme of emptiness and fullness is repeated here (1:21).

3:18 Naomi was confident that Boaz would see the **matter** through to its conclusion the same day. Boaz had repeatedly demonstrated that he was an upright and compassionate man by his continuing provision for the two women.

4:1, 2 Official and legal business typically occurred at the **gate** of a city, so it was natural for Boaz to speak with the other **close relative** there in the presence of the elders of the community.

4:3 One of the duties of the **close relative** was to redeem land that had been sold by the family because of poverty. **sold:** Verse 9 states that Boaz purchased the land from Naomi.

4:4 Boaz offered the land to the closer relative first; this man initially agreed to purchase it. The Law provided for land to stay within a family, even if it had to be sold temporarily because of poverty. The seller could redeem the land later, or a close relative could redeem it. Land was not sold permanently because it ultimately belonged to God (Lev. 25:23).

4:5 To perpetuate the name of the dead makes it clear that the close relative was needed to buy the land but also to take Ruth as his wife. Here the **dead** relative was Mahlon, Ruth's husband (4:10). In carrying on the name of Mahlon, the line of Elimelech would continue.

4:6 When the close relative discovered that he was expected to marry Ruth, he declined his **right of redemption** because his **own inheritance** might be ruined.

4:7, 8 The removal of a **sandal** was part of a legal transaction in ancient Israel (Deut. 25:8–10). By handing over his shoe, the **close relative** was symbolically handing over his right to walk on the land that was being sold.

4:9 The **witnesses** at the gate played a significant role in validating the transaction. **from the hand of Naomi:** The land was bought from Elimelech's widow, Naomi.

4:10 acquired: In addition to redeeming the land, Boaz also redeemed Ruth by taking her as his wife. He willingly chose to be her redeemer.

4:11 The **people and the elders** affirmed the legal proceeding with their response, **we are witnesses.** Then the crowd gave Ruth a remarkable blessing by asking that **the LORD** make her like **Rachel and Leah,** Israel's founding mothers (Gen. 35:23–26). In this exceptional case we see a beautiful example of the spirit of the Law being maintained. Both the loyal love of Ruth and of God are demonstrated in this story. Ruth loyally loved Naomi by leaving her homeland and serving her mother-in-law even in the worst of circumstances. In turn, God rewarded Ruth by extending His loyal love to her. He gave this foreigner a godly husband, accepted her as one of His people, and gave her a child who would be an ancestor of King David and ultimately of Jesus (vv. 13, 22).

4:12 The Book of Ruth is replete with allusions to the Pentateuch. Here the name of **Tamar** refers to another story about the spirit of the Law (Gen. 38). One more woman had an experience strikingly similar to Ruth's: That woman was Rahab, the mother of Boaz (Matt. 1:5). Like Ruth, Rahab was a Gentile woman. Yet God extended His loyal love to Rahab because of her faith in Him and included her in the messianic line.

4:13 the LORD gave her conception: Children are a gift from God. He fashions every person in the womb of the mother (Ps. 139:13).

4:14, 15 Here the **close relative** is not Boaz but his newborn son, the grandson of Naomi. **The women** praised God for His provision for Naomi. They offered a blessing for the child, asking that his fame be extended throughout **Israel** and that he would comfort Naomi and nourish her in her **old age.** Naomi's emptiness had been replaced with fullness through the birth of this boy.

4:16, 17 The theme of Naomi's fullness continues to dominate as the **neighbor women** declared that a child was born to Naomi. His name was **Obed,** signifying "One Who Serves." The author at last reveals how Ruth, a Moabite woman, had become part of the royal Davidic line.

4:18–22 The story concludes with David's genealogy, beginning with **Perez,** the son of Judah and Tamar. This genealogy could have been added to the book long after the original writing was complete, but more probably the book as a whole was composed at a later date than the events described.

1 Samuel

Introduction

First Samuel recounts King Saul's extraordinary rise to power and influence and his subsequent tragic fall. The author of First Samuel highlights Saul's tragic flaw—his disobedience to God's commands (13:7–12; 15:10–26). Because of his disobedience, God rejected him.

First Samuel is appropriately named after Samuel, the principal character of the early narratives and the one who anointed Israel's first two kings, Saul and David. The Jewish tradition suggests that Samuel was the author of the first part of the book (chs. 1—24), and that the prophet Nathan and the seer Gad were the authors of the remainder, including Second Samuel.

At the beginning of First Samuel, the nation of Israel was at a religious low point. Even the priesthood was corrupt (2:12–17). During this time, the Israelites became dissatisfied with the rule of the judges (8:3). The people longed for a monarchy such as they saw in the surrounding nations. So the Lord allowed the Israelites to have their way. He gave them a king like the other nations: the handsome and tall King Saul (10:1).

The second half of First Samuel and first half of Second Samuel amount to an apology for David's rise to the throne. It gives irrefutable evidence that God Himself had chosen David for the throne (16:1–13). Initially, David was a surprising choice—an undistinguished member of a rural family. Yet his remarkable faith in the Lord distinguished David from his fellow Israelites and from Saul (17:1–51). God shaped David's character while he was on the run from Saul's erratic wrath. In these distressing times, David learned to trust in God for deliverance. Although he made mistakes, he always turned back to God for mercy. For this reason, David was called the man after God's own heart (13:14).

1:1, 2 Ramathaim Zophim is another name for Ramah (v. 19), a village about five miles north of Jerusalem. **The mountains of Ephraim** refers to the hill country primarily occupied by the tribe of Ephraim. **Elkanah,** whose Hebrew name means "God Has Created," was a Levite (1 Chr. 6:26, 34). He is referred to as an **Ephraimite** since he lived in the territory of Ephraim.

1:3 yearly: God's law called for the Israelites to attend three annual pilgrim festivals in Jerusalem (Ex. 34:23; Deut. 16:16). **The LORD of hosts** is a military designation referring to God as the One who commands the angelic armies of heaven (1 Kin. 22:19; Luke 2:13; Rev. 19:14) and the armies of Israel (17:45). **Shiloh,** located about twenty miles north of Jerusalem, was the religious center for the nation at this time and the location of the tabernacle (Josh. 18:1). **Eli, Hophni,** and **Phinehas** served as priests at Shiloh, officiating at the sacrifices presented in the court of the tabernacle.

1:4, 5 The **double portion** was designed to compensate Hannah for her lack of children and demonstrate Elkanah's love for her.

1:6 Her rival refers to Peninnah, Elkanah's other wife, who took every occasion to flaunt her children before Hannah.

1:7 she went up: God's law demanded that the men of Israel appear before Him on three festival occasions. This verse shows Hannah's devotion to the Lord in that she also made annual treks to Shiloh to worship God.

1:8 While Peninnah provoked Hannah, Elkanah sought to encourage her. He suggested that his love for Hannah was a greater blessing than having **ten sons.**

1:9, 10 eating and drinking: The worship of God involved not only the sacrifice of animals, but also lavish banquets of meat and wine. **Eli,** Israel's high **priest** and judge (4:18), was from the family of Ithamar, Aaron's fourth son (1 Kin. 2:27; 1 Chr. 24:1, 3). **The doorpost of the tabernacle** refers to the entrance of the place of worship, where people would approach Eli for judicial rulings.

1:11 Hannah **made a vow** to God. She promised that if God would give her a son, the child would be given back to God. Levites customarily served from age 25 to 50 (Num. 4:3; 8:24–26). Yet Hannah dedicated her son for lifelong service. The words **no razor shall come upon his head** refer to the law of the Nazirite (Num. 6:2–6). The Nazirite vow involved a designated period of time (usually no more than a few weeks or months) during which there was a commitment to refrain completely from wine, from cutting the hair, and touching any dead body. Hannah promised that her son would be a Nazirite for life.

1:12–14 Eli watched her mouth: From a distance, Eli was unable to understand what Hannah was saying. Because of the long time she spent in prayer, Eli assumed that she had drunk too much wine.

1:15 Intoxicating drink is an older translation of the word meaning "beer." **Poured out my soul before the LORD** is an excellent description of fervent prayer (see Ps. 62:8; Phil. 4:6, 7; 1 Pet. 5:7).

1:16 The Hebrew for **wicked woman,** literally "daughter of Belial," means "without value."

1:17, 18 Go in peace: Hannah's changed countenance seems to indicate that she experienced God's peace (see Phil. 4:6, 7) as she waited for the answer to her prayer.

1:19 Elkanah knew Hannah means that he slept with her (see Gen. 4:1). The word **remembered** indicates that God began to intervene on Hannah's behalf to answer her prayer.

1:20, 21 The birth of Hannah's son is part of a long history of godly women and men praying for a child as God's gift (see Gen. 12:1–3). When Hannah gave birth, she named her son **Samuel,** which means "Name of God."

1:22 until the child is weaned: Hebrew children were normally weaned when they were two or three years old.

1:23 According to the law, Elkanah might have declared Hannah's vow a rash promise and prohibited her from fulfilling it (Num. 30:10–15). The fact that he did not do so shows his love and esteem for Hannah.

1:24, 25 three bulls: God's law required that a burnt offering be given at the completion of a special vow (Num. 15:3, 8). Two of the bulls likely served as a present for Eli and the third one was sacrificed.

1:26, 27 Hannah offered a testimony of what God had accomplished on her behalf. By telling others, she exalted God and praised Him for His gracious acts toward her.

1:28 lent him to the LORD: The Hebrew word translated *lent* has the idea of a complete giving up of the child to God. **they worshiped:** The Hebrew word for *worship* means "bow down."

2:1 Hannah began her prayer by rejoicing in the Lord for having been given a child. **My horn is exalted:** Used figuratively, a horn represents power and strength, like that of an ox (see Dan. 7:21; Zech. 1:18–21). Hannah's sense of strength was in God, who had answered her prayer.

2:2 No one is holy like the LORD: That which is holy is marked off, separated, and withdrawn from ordinary use. *Holy* is the opposite of *profane* or *common.*

2:3 Since **the God of knowledge** knows all things, He will appraise our performance along with our words and our promises.

2:4, 5 Hannah mentioned three examples—military power, wealth, and the birth of children—of how God reverses human circumstances, humbling the proud and exalting the lowly.

2:6 The word **grave** refers to the place of the dead for both the righteous and the wicked (see Gen. 37:35). The sovereign God who brings death also **brings up** from the grave.

2:7, 8 dust … ash heap: These parallel terms describe the festering compost piles outside the city walls where people dumped their refuse, including the ash from ovens. Hannah used the image to indicate the deepest degradation: God assists those in the worst circumstances (see Ps. 113:7–9).

2:9, 10 The Lord would keep **His saints** from stumbling, but the **adversaries of the LORD** would face certain calamity. The Hebrew word for **anointed** means "Messiah." This phrase points to the ultimate **King,** before whom every knee shall bow (see Phil. 2:10). Hannah saw the work of God in granting her a child as another step in the fulfillment of His promise to the mothers of Israel, that He would one day provide through them a Messiah.

2:11, 12 Were corrupt is literally "sons of Belial," persons of no value (30:22). **did not know the LORD:** They had no personal, intimate knowledge. The priests were teachers of God's law and officiated at His sacrifices.

2:13–15 The priests' rightful share of a sacrifice was the breast and the right thigh of the animal (Lev. 7:34). Eli's sons sinned by taking any part they wanted and demanding the meat before **the fat,** had been burned on the altar (Lev. 3:3, 5).

2:16 if the man said: In this instance, the layperson knew God's Word and the importance of obedience better than the priests.

2:17 abhorred: Eli's sons dishonored God by doing their priestly duties with irreverence and disrespect.

2:18 The **linen ephod** was a sleeveless garment that was worn by priests, especially when officiating at the altar (see 2:28; 22:18; Ex. 28:6–14).

2:19 The **little robe** made by Hannah is different from the ephod mentioned in v. 18. The fact that Hannah made such a robe indicated her love for her son.

2:20 the loan that was given: The word *loan* here indicates a complete giving up of the child to God (1:28).

2:21 visited Hannah: God came to Hannah to grant her request, as He had to Sarah (Gen. 21:1). In His gracious condescension, He comes near to His people to meet their needs (see Ruth 1:8).

2:22–24 Eli's protests seem weak in view of the enormity of his sons' sins.

2:25, 26 Compare the description of Samuel childhood with that of Jesus (Luke 2:52). The contrast between Samuel and Eli's sons is inescapable.

2:27, 28 The **man of God** was an unidentified prophet or spokesman for the Lord. **Your father** is a reference to Aaron the divinely appointed founder of the priestly house in Israel.

2:29 Eli had warned his sons of divine judgment (v. 25), but he had never really rebuked them for their sins (3:13).

2:30 I said: As descendants of Aaron, Eli's family benefited from the promise God had given to Aaron and his sons that they would be a priesthood forever (Ex. 29:9).

2:31–33 The prophet predicted the destruction of the priestly family of Eli.

2:34 The deaths of **Hophni and Phinehas** would validate the truth of the prophecy (4:17).

2:35 The **faithful priest** refers to Zadok, who was faithful to God and to the line of David and Solomon (1 Kin. 1:7, 8; 2:26, 27, 35). To **build him a sure house** means to guarantee a long line of succession for this faithful priest.

2:36 The impoverishment predicted here was probably fulfilled when Abiathar, a descendant of Eli, was dismissed from the priesthood by Solomon (see 1 Kin. 2:27).

3:1 rare in those days: Samuel was called at a time of limited prophetic activity.

3:2 lying down in his place: Eli apparently was quartered in the court of the tabernacle, where cells were built for the priests who served the sanctuary.

3:3 The lamp of God is the gold lampstand that was located in the holy place of the tabernacle (see Ex. 27:20, 21; Lev. 24:2–4). Samuel's call took place just before dawn.

3:4–8 Three times Samuel mistook God's voice for the voice of Eli. Samuel did **not yet know the LORD** in an intimate and personal way. He had not received **the word of the LORD**.

3:9 Eli realized that God was speaking to Samuel and advised him what to do.

3:10 the LORD came and stood: These words reflect Samuel's very real sense of God's presence. This appears to have been a theophany, a visible appearance of God.

3:11, 12 from beginning to end: The judgment would extend from the death of Eli's sons and continue until the whole prophecy given by the man of God (2:27–36) was fulfilled.

3:13 made themselves vile: These were the esteemed priests of God, but they turned their privilege into disaster. **he did not restrain them:** Eli's personal failure as a father.

3:14 shall not be atoned: Eli and his sons were guilty of presumptuous sin (see Num. 15:30, 31). For such a sin, there was no atoning sacrifice.

3:15, 16 The doors of the house refers to the entrance of the court of the tabernacle.

3:17 The phrase **God do so to you, and more also** is an oath. Eli was saying, "May God do something terrible, and worse, if you don't tell me the truth."

3:18 Let Him do: Eli submitted to God and accepted God's judgment. Even with all his failures as a father, Eli remained faithful to God.

3:19 the LORD was with him: This was the key to Samuel's success as a prophet (see Matt. 28:20).

3:20, 21 The expression **Dan to Beersheba** denotes the whole territory of Israel. The term **prophet** means "spokesman" and refers to one who speaks for another (see Ex. 7:1, 2).

4:1 The **Philistines,** known in Egyptian texts as the "Sea Peoples," were Indo-Europeans who migrated from the Aegean Islands and Asia Minor to the eastern Mediterranean coastal region in the twelfth century B.C.. The **battle** mentioned here took place between **Ebenezer** and **Aphek.**

4:2 The field refers to the flat coastal plain where the Philistines were able to use their chariots to great advantage (13:5).

4:3 In preparation for their next battle with the Philistines, the Israelites brought the **ark of the covenant** from the tabernacle in **Shiloh** to the battlefield. **it may save us:** It seems that the Israelites viewed the ark superstitiously, believing divine power to be in the ark itself rather than in God.

4:4 who dwells between the cherubim: Cherubim are angels generally regarded as guardians of God's holiness. Two cherubim were mounted on the **ark of the covenant** (Ex. 25:22; Num. 7:89).

4:5–7 the earth shook: The presence of the ark gave the Israelites a false sense of victory. **God has come into the camp:** The shouting of the Israelites at the sight of the ark struck fear in the hearts of the Philistines.

4:8–10 these mighty gods: The Philistines were polytheists, and they assumed that the Israelites also had many gods.

4:11 The loss of the **ark,** symbolic of God's presence among His people, was a great tragedy for Israel—even worse than the loss of life (v. 10). The ark probably never returned to Shiloh.

4:12 Torn clothes and dirt on the head were traditional signs of mourning (see Josh. 7:6).

4:13–17 by the wayside: Eli was sitting by the city gate (v. 18), anxiously awaiting news of the battle.

4:18, 19 The loss of the **ark** was a catastrophic blow. In response, Eli fell off his chair and died—another sign of God's judgment on the house of Eli (2:33–36).

4:20 The wife of Phinehas died in childbirth. The words **you have borne a son** were spoken to comfort her as she was dying.

4:21, 22 She possibly refers to the midwife attending the birth of Eli's grandson. The name **Ichabod,** meaning "No Glory." The loss of the ark meant the absence of God's glory in Israel.

5:1 Ashdod, one of the five chief Philistine cities, was about three miles inland from the Mediterranean Sea and about 22 miles south of Joppa.

5:2 Dagon, the chief god of the Philistines, was thought to control the weather and the fertility of the land. The worship of Dagon was thought to ensure a good crop.

5:3, 4 Twice the idol of Dagon fell prostrate before the ark—as if worshiping the Israelite God.

5:5 The destruction of Dagon's idol resulted in the Philistine custom of stepping over the **threshold** of Dagon's temple (see Zeph. 1:9).

5:6, 7 The Hebrew word translated **tumors** literally means "swellings" and may refer to any kind of tumor, swelling, or boil.

5:8, 9 Lords refers to the rulers of the five cities of Philistia (6:4). To free themselves from the plague they sent the ark to **Gath,** one of these cities.

5:10 The ark was sent next to **Ekron,** about six miles north of Gath. **to kill us:** The citizens of Ekron were not enthusiastic about receiving the Israelite war trophy into their city.

5:11, 12 The Hebrew word **cry** means a cry for help (see Ex. 2:23).

6:1, 2 Diviners claimed to be able to predict the future and determine the will of their gods by observing such omens as the flight pattern of birds or the liver of a sacrificed animal.

6:3 The priests and diviners warned against the Philistine leaders to present an offering to appease the God of Israel in order to end the plague. In their understanding, the God of Israel was one deity among many, who had won some sort of contest with their god Dagon.

6:4 The offering of gold was fashioned to resemble the **tumors** and **rats** that plagued the people. **the number of the lords of the Philistines:** The offering corresponded to the number of Philistine cities and their respective lords or kings.

6:5 give glory to the God of Israel: By sending the gifts back with the ark, the Philistines acknowledged that it was God who had afflicted them with tumors.

6:6 The Philistine priests and diviners recalled the experience of **the Egyptians and Pharaoh,** who **hardened their hearts** against God at the time of the Exodus.

6:7 The use of a **new cart** and cows that had **never been yoked** was designed to show special reverence for God on the part of the Philistines. **take their calves home:** The natural inclination of cows would be to return home with their calves.

6:8, 9 if it goes up the road: If the two cows left their calves this would be a clear sign to the Philistines that the plague of tumors had been the judgment of Israel's God.

6:10–12 along the highway: The Hebrew literally reads "along one highway," indicating that the cows did not deviate onto any side roads. The **lowing** of the cattle was their plaintive crying for their calves.

6:13 wheat harvest: Wheat planted in the fall and harvested in the spring.

6:14 offered the cows as a burnt offering: Although Deut. 12:4–14 required that sacrifices be offered only at the central sanctuary, it seems that this law would not have been applied in view of the recent destruction of Shiloh.

6:15 Mosaic law stipulated that only the Levites could handle the ark, and even they could not touch it directly (Num. 4:5, 15).

6:16 The **lords** or kings of the Philistine cities had followed the ark at a distance to see what would become of it.

6:17 Although there is no indication in the text that the ark was ever in **Gaza** or **Ashkelon,** these cities apparently fell under the same plague as the other Philistine cities.

6:18 Abel here is unrelated to the name of Adam and Eve's son (see Gen. 4:2). This term may be a place or site name that more precisely locates the large stone.

6:19 The Lord brought judgment upon certain **men of Beth Shemesh** who were guilty of the presumptuous sin of gazing into the ark.

6:20 Who is able to stand: Since God is holy, He requires those who minister or serve Him to be separated from all that is contrary to His holy character. The people responded in terror and frustration. They knew of the troubles that the ark had brought to the Philistines; now, they believed, they were next.

6:21 The people of Beth Shemesh were so disturbed by the tragedy that they requested the inhabitants of **Kirjath Jearim** to remove the ark from their city.

7:1 Eleazar, whose name means "God Is Help" or "God Is Power," was **consecrated** (lit. "set apart") to care for the ark. Eleazar was probably a member of the priestly family since there was no judgment on his ministry before the ark.

7:2 it was there twenty years: Most likely, it was twenty years before Samuel called the assembly at Mizpah (v. 5). The ark remained at Kirjath Jearim for about a hundred years. It was taken there just after the battle of Aphek around 1104 B.C. and remained there until David brought it to Jerusalem (2 Sam. 5:5; 6:1–18).

7:3 If you return to the LORD: Repentance from sin and expressions of loyalty to God were prerequisites for the restoration of divine blessing (Deut. 30:1–10; 2 Chr. 7:14). The expression **foreign gods** is a general term for the idols of Canaan. **Ashtoreths** is the plural form of the name of the Canaanite goddess of fertility, sexuality, and war.

7:4 the Baals: In ancient sculptures, Baal was depicted with a horned helmet. In one hand he grasped a club or mace and in the other a shaft of lightning or a spear with leaves.

7:5 Samuel gathered the people for a prayer meeting at **Mizpah,** about eight miles north of Jerusalem. **I will pray:** Samuel repeatedly exhibited a commitment to prayer (8:6; 12:19, 23; Ps. 99:6; Jer. 15:1).

7:6 Samuel judged: Samuel acted as chief magistrate, rendering decisions and settling disputes.

7:7 The Israelite gathering at Mizpah alerted the Philistines of a potential uprising. They immediately organized an attack.

7:8 Do not cease to cry out to the LORD: The Israelites did not want to engage in battle unless Samuel was praying for victory. The Israelites wanted to depend solely on the power of God through prayer.

7:9–11 a suckling lamb: According to Lev. 22:27, no animal could be sacrificed until it was at least eight days old.

7:12, 13 To commemorate the victory and acknowledge the Lord's intervention, Samuel set up a memorial stone on the battlefield and named it **Ebenezer,** meaning "Stone of Help." The victory at Ebenezer was so decisive that the Philistines made no more attacks against the Israelites during Samuel's judgeship.

7:14 Ekron and **Gath** were Philistine cities near Israel (5:8, 10). The frontier settlements which the Israelites had been forced to evacuate could now be taken again.

7:15–17 In addition to his religious duties as prophet, Samuel served as a circuit judge. **Ramah** was about five miles north of Jerusalem.

8:1 made his sons judges: It was highly unusual for Samuel to appoint his sons to assist him in judging cases. Judges were individually appointed by God, not by their fathers.

8:2 Joel means "The Lord Is God." **Abijah** means "My Father Is the Lord." **Beersheba** was at the southern extremity of Israel

---

 IN DEPTH   ## The King of Israel

Was it God's will for Israel to have a king? Certainly it was, for God had indicated that the kingship was part of His plan for Israel in a number of prophecies (Gen. 49:10; Num. 24:17; Deut. 17:14–20).

Although kingship for them was not wrong in itself, the way the Israelites were demanding it was wrong. The people clearly stated their motives for wanting a king. First, they wanted to follow the practices of the neighboring nations (8:5). Second, they wanted a king to lead them into battles (8:20). Both motives amounted to a rejection of the God of Israel as their King (8:7).

The Lord had demonstrated on numerous occasions that He would fight the Israelites' battles. From the miraculous collapse of Jericho's walls (Josh. 6:20) to Gideon's rout of the massive Midianite army (Judg. 7:19–22), God had delivered His people again and again from their enemies. Why did they need a king now to lead them into battles?

What is more, God had given the people His Word, the prophets, and the judges to guide them. But as the tragic history of Judges demonstrates, the people ignored God's guidance and followed the practices of their neighbors (Judg. 3:7). Now, once again, the people were following their neighbors instead of the living God and the Word He had given them. Although Samuel clearly communicated God's warning to the people, they stubbornly preferred their will to God's.

In the end, God allowed the Israelites to have what they wanted. He gave them a king like those of the other nations. The tall and handsome Saul would have been the perfect choice for a king. But through Saul's tragic reign, God taught the Israelites that they needed a king who was *not* like the kings of the other nations.

They needed a king who would obey God's word instead of following his own will, a king who would trust in God instead of himself. In the shadow of Saul's mistakes, God trained young David to walk in His ways so that He could eventually lead the nation in righteousness.

(3:20), about 48 miles south of Jerusalem.

8:3–5 make us a king: Two factors contributed to the elders' request for a king: (1) the corruption of Samuel's sons, and (2) their desire to follow the pattern of **all the nations.**

8:6 There is nothing wrong with the concept of a monarchy. Yet Samuel was **displeased** because he felt that the demand for a king indicated a rejection of his own leadership.

8:7, 8 they have rejected Me: The error of the elders of Israel was their failure to recognize God as their true King (12:12).

8:9, 10 forewarn them: Samuel was called to warn the Israelites that a king would not solve all of their problems. In fact, having a king would create many hardships.

8:11–17 First, a king would draft young men to serve in the military, farm his fields, and prepare for war. **Run before his chariots** is a reference to the king's state carriage. Second, a king would draft young women to work in his palace and serve in his court. Third, a king would tax the people's crops and flocks. Fourth, a king would appropriate the servants of the Israelites and their **finest young men** and **donkeys.** Fifth, the king would take away the people's personal freedom.

8:18, 19 cry out … not hear: Since the Israelites were deliberately choosing their own path, they could not expect God to deliver them from the trouble that would inevitably result.

8:20 and fight our battles: The Israelites were looking for human leadership on the battlefield, instead of recognizing that God would lead them in battle (see Ex. 15:3).

8:21, 22 Samuel heard … and he repeated them: Samuel acted as mediator between the people and God.

9:1 Saul's father, **Kish,** was from the tribe of **Benjamin.** The term **a mighty man of power** suggests that he was a wealthy landowner and a leader in time of war.

9:2, 3 Saul means "Asked For." **Choice** suggests that Saul was in the prime of manhood. Both his physical stature—**taller than any**—and personal appearance—**handsome**—were striking. Saul was endowed

with what seemed to be great potential for leadership and service.

9:4, 5 The search for his father's donkeys took Saul north from his home at Gibeah (10:26), through the **mountains of Ephraim.**

9:6 This city refers to Ramah, Samuel's home after the destruction of Shiloh (1:1; 8:4). The term **man of God** here refers to Samuel.

9:7, 8 Saul's servant unexpectedly produced **one-fourth of a shekel of silver,** which would serve as adequate compensation for the prophet's ministry.

9:9–11 Seer refers to one who is able to see what is hidden from the eyes of ordinary people. **Prophet** refers to one who speaks for God (see Ex. 7:1).

9:12–15 A **high place** was an elevated site of worship located on a hill or on an artificial platform in a temple. The Canaanites were known for building their places of worship on hills.

9:16, 17 It seems significant that Saul is referred to here as **commander** rather than as king.

9:18 Asking **Samuel** directions to the **seer's house** at the was the final step in a remarkable sequence of events which God brought about to have Saul anointed as king.

9:19, 20 All that is in your heart does not seem to refer to the matter of the donkeys, for Samuel immediately assured Saul that the donkeys had been found.

9:21 smallest of the tribes: The tribe was reduced to six hundred fighting men during the punishment of Benjamin for the atrocity at Gibeah (see Judg. 19; 20).

9:22 The hall was where local dignitaries sat for sacrificial feasts at the high place.

9:23 which I gave you: Samuel had been instructed by God to be prepared for this special encounter.

9:24 Giving Saul **the thigh** was intended to honor him in the presence of the other guests (see Gen. 43:34).

9:25, 26 A **house** in ancient Israel usually had a flat roof which could be used as a place to relax. It appears that Saul slept on the roof (v. 26).

9:27 Tell the servant to go on: The anointing

of Saul was private. Later, he would be publicly installed as king before all Israel (10:17–27).

10:1 the LORD has anointed you: The anointing of a ruler was a religious act. That is why David had such regard for Saul, refusing to lift a hand against "the LORD's anointed."

10:2 Rachel's tomb: Rachel had died giving birth to Benjamin on a journey from Bethel to Bethlehem. **in the territory of Benjamin:** Rachel was buried near Bethlehem.

10:3 The terebinth, refers to a tree, native to the land of Israel, which grows to a height of around 35 feet. **Tabor** is an apparent reference to Mount Tabor, in the Valley of Jezreel, where these trees were prominent.

10:4 For strangers to offer Saul **two loaves of bread** would have been a remarkable sign. Their bread would have been for use in the worship of God.

10:5 The Hebrew word translated **hill** probably refers to Gibeah, Saul's hometown (11:4). **Philistine garrison:** The Philistines dominated the land and had set up a military outpost in Saul's hometown. **A group of prophets** may refer to members of the "school of the prophets," which was probably instituted by Samuel for the purpose of preparing young men for prophetic ministry.

10:6–8 The Spirit of the LORD refers to the Holy Spirit. The expression **be turned into another man** may mean spiritual regeneration or a marked advance in spiritual growth.

10:9 God gave him another heart: In Hebrew this expression literally reads, "God changed him for another heart."

10:10 God worked through His Spirit in Saul's life so that he was able to exercise a prophetic gift.

10:11 As a result of the Spirit's mighty working in Saul, the people asked, **Is Saul also among the prophets?** The question expresses surprise at Saul's sudden change in character.

10:12–16 But who is their father: The implication of this question is that the fathers of the prophets were not important people. The prophets in any case did not obtain their gift by inheritance, but by God's will.

10:17, 18 Mizpah was where the Israelites had gathered for a time of spiritual revival before their victory over the Philistines (7:5).

10:19 rejected your God: Samuel reiterated his earlier admonition (8:10–18), warning the people of their attitude—which was actually a rejection of God's kingship.

10:20, 21 The choice of Saul as Israel's first monarch was made by casting lots, a means of determining God's will in answer to "yes" and "no" questions. The lots were cast like dice.

10:22, 23 hidden among the equipment: This may reflect Saul's modesty, or perhaps his hesitancy and self-doubt over assuming the position of national leader.

10:24 The phrase **him whom the LORD has chosen** reflects the sovereignty of God. Although the Israelites decided to have a king, it was the Lord who selected Saul.

10:25 the behavior of royalty: Samuel taught the people what to expect from a king, possibly reviewing his instruction in 8:11–18 and God's laws for kingship in Deut. 17:14–20.

10:26 Gibeah, three miles north of Jerusalem, served as the first capital of the Israelite monarchy.

10:27 Some rebels questioned Saul's military leadership and refused to honor him with the gifts customarily given a king. But Saul **held his peace** in order not to provoke the situation.

11:1 Nahash, whose name means "Serpent," was commander of the Ammonites, descendants of Lot who occupied the fringes of the desert east of Gad and Manasseh.

11:2 put out all your right eyes: The condition of surrender demanded by Nahash was not only cruel and humiliating but would have made the Israelite warriors unable to fight.

11:3, 4 The elders of Jabesh Gilead asked for **seven days** in which to find help before conceding defeat. Nahash agreed to the proposal, since he apparently was not prepared to take the city by force and wanted to avoid a long and costly siege.

11:5 Saul, coming behind the herd: Although Saul had been appointed king, he did not assume governmental authority at once. Saul continued farming until he could answer Israel's expectations of him as king by delivering the Israelites from their enemies (8:20).

11:6 the Spirit of God came upon Saul: The Holy Spirit empowered Saul to deliver the citizens of Jabesh.

11:7 Two **oxen** were customarily yoked together for work. Saul's call to arms was accompanied by a threat.

11:8 Bezek was due west of Jabesh Gilead on the other side of the Jordan River.

11:9 by the time the sun is hot: The sun becomes hot before noon.

11:10 The message to Nahash may have been designed to lull the Ammonites into a false sense of security.

11:11 Saul divided his forces into **three companies** so he could attack at the same time from different directions.. **the morning watch:** Saul's attack probably took place at dawn, before the Ammonites had armed themselves for battle.

11:12 Saul's victory over the Ammonites gave him the support and allegiance of the people of Israel.

11:13 the LORD has accomplished salvation: Saul recognized that the victory over the Ammonites belonged God alone and refused to heed the suggestion of his zealous supporters.

11:14, 15 Samuel called the tribes to **renew the kingdom.** As a result of Saul's victory over the Ammonites, the Israelites enthusiastically endorsed his kingship.

12:1, 2 walking before you: Saul was leading Israel and attending to the nation's needs. Samuel referred to the two reasons cited by the elders of Israel in their demand for a king: (1) Samuel's **old** age and (2) his **sons,** who had demonstrated their unworthiness for public office.

12:3–5 before the LORD and before His anointed: Samuel asked whether anyone wanted to accuse him before God and His anointed king. Samuel's past record was established to inspire confidence in his present exhortation.

12:6, 7 Righteous acts refers to the benefits that God had bestowed on His people.

12:8 Samuel summarized the descent of Jacob's family into Egypt (Gen. 46), the Egyptian oppression (Ex. 1:8–22), the Exodus from Egypt (Ex. 2—15), and the conquest of Canaan (Josh. 1—12).

12:9 Samuel recounted the nation's apostasy and subsequent divine discipline. **Moab:** The Moabite oppression is recorded in Judg. 3:12–30.

12:10 After a period of oppression, the Israelites repented and cried out to the Lord for deliverance.

12:11 Jerubbaal, also known as Gideon, delivered Israel from the Midianites (see Judg. 6—8). **Jephthah** defeated the Ammonites (see Judg. 11).

12:12 The threat of **Nahash** was probably felt long before the threatened attack of Jabesh Gilead (11:1–3) and was probably a factor in Israel's request for a king (8:20).

12:13, 14 The **fear** of **the LORD** is not just a pious attitude but a serious and obedient response to the revelation of God's holy character.

12:15, 16 The consequences for disobeying God's covenant are outlined in Deut. 28:15–68.

12:17, 18 The season for **wheat harvest** in Israel is the months of May and June. **send thunder and rain:** For rain to fall during the wheat harvest would be most unusual. The miracle was intended to convince the people of their great **wickedness** in demanding a king.

12:19, 20 Do not fear: By this Samuel meant, "Do not fear the death penalty for disobedience."

12:21 Empty things refers to false gods and idols (see Is. 44:9–20).

12:22 His great name's sake: In ancient times, one's name stood for one's character. The name of God speaks of His reputation and attributes.

12:23, 24 Samuel assured the people that he would not forget **to pray** for them. For Samuel, a lack of prayer was a moral compromise, a sin.

12:25 The words **swept away** anticipate God's ultimate judgment of captivity and exile from the land (Deut. 28:41, 63, 64).

13:1 one year ... two years: This verse

provides a chronological note recording the date of this encounter with the Philistines relative to Saul's reign as king.

13:2 Saul selected and trained a regular, standing army.

13:3 While Saul was in Michmash, his son Jonathan attacked the Philistine garrison at **Geba,** about a mile southwest of Michmash. The two sites are separated by a deep ravine. The **trumpet** was a ram's horn used to signal and summon the military.

13:4 Saul had attacked: Either Jonathan had been acting under Saul's orders or Saul took credit for his son's victory. Saul withdrew his army to **Gilgal** in keeping with Samuel's instructions to him at his anointing (10:8).

13:5 Beth Aven was about one-half mile west of Michmash.

13:6 the people hid in caves: The limestone of the hill country region contains many natural caves which could be used as hideouts in time of attack.

13:7 Gilgal, located northeast of Jericho in the Jordan valley, was the appointed place of Saul's meeting with Samuel (v. 8).

13:8, 9 Waited seven Samuel had told Saul to wait seven days at **Gilgal** until Samuel came to offer sacrifices. Concerned that the people were losing courage and starting to scatter, Saul assumed priestly prerogatives and offered the **burnt offering** himself (see Lev. 1).

13:10–12 as soon as he had finished: Samuel's delay may have been intended as a test of Saul's obedience.

13:13 Saul's sin was failing to keep **the commandment** God had given through Samuel.

13:14 your kingdom shall not continue: Although Saul would retain his throne, his descendants would not carry on his dynasty. **A man after His own heart** is God's description of David, a man with many faults, but a man whose spirit was sensitive to God's will.

13:15, 16 Saul's army had dwindled from three thousand (v. 2) to only **six hundred men.**

13:17 The Philistines sent their raiders to harass the Israelites in the hopes of weakening Israelite resolve or of forcing a decisive engagement.

13:18 The twin towns of **Beth Horon** (Upper and Lower) were located west of Geba, about two miles apart on a ridge guarding the approach to the hill country from the coastal plain.

13:19 no blacksmith: The Canaanites and Philistines learned how to forge iron from the Hittites. Although they were not great in numerical strength, the Philistines were able to dominate Israel.

13:20 Sharpen may also be translated "to forge." The **plowshare** is the metal part of the plow that breaks up the soil. A **mattock** is like a pickax but has blades instead of points. It is used for digging and breaking up soil that cannot be reached by a plow.

13:21 The **pim** was approximately two-thirds of a shekel. Based on what is known of ancient Israel's economy, the charge was exorbitant. **The points of the goads** refers to the sharp ends of prods used to direct cattle.

13:22 The weapons available to the Israelite soldiers would have included slings, bows and arrows, and numerous instruments made of bronze.

13:23 The pass of Michmash is the deep gorge that separated Michmash and Geba.

14:1 he did not tell his father: Saul would have thought Jonathan's plan was reckless.

14:2 Gibeah, Saul's home, was about three miles southwest of Geba, where Jonathan was camped at the Philistine garrison he had captured (13:3, 16).

14:3–5 The genealogy of **Ahijah,** the high priest and descendant of **Eli,** is given in full.

14:6–8 The term **uncircumcised** was an Israelite designation for the Gentiles, who did not share the distinctive mark of God's people under the Old Covenant (see Gen. 17:10–14).

14:9–13 The assault of Jonathan on Michmash was an act of faith. The response of the Philistines, **come up to us,** was taken as a sign that God would grant them victory.

14:14 about half an acre: The Hebrew text reads "half a yoke of land." A yoke of land was the area a pair of oxen could plow in one day.

14:15, 16 The defeat of the garrison at Michmash left the Philistines in a state of panic. **The earth quaked** may refer to an actual earthquake, which added to the panic and confusion.

14:17 call the roll: Saul had to have the troops mustered before he realized that his own son was not present.

14:18, 19 Bring the ark of God here: According to 7:2, the ark at this time was at Kirjath Jearim. There is no mention of its being moved before it was brought to Jerusalem by David.

14:20 against his neighbor: There was such confusion in the Philistine camp that it was hard to tell friend from foe.

14:21 The Hebrews who were with the Philistines were deserters or mercenaries.

14:22, 23 The mountains of Ephraim refers to the mountainous region occupied by the tribe of Ephraim, just north of Benjamite territory.

14:24 Cursed is the man: Saul foolishly ordered that none of his soldiers should eat until he had **taken vengeance** on his **enemies.**

14:25, 26 The bees had produced so much **honey** that it had flowed from their combs in the trees to the **ground.**

14:27 Because of his absence (vv. 1–17), Jonathan had not heard his father's oath. He did what any soldier would do and helped himself to some honey as he pursued the Philistines.

14:28–31 Aijalon was located about 18 miles west of Michmash.

14:32 ate them with the blood: The Israelite soldiers began to eat the captured Philistine livestock without first draining the blood, in violation of God's law (Lev. 17:10–14).

14:33, 34 roll a large stone: Saul realized the serious nature of the offense and had a stone table set up to slaughter the animals and drain the blood properly.

14:35 Saul built an altar to thank God for his victory over the Philistines.

14:36–38 Let us draw near to God: Saul decided to ask for God's counsel about it. God's silence was taken by Saul as an evidence of sin in the camp.

14:39–45 he shall surely die: This was Saul's second foolish oath (v. 24).

14:46 their own place: As a result of Israel's victory, the Philistines left the hill country and returned to their settlements on the coastal plain.

14:47 Zobah was the Aramean kingdom in the Bekah Valley. The **Philistines** occupied the coastal plain west of the hill country.

14:48 The victory over the **Amalekites,** nomadic desert tribesmen who lived south of the hill country, is recorded in 15:1–9.

14:49 In 1 Sam. 31:2 and 1 Chr. 8:33, the names of Saul's four sons are given as Jonathan, Abinadab, Malchishua, and Esh-Baal. **Jishui** is probably a second name for Abinadab.

14:50, 51 Ahinoam means "My Brother Is Pleasant."

14:52 took him for himself: Saul drafted the strong and brave young men into his army.

15:1 The LORD sent me: Samuel referred to his part in Saul's appointment to add weight and authority to the command that he was about to give.

15:2 The Amalekites were a nomadic people who lived in the region of the Negev, the dry land south of Judah (see Num. 13:29).

15:3 The expression **utterly destroy** is literally "to put under a ban," similar to the ban placed on Jericho at the time of the conquest (Josh. 6:17, 18).

15:4 men of Judah: Early in the period of the united monarchy, the distinctions between the northern tribes of Israel and the southern tribe of Judah began to be noted (11:8).

15:5 The Amalekites were a nomadic people. The term **city** must refer to their main settlement.

15:6 The Kenites, who had been loosely associated with the Israelites since Moses' marriage to the daughter of Jethro, a Kenite were a nomadic offshoot of the Midianites.

15:7 Havilah refers to a district of northeast Arabia. **Shur** was the western part of the Sinai peninsula bordering Egypt. The campaign against the **Amalekites** covered extensive territory.

15:8 took Agag king of the Amalekites alive: This was a direct violation of the Lord's command (v. 3). Saul devoted the rest of the people to the ban but saved the life of the king.

15:9–11 By sparing **Agag** and the **best** of the spoil, Saul was following his own desires instead of serving as an agent of God's judgment.

15:12 The **monument** that Saul set up was probably intended to commemorate the victory over the Amalekites. Saul then returned to **Gilgal**, where the Israelites had convened before their war with the Philistines (13:8–15).

15:13 Saul's words **I have performed the commandment of the LORD** are the exact opposite of God's evaluation (v. 11).

15:14–19 When confronted by Samuel, Saul excused his disobedience by blaming **the people.** He also sought to justify sparing **the best of the sheep and the oxen** by suggesting that he intended them for sacrifice.

15:20, 21 I have obeyed the voice of the LORD: Given another chance by Samuel to get things right with God, Saul persisted in affirming his innocence.

15:22 to obey is better than sacrifice: Samuel emphasized that sincerity and obedience were the prerequisites for worship that pleased God.

15:23 Saul's stubborn disobedience was essentially an act of **idolatry** because it elevated his will above God's will. **He also has rejected you:** Saul failed to realize that he was not a sovereign and independent ruler like other monarchs.

15:24, 25 I have sinned: In response to Samuel's rebuke, Saul confessed his sin and explained that because he **feared the people,** he **obeyed their voice.**

15:26, 27 Saul had disobeyed God one time too many; for him, there was no return.

15:28 The tearing of Samuel's robe (v. 27) served as a sign that God had **torn the kingdom** from Saul. The **neighbor** who would receive the kingdom was David (16:11–13).

15:29 the Strength of Israel: This designation of God occurs only here in the Bible. **will not lie nor relent:** God's decision to reject Saul was irrevocable.

15:30, 31 Saul's requests for forgiveness and desire to worship God suggest that, despite his flaws, he was a sincere believer in God.

15:32, 33 Bring Agag: Samuel executed Agag in order to obey God's clear command (v. 3).

15:34, 35 See evidently means "to give attention" or "to regard with interest." The point is that God was through with Saul as king, and so was Samuel.

16:1 Fill your horn: The ram's horn served as a vessel for the anointing **oil** (10:1). **Jesse the Bethlehemite** was the son of Obed, the son of Ruth and Boaz. **I have provided Myself a king:** God made it clear to Samuel that this king would be of His choosing.

16:2, 3 Samuel's concern for his life was not unwarranted in light of Saul's suspicious nature and spiritual degeneracy (18:11). **say, 'I have come to sacrifice':** God did not instruct Samuel to lie, but instead He provided a legitimate opportunity for Samuel to visit with Jesse and his family.

16:4 Because Samuel's visit was unexpected, **the elders of the town** wondered if he had come to execute judgment (7:15, 16).

16:5 The Hebrew word for **peaceably** means "things as they ought to be." The word **sanctify** means "to set oneself apart" by means of ceremonial washings and purifications.

16:6, 7 The **appearance** and **stature** of Jesse's oldest son, Eliab, commended him to leadership. Instead of looking at appearances, God searched the **heart.**

16:8, 9 The parade of sons began with the oldest. The assumption was that the firstborn would receive a higher rank than his brothers. God's way surprisingly reversed this expectation.

16:10, 11 Are all the young men here: After looking at Jesse's seven sons, Samuel wondered if someone had been left out. In fact, **the youngest** was out in the field, caring for his father's flock. **keeping the sheep:** In ancient times, both divine and human rulers were frequently compared to shepherds (see Ezek. 34).

16:12 Ruddy means "reddish," referring to complexion and perhaps hair color. **bright eyes:** The Hebrew words may also be rendered *beauty of eyes.* **anoint him:** David was anointed with olive oil. This religious ritual consecrated him to the kingship.

16:13 David was empowered by God's Holy **Spirit** for the work of ruling God's people.

16:14, 15 distressing spirit from the LORD:

This affliction has been understood in various ways: (1) demon possession as divine punishment; (2) demonic attack or influence; (3) an evil messenger, like the one sent to entice Ahab (1 Kin. 22:20–23); or (4) a spirit of discontent created by God in Saul's heart (see Judg. 9:23).

16:16, 17 Whatever Saul's problem was, it was temporarily relieved by music (v. 23). It was generally believed that music had a beneficial influence on those with morbid natures.

16:18 a mighty man of valor, a man of war: David the shepherd boy had not yet demonstrated his military abilities.

16:19–21 David's appointment as Saul's **armorbearer** may have taken place after his victory over Goliath (17:55–58).

16:22 Stand before me is an expression for entering the king's service (see 1 Kin. 10:8).

16:23 Empowered by the Spirit of God, David was able to drive away the **distressing spirit** (v. 14) from the king with his soothing music (18:10).

17:1 The Philistine and Israelite armies were gathered in the Elah Valley, about 15 miles west of David's hometown of Bethlehem.

17:2, 3 The Valley of Elah is an east-west valley leading from the hill country of Judah toward the lowlands of the Philistines.

17:4 champion: The Hebrew expression is literally "a man who is a go-between," meaning a warrior who will fight in single combat as a stand-in for the entire army. The **cubit** was about 18 inches and **a span** was nine inches. Thus **Goliath** stood nine feet, nine inches tall.

17:5, 6 bronze helmet: Goliath's **coat of mail** was made of overlapping plates of bronze sewn on leather and weighed **five thousand shekels** or about 125 pounds. **Bronze armor** refers to the greaves that protected his legs. **bronze javelin:** This weapon was designed for hurling.

17:7, 8 The **spear** was a weapon designed for hand-to-hand combat, like a long sword. **shieldbearer:** There are two different Hebrew words for "shield." One refers to a small round shield usually worn on the left arm. The other, used here, refers to a much larger, oblong shield, often carried by the

shield-bearer as the soldier moved into battle.

17:9, 10 Defy is a harsh word, meaning "to put under reproach" (vv. 25, 26). The defiant taunts of Goliath were as much against the God of Israel as against the fighters (vv. 26, 36).

17:11 they were dismayed and greatly afraid: The army was sick with dread. Perhaps the Israelites had forgotten the victories God had given Israel in times past.

17:12–16 that Ephrathite: Ephrathah was a family name in the tribe of Judah, the area where **Bethlehem** was located (see Mic. 5:2).

17:17–19 Jesse sent David with provisions—**grain, loaves,** and **cheeses**—for his sons and their officers.

17:20–23 going out to the fight: The soldiers were going out to the battle line, but only to shout their taunts.

17:24 fled ... afraid: The fear of the Israelite army was shameful. Perched on the fortified hillside, none of them was in immediate danger.

17:25 Saul promised riches, exemption from taxes and the duty of public service, and his daughter's hand in marriage to the person who would defeat Goliath.

17:26 Uncircumcised is used as an expression of contempt for a pagan person.

17:27, 28 David's oldest brother, **Eliab,** was abrupt with David. **pride ... insolence:** This language is similar to that used to describe the rage of Joseph's brothers against him (Gen. 37).

17:29 Is there not a cause: There was reason to be agitated—not at David, but at the Philistine.

17:30–32 your servant will go: David weighed the difficulties from a divine perspective. Here was an opportunity for God to display His power.

17:33–37 David's past victories over **a lion** and **a bear** gave him the faith to trust God for victory over Goliath.

17:38, 39 Saul's armor was designed for a large man. David could not even **walk** in it, much less fight in it.

17:40, 41 A **sling** was the typical equipment of a shepherd. It was a hollow pocket of leather attached to two cords. Putting a stone in the pouch, the slinger would whirl it around his head to build up momentum. Releasing one of the cords would hurl the stone at its target.

17:42 David lacked the signs of age and the scars that one would expect of a battle-seasoned champion. Unlike most soldiers of Israel, he had not yet grown a beard.

17:43, 44 The appearance of a boy as his challenger offended the pride of Goliath. Goliath saw the shepherd's staff and was angry because David appeared as if he were out to beat a **dog.**

17:45 The name of the LORD speaks of God's covenantal relationship with the Israelites. David was depending on the power of God as the Warrior and Defender of His people.

17:46, 47 David's victory demonstrates to **all the earth** that God delivers His own against overwhelming odds. **the battle is the LORD's** put the contest into proper perspective.

17:48, 49 hurried and ran: Part of David's strategy was to rush the giant. Guided by the Lord, David skillfully hit the right spot on **his forehead** with a powerful blow.

17:50, 51 cut off his head: This was an indignity to a fallen foe and the decisive sign that he was dead. It filled the Philistines with terror.

17:52, 53 The Israelites pursued the Philistines north toward **Ekron** and east toward **Gath.**

17:54 A part of **Jerusalem** was occupied by Israelites, but the citadel was still in the hands of the Jebusites. David took Goliath's **head** to the part of the city that was under Israelite control.

17:55 whose son is this youth: Saul would need to know name of David's father in order to reward David's family (v. 25).

17:56–58 your servant Jesse: David likely intended to emphasize that Jesse a loyal *servant* of Saul.

18:1, 2 Saul was captivated by David. He conscripted him anew to his court (16:19–23).

18:3 This **covenant** was a mutual agreement in which David and Jonathan were bound to care for the needs and attend to the

interests of each other. **as his own soul:** These words, repeated for emphasis (v. 1), describe the unselfish nature of Jonathan's love for David.

18:4 sword ... bow ... belt: These were treasured items that would not have been casually surrendered. With these gifts Jonathan ratified his covenant with David.

18:5 behaved wisely: This description is a part of an ongoing subtle contrast between David and Saul. The phrase reveals that David was acting with skill and achieving success.

18:6 when David was returning: Women came together from across the land to celebrate the national victory and their new national champion.

18:7 thousands ... ten thousands: The poetic use of exaggeration is evident here. David had not yet killed even a dozen people, much less thousands.

18:8, 9 the saying displeased him: Saul saw David's achievements as undercutting his own prominence among the people. **the kingdom:** To Saul, there appeared to be no honor left for David except for him to take the throne.

18:10–13 The expression **he prophesied** can be used of legitimate prophecy or the erratic prophetic ecstasy associated with the ravings of false prophets and pagan priests (1 Kin. 18:29; 22:12). Whatever the case here, God was judging Saul for his previous disobedience by allowing his mind to become troubled.

18:14, 15 the LORD was with him: David's relationship with God was the key to his success.

18:16 he went out and came in before them: David's military activities elevated him to prominence before the people.

18:17–20 While Saul had previously promised to give his daughter to the man who killed Goliath (17:25), here he linked the marriage to future conquests, hoping that David would be killed by the Philistines.

18:21–23 that she may be a snare to him: Saul hoped that offering Michal in marriage would lead to David's death. **I am a poor ... man:** David did not have the resources to bring a wedding dowry fit for a king (v. 25).

18:24, 25 In many cultures of the ancient Middle East, a **dowry** was paid by the bridegroom to the father of the bride as economic compensation for the loss of a daughter. **one hundred foreskins:** The foreskins would be proof that David had killed that many Philistines.

18:26, 27 the days had not expired: Apparently there was a time limit during which David had to fulfill the conditions of the dowry.

18:28–30 The war with the **Philistines** continued, as did David's brave exploits. **behaved more wisely:** This significant phrase meaning "to act with skill" is again contrasted with the phrase meaning "to play the fool," used of Saul in 13:13. David's successful military engagements gained him increasing honor and recognition.

19:1 When Saul's scheming efforts failed, he brought **Jonathan** and **all his servants** into the plot. Apparently, Saul did not know about the friendship of David and Jonathan.

19:2, 3 Loyal to his covenant of friendship, Jonathan pledged to intervene on David's behalf before his father (18:3).

19:4, 5 his servant: Jonathan's strongest argument was that David's actions demonstrated loyalty to Saul. **innocent blood:** By having David killed, Saul would incur the guilt of bloodshed.

19:6, 7 Saul swore: Following the normal form for making such an oath, Saul says literally, "If he would die!" He means, "I will not allow him to die."

19:8–10 Each time there was **war** with the Philistines, David had opportunities for great exploits. Saul himself no longer went to war. He stayed at home sulking about David's victories.

19:11 tomorrow you will be killed: Because of her great love for her husband, Michal told David about Saul's plot.

19:12, 13 The **cover of goat's hair** and **clothes** was used to make it appear that David was still in bed.

19:14 He is sick: Michal loved her husband so much that she was willing to go against her father's wishes, to lie for David and even to die for him.

19:15–17 Saul feared and hated David so much that he was willing to murder a man lying sick in his bed.

19:18, 19 Facing a serious personal crisis, David **went to Samuel at Ramah** for help. Together David and Samuel went to **Naioth** a community within the city of Ramah.

19:20, 21 The working of God's **Spirit** distracted Saul's messengers from their purpose and protected His servant David.

19:22, 23 Sechu was probably north of Jerusalem in the region of Gibeah and Ramah.

19:24 lay down naked: Ancient Israelite culture looked with disdain on nudity in public. Saul's plan to kill David was totally thwarted by God's protective hand.

20:1, 2 You shall not die: Jonathan was certain that Saul would not kill David. It is possible that Jonathan was unaware of the events of 19:8–24 and was trusting in Saul's solemn oath not to kill David (19:6).

20:3 Do not let Jonathan know this: David suggested that Saul had kept his plans from Jonathan to avoid causing his son grief.

20:4 Jonathan's words reflected his covenant of friendship with David (18:3). He had vowed to help David.

20:5, 6 The first day of the month, **the New Moon,** was observed as a religious festival (Num. 10:10; 28:11–15). **yearly sacrifice:** Apparently Jesse's family gathered for a special time of worship during the New Moon celebration (v. 5).

20:7–11 The words **deal kindly** may also be rendered "show covenant loyalty." In other words, David was asking Jonathan to be faithful to his **covenant** of friendship (18:3).

20:12, 13 If the news was **good toward David,** Jonathan would send a messenger to inform his friend. If the news was **evil,** then Jonathan would inform David personally.

20:14, 15 the kindness of the LORD: Jonathan used the same Hebrew word meaning "covenant loyalty" that David had used earlier (v. 8). Both Jonathan and David were appealing to their covenant of friendship as a basis for acts of kindness. Jonathan appealed to David to protect his own life and the lives of his descendants. Jonathan knew that

David might someday take the throne—and he was aware of the custom of a new king killing the offspring of his predecessor.

20:16–18 Let the LORD require it: Jonathan prayed that the Lord would hold David accountable to the obligations of the covenant.

20:19 The stone Ezel was likely a familiar landmark.

20:20–24 Jonathan declared that **the LORD** would be a witness to the covenant of protection which he had arranged with David (vv. 14–16).

20:25–29 he is unclean: Noticing that David's seat was empty, Saul assumed that ritual uncleanness must have prevented his participation in the feast. Saul's suspicions were aroused when David was absent on the second night of the feast.

20:30, 31 your mother's nakedness: Saul suggested that Jonathan and his mother with him were shameful because of Jonathan's apparently despicable behavior.

20:32–34 his father had treated him shamefully: Jonathan, the loyal friend of David, was so upset he would not eat because of how David had been insulted by his father.

20:35–40 On the third day, Jonathan went to the field to signal to David that he should flee the court of Saul. He got rid of his servant on a ruse and at great personal risk went to meet David one last time.

20:41, 42 David and Jonathan **wept together.** Both were warriors but also men of tender hearts. They were loyal friends and committed to each other even in difficult circumstances.

21:1 Ahimelech, the great-grandson of Eli (1:9), was serving as high priest. His name means "My Brother Is King." **was afraid:** His fear may have been due to rumors of a breach between Saul and David.

21:2 The king has ordered me: David deceived Ahimelech into believing that he was on a secret mission for the king. His lie unwittingly precipitated a tragedy for the priests of Nob (22:6–19).

21:3–5 no common bread: Ahimelech explained that the only bread available was **holy bread,** sometimes called the "showbread." According to God's law, this bread could be eaten only by priests.

21:6 the priest gave him holy bread: The Talmud explains this apparent breach of the law on the basis that the preservation of life takes precedent over nearly all other commandments in the Law. The spirit of the Law was kept by Ahimelech's compassionate act.

21:7, 8 Doeg, an Edomite, witnessed the encounter between David and Ahimelech and passed the word along to the king.

21:9 Having fled Gibeah without weapons, David laid claim to **the sword of Goliath,** whom David had **killed in the Valley of Elah** (17:40–51).

21:10 Achish ruled the city of **Gath,** one of the five major cities of the Philistines (6:17).

21:11 David the king: The popular song sung in his honor after his victory over Goliath had reached the ears of the Philistines (18:7; 29:5).

21:12, 13 These verses provide the background for Ps. 34 and perhaps Ps. 56. In Ps. 34, **Achish** is referred to as Abimelech, which was apparently a dynastic title used by the Philistine rulers (Gen. 20:2; 26:1). **very much afraid:** If the superscription of Ps. 56 relates to this incident, David was seized by the Philistines. **Madness** was associated in ancient times with being controlled by a powerful spirit. David changed his demeanor and behaved as though he were insane, writing graffiti on the doors of the gates and drooling.

21:14, 15 Achish had no interest in adding an insane soldier to his army. The title of Ps. 34 indicates the conclusion of this incident. The king "drove him away, and he departed."

22:1 After David's escape from Gath, he gathered his family and followers at a cave near the city of Adullam. **The cave of Adullam** was where David composed Ps. 142 and possibly Ps. 57.

22:2 David soon attracted a considerable following of those who were oppressed and discontented with Saul's rule. **Everyone who was in debt** apparently refers to those who were in danger of being sold into slavery by their creditors (2 Kin. 4:1). **Captain** is a general term for a political, military, or religious leader. The **four hundred men** soon grew to six hundred (23:13).

22:3, 4 The name **Mizpah** means "Watch-tower"; this was probably a fortress in **Moab.** David's family connection with the Moabites is related in the story of Ruth (Ruth 1:4–18; 4:21, 22).

22:5, 6 Following the advice of the **prophet Gad** (2 Sam. 24:11), David left the **stronghold** and hid in **the forest of Hereth,** the location of which is unknown.

22:7, 8 the son of Jesse: Saul perhaps was unwilling to refer to David by name (20:30, 31). Saul suggested that the Benjamites could not expect blessings under the rule of David, who was from the tribe of Judah.

22:9–13 Doeg sought to ingratiate himself with Saul by betraying **Ahimelech,** the high priest who gave David provisions and a weapon (21:1–9).

22:14–16 as faithful as David: In answering the charges against himself, **Ahimelech** inadvertently defended David. **knew nothing:** Ahimelech made a case for his innocence by declaring his ignorance of the breach that had occurred between Saul and David.

22:17–19 would not lift their hands to strike the priests: The soldiers attending Saul knew better than to raise their weapons against the priests of the living God. Seeing a further opportunity to win Saul's favor, **Doeg,** a Gentile, carried out the slaughter of the 85 priests.

22:20, 21 Abiathar had not been among the 85 priests killed by Doeg at Gibeah. He escaped from Nob before the massacre. According to 23:6, he met up with David at Keilah.

22:22 I have caused the death of all the persons: David recognized that his deception led to the massacre of the priests and their families (21:1–9). The destruction of the priests of Nob was a partial fulfillment of the prophesied judgment on Eli's house (2:27–36).

22:23 he who seeks my life seeks your life: David and Abiathar were both regarded as enemies by Saul. **safe:** David offered Abiathar protection. He brought the ephod with him and inquired of the Lord for David (23:2, 6).

23:1 Instead of turning to Saul, their king, the people of **Keilah** appealed to **David** for deliverance from the **Philistines.** Located in a region of Jerusalem, Keilah belonged to the tribe of Judah (Josh. 15:44).

23:2, 3 David inquired of the LORD: David sought the will of God about whether the Lord had called him to deliver Keilah. **here in Judah:** The men had taken risks in associating themselves with David in Israelite territory, but they sensed that there would be increased risks if they left the hill country of Judah.

23:4–6 Abiathar did not join up with David until he was at **Keilah.** The account of this meeting was apparently included earlier to complete the narrative of what happened to the priests of Nob (22:20–23). The **ephod** was the outer vest of the priest. By means of the Urim and Thummim, God could be consulted and His will determined (see Ex. 28:30; Num. 27:21).

23:7, 8 a town that has gates and bars: Saul assumed that it would be easier to capture David in a fortified city than to chase him all over the wilderness. In an attempt to capture David, he was willing to destroy an entire Jewish town.

23:9–12 Bring the ephod here: David sought the will of God through the Urim and Thummim, which were attached to or inside the breastplate of the ephod (v. 6). David used the ephod to find out whether he was safe staying in Keilah.

23:13, 14 Strongholds refers to the various hideouts where David and his followers found refuge. The **Wilderness of Ziph** is the barren region about four miles southeast of Hebron.

23:15–18 Jonathan ... went to David: This was the custom between the two; Jonathan initiated their friendship. **his hand in God:** Both men had a fervent love for God, and Jonathan encouraged David to continue his obedient walk with the Lord. Jonathan recognized that David was destined to be Israel's next **king** and was content to take second place beside him because it was God's will.

23:19 Jeshimon may not be a proper name but a term meaning "waste" or "desert." The term is used here of the barren wilderness of Judah, which is in the vicinity of Ziph.

23:20–23 crafty: David's boyhood work as a shepherd gave him plenty of opportunity to learn the geography of the region and to become familiar with the hiding places of the wilderness.

23:24 By the time the Ziphites returned to **Ziph,** David and his men had moved to the **Wilderness of Maon,** a desert region to the south.

23:25–28 Although Saul and his men managed to surround David's hideout, a report of a raid by the **Philistines** forced Saul to withdraw, allowing David to escape. The place of David's near capture was named **the Rock of Escape** to commemorate his deliverance.

23:29 En Gedi, meaning "Spring of the Kid," was an oasis east of Hebron. The site was noted in biblical times for the fresh water spring and lush vineyards (see Song 1:14).

24:1, 2 The Rocks of the Wild Goats is another name for the area of En Gedi.

24:3 sheepfolds: At night, shepherds in this wild area would gather their sheep into a protective rock enclosure. The shepherd would position himself at the entrance of the sheepfold to guard against animals of prey and thieves.

24:4 the LORD said to you: These words are not recorded elsewhere in Scripture. **corner of Saul's robe:** Saul may have laid his robe aside, enabling David to cut off a piece unobserved. The piece of cloak would serve as proof that Saul had been at David's mercy.

24:5 David's heart troubled him: David was conscience-stricken. He knew it was wrong to assault the Lord's anointed king. Even though David had not really done anything to hurt the king physically, the fact that he had reached out with his knife troubled him.

24:6, 7 The LORD forbid: To cut off a portion of Saul's robe constituted for David an act of disrespect for God's representative, even though that man was seeking to take David's life.

24:8, 9 My lord the king: These words of respect from the voice that Saul knew well must have been quite stunning to him. **and bowed down:** This was an act of respect for

Saul's position as king. **David seeks your harm:** Some people in Saul's court were falsely accusing David of trying to overthrow Saul.

24:10 the LORD delivered you today into my hand: David recognized God's sovereignty in bringing about the circumstances that gave him an opportunity to kill Saul.

24:11 My father is a warm term of affection and respect. **your robe:** There could be no clearer evidence that David was not out to harm the king.

24:12 David dedicated to **the LORD** the matter of his relationship with Saul. God alone could settle the matter and bring about perfect justice (see Deut. 32:35; Rom. 12:17–21).

24:13 Wickedness proceeds from the wicked: The meaning of the proverb is that only a wicked man would seek to do evil against another. Since David did not take advantage of the opportunity to kill Saul, he was most certainly a good man.

24:14, 15 David likened himself to a **dead dog** and a **flea** in contrast with **the king of Israel.** How could a dead dog or a flea be of any danger to Saul?

24:16–18 Saul lifted up his voice and wept: Saul's tears reflect his remorse at seeking to do David harm. However, it was a short-lived remorse (26:2).

24:19 may the LORD reward you with good: Saul prayed for God's blessing on David.

24:20, 21 swear now to me by the LORD: Saul asked David to commit himself by oath to (1) preserve Saul's family and (2) preserve Saul's name.

24:22 David swore to Saul: David agreed to Saul's requests. While Saul returned **home** to Gibeah (10:26), David remained in hiding. He apparently had no confidence in Saul's expression of remorse.

25:1 Then Samuel died: Samuel's death may have taken place while David was in the Wilderness of En Gedi (24:1). Samuel's popularity was evidenced by the fact that the nation of Israel assembled at **Ramah** to honor him at his burial.

25:2 Carmel was located on the edge of the Judean wilderness, about a mile north of **Maon.** Like the times of harvest, the **shearing** of the sheep was a festive occasion.

25:3 The personal conduct of **Nabal** suggests that his name, meaning "Fool," was appropriate (v. 25). Nabal was a descendant of the **house of Caleb,** which had occupied the area at the time of the conquest (see Judg. 1:20). **Abigail was** a woman of wisdom and beauty.

25:4–9 Nabal lived in a wilderness area and owned thousands of sheep and goats, and so was a prime target for thieves. David and his men had protected Nabal's flocks and possessions. **nor was there anything missing:** David and his men had provided protection and had not taken advantage of their position or authority. David sent his men on a **feast day,** when most people display an extra measure of generosity. **Please give whatever comes to your hand:** Apparently, no price had been set for the services rendered.

25:10 Who is David: Nabal pretended not to know David. He added insult to injury by suggesting that David might be just another runaway servant.

25:11–14 Nabal lived in a region where **water** was scarce (see Josh. 15:19).

25:15, 16 Nabal's own men testified to the care and protection they received from David and his men.

25:17 For he is such a scoundrel: The servants were so angry at their master that they spoke this way of him to his wife!

25:18 Abigail gathered an abundance of goods to compensate David and his men.

25:19–21 Go on before me: Abigail wisely sent the provisions ahead to forestall any hostility caused by her husband's insulting behavior.

25:22 May God do so, and more also: David made an oath calling down God's judgment on his enemies should he fail to kill everyone who worked for Nabal.

25:23, 24 Abigail did everything she could to show respect to David when he was angry and to obtain his forgiveness for the wrong Nabal had committed against him.

25:25 For as his name is, so is he: Abigail's humor at her husband's expense was designed to save his life (vv. 21, 22).

25:26 as the LORD lives: Abigail showed herself to David to be a woman of faith.

25:27 This present means the provisions mentioned in v. 18. These gracious gifts expressed Abigail's desire to make things right.

25:28 an enduring house: Abigail's words indicate that she expected David to succeed Saul and enjoy a lengthy line of successors (v. 30).

25:29–31 bound in the bundle of the living: This metaphor reflects the custom of binding valuables in a bundle to protect them from injury. **no grief to you:** Abigail sought to show David that the present slight was nothing compared to his future glory.

25:32–35 respected your person: A literal translation of this phrase would be "I lift up your face." This is the opposite of Abigail's bowing before David when she first met him (vv. 23, 24).

25:36–38 his heart died within him ... like a stone: Nabal apparently suffered a stroke and became paralyzed. His death was the result of God's judgment.

25:39, 40 David gave praise for it was God who had exacted justice and not David himself.

25:41, 42 to wash the feet of the servants: Washing the feet of others was a servant's task. Abigail expressed her willingness to do the most menial jobs.

25:43 Ahinoam became the mother of David's oldest son, Amnon (2 Sam. 3:2). **Jezreel** is not the city in the north, but a town in the hill country of Judah (Josh. 15:56).

25:44 David was without **Michal,** his wife. Saul had given her to another man.

26:1 The Ziphites were from Ziph, four miles southeast of Hebron. They traveled about 25 miles north to report to Saul at **Gibeah.**

26:2–4 Apparently forgetful of the events of 24:16–22, Saul led his men into the wilderness in pursuit of David. The similarities between the events of ch. 24 and the events here are striking.

26:5 Abner the son of Ner had served as a very successful commander of Saul's army.

26:6 Ahimelech the Hittite was a non-Israelite who had joined David's force, probably as a mercenary soldier.

26:7 Saul's **spear** was a symbol of his authority (18:10; 19:9).

26:8 Abishai seems to have had a bloodthirsty nature (see 2 Sam. 16:9; 19:21). He promised not to strike Saul **a second time**—meaning that his first blow would be fatal.

26:9, 10 David once again refused to **stretch out his hand against the LORD's anointed** (ch. 24). **the LORD shall strike him:** David knew that God would remove Saul from office according to His own perfect timing.

26:11, 12 take now the spear and the jug of water: These items would prove that David had been close enough to Saul to kill him but had refrained from doing so. David's visit to Saul's camp went undetected because the Lord had caused **a deep sleep** to fall upon the soldiers.

26:13, 14 calling out to the king: David did not shout directly to Saul; instead, he taunted Abner, Saul's general.

26:15, 16 The **spear** and the **jug of water** served as evidence of Abner's negligence and proof of David's goodwill.

26:17, 18 Is that your voice, my son David: Saul recognized the familiar voice, as he had near the cave at En Gedi (24:16).

26:19 If the LORD has stirred you up against me: David contemplated the possibility that God was using Saul as an agent of divine discipline. On the other hand, he called for God's judgment on any evil men who had stirred up Saul against David.

26:20–22 David likened Saul's actions to pursuing **a flea** (24:14), hardly fitting for a royal figure. Saul once again confessed his sin promising not to make another attempt on his life.

26:23 Righteousness and **faithfulness** are characteristics of God Himself, which believers may share.

26:24, 25 David requested that his **life be valued** as much as he valued Saul's life. As the two parted, Saul recognized that David would eventually **prevail** (24:20). This was the last meeting between Saul and David.

27:1 Now I shall perish someday by the hand of Saul: As he had done earlier in fleeing from Saul, David journeyed toward the coastal plain and entered **the land of the Philistines.**

27:2 Achish seems to have welcomed David. Perhaps he had heard of the split between David and Saul and was anxious to strengthen his own army with David's **six hundred** fighting men.

27:3, 4 David dwelt with Achish at Gath: David's move to Philistine territory delivered him from the immediate danger of Saul and provided him an opportunity to further develop his leadership and military skills (vv. 8–12). His time in Philistia also gave David knowledge of the geography of the region, which would serve him well during his later Philistine wars.

27:5 why should your servant dwell in the royal city: David suggested to Achish that it was too great an honor for him to continue to dwell in Gath, the city of the king.

27:6 Achish established David as his vassal over **Ziklag,** one of the cities of the Israelite Negev.

27:7 Ziklag remained David's headquarters until Saul's death, when David moved to Hebron (2 Sam. 1:1–4).

27:8 David convinced Achish that he was serving the Philistines. Yet he used Ziklag as a base for raids on desert tribes who were enemies of the Israelites.

27:9, 10 Where have you made a raid today: Although David pretended to serve the interests of Achish, he was actually attacking the enemies of Israel.

27:11 The complete destruction of human life seems to be the only way David was able to avoid discovery.

27:12 he will be my servant forever: David's deception was so effective that **Achish** concluded that his switch in allegiance was permanent.

28:1 in those days: The events of ch. 28 occurred during the time David was living at Ziklag as a vassal of the Philistine king. **you will go out with me:** Since David was a vassal of **Achish,** the Philistines expected him to join them in their campaign against Saul. David faced a terrible dilemma.

28:2 Surely you know what your servant can do: The words of David were deliberately ambiguous. His life would have been at risk had he refused to join Achish so he was forced to wait for God's deliverance. **one of my chief guardians:** David found himself not only in the Philistine army but assigned as one of the king's chief bodyguards.

28:3 Samuel had died: He could no longer be counted on to bring forth a word from the Lord. The term **mediums** refers to necromancers, those who presume to communicate with the dead. **Spiritists** is a general term for those who have contact with spirits. The medium at En Dor was one of the few such persons still known to live in the land (v. 7).

28:4 The village of **Shunem** was situated in the Valley of Jezreel, on the south slope of the Hill of Moreh. The Israelite forces were camped about five miles south of the Philistines on the mountain range of **Gilboa.**

28:5 Saul was so **afraid** of the forthcoming battle that his **heart trembled greatly.** Saul's persistent disobedience had left him completely without God's presence and protection.

28:6 God did not answer **Saul** by **dreams** as He had Joseph (Gen. 37:5–10); nor by the **Urim** and Thummim as He had the high priest (Ex. 28:30; Num. 27:21); nor by prophetic revelation as He had Samuel (3:10–21).

28:7 Find me a woman who is a medium: Saul turned to a forbidden source of counsel.

28:8 Saul disguised himself: Saul could not expect much help should his identity be known. **Conduct a séance for me** literally means "bring up for me."

28:9 Why then do you lay a snare for my life: The woman recognized the risk of being punished with death for practicing necromancy (see Ex. 22:18) and sought to make sure that her visitor was not laying a trap.

28:10 Saul swore to her by the LORD: While engaging in a practice that was a denial of God's sovereign control, Saul swore in God's name that he would protect the woman.

28:11 Saul sought the help of **Samuel** because he had anointed him as king and had spoken God's word to Saul before (10:1).

28:12 When the woman saw Samuel: When her seance really worked, the seer finally saw that her client was Saul. It seems best to follow the early view that this was a genuine appearance of Samuel which God Himself brought about.

28:13, 14 The **mantle** was a prophet's robe, such as the one Samuel had worn. It was this robe that Saul once had torn (15:27).

28:15 The words **bringing me** mean simply "up from the grave." This phrase indicates that the Israelites believed in life after death.

28:16, 17 the LORD has departed from you: Samuel was not so much making an affirmation as he was pointing out the contradiction between Saul's words and actions.

28:18 Samuel traced Saul's disobedience and judgment back to his failure to destroy the Amalekites, particularly Agag (15:2–9).

28:19–23 Saul and his sons would die in the battle with the Philistines the very next day. The words **with me** simply refer to the grave. **no strength:** Saul's sinful actions in seeking out a medium resulted in his complete collapse.

28:24, 25 Unleavened bread was baked without yeast and could be prepared without waiting for it to rise.

29:1, 2 a fountain which is in Jezreel: The Israelites gathered at a prominent but unidentified spring in the Valley of Jezreel. **passed in review:** Apparently the Philistine troops convened at an agreed-upon rendezvous to be reviewed and arranged in companies.

29:3 David was in a predicament, for he would not fight against his own people. He could do nothing but wait for the Lord to provide him with a means of escape from this dangerous situation. **Achish** had **found no fault** with David since his "defection" from Saul.

29:4 Make this fellow return: Achish was unsuccessful in persuading his fellow princes and soldiers to accept David and his men as part of the Philistine forces.

29:5 Saul has slain his thousands: The popular Israelite taunt song (18:7) continued to echo in the ears of the Philistines (21:11).

29:6 Achish was thoroughly deceived by David's display of loyalty. **as the LORD lives:** Achish swore by the name of the God of Israel to impress David with the sincerity of his confidence in him.

29:7–9 go in peace: This farewell was more than a courtesy. Achish was releasing David from any obligation that he had incurred when Achish had made David a vassal king in Ziklag.

29:10 your master's servants: Achish was referring to Saul as David's master.

29:11 After the departure of David and his men, the Philistines marched north from Aphek (v. 1) to the Valley of **Jezreel.**

30:1 The attack on **Ziklag** took place **on the third day** after David and his men left the Philistine army at Aphek. **The Amalekites** were placed under divine judgment for their attack on the Israelites after the Exodus from Egypt (Ex. 17:8–13), they (Deut. 25:19).

30:2–5 carried them away: The Amalekites probably intended to make them slaves. Among those who were taken captive were David's wives and the wives and children of his men.

30:6 David was **distressed** not only because of his personal grief but by the difficult situation pressing on him. **the people spoke of stoning him:** It is often the nature of unhappy people to vent their frustration through acts of hostility against their leaders (see Ex. 17:4). **strengthened himself in the LORD his God:** David knew where to turn in a time of crisis. He had learned to wait on God's eventual deliverance (see Ps. 40:1–3).

30:7, 8 Abiathar was the son of **Ahimelech,** the high priest from whom David had received provisions at Nob (21:1–9). The Urim and Thummim were attached to the breastplate of the **ephod** that David requested be brought to him (see Ex. 28:30).

30:9 The Brook Besor emptied into the Mediterranean Sea just south of the Philistine city of Gaza (6:17).

30:10 weary: The weariness of David's men was due to the fact that they had traveled about 80 miles from Aphek to Ziklag (29:1; 30:1), only to set off immediately in pursuit of the Amalekites.

30:11–13 found an Egyptian: A sick slave had been left by the Amalekites to die in the wilderness (v. 13).

30:14 The Cherethites (see 2 Sam. 8:18; 15:18; 20:7, 23) were a clan closely related to, if not actually a part of, the Philistines (see Ezek. 25:16; Zeph. 2:5).

30:15 In exchange for protection, the Egyptian agreed to lead David and his men to the Amalekites.

30:16 eating and drinking and dancing: The Amalekites were enjoying the booty they had taken from Philistia and Judah, including Ziklag.

30:17–21 Twilight here probably means just before first light in the morning. God was faithful to His earlier promise (v. 8); David's men were able to recover their wives and possessions.

30:22, 23 wicked and worthless men: These men insisted that the spoil captured from the Amalekites should not be divided with the men who stayed at the Brook Besor with the supplies.

30:24, 25 they shall share alike: David's band of warriors were one, although they had different strengths and abilities. They would share equally in the fruits of victory.

30:26 David also shared the booty taken from the Amalekites with the **elders of Judah**. This goodwill gesture helped David reestablish his relationships among the leaders of Judah after his stay in Philistine territory.

30:27 Ramoth of the South may be the same city as Ramah of the South (Josh. 19:8), whose location is uncertain. **Jattir,** a Levitical city (see Josh. 21:14) allotted to Judah (see Josh. 15:48), was about 13 miles southwest of Hebron.

30:28 Eshtemoa was a Levitical city (see Josh. 21:14) in the hill country of Judah.

30:29 The **Jerahmeelites** were one of the clans of Judah (1 Chr. 2:9).

30:30 Hormah was where the Israelites were first defeated by the Canaanites (Num. 14:45). **Chorashan** and **Athach** are also of uncertain location.

30:31 Hebron was soon to become David's capital. It was a Levitical city and a city of refuge.

31:1 Mount Gilboa was a small mountain range in the eastern part of the Jezreel valley.

31:2, 3 Saul's fourth son, Ishbosheth, was apparently not present at this battle, since Abner promoted him to king after Saul's death (2 Sam. 2:8–10).

31:4 Saul took a sword and fell on it: This account of Saul's death is different from that given by the Amalekite in 2 Sam. 1:6–10.

31:5 Saul's **armorbearer** joined his master in death.

31:6 all his men: This refers to men particularly associated with Saul, perhaps his royal bodyguards.

31:7 they forsook the cities and fled: As a result of Israel's defeat, many of the cities of northern Israel were abandoned.

31:8, 9 the Philistines came to strip the slain: The victors gathered clothes, weapons, and armor from the dead.

31:10 The armor of Saul was placed in the **temple** dedicated to the worship of Ashtoreth, or Ishtar, the Canaanite goddess of fertility and war. Although Saul's body was fastened to the wall of the city of **Beth Shan,** 1 Chr. 10:10 records that his head was displayed in the temple of Dagon.

31:11 The inhabitants of Jabesh Gilead had been delivered from the threats of Nahash the Ammonite by Saul in his first military campaign as king of Israel (11:1–11).

31:12 the valiant men arose: Out of gratitude to Saul the men of Jabesh Gilead risked their lives to recover the bodies of Saul and his sons and to give them a proper burial.

31:13 Although the bodies of Saul and his sons were burned, the **bones** were recovered and **buried.** Later, David exhumed the bodies of Saul and Jonathan and had them reburied in Benjamin (2 Sam. 21:11–14). **fasted seven days:** With their fasting, the men of **Jabesh** showed their respect for Israel's first king.

2 Samuel

Introduction

Second Samuel recounts the triumphs and defeats of King David. From his rise to the throne to his famous last words, this biography describes a remarkable, divinely-inspired leader. As king, David took a divided and defeated Israel from his predecessor King Saul and built a prominent nation.

Second Samuel is named after the prophet Samuel, even though he does not appear in the narratives of the book. Jewish tradition holds that the prophet Samuel wrote 1 Sam. 1—24, and that the prophets Nathan and Gad composed the rest of First Samuel and all of Second Samuel.

Second Samuel covers the period from the death of Saul (c. 1010 B.C.) to the end of David's career (c. 970 B.C.). During the forty years of his reign, David welded the loose-knit tribes together into a strong monarchy and transformed the youthful nation into a military power able to dominate surrounding nations. His conquests and alliances gave him control of territory from the border of Egypt to the Euphrates. For a brief period, Israel was as strong as any nation of the ancient world.

The key to David's successful reign was his relationship with the Lord. In his youth, David had demonstrated his strong faith in God by challenging a giant with only a few stones and his faith in God's strength (1 Sam. 17:45–51). In his adulthood, he continued to rely on God for guidance and strength (2:1; 5:19). Even when David sinned, he demonstrated to the people his repentant heart before the living God (12:13–23; 24:17–25). In the final analysis, his religious leadership was the most significant part of his reign.

The Lord gave David a glimpse of His ultimate will through the Davidic covenant (7:12–16). In this unconditional covenant, God promised David an eternal dynasty, an eternal throne, and an eternal kingdom. Ultimately, a righteous King greater than David was coming. He would be David's son and would rule from David's throne forever

(Is. 9:7). This promised King is Jesus (see Luke 1:31–33; John 1:49).

1:1 The death of Saul is recorded in 1 Sam. 31:3–5. **The Amalekites** were a nomadic, marauding people who roamed the southern part of Canaan. They were fierce enemies of Israel until they were brought under Israelite control in the time of David. **Ziklag** was one of the Israelite cities of the southern desert or Negev, originally assigned to Judah (Josh. 15:31).

1:2 clothes torn and dust on his head: The man was in mourning (1 Sam. 4:12). He **fell to the ground** to show his support for David as Saul's successor to the throne of Israel.

1:3 escaped from the camp of Israel: The army of Israel had fallen in defeat to the Philistines, but the man had escaped from the battlefield.n had escaped from the battlefield.

1:4–8 The Amalekite's report of Saul's death is different from the account in 1 Sam. 31:4, which states that Saul died by falling on his sword.

1:9 In this context, **anguish** refers to the agony of death.

1:10 I was sure that he could not live: According to the Amalekite's story, since Saul had no hope of recovery, there was justification in putting him to death. The **crown** was a mark of royalty. The **bracelet** was an ornament worn on the upper part of the arm. The Amalekite brought these items to David in order to substantiate his story.

1:11 tore them: Tearing one's clothes was a traditional expression of mourning in ancient times (3:31; see Gen. 37:34).

1:12 the people of the LORD: David and his associates mourned not only for the fallen king and prince, but also for those who had died from the ranks of Saul's army. David did not see them as enemies, but as members of God's family.

1:13 Where are you from: David's question might have been designed to determine whether the Amalekite resided in Israel or in Amalekite territory to the south.

1:14 David's use of the phrase **the LORD's anointed** indicates that even though Saul was his enemy, David respected Saul's divine right to be king. Saul as king served as God's representative and ruler over His people. David repeatedly refused to harm him because of this (1 Sam. 24:6; 26:9).

1:15 execute him: David's execution of the Amalekite was a strong statement to those under his command that he had no part in Saul's death and did not reward it in any way.

1:16, 17 Your blood is on your own head: The Amalekite, not the executioner, was morally accountable for the shedding of his own blood.

1:18 The Hebrew phrase **the children of Judah** means not young people but the descendants or tribe of Judah. **The Book of Jasher** was perhaps a collection of hymns about of Israel's wars, in which important events and national figures were commemorated in poetry.

1:19 The beauty of Israel refers to Saul and Jonathan. **High places** alludes to Mt. Gilboa (v. 6), where the warriors died.

1:20 Gath and **Ashkelon** joined with Ekron, Gaza, and Ashdod to form the Philistine pentapolis, or five-city league.

1:21, 22 no dew nor rain: A curse was pronounced on the mountains of Gilboa, the scene of the military disaster (1:6; 1 Sam. 31:8). **not anointed with oil:** Saul's shield was declared useless because it had not protected him from death.

1:23, 24 Eagles and **lions** were poetic symbols of speed and strength. **weep over Saul:** David invited the women of Israel to lead in public lamentation for Saul.

1:25 How the mighty have fallen: The poetic repetition of these words from v. 19 prepares the reader for the shift in focus of the poem to Jonathan.

1:26 Your love: David compared Jonathan's love with that of women in its depth and loyalty. David was not afraid to speak of his deep and genuine love for his friend.

1:27 How the mighty have fallen: The third repetition of this phrase (compare vv. 19, 25) brings the psalm to its painful conclusion. The phrase **weapons of war** is a figurative reference to the fallen warriors.

2:1 David inquired of the LORD: Before taking an important step, it was David's custom to

seek the will of the Lord (1 Sam. 23:2; 30:8). The Lord directed David to **Hebron**. Its central location made it a suitable capital for David.

2:2 his two wives: David's marriages to Abigail and Ahinoam are recorded in 1 Sam. 25:2–43.

2:3 The ancient name for Hebron was Kirjath Arba (see Gen. 23:2), meaning "Town of Four." Apparently, the town had four suburbs, one of which must have been Mamre (Gen. 35:27); hence, one may speak of **the cities of Hebron** (Josh. 21:11).

2:4 anointed David: This is actually the second anointing of David. The first anointing was a mark of God's intention; this second anointing was the recognition by the people of Judah that David was truly the Lord's anointed (5:3).

2:5–7 sent messengers: David's sincere action of appreciation for the kindness of the men also announced to them that he was ready to act on their behalf, because he was now the anointed king of the tribe of Judah. **let your hands be strengthened:** David made an appeal to the men of Gilead for their strong support of his kingship. However, their loyalty to Saul's dynasty prevailed, and Jabesh Gilead became the headquarters of Ishbosheth, David's rival.

2:8 Ishbosheth means "Man of Shame." His original name Esh-Baal, meaning "Man of the Master" or "Man of the Lord," was changed because "Baal" suggested Baal worship (1 Chr. 8:33, 9:39). **Mahanaim,** the capital of Gilead, was north of the Jabbok River (1 Kin. 4:14).

2:9 Gilead usually refers to the central part of the Israelite territory east of the Jordan River.

2:10, 11 While David was king in Hebron for seven and one-half years, Ishbosheth reigned for only **two years.** The difference may mean that Ishbosheth took about five years to recover the northern territory from the Philistines after Saul's defeat.

2:12, 13 pool of Gibeon: A rock-cut pool 37 feet in diameter and 82 feet deep. A spiral staircase of 79 steps cut in the rock leads to the bottom. The pool was meant either to store rainwater or to provide access to the water table. **Joab:** David's nephew became a competent military commander of David's forces (10:7–14; 12:26–28).

2:14–17 Abner proposed a contest between champions to determine the outcome of the conflict between Ishbosheth and David (1 Sam. 17:38–54). The two groups of **twelve** faced each other. Two champions contended at a time, each killing the other, until all twenty-four had died.

2:18 Joab, Abishai, and **Asahel** were brothers, all sons of David's sister **Zeruiah** (1 Chr. 2:13–16). The **wild gazelle** was renowned in Israel for its beauty and swiftness.

2:19, 20 Asahel knew that if **Abner** was dead, Ishbosheth's power base would dissolve, and the tribes could be united under King David.

2:21, 22 Abner, confident that he could defeat Asahel, wanted to avoid the blood feud that would likely develop if he were to kill Joab's brother.

2:23, 24 Unable to deter Asahel from pursuing him, Abner stabbed him with the **blunt end** of his spear, which was the end opposite the spear head. It was probably pointed so that it could be stuck in the ground (1 Sam. 26:7).

2:25 the children of Benjamin: The men of Saul's tribe were among the strongest supporters of Abner and Ishbosheth.

2:26–28 devour forever: Recognizing that continued fighting would only result in further loss of life and deepened hostility, Abner and Joab agreed to call off the conflict. Here, the **trumpet,** a ram's horn or shofar, was used to mark a truce between the warring sides.

2:29–31 Abner's army retreated across the Jordan River and returned to **Mahanaim,** Ishbosheth's headquarters (vv. 8, 12).

2:32 After burying Asahel at **Bethlehem,** six miles south of Jerusalem, Joab and his men marched another fourteen miles to **Hebron,** David's capital (v. 1).

3:1 a long war: Hostilities continued between the two royal houses, with David gradually gaining ascendancy.

3:2 David began his reign in Judah with two wives, Ahinoam and Abigail. In Hebron, he married four more wives, each of whom bore him a son.

3:3 Chileab is called Daniel in 1 Chr. 3:1. The story of his mother, **Abigail,** is found in 1 Sam. 25. She is not the same as Abigail the mother of Amasa (17:25). **Absalom** died at the hands of Joab (18:14). Absalom's mother, **Maacah,** is identified as **the daughter of Talmai, king of Geshur.** David used marriage alliances to conclude treaties and cement relations between Israel and foreign nations.

3:4 Adonijah attempted to take his father's throne just before David proclaimed Solomon king (1 Kin. 1).

3:5 in Hebron: These six sons, each from a different mother, constituted the royal family during David's reign over the house of Judah.

3:6, 7 The phrase **strengthening his hold** implies that Abner was usurping Ishbosheth's authority, becoming the power behind the throne. **father's concubine:** Ishbosheth's charge, that Abner was having sexual relations with one of Saul's concubines, was serious. The royal harem was the property of the king's successor. Taking a king's concubine was tantamount to claiming the throne (16:20–22).

3:8 Am I a dog's head: In the ancient Middle East, dogs were scavengers, living off dead animals and garbage, and were viewed with contempt.

3:9, 10 The phrase **may God do so to Abner** is a prayer for divine judgment should Abner fail to keep his oath. The words **as the LORD has sworn** indicate that Abner knew that David had been divinely chosen to succeed Saul (vv. 17, 18).

3:11, 12 Whose is the land: The implication here is that the land could be David's if he entered into a binding agreement with Abner who actually held all the power.

3:13 David's first wife **Michal** was left in Gibeah when David fled from Saul's court. She was later given by Saul to a man named Palti (1 Sam. 25:44).

3:14, 15 David's request for Michal was formally addressed to Ishbosheth. **a hundred foreskins:** David mentioned the number which Saul had originally asked for; David actually paid him double (1 Sam. 18:25–27).

3:16 Michal's second husband appears brokenhearted at her forced removal from his home.

3:17, 18 For the LORD has spoken: The Bible does not record elsewhere the divine promise quoted by Abner and referred to in vv. 9, 10.

3:19–21 David faced the most opposition from Saul's tribe, **Benjamin.** Abner personally campaigned for David's kingship in this tribe. After winning support for David in Israel, Abner proceeded to **Hebron** (2:1) to announce the people's decision to acknowledge David as king.

3:22, 23 The words **gone in peace** are repeated (v. 21), to emphasize that the hostilities between David and Abner had been resolved.

3:24, 25 What have you done: Learning of Abner's visit, Joab challenged the king for allowing the commander of a hostile army and a cousin of Saul to come and go from Hebron without being apprehended and put to death.

3:26, 27 stabbed him: This was an act of treachery, especially in Hebron, a city of refuge (Josh. 20:7). In a city of refuge, a blood avenger could not slay a murderer without a trial (Num. 35:22–25). Joab wanted to avenge the death of **Asahel his brother,** who was killed in the course of a battle (2:18–23).

3:28, 29 My kingdom and I: David issued a public proclamation denying any involvement in the murder of Abner. The death of Abner was not only an act of treachery, but also a great blow to David's hopes for a peaceable unification of the nation under his control. **Let it rest on the head of Joab:** This verse forms a strong curse on the household of Joab.

3:30 Abishai was Joab's other brother (2:18). His involvement in the murder of Abner is mentioned only here.

3:31, 32 Tear your clothes: These actions were associated in ancient times with mourning the dead (1:11; Gen. 37:34).

3:33, 34 as a fool dies: Certainly a warrior like Abner deserved a more noble death.

3:35 The murder of Abner had the potential of breaking the fragile union of the twelve tribes. David refused to participate in the meal that was customarily served to mourners after the burial as evidence of his genuine remorse.

3:36, 37 All Israel All the people became confident of David's innocence.

3:38, 39 The words **a prince and a great man** reflect how highly David regarded Abner.

4:1 Saul's son Ishbosheth lost the **heart** to act as king, since Abner, his primary supporter, was gone.

4:2, 3 The fact that **Baanah** and **Rechab** were from the tribe of **Benjamin,** the tribe of Saul, makes their actions all the more reprehensible. **Beeroth** was one of the four cities of the Gibeonites (Josh. 9:17), with whom Joshua had made a covenant.

4:4 Merib-Baal, which means "The Master Is Advocate," was the original name of Jonathan's son (1 Chr. 8:34; 9:40).

4:5, 6 The **house of Ishbosheth** was at Mahanaim. Ishbosheth was taking his midday rest, as perhaps were the members of the palace guard.

4:7 The murderers fled by way of **the plain,** meaning by way of the Jordan valley.

4:8–10 Rechab and Baanah **brought the head of Ishbosheth to David,** perhaps in hopes of receiving a reward. They used the spiritual language **the LORD has avenged** to describe their despicable actions. Yet their lofty words did not fool David. The oath **as the LORD lives** implies that David was under God's protection. There was no need to kill Ishbosheth to defend David's life.

4:11 Ishbosheth was viewed as a **righteous person** since he was innocent of any wicked deed or crime. He had simply assumed royal power after the death of his father Saul.

4:12 The execution of the assassins was justified on the basis of Gen. 9:5. Their corpses were **hanged,** or impaled, **by the pool in Hebron,** which was frequented daily by the people of the city.

5:1 All the tribes refers to tribal leaders, such as elders and heads of clans (v. 3). **We are your bone and your flesh** means "we are your relatives."

5:2 The words **led Israel out** speak of David's service as a military leader during

Saul's reign. The word **shepherd** is a vivid metaphor of the relationship between a king and his people.

5:3–5 before the LORD: Making a covenant was not just a civil arrangement but a sacred occasion. **they anointed:** This was David's third anointing (2:4; 1 Sam. 16:13).

5:6 David's first move as king was to conquer Jebus, which came to be known as **Jerusalem.** The city was strategically located in the hill country near the border of Judah and Benjamin, making it a foreign wedge between the northern and southern tribes.

5:7 Jerusalem is referred to as the **stronghold of Zion.** The word Zion originally applied to the Jebusite stronghold, which became **the City of David** after its capture.

5:8 The **water shaft** extended about 230 feet up from the Gihon spring to the top of the hill where the Jebusite fortress was situated (2 Chr. 32:30). The tunnel gave the city a secure water supply in the event of a siege.

5:9 The term **City of David** is used in Luke 2:11 to refer to Bethlehem, the city of David's birth. Here the term refers to Zion, the city from which he ruled Israel.

5:10 God of hosts may also be translated "God of Armies" (6:2). The hosts are the armies of angels that are at the Lord's command (v. 24).

5:11, 12 Tyre, located on the Mediterranean coast north of Israel, was a Phoenician city noted for its commerce, craftsmen, and wealth. Hiram's kindness toward David was probably prompted by economic interests. The **house** that Hiram had built for David must have been sumptuous for the place and time.

5:13 These marriages reflect David's involvement in international treaties and alliances which were sealed with the marriage of a king's daughter to the other participant in the treaty.

5:14 Shammua is known as **Shimea** in 1 Chr. 3:5. Shammua, Shobab, Nathan, and Solomon were David's sons by Bathsheba (1 Chr. 3:5), the wife of Uriah. David planned Uriah's death so that he could marry Bathsheba (ch. 11). The child born of David and Bathsheba's affair died in infancy (12:15–23).

5:15, 16 The lists in 1 Chr. 3:5–9 and 1 Chr. 14:4, 5 record two additional sons, Nogah and another Eliphelet (Elpelet in 1 Chr. 14:4).

5:17 The Hebrew word translated **stronghold** means "mountain fortress," suggesting a fortress other than Jerusalem.

5:18 The Valley of Rephaim, or "Valley of the Giants" (21:15–22), extends southwest from Jerusalem toward the coastal plain.

5:19, 20 As was his custom, **David inquired of the LORD** before engaging the Philistines in battle (see 2:1; 1 Sam. 23:2; 30:8).

5:21–23 The **images** which the Philistines had taken into battle to assure them of victory were captured and carried away by David's men.

5:24 God was suggesting that the sound of rustling leaves in the treetops was in fact the sound of His angelic army going forth to attack (see 2 Kin. 6:17).

5:25 The **Geba** mentioned here is most likely located south, in the Valley of Rephaim.

6:1 The **thirty thousand** men were not all the men of Israel capable of bearing arms, but the best of them.

6:2 The Name, the LORD of Hosts: At times the Name of God is accompanied by the designation "of Hosts" (5:10), referring to the angelic armies of the universe (see 1 Kin. 22:19; Luke 2:13) as well as the armies of Israel (1 Sam. 17:45).

6:3, 4 they set the ark of God on a new cart: The law was specific that the ark was to be carried by the sons of Kohath, not by a cart. David was doing what the Philistines had done.The ark had been taken to the **house of Abinadab** after its recovery from the Philistines (see 1 Sam. 7:1, 2).

6:5 Played literally means they "made merry" with dancing and music (v. 21). **Sistrums** refers to Egyptian instruments consisting of rings hanging loosely on metal rods that make a rattling sound when shaken.

6:6 In order to steady the ark when it seemed it would fall, **Uzzah put out his hand.**

6:7 Although Uzzah's violation was unintentional, his error cost him his life. God had warned His people that not even the Levites could touch the holy objects of the tabernacle.

6:8 David became angry at God. He named the place of the tragedy **Perez Uzzah,** recalling what had happened.

6:9 David was afraid of the LORD: The tragedy of Uzzah rekindled a necessary "fear of God" in the heart of David.

6:10, 11 Obed-Edom was a Levite of the family of Korah, and later one of the doorkeepers for the ark (see 1 Chr. 15:18, 24; 26:4–8). He was called **the Gittite** because he was from the Levitical city of Gath Rimmon (see Josh. 21:24).

6:12, 13 This time the ark was carried (see Ex. 25:14, 15), rather than transported by cart. Some interpreters think that the procession was halted and sacrifices were offered every **six paces.**

6:14 The Hebrew word translated **danced** literally means "whirled." The **linen ephod** was a short, sleeveless garment worn by priests (see 1 Sam. 2:18).

6:15, 16 Shouting was an expression of celebration and triumph (see Is. 44:23). The **trumpet** refers to the ram's horn or the shofar (2:28).

6:17 David erected a tent, no doubt patterned after the **tabernacle** of Moses, to serve as a shelter for the ark until a more permanent building could be constructed.

6:18 he blessed the people: David is a type of the Savior Jesus who is the great King and Priest.

6:19 A distinctive feature of the peace offering (v. 17) was that a portion would be eaten by the worshiper as a fellowship meal before the Lord. David shared this meal with those who participated in the celebration.

6:20 to bless his household: At the moment of his greatest spiritual experience, David took pleasure in the prospect of bringing God's blessing to his home, only to be met by the curses of his wife. The scornful remark about David's **uncovering himself** refers to the priestly attire worn by the king. David had exposed more of himself than Michal thought appropriate.

6:21 David rebuked Michal by reminding her that God had chosen him in place of her **father** Saul, an evidence of divine blessing on his religious commitment and enthusiasm.

6:22 David declared that he would gladly be **even more undignified** and **humble** to worship the Lord and to be **held in honor** by those who shared his spiritual values.

6:23 Michal's childlessness was the result of either estrangement from David. Thus there was no successor to the throne from the house of Saul.

7:1 The **house** refers to the palace that the Phoenicians had built for David (5:11). **Rest from all his enemies** probably refers to the peace that prevailed after David's defeat of the Philistines (5:17–25).

7:2 Nathan was a personal advisor to David. As a **prophet** (Ex. 7:1, 2), he spoke for God, advising David on religious matters.

7:3, 4 Nathan encouraged the king to build a temple for the ark. However, he spoke on the basis of his own understanding and not as a word from the Lord.

7:5 Although Nathan had encouraged David to build a temple for the ark (v. 3), the Lord revealed that this was not His intention at all.

7:6 A tent was a traveler's dwelling.

7:7 Throughout the history of God's dealings with the Israelites, never once did He reprove them for failing to build Him a permanent sanctuary.

7:8 God reminded David of His gracious dealings in taking him from the humble role of a shepherd to serve as king over His people.

7:9 A great name or reputation was highly valued by the Hebrews. As God promised to make the name Abram great (see Gen. 12:2), so He promised David that his name would be renowned.

7:10 God promised to provide Israel a secure dwelling place in the land of Israel.

7:11 house: David wanted to build God a house (vv. 2–7). Instead, God intended to build David a house—that is, a dynasty of long duration.

7:12 The first provision of the Davidic covenant was that David would have a son for whom God would establish a **kingdom.**

7:13 House here refers to the temple (see 1 Kin. 6). God also promised **to establish the throne of** Solomon's **kingdom forever** (see 1 Chr. 22:6–10).

7:14 iniquity: The sins of David's sons would require divine chastening (1 Kin. 11:1–13).
7:15 Although Solomon's sins would justify chastening, God promised that His **mercy** would not be removed, as was necessary in the case of Saul (1 Sam. 13:13, 14; 15:22, 23).
7:16–18 The words **sat before the LORD** indicate that David was in the tent which served to house the ark. **Who am I, O Lord GOD:** David's rhetorical question reflected his sense of unworthiness to have been extended such a gracious promise (vv. 12–16).
7:19, 20 David acknowledged that what God had done for him so far was far greater than anything he deserved. As if this were only **a small thing,** God now extended the promise about David's dynasty far into the future.
7:21–23 All that we have heard with our ears refers to the shared tradition about God's

work in history (Deut. 4:32–40).
7:24 Your people Israel: At the heart of God's promise to David was the continuation of His promise to the nation of Israel (see Gen. 12:1–3).
7:25 Having praised God for His gracious works, David prayed for the fulfillment of the promise.
7:26, 27 The **name** of God refers here to His reputation. David wanted God's reputation to be magnified through the fulfillment of His promise.
7:28, 29 You are God, and Your words are true: David acknowledged that God could be trusted to fulfill His promise.
8:1 The Philistines were a major threat to Israel during the reigns of Saul and David.
8:2 The Moabites occupied the land opposite Judah, east of the Jordan River and the Dead Sea.

 ## David's Cabinet

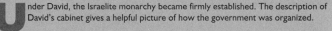

Under David, the Israelite monarchy became firmly established. The description of David's cabinet gives a helpful picture of how the government was organized.

* Administrative duties were supervised by David's sons (2 Sam. 3:2–5; 5:13, 14). David also governed through garrisons, governors, and vassal kings (8:6, 14). This system was later streamlined by Solomon, who named twelve district governors, two of whom were sons-in-law.

Like other kings in the ancient world, David had an official recorder, Jehoshaphat, whose main role was to keep a written record of David's exploits and decisions for history's sake.
A man named Seraiah functioned as David's scribe. In later years, scribes were mainly concerned with copying, editing, and teaching the Law. But during the monarchy, scribes were similar to secretaries of state or chancellors.

* Legal matters were mainly David's responsibility. As king, he took over a role handled by the judges prior to the monarchy. It was his job to set the tone for administering justice by setting policy, deciding legal questions, prosecuting offenses, and appointing judges (1 Chr. 26:29).
* The military was under Joab's command. However, Benaiah was placed over the Cherethites and Pelethites (2 Sam. 8:18), who probably acted as David's personal bodyguard.
* Religious matters were handled by Zadok and Ahimelech, the priests. The latter was the grandson of Ahimelech, the priest at Nob who had shown kindness to David, for which he and his fellow priests were massacred by Saul (1 Sam. 21, 22).

8:3 David's campaign to the north resulted in the defeat of **Hadadezer,** who ruled the Aramean kingdom of **Zobah,** which extended north of Damascus.

8:4 hamstrung: David disabled the horses by cutting the back sinews of the hind legs to prevent them from being used for military activity (see Josh. 11:6, 9).

8:5 Damascus, located at an oasis near the foot of the Anti-Lebanon mountains, was one of the most strategically located cities of the ancient world.

8:6 The **garrisons** of Israelite soldiers were intended to keep the **Syrians** of **Damascus** under David's control.

8:7 Shields of gold were splendid trophies of war (see 1 Kin. 10:16, 17).

8:8 Betah, an Aramean city, was also known as Tibhath (see 1 Chr. 18:8). **Berothai,** also known as Berothah (see Ezek. 47:16), was about 30 miles northwest of Damascus.

8:9 Hamath was about 100 miles northeast of Damascus.

8:10 The rich gifts of **Toi,** king of Hamath, reflect his desire to establish friendly relations with his powerful new neighbor.

8:11, 12 The **silver and gold** that David received from the nations he conquered were turned over to the priests to be used in building the temple (see 1 Kin. 7:51).

8:13 Name refers to the reputation **David** gained as a result of his military exploits.

8:14, 15 David reigned over all Israel: As a result of David's conquests, the sovereignty of Israel extended from the Gulf of Aqaba and the River of Egypt to the Euphrates River—the very region God had promised Abraham in Gen. 15:18.

8:16 Joab, the commander-in-chief of David's army, had led the successful attack on the city of Jebus, which became David's capital Jerusalem (see 1 Chr. 11:6, 7). Joab was David's nephew; **Zeruiah,** his mother, was David's sister (see 1 Chr. 2:13–16). **Jehoshaphat** the **recorder** kept track of state business.

8:17 Zadok and **Ahimelech** are mentioned as the principal priests during David's reign (see 15:24; 1 Sam. 22:20–23; 1 Kin. 1:7, 8). **The scribe** served as secretary of state, drafting official documents, handling correspondence, and maintaining court records.

8:18 Chief ministers were confidential advisors.

9:1 for Jonathan's sake: David and Jonathan had entered into a covenant of friendship that was to extend to their offspring.

9:2 Ziba was a servant of king Saul (16:1–4; 19:29).

9:3 The kindness of God recalls the words of the oath that Jonathan had David swear (see 1 Sam. 20:14).

9:4 Machir the son of Ammiel was a man who extended hospitality to David during Absalom's revolt (17:27–29).

9:5, 6 Once he was made aware of Jonathan's son, David immediately sent for Mephibosheth to be brought to Jerusalem.

9:7 Do not fear: Mephibosheth had good reason to be afraid. It was usual in the ancient Middle East for founders of new dynasties to kill the children of former rulers. **The land of Saul** refers to the house and property at Gibeah which was claimed by David when he took the throne (12:8). To **eat bread** at the king's table meant that he would have a pension from the king. **continually:** These privileges and provisions would continue throughout Mephibosheth's life.

9:8, 9 such a dead dog as I: Dogs in Israel were regarded as unclean scavengers, and were generally viewed with contempt. The remark reflects Mephibosheth's low self-image.

9:10 your sons and your servants, shall work the land for him: The size of Saul's estate is reflected in the fact that Ziba had 15 sons and 20 servants. **that your master's son may have food to eat:** Although Mephibosheth would always have a place at David's table as a member of the royal court, the income from Saul's estate would provide for his house and family in Jerusalem.

9:11 In his dealings with Mephibosheth, David exemplified God's grace. Mephibosheth was wonderfully blessed because of David's faithfulness to a covenant promise.

9:12 The family of Saul continued through **Micha** for several centuries (1 Chr. 8:34–40).

9:13 Mephibosheth had become **lame** as a result of a fall that had occurred when his nurse was fleeing from Gibeah after the report of the deaths of Saul and Jonathan (4:4).

10:1 The king of **Ammon** was Nahash (v. 2), probably the same Nahash who was defeated by Saul at Jabesh Gilead (see 1 Sam. 11:1–11).

10:2 as his father showed kindness to me: The occasion of Nahash's kindness is not recorded. One possibility is that Nahash, an enemy of Saul, had given aid to David during his war with Ishbosheth (2:8—4:12).

10:3 David's gesture of kindness was met with suspicion by the king's advisors, **the princes.** They suspected that David had sent the men as spies for the purpose of planning an attack on **the city** of Rabbah (11:1).

10:4 David's servants were abused and humiliated. The beard was regarded in Semitic culture as a significant aspect of a man's appearance. Cutting off half the beard was a very serious insult. **Hanun** doubled the insult when he **cut off their garments,** leaving the soldiers indecently exposed.

10:5 To prevent their further humiliation, David ordered the messengers to remain in **Jericho** until their beards grew back.

10:6 To protect themselves against Israelite revenge, the Ammonites hired 33,000 mercenary soldiers from several Aramean states to the north.

10:7 Although **mighty men** is used elsewhere to mean a select group of David's warriors (16:6; 20:7), the context here suggests that the whole army of Israel is intended.

10:8 The gates of fortified cities usually had towers which gave the defenders an advantage over enemies seeking to break through.

10:9 before and behind: Joab had allowed himself to become trapped between two enemy forces—the **Syrians** and the Ammonites. If he attacked either enemy separately, his rear troops would be exposed to the other. Joab decided to risk attacking both forces at the same time.

10:10, 11 Abishai, Joab's brother, was placed in command of the rest of the militia in order to attack the **people of Ammon.** Abishai was one of David's mighty men (23:18). He was a brave warrior and a successful commander

but was impetuous and perhaps even bloodthirsty. He had played a part in the murder of Abner (3:30).

10:12, 13 Joab's exhortation, **be of good courage, and let us be strong,** is reminiscent of God's charge to Joshua at the beginning of the conquest (see Josh. 1:6, 7).

10:14, 15 As the battle turned against the **Syrians,** the **people of Ammon** fled for shelter behind their city walls.

10:16, 17 Hadadezer ruled the Aramean kingdom of Zobah. **The River** refers to the Euphrates.

10:18 seven hundred charioteers: According to 1 Chr. 19:18, "seven thousand" charioteers were killed. One of these texts must be the result of a copyist's error.

10:19 All the kings who had been vassal rulers under **Hadadezer** transferred their allegiance to David.

11:1 Kings went to battle **in the spring of the year,** when they could be assured of good weather and an abundance of food along the way. **David sent Joab** and his army to besiege the Ammonite capital of **Rabbah.** But instead of going to war, **David remained at Jerusalem.**

11:2 from the roof he saw a woman bathing: Bathsheba was actually in her own house. **very beautiful:** Scripture describes Bathsheba as being of exceptionally fine appearance.

11:3 Bathsheba means "Daughter of Sheba." In 1 Chr. 3:5, her name is given as Bathshua.

11:4 she came to him: David was using his power as king to take advantage of Uriah's wife. It is difficult to know what Bathsheba's part was in all of this.

11:5, 6 told David: In Lev. 20:10 the command is clear that both parties in an adulterous relationship were to be put to death. But in practice, a woman who became pregnant might be forced to bear the shame and guilt alone. Bathsheba's situation was precarious because it would have been known that her husband was off at war.

11:7–10 Go down to your house and wash your feet: David encouraged **Uriah** to visit his wife. It is likely that David's words, "wash your feet," meant that Uriah should sleep with his wife that night. The **gift of food** was given by David for Uriah and

Bathsheba to enjoy together, to encourage them to be intimate.

11:11–13 The **ark** accompanied the army on their military campaign (see 15:24; 1 Sam. 4:3).

11:14, 15 How sad that David would use the dangers of war to achieve his own ends, that he would kill an innocent man, and that he would have no thought of God, while Uriah was righteous.

11:16–18 David sent Uriah to where he thought the fighting would be fiercest.

11:19, 20 charged the messenger: Joab anticipated David's anger over the loss of life and the questions he would ask about why this was allowed to happen.

11:21, 22 Abimelech's death during the siege of **Thebez** is recorded in Judg. 9:50–55.

11:23, 24 David had told Joab to have Uriah killed by withdrawing soldiers from around him, leaving him to face the enemy alone. Instead, he devised a plan to have the soldiers fight near the wall. This maneuver endangered more soldiers and resulted in greater loss of life.

11:25–27 when her mourning was over: Ordinarily, Israelites mourned a death for seven days (see 1 Sam. 31:13).

12:1, 2 There were two men: The words **one rich and the other poor** present the story as a morality tale that would gain David's attention without raising his suspicions.

12:3 The poor man's **ewe lamb** was more a dearly loved pet than a farm animal. The details about sharing **food** and drink emphasize how precious the lamb was to the poor man.

12:4 he took the poor man's lamb: These words are reminiscent of 11:4, "David sent messengers, and took her."

12:5 David's anger was greatly aroused at the loathsome injustice that had been done. **the man who has done this shall surely die:** Ironically, it was David who deserved to die for the crimes of adultery and murder.

12:6 he shall restore fourfold: David demanded that restitution be made to the poor man according to the law of Moses (see Ex. 22:1).

12:7 You are the man: It took courage for Nathan to speak these words to the king.

12:8 I also would have given you much more: The grace of God to David was not something that was about to be exhausted; all David had to do was ask, and God would have granted him favor upon favor.

12:9 you despised the commandment of the LORD: David had broken the tenth, the seventh, and the sixth commandments the ones about coveting, adultery, and murder. **killed him with the sword of the people of Ammon:** Although David's own sword was clean, there was still blood on his hands.

12:10, 11 The judgment pronounced on David and his family was threefold: (1) Bloodshed would persist all the days of David's life; (2) David's own family would bring **adversity** against him; (3) David's wives would be taken by another.

12:12 David's sin was private, but God's discipline and correction were public.

12:13 I have sinned against the LORD: David did not attempt to rationalize his sin or to make an excuse for himself. A fuller expression of David's confession is found in Ps. 51. **The LORD also has put away your sin:** God accepted David's confession and extended divine forgiveness. **you shall not die:** This is an evidence of divine grace.

12:14 Although David's sin was forgiven, **the child** born of his adulterous relationship with Bathsheba would die. While God forgives sin, He does not necessarily remove its consequences (Gal. 6:7).

12:15 the child: The baby seems not to have lived long enough to be named.

12:16 pleaded: In this verse, we sense the heart of David in anguish before the Lord. **fasted:** Fasting is an expression of the intensity of a petitioner's concern. It says, "This matter is more important to me than food."

12:17 The elders of his house were the senior officials and advisors of David's royal court.

12:18, 19 the servants of David were afraid: Those who had observed the intensity of David's grief *before* the death of his child expected that his rage would be uncontrollable when he learned that the baby had died.

12:20, 21 So David arose from the ground: In David's case, his grieving began when the child became ill. Once the child was dead, there was nothing he could do but worship the Lord. **he went into the house of the LORD:** David left his palace and ascended Mount Moriah to worship at the tabernacle.

12:22 Who can tell: These words give us a remarkable insight into the meaning of prayer. As long as there is any possibility of God intervening in a new way, prayer should continue unabated.

12:23 I shall go to him, but he shall not return to me: The child could not return to life, but David would someday join his son in death.

12:24 The name **Solomon** is related to the Hebrew word for *peace,* and means "Peaceable" or "Peaceful." **the LORD loved him:** God was not going to strike this child as He had the first one (v. 15). This child was God's choice.

12:25 Nathan the prophet was sent by the Lord to give Solomon the name **Jedidiah,** meaning "Beloved of the Lord" (v. 24). The divinely sanctioned name was the final symbol of God's forgiveness in the lives of David and Bathsheba.

12:26, 27 taken the city's water supply: Joab assured David that once he had done this, the city could not hold out against a siege.

12:28, 29 lest I take the city: Joab wanted David to have the credit for defeating Rabbah and conquering the people of Ammon. So it was that David arrived with his elite corps and won the victory that was years in the making.

12:30 a talent of gold: The crown weighed about 75 pounds.

12:31 saws and iron picks and iron axes:. David punished the Ammonites in forced work parties with various tools and implements.

13:1 Absalom and **Tamar** were children of David and Maacah, daughter of Talmai, king of Geshur (3:3). **Amnon,** David's firstborn son, was the child of Ahinoam, the woman from Jezreel (3:2).

13:2 it was improper for Amnon to do anything to her: Marriage to a sister or half sister was forbidden by the law of Moses (see Lev. 18:11).

13:3 Jonadab was a cousin to both **Amnon** and Tamar. The Hebrew word translated **crafty** is the same one used elsewhere for those who are "wise," "technically skilled," or "experienced."

13:4–6 pretend to be ill: Jonadab, Amnon's shrewd cousin, devised a plan to lure unsuspecting Tamar into Amnon's bedroom. Feigning illness would be a means of gaining sympathy and avoiding the usual proprieties.

13:7–11 your brother Amnon's house: Apparently the royal princes had separate residences.

13:12 While Canaanites and foreigners might have condoned such practices, incest was forbidden among Israelites (see Lev. 18:9, 11; 20:17).

13:13 The word translated **fools** is related to the word translated *disgraceful thing* in v. 12. **he will not withhold me from you:** While the law forbade incestuous marriage (see Lev. 18:11), this regulation may not always have been strictly observed.

13:14 he forced her: The word can also mean, "he humiliated her." Victims of rape sometimes speak more strongly of their humiliation than of the physical pain they were made to suffer.

13:15 Amnon hated her exceedingly: Amnon's lust, once gratified, turned to hatred.

13:16 The words at the end of the verse, **but he would not listen to her,** repeat the phrasing of v. 14.

13:17 It is difficult to translate the contempt which Amnon had for Tamar. Referring to Tamar, Amnon commanded his servant in a tone one might use to speak of dumping trash.

13:18 she had on a robe of many colors: The exact meaning of this phrase is debated; recent study suggests that it refers to a long garment with sleeves.

13:19 Tamar put ashes on her head, and tore her robe: The traditional signs of grief and mourning. **laid her hand on her head:** This is another expression of mourning. Tamar had much to mourn. She had lost her virginity.

13:20 hold your peace ... do not take this thing to heart: Absalom's words seem cold and heartless. Absalom planned to take revenge, but wished to conceal his plan at that time.

13:21, 22 David was **very angry** over Amnon's violation of Tamar, but did nothing to punish his son. This may have been because Amnon was David's firstborn (3:2) and was expected to succeed him on the throne.

13:23, 24 Absalom delayed his revenge **two full years,** evidently to catch Amnon off guard. Absalom planned to murder his brother to avenge his sister's rape. Absalom invited the **king's sons** to a sheepshearing festival at **Baal Hazor** about 15 miles north of Jerusalem.

13:25 David declined the invitation, offering the excuse that he did not want to be a burden on Absalom. **he blessed him:** David's memory of his blessing on Absalom must have been a grief to him (v. 36).

13:26, 27 Why should he go with you: Absalom persuaded his father to allow Amnon and the rest of the king's sons to attend the celebration.

13:28 Absalom's servants were to attack Amnon when his **heart** was **merry with wine.**

13:29 Fearing for their own lives, the king's sons fled. A **mule,** the offspring of a donkey and a horse, combines the size and strength of the horse with the surefootedness and endurance of the donkey.

13:30 Absalom has killed all the king's sons: The report that reached David was greatly exaggerated. This news must have been utterly shattering to David.

13:31 tore his garments: Tearing one's clothes was a sign of grief and mourning (1:11; 13:19).

13:32 Jonadab had helped Amnon plan his encounter with Tamar. Jonadab knew that Absalom's had planned revenge ever since the violation of his sister by Amnon.

13:33–36 The statement **Absalom fled** is repeated three times.

13:37, 38 And David mourned for his son: This mourning must refer to Amnon, who had been killed.

13:39 As David's grief over Amnon's death gradually diminished, he **longed to go to Absalom:** Apparently, David wanted to see Absalom, but thought it inappropriate in view of the circumstances.

14:1 the king's heart: Joab was aware that the king longed to be reconciled with his son, but that apart from some external

prompting, he would not make the first move.

14:2 do not anoint yourself with oil: Olive oil was used in ancient times as a soothing lotion that made the skin and hair shine.

14:3–5 Joab gave the woman the story to tell to the king. As a wise woman (v. 2), she would know how to reply to David's responses and questions. **fell on her face:** The woman bowed before the king as a preliminary sign of her request for help. **my husband is dead:** Although she had already described herself as a **widow,** these words may have been added for emotional effect.

14:6 The mention of **two sons** must have struck a chord in David; certainly he could not have been impassive when she described the one killing the other.

14:7 that we may execute him: The punishment for murder was death. The issue seemed clear, but the consequences for the woman were intolerable. **So they would extinguish my ember:** The woman used a graphic picture of the extinction of her family. The demise of a family name and the end of a family line were crucial matters to the Hebrew people.

14:8 David apparently wanted to put the woman off with a promise of future action.

14:9, 10 let the iniquity be on me and on my father's house: The persistent woman expressed her willingness to bear any guilt if David would let the blood of her son go unavenged.

14:11, 12 The protector of the family would be expected to bring vengeance on one who had taken the life of a family member. In this case, the woman pressed David to the limit with respect to her son. David promised that **not one hair** of her son's head would **fall to the ground.**

14:13 you schemed such a thing against the people of God: She accused David of doing to the nation what her enemy was trying to do to her, taking away the heir to the throne. **his banished one:** Although not formally banished, Absalom was in his extended exile from Israel.

14:14 Amnon was dead, and no amount of punishment against Absalom would bring him back to life.

14:15 After speaking of David's treatment of Absalom, the woman returned to her story about her own family. **the people have made me afraid:** The woman said she was afraid that she would lose her own son to the avenger of blood (v. 7).

14:16 the man who would destroy me: The death of the son would mean the extinction of her family, depriving her of a future share in the workings of God among His people.

14:17, 18 as the angel of God: The woman suggested that the king had superhuman ability in the exercise of judgment.

14:19, 20 David recognized **the hand of Joab** in the woman's charade.

14:21, 22 the king has filled the request of his servant: Apparently, Joab had made other attempts to bring about the reconciliation of David and Absalom.

14:23 David's unwillingness to go himself may reflect some reluctance to forgive his son.

14:24–26 do not let him see my face: David refused to grant an immediate audience to his son because he had not forgotten Absalom's crime. **his good looks:** By his charm and personal appeal, he later was able to lead the nation in a rebellion against his father (15:1–12). The reference to Absalom's long **hair** provides the background for the account of his death (18:9).

14:27, 28 In addition to three sons, Absalom had a daughter whom he named **Tamar,** perhaps after his sister (13:1). Apparently, Absalom's sons died in infancy. When he set up a pillar in Jerusalem to memorialize his name, he mentioned having no sons (18:18).

14:29–31 Joab's refusal to go to Absalom no doubt contributed to Absalom's simmering resentment of the royal house.

14:32 if there is iniquity in me, let him execute me: Absalom pleaded that his offense either be punished or completely forgiven.

14:33 the king kissed Absalom: The kiss was the symbol of their reconciliation. But, the seeds of bitterness that had been sown would soon bear the fruit of conspiracy and rebellion.

15:1–3 chariots and horses, and fifty men to run before him: This royal treatment was intended to attract attention to Absalom and to remind the people of his relationship to David as heir to the throne. **no deputy of the king to hear you:** The implication of Absalom's remark was that David was too busy to hear the case, yet unwilling to delegate someone to deal with the concern.

15:4 Absalom was playing on the people's emotions when he presented himself as the answer to their need for justice.

15:5, 6 Absalom stole the hearts: Through flattery and promises, Absalom managed to win the affection of the Israelites.

15:7, 8 Absalom sought David's permission to move to **Hebron,** about 20 miles south of Jerusalem, where he would have more freedom to start a rebellion.

15:9, 10 sent spies: Absalom began to enlist conspirators and sympathizers to join him in the forthcoming revolt.

15:11 Absalom invited **two hundred** unsuspecting men to join him in Hebron.

15:12 Ahithophel was from Giloh, a city in the mountains of Judah (Josh. 15:51).

15:13 The hearts of the men of Israel: By his deceptive practices, Absalom had gained the sympathy and support of the Israelites.

15:14 Arise, and let us flee: David fled from Jerusalem to avoid unnecessary risk of life and the tragedy of a military assault on the capital city.

15:15, 16 The loyalty of David's **servants** must have been a real encouragement in a time of such disloyalty from David's own family.

15:17 After leaving Jerusalem, David and the royal family stopped at the east edge of town before crossing the Kidron to allow his royal bodyguard to pass before him.

15:18 The **Cherethites** and **Pelethites** were elite units of David's army. These trusted troops of David were not Israelites, but mercenaries from a variety of nations, possibly Crete and Philistia. They had been with David for years, owed him their loyalty, and would defend him and his family to the death. **Gittites** were either Philistine mercenary soldiers whom David had recruited during his stay in Gath (see 1 Sam. 21:10–15) or David's original followers from Gath (1 Sam. 23:13).

15:19 remain with the king: David gave his foreign mercenaries the chance to leave him. As foreigners, they were not obligated to fight in the coming civil war.

15:20 you came only yesterday: This is an obvious exaggeration, but reflects the fact that Ittai's association with David had been brief. He did not have the long-term relationship with David that the troops mentioned in v. 18 had.

15:21, 22 As the LORD lives: With these words, the foreign military officer declared his abiding faith in and commitment to the God of Israel. **whether in death or life:** Ittai's later appointment as commander of a third of the army was David's way of showing his gratitude for such loyalty.

15:23 The **Brook Kidron** is a small stream that flows through the valley separating Jerusalem and the Mount of Olives during the rainy season (October through March). The **way of the wilderness** refers to the road leading through the wilderness of Judah to Jericho and down to the fords of the Jordan River.

15:24–26 Zadok and **Abiathar** were the priests functioning during David's reign. They were loyal to David. **He will bring me back:** David committed the entire situation to the sovereign care and will of God.

15:27 Are you not a seer: A prophet could come from any tribe, even from among the sons of Aaron. David wanted the priests to remain in Jerusalem to minister in the tabernacle and intercede before God for him.

15:28 until word comes from you to inform me: Zadok and Abiathar were to remain in Jerusalem to gather information for David.

15:29, 30 head covered ... barefoot: These were outward signs of mourning.

15:31 Ahithophel was **Bathsheba's** grandfather (11:3). A wise counselor (16:23), he had been in David's service (v. 12) but had switched his allegiance to Absalom. David's prayer was for his enemy to be confused.

15:32–34 Hushai proved to be a loyal friend of David. He was directed to return to Jerusalem to thwart the counsel that Ahithophel would be giving to Absalom.

15:35, 36 Hushai was given a key role in relaying information to David through **Zadok** and **Abiathar** and their sons, **Ahimaaz** and **Jonathan.**

15:37 The word **friend** can mean a counselor or an advisor (see 1 Kin. 4:5).

16:1 Ziba, a long-time servant of Mephibosheth, assisted David with provisions for the initial flight.

16:2 The donkeys are for the king's household: They might have been intended for David's wives to ride in turn.

16:3, 4 Ziba had been in the service of Jonathan, father of Mephibosheth (9:2, 9). **Today the house of Israel will restore the kingdom of my father to me:** According to Ziba, Mephibosheth was staying in Jerusalem in hopes that Absalom's rebellion would result in his elevation to the throne.

16:5 Shimei the son of Gera was a distant relative of Saul (see 19:16–23; 1 Kin. 2:8, 9, 36–46). **cursing continuously:** These were not simple insults or just the words of someone with a foul mouth. Shimei was asking God to destroy David (see Num. 22:6).

16:6 threw stones: Throwing stones is a gesture of contempt, as if the fleeing king were no more than a stray dog. **All the mighty men** refers to David's royal troops and bodyguards (17:8).

16:7, 8 Come out might be rephrased, "Go out" (into banishment and exile) or "Be gone!" **You bloodthirsty man:** Shimei blamed the demise of Saul's family on David (v. 5)—an unjust charge (ch. 1). **You rogue,** literally "man of Belial," is an expletive against David that means worthless or useless.

16:9 Abishai was a nephew of David, the son of David's sister **Zeruiah** (1 Chr. 2:16). He was consistently devoted to David.

16:10 What have I to do with you: This idiom means that David did not share the feelings and views of Abishai.

16:11 David argued that if his own **son** showed him no loyalty, there was no reason to expect respect from the **Benjamite,** that is, a person from the tribe of Saul.

16:12–14 the LORD will repay me with good: David hoped that the Lord would look upon his repentant heart and render a blessing to compensate for Shimei's curse.

16:15 Ahithophel had switched his allegiance to Absalom (15:31). In this context, **the men of Israel** refers to Absalom's followers.

16:16–18 Long live the king: Hushai deceptively professed loyalty to Absalom. In fact, these words could easily have applied to David for he was still the divinely sanctioned king. By using his words carefully, Hushai was able to lead his hearers to think he was praising Absalom, when in fact he was shouting for David.

16:19–21 in the presence of his son: Hushai wished to imply that his allegiance to Absalom was the natural outgrowth of his loyalty to David. It was appropriate for a son to succeed his father, and for supporters of the dynasty to give their allegiance to the new king.

16:22 In ancient times, taking over a king's harem was a recognized means of claiming the throne. When Ahithophel advised Absalom to have sexual relations with David's concubines, he knew that this would finalize the breach between Absalom and David.

16:23 at the oracle of God: Ahithophel had acquired such a reputation that his counsel was taken to be equivalent to a word from the Lord.

17:1, 2 Ahithophel realized that the fleeing king was in a vulnerable situation. He counseled Absalom to pursue and kill David and his followers in order to eliminate any chance that David would regain the throne. The **twelve thousand men** that he asked for would likely have had an easy time defeating the weary troops of David.

17:3, 4 I will bring back all the people: Ahithophel tried to persuade Absalom that if he killed only David, the people would align themselves with Absalom, and **peace** would be restored in the land.

17:5, 6 Although Absalom was pleased with Ahithophel's counsel (v. 4), he did not accept it immediately. He summoned **Hushai** (16:16) to get a second opinion on the matter.

17:7 Hushai, David's confidant, set about to frustrate Ahithophel's wise counsel. The words **at this time** leave room for an appreciation of Ahithophel's past counsel and

might have been intended to deter suspicion over his critical evaluation.

17:8 like a bear robbed of her cubs: Hushai used a strong simile to depict the ferocity of David and his men. **will not camp with the people:** Hushai suggested that David, as an experienced warrior, would not camp with the civilian refugees.

17:9 hidden in some pit: The countryside of Judah was riddled with caves, ravines, and hiding places. **a slaughter:** Hushai suggested that David could not be taken without some loss of life, and this would give rise to the rumor that Absalom was suffering a severe defeat.

17:10 will melt completely: Hushai suggested that even the bravest of Absalom's soldiers would yield to panic when facing David and his veterans.

17:11, 12 all Israel: Hushai advised that Absalom was going to need a larger army than he presently had, and that Absalom himself should lead the force into battle. Hushai knew it would take time to gather so many men, and that time was what David needed the most.

17:13 The river means any river, not necessarily the Jordan River.

17:14, 15 Zadok and Abiathar the priests had stayed in Jerusalem at David's request to gather information about Absalom's activities and forward it to him through their sons.

17:16 Hushai told David to cross the Jordan River since he could not be sure that Absalom would act on his counsel.

17:17, 18 a female servant: The young men would arouse suspicion by coming into the city, so a woman servant served as an intermediary. **a lad saw them:** The efforts of Jonathan and Ahimaaz to avoid detection were unsuccessful.

17:19–22 Crossing **the Jordan** could be dangerous, even at the fords. David was safer once he got his family and followers across that barrier. David was truly in exile.

17:23 Ahithophel committed suicide when he learned that his advice was not being followed.

17:24 Mahanaim was east of the Jordan River and north of the Jabbok.

17:25 Absalom put his army under the command of **Amasa,** since Joab had remained loyal to David.

17:26 Gilead was famous for its forests (Jer. 22:6), pasture lands (Num. 32:1–4), and the medicinal balms made from its plants (Jer. 8:22; 46:11).

17:27, 28 When David arrived in the fortified city of **Mahanaim,** he found a gracious reception. **Shobi** was a vassal king under David who ruled **Rabbah,** the capital of **Ammon. Barzillai** was an old man of great wealth (19:31–39; 1 Kin. 2:7).

17:29 The rulers showed compassion to David and his **weary** followers.

18:1 David counted and reviewed his fighting forces. **captains of thousands:** Although only a small contingent of troops left Jerusalem with David, other loyal followers soon rallied to his cause.

18:2 David divided his men into three companies—a frequent military tactic in ancient times. **Abishai,** the oldest son of David's sister **Zeruiah** (1 Chr. 2:16), was noted for his brave but impetuous spirit (3:30; 16:9; 1 Sam. 26:6–9). **Joab,** the younger brother of Abishai, had become commander of David's army as a result of his heroic leadership in the capture of Jerusalem (1 Chr. 11:4–6). Little is known of **Ittai** except that he was strongly committed to serving David and the Lord (15:19–22).

18:3, 4 you shall not go out: Although David wanted to accompany his men into battle (v. 2), he was persuaded not to go, both for his own protection and for the safety of Mahanaim (17:27).

18:5, 6 the woods of Ephraim: The battle took place in a dense forest north of the Jabbok River, east of the Jordan.

18:7, 8 Absalom's newly organized army were no match for the experienced soldiers of David. **the woods devoured:** Because of the rugged nature of the terrain and dense growth in the forest, more deaths resulted from the pursuit than from actual combat.

18:9, 10 The **terebinth,** sometimes translated *oak* or *elm,* was a strong tree, native to the land of Israel. It grows to a height of around 35 feet.

18:11 ten shekels: The shekel was the basic

unit of weight, equal to 11.3 grams or about one-half ounce. The **belt** was part of a soldier's equipment (1 Sam. 18:4; 1 Kin. 2:5).

18:12–15 against the king's son: The soldier had not forgotten David's command not to harm **Absalom** (v. 5). Since the spears did not kill Absalom immediately (v. 15), the word translated **heart** may refer to Absalom's trunk.

18:16 Joab blew the trumpet to signal the army to stop its pursuit. The death of Absalom meant the end of the rebellion. The trumpet was a ram's horn or shofar (2:28; 6:15).

18:17 Rather than returning Absalom's body to Jerusalem for honorable burial, Joab had it buried in **a large pit** in the forest. The heap of stones that covered the grave may have been symbolic of a stoning, the legal penalty due a rebel son (Deut. 21:20, 21).

18:18 The King's Valley was near Jerusalem (Gen. 14:17). **to this day:** The great monument that Absalom had erected for himself was still in existence when the narrator wrote this section of 2 Samuel.

18:19, 20 Ahimaaz with Jonathan had carried the message from Zadok and Abiathar, urging David to flee across the Jordan River (17:20, 21). The word **avenged** is used here in the sense of "delivered."

18:21–23 Cushite means someone of the land from Cush, the remote region of what is today southern Egypt and Sudan. **let me also run:** Ahimaaz could not be restrained from also running to David with the good news of victory.

18:24 two gates: The city of Mahanaim evidently had a double gate. The **watchman** at the gate was responsible to warn the city of an approaching army and to announce the arrival of important visitors.

18:25, 26 If he is alone: The fact that only one runner was approaching led David to assume that the news was good.

18:27, 28 All is well: The messenger's greeting was *shalom,* the word usually translated *peace.* **your God:** Ahimaaz recognized God's strong association with David.

18:29, 30 Is the young man Absalom safe: David expressed his first concern, his interest in the welfare of his son.

18:31, 32 the LORD has avenged: The Cushite gave God credit for delivering David. Furthermore he gave an honest answer to David's question about Absalom, although his words were carefully worded to soften the blow.

18:33 Was deeply moved can mean "quaked" or "quivered." David was overcome with sorrow. **O Absalom my son, my son:** The repetition of these words expresses clearly David's anguish.

19:1–3 the victory that day was turned into mourning: David's unrestrained expression of grief over the death of his son turned the well-deserved victory celebration into a day of mourning, not so much for Absalom himself, but for the grief brought upon David by his death (18:33). **the people stole back into the city:** What a description for the return of victorious warriors! Like cowards who had fled from battle, David's soldiers crept back into the city of Mahanaim (17:27), hoping to escape notice.

19:4 David **covered his face** as an expression of mourning (15:30). **my son:** His words, which were so touching when first announced (18:33), take on a grating sound when repeated many times.

19:5, 6 you have disgraced all your servants: Joab argued that by honoring his rebel son and neglecting his loyal soldiers, David had shamed and embarrassed those who had served him well. The words **your enemies** is literally "those who hate you." The words **your friends** is literally "those who love you."

19:7 Speak comfort may be rephrased "speak to the heart." David would have to speak words of encouragement if he expected his troops to continue their support of his kingship.

19:8 The gate was the primary meeting place in ancient cities. **So all the people came before the king:** The context implies that David followed Joab's counsel by expressing appreciation to his loyal troops and faithful followers.

19:9, 10 The movement to restore David to power was not unanimous. Some Israelites thought that because he had **fled from the land,** David lost his right to rule. There may also have been some fear that David would

avenge himself on those who had supported Absalom.

19:11 The **elders of Judah** were reluctant to call David back to Jerusalem, perhaps because of their part in Absalom's insurrection (15:10, 11). David asked his friends, the priests, to begin the movement to invite David back to his throne. Apparently, he did not want to come into Jerusalem without public support for his rule.

19:12 My brethren refers to the elders of Judah (v. 11). David knew that he needed the support of his own tribe and its leaders to resume his leadership over the nation.

19:13 Amasa, David's nephew, had commanded the army of Absalom (17:25). David offered him Joab's position as commander-in-chief of David's army. This offer was intended to secure the allegiance of Amasa and the rebel army, as well as to discipline Joab for killing Absalom against his orders (18:14, 15).

19:14 David's acts of diplomacy were effective; he was invited to return as king. The fact that David was the anointed of the Lord meant that God would ensure that David would be restored. But David could not simply wait in exile in a foreign land. He had to act on the belief that God would continue to work His will.

19:15 Gilgal, was about a mile from Jericho.

19:16 Shimei, who had cursed David when he was forced to leave Jerusalem, no doubt feared that David would punish him for this outrageous behavior (16:5–8). He hurried to meet the king so he could make amends.

19:17 a thousand men of Benjamin: This large contingent was a good sign to David that his old hostilities with the family of Saul were over at last. **they went over the Jordan:** Ziba and his sons forded the Jordan River to assist David and his family in crossing.

19:18, 19 what wrong your servant did: Shimei's confession showed genuine repentance and godly sorrow. He added no excuse, self-justification, or explanation.

19:20 The designation **house of Joseph** was sometimes applied to the northern tribes (Ps. 78:67; Ezek. 37:16) since Ephraim, the tribe of Joseph's son (see Gen. 48:5, 13–20), was the largest and most powerful tribe in the north.

19:21–23 Abishai once again (16:9, 10) called for the death of Shimei for cursing God's **anointed** (23:1). **What have I to do with you:** David often had to quell the fiery spirit of his nephew (16:10). David had spared Shimei's life once before because of the timing of his attack on him; here he spared his life again because of the timing of Shimei's repentance.

19:24, 25 Mephibosheth was actually the **son** of Jonathan and the grandson **of Saul** (4:4; 9:1–13). Ziba claimed that Mephibosheth sought to advance the cause of the house of Saul (16:1–4). **cared for his feet:** The personal neglect of Mephibosheth must have been striking. He intended his personal appearance to be a sign of mourning David's absence.

19:26–31 Mephibosheth claimed that Ziba had taken advantage of him, since he was not able to saddle or mount his donkey without help. **he has slandered your servant:** At this point, David faced a dilemma. Who was telling the truth—Mephibosheth or Ziba? David found the whole issue too complex to sort out. **divide the land:** In this way, both Ziba and Mephibosheth would be provided for in a generous manner (see 16:14).

19:32–34 very aged: The eighty-year-old Barzillai had proven himself to be an extraordinary help to David during David's exile. This was an opportunity for David to repay his kindness. **very rich:** Barzillai did not need money; David's offer of a royal pension was based on his loyal friendship.

19:35, 36 Can I discern between the good and bad: There was no effective contrast between the opportunity David offered and Barzillai's present living situation at Mahanaim. What real difference would the change make in his life, since he was too old to enjoy the pleasures of the court?

19:37, 38 Chimham was later identified by the historian Josephus as Barzillai's son (see 1 Kin. 2:7). **I will do for him:** Because of his love for Barzillai, David promised to give a royal patronage to Chimham. This was

similar to the provision David had made for Mephibosheth because of his love for Jonathan (ch. 9).

19:39, 40 The term **all** is figurative. It means that as a whole Judah supported David. **Half** means that the people of Israel were less enthusiastic.

19:41, 42 stolen you away: The people of Israel were annoyed by the fact that David's supporters in Judah had the greater part in bringing the king back from exile in the Transjordan. **The men of Judah** pointed out that even though they had a tribal relationship with David, they had never taken advantage of their privileged position.

19:43 The people of Israel were claiming a greater share in David's kingship since Israel's northern territory was formed by **ten** tribes.

20:1 Sheba was from Benjamin, the same tribe as Saul. The term **rebel,** which also means "worthless person," suggests that Sheba was a scoundrel. **trumpet:** Sheba sounded a shofar or ram's horn. **We have no share in David:** The campaign slogan or song of rebellion.

20:2, 3 every man of Israel: There was a general rebellion among the northern tribes.

20:4 Amasa, who had commanded Absalom's army (17:25), had been offered Joab's position as commander in chief of David's army (19:13). Apparently, he accepted the offer and was commissioned to put down Sheba's rebellion.

20:5, 6 Abishai, Joab's older brother (1 Chr. 2:16), was enlisted to take command of the soldiers of Judah and put down Sheba's revolt. David knew that Sheba's revolt was potentially more dangerous than Absalom's.

20:7 Joab's men are distinguished from the rest of David's army.

20:8, 9 Joab took Amasa by the beard: This friendly greeting, a preliminary to a kiss, was now a preparation for killing him.

20:10–12 wallowed in his blood: The bloody spectacle of Amasa lying on the road caused the soldiers to stop and think about what it might mean to follow Joab.

20:13, 14 He probably refers to Sheba, who traveled the land attempting to raise popular support for his rebellion.

20:15 A siege mound was used in ancient warfare to allow soldiers to reach the top of a city wall. The mound consisted of dirt and debris placed against the wall.

20:16–20 The wise woman explained to Joab that **Abel** was famous for the wisdom and counsel offered by its citizens. The citizens had done nothing to deserve the city's destruction.

20:21, 22 his head will be thrown to you: To end the siege, the people of Abel cut off **Sheba's** head and threw it **over the wall** to Joab.

20:23 Joab was the overall commander of David's army, while **Benaiah** was in charge of **the Cherethites and the Pelethites,** foreign mercenaries who fought for David.

20:24, 25 Revenue may refer to forced labor (see 1 Kin. 12:18). The **recorder,** meaning "one who causes to remember," was responsible for keeping official records. The **scribe** was the king's official secretary.

20:26 Ira replaced David's sons (8:18) as **chief minister,** a word customarily translated *priest.*

21:1 he killed the Gibeonites: Saul had broken covenant by putting some Gibeonites to death (v. 9). This incident was not recorded elsewhere.

21:2 Saul's **zeal for the children of Israel and Judah** led him to attempt to exterminate the foreign element from the land of Israel.

21:3 make atonement: Means to remove sin or defilement by offering a substitute or paying a ransom. David offered to make a settlement with the Gibeonites for the wrong Saul had done.

21:4–6 The Gibeonites asked David for royal authority to execute **seven** of Saul's **descendants.** The words **before the LORD** indicate that the judgment was intended to satisfy divine justice (v. 1).

21:7 because of the LORD's oath: Because of David's covenant of friendship with **Jonathan,** his son **Mephibosheth** was **spared.**

21:8 Rizpah was Saul's concubine.

21:9 they hanged them: God's law explicitly prohibited the punishment of a son for the sins of his father. Since there is no condemnation of David in the text it is possible that

those who were executed had been implicated in the killing of the Gibeonites.

21:10, 11 Rizpah remained near the bodies, protecting them from scavengers, from the barley harvest to the early rains (late April to October).

21:12, 13 Those who had been hanged refers to the seven sons of Saul in vv. 8–10.

21:14 God heeded the prayer for the land: Divine justice had been satisfied. God responded to the prayers of His people, bringing an end to the famine.

21:15, 16 The **spear** of Ishbi-Benob weighed **three hundred shekels,** or approximately seven and one-half pounds.

21:17 You shall go out no more with us: David's men did not want him to risk his life in battle. The **lamp of Israel** refers to **David,** whose life and leadership provided righteous guidance for the people of Israel.

21:18 Sibbechai the Hushathite is listed in 1 Chr. 11:29 with David's mighty men.

21:19–22 Jonathan was David's nephew, the son of **Shimeah.**

22:1, 2 While this psalm later became part of the congregational worship of Israel (Ps. 18), it began as David's personal and earnest expression of praise **to the Lord.** This song was composed when God delivered David **from the hand of Saul** during David's wilderness exploits.

22:3 the horn of my salvation: The horn of an animal was used for protection and defense. Hence, the horn stands for might and power.

22:4, 5 To be praised means "to be boasted about joyfully." God is not only worthy of our contemplative worship, but also to be celebrated for what He does for us.

22:6 In the Old Testament, **Sheol** is described as a place of "dust," referring to death as a place of "corruption" and as a "Pit."

22:7–15 These verses describe God's active intervention in terms reminiscent of His appearance to Moses at Mt. Sinai, with earthquakes, thunder, darkness, and lightning (Ex. 19:16–20; Ps. 68).

22:16–20 The imagery used here recalls the miraculous parting of the Red Sea (see Ex. 14).

22:21 according to my righteousness: David believed that God would deal with people according to their conduct, punishing the wicked and blessing the righteous (Deut. 30:15–20).

22:22, 23 I have kept the ways of the Lord: David was forgiven his sins when he acknowledged them to the Lord. He could stand in a *position* of righteousness even as he strove, by the power of God's Spirit, to *live* in righteousness.

22:24–29 David did not claim sinless perfection. The word **blameless** is used of a person who is sound, wholesome, and has integrity (Gen. 17:1).

22:30–31 run against a troop: David refers to a successful military pursuit (see 1 Sam. 30:8).

22:32–33 who is God: The rhetorical question emphasizes the reality of God in contrast with false gods and idols (see Is. 40:25).

22:34 Deer are noted for their swiftness, agility, and surefootedness. They are also a picture of graceful beauty.

22:35–40 It would take unusual strength to **bend a bow of bronze** (see Job 20:24).

22:41–43 the necks of my enemies: The custom of a victorious king putting his foot on the neck of a defeated foe as a sign of complete overthrow.

22:44–46 as the head of the nations: Through his military exploits and international agreements, David was able to exercise control over many surrounding nations.

22:47–49 The Lord lives: This shout of faith became a motto in biblical times, particularly when shouted in contrast to the false gods of other nations, who had no life. Like a **Rock,** God is strong, steadfast, and a place of refuge (see Ps. 91:1–3).

22:50 Because God delivered His own (vv. 48, 49), David vowed to praise Him. The word translated **give thanks** means "to confess publicly" or "to give public acknowledgment."

22:51 His anointed: David referred to himself.. But the word *anointed* also points to David's descendant. Jesus is the ultimate Anointed One, the meaning of the name Messiah.

23:1 The Hebrew word for **thus says** adds significance to what is said and may be translated "the solemn utterance" or "a revelation." **raised up on high:** David recalled his humble origins as a son of Jesse, whom God sovereignly exalted to the throne of Israel. **the sweet psalmist of Israel:** Of 150 psalms in the Book of Psalms, 73 are attributed to David by the text. No person in the Scriptures is more closely associated with music in the worship of the Lord than King David.

23:2 The spirit of the Lord spoke by: David claimed to speak the words of God through his inspired poetry (see Ps. 139:4). This is a claim to the divine inspiration of the Scriptures, just as much as are these New Testament passages: 2 Tim. 3:16; Heb. 1:1, 2; 2 Pet. 1:19–21.

23:3, 4 He who rules over men: David voiced God's expectations for rulers. The function of the king was not to impoverish the nation. Instead, the king was to ennoble the people as he presented to them the refreshing will of God.

23:5 The establishment of the **everlasting covenant** that God made with David is recorded in 7:12–16. Here and in Ps. 89 are David's celebrations of the covenant in song. **Will He not make it increase:** This rhetorical question expresses David's faith that God would carry out His promise.

23:6, 7 sons of rebellion: The Hebrew word used here is one of contempt and scorn.

23:8–12 The term **mighty men** suggests these men were heroes in the full sense of the word.

23:13, 14 The Valley of Rephaim was a route to Jerusalem (5:18). **Bethlehem,** David's hometown (1 Sam. 16:1–13), was about six miles south of Jerusalem.

23:15, 16 poured it out to the Lord: The water had been provided at such great risk that David regarded it as too precious to drink, and offered it as a sacrifice.

23:17 David calls the water **blood** because it was brought to him at the risk of life.

23:18, 19 The exploits of **Abishai,** the brother of Joab, are detailed in the record of the life of David (2:18; 10:10; 1 Sam. 26:6–9).

23:20–23 Benaiah served as commander over

the Cherethites and the Pelethites (8:18). He was in charge of David's personal bodyguards. The term **his guard** means "his obedience"—that is, those who were bound to obey and protect David.

23:24–38 thirty: The list actually contains thirty-one names. Apparently, the number of active soldiers in this unit was kept close to thirty. With minor variations, this list is also recorded in 1 Chr. 11:26–41.

23:39 thirty-seven: This figure includes **the three** (vv. 8–17); **Abishai** and **Benaiah** (vv. 18–23); the thirty-one (vv. 24–39); and David's commander, **Joab** (v. 37).

24:1, 2 The expression **from Dan to Beersheba** denotes the whole territory of Israel from its northern to its southern extremity, a distance of about 150 miles.

24:3, 4 why does my lord the king desire this thing: Joab, for all his faults, saw the error in David's plan (1 Chr. 21:3) and raised his protest in the form of a question.

24:5 The numbering began in the territory east of the **Jordan. Aroer** was about 14 miles east of the Dead Sea on the north bank of the Arnon River. **Jazer** was east of the Jordan River, about six and one-half miles west of present-day Amman.

24:6 Gilead was east of the Jordan River between the Jabbok and Yarmuk rivers. **Dan Jaan** is thought to refer to the city of Dan, about 23 miles north of the Sea of Galilee. **Sidon** was on the Mediterranean coast north of Tyre.

24:7, 8 The Hivites were Canaanites who occupied the region of Lebanon (Judg. 3:3), Shechem (Gen. 34:2), and Gibeon (Josh. 9:3). **Beersheba** was in the desert parts of Judah about 28 miles southwest of Hebron.

24:9 men who drew the sword: The numbers given refer only to men of military age.

24:10 David's heart condemned him: David fell into sin on several occasions, but his heart was always sensitive to God's righteous will. He quickly confessed his wrong and sought restoration with the Lord.

24:11, 12 Gad, David's prophet or **seer,** is first mentioned in 1 Sam. 22:5. He may have been one of the writers or contributing editors of 2 Samuel.

24:13 David was given a choice of three punishments for his sin: (1) **seven years of famine,** (2) **three months** of flight, or (3) **three days** of plague. Moses warned of all of these punishments for those who broke God's covenant (Deut. 28:15–68).

24:14 let us fall into the hand of the LORD: David calculated that God would be more merciful than a person. He apparently took the third option, a plague.

24:15 The nature of the **plague** is not specified, only that its origin was from the Lord. The number of those who died was very high.

24:16 The judgment was carried out by **the angel of the Lord.** In a demonstration of divine grace, God withheld the plague from destroying the people of Jerusalem.

24:17–21 David interceded on behalf of the people—**these sheep**—about the plague. He once again confessed his sin (v. 10) and asked God to hold him, rather than the people, accountable.

24:22 Threshing implements refers to the heavy, wooden sleds which were dragged over wheat during the threshing process to break it up.

24:23, 24 Araunah wanted to *give* David the threshing floor and the oxen for sacrifice. David was unwilling to offer to the Lord that which cost him nothing. **the threshing floor:** The threshing floor was located on Mount Moriah, where Abraham had bound Isaac. Later, Solomon would build the temple at this site.

24:25 The preservation of Jerusalem and the purchase of the temple site prepared the way for the coming of David's successor, King Solomon. He would build the temple for the true worship of Israel's God.

1 Kings

Introduction

First Kings is a story of good kings and bad kings, true prophets and false prophets, and of disobedience and loyalty to God. Most importantly, it is a story of Israel's spiritual odyssey and God's faithfulness to His people.

Traditionally, Jeremiah has been identified as the author of First and Second Kings. Evidence for his authorship include his priestly origin, his prophetic activity, his access to governmental authorities at the highest level, and his great personal involvement in the complex religious, social, and political activities that occurred during the collapse and fall of Judah in the early sixth century B.C.

Nevertheless, differences in writing style between the books of Jeremiah and Kings, as well as distinctions in the use of the names of Judah's kings make any final determination of the authorship of the books of the Kings uncertain. The author of First and Second Kings was heir to a long history of God's dealing with His people. In the books of Kings, the narrator presents a selected rehearsal of the events of the nation covering the period from the death of King David in the early tenth century B.C. to the fall of Jerusalem around 586 B.C. The author's focus is on the spiritual successes and failures in Israel's history.

The author's purpose in writing First and Second Kings was to evaluate Israel's spiritual odyssey that resulted in God's chastisement (2 Kin. 17:7–23; 24:18–20). As a result, the author devotes considerable attention to evaluating the kings according to the way they responded to the responsibilities detailed in the Mosaic and Davidic covenants. The author notes specifically those who handled such responsibilities well, such as Hezekiah and Josiah. Moreover, the ministry of the prophets as God's authoritative messengers is highlighted. Particular attention is given to the ministries of Elijah (1 Kin. 17–19; 21; 2 Kin. 2:1–11) and Elisha (2 Kin. 2:12—8:15).

1:1–4 David was about seventy **years** old at the time of his death (2 Sam. 5:4; 1 Chr.

29:26–28), and the long years of warfare had taken their physical toll. **warm:** Using a healthy person's body warmth to **care** for a sick person is a medical procedure noted by the second-century Greek physician Galen and the Jewish historian Josephus.

1:5 I will be king: Adonijah, the oldest surviving son, might have assumed that he would inherit the crown even though Solomon had been designated as successor (1:13, 17, 30; 2:15; 1 Chr. 22:9, 10).

1:6 rebuked: While David had been a capable leader and a man of deep spiritual sensitivity, he had not exercised proper parental discipline of his children (2 Sam. 13:21–39; 14:18–24).

1:7 In gaining important allies to support his quest for the crown, Adonijah sought the assistance of **Joab,** David's general, and **Abiathar,** the high priest.

1:8 Zadok was descended from the priestly line of Eleazar (2 Sam. 8:17). **Benaiah** served as the commander of the king's bodyguard and was considered one of David's mighty men (2 Sam. 23:20–23). The prophet **Nathan** had long been David's confidant, spiritual advisor, and conscience (2 Sam. 12:1–25). **Shimei** is probably the man who later became Solomon's district governor (4:18); he should not be confused with David's foolish enemy, Shimei the son of Gera (see 2:8; 2 Sam. 19:18–23).

1:9, 10 Zoheleth means "Serpent." Perhaps this was the shape of an outcropping of rock that was a well-known rendezvous point. Adonijah's ceremonial meal was held at **En Rogel** near the intersection of the Hinnom and Kidron valleys, a place situated for Adonijah's purposes. En Rogel had positive associations with David (2 Sam. 17:17).

1:11 The prophet **Nathan** went to Bathsheba because she would not want to see Adonijah displace her son Solomon as heir to the throne. If Adonijah became king she and Solomon could probably expect to die in a royal purge of all potential claimants to the throne.

1:12–28 Nathan and Bathsheba planned together how Nathan could confirm Bathsheba's report to the king. Nathan was concerned that David might fail to act quickly against

Adonijah's attempted usurpation of the crown. Giving the names of **Abiathar,** who was with Adonijah, and of **Zadok, Benaiah, and Solomon,** who were not, helped David see the situation that was developing. **Has this thing been done:** Nathan's question was both respectful and tactical. David had to act to oppose his rebellious son.

1:29, 30 An oath in the name of **the LORD** was the strongest oath a faithful Israelite would take (see 17:1). **who has redeemed my life:** In these words of praise, David celebrated the innumerable times that the Lord had acted on his behalf, to deliver him from his enemies and from his own sins. Some of David's psalms were written in connection with those times of God's deliverance (Pss. 40; 142).

1:31 King David live forever: Bathsheba put her seal on the occasion by bowing before the king and expressing the hope that his kingdom would never end.

1:32, 33 David summoned the leaders in Israel who had not been party to the conspiracy (vv. 8, 10, 26) to lend their support to the coronation of Solomon. Solomon's prestige would be enhanced by riding upon the royal mule. **Gihon** was a spring, the principal water supply for Jerusalem.

1:34–37 The plans for public proclamation, with David's sanction and with a priestly blessing, were designed to let the people of the city know that Solomon was to be the next king of Israel.

1:38 The **Cherethites** and **Pelethites** were David's bodyguard (2 Sam. 8:18; 15:18; 20:7). Their association with David went back to his days among the Philistines.

1:39, 40 Solomon's anointing by the priest **Zadok** was normal procedure for an uninterrupted succession to the throne. The anointing announced that the anointed one was now the adopted son of the living God. The blowing of the **horn** celebrated and announced the anointing of a new king.

1:41–49 The **noise** first, and then the news of the anointing of Solomon at Gihon, quickly reached Adonijah and his party at En Rogel just a few hundred feet further south (v. 9). This led to the complete demoralization of the coconspirators of Adonijah.

1:50–52 Adonijah's quest for mercy at the bloodstained (Lev. 4:7, 18, 25, 30) **horns of the altar** was in keeping with the traditional function of the altar as a haven of refuge for those who had committed unintentional crimes (Ex. 21:12–14).

1:53 Even though David was still alive (see 2:1–12) and the coronation had not yet taken place, the public celebration at his prophetic anointing at Gihon (1:38–40) was basically the same as declaring **Solomon** Israel's king. The name Solomon is related to the Hebrew word for "peace," and the verb meaning "to be complete." **Go to your house:** Solomon gave temporary clemency to his half brother, likely out of respect for his father.

2:1–3 he charged Solomon: David was following spiritual precedent as well as the custom of the ancient Middle East by passing on instruction to his son (see 1 Chr. 28; 29). The specific instructions given here echo the standards of righteousness associated with the Mosaic covenant (Deut. 5:33; 8:6, 11; 11:1, 22).

2:4 not lack a man: God had made an unconditional covenant with David (2 Sam. 7:12–16; 1 Chr. 17:11–14), granting to him a continual posterity and a royal dynasty. God's prophets predict that the heir of the throne of David will yet reign over a repentant, regathered, and restored Israel (see Jer. 33:19–26; Ezek. 34:22–31) in fulfillment of the promises contained in the Abrahamic, Davidic, and New covenants (Ezek. 37:21–28; Mic. 7:18–20). The New Testament reveals that all this will be realized in Jesus Christ, the Savior King (Acts 3:25, 26; 15:16, 17; Gal. 3:26–29; Rev. 3:21), who is David's Heir in the ultimate sense (Acts 2:22–36).

2:5–9 David's parting advice singled out some problems that had not been solved. One concerned Joab. The bold, headstrong Joab had murdered two generals (2 Sam. 3:27; 20:10), and he had killed David's son Absalom (2 Sam. 18:14). Another problem concerned Shimei, who had treated the king shamefully on a previous occasion (2 Sam. 16:5–13; 19:16–23). **gray hair:** Both Joab and Shimei had lived a long time without requital for their wicked deeds. The aged king knew that these men would likely continue to be a problem to Solomon even as they had been to him. David also included directions of kindness for the household of Barzillai, who had stood by him throughout Absalom's rebellion (2 Sam. 17:27–29; 19:31–39).

2:10, 11 There is a so-called tomb of David today on Mt. Zion in Jerusalem marking approximately where he might have been **buried.**

2:12 Solomon sat on the throne: The dramatic anointing marked him out as his father's true and only successor (1:38–40).

2:13–17 come peaceably: Adonijah would have Bathsheba believe that his request for Abishag was simply compensation for not receiving the crown that he had expected to go to him. Yet Adonijah's plea carried with it serious ramifications. Taking a member of the king's harem would normally be interpreted as a claim to the throne (2 Sam. 3:7–10; 12:8; 16:21–22). **Abishag** had cared for David in his old age (1:1–4, 15).

2:18–22 the kingdom also: Solomon not only saw through Adonijah's plot, but recognized Joab and Abiathar as fellow conspirators. All three were dealt with severely (vv. 23–35).

2:23–25 hand of Benaiah: This mighty man of David did not participate in Adonijah's plots (1:8, 26). Furthermore, he participated in the anointing of Solomon at Gihon (1:38).

2:26, 27 When **Abiathar** was **removed** from office as a priest, his influence was greatly restricted.

2:28–34 Because Joab was a murderer (2 Sam. 3:27; 18:14; 20:10), he could not claim the protective sanctity of the **horns of the altar** (1:50). Therefore, he could not escape execution (vv. 29–31).

2:35 Solomon then appointed his two loyalists to the positions vacated. **Benaiah** became the captain of the army and **Zadok** became the high priest.

2:36–46 At first Solomon placed **Shimei** under an extended house arrest rather than executing him outright for his shameful treatment of David (see 2:8, 9). However, Shimei felt he must pursue **two slaves** that

had run away. This disobedience led to his death.

3:1 married: Political alliances were often ratified by the marriage of the son of one king to the daughter of another. Therefore, the giving of Pharaoh's daughter to Solomon attested to the Israelite king's growing prestige and importance to the Egyptian king.

3:2, 3 Whether the worship ceremonies took place in specially constructed enclosures or at an open-air sanctuary (13:32), such hilltop areas or **high places** provided a setting where Canaanite religious rites could be infiltrated into Israel's worship (11:7; 2 Kin. 16:4).

3:4, 5 Gibeon is a hill about six miles northwest of Jerusalem.

3:6, 7 The term for **child** often refers to a servant or to an inexperienced person still in training for a profession (see 19:21; 20:14–15; 2 Kin. 4:12). With proper humility, Solomon emphasized his relative youth and inexperience.

3:8, 9 an understanding heart: The phrase suggested not only the willingness and patience to listen to all sides of an issue, but also the desire for the ability to reason.

3:10–12 God answered Solomon's request, granting him not only an **understanding heart,** but one that was **wise** for handling the crucial affairs of life in a fair and skillful manner.

3:13, 14 what you have not asked: Because Solomon chose a greater gift than riches and honor, God promised him everything else as well (Matt. 6:33).

3:15 a dream: Dreams were one of the ways that God revealed His will (Gen. 20:3; 37:5; Dan. 2:3). Although David had brought the **ark of the covenant** to Jerusalem (2 Sam. 6), the tabernacle and its furnishings remained in Gibeon, which served as an important worship center (v. 4; see 2 Chr. 1:3–5).

3:16–25 The fact that **harlots** could appear before Solomon suggested that he made himself available to persons of all stations of life who had a legitimate claim for justice.

3:26, 27 yearned with compassion: Her love as a mother made her give up her own child rather than see it die.

3:28 wisdom ... justice: These important qualities which marked Solomon's reign from the beginning would characterize the rule of Israel's Messiah in a far greater way (Is. 11:1–5).

4:1–6 Solomon's wisdom was also demonstrated in his appointment of proper officials for all the needs of state. For civil affairs, Solomon appointed **scribes** and a chief officer over the district officials (Azariah). He chose **Benaiah** to replace Joab as commander for **the army** (see also 2:35) and a head of forced **labor.** As a part of his personal staff, he appointed a special advisor, **the king's friend;** a chief of protocol, **the recorder;** and a minister of palace and state, to be **over the household.**

4:7–19 These **twelve governors** were in charge of Solomon's districts. They were responsible for handling lesser administrative tasks and raising revenue for the crown.

4:20, 21 numerous as the sand: God fulfilled His promise to make Abraham's descendants numerous, a great nation (Gen. 15:5, 18).

4:22 kors: The kor was the same size as the homer (Ezek. 45:14), six and a quarter bushels, a normal load for a donkey.

4:23 oxen ... fowl: Meat was a rare item in a person's diet, suggestive of a feast (Prov. 9:1).

4:24, 25 The name Solomon is related to the word **peace.** The **vine** and **fig tree** are symbols of God's blessing for those who obey His covenant.

4:26 forty thousand stalls: Some Greek manuscripts read 4,000 (a figure also found in 2 Chr. 9:25). According to 10:26 and 2 Chr. 1:14, Solomon had 1,400 chariots. Since 3 horses were considered a chariot team and would be quartered together, 4,000 would be about the number of horses Solomon needed.

4:27, 28 The provisions needed for the royal house (vv. 22, 23) were supplied monthly by each of the twelve **governors** (see 4:7–19).

4:29 In addition to giving Solomon a discerning heart (3:12), God gave him **largeness** (or breadth) **of heart.** These terms underscore Solomon's understanding.

4:30 The term **men of the East** has been associated with Mesopotamia (Gen. 29:1), the east bank of the Jordan River (Is. 11:14), or with Arabia in general (Judg. 6:3, 33; 7:12).

4:31 Ethan the Ezrahite: See the title of Ps. 89. **Heman:** See 1 Chr. 16:42 (where Jeduthun may be the same as Ethan).

4:32–34 proverbs ... songs: Solomon was the author of a large part of the Book of Proverbs. He is also traditionally assigned the authorship of the Song of Solomon, Psalms 72 and 127, and Ecclesiastes.

5:1, 2 Hiram: This Phoenician king ruled over Tyre for 34 years (978–944 B.C.). **Loved** reflects traditional Middle Eastern diplomatic vocabulary for political alliances and reinforces the biblical evidence that Hiram was David's friend and ally (v. 12; see 2 Sam. 5:11, 12). Hiram initiated the relationship with Solomon, based on his earlier relationship with David.

5:3 house: Although God did not allow David to build the temple (2 Sam. 7:13), David made preparations for it (1 Chr. 21:18—22:19; 28:9—29:19). **name:** God's name was associated with His revealed character and reputation (see Ex. 3:14, 15), as well as His sovereign ownership of everything (Ex. 20:24; Ps. 22:22).

5:4, 5 The shift from "the Lord his God" (v. 3) to **the LORD my God** demonstrates that Solomon and his father had the same faith.

5:6 cedars ... Lebanon: In addition to the Bible, other ancient literature attests to the extensive use of wood from the cedar trees of Lebanon for building and furnishing temples and palaces. **none among us:** Since Israel did not have cedar forests like those in Lebanon, the Israelites did not have workmen skilled in building with it.

5:7 Blessed be the LORD: The acknowledgment of another people's deity is well known both in the Bible (10:9; Dan. 3:28) and in other ancient Middle Eastern literature.

5:8–11 Hiram's reply indicates that he was a shrewd businessman. Not only would Solomon pay the wages of Hiram's **servants,** but he would make the payments to Hiram (vv. 6, 11; 2 Chr. 2:10). In addition to men and material, Hiram also supplied gold to Solomon, for which he apparently demanded collateral (9:10–14), and which Solomon could later redeem.

5:12–14 labor force: The workmen were put to work as forced labor gangs on public projects.

5:15–18 quarried stone: Stonecutters were common laborers who cut rocks from a quarry.

6:1 four hundred and eightieth year: Many scholars take this date as the key date for establishing the time of the Exodus. The division of the kingdom at the death of Solomon can be dated at 930 B.C. (11:41–43). Allowing forty years for Solomon's rule (11:42), the fourth year of his reign would be 966 B.C. If the Exodus took place 480 years before 966 B.C., its date was 1446 B.C.

6:2, 3 house ... for the LORD: For the interior of the temple Solomon followed the floor plan of the tabernacle but doubled its dimensions. **sixty cubits:** The standard cubit was about 18 inches. The dimensions here are approximately 90 feet long, 30 feet wide, and 45 feet high. Solomon's temple was constructed on Mt. Moriah (2 Chr. 3:1; see Gen. 22:2) at the threshing floor of Ornan (or Araunah, 2 Sam. 24:24). Like the tabernacle, the temple was divided into the Most Holy Place, the holy place, and an outer courtyard. The outer court contained a bronze altar for sacrifices and a brass basin set on the backs of twelve bulls. On the east end of the temple there was a porch. Before the entrance to the porch were two freestanding pillars: Jachin (to the right) and Boaz (to the left; see 7:21). Passing over the front porch, one would enter the holy place. Here was the holy furniture so symbolic of Israel's religious experience: the gold plated table of the bread of the presence, ten golden lampstands, and the portable altar of incense. A veil separated the holy place from the Most Holy Place, in which were housed the ark and the mercy seat guarded by two cherubim. Only the priests could enter the temple itself to minister before the Lord.

6:4–6 Three-storied **chambers** were built along the temple's outer walls. A series of ledges served as resting places for the beams of the floors. This meant that the three floors were progressively wider.

6:7–10 The rock was precut at the quarry for its proper fit in the temple building. This required great skill in measuring, cutting, and fitting the immense stones in place.

6:11 word of the LORD: This message to Solomon might have come by means of a prophet. On other occasions, Solomon had more personal encounters with the Lord (3:5; 9:2; 11:11).

6:12, 13 The most important work of Solomon was certainly the building of the temple. God promised to bless Solomon and his work if he obeyed His commands.

6:14–19 The ark of the covenant of the LORD (Deut. 10:8; Josh. 3:11) is so named because it housed the two stone tablets of the covenant—the Ten Commandments (Deut. 10:1–5). The ark symbolized the presence of the sovereign God in the midst of His people (8:10, 11; Josh. 3:13).

6:20–22 the inner sanctuary: The Most Holy Place was a cube of thirty feet. **with pure gold:** The amount of gold is given as six hundred talents, or about 21 tons, in 2 Chr. 3:8.

6:23–26 The two **cherubim** were overlaid with gold and set so as to face the door to the holy place (2 Chr. 3:12, 13). These cherubim were large, standing fifteen feet high. They were in addition to the two cherubim on the mercy seat (8:6–8). These creatures had a human face, a lion's body, and wings (see Ex. 25:19).

6:27, 28 The **inner room** symbolized the dwelling place of the living God among His people. Only the high priest could enter this room—on one day of the year.

6:29, 30 The decoration of the temple must have been exquisite. **cherubim, palm trees, and open flowers:** The beauty of the building was a symbol of the beauty of God's presence.

6:31, 32 The **entrance** to the inner sanctuary consisted of two doors made of olive wood.

6:33, 34 Double-leaved, foldable doors made of cypress wood gave access to the holy place.

6:35, 36 The use of the **inner court** was restricted to the priests.

6:37, 38 seven years: The period of time was necessary because of the greatness of the task. Solomon had large crews of workmen engaged in the building of the temple (see 5:13–18).

7:1, 2 Solomon's desire to complete the Lord's house before building his own **house** is commendable. **House of the Forest of Lebanon:** Rows of cedar pillars, as well as the free use of cedar throughout this building, gave a forest-like appearance to it.

7:3–7 The **Hall of Pillars** was a colonnaded entry hall to the Hall of Judgment. The **Hall of Judgment** was where the king could hear and decide cases too difficult for lesser officials.

7:8 house where he dwelt: Solomon's own house and that of Pharaoh's daughter are mentioned last. The gate between the palace complex and the temple area is called "the gate of the escorts" (2 Kin. 11:19).

7:9–11 costly stones: Exquisitely dressed blocks of the best quality limestone.

7:12 The **great court** was an outer court enclosing the entire temple and palace complex.

7:13, 14 Huram was of mixed parentage. His father was a Phoenician artisan who had married a widow from the tribe of Naphtali (2 Chr. 2:14). Like his father, Huram had become a master craftsman; his contributions to the work on the temple were extensive (7:40–47).

7:15–20 Among the major works of Huram were the freestanding **pillars of bronze** near the entrance of the temple. These were objects of great beauty and gave the appearance of formidable strength. These pillars spoke of the power and might of God.

7:21, 22 Jachin … Boaz: Giving symbolic names to the pillars helped teach their meaning in the true worship of the living God. Jachin means "He Will Establish." Boaz may mean "In Him Is Strength." These two free-standing pillars were placed near the porch in front of the temple (2 Chr. 3:17).

7:23–26 Cast in one piece and set upon twelve bronze oxen, the **Sea of cast bronze** replaced the laver of washings for the tabernacle (Ex. 30:17–21). While the quantity of

water held by the Sea is given here as two thousand baths (about 11,500 gallons), three thousand baths (17,500 gallons) is recorded in 2 Chr. 4:5.

7:27–38 The **ten carts** each containing a bronze laver (v. 38) were arranged beside the molten Sea, five on either side, and were used for rinsing the burnt offerings (2 Chr. 4:6). These carts were both functional and ornamental.

7:39–48 The furnishings of the temple were designed to correspond with similar furnishings in the tabernacle. The golden altar replaced the altar of incense (Ex. 30:2–4), ten golden tables (2 Chr. 4:8) took the place of the table of the presence (Ex. 25:23–30), and ten lampstands were substituted for the one golden lampstand (Ex. 25:31–40). Although there were ten tables and lampstands where before there was one, their functions remained the same, all ten being considered one unit (see 2 Chr. 29:18).

7:49–51 The gifts of **David** dedicated to service in the temple were probably stored in one of the side chambers. David's personal example of giving (see 1 Chr. 29:1–9) provided a model of godly leadership.

8:1, 2 Having been brought to Jerusalem previously (2 Sam. 6), **the ark of the covenant** was now put in its place in the temple. Because the temple was completed in the eighth month of Solomon's eleventh year of reign, Solomon must have waited about eleven months for the dedication of the temple.

8:3, 4 The holy **ark** was carried by the priests; all was done as God's law demanded.

8:5–7 The joy of the people is seen in the abundance of sacrifices of **sheep and oxen.** The placement of the holy **ark** in its proper place without incident was truly a reason to celebrate.

8:8 poles could be seen: This statement probably means that the carrying poles of the ark, which were not to be removed from their rings (Ex. 25:15), were so long that if one were to attempt to see their length, one would have to look into the Most Holy Place to see their ends.

8:9 The **two tablets of stone** upon which the Ten Commandments were inscribed were known as the "tablets of the covenant" (Deut. 9:9) and were kept in the ark (Deut. 10:1–5, 8) along with the jar of manna (Ex. 16:33, 34) and Aaron's rod that budded (Num. 17:10).

8:10, 11 As a **cloud** had covered the tabernacle and God's glory had filled it when it was inaugurated (Ex. 40:34,35), so now a cloud filled the temple. This visible presence of God's dwelling with His people—sometimes called the "shekinah glory"—gave the people incentive for holy living.

8:12, 13 Then Solomon spoke: God's dwelling in dark clouds is often mentioned in the Scriptures (Ex. 19:9; 20:21). This is a sign of His transcendence.

8:14–21 Here is a model for public declaration in a formal setting. Throughout there is glory given to the Lord, as well as a fair assessment of the work of His people in accomplishing His will. **the LORD has fulfilled:** Israel's God is a keeper of promises. His promise to give Abraham's descendants a land had been provisionally realized (Josh. 21:43–45). Solomon also appropriated God's promise to David (see 2 Sam. 7:12–18). Subsequent kings in the Davidic line could likewise by faith enjoy the blessings of God promised in the Davidic covenant (see Ps. 89:3, 4, 19–24, 27–37; see Ps. 2).

8:22–29 In his prayer of dedication for the temple, Solomon emphasized that the God of Scripture is infinite; all that He has made, vast as creation may be, finally has its limits. No mere building, no matter how wonderful, can be thought of as the dwelling place of God. Yet in His grace the Lord condescends to be viewed as having His dwelling among men.

8:30 Since God was present in the temple in Jerusalem, prayer was to be directed toward **this place** (see Ex. 15:17; Dan. 6:10).

8:31, 32 Solomon's first request asks for righteous judgment. In such situations where there was insufficient evidence to establish a charge, the accused was obliged **to take an oath** declaring his innocence.

8:33, 34 sinned against You: Solomon's second request asks for forgiveness of sin, where sin against God has caused Israel to be defeated.

8:35–40 Solomon's third and fourth requests deal with healing the land after distress or drought because of the people's sin.

8:41–43 Solomon's fifth request deals with prayer by a **foreigner.** Unlike God's people or resident aliens within the commonwealth of Israel (see Deut. 10:18, 19), foreigners have no particular claim on the ear of God. But God's people expected foreigners to be drawn to Him through the worship of His people.

8:44–53 Solomon's sixth and seventh requests concern matters relative to wartime situations. **Battle** (v. 44) was to be waged in accordance with divine directions (Deut. 20; 21:10–14) and could be lost by disobedience (see Deut. 28:64–68; Josh. 7).

8:54–59 he arose … from kneeling: The parallel account in 2 Chr. 6:12–42 records that Solomon knelt on a tall platform that he had built for the occasion in order that all might see him praying before God. Chronicles reports that Solomon closed his prayer with a plea (see Ps. 132:8–10) that God would continue residing with His people and remembering His promises to David (2 Chr. 6:41, 42).

8:60 all the peoples: This verse does not limit God to the Jews only but includes Gentiles as well.

8:61 The Hebrew term translated **loyal** basically means "at peace with," hence, "complete" or "perfect" (see also 11:4; 15:3, 14).

8:62–66 The ceremony concluded with many special **sacrifices** (v. 62) and ended on a high note of **joyful** (v. 66) praise and thanksgiving to God for His goodness.

9:1–9 the second time: God had appeared previously to Solomon in Gibeon (3:4–15). The Lord's warning was a necessary reminder for Solomon, who would come to compromise the conditions required for enjoying God's blessing. Solomon would have to endure the consequences of disobedience (see 11:1–11).

9:10–13 These **twenty cities** (v. 11) lay east and southeast of Acco in the tribal allotment to Asher. Apparently they had been ceded to Hiram as collateral for the gold necessary for furnishing the temple and palace complex. Hiram's displeasure with them would later result in Solomon's redeeming the towns by repaying the debt in some other manner (see 2 Chr. 8:1, 2).

9:14 one hundred and twenty talents of gold: This is an immense amount (see also the gift of the queen of Sheba in 10:10). **A talent** was said to be the full load one man could carry (see 2 Kin. 5:23). It was equal to three thousand shekels, or about 70 pounds.

9:15 The identification and location of the **Millo** are uncertain. Probably the word refers to architectural terraces and buttressing on the slope of the eastern hill of Jerusalem.

9:16 Gezer, which had been a strong Canaanite city, was part of Ephraim's territorial assignment. Ephraim had never taken Gezer; however, Egypt had conquered the city. It made it a splendid gift for Pharaoh to give on the occasion of his daughter's marriage to Solomon.

9:17–19 Three cities were key to Solomon's defensive strategy. **Lower Beth Horon** and **Baalath** served to defend Judah's western front. **Tadmor** is probably the important commercial city in Syria, later known as Palmyra.

9:20, 21 The five nations listed here are peoples who constituted the early inhabitants of Canaan. **Solomon** assigned their surviving members to work on public projects in accordance with the principle of compulsory labor (see 5:13).

9:22–25 These **three times a year** included the Feasts of Unleavened Bread, Pentecost, and Tabernacles (see Deut. 16:16). Not only did Solomon show himself a faithful spiritual shepherd by leading His people in worship, but continual attention to prescribed religious duties would keep the temple **finished,** or properly maintained.

9:26, 27 Ezion Geber was at the head of the modern Gulf of Aqaba. Its key location as an outlet to the Red Sea and the regions beyond made it commercially important to Solomon and to Hiram, his Phoenician trading partner (2 Chr. 8: 17, 18).

9:28 Ophir may have supplied gold for Solomon to repay his debt to Hiram (see 5:8–11; 9:11–14).

10:1, 2 Located in southwestern Arabia (present-day Yemen), **Sheba** was the homeland of the Sabeans. The Sabeans dealt in such precious commodities as gold, gemstones, perfumes, and rare spices. The **queen of Sheba** came to ask Solomon **hard questions** to satisfy her own mind and to examine his wisdom.

10:3–9 Solomon's brilliant replies to the queen of Sheba's difficult **questions** (v. 3), as well as the skillful use of his wisdom for the needs and interests of his kingdom, convinced her that such wisdom must be divinely bestowed.

10:10–15 one hundred and twenty talents: Solomon used the gold not only to furnish the temple (6:20–35; 7:49–51) and palace (10:18–21) but also to make five hundred ornamental shields, which were placed in the House of the Forest of Lebanon (10:16, 17).

10:16, 17 Made of wood (or basketwork) and covered with gold plating, these **shields** were intended for ceremonial occasions.

10:18–21 The **throne of ivory** was probably made of wood inlaid with ivory, as well as being overlaid with finest gold. Solomon received ivory as a result of his trading ventures with Hiram (v. 22).

10:22, 23 Solomon's **merchant ships** are linked to his commercial arrangements with Hiram.

10:24, 25 all the earth: This phrase refers to the international reputation of Solomon's wisdom.

10:26 one thousand four hundred chariots: The reasonableness of the figure given here may be seen in that Shalmaneser III of Assyria reports that at the Battle of Qarqar (853 B.C.) he faced a combined enemy chariot force of 3,900, some two thousand of whom were supplied by Israel.

10:27 silver ... cedar: Israel under Solomon enjoyed its greatest period of prosperity. This time of prosperity and peace also must have allowed for the growth of scholarship and for arts and music.

10:28, 29 Keveh is probably the city of Que attested in a ninth century B.C. inscription found in southern Asia Minor.

11:1 many foreign women: The word order in the Hebrew text emphasizes the word *foreign,* with a secondary emphasis on the adjective *many.* Taking many wives violated the standard of monogamy established at the beginning (Gen. 2:24, 25), and resulted in rampant polygamy, something God had also forbidden to Israel's kings (Deut. 17:17). Solomon's yielding to the customs of the day would have serious spiritual consequences for himself (vv. 3–13) and his people (2 Kin. 17:7–20).

11:2 clung to these in love: Our harsh assessment of Solomon's many wives is mitigated somewhat by the use of this phrase (compare also, "King Solomon loved," in v. 1).

11:3 seven hundred … three hundred: If the reference to 60 queens and 80 concubines in Song 6:8 is to Solomon's wives, it represents a much earlier period in Solomon's reign.

11:4 Because of the influence of his many wives, Solomon compromised his faith by worshiping foreign gods.

11:5, 6 Ashtoreth was a Canaanite goddess of love and war. **Milcom** was the national god of the Ammonites.

11:7, 8 The use of a **high place** in association with the worship of foreign gods shows the danger that the high places presented to Israel (see 3:2–4; 14:23; see also Mic. 1:3). **Chemosh** was the national god of Moab. His worship was practiced repeatedly by God's people (see 2 Kin. 23:13). **Molech** is associated with human sacrifice and with Baal (Jer. 7:31, 32; 19:5, 6; 32:35).

11:9–13 God had appeared twice before to Solomon (3:5; 9:2). Solomon's spiritual odyssey may be seen in the details of his three audiences with God. While God graciously postponed the division of Solomon's kingdom until after his death, internal troubles appeared while he was still alive (vv. 14–40). **your servant:** That is, Jeroboam the son of Nebat (see 11:26; 12:20). **one tribe:** The tribe is Judah, the principal tribe of the southern kingdom. Simeon had assimilated with Judah by this time (see also at 12:17, 20, 21).

11:14–22 Hadad the Edomite was one of the survivors who had escaped when David defeated the Edomite army (see 2 Sam. 8:13, 14). Pharaoh's ready reception and favorable treatment of Hadad probably had political ramifications.

11:23–25 Having escaped David's earlier campaigns against the Arameans (2 Sam. 8:3–6), **Rezon** would later become king of Damascus and his people would remain a constant threat to Israel.

11:26 The Ephraimite **Jeroboam** fled to Egypt where he found refuge. He became the first king of the northern kingdom (12:20).

11:27 this is what caused: The phrasing suggests that there was a problem in the building projects that led to Jeroboam's rebellion. These two verses explain something about Jeroboam's background. He was a major officer of one of the large work groups. Among the projects to which Jeroboam had been assigned were the building of the **Millo** (see at 9:15), and the repair of the **City of David.**

11:28, 29 The prophecy of **Ahijah** of Shiloh was fulfilled literally (12:1–20). Ahijah would remain God's loyal prophet into his old age (14:1–18).

11:30–32 God had already warned Solomon that all but **one tribe** would be taken away from Solomon's heir (v. 13; see 12:20). Only ten tribes, however, are promised to Jeroboam.

11:33–35 they have forsaken Me: See the list of particulars in vv. 4–8.

11:36 This is a biblical image of one of the divinely intended functions of Davidic kings in ancient Israel. In the midst of the darkness of a pagan world, the Davidic kings were to be **a lamp** to the nations, in anticipation of the Coming One who is the Light of the World.

11:37, 38 an enduring house: Although God gave Jeroboam the opportunity to establish a lasting dynasty, he proved unworthy (see 12:25–33; 14:10–18). Jeroboam's name would forever be associated with the spiritual infidelity that would ultimately bring the northern kingdom to ruin (see 2 Kin. 17:21–23).

11:39, 40 Solomon, whose reign was characterized by peace more than that of any other king in Jerusalem (see again 4:24), ended his life in strife as he sought **to kill Jeroboam.**

11:41–42 Because of his considerable sin, the golden era that Solomon initiated would die with him. Had he lived out his life in righteousness, and had he taught his son Rehoboam to succeed him in true justice, the golden era might have endured for generations.

11:43 rested with his fathers: The meaning of this idiom in the Hebrew Bible is burial in the same place as one's ancestors. **Rehoboam his son:** It is usual in a royal obituary to state who it was that followed the deceased on the throne. This provides a sense of continuity.

12:1–3 Rehoboam: Rehoboam became a means of harming the expansion of God's people, even prompting civil war and the secession of the ten northern tribes. Situated in Ephraim, **Shechem** was an important center of Israelite activity. By going for his coronation to a place with ancient ties to the history of his people, and which was situated in the region of the northern tribes, Rehoboam believed he was making a strategic move.

12:4, 5 A system of forced labor had been imposed by Solomon to accomplish and maintain his building projects (see 5:13–18). Because this **burdensome service** was especially hateful to the northern tribes, relief from it was a crucial issue.

12:6, 7 By **elders** is meant the chief government officials who had advised Rehoboam's father Solomon (see 4:1–19). Their advice was to show moderation and temperance.

12:8, 9 The **young men** were men of Rehoboam's generation whom he had appointed to government office.

12:10, 11 little finger … father's waist: The advice of Rehoboam's own advisors was that the system of forced labor should be intensified until their sting become like that of a scorpion.

12:12–14 Foolishly, Rehoboam followed the advice of the hot-headed **young men.**

12:15 from the LORD: Even at this crucial time of national schism, God was sovereignly working through human events to accomplish His will, which had been made known through earlier prophecy (11:29–39).

 IN DEPTH | **The Divided Kingdom**

Tensions had existed between the tribes since the time of the judges, especially between Judah in the south and Ephraim, the most influential tribe in the north. Many of Israel's leaders, such as Joshua and Samuel, had come from the tribe of Ephraim. But David was from the southern tribe of Judah. These factors, along with the moving of the capital and the center of worship to the southern city of Jerusalem, strained the relationship more. Solomon's taxation to fund building the temple and palace in the southern city of Jerusalem alienated the northern tribes even further.

After Solomon's death, his son Rehoboam was approached by the people of Israel with a request that the taxes that they had been forced to pay under his father's numerous building programs be lessened. Rehoboam rejected his elders' advice to be lenient, and he insulted the people by threatening to make their burden even heavier (12:14). This was the final event that split the nation into two kingdoms. Rehoboam remained king of the southern kingdom while Jeroboam became king of the northern kingdom.

Citing the example of the calves created by Aaron near Mount Sinai, Jeroboam erected statues of two golden calves for worship so that his people would not be forced to travel the great distance to Jerusalem. With these idols, Jeroboam led his people away from the worship of the one true God, by combining true worship with the false worship of their neighbors.

The northern kingdom, known as Israel, and the southern kingdom, known as Judah, existed separately for another two hundred years. At times, the two fought each other; at other times, they cooperated in a friendly alliance against threatening neighbors. However, the period would become known more for the great prophets who rose up during times of spiritual instability than for either side's political success.

12:16 What share have we in David: The ancient rivalry felt by the northern tribes now came to a peak in resentment against the tribe of Judah and the house of David.

12:17 cities of Judah: The southern section also included the tribal allotment of Simeon. But Simeon was absorbed by Judah; their allotment was "within the inheritance of the children of Judah" (Josh. 19:1).

12:18 The resistance of the northern tribes to the king's agent **Adoram** was forceful and decisive—they killed him!

12:19 That is, to the **day** of the narrator. In the end, Israel's rebellion was its own destruction.

12:20 Jeroboam ... king: The coronation of Jeroboam apparently was done apart from priest or prophet of the Lord; there was no divine anointing, no true religious ceremony.

12:21 Rehoboam's first inclination when he arrived in Jerusalem was to lead a war of reprisal against Israel. **Benjamin:** People of the border tribe might have gone either direction.

12:22 Iddo the prophet and **Shemaiah** together wrote a history of Rehoboam's reign.

12:23, 24 this thing is from Me: The foolish behavior of Rehoboam brought about God's judgment in dividing the nation into two new kingdoms.

12:25 built Shechem: This strategic and historic city became the first capital of the northern kingdom.

12:26, 27 However, Jeroboam knew **in his heart** that just having a new presence in Shechem and Penuel would not in itself make the people of the northern kingdom forget the glories of the temple in **Jerusalem.**

12:28 Not only would they strike a familiar chord from Israel's history, but the **two calves of gold** would arouse the interest of the remaining Canaanites in the northern kingdom. The result of Jeroboam's action was religious confusion and apostasy; it would bring God's sure condemnation (see 14:9).

12:29 Bethel was north of Jerusalem in Benjamite territory, although its precise location is uncertain. This city had enjoyed a prominent place in Israelite history throughout the earlier patriarchal (Gen. 28:10–21) and post-conquest (Judg. 20:26–31) eras. **Dan** was in the northern portion of Israel.

12:30 The divine declaration is simple: **this thing became a sin.** The exclusive claim of Jerusalem as the central place of the worship of God in the holy temple (see 6:1) was now being ignored by the people of Israel.

12:31–33 Jeroboam's new religious institutions included starting a new religious order that did not include the Levites; setting up shrines at high places (see 3:2, 3); and replacing the Feast of Tabernacles with a fall festival in the eighth month. His various attempts at religious innovation would quickly incur God's denunciation (ch. 13) and earn him a reputation that would live in spiritual infamy (13:33, 34; 22:52).

13:1, 2 man of God: This prophet is unknown to us. The phrase **by the word of the LORD** emphasizes that the man of God was functioning at the command of God and in God's power. **Jeroboam ... altar to burn incense:** Having established his own deviant religion and his apostate priesthood, Jeroboam hardly had compunctions about serving priestly functions.

13:3 The word **sign** indicates something miraculous (Ex. 4:21; Jer. 33:20, 21). Miraculous signs may indicate either the intended purpose of the deed or its wondrous effects, both ideas often occurring together (see Deut. 6:22; Ps. 78:43).

13:4, 5 Unlike David, who confessed his sin when he was accused by Nathan the man of God (see 2 Sam. 12:13), the wicked Jeroboam sought to **arrest** his accuser. Instead he found his own arm "arrested" and the altar destroyed.

13:6, 7 the LORD your God: This language may be simply deferential to the prophet, but here it may indicate a recognition by Jeroboam that he was no longer really serving the living God.

13:8–10 not go in: The prophet did not want his act of mercy to suggest that God accepted Jeroboam's deviant worship.

13:11 Besides being an important cult center (see 12:29), **Bethel** may have had one of the early prophetic schools (see 2 Kin. 2:3–7).

an old prophet: Perhaps the aged prophet had been previously associated with such a group. Whatever his status then, at this point he clearly tells lies (see v. 18).

13:12–18 The **prophet** was clearly an apostate. He had not spoken against Jeroboam; instead, he boldly lied to the Lord's true prophet.

13:19 went back with him: The man of God had withstood Jeroboam's attempt to save face by having the prophet stay with him (v. 7), yet now the prophet failed to discern the deception and plainly violated God's clear instructions (v. 9).

13:20–23 Whatever his motives were for bringing the man of God to his house, the aged **prophet** now received a true word from God.

13:24–28 The way **the lion** stood by both the man of God and his donkey shows that the lion did not kill for food but was God's executioner (see vv. 25, 26, 28).

13:29–32 The old prophet was brought back to biblical faith at the sight of the death of the true prophet from Judah. **the saying … will surely come to pass:** This confession proclaims renewal of faith in God's word by the prophet who had become deceitful. **cities of Samaria:** The city of Samaria did not in fact come into being for nearly one-half century (see 16:24), but the author mentions it here from his own later perspective.

13:33, 34 Rather than learning from the report of this incident, Jeroboam became even more set in his **evil way.** His apostasy would earn for him his reputation as the one who "made Israel sin" (16:26).

14:1 Abijah: The name means "My Father Is the Lord."

14:2 In a time of distress Jeroboam turned not to one of his own prophets but to the true prophet of God who had predicted his kingship (11:29–39). Although **Ahijah** was now old (v. 4), his spiritual insight was not so dim that he could not see through disguised human intentions (v. 5).

14:3 ten loaves: The gifts that Jeroboam's wife took along are not those customarily given by a king (see 2 Kin. 8:7–9) but rather were common fare (see 1 Sam. 9:6–8).

Jeroboam no doubt was hoping he could deceive the prophet by sending a simple gift.

14:4–6 Located about twenty miles north of Jerusalem, **Shiloh** had been the religious center for the nation during the time of the judges and was the location of the tabernacle (Josh. 18:1; 1 Sam. 1:3). Although he **could not see,** Ahijah could "see" by means of the revelation of the living God.

14:7–10 bond and free: Like "heaven and earth" in Gen. 1:1, the two opposites together mean totality, or all kinds and classes of people (see 2 Kin. 14:26).

14:11, 12 Dogs were scavengers and came to symbolize the dregs of society (see 2 Kin. 8:13).

14:13 something good: Abijah's character receives special divine consideration. Although the age of Jeroboam's son is not certain, he may have been quite young.

14:14 cut off the house: As prophesied here, the end of Jeroboam's line would soon be accomplished (15:27—16:7).

14:15, 16 God had promised that He would **uproot** Israel should it violate its covenantal obligations (Deut. 28:63, 64). **wooden images:** The worship carried on here concerns the goddess Asherah.

14:17 Famed for its beauty (Song 6:4), **Tirzah** was a royal retreat and the capital of the northern kingdom's first two dynasties (see 15:33).

14:18 all Israel mourned: The sorrow of the people was also part of Ahijah's prophecy (v. 13).

14:19 The book of the chronicles of the kings of Israel is mentioned often in 1 Kings as an early sourcebook for the history of the northern kingdom. These chronicles should not be confused with the biblical books of 1 and 2 Chronicles.

14:20 Each of the subsequent kings of Israel would be judged against the example of the wickedness of **Jeroboam** (see 15:34). Only with Ahab (see 16:31) was a worse pattern set.

14:21 the city which the LORD had chosen: These words celebrate not only Jerusalem (Deut. 12:1–19) but also the Davidic kingship.

14:22 Judah did evil: Although Rehoboam apparently began his reign well (see 2 Chr.

11:5–17, 23), his spiritual condition soon deteriorated (2 Chr. 12:1).

14:23 The **high places** were a problem throughout the history of Judah and Israel (Mic. 1:3). These were the places in which Canaanite worship rites were practiced in honor of Baal and where other foreign gods were worshiped as well.

14:24 perverted persons: Male prostitutes were part of the fertility rituals of ancient Canaan (see Deut. 23:18). Here the word is a term that means "devoted to sacred service." **abominations:** This is an exceedingly strong term; it describes perverted activities that impelled God to dispossess the Canaanite peoples from their land (see Deut. 18:9, 12).

14:25 Shishak: Although Jerusalem and Judah were spared total annihilation at this time because Rehoboam repented, Jerusalem was looted as a result of the sins that took place "on his watch" (2 Chr. 12:1–9). Egyptian records confirm that Shishak' s invasion was widespread and highly successful.

14:26–28 The sacking of **treasures of the house of the LORD** (v. 26) is particularly shocking, when we think of the long and detailed description of Solomon's greatest accomplishment, the building and furnishing of the holy temple in Jerusalem (chs. 6—8). **bronze shields:** A compelling symbol of the ruin of the temple treasures is seen in the change from shields of gold (v. 26; see 10:16, 17) to bronze.

14:29 The book of the chronicles of the kings of Judah is mentioned 15 times in Kings. Apparently it was an official record of events in the southern kingdom down to the days of Jehoiakim. Neither this work nor "the chronicles of the kings of Israel" (v. 19) is to be confused with the biblical books of Chronicles.

14:30–31 The early history of Rehoboam and Jeroboam (see 11:26—12:17) led to their continuing enmity and **war.**

15:1 Although it may reflect a popular name for Abijah (2 Chr. 12:16), **Abijam** is a strange name for a king of Judah, as it ties together the Hebrew word for "Father" with the Hebrew word for "Sea"—normally a deity of Canaan.

15:2 Maachah was the granddaughter of Abishalom and the favorite of Rehoboam's eighteen wives. A woman of strong will, she wielded a good deal of influence during the reign of her son Abijam and her grandson Asa.

15:3 The word translated **loyal** here denotes one who is wholly devoted to God.

15:4 for David's sake: That is, because of God's love for David and the promise He had made to him (see 2 Sam. 7). **lamp:** This is one of the lovely images of God's intended blessing on the Davidic house.

15:5 The quality of David's reign is celebrated. **Uriah:** At the same time, his most grievous sin is not omitted (2 Sam. 11, 12).

15:6 Because Rehoboam reigned until his fifty-eighth year (14:21), Abijam probably knew little respite from **war** (see 14:30). Abijam did at least trust God during the war against Jeroboam, and God gave him a decisive victory (see 2 Chr. 13:2–20).

15:7, 8 This follows the pattern established for recording the obituaries of the kings of Judah.

15:9–11 Asa: The meaning of his name is perhaps "Healer."

15:12 perverted persons: This term is used for sacred prostitutes in the Canaanite religious practices (22:46; 2 Kin. 23:7).

15:13 removed Maachah: Asa's many spiritual activities (see 2 Chr. 14:2–5; 15:1–18) are telescoped into a few statements here (vv. 11–15). Although the reforms mentioned in vv. 11, 12 took place early in Asa's reign (see 2 Chr. 14:2–5), the chronicler indicates (2 Chr. 15:16) that the deposing of Maachah took place in the fifteenth year of his rule (895 B.C.). Maachah's removal came as a result of a time of covenant renewal (2 Chr. 15:1–15) and a consequent reaction against her vile idolatry.

15:14, 15 In some instances the **high places** were intended as places where the Lord was worshiped (see 3:2; 1 Sam. 9:12); in other cases they were used for pagan purposes (see 2 Chr. 14:2–3).

15:16 war: There were periods of peace between the two nations (see the league of Ahab and Jehoshaphat in ch. 22). But this was a period of warfare, particularly in the border areas.

15:17 Ramah was about five and one-half miles north of Jerusalem on the main north-south commercial route through the land, and it was therefore of great importance to both kingdoms. It gave east-west access to both the foothills of Ephraim and the Mediterranean coast, so it was of strategic military importance as well. Baasha was striking a blow for control of the center of the land.

15:18 To stave off the penetration of Israel into Judah, King Asa plundered the temple for money to try to make a military alliance with Damascus.

15:19, 20 Asa apparently suggested that for all practical purposes **a treaty** between the house of David and Damascus had been in effect since the days of Solomon.

15:21 The retreat of **Baasha** from Ramah was because of the renewed treaty between Asa of Judah and Ben-Hadad of Damascus.

15:22 Asa's swift action in taking Ramah allowed him to dismantle its fortifications and the use of the material to fortify two nearby strategic Benjamite towns, **Geba** and **Mizpah.** The control of these three sites afforded advanced defensive protection for Jerusalem and northern Judah.

15:23, 24 diseased in his feet: Here is another case of a godly leader who did great exploits for the Lord but ended badly.

15:25, 26 Nadab: His name means "Generous" or "Noble," but he did not live up to his name.

15:27, 28 Baasha killed him: As Baasha, a military commander for Nadab, had done to his master, so it would be done to his own house. Zimri, one of the commanders of his chariot corps, would conspire against Baasha's son Elah and kill him (16:9, 10).

15:29, 30 The death of Nadab was in line with prophetic fulfillment, an act of God's judgment on the **house of Jeroboam** I (see 14:9, 16). Nonetheless, the manner of his death was condemned by God through His prophet Jehu (see 16:2, 7).

15:31–33 Baasha … in Tirzah: The second capital of Israel (see 14:17) was located in the highlands of Ephraim between Shechem (the first capital, see 12:25) and Mount Gilboa.

15:34 did evil: Political exchange had not signaled any improvement in the spiritual climate of Israel.

16:1–7 As the son of the prophet Hanani whom Asa had executed (2 Chr. 16:7–10), **Jehu** (not to be confused with Jehu the king of Israel; see 2 Kin. 9:2) came from the southern kingdom. His long prophetic ministry lasted into the days of Jehoshaphat. Like his father before him, he confronted sin fearlessly—even in the royal house.

16:8, 9 The first two dynasties of Israel ended in tragedy. Like Jeroboam's son Nadab (15:28), Baasha's son **Elah** was assassinated. There were three more claimants to the throne before the year 885 B.C. was finished: Zimri, Tibni, and Omri. With the advent of Omri, Israel's third dynasty would be established.

16:10–12 The assassination of Elah and the annihilation of his house by **Zimri** (v. 12), while treacherous, had prophetic sanction because of the wickedness of Elah and his father Baasha.

16:13, 14 idols: Here the plural of the term for "vapor" is used. This is a contemptuous term describing the deities of false, pagan theology.

16:15–17 As Baasha had done (15:29), so **Zimri** also fulfilled prophecy against a royal house (vv. 8–14).

16:18–20 Because he **burned the king's house** in Tirzah, Zimri may have contributed to Omri's building of a new capital city and royal residence (v. 24), perhaps one that could be defended better.

16:21, 22 The source of Omri's political base is not certain. According to Josephus, **Tibni** was killed in the dynastic power struggles that brought in the dynasty of Omri.

16:23–28 The short reign of twelve years is not indicative of what **Omri** accomplished. He invaded Moab and figured prominently in an alliance aimed at stopping the westward advance of the rising power of Assyria. Yet the author of Kings describes little of Omri's achievements, because he **did evil in the eyes of the LORD.** Omri's choice of **Samaria** as the site for his new capital city was motivated by several factors: its central geographic setting, its commercial location, and its defensive potential.

16:29–31 The first level of evaluation of **Ahab** is the same as that given to his father (compare v. 30 with v. 25). **a trivial thing:** By these words we realize that in Ahab we come to the very lowest point in the degeneration of the spiritual life of the kings of Israel. Ahab's marriage to the Phoenician princess **Jezebel** produced tragic results. Jezebel was exceedingly evil. She could influence Ahab to be wicked (ch. 21). Her father was both king and priest of Baal in Sidon; similarly, Jezebel was princess and priestess of Baal. **he went and served Baal and worshiped him:** He became a full-fledged worshiper of Baal for whom his wife Jezebel was a priestess.

16:32, 33 Further, Ahab established an **altar for Baal,** a **temple of Baal,** and a **wooden image.** In these actions Ahab went a considerable distance in establishing the Baal cult as the state religion of Israel.

16:34 In defiance of Joshua's curse (Josh. 6:26, 27), Hiel **built Jericho.** Either Hiel offered his sons as foundation sacrifices (following ancient custom) or they died in some mishap.

17:1–4 The prophet **Elijah** would speak for God fearlessly in the midst of the spiritual vacuum that gripped the northern kingdom throughout the days of Ahab, Ahaziah, and Jehoram. His ministry and his stand against the Baalism of the land reached the highest circles of government in Israel. **dew nor rain:** Because the Canaanite belief was that only Baal could govern the dew and the rain, Elijah's pronouncement was as an immediate challenge: Who is really God, Baal or the Lord?

17:5 The Brook Cherith was across the Jordan River, far from the palace in Samaria.

17:6–8 The Lord of all creation may use any means He wishes to feed His prophet, even **the ravens.**

17:9–11 Zarephath was in Phoenician territory. The Lord's sustaining Elijah first by a raven and then by a **widow** provided the prophet with a test of faith.

17:12 the LORD your God: The widow of Zarephath was a woman of faith in the living God, even though she lived in a foreign land. **Bread** here denotes a round cake. The flour **bin** was a large earthenware container (Gen. 24:14), while **jar** denotes a smaller, portable container such as a jug or flask.

17:13 me … first: Elijah's challenge to the widow would call for faith in the midst of her desperate circumstances.

17:14 The LORD God of Israel acknowledges the woman's identification of the Lord as Elijah's God (v. 12), but also points the widow directly to Him who is the Sustainer of all.

17:15–17 The fresh supply of oil and flour each day would be a reminder to both the prophet and the widow of the value of trust in Him who alone is sufficient to meet every need.

17:18 Sin is not always the immediate cause of suffering (see John 9:3; Heb. 12:7–11).

17:19, 20 Elijah stayed in an **upper room,** on the roof accessible from outside the house.

17:21–23 Elijah's stretched out on the dead lad **three times.** Elisha later would perform a similar act (2 Kin. 4:34; see also Acts 20:10). **cried … heard:** The scriptural motif of crying and being heard or calling and being answered is a theme that emphasizes intimacy of fellowship or communion.

17:24 now … I know: The widow's belief had now grown into fullness of faith. That Elijah was indeed a "man of God" (v. 18) had been proved by word and deed.

18:1, 2 The New Testament indicates that the drought ended in the fourth year (Luke 4:25; James 5:17). If the point of reckoning here is late **in the third year,** the end of the drought may not have occurred until about three and one-half years after its inception.

18:3 Obadiah here is a highly sympathetic figure, whose great faith in God and heroic actions help us gain a more balanced picture of the situation of people of faith in Israel at the time. **in charge of his house:** Obadiah was Ahab's palace official and minister of state, serving as the king's personal representative.

18:4 That there could be **one hundred prophets** for Obadiah to hide may be seen from the fact that associations of prophets who met and may even have lived together are known from this period onward.

18:5–11 Keeping **horses** alive was important to maintain military preparedness in a world where there was always the threat of new hostilities.

18:12–14 Obadiah was not quite sure whether he could trust the Lord's prophet. Obadiah had already jeopardized his life in hiding God's prophets. Reporting Elijah's presence without producing him to an infuriated Ahab might well cost him his life (vv. 9, 14).

18:15–18 Baals: The wording indicates that Ahab had a practice of attending services at various local shrines where this deity was worshiped.

18:19–21 The wife of Ei, **Asherah** was a fertility goddess whose exploits and veneration were linked with Baal.

18:22, 23 Elijah focused on the fact that he **alone** stood ready to confront the 450 prophets of Baal.

18:24–26 The contest between the Lord and Baal would reveal who was the true god of storm. Such a god would have lightning in his arsenal of weapons (see Ps. 18:12–14; Hab. 3:11). Sending **fire** for the wood and the offering would be a reasonable test of the power of the rival deities.

18:27, 28 The sharp words **for he is a god** were mocking and derisive. Perhaps their god was lost in thought, **meditating,** and simply needed them to call louder. **Is busy** is a euphemism. In his harsh attack on the folly of idolatry, Elijah suggested that the reason their god did not answer was that he had gone to a celestial men's room.

18:29 no voice: Nothing the priests did elicited a response from their supposed god.

18:30 repaired the altar: This was an earlier altar that had been used by the true people of God on a legitimate high place (see 3:2–4). Elijah avoided all contact with the altar that was associated with Baal.

18:31 The numerical symbolism of **twelve stones** cannot be missed. The people of Israel had descended from twelve tribes.

18:32 The rebuilding of the **altar in the name of the LORD** would be a reminder that the Lord had not abdicated His position; He was still the God of all Israel, including the northern kingdom, where pagan syncretism and Baal worship prevailed.

18:33–35 third time: The three applications

of water not only made the sacrifice thoroughly soaked and beyond human trickery but may again attest the power of the thrice holy God (see 17:21).

18:36 The phrase **LORD God of Abraham, Isaac, and Israel** so characteristic of worship in the early period (see Gen. 50:24; Ex. 3:6, 15, 16) reminded Elijah's hearers of the inviolability of the Abrahamic covenant.

18:37 Elijah prayed that the Lord would demonstrate clearly to the **people** that He alone is the living God. He also prayed for the full revival of God's people.

18:38 Showing who really was the god of storm, Baal proved impotent, while **the fire of the LORD** destroyed everything on the site.

18:39 God's power over fire, water, and rain (v. 45) demonstrated that He, not Baal, is **the LORD, He is God!**

18:40 The prophets were **executed** because of their blatant sin and the ruin they had brought upon the nation.

18:41, 42 The respective reactions of the king and the prophet are enlightening. A compromising king, as bidden, gladly celebrated, while a faithful prophet **bowed down** and prayed for the promised result of the Lord's miraculous victory.

18:43, 44 This cloud may have seemed **as small as a man's hand** when it was first visible from Mount Carmel's height, but Elijah sensed the approach of the growing storm and warned Ahab that he had better hurry.

18:45 Elijah had announced more than three years earlier that there would be no more **rain** unless it came from the hand of the living God (see 17:1).

18:46 girded up his loins: Elijah tucked his garment into his sash, enabling him to run freely the 13 miles to Jezreel.

19:1, 2 The report **Ahab told Jezebel** did not cause her to repent or to turn from Baal to God. Ahab merely reported the facts that led to her personal embarrassment. Her response was to issue a death warrant for Elijah.

19:3 Elijah understood Jezebel's intentions **when he saw** her response, and he realized that the Lord's victory on Mount Carmel would not bring a quick end to the paganism that was rampant in the land. He saw that nothing really had changed.

19:4 The **broom tree** has sufficient foliage for shade and often grows to a height of ten feet. It grows abundantly in Israel.

19:5, 6 God brought Elijah a **cake** and **water,** even as He had provided for him in earlier days (see ch. 17).

19:7 Although **the angel of the LORD** can at times refer to God Himself (Ex. 3:2–6), in the Book of Kings it means a supernatural messenger (2 Kin. 1:3; 19:35).

19:8 As it frequently does in the Scriptures, **Horeb** refers to Mount Sinai, "the mountain of God" (see Ex. 3:1).

19:9, 10 zealous: Like Phinehas of old (Num. 25:7–13), Elijah had a passion for God that made him stand against the idolatry he saw all around him. **I alone am left:** In his depression, he thought he alone was faithful to God. When he was killed, there would be no one left to serve God.

19:11, 12 the LORD was not in: Although each of the things mentioned in vv. 11, 12 could signal God's presence (see Ex. 40:38; Zech. 14:4, 5; Acts 2:2, 3), Elijah learned that God is not just a God of the spectacular. At times, the work of God is experienced in **a still small voice,** "the sound of a gentle stillness."

19:13–16 Elijah's work for God was far from complete, but it would now take a new direction. Elijah would **anoint** Elisha (vv. 19–21), Elisha would anoint **Hazael** (2 Kin. 8:7–15), and Jehu would be anointed by Elisha's servant (2 Kin. 9:1–10). The importance of Elijah's task may be seen in that Elisha became Elijah's designated successor, and Jehu and Hazael became kings.

19:17 The three individuals, **Elisha, Jehu,** and **Hazael,** were instruments of God.

19:18–20 There were still many people who were faithful to the living God. **Seven thousand** had not stooped to worship Baal.

19:21 Elisha turned back to his home only to break fully with his past. Elisha would humbly serve Elijah until he was taken into heaven (2 Kin. 2:1–12).

20:1 One of the distinctive features of the ancient Middle East was the practice of forming alliances. Coalitions such as the **thirty-two kings** were common in times of war (Gen. 14:1–16).

20:2 When he is associated with his wicked wife Jezebel, **Ahab** appears as thoroughly evil. But in this chapter he appears as a capable leader in a time of international turmoil, and as a person who had some sense of the power and presence of God (see vv. 13, 14).

20:3, 4 Taken by themselves, Ben-Hadad's words **are mine** meant no more than that Israel was a client state to the more powerful Aramean state. Ahab's reply **All ... are yours** would then have been acceptance of such a treaty, in which Israel was the subservient party.

20:5, 6 This was a demand for complete surrender of everything of value, of any person of worth, of **whatever** was **pleasant** in Ahab's eyes, to be handed over to the foreign monarch.

20:7, 8 Ahab apparently held out little hope of withstanding so vast an enemy host. His **elders** (v. 8) counseled him against submitting.

20:9, 10 Ben-Hadad's boast was that his striking power was so great that Samaria would be ground to a powder.

20:11 Ahab's proverbial reply reminded Ben-Hadad that a **boast** alone would not get the job done.

20:12 The notice that **Ben-Hadad** was **drinking** during the time he should have been preparing for battle shows his arrogance. He was celebrating victory before he had begun fighting (see v. 16).

20:13 I will deliver ... you shall know: Just as God had demonstrated His person and power on Mount Carmel (ch. 18), He would now make Himself known to Ahab in the coming battle.

20:14, 15 The prophet revealed the outlines of the strategy Ahab should use. To his credit, Ahab obeyed the divine command and **mustered** his force.

20:16 This was an alliance of **thirty-two kings** from small areas in Aram and the surrounding territories. But they were all **getting drunk**—an arrogant act before the battle had even begun.

20:17–21 Ahab followed up his probing skirmish with a well-timed charge by his main striking force. Ben-Hadad, the king of the Arameans, barely **escaped** (v. 20) with his life. The resulting **great slaughter** (v. 21) was a tremendous victory for the army of Ahab.

20:22 The period of late **spring** to early summer was one of the two main seasons for military expeditions. Provisions were readily available for men and cattle. The end of the rains allowed for more efficient movement of troops and provisions.

20:23-25 The Aramean advisors reflected traditional ancient Middle Eastern theological conceptions. Their gods' powers, such as their **gods of the hills,** were limited to particular locations. But the living God is not limited by time (Ps. 90:2) or space (Ps. 139:7-12).

20:26-30 Apparently the Arameans were launching their second campaign in the Jordan valley. The Arameans would learn that the living God can deliver His people in the valley as well as the hills (see Ps. 23:4; Joel 3:12-14).

20:31 Ben-Hadad now appealed to Ahab's **merciful** nature. The Aramean king sent his servants to Ahab in the traditional attire of submission and repentance.

20:32-34 The term **brother** was commonly used when relations between kings were cordial (see 9:13). Ben-Hadad might have been implying, "We are both kings."

20:35-41 This **certain man** is probably a different prophet than the one mentioned earlier in the story (see vv. 13, 22). **sons of the prophets:** Although this term first occurs here, prophetic associations were known at least from Samuel's time (1 Sam. 10).

20:42-43 The prophet's dramatic tale is symbolic; as Ahab had judged the case, so he would be judged (see 22:29-37). Ahab resorts to human reason and adamantly refuses to change his ways.

21:1 Samaria was Ahab's capital city; its name is used to represent all of Israel (see 2 Kin. 1:3; 2 Chr. 24:23; Jon. 3:6).

21:2, 3 Ahab therefore negotiated with Naboth for his property.

21:4-7 In reminding Ahab that he was king and could do as he pleased, **Jezebel** reflected her Canaanite background where kings ruled absolutely.

21:8-12 Such **letters** would be written by royal scribes on scrolls or tablets and then **sealed** with the sender's personal sign.

21:13, 14 two men, scoundrels: The charge against Naboth was serious (see Ex. 22:28). Although two witnesses were required in capital cases (Deut. 17:6), these **two men** were **scoundrels,** easily bribed into giving false testimony (Prov. 19:28). Naboth was executed **outside the city** as the Law required (Lev. 24:14). God's law was followed in the manner and place of his death, though his execution was an outrage against the spirit of the Law.

21:15-18 Because **Naboth ... was dead,** the property was confiscated by the throne. Although Ahab apparently was unconcerned about how this took place, he could not escape his guilty conscience (v. 20).

21:19-24 Soon Ahab's blood would be licked by **dogs** at the pool in Samaria (22:37, 38). Ahab had lost all sense of God's law, the basic teaching of which was always love for God and for neighbor (see Matt. 22:37-40).

21:25-29 The vacillating nature of Ahab's complex character is seen here. He could all too easily be led into **wickedness** by his **wife.** Nevertheless, he could at times display courage (22:34, 35) and even real humility before God (v. 29). Unfortunately, he never really entered into a genuine spiritual relationship with God.

22:1-3 Faced with the rising threat of Assyria, Ahab had failed to press his advantage of three years before. He had not reoccupied the strategic highlands of **Ramoth in Gilead.** Now that Aram and Israel as allies had successfully turned back Shalmaneser III of Assyria at Qarqar (853 B.C.), control of Ramoth Gilead was crucial.

22:4 Jehoshaphat was the fourth king of the southern kingdom. He was related to Ahab through the marriage of his son Jehoram to Ahab's daughter Athaliah (2 Kin. 8:18, 27). Jehoshaphat's relation to Ahab now placed him in the precarious position of going to war with Ahab against the Arameans.

22:5-8 Kings in the ancient Middle East commonly sought the will of the gods before entering battle (see Judg. 20:27, 28; 1 Sam. 23:1–4). Jehoshaphat did not rely on Ahab's false prophets; he desired a true **word of the LORD.**

22:9 The prophet **Micaiah** is not known except in connection with this incident (see 2 Chr. 18:8–27).

22:10 A threshing floor was often used by the Canaanites for holding court. Threshing floors could also be scenes of spiritual importance (see Judg. 6:36–40; 1 Chr. 21:15–22:1).

22:11–16 Zedekiah tried to validate his prophetic pronouncement with symbolic magic. The **horns** symbolize great strength (Num. 24:8; Ps. 18:2), an idea reinforced by the use of **iron.**

22:17–22 The imagery of **sheep** and **shepherd** was familiar to Micaiah's hearers (see Ezek. 34:12; Mark 14:27). Micaiah's words are dramatic, emphasizing the gravity of Ahab's projected venture and counteracting Zedekiah's lies.

22:23–29 lying spirit: These prophets prophesied under the influences of evil, but their false predictions were just what Ahab wanted to hear.

22:30–33 By hiding himself behind a **disguise,** Ahab hoped he could thwart Micaiah's prophecy of doom. Ben-Hadad tried to shorten the battle by finding and killing Ahab. Jehoshaphat's life was spared not only by his timely cry but by God's direct intervention (2 Chr. 18:31).

22:34–37 The phrase **at random** indicates that the bowman did not realize that he was aiming at Ahab. Ahab's wounded body was propped up in his chariot so his soldiers would keep on fighting, and not give up immediately as Ben-Hadad hoped.

22:38 The fulfillment of Elijah's grisly prophecy (see 21:19–24) about the house of Ahab unfolds here as **the dogs licked up his blood.**

22:39–42 Archaeological excavations at Samaria have illustrated the nature of Ahab's **ivory house,** a house with luxurious decorations made of ivory.

22:43, 44 Jehoshaphat continued in his father Asa's spiritual footsteps. These **high places** were often used in the worship of Israel's God (see 3:2–4).

22:45 made war: In addition to the campaign at Ramoth Gilead, Jehoshaphat's military ventures included strengthening his forces and borders (2 Chr. 17:14–19), repelling an invasion (2 Chr. 20:1–30), and conducting an Edomite campaign (2 Kin. 3:6–27).

22:46, 47 perverted persons: See 14:24 for a description of these Canaanite cultic prostitutes, who were a part of the debased religious practices of Baal worship.

22:48–50 The destruction of the **merchant ships** sponsored by Jehoshaphat and Ahaziah ended the projected commercial enterprise. The prophet pronounces God's displeasure with the whole project (see 2 Chr. 20:35–37).

22:51–53 A wicked king of the northern kingdom, **Ahaziah** followed in the path of his father Ahab, much as Amon of Judah would later follow in the path of his wicked father Manasseh (see 2 Kin. 21:19–22). The story does not end here but is continued in 2 Kings.

2 Kings

Introduction

From the ascension of the prophet Elijah to heaven through the eventual fall of Israel and Judah, Second Kings continues the history begun in First Kings of one people and two kingdoms. The narrative displays both high and low points in the history of Israel and Judah. While it is true that few of the kings of the northern kingdom of Israel are spoken of highly, the kings of the southern kingdom of Judah do not fare much better. The books describe a people without direction, leaders who failed to lead, and a God who was forced to discipline His rebellious people.

Like First and Second Samuel, First and Second Kings were originally one book in Hebrew. Hence debate over the authorship of First Kings applies equally to the authorship of Second Kings. Many evangelical biblical scholars continue to endorse the traditional view that Jeremiah wrote the books of the Kings. But the actual author is unknown.

Second Kings describes details especially relevant to the prophetic ministries of Elijah and Elisha (1:1—9:37). During this period, the northern kingdom faced continued pressure from Aram (Syria) under its kings Ben-Hadad II and Hazael, as well as new threats from the rising state of Assyria with its powerful King Shalmaneser III (858–824 B.C.). Eventually the northern kingdom was overrun by the Assyrians in 722 B.C.

The remainder of Second Kings deals with the varying fortunes and spiritual pilgrimage of the southern kingdom, tracing Judah's history from the righteous Hezekiah (chs. 18—20) to the wicked sons of Josiah, under whom Jerusalem faced three invasions and deportations, the last in 586 B.C. Thus Judah was increasingly caught up in the complex international events that took place from the late eighth to the early sixth century B.C.

Judah was led away captive by Babylonia, and their exile would last seventy years. Second Kings ends on this tragic note. Only the final word of Jehoiachin's release provides a ray of hope in the darkness of captivity (25:27–30). The symbolic message is clear: the Lord would still fulfill His promise to restore His people (see 1 Kin. 8:46–53).

1:1 Moab rebelled: This chronological notice likely relates to the rebellion of Mesha, the king of Moab. Its placement here may serve as an indicator of the problems that would soon fall on Israel.

1:2 Ahaziah: The account of his brief, wicked reign begins in 1 Kin. 22:51. The division of the Book of Kings into two parts was for the convenience of the translators, as is indicated by the fact that Ahaziah's reign carries over from one book to the other without a break.

1:3 the angel of the LORD: At times this phrase is used as a way of referring to God. **god of Ekron:** Ahaziah followed the Baal worship of his father. The cult of Baal was strongly identified with Ekron, a city well known for its practice of divination (1 Sam. 6:2; Is. 2:6). Ahaziah probably sent his messenger to Ekron because he hoped to keep the nature and extent of his injury secret.

1:4 The determination of God was that the king would die for his sins. The king had sought a divine message from a foreign god, but received the Lord's word nonetheless.

1:5, 6 The **messengers** of the king were prevented by Elijah from completing their errand. God did not want any sham message encouraging the wicked king. He had already received the word of the living God (v. 4).

1:7, 8 Although *hairy* may refer to Elijah's garments, the usual translation **hairy man** is supported by the ancient versions. Ahaziah knew the man was his opponent, **Elijah the Tishbite** (see 1 Kin. 17:1).

1:9, 10 fire … from heaven: Heavenly fire could signal divine judgment (see Gen. 19:24). Elijah had already called down such fire in his contest with the prophets of Baal (1 Kin. 18:36–38). This fire was likely lightning. Baal was not the god of the storm he was reputed to be. The God of Israel was—and is—the Lord of creation.

1:11–13 Fifty men were a military unit attested elsewhere in the literature of the ancient Middle East. Each **captain of fifty** approached Elijah with a growing fear of the power of God associated with this great prophet.

1:14–17 So Ahaziah died: The prophetic word was fulfilled as announced. **no son:** This meant that the dynasty had ended. A king named **Jehoram** thus ruled in both kingdoms.

1:18 the rest of the acts: This follows the usual pattern for recording the obituaries of the kings of the northern kingdom.

2:1 about to take up Elijah into heaven: The story that follows is so extraordinary that the narrator introduces its subject early.

2:2–6 Stay here: The tripling of these incidents is similar to the tripling of the incidents of ch. 1 (the three bands of fifty soldiers who came to seize Elijah). **As the LORD lives:** Elisha made a solemn promise three times in these same verses; he determined that he would remain by his master Elijah no matter what might occur. **take away:** The same Hebrew verb is used for Enoch's entrance to heaven (Gen. 5:24).

2:7, 8 The water was the Jordan River (vv. 7, 13), somewhere near Jericho. Elijah was like Moses in that his life and ministry show many parallels to that of Israel's greatest prophet. As Moses had divided the waters of the Red Sea in the final act of the redemption of Israel from Egypt (Ex. 14), so now Elijah replicated this miracle by dividing the waters of the Jordan River.

2:9 double portion: Although the narrative reports twice as many miracles for Elisha as Elijah, that was not the point of Elisha's request. His real request was that he would be Elijah's spiritual successor (Deut. 21:17). Elisha wanted a double portion of his spirit.

2:10, 11 In one of the most dramatic scenes in the Bible, heaven opened, a fiery chariot with fiery horses appeared, a whirlwind blew, and the prophet of God vanished alive into heaven. The **fire** associated with the **chariot** and the horses indicate the presence of God.

2:12 The term **my father** underscores Elijah's relationship to Elisha as his spiritual mentor as well as the greatness of Elijah's reputation.

2:13 took up the mantle: Elijah had once laid this mantle on Elisha as a symbolic action (1 Kin. 19:19); now Elisha took up the prophetic status and ministry that the mantle symbolized.

2:14 The mantle in the hands of Elijah it had been an instrument for the power of the living God. It became the symbol of God's power in the hands of Elisha.

2:15 the spirit of Elijah: The prophets witnessed both the miracle of Elijah (v. 8) and the similar miracle of Elisha. In this way there would be common agreement that Elisha was the successor of Elijah.

2:16 fifty strong men: Groups of fifty men were often called upon to perform an arduous task (see 1:9–15). The men decided they needed a search party. Even though they had received a revelation from God that Elijah would be taken to heaven (see v. 3), still they checked things out.

2:17, 18 he was ashamed: Although these words may indicate Elisha's sense of shame on behalf of his disciples for their disbelief, the use of the phrase elsewhere indicates that it means Elisha was worn out, no longer willing to resist (8:11; see Judg. 3:25).

2:19–22 The salt taken from a new bowl and cast into the water symbolized the cleansing of the water for new use. The miracle was done in the name of God; Elisha was only His instrument. **to this day:** That is, at the day of the writing of the account.

2:23, 24 Go up, you baldhead: While the severity of the sentence has been questioned, the words of the youths indicated their disbelief of Elijah's "going up" into heaven (see v. 11) and their disrespect for God's prophet. God did not tolerate blasphemy against Himself by the demeaning of Elijah's departure, or the abuse of His prophet.

2:25 Elisha made his home on **Mount Carmel** (see 4:25), as well as in **Samaria** (see 5:3).

3:1, 2 sacred pillar of Baal: Probably this was a stone pillar or statue erected by Ahab and bearing an inscription and image of the god Baal. Although it was put away temporarily, it apparently was not destroyed, because it later became one of the objects of Jehu's purge (10:26, 27).

3:3, 4 Mesha king of Moab: The existence of this Moabite king is confirmed by an inscription on a pillar known as the Moabite Stone.

3:5, 6 The rebellion of Moab provoked **Jehoram** into a punitive war.

3:7, 8 Will you go with me: Because Jehoshaphat was related to the throne of the northern kingdom through the marriage of his son Jehoram to Ahab's daughter Athaliah, it could be presumed that he would be available as an ally.

3:9, 10 no water: In such a military campaign as this, both men and animals needed more water than they could carry with them.

3:11, 12 prophet of the LORD: The crucial role of Elisha in the story emphasizes the importance of the prophetic office in ancient Israel.

3:13 prophets of your father: Elisha spoke scathingly about the wicked kings of the north consulting with prophets of Baal (1:2, 3).

3:14 I would not look at you: As a devotee of Baal, Jehoram had no claim on the favor of God. Nevertheless, he would enjoy the benefits of God's grace toward Jehoshaphat.

3:15 Elisha's call for a **musician** is an effort to achieve an atmosphere free of war and strife so that he might concentrate on the anticipated divine revelation.

3:16–19 As in connection with many Old Testament miracles, the prophet's words carry instructions for human participation (4:3, 4, 41; 6:6), in order that man's faith and the divine provision may each have their proper part.

3:20–22 filled with water: The dry stream beds can easily overflow their banks in downpours of rain.

3:23–27 This is blood: The red water looked like blood and the Moabite king assumed falsely that the former enemies had once again fallen out with each other. It was a tragic miscalculation.

4:1 A certain woman: The fate of widows was perilous in the ancient Middle East. **creditor:** Both the Bible (see Lev. 25:39–45) and other ancient laws permitted selling one's family members into slavery for payment of debts. God's law worked toward limiting the abuse and the length of time in such a situation.

4:2 The small flask held olive **oil** intended for anointing, rather than food or fuel. Such a small flask was not very valuable.

4:3–7 Elisha is called **the man of God** throughout this section (vv. 16, 21, 22, 25, 27). The word God in Hebrew is literally "the God," meaning the true or genuine God.

4:8, 9 holy man of God: The adjective describes Elisha, a man she perceived was set apart for the ministry of God.

4:10 upper room: Such quarters were commonly on the roof and could be reached from the outside. This accommodated the guest while providing privacy.

4:11, 12 The term for **servant** often means a person engaged in a period of training. The same word was also used of Elisha's own relation to Elijah (1 Kin. 19:21).

4:13–16 Elisha decided that the best thing he could do for the woman was promise her the birth of a son, despite her years of frustration about this. **do not lie:** The Shunammite woman felt that even Elisha could not fulfill such a promise.

4:17 The birth of the son to the **woman** was similar to the fulfillment of the promise of God in the birth of Isaac to Abraham and Sarah (Gen. 21).

4:18–21 the bed of the man of God: The Shunammite's action speaks strongly of her faith. Placing the body on the bed of the man of God kept his death a secret until she could reach Elisha, from whom she had once seen the impossible accomplished.

4:22, 23 New Moon ... Sabbath: There was no work on these days, so they would be most suitable for seeing the prophet (see Ex. 20:9–12; Amos 8:5).

4:24–27 Elisha knew that something was wrong by the furious way she drove (v. 24), but God had not made the particular issue known to the prophet. **caught him by the feet:** This action is a mark of humility and reverence (see Matt. 28:9).

4:28 Did I ask: Her pain in the death of her child was worse than the emptiness she had felt before he was born. It was the prophet's fault, she charged. Yet it was the prophet to whom she had come for help.

4:29 Elisha's **staff,** like Elijah's mantle (see

2:13, 14), was symbolic of the power of God and the authority of the prophet. Laid upon the body of the child, the staff would signify that the prophet intended to come, and that he had faith that God would restore the boy.

4:30, 31 As the LORD lives: With this oath, the woman asserted her faith in the living God (1 Kin. 17:1). Elisha had used similar language when he refused to leave Elijah (2:2, 4, 6).

4:32–37 Elisha's actions demonstrate that his faith was in the person and power of God alone, and not in the staff that symbolized his prophetic office. He sought God who alone can grant life and perform the miraculous.

4:38 Gilgal was the first place the Israelites camped after crossing the Jordan River into Canaan (Josh. 4:19, 20). Gilgal was probably about one mile northeast of Jericho. **sitting before him:** Elisha sat at the head of the sons of the prophets.

4:39, 40 The **wild gourds** were poisonous. **death in the pot:** The reaction of the hungry men was immediate and frightening.

4:41 The **flour** had no magical properties, of course. Elisha's faith in the living God effected the miraculous cure.

4:42–44 Baal Shalisha was near Gilgal. The **firstfruits** were to be presented to God and His priests (Lev. 23:15–17, 20). With an entrenched false priesthood and a debased state religion prevailing in the northern kingdom, the man brought his offering to Elisha. The faithful prophet miraculously multiplied the loaves—with some left over.

5:1 This Aramean general **Naaman** was a remarkable figure in biblical history. This verse is filled with phrases describing his character, honor, and ability. The Hebrew word translated **leper** refers to any of several serious skin diseases (Lev. 13:1–46; Num. 5:1–4), including certain fungi (Lev. 13:47–56; 14:33–57). The **king of Syria** was Ben-Hadad II (860–842 B.C.). He was a constant threat to the northern kingdom.

5:2 captive … young girl: God used the testimony of a Jewish servant girl and brought the commanding general of Israel's greatest military foe to biblical faith.

5:3 the prophet … in Samaria: Although

Elisha traveled frequently and may sometimes have lived at Mount Carmel (see 4:25), he apparently maintained a residence in the capital city of Samaria (see vv. 9, 24; 2:25; 6:9—7:20).

5:4, 5 It is a measure of the respect that the Aramean king had for his general that he granted his unusual request. Naaman's gifts are a measure of his wealth—and of his great personal need.

5:6, 7 While such letters of introduction were common in the ancient Middle East, Ben-Hadad's frequent forays against Israel made the **king** suspicious that the Aramean king was seeking a pretext for yet another invasion of Israelite territory (see v. 2).

5:8 torn his clothes: Tearing a robe could be a sign of grief or agitation (see 11:14), as well as a mark of the sorrow that leads to repentance (Joel 2:13).

5:9 at the door: For some reason Elisha did not meet with the general face to face.

5:10 Elisha's instruction for Naaman to wash **seven times** in the Jordan River emphasizes that the full cure for Naaman's condition could be effected solely by the power of Israel's sovereign God.

5:11, 12 Understandably, Naaman's initial response was disbelief and anger. This seemed a strange and humiliating command for a general in the army of Aram. What, after all, was the Jordan River compared to the greater **rivers** of Aram?

5:13, 14 Naaman listened to his advisors, did as he was commanded, and was healed. **clean:** The word suggests that the problem of skin diseases causing *uncleanness* was an issue in his country as well.

5:15, 16 stood before him: Now that Naaman was clean, he could stand in the presence of the prophet Elisha (compare vv. 9, 10). **no God in all the earth:** Naaman stands as a wonderful example of a foreigner who came to faith in God.

5:17 earth: Although ancient Middle Eastern custom associated the identity of a god with the location where he was worshiped, Elisha might have felt in this instance that Naaman's newly-gained acquaintance with Israel's God might be benefited with this tangible reminder of the land of his cure.

5:18, 19 The name **Rimmon** is an example of a deliberate corruption of a name of a foreign god by the Hebrew scribes. Instead of writing *Ramman*, meaning "Thunderer," a name for the storm god Hadad (see Zech. 12:11), they wrote *Rimmon*, meaning "Pomegranate."

5:20–22 Gehazi: The sad story of Gehazi's greed serves as a contrast to the principled behavior of his master Elisha (vv. 15, 16).

5:23 talents: A talent was an enormous amount of silver—equal to 3,000 shekels, or about 70 lbs. **two of his servants:** Each would have been carrying a heavy load.

5:24 the citadel: The Hebrew word can refer to a hill or mound, or a building such as a citadel (see 2 Chr. 27:3,4; Mic 4:8). Gehazi dismissed the men before coming to a place where his greedy gain might be observed by people who would know about Naaman and Elisha.

5:25 Since he had lied first to Naaman (v. 22), now he must lie to **Elisha.**

5:26 Did not my heart go: The use of the term *heart* suggests not only Elisha's knowledge but also his strong feeling for Gehazi.

5:27 The irony of justice punished Gehazi's sin with the **leprosy of Naaman.**

6:1–5 The details of this building program set the stage for the loss of the **iron ax head.** In a time when most tools were still made of bronze, an iron blade was valuable.

6:6, 7 he ... took it: The man must have been impressed with what he saw, but the ax head could be of no use to him until he actually reached out and took it.

6:8–12 This remarkable narrative takes the reader into the tent of Ben-Hadad, the king of Aram, and to the meetings he had with his general staff. Ben-Hadad suspected a spy, and he was right. The spy was Elisha, who had never left Israel.

6:13–15 Dothan was in the central highlands of Israel. It is mentioned only here and in Gen. 37, when Joseph was sold to the Midianites (see Gen. 37:17). **the servant of the man of God:** Since Gehazi had become a leper (see 5:27), it is possible that this is another servant. However, Gehazi is mentioned again in 8:4 as one who was still faithfully representing the miracles done through Elisha.

6:16 those who are with us: Elisha knew that God's unseen army was far more powerful than any visible army.

6:17, 18 horses and chariots of fire: In answer to his prayer, Elisha's reassuring words to his servant (v. 16) were validated by letting him see the spiritual realities that lay beyond normal human sight. Such a fiery scene had accompanied Elijah's translation into heaven (2:11).

6:19, 20 I will bring you: Elisha's words are technically true, although he used tactics common in times of war to lead the Arameans to Samaria rather than Dothan.

6:21–23 The end of this story is even more amazing than the beginning. The blind soldiers were brought within the capital city of Israel where they easily might have been slaughtered. Instead, they were given a banquet and were sent back to Ben-Hadad unharmed. **bands ... came no more:** That is, for a period of time. The wars between the two nations revived after a period (see 6:24).

6:24 The siege of **Samaria,** the capital of Israel, was Ben-Hadad's final attempt to destroy his rival Jehoram of Israel.

6:25–27 The desperate conditions in besieged Samaria had made food and commodities scarce and expensive. The **dove droppings** may have been used for fuel or even as a substitute for salt.

6:28, 29 eat him: Israel had been warned that national disobedience could reduce the people to such a loathsome deed (Lev. 26:29; Deut. 28:53, 57).

6:30 The king was moved by the plight of his people. He tore his garments and wore **sackcloth** to attest to his concern.

6:31–33 if the head of Elisha: The phrase is an oath expressing the enraged king's will to kill Elisha, whom he blamed for the severe conditions.

7:1 Public business was conducted at the city **gate** (see Gen. 19:1; Ruth 4:1). Elisha's words were good news: Although costly, food would once again be available.

7:2 an officer: The Hebrew term for *officer* originally designated the third man in a chariot, who held a large shield. By this time it meant a high military official serving as adjutant (9:25; 10:25). The officer's doubt brought judgment on him. Although the food did come, this officer ate none of it.

7:3, 4 Because **leprous men** were excluded from the city and avoided by all, they concluded that they had nothing to lose by going to the other side.

7:5, 6 the noise of a great army: Doubtless, the army was God's (see 6:16–18).

7:7, 8 In their joy, the **lepers** took advantage of their good fortune.

7:9–11 Good news and good fortune had to be shared (Prov. 15:27; 21:17, 18), and the men feared that failure to do so might bring divine **punishment.**

7:12 what the Syrians have done: The Israelite king suspected that another military trick was being played on him. He did not connect the good news with Elisha's prophecy of good times.

7:13–16 At last the king sent a scouting party, which confirmed the good news. The prophecy about the restoration of food for the city was fulfilled (see v. 1).

7:17–20 you shall not eat of it: All of Elisha's prophecy came true. The sudden miraculous flight of the Arameans had provided goods aplenty, but the doubting officer would not enjoy them.

8:1 God again instituted a **famine.** God in His kindness spared the family of the Shunammite woman to whom Elisha had ministered (see 4:8–37). It appears that she may have become a widow by the time of this incident.

8:2, 3 to make an appeal: The Shunammite woman had not renounced or sold her property, but merely had left during the previous famine. Moreover, she had returned within seven years (see Deut. 15:1–6; Ruth 4:3, 4). Since the property was still legally hers, she pressed her claim to the king himself.

8:4, 5 Just as the Shunammite woman arrived, **Gehazi** was telling Jehoram about her. At this point, Gehazi was still faithful to the ministry of Elisha.

8:6 Restore all: We get a complex picture of King Jehoram. At times he was so angry at Elisha that he wished him dead (6:31), yet even then he was in mourning for his people. He acknowledged Elisha's spiritual leadership

at other times (see 6:21), but he knew that Elisha did not hold him in high regard (see 3:14).

8:7 Although Ben-Hadad felt that Elisha's arrival was accidental, God's prophet had come to **Damascus** in fulfillment of the instructions originally given by God to Elijah (1 Kin. 19:15–17).

8:8, 9 Ironically, a sick king of Israel had inquired of a false god about the nature of his illness (1:2); here, the pagan king of a foreign nation inquired of the living God about the nature of his illness.

8:10 You shall certainly recover: Left to natural circumstances, Ben-Hadad would recover. Yet Elisha knew that Hazael would seize both the opportunity of the king's illness and fulfill Elisha's prophecy by assassinating the king and taking the throne.

8:11, 12 ashamed: He had reached the end of his ability to resist his emotions. **the man of God wept:** Elisha wept over the suffering that Hazael would bring upon Israel.

8:13, 14 In the ancient Middle East, the **dog** was despised because it was a scavenger (see 1 Kin. 14:11; 21:23). Appropriately, Hazael would similarly be held in disdain.

8:15 Having succeeded Ben-Hadad as king, **Hazael reigned** for about 40 years (842–802 B.C.). He remained a staunch foe of God's people (see 10:32, 33; 13:3, 22). Yet like Elisha and Jehu, Hazael was an instrument of God's judgment on His sinful people (1 Kin. 19:15–17).

8:16–17 Jehoram: The name Jehoram means "The Lord Is Exalted" and can be spelled Joram. **eight years:** Joram of the northern kingdom ruled from 852–841 B.C.; Jehoram of the southern kingdom from 848–841 B.C. Although he had served alongside his father Jehoshaphat for the previous four years, Jehoram now ruled in his own right. With his father's death, he killed all his brothers and any claimant to the throne (2 Chr. 21:2–4). A wicked ruler (2 Chr. 21:11), he was greatly influenced by Queen Athaliah (2 Chr. 21:6).

8:18 the daughter of Ahab: Athaliah (see 11:1) was established as the queen of Judah and the wife of a descendant of David. The marriage of a daughter of the king of Israel to the king of Judah was a strategic event that could ease hostility between the two nations. But from a spiritual standpoint, this marriage was a disaster for Judah.

8:19 Despite Jehoram's infidelity and wickedness, God remained faithful to the Davidic covenant (see 2 Sam. 7:12–16; Ps. 89:30–37). **a lamp:** This was a figure of the hope of the Davidic promise in the darkest of times.

8:20–24 Judah's struggles with **Edom** were often accompanied by trouble with the Philistines (see 2 Chr. 21:16; Joel 3:4–8). Edom would remain a constant menace with the result that although Amaziah would later defeat Edom (14:22), they would renew armed hostilities against Judah in the days of Ahaz (2 Chr. 28:17, 18).

8:25 Ahaziah means "The Lord Has Grasped."

8:26 twenty-two years old: This figure is correct; compare 2 Chr. 22:2. **granddaughter of Omri:** The Hebrew word translated *granddaughter* is literally "daughter." Athaliah, Ahab's daughter, is the person meant (v. 18; 2 Chr. 21:6).

8:27 the way of the house of Ahab: The lowest point of Israel's religious apostasy was reached in the reign of Ahab and his wicked wife Jezebel (see 1 Kin. 16:31). Most likely because of the role of Athaliah, the evil that had spoiled Ahab affected the house of the king of Judah.

8:28 Hazael had recently been crowned in Damascus, and the year 841 B.C. would witness a change in the royal houses of both Israel and Judah.

8:29 Ahab had one of his palaces at **Jezreel,** a site between Megiddo and Beth Shan (1 Kin. 18:45). Both Joram and Ahaziah came to Jezreel for a most fateful meeting (ch. 9).

9:1–3 The selection of **Jehu** as the next king of Israel was by prophetic designation; contrast 1:17. The instructions given by Elisha to one of his associates were marked by secrecy and intrigue. The action of the prophet was seditious in the eyes of the current king.

9:4, 5 for you: The servant was obedient to Elisha and was daring in his approach to Jehu.

9:6 poured the oil: Elijah personally fulfilled the divine directive about Elisha (see 1 Kin.

19:19–21). Elisha carried out the order with respect to Hazael. One of the sons of the prophets serving under Elisha handled the case of Jehu.

9:7–10 The prophetic words to Jehu indicate that he would destroy the evil of the house of Ahab. **Jezebel:** The wicked wife of Ahab is given special attention; her gruesome end is predicted.

9:11, 12 A lie: Jehu's attempt to brush off the questions of his servants was not successful. He finally reported to them the fact of his prophetic sanction and divine anointing.

9:13 Placing a **garment** under a person is a mark of homage fit for a king (see Matt. 21:8). The actions taken here are like those performed at the anointing of King Solomon (1 Kin. 1:34).

9:14, 15 Jehu lost no time in planning the assassination of the king. These verses also remind the reader of the situation at Jezreel (see 8:28, 29).

9:16–18 The question about **peace** was a standard step in ancient negotiations. Jehu's reply indicates that he refused to negotiate.

9:19–21 the property of Naboth: Ahab's dynasty ended on the very stolen property that occasioned the divine sentence of judgment.

9:22 Is it peace … What peace: Perhaps the king met Jehu with the thought of making him realize that his plans would be acts of sedition against the legally constituted king.

9:23, 24 The frightened Joram shouted to Ahaziah, **Treachery.** But it was he and Ahaziah who were the true traitors. And they would be executed by Jehu, a man who served as the "terrible swift sword" of the Lord.

9:25, 26 remember: Jehu rehearsed to Bidkar the gist of the curse against Ahab's house (1 Kin. 21:21–24). In this way, Jehu cited this curse for justification of his actions. He proclaimed himself God's avenger.

9:27–29 The wounded Ahaziah apparently made it to Samaria where he at last was apprehended by Jehu's men (2 Chr. 22:8, 9) and taken to **Megiddo** where he died. His body finally was buried in the royal tombs in Jerusalem (v. 28).

9:30, 31 Jezebel knew that her end was near; she had heard about the deaths of the kings of Israel and Judah. Yet she brazenly spent time putting on her makeup and adorning herself. Defiant to the end, Jezebel called Jehu a **Zimri,** a traitor who had killed his master in order to seize the throne (1 Kin. 16:11, 12).

9:32, 33 Jehu had Jezebel's servants throw her out the window. Her death was particularly gruesome.

9:34–37 bury her: After Jehu had Jezebel killed, he ordered that her body be given a proper burial. However, she had become food for **dogs.** This was the grisly fulfillment of Elijah's prophecy (1 Kin. 21:23). **as refuse:** There was to be no marker, no mourning, no memorial, no sadness for this evil woman.

10:1 Ahab's **seventy sons** included children and probably grandchildren. Jehu wanted to eliminate all rivals to his kingship. The **rulers of Jezreel** were Samaritan officials, who often visited the royal residence in Jezreel.

10:2–5 Jehu's first **letter** was written to determine who might be the greatest risk to his reign. **two kings:** The deaths of Joram (9:14–26) and Ahaziah (9:27, 28) were fresh in the rulers' minds, so the response of the leaders was a fearful submission to Jehu's power.

10:6–9 killed all these: Jehu pretended that his message was misunderstood and that in any case it was Ahab's wickedness that ultimately had brought about the divine judgment of these men.

10:10 Evaluating Jehu is difficult. His praise for the ministry of the prophets of God and his stated respect for the word of God are commendable. But he did not balance his judgmental actions on Ahab's family with mercy and justice for the poor and the oppressed. He was God's instrument of judgment, but he himself also stood under God's judgment (see 10:31).

10:11 Jehu ... left him none remaining: In killing the house of Ahab, his supporters, as well as the surviving descendants of Ahaziah (vv. 13, 14), Jehu exceeded God's judgment. But he used the power God had given him for his selfish ends. Accordingly, no contradiction exists between the divine commissioning of Jehu (9:6–10) and the divine condemnation of him (10:31; see Hos. 1:4).

10:12–14 Beth Eked means "Binding House," a site near Mount Gilboa. Here Jehu slaughtered **forty-two men** of the house of Ahaziah.

10:15, 16 Jehonadab came along with Jehu as an observer. **son of Rechab:** Jehonadab was a Rechabite. These people were known for their faithfulness to God and to the austere regulations laid down by Jehonadab (see Jer. 35:1–16).

10:17 according to the word of the LORD: Jehu's action was by prophetic sanction (v. 10).

10:18–20 Finally, Jehu attacked Baal worship. With a lie, Jehu gathered all the principals of Baal worship to one place, the temple of Baal in Samaria (see v. 21; compare 1 Kin. 16:32). He pretended that he was an even more ardent champion of Baal than Ahab. He issued a royal decree for a national **solemn assembly for Baal.**

10:21–23 temple of Baal: The temple that had been constructed by Ahab (see 1 Kin. 16:32). **vestments:** By having the Baal worshipers wear distinctive clothing, Jehu marked them for death. **no servants of the LORD:** Jehu carefully distinguished the enemy, in case some of the Lord's true priests might have gathered with the priests of Baal.

10:24–28 as soon as he: It is not clear whether a Baal priest or Jehu himself was making the offering. If it was Jehu, it would have been the most effective way of keeping the priests from suspecting any danger. **kill them:** Jehu followed Elijah's example on Mount Carmel (see 1 Kin. 18:40). Yet Jehu's executions were more thorough, for he had gathered all the priests and prophets of Baal in the nation. **to this day:** That is, at the time of writing. The suggestion is that even after the fall of Samaria one could see the foul place where the temple to Baal once had been.

10:29 Jehu's destruction of Baal worship (vv. 18–28) was a political act. His continuing the state worship policies established by Jeroboam I clearly shows his disregard for true spiritual revival in Israel.

10:30, 31 done well: The evaluation of Jehu is one of limited obedience (see v. 31). Nonetheless, he accomplished a great deal and received God's commendation for his work. Most likely, a prophet communicated God's message to Jehu.

10:32, 33 Because Shalmaneser III was occupied with political pressures in the east, Hazael took advantage of the situation, harassing Israel throughout his long reign. After Jehu's death, Hazael marched freely into Israel and even into Judah (12:17, 18; 13:22). The attacks of Hazael were part of God's judgment on Israel.

10:34–36 The record of **Jehoahaz** is given in 13:1–9. He was followed by Joash (also called Jehoash; 13:10–13), Jeroboam II (14:23–29), and very briefly by Zechariah (15:8–12). The assassination of Zechariah by Shallum after a reign of only six months ended the line of Jehu in the fourth generation, just as the Lord had said (10:30).

11:1 Athaliah means "The Lord Is Exalted." Sadly, she did not live up to her name. **all the royal heirs:** Jehu had executed King Ahaziah of Judah, Athaliah's **son,** shortly after he had executed Joram of Israel (see 9:27–29). Ahaziah's older brother had been killed in an Arabian raid (2 Chr. 22:1). Further, Jehoram had killed his brothers and other royal relatives when he took the throne (2 Chr. 21:4), while Jehu had murdered still more of the royal house (10:14). Therefore, Athaliah's destruction of all of the royal heirs must have concentrated on her own grandchildren. None of the usual details relative to accession to the crown in Judah are given here. Athaliah clearly usurped the office, setting aside the precepts of the Davidic covenant (see 2 Sam. 7:12–16; Ps. 89:35–37).

11:2, 3 As the wife of the high priest Jehoiada, **Jehosheba's** marriage and her relation to the royal house made it possible for her to rescue and hide the young Joash. **Joash** (or Jehoash; see 12:1) was the son of Ahaziah. He apparently was an infant at this time. Athaliah might not have known of his existence and for this reason failed to kill him in her purges. The unthinkable was happening: The daughter of Jezebel was now the queen of Judah. A worshiper of Baal was in power in the nation of God's promise. She built in Jerusalem a temple to Baal (v. 18).

11:4 the **seventh year,** that is, of the reign of Athaliah and the life of Joash

(v. 21). **Jehoiada:** The name of the high priest means "The Lord Knows." Other details about Jehoiada's careful preparations are given in 2 Chr. 23:1–11. Jehoiada's plan included the royal guard: the presentation and crowning of the legitimate royal heir coincided with the changing of the guard on the Sabbath. **bodyguards:** The men of the royal guard are identified as the Cherethites and Pelethites in 2 Sam. 20:23; 1 Kin. 1:38. **showed them the king's son:** The revelation of this young prince was the critical moment. A zealous guard might easily have put him to death at once. There must have been a great deal of preparation on Jehoiada's part—and considerable prayer—for this moment.

11:5–9 The fact that the men of the royal guard followed the commands of Jehoiada the priest was remarkable. It must have been because they were utterly disgusted by the wickedness of Athaliah.

11:10, 11 spears and shields: David had dedicated these weapons to the temple after his campaigns against Hadadezer (2 Sam. 8:11). Since they were not gold or silver, they had apparently been ignored by Shishak when he looted the temple and palace in the days of Rehoboam (1 Kin. 14:26).

11:12 By putting a copy of the law in Joash's hand and the **crown** on his head, Jehoiada presented him as the rightful heir to the throne. The term **Testimony** recalls the covenant, emphasizing that Joash's coronation was given both its scriptural warrant and its rightful connection to the Davidic covenant.

11:13–16 in the temple of the LORD: The temple was the appropriate place to crown the king of God's appointment. It was also probably a good place to hide from a queen whose god was Baal. **there was the king:** What a shock this must have been to Athaliah. There stood a little boy who represented the end of her reign. Her words **Treason! Treason!** were technically correct. But it was she who had committed treason by murdering all the survivors of the Davidic house—except for the one who was now king. **killed:** The priest would not allow her execution in the temple, but her death was necessary. With her dead, the young Joash was safe.

11:17 Covenant renewal was particularly necessary after the unholy usurpation by the wicked Athaliah.

11:18 As Jezebel had seen her wicked husband Ahab build a **temple** to **Baal** in Samaria (see 1 Kin. 16:32), so her daughter Athaliah was behind the building of a temple to Baal in the holy city of Jerusalem. **Mattan the priest of Baal:** The very fact that there was a priest of Baal in Jerusalem is astonishing. If Athaliah and her associates had not been stopped, the sins of Samaria would have paled beside the sins of Jerusalem.

11:19–21 The young child was established as king before the nation. **rejoiced ... quiet:** The joy of the people and the peacefulness of the land were marks of God's blessing to the restored Davidic dynasty.

12:1, 2 All the days in which Jehoiada the priest instructed him has an ominous tone. After Jehoiada's death, the king's activities would take a different turn, for Jehoash would become dependent upon counsel of a different sort (see 2 Chr. 24:17–19). Nonetheless, among the kings of Judah, he was one of the few who showed some signs of righteousness.

12:3 Although God Himself might be worshiped in such **high places,** the setting provided an association with Canaanite religious rites that could too easily lead to spiritual compromise (1 Kin. 3:2–4; see also 14:23). Apostasy would become a besetting sin later in Jehoash's reign (2 Chr. 24:17–19, 24).

12:4, 5 Money collected from special taxes and voluntary offerings was designated for repairing **the temple.** Thus, renewed concern for spiritual things was evidenced after the neglect and abuse of the previous seven years (2 Chr. 24:7).

12:6–12 a chest: When the priest failed to do the work (vv. 6, 7), the king took a personal hand in seeing to its accomplishment. The chest he prepared was set against the wall at the entrance facing the right side of the altar. Because the people responded generously (2 Chr. 24:10), the work proceeded and was soon completed (vv. 11, 12; 2 Chr. 24:11–13).

12:13, 14 At first no funds were used for fashioning the sacred vessels, but there was **money** left over after the completion of the building repairs, so the sacred vessels could be completed as well (2 Chr. 24:14).

12:15, 16 dealt faithfully: Joash had commissioned such trustworthy men that no accounting of their use of the funds was necessary.

12:17, 18 The Aramean invasion recorded here took place late in Joash's reign. The **king** fell into apostasy after the death of his godly counselor, the high priest Jehoiada (2 Chr. 24:17–19, 23, 24), and this invasion came as a judgment of his wickedness.

12:19–21 Joash was severely wounded in Hazael's invasion (see 2 Chr. 24:24, 25), then he fell victim shortly afterward to the dissent and unpopularity that culminated in his assassination. Because of Joash's apostasy and murder of Zechariah, Jehoiada's son (2 Chr. 24:17–22), the king was not laid to rest in the royal tombs (see 2 Chr. 24:25).

13:1 The name **Jehoahaz** means "The Lord Has Grasped." His 17-year reign lasted from 814 to 798 B.C.

13:2, 3 evil ... sins of Jeroboam: After the end of the house of Ahab in Jehu's purge (chs. 9; 10), the kings of Israel reverted to the level of syncretism that had been established by Jeroboam I. The mention of Hazael's son **Ben-Hadad** III (802–780 B.C.) may refer to his serving as a commander in his father's army or to his growing prominence in his father's later years (v. 24).

13:4 Although Jehoahaz did not follow the Lord exclusively (v. 6), God graciously heard his genuine plea for help.

13:5 Israel's **deliverer** has been variously identified. Probably it was the Assyrian king Adad-Nerari III. Referring to an Assyrian king as a divinely commissioned deliverer of Israel is similar to the words of God in Isaiah describing the Persian King Cyrus as "His anointed" (see Is. 45:1; compare Is. 44:28).

13:6–9 the wooden image: The Hebrew word for *wooden images* is a reference to the Canaanite goddess Asherah. The image itself was a sacred tree or pole that was perceived perhaps as some sexually-oriented symbol of the fertility religion of Canaan.

13:10–13 At first, the 16-year reign of Jehoash of Israel appears to be recorded without further elaboration (vv. 10–13). But three stories are added: the death of Elisha during his reign (vv. 14–21), his military victories over the Aramean forces (vv. 24, 25), and his war with Amaziah of Judah (v. 12; 14:8–14).

13:14 O my father: Jehoash's cry over the aged Elisha repeats the words of Elisha spoken when Elijah was taken up to heaven (2:12). Thus, at the beginning of his ministry and at its conclusion, Elisha is unmistakably linked to his mentor Elijah. The grief of Jehoash at the impending death of Elisha shows that, like his father Jehoahaz (see vv. 4, 5), this Israelite king possessed some genuine spirituality.

13:15–19 Elisha's symbolic act of putting his hands **on the king's hands** should have alerted the king that the aged prophet was conveying a divine blessing on him. Jehoash's halfhearted compliance with Elisha's instructions exposed his weak faith and illustrated God's unfavorable evaluation of his character (v. 11). God's dying prophet was disturbed. Although God would allow Israel to defeat the Aramean army three times, their victory would be incomplete.

13:20 Elisha died: The supernatural translation of Elijah (ch. 2) was an unusual example of God's power; Elisha died a normal death. **bands from Moab:** The mention of invasions such as this reminds us of how perilous life was during much of Israel's history.

13:21, 22 the man ... revived: Even in death the mere presence of Elisha's body was sufficient for a miracle. There was no magic in Elisha's bones, but a demonstration of the power of God associated with His servant. This miracle should have reassured Jehoash that God intended to rescue Israel from Aramean domination (see v. 25).

13:23 This verse is one of those dazzling lights that burst from the pages of the Bible, describing the wonderful mercy of the living God (see 14:26, 27). **His covenant:** God's faithfulness to His promise is a theme of the Old Testament (Ex. 2:23–25).

13:24 This **Ben-Hadad** is the son of Hazael (v. 3). After his father's death, he reigned as Ben-Hadad III (802–780 B.C.).

13:25 In accordance with Jehoash's striking the ground **three times** with arrows (v. 18), God gave Jehoash victory over the Arameans only three times. Yet God graciously overruled Jehoash's inadequate faith by granting Israel victory over the Arameans during the reign of his son Jeroboam II.

14:1–3 did what was right: Amaziah was one of the few godly kings in the kingdom of Judah; the best kings were Hezekiah (see 18:1) and Josiah (see 22:1).

14:4 Like his father Jehoash (see 12:3), Amaziah allowed worship at the **high places.** This practice would blossom into open idolatry in the reigns of subsequent kings (16:4; 21:3).

14:5, 6 executed his servants: The principals are named in 12:20, 21. These men were guilty of assassinating his father and might have been a threat to his own reign. **Book of the Law of Moses:** Amaziah followed the law laid down in Deut. 24:16.

14:7 A more detailed account of Amaziah's defeat of the **Edomites** is given in 2 Chr. 25:5–13. Edom had regained its independence during the reign of Jehoram (see 8:20–22). Amaziah's conquest of the formidable city of **Sela** atop the seemingly unapproachable cliffs of the Wadi Musa was a monumental accomplishment. Rather than recognize God's hand in this feat, Amaziah became proud and fell into spiritual compromise (2 Chr. 25:14–16).

14:8 let us face one another: Amaziah's pride over his accomplishment (v. 10) and his anger over the looting of Judean cities by Israelite mercenaries dismissed before the Edomite campaign (2 Chr. 25:6–10, 13) clouded his thinking.

14:9, 10 Jehoash replied to Amaziah in the form of a fable—a story designed to teach a lesson. By speaking of Amaziah as a **thistle** in comparison with the **cedar** of **Lebanon,** Jehoash tried to help Amaziah be more realistic about his recent victory.

14:11 Beth Shemesh: The name of the city means "House of the Sun," indicating that there had once been a temple to the sun god there in Canaanite times. The tragedy of the battle between Amaziah and Jehoash was heightened by the fact that the proud

Amaziah forced a battle in his own territory, **Judah.**

14:12 Judah was defeated: Jehoash's forces were seasoned warriors and had defeated the Arameans (see 13:25). Amaziah's pride spelled not only his own downfall (v. 13) but that of his capital city (14:13, 14).

14:13 The damage to Jerusalem's northern walls extended from the **Corner Gate,** at the northwest corner of the city wall, east to the **Gate of Ephraim.** The northwest corner of Jerusalem had always been the city's most vulnerable point (18:17). A breach in the wall of **four hundred cubits** (600 feet) was a huge gap through which the invading army could enter the holy city.

14:14–16 gold and silver ... articles: The looting of precious objects from the temple, as well as from the palace—**the king's house**—shows the humiliation that Judah suffered as the result of this disastrous war fueled by Amaziah's pride. **hostages:** People as well as goods were carried off by the king of Israel.

14:17, 18 The notice of **fifteen years** of life for Amaziah suggests he was released after the death of Jehoash for an additional period (782–767 B.C.). If so, he reigned alongside his son Azariah (or Uzziah), whose 52-year reign began in 792 B.C. (15:2).

14:19, 20 Amaziah not only reproduced his father's spiritual problems (see 14:3); he also died as his father had, at the hand of an assassin (12:20, 21).

14:21, 22 Elath is the famous seaport on the Gulf of Aqaba. During the reign of Ahaz, Elath was captured by Rezin of Aram and became an Edomite holding (see 16:6).

14:23 Jeroboam: This is the second king of Israel to have this name. Jeroboam I was the founder of the northern kingdom at the time of the death of Solomon (930 B.C.; see 1 Kin. 11; 12). **forty-one years:** Jeroboam II had a long reign. His 41 years included ten years as coregent with his father Jehoash (792–782 B.C.).

14:24 did evil: The assessment of his reign is like that of all the kings of Israel, except for the worse assessment given to the house of Ahab (see 10:29–31).

14:25 restored the territory: The first half of the eighth century B.C. was a period of

prosperity and strength for the northern and southern kingdoms. Jeroboam II extended Israel's influence from the entrance of Hamath down the eastern side of the Jordan River to the southern end of the Dead Sea. Since Azariah also campaigned in the southern territory, the two kingdoms must have been living in harmony and enjoying mutual cooperation. **Jonah:** Once again a prophet of God gave direction to a king. The reference to Jonah here provides the historical setting for the famous prophet.

14:26, 27 no helper: The living God saw that His people needed His help, and He became the helper of His people. God used Jeroboam II to bring Israel to a new period of greatness.

14:28 The Scriptures emphasize Jeroboam's military prowess. Yet Jeroboam's **might** may have also been economic. The Samarian Ostraca, which may date from this period, record the delivery to Samaria of fine oil and barley produced on the royal estates.

14:29 The brief reign of **Zechariah** is noted in 15:8–12. He was the fourth in the line of Jehu to reign in Israel, in fulfillment of God's promise to Jehu (see 10:30).

15:1, 2 Azariah (or Uzziah, 2 Chr. 26:1; Is. 1:1) is credited with 52 years of reign. This figure includes 10 years during which his father Amaziah was held captive (792–782 B.C.), 15 years of coregency with Amaziah upon his release from captivity (782–767 B.C.), and 27 years of sole reign (767–740 B.C.). The latter part of Azariah's reign was tainted by his intrusion into the priestly office (2 Chr. 26:16–19), an act that resulted in his being stricken with leprosy (v. 5). This condition put his son Jotham on the throne to rule with him. The nature of Jotham's duties (v. 5), the assigning of a full 52 years of reign to Azariah, and Isaiah's dating of his call to the year of Azariah's (or Uzziah's) death (Is. 6:1) may indicate that Azariah retained the power of the throne until the end.

15:3, 4 Azariah was another of the good kings in Judah and received some of the same evaluation that was given to Jehoash in 12:2, 3 and to Amaziah in 14:3, 4.

15:5–7 leper: The events that brought about this affliction are described in 2 Chr. 26:16–21. **over the royal house:** Jotham assumed the office of senior administrator, handling the business of state during his father's period of isolation.

15:8–12 fourth generation: Jehu had been promised a continuing posterity into the fourth generation as a reward for carrying out his divine commission (see 10:30). Unfortunately, Jehu and his house proved unworthy of their God-given opportunities so that they repeatedly earned the condemnation of God's prophets (13:18, 19; Hos. 1:4; Amos 7:9). After the death of Zechariah in 752 B.C. and the end of the fourth dynasty, Israel plunged into a period of degeneracy, bloody conspiracies, and international intrigue that would bring about its demise in 722 B.C. So Zechariah was the last of the effective kings of Israel.

15:13–15 The short reign of **Shallum,** only one **month,** was indicative of the emerging collapse of the nation. **the rest of the acts:** This follows the normal pattern for the obituaries of the kings of the northern kingdom. Even though Shallum was king for only one month, he still received the complete royal obituary.

15:16 Because of its beauty (Song 6:4), **Tirzah** served as a royal retreat (see 1 Kin. 14:17). It also was the national capital during Israel's first two dynasties. **ripped open:** Such inhuman atrocities were common in times of warfare in the ancient world (see 8:12; Amos 1:13). Israel's sin placed it in danger of such barbaric acts (see Hos. 10:13, 14; 13:16).

15:17, 18 Menahem: This wicked king came to power by assassination and established his authority by brutal acts against humanity (vv. 14, 16). Ironically, his name means "Comforter."

15:19–22 Pul is a second Babylonian name for the Assyrian king Tiglath-Pileser III (745–727 B.C.; see v. 29; 1 Chr. 5:26). Although he came to the throne as a usurper from the ranks of the military, he would prove a competent king. Under Tiglath-Pileser III and his successors, Assyria became the dominant power in the Middle East for well over a century (747–612 B.C.). It was a period of repeated Assyrian interference in the affairs of Israel and Judah.

15:23–26 Pekahiah means "The Lord Has Opened the Eyes." After an evil reign of two years, a usurper "closed his eyes" for him.

15:27, 28 Like Shallum and Menahem before him, **Pekah** sat on the throne through usurpation and bloody deeds. Because Hoshea's nine-year reign (17:1) began in 732 B.C., Pekah's **twenty years** must have included a time of kingship in his own district during the unsettled days of Shallum, Menahem, and Pekahiah (752–740 B.C.). Apparently Pekah rode the crest of anti-Assyrian sentiment. That same political stance ultimately brought about his downfall.

15:29, 30 Hoshea ... killed him: Tiglath-Pileser III's campaign of 734–732 B.C. apparently caused a pro-Assyrian reaction within Israel that brought about both Pekah's death and Hoshea's ascension to the throne. The annals of Tiglath-Pileser III record Hoshea's heavy tribute and the Assyrian king's claim that he himself set the new Israelite king in office.

15:31–33 Jotham means "The Lord Is Perfect." Jotham's reign of **sixteen years** (752–736 B.C.) includes a 12-year coregency with his father Azariah. Since Jotham is earlier credited with 20 years (v. 30), it may be that he turned over the reigns of government to his son Ahaz in 736 B.C., even though he lived on for four more years.

15:34, 35 Jotham's reign was partly righteous. After the purge of Ahaziah and Athaliah (9:27–29; 11:13–16), the kings of Judah who reigned in relative righteousness were Joash (Jehoash) (12:2, 3), Amaziah (14:3, 4), and Azariah (Uzziah) (15:3, 4). A positive righteousness would be modeled by Hezekiah (see 18:3–6) and again by Josiah (see 22:2).

15:36 The author of Chronicles indicates that Jotham did extensive building in Jerusalem and Judah (2 Chr. 27:3, 4) and engaged in a war against the Ammonites (2 Chr. 27:5). Jotham apparently carried out the practices that brought Judah power and prosperity during the years of his father Azariah (Uzziah).

15:37, 38 Rezin ... Pekah: These two adversaries were even more prominent in the time of Ahaz (see ch. 16; see also Is. 7).

16:1, 2 The name **Ahaz** means "He Has Grasped." The **seventeenth year of Pekah** was 736–735 B.C. Ahaz's sixteen-year reign apparently ended in 720 B.C. If so, like Jotham before him, Ahaz must have lived on another four years after giving up his rule. Hezekiah's first year of independent rule began in 715 B.C., 14 years before Sennacherib's invasion of Judah and his siege of Jerusalem in 701 B.C. (18:13). If Ahaz was 20 years old at his accession in 736 B.C. (v. 2), he would have lived to be around 40. Since Hezekiah was 25 years old at his accession to coregency in 729 B.C., Ahaz was in his early teens when Hezekiah was born.

16:3, 4 After a series of kings in Judah who demonstrated a relative righteousness, Ahaz followed the evil ways of the kings of the northern kingdom. The author of Chronicles reports that the rite of making one's son **pass through the fire** was connected with the Baal worship practiced in the Valley of the Son of Hinnom (23:10; 2 Chr. 28:2, 3). Ahaz was an apostate who led his people in the religious worship practices of Canaan (v. 4; see 2 Chr. 28:2–4).

16:5 Because of Ahaz's sin God delivered him into the hands of an alliance of the two kings **Rezin** and **Pekah** (see 15:37). A great slaughter followed, and a complete deportation of Judah was averted only by divine intervention (2 Chr. 28:5–15).

16:6 Azariah had recovered **Elath** for Judah (see 14:22). Now this major port city (see 1 Kin. 9:26) was taken from Judah. **to this day:** That is, the day of the narration of these events.

16:7–9 Ahaz's request of **Tiglath-Pileser** III coincides with the Assyrian king's second western campaign (734–732 B.C.) that eventually brought about the fall of Damascus in 732 B.C. and the replacement of Pekah with Hoshea on the throne of Israel in the same year.

16:10–20 Having been summoned to Damascus by Tiglath-Pileser III, Ahaz saw a pagan **altar** that suited his tastes. His use of the altar to make sacrifices to God underscored Ahaz's paganism. Ahaz went so far as to shut the doors of the temple (2 Chr. 28:24).

17:1, 2 twelfth year: Hoshea became king in 732 B.C., so the twelve years of Ahaz indicate a period of coregency with his father Jotham, perhaps arranged due to the pressures of Tiglath-Pileser's first western campaign (744–743 B.C.).

17:3 Shalmaneser V succeeded Tiglath-Pileser III as king of Assyria in 727 B.C.

17:4 conspiracy by Hoshea: Several elements of intrigue and international affairs may have entered into the picture here. Transitions in power were often occasions for rebellion or attempted overthrow. Further, a new strong man had appeared in Egypt—Tefnekht, a pharaoh of the twenty-fourth dynasty. The time may have seemed ripe for Hoshea to enter into an anti-Assyrian coalition.

17:5, 6 After a three-year siege, Samaria fell to the Assyrians in 722 B.C. Sargon, the field commander of Shalmaneser V who succeeded him to the throne, would later claim that it was he who **took Samaria.** It was ancient practice to deport large numbers of influential citizens of a conquered country or city to decrease the possibility of rebellion (see 25:11, 12; Ezek. 1:2, 3).

17:7–20 Israel had sinned: The reason for the fall of Samaria and the end of the northern kingdom is clearly stated to be its spiritual failure, in turning from the living God to worship pagan gods. Despite repeated warnings (vv. 13, 14, 23), Israel had persisted in every form of idolatry and licentious worship (vv. 10–12, 16, 17).

17:21 Jeroboam ... made them ... sin: Jeroboam I had initiated the state worship that in effect set the standard for all of Israel's idolatrous activities. The worship of the calves at Dan and Bethel, and Israel's fascination with Baal (v. 16; see 1 Kin. 12:28, 29; 16:32, 33), are repeatedly cited as the chief causes of Israel's spiritual defeat and political collapse.

17:22–24 The **king of Assyria** was probably Sargon II (722–705 B.C.), although the practice described here was continued by later kings as well. Such a mixing of populations would break down ethnic distinctions and weaken the loyalties that the people had. The inhabitants would eventually be called Samaritans.

17:25–28 one of the priests: Although a deported Israelite priest was sent back to instruct the Samaritan population in the worship of the Lord, the end result was a mixture of various forms of paganism with the apostate religion of the northern kingdom (vv. 30–33, 40, 41).

17:29–41 A double charge is laid against the Samaritans: They did not worship the Lord, and they did not keep the laws and ordinances laid down by the Lord of the covenant.

18:1, 2 The **third year of Hoshea** is 729 B.C. The 29 years of Hezekiah's reign thus include a period of coregency with his father Ahaz before he ruled independently (715–699 B.C.).

18:3 The assessment of Hezekiah begins similar to that of his predecessors, but it goes on to transcend the evaluations of "relative righteousness" that are typical of the other kings of Judah (see 15:34, 35).

18:4 Consistently, the kings who preceded Hezekiah are criticized by the author for not destroying the **high places** (15:34, 35). While there were traditions of worship of the true God at these locations, far too often they became sites for the licentious worship of Baal and Asherah. Hezekiah's reforms included not only the destruction of the pagan cult objects introduced in the days of his apostate father Ahaz, but the **bronze serpent** that had been preserved since the days of Moses (2 Chr. 29—31). This symbol had become an object of veneration.

18:5, 6 none like him: Hezekiah's faith was unparalleled by any other king who had preceded him after the time of David. Because Hezekiah trusted the Lord, he could courageously withstand Assyrian tyranny. The northern kingdom fell to King Shalmaneser V in 722 B.C. because it did not keep God's holy standards (vv. 9–12), but Hezekiah's trust and faithfulness would let him face the later invasion of King Sennacherib (701 B.C.) and receive divine help (19:32–36).

 IN DEPTH | **The Danger of Relics**

Jesus said that God is Spirit, and that those who worship Him must worship in spirit and truth (John 4:24). This means that we worship and serve a God whom we cannot see with our eyes, but must believe with our hearts. As a result, God is a bit of an abstraction for some people. One way that they have tried to make Him more real and present is through artifacts that they have associated with Him.

As understandable as the veneration of relics may be, it is a dangerous practice. It can easily tempt people to worship the object rather than the God whom the object is supposed to point to. In essence, the relic becomes a focus of idolatry.

That happened with a number of items that the Israelites venerated, including the bronze snake that Moses had made during the Exodus journey (2 Kin. 18:4; Num. 21:8, 9). Originally, the serpent on the pole served as a means of healing for snake-bitten people, by causing them to look to the Lord for help. But after the people settled in the Promised Land, they apparently turned this standard into an idol, as if the bronze snake itself had power to heal. They burned incense to it and even gave it a name, Nehushtan.

In a similar way, the Israelites turned a ceremonial robe, or ephod, that Gideon made from the spoils of his victory over the Midianites, into an idol (Judg. 8:25–27). Later they tried to use the ark of covenant as a charm against the Philistines, with disastrous results. And in Jeremiah's day, the citizens of Jerusalem cared more about their temple than they did about the Lord of the temple (Jer. 7:12–15).

These examples show the dangers of making too much of objects and places that have had a close association with the work of God. As human beings, we live in the natural world, but we worship a supernatural God. Therefore, we need to treat shrines and relics merely as means toward that end, never as ends in themselves.

18:7, 8 In addition to refusing to serve any longer as a vassal of **Assyria,** Hezekiah also conquered the **Philistines.** This helped establish Judah as an independent nation and new power in the region.

18:9–13 Hezekiah's **fourteenth year** of sole rule was 701 B.C. The details of the generally rebellious situation that provoked Sennacherib to invade the western portion of his empire are recounted in his annals.

18:14 I have done wrong: Literally, "I have sinned." Hezekiah had refused to be a vassal of Assyria and was now threatened by their army. With the Assyrian army already at Lachish, Hezekiah felt an overwhelming sense of doom. One of Sennacherib's inscriptions describes the siege of **Lachish** and reports the heavy tribute demanded from Hezekiah. His fulfillment of Sennacherib's demands (vv. 14–16) whetted the conqueror's appetite for additional booty. Therefore Sennacherib placed Jerusalem under siege (18:13–19:36).

18:15, 16 This removal from the temple of immense amounts of **silver, gold,** and precious objects followed an earlier despoiling in the days of Amaziah (see 14:14).

18:17 a great army: The accounts of the Assyrian kings suggest that they had mounted the largest armies known in the ancient Middle East. This huge army was stationed in the land of Judah.

18:18 Eliakim was the senior palace administrator (see 15:5), and **Shebna** was the royal scribe.

18:19 The term **great king** was reserved for a king of a major power. Here the Assyrian delegation delivered an ultimatum from the "great king" of Assyria to Jerusalem.

18:20 The Rabshakeh questioned the object of Hezekiah's **trust.** Perhaps Hezekiah's reputation for trusting in God was already widely known (v. 5). Trusting became the focal point of the Assyrian's psychological warfare (vv. 19–22, 24, 30).

18:21 Because Egypt depended on the life-giving Nile River with its reeds, the figure of a **broken reed** is most appropriate. Actually Sennacherib's warning against confidence in Egypt was well taken, the point having been made previously by Isaiah (Is. 30:3–5; 31:1–3).

18:22, 23 if you are able: The Assyrian official's taunt is that the Israelites do not have enough men and that the soldiers they have are not trained for the coming conflict.

18:24, 25 The LORD said: The Assyrians may have been aware of prophecies about the judgment of Judah and Jerusalem and Assyria's own role as God's avengers (Is. 10:5–11). The remark was intended to introduce terror into the hearts of the people of Jerusalem (see 2 Chr. 32:18) by pointing out that now even their God was against them.

18:26 Since **Aramaic** was by this time the language of international communication, it might be expected that the Rabshakeh would carry on diplomatic negotiations with officials in Judah and avoid speaking the Hebrew of the common citizens. But the Assyrians loved speaking to people in their native dialect to make the intimidation more effective.

18:27, 28 their own waste: The Rabshakeh portrayed the potential horror of the coming siege by using an obscene expression. The words were drawn from street language.

18:29–32 trust in the LORD: The matter of trust (vv. 19–24) continued as an issue. The Rabshakeh tempted the Israelites to abandon their trust in the Lord and trust in Sennacherib instead. Then the promised covenantal blessings (vv. 31, 32; see Deut. 8:8; Mic. 4:4; Zech. 3:10) could all be theirs. The repeated use of the words **Do not listen to Hezekiah** (vv. 22, 29, 30) was designed to lead the people to rebel against their king.

18:33–37 The Rabshakeh's assertion that none of the **gods of the nations** who had opposed Assyria had withstood the Assyrian king is another aspect of the continued psychological warfare.

19:1 he tore his clothes: Tearing of clothes was often a sign of grief (6:30) or of repentance (see Joel 2:12, 13). The humility of the king was evidenced in this action, one already performed by his trusted servants (see 18:37). In addition to humbling himself, the king sought guidance from God.

19:2 The ministry of the great prophet **Isaiah** had begun in the year that Uzziah or

Azariah died (see Is. 6:1), nearly four decades earlier (740 B.C.). Once Isaiah had sought out Judah's godless King Ahaz to minister to him (Is. 7:3); now the prophet was being sought by the godly Hezekiah.

19:3 day of trouble: The Hebrew phrase translated here indicates not only the great danger of the present Assyrian crisis, but the distress that Hezekiah felt. The king realized that the Lord's corrective chastisement had come upon Judah and Jerusalem. The closing proverb using the imagery of **birth** (see Hos. 13:13) emphasizes the need for God's intervening strength if Jerusalem were to be delivered.

19:4, 5 hear ... reproach: The first verb does not suggest that God might not be aware of the words of the Rabshakeh. Rather, the words describe God as determining to redress the wrong.

19:6, 7 Isaiah's prophecy was one of comfort. Not only would Sennacherib fail to conquer Jerusalem, but he would face a violent death upon his return home. Both points of the prophetic message would come true, although Sennacherib was not assassinated until 20 years later (c. 681 B.C.).

19:8 returned ... departed: The Rabshakeh had been trying to persuade Jerusalem to surrender without being attacked. But when he returned with his report, he found that his king was already distracted with another war and had already moved his army away. Still, the Rabshakeh did not give up, as v. 9 describes.

19:9–11 Since **Tirhakah** did not become **king** until 690 B.C., there is an apparent problem in the chronology of this verse. However, it is possible that the biblical author just calls Tirhakah by the title he was best known by at the time of writing.

19:12, 13 This is not the **Eden** of Genesis, but an area known today as Bit-Adini, south of Haran (see Ezek. 27:23; Amos 1:5).

19:14 In a great act of faith, Hezekiah brought Sennacherib's threatening letter **before the LORD.** Of course, Hezekiah understood that the Lord already knew the contents of the letter. But by this symbolic action, Hezekiah expressed his own dependence on God for deliverance.

19:15–19 Hezekiah prayed: Hezekiah knew that there is a greater King than the king of Assyria (18:19). Hezekiah's trust in the Lord was demonstrated in his habit of prayer (see 20:2), and his prayer was answered favorably (vv. 20–34).

19:20 Isaiah gave him a direct answer from the Lord. This helps explain one of the ways in which the Lord spoke to the kings during the monarchy. Prophets could communicate the message from God to the king.

19:21 The virgin: Here we sense God's approval of Jerusalem. When God speaks to His people about their sin, His speech can be direct, confrontational, and sometimes scathing. But when He speaks to others about His people and His city, He uses favorable language. They are, on the ideal level, like a virgin daughter to Him. **the daughter of Zion:** This phrase should be written "daughter Zion," without the "of." Zion (Jerusalem) is God's daughter whom He will guard and protect like a father.

19:22–24 God's answer to Hezekiah's prayer came once again (see vv. 6, 7) through Isaiah (vv. 20, 21). **Holy One of Israel** is characteristic of Isaiah's own manner of referring to God. He uses the phrase 26 times (see Is. 6:3). Sennacherib needed to know that his boastful pride blasphemed the sovereign and holy God of all nations. The verses that follow indicate that God knew not only the boasts, but the most inward thoughts of the Assyrian king.

19:25, 26 Did you not hear: Here the Lord answered the sarcasm of the Rabshakeh (18:17–25). In the manner of an ancient insult, God asserted His own work on behalf of Judah and ridiculed the enemy.

19:27, 28 But I know: The Assyrians had a great gap in their understanding of reality; they did not include the living God in their processes. But they, in turn, were fully known. **Hook** and **bridle** are used to restrain animals (see Ps. 32:9; Ezek. 19:4). Because the Assyrian kings often treated their prisoners of war in such fashion, Sennacherib would understand the threat only too well.

19:29 God graciously gave Hezekiah a **sign** (see also 20:9–11) of His good intentions for His people. Despite the fact that the Assyrian invasion had adversely affected the crops for that year and the next, by the third year the fields would again yield a plentiful harvest. Even as a natural growth would remain for the two years preceding the harvest of the third year, so God left in Israel a spiritual remnant that would in a future day swell into a mighty harvest of souls (see Joel 2:12–14; Mic. 2:12, 13; Zeph. 3:8–20).

19:30, 31 The promises in these verses were both for the immediate situation, for more remote times of regathering, and ultimately the final regathering of the Jewish people into their land in the time of the coming Messiah.

19:32, 33 not come into this city: While Sennacherib later boasted of taking some 46 Judean cities, with reference to Jerusalem he could only report that he made Hezekiah "prisoner in Jerusalem, his royal residence, like a bird in a cage." God's defense and deliverance of Jerusalem demonstrated his faithfulness to the Davidic covenant.

19:34, 35 I … My own sake: As in the case of the redemption of Israel from Egypt at the time of the Exodus, so in the deliverance of Israel from the present trouble, God Himself would do it. He would not delegate the work of salvation to a lesser power.

19:36 departed: As God had promised through His prophet Isaiah (vv. 32–34), Sennacherib did not attack the city of Jerusalem.

19:37 The name **Nisroch** has been identified as the god Nusku or a corrupted form of Marduk, the traditional god of Mesopotamia. The events depicted here took place 20 years after God's deliverance of Jerusalem. When his father was assassinated, Esarhaddon took the throne and ruled from 681 to 668 B.C.

20:1–3 Contrast the action of the sick Hezekiah with that of Ahaziah in 1:1, 2. Hezekiah was a great man of prayer (see also 19:1, 14, 15). **I have walked before you:** Hezekiah's prayer recognized that although all of life is in God's hands, God is also a Rewarder of those who faithfully serve Him (see Deut. 5:30–33; 30:15, 16). Hezekiah's habit of prayer would once again serve him well (see vv. 5, 6; 19:14–19).

20:4–6 The pattern of divine revelation to Hezekiah was through His prophet Isaiah. **defend this city:** The Lord promised deliverance for Jerusalem.

20:7, 8 The practice of applying **figs** to an ulcerated sore is attested in the records of the ancient Middle East, being mentioned as early as the Ras Shamra (Ugaritic) tablets of the second millennium B.C.

20:9, 10 Once more the Lord provided a **sign** of His intervention (see 19:29–31). Unlike his father Ahaz who cared little about a divine sign (see Is. 7:12), Hezekiah welcomed it (see vv. 10, 11). Hezekiah's trust in the Lord (see 18:5) surfaced repeatedly throughout his reign.

20:11, 12 Berodach-Baladan, or more properly Merodach-Baladan, was a Chaldean king who twice ruled in Babylon (721–710, 703 B.C.). A perennial enemy of Assyria, he was twice defeated by them and cast out from Babylon. His search for allies in his resistance to Assyria may have occasioned the embassy to Hezekiah, especially because he had heard of Hezekiah's miraculous deliverance from the Assyrian army (2 Chr. 32:31).

20:13–15 This account of the foolishness of Hezekiah follows immediately on the narrative of his great trust in the Lord (vv. 1–11).

20:16–18 Isaiah's messages of judgment were as important as his messages of mercy (see ch. 19; 20:1–11). **all … shall be carried to Babylon:** Hezekiah's enthusiastic reception of Merodach-Baladan's ambassadors and disclosure of his wealth to them would be remembered in a future time when Babylon was no longer Judah's friend.

20:19 The word …is good: Although Hezekiah recognized that Isaiah's dire prophecy was for a future day, he acknowledged his folly in putting his people in danger.

20:20, 21 a pool and a tunnel: Hezekiah dug a tunnel between the spring of Gihon and the Pool of Siloam to bring water within the eastern wall of Jerusalem, a deed that would prove especially helpful in time of siege.

21:1, 2 Manasseh: This wicked king bore the same name as the older son of Joseph (Gen. 41:51). His reign of **fifty-five years** (697–642 B.C.) was the longest of any of the kings of the divided kingdom. Externally, the period was one of political stability. It is known as the Assyrian Peace, an era in which the kings Esarhaddon (681–668 B.C.) and Ashurbanipal (668–626 B.C.) reigned and brought the Assyrian Empire to its zenith.

21:3 high places ... Baal ... wooden image: All that Hezekiah had done removing the wickedness of Canaanite religion from Israel was reversed by his son. The wording suggests not simply that he allowed the rebuilding of these obscene images, but that he actively directed their construction.

21:4–9 Manasseh brought objects of pagan worship and obscene symbols of the fertility religion of Canaan into the temple (see vv. 4, 5, 7). All that had been accomplished by the godly kings following the purge of Jehu (see 15:34), including King Hezekiah (see 18:4–6), was undone by this reprobate. But wicked as Manasseh was, God heard his prayer when he repented and did good (see 2 Chr. 33:12–16).

21:10, 11 The author of Chronicles (2 Chr. 33:10, 11) reports that Manasseh's failure to heed **the prophets** of God led to his being taken prisoner by the Assyrian king. The chronicler also reports Manasseh's repentance, restoration, and subsequent reform efforts (2 Chr. 33:12, 13, 15, 16), all of which came too late to stop Judah's ongoing apostasy. As a result, with the accession of Manasseh's son Amon (642–640 B.C.), Judah's spiritual wickedness surfaced again (vv. 20–22).

21:12 his ears will tingle: The announcement of such a fearsome judgment was designed to bring the king to repentance.

21:13 the measuring line of Samaria: If the people had any realization of the horrors that had befallen their sister city to the north, they would not want to be measured by the same implements that had designed Samaria's destruction. **as one wipes a dish:** God would soon bring a judgment so terrible that it would never be forgotten.

21:14 God's declaration that He would **forsake the remnant** does not mean He would abolish the Davidic covenant (see Ps. 89:30–37). Rather, Judah, the political remnant of God's kingdom (17:18), would also know chastisement for its sin.

21:15 since the day: The story of the Old Testament is not a record of God's anger, but of the *delay* of the exercise of His wrath.

21:16, 17 innocent blood: In times of wickedness, true believers often lose their lives (see Joel 3:19). Innocent blood may also refer to human sacrifice (v. 6; 2 Chr. 33:6).

21:18 garden of Uzza: His burial place apparently was not among the other kings of Judah. Some have suggested that the garden of Uzza was a sacred shrine to deity of the stars.

21:19–22 Amon: This wicked king followed in the path of his father Manasseh, much as Ahaziah of Israel followed in the path of his father Ahab (see 1 Kin. 22:51–53).

21:23–26 conspired against him: No reason is assigned for the conspiracy that brought about Amon's assassination. While it may have had some connection with the international crisis that precipitated Ashurbanipal's renewed attention to the west, Amon's own wickedness may have provided a sufficient cause.

22:1 The name **Josiah** means "The Lord Supports." Like the name of Cyrus (Is. 44:28; 45:1) and of the city of Bethlehem (Mic. 5:2), the name Josiah was announced by a prophet long before the time of his birth (see 1 Kin. 13:1, 2).

22:2 what was right: The young Josiah apparently was in the hands of godly advisors, one of whom may have been the prophet Zephaniah. His concern for righteousness led to reform early in his reign (see 2 Chr. 34:3–7).

22:3 In his **eighteenth year** of reign (c. 622 B.C.), Josiah began extensive repairs on the temple (vv. 4–7; 2 Chr. 34:8–13).

22:4 Hilkiah the high priest: This man was a major figure in the revival of true religion that young Josiah accomplished. The work of restoring the temple was under his direction.

22:5–7 The careful accounting for the money used in the restoration of the temple is similar to that in the time of King Joash of Judah and of the high priest associated with him, Jehoiada (12:9–16).

22:8, 9 By **the Book of the Law** may be meant either parts or all of the Pentateuch.

This book may have been lost, set aside, or hidden during the wicked reigns of Manasseh and Amon.

22:10–13 read it before the king: This is the dramatic event that shaped Josiah's reign. Imagine what it must have been for the young king to hear the Word of God read for the first time. **tore his clothes:** Once again (see 19:1) a godly king tore his clothes in genuine remorse. Josiah's great qualities are seen in his desire for prophetic sanction for his new walk.

22:14 Although **Huldah the prophetess** is mentioned only here (and in 2 Chr. 34:22–28) in the Scriptures, some have suggested that her husband Shallum was related to Jeremiah (see Jer. 32:7–12).

22:15 Huldah takes her place beside several prophetesses recorded in the Scriptures, such as Miriam (Ex. 15:20) and Deborah (Judg. 4:4). This woman was an authoritative agent for the transmission of the word of God to the highest authorities in the land of Judah.

22:16 all the words: The threat of calamity for apostasy that the king heard may have been intended to reinforce the message of the parts of the Book of the Law that were found when the temple was being repaired and were read to the king (Deut. 28:15–68).

22:17–19 First was the bad news, addressed principally to the wicked who had forsaken God. Second was the good news, that Josiah would be delivered from impending judgment because of his piety in a difficult time.

22:20 in peace: Huldah's good word for Josiah personally was that he would not see the calamity that God would bring upon the people. Josiah's subsequent death in battle (23:29, 30) was not at issue in Huldah's prophecy. Like his godly grandfather Hezekiah, the righteous Josiah would not live to see God's future judgment of Judah (see 20:19).

23:1 all the elders: We may contrast Jehu's gathering of the priests and prophets of Baal, in anticipation of his great "sacrifice" (see 10:18–31).

23:2, 3 he read … the Book of the Covenant: Like Moses (Ex. 24:3–8) and Joshua (Josh. 8:34, 35) before him, Josiah followed the ancient standard for godly leadership (Deut. 17:18–20; 31:9–13) and assembled the people to renew the covenant (see also Josh. 24). The king's own spiritual reaction and the reforms that he enacted (see 2 Chr. 35:1–19) suggest that the texts dealing with covenant obligations and sanctions (Lev. 26; Deut. 28) were a part of the public reading.

23:4 Articles of pagan worship had been taken to the **fields of Kidron** in the reforms of Asa (1 Kin. 15:13) and Hezekiah (2 Chr. 29:16; 30:14). **to Bethel:** Carrying the remaining ashes of burned religious articles to Bethel was a bold condemnation of both the pagan religious rites and the place associated with them (see 1 Kin. 12:28–30; Amos 4:4, 5). Thus Josiah's reforms spilled over into the northern kingdom as well.

23:5 idolatrous priests: The term used here is also used by Zephaniah, who uses it of those priests who led the rites associated with Baal and with star worship of various kinds (Zeph. 1:4). These priests had been appointed by Judah's past kings but functioned outside the divinely established priesthood.

23:6 Although destroyed by Hezekiah (18:4), **wooden images** associated with the worship of Asherah had been reintroduced by Manasseh (21:7) and also by Amon (21:21; see also 13:6).

23:7–9 perverted persons: Sacred prostitution was part of the debased practices of Canaanite religion (see 1 Kin. 14:24 and also 15:12; 22:46). The horrible thing here is not just that these perverted persons were practicing their trade in Jerusalem, but that they actually had places for their **booths** in the temple precincts.

23:10 Topheth … Molech: Some scholars equate Molech with a pagan deity such as the Ammonite god Milcom (1 Kin. 11:5) or an individual Canaanite god (Lev. 20:1–5), whose worship was carried on in Jerusalem. Other scholars think that Molech was the name of a type of child sacrifice associated with Baal (see Jer. 7:31, 32; 19:5, 6; 32:35).

23:11–14 horses … dedicated to the sun: Excavations at Jerusalem have uncovered a sacred shrine used in solar worship and dating from the time of Jehoshaphat. Small horses with solar disks on their foreheads have been found at Jerusalem and Hazor.

23:15–17 Josiah's actions were prophesied long ago by a prophet who denounced Jeroboam I's **altar that was at Bethel** (1 Kin. 13:26–32). The literal fulfillment of that prophecy confirms that this earlier man of God was a true prophet (see Deut. 18:22).

23:18, 19 the prophet … from Samaria: The prophet from Samaria was the old prophet of Bethel (1 Kin. 13:11). Samaria is the name for an entire area, not just the city that was later the capital of the northern kingdom (see 1 Kin. 13:32; 16:23, 24). After the death of the man of God who had denounced Jeroboam I's altar at Bethel, the aged prophet of Bethel requested that at his death he should be buried in Bethel beside that prophet of Judah.

23:20 priests of the high places: Because these priests were not Levites, they were executed as God's law demands (Deut. 17:2–7). True priests of the Lord who officiated at the high places in Judah were spared.

23:21, 22 the Passover: The restoration of religious places was part of the revival of spiritual worship. **since the days of the judges:** Although Hezekiah had held a Passover (see 2 Chr. 30), he had done so with some modification of the Law (2 Chr. 30:13–20). Accordingly, Josiah's meeting of the strict requirements of the Law (see 2 Chr. 35:1–19) was truly unparalleled since the days of the judges. Moreover, God's law was observed by believers from Judah and Israel alike (2 Chr. 35:18).

23:23–25 no king: Josiah's following of the Law was unparalleled among the kings of Israel and Judah. Like his grandfather Hezekiah, who was without equal in his trust of the Lord (18:5), Josiah was truly a righteous king.

23:26, 27 Despite their efforts, Judah's sin was so entrenched that judgment was inevitable (17:18, 19; 23:26, 27; Lam. 1:5). Even though Manasseh repented, he still reaped the results of his sin.

23:28–30 Pharaoh Necho (609–594 B.C.) was the recently crowned king of Egypt's twenty-sixth dynasty. During the long years

of Josiah's reign (640–609 B.C.), Assyrian power had steadily crumbled until its capital, Nineveh, had fallen (612 B.C.) to a coalition of Chaldeans, Medes, and others. The surviving Assyrian forces had regrouped at Haran. Because Egypt was a long-standing ally of Assyria, Necho journeyed northward to help the beleaguered Assyrians. Josiah's deployment of his forces in the Valley of Megiddo was an attempt to prevent the Egyptians from aiding the Assyrian forces at Haran. Although Pharaoh Necho would be delayed sufficiently so that Haran would be lost to the Assyrians, Josiah's action ultimately cost him his life (2 Chr. 35:20–25).

23:31–36 Jehoahaz (called Shallum in Jer. 22:11) was Josiah's third son (see 24:18; 1 Chr. 3:15). His reign of **three months** came to an end with the return of Pharaoh Necho from Haran. Jehoahaz was summoned to Riblah, Necho's headquarters in Syria. Then he was led away to die in Egypt. His brother Eliakim was installed on the throne with his name changed to Jehoiakim. Judah thus became no more than a vassal of Egypt. The punishment for Judah's disobedience was about to fall (see Deut. 28:64–68).

23:37 did evil: Jehoiakim's short reign (608–598 B.C.) was noted for its extreme wickedness (2 Chr. 36:5, 8). Jeremiah depicts him as a ruler who took advantage of his people (Jer. 22:13, 14, 17), filled the land with vice and violence (Jer. 18:18–20), and opposed all that was holy (Jer. 25:1–7). Unlike his father Josiah, who led the nation in reformation at the hearing of the Word of God (22:11; 23:1–25), Jehoiakim went so far as to cut up and burn a scroll of Scripture (Jer. 36:21–24) and to kill Urijah, a true prophet of God (Jer. 26:20–23).

24:1 After defeating the Assyrians and Egyptians at the Battle of Carchemish (605 B.C.), King Nebuchadnezzar of Babylonia invaded Judah and made the country his vassal. He took Daniel and other notables to Babylon as spoils of war. Jehoiakim served Nebuchadnezzar **three years** and then rebelled, perhaps finding courage to do so when Pharaoh Necho succeeded in turning back the Babylonians at the Egyptian border in 601 B.C.

24:2 The name **Chaldeans** originally applied to certain inhabitants of southern Mesopotamia. But by the neo-Babylonian period, this term had become identified with Babylonians, and Babylonia was called Chaldea. Not only Chaldeans but raiding parties from nearby countries harassed Judah.

24:3–7 Because Jehoiakim and Judah had reproduced **the sins of Manasseh** (see 21:1–17), God's judgment was inevitable. Jehoiakim himself would die soon, even as Nebuchadnezzar was launching a second campaign into Judah (598 B.C.).

24:8–11 The name **Jehoiachin** means "The Lord Has Appointed." **eighteen years old:** Because the scriptural descriptions of Jehoiachin seem to represent him as a mature young man (Jer. 22:24–30; Ezek. 19:6), Jehoiachin's age at accession was probably eighteen rather than eight, as given elsewhere in some manuscripts (compare 2 Chr. 36:9).

24:12, 13 Jehoiakim apparently had died before Nebuchadnezzar arrived at Jerusalem, because it was **Jehoiachin** who was carried off captive with other leaders of Judah (such as Ezekiel, see Ezek. 1:1). He had reigned only three months (v. 8); the year was 598 B.C. Jeremiah called him "Jeconiah" and "Coniah" (Jer. 22:24, 28).

24:14 Ten thousand is probably a round number for deportees of all types from Judah and Jerusalem. The figure probably includes various categories of exiles, such as those mentioned in v. 16.

24:15 carried Jehoiachin captive: Jehoiachin's captivity (see 2 Chr. 36:9, 10) was prophesied in Jer. 22:24–27. Unlike Jehoahaz, who was carried off into Egypt previously (23:33) and disappears from the pages of sacred history, Jehoiachin's eventual release is recorded twice (25:27–30; Jer. 52:31–34).

24:16, 17 Mattaniah is Josiah's youngest son. His name means "The Gift of the Lord."

24:18, 19 Mattaniah, who reigned under the name **Zedekiah,** came to the throne in 598 B.C. This was the year of Jehoiakim's death and Jehoiachin's captivity. He was king at the time of the fall of Jerusalem in 586 B.C.

24:20 Zedekiah rebelled: The king of Judah foolishly relied on the Egyptians under Pharaoh Apries (or Hophra, Jer. 44:30) for help (see Ezek. 17:15–18). Although Apries challenged Nebuchadnezzar by attacking Phoenicia and coming to Zedekiah's assistance (Jer. 37:5), he was not able to deliver Judah (Jer. 37:7, 8). His own reign ended in a coup that ultimately cost him his life.

25:1, 2 eleventh year: The siege of Jerusalem lasted for nearly two years (see v. 1).

25:3, 4 Zedekiah's escape route lay between **two walls** near the royal garden at the southeastern corner of the city.

25:5, 6 After his capture, Zedekiah was taken to **Riblah** on the Orontes River in Syria, which was the field headquarters for Nebuchadnezzar's western campaigns.

25:7–9 put out the eyes: The annals of the ancient Middle East often mention putting out the eyes of conquered people. The last thing Zedekiah saw was the reward of his sinful folly—the horrible spectacle of his own loved ones being put to death. He would carry this picture with him until his own death in a Babylonian prison (Jer. 52:11).

25:10–17 The walls of Jerusalem would lie in a ruined condition for about 150 years (see Neh. 2:11—6:16).

25:18–20 Although **Seraiah** was executed at Riblah (v. 21), his son Jehozadak was simply deported (1 Chr. 6:15). Through Jehozadak's line would come Ezra, the priest and great reformer, who would return to Jerusalem one day and take up Seraiah's work (Ezra 7:1). The second martyred priest **Zephaniah** may be the priest mentioned by Jeremiah (Jer. 21:1; 29:5). Jerusalem would be less prone to future rebellions with the chief religious and civil officials gone.

25:21 Like Israel before it (17:18), Judah was **carried away** captive because of its sinful apostasy.

25:22 Gedaliah: Gedaliah's father Ahikam had supported Jeremiah in his struggles with the apostate officials of Judah (Jer. 26:24). Gedaliah's training and his descent from a family noted for its anti-establishment stance doubtless made him acceptable to the Babylonians. The prophet Jeremiah, spared by the Babylonians (Jer. 39:11–14; 40:1–5), was allowed to stay and assist Gedaliah in the process of reconstruction in Judah (Jer. 40:6).

25:23–26 Mizpah had long been a center of spiritual and political prominence (1 Sam. 10:17; 1 Kin. 15:22). It was an ideal location for the provincial government. **Jaazaniah:** This name appears on a seal impression found in Mizpah. The murderous deeds of **Ishmael** and the role of **Johanan** in the events are detailed by Jeremiah (Jer. 40:7—43:7).

25:27 Evil-Merodach succeeded Nebuchadnezzar and reigned a short time (561–560 B.C.). Tablets from the reign of Nabonidus (555–539 B.C.) record the daily rations of Jehoiachin who is called "Yaukin, king of the land of Yahud (Judah)."

25:28–30 spoke kindly: Evil-Merodach's kindness toward Jehoiachin brings the Book of Kings to an end—on a ray of hope. Exile is the end neither of Israel nor of the Davidic line.

1 Chronicles

Introduction

First Chronicles is an inspirational history. Writing after the Exile, the author sought to inspire the remnant of Israelites with their extraordinary spiritual heritage. Appropriately, the book focuses on David. He was not only Israel's great king, but also one of Israel's greatest spiritual leaders.

Originally both First and Second Chronicles were one book. The overall consistency of style in the book indicates that although several contributors might have worked on it at various stages, one editor shaped the final product. Jewish tradition identifies the editor as Ezra. This view finds support in the common themes and emphases of Chronicles and the Book of Ezra. Both books focus on the building and dedication of the temple.

It is evident that Chronicles is the result of a compilation process. The chronicler made use of the books of Samuel and Kings for about half the narrative. Also, the genealogies in the beginning of the book are largely derived from the Pentateuch. The compiler even cites some of the sources. Among these are the genealogical records of the various tribes (7:9, 40), the book of the kings of Israel (9:1), and the books of Samuel, Nathan, and Gad (29:29).

Writing approximately when the Israelites returned from captivity, the chronicler wanted to emphasize the Israelites' continuity with their past. The remnant was returning to Jerusalem to rebuild the temple because of the promises God had given to David many years before (see Ezra 7:10–23). God's promises were still in effect—even though the people had been in exile.

At a time when the Israelites were rebuilding the nation and the temple (Ezra 3:7–13), the chronicler painted a picture of David's kingdom as a kingdom founded on the true worship of God. Not the throne, but the tabernacle and temple were the focus of David's kingdom. Chronicles extensively describes how David moved the ark of the covenant to a suitable place of worship (13:1—16:3), appointed appropriate religious personnel (16:4–6, 37–43; 23:1—26:32), and made plans for building a permanent temple (chs. 22; 28; 29). The theme of Chronicles is that God Himself established David's kingdom (29:10, 11) in fulfillment of His promises to Abraham, Isaac, and Jacob. Through the Davidic covenant, David's kingdom itself embodies the promise of the future kingdom whose ruler is the great Son of David, Jesus Christ.

1:1–6 Adam, Seth, Enosh: The names of these ancient, pre-Flood characters were included in the genealogical record with people whose historical identities have never been questioned, such as David (2:15) and Zerubbabel (3:19). This indicates that the chronicler had no question as to their historicity.

1:7, 8 Rodanim referred to the Rhodites, natives of the Greek island of Rhodes. **sons of Ham:** Great nations were indicated by some of the names here: **Cush** referred to the Ethiopians, **Mizraim** to the Egyptians, **Canaan** to the Canaanites.

1:9–11 Cush begot Nimrod: It seems that the chronicler used the genealogy of Gen. 10 as the primary source for this genealogy. However, he used it selectively. For example, Gen. 10:9–12 was not included. The apparent purpose of this genealogy was to establish the line between Adam and David, and between David and the reigning Davidic monarch.

1:12 Caphtorim: These people lived in Caphtor (Deut. 2:23), known in ancient Akkadian texts as Kaptara and probably to be identified as Crete. The Caphtorim were related to the Philistines, or the two terms might even be interchangeable (see Jer. 47:4; Amos 9:7).

1:13–17 Heth founded the nation of the Hittites, a people in what is now central Turkey who achieved great power and prominence in the middle of the second millennium B.C. After the Hittite kingdom fell to the Sea Peoples around 1200 B.C., many Hittites settled in enclaves in Syria and Palestine.

1:18 Eber was the ancestor of Abraham, Isaac, and Jacob. The name Hebrew, a derivative of

Eber's name, was applied to the Israelites. The central place Eber occupies in the genealogies of Abram in Genesis and 1 Chronicles suggests a connection between the names Hebrew and Eber (1:24–27; see Gen. 10:21; 11:10–26). Indeed the name Hebrew may simply mean an "Eberite."

1:19–27 the earth was divided: This refers to the division of the earth's population by the scattering of the human race following the judgment of God on the Tower of Babel. Chronologically, **Peleg** apparently fits about halfway between Shem and Abram (1:24–27), a most suitable place for the Tower of Babel episode.

1:28–31 Isaac was the son of the covenant, so his name occurs first when the names Isaac and Ishmael are mentioned together, even though **Ishmael** was born first.

1:32, 33 Both Ishmael and **Midian** were descendants of Abraham, Ishmael by a concubine and Midian by another wife Abraham married after Sarah's death (Gen. 25:1, 2).

1:34–36 Timna was Eliphaz's concubine (Gen. 36:12). Timna's son Amalek was the founder of the Amalekites, a people that became one of Israel's most persistent enemies (Ex. 17:8–16; Deut. 25:17–19; 1 Sam. 15:1–3).

1:37–38 Seir was the patriarchal name of the pre-Edomite population of the region east and south of the Dead Sea (Gen. 36:20–30). Esau's daughter-in-law Timna (vv. 35, 36) was the sister of Lotan and daughter of Seir. Thus the people of Seir and the descendants of Esau were related by marriage, and together these two people groups became the kingdom of Edom (v. 43).

1:39–43 the kings ... of Edom: Compare Gen. 36:31–39. These kings were apparently descendants of Esau. The Edomites were ruled by kings several centuries before the Israelites. This fact helps explain Israel's later demand to have "a king to judge us like all the nations" (1 Sam. 8:5).

1:44–54 The Hebrew word translated **chiefs** usually referred to military leaders. Compare Gen. 36:40–43.

2:1, 2 Compare the order of the **sons of Israel** with Gen. 35:23–26.

2:3 Though he was the fourth son of Jacob

(v. 1), **Judah** appears first in the detailed genealogy because the messianic promise was to be channeled through him (Gen. 49:10). Thus the chronicler reveals that his genealogy and his presentation of the events are controlled by theological concerns rather than strict chronology.

2:4–9 Though the line to David passed through Zerah's brother Perez, Zerah's descendants are mentioned here because of the prominence of Achar (v. 7), called Achan in the narrative of Josh. 7:10–26. **Ethan, Heman, Calcol,** and **Dara** are mentioned because of their role in temple music under King David and their distinction as poets and sages (15:16–19; 1 Kin. 4:29–31).

2:10–15 This genealogy is selective, focusing on only those members important to the lineage. For example, **Nahshon** was head of the tribe of Judah at the time of the wilderness march from Sinai to Kadesh Barnea (Num. 1:7, 2:3; 7:12). He was more than five generations removed from Judah himself (2:4–10).

2:16, 17 Sisters are rarely mentioned in ancient genealogies. However, this genealogy pays particular attention to the family of David and thus to David's sisters.

2:18–24 This **Caleb** was not the famous companion of Joshua (Num. 13:6; Josh. 14:6, 7), who lived several centuries later, during the conquest of Canaan. In fact, one of this Caleb's descendants Bezalel (v. 20) was a craftsman charged with constructing the wilderness tabernacle (Ex. 31:2).

2:25–41 The sons of Jerahmeel would eventually occupy the Negev, the desert area of southern Judah.

2:42–48 This was the same **Caleb** as that of vv. 18, 19. Here his genealogy is much longer, apparently transmitted through other wives.

2:49–50 The Caleb of Joshua's time had a **daughter** named **Achsah,** who became the wife of Israel's first judge, Othniel (Judg. 1:12, 13). It might appear that the **Caleb** here in Chronicles must be the same as the later Caleb, but this is ruled out by the consistent use of Caleb throughout the chronicler's genealogy to refer to an earlier individual by that name. The meaning probably is that Achsah is the "daughter" of the earlier Caleb in the sense that she is his descendant. The later Caleb was doubtless a descendant of the early one, a conclusion supported by the record that both were from the tribe of Judah (2:4, 5, 9, 18, 42; Num. 13:6).

2:51–54 The chronicler recorded Caleb's genealogy because of the significance of Bethlehem, the birthplace of King David. One of Caleb's descendants, Salma, was the founder or **father of Bethlehem.**

2:55 Since the compiler of Chronicles was obviously a scribe, he was interested in tracing, if only briefly, various **families of the scribes.** These families are otherwise unknown, as is **Jabez,** the place they lived. They were **Kenites,** a people related to Israel through Moses' marriage to a Kenite, sometimes referred to as a Midianite (Judg. 4:11). Naming the Kenite scribes here suggests that they were descended from Judah.

3:1–5 The fact that David had six **sons** by six wives in Hebron does not condone polygamy. David had fallen into the ancient custom among kings of marrying the daughters of neighboring kings in order to create allies. Negative results inevitably followed such multiple marriages. David's first son, **Amnon,** raped his half sister Tamar (2 Sam. 13:14)—a deed for which he paid with his own life at the hands of his half brother **Absalom.** Later **Adonijah** tried to usurp the throne from **Solomon** to whom it had been promised (1 Kin. 1:5–10).

3:6–9 Tamar: The fact that only one daughter of David is named does not mean that he had no other daughters. Tamar appears in this genealogy because of her prominence in the story of King David's family (2 Sam. 13:1–39).

3:10–18 Shenazzar was probably the same man as Sheshbazzar, leader of the first group of Jews to return from Babylonian captivity (Ezra 1:8, 11) and builder of the foundation of the second temple (Ezra 5:15–17).

3:19 Zerubbabel here is designated as a son of **Pedaiah,** but elsewhere (Ezra 3:2, 8; 5:2; Neh. 12:1; Hag. 1:12, 14; 2:2, 23) as a son of Pedaiah's brother Shealtiel (v. 17). It is likely that Shealtiel had died while Zerubbabel was young and that the youth was reared by his uncle Pedaiah, thus becoming Pedaiah's son.

3:20–24 Pelatiah and **Jeshaiah** seem to be the only two **sons of Hananiah. Rephaiah … Shechaniah:** These names were detached from the Zerubbabel genealogy and may be other Davidic families. **The sons of Shechaniah:** Four generations of Shechaniah, ending in **Anani,** are listed. Hence the genealogy of vv. 17–24 presupposes about seven generations.

4:1–3 Although the genealogy of **Judah** leading up to David has already been recorded (2:3–17), the chronicler here refers to other persons and events relative to that genealogy. In the list of this verse, only **Perez** is Judah's own son. **Hezron** is his grandson, **Carmi** his nephew (2:5, 6), **Hur** the grandson of Hezron (2:18, 19), and **Shobal** the grandson of Hur (2:50).

4:4–12 Ephrathah has already been identified as Ephrath, a wife of the early Caleb (2:19) and mother of Hur. She was therefore the "great grandmother" of **Bethlehem,** since her son Hur was the "grandfather" of Bethlehem (2:50, 51). Elsewhere the names Bethlehem and Ephrath are closely connected. When Jacob was on the way to Mamre, his wife Rachel died near Ephrath, identified also as Bethlehem (Gen. 35:19).

4:13 Othniel, the first of Israel's judges (Josh. 15:17; Judg. 1:13; 3:9), was son-in-law of the later Caleb—the friend and colleague of Joshua.

4:14, 15 Kenaz was the name of Othniel's father (v. 13) and Caleb's brother (Josh. 15:17), as well as of Caleb's grandson. It is clear that Othniel had married his own first cousin, a practice that was common in the Old Testament.

4:16–21 The fact that **Shelah** named his son **Er** indicates that he followed the levirate custom of raising up a child in the name of a deceased brother. Er, son of Judah, had died because of some unspecified sin, but had left no children by his wife Tamar (Gen. 38:6–11). His brother Onan refused to honor the levirate practice on Er's behalf, so Tamar seduced Judah, her father-in-law, and bore the twin sons Perez and Zerah (Gen. 38:27–30). Shelah, the third son of Judah, apparently did honor his oldest brother by taking the widow Tamar as his wife and rearing a son in Er's name.

4:22 The chronicler made the point that his documentation rested on **ancient** texts. Even in the chronicler's own day, there were skeptics who questioned the accuracy of the genealogies.

4:23, 24 The genealogy of **Simeon** appears next because the Simeonites were a small tribe (v. 27) and had no land allocated to them (Josh. 19:1–9). They settled in the territory of Judah, and their genealogy is attached to his.

4:25–38 Because the tribe of Simeon was so small and had settled within Judah's territory, the tribe lost its identity and was considered a part of Judah when **David** became king.

4:39–41 The chronicler describes how the Simeonites lived as shepherds in Gedor. This was an area next to Egypt, possibly the same as Gerar (Gen. 26:17–20). The Hamites, who were Egyptians, had lived there at one time (v. 40), but were replaced by **Meunites.**

4:42, 43 The Simeonites pursued the Amalekites into Mount Seir, or Edom. **to this day:** That is, to the time Chronicles was written. The Simeonites had lived in Edom from Hezekiah's time.

5:1, 2 The chronicler explains why he does not trace the genealogies of Jacob's sons in birth order. Usually the oldest son of an ancient family became head of the family upon his father's death and also received a larger share of the inheritance than the other children. But Reuben, the firstborn of Jacob, had slept with his father's concubine—perhaps hoping in this way to guarantee his rights as the firstborn son (Gen. 35:22). Because of this despicable act, he lost the **birthright.** Instead, Jacob blessed the **sons of Joseph,** Ephraim and Manasseh (Gen. 48:15–22), thereby transmitting the birthright to Joseph and his sons. The birthright assigned to Joseph did not carry with it the right to rule the tribes and nation; that privilege was granted to Judah. **Judah prevailed** in the sense that God freely chose them as the tribe through which His messianic Deliverer and

King would come (Gen. 49:10). The **ruler** from Judah was David and his dynasty, a fact well known to the ancient Israelites.

5:3–6 Though the tribe of Reuben virtually disappeared from the historical record by the time of the monarchy, there still remained people who identified themselves as **Reubenites,** as this verse makes clear.

5:7–9 Part of the reason for the absence of Reuben in the historical account was the tribe's need to seek greater pasture lands for their animals. They had pushed east into the wilderness as far as the **River Euphrates.** For this reason, the Reubenites were the first to be deported by the Assyrians (see v. 6).

5:10, 11 Gad lived near Reuben and the half tribe of Manasseh. Gad was one of the tribes that sought permission from Moses to settle east of the Jordan River rather than west (Num. 32:1–42). Reuben occupied the area just east of the Dead Sea and the lower Jordan valley; Gad, the **land of Bashan** due east of the river; and Manasseh, the land to the east and north of the Sea of Galilee.

5:12–17 Once more the chronicler alludes to his sources, this time to genealogical records from the time of **Jotham** (750–735 B.C.) and **Jeroboam** II (793–753 B.C.). He wanted to emphasize that the genealogies are based on solid documentary research in texts that preceded his own time by more than 300 years.

5:18, 19 The **Hagrites** and their allies were probably desert peoples who felt increasing pressure from the expanding Israelite population. Their efforts at resisting the Israelites took place in the days of Saul (v. 10), though the narratives of Saul do not mention them.

5:20 they were helped: The help here came from God Himself in answer to their prayers. The people of Reuben, Gad, and Manasseh fielded an army of more then 44,000 men (v. 18), but ultimately it was God who brought success.

5:21, 22 the war was God's: This confirms the statement about God helping the Israelites in v. 20 and goes beyond it by referring to a practice of Old Testament times known as "The Lord's War." At times, God commanded an offensive war as a means of achieving His purposes of conquest and occupation of the Promised Land (Deut. 20:1–20). At those times, God made it clear that the battle was by His initiative and that He would ensure its success.

5:23–26 Tiglath-Pileser, the famous king **Tiglath-Pileser,** who reigned around 745–727 B.C., has gone down in Assyrian annals as one of the most powerful rulers of the neo-Assyrian period.

6:1 Levi: All religious personnel involved in tabernacle or temple ministry had to be members of the tribe of Levi. Aaron was himself a Levite, and from the beginning of the priesthood his descendants were designated as the only ones who could serve as priests (see 6:16–25; Ex. 28:1). Later the Levites were especially set apart for service in the tabernacle in a role subsidiary to the priests (Num. 18:1–7). Anyone who wanted to serve in the temple had to establish his Levitical credentials. The present genealogy was designed at least in part to meet that need.

6:2 Kohath: This son of Levi was the one to whom the office of priest became exclusively connected. Hence, every priest had to be a Levite, but not every Levite could become a priest.

6:3, 4 Beginning with **Eleazar,** the genealogy traces the line of high priests through Jehozadak, the priest who went into Babylonian exile with his people (v. 15). Including Eleazar and Jehozadak, there were at least 22 high priests in unbroken succession. Another line of priests began with **Ithamar,** including such persons as Eli, Ahimelech, and Abiathar. In the days of David, priestly service was divided between the Eleazar and Ithamar priests, with the Eleazar serving two-thirds of the time and the Ithamar one-third because of the difference in their numbers (24:1–5). Solomon rejected the Ithamar priesthood, reserving the honor of the priesthood exclusively for the priests descended from Eleazar (1 Kin. 2:26, 27).

6:5–8 Zadok: This priest, not the same person as the Zadok of v. 12, was the one selected by David to serve along with Ahimelech the son of Abiathar as high priest (2 Sam. 8:17). Eventually Zadok became sole high priest because of Abiathar's rebellion against Solomon (1 Kin. 2:26, 27).

6:9, 10 The detail that this **Azariah** ministered in Solomon's **temple** distinguishes this priest from his grandfather of the same name (v. 9).

6:11–14 Jehozadak: This last priest in the list was carried into exile in Babylon (v. 15). He was the father of Joshua, the priest who returned from Babylon with Zerubbabel to rebuild the temple (Hag. 1:1, 12, 14).

6:15–17 Gershon: The purpose of the following genealogy was to list the principal offspring of the sons of Levi who were not priests, but regular or "ordinary" Levites.

6:18–21 Amram was the father of Aaron and the whole line of high priests. All other priests had to trace their lineage to Kohath through his other sons **Izhar, Hebron, and Uzziel.** Descendants of Levi who were not sons of Kohath could not be priests at all.

6:22 Amminadab is another name for Izhar (v. 18), who otherwise appears as the father of Korah (6:37, 38; see Ex. 6:21; Num. 16:1).

6:23–32 Samuel: Samuel's ancestors were described elsewhere as Ephraimites (1 Sam. 1:1). Although Samuel was an Ephraimite by virtue of his residence in Ramathaim Zophim, a city in the tribal territory of Ephraim, this genealogy makes it clear that he was in fact a Levite. This explains why he could be trained in the tabernacle under Eli the priest (1 Sam. 2:11) and later officiate at public services that included sacrifices (1 Sam. 9:13; 10:8).

6:33–47 The temple musicians also were Levites and were divided into three groups according to their descent from Levi's three sons. The **Kohathites** in David's time were led by **Heman,** grandson of **Samuel;** the Gershonites by **Asaph** (vv. 39, 43); and the Merarites by **Ethan** (vv. 44, 47).

6:48, 49 In contrast to the Levites just listed, Aaron and his descendants had the privilege and responsibility of the office of the high priest. What set them apart from the other Levites was their access to the **altar of burnt offering** and **incense** and their work of making **atonement for Israel.** Levites could assist in this ministry and could officiate at local sacrifices. However, only priests in the line of Aaron could present sacrifices at the tabernacle or temple.

6:50–53 sons of Aaron: The genealogy of vv. 50–53 is the same as that in vv. 4–8, but this list ends with Ahimaaz. This list recites the line of Aaron only until the time of David (v. 31). Zadok and Ahimaaz were the last of the priests in the line of Eleazar under David's administration (2 Sam. 15:35, 36).

6:54 dwelling places: The remainder of the chapter describes the allocation of cities and towns to the priests (vv. 54–60), the rest of the Kohathites (vv. 61, 66–70), the Gershonites (vv. 62, 71–76), and the Merarites (vv. 63, 77–81).

6:55 Because the priests were all Kohathites, the cities of the priests were within the districts assigned to Kohath. **Hebron,** located in Judah, is the first of these cities. **surrounding common-lands:** The priests and Levites occupied not only houses within the city walls, but they owned and worked fields immediately adjacent to the cities as well. These common-lands extended out from the perimeters of the city walls for a thousand cubits (about 1,500 ft.) in every direction (Num. 35:4, 5) and could be used for farming and grazing (Num. 35:3).

6:56 Hebron had originally been assigned to the faithful spy Caleb as part of his inheritance (Josh. 15:13). However, Caleb's inheritance was further defined as not the city proper, but the nearby **fields** and **villages** (Josh. 21:11, 12). Caleb's fields were outside the thousand-cubit circumference that belonged to the priests of Hebron.

6:57–59 The Law specified that in the event of an unintentional killing, the perpetrator could find sanctuary in one of six **cities of refuge** scattered throughout the land (Num. 35:9–15). He or she could remain there in safety until the case came to trial (Num. 35:16–28). These six cities were included among the 48 Levitical cities, and **Hebron** was one of them.

6:60 The number **thirteen** refers to the original allotment of cities in Josh. 21:13–19. The chronicler was listing the priestly cities that existed in his own day, nearly a thousand years after the original distribution. This accounts not only for two missing cities, Juttah and

Gibeon, but also for the variation in the spelling of some of the names as well. The priestly cities were concentrated in the areas of Judah and Benjamin, conveniently located near the temple in Jerusalem.

6:61–65 rest of … the Kohathites: These were the Levites who were not priests. Their cities were situated mainly in the **half tribe of Manasseh** on the west of the Jordan River (see v. 70), just south of the plain of Jezreel.

6:66 Beginning here, there is a continuation of the description of non-priestly Kohathite cities begun in v. 61. Some of these cities were in **Ephraim,** with Manasseh to the north and Benjamin to the south.

6:67–70 Like Hebron, **Shechem** was both a Levitical city and a city of refuge. Shechem was especially significant in Israel. It was the site of Abraham's first altar in Canaan (Gen. 12:6, 7), the place where Jacob bought a piece of land (Gen. 33:19), and the location of the first capital of the northern kingdom (1 Kin. 12:25).

6:71–75 Gershon: The tribal areas containing the cities of the Gershonite Levites were East Manasseh; Issachar, north of West Manasseh (v. 72); Asher, on the Mediterranean coast north of Mount Carmel (v. 74); and Naphtali, west and north of the Sea of Galilee (v. 76). **Golan:** This city in Bashan east of the Jordan River was a city of refuge.

6:76 Kedesh was another of the six cities of refuge. It was the most northern of the three west of the Jordan River.

6:77 The third Levitical order, that of **Merari,** occupied cities in Zebulun. Reuben was east of the Dead Sea (v. 78), and Gad was east of the Jordan River from the Dead Sea almost to the Sea of Galilee (v. 80).

6:78, 79 Bezer was also a city of refuge, the farthest south of those east of the Jordan River.

6:80, 81 Another city of refuge, **Ramoth in Gilead,** was directly east of the Jordan River. In this way the cities of refuge were distributed throughout the land so that any Israelite would be within a few miles of one of them. All six cities of refuge were assigned to the Levites, with Hebron designated for the priests (v. 55). The cities of refuge were assigned this way because the priests and Levites had judicial responsibilities in the cases involving unintentional homicide (Num. 35:25, 28; Deut. 17:8–13; 19:17–21).

7:1, 2 The total here was limited to the **sons of Tola.** Undoubtedly there were thousands of other tribesmen of Issachar at that time, descendants of the three other sons of Issachar (v. 1).

7:3–5 thirty-six thousand: These appear to be the offspring of Uzzi (v. 3), the son of Tola (v. 2). Since the figure is much greater than the 22,600 of v. 2, it must reflect the population of a much later time, perhaps as late as the period just before the fall of Samaria in 722 B.C. At that time, Issachar would have had its largest population.

7:6–12 The chronicler recounted the genealogies of **Benjamin** in some detail because King Saul was a Benjamite (7:6–12; 8:1–40; 9:35–44). Saul was an important figure even though his reign ended tragically. The complexity of the biblical genealogies can be illustrated by comparing the list of Benjamin's sons here with that in 8:1, 2; Gen. 46:21; Num. 26:38, 39. The differences in these genealogies are most likely due to the listing of principal descendants of different time periods.

7:13 The unusual brevity of the genealogy here may reflect the greatly reduced size and importance of **Naphtali** following the maraudings of the Assyrians under Tiglath-Pileser III. Naphtali's tribal area was specifically pointed out as the object of the Assyrian campaigns (2 Kin. 15:29).

7:14 Manasseh was the son of Joseph. **Machir:** Machir's daughter became the wife of Judah's grandson Hezron, thus joining the two tribes of Manasseh and Judah (2:21).

7:15–19 If the **Huppim** and **Shuppim** here are the same as in v. 12, the tribe of Manasseh and the tribe of Benjamin were connected through the marriage of Machir and **Maachah. Zelophehad:** Apparently a grandson of Gilead (Num. 26:30–33), this man had no sons. This situation prompted Moses to announce God's provision for the inheritance rights of daughters in such cases (Num. 36:1–9).

7:20–22 The genealogy of **Ephraim** follows the genealogy of his brother Manasseh. **Tahath:** This name and **Shuthelah** both occur twice, illustrating the custom of sons being named for their grandfathers or more remote ancestors. **The men of Gath** were probably the pre-conquest Philistines (see Gen. 21:32, 34; Ex. 13:17). Since the story involves Ephraim's sons in particular and not just the tribe of Ephraim, this verse establishes that Jacob's family before the Exodus had not completely lost contact with the land of Canaan.

7:23, 24 Lower and Upper Beth Horon: These places were in Ephraim near the border with Benjamin.

7:25–27 The fact that there were nine generations between **Joshua,** the famous successor to Moses, and Ephraim (vv. 23–27) supports the view that the story in vv. 21, 22 occurred before the Exodus.

7:28, 29 children of Joseph: As this phrase makes clear, vv. 28, 29 include the cities of both Ephraim and Manasseh. The cities of Beth Shean, Taanach, Megiddo, and Dor were located in Manasseh.

7:30–39 Asher: This is the last tribal genealogy in 1 Chronicles. It may be compared with the genealogies of Asher in Gen. 46:17; Num. 26:44–46.

7:40 twenty-six thousand: This number of fighting men would place the completion of this genealogy in the period of David, as stated in v. 2.

8:1, 2 The reason for this second and much more detailed genealogy of **Benjamin** was its climactic focus on the genealogy of King Saul (vv. 29–40).

8:3–8 A grandson of Jediael (see 7:10) or Ashbel (see 7:6), **Ehud** apparently was the link between Benjamin and Saul. The sons of Ehud moved the Benjamites from **Geba** to **Manahath.** The former town was a Benjamite site on the border of Judah, about six miles northeast of Jerusalem.

8:9–11 There was a well-known Moabite king named **Mesha.** Both the Scriptures (2 Kin. 3:4) and the Moabite Stone attest to this fact. The reference here to Mesha as a son of Shaharaim and Hodesh, a Moabite wife (see v. 8), suggests that the illustrious

Moabite king may have had a Benjamite father, but the evidence is not conclusive.

8:12 Ono and Lod were ancient towns southeast of Joppa. The sons of Elpaal probably rebuilt these ancient cities.

8:13–27 Aijalon and **Gath** were two places in the western lowlands of Israel, about seventeen miles apart.

8:28 These dwelt in Jerusalem: This means that the last generation in the preceding genealogy lived in Jerusalem. This city was not taken by David until approximately 1004 B.C., so the line of Benjamin was traced to at least that time. Moreover, the fact that David succeeded Saul did not mean that all Benjamites were excluded from Jerusalem or for that matter from David's favor. For example, David was careful to attend to Jonathan's survivors (2 Sam. 9:1–13), and he gave other Benjamites positions of responsibility in his new government (11:31; 12:1–7, 29).

8:29 A comparison of this genealogy (vv. 29–40) with that of 9:35–44 shows that the **father of Gibeon** was Jeiel. The city of **Gibeon** was a prominent city that existed long before this time, as the conquest narrative makes plain (Josh. 9:1–27).

8:30, 31 Kish was the father of Saul (v. 33; 9:39). In this passage the relationship between Jeiel and Kish is unclear, because Kish is also named as the son of Ner (v. 33). However, in 9:35–39 the lineage is clearly traced from Jeiel to Ner to Kish and finally to Saul.

8:32 Since Saul was not yet born at this point in the genealogy, the **Jerusalem** here is the city of pre-Davidic times. Jerusalem remained under Jebusite control until David conquered it (2 Sam. 5:6–10). Perhaps at this time the Benjamites lived among the Jebusites.

8:33 Abinadab was eventually killed with his father on the battlefield at Gilboa (see 10:2; 1 Sam. 31:2). **Esh-Baal** evidently was Saul's youngest son, since he was not named in the genealogies of the beginning of Saul's reign (1 Sam. 14:49). He succeeded Saul as king of the northern kingdom after the five-year period in which Abner was in charge (2 Sam. 2:10; 5:4, 5). The pagan name Esh-Baal demonstrates the degree to

which Saul had succumbed to religious syncretism.

8:34–40 The same pagan tendency appears in the name of Jonathan's son. **Merib-Baal** means something like "Baal Is My Advocate."

9:1 The **book** or scroll mentioned here was not the canonical books of Kings, because those contain no genealogies. The reference must be to genealogical sources compiled and collected by the scribes of the kings of Israel. **carried … to Babylon:** This reference to the Babylonian captivity prepares the way for the genealogies and lists that follow (vv. 3, 4).

9:2 Israelites: The deportation of Israel by the Assyrians from 734 to 722 B.C. resulted in Israel's dispersion throughout the eastern Mediterranean world. However, it is apparent from this verse that some of them joined their Judean brethren in the return from Babylon after 539 B.C. The word **Nethinim,** derived from the Hebrew verb "to give" and thus meaning "the ones given," refers to temple slaves. Since the Nethinim were distinct from the **priests** and **Levites,** these temple slaves must have been from other tribes (see Ezra 2:43; 7:7; Neh. 7:46, 60, 73; 10:28).

9:3 Ephraim and Manasseh: These two tribes descended from Joseph and were especially blessed by the Lord (Gen. 49:22–26; Deut. 33:13–17). However, these two tribes did not belong to the nation of Judah. This is another confirmation that the community included Israelites as well as Judeans.

9:4–16 The normal pattern of dividing the genealogy of the **Levites** according to the three sons of Levi is not followed here (see 6:1). Rather, there are seven families listed in vv. 14–16, six of them living in Jerusalem and the seventh in Netophah. **Merari** is mentioned, but not Kohath or Gershon. In place of Gershon stands his descendant **Asaph** (6:39–43). **Jeduthun:** This is another name for Ethan, descendant of Merari (6:44–47). Both vv. 14 and 16 appear to list Merarites. **Elkanah:** The presence of this name suggests that this family is Kohathite (6:33–38). **Netophathites:** This refers to the inhabitants of the village of Netophah, a little over three miles southeast of Bethlehem. The Gershonites and Merarites evidently lived in Jerusalem in the postexilic period, while the Kohathite or the Korahite Levites lived in Netophah.

9:17, 18 King's Gate on the east: This was the famous gate just east of the temple (Ezek. 46:1, 2). After the days of the wilderness tabernacle (Num. 3:27–31), and since the time of Zechariah and the temple of Solomon (v. 21; see 26:1, 2, 14), the Korahites had been responsible for keeping the gates and attending to the place of worship.

9:19–21 As descendants of Kohath (Ex. 6:18, 21), **Korah** and his line had close connections with the priesthood. However, they could not be priests since they were descended from Izhar rather than Amram. Their close connection explains why these particular Levites ministered within the precincts of the temple.

9:22–24 The **gatekeepers** had been appointed in the days of **David and Samuel** (see 26:1–19). Since Samuel died long before David made his appointments, the chronicler must be saying that David was encouraged and instructed by the prophet from the days of his youth. In a sense, Samuel **appointed** the gatekeepers through David.

9:25 The gatekeepers lived in villages surrounding Jerusalem (v. 22). They came to Jerusalem on a rotating schedule to attend to their temple duties, serving for periods of **seven days.**

9:26 chief gatekeepers: Since there were four sides to the city and temple (v. 24) and four main gates, there must also be four **Levites** responsible for the oversight of these portals. They opened and closed the gates and provided security (v. 27). However, they also oversaw all the various rooms and other facilities of the temple. **treasuries:**

 IN DEPTH | **The Arameans**

Some of the forces opposing general Joab were Syrians (1 Chr. 9:10), members of an ethnic group also known as the Arameans. They controlled the region northeast of the Sea of Galilee, from the Lebanon Mountains on the west to the Euphrates River on the east and northward. Their principal city was Damascus.

The Arameans were among the ancient peoples believed to have migrated into the Middle East from the west as early as 2250 B.C. They became fully established as a kingdom during the period of the Israelites' conquest of Canaan (c. 1200 B.C.). During the period of the judges, they overran Israel and oppressed it for eight years (Judg. 3:8–10). However, after David became king of Israel, he extended his nation's boundary north to the Euphrates River (2 Sam. 8:1–13). It was at this time that an Aramean official named Rezon fled to Damascus and founded a strong Aramean city-state there (1 Kin. 11:23, 24). This kingdom remained a bitter foe of Israel for many generations.

One strategy that the Arameans used to advantage was to side with one Israelite state or the other during the divided monarchy (15:18–20; 2 Kin. 16:5). However, when Judah eventually joined with Assyria against Israel and Aram in the eighth century B.C., the result was the downfall of Damascus (c. 732 B.C.; 16:7–18). Many Arameans were exiled to other lands, as was the Assyrian policy, and the kingdom of Aram came to an end.

Nevertheless, through their language the Arameans left behind a legacy that can still be felt today. Aramaic, which had been spoken from at least 2000 B.C., eventually became the language of trade, commerce, and diplomacy throughout the ancient Middle East. As a result, Aramaic (a language closely related to Hebrew) came to have an important influence on the Bible. Portions of the Book of Daniel were written in Aramaic, and it was the language commonly spoken by Jews in Palestine during the time of Jesus.

This referred to the places where money was kept and to storage rooms in general.

9:27–29 they lodged: Whereas the Levites who tended the gates lived in surrounding villages, those in charge must have lived in the city, probably near the gates of the temple. They had to be nearby in order to supervise temple affairs, including the **opening** and closing of the gates.

9:30–32 Although the Levites could handle such matters as the serving vessels (v. 28), furnishings, implements, and even materials for an offering (such as flour, wine, incense, and spices, v. 29), they were not allowed to prepare the **ointment of the spices.** This was reserved for the priests alone, as Ex. 30:23–25, 33, 37, 38 states.

9:33, 34 The head **singers,** like the chief gatekeepers (vv. 26, 27), lived in Jerusalem to be constantly on hand to supervise the ministry of the temple musicians.

9:35–44 The interest the chronicler has in the genealogy of **Jonathan** probably springs from Jonathan's close friendship with David (1 Sam. 18:1).

10:1 Some 1,700 feet in elevation, **Mount Gilboa** lies in the southeastern part of the plain of Jezreel. This was Philistine territory from the time they arrived there in about 1200 B.C.

10:2, 3 Saul's sons: There was a fourth son, Ishbosheth. He survived this battle and became king of Israel five years after Saul's death.

10:4, 5 Most Semites practiced circumcision for either hygienic or religious purposes, but for the Hebrews it was the sign of God's promise through Abraham to them. The **uncircumcised** were those outside, often their enemies the Philistines. **abuse:** The Philistines could not only harm Saul personally, but bring shame on the nation that had him as their leader. Saul was driven to an extreme course of action.

10:6 all his house died: This statement was written in anticipation of the death of Ishbosheth, the last of Saul's sons. With Ishbosheth's death (see 2 Sam. 4:5, 7), Saul's dynasty came to an end.

10:7–9 Though the **Philistines** had long dominated the Jezreel-Esdraelon Valley,

there were Israelite cities in the region for some time. With Saul's death, even these were lost to the Philistines, who took them over when the Israelites abandoned them.

10:10 Dagon was worshiped by the Philistines and other peoples in Syria and northwest Mesopotamia as the god of grain.

10:11 Jabesh Gilead was just east of the Jordan River, not far from Beth Shan. The care the people of this town took in retrieving Saul's corpse from Beth Shan was doubtless in memory of Saul's quick response to their cry for help early in his reign (1 Sam. 11:1–11).

10:12, 13 Saul's untimely death was the result of disobedience to God's **word.** He had disobeyed God by not waiting for Samuel to perform a sacrifice and by not utterly destroying the Amalekites (1 Sam. 13:1–15; 15:10–23). **consulted a medium:** Before the battle, Saul had asked for Samuel's advice through the witch of En Dor (1 Sam. 28:3–25).

10:14 He killed him: This statement is shocking in its bluntness. In the final analysis, Saul's death was not by his own hand but by the hand of God. The Lord let Saul pursue a course that led to death.

11:1, 2 Hebron was a Levitical city (6:54, 55). David made it his capital following Saul's death (2 Sam. 2:3) and reigned there until Ishbosheth's death seven years later (2 Sam. 4:1–12; 5:5). David's legitimacy as successor to Saul was confirmed by the support he received from **all** the tribes. **You shall ... be ruler:** The crowds were very much aware of the promise God had made to David (1 Sam. 16:12; 24:20; 28:17).

11:3 The **covenant** refers to mutual pledges made between a king and his people, ensuring stable and successful government. The Law of Moses made provision for such a covenant (see Deut. 17:18–20). **according to ... Samuel:** Years before, Samuel had anointed David (1 Sam. 16:1, 3, 12, 13). This second anointing confirmed the first one.

11:4 Jebus was another name for Jerusalem. The name was coined by the Israelites because the city belonged to the **Jebusites.**

11:5 Another name for Jerusalem was **Zion.** The original Canaanite city, surrounded by high, thick walls, was considered a stronghold. After David took the city and made it his capital, it became known as **the city of David.** When the temple was built on Mount Moriah (2 Chr. 3:1), a hill just north of the city, that area and sometimes the whole city was called Mount Zion.

11:6, 7 The stronghold of Zion (11:5) seemed impregnable until **Joab** found a means of access. As a result, Joab was rewarded with the command of Israel's army.

11:8, 9 Once David occupied Mount Ophel, the original and very small area of Jerusalem, he enlarged it by building retaining walls along the Kidron valley to the east and south and the Tyropoeon valley to the west. Between these walls and the top of the hill he built terraces, so that various buildings could be constructed there.

11:10–12 the mighty men: This phrase applied to three persons, Jashobeam, Eleazar (v. 12), and Shammah (see 2 Sam. 23:11, 12). They were distinguished for their bravery and their service to David. Joab, already singled out as "chief" (v. 6), was above them in rank. **Jashobeam:** This first of the mighty men, known in 2 Sam. 23:8 as Josheb-Basshebeth, showed his heroism by slaying **three hundred** of the enemy single-handed.

11:13–15 Another elite group of **three,** not named in this episode, penetrated the defenses of the Philistines. **The cave of Adullam** was about 12 miles southwest of Bethlehem and was one of David's favorite hiding places in the days of his flight from Saul (1 Sam. 22:1).

11:16–19 David would not drink it: This was not an act of ingratitude. To the contrary, David expressed his deep appreciation. His men had risked their lives to bring water to David, and now in the face of their selflessness he felt unworthy to drink it. He **poured it out to the LORD** as though it were an offering of blood (v. 19).

11:20 Abishai was a brother of **Joab** and a son of David's sister Zeruiah (2:16). Like Joab, Abishai was chief over other warriors because of his great exploits.

11:21, 22 the first three: This refers to Jashobeam, Eleazar (vv. 11, 12), and Shammah. Chronicles does not mention

the third one by name (see 2 Sam. 23:11, 12) but does acknowledge his existence (v. 12).

11:23 Five cubits was about seven and one-half feet.

11:24 three mighty men: Only Abishai and Benaiah were named as members of this group.

11:25 The next level below Joab, the commander, and the two groups of "three mighty men" was **the thirty.** Their names appear in vv. 26–47 and also in 2 Sam. 23:24–39. The term *thirty* may denote an elite military unit that consisted of approximately thirty men. The term does not indicate a literal number, because the list in vv. 26–47 includes more than thirty names.

11:26–38 Asahel was the third son of David's sister Zeruiah (2:16). Apparently he was not one of the "three mighty men," but his position as first in the list of "the thirty" suggests that he had a high rank.

11:39–40 Ammonite: Some of David's heroes were not Israelites. They may have been immigrants or mercenaries.

11:41 Uriah the Hittite: The irony of including this warrior in the list is obvious from the story of his death at the hands of David and Joab (2 Sam. 11:6–17).

11:42–47 Adina the Reubenite also appears to have led a group of the **thirty.** Though there are only sixteen names from Zabad through Jaasiel (vv. 41, 47), these sixteen might have formed the nucleus of such a military unit.

12:1 Ziklag became David's private possession. He received it after he had crossed over into Philistia to get away from Saul and had placed himself under the lordship of Achish, the ruler of the city-state of Gath (1 Sam. 27:1–7). As an ally and vassal of Achish, David was required to pay tribute and show his loyalty and submission. Therefore, he made raids from Ziklag against various desert tribes, seizing their properties and bringing some of the plunder back to the Philistines. David was joined at Ziklag by many other "outlaws" and refugees from Judah until he had a sizable number of **mighty men** there (1 Sam. 27:8–12).

12:2, 3 Included among his warriors were

ambidextrous Benjamites, some of Saul's own fellow tribesmen. This shows the extent of dissatisfaction with Saul's rule.

12:4, 5 This may suggest that the Benjamites listed here formed a unit known technically as **the thirty** (see 11:25), although not exactly thirty names are recorded here.

12:6, 7 Since the other heroes such as the Gibeathite in v. 3 were listed by their place of origin, Korah was probably the name of a place in Benjamin. These **Korahites** should not be confused with the Levites of that name (9:19).

12:8–13 David had attracted a following from all over Israel. The **Gadites** came from the far northern and central areas east of the Jordan River (5:11–17) to join him. **The stronghold** was the cave of Adullam, David's principal place of refuge in the Judean wilderness (see 11:15; 1 Sam. 22:1).

12:14 hundred ... thousand: These were terms for military units which may or may not have had precisely that many men. The Gadites were so famous for their valor and leadership skills (v. 8) that they rose to high ranks in David's army.

12:15–17 The **first month** was Nisan, corresponding approximately to April. This was the time of the spring rains (Deut. 11:14), when the rivers were often at flood stage (see Josh. 3:13; 4:18, 19). Ordinarily a person could not cross the Jordan River at such times, but the Gadites were not deterred by such obstacles. They crossed the flooded Jordan pursuing their enemies in all directions.

12:18 Amasai was probably an alternative spelling of Amasa, the son of David's sister Abigail (2:17). He became David's army commander after Joab had fallen from favor (2 Sam. 19:13), but he held the post for only a short time before being assassinated by Joab (2 Sam. 20:4–13).

12:19, 20 Manasseh defected: This incident reveals how compromised David's position was when he, as vassal to Achish of Gath (see v. 1), was pressed into joining the **Philistines** against Saul at Gilboa (1 Sam. 29:1–11). As it turned out, the other Philistine rulers outvoted Achish and sent David back to Ziklag before he had to go to war against his Israelite countrymen.

12:21 When David returned to Ziklag, he found that Amalekites had attacked the city and carried off his family with other prisoners (1 Sam. 30:1). Those who had abandoned David in his march to Gilboa (v. 19) now joined him in his pursuit of these **raiders** (1 Sam. 30:2–25).

12:22–27 The **army of God** refers to the angelic hosts, too vast to count. David attracted so many recruits while he was in the wilderness in flight from Saul and at Ziklag that they were beyond counting.

12:28 This **Zadok,** apparently an Aaronite (v. 27) and therefore a priest, was probably the same Zadok who was first appointed by David as priest at Gibeon (16:39), and then by Solomon at Jerusalem (1 Kin. 2:26, 27, 35). The office of priest was not incompatible with that of warrior, as Phinehas clearly demonstrated (Num. 25:6–9; Josh. 22:30).

12:29–39 eating and drinking: Besides the normal festivity that accompanied such a grand occasion as the installation of a king, this phrase alludes to a covenant meal (Gen. 31:43–55; Ex. 24:11)—a meal that solemnized a covenant between David and the people (11:3).

12:40 Issachar, Zebulun, and **Naphtali** were geographically the most distant of the tribes. The phrase **near to them** was a way of speaking of the common identity of God's people.

13:1, 2 David consulted: Though David was king and therefore could have acted independently, he understood the importance of godly counsel. He sought the advice of his subordinate leaders.

13:3 This **ark** was the ark of the covenant that contained a copy of the Ten Commandments (Ex. 25:10–22). **since the days of Saul:** During Saul's reign, the people of Kirjath Jearim had kept the ark in their city for safekeeping. Besides holding the Ten Commandments and serving as a throne for God, the ark represented the presence of the living God among the Israelites. David wanted to unify the Israelites around their God, so he brought the ark to the nation's new political center, Jerusalem.

13:4 Again the chronicler highlighted the unity of the nation by saying that **all the**

people agreed with David's decision to bring the ark to Jerusalem.

13:5 Shihor in Egypt: This was another way of referring to the Wadi el-Arish or "River of Egypt" that marked the boundary between Egypt and Canaan. This was Israel's most southwestern point (see Num. 34:5; Josh. 13:3). **entrance of Hamath:** This was the most northern point of the kingdom under David, about one hundred miles north of the Sea of Galilee.

13:6 A major feature of the Most Holy Place in both the tabernacle and temple was the **ark.** Above and behind the ark of the covenant, **cherubim** extended their wings over the cover (also called the mercy seat) of the ark (Ex. 25:17–22). The glory of God was perceived as sitting upon the top of the ark as a king sat on a throne.

13:7, 8 Only the Levites **carried the ark.** They carried it on their shoulders with poles passing through rings on the ark's corners (Num. 4:1–16).

13:9 Chidon's threshing floor is also called "Nachon's threshing floor" (2 Sam. 6:6). A threshing floor was a flat rocky surface on which grain was crushed by threshing sledges drawn by oxen. The floor was probably in or near Kirjath Jearim.

13:10 God struck Uzza dead because of the sacred inviolability of the ark. It was a holy object, representing the presence of God Himself (Ex. 25:21, 22), so it had to be handled in accord with the strictest regulations (Num. 4:5). Handling the ark in any other way, even with the best intention, invited God's anger (Num. 4:15).

13:11, 12 The threshing floor of Chidon was renamed **Perez Uzza,** meaning "Outburst Against Uzza." From that time forward, the name of this place would remind people that violating God's holiness meant inviting His wrath.

13:13, 14 A **Gittite** means someone from Gath, the name of several cities. Since **Obed-Edom** was a Levite (15:18, 24), he was probably from the Levitical city of Gath Rimmon in Dan (Josh. 21:25).

14:1, 2 A powerful ruler of the Phoenician city-state of Tyre, **Hiram king of Tyre** was a contemporary of both David and Solomon.

His work for David, constructing a royal palace, must have begun late in David's reign. Moreover, Hiram supplied material for the temple and other buildings, a project not completed until Solomon's twentieth year (1 Kin. 9:10). **build him a house:** Once a king in the ancient Middle Eastern world had firmly established himself, he built a palace to publicize that fact. David built his palace with the understanding that God alone had put him in power and **exalted** him.

14:3 In addition to the wives he had taken in Hebron (2 Sam. 3:2–5), **David** married others in **Jerusalem.** Although the Bible never justifies polygamy, ancient kings frequently undertook multiple marriages for political reasons. A king would marry the daughter of another king in order to create a stronger alliance.

14:4 The four **children** listed here were all sons of Bathshua (Bathsheba; see 3:5).

14:5–9 the Valley of Rephaim: This was the scene of many battles between Israel and the Philistines (11:15, 16; see 2 Sam. 5:17–22; 23:13–17). The conflict here was a preemptive strike by the Philistines designed to prevent David from taking Jerusalem and making it the capital of Israel (11:4–9).

14:10–15 God has gone out before you: The strategy for this battle was different (vv. 10, 14) because God wanted David to understand that the battle was His, not David's.

14:16, 17 Gibeon was about six miles northwest of Jerusalem, and **Gezer** was about sixteen miles west of Gibeon. The Philistines evidently left the Valley of Rephaim, fled north to Gibeon, and then were pursued all the way to Gezer, a town close to their own territory.

15:1 The **place for the ark** was in the tabernacle in the City of David. The original tabernacle built in Moses' day had been placed at Shiloh, in central Manasseh (Josh. 18:1). It remained there until the capture of the ark by the Philistines (1 Sam. 4:1–11), when it evidently was moved to Nob, just two miles from Jerusalem (1 Sam. 21:1–6). Next, the tabernacle was moved to a high place at Gibeon (2 Chr. 1:3), about two miles north of Saul's city Gibeah. When David became king, he left the Mosaic tabernacle at Gibeon and appointed the priest Zadok to attend to its ministry (16:39). Even after he had built a new tabernacle on Mount Zion and brought the ark into it, the original tabernacle remained at Gibeon. Finally, Solomon brought the ark from Mount Zion and the "tabernacle of meeting" (the tabernacle of Moses) from Gibeon and stored them in the new temple (2 Chr. 5:4, 5). The **tent** of David was a transitional home for the ark between the wilderness tabernacle and Solomon's temple.

15:2–4 Having learned his lesson from the incident with Uzza (13:10), David commanded that the **ark of God** be moved this time according to the provisions of the Law. It was to be carried by **Levites** by means of poles inserted through corner rings (Num. 4:14, 15).

15:5–7 David divided the Levites into divisions according to their genealogies. **Uriel** was head of the Kohathite clan (6:24), Asaiah was chief of the Merarites (6:30), and Joel was leader of the Gershonites (23:8).

15:8–10 All three of the following families were subclans of the Kohathites. **Elizaphan** was a grandson of Kohath (Ex. 6:18, 22), **Hebron** was a son of Kohath (Ex. 6:18), and **Uzziel** was another son of Kohath (Ex. 6:18).

15:11–16 The transition from the rule of Saul to David involved a transition from the old Mosaic tabernacle to the new place David had established on Mount Zion in preparation for the temple (see v. 1). The father of **Abiathar,** the priest Ahimelech, was in charge of the old tabernacle when it left Shiloh and was moved to Nob (1 Sam. 21:1). Ahimelech (also known as Ahijah; see 1 Sam. 14:3; 22:9) was Eli's greatgrandson. Eli must have been a descendant of Aaron's son Ithamar, for the priesthood was taken from his line and given to the line of Eleazar, another son of Aaron (6:3, 4; see 1 Sam. 2:22–36). The line of Eleazar produced **Zadok** (6:8).

15:17 The musician **Heman** was a grandson of the prophet Samuel (see 6:33), a Kohathite. He is probably the same Heman who appears in the superscription of Ps. 88. **Asaph** was

leader of the Gershonite Levites (6:39, 43). Asaph and his sons ministered primarily as singers (25:1, 2; 2 Chr. 20:14) and composers, as their superscriptions suggest (Pss. 50; 73—83). **Ethan** was the head of the Merarite division of musicians (6:44). Ethan might be the same as "Ethan the Ezrahite," composer of Ps. 89 and known as a wise man (1 Kin. 4:31).

15:18, 19 second rank: The musicians apparently occupied a place of higher status than the gatekeepers, who are mentioned next (see 9:17–27).

15:20 strings according to Alamoth: The musicians listed here are the same as the gatekeepers of v. 18. Since gatekeeping was on a rotating basis and might not have required full-time attention, these two responsibilities could have been combined.

15:21, 22 The word **Sheminith** might be derived from the Hebrew word for "eighth," referring to the musical scales.

15:23 The responsibility of the **doorkeepers for the ark** appears limited to the task of moving the ark from the house of Obed-Edom to the Davidic tabernacle.

15:24–28 It is likely that **Obed-Edom** in this verse was the same person who had custody of the ark in the months just before it was brought to Jerusalem (13:13, 14).

15:29 David had married **Michal the daughter of Saul** at the beginning of his time of service in Saul's court (1 Sam. 18:27). Their relationship had been stormy, perhaps in part because David had spent at least ten years in flight from her father. For the transfer of government from Saul to David to be complete, it was necessary for Saul's daughter to be transferred back to David—even against her will. When Michal saw David rejoicing at the return of the ark, she despised him out of loyalty to her father and anger that she had been forced to return.

16:1–3 he distributed: David's distribution of food was in line with the nature of the peace offerings of vv. 1, 2. Such offerings often accompanied occasions of praise and thanksgiving such as this one. They provided a common meal in which all participated—the offerer, his family and friends, the priests, and even God (Lev. 7:11–14, 28–34; Deut. 12:17–19).

16:4–6 The appointment of **Levites** described here was of a more permanent nature than that of 15:1–24, which concerned the immediate task of moving the ark into Jerusalem. Some of the same persons were involved, as vv. 5, 6 make clear.

16:7–11 This implies that David himself composed the **psalm.** David's musical abilities were well attested (2 Sam. 22:1; see the superscriptions of Ps. 3—9).

16:12 His marvelous works: David appealed to the nation to reflect upon God's faithfulness as manifested in the nation's history. The God who had proved Himself in the past was the One upon whom the unified nation could depend in the years to come.

16:13, 14 servant ... chosen ones: These words reflect the role of Israel as an elect nation called by God to serve Him as "a kingdom of priests and a holy nation" (Ex. 19:6). David was aware of the importance of God's calling of Israel and of his responsibility as leader of this privileged nation.

16:15 The instrument that bound God and Israel together legally and formally was the **covenant.** This was an arrangement between two parties—in this case, a superior party and an inferior party—by which the two made solemn pledges of mutual loyalty and commitment. God's promises in the covenant were based on His faithful character.

16:16–18 To **Abraham,** God promised land (Gen. 12:7) and innumerable descendants (Gen. 15:5; 17:5–8). God designated Abraham's descendants as the people through whom He would bless all nations (Gen. 12:2, 3). In his psalm, David was reflecting on the reliability of God's promise to Abraham—a promise renewed to Isaac and confirmed to Jacob. Having just become king over all Israel, David was aware of God's faithfulness in granting the Israelites the land over which he had dominion.

16:19 very few: This refers to the time of the patriarchs. When Jacob went to Egypt, his extended family consisted of only seventy persons (Gen. 46:27).

16:20, 21 one nation to another: In patriarchal times, God's people moved about in Canaan and occasionally lived among other peoples such as the Egyptians (Gen. 12:10), Philistines (Gen. 20:1; 21:34; 26:1), and even the Hittites (Gen. 23:4, 17–20). **reproved kings:** This is a reference to God's judgment on Pharaoh (Gen. 12:17) and particularly his rebuke of Abimelech, the Philistine king of Gerar (Gen. 20:3–7).

16:22–24 Abraham and the patriarchs were not literally anointed with oil as though they were entering the priesthood or kingship. In this context, **anointed ones** means those set apart for God's service. **prophets:** Though the office of prophet as a "professional" calling began with Samuel, there were individuals from the earliest days of biblical history who were known as prophets. The reference here is specifically to Abraham, who is called a *prophet* in Gen. 20:7.

16:25 above all gods: This refers to the various "gods" in which the pagans believed. The heathen might fear nonexistent gods, but the living Lord was to be feared more than them all.

16:26–32 The phrase, **the LORD reigns,** is an appeal for the universal recognition of the sovereignty of the God of Israel. The Lord had called Israel into a special covenant relationship with Himself, but He did not thereby reject the other nations. Indeed, the whole purpose of Israel's election was that Israel might be the light to the nations that would cause them to turn to the one true God (Is. 42:5–7; 43:8–13).

16:33–36 trees ... rejoice: This is a figure of speech called "personification," in which inanimate things are spoken of as if they had human characteristics. Because the whole creation was negatively affected by the fall of humanity into sin, it could not be restored to perfection and could not truly **rejoice** until humanity was redeemed.

16:37 David appointed **Asaph** to be the supervisor of worship before the Lord (see v. 5).

16:38 Obed-Edom: There are two men by this name in this verse. The first is the Obed-Edom whose house sheltered the ark for three months (13:14) and who was a chief doorkeeper (15:24). The second, also a gatekeeper, was a **son of Jeduthun** (perhaps the one known as Ethan; see 6:33, 39, 44).

16:39 Until the temple of Solomon was completed, there were two legitimate places for community worship—the Mosaic tabernacle at Gibeon and David's tabernacle on Mount Zion. **Zadok,** a descendent of Eleazar, served at Gibeon, while Abiathar, a descendant of Aaron, served at Jerusalem (see 15:11).

16:40 There must have been such an **altar** on Mount Zion, but the one at Gibeon was apparently considered more "official," no doubt because it had been built under Moses' leadership (2 Chr. 1:3, 5, 6). Zadok and his fellow priests officiated at the regular morning and evening sacrifices in Gibeon.

16:41 Jeduthun: This was probably another name for the musician Ethan, who is usually named together with Asaph and Heman (see 15:17, 19; 6:33, 39, 44).

16:42, 43 instruments of God: This expression refers to instruments that play songs or praises to God. It is difficult to overemphasize the importance of music in Old Testament worship. The Book of Psalms in itself and constant references to choral and orchestral ministry demonstrate the significance of music (9:33; 15:16–24; 16:4–6; 25:1–31).

17:1–4 Nathan the prophet: This is the first time in this book that a prophet's name appears. Nathan apparently served David and Solomon as a private chaplain or counselor. One of his written works, "the book of Nathan the prophet," provided a source for the composition of the books of Chronicles (29:29; 2 Chr. 9:29). A **house of cedar** indicates David's wealth, because cedar paneling was too expensive to be used in ordinary homes.

17:5 from tent to tent: This refers to the movement of God from the provisional "tabernacle of meeting" (Ex. 33:7), to the Mosaic tabernacle (Ex. 40:34–38), and then to the tabernacle David erected on Mount Zion (16:1).

17:6 In addition to having "lived" in modest surroundings, God had also "lived" like a nomad, as the house of worship moved from one place to another. In the time of the **judges,** the tabernacle was at Shiloh (Josh. 18:1) and possibly Nob (1 Sam. 21:1). Before that, it had wandered with Israel through the Sinai desert before being set up at Gilgal (Josh. 4:19; 5:10). At this time it resided at Gibeon.

17:7 In the ancient Middle East generally, kings were often compared to shepherds (Is. 44:28; Zech. 10:3; 11:4–17). It was most fitting that David, who had literally shepherded **sheep,** should be called by God to shepherd His flock, Israel.

17:8 made you a name: David's reputation as a leader had become internationally known. He ranked with the great rulers of other nations.

17:9 appoint a place: This phrase did not suggest that Israel would move to a land other than Palestine, for that was the land of promise from the beginning. **sons of wickedness:** This was a general term for the Israelites' enemies—those who had persecuted them and taken them from their homeland.

17:10–12 As used here, **house** meant dynasty. David had said that he would build a house—that is, a temple—for God, but God told David that He would build a house—that is, a dynasty—for David. God's promise to establish David's dynasty forever was unprecedented.

17:13 Father ... son: This remarkable statement affirmed that the dynasty of David had such an intimate relationship with God that its kings would be considered God's sons in an extraordinary way.

17:14, 15 The focus clearly shifts here from David's immediate successor, Solomon, to the entire succession of kings in David's line. It was the **kingdom** and **throne** of the dynasty that would endure forever, a promise made possible only by the reign of Jesus Christ, the Son of David (Luke 1:32, 33).

17:16–18 house: David asked what made him the object of God's grace. He did not have any credentials to deserve God's amazing promises of an eternal kingdom. **small thing:** David's lack of pedigree and royal ancestry were of no consequence to God, because He was not impressed by such things. **What more can David say:** Once the truth of the promise sank into David's understanding, he found himself speechless.

17:19, 20 any God besides you: This is a clear assertion of the uniqueness of Israel's God. Statements such as "all gods" and "the gods of the peoples" in David's song of thanksgiving (16:25, 26) must be understood in light of this clear confession that there is only one living God.

17:21 As David continued to praise God, he expressed a theology of the election of Israel. God had chosen Israel, His treasured possession, by His will alone. The Israelites had nothing by which they could commend themselves to God. In fact, they were an insignificant and enslaved people (Deut. 7:6–11). Israel's prominent place among the nations was due to the Lord's abundant mercy.

17:22 Your very own people: This expression is clearly based on Ex. 19:5; Deut. 7:6; 14:2, where Israel is described as "a special treasure." The statement lies at the very center of the Mosaic covenant. At Mount Sinai, God had become the God of Israel; and Israel, in turn, had become the people of God.

17:23–27 the word which You have spoken: David's appeal to God to establish His word came immediately after his reference to the Exodus and the Mosaic covenant. David knew that God's covenant with him was founded on God's previous promises to Abraham.

18:1 This is the only record of David taking a Philistine city, although he had defeated the **Philistines** many times in battle. **Gath** was the Philistine city closest to Israelite territory, so it offered the greatest threat to Israel.

18:2 It must have been with mixed feelings that David undertook a campaign against the Moabites, for he had strong emotional links with **Moab.** His great-grandmother Ruth came from Moab (Ruth 4:13–17) and David had sent his own family there for protection when he was hiding from Saul (1 Sam. 22:3, 4).

18:3, 4 The campaign here may be connected to the Aramean war more fully outlined in 19:1–19, because **Hadadezer** is mentioned in both places. His kingdom, **Zobah,** lay immediately north of Damascus. David pursued

him as far as Hamath, a hundred miles beyond Damascus, in an effort to extend the Israelite empire all the way to the River Euphrates. David's justification may have been God's promise to Abraham that the land He was giving him would extend "from the river of Egypt to the great river, the River Euphrates" (Gen. 15:18).

18:5 The capital of the Aramean kingdom just north and northeast of Israel was **Damascus.**

18:6, 7 servants ... tribute: These technical terms, as in the case of Moab (v. 2), suggest that Damascus became a vassal state under Israel. Very quickly, Moab and Damascus became client states and Zobah an occupied territory.

18:8, 9 To the two cities **Tibhath ... Chun,** Samuel added a third Berothai (2 Sam. 8:8). All three are referred to in Egyptian texts. They were northeast of Baalbek in central Lebanon.

18:10 greet ... bless: This apparently casual language covers a more formal situation in which **Tou,** king of Hamath, was approaching David in willing submission to him as king. In other words, what Moab and Damascus did involuntarily, Hamath was doing voluntarily, making itself a vassal state under Israel.

18:11 The fact that David **dedicated** all the spoils of war to God suggests that he viewed the battles as campaigns of holy war. In such war, initiated and led by God, all proceeds of the victory belonged to Him. Such spoils were said to be "doomed to destruction" or "accursed" (Josh. 6:17, 18), meaning that they could not be used for secular purposes but were consecrated to God.

18:12 One of David's nephews (2:15, 16), **Abishai,** was included in one of the groups of David's "three mighty men" (11:20). **Valley of Salt:** This was a few miles east of Beersheba.

18:13, 14 The term **servants** suggests that Edom became not just a defeated foe, but also a vassal state under Israel's control. This allowed Edom to retain its own leadership, but it was under David's close supervision, as the reference to Israelite garrisons makes clear.

18:15 David awarded his nephew **Joab** (2:15, 16) the rank of commander of the **army** for his success in penetrating the walls of Jerusalem (11:4–9). **recorder:** Jehoshaphat was the keeper of the royal archives or records. The chronicler himself may have had access to such documents when he composed the present work (see 27:24).

18:16 Zadok descended from Aaron through Eleazar (16:39). **Abimelech:** Abiathar, a descendant of Aaron's son Ithamar, had served as David's priest in the wilderness (1 Sam. 22:20) and later at Jerusalem (15:11). But he was disloyal to Solomon and was removed from office, leaving Zadok alone as high priest (1 Kin. 2:27, 35).

18:17 Cherethites … Pelethites: These were elite companies of soldiers, probably mercenaries. They were commanded by Benaiah, a member of one of the groups of "three mighty men" (11:24). There were Philistines known as Cherethites (Ezek. 25:16; see 1 Sam. 30:14), and the connection between Pelethites and Philistines elsewhere (2 Sam. 15:18) leads to the conclusion that they were all from Philistia.

19:1–3 Since **Nahash** was reigning in Saul's earliest years (1 Sam. 11:1), the present incident must have occurred early in David's reign at Jerusalem. **Nahash** evidently reigned for over 50 years (40 years of Saul, plus seven of David in Hebron, plus whatever years had passed in Jerusalem).

19:4, 5 shaved … cut off: Ancient Semitic men were proud of their beards and scrupulously modest in their attire. The Ammonites humiliated David's men in the most offensive way possible.

19:6 made themselves repulsive: The Ammonites realized that David would surely retaliate for the way they had offended his delegation. **Mesopotamia:** This was not the great land between the Tigris and the Euphrates inhabited by the Assyrians and Babylonians, but a district on the upper Euphrates known as Aram Naharaim.

19:7 The parallel account in 2 Sam. 10:6 does not mention **chariots** but says there was a total of 33,000 men. The chronicler does not mention the number of men, but only the chariots. Both writers gave different sources of the manpower and material, so clearly they were arriving at their totals from different perspectives or with different purposes in mind. **Ammon gathered:** The Israelites were apparently between the Aramean armies and the city of Rabbah (see v. 10), so when the Ammonites attacked from the city, the Israelites were pinned between two forces.

19:8–10 Completely surrounded, Joab split up his forces so that half faced those **before** and half faced those **behind.** Joab led the section that opposed the Syrians, and Abishai commanded the section that opposed the Ammonites (v. 11).

19:11–13 may the LORD do what is good in His sight: Joab understood enough of the sovereignty and omniscience of God to know that after all human effort and energy had been expended, the battle was still God's.

19:14, 15 The Syrians were mercenaries and had no real commitment to the task at hand. When it appeared that they were in danger of defeat, they **fled.** Their retreat so demoralized the Ammonites that they withdrew into the safety of their city.

19:16–18 Samuel located the setting of the **battle** at Helam (2 Sam. 10:17), about 40 miles east of the Sea of Galilee.

19:19 The defeat of Hadadezer and all his vassal kings brought about a shift in allegiance, so that all the Aramean states that had paid tribute to Zobah came under tribute to Israel. In this context, **servants** did not signify household slaves but national subservience to a greater power, in this case Israel. This effectively eliminated all the Arameans as allies of Ammon and precluded their being a further threat to Israel. With the subjugation of everything from Aram Maachah to the Euphrates, David occupied all the boundaries of the land of promise as outlined in the Abrahamic covenant (Gen. 15:18–21).

20:1 Great military operations were conducted **in the spring of the year** for two main reasons: (1) the latter rains were over and the dry months of summer, most suitable for military activity, were at hand; and

(2) the barley harvests were in and the wheat harvests sufficiently well along to free men of military age for battle. **besieged Rabbah:** Having defeated the Aramean allies of Ammon at Helam (19:17, 19), Joab led Israel's armies against the main enemy and principal objective, the capital of the Ammonite kingdom, Rabbah. **David stayed at Jerusalem:** This agrees with Samuel's account, but Samuel also related the sordid story of David's adultery with Bathsheba, the plot to kill her husband Uriah, and the birth of David's son—all of which took place while Joab was laying siege to Rabbah.

20:2 David did not participate in the initial attack on Rabbah, but he did join Joab when it fell, because Joab earnestly entreated him to come share the credit for the victory (2 Sam. 12:27, 28). The **crown** David took was ceremonial and not for wearing, since it weighed a **talent** (about 75 pounds). **set on David's head:** This was only for this ceremonial occasion. David put the crown on his head to demonstrate that he had vanquished the Ammonites and now reigned over them as well.

20:3 It was common in Old Testament times for **people** defeated in war to be consigned to forced labor, particularly if they had been coerced into some kind of vassal relationship (see Josh. 9:22–27; 1 Kin. 9:20, 21).

20:4, 5 The city of **Gezer** was on the frontier between Israel and Philistia, and was constantly a bone of contention between them. **Sibbechai the Hushathite:** He was one of the thirty warriors who formed an elite corps (see 11:29). **the giant:** This apparently did not refer to a single individual, but to a giant race indigenous to the country east of the Jordan River (Deut. 2:10, 11, 20, 21).

20:6, 7 Shimea: This was David's older brother, the third son of Jesse (2:13).

20:8 the giant: As in v. 4, this likely referred to a giant race living in and around **Gath,** though it is possible that a particular giant was in view. The Goliath killed by David was from Gath (1 Sam. 17:4).

21:1 The word **Satan** means "Adversary." While at first he was called "the Satan," this later came to be used as a proper name, Satan (see Zech. 3:1, 2). The New Testament identifies him as the evil one, the devil, and the dragon, thus linking him to the serpent in the Garden of Eden (Gen. 3:1). **moved David:** Samuel attributed David's impulse to number the people to God Himself (2 Sam. 24:1). The apparent contradiction can be resolved by recognizing that though Satan is the author of all evil, he cannot exercise his evil intentions apart from the permission of God. Moreover, God could use him to accomplish His own purposes of judgment (1 Kin. 22:19–23) or discipline (as here with David).

21:2 Go, number: David's plan to take a census was not evil in itself, for the Lord Himself at other times had commanded the Israelites to be counted (see Num. 1). What was wrong with David's census was David's attitude—his pride. He wanted to **know** the number of the Israelites so that he could glory in the extent of his reign (see 2 Sam. 24:1).

21:3–5 Joab was concerned that David's arrogant command for a census would bring punishment, not only on the king but on innocent citizens, whom Joab described as David's **servants.** David's position as king and shepherd of his people implicated them in whatever he did. **cause of guilt:** Joab pointed out that if David's decision was put into effect David would be personally accountable for whatever followed.

21:6, 7 The men of **Levi,** dedicated as they were to priestly service, were ordinarily exempt from military conscription (Num. 1:47–49). **Benjamin:** The reason this tribe was excluded may be that the judgment of God commenced before the task was completed (27:24). Perhaps Joab simply abandoned the task before he finished.

21:8 I have sinned: To his credit, David blamed no one but himself for the judgment of God that fell on the nation. He believed that if God would forgive him, the affliction of the nation would also cease.

21:9 Gad is the second prophet named in the book (see 17:1). Here the chronicler calls Gad a **seer,** a person who sees or receives revelations from the Lord.

21:10–12 I offer … three things: This is the only place in the Bible where God offers someone a choice of punishments.

21:13, 14 David knew that the Lord is merciful—a God who forgives. David's willingness to fall into **the hand of the LORD** demonstrated his complete trust in the grace of God. Even when God was punishing him, David trusted God rather than **man**—God's forgiving nature over any leniency people might offer.

21:15 God sent an angel to destroy Jerusalem, but when He saw David's repentance and heard his intercessory prayer (v. 17), He **relented.**

21:16 Sackcloth was a rough garment usually made of goat's hair (Is. 50:3), worn by mourners to express grief (1 Kin. 21:27; Is. 32:11). David and the elders of Israel were dressed in such a manner because of the terrible calamity brought on the nation by the plague.

21:17 By calling his people **sheep,** David was acknowledging himself as their shepherd (17:7). He was supposed to be the one who guided the flock to safety and security, but by his arrogance in numbering the people he had brought them harm.

21:18, 19 Building **an altar** in a time of judgment or impending judgment was for the purpose of offering propitiatory sacrifices. Sin had caused a breach between God and His people. The presentation of appropriate burnt offerings and peace offerings (v. 26) would be the occasion for reconciliation, as the Law explained (Num. 15:1–10). **threshing floor:** The altar was located precisely where the angel of the Lord stood with sword in hand to destroy Jerusalem (v. 15). This place of judgment would thereby become the place of grace and forgiveness.

21:20–23 Grant me … this threshing floor: David wanted the altar at precisely this place because this is where the angel stood with drawn sword (v. 15), and as was certainly known to David, this was where Abraham had prepared to offer Isaac as a sacrifice to God (Gen. 22:1, 2; see 2 Chr. 3:1). It is fitting that this holy place should be the site of an altar where David could make atonement for his sins and thus effect the withdrawal of the plague.

21:24 David again showed a clear perception of the essence of sacrifice. Until he owned what Ornan had, and until he had expended his own resources for it, he could not use it as an offering to God. **which costs me nothing:** While David could have rightfully accepted these gifts without paying for them, he felt that this would not suffice as sacrifice. A true sacrifice to God required labor and investment on David's part.

21:25 The chronicler referred to the price for the whole **place,** probably several acres of valuable property. The fact that the temple was later built here suggests a large area.

21:26, 27 Just as a three-year drought ended in the days of Elijah when the prophet called down **fire** on a sacrifice at Carmel (1 Kin. 18:38, 41), so the three-day plague God brought on Israel ended with the sacrifice at Ornan's threshing floor.

21:28 he sacrificed there: Once David saw that God had sanctified the spot by setting fire to the sacrifice, he continued to use the altar as a regular place of offering.

21:29 This verse teaches explicitly that the original **tabernacle** and **altar of the burnt offering** had not been destroyed when the ark was taken from Shiloh. The Old Testament account does not trace their movement fully after Shiloh, but they did end up at Nob and finally at Gibeon (see 15:1).

21:30 David could not go before it: It was David's custom to offer burnt offerings on the altar at Gibeon rather than on the one in Jerusalem. He did not dare go to Gibeon this time because of the judgment that God was about to pour out on the land. He understood that his offerings had to be offered where he was—at the threshing floor of Ornan.

22:1 This observation by David marks a significant turning point in the history of the central sanctuary. As long as the ark remained at Kirjath Jearim and the Mosaic tabernacle was at Nob and Gibeon, it was impossible for worship to be carried out in the manner originally intended. David had taken the first steps toward remedying that by bringing the ark to Jerusalem and placing it in a tent that he provided on Mount Zion. The **house of the LORD God** and the **altar**

of burnt offering would be built on the threshing floor of Ornan.

22:2, 3 The fact that David could not **build** the temple did not prevent him from providing building materials for the use of Solomon's craftsmen.

22:4 Cedar trees came from Lebanon, the principal supplier of timber in the ancient Middle Eastern world.

22:5–7 Solomon was born about halfway through David's reign. He reigned with his father for about two years (23:1; 28:1; 29:22). Since David was only beginning to gather building materials for the temple, Solomon could not have been over 18 years old. It was precisely because Solomon was so **young and inexperienced** that David found it necessary to provide guidance for his son.

22:8, 9 You have shed much blood: The reason that God did not allow David to build the temple comes to light—David was a man of war. Until the enemies of Israel were subdued and an era of peace inaugurated, God determined that He would not "live" in a temple. David's son Solomon would **be a man of rest;** that is, a king whose reign would be free from constant warfare. At that time of peace, God had resolved that a temple would be built for Himself.

22:10–12 Having just observed the youth and inexperience of Solomon (v. 5), David knew that his son needed **wisdom** more than any other single gift. **the law of the LORD:** This cannot be limited to only the sections of the Law pertaining to kingship (see Deut. 17:14–20), although this is the central focus. David must have had in mind the covenant of kingship to which he himself had subscribed when he became king at Hebron (11:3).

22:13–18 Rest, or peace, was a precondition for building the temple (22:8, 9). **subdued before the LORD:** In the final analysis, the conquest of the land begun in Joshua's time and completed under David, was a divine and not a human matter. The land was the Lord's and His people were His tenants. Therefore, only when God Himself brought the land into subjection would He authorize construction of a temple.

22:19 David's dreams and desires are encapsulated in this brief verse. At that time, the **sanctuary** was divided—at Gibeon and Mount Zion—and the ark was not united with the altar at Zion (see v. 1). More than anything else, David wanted the Israelites to worship the Lord as He had instructed them.

23:1, 2 made ... Solomon king: The phrasing suggests that this is an official appointment of Solomon to be coregent with David, a choice that had to be accepted and later ratified by the whole nation (see 29:22).

23:3 A Levite normally entered service at age 25 (Num. 8:24, 25). However, exceptions were made (Num. 4:3) to answer the needs of various time periods and ministries. Evidently in David's time enough Levites could be found aged **thirty** and over that there was no need to call younger Levites into service.

23:4–7 the work of the house of the LORD: The work clearly involved anything around the temple except the work of gatekeepers and musicians, who had their own divisions (v. 5). **officers and judges:** To provide ready access to the Levites in matters of religious questions and activities, six thousand Levites were distributed throughout the land (see 26:29–32), presumably in the Levitical cities (6:54–81).

23:8–13 give the blessing: This referred to the priestly benediction of Num. 6:24–26.

23:14 sons of Moses: Because the priesthood was limited to Aaron, brother of Moses, and his descendants, Moses and his sons could not have served as a priests. However, they could assume other responsibilities of Levites (see Judg. 18:30).

23:15–20 Uzziel was the fourth son of Kohath (v. 12). There were nine Kohathite divisions of Levites: two from Amram, one from Izhar, four from Hebron, and two from Uzziel.

23:21, 22 Eleazar, son of Mahli, left no sons, so his **daughters** married their cousins, **the sons of Kish.** This resulted in a merger of the two lines of Mahli into one, so there was only one Levitical division through this branch of the Merarites.

23:23 The Mushi branch of Merarites produced **three** Levitical divisions in David's temple organization, making four in all, including the one traced to Mahli.

23:24–26 These were the sons of Levi: All three Levitical lines resulted in a total of twenty-two divisions, nine Gershonite, nine Kohathite, and four Merarite (24:18; 25:31). **twenty years and above:** At the beginning of the lists of divisions, the minimum age of the Levites was thirty (v. 3). The number *twenty* here was not a contradiction, for as v. 27 makes clear, the lower age was set by David in his last words. It seems that as time went by even 38,000 Levites were not sufficient, so that within two years or so it was necessary to lower the minimum age requirement.

23:27–29 To free the priests for the work of offering sacrifices, the Levites prepared elements for the sacrificial ritual, such as **fine flour** and **unleavened cakes,** and in other ways assisted the prescribed services.

23:30 thank and praise: This ministry fell to the Levites engaged in choral and orchestral duties (25:1–31).

23:31 burnt offering: Though Levites outside the priestly line could not officiate at the sacrifices of the central sanctuary, they could assist the priests, for example by helping to skin the animal and cut it up. **Sabbaths:** The reason for the plural was not only because there were many Saturdays in a year, but other days as well could be called a "Sabbath." For example, the eighth day of the Feast of Tabernacles was considered a Sabbath no matter what day of the week it was (Lev. 23:39). **New Moons:** This referred to the first day of every month, otherwise known as the Feast of Trumpets (Num. 28:11–15). **set feasts:** These would be Passover and Unleavened Bread (Lev. 23:4–8), the Feast of Weeks or Pentecost (Lev. 23:9–22), and the Feast of Tabernacles (Lev. 23:33–43).

23:32 tabernacle of meeting: At this point the temple had not yet been built, so David's regulations for the Levites pertained to their service in the intermediate tabernacles at Gibeon and Mount Zion. **holy place:** This referred to the outer room of the tabernacle as opposed to the Most Holy Place, to which only the high priest had access.

24:1 In order for the priests to serve in rotation and have time off from their duties, they were assigned to shifts or **divisions.** For this rotation, David divided the priests by their lines of descent from Aaron (see v. 3).

24:2 Nadab and Abihu died: This referred to the incident in which these two sons of Aaron incurred the wrath of God by offering up incense kindled with improper fire, that is, fire that did not originate from God (Lev. 9:23–10:2).

24:3 The **Ahimelech** here was the son of Abiathar (see v. 6), the young priest of Nob who had joined David in the wilderness many years before (1 Sam. 22:20). It is clear from this passage that his ancestry was from Aaron through **Ithamar.**

24:4, 5 When the descendants of the two lines were identified, there were **sixteen** family divisions from Eleazar and only **eight** from Ithamar. This complicated the process of dividing the service assignments fairly. The solution was to assign the duties by casting lots.

24:6 Shemaiah … wrote them down: In order to arrange the schedule for the priests' service and to keep it functioning properly, it was necessary that records be kept of all the names of the Levites by family and the shifts they were to fill in their rotation.

24:7–9 first lot: Since Eleazar and Ithamar are mentioned in that order in v. 6, it may be assumed that this list of names gives first someone from Eleazar, next someone from Ithamar, and so on alternately through the list.

24:10–19 This **Abijah** may be the ancestor of Zacharias, father of John the Baptist, who is named in Luke 1:5.

24:20, 21 sons of Levi: The non-priestly Levites also were divided by clan to determine their service rotation. The first division is Kohath, whose name does not appear but is implied in the mention of his son Amram. **Jehdeiah** and **Isshiah,** who were direct descendants of Moses (23:14–17), were omitted from the earlier list of Levites (23:16, 17).

24:22–24 The **Izharites** were Kohathites (see 23:12). **Hebron** was the third of the Kohathite clans (see 23:12). **Uzziel** was the last division of the Kohathites (see 23:12).

24:25, 26 Founder of the entire clan that bears his name (see 23:6), **Merari** was the third son of Levi. **Jaaziah:** This descendant of Merari appears for the first time here.

24:27–31 To assure the fairness of the Levites' assignments, they were selected by their divisions through the casting of the sacred **lots** (see v. 5). **fathers ... younger brethren:** There was no age discrimination in the work and shifts allocated to each. All served equally no matter what their age or status.

25:1 The involvement of **captains of the army** in the selection of Levitical musicians may at first appear strange. However in the conduct of God's battles against those who opposed His people, music was frequently an important element. **prophesy:** The role of a prophet was not limited to prediction or proclamation in words. Any divinely authorized utterance or deed from a prophet was a form of prophesying.

25:2 according to the order of the king: This underscored the leading role David took in the religious life of the nation (see 23:27). Even as king, David ordered that proper worship be given to the Lord.

25:3–5 Like Nathan (17:1) and Gad (21:9), **Heman** enjoyed a close relationship to David. **fourteen sons and three daughters:** The sons were accounted for in vv. 4, 13, 23–31. The daughters were not named but clearly participated along with their brothers in the public worship of God.

25:6, 7 the authority of the king: Once more the chronicler insisted that even the religious life of the nation was under the king's supervision. Israel was a theocracy in which God was the ultimate King and therefore head over all aspects of national life.

25:8–31 small ... great ... teacher ... student: The equality of all these servants of God is seen in the equal distribution of their assignments, a principle that had determined the nature of the ministry of the priests as well (24:31).

26:1 There were four **divisions of the gatekeepers,** but they came from only two of the Levitical clans, Kohath and Merari.

26:2, 3 In both 9:21 and here, **Zechariah** is the son of Meshelemiah. This means that the lists of 9:17–27 and 26:1–19 refer to the same time and circumstances.

26:4, 5 This **Obed-Edom** was probably not the Obed-Edom of 13:14, but a gatekeeper, the son of Jeduthun (16:38).

26:6–9 The oldest son of Obed-Edom (v. 4), **Shemaiah,** gave rise to a subclan of gatekeepers whose total number is given in v. 8.

26:10–13 The foregoing list appears to have identified the head gatekeepers only, that is, the **chief men.** Like their Levitical brethren in music (25:7) and the priests (24:31), these officials served right along with the four thousand others who made up the whole contingent of gatekeepers (23:5). They were not excused from such work because of their leadership positions.

26:14 The **East Gate** was the most important because it led straight into the main entrance of the temple (see 9:17, 18). It was therefore assigned to Shelemiah (or Meshelemiah, v. 1) himself. **North Gate:** This was the responsibility of the oldest son of Shelemiah.

26:15 South Gate: Obed-Edom was in charge of the gate itself, and **his sons** (vv. 4, 5) took charge of the **storehouse.** This was undoubtedly the same as the treasuries (v. 20).

26:16–20 house of God: This likely referred to the storage area where regular tabernacle or temple paraphernalia were kept at hand for the worship services (see 9:28, 29). **dedicated things:** The second storehouse would contain the items taken as spoils of war that were used exclusively for holy purposes. David had already obtained a great amount of these (vv. 26–28).

26:21–24 The Levites listed in vv. 21–23 were in charge of the regular storehouse (v. 22; see 23:8). **Shebuel** seems to have had general oversight of the regular storehouse. The Gershonites and other Kohathites of vv. 21–23 were under his direction.

26:25 The descendants of **Eliezer** became directors of the second storehouse, that of "the dedicated things" (v. 20). All the Levites who attended to the affairs of the tabernacle and temple treasuries traced their lineage back to Moses.

26:26, 27 The treasuries of the dedicated things fell under **Shelomith's** jurisdiction.

These spoils of war were kept in storage until they could be used in the building and decoration of the temple (22:14; 29:2; 2 Chr. 5:1).

26:28 Showing the long-standing commitment of the nation to build and furnish the house of God, the chronicler listed leaders of the past who had **dedicated** spoils of war as readily as David had done.

26:29, 30 This third Kohathite clan was responsible specifically for Israel **on the west side of the Jordan.**

26:31 Since Hashabiah directed the Hebronites on the west (v. 30), **Jerijah** took charge of those on the east. He must have been over Hashabiah as well because he is called here **head of the Hebronites.**

26:32 Reubenites … Gadites … half-tribe of Manasseh: These were the tribes of Israel who occupied the east side of the Jordan River, often called the Transjordan.

27:1 heads of fathers' houses: This probably referred to tribal units, since the order appears to be in decreasing size through thousands and hundreds. **month by month:** Apparently a professional standing army is being described here, one broken up into twelve corps that served a month at a time on a rotating basis. **twenty-four thousand:** The total available manpower throughout Israel would be 288,000.

27:2, 3 A connection can be made here to the list of David's mighty men, which is also headed by **Jashobeam** (11:11). He was one of "the three," which meant he was regarded as unusually heroic.

27:4 Dodai's son Eleazar was the second of the mighty men included in the first trio along with Jashobeam (11:12).

27:5, 6 As the son of a priest, **Benaiah** was from the tribe of Levi. In the earlier list of mighty men he was celebrated for having killed a lion and a gigantic Egyptian (11:22, 23). Because of this kind of courage, he became part of the second group of "the three" (11:24). Later he was named commander of the entire Israelite army (1 Kin. 4:4).

27:7 David's nephew **Asahel** (see 2:15, 16) was among the thirty mighty men but did not achieve a position among "the three" (11:26).

27:8–9 A **Tekoite** was a person from the village of Tekoa. This would make Ira a member of the tribe of Judah. It is clear that even if the military divisions were made up along tribal lines, their commanders were often David's own fellow Judeans.

27:10 Helez: The leadership of the army was not limited to Judeans (27:9), since Helez was an Ephraimite in such a position.

27:11 Since Husha was a Judean (4:4), **Sibbechai** also came from the tribe of Judah. **Zarhites** likely referred to descendants of Zerah, a son of Judah (2:4; see Num. 26:20). Sibbechai was one of the thirty heroes, having distinguished himself by killing a Philistine giant (11:29; see 2 Sam. 21:18).

27:12 A Benjamite commander, **Abiezer** came from the Levitical town of Anathoth, just north of Jerusalem. He was also a member of the elite thirty (11:28).

27:13 Since Netophah was a village near Bethlehem, **Maharai** was still another of David's fellow tribesmen named as commander of a **division** and member of the valorous thirty (11:30).

27:14 Another Ephraimite, this **Benaiah** (see v. 5) came from Pirathon, five miles south of Samaria. Like the others he was one of the thirty mighty men (11:31).

27:15 Like Maharai (v. 13), this captain came from Netophah. Besides being one of the thirty (11:30), **Heldai** could claim descent from Israel's first judge, **Othniel.**

27:16, 17 officer: The list that begins here (vv. 16–22) is clearly nonmilitary and tribal in nature. The description of these officers is much more political than the descriptions of the captains and officers of the military divisions (see v. 1).

27:18, 19 Elihu: This brother of David is usually called Eliab (1 Sam. 16:6).

27:20–23 take the number: This ties in the previous list of tribes and leaders with David's ill-fated census near the end of his reign (v. 24; 21:1–17). So confident was David that his military might would be sufficient for any encounter, he omitted from his census all **those twenty years old and under.** Even so, the result of this census was over a million men (see 21:5), a multitude very much like **the stars of the heavens**—the words of God's promise to Abraham (see Gen. 12:2; 15:5).

27:24 Joab's count included all the tribes but Levi and Benjamin (see 21:6). Although these two tribes are included in the present list (vv. 17, 21), nothing is said of their being counted. On the other hand, Asher and Gad, missing in this list (see vv. 16–22), must have been included in Joab's **census.**

27:25 As opposed to the "treasuries of the house of God" and the "treasuries of the dedicated things" (26:20), the **king's treasuries** were the royal storehouses. They contained the revenues of the state in the form of precious metals (29:3–5) and other goods and commodities gained through taxation, tribute, and other means (see 2 Chr. 9:13, 14). **storehouses:** These were regional collection facilities ranging no doubt from granaries to warehouses to places of safe deposit of valuables.

27:26, 27 vineyards: This industry was in two divisions, one to grow the grapes and the other to make **wine.**

27:28 sycamore: This word refers to a tree that yielded figs. It could also be a kind of mulberry.

27:29 A fertile plain between Israelite and Philistine territory, **Sharon** was ideal for grazing cattle and sheep. It is appropriate that someone from Sharon, who knew the land and all its seasonal changes, should be in charge of the livestock of that region.

27:30 Inhabitants of the desert were at home with the breeding and use of camels (Gen. 37:25), so naturally an **Ishmaelite** would be in charge of such animals.

27:31 Since there was no essential difference between the king and his state, the **property** of the king consisted of the assets of the nation.

27:32–34 Jehoiada the son of Benaiah: In the list of military officers there was also a "Benaiah who was a son of Jehoiada" (see v. 5). This is probably an example of the custom in which a man is named after his grandfather. The counselor Jehoiada was probably the grandson of Jehoiada the priest and son of the famous warrior Benaiah (v. 5). **Joab:** From the days of David's conquest of

Jerusalem, Joab held the position of commander of the army of Israel (11:6), a post he kept until Solomon became king (1 Kin. 2:28–35).

28:1 These were the individuals of 27:1–34, plus others who were **the leaders** of all the branches and extensions of Israel's government. The occasion was of such significance that a total assembly of dignitaries was essential.

28:2–4 The word **footstool** is a metaphor describing either the ark of the covenant or the tabernacle as the earthly base of God's activity. He sits on a throne in heaven, and His connection with the earth is focused in his earthly dwelling place, the tent or the ark.

28:5 The call to rule was not limited to David, but included his descendants (see 17:11). Only one of his **sons** could reign in his place. God chose Solomon to succeed David as the king of Israel (22:9, 10; see 2 Sam. 12:24; 1 Kin. 1:13, 30).

28:6 My son ... his Father: This remarkable statement not only shows that the Davidic kings enjoyed unparalleled access to the Lord as His adopted sons (see 17:3; Ps. 2:7), but it anticipates the absolute sonship of the Son of David, Jesus Christ (Acts 13:33; Heb. 1:5).

28:7, 8 The conditional aspect of the covenant with David and his dynasty is real, not hypothetical. Not one of the kings, including David, was able to **observe** the **commandments** and **judgments** perfectly. Therefore they were unable in themselves to reign forever or even set the stage for an everlasting rule. But One would come who would be able to do so and who would fulfill the covenant perfectly.

28:9, 10 True service of God is more than rational and intellectual. It requires a commitment of the emotions as well. This was precisely where Solomon failed. Even though he had great wisdom (2 Chr. 1:12; 9:3, 22, 23), he allowed his **heart** to turn aside from God because he loved foreign women (1 Kin. 11:1–4).

28:11 The **plans** for the temple, as v. 12 makes clear, were not from David's own creative imagination but from the Spirit of God.

vestibule: This was a porch in front of the temple (see 2 Chr. 3:4). **treasuries:** These, also called storehouses (26:15, 17), included "treasuries of the house of God" and "treasuries of the dedicated things" (26:20).
upper chambers: Besides the main temple building, there were rooms of all kinds attached to it to accommodate the priests, the Levites, and all the equipment and items they needed to carry out the temple worship (see Neh. 13:4, 5). **the place of the mercy seat:** This was the Most Holy Place, the inner room that housed the ark of the covenant, the cover of which was known as the mercy seat (Ex. 25:17).

28:12, 13 by the Spirit: Moses had received the plans for the tabernacle by direct revelation from God (Ex. 25:8, 9). David explained that he received the plans for the temple in the same way. David wanted it to be known that even the assignments he gave to the **priests and the Levites** (23:1—26:32) were revealed to him by God.

28:14–18 The chariot was a way of referring to the cherubim who hovered over the ark with outstretched wings, symbolizing the holiness of God.

28:19 David asserted that **all the works of these plans** existed in written form from the hand of the Lord. David himself may have been the scribe, for he said that God's hand was upon him in the production of the plans.

28:20, 21 Be strong and of good courage: David's charge to Solomon is very similar to the charge given to Joshua when Moses handed over the leadership of Israel to him (Deut. 31:7, 8).

29:1, 2 God Himself had **chosen** David out of all his brothers (28:4). Now He chose Solomon out of all of his brothers to succeed David on the throne (28:5). **the work is great:** The project was great not only because of its size and complexity, but because it was for God Himself. Since the very plans and specifications had been revealed to David by God (28:19), David was fully aware of the significance of his charge to Solomon. God's work could not be undertaken lightly.

29:3, 4 my own special treasure: As a testimony to his professed affection for the house

of his God, David pledged generous gifts from his own resources.

29:5, 6 This magnanimous gesture by David gave him the boldness to solicit a similar response from those under him. David asked the others to **consecrate** themselves, not their treasures. David knew that those who first consecrated themselves to God would have no difficulty in being generous in the work of God.

29:7 five thousand talents: About 190 tons. **ten thousand darics:** About 185 pounds of gold. **eighteen thousand talents of bronze:** This was equivalent to about 675 tons. **one hundred thousand talents of iron:** This was approximately 3,750 tons.

29:8 These **precious stones** provided the adornments worn on the shoulders and breastplate of the high priest (Ex. 28:9–12, 17–21).

29:9 loyal heart: The Hebrew is literally "with a fullness of heart." This parallels the word **willingly,** and the two words together suggest that coercion played no part in the offering.

29:10 David blessed the LORD: Upon the completion of the offerings, David offered praise, using a song no doubt composed especially for this occasion (vv. 10–12), followed by a prayer of confession and petition.
29:11 The purpose of the temple was to exalt the **LORD** and to acknowledge the universality of His **kingdom.** David modeled before the people the worship of the living God. It typically starts with praise for God's eternity, His complete control over the universe, and His great power. He is the glorious Master over all (see Ps. 134:3).

29:12–14 David confessed that the **riches and honor** he enjoyed had come from God's generosity. The offerings he and his people had just made were possible only because God first had given to them.

29:15 aliens and strangers: David asserts that life on earth is transitory and even nomadic. Only when a person becomes conscious of his or her place within the care and blessing of a sovereign God does life become more than a **shadow.** Suddenly the **hope** of a future with God illuminates that person's journey on this earth (see Heb. 11:13–16; 13:14).

29:16, 17 With gifts, offerings, and sacrifices, a person demonstrates not only gratitude to God, but trust in Him (see 1 Sam. 15:22). A righteous life always produces a generous spirit. For this reason, David could proclaim that his giving was only out of the uprightness of his heart. Moreover, his **joy** was heightened all the more when he saw that his people also understood this principle of true giving.

29:18 This formula **LORD God of Abraham, Isaac, and Israel** was associated with God's covenantal promises to the Israelites (see Ex. 3:6, 15; 6:3, 4; Deut. 6:10). With this name of God, David was petitioning God to keep His people always in covenant fellowship with Himself.

29:19 In his prayer, David used the language of the covenant—**commandments, testimonies,** and **statutes** (see Deut. 6:1, 2, 20; 8:11; 11:1). Unlike v. 18, David uses this language not as much for the nation as a whole as for his son Solomon. God had already made a covenant with David (17:7–14) and promised to renew it with his descendants. David prayed that God would give Solomon a **loyal heart** to be obedient.

29:20–22 the second time: This unusual phrase can only refer to the ratification of Solomon's kingship, not to its original establishment. David had appointed his son to be king at least two years earlier (see 23:1), an appointment that made Solomon a coregent rather than a true king, since he ruled alongside his father David.

29:23, 24 Once more the chronicler ties the kingship of David and that of God closely together. As God's son (see 17:13), Solomon would sit on the throne as God's representative. In that sense, the royal throne was also **the throne of the LORD** (see also v. 20).

29:25, 26 any king before him: Obviously this included only Saul and David, but it is still a remarkable statement in light of David's widely recognized power and magnificence (11:9; 14:2; 18:1–13; 29:28).

29:27, 28 In comparison to the patriarchs and even to such men as Eli and Samuel, David's 70 years seem short. However, in his time this was a **good old age.** Moses used it as the standard for reasonable longevity (see Ps. 90:10).

29:29, 30 Here the chronicler revealed three sources he used in writing. The reader interested in more information about **the acts of King David** is referred to those books. This note shows that the author of Chronicles did not invent the account or depend on oral tradition. Instead the chronicler cited texts available in his day.

2 Chronicles

Introduction

When it was first written, Second Chronicles brought a ray of hope to a people in need of encouragement. The Israelite community, reduced to a tiny minority in exile among the Babylonians, was struggling to understand its place. Had God's promises to Abraham and David been revoked because of the nation's sins? Was there any hope of reviving David's dynasty? Could God's people survive without the temple? Second Chronicles answered these questions with a historical review of God's faithfulness to the Israelites. Although the nation had steadily declined over the centuries, God had always been faithful to those who remained true to Him. God would keep His promises to the Israelites.

First and Second Chronicles were at first a single book. The book itself does not state who wrote it, but the overall consistency of viewpoint and style indicates that it was probably the work of one person. Most commentators refer to this person as the "chronicler." One Jewish tradition identifies him as Ezra (c. 460–430 B.C.) because Chronicles and Ezra share common themes like extensive lists, the Levites, and the temple. The chronicler had access to many official documents, which he often mentions by name (9:29; 12:15; 33:19).

The details of the history of Israel and Judah in Second Chronicles communicate the great message of redemption—particularly God's blessing on David and his successors. First Chronicles focuses on the Davidic covenant during David's time, and Second Chronicles continues that theme in the period after David's death. Even though Second Chronicles relates the experiences of Solomon and his successors, it continues to emphasize God's promise of an everlasting dynasty to David. Successors to David came and went. Some were true to the requirements of that covenant, and others were not. But God's commitment to the household of David continued throughout, even after the exile to Babylon.

The centrality of the Davidic covenant also explains why Second Chronicles devotes more attention to Judah than to Israel. Ever since the division into southern and northern kingdoms (10:16–19; see 1 Kin. 11:9–13), Judah had become the inheritors of God's promises to David. Though David's successors ruled only the smaller kingdom of Judah, God had remained faithful to His unconditional covenant with David. Judah was the nucleus through which God would accomplish His work of redemption.

1:1, 2 exalted him exceedingly: This repetition of the wording 1 Chr. 29:25 shows how 1 and 2 Chronicles were originally one book, even though it is customary to print the two parts separately.

1:3, 4 The term **high place** comes from the fact that many ancient worshipers used hills for their sacred rites. Over time, *high place* came to mean any worship center, whether it was on a hill or not. In the Old Testament, the high places were usually associated with pagan, particularly Canaanite, religion, but there was nothing inherently evil about using a hilltop as a place of worship. Thus the patriarchs (Gen. 12:8; 22:2) and other worshipers of God offered their sacrifices on high places (1 Sam. 9:12; 1 Kin. 18:19, 36–38). The evil was not in the place itself but in the pagan rituals that were usually practiced there.

1:5 Bezalel was one of the two men chosen especially by God to build the tabernacle in the wilderness (Ex. 31:1–11). Aholiab was the other. The text here mentions Bezalel alone apparently because he was the master craftsman, while Aholiab was his assistant. **the assembly sought Him there:** This phrase is important because **Solomon** and the people, as a congregation, usually worshiped God at Gibeon.

1:6 went up: Solomon's worship at Gibeon affirmed the covenant that bound God and the Davidic dynasty together (1 Chr. 17:7–14) and showed that Solomon accepted the religious responsibilities of his office (v. 3).

1:7–9 Solomon knew about the Abrahamic covenant and God's promise to make Abraham's descendants like **the dust of the**

earth (Gen. 13:16). Solomon believed that the promise had come to pass, and he was confident that God would fulfill His **promise to David** as well. This meant that he saw his own succession (1 Chr. 17:11) and the building of the temple as fulfillment of God's promises (1 Chr. 17:12, 13).

1:10 go out and come in: This figure of speech refers to the totality of Solomon's life. As king he would lead by example as well as by edict.

1:11, 12 Solomon's request for wisdom centered on God's **people** and how he could best serve them, not on his own gain. Once Solomon had demonstrated this spirit of servanthood, God granted many unsolicited blessings.

1:13, 14 Solomon located his **chariots** in other **cities** besides Jerusalem, possibly in Hazor, Megiddo, and Gezer (1 Kin. 9:15,

19). The 1,400 chariots 12,000 horsemen here compare to 4,000 stalls for horses and chariots and 12,000 horsemen in 9:25. A chariot force of 1,400 units was a significant achievement for Israel, a nation located primarily in hilly terrain where chariots were of limited value.

1:15, 16 Keveh was probably an ancient name for what later came to be known as Cilicia. This city was on the northeast Mediterranean coast, a region famous for horses.

1:17 six hundred shekels of silver: This verse suggests that a chariot cost as much as four horses. **they exported them:** Solomon had a thriving business in horses and chariots. Because Israel was on the route between Asia and Africa, such goods would go through Israel and become subject to Solomon's import and export taxes. **Hittites** were the peoples of the ancient

---

IN DEPTH | **Solomon's Temple**

Solomon's temple was the first of three temples that Israel built in its long history. David wanted to build it, but as a man of war he was unqualified to build such a holy place. So with the plans that God gave David and which David passed on to him, King Solomon built the house of God. As God had instructed, Solomon built it on Mount Moriah just north of the ancient City of David.

Solomon wanted to build a temple worthy of being the center of worship for the entire nation, so he used only the best craftsmen and materials. The materials included cedar and algum logs, gold and silver, cut stone, and fine linen. Most of the temple's beams, posts, walls, and doors were overlaid with gold, decorated with carvings of palm trees, garlands, and cherubim. The Most Holy Place alone was overlaid with twenty-three tons of fine gold. In this room two giant gold cherubim, with seven-and-a-half-foot wings overshadowed the ark of the covenant. A veil of crimson and fine linen separated the Most Holy Place from the holy place. The temple's furnishings included ten lampstands of gold, ten tables, and one hundred bowls of gold. Only the most skilled craftsmen worked on these details. The temple was sixty cubits long and twenty cubits wide or ninety by thirty feet.

It took seven years for Solomon's workers to complete this grand building, and the finished structure dazzled all who saw it. Yet for all its beauty, Solomon knew that no manmade building could contain God, as heaven itself could not contain Him (6:18). The temple served mainly as a reminder of God's covenant. To all who came and worshiped there, God held out his promised presence. However, the temple was no guarantee of that presence. God had promised to live among the Israelites forever, and the temple was God's so-called "dwelling place," but for the Holy God to live among His people they had to remain faithful to Him. Unfortunately they did not remain faithful, and consequently the temple was looted and destroyed as were the second and third temples after it.

nation of Hatti in central Asia Minor. They reached the height of their power at about 1350–1300 B.C., but were nearly exterminated by the Sea Peoples in about 1200 B.C. There were pockets of Hittites in Solomon's day, mainly north of Israel among the Syrians.

2:1, 2 a royal house for himself: It was customary for a new king to build a palace as a sign of his newly won sovereignty, though this usually was done after a military conquest (see 1 Chr. 14:1, 2).

2:3, 4 Hiram king of Tyre was the same Phoenician ruler who had provided men and materials for David's palace (1 Chr. 14:1).

2:5 Solomon's statement that **our God is greater than all gods** means that God is the only true God, not that He is the greatest one among many lesser ones.

2:6 Solomon could not **build** a dwelling place for God because God could never be contained within any physical structure. The **temple** provided a place for God's people to go and offer sacrifices of worship to the Lord.

2:7, 8 The skillful men ... with me refers to the people **David** had already selected and organized for the purpose of building the temple (1 Chr. 22:15, 16). The chronicler emphasized David's interest in the temple and the elaborate steps he took to prepare for its building (1 Chr. 22:1–19).

2:9, 10 The amount of **ground wheat** here is about 125,000 bushels or 3,750 tons. **Twenty thousand baths** is approximately 115,000 gallons.

2:11, 12 Blessed be the LORD God of Israel: Most likely a polite salutation to Solomon rather than a sincere recognition of God as the one true God. **a wise son:** It is clear from his letter that Hiram knew a great deal about Solomon, including the background of his request for materials and workmen, his selection by God to be king, his unusual wisdom, and his call to build the temple. Apparently Hiram, David, and Solomon maintained close contact.

2:13, 14 Hiram had an Israelite mother and a Phoenician **father.** Moses had warned the Israelites not to take spouses committed to pagan religions (Deut. 7:1–5).

2:15, 16 Joppa, now known as Jaffa, was the only seaport on the Israelite Mediterranean coast between Dor on the north and Philistia to the south. Though Hiram's rafts helped transport the timber from Lebanon to Israel, the route from Joppa to **Jerusalem** was not so easy—it was a winding, steep ascent of nearly 40 miles.

2:17, 18 Solomon's policy of forced labor drafted **aliens** first into the hard work of carrying loads and quarrying stone (v. 18). The term suggests any persons living in Israel who were not native Israelites. **The census** refers to David's ill-advised count in the closing years of his reign (1 Chr. 21:1–5).

3:1 Mount Moriah was sacred and therefore an appropriate place for the temple not only because the **threshing floor of Ornan** was there (see 1 Chr. 21:18–30), but also because it was the "land of Moriah" to which Abraham took Isaac for sacrifice (Gen. 22:2). David had received explicit instructions from the Lord that the very site that he had purchased from Ornan, and where he had already built an altar, should be the location of the future temple (1 Chr. 21:18, 26). Mount Moriah is known today as the temple mount and the site of the Muslim Dome of the Rock.

3:2 The **second day of the second month** fell in April of the modern calendar. Making arrangements for the building, amassing building materials, and clearing the site could easily have required four years. This explains why Solomon did not begin the project in his first year.

3:3, 4 The Israelites had two standard **cubits,** one about 17.4 inches long and the other about 20.4 inches. Probably **the former measure** mentioned here was the 17.4-inch cubit, making the temple **foundation** about 90 feet long and 30 feet wide. The Mosaic tabernacle was 45 feet long and 15 feet wide (Ex. 26:15–37).

3:5–7 The **larger room** was the holy place or "sanctuary" (1 Kin. 6:17).

3:8 The Most Holy Place was the inner sanctuary, where the ark of the covenant (1 Kin. 6:19) was kept. This room was cubical in shape, **twenty cubits** (30 ft.) on a side (see 1 Kin. 6:20 for the height). **Six hundred talents** is approximately 23 tons of **gold.**

3:9 Gold by itself is too soft to use for **nails,** so the nails mentioned here must have been decorative or else some other metal plated with gold. The weight **fifty shekels** (about 1.2 lbs.) implies that they were plated nails.

3:10 The **cherubim** that Solomon had fashioned for the Most Holy Place were not the ones carved into the walls of the holy place (see v. 7), but additional ones carved and plated with **gold** here in the Most Holy Place.

3:11–13 The **cherubim** stood side by side with outstretched wings **touching** in the middle and overshadowing the ark. Since each wing was **five cubits** long and the room was twenty cubits across, the cherubim's wings spanned the entire width of the room. Facing **inward** meant that the cherubim were facing the veil and the holy place.

3:14 The veil was a heavy curtain between the holy place and the Most Holy Place. It shielded the ark and cherubim from view (see 5:9). Cherubim were woven into the fabric of the veil.

3:15 The **two pillars** in front were freestanding and did not support any part of the temple. **Thirty-five cubits** was about 53 feet, and with the **five cubit capitals on top,** the pillars were about 60 feet tall.

3:16 As in v. 5, **chainwork** appears to be a network of fruits and plants, as the presence of **pomegranates** indicates.

3:17 The names **Jachin** and **Boaz** mean "He Establishes" and "In Him Is Strength." Thus the two pillars were constant reminders of the presence and power of God.

4:1 The **bronze altar** was for burnt offerings in the courtyard of the temple.

4:2 The Sea was a receptacle for water corresponding to the much smaller bronze laver of the Mosaic tabernacle (Ex. 30:17–21). That laver provided water for the priests to wash their hands and feet in preparation for ministering at the altar. The Sea served the same purpose (see v. 6). It was huge—15 feet in diameter and 45 feet in **circumference.**

4:3 The **oxen** stood for strength and fertility. Other Bible passages use the ox's horn to signify this (see 1 Sam. 2:10).

4:4 The **twelve oxen** were in addition to the ones engraved on the outside of the Sea,

and like them they symbolized strength and productivity. Their number corresponds to the twelve tribes of Israel.

4:5 The **Sea** was very heavy even when empty. When filled with **three thousand baths** (about 27,000 gallons) of water, it would have weighed about 110 tons more.

4:6 The **ten lavers** were arranged in two rows of **five,** on the north and south sides of the Sea. According to 1 Kin. 7:38, each held 40 baths or about 230 gallons. They could accommodate large animals such as oxen. The law of **burnt offerings** required that certain parts of the animal be washed in water before being placed on the altar (see Lev. 1:9, 13).

4:7 Whereas the wilderness tabernacle had only one lampstand, this temple had **ten** (see Ex. 25:31), five on the north side of the holy place and five on the south. They symbolized the light of God's creation (Gen. 1:3–5) and the fact that God Himself is light (see John 8:12).

4:8 There had been only one **table** in the tabernacle (Ex. 25:23), but the temple had **ten.** They held the loaves of showbread (Ex. 25:30). **bowls of gold:** The word for bowls here is derived from the Hebrew verb meaning "to sprinkle." The priests used the bowls to hold liquids that were sprinkled.

4:9 There were areas in and about the temple that only the priests could enter. One of these was the area immediately surrounding it and enclosed by a separating wall, the **court of the priests.** The **great court** was an outer area where the people in general could go.

4:10–13 The **Sea** was placed to one side of the entrance to the temple, to the **southeast.** The temple faced east.

4:14–16 Carts were mobile stands designed as bases for the ten **lavers** referred to in v. 6. They were four cubits on a side and three cubits high, had four bronze wheels, and were covered on the sides by richly decorated panels (1 Kin. 7:27–37).

4:17, 18 Many bronze products were made at a place in the Jordan valley about 35 miles north of the Dead Sea. Archaeologists have uncovered evidence of this work in an area where the **clay** is suitable for bronze casting.

4:19–21 This is the first mention of the **altar of gold** in Chronicles (see Ex. 30:1–10; 1 Kin. 7:48). This altar was used for offering incense. It was in the holy place just in front of the veil (see 3:14).

4:22 inner doors: The tabernacle had only a veil between the holy place, here called **the sanctuary,** and the **Most Holy Place** (Ex. 26:31–33). Solomon's temple had a set of doors there as well.

5:1 The treasuries of the house of God listed here were dedicated by David in the sense that he had allotted them to the building and maintenance of the temple (see 1 Chr. 18:7, 8; 29:3–5).

5:2 Though David had built a tabernacle on Mount Zion to house the **ark** (1 Chr. 15:1), it was still separate from the original tabernacle at Gibeon and thus was not yet in a permanent location. Completing Solomon's temple made it possible at last to place the ark in its proper setting.

5:3, 4 Since this was in the **seventh month** (that is, Ethanim or Tishri; 1 Kin. 8:2), the feast was Tabernacles. This feast was an appropriate occasion for moving the ark to a permanent location, because the Feast of Tabernacles commemorated Israel's wandering in the wilderness, when the ark had no permanent place (Lev. 23:39–43).

5:5 The term **tabernacle of meeting** refers to the Mosaic tabernacle. Solomon ended worship at the high place at Gibeon by dismantling the Mosaic tabernacle located there (see 1:3) and by bringing it and all its **furnishings** to Jerusalem.

5:6, 7 Like David before him, Solomon, a priestly **king,** exercised the privileges of his office by offering sacrifices (see 1 Chr. 16:1–3).

5:8 According to Moses' instructions (Ex. 25:12–15; Num. 4:6), the ark had rings attached to each corner, through which carrying **poles** were inserted. These poles were about 20 cubits (30 feet) long, since those who ministered in the holy place could see them at either end of the veil (v. 9).

5:9 to this day: This statement would be charged with emotion for any Israelite who lived through the Babylonian exile years later, when Nebuchadnezzar's army destroyed

Solomon's temple and carried away many of its furnishings.

5:10, 11 On this day of inaugurating the temple, **all the priests** participated in the services regardless of their priestly **divisions.** From then on they would serve in rotation according to their division (see 1 Chr. 24:1–19). **The Most Holy Place** was normally restricted to the high priest only (Lev. 16:15; Heb. 9:7); on this occasion the regular priests had entered it to bring in the ark (v. 7).

5:12 Asaph, Heman, and Jeduthun were the heads of the divisions of Levitical musicians (see 1 Chr. 6:33, 39, 44; 15:17; 16:37, 42; 25:1). The **east end of the altar** was between the east gate of the inner court and the great bronze altar. Altogether there were far more than **one hundred and twenty priests;** the ones numbered here were probably a select group of instrumentalists.

5:13, 14 As v. 14 suggests, the **cloud** was a manifestation of God's glory. In a sense, the cloud both revealed and concealed the glory of God, which is too awesome for human eyes to see (see Ex. 19:16, 18; 20:18, 21; 24:16–18; 33:9, 10, 22; 40:34–38).

6:1, 2 The dark cloud which had represented the glory of God now filled the temple (5:14). This was in line with God's own promise to David when He said, in response to David's decision to build a temple, that He had lived in a portable tabernacle (1 Chr. 17:5). Although David's son built a temple for God, the time would come when God would build David an eternal **house** or dynasty. With David's permanent dynasty would come God's permanent relationship with His people (1 Chr. 17:7–14). Thus Solomon built the "house" in which God could live among them.

6:3, 4 fulfilled with His hands: A direct reference to the covenant that God had made with David, when He promised him an everlasting house (see 1 Chr. 17:11, 12). Solomon, as David's chosen heir, had lived to see God's words of promise come true. God had made Solomon king and built the temple.

6:5, 6 I have chosen Jerusalem: This refers not so much to Jerusalem as a political capital, as it was for David and Solomon

(1 Chr. 11:4–8), but as a place for God's name. This emphasis is unmistakable in the narrative about Ornan's threshing floor (see 1 Chr. 21:18–22:1). Only Jerusalem would be acceptable as a place for God's earthly dwelling.

6:7–11 The covenant of the Lord refers to the stone tablets of the Ten Commandments (see 5:10).

6:12, 13 The **bronze platform** was not a regular feature of the temple but a stage constructed for Solomon's speech, so the assembly outside the walls of the courtyard could see him.

6:14 no God … like You: God is different from all other "gods." He alone made and kept a **covenant** with His people, something unheard of in the religious traditions of the nations. **covenant and mercy:** The word for *mercy* here connotes loyalty; it means that God is faithful to His **servants.**

6:15, 16 Solomon's position as king attested to God's having fulfilled His **promise** (see v. 10). But portions of God's promise depended on God's people obeying God's law. **Only if** David's **sons** took **heed to their way** would they enjoy the full benefits of God's favor. So Solomon prayed that his people would stay faithful to God.

6:17, 18 will God … dwell with men: God is altogether separate from humanity (2:6), but He accommodates Himself to the low position of human beings in order to fellowship with them (see Gen. 2:8; 11:5; 18:1, 2; Ex. 23:20–26).

6:19–21 The temple was God's **dwelling place** in the sense that it gave God's people a place to pray to the living God. Yet God could not be contained within the four walls of a building (see v. 18).

6:22 comes and takes an oath: A reference to legal oaths in which people swore their innocence before God (see Ex. 22:8–11; Deut. 17:8, 9). Such oaths had to be sworn in the temple and before the **altar.**

6:23, 24 Solomon's request that God **hear from heaven** underscored God's transcendence. Although God had chosen to be present on earth at the temple, He also transcended the temple building.

6:25–28 bring them back: A hint of the future

captivity and deportation of God's disobedient **people** (Deut. 28:29, 30). When the exile to Babylon became a reality, the temple was destroyed and no one could pray at that place as before.

6:29–31 Israel was a community and could pray together as a nation. But each member was also responsible for his or her own sin (Ezek. 18:1–4) and each needed to seek God's forgiveness. Prayer toward the temple could be national or individual.

6:32, 33 God made His covenant exclusively with Israel, the nation descended from Abraham, but He did so for the purpose of attracting the nations to Himself, the Creator of all people. A **foreigner** who embraced the Lord as God would be numbered among God's people.

6:34–36 take them captive: Solomon's speech anticipated the possibility of exile (v. 25), something that had already taken place by the time Chronicles were written.

6:37–40 Let Your eyes be open: God is Spirit (John 4:24) and doesn't have physical eyes and ears, but He is a Person who intimately knows us and hears our prayers. Solomon was praying that God would not ignore His people.

6:41 In light of Ps. 132:8, 9 (the passage quoted by Solomon), the **resting place** is the temple. **Ark** is a synonym for the presence of God.

6:42 Your Anointed: A reference to Solomon, which shows that he understood his unique role as one set apart by God for royal service (see 1 Chr. 22:10, 11). Like David, Solomon was a messianic figure who anticipated the goal of his royal line, the true Anointed One, Jesus Christ.

7:1, 2 God responded positively to Solomon's prayer by igniting the sacrifices with heavenly **fire.**

7:3–5 The people saw in God's **glory** His acceptance of the king and the temple, two central elements in His covenant promise to David (see 1 Chr. 17:11, 12).

7:6–8 The **feast** was the Feast of Tabernacles, which began on the fifteenth day of the seventh month and continued through the twenty-second day (Lev. 23:34–36). **Hamath** and **Brook of Egypt** specify the extent of Solomon's early kingdom from north to south.

7:9 The Feast of Tabernacles ended with an **eighth day** assembly, which fell always on the twenty-second day of the seventh month, Tishri. The seven-day **dedication of the altar** is the one referred to in 5:3.

7:10 he sent them away to their tents: Probably a reference to the huts or booths in which people stayed as part of the Feast of Tabernacles (Lev. 23:42, 43).

7:11 The king's house refers to Solomon's own palace, a project much more elaborately explained in 1 Kings (see 1 Kin. 2:1; 7:1, 8). It took Solomon 13 years to build his palace and 20 years in all to build it and the temple (8:1).

7:12 In the next several verses (vv. 13–15), the Lord reviews and answers the petitions of **Solomon** (6:14–42). Solomon's prayers had been **heard** and would be answered, but there were conditions (see v. 14).

7:13, 14 If God's people would do three things, God would respond in three ways. The Lord's people needed to become **humble,** that is, confess; they needed to **pray,** or repent; and they needed to **turn,** or come back to Him. If they did, God would **hear, forgive,** and **heal** them.

7:15–18 I will establish the throne: The conditions for God's blessing on David and his line did not extend to the ongoing existence of that dynasty. The covenant promises to David were unqualified. The Lord had told David that if his son—that is, Solomon—sinned he would be disciplined, but "my mercy shall not depart from him," and "your house and your kingdom shall be established forever before you" (2 Sam. 7:15, 16; see 1 Chr. 17:13, 14). Solomon might sin and be disciplined, but God's promises would stand. David's dynasty would go on.

7:19 if you turn: Here the word for *you* is plural. The Lord was speaking to the nation as a whole.

7:20, 21 proverb: The nation of Israel would become an object lesson to other nations, who would see the temple lying in ruins and understand the clear message about sin and its cost.

7:22 embraced other gods: Idolatry would

be the downfall of the nation (Deut. 28; 29).

8:1, 2 This compressed account of transactions between Solomon and **Hiram** is more fully spelled out in 1 Kin. 9:10–14. In payment for the timber and gold that Hiram provided for Solomon's construction projects, Solomon gave twenty Galilean cities to Hiram. The Phoenician did not like the cities, but he took them anyway and even paid 120 talents of gold for them. Eventually Solomon took back the cities, rebuilt them, and settled Israelites in them once more.

8:3, 4 Solomon **built** and fortified cities such as **Tadmor** because they were on vital caravan routes. These fortified cities provided protection to his own caravans and became the customs points at which Solomon collected taxes. **storage cities:** Facilities were scattered throughout Solomon's outlying provinces to provide warehouses for his armies and merchantmen, as well as to store produce and other tribute paid by the vassal states (see 1 Kin. 9:19).

8:5 Upper Beth Horon and **Lower Beth Horon** were strategically located near the border between Judah and the northern tribal districts, along a major mountain pass to the Mediterranean Sea (see Josh. 10:10; 1 Sam. 13:18).

8:6–8 The people groups named were remnants of the population of Canaan who survived the conquest. **Israel** reduced many of them to **forced labor** (see 2:17).

8:9–11 The daughter of Pharaoh is not named here. Solomon had married her early in his reign (1 Kin. 3:1) and had provided her housing near **David's palace** on Mount Zion.

8:12, 13 The daily rate refers to the morning and evening sacrifices of lambs, one on each occasion (Ex. 29:38–42).

8:14, 15 Solomon, like all kings in David's line, had jurisdiction over **the priests and Levites,** as well as over civil, military, and political affairs.

8:16, 17 Ezion Geber and **Elath** were cities located close together at the northern end of the east branch of the Red Sea.

8:18 The Phoenicians were world-famous mariners, so when Solomon undertook a merchant marine enterprise he called once more on his good friend **Hiram,** the King of

Tyre. The land of **Ophir,** located apparently in South Arabia (see 1 Chr. 29:4), was a source of finest **gold.**

9:1–3 Sheba was more than a thousand miles south of Israel, at the southern end of the Arabian peninsula. **hard questions:** Solomon was known for his great wisdom (1:10–12; 1 Kin. 4:29–34), a trait much prized and admired in the ancient Middle East.

9:4–12 Blessed be the LORD your God: This was the language of politeness in the ancient world and does not suggest that the queen of Sheba was converted. Visiting dignitaries customarily praised the god of the host nation.

9:13 Solomon's annual income in **gold** through taxes alone amounted to 25 tons. Since king and state were identified, this figure reflects the annual revenues of the entire nation through taxes.

9:14 The **gold and silver** that the **kings** and **governors** brought to Solomon was tribute—a form of taxation on vassal states, not a voluntary gift.

9:15, 16 The **shields of hammered gold** were for decorative or ceremonial purposes, not the armory. Gold was too expensive, too heavy, and too soft to use in battle.

9:17–22 To Tarshish is possibly a figure of speech, meaning "a great distance" or "to the ends of the earth."

9:23 In the context of Solomon's own time and place, **all kings** referred to the kings of the eastern Mediterranean world.

9:24, 25 each man brought his present: Ordinary presents are not given and received at a **set rate** so these presents were tribute paid to the king by vassals.

9:26, 27 Most of the kings of Israel had continuing trouble with the **Philistines,** even though they were able to subdue every other surrounding neighbor. David had some success against the Philistines (1 Chr. 18:2), and later Jehoshaphat managed to exact tribute from some of them (see 17:11).

9:28, 29 Nathan the prophet had rebuked David for his adultery and murder (2 Sam. 12:1) and had become a confidant and counselor to both David and **Solomon** (1 Kin. 1:8, 11). **Ahijah the Shilonite** would select

Jeroboam as the first king of the northern kingdom of Israel (1 Kin. 11:26–40) and later would announce God's judgment on him (1 Kin. 14:1–16). **Iddo the seer** was a contemporary of Ahijah who compiled accounts of both Jeroboam and Rehoboam (12:15).

9:30, 31 Rehoboam was a son of Solomon by his wife Naamah of Ammon (12:13). Rehoboam was 41 when he began to rule, so he must have been born during the period when Solomon ruled alongside David (see 1 Chr. 29:22, 23).

10:1 Why did Rehoboam go **to Shechem** to be crowned? Shechem had a rich history dating back to Abraham's travels in the land (see Gen. 12:6, 7; 35:4; Josh. 24:1–28). But more importantly, a rift had begun to develop between the northern and southern tribes (1 Kin. 11:26–40), and Shechem would be a more neutral place than Jerusalem.

10:2, 3 As head of all of Solomon's forced labor in the district of Ephraim, **Jeroboam** enjoyed great favor with the king. But the prophet Ahijah informed him that he would become ruler of the ten northern tribes because of Solomon's idolatry (1 Kin. 11:26–33). When Solomon heard of this he tried to kill Jeroboam (1 Kin. 11:40), but Jeroboam fled to **Egypt.**

10:4, 5 Solomon's heavy **yoke** included taxation and forced labor (see 1 Sam. 8:11–18; 1 Kin. 4:7; 9:15).

10:6–11 Rehoboam promised that even the lesser evils of his reign—his **finger**—would be as hard as anything they knew under Solomon. The young men compared Solomon's rule to a **whip** and Rehoboam's to a **scourge,** a whip with sharp bits of metal that cut the flesh and caused excruciating pain.

10:12–15 the turn of events was from God: Human foolishness and decisions achieved God's purposes. Solomon's defection from God late in his reign had already disqualified his descendants from ruling over all Israel (1 Kin. 11:9–13). Rehoboam initiated the split with his own foolish actions.

10:16, 17 In the people's poem, **Israel** referred to the ten northern tribes, **David** to the southern kingdom of Judah.

10:18, 19 Hadoram, called Adoniram in 1 Kin. 4:6, was Jeroboam's counterpart in Judah as officer in charge of forced labor.

11:1 Shortly after the kingdom divided, the tribe of **Benjamin** joined Judah to form the southern kingdom. This is ironic because Saul was a Benjamite. However, Benjamites had shown great loyalty to David many years before (see 2 Sam. 19:16–20, 40–43). Also, Benjamin was closer geographically to Judah than to the northern tribes.

11:2–4 Like Nathan, Ahijah, and Iddo (9:29), **Shemaiah** was a writing prophet. The writer of Chronicles depended on Shemaiah's writings for some of his information (see 12:15).

11:5–14 all their territories: Though Israel and Judah had split into two kingdoms, **the priests and the Levites** of Israel sided with Judah. They knew that Rehoboam was David's offspring, and therefore the heir of God's covenant promise to David.

11:15 The **calf idols** were the golden calves that Jeroboam had installed at Bethel and Dan.

11:16 Once the legitimate religious leaders had **left** Israel, the worshipers of God in the northern kingdom could no longer worship in good conscience, so they made pilgrimages **to Jerusalem** three times a year (see 1 Kin. 12:27, 32, 33).

11:17 Jeroboam's program of establishing a new religious structure in Israel apparently took at least **three years.** Meanwhile, the pilgrimage of godly Israelites from the north to Jerusalem **strengthened** Rehoboam and weakened Jeroboam (1 Kin. 12:27).

11:18, 19 Mahalath may have been David's greatgranddaughter. **Rehoboam** was David's grandson, so in any case this marriage was within the larger royal family.

11:20 Rehoboam's claims to legitimacy took further support from his marriage to **Maachah,** granddaughter of David's son Absalom. Their son **Abijah** would eventually succeed Rehoboam (see 12:16).

11:21–23 Rehoboam named his son Abijah as the next **king** to ensure a smooth succession following his death. Abijah probably served under or alongside Rehoboam, just as Solomon had served under David (1 Chr. 23:1).

12:1 the law: The normal Hebrew word for

the Mosaic covenant, the Ten Commandments.

12:2, 3 Egypt was beginning to recover from a long period of decline and wanted to reestablish control over Palestine. God used their ambitions to discipline Rehoboam for abandoning the Lord. **The Lubim** were the Libyans. **The Sukkiim** were other desert tribes, perhaps from western Libya. **Ethiopians:** Sometimes referred to as Cushites, these famous warriors originated in the lands south of Egypt.

12:4–8 In order that the Judeans might understand how privileged they were to serve God, He would allow them to become **servants** to the Egyptians. Only then would they appreciate again the joy of being God's servant people.

12:9–11 The **treasures of the king's house** that the Egyptians seized had been spoils of war captured by David and dedicated to God (1 Chr. 18:6–8; 22:14). Judah was now a vassal state of Egypt.

12:12, 13 The king's conduct had inevitable consequences on the nation. When a king obeyed God, the Lord would bless the nation. When the king turned away from the Lord, his subjects would suffer. But when the king repented and **humbled himself** before God, God's forgiveness and restoration would cover both him and his kingdom.

12:14–16 did not prepare his heart to seek the LORD: Note the differences between David, Solomon, Rehoboam, and Abijah (in ch. 13). David, a man of God (see 8:14), died at a very old age with riches and honor. Solomon died wise, rich, and powerful. But Rehoboam **did evil.** As a result, he fought wars throughout most of his troubled reign. Abijah followed Rehoboam's example of not honoring God (13:8–18).

13:1–4 Mount Zemaraim was a few miles southwest of Bethel (see Josh. 18:22).

13:5 covenant of salt: Salt was a preservative and symbolized durability—an apt description of the eternal Davidic covenant (see Lev. 2:13; Num. 18:19).

13:6 Abijah blamed the division of the kingdom on **Jeroboam,** not Rehoboam, or even Solomon (see 10:16). But Jeroboam's rebellion was fueled by Solomon's disobedience to the covenant and his harsh policies.

Moreover, Rehoboam's foolish plan to increase the severity of those abuses infuriated the Israelites even more. The blame lay with all three—Jeroboam, Rehoboam, and Solomon.

13:7, 8 Abijah's version of the nation's division put his father in a relatively good light. According to Abijah, if Rehoboam had made any mistakes, it was just because he was **young and inexperienced.** Abijah further equated the kingdom of Judah with **the kingdom of the LORD,** making the victory of Judah over Israel sound like a foregone conclusion.

13:9 Jeroboam's illicit religion filled the priestly ranks with anyone who had the means to purchase the office. Thus Abijah asserted that all a person had to do to **consecrate himself** was to come with the appropriate sacrifices (1 Kin. 12:31; see Lev. 8:2). But Abijah's words were hypocritical, for the same evil deeds were going on in his own kingdom (see 14:2–5).

13:10, 11 The **priests** of Judah were true priests who traced their ancestry to **Aaron** as the Law required (see 1 Chr. 6:1–15). Throughout the passage the contrast is between the authorized worship at Jerusalem and the illicit practice of religion at Dan and Bethel.

13:12–19 Among the Israelite cities that fell to Judah was **Bethel,** the southern center of the false religious cult that Jeroboam had established (see 1 Kin. 12:29).

13:20–22 One of the gauges of a king's power and prosperity was the size of his family.

14:1, 2 Abijah's son **Asa reigned** for 41 years, until 870 B.C. (see 16:13). **ten years:** This suggests that during the first ten years of Asa's reign there was peace between Judah and Israel (see v. 6).

14:3–5 **Sacred pillars** were stone posts associated with Canaanite fertility rites. **Wooden images** were fashioned from live evergreen trees, which were regarded as a fertility symbol, since they retain their leaves throughout the year. Eventually, cut poles took the place of live trees.

14:6–8 Rehoboam had **built fortified cities** in his time, but Shishak of Egypt had destroyed

them (11:5–12; 12:2–4). It is likely that Asa just rebuilt them. The phrase **in those years** refers to the first ten years of Asa's reign, the years of peace (v. 1).

14:9 Since Egypt was strong at this time (12:3) and fully in control of its own territory, it is likely that **Zerah** and his large army were mercenaries of the Egyptian king Osorkon I (914–874 B.C.), successor to Shishak. **Mareshah** was one of Asa's important fortified cities, about 25 miles southwest of Jerusalem (11:8). It was near the Via Maris, the coastal highway connecting Egypt and Canaan, making it strategically important.

14:10 The **Valley of Zephathah** was on the north side of Mareshah.

14:11, 12 it is nothing for You to help: Asa showed great faith in his prayer before the battle against Zerah's huge army. **in Your name:** Asa believed that God was on his side and that Zerah's attack was aimed at the Lord as well as at God's people (see 13:8, 12, 14, 15).

14:13–15 Gerar was on the frontier between Egypt and Canaan and might have been in Egyptian territory at this time.

15:1–5 in their trouble: The Israelites were constantly being invaded and harassed. But when circumstances looked hopeless, the people cried out to God in repentance, and He delivered them (see Judg. 2:11–19). **no peace:** Beside the dangers of war, the continual perils of robbery and crime plagued the nation.

15:6–9 Along with godly priests and Levites (see 11:13–17), many of the ordinary citizens of Israel **came over to** Judah when they saw Asa's zeal for God, and God's blessing upon him.

15:10 The **third month** probably locates this festival at the time of the firstfruits, the Feast of Pentecost (see Lev. 23:15–21; Num. 28:26–31).

15:11 Spoil likely refers to the animals taken from the Ethiopians after Asa's victory over Zerah (14:15). If so, the battle of Mareshah (see 14:9, 10) must have taken place right before this event.

15:12, 13 Asa gathered an assembly to reaffirm Israel's **covenant** (or promise) to seek the Lord. The nation had assembled before to renew their commitment to God (Deut. 27:9, 10; 29:1; 31:10–13; Josh. 8:30–35; 24:1–28).

15:14 Taking **an oath** was an essential part of covenant-making (Ex. 24:7, 8; Deut. 27:11–26; 29:12). The people declared their determination to keep the covenant.

15:15 The conflict with Zerah the Ethiopian (14:9) had broken the ten-year period of peace at the start of Asa's reign (14:1). After winning the war and renewing the covenant with God, Judah once again had **rest all around.**

15:16 Maachah is called Asa's **mother,** a Hebrew word that can also mean *grandmother.* Still, Asa demoted her **from being queen mother** because she had set up pagan idols.

15:17 high places were not removed from Israel: Asa destroyed the high places of Judah, but not those of Israel (see 14:3, 5).

15:18, 19 silver and gold and utensils: These items were taken as spoils of war and **dedicated** to the worship of God; they could not then be used for any other purpose (1 Chr. 18:8; 26:20).

16:1–3 The **treasuries of the house of the LORD** were items of value stored in the temple as ordinary revenue (see 1 Chr. 26:20). They did not include things dedicated to the Lord (see 15:18). Asa used these treasuries to secure Ben-Hadad's assistance against **Baasha king of Israel.**

16:4 Ijon was in the tribal territory of Naphtali, some ten miles north of **Dan** and thirty-five miles north of the Sea of Galilee. **Abel Maim** was only three miles west of Dan. **Naphtali** was the most northern tribal territory of Israel, very close to Damascus.

16:5, 6 Diverted by attacks from the north, Baasha left **Ramah** unfinished (v. 5). Asa, the king of Judah, took advantage of the situation and built his own fortifications at **Geba,** just east of Ramah, and at **Mizpah,** between Ramah and Bethel. Ramah ended up between Asa's fortresses and the Israelites could not rebuild it.

16:7–9 Hanani the seer was probably the father of another prophet Jehu, who once challenged King Jehoshaphat of Judah (see 19:2; 20:34).

16:10–13 diseased in his feet: Asa may have been suffering from gout, a common disease in the ancient world. For his malady Asa **did not seek the LORD, but the physicians.** He failed to turn to God during his sickness.

16:14 great burning: This had nothing to do with cremation, but was the burning of spices and perfumes to mourn a king's death (see 21:19).

17:1, 2 cities of Ephraim: Ephraim is a synonym for Israel. The cities referred to here are mentioned also in 15:8; they could include Ramah, Geba, and Mizpah as well (16:6), depending on fluctuations of the border between Israel and Judah.

17:3–8 Jehoshaphat was the first king since David who **walked in the former ways of his father David.** He obeyed God's commandments and took delight in the Lord's ways.

17:9 The Book of the Law refers to the five books of Moses, the Pentateuch. When Moses passed the leadership of Israel on to Joshua he instructed him never to let "this Book of the Law" depart from his mouth (Josh. 1:8). Unfortunately, Jehoshaphat's initiative in sending out teachers to instruct the nation in God's laws was not the norm (see 15:3).

17:10, 11 There is no record of Jehoshaphat conquering Philistia, but he was powerful enough to compel at least some of the **Philistines** to pay **tribute** to his sovereignty.

17:12–18 Jehoshaphat's **men of war** were grouped into three divisions of Judeans with a total number of 780,000 (vv. 14–16), and two divisions of Benjamites numbering 380,000 (vv. 17, 18). The Hebrew word for **thousand** can also mean "clan" (as in Judg. 6:15; 1 Sam. 10:19) or "village" (as in Mic. 5:2), and possibly "company" in a military context. Thus, 780,000 may refer to 780 companies and 380,000 to 380 companies.

17:19 Jehoshaphat's troops were stationed at Jerusalem. He had additional forces **in the fortified cities** throughout the countryside.

18:1 Jehoshaphat **allied himself with Ahab** by arranging for his son Jehoram to marry Ahab's daughter Athaliah (see 21:5, 6; 22:2).

18:2 Ahab died in battle a few days after Jehoshaphat's **visit** (v. 34). **Ramoth Gilead:** This important city some 35 miles east of Beth Shan was controlled by the Arameans. It was also one of the Israelite cities of refuge (Josh. 20:8; 1 Chr. 6:80).

18:3, 4 I am as you are: Jehoshaphat was referring to the intermarriage of their families (v. 1).

18:5 The prophets were probably prophets of Asherah, the Canaanite goddess worshiped by Ahab's wife Jezebel (see v. 6; 1 Kin. 18:19).

18:6–9 the entrance of the gate often led to a large open place in Israelite cities. Public assemblies could convene there or in rooms built into the sides of the gateway. The **threshing floor** was a large, flat area where grain was separated from straw (see 1 Chr. 21:15). The threshing floor of Ornan was just outside the walls of Jerusalem, where the winds could blow away the chaff. This is probably where the kings had set up their thrones.

18:10 Horns symbolize strength in the Old Testament, so **horns of iron** would represent great strength (see Zech. 1:18–21).

18:11, 12 In this context, **prophesied** suggests rantings and ravings typical of the demon-possessed false prophets of Canaan (see 1 Kin. 18:26–29), not true prophecy.

18:13, 14 whatever my God says: The true prophets' prophecies come directly from God. Their words are God's words.

18:15 Ahab knew from experience that his prophets told him what they thought he wanted to hear, not **the truth.** Because their prophecies agreed with Micaiah's, he knew that Micaiah must have been lying when he prophesied success.

18:16, 17 The Bible often uses **sheep** and **shepherd** as metaphors for the people of a nation and their king (see 1 Chr. 17:6, 7).

18:18, 19 Micaiah saw **the LORD** in heaven. Here we see God's sovereignty over all. The spirits who stood before Him were both angels and demons, and none could act without God's permission.

18:20–22 A lying spirit was a demon whom the Lord allowed to deceive the prophets. God cannot lie (see Num. 23:19), but He

does allow others to do so. In this sense, God **put a lying spirit in the mouth of** Ahab's prophets.

18:23–28 A real prophet's predictions always came true (Deut. 13:1–3; 18:22). Micaiah staked his reputation on the fact that Ahab would not come home **in peace**—that is, alive.

18:29–34 at random: This is the human perspective. The wounding of Ahab, disguised as he was, appeared to be an accident. But from God's perspective, chance had no part in it. The arrow reached its true destination. Micaiah's prophecy had come true (see v. 16).

19:1, 2 The prophet Hanani had once chastised King Asa for depending on the Arameans to defeat Baasha, king of Israel (see 16:7). **Jehu the son of Hanani,** also a prophet, now went on a similar mission to Jehoshaphat.

19:3, 4 Originally the land of Israel stretched "from Dan to **Beersheba**" (see Judg. 20:1). Dan refers to the town of Dan just north of the Sea of Galilee, not the tribe of Dan near Judah. But after the division into two kingdoms **the mountains of Ephraim** became the northern border of Judah. Thus this verse asserts that Jehoshaphat restored the people of Judah to more faithful observance of the covenant. This was admirable, but it was also a basic duty of the Davidic monarch (see 14:4; 15:9; 17:7–9). Jehoshaphat was only doing his job.

19:5, 6 The role of Jehoshaphat's **judges** differed from that of the heroic leaders who led Israel before David's time (Judg. 2:16). The judges that Jehoshaphat appointed served as local officials in the **fortified cities.**

19:7, 8 Matters too difficult for the local judges or those that required appeal went to the high court **in Jerusalem** where the **Levites, priests,** and **chief fathers** sat.

19:9–11 As chief priest, **Amariah** held jurisdiction over all **matters of the LORD,** that is, religious cases. **Zebadiah,** the **ruler of the house of Judah** (see 1 Kin. 4:7), ruled over **all the king's matters**—that is, civil cases.

20:1 Moab went **to battle against Jehoshaphat** under the leadership of Mesha, who had gained Moab's independence from the

Omri dynasty of Israel soon after Ahab died (see 18:34). The battle mentioned here took place when Ahab's son Ahaziah was king of Israel (20:35). The defeat of Jehoshaphat's enemies in Israel only meant the rise of other enemies outside Israel. This situation would test Jehoshaphat's faith.

20:2 Hazazon Tamar is on the western shore of the Dead Sea, a few miles south of Qumran. It was David's hiding place in the days of Saul (1 Sam. 23:29).

20:3, 4 seek the LORD: Jehoshaphat's reforms (see 19:4) were not hollow religiosity, and they did not break under the strain of sour circumstances. As soon as he heard of bad news from the north, Jehoshaphat sought God and **proclaimed a fast.** He knew that success required God's favor. And if God was for them, they could not lose (vv. 6–12; see 13:5, 12).

20:5–7 Jehoshaphat recalled God's care for His **people Israel** in the past, when He had led them to victory over their Canaanite foes.

20:8–14 As a member of the Asaph division of the Levites (1 Chr. 6:39; 15:17, 19; 16:7), **Jahaziel** was probably a musician. Music was an important part of Israel's religious life (see 13:12). The people would go into battle praising God with instruments and voices (vv. 19, 21, 22, 28).

20:15–17 The **ascent of Ziz** was a dry stream bed just north of En Gedi. The **Wilderness of Jeruel** lay between Hebron and the Dead Sea.

20:18, 19 The **Kohathites** were members of the Levitical division of Heman (1 Chr. 6:33). The **Korahites** were a subclan of the Kohathites (1 Chr. 6:37, 39), who were employed as gatekeepers for the temple (1 Chr. 26:1–19). Their positive response to Jahaziel's speech and their praise to God (see vv. 15–17) was as important as any military preparation.

20:20 Tekoa was a town about 10 miles south of Jerusalem. The **Wilderness of Tekoa** was between the town and the Ascent of Ziz (v. 16).

20:21, 22 sing ... praise: The battle was the Lord's and its outcome was certain. The people celebrated God and His victory (see Ex. 15:1, 20, 21; Judg. 7:18–20; Ps. 47; 98).

20:23, 24 Before Judah's armies could even reach the battlefield, the Ammonites and Moabites attacked their Edomite allies and destroyed them, then they turned against each other. As a result, Judah won without even having to fight.

20:25 Spoils of war, like **valuables** (precious metals) and **jewelry,** became God's property, because God Himself had triumphed and therefore deserved the fruits of war (Josh. 6:24; 1 Chr. 18:7, 8).

20:26–28 After they experienced God's blessing and protection in the wilderness, the Judeans renamed Ziz the **Valley of Berachah,** meaning "Blessing," to remind themselves of God's goodness.

20:29–33 the LORD had fought: The spectacle of Jehoshaphat's enemies in defeat, like the battles that Joshua had led years before, struck fear in the hearts of enemy nations because it involved a miracle. No human army could prevail over God's omnipotence.

20:34 For a complete account of Jehoshaphat's reign the chronicler recommended the **book of Jehu,** which itself was cited in **the book of the kings of Israel.** Jehu was the son of the prophet Hanani and was a prophet himself (see 19:2). He is mentioned in 1 Kings in connection with the kings of Israel (see 1 Kin. 16:1, 7). He was therefore a good source of information about both the northern and southern kingdoms.

20:35 Ahaziah was the son of Ahab; he succeeded his father and reigned for two years (1 Kin. 22:51). Ahaziah was injured in a fall and turned to the Philistine gods rather than to the Lord for healing (2 Kin. 1:2).

20:36, 37 Tarshish was in the western Mediterranean. The name came to represent any place far away. Ships of Tarshish were large vessels that transported heavy cargo over long distances (see 8:17, 18; 9:21). **Ezion Geber** was a port on the Gulf of Aqaba (or Elath), the eastern arm of the Red Sea (see 8:17).

21:1, 2 The names of Jehoram's **brothers** highlight Jehoram's choice as king emphatically, as if to say, "Not these brothers, but this one." We soon learn how significant for all of them this choice turned out to be (see v. 4).

21:3 gifts ... fortified cities: Jehoshaphat did what his great-grandfather Rehoboam had done. He gave the kingdom to his firstborn and then distributed extravagant gifts to his other sons (11:23). He wanted to satisfy each of his sons, since only one of them could succeed him as king.

21:4–6 princes of Israel: Jehoram extended his bloody purge as far as his distant relatives in Israel (see 18:1). He was so evil that not even blood ties restrained his lust for power.

21:7 Individual kings such as Jehoram committed evil and scorned **covenant** obligations, but the promise of God to **David** (Ps. 89:30–37) about his house remained intact (see 1 Chr. 17:7–14).

21:8, 9 Edomites revolted: Jehoram's father Jehoshaphat had conquered Edom (20:22, 36).

21:10 In the western lowlands of Judah, **Libnah** was close to the border with Philistia.

21:11 commit harlotry: Israel's covenant with God was like a marriage relationship, and to violate it was to commit spiritual unfaithfulness (see Ezek. 16:15–43; 23:1–21; Hos. 4:11–19). Like Solomon before him (1 Kin. 11:1–8), Jehoram failed to provide godly leadership.

21:12–15 Though 1 and 2 Kings pay considerable attention to **Elijah the prophet** (1 Kin. 17:1–2 Kin. 2:18), the books of the Chronicles mention him only here. He had been taken up into heaven after King Ahaziah's death (2 Kin. 1:17; 2:1).

21:16–19 The Arabians were from the southwestern part of the Arabian peninsula, probably near present-day Yemen. They lived across the Red Sea from the **Ethiopians.**

21:20 The tombs of the kings was a royal cemetery in Jerusalem where most of David's dynasty were buried (Asa was an exception; see 16:14). Jehoram was not buried there, but in Jerusalem, the **City of David.**

22:1–4 Ahaziah of Judah was the namesake of his uncle from Israel. Ahaziah's father Jehoram had married a sister of Ahab's son Ahaziah (see 1 Kin. 22:40; 2 Kin. 1:17; 8:18).

22:5 Jehoram the son of Ahab succeeded his brother Ahaziah because Ahaziah had no sons of his own (2 Kin. 1:17). He is also called Joram, a short form of Jehoram, to distinguish him from his brother-in-law Jehoram, who was king of Judah. **Hazael** was the king of Damascus who came to power after assassinating Ben-Hadad (2 Kin. 8:7–15). Elijah had prophesied that this would come about and had even commissioned Elisha to anoint Hazael to his new position (1 Kin. 19:15).

22:6 Jezreel was a royal city located in the Plain of Jezreel and frequented by the kings of Israel. It was about 10 miles west of the Jordan River and 25 miles west of Ramoth Gilead (see 1 Kin. 21:1–4). In this instance **Ramah** is an abbreviated form of Ramoth Gilead.

22:7, 8 Ahaziah's visit to his dying uncle turned out to be **God's occasion for Ahaziah's downfall.** Jehu was an officer in Israel's army who participated in the campaign against Ramoth Gilead and who was anointed there as king by a servant of Elisha (2 Kin. 9:1–6). Elijah had prophesied that Jehu would become king of Israel (1 Kin. 19:16). Elisha carried out the commission through his servant, telling Jehu to remove Joram from the throne and to eradicate the entire Omri dynasty (2 Kin. 9:7–10).

22:9 When Ahaziah became aware of the slaughter of the northern dynasty and even some of his own relatives who happened to be in Jezreel (see v. 8), he fled to Israel's capital, **Samaria.** But Jehu found him there and murdered him. In one day, both kingdoms lost their rulers. **they buried him:** The people honored him in this way only because Ahaziah was the grandson of the godly Jehoshaphat.

22:10 Most of **the royal heirs** Athaliah murdered were her own grandchildren. She wanted to stamp out the Davidic dynasty and bring Judah back under Israelite control. But this could not happen as long as Jehu was in power in the north.

22:11 It was Ahaziah's own sister **Jehoshabeath** who rescued her nephew Joash from her mother Athaliah.

22:12 Though **Athaliah reigned** for **six years,** she was not a descendant of David and therefore was never listed among the kings of Judah. Meanwhile, her grandson Joash remained the sole survivor in the Davidic line.

23:1, 2 The **Levites** were the religious leaders of the nation; the **chief fathers** were the civil leaders. Jehoiada needed support and help from both civil and religious leaders to overthrow Athaliah.

23:3 covenant: This was a solemn pledge to restore the throne to Joash and to submit to him as David's rightful heir (see 1 Chr. 29:21–24).

23:4, 5 one-third: Jehoiada was referring to the changing of **priests and the Levites** for the week to come (see 1 Chr. 24:3). The coming and going of so many men at once would disguise the plot.

23:6–8 Though one division of priests and **Levites** would normally replace the other, both **divisions** remained at the temple so they would have enough men to place Joash, the true heir, on David's throne.

23:9, 10 The temple contained **spears** and **shields** that David himself had assembled over 150 years before. Jehoiada distributed these among the soldiers, who could not have carried their own weapons into the area without arousing suspicion.

23:11, 12 The Testimony was a copy of the Law of Moses, part of which outlined the king's covenant privileges and duties (see Deut. 17:18–20; 1 Chr. 29:19). **anointed him:** An anointing was the sign and seal of the king's appointment by God and a symbol of the Spirit of God upon him (see 1 Sam. 16:13; 1 Kin. 1:39).

23:13 The **pillar** was probably one of the two that stood in front of the temple (see 3:15).

23:14 not ... in the house of the LORD: The temple was regarded as a place of sanctuary from violence.

23:15 The Horse Gate in the temple provided access to the royal palace. There was another Horse Gate in the city wall.

23:16–19 killed Mattan: The Law required that leaders in the worship of false gods be put to death (Deut. 13:6–11). This sort of execution had been carried out before (see 1 Kin. 18:40; 2 Kin. 10:25–28).

23:20, 21 The Upper Gate joined the temple

to the royal palace on the north side of the temple (see 27:3).

24:1, 2 Joash could not rule alone at the age of **seven,** so his uncle Jehoiada acted as his guardian and counselor (see v. 3). As long as Jehoiada was alive, **Joash did what was right.**

24:3, 4 Repairing the house of the LORD was necessary because of the neglect it had suffered during the evil reigns of Jehoram, Ahaziah, and Athaliah (see v. 7).

24:5, 6 the collection: This was the "atonement money" that the Levites collected for the temple and its services (Ex. 30:11–16).

24:7, 8 The **dedicated things** included gold, silver, and other valuables collected as tribute from defeated enemies and presented to God as spoils of war (2 Sam. 8:10, 11).

24:9–12 The priests and Levites who supervised various ministries such as music, gatekeeping, and maintenance did **the work of the service.**

24:13, 14 The people had been so generous (see v. 11) that **money** remained after all the work had been done. This extra money allowed for a complete restocking of the temple with the **gold and silver** implements needed for its services. As long as **Jehoiada** remained alive, Judah enjoyed a revival of the true worship of God.

24:15, 16 Jehoiada was buried **among the kings** because of his service to God and to Joash.

24:17–19 The extent of Jehoiada's positive influence on Joash became obvious soon after the priest's death. King Joash became a proponent of idolatry and **would not listen** to God's rebukes.

24:20, 21 Jesus spoke of "Zechariah, son of Berechiah" as one of a series of prophets who was murdered in the temple court (Matt. 23:34, 35). This could be the Zechariah who wrote the Book of Zechariah (Zech. 1:7), which says nothing about his death. **Zechariah the son of Jehoiada** also died a martyr in the temple court, as described here. Either (1) the chronicler's Zechariah was actually the grandson of Jehoiada and the son of an unmentioned Berechiah, or (2) the prophet who wrote the Book of Zechariah was also killed in the temple precincts, a fact recorded only in the Gospels.

24:22 killed his son: Besides forgetting all the good Jehoiada had done for him, Joash had killed his own cousin (see 22:11; 24:20). This once-good king had sunk to the level of his evil grandmother Athaliah (see 22:10), despite decades of past faithfulness to God. As long as he received good advice, he did well. But once it was gone, he abandoned God.

24:23–27 God arranged for Israel's defeat and Joash's death in fulfillment of Zechariah's dying cry for justice (v. 22). **tombs of the kings:** Like his grandfather Jehoram, Joash was excluded from the royal cemetery because he fell far short of the Davidic ideal (see 21:20).

25:1–4 Amaziah did what was "right in the sight of the Lord" (v. 2) by obeying the **Book of Moses** with regard to the innocent children of lawbreakers (Deut. 24:16).

25:5, 6 The king of **Israel** was Jehoash (or Joash; v. 17). The hiring of Israelite mercenaries here, though judged evil (v. 7), implies that good relations existed between the two kingdoms.

25:7 As the breakaway kingdom that no longer stood within the Davidic covenant, **Israel** had disqualified itself as the people of the Lord. It was therefore improper for Judah to form alliances with the northern kingdom (see 19:2; 20:36, 37; 22:7).

25:8, 9 If this war had been sanctioned by the Lord, victory would have been certain. But Amaziah had made his own decision to go to **battle** (v. 5) and had no assurance of God's help.

25:10 Amaziah heeded the prophet's advice and sent the Israelites back without even demanding the return of the hundred talents of silver he had paid them (v. 9). This **greatly aroused** the Israelite mercenaries because they thought their share of the spoils would have been much more than that.

25:11, 12 The **Valley of Salt** probably refers to the desert south of the Dead Sea. The **people of Seir** were the Edomites (see 20:10). Amaziah wanted to recover Edom as a Judean province, but he only succeeded in part (see 21:8, 10; 26:2).

25:13 The **soldiers** who attacked and sacked cities of Judah were those from Israel whom Amaziah had hired and then released (vv. 6, 10). Having been denied a part in the spoils of Edom, they set out to get them from Judah.

25:14 Amaziah had listened to the prophet of God, only to succumb to false worship later. This is why the chronicler said that Amaziah served God, "but not with a loyal heart" (v. 2).

25:15–18 The **thistle** here represents Amaziah, and the **cedar** Joash. It was arrogant for the weak, insignificant Amaziah to suppose that he could defeat Joash. The **wild beast** that passes by and tramples the thistle represents the war that Amaziah was so eager to pursue. Such a war would crush him.

25:19, 20 it came from God: As we find several times in 2 Chronicles, what appears to be a purely human decision or action turns out to be part of God's plan of blessing or judgment (see 22:7).

25:21 Beth Shemesh was 18 miles west of Jerusalem. The ark of the covenant came here when it returned from Philistia (see 1 Sam. 6:12–14).

25:22, 23 Since Ephraim lay north of Jerusalem, the **Gate of Ephraim** was probably in the northern wall of the city, perhaps the same as the later Damascus Gate. The **Corner Gate** was at the east or west end of the north wall.

25:24 One reason Joash's forces demolished the north wall was to gain access to the temple and its treasures. Obed-Edom's sons had been put in charge of the storehouse of the temple, probably meaning both the treasuries of the house of the Lord and the treasuries of the dedicated things (see 1 Chr. 26:15, 20). The **treasures of the king's house** refers not only to the king's private wealth but also to the state coffers.

25:25–27 The word **they** must refer to those who decried the defection of Amaziah from the Lord and who wanted to restore a godly regime. Thus Amaziah, like his father Joash (24:25), was assassinated. The fact that Amaziah reached the city of **Lachish** on the border with Philistia, some

25 miles from Jerusalem, suggests that he may have been seeking sanctuary among the Philistines.

25:28 City of Judah: This is an unusual way of speaking of the City of David. Since there is no note that he was buried with his **fathers** in the royal tombs, he probably was not.

26:1, 2 On the eastern arm of the Red Sea, **Elath** was technically in Edomite territory (see 8:17) but regularly was under Israel or Judah throughout Old Testament times (20:36; 21:8–10). Some time after Amaziah's death, Uzziah rebuilt Elath.

26:3–5 The **Zechariah** named here may have been the son of Jehoiada (24:20, 21).

26:6 Also known as Jabneel (see Josh. 15:11), **Jabneh** lay near the Mediterranean coast, less than 10 miles north of **Ashdod.** The geographical pattern of Uzziah's campaigns suggests that he was trying to gain access to the Mediterranean Sea and neutralize Philistine influence.

26:7 Gur Baal was most likely at present-day Tell Ghurr, about eight miles east of Beersheba. The **Meunites** were a desert tribe living mainly in Edom, south and west of the Dead Sea (see 1 Chr. 4:39–41).

26:8 The last recorded contact of Judah with Ammon was almost a hundred years earlier, in the days of Jehoshaphat. The **Ammonites** and Moabites had defeated the Edomites, but then began to fight each other (20:1, 22, 23). Evidently they still had not recovered sufficiently to prevent **Uzziah** from dominating them and extracting tribute from them.

26:9 The **Corner Gate** was at one end of the north wall of **Jerusalem** (see 25:23). The **Valley Gate** was on the west side of the city near the temple mount (see Neh. 2:13, 15).

26:10–14 Archaeological research has uncovered many **towers in the desert** that date from the time of Uzziah. **Carmel** was a region south of Hebron, not the famous mountain where Elijah confronted the prophets of Baal.

26:15 devices: This is one of the earliest references to catapults, which seem to have been defensive weapons, since their users

were **on the towers and the corners.**

26:16 Uzziah, swollen with pride, entered **the temple.** Uzziah was a descendant of David, but there were strict limits on his role in worship.

26:17 The **Azariah** named here may be the same as Azariah the son of Johanan (1 Chr. 6:10).

26:18 the priests, the sons of Aaron: Uzziah sinned when he exercised priestly privileges that were reserved for the Aaronic order (see Num. 16:39, 40).

26:19 Leprosy was any kind of serious skin condition (see Lev. 13:1—14:32).

26:20 The urgency of the priests to **thrust him out,** as well as Uzziah's own haste to leave, came from the strict requirements of the Law (see Lev. 22:2–6; Num. 12:10, 15). The Law viewed leprosy as a breach of God's holiness; it was a graphic symbol of defilement.

26:21 isolated house: Because of his uncleanness, Uzziah had no access to the temple either as a worshiper or as king. **was over the king's house:** Control of the temple and the state now passed to Jotham. This implies a coregency. As long as Uzziah lived, Jotham exercised power on his behalf.

26:22 Isaiah the prophet witnessed the last years of Uzziah but wrote virtually nothing about him in his book.

26:23 reigned: This simply means that Jotham made the transition from coregent (v. 21) to full and independent king.

27:1, 2 Jotham's **sixteen years** began eleven years before Uzziah died. This suggests that Uzziah had leprosy for more than a decade before he died.

27:3 The **Upper Gate** connected the temple and the royal palace (23:20). Jotham repaired or rebuilt it. **the wall of Ophel:** Ophel was the original Jebusite area of Jerusalem. Its walls dated back hundreds of years and must have required regular maintenance.

27:4 cities ... fortresses and towers: From the earliest days, the kings of Judah had built defense works and facilities for storing food and supplies. In Jotham's time the Assyrians and other potential enemies were becoming a threat, so this building was necessary.

27:5–9 Uzziah had reduced the Ammonite **people** to tributary status, but evidently they had broken free. Jotham therefore reasserted his control and forced renewed payments. **second and third years:** After three years the tribute ended, suggesting that Ammon once more regained its independence.

28:1, 2 Ahaz's reign of **sixteen years** could mean that he came to the throne about four years after the sixteen-year tenure of his father Jotham (see 27:1).

28:3 The **Valley of the Son of Hinnom** was just outside the western wall of Jerusalem. It was a dumping ground for all kinds of refuse, much of which was burned. The valley itself became a symbol of impurity. It was used as a site of pagan worship, including human sacrifice (see 2 Kin. 23:10; Jer. 7:31, 32; 19:2–6; 32:35).

28:4 every green tree: Canaanite nature cults focused on evergreens, probably as symbols of perpetual fertility.

28:5 king of Syria: Rezin (2 Kin. 16:5).

28:6 Pekah, who assassinated Pekahiah son of Menahem so he could become king of Israel (see 2 Kin. 15:23–25), reigned for 20 years (2 Kin. 15:27). He was murdered in a plot headed by Hoshea, the last king of Israel.

28:7 The **officer over the house** was a manager of the palace and all of its staff and activities.

28:8, 9 This prophet **Oded** is mentioned only here. **killed ... in a rage:** God used the Israelite armies to carry out his judgment on Judah (v. 6), but He never intended for the Israelites to enjoy it. Oded condemned their malicious and self-serving attitude.

28:10–12 The Israelites intended to make the survivors of Judah their **slaves,** although this was forbidden by the Law of Moses (Lev. 25:39–46).

28:13, 14 offended the LORD: This admission by Israel's leaders applies not only to the outrageous slaughter of their brethren from Judah (v. 6) but also to the whole course of their history until then. The Israelites could see from the rise of the Assyrians and their encroachment on Israel that the end was near.

28:15 anointed them: They applied balms and oils to the wounded.

28:16 The **kings of Assyria** were Tiglath-Pileser III, Shalmaneser V, and Sargon II.

28:17 The relationship between **Judah** and the **Edomites** changed often. Judah usually dominated Edom and was never under its control, but the extent of domination varied from one generation to the next. Now Edom was independent once again and powerful enough to invade Judah and take prisoners.

28:18, 19 lowland: This region between the hill country of Judah and the coastal plain is commonly called the Shephelah. **The South** was the Negev. **Beth Shemesh** was eighteen miles west of Jerusalem near the Philistine border. **Aijalon** was in the Aijalon valley seven miles north of Beth Shemesh. **Gederoth** was possibly the same as Gederah, located about three miles west of Aijalon. **Sochoh** was in the southern lowlands, about ten miles southwest of Hebron. **Gimzo** was eight miles northwest of Aijalon. All these places were near valleys that led up to central Judah from the surrounding plains. Control of them meant control of Judah itself. Because Ahaz understood this, he appealed to Assyria.

28:20–22 Tiglath-Pileser brought Mesopotamian influence over the countries of the eastern Mediterranean to its highest point. He undertook a campaign against Arpad in Syria and terrorized Menahem of Israel so much that Menahem paid him a huge bribe to be left alone (2 Kin. 15:19). Tiglath returned to the west again, and Ahaz scrambled for protection against Syria and Israel (2 Kin. 16:5–7; Is. 7:1, 2). The Assyrians overran Damascus and replaced the assassinated Pekah of Israel with Hoshea (2 Kin. 15:30), but they **did not assist** Ahaz. The king of Judah's troubles with the Edomites, Philistines, Arameans, and even Israelites (Is. 7:1) were over for the time being, but at great cost.

28:23 King Ahaz's idolatry and unfaithfulness to God (v. 19) led to God's judgment. Rather than repent, Ahaz sought to appease the gods who **had defeated him,** the **gods of Damascus.**

28:24 The account in 2 Kin. 16:10–18 relates how Ahaz, having seen an altar in

Damascus, ordered one like it built in Jerusalem. On this altar he offered regular burnt offerings.

28:25 If destroying **high places** is a sign of a godly reign (see 14:3, 5; 15:16; 16:6), then constructing them is a clear sign of the opposite.

28:26, 27 The term **kings of Israel** refers not just to the northern kingdom, but to the entire nation under God.

29:1, 2 Hezekiah was the only king of Judah who was as faithful to the Lord as **David** had been.

29:3 The **first year** of Hezekiah's independent rule began in 715 B.C. Hezekiah had ruled alongside Ahaz since 729 B.C. The fact that Hezekiah began his work on the restoration of the temple in his **first month** testifies to his zeal for God's work. Hezekiah **opened the doors** of the temple as a step toward spiritual renewal. Ahaz had closed the doors as an expression of hostility to God and the covenant (see 28:24).

29:4, 5 The **East Square** was the courtyard directly in front of the portico of the temple (see 4:9, 10; 6:13; 7:7).

29:6–9 captivity: This could refer to the fall of Samaria and deportation of the northern tribes just seven years earlier (2 Kin. 17:6). But under the wicked leadership of Ahaz, many of the people of Judah had been taken captive by Rezin of Damascus and Pekah of Israel (see 28:5–8).

29:10, 11 Hezekiah's **covenant** placed him and his people under the authority of God. Hezekiah pledged himself to lead the nation in faithfulness, as the terms of the original Davidic covenant demanded.

29:12 Kohathites ... Merari ... Gershonites: Hezekiah summoned the leaders of the three major Levitical clans, two leaders from each clan.

29:13 The family of **Elizaphan** was part of Kohath (1 Chr. 15:8).

29:14 Asaph was the father of a division of Levitical musicians (see 1 Chr. 25:1, 2). **Heman** and **Jeduthun** were musicians (see 1 Chr. 25:1, 3–5).

29:15 The phrase **at the words of the LORD** means that Hezekiah undertook his reformation at God's direction.

29:16 The **inner part** apparently refers to the Most Holy Place, and the term **temple** must refer also to the larger chamber, the holy place (3:5–7; 4:7, 8). The **court** was the inner court just outside the temple, the area restricted to the priests and Levites (4:9). The work of temple repair and restoration began in the Most Holy Place and then continued until it reached the courtyard.

29:17, 18 The work began on the **first day of the first month** of Hezekiah's reign, not of the calendar month (v. 3). **Sanctify** means to "cleanse or purify" or "to set apart for a holy purpose."

29:19 articles: Ahaz had destroyed some but not all of the temple implements (see 28:24).

29:20, 21 bulls ... rams ... lambs: The Law required the sacrifice of these animals for atonement of **sin** in general (see Lev. 1:3–13). On the other hand, the sacrifice of **goats** atoned for specific sins (Lev. 4:1–5:13). Here the priests offered **seven** of each kind to signify the wholeness of their repentance.

29:22–24 The repetition of **all Israel** here suggests that Hezekiah meant to include all twelve tribes, including the northern kingdom (see 30:1–9).

29:25 King David was responsible for religious as well as civil and political matters. He had exercised that responsibility by appointing Levitical musicians and instructing them about their temple ministries (see 1 Chr. 23:2, 27; 25:1–31). He was guided and advised by two of God's faithful prophets, **Gad** and **Nathan.**

29:26 The **instruments of David** were those deemed appropriate for temple worship (see 1 Chr. 25:1, 3, 5, 6).

29:27–30 The words of David and of Asaph refers to the psalms of David and Asaph (1 Chr. 6:39; 15:17; 16:5), many of them in the Book of Psalms. The people of Judah used these psalms for community worship and private meditation.

29:31, 32 Sometimes called "peace" or "fellowship" offerings, **thank offerings** celebrated the relationship gained by the offerings of atonement (vv. 21–24; see Lev. 3:1–17; 7:11–36). **willing heart:** People gave these gifts to God not out of compulsion but as a joyful response to the grace of God.

29:33 The thank offerings included people, priests, and God Himself. In effect, the **consecrated things** made up a banquet at which everyone gathered before the Lord for fellowship and communion.

29:34–36 Under Ahaz the **priests** and **Levites** had been stripped of their duties. Now, 20 years later, there were not enough priests. Hezekiah had to reconsecrate the older priests and commission new ones.

30:1–3 Though the kingdom of **Israel** had split more than two centuries before, **Hezekiah** never lost sight of the fact that God's covenant was made with all twelve tribes and that His promises included them all (see Ezek. 37:15–28). **The Passover** was ordinarily celebrated in the first month of the religious year (Ex. 12:6, 18). But this year the repair and consecration of the temple was still underway (see 29:1–17). The Law made provision for the Passover to be postponed if a person was absent on an important journey or was ritually defiled (Num. 9:9–12). Hezekiah interpreted this Law to include the priests who had not yet consecrated themselves to ministry (see 29:34). All the people of Israel had not had time to gather **together at Jerusalem** in any case, so they delayed the celebration until the **second month.**

30:4, 5 The fact that **all Israel** was included reveals that there were many followers of God left in the northern kingdom, despite more than 200 years of backsliding and the Assyrian conquest (see 29:24).

30:6, 7 the LORD God of Abraham, Isaac, and Israel: Hezekiah appealed to the nation on the basis of the ancient Abrahamic covenant (see 29:5). Even though the kingdom was divided and many of its people languished in exile far from home, God's promise could not change, and it bound them all together as God's people. They still had time to return to the Lord.

30:8 People who were not priests were not allowed to enter the temple, so **enter His sanctuary** is a figure of speech for serving the Lord.

30:9 The **brethren** and **children** were Israelites who had been carried away into Assyrian captivity. Hezekiah pleaded with the remnant left behind to repent, promising that this would result in better treatment of those in captivity and would guarantee their return to the **land.**

30:10 Zebulun was probably the northernmost territory of Israel at this time because Naphtali had been taken by Tiglath-Pileser III (2 Kin. 15:29).

30:11, 12 In Judah the reaction to Hezekiah's invitation was totally different from Israel's (vv. 10, 11), because God had put His **hand on Judah.** God's grace is always a part of a person's efforts to please Him.

30:13 Because the **Feast of Unleavened Bread** immediately followed the Passover and was connected to it (Lev. 23:4–8), the Feast of Unleavened Bread sometimes referred to the Passover as well (Ezra 6:22).

30:14 The debris removed from the temple had already been hauled off for burning (29:16), but the burnt offering and **incense altars** still remained in Jerusalem until the time of the Passover.

30:15, 16 The Levites killed the animals and then handed the **blood** over to the priests to apply it. Usually burnt offerings were sacrificed by the individual worshipers who gave the blood to the priests (Lev. 1:4, 5).

30:17 Traditionally the **slaughter** of the Passover lamb was performed by the head of the family (Ex. 12:3–6). But on this occasion many were not ritually purified, and the Levites acted on their behalf.

30:18–20 not cleansed … yet they ate: Those who came from distant parts of Israel were disqualified from sacrificing and did not do so. Still, they ate the Passover meal, in violation of the Law of Moses (see Ex. 12:43–49). They felt it more important to obey the spirit of the Passover than its letter. Hezekiah prayed for them, asking God to observe the desire of their hearts.

30:21, 22 taught the good knowledge of the LORD: Because of Ahaz's many years of wicked rule (28:23–25), the people of Judah must have become ignorant of the truths of their faith. The people from the north (v. 18) had virtually no preaching of God's revelation for

200 years, apart from the witness of the prophets such as Hosea and Amos. But the Levites' ministry included teaching (17:8–10; Deut. 17:18; 31:9–13; 33:10), and this great Passover was an opportunity to explain the history and purpose of God's covenant with Israel.

30:23, 24 Like Solomon before him (7:8–10), Hezekiah found it impossible to limit the festivities to eight days (including the Passover). Their common consent to celebrate **another seven days** was a sign of renewed spiritual vitality.

30:25, 26 The **sojourners** were aliens who lived in Israel and Judah and who could come to the festivals because they followed God and the Law (see Deut. 16:11; 26:11; 29:11; 31:12).

30:27 blessed the people: This may have been the formal blessing of Num. 6:24–26.

31:1 The phrases **all Israel** and **all the children of Israel** refer to the entire nation, north and south, Israel and Judah.

31:2 The long interruption (28:24) of Judah's official worship in the time of Ahaz brought chaos to their religious life. They abandoned the system of priestly and Levitical **division.** Just as David had originally organized the Levitical system (see 1 Chr. 23:1—26:28), so now Hezekiah had to reorganize it.

31:3 The **New Moon** celebrations came at the appearance of the new moon, the beginning of another month (see Num. 28:11–15). The feasts in view here were the Passover and Feast of Unleavened Bread (Lev. 23:4–8); the Feast of Firstfruits or Pentecost (Lev. 23:15–22); and the Feast of Tabernacles (Lev. 23:33–43).

31:4 The Law stated clearly that the people were to **contribute support** by their tithes and offerings so the work of the temple could go on (see Num. 18:8–24).

31:5 The early harvests of grain, particularly barley, were being reaped at this time. The Passover had been held in the second month (30:2) and it was now already the third (v. 7). The **firstfruits** began appearing at the time of the Feast of Passover and Unleavened Bread, and the harvests were fully gathered in some 50 days later, at the time of the Feast of Weeks or Pentecost (Lev. 23:9–22). **the tithe:** A

tenth of the harvest belonged to the Levites, whose sustenance depended on it (v. 4; see Num. 18:21–24).

31:6 The **holy things** were likely metals and other nonperishables (24:10, 11; see 1 Chr. 29:2, 7, 8) which were **consecrated to God** for use in worship and service.

31:7–9 The **third month** was the month after the delayed Passover (30:2) and the time of the early harvest (v. 5). The **seventh month** was Tishri, the month of the final annual harvest of fruits. The Feast of Tabernacles celebrated the year-end harvest (Lev. 23:39; Deut. 16:13) at this time. There was a continual ingathering from the third to the seventh month, and the people brought their tithes to the temple as an expression of renewed devotion.

31:10 The **chief priests** from Solomon's time onward were Zadokites (see 1 Kin. 2:27, 35).

31:11 prepare rooms: Places already existed in the temple for storing food supplies and other materials (see 1 Chr. 26:15, 20).

31:12–14 At the front of the temple the **East Gate** led to the great courtyard and the Kidron valley beyond (see 1 Chr. 26:14).

31:15 Because most of the priests lived in the cities allotted to them and not in Jerusalem (see 1 Chr. 6:54–60), Kore and his **assistants** took provisions to them (v. 14).

31:16 three years old: The boys described here were young apprentice priests dedicated to the office by their parents. Samuel had such a ministry (see 1 Sam. 1:24, 28; 2:18).

31:17 All religious personnel had to descend from Levi, but the priests as such had to trace their **genealogy** specifically to Aaron (see 1 Chr. 6:49–53).

31:18–21 all who were written in the genealogy: This is an all-inclusive way of designating both priests and Levites. Anyone whose lineage was Levitical could draw upon the tithes and offerings raised for their support.

32:1, 2 In Hezekiah's fourteenth year, **Sennacherib** invaded Judah and eventually laid siege to Jerusalem (2 Kin. 18:13–17). The **fortified cities** that he took had first been built and equipped by Solomon

(8:2–6), and then rebuilt and enlarged by Solomon's successors down to the time of Hezekiah (see 11:5–12; 14:6, 7; 17:12; 26:9, 10; 27:4; 32:29).

32:3 With the help of 2 Kin. 20:20 we learn that Hezekiah managed to **stop the water** by concealing the springs **outside the city** and then digging a tunnel to bring them to the Pool of Siloam inside the city walls. Hezekiah hid the source of water and made it unavailable to the enemy.

32:4 The brook was the Wadi Kidron, east of Jerusalem.

32:5 Millo means landfill and refers to extensive terracing that surrounded the ancient hills of Ophel and Mount Zion.

32:6 The main **city gate** was where the population could assemble and where court and other official functions were held (see 6:12; 29:4).

32:7, 8 more with us: This is not Judah's army; Hezekiah meant the armies of heaven (see 2 Kin. 6:14–17).

32:9 Both the Old Testament and Assyrian inscriptions document the **siege against Lachish,** an important fortified city west of Jerusalem and near the great coastal route (see 11:9). Its capture by Assyria would cut off access to Jerusalem from the west and would give Assyria control of the coast.

32:10, 11 The **siege** of **Jerusalem** had not actually begun, but Sennacherib's envoys spoke of it as already underway. Jerusalem was under siege psychologically.

32:12–16 Sennacherib's messengers tried to destroy the peoples' faith in God by pointing out that the other nations, despite their many gods and many altars, had been powerless to resist the Assyrians.

32:17 Sennacherib **also wrote letters** because he wanted to avoid a long and costly siege.

32:18, 19 Aramaic had become the language of international communication and diplomacy. The Judean negotiators wanted the matter discussed in Aramaic because they felt that they deserved to be addressed in regular diplomatic language. The Assyrians continued the dialogue in Hebrew to **frighten** and **trouble** the people.

32:20 By now **the prophet Isaiah** had been involved in public ministry to the kings of Judah for nearly 40 years (see 26:22; Is. 6:1). He had considerable prestige and was especially important as a counselor of young Hezekiah (see Is. 37:1–7).

32:21–23 Sennacherib **returned shamefaced to His own land,** Assyria, and its capital Nineveh. The same Sennacherib who had mocked God's ability to preserve Hezekiah and Judah (vv. 17, 19) now died a violent death while in the very act of worshiping **his god.** His two sons assassinated him 20 years after the siege of Jerusalem and fled for their lives. Then a third son Esarhaddon became king.

32:24 Hezekiah was sick: His sickness struck shortly after Sennacherib's defeat (see 2 Kin. 20:1, 12) and involved affliction with boils (see Is. 38:10–21). **a sign:** When Isaiah told Hezekiah he would recover, the king wanted confirmation. The sundial moved backward for him ten degrees, adding forty minutes to the day (Is. 38:8).

32:25–29 God had given Hezekiah an extraordinary **favor**—15 additional years of life (2 Kin. 20:6). But his **heart was lifted up:** Hezekiah had received Babylonian envoys who had come to congratulate him on his recovery and probably to enlist his support in their struggle against Assyria (2 Kin. 20:12–19). Their visit ignited his desire to show off all the treasures of his kingdom. Because of this indulgence in pride, God's **wrath was looming.** The account in Kings reveals Isaiah's response to Hezekiah's pride. The time would come, the prophet said, when all the wealth that **Hezekiah** had used to impress his visitors would be seized by the same Babylonians (2 Kin. 20:16–18).

32:30 Upper Gihon was a spring in the Kidron valley near the Water Gate.

32:31 The **test** was not for God's benefit, but for Hezekiah's.

32:32 The vision of Isaiah is the prophetic Book of Isaiah (Is. 1:1).

32:33 The term **upper tombs** probably refers to the royal cemetery where all the godly descendants of David were buried. Others were entombed in the City of David, but not in the same area (see 28:27).

33:1, 2 Manasseh was not the only king who lived according to the **abominations of the nations.** Ahaz did too (see 28:3).

33:3 The host of heaven were the gods of the sun, moon, and stars. The Babylonians especially revered these deities (see Deut. 4:19; Ezek. 8:16).

33:4 In Jerusalem shall My name be: The point was that God had the exclusive right to inhabit the temple, as opposed to the deities Manasseh introduced (v. 5).

33:5 In addition to altars inside the temple (v. 4), Manasseh erected altars to his star deities in the **two courts**—the court of the priests and Levites and the one open to the public (4:9; see 1 Kin. 7:9–12).

33:6 Valley of the Son of Hinnom: Like Ahaz, Manasseh practiced human sacrifice, going so far as to offer up his own children (28:3). **Soothsaying** is an attempt to determine the plans and purposes of the gods so as to avert their hostility or take advantage of their favors. **Witchcraft** and **sorcery** attempt to bring about desired results by using magical or mystical rituals. **Mediums** are those who claim to contact and consult with the dead. **spiritists:** These are "knowing ones" whose specialty also is communication with the dead in the hope of acquiring information inaccessible to the living. All such practices were common among Canaanite and other pagan religions and were to be strictly avoided by God's people (see Deut. 13:1–6; 18:9–14).

33:7–9 God's ancient promise never to remove the people of Israel from the land they had inherited was conditioned on their obedience to all the covenant stipulations—**law, statutes, and ordinances**—to which they had sworn (see Gen. 17:7, 8; Lev. 26:27–35, 46). Manasseh's behavior had jeopardized the presence of the people in the land.

33:10, 11 For some time **Babylon** had been part of the Assyrian empire, though it had broken free on occasion, especially under the leadership of Berodach-Baladan, Hezekiah's contemporary (see 2 Kin. 20:12). Ashurbanipal brought Babylon back under Assyrian domination. He was the king who took Manasseh to Babylon as a prisoner.

33:12–14 The term **City of David** originally referred to Mount Zion alone (see 1 Chr. 11:5) but eventually designated the entire city including Mount **Ophel,** the original Jebusite settlement. **Gihon** was the spring that was the main source of water for Jerusalem (see 32:3, 4, 30). Manasseh's construction of a water tunnel began at Gihon and went north past Mount Ophel to the northeast corner of the temple mount. Then it went west to the Fish Gate. This was a total distance of about 750 yards. These **fortified cities** were the same ones that had been captured by Sennacherib.

33:15, 16 Manasseh **took away** the old idols—a sign of true conversion and devotion to God (v. 13).

33:17–19 The sin of worshiping at **high places** was in their association with paganism (see Deut. 12:2, 3). God wanted all worship by the people as a community to take place at the temple. This is what is meant by the exclusiveness of the central sanctuary (see Deut. 12:5–28).

33:20 in his own house: Manasseh had truly converted (v. 13), but his prior sin had been so heinous that he was denied burial in the royal cemetery (see 32:33).

33:21, 22 The **carved images** were in addition to the wooden images he had made (v. 3). The images were representations of deity carved from wood or stone. The carved image to which **Amon sacrificed** had been set up in the temple as an idol (v. 7). It was later removed from the city (v. 15) but apparently not destroyed, since Amon set it up again.

33:23–25 At this time **people of the land** was a technical term that indicated a certain level of leadership, perhaps a council of elders. In crises like the assassination of Amon they could assume interim powers until proper government could be restored (see 22:1; 26:1; 36:1).

34:1–3 The **wooden images** were poles dedicated to Asherah, the Canaanite fertility goddess (see 33:3). The **molded images** were like the **carved images** except that they were made of molded metal (see Ex. 32:4, 8; Is. 42:17; Hos. 13:2).

34:4 Josiah's destruction of the altars and idols built by his grandfather Manasseh and father Amon recall Moses' grinding up the golden calf and scattering its **dust** upon the waters (Ex. 32:20).

34:5 burned the bones of the priests: This act of Josiah, which took place at Bethel, fulfilled the words of the prophet of Judah in the days of Jeroboam I, king of Israel (see 1 Kin. 13:1, 2; 2 Kin. 23:15, 16). The prophet had mentioned Josiah by name three hundred years before.

34:6, 7 Josiah's purge of the idolatrous cults was not limited to Judah and Bethel but extended from the south—**Simeon**—to the north—**Naphtali.** Israel had been subject to Assyria for a century, and new religious movements such as that of the Samaritans had gained a foothold in the region (see 2 Kin. 17:24–31; 23:19).

34:8 Shaphan was a scribe or secretary of the king (v. 15). He was responsible for state records that must have included the original temple plans and specifications. The temple was repaired strictly according to its original pattern. The office of **governor** was like that of the modern mayor (see 18:25). A **recorder** kept the royal diaries. The work of men like **Joah** provided sources for later historians such as the author of Chronicles (see 1 Chr. 18:15).

34:9 Hilkiah was probably the **high priest** of the genealogy of 1 Chr. 6:13 (see Ezra 7:1).

34:10, 11 Josiah's work of restoring what was destroyed included not only repairs to the temple and related buildings, but repairs to the fortifications (see 15:8; 24:5; 28:24; 29:6, 7; 32:5).

34:12–16 The **sons of Merari** and the **Kohathites** were two of the three clans of Levi (see 1 Chr. 6:1, 16; 23:6). **Shaphan** delivered the scroll because he was the king's scribe. He would know how to assess the authenticity of the text and tell the king whether it was important.

34:17–21 Josiah knew that the scroll contained the Book of the Law of the Lord, but he did not know what to do about the words of **wrath** and judgment that it contained. **our fathers have not kept … all that is written:** Josiah wanted to know what God demanded of him because he intended to comply.

34:22 Huldah the prophetess is one of four female prophets named in the Old Testament, the other three being Miriam (Ex. 15:20), Deborah (Judg. 4:4), and Noadiah (Neh. 6:14).

34:23 Thus says the LORD indicates that Huldah's words were a prophecy.

34:24, 25 written in the book: Both Deuteronomy and Leviticus have long lists of blessings and **curses** attached to the covenant with Israel (see Deut. 28; 29).

34:26–28 gather you to your fathers: This was a promise that Josiah would die and be buried among his own people, not in a foreign land. Huldah's promise that Josiah would die **in peace** meant that he would be spared the **calamity** by which Judah would be judged.

34:29, 30 The term **Book of the Covenant** refers to the Book of the Law of the Lord (v. 14), the Pentateuch. Josiah was about to lead the community in renewing the covenant. His reading of the scroll was part of his duties as king (see Deut. 17:18–20).

34:31 Very few of the kings of Judah promised to **follow the LORD** as Josiah did. After David, only Joash, Hezekiah, and Josiah made such public commitments (see 23:3; 29:10; 1 Chr. 17:7–14). They stand head and shoulders above the other kings of Judah and Israel.

34:32, 33 Josiah's commitment to the Lord was real because he **removed all the abominations.** This included all idols that had been introduced by earlier kings.

35:1–3 Josiah's command to **put the holy ark in the house** means that the ark of the covenant had been removed from the temple. Who removed it and when is not known, but there were plenty of wicked kings who could have done so. **no longer … on your shoulders:** The only proper way for transporting the ark was by means of poles thrust through corner rings of the ark and borne on the shoulders of the Levites (see Num. 4:5, 6; 1 Chr. 15:2). The fact that they were carrying it about shows that it had no regular place of storage. But once the temple had been cleansed and repaired, the ark could be returned to its place.

35:4 In preparation for the Passover the priests and Levites had to organize themselves by their assignments within **divisions.** The divisions were determined by the genealogical registers (see 1 Chr. 6:1–30).

35:5 The term **holy place** refers to the whole temple area. The **lay people** could not enter the area where the great bronze altar stood, so the Levites represented them there by tribe, clan, and family units. In former times the heads of families offered their own Passover lambs and thus had access to the altar (Ex. 12:3), but by Josiah's time the responsibility for slaughter rested upon the Levites alone (see 30:15–20).

35:6 prepare them for your brethren: The Levites were standing in for the people in the sacrifice of the **Passover** lambs. This became the tradition from that time on, with the result that the priests gained influence and power.

35:7 Normally the people provided the Passover **lambs and young goats** from their own flocks (Ex. 12:3, 5), but Josiah was being generous (see 30:24). That Josiah gave **thirty thousand** of them means that the total number of people must have been 150,000 or more, as each household offered its own lamb or goat.

35:8 Hilkiah was the chief priest under Josiah (see 34:9).

35:9–11 The way the **priests** and **Levites** prepared **the animals** was in accord with Moses' instructions (Ex. 12:4, 8, 9, 21, 22).

35:12 This particular Passover included a time of fellowship and praise. The **cattle** were used for **burnt offerings** (vv. 7–9) for the celebration of the thank or peace offerings (see Lev. 3:1–5). The offerer, his family, and the priests and Levites could eat any Passover animals and burnt offerings that were sacrificed as thank offerings. The Passover of Josiah was an occasion for recalling the deliverance of Israel from Egypt (Ex. 12:24–27), and a time of great festive celebration of God's goodness in bringing reformation and renewal.

35:13 The **other holy offerings,** distinguished from the Passover offerings, were the cattle slaughtered for thank or peace offerings (v. 7).

35:14 Themselves refers to the **Levites,** who had helped the priests.

35:15 Asaph, Heman, and Jeduthun headed up the Levitical musical divisions in the days of David (see 1 Chr. 15:17; 25:1). The day-long Passover celebration was accompanied by music.

35:16 It was most unusual to have such a combination of festivals and offerings all on **the same day.**

35:17 The Passover was held on the fourteenth day of the month Nisan (see v. 1) and was followed for the next **seven days** by the Feast of Unleavened Bread.

35:18 It had been almost four hundred years since the **days of Samuel the prophet** (see 1 Sam. 7:15–17). **None of the kings** had held so great a Passover in all that time (30:26).

35:19 Josiah was twenty-six years old (see 34:8) in the **eighteenth year** of his reign.

35:20 Located on the upper Euphrates River, **Carchemish** was one of the last strongholds of Assyria to resist the onslaught of the rising neo-Babylonian kingdom. Necho, more afraid of the Babylonians than the Assyrians, was hoping to get to Carchemish in time to assist his Assyrian allies in their time of peril. Josiah was an ally of Babylon, so he went to Megiddo (v. 22) to intercept the Egyptians and allow for the Babylonians to attack Haran and Carchemish without Egyptian interference.

35:21 The house is a reference to the Babylonians. **God commanded me:** God sometimes spoke to pagan rulers about a course of action He wanted them to take (36:22; see Gen. 20:6; 41:25; Dan. 2:28). Necho did not know that the source of his divine leading was the God of Israel and not one of his own Egyptian deities. But God did direct him, displaying His sovereignty over even the wicked and unbelieving powers of this world (see Is. 44:28—45:1).

35:22 The major route from Egypt to the upper Euphrates was the Via Maris or the Way of the Sea. This route went up the coast of Palestine before turning inland through the mountain pass at **Megiddo.** It crossed the Plains of Jezreel or Esdraelon, crossed the Jordan River near the Sea of Galilee, and passed through Damascus where it joined the north-south route to upper Syria. Josiah's objective was to control the pass at Megiddo and dictate the movement of traffic through that vital point.

35:23, 24 As a godly successor of David, Josiah was buried with full honors in the royal **tombs of his fathers** in the City of David (see 32:33).

35:25–27 The book of the kings of Israel and Judah may have been the canonical book of 1 and 2 Kings.

36:1, 2 The people of the land was a technical term that referred to a body of leaders such as a council of elders or a kind of informal parliament (see 33:25). This group acted in time of crisis, such as the death of Josiah in battle. His loss was made worse by the fact that he had at least four sons who could succeed him. Josiah may not have made his choice of successor clear.

36:3 The **king of Egypt** was Necho (see 35:20). After Assyria's defeat at Haran and Carchemish, the Egyptian army withdrew south of the Euphrates River to dominate Syria and Palestine. Judah became an Egyptian vassal state, which explains why Necho could depose Jehoahaz and require **tribute.** Judah had become a poor and weak nation.

36:4 Necho required the change of name in order to display his power over **Eliakim.**

36:5, 6 Nebuchadnezzar was the son of Nabopolassar, founder of the Neo-Babylonian or Chaldean Empire. He was leading a campaign against Carchemish when he succeeded his father. He drove Egypt out of Syria and Palestine and took some Jewish captives, including Daniel, back to Babylon (see Dan. 1:1). At the same time, Jehoiakim changed his loyalty from Necho to Nebuchadnezzar and remained a trusted vassal for three years (see 2 Kin. 24:1). But then Jehoiakim rebelled against Babylon, and in about 602 B.C. Nebuchadnezzar returned to Jerusalem to punish him. Nebuchadnezzar **bound** Jehoiakim **to carry him off to Babylon.** He did not actually take him away, since Jehoiakim reigned until about 598 B.C. and died of natural causes in Jerusalem (see 2 Kin. 24:6; Jer. 22:18, 19).

36:7–9 Nebuchadnezzar ... carried off: The Babylonian king looted the temple of its treasure, fulfilling the prophecy made to Hezekiah a century earlier (see 32:31; 2 Kin. 20:17).

36:10, 11 Zedekiah was the youngest of the four sons of Josiah and the third to rule over Judah (see v. 1). He became king by Nebuchadnezzar's appointment.

36:12 Jeremiah was the famous **prophet** who composed the Book of Jeremiah, which includes his words to Zedekiah (Jer. 21:3–7; 32:5).

36:13 By 588 B.C. Zedekiah **rebelled against King Nebuchadnezzar** and, like his brother and nephew before him, invited swift Babylonian retribution. Nebuchadnezzar captured Jerusalem after a two-year siege (see 2 Kin. 25:1–3).

36:14 The abominations of the nations refers primarily to idolatry and all the immorality and perversity that went with it. God's covenant with Israel required them to be different from the nations in this respect (see Ex. 23:24; Lev. 26:1; Deut. 4:15–20, 25–28, 18:9–14; 27:14, 15).

36:15, 16 messengers were the prophets He had sent from the beginning of Israel's history.

36:17–19 The **king of the Chaldeans** (Babylonians) was Nebuchadnezzar, who became an instrument of God's judgment all through Judah's last years and well into the Exile (see Dan. 2:37, 38; 5:18, 19).

36:20 until the rule of the kingdom of Persia: Cyrus of Persia conquered Babylon in 539 B.C. and allowed the Jews to return to Jerusalem the following year.

36:21 In two places (Jer. 25:12; 29:10), **Jeremiah** predicted the Exile and its length (see Dan 9:2). **Sabbaths:** According to the Law of Moses the land was to lie fallow every seventh year (Lev. 25:4). This became known as the sabbatical year. Judah's exile in Babylon allowed the land to enjoy the Sabbaths it had missed (see Lev. 26:33–35).

36:22 The **first year of Cyrus** refers to his first year of rule over Babylon, not his first year over Media and Persia. He began to rule Media and Persia in 550 B.C. Twelve years later he brought Babylon under his control and issued his famous decree, known from the Old Testament (here and Ezra 1:2–4) and from the Cylinder of Cyrus. **the LORD stirred up:** Cyrus was both a mighty monarch and the instrument by whom God delivered His people from exile, returned them to their land, and rebuilt the temple (see Is. 44:28—45:1).

36:23 the LORD God ... has given me: According to his own account on the Cylinder of Cyrus, the god who called and blessed Cyrus was Marduk, chief deity of the Babylonian pantheon of gods. Since that document was for Babylonian readers, his reference to Marduk is understandable. The Bible attributes his success to the living Lord. It was God Himself who gave Cyrus sovereignty, who commanded him to rebuild the **Jerusalem** temple, and who had inspired him to release the Jews to their own country. The temple and the holy city lay in ruins, but God was not done yet. He was about to bring His people back to the land and to revive His promises to save and restore them.

Ezra

Introduction

The Book of Ezra is a remarkable witness to God's faithfulness to His people. Ezra describes the events leading to the return of the Israelites from captivity in Babylon and the discouraging experiences of that small community in the harsh world of the Promised Land. But through every experience God proved Himself faithful. Through the leadership of Ezra and Zerubbabel, God fulfilled His promises announced by His prophets to restore His people from Babylon, to rebuild the temple at Jerusalem, and to renew their hope that the Davidic kingdom would be restored.

Jewish tradition ascribes the book to Ezra along with the books of Chronicles and Nehemiah. Modern scholars generally agree with this tradition. The fact that Ezra is the principal character of major sections of Ezra lends some credibility to his authorship of this book. Ezra participates in the events described in the second half of Ezra (chs. 7—10). These chapters are written in the first person, provide detailed descriptions, and point to an eyewitness as the author.

The books of Ezra and Nehemiah should be studied together for a better understanding of the return of the Babylonian exiles to Jerusalem. The combined narrative presents the story of the exiles' return in two time periods, each marked by two prominent leaders: rebuilding the temple, under Zerubbabel and Joshua the priest (538–515 B.C.); and restoring the worship of God and rebuilding Jerusalem's walls, under Ezra and Nehemiah (458–420 B.C.).

Yet the Book of Ezra is not simply a string of historical facts about the returning exiles. Instead, the narrative shows how God fulfilled His promises announced by the prophets. He brought His people back from Babylon, rebuilt the temple at Jerusalem, restored the patterns of true worship, and even preserved the reassembled community from fresh relapses into heathen customs and idolatrous worship. Through the prophets and leaders He had called, the Lord had preserved and cultivated a small group of returning exiles, the remnant of

Israel. With godly determination, they rebuilt the temple. Then the Lord sent Ezra and Nehemiah to exhort them to obey His law wholeheartedly. While the people were rebuilding Jerusalem's walls, God was rebuilding their hearts so that they would truly obey and worship Him.

1:1 The first year of Cyrus is the first year of his rule over Babylon. In 539 B.C. Cyrus the Great, founder of the greater Persian empire, conquered Babylon without a struggle. He ruled as king of Persia from 559–530 B.C. **the word of the LORD by … Jeremiah:** Jeremiah had prophesied that the Babylonian captivity would last 70 years (see Jer. 25:11; 29:10), after which the Lord would judge Babylon (see Jer. 25:12–14). Cyrus's **proclamation** was probably shouted by heralds in the principal towns of the empire and posted in public.

1:2 the LORD God of heaven: After the destruction of Jerusalem, God was no longer identified with the temple as the One who dwelt between the cherubim (see 1 Sam. 4:4; 2 Sam. 6:2). The Persians could understand that there was a particular "God of Israel," but they would have recognized Him as simply one god among others. However, the phrase *God of heaven* indicates that the Lord is not just another god, but that only He is God. The fact that Cyrus used this title for the Lord suggests that He was prompted by Jewish advisors.

1:3 He is God: It is likely that Cyrus was speaking as a polytheist who merely recognized that the **God of Israel** should be worshiped **in Jerusalem.**

1:4 let the men of his place help him: The assistance that the Israelites were to receive from their non-Jewish neighbors in rebuilding the temple is reminiscent of the help an earlier generation received from the Egyptians before the Exodus (see Ex. 12:35, 36).

1:5 Moved here translates the same Hebrew word as *stirred* in v. 1. The verb means "to rouse" or "to stir up" (see Is. 45:13; Hag. 1:14; Zech. 4:1).

1:6 All those who were around included non-Jewish neighbors (v. 3) as well as Jews who wanted to stay in Babylon.

1:7 King Cyrus also brought: The people who returned to Jerusalem were helped not only by their neighbors, but by the king himself. Cyrus ordered the return of the temple articles that had been taken by **Nebuchadnezzar** (see 2 Kin. 24:1–7, 11–13; 25:8–17; 2 Chr. 36:5–7, 9, 10, 13–19; Dan. 1:2).

1:8 Mithredath the treasurer: not the same as the Mithredath in 4:7. The name **Sheshbazzar** occurs only in two passages (vv. 8–11; 5:14–16), both related to official Persian actions. On the other hand, the name Zerubbabel is used in passages related to Jewish activity. Ezra 5:2, 16 appear to identify Sheshbazzar and Zerubbabel. It is possible that Sheshbazzar was a name by which Zerubbabel was known in Persian circles. **The prince of Judah** means Zerubbabel was in the Davidic royal line. Zerubbabel was the grandson of King Jehoiakim. In 1 Chr. 3:17–19 he is called the son of Pedaiah instead of Shealtiel. It

may be that Shealtiel died childless and his brother Pedaiah married his widow, following the custom of levirate marriage (see Deut. 25:5–10; 1 Chr. 3:18).

1:9–11 The separate items listed in vv. 9, 10 total 2,499. However, the total for **all the articles** given in v. 11 is 5,400. Probably vv. 9, 10 list only the larger and more important items that were transported back to Jerusalem.

2:1 The people of the province refers to the Jewish people of Judah (see 5:8; Neh. 1:2, 3; 11:3). The use of this phrase probably indicates that the register of ch. 2 was compiled in Babylon. Nehemiah's list in Neh. 7:4–73 would have been compiled after he arrived in Jerusalem, which could account for some of the differences between the two registers.

2:2 The men listed in this verse were the leaders of the expedition. Those who returned to Jerusalem are called **the people of Israel** and not Judah, because all twelve tribes of Israel were represented.

🔨 IN DEPTH New Reasons for Taking a Census

Census data has been used by governments throughout history for a variety of purposes: for example, to draft soldiers for military service, to collect tax revenue, and to conscript laborers for public works projects. When a census was taken of the Jews who returned to Palestine from Babylon (Ezra 2:1), the results were put to several new and interesting purposes:

(1) To return properties to their rightful owners. Generations earlier, Moses had taken a census of the Israelites as they prepared to enter Canaan, to obtain data to be used to divide the land among the tribes of Israel (Num. 26). Later, when the people took possession of the land, they settled in their allotted territories (Josh. 13—19).

From that time forward, each family's land was intended to stay in the family. In fact, an intricate set of laws was established to ensure that no family lost its land permanently. Thus when the exiles returned, it was important that they be able to trace their lineage in order to verify their claims to family lands or, in the case of priests and Levites, to Levitical cities (Ezra 2:3–58). Certain priests who could not prove their heritage were made to wait until a priest could consult God as to their status (2:59–63; Neh. 7:61–65).

(2) To collect resources for rebuilding the temple. Indirectly, the census became an occasion for the returnees to give a freewill offering that was used toward the building of a new temple (Ezra 2:68, 69).

(3) To redevelop and repopulate Jerusalem. Several years after this census was taken, Nehemiah reviewed it when he realized how empty Jerusalem was (Neh. 7:4, 5). Then the people cast lots in such a way that one-tenth of the population of Judah was relocated to the capital city in order to reclaim its public life (11:1, 2).

2:3–20 These verses contain the names and numbers of the families who returned to Jerusalem. It may be that these were the people whose homes were in the city of Jerusalem itself.

2:21–35 These verses list the returnees according to their cities. Note that Jerusalem is not listed. Perhaps the registry dealt first with the inhabitants of Jerusalem (vv. 2–20) and then focused on those outside Jerusalem.

2:36–39 The total number of **priests** listed is 4,289. This was about ten percent of the returning remnant.

2:40 The Levites assisted the priests in the temple and in teaching the people the Law (see Neh. 8:7–9). Compared to the number of priests who returned to Jerusalem (vv. 36–39), it is striking how few Levites were with them (other Levites are included in the special lists of vv. 41, 42). According to 1 Chr. 23:4, 24,000 Levites were involved in the worship of God during the time of David.

2:41 The singers were Levites who had the responsibility of praising God with music (see 1 Chr. 15:16). Though only 128 singers returned to Jerusalem, at one time there had been as many as four thousand people who "praised the Lord with musical instruments" in Solomon's temple (1 Chr. 23:5).

2:42 The gatekeepers, who were also Levites (see 1 Chr. 26:1–19), prevented unauthorized people from entering the restricted area of the temple. There were 139 gatekeepers in the return to Jerusalem under Zerubbabel; compare that figure to the four thousand gatekeepers who guarded the temple during the time of Solomon (see 1 Chr. 23:5).

2:43–50 Nethinim means "Given Ones" or "Dedicated Ones." In 1 Chr. 9:2, the Nethinim are distinguished from the priests and the Levites. Jewish tradition identifies the Nethinim with the Gibeonites who had been assigned by Joshua to assist the Levites in more menial tasks (see Josh. 9:27).

2:51–55 The sons of Solomon's servants are linked with the Nethinim (v. 43). The sons of Solomon's servants were probably descendants of the inhabitants of Canaan at the time of Solomon—that is, descendants of the Amorites, Hittites, Perizzites, Hivites, and Jebusites whom Solomon had hired to build the temple (see 1 Kin. 5:13).

2:56–63 Although these people could not prove their Jewish origin, they were permitted to return to Jerusalem. But without genealogies they were **excluded from the priesthood,** according to the Law of Moses (see Num. 16:1–40). **The governor** Zerubbabel was careful to follow the Law by declaring that the would-be priests **should not eat of the most holy things,** meaning that they should not participate in priestly functions.

2:64 forty-two thousand three hundred and sixty: The individual numbers listed in ch. 2 add up to only 29,818. It is possible that the larger total includes women, who are not named in the lists.

2:65 The **singers** listed here were not the temple choir of v. 41. These were professional singers employed for banquets, feasts, and funerals (see 2 Chr. 35:25; Eccl. 2:7, 8). Their presence could be an indication of luxury (see 2 Sam. 19:35). It appears that many of the Jewish people had achieved some prosperity while living in Babylon.

2:66 The large number of **horses** listed here also suggests affluence among those who returned to Jerusalem. Prior to this time, horses in Israel had been used only for war and ceremonies. Only the very rich and well-armed owned horses.

2:67 The beasts of burden were **camels** and **donkeys.** Camels were expensive; the poorer classes rode donkeys.

2:68 when they came to the house of the LORD: The first thing that many of the returnees did when they reached Jerusalem was to contribute to the rebuilding of the temple.

2:69, 70 Ezra records the amount of gold, silver, and garments given for the rebuilding of the temple, as does Nehemiah (see Neh. 7:70–72). However, the two sets of figures do not match. Apparently Ezra's list rounds off the figures, while Nehemiah's list presents them in more precise detail. It is also possible that the two lists give totals from different times of collection—perhaps in Babylon and then later in Jerusalem.

3:1 The seventh month was sacred to the Jewish people. The first day of the month was the Feast of Trumpets (see Num. 29:1–6), the tenth day was the Day of Atonement (see Num. 29:7–11), and the fifteenth day was the Feast of Tabernacles (see Num. 29:12–38).

3:2, 3 Jeshua was the same person as the priest Joshua (see Hag. 1:1; Zech. 3:1).

3:4 In obedience to God's Word, the Israelites observed **the Feast of Tabernacles** or Booths, which commemorated the earlier generation's wanderings in the wilderness (see Num. 29:13–38).

3:5–7 When Solomon built the first temple, he purchased materials from **Sidon and Tyre,** had them shipped to **Joppa,** and paid for them with grain, wine, and oil (see 2 Chr. 2:10–16).

3:8, 9 The construction of Solomon's temple had begun in the second month of the year (see 1 Kin. 6:1). Likewise, construction of the second temple began in the second month. **from twenty years old and above:** The Law had required that Levites be at least thirty years old before they entered into service (Num. 4:1–3). Later, the minimum age was reduced. The lower minimum age allowed more Levites to enter into temple service. This provision was vital in view of the small number of Levites who made the trip back to Jerusalem (2:40).

3:10, 11 The returnees to Jerusalem celebrated laying the temple's foundation in almost the same way that the previous generation had celebrated the first temple (see 2 Chr. 5:13).

3:12, 13 Solomon's temple had been destroyed in 586 B.C., and this scene took place fifty years later. The **old men** could remember the grandeur of the first temple, and they **wept.**

4:1 The adversaries of Judah were the Samaritans. Esarhaddon (v. 2), who ruled Assyria from 681–669 B.C., had transported the conquered people of the northern kingdom to other lands. He then brought people from other lands into Palestine. These foreigners intermarried with the Hebrews who were left in the land. Their offspring became the Samaritans.

4:2 we seek your God as you do: The Samaritans did not use the proper name for God—that is, Yahweh—perhaps suggesting that their understanding of the Lord was still quite poor. As a result, they presented the threat of syncretism, or mixing true worship of God with the worship of false gods.

4:3 You may do nothing with us is not a rude rebuff; it is a righteous refusal. The people offering help were not friends, but adversaries (v. 1). They may have sacrificed to the Lord, but they were idolatrous at the same time (see 2 Kin. 17:29–35).

4:4, 5 The people of the land is another way of referring to the Samaritans, who became active enemies of Israel's rebuilding program for the next several years. The Samaritans **troubled** the Jewish people, perhaps with threats and attempts to cut off their supplies. The Samaritans then **hired counselors,** or lawyers, probably to represent them against the Jewish community at the Persian court.

4:6 When Darius I died (486 B.C.), his son **Ahasuerus** reigned (485–465 B.C.). He is the same king who appears in the Book of Esther. At the beginning of his reign, the Samaritans wrote him a letter hoping to stop the Jews from completing work on the temple. Apparently nothing was accomplished by the letter.

4:7, 8 Artaxerxes Longimanus (464–424 B.C.) succeeded his father Xerxes. He too received a letter from the Samaritans against the Jews (v. 6). The letter was **written in Aramaic script, and translated,** or read aloud in Aramaic. Like the Samaritans' letter to Ahasuerus, this letter evidently was ignored.

4:9, 10 The point of these two verses is that the Samaritan letter reflected the views of the whole province. The beginning of the letter, filled with rhetoric and flourish, was designed to bring political pressure on the Persian king. **Osnapper** was probably another name for Ashurbanipal, the king of Assyria (669–626 B.C.) who completed the transplanting begun by Esarhaddon (v. 2).

4:11 Your servants is a technical term for vassals. By including this term in the introduction of the letter, the men were assuring the king of their allegiance and were reporting the rebellion of the Jewish people.

4:12, 13 the rebellious and evil city: The rebellion to which the Samaritans referred was the long period of siege the armies of Babylon were compelled to undertake against Israel. **finishing its walls:** The Jews perhaps had begun construction on the walls but were nowhere near completing them.

4:14, 15 The Samaritans suggested that the king search his official records to see if Jerusalem had been destroyed in the past because of rebellion. Indeed it had. Nebuchadnezzar had conquered Jerusalem years before because it had rebelled against him.

4:16 The Samaritan letter concluded with a warning that if the king did not stop the Jews, he would lose not only income, but also dominion over Jerusalem and the region beyond the Euphrates River.

4:17, 18 In this context, the word **peace** is used of the treaty relationship that existed between the king and his vassals (5:7).

4:19 A search of the king's official records confirmed the Samaritans' allegation of **rebellion** and **sedition** on the part of the people of Jerusalem, no doubt referring to the revolts under Jehoiakim, Jehoiachin, and Zedekiah (see 2 Kin. 24:1–20). The fact that these revolts were against the Babylonians and not against the Persians was not important. The Persians had become the heirs of the Babylonian empire, and they would take such a report seriously.

4:20 The Persian king also found out that Jewish kings had **ruled over** a large region. David and Solomon had both possessed a great sphere of rule. Subsequent kings had aspired to the former glory of David and Solomon.

4:21, 22 The Persian king Artaxerxes ordered the Jewish people to **cease** their work on the temple. However, he left open the possibility of a future change in policy. Years later at the request of Nehemiah the decision was reviewed (see Neh. 2:1–8).

4:23, 24 By force may suggest that the enforcers of the king's edict demolished the part of the wall that had been repaired. This would have been part of the rubble that Nehemiah discovered when he arrived in Jerusalem (see Neh. 2:12–16).

5:1 Haggai, who wrote the Old Testament book that bears his name, began his ministry in August, 520 B.C. (see Hag. 1:1). **Zechariah,** the prophet who also wrote an Old Testament book, began his prophetic ministry in October or November of the same year (see Zech. 1:1). The Jews had been forced to stop working on the temple (4:24). Now years later, God revived His work. He instructed His prophets to prophesy, and He expected His people to respond in faith and action.

5:2 Zerubbabel the civil governor and **Jeshua** (also known as Joshua) the high priest led the people once again in rebuilding the temple. The prophets Haggai and Zechariah joined in this call to action.

5:3 When the temple rebuilding resumed, resistance renewed. **Tattenai** was a regional **governor.** Since there were only twenty regional governors called satraps in the Persian empire (8:36), it may be assumed that Tattenai was a very powerful man. Zerubbabel, as governor of the small district of Judah, was under the authority of Tattenai (1:8). The regional governor and his staff personally visited Jerusalem.

5:4 The official delegation of Tattenai asked who had commanded the work on the temple to be done (v. 3). The answer in this verse gives **the names of the men who were constructing** the temple, but not the name of the one who commanded the work to be done.

5:5 The eye of their God is a way of speaking of the sovereignty and providence of God (v. 1): God was protecting and watching over those who obeyed His command. The governor decided that he would not stop the work on the temple until an **answer was returned** from the king.

5:6 The governor sent his inquiring letter to King **Darius** (who ruled from 521–486 B.C.). The fact that Tattenai contacted the emperor shows that despite his own considerable power, he still had to proceed under the process of Persian custom and law.

5:7, 8 The walls described in Tattenai's letter were the walls of the temple, not the walls of the city. **Timber** was used for the beams of the temple floor and roof.

5:9–11 In his report to Darius, Tattenai indicated that he had learned a great deal from the Jews about their history and destiny, including a reference to a **great king,** that is, Solomon.

5:12 Though the Jewish people acknowledged that **Nebuchadnezzar** destroyed the first temple, they traced the cause not to his power, but to their sin and ultimately to God's judgment. Tattenai's use of the title **God of heaven** is perhaps an unwitting acknowledgment of the reality and sovereignty of God.

5:13–16 This portion of Tattenai's letter to King Cyrus describes the events that led to the official Persian decree to rebuild the temple (1:1–4). Note that the delay described in ch. 4 is not mentioned here.

5:17 Apparently **the king's treasure house** contained the official records as well as the treasury. Tattenai's request to find the original decree **issued by King Cyrus** delayed the rebuilding.

6:1, 2 At the suggestion of Tattenai and his aides (5:17), **King Darius** ordered his staff to search the official records in the **archives,** or "house of the books," to see whether Cyrus had authorized the rebuilding of the temple at Jerusalem. Apparently nothing was found in **Babylon,** and the search moved on to **Achmetha,** the summer residence of the Persian kings.

6:3–5 King Darius began his reply to Tattenai by quoting from the **decree** of **King Cyrus.** Cyrus's public proclamation can be found in 1:2–4. **its height sixty cubits and its width sixty cubits:** Though the complete dimensions are not given, it is likely that the second temple was built on the foundation stones that were still in place from the time of Solomon (see 1 Kin. 6:2). The **three rows of heavy stones and one row of new timber** describes the construction of the wall of the inner court (see 1 Kin. 6:36). The heavy stones that had aroused Tattenai's suspicion (5:8) were expressly authorized.

6:6, 7 therefore: Based on the discovery of the decrees of Cyrus, King Darius issued an order of his own. He concluded that what the Jewish people were doing was legal and that the regional government should stop opposing them.

6:8–10 Moreover: King Darius endorsed Cyrus' order and added his own decree. **taxes on the region beyond the River:** Not only could Tattenai not stop reconstruction of the temple; he also had to fund its completion.

6:11, 12 Also I issue a decree: To ensure obedience, Darius decreed that violation of his order would be punished by death.

6:13 Tattenai **diligently** carried out the king's orders. There is no indication that Tattenai mistreated the Jews in any way.

6:14 and they prospered: God blessed the people because they listened to the prophets and the preaching of the Word of God. **Artaxerxes** (464–424 B.C.) did assist the rebuilding of the temple, although it was completed years before Artaxerxes came to power. Artaxerxes contributed to the welfare of the temple by issuing a decree about its maintenance (7:15, 21).

6:15 The temple was completed in 515 B.C. in **Adar,** the month of February-March.

6:16 celebrated … with joy: Some people have suggested that Pss. 145—148 were used to celebrate the completion of the rebuilding of the temple.

6:17 As was the case with the dedication of the first temple, this dedication was celebrated with an abundance of **sacrifices.**

6:18 The Law laid down the duties of the **priests** and **Levites** (see Num. 18). Later the **divisions** of priests and Levites were instituted by David.

6:19 This celebration of **the Passover** must have been memorable; it was the first time since the captivity that the people were able to celebrate according to the Law—with sacrifices offered in the temple (v. 20).

6:20 The priests and the Levites … purified themselves so they could perform the duties of their office. The Levites **slaughtered the Passover lambs** for themselves and others.

6:21 The nations of the land evidently refers to the people who had been transplanted into Palestine by the Assyrians (4:4). Those **who had separated themselves** were Israelites who had remained in the land during the captivity. The **filth** from which they separated themselves was the idolatry practiced by the pagans and perhaps their intermarriages with foreigners.

6:22 The Feast of Unleavened Bread imme-diately followed the Feast of Passover. **The king of Assyria** is a reference to Darius. Even though he was actually the king of Persia, Darius could be called the king of Assyria because he was the ruler of the former realm of Assyria. The title **God of Israel** was probably effective in helping the Jewish people recapture a sense of their heritage and re-kindle their hope.

7:1–5 after these things: The events of ch. 6 took place during the reign of King Darius; more specifically the temple was completed and dedicated in 515 B.C. Chapter 7 jumps forward many years to the reign of **Artaxerxes** (464–424 B.C.), for Ezra re-turned around 458 B.C. Thus between chs. 6 and 7 there is a gap of approximately 60 years. During this period, the events of the Book of Esther took place. **Ezra,** the leader of the second return to Jerusalem, is intro-duced with a long genealogy, demonstrating that he was from a priestly family—the fam-ily of **Aaron.**

7:6, 7 Ezra was not only from a priestly fam-ily; he was also **a skilled scribe**—one who copied and studied the Law. After the Exile, the office of scribe came into prominence, in some ways replacing the prophet in impor-tance, and eventually eclipsing even the role of the priest. **The Law of Moses** refers to God's law. Moses may have been the person most closely associated with the Law, but it was the Law that **the LORD God of Israel had given.**

7:8, 9 The first month is March-April; the **fifth month** is July-August. The route trav-eled by Ezra was dangerous because a rebel-lion had broken out in Egypt and spring was the time when ancient armies began their campaigns.

7:10 Throughout his life, Ezra had concen-trated fully on the study, practice, and com-munication of the Word of God. **Heart** indicates the whole of one's being. Ezra dili-gently searched the Scriptures so that he could live by them and teach them to Israel. Because of this, the gracious hand of God empowered him (v. 9).

7:11 the priest, the scribe, expert: These words describe Ezra with exceptional praise. Ezra is referred to as "the scribe's scribe" or the teacher of scribes.

7:12 Ancient Middle Eastern monarchs com-monly took self-aggrandizing titles such as **king of kings** (see Ezek. 26:7; Dan. 2:37). The Persian kings were literally kings over many kings because the Persian empire in-cluded many conquered kingdoms.

7:13–19 Three sources of offerings for the temple are listed: (1) **the silver and gold** of **the king and his counselors,** (2) **the sil-ver and gold** of the people of Babylon, and (3) **the freewill offering** of the Jewish **peo-ple** who remained in Babylon. The **dwell-ing** of God **in Jerusalem** is a reference to the temple.

7:20 And whatever more may be needed: Ezra had what amounted to a royal blank check.

7:21–23 The decree of Artaxerxes included an order to the provincial **treasurers** to al-low Ezra to claim extra supplies from them. However, there were limits on the supplies. Ezra could take no more than one hundred talents of silver (nearly four tons), one hun-dred kors of wheat (about 625 bushels), and one hundred baths each of wine and oil (about six hundred gallons each).

7:24 All temple officials were exempt from every form of **tax.** Artaxerxes, like Cyrus (1:2–4) and Darius (6:1–10) before him, wanted to win the goodwill and avoid the wrath of the gods that were worshiped throughout the empire.

7:25, 26 Ezra was given authority to set up a judicial system with the power to punish. Al-though the **magistrates and judges** had authority over only Jewish people, their au-thority extended beyond Jerusalem to Syria, Phoenicia, and Palestine.

7:27, 28 To beautify the house of the LORD is a reference to the reestablishment of moral, spiritual, and religious life. **I was encour-aged:** With renewed vigor, Ezra gathered **leading men of Israel** to return to Jerusa-lem with him.

8:1 These are the heads of their fathers' houses: The list of people who returned to Jerusalem recalls the list of the men for war at the time of the anticipated conquest of the land of Canaan (see Num. 1; 26).

8:2–14 In this list, twelve families are represented by their chiefs and the number of males in each family is given. The total number of the heads of families who accompanied Ezra back to Jerusalem was 1,496.

8:15, 16 Ezra discovered that there were no **sons of Levi** among the returnees who accompanied him back to Jerusalem. Zerubbabel had faced a similar problem. Over four thousand priests returned with him to Jerusalem, but only 74 Levites were among the returnees (2:36–42).

8:17 The location and significance of **Casiphia** is uncertain. It has been suggested that this is Ctesipon on the Tigris River, near modern Baghdad. The Hebrew word for **the place,** a synonym for the holy place (see Deut. 12:5), may mean that there was a Jewish sanctuary or temple in Casiphia.

8:18–21 On the road to Jerusalem, the large Jewish caravan would have been an easy target for robbers. Knowing that the returnees needed the Lord's help, Ezra **proclaimed a fast** as a symbol of their submission to God.

8:22, 23 To persuade the king to let him return to Jerusalem, Ezra had told him about the **power** and **wrath** of God. So when Ezra received the king's permission to return, he was **ashamed** to ask for an armed **escort.**

8:24–30 Before the returnees departed, Ezra entrusted the load of valuables to twelve people. Although v. 24 reads as though **Sherebiah, Hashabiah,** and their **brethren** were **priests,** v. 18 indicates that they were Levites. Verse 30 confirms that the treasure was entrusted to priests and Levites. Ezra followed the Law, which taught that the priests were to handle the sacred objects and the Levites were to carry them (see Num. 3:8, 31, 45).

8:31 According to 7:9, the returnees began their journey on the first day of the first month. According to v. 15, the returnees camped at the river for three days. Yet this verse speaks of the departure on **the twelfth day of the first month.** These time discrepancies may be explained as follows: The people began to assemble at the river on the first day of the first month. During the course of the first three days,

Ezra discovered that there were no Levites among the travelers. During the next eight days, Ezra enlisted Levites (vv. 15–20), entreated the Lord (vv. 21–23), and entrusted the travelers' considerable load to the priests and Levites (vv. 24–30). The returnees then departed from the river on the twelfth day. So from their point of view, the journey to Jerusalem began on the first day of the first month, when the people left their homes in Babylon. The group departed from the river on the twelfth day of the first month.

8:32 The returnees arrived in **Jerusalem** on the first day of the fifth month (7:9). The trip took about three and one-half months (compare 7:9 with 8:31).

8:33, 34 After three days rest, the returnees deposited their treasury in the temple (see Neh. 2:11). Four men—two priests and two Levites—counted and **weighed** everything. A **written** inventory was then put on file.

8:35 The **sin offering,** which consisted of **twelve male goats,** one for each tribe of Israel, was for the atonement for sins. The **burnt offerings** signified the surrender of the entire nation to the service of the Lord.

8:36 The king's orders were the authorization for Ezra to administer the Jewish law among the Jewish people of the province. Satraps, or "protectors of the realm," were highly placed individuals who ruled under the emperor in various regions of his empire (5:3).

9:1 When these things were done: These words seem to imply that **the leaders came** to Ezra immediately after the events of ch. 8. Actually, over four months passed between the events of ch. 8 and those of ch. 9. Ezra arrived on the first day of the fifth month (7:9) and he deposited the treasure in the temple on the fourth day of the fifth month (8:33). The assembly that took place soon after the leader's report occurred on the twentieth day of the ninth month (10:9). The delivery of the royal orders to the regional governor (8:36) may have taken weeks or even months. Ezra did not just deliver the decree; he secured the support of the king's satraps and governors. **The people ... have not separated themselves**

from the peoples of the land: Both the leaders and the people of Israel had failed to remain separate from the Gentiles who lived in the land.

9:2 The Jewish returnees were marrying the pagan peoples of the land, a practice that the Law of Moses expressly prohibited (see Ex. 34:16; Deut. 7:3).

9:3–5 knees ... hands: Physical postures of prayer are often described in the Bible. Kneeling is a sign of humble respect. Raising one's hands is a sign of openness to God and recognition that all gifts are from the Lord's hand.

9:6 ashamed and humiliated: Ezra felt an overwhelming sense of shame. His prayer was one of confession. Though Ezra had not participated in this sin himself, he identified with the sins of the people.

9:7 Ezra further acknowledged that the people's sinful actions were part of their history. The whole nation—**kings** and **priests,** as well as the people—had sinned in the past, and they had suffered for it at **the hand of the kings of the lands.**

9:8, 9 a peg in His holy place: This metaphor refers to a peg in the wall on which a utensil is hung (see Eccl. 12:11). God's mercy had permitted the remnant to be fixed in the place God had chosen. **enlighten:** God had given the light of His will to those who were in the darkness of sin. **bondage:** The people were no longer slaves; they were free.

9:10–12 Ezra confessed the sins of the nation by referring to what **the prophets** had preached. The prophets prohibited intermarriage with Gentiles (see Deut. 7:1–3; 23:7; Mal. 2:10–16).

9:13–15 Ezra ended his prayer not by asking for forgiveness, but by declaring that God was **righteous** (see Deut. 32:4; Ps. 119:137; Zeph. 3:5). Israel was guilty and deserved whatever justice God gave them.

10:1, 2 Many people in Israel were concerned about the sin in their midst. So while Ezra wept, prayed, and confessed, these people **gathered** around him and **wept very bitterly.**

10:3 Making a **covenant** with God means binding oneself by an oath to God to do

something. It was the most binding form of commitment a person could make.

10:4 Arise: Shechaniah (v. 2) reminded Ezra that it was his **responsibility** to teach Israel the law of God (7:25).

10:5–8 within three days: This was a reasonable demand because Bethel (2:28), Lod (2:33), and Jericho (2:34) were some of the more distant Jewish cities, and they were all within three days' journey. According to the Law, the money from the sale of **confiscated** property went into the temple treasury (see Lev. 27:28, 29, where *devoted* means "confiscated").

10:9 The ninth month (Chislev; see Neh. 1:1) is November-December.

10:10–14 The people faced two problems: (1) There were too many of them for the investigation to be done in a day or even two days. (2) The weather would not permit them to stay in Jerusalem. The people who had traveled from a distance could not stay in the city, living and sleeping in the open air, during the cold, rainy period. Therefore they requested that the investigation be organized by their officials.

10:15–17 Two men, with the support of two Levites, opposed Ezra's plan. The reasons for their opposition are not given. Apparently their objections had no effect (vv. 16–18). **Meshullam** is likely the same man who was part of the group of learned teachers that Ezra had recruited (8:16); however, he is not the same man who is mentioned among the repentant offenders in v. 29.

10:18–24 They gave their promise may also be translated "they gave their hand." The symbol of raising a hand to take an oath is still practiced in many cultures. With this sign, the Israelites agreed to put away their unlawful wives and offer a sacrifice according to the requirements of Lev. 5:14–19. Although this promise and sacrifice are mentioned only in connection with the priests, it is likely that everyone on the list fulfilled these requirements.

10:25–43 Others of Israel refers to the people, as opposed to the leaders.

10:44 Even though some had had **children** with their pagan wives, they still separated themselves from them.

Nehemiah

Introduction

This book is principally the story of gifted leadership in the person of Nehemiah. Facing criticism and opposition, Nehemiah resolutely led the small Israelite community as they rebuilt the walls of Jerusalem for its physical protection. But he also did not hesitate to guide the Israelites spiritually. By demanding that the Israelites obey God's law, Nehemiah pursued their spiritual as well as their physical welfare.

Many readers conclude that the book was written by Nehemiah because of the words of the first verse, "The words of Nehemiah the son of Hachaliah." In fact, it is widely believed that Nehemiah originated the following passages: 1:1—7:5; 12:27–43; 13:4–31. But there are two different views of the authorship of the rest of Nehemiah. Some believe that Nehemiah wrote the whole book, relying on his own memories. Others believe that Ezra wrote the book, using Nehemiah's memoirs, for the passages listed above.

After the exile of the Jewish people, Nehemiah occupied a prominent position in the court of the Persian king. He was the trusted cupbearer of King Artaxerxes I. In 444 B.C., Artaxerxes allowed Nehemiah to go to Jerusalem and rebuild its walls. Nehemiah stayed in Jerusalem for twelve years and then returned to Persia in Artaxerxes' thirty-second year. Around 425 B.C., Nehemiah left Persia and returned to Jerusalem for the last time (13:6). Nehemiah's memoirs could not have been completed until after his second visit to Jerusalem. Thus, the earliest that the Book of Nehemiah could have been completed would be around 425 B.C.

The Book of Nehemiah records the restoration of Jerusalem under the leadership of Nehemiah. In the book, the returning Jews showed spiritual lethargy and a coldhearted indifference toward God. It took a determined, godly leader like Nehemiah to motivate this group to act on God's promises and rebuild Jerusalem's walls.

The Book of Nehemiah makes it clear that God did not restore His people only one time; rather, He repeatedly, constantly, and continually restored His people. In spite of their unfaithfulness, God accomplished His will. The restored walls of Jerusalem, the repopulation of Jerusalem, and the repeated reformation of the Israelites was clearly God's work. In the end, His name would be glorified.

1:1 Nehemiah, whose name means "The Lord Comforts," was a highly placed statesman associated with Ezra in the work of reestablishing the people of Judah in the Promised Land. **The month Chislev** corresponds to our November-December (see Ezra 10:9). **The** twentieth year refers to the twentieth year of the rule of Artaxerxes I Longimanus (464–424 B.C.)—that is, 444 B.C. Artaxerxes was the same Persian king who had commissioned Ezra to return to Jerusalem (see Ezra 7:1). **Shushan the citadel** was about 150 miles north of the Persian Gulf, in present-day Iran.

1:2 Nehemiah's brother **Hanani** (7:2) had visited Jerusalem and returned to Shushan. This journey, which covered nearly a thousand miles one way, would probably have taken at least four months. Nehemiah was concerned about the Jewish people and Jerusalem.

1:3 Life was difficult for the people in Jerusalem. This difficulty was due in large part to the condition of Jerusalem's **wall.** In the ancient Middle East, a city wall provided protection for the inhabitants. The condition of a city wall was also seen as an indication of the strength of the people's gods. The ruined condition of the wall of Jerusalem reflected badly on God's name.

1:4 wept ... mourned: Nehemiah was deeply disturbed. Without a wall, Jerusalem was vulnerable to attack. The riches of the temple treasury (see Ezra 8:15–36) would have been quite a temptation for Israel's enemies.

1:5 God of heaven: Nehemiah acknowledged God's government of the world, including His sovereignty over the pagan king who was over Nehemiah, the Jewish people, and the city of Jerusalem. **covenant and mercy:** By using these two words together, Nehemiah was holding God to His promises. The Lord had staked His character on His loyalty to His covenant with His people.

1:6 let Your ear be attentive and Your eyes open: Nehemiah asked God to look at him and listen to him as he prayed. These words were designed to encourage the one praying, for God does not turn His ears from or close His eyes to His people (see Ex. 2:23–25). **the children of Israel:** By using this ancient name for the Jewish people, Nehemiah indicated the continuity of the Jewish people of his day with the Israelites of the past: Nehemiah then confessed the sins of his father's house as well as his own.

1:7 Israel had sinned against the Lord and against His **commandments.** By using the word **we,** Nehemiah included himself among the sinful people. **commandments … statutes … ordinances:** These words describe the totality of God's law (9:13, 14).

1:8 Remember: After confessing his sin and the sin of the people, Nehemiah reminded God of what He Himself had said. **I will scatter you among the nations:** This is an allusion to God's covenant in Lev. 26:27–45 and Deut. 30:1–5. Nehemiah himself was born in Persia, a distant nation, because of God's fulfillment of this promise.

1:9 The Lord had promised that if the nation of Israel would **return** to Him in obedience, He would regather them to their land. Nehemiah addressed the Lord as a covenant-keeping God. He confessed his and the people's sin because the Law demanded confession (see Lev. 16:21). Then he held God to His covenant to return Israel to the land. **bring them to the place which I have chosen as a dwelling for My name:** The ultimate intent of God's covenant was not just to return the people, but to return them to the place where God had established His name. For that to be accomplished, much needed to be done.

1:10 Your servants and Your people: By using this phrasing, Nehemiah was suggesting to the Lord that the time was right, the people were right, and the task was right to restore Jerusalem. **Your strong hand** is one of the phrases associated with God's deliverance of Israel from Egypt (see Ex. 6:1; 13:14; 15:6; Deut. 6:21).

1:11 Your servant … Your servants: Nehemiah and the godly people of Israel shared common concerns before God. **let Your servant prosper:** Nehemiah requested permission to return to Jerusalem, rebuild the wall, and restore the community. He enjoyed the comfort and convenience of a royal palace and a position of honor and responsibility. There were many compelling reasons for him to stay where he was, but he asked for permission to do God's work. As **the king's cupbearer,** Nehemiah held an honored position. His constant proximity to the king of Persia made him privy to the state secrets and personal affairs of the king.

2:1 Nisan corresponds to March-April. **sad in his presence:** Four months after hearing the report from his brother about Jerusalem, Nehemiah was still grieving over the conditions in Jerusalem.

2:2 The king noticed Nehemiah's sad expression and concluded that it was caused by **sorrow of** heart rather than physical illness. **I became dreadfully afraid:** Persian monarchs believed that just being in their presence would make any person happy. Yet, Nehemiah was about to request the emperor's permission to go to Jerusalem, suggesting that he would rather be somewhere other than in the emperor's presence. On top of that, it was Artaxerxes himself who had ordered the work on the wall to be stopped (see Ezra 4:21–23). Nehemiah had reason to be afraid.

2:3 live forever: Addressing the king with proper respect, Nehemiah related the burden of his heart. **the place of my fathers' tombs:** It is possible that this phrase was designed to catch the king's attention. In many Asian cultures, a connection with the burial places of one's ancestors was a matter of great importance.

2:4 I prayed: Even though Nehemiah had come into the presence of **the king,** he had never left the presence of the true King of kings.

2:5 After his silent prayer (v. 4), Nehemiah spoke boldly, asking for permission to leave the king's palace to travel to Jerusalem to rebuild the wall.

2:6 How long will your journey be … when will you return: In responding to Nehemiah's request (v. 5), the king might have had

Nehemiah executed on the spot; or he might have dismissed Nehemiah with a laugh. However, his questions implied that the request was already granted. **I set him a time:** The fact that Nehemiah responded quickly to the king's request for specific details indicates that he had been planning the trip.

2:7 Nehemiah knew that he needed safe passage for his journey to **Judah,** so he requested **letters** from the king to show to **the governors of the region beyond the Eu-phrates River.**

2:8 Nehemiah's plans were detailed. He asked the king for permission to go to Jerusalem (v. 5), for letters to ensure safe passage (v. 7), and also for provisions. Nehemiah requested a letter addressed to **Asaph, the** man in charge of **the king's forest,** to enable him to obtain supplies of lumber for three projects: (1) the **gates of the citadel,** (2) **the city wall,** and (3) his personal **house.** Jerusalem had plenty of limestone for building projects. But timber, necessary for making roofs and other parts of large building projects, was scarce. **according to the good hand of my God:** The king graciously granted Nehemiah all that he had requested, but Nehemiah knew that the ultimate source of his provisions was God.

2:9 captains of the army and horsemen: Nehemiah had a military escort to Jerusalem. In 458 B.C. Ezra had journeyed to Jerusalem with 1,800 people carrying valuable treasures, and had refused a military escort (see Ezra

8:22). Fourteen years later, Nehemiah made the same trip with a smaller company and no valuables, but the king sent an escort with him.

2:10, 11 Sanballat was the governor of Samaria. **Horonite** refers to Sanballat's city Beth-Horon. **Tobiah** was probably Sanballat's secretary and confidential advisor. **Ammonite:** At the time of Nehemiah, the Ammonites (see Gen. 19:38) had pushed west into the land vacated by Judah. The prospect of a strong Jewish community in newly fortified Jerusalem would have seemed threatening to the Ammonite power.

2:12–15 Since Nehemiah had arrived in Jerusalem from the north, he would have seen that side of the wall as he approached the city. If he lived in the southwestern part of the city, he would have had ample time for viewing the western wall. Nehemiah seems to have been concerned with inspecting the southern and eastern walls of Jerusalem. With a few servants, he passed through **the Valley Gate** into the Valley of Hinnom. He then traveled along the south wall. When the piles of stone and heaps of rubble obstructed his passage, he dismounted his animal and continued on foot up the Kidron valley in order to view the eastern wall.

2:16 the officials did not know: The only people who knew Nehemiah's plans were the few men who had made the secret night ride with him (v. 12).

2:17 we: Nehemiah encouraged all of the

IN DEPTH — Nehemiah's Religious Reforms

Although Nehemiah is usually remembered for what is considered his greatest accomplishment, rebuilding Jerusalem's wall, he was also a religious reformer. Like Ezra, Nehemiah was a purist in religious matters. True worship was only possible to the undefiled, and to Nehemiah that disqualified all of the people who had remained in the land during the Exile. Only the returned exiles, who had kept the faith pure while in captivity, were acceptable. When Nehemiah found that Tobiah, one of his enemies and an Ammonite official (Neh. 2:19), had been given rooms in the temple itself, he was aghast and removed Tobiah promptly (13:7–9). Nehemiah also restored official support of the Levitical ministers (13:10–14) and resumed enforcement of the Sabbath laws (13:15–22).

people to assist in rebuilding the city's walls.

2:18 Nehemiah emphasized that it was not just *his* idea to rebuild the wall of Jerusalem. Rather, the idea had come to him from the Lord (vv. 8, 12). In response to Nehemiah's challenge, the people replied, **Let us rise up and build.**

2:19 In v. 10, Nehemiah mentioned two men who were unhappy about his coming—Sanballat and Tobiah. Here the opposition grows to three. **Geshem** was the leader of a company of Arab troops maintained by Sanballat. In v. 10, Nehemiah's opponents were grieved; here **they laughed.** They accused Nehemiah of false motives, of plotting rebellion against the king.

2:20 Nehemiah ignored his opponents' accusation that he was rebelling against the king. He asserted that God was involved in what he was doing. Nehemiah's motive was not rebellion against the king, but submission to God.

3:1 Eliashib the high priest and the other **priests** were the first people to start rebuilding Jerusalem's walls. At this point in Israel's history, the priests were the leaders. There were no kings or judges, so the people looked to the priests for leadership. It is significant that the high priest and the priests **built the Sheep Gate.** The Sheep Gate was on Jerusalem's northeast side, just north of the temple and was used for bringing sheep to the temple for sacrifice. **they consecrated it:** The priests dedicated the repaired gate, wall, and tower to the Lord. They knew that unless God blessed the city with His presence, no walls and gates would keep the people safe (see Ps. 127:1).

3:2–4 Next to: The idea here is that the people worked together—not just in the same place, but in cooperation.

3:5–8 The Broad Wall was probably built in the seventh century B.C. by Hezekiah to accommodate the influx of refugees from the fall of Samaria in 722 B.C. (see 2 Chr. 32:5).

3:9–14 This verse describes the rebuilding of the southern portion of Jerusalem's wall.

3:15 The Fountain Gate probably faced the En Rogel spring. **The Pool of Shelah** is also known as the Pool of Siloam or Shiloah.

3:16–28 In the easternmost part of the city,

the Horse Gate was the gate leading to the Kidron valley.

3:29–32 Goldsmiths and **merchants** also labored on the wall. They were not bricklayers, but they worked just the same.

4:1 furious … indignant: These two words together mean "burning with rage."

4:2 Sanballat gathered men from the **army of Samaria,** his local militia, and then mocked the Jewish people with sarcastic questions. **these feeble Jews:** The verb from which the adjective *feeble* is derived is used of a woman who is no longer able to bear children (1 Sam. 2:5). **fortify … offer sacrifices … complete it in a day … revive the stones:** Sanballat poured contempt on the Jewish people and on their God. The reference to reviving the stones came from the fact that the stones of the former wall had been **burned.** When limestone is subjected to intense heat, it becomes unsuitable for building.

4:3 Tobiah, the aide of Sanballat (2:10, 19), carried Sanballat's jest (v. 2) even further. Tobiah declared that if a small creature like **a fox** jumped on the wall, the wall would collapse because of its flimsy construction.

4:4, 5 Nehemiah did not respond to his opponents (vv. 2, 3). Instead, he prayed that the Lord would not forgive them. Nehemiah believed that when the people of God were involved in the work of God, any assault on them was an assault on God.

4:6–8 When their ridicule did not stop the work on the wall, Nehemiah's opponents tried a threat of attack. The opposition against Nehemiah had started with two people (2:10) and had grown to three (2:19). Here it had become a multitude, one which surrounded Jerusalem. **Sanballat** was a Samaritan; Samaria was north of Jerusalem. **The Arabs** were to the south, **the Ammonites** to the east and **the Ashdodites** to the west.

4:9 Prior to this verse the prayers recorded in the Book of Nehemiah are individual prayers. This one was a group prayer. Nehemiah's spirit had affected the entire group of workers. They not only prayed, but they set a **watch** and did what was humanly possible to protect themselves from attack.

4:10 Under the circumstances, some of the workers became discouraged. The wall was half finished (v. 6), but the task was taking its toll. The words of the fatigued **laborers** appear as a song or poem in the Hebrew text.

4:11, 12 While the Jewish workers became discouraged (v. 10), the opposition intensified. The **adversaries** began a whispering campaign among the Jewish people to stop the building of the wall.

4:13 I positioned men: Because there was no Jewish army, the people had to defend themselves. Nehemiah placed men strategically on the wall. From the high places on the wall, men could see the approaching enemy. Other men defended the low places of the wall.

4:14, 15 nobles ... leaders ... rest of the people: Nehemiah's strategy was to address both leaders and laypeople. In this way, all the community would have "ownership" of the same ideals. **fight for your brethren:** Nehemiah reminded the Jewish people that they were not mercenary soldiers earning a salary or hoping for loot. Not only were their own lives at stake, but so were the lives of their loved ones. God answered Nehemiah's prayers. The people were inspired by his wise words and **returned** to their tasks.

4:16–18 Nehemiah armed the workers and divided his own **servants** into two groups. Half of them worked on the wall and half of them stood guard. Since the builders needed both hands to work, their swords were hung on their sides. Those who carried baskets of debris on their heads held their weapons in one hand and supported the load with the other.

4:19, 20 Nehemiah instituted an alarm system for those who worked on the wall. Apparently the workers were scattered all over the wall and separated so far from each other that some were beyond the reach of the human voice. For that reason, a trumpeter with a ram's horn stood near Nehemiah wherever he went. If the wall was attacked, the alarm would gather all of the people quickly to the danger spot.

4:21–23 Nehemiah instituted a twenty-four hour work and watch program. The people worked during the day and stood guard at night. Workers living out of town were asked to remain in the city rather than return home.

Except for **washing,** Nehemiah and his men never took off their **clothes.** They worked day and night.

5:1–5 The prolonged period of working, watching, fear, and weariness inevitably led to trouble among the people in Jerusalem. There were three groups of complainers, each introduced with the phrase **there were those who said.** The first group had large families, and did not have enough food to eat. The second group had large mortgages to pay and could not buy food. The third group had large taxes to pay and had been forced to mortgage their land and even to sell their children. While hunger, shortages, taxes, and money were the immediate results of the people's circumstances, they were not the heart of the problem. The people's basic problem is pinpointed in the words **against their Jewish brethren.** The people were not complaining just about poverty and high taxes; they were grumbling about each other. In v. 1 the **people** refers to the poor; the *brethren* refers to the rich rulers (v. 7). In short, this was a class conflict. The poor people had **mortgaged** their **lands and vineyards and houses.** They had **borrowed money** and even had sold their sons and daughters into slavery. From the perspective of the Law, there were two problems here: (1) usury, lending money and charging interest, and (2) slavery. It was not wrong for a Jewish person to lend money with interest to a non-Jewish person (see Deut. 23:19, 20), nor was it wrong for a Jewish person to lend money to a fellow Jew. However, the Law did prohibit usury (see Ex. 22:25). Interest rates were exorbitant and could easily lead a person into poverty and enslavement. This leads to the second problem. According to the Law of Moses, a Jewish person could hire himself out to someone, but not as a slave (see Lev. 25:35–40).

5:6 I became very angry: Nehemiah's first response to the sins of the Jewish people was anger. Deliberate disobedience of the Word of God ought to make a person indignant toward the sin—but not toward the sinner.

5:7–10 After getting angry at the sins of the Jewish people (v. 6), Nehemiah spent some time in **serious thought.** He then confronted the guilty people. After rebuking the guilty parties privately, Nehemiah confronted them in public with the same charges. When Israel, a nation called by the Lord, stopped honoring and obeying Him, it became a scandal because God's name was being dishonored.

5:11, 12 Nehemiah challenged the lenders to **restore** what they had taken with interest. The **hundredth of the money** is probably a reference to the interest they had been charging.

5:13 Nehemiah **shook** his **garment** as if he were getting rid of what he was carrying. In doing so, he dramatized what God would do if the people broke their promise. God would shake them loose from their houses and their possessions.

5:14 During his twelve-year administration (444–432 B.C.), Nehemiah did not collect taxes from the people, although as governor he had that right.

5:15 Several **former governors** had paid their own expenses with the people's taxes. **laid burdens:** The former governors had made life difficult for the people. **Rule** here indicates an arbitrary, oppressive rule—the abuse of power through extortion.

5:16–18 Nehemiah had not acquired mortgages on **land.** As governor, he could easily have acquired real estate and sold it at great profit. But instead of making money for themselves, Nehemiah and his servants worked on the wall of Jerusalem for the protection of the people and the glory of God.

5:19 Nehemiah's motives were pure. He was not doing **good** for the praise of men, but to please God. His prayer is repeated at the end of the book (13:31).

6:1, 2 Nehemiah's enemies, realizing that open opposition had not worked and that the wall was close to being finished, suggested a conference. Somehow, perhaps by a word from the Lord, Nehemiah was warned of his enemy's intent.

6:3–7 The evidence that was used to accuse Nehemiah of rebellion was the assertion that **prophets** were proclaiming Nehemiah to be king. Nehemiah's enemies threatened to take

the matter to the king of Persia. They used this threat as leverage to force Nehemiah to attend their proposed meeting. Although they had no real intention of going to the king (v. 9), they hoped their threats would ruin Nehemiah's reputation so that the workers would lose their resolve.

6:8, 9 Nehemiah would not allow himself to get sidetracked. Instead, he committed his enemy's accusations to the Lord (see Ps. 31:13, 14).

6:10 Evidently **Shemaiah** was a priest. When Nehemiah visited him, Shemaiah proposed that they enter the holy place to be safe from assassins. Shemaiah's suggestion was for Nehemiah to flee into the sanctuary. It was lawful for an Israelite to seek refuge at the altar outside the temple (see Ex. 21:13, 14), but only a priest could enter the holy place. Nehemiah's enemies were subtly tempting him. If they could trap him in sin, this would discredit him and the work.

6:11–16 God gave Nehemiah the wisdom to discern the error in Shemaiah's counsel. **Tobiah and Sanballat** were the principal instigators behind Shemaiah. Nehemiah indignantly rejected Shemaiah's counsel for two reasons. A man such as himself should not **flee.** Nehemiah was the governor, a leader of the people. He was responsible to the king and ultimately to the King of kings. A man in his position should not run and hide out of fear.

6:17–19 Here is a postscript. It turns out that during the building of the wall, a number of personal letters had been exchanged between some of the **nobles of Judah** and **Tobiah.** Tobiah and his son **Jehohanan** had married Jewish women. Some of the nobles sang Tobiah's praises to Nehemiah and then reported back to Tobiah everything they learned from the governor. With these letters, they hoped either to entrap Nehemiah in his own words or to intimidate him.

7:1 The Levites were assistants to the priests (Num. 18:1–4) and guarded and cleaned the sanctuary. Nehemiah **appointed** the Levites to their duties in the temple. **The gatekeepers** and **singers** were numbered among the Levites. The gatekeepers kept watch over the house of God and opened and closed the gates of the temple court (see 1 Chr. 9:17–19; 26:12–19). The singers led the people in their musical worship of God.

7:2 Nehemiah appointed two guards over the city as municipal officers in charge of security, each guard responsible for half of Jerusalem (3:9–12). One of the guards was Nehemiah's brother **Hanani,** who had visited Jerusalem and brought back a bleak report to Nehemiah in Shushan (1:2). The other guard was **Hananiah.**

7:3 Nehemiah not only established guards over Jerusalem (v. 2); he also established guidelines for protecting the city. **The gates** of a city normally opened at sunrise, but Nehemiah ordered Jerusalem's gates to be kept closed until the sun was high. This extra precaution would have discouraged enemies from mounting a surprise attack at sunrise. Gates were critical to the defense of an ancient city.

7:4 For the size of the **city,** Jerusalem was underpopulated. Even though it was 90 years since people had returned under Zerubbabel to live there, there was still much undeveloped space within the walls renewed by Nehemiah.

7:5 my God put it into my heart: Nehemiah attributed to the Lord the idea of a census that would show the distribution of the population. If he knew the population pattern in the capital and the countryside, he could then determine which districts could best afford to lose a portion of their inhabitants to Jerusalem.

7:6–73 Nehemiah discovered a list, recorded by families, of the names of the Jewish people who came from Persia to Judah in 536 B.C. under Zerubbabel. This long list consisted of the names of leaders (v. 7), people by families (vv. 8–25), people by cities (vv. 26–38), priests (vv. 39–42), Levites (vv. 43–45), Nethinim or temple servants (vv. 46–56), Solomon's servants (vv. 57–60), returnees without a genealogy (vv. 61–65), the total number of people (vv. 66, 67), their animals (vv. 68, 69), and the gifts given for the support of the work (vv. 70–72). This same list is found in Ezra 2 with some minor variations. One thousand gold **drachmas** would weigh about nine pounds.

8:1 The phrase **all the people** indicates that people gathered together from the cities and the countryside of Judah. The **open square** was presumably located between the southeast part of the temple and the eastern wall. The leader—in this case, the reader—was **Ezra.** This is the first time Ezra is mentioned in the Book of Nehemiah. The people instructed Ezra to get the Book of the Law, which Ezra had brought to Jerusalem as much as 13 years before. What had been confined to private study among learned men was made public to everyone.

8:2 In Scripture, **women** are often presumed to be present in group gatherings; here they are mentioned explicitly. Everyone **who could hear with understanding**—that is, older children as well as adults—gathered **on the first day of the seventh month.** The wall had been completed on the twenty-fifth day of the sixth month (6:15) so this event took place just a few days after the completion of the wall.

8:3, 4 morning until midday: This would have been a period of about six hours.

8:5 As Ezra unrolled the scroll, **the people stood,** signifying their reverence for the Word.

8:6, 7 Before reading the Book of the Law, Ezra led the people in prayer. **Blessed** here indicates identifying God as the source of the blessing of the people (see Ps. 103:1). The people answered **Amen** and lifted their hands, indicating their participation with Ezra in prayer.

8:8 they read distinctly: The Levites explained fully the meaning of the Law of God. **they gave the sense:** The Levites explained the Law so that the people got the sense and insight of what was being read.

8:9–11 Once the people understood the Word of God, they **wept.** They had heard the high standard of the Law and recognized their low standing before the Lord, and were convicted. Nehemiah, Ezra, and the Levites were undoubtedly glad to see the people's conviction. However, they urged the people to stop crying and reminded them that this **day** was **holy to the LORD.** The first day of the seventh month (v. 2) was the Feast of Trumpets. It was not a time to weep, but to celebrate. The people were instructed to celebrate the feast with eating, drinking, and sharing. **Strength** here means "place of safety," a "refuge," or "protection." The people's refuge was God: They had built a wall and they carried spears and swords, but He was their protection.

8:12 The people went to their houses **to eat and drink,** to share and **rejoice,** because they took to heart the words of Nehemiah, Ezra, and the Levites (vv. 1–9). They obeyed the Word of the Lord and celebrated the Feast of Trumpets.

8:13 The **heads** of families, **the priests,** and the **Levites** came back the next day to hear more teaching from God's Word. **understand:** Even the leaders gathered to gain the sense of the Scriptures and how they should act.

8:14, 15 By this time, the reading of the Law had advanced to Lev. 23. The listeners discovered that they were to observe the Feast of Tabernacles from the fifteenth to the twenty-second day of the seventh month. During this time, the people were to live in **booths** made of fresh branches of fruit and palm trees. This feast was observed in memory of their ancestors' living in booths—that is, tents—after the Exodus (see Lev. 23:40).

8:16 The people observed the Feast of Tabernacles according to the Law. Those who lived in cities built their **booths** on the flat tops of their houses or **in their courtyards.** The priests and Levites built their booths in **the courts** of the temple. The people from the country constructed huts in the street before the **Water Gate** and the **Gate of Ephraim.**

8:17 since the days of Joshua ... the children of Israel had not done so: The reference here is to the construction of booths. The people of Israel had certainly celebrated the Feast of Tabernacles since the days of Joshua. In fact, those who had returned with Ezra kept the feast the first year of their return (see 1 Kin. 8:65; 2 Chr. 7:9; see especially Ezra 3:4).

8:18 The reading of the Law was required during the celebration of the Feast of Tabernacles, which occurred on the Sabbath year (see Deut. 31:10, 11).

9:1 the twenty-fourth day of this month: The people's public worship had begun on the first day of the seventh month (8:2). More than three weeks later, the people were still engaged in public worship.

9:2 Of Israelite lineage means "the seed of Israel." The separation **from all foreigners** was a sacred separation from foreign persons who worshiped other gods and whose practices might have brought harm to the integrity of the Lord's worship by His people. **their sins and the iniquities of their fathers:** The confession of the people's own sins was for personal and corporate forgiveness; the confession of their father's sins was for remembrance, that they might not continue in past evil actions and attitudes.

9:3, 4 As in 8:5, the people **stood** in reverence at hearing the reading of the Scriptures. **one-fourth of the day:** Approximately three hours (compare 8:3) were spent in public reading and three hours were spent in corporate worship.

9:5 Your glorious name: The importance of the name of God can scarcely be overestimated. This psalm is solidly based on the theology of the Law (the books of Moses) as would be expected following the three-week reading of the Scriptures (8:1, 2). Thus this poem's exaltation of the Lord's name is based on God's own revelation of His name recorded in the Book of Exodus (see Ex. 3:14).

9:6 One of the fundamental teachings of Scripture is that God is not one among many; He **alone** is the living God (see Deut. 6:4). **heaven ... earth ... seas:** God alone has made all things, and He alone preserves all things. Therefore, worship is due Him.

9:7, 8 You are the LORD God: The use of the definite article on the word God marks Him as "the true God." **Abraham:** The point here is to emphasize God's grace. Abraham did not seek out the Lord. Instead God sought him. **You found his heart faithful:** The subsequent history of the people of Israel was not marked by the steady faithfulness seen in Abraham, much to the displeasure of the Lord. The Promised Land, **the land of the Canaanites,** was populated by diverse groups of people who had all lost their right to the land because of their sinfulness (see Gen. 15:18–21; Ex. 3:8, 17; 23:23; 33:2; Deut. 7:1; Josh. 3:10).

You have performed Your words: This is the essence of the psalm. God's faithfulness to His people cannot be challenged.

9:9 The Book of Exodus tells about the plight of the Israelites in Egypt and their complaint to the Lord for deliverance. It then speaks of God's mercy in His response to the people's need. This verse suggests that before the people expressed their hurt, the Lord was already aware of their troubles.

9:10 The **signs and wonders** were the ten plagues of Ex. 7—12. These great acts of God were directed primarily against Pharaoh. **acted proudly:** In Ex. 18:11, Jethro, the father-in-law of Moses, used this same phrase to describe the presumptuous actions of the Egyptians. It was the proud actions of the Egyptians that brought God's judgment on them.

9:11, 12 Note the simile of Pharaoh's troops sinking **as a stone** (compare Ex. 15:5). **cloudy pillar ... pillar of fire:** The continued presence of God in the lives of His people was indicated by these symbols.

9:13, 14 The significance of the **Sabbath** in God's law for Israel is celebrated here (see Ex. 20:8–11; 23:10–13; 31:12–18). **By the hand of Moses:** The Law came from the Lord, but it was given by the agency of Moses (see John 1:17).

9:15 The gifts of **bread,** or manna (see Ex. 16:9–35), and **water** (see Ex. 17:1–7) demonstrated God's care for His people in their journey to the Promised Land.

9:16, 17 The sin of the Israelites was that they **acted proudly**—that is, they behaved toward God in the same way that the people of Egypt had behaved toward them. The primary reference here is to the rebellion of Israel against the Lord at Kadesh (see Num. 13; 14). The people's rebellion went so far that they **appointed a leader** to take them back to Egypt. **Ready to pardon** means abounding in forgiveness. **Slow to anger:** This phrase translates a Hebrew idiom ("long of nose") that has the same meaning as the English expression "to have a long fuse." Because of the God's loyalty and steadfastness, He **did not forsake** His people.

9:18–21 In these verses, the poet describes the faithfulness of God to the Israelites in the wilderness despite their wretched behavior. **Molded calf** is a reference to the act of rebellion described in Ex. 32. **Manifold mercies** describes deep feelings like those of a mother for her child. **You did not forsake them** is repeated from v. 17. God would have been justified in abandoning His people because of their extreme sinfulness and wicked rebellion; yet He was compelled by His character not to do so.

9:22–25 The poet describes the mercies of God in Israel's conquest of the Promised Land and in God's continuing provision for them. **kingdoms and nations:** The Bible celebrates the conquest of the land east of the Jordan River, as well as the conquest of Canaan itself. **as the stars:** The miraculous growth of the people is described in this familiar hyperbole (see Gen. 15:5; 22:17). **strong cities ... rich land ... houses:** With few exceptions, the people of Israel conquered the inhabitants of Canaan in such a way that they were able to move into the Canaanites' undamaged homes and cities. The Israelites were also able to enjoy crops and wells for which they did not have to work. All of this is testimony to God's **great goodness.**

9:26–29 The rebellion of the people was expressed during the period of the judges and throughout the period of the kings. **Cast Your law behind their backs** is a graphic metaphor for rebellion. **You delivered them into the hands of their enemies** refers to the experiences of the Israelites during the period described by the Book of Judges. **he shall live by them:** Salvation in any period is only by grace through faith (see Eph. 2:8, 9). Keeping the Law was never a means of salvation, but a guide for living a life that pleases the Lord.

9:30, 31 God continued to be faithful to His disobedient people. **For many years** refers to the history of the people of Israel from Saul to the last of the kings. **Your spirit in Your prophets** speaks of God's work in inspiring the words of the prophets of Israel (see Jer. 1:9). **You gave them into the hand of the peoples of the lands** refers to the captivity of Israel.

9:32 Now refers to the time of the great revival

under Ezra (8:1, 2). **covenant and mercy:** God's covenant loyalty is unbreakable (see Heb. 6:17, 18). **Do not let all the trouble seem small:** In view of the unspeakable wonder of God, the hardship of His people might seem too small a matter to be noticed. **kings ... people:** The effects of Israel's trouble were all-inclusive.

9:33–35 You are just: The poet affirms the righteousness of God. **You have dealt faithfully ... we have done wickedly:** This is the basic reality not only of this chapter, but of the history of God and His people.

9:36, 37 Servants is used as a term of irony here. The people of Israel had been called to be the servants of God (see Lev. 25:55), but here they were servants of foreign rulers. The produce of the land did not belong to them; it went to **kings.** The people were taxed by Persians for the produce of the land that was God's gift to them.

9:38 The psalm ends in action, not just sentiment. The intent was changed behavior. The pledge was to mirror God's faithfulness. The new **covenant** community desired to demonstrate the faithfulness of Abraham and Sarah.

10:1 The way someone "signed" a **document** in the ancient world was similar to the use of a wax **seal** in more recent times. A distinctive seal was pressed into soft clay. The pattern of the seal showed what authority issued that document.

10:2–8 The **priests** who sealed the covenant are listed here. Some of these names appear in a later list as heads of priestly houses (12:11–20). Twenty-one priests who were heads of households signed the agreement in the name of the houses and families of their respective classes.

10:9–13 The **Levites** also signed the covenant. Some of these names appear later as heads of the orders of Levites (12:8).

10:14–27 Forty-four **leaders** also signed the covenant. In contrast to the religious leaders, these were the political leaders of the Jewish community (compare 7:4–63; Ezra 2).

10:28 Not only leaders, but laypeople signed the covenant. **The Nethinim** were temple servants who did menial work in the sanctuary (see Ezra 2:43). **Those who had separated themselves from the peoples of the lands** were the descendants of those Israelites who had been left in the land and who joined the returning remnant. Men, women, and children of sufficient age signed the covenant.

10:29 entered into a curse: The phrase points to the penalties for failure to comply with the covenant. The people took an oath to live by the Word of God. **God's Law:** The Law was a gift of God, **given by Moses.** The Israelites swore that they would observe the law of God.

10:30 The Israelites' decision to obey the Word of God in every area of their lives (v. 29) was not just a general statement. The people specifically vowed to obey the Word of God in their marriage relationships. Marriage with non-Jewish people was clearly forbidden in the Scriptures (see Ex. 34:12–16; Deut. 7:3; Josh. 23:12; Judg. 3:6). **We would not give our daughters ... nor take their daughters:** The parents of Israel decided that they would not permit their children to marry non-Jews. In the ancient world, marriages usually were arranged by the parents.

10:31 This verse deals with **Sabbath** observance. Three particulars about the Sabbath are mentioned. First, the people promised to stop all buying and selling from foreigners on the Sabbath. Second, they pledged to observe the Sabbatical year—that is, to leave their fields uncultivated during every seventh year (see Lev. 25:1–7). Third, they decided not to collect debts during the Sabbatical year (see Deut. 15:1–6).

10:32–39 The remainder of the chapter covers the people's promise to obey the Word of God about the temple. In this area, the people made four promises: (1) They promised to pay a temple tax to defray the expenses of the worship services in God's sanctuary. (2) They promised to provide a **wood offering.** The Law prescribed that wood should be constantly burning on the altar (see Lev. 6:12, 13). (3) They promised to offer their **firstfruits** at the temple. The firstfruits of the ground were given to the Lord as an acknowledgment of His status as landowner (see Ex. 23:19; 34:26; Deut. 26:2). (4) They promised to pay **the priests.**

11:1–3 Nehemiah **cast lots** to repopulate Jerusalem. Here the casting of lots was to determine God's will. **one out of ten:** This was the proportion demanded in order to bring the population of Jerusalem to the level deemed necessary for its strength and viability.

11:4–9 Four hundred and sixty-eight men from the tribe of Judah lived in **Jerusalem; nine hundred and twenty-eight** men from the tribe of **Benjamin** also lived there. According to 1 Chr. 9:3, descendants of Ephraim and Manasseh also made their home in Jerusalem.

11:10–12 The work of the house refers to the work of the temple—specifically, attending the sacrifices of the temple.

11:13–15 Mighty men of valor refers to the men who guarded the city of Jerusalem.

11:16–18 The oversight of the business outside of the house of God refers to the maintenance of the temple, including repairs.

11:19 The gatekeepers were also defenders of the city.

11:20–22 the overseer of the Levites: Uzzi was a principal administrator of the temple.

11:23, 24 The king's deputy was the representative of the people. This individual may have received and forwarded petitions and complaints to the king.

11:25–36 These verses record the residents outside Jerusalem—namely the tribes of Judah (vv. 25–30) and Benjamin (vv. 31–36). The people of Judah lived in 17 towns and their surrounding villages. The descendants of Benjamin occupied 15 sites. **Kirjath Arba** is another name for Hebron.

12:1–8 The return of **Zerubbabel** is recorded in Ezra 1—6. **Jeshua** is Joshua the priest. **Ezra:** This is not the priest who wrote the book of the same name (see Ezra 7:1).

12:9 stood across from them: The singing was conducted with two choirs standing opposite each other.

12:10, 11 The listing of the descendants of **Eliashib** all the way to **Jaddua** may indicate that someone who lived after Ezra and Nehemiah added some of these names.

12:12–21 In vv. 1–7, the names of twenty-two **priests** are listed. Here only twenty names are recorded. Hattush (v. 2) and

Maadiah (v. 5) are not mentioned in this list.

12:22 Darius refers to Darius II (Nothus), who ruled Persia from 423 to 405 B.C.

12:23 The book of the chronicles was not the biblical book, but an official record of **the heads of the fathers' houses.**

12:24–29 After the completion of Jerusalem's wall (ch. 6), a revival of the people broke out (see chs. 8—10). After the revival, Nehemiah took steps to repopulate the city (see 7:4, 5; 11:1, 2). These two factors explain why the dedication of the wall was delayed. The people celebrated the dedication of the wall **with gladness,** referring not only to their festivity but to the worship of God.

12:30–35 The method of purification is not stated, but the order is—**the priests and Levites,** followed by **the people, the gates, and wall.** Those who bore the vessels of the Lord had to be cleansed first.

12:36–42 The association of the name **David** with **musical instruments** was a reference to Israel's glorious past.

12:43 The **sacrifices** offered at the dedication of the wall probably were not burnt offerings, but peace offerings in which the people shared a common meal.

12:44–47 After the dedication of the wall, the people took steps to provide for the **priests, Levites, singers,** and **gatekeepers** who served in the temple. The joy of the Lord should produce service for the Lord. In this case, the people's joy overflowed into providing for the temple. Men were appointed as custodians of the firstfruits and tithes.

13:1–3 The first area of backsliding for the **people** was their relationship with foreigners. Even though 9:2 states that "those of Israelite lineage separated themselves from all foreigners," the people once again allowed foreigners into the congregation. Relationships between the Jewish people and the foreigners in the land had caused them to violate God's command (see also 1 Cor. 15:33).

13:4, 5 The second major area of backsliding dealt with in this chapter (vv. 1–3) was that the high priest was allowing God's enemy to live in God's house. **Eliashib** was the high priest (vv. 4, 28). **Tobiah** was one of the men who had tried to stop the building of the wall (2:10, 19; 4:3; 6:10–12, 17, 19). Eliashib allowed Tobiah to stay in the large room of the temple that had previously been used for storing grain. In fact, Tobiah had been given access to several rooms of the temple.

13:6–9 When Nehemiah returned to Jerusalem, he immediately initiated reforms. He removed Tobiah's furniture from the chamber and then ordered that the room be cleansed. When the washing, scouring, and sprinkling with blood were completed, the chamber was once again filled with **grain** and the other items that had been there before.

13:10, 11 Contended is a term used often in the prophets to refer to God bringing a legal case against His errant people (see Jer. 2:9). Nehemiah was acting like a prophet, bringing a legal case against an apostate person. He contended for what was right.

13:12, 13 Then all Judah brought the tithe: The gifts that should have been brought earlier were finally being brought by the people. **treasurers:** Nehemiah chose faithful men (see 7:2; 1 Cor. 4:2; 2 Tim. 2:2) to make sure the gifts were distributed properly.

13:14 Normally prayer is offered to the Lord before or during an event. In this case, Nehemiah's prayer followed his **good deeds.** Nehemiah was saying, "What I did, I did in accordance with Your will; now preserve it and protect me."

13:15–22 Another difficulty that Nehemiah faced concerned **the Sabbath.** The Jewish people in Judah were working on Saturday. People were buying and selling produce in Jerusalem. **Men of Tyre** brought fish and other things to be sold both in **Judah** and **Jerusalem.** The people had put their business ahead of obedience to God's command about their day of rest. **I commanded the gates to be shut:** Nehemiah took charge, ordering the gates to be closed from Friday evening to Saturday evening and even posting his own servants as guards. When the **merchants** set up outside the wall, Nehemiah **warned** them that if they stayed around again **on the Sabbath,** he would himself attack them.

Awed by the threat of the one-man army, the merchants left.

13:23, 24 The problem of Jews marrying foreigners had been dealt with thirty years before by Ezra (see Ezra 9:1–4). The people had then made a covenant, vowing that they would not do this (10:30). In this case Nehemiah found children of the mixed marriages who could not speak Hebrew, the **language** of Scripture. Without knowing Hebrew, these children could not learn the Law in their homes or worship in the holy temple. The Jews were raising children who did not know or worship the living God.

13:25–27 Nehemiah's attack on the Jews who had married non-Jews was confrontational, direct, and even brutal. **contended ... cursed ... struck ... pulled out their hair:** It is unnerving to read this list of verbs and imagine the scene. These were not the dispassionate remarks of someone giving a seminar. Nehemiah used everything he could, including his hands, to enforce obedience to the Law. **made them swear:** Nehemiah forced them to comply to the will of God in this matter. After all, this was the principal issue that had led to Israel's captivity in the beginning. Nehemiah simply could not allow such a disaster to happen again.

13:28, 29 I drove him from me: This action was taken against the most prominent offender, the grandson of the high priest Eliashib. This young man had married the daughter of Sanballat (2:10), the governor of Samaria and the archenemy of the Jewish people. The marriage was particularly offensive because it formed a treasonable alliance with Israel's enemies and compromised the purity of the high priesthood (ch. 12). Nehemiah expelled the young man from the community, praying that God would remember those who had defiled the priesthood.

13:30, 31 I cleansed them of everything pagan: Nehemiah's testimony was that he had done everything he knew how to bring about righteousness in the priesthood and among the Levites, including their offerings and service.

Esther

Introduction

The Book of Esther has all the elements of a great novel. There is the beautiful young orphan girl who rises from obscurity to become queen. She even hides a secret that could bring about her demise. Then there is the ambitious villain whose passion is to destroy the innocent. Finally the story line involves a power struggle, romantic love, and a startling exposé. But in the end, the point of this true story is clear: once again the Israelites' God had miraculously saved them from certain destruction.

The identity of the author of Esther is unknown. However the writer was probably Jewish and lived in Persia. A strong Jewish spirit pervades the book, particularly evident in the account of the establishment of the Jewish festival Purim. Moreover, the author was acquainted with Persian culture, as the extensive descriptions of the palace complex at Shushan (also called Susa) and the domestic details about the reign of King Ahasuerus indicate. For these reasons, some Jewish rabbis have ascribed the authorship of the book to Mordecai, one of its principal characters. The Book of Esther was probably written shortly after the reign of Ahasuerus, no earlier than 465 B.C. The events of Esther span a decade during the reign of Ahasuerus, or Xerxes, who succeeded his father Darius as ruler of the Persian Empire in 486 B.C.

The Book of Esther has held an important place in the canon because of its strong testimony to God's providence and protection of His people. Through the twists and turns of this story line, the author weaves an underlying story about God's character. The narrative demonstrates God's providence and sovereignty in a situation that seemed hopeless. The Israelites were living among foreigners who did not fear God and who did not care about them. An implacable enemy of the Israelites had gained power at court and was laying a plan to destroy the Jews. But at a time when God seemed so distant, He was actually preparing to deliver His people.

1:1 The kingdom of **Ahasuerus** extended from **India** to **Ethiopia** (Cush, or northern Sudan). **provinces:** The Persian kingdom under Ahasuerus was divided into small areas called provinces and larger divisions called satrapies.

1:2 The capital of ancient Elam, **Shushan** (or Susa) was one of four royal residences for the Persian emperors. Shushan was 150 miles north of the Persian Gulf. It was the location of one of Daniel's visions (Dan. 8:2), and it was where Nehemiah served as cupbearer to King Artaxerxes I (see Neh. 1:1, 2).

1:3–5 In **the third year** of his reign, Ahasuerus displayed the riches of his kingdom for six months. **made a feast:** There is some uncertainty about whether the king gave one feast or two. It is possible that v. 3 introduces the idea of the grand banquet and v. 5 records the specifics of what turned out to be a seven-day festival. It is not likely that the feasting itself extended for 180 days. **Persia and Media:** Previously the Medes had been the stronger of the two nations. Beginning with the reign of Cyrus, the Persians dominated the kingdom. Together they established a powerful empire (see Dan. 5:28).

1:6, 7 white and blue: These were the royal colors of the Persians. The Persian custom was to recline on couches at the table.

1:8 The monarch **ordered** that guests could drink as much or as little as they pleased. This differed from the usual Persian custom by which people at a banquet were required to drink each time the king raised his cup.

1:9 Vashti: The queen gave a separate banquet for the women guests.

1:10–12 Castrated men, or **eunuchs,** were assigned to act as harem attendants and as agents of communication between the king and his harem (6:14). Because of the level of trust these men could attain, they might also function as administrators in the kingdom as well.

1:13 men who understood the times: Court astrologers and magicians gave advice and predicted the future on the basis of what they pretended to know about the supernatural. The prophets often looked upon such charlatans with derisive scorn (see Is. 44:24, 25).

1:14, 15 The **seven** counselors of Ezra 7:14 were probably the same group of men. These men enjoyed the unusual privilege of speaking personally with the king.

1:16–18 Acting as spokesman for the others, **Memucan** responded shrewdly by enlarging the offense beyond a personal affront to the king. **contempt:** The Hebrew word used occurs only here in the Old Testament. It is related to the verb translated *despise* in v. 17.

1:19–21 royal decree: Memucan urged the king to take immediate action against Vashti. The queen would be given what amounted to a divorce. This would have the effect of demoting her from her privileged position as the chief wife of the king.

1:22 sent letters: The Persians were known for their excellent postal system. **speak in the language of his own people:** This suggests the respect that was held for local languages and dialects in the Persian empire.

2:1–3 It was customary for the virgins of the king's harem to spend a year in **beauty** treatments and purification rites before going to see the king (see v. 12). Again we see the exaggerated sense of power of the king contrasted with the fragile status of women. **Beautiful young virgins** were seen to exist just to bring pleasure to the king.

2:4, 5 The name **Mordecai** is related to the name of Marduk, the principal Babylonian deity. The phrase **a certain Jew,** along with the genealogy and the tribal name Benjamite, prepares us for the upcoming conflict with Haman in ch. 3. **Shimei** may refer to the man from the family of Saul who cursed David (see 2 Sam. 16:5–13). **Kish** may be the father of Saul (see 1 Sam. 9:1, 2). If these figures are the ones intended, they are Mordecai's remote ancestors from the tribe of Benjamin.

2:6 This verse is difficult to interpret, as the Hebrew text does not indicate the subject of the verb **had been carried away.** The subject could not be Mordecai. If he had been among those carried away into captivity, he would not likely have lived until the time of Ahasuerus. The subject might be Mordecai's ancestor Kish, understood to be a different person than the father of Saul. It is also possible that the original phrasing just means that Mordecai and his family were among those descended from the captives who were taken to Babylon in the days of Nebuchadnezzar.

2:7 Hadassah is a Hebrew name that means "Myrtle." Esther is a Persian name meaning "Star." Like the name of her cousin Mordecai, the name **Esther** was related to that of a local deity, the goddess Ishtar. Jewish people in antiquity customarily had two names when they lived in regions distant from Israel. One would be their secular name, a name understandable in their adopted culture, and the other would be their sacred name given in Hebrew.

2:8 We cannot determine whether Esther went willingly or reluctantly to the king's palace. She was brought into the palace complex, but not yet into the living quarters of the king.

2:9 obtained his favor: This phrase characterizes Esther's relationships with all who knew her, including the king (see v. 17). Esther found favor with many, as is demonstrated throughout the chapter. **her allowance:** Hegai made certain that Esther received choice food in liberal portions. He also gave her seven personal attendants and the most desirable place to live within the quarters of the harem.

2:10–13 Many reasons have been suggested about Esther's hesitation to **reveal**

 IN DEPTH   **The Persian Empire (500 B.C.)**

 y Esther's time the Persian empire stretched from India in the east through Asia Minor to Greece in the west and included Egypt and some of coastal Africa to the south.

her national origin. The time does come when Esther would identify herself and her people (see ch. 8). In fact, her self-disclosure would come at the point when the danger to her person was highest.

2:14 concubines: These women lived unfortunate, though highly pampered, lives. If the king never **called for** them again, they were destined to live as though they were widows for the remainder of their years (see 2 Sam. 20:3). The point made here emphasizes how courageous Esther was when she later made her appearance before Ahasuerus (see 4:11; 5:1).

2:15 Again we see the providence of God at work. Esther found favor with everyone she encountered.

2:16 Esther became the principal wife of the king four years after Vashti was divorced. The month **Tebeth** corresponds to our December-January.

2:17 The king apparently was so delighted with Esther that he **made her queen** right away. The nouns **grace and favor** together mean "abundant favor."

2:18, 19 sat within the king's gate: This phrase has a special significance; it means that Mordecai had an official position. Shortly after Esther became queen, she gave Mordecai a position within the king's gate where official business took place (see Deut. 22:13–15).

2:20–23 Mordecai learned of a plot by **two** angry **eunuchs** to take the king's life. Mordecai not only used this information to save the king, but eventually his own people.

3:1 Some believe **Agagite** is a reference to the historical district of Agag within the Persian empire. Others believe this term more likely linked Haman's descent with the Amalekites. These people, descendants of Esau (see Gen. 36:12), were ancient enemies of the Hebrews (see Ex. 17:8). Agag, a king of the Amalekites, was captured by King Saul (see 1 Sam. 15:8).

3:2–4 All the officials of the king were on duty within the king's gate. **Mordecai would not bow or pay homage:** To comprehend the force of this verse, we need to look at v. 4. There Mordecai reportedly told the king's servants that he was a Jew. It is not known whether the bowing was required as an act of

worship to the king's man or just as an overt sign of deep respect. As a Jew, Mordecai may have not been able to bring himself to show this sign of respect to one who was an ancestral enemy.

3:5, 6 Mordecai's daily refusal to bow down to **Haman** filled the official with such rage that he sought to kill all Jewish people in the Persian empire. Haman's Amalekite ancestry would account for his deep hatred.

3:7 Nisan: This, the first month of the ancient lunar calendar, corresponds to March-April. The twelfth year of the king's reign was 474 B.C. **they cast pur:** The word *pur* was the basis for the name of the Feast of Purim in ch. 9. The casting of lots was common in ancient times. The fact that the lot was cast at the beginning of the year to determine the best time to destroy the Jewish people fits with the culture of the day. The Babylonian religion maintained that the gods gathered at the beginning of each year to establish the destiny of human beings.

3:8, 9 Haman did not identify the **people** at first. He may have played on the Persian emperor's native sense of superiority to other peoples. Haman acted as if his motive were no more than proper concern for the welfare of the king. He implied that this unnamed group was rebellious, a present danger to the king.

3:10 The king's **signet ring** symbolized his authority. When he gave this ring to Haman, he was passing to him a symbol of his own royal person. This meant that Haman could proceed with his plan.

3:11 It might seem that the king was refusing to accept **the money.** However, this is difficult to harmonize with Mordecai's words to Esther in 4:7 and her comments about being "sold" in 7:4. More likely, the king was engaging in the common method of bargaining (Gen. 23:7–18).

3:12 scribes: The king had secretaries who put into writing the official documents. This verse gives us a picture of the comprehensiveness of the decree. It was given to officials in the provinces, making sure it was distributed everywhere. It was also written in the language of each people group within the realm.

3:13, 14 The **couriers** were royal messengers stationed at various spots along the main roads who would carry messages on horseback. The plot to **kill** the Jewish people included the slaughter of those of all age groups and both sexes.

3:15 The contempt of the king and Haman who **sat down to drink** while this message was being delivered cannot help but strike a responsive chord of empathy for the Jewish people among the readers of this book. The text notes that even the people in the city of Shushan were perplexed.

4:1, 2 In the ancient Middle East, **sackcloth and ashes** were used as a visible sign of mourning, indicating a sense of desolation.

4:3 In this book **fasting** connotes a strong but veiled appeal to God to intervene in a time of severe crisis. In v. 16 Esther commanded a three-day fast among Shushan's Jews. The queen herself, along with her maids, undertook a fast at this time before she approached the king.

4:4 The verb **distressed** is strong, suggesting the idea of writhing in severe pain or anguish. Certainly Esther was deeply disturbed by Mordecai's appearance and agony, though she did not as yet understand what had happened (see v. 5).

4:5, 6 city square: Many events took place in the plaza of a city, including gatherings, proclamations, and public lamentation.

4:7 If Mordecai had not been appointed as a high official at the **king's** gate, it is unlikely that he would have known about Haman's bribe to the king. He was providentially placed by God in an exalted position in a foreign government, as were Joseph (see Gen. 41), Daniel (see Dan. 2:48), and Nehemiah (see Neh. 1:11).

4:8, 9 Mordecai recognized the decree as a threat to the existence of his people, so he boldly commanded Esther to intercede for her people before the king, knowing that this could only be at the risk of her life (see v. 11). If she was not identified as a Hebrew woman, she might possibly escape the fate of her people—but only if her association with Mordecai (see 2:7, 15) was not remembered by their enemies. In any event, she would be in a most risky position. **make**

supplication: The word means to ask for a gracious response. It is a term that often is used of coming to the Lord for deliverance; here it is used of coming to a king for mercy.

4:10, 11 Esther understood that Mordecai was asking her to risk her life. She was understandably fearful. Her fear was compounded by the fact that the king had not summoned her for **thirty days,** implying that she had not been enjoying the king's favor recently. Who knew if he would still have regard for her at all?

4:12–14 Mordecai, by his confidence that **relief and deliverance** would come from **another place,** was strongly asserting his faith in God and His promised protection of the Jewish people. God would intervene with or without Esther. If she refused to help, she would perish, along with her **father's house.** Mordecai may be referring to divine judgment here. In the closing appeal, Mordecai suggested a providential reason for her becoming queen at this precise time in history; that is, Esther was acting as God's agent in delivering the Jewish people.

4:15–17 Esther agreed to intervene with the king on behalf of her people. The fasting **for three days** implies a period of earnestly seeking God in prayer at this critical juncture. But even at this point, the narrator did not use the name of God—something that is most remarkable. Esther was also looking for the support of the Jewish community by asking them to join in this fast.

5:1, 2 she found favor in his sight: Again we are struck by the providence of God, demonstrated by the king's response to Esther. To indicate his approval, the king held out the **golden scepter** to her.

5:3 The king, knowing that Esther must have had an unusual reason for daring to approach him, asked her what she wanted. He promised her **up to half** his **kingdom.** Perhaps the phrase was a common form of exaggeration among royalty. Although it probably was exaggerated, the statement certainly showed the king's favorable attitude toward her.

5:4, 5 If it pleases the king: This expression is found frequently throughout the book. It was a formula of polite address. Esther made her initial request; she invited the king and Haman to come to her **banquet** that same day.

5:6–8 The king continued examining Esther for the real **request.** She delayed and asked the two back for a second banquet the following day. One may ask why Esther waited instead of disclosing what was on her mind. The delay providentially allowed time for the king's sleepless night and the events that followed (ch. 6).

5:9 Haman's good spirits on the way home from the banquet were from the wine he had drunk and from the honor of being invited along with the king to the feast at Esther's table. However, his mood changed quickly when he encountered Esther's cousin. This time **Mordecai** did not even rise in his presence. Further, Mordecai showed no sign of fear before him, despite the death decree against the Jewish people.

5:10–12 Haman's vanity matched that of the king he served. He bragged to his wife and friends about his wealth, his sons, and his status in the kingdom. It was considered a great blessing among ancient Semitic peoples to have many sons. In Persia, the man with the most sons would receive presents from the king himself.

5:13, 14 gallows: This word is the usual word for wood, the material the gallows were made of (2:23).

6:1 This verse marks the turning point of the book. Within this chapter we observe a series of events that unmistakably point to God's sovereign hand controlling all events. Only because of his sleepless night did the king learn of Mordecai's past bravery on his behalf. **the book of the records of the chronicles:** This would be the official record of the events of the Persian empire. It is referred to in 2:23 and again in 10:2. Ezra 4:15 also mentions such a work. Apparently the chronicles **were read before the king** for an extended period.

6:2, 3 The king might have been aware to some extent of Mordecai's deed when it originally occurred. In 2:23 the author says that the events were written down "in the presence of the king." Now the Lord led the

king to this very text. It was customary for the Persian kings to reward promptly those who performed some noteworthy act of service.

6:4, 5 Again we see the hand of God sovereignly at work on behalf of his people. No sooner had Mordecai's reward been discussed than Haman appeared in the king's **court.** Ironically, Haman, who knew nothing of the recent discussion, was coming to recommend that Mordecai be hanged.

6:6–11 One cannot miss the irony and humor of this turn of events. In his arrogance, Haman presumed that the king desired to honor him. He suggested a course of action that he would most enjoy, a royal parade through the city plaza so that everyone could see and hear about the king's delight in him. The king obliged, but was planning the reward for a man Haman regarded as his enemy. Worst of all, it was Haman who had to lead Mordecai through the square and proclaim the king's pleasure in Mordecai. The **royal crest** on the head of the horse was a crown that formed from the forelock of the horse. The term **Jew,** derived from Judah, came into use during the exile because the people were principally from the southern kingdom of Judah.

6:12, 13 Haman's wife and friends told Haman that he would **not prevail,** for the very reason of Mordecai's Jewish descent. The Hebrew wording is quite strong: the meaning is that he will most certainly fall.

6:14 The role of **eunuchs** as royal messengers is portrayed again in this verse (1:10). They were the ones who came to take Haman briskly to Esther's second banquet.

7:1–4 Esther repeated her address of 5:8 and now added her request. **let my life be given:** Esther asked the king to spare her life and the lives of her people. This latter appeal was an impassioned plea to the king in which she also disclosed her true identity to him for the first time. Esther told the king that she and her fellow Jewish people **have been sold,** referring to Haman's bribe to the king in 3:9.

7:5 Esther's speech had a dramatic effect on the king. She had aroused more than his curiosity. He was angry. The life of his own queen was in danger because of a plot by one of his trusted men.

7:6 Esther finally exposed the culprit. It was none other than Haman, the **adversary** and **enemy,** "the fierce enemy." It is no wonder that Haman was **terrified** before Esther and the king. In his evil plan to kill his enemy, he had unwittingly threatened the queen's life.

7:7 The king was astonished and furious. He left the room and went out to the **palace garden.** This must have been a very unusual act for an autocrat. Usually, he would be expected to respond immediately and rashly. However, this time he was so taken aback by the turn of events that he needed time to think.

7:8 Haman was draped over the queen's **couch** in a compromising position. Presumably, he was grasping at her with a desire to implore her favor. The king, on discovering this outrageous situation, wondered aloud if Haman intended to ravage the queen. The Persians had strict rules about contact with the harem by any male other than the king. The eunuchs were the only persons who had access to the rooms of these women. Haman was in danger just by being near her. This sight enraged the king. As he spoke, **they covered Haman's face.** It is likely that it was the eunuchs who came and did this. The covering of his face signified that he was condemned to death.

7:9, 10 Harbonah: This eunuch, first mentioned in 1:10, spoke at a critical moment to the ruler. He disclosed the story of the **gallows** which Haman had prepared for Mordecai and told the king where it was located. He reminded the monarch of Mordecai's bravery on behalf of the king. Ahasuerus took Harbonah's cue and commanded his servants to **hang** Haman on those very gallows.

8:1 On the same day as Haman's execution, the king gave his queen **the house of Haman.** The term *house* here refers to his estate. This was in keeping with Persian law, which put the estate of a traitor into the custody of the crown.

8:2 Mordecai was given Haman's position as the prime minister. He received the full authority of the king, as evidenced by the transfer of the **signet ring** to him. Esther also put Mordecai in charge of Haman's estate, which gave him great wealth.

8:3–6 Esther, knowing that danger still lurked ahead for her people, pleaded passionately for their lives before the king. The queen continued to receive the blessing of the monarch as he again extended the **golden scepter** to her. Courageously Esther implored the king to **revoke** Haman's hateful decree against all the Jews in the empire. The parallel statements in v. 6 reinforce Esther's poignant and personal plea to her king.

8:7 Mordecai had heard Esther's entire presentation to the king. Ahasuerus, by reiterating what he already had done, communicated his support for Esther and her people.

8:8 In the Persian empire, a royal **decree** could not be altered, but a second one could invalidate it. Thus, the king instructed Mordecai and Esther to write a second decree. The second decree would carry all the weight of the former one—but would reverse the expected results.

8:9, 10 Sivan: This would be May-June. The date would give the Jewish people approximately eight months of preparation for any attack (see 3:13).

8:11–14 These verses have occasioned controversy about whether the Jewish people were unethical toward their enemies. Some commentators understand the verse to mean that the Jewish people were given permission to slaughter even the wives and children of any people that would attack them. Another view is that the Jewish people may not have carried out what was permitted, but killed only the men who attacked them (see 9:6). There is another possibility, that the verse refers to the women and children of the Jews. That is, the assault mentioned in the verse was expected to be directed against the men, women, children, and possessions of the Jews. Against such assault, the Jews were to arm themselves and make proper defenses (see 9:5, 6). **plunder their possessions:** This concluding phrase could be a citation of Haman's decree (see 3:13). If so, it would explain why the Jewish people did not take any plunder (see 9:10), but simply defended themselves against their enemies.

8:15, 16 Mordecai, dressed in royal attire, received a joyful welcome from the **city of Shushan,** which included both Gentiles and Jews. The residents of this city **rejoiced** that Mordecai had been appointed as prime minister. The word **light** conveys the sense of happiness.

8:17 Note the marked contrast of the reaction of the Jewish people to this second decree as compared to the first one (see 4:3). The reality of their deliverance influenced the Gentiles in the empire as well. **became:** This is the only place in the Old Testament that this Hebrew word is used of conversion to Judaism. The unexpected turn of events in favor of the Jewish people greatly moved their neighbors.

9:1, 2 The Jewish people assembled throughout the kingdom to **lay hands on** or kill (see 2:21) their foes. The enemies of the Jewish people could not succeed in their assault against them due to a **fear** of them.

9:3, 4 In addition to a fear of the Jewish people, there was also a **fear of Mordecai** among the leaders, which caused them to assist the Jewish people. Their motive may have been to protect themselves politically in light of Mordecai's power and popularity.

9:5, 6 The defense of the Jewish people against their enemies was strong and certain. They **killed** five hundred of their enemies in Shushan alone.

9:7–10 The author returns to the conflict with Haman by recording the death of his ten sons. The patterns of reprisal and vengeance were so deeply ingrained in the cultures of the ancient Middle East that the survival of even one of these sons might mean trouble for the next generation of Jewish people.

9:11–14 Esther renewed her original request (8:11) for the Jews to have the authority to protect themselves against attack. The king

assented. He also ordered **Haman's ten sons** to be exposed on the gallows. The men were already dead (v. 10). Their bodies were displayed as a warning to anyone who planned evil toward the Jews.

9:15, 16 In Deut. 25:17–19, Moses linked the people's continued **rest from their enemies** with the command to "blot out the remembrance of Amalek from under heaven." In this chapter, the blessing of rest for the Jewish people is associated with the destruction of their enemies (vv. 18, 22). This similarity with Deuteronomy reinforces the argument that Haman was a descendant of the Amalekites.

9:17–19 These verses summarize the days of deliverance for the Jewish people. In Shushan, they had two days of fighting, then they rested and celebrated on the fifteenth day of **Adar** (February-March; see 3:7, 12). The Jewish people in the remainder of the Persian provinces fought for one day and fasted on the fourteenth day of that month.

9:20–25 In light of the difference of timing between the Jews in Shushan and Jews in the rest of the kingdom, Mordecai told the people by **letter** that they should designate both the fourteenth and the fifteenth of Adar as annual holidays.

9:26–32 Purim: This verse explains the name of the two-day festival. The name is derived form the word *pur,* meaning "lot," the lot that was cast to determine the day of the Jewish people's death. Purim reminds the Jews of God's deliverance from their day of destruction. The feast was established as an annual festival.

10:1 tribute: This word may refer both to taxation and forced labor that the king imposed on all his territory.

10:2, 3 The Book of Esther concludes with high praise of Mordecai, whose deeds were recorded in the official chronicles of the Persian empire. Mordecai held the **second** highest rank in the land, a note that recalls Joseph's ascendancy in Egypt (Gen. 41:37–45).

Job

Introduction

The Book of Job records the troubling questions, the terrifying doubts, and the anguish of a sufferer. It can help us in the time when we are surrounded with troubles by giving us a glimpse of God's perspective on our suffering.

There is no consensus about who wrote the Book of Job or when it was written. Suggestions for an author include Job, Elihu, Solomon, and even Moses. The text indicates that the events of Job occurred in the land of Uz (1:1), but the location of Uz is unknown. That Job was the greatest among the people of the East (1:3) indicates that Job lived east of the Jordan River. Some have concluded that Uz was located in Syria or northwest Mesopotamia. However, most writers think Uz was located near Edom, because many of the proper names in the Book of Job occur in the genealogy of Esau, the father of the Edomites (see Gen. 36).

As for the time of writing, there is strong literary evidence that the Book of Job was compiled and written during the time of Solomon, when wisdom literature flourished. The mention of iron tools and weapons (19:24; 20:24; 40:18) and even mining (28:2) implies a date during the Iron Age (after 1200 B.C.). Moreover, the description of a horse in a military context (39:19–25) may indicate the mounted warhorse, which was used at the earliest around the tenth century B.C.

The uniqueness of the Book of Job is not in its approach to the problem of suffering, but in its revelation of the sovereign God to whom everyone must properly relate. Sufferer and non-sufferer alike must humbly trust in God's sovereign grace. Because Job and his friends were ignorant of Satan's challenge to God, the Book of Job contains much bad theology and misapplied truth. It is important to read passages in the Book of Job in light of the message and purpose of the entire book. The only proper response to the omnipotent God is submission and faith.

The Book of Job teaches that the Lord is not bound to anyone's preconceived

theological system. He is completely free, but also truly good. He is the sovereign and benevolent Creator who continues to determine the course of the universe according to His own hidden plan. Just like Job, we must learn to submit to the Almighty God and accept by faith that He has a good plan for us.

1:1 The dramatic events of the prologue of the Book of Job set the stage for the intricate dialogues of the main body (3:1—42:6). **Uz:** The precise location is unknown but may have been near Edom. Two aspects of Job's character and actions are highlighted. **Blameless** and **upright,** meaning "straightforward" and "ethically straight," emphasize his spotless character. Like Daniel (see Dan. 6:4), Job was blameless before his human critics, but not completely sinless before God. Job **feared God and shunned evil,** an indication that his right relationship with God motivated him to turn away from evil.

1:2, 3 Job had an ideal family consisting of **seven sons and three daughters.** The number seven was the biblical number of completeness. In the ancient Middle East, having many children was considered a sign of God's blessing (Ps. 127:3–5).

1:4 Each of Job's sons would participate in a feast with his siblings on **his appointed day.** The term could refer to a birthday celebration. However, the context of v. 5 may indicate a regular, perhaps weekly or seasonal, cycle of celebration and feasting.

1:5 When Job undertook to **sanctify** his children through **burnt offerings,** he performed an intercessory role that corresponds to what he did when he prayed for his friends in the epilogue (42:10). **cursed God:** The Hebrew text has "blessed God," which is probably a euphemism—a reverent substitution of a milder word by a Hebrew scribe because he could not bear to have the word *cursed* next to the divine name.

1:6 The sons of God are celestial beings or angels who were created by Him and who serve Him (4:18; Ps. 103:20, 21) as his "holy ones" (5:1). Compare the expression "sons of God" in Gen. 6:1, where the phrase is used of angels who were enemies of the Lord. The imagery seemingly indicates a heavenly council over which the Lord sits as Supreme King (Ps. 89:5–7; Dan. 7:9, 10). Strictly speaking, **Satan** may be a title rather than the personal name of the leader of all evil forces. The Hebrew word was not clearly used as a proper name until 1 Chr. 21:1, chronologically one of the last Old Testament books written. Nevertheless, the characteristics of the "Adversary" in the Book of Job imply that he was in fact Satan. He answered God's questions in an antagonistic manner and accused Job of ulterior motives.

1:7 The Hebrew word Yahweh, usually translated **the LORD,** is the personal name of the true God of the Old Testament (see Ex. 3:14, 15). It is the particular name of God in covenantal relations with His people Israel (see Ex. 6:1–6; 19:3–8). This indicates that though Job was not an Israelite, he had a relationship with the true God (see v. 21 where the Lord's name is used). **From where do you come:** God's inquiry does not imply an ignorance of Satan's behavior but was part of the conversation with Satan.

1:8 My servant refers to the proper relationship every person should have with God—a joyful and reverent trust in God. Job was a model of this type of relationship with the Lord.

1:9 Satan, always "the adversary," questioned Job's motives for fearing and serving God. The expression **for nothing** is emphatic in the Hebrew text. The question may be paraphrased, "Is Job really free of ulterior motives?"

1:10 God had placed a **hedge** of protection **around** Job and **his household.** No harm could come to him unless the Lord permitted it (v. 12; see 2:4–6).

1:11 Satan ignored customary court etiquette that would not permit him to address God directly as **You,** or use the personal references **Your hand** or **Your face.** Such irreverence was part of his constant strategy to demean God. **curse:** The sin of cursing God is a pivotal issue for the Book of Job. Job feared that his children might think or speak irreverently of God (v. 5). But Satan asserted

that Job would **surely curse** God if his prosperity and blessings were removed.

1:12 That **Satan** must receive permission from the Lord to **lay a hand on** Job (see v. 11) indicates that God limits Satan's power. Believers can find strength and assurance from the fact that Satan's actions are limited by God's sovereign control. After the prologue, Satan is never mentioned directly again in the Book of Job; he is only a minor character compared to the Lord of the universe.

1:13–16 In one **day** Job plummeted from the pinnacle of prosperity to the pit of poverty. He must have felt that all heaven and earth had turned against him. The four rapid disasters that struck him came alternately from earth and heaven. First was the raiding of his livestock and **servants;** then from heaven, **the fire of God;** then again from earth, the loss of his **camels** and **servants;** and then the climactic blow again from heaven, **a great wind** that demolished his **house** and killed his children. The **Sabeans** were nomadic raiders from Sheba. They were probably the people of the queen of Sheba (see 1 Kin. 10:1–13). Her homeland was probably southwestern Arabia, present-day Yemen.

1:17–19 The Chaldeans were part of various west Semitic marauding tribes active in the middle Euphrates from the twelfth to the ninth century B.C. They migrated eastward into Assyria and then into Babylonia, and were the forerunners of the Chaldean or neo-Babylonian dynasty established by Nebuchadnezzar's father.

1:20 Finally the spotlight focuses on Job's reaction to his trials. Did he serve God for profit as Satan had alleged (1:9)? Job passed the first test with a model response. He showed intense grief according to the accepted custom of his day (v. 20). Then he humbly accepted God's will without complaining or blaming God for his tragedies. Job acknowledged God's sovereign control over all circumstances when he **fell to the ground and worshiped.** The context indicates that Job's fall was not an involuntary reflex of despair but a deliberate act of humility before God.

1:21, 22 Having fallen on the ground, Job uttered words that were consistent with his posture. First he gave a realistic appraisal of his status: Just as he came into the world **naked,** so would he leave it **naked.** Then he repeatedly acknowledged the control of **the LORD** over all circumstances. The name Yahweh is used three times in this verse to emphasize Job's dependence on the true God.

2:1–3 The first sentence of this verse repeats 1:8 verbatim, emphasizing that Job's character had remained flawless despite Satan's assaults. In the second sentence the Lord affirms that Job had maintained **his integrity** (the same Hebrew root as *blameless* in 1:1, 8), although **Satan** had **incited** Him to destroy Job **without cause.** "Without cause" translates the same Hebrew word Satan had used in insinuating that Job did not serve God "for nothing" (1:9). Now the Lord throws it back in his face.

2:4 The origin of the proverb **skin for skin** utilized by **Satan** is disputed. Some think it may have originated from the practice of bartering animal skins. Others believe that the phrase is similar to the proverb "life for life, eye for eye, tooth for tooth" (Ex. 21:23–25). In the last half of the verse Satan charges that Job would be willing to lose his possessions or even his family, as long as **his life** was spared.

2:5, 6 When the Lord placed Job into Satan's **hand,** it is extraordinary that He commanded Satan to **spare his life.** Ironically, the word *spare* normally refers to God's role in His providential care of people (see 29:2).

2:7 The disease that inflicted Job with **painful boils** from head to toe is difficult to identify. The term for *boils* was used to describe the plague of boils in Egypt (Ex. 9:9–11). The same phrase *painful boils,* as one of the covenant curses for the disobedient (see Deut. 28:35), denoted an incurable illness.

2:8, 9 The words of Job's wife—**curse God and die**—were probably Job's most severe trial. Ironically, her question **do you still hold fast to your integrity** uses almost exactly the same wording the Lord had used (see v. 3). The wording emphasizes Job's perseverance, which his wife misconstrued as religious fanaticism. She thought he was

blindly refusing to face the reality of his desperate situation.

2:10 Job's response to the second test, the loss of his health and alienation from his wife, was once again commendable. His rhetorical question, urging the acceptance of both **good** and **adversity from God,** anticipates one of the central messages of the Book of Job: The person of faith will trust in God through prosperity or adversity, even while unable to understand why bad things happen.

2:11 **Eliphaz the Temanite** was apparently an Edomite from Teman in northern Edom (Gen. 36:11). The term **Shuhite** may refer to Bildad's ancestry, or more likely to his geographical origin, since the other two friends seem to be identified by their home towns. **Zophar the Naamathite** may have come from Naameh, a mountainous area in northwestern Arabia.

2:12–13 These friends truly cared for Job because they **wept** and stayed close by him for **seven days and seven nights.** Yet later they would fail Job miserably by not listening to him (see 8:4–6; 13:5–13).

3:1, 2 When **Job cursed the day of his birth,** he came close to blasphemy. The Hebrew word for *cursed,* meaning "to hold in contempt," is elsewhere used of cursing God (Ex. 22:28; Lev. 24:15) or cursing one's parents (Ex. 21:17). Job's pain had driven him to express a very strong malediction against the day of his birth and the night of his conception, which were personified as those responsible for his existence (see vv. 3–6). However, Job did not commit blasphemy. He did not curse the Chaldeans or Sabeans, much less God. Neither did he express thoughts of suicide.

3:3–19 Job's wish that he had never been born because his life was full of **sorrow** (vv. 3, 10) reflects a serious misunderstanding about the basic meaning of human existence. The Bible teaches that the purpose of life is not happiness but the praise of God's glory (Eph. 1:3–14). Job used two separate Hebrew words translated *curse,* different from the Hebrew term in v. 1. He wished that the popular magicians who cast spells on the day for their clients could have cast a spell on his day so that he would never have been born. Job's belief in one God (see 31:26–28) indicates that he was speaking poetically and dramatically. He was not endorsing any kind of pagan magic, but using vivid and forceful language to express the intensity of his agony and despair.

3:20–22 Even though Job longed for **death,** he was not considering suicide. The context of other passages indicates that Job only wished that the Lord would let him die (see 7:15–21; 10:18–22).

3:23–26 Job bemoaned that God had **hedged** him **in** so that he could not die. The irony is that Job perceived God's protective hedge around him as keeping him from a desirable death.

4:1 Since **Eliphaz the Temanite** spoke first, he was probably the oldest and therefore presumably the wisest of the three. Eliphaz was a little more courteous to Job than were his other two friends. However, his observations were distorted. Eliphaz firmly believed that God would never punish the righteous and would not preserve the sinner. He concluded that since Job was suffering, he must be a sinner (see 22:4–11, 21–30).

4:2–6 Though Eliphaz seems surprised at Job's response (ch. 3), his initial remarks are complimentary and courteous. The content of vv. 7–11 suggests that v. 6 probably contains at least a mild rebuke. The phrase **you are weary** translates one word in the original Hebrew and repeats the same root word found in the phrase "will you become weary" in v. 2. This repetition indicates that Eliphaz had already recognized the apparent contradiction between the patient Job of the prologue and the impatient Job of the dialogue.

4:7–9 Eliphaz highlights the retribution doctrine—that is, God supports the righteous but abandons the wicked—with two rhetorical questions. He supports his belief by an appeal to his experience; that is, "you reap what you sow." Because the word **trouble** is the same word used by Job to describe his own plight as full of "sorrow" (3:10) and "misery" (3:20), Eliphaz may be equating Job with the wicked **who plow iniquity.**

4:10, 11 To the reader it may seem that Eliphaz suddenly adds illustrations of God's retribution on animals. But probably these are proverbial sayings with a double meaning. Eliphaz may have been implying that Job's "groanings" or "roaring" made him comparable to the old lion, symbolizing the wicked, whose sins were now being repaid with suffering.

4:12–18 Eliphaz appeals to a vision to authenticate his theology. He claims that he **heard a voice** that told him that no one was **righteous** compared to **God,** implying that Job was not righteous.

4:19, 20 The description of people as living **in houses of clay** with their **foundation in the dust** emphasizes the mortality and fragility of human existence. Like the temporary houses they live in, people can perish without anyone knowing. Since the body is fashioned from clay, God the potter who fashioned it can easily turn it back to dust (see 10:8, 9; 33:6).

4:21 The Hebrew word for the phrase **their own excellence** may mean "tent cord." Thus the text may be stating that humanity's existence is as precarious as a tent in the midst of a windstorm.

5:1 Eliphaz's warning against appealing to **holy ones** or angels anticipates Job's later desire for a "mediator" (see 9:33).

5:2–6 Eliphaz begins another appeal to personal observation and experience. Eliphaz uses a play on the words **ground** and **man,** along with the repetition of the word **trouble,** to aid his argument that Job's trouble did not come out of nowhere—that is, **spring from the ground.**

5:7 The word **sparks** may allude to the Ugaritic god of the underworld who was supposedly responsible for plagues and lightning. A reference like this to mythology does not imply or endorse a belief in other gods. Eliphaz is saying "just as a plague springs up from the demonic forces of hell, so does trouble come from person's nature."

5:8–17 Eliphaz insinuates that since Job's suffering was a result of God's **chastening** for his sin, he should **not despise** or reject what God was trying to teach him. Though it is true that God sometimes disciplines people for their sin through pain and suffering (32:1—37:24; Prov. 3:11; Heb. 12:7), Eliphaz was wrong to suggest that this was necessarily so in Job's case.

5:18–22 Eliphaz states that God is the author of both pain and healing. God would heal the **wounds** he inflicted for discipline. When God does allow pain to come into our lives, it is not to harm us, but to make us better.

5:23–27 The presence of stones in a field could make land impossible to farm (see 2 Kin. 3:19, 25). Thus the expression **covenant with the stones of the field** would mean being **at peace** and harmony with even the destructive forces of nature.

6:1 When Job **answered,** he did not respond directly to Eliphaz. This may be the reason the text does not specify a name here. Job usually responded to all three of his friends, not to one individually (see 6:24–30). His friends in turn did not respond point-by-point to what Job said. Consequently the dialogue is not so much a conversation between friends as it is a speech contest in which one speaker tries to win a debate and impress his audience with his rhetoric.

6:2–4 Job's suffering was so intense that he portrayed it as caused by **arrows of the Almighty** that were dipped in **poison.** The arrows of the Lord are generally symbolic of His judgment (Deut. 32:23, 42) or wrath (Ps. 38:1, 2). Job also assumed that God was required to reward the obedient and punish the guilty in this life, and he may have presumed that the Lord was punishing him unjustly.

6:5–13 Though the exact translation is disputed, the overall context of these verses seems to indicate that Job was more concerned to preserve his relationship to **the Holy One** than to have God remove his pain and **anguish** through death (vv. 8, 9).

6:14 The exact meaning of the Hebrew word translated **afflicted** is disputed. It may mean "to melt"; thus the idea could be "failing" or "despairing." Verse 14 seems to be transitional, linking Job's despair of vv. 8–13 with his disappointment of vv. 15–21.

6:15–17 Since the friends are called **my brothers,** Job apparently at one time had a close relationship with them. This only intensified his feelings of disappointment. He compares them to **the streams of the brooks,** the torrents of water that fill the ravines during the rainy season and **pass away** in the summer.

6:18 The word **paths** in this verse concludes the imagery of empty ravines left by the seasonal streams called "wadis" (vv. 15–18) and links this section to the next (see v. 19).

6:19, 20 Job compares his intense disappointment with his friends to the thirsty **caravans of Tema** and **the travelers of Sheba,** whose hopes for water were dashed by reaching the dry stream beds.

6:21 When Job hoped to receive help from his three friends, they offered **nothing.** This was like a desert wadi, a seasonal stream that vanishes in the time of greatest need.

6:22–26 Job pleads with his would-be counselors to have understanding rather than an argumentative spirit. The friends' demeanor degenerates into arguments and reproofs as they overreact to Job's words, which even Job admits belonged to the **wind.**

6:27–30 The repeated word **injustice** in these verses is the same term used by Eliphaz in 5:16. Eliphaz argued that God "saves the needy" from the unscrupulous tactics of the wicked (5:12–15), so "that the poor have hope and injustice shuts her mouth." Job responds by implying that the words of Eliphaz deal injustice to him in his time of need (see 6:14–21) by assuming that he is not righteous.

7:1, 2 Job argues that his own lot is worse than the **hard service** of the hired laborer or the common slave. Job's use of the word **servant** is an ironic indicator that his life as God's servant (see the same Hebrew term in 1:8) has now become full of drudgery and slavery rather than joyous trust in the Lord.

7:3–5 Although the Book of Job does not record how long Job suffered, the phrase **months of futility** implies that it was a considerable time.

7:6 Job's choice of the word **hope** in the context of the **weaver's shuttle** may convey a double meaning (see also 11:18). The Hebrew word for *hope* sounds like the Hebrew word that means "thread" or "cord" (see Josh. 2:18, 21). Not only did Job believe his days were without *hope* but that he had not even a *thread* of hope left. As if he were regarding a thread in a weaver's shuttle, Job could not see the design that God had for his life through the suffering that he was experiencing.

7:7–10 Job describes **the grave** (sometimes rendered Sheol) as a place from which one **shall never return** (see 10:21). The focus here is on death. Though the dead person would **never return to his house** on earth, there was a belief in a meeting "house" in the underworld for those who had been on earth (see 30:23).

7:11 Job speaks frankly with God as he begins to pour out his **anguish** and to **complain** in **bitterness.** He had no fear that the Lord would misinterpret him as his human counselors had.

7:12–14 The **sea** and its terrifying inhabitant the **sea serpent** symbolized chaos and the forces of evil and were even considered gods in the pagan religions of the ancient world. Once again Job uses mythological imagery to express his frustration and deep anguish.

7:15, 16 Job is not considering suicide when he states that he would choose **strangling and death rather than** to live in his **body** (see 3:20–22). Strangling may refer to the symptoms of his disease, such as coughing or choking, that he wishes God would use to kill him.

7:17–19 These verses sound similar to Ps. 8:4. Whereas the psalmist marvels that God should "visit him," Job uses the same word in a negative sense to complain that He **should visit him** all the time.

7:20, 21 Job appeals to God to show him what he has done to deserve being made a **target** for God's persecution. When Job calls God the **watcher of men,** he uses a participle that normally describes God in a positive role as one who preserves His people (Ps. 31:23).

8:1, 2 Bildad twists Job's words of 6:26. Job had acknowledged that he had overreacted with words that belonged to the **wind.** To paraphrase Bildad's sarcastic response: "Yes, you're right, Job! All your **words** are like a mighty wind; you are full of hot air!"

8:3 Bildad argues that God could never **pervert justice.** The only possible conclusion

was that Job and his children received what they deserved as sinners (see vv. 4–7, 20).

8:4–6 The repetition of the word **if** in these three successive verses illustrates the presumptive nature of Bildad's statements (vv. 8–22). In his zeal to defend orthodox doctrine, he fails to listen to Job's pain. Bildad admonishes Job to **seek God** now so that God will restore Job's prosperity, rather than talking about how God will seek him unsuccessfully once he is dead (7:21). Bildad uses the words **pure and upright,** the same words the Lord has already used in affirming Job's blameless character (see 1:8; 2:3).

8:7–10 The advice that Job's **latter end would increase abundantly** anticipates Job's restoration in the epilogue (42:10–17), though it came about in a way quite different from what Bildad envisioned.

8:11–19 Bildad uses illustrations from nature to support his belief that God punishes only the wicked and always rewards the righteous in this life. He falsely deduces that one can always determine the cause by looking at the effect. The metaphor of the **spider's web** implies that Job had trusted in his house and riches, which were no more permanent than the web.

8:20–22 Bildad's dogmatic statement about how **God will not cast away the blameless** is undermined by the fact that he uses the word *blameless* in the same way the Lord used it in the prologue (1:1, 8; 2:3) to describe Job.

9:1–7 The verb **to contend** indicates that Job was considering the idea of entering a legal case against God. The prophets often used this word when speaking of God bringing a legal case against Israel (Is. 1:2; Mic. 6:1). The Hebrew for *contend* is almost always used metaphorically in Job, referring to a "lawsuit" between Job and God. Job calculates that the chances of answering God's interrogation are very slim, **one** in **a thousand**—something God later verifies (see 38:1—42:6).

9:8 spreads out the heavens: Job attributes this phenomenon to God **alone.** The fact that the Lord **treads on the waves of the sea** shows his unique control over the alleged forces of evil (see 38:8–12). The word *waves* emphasizes that the Lord **treads** the supposed sea god Yamm under his feet (see also v. 13). This verse emphasizes that the sea is no more than a natural force under the control of the omnipotent God.

9:9–16 the Bear, Orion ... the Pleiades: God's creation of the wonders of the heavens is also celebrated by Amos (see Amos 5:8). Indeed, these words come back on Job's head (38:31–33). **great things ... wonders:** The works of God are so amazing and numerous that the human mind cannot comprehend them.

9:17–20 This verse teems with possible ironic innuendoes. Job's statement that God **crushes** him **with a tempest** anticipates the appearance of the Lord "out of the whirlwind" in 38:1, but with a different result. Job blames God for crushing and wounding him **without cause,** when actually it was Satan who had sought to destroy him without cause (2:3).

9:21 The phrase **I do not know myself** means "I do not care for myself" according to the clarification given in the rest of the verse.

9:22–24 Job contradicts Bildad's claims of 8:3, 20 by accusing God of unjustly destroying both the blameless and the wicked (see 8:20, 21). Thus Job accuses God of being an unjust Judge who blindfolds earthly judges (v. 24).

9:25–28 Job desires to stand before God as an **innocent** man—not absolutely sinless, but innocent of any sin comparable to his suffering.

9:29–35 Job complains that God is **not a man** who would **go to court** with Him (see 9:3). Neither does Job have an impartial **mediator** between God and himself—a mediator who can present his case before God.

10:1, 2 Show me: Job dares to speak to God as an equal. Again using legal language (see 9:3), Job demands that God give him a fair trial through proper court protocol. Here Job comes close to unjustified indignation at God's sovereign will for his life.

10:3–7 This verse serves as a transition from Job's complaint (vv. 1–6) to his brief description of how God had lovingly created him (vv. 8–12). Job knows that he is **not wicked,** and he thinks that God is unjust in oppressing him. Yet Job also realizes that there is **no one who can deliver** him from God's **hand.**

10:8–16 In these verses, Job paints a portrait of the apparently contradictory nature of God, contrasting His loving character with His judgment. Job wonders how the God who had so carefully **fashioned** him in the womb can turn against him like a **fierce lion.** Not being able to **lift up** his **head** expresses Job's shame and **disgrace** (see Judg. 8:28; Lam. 2:10). Job's **misery** was so deep that although he believed he was innocent, he felt like a criminal with no self-esteem or dignity.

10:17 The phrase **you renew your witnesses against me** is a legal metaphor that may refer to each new aspect of Job's illness. In the equivalent **war** metaphor, the Lord was sending **changes** or troop reinforcements against him.

10:18–22 Job asks why he was ever born (vv. 18, 19; see 3:3–10). Then, he wishes the Lord would **leave** him **alone** to die (vv. 20–22; see 3:20–26; 7:16–21). In contrast to 3:17–19, where the grave is described as a place of rest and freedom, the grave here is **the land of darkness** lacking **any order.** Job amplifies his wish that he could have gone straight from **the womb** to the tomb by linking the darkness of the grave with the dark day of his birth (3:3–9).

11:1–4 Zophar the Naamathite (see 2:11) was even more rude than Bildad (vv. 2–6; 8:1–13). He was a brash dogmatist who based his arguments on misapplied theology coupled with simplistic reasoning. Zophar exaggerates what Job has said about his innocence (see 9:14–21) to make Job look foolish. Job never stated that his **doctrine** was **pure.**

11:5–9 When Zophar interrogates Job about the impossibility of comprehending the **deep things of God,** he uses for **search out** the same term Job used to describe God's wonders as beyond "finding out" (9:10). Thus Zophar may be trying to turn Job's words against him by saying that Job's actions are inconsistent with his theology. Since these verses anticipate portions of the Lord's speeches (see 38:16–18, 34–38), Zophar's doctrine is correct, but the application is wrong.

11:10–12 Zophar's rhetorical question about God, **who can hinder Him,** echoes Job's sentiments in 9:12 verbatim. However, Zophar denies Job's allegation that God does not know the difference between the righteous and the wicked (v. 11; see 9:22). As a retort to Job's rhetorical question (6:5) in which he compared his own cries to the braying of the "wild donkey," Zophar uses what may be a proverbial statement about the wild donkey. He could be implying that Job's "empty talk" indicates that he is **empty-headed** (vv. 3, 12).

11:13, 14 stretch out your hands: Stretching out the hands was a posture of prayer as well as of praise (see Ps. 134:2). Assuming that Job is suffering because of his **iniquity,** Zophar rudely repudiates Job's assertion that he has no "injustice" on his tongue (6:30) by alleging that, in fact, it is Job's **tents** that are full of **wickedness** or injustice. The implication may be that Job had acquired his wealth by wrong means or had tolerated evil in his household.

11:15, 16 as waters ... passed away: This is similar to our expression "water under the bridge."

11:17–20 The phrase **dig around you** is a literal rendition of a Hebrew root that may mean "to look carefully about" with "eagle eye" scrutiny.

12:1–4 mocked by his friends: The verb Job uses is also found in a similar negative context in Ps. 2:4. In those contexts, the verb indicates ridicule. But in other passages, this word expresses joy and laughter (Gen. 21:6).

12:5–22 God's reversal of **darkness** to **light** was precisely what Job needed (see 10:21, 22).

12:23–25 God's coming reversal of human wisdom is desired by all who presently suffer the arrogance of people who prate their knowledge with no fear of the living God (see Prov. 1:7).

13:1–4 Job desires to **reason** or argue his cause before God. He rejects the incompetent counsel of his three friends who, like **worthless physicians,** have made a wrong diagnosis about the cause of his disease and suffering. In fact they were **forgers of lies,** literally "falsehood-plasterers."

13:5–13 In response to Zophar's derisive question about Job's words (11:3), Job expresses the desire that his friends would be absolutely **silent.** Indeed, that would have been the friends' wisest action (Prov. 17:28). Using the vocabulary of a wisdom teacher, Job explains his reason for insisting on silence. He wants them to **hear** and pay attention to his words. He urges them to listen diligently to his words instead of trying to defend God. Their pious **platitudes** are as worthless as **proverbs** composed of **ashes.**

13:14 The latter half of the verse seems to clarify **take my flesh in my teeth** to mean risking loss of one's **life** like an animal who tries to defend itself while carrying its prey in its mouth.

13:15–17 trust Him: While this verse is widely known as a powerful statement of Job's trust in God, it is not without difficulties. The Hebrew word translated *Him* is similar in sound to the Hebrew word for *no.* Thus some have translated the verse as follows: "Behold, He will slay me; I have no hope." Yet the positive translation of the verse as it is here seems preferable because it follows the flow of the section (vv. 13–19), which has other positive elements (see vv. 16, 19). It also makes wonderful sense within the verse. Job believes that God is in the process of slowly taking his life. But in a bold declaration of faith, Job declares his absolute trust in God.

13:18–28 Since Job is still in this life of pain (see v. 15), he turns to God as best he can and appeals his case directly to Him. Job requests that God, as plaintiff, list the specific charges He has against him rather than continue being his Judge. The Hebrew terminology resembles vv. 20, 21. Job asks **why** does God **hide** His **face,** a Hebrew idiom indicating the absence of God's favor and blessing. In a portrait of God's "malevolent activities," Job uses the verb **watch.** The word normally describes God's benevolent care over a person's life, but in the Book of Job it depicts the role God gives to Satan (in 2:6).

14:1–6 Job agrees with Eliphaz's assessment that a person is born for trouble. He emphasizes life's misery and brevity through two vivid metaphors: a fading **flower** and a fleeting **shadow.** That God has **determined** the length of a person's life (see Ps. 90:10) emphasizes God's sovereign power and wisdom, and conversely the impotence of human beings.

14:7–9 hope for a tree: Job implies that life is better for trees than for people. When a tree falls, it can sprout again.

14:10–13 Job's wish for **the grave** to be a temporary hiding place from God's **wrath** differs dramatically from his earlier remarks about the grave (see 7:9, 10; 10:18–22). He attributes the cause of his suffering to God's wrath because he assumes the retribution dogma that the righteous are always blessed and the wicked will eventually experience God's judgment.

14:14–22 Job's question **if a man dies, shall he live again** is answered with an emphatic "Yes" by Jesus and the New Testament authors (see John 11:23–26; 1 Cor. 15:3–57; see also Is. 26:19; Dan. 12:2). But Job responds to his own question by a determination to **wait** for his **change** to come. Since Job considers life hard (see 7:1), perhaps he is implying that he will wait for relief from his suffering through death to find out the answer.

15:1–3 The insinuation that Job had filled himself **with the east wind** is an allusion to the violent and scorching wind from the desert that brought no rain. Thus Eliphaz is implying that Job's arguments were destructive (see vv. 12, 13) and without substance.

15:4–6 Eliphaz's statement **your own mouth condemns you** expresses ironic agreement with Job's earlier words (9:20). But Eliphaz deliberately twists Job's words to say that Job no longer needs a day in court since his own mouth has already incriminated him.

15:7 Are you the first man who was born: This sarcastic question anticipates a theme developed in the Lord's speeches (see 38:4–21).

15:8–12 wisdom ... know: Eliphaz throws Job's words of 12:3 and 13:2 back into his face. He counters Job's sarcastic rebuttal to Bildad that wisdom comes only with age (12:12) by saying that people **much older than** Job's **father** are on their side. Since Job was already a mature man who had raised ten grown children, this may be an exaggeration for effect.

15:13 The Hebrew word translated **spirit** may also be translated "temper" or "anger," as in Prov. 16:32.

15:14, 15 Eliphaz rephrases his thought of 4:17, 18 by interweaving an apparent gibe at Job's complaint of 14:1 about man "born of woman."

15:16–18 The phrase **what I have seen** shows that Eliphaz bases his instruction on experience and observation (see 4:1). He also appeals to the wisdom tradition as Bildad has done in 8:8–10.

15:19, 20 hidden from: The Hebrew could also be translated "stored up for."

15:21, 22 dreadful: Eliphaz begins his subtle argument to prove that Job is a wicked man. He alludes to Job's *dread,* the same word translated *feared* in 3:25, as an implicit indicator that Job is wicked.

15:23, 24 By using the phrase **make him afraid** in the context of **a day of darkness,** Eliphaz twists the words of Job's lament about the day of his birth (3:4, 5) to fit the dark day of his death (10:18–22). Then in contrast to 14:20 where Job blames God for *prevailing* against people, Eliphaz says that the wicked man's own fears **overpower** him.

15:25–33 The imagery of the **fat** man who eventually loses his **wealth** and **possessions** by divine punishment for his wickedness, insinuates that Job's calamities have occurred because of his own self-indulgence.

15:34, 35 In mentioning the **fire** that **will consume** the tents of the wicked, Eliphaz uses the same two words that describe the fire of God that devoured Job's sheep and servants (see 1:16).

16:1, 2 I have heard many such things: Beginning with a rare direct allusion to what the previous speaker just said, Job belittles his friends as **miserable comforters.** To paraphrase Job: "Rather than comforting me in my troubles, you have increased my trouble."

16:3 The phrase **words of wind** is a caustic comeback to Eliphaz's words in 15:2 and Bildad's in 8:2. Both had twisted Job's words of 6:26 (see 8:2; 15:2, 3).

16:4, 5 The phrase **shake my head at you** indicates a mocking posture (as in Ps. 22:7).

However, the word **comfort,** meaning "to nod the head sympathetically," is used in 2:11 of the friends who came to console him. In effect, Job is saying: "Please nod your head with understanding instead of mocking and ridiculing me."

16:6–10 strike me: Those who mocked and mistreated Job were probably various passersby (30:1, 9–12).

16:11–22 The identity of Job's **witness** is disputed. One's understanding about Job's "Redeemer" in 19:25 will affect one's understanding of Job's *witness* (see 19:25). Some argue that Job was referring to God. However, the context of 9:33, where Job wished for an impartial mediator between God and himself (see 9:32, 33), and the immediate context of v. 21 suggest that Job was using a legal metaphor to express his wish for an advocate who would **plead for him with God, as a man pleads for his neighbor** on earth. This anticipates Jesus Christ, who is our Intercessor (Heb. 7:25) and Advocate (1 John 2:1).

17:1–11 In another legal metaphor, Job appeals to God to act as his advocate by laying down **a pledge,** that is, providing bail. The use of the same metaphor in Ps. 119:121, 122 to indicate the psalmist's request for relief from his "oppressors" may suggest that Job was pleading for God to demonstrate confidence in his innocence.

17:12 This verse may be a caricature of the friends' false assurances that if he would repent, his **darkness** would soon become **light.**

17:13–16 Job counters the false assurances of his friends with a facetious statement about waiting for **the grave** as one who longingly desires to go home to his **house** and his long-lost relatives, **corruption** (or "the pit") and the **worm.**

18:1–3 When Bildad asks why he and his friends are **counted as beasts,** he apparently resents the implication of Job's words in 12:7–9.

18:4 The phrase **you who tear yourself in your anger** seems to be Bildad's answer to Job's allegation that God had torn Job in His anger (16:13).

18:5–10 net ... trap: Six different Hebrew synonyms for various types of nets and traps

emphasize the many imminent dangers that God has designed for the wicked.

18:11–14 Bildad attributes Job's disease to **the firstborn of death,** a reference to the demon of plagues and disease (see 3:8).

18:15–19 In describing **roots** as being **dried** or withered, Bildad contradicts Job's previous argument about the tree that is cut down but sprouts up from its roots (see 14:7, 8). There seems to be no hope for Job's family tree because God, who is about to wipe **the memory** of Job **from the earth,** has already removed his descendants or **posterity.**

18:20, 21 In this summation of the evidence, Bildad uses the word **wicked,** in Hebrew literally the "unjust one," to suggest that he is refuting Job's allegation that God has turned him over to the "ungodly." Bildad believes that the evidence he has exhibited in vv. 5–20 implicates Job himself as the culprit, the wicked one.

19:1, 2 How long will you torment: Job is tired of hearing Bildad's rude questions and the tormenting words of all his friends.

19:3–8 Job's friends have used the **disgrace** associated with his disease to **plead** the case that he is guilty of sin (10:17; 16:8, see 17:3). With the statement **God has wronged me,** Job responds to Bildad's implication in 8:3 that God does not subvert justice. He argues that Bildad's theory about God does not fit the facts. Instead he asserts that God has wrongly entrapped him as though he were a wild animal or criminal.

19:9, 10 Job compares his removal from the respected position of judge or city councilman (see 29:7–25) to being dethroned like a king whose **crown** is taken from his **head.** Job's **hope,** which had once sprouted up like a new tree from a stump (see 14:7–9), has been totally **uprooted.**

19:11–17 The mention of **the children of** Job's **own body** is problematic since the book seems to document the loss of all ten of his children (see 1:2, 18, 19). It is possible this is a rhetorical statement: "I would be repulsive even to my children" (compare v. 18).

19:18–20 The meaning of the phrase **skin of my teeth** is uncertain. It may imply that his body was so devastated by disease that his teeth had fallen out and only the *skin* or gums of his teeth were left intact.

19:21, 22 That Job believed **the hand of God has struck** him is ironic, since in fact, God had refused Satan's request to "stretch out His hand" against Job (1:11; 2:5).

19:23–26 Job expresses his confidence in his living **Redeemer,** which in this legal context may be translated "Vindicator" or "Protector of the Family Rights" (see Ps. 119:154; also Ruth 4:1 where the word is translated *close relative*). Some interpreters believe that Job was referring to God, a view supported by the context of 17:3 and possibly by the mention of **God** in v. 26. However, the context of the Book of Job—Job's longing for a mediator (9:33) and his desire for someone to plead on his behalf with God (16:19–21)—may suggest that he was thinking of someone other than God.

19:27, 28 Again, the redundant, emphatic pronoun **I** in the Hebrew text (as in v. 25) indicates a strong belief and deep conviction. This is a wonderful example of a sufferer passionately expressing his resolute faith even in the middle of a horrible situation.

19:29 Job's warning to his friends to be **afraid of the sword for yourselves** may have been his rebuttal of Eliphaz's remarks about the wicked person watching in dread for the sword (15:22).

20:1–6 Zophar confronts Job's confident statement in 19:25 with a sarcastic rebuke. Since Job supposedly knew so much about his Redeemer, surely he knew the wisdom teaching that the **wicked** prosper only for a **short** time.

20:7 The word **refuse** may also be translated "dung."

20:8–19 Though **evil** may be **sweet** to the wicked for a while, the certain consequences of their behavior will bring about their downfall.

20:20–26 In stating that the wicked person **knows no quietness,** Zophar implies that Job has received what he deserves. Zophar's statement that the **well-being** or "prosperity" of the wicked **will not last** fits Job's circumstances: Job has lost everything. In essence, Zophar is confirming

Job's complaint in 7:7 that he will "never again see good."

20:27, 28 Zophar apparently reverses Job's appeal to the earth and heavens (16:18, 19) for vindication. He argues that the **heavens** and **the earth** will bear witness not to Job's innocence but to his **iniquity.**

20:29 In this summary verdict, Zophar suggests that it is too late for Job to repent (contrast his previous words in 11:13–20). God would have no clemency for such a **wicked** person.

21:1, 2 your consolation: Job tells the three friends that if they will **listen carefully,** they will finally be of some consolation, or comfort, to him.

21:3–6 keep mocking: Perhaps Job turned directly to Zophar to rebuke the most offensive of his friends. Zophar had not only claimed that Job mocked, but he mocked Job's words.

21:7 Why do the wicked live: With a rhetorical question, Job begins exposing the loopholes in the retribution dogma—the belief that suffering always indicates God's punishment of a person.

21:8–16 Job reacts to Eliphaz's argument in 15:21–24 that although the wicked live peacefully for a while, they live in terror of inevitable destruction. Job contradicts this by saying that the wicked even live in their **houses** safe—without **fear.** The wicked simply deny God's existence, so they live without any fear of His judgment.

21:17 The rhetorical questions introduced by **how often** expect the answer "not very often." With the first question about **the lamp of the wicked,** Job challenges Bildad's belief that the wicked person's light does go out (see 18:5, 6). The second question opposes Zophar's dogmatic statement in 20:23 that God will judge the wicked before they find enjoyment in life.

21:18–29 Job denies the dogma that even if a wicked person prospers temporarily, his children will be punished. Job's position is sustained by other passages in the Bible (see Deut. 24:16; Ezek. 18:1–28; John 9:1–3).

21:30–32 Job may be quoting his friends' position that the **wicked** are doomed. However, the Hebrew words translated **reserved for** could also be rendered "spared from," which would indicate Job's own contrary belief. This latter view is supported by the Hebrew word translated **brought out.** This word reappears in v. 32 in the context of a wicked person being *brought* to the cemetery without being repaid for what he has done (see v. 31).

21:33, 34 shall be sweet: Job uses the same Hebrew word Zophar used (in 20:12) in arguing that evil is sweet to the wicked person but will become bitter in his stomach (20:14). Job contradicts this by saying that things are sweet for the wicked even in the grave.

22:1, 2 The implication of Eliphaz's rhetorical question—that a human being cannot put God under any obligation that God must repay—is a valid theological principle that the Lord Himself corroborates in 41:11. However, his application of that principle to Job's circumstances (vv. 3–5) was invalid, for it was based on the faulty assumption that the righteous are always blessed and the wicked always experience God's judgment on earth.

22:3, 4 The same Hebrew root words for **blameless** and **fear** had earlier been used by Eliphaz in his courteous remarks about Job's "reverence" and "integrity" (4:6). In these verses, Eliphaz is being sarcastic.

22:5–9 naked ... weary ... widows: Eliphaz lists some trumped-up charges about the way Job gained his great wealth: greedy exploitation of the poor in business dealings; lack of hospitality or charity; and lack of compassion to the bereaved. Job categorically denied these charges (see 29:11–17; 31:13–22) and God's own witness to Satan reveals to the reader that the charges were false (1:8).

22:10–14 Can He judge: Eliphaz misrepresents Job's position. Although he accuses Job of not understanding God, it is Eliphaz who has the greater misunderstanding.

22:15–17 Eliphaz twists Job's words recorded in 21:14–16 to support his own view that Job was walking in **wicked** ways. Because of this, Job's prosperity was only temporary.

22:18 The phrase **but the counsel of the wicked is far from me** (quoting Job in 21:16) may be an example of innuendo,

mocking Job for what he was saying and also expressing Eliphaz's own sentiments.

22:19–21 The Hebrew word translated **acquaint yourself,** or sometimes "yield," is derived from the same root as "be profitable" in v. 2. This might be a play on words: "Although you cannot be profitable to God through your efforts, you can acquaint yourself with or yield to Him."

22:22, 23 Eliphaz issues another call for repentance (5:8–17) by asking Job to **return to the Almighty.** Then he suggests that Job **remove iniquity from** his **tents.**

22:24–29 Eliphaz implies that Job has been trusting in his riches rather than in God. Then he urges Job to trust in **the Almighty** God as he does in **gold.**

22:30 Eliphaz's prediction that God would **deliver one who is not innocent** through the **purity** of Job's **hands** would be fulfilled ironically through Job's prayer for the three friends (42:8–10).

23:1–12 Job's use of the metaphor about **gold** to express his assurance of being found pure from guilt may be a rebuttal to Eliphaz's brazen words of 22:24, 25. When Job asserts that he has **kept** God's **way,** he rejects Eliphaz's accusation that he has kept the way of the wicked (see 22:15).

23:13–16 When Job contemplates the **unique** power and sovereign freedom of God, he is **terrified.** To him, God seems to be a capricious despot who does as He pleases (see 9:12, 34).

23:17 This verse likely describes Job's **deep** depression, not only because of his losses, but also because of his failure to understand God's purpose.

24:1 Since times are not hidden from the Almighty might also be translated, "Why are not times stored up by the Almighty?" The parallelism of the second line may indicate that the word *times* alludes to the set **days** for God's judgment.

24:2–8 Removing **landmarks** in the ancient Middle East was tantamount to stealing land. It was a serious crime that placed a person under a divine curse (see Deut. 27:17).

24:9–11 It is ironic that Job complains about God allowing people to **snatch** an infant from its mother's **breast.** Previously he had complained that God had not taken him from his mother's breasts after his own birth (see 3:12).

24:12, 13 In this transition between lists of social crimes and criminal acts, Job protests against God ignoring those who **cry out** for help, since God was supposedly ignoring his own cries for help.

24:14–16 Thieves would **break,** literally "dig," **into houses** by night. The walls of houses were built of mud bricks through which thieves could dig.

24:17–25 These verses about the ultimate fate of the wicked are problematic. They sound more like the friends' words than Job's (see 15:1—21:34). But Job was probably quoting his friends' viewpoint in order to refute them.

25:1, 2 In referring to God's **dominion and fear,** Bildad seems to be responding to Job's comments (in 23:13–17) that the very thought of God's sovereignty made him afraid.

25:3, 4 Bildad repeats the previous rhetorical questions posed by Job (see 9:2) and Eliphaz (see 4:17; 15:14) to emphasize that a person cannot **be righteous** or **pure** before the Lord.

25:5, 6 Bildad's view of God's dominion and majesty in the heavens causes him to devalue mortal **man** as a **maggot.** He responds insensitively to Job by suggesting that Job does not need to wait until he dies to be grouped with the maggots.

26:1–4 How have: Rather than presenting genuine questions, these verses are probably sarcastic exclamations by Job to imply how little Bildad has helped him.

26:5, 6 The words of these verses echo the thoughts of God's omnipotence found in the Psalms (see Ps. 139:7–12). While **Sheol** and **Destruction**—that is, death or the place of the dead—were fearful, hidden concepts to Job and his contemporaries, they caused no fear and held no secrets for the all-knowing God.

26:7, 8 the north over empty space: The Hebrew word translated *north* probably does not refer to a geographical designation (see Ps. 48:1, 2, where the same Hebrew term describes God's mountain), but to God's dwelling place in the heavens (see v. 9,

which mentions God's throne). If the statement that God **hangs the earth on nothing** (see Gen. 1:2) refers to the suspension of earth in space, it preceded Newton's concept of gravitational attraction by thousands of years. Job probably thought, as did other ancients, that the earth was a circular disk (see v. 10) supported by nothing.

26:9–11 Job's graphic description of the **circular horizon** and the pillars of heaven—probably the mountains that held up the heavens in ancient cosmology—pictures the way the earth appears to the human eye.

26:12, 13 With his power God controls **the sea,** which was a symbol of evil and chaos. The highly figurative language may express the power of God over creation in a wide variety of ways.

26:14 This is one of the most stunning of all the verses in the Bible that describe the **power** of God. Job asserts that if we truly considered God's great power, we would know that what we observe of creation represents **the mere edges** of His garment.

27:1 Moreover Job continued his discourse: The different editorial formula for introducing the speaker (as in 29:1) suggests something unusual. Perhaps Job had paused briefly to wait for Zophar before he continued speaking.

27:2, 3 As God lives: These words reflect part of an oath formula used in ancient courts. Job paradoxically combines these words with two accusations against God. According to Job, the living God is the very one who has denied him **justice**—his legal right to due process. Job swears in the name of the divine Judge who, as his opponent, has perverted justice in His own favor. He alleges that God has **made** him **bitter.**

27:4 Job denies that he would use the tactics of his so-called friends (see 13:7). He not only refuses to **speak wickedness;** he will not lie or attempt to defend himself.

27:5, 6 you: This Hebrew plural (also in vv. 11, 12) refers to all of Job's three friends. Job maintains that they are erroneous in their reasoning, and to agree with them would be to compromise his integrity. Job's determination to **hold fast** his **righteousness** and

integrity was remarkable. Though he believed that God had taken away a fair trial (v. 2), he would not **put away** his integrity. He persevered despite the discouraging words of his wife and friends.

27:7–12 In this imprecatory prayer, Job wishes that his **enemy** would receive the fate reserved for the **wicked.** Since he turns the words of his friends back against them, he may be alluding to his friends collectively as an enemy. Job returns Eliphaz's own advice back to him (in 22:22–27). Whereas Eliphaz counseled Job to turn to the Almighty for instruction and to delight in Him, Job denies that a godless person would turn to God, much less **delight himself in the Almighty.** Therefore, Job insists that Eliphaz and his friends should turn to the Almighty and receive instruction.

27:13–23 Since these verses sound more like the friends' words than Job's, some scholars assign them to Zophar or Bildad. However since Job had a fondness for turning the words of his friends back in their faces, these verses may be a satirical paraphrase of the friends' teaching about the fate of the wicked (see 24:18–25). Job's prediction that the **innocent will divide the silver** may foreshadow what happens to Job himself in 42:11.

28:1–4 The mention of **iron** being mined **from the earth** implies a time after the beginning of the Iron Age (around 1200 B.C.) for the writing of the Book of Job.

28:5, 6 The term translated **sapphires** probably means lapis lazuli.

28:7, 8 The **bird,** the **falcon,** and the **lions** represent all animals of every kind. No animal is familiar with the treasures hidden in the earth that human beings can discover (see vv. 2–11).

28:9–11 The streams from trickling may be rephrased "the sources of the rivers."

28:12 The word **wisdom** (see also v. 20) may emphasize the true wisdom that only the Lord knows (see vv. 23–27) and that people may learn in relationship with Him (see v. 28).

28:13–19 Every verse in this whole stanza has the Hebrew word for **not** at least once, emphasizing the absence of wisdom and even the

desire for wisdom. Thus the rhetorical questions about the whereabouts of wisdom and understanding (v. 12) receive an emphatic answer: **not** anywhere in **the land of the living** or of the dead (see v. 14 and its parallel in vv. 21, 22).

28:20–27 Only **God understands** the **way** of wisdom and **knows** the **place** of understanding. God alone is the master and source of wisdom (see vv. 27, 28).

28:28 This verse vindicates Job's stance and marks a transition from the dialogue to the discourses. The words **He said** may introduce a reference to the Book of Proverbs (see Prov. 3:7; 9:10).

29:1, 2 Job's wish for the prosperity of **months past** suggests how long it was since his suffering began (see 7:3).

29:3–5 The picture of God's **lamp** shining on Job's **head** symbolizes divine blessing and success (contrast 18:5, 6; 21:17; see also Ps. 18: 28, 29).

29:6, 7 The gate of **the city** with its nearby **open square,** similar to the modern courthouse square, was a place where town business and court proceedings were held (see Ruth 4:1).

29:8–11 saw me and hid: Job describes the respect he had received from young and old alike because of his position in the city.

29:12–14 The vivid portrait of Job being **clothed** in **righteousness** and wearing **justice like** a judicial **robe** is a stark contrast to his present condition, with his flesh being "clothed" with worms and dust.

29:15–17 broke the fangs: Job had rescued the poor (see v. 12) and the helpless from the wicked. Functioning much like a judge, Job had established justice and righteousness (see v. 14). This explains his frequent use of legal metaphors in his speeches (see 9:3).

29:18–25 Job reminisces about his past days of **glory.** The phrase **bow is renewed** apparently symbolizes a rejuvenation of vigor and might (see Gen. 49:24).

30:1–6 But now introduces Job's lament (ch. 30) about the complete reversal of his former prosperity (ch. 29). Rather than everyone respecting him (see 29:8–11, 21–25), even young ruffians were daring to **mock**

him (see 29:24). These young people were so base that Job had **disdained to put** their **fathers,** who were presumably better than they, with his **dogs.** His words not only emphasize how low they are but also how humiliated he feels as an outcast among outcasts (see vv. 9–11).

30:7 brayed: Job's use of this verb emphasizes not only that the ruffians are poor (see 24:5, where the poor are called "wild donkeys"), but also that they act more like animals than human beings.

30:8–15 When Job says God **loosed** his **bowstring,** he apparently expresses a meaning opposite to that in 29:20. Here the words mean that God had put him "on the shelf," as a bow is set aside when it is unstrung.

30:16, 17 When Job says that his **soul is poured out** like water, he means being emotionally and physically drained of strength (see Lam. 2:11, 12) because of his **days of affliction** (see vv. 1–31).

30:18, 19 Job compares the terrible effects of his suffering and disease (see vv. 16, 17) to being choked by a powerful **force.** Then he identifies God as the One who abuses His great power by harming Job for no apparent reason (see 9:19; 24:22). To the suffering Job, God seems like a gangster who grabs a person by the neck and flings him into the **mire.**

30:20, 21 Ironically, Job blames God's strong **hand,** which Satan could not move, for calamities that have actually been caused by the hand of Satan (see 1:11, 12, 18, 19).

30:22, 23 I know: Job declares his frustration with God almost as directly as he had expressed his confidence in the Redeemer (19:25). Just as surely as he knows that God will vindicate him, he also knows that God will **bring** him **to death.**

30:24, 25 Job builds on the image of the helpless (v. 24) by remembering his own compassion for the **poor.** Now that he is

---

IN DEPTH   Worshiping the Sun and Moon

A s Job takes an oath of innocence (Job 31), he swears that he has never been enticed to worship the sun or moon (31:26, 27), Possible worshipers threw kisses to these celestial deities, since kissing was part of idol worship (1 Kin. 19:18; Hos. 13: 2). Job again swears that he has not gestured such kisses (Job 31:27). Job's oath reflect the popularity of both sun and the moon as deities in Syria-Palestine.

Yareah, the moon god , is mentioned in the Ugaritic ritual and mythological texts, dating around 1400 to 1200 B.C. In one narrative Yareah is a guest at a drinking feast of the gods, but there is little mention of him otherwise. The moon god Sin of Haran was worshiped throughout Syria-Palestine and Mesopotamia from the third millennium through at least the Hellenistic period (332–37 B.C.). The characteristic crescent moon with dangling tassels, which symbolized this deity, has been found on numerous inscriptions and steles (stone slabs), including some discovered in Judah and Israel.

Much more is known about Shemesh. This deity, who could appear as either feminine (sun goddess) or masculine (sun god), was important in all ancient Near Eastern pantheons. In Ugarit the goddess Shapsu (meaning "sun") was the arbiter of divine judgment as proclaimed by the chief god El in this she mirrored an image, found from Egypt to Mesopotamia, of the sun as god of justice. [L&T, 1089]

People of the ancient Near East believed that the sun god rode through the sky by day and the netherworld at night, and thus saw and knew all human activity. Such knowledge made Shemesh useful for locating anyone who was to receive a message from El. In the Ugaritic text, El sends Shapshu to Baal and Mot to stop fighting. In Egyptian thought, the sun god (who had several names, including Re and Aton) was believed to be the creator of the universe each morning.

downcast, why does God not sympathize with him?

30:26–31 In light of the nearby reference to Job's dark, diseased skin (see v. 30), the word **mourning** might mean "darkened," as in 6:16. When Job cries **out for help,** both God (see v. 20) and people of all social classes ignore him. His loud cries for justice are as futile as the wails of **jackals** and **ostriches.** Because of his diseased condition (see v. 30), Job feels ostracized, like these animal inhabitants of desolate places.

31:1 This verse begins Job's oath of innocence (ch. 31). When Job made a **covenant with** his **eyes,** he wisely recognized that the eye is the main avenue for temptation (see vv. 7, 9, 26, 27).

31:2–5 The word **if** was part of a formula used by accused persons to swear their innocence. The full oath formula was, in effect, "If I am guilty of this crime, may God impose that curse." Because of hesitation about speaking a curse, the person swearing the oath would normally use an abbreviated version. By contrast, Job's daring use of the full formula four times (see vv. 7–10, 21, 22, 38–40) demonstrates his confidence that he would be acquitted.

31:6–13 Job implies that he had been fairer in listening to the lawsuit or **cause** (see Mic. 6:1) of his own servants than God was being with his complaint.

31:14–16 Job claims to have satisfied the **desire** of the **poor,** possibly in contrast to God's refusal to give Job a fair hearing before Him.

31:17–22 The loss of an **arm** in ancient society usually meant the loss of income, respect, and even life itself.

31:23–27 The phrase **my mouth has kissed my hand** reflects the apparent ancient custom of kissing the hand as a prelude to the superstitious and idolatrous act of throwing a kiss to the heavenly bodies.

31:28–34 God who is above: Job was resolute in his belief in the one, living God. Though he lived in a world filled with notions of many gods, Job believed in one God.

31:35 Job's wish for **one to hear** him seems to express his continued desire for an impartial mediator or judge (see 9:32, 33; 16:19;

19:25). Job's **mark** refers to his written signature attached to his oath of innocence (ch. 31). He seeks a subpoena to compel God the **prosecutor** to **answer** him with specific charges, or perhaps an acquittal in a **book,** that is, a legal document.

31:36 Job believed that the written charges would be so few, if any, that he could wear the document proudly on his **shoulder.**

31:37–39 Job's idea of approaching God **like a prince** shows his confidence that he will be vindicated but reflects a lack of humility.

31:40 the words of Job are ended: For the second time, the dialogue comes to a close (see 27:23), ending in a stalemate. Job has finished his words, and his three friends have nothing more to say. This leads to the voice of a new speaker, Elihu.

32:1 The phrase **these three men** seems to emphasize the distant relationship between Job and his so-called friends. A gulf existed partly because the trio had been accusing Job of self-righteousness.

32:2, 3 Elihu was of the tribe of Buz and of the **family of Ram,** perhaps an ancestor of King David (see Ruth 4:19). His name means "He Is My God." Elihu was angry about what both Job and his friends had been saying. Like the other friends, Elihu thought that Job had only **justified himself.**

32:4, 5 The editorial introduction (vv. 1–5) emphasizes the **wrath** of the young man against Job (v. 2) and against his three friends (vv. 3, 5). The word *wrath* is found four times in these verses.

32:6–22 I am young: Elihu introduces himself and his four speeches as he explains why he has waited to speak but feels compelled to speak out at the present time. As a reassurance to Job about his complaint that the friends are partial to God (see 13:7–10), Elihu promises not to **show partiality** in his role as an arbiter (see vv. 12–14).

33:1–8 Elihu responds to Job's **fear** of God (see 9:34; 13:21). Elihu reassures Job that he has nothing to *dread* since his **hand** will not **be heavy on** him.

33:9–13 In vv. 9–11, Elihu summarizes Job's position as he perceives it. Then he confronts Job by saying that Job is **not righteous** in attacking God. With great perception, Elihu cuts straight to the heart of Job's problem. Job has been treating God as though he were God's equal. Since **God is greater than man,** Elihu asks: **Why do you contend** or "file a lawsuit" against God?

33:14–22 In response to 7:14 where Job complained of nightmares, Elihu suggests that God may have been trying to teach Job something through a **dream** or **a vision of the night.**

33:23–28 The precise identity of the **messenger** or angel is disputed. God may have used this figure as **a mediator** to address Job's need for an impartial arbiter (9:32, 33; 16:19) and to contradict Eliphaz's counsel of 5:1.

33:29–33 This conclusion to vv. 14–30 succinctly states God's primary purpose in getting a person's attention through dreams and suffering: He wants to keep him from **the Pit**—that is, the grave and hell—and give that person **the light of life.**

34:1, 2 In vv. 2–15 Elihu addresses **you wise men,** probably a sarcastic reference to the three friends whose wisdom he had belittled in 32:12–16.

34:3–15 Surely God: Perhaps in response to Job's charges in 9:22–24, Elihu defends God's impartiality according to the traditional retribution dogma: God will justly punish the wicked. Elihu defends God's justice by siding with Bildad (see 8:3) against Job (see 19:6).

34:16 Elihu addresses Job directly in vv. 16–33, as indicated by the singular Hebrew verb translated **hear.**

34:17 The two rhetorical questions in this verse seem to rephrase Job's complaints of 9:14–31 and 24:1–17 in order to refute them. **Will you condemn Him who is most just:** The second question anticipates the Lord's own rebuke of Job in 40:8.

34:18–28 Elihu responds to Job's complaints about God ignoring the plight of the poor and afflicted (see 24:1–12) by asserting that God does hear **the cry of the poor** and **the cry of the afflicted.**

34:29–37 Elihu's conclusion mixes sound analysis with an unfair representation of Job's position. His statement that Job's words are **without knowledge** anticipates the Lord's own words (see 38:2).

35:1–3 By reading between the lines of Job's many complaints, Elihu exaggerates Job's position: "What benefit do I receive for being good?" Though Job had never made a bargain to serve God for mutual benefit, as in the religions of his day, Job's actions and words may have seemed to reflect that pagan attitude.

35:4–8 God was not under any obligation to Job for any work or deed (see 41:11). Therefore, it was logically inconsistent for Job to demand that God must appear in court (see 31:35).

35:9–16 One reason God **does not answer** when people **cry out** is that they are full of **pride** and devoid of pure motives (see James 4:3). Elihu implies that Job's prayers have not been heard because of his pride (see also 33:17).

36:1–6 Elihu states his thesis: God is both **mighty** and just in His dealings with humankind (see 36:1—37:24). Elihu challenges Job's assertion that the wicked are not punished by God (21:7) and his subsequent arguments (see 21:27–33). Then Elihu counters Job's complaints of 24:1–17.

36:7–15 Affliction will also reveal **the hypocrites** who, because their hearts are incorrigibly wicked, **do not cry** to God **for help.** The warning is clear: Do not reject God's message by failing to cry out to Him for help (see Rom. 1:18–32).

36:16–29 Take heed: Elihu says that God intended to teach Job something through his affliction. Rather than trying to correct the Teacher, Job should **remember to magnify** God's **work** as Maker of all things. Thus, Elihu is setting the stage for the Lord, who will emphasize this concept in His speeches (see 38:1—42:6).

36:30–33 God the sovereign warrior **commands** the thunderstorm as He dispenses **lightning** from **His hands** like arrows (see 16:12, 13). The Book of Job makes clear that God alone controls the unpredictable changes of the weather (see 38:22–30, 34–38).

37:1, 2 The plural Hebrew verb **hear attentively** indicates that Elihu appeals to Job and his friends and perhaps to any bystanders listening.

37:3, 4 The **voice** of God **roars.** The Hebrew word for *roars* seems to compare thunder to

God growling like a lion, the majestic king of beasts.

37:5–7 He says: As God once spoke and brought forth light, land, and all manner of life (see Gen. 1:3, 9, 14, 20, 24, 26), so now He speaks and controls all that He has made (see Ps. 147:15–18). God uses the winter storms to stop **the hand of every man** so that he cannot work but instead **may** recognize the **work** of God.

37:8, 9 Elihu continues to praise the all-powerful God with a series of metaphors. He describes God as keeping the wind in a **chamber** just as He does the snow and hail (see 38:22, 23).

37:10 In a poetic figure of speech, Elihu speaks of the **breath of God** causing **ice** to form and **waters** to freeze. All of this is spoken with joyful delight, for Elihu is celebrating God's control of the world.

37:11, 12 The nautical term **guidance,** literally "steerings" or "rope-pullings" (see the usage of this word in Prov. 1:5), portrays God as the wise Captain who skillfully charts the course for the clouds, which respond obediently to His hand at the helm.

37:13–17 God **causes** the storm **to come** for three specific reasons: (1) for punishment for people's wickedness, (2) for the nourishment of the earth, and (3) for supplying the needs of His people. **For correction** presents the idea of judgment by His rod or scepter.

37:18 Strong as a cast metal mirror: Ancient mirrors were firm and unbreakable because they were made of polished bronze.

37:19–22 If people **cannot look at** the bright **light** of the sun **in the skies,** how much more difficult is it to approach God (see v. 20), who appears in His own **golden splendor** and **awesome majesty?** See the experience of Moses described in Ex. 34. **the north:** In ancient times, north was viewed as the direction of God's abiding place (see Is. 14:13).

37:23, 24 Elihu's concluding words offer praise to the living God who is at once elusive—**we cannot find Him**—and merciful—**He does not oppress. Judgment** means "justice." **Justice** means "righteousness." **fear:** Finally Elihu speaks of the

reverential awe and worshipful wonder that all people should have for their omnipotent Creator.

38:1 out of the whirlwind: Though Job feared that God would crush him in a tempest (see 9:17), God does not come to destroy Job; rather God overwhelms Job into submission in order to restore him to his proper role as the Lord's servant.

38:2, 3 The theme of the first speech of the Lord is given here: Job **darkens** the **counsel** of the Lord—that is, God's plan or design for the universe. Ironically, God challenges Job to teach Him (v. 3; 40:7). These challenges are designed to alert Job to the consequences of his complaints and demands. Job's defiant attempt to meet God on equal footing in a law court (see 31:35–37) amounts to a rival claim to His throne (see 40:10–14).

38:4–7 Perhaps partially in reply to Job's words about the Lord shaking the pillars of the earth (9:5, 6), the Lord asks Job if he was an eyewitness when He laid the earth's **foundations.** The joyful response of the **morning stars,** personified as singing, and **the sons of God** (see 1:6) as eyewitnesses to the earth's creation contrast with Job's complaints that were spoken in ignorance.

38:8–11 The Lord emphasizes His control of the **sea** and its **proud waves.** These forces, which ancient society considered to be chaotic and threatening, were allowed to exist only within divinely set limits (v. 10). Though Job knew this in theory (see 26:12, 13), he needed to apply this truth to his life.

38:12–15 The Lord answers Job's complaints that wickedness is rampant at night (24:13–17). Using personification, the Lord describes how He alone commands **the morning** to get out of bed and **the dawn** to pull off the covers of the night in order to shake out the wicked like bedbugs. God implies that only because of His control of the darkness are the activities of the wicked curbed at all.

38:16–18 Has Job ever been to the bottom of the sea, or taken a trip through the **gates of death?** Perhaps in response to Job's desire for a respite in the darkness of

Sheol (10:18–22), the Lord wants to know if he has ever been there.

38:19–21 Since Job had spoken intelligently about the distant horizons (see 26:10), the Lord exposes Job's limited knowledge by asking him to lead a guided tour to the abode of **light** and **darkness**. Since Job had stated that the wicked "do not know the light" or "abide in its paths" (see 24:13, 16), the Lord reveals the deficiencies of Job's secondhand knowledge. Had Job been there in person, he would have understood that the Lord has a **place** for both **darkness** and dawn, as well as for good and evil.

38:22–30 By asking if Job understands the unpredictable weather phenomena, the Lord reveals that His designs are not centered on humanity alone. Though God utilizes meteorological elements to intervene in human affairs (vv. 22–24), He also uses them to limit the chaotic wilderness and sea (vv. 25–30) that lie outside the human realm. The graphic metaphor of **the treasury** for **snow** and **hail** portrays these elements as weapons in the arsenal of God. He uses hail as slingstones (see Josh. 10:11). He prepares other weapons, including snow (see Ps. 68:14), thunderstorms, lightning (see v. 24), and winds (see 37:9). **frost of heaven:** Since frost is water vapor from the atmosphere that has condensed on cold surfaces, the word *heaven* may refer to the atmospheric heavens.

38:31, 32 The **Great Bear with its cubs** is a reference to the constellation known as Ursa Major.

38:33–38 In asking whose command the clouds obey, the Lord implies Job's impotence and ignorance of these matters, as well as His own sovereignty and omniscience.

38:39, 40 The Lord interrogates Job about the animal kingdom to demonstrate Job's impotence to govern it and his ignorance of God's providential plan (see 38:1—40:5). The wild animals listed were either favorite game animals of kings or used by royalty. Before Job could validate his claims to be able to run the universe better than the Lord, he would need to prove that he could control these hostile forces.

38:41 If the Lord provides for the young **raven** who cries out for help, how much more

will He hear and provide for people when they cry to Him?

39:1–4 God, who provides the prey for the predators (see 38:39–41), also takes care of that prey, which includes the **mountain goats** and **deer.** By taking care of them in their most vulnerable moment of giving birth, the Lord provides for order and balance in nature. The Hebrew word translated **with grain** may also be rendered "in the open field."

39:5–12 The **wild donkey,** the symbol of the exploited poor in 24:5, finds satisfaction where God has placed him on earth free from the **shouts of the driver** or "slave driver." This contrasts with Job's complaints about the voice of the oppressor (3:18). True freedom is found in being content where God has placed us (see Phil. 4:10–12).

39:13–25 Job had identified himself closely with the **ostrich** (see 30:29). Therefore, the Lord ironically agrees that there are similarities. Both are deficient in knowledge (see v. 17; 38:2). But although the ludicrous-looking ostrich is no doubt laughed at (as was Job; see 30:1) and experiences misfortunes (see vv. 14–16), the ostrich is not concerned about the situation. This contrasts with Job, who has been full of worry (see 3:25; 15:24).

39:26–30 God asks Job if he designed the majestic birds—the **hawk** and the eagle—by his aerodynamic genius. **eagle:** The context of v. 30, where the young birds feast on the blood of the dead, suggests that a vulture is in view. However, the traditional translation *eagle* conveys the royal and majestic qualities associated with the vulture in the ancient Middle East (vv. 26–30), in contrast to the revulsion its name brings to many modern readers. The implication is that God allows the young vultures to feed on the **blood** of **slain** people to help prevent the spread of disease. This is an answer to Job's complaint about God's failure to stop the exploitation of the helpless (24:1–17) and His ignoring of the pleas of the dying. The Lord demonstrates to Job again that He limits evil.

40:1–3 Moreover the LORD answered: The Lord reinforces His initial thematic challenge (see 38:2, 3) with a dynamic question loaded with legal terminology. The word **contend** means "to bring a lawsuit" (see 9:3). God reverses Job's accusation that God has brought a lawsuit against him. It really has been Job accusing God, not the other way around. The Lord reprimands Job for his error. Who is Job to judge God?

40:4 vile: Job's placing his **hand over** his **mouth** is probably a gesture of respect (see 29:9) as God's subordinate.

40:5–7 prepare yourself: But God has not finished speaking. The words of v. 7 are repeated from 38:3; but the stakes are even higher now.

40:8 The Lord confronts Job with critical errors in his speeches. Job has dared to **annul** God's **judgment** or justice. The context of Elihu's speeches, where Elihu used this same word about the Lord's kingship over the universe (see 34:17; 37:23), suggests that Job has maligned God's justice by claiming that God rules without establishing moral or social order in the universe (see 24:1–17). Because Job had assumed the inflexible retribution dogma, which views suffering in this world as God's punishment for sin, Job had to **condemn** God in order to maintain his own innocence.

40:9–14 The absurdity of Job's defiant criticism of the way the Lord runs the universe is forcefully brought to his attention by God's ironic invitation to become "king for a day" over the whole universe. If Job had the power, let him don the royal regalia of God's majestic attributes and **humble** the **proud** and **wicked** forces in the world.

40:15–24 The identity of **the behemoth,** meaning the "great beast," is disputed. Suggestions include the elephant, some sort of dinosaur, or a purely mythical monster. The hippopotamus, which had overtones of cosmic evil, seems to fit the biblical and cultural evidence best. Job could not approach, much less subdue, this massive beast; how could he force his way to the Almighty with his case (see 40:15–41:34)? The clause **though he takes it in his eyes** is one possible translation of the Hebrew. However, it might also be construed as a question: "Can one take him by his eyes?" The phrase *in his eyes* may refer to the difficulty of capturing

the hippopotamus when it is submerged, with only its eyes above the water. Also, because of the thick hide of the hippopotamus most weapons are ineffective unless one is shot through its eyes.

41:1 The identity of **Leviathan,** basically a transliteration of the Hebrew word for "sea monster" or "sea serpent," is disputed. The traditional view is that it is the crocodile. As in the case of the behemoth (40:15–24), the description of Leviathan begins as a grand, poetic description of a well-known, formidable beast. But by the time the description is complete (see vv. 18–21), Leviathan has become a fire-breathing dragon, a powerful symbol of chaos, evil, and destruction. Ultimately, Leviathan's image is a portrait of chaos at the beginning of God's creation and of Satan at the consummation of the ages (see Ps. 74:2–17; Is. 27:1; 51:9). Only God can control and destroy Leviathan.

41:2, 3 The **reed** indicates the material that was twisted or spun into a cord or rope, perhaps to "string" the Leviathan like a fish. However, the clause **pierce his jaw with a hook** may suggest the picture of Leviathan as a prisoner of war with a hook or ring in his jaw or nose (see 2 Chr. 33:11).

41:4–9 The Lord continues to confront Job with a series of rhetorical questions. Can Job make Leviathan an eternal **servant** or vassal? The Lord's mention of the **covenant** implies that perhaps Job could offer it a peace treaty, like a great king subduing a lesser king in battle (see v. 34).

41:10 When the Lord says **no one** would be so foolish as to **stir** Leviathan **up,** he is replying to Job's desire that this monster be roused (see 3:8). In effect, the Lord questions Job: "What would you do, Job, if he were provoked?" (see vv. 8, 9).

41:11 Who has preceded Me could also be rendered "who has confronted Me?" **that I should pay:** The Hebrew verb means "to pay a debt" or "to make restitution for something lost or stolen." The Lord confronts Job for implying that God owed him something for being righteous (see 34:5–8) or that God had to make restitution for the property and posterity He had allegedly stolen from Job (see 10:3). Thus the Lord plainly refutes Job's misconception that God is obligated to reward a person who is obedient.

41:12–34 mighty power: The Lord reinforces the argument of vv. 1–11 by describing the invincibility and terrifying splendor of Leviathan's bodily features. Using poetic exaggeration (see v. 18), the Lord gradually transforms the physical Leviathan to the mythological dragon (see 7:12), which breathes **fire** and **smoke** (vv. 19–21). Even though the Leviathan was God's creature, it terrified the Egyptians so much that they worshiped it as a god. The phrase **he beholds every high thing** could also be translated "he looks down on everything haughty." **King** Leviathan, who is **over all** who have **pride,** gazes with a look of superiority at the haughty. Therefore Job, whose pride had been exposed, could never succeed in subduing the mighty Leviathan or validating his claim to be able to rule the world better than God.

42:1–6 The phrase **I abhor myself** means "to reject" or "to recant." Job repents of his words and accusations that were based on the false belief that God always rewards the righteous in this life. Instead of accusing God of injustice, Job submits to the will of the sovereign Lord of the universe.

42:7, 8 In contrast to his friends, Job had **spoken** of God **what is right.** Unlike the friends, Job had recanted his false belief, repented of his pride (v. 6), and affirmed God's unconditional sovereignty over his life (v. 2). Job had been right in maintaining his innocence in the face of his friends' false accusations.

42:9–11 Since Israelite law required a thief to restore double for stealing "an ox or donkey or sheep" (Ex. 22:4), it was ironic that **the LORD gave Job twice** the amount of livestock he had before (see v. 12). Clearly, the Lord was not admitting that He owed Job anything (see 41:11), but He was expressing His benevolent mercy.

42:12–17 The restored prosperity of Job should not be seen as compensation for his piety (see 41:11). After Job had given up his demand for his former prosperity, the Lord could give it to him as a free gift. This conclusion shows that the Book of Job does not totally reject the principle of divine retribution but only its false application. It concurs with the Book of Proverbs that the fear of the Lord normally leads to an abundant and long life. But we cannot presume that God will always operate in this manner, as Job's friends had done.

Psalms

Introduction

As one of the greatest collections of songs, prayers, and poetry, the Book of Psalms expresses the deepest passions of humanity. The psalms lead us through the valleys and peaks of human experience, but in the end they guide us to the praise of our loving Creator.

The introductory words found before the first verse in most psalms often attribute the following psalm to King David, the "sweet psalmist of Israel" (2 Sam. 23:1). These superscriptions were probably not part of the psalms when they were originally composed but were added by editors to aid in the interpretation of the poems. Nevertheless, the historical books of the Bible speak of David's accomplishments as a musician, singer, and composer of poems (1 Sam. 16:19–23; 18:10; 1 Chr. 29:10–15). Moreover, one of David's psalms is recorded in 2 Sam. 22 and reappears with only slight variation as Ps. 18. Thus, the connection between King David and the Psalms is well documented.

Of course, David is not the only composer of the Psalms. Others include contemporaries of David whom he placed in charge of worship in Jerusalem: Ethan, Heman, and Asaph. Solomon followed in his father David's footsteps by writing psalms as well as proverbs. Some of the earliest psalms were written by Moses, five centuries before the time of David. One priestly family, the sons of Korah, continued to write psalms for centuries. However, the composers of many of the psalms remain anonymous.

Many of the psalms can be identified as certain types by their theme.

The royal psalms emphasize God as King, often using the words "the Lord reigns." These psalms often point forward to the coming rule of the Savior King, the Lord Jesus. The psalms of Zion focus on Jerusalem, using its endearing name Zion. These psalms rhapsodize on the city as God's choice for the site of His holy temple. The penitential psalms are poems in which the psalmist confesses sin to the Lord, asks for and receives forgiveness, and then praises God for the renewed relationship that God's forgiveness provides.

The wisdom psalms focus on some of the same issues that are found in the Book of Proverbs. These psalms present sharp contrasts between the righteous and the wicked, address God's blessing and cursing, and often focus on righteous living. One subcategory of the wisdom psalms is the Torah psalms. These focus on the beauty, truth, and sufficiency of the Law of God. Two other subcategories of the wisdom psalms are the creation psalms and the history psalms. In the creation psalms, the psalmist calls for the believer to praise God as the Creator of the universe and the Savior of His people. In the history psalms, the psalmist recounts the history of Israel and asks for a renewed commitment to God.

Some of the most troubling psalms are those that contain prayers asking God to curse the wicked. These imprecatory psalms are sometimes thought to conflict with the sentiment of the gospel, but in fact they accurately reflect God's abhorrence of evil. In contrast to the imprecatory psalms are the joyful and prophetic Passover psalms that became a part of the Passover celebration in Judaism. These psalms are a remarkable celebration of the great acts of the Lord in delivering His people from Egypt, the theme of the Passover celebration. They point forward to the deliverance that would come through the Savior Jesus.

A final group of psalms is clustered at the end of the book. These are the Hallel psalms, named for the principal Hebrew word for praise, *hallel*. As their name suggests, these psalms praise God for His character and saving works.

Psalm 1, a wisdom psalm, presents a vivid contrast between the way of the righteous (vv. 1–3) and the way of the wicked (vv. 4–6). No author is named nor is any circumstance given for the writing of this poem. It was probably written late in Israel's history. With its focus on the distinctions of character and the different destinies of the righteous and the wicked, this psalm serves as an introduction to the entire Book of Psalms.

1:1 Who walks not: The parallelism in this

verse speaks of an increasingly deeper involvement with wickedness: "walking beside," "standing with," "sitting beside." Similarly, the terms for the wicked are progressive: **ungodly, sinners,** and **the scornful.** The imagery of this verse presents an ideal righteous person—one who is *in* the world, but quite unaffected *by* the world.

1:2 But his delight: Instead of finding enjoyment in entanglements with wicked persons, the godly person finds his or her deep enjoyment in the things of God, particularly the Word of God. **The law of the LORD** refers specifically to the Pentateuch, the first five books of the Old Testament. The Hebrew word for *law* expresses the idea of God pointing out the path for life in fellowship with Him (19:7–11). **Meditates** means "to mumble" or "to speak to oneself" (4:4). Biblical meditation is focusing the mind on Scripture.

1:3 like a tree: This simile presents an image of a desert date palm that has been firmly planted in a well-watered oasis (Jer. 17:8). Everything about the tree is valuable and productive. Likewise, the righteous are valuable and productive to God—people in whom He finds pleasure (33:15; 147:11). **Shall prosper** is not a guarantee of the future financial worth of the righteous; rather, the righteous person is always useful and productive to the Lord.

1:4, 5 Like **chaff,** the refuse that is blown away by **the wind** after the grain harvest, **the ungodly** have no stability (35:5; 83:13). When the judgment comes, the ungodly will no longer **stand** (5:5).

1:6 The Bible speaks of two ways (Prov. 2:8; 4:19), only one of which leads to God. This is a consistent biblical theme, culminating in the celebrated words of Jesus, "I am the way" (John 14:6). The verb **knows** in this context refers not just to God's awareness, but to an intimate, personal knowledge (101:4). God is intimately involved with the way of the righteous, but has no connection with the way of the ungodly, except in judgment (146:9).

Psalm 2, a royal psalm, focuses on the coming glorious reign of the Lord's Messiah. The author is anonymous in the Hebrew text, but the New Testament apostles assign it to David (Acts 4:24–26). This psalm should be read in conjunction with Ps. 110. Both psalms point prophetically to the coming rule of Jesus (see Acts 13:33; Heb. 1:5, 6; Rev. 12:5).

2:1 Why do the nations rage: Originally this passage referred to the nations that confronted David and his legitimate successors. But the Davidic kings were mere shadows of the coming great King, the Savior Jesus. Consequently, the verse also refers to any attack on Jesus and His divine kingdom. This assault by the nations occurred in its most dramatic form at the Cross, but resistance to God's kingdom has continued.

2:2 LORD refers to the Father. **His Anointed** (18:50; 132:10) refers to the Son. The word conveys a sense of royalty, for kings were anointed (see 1 Sam. 10:1; 16:13). **The kings of the earth** would attempt to withstand the King of the universe.

2:3–5 hold them in derision: God laughs scornfully at an attack on His Son (37:13). The idea of "fighting off" the will of God is truly preposterous. **He who sits in the heavens:** God is King of the universe (Ps. 93). What are the kings of the earth compared to Him?

2:6 My King: David and his legitimate heirs were given a divine promise that they would rule the Israelites under the Lord's blessing. Any attack on the king of Israel was an assault on God's promise. **Zion** is another name for Jerusalem. **My holy hill:** The site of Zion was "holy," for it was declared to be so by God. It was the place where Abraham bound his son Isaac (Gen. 22), where the holy temple was built (2 Chr. 3), and where the Savior Jesus would die (Matt. 27).

2:7, 8 You are My Son: Each time a legitimate son of David was crowned king as the successor to his father in the city of Jerusalem, these words could be used of him. The new king was adopted by God as his "son"; he would look to God as his "Father" (see 2 Sam. 7:5, 14). This formula of adoption was announced in a solemn ceremony of coronation attended by priests and prophets, with pomp and celebratory worship of God. In the New Testament, the Son of God is also declared to be the King, the true Anointed, the Christ (see Matt. 3:17; Acts 13:33; Heb. 1:5; 5:5).

2:9 rod of iron: The future rule of the royal Son would be absolute. There would be no rebellion.

2:10, 11 be wise: Potentially rebellious kings would avoid terrible judgment only by submitting to the Anointed of God. **rejoice with trembling:** Only with the proper fear, adoration, reverence, and awe of the Most Holy God could there be genuine joy in the coming kingdom.

2:12 Kiss the Son: The kings and all peoples could either love and respect the Lord's Anointed and so experience His great blessing, or they could refuse to submit, and incur God's wrath.

Psalm 3 is a lament psalm ascribed to David. The superscription indicates a precise setting: the period of David's flight from his son Absalom (2 Sam. 15). This is one of the few psalm titles that ties a psalm to a specific incident in the life of David.

3:1, 2 Many: At this point in David's life there was one specific foe who troubled him greatly—his son Absalom. However, David's friends had also become his foes because they were advising him that no one would help him, not even God. **Selah:** This is a musical term, perhaps indicating a pause in the lyrics for a musical interlude. **3:3, 4** The phrase **but You, O LORD** changes the mood of the psalm from dejection to confidence. David says three things of the Lord: (1) When no one would help David, God was his **shield.** (2) When David had nothing to treasure, God was his **glory.** (3) When no one would encourage him, God Himself would encourage him and lift his **head.**

3:5, 6 I lay down and slept: Given the stress that David faced, it is remarkable that he was able to enjoy a night's rest. This was possible only because of God's sustaining power. **I will not be afraid:** When God is one's protector, there is no need to fear (23:4; 27:3; 118:6).

3:7, 8 David calls out for God to **arise,** to move on his behalf, to incline to his prayer (40:1). **on the cheekbone:** In the poetic

imagery David uses, his enemies are like powerful beasts whose strength is in their jaws and whose terror is in their teeth. But they are no longer a threat because of God's protection. **Salvation,** in this instance, refers to deliverance from the immediate pressure that the psalm has already described. One meaning of the Hebrew word translated *salvation* is "room to breathe."

Psalm 4 is linked to Ps. 3 in mood and concept. Both speak of the possibility of finding such peace in God's presence that even when torn by physical and emotional pain, a person may still have restful sleep (3:5; 4:8). This is a lament psalm of the individual, but one in which there is an unusual degree of confidence. To the wicked there is a proclamation of hope rather than a pronouncement of doom. Psalm 4 is the first of the psalms to have a superscription that focuses on its musical nature. **To the Chief Musician** is a notice that indicates that this psalm is from an early collection of psalms used in temple worship. **With stringed instruments** specifies the musical setting for the psalm. **A Psalm of David** serves not only as a notice of authorship, but also as a reminder that the poem was to be sung.

4:1 O God of my righteousness can also be translated "O my righteous God." The phrase has two meanings: (1) Only God is righteous. (2) All of a person's righteousness is found in Him alone. The psalmist is facing a very pressing need, but his confidence in God remains strong. He addresses God in terms of His character—His "righteousness."

4:2 How long: The psalmists often use these words to question God (13:1, 2). Here they are addressed to the wicked. **my glory:** For the believer, one's sense of glory or honor is found in relationship to the Savior.

4:3 set apart: This is the central point of this psalm. God has identified the **godly**—those who are devoted to God and His ways. He exercises special care over them and listens to their prayers.

4:4, 5 Be angry, and do not sin: These words are cited by Paul in the New Testament to describe "righteous indignation" (Eph. 4:26). Here the psalmist exhorts his reader not to let anger or anxiety erode trust or faith in the Lord. **put your trust in the LORD:** The psalmist calls on his neighbors to put their faith in God (Ps. 67).

4:6 any good: Although our lives often seem to be filled with uncertainty, there is never uncertainty with God. **light of Your countenance:** This phrase recalls the Aaronic benediction (Num. 6:26) and indicates God's favor. Those on whom the Lord shines His face are truly blessed.

4:7 grain and wine: The joy God gives transcends the joy of the harvest. Agricultural produce, the result of abundant rain on fertile soil, was a blessing of God on His people. But there is something greater than full barns and overflowing cisterns—the joy of God's presence.

4:8 The peace that God gives is far from a relaxation technique. It is a peace that enables an anxious person to lie down **and sleep** (3:5).

Psalm 5, a lament psalm, speaks of an unspecified but distressing period of David's life, a time marked by enemies who verbally opposed him and his rule. In the culture of the Old Testament, a blessing or a curse was an appeal to God to *do* what the curse or blessing specified. So when David's enemies hurled curses at him, they believed that those curses called on divine power to destroy him. In this psalm, David is in distress because of the lies and boasts of his adversaries (101:7). He identifies his own cause with that of the Lord, so that attacks on him became attacks on God Himself.

5:1–3 Give ear: This is the language of a person who believes that God has forgotten his plight. The sufferer calls on the Lord to listen, even though the Lord has been continually listening and caring. **My King:** The psalmists often address God in heaven as King, the ruler over all. At times, the psalms focus on prayer **in the morning** (88:13)—a commendable habit that helps a person to dedicate all the activities of the day to God.

5:4–6 Takes pleasure means to find enjoyment or reason for laughter. There is no enjoyment to be found in evil. The Hebrew word for **boastful** is the same one used to describe the praise of God. The praise of God

is the focus of the psalms; but praise of self—a mere boast—is a twisted, human perversion of true praise. **not stand:** This psalm speaks of final judgment on the wicked (compare 1:5). They will not be allowed to stay in His glorious presence. The phrase **workers of iniquity** occurs often in the psalms to describe those who practice evil (14:4).

5:7, 8 But as for me: In the Hebrew text, these words indicate a sharp contrast with the previous description of the wicked. The Hebrew word **temple** can be used of any very large structure—"palace" or "big house." David was a leader in reforming the worship of God in Jerusalem, and he established a structure for the worship that would take place in the temple to be built by Solomon. David uses the word *temple* in anticipation of the future glorious building; all later generations of Hebrew worshipers would understand their own worship better because of the use of this word in these psalms. **Make Your way straight:** David prayed that God would make clear His will for him.

5:9, 10 Their throat is an open tomb: These words describe the perverse language used by people in opposition to God. Paul used the words of these verses to argue for depravity of all people (Rom. 3:13).

5:11, 12 rejoice: Here the psalmist describes the joy of the saved, the ecstasy of the ones whom God saves from their own deserved destruction.

Psalm 6 is a lament psalm that shares elements of the penitential psalms. David was experiencing what he feared to be a mortal illness. He sensed that this illness may have fallen on him because of his own sinfulness. The title of the psalm is similar to those of Ps. 4 and 5. The specification of instruments is a reminder that this very personal psalm became part of the worship of the community when the temple was built.

6:1–3 in Your anger: The psalmist suffers from a grave physical illness, one from which he fears he might not recover (v. 5). His principal concern is not only that his suffering might be more than he could stand, but that it comes as a result of God's severe anger. In his mourning, David cries out to God (as in 38:1). **My bones** is a poetic way of describing a deeply troubling illness; David's entire being is in torment. **6:4, 5 Return:** This is a typical part of a petition in the psalms of lament (Ps. 13). The call for God to act is based on faith. **Your mercies' sake:** Perhaps the most significant single term in the Hebrew text about the character of God is the word rendered *mercies* here. The Hebrew word describes what some call the loyal love of God. **In the grave:** When a believer dies, his or her voice is lost from the singers of God's praise in temple worship. If God still desires to hear David's voice in worship, He must keep David alive. He would be of no use to God dead; alive he could sing, shout, and testify to God's love and His mercy (94:17).

6:6–10 Depart: The change of mood in the psalm is due to the Lord's response. David who has been so ill is now healed. The Lord has answered David's prayer. **Let all my enemies be ashamed:** The psalmist speaks in righteous indignation against those who have reviled him, and more importantly have ridiculed his God.

Psalm 7 is a lament psalm, featuring David's protests of innocence. In some psalms, the psalmist indicates that his suffering is deserved. Such cases lead to confession of sin. But in other cases, psalmists, like David in this psalm, do not believe they deserve the suffering or the feeling of being abandoned by God. Hence this psalm expresses David's extreme sorrow.

7:1, 2 I put my trust: The verb here can describe the action of a bird seeking refuge in the wings of its mother. **Tear me like a lion** vividly conveys the psalmist's fear. David had witnessed a lion who had captured its prey, and he compares his own fate to being captured and torn apart.

7:3–5 if I have done this: David protests that he is innocent of whatever charge his enemy has brought against him (Ps. 94). **let him trample my life:** These solemn words are spoken to God. The Lord can enact His judgment through David's enemies if his protest of innocence is false.

7:6–8 in Your anger: This is a plea for God to display His anger against the psalmist's adversaries, to judge them for their slander against David. **Lift Yourself up:** David implores the Lord to rise from His throne to intervene on his behalf, to bring justice in the intolerable situation (3:7). **Judge me:** Only someone confident of his own innocence would dare to pray these words before the Lord. David was innocent of the charges. He had not attacked someone without cause (see vv. 3–5).

7:9, 10 In the Hebrew, **hearts and minds** is literally "hearts and kidneys"—an ancient way of describing the innermost person. **My defense** means "my shield." God hovers over the believer like a military shield, an invisible defense (33:20).

7:11–13 God is angry: The indignation of God is directed at the enemies of His people. **sharpen His sword:** The imagery in vv. 12, 13 is of a great warrior preparing for battle. The Warrior is the Lord and the battle is against the wicked (37:9; 118:10).

7:14–16 conceives trouble: The wicked become "mothers" to trouble. They will give birth to their own destruction.

7:17 Most High is a term often used to describe God's authority over the nations (Deut. 32:8). The God of Israel is not just another national deity; He rules all nations.

Psalm 8, a psalm of praise with wisdom connections, is a poetic reflection of the great creation text of Gen. 1. This psalm expresses wonder at the majestic and sublime nature of God. However, the center of the psalm focuses on human beings, a rarity in Scripture. But even this focus leads to the praise of God, the Creator of humanity. Thus the psalm sets to music the significance of the phrase "in His image" in Gen. 1:26–28.

8:1 How excellent is Your name: The name of God and the glory of God are alternate ways of describing who He is. This psalm ends with the same words it begins with. These words of praise to the name of God form a frame for its central subject—the praise of man as male and female, whom God has made to reflect His majesty.

8:2 mouth of babes: This verse was quoted by Jesus (Matt. 21:16) to the priests and scribes who wanted to squelch the people who were speaking the words of 118:26 in praise of Jesus.

8:3, 4 Your heavens: David is in awe at the splendors of creation; the wonders of nature lead him to praise its Creator. Even the universe with its infinite distances was the work of the Lord's fingers (19:1). **What is man:** In view of the vastness of creation and the surpassing glory of God the Creator, who are we to presume upon Him?

8:5–8 You have made him a little lower than the angels: The response to the rhetorical questions of v. 4 is stunning. Man, as male and female, stands at the summit of God's creation. The Hebrew text is "You have made him to lack little of God." God made human beings in His image, just a little lower than angels. The words **crowned him with glory** fill out and explain the parallel phrase "a little lower than the angels." God created human beings as majestic creatures who were to rule over His creation. But in our fallen state, we are profoundly disfigured, a perversion of the majesty God has intended (9:20). However, Jesus restores those who put their trust in Him. In Christ, we recover majesty; in Him, we become the people that God wants us to be. We are valuable because God Himself created us in His own image.

8:9 O LORD, our Lord: The first word is the divine name Yahweh. The second Hebrew word translated *our Lord* speaks of the One in control: "our Sovereign."

Psalm 9 may have been originally one poem with Ps. 10. Indeed, there is evidence that several of the psalms have been restructured in varying ways (see Ps. 42; 43). Note that Ps. 10 does not have a new superscription and that the two psalms deal with the same theme. Moreover, the psalms in the Hebrew text form a partial acrostic pattern. Ten of the initial letters of verses in Ps. 9 follow the order of the Hebrew alphabet, and seven initial letters in Ps. 10 continue the same pattern. In Hebrew, this pattern is pleasing to the listener and attests to the skill of the psalmist.

9:1, 2 with my whole heart: Real praise is not halfhearted; it involves one's whole being (146:2). The words of these two verses are characteristic of the praise of God in the

Psalms. He is to be praised for His works and His name. His name represents who He is; His works stand for all He does. **Most High** is a designation for the Lord, especially as He rules the nations (47:2; 78:35; Deut. 32:8).

9:3–5 The **enemies** are not identified. All subsequent readers can fill in their own list of those who trouble them. The psalmist has confidence that God is in control (v. 4) and that He executes judgment (v. 5). Therefore in the middle of trouble, the psalmist is able to foresee the end of his enemies (vv. 17, 18).

9:6–8 One day even the names of the enemies of God will be forgotten. But the name of God will **endure forever.**

9:9, 10 Refuge speaks of a secure height, something inaccessibly high. David was often outdoors, and he used images from physical geography to describe the wonder of God's protective care (91:1, 2). **who know Your name:** To know the name of God was the Old Testament equivalent of saving faith in the New Testament. **have not forsaken:** This is a further explanation of the meaning of God's name. He is a faithful God—a God who never gives up on His people.

9:11, 12 He avenges blood: God is the Avenger, not any person (Deut. 32:35). One day God will judge the wicked. In the end, He will establish His just rule.

9:13–16 David asks that his life be spared **from the gates of death** so that he might praise the Lord in the **gates** of the temple. Only God could accomplish such a sudden reversal; only the Lord could lift him from such depths. **Daughter of Zion** was an endearing term for Jerusalem. As Jacob was God's "son," so Jerusalem was God's "daughter" (Ps. 48). **In the net:** David prays that the evil the wicked intend for him will become their own trap (7:15, 16; 35:7, 8).

9:17, 18 hell: Just as the Psalms speak of heaven as the destiny of the righteous (see 23:6), so they also speak of hell as the destiny of the wicked (see 1:6). It is a place from which the righteous want to be delivered (86:13). Passages like this one confirm the New Testament affirmation of a day of final judgment in which the righteousness of God will be displayed and the wickedness of unrepentant humankind will finally receive punishment (see Matt. 25:31–46).

9:19, 20 Do not let man prevail: Although human beings are made in God's image as described in Ps. 8, the wickedness of fallen humanity is profound. Humanity in rebellion against God is a gross perversion of God's plan. The Lord cannot allow this arrogance to go unchallenged.

Psalm 10 was originally part of Ps. 9. The two are found as one psalm in the Septuagint, the ancient Greek translation of the Hebrew Scripture. Psalm 10 reiterates the desire expressed in Ps. 9, that the Lord would deal with the wicked enemies of the psalmist. This psalm reflects a sense of urgency: the psalmist pleads for immediate deliverance from his enemies.

10:1, 2 Stand afar off are classic words of lament or mourning (13:1–3). As the psalmist views the actions of the wicked, he finds himself angry at wickedness and wondering how God can remain apathetic and inactive. But even with his doubts, he continues to pray to the only God who can deliver him from his troubles.

10:3, 4 God is in none of his thoughts: For the psalmist, this is the most difficult part of his circumstances (14:1). With no thought of God, his wicked enemies are able to boast in themselves. They turn reality upside down by praising evil and spurning God.

10:5–7 Only those who stand on the sure foundation of God's Word can confidently say, **I shall not be moved** (see 15:5). The wicked who have lost all sense of God assume that they can use these words themselves. But eventually they will be swept away by the turmoil and troubles of this world (see Matt. 7:24–27).

10:8–10 sits in the lurking places: The psalmist views the wicked as oppressors. They are similar to lurking beasts, ready to pounce on their prey.

10:11 God has forgotten: The wicked behave the way they do because they doubt that the Lord knows, cares, or will act. They want to believe that there will be no final judgment, so they feel free to do as they please. But the truth is that God will establish justice (see vv. 14, 15).

10:12, 13 Arise, O LORD: The psalmist returns to his call for God to act (see 9:19, 20).

10:14, 15 You have seen is the classic confession of trust in God in the psalms of lament. God does know; He does see; and He will act. God protects those like **the fatherless** who have no other protection (27:10). **Break the arm:** As in 3:7, this is a call for God to destroy the power of the wicked.

10:16–18 The LORD is King: These words suggest that Ps. 9 and 10 are royal psalms. Usually the royal psalms have a more positive viewpoint. They take the stance that God is King and the world is established and will not be moved. On the other hand, Ps. 9 and 10 question how there can be such distress in the world with God as King. But since God *is* King, this psalm concludes with the fervent prayer that the will of God may be done on earth as it is in heaven (Rev. 19:1–6).

Psalm 11 is a psalm of trust. The title ascribes the psalm to David. In the middle of the psalms of lament (see Ps. 9; 10; 12), this psalm expresses great trust in the Almighty Lord. It is the context of adversity that makes this psalm of trust all the more impressive.

11:1–3 The phrase **I put my trust** describes seeking refuge, similar to a bird under the wings of its mother (Ruth 2:12). **Flee as a bird:** Here is the contemptuous challenge of the wicked. They are like their father, the devil (John 8:44; 2 Cor. 11:13–15). They view the righteous as helpless birds flying to their mountain home. They do not realize that their mountain home is protection in the Lord Himself. **bend their bow:** This is a picture of the wicked on the hunt for the righteous (10:8–10).

11:4–6 The words **in His holy temple** prove that the charge of v. 3 is false. God *is* in control; the foundations are not destroyed. **His eyes behold:** It may appear that God is not involved (10:11), but He does see and He will act (Ex. 2:23–25; 3:6–15). **tests the righteous:** There are times when the Lord allows trials to come into the life of the righteous as a test. But God's actions are more severe toward the wicked, whom He **hates.** The Hebrew word for *hates* is a strong term that speaks primarily of rejection (5:5).

11:7 Because the LORD is righteous, the believer who is under stress can continue to trust in Him. Such faith allows him to ignore the taunts of the wicked. The believer needs only to return to the wings of God to renew strength and purpose in the midst of a troubled day.

Psalm 12, a psalm of lament, begins with a focus on the power of the wicked's perverse mouth (Ps. 52; 120). It concludes powerfully with an assertion of the power of the pure and truthful words of God. The title ascribes the poem to David.

12:1–3 godly man ceases: David wonders if there are any righteous people left. **speak idly:** This psalm charges the wicked for using words to destroy and hurt others.

12:4 With our tongue: Because the wicked do not submit to any authority over them, they believe they can say anything they want.

12:5–7 Now I will arise: With these dramatic words, God speaks to David and reveals His righteous character. He will not linger; He will judge the speech of the wicked. **pure words:** In contrast to the idle words of the wicked (vv. 1–4), the words of God are altogether trustworthy. The eternal and steadfast nature of the Lord Himself stands behind His words.

12:8 The wicked prowl: Even with God's words of judgment, there are still wicked people looking for those whom they might destroy. One day there will be full punishment (10:16–18). For now, we still struggle with the help of the Holy Spirit against the evil in our own souls and the pervasive wickedness in our world.

Psalm 13, is a psalm of lament, an impassioned cry to the Lord for help. It is ascribed to David. The psalm is brief, even terse; but it is remarkably powerful in its tone and imagery. There are similarities between this psalm and Ps. 142.

13:1, 2 These two verses present all three pronouns that occur in a typical lament psalm: (1) *I* am hurting; (2) *You* have forgotten; (3) *they* are winning. Four times in two verses David screams out **how long** (4:2; 6:3). The Lord allows David to pour out his anxiety before Him. But by the end of David's prayer, the Lord has granted

him a correct perspective on his situation. David's only option is to trust in the sovereign mercy of his loving God.

13:3, 4 Enlighten my eyes: As a person who is nearing death might sense the dimming of his vision (38:10), David also senses his death and pleads with God to intervene before he dies. **Lest my enemy say:** If God does not intervene, not only will the psalmist be lost from the community that praises the living God (6:5), but his enemies will also claim a victory over him and his God. The Lord's honor is at stake.

13:5, 6 The tone of the psalm abruptly changes from despair to hope. In this verse, David recalls his commitment to trust God completely. The term **mercy** describes God's *loyal love,* His faithfulness to His commitment to take care of His people. **I will sing** was the psalmist's vow to praise God in the worshiping community. Based on the assurance that God will deliver him, David resolves to tell the people about it.

Psalm 14, which is closely allied with Ps. 53, is a wisdom psalm attributed to David. It speaks of the foolishness of living as if God did not exist.

14:1 The word **fool** refers not to mental inability but to moral and spiritual insensitivity. The phrase **no God** suggests "practical atheism," the view that if there is a God, it really does not matter to a person's life. This is the viewpoint stated in 10:4, 11; 12:4. The Hebrew word for **corrupt** has the idea of soured milk. Those who cease to believe in God will eventually "sour"; they will degenerate into doing evil.

14:2, 3 The LORD looks down: Here the Lord's inquiry leads to judgment (as in Gen. 6:12). The pictorial language is a way of describing the omniscience of God, the fact that the Lord knows everything. **No, not one:** The biblical teaching on depravity is not that each individual is as evil as he or she could possibly be, but that sin is present in every individual (Rom. 3). Since no one is perfect, all must ask God for His forgiveness.

14:4, 5 The wicked lack **knowledge** of God's truth. Although people may be brilliant in their chosen fields, they can still be morally insensitive and spiritually closed to the issues that have eternal consequences. **My people** refers to those who are faithful to God. God has delivered a group of people from the prison of wickedness. These people are His people and must follow His ways.

14:6 His refuge speaks of shelter, as in the shadow of a tree. David as an outdoorsman had experienced the urgent need of shelter from the fierce elements. He uses this common experience to describe the various ways in which God protects His people from the storm of evil that surrounds them (9:9).

14:7 The salvation of Israel refers to a future salvation, the coming reign of God (Ps. 2; 89).

Psalm 15 may be a wisdom psalm, but its principal focus is on the proper approach to the worship of God. The psalm asks the question, Who is righteous enough to approach God? Certainly no one is except Jesus, the Messiah. But there have always been those who stand before God as forgiven sinners, whose righteousness comes as a gift from God. This psalm is ascribed to David.

15:1 who may abide: Except for priests, people did not live in the precincts of the temple. These words describe an approach to God's presence in which one might feel accepted, even "at home." **holy hill:** This phrase is used of the presence of God in the temple or the tabernacle. The Hebrew term is a general one that refers to wherever the tabernacle was in David's day; later singers of this psalm applied the word to the temple built in Jerusalem.

15:2–4 He who walks uprightly speaks of relative righteousness, not absolute righteousness, for no one is innocent before God. The Lord commands us to be holy (see 1 Pet. 1:15, 16), and He also gives us the power to become holy (2 Thess. 2:16, 17). **vile person is despised:** The righteous hate what God hates (vv. 4, 5). The point is not so much the emotion of hatred as the deliberate rejection of wicked ways (1:1).

15:5 never be moved: The promise of God for the righteous is for this life and for the life to come. The Lord is the righteous person's sure foundation.

Psalm 16, a psalm of lament, has a remarkable prophetic aspect that parallels many of

the messianic prophecies about the Suffering Servant (Is. 53). This poem of David became central in the preaching of the apostles in the early church (Acts 2:22–31).

16:1–4 I put my trust: David uses the expression of a bird seeking refuge under its mother's wing to indicate his complete trust in the Lord (compare 7:1; 11:1). From this strong stance of confidence, he is able to boast that his goodness comes only from God.

16:5–8 My inheritance refers to the Promised Land. God had given this inheritance to His people (Deut. 6:1–3). However there was a greater inheritance for the Levites, who did not receive a share in the land (Num. 26:62); their share of the inheritance was in the Lord. David as king had extensive royal holdings. But he realized that no inheritance was greater than his relationship with God.

16:9–11 path of life: With this phrase David speaks of his escape from death at a critical point, but he also indicates the eternal life given by the resurrected Savior to all who trust in Him.

Psalm 17 is a special use of the psalm of lament; it is a protest of innocence (Ps. 26; 35; 43; 69). The psalm is ascribed to David. At times, David suffers under the heavy hand of God's anger because of unconfessed sin in his life. But there are other occasions where he insists that his present troubles are not caused by any fault in his life. In such a case, he calls upon God to vindicate him. God indicates through these psalms that He has a special concern for people who experience undeserved suffering, even though He allows the trouble to come for reasons that may never be known in this life.

17:1, 2 a just cause: With these words, David sets the tone of the psalm. By protesting his innocence, he hopes to convince God to move on his behalf and deliver him from his trouble. He asks for God to search him thoroughly and to declare his **vindication,** often translated "justice" or "judgment."

17:3–5 tested my heart: David knows that God has done what he is requesting even before he asks. That is, God knew David's needs and what was in his heart. David's prayer helps David to focus on the source of his strength and reaffirm his determination to live a pure life (1:1–3; 19:14).

17:6–9 Incline Your ear is pictorial language describing the mercy of God (40:1): God will stoop down to earth to hear David's plea. **lovingkindness:** This significant term for God's loyal love is enhanced by the Hebrew term for **marvelous,** a word used in the Bible only with reference to God. **The apple of Your eye:** Just as a person has an instinctive response to protect the eye, so God cares instinctively for His servants. **shadow of Your wings:** Chicks who flee for protection to the wings of their mother find safety and warmth and love as well. In the same way, God protects us.

17:10–12 The words **fat hearts** are a description of insensitivity, similar to the language of Is. 6:10. **As a lion:** The wicked are insensitive to human needs; they are like lions who wait for the right opportunity to destroy their prey.

17:13, 14 their portion in this life: The wicked live their lives with only the pursuit of the pleasures of this world in mind. The righteous should not try to obtain what this life can offer, but instead pursue God and His ways.

17:15 when I awake in Your likeness: This verse is a key text on biblical immortality in the Old Testament. Having rejected the idea that the pleasures of this life are ultimately fulfilling, David anticipates the day when he will awake in glory and be made in the likeness of God.

Psalm 18 is attributed to David. The text of this psalm is found in 2 Sam. 22 with some variations. The superscription indicates that this psalm was David's hymn of celebration to the grace of God. This may be a psalm of trust.

18:1 I will love You, O LORD: Twice in the Psalms the psalmist declares a love for God (116:1). Here an unusual word for *love* is used, referring to compassion as deep as a mother's love.

18:2, 3 The Hebrew word for **my rock** is balanced by its parallel Hebrew word **my strength,** meaning also "my rock." References to God as a mountain fortress that

protects the believer are found many times in the Psalms (91:1–3; 144:1). This is a particularly apt image for David, who many times had to hide in the mountains for security (see 1 Sam. 26:1, 20). The words strength and **stronghold** reinforce the image of God as Protector.

18:4–6 In these verses, David describes how his life is endangered. Using strong language, he expresses the pain he feels as he watches death come near: **sorrows of Sheol.** But even in the great depths of his trouble, he cries out to the Lord and the faithful God answers him.

18:7–9 the earth shook … He bowed the heavens: Underlying these poetic words is the understanding that the Almighty will turn the universe inside out, if necessary, to deliver His servant.

18:10–14 The language **He rode upon a cherub** is similar to the descriptions of Baal in Canaanite poetry. Thus David is taking the words typically used to praise Baal and applying them to the living God, the only One who truly deserves such praise. The *cherub* is a royal symbol and thus speaks of God's power and glory (80:1). The references to **darkness** speak of the hiddenness of God. He cannot be completely understood by those whom He has created. The references to **brightness** speak of God's holiness.

18:15 the channels of the sea: This culminates the picture of God's turning the universe upside down (v. 7). Even the most hidden passages of the sea are exposed, as are the elements that hold the earth together. The Lord God does all this to rescue His servant David (v. 16). All of the Lord's fearsome power is used to save the one who worships Him.

18:16–19 He drew me out of many waters: Again, David draws from the language of the Canaanites, turning it to the praise of God. The *waters* were regarded as dark gods in Canaan. But according to David, God is Lord of all, and the waters are His creatures. He delivers His servant David from any power that might hold him.

18:20–24 cleanness of my hands: David pleads his integrity, as in Ps. 17. Contrast this language with the description of the bloodied hands of unfit worshipers in Is. 1:15. **blameless:** No one is completely innocent before God. But God enables His servants to pursue godliness in this life.

18:25–30 With the merciful: The psalmist describes the actions of God in terms of the people to whom He relates. God deals with each person according to his or her attitude. He opposes the proud but delivers the **humble,** for the humble turn to Him for strength.

18:31 who is God: With a question, David confesses that he cannot compare God to any person, god, or object (113:5; Is. 40:25).

18:32–36 The use of battle armor, such as a **shield,** as an image of God's provision for the righteous is found in both the Old and New Testaments (Eph. 6:10–20).

18:37–41 pursued my enemies: God gives David strength to complete the battle against his enemies. God Himself is a Warrior (Ex. 15:3) and He outfits His servants for battle. **to the LORD:** Apparently in the extremes of battle, the enemies of David found no help from their gods, so they screamed aloud to David's God for deliverance. But God would not answer them. There is only one prayer from the wicked to which He gladly listens—the prayer of repentance.

18:42, 43 Head of the nations is language that prophetically speaks of the reign of the Messiah. David gained his empire by the work of the Lord on his behalf. But David's empire was only a picture of the kingdom of God that will one day be governed by David's greater Son, the Lord Jesus.

18:44–50 Ordinarily, praise to the Lord was given in the congregation of the Israelites. On occasion the poets speak of God's victories **among the Gentiles** who still worship other gods (138:1). This was a form of mission activity during the Old Testament period (117:1). By proclaiming the victories of God to the nations, the poets were calling for the nations to respond in faith. How fitting that Paul would cite this verse (or its parallel in 2 Sam. 22:50) in Rom. 15:9 as an indicator of God's ongoing intention to bring His salvation to all people. **to His king:** David's victories are prototypes of the victories

of the great King to come. The use of the word **anointed** is appropriate for David, but it points forward to the Savior who is *the* Anointed One (2:2).

Psalm 19, a wisdom psalm, celebrates the Word of God in the context of creation. Thus it is both a creation psalm and a Torah psalm. Both the creation psalms and the Torah psalms are regarded as subgroups of the wisdom psalms. The poem begins with the heavens, centers on the Word, and culminates in the heart of the servant of God.

19:1–6 All of creation including the **heavens** reveals God's glory and majesty (Rom. 1:18–20). **Firmament** is another word for heaven (Gen. 1:6). The vast expanse we see is testimony to the craftsmanship of God (8:3). From the vantage point of earth, there is no heavenly body so wonderful as **the sun.** In the ancient Middle East the sun was often thought of as a god. In this poem, the sun is only a stunning symbol of the Creator.

19:7–11 The law is the Torah, which means "instruction" or "direction." This passage (vv. 7–9) presents six words for the law of God—**law, testimony, statutes, commandment, fear,** and **judgments;** six evaluations of the law—**perfect, sure, right, pure, clean,** and **true;** and six results—**converting the soul, making wise the simple, rejoicing the heart, enlightening the eyes, enduring forever,** and **righteous altogether.** The Scripture provides the key to wisdom, joy, and eternal life.

19:12–14 his errors: The discussion of the nature and perfection of the law of God leads the psalmist to consider his own imperfection. He is aware of both hidden **faults** and **presumptuous sins;** he asks to be delivered from both. **My Redeemer** describes God as the One who purchases our freedom from bondage. The principal meaning of the word is "defender of family rights."

Psalm 20, a royal psalm, is a psalm of trust ascribed to David. The tone of the psalm is one of blessing, such as a king might bestow on his people, perhaps on the eve of battle.

20:1–5 The day of trouble likely refers to the day of battle. But it has wide application for any troubled day in the life of the believer.

sanctuary: Help from God was perceived to come from the temple in Jerusalem. Ultimately it comes from God's dwelling in heaven, of which the earthly sanctuary was a symbol. In the immediate context, **salvation** is used to describe daily deliverance from the rigors of the battle and the victory over the enemy. But the Lord's deliverance of us from our spiritual troubles should prompt the same type of praise.

20:6 King David was the **anointed** of the Lord (18:50). **His right hand:** This is a slogan that describes God's powerful deliverance of the Israelites from Egypt (17:7; 44:3; 118:16; see also Ex. 15:6).

20:7–9 Chariots were the leading weapon on the ancient battlefield. The implements of warfare are mere tools in God's hand. The wise trust in God because the battle belongs to Him. **May the King answer:** Above King David was God the Great King; moreover, one day King Jesus would rule from sea to sea.

Psalm 21 is another of the royal psalms of David. Psalm 20 is a prayer of the king for God's blessing on his army. Psalm 21 is an assurance of God's blessing on the king. Both psalms, as is the case with all the royal psalms, speak ultimately of the great King to come, the Lord Jesus.

21:1, 2 joy in Your strength: An ancient king would tend to find joy in his own strength and power (20:7, 8). But a wise king would find pleasure in the Almighty, for all power comes from Him. **Your salvation:** One meaning of the Hebrew word *salvation* is "room to breathe." God had given King David a release from the pressures and constraints that bound him. **his heart's desire:** The Lord gives people their aspirations when they come from a desire for God's honor and glory (20:4; 37:4; 145:19).

21:3–7 blessings of goodness: King David acknowledges that all he has is God's gift; his kingship itself (the **crown**) is a gift from the Lord. But God's greatest gift is **life**—temporal and eternal. In response to God for His many gifts, David trusts **in the LORD.**

21:8–12 As is customary in the Psalms, the **enemies** of the king are the enemies of the Lord. Therefore the curse on the enemies is provoked by holy zeal for the glory of God (Num. 25). **The time of Your anger** may refer to any period of God's judgment, but compare to "the day of the Lord" (Joel 2:1; Zeph. 1:14). **Their offspring:** The wicked intend evil against the Lord; but He will prevail, causing them to flee from His anger.

21:13 Be exalted: The psalmist concludes with a shout of joy as he leads the faithful people in praising God for the promise of His final victory.

Psalm 22 is a profound lament psalm that concludes as a triumphant psalm of praise for God's deliverance. Although this psalm speaks of David's own distress and the Lord's deliverance of him, it also prophetically describes in remarkable detail Jesus' crucifixion and resurrection. The language David uses to describe his own predicament is prompted by the Holy Spirit. Thus it could span a thousand years to describe precisely the experiences of the Savior Jesus—both His excruciating death and victorious resurrection.

22:1–3 With the words **My God, My God,** David expresses a painful sense of separation from God at a time of great trouble (38:21). These words were quoted by Jesus while in agony on the Cross (Matt. 27:46; Mark 15:34).

22:4 Our fathers trusted in You: Even in the midst of great pain, David confesses His faith in the God of his fathers. God has been faithful to earlier generations; surely He will continue to be faithful to those who call upon Him.

22:5–8 David's suffering makes him feel as though he were no longer human; instead he feels like a **worm.** When David was at his lowest, his enemies ridiculed his faith in the Lord. These words also describe the experience of the Savior who endured the verbal abuse of His tormentors (Matt. 27:27–31, 39–44).

22:9, 10 You made Me trust: With troubles and taunts swirling around him, David places his trust in the Lord—the One he has trusted throughout his entire life. Instead of doubting God's goodness, David reaffirms his lifelong faith in the Almighty.

22:11 Be not far from Me: David repeats his original plea (v. 1) for emphasis (vv. 19–21). He cannot endure his suffering without divine support.

22:12–15 David uses striking imagery to describe his distress. He is surrounded by animals—**bulls** and **lions.** Moreover, David's distress is so profound that he feels as if his life has been drained from him. These words become even more poignant when they are applied to the sufferings of Jesus on the Cross (see John 19:34). **My tongue clings to my jaws:** Jesus' words "I thirst" (John 19:28) expressed the pain of terrible thirst. **the dust of death:** For David, death would be avoided at this time (as in 16:9, 10). For the Savior, however, there was no reprieve.

22:16, 17 dogs: This is the third animal portrayal of the psalmist's enemies (vv. 12, 13). **They pierced My hands and My feet** explicitly predicts the crucifixion of the Lord Jesus Christ. The words are just a figure of speech for the terrifying experiences of David; but as a prophet (Acts 2:30), David spoke accurately of the sufferings of Jesus.

22:18 The soldiers at Jesus' crucifixion gambled for His **garments,** in direct fulfillment of this text (Matt. 27:35).

22:19–21 Up to this point, the focus of this psalm has been on the suffering of the psalmist. The Lord God, who seemed so distant (vv. 1, 11), is now petitioned to draw near, to **help, deliver,** and **save.** The Lord is the only source of **strength** to help David fight off the attacks of his tormentors.

22:22–24 Not only does the psalm describe David's pain and prophetically Jesus' suffering on the Cross; it also depicts God's deliverance. The Lord has answered, and David who has suffered so much promises to sing the praises of the Lord, his Deliverer. **Nor has He hidden His face:** The psalm begins with a sense of desperation based on a feeling of separation from God (v. 1). But the psalm ends with praise and gratitude: in reality God is near, He has answered, and He does save.

22:25, 26 David promises to praise the Lord for His miraculous salvation among other believers—in the **great assembly** at the temple (13:6). This public proclamation would

encourage others to place their trust in the Lord.

22:27–30 All the ends of the world: For David, these words refer to the spread of the news of his deliverance to places outside of Judah. For the Savior Jesus, these words speak of the eventual spread of the gospel of redemption to **all the families of the nations,** a fulfillment of God's promise that He would bless all nations through Abraham's descendants (Gen. 12:3).

22:31 to a people who will be born: The gospel message of the death and resurrection of Jesus will spread not only geographically but also throughout all time. All people will hear the clear message of what **God has done.**

Psalm 23 is a psalm of trust. David has no fear or concern, for the Lord is his Shepherd. On the one hand, David is the "sheep" whose Shepherd is the Lord. At the same time, one of the most common descriptions of kingship in the ancient world is that of shepherd. In this sense, David as king was shepherd over the flock of Israel. This means that Ps. 23 is also a royal psalm. Moreover, the psalm prophetically speaks of Jesus. He is the Good Shepherd whose flock trusts in Him (John 10) and the King whose perfect rule will be established (Luke 23:2, 3; Rev. 17:14).

23:1 The LORD is my shepherd: The word pictures David uses for God come from his own life and experience. He had been a shepherd in his youth (1 Sam. 16:19).

23:2 Any disturbance or intruder scares sheep. They are very fearful animals and **cannot lie down** unless they feel totally secure. **green pastures:** David uses eloquent language to express his view of the abundant care God gives to His people. **still waters:** Sheep are afraid of fast-flowing streams. God's provision of *still waters* has a soothing effect and calms the sheep.

23:3 He restores my soul: God refreshes His people with His quiet voice and gentle touch. For this reason, the sheep know the Shepherd and are known by Him (John 10:14). **For His name's sake:** The loving actions of the Shepherd proceed from His nature.

23:4 The valley of the shadow of death can refer to any distressing time in our lives. The awareness of our own mortality often comes with sickness, trials, and hardship. But the Lord, our Protector, can lead us through these dark and difficult valleys to eternal life with Him. There is no need to fear death's power (1 Cor. 15:25–27). **You are with me:** The Good Shepherd is with us even in what seem the most difficult and troubling situations. **Your rod and Your staff:** Ancient shepherds used the *rod* and *staff* to rescue, protect, and guide the sheep. Thus, they become symbols of the Good Shepherd's loving care over His flock.

23:5 a table before me: God's provision is so luxurious, it is as though He has prepared a banquet. **anoint:** Typically an honored guest in the ancient Middle East was anointed with olive oil that contained perfumes. **My cup:** God's provision is as abundant as the wine offered to a guest by a generous host. The lavish treatment of the guest is indicative of the loving care of God for His people.

23:6 The use of both **mercy** and **goodness** to describe God's loyal love intensifies the meaning of the two words. What is described in v. 5 is God's overabundant mercy—love that is in no way deserved. The Hebrew verb **follow** describes an animal in pursuit. When the Lord is our Shepherd, instead of being stalked by wild beasts we are pursued by the loving care of the Lord. **the house of the LORD forever:** God's promise for the Israelites was not just for the enjoyment of this life in the land of promise (see 6:1–3); it was also for the full enjoyment of the life to come in His blessed presence (16:9–11; 17:15; 49:15).

Psalm 24, a psalm of David, is one of the royal psalms. The psalm describes the Lord's entrance into the holy city. It may have been sung when David brought the ark of the covenant to Jerusalem (2 Sam. 6:15). This psalm is often linked with Ps. 22 and 23, for all three psalms speak prophetically of the Lord Jesus. Psalm 24 also has some affinities with Ps. 15, for both ask and answer the question of who is fit to come into the presence of the Lord.

24:1, 2 The earth is the LORD's: The psalmist praises God as Sovereign over all He has created. These words also set the stage for the question of vv. 3–5: If God is Lord over all,

who then may approach Him? **those who dwell therein:** God's rule extends to all people, even those who do not acknowledge His power. **founded it upon the seas:** Drawing on the language of Gen. 1 in which God calls the dry land to rise from the watery abyss (Gen. 1:2, 9), David describes God's continued control over the waters.

24:3 Who may ascend: As in Ps. 15, those who approach the Holy One to worship Him in the temple in Jerusalem—**His holy place**—must approach Him in righteousness. This verse highlights the inability of any person except the King of glory to stand before God.

24:4, 5 Clean hands refers to a person's actions; pure heart refers to inner attitude.

24:6, 7 Lift up your heads: The gates of the city seem to sag; the doors appear loose. But they must rouse themselves for **the King of glory.** One is coming who is worthy to stand in the holy place. As He nears, the gates raise themselves to honor His entry.

24:8 Who is this King: This is praise for the King who is fresh from battle. This is the One who may enter the city, the Lord Himself. Only with the coming of Jesus did the meaning of this ancient poem become clear (see Matt. 21:1–10; Rev. 19).

24:9, 10 The LORD of hosts: The repetition in these verses is for effect and emphasis. This is praise for the coming King.

Psalm 25 is a psalm of lament. But in the middle of his sorrow, David petitions the Lord to forgive him. Although the psalm contains elements of a lament psalm and a penitential psalm, the mixture of the two forms makes the psalm unique. The psalm is an acrostic, with one poetic line for each successive letter of the Hebrew alphabet.

25:1–3 Let me not be ashamed is the opening and closing appeal of Ps. 25 (v. 20). Shame is the intended end of the enemies of God (35:26), but not of the faithful. **who waits:** Waiting on the Lord is the equivalent of hoping in Him (25:5; 40:1).

25:4–7 Show me is an appeal to God to enter into David's life more directly, to help him become conformed to the character of God (Rom. 12:1, 2). **sins of my youth:** Both the sins of immaturity and the **transgressions**

of adulthood need forgiveness (see 1 John 1:9).

25:8 Good and upright is the LORD: In the midst of David's plea for forgiveness, he praises God by speaking of two of God's characteristics. God *must* be both good and upright. Because He is both, the Lord extends mercy to repentant believers and at the same time promises not to allow the guilty to go unpunished.

25:9–14 Pardon my iniquity: David returns to the subject of his own sinfulness, summarizing vv. 4–7 as well as expressing his desire for the Lord to teach him. **fear Him:** Those who fear the Lord pay attention to His instructions and thus learn the secrets of God's wisdom (111:10; Prov. 1:7; 3:32).

25:15–20 Let me not be ashamed is a reprise of the opening verses, with emphasis both on David's **enemies** (v. 2) and on his continuing stance of waiting in expectant hope (v. 5).

25:21, 22 Redeem Israel: This concluding verse is outside the general acrostic pattern of the psalm. Here David petitions the Lord to be compassionate with the nation Israel just as He has been with David.

Psalm 26 is a psalm of lament in which there is a protest of innocence (Ps. 17; 35; 43; 69).

26:1, 2 The Hebrew word for **vindicate** usually means "to judge"; however, here it means "to declare righteous." **my integrity:** This is the prayer of a forgiven sinner who is living in the fear of God but whose life has been plagued by undeserved evil.

26:3–5 Your lovingkindness: The loyal love (13:5) of God is the recurring focus of the Book of Psalms. **have not sat:** As in the description of righteousness in 1:1, David declares that he has no part with men of wickedness or idolatry. Instead he has continually sought the Lord.

26:6–8 go about Your altar: The heart of this psalm is the desire to worship God in integrity. In this regard, the poem shares the spirit of Ps. 15. **where Your glory dwells:** The place where God chose to reveal His glory to His people. The priests interceded for the people with the required offerings. Today "the Most Holy Place" is in the presence of God, where our Savior pleads our case (see Heb. 7:25).

26:9–11 Do not gather: On the basis of his protests of integrity (vv. 1, 2), David prays for divine discrimination (4:3). God distinguishes those who have responded to His grace from those who have not.

26:12 As always in the Psalms, praise is a public and vocal action that has its proper place in the **congregations** of believers.

Psalm 27, a psalm of trust (Ps. 23), begins with David's affirmation of the reality of God in his life. The poem presents a strong desire to live in the presence of God and points to the ongoing need for believers to continue to "wait" on the Lord.

27:1–3 Light indicates deliverance from darkness (Gen. 1:3), which is a biblical symbol of evil. The word **salvation** combined with the word *light* means "saving light" (3:8). **to eat up my flesh:** David pictures his enemies as ravenous beasts who would shred his flesh (10:8–10; 22:12–16).

27:4, 5 The phrase **dwell in the house of the LORD** expresses David's desire to be always nearer to God's presence. **The beauty of the LORD** speaks of God's "pleasant nature."

27:6 Sacrifices of joy are praise offerings the believers bring to God to celebrate the blessings He gives them (Heb. 13:15).

27:7–13 Throughout this psalm, seeking the presence of God (His **face**) was the psalmist's highest purpose. **Enemies** might dissuade the righteous from seeking the presence of the Lord. But the psalmist wants to know God's presence in this life—**in the land of the living.**

27:14 To **wait on the LORD** is to demonstrate confident expectation. The Hebrew word for *wait* may also be translated "hope." To hope in God is to wait for His timing and His action (40:1; Is. 40:31).

Psalm 28, a psalm of lament, is attributed to David. The psalm includes a prayer against David's enemies and a royal invocation of praise to the Lord.

28:1, 2 Do not be silent: One of the ways David senses the distance of God is His "silence" (13:1; 22:1). David might be referring only to his lack of a sense of intimacy with God (27:4, 5), but it is also possible that he is awaiting a specific word from the Lord through a prophet or a priest. **The pit** is one of the terms for death in the Psalms (9:17, 18; 16:10; 143:7). David asks to be rescued from death so that he might live to praise God.

28:3–5 Do not take me away: Again, the psalmist is asking to be delivered from death (6:5). **according to their deeds:** David pronounces his curse on the wicked, from whom he wishes to be distinguished (4:3). **they do not regard:** The language here is similar to that of Paul in Rom. 1:18–32. One day even the wicked will have to acknowledge God as their Creator and give Him the glory He deserves.

28:6, 7 Because the plea of the psalmist has been **heard,** the last section of the poem is a hymn of praise (138:1).

28:8, 9 The term **His anointed** acknowledges God's covenant with David, His promise that He would be David's God and David would be His representative. This passage became a heritage of the monarchy, a treasure for each godly king in the Davidic line to go back to for strength and encouragement. **Shepherd them:** As in Ps. 23 and 80, the comparison of God with a shepherd is an image of the loving care of a great king (Eccl. 12:11).

Psalm 29 is a worship psalm (see also Ps. 15). But it is also a royal psalm that uses striking language to assert the sovereign reign of the Almighty. David has taken over some of the vocabulary and poetic style of the Canaanites and used it to praise the living God. As in the case of Ps. 93, the result is both a debunking of Baal and an unusual way of praising the true God of Israel.

29:1 Give here means "to ascribe." **O you mighty ones** means "O sons of gods." This Hebrew phrase refers to spiritual beings who are in the presence of God. We know these beings to be angels.

29:2 glory due to His name: The call is for the angelic hosts to acknowledge fully the wonder of God. The poets of the Bible delighted in taking the ideas of the Canaanites and then stripping them of their essentials. See the scathing attacks on idolatry in 115:4–8; Is. 41:21–29. Here the psalmist takes a treasured image of Canaanite thought—Baal with other gods bowing before him—and turns it inside out. It is not Baal, but the true God who is worshiped. He is worshiped not by gods who do not even exist, but by His own angels.

29:3, 4 The voice of the LORD: Both the language and the parallelism of this verse directly reflect Canaanite poetry. Baal was believed to be the god of the storm who thundered in the heavens. Here the sound of thunder is a symbol of the voice of God.

29:5–9 cedars of Lebanon: There is a dramatic energy to these verses as they trace the movement of the storm from the north of **Lebanon and Sirion,** an ancient name for Mount Hermon (Deut. 3:9) to **Kadesh** in the south. Nothing stops the advance of the storm. All the angels in the heavenly sanctuary acknowledge the surpassing **glory** of the omnipotent God.

29:10, 11 As Baal was supposed to have been victorious over the waters, here it is God who is the true victor over all. He even controls the waters at the height of their destructive power, the **Flood.** There is no one to oppose His glorious rule; He is King forever. **The LORD will give strength:** Since He is the true God, there is none other. Only He can empower His people.

Psalm 30, a psalm of declarative praise, commemorates a time when God delivered David from mortal illness.

30:1 I will extol You: David begins his song with a strong determination to praise God.

30:2, 3 up from the grave: David is not reporting a resurrection, but a deliverance from a nearly fatal illness. As in 28:1, the psalmist describes death as a great **pit** into which a person drops into the enveloping darkness of the unknown.

30:4, 5 in the morning: For a sick person, nothing is so long as a painful, sleepless night; few things are as desired as the coming of morning (5:3; 130:6; 143:8).

30:6–10 As in 6:5, the psalmist pleads with God to save his life so that he can fulfill his promise to **praise** God in the worship of the community. The emphasis is on singing praise to God in this life. **Helper** can be translated "power" or "strength" (33:20). What a sick person needs is strength for recovery. God is that powerful force.

30:11, 12 mourning into dancing: The psalmist has been transformed and renewed because of God's blessing on his life. He boasts in God as he fulfills his vow of praise.

Psalm 31 is a psalm of lament, but it has such a strong element of trust that it can also be classified as a psalm of trust (see Ps. 23 for an example). The psalms of trust grow out of the confession of trust that occurs in the psalms of lament. In this psalm, the relationship between the two classifications is apparent.

31:1–3 The phrase **I put my trust** pictures the action of a bird seeking refuge under its mother's wings (11:1; 17:7; 91:1–4). The imagery of God as the **rock** and fortress for the believer recurs often in the Psalms (91:1–3).

31:4, 5 With the words **into Your hand I commit my spirit,** David expresses a complete dependence on God—his life is in God's hands to do with as He pleases. These words were spoken by Jesus on the Cross shortly before His death (Luke 23:46) and by Stephen before his death (Acts 7:59).

31:6–11 I am in trouble are classic words of lament and thus begin the lament section of this psalm. **My eye wastes away:** David uses similar language in 6:7 to express his sorrow. **a reproach:** As in the case of Ps. 30, it is possible that what faces the psalmist is a terrible illness—perhaps a physical condition that makes him repulsive to others.

31:12–18 my times are in your hands: David petitions the Lord, who is in complete control of his life, for deliverance. **Your face shine:** This expression grows out of the words of the Aaronic benediction in Num. 6:24–26. It is a plea for God to "smile" in favor on David.

31:19–22 This verse begins the praise section of the psalm. David affirms that the delights of knowing God outweigh any other kind of pleasure. **the secret place:** God makes His people safe in the intimacy of His friendship (27:5). **I said in my haste:** The psalmist says things in his pain that he would not say under normal circumstances.

31:23, 24 David encourages the community to join him in praising God. Of all the sacrifices offered in the Old Testament period, only the sacrifice of praise continues in New Testament worship (Heb. 13:15).

Psalm 32, a wisdom psalm, is also one of the great penitential psalms. It is generally believed that this psalm—like Ps. 51—has its origin in David's response to God following his infamous affair with Bathsheba (2 Sam. 11).

32:1 Blessed, the word that begins the Book of Psalms (1:1), means "to be happy." It is appropriate that this term is used of both the righteous person of the first psalm and the confessed sinner in this psalm. **sin is covered:** The psalmist describes God's dealing with sin in various ways. Sin can be taken away, the basic meaning of the word **forgiven,** and covered, the basic meaning of atonement.

32:2–5 I kept silent: The silence was a stubborn resistance to admitting guilt, a hope that in time the sin and its penalty would go away. The more David delayed his confession, the more he suffered. David realized it was not just his conscience or his feelings that were assaulting him, but the heavy **hand** of God (38:1, 6–8). No matter who else is hurt, the principal offense of any sin is always against God. **You forgave:** The consequences of David's sin with Bathsheba remained despite God's forgiveness (2 Sam. 12:13–20). But at this point, the greater news was God's forgiveness. God had restored His relationship with David.

32:6 who is godly: On the basis of his own experience, David instructs the congregation. They can also experience forgiveness if they will come to the Lord in faith.

32:7 The psalm has quick and dramatic shifts. After addressing the congregation, David speaks directly to God: **You are my hiding place.**

32:8, 9 I will instruct you: The Lord "comes into the psalm" to instruct the people. He exhorts the people not to be like a **horse** that will not go where its rider wants it to go; it has to be disciplined because it is stubborn. God does not want to muzzle or bridle His people like a horse. He expects

His servants to respond promptly to Him of their own accord.

32:10, 11 The psalmist resumes his song by contrasting the **many sorrows** of the wicked with the joy of the forgiven sinner. He then calls for all the righteous to join him in public praise of the wonder of God's mercy.

Psalm 33, a psalm of descriptive praise, calls for all people to join Israel's faithful in praising God and waiting on (trusting in) the Lord.

33:1–3 God sees the praise from believers as **beautiful** (147:1). **harp:** Throughout the Psalms, many instruments are used to praise the name of the Lord (98:5; 150:3–5). **to Him:** Praise is always directed to the One who deserves all praise, the Lord Almighty.

33:4, 5 Although the world is filled with evil and with people who have no thought of God (Ps. 14), believers must look beyond the apparent confusion of the world to see God's **goodness**—the goodness that manifests itself as the sun rises, a bird sings, and a mother lovingly embraces her child. Out of His goodness, God holds together the earth and provides for the sustenance of all people.

33:6, 7 The reference to God's control of the **waters of the sea** grows out of the creation story in Gen. 1, in which God brings dry land from the waters and establishes His place for the waters that remain (Gen. 1:6–10). The idea also grows out of Canaanite religious ideas, for the Canaanites considered the seas as malevolent deities. No power—no matter how evil—is a threat to God's control (Job 26:10; Prov. 8:28, 29).

33:8, 9 The Bible presents the **fear** of the Lord as a mark of reverence and awe by those who recognize Him as Lord (40:3). **He spoke:** The account of creation in Gen. 1 describes God's word as the sole source of creation. This psalm emphasizes God's word as the controlling element in creation (vv. 4, 6). It was by God's "breath" (v. 6) that He made all things.

33:10–12 In contrast to the ineffective **counsel of the nations,** the counsel of God is wise counsel that lasts forever. **Blessed** means to be manifestly happy; the same word is used at the beginning of Ps. 1. Those who listen to God's counsel will be happy.

33:13–15 The Lord looks on humankind with a sense of discriminating pleasure. The emphasis of this section is not condemnation, but discrimination.

33:16, 17 army: People should not rely on physical strength or material resources to save them. Salvation belongs to the Lord (3:8), both for spiritual deliverance and for physical strength.

33:18, 19 eye of the Lord: This is a particularly warm image of God's care for His people. God watches all people, but He looks with delight on **those who fear Him** and **hope in His mercy** (147:11).

33:20–22 waits: To wait on God is to adopt a stance of resolute faith (40:1). **Just as we hope:** The psalm concludes with a phrase similar to "Amen." This is a "yes" to God's mercy, a statement of agreement with His provisions.

Psalm 34 is a wisdom psalm and a psalm of praise. It is written in the form of an acrostic, with one verse for each letter of the Hebrew alphabet. One verse appears to have dropped out at some point; there is no verse for the Hebrew letter *waw*, that would otherwise appear after v. 5. The title of the psalm ascribes it to David and specifies that it was written to commemorate his escape from Abimelech the king of Gath (1 Sam. 21:10–15). The name of the king in 1 Sam. 21 is Achish. It is believed that Abimelech was a throne name and Achish a personal name.

34:1–3 at all times: The determination of David to praise God is similar to the words of Paul in 1 Thess. 5:18. **Exalt His name together** is David's call for the congregation to join him in his praise of God.

34:4–7 He heard me is a classic statement of praise in the psalms. God is praised for the deliverance He provides in response to the prayers of His people (40:1). **were radiant:** Those who came to God in prayer as David did found themselves transformed; it was as if they also experienced what Moses had on Mount Sinai (Ex. 34:29; 2 Cor. 3:18). **Poor man** refers to the needy as well as the humble, whom the Lord delights to deliver (147:6).

34:8, 9 The center of biblical mission in the Old Testament is found in the words **taste and see.** The task of Israel was to attract the nations to their God. For their faithfulness to Him, God had promised to bless them abundantly, and when the nations saw this blessing they would see that the living God was with them. In the midst of a world of gods who were not good at all, there was one living God, and He was altogether good (100:5). **Fear:** To fear God is to respond to Him in piety and obedience.

34:10 shall not lack: As is true of 23:1, this is not a categorical statement. Time after time, however, the believer is able to attest to the ways God has met needs.

34:11–14 Come, you children: David took on the role of a wisdom teacher addressing the young people who are in his charge (Prov. 3:1–12). **Depart from evil:** The same sentiment is found in 37:27.

34:15, 16 In this context, **the eyes of the LORD** symbolize His care and protection.

34:17–19 the LORD hears: With slight variations, this is a reprise of v. 6. **The LORD is near:** When the Scriptures speak of God being near, it is to comfort the believer with a sense of His care.

34:20, 21 guards all his bones: This verse, which speaks of the Lord's preservation of the righteous, notes that not a bone is broken. John 19:33–36 shows that the words of this verse were fulfilled in detail in the death of Jesus. Despite the terrible suffering the Savior endured, none of His bones were broken. When the Roman soldiers came to break Jesus' legs to hasten His death, they found that He had already died.

34:22 This verse is outside the acrostic pattern; it summarizes the psalm, giving appropriate praise to the Lord who saves those who put their faith in Him (see 1 Tim. 4:10).

Psalm 35 is a psalm of lament and a protest of innocence (Ps. 17; 26; 43; 69). Like Ps. 94, this poem by David places an unusual emphasis on the role of his enemies. Sometimes it is called an imprecatory psalm.

35:1–3 Plead my cause is the classic protest of innocence (Ps. 17; 26; 43; 69). David has been wrongly attacked, so he prays that God will deliver him from these assaults (see Ps. 94). **stand up for my help:** David is not afraid to ask God to take up arms like a soldier and fight for him.

35:4–9 David's first petition calls for **shame** on his enemies (v. 26). This is not just a call to embarrass them; it is a call for final judgment. **without cause:** Here is the heart of David's position: he has not done anything to bring on this evil attack.

35:10 These two verses are the first prayer of confidence in this psalm (vv. 17, 27). **All my bones** refers to the inner being, the total person. **who is like You:** There is nothing in all the universe to be compared with God.

35:11–17 The psalmist begins his second cycle of petition with reference to treacherous **witnesses,** like the false witnesses in the story of Jezebel and Naboth in 1 Kin. 21. The actions of these witnesses are even more shameful because they had received the help of the psalmist in their own times of need.

35:18 give You thanks: This is the second of the vows of praise that follow each cycle of petition in this psalm (vv. 9, 10, 27, 28). The Hebrew word for *thanks* means "to make public acknowledgment," to praise God in the community (122:4; 136:1).

35:19–21 The enemies would **rejoice** if someone like David fell. **hate me without a cause:** Again, David asserts his innocence (v. 7). The fact that he is hated for no cause is baffling and discouraging. The passage also predicts the suffering of the Savior Jesus (John 15:23–25). **peace:** Far more than simply an absence of war, the biblical *peace* has the idea of wholeness, things as they ought to be. Note that the contrasting opposite here is not war, but deceit. **Aha, aha:** These contemptuous sneers are similar to the assaults in 22:7.

35:22–25 You have seen: The wicked were not the only ones who have seen David's grave distress (v. 21); God has also seen his pain. **Stir up Yourself:** The people of Israel know that God, unlike the false gods (1 Kin. 18:27), never sleeps (121:4; Is. 40:28). Yet for David, it seems as though God is napping (44:23).

35:26–28 The phrase **be ashamed** refers not to simple embarrassment, but to the revelation of the complete emptiness of wickedness before the judgment seat of God (14:5; 31:17; 36:12). **Who favor:** We learn that

David has defenders. Those who are on his side will share his joy when he is saved.

Psalm 36 is a wisdom psalm that gives a revelation of the nature of sin and an exaltation of God's unfailing love (see also Ps. 14; 53).

36:1–4 The term **oracle** was used by the prophets of the Old Testament to mean a divine utterance. In this psalm, David "the prophet" (Acts 2:30) has received a prophetic revelation as striking as any among the sons of the prophets. He has received divine insight into the nature of wickedness. **no fear of God:** Underlying wickedness is a complete disregard for the reality of God in a person's life and in the world. **flatters himself:** With no sense of God or of final judgment, the wicked become egotistical. **words of his mouth:** The theme of the wicked mouth is developed in Ps. 12. **ceased to be wise:** The wisdom that the psalmist observes here is the practical outworking of the skill of sound living. **Wickedness** is crookedness and perversity.

36:5, 6 The contrast of these verses with the previous ones is extreme. Just as the revelation of depravity in vv. 1–4 is awful, the revelation of the Lord's love is even more wonderful. **great mountains ... great deep:** The height of the great mountains can be compared to how great God's righteousness is; the depth of the seas can be compared with how mysterious and inaccessible God's true judgments are.

36:7–9 their trust: Because of God's nature, righteous men and women come to Him like nestlings seeking shelter under the wings of the mother bird (7:1; 11:1; 16:1; 31:1). Although the wicked are never **satisfied** (Prov. 27:20), the one who trusts in the Lord can find ample satisfaction. **fountain of life:** God's salvation and continuing mercy to His people are often described in terms of life-giving water (Is. 12:3; Jer. 2:13).

36:10–12 continue: On the basis of two of the revelations this psalm presents—the nature of the wicked (vv. 1–4) and the nature of God's loyal love (vv. 5–9)—David prays that God's loyal love will continue in the lives of His people. **There the workers of iniquity have fallen:** This is the third

revelation in this psalm. David is given a glimpse of the horror of divine judgment on the wicked. In effect, the psalmist "sees" the judgment scene and shudders.

Psalm 37 is a wisdom psalm written as an acrostic. Its simple message is to maintain patience in the midst of troubles. God's people can have such patience because they know that their eternal reward will abundantly surpass any temporal troubles.

37:1–4 Do not fret is the theme of this psalm. When the wicked seem to prosper, the psalmist calls for patience, a renewed sense of dependence on the Lord, and a new sense of pleasure in knowing Him.

37:5, 6 To **commit your way** means "to roll it over on" the Lord. What a splendid picture of trusting in Him.

37:7, 8 Rest ... wait patiently: These commands reemphasize the major point of the psalm, "do not fret" (v. 1). This is not a call to be inactive, but to depend actively on the living Lord. The psalm gives us a commandment to cease from worry.

37:9–12 the meek shall inherit the earth: Jesus quoted these words in Matt. 5:5, confirming the Old Testament and showing the importance of the Psalms in His life.

37:13–17 The LORD laughs: These words recall the scornful laughter in 2:4. What sheer horror for the wicked to hear God's laughter directed against them! Contrast this laughter with the delight that the Lord finds in the ways of the righteous (see v. 23).

37:18–20 The phrase **the LORD knows the days of the upright** has several meanings: (1) God knows our circumstances and provides for us; (2) God knows how long we will live and will sustain us to the end (90:12); (3) God knows that our days on earth are only the beginning of our days with Him in eternity.

37:21–23 the righteous shows mercy: There are many contrasts between the wicked and the righteous in the wisdom psalms; this one is based on contrasting attitudes toward possessions (15:5; 112:5). Of all the things on earth that God has created, only one will last—people. All material things will pass away (2 Pet. 3:10–12).

37:24 upholds him: The righteous know that when they fall, they are never left lying there; when they stumble, they are never completely forsaken.

37:25 begging bread: These words may be viewed from two perspectives: (1) The hunger of the righteous is temporary and will be replaced by fullness in the days to come; and (2) there is a hunger that the righteous never need to suffer: they are never deprived of the Lord's presence (see John 6:35). Perhaps this is also a call to help the righteous when they do suffer hunger in this world.

37:26–29 The same command to **depart from evil** is found in 34:14. In this life people must choose either to cling to God and righteousness, or to pursue evil. The way of God leads to everlasting life. **the LORD loves justice:** Because God stands opposed to injustice, God's people ought to love the things that He loves and detest the things that He hates.

37:30, 31 in his heart: At numerous places in the Psalms, the psalmist declares his love for God's law and his effort to make it integral to his life (1:2; 19:7–11; 119:1–176).

37:32–35 To **wait on the LORD** is an act of faith; not to wait on Him is foolishness. **like a native green tree:** David admits that the wicked might prosper, but he also affirms that they will not enjoy success forever.

37:36, 37 In this context **peace** suggests "everything as it ought to be." The destiny of the righteous is in sharp contrast to the fate of the wicked (1:4–6).

37:38–40 salvation: The principal issue here is not regeneration but sanctification—the daily deliverance of God's people from temptation and evil.

Psalm 38 is a psalm of lament, specifically a penitential psalm. In it, David pleads earnestly for the mercy of God even when he senses God's discipline. The psalms of penitence are a model for our own prayers of confession and a warning against the type of behavior that will lead to God's correction.

38:1–5 As in 6:1, David has two concerns. His first concern is the painful distress he feels during the time of God's discipline on his life (32:4). David's second concern is that God might be placing His heavy hand

on him in **wrath,** as He does on the wicked (37:22). **my iniquities have gone over my head:** David uses expressive language to describe his loss of control: he cannot free himself from the burden of sin (69:5). This is similar to Paul speaking of himself as the "chief" of sinners (1 Tim. 1:15).

38:6 I am troubled: David feels he is carrying an immense load. In this case, the heavy load is guilt.

38:7–12 light of my eyes: As in 13:3, David complains that he is about to lose his vision: probably he means that an oppression like death seems about to overcome him. **My loved ones:** David expresses sorrow because even those closest to him are leaving him. See Job's similar experience in Job 2:9, 10.

38:13–17 David is determined, even in the gravest suffering, not to present an opportunity for his enemies to condemn the name of the Lord. In this, David's silence foreshadows the silence of the Savior Jesus before His accusers (see Mark 14:61).

38:18–20 I will declare: David's silence is only before his enemies (vv. 13–16); to the Lord he willingly confesses his sins. He expects that the merciful God will forgive and restore him (Ps. 32).

38:21, 22 be not far from me: These words echo the sentiment of 22:1. All that is left for David is to trust in God. In that sense, David was in the right place, for confidence in any person or thing other than God Himself is misplaced trust.

Psalm 39 is a wisdom psalm in the form of a psalm of individual lament. The title indicates that this is a psalm of David composed for Jeduthun. Psalm 39 is unusual in many respects. It speaks of a determination to be silent against foes, whereas most psalms speak boldly against enemies. Moreover, it ends with a request that God leave the psalmist alone, a stance that is remarkably like sections of the Book of Job.

39:1 I will restrain my mouth: David determines to be silent in suffering so that he will not speak out foolishly.

39:2–5 Make me to know my end is an appeal to God to deliver the psalmist before his life passes him by (90:7–12). **Vapor** refers to something that passes quickly, not something that has no meaning.

39:6–8 My hope is in You: David is in a quandary. Should he ask for God's help or should he ask God to leave him alone? Unlike most of the psalms of lament, there is noticeable difficulty in moving into a posture of praise. **my transgressions:** David acknowledges his sin and throws himself on the mercy of the Lord (Ps. 32).

39:9–13 Hear my prayer: David has been silent for a period of his distress (vv. 2, 9) but can remain silent no longer. Here he cries for God not to be silent, but to deliver him. **Remove Your gaze:** If God is not going to deliver him, the despondent psalmist asks God to just leave him alone. Sometimes the pain of the psalmist was so far from being resolved at the time when he composed his poem that he remained on the edge of despair to the last verse. Yet the fact that God saves those who call upon Him is described again and again in the Book of Psalms (22:21; 118:21)

Psalm 40 is a psalm of declarative praise that moves into a psalm of lament. This psalm is a remarkable example of how troubles and difficulties forced David to depend continually on the Lord.

40:1 The Hebrew translated **I waited patiently** is literally "waiting I waited." The emphasis of this phrase is not really on patience, but on the fact that David waited solely on the Lord. The verb "to wait" expresses a confident trust or faith in the Lord (130:5). The words **He inclined to me** present the image of the Creator of the universe stooping from His throne to save the helpless.

40:2, 3 horrible pit: David writes this poem during a period of terrible stress; he feels as if he is stuck in a pit or swamp. No matter how hard he tries, he cannot get out. But David turns his frustration over to the Lord and trusts in His strength. **a new song:** The Lord's salvation prompts David to praise God. The music is new because God's salvation is fresh and new to David.

40:4, 5 The proud refers to idolaters who will not bow in humility before the Lord (147:6). **Lies** refers to idols. Not only are the

works of God directed toward the people of faith, but so are His **thoughts.** He is thinking about us.

40:6 The Lord takes pleasure in those who obediently come to Him with praise on their lips (1 Sam. 15:22, 23). **My ears You have opened:** The Lord not only gives us ears to hear His word, but also grants us understanding so that we can obey Him.

40:7, 8 Behold, I come: David brings his sacrifice, but his focus is on presenting his own life to the Lord (Rom. 12:1, 2). According to the Book of Hebrews, Jesus spoke these words to the Father (Heb. 10:4–6). **Delight** is related to the word *desire* in v. 6. What brings pleasure to God will also bring delight to His people.

40:9–12 Do not withhold: Even after the experience of deliverance with which the psalm begins, David has another reason to turn to the Lord in renewed prayer. The Hebrew for **your tender mercies** (which can also mean "womb") refers to God's affection for us. In effect, David is asking the Lord to surround him with warmth and comfort that is practically maternal.

40:13–15 deliver me: David does not ask for forgiveness of sin here (contrast 51:3, 4), but for deliverance from powerful enemies. **Aha, aha:** David's enemies are all around him, taunting him mercilessly (35:21).

40:16, 17 The LORD be magnified: With these great words of praise, David encourages others in the community to glorify the Lord (35:27). **poor and needy:** The psalmist is still in trouble, pleading with God to deliver him anew.

Psalm 41 is a lament psalm. Since it begins and concludes with words of praise to God, it may also be called a psalm of praise. The poem is ascribed to David and speaks of the plight of a person suffering from serious physical illness. Ultimately, it presents the victory of the Savior Jesus over His enemies, especially the great enemy Satan.

41:1 Blessed: When the verb *blessed* is used with God as its object (as in v. 13), it serves as a word of praise (103:1, 2). To bless God is to identify Him as the source of our blessings. **The poor** refers not only to those who do not have enough money, but also to those who suffer illness or misfortune through no fault of their own. For such persons, God is Defender, Deliverer, and Sustainer.

41:2, 3 Blessed on the earth refers to the acts of God's goodness in a person's life, including health, wealth, longevity, spiritual vitality, and harmony with God and people (Prov. 3:1–4). **bed of illness:** The distress in this psalm is the psalmist's serious physical illness.

41:4 for I have sinned: In the context of the psalm, this is a general acknowledgment of sin and the need for God's forgiveness and restoration (1 John 1:9).

41:5–8 At times, the psalmist's **enemies** are indicated (3:1), but more often these enemies are left unspecified in the psalms, allowing others to think in terms of their own situations. **his name perish:** In ancient cultures, for a person not to be remembered was like saying that he or she had never existed. The righteous in Israel hoped that their names would endure after them, that they would have a "great name" (Gen. 12:2). **he speaks lies:** David charges his enemies with visiting his sickbed on the pretext of mercy but with malice in their hearts.

41:9 Familiar friend describes a close, intimate relationship. The outrage of betrayal by one so close is nearly unbearable (Matt. 26:14–16). The fulfillment of this verse in the experience of Jesus and Judas is remarkable. Not only did the two eat a meal together (Mark 14:18–21), but Jesus also called Judas a "friend" at the moment of betrayal (Matt. 26:50). Moreover Jesus quoted this verse, noting its fulfillment in Judas (John 13:18).

41:10–12 Raise me up was David's prayer for healing from the disease that had him bedridden (v. 3). In another sense, these words look forward to Jesus' resurrection (16:10, 11; 118:17, 18). **does not triumph:** The failure of David's enemy to destroy his life was an indicator of God's pleasure in David's life. **my integrity:** These words suggest that it is the righteous person who is suffering in this psalm, not an unrepentant sinner (26:1). **before Your face forever:** David prays not only for a long life on earth (v. 2), but also for eternal life in God's presence (23:6).

41:13 Blessed: This psalm begins with a blessing of God on the righteous; it ends with the righteous blessing their Lord. The word here for *blessed* is different from the word in v. 1. Here the word identifies the Lord as the source of our blessing. The word **Amen**, meaning "surely" and "let it be," is an affirmation of faith in God. It is simply saying "yes" to God.

Psalm 42 and Ps. 43 were probably originally one poem, like Ps. 9 and 10. Note that Ps. 43 does not have a superscription and that 43:5 repeats the refrain of 42:5, 11. Apparently a longer psalm was divided into two sections for use in temple worship. As an independent poem, Ps. 42 is an individual lament with a strong emphasis on trust (see Ps. 23). The psalm is attributed to the sons of Korah, a musical family in Israel. They descended from the priest who had led an abortive rebellion against the leadership of Moses and Aaron (Num. 16).

42:1–4 pant: The verb "to pant" is unusually expressive of a spiritual thirst for God. The psalmist describes his experience of being cut off from the worshiping community. He feels distant from God's presence among His people and he longs for intimacy with God (see v. 4). For the believer who lived during Old Testament times, there was only one place where the true worship of the Lord was possible—the temple in Jerusalem. **go with the multitude:** The psalmist was consumed with thoughts of the worship of God that he had experienced at the temple in Jerusalem among throngs of joyful believers (Ps. 100).

42:5 Why are you cast down: These words are repeated in v. 11 and 43:5. The psalmist reminds himself that one day he will experience anew the presence of God. In the end, his hope in the Lord will not be misplaced. **praise Him:** The psalmist is not describing an act of private devotion, but of public praise of the goodness of God. This is praise in words and songs that would be repeated in the midst of the congregation (22:22; Eph. 5:19; Heb. 13:15).

42:6 The land of the Jordan and **the heights of Hermon** refer to the Promised Land, from which the people were exiled.

42:7–11 Why have You forgotten me: The psalmist asks these troubling questions in faith, for he remembers that God is his **Rock,** his protector and foundation. He cannot help but **hope** in Him in the middle of difficult circumstances.

Psalm 43 is a continuation of Ps. 42. The original poem was separated into the two psalms we have today so they could more easily be used for worship in the temple. As it stands, Ps. 43 shares features of a psalm of lament and a psalm of trust.

43:1, 2 Vindicate me is a protest of innocence (Ps. 17; 26; 35). The psalmist takes the stance of a person wrongfully attacked. **Why do You cast me off:** More hurtful than the words of the psalmist's enemies is the sense that God has rejected him (Ps. 13).

43:3, 4 Your light and Your truth: The psalmist asks God for deliverance. Only the "true light" of God could save the psalmist from the lies and darkness all about him. **Your tabernacle:** More than anything else the psalmist desires to rejoin the worshiping community in praising God (149:1).

43:5 Why are you cast down: These words are the refrain of this and the previous psalm (see 42:5, 11). In time of doubt and stress, the psalmist urges his inner being, by the power of God, to keep believing. He knows that one day, by God's grace, he will return to the place of praise to God, the center of worship in Jerusalem.

Psalm 44 is a lament of the community, a collective sigh of the people of Israel for God to help them in a time of great national stress. The psalm also presents an occasion for a rehearsal of God's great deeds in the Exodus, the major saving action of the Lord in the Old Testament period (Ps. 105). This psalm is attributed to the sons of Korah, the descendants of the rebellious priest mentioned in Num. 16.

44:1–3 heard with our ears: God's marvelous intervention in history to deliver the Israelites from Egypt was the cornerstone of Old Testament faith (17:7; 118:16; Ex. 15:6). Each generation of Israelites was obligated to tell the next generation about what God had done for them. The story that they told was not just a national history, but also a description of the loving character of God (Deut. 8). **You favored them:** The selection of Israel as the people of God came by His grace alone (4:3; Rom. 11).

44:4, 5 my King: In this community lament, it is striking that here the speaker is singular. It may be that these words are spoken by Israel's king to the King of glory. As the king of the nation, it was appropriate for him to lead the people in asking for God's renewed favor.

44:6–12 The words **cast us off** begin the lament section of the psalm. The army of Israel was not to be regarded as just a group of warriors—they were the warriors of the Almighty (Ps. 144). Their victories were the victories of God and their defeats were losses that He allowed them to endure. **You sell Your people:** When the people suffered loss, it was as though God had "sold" them. But God's deliverance of them from suffering is depicted as His purchase of His people—the meaning of the word *redemption* (see v. 26).

44:13–20 we have not forgotten: The people protest that they have not rejected God. The implication is that their troubles would be deserved if they had rejected him. **Stretched out our hands** refers to a posture of prayer (Ps. 134). They protest that they have not prayed to the idols of the nations, but have been faithful to the only living God.

44:21, 22 as sheep: These words predict another beloved Son of the Most High who would also feel cast off by the Lord (Is. 53:7; see also Rom. 8:36).

44:23–26 Israel's God does not sleep (121:3, 4; Is. 40:28). The cry to **awake** is an appeal for God to act on behalf of His people. The cry is based on the people's faith that the Lord will forgive. **redeem us:** In v. 12, the people suggested that God had sold them; here they ask Him to redeem them—to buy them back for Himself.

Psalm 45 is a royal psalm—a royal wedding song that celebrates human marriage in such a grand manner that the New Testament writers applied it to the great King Jesus as well (compare vv. 6, 7 with Heb. 1:8, 9). Like many other psalms, this one not only portrays the joy of human marriage, but also describes prophetically the glorious reign of

Jesus (see Ps. 2; 22; 69). This psalm was composed by the sons of Korah.

45:1-5 You are fairer: This psalm's cultural setting is the opulence of an ancient eastern royal court. The profuse description of the royal groom would be appropriate in that culture. **O Mighty One:** In the ancient Middle East the king was supposed to be a great warrior. The model in Israel was David, the celebrated champion who defeated the giant Goliath (1 Sam. 17). The term Mighty One is also a messianic title. **Your glory and Your majesty** can be rephrased as "Your majestic glory."

45:6-9 The words **Your throne** indicate the messianic direction of the psalm. Here the King is addressed as **God,** yet it is "God, Your God" who anointed Him. Thus these verses describe the interaction of the Father and the Son, for both are called "God." The writer of Hebrews used these verses to assert Jesus' deity (Heb. 1:8, 9). **anointed You:** Anointing set aside a particular person for special service to God. In Old Testament times, those who were anointed for special service foreshadowed the Anointed One, the meaning of *Messiah* and *Christ.* As symbols appropriate for divine service, the **garments** of a priest or king had to be clean and luxurious. The king was surrounded by radiant women; his bride the queen was resplendent in her precious golden garments. This is a portrait of heaven, with God as King and the church as His radiant bride (Rev. 19:1-10).

45:10-11 O daughter: The beautiful bride forsakes her own family and relationships as she becomes part of the family of her king and husband. **worship Him:** The bride is to give homage and worship to the great King. **robes of many colors:** In the ancient world, the beauty of the bride's gowns might be an expression of her family's wealth, their pride in her, and their love for her.

Psalm 46, as a psalm of trust (Ps. 23), rejoices in the deliverance that the Lord gives His people in the midst of a fearsome battle or siege. Psalm 46 was Martin Luther's basis for the Reformation hymn "A Mighty Fortress Is Our God." The psalm is also called "A Song for Alamoth," a word that may refer to soprano voices.

46:1 Our refuge and strength may be rephrased "our impenetrable defense." The psalms regularly use imagery of a fortress to describe God. In the ancient Middle East, cities were built on heights with high walls for defense. Yet there was no city and no defensive structure that was impenetrable. However, the psalmist describes here the One who is a sure defense.

46:2, 3 earth be removed: The wording of vv. 2, 3 moves the action to a cosmic level. What if the struggle were not just an ordinary war with ordinary weapons? What if the war involved even shaking the mountains and causing the seas to roar? It makes no difference. God is a refuge for His people against everything actual or imagined.

46:4, 5 God is in the midst of her: The people do not have an absentee deliverer, a defense that is only sometimes present. The Lord lives with His people. Consequently, His protection can be counted on.

46:6, 7 The LORD of hosts is with us: These words form a refrain (see v. 11). The pairing of the words "the Lord of hosts" with "the God of Jacob" is notable in both this verse and v. 11. This refrain praises the Almighty, the Commander of heaven's armies, for choosing to live with the descendants of Jacob, His people.

46:8-11 desolations: The picture here is of final judgment (Ps. 1; 110). **Be still:** The call for stillness before the Lord is not a preparation for worship, but for impending judgment (Hab. 2:20; Zeph. 1:7; Zech. 2:13). God will be exalted. All the earth will bow before Him.

Psalm 47, a royal psalm attributed to the sons of Korah, presents the grand ascent of the King of kings to His throne. The psalm also presents the joy of the people over the fact that the great King's rule means the end of all inequity, warfare, and trouble (Is. 11:3-5).

47:1-3 clap your hands: There are many ways in which the people of God express their joy in Him; one is the clapping of hands in joyful adoration. **all you peoples:** It is principally the people of God who will praise the great King; but the call for the nations was always a part of the larger picture in the theology of the psalms (Ps. 67; 117). **the LORD Most High:** The divine name usually translated "the LORD" is buttressed by the term *Most High,* which speaks of God's power over all nations (7:17; 77:10; 78:17, 35, 56; 82:6; 107:11; Deut. 32:8). **Awesome** is related to the word for "fear" and suggests reverence for Almighty God (147:11). **Great King** is the key phrase of this psalm. All kings have derived authority; only one King, the great God of heaven, is absolute in power and righteousness.

47:4 The words **whom He loves** are perhaps the most significant contribution of this psalm to our understanding of God's purposes. To love means "to make one's choice in." God had chosen the Israelites to be His holy people and in that way He loved them.

47:5–7 God has gone up: This psalm speaks of an anticipated enthronement of God. As He seats Himself on the throne, all who see Him in heaven and earth shout aloud in triumph. **Sing praises:** The repetition of this command in vv. 6, 7 is similar to the angelic voices singing of the holiness of God in Is. 6:3. The reason for the call to sing is clear: **God is the King of all the earth;** He deserves our praise.

47:8, 9 The people of the God of Abraham: This is the prophetic picture of the ultimate fulfillment of the Abrahamic covenant (Gen. 12:1–3). One day all the peoples of the earth who have come to faith in God through Jesus will discover that they are one people. They are all the true seed of Abraham, because they, like Abraham, believed in God (Gen. 15:6; Gal. 3:5–8). Then all **shields** will belong to God; there will be no other power on earth or in the universe apart from the power of God.

Psalm 48 unites with Ps. 46 and 47 to form three great psalms of praise to God for His kingship and His love for the holy city of Jerusalem. This emphasis on Jerusalem has led many scholars to speak of these psalms as "Songs of Zion." Attributed to the sons of Korah, this psalm calls the people to offer reverent praise to their Lord.

48:1 Great is used often in the Psalms to describe the person of God (21:5; 77:13; 95:3; 96:4; 145:3; 147:5). **city of our God:** The city of Jerusalem had a particularly dear place in the heart of God's people (see 1 Kin.

14:21). The city was holy because of the presence of God in the temple.

48:2, 3 The joy of the whole earth: The purpose of God's work in Israel was to draw all nations to Himself (117:1). **sides of the north:** This phrasing is likely borrowed from Canaanite poetry. In Canaanite thought, the great gods resided in some remote northern location. For Israel, God's dwelling was the physical city of Jerusalem. **The city of the great King:** Jesus quoted these words in Matt. 5:35 and identified the city as Jerusalem. **God is in her palaces:** These words express a prayer for the present and hope for the future. The beauty of the city of Jerusalem comes from the presence of the Lord, who has made His dwelling there.

48:4–7 This section describes from a different point of view the final battle referred to in Ps. 2 and 110. Psalm 48 describes the approach and hasty retreat of the errant **kings.** The connection between this text and Ps. 2 is heightened by the use of an unusual Hebrew word for **fear**—a term meaning "trembling" or "quaking terror"—which is found in both places (2:11).

48:8 as … we have seen: The people who first sang this song knew the presence of God in temple worship. They knew that they were in the city where God had chosen to establish His blessing.

48:9 We have thought: The verb is an unusual one in Hebrew. It refers to making comparisons and looking for similarities, thinking and considering with discrimination. The point is that nothing can be compared to the loyal love of God.

48:10–14 Praising the city of **Zion** is another way of praising God, whose dwelling was there. To be a **guide** describes the work of a shepherd (78:52).

Psalm 49, a wisdom psalm attributed to the sons of Korah, has many similarities with Proverbs and Ecclesiastes. The psalm calls for the wise person to realize that there is nothing to fear from the oppressive rich: like animals, they too will die. But the righteous will live forever. This psalm is quite different from a psalm of praise; it is an instruction text set to music.

49:1–5 Hear this, all peoples: The call for

wisdom and understanding goes to everyone, similar to the calls for universal worship of the Lord (Ps. 117). **Dark saying,** which may be translated "riddle" or "enigma," refers to a perplexing moral problem: how do the righteous come to terms with oppressive rich people who seem to have no thought for God?

49:6–9 Those who trust in their wealth: As in the teaching of Jesus (Mark 10:24), there is a warning against trusting in wealth, for wealth can achieve nothing of lasting value in this life or the life to come. **Nor give to God a ransom:** Wealth cannot buy redemption. **Pit** refers to the power of death in its dark aspect (16:10). Only God has the power to deliver us from death and hell.

49:10 The theme that **wise men die** is developed in Ecclesiastes. The rich and the poor, the wise and the fool, all have the same fate—physical death.

49:11–20 These verses vividly describe both the power of death and the greater power of God. **their beauty shall be consumed:** Death is the great leveler. People who have beauty, riches (vv. 16, 17), and power in this world will lose them all at death. They will be stripped of everything except their character or soul. This is why the Scriptures exhort us to pursue character development—God's law, holiness, wisdom, and knowledge—more than anything else. Each use of the word **grave** in these two verses is a translation of the Hebrew word Sheol, meaning death (16:10). **God will redeem my soul:** The psalmist trusts in God to deliver him from the power of death.

Psalm 50, a wisdom psalm, is the first of twelve poems attributed to Asaph, one of the music leaders appointed by David. This psalm contrasts the distinctions of the righteous and the wicked in the eyes of God, a constant theme of the wisdom writers. True wisdom in biblical thought is based on the "fear of the Lord," a proper response to the awesome nature of God. In this psalm, God is portrayed as the great Judge (Ps. 96—98).

50:1, 2 The Hebrew text uses the three terms **the Mighty One, God,** and **the LORD** as a stunning introduction to this poem. This language suggests a grand display of God Himself

in the midst of His people (18:7–9). **Out of Zion:** The glory of God shines from His sanctuary in Jerusalem.

50:3–6 Our God shall come: This prophetic language speaks of the coming kingdom of God (Ps. 96—98). **God Himself is Judge:** This is the point of this psalm; God is the great Judge. When used of God, the Hebrew word for Judge has connotations of royalty (94:2). Thus this wisdom psalm is also a royal psalm, because it speaks of the coming of the great King who both rules and judges.

50:7–10 not rebuke you: The sacrifices were commanded by God in Leviticus, but the people had difficulty keeping a godly perspective on the nature of sacrifices. **every beast of the forest:** The people were not doing God a favor by bringing their animals, for everything belonged to Him anyway. He knows every bird and beast.

50:11–15 If I were hungry: The God of Israel does not hunger for food; however, He does "hunger" for righteousness of His people.

50:16–21 The attention of the psalm turns from the righteous who need instruction to the **wicked** who merit judgment. This section announces God's judgment not against the nations, but against the people of Israel who heard but spurned God's word. **You give your mouth to evil:** God offered truth, but these people chose falsehoods. They had seen the light but preferred to live in darkness (John 3:16–21). **your own mother's son:** There was no sense of decency remaining in these wicked persons; even normal bonds of family relationships were disregarded.

50:22, 23 In the climax of the revelation of the coming judgment in this psalm, the Lord offers an opportunity to repent and receive forgiveness. This is an indicator of His grace. The Lord wants to save; His warnings are another expression of His mercy.

Psalm 51 is associated with one of the hardest experiences of David's life, the aftermath of his affair with Bathsheba. This is one of several psalms of David in which the title specifies the incident that inspired the poem. For the account of David's sin and Nathan's rebuke, see 2 Sam. 11; 12:1–15. David's response to Nathan was immediate: "I have sinned against the Lord" (2 Sam.

12:13). Sometime later, he wrote this memorable, penitential psalm.

51:1, 2 David's call for **mercy** is the only appropriate request for a confessing sinner. No sinner should ask for justice, for that would mean judgment and ruin. Mercy and forgiveness is God's gift to the confessing sinner. Even when the Lord forgives, He does not tarnish His just character. Confessed sins are covered by the sacrifice of His Son on the Cross (see 2 Cor. 5:21). The phrase **according to Your lovingkindness** expresses God's loyal or covenantal love to His people (13:5).

51:3, 4 The months of agony that David suffered because of his guilt are expressed in the striking words—**my sin is always before me. Against You:** David had sinned against Bathsheba, Uriah, and the nation he was called to rule. But none of these indictments were as serious as David's offense against God. The first few verses use several different words to describe sin—"transgression," "iniquity," and "sin." The words for forgiveness are all pictorial words: "blot out" (v. 1), "wash," and "cleanse" (v. 2). All these words express the seriousness of sin and the great lengths God goes to in removing our sin.

51:5, 6 brought forth in iniquity: Sin was found in David from the beginning; from birth he was inclined toward sin (see Rom. 5:12). **Inward parts,** a rare word in the Hebrew Bible, indicates something clouded over, difficult for anyone but God to see. The Lord's penetrating gaze searches the innermost recesses of a person's mind and heart.

51:7–9 hyssop: Here David refers to the ritual acts of cleansing described in the Law of Moses (Lev. 14:4; Num. 19:6). David repeatedly calls for his cleansing (see also v. 9). By this, he expresses his profound sense of guilt.

51:10 The verb translated **create** is the same one used in Gen. 1:1 and refers to what only God can do. David was asking that his heart be renewed, restored, and transformed. God is the only source of such a renewal.

51:11–15 David calls **sinners** to salvation in this verse. He vows that he will use his experience of God's grace as a renewed motivation

to bring others into the knowledge of the love and mercy of God (40:3). **my tongue shall sing:** David desires to be forgiven for several reasons: (1) for his own peace, (2) for the message of hope that he could communicate to others, and (3) for the praise he would be able to give in the community of the faithful.

51:16, 17 You do not desire sacrifice: The key term here is the verb *desire,* which means "to find pleasure in." God's pleasure is not in the sacrificed animal, but in the restored person. He demanded sacrifices, even from David; but His pleasure is in the person who comes obediently to Him (Gen. 4:1–7; Rom. 12:1, 2).

51:18, 19 Do good: David declared God's goodness to the whole community in their collective worship (125:4). The Hebrew verb translated **pleased** is the same verb translated *delight* in v. 16. God took pleasure in those whose hearts were humble before Him. Their sacrifices were a source of joy.

Psalm 52, a psalm of lament, strongly emphasizes judgment of David's enemies. The title of this psalm specifies the incident in David's life that prompted him to write it. Doeg, an official of Saul, had spied on David when he fled to Ahimelech, the priest at Nob, for provisions and guidance (1 Sam. 21:7). Doeg's report angered Saul so much that he destroyed the priestly family at Nob (1 Sam. 22). This incident must have been disheartening to David. His actions had caused the death of others, and his enemies were determined to destroy him.

52:1–4 Boast is related to the word meaning "praise"; however, boasting in evil is no more than a perversion of praise. **Mighty** is likely used here sarcastically; the only Mighty One is the Lord. **The goodness of God** is His "loyal love." The contrast is between a wicked man who boasts in evil and the Lord who is constant in His supreme character. **Your tongue** refers to more than just words. These people used language as a weapon, for they believed that the gods could empower their words to a devastating effect.

52:5–7 God shall destroy you forever: The psalmist uses the strongest terms to describe divine judgment on those who practice evil.

Uproot you from the land of the living refers to death, but not eternal death. **The righteous also shall see and fear:** This fear is a deepened respect for God and a sense of awe before His throne.

52:8, 9 A green olive tree is a symbol of beauty. In Rom. 11, the olive tree is used as a symbol of the Gentiles who are grafted into the root, the people of God or the church. The Hebrew word for **mercy** is the same term, meaning "loyal love," that is translated "goodness" in v. 1.

Psalm 53 is a recasting of Ps. 14 with only slight differences, particularly in the ending.

53:1 In the Bible, the term **fool** does not mean mental incompetence, but moral and spiritual insensitivity. The fool is the one who ignores God.

53:2–6 God has scattered the bones: This is a prophetic pronouncement of the final judgment on the wicked. Those who did not fear God will be filled with **great fear,** for God will come in His glory and power. One day there will be no more wickedness to contaminate the earth or to compromise the people of God.

Psalm 54 is a psalm of lament in which the answer to the prayer is declared before the end of the poem. This is another of David's psalms in which the title indicates the specific situation that gave rise to the poem (Ps. 51; 52). Twice the people of the Wilderness of Ziph had informed Saul that David was hiding in their region (1 Sam. 23:19–23; 26:1–3). David's distress is understandable; yet from the Ziphites' viewpoint, their actions were warranted. After all, Saul was the king and David was a fugitive.

54:1–3 Save me, O God, by Your name: The poets of the Bible knew the significance of God's name even when they did not use it. The people of Ziph probably are indicated by the words **strangers** and **oppressors.** David makes the point that they are not pious people. Since he is God's servant, he expects that God will deliver him.

54:4, 5 Helper could also be translated "power." The Lord was David's strength in his time of need. **Cut them off** is David's curse on his enemies, an imprecation. Even so, David did not take vengeance into his own hands. Only the Lord can take revenge.

54:6, 7 I will freely sacrifice to You: The prayer has been answered, and God is honored. Thus David expresses his willingness to fulfill his vow.

Psalm 55 deals with life and death, deliverance from hell, and the abiding presence of God. It speaks prophetically of the experience of the Savior Jesus. This psalm consists of many short sections, and its choppy quality shows the deep emotion behind it.

55:1–3 Give ear to my prayer: This psalm begins in a way that is common in the lament psalms. There is a call to God, a reference to the psalmist's distress, and a notice about his enemy. David's shock is not that he is in distress again or even that he has more enemies. The great shock is that the enemy is his own friend (vv. 12–14).

55:4–8 David's intense pain can be felt in his strong language. The phrase **terrors of death** is unusual. The Hebrew word for *terror* or "dread" is first used in Scripture to describe the horror that Abraham felt in the unnatural darkness that seized him as God was about to come near (Gen. 15:12). The word also described the horrors that would fall on the people of Canaan when the Lord gave the land to the Israelites (Ex. 15:16).

55:9 David calls for God's judgment on the wicked; he renews this call in vv. 15, 23.

55:10–14 Here is the reason for David's terrible pain in this psalm. It was not an ordinary enemy who had risen up against him; it was his **companion,** his confidant and friend. The one who betrayed him was not only a close friend, but a person with whom David had worshiped the Lord.

55:15 In rage, David cries: **Let death seize them.** His words are directed against the wicked generally, and not personally against the one who had distressed David (vv. 13, 14). David could express his emotions to God in prayer, but judgment or revenge was in God's hands (see Rom. 12:19).

55:16–19 The words **as for me** mark a dramatic turning point in the psalm. David reverts to a stance of faith; He declares his trust in the omnipotent Lord. **God will hear:** David reminds himself of the great acts of deliverance that God has done on his behalf in the past and the work that God will continue to do in the future.

55:20 He has put forth his hands: David turns to describe his former friend, now his enemy (vv. 13, 14). He had been completely taken in by the man's lies.

55:21–23 To anyone who has experienced grief or desolation, the command to **cast one's burden on the LORD** is refreshing. The Lord is the one constant in life (v. 19) and the one true friend (27:10). He can always bear the burden.

Psalm 56 is a psalm of lament. This poem of David has the same setting as Ps. 34—the flight of David to Achish at Gath. In Ps. 34, Achish is referred to as "Abimelech," his royal designation. The fact that two of David's psalms are tied to this one event demonstrates how devastating the experience was to David. Cut off from all he had known, David tried to find refuge among the Philistines. When they turned on him, he was forced to escape by pretending to be insane (1 Sam. 21:10–15). This psalm was sung in corporate worship, for it is addressed to the "Chief Musician" and is set to the tune "The Silent Dove in Distant Lands."

56:1 Be merciful to me: David cries out to God because of his overwhelming sense of loss during his time as a fugitive in a foreign land (see 1 Sam. 21:10–15).

56:2–4 I will trust are words of abiding confidence, even in times of distress. Alternating passages of pain and faith are a characteristic of the lament psalms (Ps. 13). **I will praise His word:** This insert is also found twice in v. 10. The idea of **what can flesh do** is repeated in v. 11 and is developed more fully in 118:6.

56:5 All day they twist my words: In lament psalms, the psalmist typically complains about lies, the misuse of language, and deceitful speech (Ps. 12).

56:6–11 You number my wanderings: The psalmist is confident that God has a particular interest in his every pain, even his every tear. He also knows the great truth that comes from the meaning of God's name, that the Lord is *for* us. **I will praise His word:** The double insert of this shout of praise shows the psalmist's great enthusiasm for the praise of God.

56:12, 13 Vows made to You: The psalmist takes very seriously His determination to praise the Lord. **You have delivered my soul:** Here is the psalmist's report of deliverance. In the congregation of believing people, David rejoices in the Lord.

Psalm 57 is another of David's poems in which the title gives the specific setting of the psalm. The narrative of David's life indicates that he once hid in a cave in En Gedi (1 Sam. 24:1–7), the setting of this poem. In En Gedi, David spared Saul's life even though Saul had become an easy target. Rather than killing Saul while he had the chance, David cut off a piece of the king's garment. David later repented even of that act against Saul. This psalm is one of four that were set to the tune "Do Not Destroy" (Ps. 58; 59; 75).

57:1–3 The opening cry **be merciful to me** is similar to many in the lament psalms, but here it is followed immediately by a confession of trust in the Lord. **in the shadow:** The picture of hiding under the wings of a mother bird is a familiar theme in the Psalms (91:1–4). Here the psalmist vows that he will pray only to his God, for God alone can deliver him from trouble.

57:4–6 The psalmist's foes are like **lions** prowling about for prey. **Be exalted:** In the midst of his distress, the psalmist shouts his praise to God (v. 11). One of the ways in which God exalts Himself is by graciously delivering the needy. **They have prepared a net:** The psalmist is like a bird that is easily caught; yet by God's mercy, his enemies will fall into their own pit.

57:7 Near the end of his life, Paul was able to say that he had kept the faith (2 Tim. 4:7). With the words **my heart is steadfast,** David is assuring God of much the same thing: he has remained faithful to the God who has provided for Him from the beginning.

57:8–11 I will praise You: As is common in the Psalms, the conclusion is a vow to praise the Lord. Such praise would be centered on the Lord's saving acts. In this poem, the praise of the Lord revolves around His **mercy** and **truth** (86:15).

Psalm 58, an imprecatory psalm, might have been provoked by a very strong attack on

David. This is one of the four psalms set to the tune "Do Not Destroy" (Ps. 57; 59; 75).

58:1, 2 You silent ones is a derisive term for the wicked judges. Although they were just humans, they were behaving as though they had divine power. **wickedness ... violence:** Instead of establishing righteousness, these wicked judges were producing havoc. They thought they had all power **in the earth.** But they would soon learn that God "judges in the earth" (v. 11).

58:3–5 The effects of the wicked in powerful places are as deadly as the effects of poisonous snakes that are out of control. The word **charmers** refers to those who have the ability to "control" the behavior of snakes; but in this case, not even the equivalent of charmers could control the

destruction and evil that resulted from wicked people in high places.

58:6, 7 In 57:4, the wicked are described as having powerful **teeth,** as though they were carnivores, eating the righteous alive. Here David asks God to shatter their teeth, symbolizing the destruction of the power of the wicked over the poor and defenseless (3:7).

58:8 The ancient Israelites desired children so much that a live birth was considered extremely precious. Alternatively a **stillborn child** would cause great sorrow.

58:9 In this verse, David speaks of the certainty of divine judgment. **Before your pots can feel:** It takes some time for a pot to boil. But the judgment of God will come suddenly—even before a pot would feel the heat.

IN DEPTH   **Lessons in Music**

The Book of Psalms is the hymnal of ancient Israel. The psalms are ancient lyrics preserved with occasional musical notations. Most of these musical notations are found in the superscriptions or titles. For instance, many are directed "To the Chief Musician" (Pss. 51—62). Others call for musical accompaniment. For example, Ps. 4 calls for stringed instruments, Ps. 5 for flutes, Ps. 6 for the eight-stringed harp, and Ps. 8 for the instrument of Gath. The titles sometimes specify the tune to be used, such as "of the Son" in Ps. 9 and "The Lilies" in Ps. 45. In this way the superscriptions contain hints of the musical nature of the psalms.

The psalms present a balanced picture of the use of music in worship. In particular, the first three verses of Ps. 33 are instructive. As v. 1 suggests, the purpose of godly music is to rejoice in the God who has given us new life. As the psalmist notes with his directive to the "righteous," this type of praise can come only from those who have been cleansed by God's grace and renewed by His Spirit. Indeed the psalmist describes this praise from the righteous as "beautiful," for God enjoys receiving praise from His people. For this reason, worshipful music is always directed "to Him" (vv. 2, 3). That is, God is always the audience for the music performed in His name.

What kind of music can we present to God? The psalmist describes a variety of instruments, such as the harp and the instrument of ten strings, that join the human voice in giving praise to the Lord. But his exhortation to sing "a new song" (v. 3) is not merely a call for new music and new hymnals. The phrase new song means to sing to God with a renewed sense of wonder at all He has done for us. The worship of God should never degenerate into something that we just do; we should always approach God with rejoicing. With the phrase "play skillfully" (v. 3), the psalmist exhorts us never to approach our worship with a casual attitude. We are to "play skillfully" because we are playing to the Lord, and we must offer Him only our best. But skill is not the only criterion of worship music, for the psalmist's final exhortation in v. 3 is to play "with a shout of joy." Since God always considers our attitudes, genuine joy in the presence of our caring Lord is required for music to be truly worshipful.

58:10 The destruction of the wicked brings sadness at the thought of the waste of human dreams, lives, and hopes. But there is great joy for **the righteous** in the recognition that the Savior King has won the victory (Rev. 19:11–21). There is also joy in knowing that wickedness will no longer anger the Lord of the universe (68:3). Justice will be established forever.

58:11 a reward for the righteous: See 1 Cor. 3:11–15 for further development of this theme. **in the earth:** This is the fitting arena of divine judgment, for the wicked judges thought they possessed all authority on earth (v. 2).

Psalm 59, a psalm of lament, contains strong assurance of the final judgment of the wicked. The superscription refers to the story found in 1 Sam. 19:9–17: David escaped Saul's anger with help from his wife Michal. She showed unusual heroism and great devotion to David—actions that resulted in a strained relationship with her father Saul.

59:1, 2 The repetition of the phrase **deliver me** is for emphasis, meaning "to bring one out" of trouble and distress. The verb translated **defend** means "to set on high" or "to place out of reach of trouble" (91:14). **Save me:** This is the most common of the Hebrew verbs for salvation. It suggests "to give room to" or "to expand an area to breathe."

59:3, 4 they lie in wait: Enemies become like wild animals on the hunt or enemy soldiers lurking along one's paths. **Not for my transgression:** There were times in David's life when he knew that he was suffering because of sin in his life (Ps. 32). There were other times when he believed himself to be innocent of sin, but still he was hounded by wicked persons. Here he shouts his protest aloud: **through no fault of mine.** He was guilty of no wickedness that would cause such merciless attacks on him.

59:5 David's call for the Lord to **awake** is another way of asking God to pay attention to his plight (7:6; 35:23; 44:23; Is. 51:9). To ensure God's reception of his bold shout, David uses the "full name" of God. **Do not be merciful:** The righteous constantly experience the mercy of the Lord, but His mercy is not extended to those who constantly oppose Him.

59:6, 7 A dog in the ancient Hebrew culture was considered a scavenger, not the beloved pet of our own day. **Who hears:** Like those described in Ps. 9; 10, the wicked here believe that they will face no punishment for their evil. They are profoundly mistaken (75:7, 10; 92:6).

59:8 But You: This is a complete turnaround in the psalm—from thoughts about the wicked to an acknowledgment of the reality of God in human affairs. **shall laugh ... in derision:** The wording is the same as in 2:4 (Job 9:23; Prov. 1:26). There is the pleasurable laughter of God in joy with His people (see 147:11; Zeph. 3:17). But this is the laughter of contempt.

59:9 Wait can also mean "watch." The enemies of David had come to watch for him; but David was determined to "watch" for God. The noun **my defense** means "a high place of refuge" and is related to the verb in v. 1.

59:10 My God of mercy: The term *mercy* is sometimes translated "loyal love" (13:5). The Lord is the "God of my loyal love."

59:11 This verse begins the second round of the petition in the psalm. The imprecation or curse in this verse is unusual. Instead of asking for the destruction of the wicked, the psalmist asks for them to be scattered, to be made fugitives. This would be a constant reminder of the consequences of evil.

59:12, 13 The repetition of this verbal phrase **consume them** is similar to the repetition of the phrase *deliver me* in vv. 1, 2. **that God rules in Jacob:** The idea is similar to 58:11.

59:14–17 But I: The words of these verses capture the positive thrust of this psalm. David sings with joyful abandon of his relationship with God, despite the presence of wicked persons. There are two verbs translated **I will sing;** together they capture the idea that singing in the name of the Lord is a wonderful act of faith (Ex. 15:2). **You, O my Strength** is repeated from v. 9. In God, the believer finds strength, **defense,** and **mercy.** This psalm ends in a grand manner with bold faith in the living God.

Psalm 60, a psalm of community lament (Ps. 80), expresses David's great faith in the eventual victory he would find in the Lord. Since the tone of the psalm is military in nature, it is possible that this poem was used in military training. The campaign of David and his general Joab against Hadadezer, the king of Zobah, did not succeed at first (2 Sam. 8:3–8). This psalm describes the feelings of David and his army at the time of their defeat. But it also records their confident expectation that they would eventually succeed.

60:1–3 David accuses God of having **broken** them **down.** This is a poetic description of an otherwise unknown defeat of the armies of Israel in a battle that was part of the campaign against Aram of Zobah and Mesopotamian allies (2 Sam. 8). The defeat was so startling that it caused the people of Israel to feel as though God had **made the earth tremble,** a metaphor for devastation.

60:4, 5 a banner: Despite the recent defeat, the people still had reason to hope in a final victory for Israel over its foes. The term **beloved** (127:2; Is. 5:1; Jer. 11:15) is particularly endearing. God had a reason to act on behalf of His people: He loved them.

60:6–9 At this point in the psalm, God speaks (75:2–5, 10; 91:14–16). The Lord affirms that He is in charge, that the land belongs to Him, and that He will give victory to His people. **Shechem** and **the Valley of Succoth** represent regions west and east of the Jordan River in the central parts of the land. **Gilead** and **Manasseh** are also regions east and west of the Jordan River; **Ephraim** and **Judah** are regions in the north and south. The Lord was asserting His sovereignty over the entire land of Israel. **Moab ... Edom ... Philistia:** These traditional enemies of Israel were also enemies of God. The Lord would not allow them to disturb His people.

60:10 Is it not You: The very One the people thought had **cast** them **off** (v. 1) would lead them to final victory.

60:11, 12 Ultimately, true **help**—the Hebrew word means "salvation"—comes only from God. **we will do valiantly:** David's general Joab led the battle, and under God's hand Israel's enemies were defeated. When **the help of man** proves **useless,** often God

dramatically provides strength and power so that our boast is solely in Him.

Psalm 61, a royal psalm attributed to David, has elements of lament (Ps. 13) and trust (Ps. 23). In this psalm, the king of Israel points to the great King who is to come. The title includes the words "On a stringed instrument" (see the titles of Ps. 4; 6; 54; 55; 67; 76).

61:1 Hear my cry is classic language of a lament psalm. David calls on the Lord to hear the prayer of the troubled believer (5:2, 3; 17:1; 55:2; 66:19; 86:6; 142:6).

61:2 From the end of the earth: David describes his sense of being far from God's presence in his time of need. His prayer is that he might be brought back to **the rock that is higher** than he. The imagery of God as a Rock for the believer was introduced by Moses (see Deut. 2:4) and is developed elsewhere in the Psalms (62:2; 71:3; 91:1, 2; 144:1).

61:3 The idea of God as one's **shelter** or refuge is seen in a number of passages in the Psalms (14:6; 46:1; 62:7, 8; 71:7; 91:2, 9; 94:22; 142:5). Such verses present the psalmist's strong affirmation of the protection and deliverance to be found in God.

61:4 I will abide implies strong determination. It is used of a worshiper in God's house in 15:1. Elsewhere, the psalmist compares himself to (1) an everlasting guest in the tent of the Lord (Ps. 15) and (2) a chick who has complete **trust** under its mother's wings (63:7; 91:4).

61:5 The pronoun **You** is emphasized in this verse as David celebrates the work of God in his life and in the life of his people. **the heritage:** God had given the nation to David for him to rule responsibly. These words also refer to the greater reality of the Savior King who would receive the nations as His inheritance to rule forever. **who fear Your name:** To *fear* is to hold the name of God in awe and wonder, in worship and obedience (see 147:11; Ex. 20:20).

61:6, 7 The terms **many generations** and **forever** refer to David's long rule but more literally prophesy the eternal rule of Jesus, the King of kings. **Mercy and truth** together mean "loving loyalty." Psalm 23 presents the believer pursued by God's "goodness and mercy" (23:6); but here the king is guarded by God's loving loyalty.

61:8 My vows refers to the vows of praise to God mentioned in v. 5 (see also 22:22–26; 66:13; 76:11).

Psalm 62 is a wisdom psalm that eloquently urges silent confidence in the victory of God over all enemies because salvation is found only in Him. Jeduthun in the superscription was the chief of one of the choirs in the temple (1 Chr. 9:16) whose descendants founded a temple choir (1 Chr. 16:41, 42). The superscription "To Jeduthun" is also found in Ps. 39 and 77.

62:1, 2 In these two verses, David declares his complete dependence on God. **silently waits:** David expresses silent resignation before the sovereign will of the living God.

62:3 How long: David addresses his tormentors directly, expecting that they will soon be judged. **attack:** The word means to threaten or shout at someone.

62:4, 5 wait silently: A different Hebrew word is used here, but the concept of v. 1 is restated. **My expectation** may also be translated "hope" (71:5).

62:6, 7 Verse 6 is a restatement of v. 2, but strengthened by dropping the word *greatly*. **My salvation and my glory** may be rephrased "my glorious salvation."

62:8–10 Trust: David addresses the righteous (contrast v. 3) with his lesson of reliance on God (40:3). What is true for David (v. 7) is extended to everyone in the believing community.

62:11 once, Twice: It is a convention of wisdom literature to use a number and then raise it by one (Prov. 30:11–33). The point here is that David has heard the message with certainty.

62:12 Mercy can be translated "loyal love," the covenantal love of the Lord (13:5). **to each one:** God is the true Judge; He will repay and reward every person (Eccl. 12:13, 14).

Psalm 63 is a royal psalm with elements of the psalms of trust (Ps. 23). The brief biographical note in the title "when he was in the wilderness of Judah" possibly refers to an incident during the period when Saul was chasing David (1 Sam. 22—24).

63:1, 2 O God, my God: The opening words indicate faith in God, but they also suggest a time of trouble (22:1). **thirsts ... longs:** The psalmist is away from the place of God's worship and feels the distance keenly (42:1, 2). **The sanctuary** had been at Nob (1 Sam. 21:1), and it was there that David had sought the presence of the Lord. Later it was moved to Jerusalem (76:1, 2).

63:3–5 The psalmist expresses his joy in knowing God and his determination to continue praising God throughout his life. **Lovingkindness** may also be translated "loyal love" (13:5). **bless ... hands:** Praise (the meaning of *bless* here) and raising the hands in worship are often associated in the Psalms (134:2). To lift the hands to the Lord expresses dependence on Him, coupled with an acknowledgment of His power, wonder, and majesty (77:2).

63:6 From his **bed,** David continues to fix his thoughts on God (77:6). **night watches:** The Israelites counted three watches to the night. Evidently David is having difficulty sleeping, and he directs his thoughts to worship.

63:7, 8 in the shadow of Your wings: See 91:4 for this expression of faith in God. **Your right hand:** The same power of God that delivered Israel from Egypt (Ex. 15:6) would support David—and all other believers in their daily life (74:11).

63:9, 10 David predicts the destruction of his enemies. They will be driven to barren places where only **jackals,** wild dogs of the desert, roam.

63:11 The king refers to David. When he finally became king, David would find his true pleasure in God. **Everyone who swears by Him** refers to those who believe in the Lord.

Psalm 64 has elements of lament (Ps. 13) and imprecation (Ps. 137), but it appears to be basically a wisdom psalm. It contrasts the righteous and the wicked, compares their destinies, and is itself a "meditation" (v. 1).

64:1 The initial cry of the psalmist expressed with the verbs **hear** and **preserve** resembles the psalms of lament (Ps. 13), but the term **my meditation** suggests that this is a wisdom psalm. In other passages the term *meditation* has the idea of "complaint" (55:2; 102:2; 142:2). But in this psalm the word indicates contemplation, for David contemplated the wicked and their end (see also 73:17).

64:2–6 The arrogance of the wicked in their plots against the righteous is a continuing theme in the Psalms (Ps. 9; 10; 12). **Who will see:** The wicked do not know, or do not care, that there is One who sees (73:11), and who will repay (75:7).

64:7–10 trust: By placing our problems into God's hands, we can rest in His sovereign will for our lives. **All the upright in heart** is another designation for **the righteous** or "the blameless" (v. 4). Their **glory** is their exuberant praise to God (63:11).

Psalm 65 is a wisdom psalm and more particularly a creation psalm (as Ps. 19). It celebrates rainfall, sharing the mood of Ps. 104. But this is also a prophetic psalm. The prophetic element is signaled in the first verse, the vow of praise yet to be paid—that is, all creation is waiting to praise the Lord when He finally appears in glory (see Rom. 14:10, 11; Rev. 19:5).

65:1 Praise is awaiting You: There is still a vow of praise to be performed (v. 3). In the background of this psalm is an idea not far from that of Paul in Rom. 8:22, the groaning of creation for its release from the curse brought on it by humanity's fall (Gen. 3:17). The point of the psalm is twofold: (1) Every good rain and every full harvest is a blessing from God, showing His delight in His creation. (2) A day of God's goodness is coming in which good rains and harvests will be greater than ever before.

65:2, 3 atonement: David speaks of a coming day when sin will be dealt with fully, when redemption will be completely paid. This took place in the death and resurrection of Jesus Christ (see Eph. 1:7).

65:4 shall be satisfied: In other psalms, David expresses his desire to live in the presence of God (27:4, 5). The fulfillment of this desire in David's day came through the sacrificial services of worship in Israel.

65:5–8 The **awesome** power of God at creation in the beginning (Job 26) will one day be seen anew in the restoration of all things.

noise of the seas: God's power over the "dark powers" of the seas is a regular theme in the royal psalms (Ps. 93).

65:9, 10 You visit the earth: Rainfall is seen here as a gracious visitation of God. This is in keeping with the provisions of God's covenant with Israel (Deut. 28:12).

65:11–13 Your paths: The picture is of wagon tracks across the heavens, where the "cart" of God's mercies sloshes abundance on the earth below. **they also sing:** The "singers" here are the pastures and the valleys. The coming of God's kingdom to earth will be a magnificent time of productivity (67:6). This is the vow that remains to be performed (v. 1).

Psalm 66, a psalm of praise, offers significant contributions to our understanding of the values of biblical worship. In the course of the psalm, the psalmist offers *descriptive praise,* praising God for who He is and what He does, as well as *declarative praise,* praising God for specific answers to prayer.

66:1, 2 The call is not only for the people of Israel, but for peoples of **all the earth** to join in the praise of the living God, the Most High (Ps. 87; 96; 117). **Sing out the honor of His name:** The Lord is pleased with music that praises His glorious name (Ex. 15:2).

66:3, 4 How awesome: The **works** of God are designed to bring a sense of awe to people (19:1, 2). In this context, **submit** means "to cringe" before God. The term translated **worship** means "to kneel" or "to bow down." The opening verses of this psalm present a call and an expectation that one day all the earth will worship God.

66:5–9 To **bless** God is to identify Him as the source of our blessing (see 103:1, 2). **you peoples:** The call is to all the nations of the earth (vv. 1, 4, 5). God's preservation of His people is one of many reasons to bless Him.

66:10–15 Your house refers to the temple in Jerusalem where God lived among His people. During periods of distress in his life, the psalmist made **vows** that when God brought him out of distress, he would publicly acknowledge God's deliverance (40:1–3; 61:5, 8; 76:11). Each of the **sacrifices** would be accompanied by the heart attitude of the true worshiper (see John 4:23, 24).

66:16–19 You who fear God refers to those who respond in awe and wonder to the Lord (v. 4). **iniquity:** Among the things that can block effective prayer is ongoing sin in a believer's life (Ps. 32). But the psalmist here confesses that God **has heard.**

66:20 The concluding words of the poem are an affirmation of the psalmist's blessing of the Lord (v. 8) based on his realization of God's continuing goodness in his life.

Psalm 67, a psalm of praise, serves as a marvelous invocation and doxology in worship. The poem calls the nations of the world to praise God, to join Israel in honoring the Creator.

67:1, 2 cause His face to shine: In the language of the Aaronic benediction (Num. 6:24–26), the psalmist calls for God to smile on His People (Ps. 80). From the beginning, God had intended to bring His blessing to **all nations,** in fulfillment of the provisions of the Abrahamic covenant (Gen. 12:3). This passage anticipates the thrust of world mission that is found in the New Testament (Matt. 28:18–20; Acts 1:8).

67:3, 4 Let the peoples praise You: God's desire is for all people to praise Him, for He is their Creator and their Provider (2 Pet. 3:9). This should also be the desire of God's people.

67:5–7 yield her increase: As in the prophetic aspect of Ps. 65, the coming of God's kingdom on earth will be marked by a magnificent increase in production. The curse on the land (Gen. 3:17–19; Rom. 8:22) will be lifted in "the year of God's goodness" (65:11).

Psalm 68 is based in part on the Song of Deborah in Judg. 5. It speaks with great power of the glory of God. The first and last verses of the psalm (vv. 1, 35) capture its essence. The title refers to it as both a "Psalm" and a "Song," indicating its musical nature.

68:1–3 Let God arise … flee before Him: The presence of the wicked on the earth is an assault on God's holiness and a constant threat to the righteous. Only God's mercy compels Him to delay His judgment (75:2). But when God awakes, His enemies will be scattered; they will disappear like **smoke.**

68:4 Extol Him who rides on the clouds: A well-known description of Baal was as "the rider of the clouds." Here the title is stripped from the supposed "god" Baal and given to the living God of Scripture. The fact that the Lord is the Rider of the clouds indicates that He is the One who brings rain and controls the powerful forces of a storm (147:8, 9, 15–18). **YAH** is a shortened form of the divine name Yahweh (Ex. 3:14, 15).

68:5 The Lord is not limited to clouds and storms; He also meets the needs of the helpless. For all people, He is **in His holy habitation,** dispensing justice.

68:6–10 The psalmist describes the work of God on behalf of His people in poetic terms that recall the Exodus events and draw on the Song of Deborah (Judg. 5:4). The language of this section is also an expansion of the description in v. 4; this is the march of God as the true God of the Storm.

68:11 The term translated **word** refers to a command rather than a revelation. The command was that God's works would be made known among the peoples. **Those who proclaimed it** translates a feminine participle. Thus the people who made the proclamation were women, most likely the women who gave praise to God under the direction of Miriam (Ex. 15:20, 21).

68:12–14 The Almighty is the name Shaddai, a title that refers to the majesty and strength of the Lord (91:1). The scattering of **kings** refers to the early battles won by Israel during the wilderness period and at the time of the conquest of the land of Canaan.

68:15, 16 Bashan was a very fertile area northeast of the Sea of Galilee, a part of the former territory of Og. It is possible that the connotation of Bashan as a place of plenty is transferred poetically to Jerusalem in these verses, for it was only in Jerusalem that the Lord had sworn that he would **dwell.**

68:17, 18 When God delivered His people from Egypt, He brought them out with great treasures from the Egyptians (Ex. 12:35, 36). These gifts were used by the people of Israel to build the tabernacle (Ex. 35) **that the LORD God might dwell there.**

68:19, 20 This section is a benediction, a blessing on the Lord, for His **daily** mercies in the lives of the people of faith. **The God of our salvation** is a great title for the One who saved Israel from Egypt, who saved Israel from their sin, who continues to save His people in their daily lives, and who will glorify His people in the future.

68:21, 22 The Lord is the Victor over the **enemies** of His people. None shall escape, whether near—**Bashan**—or far—in **the sea.** Like grapes they will be crushed, and justice will finally be served (58:10)

68:23-27 The **procession** of God could refer to one of three things: (1) carrying the ark of the covenant through the wilderness during the time of the Exodus; (2) God leading as the Commander of His armies in Israel; (3) the grand procession of the Savior King as He comes to establish His reign on earth (Rev. 19:14-21). **Timbrels,** or tambourines, often played by women, were used for both sacred and secular occasions. Associated with dance, they suggested joy (81:2; 149:3; 150:4). **little Benjamin:** The role of Benjamin, one of the smaller tribes, was significant. Saul was from this tribe, and the city of Jerusalem was located within its borders.

68:28-30 Kings ... presents: The term *presents* means "gifts offered in homage." Royal guests came to Solomon with gifts (1 Kin. 10:1-10); but the ultimate prophetic fulfillment of this verse was in the kings who came to Jerusalem to bring gifts to the infant Jesus (Matt. 2:1-12). One day all kings will show their obedience and humility before Jesus, the great King (2:10-12; 76:11).

68:31-35 The psalm ends with a celebration of the presence of God in the midst of His people. This section looks forward to the reign of Jesus the Savior King (Zeph. 3:14-17). **Him who rides on the heaven of heavens** is a development of the phrase found in v. 4. The Lord's **voice** is the thunder; God is the true God of storm (77:16-20) and Creator of the universe.

Psalm 69, a psalm of lament, is more specifically a protest of innocence. This highly messianic psalm presents a remarkable description of the suffering of Jesus Christ. Whereas Ps. 22 describes Jesus' physical sufferings, Ps. 69 focuses more on His emotional and spiritual suffering. Yet like Ps. 22, this psalm was written by David approximately a thousand years

before the events it describes. Both psalms begin with the sufferings of David but have their full meaning in the sufferings of Jesus.

69:1-3 I sink in deep mire: The opening words of this psalm of anguish use the strong image of a person about to drown—not just in deep waters, but in muck (40:2). This powerfully descriptive language expresses extreme mental anguish. **I am weary:** As a drowning man might exhaust his voice entirely, so David is worn out from praying and crying out to the Lord (6:6).

69:4 hate me without cause: These words describe David's experience in a difficult period of his life. It seems that his foes are innumerable; but more devastating to him than their number is the fact that he has not caused their attack. Any attack is difficult; an unprovoked attack is intolerable.

69:5-12 zeal for Your house: Like Phinehas in Num. 25, David describes himself as a zealot for the house of the Lord. Jesus' cleansing of the temple was a fulfillment of these words (see John 2:17). **When I wept:** Even the piety of David has become a reason for his enemies to chide him. **Those who sit in the gate:** The elders of the cities looked with contempt on David.

69:13-19 The words **deliver me out of the mire** tie the psalm together; compare the words of vv. 1-3. **Hear me:** This renewed plea to God is based on the character of the Lord; His lovingkindness or loyal love, and His tender mercies compelled David to keep looking to the Lord for deliverance.

69:20, 21 for my thirst: At one point during Jesus' suffering on the Cross, He was offered vinegar to soothe His thirst (Matt. 27:34; John 19:28-30).

69:22-28 Pour out Your indignation upon them may refer to the Lord's judgment on His foes in this lament over Jerusalem. The words of v. 25 were fulfilled in Judas Iscariot. See Acts 1:20, in which the words of this verse are joined to the words of 109:8.

69:29-36 The phrase **I am poor** refers to a brokenness of spirit and sense of worthlessness caused by the assaults of the wicked. **I will praise:** David praised God in exuberant joy when the Lord saved him from the depths of despair.

Psalm 70, a psalm of lament, is a reprise of 40:13–17. The description of the poor and needy was such a necessary element in the encouragement of people enduring troubles that this section was selected for individual use as a freestanding poem.

70:1, 2 Let them be ashamed and confounded: David prays that those who rejoice in his misery will be proven wrong in their assumption that the Lord is unable to help His people. In this way, the Lord's deliverance of David will result in God's name being glorified.

70:3–5 The last three words of the psalm **do not delay** indicate the near-desperation of David. The cry echoes David's plea in v. 1 for the Lord to "come quickly" to save him. Even in panic-stricken despair, David reminds Himself that the Lord is his only source of strength, help, and deliverance.

Psalm 71 is a psalm of lament with a major focus on the psalmist's trust in God. The psalm alternates between expressions of desperate need and resolute trust in the Lord. In this interplay, the psalmist models the way believers should react to suffering. A believer should completely trust the Lord in a difficult situation, but at the same time cry out to Him for deliverance. The psalmist describes himself as an old man who has trusted in God for a long time (vv. 9, 18). In his great time of need, he asks God to be faithful to His servant.

71:1 The theme of the psalm is stated in this verse. On the basis of resolute **trust** (61:4; 91:3), the psalmist asks that he **never be put to shame.** Trusting in God is never foolish (4:2; 119:31).

71:2, 3 in Your righteousness: The psalmist is concerned not only with his own plight but with the character of God (vv. 15, 16, 19, 24). The psalmist's point is that God could display His righteousness by answering the needs of the psalmist, whose life had been lived in constant trust in God. **strong refuge:** The Lord is the only source of continual protection for the psalmist.

71:4 The Hebrew root of **deliver me** means "to cause to escape" (17:13; 37:40; 144:2). After asking for deliverance, the psalmist reasserts his strong faith in God, calling Him

his **hope** and his **trust,** the One who has sustained him from his birth (22:10).

71:5–7 a wonder: The psalmist declares that the work of God in his life has made him a special sign to the people, similar to the great miracles of God through Moses and Aaron in Egypt (Ex. 7:3; 11:9).

71:8–11 The psalmist uses familiar images in the psalms of lament (Ps. 13) to encourage God to respond to his need. **in the time of old age:** The psalmist has trusted in God his entire life (v. 6); it would be sad if he were dismissed by the Lord late in life (v. 18). Not only was the psalmist's own life and comfort at stake, but so was the reputation of God. If the enemies concluded that **God has forsaken him,** then the reputation of the Lord would be tarnished in the world.

71:12, 13 do not be far: These words evoke the language of 22:1, 19. **confounded:** The language of this verse is imprecatory (Ps. 137); the psalmist calls for justice and vengeance against his enemies, for they are in fact enemies of the living God (v. 24).

71:14–16 I will hope: The Hebrew text has an emphatic pronoun meaning "as for me," bringing determination to the psalmist's words. The Hebrew verb translated *hope* describes a confident expectation that God will intervene and deliver (147:11).

71:17, 18 youth … old and grayheaded: The psalmist has trusted in God all his life. In his old age, he faces a crisis. He fully expects that God in His righteousness (vv. 2, 15, 16, 19, 24) will respond favorably to his request to deliver him and preserve him from shame (v. 1).

71:19, 20 The psalmist speaks of the **great things** that God had done, for which He is worthy of praise. He also speaks of the **great and severe troubles** that he has experienced at God's hand, and from which he seeks relief. **Depths of the earth** is a metaphor for the psalmist's despondency (40:2); he feels as though he has already dropped headlong into a pit.

71:21–23 The poem concludes with a bold vow of praise, in confident expectation that the psalmist's prayer will be answered. The psalmist praises God with **the lute,** but also with his **lips.** At the same time, his inner being, his **soul,** is filled with praises to the living God.

71:24 brought to shame: The psalm comes full circle with the word *shame.* The psalmist begins by asking the Lord to prevent him from becoming shamed (v. 1), and he ends the poem with a declaration that the wicked have been shamed. The Lord has answered his prayer; He has protected His righteous servant.

Psalm 72, a royal psalm, is one of two psalms (see also Ps. 127) ascribed to Solomon, the son of David. King Solomon might have arranged David's psalms in something like their present order, then appended his own psalm to the group (see v. 20). This psalm is intensely messianic, speaking in ideal terms of the coming of the great King. On the basis of the ideals of ancient Middle Eastern royalty, the psalm calls for a good king to govern Israel under God's blessing. Ultimately this King is the Savior Jesus.

72:1–7 Fear You is an expression of wonder, awe, reverence, worship, and obedience. **He shall come down:** The great King is pictured as the gentle rains of God's blessing on the earth. His reign will lead to true **peace,** the state of things as they really ought to be.

72:8–12 The promises of God to Abraham included a promise that his descendants would have **dominion** over the land of Canaan (Gen. 15:18–21). These verses expand the geographical dimensions to include the entire earth. **The River** refers to the Euphrates—a distant, significant waterway that many Israelites hoped would become the extent of their kingdom. The glorious coming King will have the river as a *near* border; His territory will extend **to the ends of the earth.** No one will escape the power of His reign. **Tarshish** and **Sheba** were the most distant places known to the Israelites; they suggest distances beyond Solomon's imagination.

72:13, 14 This section emphasizes the work of the King on behalf of the **poor** and **needy. precious shall be their blood:** The blood shed by the needy points to the blood the Savior shed on the Cross (see Heb. 12:24).

72:15–17 The promise of life in the words **He shall live** is a messianic theme (16:10,

11; 91:16; 118:17, 18), for the coming Savior is the only One who grants true life (John 11:25). The **name** of the great King will be regarded as the greatest name in the universe.

72:18, 19 The repetition of the word **blessed,** the focus on the **name** (as in 89:16), and the double **Amen** all indicate that this psalm was used in the worship of God in His temple.

72:20 The prayers of David: The superscription of Ps. 72 attributes the psalm to Solomon. It is possible that Solomon wrote this poem in honor of his father David at the end of an early edition of the psalms so far collected. Other psalms were added later to this original collection.

Psalm 73 is a psalm of trust with some features of the wisdom psalms. The psalm is unusual in that it tells a story about the psalmist's struggle with envy, doubts, and his faith in God. But through his struggles, the psalmist Asaph learned to trust in God.

73:1–4 In the opening verses Asaph describes the crisis of faith he experienced. He begins with one of the basic elements of biblical theology, that **God is good to Israel** (100:5; 106:1; 107:1). But then he confesses that he almost **stumbled** when he became **envious** of the success and wealth of the **wicked.**

73:5, 6 Asaph observes that the attitudes and actions of the wicked seem to place no constraints upon them. They appear not to have **trouble.** Their **pride** and **violence** are not hidden but are displayed like jewelry. They fulfill their lustful appetites and boast about their wicked accomplishments.

73:7–12 Asaph describes the apathy about God characteristic of the wicked, who had concluded that God—if there was a God—was disengaged from people's lives. Asaph is bothered by the fact that with this aberrant view of life the wicked are still able to enjoy life, drink their fill, and live **at ease.** Thus the psalmist feels that his own acts of righteous living are without meaning or purpose.

73:13–18 untrue: Asaph realizes that if he continued on this path, he would be abandoning the faith. He finds the issue **painful** to consider until he comes to a new sense of enlightenment in **the sanctuary,** the temple in Jerusalem. He rediscovered something he probably knew but had not really considered: the prosperity of the wicked will not last.

73:19 Asaph remembers that the wicked are just a step away from disaster. **In a moment** they could find all of their wealth valueless and their pleasure vanished as they face an eternity separated from the presence of their Creator.

73:20–24 Asaph **was grieved** because of his own lapse of faith (vv. 1–3). In the manner of a wisdom psalm, he speaks of his own foolishness. **like a beast:** An animal has no sense of eternity and a divine perspective. The psalmist was making an animal-like decision when he began to wonder about the wicked (vv. 1–3). But God had never left him, even when he struggled with doubts. **And afterward:** What helped the psalmist gain a proper perspective on this life was the afterlife. The righteous will have the glorious privilege of living with God forever.

73:25–28 The contrast between the words **shall perish** and **draw near to God** explains the heart of the psalm. There are those who may enjoy great wealth and notoriety today, but nothing they have or do will last forever. Therefore, Asaph concludes he has **put** his **trust in the Lord GOD.**

Psalm 74 is a lament psalm of the community (as is Ps. 80) and a powerful presentation of Hebrew poetry at its best. The poem describes God's actions in the past and the desire of His people for Him to act in the present. This is one of eleven psalms attributed to Asaph (Ps. 50; 73—83).

74:1, 2 O God, why is a classic lament in the Psalms (13:1). The invasion of a foreign power into Judah and Jerusalem had devastated the people. The foreign invader was viewed as an expression of the **anger** of the Lord. The principal call of the psalm is for the Lord to **remember** His people and the foolish ridicule of their enemies (vv. 18, 22). In his appeal to God the psalmist uses a series of endearing terms to describe the people of God: **the sheep of** Your pasture, Your congregation, the tribe of Your inheritance, and **this Mount Zion.**

The psalmist also focuses on the loving actions of God for His people in the past. In the context of God's past faithfulness to the people He has chosen, the psalmist calls upon God to deliver His people in their time of need (vv. 20, 22).

74:3–10 Lift up Your feet is a call for God "to get up and walk" to see what is going on. The worst part of the enemy invasion was the desecration of the temple in Jerusalem.

74:11 The psalmist calls on God to fight against the enemy, to extend His **right hand** to protect and deliver the people as He had during the Exodus (63:8; see also Ex. 15:6).

74:12 The Lord is **King** by virtue of His creation of the earth (Ps. 93). He is King because of His special relationship with Israel (44:4; 99:1–3). And He is the coming King who will reign over all (96:13; 97:1–6; 98:6–9). **from of old:** The psalmist recalls the ancient victories of the Lord over the dark forces in a poetic recasting of the events of creation.

74:13 the sea ... the heads of the sea serpents: In Canaanite mythology, the sea and its serpents joined together as enemies of Baal. Supposedly Baal was victorious over these enemies and subsequently became king. The psalmists of the Bible use the language of Canaanite myth to describe the victories of God in the formation of the earth, in the deliverance of His people from Egypt, and in future battles (77:16–20; 93:1–5; Is. 27:1; 51:9, 10).

74:14 One of the enemies of Baal was the sea monster Lotan. In Hebrew literature this figure became the **Leviathan.** The name speaks poetically of various evil forces over which God has ultimate control and victory. Eventually the Leviathan became a symbol for Satan (Is. 27:1) who is "the dragon, that serpent of old" (Rev. 20:2).

74:15 the fountain: The Lord gave water to the people of Israel in the wilderness (Ex. 17:5, 6; Num. 20:8–13). **mighty rivers:** He also enabled His people to cross over the Red Sea (Ex. 14) and the River Jordan (Josh. 3).

74:16, 17 In His great works of creation (Gen. 1) God established His rule over **day, night, light,** and **the sun.** In addition, He established the seasons and set **borders, a**

reference to the limitations He placed on the waters (Prov. 8:27–29).

74:18–21 Three times in this poem the psalmist calls upon God to **remember** (vv. 2, 22). In addition to appealing to the honor of God's **name** (v. 10), the psalmist uses endearing terms for God's people who are in distress: **Your turtledove, Your poor, the oppressed,** and **the poor and needy.** These were the people with whom the Lord Himself had chosen to make a **covenant.**

74:22, 23 The phrase **plead Your own cause** refers to a legal complaint and is often used by the prophets in contexts of impending judgment on Israel (Mic. 6:1). For the third time in this poem (vv. 2, 18), God is asked to **remember** His stake in Israel and His need to defend His own reputation against **foolish** people.

Psalm 75 a grand psalm of praise (Ps. 100), contains a lively interchange between the people, the psalmist, and the Lord.

75:1 Thanks indicates public acknowledgment of God. **Your wondrous works** speaks of the actions only God can perform, those that instill a sense of awe on the part of His people.

75:2 When I choose the proper time: God will not be rushed—not even by His people.

75:3 The earth ... dissolved: In times of great stress, it may seem that the world is falling apart (60:2). God's response is **I set up its pillars firmly.** God has not abandoned His people, nor has He given up His authority.

75:4, 5 On the basis of God's determination to wait until the "proper time" (v. 2), there are strong warnings to **boastful** and **wicked** people who misinterpret God's delay and think there will be no judgment. **The horn** is an ancient symbol of strength. The wicked strut around like powerful animals, brandishing symbols of power with no thought of God. But the power of the wicked is feeble compared to the strength of the Almighty (v. 10).

75:6, 7 The words **God is the Judge** establish the fact that He is the true ruler of the universe (50:6; 58:11). **He puts down ... exalts:** As Daniel declares in his prayer (Dan. 2:20–22), God is sovereign in the world's affairs.

75:8, 9 This is not a cup of blessing, but of the Lord's wrath. The biblical image of **wine** and judgment goes back to Jacob's blessing on Judah (Gen. 49:11) and is referred to in Christ's judgment as depicted in Rev. 19:13–15.

75:10 The psalm concludes with the words of God. Here God depicts the contrasting fates of the **wicked** and the **righteous. horn:** The wicked have proudly lifted up their horn (vv. 4, 5) by boasting in their strength. The Lord will take away the very strength in which they have boasted.

Psalm 76 is a psalm of praise with a strong focus on the fear of God.

76:1–3 The word translated **tabernacle** is literally a "lair," like that of a great lion. **Salem** is the shortened form of the name Jerusalem.

76:4–6 more glorious and excellent: Nothing in all the universe or in all eternity can be compared with God (77:13). His glory and beauty are unsurpassed and His power is unassailable.

76:7 The repetition of pronouns **You, Yourself** is for emphasis: Only the Almighty is **to be feared.** For the righteous, the fear of God is a response of awe, wonder, adoration, and worship. For the wicked, the fear of God is terror, for there is no escape from Him (14:5).

76:8–10 judgment to be heard: In God's victories over the enemies of His people, word of God's glory and justice would spread to the entire world. Even the **wrath of men** will praise God because any anger against God is utterly futile.

76:11, 12 The psalmist instructs the righteous in the true worship of the sovereign Lord of creation. **Make vows:** These are vows of praise, sacrifice, and faithful living (61:5, 8; 66:13; Heb. 13:15). As one might **bring presents** to a king (72:10), so the righteous should bring their gifts to God—the ultimate gift being the dedication of their lives to the service of God (Rom. 12:1).

Psalm 77 is a psalm of a troubled believer. It is marked by a sense of inward trouble and reflection. Key terms in the psalm are the verbs "to remember" and "to meditate."

77:1, 2 stretched out: Asaph was in such need that he held his **hand** out before the Lord throughout the **night** (63:4; 134:1, 2).

All the while, he groaned and complained as he remembered God. What he knew of God contrasted with what he was experiencing. The more the psalmist thought about these things, the more troubled he became.

77:3–6 You hold my eyelids open: Asaph could not sleep (63:6). Through the night he thought about his situation and his past (vv. 4–6), but most importantly he turned to God. First he cries out to the Lord in anguish (vv. 7–9). But then his focus changes; he reminds himself of the power of God and all the miraculous things the Lord has done (vv. 10–20).

77:7–9 Wondering if God is finished with him, Asaph asks if the Lord will ever show mercy to him again. Each of the verses presents painful questions; perhaps none as difficult as the one in v. 9: **Has God forgotten to be gracious?** Asaph was at the depths of despair.

77:10–13 I will remember the works of the LORD: Asaph made a conscious decision to turn from his pain and focus his thoughts on the person, works, and wonders of God. His first focus is on the incomparability of God. **Who is so great a God as our God?** With this question Asaph reminds himself that the living God cannot be compared to any other god or power.

77:14–18 Asaph now turns his thoughts to God's sovereignty over the powers of the sea, His control over the **waters** and the **depths** (74:12–15; 93:1–5). Moreover, the Almighty controls the **skies,** for a storm as depicted in these verses is just a response to His strength. **Your arrows** is a poetic description of lightning.

77:19 This verse presents images of God as the Lord of the storm (vv. 16–18) and the sea, walking on the waters. The term **great waters** may be rephrased "many waters" (18:16; 32:6; 144:7). The point is that the waters are no threat to God, for they are just another pathway for Him to walk.

77:20 God is Lord of His people. He is the Shepherd who leads His **flock,** as He has done from the time of **Moses and Aaron.** Lost in contemplation of the greatness of God, the psalmist seems thoroughly distracted from his pain. He does not mention it again, not daring

to compare it to the greatness of the Almighty.

Psalm 78, a wisdom psalm, relates the early history of Israel in a dramatic poetic alternation between reports of the faithfulness of God to His people and of their periodic outbreaks of stubbornness, willfulness, and rebellion against Him. Asaph expresses an intense desire that the present generation not repeat the failures of so many past generations.

78:1, 2 The psalmist uses the vocabulary of the wisdom school to establish himself. **My law** is the familiar word *Torah.* The wisdom writers use this word to connote insight; their instruction is always in accord with the "instruction" of Moses (Prov. 1:8; 3:1; 4:2). The terms **parable** and **dark sayings** or riddles indicate sayings with "deeper meanings" or "teachings with a point" (Prov. 1:6). With the words **my people** the psalmist shows himself to be one with them even though he stands over them as their teacher.

78:3, 4 Asaph explains that the teaching was designed to be passed from one generation to the next, so that each generation would contribute to **the praises of the LORD.** The phrase **His strength and His wonderful works** means "His extraordinarily wonderful works."

78:5, 6 The **testimony** God **established** was a lasting procedure, a means whereby one generation would pass on to the next the need to know the Lord.

78:7, 8 Because **their fathers** did not believe in God, the present generation needs to be different from their predecessors.

78:9 Asaph's first illustration of the faithlessness of previous generations is taken from an incident in which the people of **Ephraim** rejected God. The psalmist may be referring to Ephraim's conflict with Jephthah (Judg. 12:1–7).

78:10–16 The psalmist celebrates the **marvelous things** God did for Israel in delivering them from Egypt, especially at the crossing of the Red Sea (Ex. 14), the signs of God's presence with His people (Ex. 13:21), and the bringing of water from the rock in the wilderness (Ex. 17:1–7; Num. 20:1–13).

78:17, 18 The Hebrew word translated **rebelling** here is translated *provoked* in two other places in this poem (vv. 40, 56). **food of their fancy:** This derisive language is used to describe the outrageous ungratefulness of the Israelites as they clamored for food and water in the wilderness.

78:19–28 God's **anger** against His people centered on their lack of faith and **trust** in Him, evidenced by their contempt for the manna He gave them. The psalmist refers to God's manna as the **bread of heaven** and **angels' food.** The Israelites audaciously rejected the food of angels.

78:29–31 For He gave them their own desire: People of true faith will seek God's will and respond in grateful praise. Self-centered people will simply complain and suffer the result.

78:32, 33 In spite of this: The psalmist says that the people had suffered enough from their ingratitude to have learned the lesson of faith. Unfortunately, they had *not* learned. So God determined that they would not enter the land of Canaan but would spend their days **in futility.**

78:34–37 The people tended to remember the true character of God only when pressed to do so by His judgments; but God always **remembered** (v. 39) the frail nature of the people. The image of God as a **rock** is found in Moses (Deut. 32:4) and is developed elsewhere in the Psalms (61:2; 62:2, 7; 91:1, 2; 144:1). God as **Redeemer** is the Savior, who rescued Israel from Egypt just as He also delivered them from their sins (19:14; Is. 41:14; 44:6). The title **Most High God** emphasizes the majesty and power of God. God surpasses all powers, all creation, and nothing can be compared to Him.

78:38 full of compassion: The awesome transcendence of the Lord is complemented in this section (v. 35) by an emphasis on His compassionate mercy.

78:39–42 The verb translated **provoked** here is used three times in this psalm (*rebelling* in v. 17; see also v. 56). Even though God had showered blessings on His people, they provoked Him with their contempt and ingratitude.

78:43–55 This section is a poetic retelling of the way God helped Israel in Egypt during the wilderness years. Verses 43–51 recount

the ten plagues of Ex. 7–12, and vv. 52, 53 speak of the deliverance of Israel at the Red Sea (Ex. 14). Verse 54 speaks of the experience at Mount Sinai, and v. 55 summarizes the conquest of the land of Canaan.

78:56 Tested and provoked may be rephrased "thoroughly provoked." The title **Most High** is used three times in this poem (vv. 17, 35), as is the Hebrew word for *provoked* (vv. 17, 40). The two words emphasize the seriousness of the Israelites' action; they were rebelling against their Creator, the Ruler of the entire universe.

78:57–67 High places refers to the places where the Canaanites worshiped Baal and other fertility gods. **Carved images** were fertility symbols from Canaanite cults. The reference to **Shiloh** places this period of Israel's apostasy in the latter period of the judges (1 Sam. 1:3). **His strength** and **His glory** are unusual ways of speaking of the ark of the covenant, which was lost to the Philistines during the battle of Aphek (1 Sam. 4:1–11).

78:68–71 The choice of **Judah** over the other tribes and of **Zion** over other cities is explained only in terms of God's sovereignty and love. The description of the **sanctuary** suggests that this psalm was written after Solomon's temple was built.

78:72 The words of praise for **David** in v. 72 are very close to 1 Kin. 9:4, suggesting some connection between the two passages. The shepherding attributed to David is an ideal; it will be fully realized in the Savior King, Jesus, the true Good Shepherd (Ps. 23; John 10).

Psalm 79, a lament of the community (see Ps. 80), was written in response to an attack on the city of Jerusalem and the sacking of the holy temple. In these respects this psalm is similar to Ps. 74. The event behind the psalm may have been the destruction of Jerusalem by the Babylonians.

79:1 Your holy temple: It is not clear whether the destruction described in this verse was what the Babylonians did in 586 B.C. The ruin of Jerusalem—it was **in heaps**—may indicate an invasion of the land prior to its total destruction.

79:2–4 The lament over the dead defenders of Jerusalem is similar to the words of Jer. 7:32–34; Lam. 4:1–10.

79:5 The question **how long** is a standard element in the lament psalms (13:1, 2; 80:4). The question is based on the Lord's eternal character. Since God is eternal, Asaph asks, will He be **angry forever?**

79:6, 7 Pour out Your wrath: An imprecation or curse on one's enemies is often found in the psalms of lament (Ps. 137). Vengeance is left to the Lord, but such a call for vengeance is based in part on the covenant provisions God had established with Abraham. God had promised to curse those who cursed Abraham's descendants (Gen. 12:2, 3).

79:8–10 The appeal is based on the character of God as expressed by His name (Ex. 3:14, 15; 6:2, 3). Another basis for the psalmist's appeal is the international reputation of God (42:10). If God delivered the Israelites, His power would be demonstrated to all the nations.

79:11, 12 Groaning may also be translated *crying.* **Your power** refers to the powerful, outstretched arm of God that had delivered Israel from Egypt (Ex. 6:6). **Reproach** refers to an insult or taunt (74:10, 18, 22).

79:13 Sheep: God's care for the Israelites was so great that they were called His sheep (77:20; 95:7; 100:3). The people vowed to bring **thanks,** or public acknowledgment (35:18; 105:1), and **praise** to God.

Psalm 80, a lament of the community, has especially powerful imagery. The psalm is marked by two metaphors for Israel in its relation to God: (1) the flock of the Good Shepherd; (2) the vine of the True Vinedresser. Both of these metaphors are used by Jesus of His people in the New Testament (John 10; 15). This is one of Asaph's psalms (Ps. 50; 73—83) and is set to the tune "The Lilies" (Ps. 45; 69).

80:1, 2 O Shepherd of Israel is reminiscent of the teaching of Ps. 23 and points forward to the teaching of John 10. God's pattern is to **lead** His people as a shepherd might lead **a flock. between the cherubim:** In the Most Holy Place, the ark of the covenant was topped by the mercy seat on which were two cherubim, heavenly symbols of the throne of God (Ex. 25:22). **shine forth:** After Moses had been in close proximity to

the Lord, his own face was transformed by a resplendent glow (Ex. 34:29–35). Here the appeal means that the Lord should make His presence known in a saving manner.

80:3 Cause Your face to shine is reminiscent of the priestly benediction, "The Lord make His face shine upon you" (Num. 6:25).

80:4, 5 Since their request for deliverance has seemed to go unanswered, the people ask whether God's anger is directed even **against their prayer.** The phrases **bread of tears** and **tears to drink** refer to the manna and water that God provided for Israel in the wilderness. God had given the people of past generations nourishing food; but the people of this generation have only their tearful despair.

80:6–11 God's bringing the Israelites from **Egypt** to Canaan is compared to transplanting **a vine.** The vine grew rapidly, so that it **filled the land** and reached to the Mediterranean **Sea** and the Euphrates **River.** These expansions of the Lord's vine occurred during the reigns of David and Solomon.

80:12 But then there came a dramatic change. The Lord broke **down her hedges**—that is, He removed Israel's protective walls. Israel became weak, subject to all kinds of assaults.

80:13–17 Look down from heaven: The appeal is for the heavenly Vinedresser to observe the sorry state of His vine. The Hebrew word translated **visit** can describe a gracious visit of the Lord (65:9) or a visit in judgment. Of course, the prayer offered is for a merciful visit from Israel's Protector. The appeal is for God to use His **right hand** (Ex. 15:6) to restore what He had **planted.**

80:18–19 Revive us is a call for new life from God's Spirit. **We will call upon Your name:** In response to God's work of deliverance, the psalmist promises renewed praise centered on the *name* of God.

Psalm 81 begins as a psalm of praise and becomes a psalm of admonition (Ps. 50), in which the voice of the Lord Himself is heard (Ps. 75).

81:1 Sing aloud ... Make a joyful shout: The energy level of this psalm is similar to that of other psalms of praise. The use of voices and instruments to praise God is a standard element of joyful worship in the Psalms (Ps. 149; 150).

81:2–5 The **New Moon** festival is mentioned in association with the Feast of Trumpets (Num. 29:6). Regulations for this festival can be found in the instructions to the Levites during the time of David (1 Chr. 23:31) and Solomon (2 Chr. 2:4). This psalm seems to be a basic instruction on the festival.

81:6, 7 his shoulder ... His hands: This is a poetic way of describing how God delivered His people from the Egyptian taskmasters (Ex. 1). **I answered you:** The Lord's appearance to Moses on Mount Sinai was God's great revelation of Himself (Ex. 19; 20).

81:8–10 The phrase translated **I will admonish you** is also found in 50:7, where it is translated "I will testify against you." The basic stipulation of the first commandment is repeated: there must be **no foreign god** among the Israelites (Ex. 20:3).

81:11–16 The people's resistance to obeying God led to their punishment. God identifies the root of the people's problem as **their own stubborn heart.** They wanted to follow their own ways and refused to listen to God.

Psalm 82 is a wisdom psalm.

82:1, 2 The congregation of the mighty refers to an assembly before God. As a wisdom writer, the psalmist Asaph uses the language of Job 1, Ps. 110, and Is. 6 as a teaching device to present a morality tale. Asaph describes the wicked judges of all time gathering before God and His angels to give an accounting of themselves. **Gods:** The Hebrew word may refer to the true God or to false gods. Here it is the judges of the earth (see also v. 6). Asaph uses this honorific term sarcastically to express his contempt for the evil judges.

82:3 do justice: God expects all judges to administer true justice. His basic desire was that the defenseless would find a haven of justice in the courts.

82:4, 5 They do not know is the collective sigh of oppressed people of all ages. Wicked judges act as if they did not care about their official responsibility or the judgment they will face for abusing it. **All the foundations of the earth are unstable:** In 11:3, the taunt of the wicked is that the earth's foundations are destroyed. This is said to be untrue, for God is

still in control. In this psalm, however, the situation *is* deemed unstable because of the profound wickedness of the judges.

82:6, 7 die like men: Jesus quoted these verses in His exchange with the religious authorities who wanted to stone Him for declaring Himself to be the Son of God (John 10:31–35).

82:8 Arise, O God: In view of the overwhelming disaster that wicked judges have created, the poor and afflicted of all time call out for the true Judge, God Himself to come. Their cry will not go unheeded. The righteous Judge is coming, and He will establish justice (96:13; 98:9).

Psalm 83 is a psalm of lament in which particular attention is given to the wicked. The curse that Asaph utters against the wicked puts this psalm in the category of the imprecatory psalms. When we read the strong words in this psalm, we need to keep in mind that the intent of the psalmist Asaph is to vindicate the glory of God.

83:1 Do not keep silent: Calls for God to awaken, to rouse Himself, to turn and look, and to speak, are all ways the psalmists prayed for God to act. They believed that God as the Holy One would root out all evil. What they did not always recognize was that God's delay in judgment was an expression of His mercy.

83:2, 3 Asaph feels revulsion against the **enemies** of the Lord. He hates what God hates (101:6–8). The attacks of the wicked are not only against God, but also against the **people** of God.

82:4 let us cut them off: God's attitude toward those who plot the destruction of His people is clear: His curse will rest on them (Gen. 12:2, 3).

83:5–8 consulted together: Throughout history, many nations have conspired to bring about the ruin of Israel and Judah. All such endeavors are condemned in this psalm. **against You:** In conspiring against the people of God, the wicked actually resist God Himself. **The tents of Edom:** The place names in this passage refer to nations on the borders of Israel and Judah. The **Hagrites** may have come from Arabia (1 Chr. 5:10, 19, 20). The people of **Gebal** may have lived in a mountainous region south of the Dead Sea; alternatively, Gebal may have been another name for Byblos, a city near Tyre.

83:9–12 Asaph recites God's great victories against the formidable foes of Israel. God's victory at **Midian** was accomplished through Gideon (Judg. 7). God's victory over **Sisera** was accomplished through Deborah and Barak (Judg. 4; 5). The same God who had battled Israel's enemies in the past would fight all those who might oppose His people in the future.

83:13–15 In a culture in which remembering a person was very important, an ultimate curse would have been to regard a person's memory as **whirling dust** or windblown **chaff.**

83:16–18 seek Your name: Asaph's first call for God to shame Israel's enemies is redemptive—that the nations might hear, feel shame, repent, and seek the face of the Lord. Yet if they continued in their wicked path, they would face further confounding and would one day face God in judgment.

Psalm 84 is one of the psalms of Zion. These psalms celebrate God's presence in Jerusalem, the city where His temple was built. This psalm was composed by the sons of Korah (see Ps. 42; 44—49; 85; 87; 88).

84:1, 2 Tabernacle is used here as a poetic term for the temple that was built by Solomon. **the living God:** All other "gods" are nonentities; but He who created the universe, who chose Israel as His people, and who provided salvation for the world lives forever in great glory.

84:3, 4 sparrow … swallow: By describing the approach of birds to the courtyards of the temple, the psalmist expresses his own great joy.

84:5–7 The phrase **whose heart is set on pilgrimage** refers to those who make their way to the temple not out of obligation, but out of a wellspring of joy. **The Valley of Baca,** or "Valley of Weeping," refers to the various difficulties that one might face on a pilgrimage. The person on a pilgrimage might discover that the once-dark valley is filled with springs, **rain,** and **pools**—all signs of God's blessing. **strength to strength:** As

one nears the temple, the rigors of the journey become tolerable, for the joy of the approaching arrival strengthens the soul.

84:8 LORD God of hosts, literally the "God of armies," speaks of God's transcendence. The *hosts* are the angelic armies of the heavens. This title is balanced by the phrase **God of Jacob,** referring to the covenant relationship God established with the patriarchs of Israel.

84:9 The two phrases **our shield** and **Your anointed** both point to the same person, the king of Israel (see 89:3, 4). Each person who was anointed in the Old Testament foreshadowed the coming Anointed One, the Messiah.

84:10–12 a day … a thousand: Nothing in the pilgrim's daily experience can be compared to a day spent in the worship of God in the holy temple. **a doorkeeper … dwell in the tents:** The role of a menial servant in the **house of** his **God** is more desirable than a life of luxury with those who practice **wickedness. No good thing will He withhold:** This is the observation of a wise and righteous person; time after time, God gives good gifts to His people.

Psalm 85 is a prayer for restoration that is rooted deeply in trust in God. The setting for the psalm appears to be the restoration of the people of God following a great catastrophe—perhaps the Babylonian captivity. With this psalm, the people prayed for a revival of their spirits and a renewal in their land. The ultimate fulfillment of their prayer would be in the coming glorious kingdom of the Savior Jesus. This is one of the psalms composed by the sons of Korah (see Ps. 42; 44—49; 84; 87; 88).

85:1 You have brought back the captivity may refer to the return of the exiles from Babylon. But it also may be a more general reversal of fortune (14:7).

85:2–7 God of our salvation may be rephrased as "our Saving God." **Your anger:** The first section of this psalm already says God's anger has turned away from the people (v. 3). Yet until the restoration is complete, the people still feel the effects of God's wrath. This suggests an understanding that the people's troubles were because of their own sin disciplined by God. **revive us:** The people prayed for their own welfare and for renewed ability to praise God.

85:8, 9 The speaker here may be a priest expecting to **hear** a direct revelation from the Lord. Such a revelation would be consistent with God's character. **Peace** suggests wholeness, fullness, things as they ought to be. The word **saints** is related to the term translated *mercy* in v. 7; these are people who reflect the love of God in their own lives. **not turn back to folly:** God's blessing would continue only as long as the people remained faithful to Him.

85:10–13 mercy and truth ... righteousness and peace: The union of God's mercy and truth and His righteousness and peace describes the way things ought to be, or the state of *peace* spoken of in v. 8. The blending of the ideals of **truth** and **righteousness** in v. 11 suggests a vision of the kingdom of God (see Is. 11).

Psalm 86 is a psalm of lament in which David expresses grave concerns about his lowly state, as well as joy in the God who alone is merciful.

86:1–5 Bow down Your ear: As in 31:2, David uses a dramatic phrase that captures the grandeur of God on high and David's humble position on the earth below. The phrase **I am holy** speaks of the faithfulness and godliness of a righteous person who, by God's grace, is living in accordance with God's law. It is another way that David describes himself as a **servant** of the Lord.

86:6–9 Among the gods: The ancient nations took their sense of identity in part from their ties to their supposed gods. When the nations found out that their "gods" did not exist, they would have to acknowledge that the Lord alone is God. Here David envisions other nations worshiping the true God and thus anticipates the missionary thrust of the New Testament (Ps. 117; Matt. 28:18–20).

86:10–13 Teach me Your way: David asks the Lord to teach him so that he will be able to praise God in the midst of the congregation. **Mercy** is the "loyal love" of the Lord. **depths of Sheol:** David describes the Lord as mercifully delivering him from certain death (9:17; 116:3, 4).

86:14 The Psalms consistently describe God as the enemy of **the proud** and the friend of the humble (138:6; 147:6).

86:15 The phrase **abundant in mercy and truth** is a precursor of the New Testament phrase "full of grace and truth" (John 1:14). The Lord upholds the truth so that He can mercifully free those caught in falsehoods.

86:16, 17 save the son of Your maidservant: The idea here may be that since David's mother was a pious woman, the Lord ought to save David from his lowly state (116:16).

Psalm 87, a psalm of Zion, is also an intensely evangelistic psalm that anticipates the New Testament mission to present the gospel to the entire world (see Matt. 28:18–20). This psalm is one of the collection from the sons of Korah (Ps. 42; 44—49; 84; 85; 88).

87:1 His foundation: God Himself established Zion or Jerusalem as the center of true worship. He ordained Solomon to build a temple there so that He could live among the Israelites (1 Kin. 6:13). Zion is holy because of God's declaration (1 Kin. 11:13), His promise, the worship given Him there (1 Kin. 8:14–66), the future work of the Savior there (Matt. 21:4–11), and the future rule of the King there (Rev. 21).

87:2, 3 God has a special love for the place where His name is worshiped. **The gates of Zion** are the conspicuous entrance to the city. The verb **loves** includes the idea of choice (see Deut. 6:5) as well as emotion. God chose Jerusalem; and He also has an enduring affection for the city.

87:4 I will make mention: In this verse, God Himself speaks. **Rahab** is a symbolic name for Egypt (Is. 30:7) that has negative connotations. It alludes to the arrogance of the Egyptians. **Babylon** was the proverbial seat of apostasy and idolatry (Gen. 10:10). **To those who know Me** may be rephrased "*as* those who know Me." Thus the verse anticipates a time when foreigners would know and worship the living God.

87:5 And of Zion: Despite their foreign heritage, the people who worshiped God were considered as having been **born in** Zion. Thus this psalm anticipates the New Testament teaching of the second birth (John 3). The title **Most High** is used particularly with reference to God's power over the nations (47:2; 78:35; 82:6). **shall establish her:** Zion would become the place where people from other nations would come to worship the living God. This is prophetic of the coming of the gospel of Jesus, the spread of that gospel, and the culmination of the gospel in the rule of the Savior King (Is. 2:1–4).

87:6 The LORD will record pictures God making a register of the people of the nations. All believers will find their true identity in the Lord.

87:7 The singers and the players are called to celebrate together the joy of the Savior God. The image of **springs** indicates salvation, which is found only in the Lord (Is. 12:3). This anticipated the salvation that God would offer through Jesus Christ (Titus 2:11).

Psalm 88 begins as a psalm of lament but never comes to the resolution of trust and praise that is the hallmark of those psalms. Thus Ps. 88 can be considered a psalm of complaint. The title ascribes the psalm to Heman the Ezrahite. Heman is identified in 1 Kin. 4:31 as a gifted wise man, and in 1 Chr. 15:16–19 as one of the musically gifted Levites who ministered in worship during the time of David. The name of the tune perhaps means "A Dance of Affliction."

88:1, 2 Even in the midst of despair, Heman confesses his faith in God's saving goodness—**O LORD, God of my salvation** (vv. 9, 13). **cried out … my cry:** This language of desperate weeping is not unusual in the psalms of lament. The Hebrew word for *cried* indicates a loud scream.

88:3–5 Grave here is the familiar word Sheol (86:13), which is often linked with the term **pit** as a symbol of death (30:3; 143:7; Prov. 1:12; Is. 14:15; 38:18). Heman feels so near to death that he describes himself as **adrift among the dead.**

88:6–8 Heman feels as though he were in **the lowest pit** and the deepest darkness. His most vexing problem, however, is his belief that God has brought this trouble on him. **put away … from me:** Not only does he feel troubled by God; he is also alone, separated from all of his friends.

88:9 Verses 9 and 13 are a reprise of v. 1. Heman continues to pray. Even though his eyes are strained and bloodshot from constant weeping, he continues to call out to the Lord for salvation.

88:10–16 The context of these verses is the worshiping community in Jerusalem (Ps. 6). If God allows Heman to die, Heman's voice will never again be heard in the temple giving praise to God.

88:17, 18 Loved one: In v. 8, Heman describes himself as removed from his friends; now he says his friends are removed from him. At the close of the psalm, Heman still feels alone, even though the psalms consistently describe a Lord who hears and answers those who call on Him (see 28:6).

Psalm 89 begins as a psalm of praise but ends as a psalm of lament. It celebrates God's covenant with David (2 Sam. 7) and then laments how David's descendants had not remained faithful to the provisions of that covenant (see 2 Sam. 7:14). Yet even in the face of unfaithfulness, this psalm reaffirms God's faithfulness to His covenant and its ultimate fulfillment in David's greater Son, the Messiah (vv. 33–37). The title attributes the psalm to Ethan, who was also known as Jeduthun (1 Chr. 25:1, 3, 6).

89:1, 2 The **mercies** of the Lord in this psalm center on the covenant He made with David, promising him an eternal dynasty (see 2 Sam. 7). **Mercy,** which may be translated "loyal love," refers to the exact words of God's promise to David (2 Sam. 7:15). The Lord had promised that His mercy would always rest on David's son.

89:3, 4 Ethan quoted God's words to David in 2 Sam. 7. David is referred to as **My chosen** and **My servant** (v. 20)—names that describe his intimate relationship with the Lord (see 2 Sam. 7:7). **Your seed … your throne:** God had promised David a line of descent and an enduring throne (2 Sam. 7:12, 13).

89:5, 6 All praise in heaven and earth belongs to God, who is incomparable. No one, not even the supposed gods, can match His strength and love. This is the point of the question, **Who in the heavens can be compared to the LORD?**

89:7–10 Rahab is a title for Egypt (87:4). **The sea** and Rahab refer to God's great victories: in the beginning, His control of His creation; in the historic past, His victory over Egypt; and in the future, His complete triumph over Satan, sin, and death (Is. 27:1; 51:9). The psalmists regularly assert God's complete control of creation (see 24:1).

89:11–14 God is the great Deliverer; He brandished His **arm** and **hand** in delivering His people from Egypt (Ex. 6:6; 15:6).

89:15–18 To exalt the **horn** of the people (75:4, 5; 92:10; 132:17) means to give them power and eventual triumph. **The Holy One of Israel** (78:41) is the title Isaiah uses to describe God, following his experience of God's holiness in his memorable vision of God's throne (Is. 6).

89:19 The psalm recounts God's remarkable intervention in the life of David and the specifics of His covenant with David. **Your holy one:** David had been singled out as holy to the Lord. Yet his beginnings were not spectacular, for he was **from the people:** he had been an ordinary shepherd (2 Sam. 7:18). In these respects, and in many others, David was a type, or a divinely intended portrait, of the Savior. In a similar way, Jesus came from humble origins as the son of a carpenter. Yet He was the Holy One, the Son of the Most High.

89:20–25 My faithfulness and My mercy: God will remain true to His word and demonstrate His love to His servant. **sea ... rivers:** The possible reference here is to Israel's expansion of its borders. But note the language used to describe God's control over creation (vv. 9, 10). The Lord is extending to His servant the authority He has over creation.

89:26–33 Father ... firstborn: This wording is derived from God's covenant with David (2 Sam. 7:14). **his sons:** The provisions of the Davidic covenant in 2 Sam. 7 included the discipline of errant sons.

89:34–38 The words **my covenant I will not break** and the wording of v. 35 assure the reader that the will of the Lord is quite settled in this matter. The people might become faithless, but God cannot deny Himself. In spite of errors, rebellions, sins, and apostasies in the lives of many of the kings of Judah, God is determined to complete, fulfill, and accomplish His grand plan for David's dynasty (2 Sam. 7:1–24).

89:39 The occasion of this psalm was probably the defeat of Israel's armies, accounting for the psalmist's strong sense of consternation before the Lord. **You have renounced the covenant of Your servant:** The military defeat that likely sparked this psalm was a temporary situation; a victory was still to come. Nonetheless, the psalmist presses his claim to God: This is the covenant that the Lord has established, that He has sworn Himself to uphold.

89:40–45 As a result of the military defeat, the people were despondent and disillusioned. The psalmist voices their feelings and thus allows the process of healing to begin, even as the people wait for their deliverance from the Lord.

89:46–51 The writer complains that God has not been keeping His promises to David (2 Sam. 7:1–24). As a result, His people are experiencing undeserved **reproach** from their enemies. There is no resolution to this psalm; it ends with the people, the king, and the psalmist in distress. Yet the inclusion of this psalm among the praises of Israel suggests that God *did* answer this prayer of His beleaguered people, just as He did in the case of Ps. 60.

89:52 This verse is an editorial addition to Ps. 89, the concluding line of praise for Book III of the Psalms.

Psalm 90 is a psalm of lament in which the community complains of God's judgment and the brevity of life. But even in the midst of sorrow, the people acknowledge the security they have in the Lord and pray for renewal. This is the only poem in the Book of Psalms attributed to Moses.

90:1, 2 Lord here is not God's personal name (Ex. 3:14, 15), but a Hebrew word celebrating His majestic authority. The word suggests a title similar to "my Supreme Master." **Dwelling place** refers to the Lord as the "refuge" of His people (71:3; 91:9).

90:3–5 Even if people lived **a thousand years,** they would pass away like **a watch in the night.** A thousand years may seem long at the time, but not in comparison to God's eternal existence.

90:6, 7 wrath: The allusion is to the anger of God against the unbelieving Israelites in the wilderness (see Num. 13; 14). An entire generation spent their lives wandering in the wilderness because of their unbelief and rebellion.

90:8–10 seventy ... eighty years: The point here is not to set a maximum, but to present a context for the brevity of human life. No matter how long people live, it is inevitable that they will **fly away** to death.

90:11, 12 These verses are the key of the psalm. Moses had experienced a sufficient measure of God's **anger** (Ex. 32; Num. 14:11–25; Deut. 3:23–28). **teach:** What Moses needed was a new understanding of the meaning of his own life. **number our days:** This is more than just having a sense of mortality; it means valuing the time we do have by using it for eternal purposes.

90:13–15 Moses uses the word **return** in v. 3 to refer to God's call for his death. Here he asks God to *return* for a renewed sense of life. **compassion ... mercy:** Moses is asking God for new meaning in his life in the days that remain.

90:16, 17 Your work ... Your glory: Moses asks God to give him a sense of lasting meaning in life, something that will continue to the next generation.

Psalm 91, a psalm of trust, does not identify its author. The psalm is sufficiently similar to Ps. 90, a psalm of Moses, that it might also be by him. Alternatively, the experiences and ideas of Moses could have been used by an anonymous writer. This poem has a very strong messianic thrust, and God Himself speaks in vv. 14–16 (see also Ps. 12; 60; 75; 87).

91:1, 2 in the secret place: The person who trusts in God is the one who lives close to Him. The title **Most High** emphasizes God's majesty (92:1) and is parallel to the term **Almighty,** a translation of the divine title Shaddai. Together the terms Most High and Shaddai speak of God as a mountain-like majesty, in whose presence there is a "secret place" or a **shadow.**

91:3 fowler ... pestilence: The images of a bird trap and various types of disease are a general description of dangers that might come to helpless people.

91:4 His feathers ... His wings: God is described as a mother hen under whose wings the psalmist can come for refuge (61:4; 63:7). **Shield and buckler** indicates complete protection from all harm. God is a protective shield for the believer.

91:5, 6 The interplay of words for **night** and **day** in these verses indicates the universal nature of God's protection. **Terror, arrow, pestilence,** and **destruction** together refer to evil in general.

91:7, 8 A thousand ... ten thousand: Like the Israelites in Egypt who were spared the danger that touched their neighbors (Ex. 9:26; 10:23; 11:7), believers in the Lord are protected from any assault. **look ... and see:** The punishment of the wicked is as sure as the deliverance of the righteous.

91:9, 10 In vv. 14–16, God describes the same person addressed by the psalmist in vv. 9–13. This person is the coming One. **Most High:** The psalmist indicates that the coming One's faith in God is the same as the psalmist's.

91:11–13 His angels ... a stone: These words were used by Satan to tempt the Savior (Matt. 4:5, 6). **the lion and the cobra:** The animal and snake imagery in this verse pictures all kinds of evil that might threaten the coming One. The Father will protect Him no matter what the danger.

91:14–16 The verb used here for **love** here has the idea of "holding close to," even "hugging tightly in love" (Deut. 7:7; 10:15). **He has known My name** speaks of an intimate, experiential knowledge of the Father (John 1:18).

Psalm 92, a psalm of descriptive praise (Ps. 113), celebrates the person and work of God in an exuberant way. The psalm also includes several wisdom themes. The title is unusual in that it attaches the designation "for the Sabbath day."

92:1–5 To give thanks means "to give public acknowledgment" or to praise God verbally in a public setting (35:18; 105:1).

92:6 A senseless man ... a fool: In contrast to the limitless wisdom of God is the shallow nature of the fool (14:1).

92:7–9 The Lord's eternality is contrasted with the brevity of the lives of His **enemies.**

Because of God's patience, He allows evil to occur (2 Pet. 3:9)—but He will not allow it to flourish forever.

92:10 My horn you have exalted (75:4, 5; 89:17, 24; 132:17) is a figure of speech for the psalmist's eventual triumph, the celebration of the psalmist's strength. **I have been anointed with fresh oil** is not just a general statement of God's interest in the psalmist, but a prediction of the coming One, the Lord's Anointed.

92:11–15 The language of this section speaks of God's continuing blessing on the believer not only in this life but also in the life to come (Ps. 23). The **tree** image recalls the words of 1:3.

Psalm 93, a royal psalm, focuses on the reign of God over the earth, making use of a distinctly Canaanite perspective. The psalmist denies Baal and shouts exuberantly in praise of God. God is King of all. To whom may He be compared (Is. 40:25)?

93:1, 2 The phrase **girded Himself with strength** describes the victor of one-on-one combat. God is dressed in the garments of victory. This is a celebration of God as the Creator. **cannot be moved:** There is no power on earth or in the universe that can wrench control of the earth from God. **from of old:** Unlike Baal, who was a recent "upstart" in the myths of Canaan, the rule of God is from antiquity. The living God is eternal.

93:3, 4 The floods: Baal was supposed to have been victorious over the waters; thus, this section of the poem is a continuing refutation of Baal worship while it joyfully celebrates the power of God. **The LORD ... is mightier:** The Creator King is infinite in power; no force in the universe competes with Him.

93:5 While this psalm uses language resembling the worship of Baal to emphasize the greatness of God (Ps. 29), it also glorifies God with praises never attributed to Baal. None of the accolades of Baal speak of his **testimonies.** But God is superior to Baal, for He is faithful to His word. He is the gracious God who speaks to His people; He is the holy God of Scripture who is approached by His people; and He is the eternal God whom we worship.

Psalm 94 is a royal psalm, since the phrase "Judge of the earth" (v. 2) is equivalent to "King" (50:4–6). The righteous call for the divine Judge to punish evil in the world (82:8; 96:13; 98:9). Psalms 93—99 are a splendid list of psalms focused on the eternal reign of God.

94:1–3 Even when the psalmists call out for divine **vengeance,** they recognize that God decides when to exercise His wrath and judgment. God's law clearly states that vengeance belongs to Him (Deut. 32:35). **How long will the wicked triumph:** This question is based on a concern for the glory of God. The answer, of course, is in God's mercy. The Lord may delay this judgment, but in His own timing He will come to establish true justice (2 Pet. 3:9).

94:4–6 The Psalms often describe the wicked in terms of their evil **speech** (Ps. 12). **They slay the widow and the stranger:** The Israelites had been commanded to comfort widows and orphans and to welcome strangers as long as those strangers obeyed the Law of God (Ex. 22:22). Thus the wicked were brazenly disobeying God's commands.

94:7–11 The command to **understand** is for fools to abandon their foolishness. Surely, the psalmist argues, the Creator of the earth is not deaf, nor is the Fashioner of the eye blind. Although idols do not have real eyes and ears (115:3–8), the God of heaven does see and hear. **The LORD knows:** The difference between the thoughts of God and the thoughts of human beings is beyond comprehension.

94:12 Blessed is the man: This beatitude uses the word with which the Book of Psalms begins, a term meaning "manifest happiness."

94:13, 14 Pit is one of the words used as a synonym for Sheol (16:10). Digging the "pit" is a way of describing the preparations for the final judgment of the wicked (Rev. 20). **will not cast off His people:** God will not forget His people any more than He will forget or deny Himself (2 Tim. 2:13).

94:15–19 Who will rise up for me is an appeal to the Lord who alone is the sure defense of the believer. **settled in silence:** The psalmist exclaims that if the Lord had not delivered him, he would have died. The comforts of God extend from His hearing the call of the righteous to His meeting their needs even when they are not aware of them.

94:20–23 Throne of iniquity is a description of the wicked who have great power. The holy Lord cannot tolerate evil in His presence. **The LORD … shall cut them off:** Final judgment will one day come to the wicked.

Psalm 95 places particular emphasis on the worship of God, making it a worship psalm. But it is also a royal psalm because of the way it acknowledges God as the great King (v. 3).

95:1–5 Oh come: The psalm begins with energy and delight at the prospect of worshiping God in the temple (Ps. 100). The use of the **psalms** in worship is indicated in this passage. **In His hand** refers to God's control over all that He has made.

95:6, 7 Each of the key verbs in this sentence describes a physical posture of humility before the Lord. The Hebrew word translated **worship** means literally "to prostrate oneself." When **bow down, kneel,** and **worship** occur together as in this verse, they amplify each another and call for a reflective, humble approach to God. Worship is joyful and can be done with abandon (vv. 1–5); but at other times worship may be quiet reverence of the Almighty (see Ps. 134).

95:8–11 The third movement of this psalm is a call for obedience in worship and a reminder of God's judgments in past times on people who did not take Him seriously. The word **rebellion** is literally "Meribah," a word that would remind the Israelites of the times they had doubted the Lord's provision for them (Ex. 17:7; Num. 20:13). The event of Meribah was the rebellion of the first generation at Kadesh (Num. 14). By refusing to enter Canaan, the entire generation of Israelites lost their opportunity to enjoy the promises of God in the land of blessing.

Psalm 96, a royal psalm, is part of the set that begins at Ps. 93. This psalm emphasizes world mission, specifically the prophetic fulfillment of the mission provision of the Abrahamic covenant (Ps. 67).

96:1–3 Among the nations is a bold declaration that one day the message of God's mercy will be known the world over. One day the message of God's salvation will be known **among all peoples.** This declaration depends on God's promise to Abraham that through his descendants all nations of the earth will be blessed (Gen. 12:1–3).

96:4–6 The mention of other gods in v. 4 is clarified by the words of v. 5: These gods are just **idols.**

96:7–9 families of the peoples: The allusion to the Abrahamic covenant continues (vv. 2, 3; see Gen. 12:1–3). One day, the praise of God will come gladly from people of all nations.

96:10 The LORD reigns is the key phrase of the royal psalms (93:1). It was the countercultural cry of ancient Israelites in a world that believed that gods could rise and fall. In contrast, the living God remains Ruler for all eternity.

96:11–13 Let the heavens rejoice: This poem calls for all of creation to respond to the coming of the King of glory. **He is coming … He is coming:** Like the echo of approaching footsteps, the words echo each other.

Psalm 97, one of the series of royal psalms (Ps. 93—99), has a particularly apocalyptic tone in its description of God's final judgment on the wicked before He establishes His great kingdom.

97:1 The earth as a whole and its smallest parts—the **isles**—join together in rejoicing at the prospect of God's reign on earth.

97:2 Clouds and darkness may be rephrased "impenetrable clouds," an indicator of the final judgment and God's awesome power (Joel 2:2; Zeph. 1:15). **Righteousness and justice** may be rephrased as "absolute righteousness." The foundation of God's coming judgment will be His integrity; His judgments will be correct.

97:3–6 fire: The psalmist uses the imagery of the storm god Baal to describe God's judgment. This poetic language attempts to describe the final judgment of God upon the earth before He establishes His kingdom.

97:7, 8 The continuing practice of idolatry throughout world history is a grave offense against the Lord. Such behavior will finally end in **shame** and terror (14:5).

97:9–11 To **hate** means to reject; to **love** means to choose. Since both are an expression of the will and not just an emotion, the Bible commands both love and hatred. **Light is sown:** The picture is that of someone sowing seed, with the seed being light and joy. This speaks of the restoration of the earth (Ps. 110).

97:12 rejoice: The psalm begins and ends on a note of rejoicing.

Psalm 98 one of the set of royal psalms that includes Ps. 93—99, is an exuberant psalm of praise. This poem shares the same joy as Ps. 96.

98:1–2 The term **marvelous things** is used only to describe the actions of God in the Bible. The **right hand** of the Lord is a way of referring to His great salvation of Israel from Egypt (Ex. 15:6; Deut. 4:34). The phrase is like a slogan for the Lord's redemption (118:15, 16).

98:3–8 In Canaanite thought, **the sea** represented a dark deity. In the Psalms, the sea is a part of creation that God completely controls (Ps. 93). The **clapping** of the **hands** of **the rivers** and the rejoicing of the **hills** represents the praise of creation at the establishment of God's kingdom on the earth.

98:9 He is coming: This verse and 96:13 answer the call for justice found at many points in the Psalms. At last the Lord will put an end to cruelty, evil, and injustice.

Psalm 99 the last of the set of royal palms that began with Ps. 93, praises God as the King of His people.

99:1, 2 The cherubim are the angels most closely related to the glory of God. Two gold cherubim graced the mercy seat of the ark of the covenant (Ex. 25:18–22). **Let the earth be moved:** Since God is the great King, the stability of the earth depends on Him; He can shake the world to demonstrate His power over it (Matt. 24:29). **great in Zion:** The holy temple in Jerusalem was the earthly structure for God's heavenly presence. But His reign extends throughout the entire world.

99:3 awesome name: The name of God is a blessing and comfort; it also evokes awe and wonder. **Holy** means to be "distant" or "distinct from." This is the principal Hebrew word used to describe the transcendence of God (113:4–6).

99:4, 5 The **footstool** of the Lord is sometimes said to be the earth (Is. 66:1); but

more specifically, Zion is the Lord's footstool (132:7; Is. 60:13). When the Israelites came to the temple in Jerusalem to worship, they pictured themselves as being at the feet of the Creator.

99:6 The psalmists worshiped God by recalling His saving acts to their predecessors. **Moses** is mentioned by name in the Psalms several times (77:20; 103:7; 105:26; 106:16, 23, 32), as is **Aaron** (77:20; 105:26; 106:16; 115:10, 12; 118:3; 133:2; 135:19). This psalm is the only one to mention **Samuel** by name. **He answered:** The Lord heard their prayers and did not remain silent. Since God answered the prayers of our ancestors, surely He will continue to answer the prayers of those who call upon Him.

99:7–9 His holy hill: The site of Zion is "holy" because of the presence of the Lord. This holy hill is also His "footstool" (see v. 5).

Psalm 100 is a psalm of descriptive praise that follows a set of royal psalms (Ps. 93—99). The phrase "A Psalm of Thanksgiving" refers to public acknowledgment of the Lord.

100:1, 2 The Hebrew verb for **make a joyful shout** is a highly charged command for public praise. The command is addressed not just to Israel but to all the earth. The Israelites were to be a people who would attract the nations to worship God.

100:3 The words **the LORD, He is God** reflect the great confession of faith in Deut. 6:4–9. To **know** that the Lord is God is very similar to the command to "hear" in Deuteronomy.

100:4 Enter: The commands of vv. 1, 2 are reiterated. The people of the Lord may actually come into His presence and bring Him worship that pleases Him.

100:5 the LORD is good: The shout of the goodness of God in this verse is buttressed by an appeal to **His mercy** and **His truth.** The Hebrew word for *truth* comes from the root meaning "to be established" or "to be confirmed." From this root also comes the word *amen,* meaning "surely" or "truly." God's goodness is based on His loyal love and His truth.

Psalm 101 is a royal psalm. David the king declares his purposes and asks for God's help in maintaining righteousness. This brief psalm has a tone of strong judgment, indicating a desire not only to preserve the innocent and protect the needy, but also to maintain the reputation of God against the attacks of His foes.

101:1, 2 Mercy and justice may be rephrased as "gracious justice." There is a harshness to the tone of the psalm that might emphasize the *justice* element of this phrasing; but underlying the justice is God's "mercy" or "loyal love."

101:3, 4 The Hebrew expression for **wicked** implies utter worthlessness. The phrase **I hate** indicates utter rejection (5:5). David hated what God hated and loved what God loved.

101:5–8 David made a covenant with his **eyes** (Job 31:1) to observe the righteous and sustain them in their walk. Alternatively, his eyes were also directed *against* the wicked. **the evildoers:** Elsewhere, this Hebrew phrase is rendered *workers of iniquity* (14:4).

Psalm 102, a penitential psalm, has an unusual inscription. The title describes a person in distress but does not name him.

102:1 In its entreaty for the Lord to **hear,** the beginning of the psalm reflects a pattern of lament (see 13:1, 2). The next section (vv. 3–7) reflects a pattern of penitence (see 32:3–5).

102:2, 3 my days are consumed: This description of the psalmist's sense of his own frailty is matched by the words of 144:4, "like a passing shadow."

102:4–8 The psalmist names birds—**a pelican, an owl,** and **a sparrow**—who live in distant, lonely places. The psalmist felt isolated, alone, and vulnerable, an isolation intensified by the harsh ranting of his enemies.

102:9–12 Shall endure may also be translated "sits enthroned." God is King forever. He is gracious, loves His people, and promises to favor them.

102:13–15 The psalmist anticipates a time when the Lord will reign over all the **nations** (Ps. 96—98); but his prayer is for God's answer to his own cry for deliverance.

102:16–19 The psalmist realizes that the Eternal One has stooped from heaven to meet his need, that the King of kings has come to his aid. His joy is such that he wants

people who have not yet been born to learn what God has done.

102:20–28 midst of my days: The psalmist remembers his troubling experiences and contrasts the brevity of his own life with the eternity of God. **Of old:** God is eternal and His works are from ancient times.

Psalm 103, a wisdom psalm attributed to David, is also a psalm of praise. The poem begins with the psalmist speaking in the singular (v. 1), but then moves to include the community, both angels and people (vv. 20–22).

103:1 To **bless the LORD** is to remember that He is the source of all our blessings. The psalmist blesses the Lord with his entire being (146:2).

103:2–5 heals all your diseases: Even though God is not bound to heal every disease, every healing does come from Him. **Who satisfies your mouth:** In addition to being a healer, God provides food as well as other blessings (111:5).

103:6 God is *for* the helpless and the **oppressed.** He is not unfair, for He is the One who will restore justice to the earth.

103:7 made known His ways to Moses: God blessed His servant Moses in a special way by revealing the Law to him. **His acts:** During the Exodus and the wilderness wanderings, God saved the Israelites from Pharaoh's army, provided them with water and food, and revealed the Law to them.

103:8–14 The LORD is merciful: This is a basic description of God in the Old Testament (see 86:15; Ex. 34:6, 7). If God dealt with us **according to our sins,** no one could stand before Him (130:3). There is no way to compare the divine with the mortal; the mercy of God is greater than **the heavens.** He removes our sins completely (Mic. 7:19) and cares for His people as a good **father** cares for his **children.**

103:15–19 Mercy may be rephrased as "loyal love." God's anger is for a moment (v. 8); His loyal love is forever. His blessing is on those who keep faith with Him (147:11). **His throne:** The Lord is King of all and King forever.

103:20–22 Bless the LORD: The psalmist began the psalm with a call to his own inner being to respond with praise to God (v. 1);

he concludes the psalm with a call to heaven and earth to join him in joyful praise.

Psalm 104, a wisdom psalm, is also a creation psalm (Ps. 19). It is an exuberant poetic recasting of Gen. 1, a joyful celebration of the world as the creation of God.

104:1, 2 God is Spirit (see John 4:24), and descriptions of Him vary through the Bible. One strong description of Him is **light** (see 1 John 1:5). Here light is described as the garment that enfolds His wonder. The first act of God in Genesis was the command for light (Gen. 1:3).

104:3, 4 beams of His upper chambers: With these poetic words, the psalmist alludes to the heavenly dwelling place of God, a place beyond human understanding. **makes the** clouds His chariot: Idolaters used similar language of Baal. The psalmist strips Baal of these honors and applied them to the living God (Ps. 93).

104:5–7 You who laid the foundations of the earth is a poetic way of describing how God created the heavens and the earth. **The deep** is the same term used in Gen. 1:2. **At Your rebuke:** The psalmist recalls that God brought dry land from the watery abyss in Gen. 1:9, 10. The word of God is referred to as a "rebuke" or a "thundering."

104:8, 9 A boundary is a regular theme in wisdom literature (Prov. 8:29). God's control over the turbulent waters (Ps. 93) is proof that He, not Baal, is the true Sovereign.

104:10–15 vegetation: The basis for this section is Gen. 1:11–13, the creative acts of God on the third day. Here the psalmist indicates the specific purpose of God's creation: to provide for the needs of human beings.

104:16–19 seasons: The events of the fourth day of creation are reviewed here (Gen. 1:14–19). The point is that God has established the patterns of life.

104:20–24 The Hebrew wisdom writers looked at the world with a sense of wonder and reverence because it reflected the **wisdom** of its Creator.

104:25, 26 References to the **sea** in the psalms are generally in the context of Canaanite ideas. The Canaanites said that Baal controlled the powerful gods of the seas. But the psalmist asserts in the face of

this falsehood that God created the waters and everything in them—even Leviathan, the great sea monster (see Job 41).

104:27–30 These all wait: All creation depends on the Creator for birth, life, and sustenance. Even death is controlled by the Sovereign One.

104:31 God continues to **rejoice** in His creative work on earth (Prov. 8:30, 31). The Lord considered His creation "good" from the beginning (Gen. 1:31), and His pleasure in it remains.

104:32–35 my meditation: The psalmist wants to respond properly to God's creation. **Bless the LORD** echoes the beginning of the psalm (v. 1).

Psalm 105, a psalm of praise (compare Ps. 113), focuses on the positive experiences of Israel in their early history. Contrast Ps. 106, which reviews the same period of history but with an emphasis on the faithlessness of the people. This poem celebrates God's faithfulness to His covenant with Abraham in the lives of His people. The people needed to remember to be faithful to God, who had never forgotten to be faithful to them.

105:1–6 The psalmist calls to memory what God did for His people in fulfillment of the covenant with Abraham. **Remember** is the key idea of the psalm: The psalmist wanted to remind God's people of His goodness.

105:7, 8 The psalmist assured his audience that even if they did not *remember,* God does remember. **He remembers:** The words of the original promise to Abraham set out the Lord's obligation in strong terms (Gen. 12:1–3). These ideas are reinforced by the dramatic encounter with Abraham in Gen. 15. In the story of the binding of Isaac in Gen. 22, the Lord undertakes an irrevocable oath of obligation (Gen. 22:16–18).

105:9–15 When they went: This section is an overview of the history of Israel, probably written after the return of the exiles from Babylon (Ps. 147). The major theme of the poem is God's faithfulness to His people in their early history.

105:16, 17 The experiences of **Joseph** occupy a long section of the Book of Genesis (Gen. 37—50). Here Joseph's story is recounted as poetry and song.

105:18–26 The psalmist recites the history of the plagues to demonstrate the Lord's power. The plagues took place within time and space; they were the action of God with humans in the real world. The order of the plagues is not followed strictly, and only eight of the plagues are mentioned (Ex. 7—11).

105:27–45 with gladness: This poem celebrates the joy of the Lord in His acts of deliverance. **gave them the lands:** The psalm was probably composed after the exile in Babylon. A celebration of God's gift of land would have been a great source of encouragement to the people who had just returned to the land.

Psalm 106, a wisdom psalm, rehearses much of the same history covered in Ps. 105. The two poems are companions, although their perspectives are different. Psalm 105 is about God's faithfulness; Ps. 106 is about forgetting—specifically God's people forgetting His mercies. This psalm calls for the praise of God despite the short memories of His people.

106:1–5 Oh, give thanks to the Lord: The words of v. 1 and the general language of **praise** in v. 2 connect this poem with Ps. 105 as a set (105:1, 2). Possibly both psalms were written by the same psalmist and were designed to go together, since this psalm builds on the theme of remembering.

106:6 We have sinned with our fathers: This is a psalm of community penitence. The connection of the present generation to the sins of the fathers is ominous. Would the present generation have to suffer the misfortunes and judgments that God brought upon their fathers?

106:7–12 God knew that His people would be faithless repeatedly, yet He **saved them for His name's sake. Then they believed:** The people were often faithless; but they had moments of true faith and performed actions of true praise.

106:13–16 They soon forgot: These words contrast dramatically with the emphasis of Ps. 105, which may indicate that the two psalms were written by the same psalmist and designed to go together. **He gave them their request:** Several times God gave the people what they thought they wanted, but with the gift came His judgment on their sin.

106:17 The rebellion of **Dathan** and **Abiram** is described in Num. 16.

106:18–23 The story of the gold **calf** is recorded in Ex. 32. **changed their glory:** In exchange for the living God, the people accepted an image of an ox.

106:24 The fact that **they despised the pleasant land** is regarded as a result of their unbelief and rejection of God's good gift. God's judgment (Num. 13; 14) was fully deserved.

106:25–30 Baal of Peor refers to the incident described in Num. 25, following the encounter of Balaam and Balak at Moab. However, this psalm adds a new detail to the story: eating sacrifices offered to the dead. **Phinehas,** one of the great champions of God in the Old Testament, is celebrated in this poem. As Abraham's faith was accounted to him for righteousness (Gen. 15:6), so was the action of Phinehas (Num. 25).

106:31–33 Waters of strife is a reference to Meribah (95:8; Num. 20:1–13). Here the sin of Moses is called "speaking **rashly**." In Num. 20:12, God specifically identified Moses' sin as dishonoring Him before the people by not trusting Him. By not following God's command "to speak" to the rock, Moses had not modeled proper obedience and respect for God's command.

106:34–39 God's judgment on Israel in Canaan was a result of the Israelites' failure to **destroy the peoples.** If the Canaanites had been driven out of the land, the people of Israel might never have succumbed to the idolatry that marked their existence for hundreds of years. Instead, the Israelites learned to worship the Canaanite idols.

106:40 The wrath of the Lord must be viewed in the context of His long-standing mercy and forbearance. There was a long history of rebellion in the face of His gracious provision before God became enraged. Yet even in the midst of His wrath, God's merciful nature was evident.

106:41–47 The words of appeal **save us** are buttressed with the words **O Lord our God.** Though the people had been faithless, the Lord was still their God. If they would return to Him, they would have a home in His mercy and a promise of eventual triumph.

106:48 Blessed be the Lord God of Israel: This verse is an addition to Ps. 106 that forms the concluding verse of Book IV of the Psalms. It is a beautiful liturgical call for the people together to bless their faithful God.

Psalm 107, a wisdom psalm, shares the form and many of the same themes as Ps. 105 and 106. Psalm 107 reviews God's actions in the experiences of His people. The psalm begins and concludes with appeals to trust in the "loyal love" of God.

107:1 Oh, give thanks to the Lord: The beginning of this psalm links it to the two preceding psalms (105:1; 106:1). The key point of this psalm is that God's **mercy endures forever.** He is always willing to restore those who call on Him.

107:2–9 They wandered in the wilderness: This may refer to the historical experience of Israel in the desert of Sinai. It also can apply to any group of dispersed Hebrew people away from the mercies of God. **He satisfies:** This is the point that every generation of believers needs to remember. We will never discover anything more satisfying than the Lord, who will meet all our needs.

107:10 Those who sat in darkness refers to prisoners. Those who know the Lord will call out to Him in their distress, even though it may have been their own rebellion that caused the distress. The mercy of God is demonstrated in His acts of deliverance.

107:11–17 Fools is a harsh word that emphasizes moral failure (Prov. 1:7; 15:5). These people deserved the trouble they suffered. Yet they too may call upon the Lord, and He will deliver and restore them.

107:18–35 He turns rivers into a wilderness: Because of the people's sinfulness, God may bring curses on the land and afflict people with harsh circumstances in order to drive them back into His loving arms (1 Kin. 17:1–7). **turns a wilderness into pools of water:** When His people cried to Him for assistance, God restored the fertility of the land (Deut. 30:1–10; Ruth 1:6).

107:36–43 Whoever is wise: There is no wisdom apart from centering in and responding to the love of God. The psalmist exhorts the readers to review God's history of delivering those in trouble, and to praise His great love.

Psalm 108, a psalm of trust, reveals the assurance a person can have when the Lord is his or her God. The psalm is actually a medley of two other psalms of David. Verses 1–5 are from 57:7–11, and vv. 6–13 are from 60:5–12. As this psalm shows, there was considerable reworking of some parts of the Book of Psalms so that the psalms could be used in the varying circumstances of temple worship.

108:1, 2 I will awaken the dawn: The psalmist wanted to sing to the Lord before the sun rose. The prospect of a sleepless night did not deter him from praise and thanksgiving.

108:3–13 The remarkable fact about the words **I will rejoice** is that they are spoken by God. The Lord has pleasure in delivering His people and giving them victory.

Psalm 109, a psalm of lament, pays particular attention to the psalmist's enemies. As a result, this poem may also be regarded as an imprecatory psalm.

109:1–3 The call to **not keep silent** is a regular feature of the lament psalms. **fought against me without a cause:** The psalmist declares his innocence and insists that his enemies have rewarded his prayers with evil, his love with hatred.

109:4–8 Set a wicked man over him: Here the psalm takes a decidedly negative tone. The description of the wife of the enemy becoming an impoverished widow and the children becoming beggars seems particularly harsh. However, the psalmist directs these strong requests to the Lord; he does not actually take the sword into his own hand. He may feel compelled to vent his anger in words, but the psalmist understands that vengeance itself belongs to the Lord.

109:9–16 Let the iniquity of his fathers be remembered: Although the psalmist's words may seem extremely hostile, he is simply asking that his enemy's evil actions be judged. **The poor** are not those without wealth so much as those without protection or defenders.

109:17–21 The psalmist asks for action that would befit God's **name,** a name associated with righteousness (23:3). His appeal is to God's **mercy** or "loyal love." The psalmist describes himself as a wasted, hollow shell of a man, as in 22:6–8. The intensity of the psalmist's attacks on his enemies can be explained in part by the intensity of his own afflictions.

109:22–27 That they may know: Even in the psalmist's intense emotional state, he wants to see the name of God defended, proclaimed, and honored.

109:28–31 The psalmist makes his vow of **praise** for the deliverance he knows that the Lord will provide. This vow to praise God is a characteristic of many of the psalms.

Psalm 110, a royal psalm, is one of the most directly messianic of all the psalms. Jesus Himself identified David as the writer of this psalm, as the title also indicates. The interpretative key to the psalm lies in the identification of "my Lord" in v. 1. Jesus asserted that in v. 1, David was speaking of someone greater than himself. Since no ordinary son of David could be greater than him, "the Lord" of v. 1 refers to the coming Messiah, God's Son. Hence this psalm describes a conversation between God the Father and God the Son (v. 1), in which the Father grants the Son royal and priestly honors.

110:1 to my Lord: According to Jesus' interpretation of the passage (Mark 12:35–37), this is a reference to the Son of God in heaven in the presence of the Father. David himself confesses the Son to be his Lord, that is, his master or sovereign. **at My right hand:** This position of high honor beside the Father was given to the Savior upon His resurrection and ascension (Acts 2:33–36; Heb. 1:13). The Savior's placing His **feet** on His foes depicts the utter defeat of the enemies of Christ.

110:2, 3 Rule: The Father commands the Son to take His kingdom back from His enemies. The outcome of this final battle was determined long ago (47:3). **your people:** The description in vv. 2, 3 of the people who join the coming King in His great battle accords well with that in Rev. 19:14.

110:4 priest: David himself had performed some priestly functions, especially when he led the worship surrounding the arrival of the ark of the covenant (2 Sam. 6:12–19). He even exercised some authority over the priests by supervising the Levites (1 Chr.

23:1–6). But here David envisions God appointing the coming Messiah to be a priest (Heb. 7). This was a source of confusion for Jews, as evidenced by the questions the New Testament Jews had about the Messiah. Some Dead Sea Scrolls give evidence that more than one Messiah was anticipated. According to Scripture, the Messiah would be a descendant of David (Is. 9:7), but this prophecy presents Him as a priest. The solution to this problem is that the Messiah was a priest by divine declaration—not human descent. **Melchizedek** became a prototype of the Messiah, whose priesthood was not based upon connection with the line of Aaron, but was by divine decree (Heb. 5:5–11; 7:1–28).

110:5–7 The Savior King is in battle (vv. 2, 3), and the Father is His shield at His **right hand** (16:8; 142:4). God the Father assists the Son in the battle. **execute kings:** The rule of the King will be absolute, dramatic, and forceful. **He shall lift up the head:** As the great Victor, the Son will hold His head high in triumph over all His enemies (3:3).

Psalm 111, a wisdom psalm, also serves as a psalm of praise. This psalm and the next are written as acrostics.

111:1–9 The distinctive message of this section of the psalm is an appreciation of **the works of the Lord** for the way they cause the psalmist to glorify God. Creation calls attention to the Creator (19:1–6; 104:1–35). Faith understands **food** and all other provisions as gifts of God. **redemption:** The psalmists constantly look back to the Exodus, but they also speak of that which was still to come—redemption in the Savior Jesus.

111:10 The fear of the Lord describes an obedient response of wonder and awe before the Most High God.

Psalm 112, a wisdom psalm, is very similar to Ps. 111; together they form a matched pair of acrostic poems.

112:1 Praise the Lord: Like Ps. 111, this psalm begins with the Hebrew word *hallelujah.* It then picks up where Ps. 111 left off. **Blessed,** a word meaning "one who is manifestly happy," is the same term with which the Book of Psalms begins.

112:2–9 His descendants will be mighty: Compare the blessings of vv. 2, 3 with the strong curses placed on the wicked in 109:6–13 to see the vivid contrast the Psalms make between the destinies of the wicked and the righteous. This distinction is characteristic of the wisdom writers in Israel. The description of the **good man** in v. 5 is similar to the description in Ps. 15.

112:10 Here as in Ps. 1, the contrast between the righteous and the wicked is sharp and uncompromising. The desire of the righteous will prevail (v. 8), but the desire of the wicked will **perish.**

Psalm 113, a psalm of descriptive praise, begins and concludes with the words "Praise the Lord!" (in Hebrew, *hallelujah*). This psalm and Ps. 114 are regularly recited at the Passover Seder, a celebratory meal before the serving of the dinner. Ps. 115—118 are recited following the dinner.

113:1–3 The name of the LORD refers to the person of God. In biblical times there was a close association between a person's name and his or her identity. The name symbolized the person. Therefore, praising the *name* of God centers one's thoughts on God's character.

113:4–6 high above all nations: Unlike the man-made gods of the ancient Middle East, the Lord is not limited to a certain tribe or territory. He is sovereign over all; He is Most High (7:17; 47:2). **glory above the heavens:** Not only is God supreme over all nations, His glory cannot be contained in the universe. His glory is not only beyond the universe, it is beyond the capacity of human language to fully describe.

113:7 The poor might try to eke out their existence by scratching at rubbish heaps outside the city wall, that is, **out of the dust.** God's care for the poor and needy is a special interest in the Psalms. In this psalm we see a marvelous picture of salvation. While we scavenge about for significance, God's mercy in Jesus makes us citizens of heaven.

113:8, 9 No image better conveys human emotional suffering in biblical times than that of the **barren woman.** In that time and culture, a barren woman was without significance and without joy. Note that God stoops down to bring her the joy for which she craves—happy children.

Psalm 114 celebrates Israel's deliverance from Egypt. There is a light, lively spirit to this poem that balances the heavier pacing and stronger theology of the first song of deliverance in Ex. 15. This poem is recited with Ps. 113 at Passover before the dinner is served.

114:1, 2 The newly freed slaves left Egypt still refusing the **strange language** of their long-term captors. With this slight, Israel affirmed that true values in life were not to be found in the "glories of Egypt," but in the presence of the Lord. **sanctuary:** This verse anticipates the New Testament sense of God living among His people rather than in a shrine (Ezek. 37:26, 27; 2 Cor. 6:16–18).

114:3–6 The sea and the **Jordan,** the **mountains** and the **hills,** all appear as frightened animals before the awesome presence of the Lord.

114:7, 8 God not only delivered His people from Egypt; He also provided for their needs by bringing water from a **rock** (Ex. 17; Num. 20). Water was a physical blessing, but also a spiritual symbol of His salvation.

Psalm 115, a community psalm of praise, focuses on the glory of the Lord in the salvation of His people. Several sections of this psalm are used in Ps. 135.

115:1, 2 Not unto us: People have a natural tendency to divert to themselves glory that belongs to God. This psalm redirects the glory to its proper focus, the Lord Himself. The **Gentiles,** who do not know God, are prone to insult believers in times of testing when God's activity is not apparent (42:3).

115:3–8 Like the prophets (Is. 40; Jer. 10), the psalms are derisive toward the **idols** of the nations. The psalmist denies any reality to the false gods created by people (135:15–18). In contrast to these "gods" that have to be carried about, propped up, and coddled, Israel exalted the **God** who **is in heaven** and who **does whatever He pleases.** He is the only God who can demand our worship.

115:9–11 On the basis of the confession of the reality of God, the psalm begins a litany that encourages trust in God alone. With this litany the choir leader would exhort first **Israel,**

then the **house of Aaron,** and finally all **who fear the LORD** to trust God. The refrain proclaims God's protective care over them.

115:12–15 A second litany focuses on God's blessing. Not only is He the only God who is trustworthy; He also desires to bless all those who trust in Him.

115:16–18 The plural **heavens** may refer to the dwelling place of God (2 Cor. 12:2). **The dead:** As in 6:5, this is not a theology of death, but of praise. It is the work of the living to praise God. When anyone dies, that voice is lost from the living choir.

Psalm 116, a messianic psalm, is one of the Passover psalms (Ps. 113—118). This psalm most likely was recited by Jesus on the night of His arrest, the night He celebrated Passover with His disciples (Luke 22:15).

116:1, 2 The wording of **I love the LORD** in Hebrew suggests deep excitement and emotion. **He has inclined His ear to me:** As in 40:1, these words speak of the love of God. He bends from His place of glory to meet the needs of His people.

116:3–5 Pains of death describes the psalmist's harrowing experience of suffering that brought him seemingly to the brink of death (86:13). These words point prophetically to the Savior's anguish on the Cross (Matt. 27:27–35).

116:6 In this context, **simple** means innocent, clean, or untarnished. In the Book of Proverbs, the word usually means naive or untested (Prov. 1:22).

116:7–10 Paul quotes the words **I believed, therefore I spoke** in 2 Cor. 4:13, 14 as proof of the scriptural hope of the resurrection of the Savior Jesus.

116:11–13 With the phrase **what shall I render,** the psalmist vows to praise God in an audible and public manner among the people of faith. At Passover this psalm is read after the meal, immediately following the third cup of wine, called **the cup of salvation.** How appropriate that this Passover psalm would call to mind God's cup of salvation the very night that the Savior was betrayed (Matt. 26:27; Luke 22:14–22).

116:14–17 The psalmist declares that he is God's **servant.** As Jesus demonstrated in the Upper Room celebration of the Passover,

every true follower of Christ must become a servant. Just as Jesus the Son of God became a servant to His disciples and washed their feet, so every believer needs to serve others (John 13:1–17).

116:18, 19 I will pay my vows: These words are evidently the concluding words of the psalmist, declaring his intention to make good on his promise to bring his offering of praise to the temple court.

Psalm 117 is a descriptive psalm of praise. It is the shortest psalm.

117:1 Laud, which means "to speak well of," nicely parallels the term **praise,** which means "to be excitedly boastful about." The Hebrew word for Gentiles means all people except Jews; the word for **peoples** speaks of smaller groups of people, along ethnic and language lines.

117:2 Merciful kindness, or "loyal love," refers to God's faithfulness to His covenant promises to His people. The reason the nations are to give praise to God is found in His relationship with Israel.

Psalm 118, a psalm of declarative praise, is the climax of the group of psalms called the Passover psalms or Hallel psalms, after the Hebrew word for praise, *hallel. Hallelujah* comes from this word. These psalms were probably sung by the Savior on the night before His death.

118:1, 2 The liturgical instruction **let Israel now say** appears from time to time in the Psalms (Ps. 124; 129). This psalm was recited in antiphonal responses. The refrain praises God's mercy: **His mercy endures forever.**

118:3–8 The idea of **distress** in these psalms is a picture of constraint, constriction, or lack of room. Even when surrounded by impossible circumstances, the believer can proclaim **the LORD is on my side.** And if so, **what can man do to me? confidence in princes:** Although relying on other people is part of living, our ultimate trust can only be placed in the Lord God. Even powerful rulers are limited by their mortality (146:3).

118:9–11 The psalmist feels that he is alone and that the whole world is arrayed against him. The words **I will destroy them** are used three times in vv. 10–12; the repetition is for emphasis and finality. Even though the

psalmist is completely encircled by his enemies, he knows that God will help him triumph over them.

118:12–14 You pushed me: Translated literally, the Hebrew phrase means "pushing,
you pushed me to make me fall." **But the
Lord helped me:** Deliverance always
comes from God. The Lord is not only our
Helper, but also our **strength and song.**
These words are a quotation from the "Song
of Moses" (Ex. 15:2); they are also quoted
in Is. 12:2.

118:15–17 The voice of rejoicing: The psalmist
summons the people of God to join him in
praise, just as in the days of the Exodus from
Egypt. The slogan of redemption, **the right
hand of the Lord,** is again a quotation from
the Song of Moses (Ex. 15:6). It depicts God
using His limitless strength to save the psalmist.

118:18–21 Open to me the gates: The psalmist draws on the wording and imagery of Ps.
24. There is only One who can enter the
gates of the Lord of His own accord—the
perfect King of glory. **gate of the LORD:** It is
possible that the literal reference is to the
gate of Jerusalem, the city of God—or even
to a gate of the temple.

118:22 The Savior is pictured as a discarded
stone that is then reused as the most significant stone of all, the **chief cornerstone.**
This potent imagery depicts Jesus' rejection
by many (Is. 53:3; Luke 9:22; 17:25). Jesus
elaborated on this prophetic verse with the
parable of the vineyard owner. In this parable, the rejection included the murder of the
owner's son—a reference to God's only Son
(Mark 12:1–12). But even though the Savior
was rejected, He was elevated to the right
hand of God (Acts 7:56).

118:23–26 The words **save now** in Hebrew
are more familiar in the transliteration "hosanna." These words are so significant that if
the children had not shouted them aloud
(see Matt. 21:16) when Jesus entered Jerusalem, the stones would have had to shout
them (Luke 19:40). The words **blessed is
he who comes** are the words the people
used to bless Jesus on his triumphal entry
into Jerusalem (Matt. 21:9; Mark 11:9; Luke
19:38). As God's only Son, Jesus is the One

who comes **in the name of the LORD;** He
reveals God the Father (John 14:8–11).

118:27–29 The closing words call the community to end the psalm as it began (v. 1)—with
praise for the goodness and love of the Most
High God.

Psalm 119, a wisdom psalm, is the premier
song about the Torah (Ps. 19). It celebrates
the Word of God in a way that is almost exhaustive. This very lengthy poem is an acrostic: For each of the twenty-two consonants
in the Hebrew alphabet, there are eight
verses beginning with that letter. Within the
psalm, eight words for God's Law occur
again and again: law; testimonies; promise;
precepts; statutes; commandments; judgments; word. The psalm uses the full meaning of all these words as it elaborates on the
application of the Law of God to both daily
life and Israel's destiny. The Law is specific
and general, directive and restrictive, liber-
ating and opening, gracious and solemn.

119:1–15 The Hebrew word *torah,* translated
law, basically means "instruction" or "direction." Broadly it refers to all God's instructions from Moses to the prophets. More
strictly it refers to the first five books of the
Old Testament. The Law was never designed as a means of salvation; no one could
be saved by keeping it. The Lord gave His
law to a people with whom He had already
graciously established a covenantal relationship (Ex. 20:2). Instead, the Law was the
means for the Israelites to learn how to live
as God's holy people.

119:16 The Hebrew word for **statutes** refers
to something marked out as a boundary,
something inscribed or engraved. Hence the
word speaks of the permanence of the Law.
Indeed God Himself had engraved it in stone
(Ex. 24:12). The same word is often translated "decree" (2:7).

119:17–22 The Hebrew word translated **testimonies** is derived from the Hebrew verb
meaning "to witness" or "to testify." It refers
to the Ten Commandments, called the "two
tablets of the Testimony" (Ex. 31:18). The
commandments were a testimony because
they were a witness to the Israelites of their
faithfulness or unfaithfulness to the covenant
(Deut. 31:26).

119:23–37 The phrase **Your way** describes the will of God as a path, distinguished from other paths that lead to destruction (compare Prov. 2:8). God's path leads to life, and His ways are a reflection of His good character.

119:38–45 at liberty: The psalmist celebrates the freedom that is found in obeying God's instruction. Although many think of laws, instructions, and commandments (v. 47) as limiting and restricting, the Law of God paradoxically frees us. It frees us from sin (v. 133) and gives us the peace that comes from following the Lord's instructions (v. 165).

119:46–56 precepts: This Hebrew word means "an appointed thing," "something for which one is given charge." The word has the same idea as a commandment (v. 4). Both words assume that the One who commands has the authority "to take charge" or "to appoint."

119:57–62 the wicked have bound me: The psalmist describes a hostile world in which even rulers persecute him (v. 161). His enemies not only fabricate lies about him (v. 69), but also seek his death (v. 87). Yet in the same breath by which the psalmist voices his concerns, he proclaims his allegiance to the Law. He will not abandon the truth even under pressure.

119:63–72 The psalmist regularly affirms his **delight** with the Law (vv. 25, 35, 47, 174). This is not the delight of a passive observer, but the delight of a disciple who has staked his life and security on a cause or principle. The psalmist maintains this type of complete commitment to the Law.

119:73–82 The Hebrew term for **promise** is derived from the verb "to say." The term is a general word for God's Law, encompassing everything that the Lord has promised and spoken.

119:83–91 The stability of the universe, or the **heaven,** mirrors God's **faithfulness,** love, and care. But even more important, it reflects the permanence of God's laws and the fact that the universe serves Him.

119:92–103 The psalmist again and again proclaims his **love** for the Law (vv. 47, 119, 127, 159, 167). He compares his desire to a thirst for water (v. 131) and a craving for honey (v. 103). His attraction to the Law is the result of his love for God Himself, his Teacher (vv. 102, 132).

119:104, 105 Word means the utterance of the Lord God. That God speaks at all to His people indicates His grace. The psalmist describes God's Word as **light,** a guide for living.

119:106–127 Commandments pertain to anything the Lord God has ordered. The word alludes to God's authority to govern His people. The commandments of God are positive and negative, specific and general, restrictive and permissive. Yet most important, they help a person to identify his or her way in a world that is filled with confusion, sin, and error.

119:128–132 as Your custom: Here the psalmist identifies himself as a servant of the Lord and asks to be treated as one of His own. The psalmist's reference to God's mercy in this verse alludes to God's promise to show mercy to those who love Him (Ex. 20:6).

119:133–149 To **revive** means "to cause to live." With this word the psalmist begs God to transform his life, to breathe new life back into his soul. The psalmist does not want his obedience to be mechanical; he asks for a renewed spirit.

119:150–160 The word **judgments** is derived from the Hebrew word meaning "to judge." God has given decisions that are like the calls of a referee or the legal rulings of a judge; He has rendered judgments on what is acceptable behavior and what actions will receive His blessing.

119:161–176 come before: This term usually refers to the presentation of an offering before God. The only offering the psalmist can present here is his **cry** for help. Although he has **chosen** the Law of God to live by, he has not always kept it. Therefore, the psalmist ends his lengthy poem with a confession and a plea for salvation.

Psalm 120 is the first of a group of psalms called the Songs of Ascent (Ps. 120—134). This group of hymns was likely used by pilgrims making their way to Jerusalem to worship the Lord during the three annual national feasts—Passover, Pentecost, and Tabernacles (Lev. 23). As pilgrim families made the arduous journey to the holy city for festive worship, they would use these psalms as encouragement along the way. It is also possible that once they arrived in Jerusalem, they would sing these songs anew as they drew near the temple, reenacting their journey and affirming God's blessing on their path. Ps. 120, a psalm of lament, focuses on the lies of the wicked that affect the righteous.

120:1–3 lying lips: In the context of these psalms, the lying lips belong to those who assault the believers for their trust in the Lord (40:4). **You false tongue:** The psalmist is distraught at the seeming power of the words of the wicked.

120:4–7 This section of the psalm reveals the intensity of the psalmist's distress—**woe is me.** His environment was hostile even to his faith. **Meshech** and **Kedar** are random examples of the pagan peoples among whom the psalmist had to live.

Psalm 121, a psalm of trust (Ps. 23), is the second song of ascent. Ps. 120 sets the stage for the Israelites' journey to the Holy City; this poem is a song "for the road."

121:1, 2 The words **lift up my eyes** dramatically picture a traveler approaching the city of Jerusalem. On first sight of the city walls and the temple, the singer asks rhetorically where help is to be found. The answer is the strong affirmation: **Help comes from the Lord.**

121:3–7 He will not allow: It is possible that several sections of this brief poem were recited back and forth by small groups of pilgrims; there is an antiphonal quality to these verses (also Ps. 124). **will not slumber:** On the long journey to Jerusalem the people would have to stop and sleep, yet they would still be cared for by God. The language of confidence in this psalm indicates that it is about the psalmist's trust in the living Lord, his Protector.

121:8 and even forevermore: In what appears to be an antiphonal response to the words of vv. 6, 7, the poem concludes with a renewed affirmation of God's ongoing protection in this life and the life to come (23:6).

Psalm 122, a psalm of Zion, is the third song of ascent. This poem describes the joy of the pilgrim on arriving at Jerusalem to worship

God. This is one of four songs of ascent attributed to David (also Ps. 124; 131; 133).

122:1 I was glad: The Hebrew verb for laughter and delight is used to describe the attitude of the pilgrim who arrives in Jerusalem to worship the Lord. The joy of the pilgrim in this psalm contrasts strongly with the sorrow of those who were not able to come to worship God, because of personal (42:1–3) or national exile (137:1–3).

122:2, 3 The visitor is overwhelmed not just by the buildings of **Jerusalem,** but by the fact that the city was the place for the worship of God. **Where the tribes go up:** This refers to the three annual feasts of ancient Israel (Lev. 23), as well as to any time that an individual or family needed to worship the Lord in the Holy City.

122:4 The Testimony of Israel may refer to the ark of the covenant (Ex. 16:34). **To give thanks** means "to make a public declaration" or "to give public acknowledgment" (105:1). The people of God would praise God for His goodness in their lives.

122:5 thrones: Jerusalem was not only the central place for worship; it was also the site where civil judgments and decisions were made. Religious and civil issues were closely intertwined in the Law of God.

122:6–9 peace of Jerusalem: In the process of praying for the good of the city, the people came under God's blessing. It is God's desire for the city to have peace (125:5; 128:6). True peace will only come when the Prince of Peace returns to establish His rule (Ps. 98). **Because of the house:** The determination of the pilgrim to seek the good of Jerusalem was based on the fact that the site was the central location for the worship of the Lord and the place God had chosen for Himself (1 Kin. 11:36).

Psalm 123, an individual psalm of lament, is the fourth song of ascent.

123:1–4 The people who prayed for God's **mercy** had to endure the **contempt** of their neighbors. Perhaps they were being mocked for their resolute faith in God at a time when it seemed that God was not answering their prayers.

Psalm 124, a psalm of declarative praise, is one of four songs of ascent attributed to

David (see also Ps. 122; 131; 133). This psalm was likely designed to be read aloud as an antiphonal response (see also 118:1–4; compare Ps. 121; 129; 134; 135; 136).

124:1, 2 The LORD who was on our side amplifies the meaning of the divine name of God (Ex. 3:14, 15). The priests may have spoken the words **let Israel now say** as encouragement for the people to rehearse aloud their national experience (Ps. 129).

124:3 swallowed us alive: The psalmist describes his enemies first as ravenous beasts, then as raging waters; but God has defeated them all. The reference to raging **waters** has a double source—the story of creation and the Canaanite myths about evil gods who were believed to be water deities (Ps. 93).

124:4–7 Blessed be the LORD: Blessing God means identifying Him as the source of our blessing (103:2). **as prey:** The animal imagery of the enemies (v. 3) continues in this praise of God. The image of a helpless **bird** that has escaped a trap is common in the Psalms (11:1–3).

124:8 The words **who made heaven and earth** are similar to the words in 121:2; 134:3. These liturgical phrases were recited by the worshiping community during their journey to Jerusalem and when they arrived for corporate worship.

Psalm 125 a psalm of trust (Ps. 23), is also a song of Zion. This anonymous poem is the sixth song of ascent.

125:1, 2 As in the other songs of Zion (Ps. 48), there is a deep belief in the invincibility of the city of Jerusalem because of the Lord's choice of **Mount Zion** (1 Kin. 11:36). Likewise, the psalmist proclaims that those who trust in the Lord will endure. **the mountains surround Jerusalem:** Jerusalem is built on one of seven mountain peaks in the region. The mountains provide some protection for the city, since any invading army would have to march through arduous and dangerous mountain paths. Yet the city's true protection comes from the Lord.

125:3 The scepter of wickedness is a symbol of the power of evil. This verse recalls the Lord's promise that the gates of hell will not prevail against His church (Matt. 16:18). In

this way, God in His mercy protects His people from participation in evil.

125:4, 5 The phrase **workers of iniquity** is often found in the wisdom psalms (14:4); the Lord will oppose those who do evil. **peace:** The psalm concludes with a prayer for God's peace to rest on His people.

Psalm 126, a song of Zion, is the seventh song of ascent. The distinctive element of this poem is that it comes from the time of the restoration of Jerusalem following the Babylonian captivity (compare Ps. 137). The mood of this psalm is one of sweet joy following the sorrows of long separation.

126:1–3 The return from Babylonian **captivity** had been anticipated for so long that it seemed like a dream to the returnees. Some of the people had waited an entire lifetime. The joy of the people could not be contained; their praise to God was unstoppable.

126:4 The people who returned were a small percentage of those who had been exiled. **Bring back** is the beginning of the prayer that God would complete the restoration of His people to their land. Ultimately, this is a prayer for the coming of Jesus, who will complete God's work among His people.

126:5, 6 The people of Judah had gone to Babylon in **tears.** Yet their sorrow reaped tremendous rewards; the Lord came to the rescue of His humbled people (34:18; Is. 66:2; Matt. 5:4). Upon their return to Jerusalem and Judah, they were reaping a harvest of rejoicing.

Psalm 127, a wisdom psalm and the eighth song of ascent, is one of only two psalms attributed to Solomon (the other is Ps. 72).

127:1, 2 With the words **unless the Lord builds,** the psalmist asserts that life lived apart from God is not worth living, a view that this psalm shares with the Book of Ecclesiastes. Even building a house is useless if the Lord is not in the process.

127:3–5 children are a heritage: Children are God's gifts (128:3). **Like arrows:** In ancient times, having many children was regarded as a symbol of strength. This was particularly true in an agricultural economy, since the extra hands of children increased the productivity of the farmer. A full **quiver**

was a mark of God's blessing. The blessing of a home in ancient times gave a person a measure of pride in the community.

Psalm 128, a wisdom psalm, is also a psalm of Zion. Like Ps. 127, this poem addresses God's blessings in the home and family. As families made their way to the holy city for the annual festivals, they would encounter other families and mutually celebrate the goodness of God in their lives. Psalm 128 is the ninth song of ascent.

128:1 The word **blessed** describes the happiness of those who trust in the Lord and do His will (127:5). **who fears the LORD:** The fear of God is an attitude of respect, a response of reverence and wonder.

128:2, 3 labor of your hands: There is a reward in work and a satisfaction in labor that is a blessing of God (Eccl. 3:9–13). **Your wife:** This psalm focuses on the godly man in ancient Israel. Bearing children was a mark of God's blessing on his wife. His children were regarded as precious provisions, like **olive plants,** in his home (127:3–5).

128:4–6 The LORD bless you: This is the psalmist's prayer for the man who desires for his own family the blessings described in the psalm. **children's children:** This priestly prayer of blessing includes a desire for longevity and for happy posterity in the land. Only when God grants His **peace** on His people will the ideal conditions of family life be realized. Therefore, whoever prays for the blessing of God on a family also prays for the blessing of God's peace on the community as a whole (122:6–9; 125:5).

Psalm 129, a psalm of trust (Ps. 23), has its roots in the psalms of lament, for those psalms contain a section proclaiming trust in the Lord. The psalm has an antiphonal quality, calling for response and counter-response (compare 118:1–4; 124:1–5). This is the tenth song of ascent.

129:1–4 Many a time: The psalm begins with a liturgy of suffering, as the people of God acknowledge that throughout their history in the land they have been under constant assault by various peoples. With the words **let Israel now say,** the priest calls for the people to rehearse their history aloud (124:1). **The plowers plowed:** This imagery of the

brutal treatment they suffered was especially vivid in an agrarian setting. Even in the midst of such cruel circumstances, the Lord was **righteous.** He remained faithful to His promises to His people and He fought for them.

129:5–8 those who hate Zion: This begins the imprecation or cursing of the foes of Jerusalem. **Shame** is the intended end of the wicked (35:26). **as the grass on the housetops:** Sod was sometimes used on the roofs of houses. After a spring rain, there might be grass growing on the housetop. But this was not grass that flourished; it soon withered under the summer heat. The curse here is strong: May the enemies wither as quickly as rooftop grass.

Psalm 130 is a penitential psalm. Its placement following a psalm of imprecation (Ps. 129) is fitting. After all, a person might take such joy in the destruction of the wicked that he or she no longer would consider his or her own heart before the Lord. This psalm is the eleventh song of ascent.

130:1, 2 The psalmist shouts aloud to God from **the depths** of his own despair (Ps. 32; 51). In this case it was not enemies who were plowing his back (129:3), but his own sense of sin that was eating at the depths of his soul.

130:3, 4 God does not **mark** or keep count of our sins. Through the sacrificial system and ultimately in the provision of Jesus Christ, God dismissed His people's sins altogether (Mic. 7:19); He does not keep track—as an accountant would—of their sins.

130:5, 6 I wait … I do hope: In these two verses, the psalmist repeats five times that his hope is in the Lord. This was a confident expectation in the God who is always faithful to His promises.

130:7, 8 After proclaiming his own hope, the psalmist exhorts the community of **Israel** to **hope in the LORD.** God is not only capable of delivering the individual; He also delivers the community of believers who hope in Him (131:3). **He shall redeem:** In the Old Testament, the redemption of God's people refers to God's deliverance of His people from Egypt and from all other national foes, as well as to God's forgiveness of sins through the sacrificial system. The final redemption of all God's people came only in the death and resurrection of the Lord Jesus Christ (Gal. 3:13).

Psalm 131, a psalm of trust, is one of four songs of ascent attributed to David (also Ps. 122; 124; 133).

131:1 my heart is not haughty: David presents himself with genuine humility, a delicate balance between self-abasement and arrogant pride. From the life of David we know that he was not always able to keep this balance. But it was his desire, and at times—by God's grace—a reality in his life.

131:2, 3 Like a weaned child: The image is that of a child who is no longer unsettled and discontented, but one who is at peace and trusting in his mother, who is there to comfort and to meet his needs.

Psalm 132 a royal psalm, is the thirteenth song of ascent. Like Ps. 89, this poem reflects God's covenant with David (2 Sam. 7), in which He promised David a royal house—a promise that would be fulfilled in the coming of the great Savior King. It is possible that this psalm was written late in Israel's history, after the exile in Babylon. This would explain the people's call for God to remember His covenant with David. With no king on the royal throne of David, the people had great reason to call upon God to remember His promise.

132:1 If this psalm was written during the postexilic period, the words **remember David** have a significant meaning. During the years between the return of the people to Jerusalem and the birth of Jesus, there would have been a growing desire on the part of godly people for the Lord to restore David's kingdom in fulfillment of the Lord's promise.

132:2 The Mighty One of Jacob is a rare designation for God. Identical or similar expressions are found elsewhere in the Bible only in Gen. 49:24 and the Book of Isaiah (Is. 1:24; 49:26; 60:16).

132:3–8 Ephrathah refers to the region of Bethlehem (Ruth 1:2). The temple in Jerusalem was regarded as the **footstool** of God, whose dwelling is in heaven (99:5). The call **arise, O LORD** is a prayer for God to fulfill

His covenant promise to place a great king on David's throne (v. 1).

132:9, 10 Do not turn away: Based on God's promise to David (2 Sam. 7), the psalmist calls for God to fulfill His word to send His Anointed. This is a clarion call for the coming of the Savior King, Jesus.

132:11, 12 The words **the LORD has sworn** are a poetic recasting of the central words of the Davidic covenant in 2 Sam. 7:8–16 (see also 89:3, 4, 26–29). The ultimate fulfillment of these words is in Jesus Christ, the Son of David (Luke 1:32, 33; Acts 2:30).

132:13 God's choice of the Davidic line was also a choice of **Zion** as His dwelling place.

132:14–18 This verse celebrates God's covenant to send His **Anointed** One (v. 10). The words **horn** and **lamp** speak of the Messiah's authority and righteousness (Is. 11:1–5). **His crown:** The Messiah's kingdom will be established forever (Is. 9:7).

Psalm 133 is one of four songs of ascent attributed to David (see Ps. 122; 124; 131). With its emphasis on the unity of the believers, this poem anticipates Jesus' prayer in John 17.

133:1, 2 Good and … pleasant may be rephrased as "great delight" or "good pleasure." There is a sense of serene wonder in these words describing the unity of God's people. **like the precious oil:** Priests were anointed with a fragrant oil as a symbol of God's blessing on their holy office (Ex. 30:22–33).

133:3 like the dew of Hermon: This high mountain to the north of Israel received such large amounts of water that it seemed to be a source of moisture for the lands below. Similarly, the blessings of God flow to His people. **the blessing:** The intent of God is for the good of His people in this life and in the life to come.

Psalm 134 concludes the songs of ascent. This psalm was likely read as a responsive poem of praise (see also Ps. 118; 121; 124; 129; 135; 136).

134:1, 2 To **bless the LORD** is to identify Him as the source of all blessing (103:2). In this context, **servants of the LORD** refers to the priests of Israel who conducted their ministry at all hours in the temple (135:1, 2).

The idea behind this blessing was that the people who had come to worship at the temple were getting ready to go home. They had come for a great festival but had to return to their regular work and routine. However, the priests remained at the holy temple. It was their continuing worship of the Lord that allowed God's blessing to continue on the nation as a whole.

134:3 Bless you from Zion may have been the grateful response of the priests to the people, their own blessing on the people from the holy temple.

Psalm 135, a psalm of descriptive praise that recalls ideas and motifs from several earlier psalms, may have been composed after the exile in Babylon. The psalm presents God's saving works during the Exodus and contains a scathing attack on idolatry, taken from Ps. 115. The beginning and ending of this poem are written in the pattern of liturgical praise.

135:1–5 you servants of the LORD: This psalm begins with a call for the priests of Israel to praise God in the temple (134:1, 2). The endearing term **special treasure** is used only here in the Psalms (see also Ex. 19:5; Deut. 7:6; 14:2).

135:6, 7 Whatever the LORD pleases: These words are adapted from 115:3. The words **lightning for the rain** appear to be a citation of Jer. 10:13, indicating that this psalm was written after the exile in Babylon. God is active in creation. Conversely, the gods of the nations are impotent (vv. 15–18).

135:8 firstborn of Egypt: This psalm rehearses the saving events of the Exodus, culminating in the events of the Passover (Ex. 12:12). The defeat of Egypt was the work of the Lord.

135:9–14 God's saving actions established His reputation. Because of them, His **name** and His fame spread throughout the world. **He will have compassion:** Those who faced the hardships of restoring themselves in the land needed to know of God's continuing promise of mercy (Ps. 132).

135:15 The idols of the nations: This verse is a devastating satirical attack on pagan idolatry. The people who returned from Babylon had had their fill of the worship of idols;

finally, the people of Israel were ready to worship the only true God.

135:16–21 To **bless the LORD** is to identify Him as the source of all blessings (103:2) and to be grateful for all that He has given.

Psalm 136 is the quintessential psalm of descriptive praise. The worship leader, perhaps a priest, would read the first part of each verse. The people would then respond with their praise centering on the mercy of God: "For His mercy endures forever." This psalm, known as the "Great Hallel," was often recited in the temple as the Passover lambs were being killed.

136:1, 2 Give thanks means "to give public acknowledgment"; it is one of the principal words for praise in the Psalms (35:18; 105:1; 122:4). **Mercy,** which may also be translated "loyal love," is the most significant term used in the Psalms to describe the character of God. His mercy is "forever"; it is part of His eternal character.

136:3–5 In the Old Testament, the term **great wonders** is used exclusively for the awe-inspiring actions of God. His creation of the universe is the grand display of His **wisdom.** The heavens give a clear presentation of the glory of God (19:1–6).

136:6–13 struck Egypt: The psalmist refers to God's great acts of deliverance in bringing Israel from Egypt at the dawn of Israel's redemption (Ps. 78; 105; 135:8–12). **strong hand:** This is a slogan of redemption (118:15, 16; see Ex. 15:6). It has been said when God created the universe, it was the work of His fingers (8:3); but when He battled for the salvation of His people, it was with His strong right hand.

136:14–20 The psalmist's recital of Israel's history includes the capture of the lands east of the Jordan River, including the territories of **Sihon** and **Og** (Num. 21). The result was the gift of the land of Canaan to the people of Israel.

136:21–23 It is possible that the words **remembered us** suggest the return of the people of Judah and Jerusalem to their land following the Babylonian captivity. Like Ps. 135, Ps. 136 may have been written after the Exile.

136:24–26 Oh, give thanks: The psalm ends as it begins, with celebration of God's continuing faithfulness to His people Israel and a call to thank Him for His goodness.

Psalm 137, a song of Zion, is also a particularly impassioned imprecatory psalm. Although no author is named, the psalm clearly shares with the Book of Lamentations the despair of those who suffered the destruction of Jerusalem by the Babylonians in 586 B.C.

137:1–4 Babylon was one of the great empires in world history. When this psalm was written, the Jews were living there in exile. **we wept:** The emotions of the psalm are clearly indicated. The memory of Zion was painful for those in a foreign land (42:1–3). **hung our harps:** Making joyful music to the Lord in a foreign land was so difficult that the captives refused to make music at all. They took the words of their captors as taunts.

137:5, 6 If I forget you: It is difficult for the modern reader to appreciate the love for Zion among the people of Old Testament faith. This love was not just for a place but for its function in their lives. It was in **Jerusalem** that the temple had been built. The place was holy because of God's presence there (2:6).

137:7 Remember, O Lord: After speaking with great passion about his own remembering and forgetting (vv. 4–6), the psalmist calls upon the Lord to remember the abominable actions of the people of Edom in the day of Jerusalem's trouble. **Raze it:** The men of Edom leered and jeered as Jerusalem was shamefully leveled.

137:8, 9 Happy is the same term of blessing that begins the first psalm (1:1; 146:5). The blessing would come on the army that finally destroyed the wicked city of Babylon, that had itself been used as a tool of judgment in the hands of Almighty God (Hab. 1:12–17).

Psalm 138 is a psalm of declarative praise attributed to David. The mood of this psalm contrasts strongly with that of Ps. 137.

138:1, 2 The psalmist begins his praise with a determination to involve his **whole** being (146:1). **Before the gods:** David is so confident in his faith in the Lord that he is determined to take the name of God into foreign territory.

138:3–6 David, as a king who believed in God, looked forward to a day when **all the kings of the earth** would share his experience. **regards the lowly:** God comes to the humble because they will have regard for Him. Conversely, He distances Himself from the proud (86:14; 147:6).

138:7, 8 Though I walk: The psalmist is aware that new troubles will confront him. He has confidence that God, who has blessed him in the experience of this psalm, will continue to bless his path. **perfect:** The same Hebrew verb is translated "perform" in 57:2. The point of the word is that God acts on behalf of His servants.

Psalm 139, attributed to David, is a wisdom psalm of descriptive praise. This mixture of wisdom and praise is not uncommon in the Psalms (see Ps. 145; 146). This poem describes the attributes of the Lord not as abstract qualities, but as active qualities by which He relates Himself to His people.

139:1–5 You have searched me: God is active to search and test His servants. He knows our motives, desires, and words before they are expressed. In short, He knows His servants completely. But as v. 5 makes clear, the purpose of His intimate knowledge of His servants is protective and helpful, not judgmental and condemning.

139:6, 7 There are two different ways in which the words **where can I go** can be understood. One is that David *wanted* to flee from the presence of God, but could not. The second view takes the words as a celebration of God's mercy, that there was no place in all creation where David, the servant of God, would find himself separated from God's presence.

139:8–12 Your hand: The wording of v. 10 seems protective, suggesting that the psalm speaks of God's helpful presence. **darkness:** Here David stretches his imagination to the brink. Darkness refers to death or the "pit" (16:10). This is an expansion of the words of v. 8, "If I make my bed in hell." David suggests this as the one place in the universe where God would not be present. But even though God is opposed to all darkness, God would turn the darkness into light in order to find His servant David.

139:13–16 You formed my inward parts: David affirms that the work of God in his life extended back to his development in his mother's womb. **You covered me** may also be translated as "You wove me together," a description of the work of God creating the person in the mother's womb. **I am fearfully and wonderfully made** might be rephrased as "I am an awesome wonder" (Ps. 8). **skillfully wrought:** The development of the fetus was something quite mysterious to the ancients. To them, it was as though the fetus were being developed in the middle of the earth. The Hebrew word **my substance** indicates the embryo.

139:17–21 slay the wicked: David desires a world in which there is no more evil, no more distraction, no more destruction. The enemies of God are David's enemies because his life and thoughts are so closely tied to the Lord.

139:22–24 Search me, O God: These words are similar to those of 19:14. David asks God to examine his thoughts and purge him of sin so that he might enter into everlasting life.

Psalm 140, a psalm of individual lament ascribed to David, is particularly concerned with the wicked. David's desire for the judgment of the Lord to come upon the wicked identifies this poem as an imprecatory psalm.

140:1–3 Deliver me: David cries out to the Lord for deliverance from the wicked, who continually harm the innocent.

140:4–6 With the words **You are my God,** David confesses his complete trust in the Lord even though he is surrounded by people plotting his destruction. On the basis of his trust, he now pleads with the Lord to deliver him.

140:7–10 Let burning coals fall upon them: David recalls the judgment of Sodom and Gomorrah (11:6; Gen. 19:12–29) and asks God to use this particular judgment on his enemies.

140:11–13 The **cause** of the **poor** and the **afflicted** is of special interest to the Lord. He promises to uphold and comfort them (41:1; 72:4; 109:31; Luke 4:18; 6:20).

Psalm 141, an individual psalm of lament, is ascribed to David. In this case no particular

event is cited as the cause for David's distress. Because this poem records David's desire for the judgment of his enemies, it falls into the category of the imprecatory psalms.

141:1, 2 Lord, I cry out to you: David asks to be heard as he prays in the assembly of the righteous. As the smoke and aroma of **incense** rises to the Lord as something sweet and compelling, so David desires that his prayer will not be ignored.

141:3 Set a guard: This is a prayer for wisdom, for restraining evil language, and for knowing the correct words to speak. David wanted to avoid any act of impiety, irreverence, or even idolatry; he did not want to offend God with anything he said.

141:4–7 With the words **let the righteous strike me,** David expresses his willingness to accept the judgment of the righteous; what bothers him is the instruction and judgment of the wicked. **against the deeds of the wicked:** The wicked have brought David to his state of distress. He envisions a day when the wicked will be destroyed.

141:8–10 In light of the wicked's strength, it is easy for us to fix our eyes on, or worry about, the wicked. It is also natural to focus on ourselves. We either become self-absorbed in our difficulties or exalt ourselves in our victories. But David fixes his **eyes** only on the Lord (2 Cor. 3:18; Heb. 12:2, 3).

Psalm 142, a psalm of individual lament ascribed to David, provides a specific reference for the setting of the poem. The term *the cave* may refer to one of two occasions on which David hid from King Saul in a cave. One occurred in En Gedi (Ps. 57; 1 Sam. 24); the other at Adullam (1 Sam. 22:1, 2). The second may well be the setting for this poem of deep anguish. This was a time in David's life when it appeared that he was totally alone. In fact, he began to doubt whether even God was truly for him. But as the superscription indicates, David turned to the Lord in prayer.

142:1, 2 I cry out: There is a significant emphasis on the vocal and desperate nature of David's lament in this psalm. **With my voice** may also be translated "aloud."

142:3–5 In the midst of his distress, David

makes his preliminary confession of trust—God **knew** his **path** from the beginning. **Look on my right hand:** With enemies on every path, David screams aloud to God that he is defenseless. **You are my refuge:** In the midst of his pain, David renews his confession of trust that somehow God must be near. He then pleads with God to deliver him from his foes.

142:6, 7 The cave that was intended as a place of refuge has become a place of confinement—**a prison.** The psalm ends with a vow that when God would deliver him from his awful experience, David would bring renewed **praise** to God in the worshiping community.

Psalm 143, a psalm of individual lament ascribed to David, is similar in tone to other psalms of distress, particularly Ps. 6. Some scholars categorize Ps. 6 and 143 as penitential psalms.

143:1–3 David asks God not to bring him **into judgment,** yet he does not confess his sins as in Ps. 32; 38. **no one living is righteous:** This is not so much a confession of sin as an observation that everyone is sinful. **in darkness:** To live in darkness is similar to being in the pit (v. 7); this is the reason for the parallel to those who are already dead (Job 10:21, 22).

143:4–6 the days of old: This is similar to 42:4, in which the psalmist remembers rejoicing in temple worship in times gone by. **spread out my hands:** This was one of the traditional postures for prayer in biblical times.

143:7, 8 the pit: Without a renewed sense of God's presence, described by the words, **Your face,** David believes that he is as good as dead. **in the morning:** Often in the psalms there is an expectation that an answer from God might come with the morning light (5:3; 30:5; 130:6).

143:9–12 for Your name's sake: The requests of the psalmists are often tied to various character traits of God. When we pray "in Jesus' name," we pray both in the authority of His name and in the character it represents.

Psalm 144, a psalm of descriptive praise with overtones of lament and petition, is ascribed to David. This poem is similar to Ps. 18 in that it describes the salvation acts of the Lord in terms of great heavenly phenomena.

144:1, 2 The LORD my Rock is often used in the Psalms to describe God as the fortress of His people. At times, the word is translated *strength* (18:1). David found in the Lord the protection and preparation he needed in times of battle.

144:3, 4 what is man: This is a quotation from 8:4, but without the stunning answer presented in 8:5. Here the rhetorical question is used to speak of the frailty of humans who are in need of God's help. **passing shadow:** The sense of human frailty is illustrated dramatically in these words (102:2, 3).

144:5, 6 The lightning of the Lord is a symbol of His judgment (97:4). David celebrates God's righteous judgments, which he prays will be exercised against his evil foes.

144:7–10 I will sing a new song is David vows to respond to God's deliverance with renewed worship and praise (149:1). **David:** It is rare for these poems to mention the psalmist by name (18:50). David's use of his own name indicated to later generations that this psalm arose out of actual experiences in his life.

144:11 lying words: The principal lie of the enemy was that the Lord could not save His people (Ps. 12).

144:12–15 The image of **pillars** seems to indicate health, beauty, and dignity. **barns:** Agricultural productivity was possible only in times of peace and would be meaningful only in times of national freedom. **Happy:** The happiness that David describes refers both to external well-being—**in such a state**—and to internal peace—**whose God is the LORD.**

Psalm 145, a wisdom psalm, is also a psalm of declarative praise. The poem is written in the form of an acrostic, with one verse for each letter of the Hebrew alphabet.

145:1–3 The familiar words **great is the Lord** express God's grandeur in the universe and remind us of how small we are in His presence. The fact that frail humans are used to praise God is a marvel to the psalmist.

145:4–6 One generation ... to another: The expectation is that the message of God's wonder and mercy will be known throughout the land and will be taught for generations.

145:7 The word **memory** may refer to the divine name of God. The Hebrew term for *memory* is translated "memorial" in Ex. 3:15.

145:8 God had described Himself as **gracious and full of compassion** (Ex. 34:6, 7; Num. 14:18). David uses God's own words to praise Him for His merciful character (86:5, 15; 111:4; 112:4).

145:9–13 All Your works echoes the words of 19:1–3. All that God has made bears the marks of His wonder (111:2). **They shall speak:** The task of the righteous is to declare the works of the Lord to all people. **an everlasting kingdom:** Because the rule of God is eternal, the message of His wonders needs to be delivered to all people in the present time.

145:14 The words **upholds all who fall** describe the ongoing actions of God on behalf of the needy in a way that may suggest that these words are absolute and invariable. Yet the same people who sang the songs of praise also cried out to the Lord with the psalms of lament. In a world in which life is tough, the psalms delight in affirming that God is good and that there is no limit to His power, His love, and His concern for His people.

145:15–17 The pairing of **righteous** and **gracious** is a powerful demonstration of the character of God. His righteousness leads to His discriminating judgment; His grace leads to His saving works and forgiving actions. God both preserves and destroys based on His infallible insight into human intent and purposes.

145:18–21 My mouth: David resolved to be faithful in praising the Lord (146:1), but he also saw his praise as one part of the praise of all creation—that is, **all flesh.**

Psalm 146, a psalm of descriptive praise, is part of the grand pinnacle of praise in this book of praises. Each of the last five psalms begins and ends with the Hebrew word "Hallelujah!" This final set of praise psalms

forms an exuberant ending to Israel's orchestrated responses to the wonder of God and His gracious works on their behalf. Psalm 146 also shows some similarities with wisdom literature.

146:1, 2 My soul is another way of speaking of one's inner being and is often used as a substitute for the pronouns "I" or "me." **while I live:** The psalmist makes a strong vow to praise the Lord for the rest of his life.

146:3 in princes: The point is that even the best of people are not adequate help in times of terrible stress. Even princes are mortal, and are not able even to help themselves (118:9). In contrast is the individual who finds ultimate help in God who lives forever (vv. 5–7).

146:4–6 Happy indicates a deep and abiding pleasure, a manifest joy. This is the proper description of one whose help and hope is in God. **Who made heaven and earth:** Creation themes pervade the hymns of Israel (Ps. 104); here the point is that the Creator of the universe is the One who comes to the aid of the righteous.

146:7–9 the eyes of the blind: In these two verses there is a special focus on the gracious actions of God on behalf of the impaired, the helpless, the lonely, and the needy (38:6).

146:10 The Lord shall reign forever: The Bible presents several dimensions of the rule of God: He is King as Creator (Ps. 93); He is King as Savior of His people (Ps. 99); and He is King as the coming One (Ps. 98). This verse speaks of God's present and eternal reign rather than specifically of His coming rule at the end of time.

Psalm 147, a psalm of descriptive praise, places a strong emphasis on creation themes. This anonymous poem was likely written following the return of the Jewish people to Jerusalem from the Babylonian captivity (also Ps. 126; 132; 135).

147:1 The sentiment **praise is beautiful** is also expressed in 33:1. The people of God may bring their offerings of praise and worship to the Lord.

147:2, 3 builds up Jerusalem: The few people who had returned from captivity faced an immense task. But they needed to know that because the work was God's, He would see that it was accomplished. **He heals the brokenhearted:** God's principal work is within the human heart (51:10–12).

147:4–6 He counts the number of the stars: Quoted from Is. 40:26, these words describe the infinite knowledge of God. But the words signify more: God's principal interest is not in stars or insects; God's interest is in His people (v. 11). **lifts up the humble:** God's greatness may be approached only by the humble; He resists the proud, but He comforts the lowly (86:14; 146:9; James 4:6).

147:7–9 rain for the earth: A regular part of God's covenantal mercies is the bringing of rain for produce and livelihood (Lev. 26:1–13). More than that, God sends rain on the just and the unjust because of His continuing mercy to all.

147:10, 11 He does not delight: The enjoyment God finds in His people is greater than any pleasure He may find in horses or runners. To **fear** God is to be properly responsive to Him in awe and wonder.

147:12 The words **praise the LORD** introduce the third movement of the psalm. This section was a reminder to the new settlers in the land of promise that God had blessed them in numerous ways. He had given them protection, posterity, peace, and productivity.

147:13–20 God's word goes throughout His creation, causing snow, frost, hail, wind, and every other aspect of weather to obey His command. Here He gives His word to His people. Shall we obey as does the wind? Or shall we be the only element of creation that is unresponsive to the divine will?

Psalm 148 is a complex psalm. Because of its many references to the creation, it can be labeled a wisdom psalm, and more particularly a creation psalm (Ps. 19; 104). It is also highly charged with praise. Like Ps. 19, this psalm moves from the heavens to the human heart.

148:1–6 Praise Him: All of the universe is called to boast of the wonder of God. In this first section, praise is commanded from all aspects of the heavens above, including the angelic hosts. The language **waters above the heavens** comes from the creation story

in Gen. 1:7. **He commanded:** Genesis 1 describes creation as a spontaneous response to the word of God (33:9; 147:15).

148:7, 8 The focus of the psalm switches to **the earth.** All hosts above and all creatures below are to praise our great God. **great sea creatures:** This includes real sea creatures that inspired awe and wonder, as well as creatures of mythology that the Canaanites had made into gods. Israel called on all creatures to praise God—both those that are His creation and those that their neighbors believed to be gods.

148:9–14 the horn of His people: The people are pictured here as an animal whose strength is in its horn. **near:** When we consider the meaning of God's holiness (99:1; Is. 6:3), the marvel that He approaches us to mercifully provide for us becomes overwhelming.

Psalm 149, an exuberant call to praise God, was used by the army of Israel as well as by the people in their worship of God.

149:1 The call for **a new song** comes at several points in the Psalms (33:3; 40:3; 144:9). These words encourage more than just novelty; they call for freshness and integrity in performing music.

149:2–5 Maker: Not only is God the Creator of the universe (8:3; 19:1; 104:1–35), He is particularly the Creator of His people (100:3) and their great King (Ps. 93). In the temple of the preexilic period, sacred **dance** was an integral aspect of worship (150:4). **Saints** refers to the redeemed who have been made God's people by His grace. The Hebrew word is related to the term meaning "loyal love" (13:5). The *saints* are those who demonstrate in their lives the characteristics of God whom they serve. **on their beds:** In some of the festivals of Israel, such as Passover, the people would recline at feast tables as a vivid symbol that they had been redeemed. In the first Passover (Ex. 12), the people were to eat standing, ready to travel. The custom had developed for the people to recline at the table, symbolizing their redemption and enjoyment of God's work in their lives.

149:6–8 two-edged sword: The focus of the psalm switches from the congregation at worship to the army in training. Israel's army was to be the vanguard for the battle of the Lord. Their training was to have a strong component of praise and worship to God.

149:9 the written judgment: It is likely that this is a direct reference to the Law (perhaps Deut. 7:1, 2) in which God decreed His judgment on the peoples of the land of Canaan.

Psalm 150, a psalm of praise, is a development of the Hebrew word *hallelujah,* meaning "Praise the Lord." How fitting that this book of praises—the meaning of the name of the Book of Psalms in Hebrew—ends in repeated commands to praise the Lord.

150:1–5 The varied instruments in this section include horns, reeds, strings, and percussion, encompassing many of the instruments known in Israel at that time (33:2, 3; 98:4–6).

150:6 everything that has breath: The very breath that God gives us should be used to praise Him. By His breath God created all things (33:6), and by our breath we should adore Him. The Book of Psalms begins with God's blessing on the righteous (1:1) and concludes with all of creation blessing its loving Creator.

Proverbs

Introduction

The Book of Proverbs passes on a core of knowledge and experience that God says we *must* have if we are to live successfully. These proverbs are universal principles that speak to modern problems as much as to ancient ones because they concern human nature and God's ways.

The title of the Book of Proverbs (1:1) and two collections of maxims within it (10:1; 25:1) identify King Solomon as their author. First Kings confirms this by attributing three thousand proverbs and more than a thousand songs to him (1 Kin. 4:32). Although Solomon was the main writer of the Book of Proverbs (10:1—22:16), some proverbs were written by other writers, and some of Solomon's were not added to the book until after his death. Agur wrote ch. 30, and Lemuel wrote 31:1–9. We have no information about Agur (ch. 30) or Lemuel (31:1–9) besides their names.

Solomon's 375 proverbs (10:1—22:16) appear as a large collection with no particular organization. In places a few sentences on one theme appear together, but other sentences on that theme often appear elsewhere as well. Many other topics are interspersed throughout the collection.

The purpose of the Book of Proverbs is to give a course of instruction in wisdom, preparation for life, and the ways of life in God's world. Israel's contribution to wisdom literature was to place all wisdom in the context of faith in the Lord. The words "The fear of the LORD is the beginning of knowledge" (1:7) set the record straight. This is the foundation on which all other wise sayings stand. It is the Book of Proverbs' central idea: Fear of the Lord motivates us to obey God's commandments, and obedience to them constitutes true wisdom.

1:1, 2 Verses 2–6 explain the purpose of the Book of Proverbs. The verbs **to know, to perceive,** and **to receive** refer to the ways we acquire wisdom. **Wisdom** refers to skill. **Instruction** could also be translated *discipline;* it refers to the process of receiving knowledge and then applying it to daily life.

1:3 The word for **wisdom** in this verse is different from the word used in v. 1. This word denotes applied skill, such as that of an artisan or a musician. That is, wisdom affects living much the way the skills of artists affect the practice of their craft. The words **justice, judgment, and equity** give wisdom, discipline, and words of insight a moral context.

1:4 The simple or "naive" is young, inexperienced, and likely to make mistakes. The terms **prudence** and **discretion** include the harsh facts of life. A wise person has learned by experience how to distinguish what is true, praiseworthy, and good from what is false, shameful, and bad (see Rom. 12:1, 2).

1:5, 6 increase learning: No one finishes the study of wisdom; there is always more to learn. Verse 6 speaks of the lessons that a more mature person gains from the study of a **proverb, an enigma, words of the wise,** and **riddles.**

1:7 The fear of the LORD is the most basic ingredient in wisdom. All wisdom depends on knowledge of God and submission to His will. To know something but not to know God overturns the value of having knowledge in the first place.

1:8, 9 The opening words of wisdom's instruction come as an appeal from parents to their **son** (a generic term for child)—a theme that continues throughout the book. Both **father** and **mother** teach.

1:10–14 if sinners entice you: This is the first of several texts in which wisdom teaches by means of a story.

1:15–18 The parents speak words of caution. One step on this precipitous path is a step toward destruction. Spreading a **net** in the sight of the bird one wishes to trap would be a fruitless task. Yet the fool is less sensible than the bird; he will watch the trap being set and get caught in it anyway.

1:19 It takes away the life: These words conclude the story and introduce a theme that the following passages develop further: The study of wisdom is a matter of life and death.

1:20, 21 The word **wisdom** is plural but the verb **calls** is singular. The plural is intensive—it calls attention to the word and heightens its meaning.

1:22–27 Wisdom addresses the **simple ones,** or "open ones," the naive. These are young people who have not yet made up their minds about life or the direction they will take. Wisdom ridicules those who reject her when they come to face the inevitable judgment of their foolishness (see Ps. 2:4). Yet Wisdom laughs with joy at God's works and has delight in the people of God (8:30, 31).

1:28–33 I will not answer: When fools despise wisdom, they must face the results of their choice. Their hatred for wisdom arises out of a refusal to fear God (v. 29). Fools bring about their own destruction. Rejection of wisdom **will slay them.**

2:1–4 These verses begin the second of the **my son** passages and tie the concepts of wisdom and the knowledge of God more closely together. On the one hand, wisdom is near and available. Yet it is not easy to embrace.

2:5–7 When a person seeks wisdom, he or she finds it in **the fear of the LORD,** or **the knowledge of God.** Those who know God fear (revere) Him. **sound wisdom:** Here is another word for wisdom, a word that may be translated "abiding success" or "victory."

2:8, 9 The phrase **paths of justice** (v. 8) contrasts strongly with ways of darkness (v. 13). This contrast introduces one of the dominant themes of Proverbs, the contrast of two roads. Jesus spoke of two roads, one narrow and the other broad (Matt. 7:13, 14). The right road is marked by demands of **righteousness, justice,** and **equity** (see 1:3).

2:10, 11 enters your heart: These words emphasize the internalization of wisdom. The proverbs do not just provide knowledge; they provide insight to be learned and practiced.

2:12–15 The way of evil (v. 12) contrasts directly with the way of wisdom. It is characterized by **perverse things,** by lies and distortion, by twisting and deception, and by darkness and deviousness.

2:16–22 The immoral woman is literally "the strange woman." Adultery was foreign and strange to the ideal of God's law. "Adulteress" also connoted prostitution, because the "foreign women" of the ancient Middle Eastern fertility cults included sexual practices in their worship rituals.

3:1, 2 Law and **commands** are words that, as in 1:8, draw attention to the connection

---

IN DEPTH | **What Kind of Wisdom?**

The purpose of Proverbs is straightforward: "to know wisdom" (Prov. 1:2). It is common to conceive of wisdom as either an advanced form of knowledge or learning, or else as a rare sense of deep understanding and insight. This view of wisdom has a touch of the mystical about it, as if those who possess it had in some way tapped into profound, enigmatic truths from ages past.

However, there is no mystery about the wisdom talked about in Proverbs, nor is it necessarily limited to a privileged few. The wisdom that Proverbs mentions more than forty times and that Ecclesiastes mentions twenty-seven times is the Hebrew *chokmah*, which means something like "the skill of living." This wisdom is practical, not esoteric. It means that a person knows how to live in a responsible, productive, and prosperous way.

From that standpoint, the wisdom of Proverbs has a lot in common with what we might call common sense, or even "street smarts." It is an understanding of the way the world works. The issue is not so much what one knows intellectually but what one does practically. It is truth applied.

That is why Proverbs deals with so many day-to-day issues of life, especially those involving moral choices and other decisions that affect the future. The wise person (Hebrew *chakam*) avoids evil and promotes good by observing what others have chosen and then pursuing a course of action based on the outcomes. Thus the Proverbs are not so much promises of God as they are observations and principles about how life works.

between wisdom and the Law of Moses. The proverbs are an application of the Law.

3:3, 4 Mercy and truth is an important pair of words in the Bible, describing God's character (see Ps. 100:5) and the demands He makes of His people.

3:5, 6 The words **trust in the LORD** echo the command of Deut. 6:5 to love God with all our being. Trusting in God is a conscious dependence on God, much like leaning on a tree for support. The idea is reinforced here by the command to **acknowledge Him,** which means to observe Him and get to know Him in the process of living.

3:7–10 The command to honor God with wealth and to give to Him from the **firstfruits** of all income is a part of what it means to worship God. In God's covenant with Israel, fullness of **barns** and **vats** was God's blessing, a part of God's covenant promise. Yet these verses should not be taken as a formula for getting rich. They speak of what righteous people can reasonably expect in life, not what God promises to return on investments.

3:11, 12 The discipline of the **LORD** is the other side of His grace. We should cherish God's correction in our lives, because God disciplines only those He **loves** (see Heb. 12:7–10).

3:13–18 Happy: The Hebrew term **blessed** implies that God is truly pleased. The person who has discovered wisdom has found a priceless treasure. Adam and Eve were expelled from the Garden and forbidden access to the tree of life (Gen. 3:22–24), but wisdom is another **tree of life** and will begin to restore the lost happiness of Paradise.

3:19, 20 by wisdom founded the earth: One central theme in Proverbs is the association of wisdom with creation. Chapter 8 is devoted to this theme.

3:21–27 let them not depart: This verse encourages the **son** to keep faith with wisdom. The intent is much like that of the Shema (see Deut. 6:4–9). It also resembles the basic ideas of Ps. 91 (compare v. 26 with Ps. 91:10–13).

3:28 This verse introduces a passage that explains the proper treatment of **your neighbor,** a theme that Jesus also developed (Luke 10:25–37).

3:29–35 There is no benefit in feeling **envy** for **the wicked,** because God detests wickedness. Only a fool would wish to be detestable to God!

4:1–4 In most of the ancient Middle East, instruction in wisdom was primarily a matter of training for the court. The masters were regarded as "fathers" of the students. But in Israel, training in wisdom extended to the home. **Instruction of a father** implies warmth and affection, as well as a parent's concern and discipline. Verse 1 begins a little like the first parental section (1:8), but the addressee is now plural, **my children.** As his father had taught him, so the son now teaches his own sons.

4:5–7 Verses 5–9 present an impassioned plea from the father to his sons to **get wisdom** whatever the cost. The presentation in these early chapters of Proverbs follows the pattern: statement, restatement, embellishment. By making generous use of creative restatement, the ideas come through all the more strongly. Particularly striking are the words of v. 7: **Wisdom is the principal thing.**

4:8, 9 These verses emphasize the supreme value of wisdom. The person who holds wisdom in highest esteem and embraces it fully will be exalted and honored; its very presence becomes an **ornament of grace** and a **crown of glory.**

4:10–19 These verses present a renewed appeal from father to son to walk in **the way of wisdom** and to avoid **the path of the wicked** at all costs. The contrast of the two **paths** is profound. The way of wisdom is straight, unencumbered, and safe. The way of the wicked is tortuous, hazardous, and marked by violence.

4:20–27 This section demands constancy of **heart** and purpose, honesty in speech, steadiness of gaze, and a right goal in walk and **life.** Setting off on the path of wisdom is no casual thing.

5:1–6 Chapter 5 returns to the theme of the **immoral woman** (see 2:16–19). This passage speaks strongly for marital fidelity against any and all pressure to the contrary.

5:7–14 The Bible teaches that temptation in general is unavoidable, but some temptations should be avoided at all costs. A wise son knows this and will **not go near** an immoral woman.

5:15 In an arid country like Israel, a **well** was a prized possession and a privilege to be cared for. So was (and is) a spouse. **Drink water** is an oblique reference to sexual union (see 9:17), and **from your own cistern** is a clear call to marital fidelity—one man, one woman, together in marriage.

5:16–23 The words **rejoice with the wife of your youth** comprise a command and an encouragement to find pleasure in the mutual joy of married love.

6:1–5 These verses warn against putting up **surety** (see 11:15), or cosigning a loan. This does not mean we should never be generous or helpful if we have the means, only that we should not promise what we cannot deliver. In Solomon's day, a cosigner who could not pay could lose all he had and be reduced to slavery besides. Even though laws differ today, inability to pay a debt is still a form of bondage and can be a serious problem.

6:6–11 This passage warns against the trap of laziness. The **sluggard** or lazy person is held captive to leisure. He can learn all he needs to know by studying the **ant,** a humble creature that busies itself with storing food during the summer against the winter that lies ahead. Like the ant, a wise person works hard. By contrast, the lazy person is addicted to sleep and has lost all interest in work (see 26:13–16).

6:12–15 **A wicked man** is a troublemaker. Unlike the sluggard, whose only desire is another place to nap, the troublemaker cannot wait to cause more problems or to get into more mischief. Unlike the sluggard (see v. 6), he is too busy, though he is doing the wrong things. He delights in bringing dissension. But like the sluggard, he does not realize that **calamity** awaits him.

6:16–19 This passage is a numerical proverb (see 30:15–31) that describes **seven** things that **the LORD hates.** The use of numerical progression—six, even seven—in these proverbs is a rhetorical device that embellishes the poetry, provides a memory aid, and builds to a climax. In a list of this type,

the last item is the most prominent. Thus, the reader knows that causing **discord among brethren** (see v. 14) causes God's greatest disapproval. Contrast the blessing of God on brothers who live together in peace (Ps. 133:1).

6:20–24 This passage links the teaching of the father with that of the **mother** (see 1:8). The mother's instruction should be bound about one's **heart** and **neck,** a constant companion and a trusted guide—just like God's law.

6:25–35 **steals to satisfy:** This passage does not condone theft. It contrasts theft, which can be an understandable course of action, with adultery, which never makes sense. Throwing away one's commitment to one's lifelong companion is pure folly. For the ancient Israelites, marital fidelity was a mark of one's fidelity to God.

7:1–5 The problem of immorality (see 2:16–19; 5:1–23; 6:20–35) does have a solution: **Keep my commands ... as the apple of your eye.** People should guard wise words as instinctively as they protect the pupil of the eye.

7:6–13 The **young man** who gives in to the immoral woman is described as **simple,** a term that pegs him as naive, inexperienced, and **devoid of understanding** (see 1:4; 9:3). He has no idea how foolish he is. He thinks he makes his way to the **woman,** but she in fact seduces him.

7:14–21 The adulteress begins her proposition by talking about her supposedly righteous actions that day. Since the offerings she presented to the Lord were fellowship or **peace offerings,** she could bring part of them home for a feast before the Lord. But here she presents the offering as a feast for the young man she plans to entrap. She overcomes her target's fear by assuring him that her husband will not come home and discover them together.

7:22–27 The passage here uses several unflattering metaphors to describe how a young fool falls into immorality. The phrase **as a fool to the correction of the stocks** could be translated "as a stag prances into captivity." The idea is that the young man is oblivious to his fate.

8:1–11 Chapter 7 focused our attention on the fool and the traps that catch him; ch. 8 shifts to wisdom. It is a hymn of praise about how wonderful wisdom is. **Does not wisdom cry out:** Wisdom wants to reach everyone and therefore broadcasts her message publicly, unlike the immoral woman, who uses privacy and deception to achieve her goals. Wisdom's words of **truth** contrast with the lies of **wickedness** 7:21–23; wisdom will deliver on her promises; she is not a tawdry tease. What wisdom offers is of inestimable worth, far more valuable than **silver** and **gold.**

8:12, 13 The words **I, wisdom, dwell with prudence** introduce the second section of this passage about the excellence of wisdom (vv. 12–21). Again in this context we see wisdom tied directly to **the fear of the LORD.** The offer of wisdom is held out only to those who fear God. Coming to wisdom requires coming to God, and coming to God means turning away from all that God hates.

8:14–21 princes … nobles … judges: Power and authority require the use of wisdom; this is one of its loftiest appeals. What's more, wisdom leads those who follow her to **riches and honor** (see 9:1–6). These contrast directly with the shameful fate of the fool (6:33, 35).

8:22–31 This section of ch. 8 describes wisdom's role in creation. **The LORD possessed me at the beginning of His way:** The Hebrew verb for *possessed* can mean "brought forth" or "created." Melchizedek used the same word to identify God as creator of the universe (see Gen. 14:19). God, who is ever wise, produced wisdom; God, who possesses all knowledge, brought forth knowledge. Wisdom had a **beginning** only in the sense that God singled it out for special display at that time; insofar as it is one of God's perfections, it has always existed. The term **master craftsman** speaks of an artisan or of a darling child. Wisdom is both. With wisdom's skill, God created the universe. **delight:** In her playful, childlike exuberance, Wisdom is a darling child. And her greatest joy comes in the finest of the work of God—**the sons of men**—that is, humankind.

8:32–36 Now therefore, listen to me, my children: This section is the epilogue of the ch. 8 hymn of praise. It calls everyone to listen. Wisdom offers blessing and life to those who heed her, but cursing and death to those who hate her. Wisdom's gracious invitation is more desirable than anything and an invitation to a **blessed** life.

9:1 Here is the final contrast between wisdom and folly. Each holds a banquet, one for life (vv. 1–6) and one for death (vv. 13–18). Between the two banquet descriptions is a section (vv. 7–12) that speaks of consequences of the life of wisdom and of the plight of folly. **Seven pillars:** The number seven represents completeness, as it often does in Semitic poetry. That is, it is not that there were precisely seven pillars so much as that the house of wisdom was solidly built and substantial in character.

9:2, 3 The meal at wisdom's banquet includes **meat** and **wine** and a lovely **table** (see 7:14). Freshly butchered meat was a mark of a feast in biblical times. **mixed her wine:** Wine was a staple in ancient Israel; but when a feast was special, a homemaker would add aromatic spices to the wine, enlivening the bouquet and improving the taste (see Song 8:2). This all sets up a contrast with the foolish woman. While wisdom is busy, attending to every detail like a gracious hostess, the foolish woman sits at the entrance of her house with very little to do (v. 14). Wisdom sends her trusted **maidens** throughout the city, inviting people to come and dine.

9:4–6 Wisdom makes a point of inviting the **simple,** meaning those who have not yet made up their minds about their course in life (see 1:4; 7:6). **Forsake foolishness:** The person who comes to wisdom has nothing to lose but naivete. See Heb. 5:14, which speaks of a mature person as one who is able to eat and to enjoy solid food, in contrast to the naive who is able only to drink milk (Heb. 5:13).

9:7–9 A **scoffer** or mocker is thoroughly set against wisdom (see 1:22) and scoffs at the things of God (Ps. 1:1). How should a person respond to a mocker? It is best not to respond at all. By contrast, a **wise man**

accepts correction and responds with gratitude to the one who points out his error.

9:10–12 fear of the LORD: This is the central theme of the Book of Proverbs (see 1:7). The only appropriate way to approach the holy God is with fear, or reverence. The term **Holy One** is an intensive plural of the Hebrew word for *holy:* "the most Holy One" or "the quintessence of holiness."

9:13–18 This section is a parody of vv. 1–6. Like personified wisdom, the **foolish woman** calls out an invitation. But she is brash, loud, undisciplined, and **knows nothing** (see 7:10–12). She cries out in the same words that wisdom has used (compare v. 16 with v. 4), but with a twist: she has no marvelous banquet for her guests, only shabby food, stolen and meager.

10:1, 2 The proverbs of Solomon focus on the **wise son**, as in chs. 1—9, and contrast him with the **foolish son.** The term *son* is generic—the central issue is not that he is a son rather than a daughter, but that he is wise or foolish. The child's behavior affects both parents. Both parents find their joy or sadness in their child who demonstrates skill in life.

10:3 This verse speaks of God's gracious provision of food for the **righteous** and His retributive justice on the **wicked.** Proverbs such as this emphasize (1) circumstances as they ought to be and (2) the *end* of the wicked (see Ps. 73:17). They do not necessarily indicate circumstances as they always are, nor what the wicked are experiencing right now.

10:4 slack hand ... poor: Proverbs often link laziness with poverty, and hard work with riches, but not always (see v. 2). This proverb states the norm.

10:5 Gathers in summer contrasts a skillful person with a shameful person, based on whether he works hard during the harvest season.

10:6, 7 In biblical times, a person's **name** was significant and important. When a person's name was remembered by future generations for good, that person's life was believed to have been of great value. But when the memory of a name rotted away, it was as though that person had never lived.

10:8 The Hebrew verb for **will fall** means "is ruined" and comes from the same root as the verb *will rot* in v. 7.

10:9 Many of the proverbs contrast two paths of life. **Walks with integrity** means conforming to God's law as a course of life. Choosing crooked paths is willfully to disdain the Law God so graciously provided.

10:10 winks with the eye: Although many proverbs contrast two behaviors, both units of this proverb speak of evil actions. Moreover, the second unit of this verse is identical with the second unit of v. 8; this is a connective link that ties the passage together.

10:11, 12 Hatred ... love: This verse describes interpersonal relationships, not salvation. When people respond in love to each other, they cover over the **sins,** or offenses, that would otherwise come between them.

10:13 This proverb tells of the positive role that speech can have—that of speaking wisdom. The **rod** refers to punishment, in this case deserved. The term **devoid of understanding** comes from the Hebrew idiom "lack heart." The one who "lacks heart" is contrasted with the one who is "wise in heart" (see v. 8).

10:14, 15 These verses contrasts the wise person's pursuit of knowledge with the empty talk of a fool. **Wealth** is like a **strong city.** In biblical times only walled cities had any defense against enemy armies; likewise, a wealthy person is able to withstand the assaults of others.

10:16, 17 These verses present the doctrine of the two ways: The righteous is on the **way of life,** but the wicked wander from it.

10:18–21 These verses tell of the dangers of speech, particularly **lying** and **slander.** The way to avoid these sins is to exercise restraint.

10:22–24 For the fool, wickedness is only a game. He makes up the rules as he goes along; for him losing is only in getting caught. But a person who has understanding takes a longer-term perspective. In the end he gets his way while justice comes upon the **wicked.**

10:25, 26 The short-lived nature of the wicked is contrasted with the stability of the righteous.

As in Ps. 1:3, 4, where the righteous are compared to a tree and the wicked to chaff, so in this proverb the storm blows away the wicked but cannot dislodge the righteous. The **everlasting foundation** of the righteous is faith in God.

10:27 This verse contains the first instance of the phrase **the fear of the LORD** in chs. 10—22 (see 1:7, 29; 2:5; 8:13; 9:10). The tie of piety to long life and of wickedness to an early death is another common theme in Proverbs (see 3:1, 2).

10:28 hope ... expectation: The **righteous** have something to look forward to; the **wicked** do not (v. 24).

10:29 Different people see the **way of the LORD** differently. Those who are innocent see it as a shelter from the storm and the heat of the day. Those who practice iniquity see it only as a source of terror.

10:30 This proverb presents a confident hope in the ultimate survival of the righteous and the final judgment of the **wicked.** In our limited experience, we might see the wicked succeeding and the righteous only struggling to live. But the final judgment (see Ps. 73) will reverse their fortunes.

10:31, 32 These verses form another pair of sentences about true and false speech. They may be compared to vv. 11, 13, 20, 21 and James 3. This repetition with variation indicates the significance of truth and falsehood in both ancient Israel and in the modern world as well.

11:1 Dealing fairly with one another is an outgrowth of the command to love one's neighbor as oneself (see Lev. 19:18), which in turn is an outgrowth of the central command given to Israel, to love God alone (see Deut. 6:4–9). That is why false balances are an **abomination** to God.

11:2 Many proverbs contrast the arrogant with the humble, as this one does. The Hebrew word for **pride** comes from a root that means "to boil up"; it refers to a raging arrogance or insolence. The image pictures the presumptuous or arrogant behavior of the godless person.

11:3–6 These verses form a series of proverbs that contrast the results of righteousness and perversity in people's lives. As pride

and humility are contrasted in v. 2, so **integrity** and **perversity** are contrasted in v. 3.

11:7–9 From time to time the proverbs speak of **death** as a time of reward and punishment. **Riches** cannot help with this. Only righteousness has meaning and power beyond the grave.

11:10, 11 Truly **righteous** people bring justice to all the inhabitants of a **city,** and the city experiences true peace—that is, *shalom,* meaning "things as they ought to be." Many Psalm writers cried for vindication of the righteous and for a cessation of evil (see Ps. 69:22–28).

11:12 Patience and control are part of wisdom. A person who is **devoid of wisdom,** who "lacks heart" (see 10:13), despises his neighbor. But the understanding person knows enough to control his passion and to keep silence (see 17:28).

11:13 A **faithful** friend **conceals** delicate matters that an unfaithful person reveals. "Love covers a multitude of sins" (see James 5:20).

11:14 In modern times as much as formerly, leaders of nations need adequate **counsel.** So do all individuals. We all need to seek advice from wise and trustworthy people.

11:15, 16 These two proverbs balance each other. The first warns against rashly giving **surety** or a pledge for a stranger. The second praises generosity; generosity begets honor. One of the greatest virtues is to be freed of possessiveness.

11:17–19 Proverbs such as this remind us that the pursuit of righteousness is a matter of **life** and **death.**

11:20, 21 The term **join forces** is literally "hand for hand." Collective opposition to God's purposes makes no sense at all (Ps. 2:1–4).

11:22 A golden **ring** would be ludicrous on a pig's **snout.** To the ancient Israelites, pigs were unclean and repellent. The immoral person is compared to such an animal.

11:23 The term **desire** is used in some of the proverbs in a negative sense (see 13:12, 19; 18:1; 19:22), but here it has a positive meaning. The righteous desire good.

11:24–27 These proverbs should shape our attitudes toward wealth: it should be shared. Stinginess may lead **to poverty.** Generosity has the opposite effect. Selfishness is foolish because it only creates enemies and dishonors God.

11:28 This proverb addresses the folly of trusting in **riches.** The second line can easily be misinterpreted to mean that righteousness always leads to success. The proverb actually addresses a person's attitude toward wealth. It is foolish to trust in riches instead of God.

11:29, 30 The image of the **tree of life** denotes the tree in the Garden of Eden (Gen. 2; 3). Righteousness and wisdom are ways of recovering the lost tree of life.

11:31 Here is a **how much more** proverb, one that argues from a premise to conclusion. Since the righteous will finally find their reward (see 2 Cor. 5:10), it follows that the wicked, who are defiant toward God and in conflict with His works, will certainly receive judgment.

12:1 The wise person knows that discipline and instruction will bring its own reward. Yet the person who hates a reprimand is **stupid,** literally "stupid as a cow."

12:2 He will condemn: John's Gospel speaks of one being condemned already because of evil deeds, and deliberately clinging to the darkness even though the light has come (see John 3:16–21).

12:3 Contrasts such as the one in this proverb speak of a person's ultimate end; otherwise they would be proven false by countless examples of wicked persons who flourish while the righteous suffer. *In the end,* the righteous will stand sure.

12:4 Excellent wife, or "noble woman," are the same Hebrew words used in the famous acrostic in 31:10–31. A husband whose wife is like the woman described in ch. 31 should rejoice in her, because her noble character brings him honor.

12:5, 6 Our **thoughts** do matter. At the very least, they must not be **deceitful.** A person's thoughts determine what he or she says and does. The **words** of wicked persons are like a deadly ambush.

12:7–9 A **better ... than** proverb, this verse contrasts a person who is a "nobody" but has a servant with a person who makes a great display but does not even have food on the table.

Pretension and arrogance destroy those who indulge in them.

12:10, 11 tills his land: Many proverbs contrast hard work with laziness. Wise people work hard while fools waste time.

12:12, 13 yields fruit ... is ensnared: Wickedness hurts the wicked; righteousness helps the righteous (see v. 14). This is another way of saying "whatever a man sows, that he will also reap" (Gal. 6:7).

12:14–17 at once: Careless words can make a fool out of us, so we are wise to think before we speak.

12:18, 19 Many proverbs praise people who speak carefully and truthfully. Speech reflects a person's character.

12:20–23 An **abomination** is something that "nauseates" God (see 11:20). The term conveys extreme hatred. Thus it is better to remain silent than to have **lying lips.**

12:24 Anyone who wants to have a position of authority cannot dare to be **lazy** (see vv. 11, 14).

12:25 Anxiety loses some of its force in the face of a positive, encouraging **word.**

12:26 Our **friends** help to determine who we will become (see 1 Cor. 15:33).

12:27, 28 Lazy people do work; they just don't finish what they start. The cure for their laziness is **diligence**—to follow through to the end.

13:1–4 A **wise son** listens to instruction (see 10:1, 17) and is better off than the **scoffer**—the worst kind of fool (see Ps. 1:1). Some fools are naive and inexperienced, but open to suggestions; sometimes even those established in folly may rethink their position. But scoffers laugh at righteousness.

13:5 The person who **hates lying** does not just feel bad about it; he avoids it like the plague.

13:6 In the proverbs, **righteousness** is portrayed as a friend and **wickedness** as an enemy (see 11:27). Wickedness hurts us but righteousness helps.

13:7 rich ... nothing: The paradox of greed causing poverty, and of generosity causing wealth, is a recurring theme in Scripture (see 11:24; Matt. 6:19–21). The point is not how much money you have, but what you do with it.

13:8, 9 For an ancient Israelite, an oil **lamp** would be the only source of light at night. Without it, a person had no way of seeing the path in front of him (see 20:20; 24:20).

13:10 The word **pride** (see 11:2) does not refer to self-esteem or to a positive mental attitude, but to arrogance and a refusal to glorify God. Such pride is self-serving and leads to conflict.

13:11 This proverb describes the natural long-term consequences of cheating. People who compromise their honesty to get rich only postpone the inevitable need to earn their keep. The day comes when their cheating catches up with them, but by then their honest colleagues have become far better at obtaining **wealth.** Cheating doesn't work anymore, and the wealth of the dishonest is **diminished.**

13:12 The **tree of life** (see 11:30) symbolizes the achievement of a deeply felt desire. It is like coming back to the Garden of Eden.

13:13 will be rewarded: A person can either despise instruction or respond in reverence, understanding that the ultimate Giver of instruction is God. Correction is only for one's good.

13:14 fountain of life: In an arid land such as ancient Judah, a fountain provided water for oneself and for one's flocks. It was a necessity—a source of life. That is a very strong endorsement for **the law of the wise.**

13:15 Favor with God and other people—a good reputation—is highly desirable because it ensures that you won't be alone in life. It comes from **good understanding.**

13:16 Many proverbs pit the **fool** against the **prudent** person.

13:17 A ... messenger who acts wickedly will be discovered and his sentence will be harsh indeed. But a messenger who acts in faithfulness brings healing as he goes. In ancient times it was not unusual for a monarch to lash out against the bearer of bad news. This proverb is a lashing out against a wicked messenger.

13:18, 19 Few things are as **sweet** as accomplishment. But the folly of the fool is so deeply entrenched that he becomes ill if he leaves his self-destructive path.

13:20 walks with: The selection of friends

(see 12:26) is extremely important. Pressure from peers is much stronger than many people realize.

13:21 Evil is a sinner's enemy (see v. 6), not a friend; a pursuer, and not a companion.

13:22 In the Book of Proverbs, **wealth** is a topic with many themes. Wealth may come as a benefit of righteous living (v. 11; 10:22); but there is no guarantee of this (28:6). Wealth cannot make a person good (11:4), and in the end it matters less than God's favor anyway (11:28). **A good man** knows this and trusts in God to meet his needs; **the sinner** tries to acquire and keep wealth and in the end fails.

13:23–25 hates ... loves: This is the first of several proverbs on parental discipline. A parent's loving discipline is modeled after God's loving correction (see 3:11, 12).

14:1 A **wise woman builds her house;** that is, she develops a peaceful setting for family nurture.

14:2 Fears the LORD contrasts starkly with **despises Him.** Love for **uprightness** will naturally coincide with love and respect for the most upright One of all, God Himself. Fear of the Lord as the beginning of wisdom is the central theme of Proverbs (see 1:7).

14:3 rod of pride: This proverb addresses the dangers of foolish speech and the rewards of sensible speech. The words of the fool shape themselves into a rod that is ready for his enemies to use on him. This proverb calls to mind that many people are their own worst enemy; given enough rope, they prepare a noose for their own hanging.

14:4 clean: A farmer has to put up with some disorder in the barn if he wants the help of an ox. This is not an excuse to be slovenly, but an encouragement to work hard.

14:5 This proverb is a restatement of God's law: "You shall not bear **false witness** against your neighbor" (Ex. 20:16; Deut 5:20).

14:6–8 This proverb contrasts prudent and foolish people. Wise people know what they are doing and why they are doing it. They have wise reasons for what they do, based on a knowledge of their choices. **Fools,** on the other hand, deceive so often that they deceive themselves. They do not know where they are headed.

14:9–12 Only when it is too late does the deluded person discover that he is on the crowded highway to **death.** The implication is not that he was tricked, but that he relied too heavily on his own "wisdom" rather than turning in humility to God.

14:13–15 A characteristic of the naive person is gullibility. A **prudent** person is careful.

14:16 The phrase **fears and departs from evil** suggests fear of God (see v. 2).

14:17–19 Controlling the gate of a city meant controlling the city; submitting at the gate meant an inability to overcome its defenses. In the end, the wicked will submit at the **gates of the righteous.**

14:20, 21 despises … sins: Jesus identified the command to love others, and not hate them, as second only to loving God (see Matt. 22:39).

14:22 One of the most significant pairings of words of piety in the Bible is the phrase translated **mercy and truth.** Together the words mean "constant faithfulness" or "true loyalty." In the New Testament, the Greek equivalent of this phrase is translated "grace and truth" (John 1:14) and is used of the Savior Jesus.

14:23–27 These proverbs interject the central idea of the Book of Proverbs—the **fear of the LORD** (see 14:2). The fear of God provides both protection and a **fountain of life** (see 13:14; 18:10), an image that recalls the Garden of Eden.

14:28–31 oppresses … honors: The theme of "as you treat people, so you treat God" is central to Scripture (Ex. 22:22–24; Matt. 25:31–46; 1 John 4:20).

14:32 Some of the proverbs describe deliverance from **death** (see 11:4). The teaching of life after death is not a major teaching in the Old Testament, but neither is it altogether neglected.

14:33–35 Righteousness exalts a nation: Although each individual is responsible for his or her actions, the effects extend to the whole community.

15:1, 2 Often it is not so much what we say but the way we say it that prompts such varied responses as acceptance and **wrath.**

15:3 That the **eyes of the LORD** are in every place watching everything chills those who do evil and comforts those who submit to Him (see Eccl. 12:14).

15:4 The soft answer of v. 1 is now a soothing tongue, and the hurtful word of v. 1 is now crooked dealing. The former is like a **tree of life,** taking us back to Eden (see 3:18; 11:30; 13:12); the other **breaks the spirit,** recalling the expulsion from the Garden (Gen. 3:23, 24).

15:5 The truly wise person profits from **instruction.** The term for the *prudent* in the second part of this proverb means "to be shrewd." Shrewdness can be evil, but here it has the positive sense of "street smarts" (see 1:4).

15:6 The house of the righteous contains great treasure because it is founded on wisdom and a proper response to God. On the other hand, the wicked never gain enough to suit them, and lose what they have because of their deceptive ways.

15:7 People reveal who they are by what they say. The **fool** cannot help but speak foolishness.

15:8, 9 From time to time the proverbs touch on the subject of worship (see 16:6). Worship from those who are not contrite or humble is an **abomination** to God (see 11:20). Verse 9 speaks of yet another **abomination to the Lord**—the course of life taken by the wicked.

15:10 This proverb promises **harsh discipline** for any person who **forsakes the way** of God. That is, discipline comes as a means of correction, not punishment. Only the person **who hates correction**—the one who stubbornly refuses to listen, time and time again—**will die.**

15:11 This is a "how much more" proverb (see 11:31), which impresses on the reader the clarity with which the Lord sees people's hearts. The Hebrew word *sheol,* translated **Hell,** in this proverb connotes the fear of the unknown (see 9:18). When used with the word for **Destruction,** *sheol* means "the mysterious realm of death," a dark and scary condition. Yet death is no mystery to the Lord. And if the mysterious realm of the dead is known to Him, then surely a person's heart is transparent to Him. Such arguments from the greater to the lesser appear in both Testaments.

15:12 The **scoffer** (see 14:6) is used as a foil or comparison in Proverbs to expose more sharply the character of the wise. Whereas the sluggard is a comic figure in Proverbs, the scoffer is a villain. He delights in scorning the things of God (1:22) and is incapable of responding to discipline (9:7), reproof (9:8), or rebuke (13:1). He cannot find wisdom (14:6) and should be avoided (see Ps. 1:1).

15:13, 14 The person with an **understanding** heart, another description of the wise, is never satisfied with what he or she knows. The pursuit of wisdom and **knowledge** are life-long occupations—never fully realized in this lifetime. But fools, not knowing the extent of their ignorance, continue to pursue folly.

15:15–18 A **wrathful** person can stir up strife where there is none; but a person who has a slow fuse—who is **slow to anger**—soothes contention (see v. 1).

15:19, 20 despises his mother: This proverb is like the fifth commandment: "Honor your father and your mother" (see Ex. 20:12). Honoring and listening to parents is a favorite theme of Solomon's proverbs; this collection begins with the same exhortation (see 10:1).

15:21, 22 The greater the decision, the greater the need for advice. Even wise, capable decision-makers—whether common people or rulers—need **counselors** (see 13:10).

15:23 Solomon devoted many of his proverbs to the consequences of speech (see v. 4; 14:23). Just as foolish words can bring about a person's own destruction (see 14:3), a wise **word** can bring joy to all who hear it.

15:24, 25 God will bring about justice in the end. To the haughty, God will give a dose of humility. But for the **widow,** a completely defenseless person in ancient times, God will provide protection.

15:26 Many proverbs focus on what God hates (see vv. 8, 9). Evil **thoughts** disgust Him. There is no such thing as "private thoughts." We should pray with David that our words and the meditation of our hearts would be acceptable in God's sight (see Ps. 19:14).

15:27–32 He who disdains instruction despises his own soul: The natural instinct for self-preservation is dangerous when it is time to listen to a necessary rebuke.

15:33 Knowledge alone does not make a person wiser; **the fear of the LORD** must accompany it. The same is true of **honor.**

16:1, 2 These verses contrast human limitations with the sovereignty of God. **Man** can plan, dream, and hope, but the final outcome is **from the LORD.** Rather than "resign ourselves to fate," we should trust in God. Our loving Lord is in control of our seemingly chaotic situations. In addition to being sovereign, God is the final Judge. All the injustices of this world will be corrected some day.

16:3 The verb **commit to** is from a word meaning "to roll." The idea is to "roll your cares onto the Lord." Trusting the Lord with our decisions frees us from preoccupation with our problems (see 3:5, 6).

16:4, 5 proud in heart: Pride has everything backwards. It takes credit away from the Giver who gives graciously and awards it to the receiver who takes without thanking. That is why God sees it as an **abomination,** a word that throughout Proverbs refers to God's revulsion (see 15:26).

16:6 In mercy and truth can also be translated "by genuine piety." **Atonement** probably alludes to a sacrificial offering, but not apart from a contrite heart (as in Ps. 40:6–8). **fear:** Respect for God turns a person away from evil (see 3:7).

16:7, 8 The Book of Proverbs often speaks of wealth as the reward of wisdom and virtue (see 14:11), but not always. **Righteousness** is the real treasure.

16:9, 10 This verse begins a section that relates to kings (vv. 10–15). The word **divination** refers to judicial decisions. Because the nation rested in the king's hands, his first responsibility was to obey God. Even the king had to submit to the dictates of justice.

16:11 Honest weights and scales matter to God because God is perfectly true. Falsehood and dishonesty do not just cheat people; they also offend God.

16:12–15 life … his favor: Successfully courting a powerful person's favor is like seeing rain clouds in a dry land. The phrase about the light of the face in this proverb helps us understand Aaron's benediction in Num. 6:24–26.

16:16, 17 A **highway** is a thoroughfare, a metaphor for the way a person lives habitually. An **upright** person's "highway," or habit, is to **depart from evil.** He does not compromise; he consistently strives to do good.

16:18, 19 the proud: Destructive pride brings down many winners and is contagious.

16:20, 21 This verse begins a small section of proverbs on the superiority of wisdom (vv. 21–24). Wisdom is never easily gained or quickly achieved; that is why a wise person **increases learning.**

16:22, 23 Those who have **understanding** have access to a fountain of life that constantly renews itself and is available to everyone. The phrase **wellspring of life** is an image of salvation; water was essential for life in the arid regions of ancient Israel (see Ps. 36:8–10; Jer. 2:13).

16:24 The Hebrew word for **honeycomb** is also used in Ps. 19:10, 11 with regard to the Word of God. The Israelites saw honey as a healthy food as well as a sweetener. Any comparison to it would connote positive, healthful effects.

16:25 Contrasts of God's **way** with the way of the wicked figure in the teaching of Jesus as well as the proverbs (Matt. 7:13, 14). This proverb likens the wicked to being on the wrong road. They think they are going the **right** way, but in the end it leads to **death** (see 14:12). Death refers to physical death (as in 1 Cor. 11:29, 30).

16:26–29 These verses all begin in a similar way, describing three different types of wicked people. The word **ungodly,** or "scoundrel," means "a man of Belial"; this person is a muckraker who uses bad information for evil purposes; he destroys people on purpose. The **perverse** person starts fights between friends. The **violent man** uses his power of persuasion to recruit others to join in his attacks.

16:30, 31 Old age becomes **a crown of glory** to those who walk the **way of righteousness**—one of the rewards of pursuing wisdom.

16:32 One of the most favored persons in the ancient Middle East was the military hero. Yet this proverb suggests that one **who is slow to anger** and **who rules his** speech is a greater hero than a returning warrior.

16:33 The use of lots in ancient Israel (see v. 10) could easily be confused with luck. But when a **lot** was cast as a means of determining God's will, the people knew it did not fall indiscriminately. God exercises sovereignty over human affairs (see 16:4).

17:1 The expression **a dry morsel** means "very little," especially in comparison to **feasting.** But the feasting in this verse is tainted by contention. *Feasting* could also be part of a sacrifice to God, but even such a feast could be ruined by angry disputes between believers.

17:2 Reversals of fortune could happen if the **wise servant** was sufficiently skillful and the **son** and his brothers were undeserving. Much of the Book of Genesis describes the rise of an unexpected younger son over his older brother (see Gen. 25:23–34).

17:3 The refining of **silver** and **gold** is an exacting process, involving skill and considerable heat and stress. The refining work of God on His people often requires stress as well.

17:4 This proverb presents the **evildoer** and the **liar** as a parody of the wise. As the righteous person listens with care to the instruction of a teacher, so the wicked person **listens** with care to the ruinous speech of the unrighteous.

17:5, 6 Only a grandmother or grandfather can appreciate this verse fully. Yet all of us can see its central point: Grandparents adore their grandchildren, and **children** adore their parents. It is this strong bond of family ties that keeps generations together.

17:7 It is a contradiction in terms for a **fool** to speak well or for a **prince** to be a liar. It is **not becoming** for such inappropriateness to exist.

17:8–12 Nothing matches the rage of a mother **bear** who has been separated from her **cubs;** yet there is nothing in life more dangerous than the **fool** in the midst of his **folly.**

17:13–15 abomination to the Lord (see 16:5): Since God is a God of justice, He detests those who pervert justice—both those who declare the innocent guilty and those who declare the guilty innocent.

17:16, 17 This proverb lauds faithfulness. Unlike fickle friends (see 14:20), a true **friend** is constant, and a real **brother** helps in times of stress.

17:18 Making a **pledge** for another person is not wrong, but this proverb does call for caution in such transactions (see 11:15). The one making the loan may lose his independence.

17:19–21 The foolish child is one of the hardest realities to face (see 10:1). There is no heartache so grievous as the pain of realizing that one's child is a **fool,** obdurate to God, and useless in life.

17:22, 23 Like false weights (see 16:11), skewed justice destroys a culture. A **bribe** is literally a "gift." In v. 8, the same Hebrew word is translated positively as *present,* but in this verse the meaning is negative because they purpose of the gift is to pervert justice.

17:24 Wisdom produces a satisfied life. The fool continues searching without finding any satisfaction.

17:25–28 Only a perverse population would **punish the righteous.** Like several other proverbs, this one describes what is to be recognized as an outrage.

18:1 This proverb condemns any person who **isolates himself** from the community for selfish reasons. Such a recluse is so intolerant of anyone who disagrees with him that he finds fault with **all wise judgment.**

18:2 A compulsive talker never listens, only pausing to plan what he will say next. Every speech confirms what a **fool** he is.

18:3, 4 wellspring of wisdom: This image is similar to the phrase "a fountain of life" (see 10:11; 13:14; 14:27; 16:22).

18:5 show partiality: Distortion of justice is all too common; many proverbs condemn it (see 17:23).

18:6–8 The words of a talebearer (see 16:28) are like delicious sweets. Although they are fun to eat, they ruin the person's health. Gossip is fun to listen to, but the stories damage the listener's **inmost body,** or soul.

18:9 The word **slothful** means a person who is "known to be slack." It refers to a lazy

person (see 15:19). **Destroyer** means "lord of destruction."

18:10, 11 The phrase **name of the LORD** (v. 10) is a way of speaking of God's person. The **righteous** turn to God for security. Rich people, by contrast, tend to trust in their **wealth** (v. 11; Luke 12:13–21).

18:12 The Hebrew word for **haughty,** ordinarily negative, can also be used positively to mean courage and daring (see 2 Chr. 17:6). The path to **honor,** which the proud so covet, is **humility.**

18:13, 14 This proverb affirms the value of coping skills. **Sickness** can be overcome, but there is no medicine for a **broken spirit** (see 15:13; 17:22; Is. 66:2).

18:15–18 Whenever both sides agree on the method of settling a dispute, that method is a means to peace. The **casting** of **lots** was a biblical pattern for assistance in decision-making (16:33). Behind the lots was the sovereign power of God.

18:19–21 stomach ... mouth: Inner satisfaction comes from true and good speech. **Death and life:** The words people say wield great power (see James 3:2).

18:22, 23 favor: Problems in marriage arise from breakdowns in communication or mutual respect, not from some flaw in marriage itself (see 12:4).

18:24 This is a difficult verse to translate because of confusion over an ambiguous Hebrew word translated here as **be friendly.** This translation takes it to mean "to make oneself pleasing" as in 1 Sam. 29:4. To have friends one must be friendly. But the word could also mean "to beat each other up" as in Is. 24:19. Then the verse could be translated, "Sometimes even friends destroy each other, but there is a Friend who loves more faithfully than a brother."

19:1 This proverb, one of the "better than" proverbs (see 17:1, 10), presents a **poor** person in a more favorable light than a rich person (see 28:6). In this case, the poor person's life is marked by **integrity,** whereas the successful person has gained his wealth through cheating and deception. The Book of Proverbs does not place a premium on health and wealth. It gives that honor to *integrity* (see 3:1–12).

19:2–4 This proverb speaks of the effects of **wealth** and poverty on friendship. It does not describe how friends ought to behave, but how many friends actually do. Like a faithful spouse, a faithful friend is priceless (see 14:20).

19:5–7 The behavior of **brothers** and **friends** who abandon a friend because of poverty should be contrasted with the true friend in such texts as 17:17; 18:24.

19:8 Ultimately, to **find good** means to find the Lord in His Word (see 16:20).

19:9, 10 The phrase **is not fitting** might also be rendered "is not a pretty sight" (see 17:7). For the wrong people to rule is an outrage.

19:11 discretion: Patience and restraint are virtues of wisdom (see 16:32); rashness and violent outbursts of rage are not.

19:12 The descriptions of a lion's **roar** and **dew on the grass** are especially fitting when a monarch has all power. His rage may be violent and unpredictable, his pleasure gracious and restorative. A good king will display rage and spread favor for the right reasons.

19:13, 14 Continual dripping speaks of constant dissension within a family. **A prudent wife** is a woman who demonstrates wisdom or skill. Finding the right spouse is a blessing from God (see 18:22).

19:15 The proverbs have no kind words for **slothfulness,** the habit of the sluggard (see 6:6, 9). The proverbs call for mercy and compassion on the poor and the weak, but only contempt for the lazy (see v. 17; 10:4, 5).

19:16–18 on his destruction: Refusal to discipline dooms a child's future (see 13:24).

19:19–21 A wise person commits his or her **plans** to the Lord (see 16:3). A person whose plans oppose the Lord (as in Ps. 2:1–3) may actually become God's enemy. But the person whose ways are from God will certainly succeed (see also 16:1, 9).

19:22 The poor person who has integrity has more honor than the successful person who has achieved his station or rank by deception (see v. 1).

19:23 This proverb emphasizes the lifelong nature of genuine piety and the abundant rewards that it gives. **The fear of the LORD** is contrasted with all other pleasures (see 15:16, 33), because it alone keeps the believer innocent and provides lifelong satisfaction.

19:24, 25 The **simple** person, the one who has yet to set his or her course in life, can learn by watching the **scoffer** suffer. The scoffer himself may not learn from his punishment, but anyone who is ready to learn surely can.

19:26–29 The desire for a good **son**—or daughter—is the subject of several proverbs (see 10:1). A child who is abusive to his parents shames them and violates God's command (see 20:20; Ex. 20:12; Deut. 5:16). As an abusive son is shameful, so an obedient son is faithful and successful.

20:1 This chapter begins with a warning against the abuse of **wine,** or excessive drinking (see this theme more extensively in 23:29–35). A wise person takes the danger seriously. There is no wisdom in drunkenness, only **brawling** and confusion.

20:2–4 Because the **sluggard** (see 19:24) does not plow his field on time, he has nothing to harvest (see 10:5).

20:5 draw it out: The wise of ancient Israel knew something that modern counselors rediscover in their training and experience, that motivation for behavior is complex. A gifted counselor is able to draw out from a person genuine feelings and motivations, just as someone draws water from a deep well.

20:6–9 Who can say: This proverb is a rhetorical question. Everyone sins, a theme that Paul addresses at length in Rom. 3:10–23. Anyone who claims never to sin is a liar (see 1 John 1:8, 9). But those who confess their sin obtain forgiveness (see Rom. 4:7).

20:10 The repeated emphasis on crooked weights and **diverse measures** (see 11:1) reminds us that cheating is a chronic problem.

20:11 by his deeds: A pattern established early in life may continue to mark a person for his or her lifetime. Even at a very early age, a person's moral character may be revealed.

20:12 This proverb speaks of what **the LORD has made.** We can use both our ears and our eyes to learn about God's law (see Ps. 40:6; 119:18). They are physical means to getting the guidance we need.

20:13, 14 Sleep is a gift from God that restores a person's energy and vitality. Yet sleep can also be a matter of excess and laziness. Hard work is necessary to make a living; laziness leads only to poverty (see 6:6, 9).

20:15 This verse is not a comment on the morality of wealth, but a statement about the comparative value of wisdom and money. Wisdom is simply worth more. Thus, being poor and wise is more **precious** than being rich and foolish (see 19:1).

20:16 It is foolish to lend to **a stranger** without securing a **pledge,** or promise, of repayment (see 11:15). The Israelites were not allowed to exact such pledges from other Israelites (see Ex. 22:25–27).

20:17 afterward: The Scriptures do not say that there is no pleasure in sinning, only that the reward doesn't last (9:17, 18).

20:18 This proverb is a maxim that moves from the lesser to the greater (see 15:11). We should always think before we act, and serious matters like **war** require a maximum of forethought.

20:19, 20 This proverb is about breaking the fifth commandment, "honor your father and your mother" (Ex. 20:12; Deut. 5:16). The statement **His lamp will be put out in deep darkness** is a symbol of eternal damnation.

20:21 at the beginning: Sometimes what seems to be sudden luck turns out to be a dismal turn of fortune. What seems too good to be true often is.

20:22 Because of our limited understanding and imperfection, we are not qualified to **recompense evil.** Instead we must commit our cause to God, whose vengeance is certain and perfectly just.

20:23, 24 Even a man with great strength does not fully control his **steps.** His life and his very breath are gifts from God. Since life itself is God's gift, only a fool assumes he knows its full meaning.

20:25 Several proverbs warn against making rash promises about **holy** things, then withdrawing the promises later (see Eccl. 5:1–7). It is better never to vow than to vow and then change one's mind.

20:26 This royal proverb (see v. 8) presents discipline as a merciful act. To punish wickedness is entirely appropriate. When the **wicked** are sifted out and punished with the severity that their crimes demand, all of society benefits.

20:27–29 Each stage of life has its own advantages. The **young** have their youth and vigor; the aged have their wisdom (see 16:31).

20:30 Suffering cleanses. No one wants to be **hurt,** but God can bring good out of any evil and make us better through hardship.

21:1 A person can look at a river and think that it is following a random pattern, but the water is following the direction of God's hand. So is the king. This world's apparent chaos is God's work.

21:2 in his own eyes: A person's own defense of his life, manner, or way may convince himself, but the final evaluation belongs to God (see 17:3).

21:3 The proverbs occasionally touch on the subject of worship (see 15:8; 16:6). This proverb affirms, as do Ps. 40:6–8; Mic. 6:8, and numerous other passages in the Bible, that righteous living is more important than **sacrifice** (see 1 Sam. 15:22).

21:4 haughty ... proud: See 16:18. The second unit of the verse is difficult to translate. Some versions render the problematic Hebrew word for **plowing** as *lamp.*

21:5 Planning typically leads to **plenty,** and haste to **poverty** (see 20:21). It is not wrong to plan, but it is wrong to plan what the Lord has expressly forbidden (see also 16:1).

21:6, 7 Some prosperity is good and some is bad. The difference lies in how one gets it. **A lying tongue** has a total return of zero.

21:8 The way: This antithetical proverb takes us back to the very beginning of the study of wisdom, the contrast between the righteous and the wicked (see chs. 1—9; Ps. 1).

21:9 Ancient Israelite roofs were flat and could be used as a deck or terrace. On occasion people would build a temporary shelter on a part of the roof. Here, the harried husband finds he prefers to live on the

housetop rather than below with the nagging words of his wife.

21:10 Here is a person whose passion is **evil;** hence, he has no compassion for anyone.

21:11 The fool in this text is the worst sort, the **scoffer** (see 19:25); a person who is **simple** has enough sense to learn from seeing the scoffer punished. The **wise** always learn, the simple sometimes learn, but the scoffer is a lost cause.

21:12, 13 cry himself: A person who is indifferent to people in need will find no one helping him when he calls out for help.

21:14, 15 Justice is not a heavy obligation that weighs a person down. For the righteous, promoting justice is a **joy.** For the wicked there is no joy in justice, nor will there be joy in their final end (see 10:29).

21:16 The congregation of the dead: The term *dead* is a frightful one, meaning "shades" (see 9:18). Death in these verses may speak of physical death rather than spiritual death (as is the case in James 1).

21:17–20 This proverb contrasts the prosperity of **the wise** with the poverty of the fool (see 20:15). The key lies in the way they treat their possessions. Fools abuse or neglect their own property.

21:21 life, righteousness and honor: It is possible that these three ideas go together to mean "a more abundant life." The pursuit of righteousness is its own reward. But added rewards are found in fullness of life, achieving righteousness, and receiving honor.

21:22, 23 This proverb has a pun on the word "to keep." If a person **guards** or "keeps" his mouth, he will **keep** or preserve his soul. The converse of this is seen in the many troubles a person brings on himself by careless speech.

21:24 This proverb applies four different Hebrew words for arrogance to the **scoffer** (see v. 11). The first two words, **proud** and **haughty,** mean "profoundly arrogant" (see v. 4). The second two, **arrogant** and **pride,** mean "boundless arrogance."

21:25 The longing of the lazy man **kills him;** he is devoured by his own passions because he will not expend the energy to fulfill them. Verse 26 describes further the insatiable greed of the lazy person by contrasting it with the generosity of the righteous.

21:26–28 A large number of proverbs focus on the **false witness** (see 19:28). The problem with a false witness is that his lies pervert justice for others. Even if he lies only once, the lie may be circulated by others.

21:29, 30 Usually the proverbs use the word **wisdom** positively. But in this verse the word is paired with conjurers' tricks. These tricks have no power over God, as Balaam the pagan prophet discovered in his encounter with the Lord on the plains of Moab (see Num. 22—24). True wisdom can be found only in God.

21:31 A soldier can do all within his ability to prepare for **battle** (see 20:18), but in the end no preparation can override God's power. Victory is in God's hands.

22:1 This proverb points out that a reputation has more value than possessions or wealth. A **name** cannot be replaced easily, not even with lots of money.

22:2 This sentence eloquently repeats the theme of riches (v. 1): God makes both **the rich and the poor.** This means that those who favor the rich over the poor (see James 2) have not only missed the point of creation; they have insulted the Creator (see 14:31)

22:3 The term **prudent** means "shrewd" (see 1:4 for a related word). There is no wisdom in being reckless.

22:4 The route to the good life—**riches and honor and life** (see 21:21 for a similar triad)—is humility (see Mic. 6:8) and the fear of God.

22:5–8 The idea of just retribution is significant (see 21:7). A person who lives by violence is likely to die violently; a person who lives wickedly should not be surprised if he falls victim to crime (see Matt. 26:52).

22:9 The words expressing the idea of generosity in this verse are "a good **eye.**" A good eye observes the needs of others first. A bad eye sees only its own self-interest.

22:10 The **scoffer** (see 21:24) should be expelled from the community because his influence is harmful to everyone. The wise know that the scoffer is not a laughing matter, because he is laughing at holy things, at God Himself.

22:11 A person who is marked by **purity** of

speech and heart becomes the confidant of a good king. Compare this proverb with Ps. 15, which describes a person who wants to become a friend of the Lord.

22:12 The eyes of the LORD (see 15:3; 21:2) are the final arbiters of knowledge and justice. The eyes of human beings are simply not trustworthy. When the king takes his position seriously, he also makes decisions that are proper and upright (see 20:8).

22:13 The proverbs about **lazy** people (see 19:15) provide comic relief by poking fun at how the lazy invent all sorts of excuses for avoiding work and risk. They will do anything to avoid doing anything.

22:14 This proverb takes us back to the **immoral woman,** or the "strange woman" (see 2:16). Her mouth is an open pit, destruction to anyone who falls there (see 9:18).

22:15, 16 The last of the proverbs of Solomon in this collection deals with social justice. Ultimately, all human affairs are in God's hands, even though at times the wicked prosper. God made both the **poor** and the rich (v. 2) and He will justly determine their destinies (24:12).

22:17–21 Incline your ear: These introductory words call the reader to pay attention and to prepare to learn about and worship God. The advice emphasizes strongly that a person's **trust** must **be in the LORD.**

22:22, 23 Most violations of justice target **poor** and **afflicted** people because they are weak and defenseless. But anyone who does this makes an enemy of God, who **will plead their cause.**

22:24, 25 friendship with an angry man: Whereas the words of vv. 22, 23 are based on Hebrew faith, these ideas are derived from observation of human behavior and interaction. The Book of Proverbs includes both types of insight: revelation of truth about God, and observation of human experience (see 1 Cor. 15:33).

22:26–29 The ancient Israelites regarded respect for the posted **landmark** as more than a question of private property. They saw it as a basic part of civil life. People must feel a certain sense of public trust and fairness for society to function.

23:1–3 A big part of the training of the courtier would be in proper manners at state dinners and formal occasions. The comment on a **knife to the throat** is prompted by two concerns: (1) rude behavior was to be avoided at all costs, and (2) too many royal dainties would likely make a person ill.

23:4, 5 These verses call for moderation in work. **do not overwork to be rich:** Although the proverbs discourage laziness (see 22:13), they also discourage any overworking whose purpose is greater wealth.

23:6–11 their Redeemer is mighty: The tendency of evil people in all ages is to take advantage of the helpless. But the destroyer of persons needs to know that the widow and the orphan have a Redeemer, a protector of family rights. His name is the living God.

23:12 The Hebrew word for **instruction** can also be translated "discipline."

23:13–16 he will not die … beat him: This language was designed to motivate overly permissive parents, who were afraid of damaging young children with any kind of discipline, or of making rules and enforcing them. There is no call here for abuse. Loving discipline does not destroy rebellious children; it does them a big favor.

23:17, 18 The first proverb here sharply contrasts the vain **envy** of **sinners** with the **fear of the LORD,** the expression of piety that the proverbs repeatedly encourage (see 1:7). The second gives the perspective that everyone needs: present success—or lack of it—is not the final outcome. There will be a future state fundamentally different from this world.

23:19–23 The drunkard and the glutton have no self-control, and this fact plagues them. Hebrew culture gave a prominent place to eating and drinking, but it had little tolerance for drunkenness and gluttony.

23:24, 25 the father of the righteous: Joy comes to parents who see their children succeed. But when those parents have faith in the Lord, the greatest joy comes from seeing their children be faithful to Him.

23:26–35 Who has woe: Along with Isaiah's celebrated description of debauchery (Is. 19:11–15), this section is one of the sharpest attacks on drunkenness in the Bible (see vv. 19–21; 20:1). The satire is razor sharp and the imagery vivid.

24:1, 2 Do not be envious of evil men: Whereas 23:17, 18 tells about the future to discourage envy of the wicked, this set of verses points out how unworthy the wicked are of any admiration at all.

24:3–11 These verses speak with a certain confidence and understanding of life beyond the grave (23:17, 18). This verse is a prayer to God as **death** approaches.

24:12 according to his deeds: Jesus' words about eternal rewards open and close the New Testament (compare Matt. 5:11, 12 with Rev. 22:12). Yet Jesus' action on the Cross will deliver those who believe in Him from any condemnation (see Rom. 5:18; Rev. 22:17).

24:13, 14 Here is one of the associations in the Proverbs of **honey** and the **honeycomb** with wisdom (see 16:24). Wisdom and its pursuit, while rigorous, is good for the soul and can be pleasant.

24:15, 16 Ultimately the **wicked** will fall. The righteous can be assured of this not because they are strong, but because they have a Redeemer (see 23:10, 11).

24:17–22 fear the LORD and the king: The Hebrew text breaks the phrasing: "Fear God, my son, and the king" (see Rom. 13:1–7). This proverb relates most fully to the Davidic kings, who were God's regents on earth; one way the ancient Israelites could show respect for God would be to respect the king. But the duty to honor civil authorities still applies to all people of all times (Rom. 13:1).

24:23–34 These things also belong to the wise is a sectional heading that corresponds to the one in 22:17. Verses 23–34 serve as an appendix to the preceding section (22:17—24:22). Israel's basic concern with equity in **judgment** was not unique; but in Israel a concern for equity was tied to God's character. Since God does not show partiality, neither should we. The lazy person is judged on the basis of the shambles of his field. From this sorry state of affairs the wise take a lesson. The only concern the lazy have is for **a little sleep.**

25:1 After the first collection of proverbs from **Solomon** (10:1—22:16) and proverbs from foreign sources (22:17—24:22; 24:23—34) comes a collection of proverbs attributed to

Solomon, but which were not compiled until the time of King **Hezekiah.**

25:2–5 Silver is valuable only after the impurities have been removed. Similarly, wickedness needs to be removed from a king for his throne to be established rightly.

25:6, 7 Do not exalt yourself: Knowing your place is a recurring theme in the Bible. It is humiliating to be told to remove yourself from a seat of honor. **Whom your eyes have seen:** This phrase reflects the custom in the ancient world of never looking directly in the eyes of a superior until told to do so (see Is. 6:5).

25:8–15 hastily to court: In our own litigious age, this group of verses has unusual relevance. Seek to deal with complaints outside the court on a private level or even with an arbiter.

25:16 found honey: Too much of a good thing can cause illness and distress.

25:17 neighbor's house: The issue is moderation. Too much "neighborliness" becomes an imposition.

25:18–26 An **unfaithful man**—annoying and undependable—cannot be trusted at all. **Coals** of fire speaks of God's judgment (see Ps. 120:4; 140:10); the idea is that an act of kindness to your enemy may cause him or her to feel ashamed. This is just one way to overcome evil with good (see Rom. 12:20).

25:27 much honey: Moderation in good things (see v. 16) goes with humility.

25:28 rule: Self-control is a key part of obedience to God (see Gal. 5:22, 23).

26:1, 2 snow in the summer: A most unlikely happening in Israel. **Rain in harvest** is not only unusual, but disastrous, because rain at that time would cause the crops to rot.

26:3 rod for the fool's back: The fool has no motivation to do anything. He is no better than a brute beast whom someone else has to motivate.

26:4, 5 Some people have called the two proverbs here contradictory, but that is not necessary. The phrase **according to his folly** appears twice as a play on words with two shades of meaning. On the one hand, it means "avoid the temptation to stoop to his level"; that is, don't use his methods, **lest you also be like him.** On the other hand, it means "avoid the temptation to ignore him altogether"; that is, respond in *some* way, or else he will become **wise in his own eyes** and his folly will get worse.

26:6–11 dog ... vomit: A fool does not learn from his mistakes.

26:12 Being haughty is even worse than being a **fool.** Egotism is the epitome of folly (see 28:11).

26:13–15 These proverbs about the **lazy man** have a "can you top this" quality that provides comic relief; the lazy man is the object of many jokes in Scripture. This set of verses includes several (see 19:15). Each one belittles laziness and the many outrageous excuses people often use to justify it.

26:16, 17 The problem with taking a **dog by the ears** is that the dog will probably bite. The same is true of getting involved in another's quarrel. It's an invasion of privacy.

26:18–21 Fires do not burn without fuel; **strife,** or fighting, works the same way.

26:22 The slanderer looks upon his nasty words as **tasty** tidbits, delicious morsels of raw gossip. Many people have an insatiable hunger for malicious gossip.

26:23 The meaning of this proverb is not far from Jesus' remarks to His enemies that they were like whitewashed tombs (Matt. 23:27). No amount of painting on the outside changes the value of the rotten interior.

26:24–28 A person who hates says one thing but stores up anger **within.** He may find that his hatred hurts him, when in his life there is so much falsehood that no one believes him no matter how gracious and truthful he might be at times.

27:1–5 The wise of ancient Israel warned about a concern for **tomorrow** that overshadows the needs of today.

27:6 Correction given in love by a **friend** is better than insincere acts of affection (see Ps. 141:5).

27:7 Those who are full do not appreciate what they have, while to those who are **hungry** anything tastes good.

27:8–10 from its nest: Straying from home can mean losing security and becoming open to new and powerful temptations (see the parable of the prodigal son, Luke 15).

27:11 This is the first **my son** proverb in this

collection; it is very similar to those in the earlier parts of Proverbs (see chs. 1–9). A child who grows up wise confirms that the parents who taught him or her were themselves wise (see 10:1).

27:12–16 Normally a **garment given in pledge** was only a symbolic collateral and was returned immediately, but not if the one making the pledge was unreliable or a stranger (see 20:16).

27:17 iron sharpens iron: A famous proverb, this verse may also be translated as applying to the will: "Let iron sharpen iron, and so let a person sharpen his friend." The idea is that people grow from interaction with one another.

27:18 keeps the fig tree: This proverb speaks of faithfulness and reward. The word **master** may refer to God.

27:19 a man's heart: Thoughts reflect a person's true character.

27:20–22 Hell and destruction are used often in the Bible to describe the fearful aspect of death. They are like ravenous monsters. Compare this proverb with the image of Satan as a roaring lion (see 1 Pet. 5:8).

27:23–27 These verses affirm diligence and describe its practical rewards. The model is that of the farmer who cares for his **flocks and herds;** if he diligently cares for them, in time they will care for him.

28:1–3 The wicked **flee** when there is no cause (see Ps. 53:5) because of guilt and the fear of getting caught that goes with it.

28:4, 5 When a person abandons God's **law,** he or she loses all sense of right and praises **the wicked** (see Rom. 1:28–32). And since true **justice** is from God, the ungodly have trouble understanding it. This is why the fear of the Lord is the beginning of wisdom (see 1:7).

28:6 The proverbs balance their words on **poor** and **rich** people; they do not assume that godliness leads to wealth or that wealthy people are necessarily godly. As this proverb points out, sometimes we must choose between doing good and getting rich.

28:7 To be a **companion of gluttons** (see 23:20, 21) is to break God's law. This is why Jesus' enemies charged Him with associating with gluttons: such accusations were attacks on His faithfulness to God (see Matt. 11:19).

28:8, 9 Profit taken by **usury** is unjust. God will help the poor eventually, at their exploiters' expense.

28:10–13 causes the upright to go astray: These words resemble Jesus' warning against leading his disciples astray (Matt. 18:6). Paul vividly captures this kind of evil: "If anyone defiles the temple of God, God will destroy him" (see 1 Cor. 3:17).

28:14 Happy is the man is a beatitude (see Ps. 1:1) about the person who is in awe of God. The person who never thinks of God faces calamity.

28:15–19 Tills his land is a call to hard work, a promise of reward, and a warning against **frivolity** or overindulgence in fun.

28:20 A faithful man succeeds. That is, faithfulness to God, not greed, determines success in life.

28:21, 22 To exercise **partiality** (literally "to recognize faces") means to judge on the basis of favors or bribes instead of what is right.

28:23 rebukes a man: Constructive criticism has more value than flattery, which aims only to win people's affection.

28:24 robs his father: This proverb condemns breaking the fifth commandment, "Honor your father and your mother" (Ex. 20:12). Respect for parents as a duty is a common theme in the Book of Proverbs.

28:25–28 One of the main causes of **strife** is pride; trust in God leads to blessing. **walks wisely:** Security can only come by trusting God, not by relying on oneself.

29:1 The Hebrew phrase for **often rebuked** is "a man of rebukes." The judgment on a person who stubbornly rejects God's correction is swift and final.

29:2–4 The words **righteous are in authority** can also be translated "righteous are great." People will always respond to good government and justice. Justice is not served by **bribes,** nor is good government established that way.

29:5, 6 Spread a net: Lies entrap liars (see 10:8). Moreover, the evil person is trapped by his own actions. Both the liar and the wicked are contrasted with the righteous, who run happily because they are innocent of any wrongdoing.

29:7–12 Righteous people are concerned for **the poor** and help them (see 22:22); the wicked do not even consider the needy.

29:13, 14 God is responsible for giving life to both the **poor man and the oppressor.** Jesus attested that God causes rain to fall on the just and the unjust (Matt. 5:45).

29:15–17 The words **rod and rebuke** both speak of correction or discipline. An undisciplined child shames everyone, especially his or her parents (see v. 17). Verse 17 places the burden of correction on the parents. The word translated **delight** speaks of rich, delicious food (see Gen. 49:20).

29:18 where there is no revelation: The Hebrew word for *revelation* speaks of revelatory vision, a word from God. Without God's revelation of the Law, the people flounder. True happiness is discovered within the constraints of revelation, in the counsel of the Savior.

29:19, 20 hasty in his words: Even a wise person may become foolish by speaking too quickly. It is better to be silent or to choose words carefully than to speak whatever first comes to mind.

29:21–23 See Ps. 147:6; God raises the **humble** and puts down the arrogant. Mary praised God for doing this marvelous thing (see Luke 1:46–55).

29:24–27 God controls human affairs. Therefore it makes more sense to **seek** the Lord first before stooping to seek the favor of human rulers.

30:1 A new section of the Book of Proverbs begins with **the words of Agur.** Like Lemuel (31:1–9), Agur was a non-Hebrew contributor to the Book of Proverbs. He came to faith in the God of Israel in a foreign land. We know nothing about his father **Jakeh,** but the word translated **his utterance** may be a place name. **Ithiel and Ucal** were probably Agur's pupils. Since the back-to-back repetition of the name Ithiel is unusual, some construe the Hebrew letters differently and translate the text "I have wearied myself, O God; I have wearied myself, O God, and am consumed." This would fit the context of the following verses.

30:2, 3 more stupid than any man: Agur means he was at a loss. Similarly, his denial of **knowledge of the Holy One** is a rhetorical flourish as well. Agur was stating with dramatic irony that he could not explain the puzzle before him.

30:4 This verse gives the riddle that perplexed Agur. The questions are enigmatic. They culminate in **What is His name, and What is His Son's name, If you know?** At this point, the riddle has no answer. The Old Testament would answer that "His name" is the Lord God, but did not have a name for His Son. This riddle was to remain unsolved until Jesus answered it for Nicodemus (see John 3:13). These verses are one of the most straightforward messianic texts in the Bible.

30:5–9 two things: This was all Agur needed.

30:10 This proverb is unusual in warning against slandering a **servant.** Slaves in ancient times were often regarded as less than a full person.

30:11–16 Agur wrote about **a generation** plagued by social ills such as lack of respect for parents, self-righteousness, greed, and selfishness. Such evils have plagued every generation.

30:17 mocks his father: The lack of parental respect spoken of in v. 11 leads to this curse. The language is strong and violent, as is the punishment of the one who abuses his or her parents.

30:18, 19 The term translated **virgin** could also read "young woman" in this context.

30:20 This verse contrasts with the way of v. 19; this **way** is awful whereas the former is wonderful. The **adulterous woman** regards her illicit sexual relations without remorse, as if she were finishing a plate of food.

30:21–23 Contrasting with the four wonderful things of vv. 18, 19 are four things that are grievous, an upsetting of order. Three are clear: the **servant,** the **fool,** and the **maidservant** are all in unexpected positions of power. The **hateful woman** describes the sorry lot of a woman whose husband hates her.

30:24–28 This numerical proverb speaks of **four** creatures that are small in size but amazing in behavior. Each of these small creatures has a behavioral trait from which wise people can learn.

30:29–33 The proverbs of Agur conclude with warnings against boasting and troublemaking. The phrase **put your hand on**

your mouth means "stop it." The idea is if you are in the middle of making trouble and suddenly realize your foolishness, stop right then before things get worse.

31:1 This verse begins a new section of material from a non-Israelite source. Some have thought that the name **Lemuel,** meaning "Belonging to God," is a pseudonym for Solomon, but this is only a guess.

31:2–7 Lemuel's mother advised him not to **give** his **strength to women.** Often in the ancient world a king would amass a large harem or involve himself sexually with many women. The wisdom of Lemuel's mother was that such behavior destroys rulers. She likewise advised him to avoid **intoxicating drink,** so that he could always have a clear head.

31:8, 9 for the speechless: The duty of a king in the ancient world was to defend the weak, to uphold the helpless. These ideals were rarely realized in that age or even in our own. But one day a King who is the Defender of the helpless will establish his righteous reign (see 23:10, 11).

31:10–12 Proverbs 31:10–31 is an acrostic poem; each verse begins with a successive letter of the Hebrew alphabet. Some have thought that it continues the teaching of King Lemuel's mother (vv. 1–9), but it may also be an independent, concluding unit. As the Book of Proverbs begins with the Prologue (1:1–7), which gives the goals of wisdom in general terms, so now it concludes with this Epilogue (vv. 10–31), which presents them in a case study. The opening words **who can find** position this woman as an ideal. The phrase **a virtuous woman** speaks of excellence, moral worth, ability, and nobility, not just marital fidelity (see also 12:4). Such a woman is the ideal of wisdom in action.

31:13–15 These verses emphasize both hard work and skill. The woman they describe does things she enjoys, finding her fulfillment in varied tasks. The words **she rises early** describe her concern for others; she gives herself to care for her family and servants.

31:16, 17 She considers a field; that is, she buys and sells and builds her own resources.

These words are remarkable in light of the many restrictions placed on women in the ancient world.

31:18, 19 her merchandise is good: One of the avenues the woman exploits is a "cottage industry" in which she acts independently.

31:20–22 The virtuous woman works not to get rich, but to give **to the poor.** She can be concerned for others because she has provided for her family.

31:23 The virtuous woman's husband has a position **in the gates** as an elder of the city; some of his status comes from his wife's reputation, not just his own.

31:24 Linen garments probably indicates clothing for women.

31:25 The virtuous woman's own **clothing** is far richer than linen or silk; she is dressed in strength and honor.

31:26, 27 Any woman who **opens her mouth** with wisdom deserves praise, given all the information on the use and misuse of speech in the Book of Proverbs. A virtuous woman takes care to speak well (James 3:2).

31:28, 29 The virtuous woman is blessed by her family—by her **children** as well as her husband. The words of v. 29 are the blessing of her husband.

31:30, 31 Charm may be used for good or for evil; it is not necessarily bad. But its good use requires the fear of the Lord—the main theme of the Book of Proverbs.

Ecclesiastes

Introduction

The Book of Ecclesiastes is one of the most misunderstood books in the Bible. Christians have tended either to ignore the message of the book, or to regard it as the testimony of a man living apart from God. This is unfortunate, for the book asks relevant questions about the meaning of life, and it declares the futility of an existence without God.

The writer says that he was "the son of David, king in Jerusalem" (1:1, 12, 16), words that have led many to assume that the writer was Solomon. Evidence in the book itself points to Solomon: (1) the author had "more wisdom than all who were before" him (1:16; see 1 Kin. 3:12); (2) he gathered for himself "silver and gold and the special treasures of kings" (2:8; see 1 Kin. 10:11–23); (3) he "acquired male and female servants" in great numbers (2:7; see 1 Kin. 9:20–23); and (4) he engaged in extensive building projects (2:4–6; see 1 Kin. 9:1–19).

Solomon probably wrote this book toward the end of his life, after he had repented of idolatry and his pursuit of foreign wives. Thus the Book of Ecclesiastes is both a monument to Solomon's recommitment to the living God and a guide for others through the perils of life.

Ecclesiastes should be interpreted in light of its conclusion: "Fear God and keep His commandments, for this is man's all" (12:13). To fear God means to revere, worship, and serve God—to turn from evil and turn in awe to the living God. Why should we respect and obey God? Because God will judge everyone—both the righteous and the wicked (12:14). He will call forth all men and women to account for their actions. The admonition to fear God and the expectation of divine judgment are the two great themes that conclude the book and provide an interpretative framework for the rest of it (see 12:13, 14).

The journey of Solomon to his conclusion "to fear God" is founded on the human search for meaning in life. Money or fame will only leave us empty-handed, because our souls yearn for something that will last.

Our frustration arises from a hunger to fellowship with our eternal Creator. In Ecclesiastes, Solomon takes us on a tour of all of life and concludes that all of it is vanity. Pleasures and riches lead to boredom and despair. Only a relationship with the One who created us and continues to care for us will truly satisfy.

1:1 The title **Preacher** denotes a function or a profession. It literally means "one who assembles" or "one who gathers people together." Thus the word refers to Solomon as a person who convened an assembly of the wise in order to explore in a formal manner the meaning of life. It might be better to transliterate the Hebrew word *Qohelet* rather than to translate it, for it seems to be Solomon's pen name.

1:2 Vanity of vanities: This phrase translates the Hebrew superlative, familiar from such phrases as "song of songs" and "holy of holies." Here it might express "the ultimate absurdity" or "utter emptiness." The word *vanity* means "breath" or "vapor" and thus speaks of life as "quickly passing." Life is like a vapor. Wherever we read the word *vanity* in Ecclesiastes, we should think not of what is "meaningless," but of what is "quickly passing" (v. 14; 6:12). This is one of the key terms in the Book of Ecclesiastes. The teaching of the Preacher is to realize that life is a fleeting thing that needs to be savored and enjoyed as a gift from God.

1:3 The senses of the term **profit** are: (1) "advantage" and (2) "adequate gain." Here it refers to compensation or gains, usually in the commercial realm. The question is: What is left after all expenses are taken into account? **labor:** Both the noun and the verb carry negative connotations, referring to activities requiring exertion. **under the sun:** This phrase (also translated as "under heaven" in v. 13; 2:3; 3:1) describes *life* lived here on this earth, as God has been pleased to place us. In these two verses (vv. 2, 3), the Preacher has established one of his principal ideas: Life may seem pointless because it is quickly passing. It is the burden of the rest of his book to help the assembly of the wise understand how to truly value life because it does pass so quickly.

1:4 The term **generation** suggests both the human actors and the natural phenomena as well. With the verb **passes away** we have the first of a series of antitheses in Ecclesiastes. **the earth abides forever:** Only God is eternal and everlasting in the fullest sense. But compared to the lives of humankind, the earth abides with little change.

1:5–7 The sun ... The wind ... the rivers: These three elements of God's creation are seen to be going about in their expected courses, with little change and little effect.

1:8, 9 all things are full of labor: What is true of the sun, wind, and rivers (vv. 5–7) is also true of all other temporal things. The whole world is made up of what could be called "the restless ones." **The eye is not satisfied:** Here a proverb is quoted describing insatiable appetite in depicting the seeming pointlessness of the courses of natural phenomena.

1:10, 11 If it appears that something **new** does happen from time to time, it is only because people's memories are short.

1:12 I, the Preacher, was king: There is a shift from the third person of vv. 1, 2 to the first person here. The writer, or perhaps a later editor, returns to the third person in the epilogue, 12:8–14. This is most likely a reference to Solomon as the author of the book.

1:13 under heaven: This is a synonymous expression for "under the sun" (vv. 3, 9); it refers to life as it is lived by people on earth. **God:** Ecclesiastes does not use the divine title Yahweh, God's covenantal name (Ex. 3:14, 15). Instead, the book uses the word *Elohim* for God 28 times, a word that emphasizes His sovereignty over all creation. The wisdom writers often use *Elohim* when they wish to speak of universal truth instead of truths that are peculiar to God's covenantal relationship to Israel. **sons of man:** This is a way of speaking of human beings in a very general sense.

1:14 grasping for the wind: This phrase does not occur in the Hebrew Bible outside of Ecclesiastes. Seven of its nine occurrences (v. 14; 2:11, 17, 26; 4:4, 6; 6:9) follow "vanity" statements. The phrase explains the nature of life according to the Preacher. Life is real, but quickly passing; any attempt to seize it is as futile as grasping the wind.

1:15 Solomon is not claiming that there is no

use trying to straighten out or change anything. Rather, he explains that no amount of investigating or using the resources of earth will ever straighten out all that is **crooked,** twisted, perverted, or turned upside down (7:13).

1:16 all who were before me in Jerusalem: This phrase does not rule out Solomon as the author of the book just because he was preceded in Jerusalem only by his father David. There were other kings including Melchizedek (Gen. 14:18) and Adoni-Zedek (Josh. 10:1). The city of Jerusalem had existed for hundreds of years before Solomon became its king.

1:17 It was not **wisdom** that Solomon judges absurd, but rather becoming "more wise" (2:15) and "overly wise" (7:16).

1:18 much wisdom is much grief: For all of wisdom's other advantages, Solomon confesses that much wisdom and learning are the source of pain, chagrin, and sorrow. It is well known that the very process of learning is an expansion of the awareness of our ignorance. For mortals, an increase of wisdom may only increase pain (12:12).

2:1 The Preacher uses a literary device of conversing with himself as a way of describing his thought processes. **mirth:** A new test is proposed, following the test of wisdom. It is the test of "joy," or "pleasure."

2:2 Solomon labels the lighter side of pleasure and joy as sheer **madness,** but even the weightier aspects of laughter cause Solomon to ask if anything substantial is really achieved.

2:3 flesh with wine ... heart with wisdom: Here the test is an attempt to balance excess on the one side with learning on the other.

2:4–6 I built myself houses: Solomon worked for 13 years building "the king's house" (1 Kin. 9:10), then he built "the house of the Forest of Lebanon" (1 Kin. 10:17), and another house for his wife, Pharaoh's daughter (1 Kin. 9:24). **vineyards ... gardens and orchards:** Solomon's interest in the natural world (God's creation) was prodigious (1 Kin. 4:33).

2:7, 8 Maintaining the various buildings and gardens of the king must have demanded an extensive staff of servants. **silver and gold:** Solomon's riches were unsurpassed by the kings of the ancient world (1 Kin. 10:14–29).

2:9, 10 my eyes desired: Solomon had limitless ability to fulfill any and all of his desires. **labor:** One of the Preacher's favorite words occurs here for the third time. It appears in the book about 31 times.

2:11 At the end of his grand quest for possessions and experiences, Solomon concluded that it was **vanity** or "vapor," a **grasping for wind.** That is, even with all he had done and experienced, there was still a sense that nothing lasting or enduring had been achieved.

2:12 madness and folly: This topic was introduced briefly in 1:17. The two words together express a single concept, "senseless folly."

2:13 There is a relative value of **wisdom** over **folly,** but both have their limitations (vv. 19, 21).

2:14 the same event: Some versions incorrectly render this Hebrew term which means "happening," or "event" as the word *fate.* This is one of the Preacher's favorite words (vv. 14, 15; 3:19; 9:2, 3, 11). Here, the inevitable *event* is death. Both the wise and the foolish must die.

2:15–19 Such hatred of **life** is astonishing since the one who finds wisdom also finds life, according to Prov. 3:16; 8:35. But the Preacher's dissatisfaction was related to the quickly passing nature of everything (1:2), including even the good things; they were a **grasping for the wind** (1:14).

2:20 labor in which I had toiled: This could refer either to all the toil he had undertaken or, more probably, to the "earnings" he had gained.

2:21 The noun **skill** is found only in Ecclesiastes (v. 21; 4:4) It depicts one who is expert at a craft. **great evil:** The term *evil* often has a sense of moral evil; here however it may mean "calamity" or "ruin." There is a sense of sadness that runs through this section. Nothing that we gain in this life can be carried on into the life to come.

2:22–24 The Preacher concludes that all good is located only in God. **eat and drink ... good in his labor:** This repeated refrain marks one of the central affirmations of Ecclesiastes. In the midst of a world of trouble, a believer is able to seize the moment in joy from God. Only God supplies the key to

the meaning of life. Without Him, genuine meaning, satisfaction, and enjoyment in life are ultimately elusive. **from the hand of God:** This figure of speech announces that even such mundane acts as eating, drinking, and earning a paycheck are gifts from God.

2:25 more than I: An alternative meaning of this phrase, "apart from God," may be more appropriate in this context. Believers pray before their meals in order to affirm that God is the great Giver of all good gifts. They can enjoy the food on their plates only when they recognize that fact.

2:26 God gives: One of the words used most frequently in Ecclesiastes to describe God's relationship to individuals is the verb "to give." It appears 11 times with God as subject.

3:1 a season ... a time: Both words are usually regarded as being specific points in time rather than a continuity of time. **under heaven:** That is, life "under the sun," the sphere in which human life is lived.

3:2 born ... die: The pairs of words in these verses are natural events in human life, and all are under the hand of the living God.

3:3 a time to kill: In the plan of God, there is a time for executing murderers (Gen. 9:6) and for going to war against enemies designated by God. **a time to break down:** There is a time for dismantling walls, stone buildings, or even nations (Is. 5:5; Jer. 18:7, 9).

3:4 weep ... laugh: God's plan includes both sorrows and joys. Believers do not mourn in the same way as unbelievers (1 Thess. 4:13), but we do mourn (Matt. 5:4). Dancing and leaping are natural ways of expressing laughter, pleasure, and joy in the presence of the Lord (Ex. 15:20; Ps. 149:2, 3; 150:4) and in times of personal happiness (Luke 15:25).

3:5 In times of peace, **stones** were cleared from the fields, allowing for cultivation. In wartime, the rocks were thrown on the fields to make them unusable (2 Kin. 3:19, 25). **to embrace:** In this context the words describe the sexual embrace.

3:6 to keep ... to throw away: There is a period of life in which one wishes to accumulate things for enjoyment and memories; later in life, one needs to work out ways to dispose of what has been accumulated.

3:7 When bad news came, it was customary to rip one's garments to show grief (2 Sam. 13:31). When the problem passed, it was just as well to **sew** the garment back together.

3:8 In this verse the first part names the positive **love** first, then the negative **hate.** The second part uses the reverse order, negative then positive, to end with **peace.**

3:9 What profit: All of life unfolds the appointment of God. All the toiling of man cannot change the times, circumstances, and control of events that God has reserved to Himself.

3:10 One of the words that is unique to the Book of Ecclesiastes, **task** may have a neutral connotation as here (see 5:3; 8:16) or a negative connotation (something burdensome, as in 1:13; 2:23, 26; 4:8; 5:14).

3:11 All of God's creation is **beautiful.** The point is that God makes everything that way **in its time.** From the divine perspective, there is no ugliness in the events of our lives (3:1–8). **Eternity in their hearts** refers to a deep-seated, compulsive drive to transcend our mortality by knowing the meaning and destiny of the world. Because we are made in the image of God, we have an inborn inquisitiveness about eternal realities. We can find peace only when we come to know our eternal Creator. Even then, we know God only in part (1 Cor. 13:12).

3:12, 13 nothing better: The advice of the Preacher is to seize the day in the joy of God. **rejoice ... enjoy:** Biblical faith is a call for joy, even when we live in a wicked world and under terrible stress; this is because we find true joy in the living God.

3:14, 15 God's works have a durable quality to them. As Deut. 4:2; 12:32; Prov. 30:6 advise, **nothing** may be **added** and nothing **taken** away. **should fear:** The "fear" of God in wisdom literature refers to true piety, not terror (5:7; 12:13).

3:16, 17 The term **judgment** may also be translated "justice," giving an even more striking contrast to these words. It was outrageous that in the very establishments where people should expect justice, they could find only **wickedness.** The Preacher warns the wicked judges that God, the final

judge, will come, rectify all wrongdoing, and bring true justice.

3:18 tests them: The basic meaning of the verb is "to choose, select, purify, test." Death is the great leveler of all persons. In that regard, humans are no different than animals.

3:19 one breath: The Hebrew expression might be translated "one spirit" or "one wind." The phrase in this case describes breath as the sign and symbol of life (see 8:8; see also Gen. 6:17; 7:15, 22). In this, humanity and animals are alike (but see v. 21).

3:20, 21 all go to one place: Both humans and beasts die and go to the grave. But this is not the end for human beings—they will face eternal life or death. People and animals differ; their bodies go back to the dust from which they came, but the human spirit is immortal.

3:22 better: As in v. 12 and 2:24, there is a blessing given to humankind in terms of ordinary pleasures. **his heritage:** The allotment that God has designated may include material possessions (2:21; 11:2) or the pleasures that come from them (2:10; 3:22; 5:17, 18; 9:9).

4:1 Here is another complaint that threatens the plan of God. So much pain can come to the downtrodden that they may even despair of life (1 Kin. 19:4; Job 3:3–10). Only when the oppressed go into the house of God will they gain perspective for possible recovery (5:1–6; Ps. 73:17). **they have no comforter:** The absence of anyone to offer comfort only increases the pain and frustration.

4:2 I praised the dead: Being without a comforter is often worse than death itself.

4:3 he who has never existed: So powerfully wrong and so lonely is the suffering of the oppressed, that Solomon argues that nonexistence could be preferred over existence.

4:4 a man is envied by his neighbor: To the previous obstacles to accepting that God's plan encompasses everything is now added a fourth: the envy and cruel competition found in the world.

4:5, 6 the fool: There are numerous statements in the Book of Proverbs about the self-destructive nature of laziness. **a handful:** Moderation is preferred to overexertion. In place of the sometimes cruel competition of the marketplace, Solomon recommended: "Better is a little with righteousness, than vast revenues without justice" (Prov. 16:8).

4:7, 8 The problem of sadness and loneliness is another obstacle to accepting the fact that God has a plan that embraces everything. Consider the person who has no family, not even an heir to whom he can leave all for which he has worked so hard. In 4:1 there is "no comforter." In 4:4–6 there is no rest. In 4:8 there is no companion. **grave misfortune:** This literally refers to an evil or burdensome task (3:10).

4:9–12 Throughout this section there is an emphasis on the obvious benefits of companions. The intimacy and sharing of life brings relief for the problem of isolation and loneliness. A companion can offer assistance, comfort, and defense.

4:13, 14 Popularity, even in the form of royal power, is elusive. In one case, an old **king** had been born to the throne but becomes so **foolish** and senile that he cannot discern that his days for ruling are over. In another case, a young man, like Joseph, may rise from prison to take the throne (Gen. 41:14, 37–41).

4:15, 16 those who come afterward: Even the young man who replaces the old king's predecessor will share the old king's fate. Today's hero may become tomorrow's beggar.

5:1 Walk prudently: Literally, this phrase is "guard your feet" when you go to worship God. It means to behave yourself. **to hear:** As is common in the prophets, there is a warning to be circumspect about sacrifice. God has no pleasure in those who do all the right things for all the wrong reasons (Is. 1:10–15).

5:2, 3 God is in heaven ... you on earth: The essential contrast between God's righteous might and our sinful mortality should cause us to revere the Almighty (see v. 7).

5:4, 5 One should not attempt to bribe God with a hasty **vow.** The first part of this verse is almost identical to Deut. 23:21. See the later example of the lie of Ananias and Sapphira (Acts 5:1–11).

5:6 A priest or prophet or one of God's angels is the **messenger of God** who would hear such excuses for unfulfilled vows (Hag. 1:13; Mal. 2:7).

5:7 To **fear God,** a central theme of the Book of Ecclesiastes, does not mean to be afraid of God (Ex. 20:2). It means to have reverence, awe, and wonder in response to His glory. For the wisdom writers (Job 1:1; Ps. 111:10; Prov. 1:7), "to fear God" means to respond to Him correctly, in true piety.

5:8, 9 for all ... king: All people live by God's grace in His provision for the earth.

5:10 not be satisfied: The topic of an insatiable appetite is addressed for the third time (1:8; 4:8). Desire always outruns possessions, no matter how vast acquisitions may grow.

5:11, 12 There are few things so satisfying in life as **sleep** following a hard day's work; but the greedy rarely enjoy decent rest.

5:13, 14 Misfortune literally refers to a "worthless task" (compare 3:10).

5:15 naked shall he return: The maxim that "you can't take it with you" is affirmed here (2:21).

5:16 labored for the wind: The wording is similar to "grasping for the wind" (1:14).

5:17 darkness ... anger: The frugal lifestyle of the covetous prevents them from enjoying what they *do* have (contrast 2:24–26; 3:12, 13).

5:18, 19 God has separated the **gift** of enjoying something from the gift of the object itself so that we might be driven back to the Giver.

5:20 keeps him busy: God keeps a person occupied and delighted primarily with Himself and then with the gifts He gives. **joy of his heart:** The Preacher uses the word *joy* in two ways: (1) "enjoyment," an internal sense of pleasure (2:10, 26; 4:16; 9:7; 10:19) and (2) "pleasure," pleasurable actions (2:1, 2, 10; 7:4; 11:9).

6:1, 2 God does not give him power: Prosperity without the divine gift of enjoyment amounts to nothing (5:19).

6:3 Sometimes the achievement of the greatest of goals becomes hollow when there is no decent end to life. **stillborn child:** Ordinarily a great sadness, the child who does not live is considered to be better off than the person who has lived poorly. If life is nothing more than a meaningless journey to death, then a stillborn is better off, for that child reaches the end of the worthless journey with less pain (vv. 4–6).

6:4–6 That one **place** is, as 3:20 argues, the grave. If a long life terminates in death with no prospect of anything else, will that life have been worthwhile? Long life without knowing God and without the power to enjoy it is frustrating and useless.

6:7, 8 The Hebrew word for **soul** can also be translated *appetite*. If it is meant to parallel the word *mouth* in the first line, then *appetite* may be appropriate in this context. Yet the translation *soul* fits well in the argument of the gift being kept separate from the power to enjoy the gift (5:10).

6:9 The meaning of this proverb is that it is **better** making do with what we can look on and enjoy than fantasizing about desirable things that are beyond our grasp.

6:10 Whatever happens has been already known, because to name something is to know it (1:9–11). All things are foreknown and foreordained by God (see also 1:9–11).

6:11, 12 like a shadow: This phrase is a confirmation of the meaning of the Hebrew word translated *vanity.* Life passes away quickly, like a vapor. **what will happen after him:** The implied answer is that only God knows what will happen to us after death. Rather than imply that nothing exists beyond the grave, this book teaches that each person's life will be reviewed by God after death.

7:1 A person's death may be **better** than the day of birth if the name of that person has merited a lasting reputation and influence.

7:2–4 These verses expand upon the idea of v. 1. We may learn more about the meaning of life in the **house of mourning** than in the **house of feasting.**

7:5, 6 Burning **thorns** will provide quick flames, little heat, and a lot of noise, just like the sudden outbursts of laughter among fools; there is more noise than substance.

7:7, 8 bribe: Another form of this maxim is found in Ex. 23:8; Deut. 16:19. See also Matt. 28:11–15; Luke 22:4–6.

7:9, 10 The temptation to glorify the past at the expense of the present must be resisted. The pleasures or advantages of those **days** may be more imaginary than real.

7:11 Those who find **wisdom** find life, argues Solomon (Prov. 8:35). Wisdom is as good as an inheritance; in fact, wisdom is even more advantageous or profitable.

7:12 The word translated **defense** literally means "shade" or "shelter," a kind of protection.

7:13 The **crooked** that needs straightening (1:15) is the presence of afflictions and adversities in life. Both prosperity and adversity come from the hand of God. For prosperity give thanks, but in adversity reflect on the goodness and comprehensiveness of the plan of God.

7:14 find out nothing: If mortals do not come to know God and His plan, they will not be able to discern anything about life (3:11) or about what will happen after they are gone.

7:15 just man: There are inequities in life that will always be a mystery (3:16–4:3; see also 8:14).

7:16 do not be overly righteous: Few verses in Ecclesiastes are more susceptible to incorrect interpretation than these (vv. 16–18). This is not the so-called golden mean that advises: "Don't be too holy and don't be too wicked; sin to a moderate degree." The Preacher was warning instead about pseudo-religiosity and showy forms of worship. To "be overly righteous" would mean "righteous in your own eyes" (see Prov. 3:7).

7:17, 18 The **this** that Solomon refers to is the true wisdom that comes from the fear of God. The **other** is the folly of fools. **fears God:** True piety in reverence and awe is the best protection against either absurdity.

7:19, 20 not a just man on earth: This language recalls Solomon's prayer when he dedicated the temple (1 Kin. 8:46; see also Ps. 14:2–4; 143:2).

7:21, 22 take to heart: At times you may find another doing to you the same harmful thing that you have done to someone else.

7:23 proved by wisdom: The verb means "to put to the test."

7:24 The theme of wisdom's inaccessibility also appears in Job 28. The answer to this search for wisdom is that God **can find** wisdom (see Job 28:23–28).

7:25, 26 Wisdom literature is filled with warnings about the loose **woman** (see Prov. 7). However, this is balanced by the Preacher's praise for a spouse as a gift from God (9:9).

7:27, 28 The truth that all persons are sinners is put in a deliberate exaggeration. **Man** and **woman** mean "a good man" and "a good woman." In the Book of Proverbs, Solomon asked the same question: "Who can find a faithful man?" (Prov 20:6).

7:29 Even though God made everything beautiful (3:11) and **made** human beings **upright** (see Gen. 1:31), Solomon's search for the "sum" had failed. Yet humankind's search for wicked devices and intrigues had succeeded wonderfully.

8:1 The idiom "to cause one's **face** to **shine**" (see also the Levitical blessing of Num. 6:25) is an image of a person who is stable. Out of the depths of experience and understanding, that person is able to enjoy life and build up others.

8:2, 3 Subjects are obligated by an **oath** of allegiance to render their obedience to "the powers that be" (Rom. 13:1–5). **not ... stand for an evil thing:** Even before a king, evil is to be resisted (Acts 5:29).

8:4, 5 What are you doing: This same question is asked of those who pretend to be able to rebuke God (Job 9:12; Dan. 4:32). The rhetorical question amounts to a firm denial of the king's power.

8:6, 7 time and judgment: The phrase means an "appropriate time of judgment." God will judge everyone; every matter, including judgment, has its set time (12:14).

8:8, 9 Since the word **spirit** is paralleled by the "day of death," the term *spirit* in this context means "life force" (3:19).

8:10 It was difficult to see the **wicked** receiving a funeral procession from the city to the cemetery while the righteous were **forgotten.**

8:11 sentence ... is not executed: There are cases when God postpones punishment, letting the guilty person live longer.

8:12, 13 The sharp contrast of the righteous and the **wicked** in these verses is a hallmark of Hebrew wisdom literature (Ps. 1).

8:14 according ... righteous: Although there seem to be some glaring inequities in this present life, we know that God is working out His good purposes (3:16—4:3; 7:15).

8:15 In contrast to the mad search for the meaning of all things is the contentment that a wise, loving God gives to those who will receive His gifts of **enjoyment.** Here is one of the central themes of Ecclesiastes. **eat, drink, and be merry:** The Preacher marks the end of the third major section of his book with this refrain. The wicked person (the fool) decides that the best thing to do is to "eat, drink, and be merry" with no thought given to the living God. But the righteous person (the wise) can enjoy life while thinking of God and His good gifts.

8:16, 17 Solomon equates God's work with the activity that takes place on earth. Therefore it should not be surprising that humans cannot fathom God's activity (3:11; 7:25–29; 11:5–8). The Hebrew word translated **attempts** can also be translated *claims* or *thinks* in this context (see 2 Chr. 13:8 where the word is translated *think*).

9:1 In the hand of God means "in God's control and possession." **love nor hatred:** Sometimes in Hebrew two opposites together are a way of saying "everything." Love and hate are best viewed as words for God's favor and disfavor.

9:2, 3 Some versions translate the word **event** as "fate" (see 2:14). However, there is no hint here of the power of fate as some people in antiquity believed. The word simply refers to an outcome determined by God.

9:4 In this verse, Solomon uses a proverb that says a living lowly creature is preferable to a dead exalted creature. The point is not that death is the absolute end of all things; instead, while there is life, there is **hope** of doing something to the glory of God.

9:5, 6 This, again, is not a flat denial of any hope beyond the grave. The point of view is limited to what can be known strictly from a human point of view, "under the sun." **they have no more reward:** A person must work while it is still day (that is, while one is still alive), for the night will come when no one can work (John 9:4).

9:7 God meant for all His gifts to be enjoyed. The image of **bread** and **wine** is frequently used in Scripture as a symbol of the fact that God gives comfort and cheer to people (Gen. 14:18; 1 Sam. 16:20; 25:18; Neh. 5:15; Lam. 2:12).

9:8 It was difficult in ancient times to keep white **garments** clean (see the analogy in Is. 1:18). White garments and ointments—**oil**—were symbols of joy and purity.

9:9 Marriage is the gift of God. "Marriage is honorable" and the marriage bed "undefiled," instructed the writer of Hebrews (13:4). Marriage is to be cherished (Prov. 5:15–20) and unfaithfulness avoided (Prov. 5:1–14). **vain life:** That is, life that passes so quickly.

9:10 no work ... in the grave: This affirmation is not a denial of a personal future state after death. Yet in relation to this world, the possibilities of working and learning have ceased. If we plan to do anything to the glory of God in this world, we had better do it while we still have time (John 9:4).

9:11–13 We would like to think that the best always win. But our experience shows that these expectations are not always realized. **not to the swift ... strong ... wise ... men of understanding ... men of skill:** These five assets were enjoyed by individuals. But while some planned and counted on their assets, God in the end determined their lot.

9:14–18 Here is a parable about how an unstoppable military operation against a small city was prevented by the wisdom of one **poor,** but **wise man.** The conclusion is that wisdom is preferable to strength, and should be heeded.

10:1 Just as one fly can ruin a whole batch of **ointment,** so an ounce of folly will spoil a pound of wisdom.

10:2 In ancient thought, the **right hand** was the place of honor and favor, while the left hand was the reverse.

IN DEPTH — **Death and Life**

A ncient people reflected on the inevitability of death. As the Book of Ecclesiastes expresses: "No one has power in the day of death" (Eccl. 8:8). Similar reflections are found in the Gilgamesh Epic, the adventures of Gilgamesh, king of Uruk around 2600 B.C.

The Gilgamesh Epic, composed in Akkadian, has been preserved in two major versions, one from late in the Old Babylonian period (1750–1600 B.C.) and a second by Neo-Assyrian scribes (750–612 B.C.). The Neo-Assyrian version contains a scene in which Gilgamesh, in his search for immortality, passes by Siduri, the divine alewife (who is tending her beer stand on the seacoast). Her advice (in the Old Babylonian version) on the futility of his quest is quite similar to the advice of Ecclesiastes: "Live joyfully" (Eccl. 9:9).

Siduri begins by reminding Gilgamesh that it is impossible for humans to find eternal life, which the gods have reserved for themselves. Her advice to Gilgamesh is to eat, make merry, and rejoice in the feasting while he can. She tells him to enjoy the daily rounds of life: Wear clean clothing, bathe himself, play with his children, and enjoy his wife. That is all, she tells him, that is allowed by the gods. Old age and death will overtake everyone. Gilgamesh continued on his search, but found that Siduri's words reflected reality.

The writer of Ecclesiastes offers readers much the same advice: Eat and drink with joy, wear clean ("white") garments, attend to your body ("oil on your head"), and enjoy your wife (Eccl. 9:7–9). The passage in the Gilgamesh Epic shows that these ideas of Ecclesiastes were known in the ancient Near East as early as the Israelite and Judean kingdoms. Siduri's speech proves that the idea of resignation to mortality was pondered in the ancient Near East in almost the same terms as it was by the preacher of Ecclesiastes.

10:3 There are times when even **a fool** acts appropriately; yet he remains a fool.

10:4, 5 conciliation pacifies: This proverb is similar to many ancient sayings that were used to train courtiers and diplomats.

10:6 folly … dignity: Things are simply not always what we think they ought to be (9:11); but God is still in control, and He works His good purposes through events we do not understand.

10:7 servants on horses: In the ancient Middle East, such a reversal of the normal roles of servant and master was felt to be an outrage against society.

10:8–10 The wise person will sharpen the **ax.** A person of limited training will have to work harder, as though with a dull ax, than someone wiser whose tools are in order.

10:11 a serpent may bite: Along with the preceding verses, the point made here is that an unused skill is wasted.

10:12, 13 It is the inability of the **fool** to choose his words carefully that will bring about his own destruction.

10:14 Who … after him: This rhetorical question about the fool's lack of knowledge about the future is one of the repeated themes of Ecclesiastes. The same question is asked in 3:22; 6:12; 8:7; in part in 9:12; and especially in the grand conclusion of 12:14.

10:15 go to the city: If **fools** are so untrustworthy in ordinary affairs, how can they be trusted when they express their opinion about the hereafter?

10:16 Pity those leaders so young or inexperienced that they lose control over their areas of responsibility, or who spend their nights partying into the early **morning.**

10:17 Useful nobility expresses itself in a sense of responsibility and deference to social order. This verse is an argument for propriety. **proper time:** Here is Solomon's case for moderation and orderliness.

10:18 All forms of **laziness** bring houses and lives into disrepair.

10:19 money answers everything: Rather than being cynical or critical about wealth or the rich, this comment is to be taken in the context of the dissolute nobles (v. 16) and banqueters (v. 17). Wealth for them is only pleasure and a means of having fun.

10:20 a bird of the air: We should watch what we say, for we never know who is listening.

11:1 cast your bread upon the waters: Verses 1–6 emphasize the element of risk and uncertainty in commercial and agricultural enterprises. Thus if the preceding proverbs in ch. 10 deal with royalty and leaders, these in vv. 1–6 deal with common people. Men and women must venture forth judiciously if they are ever to realize a gain, even though there is always a certain amount of risk.

11:2 seven, and also to eight: This urges us to be generous to as many as possible—and then some.

11:3 Regardless of which way a **tree falls,** someone is going to get the use of its wood, so stop worrying that it did not fall on your side (or even hoping that it will).

11:4 will not sow: The person who is so cautious that he must wait for the ideal time before he makes a move is doomed to fail.

11:5 Some works of God defy explanation. **who makes everything:** The concept of God as Creator in Ecclesiastes is not limited to 12:1. The inability of humans to know God's works apart from knowing Him is one of the themes of this book (3:11; 8:17; 9:12).

11:6 which will prosper: Do not hold back from getting involved. Let the success or failure of a task rest in the hand of God—but get to the task.

11:7 light is sweet: An affirmation of the joy of life, despite all the troubles that the book has presented.

11:8 remember the days of darkness: In appreciating the opportunities of life, we must think more seriously about death. This is contrasted with the joy of working while it is still light.

11:9 Solomon was speaking to young people (see Prov. 1:8; 2:1; 3:1), encouraging them to learn the lessons that he had learned over the course of his life. **Walk in the ways of your heart:** This verse is not an invitation to live sinfully in sensual pleasure (as Num. 15:39 describes). Instead, it urges young people to enjoy themselves while not forgetting that God will review the quality of their life (3:17; 12:14).

11:10 Tragically, **youth** does not last; it too passes like a vapor. We all seem to discover that "we get old too soon and smart too late."

12:1, 2 The person is losing his sight because of the ravages of age.

12:3 Verses 3–6 list the bodily infirmities that increasingly hinder an older person from serving God. If the **house** stands for the aging body, then the **keepers** are the arms and hands. **strong men bow down:** The legs are bent in feebleness and the knees cannot be depended on for support. **grinders cease:** The teeth, now fewer than before, cannot chew the food as well as they once did. **those that look through the windows grow dim:** The eyes begin to lose their sight.

12:4 doors are shut in the streets: Just as the jaws of Leviathan are called the "doors of his face" (Job 41:14), so the lips and jaws are possibly intended here. **sound of grinding is low:** A depiction of toothless old age when eating only soft foods makes little or no noise. **daughters of music are brought low:** The ability to hear—and thus the ability to make and enjoy music—wanes.

12:5 afraid of height: Things that used to be a regular part of life now become threatening. **almond tree blossoms:** Hair turns white. **grasshopper is a burden:** This may refer to the halting step of the elderly as they hobble along on their canes. **desire fails:** This is generally understood as a reference to a vanishing sexual desire. Then comes death: **eternal home.**

12:6 Some suggest that **silver cord** refers to the spinal cord. **golden bowl is broken:** This may refer to the brain. **pitcher shattered at the fountain:** One suggestion is that this is a failing heart. **wheel broken at the well:** The system of veins and arteries radiating out from the heart might have appeared to the ancients like the spokes on a wheel. An alternative explanation of this verse is that each of the four images represent death. That is, there is no physical representation intended in these images as in those of vv. 3–5. Instead, this verse describes the destruction of four significant objects—a demonstration of the finality of this life.

12:7 dust will return: These words refer clearly to the universal fate of the descendants of Adam and Eve. **spirit will return:** This is a clear allusion to Gen. 2:7. The term *spirit* is the same used in earlier passages (3:19, 21; 8:8).

12:8 The refrain of **vanity**—the brevity life—is here repeated. It is possible that the book originally ended with these words.

12:9 Early on in his book, **the Preacher** speaks of his pursuit of wisdom (1:12—2:26). It is possible that he speaks of himself here in the third person (as in 1:1, 2). Probably it was an editor under the guiding hand of God who wrote these evaluations of Solomon, much as Joshua or some other editor wrote an evaluation of Moses under the influence of God's Spirit (Deut. 34). **pondered ... sought out ... set in order:** The three verbs that describe Solomon's activity may also be translated "weighed ... examined ... and arranged."

12:10 The Preacher devotes special care to write **acceptable** words—pleasant words, words of grace—and **words of truth.** The truth referred to here is the truth from God.

12:11 Just as an ox goad prods an animal in the right direction, so will the words of this book when they are properly understood. **by one Shepherd:** Kings were typically compared to shepherds, and Solomon is claiming that the source of his ideas is God, the Shepherd of Israel (Ps. 80:1).

12:12 Many other **books** may weary their readers. Careful study of Ecclesiastes will have the opposite effect as it instructs, warns, and admonishes its readers.

12:13 To **fear God** is one of the major themes of this book and of wisdom literature in the Old Testament. To fear God is to respond to Him in awe, reverence, and wonder, to serve Him in purity of action, and to shun evil and any worship of anything else in His universe. **man's all:** We are whole or complete only when we fear God and obey His commandments. If we follow what this book has said, we will have a relationship with God and find life in Him.

12:14 judgment: This same teaching is echoed by the apostle Paul in 2 Cor. 5:10. Death is not the end. All of life will be reviewed by our righteous Lord (see at 3:17). Life must be lived through faith with the values of the eternal God in view.

Song of Solomon

Introduction

The Song of Solomon is a moving love story between a young country girl and King Solomon. In delicate poetry, the lovers express intense passion and deep longing for each other. The young girl compares her love for her husband to the anticipation of a frantic search, while Solomon likens his bride's beauty to picturesque gardens and delicious fruit. Yet even in this eloquent expression of the passion between a bride and bridegroom, there is an exhortation to remain sexually pure before marriage (2:7). In this way, the book celebrates human sexuality within the context of marriage.

The author of the Song of Solomon is Solomon, the son of David and the third king of Israel. He is named as the author and his name appears seven times in the book (1:1, 5; 3:7, 9, 11; 8:11, 12). The fact that Solomon was known for his wisdom and poetry (see 1 Kin. 4:29–34) partially substantiates his authorship of this book.

The Song of Solomon retells the romance between King Solomon, the richest king ever to rule Israel, and his beloved bride, who came from a small village in the region of Galilee. Strangely we never learn her name. She is called simply the Shulamite. For some time he pursued her and made periodic visits to her country home to see her. Finally, he proposed. The Shulamite gave much thought to whether she really loved Solomon and could be happy in the palace of a king. Finally she accepted.

The Song of Solomon provides an example of how God created male and female to live in happiness and fulfillment. Because of its emphasis on human love, this book presents an extraordinary variety of expressions for love. But within this celebration of love, the book condemns unchaste relations outside of marriage—and in particular, sexual experimentation before marriage. We cannot ignore the sexual content of the book, but we can appreciate the context in which it is placed—a godly marriage. The Song of Solomon is necessary reading not only for the married, but for young people who want to understand God's design for marriage.

1:1 Like the superlative expressions "holy of holies" or "king of kings," **song of songs** means "the loveliest of songs." **which is Solomon's:** There are two principal speakers in this book, the woman (the Shulamite) and the man (Solomon). Even though Solomon wrote this book, interestingly enough the point of view presented is largely that of his bride.

1:2 This prologue to the book forms the emotional setting for all that follows. **love:** The Hebrew noun used here means sexual love, as it clearly does in Ezek. 16:8 (also Prov. 7:18; Ezek. 23:17). This is the Hebrew word that most approximates the Greek word *eros.* In the Song of Solomon, this plural word (a mark of intensity) speaks of divinely blessed lovemaking (used also in v. 4; 4:10; 7:12; compare 5:1).

1:3 ointments: It was customary in biblical times to rub the body with fragrant **ointments** (oils) after a bath in preparation for a festive occasion (Ruth 3:3). **your name:** The Shulamite speaks of her beloved's reputation as akin to a lovely aroma; he was an object of desire to young women everywhere. The term **virgins** is the same word used at Is. 7:14. The word means women of marriageable age (they are the same as the "daughters of Jerusalem" in v. 5).

1:4 The complexity of the interchanges in this book are illustrated in this verse. The headings help sort out the speakers. **the king:** This is Solomon; yet aside from the title (v. 1), he is not identified by name as a protagonist until 3:7, 9, 11 (his name in v. 5 is part of a descriptive phrase). **chambers:** This means the bridal chamber. The verse ends with the thoughts of the young woman as she gazes at her lover.

1:5 The Shulamite compares her **dark** coloring, acquired from long hours working in the vineyards (v. 6) with the lighter complexion of the city maidens. Unlike the young women of the court in Jerusalem who had been raised in comfort and conditions of ease, this woman had worked as a field hand under the blazing sun. **but lovely:** She knows that her beauty is not diminished by her more rugged manner of living. Her groom assures her that this is truly the case (v. 8). The rare term *lovely* is used to describe physical beauty in this book (see v. 10; 2:14; 4:3; 6:4; compare the word in v. 8). **O daughters of Jerusalem:** These are women who serve as the attendants of the bride. These woman also serve as the chorus in the book. They are the same as the "virgins" of v. 3.

1:6 Her **own vineyard** refers to her appearance. Unlike the beautiful women of the royal court, the Shulamite had not had the lifestyle or the resources to take much time for her appearance. Still, it was she who swept away the king's heart.

1:7 you whom I love: A more literal rendering might be, "whom my soul (my inner being) loves." Here the young woman mentally addresses Solomon, her husband. She pictures him as the shepherd of Israel. **one who veils herself:** Solomon, as king, was busy with affairs of state. The young bride does not want to veil herself as a prostitute would in order to get his attention, nor does she want to be left alone. She desires to be his true companion.

1:8 If you do not know ... feed your little goats: It would be better if she returned to the borders of Lebanon and the life of the farm rather than live alone and anxious in Solomon's palace. The point of this verse is that one should always count the cost of marriage to a particular person *before* the marriage.

1:9 Here is yet another term for **love** in the book, the rarer word meaning "dear companion" (compare at vv. 2, 3). **my filly:** In Solomon's time the horse was the companion of kings. Solomon loved horses, particularly those from Egypt. Eventually he had a stable of twelve thousand horses with 1,400 chariots (1 Kin. 10:26).

1:10, 11 ornaments: These are kind words from the women of the court (see 1:4). Their kindness is remarkable, since each of these women may have hoped to be chosen by the king (as v. 3 indicates).

1:12 his table: That is, the setting of the wedding banquet.

1:13, 14 This verse refers to an oriental custom for a woman to wear a small bag of **myrrh,** a perfumed ointment, around her neck at night. All the next day a lovely fragrance would

linger about her. The young woman says that beginning that night, it would be her husband who would lie with her. **my beloved:** Here the noun *beloved* is related to the word translated "love" in v. 2, referring to sexual love.

1:15 Behold, you are fair: The word *fair* means "beautiful" (as in v. 8). **my love:** This term is used for the first time in the book; it means "dear friend." **dove's eyes:** The idea is purity, innocence and beauty (see 4:1; 5:12; compare 2:14; 5:2).

1:16 The word **handsome** used here is the masculine counterpart of the term translated "fair" in v. 15.

1:17 beams of our houses are cedar: *Houses* may mean "grand house" or "mansion." As the Shulamite lies on their wedding bed (v. 16), she observes the marvelous cedar beams above her head. The opulence of Solomon's personal and public buildings in Jerusalem is well documented (1 Kin. 7:1–12).

2:1, 2 Solomon takes the young bride's words (v. 1) comparing herself to a simple flower and assures her that, beside her, the fancy women of the city are but **thorns.**

2:3 The **apple tree** and the raisin cakes (v. 5) are symbols for sexual passion in ancient love songs.

2:4 the banqueting house: The literal meaning of the phrase is "the house of wine," used because of the role that *wine* plays not only in feasting, but especially in weddings in biblical cultures (1:2). In the Bible, wine is a symbol of joy (see Ps. 104:15) and the drinking of wine is associated with joyful occasions. **his banner:** This may be the same term as used in Num. 1:52, meaning "standard" or "flag." Even today, Jewish weddings take place under a "banner" or covering.

2:5, 6 These verses describe the joy of sexual expression between a husband and wife. **raisins ... apples:** Ancient symbols of sexual passion (see v. 3). **lovesick:** These are the words of one overwhelmed with love.

2:7 Here the Shulamite speaks to her attendants in their virginity and entreats them (**I charge you**) to maintain their sexual purity until marriage (see 3:5; 8:4).

2:8, 9 leaping ... skipping: This is the young bride's imaginative way of recalling the joy she experienced at her husband's arrival.

The same is true of her words for him: **gazelle ... stag,** animals that symbolize virility. **windows ... lattice:** That is, Solomon was looking at *her* through an opening in the wall.

2:10 my love: A term of endearment meaning "my dear friend" (see 1:15). **my fair one:** Solomon describes his bride as "beautiful" (see 1:8, 15).

2:11–13 the winter is past: By this Solomon means that the time of joy has come; it is the summer of their love. Solomon may have come at a time of great beauty in the fields and forests where the young woman lived; he uses the beauty of creation to describe the ripeness of time for their love.

2:14 Solomon's great find in this young woman is occasioned in part by her shy charm. **in the clefts:** Solomon speaks of the Shulamite using a figure of speech describing her isolated home in the mountains.

2:15 The Shulamite's brothers called on Solomon to **catch** them **the foxes.** Many times they had seen **little foxes** creep into the vineyards they tended and destroy the roots by gnawing on them. The **vine** of the budding love of the couple was tender and needed to be protected from these "little foxes," which symbolize the problems of life that may gnaw away at a relationship.

2:16 My beloved is mine, and I am his: The expression describes the mutual intimacy that a married couple experiences. Both belong to each other (see 6:3; compare 7:10).

2:17 until the day breaks: Here the woman wishes the king to leave for the night. The book is pervaded with the sense of doing what is right at the appropriate time. Here, she wishes him to flee like a **gazelle.** Later, she will want him to rush to her like one (8:14).

3:1 on my bed: This is a dream that took place before they were married. The young woman was becoming concerned about what she would be getting into in this royal marriage.

3:2, 3 Her frantic search for her beloved is initially unsuccessful. Twice in these verses she describes him as **the one I love.** In each case, the wording is "the one whom my soul (or my inner being) loves."

3:4 At last she finds him, using the same phrasing (**the one I love**) of vv. 2, 3. In her dream she takes him to her mother's **house.** That is, the worry of his absence is intolerable to her; she wants him to move back with her to her familiar home and life-style.

3:5 do not stir up: Again there is a strong warning against premarital sex. People should not allow sexual passion to stir before they have gotten to know each other in other ways (2:8–17), until they have worked out the problems of their relationship (the "little foxes," see 2:15–17), and until they have counted the costs of marriage (3:1–4).

3:6 Who is this coming: Contrast the bold, royal journey here with the earlier, playful approach in 2:8. **perfumed:** The precious ointments here are marks of luxury and royalty; later, on the woman, these elements would be symbols of love (4:6).

3:7, 8 The **couch** was a sedan chair with poles projecting from the front and back so that a person could be carried by several bearers (vv. 9, 10). The Shulamite was being carried to the wedding and to her groom on Solomon's own couch.

3:9, 10 Apparently Solomon had ordered this couch (vv. 7, 8) to be designed and built especially for the wedding. To the Shulamite, the couch's rich ornamentation of **silver** and **gold** is less significant than the fact that the couch represents Solomon's **love** and care for her (2:4).

3:11 O daughters of Zion: These are the Daughters of Jerusalem (see 1:5). **and see:** For a wedding to be recognized in ancient Israel, it had to be a public event. Such a day has always been regarded as a day of **gladness** (Ps. 19:5). **the crown:** Solomon's royal symbol was appropriately worn at this wedding.

4:1 Solomon lavishly praises his bride's great beauty. He uses verbal symbols of loveliness to paint a picture of the breathtaking charm of the Shulamite. **Dove's eyes** (2:14) are a picture of purity, innocence, and beauty (as in 1:15). The bride's **veil** would have covered the rest of her face, leaving only her beautiful eyes to be seen (see at 2:14; see also 5:7). The king compared the movement of her flowing **hair** to the graceful movement of **a flock of goats** in their descent **down from Mount Gilead.**

4:2–5 The king rhapsodizes on the perfection of his bride's **teeth,** her **lips** and facial features, her **neck,** and at last her **breasts.** Scarlet (v. 3) describes luxuriance and beauty; the **pomegranate** speaks of sweetness; the term **lovely** is the same rare word used first in 1:5. The **tower of David** (v. 4) pictures strength and grace; the **fawns** (v. 5) have exquisite loveliness.

4:6 until the day breaks: The couple's first night together was a precious time (see 8:14).

4:7 fair: The king has used this term for beauty before (v. 1). However, the difference here is in the word **all.** Now he rhapsodizes on how perfect his bride is; every part of her is attractive.

4:8 These words demonstrate Solomon's sensitivity to his new bride's emotions at this point. He calls her mind back from thoughts afar off. He says, "**Come** back **with me.**" His use of the word **spouse** for the first time is appropriate here on their wedding bed.

4:9 My sister, my spouse: This strange pairing of words was based on the idea that in marriage a couple became "related." The woman was dignified as a member of the king's family.

4:10 your love ... your love: That is, erotic love.

4:11 lips ... honey and milk: The sweetness of his bride's kisses is like food to him (see 5:1; compare 1:2).

4:12 spring ... fountain: Solomon evokes thoughts of refreshment and delight. His use of the words **enclosed ... shut up ... sealed** indicate, in a poetic manner, his

wife's virginity on their wedding night. This was the treasure she brought to him, and which she adjured the other young women in the court to maintain for their wedding nights as well (2:7).

4:13–15 pleasant fruits: These verses expand the images of the garden and the fountain for sexual love from v. 12.

4:16 The bride is now ready to accept her lover for the first time to her **garden.** She calls on the **wind** to blow through. That is, she is ready to make love to her husband for the first time.

5:1 drunk my wine: This verse is a necessary part of the preceding chapter. At the conclusion of their lovemaking, the groom speaks of his complete satisfaction in his beautiful bride.

5:2–7 I sleep: These words begin a section (vv. 2–8) that most likely is another dream sequence (see 3:1–5). The bride dreams that her lover is coming to her, but she has already washed, removed her **robe,** and gotten into bed (v. 3). She finally goes to the **door** to let him in, but he is gone. Her sorrow at this drives her into the **city** to search for him. The **watchmen** find her and are hostile toward her.

5:8, 9 The bride asks the **daughters of Jerusalem** to help her in her search. But they question what is so special about the one for whom she seeks.

5:10–16 The bride responds to the question of v. 9 with a poem extolling the handsomeness of her husband, beginning with his **ruddy** complexion and ending with the sweetness of his **mouth.**

6:1 The chorus members now join in the search. In the dream sequence, we suspect that the chorus is well aware of his location.

 IN DEPTH   ## Places Named in the Song of Solomon

From the peaks of Lebanon to the streets of Jerusalem (4:8; 6:4), the love story in the Song of Solomon takes place in a variety of settings. The lovers speak of, and to, each other with several word pictures, including "the rose of Sharon" (2:1), "the lily of the valleys" (2:1), and "the vineyards of En Gedi" (1:14).

It is only the bride who needs to discover his whereabouts.

6:2 his garden ... his flock: This is a change of language from 4:12–16. On their wedding night, the bride presented herself to Solomon as his garden. But he has another "garden" to tend as well, and it is one in which he also takes great pleasure. This is the "garden" of his work, his responsibility as the king of Israel. The flock is the people; the lilies represent the produce of the land. This realization leads to the strong affirmation in the next verse that the husband and wife belong to each other.

6:3 He feeds his flock among the lilies: With these words the bride comes to terms with the reality that, as much as she and the king are in love, he still has other responsibilities and so does she. His work as king makes him the shepherd of his people, yet his love for her does not necessarily diminish because of his devotion to his work.

6:4–7 Tirzah ... Jerusalem: Solomon idealizes the beauty of these cities, even as people speak of beautiful cities in our own day. **army with banners:** From a distance, there is a kind of beauty in the sight of an army, especially for a king.

6:8, 9 sixty ... eighty: This use of numbers is a rhetorical device to emphasize that the bride alone is Solomon's love. **praised:** Here is a use of this verb in a context other than the worship of God.

6:10 morning ... moon ... sun: The king's rapture at the very thought of his wife lifts his soul to the heavens.

6:11 Here the term **garden** refers to the Shulamite's homeland.

6:12, 13 Shulamite: The term may mean "a woman from the village of Shulam." However, the hometown of the woman is usually thought to be Shunem. Her title sounds very much like the Hebrew pronunciation for the name Solomon. Both words are related to the Hebrew word for peace (*shalom*). **the dance of the two camps:** In Hebrew, the word is Mahanaim. The woman offers to dance before her beloved so that he might enjoy her beauty in lovely motion.

7:1–5 Solomon rhapsodizes on the beauty of his bride. In the eyes of love, one's lover has a beauty that transcends what others might see. **prince's daughter:** Although of common birth (1:2), the Shulamite has regal beauty. **the curves of your thighs:** The Hebrew wording suggests not only her form but the fluid motion of her dance (6:13).

7:6 This verse summarizes the king's joy in her beauty.

7:7, 8 palm tree: This is a sexual image that has its basis in the pollination of palm trees. To fertilize a female palm tree, the gardener climbs the male tree and takes some of its flowers. Then he climbs the female tree and ties the pollen-bearing flowers among its branches.

7:9, 10 desire: This word is used only three times in the Bible. Here it clearly means "sexual longing."

7:11, 12 She was familiar with all the environs, but especially the **vineyards** (see 1:6; compare 8:12). **my love:** This refers to a sexual embrace; see 1:2 where the same word is used.

7:13 From early times, **mandrakes** were associated with fertility (Gen. 30:14).

8:1, 2 like my brother: The love of the bride for her beloved was so intense that she wished that she had known him his entire life. **spiced wine:** The wines of the ancient world were often flavored with aromatic spices on special occasions (Prov. 9:2).

8:3, 4 left ... right: The repetition of 2:6, 7 punctuates both the joy of sexual intimacy within marriage and the warnings against sexual activity before marriage.

8:5 The king takes his bride back to her home country for a visit. The **apple tree** symbolizes the place where the Shulamite had been awakened sexually and where her mother had given birth to her.

8:6 A **seal** is a symbol of possession or ownership. The Shulamite wants the king to feel a total ownership of her in his **heart.** She is committed only to him; and she wants him to be completely committed to her. As long as she resides in his heart, she feels secure. She knows that love deeply rooted in a heart commitment is intense—**strong as death**—and passionate—like **flames of fire.**

8:7 quench ... despised: The point of this powerful verse is that true love cannot be destroyed, and neither can it be purchased.

8:8 The Shulamite came from a fatherless home where she had been raised by her mother and brothers (1:6). They alternated between protective concern for her and anger with her. But in her growing up, her brothers had protected her.

8:9 if … a wall: By this the brothers meant that they would praise her for virtue and strength during puberty. **if … a door:** However, if she were loose, like a swinging door, they would have to protect her from herself and from untoward advances by young men.

8:10 The woman explains that she has been virtuous in her youth—**a wall**—and she will remain faithful in her adulthood—**towers.** In this way she discovers **peace.**

8:11, 12 Solomon owned many vineyards, some in areas remote from Jerusalem. **Baal Hamon** ("Lord of Hamon") was a site near Shunem, the town near where the Shulamite may have grown up. It was customary for an absentee owner to lease out a vineyard. As Solomon's vineyard had been entrusted to the Shulamite's brothers, so had the Shulamite. After caring for this vineyard, the brothers earned one thousand shekels profit. But they also cared for and protected the king's other "vineyard," the Shulamite. Now, she requests that her brothers be rewarded with two hundred shekels profit. **My own vineyard:** Here she sees that vineyard of old (see 7:12), but indicates that she now has another "vineyard" to tend—her dear husband.

8:13 The companions: This may be a reference to the woman's friends living nearby.

8:14 Make haste: During the period of courtship, the young woman had asked her suitor to run away like a **gazelle … stag,** lest they become entangled with passion too soon. Now, in their married love, she wishes he would rush to her (see 4:6). **the mountains of spices:** That is, she wants him to return to her loving embrace (see 1:13; 4:6).

Isaiah

Introduction

The Lord called the prophet Isaiah to warn His people of their headlong rush into disaster because of their rebellion and idolatry. The Book of Isaiah records these prophetic words of warning, but it also records Isaiah's words of promise and hope. One day, a Messiah would come who would save, comfort, and bless His people. Isaiah the son of Amoz has traditionally been identified as the author of the entire book that bears his name (1:1).

Understanding Hebrew prophetic literature involves recognizing and interpreting parallelism. The Hebrews used parallelism in poetry and prophecy as a literary technique to emphasize a particular thought. Here is an example: "The ox knows its owner / and the donkey its master's crib; / but Israel does not know, / My people do not consider" (1:3). In the first part of this verse, both the ox and the donkey intuitively know the objects that they depend on, the owner (provider) as well as the "master's crib" (provision). The second part of the verse contrasts the intuition of animals with the behavior of the Israelites. Israel does not know "its Owner," and even though they are God's "people," they "do not consider" God's provision. Thus the second half of the verse creates the analogy in parallel with the first half.

Unlike prose which addresses historical realities more directly, prophetic poetry draws its readers into spiritual realities with the use of evocative language. Thus in 42:15, the images of "mountains and hills" represent both physical and spiritual obstacles to the exiles' return to Jerusalem. The promise that the Lord would "dry up" these obstacles means that He would eliminate all impediments to the exiles' return, just as He had dried up the Red Sea long before.

Another major element in understanding prophetic literature is recognizing that the prophecies themselves and their arrangement often lack chronological perspective or have multiple fulfillments. For example, the same prophecy may speak of both Jesus' First and Second Comings (63:1, 2). Likewise, one

prophecy may speak of both the virgin birth of Jesus as well as the birth of Isaiah's son during Pekah's invasion. Ultimately, the interpretations of Jesus and the New Testament authors provide a guide for interpreting Old Testament prophecies.

Isaiah predicted that the complete restoration of Israel was still to come (49:8–26). The promised Messiah would appear in the future (61:1–3). Then Gentiles would join Israel's godly remnant to become the "servants" of the Lord (56:3; 65:1, 15, 16) in a new nation (65:1; 66:8). The ultimate triumph of good over evil would have to await the new heaven and the new earth (65:17–19).

1:1 God mediated His message through the godly **Isaiah** to **Judah,** specifically to their magistrates, priests, and prophets in **Jerusalem.** The nation of Israel had been divided into two parts: Judah (the southern kingdom) and Israel (the northern kingdom). The entire nation was heading down a path of sin and idolatry that would end in destruction. Thus in this book, the word Israel sometimes refers to both the southern and the northern kingdoms. Isaiah lived to see the nation of Assyria take the northern kingdom into captivity in 722 B.C. Therefore this record of Isaiah's visions contains the revelations that God graciously gave during the reigns of **Uzziah** (792–740 B.C.), **Jotham** (752–736 B.C.), **Ahaz** (736–720 B.C.), and **Hezekiah** (729–699 B.C.). Because God never changes, this revelation is still relevant for His people today.

1:2 God's relationship with His people is personal; He likens Judah to ungrateful **children** (63:8; Ex. 4:22; Hos. 11:1). The Hebrew term translated **rebelled** means "to refuse to submit to someone's authority and rule" (63:10; 66:24).

1:3 Even an **ox** and a **donkey** recognize the **owner** who feeds them, so they do not rebel against him. But Israel, God's own children whom He "nourished and brought up" (v. 2), had rebelled against Him.

1:4 sinful nation: Despite God's divine parenting, the people had turned to sin. **The Holy One of Israel** is Isaiah's favorite title for God. The Lord is holy because He is profoundly different from all of humanity, is the Creator exalted in heaven (6:1–3) and without sin (6:4–7). He alone is the righteous Judge (v. 20) and Protector of the faithful (10:20; 43:3).

1:5 Isaiah answers his own indignant question, **Why should you be stricken again?** The people would only **revolt more and more.** More preaching would only make their hearts hard (6:9, 10). In 53:4–6 Isaiah reveals God's gracious response to their hard hearts: the Lord will strike His Servant instead of sinners (53:4–6). Such love can win over even the toughest rebel (Rom. 5:8).

1:6 From **foot** to **head** means everyone and everything. Judah's wounds were not **closed, bound up** (bandaged), or **soothed,** because the people had refused to repent.

1:7, 8 Daughter of Zion is a beautiful personification of Jerusalem (37:22; 60:14). **Booth** and **hut** refer to lean-to shelters used by farmers and watchmen during the harvest.

1:9 The title **LORD of hosts** is a favorite of Isaiah, for it speaks of God's holiness and sovereignty. Judah's survival was not because of an enemy's weakness but to God's power. Though God punished His sinful people, He always preserved a **remnant** (6:13; 10:20; 11:16) because He was faithful His promise to Abraham. The word *remnant* means "survivor."

1:10–15 God desired **sacrifices,** but not from people who disobeyed Him and mistreated others, even if the sacrifice presented was the best. "To obey is better than sacrifice," said Samuel (1 Sam. 15:22, 23). God judges not only our acts, but the attitude of our hearts (1 Cor. 4:5). Verses 13–15 contain an itemized condemnation of the people's sacred seasons: **New Moons** (Num. 28:11–15), **Sabbaths** (Ex. 31:14–17), and **appointed feasts** (Ex. 23:14–17). These feasts are condemned as **futile** because the people did not celebrate them out of love for God.

1:16–18 Reason together means "to come to a legal decision." The people were to come to an agreement with God about the enormous gravity of their sin. God was prepared to pardon their sins if they would repent and turn to Him. **Says the LORD:** The verb form

suggests a repeated offering of grace. **Scarlet** recalls the picture of "hands … full of blood" (v. 15). God's grace and power can make such bloodstains as **white as snow** (Rom. 3:21–26).

1:19, 20 There was another side to God's offer. If the sinful people did not repent, instead of the promise that they **shall eat the good of the land** (3:10) stood the threat that they **shall be devoured by the sword.** The promise and threat were certain because **the LORD** had spoken them. Here the verb **has spoken** indicates finality (contrast the verb *says* in v. 18). While God had graciously extended His offer of mercy over a significant period of time, this was the only offer God made. They could not "cut another deal" with Him (40:5; 55:11).

1:21–24 The debased **silver** and **wine** refer to Jerusalem's unjust rulers.

1:25 God's **hand** had delivered Israel from Egypt. Now that same hand was against the people in judgment.

1:26 God's goal for Jerusalem was to become a **city of righteousness,** a city where the Lord would be faithfully worshiped.

1:27, 28 The Hebrew word for **redeemed** means "ransomed" or "freed someone from another's ownership through the payment of a price." Zion's **penitents,** those who turned their back on idolatry and injustice, would find freedom from sin and judgment.

1:29 Idolaters **shall be ashamed** because the **terebinth,** a sacred tree, and the **gardens,** sacred groves for fertility rites or the worship of spirits, would fail to save them in the time of judgment (65:3).

1:30, 31 Terebinth represents both the sacred trees (v. 29) and the **strong,** dominating rulers of Israel. **The work of it** is perhaps a reference to the injustice of Israel's tyrants (v. 23), which was the opposite of the Lord's righteous work (5:12). **no one shall quench:** God will rid His creation of the proud through His gracious, purifying judgment.

2:1, 2 Some have interpreted the phrase **in the latter days** as pointing to the new epoch initiated by the saving work of Christ and the coming of the Holy Spirit at Pentecost (see Acts 2:17). Just as **the LORD's house** (the temple) was a type of the heavenly sanctuary (Heb. 9:24), so presumably **the mountain** (Mount Zion) was a copy of a heavenly reality (Heb. 9:23, 24; 12:22–24).

2:3 By quoting the people's words, **let us go up to the mountain of the LORD,** Isaiah vividly depicts their regenerated hearts, since the unregenerate do not seek God (see Rom. 3:11).

2:4 Plowshares probably means "hoes." One day there will be an end to all weapons, and to all warfare because of the reign of the Prince of Peace (9:6), the Savior King whose name is Jesus.

2:5 Isaiah includes himself with the godly remnant: **let us walk.** Even though they could not see the glorious future of Zion, they continued to place their faith in God and obey His law. **Light** is a metaphor for God's law.

2:6–7 The exhortation to **the house of Jacob** was necessary (v. 5), for God had handed it over to destruction. **You have forsaken** was a present, but not a permanent, condition for the Israelites. To renounce **eastern ways** and **soothsayers,** the customs of Mesopotamia, was a hallmark of faith in the God of Israel.

2:8 The work of their own hands refers to man-made idols in particular.

2:9 Each man humbles himself before things that are themselves debased—idols. Isaiah implored Him **not** to **forgive** those who had turned to idols.

2:10 Dust symbolizes the abject humility of the defeated (47:1; Gen. 3:14; Ps. 44:25). The wicked among the Israelites would grovel in the dust before the righteous Lord.

2:11 Lofty looks are the outer manifestation of proud hearts. The refrain **the LORD alone shall be exalted** highlights the theme of this prophecy. **In that day** the Savior will be exalted above all other proud contenders.

2:12 Lifted up is translated "exalted" in v. 2. Any rival to God's exaltation will be dwarfed. **The day of the LORD** has two sides: (1) the night of God's judgment and (2) the daylight of His salvation after judgment. Isaiah used the term to describe either or both aspects.

2:13–17 The cedars of Lebanon and **the high mountains**—the exalted things of creation—

as well as the **high tower** and the **fortified wall**—the exalted things made by humanity—will be humbled so that the arrogant can see the greatness of God. **The ships of Tarshish** prized objects which the arrogant made and considered to be more important than God.

2:18 The term **idols** means "worthless things."

2:19 holes ... caves: People will scurry like frightened animals with no place to hide (Matt. 24:16). **Terror** refers to the dread of the wicked at the sight of God (Ps. 14:5).

2:20–22 Sever yourselves: Since God will reject proud idolaters, it follows that the faithful should also reject them. How ludicrous to trust in transitory, impermanent man, whose **breath is in his nostrils,** instead of in the One who gives everyone breath.

3:1 God **takes away** Judah's leaders through the sword and exile.

3:2, 3 Judah's administration was organized around warriors—**mighty man, man of war, captain of fifty;** sages—**judge, elder, honorable man, counselor;** religious mediums—**prophet, diviner, enchanter;** and craftsmen—**artisan.**

3:4 Because of the Lord's judgment on Judah, the shrewd, ungodly leaders would be replaced by **children** and **babes,** meaning inexperienced and incompetent leaders.

3:5 For **every one** to be oppressed **by another** describes a state of anarchy. In such an upside-down world, **child** insults the **elder, the base** ignores **the honorable.** In His judgment, the Lord has given over the wicked to their own evil ways.

3:6, 7 During this period of deprivation, a man would qualify for leadership just by having **clothing.**

3:8, 9 The people's **tongue** and **look** betray their arrogance against God. Judeans were parading their defiance against God just like the Sodomites.

3:10, 11 eat the fruit: Compare this idea with 1:19.

3:12 The lamenting words **My people** (see v. 15) are reminiscent of David's pain over his erring son Absalom (2 Sam. 18:33).

3:13 to plead: This is a judicial term meaning to plead a case (Mic. 6:1).

3:14 The vineyard represents the nation (5:1–7), used here as a term parallel to **the poor.** The leaders had taken advantage of the weak in order to plunder them (v. 15).

3:15 Lord GOD of hosts: See the similar usage in 1:9.

3:16 The plural **daughters of Zion** suggests the women of the city as well as a personification of Jerusalem (see 1:8). The prophet shows his scorn for pretense and flagrant display.

3:17 The term **secret parts** and its parallel **head** may mean "forehead."

3:18–26 Rope ... baldness ... sackcloth refer to the conditions of the people who are going into exile. **Your men** refers to the men of Jerusalem. The **gates** of Zion **mourn** because its inhabitants have gone into exile for their sins.

4:1 in that day: This phrase connects this verse with the preceding unit (3:16–26). The women of Jerusalem would have to beg a **man** to father their children and **take away** their **reproach**—the fact that they have no children.

4:2 In that day speaks of the future revelation of the glory of the Lord on the earth (2:2–4). **The Branch of the LORD.** Christ, will be glorifed, so the earth will be released from its curse, producing all that God intended it to produce in the beginning (Ps. 65).

4:3 recorded: The record of births in Jerusalem (Ps. 87:5, 6) may be related to the "heavenly book" (Ex. 32:32; Ps. 69:28; Dan. 7:10; Rev 20:12).

4:4 The spirit of judgment ... burning means "a fiery judgment." Through the processes of a purging fire, which outwardly consumes the faithless and inwardly purifies the faithful, God will produce a holy city.

4:5 Cloud and smoke: God's protective **covering** over the restored and sanctified Mount Zion.

4:6 Over the cloud and smoke on each dwelling will be the **tabernacle,** manifesting God's protection of His people (Ps. 91:1; Rev. 21:3).

5:1–3 Judah is like a vineyard that has every advantage. Its failure to produce justifies God's judgment (1:2, 3). **Well-beloved ... my Beloved:** Isaiah speaks of the Lord in endearing terms. The term **wild grapes** means "stinking

things" (v. 4). **My vineyard:** The pronoun indicates God's love and pride over His possession—the nation of Israel.

5:4 What more could have been done: When it comes to the failed relationship between God and His people, the blame falls solely on the people. The Lord did everything He could—from instructing His people to giving them the Promised Land.

5:5 Please let Me tell you may be translated more forcefully as "Now I *will* tell you." God was warning His people.

5:6 Briers and thorns symbolize the anarchy that will overtake the land during the Exile. **clouds:** God would command the clouds to with the rain because the people were rebellious.

5:7 justice ... oppression: These words have similar sounds in Hebrew. Choosing similar sounding words is a technique of Hebrew poetry.

5:8 Till ... land: The greedy land barons aimed to control all of the choice land of Israel. God gave the fields, which "shall not be sold permanently, for the land is Mine" (Lev. 25:23) as a patrimony to all His people (Num. 27:7–11). Deprived of these ancestral lands, Israel's citizens had become day laborers or slaves on what had formerly been their family inheritance.

5:9, 10 While invaders could destroy the houses, only God could bring the drought. Yet both were judgments from His hand. **One bath** is about six gallons. **A homer** is about six bushels. **One ephah** is one-tenth of a homer. The produce of the land would be meager in the time of divine judgment.

5:11 This verse is a strong condemnation of the abuse of **intoxicating drink** (beer) and **wine** (v. 22).

5:12 The harp and the strings: Music was played in ancient Israel both in the worship of the Lord and in times of feasting. Here **their feasts** means "their drinking parties." **do not regard ... consider:** The people were oblivious to the reality of the **work of the LORD** in their midst.

5:13 have gone into captivity: Although the verb is in the past tense, here it refers to future captivity. **Knowledge** refers to a personal involvement with someone or something.

thirst: The judgment matches the crime of indulging in alcoholic beverages.

5:14 Sheol is the word for "grave," which is compared to a gaping jaw that devours the elite rich and the common masses alike.

5:15, 16 the eyes of the lofty: Proud people get little respect from God (Ps. 147:6).

5:17 What were formerly mansions surrounded with lush vineyards would become **waste places,** where **lambs** and **fat ones,** those prepared for sacrifice, feed.

5:18, 19 Those who mocked Isaiah's proclamation of the day of the Lord were not simply "falling" into sin; rather, they labored to **draw iniquity** along, as on **a cart.**

5:20 call evil good: Those who pervert God's evaluation of what is good by calling evil good are heading down a path to judgment.

5:21 At the root of the moral, social, and theological corruption denounced in this prophecy is being **wise** in one's **own eyes**—an insensitive, arrogant egotism.

5:22 mighty at drinking wine: The **intoxicating drink** was probably beer.

5:23 bribe: The perversion of **justice** by bribery is a serious evil that undermines society.

5:24 As the vineyard yielding only sour grapes is finally judged, so the wicked will finally be cut off without hope.

5:25 The hills that seem permanent **trembled,** even as the sea "fled" before the anger of the Lord. The Lord's **anger is not turned away** even after the horrible judgments of vv. 24, 25. **His hand** is stretched out to punish His people.

5:26 The Assyrian army literally "trampled down" (v. 5) the pleasant land of Israel. **whistle:** The Lord would control this army of judgment, for He would give them their signal to invade (see 7:18).

5:27–29 The preparations of the Assyrian army were complete; the soldiers were thoroughly ready for war (see 40:30, 31).

5:30 The clouds symbolize judgment.

6:1 King Uzziah died in 740 B.C. This good king would eventually be replaced by wicked Ahaz (7:1). The **throne** where **the Lord** is seated, **high** and exalted. He is high above all other kings, but at the same time

He is concerned about the welfare of His people.

6:2 The **seraphim** live in the presence of God.

6:3 Holy, holy, holy: To say the word *holy* twice in Hebrew is to describe someone as "most holy." To say the word *holy* three times intensifies the idea to the highest level. To be *holy* means to be different, distant, or transcendent. The Lord is perfect but in His mercy He still reaches down to take care of us. **The whole earth is full of His glory:** We know that the glory of God transcends the universe.

6:4 The doorposts of the temple shook in response to the voice which cried out exalting the Holy Lord.

6:5 Confronted with this vision of the Lord, Isaiah was **undone. I am a man of unclean lips:** Isaiah knew that he was a sinner. **a people:** Isaiah's plight is the plight of every person. No one, in his or her present state, is capable of standing before the Holy One (Ps. 24:3). **the King, the LORD of hosts:** After contemplating the death of Uzziah (v. 1), Isaiah had seen the King who will never die.

6:6 The **live coal ... from the altar** symbolizes both the purification of the fire of the Spirit that enabled the prophet to speak. From that point on, his words would be light to his hearers and power to those who would listen. A coal from the altar was used to reminds us that all sin is forgiven because of a sacrifice. God sovereignly and graciously cleansed Isaiah's sin.

6:7 taken away: Sin is removed as far as the east is from the west. The Hebrew word translated **purged** means "covered" and is the same word that is translated *atonement.*

6:8 Here the Lord uses the pronoun **Us** to mean the Triune God. **Send me:.** Isaiah's willingness proceeded from a grateful heart; he wanted to serve the God who had forgiven him (v. 7).

6:9, 10 The people were cursed with spiritual deadness. Isaiah's preaching was destined to **make ... their ears heavy.** Paul quotes this proclaimation to the Jew in Acts 28:26-27 as he turns to minister to the Gentiles.

6:11, 12 Understandably, Isaiah's third question to the Lord was **how long** would the people continue to be unresponsive to his words of truth from God. The answer was grim. **waste … desolate:** These words describe the coming judgment of God on Judah that would lead to the nation's captivity under the Babylonians.

6:13 A tenth is one of Isaiah's expressions for the "remnant"; it is only a small percentage of the Israelites. From Israel's blasted **stump,** God would produce a **holy seed** (11:1).

7:1 The Book of Isaiah was written over the period of the prophet's lifetime; but chapters 7–12 were set in the context of the Syro-Ephraimite wars.

7:2 The phrase **house of David** is the king of Judah, Ahaz. The word **Ephraim** represents the northern kingdom, Israel. The **heart** of the nation was **moved** because Syria had defeated Ahaz earlier (2 Chr. 28:5).

7:3 Shear-Jashub means "A Remnant Will Return." The name of Isaiah's son spoke of a coming Exile and then the salvation of the remaining faithful. Ahaz was probably standing at the **aqueduct** at the time of this encounter.

7:4 God contemptuously dismissed the arrogant kings of Israel and Syria. What Ahaz greatly feared, God considered no more than **stubs of smoking firebrands** drawn from a bonfire. The **son of Remaliah** is Pekah, king of Israel (see v. 1).

7:5, 6 The plotting of Syria and Ephraim was no secret to God, who made it known to His servant Isaiah. **Tabel** means "Good for Nothing." Syria and Israel wanted to place an incompetent puppet king over Judah.

7:7, 8 It shall not stand: The plans of humankind are futile when they oppose the will of God. **Within sixty-five years** suggests that God will fulfill His promises on time.

7:9 You is plural. The prophet was speaking to the royal family and the nation. **Believe** and **established** are a play on the same Hebrew word from which we get our word *amen.* Believing entails having knowledge of God's Word, accepting that it is true, and placing our trust in the Lord to help us keep it.

7:10 While Isaiah's prophecy was principally addressed to King **Ahaz,** it was directed to others in v. 13.

7:11 The **sign** pertains to the prediction in vv. 7–9, the demise of the power of Samaria. **In the depth or in the height** indicates that Ahaz could ask for any sign he wished.

7:12 not ask … test: In the mouth of the wicked Ahaz, these arrogant words rang hollow.

7:13 Will you **weary my God?** This stuborn and arrogant king dared to trust in God even when his enemies surrounded him (see v. 12).

7:14 . The **sign** would be chosen by God Himself. The word **Lord** speaks of the sovereignty of God, of His great control over all His creation. The pronoun **Himself** adds an absolute certainty to the impending sign. The Hebrew word rendered **virgin** means "a young woman of marriageable age." But the Septuagint translates the Hebrew word with a Greek word that specifically means *virgin.*

7:15 Curds and honey represent the Judean's simple diet after the Assyrian invasion. Thus the Child, similar to Isaiah's son Shear-Jashub (see v. 3), would be identified with the remnant.

7:16, 17 For before: Similar prophecies were spoken of the Child's birth and Isaiah's other son Maher-Shalal-Hash-Baz (8:3): Israel and Syria would be destroyed before this child and Isaiah's son would reach maturity (see 8:4 where Syria is referred to as Damascus and Israel as Samaria).

7:18, 19 The invading hordes are likened to swarming insects—**the fly** and the **bee**—blanketing Judah, a condition fulfilled in the Assyrian invasions.

7:20 shave … the hair: This was a symbol of humiliation. **Hired** refers to Ahaz's foolish idea of paying Assyria to save him from the alliance of Syria and Israel.

7:21, 22 A young cow and two sheep out of what used to be large herd indicates impoverishment in the time of trouble.

7:23–25 vines … thorns: The productivity of the land would be greatly reduced in the period of God's judgment. The repetition of **briers and thorns** in vv. 23–25 is emphatic; in other words, the land would no longer be cultivated.

8:1 large scroll: This message from the Lord was intended to be read and pondered by many people.

8:2 Just as the wicked Ahaz was forced to be a party to the sign about the birth of Immanuel (see 7:10–17), **Uriah,** an apostate priest and **Zechariah,** presumably a false prophet (not the prophet who wrote the Book of Zechariah), were witness to this prophecy.

8:3 Isaiah's wife was a **prophetess** in her own right.

8:4 spoil of Samaria ... king of Assyria: This is a specific prediction of the fall of Samaria to the Assyrians in 722 B.C. This prophecy has to have been written shortly before that time, as the fulfillment would come before the new child would be able to speak.

8:5 The LORD also spoke to me again: This phrase introduces a new prophetic section and reminds the reader of the source of the prophetic images in the Book of Isaiah.

8:6 The gentle waters of **Shiloah** picture the sustaining presence of the Lord. Shiloah may have been a little stream that flowed through an aqueduct to the Pool of Siloam. **rejoice:** The Judeans looked for the salvation that a mere king could offer instead of appealing to the King of kings for protection.

8:7, 8 The River refers to the Euphrates. **neck:** Assyria would devastate Judah, but not completely annihilate it (ch. 37). **wings:** In the middle of v. 8 the image of Assyria changes to the image of a bird of prey. Isaiah bestows the name of the promised Child, **Immanuel** (7:14), on Judah, because it would be preserved only because God was with that nation (see v. 10).

8:9 Far countries refers to the many nations that made up Assyria's international army (5:26; 7:18). **Gird yourselves ... be broken:** The nations would do the will of God, but in turn would be destroyed.

8:10 It will not stand: The Lord would defeat the purposes of Judah's enemies; all their councils would come to nothing. The Child whose name would mean **God is with us** (v. 8; 7:14), was a sign not only of the destruction of Syria and Israel (7:17), but of all of God's enemies, including Assyria.

8:11 Strong hand signifies a powerful sense of the Lord's inspiration (Ezek. 1:3).

8:12 Do not say: The commands in vv. 12, 13, 15, 19 are in the plural. Perhaps Isaiah's adversaries were labeling his rejection of an alliance with Assyria a **conspiracy.**

8:13 Hallow means to treat as holy. **Your fear** indicates a sense of reverence, awe, and wonder. **Your dread** indicates fright and terror.

8:14 God is a **sanctuary** for believers, but a **stone of stumbling** for unbelievers. **Both the houses** designates both Israel and Judah.

8:15 stumble ... broken: The wicked will not prevail for long (v. 10).

8:16 Testimony refers to a legal transaction. **Law** refers to God's instruction revealed through Isaiah. Isaiah's disciples put his prophecies in the form of a legal transaction.

8:17 wait ... hope: These words indicate a confident expectation that God would meet the needs of His people and deliver them from disaster (40:31; Ps. 40:1).

8:18 children: Isaiah's two sons, whose names speak of the impending judgment of God, were **signs and wonders in Israel.** (20:3). **Mount Zion:** The place of the holy temple was a mirror of God's dwelling in the highest heaven.

8:19, 20 In the fertility religions of Canaan **mediums and wizards** would deliver divine revelations. **who whisper and mutter:** But the best one could get from these perverted "prophets" was garbled muttering. **Seek the dead** indicates necromancy, the practice of conjuring up the spirits of the dead in order to influence events (29:4; 65:4).

8:21 They refers to the wicked who refuse to revere God (v. 13). **It** refers perhaps to the implied **darkness** of v. 20. **curse:** For similar usage, see Ex. 22:28; Lev. 24:15, 16.

8:22 The prophets commonly used the imagery of **darkness** to indicate judgment (5:30). The synonyms for *darkness* in this verse describe not only moral and spiritual blight, but also the invasion of Assyria that took away liberty and brought foreign oppression.

9:1 Nevertheless the gloom: This line completes the thought of 8:22 and promises a dramatic change to come. The ancient tribal allotments of **Zebulun** and **Napthali** which included **Galilee,** were the first to feel the brunt of the Assyrian invasions (2 Kin. 15:29). The three phrases at the end of the verse—**the way of the sea, beyond the Jordan, Galilee of the Gentiles** or "nations"—indicate administrative districts of the Assyrian conqueror Tiglath Pileser III.

9:2 Have seen: The future event is described by the prophet, under the impulse of the Spirit, as having already occurred. **Light** stands for the incarnate Jesus. **Shadow of death** means "deep darkness" (compare 60:2; Ps. 23:4). Here this Hebrew word complements the more commonly used word for **darkness.**

9:3 joy of harvest ... divide the spoil: The agricultural society knows no greater joy than that of harvest. A soldier knows no greater joy than that of a finished battle when his side has won, he is still alive, and there is now booty to divide.

9:4 yoke ... staff ... rod: These three images of oppression emphasize the suffering of the people during the period of foreign domination.

9:5 warrior's sandal: Assyrian armies were marked by the noise of the marching of many feet. **Garments rolled in blood** from past battles was a deliberate scare tactic to frighten enemies in an impending battle. All of these emblems of warfare were to be burned in the coming day of the reign of the divine Child (v. 6).

9:6 Born speaks of the Child's humanity and **given** of His deity. **Wonderful, Counselor** is one name, meaning "wonderful divine Counselor" (11:1–5). **Mighty God** indicates that the Lord is a powerful Warrior (10:21). **Everlasting Father** describes a King and Father who provides for and protects His people forever (40:9–11; Matt. 11:27–30). Thus the word Father is used here of the Savior's role as an ideal king. **Prince of Peace** is the climactic title. The Child is the true Prince—the One who has the right to reign and who will usher in peace. The four double names combine aspects of Jesus' deity and His humanity. Together, these four double names assert the dual nature of the Savior: He is God become man.

9:7 Of the increase may be translated "to Him will increase." **Government and peace** may be rephrased as "peaceful reign." The risen Lord Jesus brings His rule of peace to the believer's heart in the present age. Moreover, He will establish the kingdom of God which will be His reign of peace. The fact that this coming Child will occupy **the throne of David** forever fulfills God's promise to David (2 Sam. 7:8–16; Ps. 89:19–37; Luke 1:32, 33).

9:8–10 Bricks refers to the mud brick walls common in ancient Israel. The people were planning to make their buildings more grandiose, not taking into account the fact that the Lord was about to destroy the buildings because of His judgment on their sins.

9:11 The adversaries refers to the Assyrians who were used by **the LORD** to punish the northern kingdom.

9:12 The Syrians were to the east of Israel and the **Philistines** to the west.

9:13 Turn indicates repentance and a desire for restoration.

9:14, 15 Head and tail is a figure of speech for all leaders.

9:16 cause them to err: For a similar usage, see 3:12.

9:17 Young men ... widows denotes every person. Everyone had turned from the faithful worship of God. All of Israel had been contaminated with evil, hypocrisy, and foolishness.

9:18–20 The **fire** of **wickedness** is matched by the **fire** of **the wrath of the LORD. Wickedness** refers both to the sin itself and to its destructive consequences. **No man shall spare his brother** refers to anarchy (3:4, 5). **right hand ... left hand:** These figures of speech indicate an insatiable hunger and the consequent ruin that would occur in the day of judgment.

9:21 Manasseh fought **Ephraim** (see Judg. 12:4); then together they fought **Judah** (but see 11:13).

10:1 Woe is a chilling word when spoken by God (5:8–23; 10:5; 18:1); here the Lord condemns the leaders who write laws that perpetuate evil in the community.

10:2 The **needy** are regularly seen in Scripture as those to whom the righteous should show true piety. When godly people reach out to help those who cannot help themselves, they display pure, biblical religion (James 1:27). Conversely, the mark of the ungodly can be seen in their oppressive actions against people who cannot help themselves.

10:3 From afar refers to Assyria. **To whom:** The wicked could not turn to God, for they had refused to do so before and had ignored God's warnings (see 8:6).

10:4 Prisoners refers to the Israelites being led away into exile.

10:5 And ... indignation may also be translated "even the staff in My indignant hand." **rod of My anger:** Though God sovereignly uses sinners as instruments of His will (7:17; 13:5), they will be held accountable for their own wickedness.

10:6 The **ungodly nation** is Judah (vv. 11, 12).

10:7, 8 in his heart: The purpose of the arrogant Assyrians was to continue their path of uninterrupted conquest. But God had different plans for them (see v. 12).

10:9 Calno ... Damascus: This is a list of cities that had already fallen to the Assyrians.

10:10, 11 idols ... images: The Assyrians had conquered the nations who had false gods; surely, they believed, they would also have an easy time against **Jerusalem and her idols.**

10:12 The **fruit** is the king's speech cited in vv. 13, 14. **arrogant heart ... haughty looks:** For a similar idea, see 2:11; 3:9; 9:9.

10:13 By the strength of my hand: The wicked are quick to take credit for their successes. The righteous correctly give praise to God for their accomplishments.

10:14, 15 An implement in the hand of its user has no reason for boasting; Assyria was just a tool in the hand of God. It had no reason to **boast.**

10:16 leanness ... burning: These words describe the coming judgment of the Assyrians, who had become **fat** because of their acts of conquest.

10:17, 18 The Light of Israel is a wonderful title for God (see 9:2; 58:8; 60:1, 19, 20). The Lord Jesus is described as a "Light" of Israel as well (see John 1:1–13). **His thorns ... his forest** refers to all persons and possessions in the Assyrian Empire.

10:19, 20 The remnant is the portion of Abraham's offspring that God preserved. The Hebrew word used here for *remnant* is different from the words used in 1:9; 6:13.

10:21, 22 as the sand ... A remnant: Most of the people of the northern kingdom were carried off into captivity. But some Israelites made their way to Judah and became part of the southern kingdom. These people and their descendants would act as a remnant by preserving the names of the northern tribes among the people of God.

10:23, 24 O My people: The language here expresses the loving care of the Lord for His people. They need not fear the armies of the Assyrians.

10:25 a very little while: From the viewpoint of eternity, the period of trial is exceedingly brief.

10:26 On the sea refers to God's great triumph over Pharaoh at the Exodus (Ex. 14; 15).

10:27 The **anointing oil** was used to initiate both priest and king of God choosing.

10:28, 29 The cities as listed in these verses are closer and closer to the capital at Jerusalem. Each town conquered was another step toward the impending defeat of the holy city.

10:30, 31 Lift up your voice: The language turns to that of panic. The actions are those of a frightened people facing defeat and disaster.

10:32 daughter of Zion: The army was near **Jerusalem** itself. The pronoun **he** refers to Assyria, the enemy.

10:33, 34 The **bough** is the king of Assyria and the **thickets** are his army. The point is that God will bring judgment on the instruments He used to judge Israel.

11:1 A Rod from the stem of Jesse will inaugurated a kingdom of righteousness and peace and will establish an incomparably greater kingdom. The words Rod and **Branch** are messianic terms.

11:2 Spirit: Messiah would be empowered by the Holy Spirit, the Agent for establishing God's kingdom. **wisdom and understanding:** The seven distinct ministries of the Holy Spirit are listed here. The Messiah will embody all this; He will be the ideal King (33:6).

11:3 Delight refers to the sense of smell. There may be an allusion to the incense burned at a coronation ceremony. **the fear of the LORD** may refer to the standard of moral conduct known through special revelation and accepted by the faithful.

11:4, 5 In this context, **judge** means to act on their behalf. As the judge of His people, God is not dependant on seeing and hearing the external. **rod of His mouth:** The Messiah will conquer by His words (49:2; Heb. 4:12; Rev. 19:15).

11:6–8 a little child shall lead them: In the coming kingdom, a youngster will be able to lead formerly wild animals. This is a way of emphasizing the complete peace in the coming kingdom.

11:9 In ancient times, **the knowledge of the LORD** was limited and spotty; there is coming a glorious age in which there will be no limit to access to divine truth. **As the waters cover the sea** means "thoroughly." God will make Himself known throughout the earth.

11:10 in that day: This verse forms a single prophetic vision. The exalted **Root of Jesse** will attract the **Gentiles** to **His resting place** (2:3). This is a prophecy of the coming of people of all nations to the knowledge of God. Thus in the Old Testament, the Lord expresses His concern for the salvation of other nations (see Gen. 12:1–3). **Banner** is a rallying symbol. Jesus the Messiah is the *banner* for the gathering of peoples from all over the earth.

11:11 The **second time** may refer to the remnant coming back to the land in 538 B.C., in contrast to the first Exodus from Egypt.

11:12 the four corners of the earth: The Messiah will gather disciples from all over the world.

11:13 Ephraim … Judah: Not only will God destroy the enemies of the Israelites and Judeans, but He will also remove their ancient enmities (9:20, 21).

11:14 upon the shoulder: The image is that of a bird of prey attacking another bird. **The Philistines, Edom, Moab,** and **Ammon,** Israel's traditional enemies, may represent the adversaries of the Messiah's kingdom.

11:15 Mighty wind is an allusion to Ex. 14:21–27. **The River** refers to the Euphrates. **dry-shod:** As God had provided a dry passage across the Red Sea in the first Exodus, so in the second Exodus He would remove any physical barrier that would hinder the return of His people.

11:16 A highway symbolizes the certainty of the return, for no obstacles would hinder the Lord's returning exiles (35:8–10; 40:3, 4; 57:14; 62:10).

12:1 The first **you** is singular, representing the remnant as an individual. **angry:** The anger of God had caused the people to be dispersed among the nations (5:25; 9:12); His grace would lead to their regathering.

12:2 God is my salvation: This psalm of redemption is based on the first psalm of redemption in Exodus (Ex. 15:2; Ps. 118:14). **YAH, the LORD,** by its repetition, emphasizes that Israel's covenant-keeping God—and not the nations—brings salvation (26:4). **My strength and song** may be rephrased as "my strong song" or "my song of strength" (Ex. 15:2).

12:3 You in vv. 3–5 is plural. The Hebrew poets often associate the concept of **water** with salvation (Ex. 17:1–7). In an arid land, the provision of **wells** and springs was regarded as a divine gift (55:1).

12:4 As in the Psalms, this hymn uses several terms for the praise of God. **Praise** means "to give public acknowledgment" or "to declare aloud in public." **Call upon His name** may be rephrased as "proclaim in His name." **Declare** means "to make known." **Make mention** means "to cause to remember." Each of these verbs designates public, vocal acknowledgment of the wonders and works of God.

12:5 Sing to the LORD: The principal audience of sacred songs is God Himself (Ps. 33:1). **all the earth:** This emphasis fits the same line of thought found in Ps. 19:1.

12:6 Cry out and shout may be rephrased as "shout aloud in great joy." **Inhabitant of Zion** refers to the people who returned from captivity in Babylon.

13:1, 2 The word **burden** comes from the root meaning "to lift up" or "to bear." It is as though the prophet were heavily laden with a message from God that he must deliver because of its sheer weight (Nah. 1:1; Hab. 1:1). **Babylon** was the crown jewel of the Assyrian empire. This oracle may refer to its destruction around 689 B.C. when Sennacherib quelled a rebellion there. Yet the Lord's overthrow of **Babylon,** "the glory of kingdoms" (v. 19), symbolizes His triumph over the world (v. 11).

13:3, 4 Sanctified ones refers to the victorious armies of the earth **who rejoice,** wittingly or unwittingly, in the Lord's **exaltation** (45:1–7; Joel 2:11). **Many people** represent all nations, who will be instruments in God's hands for judging sinful nations, though they themselves are sinners.

13:5 Far country ... end of heaven refers to the whole earth (11:11, 12). **His weapons of indignation:** The nations are the tools God will use to vent His wrath against Babylon.

13:6 The day of the Lord is **at hand**—able to happen at any time—not because people have almost reached it as a destination, but because it may burst in upon people without further warning.

13:7, 8 limp ... melt ... afraid: These images describe the depth of the people's fear. **a woman in childbirth:** This is a familiar image of stress in the poetry of the Bible.

13:9–11 iniquity ... arrogance ... proud ... haughtiness ... terrible: The common element is pride, which brings the nations down (2:6–22).

13:12 mortal: The Hebrew word speaks of the inherent weakness of humanity (Ps. 8:4).

13:13, 14 heavens ... earth: The shaking of the cosmos, including the sun, moon, and stars—which were worshiped by the pagans—symbolizes the overthrow of all that unbelieving humans exalt as rivals to God (2:12–18).

13:15, 16 Everyone ... children ... houses ... wives: In the ancient Middle East, the brutality of war extended to everyone, regardless of age, gender, or station.

13:17, 18 The Medes, who lived in what is today northwest Iran, were fierce enemies of the Israelites. Significant for dating this prophecy is the fact that Persia, which conquered the Medes in 550 B.C. and in conjunction with the Medes conquered Babylon in 539 B.C., is not mentioned.

13:19 In 4:2, the same Hebrew word translated **glory** here is translated "beautiful" to describe the Branch of the Lord.

13:20 It will never be inhabited: Places that once were fabled for their great structures will become so desolate that even desert peoples would not **pitch tents there.**

13:21, 22 The language of these verses is that of the ancient Middle Eastern curse. The animals named in these verses ominously represent that which is unclean, unholy, uncivilized, and unsettled.

14:1 Still may also be translated "again," in which case it refers to the second Exodus, the return of the remnant from Babylonian captivity (see 11:15, 16). **choose:** The Lord will make His choice in Israel. **Strangers** will join the returning Israelites as they did in the first Exodus (Ex. 12:38). But in this case, the strangers will be loyal adherents of the Lord.

14:2 people will take them: For the development of this idea, see Ezra 1:1–8. **captive:** For the development of this theme, see Eph. 4:8.

14:3 Hard bondage is an allusion to the first Exodus (ch. 12). **Rest** recalls the freedom from Egyptian servitude (Deut. 5:12–15).

14:4 Proverb refers to a highly figurative poem. **oppressor:** This is the same term used in 9:4 of an unnamed Assyrian tyrant.

14:5, 6 The staff and **the scepter** were symbols of authority and power in the ancient Middle East (9:4). **struck:** The Babylonian kings had paraded their tyranny, but now the Lord in judgment was breaking their instruments of oppression.

14:7, 8 At rest and quiet may be rephrased as "utterly quiet." This is the security that comes after the tyrant is dead. **cypress trees rejoice:** The trees are personified, describing the joy of the formerly oppressed people (35:1; 44:23; 55:12).

14:9–11 excited: The commotion in hell when the king of Babylon arrives contrasts sharply with the rest on earth when he is gone. The defeated subjects of the Babylonian tyrants are pictured as sitting on **thrones,** while the king is given a blanket of **worms.**

14:12 Fallen from heaven is a figure of speech meaning cast down from an exalted political position. The name for **Lucifer** in Hebrew literally means "Day Star," or the planet Venus. This is an apt summary of the failed goal of the king of Babylon (v. 4) who wanted to grasp universal and eternal domination.

14:13 above the stars of God: In this highly poetic language, Isaiah describes a king whose longing for glory was unlimited.

14:14 I will be like the Most High is the most outrageous of the arrogant desires of this Assyrian or Babylonian king. He wanted to surpass the Most High, a term for the Lord that is often used in connection with the nations of the world (see Ps. 87:5; 91:1, 9; 92:1).

14:15 The word **lowest depths** renders the same Hebrew word translated "farthest sides" (in v. 13). This is an example of comic justice for this king who wished to ascend to the heights of the gods and even the Most High Himself.

14:16 man ... tremble: Isaiah compares this king to the One who can truly shake the earth (see 13:13).

14:17, 18 The house of his prisoners refers to exile. Unlike Cyrus, who sent the exiles home, the king of Babylon kept them captive.

14:19 out of your grave: The ancients believed that a proper burial was very important. **abominable branch:** Contrast this with the Beautiful Branch, the Messiah (11:1). This is an "anti-Messiah" figure.

14:20 The brood ... shall never be named: This evil king's posterity will not be remembered.

14:21, 22 I will rise: The Lord Himself is behind the destruction of this arrogant king (v. 5).

14:23, 24 porcupine ... marshes: The former beautiful city of Babylon (13:19) would become a wild, inhospitable place.

14:25 My land ... My mountains: The Lord asserts His sovereignty. **yoke ... his burden:** In 9:4, these same terms are used of the Assyrian menace.

14:26–28 King Ahaz died in 720 B.C.

14:29 Rod is probably a metaphor for the Assyrian king (10:5). **its offspring will be ... serpent:** More trouble would come upon

Philistia; it would have nothing for which to **rejoice.**

14:30 Like Babylon (v. 22)—but unlike Israel—Philistia would have no future, because it would have no **remnant.**

14:31 The **gate** of a walled **city** was its weakest point. When the gate fell, the city could be taken. **No one will be alone** speaks of the close ranks of the Assyrian army.

14:32 founded Zion: The destruction of Philistia would leave no refuge for the Philistines. The only place they could go to be saved would be Jerusalem, the city built by God.

15:1 burden: For similar phrasing, see 13:1. **Ar** and **Kir** were cities of Moab (16:7, 11; Deut. 2:9; 2 Kin. 3:25).

15:2 High places were sites of pagan worship (16:12). **weep ... wail:** This refers to the mourning over the destruction of the cities of Moab. **Baldness** and having one's **beard cut off** were aspects of mourning rituals.

15:3 Sackcloth and **weeping** were part of Middle Eastern mourning rites (Gen. 23:2; 37:34; 2 Sam. 1:11, 12).

15:4 Heshbon, Elealeh, and **Jahaz** were cities in Moab. **armed soldiers:** The weeping would extend even to hardened fighting men.

15:5 My heart refers to Isaiah, who felt sympathy for Moab (16:9–11). **Zoar** was a southwestern border city of Moab on the south end of the Dead Sea.

15:6–8 The **waters** and **green grass** of the oasis could not survive the numerous refugees.

15:9 The term **Dimon** sounds like **blood** in Hebrew. **Lions:** Fleeing from one tragedy after another in their flight southward, the refugees turn to Judah in the west for asylum (16:1–5). As would be the case with Israel a **remnant** would survive in Moab.

16:1, 2 Wandering bird is a sad description of the hopeless condition of the **daughters of Moab,** the women of the nation.

16:3 Take counsel may also be translated "make plans." Moab would find salvation in the **shadow** of Zion (2:2–4).

16:4, 5 Moab's salvation ultimately lies in the coming One, Jesus the Messiah, whose **throne will be established** (9:1–7; 11:1–5; Amos 9:11, 12; Acts 15:16, 17).

16:6 Pride is a regular target of the Lord's judgment (2:5–22; 13:11).

16:7 Kir Hareseth is another name for Kir (15:1).

16:8 Vine is a figure of speech for Moab (compare Israel's description as a vine in 5:1–7). **Sea** may refer to the Dead Sea because it is the nearest large body of water to Moab.

16:9 Heshbon and Elealeh were among the principal settlements in ancient Moab (15:4).

16:10 Contrast the lack of **gladness** in this verse with the ecstatic joy of 9:3.

16:11 Isaiah the prophet expresses his determination to one day rejoice over Moab. This is a promise of its future restoration.

16:12 high place ... sanctuary: As long as the people worshiped false gods, they would be doomed to pain, judgment, and recurring trouble (15:2).

16:13, 14 A former prophecy against Moab (see 15:1) would be realized **within three years,** perhaps referring to the quelling of a rebellion against Sargon in 715 B.C. However, a **remnant** would remain (15:9). Moab had far more hope for salvation than did either Babylon or Philistia.

17:1, 2 cities ... flocks: Where people once lived, conditions would be suitable only for flocks (14:23).

17:3 Ephraim designates northern Israel. Since **Damascus,** the capital of Syria, was allied with Ephraim, the oracle of God's judgment was against both nations.

17:4 In that day: For a similar phrase, see 2:12.

17:5 harvests: The nation of Syria would be "harvested" of its people. The word **Rephaim** is the Hebrew word for "shades" or "ghosts." Thus the Valley of Rephaim is the Valley of Death.

17:6 A remnant would be **left** (10:20) even though it would be pitifully small.

17:7 The verb translated **look** means "to look with interest" or "to look with favor." **Holy One:** For a similar idea, see 6:3.

17:8 Altars refers to pagan worship. **work of his hands:** For similar wording, see 2:8; 31:7.

17:9 His strong cities will become as fragile as a little **branch.**

17:10 You refers to the northern kingdom. **forgotten** The people had forgotten the God who had saved them from slavery. The language recalls the first Exodus; the Lord is called **the God of your salvation** and **the Rock** (compare Ex. 15:2; Deut. 32:4).

17:11 Make your plant to grow may allude to the ancient practice of force-blooming potted plants and allowing them to die. Pagans believed that this reenactment of the life cycle would secure fertile fields. Just as the choice vines of the Lord's vineyard disappointed Him (5:1–7), so His people would find their harvest hopes shattered.

17:12 Seas and **mighty waters** speak of chaos and death (8:7; Ps. 46:3).

17:13 Chaff, which lacks life, value, and stability, was threshed and winnowed on windy **mountains** or hilltops. When God judges the unrelenting, roaring seas—the nations that plundered God's people—they will become mere tumbleweed **rolling** before **the whirlwind** of God's judgment.

17:14 Sennacherib's army would be destroyed between **eventide** and **morning** (37:36–38).

18:1 Ethiopia, called Cush in the Bible, was at the southern end of Isaiah's world.

18:2 Sea may refer to the Nile River, from which small **rivers** branched. **Tall and smooth** (v. 7) probably designates the peoples along the entire stretch of the Nile River. Perhaps the term *smooth* refers to the ancient Egyptian custom of shaving the whole body.

18:3 banner: For the use of this word to refer to salvation instead of judgment, see 11:10, 12.

18:4, 5 The figure of God working in **rest** speaks of His indescribable power and unlimited sovereignty. God is steady in His work. His judgment will be felt **like clear heat in sunshine.**

18:6 God's judgment will be so extensive that the carcasses of His victims will be devoured in the **summer** and **winter.**

18:7 the place of the name: Note how closely the Lord identifies with Mount Zion. This was the one place for the true worship of God.

19:1 the LORD rides on a swift cloud: For similar imagery, see Ps. 18:10; 68:4; Matt. 26:64.

19:2 The political anarchy of **Egyptians against Egyptians** has religious roots; their many gods failed them.

19:3 The spirit of Egypt: The principal key for understanding the world of ancient Egypt is the concept of *ma'at,* an Egyptian word for "order." When God brought Moses to confront Pharaoh (Ex. 5–14), it was *ma'at* that was under attack.

19:4 Cruel master may be an allusion to Pharaoh's tyranny against Israel (Ex. 6:9).

19:5–10 The disruption of the **waters** and all that is related to them marks God's attack on the nation. The **foundations** and those **who make wages** together may be a figure for the whole economic spectrum.

19:11 Zoan was the capital of Egypt at this time. **Son** here refers to a member of a guild.

19:12 Where are your wise men: The Lord taunts those who consider themselves wise and learned. True knowledge comes from the fear of the Lord.

19:13–17 Noph or Memphis was Egypt's ancient capital.

19:18 Five cities will **speak the language of Canaan and swear by**—take an oath of allegiance to—**the LORD of hosts.**

19:19 Altar and **pillar** may allude to the patriarchs Abraham and Jacob respectively (Gen. 12:8; 28:22).

19:20–22 The Egyptians will know probably alludes to Israel's experience in the Exodus (Ex. 6:7; 7:5).

19:23, 24 A highway signifies the removal of alienation and separation (11:16). Historically, **Egypt** and **Assyria** were enemies.

19:25 My people and **the work of My hands,** titles for Israel (10:24; 60:21), are applied here to the converted Gentiles, symbolized by Egypt and Assyria (56:7; 65:1).

20:1 Tartan was one of the three chief officers of the Assyrian Empire (2 Kin. 18:17).

20:2, 3 Isaiah replaced wearing **sackcloth,** the garb of spiritual mourning, with walking **naked and barefoot,** signs of being exiled into captivity.

20:4 Esarhaddon, **king of Assyria,** conquered Egypt and fulfilled this prophecy in 671 B.C.

20:5, 6 They and **this territory** probably refer to the nations bordering the eastern

shore of the Mediterranean Sea, who looked to Egypt to save them from Assyria. This would include Judah.

21:1 Wilderness means "desert." The phrase **Wilderness of the Sea** may be a sarcastic parody of Babylon, whose southern region on the Persian Gulf was called the "Land of the Sea."

21:2 Its sighing may refer to the sighing Babylon inflicted on others, or to its own sighing under Assyrian oppression.

21:3 Perhaps Isaiah was **distressed** by the report of Babylon's fall because it meant that Babylon could not save Judah from the Assyrians.

21:4 Although Isaiah **longed** for the fall of Babylon, he feared its consequences to Judah.

21:5 Having summoned Babylon's princes to **eat and drink,** Isaiah summoned them again to **anoint the shield** in preparation for battle (Dan. 5).

21:6 Lord here means "Master." The **watchman** is probably Isaiah.

21:7 A chariot of donkeys probably means "donkey riders" and **a chariot of camels** probably means "camel riders." The Persian army used donkeys and camels.

21:8, 9 In the daytime ... every night suggests "continually"—a display of Isaiah's faithfulness to His calling.

21:10 My threshing is a metaphor for the punishment coming on Judah.

21:11 Dumah was located at the intersection of the east-west trade route between Babylon and Edom and the north-south route between Palmyra and Edom. **Watchman** refers to the night patrol who kept watch on the city. The metaphor refers to the prophet Isaiah, who as a guard on the walls could see the dawn of salvation—in the east before others.

21:12 and also the night: Dumah's future was grim. Relief from Assyrian domination would be followed quickly by Babylonian domination.

21:13 Dedanites may be the refugees described in v. 15.

21:14 Tema was about two hundred miles southeast of Dumah (v. 11).

21:15 The **drawn** swords are those of the Assyrians and Babylonians.

21:16, 17 Kedar was a fertile region in the northwestern part of the Arabian desert in which Dedan and Tema were located (60:7). Its refugees would be driven deeper into the desert.

22:1 Valley of Vision sarcastically describes Jerusalem. Mount Zion is ironically personified in its valleys from which it could see nothing. Instead of partying on **housetops,** the ailing city should have been in its prayer closets.

22:2, 3 In the prophet's vision, the rulers are **not slain with the sword** while heroically defending the city, but are **captured** while fleeing to save their own skins (2 Kin. 25:4–6).

22:4, 5 daughter of my people: For a similar reference, see 1:8.

22:6, 7 Kir is **Elam.** The Elamites may have been part of the Assyrian army (5:26). **gate:** The same army that plundered Babylon (21:2) will arrive at Jerusalem's gates.

22:8 The House of the Forest is the nation's armory (39:2).

22:9–11 The defense of the city depended upon the availability of **water** within its **walls.** Hezekiah addressed this need by digging a tunnel beneath the city, connecting the **lower pool** in Jerusalem's southwestern valley with the **old pool,** the source of water in the eastern valley.

22:12–14 Called for weeping and for mourning … But instead, joy and gladness: God demanded repentance and renewal; the people instead turned to pleasure and parties.

22:15 Steward refers to a high government official who was responsible for caring for the king and his dominion.

22:16 By hewing himself **a sepulcher on high,** Shebna rivaled the king (2 Chr. 16:14), to whom he should have been a father (v. 21).

22:17 throw you away: An impressive grave is no defense against God.

22:18, 19 drive you out: Shebna was demoted to a secretary by the time of the Assyrian siege (36:3, 22).

22:20 Eliakim was an official whom God would honor in place of the arrogant Shebna (v. 15).

22:21 The word **father** suggests the self-sacrificing love of Eliakim for citizens of Jerusalem.

22:22 The steward had the **key** that gave him an audience with the king.

22:23 A peg suggests one who is firmly in place, a reliable person (but see 22:25). **Glorious throne** suggests that Eliakim will bring honor to the memory of his **father's house** in contrast to the shame Shebna had brought to his master (see v. 18).

22:24 All vessels is a metaphor for all of the inhabitants, both the influential and the insignificant.

22:25 the peg that is fastened in the secure place: The reference here appears to be Eliakim (v. 20). Even the noble Eliakim could not sustain the **burden** of government. Only Immanuel could do that (9:6, 7).

23:1, 2 Tyre was besieged several times over a period of about four hundred years before it was finally **laid waste** by Alexander the Great in 332 B.C. **Cyprus** had close commercial ties with Tyre (Ezek. 27:6), as did Solomon (1 Kin. 5:1, 8–11).

23:3, 4 Shihor, a synonym for Egypt (see Jer. 2:18), brought its coveted **grain** to Phoenicia, bringing **revenue** to Tyre, the **marketplace for the nations.** Sidon, the other prominent city along with Tyre, depended on the Mediterranean Sea for its livelihood, which is personified here as a bereft father.

23:5 Egypt would be in **agony** because its profitable trading partner was gone.

23:6, 7 Tarshish is Tartessus in Spain and represents the most distant place to the ancient Israelites (2:16). **Whose feet … to dwell** is a personification of Tyre's colonies. Tyre's large merchant fleet transversed the Mediterranean Sea. Their colonies were sprinkled throughout the Mediterranean world in support of their shipping empire.

23:8 crowning: Tyre crowned its trading merchants with wealth and prestige.

23:9 dishonor the pride: For a similar idea, see 2:12–19.

23:10–12 Oppressed suggests "crushed" in war. **virgin daughter of Sidon:** It is possible that this phrase is used as a parody. Jerusalem is the Lord's daughter; Tyre is just a pretender.

23:13, 14 Since **the Chaldeans** had not escaped the siege **towers** of the Assyrians who **raised up** or laid bare the foundations of Babylon's **palaces,** neither would Tyre.

23:15 Seventy years symbolizes a full measure of time, a lifetime.

23:16 The **forgotten harlot** who, in her old age, sings **songs** to be **remembered** is a metaphor for the restoration of Tyre.

23:17 Will deal is a translation of the Hebrew verb "to visit." Although the verb can express God's merciful visitation on His people, here the verb is used to express God's judgment (24:21). **Commit fornication** is a metaphor for Tyre's forming economic alliances with anyone that enriched her, regardless of ethics.

23:18 Tyre's **pay** would be **set apart,** or "regarded as holy," **for the LORD** (18:7; 60:5–11). This was not a violation of Deut. 23:18, which forbade bringing a harlot's pay to the temple.

24:1 Scatters is an allusion to Gen. 11:9. The Lord had scattered the **inhabitants** of the earth in the past at the tower of Babel; He would do so again.

24:2, 3 As ... debtor: Wealth and power will make no difference. Both will suffer for wickedness before God.

24:4 The earth mourns: For a similar idea, see Rom. 8:22.

24:5 laws ... ordinance ... everlasting covenant: The usual language about a breach of the covenant is applied more generally to the wicked nations. Perhaps these words speak of that innate sense of right and wrong—the conscience—that God has given to all humankind, but which everyone violates (Rom. 1:18–32; compare Acts 24:16).

24:6 Left may also be translated "remnant" (10:20, 21).

24:7 New wine is simply a synonym of the standard word for wine.

24:8, 9 Mirth and **joy** represent the same Hebrew word.

24:10 Confusion is translated "without form" in Gen. 1:2.

24:11, 12 cry for wine: For a similar image, see Zeph. 1:13.

24:13 shaking ... gleaning: People in desperation continue to seek for a single **olive** or for **grapes.**

24:14 They refers to those who love God's law and who have suffered for righteousness.

24:15 dawning light ... the sea: The imagery suggests the east (the dawn) and west (the Mediterranean Sea). From east to west, everyone should give the Lord the praise that is due Him.

24:16 But I said: The prophet could not join the oppressed's hymn of praise because he saw the treachery that would precede the rejoicing (33:1; Dan. 7:28; 8:27).

24:17, 18 Windows may be an allusion to the Flood (Gen. 7:11). In the Old Testament the word means "openings."

24:19–21 The Hebrew word to **punish** means "to visit" (23:17). The **host** of stars (Jer. 33:22) is identified with fallen angels (Matt. 24:29; Rev. 12:4, 9).

24:22 prisoners: For a similar idea see 2 Pet. 2:4.

24:23 His elders may be a reference to angelic beings who attend God's majesty.

25:1 Wonderful things refers to the wonders only God can do. **Faithfulness and truth** may be rephrased as "absolute truth."

25:2 Any proud **city** is in view here (24:10). **never be rebuilt:** For a similar idea, see 24:20.

25:3 The terrible nations are those addressed in chs. 13–23. The pairing of **glorify** (24:15) and **fear** speaks of the absolute submission to God of all people (Phil. 2:10).

25:4 The repetition of the word **strength** and the use of the terms **refuge** (57:13) and **shade** is similar to the listing of terms for protection in Ps. 91:1–3.

25:5 The use of the term **terrible ones,** or nations, three times in vv. 3–5 emphasizes divine judgment on the nations represented.

25:6 A feast of wine on the lees refers to the best wine. **Fat things full of marrow** refers to the choicest food.

25:7 The surface of the covering and **veil** refer to a "shroud." This is a promise of the end of death (v. 8).

25:8 Lord **will swallow up death. wipe away tears:** This promise is given anew in Rev. 7:17; 21:4. **the LORD has spoken:** The promises are as sure as the eternal character of God (1:20).

25:9 Note the change from "my God" (v. 1) to **our God.** This verse is the faithful's song of praise. **Be glad and rejoice** may be rephrased as "be exceedingly happy." **Salvation** is deliverance from constraint, whether it is falling into a pit (Ps. 40:2) or the constraint of sin and death.

25:10, 11 Moab symbolizes the proud. **for the refuse heap:** This phrase refers to water mixed with dung—a very unpleasant image.

25:12 He will bring down: This will be the work of the Lord.

26:1 In that day: For a similar phrase, see 2:12. The pilgrim's **strong city** presumably is Mount Zion (2:2; 60:14).

26:2 Open the gates is the language of a pilgrim song (Ps. 118:19, 20).

26:3 The Hebrew expression translated **perfect peace** is literally "peace, peace"; compare the word *holy* in 6:3. Immanuel will inaugurate this superior kind of peace (9:6; 11:6–9).

26:4 Trust means "to commit oneself fully to." **YAH, the LORD** is an emphatic designation of God (see 12:2).

26:5, 6 Line after line asserts the destruction of the **lofty city** (v. 1) by the power of God.

26:7 uprightness; O Most Upright: The relative uprightness of the righteous is put into the context of the absolute uprightness of the Holy One.

26:8 waited: For a similar idea, see 40:31 (compare Ps. 40:1).

26:9 in the night ... early: The prophet describes his relentless search for God.

26:10 The wicked show contempt for God's grace (Rom. 2:4). **Majesty is translated "excellent things" in 12:5.**

26:11 Your hand: The works of God are ignored by the wicked (5:12). **The fire of** may also be translated "the fire upon."

26:12 True **peace** comes only from the Lord (26:3; John 14:27).

26:13 Other **masters** included rulers of Egypt in the past, rulers of Assyria in the present, and rulers of Babylon in the future.

26:14 They are dead: The prophet saw the future demise of the enemies of God's people.

26:15 You have increased the nation: The repetition of this expression emphasizes both its certainty and its magnitude.

26:16 The pronoun **they** refers to the faithful nation.

26:17, 18 a woman with child: A woman can endure labor pains for the sake of the joy that follows. The faithful remnant of Isaiah's time endured oppression, but **brought forth wind,** a metaphor for meaningless labor.

26:19 Isaiah, addressing his faithful peers, assures them that their **dead** will rise in resurrection.

26:20 My people refers to the faithful, righteous remnant. Their sufferings under the Assyrian tyrants were but **for a little moment.**

26:21 Comes can also be translated "is about to come." When **the earth** discloses the **blood** of the poor and needy that it has swallowed from the hands of ruthless tyrants, it will bear testimony against those evil people; the Lord will avenge them (Gen. 4:10).

27:1 Leviathan was a mythological, dragonlike deity who symbolized chaos and who battled unsuccessfully against God. God will triumph over all who oppose Him.

27:2 The **vineyard** is Israel. God wanted them to produce delectable wine.

27:3 I ... keep it contrasts with "I will lay it waste" (5:6). **Water it every moment** contrasts with "no rain on it" (5:6). **Lest any hurt it** contrasts with "I will take away its hedge" (5:5). This passage is a complete reversal of the judgment recorded in ch. 5.

27:4 Fury is not in Me contrasts with "For all this His anger is not turned away" (5:25). **Who would set briers and thorns** contrasts with "there shall come up briers and thorns" (5:6).

27:5 peace: For a development of this theme, see 9:6; 11:1–16; 26:3.

27:6 Those who come refers to the regathered exiles (v. 13).

27:7 Has He: The two questions that begin with these words expect a negative answer.

27:8 Sending it away refers to the Exile (v. 13).

27:9 iniquity ... covered: See 40:2 for another statement that Israel's punishment atoned for its guilt.

27:10, 11 the fortified city will be desolate: For a similar idea, see 25:2, 10–12; 26:5, 6.

27:12 Thresh refers to harvesting a crop by flailing, such as beating an olive tree. **the River to the Brook of Egypt:** These geographical references mark out Israel's ideal homeland.

27:13 The great trumpet is a figure of speech for assembling troops (Ex. 19:16, 19; 1 Sam. 13:3; 2 Sam. 6:15; Matt. 24:31; 1 Cor. 15:52; 1 Thess. 4:16).

28:1 The crown of pride refers to Samaria.

28:2 The **strong one** refers to Assyria, which is likened to **hail** that strips a plant of its leaves and **mighty waters** that sweep away the stalks (8:7, 8; 17:12, 13).

28:3, 4 crown of pride: This phrase is repeated from v. 1.

28:5 In that day: For a similar phrase, see 2:12. The true **crown of glory** (29:17–24; 30:18–33; 32:1–33:24) stands in contrast to the false one (vv. 1–4).

28:6 The **spirit of justice** will prevail in the messianic age (11:1–5; 42:1–4).

28:7, 8 They also refers to the religious leaders, **the priest and the prophet.**

28:9, 10 Will he teach was spoken by the hardened leaders against Isaiah. A child was **weaned** between the ages of three and five, the time for elementary moral education, which is described in v. 10.

28:11 The **stammering lips** were those of the Assyrians, who would become the teachers of Israel.

28:12 In place of the **rest** that comes from faith, Israel's oppressors would teach with a rod.

28:13 The word of the LORD would take the shape of discipline in the form of foreigners teaching their morals to Israel, who should have learned from God.

28:14 Scornful men are worse than "fools"; beyond choosing what is bad, they despise what is good (Ps. 1:1).

28:15 covenant with death ... lies ... falsehood: These phrases are probably Isaiah's way of describing the people's covenant with Egypt. **Overflowing scourge** is likely the prophet's way of describing the Assyrian reprisals.

28:16, 17 Therefore: In response to the people's

scoffing, **the LORD** promises to establish His future kingdom on the **sure foundation** of justice and faith.

28:18, 19 As often as: The Assyrian army trampled through Israel many times.

28:20 The too-short **bed** and the too-narrow **covering** give a false promise of security and comfort, an apt figure for the people's ill-advised, obstinate alliance with Egypt.

28:21 At **Mount Perazim,** God broke forth like a mighty flood. In the **Valley of Gibeon,** He brought forth hail (Josh. 10:10, 11).

28:22 Mockers comes from the same Hebrew root as "scornful men" in v. 14.

28:23–29 The wisdom that the farmer uses in vv. 24–28 to tend his crops comes from God, the source of all good counsel.

29:1 Ariel probably means "altar hearth" (Ezek. 43:15, 16). The destruction and bloodshed in Jerusalem would make the city appear like an altar. **where David dwelt:** David made Jerusalem his capital and planned the temple that Solomon would later build in that city.

29:2 Heaviness and sorrow may be rephrased as "grievous sorrow."

29:3 Siege refers to the Assyrian siege of the city in 701 B.C.

29:4, 5 Voice ... like a medium's refers to the forbidden, deceptive "voices" for which the medium supposedly served as a channel.

29:6 thunder and earthquake and great noise ... storm and tempest ... fire: The Lord's coming to His people is described using the imagery of the elements that accompanied Him at Sinai.

29:7, 8 As a dream means "quickly passing," almost "unreal."

29:9, 10 Pause ... Blind: Whereas the religious leaders of Israel were physically **drunk** (28:7), those of Jerusalem **stagger** not from intoxicating drinks, but from ignorance of the Lord and His ways.

29:11, 12 The **literate** represent the religious leaders who found Isaiah's prophecies **sealed** because of their own spiritual blindness. The **illiterate** represent the common people.

29:13 The people's **mouths** and **lips** spoke the right things, but their inner nature was far from God.

29:14 God's **marvelous work** includes both judgment on the proud and salvation for the lowly (vv. 17–24).

29:15 The word **counsel** refers to making alliances instead of running to God for assistance.

29:16 potter ... clay: For a similar idea, see 45:9.

29:17 Lebanon is a symbol of the earth's might. **Fruitful field,** or "garden," is the opposite of Lebanon, a forest.

29:18 Those who were once **deaf** and **blind** to **the words of the book** will miraculously understand it (vv. 9–12).

29:19 poor: For a similar usage, see 61:1.

29:20 terrible one: For similar references, see 13:11; 25:3, 4; 49:24. **scornful:** For a similar reference, see 28:14.

29:21 By a word refers to false testimony. **Lay a snare** may include the miscarriage of justice through legal technicalities. **By empty words** refers to winning a case through lies or clever arguments.

29:22 Jacob shall not now be ashamed: Based on God's covenant with the patriarchs, the Lord gave a renewed promise of deliverance and blessing to the Israelites.

29:23, 24 My hands: God Himself will bring about the redemption of His people. **Holy One of Jacob** refers to the One whom Jacob regarded as holy.

30:1 This is the fourth **woe** in 28:1–35:10. **The rebellious children** are Hezekiah's advisers. To the sin of injustice they **add** the **sin** of devising plans independently of God.

30:2 the shadow of Egypt: The contrast, of course, would be trusting in the "shadow of the Almighty" (Ps. 91:1).

30:3 Shame refers to deep humiliation.

30:4 His ambassadors may be the people from Judah who went from **Zoan** (19:11–13) in the Delta to **Hanes,** some 50 miles south of Cairo.

30:5 Shame and **reproach** speak of an intolerable humiliation.

30:6 The burden against the beasts was because of the fact that they vainly carried Judah's gifts through the wilderness to Egypt (vv. 7–11).

30:7 Rahab, which means "Storm" or "Arrogant," was a dragon from pagan mythology that was pictured as resisting creation.

30:8, 9 That can mean "because." **Law** refers to the prophet's instruction, which is from the Lord Himself (see v. 15).

30:10 Do not see: For a similar usage, see Mic. 2:6.

30:11 To cease: This was the most flagrant of the people's wicked words.

30:12 To not choose to obey the Lord is to reject Him, even to **despise** His message. **trust in oppression:** For a similar idea, see 1:15–17; 29:20, 21.

30:13, 14 A bulge in a high wall and **the breaking of the potter's vessel** signify that judgment would come **suddenly** and completely. **A shard** is a piece of broken pottery.

30:15 Returning entails repentance. **Quietness and confidence** may be rephrased as "utter trust." Trusting in God's strength is the only way we can find true rest.

30:16 Instead of trusting in the Lord, the people were depending on Egypt for **horses** and chariots to defend the land (31:1; contrast Ps. 20:7).

30:17 One thousand shall flee: The point is that the nation will be utterly routed (Deut. 32:30).

30:18 God's **justice** demands that the Assyrian oppressors be punished (Judg. 2:16).

30:19 You shall weep no more: A similar promise is given in 25:8.

30:20 bread of adversity: The Lord was giving the Israelites meager rations as though they were in prison (1 Kin. 22:27). But after judgment the Lord would provide salvation: Israel's **eyes** would **see** (29:24).

30:21 The people had been living in such a way that they were oblivious to their spiritual teachers (v. 20); now they would be taught by the Spirit of the living God.

30:22 Defile means "to desecrate by destruction." **Unclean thing** refers to something soiled by menstruation.

30:23, 24 The promises that were part of the original Mosaic covenant were in force again.

30:25, 26 on every high mountain ... light of the sun will be sevenfold: These phrases emphasize the magnitude of the coming salvation. **When the towers fall** is associated with the collapse of human pride (2:12–17).

30:27 The name of the LORD refers to His character, as memorialized in His saving acts throughout history.

30:28 His breath describes the sound of the Lord's voice as a roaring, overflowing river.

30:29 song ... in the night: In times of festivals, singing would extend long into the evening. **The Mighty One** literally means "Rock" (Ps. 144:1).

30:30, 31 Here God's **voice** is compared to the thunder (Ps. 29:3, 4; contrast v. 28). **descent of His arm:** The strong arm of God would descend in judgment. **Assyria:** Only is the enemy nation mentioned by name.

30:32 And in battles: These were soldier-musicians; they were to be ready to fight or to play music as the occasion demanded.

30:33 Tophet was probably a deep, wide pit containing a bonfire of blazing wood, where children had at times been burned to death as offerings to pagan deities **Brimstone** is a reminder of the fiery destruction of Sodom.

31:1 Look means "to look with interest" or "to look with respect." **Seek the LORD** entails consulting His prophets for direction (29:9, 10; 30:1).

31:2, 3 The house of evildoers refers to Judah. Their **help** refers to Egypt. Both Egypt and Judah **will perish together.**

31:4, 5 Lion connotes **the LORD of hosts** and His resolve to **fight** the enemy. The **multitude of shepherds** refers to the Assyrian officers.

31:6, 7 revolted: For an explanation of the rebellion, see 30:1. **throw away:** For a similar idea, see 30:22.

31:8 Not of man refers to the death angel that destroyed Sennacherib's vaunted army (37:36).

31:9 A **banner** was a rallying point for a battle. The **princes** would be too dispirited to rally for the cause.

32:1 The prophecy about this **king** is fulfilled in the Lord Jesus Christ (7:14; 9:1–7; 11:1–5; 28:16; John 10:11, 16). The **princes** are His "undershepherds" (1 Pet. 5:2–4).

32:2 The four similes for the future King's protection and provision of His people contrast with Israel's present incompetent leadership (28:7; 29:9, 10; 30:1, 2; 31:1, 2).

32:3, 4 Clear **eyes** and listening **ears** are

figures for the future sensible leadership, in contrast to the present senseless, foolish leadership. The people would have a **heart** that is understanding and a **tongue** that speaks **plainly.**

32:5–7 The contrast between the way the noble and foolish **speak** comes from the person's **heart** (v. 4). If a person meditates on evil, that person will speak and act treacherously.

32:8, 9 The term **complacent** is used three times of these women (vv. 9, 10, 12); it is derived from the verb meaning "to trust." Although the wicked erroneously relied on Egypt for their security (see 31:1), the righteous placed their trust in the Lord.

32:10–12 Mourning women in the ancient Middle East removed their clothing and wore **sackcloth** around their **waists** (Gen. 37:34).

32:13, 14 palaces ... pasture: These images speak of the complete ruin of Jerusalem in the day of God's judgment.

32:15 The new age depends on the creative work of **the Spirit** (11:2; 42:1; 61:1; Ezek. 36:26, 27; Joel 2:28, 29) who originates **on high,** in God's dwelling (33:5). This is in contrast to going "down to Egypt" (31:1).

32:16 fruitful field: This is a reversal of the judgment predicted in 29:17.

32:17, 18 The Hebrew words translated **assurance** and **secure** are related to the Hebrew word translated "complacent" in v. 9.

32:19, 20 Hail may refer to Assyria (28:2).

33:1 You refers to Assyria, who **treacherously** (21:2; 24:16) broke its treaties (2 Kin. 18:13–37).

33:2 The besieged remnant, including Isaiah, had **waited** for the Lord in prayer (37:14–20) and in confident expectation (40:31).

33:3 When You lift Yourself up speaks of the heavenly King (vv. 5, 10) as He rises to demonstrate His glory and vindicate His justice.

33:4 The **plunder** of God's war will be **gathered** as swiftly and completely as **the caterpillar** and **locusts** can strip a field, since the Lord's judgment will come quickly without warning (1 Thess. 5:2).

33:5 exalted ... on high: This chapter presents the "rising glory" of the Savior King over His people. **Justice and righteousness** may be rephrased as "true justice."

33:6 Wisdom and knowledge … fear of the LORD: The Messiah's characteristics (11:2) will also characterize His city.

33:7, 8 Valiant ones may sarcastically refer to three officials of Judah who conferred with the Assyrians (36:3, 22). Judah's **ambassadors** wept **bitterly** because Assyria took their gifts, but continued to besiege Jerusalem (v. 1). With the treaty between Assyria and Judah broken, the **highways** were not safe.

33:9 Sharon was on the western coastal plain. **Bashan** was on the east side of the Jordan River.

33:10 Now … Now … Now: The King is about to assert His authority (vv. 5, 16).

33:11 You refers to Assyria (v. 1). **chaff … stubble … fire:** The grandeur of Assyria would be consumed quickly.

33:12 The burnings of lime—all that is left from burning lime is dust—and **thorns … in the fire** indicate the thoroughness and swiftness of Assyria's destruction (27:4).

33:13 Hear: For a similar call for all to acknowledge the Lord as Sovereign, see 34:1.

33:14 burnings: For a description of God as a consuming fire, see Deut. 4:24; 9:3; Heb. 12:29.

33:15, 16 Who stops … shuts: These words do not advocate ignoring social evil, but refusing to take part in it.

33:17 The **King** is the Lord (v. 22).

33:18 The scribe … who weighs refers to those who took the tribute (2 Kin. 18:14).

33:19 stammering tongue: For a similar idea about Israel's enemies, see Deut. 28:49.

33:20 The **feasts** were celebrated from the heart (30:29), and not perfunctorily (29:1). **Not be taken down** implies that the Exile is over. Judah's immediate salvation merges with its ultimate deliverance.

33:21 Judah would be protected figuratively by **broad rivers,** like those at Tyre (23:1–3) and Thebes (Nah. 3:8). However, no intimidating ship would be on the rivers, because God Himself would defend Judah.

33:22, 23 Note that the **Lawgiver** is associated with other acts of mercy.

33:24 Sickness and sin will be removed in the coming kingdom of the glorious Savior.

34:1 Let the earth hear: For similar calls for all the world to listen to Isaiah's prophecy, see 1:2; 33:13.

34:2 Indignation is a strong term used to describe the wrath of God. **Destroyed** means "to devote to destruction." Because the Lord had defeated His enemy, the spoils were to be devoted totally to Him by burning them (23:18).

34:3 The **blood** of the dead would be so great that it would create mudslides.

34:4 The host of heaven refers to pagan deities (24:21; 2 Kin. 17:16). **heavens … rolled up like a scroll:** The old cosmos will give way to the new (51:6; Matt. 24:29; Rev. 6:13, 14; 21:1).

34:5 The Lord's avenging **sword** moves from demolishing the pantheon of **heaven** (v. 4) to **Edom** (63:1) in particular.

34:6 Sin must be atoned for by **sacrifice,** either of the sinner himself as here (Ezek. 33:10), or by the substitutionary sacrifice of Christ (52:13–15).

34:7 Oxen and **bulls** may represent Edom's troops or leaders.

34:8 vengeance: The Lord secures His sovereignty and keeps His community whole by saving His wronged subjects and punishing their guilty oppressors.

34:9, 10 Brimstone and **burning pitch** may be allusions to Sodom and Gomorrah (30:33; see Gen. 19:24; Ezek. 38:22).

34:11 The pelican, porcupine, owl, and **raven** are all unclean creatures of remote, uninhabited places. The Hebrew words translated **confusion and emptiness** are translated "without form and void" in Gen. 1:2.

34:12 There will be no **nobles** or **princes** in the desert.

34:13–15 For a similar description of these unclean desert creatures, see 13:21, 22.

34:16 The book of the LORD may refer to the prophecy found in vv. 1–15.

34:17 As God gave Israel the Promised Land by **lot,** so in judgment He **divided** Edom **among** the unclean animals.

35:1 wilderness … desert: The Spirit of God will make the earth fruitful again (32:15).

35:2 The glory of the LORD would be seen in the return of the captives from Babylon (40:5).

35:3 Strengthen the feeble hands: This phrase is cited in Heb. 12:12.

35:4 save you: When the Lord comes, He will offer salvation (see Luke 19:10).

35:5, 6 eyes ... ears ... lame ... tongue: This prophecy of healings was fulfilled in Jesus.

35:7 The habitation of jackals speaks of the coming reversal of the devastation God had brought on the land (see 34:14).

35:8, 9 ravenous beast: Ferocious animals could make traveling dangerous in the ancient world.

35:10 the ransomed: The Lord would come to rescue them from their tragic predicaments.

36:1 The **fourteenth year** of King Hezekiah's sole reign was 701 B.C.

36:2 The Rabshakeh may have been the king's personal advisor.

36:3 Eliakim ... Shebna: For further details, see 22:15–23.

36:4, 5 Only the Assyrian leader is referred to here as **king,** not **Hezekiah.**

36:6 Judah had refused to listen to Isaiah's insistence that reliance on **Egypt** was worthless (19:14–16; 30:3, 7; 31:3). Here they were given the same warning from their enemy.

36:7 taken away: Hezekiah had destroyed the idolatrous high places and altars that his father Ahaz had built (see 2 Kin. 18:1–5; 2 Chr. 31:1–3).

36:8 riders: Micah referred to Jerusalem's soldiers as just a "troop" (Mic. 5:1) compared to the enormous army of Assyria (Mic. 4:11).

36:9 one captain of the least: Judah had no hope of defeating the force that surrounded him.

36:10 The LORD said to me: These words about the Lord were no more than a boast.

36:11, 12 Aramaic was the language of international diplomacy during this period.

36:13, 14 The Rabshakeh spoke **in Hebrew** so his words to be understood by the citizens of Jerusalem. **deceive you:** He structured his speech to quickly discourage those who heard it.

36:15–17 take you away: The Assyrians commonly exiled the people groups they conquered (see 2 Kin. 15:29; 17:6).

36:18–21 The Rabshakeh assumed that different gods were worshiped in **Samaria** than in Jerusalem, so he repeated some of the same sentiments articulated by the Assyrian king in 10:10, 11.

36:22 The words of the enemy would not bring pleasure **to Hezekiah.** The torn **clothes** indicated that the messengers were bearing bad news (37:1).

37:1 Sackcloth was a sign of mourning, repentance, and humiliation (20:2, 3; 1 Kin. 20:31; Neh. 9:1; Dan. 9:3).

37:2, 3 Eliakim ... Shebna: One of Isaiah's prophecies condemns Shebna for his arrogance (see 22:15–23).

37:4, 5 For more references to the **remnant,** see 1:9; 10:20.

37:6–10 The Lord commonly reassured His servants with the words: **Do not be afraid.**

37:11 utterly destroying: See 34:2 for another use of this term.

37:12–15 Hezekiah prayed: Hezekiah had learned to turn to God for help in his times of need.

37:16–21 Because you have prayed to Me: God's gracious response was a direct answer to the prayer of a godly king.

37:22 virgin: Cities are often personified as female in the Scriptures. This imagery speaks of Jerusalem as a "daughter" being threatened by an attacker.

37:23 reproached and blasphemed ... raised your voice ... lifted up your eyes on high: The folly of the wicked of all ages is epitomized here.

37:24 Chariots were the most prized military hardware of the time.

37:25 dug and drunk water: Deserts cannot stop Assyria's king; he presents himself as invincible.

37:26–29 The Assyrians dragged prisoners away with a **hook in** the **nose;** soon *they* would get the hook!

37:30–32 Assyria had promised to feed the Judeans; but only God could guarantee that the people would **eat** (36:16, 17).

37:33 thus says the LORD: God gives His final sentence against the Assyrian tyrant.

37:34, 35 for My own sake: The Lord would save and protect the city for His own honor, for He had established the city for the worship of His holy name.

37:36 This verse is the fulfillment of God's promise to take vengeance on those who trouble His people (34:8). **the angel of the LORD:** Here the angel of the Lord delivers His people by fighting for them (see Ex. 15:3).

37:37–38 Death **in the house of Nisroch** contrasts with life in the house of the Lord.

38:1 In those days refers to a time before the events recorded in chs. 36 and 37 (v. 6).

38:2 prayed: Hezekiah turned to the Lord in prayer.

38:3–6 Hezekiah wept bitterly because apparently at that time he had no male heirs. Hezekiah lived an additional fifteen years (v. 5); Manasseh, the successor to his throne, was twelve when Hezekiah died (2 Kin. 20:21–21:1).

38:7 sign: For a related reference, see 7:11–14.

38:8 Bringing **the shadow on the sundial … backward** symbolized the divine extension of Hezekiah's life.

38:9 the writing of Hezekiah: Scriptures attest to King Hezekiah's interest in devotional literature. Apparently he instructed his scribes to compile some of the proverbs of Solomon (see Prov. 25:1). Furthermore, he ordered the Levites to worship God with the psalms of David and Asaph.

38:10, 11 Hezekiah was mourning the fact that he was dying at an early age.

38:12 Pulling up a **tent** represented impermanence.

38:13–17 for my own peace: Hezekiah accepted trials as part of God's good plan for him. **sins:** The forgiveness of sin and healing are aspects of salvation.

38:18 cannot thank: Praise for healing can only be offered while a person is alive (Ps. 6:5).

38:19 father … children: The righteous teach their children of God's faithfulness.

38:20 sing: For a song of praise to God our Savior, see 12:1–6.

38:21 poultice: All healing is of God, who may use medicine and the skills of health care professionals.

38:22 Depending on one's attitude, the request for a **sign** may express either unbelief (Matt. 12:39; John 6:30) or faith (v. 7). The

healing of a boil would be the sign that the Lord would save Hezekiah (see vv. 20, 21).

39:1 recovered: The miracle of the sundial (38:8) would have held special interest for the astronomy-minded Babylonians.

39:2–4 The fact that Hezekiah showed **his treasures** instead of praising God suggests that he was trusting in his might and the armies of the nations like Babylon, instead of in the Lord.

39:5, 6 LORD of hosts: This title describes the Lord as Commander in Chief of the angelic armies.

39:7, 8 Eunuchs were royal officials or servants who were often castrated to keep them from being a threat to the king's harem.

40:1 Comfort is repeated for emphasis, and is an announcement of an end to the people's suffering.

40:2 Here the word **Jerusalem** represents the exiles. The Lord would end their period of exile and restore them to the city of Jerusalem.

40:3 crying in the wilderness: The voice is heard in the wilderness, calling the people there to ready themselves for the coming of the Lord. **Prepare** means "clear away the obstacles" (57:14; 62:10). **Highway** represents the hearts of people who must be spiritually prepared by repentance for God's glory to be revealed on the earth (Luke 3:3–20).

40:4 While the highway of v. 3 was to be prepared by the people of the Lord, the changes required in v. 4 could be accomplished only by divine action.

40:5, 6 The glory of the LORD began to be **revealed** in the restoration of the captives of Judah from the Exile (44:23). More grandly, the glory of the Lord would be displayed in the coming of the Lord Jesus Christ. **the mouth of the LORD has spoken:** The importance of this prophecy is underscored by the language of divine oath.

40:7, 8 But the word of our God stands forever: These words offer full assurance of the eternal nature of the divine word.

40:9 Zion is an endearing term for the remnant who have remained faithful to God. The **good tidings** are that God has come to rescue His enslaved people.

40:10 The Lord GOD might be rephrased "the LORD, the Master." **Reward** describes the spoils of victory—namely, the delivered people.

40:11 Gather the lambs with His arm is a description of the Father's love for His people (Mic. 5:4).

40:12 Who: The answer is "God, Creator of the cosmos, and Israel's Lord" (vv. 15–17). **A span** is the width of a stretched-out hand. The verse dramatically imposes images of God's might.

40:13, 14 directed: These questions are an attack against Marduk, a Babylonian deity, who needed the assistance of other gods in creating the world.

40:15, 16 a drop in a bucket: Wicked nations have no power to thwart the purposes of God (Ps. 2:1–6). The word **scales** links the answer in this verse to the question in v. 12: Who has measured the dust of the earth? Its sovereign Creator has.

40:17 Worthless is the same term used to describe the primeval chaos (Gen. 1:2).

40:18 liken God: The God of Scripture is incomparable; there is no one else like Him (40:25; 46:5; Ps. 113:4–6).

40:19 goldsmith: Many idols were made with wood, then overlaid **with gold** (41:6, 7; 44:9–20; 46:6, 7). **Silver chains** kept the idol from moving or falling.

40:20 too impoverished: The poor had to choose the best wood available and then hope it was good enough. What is the value of the prayer of a poor man to a plain idol? What is the value of the prayer of the rich to one covered with gold? To both questions, the answer is "none."

40:21, 22 Have you not known: The questions express God's incredulity at worshipers of idols. **stretches out the heavens:** Creation is the work of the God of Israel.

40:23, 24 nothing ... useless: For a similar expression of the insignificance of entire nations before the might of the living God, see v. 17. **planted ... blow ... wither:** This imagery describing God's judgment is similar to that in vv. 6–8.

40:25 To whom then will you liken Me: This is part of an important biblical theme, the incomparability of God.

40:26 Lift up: Human beings are responsible to discern the greatness of the Creator in His creation. **These things** refers to the heavenly bodies. **by number:** Each of the stars is known to the Creator; to each He has given a **name** (Ps. 147:4).

40:27 My way is hidden from the LORD does not question God's omniscience, but His good will.

40:28, 29 Have you not known: The Lord repeats this rhetorical question for emphasis (see v. 21). God is **everlasting** omnipotent and inscrutable. **Neither faints nor is weary:** the Lord will never let His people down (Ps. 121:3, 4).

40:30 youths: The point is that human strength cannot compare with the power of God.

40:31 To wait entails confident expectation and active hope in the Lord. **Mount up ... run ... walk** depicts the spiritual transformation that faith brings to a person. The Lord gives power to those who trust in Him. **eagles:** The eagle depicts the strength that comes from the Lord.

41:1 Keep silence: Divine calls for silence usually anticipate judgment (Zeph. 1:7). **Renew their strength** contrasts strength that results from faith with unassisted human strength.

41:2 One from the east refers to Cyrus, king of Persia. God, who has authority over the nations, **gave the nations** to Cyrus as a ransom for Israel (43:3).

41:3 Cyrus advanced so fast it was as though **his feet** did not touch the ground.

41:4 first ... last: The Lord is eternal not only in that He is not bound by time, but also in that He is Master of time.

41:5 The pronoun **it** refers to the conquests of Cyrus (vv. 2, 3).

41:6, 7 This verse satirizes assistance from idols in contrast to the sure help from the living God (vv. 10–16).

41:8 Servant refers to one highly honored by the Lord. In chs. 40–55, the title of servant is bestowed implicitly on Cyrus (45:1–4) and explicitly on God's prophets (44:26), the nation of Israel (44:21; 45:4) and particularly on the Lord Jesus Christ (42:1–4; 52:13).

41:9 The ends of the earth indicates God's sovereign rule over the earth (v. 4).

41:10 The Lord's command to the Israelites to **fear not** contrasts with the fright of pagans in vv. 5, 6.

41:11, 12 The people of God are given renewed assurance that their formidable enemies will be brought to **nothing** (40:17, 23).

41:13 The Lord will hold the exile's **right hand** (42:6) just as He held the hand of Moses (63:12). The Lord is with them; they have nothing to fear.

41:14 Redeemer refers to the family protector who would avenge murders (Num. 35:19) and redeem indentured slaves (Lev. 25:47–49). When the Lord is called the Redeemer, the title highlights His zeal to purchase back His people (49:26).

41:15 The lowly "worm" (v. 14) would be transformed into a **threshing sledge** (28:27) that removes **mountains,** the symbols of opposition.

41:16 winnow Threshed grain is tossed in the air to separate the chaff from the grain.

41:17 The poor and needy refers to the exiles moving homeward across the desert. **thirst:** God will meet the people's most basic needs.

41:18 rivers ... fountains ... pool of water ... springs of water: The returning exiles would need water, but God's provision would be bountiful.

41:19 in the wilderness ... tree: The abundant water supply would also lead to the Lord's massive plantings of trees and vegetation (35:1, 2).

41:20 the hand: God's hand indicates His power and strength (40:10; 41:10).

41:21 King of Jacob: This title for God pictures His special relationship with His people.

41:22 The phrase **things to come** may refer to the mighty acts God would do through Cyrus. Idols cannot tell the past or the future, but the Lord God can.

41:23 that you are gods: This is part of the satire (vv. 21, 22). **Do good or do evil** is a way of saying "do anything."

41:24 The word **indeed** assumes a period of silence between v. 23 and v. 24. The supposed "gods" were mute. An **abomination** causes revulsion.

41:25, 26 from the north ... From the rising of the sun: The conquest of Media by Cyrus (550 B.C.) made him master of the territories north of Babylon.

41:27 The pronoun **they** refers to the "former things" and "things to come" (of v. 22). **One who brings good tidings** refers to the prophet Isaiah.

41:28, 29 These verses present the futility of the nations; they do not have true understanding of reality—past, present, or future (41:26).

42:1 Behold: The Lord formally presents His Servant. The title **My Servant** is identified with Jesus Christ in the New Testament (Matt. 12:15–21). **uphold:** When God upholds a person, nothing can bring him down. The Servant—that is, Jesus—was filled with the Holy **Spirit** (59:21; 61:1; Luke 3:22) which empowered Him to bring **justice** to the world.

42:2 The Hebrew word rendered **cry out** means "to cry out in distress." The phrase **cause His voice to be heard in the street** suggests the same idea; the Servant's rejection is heard for the first time (49:4; 50:5, 6; 53:4–9).

42:3 The phrase **a bruised reed** represents the poor and needy (41:17; 42:7). A **smoking flax** represents those who have almost lost their faith and hope in the Lord.

42:4 law: The Servant will mediate the New Covenant (2 Cor. 3:3; Heb. 8:7–13).

42:5 The Lord God introduces Himself as the source of all life—**breath** and **spirit**—for He will enable the Servant to free people from death and spiritual darkness (vv. 6–9).

42:6 The Servant **in righteousness** will deliver Israel from sin, and institute a new **covenant** binding Israel to the Lord (49:8). The prophets refer to this new covenant as a "covenant of peace" (54:10; Ezek. 34:25); an "everlasting covenant" (55:3); a "new covenant."

42:7 To open ... darkness Christ gave sight to the blind to show that He had the power to give everyone spiritual insight (v. 16).

42:8 My name: That God reveals His name to His people is an indication of His wondrous grace.

42:9 former ... new: God through Isaiah was announcing new prophecies, and these too would come to pass.

42:10, 11 You who go down to the sea ... the wilderness and its cities: The command is for all people to **sing.**

42:12 Glory links this hymn with the Servant's Song (v. 8).

42:13 man of war: The zeal of the Lord. **He shall prevail against His enemies:** A similar promise that the Lord will eventually triumph is found in 41:11, 12.

42:14 held My peace describes the Lord's patient delay in acting (48:9; 57:11). **A long time** most likely refers to the 70 years of captivity (2 Chr. 36:21). **woman in labor:** The words not only speak of her **cry,** but of the timely bringing forth of the new age begun with the restoration.

42:15 mountains ... rivers: These words refer to all obstacles in the way of returning to the land from Exile.

42:16, 17 Blind refers to the state of the exiles, forming a link with the Servant's task (v. 7) and the Lord's accusation against Israel (v. 18).

42:18, 19 The people were **deaf** because they would not listen and **blind** because they would not see. **My servant:** Isaiah uses the title *servant* for Israel because that nation was to be God's **messenger** to the nations.

42:20, 21 for His righteousness' sake: In punishing Israel for its sin, the Lord exalted His **law.**

42:22–24 Israel was **robbed and plundered** by the Assyrians and the Babylonians. No one said **Restore** until Cyrus commanded the exiles to return to Jerusalem (Ezra 1:2–4).

42:25 For similar descriptions of God's **anger,** see 10:5; 28:21.

43:1 The Hebrew verb translated *created* means "to fashion anew"—a divine activity. The second verb *formed* means "to shape," to fashion as a potter, and is used in Gen. 2:7 of God fashioning the body of the man from the dust of the earth.

43:2 Walk through the fire is a metaphor for protection in danger (Ps. 66:12).

43:3 LORD your God: The God of all creation declares Himself to be the God of the Israelites.

43:4 Israel is considered **precious** because of God's sovereign grace (Deut. 7:6–8).

43:5, 6 Fear not: God's people are to *fear* Him. Being sure of His presence, they need not be afraid of anything or anyone.

43:7, 8 As a **blind** and **deaf** witness, the nation Israel did not fulfill the prophecy of restoration (42:18–20).

43:9, 10 witnesses: The people of Israel had witnessed the great works of God.

43:11–13 The Lord was always at work—saving, protecting, guiding, and disciplining His people.

43:14 The Chaldeans were a people who settled in lower Mesopotamia and founded the Neo-Babylonian Empire.

43:15–17 With the titles **the LORD** (Ex. 3:14, 15), **Holy One** (1:4), **Israel's Creator,** and **your King,** the living God declared His intimate relationship with the Israelites.

43:18 The Lord commanded the people not to **remember** the past (46:9, 10). The kingdom of Israel inaugurated at the first Exodus and the conquest of the Promised Land would be insignificant compared to the new kingdom God would establish. **former things** refers to the prophecies of judgment by Isaiah and other prophets (see 42:9, 21–25; 43:9, 10; 46:8, 9; 48:3).

43:19, 20 a road in the wilderness: The Lord would give the exiles an unobstructed route back to the Promised Land. **rivers in the desert:** Even in desolate regions the Lord would refresh His people.

43:21, 22 The Lord's accusation was that the people had not worshiped Him in the way He prescribed and with the motivation He demanded.

43:23, 24 The exiles' ingratitude—**Nor have you honored Me**—contrasts with the Lord's forbearance—**you have burdened Me.**

43:25 for My own sake: The Lord chooses to save and forgive. This arises out of His character.

43:26 State your case: The Lord asks Israel to answer His charges.

43:27, 28 First father refers to Abraham (51:2). **Princes of the sanctuary** refers to the leaders of the priests in Jerusalem (1 Chr. 24:5).

44:1 Now: The call to listen immediately is featured in 42:14; 43:1.

44:2 Thus says the LORD: This emphatic statement emphasizes that God authored the prophecy and thus it is certain to come to pass. **Jeshurun,** meaning "Upright One," is a poetic word for the nation of Israel (Deut. 32:15).

44:3 pour My spirit: Moses prayed for the Lord's Spirit to come on all Israel (Num. 11:29); the prophets foretold it (Joel 2:28–32), and Christ fulfilled it (Acts 2:14–36).

44:4 Luxurious **grass** symbolizes prosperity.

44:5 The repatriated would proudly identify themselves with the Lord. **The name of Israel** would no longer be associated with a worm (41:14).

44:6, 7 Redeemer: This term is also used in 41:14 and refers to the zeal with which the Lord acts to defend his people. **First ... Last:** God is completely sovereign over time (41:4).

44:8 Do not fear: When God is on your side, you do not need to fear anything or anyone else. **Rock:** The image of a rock represents stability and protection (Ps. 62:2, 6, 7).

44:9 an image: This is the term used in the Second Commandment to describe an idol (Ex. 20:4). **Useless** is translated "without form" in Gen. 1:2.

44:10 The Hebrew has the words **god** and **image** together, emphasizing the absurdity of worshiping an image molded by human hands.

44:11, 12 be ashamed: When all people come face to face with God, it will be a day of shame for those who rejected Him in this life.

44:13, 14 While people were made in the image of God (Gen. 1:26–28), idolaters made gods in **the figure of a man**.

44:15, 16 Isaiah was struck by the absurdity of using one part of a log for burning and the other part as an object of worship.

44:17, 18 you are my god: This is a scene of complete hopelessness. Worshiping and depending on any object made by human hands—such as money—is just as hopeless.

44:19 a block of wood: The awful truth was that people were worshiping objects made from God's creation instead of the Creator Himself.

44:20 He feeds on ashes: Compare the two banquets in Prov. 9:1–6, 13–18.

44:21 not be forgotten: Although the exiles might have thought God had forgotten them (see 49:14, 15), the Lord declared that He would remember the nation He had created.

44:22 blotted out: The idea of total forgiveness of sins is also found in 40:2; 43:25.

44:23 The songs (12:1–6) of the **heavens** and **earth** (1:2; 49:13), the **forest** (35:1, 2) and **every tree** (14:7, 8; 55:12) mirror the joy of God's people at the arrival of salvation.

44:24 Thus says the LORD: Because the Lord says this, it will come to pass (43:1, 14; 44:2, 6, 24.

44:25 Babblers refers to the **diviners**. **wise:** People wise in their own eyes, but not wise toward the Lord.

44:26 built: The rebuilding of the temple and the resettlement of the land after the devastation by Babylon inaugurated the new age (58:12; 61:4).

44:27 Deep refers either to the moat protecting Babylon or to the obstacles blocking the returning exiles (42:15).

44:28 Cyrus: Isaiah mentions by name the king of Persia who would allow the Israelites to return to Jerusalem in 538 B.C.

45:1 To be **anointed,** literally to be "Messiah," indicates appointment to an office, usually as king (61:1). The bestowal of this unique and exalted title on the Persian king, after it had been used in Israel of such notables as the patriarchs (Ps. 105:15), David (Ps. 2:2), and the coming Messiah (Dan. 9:25), must have shocked Isaiah's Israelite audience (vv. 9, 10).

45:2 I will go before you: This was the Lord's promise to Cyrus, similar to His promise to His people of old. Babylon had one hundred **gates of bronze.**

45:3, 4 have not known Me: Cyrus knew that the Lord had appointed him, but he did not know the Lord God personally (see Ezra 1:2). **Who call you by your name** refers to the specific naming of Cyrus by the Lord before Cyrus became king (compare 43:1). God anointed Cyrus to establish again the people whom He loved (43:1).

45:5, 6 From the rising of the sun to its setting means everywhere (Ps. 113:3).

45:7, 8 Because Cyrus was anointed by the true God, heaven would shower its blessings on earth.

45:9, 10 potsherd: Why should a created being question the Creator? A piece of pottery does not question the potter.

45:11 Thus says the LORD: This statement points to the certainty of these words.

45:12 Created is the same verb used in Gen. 1:26–28 (see 43:1).

45:13 The pronoun **him** refers to Cyrus.

45:14 After the Lord handed over **Egypt, Cush,** and **the Sabeans** to Cyrus as a ransom, they would hand themselves over to Israel and its Lord.

45:15, 16 God hides Himself in His wrath, but He reveals Himself in the Scriptures.

45:17 an everlasting salvation: These words of divine promise are echoed in 51:6.

45:18 The Lord created the earth **to be inhabited,** not to be desolate, as the Assyrians and Babylonians had left the land of Israel (33:9; 44:26, 28).

45:19 Pagan diviners pronounced their oracles **in secret** and **dark** places. The Lord's prophets proclaimed the truth openly to all who would listen.

45:20 Draw near together: For similar ideas see 41:1, 21, 22; 43:9; 44:7.

45:21 The pronoun **this** refers to the universal salvation begun with Cyrus's decree that Israel return home (44:24–45:13).

45:22 no other: For additional references to God's incomparability see 40:25; 45:5.

45:23 I have sworn by Myself: The certainty of the Word of the Lord is emphasized strongly in the Book of Isaiah (40:8). The Lord's promise **that to Me every knee shall bow** will be fulfilled in Jesus Christ (see Phil. 2:10, 11).

45:24, 25 Those **who are incensed against** God will have no share in His eternal kingdom (50:11; 66:24).

46:1, 2 Bel, meaning "Lord," was a title of Marduk, Babylon's chief deity. **Nebo,** Marduk's son, was the god of fate, writing, and wisdom. The heavy idols that were expected to bring deliverance were **themselves** dragged away into **captivity.**

46:3 An unbelieving **remnant** (1:9; 10:20) is likely being referred to here.

46:4, 5 Old age indicates the Lord's never-ceasing care. **I am He:** The Lord Himself and no one else would save Israel (41:4).

46:6, 7 The pronoun **they** refers to the idol makers. **They bear it:** God carries and supports His people; idols are carried by those who worship them.

46:8 Transgressors refers to the unbelieving remnant (v. 3).

46:9, 10 the end from the beginning: As the Sovereign of the cosmos, God knows the outcome before the beginning.

46:11 A bird of prey from the east refers to Cyrus (41:2) and to the speed and power of his conquests.

46:12 There would be those who refused to leave the comfort and security of Babylon and Persia.

46:13 Righteousness is a synonym for **salvation** in Isaiah. **Israel My glory:** God loves His people Israel and has never utterly cast them aside.

47:1 O virgin daughter of Babylon She was about to discover that she was the **daughter of the Chaldeans.**

47:2, 3 Grinding **meal** was usually work for female slaves. Babylon would lose its status and privilege. **Nakedness** indicates disgrace, impropriety, lack of dignity, and vulnerability.

47:4 In contrast to the humiliated Babylon, Israel had a **Redeemer.**

47:5 The similar structure of vv. 1, 5 link the first stanza (vv. 1–4) with the second stanza (vv. 5–8).

47:6, 7 Babylon's cruel abuse of Israel when the Lord had **given them into** Babylon's **hand** would be avenged. **a lady forever:** Babylon arrogantly boasted that it would remain an empire, "the Lady of Kingdoms" throughout all time.

47:8, 9 Babylon had deified itself with the statement **I am.** This wicked self-deification mirrors the boasting of the king of Tyre (Ezek. 28:11–19). Babylon is no longer considered a virgin (v. 1), but is a **widow.** The **loss of children** suggests the loss of hope in the future.

47:10 Wickedness, wisdom, and **knowledge** refer to the same idea as "sorceries" and "enchantments." **No one sees me:** The wicked believe that there is no all-knowing, all-seeing God.

47:11 The word **therefore** links Babylon's pretensions of "knowledge" (v. 10) with the just judgment that the nation did **not know.**

47:12–14 The command to **stand** matches the Lord's introductory commands in vv. 1, 5. The word **sorceries** links the final stanza with the earlier ones (vv. 9, 10).

47:15 Babylon's fate would also overtake those **with whom** it had **labored,** its ancient **merchants,** on whose trade it depended for its wealth.

48:1 Hear is an appeal to "deaf Israel."

48:2, 3 The citizens of the **holy city,** Jerusalem, professed to **lean on the God of Israel** (Rom. 9:6).

48:4 Obstinate means "hard." **Iron and bronze** are metaphors for rebelliousness.

48:5 Despite Israel's knowledge that no **idol** had helped them, in the future they would attribute their salvation to some other god than the one Lord.

48:6 To **declare ... hidden things,** the Lord must know and control the future.

48:7, 8 As God unfolded His plan of redemption, He **created** events that Israel had **not heard** about before.

48:9 Defer My anger means to be "longsuffering" (Ex. 34:6).

48:10 Refined, a reference to judgment (1:25; 4:4), refers to the Babylonian captivity. **Furnace** is an allusion to Israel's suffering in Egypt (Deut. 4:20; Jer. 11:4).

48:11 For My own sake: The Lord shows His settled will to maintain the integrity of His great name (v. 9).

48:12 called: For a similar reference to God's calling of Israel, see 42:6.

48:13 Earth and **heavens** refer to the entire cosmos (13:13; 40:21, 22; 51:6, 13).

48:14 Assemble yourselves probably was addressed to the nations.

48:15 I, even I draws attention to the source of this prophecy: the living God.

 IN DEPTH   The Purpose of Prophecy

Perhaps you think of prophecy as having mainly to do with predictions about the future. That's understandable, since prophets in Bible times sometimes foretold what would happen in the future (for example, Is. 7:14–17; 45:1–7; Jer. 28:12–17). However, the purpose of prophecy goes beyond merely informing people about things to come. There are at least two additional reasons why God spoke through the OT prophets:

First, *prophecy shows that the Lord is God.* A god who cannot reveal himself to human beings is unlikely to command much respect. But through prophecy, the Lord has made Himself known in compelling ways. For example, He demonstrated His omniscience by revealing to the Israelites what would happen in the future, something no pagan idol could do (48:5). He also demonstrated His power through the prophets in ways that left no doubt about who He is (1 Kin. 18:36–39).

Second, *prophecy announces God?s word.* Closely related to God's revelation of Himself through prophecy is His communication of truth that He wants people to know. Prophecy is often referred to as the "word of the Lord" (Is. 1:10; 28:14; 38:4); in fact, it is often prefaced by the words, "thus says the Lord God" (7:7; 10:24; 22:15). Thus prophecy is revelation from God. It brings to light truth that would otherwise would remain unexpressed.

The point of these revelations is not merely to inform, but to declare what is true, and then to tell people how they should live in light of what is true. Sometimes prophecy helps to warn people about the consequences of their actions, and sometimes it encourages them when circumstances appear to be desperate. But whatever its effect on people, the purpose of prophecy is to proclaim God and His word.

48:16 Me refers to the Servant, Jesus (42:1–13; 61:1), who has **spoken** through His prophets (1 Pet. 1:10, 11).

48:17 The Lord **teaches** and **leads** through His servants (Deut. 5:27), His prophets, and His Son.

48:18 A river supplies water to produce luxuriant growth. **The waves of the sea** speak of power, constancy, and increase.

48:19 Sand recalls God's promise to the patriarchs that the Israelites would become very numerous (Gen. 22:17; 32:12).

48:20 Go forth: The people are told to leave Babylon, forsaking its comforts.

48:21, 22 They did not thirst is an allusion to God's provision of water.

49:1 Matrix means "womb" (Ruth 1:11).

49:2 Through the preaching of His **mouth,** the Servant will conquer the earth (11:4). **Shadow** suggests protection.

49:3 In whom I will be glorified: In partial fulfillment of this prophecy, Jesus prayed to His Father, "I have glorified You on the earth." (John 17:4).

49:4 reward: The Servant will be vindicated (50:8) and will be rewarded after His death (53:8) and resurrection (53:10).

49:5 The political mission of Cyrus **to bring Jacob back** from Babylon (44:28; 45:13) foreshadows the spiritually redemptive mission of the Servant to free His people from their captivity to sin (42:7).

49:6 light to the Gentiles: After Jesus' death and resurrection, the great commission of global evangelism is carried on by His apostles (Acts 13:47; 26:23) and those who succeed them to the end of the age (Matt. 28:18–20).

49:7 Paradoxically, the King who humbles Himself to become the **Servant of rulers** will Himself receive homage from them.

49:8 In an acceptable time, in contrast to the day of vengeance (34:8; 61:1; 2 Cor. 6:2), the Lord will hear the Servant's complaint that His mission toward Israel was in vain.

49:9 The imagery of feeding in pastures implies that the Servant would be Israel's Shepherd-King (40:11).

49:10 The word **thirst** is an allusion to 48:21. **Heat** and **sun** may be allusions to Ps. 121, a psalm of pilgrimage.

49:11 Mountains, which were once barriers, will become **highways,** the means of salvation (vv. 22, 23).

49:12 These oracles are addressed to all Israel and all the earth (48:1; 49:1).

49:13 Sing: The Lord is the Creator of music (12:1–6; 44:23).

49:14 The complaint **The LORD has forsaken me** resembles that in 40:27–31.

49:15 The Lord says: **I will not forget you.** The verb suggests an even stronger assurance, "I am *unable* to forget you."

49:16 inscribed: This may refer to the Lord's command for the names of the tribes of Israel to be inscribed on the stones of the priest's ephod (see Ex. 28:9–12). When the priest was in the temple, the engraved names would remind God of His covenant with Israel. **Your walls are continually before Me:** The Creator God has His thoughts focused on the welfare of His people (see Ps. 40:5).

49:17 The restored **sons** of Zion would carry out the decree. Zion's would-be **destroyers** were the Babylonians.

49:18 As I live: This is an oath formula. Zion's "sons" were a splendid **ornament,** like the jewels of a **bride** (61:10).

49:19 Desolate means "childless" (54:1).

49:20, 21 the place is too small: This prophecy points to the return of the exiles to Jerusalem; under Ezra and Nehemiah the exiles built a relatively small city (see Ezra 2; Neh. 7).

49:22 I will lift My hand in an oath: God swears by His own character. **Standard** is often translated "banner" (11:12).

49:23 The nations that enslaved Israel had served as **foster fathers** and **nursing mothers** (60:9).

49:24, 25 Israel asks rhetorically: **Shall the prey**—captive Israel—**be taken from the mighty**—Babylon? Apparently Israel expects a negative answer to this question, but the Lord responds affirmatively. He would **contend** with the mighty, terrible Babylon (Jer 50:33, 34) and free His people.

49:26 oppress: Cannibalism was possible during the horrible famine of a siege (9:20; see Deut. 28:53–57).

50:1 Permanent exile would have required a **certificate** of **divorce.** If the Lord had issued one, He could not have taken Israel back (see Deut. 24:1–4; Jer. 3:1, 8). If the Lord had sold Israel to **creditors** He would not have any authority over their destiny. But the Israelites had sold themselves. So, God as their Redeemer could buy them back (see 41:14; 52:3).

50:2 God **came** to Israel at the Exile through the prophets. Later God came to earth through His Servant and Son, Jesus (41:9).

50:3 Blackness may be an allusion to the ninth plague of Egypt, when the Lord made darkness cover the earth (see Ex. 10:21).

50:4 The title **Lord GOD** is emphasized in this section (vv. 5, 7, 9). The Lord educated the Servant's **tongue**. The word **learned** is translated elsewhere as "disciple" (8:16). **The** Lord **awakens** the Servant's **ear to hear**.

50:5 opened: The opening of the ear canal as a symbol for hearing and obeying.

50:6 People sometimes **struck** the **back** of a fool. Pulling someone's **beard** was a sign of contempt and disrespect (2 Sam. 10:4, 5).

50:7 The Lord is the Servant's only source of **help** (41:10; 49:8). The phrase **not be disgraced** means to be honored (49:7; 52:13). **Like a flint** indicates determination.

50:8 justifies: God would view this One as completely righteous.

50:9 the Lord GOD will help Me: See the same voice of confidence in the Lord in Ps. 118:6–12.

50:10 Who ... fears the LORD: The fear of the Lord is the beginning of true wisdom (see Prov. 1:7).

50:11 Those **who kindle a fire** means those who are self-reliant, instead of walking in the light of the Lord and His Servant (2:5; 42:6).

51:1, 2 Look links the metaphor of v. 1 with its interpretation in v. 2. The metaphors **rock** and **pit** are interpreted in v. 2 as referring to **Abraham and Sarah.**

51:3 Zion replaced **Eden.** Both were places of fellowship with God, free from sin, and guarded by cherubim.

51:4 The Servant is the **light of the peoples** (42:6; 49:6; John 3:17, 18).

51:5 The day of the Lord is **near. wait:** The verb translated *wait* has to do with confident expectation and active hope (40:31; Ps. 40:1).

51:6 The old cosmos will **vanish away** and **grow old** (34:4; Heb. 1:10, 11), **and those who dwell in it will die** (v. 8). **Righteousness,** a synonym for **salvation** in Isaiah will last forever (45:17; 56:1).

51:7 In whose heart is My law refers to those who are bound to God by the provisions of the New Covenant (42:6; Jer. 31:33). The **reproach** of the exiles anticipates the rejection of the Servant (50:4–11).

51:8 righteousness ... forever ... salvation: The interrelationship of salvation, righteousness, and eternality can also be seen in v. 6.

51:9 Awake implies that the Lord appeared to be asleep (40:27; Ps. 44:23). Isaiah's prayer is based on God's promise (50:2), and addressed to God's strong **arm** (41:10; 51:5). **Rahab** was a mythical **serpent** that resisted God's creation of the universe.

51:10, 11 The Lord's miracle at the Red Sea (Ex. 14:21, 22) is probably represented by the imagery of a pagan myth in which the **sea** opposed the creating deity. The probable allusion is supported by **the ... deep,** a term used for the primeval chaotic waters of Gen. 1:2.

51:12 The Lord responds to the double imperative of v. 9, "Awake, awake," with the doubled pronoun **I, even I.**

51:13 oppressor: For a graphic depiction of the punishment of Israel's oppressors, see 49:26.

51:14 Captive exile literally refers to the exiles in Babylon.

51:15 Who divided the sea ... roared: The sea represents all that is evil and in opposition to the Lord (Ps. 93).

51:16 Your mouth refers to the words of the Servant (41:9; 44:26; 50:4).

51:17, 18 Awake, awake: The same double imperative is found in v. 9 (contrast 40:1). **drunk ... the cup:** For similar imagery see Jer. 25:15–29; Lam. 4:21; Ezek. 23:31–34.

51:19, 20 These two things refers to the desolation of the land and the destruction of the people.

51:21–23 The cause of drunkenness was not **wine,** but the **cup of trembling,** the terror of God's judgment. **those who afflict you:** Israel's oppressors would be made to drink "the cup of ... fury" (v. 22).

52:1 Holy city contrasts with **uncircumcised** and **unclean** Babylon. **Jerusalem** (1:8; 40:1, 9) is commanded to awake because she is forever free of her despicable oppressors. **Zion:** The exiles are identified by their home city (40:1, 9). Zion's **strength** is like **beautiful garments** that adorn a queen mother (61:10).

52:2, 3 Arise ... sit down evokes the image of a queen ascending her throne. **Loose yourself:** For similar images of freed captives, see 42:7; 48:20; 51:14.

52:4 to dwell there: The wording suggests that Israel was dependent on Egypt's hospitality; but the text assumes the Egyptians betrayed that trust. **Without cause** means that Israel had not wronged either **Egypt** or Assyria.

52:5 God's justice demands that those who make Israel **wail** will be punished.

52:6 Know My name: The Lord glorifies His name by predicting and fulfilling the promise of redemption pledged in v. 3.

52:7 The vision is of the **feet** of the one who runs across **mountains** to the city waiting for **good news** or **glad tidings.** The message **Your God reigns** stands behind all history.

52:8 Your watchmen refers to those who long for salvation (21:11; 62:6).

52:9, 10 The LORD has made bare His holy arm in order to fight majestically.

52:11 In the first Exodus, Israel carried out silver and gold from Egypt; in the second Exodus, the priestly nation would **bear the vessels** made from those elements (2 Kin. 25:14, 15; Ezra 1:7–11; 5:14, 15).

52:12 Before and **rear guard** are allusions to the pillar of cloud and fire that protected Israel. **the LORD ... the God of Israel:** The pillar of cloud and fire actually stood for the Lord Himself (Ex. 33:9–11).

52:13 Exalted and extolled and be very high may refer to three successive events, describing the Servant's resurrection, ascension, and glorification.

52:14 So His visage was marred ... more than the sons of men: He would be so disfigured that He would no longer look human.

52:15 The **nations** are represented by their **kings. Shut their mouths** is a token of stunned respect. **For what had not been**

told ... they shall consider: Romans 15:21 refers to this passage.

53:1 Who has believed: The word **report** is related to the verb "they heard" in 52:15. **Our** refers to the believing remnant in Israel. **Arm** refers to God's great work (40:10; 52:10; Ps. 118:22, 23).

53:2 A root out of dry ground suggests Christ's rejection by Israel (49:4; 50:6). **No form or comeliness** indicates that the Servant did not have a majestic manner.

53:3 He is despised and rejected: For related references describing the rejection of the Servant, see 42:2; 49:7; 50:6 (compare Mark 9:12). **Man of sorrows:** Because He is a "Man of sorrows," He is able to comfort those who experience sorrow.

53:4 He has borne: Jesus came to suffer and die for the sins of others. **Griefs**—or pain—and **sorrows**—or sickness—refer to the consequences of sin. The people considered Christ to have been **smitten by God** because the law said, "he who is hanged [on a tree] is accursed of God" (Deut. 21:22, 23; Gal. 3:13).

53:5 The repetition of the pronouns **He, Him,** and **His** for **our** and **we** underscores the fact that the Servant suffered in our place. **Peace** sums up the Servant's ministry of reconciliation. (2 Cor. 5:17–21). By saying that they were **healed** (v. 4), the remnant expressed its faith in what God had announced in 52:13.

53:6 All we like sheep have gone astray: For a New Testament perspective, see 1 Pet. 2:25.

53:7 Opened not His mouth speaks of the Servant's willingness to die for sinners **as a lamb to the slaughter.**

53:8 cut off from the land of the living: This language clearly indicates that the Servant would die.

53:9 Often in Hebrew poetry, **the rich** appear as synonymous with **the wicked. at His death:** The Hebrew term *death* is in the plural, as a focus on the deep significance of Christ's death.

53:10 it pleased the LORD: The Old Testament pointed to the doctrine of the atonement long before Jesus died for our sins. The Father was *pleased* that His Son should die because it would cover the sins of many and reconcile them to Himself (see v. 11). **Offering** refers to the "trespass offering," the sacrifice of a ram for the Lord's atonement for sin.

53:11 Knowledge means having insight into one's mission (see 52:13). **Justify** means to acquit from guilt and declare righteous (5:23).

53:12 As the great King, the Lord will **divide the spoil** of victory with His Servant (41:8; 52:13). **Great** and **strong** correspond to the Servant's condition after His rejection, suffering, and death.

54:1 The increase that began in the restoration from Exile (51:1–3) continues today, for the New Testament applies this verse to "the heavenly Jerusalem" (Heb. 12:22), "the mother of us all" (Gal. 4:26, 27). Salvation depends on sovereign grace.

54:2 The Lord encourages Zion, the mother of His people, to **enlarge** the family **tent** for her many children (49:19, 20).

54:3 Expand is an allusion to Gen. 28:14, where the same Hebrew word is translated "spread abroad."

54:4 The shame of your youth refers to Israel's infidelity., that led to the Egyptian and Assyrian oppression (52:4; Jer. 31:19; Ezek. 16:1–6). **The reproach of your widowhood** refers to the Babylonian exile (vv. 6–8).

54:5 The titles **LORD of hosts** (1:9), **Redeemer** (41:14), and **God of the whole earth** show that God did not Israel permanently (v. 7).

54:6 Like a woman forsaken ... you were refused refers to Zion's experience in Exile (40:27; 49:14; 50:1).

54:7 God's anger against His elect is **for a mere moment** (26:20; Ps. 30:5). **Great mercies** speaks of the affections of God in nurturing, maternal terms.

54:8 I will have mercy: That is, "I will love you as only a mother can love."

54:9, 10 As the Lord had **sworn** to **Noah** that **the waters ... would no longer cover the earth** (Gen. 9:11), so He swore to Zion after the Exile that His **covenant of peace** (42:6; Ezek. 34:25) would not **be removed.**

54:11, 12 walls of precious stones: For a more detailed description of the New Jerusalem, see Rev. 21:18–21. The **afflicted one** is Zion or Jerusalem (51:21).

54:13 The **children ... taught by the LORD** include those taught by Christ.

54:14–17 The **tongue** that speaks judgment you will **condemn.** The accusers are operating not in the Spirit of God, but in breaking unity and bringing in division. (50:7–9; 1 Cor. 1:20).

55:1, 2 Ho is an exclamation of pity. **Thirsts** is a metaphor for desiring what satisfies a person's spirit (41:17; 44:3). **Waters** is a metaphor for the enjoyment of salvation in God (John 4:10–14). **Wine and milk** are symbols of complete satisfaction (v. 2). **You who have no money ... buy** expresses that salvation is a free gift for those who desire it.

55:3 Incline your ear and **Hear** are synonyms for **come to Me.** The **everlasting covenant** (54:10) refers to the Davidic covenant and to the New Covenant. **The sure mercies of David** are God's promises of an eternal Offspring, throne, and kingdom (2 Sam. 7:12–16). The pronoun **Me** includes the Servant of the Lord, Jesus the Messiah (48:16; 61:1).

55:4, 5 God's fulfillment of the promises to the house of David serves as a **witness** to the nations (43:10, 12; 44:8). Jesus Christ is a **leader ... for the people** (42:6; 49:6; Dan. 9:25; Heb. 2:10; 12:2).

55:6, 7 To **seek the LORD** is to seek His Word (Amos 5:6, 14; Acts 17:27).

55:8, 9 God's gracious **thoughts** exceed all human imagination (64:4; Rom. 11:33; 1 Cor. 2:9; Eph. 3:20). No one can fathom the depths of His wisdom.

55:10, 11 God's **word** like rainfall produces fruit (Ps. 147:15–20). Just as water enlivens a withering rose, God's word produces life in the hearts of sinners.

55:12 The **singing** of the elements of creation is a way of describing the singing of God's people. The rejoicing of the people at the Lord's salvation will be so full that it will seem that **mountains, hills,** and **trees** join in the chorus and applause (14:7, 8; 44:23).

55:13 Instead of the thorn shall come up the

cypress tree: This symbolizes the replacement of judgment with salvation. **Everlasting sign** recalls the rainbow after the Flood (19:20; Gen. 9:8–17).

56:1 about to come: God's salvation is always near (51:5; Phil. 4:5). **My righteousness** is a synonym for **My salvation** (41:2; 45:8; 46:13; 51:6).

56:2 Keeps from defiling the Sabbath Since keeping the Sabbath revealed clear commitment to the Lord, it was closely associated with righteousness and justice.

56:3 In speaking of the proselyte **who joined himself to the LORD,** Isaiah was prophesying of foreigners who would be converted to the worship of the true Lord (see 44:5). and thus be counted among those "born in Zion" (see Ps. 87).

56:4, 5 eunuchs: Probably some of the male exiles were castrated so that they could serve in the Babylonian and Persian courts (39:7; Dan. 1:3). **A place and a name** may be rephrased as "a memorial monument." For Isaiah, this memorial is **better than that of sons and daughters** because it symbolizes an **everlasting name,** or everlasting life, in the temple.

56:6, 7 house of prayer: Inclusion in the covenant community involves intimate communion with God. **for all nations:** People of other nations who came to a living faith in God were met with a **joyful** welcome.

56:8 Outcasts refers to the exiles (11:11, 12).

56:9 The **beasts** summoned to attack the ungodly community are hostile nations.

56:10 The pronoun **His** refers to the Lord. **Watchmen,** those who ought to warn the city of approaching danger, refers to prophets (21:6; Jer. 6:17; Ezek. 3:17; 33:2–7) who do not fear God. The ungodly watchmen leave the people defenseless.

56:11, 12 greedy dogs: The dog was not highly regarded in biblical culture. **Shepherds** is a metaphor for rulers (40:11; Ezek. 34:1–6).

57:1, 2 Peace here refers to the final state of the righteous who **rest** in their deathbeds (3:10, 11; 53:5; Phil. 1:21–23). No one understood that the righteous were being spared the judgment to come (2 Kin. 22:19, 20).

57:3, 4 Adulterer and **harlot** allude to the perverse Canaanite fertility rites that threatened the culture of ancient Israel.

57:5 Green tree was associated with pagan fertility rites. **Slaying the children** was associated with the worship of Molech and with demon worship.

57:6 Immoral idolatry was the people's **portion** or **lot,** instead of the Lord (Deut. 4:19, 20; Ps. 16:5; 142:5).

57:7 A **high mountain** refers to a place for idolatrous practices (Jer. 3:6; Ezek. 16:16; Mic. 1:3–5). The word **bed** is associated with sexual aspects of idolatry (Ezek. 23:17; Hos. 4:13). **sacrifice:** Animal and grain offerings were also part of pagan worship.

57:8 Remembrance may refer to a pagan cultic symbol in the home. **made a covenant:** is here used in the context of obscene behavior associated with pagan worship. **nudity:** The Hebrew word is the regular term for "hand." Here it appears to be a euphemism for the male genitals.

57:9 King probably refers to the Ammonite god Molech (1 Kin. 11:7), whose name means "king." **Sheol** here alludes to the gods of the underworld.

57:10 There is no hope: The people found a counterfeit **life** in immorality and idolatry that would only lead to permanent death.

57:11 Lied here refers to infidelity to the Lord. The Lord **held** His **peace** by not sending judgment immediately (42:14; 48:9; 2 Pet. 3:9).

57:12 your righteousness: Here this phrase is stated in sarcasm or irony (58:2, 3; 64:6).

57:13 Let your ... idols deliver you: The thought is pitiful (44:17). **the wind will carry them all away:** The idols are like worthless chaff (Ps. 1:4). **puts his trust:** This verb is used of a little chick finding shelter under its mother's wings (4:6; 25:4; Ruth 2:12).

57:14 The phrase **one shall say** resembles "The voice of one crying" (40:2). **Heap it up** resembles "Every valley shall be exalted" (40:4). **Prepare the way** repeats the appeal of 40:3 (see also 11:16; 35:8–10; 62:10). **Stumbling block** probably refers to the idolatry described in vv. 3–13.

57:15 High and Lofty may be rephrased as

"Exceedingly Lofty" (2:11; 6:1; 52:13). God is above everyone—perfect and holy. **inhabits eternity:** Not only is God eternal, without beginning or ending, He transcends time itself. In this way He is able to give all of His time to each of His people. **High and holy** may be rephrased as "unsearchably high" (32:15; 33:5, 16). **Contrite and humble** may be rephrased as "genuinely humble," referring to those who submit and repent under God's judgment (Ps. 34:17, 18; 51:17; 1 Pet. 5:6).

57:16 God **will not contend forever** because humans will always **fail.**

57:17 Covetousness violates God's covenant (56:11; Ps. 119:36; Jer. 22:17).

57:18 I ... will heal: The Lord is the Physician (30:26). **Mourners** refers to those who lament the destruction of Jerusalem (66:10).

57:19 Peace, peace indicates "genuine peace." Contrast the false use of this phrase in Jer. 6:13, 14; 8:10, 11.

57:20 The fate of **the wicked** is also described in 56:9–12; 57:3–13. **troubled sea:** For a similar analogy comparing the wicked to turbulent waters, see Jude 13.

57:21 There is no peace ... for the wicked: This phrase is also found in 48:22.

58:1 Isaiah was to alert the people as loudly and clearly as a **trumpet. Transgression** is related to the verb translated "rebelled" in 1:2.

58:2 Ordinance is translated "justice" in 56:1. The hypocritical religionists **delight in approaching God** in ritual worship (29:13).

58:3, 4 Formerly, the nation **fasted** in times of national calamity (Jer. 36:9; Joel 1:14); later, fasting became part of the liturgical calendar. This sermon may have been delivered on the Day of Atonement when the people of Israel **afflicted** their **souls** (v. 10; Lev. 16:29). Paradoxically, Israel finds **pleasure** in fasting, but not in keeping the Sabbath (vv. 13, 14). The accusations, **you ... exploit all your laborers** and **you fast for strife and debate,** expose the hypocrisy of the people's worship. Instead of ceasing their normal pursuits and setting the day aside to fast and pray, they **strike with the fist** the laborer who does not work.

58:5 The people's fast was not **an acceptable day to the LORD** because it focused on

self-righteousness and not on justice for others. **Bow down** and **spread out** refer to the mourning ceremonies which accompanied fasting (Joel 1:13, 14). **Like a bulrush** is meant to signify humility (42:3).

58:6 To loose, to undo, to let ... go free, and **break every yoke** are synonyms of genuine righteousness (Ezek. 18:16–18). *Yoke* is a metaphor for social oppression.

58:7 The poor who are cast out refers to those whose lands and houses were expropriated in payment of debts.

58:8 The **light** dawned with the advent of Christ (v. 10; 9:2; 10:17; 59:9; 60:1–3; Luke 1:78, 79). **Righteousness** refers to salvation (56:1). **The glory of the LORD** probably alludes to the pillar of cloud and fire in the desert (4:5, 6; Ex. 13:21; 14:20). **rear guard:** A marching army needs an alert rear defense (see also 52:12).

58:9 The pointing of the finger was a sinister gesture (Prov. 6:13).

58:10 The afflicted soul here contrasts with the hypocritical affliction described in v. 3.

58:11 A watered garden and a perennial **spring** are similes for prosperity and the blessings of God's salvation.

58:12 Build the old waste places restored exiles had the spiritual and economic resources to rebuild Judah.

58:13 Doing your pleasure probably refers to commerce (vv. 3, 4; Amos 8:5). **Holy day** clearly indicates that in vv. 2–9 the Lord was not rejecting ritual altogether (see 66:23).

58:14 This blessing is based on the Song of Moses in Deut. 32:9, 13.

59:1, 2 The Lord's **ear** is able to **hear.**

59:3 your hands are defiled with blood: For similar passages on the people's guilt, see 1:15; 59:7. **Your lips have spoken lies:** For related passages, see 33:15; 59:13; Mark 7:21–23; Rom. 3:10–18; Gal. 5:19–21.

59:4 Calls for justice probably means to help the poor in the law courts. No one would **plead** the case of the poor fairly (1:17; 5:23; 59:14). **Conceive evil and bring forth iniquity** is translated "conceive trouble and bring forth futility" in Job 15:35.

59:5 Hatch ... eggs and **weave the ... web** signify the deliberate, calculated wickedness in the courts (32:7; 59:4).

59:6 Their webs will not become garments illustrates the futility and the ultimate failure of the schemes depicted in v. 5.

59:7, 8 This passage is cited in Rom. 3:15–17 to document the universality of sin. **Their feet ... make haste to shed innocent blood:** The people **run** without forethought into evil (Prov. 1:16).

59:9 With the pronoun **us,** Isaiah identified himself with his people's sins (Ezra 9:6, 7; Dan. 9:5). The words **justice** and **righteousness** refer to God's salvation (46:13). **Light** and **darkness:** The Book of Isaiah makes use of the words *light* and *darkness* as a way to contrast eternal life and death, truth and falsehood.

59:10 The people **grope ... like the blind** in fulfillment of the covenant curse on those who were disobedient (Deut. 28:29).

59:11–13 The people **growl** out of frustration. **moan:** For related images of the people's despair involving doves, see 38:14; Ezek. 7:16.

59:14 Justice and **righteousness** speak here of ethical conduct (v. 4).

59:15, 16 Justice refers here to **salvation** (vv. 9, 10). The Lord, using the first person, expresses the thought of this passage in 63:5. **no man:** God's salvation does not depend on humans (Ezek. 22:30). **His own arm** represents the Lord as a warrior. **Righteousness** refers to the Lord's victorious salvation (46:13; 51:6, 8; 56:1).

59:17 The Lord's **breastplate** and **helmet** are taken up by His saints in their battle against the devil (Eph. 6:14–17).

59:18 Recompense to His enemies is translated "fully repays His enemies" in 66:6. **Coastlands** indicates that the Lord's adversaries were distant nations (41:1).

59:19 From the west ... from the rising of the sun is another way of saying everywhere. **When the enemy comes** could also mean "when He comes as an enemy" (35:4).

59:20 The Redeemer will come in the person of Jesus Christ. **turn from transgression:** For similar appeals to turn from sin in the prophecies of Isaiah see 1:17–19; 30:15; 31:6; 59:9–15.

59:21 Them refers to the repentant (v. 20). **My Spirit:** For similar references see 11:2;

30:1; 42:1; 48:16; 61:1. **You** and **your** in this verse are singular, probably with reference to Isaiah. God's Spirit and **words** would be given to Israel. (44:3).

60:1 Arise is addressed to Zion (v. 14). **shine:** Zion is both the recipient of God's **light** and the reflector of it.

60:2 As was the case during the Exodus from Egypt, **darkness** is on the wicked while God's light is on His people (Ex. 10:23). **Deep darkness** elsewhere describes a cloud enfolding the glory of God (Ex. 20:21), and serves as a warning of His impending judgment (Jer. 13:16).

60:3 They come to heavenly Zion to bring tribute (vv. 5, 11, 13). Christ is the **light** to kings (42:6; 49:6).

60:4 .**Your sons ... your daughters:** this is addressed to the few restored exiles and looks to a greater return that is still in the future (11:11).

60:5 become radiant: See "shine" in v. 1. **wealth of the Gentiles:** For similar phrases, see Hag. 2:7; Zech. 14:14.

60:6, 7 Camels carried **gold and incense. Midian** was famous as a caravan leader and trader (Gen. 37:28, 36). **Sheba was** renowned for its wealth. **proclaim the praises:** The nations would not bring just their wealth; they would accompany their gifts with public, vocal praise.

60:8 The ships' sails resemble a fast-moving cloud and **doves** returning **to their roosts.**

60:9 The **ships of Tarshish** will bring the remnant home.

60:10 Wrath is translated "indignation" in 34:2.

60:11 Zion's **gates shall be open continually** to accommodate the great influx of the **wealth of the Gentiles** (v. 5).

60:12 The nation and kingdom that does not serve Zion **shall perish.** In the coming kingdom, there will be no opposition to the reign of the Savior-King.

60:13, 14 The **glory of Lebanon** adorned the first temple (1 Kin. 5:10, 18) so it will **beautify** the temple again (vv. 5–7). The **place of** the Lord's **feet** was the ark of the covenant (1 Chr. 28:2); later it was the temple (Ezek. 43:7), and then the whole earth (66:1).

60:15 The new sanctuary will be greater than the old one because it is **eternal,** rich, and spiritual (vv. 17, 18).

60:16 milk the breast of kings: This line, representing great wealth, demonstrates clearly that the prophet was using figurative language.

60:17 The new temple will be made of precious metals—**gold, silver, bronze,** and **iron**—symbolizing its great and enduring wealth. **Peace** and **righteousness** are personified as **officers** and **magistrates** respectively (26:3; 48:18).

60:18 God's **Salvation** and Israel's **Praise** will be the city's defense (Zech. 2:4, 5).

60:19, 20 These verses describe the new heaven and earth (Rev. 21:1, 23; 22:5).

60:21 In the new Zion, **people shall all be righteous** (4:3; Rev. 21:27). Though the exiles were back in the land (49:8; 54:3), they looked to a time, when Israel would **inherit the land forever.**

60:22 A little one shall become a thousand: The inhabitants of the new Zion will be prolific (54:3; Lev. 26:8).

61:1 the LORD has anointed: The name Messiah, or Christ in Greek, means the "Anointed One." **Poor** also means "humble," which like **brokenhearted,** indicates those who confidently hope in God in spite of their present distress (11:4; Ps. 34:18; 51:17). **Proclaim liberty** probably alludes to the official inauguration of the "Year of Release" or Jubilee (Lev. 25:10). **Captives** refers to those in bondage to wickedness. **Those who are bound** is translated "prisoners" in 49:9, here it means "captives."

61:2 The acceptable year of the LORD corresponds to "the day of salvation" (49:8) and "the year of My redeemed" (63:4).

61:3 A host lavished on a guest the **oil of joy** (Ps. 23:5; 45:7; Luke 7:46). **He may be glorified:** For similar references see 44:23; 49:5.

61:4, 5 They refers to Jews (58:12) and Gentiles (60:10). **desolations of many generations:** See 58:12; 60:10.

61:6 priests of the LORD: With Christ, they will make intercession for sinners (53:12; Ex. 19:6; 1 Pet. 2:9; Rev. 1:6). **Servants** here means "ministers," a synonym for "priests." (1 Kin. 8:11).

61:7, 8 Everlasting joy: For other references to eternal joy, see 35:10; 51:11; 60:19, 20.

61:9 Shall be known has the sense of "shall be renowned." **among the Gentiles ... whom the LORD has blessed:** This section alludes to the fulfillment of the promises made to Abraham (41:8; 51:2; Gen. 12:3).

61:10 I and the parallel **My soul** refer to personified Zion. **Rejoice** is translated "joy" in v. 3 (see also 65:18). **Clothed** signifies the Servant's new glorified status or condition (47:2; 52:1; 59:17).

61:11 spring forth: This phrase is also found in 42:9; 43:19; 45:8 to describe the coming of God's salvation. **Righteousness** here means "deliverance" (54:17).

62:1, 2 The repetition of **righteousness** (v. 1) shows that the divine oracle and the prophet's comment are linked. **A new name** signifies a new status.

62:3 Zion is **a crown of glory,** or **royal diadem, in the hand of the LORD.**

62:4, 5 The words **Forsaken** and **Desolate** are symbolic names for Jerusalem under judgement. **Hephzibah** (My Delight is in Her) and **Beulah** (Married) are symbolic names denoting blessing.

62:6, 7 I refers to the Lord (vv. 1, 8). **Watchmen** refers to prophets (56:10). **You who make mention of the LORD** is Isaiah's synonym for "watchmen" and shows that the prophets were intercessors. The phrases **do not keep silent** and **give Him no rest** relate the prophets' prayer to the Lord's promises in v. 1 (see 64:12; 65:6).

62:8 no longer: This phrase gives assurance that the covenantal blessings will outlast the curses.

62:9 in My holy courts: This phrase anticipates the rebuilding of the temple (Lev. 23:39, 40; Deut. 12:17, 18; 14:22–27; 16:9–17).

62:10 Gates probably refers to those in the "holy courts" (v. 9). The prophet commanded the worshipers of v. 9 to pass through the gates in order to praise the Lord. **Prepare the way** means to encourage the people to come to the temple for worship (40:3, 4; 57:14). **Stones** refers to any impediment to worship (57:14). **Lift up a banner** (5:26; 11:10) is an encouragement to all **peoples** to worship God.

62:11 Proclaimed to the end of the world links this verse with "a banner for the peoples" in v. 10. The verb **say** is plural, indicating that a number of people will declare this announcement of salvation to Jerusalem.

62:12 The pronoun **they** refers to the Gentiles (v. 2). **The Holy People:** For similar descriptions of the redeemed, see 4:3; Ex. 19:6.

63:1 The word **comes** links this verse with 62:11. **Edom** epitomized Israel's enemies (Ps. 137:7; Lam. 4:21, 22; Ezek. 25:12; 35:1–15; Obad. 13, 14); it was famous for its wine-making (see v. 3 for a reference to wine). Note that the text does not say God vanquished Edom, but rather the "peoples" (vv. 3, 6). **garments:** See the warrior's garments in 59:17. **Bozrah** was the chief town of Edom (34:6; Jer. 49:13).

63:2 The **apparel** will be **red** from blood-stains.

63:3 I is applied to Christ in Rev. 19:15. **The winepress** represents the battle.

63:4–6 year of My redeemed: This phrase alludes to the "law of redemption" of slaves and property (61:2; Lev. 25).

63:7 I will mention: Isaiah publicly proclaims God's saving mercies (Ps. 77:12; 89:1). The plural words **lovingkindnesses** and **praises** refer to the Lord's many acts of love and loyalty to His people. The word *lovingkindnesses* is translated "sure mercies" in 55:3 (see also Ps. 89:1).

63:8 In the Hebrew Bible, the term **My people** is used in two ways: (1) those who were united nationally to God by blood and history through Abraham's flesh (48:1; Ex. 3:7), and (2) for those who were united to Him inwardly through Abraham's faith and obedience (Lev. 26:12; Deut. 29:13).

63:9 Their affliction probably refers to God's sympathy for His people in Egypt (Ex. 2:25; 3:7) and at the time of the judges (Judg. 10:16). **He was afflicted:** God shares the hurt of His people (Ex. 2:23–25). **Bore** and **carried** are allusions to Ex. 19:4 (see Deut. 1:31; 32:10–12).

63:10 rebelled: This verb means "to be contentious" (Num. 20:10; Ps. 78:40; 106:33, 43). The **Holy Spirit** is referred to from time to time in the Hebrew Scriptures, and several times in the Book of Isaiah (11:2; 42:1).

63:11 Days of old refers to the period of the Exodus and the Wilderness. **The sea** is an allusion to the Red Sea (50:2; Ex. 14:21–29). **Shepherd,** referring to Moses, is plural. Christ is the greater Shepherd (John 10:11; Heb. 13:20; 1 Pet. 5:4). **Put His Holy Spirit within them** is an allusion to Num. 11:17, 25.

63:12 Glorious arm is an allusion to Ex. 15:6 (see also 41:13; 51:9). **Dividing the water** is a reference to Ex. 14:16, 21 (see Ps. 78:13).

63:13, 14 The account of the Exodus and settlement of the land is concluded with two images. The first is **a horse** moving sure-footedly across the sea bottom as through a **wilderness;** the second is **a beast,** meaning "a domesticated herd," returning from grazing on mountainsides **into the valley … to rest** (Deut. 12:9).

63:15 Heaven refers to God's universal rule over space and time (Ps. 11:4–6). The pronoun **me** is a personified Israel (59:9–15).

63:16 God is their **Father** because He created them as a nation (Deut. 32:6; Jer. 3:4, 19). **Abraham** and **Israel,** the people's human fathers (51:2), were limited in their knowledge by time and space, in contrast to the Lord, the people's **Father** and **Redeemer from Everlasting** (41:14).

63:17 us: Isaiah identifies himself with his people (59:9–15). The Lord, confirming the people in their sin, **hardened** their hearts (6:10; Ex. 4:21; Ps. 95:8).

63:18, 19 Called by Your name signifies the Lord's ownership of the people (Deut. 28:10; Jer. 14:9).

64:1, 2 Oh, that … You would come down: This appeal for the Lord to is based on His appearances at Sinai. The image of **fire** often symbolizes God's presence especially in judgment.

64:3 Awesome things: The appearance of God is fearsome (Ex. 19:16–21; Deut. 10:21; 2 Sam. 7:23). **for which we did not look:** God's saving acts surpass expectations (Eph. 3:20).

64:4 Paul cites this verse with some changes in 1 Cor. 2:9.

64:5 You meet him … Who remembers You in Your ways: These words reinforce the idea of v. 4. The word **indeed** provides a transition from the petition to the confession of sin.

64:6 Unclean means the people were unfit for God's presence. **Filthy rags** refers to garments stained during menstruation. **As a leaf** signifies the people's human weakness.

64:7 There is no one who calls is a phrase calling attention to the people's apathy. **hidden:** God is never really "in hiding," but does obscure His presence because of sin (1:15).

64:8 But now, O Lord: These words serve as a contrast to the preceding section, the confession of sin. **We are the clay:** For being clay in the Potter's hands, see Rom. 9:20, 21.

64:9 Do not be furious claims God's promise in 54:7, 8. **Nor remember** claims God's promise in 43:25. **Please look** refers to God's "hiding" of Himself in v. 7.

64:10 cities … Zion … Jerusalem: The prophetic picture of the devastation of the land following the Babylonian invasion is used as a means of appeal to the heart of God.

64:11 Our fathers praised You suggests that the speakers are at least a generation removed from the fall of the temple.

64:12 Will You restrain Yourself: The people use the language of love to implore God to act again on their behalf.

65:1 I was sought means "I allowed Myself to be sought." **I was found** means "I allowed Myself to be found." **A nation that was not called by My name** includes the Gentiles and the remnant who "sought" God (v. 10). Together they are the servants who will be called "by another name."

65:2 I have stretched out My hands pictures God beckoning Israel to respond to Him. **All day long** suggests patience. **Rebellious** describes Israel (63:10). **Who,** repeated six times in vv. 2–5, introduces a sorry catalogue of Israel's abominable religious practices: arrogance (v. 2), open defiance (v. 3), idolatrous fertility rites (v. 3), divination (v. 4), eating unclean foods (v. 4), and blasphemous self-righteousness (v. 5).

65:3 To My face means "openly." The people did not hide their shameful practices or restrain their evil habits.

65:4 Spend the night in the tombs may refer to the practice of seeking an oracle from the dead. The Law prohibited eating **swine's flesh** (66:17; Lev. 11:7). **Abominable things** refers to other foods prohibited to Israel (Lev. 11).

65:5 I am holier than you: The idolaters regarded themselves as better than others. **Smoke** and **fire** stand for things that provoke God's anger.

65:6 It is written refers to the heavenly records. **I will not keep silence:** For a similar phrase, see 62:1.

65:7 blasphemed Me: The Israelites rejected and offended God by offering sacrifices to the false gods of other nations on the hilltops.

65:8 New wine represents the **servants** (54:17); the otherwise unproductive **cluster** represents all Israel (5:1, 2). *Servants* include "the remnant," as well as foreigners (56:6).

65:9 I will bring forth descendants is fulfilled in Christ and in all those who are found in Him (Gal. 3:16, 26–29). **Jacob** and **Judah** represent all Israel.

65:10 Sharon, in the west, and **the Valley of Achor,** in the east, denote the whole land.

65:11 The word **who** occurs four times in this verse, introducing more (vv. 2–5) of Israel's sins. These sins involved forsaking the Lord, forgetting His place of worship, worshiping **Gad,** a god of good luck, and worshiping **Meni,** a god of fate.

65:12 When I called, you did not answer contrasts with "Before they call, I will answer" in v. 24.

65:13 Behold … But: The pattern here recalls the blessings and curses on Mount Gerizim and Mount Ebal. **Eat** and **drink:** This is a festive meal accompanied by rejoicing.

63:14 Sing here develops the idea of rejoicing in v. 13 (see also 12:1–6; 35:10; 61:7).

65:15 The **chosen** (v. 9) will use the apostates' **name as a curse** by invoking the terrible fate of the apostates upon others. "The Lord make you like apostate Israel." **Another name** signifies the launching of a new era.

65:16 He who blesses himself in the earth will invoke the Lord's name, because He is the **God of truth.**

65:17, 18 I create may also be translated "I am creating" or "I am about to create." **new heavens and a new earth:** God will fashion a new cosmos that will be ready for His presence and for the enjoyment of His people. **Former** encompasses everything up to the creation of the new cosmos (Rev. 21:4). **Be glad and rejoice** means "to be openly, deliriously happy." Saints are called upon to celebrate by faith the coming glorious salvation (66:10). **Create Jerusalem** signifies that it will be entirely new.

65:19 My people: This title for the citizens of Jerusalem is also used in 63:8. **weeping shall no longer he heard:** For similar ideas about God's coming salvation, see 25:8; 35:10; 51:11.

65:20 the child shall die one hundred years old: On one level, these words indicate a return in the coming kingdom to the extended life spans that are noted before the Flood (Gen. 5). It appears that people will not be affected by disease and aging in the same way as in our present world.

65:21, 22 houses … vineyards: The life of blessing in the coming kingdom is presented in terms that would have been readily understood by the people of Isaiah's day (Mic. 4:4). Industry will not be limited to these twin pursuits, but the happy, blessed life is indicated by them. **As the days of a tree** indicates longevity and stability and the words **long enjoy** reinforces these ideals.

65:23 They shall not labor in vain: These words speak of God reversing the curse.

65:24 Before they call, I will answer expresses the truth that there will be no delay between petition and praise.

65:25 The figures represent the restoration of nature and the coming of universal peace. **Dust shall be the serpent's food** indicates the specific curse in Gen. 3:14 will be consummated.

66:1 The Lord has no need for a man-made temple because **heaven** and **earth**—the whole cosmos—is His sanctuary (40:22). **footstool:** The resting place for the "feet" of the Lord is the earth. **Where is the house:**

No place can accommodate the transcendent God (1 Kin. 8:27). **The place of My rest** refers to the temple (1 Chr. 28:2; Ps. 132:8, 14).

66:2 Those things refers to everything in the universe. **I look:** God seeks true worshipers (John 4:24). **Contrite spirit … trembles at My word** is similar to Jesus' phrase "in spirit and truth" (John 4:24).

66:3 Breaks a dog's neck may refer to a pagan practice; in any case, the dog was regarded as an unclean animal, a detestable scavenger. The sacrifice of **a bull, a lamb, a grain offering,** and **incense** was considered to be **their own ways** because the worshipers lacked a contrite spirit. It was as if **their soul** delighted **in their abominations.**

66:4 their fears: This is the judgment spelled out in vv. 15, 16, 24. **when I called … I do not delight:** This passage echoes 65:12.

66:5 Your brethren who hated you: These words intensify the opposition encountered in ch. 65. **Let the LORD be glorified** represents the false worshiper's hypocritical righteousness (v. 17). **Cast … out** of the temple, the true worshipers went into the world and brought back Gentiles (v. 18). **Joy** is spoken sarcastically (Ps. 22:8). The persecutors **shall be ashamed** and the persecuted shall "rejoice" (v. 10).

66:6 Isaiah heard the **sound of** battle **noise** proceeding from the **city** and the **temple** (13:4). **His enemies** refers to the self-righteous idolaters persecuting God's servants.

66:7, 8 Before she … gave birth represents the birth of the community from the cast-out worshipers as coming so quickly that it will be without pain. At times, Zion is pictured as the daughter of the Lord (1:8); here she is the mother of His people. The **male child** and **her children** may refer to Christ and His Church.

66:9, 10 The rhetorical questions introduced by the words **shall I** guarantee the prophecy of vv. 7, 8. God finishes what He begins (Phil. 1:6).

66:11 Through the joyful faith of v. 10, saints before Christ's coming ate figuratively at a banquet (65:13).

66:12 The pronoun **her** refers to Mother

Jerusalem (vv. 7, 8). **You** refers to true worshipers and their offspring (v. 22), the beloved children of Mother Jerusalem.

66:13 I will comfort you: Here God Himself is the comforting "Mother" (2 Cor. 1:3, 4).

66:14 Heart and **bones** refer to mental and physical health (Ps. 6:2; 109:18).

66:15 This verse is a picture of God's judgment. **Fire** is the lightning; **His chariots** are the storm clouds (Deut. 33:26; Ps. 18:10). **Like a whirlwind** depicts the speed and strength of the Lord's coming (Jer. 4:13).

66:16 The Divine Warrior comes with **fire** and **sword** (Luke 21:24; Rev. 19:11–15). **All flesh** refers to all of the false worshipers described in this chapter (Jer. 9:2).

66:17 This summarizes the abominable practices of the false worshipers (65:2–5; 66:3).

66:18 Their works and their thoughts probably refers to the right acts and spirit of the true worshipers, on whom God looks with favor. **My glory** probably refers to God's presence in His temple (Ezek. 11:22, 23; 44:4).

66:19 The **sign** may be the deliverance of the true worshipers as judgment falls on the false. **Those … who escape** may refer to those who escape God's slaughter (vv. 16, 17), but more likely to those who escape persecution. **declare My glory among the Gentiles:** For another prophecy by Isaiah of the spread of God's glory throughout the world, see 24:14–16.

66:20, 21 horses … camels: Animals represent the diverse countries from which they come. The Gentiles are likened to **a clean vessel.**

66:22 Your descendants … remain guarantees the continuity of true Israel (65:9).

66:23 From one New Moon to another refers to all time. **All flesh** refers Jew and Gentile (vv. 16, 24). Through all time and from all the earth, true **worship** will be offered to God.

66:24 Their worm … is not quenched depicts eternal punishment (48:22; 57:20). The imagery derives from the Valley of Hinnom that was Jerusalem's garbage dump, where unclean corpses decomposed and were burned.

Jeremiah

Introduction

The Book of Jeremiah reveals the inner struggles of a prophet of God. In "confessions" such as those in 15:10–21; 20:7–18, Jeremiah reveals his inner turmoil about his call to prophetic ministry. Yet despite his anguish, Jeremiah fulfilled his ministry of proclaiming God's judgment against the people of Judah for their idolatry, their unfaithfulness to the covenant, and their disobedience of His will. Jeremiah serves to this day as an example of someone who remained faithful to the word of God despite countless hardships.

Jeremiah's writing ministry began in the fourth year of the reign of King Jehoiakim of Judah in 605 B.C. (see 36:1, 2). The book was completed sometime after the fall of Jerusalem in 586 B.C. It consists of warnings that the nation would fall to the pagan Babylonians unless the people turned from their idolatry back to worship of the one true God.

Just as the prophet predicted, Jerusalem's walls were breached in the fourth month of 586 B.C. One month later, the temple was burned, along with the palaces, houses, and other administrative buildings. An additional 4,600 Jerusalemites were deported to Babylon. Gedaliah was appointed governor of Judah at Riblah. Jeremiah, who had been imprisoned by Zedekiah, was released and sent to serve under Gedaliah. Gedaliah was assassinated and his supporters fled to Egypt, fearful of Nebuchadnezzar's revenge. Jeremiah went with them to Egypt against his will, and there he continued to confront the Jews for their idolatry and unfaithfulness.

Jeremiah was keenly aware of the provisions of the covenant between God and Israel. The covenant bound Israel to God in a special relationship. But the covenant had two sides. Faithfulness to the Lord and the covenant would bring blessing; disobedience would result in punishment, destruction, and exile (see Deut. 27:14–28:68). Jeremiah called the people to obey the covenant and to turn from their idolatry and their unjust treatment of one another (11:6, 7).

Jeremiah's message of judgment also contained hope: a righteous remnant would be restored. The land had been defiled by the people's idolatry. The leaders had brought the nation to the brink of disaster and the people were exiled. But based on His everlasting love for Israel, God promised to bring the people back from captivity and restore them to blessing (30:18–31:6). Israel's enemies would be defeated (30:16), and the people would sing of God's goodness (31:12).

1:1 The name **Jeremiah** probably means either "The Lord Exalts" or "The Lord Establishes."

1:2 The word of the LORD came literally to Jeremiah. He did not speak out of his own imagination, as did false prophets like Hananiah (28:1, 2). Jeremiah's call to ministry came in **the thirteenth year** of Josiah, who reigned 31 years.

1:3 Jeremiah's ministry as a prophet lasted from the beginning of the reign of **Jehoiakim** (608 B.C.) to **the eleventh year of Zedekiah** and the fall of Jerusalem (586 B.C.). Gedaliah was appointed governor over Judah after the Babylonians, under Nebuchadnezzar, had deported the leading citizens of Jerusalem. Jeremiah continued ministering until he was taken unwillingly to Egypt following the assassination of Gedaliah.

1:4 The word of the Lord came: A standard way of introducing a divine oracle at the beginning of a prophetic book (see Ezek. 1:3; Hos. 1:1; Joel 1:1; Jon. 1:1; Mic. 1:1; Zeph. 1:1; Hag. 1:1; Zech. 1:1).

1:5 Jeremiah was keenly aware God's call on his life had been determined before his conception. As God's word became a reality in his life, the prophet understood that God **knew** him and had called him to proclaim a critical message at a crucial point in the history of the nation. The word *knew* refers to an intimate knowledge that comes from relationship and personal commitment. Jeremiah's role was to be a **prophet** to the nation of Judah as well as a messenger of God for all **nations.**

1:6 Like Moses, who was called to **speak** to the Pharaoh of Egypt at a decisive point in Israel's history, Jeremiah was called to address the kings of Judah and leaders of Babylon. Jeremiah's doubts about his power to speak before the nations' leaders were because of his **youth.** The word *youth* can refer to a wide range of ages—from infancy up to the teen years.

1:7, 8 Jeremiah would not **go** and **speak** alone or of his own accord, but according to the word of the Lord and with His powerful presence. The term **deliver** is used in Jeremiah to indicate the saving of the people from their captors (15:20, 21), the deliverance of the poor from their oppressors (20:13), and the safety of the prophet from possible harm before national leaders. **I am with you:** Twice in his call (see also v. 19), God reassured Jeremiah of His presence and protection.

1:9 Jeremiah is commissioned for his task and the essence of his message is outlined. **I have put My words in your mouth:** The source of Jeremiah's message was clearly the Lord, but the message would be expressed through the personality, experience, and artistry of the prophet.

1:10 I have … set you over the nations: The nations were instruments in God's purpose of revealing Himself. The Lord would use Babylon to punish Judah, and then He would use the Persians to punish Babylon. With God's words in his mouth, Jeremiah had the authority to stand before any ruler. **To root out and to pull down … To build and to plant:** Judgment and restoration were the two messages of the prophet of God.

1:11, 12 God confirmed His call to Jeremiah with two visions. The first vision involved an **almond tree,** which blossoms when other trees are still dormant. The almond tree served as a harbinger of spring, as though it "watched over" the beginning of the season. In a similar fashion, God was "watching over" His word, ready to bring judgment on Israel.

1:13, 14 The second vision God used to confirm Jeremiah's call involved a **boiling pot** that was tilted toward the south, indicating the direction in which the pot's contents would be spilled. The **calamity** suggested by this vision was an enemy attack on Judah and Jerusalem from **the north.** In 20:4, Jeremiah finally identifies this enemy as Babylon.

1:15 The calamity from the north (v. 14) would involve a siege of **Jerusalem** and **all the cities of Judah.**

1:16 One of the main reasons for God's judgment on Judah and Jerusalem was Israel's worship of **other gods. Burned incense:** The Hebrew term meaning "to burn" or "to make smoke" is used 19 times in Jeremiah, all in the context of burning sacrifices to other gods. **worshiped:** The term means "to cause oneself to bow down" in honor or service of God or man. The first and foremost commandment (see Ex. 20:3) had been broken.

1:17 Prepare yourself is literally "gird up your loins," or tuck your robe in your belt so you can run (see 1 Sam. 2:4). **do not be dismayed:** If Jeremiah shrank back in terror before the men God had commanded him to confront, God Himself would bring terror into the prophet's life.

1:18 God **made** Jeremiah an impregnable **fortified city** with **bronze walls.** Jeremiah's defense system could not be battered down or tunneled under by men and armies. **kings … princes … priests … people:** This list of the various types of people in Israel suggests that the entire nation would be against Jeremiah.

1:19 The people and their leaders would **fight** against Jeremiah and his message, but they would not overcome because God Himself protects and fights for the faithful.

2:1–3 Chapter 2 is presented in the form of a covenant lawsuit, an indictment brought by God against His people (2:1—3:5). The **betrothal** period between God and Israel in the **wilderness** was a time when Israel **went after,** or worshiped, the Lord. The nation of Israel is referred to as the **firstfruits,** which rightfully belonged to God (see Deut. 26:1–11) and **holiness.**

2:4, 5 Idols means "futility," "vapor," or "worthlessness." **They … have become idolaters:** Those who serve idols, which are only vapor, become like vapor themselves.

2:6 In pursuing other gods, the people of Israel lost sight of their identity as the elect of God. They forgot how God had delivered them from oppression in Egypt and had given them food, water, and protection in the **wilderness** for forty years.

2:7 God's guiding hand had **brought** Israel into a **bountiful country,** the region of Carmel, with its luxurious trees and vineyards. Israel had enjoyed the bounty of the land flowing with milk and honey, but then turned God's beautiful **heritage** into a polluted **abomination.**

2:8 The people had not sought the Lord, nor had the **priests, rulers,** or **prophets.** Those who should have known God most intimately **did not know** Him at all. The rulers **transgressed against** God and His covenant.

2:9 Charges of apostasy and idolatry are formally presented in 2:9–13.

2:10, 11 The only nation whose god was truly God was at the same time the only nation that exchanged its God for others.

2:12, 13 God's **people** had **forsaken** (1:16) Him. God, the **fountain of living waters,** offered a limitless supply of fresh, life-giving sustenance. Instead the people chose **broken cisterns,** which were useless for storing water and useless for sustaining life.

2:14 Israel was not founded to be a **servant** or **homeborn slave.** Yet the nation that God set free from slavery and oppression had placed itself in the position of a servant, enslaved by Assyria and Egypt.

2:15 Assyria—**the young lions**—laid waste to Israel and Judah during several invasions between 734 and 701 B.C.

2:16, 17 Egypt forced Judah into a vassal relationship. The Egyptians had **broken the crown of** Israel's **head** by killing Josiah. **Noph** is Memphis, the capital of Lower Egypt. **Tahpanhes** was in the eastern Nile delta.

2:18 Sihor means "Black" and refers to the Nile River. The word **River** refers to the Euphrates, which is associated with Assyria. The people of Judah had left the everlasting fountain of God for the broken cisterns of Assyria and Egypt (v. 13).

2:19 Backslidings means "turnings." Israel had turned in every direction for help except to the true source of safety and security. The phrase **says the Lord GOD of hosts** confirms the severity of the crime and the certainty of the punishment about to befall the people of God.

2:20 Israel had **broken** its **yoke** like a beast, even though the people had promised to be faithful when they came into the land (see Josh. 24:24). The term **harlot** referrs to unfaithfulness to God, and it may also refer to the ritual prostitution of Canaanite and Phoenician fertility cults.

2:21, 22 Noble vine refers to the lush vines of the Sorek valley, which runs from Jerusalem to the Mediterranean Sea through some of the richest farmland in the country. Judah became an **alien** vine, fertilized by foreign gods (see Is. 5).

2:23–25 The picture of the wild **dromedary,** a female camel in heat, and a **wild donkey** mad with lust vividly portrays the craving of Israel for foreign gods.

2:26–30 The term **plead** recalls the charges made by God against Israel in v. 9. The people tried to *plead* their case, but Jeremiah repeated God's charge of rebellion (v. 8). God, the Sovereign Lord, **chastened** His **children** repeatedly, but they **devoured** His spokesmen the **prophets** like hungry lions.

2:31, 32 A virgin bride could hardly forget the wedding sash that was the sign of her new status. Yet God's bride Israel had forgotten her wedding adornment—God Himself.

2:33 taught the wicked women: Judah had become so skilled in adulterous ways that they could have instructed prostitutes in new methods of seduction.

2:34, 35 The blood … of the poor innocents: Provision for the poor was specifically commanded in the Law (see Deut. 15:7–11).

2:36, 37 Israel turned every direction but to the Lord. Appealing to **Egypt** would have been as fruitless as appealing to **Assyria** had been in the past. **With your hands on your head:** This was a gesture of grief and remorse—in this case, over Israel's futile pursuits.

3:1 Deuteronomy 24:1–4 forbids a man to remarry his divorced wife if she has remarried and been divorced in the meantime. The woman has been defiled by the second marriage. After forsaking God, Israel had taken many other **lovers**—that is, other gods. Yet the Lord in His mercy still extended His loving hand to His unfaithful bride.

3:2 desolate heights: This term parallels the high hills of 2:20. Upon these barren heights Israel committed physical and spiritual adultery.

3:3–5 Showers and **latter rain** refer to the two types of rain that fall in Israel in the spring, from March to early April. These rains are vital in the dry land. Even the punishment of drought did not soften Israel's **harlot's forehead.** Israel was like a prostitute who was totally unashamed.

3:6 The reign of **Josiah** (640–609 B.C.) followed the idolatrous reigns of Manasseh (697–642 B.C.) and Amon (642–640 B.C.).

3:7 Return means to "return" to God in faith (5:3). Judah had witnessed Israel's refusal to repent.

3:8, 9 Adultery is forbidden (see Deut. 5:18). Because of Israel's adultery, the Lord presented her with a **certificate of divorce** based on Deut. 24:1–4. As a consequence, in 722 B.C. Israel was taken captive by Assyria, and Samaria was destroyed. Judah looked on but did not learn from Israel's example.

3:10 Judah pretended to repent in times of distress, but did not actually turn with its **heart** to the Lord (see Deut. 6:5; 10:16). The *heart* means the people's will, mind, and emotion.

3:11 Because it had not learned from Israel's example, Judah was considered more **treacherous** than Israel.

3:12 The cry **toward the north** may indicate a summons for the northern kingdom in the days of Josiah to repent. **Return, backsliding Israel:** If the people turned in repentance (3:1, 7; 5:3), God's **anger** would not come upon them.

3:13 Iniquity refers to the breaking of the covenant commandments. Israel's rebellious iniquity is identified as the pursuit of **alien** gods, idolatry committed throughout the land.

3:14 To *marry* in this context means to become lord or master. In other words **married** describes the covenant relation between God and Israel.

3:15 shepherds: From Moses in the Old Testament to Jesus in the New, God provides faithful, devoted leaders after His own heart.

3:16 God ordained that His shepherds would lead Israel through a time of blessing,

increase in numbers, and material prosperity. In that future time, the **ark of the covenant,** would no longer be central to the true religion of Israel. God Himself would be central to Jewish worship.

3:17 Jerusalem, not the ark of the covenant, would be **The Throne of the LORD** and the focal point of the world's religion. **The name of the LORD** summarizes the essence of His character and His relationship with His people (see Ex. 3; 14; 15).

3:18 Restoration and reunification of Israel, unknown since the days of David and Solomon, would be brought about by God Himself. From the **north,** the direction from which Israel's enemies typically came, God would bring back His people and bless them in the **land** of promise, under the Lord's chosen Shepherd—the Messiah.

3:19 The possession of the **land** was always dependent on the covenant faithfulness of Israel to their God. The Lord's desire has always been to bless His people.

3:20–22 The confessions and prayers of the people were but idle words, because they had **forgotten** their God. The confession begins with acknowledgment of the Lord as God in accordance with the First Commandment (Ex. 20:2, 3).

3:23 The term **vain,** meaning "falsehood," is found thirty-seven times in Jeremiah, often in reference to idolatry and false prophecy (see 5:2; 7:4, 9).

3:24 Shame is a euphemism for idolatry, which had consumed Israel's thoughts, their flocks and fields, and even their children. The reference to children recalls the human sacrifices in the Valley of Hinnom in the days of Manasseh.

3:25 The people acknowledged the **shame** and **reproach** that they had brought upon themselves. They had **sinned against** God since their days of **youth** in the wilderness.

4:1 The term **abominations** or "detestable objects" is usually used in the context of idolatry in the Old Testament (7:30). **You shall not be moved** implies that repentant Israel would be unwavering in its faith in God.

4:2 The LORD lives: This phrase was regularly used in oaths. When spoken by those faithful to the covenant it should have been a sign of **truth, judgment,** and **righteousness.** These three terms summarize the ultimate and ideal demands of the covenant by which all men, from kings to slaves, were and will be judged. **bless themselves:** The results of Israel's justice and righteousness would have international consequences.

4:3 fallow ground: This is unused soil, not a regularly plowed field. Israel needed a new field in which to sow its seed of faithfulness, a radical departure from its ways of sin and idolatry.

4:4 Circumcise: Circumcision was a sign of the covenant relationship between Israel and God (see Gen. 17:10–14). The intent of God was always that the outward symbol should be a sign of an inward reality of total devotion to Him (see Deut. 10:12–21).

4:5 Jeremiah announced the judgment of Judah and Jerusalem with the alarming sound of a **trumpet,** literally a shofar made of a ram's horn. This was the instrument used to sound the alarm when an enemy attacked a city.

4:6 Standard may refer to signal fires that connected Jerusalem with the perimeter fortresses of Judah. Since the foe **from the north** was yet unidentified by Jeremiah, this prophecy probably dates from between 622 and 609 B.C.

4:7 Destruction would come as a terrible surprise, like a **lion ... from his thicket** pouncing suddenly upon its prey.

4:8 Sackcloth was a rough-textured fabric worn as a sign of mourning or distress (6:26). **fierce anger:** The burning wrath of God would come as an inextinguishable fire.

4:9, 10 This passage indicates the deep inner struggle Jeremiah faced in his proclamation of the divine message. Jeremiah challenged God's dealings with His people, claiming that God had **deceived** the people with a message of **peace.** False prophets like Hananiah foretold a time of peace when in reality despair was more in order.

4:11, 12 The sirocco **wind** comes from the deserts east and south of Israel, bringing scorching heat and whirling dust. The divine

winds of judgment would bring destruction to Jerusalem, the **daughter** of God.

4:13 Judah had become the foe of God, and He would use the nation's international foes to discipline them. The imagery of **clouds** and **chariots like a whirlwind** portray the thoroughness and swiftness of God's judgment.

4:14 The word **wash** is used in Leviticus and Numbers to describe the cleansing of garments that had become defiled through contact with unclean objects or diseases. Cleansing of the **heart** is foundational to salvation (see Is. 1:18–20).

4:15 Dan: The most northern city of Israel proper. Dan was conquered by Tiglath-Pileser III in 733 B.C. and was incorporated as part of an Assyrian province. **Ephraim** was in the southernmost region of the northern kingdom of Israel. The message is clear. Just as Israel had been subjugated, Judah was also in danger.

4:16–18 Jeremiah, the prophet to the **nations,** announced the attack of foreign enemies who would raise their battle cries against Judah.

4:19, 20 Soul here means "bowels" or "belly." In ancient Middle Eastern thought, the internal organs were the seat of emotions and feelings. The term describes Jeremiah's inward anguish over the coming destruction of Jerusalem. The phrase **makes a noise** depicts the "groaning" of the prophet's **heart** at the sound of the trumpet announcing Judah's destruction (v. 5).

4:21, 22 Foolish describes the character of the people. The terms *foolish* and *silly* are contrary to the terms **knowledge** and **understanding.** God described His people as impudent children. They were **wise** in the ways of **evil,** but totally deficient in knowing how to **do good.**

4:23 without form, and void: This Hebrew phrase is the same one used in Gen. 1:2 to describe the chaos before the ordering of the cosmos. **no light:** The lack of light describes the disastrous effects of sin on creation, particularly on the land of Judah.

4:24, 25 The symbols of stability and strength would be shaken as by an earthquake. **Birds** would disappear as Hosea had proclaimed (see Hos. 4:3). In Gen. 1, the creation of the birds of the heavens depicts the fulfillment of the creative process. In Jeremiah and Hosea, the removal of the birds symbolizes the reversal of creation.

4:26 The term **fruitful** refers to the region of Mount Carmel, where there were productive vineyards, olive groves, and oak trees. The term is used to symbolize the productivity of the land as a "garden of God." Yet this also would be turned to desert.

4:27 Desolate refers to the uninhabitable devastation of Judah as a result of its unfaithfulness. Yet the land would not see total destruction. God remembers His mercy in His wrath.

4:28, 29 The **black** skies associate darkness with God's judgment. The term **relent,** meaning "to repent" or "to be sorry," parallels the term **turn back.** God's judgment on sin and rebellion is inescapable (see Num. 23:19).

4:30 Instead of turning to the Lord in its time of despair, Judah would turn to the idolatrous activity which had caused its dismal plight. To **adorn** oneself in **crimson, gold,** and eye **paint** depicts the seduction of clients by a prostitute. The word **lovers** describes Judah and Israel's history of physical and spiritual prostitution.

4:31 The voice of God called for repentance; but the **voice** of the people cried out in anguish and despair, but not to the Lord their Savior. **Daughter of Zion:** The term is an endearing way of describing Jerusalem as God's beloved daughter (see 4:11; 6:2). The use of this warm phrase in such a terrible context heightens our appreciation of the horror of the moment. **My soul is weary** suggests dying words of agony and despair. Judah's lovers had become her **murderers.**

5:1 Similar to Abraham's plea that Sodom be saved on account of the few faithful people among its inhabitants (see Gen. 18:16–33), so Jeremiah summoned the people to search the city of Jerusalem for one just and righteous person.

5:2 The phrase **as the LORD lives** invokes God's name and character in the proclamation.

5:3 God always looks for **truth** (v. 1) and faithfulness. When truth was found lacking in

Judah, God punished the people of Jerusalem through foreign invasion. Rather than repenting, the people reacted in rebellion. The Hebrew term translated **correction** means "chastisement" or "discipline." Sometimes it means "instruction." In the prophets it generally refers to God's attempt to teach His children faithfulness by means of discipline or punishment (7:28). But despite the words of Jeremiah and other prophets, Israel refused "correction" and continued down the path of self-destruction.

5:4 Here the term **poor** is paralleled by the word **foolish,** a rare term used by Isaiah (19:13) to refer to the nation as deluded and deceived. Thus the word *poor* refers to those who lack knowledge of God and are insensitive to His instruction and inattentive to His will.

5:5, 6 Greatness is achieved not by wealth and power but by the knowledge of God and obedience to Him. **known:** The word refers to intimate and practical knowledge. Here the knowledge is of the **way of the Lord**—the path characterized by truth, justice, and righteousness. Jeremiah paints a picture of Judah as oxen that have **broken** their **yoke,** wandering aimlessly through the field. Because they have broken the yoke, they are exposed to the elements and the wild animals. The animals symbolize the foreign nations who would lay siege to their cities.

5:7 The message is still addressed to the leaders of Judah (v. 5). The word **pardon** means forgiveness that cannot be granted where there is no repentance, but only continual abandoning of the ways of the Lord. **not gods:** The use of this phrase, found also in 2:11 and 16:20, is tantamount to declaring the nonexistence of the foreign deities that Judah worshiped. The words **your children** refer to the children of the leaders, who are the leaders' children and not God's. **I fed:** The term means God had satisfied their every need. **adultery ... harlots' houses:** These terms refer to physical adultery, though the source of this immoral sexual conduct may have been the presence of pagan cultic prostitutes.

5:8 In the context of Josiah's reforms, the men may have turned from cultic prostitutes, whom the king had eradicated, to ordinary prostitutes. From the brothels they turned to one another's wives. Like **stallions,** their lust was uncontrollable.

5:9 The Hebrew word translated **punish,** literally meaning "to visit," can be used of the visitation of God in mercy (see Ps. 65:9) or in wrath. Here it clearly refers to wrath.

5:10, 11 An unidentified adversary is called upon by the Lord to attack Jerusalem, but not to utterly destroy her. **her branches:** The degenerate, unfaithful limbs would be pruned because they were not His.

5:12 The people **lied** about the Lord, denying that He was about to inflict a horrible defeat. They had deceived themselves into thinking that God would not punish His own city and people, forgetting the negative effects of disobedience to the covenant (see Deut. 27; 28).

5:13 False **prophets** like Hananiah (28:11) had foretold a time of peace and deliverance from the domination of their enemies. But their **word** was like an empty breeze. The very **sword** (v. 12) they denied would seal their fate.

5:14 this word: This refers to the proclamation of Jeremiah, who voices the words of the Lord with the intensity of a blazing **fire.**

5:15, 16 Jeremiah announces the imminent coming of a **mighty nation** from distant lands that will carry out the divine purpose. The nation is not named, indicating that the oracle predates the advent of Babylon under Nabopolassar and Nebuchadnezzar. The only identification is that the enemy speaks a tongue unknown to the people in Jerusalem.

5:17 The word **eat** is used four times in this verse to paint an image of the enemy as consuming field, flock, and fortifications.

5:18 In the middle of a prophecy of judgment comes a word of hope. The phrase **in those days** is indicative of the judgment God would visit upon His people.

5:19 In summary, Jeremiah repeats two key words describing the sins of Judah and Israel: **forsaken** (abandonment) and **foreign gods** (idolatry; see 1:16; 2:13). Since Judah persisted in worshiping gods from foreign lands, God would allow them to be deported and serve their enemies.

5:20 house of Jacob: Even after the northern kingdom had been destroyed, the prophets still spoke of Israel. There was not a complete destruction of the northern tribes, as is commonly assumed.

5:21 foolish: This term emphasizes the people's ignorance of the ways of God. The parallel phrase **without understanding** shows the waywardness of the mind of the nation.

5:22, 23 To **fear** God is to acknowledge His majesty and to submit to His will. The negative rhetorical questions highlight Judah's refusal to submit to and to serve God. Instead, they bowed to the many foreign gods who were entirely powerless.

5:24, 25 The **fear** of the LORD is associated here with His creation of the natural world. **our God:** This title indicates the covenant affinity between the Lord and His people which was sadly lacking in their **heart** and mind.

5:26–29 the wicked: Those responsible for the welfare of the whole populace had abused their positions. The picture presented is one of **birds,** or the poor, being ensnared by **great** men who were building wealth at the expense of orphans and the **needy** (see Deut. 10:18).

5:30, 31 Jeremiah describes the moral depravity of Judah's leaders as **an astonishing and horrible thing.** The deterioration of the leadership of the land reached to the **prophets** and **priests**. Both offices had succumbed to the temptation of abusing their power, rejecting their responsible roles as messengers and servants of God.

6:1–3 The siege alarm was sounded to the cities surrounding Jerusalem. Jeremiah called his own tribe of **Benjamin** in the north to abandon the city for more secure territory. To the south in **Tekoa,** the watchman's **trumpet** was blown; to the west in the **Beth Haccerem** region, communication signal fires were sent. The offensives of Sennacherib in 701 B.C. and of Nebuchadnezzar in 586 B.C. brought siege forces from both the north and the south. The origin of the **disaster** is the north, the direction from which most of Israel's enemies approached Jerusalem.

6:4, 5 Prepare or "make holy" speaks of ritual sanctification performed in preparation for battle. Sorcerers and diviners were called upon to perform sacrifices to determine the will of the gods and assure a successful outcome in battle.

6:6 The terminology implies that God Himself was the true combatant against Jerusalem. Though the enemies were calling on their deities for help in their siege against Jerusalem, it was the Lord who would fight for them and assure the defeat of Jerusalem. **Cut down trees ... build a mound:** A siege mound was a ramp of wood, stone, and sand that sloped toward the wall of a city. Armored siege machines could go up the ramp and attack the city walls.

6:7 Jerusalem had become a well of bitter and polluted waters. **Violence and plundering** characterized the city that was once overflowing with peace, justice, and righteousness. **Grief and wounds** describe the sickness and injury that would continually plague the inhabitants. The horrors of the siege of Jerusalem by the Babylonians in 588–586 B.C. were unspeakable (see the Book of Lamentations).

6:8 Instructed can also mean "disciplined" or "chastened." Jerusalem was advised to heed the discipline of the Lord or face imminent desolation as a result of His departure.

6:9 The LORD of hosts may also be translated "The Lord of armies" (2:19; 5:14). **Thoroughly glean** indicates the thoroughness of the punishment. Every person among the **remnant** of Israel would know God's judgment. **put your hand back:** Jeremiah had to return to his proclamation so that no one would be unaware.

6:10 Because their ears were **uncircumcised,** meaning that their lives were not devoted to the Lord, the citizens of Jerusalem were incapable of keeping the covenant. Furthermore, their rebellion had become so ingrained that the **word of the LORD** had become a disgrace to them.

6:11 Jeremiah's own emotions reveal his identification with God's feelings about Judah. The prophet was both angry and **weary** with the entire nation, from the youngest of **children** to the oldest of the **aged** men.

6:12 The entire **land** and its contents would be given to others by the power of the **hand** of God. God's hand had saved the people; it would also bring about their judgment.

6:13 The accusation of **covetousness** suggests monetary gain by means of deception and fraud. Even those called to guide the nation in its covenant relationship had defrauded God and man.

6:14 The religious leaders sought to comfort the people with a message of hope and **peace.** But such words were not the word of God.

6:15 Nor did they know how to blush: The people had lost all sense of what was right before God. **they shall fall:** Everyone would experience the harsh hand of God's judgment.

6:16, 17 Old paths probably refers to the Sinai covenant and the Book of Deuteronomy, as Jeremiah called the people back to former days of steadfast devotion. The people obstinately refused to **walk** rightly and **find rest.** They also refused to **listen** to the alarming **sound of the trumpet,** denying that any danger existed.

6:18, 19 The **nations** and the **earth** are called to witness the stubborn character of Judah (see Is. 1:2; Mic. 1:2). **My words ... My law:** The revelation of God through Moses and the prophets was rejected by the people for whom it was prepared and given.

6:20–23 Even if the people used the most expensive offerings, their sacrifices were still neither **acceptable** nor **sweet.** The **burnt offerings** were the "holocaust" offerings, in which the entire animal was consumed by fire. The **sacrifices** were those that were partially consumed by the offerers, making themselves the primary beneficiaries of their own worship.

6:24, 25 Anguish or "distress" overwhelmed the people. Their **pain** is compared to childbirth. The people were prisoners in their own city.

6:26 Daughter of my people may be rendered "O Daughter, My people" (see 4:11, 31; 6:2, 23). Jeremiah used an endearing word for Jerusalem in the middle of this warning of coming judgment. The most dreaded loss for an ancient Israelite family was that of an **only son.** To **roll about in ashes** symbolically expressed sorrow and despair.

6:27 The Lord describes Jeremiah's role. Jeremiah would act as the nation's **assayer,** the one who tests or evaluates quality or purity.

6:28 Jeremiah gives his assessment of the people. **Rebels** speaks of their defiant attitudes. **Slanderers** refers to those who tell tales. **Corrupters** refers to those who destroy.

6:29, 30 Jeremiah assesses Judah as a refiner purifies **silver,** using **lead** to remove impurities (9:7). The lead is consumed, so the dross in the silver ore cannot be purged. This results in the refiner discarding the ore because it is so impure that the smelting process is not worth the energy it takes.

7:1, 2 The word that came to Jeremiah was a direct message from God in His temple courts. **Stand in the gate:** The parallel in 26:2 suggests the proclamation was made in the outer court of the temple before a large audience. **Worship** suggests bowing prostrate in service and obedience to a god, king, or priest. In bowing down, the worshiper pledged himself or herself to obedience in adhering to the demands of the one being honored (22:9).

7:3 The LORD of hosts can also be translated "God of armies" (2:19; 5:14; 6:9). **Amend:** The call to repentance here uses a different term (26:13) from the usual word translated "return" (3:1). A complete transformation of the people's **ways** and **doings,** lifestyle and beliefs, was necessary.

7:4 Trust conveys the sense of security and confidence that the people had in their holy place. They believed that God would never allow the city or the temple to be destroyed. **The temple of the LORD** had become a talisman to the Israelites. They believed the building guaranteed their security whether or not they obeyed the provisions of the covenant.

7:5, 6 The only true hope for dwelling in the context of the temple was a radical restructuring of Judah's society. **Thoroughly amend,** or "make good" or "do good," emphasizes the necessary transformation of Jerusalem's inhabitants. **thoroughly execute judgment:** The emphatic phrase form implies the depth of corruption that existed in the land; there was no justice. **Stranger** refers to resident aliens dwelling in the land. **The fatherless** and **the widow** were accorded special treatment in the Law, but they had been abused by the leaders of Jerusalem.

7:7 I will cause you to dwell: This phrase emphasizes the will and work of God to establish the nation of Israel in the land. In order for the nation to dwell in the land, it had to be faithful to God (see Deut. 7:6–11).

7:8 The refrain of v. 4 is complemented here by the phrase **cannot profit** (2:8, 11). The idea that the temple was inviolable was as profitless as the powerless gods that Israel idolized.

7:9 The covenant stipulations that Jerusalem's inhabitants had violated are listed here (see Ex. 20:1–17). **burn incense:** Jeremiah uses this phrase 19 times in the context of worshiping deities other than God (1:16).

7:10 Stand before means "to place (oneself) in submissive service to someone." Entering the temple of God while worshiping other gods was incomprehensible. For the people to think that they were secure (**delivered**) enough to perform perverted **abominations** (2:7) was the ultimate hypocrisy.

7:11 den of thieves: Like robbers hiding in a cave, Judah attempted to hide behind the sanctuary of the temple for protection from the divine hand of judgment. But the Lord had **seen** the hypocrisy of Israel's ways.

7:12 Shiloh was the site of the tent of meeting and ark of the covenant in the days of the judges. Leaders in the family of Eli had abused their priestly position for personal gain, and idolatry was rampant in the land. When the Israelites attempted to use the ark as a victory-giving talisman, the ark was captured (see 1 Sam. 4), and the sanctuary was destroyed by the Philistines. The Philistines were instruments of divine punishment for the **wickedness** of God's **people.**

7:13 All these works are the sins listed in vv. 6, 8, 9.

7:14, 15 The earlier dwelling place of the ark, **Shiloh,** served as an example of the impending destruction of Jerusalem. The temple had to be destroyed to vindicate the name of God; the people had to be removed from the land in order to purge it of wickedness.

7:16 God's instruction to Jeremiah, **do not pray for this people,** indicates the extreme depravity of Jerusalem's inhabitants (see also 11:14; 14:11). No manner of **intercession**

was to be made on behalf of Judah. God would **not hear** Jeremiah's appeals.

7:17, 18 The queen of heaven refers to the goddess Ishtar (Astarte), who was worshiped in open-air cultic centers throughout the eastern Mediterranean region and Mesopotamia. Worship of Ishtar involved the preparation of special **cakes** that bore the goddess's image, as well as **drink offerings** (44:19). The family cooperation in the idolatrous worship of Ishtar stood in direct opposition to the covenant demands that a father instruct his children in the ways of the Lord (see Deut. 6:4–9).

7:19 Provoke, which means "to vex or irritate," describes the effects of Israel's continual unfaithfulness on God.

7:20 God's judgment on Ishtar worship is described in terms of a fire that cannot be **quenched.**

7:21 Add your burnt offerings to your sacrifices: Because the people had missed the true meaning of the Lord's worship, they could multiply their offerings as much as they liked, and it would do them no good.

7:22 All **sacrifices** were not rejected, only those offered without true repentance and a commitment to obey the Lord.

7:23 that it may be well with you: Obedience would bring blessing. When the prophets lashed out against sacrifice, it was not against the sacrificial system as God had established it, but against the corruption of that system.

7:24 The history of Israel is seen in terms of disobedience rather than faithfulness to the covenant, reflecting the people's **evil hearts** (4:14). The result was a worsening or **backward** direction rather than an improving or **forward** walk.

7:25 From the days of Moses, God sent His **servants the prophets** to call the nation of Israel to obedience. **Daily rising up early and sending them** indicates the persistence and urgency of God's message through His prophets.

7:26, 27 Incline their ear suggests eager listening and readiness to obey. **Stiffened their neck** suggests a cold rebuff to the will and work of God. Jeremiah, like Isaiah before him (see Is. 6:9, 10), was told that the people would not respond to his message.

7:28 The people were stubborn, rejecting the laws of the covenant. They were persistently disobedient to the **voice of the LORD** revealed through His prophets. **Correction** refers to the instruction of the Law and the prophets (5:3). **Truth** refers to the faithfulness and fidelity that was characteristic of God but absent among His people.

7:29 To **cut off** one's **hair** was a way of expressing mourning and grief. The act may also have symbolized that Judah had rejected the covenant relationship just as if they had broken a Nazirite vow, a sign of personal devotion that required the hair not to be cut (see Num. 6:1–21). The Lord had **rejected** this **generation,** even as they had rejected His Law (6:19) and had been rejected by their "lovers" (4:30).

7:30, 31 The **evil** doings of this generation, which had continued since the days of Manasseh, included the placing of **abominations** or "detestable objects" in the temple of God. The **Tophet** sacrifices, adopted from Phoenician and Canaanite practices, involved the ritual sacrifice of children in times of national crisis or disaster. **burn ... in the fire:** This took place in the Valley of Hinnom southwest of Jerusalem (called Gehenna in the New Testament).

7:32 days are coming: This phrase signifies the advent of a divine intervention in history, usually in judgment. With the phrase **Valley of Slaughter,** Jeremiah uses the prophetic device of changing a name to express the Lord's assessment of the Valley of Hinnom.

7:33 Unburied **corpses** left to the elements and animals were regarded as a horrible desecration in the ancient Middle East.

7:34 Prayer would avail Judah nothing on account of its great sin. The nation would be devoid of all joy and **gladness.** The **land** would **be desolate.** The word *desolate* is used extensively in Isaiah, Jeremiah, and Ezekiel to refer to the devastation in Jerusalem.

8:1–3 In the day when Jerusalem's judgment was fulfilled at the hands of its enemies, the **bones** of its people and their leaders would be desecrated by removing them from their graves. **the sun and the moon and all the host of heaven:** The gods and goddesses to whom Jerusalem looked for deliverance would stand over the people's desecrated corpses, which are pictured here as **refuse** or "dung" (9:22). Those who survived the siege as exiles and slaves would prefer **death** over **life.**

8:4, 5 The questions in these verses emphasize the absurdity of Judah's lifestyle. Instead of correcting their erroneous behavior, the people were engaged in **perpetual backsliding.**

8:6 No righteous or repentant person could be found in the city of Jerusalem. Every person pursued his or her **own course,** a lifestyle leading to destruction.

8:7 Jeremiah contrasts the citizens of Jerusalem with the birds **in the heavens** who understand the approach of the seasons and **appointed times.** Whereas the birds follow their instincts to migrate, the people of Israel refused to follow God's promptings to obey His covenant. Note that God still refers to the people of Judah as **My people,** even though they continued to rebel against Him.

8:8, 9 Jeremiah contended with fraudulent scribes and **wise men** whose understanding of the Law Jeremiah deemed **falsehood. False pen** describes the idolatry and errant beliefs of the Jerusalem's leadership. The wisdom of the scribes and wise men was folly and shame because it was not founded on a true knowledge of God's word and law.

8:10–13 The people had interpreted the Law unwisely, believing that **peace** and prosperity would be granted to them. They were grossly mistaken (6:12–15).

8:14 Assemble ... enter: Judah's inhabitants would gather within the citadel and walls of Jerusalem for protection from an oncoming army.

8:15 The search for **peace** and **health** was hopeless and full of **trouble**—"terror" or "dismay." God's hand of judgment strikes terror in the hearts and minds of those who continue in sin and rebellion.

8:16 Dan lies at the northern border of Israel. In 1:14, 15, Jeremiah warned that calamity would come from the north. The **snorting** of enemy horses would sound the fury of the impending invasion.

8:17 serpents ... Vipers: Judgment by means of poisonous snakes is described in Num. 21:6.

8:18 The hopelessness of Judah was so overwhelming to Jeremiah that his **heart** was **faint.** The word *faint* describes an illness or sickness that results from great **sorrow.**

8:19 Cry refers to great grief resulting from God's rejection, or foreign oppression (see Ps. 18:6). **Far country** or "far places" probably refers to the outer reaches of the land of Judah. **Is not the LORD in Zion? Is not her King in her:** These rhetorical questions expect an affirmative response. God had not abandoned His people; it was the Israelites who had rejected the living God for other gods. **Provoked** describes the defiant attitudes of the people toward the pure worship of God. **Carved images** generally refers to stone idols. The phrase **foreign idols** in Hebrew is "foreign futilities." The people were looking for deliverance in useless images.

8:20–22 This proverb reflects the sense of helplessness in the early fall. The **harvest** was meager and the oppression persisted. Even Jeremiah was deeply **hurt**—this translates a Hebrew word derived from the verb meaning "to break," "to shatter"; in other words, the prophet's spirit was broken over the fate of his people. **Is there no balm in Gilead:** The region of Gilead was known for its balsam ointment (see Gen. 37:25). There is no healing for a people intent on rebelling against God.

9:1 my eyes a fountain of tears: Jeremiah, who is known as the "weeping prophet," identified personally with the suffering of his people. Here he expresses his desire for a reserve of tears that would flow without stopping.

9:2, 3 Jeremiah desired a **wilderness** refuge where he would be free from the degradation of Jerusalem. The word **adulterers** refers literally to unfaithful husbands or wives, but here to idolaters as those who are spiritually faithless.

9:4 take heed to his neighbor ... do not trust any brother: The personal affairs of the people were characterized by deceit, slander, and mistrust. Ethical standards had collapsed.

9:5, 6 They weary themselves to commit iniquity: The people had literally worn themselves out with perversions. **Deceit** here is the same term used of Jacob's trickery toward Esau (see Gen. 27:35). The term refers to swindling by false speech or false scales.

9:7 Jeremiah returns to the imagery of metallurgical refining (6:28–30). God would **refine** and **try** the people by fire to see if any were faithful to Him.

9:8, 9 Jeremiah returns to the imagery of bow and **arrow** to depict Judah's deceit (v. 3). The picture is of a person speaking **peaceably to his neighbor** while lying **in wait** to ambush him.

9:10, 11 weeping and wailing for the mountains: The entire land would be laid waste by destruction. Even the animals would abandon the land because not a crumb of food would remain for the **birds** and **beasts.** The holy city of Jerusalem would become a **den of jackals** where no man or woman lived.

9:12 The wise man observes and understands the natural order and the working of God in the world He has made. No wise person could be found among the inhabitants of Judah and Jerusalem.

9:13, 14 The people's lack of adherence to the covenant they had **forsaken** is indicated by the phrase **have not obeyed … nor walked.** The word *obey,* which comes from the Hebrew word meaning "to hear," implies an active response to God's word. Instead of walking according to God's law, the people walked according to the **dictates** or "stubbornness" of **their own hearts.**

9:15, 16 Water of gall, used in 8:14 to describe God's judgment, refers to some kind of poisonous or salty drink. **scatter them … send a sword:** The people of Judah would be exiled from their promised homeland and even killed as they ran away because they rejected God.

9:17 Skillful wailing women refers to professional mourners called to weep over the collapse of Jerusalem.

9:18 make haste: There is urgency in summoning the skilled mourners to lead the people in tearful lament over the imminent destruction of Judah.

9:19 plundered: This term, which means "to devastate," is used frequently in Jeremiah to refer to the impending devastation of Jerusalem.

9:20–22 Teach your daughters wailing: The impending disaster in Jerusalem would be so great and the dead would be so numerous that multitudes of trained mourners would be needed. **children … young men … men:** Death claims its victims without respect to sex or age. Corpses would remain in **the open field** like **refuse** or dung (8:2).

9:23, 24 wise … mighty … rich: The people with whom Jeremiah contended were depending on their own capabilities rather than on God. **Glory** may also be translated *boast,* meaning "to praise oneself." People should find their real meaning and true worth in the fact that they know God and may celebrate His attributes. Three attributes of God that He demands of people called by His Name are **lovingkindness,** meaning "loyal love"; **judgment,** meaning "justice"; and **righteousness,** meaning "uprightness."

9:25, 26 God would **punish** or "visit" Judah, along with its **uncircumcised** neighboring nations. Circumcision, the sign of God's covenant with Abraham, was meaningless without a **heart** devoted to God. The point of this text is similar to the concept of temple inviolability (ch. 7). Just as God would destroy even the temple (7:12–14), so He would ignore even circumcision when it was only an outward symbol (see Deut. 10:12–22).

10:1, 2 The way of the Gentiles was worshiping natural phenomena by means of handmade icons and symbolic imagery. **The signs of heaven** were the astral deities (8:1–3) worshiped in the days of Manasseh and reinstituted following the death of Josiah and the collapse of his reforms. **dismayed:** The heavenly realms held a certain awe or terror for the nations, but Israel was to worship God who held the heavenly realm under His control.

10:3, 4 Customs refers to the practice of constructing deities for worship. **Futile,** which means "vapor," "vanity," or "worthlessness," describes the utter uselessness of idol worship.

10:5 The **upright** idols were dumb and motionless; they required attendants to care for them and carry them from place to place. **Do not be afraid:** There is no reason to fear—let alone worship—things that are completely powerless, unable to do **good** or **evil.**

10:6, 7 there is none like You, O LORD: This phrase expresses one of the great teachings of the prophets—God is not simply "better" than other gods; He alone is the living God.

10:8 Dull-hearted can mean " brutish," "stupid," or "unreceptive." The idea is that instruction received from idolaters is as worthless as the idols themselves.

10:9, 10 Silver came from **Tarshish,** which some scholars have identified with Tartessus in southern Spain. The wooden and metallic idol was adorned with **blue and purple** fabrics, whose dye probably originated with the Phoenicians. However, even the most **skillful** or "wise" craftsmen could not manufacture true gods, for there is but *one* **true, living,** and **everlasting God.**

10:11 This verse was originally written in Aramaic rather than Hebrew, the usual language of the Old Testament, but the reason for this change of language is not known. The message is clear that the helpless so-called **gods** would be destroyed.

10:12, 13 Jeremiah emphasizes the creative power of God, drawing from the imagery of Job 38 and Ps. 8. By God's **power, wisdom,** and **discretion** or "understanding," **the earth** and **the heavens** were brought into orderly existence. By the command of **His voice,** at Creation (see Gen. 1:1—2:4), the **waters, lightning,** and **wind** are summoned. Jeremiah reminded the people of Judah that their God not only created the universe but also governs its ongoing life.

10:14, 15 metalsmith: The craftsmen who used silver and gold for the images they constructed were **put to shame** by their handiwork. The lifeless and useless objects that they fashioned showed that their efforts were **futile.**

10:16 The Portion of Jacob: The Lord is the *portion* or "share" of His people, sufficient for their every need. **His inheritance:** Israel belonged to God; God is the sufficiency of His people.

10:17, 18 gather up your wares: The Assyrian stone reliefs of Shalmaneser III depict

captives transporting household goods on their heads as they go into exile in the eastern reaches of the empire. Soon, this would be the fate of the people of Judah.

10:19 Woe is me: Jeremiah personally identified with Judah and the destruction of Jerusalem. **my hurt … My wound:** The injuries inflicted upon Judah were **severe;** the Hebrew text suggests "incurable wounds." **infirmity:** Supplementing the words *hurt* and *wounds,* the word *infirmity* completes the threefold imagery of the damage done to Judah.

10:20 Like the Bedouin whose tent had been destroyed by marauding bandits, Judah lay **plundered** while its **children** were murdered or deported. No one remained to **pitch** the **tent** and reestablish the nation.

10:21 In the Book of Jeremiah, **shepherds** usually refers to the national leaders to whom God gave the responsibility of maintaining justice. Judah's leaders had become **dull-hearted,** dumbfounded by the chastisement that God had brought upon them. Because the leaders had not **sought** God with a whole heart, they would not **prosper** with the growth of their **flocks.** Instead the shepherds would lose their flocks. The people would be **scattered** like sheep.

10:22, 23 The advance of the foe from the **north** is announced (1:14, 15; 8:16). The armies of this foe would destroy the towns of **Judah,** reducing it to a **desolate … den of jackals** (9:11).

10:24 The verb **correct,** which means "to discipline" or "to instruct," has as its goal conformity to the word and will of God. Jeremiah pleaded with the Lord to deal with the nation according to His **justice,** but to withhold His **anger.**

10:25 The passage ends with a prayer to God to bring judgment upon those who destroyed Judah. Even the Gentile nations would be judged according to God's ethical standards.

11:1, 2 Jeremiah's message from the Lord here is strongly associated with the Book of Deuteronomy. The term **words** is the Hebrew name of the Book of Deuteronomy; it is also used to refer to the terms of the **covenant.** A *covenant* is a legal treaty or relationship between individuals, between nations, or—in the case of Israel—between a nation and its God. The covenant specified rights, obligations, and responsibilities of the parties entering into the agreement.

11:3 **Cursed** suggests the negative provisions of the covenant as summarized in Deut. 27:26 (see all of Deut. 27; 28).

11:4 **iron furnace:** This terminology comes directly from Deut. 4:20, which is set in a context of a warning against worshiping idols. **Obey:** Obedience is the key to blessing (see Deut. 27:10; 28:1–14).

11:5, 6 **that I may establish the oath:** The blessing of the land, as promised to Abraham, was dependent upon the covenant loyalty of the people. The words **Judah** and **Jerusalem** are a standard way of referring to the entire nation of Israel.

11:7, 8 The emphatic form of the Hebrew phrase **earnestly exhorted** highlights the history of God's continual urgent—**rising early**—pleas for loyalty from His nation, from the Exodus until the present. The message had been the same from the beginning: **obey.**

11:9, 10 **turned back:** The people had returned to the ways of **their forefathers,** who had rebelled against God and the covenant. **Gone after** means "to serve" or "to worship." Both the northern and southern kingdoms had practiced idolatry and broken the first of the Ten Commandments.

11:11 Because the heart of the nation was evil, God would **bring calamity** upon the people. Even if the people were to **cry out** in distress, God would **not listen.**

11:12, 13 Rather than accept God's punishment and repent of their evil ways, the nation preferred to **cry out** to other **gods** for deliverance. The **altars** of their **incense** (1:16; 7:9) and sacrifices would become **shameful** objects.

11:14 Judah's status was decided. Jeremiah's **prayer** would be to no avail (7:16; 14:11).

11:15 **My house:** The nation had no right to worship in God's temple while paying homage to other gods.

11:16 **The LORD** called Judah the **Green Olive Tree,** indicating its beauty and His blessing on the nation. But **the noise of a great tumult** or tempest would accompany the

attacking army that would ravage and destroy the tree with **fire.**

11:17 The term **planted** recalls the theme of 2:21, the idea that God had established Israel as His choicest vine. However, here the context is the impending **doom** that would result from the **evil** done by the Lord's people.

11:18, 19 **a docile lamb brought to the slaughter:** This imagery is reminiscent of Is. 53:7 and the sacrificial death of Jesus Christ.

11:20 Jeremiah appealed for vindication to God, as the one true righteous Judge. **Mind** is literally the internal organs of the body, and is a way of referring to the seat of human emotion. **Heart** refers to the seat of the intellect and will. **Vengeance** describes God's fury and anger against sin that demands punishment.

11:21–23 **The men of Anathoth** insisted that Jeremiah **not prophesy in the name of the LORD.** If Jeremiah had yielded to their demand, he would have repudiated his calling, his person, and his God. The threat of death to Jeremiah was answered by punishment of the **young men** as well as their children. The prediction of death by **famine** was fulfilled when the city was besieged by the Babylonians in the days of Zedekiah.

12:1 **Plead** means "contend legally." While no legal grievance can be brought against God, Jeremiah could pose legal questions to the righteous Judge.

12:2 The theme of God's establishing the nation of Israel is also found in 2:21; 11:17. The plant had **taken root,** but was producing bad **fruit.**

12:3 **You, O LORD, know me:** God's intimate relationship with Jeremiah is evidenced here. The prophet had faced becoming like a **sheep for the slaughter** (11:19); here he calls for his enemies to be judged in the same way.

12:4 **How long:** Jeremiah's question related to God's delay of judgment on the people of the land. **land mourn ... herbs of every field wither ... beasts and birds are consumed:** These three elements are recurring themes in Jeremiah and other prophetic texts (see 4:28; Is. 40:7; Zeph. 1:3). In spite of past chastisement, the people believed that God would not bring their country to an end.

12:5, 6 God's response to Jeremiah's question (v. 4) comes in the form of two metaphorical questions. The first metaphor, of foot racing, was designed to teach Jeremiah that the obstacles he faced in his hometown were meager compared to those he would encounter before the kings of Judah and Babylon (the **horses**). The second metaphor, of **peace,** was designed to remind the prophet of the impending turmoil he would have to endure in proclaiming the message of judgment to an unrepentant leadership.

12:7 dearly beloved: God's love and concern for His people does not preclude discipline when their sin makes it necessary.

12:8, 9 Judah had become like a **lion** roaring against God, resulting in His beloved becoming His **hated.**

12:10, 11 Rulers refers to the foreign kings who had come as agents of God to judge Judah. Because of sin, the land that once saw God's bounteous blessing would experience His devastating judgment.

12:12 Destruction would come to the **desolate heights** where Israel and Judah performed their idolatrous deeds (3:2; 3:21; 4:11).

12:13 The imagery turns to the fields, which the Israelites believed were endowed with fertility by Baal. Because of the people's idolatry, their fields were overgrown with **thorns.**

12:14 Evil neighbors included the powerful nations of Babylon and Assyria, as well as opportunistic kingdoms like Edom, Moab, and Ammon. These latter kingdoms seized land, crops, and hostages when Judah was weakened by invasion. **The inheritance** refers to the **land** that God gave His people under specific conditions. **Pluck ... out,** which means "to root out, destroy," is often used in the Book of Jeremiah in the context of God's retribution on evil nations. **Judah** would be "plucked out" from among those who were plucked out.

12:15 In the midst of His judgment, God would remember His covenant with Abraham. Eventually He would **return and have compassion** on His people.

12:16, 17 The nations are given a stern condition about their survival and blessing. They are advised to **learn** the **ways** of Israel more diligently than they had **taught** Israel their own ways of Baal worship. **If** the nations would do this and place themselves under His covenant—**swear by His name,** they would **be established;** i.e., share in Israel's salvation.

13:1, 2 linen sash: This article of clothing was like a short skirt or kilt worn by men. Jeremiah was not supposed to wash it.

13:3–5 Jeremiah was commanded to take his linen **sash** to the **Euphrates** River and **hide** it between the rocks.

13:6, 7 Because Jeremiah's sash was dirty and then was exposed to the elements, it was **ruined** and **profitable for nothing.**

13:8–11 As Jeremiah's waistcloth was ruined (v. 7), so Judah's **pride** would be reduced to **ruin.** *Pride* describes the self-exalting conduct that characterized Israel in its love for idols. This pride is explained in a triplet of verbal phrases: **refuse to hear ... follow the dictates of their hearts ... walk after other gods.** Jeremiah's undefiled waistcloth in v. 1 symbolized unspoiled Judah in its early days of covenant faithfulness to God. But as the waistcloth became ruined near the Euphrates, so Judah defiled itself by its allegiances to Assyria, Babylon, and their national deities.

13:12 Jeremiah's quotation of a well-known proverb on the blessing of plentiful **wine** would be met with a derogatory response.

13:13 Blessing turned to debauchery among the leaders and citizens of Jerusalem. The listing of **kings, priests, prophets,** and **inhabitants** is a means of depicting the entire religious and political nation by listing the different parts.

13:14 The wine jars of God's wrath would be smashed and broken together, a picture of a devastated nation. The triplet of synonyms for compassion—**pity, spare,** and **have mercy**—heightens the effect of hopelessness in Judah's situation.

13:15 Proud refers to self-exaltation and contempt for the **spoken** or revealed word of God.

13:16 To **give glory** to God is to exalt and

worship Him. This verse warns of the consequences of failing to glorify God. In the rugged **mountains** that dominate the landscape of Judah, where walking in the **dark** is hazardous, no hope or **light** would be discerned.

13:17 Jeremiah had been told not to pray for the rebellious and unresponsive people of Judah (7:16; 11:14; 14:11), but here he expresses **in secret** his deep lament for the **LORD's flock,** who had been carried away into exile.

13:18, 19 The king and **the queen mother** are Jehoiachin and his mother Nehushta, who were exiled by Nebuchadnezzar (see 2 Kin. 24:8–12) after only three months on the throne in Jerusalem. **Humble yourselves:** Jeremiah advised the royal household to submit to Babylon.

13:20 Those who come from the north refers to the Babylonians.

13:21 you have taught them … to be head over you: This verse seems to indicate that Judah had cooperated with its enemies as they began to dominate the nation. The metaphor of childbirth portrays Judah reaping the fruits of its labors in pain and anguish.

13:22 Your skirts have been uncovered: Judah would be shamed by its conquerors in the same way that a prostitute was publicly disgraced.

13:23 The negative rhetorical question confirmed Judah's inability to change its own ways. The nation had reinforced its habit of doing **evil** (4:22) for so long that it did not know how to **do good.**

13:24, 25 The consequence of Judah's continual rebellion would be the scattering of its inhabitants like chaff or **stubble** driven by the desert **wind.**

13:26, 27 Uncover your skirts refers to public exposure (v. 22). Since Judah had lustfully sought adulterous relationships with foreign gods and goddesses, God would expose and bring to **shame** its actions. **Adulteries** are literally sins against marriage. Applied to Israel the term means involvement with another nation's gods.

14:1 Droughts were viewed as indicators of divine displeasure, as in the idolatrous days of Ahab, Jezebel, and Elijah.

14:2 Four short clauses using four words for lament profile the mourning of the country. The Hebrew word translated **mourns** is a general word for grief over the dead. **Languish** means "to wither" or "to shrink back." The Hebrew word for **mourn** describes the dark gloom of weeping and wailing.

14:3, 4 nobles: The men of renown, who could have afforded any price for water, sent out servants to search in all the normal locations for water, but **no water** could be **found.** The rain-starved farmlands were scorched by the sun, and the farmers **covered their heads** in mourning.

14:5, 6 The drought of Judah affected even the wild animals. The doe abandoned its fawn for lack of forage. **Wild donkeys stood** on barren hills, sniffing the wind for the scent of moisture—to no avail.

14:7 Jeremiah echoes the sentiments of his people in his plea for forgiveness and deliverance for the nation. The word **iniquities** refers to the accountable guilt that results from continual unconfessed sin.

14:8, 9 Jeremiah pleaded with God on the basis of God's name and character, particularly His role as the **Hope** and **Savior** of His people. Instead of having an intimate relationship with Judah, God had become like **a stranger** or **a traveler** in the land, because the people worshiped other gods.

14:10 Unlike the troubled Jeremiah, the **people** were unrepentant. Jeremiah realized that judgment was inevitable because God offered no hint of deliverance. **they have loved to wander:** *Loved* describes voluntary desire. *Wander* describes a repetitive back and forth movement—in this case, of seeking every possible occasion for sin.

14:11, 12 Jeremiah was instructed **not** to **pray** for the **good** of Jerusalem. **fast … offer burnt offering:** These methods of expressing penitence and establishing communion with God were ineffective because of the people's disobedience. The doom of Judah was sealed.

14:13 Jeremiah complained to the Lord about false **prophets** who were proclaiming a message of **peace** instead of war and pestilence. These pretentious prophets presumed upon God's mercy and promise of deliverance as demonstrated in the days of Hezekiah and Isaiah, when Jerusalem was miraculously rescued from the siege of Sennacherib's army.

14:14 The prophet who truly speaks in the **name** of God will see his words come to pass. The false prophets who promised peace (v. 13) spoke **lies** of their own device (see 2 Pet. 1:19–21).

14:15, 16 God's condemnation would fall first on the false **prophets** because of their prophecies of peace (v. 13). Next in line for judgment would be the inhabitants of the city who had been deceived by the false prophets.

14:17, 18 The setting for this lament over the desecrated **city** may be either 597 B.C., when Judah was invaded, or 588–586 B.C., when Jerusalem fell.

14:19, 20 The people of Judah acknowledged their **wickedness,** meaning "rebellion," their **iniquity,** meaning "perversity," and the fact that they had **sinned.** This triplet of terms indicates the pervasiveness of sin in the land.

14:21, 22 The people's plea for God's mercy was based on His character—His **name's sake,** His **glory,** His **covenant** relationship with Israel, and His power over creation. At stake was God's reputation and the blessing that would come to the people, but here the obligations of the people to the Lord are disregarded.

15:1 When **Moses and Samuel** interceded with God on behalf of the nation, God responded favorably. However, not even these men of God could alter the Lord's intended purpose for the people of Judah—that they should be driven from the land.

15:2 Death, sword, famine, and **captivity** would be the outcome of God's judgment. He would use foreign armies as instruments of judgment (14:11, 12).

15:3, 4 The **four forms of destruction** describe the complete judgment of Judah. The imagery of **dogs, birds,** and **beasts** devouring human flesh vividly illustrates not only death, but desecration. The basis for this desecration is the defilement of Jerusalem that took place during the reign of **Manasseh,** when idolatry reigned in the temple courts and children were sacrificed to Molech (7:31).

15:5, 6 Forsaken means "cast down" or "rejected." The people threw off the yoke of the covenant and went **backward** instead of forward in obedience. **My hand** indicates the active power of God in accomplishing His will for His people (see Deut. 26:8). **I am weary of relenting:** *Relenting* refers to God's restraining from totally demolishing Israel and Judah for hundreds of years of idolatry and unfaithfulness.

15:7, 8 Like wheat chaff that is scattered by the **winnowing** fork and the wind, the people of Judah would be dispersed. The population would be decimated. The further ravaging of the land is revealed in the numerous **widows** who would be left in the wake of the death of the men of Judah.

15:9 The blessing of **seven** sons was the ultimate hope for ancient mothers and fathers. But the utmost horror was to lose all seven in death, resulting in the loss of an heir.

15:10, 11 Every one of them curses me: To curse someone in ancient Israel was to invoke condemnation on that person with a prescribed formula.

15:12 Iron here may symbolize Jeremiah, who was called an "iron pillar" in his call in 1:18. The iron of the north could then refer to the high quality iron from Asia Minor or the Balkans. Otherwise the imagery is that of a powerful foe from the north.

15:13, 14 Judah would be taken captive and exiled to an unknown **land,** as had happened to Israel a century before.

15:15 God's **patience** was shown in the way He endured for a long time the sin of His people. Jeremiah requested God to be patient with him and not **take … away** his life because of his own rebellion.

15:16 Eating the **words** of the Lord means to internalize them and allow their meaning to become a reality in one's life. To be **called by** the Lord's **name** is to be recognized as belonging to Him as a servant.

15:17 Jeremiah's isolation and **indignation** were the results of his obedience to the word and calling of God.

15:18 My pain refers to Jeremiah's internal agonizing over his prophetic role. The **unreliable stream** is a vivid picture of the arid regions of the Middle East, where water is at a premium and streams can run dry without warning.

15:19 The Lord responded to Jeremiah's impassioned inquiry (vv. 15–18) with a message of repentance and reassurance of Jeremiah's call. **return:** Jeremiah is admonished to "repent" (3:1, 7, 12), after which God would restore him to his prophetic position as God's spokesman.

15:20, 21 I will make you … a fortified bronze wall … they shall not prevail: Jeremiah was recommissioned with words similar to those of his original calling (1:18, 19). **The wicked** refers to people such as Jehoiakim and the men of Anathoth who had opposed Jeremiah so vehemently (11:18–23). God promises His presence in times of opposition, persecution, and imprisonment for His sake.

16:1, 2 In the case of Jeremiah, the prohibition against marriage was both a sign to the nation and a blight against his name among the people. Celibacy was abnormal; large families were indicative of God's blessing upon a household. Jeremiah faced life with God as his sole comfort and support.

16:3–5 God's prohibition against participating in the customary grief process reveals the abnormal nature of Jeremiah's life. The trio of terms for sorrow—**mourning, lament,** and **bemoan**—is followed by a trio of terms referring to God's faithful care—**peace, lovingkindness,** and **mercies**—from which Judah had been removed.

16:6, 7 The pagan mourning practices of cutting oneself and shaving oneself **bald** were strictly forbidden in the Law of Moses (see Lev. 19:28; 21:5; Deut. 14:1). The **bread** of **mourning** and **cup of consolation** probably refer to food and drink brought for the family of the deceased.

16:8, 9 The **house of feasting** was a banquet hall often used for wedding celebrations. Jeremiah was restricted from participating in all meaningful family ceremonies. Jeremiah's life was symbolic of the state of **Israel** and the estrangement between God and Judah.

16:10 The trio of questions posed by the people indicates their lack of understanding of God's word. The people of Judah had missed the purpose for which they were chosen, to show to the world the nature and character of God by living as the people of God.

16:11, 12 Judah had **forsaken** its covenant **LORD** and pursued other deities. Abandoning God and His **law** or "instruction" led to disaster.

16:13 The blessing of devotion to God was freedom, prosperity, and large families in the land. Blessing was dependent on obedience; the consequence of disobedience was a dreaded life **out of** the **land,** in a world the people did **not know.**

16:14, 15 the days are coming: The future restoration of Israel would surpass the ancient deliverance from Egypt (23:7, 8).

16:16, 17 The **fishermen** and **hunters** refer to the Babylonian armies that would scour the land for Judah's rebels.

16:18 Defiled is used sometimes to refer to combined ethical, physical, and spiritual uncleanness. God's **land** or **inheritance** had been profaned by numerous cultic objects, which Jeremiah scathingly refers to as **the carcasses of their detestable and abominable idols.**

16:19–21 A message of hope begins with a trio of honorific terms for God: **strength, fortress,** and **refuge.** *Strength* and *fortress* are related words in Hebrew, like the English "strength" and "stronghold." A *refuge* is a place of safety from danger. Jeremiah knew that His only place of strength and safety was in God.

17:1, 2 Judah's **sin** had become so deeply **engraved** that it could not be removed. The **point of a diamond** on **a pen of iron** indicates the permanence of the engraving. The **heart** of the people was inextricably entangled in stubborn rebellion against God.

17:3 Jerusalem and the other cities of Judah were demolished and plundered by the Babylonians. The remaining **treasures** of the temple of God were carried by Nebuchadnezzar's army to Babylon. Even the idolatrous cultic centers were destroyed (15:13, 14).

17:4 let go: This phrase usually refers to letting the land lie fallow during the sabbatical year (see Ex. 23:10, 11). Judah's captivity would provide rest for the land from the idolatrous activities of its people.

17:5, 6 cursed: This term is used extensively in Deuteronomy. Two different words for **man** are used in this passage. The first refers to a strong and capable male; the second is a generic term for humankind as made in the image of God (see Gen. 1:26–28). One cannot trust in both God and humankind; to turn one's **heart** toward people is to turn away from God.

17:7 The term **blessed** is used often in the Psalms and Deuteronomy to describe the benefits that accrue to the person who is devoted to the Lord and His Word.

17:8 This verse teaches that one who trusts in God will not be free from trials and adversity, but that God will bring fruit and blessing in and through those difficulties (14:1–9; 15:19–21).

17:9, 10 The heart refers to the mind, the source of thinking, feeling, and action.

17:11 The teaching of 17:1–10 is supported by a proverb based on the common belief that the **partridge** hatched eggs other than its own. When the young birds recognized that the partridge was not their mother, they would leave her. Similarly, a man who unjustly gains wealth will be abandoned by that wealth and then be known as a **fool.**

17:12, 13 A glorious high throne refers to the temple in Jerusalem and the ark of the covenant, the symbol of God's presence and sovereignty over the nation. **The hope of Israel** refers to the expectation of deliverance and the restoration of the faithful (14:8). Judah had nowhere to turn because it had **forsaken** God and His lordship.

17:14 Though Jeremiah struggled with difficulties, he continually turned in **praise** to the Lord who can **heal** and **save.** Likewise, the only hope of healing and salvation for the nation of Judah was divine intervention.

17:15, 16 Some scoffers dared to defy God and the word revealed through Jeremiah. Jeremiah pointed out that he took no pleasure in proclaiming judgment. He remained a devoted **shepherd** who was intimately concerned for his own people.

17:17 Terror may refer to physical, emotional, or mental horror. The word **hope,** meaning "refuge" or "shelter," refers to a position of safety and security in the face of danger and helplessness, such as Jeremiah faced in Judah and Jerusalem.

17:18 Jeremiah called for his persecutors to be **ashamed** and **dismayed,** to be dishonored and demoralized. The prophet also called upon the Lord to confirm the message of judgment in the **day of doom** and **double destruction.**

17:19, 20 The particular **gate** is not mentioned, though the description would place it in the area of the Davidic citadel. Jeremiah's message was to be proclaimed throughout the city.

17:21, 22 The Sabbath was a sign of creation and the covenant relationship between God and Israel. To **hallow** it is to set it apart, to distinguish it from other days.

17:23 Abuse of the Sabbath was apparently commonplace throughout the history of the nation.

17:24, 25 If the **Sabbath** was kept holy, signifying the covenant faithfulness of Israel, the nation would retain its sovereign **kings and princes.** In other words, the promise of unending Davidic succession in kingship would be fulfilled (see 2 Sam. 7:16).

17:26 If the stipulations of v. 21 were followed, the temple would once again become the center of worship for the nation.

17:27 The consequence of disobedience would be total destruction of the city. If the stipulations of 17:21 were not followed, the Lord would bring an unquenchable, destructive **fire** against the city and its **palaces** (see 4:4; Hos. 8:14; Amos 1:4—2:5).

18:1, 2 Arise and go down is a common formula for divinely directed service.

18:3–6 The potter's **vessel** was **marred** and thus unsuitable for its intended purpose. The potter's remolding of the clay into an acceptable and unblemished work symbolized God's action in reforming Israel.

18:7, 8 If a **nation** threatened with destruction would turn **from its evil,** God would **relent of the** promised **disaster.** God the Potter was more than willing to forgive Judah. Unfortunately, the people continued in their stiffnecked ways.

18:9, 10 A nation to whom God has promised His blessing may forfeit its preferred status through disobedience. In such a case, God would **relent** of the **good** He had promised and bring calamity upon the rebellious people.

18:11 God was **fashioning a disaster,** a calamity, for **Judah** if it did not repent or **return** to Him and change its actions from **evil** to **good.**

18:12 The people's response to God's warning (v. 11) is similar to that in 17:23: They rebelliously pursued their own ways. **Hopeless** describes the despair the people felt about obedience to God. These feelings were the direct result of the **evil heart** that is characteristic of people who continually turn away from the Lord and His ways.

18:13, 14 Negative rhetorical questions show the absurdity of Israel's rebellion. **The snow water of Lebanon** describes the Mount Hermon watershed that erupts in numerous springs, providing most of the water for the Jordan River. God's blessing was often demonstrated in the provision of water from rocks in arid regions (see Ex. 17:6). No one would trade cool spring water for **strange** or "alien" **waters.**

18:15 The principal indictment against Judah was idolatry, which had resulted in the people's wayward lives and the humiliating destruction of the land. **worthless idols:** Foreign deities such as Baal and Asherah were represented by empty and ineffective cultic figurines. **they have caused themselves to stumble:** The people had brought upon themselves the droughts and disaster because they had strayed **from the ancient paths,** the way of the Law and the covenant relationship to God.

18:16 make their land desolate: For similar descriptions of the destruction of Judah, see 4:27; 6:8; 9:11.

18:17 An **east wind** refers to the scorching, late-spring scirocco wind from the northern Arabian desert. **I will show them the back and not the face:** This graphic expression depicts God withholding His assistance from the nation in its day of despair (2:27).

18:18 Similar to the situation in 11:18–23, the people devised **plans** to counter the words of **Jeremiah.** They reasoned that with their own priests, wise men, and prophets in Jerusalem, they did not need to listen to Jeremiah.

18:19, 20 Jeremiah reminded the Lord how he had interceded for the people and had asked God to **turn away** His **wrath** and judgment. But instead of showing their appreciation for Jeremiah's intervention, the people **dug a pit** in anticipation of his demise.

18:21, 22 Jeremiah's cry for personal revenge may not be as easily justified as those of the psalmists (see Ps. 137). Nonetheless, he had been falsely charged with misrepresenting the truth of God.

18:23 You know: As God had known Jeremiah's heart (12:3; 15:15), so He was keenly aware of the people's plots against the prophet. The word translated **atonement** is the same Hebrew word used in Yom Kippur, the Day of Atonement. The word emphasizes total cleansing and removal of sin and its effects. The word **blot out** is also used to refer to the removal of sin and guilt by God. Jeremiah's appeal was for God to condemn in **anger** rather than to forgive his enemies.

19:1, 2 The elders were summoned to follow Jeremiah to the **Valley of the Son of Hinnom** (7:31, 32), a dumping area where children were ritually sacrificed in the days of Manasseh.

19:3 Hear: This key word of the Deuteronomic code (see Deut. 6:4) calls for a decision about the content of the message. **his ears will tingle:** This expression is used to refer to a harsh, ringing judgment announcement (see 1 Sam. 3:11).

19:4–6 made this an alien place: The people, through their idolatry, had prevented the once-holy city of Jerusalem from being the place where God chose His name to dwell. The city had become a place of alien gods and goddesses. **The blood of the innocents** refers to the murderous act of child sacrifice (7:31). This abominable practice, performed in the name of religious worship, was explicitly forbidden in the covenant (see Deut. 12:31).

19:7 Babylon was the agent who would **make void,** or "lay waste," **the counsel** of the elders who rebutted the Lord's message through Jeremiah and continued in idolatry.

19:8 God would allow Jerusalem to be made an object of derision and humiliation in order to vindicate His name (18:16). **Plagues** would strike the city according to the covenant curse of Deut. 28:58–61 (see Lam. 2:15; Zeph. 2:15).

19:9 The gruesome practice of cannibalism appears, recalling the words of Deut. 28:53. After years of siege resulting in severe famine, the people would resort to eating human **flesh** in order to survive. This prophecy was literally fulfilled in 586 B.C. when Nebuchadnezzar invaded Judah, and again in A.D. 70 when Titus destroyed Jerusalem.

19:10, 11 As pottery **breaks** into pieces when it is thrown on the hard ground, so God's judgment would shatter the city and scatter those dwelling there. Restoration would be impossible. The number of corpses would outnumber possible burial sites (7:32, 33).

19:12–15 As the **inhabitants** of Jerusalem had made the Valley of the Son of Hinnom a place of death, so the Lord would make the entire city of Jerusalem a place of death (vv. 4–6).

20:1 Pashhur … chief governor: A person in this position had to be a priest. He had oversight of the temple, the temple guards, entry into the courts, and so on. Jeremiah's proclamations against the city and the temple were of grave concern to Pashhur because of the threat to the continuation of the cult in which he was involved.

20:2 Jeremiah was beaten and confined to a stockade by **Pashhur.** This was not a normal prison or dungeon, but a holding cell for those who might defile the area by uncleanness or aberrant behavior.

20:3, 4 The name **Magor-Missabib** means "Terror on Every Side." As Pashhur had been a **terror** to Jeremiah, so he would become a terror to himself, his family, and his associates. The foe from the north described in earlier passages (1:13–15) is here identified as **Babylon.**

20:5 The four resources of Jerusalem that would be transported with the exiles to Babylon were **wealth, produce, precious things,** and **treasures.** This list is balanced by four terms for the confiscation of Jerusalem's valuables: **give, plunder, seize,** and **carry.** The use of these terms for both the plunder and the confiscation indicates comprehensiveness.

20:6 Pashhur, his family, and his close associates who had opposed Jeremiah would be deported to **Babylon** because Pashhur had **prophesied lies;** that Jerusalem would not suffer destruction.

20:7 induced … persuaded: A play on words is intended by using two forms of the same word, which means "to entice." Jeremiah claimed that the Lord had seduced him and that he had succumbed to the temptation.

20:8 Jeremiah had faithfully proclaimed the Lord's **word** of judgment and destruction, but the prophecy had not been fulfilled, thus opening the prophet up to **reproach** and **derision.**

20:9 Jeremiah decided to refrain from declaring God's word or speaking **in His name.** But the divine message could not be held within or in any way hindered from accomplishing God's purpose (see Is. 46:10, 11; 55:11). God's **word** was like a consuming **fire** in Jeremiah's **heart** and **bones.**

20:10 Jeremiah was mocked with his own words, **fear on every side** (vv. 3, 4). **Report … and we will report it:** Whatever Jeremiah announced or denounced, the leaders of Judah turned back against him until he was devastated and demoralized.

20:11 Most psalms of individual lament contain a confession of trust in God (see Ps. 13). Jeremiah turned to God in prayer and praise in his hour of deepest need. **with me:** In his call, Jeremiah was promised God's presence to deliver him (1:8, 19). **mighty, awesome One:** God was Jeremiah's powerful warrior. Jeremiah's enemies would **not prevail** (vv. 7, 10), but would **stumble** and fall before God.

20:12 You who test: God tests (6:27; 17:10) and judges **the righteous,** those who walk uprightly in His ways and truth. **see the mind and heart:** God can see the innermost being of a person and discern his or her attitude and spirit.

20:13 Jeremiah's confession of trust turns to praise as he quotes or paraphrases a psalm or hymn.

20:14, 15 In ancient Israel, to curse God or one's parents was an offense punishable by death. Jeremiah avoided committing a capital offense by cursing his conception and birth, and hence his call from God.

20:16–18 Jeremiah's intense dejection caused him to call for the death of the man who told Jeremiah's father the good news of his son's birth. **did not relent:** Jeremiah thought it would have been more merciful for him to die before birth than to endure the hardship of rejection, persecution, and imprisonment that he faced.

21:1 Pashhur the son of Melchiah had Jeremiah cast into a dungeon for the prophet's alleged disloyalty to the kingdom (38:1–6). **Zephaniah the son of Maaseiah** was a temple officer who, with others, sought divine guidance through Jeremiah's counsel (37:3, 4).

21:2 To **inquire** of the Lord means to seek His will. **Nebuchadnezzar** was king of Babylon from 605–562 B.C. **wonderful works:** This phrase is primarily used of God in His cosmic activity and mighty acts in history on behalf of Israel (see Ps. 40:5). God had delivered Jerusalem from destruction during the siege of Sennacherib of Assyria in 701 B.C.; King Zedekiah was hoping for a similar divine deliverance.

21:3, 4 Jeremiah's response to **Zedekiah** was demoralizing. Instead of turning back the forces of the Babylonians, God would thwart what little strength Jerusalem could muster against them.

21:5 Because the people of Judah had become God's enemies, God would **fight against** them. **outstretched hand … strong arm:** The divine instruments by which Israel had gained freedom from Egypt (see Ex. 15:6; Deut. 6:21) and deliverance from their enemies would be used against them.

21:6, 7 The **pestilence** that would strike **man and beast** recalls one of God's plagues on the Egyptians prior to the Exodus (see Ex. 9:1–7). **Nebuchadnezzar … enemies … those who seek their life:** Not only did the Babylonians inflict damage upon Judah, so did constant enemies like the Edomites, who raided and then settled in the dry regions to the south. God would not **spare** or **have pity** on the stubborn and rebellious inhabitants of Judah and Jerusalem.

21:8, 9 way of life … way of death: *Death*

would come to those who attempted to survive the siege of Jerusalem; *life* was possible through surrender to the **Chaldeans** (Babylonians).

21:10 I have set My face: This phrase describes the fixed intention of God, which in this context was against Jerusalem. The result would be **adversity** rather than **good.**

21:11–14 This oracle in language reminiscent of 7:6 and Deut. 17:18–20 establishes the basis for judgments against the kings of **Judah** in subsequent chapters. The **king** was to be devoted to the commandments of God and was to mete out **judgment,** or justice. The ultimate test of the king was measured in his judicial response to those who were oppressed and **plundered** (see Is. 1:17; Amos 4:1–3). **inhabitant of the valley … rock of the plain:** These phrases refer to Jerusalem. **come down:** Attacking armies generally approached Jerusalem from the north.

22:1 One goes **down** to Jerusalem by coming from the north in Anathoth and descending slightly in elevation. **The house of the king** was the royal palace located just south of the temple courtyards.

22:2 Jeremiah's prophecy was addressed to three groups: kings who sit upon the **throne of David,** the kings' **servants** (royal officials and attendants), and the **people who enter these gates.** The last phrase may refer to the citizens in general or to personnel who regularly entered the palace gates.

22:3 According to Is. 11:1-5, the ideal Davidic king would **execute judgment,** or justice, **and righteousness,** or uprightness, fairness, and conformity to standard. The wisdom and prophetic writers echoed the same sentiment about the righteousness of kingdoms—that they must be measured according to their protection of the three segments of society who were unable to defend themselves: the **stranger,** the **fatherless,** and the **widow.**

22:4, 5 If justice and righteousness characterized the leadership of the land, the continued prosperity of the Davidic dynasty would be assured. However, if the Lord's **words** were not heeded, the house of David would be made a **desolation.**

22:6, 7 Gilead and **Lebanon** were sources

for timber for the royal palaces. These luxurious residences would be reduced to deserted **wilderness** and set ablaze if the kings disobeyed the covenant.

22:8 Even the **nations**—the Gentiles—would recognize that the punishment described in vv. 5–7 was the work of the Lord.

22:9, 10 The pagan nations would recognize that the destruction of Jerusalem was the result of Judah's violation of its **covenant** with God. The people of Judah had exchanged their God for alien deities, whom they **worshiped** and **served.**

22:11, 12 This is the first of three messages directed at specific kings of Judah. **Josiah** died at Megiddo in 609 B.C. while attempting to block Pharaoh Necho of Egypt from coming to the aid of Assyria. **who went from this place:** This is a reference to Jehoahaz, also called **Shallum.** This fourth son of Josiah was placed on the throne by the people of Judah, but he was dethroned after three months by Pharaoh Necho. Shallum was imprisoned and taken captive to Egypt (see 2 Chr. 36:1–4). Eliakim (Jehoiakim), Shallum's brother, was placed on the throne as an Egyptian vassal. Necho maintained control of Palestine until Nebuchadnezzar defeated Egypt at the Battle of Carchemish in 605 B.C. Shallum (Jehoahaz) died without returning from Egypt, in fulfillment of Jeremiah's words (2 Kin. 23:34).

22:13, 14 unrighteousness ... injustice: The key terms for true, biblical leadership quality—righteousness and justice—were negated by the king's actions. **uses his neighbor's service without wages:** The king was supposed to be the guardian of his people, but Jehoiakim enslaved his fellow Israelites to build his self-aggrandizing palaces.

22:15, 16 Did not your father ... do justice and righteousness: This rhetorical question identifies Josiah, father of Jehoiakim, as a model king. **knowing Me:** Israel perished because of its lack of knowledge of God (see Hos. 4:6).

22:17 Jehoiakim did not follow in the footsteps of Josiah. **covetousness ... shedding innocent blood ... practicing oppression and violence:** This triad of sins would hammer home a resounding message to Judah about the collapse of its kingship.

22:18, 19 A king of such despicable character as **Jehoiakim** deserved no **lament. burial of a donkey:** Jehoiakim would receive an ignoble burial, like an animal, alone and unlamented.

22:20 Jerusalem was called upon to mourn its destruction in the mountainous regions of the north—**Lebanon,** in the northeast—**Bashan,** and in the mountainous regions of the southeast—**Abarim.**

22:21 God had spoken to Israel and Judah in times of **prosperity,** as in the days of Azariah, Jeroboam II, and Josiah, but the people would not **hear** and **obey** the words of the prophets, righteous kings, priests, and other leaders.

22:22, 23 The wind shall eat up: The winds of adversity and invasion would carry off Judah's leaders and allies alike. The nation would be **ashamed** that it had entered into such futile associations. **Lebanon** refers to Jerusalem here (in contrast to v. 20). **Cedars** refers to the luxuriant royal palaces in the city (see Ezek. 17:1–10).

22:24–27 Coniah, also known as Jehoiachin, succeeded his father in 598 B.C. under the threat of siege from Babylon as a result of Jehoiakim's rebellion. The king's **signet** ring, a symbol of his power and authority, was used to seal official court documents. Jehoiachin could not serve God in such a capacity because of his evil reign (see 2 Kin. 24:9). Jehoiachin reigned for three months until he and his family were exiled to Babylon by Nebuchadnezzar (see 2 Kin. 24:6–16). **Your mother** refers to Nehushta, the queen mother of the eighteen-year old Jehoiachin. Eventually Jehoiachin was released from prison, after the death of Nebuchadnezzar (see 2 Kin. 25:27).

22:28–30 childless: The king had seven sons (see 1 Chr. 3:17, 18), but the Davidic lineage of kingship would not extend to his heirs. **A man who shall not prosper:** Jehoiachin remained in prison throughout the reign of Nebuchadnezzar from 598 to 562 B.C.

23:1, 2 Woe usually introduces a harsh message of judgment. **shepherds:** In the ancient Middle East, the ideal of kingship was often presented in the imagery of a shepherd. But instead of protecting and nurturing the nation, the shepherd-kings of Israel had **scattered** and **not attended to** or "visited" the people.

23:3 The kings of Israel had caused the dispersion of the nation; but the Lord would mercifully bring about the restoration of the **remnant.** The concept of a reestablished *remnant* is prominent in the prophets (see Is. 1:9; 10:20–23; 11:16; 46:3). The blessing of restoration and prosperity as a consequence of repentance is outlined in Deut. 30:1–10.

23:4 God would raise up a new generation of kings who would place the people's welfare and God's will above all other considerations.

23:5 Branch: Beginning with Is. 4:2, this term is used of the promised Messiah (see 33:15; Zech. 3:8; 6:12). This great king will reign with **judgment,** or justice, and **righteousness.** This ideal was founded on God's promise to David (2 Sam. 7:16). The necessity for the Lord to send His own king is based on the failure of Israel's monarchs to live up to the standards of kingship (21:11, 12; 22:1–4).

23:6 The **days** of the Messiah's reign would bring salvation. Both **Judah** and **Israel** would be restored. The **name** that characterizes this ideal king is **THE LORD OUR RIGHTEOUSNESS.** Contrast that to the name Zedekiah, which means "The Lord Is My Righteousness" (21:1). Zedekiah's name was a gross misnomer compared to the One who would establish the true, righteous rule—God's appointed king (see also Is. 9:7; 11:1–10). This verse is one of the texts in the Hebrew Bible that speaks specifically and surely of the coming of the glorious Savior and King.

23:7, 8 the days are coming: The future restoration of Israel would exceed even the first Exodus, the deliverance from Egypt.

23:9, 10 Heart here refers to the mind more than the emotions. Jeremiah's dismay over the false **prophets** weakened him, so much so that he felt **drunken** from the inner turmoil. The prophet also felt unrest from his being consumed by the **holy words** of God. **adulterers:** This term could apply to those

who practiced immoral sexual behavior, those who committed spiritual adultery by pursuing other gods, and those who were involved in cultic prostitution.

23:11, 12 Prophets were to be spokesmen for God in directing the nation. Priests were to teach the Law (see Lev. 10:8–20). **My house:** Like the **prophet and priest,** the temple of God had become polluted by the **wickedness** of the spiritual leaders.

23:13, 14 The **prophets of Samaria,** rather than speaking in the name of God, **prophesied by Baal.** They **caused** the **people of Israel to err**—that is, to stray morally, mentally, and spiritually from God's norms. The leaders of Judah had supported **evildoers** who, like the kings, had abused the power of their position. The nation had become like **Sodom** and **Gomorrah** and thus deserved the same judgment those cities suffered (see Gen. 19:12–29).

23:15 Wormwood and **water of gall** refer to bitterness and death by poison. According to Deut. 18:20, the consequence of false prophecy was death.

23:16 Worthless is used to describe the futility of listening to those who **speak a vision of their own heart.** Visions were commonly understood to be a means of receiving a message from God (or the gods).

23:17 The false prophets proclaimed a false hope of **peace** and security to those who despised Jeremiah. However God's intention was to bring **evil,** or calamity (6:14).

23:18 God's **counsel** is available to those who walk in the fear of the Lord according to **His word**.

23:19, 20 God's counsel to Jeremiah's audience was not peace but harsh judgment. **Whirlwind** is used as a symbol of God's judgment (see Is. 29:6). **thoughts of His heart:** This phrase denotes God's plans and purposes by which He was bringing punishment (contrast Ps. 40:5).

23:21–24 A true prophet must be **sent** by God with a word from God. A true prophet of God calls people to repentance of sin or **evil** and to renewed faith.

23:25–27 Lies here is singular, referring to the quality of the word the false prophets spoke. **I have dreamed:** Dreams were prized among the Assyrians, Egyptians, and Babylonians as a means of divine revelation. But in Israelite law and tradition, dreams were received cautiously. **the heart of the prophets:** The character of the false prophets was based on **lies** and **deceit.** Their deception was apparent because their goal was to draw the people into idolatry, leading people to **forget** God and follow **Baal** (2:8).

23:28, 29 This poetic interlude compares **dream** and **word.** A dream is fleeting, like **chaff** in the wind. God's word has the force of **fire** and a **hammer.**

23:30, 31 steal My words: Lacking true knowledge and a word from God, the false prophets repeated false hopes and twisted God's words. They spoke on their own, lacking a true word from God.

23:32 The counterfeit spokesmen of God prophesied **false dreams,** deluding the people. **Recklessness** further indicates the perverse character of the false prophets.

23:33–36 No true **oracle** would come from the false prophets. The sharing of oracles among neighbors (v. 27) would involve perverting **the words of the living God.** The false prophets turned God's words around to their own desired benefit.

23:37–40 Speaking **the oracle of the LORD** was forbidden for the false prophets. **everlasting reproach ... perpetual shame:** The disgrace that resulted from the false prophets would last for an extended period of time; its memory would endure forever (20:11).

24:1 The LORD showed me: This phrase suggests a visionary experience like those of Amos and Joel. The historical setting is the 597 B.C. exile of **Jeconiah** (Jehoiachin).

24:2, 3 The observation of **good,** or newly ripened, **figs** in the temple would place this account in the context of the fall festival of firstfruits (see Deut. 26:1–11).

24:4–7 The **good figs** are identified with the deported exiles, including Jeconiah's royal household, whom God set apart **for good.** God would **bring ... back** the captives, establish them in the **land,** and multiply their crops. Above all, God would **give them a heart to know** Him.

24:8–10 According to chs. 28 and 36–38, the people who remained in **Jerusalem** treated Jeremiah harshly, subjecting him to beating and imprisonment. **Zedekiah** and his entourage, along with Jews who fled to Egypt, would see the **trouble,** meaning "trembling fear" or "horror," and **harm,** meaning "calamity," from the Lord.

25:1, 2 the first year of Nebuchadnezzar: In 605 B.C., Nebuchadnezzar succeeded his father on the throne of Babylon. He quickly moved his army to Carchemish and then defeated the Egyptians and some Assyrians. The following year Nebuchadnezzar's forces gained control of all of Palestine, reaching southward to the Brook of Egypt.

25:3 Starting from time he was called in 626 B.C., Jeremiah faithfully proclaimed the word of the Lord for 23 years. The idiom **rising early and speaking** describes Jeremiah's diligence and persistence.

25:4, 5 Other **prophets,** such as Habakkuk, Zephaniah, Urijah (26:20), and those of previous centuries, had persistently proclaimed the message of repentance so that the nation might remain **in the land.** Security, prosperity, and long life *in the land* were directly related to the nation's covenant faithfulness to God (see Deut. 28; 29).

25:6, 7 The phrase **go after** is used throughout Jeremiah to mean resorting to **other gods** in worship. **The works of your hands** refers to the man-made idols used in pagan worship, a breach of the covenant (see Ex. 20:3–5) that provoked God **to anger.**

25:8, 9 Nebuchadnezzar ... My servant: This expression does not imply that the Babylonian monarch worshiped Israel's God, but simply that he was used by God to fulfill His purposes (as in the case of Cyrus, who is called the Lord's "anointed" in Is. 45:1).

25:10, 11 take: This term means "cause to perish" and indicates harsh judgment. Life as they knew it would cease. **These nations** refers to Judah and the surrounding nations, such as Moab and Phoenicia, who would be subjected to enslavement and captivity. **Seventy years** is the approximate length of the Babylonian captivity.

25:12–17 The triad sequence **drink ... stagger ... go mad** depicts the judgment process by which the **sword** of the Lord subdues those opposed to Him. To drink the cup and stagger was to display one's guilt (see Num. 5:19–28).

25:18 The list of nations that would be made to drink from the cup of the Lord's judgment begins with **Judah** and **Jerusalem,** which would be made a source of derision (19:8; 25:9).

25:19 The first foreign nation condemned by God through Jeremiah was **Egypt.** The expanded oracle is found in ch. 46.

25:20 The **land of Uz** is generally interpreted as the region of Edom or northern Arabia. **Ashkelon** was captured by Nebuchadnezzar in 604 B.C. **Gaza** and **Ashdod** are also mentioned in Nebuchadnezzar's Babylonian chronicles (see ch. 47).

25:21, 22 The states of **Edom, Moab,** and **Ammon,** and the Phoenician coastal territories of **Tyre** and **Sidon,** suffered heavily under Nebuchadnezzar's attacks (see 48:1–49:22; Ezek. 27; 28).

25:23, 24 The Arabian desert kingdoms of **Dedan, Tema,** and **Buz** were condemned. Dedan and Tema were in Edomite territory (49:7, 8). The location of Buz is unknown.

25:25, 26 Elam and Media were located east of Babylon (49:34–39).

25:27, 28 The triad of terms for progressive inebriation—**drink, be drunk,** and **vomit**—emphasizes the extent of judgment that would flow from God's cup of wrath.

25:29 God's judgment would **begin** with His own people and their holy city. God would **bring calamity** on the city that was called by His **name.** In doing so, God would vindicate His name and His holiness. From Jerusalem, God's **sword** of judgment would go forth to the ends of the earth.

25:30 on high … from His holy habitation: Generally these phrases refer to God's abode on Mount Zion (see Joel 3:16; Amos 1:2).

25:31 A noise refers to a thunderous judgment resulting from God's **controversy** or "covenant lawsuit" against the nations. Though they had not received the Law like Judah and Israel, the Gentiles would be judged because they were **wicked.**

25:32, 33 As with Judah's horrifying calamity of unburied corpses (7:33), the nations would experience massive death and extensive destruction. The neglect of the dead is described in a triad of terms: **not be lamented …** (not be) **gathered …** (not be) **buried.** This desecration would be finalized by the decay of bodies into **refuse** or "dung" (8:2; 9:22; 16:4).

25:34–38 Homes and pastures that once were **peaceful** and secure would be devastated. **The Oppressor** is a surprising designation for the Lord.

26:1 In the beginning: This expression technically refers to the part of the year between the day the king ascended to the throne and the beginning of his first full year of reign, which began in the spring month of Nisan (March-April), 608 B.C.

26:2 The **court** of the temple may refer to one of the inner courts connected by the gate mentioned in 7:2. **Come to worship** describes the normal worship there or perhaps more specifically the pilgrimages to Jerusalem for festival and fast days. **Do not diminish:** Jeremiah was told to speak with unwavering boldness.

26:3–5 The introduction to the judgment oracle is expressed in conditional terms. If the people repented of **evil,** the Lord would relent from the **calamity** He was threatening to bring on them.

26:6 Shiloh was not far from Jerusalem. The people could see the effects of its destruction by the Philistines in 1050 B.C.—a destruction that overtook it even though it was the first resting place of the ark of the covenant. Jeremiah uses Shiloh as an illustration of the coming judgment of Jerusalem.

26:7–9 The priests and the prophets and all the people refers to the collective worship assembly. The religious leaders responsible for overseeing the temple considered Jeremiah's words blasphemy, for he spoke of the destruction of the temple itself. The people rejected Jeremiah's prophecy and tried to kill him.

26:10, 11 Jeremiah's words were reported to the **princes,** the royal administrators and kingdom officials, who came to the **New Gate** to carry out an official inquiry. The prophets and priests presented an accusation against Jeremiah, calling for the death sentence for speaking **against** Jerusalem.

26:12, 13 Jeremiah called the assembly to **amend,** or make good, their evil **ways** and to **obey** God's **voice,** referring to the covenant and the words proclaimed by Jeremiah.

26:14, 15 Held captive by the hostile crowd, Jeremiah pointed to the potential sin of shedding **innocent blood.** Jeremiah had already accused the leaders of Jerusalem of shedding *innocent blood* with child sacrifices in the Hinnom valley (2:34; 19:4).

26:16 This man does not deserve to die: Jeremiah's self-defense gained acceptance from the crowd, against the objections of the wicked religious leaders.

26:17–19 After Jeremiah's hearing, one of the **elders** from the people cited the precedent of the eighth-century prophet **Micah of Moresheth.** In the reign of **Hezekiah,** Micah had announced the impending destruction of Jerusalem by the Assyrians (see Mic. 3:12). Yet because of the repentance of Hezekiah and the inhabitants, the city was spared from the onslaught of the Assyrian army under Sennacherib (701 B.C.).

26:20–23 Urijah, whose name means "My Light Is the Lord," was from Kirjath Jearim, about 15 miles west of Jerusalem (see 1 Sam. 7:1, 2). Like Jeremiah, Urijah had **prophesied in the name of the LORD** about judgment against Jerusalem. When **Jehoiakim** and his administrators heard of Urijah's declarations, they sought to seize the "blasphemous" prophet, who escaped by fleeing to **Egypt.** Since Jehoiakim was a vassal to Necho of Egypt, Urijah was extradited and executed.

26:24 Jeremiah was sheltered by **Ahikam the son of Shaphan** who, along with his father, served as a scribe under Josiah when the Book of the Law was found in the temple (see 2 Kin. 22:8–14). Ahikam's brother Gemariah also opposed Jehoiakim's burning of Jeremiah's original scroll (36:25). This faithful family was supportive of Jeremiah and was instrumental in saving his life.

27:1–3 Bonds and yokes are wooden bars or beams that attach to a pair of oxen with leather bands. The symbolic act of wearing the yoke would communicate bondage, restraint, and enslavement.

27:4, 5 The foreign ambassadors were to announce to their **masters** that the God of Israel is the true sovereign Lord over creation and the affairs of humans. The whole of creation is summed up in the triad **earth ... man ... beast.** Unlike the gods of the nations, whose power was often believed to be geographically limited, the God of Israel reigned over all the earth, granting territorial rights and power to nations and kings as **it seemed proper** to Him.

27:6, 7 My servant: With all of his military might and conquests, the king of Babylon was still a servant of the God of Israel, carrying out the Lord's purposes—the judgment of Judah. **son's son ... time of his land:** Following the death of Nebuchadnezzar in 562 B.C., his heirs and successors retained control of Babylon for only 24 years. Babylon fell without a battle to Cyrus and the Persian armies in 539 B.C., and later to Alexander the Great of Greece.

27:8 The symbol of the **yoke** is explained to the foreign ambassadors. Those who would not submit as vassals to Babylon would be punished.

27:9, 10 The way kings summoned various prophet-diviners to give them direction is well known from the Book of Daniel (see Dan. 2:2; 5:7). Besides **prophets,** there were **diviners,** like Balaam (see Num. 22—24), who were prohibited from practicing their craft in Israel (see Deut. 18:9–14); **dreamers,** a class of fortune-tellers prohibited by the Law (see Deut. 13:1–5); as well as **soothsayers** and **sorcerers,** both common among the nations but forbidden to practice their trades in Israel (see Deut. 18:9–14). The collective effort of these diviners to determine the fate of their nations failed. Like the false prophets of Judah, they heralded a message of rebellion and resistance against Babylon. Only Jeremiah stood for the truth: the Lord would punish Judah through Nebuchadnezzar.

27:11 bring their necks under the yoke: To submit to Babylon was to submit to the will and purposes of God.

27:12–14 Jeremiah's message to **Zedekiah** was the same as his message to the foreign ambassadors (vv. 4–11): submit to Nebuchadnezzar and the Babylonians and **live,** or rebel against Nebuchadnezzar—and God—and **die.**

27:15 I have not sent them: Divine call and commission are prerequisites to fulfilling a true prophetic role.

27:16, 17 Do not listen: For the priests to *listen* to the false words of the prophets about the inviolability of the temple was to seal their own doom and that of the temple. Many **vessels** (v. 19) had been carried off by Nebuchadnezzar in the exile of Jeconiah (Jehoiachin). The false prophets said that Babylon would be defeated and the temple furnishings would be returned.

27:18–20 Jeremiah proposed a test to verify the words of the contentious prophets. **if the word of the LORD is with them:** If the prophets truly spoke for the Lord, their **intercession**—the survival of the remaining temple implements—would come to pass. **vessels which are left:** Many of the furnishings of the temple of the Lord were transported to Babylon in the exile of Jehoiachin and his entourage (see 2 Kin. 24:13). According to Jeremiah, the vessels that remained would be taken in the final destruction of the city. Events would demonstrate whose word was from the Lord.

27:21, 22 Jeremiah's message from the Lord is presented in detail. The remaining **vessels** in the temple, as well as in the king's palace, would be **carried to Babylon** until the Lord restored His people. In the midst of a prophetic message against the false prophets, Jeremiah spoke a message of hope and restoration. Destruction was imminent, but God would restore the righteous remnant.

28:1 The same year refers to the time of ch. 27 (593 B.C.). **The fifth month** was the month of Ab (July-August). **Hananiah** was from **Gibeon,** six miles northwest of Jerusalem and about five miles west of Jeremiah's hometown, Anathoth.

28:2–6 Hananiah spoke in the name of the **LORD of hosts,** using the name of God as Jeremiah did to introduce a solemn message of judgment against Babylon. Building on Jeremiah's imagery of the *yoke* (ch. 27), Hananiah proclaimed the contradictory message that the **yoke of ... Babylon** would be **broken** by God. Hananiah believed that God's message

for Judah was one of imminent deliverance—**within two full years**—from servitude to the king of Babylon. Hananiah also prophesied the return of the holy **vessels** taken by **Nebuchadnezzar** from the temple of God. Furthermore, Hananiah espoused the popular belief that the kingship of Zedekiah was illegitimate and that God would restore **Jeconiah** (Jehoiachin) to the throne in Jerusalem.

28:7–9 war and disaster and pestilence: Hananiah's message of peace and prosperity ran contrary to the long tradition of the genuine Hebrew prophets.

28:10, 11 Seizing the **yoke** from Jeremiah's **neck** (ch. 27) and breaking it before the people, Hananiah made a resounding proclamation: **Even so I will break the yoke of Nebuchadnezzar ... from the neck of all nations within the space of two full years.** This announcement reversed every statement by Jeremiah and advanced the cause of rebellion against Babylon by Judah and the surrounding nations, something King Zedekiah had desired all along.

28:12, 13 After an indefinite period of time, the **word of the LORD came to Jeremiah.** God's prophet was instructed to return to Hananiah with a new interpretation of the *yoke* motif. Because Hananiah had broken the original **yokes of wood,** God would replace them with **yokes of iron** that could not be broken.

28:14 All these nations against which Jeremiah originally had spoken (in 27:1–11) would serve Nebuchadnezzar.

28:15, 16 Hananiah had not been **sent** by God, but he had led the people astray with a **lie.** As a result, Hananiah would be **cast ... from the face of the earth** and **die** that very year.

28:17 The seventh month: Two months after Hananiah prophesied about Judah's captivity (v. 1), the false prophet was dead.

29:1 words of the letter: A written document was carried from Jerusalem to the Jews in Babylon. **remainder:** This may imply that some of the **elders** were executed in the 594 B.C. revolt alluded to in vv. 21–23.

29:2 This parenthetical passage provides background from 2 Kin. 24:12–16 about the deportation of Jeconiah (Jehoiachin), the royal family, and chief artisans of Judah to Babylon in 597 B.C. This method of eliminating leaders and leaving the peasant population to pay taxes to the kingdom was learned from the Assyrians and was designed to reduce the likelihood of rebellion.

29:3 The messengers were **Elasah the son of Shaphan,** perhaps a brother of the sympathetic Ahikam (26:24), and **Gemariah the son of Hilkiah,** a member of Jehoiakim's administration (36:10).

29:4 Jeremiah reminded the exiled community that ultimately it was **God,** not Nebuchadnezzar, who had caused them to be **carried away captive … to Babylon.**

29:5, 6 Jeremiah had proclaimed a period of seventy years (25:12) of Babylonian exile. For the meantime, he counseled the people to settle in and carry on their normal daily activities. The terms **build** and **plant** are significant because they fulfill the particulars of Jeremiah's call (1:10). Exile did not necessarily mean imprisonment or enslavement, but displacement and resettlement in unknown lands. **be increased … not diminished:** If the people were faithful in the circumstances of captivity, God would cause them to prosper with children and with fertile crops.

29:7 The exiles were instructed to **seek** and **pray** for the **peace,** or well-being of Babylon and the other towns where they were deported. As a result, they themselves would live in peace as beneficiaries of God's gracious sovereignty over the nations (27:5, 6).

29:8, 9 Jeremiah issued a warning against following the advice of **prophets, diviners,** and **dreams.**

29:10 The concept of the **seventy years** of Babylon captivity is reiterated from 25:12. The number *seventy* symbolizes completion and fulfillment of God's sovereign plans for creation and human history. The completion of the years of the kingdom of Babylon would also be the completion of Judah's exile.

29:11 I know the thoughts that I think: The Lord here places considerable emphasis on His unchangeable plan to bring **peace** and not **evil. a future … a hope:** God had not terminated His relationship with Judah; He

remembered His covenant promises of restoration (see Deut. 30:1–10).

29:12, 13 The promised response of the Lord to the people's prayers stands in contrast to His refusal to hear in 7:16. **all your heart:** The picture here differs greatly from the usual depiction of the heart of the people of Judah as stubborn and wicked (3:10; 4:14; 7:24). God would search the people's heart and reveal its true character (11:20).

29:14 I will be found: Those who seek God with a whole heart will find Him and experience His renewal. **I will bring you back … gather you … bring you to the place:** God was the captor, and He would restore His people from captivity.

29:15–20 The cause of Jerusalem's shame was its failure to heed the **words** of God, revealed through the covenant stipulations and the diligent—**rising up early**—proclamation of the prophets (25:3; 26:5).

29:21 Ahab the son of Kolaiah, and Zedekiah the son of Maaseiah were the prophets spoken of in 29:15. The two were accused by Jeremiah of a deplorable crime: prophesying **a lie** in God's **name.** Their *lie* was prophesying the imminent collapse of Babylon and the restoration of the captives to Jerusalem.

29:22, 23 This term **curse** may be a play on the name Kolaiah ("called of the Lord"; v. 21). He claimed to be called of God, but was cursed along with those who supported his position. These Jewish leaders had compounded their sin by doing **disgraceful things** (see Deut. 22:21).

29:24–28 Jeremiah addressed **Shemaiah the Nehelamite** about his correspondence with **Zephaniah the son of Maaseiah** and the Jerusalem priesthood. Shemaiah had challenged Zephaniah's apparent leniency in dealing with the problem of Jeremiah's prophecies about the exiles' immediate future.

29:29, 30 When **Zephaniah** received the **letter** from Shemaiah, he read it to Jeremiah, who then received a word of judgment from God against Shemaiah and his family.

29:31, 32 prophesied … caused you to trust in a lie: The accusation against Shemaiah parallels that of numerous judgment oracles in Jeremiah (5:31; 14:14; 23:16; 27:10).

The ensuing sentence against Shemaiah is like those against Pashhur (20:6), Jehoiachin or Coniah (22:30), and Hananiah (28:16).

30:1, 2 The oracles of Jeremiah were recorded by the scribe Baruch (ch. 36). **Book** refers to any type of writing medium, from a clay tablet to a parchment scroll. Jeremiah's oracles were recorded on a scroll (36:2).

30:3, 4 they shall possess it: Possession of the land, as in the original possession under Joshua's leadership, would be the responsibility of the faithful remnant living according to the covenant relationship.

30:5, 6 voice of trembling ... fear ... not of peace: Jeremiah's audience was the whole nation of Israel and Judah, which had experienced the dread and horror of the day of the Lord (see Joel 1:1—2:11; Amos 5:18–20). **Hands on his loins** symbolizes the agony of God's people, who had become like defenseless pregnant women in the midst of delivery before their enemies (4:31; 6:24).

30:7–9 The incomparable **day** of God was an ordained time of horror and distress for Israel and Judah, out of which the Lord would save them. Jeremiah expressed the hope of release from the bondage of the **yoke** of Babylon according to the Lord's timing (25:12) and not that of men (28:11). Then Israel would **serve the LORD their God, and David their king.** God would **raise up** a messianic king from David's line to rule over the nation (see Is. 9:7; 11:1; Hos. 3:5).

30:10, 11 My servant: The use of this terminology for Israel and Judah parallels that of Is. 42:1; 44:1. The hope of the nation was **rest,** tranquillity in the absence of external and internal distress, and **quiet,** security and ease resulting from trust in the Lord.

30:12 Your affliction is incurable, Your wound is severe: God's hand of judgment had brought serious harm to the nation, a mortal wound unless God intervened.

30:13 Healing here refers to the growth of new skin over an open wound.

30:14 Israel's **lovers** were nations like Assyria, Egypt, Phoenicia, Ammon, and Edom, with whom it had made political and religious alliances. These nations had quickly **forgotten** Judah; they shrank back or were defeated by Nebuchadnezzar.

30:15 iniquities ... sins: These terms are repeated from v. 14, emphasizing the character of the people and echoing the reasons for harsh judgment. The lament applied to both the sin and its results.

30:16, 17 Restoration and healing of Israel came in two forms, retribution against its enemies and healing of its wounds. Four sets of terms designate God's retributive justice: **those who devour** would **be devoured; adversaries** would **go into captivity; those who plunder** would become **plunder;** and **all who prey** would become **prey.**

30:18 Jacob's tents ... dwelling places ... city ... palace: These phrases emphasize God's work in rebuilding the homes and cities of His returning exiles, from the peasant population to the administration.

30:19 Instead of the voice of lament, fear, and trembling echoing throughout the land (4:31; 30:5), the sound of **thanksgiving** and merrymaking would reverberate.

30:20–22 Israel's leaders would no longer be appointed by foreign kings, and foreign rulers would not preside over Israel's lands.

30:23, 24 These verses are essentially a reiteration of 23:19, 20. In this context, they attest to Israel's new understanding of its God and assure the people of God's judgment on their enemies and oppressors.

31:1 Coinciding with the restoration of the nation to its land would be the fulfillment of the covenant between God and His people, **all the families of Israel.**

31:2 survived the sword ... found grace in the wilderness ... give him rest: These phrases describe Israel's deliverance from Egypt and God's victory over the army of Pharaoh.

31:3 Of old, which may also be translated "from afar," may refer to the betrothal days of Israel in the wilderness (2:1–3) or to the distant lands of Assyria and Babylon to which Israel and Judah had been exiled. The phrase **everlasting love** is paralleled with **lovingkindness,** which means "loyal love" or "covenant loyalty." Out of His faithfulness to the covenants He established with Abraham and Moses, God established the nation Israel for His glory and for hers. The

Lord would also deliver His people from captivity and reestablish them by His love.

31:4 O virgin of Israel: Earlier in Jeremiah, this expression was used sadly in depicting the departure of Israel from faith in God (2:32; 14:17). Here the image is reversed; Israel is rebuilt in the manner of her former betrothal (2:2), having become again like a virgin bride to God. **adorned ... go forth in the dances:** Joyful celebration of marriage and festival throughout villages is in view here (v. 13).

31:5 The mountains of Samaria, which were ravaged by the Assyrians in 733–722 B.C., would be replanted with vineyards. The hills would produce fruit for consumption rather than tribute for foreign powers. The plantings would be for regular, normal enjoyment—a gift of God in the lives of His people.

31:6 The day would come when the nation would be united once again, with northern kingdom Israelites making pilgrimages to **Zion** (Jerusalem) for worship, instead of continuing to visit the rival sanctuaries of Dan and Bethel (see 1 Kin. 12:27–29). The purpose of the **watchmen** would be not to warn the people about oncoming armies but to call them to come with joy to the holy city.

31:7, 8 The chief of the nations would be **Jacob,** meaning Israel. In 15:9 the **remnant** is

The New Covenant

Jeremiah is the only OT prophet who speaks about the New Covenant that Jesus inaugurated (Matt. 26:28). Some readers, desiring to celebrate what is "new" in the New Covenant, might be tempted to disparage the former covenant, the Mosaic covenant. But we should be careful to avoid any implication that there was something wrong in the covenant God had graciously bestowed on Israel.

God had never designed the Law of Moses as a means to obtain salvation. Instead, forgiveness of sins has always been God's gracious gift to those who have humbled themselves before Him in faith (Gen. 15:6; Mic. 6:6–8; Rom. 4:1—5:2; 7:13–25). The Law was God's way of pointing out the pathway that believers should walk. Thus, the problem with the covenant at Mount Sinai was not in God's provision, but in Israel's response.

The Israelites had continually broken the covenant. Time and again through priests and prophets God called His people to repent, but any change of heart they underwent they soon abandoned. In the days of Jeremiah, King Josiah destroyed the idols that were in the land. But soon after this godly king died, the people turned back to worshiping the idols of the neighboring countries. The *hearts* of the people remained unchanged. Only God Himself could change hearts and minds: thus a new covenant was needed.

The announcement of a new covenant by the prophet Jeremiah would have been alarming to godly Israelites. After all, the old covenant had come from the hand of God and had been accompanied by miracles and wonders. But the New Covenant would also be accompanied by the miracle of changed hearts and lives. The Spirit of God would enter people's lives in order to assure their adherence to the covenant (31:34; see Acts 2). No longer would intermediaries such as priests or prophets have to stand between the people and God. The Spirit would teach the people the knowledge of God—a knowledge that would demonstrated by faith, obedience, and devotion to the Lord.

Jesus fulfilled Jeremiah's prediction of the coming of a New Covenant through His work on the cross. By His death, the giving of His blood for many, redemption and forgiveness of sins were attained (31:34). While Jesus was on earth, He instructed His disciples in His Father's ways (Luke 24:13–27). But after Jesus ascended to heaven, the Sprit of God was poured out on the believers gathered in Jerusalem, fulfilling the promise spoken by Jeremiah.

described as all but vanquished. Here the restored community shouts for joy.

31:9 weeping ... supplications: Phrases from the Songs of Ascents (Pss. 120—134) are found here. In Ps. 126, those who are weeping are filled with gladness at the Lord's return of exiles from captivity. **rivers of waters:** This imagery of God's provision of life-sustaining water through the desert is like Is. 35:5–7.

31:10, 11 God would be the people's good **shepherd,** unlike past kings (23:1–4). **redeemed ... ransomed:** These two terms for redemption describe the transfer of ownership of Israel from the mighty Babylon to the incomparable God. Israel's freedom was gained by God, its great "kinsman redeemer" (see Is. 51:10, 11).

31:12 The blessings of the goodness of the Lord are bountiful crops, flocks, and vineyards (see Ps. 65). **well-watered garden:** This expression of blessing upon the crops is also found in Is. 58:11.

31:13, 14 The theme of joy is summarized in God's intention to fill the **priests** and the **people** with **abundance.** Jeremiah gave the people hope and comfort in facing the poverty and oppression of exile and captivity.

31:15–16 Rachel's **bitter weeping** was caused by the exile and captivity of her children. She refused **to be comforted** in her sorrow and loss.

31:17 Hope describes a faith that waits expectantly for God's redemptive and eternal blessing. **their own border:** Ephraim would be restored to its God-ordained territories.

31:18, 19 struck ... on the thigh: This indicates an outward demonstration of remorse over sin and change of life (see Ezek. 21:12).

31:20 My heart yearns: This phrase describes the Lord's deep love and concern for the welfare of His children.

31:21 The **signposts** and **landmarks** would point out the way to the people's homeland. More importantly, Israel was instructed to **set** its **heart** toward the **way** that is the path of faith in its God.

31:22 Backsliding was a major theme in 3:6—4:4, describing the continual waywardness of the nation. Here the Lord was bringing about the re-creation of His people. **A new thing** probably refers to the fact that

virgin Israel would **encompass** or cling to her divine Bridegroom.

31:23–26 Mountain of holiness refers to the ideal city of Jerusalem, the holy mountain home of God, the Righteous One, and Judah, His righteous remnant. As with Israel, Judah's reestablishment would see renewed productivity of its crops and flocks (31:5, 12). The people would be **satiated** (31:14).

31:27, 28 sow: God would plant and multiply the **seed of man** and animal in the land of Judah.

31:29, 30 The proverb in this passage is also found in Ezek. 18:2. The contexts in both books indicate that this proverb is not original to Jeremiah or Ezekiel. In Israel and other ancient Middle Eastern communities, corporate responsibility was emphasized in legal and moral matters (see Deut. 5:9), though individual accountability was not overlooked (see Deut. 24:16; 2 Sam. 12:1–15). In Jeremiah and Ezekiel, focus is placed on the responsibility of the individual for his or her **own iniquity.**

31:31 days are coming: In Jeremiah, this phrase usually introduces a special occasion of divine intervention in history. **new covenant:** As contrasted with the Mosaic and Deuteronomic covenant. **house of Israel ... house of Judah:** According to 11:10, both kingdoms had broken God's covenant by rejecting His words and by worshiping other gods.

31:32 fathers: From the wilderness period (see Ex. 32:1–10; Num. 25:1–9) until the days of Manasseh, the history of Israel was permeated with idolatrous activity, only occasionally broken by periods of true faithfulness to God. The people seemed incapable of acting in sustained obedience to the covenant. **husband:** As Hosea was to Gomer, the Lord had been a faithful and devoted *husband* to Israel.

31:33 I will make: The new **covenant** would be initiated by God Himself, assuring its effectiveness. **after those days:** This expression looks forward to the time of fulfillment of the new covenant, which found fruition in the life, death, and resurrection of Jesus Christ. **put My law in their minds ... write it on their hearts:** Together the *mind* and *heart* describe the total inner motivations of mind, will, emotion, and spirit.

31:34 No more shall every man teach: No longer would intermediaries like priests or prophets be needed to show the people how to **know the LORD.** From youngest to oldest, from peasant farmer to kings and princes, all would know God. He will **forgive** and will purposefully not **remember** the **sin** and **iniquity** of His people who come to Him in repentance and faith. Jesus the Messiah fulfilled this promised New Covenant through His work on the Cross (see Matt. 26:26–28; Mark 14:22–24; 1 Cor. 11:25).

31:35 sun ... moon ... stars: God, the Creator of all things, entered into covenant with His people. **sea ... waves:** God is Master of the sea, as He is Master of all things (see Is. 51:15).

31:36, 37 Ordinances here are the natural laws that govern creation. The foundation of the New Covenant is as sure as the God who maintains creation.

31:38–40 days are coming: This expression introduces a new era in the history of God's dealing with His people. A survey is made of the environs of the new Jerusalem, a city **built for the LORD** in its entirety. The **Tower of Hananel** (see Neh. 3:1) was located at the northeast corner of the city. The **Corner Gate** (see 2 Kin. 14:13) was to the northwest. The **valley of the dead bodies** is probably a reference to the Valley of Hinnom, where children had been sacrificed in times of terrible apostasy (7:32). **The fields as far as the Brook Kidron** are the slopes of Mount Zion bordered by the Valley of Hinnom. **plucked up ... thrown down:** The destructive terms of Jeremiah's call are used again (1:10). No longer would the city see devastation, for it would be **holy to the LORD.**

32:1, 2 This verse relates the chronologies of Israel and Babylon. Nebuchadnezzar's **eighteenth year** was 588 B.C., at the beginning of the siege of Jerusalem. The siege resulted from Zedekiah's revolt against Babylonian rule.

32:3–5 Jeremiah was imprisoned for his declaration that Jerusalem would fall to

the **Chaldeans** and **Zedekiah** would be taken captive. **face to face ... eye to eye:** The one-on-one confrontation with Nebuchadnezzar would result in the removal of Zedekiah's eyes (39:5–7).

32:6–8 The Lord instructed Jeremiah to purchase a field in his hometown of **Anathoth,** three miles north of Jerusalem, when Jeremiah's cousin **Hanamel** came to visit. **right of redemption:** According to Lev. 25:25–30, a man had the right to redeem property when a relative found it necessary to sell land because of debt or financial failure.

32:9 The land transaction was conducted according to the legal customs of the day. The price of **seventeen shekels** would amount to about seven ounces of **silver.**

32:10, 11 According to custom, one copy of a **deed** was **sealed** for safekeeping; a second copy was left open for future consultation.

32:12 Baruch the son of Neriah: This friend of Jeremiah is first mentioned here (see ch. 36); he may have brought the silver for the land to Jeremiah in prison.

32:13–15 shall be possessed again: Jeremiah realized that the end of the city was near (v. 2); his action in purchasing land was a remarkable demonstration of faith in God that the people of Judah would return one day to their land.

32:16, 17 There is nothing too hard for You: Affirming God's power in creation (27:5) bolstered Jeremiah's faith in God's ability to deal with the siege of Jerusalem.

32:18, 19 The Lord's mercy and devotion to His people was demonstrated in His extending **lovingkindness,** or loyal love, to **thousands** (see Deut. 5:9, 10), but the seriousness of sin is not to be overlooked (see Ex. 20:5, 6; 34:7). **everyone according to his ways:** Each man and woman will be judged individually on the basis of his or her own actions (17:10).

32:20, 21 The great historical demonstration of God's loyal love was the exodus of Israel from **Egypt.** This was accomplished **with signs and wonders** (see Ps. 78:43) by which the name of God was made known among nations such as Moab (see Num. 22–24), and peoples such as those in Jericho (see Josh. 2:8–14). **strong hand ... outstretched arm:** These expressions are found in Israel's confessional statement about the Exodus (Deut. 26:8). The addition of **great terror** indicates the mighty acts done against the Egyptians.

32:22, 23 The final step in this rehearsal of history was the gift of the Promised Land. **not obeyed:** The nation responded to God's grace with disobedience and breaking of the covenant, resulting in the **calamity** of the Babylonian siege and the eventual destruction of Jerusalem.

32:24, 25 You see it: What Jeremiah had prophesied in the name of God, the attack of the Babylonian foe from the north and the ensuing **sword, famine,** and **pestilence** (21:7), was now being fulfilled. Buying a field in a disintegrating land seemed out of line with Jeremiah's previous messages of destruction. Why buy land in a region overrun by Babylonians?

32:26, 27 God of all flesh: God was Lord over Israel and Judah, and Lord over the nations (27:1–11)—including mighty Babylon (25:15–26).

32:28–35 kings ... princes ... priests ... prophets ... men of Judah ... inhabitants of Jerusalem: This exhaustive list indicates the rebellion of the entire nation against God.

32:36–38 These verses serve as a summary of the situation in Jerusalem, described by the regular triad of devastation: **sword ... famine ... pestilence.**

32:39 one heart ... one way: Because the Lord had written on the *heart* of the people a New Covenant (31:33), no longer would they worship other deities and turn to foreign nations for help. The word *way* is often used in Jeremiah to denote the character of a person's life. **fear Me:** To fear God is to submit to His sovereign majesty and walk according to His way.

32:40 The expression **everlasting covenant** is also found in Is. 55:3; Ezek. 16:60; 37:26. In Ezekiel it is equated with a "covenant of peace" that God will establish with His people. This covenant will be everlasting, unlike the Sinai covenant which had been broken and ignored for so long. **My fear in their hearts:** This phrasing closely

parallels in meaning and purpose that of the New Covenant of 31:31–34.

32:41 plant: This term from Jeremiah's call (1:10) depicts God establishing His people back in their homeland with a restoration of peace and prosperity. **My heart ... My soul:** These terms describe God's total devotion of heart, will, and emotions to His faithful children.

32:42–44 calamity ... good: God would act to reverse the manner in which He dealt with His people after they had been punished by the Babylonians. **Men will buy fields:** Final assurance is given to Jeremiah, who had purchased a field in perilous and disastrous times. Fields would be bought and sold again throughout the land when the **captives** had been brought home.

33:1 while he was still shut up: A chronological tie is made to 32:2 (588 B.C.). Jeremiah had been placed under palace **court** guard because of what his enemies regarded as "seditious speeches," announcing the fall of Jerusalem and giving advice to Zedekiah to surrender to Nebuchadnezzar.

33:2, 3 Jeremiah urged the people to call out to the Lord, pointing out that this time the Lord would hear and **answer** (7:16) their cries. **Mighty things** has the abstract meaning of "inaccessible" or "unfathomable." God had done **great** things in creation; here the people were invited to observe anew the unfathomable greatness of God's work on their behalf.

33:4, 5 Houses that were built along the city walls could be torn down and filled with rubble to produce a wider, more solid wall. This was one means of combating the sloping earthen siege ramparts that armies constructed opposite domestic quarters rather than at heavily fortified towers or gates.

33:6, 7 Judah and Jerusalem in their idolatry and rebellion were without peace and **health** (8:15, 22). The Lord promised **healing** in response to their repentance (3:22; 30:17).

33:8 Forgiveness is described with two terms, **cleanse** and **pardon.** The word *cleanse* describes ritual purification of what is physically or spiritually unclean or defiled, like Israel and Judah (2:23; 7:30). *Pardon* means "to forgive," and in the Old Testament is used only with God as the subject as He forgives man. This fact helps us understand the reaction of the scribes when they heard Jesus forgiving sins (see Mark 2:7).

33:9 As the citizens of Moab (see Num. 22:1–6) and Jericho (see Josh. 2:8–14) were full of fear and trembling before the nation that had benefited from the Lord's mighty works, so all would **fear and tremble** in amazement at God's new masterwork.

33:10–14 The focus turns to the regions within the nation of Judah that would experience God's restoration. **desolate:** Note the parallel judgment in 7:34; 25:9. The regions listed are similar to those in 17:26. The six locations are organized around two triads: one introduced by the words **mountains** (the hill country), **lowland** (the Shephelah), and **South** (the Negev); and the second moving in a north-south direction: **Benjamin, around Jerusalem, Judah.**

33:15, 16 These verses closely parallel 23:5, 6, which focuses on the royal leadership of the nation, the combined restored Israel and Judah. **Branch of righteousness:** God would raise up a messianic king of Davidic lineage who would rule according to the divine ideal, with **judgment,** meaning justice, and **righteousness.**

33:17, 18 The Davidic covenant of divine succession is reiterated (see 2 Sam. 7:12–16). The Levitical priesthood would likewise be heirs to a divine succession in overseeing the sacrificial system in the Jerusalem temple.

33:19–24 The two families in this context are the houses of David and Levi (see Zech. 12:12, 13). Because of their sins of rebellion against the covenant and their idolatry, Israel and Judah were **despised** (6:30; 7:29) by God and ridiculed among the nations.

33:25, 26 Ordinances refers to the laws which govern the divine order of the cosmos (5:22; 31:35, 36). If day and night should cease, only then would God **cast away** the great multitude of **the descendants of Jacob.** The promise of leadership succession is extended to the nation in terms of its existence as the people of God. The evidence of that promise and God's **mercy** would be the **return** and restoration of the exiles to the land of God's inheritance.

34:1 all his army ... all the kingdoms ... all the people: Jeremiah pictured all the armed forces of Babylon and its vassals arrayed against Judah and Jerusalem.

34:2, 3 you shall not escape: Though Zedekiah attempted to flee to Jericho, Nebuchadnezzar's forces captured him and brought him to Riblah for a **face to face** meeting with Nebuchadnezzar (32:3, 4).

34:4, 5 In 21:4–7, Jeremiah proclaimed the destruction of Jerusalem and the death of its inhabitants by sword, pestilence, and famine. **Zedekiah,** the king, would **die in peace** in Babylon, meaning that he would not be executed by the **sword.** According to 2 Kin. 25:6, 7, his sons were killed before his eyes and then his eyes were put out.

34:6, 7 The background of the siege of Judah and Jerusalem is outlined. The fortifications at **Azekah** and **Lachish** in the lowlands were the avenue through which possible aid from Egypt would have come. They were the last to fall before Jerusalem was destroyed.

34:8, 9 covenant: A legal agreement was made between Zedekiah and the people of Jerusalem during the Babylonian siege to release from bondage all Hebrew slaves. **Liberty** is a technical word for the release of Hebrew slaves every fifty years in the Year of Jubilee (see Lev. 25:8–10), when slaves were freed and indebted land was returned to its original owners.

34:10, 11 The **princes** concurred with the king's covenant (vv. 8, 9) and released Jews in bondage to them, but then reversed their decision when the siege was briefly withdrawn (vv. 21, 22). This opportunism in a moment of crisis demonstrated the leaders' contempt of the covenant.

34:12–14 Jeremiah, a faithful steward of the **word** of God, began his attack against Judah's leaders by recounting the teaching of the Law on the matter of emancipating slaves (see Ex. 21:2–6; Deut. 15:12–15). He reminded the people that their forefathers were slaves in **Egypt,** and that God had freed them from slavery and oppression.

34:15, 16 When the princes of Judah emancipated their Hebrew slaves, it demonstrated their covenant faithfulness and devotion to

God (v. 10). But when the righteous decision was reversed (v. 11), the **name** of God was **profaned.** That name had been defiled by the breach of covenant in the same way that the people had defiled the land with their idolatry (16:18).

34:17 Because the leaders of Judah had disobeyed the covenant by revoking the **liberty** granted to Hebrew slaves (v. 11), the Lord declared that He would grant *liberty* to the leaders—liberty from their disobedience and liberty **to the sword, to pestilence, and to famine.**

34:18, 19 The covenant ceremony is outlined. The main ritual of the two-party covenant began with cutting the sacrificial animal in half, after which the two participants would walk together between the **parts** (see Gen. 15). The divided animal portrayed the potential fate of those who broke the covenant stipulations.

34:20 I will give them into the hand of their enemies: The slaves who had been wronged by the leaders of Judah would be vindicated by God, using the Babylonian army as His instrument.

34:21, 22 gone back: Nebuchadnezzar had withdrawn from Jerusalem to meet the Egyptian army of Pharaoh Hophra. **Zedekiah** had hopes that Hophra would be successful in delivering Israel from its impending doom. However, Nebuchadnezzar soon renewed the siege of Jerusalem and destroyed the city.

35:1 in the days of Jehoiakim: Jehoiakim reigned from 609 to 598 B.C.

35:2 The Rechabites were a tightly knit group of descendants of the Kenites (see Judg. 1:16; 1 Chr. 2:55). This group is known from the story of Jehonadab the son of Rechab, who assisted Jehu in purging the Baal prophets from Samaria (see 2 Kin. 10:15–28). The Rechabites lived as nomads. They refused to drink wine or strong drink and would not cultivate vineyards. They also would not plant any other crops. Many scholars believe that they were a clan of metalsmiths. The Rechabites were invited by Jeremiah into one of the **chambers** surrounding the courtyard of the temple.

35:3–5 Man of God refers to a number of named and unnamed prophets, emissaries

from God who delivered specific messages (see 1 Sam. 2:27; 1 Kin. 12:22; 13:1; 2 Kin. 1:9). In the temple and in the presence of leading temple personnel, Jeremiah tested the Rechabites' faithfulness to their tradition by putting **wine** in front of them and telling them to drink.

35:6–10 The Rechabites refused to drink wine, on the basis of the teaching of **Jonadab** their forefather. **obeyed the voice:** This is the language of faithfulness, often used in the negative by Jeremiah to refer to Judah's failure to obey the covenant (3:13; 7:23, 24).

35:11–15 receive instruction … obey My words: This phrasing comes from the words of the Rechabites (v. 8) and from Jeremiah's oracle in 7:28. The Rechabites had obeyed the instructions of their forefather Jonadab. In the case of Judah, though God Himself had instructed the Israelites in the covenant and had presented His message repeatedly through many faithful prophets, the people had not obeyed Him.

35:16, 17 The Rechabites had not wavered in keeping the **commandment** of Jonadab, but the Israelites had continually rebelled against the teaching of God.

35:18, 19 Blessing is pronounced over the faithful household of the Rechabites. Their complete obedience is outlined in a triad of verbs: **obeyed … kept … done.**

36:1 The narrative recounts the interaction with Jehoiakim about the word of God during the king's fourth year, 605–604 B.C. In late spring as the year began and the river was "at flood stage," Nebuchadnezzar crossed the Euphrates and defeated the Egyptians at Carchemish. **it came to pass:** The original scroll of Jeremiah's oracles, prepared with the scribal assistance of Baruch, was read in the temple in the ninth month of the fourth year of Jehoiakim in November-December 604 B.C. (see v. 9). This was at the same time as the attack of the Babylonians on Ashkelon.

36:2 scroll of a book: The usual material for a scroll was parchment (a kind of leather), though Egyptian papyrus was also available. The contents of the scroll were the oracles dating from the **days of Josiah,** at the advent of Jeremiah's ministry (626 B.C.), to **this day** (604 B.C.).

36:3, 4 Baruch the son of Neriah was a trained scribe and close friend of Jeremiah (32:12). **at the instruction:** This phrase refers to the process of dictation from Jeremiah to Baruch.

36:5 Confined can refer to physical imprisonment, being placed under guard (33:1; 39:15); a mental or spiritual constraint; or some other form of restriction. No prison is mentioned in this chapter. It is possible that Jeremiah was somehow prohibited from entering the temple courts, perhaps after his temple sermon (7:1–15; 26:1–19).

36:6, 7 The **scroll** of Jeremiah's early oracles against Israel and Judah was to be read on a **day of fasting,** a time aside by official declaration of the king or priests (v. 9) in a period of national crisis.

36:8 Baruch, a faithful disciple like Jeremiah, read from the **book** of God's words in the temple of the Lord.

36:9, 10 The official proclamation of the **fast** came in November-December of 604 B.C. People from all over Judah assembled in the temple of the Lord for the fast, providing Baruch and Jeremiah a sizable audience.

36:11–13 Gemariah's son **Micaiah** reported the occasion and words to the royal **princes,** including **Gemariah** and **Elnathan.** Elnathan's father **Achbor** also played a role in the reading of the scroll in the days of Josiah's reform. The parallels between Josiah's reform and Jeremiah's desire for national revival were included by Baruch deliberately, to remind the people of the earlier event.

36:14 Jehudi: The list of three ancestors is unusual. The last name **Cushi** may indicate that Jehudi was a Cushite, thus of foreign ancestry. Jehudi was the messenger appointed to summon Baruch to the court of the princes.

36:15–19 looked in fear: Alarmed at the words of the scroll, the princes felt impelled to inform the king. **wrote them with ink:** Baruch told the princes how and when the scroll was written. The leaders told Baruch to **go** with Jeremiah and **hide** until the matter could be investigated.

36:20–24 Baruch and Jeremiah would have learned later that the original scroll was destroyed, since they were in hiding when it

happened. **winter house:** The royal palace had rooms with fireplaces for use in the winter. As the scroll was read, Jehoiakim showed no signs of fear or lamentation, unlike Josiah when the Book of the Law was read in his hearing (see 2 Kin. 22:11–13).

36:25, 26 The king's son could mean: (1) the literal son of **Jehoiakim;** (2) the son of a man named *Hamelek,* which means "the king"; (3) or an office title for a person with the function of a deputy or policeman. The third view seems to be indicated in this context.

36:27, 28 The Lord told Jeremiah and Baruch to prepare a second **scroll** of the earlier oracles. Verse 32 notes that additional material was included.

36:29–32 Indictment and judgment against Jehoiakim is pronounced. The indictment was declared because he destroyed the scroll of the word of the Lord. First, the Davidic lineage would not continue through him. His son would rule for only three months before Nebuchadnezzar deported Jehoiachin to **Babylon,** where he died. Second, the king's body would be treated disgracefully after his death. As the king had **cast** the scroll into the fire, so his body would be cast from the royal palace. Third, the royal household would experience the destructive judgment that had been proclaimed in the words of the original scroll.

37:1, 2 Zedekiah, like **Jehoiakim** and so many other kings before him in Israel and Judah, had rejected the word of God and its warnings of judgment. The end of rebellion was in sight. Jerusalem would soon fall to the Babylonian armies, the instruments of divine discipline.

37:3, 4 Jehucal was a friend of Pashhur (21:1). Together they eventually called for Jeremiah to be executed (38:1). **Zephaniah the son of Maaseiah** was a member of the delegation who had sought a word from God at the beginning of the Babylonian siege (21:1–10). He was sympathetic toward Jeremiah, as reflected in the letter from Shemaiah (29:24–28).

37:5 In late spring or early summer of 588 B.C., Pharaoh Hophra led the Egyptian **army** into southern Palestine. The Babylonian forces withdrew their siege of Judah and Jerusalem to confront the Egyptians. Zedekiah hoped the Babylonians would be defeated, but his hopes proved to be in vain.

37:6–8 Jeremiah's response to Jehucal and Zephaniah (vv. 3, 4) was the same unchanging **word** from **the LORD** he had always proclaimed. The Babylonians would soon return to destroy Jerusalem.

37:9, 10 Do not deceive yourselves: To think that the brief respite caused by the Egyptian appearance in the southern coastal plain was proof of imminent deliverance, as the false prophets declared, was an exercise in self-deception and futile imagination.

37:11, 12 The lifting of the **siege** by the Babylonians afforded the people in Jerusalem some opportunity for movement outside the city.

37:13 Irijah, a captain of the guard and a royal military official, arrested Jeremiah at the **Gate of Benjamin** on the north side of the city. The charge of defection was not unreasonable. Jeremiah had advised the people of Jerusalem to defect to the Chaldeans so that their lives would be spared (21:9). A number of them followed his advice (38:19).

37:14–16 Jeremiah denied the accusation of defection but to no avail. Irijah arrested the prophet and arraigned him before the court of **princes**. Prison space was lacking in Jerusalem because of the crowded conditions of the siege, so a prison was devised **in the house of Jonathan the scribe. the dungeon and the cells:** Jeremiah's prison seems to have been a cistern with vaulted ceilings in Jonathan's house.

37:17–19 Fearing possible exposure and opposition from his courtiers, Zedekiah **secretly** summoned Jeremiah and asked of him a word from the Lord. The several encounters between Jeremiah and Zedekiah indicate the weak character of Zedekiah. He seems to have earnestly desired a word from God but could not come to grips with the reality and respond appropriately.

37:20, 21 Jeremiah appealed to Zedekiah's sense of justice and decency and asked to be released from prison. Zedekiah consented and committed the prophet to the **court of**

the prison, a place near the royal palace where limited mobility was possible, such as in the transaction to purchase the field (see 32:1–15; Neh. 3:25).

38:1 Jucal (Jehucal) was one of the emissaries sent by Zedekiah to Jeremiah in 37:3. **Pashhur** came to Jeremiah with a group when the Babylonian siege began in January 588 B.C.

38:2, 3 Jeremiah said the choice was between **life** under the Babylonians and death among the ruins of Jerusalem. Such a statement was treasonous, as was the statement that Jerusalem must fall.

38:4 The **princes** accused Jeremiah of demoralizing Judah and seeking the harm of Jerusalem. **weakens the hands:** This expression describes the discouragement or demoralization of soldiers (see Ezra 4:4).

38:5 the king can do nothing: Zedekiah was powerless before the court of princes. The fate of Jeremiah was placed in their hands.

38:6 Jeremiah was imprisoned in the basement cistern of **Malchiah the king's son.** Probably because of the length of the Babylonian siege, the cistern had no water for drinking, only **mire** of muddy lime clay. This cistern had a narrow circular opening, and could be entered and exited only by means of ropes. The court princes probably expected Jeremiah to die a slow death.

38:7–10 Ebed-Melech the Ethiopian: The name means "Servant of the King." **Gate of Benjamin:** Jeremiah had entered and left the city many times through this northern gate. The king was likely performing his normal function of mediating disputes and settling legal questions. **no more bread:** A siege cut off water and food supplies from a city, hoping starvation would force a surrender.

38:11–13 Ebed-Melech took special care to obtain **rags** for Jeremiah to cushion his armpits, preventing the **ropes** from cutting his skin. A foreigner, a once-despised Cushite, cared more for the prophet of God than did the king and princes of Jeremiah's own people.

38:14 This meeting between Jeremiah and Zedekiah is parallel to the account in 37:17–21.

The location of the **third entrance** is unknown. The secrecy of the meeting may indicate that it was a private access for the king from the royal palace into the temple courts. Zedekiah's request to ask Jeremiah **something** was done with sincerity. He wanted the prophet to be honest and open in his answer.

38:15, 16 will you not: Jeremiah was fearful of being returned to the dungeon, of being turned over to the Egyptian courtiers who would do him further harm, or of being executed for speaking boldly against the king. Zedekiah swore by the name of God that no harm would come to the prophet from any source.

38:17, 18 Jeremiah repeated to the king the message recorded in vv. 2, 3. **Surrender** would spare the life of the king and the city; failure to surrender would bring death and destruction.

38:19 I am afraid: Zedekiah revealed he was afraid to surrender to the Babylonians because he feared retaliation by early deserters (21:9; 39:9; 52:15) from Jerusalem. His unfitness to be king is proven by his concern for his personal safety above that of the city and its inhabitants.

38:20–23 Jeremiah tried to settle Zedekiah's fears and to resolve his moral and ethical dilemma by reassuring him that surrender would result in his personal safety. But if the king refused **to surrender** to Nebuchadnezzar, the **word** of judgment would fall. **Women** and **children** would be handed over to Nebuchadnezzar, and Jerusalem would be destroyed.

38:24–26 Zedekiah instructed Jeremiah not to tell the pro-Egyptian **princes** about their conversation lest the prophet be executed. Together they constructed an account of their meeting that might be used if Jeremiah was questioned about what had been **said.** It is clear that Zedekiah was afraid of a revolt from within his royal court.

38:27, 28 As expected, **the princes** questioned Jeremiah. The answer he and Zedekiah had prepared proved satisfactory.

39:1 The Babylonian siege began in the **tenth month** of the **ninth year** of Zedekiah's reign, that is, in December 589 or January 588 B.C.

39:2 eleventh year of Zedekiah … fourth month … ninth day: The walls of Jerusalem were breached about the time food supplies were exhausted, in June or July 586 B.C.

39:3 sat in the Middle Gate: The Middle Gate was probably in the north wall of Jerusalem, the direction from which the city was taken. The Babylonian princes sat in the gate to assert their authority in the conquered city. **Nergal-Sharezer** ruled Babylon from 560 to 556 B.C. **Nebo** may be a short form of Nebushasban. When combined with **Sarsechim,** the resulting name is probably a variation of the name Nebushasban Rabsaris (v. 13). **Rabmag** and **Rabsaris** are titles.

39:4 When **Zedekiah** saw the Babylonian officers enter the gate on the north side of Jerusalem, he and his men left at night through a **gate between the two walls,** probably near the union of the Kidron and Tyropoeon valleys on the south side of the city.

39:5–7 Zedekiah and his military escort were captured near Jericho and taken to **Riblah,** a city in Aram. **Hamath** was a region of Aram. There Zedekiah met Nebuchadnezzar, as Jeremiah had prophesied (34:3). Zedekiah's sons and his men were **killed** before his eyes just before he was blinded. **Bronze fetters** refers to the pairs of shackles placed on his wrists and ankles. Zedekiah died in prison in Babylon (52:11).

39:8–10 In addition to the royal palace and homes of the inhabitants, 52:13 includes the "house of the Lord" among the buildings burned in Jerusalem. **poor:** Typically the Babylonians deported the upper classes and left behind peasants to work the fields.

39:11 Nebuchadnezzar had given special instructions to **Nebuzaradan** about the treatment of Jeremiah. The positive teaching of the prophet about the king of Babylon had come to his attention in some way, perhaps through deserters or spies.

39:12–14 During the destruction of Jerusalem, Jeremiah was released from the court of the prison and brought to Mizpah to be under charge of **Gedaliah,** whom Nebuchadnezzar had appointed governor over the peasant population of Judah and Benjamin.

39:15–18 Ebed-Melech, who had rescued Jeremiah from the muddy cistern in the prison court (38:11–13), was promised safety and deliverance by the Lord because of his assistance to Jeremiah and because he had **put** his **trust in** God.

40:1 Ramah was about five miles north of Jerusalem, along the ancient road leading from Jerusalem to Shechem. With the destruction of Jerusalem still in process, Ramah served as a way station for captives going to the eastern provinces of the Babylonian Empire.

40:2, 3 Nebuzaradan knew of Jeremiah's predictions about the demise of Jerusalem and the victories of the armies of Babylon. Prophets whose words were deemed verified were generally treated well by peoples of the ancient Middle East. **The LORD your God has pronounced this doom:** Consider the irony of a foreigner stating the truth about the reason for Jerusalem's destruction.

40:4, 5 Jeremiah was released from bondage and given three options: (1) to go with Nebuzaradan to Babylon and enjoy special treatment and protection there; (2) to **remain** in the care of Gedaliah, the district governor at Mizpah; (3) to live in the land as he chose. Nebuzaradan gave Jeremiah rations and gifts because of the prophet's proclamations about Babylon and Nebuchadnezzar (25:9; 27:6).

40:6 Jeremiah chose to go to **Mizpah** to serve under **Gedaliah son of Ahikam,** staying with his people not far from his hometown and the property he had purchased while in the court of the prison (32:1–15). Mizpah was about eight miles north of Jerusalem.

40:7–10 The captains of the armies refers to the surviving Jewish commanders of the armies in the towns throughout Judah who had fled into the rugged hill country. Among the list of escaped leaders was **Ishmael,** a member of the royal family and a court officer (41:1); **Johanan,** who would become the leader of the assembly (vv. 13–16); and **Jezaniah** (Jaazaniah) whose father was a **Maacathite.**

40:11, 12 The Jews who had escaped the Babylonian onslaught into neighboring states returned home and began working the fields, vineyards, and orchards.

40:13, 14 Johanan led a group of leaders to Gedaliah to warn him of a plot by **Ishmael** and the Ammonite king **Baalis** to assassinate the governor.

40:15, 16 Johanan **secretly** asked **Gedaliah** permission to kill **Ishmael,** fearing reprisal from Babylon that would surely destroy the reconstruction efforts and lead to further bloodshed. Unfortunately, Gedaliah was far too trusting of Ishmael, the royal descendant who seems to have coveted Gedaliah's position.

41:1–3 The year of the assassination of Gedaliah is not given, only the month—**the seventh** month or Tishri, September-October. The murder of the **governor** could have taken place as soon as three months after the fall of Jerusalem. Others associate the third deportation of 582 B.C. with this rebellion.

41:4–9 Two days after Gedaliah's death a group of faithful pilgrims were on their way to Jerusalem, probably with grain rather than animal offerings. Ishmael and his followers massacred the worshipers and **cast** their bodies into a **pit.**

41:10 carried away: Ishmael took captives from Mizpah for future use. He then fled into Ammonite territory, probably to join forces with his ally Baalis.

41:11, 12 When **Johanan,** who had warned Gedaliah about the assassination plot (40:13–16), heard of the atrocities of Ishmael, he mustered his forces and confronted the rebel army at **Gibeon.**

41:13–15 When they saw **Johanan,** the captives Ishmael had taken from Mizpah ran over to join his forces. **Ishmael** and **eight** of his men escaped to Ammon.

41:16–18 Fearing imminent reprisal from the Babylonians on account of the rebellion, Johanan gathered the inhabitants of Mizpah, including Jeremiah, together with those he had rescued and began a trek toward **Egypt,** seeking a place of safety. Egypt was the only country in the region that was free from Babylonian control.

42:1–3 said to Jeremiah: The people asked Jeremiah to intercede with the Lord on their behalf.

42:4–6 I will pray: Jeremiah agreed to pray to God. He asked the people to agree to abide by the answer he received. The people responded with an oath of obedience, calling upon the Lord as witness.

42:7–10 after ten days: God's response to Jeremiah's prayer on behalf of the people did not come immediately. Jeremiah convened the assembly and declared the answer from God in terms reminiscent of his call: **build you ... not pull you down ... plant you ... not pluck you up** (1:10).

42:11, 12 Jeremiah assured the people with the same words the Lord had used to give him assurance in his call: **I am with you, to save you and deliver you** (1:8). God's promise to bring His people through a time of trial to experience His restorative power would show His great **mercy.**

42:13, 14 If the people disobeyed God and fled to Egypt, they would suffer the consequences. The people's hope for safety in Egypt is presented in a triad of phrases: **see no war, nor hear the sound of the trumpet, nor be hungry.** The people seem to have had their minds made up before they sought the word from the Lord (vv. 2, 3).

42:15–22 set their faces: This expression indicates the fixed intentions of the people. The announcement of judgment against the disobedient evacuees echoes Jeremiah's earlier pronouncements against Judah. The very thing they were trying to escape from would meet them in Egypt.

43:1–3 The people had already intended to go to Egypt to escape the perceived danger of Babylon. **Azariah** and **Johanan** spoke out against the counsel given by Jeremiah in 42:9–22.

43:4–9 Johanan led the migration to Egypt, against the direction of the Lord through Jeremiah. The caravan journeyed **as far as Tahpanhes,** a city on the eastern edge of the Nile Delta (2:16).

43:10, 11 This judgment oracle echoes earlier pronouncements against Judah, with Nebuchadnezzar identified as the **servant** of God (25:9; 27:6). The **stones** symbolized the strong foundation of Nebuchadnezzar's empire, the point from which he would spread his **royal pavilion** (tent, or canopy). **death ... captivity ... sword:** Severe judgment is pronounced on Egypt, including

judgment on the disobedient people of Judah.

43:12, 13 The destructive judgment was extended to the temples of Egyptian gods and goddesses. Destruction of Egyptian temples was carried out by Esarhaddon of Assyria in the seventh century B.C., and again by Cambyses of Persia in the sixth century B.C.

44:1 Migdol is a common Semitic term meaning "Watchtower." Here the term is identified with a small fortress 25 miles east of Tahpanhes. **Noph** is another name for Memphis, the capital of Lower Egypt. **Pathros** is Upper Egypt.

44:2, 3 Jerusalem was brought to **desolation** because the people broke God's covenant by worshiping other gods, rejecting the lordship of God, and thus provoking Him to anger.

44:4, 5 prophets, rising early and sending: Jerusalem had been warned time and again by faithful and tireless messengers from God (7:25; 25:4; 26:5). **they did not listen or incline their ear:** This reference is to the people's disobedience in worshiping foreign deities.

44:6–8 provoke: This term indicates willful, stubborn rebellion against God.

44:9, 10 They have not been humbled ... nor have they feared: The present generation of Jews had learned nothing from the past failures of the nation. The people were not broken in heart, only more stubborn.

44:11, 12 set their faces: God had set His face against the remnant of Judah because they had set their face to enter Egypt against His will (43:7).

44:13, 14 The Jews in Egypt would suffer the same judgment as those in Jerusalem. Only a small **remnant** would survive to tell their story.

44:15–17 The people countered Jeremiah's words with an argument from experience. They rejected God by saying that when they worshiped the **queen of heaven**—that is, the goddess Ishtar or Astarte, they **had plenty of food, were well off, and saw no trouble.**

44:18 Queen of heaven refers to Ishtar, a goddess of war and fertility who was worshiped with explicit sexual activity. The people reasoned that when they stopped worshiping the queen of heaven in the days of Josiah's reform, their king was killed and their land was overrun and destroyed.

44:19 Women were leaders in the Ishtar rites, which included incense burning, drink offerings, and special ceremonial **cakes** marked with the symbol of the goddess (7:18).

44:20, 21 remember: This term is often used in contexts describing the basis for God's judgment.

44:22, 23 no longer bear it: The longsuffering of the Lord had reached its end. The cause of the judgment was the people's **evil … doings** and **abominations.** When the covenant was broken, the covenant curses came to bear.

44:24, 25 The focus is on the stubbornness of the **women** who persisted in their idolatry. Nothing could make them abandon their **vows** to worship Ishtar.

44:26, 27 The **name** of God reveals His quality and character in dealing with humankind.

44:28–30 A small **remnant** would survive and see the fulfillment of God's word as revealed through Jeremiah. Their own hopes of prosperity in Egypt would vanish, and the sign of God's work against them would be the fall of Pharaoh Hophra of Egypt. In 570 B.C. Hophra was overthrown in a military coup by his own general Amasis. Three years later he was executed in fulfillment of Jeremiah's prophecy.

45:1 Baruch assisted and encouraged Jeremiah when he was imprisoned. In this passage Jeremiah replies with a personal word of encouragement from the Lord for his scribal friend. The date of the passage, 604 B.C., identifies it with the circumstances of ch. 36. Baruch had read Jeremiah's oracles before the temple crowd and the princes of Judah, before Jehoiakim burned the original scroll. A second scroll was prepared by Baruch, and he remained an assistant to Jeremiah throughout his ministry, including the journey to Egypt.

45:2, 3 Jeremiah addressed Baruch in light of the scribe's sorrow. **Woe:** Baruch lamented his plight in the same manner that Jeremiah had done (15:10). **added grief to my sorrow:** Baruch suffered mental anguish and

personal rejection from his people because of his association with Jeremiah (36:15–19; 43:3).

45:4, 5 great things: Baruch apparently had hopes for position, honor, and distinction. However, these dreams were lost through his association with Jeremiah. Yet Baruch would be spared the judgment that would befall the land, for the Lord would give him his life as a **prize,** or booty (21:9; 38:2).

46:1 This verse introduces a collection of oracles **against the nations.** The text moves generally from the west—Egypt—to the east—Elam and Babylon. Scattered throughout the oracles are brief messages of the restoration of Israel and Judah. The main message of these oracles is the sovereignty of God over all the nations of the earth.

46:2 Against Egypt: The background here is Nebuchadnezzar's defeat of Pharaoh Necho at Carchemish in 605 B.C. Jeremiah's proclamations about the future Babylonian invasion were no doubt based in part on this battle, which firmly established Nebuchadnezzar as the great imperial monarch of his generation.

46:3, 4 Buckler and shield are two different sizes of shields (see 1 Kin. 10:16, 17).

46:5, 6 The strong Egyptian army was overpowered suddenly by the mightier Babylonians. **fear … all around:** This expression was also the name given to Pashhur by Jeremiah in 20:3, 4, and to Jeremiah's persecutors in 20:10.

46:7–9 Egypt had been weak for three hundred years (see 1 Kin. 14:25), but was still known for producing and exporting chariots. **Ethiopians, Libyans,** and **Lydians** were apparently mercenaries under Necho.

46:10–12 The day of the LORD is described here as **a day of vengeance** in which Egypt is punished for the death of Josiah. Egypt's demise is pictured as a sacrificial feast. As there was no healing **balm** for sinful Judah, so now Egypt was mortally wounded, stumbling to its death.

46:13 This verse is a prose introduction to a poetic description of Nebuchadnezzar's attack on **Egypt.** After the battle at Carchemish, the Babylonian march through Palestine was resumed in 604 B.C. They attacked Ashkelon and then pursued the Egyptians.

46:14–17 Why are your valiant men swept away: The fall of the gods before God in judgment is a prominent theme in the oracles against the nations (v. 25). **the LORD drove them:** Babylon is depicted as the instrument of God's judgment.

46:18, 19 Tabor … Carmel: The mountains stand for the certainty of God's kingship. Like Judah, Egypt would face God's destructive judgment.

46:20–24 Egypt's destroyer invaded **from the north,** the same direction from which Judah's adversary attacked. **fat bulls:** Egypt's well-paid **mercenaries** were frail before God and the Babylonians, who came like lumberjacks cutting down the forest and chopping the fleeing serpents, the Egyptians. Egypt's demise is parallel to Israel's; the virgin daughter had been violated and stood **ashamed** (2:26), soon to be taken captive by Babylon.

46:25, 26 The **gods** and goddesses of Egypt were punished in the defeat of the people who worshiped them. **days of old:** After the Babylonian invasion and exile, normal life in Egypt would be restored.

46:27, 28 do not be dismayed: Israel would be preserved.

47:1, 2 The metaphor of rising **waters** is found in Is. 8:7, 8; 28:17 in reference to the Assyrian army; here the foe is Babylon (1:13; 4:6; 6:1, 22; 25:9). The destructive **overflowing** of the river is more typical of the Euphrates River in the north than of the Nile floods, which bring beneficial nutrients to the fertile valley.

47:3 Lacking courage is literally "from weakness of hands," describing the paralyzing terror felt by parents as they abandon their children in flight.

47:4, 5 Philistines and Phoenicians are associated through their origins among the sea peoples who came from the northern Mediterranean and Aegean islands to the coastlands of Palestine in the twelfth century B.C. **Caphtor** is identified with Crete. **Tyre and Sidon** were the largest Phoenician ports. **Gaza** and **Ashkelon** were the last of the Philistine strongholds to fall, along with Ashdod, which is not mentioned. **Baldness … cut yourself:** Shaving the head and

self-inflicted wounds were mourning customs forbidden in Israel (16:6).

47:6, 7 The image of the **sword of the LORD** is often used to portray divine judgment (12:12; 46:10, 14, 16). **quiet … Rest … be still:** The judgment had long been withheld; the long-suffering of the Lord had reached its end.

48:1–8 As the apostate people of Judah trusted in the queen of heaven (44:17, 18), Moab trusted in its patron deity **Chemosh,** a god of fertility and storm. **captivity:** Taking a deity captive was a well-known Middle Eastern custom. The national statue of the patron deity was seized, and it was believed that the captured god could no longer protect its people.

48:9–13 not been emptied from vessel to vessel: Though Moab was subject to Israel in the ninth century B.C., it had never experienced exile and had become complacent in its security. God would **empty** Moab's **vessels,** causing the Moabites to be taken captive. **break the bottles:** Moab's cities would be destroyed. **Chemosh** (v. 7), the great protector of Moab, would become powerless before God, as **Bethel** fell with **Israel** (Amos 3:14).

48:14–17 Jeremiah assured Moab that there is but one true **King, Whose name is the LORD of hosts,** the all-powerful "God of armies."

48:18–20 Dibon was the capital from which King Mesha ruled (see 2 Kin. 3:4–27). The haughty **Moab** was **shamed** by the destruction of its mighty fortresses.

48:21–25 Mephaath was one of the Levitical cities (see Josh. 21:37). **Bozrah** refers not to the capital of Edom, but to Bezer, one of the cities of refuge (see Josh. 20:8). **Horn** and **arm** are symbols of the power and strength that was broken.

48:26–29 Make him drunk: Judgment is portrayed in the form of drunkenness to the point of vomiting, the result of Moab's mockery of Israel (25:15–29). **Pride** refers to the haughtiness by which one thinks of oneself as greater than others.

48:30–33 The scene in Moab turns to mourning and intense lamentation over the failure of the crops and vineyards. **Kir Heres,** also called Kir Haraseth, (see 2 Kin. 3:25; Is. 16:11), may be a name for the capital city of Moab (Kir of Moab; see Is. 15:1). The **joy** once heard echoing from the vineyards and winepresses had vanished before the horrifying sound of horses' hoofbeats and clashing weapons.

48:34 The waters of Nimrin empty into the Jordan River opposite Jericho. A lament from **Heshbon** and **Elealeh** to **Horonaim** and **Zoar** would cover all the Moabite plateau from north to south, from the Dead Sea to the desert.

48:35–39 offers sacrifices ... burns incense: Idolatry would end; the people could no longer worship Chemosh and other deities.

48:40–44 The imagery is that of Babylon spreading its ravaging armies over Moab like an **eagle** spreading its **wings** (49:22; Deut. 32:11; Ezek. 17:7). **exalted himself:** Moab's chief sin was pride, considering itself greater than the God of Israel. Its pride would be turned to fear and terror, and then the nation would be taken captive.

48:45–47 Bring back means "restore the fortunes of." Moab would see its people restored to their homeland. Their crops and vineyards would once again be productive. Moab, Judah, and Israel returned home in 538 B.C., during the reign of Cyrus.

49:1, 2 Milcom, the patron deity of the Ammonites, is pictured as taking **possession** of the land formerly belonging to the Gadites, a process that began in the days of the judges.

49:3 Heshbon (48:2) was at one time possessed by the Ammonites, but later lost to the Moabites. **Rabbah** was the capital city of the Ammonites. The **captivity** of the patron deity **Milcom** was tantamount to his defeat, visible in the exile of leaders and people, together with his statue, from their homeland.

49:4 Valleys ... flowing valley may be a reference to the Jabbok valley on the northern border of Ammon.

49:5, 6 no one will gather those who wander off: Those who fell by the wayside during the flight from Ammon would be abandoned.

49:7, 8 Edom was known in the Bible for its wisdom (Obad. 8). **Teman** was the name of

a city or district of Edom in which the capital city Bozrah was located.

49:9–11 grape-gatherers: This imagery derives from 6:9, but there was no real remnant left in Edom. The nation had been totally ravaged and stripped bare, with only women and children left alive to work the land.

49:12, 13 drink of the cup: The imagery of the cup of divine wrath is particularly applied to Edom and more specifically to its capital city, **Bozrah.**

49:14–16 The imagery in these verses is that of **the nations** being mustered by God to besiege Edom. Edom would be reduced from a proud people of mighty mountain fortresses to one that was **small among** the nations.

49:17–19 an astonishment ... hiss: Like Israel, Judah, Egypt, Moab, and Ammon, Edom would be destroyed and would become an object of derision.

49:20–22 The two things on which Edom most prided itself, its wisdom and its fortresses, would vanish before the judgment of the Lord. As the strongholds collapsed, the earth would quake; its tremors would be felt all the way to the Red Sea.

49:23–27 Hamath and Arpad were major towns located west and north of the capital of Damascus.

49:28 The region of **Kedar** was the most important Arab tribal group in the biblical period. Kedar was in northern Arabia and was known for its sheepherding and merchant caravans (see 2:10; Is. 60:7; Ezek. 27:21). The phrase **men of the East** is associated with the Arameans, Midianites, Amalekites, and other nomadic desert tribes (see Gen. 29:1; Judg. 7:12).

49:29 The various items listed in this verse are typically those of nomadic peoples. The panic-filled shout, **fear is on every side,** is common in Jeremiah's oracles (6:25; 20:10; 46:5; 49:5).

49:30–33 Nebuchadnezzar's army would attack the tent villages of Kedar and **Hazor.** The oases would be left to the **jackals** for habitation (9:11; 10:22). The Bedouin peoples would be scattered afar, as if by the hot desert winds.

49:34–36 break the bow: The Elamites were

famous for their skilled archers (see Is. 22:6), who became an important part of the Persian army under Cyrus. The expression **four winds** indicates the military might that the Lord musters against His enemies (see Ezek. 37:9; Dan. 8:8).

49:37–39 I will set My throne: This expression depicts the establishment of the kingdom of the God of Israel, the great conquering King in the land of the Elamites (1:15; 43:10). Elam would experience the restorative power of God, as its people were returned and its fortunes restored (48:47; 49:6).

50:1 The Chaldeans, or Babylonians, were vassals of Assyria until the revolt of Nabopolassar, who gained control of Babylon in 626 B.C. Nebuchadnezzar, the son of Nabopolassar who succeeded his father to the throne in 605 B.C., was the strongest and longest-reigning Chaldean monarch. After Nebuchadnezzar died, the nation declined steadily. In 539 B.C. it was conquered by Cyrus, apparently with little effort.

50:2, 3 Bel was a title like Baal, meaning "Lord," for **Merodach,** another name for Babylon's patron deity Marduk. **idols … images:** The oracle begins with a defamation of the gods of Babylon. **out of the north:** The invading nation is not defined, yet from historical records it is known that Cyrus attacked Babylon from the north after defeating the city of Sippar.

50:4, 5 Israel and **Judah** would be restored as they sought the Lord in mournful repentance, looking for help to return home. They would enter into a **perpetual covenant** with the Lord that they would not forget or reject (see Ezek. 16:60).

50:6, 7 Shepherds refers to the national princes, priests, and prophets who led the people to sin against the Lord, their true source of hope and sustenance (23:1–4).

50:8–10 The train of thought turns to the Jews, who should flee from Babylon like **rams** of a flock.

50:11–13 Babylon's plunder would be its punishment for gloating over Judah's demise and the abuse of God's **heritage.** Great Babylon would be reduced to the **least of the nations.**

50:14–16 against her all around: Assault forces would press hard on every side, as what had been the instrument of God became the object of His wrath.

50:17–20 The Lord had used Babylon to punish **Assyria** for deporting Israel; He would use another foe from the north to inflict punishment on **Babylon.** The result would be the restoration of Israel and Judah and the pardoning of their iniquities and sins.

50:21–28 utterly destroy: The tables would be turned on Babylon, the soon-to-be-broken **hammer** and future **heaps of ruins.** The **LORD God of hosts** had launched His vengeful weapons upon the city through His anointed servant Cyrus (see 2 Chr. 36:22, 23; Is. 45:1).

50:29–34 The wise and righteous Ruler would **plead** the **case** of the oppressed children of Judah and obtain their redemption. God, the **Redeemer** of Israel (see Is. 47:4), offers to obtain the legal freedom of His people from captivity.

50:35–46 The **sword** of God would overturn all elements of Babylon's greatness—its leaders, its weapons, and its wealth. **A drought is against her waters:** Babylon was built on both sides of the Euphrates River, and the region of southern Mesopotamia was networked with irrigation canals. The Lord would carry out His judgment against Babylon as He had in the days of Elijah.

51:1–4 destroying wind: The imagery of a scorching desert wind is found in 4:11, 12; 18:17. The imagery of winnowing or scattering is found in 13:24.

51:5 Though **Israel** and **Judah** had **forsaken** the lordship of God, He had not forsaken His sinful people.

51:6–10 The imagery of Babylon's **cup** of fury from 25:15–29 is reversed. Here Babylon's cup is broken by the Lord. **balm:** As in the case of Judah (8:22), decadent Babylon was beyond healing and had to be abandoned. The destruction of Babylon was the vindication of the justice of God.

51:11–14 vengeance: The Lord would avenge Babylon's fierce abuse of Israel and other conquered nations. The **covetousness** of Babylon is typified in the taking of temple treasures from Jerusalem (see 2 Kin. 25:13–17).

51:15–26 Babylon had been God's **battle-ax** for judgment against the nations, and Judah in particular. **I will repay:** Babylon would experience God's battle-ax of punishment for the **evil** it inflicted on Jerusalem. The seemingly invincible **mountain** of Babylon would be crumbled by the power of God's outstretched arm.

51:27, 28 Ararat, Minni, and Ashkenaz were mountain tribes from what is today eastern Turkey and Armenia. **The Medes** were from the Zagros mountain region in present-day central Iran.

51:29–32 The mighty men of Babylon have ceased fighting: The Nabonidus Chronicle, a text describing the fall of Babylon, reports that "Cyrus entered Babylon without a battle." By the time Cyrus reached Babylon, he had conquered all of Babylonia except for the capital city, cutting off roads and supply routes.

51:33–35 The harvest **threshing floor** depicts the punishment of Babylon.

51:36–40 plead your case: The imagery here involves a legal proceeding. Babylon had been arraigned, indicted, and convicted. Here it is sentenced to punishment by the Lord.

51:41–44 The primeval **sea**, conquered by Marduk according to the Babylonian creation myth, would overflow Babylon in the form of enemy nations. **Bel** is an honorary title for Marduk, the patron deity of Babylon. **I will bring out … what he has swallowed:** Nebuchadnezzar had swallowed up nations like a glutton (v. 34); those very same nations would be returned.

51:45–48 The release of Israel from captivity is foreseen. The people would be called upon to flee the city because of its impending destruction. **carved images:** Babylon was known for its thousands of images of its numerous gods and goddesses. As the king claimed to conquer nations in the name of his patron deity, so the gods of the defeated would be punished along with their worshipers. The devastation of decadent Babylon would be no cause for mourning among the nations. Instead, the nations would sing joyfully of Babylon's fall.

51:49–58 slain of Israel: Babylon would be destroyed for killing so many in Israel. The remnant of Israel would be called upon to

remember their God and how He delivered them from afar.

51:59–64 Jeremiah instructed **Seraiah,** a brother of Baruch who was about to be taken captive to Babylon, to read a scroll within the walls of Babylon. The scroll that Jeremiah gave to Seraiah contained a list of the various evils that would befall Babylon as a result of God's judgment.

52:1–3 Zedekiah reigned as king of Judah from 598 to 586 B.C., until God finally cast him out of Jerusalem for doing **evil in the sight of the LORD** (23:1–4).

52:4–6 The siege of Jerusalem began on the **tenth day** of the **tenth month** (Tebeth)— probably in December 589 B.C., and it lasted over two years. In June-July 586 B.C., as food supplies were exhausted, the walls of Jerusalem were breached (39:2).

52:7–11 The attempted escape, capture, and ultimate fate of **Zedekiah** are also described in 39:1–10.

52:12–16 The entire city of Jerusalem was burned, from the temple to the royal palace to the **houses.** The city **walls** were demolished. Leading citizens and some of the poor were deported under Nebuzaradan's command, leaving only a remnant of peasant farmers to work the fields, vineyards, and orchards.

52:17–23 Sacred implements and furniture from the temple of God were taken as booty to Babylon. Most of these items are described in 1 Kin. 7:15–51.

52:24–30 Certain persons were chosen for execution. **Seraiah** was the grandson of Hilkiah, the faithful priest under Josiah. **Zephaniah** is possibly the person of the same name in 29:25. **Doorkeepers** were key temple personnel. Leaders of Judah's forces were executed.

52:31–34 Jehoiachin was released from prison soon after Nebuchadnezzar died in 562 B.C. Nebuchadnezzar's son **Evil-Merodach** became king but reigned only two years (562–560 B.C.). **lifted up the head:** Jehoiachin was pardoned by the king of Babylon. Jehoiachin was provided food and given a seat of honor in Babylon. This restoration was symbolic of the future restoration of Israel and Judah to their homeland.

Lamentations

Introduction

The Book of Lamentations reveals the broken heart of the prophet Jeremiah over the national tragedy that had unfolded before his eyes: Jerusalem, God's city, had fallen to the Babylonians. Jeremiah's sorrow and tears were not for his own personal loss, however, but for the sinfulness of the Israelites. The people of Israel had chosen to reject God. Yet even in this time of suffering there was hope. The Lord would not discipline His people forever; He would eventually restore those who waited on Him.

Although no author is named in the book, the prophet Jeremiah has been traditionally identified as the writer of Lamentations. The author seems to identify himself with Jeremiah when he says, "I am a man who has seen affliction by the rod of His wrath." In addition, there are many linguistic similarities between Lamentations and Jeremiah.

The five chapters of Lamentations are five poems with ch. 3 as the midpoint or climax. Accordingly, the first two chapters build an "ascent," or crescendo, to the climax, the grand confession in 3:23, 24: "Great is Your faithfulness. The LORD is my portion." The last two chapters are a "descent," or decrescendo, from the pinnacle of ch. 3.

Lamentations focuses on national suffering—specifically, the suffering of Judah. Along the way, the book tackles some of the toughest questions faced by God's people: How can God's love and justice be reconciled with our pain? If God is in control of history, how could a nation suffer so much so soon after it had been led by such godly leaders as King Josiah and those involved in that revival? Where was God during His people's unhappiest hour?

The Book of Lamentations offers some practical theological reflections on the purposes and results of suffering. Rather than explaining away pain, the book helps us face pain. By avoiding cheery clichés, the Book of Lamentations provides companionship for those who are suffering and plants seeds of hope for rebuilding after the suffering is over.

In fact, the anger of God is a sign that He cares. The Lord's anger is never capricious or unreasonable. His discipline is a sign that He has not abandoned us. Even in His display of anger, God is still full of mercy and grace. Come what may, God remains faithful. His faithfulness is the greatest comfort to those who suffer; His compassions are new every morning.

1:1 How: This exclamatory word is used frequently in laments and funeral songs. It expresses astonishment, sorrow, and dismay (see 2:1; 4:1; Is. 1:21; 14:4; Jer. 9:19; 48:17; Ezek. 26:17). **lonely:** This is a stranded individual, one who is **like a widow.** Jerusalem is personified, or portrayed as a person (see Is. 1:21). Beginning in v. 12, Jerusalem "speaks" of her own troubles in the first person. **princess ... slave:** This is a terrible reversal of fortune.

1:2 Among all her lovers (v. 19) describes Judah's sin of turning away from God and toward the gods of Canaan (see Jer. 3:1–6). Also, the sins of Judah often involved the sexual forms of pagan worship that characterized the Canaanite people.

1:3 The southern kingdom **Judah** is personified here as Jerusalem was in v. 1. **captivity:** The implications of v. 1 are made clear. The reference here is to the Babylonian captivity suffered by Judah following the destruction of Jerusalem in 586 B.C.

1:4 mourn: The roads "mourned" because there would no longer be throngs of pilgrims traveling to Jerusalem to worship at the temple. **her gates:** The image of sad gates is also found in Ps. 24:7–10, which indicates that the gates would not always mourn. **priests ... virgins:** These two words indicate people from all elements of the city; everyone in the city experienced **bitterness.**

1:5 the LORD has afflicted her: God punished Jerusalem because of the people's **transgressions.** The suffering described in the Book of Lamentations was fully deserved (v. 1).

1:6 Daughter of Zion is an endearing term for Jerusalem that speaks of God's extraordinary love for the city (see Ps. 87:2). **All her splendor has departed:** Israel's glory was found in the presence of the Lord (see Ps. 96:8). But that glory had been removed from the Most Holy Place (see Ezek. 9:3; 10:19; 11:22).

1:7 In this verse the name **Jerusalem** is a comprehensive term that alludes to the "widowed" city of Jerusalem in v. 1; the nation "Judah" in v. 3; and the center of worship on "Mount Zion" in v. 4. The nation, the city, and the temple were ravaged by the invading Babylonian armies in 586 B.C. The emphasis is on Jerusalem's utter helplessness as her enemies ridiculed her miseries (v. 21).

1:8 they have seen her nakedness: It was an extreme humiliation for a woman to be stripped of all her clothing in public. Such exposure was reserved for prostitutes (see Ezek. 16:35–39; 23:29), which Judah had become in a spiritual sense (vv. 2, 8, 9).

1:9 Judah is pictured as a "dirty harlot" because of her involvement with the sins of Canaanite worship. In fact, Judah was so engaged in dishonorable behavior that she had lost her sense of decorum and would not clean **her skirts.**

1:10 Since God's people had not preserved the **sanctuary** of their hearts from pollution, they had no reason to be amazed when their enemies desecrated the earthly sanctuary. As a rule, Gentiles were forbidden to enter the congregation of the Lord (Ammon and Moab are mentioned specifically in Deut. 23:3, 4; the command was extended to all nations in Neh. 13:3; Ezek. 44:7, 9).

1:11 They seek bread: Moses had predicted a famine in Deut. 28:17, 38–42. **See, O LORD:** The call for God to pay attention is very similar to those found in the Psalms of Lament (see Ps. 142:4).

1:12 Passersby are asked rhetorically to look, listen, and compare Jerusalem's grief to any other grief experienced by mortals. God's **fierce anger** is put in the context of the day of the Lord (see Joel 2:1–11; Zeph. 1:14–18).

1:13 Jerusalem's suffering is portrayed, using several metaphors: (1) **fire** from heaven, (2) a hunter's **net** spread to trap animals, (3) an animal yoke fastened about the head of a person (v. 14), and (4) the crushing of grapes in a winepress (v. 15). **turned me back:**

The purpose of Jerusalem's suffering was to bring about a turning or repentance.

1:14 yoke of my transgressions: The idea here is sinful patterns of life becoming compulsive, burdening people like a yoke on a beast of burden. **He made my strength fail:** God imposed a yoke until all of Zion's strength failed. With no power of their own left, weary people are more likely to listen to God.

1:15 The virgin daughter of Judah: Jerusalem (Judah) was supposed to be the chaste bride of God. Instead she had become a polluted harlot because her people worshiped other gods than the God with whom they covenanted (vv. 2, 8, 9).

1:16 The people of Jerusalem wept because the very fate Jeremiah had prophesied had come to pass. **comforter … Is far from me:** The real Comforter of Judah is God. But because of Judah's sin, God would not come to their assistance.

1:17 Spreads out her hands is a reference to prayer (2:19). **an unclean thing:** The Israelites were supposed to be God's holy people (see Deut. 7:6). However, they had become worse than their pagan neighbors.

1:18 The LORD is righteous: Verses 5 and 17 establish that ultimately it was the Lord who permitted Jerusalem's collapse. Yet God remained just and right in what He did (see Ex. 9:27; Ezra 9:15; Neh. 9:33; Jer. 12:1).

1:19 priests … elders: The people who should have been a help were themselves in trouble.

1:20 While the roads leading to Jerusalem "mourned" because there would be no more pilgrims traveling to the city (v. 4), the **sword** of Judah's enemies mourned because there were no more Jews to kill.

1:21, 22 All my enemies: Those who previously had been friends of Judah (v. 2) became Judah's enemies. **Bring on the day:** Several times the "day" of God's wrath is mentioned in the Book of Lamentations (2:1, 21, 22). The term is used to refer not only to the time of Jerusalem's fall in the past, but also to a future day when God would rectify all of the wrongs that the nations had committed against Israel and God.

2:1, 2 The beauty of Israel was found in its temple (see Is. 64:11) and its ark of the covenant (see 1 Sam. 4:21, 22; Ps. 78:60, 61). In

1 Chr. 28:2 God's **footstool** is identified with the ark of the covenant. Occasionally God was pictured as enthroned and seated between the cherubim that were over the ark (see 1 Sam. 4:4; 2 Sam. 6:2; Ps. 80:1; 99:1, 5; 132:7). This passage says that God, in His wrath, had abandoned His footstool.

2:3 The **horn** was a symbol of strength and power (see 1 Sam. 2:1; Ps. 75:5; 92:10; 148:14; Jer. 48:25). **drawn back His right hand:** Usually the right hand of God is understood as the instrument of help for God's people stretched out against their enemies (see Ex. 15:6; Ps. 20:6). Here God's hand is withdrawn from the enemies, leaving the people of God at their mercy.

2:4 like an enemy: The Lord did not simply relax His protection of Judah (v. 3). He purposely worked against His people **with His right hand.**

2:5 swallowed up: Sheol, or death, is sometimes portrayed as "swallowing up" people (see Prov. 1:12; 27:20; 30:16); here God is described as doing the swallowing (v. 2).

2:6, 7 Tabernacle means "booth" or "hut," a structure found in a **garden.** The point seems to be that the glorious temple of God had become similar to the dilapidated house of David (Amos 9:11). The temple of God had become a booth of branches similar to those used for the Feast of Booths (Succoth).

2:8 Four weeks after the capture of Jerusalem, Nebuchadnezzar had destroyed the temple, the palace, the homes of the people, and the city **wall** (see 2 Kin. 25:9, 10; Jer. 52:13, 14).

2:9 The Law is no more: These words do not suggest the end of the Law, but rather the ceasing of the work of the Law in the lives of the people for their blessing (see Deut. 6:1–3).

2:10 Throwing **dust** on the head (see Job 16:15; Is. 29:4; Mic. 1:10) was a common sign of mourning. **virgins of Jerusalem:** Their sadness was increased by the knowledge that this was not a time for marriage and family. Even though their lives had been spared, they had lost their futures.

2:11 My eyes fail with tears: This is the response of the author Jeremiah who suffered with the afflicted (1:2). **Bile** is literally "liver," a symbol of deep emotion.

2:12 Grain and wine are used here as a synonym for food.

2:13 How shall I console you: Jeremiah had no words to help the grieving women of Jerusalem as they looked helplessly on their dying babies.

2:14 false and deceptive visions: False **prophets** spewed forth their "utterly valueless" lies.

 IN DEPTH   **How Far Will God Go?**

The destruction of Jerusalem revealed an astonishing fact about God: He will go to great lengths to draw His people back to Himself. The people of Judah strayed far from the Lord. It was not that they were irreligious. On the contrary, they were pious and devout. For the most part they maintained the religious rituals detailed in the Law, gathering in the temple week after week to offer sacrifices and observe the Sabbath. But during the rest of the week, they ignored the Law.

In essence, the people confused means with ends. They forgot that the sacrificial system, the Sabbath, the temple, and even the Law were all merely means to a far more important end—the end of knowing and serving God (Jer. 22:15, 16). So eventually God took these means away (Lam. 2:5–9), important and valuable as they were.

God destroyed Jerusalem; God pulled down the temple and its furnishings; God did away with the religious rituals; God removed the king and the high priest; God allowed the written Law itself to be destroyed; and God stopped giving visions to the prophets.

God's people today must also beware of confusing means with ends. Religious activities and resources have value, but they are not what life is all about. God Himself is what matters, and He will go to whatever length is necessary to help us remember that.

2:15, 16 Shake their heads was a common expression of derision (see Ps. 22:7; 109:25; Jer. 18:16; see also 1 Kin. 9:8; Job 27:23; Jer. 19:8; 49:17; 50:13; Ezek. 27:36; Zeph. 2:15). Losing face in the ancient Middle East was a terrible evil. Jerusalem was supposed to be **the joy of the whole earth,** the source of spiritual blessings for all the nations of the earth (see Gen. 12:3). Now Jerusalem was profaned (v. 2) and unclean (1:17).

2:17 The LORD has done what He purposed: God had promised Moses that He would judge sin (see Deut. 28:15, 16). The destruction of Jerusalem was a fulfillment of that promise.

2:18 The **wall** of the people's hearts was more impenetrable than the wall of the city of Jerusalem (2:7, 8).

2:19 Arise: The call is for people to awaken and scream for mercy from the Lord. **Lift your hands** refers to a posture of prayer (see 1:17; Ps. 134:2).

2:20 Should the women eat their offspring: So desperate were the scenes of starvation in Jerusalem that women actually fought over whose deceased child would be eaten next (4:10).

2:21 Young and old: The punishment of Jerusalem affected everyone. **virgins ... young men:** The punishment of Jerusalem extended even to the "pride of the city" (1:18; 2:4).

2:22 The terrors that surround me: The people mocked Jeremiah with the slogan "terror on every side," because he seemed to see catastrophe everywhere.

3:1 I am the man: Jeremiah's personal testimony paralleled the experience of the city of Jerusalem as a whole (2:11). **The rod of His wrath** refers to the Babylonians as instruments of God's judgment. In Is. 10:5, Assyria is referred to as "the rod of (God's) anger."

3:2, 3 The imagery of **darkness** represents adversity and God's judgment (see Job 12:25; Is. 9:2; Amos 5:18).

3:4, 5 He has aged my flesh: This imagery suggests the ebbing and wasting away of Jeremiah's life and that of the nation.

3:6 like the dead of long ago: So hopeless did the situation seem that Jeremiah felt like he had died long ago. **Dark places** may imply the grip of death (see Ps. 88:6 where the

same Hebrew word is used in parallel to the word *pit*).

3:7 He has hedged me in: Jeremiah felt as though there was no way out of his predicament.

3:8 He shuts out my prayer: On occasion, God had forbidden Jeremiah to pray for the deliverance of Judah (see Jer. 11:14; 14:11).

3:9 He has blocked my ways with hewn stone: A common practice of the Assyrians was to wall up prisoners in confined places and leave them to die.

3:10, 11 Jeremiah compared God to a **bear** or **lion** waiting to ambush (see Hos. 13:8; Amos 5:19). God had permitted Judah to be attacked and mangled.

3:12, 13 He has bent His bow: This verse echoes Job 16:12, 13, in which Job compares God to an archer who makes human beings His target (2:4).

3:14 I have become the ridicule of all my people: Jeremiah was made the butt of scoffing and mockery (see Jer. 20:7).

3:15 Wormwood was a bitter herb used to flavor some drinks.

3:16–18 He has also broken my teeth with gravel: The people had sensed that they were so associated with dust and sackcloth—symbols of mourning—that it was as though they fed on dirt. The dust became gravel which broke the people's teeth. The people were also **covered** with **ashes,** another symbol of mourning (see Jer. 6:26).

3:19, 20 Remember: Jeremiah attempted to change his mood by recalling his past experiences. But what he remembered only made him feel worse.

3:21 This I recall to my mind: Jeremiah's remembrance of God's faithfulness brought about a change in the prophet's emotions. When we focus on the Lord, we are able to rise above, rather than to suffer under, our troubles.

3:22 This verse seems to contradict all that had been written up to this point (see 2:1–5). Yet the very fact that there was a prophet left to write these words and a remnant left to read them show that not every person in Jerusalem had been **consumed.** The fact that there was a remnant at all was because of the **mercies** and **compassions** of God.

3:23 new every morning: Every day presents us with a new opportunity to discover and experience more of God's love. Even in the midst of terrible sorrow, Jeremiah looked for signs of mercy. **Great is Your faithfulness:** Here is the heart of the Book of Lamentations. The comforting, compassionate character of God dominates the wreckage of every other institution and office. God remains "full of grace and truth" in every situation (see Ex. 34:6, 7; John 1:14).

3:24 The LORD is my portion: This expression is based on Num. 18:20, in which Aaron was denied an inheritance in the land but was told instead that the Lord Himself was his portion and inheritance. **I hope in Him:** Hope is not a wishful thought, but a confident expectation in Lord. The verb *hope* suggests the idea of a "waiting attitude" (v. 21).

3:25 those who wait: The idea here is the acceptance of God's will and His timing (see Ps. 40:1; Is. 40:31).

3:26 good: Not only is God good to those who wait and hope on Him (v. 25), but it was also good for the people. **hope and wait quietly:** A quiet confidence in the **salvation of the LORD** is always in order.

3:27, 28 Youth here refers not to age, but to strength as opposed to diminished vitality.

3:29, 30 Put his mouth in the dust is a figure of speech for conquest. The phrase pictures a captive lying face down with the conqueror's foot on his back. **Hope** refers to the confident expectation that the Lord will deliver (v. 26).

3:31, 32 The promises that God made to the patriarchs (see Gen. 12:1–3; 15:13–21; 22:15–18) were not **cast off,** but were still in force. The wickedness of God's people delayed but could not frustrate the fulfillment of His promises.

3:33–36 before the face of the Most High: God is offended when a person deprives another human being of his or her rights. God is omniscient and notices everything.

3:37–42 These verses present a plan for repentance and renewal. **turn back:** Repentance in the Old Testament prophets is often expressed by the verb meaning "to turn" (see 5:21; Jer. 3:1). **lift our hearts and**

hands: Lifting hands was a common posture in prayer (2:19).

3:43–46 So long as sin festered, God's wrath was a **cloud** (2:1) or veil through which no prayer could penetrate.

3:47, 48 Desolation and destruction may be rephrased as "utter devastation."

3:49–51 The imagery of weeping continues from v. 48 (see also 1:2; 2:11). **Daughters of my city** refers to the people of Jerusalem.

3:52–54 silenced my life in the pit: Jeremiah speaks not only of his own experience of being cast into a pit (see Jer. 38:4–6), but also of his pain and grief over the wretched condition of his fellow countrymen. The *pit* is a metaphor for the grave or extreme danger (see Ps. 28:1; 30:3; 40:2).

3:55–57 The Lord's **name** is the term by which He delights to reveal His mercies to His people (see Ex. 3:14, 15).

3:58–60 pleaded the case: Jeremiah used the terms of God's formal accusation (see Jer. 2:1–3:5); however, here the words are used *for* the people rather than *against* them. **You have redeemed my life:** Here is a hint of the light of the New Testament gospel. The only way that God would be able to *plead the case* of His people was if He Himself paid for—or redeemed them from—their sinfulness.

3:61–63 Jeremiah here turns to the **enemies** who treated God's people so poorly during their weakened state (1:21).

3:64–66 Repay them, O LORD: The request for divine vindication is an expression of a longing for God's righteousness and the success of His kingdom and His truth.

4:1, 2 The Babylonian army looted the temple and overturned all its huge **stones. precious sons:** The people of Jerusalem were of more value than the temple. Elsewhere these people are referred to as "My son, My firstborn" (Ex. 4:22) and "a special treasure to Me ... a kingdom of priests and a holy nation" (Ex. 19:5, 6).

4:3 Jackals were the dogs of the desert, disreputable beasts. However, even these animals cared for their young. **Ostriches,** on the other hand, seem to care very little for their young.

4:4 The tongue of the infant: The theme of

thirsting and starving children is revisited (see 2:11–13).

4:5, 6 People who formerly could have eaten any **delicacies** they wanted groveled in refuse **heaps** during the terrible days of the Babylonian siege of Jerusalem.

4:7, 8 Nazirites were men and women who committed themselves to God for periods of special devotion (see Num. 6:1–21). **Like sapphire … soot:** The siege of Jerusalem was so terrible that no one was exempt, not even the godly people like the Nazirites.

4:9 Dying early in the siege was perhaps **better** than living through all of its horrors.

4:10–12 This verse describes the horrible effects of the long siege that were alluded to in 2:20. **cooked their own children:** This unimaginable horror could only have occurred in the most inhumane conditions.

4:13, 14 The very people who should have been agents of righteousness became agents of sin (see Jer. 8:10; 14:18).

4:15, 16 Wherever the wicked wandered, they were treated as lepers, people who were not welcome in any place. **the LORD scattered them:** The priests and prophets were separated from **the face of the LORD** because they had helped cause the people of Judah to stumble.

4:17–19 a nation that could not save us: After the fall of Jerusalem in 586 B.C., the survivors in Judah turned to Pharaoh Hophra of Egypt to deliver them, thereby breaking covenant with Nebuchadnezzar and the specific word of God (see Jer. 42—44; Ezek. 29:16).

4:20 The heir to the Davidic line was "**the breath** of life" to the nation. But King Zedekiah was captured while trying to escape, put in chains, blinded after watching his sons massacred, and marched off to Babylon to die.

4:21, 22 It is possible that the phrase **daughter of Edom** is a sarcastic, judgmental phrase. Edom may have thought so highly of herself (see Obad. 3) that she believed she could assume the place of privilege her father Esau had lost, once Judah was destroyed.

5:1–3 The Promised Land had been a gift from the Lord to Abraham. This **inheritance** was a

kind of "down payment" on the future reign of God that would include the restoration of His people to that land. God demonstrated that He owned all nations and that Israel was to be His instrument for blessing all the nations on the earth. Yet in their present condition, the people of Israel seemed to be the most helpless of all peoples.

5:4–7 The survivors of the Babylonian siege were reduced to servitude, caught between **the Egyptians** and **the Assyrians** (4:17–19).

5:8, 9 The small harvests that were obtained from the land after the destruction of Jerusalem were vulnerable to nomads from the desert who occasionally took the **lives** of the people of Judah as well.

5:10 Our skin is hot: Disease would have been rampant during the siege.

5:11–13 The suffering of Jerusalem left no one unscathed—**women, princes, elders,** and **young men.**

5:14 gate … music: Ordinary events and pleasures were no longer appropriate or even possible for the people of Jerusalem.

5:15 joy … dance: This verse illustrates Eccl. 3:4. This was a time to weep and mourn, not to laugh and dance.

5:16 The crown has fallen from our head expresses the loss of Judah's position of honor.

5:17 our heart is faint … our eyes grow dim: The normal zest for life was gone. Death would be better than a horrible existence during the siege of Jerusalem.

5:18 foxes: The idea of wild animals roaming the holy city where the people of God once came in glad worship was the final indignity.

5:19, 20 You, O LORD, remain forever: God's eternal rule and reign are a hope and support during the bleakest moments of suffering and despair (see Ps. 80:1, 2; 89:3, 4; 103:19).

5:21 The one word **turn** (1:13; 3:40) can summarize God's message to His rebellious people.

5:22 Unless You have utterly rejected us: What is stated as a possibility actually emphasizes that the occurrence is completely out of the question: The Lord cannot reject His own people forever.

Ezekiel

Introduction

The prophet Ezekiel had the thankless job of proclaiming God's message on the crowded and hostile streets of Babylon. At the same time that Jeremiah was warning the citizens of Jerusalem of the coming destruction of that holy city, Ezekiel was preaching the same message to the exiles in Babylon. Even though these exiles were hundreds of miles away from the Promised Land and the temple, God would not leave them in the dark. Instead He sent Ezekiel to warn, exhort, and comfort the weary exiles.

Ezekiel received and reported revelations from the living God as an exile in Babylon during 593–571 B.C. All that is known of this solitary prophet comes from his written prophecy, and no compelling data exist for the acceptance of any author other than the one named in the book itself: Ezekiel, son of Buzi (a priest), who was taken captive with Jehoiachin and other Hebrews in 597 B.C.

During Ezekiel's life and ministry, Israel (the northern kingdom) was corrupt politically and spiritually. Their idolatry led to captivity by Assyria in 722 B.C. The leadership of Judah eventually fell into the idolatry of the neighboring nations. The people refused to heed the prophets' reminders about the curses and blessings promised by God in the Mosaic covenant. Ezekiel prophesied that there would come catastrophe and captivity for Judah and Jerusalem. Yet he also had a message about eventual restoration and renewal, based on God's faithfulness to the promises of all the covenants made with His people since the Abrahamic covenant.

Ezekiel's ministry was primarily to those Jews deported from Judah by the Babylonians and any Israelites that remained in exile from previous deportations by the Assyrians. Still his messages had great instructional and practical significance for the Hebrews remaining in Israel and for the surrounding pagan nations, whose fate he foretold. Although Ezekiel was transported in visions to Jerusalem (see chs. 8; 11), those revelations were always for the benefit of him and those to whom he was speaking in exile.

Ezekiel's warnings of national calamity include warnings of disease, death, destruction, and deportation. Yet in the end, the prophet concludes with the comforting news that a day would come when God's rule and practical righteousness would return with a new temple and city and a renewed land and nation (chs. 33—48).

1:1, 2 This was the **fifth day** of the fourth month (v. 1). Ezekiel's "thirtieth year" was 597 B.C., when King Jehoiachin was deported to Babylon by Nebuchadnezzar (2 Kin. 24). The year 593 as the **fifth year of … captivity** is arrived at by using the Babylonian calendar, which begins in March.

1:3 Ezekiel uses the introductory phrase **the word of the LORD came** 50 times in this book. It always introduces a divine message and sometimes a new section. The name **Ezekiel** comes from the verb meaning "to seize," "to hold fast," coupled with the term meaning "God." Thus Ezekiel's name indicates that he was a man whom God had seized. **the hand of the LORD was upon him:** The divine origin of Ezekiel's message is emphasized in these first few verses.

1:4 whirlwind … great cloud … raging fire: Compare the descriptions of divine appearance in Ex. 19:16–20; Ps. 18:7–15; Mic. 1:2–4. See also v. 13 below. The term translated **amber** may also be understood as something like "glowing metal" (v. 27)

1:5 In ch. 10, these **living creatures** are related to the cherubim—celestial beings associated with God's holiness and glory and sometimes poetically with storm winds upon which God travels (see Ps. 18:10). There are two basic approaches to understanding the *four living creatures:* as a highly symbolic representation of deity, or as highly symbolic representations of angelic beings who serve in God's presence. Probably they are angels, since God Himself is not revealed until the end of the section (v. 26).

1:6 four faces: This image may suggest complete awareness; nothing is "behind" or "beside" these creatures.

1:7 legs … feet: The imagery portrays strength and beauty.

1:8 The "humanlike" representation includes **hands** and presumably arms.

1:9 did not turn: This seems to follow from the four faces (v. 6).

1:10 man … lion … ox … eagle: Composite fantastic figures in these classic combinations have been found in Mesopotamian and Egyptian iconography. The idealized strengths of each figure were thus presumed to reside in the living creature.

1:11, 12 One pair of **wings** was stretched upwards, as if in reverence; the other pair was used to cover the body as if in submission.

1:13–15 fire … lightning: These phenomena regularly attend descriptions of the appearances of God to His people (see Ex. 19:16–20).

1:16, 17 beryl: This may be chrysolite, a yellow or gold-colored stone. **wheel in the middle of a wheel:** The composite wheels were able to go in any direction without pivoting.

1:18 rims … full of eyes: The wheels had an exquisite beauty and an animate intelligence.

1:19–21 The prophet emphasizes the association of the wheels with the living creatures, as well as the creatures' ability to travel wherever they wished. The mysterious phrase **the spirit … in the wheels** emphasizes the significance of the wheels. It appears that the wheels represented the flexibility and mobility of the living creatures. This is a pictorial representation of God's omnipresence.

1:22, 23 firmament: The same word is used in Gen. 1:6. It means an "expanse" or "platform."

1:24 Almighty: This is the divine name *Shaddai,* most likely based on a word meaning "mountain," to suggest God's omnipotence and majesty (see 10:5).

1:25 This **voice** connects with the "man" of v. 26. In Gen. 1 the voice of God summons light from the darkness (Gen. 1:3). Here above the din of angels' wings there is *a voice.* In John 1:1 is revealed the apostle's term for the Savior: the Word.

1:26 While Isaiah describes the elevation of

the Lord's **throne** (see Is. 6:1), Ezekiel focuses on its beauty. **sapphire:** This is precious lapis lazuli, a deep blue stone with golden specks. The enthroned figure with **the appearance of a man** is the culmination of this vision.

1:27, 28 Fire like burning metal (**amber,** v. 4) and rainbowlike **brightness** surrounded the One on the throne (v. 26). **the likeness of the glory of the LORD:** Human *likeness* here may reflect the personal nature of God's revelation of Himself. Further, it points forward to the plan of a more personal revelation of God coming as the Messiah (see John 1:1–18). The *glory* indicates the wonder, majesty, and worthiness of the living God. Amid the wheels, the creatures, the colors, and the dazzling light was a figure who appeared like a man (v. 26). **I fell on my face:** The prophet's response was to fall down in worship and submission.

2:1 Son of man: Ezekiel uses this phrase more than 90 times to refer to himself. It emphasizes his humanity in his God-given role as a spokesman for God. The meaning of the phrase is "human one." In the Old Testament, only Dan. 7:13 and 8:17 use this phrase. In the New Testament, *Son of Man* is used frequently by Jesus for Himself. With this phrase Jesus was calling Himself "the Human One," the long-awaited Messiah who came as God in the flesh (Luke 21:27; John 1:14; 2 John 7).

2:2 the Spirit: This reference to the indwelling of the Holy Spirit in God's prophet is of great importance. The visions and messages of Ezekiel revelations from the living God.

2:3, 4 Ezekiel was called to speak God's message to the **children of Israel.** God describes them as **a rebellious nation** and more specifically **impudent and stubborn**—literally "stiff-of-face and hard-of-heart children" (see 3:7). The Hebrew term for *rebellious* indicates a breaking of the covenant relationship. **Thus says the Lord GOD:** Like Moses (Ex. 3; 4), Ezekiel would speak in God's name only what God commanded him.

2:5 If the rebellious people refused to listen to Ezekiel's message, Ezekiel would still prove himself a true **prophet** of God by continuing to proclaim God's messages (see also v. 7).

2:6, 7 briers and thorns ... scorpions: These images portray the nature of the rebellious opponents of Ezekiel's warnings. God told Ezekiel not to allow fear to hinder his message.

2:8, 9 eat: In contrast to rebellious Israel, Ezekiel was to set an example by being receptive and listening to God's message.

2:10 The unusual feature of writing on both sides of a scroll indicates the magnitude of the nation's transgressions and its need for lengthy **lamentations** (see Zech. 5:3; Rev. 5:1). Although Ezekiel would later bring words of comfort and consolation (see chs. 33—48), his first prophecies from God contained only sorrow and sadness.

3:1–4 eat: The symbolic act of eating the scroll demonstrated that Ezekiel internalized the message in preparation for speaking to the people.

3:5–7 Although no linguistic barrier existed between Ezekiel and the nation, Israel would pay less attention to the prophet than foreigners would. Israel's rejection of the prophet's message was the symptom of a fundamental revolt against God's rule (see 1 Sam. 8:7). All Israel was characterized as **impudent**—literally "hard-of-head"—and **hard-hearted.**

3:8, 9 I have made your face strong: There may have been an intentional pun on Ezekiel's name, which means "strongly seized by God" (see 1:3) or "God strengthens."

3:10, 11 A necessary prerequisite to God sending Ezekiel as His messenger was Ezekiel's reception of God's words. God told Ezekiel that he was to make it clear that his message and authority came from the Lord, and that he must continue to **speak** regardless of his audience's responses and reactions.

3:12, 13 Blessed ... from His place: This **thunderous** acclaim in praise of the living God came from His myriad of angelic armies (compare Is. 6:3). **glory:** The word suggests "weight" or "significance," indicating the wonder, majesty, and worthiness of the living God.

3:14 Bitterness means "distress" and "anguish." Ezekiel's human perspective caused him to focus on the distasteful calling of delivering a message no one would listen to. The

prophet was angry—**heat of my spirit**—and appalled. But the **hand of the LORD** was present to help him deal with these feelings and then move him on to live and work among the captives (see v. 15).

3:15, 16 The Israelites who had been exiled to Babylon lived in **Tel Abib,** meaning "hill of flood." **Seven days** is the time normally taken for mourning the dead, as well as the time set aside for a priest's consecration (Gen. 50:10; Lev. 8:33). Ezekiel sat **astonished** with these captives for seven days as evidence that he had experienced a unique encounter with God (see Job 2:13). At the end of the seven days Ezekiel would be ordained for the priesthood and would be ready to proclaim mourning for Israel.

3:17 The **watchman** stood on the city wall guarding against any external or internal threat. He would sound an alarm upon sighting impending danger (see 2 Sam. 18:24).

3:18, 19 his blood: This severe warning given to Ezekiel was similar to that given to a military watchman in ancient times. If the watchman failed to give the alarm to the city in a time of peril, the blood of the city would be required of him. But if the watchman sounded the alarm and the city did not respond, the watchman could hardly be blamed.

3:20, 21 The **stumbling block** is interpreted by some as a death sentence. If the person continued repeatedly in sin, then death would result. The reference to "life" and "death" in this section is to physical, not eternal, realities.

3:22, 23 The word **glory** suggests "weight" or "significance." The emphasis is on the central significance and awesome wonder of the living God.

3:24, 25 Ezekiel wrote more about the indwelling of God's **Spirit** than any of the prophets (see 2:2).

3:26 The phrase **not be one to rebuke them** qualified what was meant by Ezekiel's being **mute.** The idea may be better stated as "not be a legal mediator." During his "mute" period, Ezekiel would not be allowed to speak as a mediator on behalf of the people before God, their Judge.

3:27 He who hears, let him hear: Jesus used this warning often in His teaching (see Mark

4:23). It emphasizes individual responsibility and readiness to accept the divine message.

4:1 The **clay tablet** was unfired mud or clay soft enough to be inscribed with a stylus. The term translated **portray** means to scratch or mark on the tablet.

4:2 Lay siege: The city of Jerusalem would come under *siege,* meaning that the Babylonians would surround the city and cut off its outside supplies. The purpose was to starve the inhabitants into submission (see vv. 9–12; 16, 17). By his symbolic drawing, Ezekiel may have been commanded to do what other "prophets" of the nations might do. That is, the hired "prophets" of the pagan nations might use such a drawing as a device for invoking the gods to bring about the event graphically described. In Ezekiel's case, the drawing was the opposite of what the people wanted. As they sat in captivity, the worst news would have been that the holy city had been destroyed. In this case, the drawing showed the people the horrible truth of what God had already ordained.

4:3 The **iron plate** or pan was a utensil that Ezekiel possessed as a priest; it was for baking grain for the cereal offerings (Lev. 2:5; 6:21; 7:9). Here its purpose was to represent a wall between Ezekiel and the city. The first three verses of the chapter dramatize **to the house of Israel** the inevitable siege that would come against the holy city.

4:4–6 bear their iniquity: The prophet represented Israel—the northern kingdom—and Judah—the southern kingdom—and the length of time each was going to be punished for its sin. Since Ezekiel set the deportation of Jehoiachin (597 B.C.) as his chronological reference point (see 1:2), the most straightforward interpretation of vv. 4–8 pictures the punishment of exile and Gentile rule inflicted upon the Hebrew nation over a 430-year period as extending from 597 to approximately 167 B.C. This was the time Jewish rule returned to Judah, through the Maccabean revolt.

4:7 The **arm ... uncovered,** used in connection with God's command that Ezekiel **set** his **face toward the siege** (see 4:3), most likely refers to the siege as a set and

certain event (see Is. 52:10, and the modern idiom of "rolling up one's sleeves"). The siege showed that God would punish His disobedient people.

4:8 Restrain more literally reads "place ropes on." Ezekiel was bound while lying on either side for the entire 430 days; but the activities described in 4:9–17 show that his lying down and being tied up occurred only during parts of each day.

4:9–11 The recipe of six mixed grains for the bread indicates the limited and unusual food supply while in bondage in a foreign land. The small amounts of these grains vividly picture the short supply of food in a city under siege. Because a city under siege was cut off from outside supplies, the people had to ration their **food** and **water.** If those supplies ran out, they would be forced to surrender. In Jerusalem, the people would be allowed daily only one-half pound of bread (**twenty shekels**) and less than a quart of water (**one-sixth of a hin**).

4:12–15 The bread is called **defiled** (v. 13) in light of what is said in v. 12. In order to portray the fate of the unfaithful nation, God wanted Ezekiel to temporarily eat food made unclean by being cooked over a fire fueled by **human waste** (Deut. 23:12–14). God at first commanded Ezekiel to use human excrement because it would most accurately and forcefully symbolize the horror of the coming siege of the city. But **cow dung,** a common fuel, was allowed as a substitute in light of Ezekiel's faithfulness to the ceremonial law (Deut. 12:15–19; 14:3–21).

4:16, 17 The terrible conditions of the siege of Jerusalem would fulfill Ezekiel's symbolic acts (vv. 9–12). Both **water** and **bread** would be rationed. **Anxiety** and **dread** (see 12:19) would be rampant. The people had broken their covenant with God, and He had no choice but to bring upon them the consequences of their disobedience.

5:1 Shaving the **head** was an act showing shame or disgrace in Hebrew culture (see 7:18; 2 Sam. 10:4). It also represented a type of pagan mourning forbidden by the Law (see 27:31; Deut. 14:1; Is. 15:2; 22:12). Shaving the head was a mark of defilement, making a priest like Ezekiel ritually unclean, and so unable to perform his duties in the temple (Lev. 21:5). This told the people that they were about to be humiliated and defiled.

5:2 Each citizen of Jerusalem would suffer one of the three fates depicted by each of the three mounds of the equally measured shorn hair: (1) Some would be burned along with the city or would die from plague, famine, or other **siege** conditions (5:12; 2 Kin. 25:9); (2) some would be murdered by the **sword** during the attack (5:12; 2 Kin. 25:18–21); and (3) some would be scattered in the **wind**—referring to the Exile (5:12; 2 Kin. 25:11–17, 21).

5:3, 4 a fire will go out: A remnant from the group sent into exile would be saved from death and merged into the foreign culture. Other exiles would be killed.

5:5–7 This is Jerusalem: The words were being said in anguish. The personal God of the Hebrews had given them the city as an inheritance. God loved it and established it as the center of the world, because His temple was there. Here, however, He describes the extent of its people's abominations. **She has rebelled** refers to the people of the favored city whose sin was even worse than that of the nations around them. They had failed to follow even the moral laws that were common among the pagans.

5:8 I, even I, am against you: The solemn, emphatic pronoun is sad indeed.

5:9–17 The elements in God's judgment on the people for their sins can be enumerated in this way: (1) a judgment that will be worse in extent than ever before; (2) a terrible famine that will lead to cannibalism; (3) **pestilence,** meaning plagues and diseases associated with famine; (4) violent death by sword or wild beasts; and (5) the scattering and killing of a remnant. These punishments would come as the result of the people's idolatry—they had **defiled** God's temple with **detestable things** and **abominations** (v. 11), showing their complete disregard for the Law (see vv. 6, 7; see 11:18). The disobedient and rebellious people should not be surprised at the horror they were soon to face.

6:1–3 The **mountains of Israel** may signify the land in general (see 36:1–6); however, the

hills could be especially condemned because in their wooded areas the people had built altars and shrines to Canaanite idols (v. 13). **High places** were originally elevated locations for the worship of the god Baal and other deities of the Canaanite pantheon. The term *high place* could be used of any location, whether hilltop or valley (see v. 6; Jer. 7:31) where Canaanite gods were worshiped (1 Kin. 11:4–10). The Israelites adopted the use of these and associated worship practices, including sexual misconduct, sorcery, spiritism, snake worship, and child sacrifice.

6:4–6 The phrases **cast down your slain, lay the corpses,** and **scatter your bones** refer to God's judgment. Dead people lying unburied and bones scattered around signify the ultimate defilement of the land. God would bring this upon them because they had defiled and desecrated themselves by worshiping in the pagan high places (see 2 Kin. 23:20; Ps. 53:5).

6:7 you shall know that I am the LORD: Ordinarily, one would come to *know* more to experience the reality of the living God through encounters with His mercy. But because of the evil path that the people of Judah had taken, they would experience His reality through His judgment (Is. 28:21).

6:8–10 Not only would God prove His justice and faithfulness to His past promises and warnings about the consequences of idolatry (see 5:13), but He would **leave a remnant** of His people so they would **remember** the One true God **among the nations.** God had promised that, despite any future destruction of the nation that might occur because of sin, He would always preserve a portion from annihilation (see Deut. 28:61–64).

6:11, 12 Alas: This word, also translated "Ah!" (21:15) and "Aha!" (25:3), is meant sarcastically. Either God was displaying His delight over the destruction of idolatrous places and practices (vv. 1–7, 13) or He was having Ezekiel enact the mocking role of a jealous neighbor nation, such as Ammon (25:1–7).

6:13, 14 Then you shall know that I am the LORD: The Lord states the purpose of the coming destruction of His city and many of its people. The use of God's personal name further emphasizes the intent to bring His people back to Himself.

7:1–4 The three uses of the key word **end** emphasize that the fulfillment of the prophecy was at hand. **The four corners of the land** suggests that all the people of Judah would be affected, not just those in Jerusalem.

7:5–7 Key words in these verses include **end** (used two times), in parallel with **doom.** There now is an added emphasis on **disaster** (used two times); the coming disaster will be unlike any other (5:9).

7:8, 9 Again at the end of this oracle (see vv. 4, 27), God states His purpose in disciplining Israel: to cultivate in His people a better understanding of Himself.

7:10, 11 The flowering of the **rod** and **pride** indicates that the time to bring judgment was ripe. These words describe one whose time had come, a person marked by arrogance. In this case, it pictures the chosen instrument of God (Num. 17:5) with whom He would discipline Jerusalem and Judah—namely, Nebuchadnezzar, king of Babylon and the characteristic representative of the arrogant and evil Babylonians (see v. 21).

7:12, 13 Let not the buyer rejoice: The fact of coming judgment was so certain, and its effects would be so lasting and devastating, that transactions of buying and selling would be concluded improperly or not at all.

7:14, 15 No one goes to battle for Judah because the nation and land would be so devastated by death and diseases brought on by warfare and famine (5:8–17).

7:16–19 Those left alive would hide in the hills and be characterized by four things: (1) **mourning**—moaning **like doves** in **shame,** displaying their humiliation over sin by wearing **sackcloth** and shaving their heads (see Is. 15:2, 3); (2) weakness; (3) **horror;** and (4) disgust and disillusionment over wealth.

7:20–22 This section describes the judgment that would come on the people for taking the treasures of the temple to make pagan images. The people had sinned horribly when they crafted idols out of the temple treasures and then worshiped what their hands had made (Rom. 1:25).

7:23–27 God promised to **do to them according to … what they deserve.** Because Judah had been so bloodthirsty, God would send **the worst of the Gentiles** to **possess their houses,** defile the temple, and bring **violence** to the land. This section predicts Nebuchadnezzar's desecration of the Jerusalem temple in 586 B.C.

8:1 sixth year: This second exact date given in Ezekiel is 592 B.C., when Ezekiel was acting out the siege of Jerusalem (see 1:1; 4:1–8).

8:2 The first word translated **fire** may also be read in Hebrew as the word meaning "man." In the second instance **fire** is the expected meaning.

8:3, 4 The **north gate of the inner court,** called the "altar gate" in v. 5, was near the sacrificial altar (Lev. 1:11). There Ezekiel saw the **image … which provokes to jealousy.** All idolatry was forbidden, and any idol represented a violation of the loyalty that belonged to Israel's God.

8:5, 6 to make Me go: The people thought that just because the temple stood among them, whatever wrong they might do could not bring disaster. They thought the temple guaranteed their security. They did not realize that their evil had actually caused God to leave His temple, which would then no longer be their protection.

8:7–9 A view through a **hole** in the temple **wall,** this next scene of the vision gives a glimpse of even worse idolatrous acts. The people's **abominations** (vv. 6, 9, 10, 13, 15, 17) were not limited to a periphery. They extended deeply into the hierarchy of Israel's religious leadership.

8:10 all around on the walls: In conformity with surrounding pagan nations (primarily Egypt), God's people were worshiping images of clean and unclean creatures that represented various gods.

8:11 The **seventy** elders represented the nation's leaders (Num. 11:16–25). The **censer** each man carried (a vessel for holding burning incense) and the burning **incense** would not necessarily be evil, but here they were being used to worship idols.

8:12 The emphasis is on the elders' pagan beliefs as well as their resultant secret behavior—**in the dark.** They thought of God in limited, human terms, much as their neighbors viewed the gods of the nations. They thought He was not omniscient and omnipresent.

8:13, 14 Tammuz was a fertility god. The women were crying out to the idol because they had no children or because the crops were failing. In the sixth month, August-September, Tammuz was thought to "die" with the scorched land. Worshipers would wail over his death and cry for his resurgence.

8:15, 16 The location for the sun worship was in the **inner court ... between the porch and the altar.** These 25 **men** must have been Levites if temple regulations were being followed; otherwise, the area was forbidden (see Num. 3:7, 8; 18:1–7; 2 Chr. 4:9; Joel 2:17). Whether priests or not, they were turned in the wrong direction—their backs were to God's temple and they were **worshiping the sun.**

8:17, 18 put the branch to their nose: This action is not mentioned elsewhere. In the context it appears to be (1) a ritualistic gesture used in idol worship, or (2) an action indicative of the extensive violence which was occurring in Judah as a result of idolatry.

9:1 He is the God of Israel, who has been speaking since Ezekiel saw the glory of God (see 8:5). **those who have charge over:** This is the sense given to a Hebrew word that is frequently used of a vengeful visitation (Is. 10:3).

9:2 One man among them was probably one in addition to the six, making six men equipped as executioners and one representing the presence and purity of the holy God, who is worthy to mark out some for judgment and to omit others (see vv. 3–7; Ex. 12:1–13; Rom. 9:14–29; Rev. 7:3; 9:4).

9:3 It is not clear whether the term **cherub** here indicates (1) the cherubim on the ark of the covenant in the Most Holy Place or (2) the cherubim of the throne with wheels in 10:1–5, 18. Either way, this pictures the departure of God's glory from the temple, then from Jerusalem, and then from Judah.

9:4 Mark translates the Hebrew name for the last letter of the Hebrew alphabet, which in Ezekiel's time looked like an X. Those so marked are people who **sigh and cry** over

the abominations of idolatry. Those who demonstrated a righteous attitude through true repentance and remorse were marked out from the hardened rebels. These would be the remnant (see v. 8).

9:5, 6 Go after him: The universality of this judgment is shocking to us; but this is in line with divine judgments from the time of the Flood in Genesis to the final judgment described in Revelation.

9:7 My sanctuary: The corrupt spiritual leaders had been practicing idolatry and immorality in the temple (8:3–16). Judgment would begin with them because they had led the nation astray (1 Pet. 4:17).

9:8 The prophet was horrified by what he saw. The word **Ah** was sarcastic in 6:11; here it is a sincere gasp of pain (as in 11:13). **The remnant,** a group chosen and saved from destruction by a sovereign God, is a recurring theme in the Bible (see 2 Kin. 19:31; Ezra 9:8; Is. 1:9; 10:20–23; Amos 5:15; Rom. 9:27–29; 11:1–8).

9:9, 10 Three reasons are given as to why the nation deserved this terrible outpouring of God's wrath: (1) **iniquity,** or guilt of sinful offenses (see 4:4–8); (2) **bloodshed,** or violence (see 8:17); and (3) **perversity,** or injustice.

9:11 I have done: The report of judgment was brought by one man (vv. 3, 4) appearing as a righteous accountant.

10:1 See ch. 1 for an understanding of the several terms in this verse. The **cherubim** here are the living creatures of 1:5.

10:2 Coals of fire (see 1:13) are sometimes related to a chastisement for cleansing (Is. 6) and at other times to judgment by fiery catastrophe (Gen. 19:24, 25).

10:3–5 The **cloud** represented God's glory (as in 1:4), which was seen moving from the **inner court** to the **threshold** of the temple. From there it filled the temple (**house**).

10:6 when He commanded ... he went in: These words display the man's unquestioning obedience to God (see v. 5; 1:24; 8:2–5).

10:7, 8 A particular **cherub** handed the coals to the man in linen (v. 2). Though not stated explicitly, it is implied that all the directives of v. 2 were now carried out. The coals were then scattered on Jerusalem.

10:9–17 Ezekiel describes the **wheels** (vv. 9–14) and then the **cherubim** (vv. 15–17). See ch. 1 for details in this vision. Only in v. 14 is something different from the description in ch. 1. Whereas one of the four faces in 1:10 is an ox, here it is a **cherub.** There are ancient sculptures with animal bodies and wings but human faces, sometimes called "cherubs." The difference of the faces between 1:10 and 10:14 should not be called an error; it is possible that the images which Ezekiel saw were changing from time to time.

10:18, 19 God's **glory** continued moving gradually but progressively away from the temple (vv. 3, 4): from the entrance door of the temple to the wheeled cherubim throne, and then with the throne to the **east gate** of the temple.

10:20–22 The cherubim sometimes serve as guardians (see Gen. 3:24). They are associated with God's throne and presence (the mercy seat on the ark; Ex. 25:18–22; 1 Chr. 13:6). They are also associated with God's chariot-like throne (v. 1; 1:20–26; Ps. 18:10).

11:1, 2 Ezekiel saw **twenty-five** civic leaders at the temple. **Princes of the people** denotes public and political officials often serving in judicial, military, or royal posts (see 2 Sam. 8:15–18; 20:23–26). These men had been giving **wicked counsel,** and even stooped so low as to **devise iniquity** against their own people.

11:3 The time is not near to build houses can be rephrased, "Is it not now time to build houses?" These officials were proclaiming that the inhabitants of Jerusalem were as secure behind the city's walls as meat was safe in its cooking pot (**caldron**). There was no impending doom, they said; therefore, new construction projects were encouraged.

11:4, 5 Son of man means "human one." This phrase appears 90 times in Ezekiel and emphasizes Ezekiel's humanity in his role as a spokesman for God. In the Old Testament the phrase is used also for Daniel (Dan. 8:17) and for the coming Messiah (Dan. 7:13). In the New Testament the phrase *Son of Man* is used frequently by Jesus for Himself (see 2:1).

11:6 slain: Jerusalem's official leaders had been accused of wicked activities and giving unrighteous advice (v. 2); here we discover that they had killed fellow countrymen.

11:7–12 The verdict of a death penalty is announced. Contrary to the leaders' false beliefs, the ones they killed were the godly people whose presence might have offered protection in the **caldron**—that is, Jerusalem. Those who had gained power by the sword, knowing the dread of such force, would experience defeat and death the same way. They would be dragged out of the city and killed by **strangers,** or the Babylonians.

11:13, 14 Ezekiel's reaction showed that **Pelatiah,** one of the corrupt city leaders (v. 1), was struck dead by God as undeniable proof that the prophet's message would come true.

11:15 Ezekiel's **brethren** were those in exile with him. The people in Jerusalem (representative of Judah) regarded the exiles as sinners because they had been deported to Babylon.

11:16 God explained to Ezekiel that the Hebrews taken captive and spread among foreign lands were actually the remnant whom God was protecting. God himself would continue as their **sanctuary**—a "holy place" or a "set-apart place."

11:17 I will give you the land: God promises that Israel will be restored to the Promised Land. This is in keeping with the unilateral and unconditional nature of the covenant made with Abraham (Gen. 12:1–3; 15:13–21; Deut. 30:1–6), and renewed with David (2 Sam. 7:12–16) and Jeremiah (Jer. 31:31–34).

11:18–20 When the remnant returned to the land, they would abolish idolatry. At that time, God would establish a new covenant with them (Jer. 31:31–34). Then God would pour out His Spirit (see 36:26, 27; Joel 2:28, 29) so that His people would become united in purpose and empowered to maintain their righteousness. They would finally become His people (see Ex. 6:6–8).

11:21 As with Pelatiah, God promised to continue judging idolaters whose affections were for **detestable** objects—that is, idols. Such **recompense** was fully deserved because ample warning had been given; the people were personally responsible for the choices.

11:22, 23 God's glory continued to move away from **the city** to the Mount of Olives—**the mountain.** See 10:3, 4, 18, 19. The Hebrew term for **glory** literally means "weight" or "significance" and refers to the wonder and majesty of the living God.

11:24, 25 the Spirit: Ezekiel's visions are not just dreams; they were inspired by God Himself and thus were prophetic.

12:1, 2 The exiled community among whom Ezekiel was ministering was described twice as **a rebellious house.** This is further defined by the phrases: **eyes to see … and ears to hear** (Is. 6:10). The Israelites' hardness of heart was sustained for over a year (see 1:1, 2; 8:1). They would not listen to the prophet's words or his dramatizations of coming judgment (chs. 4—6).

12:3–8 Ezekiel's next visual demonstration warned the captives already in Babylon that they should not expect a quick return to Jerusalem. He had already shown that the city would soon fall (chs. 4; 5); those not killed would be led into exile. **I did as I was commanded:** In contrast to the inattention and disobedience of the people, God's prophet Ezekiel was always obedient to Him (see chs. 2—5).

12:9, 10 Ezekiel's audience was composed of people who had already experienced exile; but the people were so rebellious and so resistant to the message they continued disdainfully to ask the prophet, **What are you doing?** The phrase **prince in Jerusalem** refers to Zedekiah (vv. 12–14), the ruler of Judah (2 Kin. 24:17–20).

12:11–14 Speaking in 592 B.C., Ezekiel predicted the deportation of Jerusalem's population to Babylon six years later, and prophesied exactly what would happen to their leader Zedekiah. The king would attempt to escape by night, secretly and in disguise (**cover his face**); but he would be caught and blinded by the Babylonians, then carried off to Babylon where he would die (see 2 Kin. 25:1–7; Jer. 52:1–11). Ezekiel was a **sign** to his audience already in exile as he foretold the fate of the Jews still living in Jerusalem.

12:15, 16 The LORD translates God's personal name. It appears in this prophecy to indicate God's special relationship to the Israelites. Ezekiel instructed the exiles that their difficult situation did have a purpose. God would use it to demonstrate that He was a personal, caring Lord. Its aim was corrective and instructive. Furthermore the Exile would be a testimony or sign to **the Gentiles.** The defeat of God's people would not indicate the Lord's lack of strength, but the serious consequences of sin against Him. Through the difficult experience, His people would learn that their God was both holy and loving. Sin offended Him, but He still would reach out to restore the sinner.

12:17–19 To the **people of the land** (that is, his fellow exiles), Ezekiel was to demonstrate and declare God's warning about the devastating conditions that would befall the people in Judah and Jerusalem.

12:20, 21 For the fulfillment of the prophecy that Jerusalem and Judah would be **laid waste,** see 2 Kin. 25:8–21; Jer. 39:8–10; 44:1–6; 52:1–30; Lam. 1:3, 4.

12:22 The **proverb** or popular saying among the exiles indicates how hardened they were to Ezekiel's prophecies. **The days are prolonged, and every vision fails:** Although already captive, the people were cynical and apathetic, mistakenly thinking that a delay in judgment meant no judgment.

12:23–25 The days are at hand, and the fulfillment of every vision: An antithetical proverb would replace the old one (v. 22), and false prophets opposing Ezekiel would cease to speak. **in your days:** The exiles would live to see the judgment on Jerusalem fulfilled.

12:26–28 The people still thought that judgment would be delayed; Ezekiel was told to assure them a second time that the judgment would not **be postponed any more.**

13:1–4 The false prophets were **foolish** and like **foxes in the deserts.** The word translated *deserts* conveys the idea of open, desolate places. In the immediate context (v. 5), the foxes are pictured roaming amid the rubble of ruined city walls. The false prophets were like foxes among the ruins because they scavenged for themselves while ignoring the human wreckage surrounding them.

They were racketeers instead of reformers.

13:5 The **day of the LORD** refers to times when God triumphs (see 7:19; 30:3). The phrase is particularly used by the prophets to describe those periods in which God is unusually active in the affairs of His people. In that day, God will bring about His purposes for the world: He will rescue the righteous and judge evildoers.

13:6, 7 The false prophets, such as Balaam, practiced **divination** (see Josh. 13:22). This was the pagan art of finding "divine" guidance through such means as astrology, reading sheep livers and other animal organs, and consulting spiritists or witches to communicate with the dead (see 1 Sam. 28:3–19). These prophets hoped to receive some kind of revelation. But they did not find the truth for they were not searching for it where God had clearly pointed it out—in the Law and the prophets.

13:8 The divine judgment on all false prophecy and knowledge is given in this verse; it is **nonsense.**

13:9 Because these false prophets had prophesied messages that contradicted God's truth (v. 10), they were condemned. The Lord would separate them from God's people, from membership in the nation of Israel, and from life in the land. **enter into the land:** The false prophets would not participate in the future restoration of the people to the Promised Land.

13:10–16 These prophets would experience God's wrath—just as the walls of Jerusalem which were being constructed at that time would be destroyed. Jerusalem would be conquered and captured for the sins of its inhabitants. The false prophets had deceived the people with false hopes of comfort and prosperity (v. 10). Their deception placed them not only at odds with God's truth, but also with God Himself. Their destruction was certain.

13:17–19 the daughters: The Hebrew women who were false prophetesses were confusing their own ideas with God's and casting magic death spells through sorcery or witchcraft (Lev. 19:26).

13:20–23 These prophetesses were sowing discouragement and doubt among those not involved in demonic divination and were offering encouragement to those already initiated: **the righteous ... the wicked.** They would be stopped through the same judgment that was to come on the rest of the false prophets.

14:1–3 God revealed to Ezekiel that this group of **the elders of Israel** consisted of double-minded men (see 1 Kin. 18:21; Matt. 6:24; James 1:5–8). Outwardly, they came to seek a word from God through His true prophet Ezekiel, but in their hearts they harbored loyalties to other gods. **let Myself be inquired:** God knows all hearts and minds (Ps. 139:1–6), and He asks Ezekiel a rhetorical question about whether He ought to give guidance to such religious hypocrites (see vv. 4, 5).

14:4 answer ... according to the multitude of his idols: God responded to these hypocrites by allowing them to experience the practical consequences of disbelief and disobedience. Their idolatry consisted not only of the theological error of worshiping other gods, but also the immorality that was a natural result of a heart turned away from the living God. Evil is never caused by God (see Ps. 5:4), but He permits the suffering it brings to the world (see Job 1; Rom. 6:23).

14:5 seize the house of Israel by their heart: These words announced God's restorative purpose (see Prov. 3:12; Rev. 3:19) in allowing sin to run its course.

14:6, 7 Idolatry was condemned whether practiced by an Israelite (one of God's chosen people) or by **strangers** (Gentiles) spending time in Israel. Anyone from any culture who had come into contact with specific revelation about the Hebrew God was held responsible for his or her response to the truth.

14:8 The unrepentant idolater would be separated not only from God but also from God's people (13:9). This experience would be a strong visual warning—**sign**—and an international example—**proverb**—of God's honoring of His promise to punish disobedience with cursing (Lev. 20:1–7).

14:9–11 God allows false preaching for His own inscrutable purposes, but the preacher is held accountable for the content of the message. These were Israelite false prophets who deliberately ignored the truth and mixed it with falsehood. Their punishment would be the same as **the one who inquired** (the elders; see vv. 1–3). But they would also have the same redemptive plan (see v. 5).

14:12–20 Jerusalem's "persistent unfaithfulness" was so offensive to God that the presence of spiritual giants could not stay judgment by famine, wild beasts, military invasion (**sword**), or disease (**pestilence**).

14:21 These **judgments,** though stated hypothetically so far, would actually come on **Jerusalem** (see Lev. 26:22–26).

14:22, 23 A remnant would be **brought out** from Jerusalem. When the exiles observe **their ways and their doings**—that is, their wicked actions—they will be reminded of God's justice and grace. This is a remarkable use of the term *remnant*. Ordinarily the term is used of the righteous. Here it is used as a sample of the wicked people, whose deeds justified the actions of God in sovereign judgment: **I have done nothing without cause.**

15:1–5 The **wood of the vine** is depicted as useless. Unlike an olive tree, whose wood is also useful, the vine has only one use, to bear grapes.

15:6–8 In this instance the vine is symbolic of the Israelites still in Jerusalem (see Ps. 80:8–19; Is. 5:1–7). God had designed the people of Israel for a particular purpose, to bring glory to His name by living faithfully to His covenant and by bringing the nations to the knowledge of the Lord. Instead, Israel had become like the pagan nations around them. Israel had **persisted in unfaithfulness** and had failed to trust in God's power. Jerusalem, and by implication the entire nation, had not faced exile before but now would be disciplined with **another fire.** This refers to additional destruction and deportation to be brought by Nebuchadnezzar.

16:1, 2 to know her abominations: What follows is an animated development of the dreary story, designed to teach errant Jerusalem the real nature of her character in the eyes of God.

16:3 your father was an Amorite and your mother a Hittite: These shocking words refer to the cultural and moral origins of Jerusalem. Ancient Canaan was inhabited by Semitic and non-Semitic peoples. The Amorites and Hittites are associated in Scripture with the southern hill country, where Jerusalem was located (Num. 13:29). The point is that non-Israelites founded this city. Jebusites controlled it when the Israelites entered the land under Joshua (Josh. 15:8, 63). Israel did not fully control the city until David conquered it (2 Sam. 5:6, 7).

16:4, 5 God reminds Jerusalem that He had rescued them from being like an abandoned newborn child, unwashed, unsanitary (not **rubbed with salt**), and exposed to the elements to die. God alone had given her glory.

16:6 In contrast to Israel's apathetic disdain—which led to disobedience including idolatry (see Judg. 1, 2)—God had wanted Israel to **live,** having purposed and planned to impart His life and glory to them.

16:7–9 breasts were formed: The city is compared to a young woman, mature and lovely. Yet the city was **naked and bare** until God covered it with a relationship of covenantal love. This began when David moved the ark of the covenant there and God established the covenant with David (2 Sam. 6:1—7:17; see Ps. 132). Jerusalem became God's dwelling place (2 Sam. 7:12–17; 1 Kin. 5; 6).

16:10–14 The adornments listed here are gifts from a groom to his bride. Figuratively they express the beauty and bounty God gave to Jerusalem under Solomon. **badger skin:** The exact meaning of this Hebrew term is unknown, but it refers to a kind of fine leather. The idea is that God clothed Jerusalem in the finest materials available. During the reigns of David and Solomon, Jerusalem achieved significant status as the capital of a nation rich in wisdom and wealth (1 Kin. 10:23). But this was only because God **bestowed** it.

16:15 trusted in your own beauty: These words indict God's people for forgetting that their fame and fortune were God's gifts and not their own doing (v. 14). They relied on themselves and their gifts instead of on God. They came to believe that their material health and wealth as a nation demonstrated God's approval of their spiritual life, even through they were becoming spiritually corrupt. **played the harlot:** This phrase refers to spiritual prostitution—idolatry, trusting in false gods.

16:16–21 These verses list the specific acts of idolatry engaged in by the spiritually unfaithful in Jerusalem and Judah. Mesopotamian and Canaanite pagan rituals are featured. The people's unfaithfulness to God consisted of: (1) building altars to idols and decorating the **high places** with their **garments** (1 Kin. 11:7, 8); (2) fashioning **male images** (phallic or sexually perverse statues) from **gold** and **silver** that God had provided; (3) giving what belonged to the true God to these false gods; and (4) practicing human sacrifice to appease these gods (2 Kin. 16:1–4).

16:22–24 The Israelites **did not remember** how much God had done for them since rescuing them from a dirty, destitute, and dying condition (vv. 1–14).

16:25, 26 Egypt is called a **fleshly** neighbor because that nation wanted alliances with Israel, who **committed harlotry** by eventually reciprocating (1 Kin. 10:28; 2 Kin. 17:4; 18:21; Hos. 7:11).

16:27–29 Jerusalem's kings had sought political alliances with Assyria (2 Kin. 15:17–20) and Babylon (2 Kin. 20:12–19) instead of relying on their God for security. Probably a part of the treaty-making ceremonies was to worship the other nation's gods. For Israel to do this would be a violation of the First Commandment. In fact, King Ahaz dared to replace the bronze altar of the temple at Jerusalem with a copy of an Assyrian altar (2 Kin. 16:5–18). In this way, foreign alliances led the Israelites away from God.

16:30–34 Jerusalem was denounced as being less like a prostitute and more like **an adulterous wife.** She was deemed worse than the typical prostitute because instead of receiving payment for services rendered, she sought out **strangers** (foreign nations) and **hired** them for the privilege.

16:35, 36 Jerusalem was filthy spiritually because the city had soiled itself by worshiping foreign idols and practicing child sacrifice (vv. 20, 21; Deut. 12:29–32).

16:37–43 As a result of its sin, Jerusalem would be punished. God would use her foreign **lovers** to expose Jerusalem's hypocrisy and bring international shame (**uncover your nakedness**). According to the Law, adultery was punishable by death (Lev. 20:10). The people deserved death because they had committed spiritual adultery and had murdered their own children through child sacrifice. The city would be looted and burned, and its people killed. The tangible material riches gained as a result of God's favor (v. 8) would be lost. All this would culminate in the Babylonian invasion of 586 B.C. led by Nebuchadnezzar.

16:44–47 This allegory describes Jerusalem as the sister of two cities—**Samaria** and **Sodom.** All three were presented as the characteristic offspring of the religiously and morally corrupt cultures in Canaan (v. 3). Thus the proverb **Like mother, like daughter** applied to Jerusalem. The condemnation of the mother—that is, the Hittites—and the sisters—Samaria and Sodom—for **loathing husband and children** is difficult to explain. It probably refers to idolatry—God being the hated husband (see Hos. 2:16)—and child sacrifice. Clearly this passage emphasizes the people's great sinfulness and the certainty of their punishment.

16:48–52 Ezekiel names the sins for which the cities of Sodom and Samaria were renowned. Jerusalem was pronounced even more guilty.

16:53–59 Jerusalem had arrogantly poked fun at Sodom, so Jerusalem would be despised by Syria and Philistia. Hope and humiliation would be hers because when the people returned from captivity, they would return alongside others whom they considered horribly wicked. Although restoration was promised, the people still had to pay for their sins by living in exile. This punishment was consistent with God's promises to repay disobedience with specific curses (see 4:16, 17; 5:8–17). The people had **despised the oath by breaking the covenant** that God had made with Moses; thus they would receive the punishments for disobedience that were written in that covenant (see Ex. 24; Lev. 26; Deut. 28; 29). Blessings or curses were dependent on Israel's obedience or disobedience.

16:60–63 Nevertheless: Despite Jerusalem's disobedience to the Mosaic covenant and the resulting punishment (v. 59), the covenant with Abraham would still be honored: **I will remember.** Fulfillment of the covenant with

Abraham did not depend on the people's faithfulness; God had made the promise and He would keep it (see Gen. 15; 17:7, 8; Lev. 26:40–45; Ps. 145:13; Phil. 1:6). The **everlasting covenant** had been made with Abraham before the Hebrew nation even existed. This covenant would be remembered and re-established with the exiled Judeans. Further, God would provide **atonement** through the New Covenant (Jer. 31:31–40), which pointed ultimately to the Cross of Christ.

17:1, 2 The Hebrew words translated **riddle** and **parable** can be used to refer to allegory. The *parable* primarily refers to a comparison between two things. A *riddle* was sometimes used as political contests of mental competition between kings, in which the loser would submit to the winner and be killed. Some take the following riddle as a contest posed by God to Zedekiah, Judah's king.

17:3–10 In light of vv. 11–21, the **great eagle** is the king of Babylon (v. 12); **Lebanon** symbolizes Canaan, of which Jerusalem (v. 12) is the major city; the **highest branch** is the king of Jerusalem and Judah (v. 12); the **topmost young twig** refers to the nobility of Judah (v. 12); the **land of trade** is Babylon (v. 12); the **seed** is a member of the royal family (v. 13); the **fertile field** is the land where this royal offspring would rule (vv. 13, 14); the other **great eagle** is the king of Egypt (v. 15); and the **vine** is the remnant and ruler left in Judah. This remnant failed to prosper because they made a treaty with the Egyptian pharaoh. As a result, even the remnant was killed and scattered by Babylon's army (vv. 15–21).

17:11–21 Since Ezekiel had preached earlier about Jerusalem's past abominations (ch. 16), the people were likely charging God with unfairness in punishing the present population. Ezekiel points out that present and past sins make God's actions just and fair. In this section, **the LORD** explains His grounds for using Babylon to judge Judah. The historical background of this story is found in 2 Kin. 24; 2 Chr. 36; and Jer. 37; 52.

17:22 I will take: The Hebrew is emphatic: "I Myself will take" In contrast to human kings,

God declared that He personally would pick out, plant, and make prominent a **tender one**—that is, a twig or a sprig. Cedar branches are symbolic of rulers on the Davidic throne (see 17:3, 4, 12, 13), and elsewhere of a line of David's descendants prophesied to produce the Messiah (see 2 Sam. 7:16; Is. 11:1–5; Jer. 22:24–30; 23:1–6; Zech. 6:9–13; Matt. 1:1–17). If not directly messianic in intention, vv. 22–24 at least have strong messianic implications. Thus, with reference to His humanity, we discover a new title for the Savior Jesus. He is the Tender One.

17:23, 24 What was accomplished in the restoration under Zerubbabel was a fulfillment of this promise. But as is often the case in biblical prophecy, the greater fulfillment is still to come in the reign of the Savior King. The establishment of the cedar twig, the Messiah, over Israel will make the nation a fruitful and **majestic cedar** where diverse people will live in unity and harmony.

18:1–3 The Hebrew word (see Eccl. 10:10) rendered **set on edge** is literally "made dull" but can refer to a sour sensation. The main idea of the **proverb** is clear: children are affected by their parents' behavioral choices just as eating sour grapes produces a bitter taste. However, the people were interpreting and applying this proverb incorrectly; therefore, God said they should not use it any longer.

18:4 Apparently the exiles were filled with despair and had a fatalistic approach to such truisms as the proverb quoted in v. 2 (as also in 16:44) and to related Scriptures (see Ex. 20:5; 34:6, 7; Deut. 5:9). Their false belief was that they were being punished for the sins of previous generations. Their sin was that of becoming insensitive and irresponsible, since they thought judgment would come regardless of what they might do. God's reply reminded them that it had always been otherwise: only the individual person **who sins** will **die.**

18:5–9 A righteous man—a father or the first generation—is **lawful.** He does what is morally right according to the Law of Moses. He does not participate in the following sins: (1) idolatrous ceremonial meals, (2) sexual misconduct, (3) mistreatment of the poor, (4) theft, or (5) **usury,** charging interest on debts owed by fellow Hebrews (Deut. 23:20). His reward is life (Ex. 20; Lev. 18:1–5; Deut. 5; 11).

18:10–13 The unrighteous son of the righteous man of vv. 5–9 (the second generation) breaks and rejects the laws and ethics that defined his father's lifestyle. His punishment is death (vv. 13, 18; see Rom. 6:23) and **his blood shall be upon him.** Clearly the point of this passage is personal responsibility for sin.

18:14–18 The grandson of the righteous man of vv. 5–9 (third generation) purposely chooses to live by God's laws, imitating his righteous grandfather and not his sinful **father.** The grandson, like the grandfather, **shall surely live** as a result of his own righteousness; but the father dies because of his disobedience and depravity (see vv. 9, 13, 18).

18:19–32 In this passage, Ezekiel further clarifies his teaching on individual responsibility for sin by answering certain questions that reflect what his audience might be thinking in response to his previous message. **turn ... and live:** Everyone is judged equitably and individually. God never enjoys condemning a person, but is just and righteous in dispensing His judgments.

19:1 The **princes** were Judah's kings. Ezekiel likely turned his attention to these kings because he had just spoken (in ch. 18) of the relationship between fathers (leaders) and children (followers), and of the sins committed in Judah by powerful people.

19:2–10 The **lioness** and the **vine in your bloodline** (v. 10) represented the nation of Israel since each was a "mother" of kings—the **cubs** and the **branches.** The vine and lion images are common symbols for Hebrew royalty and nationality. The first cub **brought ... with chains to the land of Egypt** was Jehoahaz, who was captured and imprisoned by Pharaoh Necho in 609 B.C. (2 Kin. 23:31–34; 2 Chr. 36:1–4). The second cub that was **trapped in their pit** was the destructive Jehoiachin, who gave out false hopes of revival and was taken captive by **the king of Babylon** (Nebuchadnezzar) in 597 B.C. (2 Kin. 25:27–30; 2 Chr. 36:9, 10).

19:11–14 These verses mention the fruitful monarchical period of the past, but the focus was on the present distress and promised judgment. At this time, Judah had already experienced two invasions by Babylon, called the **east wind** (see 15:1–8; 19:5–9). Ezekiel and the other exiles were presently living in that desert land. Neither the current king Zedekiah (the **rod of her branches**) nor any other leaders were fit to rule. Judah's rulers were responsible for the nation's horrible condition (see Jer. 22:10–13). The immediate source of rebellion and the cause of imminent judgment was Zedekiah, who would be deported when Jerusalem was destroyed in 586 B.C. (2 Kin. 24; 25).

20:1 The chronological note suggests a date of July-August 591 B.C. and the start of a new section and series of messages (see 8:1, which was eleven months earlier). The political context of this prophecy was Zedekiah's foolish and sinful alignment with Egypt against Babylon in hopes of deliverance from Nebuchadnezzar's attacks. The social context was that of exiled elders coming to Ezekiel to obtain a divine explanation of current events. They wanted to know if Egypt would save Judah from the Babylonians.

20:2–4 God explains to Ezekiel that the elders of Israel (v. 1) had forfeited any right to inquire of Him because of the **abominations of their fathers.** All people are responsible for their own sins, and this does not mean that these Hebrews were paying for sins their ancestors had committed. Instead, the present generation of Hebrews in exile had clearly shown their failure to learn practical lessons from history, and thus had condemned themselves to repeat many mistakes.

20:5, 6 I chose Israel: Here is the only use of this elective verb in Ezekiel. It signifies Israel's sovereign selection for God's eternal and temporal purposes. **raised My hand:** This image refers to the unconditional vows made by God to Abraham and later renewed with the nation He formed in Egypt from Abraham's descendants (v. 9). That God "raised His hand" reveals His determination to maintain His covenant promise.

20:7 abominations: Elsewhere in Ezekiel this term is translated "detestable things." See vv. 8, 30; 11:18.

20:8 the idols of Egypt ... in the midst of the land of Egypt: Here God spoke of something not explained in the Book of Exodus; that is, the Israelites had engaged in the idolatry of the Egyptians during their sojourn there. Thus, though not mentioned elsewhere, there was the threat of divine retribution against the people before the time of the Exodus.

20:9 acted for My name's sake: God vindicated His grace, power, and trustworthiness before the Egyptians by fulfilling His promises to defeat Egypt and deliver even His disobedient people (His people who were supposed to worship God).

20:10–11 Following their exodus from slavery in Egypt, God began to sanctify the Israelites by revealing to them a code of Law and entering a covenant relationship with them on a Creator-creature basis. **if a man does, he shall live:** This does not teach that eternal salvation can be earned by good works, but that the quality of the believer's physical and spiritual life on earth are related to his or her obedience to the living God.

20:12–19 My Sabbaths: The Sabbath was a day to cease all ordinary work or labor, as clearly emphasized in Ex. 20:8–11; Deut. 5:12–15. This verse explains the purpose of the Sabbath; it was to serve as **a sign** or a potent symbol of God's covenantal relationship with His people Israel.

20:20–26 hallow: This word means "to treat as holy," "to observe as distinct," and "to consecrate." God commands that His **Sabbaths** be continually maintained by His people as sacred—distinct and separate from all ordinary days.

20:27 During the conquest and settlement of Canaan, Israel inherited the Promised Land. Yet again God's people were obstinate and guilty of blasphemous disloyalty because they served false gods (Num. 15:30, 31).

20:28, 29 high hills ... thick trees: These phrases refer to the locations of altars in Canaan for idol worship. Many of the exiles had visited such places in the past, and many in Judah were still doing so.

20:30 defiling ... committing: These words emphasize the continual, ongoing nature of Israel's disobedient disloyalty.

20:31, 32 like the Gentiles: Chosen to be a nation separate from sin and secular ways—a special instrument to reveal God's glory—Israel's consistent tendency was to identify with the neighboring, ungodly nations and to take on their idolatry (see Ex. 19:5, 6; Deut. 17:14; 26:16–19; 31:21; 1 Sam. 8:5; Ps. 135:4).

20:33–36 The judgment of captivity in Babylon had begun in the deportations of 605 and 597 B.C. and would be continued with Jerusalem's fall in 586 B.C. However, God also promised to restore Judah and to judge her enemies with fury (see Deut. 4:34). This refers to the Persian conquest of Babylon in 539 B.C. and to the three returns of the Jews to their land and the rebuilding of their homeland (538–c. 330 B.C.). Yet Israel would again be taken captive and made to wander throughout the nations. **I will bring you out:** Leaving Babylon would be a second Exodus, celebrated prophetically by Isaiah as well (see Is. 40:1).

20:37, 38 pass under the rod: This is the way a shepherd counts and controls his sheep (see Lev. 27:32; Jer. 33:13). A rod sometimes speaks of discipline (Ps. 89:32), but here it is parallel to the idea of **bring you into the bond of the covenant.** God's lordship of His people for personal, purposeful relationship is in view. This future bonding with God will be a time when Israel is cleansed of spiritual idolaters (see v. 39; 16:15–34). At that time, the people will finally **know that** God is **the Lord** (see 16:63; 36:25–38; Jer. 31:31–34; Dan. 12:10).

20:39 The command **Go, serve every one of you his idols** is an ironic command; the rest of the verse indicates that God was giving the stubborn people over to what they had decided.

20:40–45 The future repentant, renewed, and regathered Israel will be characterized by: (1) a return to the land of Israel and an acceptable, sacrificial system of worship (see chs. 40—48); (2) a revived, personal knowledge of its sovereign and faithful Lord; (3) a renunciation of former sins; and (4) a recognition that God's grace governs the nation's history of sin and salvation. **My holy mountain:** Reference is made to the glorious central location for worship in Israel—Mount Zion in Jerusalem (Ps. 2:6; 78:68; Is. 35:10; 60:14).

20:46–49 The **forest land, the South** refers to the land of Judah—the southern kingdom—which had more trees then than now. **from the south to the north:** This figure of speech expresses totality, meaning "everywhere."

21:1–5 both righteous and wicked: This pairing shows that God would allow the consequences of sin to affect everyone in the land.

21:6 breaking heart: The phrase translates words that literally mean "breaking loins," suggesting great emotional upheaval.

21:7 when they say: This means "when they ask" (see 12:9).

21:8–11 The Babylonian army led by Nebuchadnezzar—the **sword**—is pictured as ready and moving swiftly. While vv. 9–17 are written as Hebrew poetry, the lines actually meant to be sung may have been limited to these in vv. 9–11. **My son:** In this context, the words refer to Judah (see "My people" in v. 12). If the people reacted with **mirth,** it would show that they mistakenly believed that such judgment would never come on God's people and must therefore be meant for an enemy nation.

21:12 Cry and wail ... strike your thigh: Ezekiel was told to add verbal groans and a physical gesture to his musical message. In that culture, these actions displayed great grief and sorrow (Jer. 31:19).

21:13 Israel failed a test. The **sword** would strike God's people, specifically the nation's rulers (the meaning of the word **scepter**). These words drew upon the messianic implications of Gen. 49:9, 10 and the promises of the Davidic covenant in 2 Sam. 7. The Jews had misinterpreted these promises to mean that their nation would never fall. Because of their sin, however, the Davidic line of kings would be interrupted. False messianic hopes related to Judah were corrected when Jerusalem was overthrown in 586 B.C. by Nebuchadnezzar (see vv. 25–27).

21:14–18 Ezekiel was commanded to clap (see 6:11). The order **the third time let the sword do double damage** was a numeric device (see Prov. 6:16) used here to emphasize the extent and effectiveness of the sword's (or Babylon's) employment against Judah. **I also will beat My fists** pictures God clapping along with Ezekiel. God would applaud the fact that even evil events can be made to serve His purposes and plans (see Jer. 27:5).

21:19, 20 Ezekiel was instructed to draw a map to depict the path of the coming conquerors. The **king of Babylon** is Nebuchadnezzar; the **same land** is Babylon. **Make a sign:** Ezekiel was to place a signpost at a fork in the road leading to the capital cities of Ammon—**Rabbah**—and Judah—**Jerusalem.**

21:21 Three ancient pagan arts for seeking divine guidance would be used by Nebuchadnezzar to determine which city to attack. **shakes the arrows:** This was a method of casting lots using arrows inscribed with names. They were shaken about in the quiver and then dropped to the ground like throwing dice. **consults the images:** This refers to the teraphim or household idols (see Gen. 31:19; Judg. 18:14; 1 Sam. 19:13; Hos. 3:4). **looks at the liver:** Sheep livers from sacrificed animals were studied. The shades and shapes of various sections of the organ were the basis for a positive or negative prediction.

21:22 That Nebuchadnezzar's answer coincided with God's promises and predictions for Jerusalem did not mean that his **divination** was acceptable. It only demonstrated that God is sovereign while individuals remain responsible for all choices, good or bad (Gen. 45:4–8; 50:20; Job 2:10; Dan. 2:20–23; 4:34–37; Rom. 8:28).

21:23, 24 The Judeans in their pride and false sense of security in the treaties (**sworn oaths**) would conclude that the king received a **false divination** (see vv. 21, 22; 2 Kin. 24:20). However, the verdict had been pronounced: Jerusalem would be **taken.** Nebuchadnezzar would be God's instrument to punish the people's rebellion (see 7:3, 4).

21:25 The **prince of Israel** Zedekiah would come to its **end** by being captured in 586 B.C. (see 7:27; 12:9, 10, 11–14).

21:26, 27 The **turban** (see Ex. 28:4, 37–39) and the **crown** stand for the priesthood and the kingship. Both would be removed from Judah. **overthrown:** This word means "wrecked" or "ruined" and is used three times consecutively in the Hebrew text to underscore the comprehensive and intensive nature of the destruction.

21:28 Ammon was east of Judah between the Jabbok to the north and the Arnon to the south. While Jehoiakim was king (608–598 B.C.; 2 Kin. 24:2), the **Ammonites** joined other nations east of the Jordan River in raiding Judean territory, in return for protection from Nebuchadnezzar. Later, during the reign of Zedekiah (c. 593 B.C.), Ammon, Moab, Edom, and others conspired against Babylon, but with false hopes of help from Egypt (Jer. 27:3–11). **their reproach:** This was the Ammonites' ridicule of Judah and delight over the destruction of Jerusalem, especially the temple (see 25:3, 6; 36:15; Obad. 10—14; Zeph. 2:8). The **sword** bringing judgment was either Nebuchadnezzar's army (see vv. 9, 10, 19, 20; 25:4) or the Ammonites who had been led to believe they would be involved in Judah's defeat (see v. 29).

21:29 Ezekiel pronounced that Ammonite prophecies of victory and security from a fate similar to Judah's were **false visions.** The dead Judeans would be joined by Ammonite corpses.

21:30 I will judge you: This is God's prediction for Ammon and the Ammonites. How it would be done is the subject of vv. 31, 32.

21:31, 32 The **brutal men** are defined as "the men of the East" in 25:4. The fall of Jerusalem meant only that Judah would be judged first. Some Judeans took refuge in Ammon (see Jer. 41:1–3). God remembered Ammon's animosity and foretold its future as a place that **shall not be remembered.** The events of Jer. 41 led to a Babylonian expedition against Ammon in which the capital city Rabbah was sacked and many inhabitants deported (see 25:1–7). Ammon was later invaded by Arabs and its autonomy ceased. Eventually it was absorbed into the Persian Empire.

22:1–5 These verses focus on the sins of Jerusalem, principally bloodshed (social sin) as a result of idolatry (spiritual sin). A problem in the vertical relationship with God inevitably leads to some degree of injustice and injury in horizontal, human affairs. **You have caused your days to draw near:** The city was ripe for judgment. When such hypocrisy is exposed and punishment is executed before the world, God's people become lasting objects of ridicule.

22:6–12 Jerusalem's **princes** had shed the blood of innocent people. These evil leaders had been: (1) taking advantage of parents and the weak (see Ex. 20:12; 22:21–24; 23:9; Lev. 19:3; Deut. 24:17); (2) rejecting God and His covenant, leading to ungodliness and inhumanity (see Ex. 20:8); (3) murdering the innocent by slandering them (see Lev. 19:16); (4) preferring idolatrous religion and its immoral rituals (see 22:1–5; Deut. 12:1–2; 16:21, 22); (5) engaging in sexual immorality with **neighbors,** family, and relatives (see Lev. 18:6–23; 20:10–21); and (6) loving money and using it to get ahead of fellow citizens (see 18:5–9; Ex. 23:8; Deut. 23:19, 20; 24:6, 10–12; Matt. 6:24; 1 Tim. 6:5–10).

22:13–16 God reveals His planned actions against Jerusalem and Judah. The expression **beat My fists** (see 21:14–17) shows great anger. **Defile yourself** refers to the desecration and destruction of Jerusalem by the Babylonians (2 Kin. 24:13; 25:9, 13–21).

22:17–23 These verses are primarily about God's chastisement of His sinful people through the burning of Jerusalem by the Babylonians (2 Kin. 25:9). Yet the verses also point to the fiery ordeals and trials that force all of us into a more perfect relationship with our Lord.

22:24, 25 This verse echoes the promises of Deut. 28:12, 24, where the abundance or absence of rain in the **land** is associated with obedience or disobedience to the Law.

22:26, 27 The **priests** were not examples of separation from worldly ways (see Ex. 19:6; Lev. 11:44; 22:32). Some at least were motivated by monetary gain (see Mic. 3:11).

22:28 plastered them: This probably refers to the prophets themselves. **untempered mortar:** The Hebrew word means "mud-plaster" or "whitewash." These prophets were involved in "whitewashing" the sins of the nation's leaders (see Matt. 23:27; Luke 11:39). If the proper antecedent for **them** is "princes" (v. 27), then the priests were also guilty of approving murder.

22:29 As go the leaders, so go the followers (see 12:18, 19). The **people of the land** were average citizens or commoners.

22:30, 31 sought for: God could not find a spiritual leader to guide the people in godliness. Why not Ezekiel? (See 3:17–21; 33:1–6.) A qualified leader is useless if people refuse to be led.

23:1, 2 The **one mother** of the two **daughters** was the Hebrew nation—Israel. The two daughters are the northern kingdom—Israel, or Samaria—and the southern kingdom—Judah. Though they did not split apart until after the death of Solomon, the allegory speaks from that later time and perspective as it presents a pictorial review of Israel's past.

23:3 It was during the formative years of the Hebrew nation in Egypt (its **youth**) that the Israelites began practicing political and spiritual prostitution by conforming themselves to the ways of the world, worshiping idols, and trusting in an earthly instead of heavenly power (see 16:26; 20:7, 8).

23:4 In Hebrew, the names **Oholah,** meaning "Her Own Tabernacle," and **Oholibah,** meaning "My Tabernacle Is in Her," seem to refer to God's sanctuaries in each land or, in a distinct usage, to the tent shrines for Canaanite idols as opposed to God's true temple (see 2 Sam. 6:17). **Samaria** is the **elder** (literally the "greater") because she first made political and idolatrous alliances with foreign nations and was the first to be punished by foreign captivity.

23:5, 6 played the harlot: This word may be used for any immoral sexual acts. Here it refers to the nation placing its faith in and seeking strength and security from alliances with political powers instead of God (2 Kin. 15:17–20; 17:1–4; Hos. 12:1–2).

23:7–10 Ezekiel reminds his audience of how God already had judged Samaria through Assyrian conquest and captivity in 722 B.C. (2 Kin. 17:5–41). **Uncovered her nakedness** means to be stripped bare and so put to great shame. **Became a byword** means

people began using the name "Samaria" as a synonym for "immoral nation."

23:11–14 Judah **increased her harlotry** by engaging in political and spiritual intercourse with first the Assyrians (vv. 12, 13; see 2 Kin. 16:7–9) and then the **Chaldeans** (a regional term used for the entire Babylonian Empire; see vv. 15, 17, 23). The last two lines tell how Judean envoys to Babylon became enamored of Babylonian rulers and their power through pictures (see Jer. 22:14) on their palace and temple walls.

23:15–18 alienated herself: This is an allusion to Judah's turning in disappointment and disgust from relying on Babylon to relying on Egypt (see 2 Kin. 23:28–24:1). God's alienation from Jerusalem is an allusion to the city's coming defeat by Nebuchadnezzar in 586 B.C.

23:19, 20 Judah renewed its alliance with Egypt (Jer. 37:5–7) which is strikingly symbolized in this verse as a lustful, illicit lover (see v. 3; 16:26).

23:21–27 God's verdict was that He would judge Jerusalem through Babylon, formerly an ally but now an enemy. **Pekod, Shoa, Koa, ... the Assyrians with them:** These were tribal vassals of Babylon that would join the assault on Judah. A **buckler** was a large rectangular shield.

23:28–31 This "lover" was one whom the Judeans came to **hate** as an enemy. God explains that He would use the Babylonians as an instrument of His wrath: (1) to expose the extreme unfaithfulness of Judah and (2) to punish Judah for its idolatry that had resulted from forbidden political alliances (see Ex. 20:1–6; 34:10–17; Deut. 18:9–14).

23:32–34 The **cup** is often symbolic of God's judgment (see Ps. 75:7, 8; Jer. 25:15–29; Matt. 20:22; Rev. 14:10). **break its shards:** The phrase portrays how completely Judah would drink the cup of wrath, breaking what was already broken.

23:35 This verse summarizes why God was going to punish Jerusalem with such vengeance: **you have forgotten Me.** The people had intentionally ignored God, pictured by the parallel phrase **cast Me behind your back.**

23:36–39 adultery ... defiled ... slain: These themes have been developed previously (see

v. 8; 16:20, 21; Ex. 20:3–13, 22–26; 22:20; Lev. 18:21; 19:30; 20:1–5; Deut. 4:15–40).

23:40–42 Sabeans: This Hebrew word may also be read as "drunkards." The nomadic peoples east and south of Israel were considered uncivilized and repugnant by the Hebrews.

23:43–49 Alarmingly, those God would use to judge Samaria and Jerusalem (Assyria and Babylon respectively) are here called **righteous.** Obviously this does not describe their standing before God or their way of life. Instead, it underlines their role as instruments of God's just judgment (see vv. 46, 47; Deut. 22:13–30).

24:1, 2 This is the fourth chronological reference given by Ezekiel (see 1:2, 3; 8:1; 20:1). The date is January 588 B.C., the **very day** that Nebuchadnezzar—**king of Babylon**—began his attack on Jerusalem (see 2 Kin. 25:1–3; Jer. 39:1, 2; 52:1–6). Ezekiel was commanded to **write down the name of the day.** This would be a bitter reminder of God's trustworthiness to do what He promised through the prophets. Nebuchadnezzar's siege was God's judgment on Jerusalem.

24:3–5 The subject of this **parable** is explained in v. 2. The audience was again **the rebellious house** (see 2:3–8; 3:5–7; 11:3–12; 12:2, 22–28). **Flock** was symbolic of God's chosen people (see ch. 34). **Bones** were sometimes used as a fuel for fire.

24:6 Bloody city explains why Jerusalem—the **pot**—must experience the heat of God's wrath (see v. 9; 22:2–12) through the Babylonian siege that had now begun. The remainder of this verse announces the verdict: exile. **no lot has fallen:** God does not play favorites; His judgment would fall equally on all inhabitants of the city, for all of them had sinned.

24:7, 8 These verses elaborate on the city's sin of bloodshed (see also v. 6). The people failed to deal with the sin, so God declares that it would remain exposed to His judgment (see Gen. 4:10; Lev. 17:13; Is. 26:21).

24:9–15 have cleansed you, and you were not cleansed: This probably refers to the deportations of 605 and 597 B.C., whose cleansing effects were incomplete.

24:16, 17 you shall neither mourn nor weep: The picture of Ezekiel's wife dying and Ezekiel not being allowed to grieve illustrated God's pain over the death of His wife—Jerusalem—and His inability to mourn because the nation deserved the punishment. Ezekiel was called by God to "be a sign to the exiles" by demonstrating what they should do (see vv. 21–23) in response to the "death" (destruction) of their desire and delight—their nation and its capital city. A long period of mourning was the normal, ritual response to the death of a loved one in the ancient Middle East (see 1 Sam. 4:12; 2 Sam. 1:12, 17; 3:31, 35; 15:30; 19:4; Is. 58:5; Jer. 16:7; Mic. 1:8, 10).

24:18 did as I was commanded: Ezekiel had been given a revelatory command that was hard for him personally. He faithfully communicated it to the people. His absolute obedience to the harshest of God's commands contrasted with the disobedience of his fellow countrymen.

24:19, 20 tell us: When obedience to God demanded unusual actions, the people's curiosity about the reasons for such behavior was aroused, creating an opportunity for verbal witness about God's revelation.

24:21 the delight of your soul: The meaning "affection" is likely intended here. The entire phrase means something like the "object of your affections." The Judeans had the wrong kind of pride about the temple. Instead of the temple being a place of worship and house of God—**My sanctuary**—the Judeans took pride in the building as a sign of their importance. Therefore, God was going to **profane** it by allowing the Babylonians to capture the city and destroy the temple (see v. 25; 2 Chr. 36:15–21; Lam. 1:10, 11). With no city or temple to boast about, the humbled Israelites could boast only in God's mercy.

24:22–24 The Judeans should respond to the death of the nation as Ezekiel had been told to respond to the death of his wife (vv. 15–18): they would not mourn their loss. The consistent purpose of divine discipline is seen again: **you shall know that I am the Lord GOD** (see 6:8–10; 12:15, 16). The trials would prompt the Israelites to depend on the Lord and know that He is holy.

24:25–27 When the **one who escapes** on the day Jerusalem falls (586 B.C.) arrives to give Ezekiel the news (perhaps about three months later), Ezekiel would be relieved of his inability to speak anything except judgment, and would be allowed to preach hope (see vv. 1, 2, 24; 3:25–27; 33:21—39:29; 2 Kin. 25:8, 9).

25:1, 2 On **Ammonites,** see 21:20, 28. Ammon corresponds roughly to the present-day country of Jordan with its capital Amman.

25:3 For further background on the Ammonites and Ammon, see 6:11; 21:15; 26:2; 36:2; Neh. 4:7–9; Ps. 35:19–21; Jer. 49:1–6; Amos 1:13–15; Zeph. 2:8–11.

25:4, 5 Men of the East is another title for the Babylonians (see 21:31). Ancient historical records mention Ammon's subjugation by Nebuchadnezzar five years after the fall of Jerusalem. Arab invaders came to dominate the territory, and Persian control began about 530 B.C.

25:6, 7 The Ammonites rejoiced at the destruction of Jerusalem and its temple; therefore, they would also be punished. The Ammonites were eventually to perish as a people.

25:8 Moab was south of Ammon, east of the Dead Sea and between the Arnon and Zered rivers. The Moabites descended from the incestuous relationship between Lot and his first daughter (Gen. 19:30–38). **Seir** (Edom) is mentioned because it was guilty of accusing Israel of being **like all the nations** (see 35:15; 36:5; Gen. 32:3; 36:8, 9). This accusation reflects Moab and Edom's malicious misinterpretation of Judah's misfortune as a proof that God was powerless (see Gen. 12:1–3; Ex. 19:5, 6; Num. 22:12; Deut. 7:6–8; Jer. 48:27; Zeph. 2:8, 9).

25:9–11 the territory: This expression, literally meaning "shoulder" or "side," describes the northwest corner of Moab, the area most difficult to conquer because of its topography (a mountain plateau high above the Jordan valley). Apparently the attack would culminate in the ruin of Moab's **glory,** its frontier cities.

25:12 Edom was located south of Moab, from the Zered River south to the Gulf of Aqaba. The Edomites descended from Esau. The

transgressions most characteristic of Edom were its perpetual animosity and repeated, vindictive acts of violence against Israel. The Hebrew words rendered **greatly offended** ("be guilty") may indicate continuous or repeated rather than intensive behavior.

25:13 The precise locations of **Teman** and **Dedan** are not known, but they probably are mentioned to convey the idea of Edom from one end to the other (see Joel 3:19).

25:14 Since Edom had taken their revenge on the Judeans and showed them hostility when they needed help, God would show Edom His **vengeance.**

25:15 The **Philistines** lived in southwest Palestine along the Mediterranean coast. They had a long history of constant competition for control of Judah (see Judg. 13–16; 1 Sam. 4; 13; 31; 2 Sam. 5:17–21). The Hebrew root meaning "to take revenge" is found three times in this verse, indicating the great vengeance of which Philistia was guilty.

25:16, 17 Cherethites: This term (probably meaning "Cretans") was used here as a substitute term for some or all of the Philistines, who migrated from Caphtor (understood to be Crete). Their more remote ancestors were Aegeans.

26:1 The date places the prophetic pronouncements against Tyre, the Tyrian monarch, and Sidon somewhere in March or April of 587–586 B.C. (**the eleventh year**). This was at or just after the fall of Jerusalem (see v. 2).

26:2 Tyre, in competition with Sidon (see 1 Kin. 16:31; Is. 23:2, 12), was a major seaport and leading city in Phoenicia (present-day Lebanon). **has said:** The past tense could refer to an event that had not yet taken place, using a Hebrew idiom which describes a future event as so certain that it can be expressed as having already been accomplished (see Is. 9:6, 7; 52:13—53:12). **I shall be filled** was evidence of Tyre's greed and materialism, desiring any wealth of Jerusalem that could be found in its ruins after the Babylonian conquest.

26:3–5 The armies (**many nations;** see vv. 4, 7–14) that would attack Tyre are appropriately compared to waves of the sea, because the city of Tyre was an island fortress.

26:6–14 The fulfillment of this prophecy of Tyre's fate began with the long siege of the city by the Babylonian army under **Nebuchadnezzar** (c. 580–570 B.C.). Nebuchadnezzar ruled the Neo-Babylonian (Chaldean) Empire from 605–562 B.C. The second phase came with the Persian conquest in about 525 B.C., followed by the final and famous siege of 332 B.C. by the Greeks under Alexander, which completed the predictions of this passage (especially vv. 5, 14; see 47:10). Alexander literally fulfilled the words **break down your walls** (see v. 5) when his army built a causeway between the shore and the city on its island. He tore down defensive walls to build the causeway.

26:15, 16 The **princes of the sea** (see 27:35) were the rulers of various settlements in Phoenicia that were connected with Tyre. They would surrender and submit to Babylonian rule when they saw what happened to Tyre: **be astonished at you.** They would mourn in song (see vv. 17, 18) after they took off their **robes** and **embroidered garments** (see Jon. 3:6).

26:17–19 The **deep** is the same Hebrew word as in Gen. 1:2. Imagery of the chaotic waters of creation picture the coming catastrophe.

26:20, 21 The **Pit** is probably a synonym for hell (see Is. 14:15; 38:18). **never be inhabited:** Ancient Tyre would cease to exist.

27:1–3 perfect: The proud citizens of Tyre saw themselves as the finest example of a merchant "ship" in the ancient world.

27:4, 5 Senir is an Amorite term used for Mount Hermon or another peak in its range. **Fir** is rendered elsewhere "pine," "cypress," or "juniper."

27:6 Bashan (see 39:18) was the broad and fertile plateau east of the Sea of Galilee and the upper Jordan River.

27:7 Elishah has coasts and is associated here with Egypt; therefore it may be Italy or Sicily.

27:8 Sidon was a Phoenician seaport about 30 miles north of Tyre. The two cities were rivals, but Tyre tended to dominate Sidon (see 28:21, 22; Gen. 10:15, 19; Judg. 18:28; Is. 23:2; Matt. 11:21, 22). Like Tyre, the city of **Arvad** was on an island off the coast of Phoenicia. It was Phoenicia's northernmost town (see 28:11; Gen. 10:18; 1 Chr. 1:16).

27:9 Gebal was another successful Phoenician port, between Sidon and Arvad (see Josh. 13:5; 1 Kin. 5:18). It was called Byblos by the Greeks and Romans, and Gubla by the Assyrians and Babylonians.

27:10, 11 Lydia and **Libya** are literally Lud and Put, usually understood to be in western Asia Minor (Lud) and Africa (Put).

27:12 Tarshish was possibly in Spain.

27:13 Javan is Greece (see Gen. 10:4). **Tubal** and **Meshech** are thought to have been in eastern Asia Minor (modern Turkey).

27:14 On **the house of Togarmah,** see Gen. 10:3. This phrase may refer to the people of Armenia in eastern Asia Minor (see 38:6).

27:15 Dedan may perhaps be understood as "Redan" (Rhodes), because the written forms of the Hebrew letters for *d* and *r* are easily confused. Rhodes was a major trading center in the southern Aegean Sea.

27:16 The Hebrew term for **emeralds** may also be translated "turquoise."

27:17 Minnith was in Ammon (see 21:28) and presumably was famous for its fine wheat. **Millet** translates a Hebrew word that apparently stands for some type of food, but exactly what kind is not known today. **Balm** was an aromatic resin or other gummy substance that may have had medicinal value (see Jer. 8:22).

27:18 Damascus was and is the capital of Syria (v. 16). **Helbon** is north of Damascus, a region still recognized for its wine production.

27:19, 20 Cassia (see Ex. 30:24; Ps. 45:8; Song 4:14) was either a type of cinnamon tree or a plant from which perfume and incense were made. **Cane** refers to an oil-producing reed found in swamps.

27:21 Kedar was a nomadic tribe in Arabia.

27:22 Sheba and **Raamah** were located near Arabia (see Gen. 10:6, 7).

27:23, 24 Ancient **Haran** was a merchant city along the important Euphrates trade route (see Gen. 11:27–32), in what is now eastern Turkey. **Canneh** (see Is. 10:9),

Eden, and Chilmad were probably in Mesopotamia, most likely south of Haran (see 2 Kin. 19:12). The verse seems concerned with cities, so **Assyria** is better translated "Asshur," a city south of Nineveh; but the term could stand for the citizens of Assyria.

27:25, 26 The **east wind** was often powerful and potentially destructive (see Gen. 41:6; Job 27:21; Ps. 48:7; Is. 27:8). Thus it symbolizes the destruction the Babylonian army would bring on Tyre.

27:27, 28 The **common-land** was the pastureland controlled by a city.

27:29–36 The final verses of the chapter present a remorseful and revengeful lament to be chanted, perhaps over and over, by Tyre's trade partners. Tyre's nearest neighbors (see 26:16–18) would be troubled by Tyre's defeat, but soon they would turn against Tyre themselves in the vain hope of escaping a similar fate at the hands of the Babylonians.

28:1–3 you are wiser than Daniel: The Hebrew name Daniel is spelled here the same way as in 14:14: *Dan-El.* It might refer to a different person otherwise unknown in Israel's ancient history.

28:4–7 The **strangers** are the Babylonians (see 7:17–19; 23:23; 30:11; 31:12; 32:12).

28:8, 9 The phrase **midst of the seas** parallels the word *Pit* and reinforces its meaning, for it too signifies the place and fact of death.

28:10 the death of the uncircumcised: This term denotes a disgraceful death (see 31:18; 32:19).

28:11, 12 Seal of perfection is more literally "the one sealing a plan" (the same Hebrew word for "plan" or "pattern" appears once more at 43:10). In effect, the king affixed the official seal of his signet ring to the plans that made Tyre one of the leading centers of commerce in that day. **wisdom ... beauty:** These descriptions mark out the king of Tyre as an exceptional ruler, displaying the ideals of kingship in the ancient Middle East.

28:13 in Eden, the garden of God: This is possibly an exaggerated comparison: this king invaded a place like Eden in its beauty. **created:** The Hebrew verb for *created* is the same as the one used in Gen. 1:1. The word emphasizes God's active work in history.

28:14 The holy mountain of God could be "the holy mountain of gods." According to Canaanite beliefs, the "seat of the gods" was in the "mountains," or the "mountains of the north" (see Ps. 48:2). The focus here seems to be on the king of Tyre's attempt to enter into the council of the gods.

28:15 The term **perfect** does not mean sinless, but complete or flawless. The king of Tyre had been in complete control and was unchallenged until he was filled with prideful **iniquity.**

28:16–19 The king's pride led to materialism, violence, and sinfulness in business and religion. **abundance of your trading:** The expression is most easily and appropriately applied to the human king who was the driving force behind the development of Tyre's commercial empire. The true God—the pronoun **I**—dethroned the king, derailed his unholy ambitions, and destroyed the source of his pride in order to make his example a deterrent to others. The king's commercial empire collapsed and his machinations to resemble a god were crushed.

28:20–23 Sidon was Tyre's sister city, but its lesser importance may explain the brevity of treatment here (see 27:8). As commercial "sisters," the cities had similar characters and concerns, so they shared similar crimes.

28:24 God would free Israel. The **brier** and **thorn** refer to the nations around Israel who had been enemies and evil influences. When the judgments were executed fully, these nations would no longer be able to harass and oppress Israel.

28:25, 26 God promised that Israel will someday be gathered from its dispersion among the nations to return and **dwell in their own land,** the land that God had given to **Jacob.** The end of the foreign nations' ability to attack Israel will lead to a time of peace, prosperity, and protection.

29:1 tenth year ... tenth month: This is December 588 or January 587 B.C. This introduction of another date by Ezekiel (his sixth) is a chronological break, but not a thematic break, with 26:1—28:26 (see 1:2; 8:1; 20:1; 24:1; 26:1).

29:2 The **Pharaoh** was Hophra (c. 589–570 B.C.; see Jer. 44:30). The prophecy against him was also a prophecy against all Egypt (see 30:22; 32:2), like the previous prophecy against Tyre and its king (see 28:1–19).

29:3 O great monster: The Pharaoh is pictured here as a crocodile. **My river** refers to the Nile. Pharaoh's arrogant pride is described by his words about the Nile River, **I have made it for myself** (compare with the words of the king of Tyre, 28:2). In the Egyptian religion the crocodile god Sebek was a protector (see 32:2).

29:4, 5 Whereas v. 3 explains why Pharaoh would be punished, these verses explain how the punishment would be accomplished. The imagery pictures a crocodile being caught, carried out of the water onto land, and left as carrion. The **fish** represent the Egyptians, who would be judged along with Pharaoh (v. 2). Pharaoh's destiny to be **food** may have been an intentional insult to the rulers famous for their burials and pyramids.

29:6, 7 God's purpose for judging Egypt was to encourage the nations and individuals to come to know Him. **Staff of reed** refers to the people of Egypt. This alludes to Egypt's weakness as an ally and the worthlessness of that country's protection (see Is. 36:6). Israel was foolish to rely on Egypt for protection. They should have turned to God for their security and strength.

29:8 sword: Here is another reference to the Babylonian army under Nebuchadnezzar, the predicted human instrument of God's coming wrath (see 21:1–7, 9–11, 19, 20; 26:7–14).

29:9 The nation was indicted as a result of what **he**—that is, Pharaoh—boasted. Often national monuments were inscribed in ancient times with the exaggerated and arrogant boasts of kings.

29:10 Migdol to Syene refers to places most likely near the northern and southern boundaries of ancient Egypt, indicating the totality of the land (see Judg. 20:1). The desolation would extend to the land south of Egypt—ancient Nubia which is modern Sudan.

29:11, 12 The Egyptians would experience a scattering to other lands for **forty years** (see 4:4–8). A Babylonian chronicle suggests that Egypt was conquered around 568 B.C.

Forty years after this date, the Persians instituted a policy of resettlement for many of the peoples who had been dispersed by Babylon.

29:13–15 The **land of Pathros** is southern Egypt. This kingdom would thereafter be **lowly** and **the lowliest,** never again to dominate other nations.

29:16, 17 came to pass: Ezekiel received this oracle from God (vv. 17–21) and apparently the following message also (30:1–19) in March-April 571 B.C., the latest date in the book (see v. 1).

29:18 labor strenuously: This recalls the difficult siege of Tyre. Heads were **made bald** and shoulders **rubbed raw** in the protracted siege, which took thirteen or more years. **yet neither:** The fact was that neither Nebuchadnezzar **nor his army received** much of a reward for their efforts.

29:19, 20 God affirms that He is sovereign over the coming fall of Egypt to Babylon to make up for the **wages** they had not received from their conquest of Tyre. God specifically named Nebuchadnezzar as his instrument (see Jer. 43:8–13).

29:21 In that day: This refers to the day when Egypt would fall to Babylon, and a prophecy about the Messiah should not be read into this text. **Cause the horn ... of Israel to spring forth** means that the nation would renew its strength. Renewal and encouragement would come to God's people in exile when they heard about Egypt's downfall orchestrated by the hand of God, who is holy and sovereign.

30:1–3 The phrase **the day of the LORD** refers to the period of divine wrath on the nation of Egypt. This term suggests God's personal involvement in His judgmental work. God would use Babylon under Nebuchadnezzar to punish Egypt and her allies (see Gen. 12:3; Jer. 25; 46). **the time of the Gentiles:** That is, the time of God's wrath on the nations.

30:4, 5 Ethiopia is the Hebrew Cush, and refers to the area south of Egypt toward modern Ethiopia. **Libya** and **Lydia** were in Africa and Asia Minor. **Mingled people** may be read as "all of Arabia." **Chub** is an obscure term that was understood as the "Libyans" by the Septuagint translators of the Hebrew Old Testament. The **allied** lands were lands to the south, east, and west of Egypt that would also fall to the Babylonian army.

30:6, 7 Migdol to Syene means the whole land of Egypt.

30:8 Fire is often symbolic of judgment.

30:9 This **day of Egypt**—the day that Egypt and her allies would be conquered—was part of a larger period of God's judgment on the nations outside Israel by means of Babylon; in fact, Ezekiel describes the Babylonians as **messengers** sent from God Himself. No one could prevent the coming day of judgment, for the Almighty had ordained it.

30:10–12 These verses add extra details to the more general predictions about Egypt's doom in the preceding verses (vv. 3–9). **Most terrible of the nations** was applied to the Babylonians because their cruelty was legendary (see 2 Kin. 25:7; 2 Chr. 33:11; 36:17; Jer. 39:4–10).

30:13–19 This fourth and final message adds more detail to the description of the coming destruction of Egypt. Emphasis seems to be placed on the fall of major cities. **Noph** was ancient Memphis, a significant city in Egypt. It was capital of the Old Kingdom in the third century B.C. **Zoan,** the classical Tanis, was a city in the northeastern delta. **No** was ancient Thebes, the capital of Upper or southern Egypt. Thebes was destroyed by the Assyrians in 661 B.C. **Sin** was ancient Pelusium, a fortress town on the northeastern border where the ruling Egyptian dynasty of Ezekiel's day had a residence. **Aven** (or Heliopolis, "the City of the Sun") was ancient On, a center for worship of the sun-god Re. Aven was north of Memphis at the southern tip of the delta. **Pi Beseth,** or Bubastis in Greek form, was once the capital of Lower Egypt (the northern or Nile Delta area). **Tehaphnehes** was also a fortress town on the northeastern border, the place where the Babylonian army would enter Egypt to bring this dark **day.**

30:20 first month: March-April 587 B.C. (see 29:1, 18–20). Ezekiel returns to a chronological sequence for the prophecies.

30:21 I have broken the arm of Pharaoh: The prophecy refers to Pharaoh Hophra's unsuccessful attempt to relieve the siege of Jerusalem just a few months earlier (see 29:2, 6, 7). God used Nebuchadnezzar to defeat the Egyptian army.

30:22–26 I will scatter: These verses predict the continued weakness of Hophra against Nebuchadnezzar and the coming catastrophe for all Egypt when its cities would be defeated and the people deported (beginning c. 568 B.C.).

31:1, 2 third month: May-June, 587 B.C. See 1:2; 8:1; 20:1; 24:1, 2; 26:1; 29:1, 17; 30:20.

31:3 Egypt was compared to Assyria in greatness and presumably in its great pride over its achievements. Ezekiel uses another allegory (see 15:1–8; 17:1–10): **Assyria** as **a cedar in Lebanon.** This image pictures the nations as trees in a forest in Lebanon (a country prized for its cedar trees; see vv. 15–18; 1 Kin. 5:7–10; 7:2, 3; Ps. 29:5). Assyria at one time was the highest tree, but it had been cut down. Its capital city Nineveh fell in 612 B.C., signaling the end of Assyrian domination and the beginning of neo-Babylonian control of the ancient Middle East.

31:4 The **waters** were the Tigris and Euphrates rivers. These mighty rivers brought agricultural fertility and fostered the development of great cities along trade routes (see vv. 8, 9; 15–18; Gen. 2:10–14).

31:5–9 The unparalleled greatness of Assyria is portrayed with vivid poetic images. There is both comparison and contrast with Egypt. Before turning to the mostly narrative explanation in vv. 10–18, the prophet indicates that although Egypt was great, it was not the greatest nation. If Assyria had fallen to Babylon, no hope would remain for Egypt (see 31:18).

31:10–14 Because Assyria gloated over her greatness, God sentenced this cruel nation to harsh treatment and subjection under Babylon. **I will deliver:** The meaning is that Babylon, the **terrible** nation, had **cut** Assyria down. The picturesque conclusion to this second message of ch. 31 indicates that all the other nations (**birds, beasts,** and **trees**) that observed Assyria's **ruin** would share its destiny of **death, depths,** and the **Pit,** and would never attain its heights of power.

31:15–17 Hell renders the Hebrew word sometimes transliterated as Sheol, which often speaks of the grave or death (see Gen. 37:35; Ps. 6:5; Jon. 2:2). God had dried up or devastated Assyria, and all the nations were caused to **mourn for it** and **shake** because of its death and burial, as it was cast into **hell, the Pit,** and **the depths of the earth.** Those nations, **the trees of Eden,** who were guilty of a similar, sinful pride in their achievements would receive the same punishment.

31:18 If Assyria, the greatest nation, had fallen to the Babylonians, surely a nation less great would also fall. This pointed to Egypt—**Pharaoh and all his multitude** (see vv. 2, 3, 5–9).

32:1 twelfth month: February-March 585 B.C. (see 31:1), after the fall of Jerusalem in 586 B.C. (see 2 Kin. 25:8), but about 20 years before the Babylonian invasion of Egypt (see 29:19–20). However, the record of the fall of Jerusalem is given in 33:21. This section (32:1—33:20) is placed before 33:21, although it reports events that follow the fall of Jerusalem. Ezekiel's arrangement is thematic. He can first record his lament, and then explain the events that inspired it. Even though the Egyptians arrogantly thought that they, unlike Judah, would not fall to Babylon's forces, they would eventually experience the same fate as the citizens of Jerusalem.

32:2 The words **lion** and **monster** depict Egypt as proud and powerful.

32:3–10 These poetic lines picture Egypt and its ruler, Hophra, as a crocodile who will experience the judgment ordained by God. Egypt will be caught, killed, and consigned to **darkness**—a recognizable element of the day of the Lord (see 30:1–5; Amos 5:18–20; Acts 2:20).

32:11–15 This section interrupts the flow of vv. 3–10. The **king of Babylon** was Nebuchadnezzar. **the most terrible of the nations:** That is, the Neo-Babylonian Empire (see 30:10–12). **rivers run like oil:** This phrase, not used elsewhere, pictures the time following massive killing when the Nile and its tributaries would experience a "deadly" calm. The **waters** will be **clear** because there will be no human or animal life.

32:16 Such a scene of judgment will produce mourning and great grief; but God is to be seen as just and doing what was necessary to stop the people's arrogance.

32:17 This is 15 days later than v. 1, still in 585 B.C.

32:18–21 Depths of the earth, the Pit, and **hell** refer to the grave or death, not the place of eternal punishment for God's enemies.

32:22, 23 Assyria was the master of the ancient Middle Eastern world until the rise of the neo-Babylonians around 612 B.C., early in Jeremiah's career and about 20 years before Ezekiel's first vision.

32:24, 25 Elam was east and southeast of Assyria, in what is now Iran. The people of Elam were descended from one of the sons of Shem (Gen. 10:22; 1 Chr. 1:17).

32:26, 27 Meshech and Tubal: These peoples were located in ancient Anatolia or Asia Minor, present-day Turkey. These names are mentioned as sons of Japheth (Gen. 10:2; 1 Chr. 1:5).

32:28, 29 Ezekiel switches suddenly to the second person singular—**you**—as a wake-up call or reminder to Pharaoh, the representative of Egypt. **Yes** is an emphatic use of the conjunction otherwise translated as "and."

32:30 The **princes of the north** are lands north of Israel such as Tyre and Sidon in Phoenicia. The **Sidonians** were from Sidon, a seaport on the coast about 30 miles north of Tyre (see 27:8).

32:31, 32 Pharaoh: Now the message (vv. 17–32) comes full circle. The point is that Egypt and Pharaoh will die like the other nations at the hand of the living God, who judges every nation with justice.

33:1, 2 The **children of your people** refers to fellow Israelites in exile with Ezekiel, now including the people of Judah deported to Babylon after Nebuchadnezzar's third invasion.

33:3–9 Ezekiel's duty as a **watchman** is defined.

33:10 pine away: This phrase means to rot, waste, or dwindle.

33:11–20 In punishing Israel God was being faithful to the covenant stipulations. This covenant had been approved by the Israelites. They had agreed to its commands and accepted the consequences of breaking them, corporately and individually (see 5:8–17; 12:15, 16; 16:60, 61; 18:19–32; 20:5; Ex. 19:1–9; Deut. 27). God presents His rationale in these verses for deciding who would be rewarded with life and who would suffer death: He would save those who repent and turn to Him, but would condemn those who trust in themselves and do evil. After presenting His rationale, God declares that His judgment is just and fair.

33:21, 22 In January 585 B.C., Ezekiel received the news that Jerusalem had been taken. The city had been under siege by Nebuchadnezzar and the Babylonians for two and one-half years (2 Kin. 25:1–10). These two verses introduce six oracles (33:23—39:29). Ezekiel received a message from the LORD and reported it to the exiles in Babylon.

33:23 Ezekiel's introductory formula—identical or similar to this verse—marks the beginning of the messages received from the LORD in this section of the book (33:21—39:29).

33:24 they who inhabit those ruins: This refers to the people who had remained in Jerusalem. They thought they were the remnant—the faithful ones. But they experienced the final siege of the city by King Nebuchadnezzar, for reasons God will give in the following verses.

33:25–29 Ezekiel confronted his people with specific examples of their past and present refusal to obey God's revealed will for their lives (see 18:6, 10; 22:11; Ex. 20:4, 5, 13–14; Lev. 7:26, 27; 17:10–14; 19:26; Deut. 12:16, 23). Was it not then reasonable that God would punish the present generation by removing them from the land, at least temporarily?

33:30–33 hear ... do not do: See James 1:21–25 for another condemnation of those who hear God's word but do not put it into practice.

34:1–6 The **shepherds of Israel** is a metaphor for Israel's political rulers, but it could include spiritual leaders also (even kings were supposed to be spiritual examples). The shepherds were accused of forsaking

IN DEPTH   Shepherds

Throughout the Bible, the image of the shepherd is important. From David, the shepherd boy who became the first king of Israel, to Jesus Christ, who said of Himself, "I am the good shepherd" (John 10:11), the shepherd represents one who loves and cares for his flock just as a leader or ruler cares for those under his charge.

Some characteristics of a good shepherd include feeding the flock, tending the weak and sick, searching for the lost, guiding with love, gathering and protecting the sheep, and giving one's best to them. On the other hand, a bad shepherd is more concerned about feeding himself, worrying about his own health, guiding with a heavy hand, abandoning or scattering his flock, and keeping the best for himself.

It's easy to see in these comparisons why the Scriptures often exhort leaders to be shepherds to their people. A good leader is concerned that the people's physical needs are being met and that care is provided for the sick and injured. A true leader looks for those who have fallen away. He leads like a shepherd by providing direction and correction, not with a fist but with a loving hand. A good leader protects those under his care and does not leave them to the wolves—to those who lead them astray. And finally, a good leader gives himself to those under his charge. He cares about them and their well-being.

Because Jesus called Himself the Good Shepherd, it's clear that He is the One about whom Ezekiel prophesied. He is the One who searches after His followers (34:11), saves them (34:12), guides them (34:13), and supplies their needs (34:14; John 10). Jesus' self-sacrificing life provides the perfect blueprint for making a good shepherd and leader.

the key feature of godly leadership: selfless, sacrificial service (see Is. 52:13–53:12; Matt. 23:11; Mark 10:45; Luke 22:24–30; Acts 20:17–38; Rom. 12:1–5; Phil. 2:1–11; 1 Tim. 3:1–7; 1 Pet. 2:18–25; 5:1–4). The results of self-serving leadership for Israel are seen in vv. 5, 6. **there was no shepherd:** This means that having leaders who seek to be served, rather than to serve, is tantamount to having no leader at all; therefore, the people of Israel were like sheep without a shepherd (Matt. 9:36).

34:7–10 did not feed My flock: The crimes of Israel's leaders come under review before their punishment is pronounced.

34:11–16 Compare the Lord's persistent shepherding and guiding of His people with the faithlessness of Israel's leaders in v. 6 (see also vv. 25–31; Jer. 23:1–6; John 10:1–30). The **cloudy and dark day** was the day Jerusalem fell (see 30:1–5; Zeph. 1:15). It may also speak of the future day of deliverance when God will **seek out** His **sheep** (see 36:16–36). Israel, though guilty and misguided, would eventually be rescued by the divine Good Shepherd and restored to the Promised Land (see chs. 33–39).

34:17–19 The **rams and goats** were the leaders of Israel who had failed to lead properly. They had used their positions of power to their own advantage and to the disadvantage of the people.

34:20–24 The change from the pronoun **I** to **he** in this verse indicates that God would continue operating as the Chief Shepherd through this chosen future ruler from the Davidic line. He is the Messiah—God's only Son and His **servant.**

34:25–31 The exiles were encouraged through this promise of a **covenant of peace** (see 37:26–28; 38:11–13; 39:25–29; Is. 54:10), characterized by these promises: (1) security from foreign aggressor nations, the **wild beasts;** (2) **showers of blessing,** meaning productivity and prosperity; and (3) the certainty that **the LORD** is Israel's God and desires reunion with His people and a lasting relationship built on a new covenant (Jer. 31:31–34; Heb. 8:6).

35:1, 2 Mount Seir is Edom (see v. 15; 25:8; Gen. 36:30; 2 Chr. 20:10).

35:3, 4 God reveals the nature and the purpose of His judgment on Edom (**Seir,** see v. 2). These verses are poetry and perhaps were used as a song.

35:5 at the time of their calamity: This refers to how Edom took advantage of the people of Judah during and after the Babylonian invasion (see Obad. 11—14).

35:6–9 Having stated why Edom deserved judgment, Ezekiel explained how the nation would be punished. The punishment would include widespread death and unrelieved destruction (see Is. 34:6–8; 63:1–6; Jer. 49:7–13; Obad. 18).

35:10–15 A second reason for God's revenge on Edom is given, in addition to that in v. 5—Edom expected to take over Judah and Israel after their destruction by the Babylonians. **These two nations** refers to Israel and Judah (see 37:15–28).

36:1–7 The land of Israel itself was addressed—**the mountains**—because the nations desired to own it and, in seeking possession, destroyed it physically and defamed it verbally. Israel was termed **the ancient heights** because of the hill country central to its geography. **Edom:** This nation was singled out because of its long history of animosity toward Israel (see 35:5). The **rest of the nations** were the others who in some way had mistreated Israel and thus received a sentence of judgment (see chs. 25—32).

36:8, 9 they are about to come: This was spoken to the land, picturing it as eagerly awaiting the quick return of its rightful and most respectful owners. The first return from exile would come under the Persian king Cyrus, about 50 years later (538 B.C.).

36:10, 11 This restoration would involve **all the house of Israel.**

36:12–14 My people Israel: Despite all their sinfulness, the nation was still referred to as the people of God. They would finally take possession of their land, symbolized by the mountains and the central hills of Palestine.

36:15, 16 The mountains addressed as **you** would no longer **cause** the **nation to stumble,** for God would make the nation secure from foreign armies. God Himself would reestablish the nation and place His prince on its throne (see 34:24).

36:17 like the uncleanness of a woman: The uncleanness of the blood of menstruation (not the woman herself) was compared to the past behavior of Israel in Canaan (see 18:6; 22:10; Lev. 12:2–5; 15:19–30).

36:18 Israel had defiled God's territorial gift in two main ways: (1) The nation had **shed** innocent people's **blood**. (2) The nation had worshiped **idols** by mixing the true worship of the Lord God with involvement in the idolatrous and immoral practices of pagan religions.

36:19 God **judged them according to their ways.** Israel had been hypocritical and unholy; they had not separated themselves or made themselves distinct from the pagan world around them (see v. 18). God had given His people the Promised Land as a place where they could show the world the difference it makes to follow the true God (see Deut. 7:1–11). They failed to follow God, so He forced them out of the land.

36:20, 21 The most tragic outcome of Israel's sin (see vv. 18, 19) was that the nation **profaned** God's **holy name.** Defeat and dispersion, especially in the ancient world, were negative reflections on the character (or the *name,* see 20:9) of a nation's god. God's reputation as wholly set apart from other so-called gods in power and purpose was compromised by Israel's refusal to trust in His ways. To rescue His holy reputation and His rebellious people, God remained faithful to His promises in the Mosaic covenant.

36:22–24 The preview of the return to the **land** in the Mosaic covenant is related to the promise of perpetual possession of the land of Canaan in the Abrahamic covenant (Gen. 12:1–3; 13:14–18; 15:12–21; Hos. 3:4).

36:25 Sprinkle clean water on you symbolizes cleansing from sin (see v. 17; 11:18; 37:23; Jer. 33:8). This is God's forgiveness based on a blood atonement (see Ex. 12:22; Lev. 14:4–7, 51; Num. 19:14–22; Ps. 51:7; Zech. 13:1; 1 Cor. 6:11; Heb. 10:22.).

36:26, 27 The ritual of purification from sin would be empty and meaningless apart from true repentance and the regenerating and empowering work of the Holy **Spirit** on the inner spirit of individuals. God would not only restore the people physically to the land, but would restore them spiritually, by giving them a **new heart** and **new spirit** to help them follow Him and do His will.

36:28–30 you shall be My people: See vv. 1–15; 34:29. The purpose of the Mosaic covenant would finally be realized (see Deut. 26:16–19; 29:13; 30:8). The Israelites would become a people dedicated to God's ways.

36:31, 32 These verses restate the reasons for the planned restoration and renewal of God's people. The restoration from the Exile would recover God's glorious reputation among the nations and erase the guilt of the Israelite's sin. This is all a product of God's favor on the Israelites—even though they had done nothing to merit such mercy.

36:33–35 The garden of Eden is mentioned here to suggest beauty, fertility, and productivity so great that people would be reminded of the "garden eastward in Eden" (Gen. 2:8; contrast 28:13).

36:36–38 Like a flock ... flocks of men: Animals offered for sacrifice had to be free from any observable impurity or disfigurement. The returned people of God will be living sacrifices (Rom. 12:1, 2), pure and unblemished. **I am the LORD:** This is the constant refrain of Ezekiel; God would make Himself known as the one true God in His judgment and restoration of His people.

37:1, 2 The wording recalls the past visionary experiences of Ezekiel (see 1:1, 3; 2:2; 3:12, 14; 8:1, 3, 7) although the word *vision* is not used in these verses. **bones:** Not only do the bones speak of death, indeed of many deaths, but for bones to be left in the open was an indignity and indecency according to Jewish custom. To leave bodies unburied until the bones were exposed was unthinkable.

37:3 You know: The prophet placed his faith in the living God. Ordinarily, one would say "no" to the question God posed. But Ezekiel did not limit God; he knew the Almighty could make bones live.

37:4 Prophesy to these bones: Ezekiel's prophecies had often been directed to people as deaf as these old, dry bones.

37:5 The word translated **breath** is translated in other places as *wind* or *Spirit.* The breath sent by God into the lifeless bodies symbolizes the Holy Spirit (see v. 14), who brings renewal, regeneration, and rebirth.

37:6 you shall live: This passage is not about resurrection from physical death, but rebirth from spiritual death brought about by divine power.

37:7, 8 The dramatic **noise** and then coming **together** of the bones with new flesh must have been chilling and thrilling to the prophet. This was a prophetic portrayal of the rebirth of Israel (see Rom. 9—11).

37:9 The Hebrew word translated **breath** is the same as the one translated **winds.** It can also be translated *spirit.*

37:10 an exceedingly great army: The dead bones in the valley (vv. 1, 2) must have looked like the aftermath of a horrible military defeat in which there were no survivors even to bury the dead. But now the army **stood upon their feet.**

37:11–15 The **bones** symbolize the **whole house of Israel.** This identification picks up on imagery already used: (1) those identified as **dry** or spiritually dead (see vv. 2–5); (2) those identified as despondent and dejected, with no apparent **hope** of being "resurrected" as the people of the living God; and (3) those described as disassembled and dispersed before being rejoined and rebuilt (see vv. 6–10). The major thrust of this passage is the coming spiritual rebirth of God's chosen people through the agency of His Spirit (see vv. 15–28; 36:22–32). The spiritual rebirth would miraculously revive and restore human beings to what God had intended them to be in the beginning.

37:16 a stick: This is Ezekiel's final symbolic drama using an object (see 4:1, 3, 9; 5:1).

37:17–22 mountains of Israel: This phrase represents the Promised Land (see 36:1–7, 12). The **one king** refers to the future ruler, the promised Messiah, also called Shepherd, Servant, and Prince (see vv. 24, 25; 7:27; 34:11–31; John 10).

37:23 The Hebrew word translated **dwelling places** is *backsliding* in other ancient manuscripts. In Hebrew, the two words differ in the placement of one letter.

37:24, 25 The title **David My servant** refers to the Messiah and King who would

come from David's line to save Israel (v. 22; see 2 Sam. 7:8–16).

37:26–28 The Lord had made an **everlasting covenant** with Abraham, the nation of Israel, and David (see 16:60, 61; see Gen. 9:16; 17:7; Num. 25:12, 13; 2 Sam. 7:13, 16; 23:5; Jer. 32:40). **My sanctuary in their midst:** The sanctuary or holy place of the living God is His dwelling place among His people (see Zeph. 3:15–18). **My tabernacle:** This term meaning "dwelling place" is a synonym for *sanctuary.* Both can be used of God's dwelling in the midst of His people in the wilderness. Here they point to the future dwelling of the living God in the midst of His people **forevermore.**

38:1, 2 Son of man is a title for Ezekiel emphasizing his humanity, even though his message was from God. The proper names in this prophecy do not have to be specifically identified for an understanding of the main message. The term **Gog** appears in only one other place in the Old Testament (1 Chr. 5:4), but not in reference to the same person (compare Rev. 20:8). The term could be a name or a title. **Magog** (or the "land of Gog"; see Gen. 10:2; 1 Chr. 1:5) is usually understood to be an area near the Black Sea or the Caspian Sea. In Gen. 10:2, Magog is one of the sons of Japheth, whose descendants occupied lands from Spain to Asia Minor, the islands of the Mediterranean to southern Russia. Some connect Magog with the Scythians.

38:3, 4 God is sovereign over the invasion (see vv. 14–17). **hooks into your jaws:** Here Gog is portrayed as a huge animal, perhaps a crocodile, that will be controlled by hooks. **horses, and horsemen:** When the biblical prophets speak of battles in the distant future, they use descriptions of weaponry and tactics known to them (see "sword" in v. 8; "bow arrows" in 39:3).

38:5, 6 Nations will ally with Gog from all directions: from the east—**Persia;** south—**Ethiopia;** west—**Libya;** and north—**Gomer.** The people of Gomer were the Cimmerians, a people from what is now southern Russia. **Togarmah** was near the Black Sea (see Gen. 10:3; 1 Chr. 1:6).

38:7–9 dwell safely: This phrase (see vv. 11, 14) indicates that the Israel of this passage is secure; the nation is not safe from attack, but it is safe from defeat. The time of the invasion is suggested by two temporal phrases—**After many days ... In the latter years**—and the overall context. The second phrase appears only here in the Old Testament. The first phrase usually denotes an indefinite time period, sometimes extending into the distant future or the end times (see Dan. 8:26). See also v. 16, where "the latter days" is used, a phrase that frequently points to messianic times or to the times when Israel is regathered. From Ezekiel's viewpoint, he was predicting a time in the very distant future—the *end times.*

38:10–13 Gog's **evil plan** will be to attack an unsuspecting, unprepared, and peaceful people in **unwalled villages**. The phrase **I will go up** demonstrates that Gog will decide to attack Israel even though God foresees, predicts, and controls Gog's evil actions. **Young lions** represent their rulers; however, a few ancient versions translate the Hebrew as "villages."

38:14–17 riding on horses: In early biblical history, horses were not ridden in battle, but were used to pull chariots (v. 4). **may know Me, when I am hallowed in you, O Gog:** These words show that God is determined to bring glory to His name in this unusual battle and even in this evil person.

38:18–23 These verses speak of God defending His nation against Gog and his army with supernatural and earth-shaking methods. Unusually strong language about the wrath of God is found in these verses. The piling up of intense phrases indicates more than an "ordinary" future battle. **fire ... brimstone:** A rare phrase, reserved only for the greatest catastrophes (see Gen. 19:24 when a similar phrase is used for the destruction of Sodom). This judgment would rival the magnitude of the judgment Sodom experienced.

39:1–3 I will knock ... out: This pictures God fighting for His people (see 38:21).

39:4, 5 mountains ... open field: The rout will be total; there will be no place for the enemies of God to flee for safety.

39:6, 7 Fire from the Lord often refers to lightning bolts (see 1 Kin. 18:38). **they shall know:** There is a significant emphasis in chs. 38 and 39 on God's purpose in demonstrating

the central truth that He is **the LORD** (see vv. 13, 21, 22, 28; 38:16, 23). God's battle with Gog will demonstrate His sovereignty and majesty in His universe.

39:8 Surely it is coming ... This is the day: The language throughout this section seems unusually grave, and the outcome is announced with unusual solemnity and certainty.

39:9, 10 The **seven years** could be, but does not have to be, equated with the "seven months" of vv. 12, 14. If symbolic, the number would suggest the completeness and finality of the war.

39:11 That day is the time after Gog's defeat. Burial will be necessary for reasons of sanitation as well as consecration (see Lev. 5:2, 3; 21:1; Num. 6:6). **East of the sea** is unclear, but because the valley will **obstruct travelers,** a likely candidate is the area of southern Galilee that leads toward the Dead Sea (called the Valley of Jezreel in Josh. 17:16).

39:12 cleanse the land: The Law of Moses prescribed the sacrifice of a heifer to cleanse the land if a murdered person was found in a region (see Deut. 21:1–9).

39:13 gain renown: This verse implies that the burial of Gog would become a memorial day to glorify God.

39:14–16 A complete purification is emphasized (see Lev. 11:45). **Hamonah** means "Horde," indicating a multitude of corpses.

39:17–20 A poem or song is addressed to the scavenging birds and beasts who come to the multitude of dead bodies (vv. 14–16). Whether figurative or not, the passage pictures God's sovereign control over the conquest of Israel's future and most ferocious enemies (see Rev. 19:11–21). The meal would be a divinely prepared sacrifice served at God's table—the land or **mountains of Israel.** The main course would be the mighty rulers of the earth. The **fatlings of Bashan** portray the might of these men. The herds of Bashan—**rams and lambs, ... goats and bulls**—were the strongest and most important animals of ancient Israel, fed in the rich pasturelands east of Galilee.

39:21, 22 My glory among the nations: The universal knowledge of the living God of

Israel will be based finally on the outcome of the battle described in chs. 38 and 39. Ezekiel followed the great theme of biblical theology begun in Gen. 12:3 that the ultimate purpose of God in His choice of Abraham and Sarah was to make His blessings known to all the families of the earth.

39:23–29 The Hebrew term rendered **captives** (see Jer. 30:3) can also mean "fortunes" (see Deut. 30:3).

40:1 This date is about 573 B.C., 12 years since the six messages of hope delivered the year following the fall of Jerusalem (33:21–39:29) and 25 years after the deportation of Jehoiachin (see 1:2; 33:21, 22; chs. 33–39).

40:2 Ezekiel was taken in a vision to a **very high mountain** from which he could see a city to the south. The sight seems somewhat vague, **something like the structure of a city.** Since the temple is there (v. 5), Jerusalem is suggested; but neither the mountain nor the city is named. Such a high mountain north of Jerusalem does not correlate with the geography of Israel, then or now. Mount Hermon, north of Galilee, is possible if the boundaries of the land are understood as extending that far.

40:3–5 The special circumstances of these final visions are noteworthy. Ezekiel saw a messenger with a **bronze** appearance (see 1:27, 28) who was equipped with tools for measuring. Ezekiel was commissioned to minister the complete revelation to **the house of Israel.** A **cubit** was about 18 inches, or the distance from fingertips to elbow. A **handbreadth,** the width of the hand across the widest part, was approximately three inches. Both a long cubit (a cubit of around 21 inches) and a short cubit (the standard 18 inches) existed. Based on these measurements, the **measuring rod** was six long cubits in length, about 126 inches or 10.5 feet, the height and width of the wall around the temple.

40:6–16 The thresholds of the eastern gate measure 10.5 feet wide; each gate-chamber or guard room is 10.5 by 10.5 feet, separated by a space 8.75 feet wide. The **stairs** apparently lead up to the outer threshold, and the rooms (three on each side) line a walkway to the inner threshold leading to a vestibule (or porch) that is 14 feet wide. The **gateposts** are 3.5 feet square; and the distance across the **gateway** of the outer threshold is 17.5 feet. The distance from the beginning of the gate through the outer threshold is 22.75 feet: 10.5 feet of this being the threshold. A space in front of each guardroom is 1.75 feet wide (21 inches or one long cubit). The overall dimensions of the east gate, and of the two identical north and south gates, are 43.75 by 87.5 feet. The gateposts are 105 feet high. These gates have some similarity to those excavated in Israel from the time of Solomon.

40:17–19 The lower pavement is equal in length to the gateway: 87.5 feet; and the distance between the outer gateway and the corresponding inner gateway (across the pavement) is 175 feet. **chambers:** Rooms, probably for storage or priests' quarters, line the inside of the northern, southern, and eastern walls.

40:20–37 The **archways** are 43.75 feet long by 8.75 feet wide (see vv. 8, 9, 14; apparently the porches of the gate systems in the inner court have different dimensions, although these gates are said to be like the others). Also in contrast to the outer gates, these have their porches (vestibules) on the outward side (entrance), where seven steps go up (see vv. 22, 26).

40:38–43 Ezekiel observes a room near the entrance of the northern gate of the inner court where animals are slaughtered and washed for sacrificial offerings. These sacrifices point to the ultimate sacrifice: the sacrifice of God's only Son on the Cross once for all.

40:44–46 On the inner side (facing the inner court) of the northern and southern inner gateways are rooms for priests whose principal work is singing (see 1 Chr. 16:4–6; 2 Chr. 29:25–30). Those housed at the northern gate serve at the sacrificial altar. These **sons of Zadok** would be the only Levites permitted to serve God directly (see 44:15–31). The priests of the southern (inner) gate minister in the temple.

40:47–49 The inner courtyard is 175 feet square. On **altar** and **temple** see chs. 41—43.

The width of the entrance—**vestibule**—to the temple sanctuary can be determined: 20 cubits (35 feet) with a three-cubit (5.25 feet) extension of the five-cubit (8.75 feet) **doorposts** on each side, leaving an entrance with a width of fourteen cubits (24.5 feet).

41:1–4 The outer area, the holy place (see Ex. 26:33) and the inner area, the **Most Holy Place** (see 1 Kin. 6:16–20) of the temple itself are described. Overall, the outer room is 70 feet long by 35 feet wide and has an entrance 17.5 feet wide. The inner **sanctuary** is 35 feet square with an entrance 10.5 feet wide. **Doorposts** for the outer room are 10.5 feet square and for the inner sanctuary 3.5 feet square. Walls on each side of each entrance protrude from the side walls 8.75 and 12.25 feet. The height of the entrance to the inner room is 10.5 feet.

41:5–11 Next the dimensions are given for the **wall** surrounding the **temple**. Its width is 10.5 feet. Running along the inside of the western, northern, and southern walls (but not attached) are three levels of ten rooms (90 total; perhaps these are storerooms), each 7 feet square with an outer wall 8.75 feet thick. They sit on a foundation 10.5 feet high. A space of 35 feet is apparently between these rooms and the priests' **chambers** north and south of the temple (see 42:1–14). A **terrace** that is 8.75 feet wide is on all three sides.

41:12 Behind the temple, between its western end and the western wall of the outer court is a **building** 122.5 feet wide and 157.5 feet long with walls 8.75 feet thick. Its purpose is not given.

41:13–26 Like the temple, the western building is 175 feet in total length (its inside length plus the width of the walls on each side plus 8.75 multiplied by 2; see v. 12). The full width of the eastern side of the temple proper is the same, as is that of the inner courtyard and the courtyard separating the temple and the western building. Various decorations are described in vv. 16–20. Some likely have symbolic meanings (see 28:13, 14 about cherubs), but no explanations are given here. A wooden **altar** (v. 22), the only piece of furniture mentioned in this passage, is 5.25

feet high and 2 feet square (see the dimensions of the stone tables of 40:42 and the altar of sacrifice in 43:13–17). The purpose and position of this altar is not known; but it is called **the table that is before the LORD,** to which some compare the altar of incense in the tabernacle (see Ex. 37:25–28).

42:1–14 To the north and south of the courtyard separating the temple and the western building (see 41:12–14) is a building for the priests 175 feet long and 87.5 feet wide, with three stories (see vv. 5, 6) and a door along the length facing the outer courtyard. The entrance has a **walk** 17.5 by 1.75 feet. Mainly the northern building is described, but apparently the southern building is the same or very similar. Parallel to the eastern wall (the width) and its door is a wall 87.5 feet long (vv. 7–9). These are places for certain priests (see "sons of Zadok" in 40:46) to eat and change clothes, indicating that the rooms also provide storage facilities for the holy food offerings and priestly garments.

42:15–20 measured it all around: Ezekiel was taken through the eastern gates outside the entire temple and courtyard structure and shown the size of the land area prescribed for the temple complex. Whether **rods** in v. 16 is correct or whether "cubits" is meant is debated by many scholars. Five-hundred rods square is 5,250 feet per side, nearly a mile, which to some seems too large. The cubit is the most frequent measure used to this point, but the rod has been introduced as the standard for measuring the temple (in 40:5 the rod is equated with six cubits). It makes sense that the larger unit should be used for the greatest dimensions. The large bordering area around the temple complex might be there in order to set it apart and to emphasize the temple's holiness (43:12).

43:1, 2 came from ... the east: In 11:23, God's glory had left the temple and gone east over the Mount of Olives as His presence left the city. Here His presence is pictured as returning to the city from the east.

43:3–6 I came is "He came" in a few Hebrew manuscripts, referring to God's judgment on Jerusalem.

43:7–9 This temple is God's residence from which He will rule and reign over **the children of Israel forever** (see 37:26–28). The second half of this verse appears to predict an absolute end of the idolatrous and immoral practices of the **house of Israel,** which had taken place around the temple (see 2 Kin. 23:1–20). **their harlotry:** This is either an allusion to their spiritual adultery in general or, more specifically and literally, to their participation in the religious prostitution of Baal worship (see 16:15). **carcasses:** This is taken by some as a metaphor ("lifeless idols," see Lev. 26:30) because of the context, but it could refer to memorial graves of kings buried near the temple mount (see 2 Kin. 23:30), perhaps near the royal houses just outside the southern wall (see v. 8; 1 Kin. 7:1–12).

43:10–12 God explains to Ezekiel the purpose of revealing the detailed description of the future **temple** (see 8, 9; 42:15–20; Lev. 20:7; Ps. 11:4; Is. 6:3).

43:13–17 The cubit described here is the long cubit—a **cubit and a handbreadth,** or 21 inches. The altar has a base 1.75 feet (21 inches) wide and high. A rim around the edge of the base is **one span,** or about 9 inches, wide. On top of the base is a lower section 3.5 feet high, having a 1.75-foot ledge. The distance between the smaller and larger ledges is 7 feet. The **altar hearth,** the top section of the altar where the sacrifice is offered, is 7 feet high. The **four horns** are on top of the corners (see 1 Kin. 1:50, 51). Overall the hearth is 21 feet square. Apparently the middle section is 24.5 feet square with a rim about 10.5 inches wide; and the lower section extends 3.5 feet beyond the middle one, 28 feet square (see vv. 14, 16, 17 where—assuming the symmetry of the altar—the middle section extends two cubits beyond the top). The height of the altar is therefore about 11 cubits or 19.25 feet. Assuming an 18-cubit square (see hearth and middle section in vv. 16–17) and one-cubit-high base, the foundation is 31.5 feet square. **Steps,** previously forbidden for an altar (Ex. 20:26), are necessary for this altar because of the great size of the structure. The huge altar is positioned in the center of the inner court in front of the temple entrance.

43:18, 19 These **ordinances** relate to the cleansing and consecration of the altar. See Ex. 29:36–37; Lev. 8:14–17 about the tabernacle altar and 2 Chr. 7:9 for the temple altar.

43:20–27 Atonement and **sin offering** suggest purification and cleansing from sin. Because of the sinlessness—**without blemish**—of the sacrifice, the people for whom the sacrifice is made are declared acceptable before God.

44:1–3 The **outer gate of the sanctuary** is the eastern gate of the outer court (see 40:6–16; 43:1) which must remain **shut.** The eastern gate known today as the "Golden Gate" dates from several centuries after Christ. It is walled shut today in accordance with an Islamic tradition. **the prince:** The identity of this prince is unknown. The Hebrew term does not always mean a king or a member of royalty (see Gen. 23:6). It is not the Messiah, since 45:22 indicates that this leader must make a sin offering for himself. He may be one of the Zadokite priests (see vv. 15, 16).

44:4–9 Ezekiel experiences another awe-inspiring vision of God's glory leading him to bow in worship (see 1:28—2:1). God demands that His renewed people follow His regulations exactly. He emphasizes the necessity of holiness and righteousness, especially in light of Israel's past **abominations** related to rules regulating who was to enter the temple **sanctuary.** Specifically, they had allowed **foreigners** without evidence of faithfulness to God to serve in the sanctuary (see Josh. 9:23–27; Ezra 8:20): these people were **uncircumcised in heart and uncircumcised in flesh.** This was in disobedience to God's commands (see Ex. 19:8; Lev. 26:41; Num. 3:10; Deut. 10:16; 30:6; Neh. 13:8; Jer. 4:4; 9:25), but was in conformity with the practices of foreign pagan religions, which God's people had been forbidden to imitate (see Ex. 34:12; Deut. 18:9; compare Rom. 12:1, 2).

44:10 See Lev. 21; 22 for a description of the duties of the **Levites.** Unfortunately, during the history of Israel, Levites had not obeyed the commands Moses had given them and had even encouraged idolatry (compare ch. 8; 14:1–11; Deut. 33:8–11; Judg. 17–19).

44:11–14 God explains to Ezekiel why the Levites would be limited to certain types of temple ministry. The Levites (with the exception of the sons of Zadok, see v. 15) could not be priests but could be **ministers** (servants or attendants). They could not serve in the inner court or temple, where the **holy things** are located; but they could oversee the general operation of the temple complex.

44:15, 16 The **Levites, the sons of Zadok** were descendants of the priest Zadok in the Levitical line who remained faithful when others did not (see 1 Sam. 2:27–36; 2 Sam. 8:17; 15:24–29; 1 Kin. 2:26–35; 1 Chr. 6:7, 8, 50–53). While salvation is never earned (Rom. 3; 4; Gal. 2; 3; Eph. 2:8, 9), God does reward faithfulness and righteousness. Here He rewarded His faithful priests and Levites with the opportunity to minister before Him. Responsibility and recognition have to be deserved, but never demanded (see 1 Sam. 26:23; Matt. 5:12; 25:21–23; Rev. 2:10). The Zadokites were honored for their special obedience. The **table** is not identified, but could be similar to the wooden altar of 41:22.

44:17–19 These verses speak of holiness as **linen garments** (see 42:14; Ex. 28:42; 29:37; 30:29; Lev. 6:11, 27; 16:4; 21:10; Hag. 2:12). Common things were to be kept distinct from what was consecrated.

44:20–22 These verses speak of holiness in conduct. These regulations continued practices already prescribed in the Law of Moses (Lev. 10:6, 9; 21:1–6, 7, 10, 14). Their aim was to help the priests avoid conformity to the immoral and idolatrous religious rituals and conduct among the pagan nations. The **priests,** then and in the future, have the responsibility of modeling and maintaining the highest standards of morality, self-control, self-denial, discipline, and obedience to God's will.

44:23, 24 they shall teach My people: The priests were to demonstrate verbally and visually before the people how to distinguish between what is godly and ungodly. They also served as judges in disputes and debates (see 22:26; Lev. 10:10, 11; 11:47; Deut. 17:9; 19:7; 21:5; 33:10).

44:25–27 This section deals with holiness regarding death among the people (Lev. 21:1–3; Num. 19:11–19; Hag. 2:13). Contact with a dead body was forbidden; however, a partial exception was made for immediate family members. The act still defiled the person, causing ceremonial uncleanness for a certain time. God's concern over purity in practice and procedures is seen in that the priest was to submit to a cleansing ritual and then personally present a sin offering. He was to publicly declare and deal with his own uncleanness, although what he had done was not forbidden. The circumstances that allowed touching a dead body did not overturn its consequences according to the Law. God was preserving the sanctity of His temple and statutes.

44:28–31 These verses explain holiness in the priests' provisions (see Lev. 17:5; 22:8; Num. 18:10–13, 20, 23–24; Deut. 10:9; 14:21; Mal. 3:8–12). **I am their possession:** God was to be the priests' possession in all respects; they were not to inherit land or cities. The **dedicated thing** (see Lev. 27:21, 28; Num. 18:14; Judg. 11:29–40) was something wholly and irrevocably devoted to God as a sacrificial gift. The giver would be blessed in giving (see also Acts 20:35). God's laws are governed by His love and goodness, and they are given as guides to holy and healthy living (see John 10:10). God is truthful and trustworthy; His codes of conduct are blessings, not burdens (see Matt. 11:28–30).

45:1–5 A distinct—**set apart, holy**—section was to be allocated for God. This area would be divided into two equal sections. One would be the portion for the Zadokites—**priests, the ministers of the sanctuary.** In the center of this part of the holy district is the holy square-mile environs for the temple—**the sanctuary, the Most Holy Place.** The other half of the holy district would be the portion given to the Levites. All this is holy; God owns it.

45:6 The city is not named, but Jerusalem is most likely. Its allotted property is 25,000 by

5,000 cubits. This area is located **adjacent** to and south of (according to 48:18) the Zadokite district—**the holy section.** See 48:15–19, 30–35.

45:7, 8 The identity of the **prince** is unknown (see 44:3). But his allotted area is on both sides (east and west) of the **holy district.** He will own this land bordering a tribal territory to the north and south, where the **west** and **east border** suggest respectively the Mediterranean Sea and the Dead Sea or Jordan River. The prince and God's **princes** of messianic period—in contrast to previous leaders of Israel (see 11:1–13; 14:1–11; 20–22; 34:1–10)—will not be greedy for riches and real estate but will give the land that remains to the people.

45:9–11 The merchants were exhorted to use accurate measures of the **ephah** (estimated to be around a bushel) and the **bath** (from six to nine gallons), both defined as **one-tenth of a homer** (five to ten bushels or 60 to 90 gallons). Merchants must not cheat when weighing produce (see Lev. 19:35, 36; Amos 8:5; Mic. 6:10–12). God called for an end to dishonesty and deceit; a time is coming when all such scheming will end (vv. 16, 17; see 37:15–28).

45:12 Ezekiel also demanded fair weights. The **shekel** weighed about 11.5 grams or four-tenths of an ounce. In Babylon, 24 **gerahs** made one shekel while Ezekiel sets the standard at 20; but 60 shekels made one **mina,** which conforms to the standard prescribed in this verse. In Ezekiel's system this mina is thought to weigh about 1.5 pounds.

45:13–17 These verses describe an **offering** to be given to the prince (v. 7) who, unlike previous rulers, will be just and truthful (see v. 8). The prince, in turn, will make offerings to God in order to **make atonement for the house of Israel** (v. 17), symbolizing cleansing from sin (see 40:38–43).

45:18–20 This is an annual day of purifying the temple sanctuary. In the light of Jesus' death on the Cross, the actions of the prince symbolize and emphasize that God has made atonement for all through the sacrifice of the Messiah (see vv. 15–17; 18–22). The forgiveness of individual sins is illustrated through daily sin offerings (vv. 23–25).

45:21–25 In this passage the feasts of **Passover** and Tabernacles are observed (see Ex. 12:1–14; Lev. 23:5–8; 33–43; Num. 28:16–25; 29:12–38). The dates are in relation to the Levitical calendar, the Jewish religious year. The procedures as well are very similar to those of the Mosaic system. These feasts commemorate God's faithfulness to His promises.

46:1–8 The prince shall enter: What the rituals signified under the Law was fulfilled by the Messiah. At the time of this prince, certain promises were being fulfilled and the covenants consummated in the messianic age (see 40:6–16, 28–37; 43:18–27; 44:1–2; Ex. 20:8–11). **hin:** This was a liquid measure about one-sixth of a bath, approximately one gallon (see 4:11; Ex. 30:24; Lev. 19:36).

46:9–11 the people of the land: This phrase describes the citizens of the Promised Land during this messianic period. The prescribed protocol was probably to ensure an orderly procession and service. Such regulations would be needed on the special feast days because of the participation of large numbers of people.

46:12 The preparation and presentation of this offering is the one exception to 44:1–3 (see vv. 1, 2). The **voluntary** or freewill offering was given beyond what was required (see Lev. 22:17–30).

46:13 shall daily make: This is a change from the provisions in the Law (see Num. 28:3–8; 2 Kin. 16:15).

46:14 perpetual ordinance: This is a change from the provisions in the Law (see Num. 28:5). God's people cannot be reminded too often of God's provisions for them; nor can they thank Him too much or too frequently.

46:15–18 The language of this passage speaks clearly and concretely about descendants, servants, and property, so a spiritual or allegorical meaning for this passage is difficult to defend (see 44:3). Likewise, the **prince** has sons and servants, so he cannot be the Messiah. Again, the prince's character is described in sharp contrast to many of Israel's previous leaders (34:1–10).

46:19, 20 The setting is one of the two buildings for the priests on the western end of the temple complex (see 42:1–14). The **place** is something like a kitchen.

46:21–24 The setting switches to the **outer court** (see 40:17–19), where each of the four corners has an enclosed kitchen court. These kitchens are distinguished from those for the priests (see vv. 19, 20); these belong to the Levites: **ministers of the temple,** see 44:11–14.

47:1 He is the "man" of v. 3 (see 40:3; 46:19).

47:2–6 One thousand cubits is approximately 1,750 feet (see 40:3–5). Four times the man uses the measuring **line** to mark off this distance across the stream, which progressively gets deeper from ankle depth, to knees, to waist, and finally too deep and wide to cross except by swimming. The water flows eastward from the south side of the temple.

47:7–12 The water becomes a river of healing and the source of abundant life for everything and everyone (see Gen. 2:8–10; Zech. 14:8; John 4:13, 14; 10:10; Rev. 22:1, 2). It continues flowing southeast: through the dry, rocky region between Jerusalem and the Dead Sea—that is, the Arabah or **eastern region**—and south along the Jordan valley and the Jordan Rift, as far as to the Dead Sea. When it **reaches the sea** (the Dead Sea), the salty sea becomes fresh and able to sustain life so that fishermen can fish there: **its waters are healed.** This is an amazing picture—the Dead Sea is the saltiest body of water (approximately 25 percent saline content) and is presently unable to support life. It is also the lowest point on earth, with its surface 1,300 feet below sea level and the water itself 1,300 feet deep. The living water that God will provide has immeasurable power to renew, restore, and resurrect life. This sea which is dead will teem with life all along its shores—**from En Gedi to En Eglaim.** Great volumes and variety of vegetation, everlasting and perpetually productive, will result from this river which **flows from the sanctuary** (see v. 1).

47:13 The priestly tribe of Levi had already received a special area (see 45:1–8; 48:8–14). The tribe of **Joseph** was divided into two tribes to replace Levi and thus maintain twelve tribes.

47:14 raised My hand in an oath: This phrase recalls 20:5; 36:28 (see Gen. 12:7; 15:7, 18–21; 17:8). The unilateral and unconditional nature of the Abrahamic covenant is suggested; this inheritance is a free gift of God's grace which God's people could do nothing to deserve.

47:15–17 The northern boundary of the land extends from the Mediterranean Sea—**the Great Sea**—to a border north of Damascus. The other place names are not certainly known. **Damascus** is the capital of Aram (modern Syria). **Hamath** is thought to have been north of Damascus, about half the distance to Carchemish. **Zedad:** This is believed to have been east of Hamath and Hazar Enan (the eastern point of this border). **Hauran** appears to be an Israelite region east of the Jordan River and north of Gilead.

47:18 The eastern border runs from the Damascus region southwest through Hauran to and along the Jordan River (see Num. 34:10–12). **eastern … sea:** The Dead Sea.

47:19 The southern border goes from the eastern side of the Dead Sea to **Tamar** (a town to the southwest) to the **waters of Meribah by Kadesh** (Num. 20:13, 24; 27:14) **along the brook** (of Egypt; the Wadi el-Arish) and on to the Mediterranean Sea (see Num. 34:3–5; 1 Kin. 8:65). This line runs from the Dead Sea southwest across the Negev to the Brook of Egypt, a river bed in west Sinai.

47:20 The western border runs along the coastline of the **Great Sea** (the Mediterranean Sea) north to a point directly west of Hamath (see Num. 34:6; Rev. 21:1).

47:21–23 The treatment of **strangers** or aliens in the land is considered. Non-Israelites who married and settled within the Jewish communities were to be accepted as native Israelites, qualified to share in the territorial inheritance of whatever tribe they joined (see Lev. 19:34; Is. 56:1–8).

48:1–7 From the northern district south to the priestly portions, the tribes in order are **Dan, Asher, Naphtali, Manasseh, Ephraim, Reuben,** and **Judah.** Each district is bordered north and south by another tribe. The east-west borders for each are the same as in 47:18, 20.

The tribes resulting from the offspring of Jacob and his wives' servants are given lands farthest from the most holy areas (see 45:1–8), while the descendants of Jacob's wives occupy a central position (see Gen. 35:23–26). The tribe of Judah is most favored, for it produced the Davidic and messianic line (see 37:18–28; Gen. 49:8–10; Is. 11). Historically, the tribe of Dan had occupied the northern limits of the land (see Judg. 20:1). Its idolatry was well known—Jeroboam had placed a golden calf there (2 Kin. 10:29).

48:8–15 The district has the **city** in its **center** surrounded by housing, farming, and grazing lands for general use.

48:16–22 The tribal territories of Judah and Benjamin are immediately north and south of the **holy district** (see vv. 1–7, 20). **Benjamin** like Judah is favored (see Gen. 35:24).

48:23–29 Continuing southward in order are the tribal allotments for **Benjamin, Simeon, Issachar, Zebulun,** and **Gad.** Gad is the southern border of the land.

48:30, 31 The gates are named after the original twelve **tribes** (see Rev. 21:12, 13). The gate for Joseph represents the two tribes of Manasseh and Ephraim (v. 32; 47:13). The northern gates are **Reuben** (the firstborn), **Judah** (the tribe of the messianic line), and **Levi** (the priestly tribe)—all descendants of Jacob and Leah (Gen. 35:23).

48:32 On the eastern side the gates represent **Joseph, Benjamin,** and **Dan.** While the first two were children of Jacob and Rachel, the third was the child of Jacob and Rachel's servant Bilhah (Gen. 35:24, 25).

48:33 South of the city, the three other offspring of Jacob and Leah have gates named for them: **Simeon, Issachar,** and **Zebulun** (Gen. 35:23).

48:34 The three western gates are named after **Gad** and **Asher**—the sons of Jacob and Leah's maidservant Zilpah—and **Naphtali**—a son of Jacob and Bilhah (see Gen. 35:25, 26).

48:35 The designated name for this city from **that day** is **THE LORD IS THERE** (see Is. 60:14; 62:2–4, 12; Jer. 3:17; 33:15, 16). The Lord was forced to depart from the city and the temple because of the wickedness of the Israelites (8:6; 10:18). But here, Ezekiel foresees the return of God in all His glory to His people, His temple, and His land.

Daniel

Introduction

In 626 B.C., Nabopolassar became king of Babylon. By the time of his death in 605 B.C. he had eliminated the Assyrian Empire and swallowed it into what became known as the Neo-Babylonian or Chaldean Empire. Judah had been largely under Assyrian domination from about 670 B.C., but now found itself serving a new master. King Jehoiakim of Judah became a vassal of Nebuchadnezzar, the son of Nabopolassar (see 2 Kin. 24:1). Nebuchadnezzar brought his father's empire to even greater heights, eventually deporting many Jews to Babylon.

Daniel lived in the midst of all these momentous events. Deported to Babylon as a teenager, he was a close confidant of Nebuchadnezzar throughout the Babylonian king's reign (605–562 B.C.). Later Daniel served King Cyrus, the Persian ruler who conquered Babylon.

Daniel claims to have written the book that bears his name (12:4) and uses the first person singular from 7:2 to the end of the book. There is no reason to doubt either that Daniel was a historical person or that he wrote the book that bears his name. A well-educated Jew, chosen for special training in the palace in Babylon, Daniel possessed all the linguistic skills and the historical and cultural knowledge needed to write a book of this depth and complexity.

Daniel wrote his book to assert that the God of Israel was sovereign, even over the powerful nations that surrounded His people. God's chosen nation had been conquered and dispersed by a mighty empire that did not acknowledge God. Had God forgotten His promises? Daniel's answer was that Babylon would fall to another empire, which in turn would fall to yet another great kingdom. History would continue in this pattern until God judged all Gentile nations and established His everlasting rule. Daniel's message was meant to uplift and encourage the weary hearts of the exiled Jews.

Yet Daniel also looked forward to the day when God would restore and reward Israel. The time was coming when God would gather His children to Him again. He would establish His messianic kingdom which would last forever. The God who directs the forces of history has not deserted His people. His promises of preservation and ultimate restoration are certain.

1:1 Jehoiakim king of Judah reigned from 608 to 598 B.C. He was an evil king who sided first with the Egyptians and then with the Babylonians until 602 B.C. when he rebelled. His independence was short-lived, however, and Jehoiakim remained under Babylonian domination until his death. The son of Nabopolassar, the founder of the Neo-Babylonian (Chaldean) Empire, was **Nebuchadnezzar,** who reigned from 605 to 562 B.C. In the summer of 605 B.C., Nebuchadnezzar besieged Jerusalem and seized loot and prisoners, including Daniel. **1:2 the LORD gave:** The Book of Daniel emphasizes the sovereignty of God in the affairs of nations. Jerusalem did not fall just because Nebuchadnezzar was strong, but because God had judged the people of Judah for their disobedience and idolatry. **some of the articles:** The remainder of the articles in the temple were removed later when Jehoiakim surrendered (see 2 Kin. 24:13; 2 Chr. 36:18). **Shinar**—that is, Babylon—was located on the Euphrates River fifty miles south of present-day Baghdad in Iraq.

1:3 eunuchs: In ancient Middle Eastern monarchies, royal harems were typically superintended by men who had been emasculated and were considered reliable to serve in that capacity. A eunuch was often regarded as a privileged royal official. **The children of Israel** refers to the general population of the nation of Israel.

1:4, 5 the language and literature of the Chaldeans: The language of most of Mesopotamia was Akkadian, which was written in cuneiform script, usually on clay tablets. Over the centuries the Babylonians and Assyrians produced a massive body of literature of all types. For Daniel and his friends to be truly educated required that they be familiar with these literary traditions. The term *Chaldeans* was commonly applied to the Babylonians in general, and also to the guild of astrologers, diviners, and other practitioners of wisdom to which Daniel was being introduced.

1:6 According to the first-century Jewish historian Josephus, all four of these young men were members of Zedekiah's royal family.

1:7 The name **Daniel** means "God Is My Judge." Daniel's Babylonian name **Belteshazzar** means "Lady Protect the King," referring to the goddess Sarpanitu, wife of Marduk. The name **Hananiah** means "The Lord Is Gracious." Hananiah's Babylonian name **Shadrach** means "I Am Fearful of the God." The name **Mishael** means "Who Is What God Is?" Mishael's Babylonian name **Meshach** means "I Am of Little Account." The name **Azariah** means "The Lord Has Helped Me." Azariah's Babylonian name **Abed-Nego** means "Servant of (the god) Nebo."

1:8 defile himself: Daniel's refusal to eat the **king's delicacies** had nothing to do with the consumption of rich food or wine. There were two problems with the king's menu: (1) It no doubt included food forbidden by the Law and food not prepared according to Mosaic regulations (see Lev. 11). (2) The meat had probably been dedicated to idols. To partake of the food would have been to recognize the idols as deities.

1:9 This verse implies that **the chief of the eunuchs** was over Daniel, leading some scholars to conclude that Daniel himself was a eunuch.

1:10, 11 In the Hebrew text, **your** is plural. Daniel's friends joined him in refusing to eat from the king's menu (vv. 7, 17, 19). **Endanger my head** suggests that the king might have had the chief of the eunuchs put to death for accommodating Daniel and his friends.

1:12, 13 Vegetables means things grown from seed and includes vegetables and grains. The request for **water** indicates that Daniel and his friends did not want to drink wine, probably because, like the food, it was dedicated to idols (v. 8).

1:14–16 Better and fatter indicates that Daniel and his friends were healthier than **the young men who ate ... of the king's delicacies.**

1:17 God gave them knowledge and skill in all literature: As Moses was educated in the knowledge of Egypt, so Daniel and his friends acquired a Chaldean education. The **wisdom** of the Chaldeans consisted of sciences current at the time, including the interpretation of omens communicated through astrology, the examination of livers, kidneys, and other animal entrails, and the examination of the organs and flight patterns of birds. **Daniel** had the additional advantage of understanding **visions and dreams.**

1:18 The end of the days refers to the end of three years (v. 5). **The chief of the eunuchs** was Ashpenaz (v. 3).

1:19–21 Daniel served as counselor to the king from the completion of his training under Nebuchadnezzar (about 603 B.C., see v. 5) until **the first year of King Cyrus** (539 B.C.). Thus Daniel held his position until the very end of the Babylonian Empire.

2:1 second year: Nebuchadnezzar's reign began in 605 B.C., so this is likely 603 B.C., given Daniel's preference for a "full-year" chronological system (1:1). The king was **troubled** because he did not know the future of his kingdom (v. 29).

2:2, 3 The word translated **magicians** refers to those who use the pen—most likely, those learned in the sacred writings of the Babylonians. **Astrologers** studied the stars. **Sorcerers** received power from evil spirits. **The Chaldeans** were probably a class of wise men.

2:4 the Chaldeans spoke to the king in Aramaic: Daniel 2:4—7:28 is written in Aramaic, the common language of the day.

2:5, 6 Cut in pieces refers to the ancient practice of dismembering a body (see 3:29; 1 Sam. 15:33).

2:7–9 tell me the dream: Nebuchadnezzar reasoned that if the wise men could supernaturally interpret his dream, they should first be able to tell him the content of it.

2:10–12 Babylon here probably refers to the city, not the whole province.

2:13, 14 they began killing the wise men: Nebuchadnezzar's penalty was excessive and extreme (v. 15).

2:15 Urgent means sharp or severe (v. 13).

2:16–18 Daniel, despite his education and

expertise, still knew that prayer to the omniscient God was the first step in a crisis situation. However, Daniel did not pray alone. He sought the counsel of friends who would raise petition to the Lord with him. **God of heaven** is a favorite title for the Lord in late Old Testament literature, emphasizing God's dominion over all nations.

2:19, 20 night vision: Normally visions occurred in the daytime (8:1–14) and dreams occurred at night.

2:21 Seasons here refers to the events of history.

2:22–27 Deep refers to something inaccessible (see Ps. 92:5, 6). What is **in the darkness** is hidden from sight.

2:28–30 The latter days is an expression used frequently in the end times when God will intervene in human history to establish His eternal kingdom (see Is. 2:2; Hos. 3:5; Mic. 4:1–3).

2:31–33 Image here means statue, not idol. **gold ... silver ... bronze ... iron:** The metals are listed in descending order of weight and value. The strength of the metals, however, increases from head to legs.

2:34 Without hands signifies supernatural activity.

2:35, 36 In biblical imagery, a **mountain** is often a metaphor for a kingdom (see Ps. 48:2; Is. 2:2; 11:9; Jer. 51:25; Ezek. 20:40; Zech. 8:3). The same is true in this case, as the later interpretation makes clear (v. 44).

2:37 God ... has given you a kingdom: The God of Israel is the God of all nations. Although the rulers of those nations may not have recognized Him as Lord, that did not nullify God's ultimate sovereignty nor did it alleviate the rulers' responsibility to Him.

2:38 The **head** is a reference to the Babylonian Empire, personified in Nebuchadnezzar.

2:39, 40 The image that Nebuchadnezzar saw (vv. 31–35) represented four kingdoms that would **rule over all the earth.** The first worldwide empire—the head of gold (v. 32)—was Babylon (v. 38). The second empire—the chest and arms of silver (v. 32)—was Medo-Persia (5:28; 8:20; 11:2). The third empire—the belly and thighs of bronze (v. 32)—would be Greece (8:21). The **fourth** empire—the legs of iron (v. 33)—is

the only one not identified within the Book of Daniel. Rome is the most likely choice, for it succeeded Greece. **Strong as iron:** The Roman Empire was marked by strength, but it was destructive strength.

2:41–45 The kingdom shall be divided may be a reference to the fourth kingdom, the Roman Empire (v. 40). Differences about what is meant by the ten toes (v. 42) and the kingdom that filled the earth (represented by the stone in v. 45) has resulted in widely varying interpretations. The **kingdom which shall never be destroyed** is the kingdom of God.

2:46–49 your God is the God of gods: One should not conclude from Nebuchadnezzar's confession that he had been converted. Since the Lord had enabled Daniel to interpret the king's dream, Nebuchadnezzar was willing to admit that Daniel's God was supreme, at least in matters of divine knowledge. The king gladly promoted Daniel as a result (v. 48).

3:1 sixty cubits ... six cubits: A cubit in Israel was approximately 18 inches; in Babylon it was about 20 inches. Therefore Nebuchadnezzar's image was 90 to 100 feet tall. The 10:1 ratio of height to width, however, suggests that the image was standing on a high pedestal so that the proportions of the figure itself would be closer to the normal ratio of about 4:1. The image most likely served as a symbol of the cohesion and monolithic character of Babylon under the rule of its glorious king Nebuchadnezzar. Since the state and its king could not be separated from its gods, to bow down before the image was to worship it. **The plain of Dura** was probably about six miles southeast of Babylon.

3:2, 3 The officials of the kingdom are listed in descending order of rank. **Satraps** were the chief officials of the provinces of the empire. Daniel was one of the **administrators** (2:48). In later times, Zerubbabel (see Hag. 1:1) and Nehemiah (see Neh. 5:14) were appointed **governors.**

3:4, 5 harp ... psaltery ... symphony: These three words appear to be Greek in origin. Greek words of a cultural or technical nature appeared throughout the ancient Middle East well before 600 B.C.

3:6–8 Accused means "ate the pieces of, devoured piecemeal." The term suggests slander and malicious accusations which devour the accused piece by piece.

3:9–12 No explanation is given for Daniel's absence.

3:13–16 we have no need to answer you: Shadrach, Meshach, and Abed-Nego were not being arrogant; they were admitting their guilt.

3:17 God ... is able: The response of the Jewish young men is a model of confidence in God and submission to His will. Shadrach, Meshach, and Abed-Nego recognized God's sovereignty and power.

3:18 But if not: While the faithful men knew that God could deliver them (v. 17), they were also aware that God may have chosen not to do so. Faith in God may not translate into victory in every circumstance (see Heb. 11:32–39). What was at stake was not God's ability or their own lives, but their faith and obedience to serve Him regardless of the cost.

3:19, 20 The **mighty men of valor** were Nebuchadnezzar's personal bodyguards.

3:21 bound in ... garments: Criminals were normally stripped before execution. The fact that the fine clothes of the Jewish men were not removed implies that the king's command was carried out with great haste (v. 22).

3:22 killed those men: The price of Nebuchadnezzar's rage was the loss of capable men.

3:23–25 walking: The enormous number of bricks demanded in Babylon required kilns large enough to permit people to walk in them. **The fire** burned off the men's bonds (v. 21), but did not **hurt** them.

3:26, 27 the fire had no power: The God of Shadrach, Meshach, and Abed-Nego saved them, so that there was not the slightest evidence that they had ever been in danger.

3:28–30 no other God: Pagan cultures did not deny the existence of other gods, even those of other peoples. Nebuchadnezzar declared only that the God of the Jews was a god who is able to deliver; the king forbade others to despise Him.

4:1–3 These verses are a royal proclamation by Nebuchadnezzar about the God of Israel in which the king celebrated what God had done for him and extolled His power and universal dominion.

4:4 rest ... and flourishing: Nebuchadnezzar had peace at home and prospered in his work.

4:5, 6 This **dream** of Nebuchadnezzar occurred thirty years after the dream in ch. 2.

4:7 I told them the dream: In ch. 2, Nebuchadnezzar did not tell his wise men the content of his dream (2:5).

4:8 My god refers to Marduk. Nebuchadnezzar was still a pagan at this point.

4:9 Daniel, also known as **Belteshazzar,** was **chief of the magicians,** a position given to him years earlier (2:48).

4:10–16 In ch. 2, Nebuchadnezzar dreamed of a great image, of which he was a part. His second dream involved a tree, which represented him (v. 22). **let him:** At this point it becomes obvious that the tree is a symbol of a person. **Seven times** could refer to years, months, weeks, days, or hours. Most interpreters take it to mean years, based on the usage of "times" elsewhere in Daniel (2:8; 3:5, 15; 7:25).

4:17 The point of Nebuchadnezzar's dream is that **the Most High rules** supreme in the world.

4:18 Spirit of the Holy God: The doctrine of the triune God—the Father, Son, and Holy Spirit—is evident in the Old Testament (see Gen. 1:26; 11:7; Is. 48:16), but is not developed (3:25). Nebuchadnezzar was saying that Daniel's ability to interpret dreams was the result of God's giving Daniel the spirit of interpretation.

4:19 astonished ... troubled: Having come to an understanding of Nebuchadnezzar's dream, Daniel was so upset by its content that he hesitated to divulge its meaning. **may the dream concern those who hate you:** Daniel wishes that the awful word of judgment were somehow intended for the king's enemies and not the king.

4:20 In the Old Testament, a **tree** is a common symbol for a ruler (see Judg. 9:7–15; Ezek. 31:2–14; Zech. 11:1, 2). Since few trees were present in Babylon, a tree of the gigantic proportions described here would have been impressive and unique.

4:21 leaves were lovely ... fruit abundant: Daniel indicates that Nebuchadnezzar was the source of abundant blessing for all. The **beasts** and **birds** represent the happy citizens of Nebuchadnezzar's realm.

4:22 heavens ... earth: These terms convey the idea of totality. Using deliberate exaggeration, Daniel says that Nebuchadnezzar's kingdom extended from heaven to the ends of the earth, and so was universal.

4:23, 24 Watcher means "a waking one," one who is constantly alert. The parallel **holy one** suggests that the watcher is either the Lord Himself or one of His angels (3:28; 6:22; 8:16; 10:13; 12:1). **stump and roots:** The tree—Nebuchadnezzar—would be cut down but not uprooted. The stump would produce suckers and the roots would produce new growth that would eventually give rise to a new tree, one as grand as before (v. 26). **Seven times** means seven years (7:12, 25).

4:25–29 twelve months: The reference here is to a "grace period" between the prediction of Nebuchadnezzar's madness and its occurrence. Perhaps Nebuchadnezzar was allowed a full year in the hope that he might repent and avert the judgment of God for his arrogant pride.

4:30–32 until you know: Nebuchadnezzar would become insane, animal-like in his habits and senses. Yet in that condition he would learn more of God than he ever had before. In fact, the purpose of the judgment was that Nebuchadnezzar might know who God is and how He creates kingdoms and distributes them to whom He wills. Nebuchadnezzar had to be humbled before he could be exalted again.

4:33–37 Nebuchadnezzar praises **the Most High,** recognizing that God **lives forever** and rules forever. The king unmistakably acknowledges Daniel's God as the omnipotent, eternal Sovereign of the universe.

5:1, 2 Belshazzar is called the **king** and the son of **Nebuchadnezzar** (v. 22). Other ancient records, however, seem to dispute both facts. These records indicate that Belshazzar was the son of Nabonidus, the last king of Babylon. Two possible explanations can reconcile these differing accounts: (1) Belshazzar served as vice-regent during his father's frequent

absences from the capital. Thus he would have been in charge when Nebuchadnezzar's insanity began. (2) Belshazzar was the grandson of Nebuchadnezzar; hence, the term *father* in v. 2 indicates that Nebuchadnezzar was an ancestor of Belshazzar.

5:3, 4 gold vessels ... from the temple: Belshazzar's use of the sacred vessels at a drunken orgy was a blasphemous act of sacrilege (v. 23). **praised the gods:** Belshazzar's actions demonstrated deliberate defiance of the true God (v. 23).

5:5–7 Nabonidus the king was in Arabia. Belshazzar was his vice-regent. **The third ruler** would have been next in line to the throne.

5:8–10 The queen was not Belshazzar's wife, but the queen mother. She was either the wife of Nebuchadnezzar or the daughter of Nebuchadnezzar who had married Nabonidus, the current king.

5:11, 12 The Spirit of the Holy God is the same expression used by Nebuchadnezzar (4:8, 9, 18).

5:13–16 This event took place in 539 B.C. (see v. 30). **Daniel** was an old man at this time, possibly 80 years old or older.

5:17–24 When Daniel refused Belshazzar's **gifts** and **rewards,** he was not being ungrateful or showing disrespect. He was simply saying that he would interpret the **writing** regardless of reward.

5:25–28 MENE means **numbered.** The repetition is for emphasis. God had numbered the days of Belshazzar's kingdom; its time was up. **TEKEL** means **weighed.** God had weighed Belshazzar, and the king did not measure up to God's standard of righteousness. **UPHARSIN,** the plural of **PERES** in v. 28, means **divided.** That very night (v. 30) Babylon would be divided and defeated by the **Medes and Persians.**

5:29, 30 That very night (October 12, 539 B.C.) Babylon fell to the Persian army.

5:31 Darius the Mede is mentioned by name only in the Book of Daniel (see 6:1, 6, 9; 9:1). He is not the famous Darius I Hystaspes because Darius I was not a Mede and he lived too late (522–486 B.C.) to be a contemporary of Daniel. There are two principal suggestions as to the identity of Darius the

Mede: (1) He was Cyrus the king of Persia. However, it is unlikely that Cyrus would be called a "Mede" since he was in fact a Persian. (2) He was Gubaru, a governor appointed by Cyrus. Both Daniel and ancient literary sources indicate that a certain official ("Darius the Mede" in Daniel, "Gubaru" in Persian texts) took over immediately in Babylon until Cyrus appointed his own son Cambyses as vice-regent around 538 B.C. This figure is most likely identified with Darius. Why he is called Darius is uncertain, though ancient rulers often took other names for themselves.

6:1, 2 Daniel had previously been appointed a governor in Babylon by Nebuchadnezzar (2:48). Here he was governor in the new Medo-Persian reign. **Suffer no loss** refers to taxes.

6:3, 4 Excellent spirit probably refers to Daniel's surpassing ability to do his job and perhaps includes a commendable attitude.

6:5–7 Daniel had been circumspect in obeying the laws of the land, but his enemies knew that when the law of the land conflicted with **the law of his God,** Daniel would break the former in favor of the latter.

6:8, 9 the law of the Medes and Persians: Once a royal decree had been issued, it could not be revoked—even by the king himself. It remained in force until its time of expiration.

6:10–12 Undeterred by the royal proclamation (vv. 6–9), Daniel resumed praying by the windows of his house that opened **toward Jerusalem.** His enemies were correct in assuming that if Daniel was forced to choose between the decree of an earthly king and the eternal word of the King of heaven, he would choose his God (v. 5).

6:13–15 Daniel's accusers did not describe him as governor (v. 2), but as **one of the captives from Judah,** in order to implicate him in a treasonous act.

6:16 The Aramaic word for **den** means "pit," implying that it was underground.

6:17–20 sealed it: To ensure that the den remained closed and that no effort could be made either by the king or his officials to intervene, the lid of the den was impressed

---

 The Medes and Persians

The kingdom of Media is first mentioned in Assyrian sources describing the ninth-century campaign of Assyria's Shalmaneser III (858–824 B.C.) into the land of the Medes. Media was apparently situated in the area of modern west-central Iran and flourished for the next two centuries, according to the same Assyrian sources. In the Assyrian texts the Medes are pictured in these centuries as comprised of a group of small autonomous tribes. The Greek historian Herodotus (484–425 B.C.) gives a legendary account of a unification of Median tribes occurring during the seventh century B.C. By the late seventh century the unified Median tribes, led by Cyaxares (around 625–585 B.C.) were allied with the Chaldeans against Assyria. The united Medes thus contributed to the downfall of the Assyrian capital of Nineveh in 612 B.C.

The Median kingdom continued under Astyages (about 585–550 B.C.), successor of Cyaxares, until the middle of the sixth century B.C. In 550 B.C., Cyrus of Persia successfully united the Persian and Median tribes, though it is uncertain whether the Medes were conquered or were peacefully incorporated into the empire of Cyrus. The ruler was apparently related to the royal house of both Media and Persia. Thus the union of the two nations may have been accomplished as a result of the legal claim of Cyrus to the throne. Media continued to be geographically distinct even under Persian government, and the Medes were second only to the Persians in the empire. So even after Persian absorbed Media in 550 B.C., the Medes continued to be recognized as a distinct people. This situation is evident in the recurring phrase "the law of the Medes and Persians" (Dan. 6:8, 12, 15).

with the royal seal and with the seals of the king's lords. The lid of the den could not be removed without breaking the seals.

6:21, 22 Though this is a standard way of greeting a king (see 2:4; 3:9; 5:10; 6:6), it is ironic here because Daniel, who has just been made alive by the God whom even Darius confesses as "the living God" (v. 20), blesses the king with the wish that he should **live forever.** That is literally possible for the king, of course, only if he comes to know Daniel's God who is the source of life.

6:23 because he believed in his God: Daniel's faithfulness got him into trouble (v. 10); his faith got him out of it (see Heb. 11:33).

6:24, 25 children ... wives: The families of the wicked conspirators were destroyed because the Persians, like the Hebrews and other Semites, considered guilt a collective responsibility, especially in families.

6:26, 27 I make a decree: Darius's original 30-day decree (vv. 6–9) had probably expired.

6:28 Daniel prospered throughout **the reign of Darius** and **in the reign of Cyrus.** Gubaru, or Darius, served Cyrus for about one year (539–538 B.C.), after which Cyrus appointed his son Cambyses as vice-regent over Babylon. Cyrus himself continued as king until 530 B.C.

7:1 the first year of Belshazzar: Chapter 5 records Belshazzar's death, indicating that the Book of Daniel is not arranged chronologically. The date of Belshazzar's first year cannot be stated precisely. However, since Nabonidus appears to have spent at least ten years in Arabia and since Belshazzar reigned for Nabonidus in Babylon during that time, a date of 550 B.C. for Belshazzar's first year cannot be far off. This date coincides with the inauguration of the Medo-Persian Empire under Cyrus, an occasion that may have prompted Daniel's vision.

7:2 Four winds seems to refer to winds from every direction, covering the whole earth. **The Great Sea** is probably a reference to the Mediterranean Sea (see Josh. 15:12; 23:4; Ezek. 47:10, 19), here used figuratively of the nations of the world (see Is. 57:20; Rev. 17:15).

7:3 The **beasts** represent kings (v. 17) or kingdoms (vv. 18, 23).

7:4 lion ... eagle's wings: It is commonly recognized that these two animals are the king of the beasts and the king of the birds respectively, a fitting description of Nebuchadnezzar and the Babylonian Empire (see Jer. 49:19, 22). There has been almost universal agreement from the early centuries until today that this beast represents Babylon. It is also agreed that the vision of ch. 7 and that of ch. 2 speak of the same four kingdoms. **Plucked off** is a reference to Nebuchadnezzar's humiliation (4:28–33).

7:5 If the lion with eagle's wings represents Babylon (v. 4), the **bear**—in line with Nebuchadnezzar's first dream—represents Babylon's successor, the Medo-Persian Empire (2:38, 39). **Raised up on one side** suggests that the Persians were greater and more powerful than the Medes. The **three ribs** represent the three kingdoms which the Medo-Persians devoured—Babylon, Lydia, and Egypt.

7:6 If the second beast of Daniel's dream represents the Medo-Persian Empire (v. 5), the **leopard** represents Greece (2:39). **Four** symbolizes universality (see "four winds," v. 2); **wings** are synonymous with speed. The Greeks under the leadership of Alexander the Great rapidly conquered the known world. **Four heads** describes "heads" of government. After Alexander's death, his empire was divided among his generals into four different parts (8:8, 22)—Macedonia, Egypt, Syria, and Thrace.

7:7 The **fourth beast** did not look like any known animal. Since this beast follows Greece (v. 6), it may represent Rome (2:40).

7:8 The **horns** here represent rulers. Even though the **little one** begins small, it would become the greatest of all (v. 20).

7:9 Ancient of Days is a reference to God the Father as certified by the submission of "the One like the Son of Man" to Him (vv. 13, 14) and His role in judgment (v. 22). **Fiery flame** symbolizes judgment. **Its wheels** refers to the chariot in which God rides to battle to exercise His sovereignty and to appear as Judge (see Ezek. 1:15–21; 10:1–22).

7:10 Ten thousand times ten thousand: The reference here is to innumerable servants. **The books** record the names and deeds of those who will be judged (see Rev. 20:12).

7:11 The horn here is the same as the one in v. 8. **the burning flame:** The idea that the fate of the wicked is fiery destruction is apparent in the Old Testament (see Gen. 19:24; Is. 66:24; Mal. 4:1, 3), but reaches its fullest expression in the New Testament teaching about hell (see Matt. 5:22, 29, 30; 10:28; 2 Pet. 2:4).

7:12 The rest of the beasts is a reference to Babylon, Medo-Persia, and Greece—the three beasts of vv. 3–6. **they had their dominion taken away:** Though these nations passed away, their "dominion" was inherited by their respective successors. **A season and a time** is an idiom for an indefinite period.

7:13 Son of Man is Semitic for "human being." Daniel saw **One like** the "Son of Man," indicating that He is not a man in the strict sense, but rather the perfect representation of humanity. Jewish and Christian expositors have identified this individual as the Messiah. Jesus Himself used this name to emphasize His humanity as the incarnate Son of God. **Coming with ... clouds:** John uses the same expression to speak of Jesus coming in judgment (see Rev. 1:7; see also Matt. 24:30).

7:14, 15 Him refers to the Son of Man (v. 13), who will reign over all things as the regent of Almighty God. In contrast to the vanishing nature of the previous empires, **His dominion is ... everlasting.**

7:16 One of those who stood by refers to an angel standing by the throne of God (v. 10).

7:17 These **kings** represent kingdoms (8:21). Thus each beast represents both a king and a kingdom.

7:18–20 saints of the Most High: Saints means "holy ones," a term that can refer either to angels (see Job 15:15; Ps. 89:5, 7; Zech. 14:5) or to redeemed men and women (see Ps. 16:3; 30:4; 31:23; 37:28; Prov. 2:8; Rom. 1:7; 12:13; Rev. 5:8). The kingdom received and forever possessed by the saints must be the same as the dominion of the Son of Man, which is also everlasting (v. 14). The Son of Man thus rules through His saints.

7:21–23 Daniel's vision reveals the hostility waged by the little horn **against the saints.**

The little horn's militaristic character is seen also in 11:38, 39 and particularly in Rev. 13:1–10. There, in the guise of a beast, this blasphemous enemy of the saints prevails for 42 months. The connection between Daniel's "little horn" and John's "beast from the sea" is unmistakable.

7:24, 25 There are three common interpretations as to the **ten kings who shall arise from this kingdom:** (1) The fourth beast is Greece and the ten horns are ten divisions of the Grecian Empire. (2) The fourth beast is Rome and the ten horns are the fragments of the Roman Empire. (3) The fourth beast is a revived Roman Empire and the ten kings are members of a future realm. **Another** refers to the little horn of v. 8 (see also vv. 20, 21). This king will **subdue three** others, blaspheme God (see 11:36; 2 Thess. 2:4; Rev. 13:5, 6), **persecute the saints** (see v. 21; Rev. 13:7), attempt **to change times and law,** and dominate the **saints** for a limited time. **time and times and half a time:** Time can refer to a year, times to two years, and half a time to one half of a year, for a total of three and one-half years. Some suggest that the expression does not indicate a specific number of years but instead a period of time that God in His mercy would shorten.

7:26 The **dominion** of the little horn will come to a violent end when he submits to the **court** of God (v. 10).

7:27, 28 the kingdom ... to the people, the saints: The kingdom of God, governed by His saints, will exercise rule over all the earth.

8:1 After writing in Aramaic from 2:4—7:28, Daniel returns to writing in Hebrew.

8:2 Shushan was about 230 miles east of Babylon. **Ulai** was an artificial canal located a few miles from Shushan.

8:3 The **ram** represents Medo-Persia (v. 20). The **two horns** symbolize the people of Media and the people of Persia.

8:4 Cyrus and his successors conquered **westward** including Babylon, Syria, and Asia Minor, **northward** including Armenia and the Caspian Sea region, and **southward** including Egypt and Ethiopia.

8:5, 6 The **goat** represents Greece (v. 21). The **notable horn** symbolizes Alexander the

Great (v. 21), who launched his attack against Persia in 334 B.C. By 332 B.C. he had essentially subdued the Persian Empire. **without touching the ground:** Alexander's conquest was so rapid that it seemed as if he flew across the earth.

8:7 The Persian forces outnumbered the Greeks. But in two decisive battles, the Medo-Persian Empire collapsed.

8:8 the large horn was broken: Alexander the Great died at the height of his career, before he was 33 years old. **four notable ones:** After Alexander's death, four of his generals carved up the Macedonian Empire. Antigonus ruled from northern Syria to central Asia; Cassander ruled over Macedonia; Ptolemy ruled in Egypt and southern Syria, including Palestine; Lysimachus ruled over Thrace.

8:9 The **little horn** here is not the same as the little horn of ch. 7. The former horn comes out of the fourth beast, Rome, whereas this one comes out of Greece. The *little horn* here refers to Antiochus Epiphanes, the eighth king of the Syrian dynasty who reigned from 175 to 164 B.C. Thus, this prophecy skips from 301 B.C., the time of the division of Alexander's empire, to 175 B.C., when Antiochus became king.

8:10 The host of heaven and **the stars** refer to God's people (see 12:3; Gen. 15:5). **Cast down some** describes Antiochus's conquest.

8:11 The Prince of the host refers to God Himself. The little horn, like Lucifer (see Is. 14:12), aspires to be like God. **sanctuary ... cast down:** Antiochus desecrated the house of God by erecting a statue of Zeus on the bronze altar.

8:12 Truth is a reference to the Mosaic Law.

8:13 A holy one and **another holy one** refer to angels (4:13, 23).

8:14, 15 Two thousand three hundred days refers to the time between Antiochus's pollution of the temple and the cleansing of it by the Maccabees.

8:16 This is the first mention of the messenger **Gabriel** in the Bible. The angel is mentioned three other times in Scripture (see 9:21; Luke 1:19, 26).

8:17, 18 The time of the end is a reference to a time that may already be underway (see

1 John 2:18) in some respects, but will not find its fulfillment until the Second Coming of Christ (see Matt. 24:14).

8:19 The indignation is that of the Lord against those who have rebelled against His dominion. **The end** (see "the time of the end" in v. 17) indicates that this judgment is against all those in rebellion against God, especially those living at the time just before the coming of Christ.

8:20 The two horns represent the two countries of **Media and Persia.** It is significant that the two are regarded as one empire, represented by **the ram.**

8:21 The first king of Greece was Alexander the Great.

8:22 not with its power: None of Alexander's four generals ruled with the strength of Alexander (v. 8).

8:23 When the transgressors have reached their fullness means when the sinful actions of the Jews have reached the point where God cannot permit them to go any further without bringing punishment (see Gen. 15:16; Matt. 23:32; 1 Thess. 2:16). **A king** refers to Antiochus IV Epiphanes, the king of Syria who made his capital at Antioch.

8:24 Not by his own power indicates that Antiochus would be energized by Satan, as will the Antichrist (see 2 Thess. 2:9).

8:25 Without human means: Antiochus died without human intervention. According to the apocryphal Book of Second Maccabees, Antiochus died of a painful disease.

8:26 seal up the vision: Most documents of Daniel's time were written on scrolls that could be rolled up and sealed to protect their contents. This document pertained to a time **many days in the future.**

8:27 I ... fainted and was sick: Daniel suffered a severe emotional reaction to the vision of ch. 8, apparently even greater than the reaction he had experienced after his first vision (7:15, 28).

9:1 The first year of Darius was 539 B.C., the year he was appointed by Cyrus as administrator of Babylon.

9:2, 3 The books refers to Scripture, specifically the Book of Jeremiah, which states (Jer. 25:11, 12; 29:10–14) that the desolation of

Jerusalem would be fulfilled in seventy years. Daniel's own captivity occurred in 605 B.C. It was now 538 B.C., some sixty-seven years after the conquest. The period of captivity was almost over.

9:4–14 This is a prayer of repentance for Israel's past sinfulness, but it is also a prayer of confidence because God was about to overthrow the Babylonians and allow the Jews to return to their homeland to rebuild it. The seventy years of captivity were almost up, and glorious things lay ahead. **the curse and the oath:** Covenant documents typically contained statements about the penalties for covenant violation. In **the Law of Moses,** such sanctions are found particularly in Lev. 26:3–45; Deut. 27; 28. In both passages the most feared and devastating curse of all—deportation from the land of promise—is emphasized (see Lev. 26:33–39; Deut. 28:36–68). Daniel pointed out that the curse had come to pass.

9:15, 16 brought Your people out of the land of Egypt: Daniel reflected on the greatest redemptive event of Israel's history, the exodus from Egypt, and prayed that God would repeat what He had done long ago.

9:17 Your sanctuary is a reference to Solomon's temple, which had lain in ruins since 586 B.C.

9:18 Your great mercies: It is important to note that the only basis for Daniel's appeal was the grace of God.

9:19 Do not delay: These words must be understood in light of Daniel's reference to the seventy years (v. 2). Daniel knew that all of God's promises had not come to pass, nor had the blessings been conferred on the regathered and restored people (see Lev. 26:40–45; Deut. 4:29–31).

9:20–23 while I was speaking: The angel was sent at the beginning of Daniel's prayer (v. 23). **The man Gabriel** is not a denial of Gabriel's angelic nature; the title simply serves to identify Gabriel with the vision of 8:15, 16. **evening offering:** Because the temple was in ruins, regular daily sacrifices were impossible. Nevertheless, Daniel observed the ritual of worship by praying at the hour of the evening sacrifice.

9:24 Seventy weeks may also be translated *seventy sevens.* Many scholars agree that the "sevens" are years, as the seventy years of captivity addressed in v. 2 implies. Leviticus 25:8 speaks of "seven sabbaths of years"; Lev. 26:18, 21 implies that Israel's punishment would be multiplied sevenfold. Therefore, a seventy "week" exile would be expected to last for seven times seventy years. Second Chronicles 36:21 suggests that the captivity was to last long enough to make up for seventy omissions of the sabbatical year, which occurred every seven years. This would amount to 490 years before God's people would experience perfect reconciliation with their God. There are many different interpretations of how these years account for the eras of world history before the Second Coming of the Messiah. Some interpreters have suggested that the use of the number seven in this verse is symbolic of completeness—that is, the completion of all of human history.

9:25 The command to restore and build Jerusalem may be a reference to (1) the decree of Cyrus in Ezra 1, (2) the decree of Darius in Ezra 6, (3) the decree of Artaxerxes in Ezra 7, or (4) the decree of Artaxerxes in Neh. 2.

9:26 One commonly held interpretation maintains that **the sixty-two weeks** can be added to the seven weeks of v. 25, resulting in a total of sixty-nine weeks, or 483 years. If these years are added to the date of the decree of Artaxerxes in Neh. 2, 445 B.C., with an adjustment to allow for the use of a 360-day year, the end of the sixty-nine weeks coincides with the date of the crucifixion of Jesus. **Messiah shall be cut off** may be a reference to the crucifixion of Jesus Christ. The fact that Jesus Christ died **not for Himself** but for the sins of the world may support the view that the Messiah in this verse refers to Jesus Himself. **The prince who is to come** may be a reference to the Antichrist (v. 27).

9:27 He may be a reference to the Antichrist, who will **confirm a covenant** with Israel. **In the middle of the week**—that is, three and one-half years later—he will break the covenant. **abominations ... desolate:** Antiochus committed an abomination of desolation by setting up an altar to the god Zeus in the temple in Jerusalem (11:31). The Antichrist will also commit an abomination of desolation against the living God (see Matt. 24:15). **the consummation … is poured out on the desolate:** The fact that this abomination does not occur **until** the consummation suggests that this verse is describing the abomination of the Antichrist and not that of Antiochus.

10:1 The third year of Cyrus's rule over Babylon was 536 B.C.

10:2, 3 Daniel **was mourning** because he wanted to understand the vision (v. 12). **Three full weeks** refers to Daniel's observance of the Passover and the Feast of Unleavened Bread, which took place during the first month of the year (see Ex. 12:1–20).

10:4 The twenty-fourth day of the first month occurs three days after the Unleavened Bread festival (v. 2).

10:5 A certain man is either an appearance of the preincarnate Christ or an angel. The description that follows suggests that this individual is Christ (v. 6).

10:6, 7 The description of the man here is very much like Ezekiel's description of the glory of God (see Ezek. 1:4–28) and John's description of the triumphant, risen Christ (see Rev. 1:9–20).

10:8–10 Vigor suggests majesty, splendor, or beauty. **turned to frailty … no strength:** Humans are weak and frail in the presence of God.

10:11, 12 greatly beloved: God loves everyone (see John 3:16); yet some people, because of their special relationship to God, are objects of unusual divine love (see 1 Sam. 13:14; John 13:23; 14:21, 23; Acts 13:22).

10:13 The prince of the kingdom of Persia cannot be a human ruler because the conflict referred to here is in the spiritual, heavenly realm, as the allusion to **Michael** makes clear. The prince, therefore, must be understood as a satanic figure who was to supervise the affairs of Persia, inspiring its religious, social, and political structures to works of evil. The "man" here says he was detained for **twenty-one days,** which equals the time of Daniel's mourning and fasting (vv. 2, 3). The wicked prince of Persia sought to detain the "man" so

that Daniel would be prevented from hearing more of God's revelation (vv. 12, 14). **Michael** seems to be one of the most powerful angels. He is mentioned three times in the Old Testament, all in Daniel (see also v. 21; 12:1), and twice in the New Testament (see Jude 9; Rev. 12:7).

10:14, 15 latter days: This expression is used throughout the books of prophecy to refer to the future. The messenger here is referring to the revelation of ch. 11.

10:16, 17 One having the likeness of the sons of men may refer to the preincarnate Christ (v. 5) or to the angel of vv. 10–15.

10:18, 19 For the third time in this chapter Daniel is supernaturally **strengthened** by one who **touched** him (see also vv. 10, 16). The first touch enabled him to arise from the ground, the second to speak, and the third to carry on a conversation.

10:20 Just as Persia was under the ultimate dominion of an evil spirit from Satan (vv. 13, 14), so also was Greece. Once the **prince of Persia** was overcome, the messenger would enter into conflict with the **prince of Greece.** The succession of world powers follows the pattern of Daniel's second vision (8:20–22).

10:21 your prince: God chose Michael the archangel to be a prince in His kingdom on earth.

11:1 the first year of Darius: This is the same year as that of the revelation of the seventy weeks, 539 B.C. (9:1). At the beginning of the Persian administration, the divine messenger **stood up to confirm and strengthen** Darius. This suggests that though the kingdoms of the world are under demonic control, their human rulers can be delivered from that control and used for a higher purpose by God as He sees fit.

11:2 three more kings will arise in Persia, and the fourth … against the realm of Greece: Darius (under Cyrus) was followed by Cambyses (530–522 B.C.); Gaumata (522 B.C.); Darius I (522–486 B.C.); and Xerxes (486–465 B.C.), who was the richest king of all because of his conquest and severe taxation.

11:3 The scene shifts to Greece (v. 2). The **mighty king** is Alexander the Great (v. 4).

11:4 The kingdom of Alexander was **divided** into **four** parts (8:22), **but not among his posterity**—that is, his heirs. **Others** refers to those outside Alexander's family. His generals ruled the empire he had conquered (see 8:8, 22).

11:5 Having predicted that there would be four divisions of the Greek kingdom (v. 4), the angel here speaks of two of them, the Syrian kingdom just north of Palestine and the Egyptian kingdom to the south. The first **king of the South**—that is, Egypt—was Ptolemy I Soter (323–285 B.C.). **One of his princes** refers to Seleucus Nicator (311–280 B.C.).

11:6 At the end of some years refers to the time period around 252 B.C. **The daughter** refers to Berenice, the daughter of Ptolemy Philadelphus (285–246 B.C.) of Egypt. **The king of the North** refers to Antiochus II Theos (261–246 B.C.) of Syria.

11:7–9 The **branch of her roots** refers to the brother of Berenice (v. 6), Ptolemy III Euergetes (246–221 B.C.), who conquered **the king of the North,** Seleucus Callinicus (246–226 B.C.) of Syria. Ptolemy III returned **to Egypt** with great booty and outlived Seleucus by six years. Seleucus attempted an attack on Egypt but returned to Syria without accomplishing his purpose.

11:10 The **sons** of Seleucus Callinicus were Seleucus III Ceraunus (227–223 B.C.) and Antiochus III the Great (223–186 B.C.).

11:11, 12 The king of the South, Ptolemy IV Philopator (221–204 B.C.), defeated **the king of the North,** Antiochus III the Great, at Raphia in 217 B.C.

11:13 The king of the North, Antiochus III, assembled a great army and attacked Egypt in 201 B.C.

11:14 Many shall rise up indicates that others like Philip V of Macedonia helped Antiochus fight **against the king of the South,** Ptolemy V Epiphanes (203–181 B.C.) of Egypt. The **violent men of your people** refers to Jews who tried to help Antiochus bring to pass what had been predicted in the vision of ch. 8, but failed.

11:15 The king of the north, Antiochus, defeated the **fortified city** of Sidon in 198 B.C.

11:16 The Glorious Land refers to Israel. The control of Palestine passed from Egypt to Syria.

11:17 Antiochus III's **daughter** Cleopatra was given in marriage to Ptolemy V Epiphanes of Egypt in order to **destroy** or undermine Egypt, but Cleopatra sided with her husband over her father.

11:18, 19 Antiochus III undertook a vigorous campaign into Asia Minor and the Aegean region. **A ruler,** the Roman Lucius Cornelius Scipio, defeated Antiochus. Having lost all that he had gained, Antiochus returned to **his own land,** where he was defeated and killed while trying to plunder a temple.

11:20 arise in his place: Seleucus IV Philopator (187–176 B.C.), Antiochus's son, took his father's place. **The glorious kingdom** refers to Israel. **within a few days:** Antiochus ruled for 37 years; Seleucus ruled for only 11 years.

11:21 A vile person refers to Antiochus IV Epiphanes (175–164 B.C.), who seized the throne through treachery.

11:22 They shall be swept away is probably a reference to the Egyptians. **The prince of the covenant** refers to Onias III, the high priest in Jerusalem who bore that title.

11:23, 24 He refers to Antiochus IV Epiphanes (v. 21). **shall disperse:** Antiochus took from the rich and gave to the poor.

11:25, 26 The king of the South at this time was Ptolemy Philometor (181–145 B.C.) of Egypt. **those who eat … his delicacies:** The trusted counselors of Ptolemy Philometor who ate at his table betrayed him.

11:27 Both … bent on evil: Both Antiochus and Ptolemy resorted to deceit and betrayal in working out truce arrangements.

11:28 The holy covenant refers to Israel. **do damage:** On his way back to Syria, Antiochus looted the temple in Jerusalem and killed many people.

11:29 return and go toward the south: After learning that Ptolemy VI and Ptolemy VII had formed a union against him, Antiochus returned to Egypt in 168 B.C.

11:30 Cyprus here refers to Rome. When the Romans forced Antiochus to depart from Egypt, he unleashed his frustration on **the holy covenant**—that is, Israel (v. 28). **Those who forsake the holy covenant** refers to the apostate Jews (v. 32) who cooperated with Antiochus.

11:31 defile the sanctuary: Antiochus polluted the altar by offering a pig upon it. He declared **the daily sacrifices** and other Mosaic ceremonies illegal and committed an **abomination of desolation** by erecting an image of Zeus in the holy place (9:27; 12:11). Jesus said a similar thing would happen just prior to His return (see Matt. 24:15).

11:32 the people who know their God shall be strong: Mattathias, father of five sons, refused to offer sacrifices in a profane manner and killed the king's agents. He and his sons then fled to the mountains and began the famous Maccabean revolt.

11:33 Many devoted Jews were killed in the Maccabean revolt (see Heb. 11:37, 38).

11:34 As some Jews were killed in the Maccabean revolt, others provided **a little help. Many** joined **by intrigue**—that is, insincerely.

11:35 Some of those of understanding refers to those who understood God's Word and were allowed to go through troubled times so they could be refined and purified.

11:36 the king: Many ancient and modern interpreters have concluded that at this point a new person, the Antichrist, is introduced. This king is distinguished from the king of the North (v. 40); therefore he cannot be Antiochus Epiphanes.

11:37 The king of v. 36 will cast aside **the God of his fathers,** the worship of his ancestors. **The desire of women** is usually taken to be either a female goddess or the desire of every Jewish woman to be the mother of the Messiah.

11:38, 39 god of fortresses: The king of v. 36 will not regard any god except the god of power. **A god which his fathers did not know** is probably a reference to self-worship (see v. 37; 2 Thess. 2:4).

11:40 The backdrop of this verse and the remainder of the chapter is the covenant the king of v. 36 will make with Israel. **The time of the end** refers to the period just before the return of Christ (see Matt. 24:14).

11:41–43 The king of v. 36 will **enter the Glorious Land** of Palestine. Edom, Moab,

and **Ammon,** the traditional enemies of Israel, will not be invaded. The king will then conquer **Egypt,** Libya, and Ethiopia.

11:44 The north here could be a reference to Palestine, a view which seems to be confirmed by v. 45.

11:45 The seas refers to the Mediterranean Sea and the Dead Sea. **The glorious holy mountain** refers to Mount Zion, the site of the temple. The **end** of the king of v. 36 is sealed at Christ's second coming (see Rev. 19:11–21).

12:1 At that time refers to the "time of the end" (11:40), the end of the evil king (11:36) at the Second Coming of Christ (11:45). **A time of trouble, such as never was since there was a nation** refers to the period of tribulation just prior to the coming of Christ. Those who **shall be delivered** are those whose names are **written in the book** of life, God's record of those who have been justified by faith (see Ex. 32:32; Ps. 69:28; Luke 10:20; Rev. 20:12).

12:2 Sleep is a euphemism for death, as the context **in the dust of the earth** illustrates. **Awake** is a reference to resurrection. Though this passage appears to refer to a general resurrection, other passages suggest that there is more than one (see John 5:25). It is not unusual for prophecy in the Old Testament to present events separated by a considerable span of time as if they occurred in immediate relationship to each other (see Is. 61:1, 2). Daniel is simply saying that after the tribulation, **many**—both righteous and wicked—will be raised. This resurrection of many of the righteous seems to be a reference to the resurrection of Israel (see "your people" in v. 1).

12:3 The **wise** not only understand salvation themselves (see 2 Tim. 3:15); they **turn** many others to the way of **righteousness.**

12:4 Knowledge shall increase is a reference to knowledge that pertains to these prophecies.

12:5, 6 As Daniel stood beside the Tigris River, he saw three persons, one on each side of the river and one above the **river.** The **two others** refers to two angels, different from the ones Daniel had already seen. **The man clothed in linen** may be the preincarnate

Christ (10:6). **How long** refers to the duration of the trials. Daniel was not asking when the events would begin.

12:7 A time, times, and half a time, which adds up to three and one-half years (7:25), may refer to the period immediately preceding the Second Coming of Christ (7:27). Others have suggested that this expression does not refer to a specific number of years but instead a period of time that the Lord would shorten because of His mercy.

12:8, 9 Daniel **did not understand** his own revelation (see v. 4).

12:10 Many will be **purified, made white, and refined** (11:35). Suffering will refine the righteous, but the **wicked** will be continue in their evil.

12:11, 12 one thousand two hundred and ninety days: Various interpretations have been suggested for this number of days. One significant interpretation is that these days refer to the middle of a seven-year period of tribulation prior to the coming of Christ. At that time, the Antichrist will abolish the idolatrous sacrifices that he had established (9:27).

12:13 you shall rest, and will arise: Daniel would die and be resurrected.

Hosea

Introduction

The Lord sometimes required His prophets to perform difficult and even humiliating object lessons to complement their messages. At the beginning of Hosea's prophetic ministry, the Lord told him to get married and announced that Hosea's chosen bride would be unfaithful to her marriage vows. Her adultery would illustrate Israel's unfaithfulness to her covenant Lord.

Israel, the northern kingdom, is the primary focus of Hosea's prophecy. He witnessed the reigns of the last six kings of Israel, although he did not name these kings in his prophecies. Hosea accused the nation of being unfaithful to its vows, just as his own adulterous wife had been unfaithful to her vows. By participating in the pagan fertility rites of Baalism, the people violated their covenant with the Lord. The Lord was prepared to bring against Israel the judgments threatened in the covenant (see Deut. 28:15–68). God's purpose, however, was not entirely punitive; He intended these severe judgments to bring the nation to its senses. Hosea proclaimed that the Lord would eventually restore His marriage with His people and again pour His blessings upon them.

Israel's covenant relationship with God is at the heart of Hosea's message. God delivered His people from slavery in Egypt, established them as a nation, and took great delight in them. He looked for a favorable response to His love and obedience to the commandments He had given to regulate the people's worship and daily activities. However, the people were ungrateful, turning to other gods, violating the religious and social standards of God's covenant, and forming alliances with surrounding nations.

The Book of Hosea presents a clear and balanced picture of God. He loves His people and desires an intimate relationship with them. He is jealous of their affections and tolerates no rivals. When they sin, He will discipline them as severely as is necessary. While God's jealousy may seem inappropriate and His discipline may seem harsh, this divine reaction to His people's sin is actually evidence of His love and commitment. He will allow nothing to ruin the relationship He has established. In the end, His devotion and mercy will win out, and His people will give Him the love He fervently desires.

1:1–3 wife of harlotry: Gomer may have been a common prostitute at the time Hosea married her, or perhaps she had participated in a ritual sexual act as part of the Baal cult. However, it is more likely that the descriptive phrase anticipates what Gomer would become following her marriage to Hosea. **children of harlotry:** If Gomer was a prostitute when she married Hosea, this could refer to children that Gomer already had and that Hosea adopted at the time of marriage. A more likely possibility is that the title anticipates children born to a mother whose reputation and escapades would make their lineage suspect. Gomer's marital infidelity is a picture of Israel's idolatry and unfaithfulness to its covenant with God.

1:4 bloodshed of Jezreel: In 841 B.C. Jehu, with God's approval, destroyed the evil dynasty of Omri by slaughtering Jezebel, the sons of Ahab, and the prophets and priests of Baal (see 2 Kin. 9; 10).

1:5 To **break** the enemy's **bow** means to destroy his military strength (see 1 Sam. 2:4; Ps. 46:9; Jer. 49:35).

1:6 Lo-Ruhamah means "Not Loved," foreshadowing the Lord's rejection of Israel.

1:7, 8 Will save them: This prophecy looks ahead to the Lord's deliverance of Jerusalem in 701 B.C., when He would miraculously destroy the Assyrian armies outside the city's walls (see 2 Kin. 19:32–36).

1:9 Lo-Ammi means "Not My People," threatening the termination of the Lord's covenant relationship with His people (see Lev. 26:12).

1:10 The Lord would not reject His people forever. God would fulfill His promise to Abraham and make the Israelites as numerous as the **sand of the sea** (see Gen. 22:17; 32:12).

1:11 One head refers to the messianic king to come (3:5). **Jezreel** means "God Plants," picturing God as sowing seed that would germinate and grow abundantly (2:23).

2:1 brethren ... sisters: God would mercifully restore His covenant relationship with His people, reversing the judgment symbolized by the names Lo-Ruhamah and Lo-Ammi.

2:2 Bring charges: The Lord formally accused Israel of unfaithfulness to the covenant. **Your mother** refers to the sinful nation of Hosea's time, symbolized by Gomer (1:2, 3). **she is not My wife:** This may be a formal announcement of divorce or a realistic confession that the relationship between God and Israel had lost its vitality.

2:3 The Lord warned that He might publicly humiliate His unfaithful wife by stripping her **naked** (see Ezek. 16:35–43). **dry land:** This simile pictures the loss of fertility, an appropriate punishment for a nation that had sought fertility by worshiping another god.

2:4, 5 Her children refers to the Israelites who lived in the land. Though the **mother** (the land) and the children (the inhabitants of the land) are distinct in Hosea's metaphor, both actually refer to the sinful nation. The Lord warned that He might disown the children because they were a reminder of their mother's unfaithfulness.

2:6, 7 chase: This word draws attention to the strong passion the people of Israel felt for Baal. These verses anticipate the Exile, when Israel would be separated from the idols of Baal.

2:8, 9 Since Israel refused to acknowledge the Lord as her source of agricultural prosperity, the Lord would **take back** His blessings and no longer provide for the nation's basic needs.

2:10 uncover her lewdness: The Lord would publicly expose Israel's unfaithfulness through judgment. **in the sight of her lovers:** The Baal idols would be unable to help Israel, proving their unworthiness to be worshiped.

2:11 New Moons were monthly celebrations (see Num. 10:10; 1 Sam. 20:5, 18, 24). Sabbath celebrations were weekly.

2:12 The people of Israel believed that the Baal idols gave them agricultural prosperity in exchange for their worship. **forest ... beasts of the field:** The Lord would break down the nation's defenses and turn them into overgrown thickets inhabited by wild animals.

2:13 The word **earrings** may refer to rings worn in the ear (see Gen. 35:4; Ex. 32:2, 3) or nose (see Gen. 24:47; Is. 3:21; Ezek. 16:12).

2:14 Having separated Israel from her lovers, the Lord would seek to win her back by making romantic overtures and wooing her with tender words of love.

2:15 Valley of Achor, meaning "Valley of Trouble," was a reminder of the sin of Achan and God's discipline of the nation of Israel for his sin (Josh. 7:24–26). This place would be transformed into a **door of hope** when the returning exiles passed through it on their return to the land.

2:16, 17 Israel would call the Lord her **Husband,** not her **Master,** because the latter title might have reminded the people of their former devotion to Baal.

2:18–20 betroth: Betrothal was a binding commitment, the last step before the wedding and consummation. **forever:** The Lord emphasized that the new marriage between Himself and Israel would be permanent. **Lovingkindness** means "devotion, commitment."

2:21–23 The heavens would provide rain for the **earth;** the earth would produce its fruit in turn. Israel is called **Jezreel,** meaning "God Plants," because the Lord would replant Israel in the land.

3:1, 2 To illustrate His intention to redeem Israel, the Lord instructed Hosea to reclaim Gomer, his unfaithful wife. **I bought her:** Gomer had become the property of another man. Hosea's purchase of Gomer symbolized God's great devotion, which moves Him to seek reconciliation even if it means subjecting Himself to humiliation (see Phil. 2:8).

3:3, 4 Gomer's isolation symbolized Israel's exile, when she lost her political independence and could no longer worship as she chose (2:6, 7). **sacred pillar:** These were stone pillars used by the Canaanites in their worship of Baal and other gods (see 2 Kin. 3:2; 10:26, 27; 17:10). An **ephod** was a priestly garment (see Ex. 28); **teraphim** were idols (see 2 Kin. 23:24). Both were apparently used for divination.

3:5 seek: This word highlights the change

that would occur in Israel's attitude (2:7). **David:** This is likely a reference to David's Son, the Messiah (see Is. 11:1–10; Jer. 23:5; 33:15).

4:1 charge: The Hebrew word refers to a formal complaint charging Israel with breaking the covenant. **knowledge:** This word does not refer to intellectual awareness, but to recognition of God's authority as Israel's covenant Lord.

4:2 This accusation mentions five of the Ten Commandments. **Swearing** refers to the misuse of the Lord's name in oaths and curses (see Ex. 20:7).

4:3–6 The failure of Israel's religious leaders, including most of the prophets, would bring about their downfall. **lack of knowledge:** The priests had failed to teach God's law to the people (see Mal. 2:7). As a result, the priests would be the special object of God's judgment.

4:7, 8 their glory: Great honor was attached to the priesthood. However, Israel's sinful priests would forfeit their prestige.

4:9, 10 The Israelites worshiped Baal in order to have good crops and many children, but they still would not have enough to eat, nor would they multiply in number. **Harlotry** refers to religious prostitution associated with Baal worship.

4:11–14 Wine was apparently used in Baal worship, along with divination, sacrifices, and ritual sexual acts. **Their staff** refers to **wooden idols** that Baal worshipers consulted for guidance. **daughters … brides:** Many of Israel's young women had participated in the sexual rites of Baal worship, but **the men** were just as guilty.

4:15, 16 Hosea warned the people of **Judah** not to follow in the sinful footsteps of the northern kingdom **Israel. Beth Aven,** which means "House of Iniquity," is a sarcastic reference to the important religious center Bethel, which means "House of God" (see Amos 5:5).

4:17–19 Ephraim, one of the largest tribes of Israel, is used here to represent the entire northern kingdom. **Let him alone:** These words have a tone of frustration and resignation, suggesting that Israel was hopelessly rebellious.

5:1 Mizpah is probably a reference to Mizpah of Gilead, located in Israelite territory east of the Jordan River. **Tabor:** Mount Tabor was in the northern kingdom, southwest of the Sea of Galilee. **snare … net:** The leaders of Israel, especially the **priests,** had promoted pagan worship at Mizpah and Tabor and in this way led the people to destruction.

5:2 The revolters probably refers to the leaders and priests who had rebelled against God's authority by rejecting His commandments. **Slaughter** may refer literally to acts of violence or to pagan sacrifices.

5:3 not hidden: God's people could not hide their **harlotry,** for it had **defiled** them. According to the Law of Moses, adultery made a person spiritually unclean or *defiled* (see Lev. 18:20, 24; Num. 5:20, 27, 28).

5:4 spirit of harlotry: The people had an uncontrollable desire to worship other gods.

5:5 Israel's arrogant attitude was self-incriminating and self-destructive. **Judah,** the southern kingdom, had followed Israel's moral example and would experience the same consequences.

5:6, 7 Though Israel had rebelled against God, many Israelites still tried to maintain a semblance of outward devotion to Him. They had **dealt treacherously** with God by worshiping other gods and participating in **pagan** fertility rites. **Their heritage,** or "portion," refers to the people's landed property and fields, which God would allow wild animals and invading armies to overrun and **devour** (2:12; 11:6).

5:8, 9 Blow the ram's horn: This act signaled an emergency and mustered the fighting men to defend the land. The towns mentioned here were north of Jerusalem, within or near the borders of Benjamin. The implication is that the enemy army had already swept through the north and was ready to invade Judah.

5:10, 11 Stones were used to mark the boundaries of property. A thief could steal a part of someone's land by moving the **landmark.** The Law warned that altering a boundary in this way would bring a special judgment from God (see Deut. 19:14; 27:17; Prov. 22:28).

5:12 As a **moth** slowly destroys clothing, so the Lord would destroy Israel (see Job 13:28; Is. 50:9; 51:8).

5:13 Both Israel and **Judah** sought protection through alliances with **Assyria,** but the cruel Assyrians were more interested in exploiting God's people politically and economically. **King Jareb** probably refers to Tiglath-Pileser III, with whom both Israel and Judah formed alliances (see 2 Kin. 15:19, 20; 16:7–9).

5:14, 15 Attacking like a ferocious, invincible **lion,** God would scatter His people as judgment for their treachery. But the purpose of the Lord's discipline was to drive the people to **earnestly seek** Him.

6:1 After being **torn** by the divine lion (5:14), the people would come to their senses and seek to renew their allegiance to the Lord.

6:2 two days … the third day: The reference here is to a short time period. When God's people truly repent, God is eager to restore His relationship with them.

6:3 God's restored presence and blessings would be like **the rain** that waters and renews the earth. **latter and former rain:** The *latter* rains of Israel came in the spring and caused the plants to grow. The *former* rains came in the autumn and softened the ground for plowing and sowing.

6:4 Any apparent **faithfulness** that Hosea's generation displayed was short-lived and disappeared as quickly as fog or dew before sunlight.

6:5 words of My mouth: The **prophets** announced God's destructive judgments, which then fell on His unrepentant people. **your judgments are like light that goes forth:** This comparison suggests that God's judgment, like bright sunlight, was obvious to all; or that like a bolt of lightning or a blinding flash of light, it came swiftly.

6:6, 7 Mercy means "loyalty" or "devotion" (4:1). **Knowledge of God** does not refer to mere head knowledge, but to a genuine recognition of God's authority that produces obedience to His commandments.

6:8, 9 Even Ramoth-**Gilead** and **Shechem,** which were cities of refuge where manslayers could find asylum, had been contaminated by bloodshed.

6:10 horrible thing: A related Hebrew word is used in Jer. 29:17 of rotten figs.

6:11 The comparison of God's judgment to a **harvest** indicates that the judgment was

inevitable and implies that it would be thorough in its destruction.

7:1, 2 Hardened sinners typically **do not consider** that God will hold them accountable for their deeds (see Ps. 73:11).

7:3 While kings should promote justice and be appalled by **wickedness** (see Ps. 101), Israel's rulers approved of the people's sin.

7:4–7 The background for these verses is the political turmoil of the northern kingdom. During a 20-year period (752–732 B.C.), four Israelite kings were assassinated (see 2 Kin. 15). The dangerous, uncontrollable perpetrators of these crimes are described here. These conspirators were like a large baker's **oven** that has been heating up for several hours while the bread dough rises. By morning, the **flaming fire** within can be quite destructive.

7:8 Instead of depending on the Lord for political stability, Israel formed alliances with surrounding nations. The destructive outcome of this policy is compared to a **cake** that has been placed over a fire and left **unturned.**

7:9, 10 gray hairs: Israel did not recognize that its power was declining and its freedom was slipping away, like a man who is gradually overtaken by old age.

7:11, 12 Israel was caught between the two superpowers, **Egypt** and **Assyria.** Israel tried to maintain its independence by playing one power against the other, but this vacillating policy was **without sense.** Israel was like a **silly dove,** flitting about from place to place. The Lord would trap them and **chastise** them for their spiritual unsteadiness.

7:13 Like a bird that flies away when frightened (see Jer. 4:25), Israel **fled** from the Lord and His standards.

7:14 God sent a drought that took away Israel's **grain and new wine.** Yet instead of turning to Him in repentance, the idolatrous Israelites demonstrated their devotion to Baal.

7:15 Strengthened their arms probably refers to God's past military help, especially during the reign of Jeroboam II earlier in the eighth century B.C. (see 2 Kin. 14:24, 25).

7:16 A treacherous bow is a bow that is damaged or flawed in its workmanship and does not shoot effectively. Such a bow would be unreliable and therefore worthless to a warrior or hunter. Though the Lord had been faithful to Israel, Israel had not been loyal to Him (see Ps. 78:57). **derision in the land of Egypt:** Note the irony in the fact that one of the nations to whom Israel had looked for help (v. 11) would make fun of Israel when judgment fell.

8:1–3 Just as an **eagle** swiftly swoops down and snatches its prey, so Assyria would invade Israel and take its people into captivity. **we know You:** Though Israel claimed to acknowledge the Lord's authority, it had violated His covenant and rejected the qualities the Lord regarded as **good,** such as justice, loyalty, and humility (see Amos 5:14, 15; Mic. 6:8).

8:4 They set up kings: This phrase alludes to the political turmoil surrounding the throne of the northern kingdom during the eighth century B.C., when four kings were assassinated during a 20-year period (7:4–7).

8:5 If the capital city **Samaria** stands for the northern kingdom in general, the reference here may be to the calf idols made by Jeroboam I (see 1 Kin. 12:28–30).

8:6 A workman made it: Hosea reasoned that anything that is made with human hands cannot possibly be a god.

8:7 This well-known proverb emphasizes the futility of Israel's alliances with false gods and foreign nations. Israel had planted **wind,** symbolizing its moral bankruptcy, and would **reap** a **whirlwind,** symbolizing the coming judgment.

8:8 swallowed up: This image vividly depicts the effects of Israel's foreign alliances, which drained the nation economically.

8:9, 10 like a wild donkey: This comparison draws attention to Israel's free-spirited attitude and desire to live unrestrained by God's standards.

8:11–13 altars for sin: The Lord regarded Israel's religious rituals as sinful because they were not supported by an obedient lifestyle. In fact, Israel treated God's **law** as if it were something **strange** or alien to them.

8:14 True security comes from the Creator, but God's people trusted instead in their own efforts, symbolized by their **temples** and **fortified cities.**

9:1, 2 Because of their association with the harvest, **threshing** floors were the site of agricultural festivals in which Israel offered up sacrifices to Baal. The Lord would take away the **joy** of the harvest by destroying the crops and leaving the threshing floors and **wine** vats empty.

9:3 the LORD's land: Israel had forgotten that their land belonged to the Lord. He alone decided who would or would not live in it (see Lev. 25:23).

9:4, 5 Because they had touched a dead body, **mourners** were ceremonially unclean and contaminated everything that came in contact with them (see Num. 19:14, 15, 22). Living in a foreign land, Israel would be ceremonially defiled and unable to worship the Lord with sacrifices and offerings.

9:6 Memphis: This Egyptian city, known for its great cemeteries, tombs, and pyramids, symbolized the unclean land of exile (Assyria) to which God's people would be taken captive.

9:7 Sinful Israel disdained God's true prophets, regarding them as raving maniacs. The Hebrew word translated **insane** is used in 1 Sam. 21:15 of David when he pretended to be a madman before the Philistine king.

9:8 A **watchman** would look for approaching armies and then warn the people so that they could secure the city and prepare for battle (see Ezek. 33:6). The prophets were like watchmen because they were sent by God to warn the people of judgment and urge them to repent (see Ezek. 3:17).

9:9 As in the days of Gibeah: The reference here is to the rape and murder of a young woman by men of Gibeah, an event that started a civil war (see Judg. 19). Those who witnessed this violent deed remarked that it was the worst crime committed in Israel's history until that time (see Judg. 19:30). However, the sins of Hosea's generation rivaled the infamous Gibeah murder.

9:10 At the beginning of Israel's history, God found great delight in His people. **Grapes in the wilderness** would be a pleasant surprise; **the firstfruits on the fig tree** were an irresistible delicacy (see Is. 28:4; Jer. 24:2; Mic. 7:1). However, Israel had quickly fallen into sin.

9:11 Their glory refers to Ephraim's (Israel's) population, especially its children. **like a bird:** Ephraim's population would dwindle as its women became barren. The punishment would be appropriate because this generation of Israelites, like an earlier generation at Baal Peor, promoted fertility by worshiping Baal (Num. 25).

9:12, 13 Any **children** who were born in Israel would be killed in the coming invasion.

9:14 miscarrying womb: Some women of Israel would be barren (v. 11); others would bear children, only to lose them to the invader's sword (vv. 12, 13). Still others would conceive, but miscarry.

9:15, 16 Gilgal had become a center of idolatry (12:11; see Josh. 5). **hated:** Marriage and divorce provide the background for the language used here. The Lord would reject (hate) His unfaithful wife (see Deut. 22:13; 24:3), **drive** her from His **house** (the land), and remove His protective care (**love**) from her.

9:17 Wanderers may allude to the fate of Cain (see Gen. 4:12), who like Israel (v. 9) was guilty of murder.

10:1 Israel empties his vine refers to God's blessings upon the nation, which contrast with the nation's ingratitude and idolatry.

10:2 divided: This verb refers to Israel's deceitful and hypocritical ways.

10:3 now they say: This verse anticipates the people's response when God's judgment came to destroy Israel's political stability and independence (vv. 7, 15).

10:4 like hemlock in the furrows of a field: This analogy refers to poisonous weeds sprouting up in a field and choking out the crops. In the same way God's judgment would replace His blessings.

10:5, 6 The Assyrians often **carried** off the idols of their defeated foes. **His own counsel** probably refers to Israel's foreign alliances, which would prove disappointing.

10:7 The comparison in this verse depicts Israel's **king** being swept away like a piece of wood in a stream.

10:8 thorn and thistle: This phrase may allude to Gen. 3:18, the only other passage in the Old Testament where this wording occurs.

10:9 Israel had persisted in sin since the day when a young woman was raped and murdered by the men of **Gibeah** (9:9).

10:10 The imagery in this verse depicts the Lord binding His people, like oxen, to a yoke. The figurative yoke is comprised of **their two transgressions,** probably referring to the ancient crime at Gibeah (v. 9) and the collective sin of Hosea's generation. The yoke imagery suggests that the people could not escape the consequences of their deeds.

10:11 pull a plow: Israel's rebellious spirit necessitated harsh treatment, compared here to a farmer binding his calf to the yoke and forcing it to do hard labor. Plowing refers to the discipline that Israel had to acquire through judgment and exile.

10:12 Hosea calls the people to repentance, reminding them that a decision could not be postponed, and that God's blessings could still be restored. In Israel's case, the people had to reestablish social justice—**righteousness**—and loyalty—**mercy**—in the land. **Break up your fallow ground:** Plowing and planting are necessary preliminary steps for growing a crop, which eventually sprouts when the rain falls. In the same way, repentance would set the stage for God's blessing.

10:13 The process of repentance and restored blessing outlined in v. 12 contrasts sharply with reality. Israel had planted the seeds of sin and reaped the inevitable consequences.

10:14 The identity of the conqueror **Shalman** and the location of **Beth Arbel** are uncertain. At any rate, the **battle** referred to seems to have been well known to Hosea's audience because of its extreme violence.

10:15 Israel's defeat would be so swift that the nation's **king** would be **cut off** before the battle had scarcely begun.

11:1 The Lord regarded Israel as His **son** and treated the nation with special care, delivering the people from bondage in **Egypt** (see Matt. 2:15).

11:2 they called them: The plural subject probably refers to God's prophets (see 12:10; Jer. 7:25, 26).

11:3 Like a father teaching his child to walk, the Lord patiently gave the people of Israel direction and cared for them when they experienced pain or injury.

11:4 The image of v. 3 changes as God is compared to a farmer and Israel to a beast of burden. The Lord had placed restraints—**cords** and **bands**—on Israel, but His regulations, rather than being overly strict or harsh, reflected His concern for the people's well-being. God did not drive them mercilessly but provided for their needs, like a farmer who periodically removes **the yoke** from an animal's neck so it can eat.

11:5 Repent is the same Hebrew word translated **return** earlier in the verse. Israel could not remain stationary. It had to return either to the Lord or to bondage. Israel's refusal to return to the Lord would result in a return to slavery.

11:6, 7 Devour: The people of Israel had rejected the gentle Master who fed them and provided for their needs. As a result, they would be devoured by the swords of the invading Assyrians.

11:8, 9 As the Lord contemplated the judgment of Israel, His **sympathy** moved Him to have compassion and stop short of totally annihilating the people. **For I am God, and not man:** When human beings get angry,

---

  Back to Baal

By Hosea's time Baalism had captured the minds and hearts of many Israelites. Baal was the most important deity in the Canaanite pantheon. Baal's followers believed that his blessing guaranteed the continuation of human life and the preservation of social order. As a fertility deity, Baal was the provider of children, a prized possession in the culture of the ancient Middle East. As the god of the storm, Baal brought the rains and made the crops grow. Baal's devotees trusted that with the elements of the storm at his disposal, he could defeat the enemies of his people. As the king of the divine realm under the ultimate authority of the high god El, Baal overcame the powerful and terrifying deities Yamm, the god of the chaotic sea, and Mot, the god of death and the underworld.

Recognizing the threat that Baalism posed for His people, the Lord actively opposed this false religious system from the beginning of Israel's history. He affirmed that He is the only living God (Ex. 15:11; Deut. 33:26; 1 Sam. 2:2) and Israel's rightful king (Ex. 15:18; 20:2–6). The Lord revealed His sovereignty over the elements of the storm (Ex. 9:23, 24; 19:16, 18; Deut. 33:26; 1 Sam. 7:10; 12:17, 18; 1 Kin. 17:1; 18:1, 45), demonstrated His authority over the chaotic sea (Ex. 15:8, 10) and the realm of death (Ex. 15:12; 1 Sam. 2:6; 1 Kin. 17:17–23), and proved that He alone could provide children to the infertile (1 Sam. 2:5). This attack on Baalism climaxed at Mount Carmel, where the Lord hurled a fiery lightning bolt down from heaven (1 Kin. 18:38, 39) to demonstrate beyond the shadow of a doubt that He is the living God. In contrast, Baal's prophets with their frenzied mourning rites could not provoke any response (1 Kin. 18:26–29). When Jehu later purged the kingdom of Baalism (2 Kin. 10:18–28), the Lord's victory seemed complete. However, less than a century later, Baalism had resurfaced as the religion of the people, forcing the Lord to confront Israel through Hosea the prophet.

How are we to explain Baalism's success? The Lord demanded obedience to strict moral and ethical standards as a basis for blessing. In stark contrast, Baalism appealed to the sensual nature. Baal's favor was gained through sympathetic magic in the form of ritual prostitution. Through these rites, young men and women supposedly could gain Baal's favor and ensure their ability to produce and bear children (4:12–14). Because of Baalism's attractions to the base side of human nature, it persisted in Israel. It promised an easy and even enjoyable road to prosperity, while God's way, the way of true life, demanded selflessness.

they are often incapable of tempering their anger with compassion, but God's emotions operate in perfect balance.

11:10, 11 In the coming judgment, God would tear Israel like a lion (5:14); in the future, God's lionlike **roar** would summon His people to return from exile. In the past, the people of Israel had flown back and forth between the nations like a dove (7:11); in the future, the people would speed back to their homeland **like a bird.**

11:12 Ephraim has encircled Me: The northern kingdom had surrounded God as if He were under siege.

12:1 The prophet focuses on the nation's social injustice and foreign alliances. Israel's wicked behavior would lead nowhere. **Oil** may have been used in a ritual ratifying a treaty or given as a sign of loyalty.

12:2 according to his ways: God judges people and nations according to their deeds.

12:3, 4 Hosea draws a lesson from the life of Jacob, the father of the nation. Jacob's greedy, self-reliant, and deceitful character was evident from birth when he grabbed **the heel** of **his brother** Esau (see Gen. 25:26). The climactic event in Jacob's spiritual growth was his wrestling match with God the night before he was reunited with his brother. Jacob acknowledged his dependence on God, begged for divine favor, and received a blessing (see Gen. 32:24–30). **the Angel:** The Genesis account refers to Jacob's foe as "a Man," but then indicates that Jacob wrestled with God Himself (see Gen. 32:28, 30). Since vv. 4, 5 seem to place **God** and the Angel in parallel, some understand the Angel of the Lord to be in view here.

12:5, 6 Just as Jacob had come to his senses and recognized his dependence on God, so Israel was to repent (**return**), reestablish justice in society, and depend (**wait**) on the Lord.

12:7, 8 The word **Canaanite** also means "merchant." Here the word may allude to Israel's dishonest economic activities. **Deceitful scales:** In violation of the Old Testament law (see Lev. 19:36), dishonest merchants sometimes rigged their scales so that they could give buyers less than what the buyers thought they were purchasing (see Prov. 11:1; 16:11; 20:23; Amos 8:5; Mic. 6:11).

12:9–11 The Lord had given Israel direction **by the prophets,** but the people had rejected the message. To teach Israel dependence, God would drive them from their homes and send them into exile. This would be comparable to dwelling **in tents,** as the people did during **the appointed Feast** of Tabernacles that commemorated the wilderness wandering (see Lev. 23:33–43).

12:12–14 God had always protected His people. He protected Jacob when he had to flee for his life to a foreign land. He used Moses to bring **Israel out of Egypt** and preserve the people on their way to the Promised Land. Israel's ingratitude, made evident by its sin, angered the Lord and made judgment inevitable.

13:1 The tribe of Ephraim had gained a prominent position in the northern kingdom and could strike fear into the hearts of the other tribes.

13:2 Kiss the calves refers to the idolatrous practice of kissing images as a sign of homage (see 1 Kin. 19:18).

13:3 God's judgment would sweep Ephraim away quickly, just as the sun dispels fog and dries up the **dew,** or as the wind blows away **chaff** and **smoke.**

13:4, 5 The Lord reminded Israel of who He is, what He had accomplished for His people, and what He expected from them. Because He alone was Israel's **God** and **savior,** the Lord expected the people's undivided loyalty. **know ... knew:** The repetition of the verb "to know" correlates God's demands with His grace. Because He *knew* (cared for) Israel in the wilderness, He had every right to expect them to *know* (be loyal to) Him.

13:6–9 God provided for Israel's needs and richly blessed the people, like a shepherd leading his flock to lush pasture lands. In return, Israel **forgot** the Lord. The Lord's relationship with Israel would change drastically from caring Shepherd to ravaging Predator. Ironically and tragically, Israel's rebellion had turned its Helper into a Destroyer.

13:10, 11 These verses recall how Israel demanded from Samuel a king like those of the nations around them (see 1 Sam. 8). Though offended by the people's request, which implied their rejection of divine authority (see 1 Sam. 8:7), the Lord granted their wish. Israel's king could not protect the people from divine judgment; in fact, he himself would be swept away.

13:12 bound up ... stored up: God had kept a careful record of Israel's sins, to be revealed as evidence of guilt in the day of judgment.

13:13, 14 This metaphor of childbirth illustrates Israel's spiritual insensitivity. When the crucial time of judgment arrived, Israel would respond unwisely, resulting in death. The nation's failure to repent is compared to a baby that is not positioned properly during labor and jeopardizes the life of both mother and child.

13:15, 16 Israel was like a fruitful, well-watered plant, but God's judgment would come like a scorching **east wind** and bring drought. **He shall plunder:** The reality behind the imagery of the wind is the Assyrian army, which would plunder Israel's riches and kill the people.

14:1–3 The final section of Hosea's prophecy begins with a call to repentance that includes a model prayer. The people of Israel were to pray for God's gracious forgiveness and renew their allegiance to Him by renouncing foreign alliances, their own military strength, and artificial **gods.**

14:4–8 The Lord anticipates a time when He would restore repentant Israel. The Lord's renewed blessing is compared to **dew.** Revived Israel is compared to a beautiful **lily,** a deep-rooted and aromatic cedar of **Lebanon,** an attractive **olive tree,** and a fruitful **vine.** The Lord Himself would be like a **green cypress tree** that provides protective shade.

14:9 The book concludes with advice for those who read Hosea's prophecy. God's **ways,** His demands and principles, are completely true. The wise person will choose to obey them, but the foolish person will ignore them and consequently **stumble** into judgment.

Joel

Introduction

Natural disasters—from rising flood waters to violent earthquakes—provoke fear and dread. With all their ingenuity, people still cannot control these powerful and destructive forces. They can only watch in awe. Joel begins his book with a description of such a natural disaster—a plague of ravenous locusts. The destructiveness of this plague becomes a vivid warning of the power of God's coming judgment.

The author of the book is Joel, the son of Pethuel (1:1) Very little is known about the author's life or circumstances. His name means "The Lord Is God," suggesting that he was reared in a home where God was honored. The references to Zion, Judah, and Jerusalem (2:15, 23, 32; 3:1) indicate that the prophet lived and prophesied in Judah and Jerusalem. His frequent references to the work of priests in the temple (1:9, 13, 14; 2:17) lead some to conclude that he was a priest. But Joel also displays considerable interest in agriculture in all of its forms. As a prophet of the Lord he could have been knowledgeable about the temple in Jerusalem without having been a priest.

Scholars have offered various dates for the writing of the Book of Joel, from early preexilic times to as late as 350 B.C. Some believe that internal evidence in the Book of Joel indicates that the book was written during the reign of Joash king of Judah (835–796 B.C.), and in the time of the high priest Jehoiada. Others believe that the Book of Joel is so close in tone and idea to the Book of Zephaniah that it is likely that the two prophets were contemporaries. Since Zephaniah's book dates from around 627 B.C., a number of scholars assign a date of about 600 B.C. for the Book of Joel.

Joel's prophecy had two purposes. First, Joel wrote to call the nation to repentance (2:12) on the basis of its experience of the recent locust plague. The recent disaster was only a token of a more devastating judgment to come. Yet that judgment could be averted by sincere and humble repentance (2:13, 14). In this, Joel shares a common message with other prophets. In the light of impending judgment, there is always a message of hope for those who will return in faith to God. Second, the prophecy was intended to comfort the godly with promises of future salvation and blessing (2:28–32; 3:18–21). Should the national disaster occur, Joel offered hope to the true believers that all was not over. God would keep His promise; the Savior would one day reign.

1:1 The word of the LORD ... came attests to the divine origin of the prophet's message. **Joel** means "The Lord Is God."

1:2, 3 Has anything like this happened: The calamity of recent days was unprecedented in the memory of the people.

1:4 Many interpreters have viewed this **locust** swarm as foreign armies that attacked Judah in successive waves—Assyria, Babylon, Greece, and Rome. Yet literal locust plagues were one of the judgments promised if the people disobeyed God and broke their covenant with Him (see Deut. 28:38, 39, 42). Further, Joel's description of the damage done by the locusts compares with eyewitness reports. The impression given is one of overwhelming devastation.

1:5 Awake, you drunkards: The vineyards had been destroyed, and the wine had been lost.

1:6 Nation may refer to a literal or figurative swarm of locusts. They came in such numbers that they were like a vast army.

1:7 Branches of trees stripped of bark by the rasping teeth of the locusts were left splintered and ghostly **white.**

1:8 The image here is of a young bride widowed on her wedding day. **Sackcloth** was worn by those in mourning in ancient Israel.

1:9 The drink offering refers to the wine offerings that accompanied the priests' morning and evening sacrifices (see Ex. 29:38–41). The devastation of the locust meant that no sacrifice could be offered.

1:10 The **land** is personified as mourning because its three principle crops—grain, grapes, and olives—had been destroyed (see Deut. 7:13; Ps. 104:15).

1:11, 12 The people had anticipated the joy of harvest, but because of the disaster of the locust plague, their **joy has withered away.**

1:13–15 The day of the LORD refers to a time

of judgment and deliverance. Joel views the locust plague as a contemporary day of judgment that was serving as a token or forewarning of an even greater, future "day of the Lord."

1:16 Is not the food cut off ... Joy and gladness: With the sudden loss of food, there was also a loss of joy at harvest (see Is. 9:3).

1:17 The seed shrivels indicates further devastation in the land and an inability to replant the following year.

1:18–20 Not only did the people of Judah suffer from the drought, so did the **animals,**

cattle, and **flocks.** Joel depicts the animals poetically as joining in the lament, groaning in their hunger and distress (see Rom. 8:22). **I cry out:** The prophet adds his own voice to the bellowing of beasts, the wailing of drunkards, and the mourning of priests. He was part of the suffering community, not an outsider looking on from a distance.

2:1 The trumpet, or ram's horn, was used in ancient times to signal danger or warn of a military attack (see Jer. 6:17; Amos 3:6). God demonstrated His grace by warning His people beforehand and providing opportunity for

---

IN DEPTH | **The Day of the Lord**

One of the central themes of the Book of Joel is "the day of the Lord" (1:15; 2:1). This language describes a period of time in which God "comes down" in a dramatic way to bring wrath and judgment on the wicked and salvation to the righteous. God is Lord of time. There is no period that is not "the day of the Lord" in a general sense. But at times God enters the space-time arena to assert in bold, dramatic ways that He is in control.

The day of the Lord is a major theme of OT prophecy. Thirteen of the sixteen prophets address this subject. The concept of the day of the Lord probably originated with the conquest of Canaan—a conquest that was in fact the Lord's war (Deut. 1:30; 3:22; Josh. 5:13–15; 6:2); that is, a day of judgment for the wicked Canaanites (Lev. 18:25; Deut. 9:4, 5).

The day of the Lord is not an isolated phenomenon or a single event in human history. Periods in Israel's early history and latter history, the coming of Jesus, and His second advent are all called "the day of the Lord" in Scripture. The predictions of a coming day of the Lord can be fulfilled in a number of different events. The invasion of locusts in the historic events of the life of Joel was the day of the Lord (ch. 2). But the day of wrath and deliverance that soon fell on Judah in the Babylonian invasion was also the day of the Lord.

While most references speak about future events, five biblical texts describe the day of the Lord in terms of past judgments (Is. 22:1–14; Jer. 46:2–12; Lam. 1:1—2:22; Ezek. 13:1–9). These texts reflect circumstances of military defeat, tragedy, and judgment. Such events may have stimulated the development of the prophetic concept of a future "day" or time of judgment for the disobedient Israel and all of the nations (1:15; Is. 13:6, 9; Zeph. 1:14–18).

However, the day of the Lord is not just a day of wrath and judgment on the disobedient. In some contexts, it also includes deliverance and restoration for the righteous. The day of the Lord speaks not only about future judgment, but also about future hope, prosperity, and blessing (Is. 4:2–6; Hos. 2:18–23; Amos 9:11–15; Mic. 4:6–8). Joel reveals that this day is to be heralded by heavenly phenomena (2:30, 31) that will bring sudden darkness and gloom on the earth (2:2). It will be a day of divine destruction (1:15) on the nations that have persecuted Israel (3:12–14) and on the rebellious and disobedient of Israel (Amos 5:18–20). Yet it will also be a time of deliverance and unprecedented blessing for God's people (2:32; 3:16, 18–21; 1 Thess. 5:2–5).

repentance before He brought His judgment upon them. **Zion** refers to Jerusalem (see Ps. 133:3). **coming ... at hand:** The Bible presents the day of the Lord as an imminent reality. At any moment, the day that is "near" may become reality.

2:2 Darkness is used as a figure for misery, distress, and judgment (see Is. 8:22; 60:2; Jer. 13:16).

2:3–5 The invasion that Joel envisioned was like a raging **fire** that transformed all that was beautiful into desolation. Joel compared the speed and strength of the invaders to galloping **horses.**

2:6–9 writhe in pain: The invading armies were locustlike in number and in their ability to penetrate any defense; but like men of war, they bring fear and death with them. The imagery of locusts (ch. 1) describes the overwhelming power of a military invasion.

2:10, 11 References to the **sun, moon,** and **stars** growing dim allude to a future outpouring of divine wrath (see Is. 13:10; Matt. 24:29; Rev. 6:12, 13). **Who can endure:** Nothing will be able to withstand the wrath of God (see Matt. 24:21, 22).

2:12 Turn to Me: As in Zephaniah (see Zeph. 2:1–3), an opportunity for repentance, remorse, and renewal was offered to the people.

2:13 rend your heart: God is not satisfied with outward acts of repentance. Tearing one's garments was a customary way of expressing grief or remorse (see Josh. 7:6; 1 Sam. 4:12). However, like all outward acts, the tearing of a garment could be done without true sorrow or repentance. God required more than external words or actions; He wanted a change of heart and sorrow over sin. **slow to anger:** God is reluctant to punish. Judgment is God's "unusual" or "foreign" task; He wants everyone to come to repentance (see Is. 28:21).

2:14 Who knows: These words suggest that even at the last moment, the Lord would withhold His wrath and display His grace if the people would truly repent. As a result, agriculture would be restored and productivity would return. There would be food and drink, for the people and for offerings to the Lord.

2:15 Blow the trumpet in Zion: The repetition of these words from 2:1 ties the chapter together and renews the urgent appeal for a proper response to God.

2:16 The urgency of the situation is apparent because all ages and classes of the population were summoned. According to Jewish tradition codified in the Mishnah, a **bridegroom** and **bride** could be excused from reciting daily prayers on their wedding day. But Joel excused no one from prayer at this time of spiritual emergency.

2:17 Spare Your people: If the leaders and the people would gather together with prayers of true repentance and genuine renewal, the horrible events that God was threatening might be averted.

2:18, 19 zealous for His land: The deep love of God for the land of Israel is coupled with His abiding love (**pity**) for the people. On every occasion in which God brought judgment on the land, there was the hope that one day His zeal for the land would lead to a renewal of blessing. In response to repentance, God would bring restoration and blessing.

2:20 The north was regarded as the direction from which misfortune generally came upon Israel. **The eastern sea** refers to the Dead Sea. **The western sea** refers to the Mediterranean Sea.

2:21 Fear not: There is coming a day (see Ps. 65) when God's restoration of the earth will be complete.

2:22 open pastures ... tree bears its fruit: The renewal of agriculture would be a sign that God had renewed prosperity and peace to His land.

2:23, 24 The former rain softened the soil for planting winter wheat. **The latter rain** fell in the spring, causing the grain to swell and ensuring a good harvest. If the rains failed, the crops would not grow.

2:25, 26 The same God who brings judgment is pleased to restore blessing to those who repent. This does not mean that sin leaves no scar, but that God can restore people to usefulness in spite of past disobedience.

2:27 I am in the midst of Israel: Ultimately, this is the promise of God's presence in the midst of His people in the coming reign of King Jesus (see Zeph. 3:14–20). However, God promises to be present at all times with the individual who is at peace with Him.

2:28, 29 Afterward indicates the prophetic future; this word is a signal that the text was pointing to the messianic age. **Pour out** is derived from the imagery of Israel's heavy winter rains; it speaks here of abundant provision. **All flesh** anticipates the inclusion of both Jews and Gentiles in one body in Christ (see Eph. 2:11—3:6). The ministries of the Spirit mentioned here were experienced in the early church (see Acts 11:28; 21:9; 2 Cor. 12:1–4; Rev. 1:1–3). **Your sons and your daughters:** The outpouring of the Spirit and the ministries done through His power will be accomplished without regard to gender, age, or class.

2:30, 31 The heavenly wonders described here will take place before the **great and awesome day of the LORD,** an apparent reference to the end times. **Blood and fire** correspond with Rev. 8:7, 8. **Smoke** corresponds with Rev. 9:18. **Darkness** corresponds with Rev. 8:12. **Moon into blood** corresponds with Rev. 6:12.

2:32 Anyone who **calls on the name of the Lord**—that is, repents and believes—will be **saved** from the judgment that will fall on the wicked and unbelieving.

3:1 In those days indicates a time in the prophetic future (2:28). The judgment will take place after the Lord has restored His people to the land (see Matt. 25:31–46).

3:2, 3 Valley of Jehoshaphat: The name Jehoshaphat means "The Lord Judges." The location of this valley is not known. Perhaps this was just a symbolic name for the location of the great battle in the end times.

3:4–6 Tyre and Sidon were Phoenician cities on the Mediterranean Sea, north of Galilee. **Philistia** was on the Mediterranean coast south of Joppa.

3:7, 8 Sabeans were people of Semitic origin who lived in the southwest Arabian peninsula.

3:9, 10 The military weapons of the Gentile nations would not be sufficient to protect them against God's judgment. Therefore, they are exhorted to beat their **plowshares into swords** and their **pruning hooks into**

spears. For predictions of the reverse, see Is. 2:4; Mic. 4:3.

3:11 Joel saw two armies assembling for battle. The one is made up of the **nations;** the other is made up of the **mighty ones** of the Lord (see Mark 8:38; Rev. 19:14).

3:12, 13 The use of harvesting imagery in the Book of Joel is complex. It begins in terms of the great scarcity resulting from the locust plague (ch. 1). Then there is a promised renewal of agriculture with the return of God's blessing to His repentant people (2:18–27). Here, the riches of renewed agriculture serve as a mocking backdrop for a world in conflict. In 3:18–21, there is a final renewal of agriculture because of the blessing of the resident King.

3:14 The valley of decision may be a symbolic name for the Valley of Jehoshaphat (3:2), or it may refer to the option before the people to continue toward certain judgment or to turn to God in repentance (vv. 12, 13).

3:15, 16 These verses parallel 2:30–32 and describe the same heavenly phenomena (see Matt. 24:29). In the midst of calamity, God was offering a **shelter for His people** (see Zeph. 2:1–3).

3:17 Joel anticipates a day when strangers would no longer pass through Jerusalem to plunder and destroy. Instead, they would worship the Lord (see Zech. 8:20–23).

3:18 In that day indicates the prophetic future (2:28; 3:1). Joel uses poetic imagery to describe the productivity of the land in the messianic age. **The Valley of Acacias** was the location of the last encampment before the Israelites entered Canaan (see Num. 25:1; Josh. 3:1).

3:19, 20 Egypt and **Edom** are mentioned as representatives of the Gentile nations that God will judge before the establishment of the Messiah's kingdom. Note the stark contrast with the eternal destinies of **Judah** and **Jerusalem.**

3:21 The LORD dwells in Zion: The Lord's presence in Jerusalem is the key to the blessing of the land.

Amos

Introduction

The Book of Amos is named after the prophet who delivered its oracles. Amos was from Tekoa, a town at the edge of the Judean wilderness, about five miles southeast of Bethlehem. Amos specifically calls himself a sheepbreeder (1:1; 7:14, 15). The Hebrew term used indicates that Amos was not a hired shepherd, but the owner of one or more flocks of sheep. The period of Amos's prophetic activity was very short. Amos went to Bethel from Tekoa, delivered his prophetic oracles, and returned home. He probably stayed in Bethel only a few days. Amos's spoken oracles should be dated around 755–754 B.C.

The main theme of the Book of Amos is God's passionate concern for justice. Justice is not an abstract issue with God. Instead, justice is relational; it promotes good relations between people and between groups of people. Injustice breeds anger, hostility, and violence. God created the human race to enjoy good relations with Him and with each other; therefore, injustice that breeds alienation in all of its varieties breaks God's heart.

During Amos's time the prosperity of Israel brought new wealth to the upper classes. They used that wealth to enlarge their land holdings and to build great houses for themselves. They violated the rights of the poor and the landed peasants, throwing many off their ancestral lands. Through God's provisions in the Mosaic covenant, the landed peasant class had been the foundation of Israel's society. But this class virtually disappeared. As the rich became richer, the poor became poorer and more numerous; many were sold into slavery. Israel's social structure became thoroughly unstable.

The immediate purpose of Amos's prophetic ministry was to call the leaders of ancient Israel to repent and reform. Amos warned them that if they did not heed his call, their injustice against the poor and the weak would destroy the nation. God would not allow them to continue in their unrighteous, unjust course. Repentance or retribution were the only alternatives. It is no accident that what we often remember from

Amos is his stirring call, "Let justice run down like water, and righteousness like a mighty stream" (5:24).

1:1 Tekoa was about ten miles south of Jerusalem, in a region well-suited for raising sheep and goats. **The earthquake,** mentioned again in Zech. 14:5, cannot be dated precisely.

1:2 The temple was on Mount **Zion,** the oldest part of **Jerusalem.** When **the LORD** roared from there, the nation dried up at the heat of the fiery blast. The fact that **the top of** Mount **Carmel,** on the coast of Israel in the north, **withers** indicates a great disaster. Carmel was a garden spot, normally lush and flourishing year-round.

1:3 Thus says the LORD: There was no mistaking by whose authority these messages were spoken: this was the word of God Himself. **For three ... and for four:** This stylistic device indicated the exhaustion of God's patience—the Syrians had continued to sin, again and again. This device is repeated as Amos speaks God's words against nation after sinful nation. The **transgressions** of the neighbors of Israel and Judah were against the general revelation, or "law of nature," that all people recognize and acknowledge. Since the neighboring nations had not received God's special revelation, as Israel had at Mount Sinai, Amos's oracles did not call them to account by that standard, but by the standard they *had* received. **Damascus** was the capital of Syria (also called Aram), a powerful kingdom that had been a frequent adversary of Israel throughout its history. Israelites listening to Amos would have been glad to hear of God's punishment of Damascus. **Gilead** was the region on the east side of the Jordan River from the Yarmuk River to the Dead Sea. It had belonged to Israel since they had taken over the land, but Aram often had fought Israel for possession of northern Gilead, gaining control there in Israel's times of military weakness. **Threshed ...** with implements of iron indicates extreme cruelty and inhumanity in warfare.

1:4 I will send a fire ... Which shall devour the palaces: Fire in an ancient city was a real threat. Cities were crowded with houses close together on very narrow streets; there was too little water to fight raging fires. **Hazael** and **Ben-Hadad** were kings of Syria who had been particularly harsh in their treatment of Israel.

1:5 The gate bar was the large timber that barred the city gate from the inside. If it was broken, the city would lose its security and could be captured easily. **Aven ... Beth Eden:** Amos may have intended a play on words here. Aven means "Sin" in Hebrew; Damascus was a verdant oasis city on the edge of the desert that could be compared to Eden. However, Amos may also have been referring to the Beth Eden region on the north bank of the Euphrates River.

1:6, 7 Gaza was one of the five principal cities of the Philistines, the traditional enemies of Israel who lived on the southwest coast of Canaan. **They took captive ... to deliver:** The principal method of acquiring foreign slaves in the ancient Middle East was capturing them in war.

1:8 Ashdod and **Ashkelon,** coastal cities located north of Gaza, were two of the five major Philistine cities. **Ekron,** also one of the five major Philistine cities, was situated inland.

1:9, 10 Tyre, the principal Phoenician city, was on the northwest coast of Canaan. The Phoenicians were master seafarers. Tyre and Israel had forged an alliance that was profitable for both. However, Tyre ignored the long-standing **covenant of brotherhood,** and sought commercial gain by selling Israelite slaves to **Edom.**

1:11 The nation of **Edom,** located southeast of the Dead Sea, controlled important caravan trade routes, and thus was deeply involved in commerce. **his brother:** The Edomites traced their ancestry to Esau, the brother of Jacob. But several times in the history of their stormy relationship, Edom took advantage of Israel's (or Judah's) misfortune to help others attack them.

1:12 Teman and **Bozrah** were principal Edomite cities.

1:13 The nation of **Ammon,** located east of Gilead on the edge of the desert, was descended from one of the sons of Lot, Abraham's nephew (see Gen. 19:36–38). Thus Ammon was related to Israel, although not as closely as Edom. **ripped open ... enlarge their territory:** The Ammonites killed pregnant women in order to prevent the increase of the Israelite population in Gilead, which they were trying to wrest from Israel's control.

1:14, 15 Rabbah was the capital of Ammon.

2:1 Like Ammon (1:13), **Moab** (located southeast of Israel) was descended from one of the sons of Lot. **burned the bones:** This act was believed to desecrate the remains of a deceased person, a heinous act in ancient times and a great dishonor to the person's memory.

2:2, 3 Kerioth was a major town of Moab. It was the site of a temple of Chemosh, Moab's national god.

2:4, 5 Judah was Israel's neighbor to the south. Israel and Judah shared a common heritage, a common language, a common faith, and a common covenant with the Lord. **the law of the LORD ... His commandments:** The basis of Judah and Israel's judgment was different from that of the nations Amos had just called to account before them (1:3—2:3). Judah and

 IN DEPTH   Places Judged by God

Though Amos was a simple shepherd, God had given him knowledge of lands and nations beyond the Judean pastures where he tended his sheep. Because God had placed prophetic messages on his lips, he knew about the tragic futures of cities as far away as the Syrian city of Damascus (1:5), but also as close as the Philistine city of Gaza (1:6). His pronouncements of doom encompassed the Phoenicians in the seacoast town of Tyre and the Edomites in the arid lands of the south.

Israel had received God's special revelation at Sinai; they were in a special covenant relationship with Him and were held to a higher standard of accountability.

2:6 I will not turn away its punishment: Here the focus shifted to Amos's audience. This was Israel, God's people who had violated their covenant relationship with Him. God was calling them to account for violations of the covenant. **sell the righteous for silver:** In His law, God had instructed the Israelites to work off their debts through indentured service—administered humanely and for a strictly limited time (see Lev. 25:39–43; Deut. 15:12). By Amos's day, those in power in Israel were taking advantage of the courts to sell debtors as slaves. **For a pair of sandals** means for little or nothing.

2:7 pant after the dust: Amos used deliberate exaggeration to portray the greed of those oppressing the poor. Not satisfied with gaining their victims' farms and selling the people into slavery for money, the greedy rich would not let the poor go until they had shaken the very **dust** from their heads. The **humble,** those without power or influence, should have been able to depend on the justice due them. Instead, justice was denied them. As a result, their life was turned to poverty, oppression, and insecurity.

2:8 Clothes taken in pledge, as security for a loan, were to be returned in the evening, since clothes were the bedding of the poor (see Ex. 22:26, 27). The powerful in Israel were spreading the clothes out as beds for themselves beside the altars, in a show of empty, merciless piety.

2:9, 10 Yet it was I: This emphatic statement underscores the fact that God had been Israel's Champion, and the nation's success had not been its own doing. **The Amorite** refers to the previous inhabitants of the land of Canaan.

2:11, 12 Prophets were especially privileged; God spoke to them and gave them messages for the people. **Nazirites** dedicated themselves to God with a vow that entailed specific responsibilities and prohibitions, either for life or for a specified period (see Num. 6:1–21). Total abstinence from **wine** was one of the prominent features of the Nazirite vow.

2:13 Weighed down by you is a powerful metaphor of the burden of Israel's sin on the Lord. This is the same God Isaiah describes as measuring the waters of the earth in the hollow of His hand, measuring the heavens with the span of His hand, and weighing the mountains in His balance (see Is. 40:12).

2:14–16 No resources of personal strength, no skill with weapons of war, not even the help of the mighty war horse would suffice for the military **men of might** to save themselves **in that day,** when God would bring His judgment upon them.

3:1 The whole family which I brought up emphasizes the personal, intimate relationship that God had with Israel.

3:2 You only have I known, in this context, means "You only have I chosen." God's relationship with Israel was not only intimate; it was exclusive. God had been faithful to Israel; yet Israel had not been faithful to God. For this reason, the nation would be judged.

3:3–6 This series of rhetorical questions illustrates the seriousness, certainty, and righteousness of God's impending action against Israel. Each question is framed so as to require a resounding "no" as its answer.

3:7 This parenthetical statement interrupts, yet underscores, Amos's point is that God is sovereign and does what He wills: therefore, Israel's judgment was certain.

3:8 Two more rhetorical questions complete the group of nine (vv. 3–6). It would do Israel no good to forbid prophecy (2:12; 7:13, 16); the true prophet *must* prophesy, just as certainly as God's judgment must come to pass.

3:9, 10 Ashdod, one of the five principal cities of the Philistines, was on the Mediterranean coast southwest of Israel. For God to call Philistia and **Egypt** to witness His judgment of Israel implies that these pagan nations were more righteous than Israel. They had not received God's revelation at Sinai; yet Israel, having received it, had violated it repeatedly.

3:11 This verse pictures a formal sentencing of Israel in the presence of the witnesses whom God had called (v. 9). Sapping Israel's

strength was exactly what Assyria did in the years following Amos's prophecies, finally putting an end to the nation in 722 B.C.

3:12, 13 The hired **shepherd** was responsible to the owner for the safety of the sheep. He had to make good any loss, unless he could prove it was unavoidable. A **lion** taking a sheep was an unavoidable loss, but the shepherd had to prove that the lion had taken it. A couple of small bones or a piece of an **ear** was sufficient; the owner would recognize the lion's work. As complete as the destruction of a sheep by a lion would be the destruction of Israel that God would bring.

3:14 the altars of Bethel: Jeroboam I had erected sanctuaries in Bethel and Dan to prevent Israelites from traveling to Jerusalem to worship and possibly returning their political allegiance to the house of David. Those sanctuaries of false worship had tempted many Israelites to be unfaithful to God.

3:15 The four houses mentioned here were all symbols of oppression. Many small inheritances had been stolen to form the large estates of the wealthy and powerful, where they built their opulent houses.

4:1, 2 Bashan, the region east and northeast of the Sea of Galilee, was (and is) a prime grassland area renowned for its cattle. **Cows of Bashan** refer to the sleek, fat, well-fed women of **Samaria.**

4:3 Broken walls were a symbol of the thoroughness of the destruction of the city and the homes that the people held so dear. In an undamaged city, the usual way in and out was the main gate. But Samaria would be so ruined that the deportees would be driven straight through the gaps in the walls of their houses and their city.

4:4, 5 This passage is a sarcastic call to Israel to worship. **Bethel,** a city on the central ridge road just inside Israel's border with Judah, was the site of the most important shrine in southern Israel. **Gilgal** refers to a site in the Jordan valley where Israel had encamped before and after the taking of Jericho (see Josh. 5:10; 9:6). Thus, Gilgal had historical connections with Israel's early faith and early life in the land. **For this you love:** Ignoring God's desires, the Israelites did what they wanted. They loved the feasting that went with the festivals of sacrifice, but not God's calls for justice.

4:6 The first calamity that God sent against Israel was famine. **Cleanness of teeth ... and lack of bread** indicated the exhaustion of all food supplies.

4:7, 8 The second calamity was drought. Lack of rain with **still three months to the harvest** meant the total ruin of the grain crops.

4:9 The third calamity was crop disease and locusts.

4:10 The fourth calamity was **plague** and warfare. **After the manner of Egypt** suggests that God was reminding Israel of the ten plagues that preceded their exodus from Egypt; these included epidemic diseases and other disasters. **The stench of your camps** resulted from lack of sanitation, from disease, from the putrefaction of wounds, and sometimes from corpses of men and of animals that could not be buried quickly.

4:11 The fifth calamity was the destruction of Israelite cities. The overthrow of **Sodom and Gomorrah** was the scale by which many subsequent disasters were measured. It meant total destruction, meted out in judgment by the hand of God Himself (see Gen. 19:24, 25). **A firebrand plucked from the burning** refers to a stick snatched from a fire with one end already ablaze. This was a vivid metaphor for God's last-minute rescue of most of Israel from the fate He brought upon some of its cities and territories.

4:12 Because Israel had not returned to God through these five calamities, it would have to meet God Himself.

4:13 Amos grounded God's right to exercise judgment upon Israel on His character as Creator and Sustainer of all the earth. God is sovereign over all the earth; on that basis He called Israel, and can call any nation, to account.

5:1, 2 The term **virgin of Israel** depicts the nation as a young maiden, cut off from her life before it had really begun. **On her land** is a reminder that the land had been God's gift to Israel. By their faithlessness, the people had turned God's gift into the place of their death and burial.

5:3, 4 The lamentation continues with a different image of Israel's destruction: the troops Israel would send out to defend its territory. Rather than saving Israel, its armies would be decimated.

5:5 Beersheba, about 50 miles southwest of Bethel, was the site of a temple in Amos's day.

5:6 The house of Joseph refers to the entire nation.

5:7 Wormwood, a plant with a bitter taste, is a metaphor for sorrow and bitterness.

5:8 Pleiades refers to a cluster of stars within the constellation Taurus, one of the twelve signs of the Zodiac. One of Israel's idolatries was astral worship. Far from being deities, Amos asserted, the constellations also were God's creations. **Orion** refers to a prominent constellation in the southern sky in the shape of a hunter. **He turns the shadow ... dark as night:** God designed and sustains the daily cycle of light and darkness through His own servant which was not a deity, the sun. **He calls ... the earth:** God, not Baal, Tammuz, or any other fertility deity, designed and sustains the atmospheric water cycle by which the earth receives its necessary rainfall.

5:9 The God who created and sustains the processes of all the universe surely can bring His judgment to bear, even upon the strong of the earth and their fortresses.

5:10 The gate was the location of the town court, where justice was to be upheld in all legal proceedings.

5:11 Taxes were collected in kind from those with few resources of silver and gold. To **take grain taxes** from the poor was to put them at risk of starvation if the harvest had not been bountiful. Yet the rich and powerful had sufficient resources to build luxurious **houses of hewn stone** for themselves. God promised that the rich would not enjoy their luxury stolen from the poor and powerless.

5:12 manifold ... sins: Israel's leaders did not sin incidentally or furtively; they sinned brazenly and habitually, as though God had never revealed Himself and His standards of justice and mercy.

5:13–15 Seek good: The prophet interrupted himself to plead with Israel to return to God and avoid the judgment He would bring upon them. **As you have spoken:** Worshiping in the Lord's name, the Israelites invoked the Lord's presence in their spoken prayers and blessings. If they began to live as God had taught them in the Law, He would indeed be with them.

5:16, 17 God's purposed action was that He would **pass through** the nation. A visit from God is a dreaded and mournful event for anyone not ready to meet Him.

5:18 The popular theology of Amos's day apparently looked forward to **the day of the LORD** as the time of Israel's restoration to military, political, and economic greatness, perhaps to the greatness of the reigns of David and Solomon. Amos declared such hopes futile, even pitiable. What the people looked forward to as a day of light and triumph would rise upon them instead as a day of darkness and ruin.

5:19, 20 The images of **a bear** and **a serpent** evoke the terror that follows when a person escapes a terrible danger and is exhausted and relieved, only to find a worse danger so close at hand that it is inescapable.

5:21–23 God had promised that if the Israelites honored Him with their lives, He would **savor, accept,** and **regard** Israel's sacrifices and **hear** their words. By stating He would no longer accept Israel's sacrifices or listen to them, God was rejecting Israel's worship as hypocritical, dishonest, and meaningless. **Feast days** and **sacred assemblies** refers, in general, to all of Israel's worship of God.

5:24 After dismissing Israel's empty worship as noisy and tumultuous, God called for the honest tumult of the rolling waters of **justice** and the perennial **stream** of **righteousness,** the only foundation for true praise and worship of the Lord.

5:25 This verse is a rhetorical question with "yes" as the expected answer; Israel *had* worshiped God **in the wilderness.**

5:26 Israel had not worshiped the Lord exclusively, even in the earliest wilderness days. **Sikkuth** and **Chiun** are pagan deities; apparently Israel had made images of foreign gods. The true believer in the Lord understood, without question, that any gods **made** by human hands were not gods at all.

5:27 Since Israel insisted on worshiping other gods, including astral deities, God would send them into exile to lands where these deities seemed to rule supreme.

6:1 Zion refers to Jerusalem, the capital of Judah (the southern kingdom). **Samaria** was the capital of Israel (the northern kingdom). At the time of Amos's prophecy, Israel and Judah together had enjoyed about a generation of military might and economic prosperity. It became natural for officials in Jerusalem and Samaria to regard themselves as **notable persons.**

6:2 It was the boast of Israel's elite that no other nation was greater than they were. Their boast came back upon their own heads, for just as Calneh, Hamath, and Gath were subjected to Assyrian rule, so Israel would also be subjugated by the Assyrians. **Calneh,** a city in northern Syria, was the capital of a small kingdom. **Hamath,** an important city in central Syria, was located north of Damascus. **Gath,** one of the five principal Philistine cities, was southwest of Israel.

6:3 You who put far off the day of doom refers to those who insisted that Israel was too strong to be destroyed.

6:4–6 This passage describes the extravagant living indulged in by the rich, and paid for with the wealth stolen from the poor. **lambs ... calves:** Meat was a luxury for most families of the ancient Middle East, consumed only on special occasions. Meat on a daily basis was the privilege only of the rich and powerful. The upper classes of Israel were so engrossed in their own privileges and luxuries that they cared nothing for the **affliction** of their fellow Israelites.

6:7 God's judgment would be both fitting and ironic. Those who had fancied themselves the leaders of the nation would lead their nation into exile.

6:8, 9 If God takes an oath, He takes it **by Himself,** for there is none greater than He. In his oracles against the seven nations (chs. 1; 2), Amos had prophesied the destruction of their palaces. Now it was Israel's turn. Luxurious palace strongholds represented both the **pride of Jacob** in their own strength and the oppression of the powerless, whose stolen

wealth had financed the construction of these palaces. **I will deliver up the city:** God personally would see to the destruction of Samaria and its proud inhabitants.

6:10, 11 This verse depicts the aftermath of God's judgment, when relatives came around to carry out the bodies. **One inside the house** may refer to the last survivor, sick but not yet dead. In this context, such a person might have been expected to invoke the name of God for help after answering, **"None."** Before he could do so, however, the questioner would silence him, fearful of getting God's further attention by using His name. People who had not believed that God would come in judgment would now be afraid of what further disaster He might bring upon them.

6:12 As absurd and impossible as horses running up steep cliffs or oxen plowing the sea was Israel's perversion of justice and righteousness. **Gall** is a bitter, poisonous herb.

6:13, 14 Israel's pride in its military strength would be its downfall. **Lo Debar** was a city east of the Jordan River that Israel regained from Syria when Assyria crippled the strength of Damascus. **Karnaim,** a city east of the Jordan River near the farthest limits of Israelite possession, was also regained when Assyria weakened Syria. God's punishment of Israel would fit its sin of pride. As the Israelites reckoned that they had extended their borders by their own military strength, God would allow them to be harassed and defeated from border to border. **The Valley of the Arabah** refers to the desert valley that was the southern limit of Israelite control. From north to south, from border to border, God would allow Israel to be defeated in battle.

7:1 locust swarms: Locusts are a kind of grasshopper. Joel 1:4—2:11 describes the devastation that locusts bring to agriculture, stripping every green leaf and twig, and even killing trees. **The late crop** refers to the last growth of crops and pastures, evidently including hay, before the summer dry season. **The king's mowings** implies that the king took the first harvest of hay as a tax. Thus a swarm of locusts devouring the late crop would leave the people with nothing for themselves.

7:2, 3 Oh, that Jacob may stand: If God carried out the threatened punishment, Jacob (the nation of Israel) might be destroyed. One function of the prophet was to serve as intercessor for the people before God. Amos prayed that the vision decreed in heaven might be halted before it was accomplished on earth. In response to Amos's intercession, and out of His love for Israel, God stayed His decree.

7:4–6 To call **for conflict** means to put on trial or to bring a lawsuit against Israel. To try **by fire** means that fire would have been both the instrument by which Israel's guilt would be judged and the instrument by which their punishment would be carried out. **The great deep** refers to the primordial waters that remained beneath the firmament after God fashioned it (see Gen. 1:6–8). For the deep to be dried up by fire means that the land would be devastated beyond hope.

7:7–9 A plumb line is a string with a weight on one end, used to establish a vertical line so a wall can be built straight. **What do you see:** Unlike the first two visions of natural disasters, the visions of the plumb line and the basket of summer fruit (8:1) were not self-explanatory. God asked Amos what he saw, then explained the vision's meaning. Also unlike the first two visions, God did not give Amos opportunity to intercede, nor did He relent. These judgments would be executed. The plumb line of God's revelation in the law had been set **in the midst of ... Israel** for many generations. Now God would stretch a plumb line to demonstrate how "crooked" the people's observance of His commands had been.

7:10, 11 Amaziah, the priest in charge of the temple at Bethel, informed the king about the prophet who was making threats against the king's house. Amaziah was reacting to Amos's third vision which ended with God's promise to bring the sword against the house of Jeroboam. Amaziah regarded Amos's words as a political threat, and reported them not as a prophecy from God, but as Amos's call to revolt.

7:12, 13 After sending his report to Jeroboam, Amaziah turned his attention to Amos himself. Since Amaziah was an official of the king, his command to Amos to return to Judah would have amounted to making Amos officially unwelcome in Israel. Amaziah was not concerned that Amos had proclaimed a message from God, only that the king's interests should be protected from this seditious prophet.

7:14–17 Amos denied being a prophet by profession. **Nor was I a son of a prophet** indicates not only that Amos's father was not a prophet, but also that Amos had not been trained in prophecy. **the LORD took me:** Amos made it clear that he had neither desired nor sought his prophetic task. **Your wife shall be a harlot:** The only way the spouse of an important official like Amaziah would be reduced to prostitution would be if all her family and all her resources were taken away and she were left to fend entirely for herself. The rest of Amos's oracle predicted that such a situation would happen to Amaziah's family. **Your land shall be divided** indicated that it would be assigned or sold to new owners. As a high official of the king, Amaziah possessed large land holdings; he would retain none.

8:1–3 summer fruit: The fruits that came at the end of the harvest in late summer included grapes, pomegranates, and figs. **The end has come:** Amos could not have discerned the meaning of this vision until God's pronouncement. Israel's wickedness was about to result in a harvest of judgment.

8:4 Fail means essentially "to have no means of survival."

8:5 The New Moon, the first day of the month on the Hebrew calendar, was a day of special sacrifices, a feast day, and a **Sabbath** day (see Num. 28:11–15; 1 Sam. 20:5). Rather than observing the New Moon and the weekly Sabbath with worship, thanksgiving, and rest, these people were impatient to resume their cheating and oppression of the poor. The ephah was the most common measure of dry volume. To make **the ephah small,** therefore, was to cheat the customer of value received for price paid. The shekel was a unit of money. To make **the shekel large** was to cheat the customer by taking too large a price (weight) of silver for value received.

8:6 The rich and powerful of Amos's day were making slaves of Israel's poor, the people they had dispossessed of their lands. **the bad wheat:** The chaff and other refuse of the threshing floor, perhaps even moldy or mildewed wheat, were mixed in with the good wheat to stretch it further and make a greater profit.

8:7 Their works refers to the economic injustices Amos spoke against in vv. 4–6, as well as other sins, including unfaithfulness to God.

8:8 The River and **the River of Egypt** refer to the Nile River. **Heave and subside:** The Nile rises and falls several feet in its annual flood. Amos may have intended to portray a severe earthquake in which the land's rise and fall would be as dramatic as the rise and fall of the Nile.

8:9, 10 God's judgment would be a great reversal—of light to darkness, and joy to mourning. **That day** probably refers to the "day of the Lord" (5:18). **Sackcloth,** a coarse cloth of goat or camel hair, was uncomfortable to wear. Thus it was worn next to the skin as a sign of mourning or great distress. Shaving the head to create temporary **baldness** was another mourning sign.

8:11 In 4:6, Amos reminded Israel that God had sent famine upon them, yet they had not returned to Him. Now the famine would be, not of food, **but of hearing the words of the LORD.**

8:12, 13 From sea to sea means from the Dead Sea to the Mediterranean. **to and fro:** Those in Israel searching for the word of God would have to circle all of Israel's territory, but in vain.

8:14 Dan in the far north and **Beersheba** in the far south were the limits of significant Israelite settlement. In Amos's day, Beersheba was in the kingdom of Judah. Israel could swear oaths by the Lord, claiming they worshiped Him from the extreme north to the extreme south of His land, but that would not relieve the famine of God's Word.

9:1 The people would have expected a vision of God **by the altar** to mean that He intended good for them, blessing them with His presence. Instead God would start at the altar, commanding that the destruction of the sinful nation begin there.

9:2 hell … heaven: In this imagery, Israel's fugitives from God's judgment could escape neither up nor down; God would find them no matter where they fled.

9:3 If the universe could not hide the fugitives, neither could the earth. The **top of Carmel** represented the highest point on the earth. Whether as high as that, or as low as **the bottom of the sea,** the earth would provide no escape.

9:4–6 Even **captivity** in enemy lands would not provide a refuge from God's judgment upon Israel. **I will set My eyes on them** usually is a formula that expresses God's blessing on Israel; here it alludes to the fulfillment of the curses for breaking the Mosaic covenant.

9:7 Ethiopia refers to the region near the southern horizon of Israel's geographical knowledge, south of Egypt. God's rhetorical question told Israel that they were not the only recipients of God's attention and care. God loves all peoples, even **the Philistines** and **Syrians.**

9:8 I will not utterly destroy: This was a glimmer of hope in a long passage of judgment and doom. God's judgment would be thorough, but a remnant would survive.

9:9, 10 Sifting grain **in a sieve** was the final operation in cleaning grain before gathering it into storage. In winnowing, all the chaff was blown away; only pebbles and small clumps of mud remained with the grain. The sieve was constructed with holes that were sized so the grain fell through when it was shaken, but pebbles and other debris were retained in the sieve. Thus the **smallest grain** refers to the smallest pebble; it would not fall to the ground with the clean grain.

9:11, 12 The tabernacle of David: Amos pictures the royal house of David metaphorically as a "booth" fallen in disrepair. Judah was a fallen, ruined shelter, incapable of protecting its people from any significant storm. **As in the days of old** reflects the nostalgia of Israel's people for the glory days of the kingdoms of David and Solomon, when they lived in strength, prosperity, and security.

9:13 Israelite farmers plowed at the beginning of the rainy season, from mid-October. They harvested the grain crop—first barley, then wheat—from late March to early June. For **the plowman** to **overtake the reaper** would mean such an abundant harvest that it would last all summer and would not be gathered until the plowing had started again. Grapes were harvested from midsummer to early fall. The grain crop was sown after the plowing in late fall. For **the treader of grapes** to overtake **him who sows seed** would mean the grape harvest would be so abundant that it would be extended for several weeks.

9:14 The promised restoration will be a total reversal of the punishment that God was bringing upon Israel.

9:15 As Israel planted vineyards, fields, and gardens, so God would **plant** the people **in their land,** never again to **be pulled up** in exile. God would do what He threatened through Amos—if Israel did not return to Him. God would also do what He promised through Amos in the last few verses of this book. God does not abandon His promises or His covenant, nor does He leave His people without hope. God's punishment is certain, but His restoration is just as certain.

Obadiah

Introduction

The Book of Obadiah is one of only two minor prophets that is addressed entirely to a nation other than Israel or Judah. It deals with the ancient feud between Israel and the nation of Edom, between the descendants of Jacob and those of his brother Esau. Through the prophet Obadiah, the Lord expressed His indignation at the nation of Edom. When they should have been helping their relatives, they were gloating over the Israelites' problems and raiding their homes. A day was coming when the Lord would bring justice to the world.

The name Obadiah means "Servant of the Lord." It is not known whether this was the prophet's personal name or whether he used it as a title, preferring to remain anonymous. Nothing is known of Obadiah's personal life or standing in Judean society.

Some scholars date the book very early, in the mid-ninth century B.C. This would make the Book of Obadiah the earliest of the prophetic books. However, most scholars date the book immediately following the Babylonian destruction of Jerusalem in 586 B.C.

In 586 B.C. Nebuchadnezzar's army crushed Judah and destroyed Jerusalem and Solomon's temple. Instead of offering sympathy and help to Judah's refugees, Edom handed them over to the conquering Babylonians. The Edomites even murdered some of the refugees. God gave Obadiah a stern message for Edom, a warning of God's judgment on them for their callous treatment of the fleeing Judeans.

While Obadiah's short prophetic oracle was addressed to Edom, it is doubtful that Edomite leaders ever heard or read it. One purpose of the oracle was to comfort and encourage the surviving Judeans with the message that God had not abandoned them. Judah would be restored to its own land after the judgment of the Exile had been accomplished, and their enemies would be punished.

In the grand scheme of the biblical message of God's redemption, the little Book of Obadiah may seem to be of little importance. But its portion of that message is vital. God is sovereign over all nations, whether they acknowledge His sovereignty or not. God desires that we show mercy and favor to our neighbors in their time of distress. Failure to do so will be judged by the God of justice.

1 Vision, a word common in the prophets (see Is. 1:1; Nah. 1:1) indicates that the prophet "saw" the revelation. **Obadiah** means "The Servant of the Lord." **Thus says the Lord GOD:** This phrasing is a strong affirmation that the prophetic oracle did not originate in the prophet's own thinking; God was and is the Initiator. A national oracle is directed against **Edom,** a country east of the Dead Sea and south of Moab. **The nations** is the standard biblical term for the larger national entities of western Asia and northeast Africa.

2 I will make you small: God would bring about a reversal of Edom's inflated self-importance.

3 habitation is high: Some of the mountain peaks of Edom reach over six thousand feet. **Who will bring me down:** Edom's presumed physical safety led the Edomites to become haughty; this would be their downfall.

4 as high as the eagle … among the stars: Edom's physical location became a metaphor for the proud and haughty spirit that the nation had displayed at the time of Judah's distress. Trusting in its high places and mountainous strongholds, Edom reckoned that no one could bring it to account for its actions.

5, 6 If thieves had come: The implication is that Edom would be stripped of everything. The nation would have been better off if thieves and robbers had come. **searched out:** Rather than being robbed randomly, the nation would be systematically pillaged (see Jer. 49:7–10).

7 In your confederacy referred to the nations who were allied with Edom in a covenant relationship, **at peace** and eating **bread** with them.

8 Edom had a reputation for having many **wise men** among its citizens (see Jer. 49:7).

9 The name **Teman** comes from a son of Eliphaz, who was the firstborn son of Esau (see Gen. 36:9–11). The word is often used as a synonym for Edom (see Jer. 49:7; Amos 1:12), and is thought to have been one of its principal cities.

10 your brother Jacob: Esau and Jacob were brothers, the sons of Isaac and Rebekah (see Gen. 25:24–26). Edom was descended from Esau; Judah was descended from Jacob.

11 In the day refers to the time of Judah's distress. **strangers ... foreigners:** These words, used to describe Judah's principal enemies, contrast with the words of v. 10, "your brother." It was one thing for the Babylonians to attack Judah; for a nation like Edom to join the Babylonians against their own brothers was unthinkable.

12 Judah's defeat and destruction should have brought sorrow to its neighbors. Instead, Judah's brother nation had laughed aloud. More than that, Edom had helped to complete Judah's destruction, taking spoil, capturing those who were trying to escape the Babylonian onslaught, and turning them over to Nebuchadnezzar's soldiers.

13 The day of their calamity, repeated three times in this verse, refers to the day of God's judgment upon Judah, carried out by the hand of King Nebuchadnezzar of Babylon.

14 stood at the crossroads: The phrasing suggests deliberate actions on Edom's part. **delivered up those ... who remained:** The Edomites had captured those who were attempting to escape the Babylonian army and then had turned them over to their pursuers.

15 The day of the LORD is a technical term used by the prophets to indicate the day of God's judgment (see Amos 5:18–20). Here the term likely refers to the time when God would judge **all the nations,** including Edom, that had participated in Judah's destruction. **As you have done:** The nature of God's judgment always reflects the nature of the sin being judged.

16 as you drank: The reference here is to the "cup of God's wrath" that was passed from Samaria to Judah, and finally to the nations—including Edom (see Jer. 25:27, 32, 33). The Lord still viewed Jerusalem as His **holy mountain** because He intended to reestablish His presence there (see Zech. 1:16).

17 Mount Zion and "My holy mountain" (in v. 16) refer to the same place: Jerusalem.

18 The references to **the house of Jacob** and **the house of Joseph** signify a unified Israel. God intends to rejoin the kingdoms of Israel and Judah as one people again.

19 The South refers to the Negev, the dry region around Beersheba, in the territory of Simeon and southern Judah. It could support some farming and shepherding. More importantly for this prophecy, the Negev bordered on Edom to the east. According to this verse, southern Judah was going to possess the land of the Edomites. **The Lowland,** or Shephelah, is the lower hills in Judah between the central hill country to the east and the coastal plain to the west. Judah and Philistia fought fiercely over this region in the early part of Israel's history. But Judah would eventually prevail over the lands contested with Philistia (see Zeph. 2:4–7). **Ephraim, Samaria,** and **Gilead** were parts of Israel during the period of the judges and most of the monarchy. Ephraim and Samaria were the heartland of the northern kingdom of Israel during the time of the divided monarchy. But at the time of Obadiah's prophecy, all three regions had passed under foreign domination and had experienced a significant influx of foreign population. In the day of the Lord of which Obadiah prophesied, these regions again would come into the possession of the Israelites. The land of Israel would be restored to its rightful inhabitants.

20 Zarephath was a Phoenician city 14 miles north of Tyre (see 1 Kin. 17:8–24). **Sepharad** was a city to which some Judeans were exiled. The restoration of Judah from exile which these verses predict was a sign to Judah and all nations that the God of Israel was not just a local God. He had not been defeated by the Babylonian god Marduk. The fact that He could allow His people to be carried into captivity in a foreign land and then bring them back to their own land was proof of His power and sovereignty over all the earth.

21 Saviors means "deliverers" or "those who will bring about salvation" (see Neh. 9:27). The Judeans who had been taken into captivity would come back as deliverers, and they would reign over the people of Edom. **the kingdom shall be the LORD's:** Edom had thought itself indestructible; but the Lord humbled that nation and restored the fallen Judah.

Jonah

Introduction

The Book of Jonah has been described as a parable, an allegory, and a satire. The famous story of the "great fish" (often erroneously thought of as a whale) has led many to dismiss the book as just a biblical "fish story." But it is a mistake to assume that the events and actions of the book are not historical in nature. While the story line is unusual, it is presented as normal history. Further, Jesus used the story of Jonah as an analogy of His own impending death and resurrection (see Matt. 12:39–41). The book does not specifically state who wrote it. But the tradition that it was written by Jonah as his own report of his foolish behavior and his final statement of coming to terms with the divine will is a likely possibility.

The prophet Jonah lived in the eighth century B.C., but we know very little about him apart from this book. He is mentioned in only one other passage in the Old Testament apart from the book that bears his name. Second Kings 14:25 announces the fulfillment of a prophecy of the living God that came through "Jonah the son of Amittai, the prophet who was from Gath Hepher." This passage locates Jonah's ministry in the northern kingdom of Israel during the reign of King Jeroboam II (792–753 B.C.).

The Book of Jonah challenges God's people not to exalt themselves. The Lord is free to bless, to be gracious, and to be patient with all the nations of the earth. Jonah's view of God was too restrictive. He believed that God was compassionate only toward Israel. Jonah failed to appreciate that the Lord may be equally forbearing with other nations as He was with Israel. The Book of Jonah shows that God is free and He can never be bound by human misconceptions.

Jonah's story contains a strong warning to all godly people. The elect may miss the blessing of seeing God's grace extended outside their own sphere because of their imposition of limits on God. While Jonah was praying anxiously for his personal deliverance, the sailors had already been experiencing the love of God for three days. Likewise, the people of Nineveh who repented of their sin rejoiced

that the impending judgment had not come. Jonah, however, was miserable. As we laugh at him, we may need to wince at ourselves. Jonah's silly sin is finally no laughing matter. We are condemned along with him if we share in his provincial folly.

1:1 the word of the LORD came: This phrase affirms the divine source of the message to Jonah (see also 1 Kin. 17:8; Jer. 1:4; Hos. 1:1; Joel 1:1; Mic. 1:1; Zeph. 1:1; Hag. 1:3). The name **Jonah** means "dove."

1:2 Nineveh, located on the Tigris River (see Gen. 10:11, 12), was the capital of Assyria (see 2 Kin. 19:36) for about a century (Zeph. 2:13–15; see also the Book of Nahum). Nineveh was over five hundred miles from Gath Hepher, Jonah's home near Nazareth in Israel. **Their wickedness** refers to Nineveh's pride, greed, brutality, and adultery (see 3:8; Nah. 2:11, 12; 3:1–4). **has come up before Me:** This figurative language pictures evil swelling up to confront the Lord (see Gen. 18:21; compare Lam. 1:22).

1:3 flee to Tarshish: The location of this port city is uncertain, but it could be Tartessus on the southeast coast of Spain. The city represents the most distant place known to the Israelites. **Joppa,** a non-Israelite port town, was west of Jerusalem and about 50 miles southwest of Jonah's hometown of Gath Hepher.

1:4, 5 But the LORD sent out a great wind: Throughout the Book of Jonah, the Lord shows Himself sovereign over all creation. The storm at sea was so ferocious that even the experienced **mariners were afraid.** The Phoenicians were the primary mariners of the ancient Middle East, so this was probably a Phoenician ship. Jonah was so sure he had averted God's will that he **was fast asleep** in the ship's hold.

1:6 your God: The ship's captain, a pagan, urged Jonah to pray to whatever god he might believe in. Of course, Jonah's "god" was the true God, who had caused the storm in the first place (v. 4).

1:7 cast lots: The sailors turned to practices common among them in an attempt to find the will of the gods. **the lot fell on Jonah:** Jonah was singled out as the guilty party (see Josh. 7:12–18; 1 Sam. 14:40–42).

1:8 The sailors fired a series of questions at Jonah, seeking to discern the reason for the storm. In regard to Jonah's **occupation,** the sailors may have wanted to know the prophet's reason for being on board.

1:9 I am a Hebrew: Jonah identified himself with the people of the Lord's covenant (see Gen. 14:13). **I fear the LORD:** *Fear* here indicates an ongoing activity of awe before the Lord, of piety in His presence, of obedience to His word, and of saving faith (see Gen. 22:12; Ex. 20:20; Prov. 1:7). Yet Jonah's actions contradicted his words. **God of heaven:** Lord is not just a local deity worshiped by an obscure people; He is the Supreme Ruler over all people and all creation (see 2 Chr. 36:23; Ezra 1:2; Neh. 1:4, 5). Jonah may have intended to distinguish God from Baal, the Canaanite "god of the sky" whom so many Israelites worshiped (see 1 Kin. 18:20–29; 2 Kin. 21:3; 2 Chr. 17:3).

1:10, 11 exceedingly afraid: This is the same term for *fear* that Jonah used in his statement of piety (v. 9). But here the word means to be in terror (v. 16). God, the Creator of the universe, was after Jonah. And because God was after Jonah, He was after the sailors as well. They had every right to be afraid (see Gen. 12:18; Judg. 15:11).

1:12, 13 throw me into the sea: Jonah knew that the only way for the storm to abate was for the sailors to toss him overboard. Jonah was ready to die. His words, **because of me,** are an admission of guilt and show a sense of resignation.

1:14 they cried out to the LORD: Ironically, the sailors prayed to the Lord on behalf of the Lord's rebellious prophet. Jonah needed God's grace as much as Nineveh did. **as it pleased You:** The narrator skillfully uses the sailors' words to express one of the book's themes: the Lord is free to act as He wills.

1:15 The sailors did as Jonah had said (v. 12), but only when they saw there was no other option (vv. 13, 14). With a sense of permission from the God of heaven (v. 9), the sailors **threw** Jonah **into the sea.**

1:16 Then the men feared the LORD exceedingly: In the Hebrew text, the words of this part of v. 16 are precisely the same as in v. 10, with one exception: the object of the

sailors' fear. In v. 10 these words described the sailors' overwhelming dread of the raging sea; in this verse they *feared the Lord,* indicating piety and believing faith. The sailors had the same reverential awe of God that Jonah had (v. 9). In spite of Jonah's failure, the sailors became converts (see Ps. 103:11, 13, 17). **offered a sacrifice:** The text does not say where this happened, but it may have been after the ship reached land. The important point is that their sacrifice was made to the God of Israel.

1:17 the LORD had prepared a great fish: God sent the fish—not a whale, as is commonly thought—to rescue Jonah, not to punish him (ch. 2). **Three days and three nights** may refer to one full day and portions of two more (see 3:3; Gen. 30:36; Ex. 3:18; 1 Sam. 30:12; Esth. 4:16; Luke 2:46; 24:21). Jesus Christ said His death and resurrection were foreshadowed by Jonah's experience (see Matt. 12:39, 40; 16:4; Luke 11:29; 1 Cor. 15:4).

2:1 Jonah prayed to the LORD his God: In his psalm (vv. 2–9), Jonah acknowledges God's help and thanks him for it. The phrase *the Lord his God* shows that Jonah, even though disobedient, was a true believer in God.

2:2 I cried … I cried: These terms come from two different verbs. The first is a more general term meaning "to call aloud," with a wide range of usage in the Bible. The second is a term that means a "cry for help," particularly as a scream to God (see Ps. 5:2; 18:6, 41; 22:24; 28:1; 30:2; 31:22; 88:13; 119:146). Jonah was terrified. **Out of the belly of Sheol:** When the sailors threw Jonah into the sea, he seemed to be "as good as dead." Thus for Jonah, the sea became like Sheol, the place of death (see Gen. 37:35; Ps. 16:10; 88:4, 5; Prov. 9:18; Is. 28:15).

2:3 Jonah's use of the pronouns **You** and **Your** in this verse are not accusations, but acknowledgments of the Lord's sovereign control of his life (see Ps. 88:6–18).

2:4 I will look again toward Your holy temple: The man who had run from God's presence (1:3) was alone, yet he clung to the hope that God would not abandon him. The temple, the sanctuary in Jerusalem (see v. 7; Deut. 12:5–7; Ps. 48; 79:1; 132; Heb. 9:24), was the symbol of God's presence.

2:5 The deep: This is the same term used in Gen. 1:2 to describe the mysterious and terrifying sea. In the Bible, the sea is described as a part of God's creation (see Gen. 1:10) that brings Him joy (see Ps. 104:24–26), but it also appears as a symbol for hostile forces (see Ps. 74:12–15; Is. 27:1) which the Lord nevertheless holds in His firm control (see Ps. 93).

2:6 Jonah pictures himself so deep in the sea that it is as if he had found **the moorings of the mountains. pit:** This term, along with *Sheol* (v. 2), is used to describe the realm of the dead (see Job 33:24; Ps. 30:9; 49:9).

2:7 I remembered: Jonah reaffirms his faith in the Lord and renews his commitment to Him (see Ps. 22:27; 63:6; 106:7).

2:8 worthless idols: This phrase (also found in Ps. 31:6) condemns every alternative to God. *Idols* here means "vapor," that which passes away quickly. These vaporous gods (see Ps. 86:8–10; Jer. 10:15; 51:18) were without value. **Mercy** (loyal love), the term that so often describes God's faithfulness to His covenant and to His people (see Ps. 13:5; 59:10, 17; 89:1–3) is used as a name for the Lord (4:2).

2:9 I will sacrifice to You with the voice of thanksgiving: This vow of praise is common in the Psalms (see Ps. 13:6; 142:7). **I will pay what I have vowed:** Jonah declares that he will keep his promise, a pledge both to sacrifice and to acknowledge God's help. **Salvation:** It is the Lord who delivers His people. God acts on behalf of His creation and the redeemed community to insure a relationship with them (see Ex. 15:2, 17, 18; Ps. 88:1; 89:26; 140:7; Is. 12:2).

2:10 the LORD spoke to the fish: The focus in the story of Jonah is on the Lord's sovereign control over creation to bring about His purpose.

3:1, 2 Jonah's new commission was essentially the same as the one he had received in 1:1, 2.

3:3 Jonah obeyed the command of the Lord the second time and made the journey to Nineveh. **a three-day journey in extent:** The city wall of Nineveh had a circumference of about eight miles, indicating that Nineveh was an exceedingly large city for the times. But the reference to "three days" likely refers to the larger administrative district of Nineveh, made up of several cities, with a circumference of about 55 miles.

3:4 Jonah proclaimed that there were only **forty days** before the destruction of Nineveh. Both the announcement and the specified delay show God's mercy. It was this mercy that bothered Jonah (4:1–3).

3:5, 6 believed God: The term used for God here is the general term for deity. In contrast, the sailors in ch. 1 proclaimed faith in the Lord, using the personal, covenant name for God (1:16). The fact that the writer does not use the personal name for God here may suggest that the Ninevites had a short-lived or imperfect understanding of God's message. History bears this out: We have no historical record of a lasting period of belief in Nineveh. Eventually the city was destroyed, in 612 B.C. **fast ... sackcloth ... ashes:** These are expressions of mourning and lamentation (see 2 Kin. 19:1; 2 Chr. 20:3; Is. 58:5–9; Jer. 36:6–9; Joel 1:13, 14; 2:12–18).

3:7 proclaimed and published: The king's edict reached all of Nineveh.

3:8, 9 God will turn and relent: The reversal of the threat to destroy Nineveh depended solely on the grace and mercy of the Lord. At times, the announced judgment of God is *not* His real intent (see 4:2; Jer. 18:7, 8; Amos 7:3). Such announcements usually include offers of mercy and forgiveness (see Zeph. 2:1–3).

3:10 God relented: The Ninevites' repentance moved the Lord to extend grace and mercy to them.

4:1 Jonah ... became angry: In contrast to God, Jonah had no compassion on the people of Nineveh. **displeased:** Jonah's irritation belied the good news that the city would be spared. Jonah himself had just been spared God's fair judgment, but he was unable to appreciate the parallel.

4:2 I know: Jonah himself had experienced the excellencies of God. **Gracious and merciful** may be rephrased as "marvelously gracious." **Lovingkindness** can also mean "loyal love." This is the same word that Jonah had used in his praise of God in 2:8. **One who relents from doing harm:** In this recital of God's blessed character, Jonah built on the revelation of the Lord to Moses (see Ex. 34:6, 7).

4:3, 4 please take my life: Contrast Jonah and Elijah: Jonah's death wish came from disgust at the people's repentance; Elijah's came from a yearning for the people's repentance (see 1 Kin. 19:4). Only a few days before, Jonah had pleaded for God to keep him alive.

4:5 till he might see what would become of the city: In his continuing stubbornness and lack of compassion, Jonah held out hope that God would judge Nineveh.

4:6 the LORD God prepared: The same verb was used in 1:17 to describe the Lord's preparation of the great fish. The term is also used in v. 7 about the worm and in v. 8 about the east wind. The repeated use of *prepared* is a subtle reference to the sovereignty of God. **a plant:** The nature of this plant is unknown. Some have speculated that it was a castor-oil tree or a bottle-gourd vine. It may have been a species that grew especially fast. **to deliver him:** The Lord had rescued Jonah from drowning (1:17); now He wished to relieve His prophet from the misery of the sun.

4:7 God prepared a worm: The Book of Jonah depicts the Lord as both sovereign and free to act in creation. God placed the worm in the plant to serve as His agent in Jonah's life.

4:8 vehement east wind: The scorching sirocco wind that blows in from the desert draws moisture from plants, causing them to wither (see Is. 40:7, 8).

4:9 The word translated **is it right** comes from the verb meaning "to be good," "to do well," or "to be pleasing." Here, as in Gen. 4:4, the expression has to do with ethical behavior (see also Lev. 5:4; Ps. 36:3; Is. 1:17; Jer. 4:22; 13:23). Jonah's anger (v. 1) did not arise from a desire for justice but from his own selfishness. He continued to justify his rebellious attitude. And again, God was merciful.

4:10 Pity describes an expression of deeply felt compassion (see Ps. 72:13; Ezek. 20:17; Joel 2:13, 14). However, Jonah pitied himself more than the plant.

4:11 pity: The same word used to describe Jonah's feeling toward the plant in v. 10 is used of God's feeling toward the people of Nineveh. People are of more value than animals, and animals of more value than plants, but the Lord has a concern that extends to all of His creation. The Lord's pity comes from His character (v. 2; compare Joel 2:13, 14). **livestock:** If Jonah could take pity on a plant, which is even less important than an animal, it only made sense that God would take pity on human beings, who are made in God's image. The Book of Jonah ends on this note of contrast between Jonah's ungracious heart and the kind heart of the Lord.

 IN DEPTH | **Why Nineveh Repented**

Many factors may have accounted for the Ninevites sudden change of attitude. Yet we know that God has a way of drawing people, and of arranging events so people are more likely to turn toward Him. Financial pressures, political turmoil, natural disasters, sickness—such things often cause people to take stock of their relationship with the Almighty. The case of Nineveh shows that this is true for nations as well as individuals.

Nineveh's repentance is instructive for Christians today. Like Jonah, we have been commissioned to take the gospel of repentance and salvation to the nations of the world (Mark 16:15, 16). In doing so, it might be well to consider a strategy of targeted evangelism. Efforts would seem likely to be more effective in areas where recent political upheaval and natural disasters have created instability and more openness to a message of grace. If God has been preparing hearts beforehand, it is reasonable to expect greater success under such circumstances.

Micah

Introduction

The Book of Micah presents an impassioned and artistic interplay between oracles of impending judgment and promises of future blessing on Israel and Judah. Both nations had broken covenant with their Lord. Through Micah, the Lord confronted His people, but He also promised to bring future blessing through the One who would be coming. This One would be the true Shepherd of God's flock.

Little is known about the prophet Micah beyond his name, his place of origin, and the personal tone of his book. Micah was born in the rural village of Moresheth Gath in the lowlands of Judah, near the region of Philistia, setting him apart from his more illustrious contemporary Isaiah, who was from Jerusalem. He probably compiled the book as an anthology of his own lengthy preaching career, which extended over the last third of the eighth century B.C., during the reigns of Jotham (752–736 B.C.), Ahaz (736–720 B.C.), and Hezekiah (729–699 B.C.) of Judah.

Micah's preaching warned Judah about an impending national disaster. Yet the religious leaders of Jerusalem were confident that no evil would come to them because of the presence of the holy temple in their midst. Micah confronted their arrogance and their mistaken notions of God: not even the temple on Mount Zion would be spared the onslaught of God's wrath (3:12).

The interplay of texts of wrath and mercy in the Book of Micah mirrors the character of God, for even in His wrath He remembers mercy. In the darkest days of judgment on the nations of Israel and Judah, there was always the possibility of a remnant being spared. Although the Lord was determined to maintain His holiness, He was equally intent on fulfilling His promises to Abraham (see Gen. 12; 15; 22). The Lord would balance His judgment with mercy. Consequently Micah also balances his oracles of judgment with oracles of promise.

According to Micah, there would be a time when the coming messianic King would gather His people together (2:12, 13), when He would establish peace (4:3), and when He

would bring justice to the earth (4:2, 3). Remarkably, Micah prophesies that this coming Messiah would be born in Bethlehem (5:2). The fulfillment of this prophecy in Jesus' birth in Bethlehem gives us confidence that the prophecies of Jesus' glorious future will also be fulfilled (see Matt. 2:1).

1:1 Micah means "Who Is Like the Lord?" The question presents a major biblical theme, the idea that God is incomparable (see 7:18; Deut. 4:32–40; Ps. 113:4–6). Micah's ministry centered on the Assyrian threat to **Samaria,** the capital of Israel that was destroyed in 722 B.C., and **Jerusalem,** the capital of Judah.

1:2 all you peoples: All the earth was to know that God was witnessing **against** His people. This announcement of judgment is based on the people's breach of covenant. The faithlessness of the people provoked **the Lord GOD** to enter into a judicial dispute with them.

1:3, 4 the LORD is coming: This is the language of epiphany, the dramatic coming of God to earth, here in a solemn procession of judgment. The expression **high places** is ironic. Jerusalem and Samaria were the "high places," or elevated capitals, of Judah and Israel; but "high places" were also sites of idolatrous worship.

1:5 Jacob is used to refer to the northern kingdom Israel, whose **transgression** was centered in its capital Samaria. Judah's sins were centered in its capital Jerusalem. In this verse, the intent of the term **high places** (v. 3) is made plain. Jerusalem, which was once "beautiful in elevation" (see Ps. 48:2), was nothing more than another platform of pagan worship, like the "high places" of the Canaanites.

1:6 a heap of ruins: God's judicial decision was to destroy Samaria so thoroughly that it would be a place fit only for vineyards among the rubble.

1:7 Idolatry is often described in the Hebrew Bible as spiritual adultery (see Jer. 3:1; Hos. 4:15). Israel is pictured as a wife who is unfaithful to her husband (see Jer. 2:20). This is not just a metaphor, however; the worship system of Canaan was sexual in nature. The word **idols** here has the sense of "disgusting images," probably referring to the explicit sexual nature of these idols. But there is comic justice at the end of the verse. The pagan symbols of Israel's worship would be reused by the nation's conquerors (Assyria) in their own debased temples.

1:8 I will wail … I will go stripped: Micah's response to God's message was an overwhelming sense of dread (7:1). **naked:** Micah's words describe mourning rites in which outer garments were laid aside in deep humility. The mourning person thought no longer about himself but only about the calamity that had overcome his senses.

1:9 her wounds: At first the reference is to the wounds of Israel, the northern kingdom. But the disease spread **to Judah.**

1:10 in Gath: The reference here is to the lament of David over the death of Saul and Jonathan (see 2 Sam. 1:20). Just as it was unseemly then to have the bad news of God's people profaned in a foreign city, so it would be in the present circumstance. **Beth Aprah** means "House of Dust"; appropriately, the inhabitants would **roll** themselves **in the dust,** an act of extreme mourning.

1:11 The name **Shaphir** means "Beautiful." Ironically, its inhabitants would be shamed by their nakedness. **Zaanan:** This name speaks of "sheep" who "go out on their own." However, this would no longer be the case for the citizens of Zaanan, who would no longer go out because of their fear.

1:12 Maroth means "Bitterness." The name **Jerusalem** suggests "Peace." The inhabitants

of the *town of bitterness* would be sickened with dread, and the inhabitants of *town of peace* would experience God's judgment.

1:13 Lachish: This famous guard city to Jerusalem was judged as being among the first places in Judah to adopt the sins of Baal worship. **daughter of Zion:** Jerusalem is the daughter of the Lord.

1:14 Moresheth Gath, which means "The Possession of Gath," was Micah's hometown (v. 1). The **presents** were farewell gifts; the city was soon to be lost.

1:15 The words **heir** and **the glory of Israel** might lead one to assume that this is a messianic verse, a promise of hope in the midst of despair. Yet the context is judgment (v. 16). The point here may be that the situation would be so bad that the proper *heir* and *glory* of the nation—the members of the royal family—would have to flee in terror to remote hiding places.

1:16 In a culture in which a man's hair was highly valued, to **cut off** one's **hair** was the ultimate sign of mourning.

2:1, 2 devise iniquity … covet: The ethical teaching of the prophets included oracles of judgment against greed, theft, and oppression. To *covet* is not just to have a passing thought; it is a determination to seize what is not one's own.

2:3 devising disaster: While the wicked devised iniquity (v. 1), God made some plans of His own.

2:4 A **proverb** was a taunt song. **To a turncoat:** God would take the property rights

---

✎ IN DEPTH	**Geographical Puns in Micah**

With With skillfully written wordplays on the names of Judah's cities, Micah prophesied of the coming destruction of Judah (1:3–16). He turned around the meaning of a number of town names as a way of describing the world being turned upside down. Shaphir, meaning "Beautiful," would be shamed (1:11); and Jerusalem, a name suggesting "Peace," would be disrupted (1:12). Lachish, a name sounding like the Hebrew word for *swift steeds*, would flee on its horses. All this agitation was caused by God's judgment on Judah for worshiping other gods on the high places. In fact, idolatry was so rampant that Micah describes Jerusalem and Samaria, the capital cities of Judah and Israel, as high places themselves (1:5).

from those who had seized them illegally and give them to people who were even more reprobate than they were.

2:5, 6 no one to determine boundaries: Land-grabbers would no longer have a legitimate claim among God's people. God would dispossess them even as they had dispossessed others. **Do not prattle:** These words may have been a strong warning to Micah not to be like the lying prophets who counseled that all was well in the land.

2:7–9 The **words** of God were different from the words of the lying prophets (v. 6). The words of God bring **good** to the righteous and judgment against the wicked.

2:10, 11 The lying prophets (v. 6) spoke of **rest** when **utter destruction** was decreed by the Lord. They spoke of **wine and drink** at a time of disaster.

2:12, 13 assemble ... gather ... put them together: The verbs are emphatic, demonstrating the certainty of God's determination to bring to pass His good pleasure on Israel (see Deut. 30:1–6). **breaks open ... break out:** These phrases speak of regathering Israel from wherever the people have been scattered.

3:1 Is it not for you to know justice: The idea here is that one might not expect justice from pagan leaders in a faraway place. But the **rulers** of the people of God were expected to emphasize justice. Justice is one of the key concepts of the Law (see Deut. 10:18; 32:4). Perverting justice was prohibited by God (see Deut. 16:19; 24:17). Yet this was precisely what the leaders of Judah were doing.

3:2, 3 Micah used an image of barbaric cannibalism to describe the horrendous actions of the leaders against the people. It was as if the leaders were eating **the flesh** from the people's **bones.**

3:4 He will not hear them: The wickedness of the people was so great that last-minute repentance would not suffice (see Jer. 11:11).

3:5–7 This oracle of judgment was presented against the false **prophets** who proclaimed **peace,** causing the people to be unprepared for trouble. These prophets would have neither true prophetic insight (**vision**), nor help from the forbidden arts of **divination.** Finally they would have nothing to say, for there would be **no answer from God.**

3:8–10 full of power: Unlike the silenced false prophets (vv. 5–7), Micah was divinely empowered (see 1 Cor. 2:13; 2 Pet. 1:21). **Justice and might** may be rephrased as "powerful justice," a contrast to the leaders of Israel (v. 1).

3:11 bribe ... pay ... money: The wicked leaders and prophets of Israel "worked" only when they could gain something. **Is not the LORD among us:** Many people of Jerusalem believed that they would not be affected by God's judgment because God Himself dwelled in the holy temple in Jerusalem. They reasoned that despite their evils, as long as God was in His temple, they were safe—even from divine judgment. It was unthinkable to them that God might *leave* His temple because of the sinfulness of the people.

3:12 This verse was quoted by Jeremiah (see Jer. 26:18). While the false prophets and the wicked rulers believed that they were untouchable and that Mount Zion was inviolable, the prophet Micah announced that **Zion** (Jerusalem) would **be plowed like a field,** indicating complete devastation of the city.

4:1 The phrase **in the latter days** is an indication of a prophecy of end times. **The mountain of the LORD's house** describes the temple in Jerusalem. Originally the temple site was located on one of several hills that make up the general area. In the *latter days* the temple site will be elevated **above the hills** (see Zech. 8:1–3; 14:1–11).

4:2 Many nations: When non-Israelites came to true faith, it would be in **the God of Jacob. we shall walk:** Unlike the people of Micah's generation who were strangers to justice (3:1), the peoples of the coming kingdom will be obedient to God.

4:3 judge ... rebuke: These are actions of the Savior King who will rule with a rod of iron (see Ps. 2; 110). **swords ... spears:** All weapons of destruction will be recycled into tools of production. There will finally be an end to conflict.

4:4, 5 The **vine** and **fig tree** are symbols of peace and prosperity (see Zech. 3:10). **no one shall make them afraid:** Fear, like war (v. 3), will become a thing of the past.

4:6, 7 In that day: This wording connects this section with the end times referred to in v. 1.

afflicted: Those whom God had driven from the land would be the people of His new kingdom. **remnant:** The majority of people in Israel did not live in faith and dedication to the Lord. However, true faith never really died out in Israel, even in the worst of times.

4:8 Tower of the flock is a description of Jerusalem in the ideal sense. A *tower* was a vantage point for protecting a flock of sheep. Likewise, Jerusalem is the **stronghold** or defense point for the flock of God (2:12).

4:9–12 Micah addressed the city of **Zion** (Jerusalem) as though it were a **woman in labor.** The troubles of the present would lead finally to the birth of a deliverer. **To Babylon you shall go** refers to the Exile.

4:13 Arise and thresh: The nations would be gathered by the Lord like sheaves on the threshing floor (v. 12). This is a way of speaking of the final victory over all of Israel's foes.

5:1 gather yourself in troops: The reference here seems to be to the assaults of the enemies of Judah on the people of God before their final defeat.

5:2 Bethlehem means "House of Bread" (see Ruth 1:1). **Ephrathah** locates the village in a known region in Judah (see Gen. 35:16). This prophecy figures significantly in the New Testament story of the visit of the wise men to the Christ child (see Matt. 2:1–12). Governments would be overturned to make it necessary for Mary while still pregnant to make the journey from Nazareth to Bethlehem. **goings forth:** The birth of this Savior King would be unlike the birth of any other, because He was preexistent. He is **from everlasting.**

5:3, 4 The future of Israel is pictured here in terms of the birth, life, and ministry of the Savior King. The two advents of the Savior are seen as one event by Micah. Whereas v. 2 speaks of the birth of the Savior in His First Coming, vv. 3–5 speak of the time of the rule of Jesus in the Second Coming. **She who is in labor** probably refers to Zion (4:10). The metaphor refers to the deliverance in the end time of those who will be able to delight in the coming of God's kingdom (4:9—5:1).

5:5, 6 When the Assyrian comes: The principal threat against Israel and Judah at the time of Micah was Assyria. Micah used the nation as a symbol of all of Israel's enemies and of God's final victory over each of them.

5:7–9 This section concerns God's blessing on **the remnant of Jacob.** The wickedness of the people would bring about God's judgment, but He would not cast them off completely. **In the midst of many peoples** describes the spread of the Jewish people throughout the earth in the time of God's judgment.

5:10, 11 I will cut off: It was God's intention to destroy the evils in Israel's society. **Horses** and **chariots** represent the pride of Israel's military power. Israel's tendency was to rely on its military power rather than on the Lord.

5:12 Sorcery and soothsaying had been strongly condemned by God (see Deut. 18:10).

5:13–15 The second commandment had forbidden the use of **carved images** in Israel (see Ex. 20:4). **Sacred pillars** refers to phallic poles used in Canaanite sexual worship rites. **Wooden images** refers to the Asherah groves. Both of these items had been condemned in the Law (see Deut. 16:21, 22).

6:1, 2 God (the Judge) calls for the people (the defendants) to **plead** their **case. The mountains** and **hills** were among the witnesses to the covenant that God made with His people (see Deut. 4:26; 32:1; Is. 1:2). **He will contend:** If the people were silent before the **mountains,** the Lord Himself would speak against their sin.

6:3 what have I done: The Lord was entirely innocent of misbehavior against His people (see Jer. 2:5).

6:4, 5 The Lord summarized His great mercies to Israel, including His saving works in bringing the people from **Egypt** in the Exodus and His deliverance of Israel from the evils that **Balak** and **Balaam** had planned (see Num. 22—24).

6:6, 7 Come before means "to make an approach in true worship" (see Ps. 15). **burnt offerings ... calves a year old:** These were among the divinely prescribed sacrifices of true biblical worship (see Lev. 1:3; 9:3). The words of v. 7 go far beyond any demand of the Law, and even go *against* the Law in the suggestion that God may not be satisfied except by an offering of one's own child. Micah uses hyperbole (deliberate exaggeration) to emphasize the necessity of a right attitude in the true worship of God.

6:8 This verse speaks of the attitudes that must accompany all true worship. **what does the LORD require of you:** The idea here is that God seeks certain characteristics of true worship from His people. **do justly ... love mercy ... walk humbly:** These phrases summarize biblical piety in true worship. The majority of the people of Israel had violated each of these standards repeatedly. The rulers did not know *justice* (3:1), had no interest in *mercy* (3:2, 3), and demonstrated no *humility* (3:11).

6:9 The rod is a messianic image. It is possible that this verse is based on Ps. 2 (see Ps. 2:9, 11, 12).

6:10–15 The people of Judah were abusing others with false measures, with **violence,** and with **lies.** Such practices were far removed from the description of true worship in v. 8. This is the divine vindication of the Lord's determination to bring judgment on Jerusalem, despite the fact that His holy temple was there (3:11, 12). The worship that was being offered, although it followed the form of the Law, did not come from true biblical attitudes and practices of piety.

6:16 The spiritual history of the northern kingdom reached its lowest point under the rules of **Omri** and **Ahab.** Whereas Jeroboam I had combined the worship of God with the nature and sexual worship rites of Baal (see 1 Kin. 12:25–33), Ahab and his wife Jezebel (in a marriage arranged by Omri) brought about the state worship of Baal and Asherah (see 1 Kin. 16:21–34). For these reasons, and despite the presence of the temple, God was about to bring utter shame on His people.

7:1, 2 Micah was moved by the oracles of judgment that God delivered through him (1:8). **no cluster:** For Micah, the harvest was over. There was nothing around him but undesirable fruit. **The faithful man has perished:** The norms of society had broken down; everyone was out to destroy someone else.

7:3–6 with both hands: The people were pursuing **evil** with gusto. The leaders of the

state were leading the way in evil (3:11). **The day of your watchman** refers to a time when people needed to be alert for the approach of an enemy army. In this context, judgment was imminent.

7:7 Therefore I will look: These words are a pun on the words of v. 4. While there would need to be a *watchman* for the coming of an enemy army, Micah was going to be a *watchman* for the advent of **the LORD.**

7:8, 9 The speaker in these verses is the nation Israel after it comes to repentance. **I have sinned** is the confession of the people in saving faith. **He pleads my case:** Here the Lord is speaking on *behalf* of the people (compare ch. 6). As God had delivered Israel in the past because of **His righteousness,** so He would deliver a repentant Israel in the future.

7:10 The people of Israel knew that they would suffer indignities at the hands of their enemies in the period of divine judgment. However, God's judgment of His people was designed to bring about their repentance.

7:11–13 In the day: These words call attention to a future day, the time of the end. **You** here is Zion (Jerusalem). This is a prophecy of the return of the remnant (2:12, 13; 4:1–4, 6–8; 5:3, 7, 8). **The River** is the Euphrates. The idea of these verses is a universal regathering of God's people in His land (see Deut. 30:1–6).

7:14, 15 Micah prayed that God the **Shepherd** would care for His **flock.** Micah requested that the greatest wonders of the relationship between God and His people at the time of the Exodus would be realized anew.

7:16, 17 The response of the wicked **nations** to the renewed mercies of God on His people would be terror. The nations would be humiliated because they had taunted Israel in the day of its trouble (vv. 8–10).

7:18, 19 Who is a God like You: These words speak of the incomparability of God. There is nothing in all of creation to compare with God (see Is. 40:25).

7:20 This last verse is reminiscent of God's promise to Abraham in Gen. 12; 15; 22 and His promises to Jacob in Gen. 32. The Lord had sworn to fulfill His promises to the patriarchs. He would not leave His promise unfulfilled (see Ps. 89:33).

Nahum

Introduction

The Book of Nahum is one of two books of the minor prophets that centers on Nineveh, the capital city of Assyria. In the Book of Jonah, written in the eighth century B.C., we behold a man of God who was called to preach to Nineveh. The people of Nineveh repented, and God demonstrated his compassion by not judging the city. In the Book of Nahum, written in the seventh century B.C., we find another prophet called by God to preach to Nineveh. Evil again reigned in the capital. Tragically, the people of Nineveh this time ignored Nahum's warning.

Nahum, the author of this book, is not known apart from the three chapters of this prophecy. Even the location of the place of his birth, Elkosh (1:1), is in doubt. However, since Nahum wrote considerably after the destruction of Israel in 722 B.C., we may assume that Elkosh was in Judah. The fall of Thebes in 663 B.C. (3:8) determines the limit for the earliest date of the book. The fall of Nineveh, which the book predicts, took place in 612 B.C., not long before the destruction of the Assyrian Empire in 609 B.C. This means the Book of Nahum was composed sometime before 612 B.C, perhaps under the reform of King Josiah of Judah in 622 B.C.

The people of the northern kingdom of Israel had been sinning against God and ignoring the warnings of punishment given through God's prophets. Finally God used the nation of Assyria, with its capital city in Nineveh, to destroy the nation and carry the people into captivity. A century after the fall of Samaria in 722 B.C., the Book of Nahum was written to express a major truth of the prophets. Even when God uses a nation for His own purposes of judgment, this does not excuse that nation from its own guilt before the Lord. It was Nineveh's turn to feel the wrath of God.

How does the mood of the Book of Nahum accord with the sentiment of the Sermon on the Mount? Although the Lord Jesus certainly spoke of loving one's enemies

(see Matt. 5:43–48), He strongly warned of the inevitability of judgment (see Matt. 5:21, 29, 30; 7:13, 23). In the conquest of the ancient world, the Assyrians were merciless and cruel. Their atrocities included everything from burning children to death to chopping off hands. Nineveh had an international reputation for bloodthirsty acts of repression, destruction, and wantonness. God could not be good if He failed to call such an evil nation to account. Judgment is God's "unusual act" (see Is. 28:21), but it ultimately arises out of His goodness and justice.

1:1 Most of the biblical prophets directed their judgment oracles against the sinning peoples of Israel and Judah. **Nahum,** however, brought the word of God's judgment **against Nineveh.** The term **burden** was sometimes used by the prophets (see Hab. 1:1; Mal. 1:1) to describe the "heaviness" of their message of judgment.

1:2 avenges ... furious: The repetition of words and the use of parallel terms are typical devices in Hebrew poetry for intensifying and sharpening the poet's message.

1:3 Slow to anger indicates the patience of the Lord (see Ex. 34:6, 7). However, God's patience is not a reason to disbelieve His final judgment (see Ps. 10). **whirlwind ... storm ... clouds:** The peoples of the ancient Middle East worshiped nature gods, particularly deities associated with storms, clouds, and rainfall. In Canaan, this fixation on storms was centered in the worship of Baal and his consorts Anat and Asherah.

1:4 sea ... rivers: The Lord's control extends to all bodies of water and to places of lush vegetation—including **Bashan, Carmel,** and **Lebanon.**

1:5, 6 quake ... melt ... heaves: The people of God had experienced such demonstrations of God's presence at the foot of Mount Sinai when the Lord descended with His law (see Ex. 19). **indignation ... anger ... fury:** Grouping these three terms causes the force of the words to be felt more deeply. In other words, God's anger burned intensely against the sinful people of Nineveh.

1:7 The LORD is good: For the righteous, this is the best news of all. Because we know that the Lord is good, we can endure the tribulations of life.

1:8 flood … end … darkness: The judgment of the Lord will be inescapable. The word *flood* is both a poetic term for overwhelming devastation and a specific reference to the actual manner of Nineveh's fall. It is believed that the invaders of Nineveh entered the city through its flooded waterways (2:6).

1:9, 10 What do you conspire against the LORD: Who is strong enough to resist God's power? No one, of course. The enemies of God will be comic figures. Their best plans will be no more than a tangle of **thorns;** their finest moves will be only the walk of **drunkards.**

1:11 Wicked is one of the harshest terms in biblical language, nearly a curse word. The term speaks of someone who is utterly worthless.

1:12, 13 Thus says the LORD: Here is an oracle of deliverance from God to His people. The present sense of safety and power that the enemy felt would not last; the past judgments of God on His nation would not continue. The Lord promised to **break off** the **yoke** that the enemy had placed on His people (see Is. 9:4).

1:14 Here God spoke to His people's enemy—the nation of Assyria typified by its capital city Nineveh (v. 1). In destroying the nation's **name,** God would remove its power. Further, the Lord swore to destroy their false religious system, with its pagan temples, idols, and disgusting practices. **You are vile:** The only thing to be done with Nineveh was to **dig** a **grave** and bury it. This prophecy came true literally. The city was destroyed so completely that its existence was questioned until its discovery by archaeologists in the nineteenth century (3:13–15).

1:15 Behold … The feet: The image is that of a herald of **peace** (see Is. 52:7). **O Judah:** With the promise of future deliverance from oppression, the prophet called for the people to live in righteousness and expectation. There is nothing better for the people of God in any age than to live in obedience to Him and in anticipation of His coming deliverance.

2:1 Man the fort: These were sarcastic words to the people of Nineveh and its leaders, as if they would be able to protect themselves against the wrath of the Lord.

2:2 the LORD will restore: The wrath of God against the enemies of His people means that one day the enemies will be destroyed and the people of God will be restored. **Excellence** means "majesty," "beauty," or "wonder" (see Is. 4:2). The ruin of Israel would not last forever.

2:3 red … scarlet … flaming torches: These images speak of blood, violence, and warfare. Isaiah refers to the custom the Assyrians had of rolling their outer garments in blood before a battle (see Is. 9:5) to strike terror in the hearts of their opponents. Here the tables would be turned. While others would have **shields, chariots,** and **spears,** the people of Nineveh would be bathed in blood—their own blood.

2:4 The chariots rage: The Assyrians used chariots as formidable war machines. The proficiency of the chariot drivers underlies the imagery of this verse. But as in the case of the shields and spears of v. 3, the chariots of Nineveh would not prevail no matter how fast they drove.

2:5 stumble: The people within the city would be so stunned to be under attack that they would appear helpless in their actions. **Nobles** may be used with sarcasm here; these people do not seem very impressive.

2:6 gates of the rivers: The destruction of Nineveh is believed to have taken place when the besiegers entered the city through its flooded waterways. The attack came at flood time, when rivers undermined the walls and defenses of the city. Archaeologists have found evidence of flood debris that may be associated with the destruction of the city. Thus the words of Nahum were fulfilled exactly.

2:7, 8 She shall be led away: The nation that had made so much of taking captives would be made a captive by others. **Halt! Halt!:** No one would listen to their shouts of panic.

2:9, 10 spoil: Assyria had despoiled many nations, including Samaria and the cities of Israel. There seemed to be no end to the loot that could be found within its walls. None-theless, even Nineveh was exhausted of its treasures. At long last, it was **empty.**

2:11, 12 Nineveh was the city of **lions** (v. 13). Yet despite all the horrors that the *lion* of Nineveh had brought to other nations, it would no longer need to be feared by anyone.

2:13 Although the Babylonians conquered the city, they were only God's instruments. Nineveh's greatest foe was **the LORD of hosts** Himself.

3:1 the bloody city: Nineveh was known throughout the Middle East as a city that excelled in violence and bloodshed.

3:2, 3 Horses and **chariots** were instruments of war. Verse 3 describes the horrors of the nation's war machine, which resulted in **countless corpses.**

3:4 Harlotries refers to paganism. Any worship of gods other than the God of Scripture is an act of spiritual prostitution. Nineveh was so adept at pagan practices that the city earned the descriptive title, **the mistress of sorceries.**

3:5 I am against you: This repetition of this phrase from 2:13 is more chilling each time it is heard. Who could survive the Lord's opposition? **lift your skirts:** The Lord would publicly humiliate Nineveh.

3:6, 7 The Lord described the fate of Nineveh as comparable to a person on whom unspeakable **filth** was cast. When Nineveh lay in ruins, no one would **bemoan her.** The nations would be glad that the city was gone.

3:8 No Amon ... the River: The destruction of the city of Thebes near the Nile River in 663 B.C. was going to be a template for the destruction of Nineveh. No Amon is the

Hebrew name for Thebes, derived from the Egyptian name meaning "City of (the god) Amon." The argument seems to suggest that before its destruction, no one would have dreamed of the fall of Thebes. But the destruction *had* happened—not long before the writing of the Book of Nahum. The city of Thebes was rebuilt only to be destroyed later during the Roman period (29 B.C.). Nineveh, however, would never be rebuilt.

3:9, 10 The city of No Amon had many powerful allies, but they were not sufficient to protect her in her hour of need. Who would ally with Nineveh to fight off the Lord's attack?

3:11 drunk ... hidden ... seek refuge: Nineveh would be like a helpless drunk hoping for refuge but finding nowhere to turn.

3:12, 13 Nahum satirically describes the **strongholds** of Nineveh as being so easily defeated that they would be like fruit trees that drop their **figs** into waiting mouths.

3:14, 15 Nahum taunted Nineveh by telling the people to prepare for their siege. The actual siege of Nineveh continued over two years.

3:16, 17 Despite the great economic and military strength of Nineveh, there was nothing lasting in the city's power. **When the sun rises:** The people of Nineveh would be like nocturnal insects that disappear at daylight.

3:18 Your shepherds slumber: When the shepherds are not alert, the sheep cannot be saved from danger.

3:19 All who hear: Every nation and people that had suffered under the abusive power of Nineveh would shout and **clap** upon hearing of the city's destruction. There would be no mourning for Nineveh.

Habakkuk

Introduction

Habakkuk was unique among the prophets in that he asked questions of God. His questions were, "Why does evil in Judah go unpunished?" "How can a just God use a wicked nation like Babylon to punish His chosen people?" Habakkuk wanted to know, just as we do, what God was doing and why. There seemed to be too much evil among the "righteous" and too much free-wheeling power among the wicked.

God did not strike Habakkuk down for these questions. He answered. The Lord Himself will establish His kingdom. He will hold all people and nations accountable. The present may be filled with wickedness and chaos, but the future belongs to the righteous—the truly righteous. God will bring in His kingdom, give rest to His children, and judge His people's adversaries.

We know very little about the prophet Habakkuk. The reference to music (see 3:1, 19; 1 Chr. 25:1–8) may mean that he was a Levite associated with the temple singers. The designation *the prophet* is an official title, showing that others recognized him as a prophet of the Lord. His name Habakkuk may mean "Embraced by God."

Habakkuk prophesied during the fall of Nineveh in 612 B.C. and the rise of Babylon as the Neo-Babylonian Empire. By 605 B.C., Assyria and Egypt had been defeated by Babylon at Carchemish. Judah's days were numbered, and Babylon's power was rapidly expanding. In addition, the death of King Josiah in 609 B.C. brought an end to an era of religious reform in Judah. It seemed that the wicked were prevailing both inside and outside Judah. Habakkuk cried out against the violence, lawlessness, and injustice he saw all around him.

According to Habakkuk, the Lord is sovereign; He sits in His holy temple watching the earth. He will eventually judge each person for his or her life (2:20). While people may be seduced into wickedness by the allure of power and success (2:6–20), a glorious future awaits those who submit to God (2:4). Habakkuk's prophetic vision (2:2) and

prayer (3:1) provide a proper perspective for viewing the injustices of this world. The Almighty is in control. He will establish His righteous kingdom in the end. In that day, all wrongs will be made right: The wicked will be judged for their sinfulness, and the righteous will be saved.

1:1 A **burden** refers to a prophetic oracle, usually addressed to a foreign nation (see Is. 13:1).

1:2 Habakkuk spoke to God using His covenant name **LORD** (see Ex. 3:14, 15). **how long:** This question is phrased as a formal complaint (see Ps. 13:1, 2).

1:3 iniquity ... trouble: The deterioration of society had become a cause of frustration and disappointment for the godly. **plundering and violence:** Abuse of power, acts of injustice, and oppressive deeds were common in Judah. **strife ... contention:** The people of Judah argued with each other and were involved in destructive litigation.

1:4 the law is powerless: The revelation of God given at Mount Sinai had little impact on the hearts of people whose lives were focused on material success. These people had little interest in living by God's definition of what is fair and humane. **righteous:** There were always people who were faithful to the Lord, a righteous remnant. Here the godly were restricted in what they could say and do because of the evil that surrounded them.

1:5 Look among the nations: The international scene during Habakkuk's lifetime was full of turmoil, with Assyria on the decline and Babylonia on the rise. **work a work:** The Hebrew words suggest that something ominous and impressive was about to occur.

1:6 I am raising up: God controls the nations for His own purposes (see Dan. 2:21), sometimes indirectly and at other times directly. **Chaldeans** is another word for Babylonians. **bitter:** The Babylonians were harsh and oppressive in their rule.

1:7 terrible and dreadful: Far from being humane, the Babylonians prided themselves on their arrogant use of raw power. They had no regard for other legal systems.

1:8 The Babylonians' use of **horses** and chariots made them fearsome. **fierce ... wolves:**

The Babylonians were powerful and tyrannical. **eagle:** The Palestinian eagle is a bird of prey, a vulture. These images from the animal kingdom present a vivid picture of the ferocious nature of this world power.

1:9 Habakkuk had observed **violence** in Judah (v. 2), but Babylon *relished* violence. **gather captives like sand:** The Babylonians resettled numerous conquered peoples with little regard for them as individuals.

1:10, 11 scoff … scorned: The Babylonians did not respect authorities and powers other than their own. **deride every stronghold:** The Babylonians mocked human systems of fortification, bursting through any defense they encountered.

1:12 Are you not … my Holy One: Habakkuk's point seems to be that God's holiness should have prohibited Him from using a "dirty" instrument like Babylon to accomplish His purposes in judging and reproving His own people.

1:13 purer eyes: Habakkuk wondered how God could look on as the wicked Babylonians perverted justice. **A person more righteous than he:** This was the ethical dilemma that faced Habakkuk: The Judeans were less corrupt and idolatrous than the Babylonians, who were being used to judge them for their sins.

1:14, 15 Habakkuk's charges against the Lord became even more daring. The prophet charged the Lord with reducing humans to the level of **fish** or insects and with causing chaos among the nations.

1:16 they sacrifice to their net: This phrase speaks of the contemptuous pride of the Babylonians in their devices of destruction.

1:17 Habakkuk wanted to know how God could allow the brazen activity of the Babylonians to **continue** unabated. The prophet reasoned that God surely had a desire to punish the Babylonians for their pride.

2:1 my watch … on the rampart: Habakkuk stationed himself as a watchman to look at the nations, as God had commanded him (1:5). The prophet also waited expectantly for God's response to his three charges in 1:12–17. **what He will say to me:** Habakkuk's faith is seen in his anticipation of a response from God.

2:2 The command to **write** the revelation is unusual. Generally prophets *spoke* the word of the Lord first. The term **vision** here is related to the verb translated "saw" in 1:1. The noun speaks of a prophetic revelation (see Is. 1:1). **he may run who reads it:** Messengers would proclaim the divine oracle.

✎ **IN DEPTH**   **Questioning God**

Some people believe that human beings should never question the ways of God. Some even feel that it borders on sin to ask God, "Why?" But the Book of Habakkuk counters that idea. It is filled with a prophet's perplexing questions—and the Lord's penetrating answers.

Habakkuk was not unlike many people today who are troubled by the world around them. They, too, sometimes wonder: Where is God? Why doesn't He do something about all the pain and suffering, the injustice and oppression, the wars and diseases that destroy humanity? If He is there, why doesn't He speak? If He is powerful, why doesn't He act? If He is loving, why doesn't He intervene? Habakkuk shows that questions like these are as old as the seventh century A.D.

So are the answers. While God may not explain everything to our satisfaction—nor are we capable of understanding everything He has told us—He assures us, just as He assured Habakkuk, that His ways are just and righteous, and furthermore, "the just shall live by faith" (2:4). This truth applies universally, as Paul and other writers of the NT realized (Rom. 1:17; Gal. 3:11; Heb. 10:38). In the end, the ultimate answer to our questions is to trust God.

2:3 An appointed time speaks of a determined time in God's eyes. God knows His plan and the outworking of all things in accordance with His purposes. **it will surely come:** The assurance of fulfillment lies in God Himself. **It will not tarry:** The fulfillment of the vision would not take any longer than God had planned.

2:4 The proud refers to the Babylonians, who exalted themselves and boasted of their conquests and power. **His soul is not upright in him:** The Babylonians had no regard for God, His commandments, or His people. **the just shall live by his faith:** True righteousness before God is linked to genuine faith in God. A proud person relies on self, power, position, and accomplishment; a righteous person relies on the Lord.

2:5 proud man: This arrogant and boastful person is a personification of Babylon (v. 4). The term **hell** is used here as a personification of death which, like a greedy person, is never satisfied (see Prov. 30:15, 16). **all nations ... all peoples:** These peoples of the earth should have been gathered together before the Lord in holy worship (see Ps. 117:1); instead, they became morsels for the rapacious appetite of Babylon.

2:6 A **woe** oracle is an oracle of judgment consisting of two parts: a declaration of the wrong and a notice of impending judgment. The judgment usually applies the principle of the law of retaliation: a wrong would come back to haunt the wrongdoer. **pledges:** The practice of pledging something as a guarantee for repayment was permitted under the Law, but with limitations to ensure the humane treatment of people (see Ex. 22:26, 27; Deut. 24:10–13).

2:7, 8 The Hebrew term for **creditors** has the idea of "those who bite," suggesting sudden, hurtful attacks (see Mic. 3:5).

2:9, 10 evil gain: Gaining property through extortion and the abuse of power was strictly prohibited in the Law of Moses (see Deut. 16:19). **his nest:** As a bird builds a nest far away from people and wild animals, so the rich work hard at avoiding threats to their fortune.

2:11 the stone will cry out ... the timbers will answer it: The whole structure of Israel's society called out for justice; every part reverberated with the need for righting wrongs.

2:12 Micah also spoke against the leaders of Judah, who were developing the **city** and kingdom at the expense of humane treatment of others, and of justice (see Mic. 3:10).

2:13 LORD of hosts speaks of God as the commander of the armies of the heavens (see Hag. 1:5).

2:14, 15 God's future kingdom on earth will feature a reign of righteousness (see Is. 2:1–4; Mic. 4:1–5). All humanity on the renewed earth will know the Lord and live in accordance with His will. **The glory of the LORD** speaks of the full manifestation of His person, significance, presence, and wonder. The true knowledge of God in the time of His kingdom on earth will be like **the waters**—all-embracing and inescapable.

2:16, 17 Only God's kingdom is glorious. The **glory** of human kingdoms, such as Babylon, will be transformed into disgrace. **be exposed:** In their nakedness the Babylonians would expose themselves as being **uncircumcised,** not part of God's people nor recipients of His mercy. **The cup of the LORD's right hand** represents the wrath of God (see Is. 51:17, 22; Rev. 14:10; 16:19).

2:18, 19 teacher of lies ... trust in it: Idolatry begins with deception, encourages deception, and calls for a commitment to deception (see Is. 44:20).

2:20 the LORD is in His holy temple: These words are not set in a context of worship of God by His people. The Lord is sovereign and holy. He looks at the nations and holds them accountable. **keep silence before Him:** The call to silence is not an invitation to worship, but a command to reflect on the terrible state of all who fall into the hands of the angry God (see Zeph. 1:7).

3:1, 2 I have heard: Habakkuk knew the stories of God's mighty acts as celebrated in song and in the feasts and festivals of Israel. These mighty acts included the Exodus from Egypt, the miracles by the Red Sea, and the conquest of the land. **afraid:** As he meditated on God's work in human affairs, Habakkuk was overcome with an awe-inspiring sense of the greatness of the Lord. **revive ... make it known:**

Habakkuk prayed for God's renewed involvement in Israel.

3:3 Teman is a poetic reference to God's appearance at Sinai (see Deut. 33:2). **Selah** is probably a musical term, but its exact meaning is unknown. It may indicate a sudden shouting of "Amen," a moment of silence, or a musical chord.

3:4 Habakkuk compared the appearance of God at Sinai (v. 3) to a thunderstorm, with its darkness and lightning (see Ps. 18:9–14). **His power was hidden:** While God reveals evidence of His power, its totality and greatness remain hidden.

3:5 pestilence ... fever: These plagues are personified as messengers of judgment (see Deut. 28:21, 22).

3:6 everlasting mountains ... perpetual hills: The prophets often portrayed nature quaking, mountains shaking, and creation in turmoil at the coming of God (see Is. 24:1–3; Jer. 4:24–26; Mic. 1:3, 4; Nah. 1:5).

3:7 Cushan ... Midian: These tribes are representative of the quaking nations.

3:8–10 rivers ... sea: The Lord had divided the Red Sea and the Jordan River for His people to cross (see Ex. 14:26—15:5; Josh. 3:14–17). **chariots of salvation:** The appearance of the Lord was for the express purpose of bringing deliverance to His people.

3:11, 12 The sun and moon stood still: This is an allusion to the battle of Gibeon (see Josh. 10:12, 13). Habakkuk portrayed God as a Warrior armed with a bow, **arrows,** and a **spear** (see Ex. 15:3; Ps. 18:14; 77:17).

3:13–15 The Lord's acts of vengeance against the nations would comfort His people, because those acts would lead to Israel's **salvation** (see 2 Thess. 1:7). The people of God as a nation were **anointed** (see Ex. 19:6; Ps. 114:2). **The house of the wicked** is an allusion to Israel's redemption from Egypt.

3:16–18 Habakkuk was overcome with a sense of awe at God, as well as a sense of his own weakness. **rest in the day of trouble:** The prophet encouraged the godly not to be anxious in adversity.

3:19 The LORD God: Here the divine name *Yahweh* is tied to the term *Adonai,* which means "Lord." **my strength:** God will strengthen those who trust in Him (see Ps. 18:32, 39). He will give those who live by faith the same confidence that a surefooted **deer** has in climbing mountains (see Mal. 4:2). Like a victorious army, the righteous with God's strength will occupy **the high hills.**

Zephaniah

Introduction

Zephaniah's first words were bad news: the day of the Lord was coming. The Israelites had acted like their pagan neighbors. They had scorned God's law, worshiped false gods, and sinned without remorse. Now it was time to repent or face the consequences. It was the "turn back to God" part of Zephaniah's message that offered a ray of hope. God would restore those who sought Him.

History tells us that it worked. The Book of Zephaniah tells about events that took place in the city of Jerusalem in the late seventh century B.C., when Josiah was king. The northern kingdom Israel had been destroyed nearly a century earlier by the Assyrians. The southern kingdom Judah had suffered under the wicked rules of Manasseh (697–642 B.C.) and Amon (642–640 B.C.). The evils of their reigns had made doom appear certain. But the godly King Josiah led an important revival that affected all Judah. Scripture reports that this revival, though short-lived, delayed God's judgment, the invasion by Babylon (2 Chr. 34:27, 28).

The prophet Zephaniah traced his ancestry back four generations to Hezekiah, most likely Judah's famous king. Zephaniah began ministering as prophet in Jerusalem in the same year as the great prophet Jeremiah (627 B.C.). They and Hulda the prophetess (see 2 Chr. 34:14–28) witnessed the religious reform that Josiah started, a reform that unfortunately did not last. After Josiah's death, the people returned to their errant ways; less than fifty years later (around 586 B.C.), God used Babylon to discipline them.

The prophet Zephaniah scolded Judah's leaders for countless acts of wickedness (3:1–7). But the last section of his prophecy contains words of hope (3:8–20): promises of protection for the remnant and promises for the future of those who truly know Him. In a future day, peoples of all nations will come to worship the Lord (2:11; 3:9). His own people will be renewed in righteousness (3:11–13). And the King of kings Himself will rule in their midst (3:15; see Rev. 21:1–6). That day of the Lord's return will be a day of song and gladness. The anger of the Lord (1:1, 2) will be replaced by His happy singing, for salvation will finally have come to His people.

1:1 The word of the LORD which came: The messages of the Old Testament prophets did not arise from the prophets' own will, but from God Himself (see 2 Pet. 1:20, 21). **Zephaniah** means "Hidden in the Lord," a name that relates to the principal message the prophet presented (2:3). **Hezekiah** probably refers to the notable king of Judah (see 2 Kin. 18–20). Thus Zephaniah the prophet was related to King Josiah.

1:2, 3 utterly consume: The message of Zephaniah begins with a pronouncement of universal judgment (see Gen. 6—8). These words not only introduce the particular judgment that would be pronounced upon Judah (v. 4), but they also speak of the final judgment that will usher in the kingdom of God on earth (see Rev. 19). **Stumbling blocks** here refers to idolatry, or substitutes for God in the life and affections of a person.

1:4–6 The message of God's impending judgment on the nation of Judah and its capital city **Jerusalem** must have been startling to those who believed that God would never destroy His holy temple (v. 12). **every trace of Baal:** Baal worship and its evils had led to the destruction of Israel and its capital Samaria in 722 B.C. Likewise, Baal worship and its associations would lead to the destruction of Judah and its capital Jerusalem in 586 B.C. **Milcom** is a reference to an Ammonite deity whose worship included acts of infant sacrifice (see 2 Kin. 23:10; Jer. 32:35).

1:7 Be silent: This call for silence was for solemn preparation for the horror of divine wrath (see Hab. 2:20; Zech. 2:13). **The day of the LORD** describes a period of unusual activity on the part of God in the affairs of His people. **sacrifice:** The people of God were expected to prepare sacrifices for the Lord as acts of contrition and celebration. But rebels, idolaters, and apostates would themselves become God's sacrifice. **His guests** may be the birds of the heavens—vultures and buzzards who feed on carrion (see Rev. 19:21).

1:8, 9 Foreign apparel here suggests two things: (1) acts of greed and extortion against the populace, amassing funds for exotic clothing;

(2) participation in foreign religious rites associated with exotic clothing. **Leap over the threshold** may refer to a pagan practice like the one mentioned in 1 Sam. 5:5. The priests of Dagon would not step on the doorway of the temple to Dagon because the hands and the head of Dagon had fallen there.

1:10, 11 On that day is a common way of referring to the coming judgment (or blessing) on the day of the Lord. **Maktesh:** Zephaniah shows his familiarity with the various quarters of Jerusalem as he mentions certain gates, sections, and districts of the city. Maktesh refers to a market district. Every area of the city would be affected by God's judgment.

1:12, 13 The LORD will not do good, nor will He do evil: The complacency of the people led them to believe that God is also complacent. They believed that the Lord would be inactive, neither blessing nor cursing, neither benefiting nor punishing His people.

1:14–16 The language of this passage is similar to Joel 2:1–11. **Near** describes the imminence of the coming judgment. The references to **clouds** and **darkness** resemble Canaanite poetry in which clouds and thunder are associated with the pagan god Baal. The poets of the Bible used this language to describe the true God, who would send forth His judgments like lightning bolts from a dark mass of clouds (see Ps. 97:2–6). The references to **fortified cities** and **high towers** speak of the extent of God's judgment. There would be no adequate defense against the Lord's searing judgments.

1:17, 18 like blind men: God's judgment would be so sudden and so overwhelming that the survivors would be in a state of shock, stumbling around in the dark.

2:1–3 The people were commanded to **gather together,** perhaps in repentance. **Seek the LORD:** This is the language of true repentance, renewal, and regeneration. **you will be hidden:** Zephaniah used a play on words with the meaning of his own name, "Hidden in the Lord." Even in the midst of the most calamitous of judgment scenes, the mercy and grace of the Lord is still available to a repentant people.

2:4, 5 Zephaniah moves from the description of God's judgment on Judah and Jerusalem to a description of divine judgment on the surrounding nations. The judgment begins with the nation to the west, Philistia, and its major cities and seafaring industries. The five main cities of the Philistines were **Gaza,** Ashkelon, Ashdod, Ekron, and Gath. All but Gath are mentioned here. **Cherethites** is another name for the Philistines. **Canaan** is the ancient name for the land of the people of Israel, derived from its prior inhabitants.

2:6, 7 The seacoast shall be pastures: The coastal cities of Philistia and the coastal plain that the Philistines dominated for so long would one day become the possession of the Hebrews. The same God who brought destruction upon the people of Judah (1:14–18) would restore their fortunes.

2:8, 9 The peoples of **Moab** and **Ammon** to the east of Judah were hostile to the Hebrews from the earliest times. **Moab shall be like Sodom:** Here is God's promise of retribution (see Gen. 19:12–29).

2:10, 11 The LORD will be awesome to them: For the righteous people of Judah and Jerusalem, there would be a response of awe and wonder before God. But for the wicked there would be a response of terror and dread. **People shall worship Him:** Not only would there be a righteous remnant in Judah; people would also come to God from the nations of the earth.

2:12–15 Assyria was to the east. But the ancient armies could not march across the desert. Therefore they went around the desert and entered the land of the Hebrews from the north. **The pelican and the bittern** were birds found in remote areas (see Is. 34:11). Their presence in the ruins of Nineveh attest to the severity of the destruction announced on these people. **the rejoicing city:** The rejoicing here is ironic, seen as an act of the city's complacency. Soon the judgment of God would fall, and the region would be useful only for herding animals.

3:1–4 The addressee of the prophecy is Jerusalem, the **city** of David. Jerusalem had become a center of oppression, rebellion, and apostasy. It would soon be marked by destruction. The expression of grief is reflective of God's own heart. The **princes, judges, prophets,** and **priests,** whom God had especially designated to work for righteousness, were more wicked than the "regular" citizens of Jerusalem. These leaders were destroying and defrauding the weak, the needy, and the helpless.

3:5–7 Because He is absolutely **righteous,** God had no place in the midst of such an evil people. **cut off nations:** God's punishment of Judah's neighbors should have brought the people to their senses.

3:8 the fire of My jealousy: God's response to the wickedness of Jerusalem was to declare His judgment. He would use other nations to punish the city for its rebellion.

3:9–13 The focus of the text moves to a time of national regeneration and restoration. **Pure language** refers to language used in the worship of God. One day human language will become a unifying element in the true worship of God. **My worshipers:** God's people would come from all nations to worship Him.

3:14–17 The people of God would be called to **sing** because their deliverance had come.

Daughter of Zion is an affectionate title for the city of Jerusalem. **In that day:** The people are first commanded to abstain from fear, to keep from hanging their arms in a posture of resignation. Instead, they were to take encouragement and strength from the new reality that their God lived among them.

3:18–20 those who sorrow: God is going to make all things right. Those who are enemies of God's truth will be gathered and removed; those who are disenfranchised will be restored. **I will give you fame and praise:** Ordinarily Scripture speaks of the praise that should be brought to God. Here we find the praise that God will bring to His people. **Says the LORD:** This is a solemn vow of God to do what He has promised. Zephaniah begins and ends with the strong assertion that the Lord is speaking. The implication is clear: "Listen and live!"

 IN DEPTH   Beyond the Rivers of Ethiopia

I f you are a Christian and of African descent, you may be interested in Zephaniah's prophecy that the Lord would restore His "dispersed ones" from "beyond the rivers of Ethiopia" (Zeph. 3:10). This was a remarkable promise, given the map of the world in Zephaniah's day. As far as we know, Ethiopia represented the southwestern limits of Judah's knowledge of the world. The interior of Africa, "beyond the rivers of Ethiopia," was literally "off the map" for the ancient Israelites. It was uncharted territory for them.

To what, then, was Zephaniah referring? The context shows that he was anticipating the day when the Lord would bring people from the ends of the earth to form a holy people who would worship and serve Him with true hearts (3:9, 12, 13). Among them would be people from "beyond the rivers of Ethiopia." The prophet called this new people "the daughter of My dispersed ones" (3:10) and "the remnant of Israel" (3:13). Thus Zephaniah's vision seems to tie in with Jeremiah's predictions of a scattering of the Jews throughout the world, followed by an eventual restoration (Jer. 30:10, 11, 18–22; 31:1–40).

Beginning in the sixth century, many Jewish colonies were established along the Nile and the Mediterranean coast of Africa. In fact, some have suggested that Zephaniah's prophecy pertains to the Jewish community in northern Abyssinia. However, the prophecy may look beyond a strictly Jewish restoration. It seems to correspond with a prediction by David that Ethiopians would someday "stretch out [their] hands to God" (Ps. 68:31). Likewise, Isaiah envisioned a day when distant lands which had not heard of God would be recruited to send representatives to the Lord at Jerusalem—a vision that appears to correspond with the mission of the church (Is. 66:18–21).

As far as we know, Zephaniah himself had no idea of the vast tribes of people living "beyond the rivers of Ethiopia." But every time one of their descendents turns to faith in Christ, Africa adds one more member to the "peoples {of} a pure language" who are called to serve the Lord "with one accord" (Zeph. 3:9).

Haggai

Introduction

Haggai was a prophet to the Jews who had returned from the Exile in Babylon. He urged the people to do what they should have done from the start: to rebuild the temple with a willing heart. To these admonitions he added the promise of God to be with them. With this promise, the people could return to their first enthusiasm and carry out God's purposes. Then their worship would be joyful and sincere.

Little is known of the prophet Haggai except what is in the book that bears his name. Ezra mentions him briefly in association with the prophet Zechariah (see Ezra 5:1; 6:14) and the rebuilding of the temple. The name Haggai means "Festival," an appropriate meaning given the prophet's work in restoring temple worship. But what is most remarkable about Haggai's ministry is its brevity; his messages were delivered in the span of only four months in 520 B.C.

When some of the Israelites returned from the Babylonian captivity beginning in 538 B.C., they planned to build a new temple in Jerusalem (see Ezra 1). But their resolve seems to have vanished. They built an altar on the original temple site and later laid the foundations for the new temple. But when enemies who lived in the vicinity applied pressure, the Persian king ordered the work on the temple to cease. A later emperor of Persia, Darius I, lifted the restrictions that had been placed on the rebuilding of the temple and told them to proceed. But even when the barriers were lifted, the people lapsed into spiritual lethargy. They had lost their early passion for worship of the living God.

Haggai exhorted the people to focus on their spiritual condition. They were focusing on insignificant matters while ignoring God's temple. The temple was more than a building. It was the symbol of the abiding presence of the Creator of the universe.

Zerubbabel the governor and Joshua the high priest, along with the people of God, responded quickly to the message of Haggai (1:12). Three weeks after Haggai gave his first message, they began their work on the temple (520 B.C.). Then Haggai came with a message of assurance that the Lord was with them (1:13). God would bless them because they had reordered their priorities. They had put the worship of the Lord before their own welfare (1:4, 14). Out of the bounty that the Lord would provide, the Israelites would be able to bring the proper sacrifices of true worship into the new temple.

1:1 second year ... sixth month ... first day: The date for this first message of God through Haggai is August 29, 520 B.C. The prophecies of Haggai are among the most precisely dated in the Old Testament. **Zerubbabel** was the governor of Jerusalem at the time of Haggai's ministry and the **governor** of the first group of returning exiles from Babylon (see Ezra 3:2; Neh. 7:7).

1:2 The time has not come: The people had decided that rebuilding the Lord's dwelling among His people was not important.

1:3, 4 The principal building material in Jerusalem was stone. Those who wanted to make their **houses** elaborate installed wood panels. The people of Haggai's time were making their homes elegant. But they did not feel that the "time was right" to begin working on the renewed temple.

1:5 Consider your ways: The people were asked to mull over their habits and activities and to ask whether their attitude was sensible before the Lord.

1:6 God asked the people to take stock of their lives. Though they ate and drank, they never seemed satisfied. Though they put on clothes, they never felt **warm.** Wage earners constantly felt as though their pockets had holes in them through which their money was lost.

1:7, 8 The people were instructed to go to great lengths to get **wood** for paneling the temple of the Lord (v. 4). **that I may take pleasure in it:** God's joy in the temple is related to His pleasure in the people who would worship Him there. **be glorified:** Clearly God does not need to receive more glory (see Ps. 24:7–10); however, He gladly receives the adoration of His people.

1:9 runs to his own house: Because of their preoccupation with personal comfort, the people were ignoring the central spiritual concerns of their lives. Their faulty principle of life was being shaken by the Lord. The Savior Jesus later proclaimed the true and abiding principle for the life of faith: "But seek first the kingdom of God and His righteousness, and all these things shall be added to you" (see Matt. 6:33).

1:10, 11 The blessing and cursing formula of the Lord's covenant with His people comes into play here (see Deut. 28). **Dew** is a poetic way of speaking of rainfall.

1:12 The remnant of the people were literally those who had made the trek back to Judah from their captivity in Babylon; it also refers to those within a larger population who were faithful to the Lord.

1:13 I am with you: God's promise to Moses was, "I will certainly be with you" (see Ex. 3:12). God's promise to the people of Judah was that the name of the Coming One would be Immanuel, meaning "God is with us" (see Is. 7:14). Here God repeated the same message of comfort and encouragement.

1:14, 15 This verse bears witness to the work of God's Spirit on the human **spirit** of His leaders and His people to accomplish His tasks. It is reminiscent of God's work in stirring up the people to build the original tabernacle (see Ex. 35:29; 36:2). **remnant:** Always within Israel a remnant of the faithful existed.

2:1 twenty-first of the month: By our calendar this would be October 17, 520 B.C. In the ancient Jewish calendar this day was the last day of the Feast of Tabernacles or Succoth (see Lev. 23:33–44). During this holiday the people of Israel lived in booths, or temporary shelters, commemorating their departure from Egypt when they lived in temporary shelters in the wilderness.

2:2 Speak now: Haggai was called again to address the leaders Zerubbabel and Joshua (1:1) and the true people of God (1:12).

2:3 The **temple** of Solomon was one of the wonders of the ancient world (see 1 Kin. 6). The older temple would have loomed large and magnificent, far superior to the present structure. So even though the building was completed, there may have been the sense among some of the people that it was **as nothing.**

2:4 I am with you: The Lord's words to the people (1:13) were the same as His great words to Moses (see Ex. 3:12). God brought the people back from Babylon as He had brought them back from Egypt. The message to the first leaders, Moses and Aaron, and to the second, Zerubbabel and Joshua, was the same: God would be with them. Finally, the mission in the Promised Land was the same—to build a place for the worship of God.

2:5 According to the word: The same covenant that related the people to God in their departure from Egypt bound them still. The events surrounding the decline of the nation and the people's captivity in Babylon had not rescinded the covenant relationship that insured God's presence with His people (see Ex. 29:42–46).

2:6 I will shake: This is another way of speaking of the day of the Lord. The purpose of the day of the Lord is to prepare the earth for the glorious reign of Jesus Christ on earth (see Matt. 24:29; Rev. 6:12–17).

2:7 Desire of All Nations: Some interpret these words as a messianic title that speaks of the joy of the redeemed of the nations at the time of the rule of King Jesus.

2:8 silver ... gold: God owns the cattle on a thousand hills, the gold in all coffers, and the wealth of all nations.

2:9 Peace includes good health, well-being, and an abundant life. The term speaks of everything being as it ought to be.

2:10 The twenty-fourth day of the ninth month corresponds to December 18, 520 B.C. on our calendar.

2:11 The responsibilities of the **priests** included leading public worship and instructing the people in the nature and meaning of God's **law.**

2:12 will it become holy: Since the role of the priest was to interpret God's law, it was reasonable that questions on holiness should be addressed to them. Haggai asked whether holiness could be transferred by contact. The answer was no.

2:13–15 It shall be unclean: The priests were asked if a religiously unclean person, someone who had touched a corpse, could contaminate someone else by touch. The answer was yes (see Num. 19:11–13). The **people** had worked hard to rebuild the temple, only to be told that their worship would be unacceptable in the new temple. The existence of the temple itself guaranteed nothing. The hearts of the people had to be in harmony with the sacrifices being made.

2:16, 17 you did not turn to Me: Despite God's acts of withholding His blessing, the people still had not turned fully back to Him.

2:18–21 from this day: God determined to bring His blessing on His people, but He demanded that they recognize Him as the source of their great productivity.

2:22 I will overthrow: Haggai focused on the power of God to do as He wills among the nations (see Dan. 2:21). These words speak both in a general way of the sovereignty of God over the nations throughout history, as well as more specifically of God's final judgment on the wicked nations at the time He institutes the rule of His Son as King of kings (see Ps. 2; 110; Rev. 19).

2:23 A signet ring was an item of great value in the ancient world. The owner used it much like we use our personal signature on checks or other important documents. God used this imagery to indicate that **Zerubbabel** was in His hand, that he was highly valued, and that he represented God's authority in his leadership of the people. Even though the people had been told they were still unclean in God's eyes (see 2:10–14), their leader Zerubbabel was encouraged to guide them through those trying times.

Zechariah

Introduction

Zechariah was one of the three prophets, along with Haggai and Malachi, who ministered to the exiles returning to Jerusalem. These exiles faced the ruins of what had once been a splendid city and a glorious temple. Zechariah encouraged the exiles with visions of judgment on Israel's enemies and of the complete restoration of the city of Jerusalem. Yet the most thrilling vision of all was the prediction of a coming King—the Messiah who would bring eternal salvation and the promised eternal kingdom.

The name Zechariah means "Yahweh Remembers." This powerful phrase communicates a message of hope: the God of Israel will remember His people. Zechariah entered his prophetic ministry two months after his contemporary Haggai had concluded his first oracle—in the second year of the Persian king Darius (522–486 B.C.). His last dated prophecy was delivered two years later, in 518 B.C.

King Cyrus of Persia decreed that the Jews could return to their homeland. The first group of Jews returned under the leadership of Sheshbazzar (Ezra 1:8) in 537 B.C. The altar for the temple was erected in the fall of that year, but construction on the temple itself did not begin until the spring of 536 B.C.

Opposition to the temple rebuilding by enemies of the Jews living in and around Judah resulted in the abandonment of the work until 520 B.C. During these sixteen years of neglect the people of Judah lost their vision and sense of spiritual purpose. In 520 B.C., the prophet called for the Israelites to recognize their spiritual priorities and rebuild the temple. Zechariah began his prophetic ministry just two months after Haggai (compare 1:1 with Hag. 1:1).

Zechariah's prophecies challenged the returning exiles to turn to the Lord, to be cleansed from their sins and to experience again the Lord's blessing (see 1:3). He also comforted and encouraged the people about the rebuilding of the temple and God's future work among them (1:16, 17; 2:12; 3:2; 4:9; 6:14, 15).

Zechariah teaches a great deal about the Messiah. He prophesied the Messiah's entrance into Jerusalem on a colt (9:9; see Matt. 21:4–5; John 12:14–16), His betrayal for thirty pieces of silver (11:12, 13; see Matt. 27:9, 10), the piercing of His hands and feet (12:10; see John 19:37), and the cleansing from sin provided by His death (13:1; see John 1:29; Titus 3:5).

1:1 The **eighth** month corresponds to October-November on our calendar. **Darius** ruled Persia from 522 to 486 B.C. Thus his **second year** was 520 B.C. The name **Zechariah** means "Yahweh Remembers," emphasizing God's faithfulness to His covenant promises and to His people.

1:2 The **fathers** refers to the ancestors of the present generation who had disobeyed God and come under His judgment (see 2 Chr. 36:15, 16).

1:3 The words **return to Me** remind us of the depth of God's unconditional love. **says the LORD of hosts:** The personal name translated LORD speaks of God's gracious nature as He relates to His people.

1:4 The **former prophets** refers to men like Habakkuk, Zephaniah, and Jeremiah, who had lived during the last years of the Judean monarchy and had warned of coming judgment.

1:5, 6 Their **fathers** had been killed or exiled and even the **prophets** had perished. The previous generation had been overtaken by God's judgment (see Deut. 28:15–68).

1:7 The **eleventh month** (**Shebat** is the Babylonian name) corresponds to January-February, 519 B.C. **the word of the LORD:** Here the phrase refers to a prophetic vision.

1:8, 9 Myrtle is an evergreen tree that was once very common near Jerusalem (Neh. 8:15).

1:10–13 The prophet overhears a conversation between **the Angel of the LORD** and God. This may be a conversation between the pre-incarnate Jesus and the first Person of the Trinity, God the Father (see Ps. 110). It is certainly an allusion to Jesus' role as Intercessor. The **seventy** years refers to the period of exile during which the temple lay in ruins (586–515 B.C.; see Jer. 25:7–14).

1:14 the angel who spoke with me: This is the interpreting angel in the dramatic vision, not the Angel of the Lord (v. 11). **I am zealous:** The passion of the Lord can be seen in His defense of His special relationship with Israel and Jerusalem.

1:15 I am exceedingly angry: Here the anger of God was against the nations that He had used to punish His unrepentant people.

1:16 God promised to show compassion on His people and to rebuild the Jerusalem temple (**My house**). **A surveyor's line** was used to make measurements in preparation for new construction. The stretching of the line was a promise that the work would begin and that the completion of the task would follow.

1:17 again choose Jerusalem: Jerusalem's election is a prominent emphasis in Zechariah (2:12; 3:2). The word **Zion** describes Jerusalem in an affectionate way (see Zeph. 3:14).

1:18, 19 Animal **horns** were symbolic of powerful nations and their kings (see Dan. 7:7, 8, 24). The horns that persecuted Israel and Judah included Assyria, Babylon, Medo-Persia, and later Greece.

1:20, 21 four craftsmen: The craftsmen or "smiths" destroyed the **horns** (v. 19). Historically, Babylon destroyed Assyria, Medo-Persia conquered Babylon, Greece conquered Medo-Persia, and Rome overcame Greece. These are dominant themes in the prophecies of Daniel (see Dan. 2; 7).

2:1–5 This young man refers to Zechariah. Here the words may indicate that Zechariah was young when he began his prophetic ministry (see Jer. 1:6). **towns without walls:** Jerusalem will have no need for defensive fortifications because God's presence will guarantee its safety and security. These words refer ultimately to the future Jerusalem under the rule of its glorious king (see Zeph. 3:15–19).

2:6 Although Babylon was east of Israel, travelers typically followed the Euphrates River and approached Israel from **the north.**

2:7 The name **Zion** may have first applied to the Jebusite stronghold captured by David (2 Sam. 5:7). It was later used for the temple mount (Ps. 78:68, 69) and became a synonym for Jerusalem (Is. 40:9; Mic. 3:12). **Daughter**

of Babylon signified the people living in the city of Babylon.

2:8, 9 The **apple of His eye** refers to the pupil, suggesting how important the Hebrew people are to God because of His covenant with them. Just as we protect our eyes from even the smallest particles of dust, so God protects and cares for His people.

2:10 daughter of Zion: This phrase is an affectionate manner of addressing Jerusalem and its people as the daughter of the Lord (see Zeph. 3:14).

2:11 Many nations refer to Gentiles who will enter into a relationship with God and become His people (Gen. 12:3; Joel 2:28; Amos 9:12; Rev. 21:24). The words **My people** are used elsewhere in the context of the renewal of God's covenant with His believing people (Jer. 31:33; 32:38; Hos. 2:23; see also Ex. 3:7; Deut. 4:20; 14:2; 26:19).

2:12 The familiar phrase **the Holy Land** occurs in the Old Testament only here. The land is *holy* because of the presence of God among His people.

2:13 God had **aroused** Himself from His heavenly sanctuary and was about to intervene on behalf of His people. Hence **be silent** was not an anticipation of worship, but calls for terror at the judgment that was about to be unleashed from God's glory (see Zeph. 1:7).

3:1 Zechariah saw a heavenly courtroom where **Joshua,** representing the people of Judah, was standing before the **Angel of the LORD** and was being accused by **Satan.** This is the high priest who returned to Jerusalem with the exiles (Ezra 3:2). **Satan:** The Hebrew is literally "the Satan," meaning "the Accuser."

3:2 The LORD rebuke you, Satan: These words presuppose an earlier conversation in which Satan made accusations against the people and their priest. Satan is not sovereign; he is subject to the Sovereign Lord. The **brand plucked from the fire** refers to Judah, delivered from the *fire* of Babylonian captivity. Joshua, their priest, represented the nation.

3:3 The high priest represented the people before God (see Ex. 28:29) and under no circumstances was to become defiled or unclean (Ex. 28:2; Lev. 21:10–15). Joshua's **filthy garments** were literally "befouled with excrement."

3:4, 5 The cleansing of Joshua was not complete with the removal of his soiled garments. God replaced the dirty clothes, dressing Joshua in clean garments that represented the gift of God's righteousness. The fact that Joshua had no part in his cleansing indicates that this work was totally by God's grace.

3:6, 7 Joshua was recommissioned as the nation's high priest. For his faithfulness he was promised the privilege of exercising authority over God's temple—**My house**—and its courts.

3:8 The coming Messiah is depicted as God's **Servant** (Is. 53:11). He is also referred to as **the BRANCH.** Isaiah used this word to describe the Messiah who will grow out of the root of the family of Jesse as a tender sprout shoots up from the ground (see 6:12; Is. 4:2; 11:1; 53:2). Joshua and his companions were a **sign** because the reinstitution of the priesthood signified God's intention to fulfill His promises to His people.

3:9 stone: Like the priest Aaron, who wore a jeweled ephod (see Ex. 25:7; 35:9), so the new priest had a lustrous stone, a symbol of the authority of his office. The **eyes** may be symbolic of wisdom and of the endowment of the Holy Spirit (see 4:10; Is. 11:2).

3:10 Sitting **under** the **vine** and **under** the **fig tree** is an image of peace and tranquility characteristic of the messianic kingdom (Mic. 4:4).

4:1 wakened me: It appears that these night visions came in the course of a single night.

4:2, 3 The **lampstand of solid gold** would remind the people of the lampstand in the tabernacle and the temple.

4:4–6 The rebuilding of the temple, which had at last begun in earnest (Ezra 5:1, 2; Hag. 1:14), would be accomplished not by human strength or resources, but by the power of God's **Spirit.**

4:7 The **great mountain** was a figurative reference to the great obstacles the people faced in rebuilding the temple (Ezra 5:3–17). The setting of the **capstone** would mark the completion of the project. The

words **Grace, grace to it** may be understood as a prayer for God's favor, or as a cry of admiration over the grace and beauty of the new temple.

4:8, 9 His hands: The promise about **Zerubbabel** is significant; the task that he began he would also complete.

4:10 These seven, a number used symbolically to represent the idea of completeness, are identified as **the eyes of the LORD** (see "eyes" in 3:9). The fact that these eyes will **rejoice** at the plumb line in Zerubbabel's hand suggests the delight of God over the rebuilding of the temple.

4:11–14 The **two olive branches** are identified as **two anointed ones,** representatives of the religious and political offices in Israel, or of priest and king. Many identify the two branches with the high priest Joshua and the governor Zerubbabel.

5:1, 2 A **scroll** was made of rolled parchment or leather and was the ancient equivalent of a book (see Jer. 36:1–8). A **cubit** was about 18 inches. The scroll measured about 15 by 30 feet.

5:3 The writing on the scroll was a message of judgment. **The curse** refers to the judgments spoken of in the Mosaic covenant (Deut. 30:7). The message on the scroll warned that the curses described in the covenant as a result of the people's disobedience would be executed upon the whole land.

5:4 And consume it: God's great love does not preclude the exercise of His judgment on those who violate His will. The judgment upon the disobedient would be certain and severe.

5:5, 6 The word translated **basket** is literally *ephah,* a unit of dry measure of about half a bushel. The word translated **resemblance** was understood as *iniquity* in some ancient versions.

5:7, 8 The woman sitting inside the basket is **Wickedness,** a personification of sin.

5:9 Next Zechariah saw **two women,** God's agents, disposing of the wicked woman in the basket.

5:10, 11 Shinar was an ancient name for the district in which the cities of Babylon (Babel), Erech, Accad, and Calneh were located (Gen.

10:10; 11:2). The fact that a **house** was built for the woman suggests that the removal of wickedness (v. 8) from Israel was permanent.

6:1 chariots: In ancient times two-wheeled and four-wheeled horse-drawn carts served as vehicles for transportation and for warfare. The war chariots usually had a crew of two or three men including a driver, an archer, and a defender who used a shield to protect the others.

6:2–5 These chariots and their teams represented **four spirits of heaven,** probably angels.

6:6, 7 The **horses** were **eager** to take the four spirits on their mission to bring divine judgment on the peoples of the earth.

6:8 The activity of the chariot teams would give **rest** to God's **Spirit** because His agents would be executing His judgment on the nations that threatened Israel. Cyrus's overthrow of Babylon in 539 B.C. may well have been a part of this judgment (Is. 13:1–22; 45:1–6).

6:9–11 The **captives** refer to the new arrivals from Babylon who brought gifts of **silver and gold** to help the restored community of Israelites. The **elaborate crown** was possibly a composite crown made up of several circlets. The crown was to be placed on the head of Joshua the high priest.

6:12 The Messiah Himself will **build the temple of the LORD.** Since the restoration temple (the second temple) was already being built and would be completed by Zerubbabel (see 4:9), the temple referred to here may be the future temple of the messianic kingdom (see Is. 2:2–4; Ezek. 40–42; Mic. 4:1–5; Hag. 2:7–9). The temple of Zerubbabel was a prophetic symbol of the temple that is still to come.

6:13 He will **sit and rule** and **be a priest:** In the Messiah the two offices of king and priest will be united (John 1:49; Heb. 3:1).

6:14, 15 Those from afar include Gentile peoples (see 8:22; see Hag. 2:7–9; Eph. 2:13).

7:1 The fourth year of Darius was 518 B.C. The **ninth month** or **Chislev** (the Babylonian name) corresponds to November-December.

7:2 The words translated **house of God** may also mean "Bethel," a town twelve miles north of Jerusalem. Over two hundred Jews from Bethel returned from Babylon in 538 B.C. (Ezra 2:28; Neh. 7:32), and the city was reoccupied during the restoration period (Neh. 11:31). It seems most likely that the people of Bethel sent a delegation to ask a question of the priests in Jerusalem.

7:3, 4 The **house of the LORD of hosts** refers to the temple in Jerusalem. The **fast** in the **fifth month** (July-August) commemorated the destruction of the temple in 586 B.C. (2 Kin. 25:8). The delegation from Bethel wanted to know if it was necessary to continue this annual fast as it had been observed during the Babylonian captivity.

7:5, 6 did you really fast for Me—for Me: The rhetorical question was designed to confront the people and priests with the selfish motives of their self-righteous fasting. Biblical fasting is meant to be time taken from the normal routines of preparing and eating food to express humility and dependence on God during a time of prayer. There was only one required fast in the Law of Moses, the fast on the Day of Atonement (see Lev. 16:29). The fast during the **seventh month** lamented the assassination of Gedaliah (2 Kin. 25:25). The **seventy years** (see 1:12; Jer. 25:11; 29:10) refer to the period of time while the people were in exile and the temple lay in ruins. **for yourselves:** Their fasting and their feasting were both motivated by self-interest rather than a desire to honor God.

7:7 The **former prophets** were those who ministered before the Exile (1:4; see 2 Chr. 36:15, 16). The **South** is the Negev, the dry region of Judah around Beersheba. The **Lowland** is the transitional region between the hill country of Judah and the coastal plain.

7:8–10 Zechariah's four admonitions highlight the practical social concerns that many of the prophets emphasized (Is. 1:11–17; Hos. 6:6; Mic. 6:6–8). **Execute true justice:** Judicial decisions must be made without partiality or bias. **Show mercy and compassion:** Loving commitment and concern should guide our relationships with others. **Do not oppress:** The helpless and less fortunate should be treated fairly. **Let**

none of you plan evil: Evil scheming against others is prohibited. Sacrifices and worship are of little interest to God if they are not accompanied by just actions.

7:11–14 Zechariah describes the response of the disobedient Judeans living in the land before the Babylonian exile. The consequence was God's judgment—they were **scattered.**

8:1–3 The Lord again states that He is **zealous** for Jerusalem (1:14; see Nah. 1:2). This theme in Zechariah emphasizes the Lord's passion for His people. He longed to bless them with His presence and in turn desired their worship. **Zion** is the poetic equivalent of **Jerusalem** (see 2:7). The label **City of Truth** will be valid only when the Messiah brings His righteous reign to that city. Then the land will be holy (see 2:12).

8:4, 5 Zechariah predicts that in the future messianic era, Jerusalem will be inhabited and secure. The longevity of the citizens and the presence of children at play **in its streets** suggests the city's future prosperity and divine blessing.

8:6 The rhetorical question implies that nothing is too **marvelous** or difficult for God.

8:7, 8 The terms **east** and **west** represent all parts of the earth. The expressions **My people** and **their God** (see 2:11) occur in the descriptions of God's covenant relationship with His people (Ex. 19:5; 29:45; Lev. 26:12; Hos. 2:23). With these words, Zechariah anticipates a renewal of God's covenant with His people (see Jer. 31:31–34).

8:9 The **foundation** of the second temple was laid in 536 B.C. (see Ezra 3:8–13).

8:10 no wages … no peace: Zechariah recounts the desperate situation in Judea before the work on the temple resumed in 520 B.C. (see Hag. 1:1, 6, 10, 11; 2:16, 17).

8:11–13 In the past, the people had been subject to God's discipline. In view of their recent obedience with regard to rebuilding the temple, they could now anticipate His blessing. **Let your hands be strong:** In view of God's gracious purposes and future plans for His people, they were called to be diligent in their efforts to serve Him with sincere hearts (see 1 Cor. 15:58).

8:14–17 Zechariah set forth the ethical obligations of a life of faith. He upheld the positive values of **truth** and **justice** and condemned evil plans and false oaths.

8:18, 19 As a result of God's blessing on his obedient people, the former fasts will become feasts. The **fast of the fourth month** commemorated the breach of Jerusalem's walls (Jer. 39:2). The **fast of the fifth** commemorated the temple destruction (2 Kin. 25:8). The **fast of the seventh** commemorated the assassination of Gedaliah (2 Kin. 25:25), and the **fast of the tenth** commemorated the beginning of Nebuchadnezzar's siege of Jerusalem (2 Kin. 25:1, 2).

8:20–23 Here Zechariah announces a great turning of the nations to God. During the messianic era, a multitude of people from many cities will go to Jerusalem to **seek the LORD.** These Gentiles will be included among the people of God by faith (Eph. 2:13–19).

9:1 The word **burden** suggests that a weighty judgment must be declared. **Hadrach** was north of Hamath on the Orontes River, southwest of Aleppo. **Damascus,** 60 miles northeast of the Sea of Galilee, was the capital of Aram (ancient Syria).

9:2 Hamath is mentioned in several places as the northern limit of the Promised Land (Num. 13:21; Josh. 13:5). **Tyre and Sidon** are port cities located north of Israel on the Phoenician coast.

9:3, 4 The complete overthrow of **Tyre** by Alexander the Great in 332 B.C. illustrates how even a powerful city can come under God's judgment.

9:5, 6 Ashkelon, Gaza, Ekron, and Ashdod were Philistine cities located on Israel's coastal plain south of Joppa (1 Sam. 6:17). The city of Gath completed the "five principal cities" of the Philistines.

9:7 The removal of **blood from his mouth** and **abominations** refer to the cessation of unlawful and idolatrous practices (Lev. 17:14; Is. 65:4; 66:17). **Ekron like a Jebusite:** The Jebusites were the inhabitants of ancient Jebus, the stronghold that became Jerusalem (2 Sam. 5:6, 7).

9:8 God will return as a victorious Warrior to the temple—**My house**—where He will set up a guard against any who would dare tramp through Judah's territory.

9:9 This prophecy was fulfilled on the day of

the triumphal entry, when Jesus rode into Jerusalem on a young donkey (Matt. 21:2–7; John 12:12–15).

9:10 Instruments of warfare—**the chariot** and the **battle bow**—will be destroyed and universal peace will be established. **Ephraim** refers to the northern tribes of Israel. **The River** refers to the Euphrates, the northeast boundary of the Promised Land (Gen. 15:18).

9:11, 12 The release of **prisoners** announced here would serve as a great encouragement for the Jewish people still in exile. Even though the prisoners were living in a well-watered place in Persia (see Ezek. 1:1), they were in a place like a **waterless pit** in terms of their opportunity for spiritual nourishment. They were exhorted to **return to the stronghold** Jerusalem.

9:13 Zechariah used a bold metaphor comparing Judah and Ephraim to a **bow** and arrow prepared by the Lord to be used against **Greece** (see Is. 66:19).

9:14 whirlwinds: This description, patterned after God's appearance at Sinai (Ex. 19), reveals God's sovereignty and power to protect His own.

9:15, 16 Zechariah describes the victory banquet of God's people in celebration of His victory over the nations and securing of Jerusalem. The people will **be filled** with drink like sacrificial basins were filled with blood, and they will be filled with meat like the corners of a sacrificial altar (see Ps. 110).

9:17 The abundance of **grain** and **new wine** suggests the prosperity and blessing of this future day (see 3:10; 8:4, 5; see also Amos 9:13).

10:1 The **latter rain** (Deut. 11:14) refers to the rain that comes in late spring which is essential for an abundant grain harvest.

10:2 Idols refers to household gods (see Gen. 31:19). **Diviners,** like Balaam, interpreted omens as a means of foretelling the future (Josh. 13:22; 1 Sam. 6:2). **no shepherd:** The metaphor of *shepherd* was often used in the ancient Middle East to represent a king or ruler (see Ezek. 34:6–8, 23, 24). Here the emphasis was on the lack of spiritual leadership.

10:3 While Israel lacked national leadership, there were plenty of tyrants seeking to rule God's people. These **goatherds** will be judged. By way of contrast, God will strengthen **the house of Judah** as an instrument to overthrow these oppressors.

10:4, 5 The poetic metaphors in these verses reflect the strength, stability, and victory that God will impart to His people (vv. 3, 6). **Cornerstone** is an image of steadfast strength or stability, coupled with beauty and honor (Is. 28:16; see also Ps. 118:22). **tent peg:** A peg firmly in place suggests permanence and endurance (Is. 22:23). **battle bow:** This image pictures the strength necessary for military conquest (2 Kin. 13:17).

10:6 The **house of Judah** indicates Israel's southern territory. The **house of Joseph** is Israel's northern territory, dominated by Ephraim (v. 7) and Manasseh, tribes named after Joseph's sons (Gen. 41:51, 52). The promise **I will bring them back** is a promise of restoration. The dispersed remnant of Israel would return to the Promised Land (see Matt. 24:31).

10:7 What was promised to Judah in v. 5 is here promised to **Ephraim. as if with wine:** Wine is used here as a symbol of abundant joy (Ps. 104:15; see Amos 9:13; John 2:1–11).

10:8 As a shepherd signals his sheep, so the Lord will **whistle** for His people to return to the land. **For I will redeem them:** God will deliver them from sin (3:4, 9) and from the bondage of captivity (Matt. 24:31).

10:9 Being sown **among the peoples** was God's punishment of the exiles for their disobedience (Deut. 28:63, 64). The words **they shall remember Me** anticipate their turning to the Lord in repentance.

10:10 Assyria is the region of northern Mesopotamia. **Egypt** and **Assyria** had been lands where Israel was captive. **Gilead** is the territory east of the Jordan River and southeast of the Sea of Galilee. **Lebanon** is the region north of Galilee. The future restoration will be so complete that the land will be filled with people.

10:11 God would remove any impediment to Israel's return. Zechariah used imagery from the Exodus—**the sea, the River**—to illustrate the kinds of obstacles God would overcome (see Ex. 14:21–31; Josh. 3:14–17).

10:12 I will strengthen them: The regathering will be accomplished by God's power as He gives strength to His people. **they shall walk ... in His name:** In the last days, Israel will return to the land as a believing nation (v. 8; 12:10—13:1; Rom. 11:26).

11:1 Lebanon was known for its beautiful cedars, trees used by Solomon in building his palace and the temple.

11:2, 3 The **cypress,** or juniper, will **wail** for the cedars of Lebanon. The **shepherds** will wail because the grazing lands will be ruined. The **lions** will roar because of the destruction of the **pride of the Jordan,** the jungle thicket that was their shelter.

11:4, 5 Zechariah was commanded to **feed** or pasture the **flock** of God's people Israel, knowing it was destined **for slaughter.**

11:6 The petty tyrants and oppressors (v. 5) will fall victim to foreign kings who **attack the land.**

11:7 In obedience to God's command (v. 4), Zechariah pastured the flock doomed for slaughter. As shepherds carried implements to guide and protect the sheep (Ps. 23:4), so Zechariah had **two staffs.** Their names **Beauty** and **Bonds** suggest that he wanted the flock to enjoy God's favor and to experience national unity. According to Canaanite legend, the god Baal was given the two clubs named Driver and Chaser to battle the dark deities of the sea. It is appropriate that God's messenger Zechariah is given shepherd's staffs to guide the people instead of clubs for fighting.

11:8 three shepherds: Some have suggested that the three shepherds represent classes of rulers in Israel: kings, priests, and prophets.

 IN DEPTH   **The Coming King**

Luke tells us that after Jesus ascended to heaven, the disciples returned to Jerusalem (Luke 24:52). They also went back to the Scriptures. The OT suddenly blossomed with good news. Everywhere they looked they found evidence that pointed toward the specifics of Jesus' life and ministry. When they wondered why they had missed the connections before, they must have also remembered Jesus' promise, "When He, the Spirit of truth, has come, He will guide you into all truth" (John 16:13).

When the Gospel writers recorded the details of Jesus' life, they often used references from the OT to illustrate how clearly Jesus fulfilled the character of the promised Savior and the prophecies regarding His ministry. They particularly enjoyed quoting OT passages that clearly predicted the suffering and rejection aspects of the Messiah's role. For them, it was the central theme that set Jesus apart from the popular ideas of a conquering and powerful political messiah.

Zechariah 9:9, 10 presents a prophecy whose fulfillment was clearly set in motion (though not completed) by Jesus' arrival in Jerusalem on a colt, the well-known Triumphal Entry. Both Matthew and John mention this passage. John even notes that the disciples saw no immediate connection between Jesus riding on the colt and His identity as the Messiah prophesied in Zechariah. After Jesus was glorified, "then they remembered that these things were written about Him" (John 12:16).

These verses in Zechariah include an important transition. The arrival of the saving King is followed immediately by a description of the effects of his long-term reign. This is an example of "prophetic compression." Viewed from the broader context of prophecy, Zechariah was mentioning together two stages in God's plan which are actually separated in time. The coming King would arrive twice. Jesus came first as a humble King of peace and salvation, accomplished in Jesus' earthly ministry and His death on the Cross. Second, Jesus will come as a victorious Ruler over all the world who will "speak peace to the nations." We should rejoice over Jesus' first coming and anticipate the complete fulfillment of Zechariah's prophecy at Christ's glorious return.

Others suggest that they refer to the last three kings of Judah or to certain high priests of the Maccabean era.

11:9 Let what is dying die: The judgment which God has decreed should be accepted, not resisted. **eat each other's flesh:** Cannibalism was one of the horrors of famine that resulted from siege warfare (Deut. 28:54–57; Lam. 4:10).

11:10 The breaking of the staff **Beauty** symbolizes the end of God's protection of His people. **break the covenant:** God's unconditional promise to Abraham (Gen. 12:1–3) or to David (2 Sam. 7:12–16) would never be broken. Like Ezekiel's covenant of peace (Ezek. 34:25), the *covenant* here may refer to an agreement with the Gentile nation on Israel's behalf.

11:11, 12 Zechariah, taking the role of the messianic shepherd, requested his wages for service rendered. His wage was calculated as **thirty pieces of silver,** the price of a slave (Ex. 21:32). This was the price paid to Judas for betraying Jesus (see Matt. 27:6–10).

11:13 The command **throw it to the potter** is further illuminated by Zechariah's action. He **threw them into the house of the LORD for the potter.** Potters may have been connected with the temple because of the continual need for sacred vessels (Lev. 6:28).

11:14 The rejection of the messianic Shepherd, represented by Zechariah, meant that the national unity the Israelites hoped for would not be achieved at this time. But one day the nations of **Judah and Israel** will be united (Ezek. 37:16–28).

11:15, 16 To take the **implements of a foolish shepherd** means to behave like one. **Eat the flesh** and **tear their hooves** expresses the savagery of a foolish shepherd.

11:17 The **worthless shepherd** will be judged. His **arm,** which should have been used to protect the sheep, will wither. **His right eye,** which should have watched over the sheep, will be blinded.

12:1 The **burden** is a weighty judgment that the prophet must discharge.

12:2 Jerusalem is depicted as a **cup** of wine or strong drink which causes **drunkenness.** The *cup* is a common metaphor for God's

wrath (see Is. 51:17; Jer. 25:15; Ezek. 23:33; Rev. 14:10; 16:19). **Siege** warfare involved encircling a city to cut off its food and water supplies.

12:3, 4 Jerusalem is compared to a **heavy stone** that brings injury to anyone who tries to move it.

12:5 The **governors** or leaders of Judah would affirm God's power to deliver through His people. The people's **strength** would be **in the LORD** (see Phil. 4:13).

12:6 Judah is compared to (1) a **firepan** used to carry hot coals for the purpose of starting a fire, and (2) a **fiery torch** that could ignite a field of cut grain.

12:7 Tents of Judah alludes to Jews living outside Jerusalem in the rural districts of the land. The **house of David** means David's descendants.

12:8 Zechariah compares David's descendants to God. The **Angel of the LORD** is clearly a divine being (Ex. 23:20; Num. 22:22; Judg. 2:1; 13:15–22).

12:9 All the nations that have attacked Jerusalem (v. 2) will be judged and destroyed (Matt. 25:31–46).

12:10 pour: This metaphor is derived from the deluge of winter rains and speaks of abundant provision (Job 36:28; Is. 44:3; Lam. 2:19). **Spirit of grace** refers to the gracious working of the Holy Spirit that leads to conviction and repentance (John 16:8–11). **supplication:** The Spirit will stimulate an attitude of repentance and prayer for God's mercy. There are many significant ministries of the Holy Spirit in the period of the Hebrew kingdom. **Me whom they pierced:** Jesus was pierced with a spear after His death on the Cross (John 19:34).

12:11 Hadad Rimmon may have been the site of some tragedy whose grief was still vividly remembered. Or the place may have been associated with religious rites involving mourning.

12:12–14 All of Israel will mourn for the Messiah, including members of the royal family and the priests, **the house of David** and **the house of Levi.** The phrase **wives by themselves** seems to indicate that each mourner will face his or her sorrow alone, without the comfort of companionship.

13:1 The **fountain** is an image of abundant, overflowing provision. Cleansing from the impurity of sin was made available by Christ on the Cross. At the time of Christ's second coming, the repentant and believing remnant of Israel will enter into the benefits of the New Covenant (Jer. 31:31–34; Ezek. 36:25–28).

13:2 cut off the names of the idols: In ancient times, a person's name reflected his or her reputation. Zechariah anticipated the removal of the reputation and acknowledgment of false gods.

13:3 According to the Law of Moses (Deut. 13:5; 18:20), a false prophet must be put to death. The startling thing here is that the false prophet's parents must confront the offender and carry out the penalty.

13:4 False prophets will deny that they are prophets for fear of punishment and will refuse to wear **a robe of coarse hair,** the traditional prophet's clothing (2 Kin. 1:8; Matt. 3:4).

13:5 Instead of laying claim to prophetic office, they will say they have been farmers from their **youth.** This seems to be a parody of Amos 7:14.

13:6 It is likely that the **wounds** betrayed the profession of an ecstatic prophet who slashed himself on the back or chest. The words **between your arms** refer to the body, either the back or the chest. Self-inflicted wounds were thought to gain the attention and blessing of the gods (see 1 Kin. 18:28). Under questioning, the man declares that the wounds were received from **friends** so that he will not be found out as a false prophet and be put to death (v. 3).

13:7 The **sword,** an instrument of death, is compared to a warrior being roused for action. The Lord commands the sword to strike the Messiah, **My Shepherd.** This clearly indicates that the death of Jesus was no accident, but was divinely determined. **My Companion:** This term is used elsewhere of one who is a near neighbor or close companion (Lev. 6:2; 18:20; 19:15). It suggests a relationship of equality.

13:8 Zechariah revealed the devastating result of God's dealing with His errant flock. The scattered flock will face a great judgment in which only **one-third** will survive.

13:9 The remnant that survives will be purged, purified, and reestablished in a covenant relationship with God. **refined:** The smelting pot uses intense heat to separate the dross from pure metal. **tested:** Once refined, precious metal must be analyzed to determine its value. The expressions **this is My people** and **the LORD is my God** recall the covenant (Lev. 26:12) and speak of a covenant renewal for a spiritually revitalized Israel (Ezek. 36:28; Hos. 2:23; Rom. 11:26, 27).

14:1 Some have suggested that this **spoil** refers to what is seized from Israel's enemies, apparently anticipating the victory mentioned in v. 14. The immediate context, however, indicates that the *spoil* was taken from Jerusalem by her enemies (v. 2).

14:2 The **remnant of the people** who survive the attack are evidently the one-third that will be brought through the refiner's fire (13:8, 9).

14:3 The **LORD** will turn Jerusalem's defeat into a victory. God the Warrior (Ex. 15:3) will intervene on Israel's behalf against the attacking nations.

14:4 Zechariah provides further details about how Jerusalem's deliverance will come about. The **Mount of Olives** is a hill located east of Jerusalem and the Kidron Valley. The Messiah will return to the Mount of Olives, the very mountain from which He will have ascended after His time on earth (Acts 1:10, 11). On the day of Messiah's return, the mount will be split by a deep valley.

14:5 The splitting of the Mount of Olives will provide a way of escape for the besieged and defeated people in Jerusalem. The site of **Azal** has not been identified but must be somewhere in the desert east of Jerusalem. The flight of the surviving remnant from Jerusalem is compared to what took place following the **earthquake in the days of Uzziah.** The **saints** are literally the "holy ones," angels who will accompany Jesus at His return (Mark 8:38; 2 Thess. 1:7).

14:6, 7 Cosmic upheaval is associated with the Second Coming. The glory of the Messiah's kingdom is preceded by dark days of judgment. **there will be no light:** The imagery of darkness as a portent of judgment is common in the prophets (Is. 5:30; 8:22; 13:9, 10; Ezek. 32:7, 8; Amos 5:18, 20; Zeph. 1:14, 15).

14:8 The term **living waters** describes running water from a spring or river, in contrast to the stale and stagnant water of a cistern (Jer. 2:13). The water will flow from Jerusalem toward the **eastern sea** (the Dead Sea) and the **western sea** (the Mediterranean). In contrast with the seasonal streams that flow only during the rainy season, these streams will irrigate the land **both summer and winter.**

14:9 Zechariah anticipates the glorious day when the **LORD** will reestablish His reign on this earth, where it was first challenged by Satan (see Rev. 20:1–3; also Ps. 93:1; 97:1; 99:1). This will be the answer to the prayers of all those who pray Jesus' words, "Your kingdom come" (Matt. 6:10). The words **the LORD is one** speak of His unity and uniqueness (see Deut. 6:4).

14:10 Geba was 6 miles northeast of Jerusalem. **Rimmon** was about 35 miles southwest of Jerusalem. The **Tower of Hananel** was probably a defensive fortification on the north wall.

14:11 people shall dwell in it: This is a contrast to the time of Nehemiah when the population of Jerusalem was sparse (Neh. 7:4; 11:1). In the Lord's coming kingdom, the city will be inhabited and its citizens secure.

14:12, 13 plague: This word was used to describe the judgments of God upon the Egyptians (Ex. 7:17—12:30).

14:14, 15 As the attackers are destroyed, the people of **Judah** will join the citizens of **Jerusalem** in recovering the spoil taken by the enemy (v. 1) and capturing additional booty (see Hag. 2:7, 8).

14:16 Repentant and believing people among those nations that had attacked Jerusalem (vv. 1, 2) will **worship the King** (Jesus the Messiah) and celebrate **the Feast of Tabernacles,** a fall harvest festival that commemorated the wilderness experience of Israel (Lev. 23:33–43). This feast of thanksgiving is the only one of the many feasts that will still be appropriate in the new kingdom. The others will have been fulfilled, but thanksgiving will be a continual theme in Messiah's kingdom.

14:17–19 The nations that are unwilling to come to Jerusalem to worship King Messiah and celebrate the feast will be subject to divine judgment. **Egypt** is used as an example, since it was a traditional enemy of Israel.

14:20, 21 In Messiah's kingdom, the people of Judah and Jerusalem will fulfill their destiny as a holy, priestly nation (Ex. 19:6). The words **HOLINESS TO THE LORD** will be inscribed on the gold headband worn by the high priest (Ex. 28:36). Holiness will so permeate Messiah's kingdom that even the lowly cooking pots will be holy.

Malachi

Introduction

Nothing is known of the prophet Malachi apart from this book. We are not sure that Malachi was the name of the prophet. The word means "My Messenger," and it is possible that the first verse should be translated, "The burden of the word of the LORD to Israel by My Messenger." Malachi's name identifying him as a messenger of God highlights one of the major themes of the book. Malachi prophesies that God would send a "messenger," a prophecy of John the Baptist, and "the Messenger of the covenant," a prophecy of Jesus (3:1).

The Book of Malachi was written during the last half of the fifth century B.C. Some even pinpoint the date between 420 and 415 B.C. This would place the Book of Malachi about one hundred years after the ministries of Haggai and Zechariah.

The history of the Jewish people is a story of a recurring pattern of captivity, exodus, and restoration into which Malachi also falls. There are two captivities in the Old Testament story, and two accounts of an exodus of the Jewish people from captivity. The first captivity and the great Exodus is Israel's experience with Egypt at the beginning of Israel's history; the second is Israel's experience with Babylon.

In the account of the first Exodus, Moses and Aaron are concerned about the proper worship of the living God, which was centered in the tabernacle. The point of the Exodus was the creation of the people of God as a worshiping community (see Ex. 5:1).

Similarly, two of the books of the second exodus, the return of God's people from Babylon, concern themselves with the proper worship of God. These two books, Haggai and Malachi, focus on worship centered on the rebuilt temple. Haggai exhorted the people to rebuild the temple in Jerusalem in 520 B.C. Thus this book parallels the Book of Exodus in which God gave instructions for the construction of the tabernacle. Similarly, Malachi parallels the Book of Leviticus in that both are concerned with how the people and the priests should act in the temple.

The priests of Malachi's time were indifferent to the rules of worship (1:6–14), and the people themselves had become apathetic about their offerings to God (3:6–12). Their apathy toward God was also reflected in their relations with other people—especially their spouses. It had become common at this time for men to divorce their wives. Such men ignored the fact that the Lord was a witness to their marriages, and as a result God ignored their offerings. The prophecy of Malachi is God's response to this "loveless" condition.

1:1 As in the case of Nahum (see Nah. 1:1), the prophetic message of Malachi was like a **burden** from which he needed deliverance (see also Is. 13:1; Jer. 23:33–38; Hab. 1:1). **to Israel:** In the postexilic period, the use of the word Israel for the people of Judah expresses the hope that the Lord was in the process of reasserting the fullness of His original promises to His people. The name **Malachi** means "My Messenger."

1:2 I have loved you: God is like a loving parent who speaks with fatherly affection. But His chosen people were like rebellious children who challenged His words of love for them.

1:3 But Esau I have hated: The contrast between the words *love* and *hate* here and in v. 2 seems much too strong. But on many occasions in the Old Testament, the verb *hate* has the basic meaning "not to choose." God's love for Jacob was expressed in His electing grace in extending His covenant to Jacob and to his descendants (see Gen. 25:21–26; Is. 44:1–5). In His sovereign purpose, God set His love on the one and not the other.

1:4, 5 Edom has said ... we will return: Edom was a nation descended from Esau, and they shared Esau's unbelief and self-confidence. Destruction made Israel reexamine her relationship to God. But destruction for Edom resulted only in continued pride and self-effort. **LORD of hosts:** This expression describes God as the supreme commander of the universe. The *hosts* are His heavenly armies.

1:6 A son honors his father: Here the Lord uses truisms: A father and a master can expect honor from those beneath them, but God was not receiving the honor due Him. **I am the Father:** The image of God as Father is common in the New Testament but less frequent in the Old Testament (see Is. 63:16; 64:8). **who despise My name:** In ancient Israel, a name was a symbol of a person's character, works, and reputation. Therefore, this charge was most serious. But the people dare to ask: **In what way have we despised Your name?**

1:7 God's answer to the question posed in v. 6 was in terms of **defiled food.** The word *defiled* describes bread that was not prepared properly. The bread (see Ex. 25:23–30) and the **table** on which it was displayed were holy symbols, but the priests were treating them like ordinary things.

1:8, 9 the blind ... lame and sick: The demands of holy worship of God had been made clear in the Law. Only the very best should be presented as an offering to the Lord (see Lev. 1:3); no one was to come with an offering that was blemished or unclean (see Lev. 7:19–21).

1:10 shut the doors: In a choice between service without gratitude and no service at all, God chose the second. **pleasure:** The word describes the desire of God to smile, even to laugh with joy at true worship from a godly people (see Ps. 40:6–8; 147:10, 11).

1:11 great among the Gentiles: God would one day receive praise from all the nations. Even the despised Gentiles would offer praise, while God's own people were profaning His holy name (see Ps. 87; 117).

1:12 you profane it: The people were treating God with contempt by their careless attitudes about their offerings.

1:13 The demands of God were neither understood nor appreciated; they seemed to be mere busywork. **stolen ... lame ... sick:** The gifts of the priests were not presentable; some were stolen goods, and others were animals that were useless. To sacrifice something of no value was not a sacrifice at all.

1:14 I am a great King: The reputation of the Lord among His people was supposed to be the means by which all the nations would be drawn to worship Him.

 IN DEPTH ## Blemished Sacrifices

Why should the condition of a sacrifice matter to God? He created all things, defective animals as well as the healthy ones. Why would He not accept gifts that were flawed? And why did God care about this enough to have his messenger Malachi speak so strongly? The imperfect sacrifices of the priests and people demonstrated the content of their hearts. The people were not sincere. To sacrifice a perfect, healthy animal looked to them like a waste, and they considered the work of preparing their gifts properly to be a foolish use of time and energy.

Malachi confronted this attitude with the Law of God, which clearly demanded unblemished sacrifices and sincere hearts (Lev. 1:3; 3:1; Deut. 17:1). Malachi also confronted the people with God's judgment of their actions. God was perfectly aware of what they were doing and the condition of their hearts. No sacrifices at all would have been better than second-rate and insincere ones. The people were not giving "sacrifices"; they were merely doing what was convenient, just enough to appear to obey God. Then they would turn around and pat themselves on the back for being righteous.

But though God's people had broken their covenant with Him, God remained true to His promises (Is. 53). He did not shrink from sending His only Son to a cruel death on the Cross. Jesus was the true, unblemished sacrifice to which the OT sacrifices pointed (Heb. 7:26–28). He was perfect—free from all sin. And through Jesus' sacrificial death the Lord provided salvation for all of our sins. In doing this, the Lord demonstrated His sincere love for us because He sacrificed the very best to save us (John 3:16).

2:1 The address to the **priests** shows that the section begun in 1:8 continues in this chapter.

2:2 If you will not … give glory: The behavior of the priests was defiling the name of God. **I will send a curse:** At the passage of the people into the Promised Land, the Levites placed before the people the blessings of obedience and the curses on disobedience (Deut. 27; 28). But the priests were not obeying the Law that they were supposed to uphold. They would therefore receive the curses.

2:3 Refuse was the dung in the sacrificed animal that should have been removed when the animal was prepared for sacrifice to the Lord.

2:4 My covenant with Levi: The Levites had been given the privilege of serving the tabernacle (Deut. 33:8–11).

2:5 The **covenant** of God was with Phinehas, a descendant of the tribe of Levi (Num. 25:1–14). **life and peace:** The basic meaning of the word *peace* is fullness, completeness, things as they really ought to be. **that he might fear Me:** The context here means holding God in reverential awe and worshiping Him in spirit and in truth (see 3:5, 16; 4:2).

2:6 the law of truth: The priests of the Old Testament period had a twofold responsibility—they were to represent the people in holy worship before the living God, and they were to teach and apply God's law to the people.

2:7 In the Old Testament, a prophet was commonly called a "**messenger** of the Lord." But this is apparently the only time in the Old Testament that priests are specifically called the messengers of the Lord (see also 3:1).

2:8 departed … caused many to stumble: The judgment on the departed religious leader would be more strict because of the ripple effect of his sin. **the covenant of Levi:** God made this covenant with the tribe of Levi and specifically with Phinehas (see v. 4).

2:9 The priests had the truth but had not **kept** it or practiced it. When they acted as judges, they showed partiality, making their sin even worse (see Deut. 17:9–11; 19:17).

2:10 one God created us: The use of the term *create* calls to mind the great creation text in Gen. 1:26–28. **deal treacherously:** Because God is the Creator of all humanity (Gen. 1:27), He requires that humans deal equitably with one another.

2:11 The term **abomination** indicates a stomach revulsion; the people had done something so awful as to make one ill. **institution which He loves:** Marriage is something God loves; divorce is something He hates (v. 16). The Lord's people had polluted something in which God takes great pleasure. **daughter of a foreign god:** The question of intermarriage in ancient Israel was not racial nor ethnic but spiritual—lack of faithfulness to God Himself.

2:12 cut off: The phrase may refer to banishment or even death. **being awake and aware:** The phrase may refer to a deliberate offense against the Lord (see Lev. 10:1–3).

2:13 the second thing: The prophets at times spoke of the compounding sins of the people (see Jer. 2:13). **He does not regard the offering:** When right things are done for the wrong reasons or with the wrong attitudes, God does not accept them (see Ps. 40:6–8). **goodwill:** The Hebrew suggests God's pleasure and enjoyment. God's pleasure is in sacrifices offered with attitudes of humility, faithfulness, and joy.

2:14 For what reason: The feigned surprise of the people fooled no one, certainly not the Lord. **wife of your youth:** These men had not only married pagan wives, but they had divorced their first wives to make room for their new ones. **by covenant:** The union of a marriage is formal, public, legal, and sacred—a binding contract.

2:15 make them one: Here the prophet recalls the words from Gen. 2:24, "one flesh." **a remnant of the Spirit:** This phrase probably indicates the work of God's Holy Spirit in the life of the married couple. God has joined them, and by His Spirit He has worked to strengthen them. **godly offspring:** God seeks godly children even as He seeks for true worshipers (see John 4:23, 24).

2:16 treacherously: To the Lord, attitudes of indifference to marriage vows and duties are the actions of a traitor.

2:17 God is **wearied** by people who do not submit to Him but who argue their points against His revelation. When **justice** comes, they will be sorry they asked (see 3:5).

3:1 prepare the way: Here is one of the great, explicit prophecies relating to the messianic age. It resembles the prophecy of Mic. 5:2 about the birthplace of the Messiah. Matthew and Mark identify the messenger of this verse as John the Baptist (see 4:5; Matt. 11:10; Mark 1:2, 3). **The Lord** refers here to Jesus Christ (as is the case in Ps. 110:1). **suddenly ... His temple:** Both the righteous and the wicked will be surprised when the Messiah arrives. **Messenger of the covenant:** This is a messianic title, referring to the One who will initiate the New Covenant (see Jer. 31:33, 34; Matt. 26:28; Heb. 12:24). **He is coming:** This dramatic wording indicates something that was just about to occur. However, it would be four hundred years before these words were fulfilled.

3:2 In this verse Malachi turns to the second coming of the Messiah. This second advent will be one of judgment and purification (Joel 2:11; Amos 5:18; Luke 21:36; Rev. 19:11–21). **refiner's fire ... launderers' soap:** These two images are vivid illustrations of the purifying process. The Savior King Himself will sift all people to prepare for His reign.

3:3 purify the sons of Levi: Since the priests had come under such strong censure in this book (1:6—2:9), and since the prophet himself was likely a priest, these words would have had a special significance for him.

3:4 The Hebrew word translated **pleasant** refers to things that are sweet and pleasing. God derives joy from the end result of His work.

3:5 judgment: The same word may be translated *justice* (see 2:17). The people had wondered where the God of justice was; now they will know. **fear Me:** Holding God in reverence and awe also means obeying Him (see 2:5; 3:16; 4:2).

3:6 I do not change: We might expect these opening words to ensure the nation's doom; instead, they give assurance of God's continuing mercy.

3:7 The history of Israel is not a record of ever-increasing obedience. Instead, it is a long, sad story of recurring departure from God. **Return:** This is the key term in the prophets for repentance, renewal, and restoration (see Is. 55:11; Jer. 4:1; Zech. 1:3).

3:8 The **tithes** were the gifts to the Lord that the Law required. There were three: two that were annual and one that came every three years. The tithe supported the priests and Levites, and also widows, orphans, and foreigners (Deut. 14:28, 29).

3:9–11 The people were **cursed** with poor production from their land and animals. The forces that caused loss of production are pictured collectively as **the devourer.**

3:12 One of the ways in which **all nations** would be drawn to the worship of the Lord was by seeing how the people of Israel fared with the Lord as their God. **a delightful land:** The adjective indicates enjoyment, life that is genuinely pleasurable. Faithfulness to God would lead to fruitfulness in the land.

3:13 In this verse God addresses not just their **words** but the thoughts that prompted them.

3:14 What profit: The people had doubts about the value of following the Lord. In fact, they had not really **kept His ordinance** anyway. The proper attitude is encouraged in 4:4.

3:15 the proud: This word refers to godless, rebellious people (see 4:1; compare Ps. 119:21; Prov. 21:24; Jer. 43:2).

3:16 There were other voices, those of people who did place themselves under the Law, those **who feared the LORD.** God did not ignore those who were faithful to Him. **a book of remembrance:** God never forgets His promises. God teaches us to remember and value the good that people do (Phil. 4:8); He does the same as He commands us. Those **who meditate** fear the Lord and ponder His significance in their lives.

3:17 The excitement of these words is that we can sense the pride God has in His children. The Hebrew word translated **jewels** could be rendered "special treasure." It is an endearing term that is used in the Old Testament only of the people of Israel as they are valued by the living God (see Ex. 19:5; Deut. 7:6; Ps. 135:4).

3:18 one who serves God: Serving God means putting Him first, obeying His commands, and finding one's chief joy in life as the advancement of the glory of His name.

4:1 Scripture consistently describes a **coming** day when God will arrive as a Judge and will deal with the wicked (see v. 5; compare Is. 13:6–10; Joel 1:15; 2:1–11; Zeph. 1:2—2:3; Zech. 14).

4:2 you who fear My name: This is the righteous remnant who held God in wonder and awe, responded to Him in obedience, and lived for Him with constant faith. **with healing in His wings:** The prophet compares the Savior to a bird whose comforting wings bring healing to the chicks that gather underneath (see Ps. 91:1–4).

4:3 trample the wicked: The victory of the righteous over the wicked is a promise of the living God that transcends the two testaments (see Ps. 110:4–6; compare Rev. 19:11–21). **On the day that I do this:** The identity of the Victor is already known.

4:4 Remember: This word means more than simply "to recall." The command is to act on the teaching that had come from the living God.

4:5 Elijah the prophet: The New Testament identifies John the Baptist as this Elijah (see Matt. 11:14; 17:10; Mark 9:11–13; Luke 1:17). There are three ways in which this prophecy might be fulfilled: (1) John the Baptist, whom Malachi had already prophesied (see 3:1), was the first to fill the promise of the Elijah figure. John, like Elijah, was a minister of the Lord calling people to repent and prepare for the coming of the Messiah (see Matt. 11:14). (2) Elijah appeared in person along with Moses at the Transfiguration, a stunning vindication of the messianic role of Jesus (see Matt. 16:28—17:8). (3) An Elijah-like figure will appear at the end times; he will call fire down from heaven just as Elijah did (see 1 Kin. 18:36–40; Rev. 11:1–7).

4:6 Malachi ends with both a promise and a warning. **fathers to the children ... children to their fathers:** As in every act of God announcing judgment, there is also an offer of His mercy (see Jon. 4:2). **a curse:** The term is one of the harshest in Scripture. The Hebrew word suggests complete annihilation. This is the term translated *doomed* in the account of the destruction of Jericho (see Josh. 6:17).

Matthew

Introduction

The Gospel of Matthew presents Jesus as the King—but King of a totally different kingdom—the kingdom of heaven. This Gospel does not name its author, but it was probably written by Jesus' disciple Matthew. As a tax collector, Matthew would have been literate and familiar with keeping records of money. Appropriately, this gospel contains more references to money than any of the others. Furthermore, Matthew's hometown was Capernaum, a village that is given special attention in this Gospel (4:13; 11:23). Matthew was probably written sometime between A.D. 50 and 60.

One purpose of Matthew's Gospel was to prove to Jewish readers that Jesus was their Messiah and promised King. Even though many Jews of Jesus' time were blind to Jesus' identity, Gentiles (such as the wise men) identified Him as Israel's promised King when He was a baby. The Gospel of Matthew also proves Jesus' legitimate authority by highlighting His wise teaching and righteous life (7:28, 29).

Another purpose of the book is to outline the characteristics of the kingdom of God, both for Israel and the church. The term *kingdom of heaven* appears thirty-three times and the term *kingdom of God* four times. No other Gospel lays such emphasis on the kingdom; the restoration of the glories of David's kingdom was a burning hope for many Jews at the time.

Matthew is the only Gospel writer who speaks directly of the *church* (16:18; 18:17). He points to the Gentile composition of this church by including several stories of the Gentiles' faith in Jesus: the wise men, the centurion, and the Canaanite woman. He records Jesus' prediction that the gospel will be preached to all nations (24:14), and the commission to the disciples to "make disciples of all the nations" (28:19). Jesus' teaching pointed to the blessings of the kingdom being extended to Gentiles.

1:1 Genealogy means "origin." Genealogies were very important to first-century Jews.

Christ's genealogy is crucial to historic Christianity. Matthew traced the lineage of Christ Jesus back to Abraham, Isaac, and Jacob to show that He was a Jew, but also back through David to inform the readers that Jesus is qualified to rule on the throne of David (see 2 Sam. 7:12), an event still in the future (19:28).

1:2–15 The mention of women in a Jewish genealogy is unusual. But in addition to Mary, four women are listed in this catalog of names. The extraordinary emphasis is underscored by the *kind* of women Matthew mentions: **Tamar,** who was involved in a scandal with Judah (Gen. 38); **Rahab,** the Canaanite of Jericho (Josh. 2); **Ruth,** who was a Moabite (Ruth 1:4); and Bathsheba, **the wife of Uriah,** who may have been a Hittite. Matthew shows how God's can lift the lowest and place them in royal lineage.

1:16 Joseph the husband of Mary was a direct descendant of David. Matthew, however, was careful not to identify Jesus as the physical son of Joseph. **Christ** and the word *messiah* both mean "Anointed One."

1:17 Abraham ... Christ: The genealogy is broken down into three groups of names with **fourteen** generations in each list. The name **David** in Hebrew has a numerical value of fourteen.

1:18 betrothed: In Jewish culture, this covenant was made about a year before the consummation of the marriage. It was during the one-year period of betrothal that Mary was found to be pregnant. The fact that Mary was a virgin at this time is clearly implied by the phrase **before they came together,** and by the righteous character of Joseph and his desire to divorce Mary when her pregnancy became known (v. 19).

1:19 Joseph wanted to divorce Mary on the grounds of infidelity. Joseph could have made the divorce a public matter, or he could have gone through a private ceremony before two witnesses. Being a gracious and **just man,** Joseph decided to keep it private.

1:20 conceived ... of the Holy Spirit: Verses 1–17 establish Jesus as a legal son of Joseph; vv. 18–25 deny that Joseph was Jesus' physical father.

1:21–24 Behold … Immanuel: This is a quotation from Is. 7:14. In this verse, the prophet Isaiah consoles King Ahaz of Judah. A coalition of two kings was opposing Ahaz. Isaiah tells the plans of his enemies would not succeed. As a sign to Ahaz, a son would be born of a woman, and before that boy reached the age where he could tell right from wrong, the two kings would no longer be a threat to Ahaz. Matthew makes it clear that Isaiah's words find their ultimate fulfillment in the virgin birth of Jesus, a sign to people of all ages that God was with them.

1:25 Joseph **did not know** Mary physically until **she** gave birth to Jesus. The clear implication of this verse is that Mary was a virgin only until the birth of Jesus. The brothers and sisters of Jesus were younger siblings born to Joseph and Mary after Jesus' birth (13:55, 56).

2:1 The events of ch. 2 probably took place some months after Jesus' birth. **Herod the king** is Herod the Great, who reigned over Palestine from 37 B.C. until his death in 4 B.C. Herod's reign was marked by cruelty and bloodshed. The word translated **wise men** refers to an honorable class of astrologers.

2:2, 3 born King of the Jews: These words would have struck terror and fury into the heart of Herod. **His star in the East** may refer to a star supernaturally introduced into the heavens.The star reappeared to guide the wise men to Christ (v. 9).

2:4 chief priests: This first mention of the Jewish council reveals that the Jewish leaders were alerted early to the coming of the Messiah. Their quick recital of Mic. 5:2 showed their prophetic astuteness about the messianic prophecies (v. 6).

2:5–9 Matthew clearly records how the Jewish religious authorities unintentionally affirmed that Jesus had fulfilled a messianic prophecy in His birth.

2:10 The wise men undoubtedly would have been discouraged by their failure to find the King in Jerusalem among the leaders. The reappearance of the star must have brought great joy and encouragement to them.

2:11 Gold symbolized royalty; **frankincense** was a fragrance; **myrrh** was the ointment of death.

2:12–14 warned in a dream: Five dreams of divine guidance emphasize God's orchestration of these events (1:20; 2:12, 13, 19, 22).

2:15 fulfilled: Jesus is the genuine Son of God; therefore, He gives fuller meaning to the prophecy of Hos. 11:1.

2:16–21 This prophecy is from Jer. 31:15; Rachel is weeping for her children led away to Babylon in 586 B.C. In the slaughter of the male infants at the time of Jesus' birth, Rachel once again is pictured as mourning the loss of her sons.

2:22 When Herod died, his kingdom was parceled out to his three sons: **Archelaus,** who ruled over Judea; Antipas, who became tetrarch of Galilee, Perea, Samaria, and Idumea; and Philip, who was tetrarch of Iturea and Trachonitis (see Luke 3:1). Archelaus was violent and cruel. Joseph, aware of Archelaus's reputation and guided by God in a dream, **turned** north to **Galilee.**

2:23 Nazareth was the location of the Roman garrison. Those who lived there were suspected of compromise with the enemy.

3:1 As Christ's forerunner, **John the Baptist** preceded the Lord Jesus in birth, ministry, and death. John is called "the Baptist" because he baptized those who came to him professing repentance.

3:2 The Greek verb translated **repent** indicates a change of attitude and outlook which well may result in sorrow for sins. **The kingdom of heaven** is most likely synonymous with "the kingdom of God." This kingdom begins with the Incarnation of Christ, continues with the inception of the church, and will be fully manifested when Christ returns. The kingdom was **at hand** because it was being offered to Israel in the person of the Messiah.

3:3–6 As roads were repaired, smoothed, straightened, and leveled before a king came, so John was preparing a spiritual road for the Messiah before His arrival. The quotation is from Is. 40:3.

3:7–9 The Pharisees and Sadducees were two prominent groups in Judaism during the time of Christ. In doctrine, the Pharisees held not only to the Law of Moses and Scriptures, but also to a whole body of oral tradition. The Sadducees were associated with the priestly caste. They based their beliefs on the Pentateuch—the Books of Genesis through Deuteronomy.

3:10 the ax is laid to the root of the trees: John likened his ministry to God's ax, clearing His orchard of dead wood—especially that which did not bear the fruit of repentance.

3:11–14 He will baptize you with the Holy Spirit: John identified people with himself and his message of repentance by water baptism; the One coming after him would unite people to Himself by means of the Holy Spirit.

3:15 to fulfill all righteousness: Jesus' baptism probably served several purposes: (1) Jesus joined with the believing remnant of Israel who had been baptized by John; (2) He confirmed the ministry of John; and (3) He fulfilled the Father's will.

3:16 the Spirit of God descending: This was God's official recognition of Jesus as the Messiah.

3:17 This is My beloved Son, a reference to Ps. 2:7, implies that others heard the voice of the Father. **In whom I am well pleased** recalls the prophecy of Is. 42:1. Matthew 3:16, 17 demonstrates the simultaneous existence of all three Persons of the Godhead.

4:1, 2 Satan did not lead Jesus to the temptation; the Holy Spirit did.

4:3, 4 It is written: Jesus' response to all three temptations was to quote the Word of God. Satan was tempting Jesus to do a miracle outside of the Father's will.

4:5, 6 throw Yourself down: Satan tempted Jesus to gain public attention through spectacle rather than through His righteous life and message.

4:7 Deuteronomy 6:16 emphasizes that a person should not test God. The Lord asked the Israelites to put Him to the test in only one area: tithing.

4:8–10 Christ rebuked the devil for asking for worship, a temptation to do exactly the opposite of what every Israelite was called upon to do (see Deut. 6:13, 15). Jesus *resisted* Satan, then He *defeated* Satan with the Scriptures (see Eph. 6:17).

4:11 angels came and ministered: Having rejected Satan's offer of bread, assistance from angels, and earthly kingdoms, Jesus was immediately visited by angels who helped Him.

4:12–14 Matthew indicates that **Capernaum,** located at the northern end of the Sea of Galilee, became Jesus' home and base of operation.

4:15, 16 The passage quoted here is Is. 9:1, 2. The ministry of Jesus in **Galilee** was a preview of what was yet to come.

4:17 The phrase **from that time Jesus began** occurs twice in the Book of Matthew. This one looks to the beginning of His earthly ministry, while 16:21 anticipates His Crucifixion and Resurrection.

4:18–22 I will make you fishers of men: This allusion to Jer. 16:16 was used to call Peter and Andrew to discipleship and a life of ministry.

4:23–25 Teaching ... preaching ... healing summarizes Jesus' earthly ministry. His *teaching* is illustrated by His discourses; His *preaching* is illustrated by the announcement in v. 17; His *healing* is illustrated by His many miracles.

5:1 Jesus *left* the multitude so that He could instruct the disciples. As He taught the disciples, the crowds came to where He was. The **mountain,** probably a high hill on the northwest shore of the Sea of Galilee, would have served as a natural amphitheater. **disciples:** From His many disciples, He selected twelve to receive special instruction and power.

5:2 He ... taught them: The Sermon on the Mount was given as the way of life for true children of the kingdom. It was instruction for those who had responded to Jesus' invitation to "repent" (4:17). These disciples were probably confused as to the true nature of righteousness and God's kingdom.

5:3, 4 Blessed are the poor in spirit: The idea of God blessing the humble and resisting the proud can also be found in Prov. 3:34; James 4:6.

5:5 Earth can also be translated *land* (see Ps. 37:3, 9, 11, 29; Prov. 2:21).

5:6–13 Pure **salt** maintains its flavor. In Israel, some salt was mixed with other ingredients, and exposed to the elements, the salt would be "leached out." Such leached-out salt was used for coating pathways.

5:14–16 Let your light so shine: The believer

does not have inherent light; rather we have *reflective* light. As we behold the glory of the Lord, we reflect it.

5:17, 18 Do not think that I came to destroy: Jesus rejected the Pharisees' charge that He was nullifying the law. **one jot or one tittle will by no means pass:** This statement of Jesus provides us with one of the strongest affirmations in the Bible of the inerrancy of Scripture.

5:19, 20 The righteousness of the scribes and Pharisees was essentially external adherence to rules. God demands more than this.

5:21 You have heard refers to the teaching of various rabbis rather than to that of Moses.

5:22–24 The scribes and Pharisees said that a person who referred to another as **Raca,** meaning "empty head," was in danger of being sued for libel before **the council** (or the Sanhedrin). Jesus said that whoever calls another a **fool** will have to answer to God.

5:25–27 It is wise not to have enemies. One should make peace as soon as possible because enemies are capable of doing great damage.

5:28 to lust for her: A man who gazes at a woman with the purpose of wanting her sexually has committed adultery.

5:29, 30 The hyperbole about tearing out one's eye is similar to the phrase in Prov. 23:2, "put a knife to your throat if you are a man given to appetite." Jesus advises removing every temptation to evil, no matter what the cost. The warning of **hell** (v. 22) indicates that those whose lifestyle is characterized by uncontrolled immorality are not heirs of the kingdom.

5:31, 32 Sexual immorality is a general term that includes premarital sex, extramarital infidelity, homosexuality, and bestiality (19:3–12).

5:33, 34 Do not swear at all: This does not forbid solemn, official oaths (see Gen. 22:16; Ps. 110:4; 2 Cor. 1:23), but only oaths made in common speech.

5:35–38 This important Old Testament law known as the *lex talionis* (the law of retaliation), covered what type of punishment and limited the retribution.

5:39–42 The Lord commands us to have a generous and compassionate attitude toward the needy. **Compels:** The Roman

government could press anyone into its service to carry a load as far as one mile.

5:43, 44 Hate your enemy is not found in Moses' writings.

5:45 That you may be sons of your Father in heaven means "that you may be like the Heavenly Father who displays His love without discrimination."

5:46–48 Jesus' followers are to be as perfect as God in the ways that they love. God gives us the power to keep His righteous standard.

6:1–4 they have their reward: The verb translated *have* was used in receipts and is similar to "paid in full." The hypocrites will receive **glory from men.** Contrast that with the heavenly rewards of Christ given to His followers (see 2 Cor. 5:10).

6:5, 6 Those who pray with improper motives **have their reward**—like those who do charitable deeds with improper motives (v. 2).

6:7 Jesus turned to *methods* of praying. *Why* one prays determines *how* one prays.

6:8–10 In this manner does not mean to pray using only these words, but to pray in this way. The prayer is composed of six requests. The first three ask for the kingdom to come (vv. 9, 10) and the last three for God to meet the needs of His people. **Hallowed be Your name:** The verb is an imperative and means "May Your name be hallowed."

6:11 Daily bread is a reminder of God's daily supply to Israel in the wilderness.

6:12, 13 The doxology at the end of the prayer is from 1 Chr. 29:11.

6:14–20 Do not lay up ... but lay up may be rephrased as "Do not give priority to this, but give priority to that."

6:21–24 Mammon refers to wealth, money, or property. No one can serve two masters because a time will come when they make opposing demands.

6:25–27 Stature here probably means "length of life," or age. **Cubit** then means a "length" of time, not a distance.

6:28–32 Gentiles refers to non-Jews. The Jewish people, because of God's revelation to them, were supposed to think differently than the Gentiles.

6:33, 34 To seek ... the kingdom of God and His righteousness means to desire God's righteous rule on this earth (vv. 9, 10).

7:1 The point of this verse is that a Christian should not have a spirit of carping criticism and fault-finding.

7:2 Every **judgment** that a person makes becomes a basis for his or her own judgment (see James 3:1, 2).

7:3–6 Dogs and **swine** refer to people who are enemies of the gospel, as opposed to those who are merely unbelievers.

7:7–12 The phrase **the Law and the Prophets** echoes 5:17. This so-called "Golden Rule" is the application of Lev. 19:18: "You shall love your neighbor as yourself."

7:13–20 Beware of false prophets: The way to tell false teachers from teachers of truth is **by their fruits.** *Fruits* here refers to more than their deeds; it includes their doctrine. A person speaking in the name of God is to be tested by the doctrines of Scripture.

7:21–23 Because so **many** people teach the wrong way, there is a tendency to ask how so many people could be wrong. However, it is important to remember that the Word of God is superior to any miracle.

7:24–27 The key difference in the two houses is the foundations. The **house on the rock** pictures a life founded on Christ (16:18). It will stand the test of Christ's judgment, but the **house on the sand** will fail the test (see 1 Cor. 3:12–15).

7:28, 29 not as the scribes: Scribes would cite authorities in order to lend credence to their statements. Jesus' words were self-authenticating.

8:1–3 The phrase **if You are willing** indicates genuine faith. Normally, touching a leper resulted in ceremonial defilement (see Lev. 14:45). But Jesus touched the leper, and the leper became clean.

8:4 See that you tell no one: Perhaps Jesus gave this command so that the healed person would first obey the Law before he became preoccupied with telling others about his healing. He would need to make the journey from near the Sea of Galilee to Jerusalem, and there offer the sacrifice required by Moses (see Lev. 14:4–32).

8:5–9 The centurion's response to Jesus indicated his clear understanding of **authority.**

8:10 I have not found ... not even in Israel: This commendation of the faith of the Gentile centurion was a strong rebuke of the Jewish people. Jesus made it clear that just being a physical descendant of Abraham did not guarantee entrance into His kingdom.

8:11 Sit down literally means "recline," as at a banquet table. The coming kingdom is portrayed in terms of a feast. (see Is. 25:6; Rev. 19:7–10).

8:12, 13 Sons of the kingdom refers to the Jews who should have been heirs of the kingdom. The idea that Gentiles would take their place in the coming kingdom was unthinkable to the Jews.

8:14–17 This verse quotes Is. 53:4. **took our infirmities ... bore our sicknesses:** Jesus had compassion on the people (see Mark 1:41; 5:19; Luke 7:13).

8:18–20 Son of Man: Jesus used this messianic title (drawn from Dan. 7:13, 14) over 80 times to refer to Himself.

8:21, 22 This man wanted to go to his home, wait for his father to die, and then follow Christ. Jesus' answer means that we must never make excuses for refusing to follow Him.

8:23–28 The country of the Gergesenes may refer to (1) the village of Khersa, near the eastern shore of the Sea of Galilee; (2) Gerasa, about thirty miles southeast of the Sea of Galilee; or (3) Gadara, about six miles away. This was Gentile territory.

8:29–34 We learn several things about demons in this passage: (1) they recognize the deity of Christ; (2) they are limited in their knowledge; (3) they know they will ultimately be judged by Christ.

9:1, 2 Their faith refers to the faith of the paralytic and of the men carrying him.

9:3–8 Though these leaders might deny Jesus' ability, or right, to forgive sins, the outward physical healing could not be denied. The healing of the paralytic was proof that forgiveness of sins had occurred as well.

9:9–11 Matthew is called Levi in Mark 2:14; Luke 5:27. **The tax office** was a toll booth set up alongside a highway to levy taxes on merchandise transported on that road. Tax collectors were despised because they worked for the Roman government.

9:12, 13 Jesus quoted Hos. 6:6 to emphasize that God is more interested in a person's loyal love than in the observance of external rituals. Jesus refers ironically to the Pharisees as **the righteous.**

9:14, 15 In referring to Himself as a **bridegroom,** Jesus was describing Himself as the Messiah. **Will be taken away from them** anticipates the violent death the Lord would experience.

9:16–30 See that no one knows it: Jesus wanted to discourage the masses from coming to Him for physical healing alone.

9:31–34 The Pharisees could not deny the reality of the miracles, so they attributed them to **the ruler of the demons.**

9:35–38 The harvest will mark the beginning of the kingdom age.

10:1–4 The **twelve** are called "disciples" in v. 1; here they are called **apostles.** The word *apostle* emphasizes delegated authority (see 1 Thess. 2:6); the term *disciple* emphasizes learning and following.

10:5, 6 Jesus focused His ministry on the Jews. After His Resurrection, He commanded His disciples to take the Good News to all the world.

10:7–10 The disciples' mission was to do a national religious survey to determine the people's response to Jesus as Messiah.

10:11 Because the testimony of the apostles was at stake, they were to seek out homes with good reputations. Furthermore, they were not to be constantly trying to find a more desirable residence.

10:12, 13 To **greet** a household was to pronounce a blessing on it, **"Peace** to you." If the occupants rejected their message, the apostles were to remove the blessing.

10:14, 15 These verses, together with 11:22, 24, imply that there will be degrees of judgment and torment for the lost.

10:16 Snakes are commonly thought of as **wise. In the midst of wolves** meant that the apostles would be exposed to hatred and violence from men.

10:17–20 God bring the gospel message to the Gentiles.

10:21–28 Fear Him refers not to Satan, but to God. **Destroy** does not indicate annihilation, but ruination.

10:29–33 To refuse to speak up for Christ because of persecution will result in the believer's loss of reward. (see Rom. 8:17; 2 Tim. 2:12).

10:34–36 To the disappointment of many Christians throughout the ages, it has often been those closest to them who have rejected them and their message.

10:37 not worthy of Me: Those who will be glorified with Christ in His kingdom are those who have suffered for Him (see Rom. 8:17; 2 Tim. 2:12).

10:38 Taking up a **cross** stands for great commitment—being willing to die for something.

10:39–42 reward: Jesus does not want His disciples to lose the joys of the next life by focusing on the pleasures of this world.

11:1, 2 John probably expected the Messiah immediately to judge Israel and establish His kingdom (3:2–12).

11:3–6 The Coming One is a title for the Messiah (see Ps. 118:26).

11:7–10 In the light of John's question, some may have questioned his commitment to the Messiah. John was **more than a prophet** in that he was the forerunner who announced the presence of the Messiah.

11:11 Born of women means that John had a human mother The **least in the kingdom** refers to those who will be living in the coming kingdom. The least person in the kingdom of heaven will have seen and understood the finished work of Christ on the Cross and through His Resurrection.

11:12 The violent take it by force in this context probably means that as Christ's kingdom advances, so do the attacks against it.

11:13 The prophets and the law refers to the Old Testament, which anticipated the coming of the Messiah.

11:14–19 Because of their hardness of heart, Israel failed to accept either the ministry of John the Baptist or that of the Lord Jesus Christ.

11:20–22 Chorazin was a village about two and one-half miles north of Capernaum; **Bethsaida** was about three miles east. Both of these cities would be judged for rejecting the Messiah.

11:23, 24 Capernaum, on the north shore of

the Sea of Galilee, was the base of operations for Christ's ministry.

11:25–30 You who labor and are heavy laden describes the Jews as suffering under a load of responsibilities laid on them by priests, scribes, and Pharisees.

12:1, 2 The Pharisees and scribes recognized that the Sabbath was the sign of the Mosaic covenant. While reaping was forbidden on the Sabbath (Ex. 34:21), the disciples were picking grain to eat, not for profit. According to the Pharisees, the disciples were "harvesting" and therefore breaking the Sabbath.

12:3–6 profane the Sabbath: On the Sabbath the priests carried out their work of ministry, showing it had priority over the Sabbath observance.

12:7, 8 For a similar use of Hos. 6:6, see 9:13.

12:9–14 Because of Jesus' view of the Sabbath, the Pharisees concluded that He was trying to overthrow the entire Mosaic system, and therefore had to be destroyed.

12:15, 16 withdrew: The Lord's ministry was characterized by opposition, withdrawal from opposition, and continued ministry to His followers.

12:17–21 This quotation of Is. 42:1–4 shows that the Messiah's quiet withdrawal was in keeping with the prophet's portrayal of Him.

12:22–24 Could this be the Son of David may also be translated "This one can't be the Son of David, can he?" The question expected a negative answer.

12:25–28 Jesus' defense was in three parts. First, a kingdom cannot continue to exist if it is divided against itself. Second, when the Pharisees exorcised demons, they claimed it was accomplished by the power of God. Third, the casting out of demons by the Messiah indicated the nearness of the kingdom.

12:29, 30 This verse shows how Jesus the King was confronting the kingdom of Satan. In His exorcisms, Jesus was binding Satan bit by bit; when He comes suddenly to establish His kingdom, He will bind Satan quickly and completely (see Rev. 20:1–10).

12:31, 32 The **sin** which **will not be forgiven** is the stubborn refusal to heed the Holy Spirit's conviction and accept the forgiveness that Christ offers. Because the leaders rejected

all proofs about Jesus as Messiah, nothing else would be given.

12:33–39 The sign of the prophet Jonah is explained in v. 40 as **three days and three night in the heart of the earth**.

12:40 Three days and three nights does not necessarily indicate three full days. In ancient Israel, a part of a day was considered a whole day (see Esth. 4:16; 5:1); so a period of 26 hours could be called "three days."

12:41, 42 The men of Nineveh and **the queen of the South** represent Gentiles who came to faith because of the words of God's prophets and kings.

12:43–50 This difficult analogy most likely describes the moral reformation that took place in Israel as a result of the ministries of John the Baptist and Jesus. The reformation, however, was not genuine (3:7–10); therefore, Israel's unbelief and hardness of heart were worse than before.

13:1–3 He spoke many things to them in parables: This teaching method, often used by the rabbis, utilized common scenes from everyday life to teach new truths about the kingdom.

13:4 Some seed fell by the wayside speaks of soil hardened by traffic that failed to allow penetration of the seed.

13:5, 6 Stony places refers to shallow soil resting on a shelf of rock. The plant could only live a short time because of the shallow soil.

13:7 Among thorns suggests good soil occupied with wild growth.

13:8, 9 Good ground refers to prepared or tilled soil that allows prosperous growth.

13:10, 11 The mysteries of the kingdom of heaven refers to new truths about the promised kingdom.

13:12 whoever has, to him more will be given: Just as the failure to respond to truth brings blindness, so a positive response is rewarded with further understanding (Luke 8:16–18).

13:13–24 The kingdom of heaven is like: This phrase introduces new truth about God's coming kingdom. It means that some truth about the kingdom is found in the story.

13:25–30 his enemy came and sowed tares: Tares are indistinguishable from wheat until the final fruit appears.

13:31, 32 The kingdom of heaven is like a mustard seed: This parable affirms that the number of people who will inherit the kingdom will be very small at first.

13:33 The kingdom of heaven is like leaven: When yeast is kneaded into the dough, it expands by itself. The kingdom of God will grow by an internal dynamic, the Holy Spirit, overcoming all opposition.

13:34, 35 Ps. 78:2 serves as a prophecy of Jesus' use of parables.

13:36 Jesus sent the multitude away. went into the house: Indicates the parables of 13:44–52 were for the disciples. Jesus explained previous stories and added four more.

13:37, 38 Sons of the kingdom refers to heirs of the kingdom.

13:39–43 The end of the age speaks of the time when the Son of Man will come to set up His righteous kingdom.

13:44 the kingdom of heaven is like treasure hidden in a field: In this story a man stumbles on a treasure which he makes every effort to obtain. The central truth is the value of the kingdom, which outweighs any sacrifice.

13:45, 46 the kingdom of heaven is like a merchant seeking beautiful pearls: Though the first person found his treasure by accident, the second found his by diligent search.

13:47–50 the kingdom of heaven is like a dragnet: Jesus describes a large seine net gathers fish **of every kind.** The work of judging or ferreting out the false catch is assigned to **angels.**

13:51, 52 Things new and old refers to truths about the kingdom that were found in the Old Testament and those that were freshly revealed in these parables.

13:53–56 carpenter's son: Carpenter basically means skilled worker. Joseph may have been a stonemason or some other type of craftsman.

13:57, 58 A prophet is not without honor except in his own country: In this second mission of Jesus to Nazareth, His hometown, He found that the people's unbelief had not abated (see Luke 4:16–30).

14:1, 2 John the Baptist had been beheaded. According to Herod, the miracles of Christ could only be explained as the work of a resurrected prophet, perhaps John the Baptist.

14:3, 4 Herod had gone to Rome where he met Herodias, the wife of his half-brother Philip. Herod divorced his wife and married her. John had rebuked the king for his sin.

14:5–21 Jesus' miraculous feeding of the crowd is so significant that it is the only one recorded in all four Gospels.

14:22–26 The fourth watch would be between 3:00 and 6:00 A.M.

14:27 It is I may also be translated "I am." Some interpret this as a claim to deity.

14:28–36 Only the Gospel of Matthew records the miracle of Peter walking on the water.

15:1 The fact that **the scribes and Pharisees** had traveled **from Jerusalem** to Galilee to see Jesus indicates that Jesus' reputation was becoming widespread.

15:2 The tradition of the elders was not the Law of Moses, it was the oral tradition based on interpretations of the law.

15:3 The scribes and Pharisees challenged Jesus for His disciples' violation of the teachings of former rabbis; Jesus challenged them for violating **the commandment of God.** The scribes and Pharisees were placing their own views above the Word of God.

15:4–6 Jesus was referring to a practice whereby people would dedicate their possessions to God so they could use their finances for themselves. For example, if parents needed money, the children could excuse themselves from helping because their resources were already "dedicated" to God.

15:7–14 Here Jesus chided the Pharaisees for being so concerned with ceremonial washings and dietary regulations that they failed to deal with character.

15:15–20 As a person thinks in his **heart,** so is he.

15:21–23 The woman was a Gentile who would have had no claims on a Jewish Messiah.

15:24 Israel: Jesus gave the Jews whom He called **lost sheep** the first opportunity to accept Him as their Messiah.

15:25–28 The "children" that Jesus referred to was Israel. **The little dogs** refer to Gentiles.

15:29–31 The scene changes from the region of Tyre and Sidon to a mountain near **the Sea of Galilee** but still in Gentile territory. **they glorified the God of Israel:** The Gentiles believed and glorified Israel's God.

15:32–39 This is not the same miracle recorded in 14:14–21. Jesus Himself identified two distinct feedings of multitudes (16:9, 10). This was a supernatural supply of food for Gentiles.

16:1–3 sign from heaven: Perhaps the scribes and Pharisees were thinking of signs such as the fire from heaven that answered Elijah's prayer (see 1 Kin. 18:36–38), the plagues on Egypt (see Ex. 7–12), or the sun standing still (see Josh. 10:12–14).

16:4 And He left them: Jesus left the Pharisees and Sadducees, meaning that He abandoned or forsook them.

16:5 The other side refers to the other side of the Sea of Galilee.

16:6–12 The doctrine of the Pharisees and Sadducees was hypocrisy, legalism, political opportunism, and spiritual hardness.

16:13, 14 Caesarea Philippi had long been associated with idol worship. **Who do men say that I … am:** Christ led His disciples into a proclamation of His deity by first soliciting from them what other people said.

16:15, 16 The Spirit of grace revealed to Peter the true identity of the Lord Jesus. **Son of the living God** refers to Jesus' deity.

16:17 has not revealed: People come to faith in Jesus Christ by the Father's revelation of the Son to them (see John 6:65).

16:18 I will build my church: Obviously the disciples did not at this point understand the doctrine of the New Testament church with its equality of Jew and Gentile. **the gates of Hades shall not prevail against it:** Jesus was saying that the forces of evil will not be able to conquer the people of God.

16:19 The keys of the kingdom may refer to Peter's opening the kingdom. The keys would open doors to lost people. In rabbinical literature, *binding* and *loosing* refers to what was permitted or not permitted.

16:20 Because the public did not understand the concept of the suffering Messiah, they were not to be told **that He was Jesus the Christ.**

16:21 The phrase **from that time** marks a new direction in Jesus' ministry. It introduces the Cross and the ultimate rejection of the Messiah. **Elders and chief priests and scribes** refer to the makeup of the Jewish council, also called the Sanhedrin. **Be killed** is the first of three predictions in Matthew about Christ's death (see 17:22, 23; 20:18, 19).

16:22 rebuke Him: Peter was attempting to correct Jesus.

16:23 To call Peter **Satan** was a very serious thing. But Peter was speaking for Satan.

16:24–28 coming in His kingdom: This verse anticipates the Transfiguration in ch. 17. In the Transfiguration, Peter, James, and John saw a preview of the kingdom.

17:1 The **high mountain** was probably a spur of Mount Hermon, which rises to about 9,400 feet above sea level.

17:2–4 Moses and Elijah represented the Old Testament, the Law and the Prophets.

17:5–8 This is My beloved Son, in whom I am well pleased were the identical words spoken at Jesus' baptism in 3:17 (see Ps. 2:7; Is. 42:1).

17:9 Tell the vision to no one: The command for silence was because the masses of Israel expected a conquering king, not a Suffering Servant.

17:10 The three disciples evidently did not understand the reference to Christ's death in v. 9. They had just seen Elijah on the mountain.

17:11 The Lord informed His three apostles that the scribes were right in their interpretation of Mal. 3:1; 4:5, 6. The fact that Christ used the phrase **will restore all things** indicates that the prophecy had a future fulfillment.

17:12, 13 Jesus indicates the prophecies about **Elijah** had their fulfillment in **John.**

17:14–18 The boy's epilepsy was caused by a demon (v. 18).

17:19–21 The disciples could not exorcise the demon because they were weak in faith.

17:22, 23 Once again Jesus predicted His death and Resurrection (see also 16:21; 20:18, 19). Once again the disciples failed to understand the Resurrection; they seemed to have heard only His words about His coming death, because they became **exceedingly sorrowful.**

17:24 The temple tax was a tax given annually by every adult Jewish male over 20 years of age for maintaining the temple. Jesus had not yet paid the tax, and the temple tax collector was following up on it.

17:25 Their sons may refer to citizens of a country as opposed to conquered peoples or **strangers.** However, citizens often pay customs and taxes. More likely the contrast is between the imperial family and the common people.

17:26, 27 In this verse, Jesus demonstrates that, as God's Son, He was free from the obligation to pay the temple tax. In fact, the temple belonged to Him (see Mal. 3:1).

18:1 Matthew 18 contains the fourth of five discourses in Matthew's Gospel (compare 5:1—7:27; 10:1–42; 13:1–53; 24:1—25:46). The theme of this discourse is humility. **Greatest in the kingdom** implies rank, a concept implied by Jesus Himself in 5:19.

18:2–5 Converted means to turn around (see Luke 22:32).

18:6, 7 Causes … to sin literally means to put a snare, trap, or stumbling block in someone's way. A **millstone** was a heavy grinding stone.

18:8, 9 One of the keys to understanding this assertion is to recognize the present tense of **causes you to sin.** This warning describes a person who has a lifestyle of sinning and needs drastic measures in order to change it (see 1 John 3:7–10).

18:10, 11 One of these little ones describes either a little child or a believer. Jesus implies that angels watch over and serve His followers on earth (see Heb. 1:14).

18:12–14 These little ones probably refers back to those who believe (v. 6). The Father watches over each of His little ones.

18:15–17 Jesus teaches His disciples about the process of restoring an erring believer. First, there should be a loving personal confrontation. The second step outlined in v. 16 is not as clear. The principle of witnesses is taken from Deut. 19:15, but what is it the witnesses attest? Evidently they witness that the offended brother is acting in good faith and the right spirit in attempting to work out

a reconciliation. If this does not bring peace, the offended brother is to report it to the assembly. The church then is to try to convince the believer who has sinned to be reconciled or to right the wrong. If the erring one will not respond, that person is to be disciplined by being cut off from the fellowship.

18:18 bind: Binding refers to things that are not permitted; loosing refers to things that are permitted (16:19).

18:19, 20 This passage is a promise for guidance for the two or three who confront, and a promise for the church to claim wisdom and restoration for the erring brother.

18:21 Peter's question was a logical outgrowth of the teachings of vv. 15–20. Actually Peter was being generous in his willingness to forgive **up to seven times.**

18:22 Seventy times seven may also mean "seventy-seven times." The point is not to keep count, but to always be willing to forgive.

18:23–31 Ten thousand talents would be sixty million day's wages, a sum that would be impossible to repay. Thus Jesus graphically portrayed this man's hopeless predicament.

18:32, 33 This parable reiterates the principle that we should forgive others because God forgives us (see the Lord's prayer in 6:12).

18:34, 35 These verses are a warning about the penalty for not forgiving others (see 1 Cor. 11:30–32; Heb. 12:5–11). All of a Christian's sins are forgiven and forgotten forever (see Ps. 103:12; Jer. 31:34; Heb. 8:12). If our forgiveness should be in direct proportion to the incredible amount that we have been forgiven (v. 22), then we must always be willing to forgive.

19:1–3 The use of the word **testing** indicates the malicious intent of the query from the Pharisees. The rabbis had been arguing about when it was permissible according to the Law to divorce. These Pharisees wanted Jesus to take one side on this controversy, thus giving them evidence to use against Him.

19:4–6 Jesus avoided the controversy over divorce by giving three reasons for why married people should remain married: (1) God made one male and one female. If God had intended more than one wife for Adam, He would have created more. (2) God ordained marriage as the strongest bond in all human relationships. A man leaves his parents and is **joined to his wife. Leave** means "to abandon"; **joined to** means "to be glued to." (3) The two become **one flesh.** The basic element in marriage is a covenant (see Mal. 2:14); part of that covenant is physical intimacy.

19:7, 8 Jesus pointed out that Moses never *commanded* divorce, he only **permitted** it. God's original ideal was that married couples would not divorce.

19:9, 10 Immorality may refer to any kind of sexual immorality—premarital sex, extramarital sex, prostitution, homosexuality, and even bestiality. **Whoever marries her who is divorced** probably refers to a man who marries a woman who has been divorced because of her immorality.

19:11 Jesus indicates that remaining unmarried is only for a few people.

19:12 Some people do not marry because they were born with no sex drive. Others do not marry because they are castrated. Still others forego marriage for the sake of serving God.

19:13–17 Why do you call Me good may be rephrased as "Why are you asking me concerning what is good?" The only One who can ultimately answer the question is God. The fact that Jesus went on to answer the question is a quiet claim to deity.

19:18–21 Jesus was proving the error of the man's claim to have fulfilled God's law (v. 20). If the young man loved his neighbor to the extent required by the Law of Moses (v. 19; Lev. 19:18), he would have had no difficulty in giving away his wealth to needy people.

19:22–24 Jesus' comment about a rich man's salvation would have been difficult for some Jewish people to accept.

19:25–27 we have left all: The instruction Jesus gave to the rich man was precisely what Peter and the other disciples had done (4:18–22). The natural question then was **what shall we have?** Jesus assured him that the life investment he and the other

disciples had made (16:24–28) would have dividends "a hundredfold" (v. 29).

19:28–30 throne of His glory: Christ is today seated at the right hand of the eternal throne of the Father. In the future kingdom the twelve apostles will **sit on twelve thrones, judging the twelve tribes of Israel.**

20:1–3 The third hour was about 9:00 A.M.
20:4, 5 The sixth hour was about noon. **The ninth hour** was 3:00 P.M.
20:6, 7 The eleventh hour was about 5:00 P.M. There would have been only one hour left in the working day.

20:8–15 The first workers complained that their wages were the same as those who had been hired late in the day. However, the owner had not cheated them; everyone received the agreed-upon sum for his work.

20:16 The workers with the contract represent Israel; they had the promises and the covenants (see Rom. 3:1, 2; 9:4; Eph. 2:11, 12). Those without an agreement represent the Gentiles, who would be made equal with the Jewish people when salvation became available to all through faith in Jesus Christ (see Rom. 11:16, 17; Eph 2:13–15; 3:6).

20:17–19 Once again the Lord Jesus anticipated His death and Resurrection (see 16:21; 17:9, 22, 23). For the first time He referred to the way He would die—crucifixion.

20:20–24 The indignation of **the** other **ten** apostles was probably because of their own desire for these lofty positions.

20:25–28 The measure of greatness is not position, power, or prestige; it is service.

20:29–34 Only Matthew mentions **two blind men;** Mark and Luke refer to one, probably the one who spoke. **Son of David,** a messianic title (see 2 Sam. 7:12–16), identifies Jesus as the heir to David's throne.

21:1 The Mount of Olives was directly east of Jerusalem, across the deep ravine of the Kidron valley. **Bethphage** was on the eastern slope of the Mount of Olives.

21:2, 3 The owner of the animals was likely a follower, or at least an admirer, of Jesus.

21:4, 5 These actions fulfill Is. 62:11; Zech. 9:9. The emphasis in these prophecies and Jesus' actions is on Jesus' humility.

21:6, 7 The disciples **laid their clothes** on both animals so Christ could ride either one.

Perhaps the mother donkey walked in front, followed by the colt on which Jesus was seated.

21:8 This **great multitude** refers not to the inhabitants of Jerusalem (v. 10), but to the large crowd that had accompanied Jesus from Jericho (20:29). The scene was a royal procession (see 2 Kin. 9:13).

21:9 Hosanna literally means "save now" (as in Ps. 118:25), but it was used as an exclamation of joyous praise. **Blessed is He who comes in the name of the LORD** is a quotation of Ps. 118:26.

21:10, 11 The city was moved is literally "the city was shaken."

21:12 bought and sold The money changers exchanged coins for acceptable coins to be used in the temple. **Those who sold doves** sold them at top prices.

21:13 My house shall be called a house of prayer is quoted from Is. 56:7. **den of thieves:** The temple had become a garrison for bandits.

21:14–16 In Ps. 8:2, which is quoted here, the infants expressed praise in the face of enemies.

 IN DEPTH **Parables: More Than Stories**

Although Jesus lived among a story-telling people, His approach to instruction was still unusual. His stories were memorable, but they were not transparent. People heard them but did not necessarily understand them. They are clearer to us because of the apostle Paul's writings, but few of those who first heard the parables understood them. At one point the disciples asked in frustration, "Why do you speak to (the people) in parables?" (Matt. 13:10). The disciples did not grasp the stories any better than the the crowd did.

Jesus' answer to the disciples reveals much about the purpose of His teaching. He quoted Is. 6:9, 10 to demonstrate that those with physical sight and hearing may still not be able to perceive the truths presented to them. For Isaiah, the "dullness" or hardness (Matt. 13:15) of the human heart directly affects spiritual insight and understanding. People need to soften their hearts, humble themselves before God, and honestly seek the truth in order to find it.

Jesus' stories are like wrapped gifts. The packaging of the story can either distract or captivate. But unless the package is opened, the gift itself remains unseen. Likewise unless one seeks the core of the parable—its truth and application—the lessons will remain hidden. Yet when discovered, these lessons prove to be extremely valuable. The testimony of millions of changed lives over two thousand years attests to this.

When unwrapped, Jesus' stories include powerful multiple applications. The same parable can strike people in different ways. For example, the parable of the Soils (Matt. 13:1–23) may be "heard" by at least four distinct people depending on their identification with one of the soils. The parable of the Lost Son (Luke 15:11–32) will affect a father quite differently than it would a rebellious son or a jealous brother.

When Jesus taught in Jerusalem during His last week, His parables focused on one's acceptance or rejection of Him. This time even the priests and the Pharisees "perceived He was speaking of them" (Matt. 21:45). They were stung by Jesus' parables, and they despised Him and His message. But they were unwilling to give up their pride, learn at Jesus' feet, and seek the forgiveness they so desperately needed. They sensed they would not appreciate what they found if they unwrapped the parables, so they refused to seek the truth any further. In doing this, they perfectly conformed to Isaiah's description of a people with dull hearts, hardness of hearing, and closed eyes. The religious leaders who should have been leading the people into the truth were the most blind to it.

21:17 The idea here is that Jesus abandoned the chief priests and scribes, the temple, and the city of Jerusalem. Instead of welcoming their Messiah, the religious authorities had rejected and opposed Him.

21:18, 19 He was hungry: Jesus desired to eat of the fruit of the fig tree one more time before He died, but could not. This miracle—the only recorded miracle of Jesus that involved judgment—illustrates God's judgment on the Israelites, who professed adherence to God but produced no fruit or spiritual reality.

21:20–22 The withering of the fig tree was used by Jesus to teach His disciples that faith works miracles and is the basis for answered prayer.

21:23 The mention of **these things** refers to Jesus' triumphal entry, the cleansing of the temple, and the acceptance of the praise of children. The fact that **the chief priests and the elders** opposed Jesus illustrates the unified antagonism of the Sanhedrin.

21:24, 25 It was a common rabbinic method to answer a question with a question.

21:26, 27 We do not know: The religious leaders' response released the Lord from having to answer their question, and it also disqualified them as spiritual leaders.

21:28–32 Tax collectors and harlots is a proverbial phrase for moral reprobates. Jesus' phrase **enter ... before you** not only established that these repentant sinners would enter the future kingdom, it also left the door open for the religious leaders to repent.

21:33–41 The **vineyard** illustrates God's kingdom (compare v. 43 with Is. 5:7). The detailed description of the vineyard indicates that the **landowner** provided for its well-being with utmost care. The owner of that vineyard was God; the **vinedressers** were the nation of Israel. The **servants** represent God's messengers, the prophets, who were so shamefully treated by the Jewish leaders. The **son** is Jesus, the Messiah.

21:42 The rejected **stone** is the Messiah, who became **the chief cornerstone** (see Mark 12:10, 11; Luke 20:17; Acts 4:11; Eph. 2:20; 1 Pet. 2:7).

21:43 In our time, **nation** refers to the church (see Rom. 10:19; 1 Pet. 2:9). This does not mean, however, that the kingdom has been

forever removed from Israel (see Rom. 11:26, 27).

21:44–46 A person may be broken with repentance as a result of falling on Christ. But if a person refuses to repent, the result is judgment.

22:1 The plural **parables** refers to the parable of the two sons (21:28–32), the wicked vinedressers (21:33–44), and the wedding feast (vv. 1–14).

22:2 The kingdom of heaven is like indicates that the story contains principles or truths that relate to the kingdom of God. **Marriage** refers to a wedding feast (see Rev. 19:6–10). In this parable, the **king** is God the Father and the **son** is Jesus.

22:3 Two invitations were sent out. The first was sent long before the celebration so that people would have plenty of time to get ready for the banquet. **Those who were invited** had received this original announcement. A second invitation was sent to them to announce that the banquet was ready and they should come right away.

22:4 The plea of this verse portrays the ministry of John the Baptist (3:1–12), Jesus (4:17), and the disciples (10:5–42).

22:5 They made light of it means "they did not care about it." They were so preoccupied with the here and now that they had no concern for God's kingdom.

22:6 These leaders approved John the Baptist's death at the hands of Herod Antipas (21:25); they instigated Jesus' Crucifixion (26:3–5, 14–16; 27:1, 2); and they initiated the persecution of the early church (see Acts 4:1–22; 5:17–40; 6:12–15).

22:7 The burning of the **city** refers to the destruction of Jerusalem in A.D. 70 under Titus (also see 21:41).

22:8–10 Both bad and good probably refers to Jews and Gentiles. Whatever their condition, people need to respond to the gospel. The important point to recognize is that this group responded to the invitation, while those who had received special invitations had spurned the king's offer.

22:11 did not have on a wedding garment: Like the others, this visitor had been invited to the wedding, but he failed to prepare himself for it (see Rev. 3:18). To come to a wedding banquet unprepared or in soiled clothing would have been insulting. In this parable, the garment may refer to the righteousness of Christ graciously provided for us through His death. Because this man was unprepared, the king declared him unworthy and sent him out of the banquet hall.

22:12, 13 Bind him hand and foot is a vivid picture of the man's inability to participate in Christ's kingdom. This man was an impostor, and when he was discovered, he was **cast … into outer darkness,** referring to the judgment (8:12; 25:30).

22:14 many are called, but few are chosen: All Israel had been invited, but only a few would accept and follow Jesus. Not all those invited will be among the chosen of God, for not all will believe.

22:15 Entangle means "to snare," like a trapper catching his prey.

22:16 The **Herodians** were supporters of the Herodian dynasty at the opposite end of the political spectrum from the Pharisees. Yet their common hatred of Christ was great enough that the Pharisees and Herodians joined forces against Him.

22:17 The dilemma is obvious: to side with the Pharisees and risk being accused of insurrection against the Roman government, or to side with the Herodians and lose the favor of the masses.

22:18 Test here means "to solicit to evil." The Lord called the Herodians and Pharisees **hypocrites** because they pretended to have good intentions.

22:19, 20 The **tax money** was a **denarius,** a silver coin with an image of the emperor and the inscription calling him "divine." The **image and inscription** were repugnant to the Jews because they hated their Roman overlords.

22:21, 22 Christ's followers have an obligation to earthly governments *and* to God. It is the believers' responsibility to obey the law of the land until it becomes sinful to do so (see Rom. 13:1–7). When the two realms are in conflict, Christians are to follow God (see Acts 4:18–20).

22:23 Some of the beliefs of **the Sadducees** are explained in Acts 23:8. These

men looked on the first five books of Moses as their authoritative Scripture.

22:24 The law that is the basis of the Sadducees' question is in Deut. 25:5, 6. It is the law of the levirate marriage.

22:25–28 This theological riddle had probably been used by the Sadducees to confound the Pharisees on more than one occasion.

22:29 Mistaken: Christ rebuked the Sadducees for denying the Resurrection.

22:30–32 Jesus quoted from the Pentateuch, Ex. 3:6, 15, to prove the doctrine of the Resurrection. The Lord is **the God of Abraham, the God of Isaac, and the God of Jacob,** a title that recalls that God is the One who gave the promises to the patriarchs. God promised them the land of Canaan (see Gen. 13:14–17). The patriarchs did not receive the land in their lifetimes. They must be resurrected in order to receive God's promises in full. That God is called **the God … of the living** indicates that there is a present spirit world over which God presides.

22:33 Jesus taught something that no one had seen clearly before—that the patriarchs are still living. The crowds were **astonished** because He appealed to His own authority when He taught them.

22:34 Undoubtedly the Pharisees were delighted to see their theological rivals muzzled; yet they were still intent on trapping Christ (v. 15).

22:35, 36 The **lawyer** was a student of the Law of Moses. He put the Lord to a test with a question designed to reveal how much Christ knew about the Law.

22:37 Jesus quoted from the great Jewish confession of faith called the Shema (Deut. 6:4, 5; 11:13–21). The **heart, soul,** and **mind** represent the whole person.

22:38, 39 People naturally love themselves. Because we love ourselves, we want the best for ourselves; likewise, we should be concerned for the welfare of others.

22:40 The Ten Commandments can be divided into two categories: those dealing with love for God and those dealing with responsibilities toward other people. The same may be said for **all the Law and the Prophets.**

22:41, 42 The answer to Jesus' question about the identity of the Messiah was in a number of Old Testament passages (see 2 Sam. 7:12–16; Ps. 89:3, 4, 34–36; Is. 9:7; 16:5; 55:3, 4). The Messiah would come from David's royal line.
22:43 This verse affirms that **David** wrote Ps. 110 under the inspiration of **the Spirit.**
22:44 This verse, which quotes Ps. 110:1, describes Christ's presence in heaven until He comes to reign on earth (see Heb. 10:11–13; Rev. 3:21).
22:45, 46 Psalm 110:1 uses two different Hebrew words for God. The first, translated **LORD,** is the name Yahweh, the proper name of Israel's God. The second **Lord** means "Master." David, the king of Israel, calls one of his offspring "Lord" a title for deity.
23:1, 2 The synagogues had an chair called **Moses' seat** (see Luke 4:20). **The scribes** were official copiers of the Old Testament Scriptures and also teachers of the Law (7:29; 8:19).
23:3 Jesus warned of the Pharisees' legalism, their tendency to value their own rules and regulations over the Scriptures. They followed external laws meticulously and appeared to be righteous. Yet the people were not to imitate their actions, because their hearts were filled with envy, hatred, and malice.
23:4 Contrast the Pharisees' actions with Jesus' call to the people in 11:28–30.
23:5 Phylacteries were small boxes containing Bible passages that were worn on the forehead or arm. This custom was based on Ex. 13:9, 16; Deut. 6:8; 11:18. **Borders,** translated *hem* in 9:20, refers to the tassels that were worn on the corners of garments in order to remind the Israelites of God's laws (see Num. 15:38; Deut. 22:12).
23:6 The best places were positions of honor at banquets. The **best** in the front of the synagogue, facing the congregation.
23:7 Greetings meant more than a passing "hello"; it was a respectful salutation given to a superior.
23:8–10 The Pharisees, or hypocrites, sought these titles for the prestige and power that went with them, and not for the purpose of using the positions to serve others.

23:11 All leadership is to be carried out humbly in a spirit of servanthood.
23:12 Exaltation will be carried out in the future reign of Christ (see Rom. 8:17).
23:13, 14 Jesus proclaimed **woe** on the scribes and Pharisees because of their opposition to the truth.
23:15 you travel land and sea: The Pharisees and scribes could not be accused of being lazy, but they were clearly misdirected and dangerous to the cause of God.
23:16–22 The religious authorities taught that oaths on **the temple, the altar,** and **heaven** were not binding. Oaths sworn by **the gold of the temple, the gift** on the altar, or **God** *were* binding. Jesus pointed out the absurdity of such teaching, and called the leaders **blind guides.**
23:23 The **scribes and Pharisees** were meticulous about tithing tiny seeds, but they failed to be obedient in more significant matters such as ensuring that all their actions were governed by **justice and mercy and faith** (see Mic. 6:8).
23:24 The Pharisees would meticulously **strain out** the smallest unclean insect—the **gnat**—with a cloth filter before drinking liquids, especially wine. However, Jesus said they would easily **swallow** a large unclean animal—a **camel.**
23:25, 26 The **inside** of the cup represents a person's character. Sometimes those who most loudly protest the sins of others are guilty of worse sins themselves.
23:27–33 The generation living at the time of Jesus had inherited all the guilt of their forefathers.
23:34 The present tense **I send** refers to the **prophets, wise men,** and **scribes** sent by God to the apostolic church.
23:35 Abel ... Zechariah: Jesus was saying that from the beginning of the Bible until the end, true followers of God had been mistreated, even murdered.
23:36, 37 Calling a name twice, as in **Jerusalem, Jerusalem,** indicates strong emotion (see 27:46; 2 Sam. 18:33; Acts 9:4). The phrases **I wanted** and **you were not willing** illustrate the opposition of Israel to Christ's will.
23:38, 39 Your house may refer to the temple,

but more likely to the Davidic dynasty (see 2 Sam. 7:16).

24:1 The discourse of ch. 23 had evidently been given in the **temple** precincts.

24:2 The devastation of the temple by the Romans in A.D. 70 was so thorough that the precise location of the sanctuary is still unknown today.

24:3 Undoubtedly the disciples were puzzled by the Lord's prophecy (v. 2); however, they held their tongues until they came to the **Mount of Olives.** When Jesus **sat,** they finally questioned Him about His statement about the destruction of the temple.

24:4, 5 Jesus' warning about being deceived was especially appropriate for the disciples. The destruction of Jerusalem did not necessarily mean the nearness of the end of the age.

24:6 False messiahs and **wars and rumors of wars** are characteristic of the fallen world in which we live. When the Lord said **all these things must come to pass,** He used a word for *must* that indicates a divine or logical necessity (see Acts 5:36, 37; 21:38).

24:7, 8 This passage describes characteristics of the end times. **Nation ... against nation, and kingdom against kingdom** seems to indicate wars on a broad or worldwide scale. The **famines, pestilences, and earthquakes** are more fully described in Rev. 6:1–8; 8:5–13; 9:13–21; 16:2–21. **Sorrows** literally means "birth pangs."

24:9–13 End here refers to the "end of the age."

24:14 this gospel of the kingdom: The final evidence of the end times will be the universal proclamation of the gospel.

24:15 The **abomination of desolation** literally means "the abomination that makes desolate." This prophecy comes from Daniel, specifically Dan. 9:27; 11:31; 12:11.

24:16 Some believe the final fulfillment of this prophecy will occur in the future desecration of the temple (see Dan. 9:27) and the subsequent setting up of an image of the "man of sin" in the Most Holy Place. When that occurs, everyone **in Judea** must **flee to the mountains.**

24:17–22 Those days will be shortened means that God will place a limit on the tribulation;

Christians will not have to endure persecution forever. Christ will intervene and prevent complete genocide.

24:23–25 The teaching of those who perform **signs and wonders** must be tested against correct doctrine (Deut. 13:1–5; 1 John 4:1–3), and by the witness of God's Spirit (see John 10:3–5, 27).

24:26, 27 Christ's return will not be confined to a **desert** or to some **inner rooms.** His coming will be so spectacular that everyone will know He has arrived.

24:28 wherever the carcass is, there the eagles will be gathered: This sweeping statement conveys an image of the horrible carnage that will take place in the judgment at the coming of the Son of Man (see Luke 17:37).

24:29 Immediately after: This verse moves chronologically to the close of the tribulation, a period that will be marked by monumental cosmic disturbances (see Is. 13:10; 34:4; Ezek. 32:7, 8; Joel 2:30, 3; Rev. 6:12–14).

24:30 The sign of the Son of Man will be seen appearing **in heaven** (see 16:1; Acts 1:11). **The tribes of the earth** probably refers to Israel. The context here is the national repentance of Israel predicted in Zech. 12:10, 12. **The Son of Man coming on the clouds** will be a fulfillment of Dan. 7:13, 14.

24:31 Gather refers to the gathering of the **elect** (God's people, both Jews and Gentiles) that will gloriously begin Christ's reign (see Is. 11:11, 12; 43:5, 6; 49:12; Jer. 16:14, 15; Ezek. 34:13; 36:24).

24:32 We can predict the coming of summer from certain signs: The branches of trees **become tender** and produce **leaves.** In the same way, we will know the end is coming when we see the signs Jesus described in this passage.

24:33, 34 Generation may mean "race," indicating that Israel as a people will not cease to exist before God fulfills His promises to them. **All these things** includes the Antichrist, the tribulation, and the appearance of Christ in glory.

24:35 The words of Christ are more certain than the existence of the universe.

24:36 Mark 13:32 indicates that even Jesus Himself did not know the **day and hour** of His return.

24:37–39 as the days of Noah were: Jesus was referring to the indifference of the people of Noah's time to the coming disaster. There is nothing sinful about **eating and drinking, marrying and giving in marriage.**

24:40–42 As Noah was vigilant in preparing for the Flood, so should people living in the tribulation be alert. They should prepare for the return of Christ.

24:43–51 These two servants (see Luke 19:11–26) illustrate two attitudes people will have toward Christ's return. The **faithful and wise** servant will be given more responsibilities in the Lord's kingdom. The **evil** servant will be **cut … in two,** a form of judgment used in the ancient world. **Weeping and gnashing of teeth** indicates the remorse of those who have suffered loss.

25:1 The **ten virgins** in this parable were waiting for the wedding procession that went from the bride's home to the home of her husband.

25:2 The parable of the ten virgins explains the need for wisdom (vv. 1–13).

25:3–9 Possessing **oil** illustrates the concept of being prepared; a lack of oil represents being unprepared for Christ's return.

25:10 The door was shut speaks of being shut out of the kingdom. The unwise virgins were not ready when Christ returned.

25:11 Lord, Lord is reminiscent of a similar cry in 7:21–23. The repetition of *Lord* indicates strong emotion.

25:12–14 The parable of the talents illustrates the faithfulness required of God's servants. The master traveled to a **far country** implies that there would be time to test the faithfulness of the servants.

25:15–17 A talent was about six thousand denarii that represented one day's wage. (20:2).

25:18–21 It was believed that money hidden in the ground was secure.

25:22–23 The first two servants received the same reward, even though they had received different amounts of money. The reward was based on faithfulness, not on the size of their responsibilities.

25:24–28 The wicked servant was unfaithful. If he had feared his master, he would have deposited the **money with the bankers.** Then the master would have **received back** the investment plus **interest.**

25:29 This proverb illustrates that a person must use what God has given or else lose it (Heb. 5:11, 12). This includes abilities, spiritual gifts and material possessions (see 1 Pet. 4:10).

25:30 The unprofitable servant is one who fails to be faithful to the tasks given by the master. This servant will not share in the rewards (8:12; 13:42, 50; 22:13).

25:31 The final section of this discourse involves judgment. Jesus focuses His attention on all the nations of the earth. **When the Son of Man comes in His glory** recalls the words of Dan. 7:13, 14, 27 and anticipates the future reign of Christ (see Rev. 5:9, 10; 19:11–18; 20:4–6).

25:32, 33 Nations here means Gentiles. **Sheep … goats:** Shepherds regularly herded their sheep and goats together, but there came a point when the two had to be separated.

25:34–39 The kingdom prepared for you from the foundation of the world indicates that this kingdom has always been God's goal for His people.

25:40–45 Three groups are referred to in vv. 31–46: sheep, goats, and **My brethren.** At the very least, these "brethren" are believers in Jesus Christ.

25:46 Everlasting and **eternal** describe both torment and **life,** indicating that one will last as long as the other.

26:1, 2 Matthew brings the discourse of the Lord to a conclusion with the words, **Now it came to pass, when Jesus had finished** (see 7:28; 11:1; 13:53; 19:1).

26:3 Caiaphas was **high priest** from A.D. 18 to 37. However, Luke 3:2 says that both Annas (father-in-law of Caiaphas) and Caiaphas were high priests. Although Caiaphas was officially the high priest, Annas still had influence over that office. Annas was so despicable that the Roman government deposed him from office. However, he continued to work behind the scenes through his wicked son-in-law.

26:4 The religious leaders knew they could not take Christ by argument or logic (22:46), or force (21:46). Their only recourse was **trickery.**

26:5 This verse is to be compared with v. 2, which speaks of Christ's full knowledge of what was coming and His acceptance of God's plan (see John 10:18).

26:6 Apparently Jesus spent His nights in the village of **Bethany,** just a few miles outside Jerusalem on the Mount of Olives. **Simon** was a **leper** who evidently had been cleansed by Jesus. He may have been the father of Lazarus, Mary, and Martha (see John 12:1, 2).

26:7–9 The **costly fragrant oil** (see Mark 14:3) was a perfume extracted from pure nard. She broke the flask and poured out the oil to cover Jesus' body (see Mark 14:3).

26:10–13 Jesus saw the pouring of the **fragrant oil** on His body as an anticipation of His death (see Mark 14:8). The perfumed ointment was placed on Jesus *before* His death; normally it would have been used after His death.

26:14 The enormity of Judas's sin is seen in the words **one of the twelve.** Jesus was betrayed by one of His inner circle.

26:15, 16 **Thirty pieces of silver** was the price of a slave (see Ex. 21:32). Zechariah had foreshadowed this sum in his prophetic actions (in Zech. 11:12, 13).

26:17–19 The first day of the Feast of the Unleavened Bread is also the day of the Passover (v. 18). **The disciples** were Peter and John (see Luke 22:8).

26:20, 21 One of you will betray Me indicates the Lord's omniscience. Repeatedly—in submission to the Father—Christ unveiled evidences of His deity to His disciples.

26:22 The disciples had already heard that Jesus was going to die in Jerusalem, but His revelation of betrayal was new. **Is it I** expects a negative response. The meaning is "I'm not the one, am I?"

26:23–25 The dish was a bowl of broth in which the guests dipped pieces of bread.

26:26 This is My body means "This symbolizes My body" (see 1 Cor. 10:4).

26:27, 28 This is My blood of the new covenant refers to the covenant that had been promised in the Old Testament (see Jer. 31:31–34; 32:37–44; Ezek. 34:25–31; 37:26–28).

26:29, 30 This verse anticipates God's kingdom when Christ will reign on the throne of David.

26:31, 32 All of you will … stumble: All the disciples, not just Peter, would fall away. **I will strike the Shepherd … the flock will be scattered:** This prophecy is found in Zech. 13:7.

26:33–35 The **rooster** crow is usually thought to refer to the third Roman watch, from midnight to 3 A.M.

26:36 Judas had already gone, so the Lord left eight of His disciples at this spot. **Gethsemane** (which means "Oil Press") was east of Jerusalem on the Mount of Olives.

26:37 This was the third time that Jesus singled out Peter, James, and John to accompany Him for a specific purpose. (see 17:1–13; Luke 8:49–56).

26:38 My soul is exceedingly sorrowful, even to death seems to look to Ps. 42:5, 6, 11; 43:5. **Watch** literally means "stay awake."

26:39 let this cup pass from Me: It was not the impending physical suffering that caused Jesus to pray this way; it was the reality of facing separation from His Father (see 2 Cor. 5:21; Gal. 3:13; Heb. 12:2; 1 Pet. 2:24). *Cup* is a figure of speech for wrath in the Old Testament (see Ps. 75:8; Is. 51:17).

26:40 Could you not watch with Me one hour: Although addressed to Peter, the question was meant for all three disciples.

26:41 The disciples needed to stay awake **and pray** because they were about to be tested themselves. The word **flesh** emphasizes human weakness.

26:42–44 The fact that Jesus **prayed the same words** indicates that there is nothing wrong with repetition from a devout heart. In obedience to His Father, Jesus committed Himself to **drink** the **cup,** whatever the cost.

26:45 Are you still sleeping: The disciples were resting while Jesus was sweating in prayer to the point of exhaustion (see Luke 22:43, 44).

26:46 Jesus did not go reluctantly, but with determination to do the Father's will.

26:47, 48 The fact that the multitude was armed **with swords and clubs** indicates that **Judas** did not really know the heart of Jesus.

26:49 The only person to address the Lord as **Rabbi** in the Book of Matthew was Judas (v. 25). **Kissed** means to kiss as a display of affection.

26:50 Friend: Jesus offered Judas friendship and an opportunity to change his mind. The words translated **Why have you come** may also mean, "Do what you have come to do."

26:51 John 18:10 informs us that the impetuous swordsman was Peter.

26:52, 53 A legion in the Roman army was about six thousand men. When one considers the power of one angel, the power of more than 72,000 angels is beyond comprehension. Jesus had all of heaven's power at His disposal, yet He refused to use it. His Father's will was for Him to go to the Cross.

26:54 If Jesus had called for angelic aid, the prophetic Scriptures foretelling His betrayal, His death, and His Resurrection would not have been fulfilled.

26:55, 56 all the disciples forsook Him and fled: Compare Peter's claim in v. 35 with Jesus' words in v. 41, "The spirit indeed is willing, but the flesh is weak."

26:57 Jesus was subjected to six trials—three Jewish trials and three Gentile trials. The first Jewish trial was before Annas, who was not the high priest, but was a powerful influence on the high priest's office. The second trial was before **Caiaphas** and the Jewish council. The council had been hastily called together in anticipation of passing judgment on Jesus. Matthew does not mention Jesus' trial before Herod Antipas (see Luke 23:6–12); he also combines the two trials before Pilate into one (27:2, 11–26). Jesus' opponents were trying desperately to find some legal basis for condemning Him to death.

26:58 Peter and John were both granted an entrance into the **courtyard** because John was known to the high priest. **The servants** were probably houseservants, not members of the mob who arrested the Lord.

26:59–61 This was a misquotation to say that Jesus had spoken against the temple, but it was an action for which they could condemn Him (see Acts 6:13, 14).

26:62 The high priest must have recognized that the accusers had no case against Jesus.

In maintaining His silence, Jesus fulfilled the prophecy of Is. 53:7.

26:63 I put You under oath by the living God: The high priest thought he needed to put Christ under oath. Christ needed no oath; He had indicated His divine nature and unity with the Father on several occasions (see John 8:58; 10:30–33).

26:64 Jesus answered the high priest's request (v. 63) in the affirmative and then fortified His answer by applying two clearly messianic passages to Himself: Ps. 110:1 and Dan. 7:13.

26:65, 66 Jesus' claim of sitting at the right hand of God (v. 64) was an assertion of deity and was, to this unbelieving high priest, a clear case of **blasphemy.**

26:67–74 swear: Peter swore under oath that he did not know Jesus. **immediately a rooster crowed:** Matthew, Luke, and John make the simple statement that a rooster would crow (Luke 22:61; John 18:27) whereas Mark, which was based on Peter's memories, emphasizes the exact number of times the rooster would crow. The number of times would be sharp in Peter's memory and interest.

26:75 He went out and wept bitterly indicates Peter's genuine repentance.

27:1 This was the third Jewish trial. The first two were illegal because they were held at night. The third held **when morning came** and was a "rubber stamp" of the one in vv. 57–68.

27:2 Pontius Pilate was **governor** of Judea, Samaria, and Idumea from A.D. 26–36. Because the Jews did not have authority to execute Jesus (see John 18:31), they brought Him to Pilate.

27:3, 4 Judas felt remorse because he had not planned for this to happen; he may have betrayed Jesus in order to force Him to take action against His enemies and inaugurate His kingdom.

27:5 Acts 1:18 says that the death of Judas was because of a headlong fall. The likely explanation is that Judas **hanged himself** on a tree, only to have the rope or branch break.

27:6 The religious leaders suddenly became very scrupulous about the Law. Because of Deut. 23:18, it was felt that blood money should not be used for religious purposes.

27:7, 8 Originally this plot of ground was known as **the potter's field,** a place where potters dug for clay. It was purchased as a cemetery for strangers who died in Jerusalem. It is likely Gentiles were also buried there.

27:9, 10 This prophecy is found in Zech. 11:12, 13; however, Matthew states that the prophecy was made by Jeremiah. The best solution to the problem seems to be that the prophecy **was spoken by Jeremiah** and recorded by Zechariah.

27:11–14 The title **King of the Jews** has not been used in Matthew's Gospel since 2:2. Clearly Pilate's charge against the Lord Jesus was prompted by Jewish religious leaders.

27:15–18 Barabbas was **notorious** because he was an insurrectionist and a murderer (see Mark 15:7; Luke 23:19, 25). Evidently Pilate assumed the Jews would choose Jesus to be released over a murderer like Barabbas.

27:19 Only Matthew records this incident about Pilate's wife. Pilate did not want to condemn an innocent man.

27:20–24 The religious authorities used a **tumult** to accomplish their goal. The tenure of Pilate had been rocked by conflicts with the Jews from the very beginning. He could scarcely have afforded another one on his record. Once again, Pilate pronounced Jesus to be innocent. The washing of **his hands** is recorded only by Matthew.

27:25 His blood be on us and on our children: The destruction of Jerusalem was one of the results of this sin (23:32–39).

27:26 when he had scourged Jesus: Scourging was a life-threatening punishment. Evidently this was an attempt by Pilate to punish Jesus so severely that the people would have pity and say, "It is enough; release Him" (see John 19:4, 5). However, the mob cried out for Jesus to be crucified (John 19:6).

27:27 The Praetorium was the official residence of the governor when he was in Jerusalem. It was originally built as a palace for Herod the Great.

27:28–30 The soldiers mocked Jesus for claiming to be a king. Note the references to the **robe,** the **crown,** the scepter (**reed**), and the praise.

27:31 crucified: Crucifixion, a practice probably adopted from Persia, was considered by the Romans to be the cruelest form of execution. The victim usually died after two or three days of agonizing suffering, enduring thirst, exhaustion, and exposure. The victim's arms were nailed to a beam, which was hoisted up and fixed to a post, to which the feet of the victim would be nailed. The body weight was supported by a peg on which the victim sat.

27:32 Compelled refers to the Roman government's right of impressment. The scourging undoubtedly left Jesus weak and unable to carry His cross, so a Roman guard ordered Simon to carry it. This **Simon** was the father of Alexander and Rufus (see Mark 15:21). **Cyrene,** located in North Africa, was home to a large number of Jews (see Acts 6:9).

27:33 The reason the site was called **Place of a Skull** is not known for certain; possibly the hill or mound looked something like a skull.

27:34 Sour wine mingled with gall would have dulled Jesus' pain and consciousness. Jesus refused it; He wanted to drink His cup of suffering fully aware of all that was happening (see Ps. 69:21).

27:35 In **casting lots** for Jesus' **garments,** the soldiers fulfilled Ps. 22:18.

27:36 Perhaps the soldiers **kept watch** to prevent anyone from trying to rescue Jesus from the Cross.

27:37 Putting the Gospel accounts together, the **accusation** probably read "This is Jesus of Nazareth, the King of the Jews" (see Mark 15:26; Luke 23:38; John 19:19).

27:38 two robbers were crucified with Him: This is in fulfillment of Is. 53:12, "He was numbered with the transgressors."

27:39 Psalm 22:7 predicted the insults that would be directed at the Messiah.

27:40 For a similar falsehood at Jesus' trial, see 26:61.

27:41–44 Jesus would not come down from the Cross *because* He was the Son of God and the King of Israel (see John 10:18). He was following God's plan for Him.

27:45 The sixth hour was noon. The **darkness** was not because of an eclipse of the sun, since the Passover occurred at full moon. This was a supernatural occurrence.

27:46 My God, My God, why have You for-saken Me: The duplication of "My God, My God" indicates Jesus' deep sorrow. The fact that Jesus spoke in Aramaic, the tongue of His birth, may be another sign of His extreme stress. He was quoting from Ps. 22.

27:47–49 Sour wine was the cheap wine used by soldiers and the lower class. Christ may have accepted this in order to give Himself enough strength to cry out again.

27:50 The **loud voice** (v. 46) indicates that Jesus was still fairly strong when He **yielded up His spirit.** This was not a cry of exhaustion, but a cry of victory. The purpose for which Jesus came was fulfilled. The verb translated *yielded* means "dismissed."

27:51 the veil of the temple was torn in two from top to bottom: The temple had two veils or curtains—one in front of the holy place and the other separating the holy place from the Most Holy Place. It was the second of these that was torn, demonstrating that God had opened up access to Himself through His Son (see Heb. 6:19; 10:19–22).

27:52, 53 many bodies of the saints … were raised: Because the Lord Jesus is the first-born from the dead (see Col. 1:18; Rev. 1:5) and the firstfruits of those who are asleep (see 1 Cor. 15:20, 23), these people could not have received their Resurrection bodies.

27:54 The centurion and those with him may have heard the exchanges between Pilate and Jesus (v. 11); they certainly witnessed the taunts recorded in vv. 40, 43. The supernatural signs convinced them that Jesus was indeed **the Son of God.** Significantly, this confession of faith came from a Gentile.

27:55, 56 Three women who where faithful to the Lord Jesus to the end are named: **Mary Magdalene; Mary the mother of James and Joses,** the wife of Clopas (see John 19:25); and **the mother** of James and John, wife of Zebedee, named Salome (see Mark 15:40).

27:57–60 Arimathea was about 20 miles northwest of Jerusalem. Mark 15:43 describes **Joseph** as "a prominent council member, who was himself waiting for the kingdom of God." Matthew describes him as **rich,** a fulfillment of Is. 53:9.

27:61 The two Marys are also mentioned in v. 56. These women were witnesses to the burial of Jesus.

27:62 The next day was the Sabbath. **The chief priests** were Sadducees. The **Pharisees** and the Sadducees' common animosity toward Jesus united them.

27:63 The Sadducees and Pharisees described the Lord Jesus as **that deceiver** when, in reality, *they* were the deceivers (26:4) and hypocrites (23:13, 15, 23, 25, 27, 29).

27:64 For emphasis, the verb **secure** is used three times in vv. 64–66.

27:65 The noun translated **guard** is a Latin word, since the soldiers were Romans and not part of the temple guard.

27:66 To emphasize the impossibility of anyone stealing the body of Jesus, Matthew emphasized that the tomb was sealed (see Dan. 6:17).

28:1 after the Sabbath: The Sabbath ended at sundown on Saturday. The events of this verse took place at dawn on Sunday morning.

28:2 An **earthquake** marked the death of the Lord Jesus (27:51); here it evidenced His Resurrection. The tomb was not opened to permit Christ to come out, but to allow others in so they could see that it was empty.

28:3, 4 Brilliance is a characteristic of heavenly beings (see 17:2; Dan. 7:9; 10:5, 6; Acts 1:10; Rev. 3:4, 5; 4:4; 6:11; 7:9, 13; 19:14).

28:5, 6 He is risen, as He said: For Jesus' predictions of His Resurrection, see 12:40; 16:21; 17:9, 23; 26:32.

28:7 The Lord Jesus made post-Resurrection appearances first in Jerusalem and Judea, then in Galilee, and then again in Jerusalem. Both ch. 28 and John 21 emphasize the appearances in Galilee.

28:8–10 Galilee was the appointed location for Jesus' rendezvous with His disciples (v. 7; 26:32) and was also the setting of the Great Commission (vv. 18–20).

28:11 The Roman guards **reported to the chief priests** because they had been assigned for duty to the religious authorities (27:65).

28:12–14 His disciples … stole Him away while we slept: Besides being a lie, this was a very weak explanation. If a guard was found sleeping at his post or if a prisoner escaped, the guard would be put to death (see Acts 12:19; 16:27, 28; 27:42).

28:15 Until this day refers specifically to the time of the writing of Matthew's Gospel.

28:16, 17 When **the eleven disciples went away into Galilee** they were probably accompanied by many more people. This may explain why **some doubted;** after all, the eleven were confirmed believers in the resurrected Christ by this time (see John 20:19–28).

28:18 All authority has been given to Jesus, although He is not yet exercising all of it (see Phil. 2:9–11; Heb. 2:5–9; 10:12, 13; Rev. 3:21). He will manifest this power when He returns in all His glory (see 19:28; 1 Cor. 15:27, 28; Eph. 1:10).

28:19, 20 Therefore shows that the Great Commission rests on the authority of Christ. Because He has authority over all, everyone needs to hear His gospel. The word **name** is singular, although it is the name of the Father, Son, and Holy Spirit together. This verse is another indication that God is one in three Persons. **I am with you always** demonstrates that Jesus is the true Immanuel, "God with us" (see 1:23; Heb. 13:5, 6; Rev. 21:3).

Mark

Introduction

Mark's Gospel is the most concise of all of the Gospels, because he omits Jesus' longer discourses. In general, Mark presents the miracle-working Jesus, not the teaching Jesus. His emphasis on Jesus' mighty and miraculous works makes this Gospel action-packed, fresh, and vivid. Mark constantly uses the present tense to create the impression of an eyewitness account—the kind presented by an on-the-spot reporter.

The Gospel of Mark does not identify its author. However, numerous documents from the early church unanimously point to Mark as the author. Mark was a cousin of Barnabas (Col. 4:10). He might have been the youth wearing a linen cloth at Jesus' arrest (14:51, 52), because only his Gospel mentions this incident, which occurred after all the disciples had fled. The fact that Peter announced his miraculous jail escape at the home of Mary, Mark's widowed mother (Acts 12:12), indicates Mark had significant contact with Peter and the other leaders of the Jerusalem church.

Peter was Mark's primary informant. In fact, the outline of events in Mark's Gospel follows precisely the outline of Peter's sermon to Cornelius at Caesarea (Acts 10:34–43; compare Acts 13:23–33). Oral preaching at that time, such as Peter's sermon, used established styles and rhetorical techniques to aid both instruction and recall; Mark's Gospel reflects these oral styles. In addition to recording Peter's memories about Jesus in his Gospel, Mark may have added his own memories and consulted other documents.

Mark probably wrote his Gospel sometime after Peter's death in A.D. 64 or 65. He wrote for Gentile Christians, especially Romans. This conclusion is based on the fact that he regularly explains Jewish customs and geography (7:2–4; 13:3; 14:12).

1:1 Mark starts his narrative with a simple declaration of the Good News about God's Son, the Lord Jesus Christ. The **gospel** refers to the basic story of the Good News to be found in Christ's life, ministry, death, and Resurrection.

Jesus, meaning "Yahweh saves," is the earthly name Jesus received at birth, whereas **Christ** is an Old Testament title that designates Him as God's chosen servant. **Son of God** makes clear Jesus' deity and demonstrates His unique relationship to God.

1:2, 3 Other than by quoting Jesus, Mark makes only one reference to the Old Testament. This quotation from **the Prophets,** retells the work of Christ's forerunner, John the Baptist. **Messenger** and **make his paths straight** call forth the image of a king visiting his realm. The quartet of Isaiah, Malachi, John the Baptist, and the writer Mark proclaims the coming of the King of kings, Jesus Christ.

1:4 John's **baptism of repentance** prepared his followers to receive the new message about Christ and His kingdom. **For the remission of sins** does not mean that one is baptized in order to receive forgiveness of sins.

1:5 John's baptizing was a recurring popular event that attracted large crowds. Mark vividly portrays the continuous stream of followers who flocked to John. As each person was baptized by John, he or she would admit to individual sin and the need for the Messiah.

1:6 The angel Gabriel announced to Zacharias that his son John would "go before Him [Christ] in the spirit and power of Elijah" (Mal. 4:5; Matt. 17:10–13; Luke 1:13–17).

1:7 The tense of the verb **preached** indicates continuous action in past time. John's characteristic message was to promote expectancy and acceptance of the Lord Jesus Christ. He said he was **not worthy** to loosen the Messiah's **sandal strap.** Students often performed menial tasks for their rabbis, but even they were not expected to remove someone's sandals. That task was left to slaves.

1:8 The prediction that Christ **will baptize you with the Holy Spirit** appears in each Gospel (Matt. 3:11; Luke 3:16; John 1:33).

1:9 Because He had no sins to repent, Jesus' baptism was unique.

1:10 Immediately occurs 41 times in Mark's Gospel to indicate the swift action required of a servant (vv. 10, 12, 18, 20, 21).

1:11 Three times during Christ's earthly ministry **a voice came from heaven.** It was the Father's testimony to Christ's unique and divine Sonship.

1:12 Mark declares that **the Spirit drove** Christ into the wilderness. The verb used for **drove** was frequently used to describe Christ's expulsion of demons.

1:13 Being **tempted by Satan** is something that all believers face, but Jesus triumphed completely over his adversary.

1:14 Mark begins his account of Christ's ministry with events **after John was put in prison,** as do the other synoptic Gospel writers.

1:15 Jesus proclaimed **the kingdom of God. Repent, and believe** are both acts of faith.

1:16 **Simon and Andrew** had been disciples of John the Baptist. They had known Jesus (see John 1:35–42), but were now being called to a lifetime of service.

1:17 Jesus called fishermen, hard-working and industrious people, to perform the most important task on earth: being **fishers of men.**

1:18–20 **James … John:** Simon and Andrew are fishing when we encounter them; James and John are mending their nets. Such details indicate the testimony of an eyewitness, probably Peter.

1:21 **Capernaum,** which sits beside the northern edge of the Sea of Galilee was Jesus' ministry "headquarters."

1:22 **astonished at his teaching:** Christ's teaching differed from that of scribes and Pharisees because His authority came from Himself.

1:23–25 The demon cried out **let us alone** because Jesus was a threat to *all* demons. About 20 percent of the approximately 35 miracles recorded about Jesus involved helping those troubled by demons. The demon acknowledged Jesus as **the Holy One of God,** but Jesus refused the testimony from such a disreputable source.

1:26, 27 **unclean spirit:** This is another term for demon.

1:28, 29 Mark notes the recognition this great miracle brought Jesus by saying **His fame spread throughout all the region.**

1:30, 31 Jesus completely healed Simon Peter's mother-in-law. Not only did the **fever** leave, but her strength was renewed so that she **served** Jesus and His followers.

1:32–36 The tense of the verb **prayed** indicates a continued action, not just a brief moment. Jesus' prayer life was successful because it was planned, private, and prolonged.

1:37, 38 Jesus' fame spread quickly, and the disciples' concern is evident in the statement **everyone is looking for you.** Jesus took seriously his mission to reach **the next towns. for this purpose:** Christ modeled singleness of purpose.

1:39–43 Jesus was **moved with compassion.** He not only healed but touched the leper.

1:44 After healing the leper, Jesus commanded him to **say nothing to anyone.**

1:45 The cleansed leper did not obey Jesus' simple injunction to keep quiet. As a result, Jesus had to remain in **deserted places** because the crowds swarmed to Him.

2:1, 2 Mark is largely a record of Christ's actions, but what Jesus said is not neglected. Here he describes how Jesus **preached the word,** the message of the coming kingdom.

2:3, 4 The throng blocked entrance into the already packed room. The determination of the men is seen in the fact that **they uncovered the roof** over the room where Jesus was preaching.

2:5 **their faith:** Not only did the four men have faith, but the paralytic himself had it too. When Jesus announced to him, **your sins are forgiven,** He was acknowledging the paralytic's faith.

2:6, 7 Mark notes the opposition of **the scribes,** who accused Jesus of blasphemy.

2:8–11 Jesus asked **which is easier** to demonstrate the truth of His claim to forgive the man's sins—something only God can accomplish. But to say **arise, take up your bed and walk** to a paralytic could be tested immediately. **Son of Man** is a term regularly used for the Messiah (see 8:31; Dan. 7:13; Mark 8:31).

2:12 **all were amazed and glorified God:** The crowd's reaction showed that they understood the significance of Jesus' miracle.

2:13 Jesus regularly taught the multitudes in retreat settings. This is indicated by the continuous tense of the verbs: They kept on coming, and Jesus kept on teaching.

2:14 Levi, also called Matthew (Matt. 9:9; 10:3), was Jewish, but he collected taxes for Rome. The Jews hated tax collectors. They had a reputation for taking more than they needed in order to add to their own wealth.

2:15–17 In this instance Jesus was speaking tongue-in-cheek when He used the word **righteous.** None are righteous, though some, such as the Pharisees, fancied themselves as such. Instead, Christ came to call **sinners to repentance.**

2:18 fast: Jesus was not against fasting, if properly observed. Here, the Pharisees' fasting is contrasted with Jesus' feasting, probably at Levi's house.

2:19, 20 Taken away from them may be a hint of Jesus' coming departure (John 14:19, 20; 16:5). After His crucifixion, Jesus' disciples **will fast,** perhaps figuratively in the sense of sorrowing over His loss.

2:21, 22 Mark records only four of Jesus' parables—two of which he includes here. The comparison implies that the newness of His message, and of the new covenant to follow, cannot fit into the old molds of Judaism.

2:23 Ripe grain can be eaten whole and is both tasty and nutritious. Plucking bits of grain from another's field for sustenance was permitted under Mosaic law (Deut. 23:25).

2:24 The point to the Pharisees' accusation against Jesus and His disciples was that they had performed work **on the Sabbath,** but their charge was dubious.

2:25, 26 Part of Jesus' defense was to recall the story of David's eating the **showbread** from the tabernacle. Since that bread was intended for the priests, it was **not lawful** for others to eat.

2:27, 28 Jesus does not declare the innocence of David or His disciples, but instead reminds His critics of the meaning of the Sabbath for humans and His own lordship over it.

3:1, 2 On the **Sabbath** Jesus visited the synagogue. The Pharisees **watched Him closely,** not to hear the words of life but to **accuse Him.**

3:3, 4 Certainly it was more consistent with the intention of the law to restore this man's afflicted hand, even on the Sabbath, than to destroy his hopes for the sake of keeping human tradition.

3:5 Jesus demonstrated His righteous **anger.** He was grieved with sin but did not sin Himself by retaliating or losing control of His emotions.

3:6 The Pharisees were religious experts who should have led the people in righteousness. Instead, they **plotted** Jesus' death **with the Herodians,** their bitter enemies.

3:7 Because of this plot against His life, Jesus withdrew with the disciples from the area. Still crowds flocked to Him.

3:8 Idumea (the Edom of the OT), the birthplace of Herod the Great, was south of Judea. **Beyond the Jordan** refers to the Transjordan, the cities on the east side of the Jordan River (10:1). **Tyre and Sidon** (Phoenicia in the OT), both on the Lebanese coast, were also cities Jesus visited during His earthly ministry (7:24).

3:9–12 Some people who met Christ were possessed by **unclean spirits,** or demons. These spirit beings have no bodily existence but frequently seek to inhabit humans or even animals. Mark says they **fell down before Him.** Jesus rebuked the demons who proclaimed **You are the Son of God** not because the demons incorrectly identified Jesus, but because their testimony was untrustworthy.

3:13 Jesus had a large group of followers. Even after the Twelve were appointed, He still had a large and continual following.

3:14 These **twelve** were Jesus' apostles—a chosen group sent out to fulfill a mission.

3:15 Christ gave **power** to the twelve apostles (Matt. 10:1–4). Christ and the apostles authenticated their ministry through signs, miracles, and wonders (Heb. 2:3–4).

3:16–19 Jesus **gave** Peter a new **name** because it was the Jewish custom to rename someone who had experienced a life-changing event. Jesus no doubt sent out His apostles in pairs. This explains the listing of the apostles' names in sets of two.

3:20, 21 Jesus' **own people,** no doubt close friends and perhaps even relatives (see vv. 31–35), heard of his teaching and assumed that He was **out of His mind.**

3:22 The **scribes** were harsh and direct in

their assessment of Jesus. They accused Him of being possessed by **Beelzebub** (literally, "Lord of the Flies"; 2 Kin. 1:3), another name for Satan.

3:23–26 Jesus' reply **in parables** was actually a threefold message that contrasted unity and disunity.

3:27 Jesus implies that He Himself has come to enter the house of the **strong man,** Satan, to seize his goods (1 John 3:8).

3:28–30 Anyone who **blasphemes against the Holy Spirit** places himself or herself outside the redeeming grace of God. It is apparently not a single act of defiant behavior, but a continued state of opposition entered into willfully.

3:31, 32 Opposition arose from Jesus' family, **His brothers and His mother.** We are not told what they wanted to say, but it likely involved concern for Jesus' safety or reputation, since He was becoming widely known as a preaching prophet and a worker of miracles (1:31; 2:12).

3:33–35 Whoever does the will of God expresses a spiritual allegiance that goes beyond loyalty to one's biological family. Spiritual kinship is determined not by blood or race but by obedience to God.

4:1, 2 Parables go beyond mere entertainment or moralizing; they teach vital spiritual truths about the kingdom of God.

4:3–9 During the planting season, it was common to see men scattering seed by hand over their small fields. They cast the seeds over the kinds of soil Jesus describes—smooth pathways running through fields, rough terrain that hid large rocks just beneath the surface, fields overgrown with weeds, and excellent, rich soil here and there. The point of the parable is that the condition of the soil determines the potential for growth.

4:10, 11 A **mystery** in Scripture is a truth God has revealed or will reveal at the proper time (Rom. 16:25, 26). Frequently, Jesus' opponents failed to understand the lessons because of their own spiritual blindness.

4:12 Not all will understand the teaching of the kingdom. Compare this statement of Jesus with Is. 6:9, 10; 43:8.

4:13–15 The pathway soil is trampled, hard, and unresponsive. The birds (v. 4) represent

Satan who quickly **takes away the word that was sown in their hearts.**

4:16, 17 The shallow soil overlaying the **stony ground** represents those who seem eager to receive Christ's message but whose commitment is superficial.

4:18, 19 The thorn-infested soil represents those **who hear the word** but lack single-mindedness and become unproductive. Worry (the normal **cares of this world**) and pleasure-seeking (**deceitfulness of riches** and the pursuit of **other things**) are both capable of producing a deadly spiritual apathy.

4:20 Only one soil produces fruit. Christ emphasizes the necessity to **hear the word, accept it, and bear fruit.** Such a person recognizes God's call, determines to follow it, and experiences a profound transformation.

4:21–23 Jesus' lesson of the **lamp** is that light reveals what it glows on. Like the lamp, Jesus' teachings reveal the motives of the human heart.

4:24 To those **who hear**—who receive God's Good News—**more** spiritual truth **will be given.** A growing believer must be receptive and teachable.

4:25 Whoever has, meaning those who have spiritual life, will continue to learn and grow. **Whoever does not have** spiritual life will lose even what little desire for God he or she seems to have.

4:26–29 Plants develop in a complex, intricate process that humans do not fully understand. God's kingdom likewise is growing, although we do not understand all that is happening. This parable presents God's kingdom in brief, from first sowing to final reaping.

4:30–32 A mustard seed is much smaller than a kernel of corn or a grain of wheat, yet its growth is more spectacular, reaching a height of ten to twelve feet. The point is the comparatively large result from such a humble and insignificant beginning. The **birds** in this parable illustrate how large the mustard plant has become.

4:33–35 To **cross over** the Sea of Galilee, a lake only eight miles wide, would not seem difficult. Yet its unique geography produces unusual conditions. The lake is situated seven hundred feet below sea level and is surrounded by mountains that rise three to four thousand feet above sea level. Tropical conditions prevail around the lake's surface. Yet the higher elevations can produce chilling night air.

4:36, 37 It is not unusual even today for a sudden **great windstorm,** produced by the mixture of warm and cold air, to appear on the Sea of Galilee during the evening hours. The resulting turbulence stirs up great **waves.**

4:38 The mention of Jesus being **asleep on a pillow** shows His true humanity. He was fully human and needed food and rest just as all people do.

4:39 Jesus' command over the wind and the sea demonstrates His full and complete deity. Only God the Creator can calm wind and sea.

4:40, 41 Mark uses the disciples' question **"Who can this be?"** to evoke a similar response in the minds of his readers. Mark relates the works and words of the One he calls "Jesus Christ, the Son of God" (1:1).

5:1 The country of the Gadarenes was on the eastern shore of the Sea of Galilee.

5:2 Right after leaving the boat Jesus was encountered by **a man with an unclean spirit** (1:23). The man was demon possessed.

5:3–13 It is not certain that the demons needed **permission** to leave the man and enter the pigs, but they may have been trying to forestall permanent bondage by Jesus.

5:14 The Old Testament forbade Jews to have any contact with pigs (Lev. 11:7, 8). The owners of these pigs might not have been Jewish, since this area was inhabited largely by Gentiles (see 5:20).

5:15–20 Jesus was not well received in this region. His presence had cost financial loss to some, although it meant liberation to the demoniac. All the people **marveled** when they heard what **Jesus had done for him. Decapolis** literally means "ten cities." This largely Gentile, Greek-speaking area was a strategic link in Rome's military defense.

5:21 Jesus' crossing **by boat to the other side** brought Him to Capernaum, although Mark does not mention that here.

5:22 Jairus, **one of the rulers of the synagogue,** was a lay leader charged with supervising services at the synagogue.

5:23 Jairus knew that Jesus could meet his need. However, he believed that Jesus had to touch his daughter before she could be healed.

5:24–26 Mark is not complimentary toward the **physicians** who had treated the woman, noting that **she had spent all that she had.** Mark adds the detail that her condition **grew worse.**

5:27 The woman **touched His garment.** Perhaps she had heard of another who was healed in a similar way. She must have feared having her embarrassing condition revealed to the crowd.

5:28 Her faith motivates her to act.

5:29, 30 The woman had no idea that Jesus had consciously healed her. While she sought to disappear into the crowd, Jesus turned and asked **Who touched My clothes?**

5:31 No one else was aware that the healing had happened.

5:32 He looked around, or literally, kept on looking around, gazing on the people crowded near Him.

5:33 Jesus' kind manner and tender words must have eased the fear this woman had of being revealed. She stepped forward **and told Him the whole truth.**

5:34 Jesus used a tender word, **daughter,** to address this woman, and He noted that her **faith** made the difference, for it was correctly placed in Him.

5:35, 36 The implication of the girl's reported death is that her condition is now irreversible and without remedy. Jesus insists that Jairus stop being **afraid** and continue to **believe.**

5:37 He permits only three disciples to join Him—**Peter, James, and John.**

5:38–40 Public mourning was loud and boisterous.

5:41 Talitha, cumi is Aramaic.

5:42 That **the girl arose** indicates that her life had been restored, just as in the case of the dead son of the widow of Nain (Luke 7:15) and of Lazarus who had been dead for four days (John 11:44).

5:43 The command to keep the miracle a

secret was a temporary measure, for certainly the girl's reappearance could not be hidden very long.

6:1 Jesus now went to minister in **His own country,** the area where He grew up, around Nazareth.

6:2 The people readily acknowledged both Jesus' **wisdom** and His **mighty works,** but with insensitive hearts and spiritual callousness they rejected Jesus' message.

6:3 The fact that Joseph is not mentioned here may indicate that he had died. Mark mentions Jesus' four **brothers** by name as well as His **sisters.**

6:4 A prophet is not without honor except in his own country is a maxim still repeated and still true today.

6:5–11 These instructions accompanied the Twelve on their assigned journey, the results of which are reported in Mark 6:30. These rules made for easier travel and encouraged the disciples to trust God for their food and shelter.

6:12 That people should repent: Repentance was necessary to cultivate the new life Christ offered.

6:13 Casting out demons and healing the sick would add authority to the apostles' message (2 Cor. 12:12; Heb. 2:3–4).

6:14 King Herod is Herod Antipas, the king who tried to kill the baby Jesus (see Matt. 2:1–18). After Herod the Great's death in 4 B.C., his kingdom was divided between Archelaus, who received Judea and Samaria; Philip, who ruled Iturea and Trachonitis, north and east of Galilee; and Antipas, who controlled Galilee and Perea from 4 B.C. to A.D. 39. Jesus ministered largely in the territory ruled by Antipas.

6:15 This verse demonstrates the contrast in expectations that Israel had for its coming Messiah.

6:16, 17 The **prison** where John was kept was at Machaerus, in the hills which overlook the Dead Sea. A complete palace and fortress occupied that site. **Herodias** was a granddaughter of Herod the Great and the sister of Herod Agrippa I (Acts 12:1–23). She was married to **Philip,** a half-brother of Herod Antipas. She divorced Philip in order to marry Herod Antipas. Herod likewise divorced his first wife, the

daughter of Aretas IV, king of Arabia (see 2 Cor. 11:32).

6:18–21 John's message to Herod was that his divorce was **not lawful** as grounds for remarriage.

6:22 Herodias' daughter, named Salome, was still unmarried at this point and danced seductively to please Herod Antipas.

6:23–26 Because she pleased him, Herod Antipas **swore to** Salome a solemn oath to give her **up to half** of his **kingdom**. Salome seized the opportunity for her mother, Herodias, who hated John the Baptist.

6:27 To keep his oath, Herod dispatched **an executioner** to kill John.

6:28–35 The Gospels record several times that when Jesus saw a need He **was moved with compassion** (1:41; Ex. 34:6). That compassion led to action.

6:36–38 The disciples sought to avoid responsibility for the hungry multitude, saying **send them away.** But Jesus' reply, **You give them something to eat,** must have startled them. Thomas calculated it would take the wages of two hundred days' labor to provide for that multitude.

6:39, 40 Details such as sitting **on the green grass,** which is possible only in late winter and early spring, and the fact that the groups were counted in **hundreds and in fifties** are indications of an eyewitness accounted of this story.

6:41 The tense of the verb **gave** suggests that the multiplication of the loaves took place in Jesus' hands as He *continued* or *kept on giving* the bread and fish to the disciples.

6:42, 43 The **twelve baskets full of fragments** were small baskets commonly carried by travelers. When we put God first, He will care for our needs and provide our daily bread.

6:44–46 Prayer was a vital part of Christ's communion with the Father and always preceded and accompanied especially difficult situations. This particular night followed a busy day when solitude was sought but not found.

6:47 In the middle of the sea does not mean the very center of the lake but simply out in the water. They were probably closest to the northern shore.

6:48 The fourth watch lasted from 3 A.M. until 6 A.M. That Jesus **would have passed them by** does not indicate that He was on His way to somewhere else. He could easily have calmed the waves, but He wanted His disciples to understand His mastery over all nature.

6:49 When the disciples saw Jesus they thought they saw a **ghost** (an apparition), a sign often interpreted as a foreshadowing of evil, even death.

6:50 Mark omits the added detail of Peter walking on the water to meet Jesus.

6:51, 52 Three miracles are contained in this brief account (vv. 47–51). Jesus: (1) saw the disciples out in the storm miles away. (2) walked on the water. (3) showed complete control over creation when **the wind ceased.**

6:53 They had set out for Bethsaida (v. 45) on the northeastern shore, but the storm apparently changed their course. The **land of Gennesaret** was on the northwest shore of the Sea of Galilee, just west of Capernaum.

6:54–56 Mark summarizes Jesus' healing ministry, noting how widespread it was. The hem of a garment was woven with tassels that reminded the wearer of God's commandments (see 5:27; Num. 15:37–41).

7:1, 2 Jerusalem was the central city of the Jewish faith. The were sent by the Jewish religious authorities to determine Jesus' position on the issues they counted important.

7:3, 4 These two verses explain the tradition of hand washing and various kinds of ceremonial uncleanness.

7:5 The tradition of the elders (see Matt. 15:2) was a series of rules meant to bolster the ceremonial law of the Jews. The question indirectly challenged Jesus, for as the disciples' teacher He was judged responsible for their actions.

7:6, 7 Jesus did not directly answer the question but instead addressed two more significant issues: (1) the superiority of God's law over man-made tradition (vv. 6–13) and (2) the difference between ceremonial and true moral defilement (vv. 14–23). Jesus enters into the argument by calling His adversaries **hypocrites.** The term originally referred to actors who wore masks on stage as they played different characters. Thus the Pharisees were not genuinely religious; they were just playing a part for all to see.

7:8, 9 In earlier times the Hebrews held the written law of God, the Torah, in such esteem that they would not write down their reflections on it, lest they should tempt later generations to consider their words as important as God's law. But as time went on, written commentaries on the law, collected in the Talmud, assumed greater authority than the Torah itself.

7:10–13 But you say shows the absolute contrast between God's will and man's empty tradition. The **corban** was a pious-sounding evasion of the requirement of honoring one's parents by supporting them financially.

7:14–23 A private question at mealtime bloomed into a controversy that now met the ears of **all the multitude** whom Jesus summoned.

7:24 Jesus' travels **to the region of Tyre and Sidon** are the farthest beyond Israel He is reported to have gone during His public ministry. Sidon is about 50 miles northeast of Capernaum.

7:25 Even in a house in faraway Sidon, Jesus could not find privacy.

7:26 The woman who approached Jesus was a Gentile, as the word **Greek** signifies here. She was a native of that area. **Syro-Phoenician** reflects the political situation of the Middle East at that time. Phoenicia (modern Lebanon) was part of the Roman province of Syria, which also included all of Palestine—Galilee, Samaria, Perea, Judea, Idumea, and other regions.

7:27 During a meal one does not stop to feed the house pets, **the little dogs.** Jesus is not attempting to insult the woman by using this metaphor.

7:28 The woman understood Jesus' test and persistently replied that even during the meal **the little dogs** consume **the children's crumbs** that fall from the table.

7:29 Because of her persistence, Jesus granted her request. He cast the demons out, although the girl was not in His presence.

7:30, 31 Jesus' route to Israel bypassed Galilee. Instead Jesus went east into the **Decapolis** region and then turned south past Mount Hermon until He reached **the Sea of Galilee.**

7:32–35 The healing of this **deaf** man (who also had a speech impediment) is one of the two miracles recorded by Mark only.

7:36, 37 Jesus' command to **tell no one** was meant to allow Him to move freely in the area.

8:1–5 Jesus desired to feed the multitude, but His disciples questioned **how.**

8:6, 7 The verb tenses for the words translated **took, gave thanks,** and **broke** specify action at a fixed moment in the past. Yet the verb translated **gave** is in the imperfect tense, which shows a continuing action. Thus we may conclude that the miracle of multiplication was a continuing process that took place, at least initially, in Jesus' hands.

8:8, 9 The **seven large baskets** contained leftovers—one basket from each original loaf.

8:10 Apparently **Dalmanutha** and Magdala (Matt. 15:39) are different names for the same region. Both are mentioned only once in the New Testament. Dalmanutha was probably on the western side of the Sea of Galilee, about five miles southwest of Capernaum.

8:11, 12 Obviously these men did not heed the many signs and wonders that Jesus had performed. It is doubtful that the Pharisees would have changed their minds even if they had seen another miracle.

8:13, 14 Having fed the four thousand on the western side of the lake, Jesus led His disciples by boat **to the other side,** near Bethsaida (v. 22).

8:15 Jesus repeatedly commanded His disciples to **beware of the leaven,** the growing corruption of the Pharisees and of Herod Antipas which was spreading throughout Israel.

8:16–21 The disciples continued to show a lack of spiritual discernment despite the miracles they had witnessed.

8:22–26 Jesus' healing of the blind man in stages paralleled the disciples' imperfect perception of Jesus. Like the man, they were no longer blind, but they could not see clearly either. Only the Holy Spirit could clear their vision.

8:27 Caesarea Philippi is about 25 miles north of the Sea of Galilee. One of the sources of the Jordan River springs from under a large rocky cliff that rises a hundred or more feet above the village. Many idols were carved into the rock facade. This was a perfect place for Christ to ask the question of v. 29.

8:28 The disciples' answers to Jesus' question about His identity restate popular misconceptions.

8:29 Jesus then asks His disciples for their understanding. Peter answers for the group when he says **You are the Christ.** Jesus wants His disciples to grasp firmly His true identity before He reveals to them His coming death and Resurrection. In Mark's Gospel, only the disciples come to understand who Jesus is.

8:30 Jesus' warning to **tell no one about Him** may seem strange. Its explanation lies in the fact that the Jews expected the Messiah to be a political liberator. Jesus' first coming was meant to accomplish another kind of liberation—release from sin.

8:31 This is the first of several clear predictions Jesus makes about His coming death and Resurrection (9:31; 10:33, 34). **He began to teach them** signals this new disclosure of His death, burial, and Resurrection to His apostles.

8:32 Jesus **spoke ... openly,** that is plainly, not in parables. **Peter** understood clearly Jesus' prediction of death and could not accept or understand it, and so he **began to rebuke Him.**

8:33 Peter's thoughts were probably well-intended, but did not take in God's eternal purposes and plan. Peter was not indwelt by **Satan,** but Satan had certainly suggested his thoughts.

8:34–36 To preserve one's life eternally, one must surrender earthly possessions and relationships held so dearly (see Matt. 16:24–27).

8:37, 38 When He comes in His glory is the key of this address to the disciples (vv. 34–38). It is the first glimpse of the fulfillment of all history (1 Cor. 15:24–28). Those who are willing to confess Jesus today will be rewarded before the Father in heaven (Matt. 5:10–12; 2 Tim. 2:11–13; Rev. 2:26–28).

9:1 After Jesus predicted His own death, Peter and the other disciples needed reassurance that Jesus would ultimately triumph. His prediction that some of them would see **the kingdom of God present with power** must have alleviated their fears.

9:2, 3 After six days links Jesus' prediction of v. 1 with the events of vv. 2–8. The **high mountain** was most likely one of the foothills surrounding Mount Hermon.

9:4 Elijah is mentioned in Mal. 4:5, 6 in connection with the future coming of Christ. This is why people asked John the Baptist if he were Elijah (John 1:21). **Moses** was the lawgiver and liberator, while Elijah was the first of the great prophets. Their presence confirmed the reality that Jesus is the Messiah of Peter's confession.

9:5–10 The voice of God the Father was heard audibly three times during the life of Christ. The other two occasions were at Jesus' baptism (1:11) and during His triumphal entry into Jerusalem.

9:11, 12 This question is based on the words of Mal. 4:5, 6.

9:13 Jesus' comment that **Elijah has also come** is a reference to John the Baptist. John was not a reincarnation of Elijah, but one who ministered "in the spirit and power of Elijah" (Luke 1:17) in preparing the way for Christ.

9:14–20 The boy had several problems. The **mute spirit** was a demon that kept the boy from speaking, but the demon also produced seizures.

9:21–24 I believe; help my unbelief expresses the dilemma that even those who believe can be nagged by doubt and hopelessness. This man took the correct course by appealing to Jesus for help.

9:25–29 Jesus said that **prayer and fasting** were required to prevail in some difficult instances.

9:30–32 For the second time (see 8:31), Jesus tells plainly of His coming death and Resurrection.

9:33–35 The disciples **kept silent,** refusing to tell Jesus about their discussion. But Jesus presented them with another paradox—that to be great in God's kingdom, one must be a servant.

9:36–41 Jesus is not endorsing all who claim to follow Him. Rather, this statement was meant to remind the disciples that God's work was not restricted to their small group.

9:42 A millstone is an extremely heavy circular stone, three to four feet across and about a foot thick, used to grind grain into meal.

9:43 Cut it off should be taken figuratively; it means to take whatever drastic action is necessary to avoid sin. The imagery of **hell** (frequently called *gehenna*) comes from a garbage dump outside the walls of Jerusalem. Jesus' hearers were familiar with the smoldering fires that always burned there.

9:44–50 The word **for** shows that Mark intended his readers to apply the preceding verses to their own lives. **Everyone will be seasoned with fire** may refer to the trials and judgments that all will face—believers with trials that purify faith, unbelievers with the eternal fire of God's judgment.

10:1 Jesus, now on His final journey to Jerusalem, comes to Capernaum (9:33). His Galilean ministry will head south to Judea and even into Perea on the eastern side of the Jordan River.

10:2 The Pharisees' question about divorce was a trap. Perhaps they hoped He would contradict Moses (Deut. 24:1–4) or offend Herod Antipas as John the Baptist had (see 6:18). The only possibility for divorce under Jewish law was **for a man to divorce his wife.**

10:3, 4 A certificate of divorce was a document signed before witnesses. In Jesus' day, the interpretation of this custom varied widely.

10:5, 6 Jesus declares that divorce was a concession to **the hardness of your heart** and then turns the argument to God's original intentions for marriage as seen in Gen. 2:21–25. God's design of **male and female** shows that He held each to be equal in value and worth, but that they fulfilled a different function and role in His design.

10:7, 8 A man is to **leave** his parents, cleave to his wife, then weave a life of beauty with her. The two become **one flesh,** and this bond is comparable to that of a blood relationship.

10:9 Jesus indicated that God's original purpose for marriage was that the union should not be broken.

10:10, 11 Whoever divorces his wife: Mark includes no exception to Christ's prohibition of divorce. Compare Matt. 5:32; 19:9, where an exception is made.

10:12 In Jewish society, it was not possible for **a woman** to divorce **her husband,** but Mark is presenting Jesus' words in a way his Roman audience would understand.

10:13–15 Children exhibit sincerity, eagerness, a trusting attitude, and total dependence on their parents. Thus childlikeness is a fitting comparison for the qualities a disciple should have.

10:16, 17 In addressing Jesus as **Good** Teacher, the rich young ruler (Matt. 19:22; Luke 18:18) meant no more than to issue a respectful formal greeting to a religious teacher.

10:18 The reply that **no one is good but one, that is, God** is Jesus' claim to deity, which He asks the young ruler to recognize.

10:19 Jesus recounts the seventh, sixth, eighth, ninth, and fifth commandments with the phrase **do not defraud** inserted just before the fifth commandment. All of these commands concern the fair and ethical treatment of other people (Ex. 20:12–17).

10:20–24 Those who have riches frequently also are **those who trust in riches,** a dangerous condition for a person seeking spiritual life.

10:25–27 This comparison of a **camel** going through a **needle** is a literal one (Matt. 19:24). But it is also impossible for anyone at all to be saved apart from God's grace and power.

10:28, 29 The **one who has left** all these things has not necessarily renounced them but has certainly reordered his priorities (see Matt. 19:29).

10:30 Spiritual rewards await those who follow Christ **in this time,** meaning during this age between Christ's first and second comings. Mark alone mentions that **persecutions** will follow as well—a point his Roman readers may have already known. After Christ's return, **in the age to come,** the incomparable reward will be **eternal life** in God's presence.

10:31 Worldly esteem, which is measured by wealth, social standing, nobility, birth, and personal achievement, will count for nothing in the world to come. Only humility and servanthood lead to greatness in God's kingdom.

10:32–34 Jesus revealed for the third time His imminent death and Resurrection as the disciples walked the road toward Jerusalem for Passover.

10:35 According to Matt 20:20, it was the mother of **James and John** who sought Jesus, but it is likely that the sons themselves encouraged her to do it.

10:36, 37 To be seated at a king's **right hand** was to take the position of most prominence; the person seated at the **left** hand ranked just below that (Luke 22:24–30). Jesus had to remind the disciples again about the price of greatness in God's kingdom.

10:38 To drink the cup and **be baptized** are references to the suffering and death that awaited Jesus (14:36). Jesus wanted His disciples to understand the suffering He would endure.

10:39–41 Jesus agreed with their response, though they had not yet understood the cost of their commitment. James would soon be executed by Herod Agrippa I in A.D. 44 (see Acts 12:1, 2). John was the last apostle to die, being exiled for a while on the island of Patmos (Rev. 1:9).

10:42–44 The point here is not the fact that Gentile rulers **lord it over them,** but the very idea that they seek to **exercise authority.** Jesus wants each of His followers to be a **servant**—one who as an attendant waits on others.

10:45 A **ransom** is the price paid to free slaves or hostages. The word is found only here and in Matt. 20:28, although it appears frequently in other documents of that time. Christ's life is given **for** others, in place of their lives.

10:46–48 Son of David is a messianic title. Mark shows us the irony of a blind man who had spiritual insight, while many who could see—including the religious leaders—were spiritually blind.

10:49, 50 Mark's account has all the graphic

details of an eyewitness account. Jesus **stood still;** then Bartimaeus was suddenly **throwing aside his garment** to rise and meet Jesus. Mark also notes the changed attitude of the crowd. They began by deriding Bartimaeus but later encouraged him.

10:51 Rabboni is a very tender Aramaic form of address meaning "master" or "teacher" (see John 20:16).

10:52 Bartimaeus **followed Jesus** for at least a short time **on the road.** He went along with the surging crowd at Jericho. Mark's mention of his name may indicate that he was known in the early church.

11:1 Bethphage and Bethany are just east of the Mount of Olives, about two miles from the gates of Jerusalem. Lazarus was raised to life at Bethany (John 12:1).

11:2–7 Christ's deity is evident in this passage. **You will find** demonstrates His omniscience. It is possible for a donkey **on which no one has sat** to be very calm and accommodating, but Jesus is also master of all nature and all creatures.

11:8–11 This was the triumphal entry on Palm Sunday. The crowd recognized Jesus' lordship by repeating a messianic psalm (Ps. 118:25, 26). Jesus retired **to Bethany** each night, perhaps staying in a friend's home. But in view of the fact that Jesus appears to have had no breakfast the next day (see v. 12), He and the twelve may have camped outside this night.

11:12 The next day would be Monday, and Mark devotes only eight verses to this day. Tuesday begins with v. 20, but the events of Tuesday and Wednesday are combined into one long section that ends at 13:37. A new chronological reference begins with 14:1, "after two days."

11:13, 14 Mark informs his readers that **it was not the season for figs.** Passover always comes in March or April, and fig season is not until May or June. However, fig trees generally produce a number of buds in March, leaves in April, and ripe fruit later on. Jesus was looking for the edible buds, the lack of which indicated that the tree would be fruitless that year.

11:15–17 Jesus quoted from the prophets Isaiah and Jeremiah (Is. 56:7; Jer 7:11) to make His point about the despicable conduct of those who bought and sold in the temple. **den of thieves** refers to the practice of cheating people.

11:18 The suspense of Mark's drama increases with the contrasting reactions to Christ. The religious leaders **sought** to **destroy Him** by plotting His death, while **the people** had just welcomed Him with a triumphal procession and **were astonished at His teaching.**

11:19, 20 Mark clearly indicates the transition from **evening** (Monday) to **the morning** (Tuesday).

11:21 Why was the **fig tree** both **cursed** and **withered?** Some have suggested that the fig tree represented Israel, which bore no fruit and would soon face the judgment of God.

11:22, 23 The illustration of casting an enormous mountain into the sea is an extreme example of the absolutely impossible. Having **faith in God** can accomplish the impossible.

11:24–26 It is doubtful that a person who cannot forgive another has ever experienced the forgiveness of his own sins by God.

11:27, 28 The religious leaders (v. 27), who were now plotting Jesus' death (v. 18), asked Jesus about the (1) nature and (2) source of His authority, perhaps because He had not openly declared that He was the Messiah.

11:29, 30 The intent of Jesus' question was to expose once again the insincerity of His detractors. The **baptism of John** refers to the authority of John's baptism. Was it **from heaven**—ordained by God and worthy of obedience? Or was it just **from men**—of human contrivance and void of any spiritual authority and reality?

11:31–33 We do not know was a dishonest reply, but perhaps the only one possible for men who wished only to save their reputation.

12:1 He began to speak to them in parables. This parable represents God as carefully preparing the nation of Israel (**a vineyard**) and leaving it in the care of others (the **vinedressers;** Is. 5:1–7). Great care was taken to fence the vineyard, to prepare a **wine vat** for crushing the grapes, and to build a **tower** in order to keep watch and protect the property from thieves.

12:2–5 The **servants,** including the **many**

others that were sent, represent the prophets who had gone before Jesus, perhaps culminating with John the Baptist.

12:6 In this parable, the owner of the vineyard represents God, but God Himself was never so mistaken as to assume they would respect His Son. God is omniscient, whereas the vineyard owner in the parable is not. This story illustrates the patience God had with Israel.

12:7–9 Jesus answered His own rhetorical question. The destruction of **the vinedressers,** the Israelites who rejected the Son of God, took place in A.D. 70 when the Romans smashed a revolt in Jerusalem and destroyed the temple. Giving **the vineyards to others** refers to the importance the Gentiles would assume in the growth of Christianity.

12:10–12 The chief priests, scribes, and elders **sought to lay hands on Him,** to arrest Jesus, and to carry out their plot to destroy Him (see 11:18). Only as the final points of the parable were made did these evil men realize that Jesus **had spoken the parable against them.**

12:13 The Herodians are mentioned in the New Testament three times, all in conjunction with the Pharisees. The Herodians wanted to kill Jesus because He threatened their authority (3:16; Matt. 22:16). Their attempt **to catch Him in His words** was their hope that Jesus would say something they could use as grounds for His arrest.

12:14 You ... care about no one was intended as a compliment. The teachers recognized that Jesus was partial to no one. The question, however, was a lose-lose proposition: a *yes* answer would alienate Jews who opposed Rome, while a *no* answer could be taken as treason against the state.

12:15 A **denarius** was worth an entire day's wages.

12:16 The **image and inscription** on the coin was **Caesar's,** the Roman emperor.

12:17, 18 The **Sadducees** were an elite group of religious leaders who denied the existence of angels, the immortality of the soul, and the Resurrection. They rejected the oral traditions and accepted only the validity of the Pentateuch.

12:19–22 The custom of marrying the widow

of one's brother was supported by Deut. 25:5, 6, but it was not absolutely binding (Deut. 25:7–10).

12:23 The purpose of this story was to discredit the doctrine of Resurrection.

12:24 Two categories support the Resurrection—**the Scriptures** and God's **power.** The Sadducees undoubtedly did know the Scriptures, but lacked spiritual insight to understand God's purposes.

12:25 Angels neither marry nor procreate. Luke 20:36 applies these restrictions to all angels without distinction.

12:26, 27 Jesus quotes from the Law—the Book of Exodus—to make His point. God said **I am** the God of the three patriarchs mentioned, not "I was their God, but now they are dead." He still is their God because they are still alive. Their souls not only live after death, but their bodies will be raised anew as well.

12:28, 29 The **Hear, O Israel** verse of Deut. 6:4 is commonly called the Shema (from a Hebrew word meaning "to hear") and is repeated by Jews the world over as expressing the essence of their faith in God.

12:30, 31 The first commandment summarizes the first four of the Ten Commandments. The **second** is the essence of commandments five through ten, which relate to the treatment of other people.

12:32–35 In the temple does not refer to the sanctuary itself, where only the priests were allowed to minister. The temple environs included a number of porticos and courts. One was designated especially for women (and included the treasury, 12:41), another for men. Gentiles could view the temple from an outer area.

12:36, 37 David himself said by the Holy Spirit is Jesus' clear affirmation of the doctrine of inspiration (see 2 Tim. 3:16; 2 Pet. 1:21). Jesus' argument about the Messiah being Lord as well as Son showed that the Messiah, even though a descendant of David, would be superior to him. In fact, He would be His Lord. He was both man and God at the same time.

12:38–40 The **scribes** of Jesus' day were teachers of the law, often dependent on people's gifts for their support. Some, however, overstepped the bounds of humility, piety, and dignity by flaunting their position of

respect and trust. They sought the glory that belonged to God and even took advantage of widows who helped feed and support them.
12:41, 42 By contrast, the widow worshiped God out of deep humility and genuine devotion. Mark notes for his Roman readers that her **two mites** make a **quadrans,** a Roman monetary unit. It was worth just a few cents.
12:43, 44 Jesus' comparison of the percentages contributed by the rich and the poor reminds us that God measures not how much we give, but how much we retain. Those with greater income have an obligation to return a larger percentage of it to God's work.
13:1, 2 The disciples' excitement over the temple's tremendous **manner of stones** was a natural reaction to splendid and majestic architecture; each stone weighed several tons. Thus Jesus' remark that **not one stone shall be left upon another** stunned His listeners. This prophecy was fulfilled in A.D. 70 when the Roman General Titus destroyed much of Jerusalem, including the temple.
13:3, 4 Only Mark, given to detail, mentions the names of the four disciples who questioned Jesus. They wanted to know about (1) chronology—the time of the prophecy's fulfillment, and (2) circumstances—the sign of its fulfillment. Their questions assumed that the temple's destruction would signal the end of the present age and the inauguration of the Messiah's reign. They wondered how near that event was.
13:5–7 The last days will include religious deception, conflict between nations, earthquakes and famines, and persecution of Christians. In the midst of this chaos, the gospel will spread over the entire world. **The end** is the end of the age (see Matt. 24:3, 6, 13, 14).
13:8 The beginnings of sorrows calls forth the imagery of birth pangs. Like labor contractions, these events, filled with great pain, will hasten the joyous birth of the Messiah's kingdom.
13:9–12 The promise that the **Holy Spirit** will guide one's speech in the hour of trial applies first to the Twelve and only secondarily to others who will experience persecution. But this promise does not assure escape from persecution or even freedom from being **put to death.**

13:13 He who endures to the end shall be saved is not referring to regeneration or justification but to physical deliverance from tribulation (vv. 19, 20).
13:14 The appearance of **the abomination of desolation,** first described by Daniel (Dan. 9:27; 11:31; 12:11), signals the onslaught of persecution. **Standing where it ought not** refers to the presence of an idol standing in the temple.
13:15–19 In those days there will be tribulation. The events of v. 14 signal an unparalleled time of suffering. Matt. 24:31 calls it a great tribulation, and Jer. 30:7 refers to it as "the time of Jacob's trouble."
13:20–23 To deceive, if possible, indicates that the deception will not overcome **the elect.**
13:24, 25 But points to a marked distinction between the false prophets of v. 22 and the true coming of Christ in v. 26. Great astronomical disturbances will accompany Christ's glorious return.
13:26 Jesus described His return as **the Son of Man coming in the clouds.** This passage recalls Dan. 7:13, 14, in which the Son of Man receives the kingdom from God the Father.
13:27–29 Jesus likened the signs of His second coming to the sprouts of growth and leaves on a fig tree. Both point to the glories to come—the full flowering of the earth and the return of Christ.
13:30 Some have argued that **this generation** refers to Jesus' contemporaries; others have suggested it means a people, such as the Jews, who are related by blood (see Luke 21:32.) Jesus' statement here may have been intended to incorporate those who would see the initial destruction of Jerusalem as well as those who would be living at the time Jesus returns—those who see the final fulfillment of **all these things.**
13:31 Concerning what Jesus foretells here about **heaven and earth** passing away, see also Is. 65:17; 2 Pet. 3:10; Rev. 21:1. Jesus' words, however, unlike this perishing planet, will never **pass away.**
13:32, 33 As one who was fully God and at the same time fully man, Jesus had all the attributes of deity, including omnipotence and omniscience. He knew what was in people's

hearts (2:8) and He could still the waves (4:39). When Jesus became a man, however, He voluntarily placed certain knowledge in the hands of the Father (Phil. 2:5–8).

13:34–37 Jesus' parable of the absent master of the house is unique to Mark. The point of the parable is that the master could return at any time, so all servants must be vigilant and watchful (Luke 19:11–27).

14:1, 2 The chief priests planned to **take** Jesus. They wanted to arrest Jesus, take Him away, and kill Him. **During the feast,** the population of Jerusalem would expand greatly as zealous Jews converged on the city to celebrate the **Passover** in accord with the Law of Moses (Deut. 16:16). Many of Christ's admirers were present too, so the religious leaders wanted to defer the arrest and avoid conflict.

14:3 Alabaster is a translucent stone still used to make ornamented jewelry boxes and other items of value. **Spikenard** was a precious perfume. Mark relates that the woman **poured it on His head,** while John identifies the woman as Mary, the sister of Martha and Lazarus, and notes that she anointed Jesus' feet and used her hair as a towel (John 12:3).

14:4, 5 The **some who were indignant** were Jesus' disciples (Matt. 26:8), but Judas Iscariot, a thief was their mouthpiece on this occasion (John 12:4–6). A single denarius represented a day's wages for a common laborer, so **three hundred denarii** was a considerable gift.

14:6, 7 Jesus' statement does not show callousness to **the poor** (Deut. 15:7–11).But He also wanted people to give freely and of their own volition. No one should criticize another's gift; and no one can read the heart of a giver. A giver's motive is known only to God.

14:8, 9 Mary had tremendous spiritual insight when she anointed Jesus. She anointed His **body for burial.** She understood that Jesus was soon to die.

14:10, 11 Judas Iscariot decided to profit even further from his association with Jesus by betraying Him. The **chief priests** changed their plans when Judas came knocking at their door.

14:12 The first day of Unleavened Bread was the fifteenth day of Nisan (Lev. 23:6). Mark clarified the precise time for his readers by adding **when they killed the Passover lamb.** The lamb was killed on the evening of the fourteenth of Nisan (March-April). Here, Mark is speaking of the events of Thursday.

14:13 Jesus had apparently already made arrangements for a place to eat. Jesus **sent out two of His disciples,** Peter and John (Luke 22:8). It was unusual for **a man** to be **carrying a pitcher of water,** since this was normally a woman's task.

14:14, 15 Although the identity of **the master of the house** is not positively known, there is reason to suspect it may have been Mark's father. The **guest room** is familiarly described as **a large upper room, furnished and prepared.** Mark may have been the young man of vv. 51, 52.

14:16–18 Two memorial meals were observed **as they sat** (lit. reclined) **and ate.** First, they ate the regular Passover commemoration meal, during which time Jesus predicted His betrayal by one of the disciples. Second, after Judas had left (John 13:30), Jesus observed the Last Supper, which anticipated the breaking of His body and shedding of His blood.

14:19 In Greek, **Is it I?,** is actually a negative question that implies a negative answer. The phrase means "It is not I, is it?"

14:20, 21 The statement that **it would have been good** for Judas **if he had never been born** points to the awful judgment that awaits him.

14:22, 23 Judas left the room after receiving the dipped portion of bread, prior to Jesus' act of breaking additional bread and explaining its significance (John 13:30). **this is My body:** Some view the broken bread as representing Jesus' body, which would soon be broken for their sins.

14:24 Some interpret **this is My blood** metaphorically, meaning that the contents of this cup represented Jesus' blood that would be shed for our sins. The sprinkling of blood was required to institute the Mosaic covenant in Ex. 29:12, 16, 20 (see Heb. 9:18–22). In the same way, Jesus' blood shed on the Cross initiated **the new covenant:** His blood was **shed for many.** He died on the Cross in the place of sinners.

14:25 Jesus came announcing the **kingdom**

of God (1:14, 15), promised the disciples rulership in it (Matt. 19:28), and will receive and administer it with the saints (Dan. 7:13, 14, 27; 2 Tim. 2:11, 12; Rev. 20:4).

14:26, 27 The **hymn** they sang was from the Psalms. Leaving the Upper Room, they crossed the Kidron Valley to the base of **the Mount of Olives.** Gethsemane is directly across from the eastern gate of Jerusalem.

14:28 This saying was repeated by one of the angels at the tomb shortly after Jesus' Resurrection (16:7). Nevertheless, the disciples remained in Jerusalem for more than a week before eventually following their risen Shepherd into Galilee (John 20:26; 21:1).

14:29 Peter, so emphatic in his denial, soon realized the emptiness of his declaration.

14:30, 31 Only Mark mentions Christ's prediction of Peter's denial occurring **before the rooster crows twice.** And only Mark records the two crowings of the rooster (14:68, 72).

14:32 Gethsemane, though famous today, is mentioned by name only twice in the Bible (here and in Matthew). John, however, informs us that Jesus and the disciples "often met there" and that it was a garden (John 18:1, 2). The admonition to **sit here** was directed to all but Peter, James, and John (14:33).

14:33 Jesus wanted His closest disciples **with Him,** to support Him with their presence and their prayers.

14:34 Exceedingly sorrowful: The crushing realization of having to bear the sin of the world and to lose the fellowship of God the Father was nearly more than Jesus' soul could bear.

14:35 Jesus must have prayed for some time. Mark records Jesus' petition that **the hour might pass from Him,** a reference to the time Jesus would bear the punishment for the sin of the world in His own body.

14:36 Abba was what a little child would call his father. Jesus' relationship to His Father was close and tender. In addition to the term **hour** (v. 35), **this cup** foreshadows Christ's impending death (10:38).

14:37, 38 Avoiding temptation demands constant vigilance, so much so that Christ included this admonition in the prayer He taught the disciples (Matt. 6:13; Luke 11:4).

14:39–42 The three apostles were exhorted

to watch and pray several times, yet physical fatigue overcame spiritual alertness.

14:43 Judas came with **a great multitude,** identified by John as a detachment of troops (John 18:3).

14:44 A **kiss,** usually a sign of affection, was now the signal for betrayal. **Lead Him away safely** is not an expression of concern for Jesus' safety, but rather an indication of how difficult it may have been to seize Jesus.

14:45–47 Only two of Jesus' disciples had swords that evening (Luke 22:38) and John tells us that Peter carried one of them (John 18:10, 26). Mark graciously avoids identifying Peter as being guilty of this well-meaning but pointless act. John, the eyewitness, identifies the servant as one named Malchus and says it was his right ear that was severed (John 18:10). Peter may have swung wildly, intending to cut off Malchus' head but succeeding only in wounding him. Luke the physician mentions that Jesus restored Malchus' ear.

14:48, 49 The swarms of soldiers, the secluded location, the cover of night, and the **swords** and **clubs** all suggested that Jesus was some violent **robber** or revolutionary. The cowardice of Jesus' captors was evident—why else would they arrest a peaceful teacher with such brute force? Jesus' statement that **the Scriptures must be fulfilled** indicates confidence all was proceeding under God's sovereign plan.

14:50–52 Jesus was abandoned. The eleven disciples were gone, but **a certain young man followed Him.** Only Mark tells of this incident, and many believe that this young man was Mark himself. If the Last Supper was at his home that evening, he could have risen from bed, pulled on **a linen cloth,** and followed Jesus and the disciples.

14:53 The high priest at that time was Caiaphas. The **chief priests** included others who had formerly been high priests, and **the elders** consisted of the heads of leading families in the community. Together this group made up the Sanhedrin.

14:54–56 The Sanhedrin was supposed to administer justice, but this council **sought testimony against Jesus to put Him to death.** The Jewish authorities had lost to Rome the right to pronounce a death sentence. Because no real witnesses could testify to any grounds for Jesus' death, **false witness** was heard, but it was contradictory.

14:57–59 Finally, some tried to accuse Jesus of plotting to destroy the **temple** (John 2:19–21), but even that testimony was too inconsistent.

14:60–62 Jesus **kept silent** in fulfillment of Is. 53:7. He remained silent before Pilate (15:3–5) and before Herod Antipas as well (Luke 23:9). Finally Jesus affirmed that He was **the Christ, the Son of the Blessed.**

14:63, 64 The trial was over, and Jesus stood condemned for **blasphemy**, which in this context means laying claim to deity.

14:65 Those who **beat** and **struck** Jesus here were not applying the dreaded scourging, which could disembowel an individual. Compare 15:15 where the scourging itself is mentioned.

14:66–72 He began to curse and swear. Peter may have told Mark to include this report. Each of the other Gospel writers tells us that the rooster crowed immediately upon Peter's

final denial (Matt. 26:74; Luke 22:60; John 18:27). This time **he thought about it, and he wept.**

15:1–3 Rather than murdering Jesus privately, the Jewish politicians decided to seek Pilate's approval so they could execute the "blasphemer" legally. Their charges included **many things** but apparently centered on treason. Jesus claimed to be a king, thus defying Caesar (Luke 23:2). This crime was punishable in the Roman Empire by death.

15:4–8 Pilate must have concluded that the charges against Jesus were groundless, for Mark tells us he desired to release Jesus (v. 9). So his readers could understand the complexity of the situation, Mark parenthetically explains the custom of releasing a prisoner during the feast as well as the facts about Barabbas. Mark classifies him with **rebels** who **had committed murder.**

15:9–14 Pilate attempted to release Jesus, for he **knew** the charges against Him were insubstantial. Pilate adeptly judged the Jewish leaders' **envy** of Jesus. He mocked them subtly by

 IN DEPTH   **"Give Us Barabbas!"**

But for a remarkable set of circumstances, Barabbas probably would have remained unknown to history. He was just another one of the sicarii ("dagger-men") who assassinated Roman officials in the vain hope of driving them out of Palestine. Occasionally, when political conditions were right, such men managed to gain a small following and create serious trouble. For example, in A.D. 6 Judas the Galilean led a tax revolt. But the Romans quickly executed him and scattered his followers.

In a similar way, the authorities had arrested Barabbas and others on charges of insurrection and murder (Mark 15:7; Luke 23:19). The prisoners knew well what fate awaited them—crucifixion, a grisly form of execution that the Romans reserved for political criminals. The public spectacle of nailing rebels to an upraised cross was a potent deterrent to political opposition.

But Barabbas was not to die in that manner. The arrest of Jesus, the political maneuverings of Caiaphas the high priest and of Herod and Pilate (Luke 23:6–12), and the custom of releasing a prisoner during the feast of the Passover (Mark 15:6) combined to open a way for Barabbas to go free.

What finally secured his liberty were the cries of the mob to have him released (John 18:40). Pilate found it hard to believe that they actually preferred Barabbas, and when they kept demanding that Jesus be crucified, Pilate asked, "Shall I crucify your king?" (19:15). At that point the chief priests claimed, "We have no king but Caesar!" and the governor released Barabbas. What a peculiar irony that a revolutionary against Rome should be released by the cry, "We have no king but Caesar!"

referring to Jesus as **the King of the Jews.**

15:15 Pilate had Jesus **scourged:** This word describes a punishment more severe than flogging or beating. The prisoner was beaten with a whip fashioned of numerous strips of leather attached to a handle. To the leather strips were tied sharp pieces of bone and metal, which could rip and tear a person's skin to shreds.

15:16 The hall called Praetorium refers to the governor's official residence. The **whole garrison,** a Roman cohort, consisted of up to six hundred men. Those who gathered on this occasion were probably only those nearby, though still a considerable number.

15:17 The **purple** robe mocked Jesus' claim to be a king. The **crown of thorns** was no doubt a twisted, dried vine with sharp thorns more than an inch in length.

15:18–21 They **led Him out to crucify Him** indicates that the place of crucifixion was outside the city itself (see Heb. 13:12). All three synoptic Gospels identify Jesus' cross bearer as Simon of Cyrene, but only Mark adds that he was **the father of Alexander and Rufus.** These men may have been known to Mark's Roman audience, and it is interesting that Paul greets a Rufus in Rom. 16:13.

15:22 Golgotha is an Aramaic word meaning **Place of a Skull.** The hill may have been called this because it was a place of death.

15:23 This potion of **wine** (or vinegar) **mingled with myrrh** was intended to numb the pain. Jesus refused it, choosing to suffer the complete pain.

15:24 Casting lots for and dividing **His garments** fulfilled the prophecy of Ps. 22:18.

15:25 The third hour was 9 A.M., using a common Jewish system of marking the day. Jesus suffered on the Cross until at least 3 P.M., the ninth hour of v. 34. **And they crucified Him** was a terse summary for Mark's Roman readers, for they knew quite well the horrors of crucifixion.

15:26 The inscription placed over Jesus' head appeared in three languages (John 19:20): Hebrew (Aramaic); Latin, the official language of government; and Greek, the common language spoken by many. If we piece together details from all four Gospels, the complete sign must have read, "This is Jesus the Nazarene, the King of the Jews."

15:27–31 Jesus was mocked and forsaken by nearly everyone—Pilate, Herod, soldiers, Jewish leaders, the crowd, even the robbers on either side (v. 32).

15:32 Jesus was called mockingly **the Christ,** or Messiah, by the chief priests and scribes. Their offer to **believe** in Christ if He would **descend ... from the cross** was empty mockery.

15:33 This **darkness** was a supernatural darkening of the skies.

15:34 Of the seven cries from the Cross, this fourth one was the most passionate. Quoting Ps. 22:1, Jesus expressed the agony of being abandoned by His Father as He alone bore the sin of the world. Jesus' spiritual agony was intense, yet He still addressed His Father personally as **My God.**

15:35, 36 Those who mistook Jesus' words as a call for the prophet **Elijah** may have been unable to understand Him. The dehydration caused by crucifixion often made speech difficult. A sip from the **sponge full of sour wine** was supplied because Jesus said "I thirst" (John 19:28). This allowed Jesus to utter His final two sayings, "It is finished" (John 19:30) and "Father, into Your hands I commit My spirit" (Luke 23:46).

15:37 Jesus **breathed His last** after a **loud** conscious statement. Frequently, crucifixion produced a coma prior to death, but Jesus was in control of all His faculties until the moment when He voluntarily gave up His life (see John 10:17, 18).

15:38 The significance of the supernatural tearing of **the veil of the temple** is that access to God is now open to all.

15:39 Only Mark uses the Latin term **centurion,** a Roman captain in charge of one hundred men. The centurion's statement that Jesus **was the Son of God** was a confession of belief in Jesus' deity.

15:40, 41 These women had ministered to Jesus' needs and would be the first witnesses of His Resurrection. Mark does not name Jesus' mother here but includes other prominent women. Three Marys were present along with **many other women,** and **Salome,** whom only Mark mentions by name (see also 16:1). Salome was the wife of Zebedee and the mother of the disciples James and John (Matt. 27:56).

15:42 Mark explains for his Roman audience, unacquainted with Jewish customs, that the crucifixion took place on **the Preparation Day,** that is, Friday.

15:43 Joseph of Arimathea (a town 20 miles northwest of Jerusalem) is identified as **a prominent council** (Sanhedrin) **member.** He "had not consented to their decision and deed." To ask Pilate **for the body of Jesus** was an act of bravery, which placed Joseph in opposition to the Sanhedrin and identified him as a follower of Jesus.

15:44, 45 Joseph's haste to remove the body could have been based on Deut. 21:23, which instructs that persons put to death on a tree should have their corpses removed and buried the same day.

15:46, 47 Joseph, assisted by Nicodemus (John 19:39), wrapped Jesus' body in **fine linen,** apparently encased with myrrh and aloes to retard decay. The **stone** used to cover the opening of the tomb may not have been more than three or four feet in diameter.

16:1, 2 The Sabbath is Saturday. The next day is **the first day of the week,** Sunday. The **spices** were a symbol of the care and concern these women had for their beloved Master.

16:3, 4 The women thought about how **large** the stone was and how difficult it would be to dislodge it from the entrance.

16:5, 6 Mark does not identify the **young man** who appeared **in a long white robe** as an angel, but he is there to explain the mystery that confronts the women. The passive voice of the Greek for **He is risen** indicates that an act of God had accomplished the raising up of Jesus.

16:7 Chosen by God as the first human witnesses to Christ's Resurrection, these women were commanded to **go** and **tell.** The mention of **Peter** signifies that Christ still accepted him, even though he had denied the Lord three times.

16:8 Initially, the women's fear caused them to say **nothing to anyone.** They recovered shortly, however, and brought word to the eleven disciples (16:10; John 20:2).

16:9 Although the women had been commissioned to tell of Jesus' Resurrection, none had actually seen Jesus until **He appeared first to Mary Magdalene.** Only this verse and Luke 8:2 mention Jesus' exorcism of **seven demons** from Mary, which would explain her strong devotion to Him.

16:10, 11 Jesus' Resurrection was evidently not expected by anyone in spite of His repeated predictions.

16:12, 13 Jesus' appearance **in another form** may indicate that He appeared differently to the two on the road than He had appeared to Jesus' followers before. The identity of the **two** who **walked** is not entirely stated, although one is identified as Cleopas (Luke 24:18).

16:14 After Judas' demise (Matt. 27:3–5; Acts 1:16–18), the disciples were known for a while as **the eleven.** Jesus rebuked these disciples for not believing the accounts of eyewitnesses, but He pronounced a blessing on "those who have not seen and yet have believed" (John 20:29).

16:15 The Great Commission is pronounced here and in each of the other three Gospels (Matt. 28:19, 20; Luke 24:47; John 20:21).

16:16 He who does not believe will be condemned. Those who believe in Christ will be saved.

16:17, 18 These signs were evident in the early church. Casting **out demons** demonstrated victory over Satan (Acts 16:18). Speaking with **new tongues** began at Pentecost (Acts 2:4–11). Healing **the sick** occurred in several instances, including Acts 28:8. Taking **up serpents** occurred in Paul's encounter with a poisonous snake, which did not produce ill effects (Acts 28:1–6). The New Testament does not record Christians drinking **anything deadly** without harm.

16:19 The final sign that Jesus was the Son of God is that **He was received up into heaven** to be seated **at the right hand** (the position of authority and power) **of God.**

16:20 The obedience of Christ's disciples who **went out and preached everywhere** challenges us to engage in that same endeavor. We can be confident that as the **Lord** was **working with them,** He will also work with us.

Luke

Introduction

Luke never met Jesus, yet chose to follow Him. An obviously educated man who was a physician (Col. 4:14), Luke learned all he could about Jesus and shared his findings with us. Thus his Gospel provides a unique perspective on Jesus' birth, ministry, death, and Resurrection. The author writes that he was not an eyewitness to the events surrounding Jesus but had gathered the reports of others (1:2).

Early Christian writings identify the author as Luke. He was an educated man capable of writing in high Greek style, and Col. 4:10–14 seems to indicate that Luke was not Jewish. If so, Luke would be the only Gentile author of a New Testament book. Tradition says that after accompanying Paul on some of his missionary journeys, Luke settled in Philippi, investing his life in the ministry of the Philippian church. He probably wrote his Gospel about A.D. 68.

The Gospel of Luke is the only Gospel that has a sequel—the Book of Acts. Both Luke and Acts include an account of the Ascension of Jesus, an event that only Luke describes in detail. Luke is also the longest of the four Gospels, and he gives us the fullest portrait of Jesus' ministry.

Luke wrote his Gospel to reassure Theophilus, a Gentile and a new believer, that God was still at work in the Christian community founded by Jesus. Luke presents God's grace as revealed in Jesus' ministry on earth. He emphasizes that this grace is available to Gentiles, even though the promises relating to Jesus' ministry stretch back into Israel's history (1:1–4). Luke also concentrates on Jesus' relationship to the nation and leaders of Israel.

1:1, 2 many have taken in hand: Luke makes it clear that he was not the first to write a **narrative** of the ministry of Jesus. The theme of God's plan is introduced with the note that the subject of such narratives was the **things which have been fulfilled.** The sources for these narratives were **eyewitnesses** who **delivered** their testimony to the church.

1:3 having had perfect understanding: This phrase represents the characteristics that describe Luke's work in this verse. Luke investigated his topic and he did it with care. **of all things:** Another characteristic of Luke's work was its thoroughness. **from the very first:** Luke was interested in even the earliest events tied to Jesus' life. **an orderly account:** Luke gave his narrative a basic structure. Not every part is chronological, but the broad sequence is Christ's ministry in Galilee, His travel to Jerusalem, and His struggles in Jerusalem.

1:4 certainty: The purpose of this term was to give assurance to Theophilus, a young believer. It is likely that Theophilus was a Gentile, since so much of Luke and Acts is concerned with Jewish-Gentile relationships (Acts 10; 11; 15). Luke assured Theophilus and his other readers that Jesus is the Messiah. He is worthy of worship because He is the Son of the living God.

1:5 King **Herod,** who was appointed by the Roman emperor, reigned from 37 to 4 B.C. over Judea, Samaria, Galilee, and much of Perea and Syria. The events of vv. 5–25 probably occurred around 6 B.C.

1:6 righteous before God: This phrase indicates that the priest Zacharias and his wife were recognized by God as believers. They walked faithfully with God and kept His law.

1:7 Being **barren** was a grave disappointment in ancient Israel (see 1 Sam. 1).

1:8, 9 Zacharias served for one week twice a year at the temple. Offering the incense was something a **priest** could do only once in his career. It was a great moment for Zacharias.

1:10, 11 The hour of incense came twice a day, at 9 A.M. and 3:30 P.M. Probably the afternoon offering is in view here.

1:12 fear fell upon him: To be afraid at the presence of God or His messenger (v. 11) is common in Scripture (see Ex. 15:16; Dan. 8:16, 17; Acts 5:5).

1:13 Do not be afraid: Angels often calmed the fears of those to whom they appeared. **your prayer is heard:** The angel was referring to the prayer for a child.

1:14 Joy is a major theme throughout the writings of Luke (see 2:10; 10:20; 13:17).

1:15 great in the sight of the Lord: John had a

great place in the plan of God. John was a prophet, and he was **filled with the Holy Spirit** from the womb (see Is. 49:1; Jer. 1:5). **wine nor strong drink:** The child was dedicated to live in special consecration to the Lord.

1:16 John promised reconciliation to God for those who responded to his call to repent (3:1–14). John's mission was to prepare Israel for its Messiah.

1:17 in the spirit and power of Elijah: John was the forerunner of the Messiah. This description recalls Mal. 3:1; 4:5. **a people prepared:** The prepared people are those whom God has drawn to Himself for His special purposes.

1:18 How shall I know: Zacharias expressed his doubt and asked for a sign, a lack of faith that is addressed in vv. 64, 65.

1:19 Gabriel was often a messenger of God's plan (see Dan. 8:16; 9:21).

1:20 mute: Zacharias unable to speak. The arrival of the child would break Zacharias's silence.

1:21, 22 The **people** at the **temple** awaited the blessing of the high priest.

1:23 Zacharias's **house** was located in the hill country south of Jerusalem (v. 39).

1:24 Why Elizabeth **hid herself** is not clear. The most likely suggestion is that she withdrew to prepare privately for the coming of her child.

1:25 my reproach: In Israel barrenness was cause for shame. Elizabeth praises the Lord for blessing her even as He moved His plan for all of human history forward.

1:26, 27 In the sixth month means six months after John was conceived. **Nazareth** was a village in Galilee, a region north of Jerusalem.

1:28–31 blessed are you: Mary was blessed because she received God's grace.

1:32, 33 The Highest refers to the majesty of God. **David:** Jesus fulfilled God's promise to David about an unending dynasty.

1:34 How can this be: This remark does not reflect unbelief. She accepts her role without question and is a model of faith even though she does not understand everything.

1:35, 36 The Holy Spirit will come upon you: This is a direct declaration of Jesus' divine conception. The Child's conception means

He is uniquely set apart, the **Holy One,** a phrase which is here not so much a title as a description of Jesus' sinless nature.

1:37 nothing will be impossible: God keeps His promises regardless of how difficult the circumstances may seem. Gabriel's statement about God should be our statement of faith.

1:38 Maidservant suggests humility before the Lord and a readiness for faithful and obedient service, which should characterize every believer.

1:39–41 the babe leaped in her womb: Mary's coming brought a reaction from John in Elizabeth's womb. The forerunner gave testimony to the Messiah even before he was born. The angel had predicted this baby would be filled with the Holy Spirit even from the womb (v. 15).

1:42–44 why is this granted to me: Elizabeth marveled at the grace that allowed her a role in God's great plan.

1:45 Blessed is she who believed: Mary's response of faith was exemplary. She was simply waiting on God to bring His promises to **fulfillment.**

1:46 The following hymn (vv. 46–55) gets its name, the "Magnificat," from the Latin word for **magnifies.** Mary's hymn is a recital of what God had done for her.

1:47, 48 all generations will call me blessed: Mary went from being a poor unknown Hebrew girl to the most honored woman in history.

1:49 He who is mighty: God protects and fights for His children. **holy is His name:** God is unique from all other beings (see Ps. 99:3; Is. 57:15).

1:50 The term **mercy** expresses the concept of God's loyal love (see Ps. 103).

1:51–53 Mary was looking forward to the day when God's people are no longer oppressed, but are blessed by the Lord. God's **strength with His arm** figuratively describes His activity and power as Savior of His people (see v. 47; Ps. 89:13; 118:15).

1:54–56 His servant Israel: Israel has a special role in serving God. **He spoke to our fathers:** God's actions in the life of Mary were based on commitments He made centuries before (see Gen. 12:1–3; 22:16–18).

1:57–59 they would have called him: It was a custom to give a family name to a newborn.

1:60, 61 John was the name that the angel told Zacharias to give the child (v. 13).

1:62–66 A writing tablet was a wood tablet covered with wax.

1:67 filled with the Holy Spirit: By the Spirit Zacharias announced God's promise. Zacharias's hymn is called the "Benedictus" from its first word in the Latin Vulgate translation. **prophesied:** Zacharias was a priest, and the Holy Spirit enabled him to prophesy.

1:68 He has visited and redeemed: As in Mary's hymn, God the Savior is the object of Zacharias's praise.

1:69, 70 The **horn** of an ox is a symbol of power (see 1 Sam. 2:10; 2 Sam. 22:3; Ps. 75:4). **David:** Jesus' royal ancestry is highlighted by Zacharias.

1:71 God had promised to deliver the Israelites from their **enemies**, both human and spiritual (4:16–30; 11:14–26).

1:72, 73 To perform the mercy ... remember His holy covenant: God's actions represented His commitment to love the Israelites faithfully (v. 50) and to fulfill His promises to their ancestors (see vv. 54, 73; Lev. 26:42).

1:74–76 you will go before the face of the Lord: Zacharias proclaimed to those gathered what the angel had told him (vv. 16, 17). John was to prepare the way for the Lord.

1:77 To give knowledge of salvation: John's task was to preach repentance (3:1–14) and prepare for coming One (3:15–18).

1:78–80 Dayspring is a reference to the coming of Messiah (see Num. 24:17; Mal. 4:2). **To give light ... To guide our feet:** As the Dayspring or the "Rising Sun," the Messiah will provide the light of truth and forgiveness to those blinded by the darkness of their sins.

2:1, 2 Augustus was the Roman emperor from 31 B.C. to A.D. 14. **Quirinius** was the governor or administrator over a major census organized to facilitate the collection of taxes.

2:3, 4 The registration took place at a person's ancestral home (see 2 Sam. 24). The journey from **Nazareth** to **Bethlehem** was about 90 miles, at least a three-day trip.

2:5, 6 his betrothed wife: That Mary made the journey with Joseph suggests they were already married. However, the marriage had not yet been consummated (see Matt. 1:24, 25).

2:7 Swaddling cloths were strips of cloth wrapped around a baby to keep its arms and legs straight. **Firstborn Son:** Jesus The **manger** was probably a feeding trough for animals. Jesus was probably born in a stable or in a cave that served as one.

2:8 The shepherds kept **watch** to protect the sheep from wild animals.

2:9, 10 Glory refers to evidence of God's majestic presence. In this scene, the glory is the appearance of light in the midst of darkness.

2:11, 12 The city of David refers to Bethlehem. **Savior ... Christ ... Lord:** These three titles together summarize the saving work of Jesus and His sovereign position. The word Christ means "Anointed," the word Lord was the title of a ruler.

2:13 Heavenly host refers to an entourage of angels.

2:14 Glory refers to praise given to God. **goodwill toward men:** The phrase means that people are the objects of God's goodwill.

2:15–21 eight days: According to the Law, a boy was to be circumcised on the eighth day (see Lev. 12:3).

2:22–24 Her purification refers to a ceremony in which a new mother of a son was declared ceremonially clean again (see Lev. 12:6). The ceremony took place 40 days after the birth. At this ceremony, the mother could offer a lamb or two pigeons (see Lev. 12:8). Jesus' family chose the pigeons (v. 24). **Present Him to the Lord** refers to the normal presentation of a firstborn son to God (see Num. 18:6; 1 Sam. 1; 2).

2:25, 26 Simeon was waiting for **the Consolation of Israel,** a hope that parallels the hope of national deliverance expressed in the two hymns of ch. 1. This deliverance would involve the work of Messiah. **Holy Spirit:** Luke highlights the presence of the Spirit.

2:27, 28 into the temple: The location within the temple is not given, but Mary's presence suggests the court of women.

2:29, 30 Simeon identified God's **salvation** as being personified in Jesus.

2:31, 32 A light to bring revelation to the Gentiles … the glory of Your people Israel: This is the first explicit statement in Luke that includes both Jew and Gentile. Salvation is portrayed as light (1:79). Jesus is the glory of Israel because through Him the nation would see the fulfillment of God's promises.

2:33–35 a sword: The image here is of a large, broad sword striking Mary. She would suffer much pain in watching Jesus' rejection.

2:36, 37 The testimony of Anna complements Simeon's testimony. Anna's work as a prophetess in the temple court suggests that she addressed all who would listen to her.

2:38, 39 Redemption in Jerusalem is another way of speaking of the Consolation of Israel (v. 25).

2:40 the Child grew: With this note, the story of Jesus' infancy ends. The narrative picks up in v. 41 some twelve years later.

2:41 The annual pilgrimage to **Jerusalem** was customary. The Law commanded three pilgrimages for the men each **year:** for Passover, Pentecost, and the Feast of Tabernacles (see Ex. 23:14–17; Deut. 16:16).

2:42–48 The teachers were Jewish rabbis. Note that Jesus was engaging the rabbis in theological discussion (v. 47).

2:49–52 about My Father's business: This is the first indication in Luke's Gospel that Jesus knew He had a unique mission and a unique relationship to the Father.

3:1 Tiberius Caesar began to rule after his stepfather Augustus died, in A.D. 14. **Judea** was a senatorial province, ruled by a **governor** or procurator. **Pontius Pilate** held this position and was responsible for administering the region and collecting taxes for Rome. **Herod** is Herod Antipas, who ruled Galilee and Perea from 4 B.C. to A.D. 39.

3:2 Annas the high priest (A.D. 7–14) was succeeded in office by **Caiaphas,** his son-in-law, around A.D. 18. Caiaphas served with brief breaks from then until A.D. 37. In addition to Caiaphas, all of Annas's five sons served as high priest at one point or another. The various rulers that Luke lists show the complexity of the political situation in Israel during Jesus' day.

3:3 Baptism figuratively means "to be identified with." As John the Baptist preached the people were baptized as an outward sign of their inward **repentance** or "change of mind."

3:4–6 Prepare the way: This citation from Is. 40:3–5 declares the coming of God's deliverance. Luke carries the passage through to its mention of **salvation** being seen by **all flesh** (v. 6), thus highlighting that the gospel is for all people.

3:7 As the **multitudes** flocked to hear John the Baptist, many people went through the outward motions of baptism, but were not genuinely interested in the kind of King and kingdom that John was presenting.

3:8, 9 John the Baptist warned that the fruits of repentance are necessary, not the claim of an ancestral connection to **Abraham.**

3:10, 11 What shall we do: The repentant were instructed to give to those in need, to work at their jobs with integrity, to refrain from abusing their power, and to be content with earning a basic wage.

3:12–14 Tax collectors were Jewish agents who collected taxes for the Roman state. Tax collectors often added interest to cover their own expenses and to pad their income. They were disliked both for their business practices and for their support of the occupying state.

3:15–17 One mightier than I: John's baptism was minor compared to what was coming from Jesus, who would bring **the Holy Spirit and fire** (see Matt. 3:11). As a result of Christ's work at His first coming, believers are placed into one family (see 1 Cor. 12:13) and commended to the care of the Holy Spirit. When Christ comes again, He will come in judgment. The **unquenchable** fire indicates the thorough nature of the judgment.

3:18–20 he shut John up in prison: John had **rebuked** Herod for divorcing his wife to marry his own niece Herodias, who already had been the wife of his brother Philip.

3:21, 22 a voice came from heaven: This is one of two heavenly endorsements of Jesus' ministry. **You are My beloved Son; in You I am well pleased:** This statement combines two ideas. The idea of God's Son from

Ps. 2:7 and the idea of God's pleasure from the image of the Servant in Is. 42:1.

3:23–38 as was supposed: People naturally assumed that Jesus was the physical son of both Joseph and Mary. Luke's genealogy is unlike Matthew's, although both go back to David and Abraham. Luke traces Jesus' line all the way back to Adam, showing Jesus' significance for all people. Luke provides the physical lineage from David through Mary to Jesus.

4:1, 2 Luke has the temptation about Jerusalem last, probably because Jerusalem is the place Jesus is headed for His decisive confrontation with Satan (13:32–35). Jesus demonstrated not only His ability to resist the **devil,** but also His allegiance to God.

4:3 If You are the Son of God: Satan was saying: "Let's assume for the sake of argument that You are the Son of God." In fact, Satan was challenging Jesus' identity and authority.

4:4 It is written: Jesus responded by quoting Deut. 8:3, refusing to operate independently of God. Eating at Satan's instruction would have shown a lack of dependence on the Father.

4:5 all the kingdoms of the world: Satan tempted Jesus to take a detour around the Cross by "taking the easy way" to power.

4:6, 7 this has been delivered to me: Satan's claim here is exaggerated. He has great authority over the earth (see John 12:31; 14:30; 16:11; 2 Cor. 4:4; Eph. 2:2), but not the authority to deliver kingdoms.

4:8 Get behind Me, Satan: In response to Satan's second temptation, Jesus cited Deut. 6:13. Jesus knew that only God is worthy of **worship,** that only God is to be served.

4:9 The pinnacle of the temple may refer to the southeast corner of the temple that loomed over a cliff about 450 feet high.

4:10, 11 He shall give His angels charge over you: Satan cited Ps. 91:11, 12, reminding Jesus of God's promise of protection. However, the use of biblical words does not always reveal God's will, particularly if they are placed in the wrong context.

4:12 You shall not tempt the LORD: In response to Satan's third temptation, Jesus cited Deut. 6:16. God is to be trusted, not tested.

4:13 until an opportune time: This was but the first of several encounters Jesus had with Satan and his forces (11:14–23).

4:14–17 Most **synagogue** services had a reading from the Law and one from the Prophets, with an exposition that tied the texts together. Jesus expounded from Is. 61.

4:18, 19 By citing Is. 61, Jesus was claiming to be a royal figure and to have a prophetic mission (v. 24). Jesus healed **the brokenhearted,** referring to those who were discouraged because of their plight in life. Jesus proclaimed **liberty to the captives.** Jesus gave **sight to the blind,** a reference to His miraculous works (7:22). Jesus **set at liberty** the **oppressed.**

4:20 Jesus **closed the book** in the middle of the sentence (see Is. 61:2). He did not continue because "the day of vengeance of our God," was not being fulfilled then.

4:21, 22 Jesus proclaimed the fulfillment of God's plan and promise in Himself, since He is the figure described in the passage.

4:23 Physician, heal yourself: The request for more signs was for Jesus to prove His claim by repeating the type of miraculous work He had done in Capernaum.

4:24 Jesus made it clear that He is God's messenger who declares God's ways. However, Jesus also knew that a **prophet** is often rejected.

4:25–27 Jesus speaks of a period of widespread unfaithfulness to God (see 1 Kin. 17; 18; 2 Kin. 5:1–14). During this period, judgment came on the nation in the form of **famine.** Jesus warned His listeners not to be unfaithful like their ancestors by rejecting His message.

4:28–32 Luke emphasizes Jesus' **teaching** (v. 15). The perception of Jesus' **authority** probably arose as a result of His discussing issues directly, rather than just noting tradition.

4:33, 34 Let us alone: The demon knew that Jesus possessed divine authority, and he wanted nothing to do with Him. **the Holy One of God:** Luke records the demon's use of this title as proof that Jesus is the promised Messiah (v. 41; 1:31–35).

4:35–37 rebuked: This term in Aramaic was a technical term for calling evil into submission.

Jesus possessed the **authority and power** to grant salvation, as well as to confront all opponents to it.

4:38, 39 The fact that Simon's mother-in- law served her guests **immediately** indicates that her recovery from **fever** was instantaneous.

4:40, 41 You are the Christ, the Son of God: This confession, unique to the Gospel of Luke, shows the close connection Luke makes between Jesus' sonship and messiahship.

4:42, 43 The **kingdom** is referred to 30 times in Luke and six times in Acts. Jesus announced the rule of God through His person, in dealing with sin (24:47), in distributing the Spirit as He mediates blessing from God's side (24:49), and in reigning with His followers according to the Old Testament promise (see Ps. 2:7–12; Acts 3:18–22).

4:44 Galilee probably refers to the whole of Palestine in this context (see 23:5; Acts 10:37).

5:1 The Lake of Gennesaret is also known as the Sea of Galilee and the Sea of Tiberias.

5:2–4 let down your nets: Jesus commanded Simon to place his nets in the water in order to depict a spiritual reality. Simon's new occupation would be fishing for people who would do the will of Jesus.

5:5, 6 at Your word I will let down the net: This is Peter's statement of faith. The fisherman noted that he had just failed to make a catch at the best time for fishing, the evening. The circumstances were not good for a catch at the time of Jesus' command, but Peter obeyed His word and let down his nets anyway.

5:7–9 Peter's confession indicates that he recognized God's work through Jesus. Peter, as a **sinful man,** was not worthy to be in Jesus' presence.

5:10 Do not be afraid: Jesus accepts the confessing sinner and offers that person the opportunity of reconciliation with God. **catch men:** Peter's commission was to rescue people from the danger of sin.

5:11 forsook all and followed Him: Following Jesus became the main priority in the disciples' lives. Such priority is the essence of discipleship.

5:12 The term **leprosy** was used broadly in the ancient world. It included psoriasis, lupus, and ringworm. Lepers were isolated from the rest of society (see Lev. 13:45, 46), but could be restored to the community when they recovered (see Lev. 14).

5:13 The disease responded **immediately** to the Creator's touch (4:39). Jesus honored the leper's humble request for health because he recognized Jesus' power and authority.

5:14 show yourself to the priest: Jesus directed that the regulation of Lev. 14 be followed.

5:15–19 The **Pharisees** were a group of about six thousand pious, influential teachers in the synagogues. They meticulously followed the Law, adhering to the traditional rules that kept a person from breaking it. The **teachers of the law** were officials trained in the Law of Moses. Also known as scribes, these men were in effect the religious lawyers of the Pharisees.

5:20 According to the Old Testament, only God was able to forgive sin (see Ps. 103:12). Jesus proclaimed that the man's sins were **forgiven.** This act was blasphemous to the scribes and Pharisees.

5:21 blasphemies: The charge of **the scribes and the Pharisees** was that Jesus' claim dishonored God. This was a serious charge; the conviction of blasphemy would eventually lead to Jesus' death (22:70, 71).

5:22 perceived their thoughts: The reference here is to prophetic insight. Jesus "knew what was in man" (John 2:25).

5:23 Jesus linked the healing to what it represented, the forgiveness of sin. Jesus forgave the man's sins and healed him at the same time.

5:24–26 Son of Man is an Aramaic idiom that refers to a human being, meaning "someone" or "I." Jesus used this idiom as a title, taken from Dan. 7:13, 14 (see 21:27; 22:69; Mark 14:62). In using the title here, Jesus claimed the authority to forgive sin, an authority that was limited to God.

5:27 Levi's job as a **tax collector** was to sit at a booth collecting taxes from businessmen. **Levi** is also called Matthew (see Matt. 9:9; 10:3).

5:28, 29 This verse describes the first of several feasts or meals in the Book of Luke.

5:30 Some believed that eating with **sinners** conveyed an acceptance of that person's sin. Jesus preferred leading sinners to God rather than "quarantining" Himself from such people.

5:31 no need of a physician: Jesus was not saying that the Pharisees and scribes had no need of spiritual healing. Instead He was saying that only those who know their spiritual need can be treated. As self-righteous people, the Pharisees would not come for aid, and in their own eyes, did not need a doctor.

5:32 Jesus' mission was to call sinners to **repentance.** In this passage, repentance is pictured as a patient who recognizes that illness is present and that only Jesus, the Great Physician, can treat it.

5:33 fast: The Pharisees fasted twice a week, on Mondays and Thursdays (18:12), as well as on the Day of Atonement (Lev. 16:29). The goal of fasting was to dedicate oneself to prayer and to focus on God.

5:34 bridegroom: Jesus compared His presence to the joyous time of a wedding. Jesus explained that while He was on earth, the time was not right for fasts.

5:35 The image of the removal of the bridegroom is the first hint in Jesus' ministry of His approaching death (see 2:35 for the first allusion). The church will (and did) **fast** (see Acts 13:1, 2; 14:23). Though such fasting returned, it was not required or regulated to the same degree as in Judaism.

5:36 the new makes a tear: Jesus pointed out that one cannot mix old things (Judaism) with new things (the new way He brings). The attempt to mix the two is compared to repairing clothes. The original cloth has already shrunk and when the new cloth shrinks, a rip occurs.

5:37 Putting **new wine** (Jesus' new way) into **old wineskins** (Judaism) would not work because as the new wine fermented, it would stretch the old skin and break it, ruining the wineskin and wasting the wine.

5:38, 39 Jesus pointed out that someone who likes **old wine** will not even try **new wine,** since such a person is satisfied with the old. This analogy explained why some people in Israel had trouble turning to Jesus.

6:1 plucked ... ate ... rubbing: According to Jewish tradition, the disciples were reaping, threshing, and preparing food, and so were violating the commandment not to work on the Sabbath.

6:2 what is not lawful: The Pharisees wanted to know why the disciples had violated the traditions surrounding the Law of Moses (see 14:3).

6:3, 4 In responding to the Pharisees' charges against His disciples, Jesus appealed to 1 Sam. 21:1–7; 22:9, 10. **David** and his men ate the **showbread** that only the priests could eat. But God did not punish David. Jesus pointed out that if David and his men could violate the Law to satisfy their hunger, His disciples could do the same.

6:5 Jesus has authority over the **Sabbath.**

6:6–9 Is it lawful: The issue was lawful conduct on the Sabbath (v. 2). Jesus chose to do good.

6:10, 11 Rage here is irrational or mindless anger. Pharisees started to plot against Jesus in earnest after this confrontation.

6:12 in prayer: Jesus spent time with God before the important events in His life (see 22:41–44).

6:13 chose twelve: Jesus selected the apostles, who would be responsible for leading the early church (see Acts 1:13).

6:14 Bartholomew is probably Nathanael of John 1:45.

6:15 Matthew is Levi of 5:27–32 (see Mark 2:14–17).

6:16 Judas the son of James is probably Thaddaeus (see Matt. 10:3; Mark 3:18). This is not the Lord's half brother.

6:17, 18 A level place probably refers to a plateau. The contents of the sermon that follows suggests a shorter version of the Sermon on the Mount. **Tyre and Sidon:** Jesus' fame extended even into Gentile regions.

6:19–20 Jesus directed the beatitudes to the **disciples.** The word **Blessed** special joy and favor that comes upon those who experience God's grace. **poor ... kingdom of God:** In general, the disciples of Jesus were not wealthy (see 1 Cor. 1:26–29; James 2:5). They were poor men who had come humbly to trust in God.

6:21 Jesus promised that God would provide the disciples with all the sustenance they needed. **weep ... laugh:** Any present suffering will be turned into joy.

6:22, 23 the Son of Man's sake: Identification with Jesus leads to rejection and hardship, but the disciple who has left all to follow Jesus understands what placing Jesus first means.

6:24 A **woe** is a cry of pain that results from misfortune. **you who are rich ... have received your consolation:** All that the rich receive is what they acquire on earth (see also Matt. 6:19–21).

6:25–28 The threat of religious persecution was very real when Jesus presented His command for extraordinary **love.**

6:29 offer the other: The one who seeks to love will always remain exposed and at risk. A **tunic** was an undergarment; a **cloak** was an outer garment.

6:30 do not ask them back: Jesus' instruction here is to forgive and forget.

6:31 as you want men to do to you: This is the "golden rule." Note that Jesus' command is stated in the positive.

6:32–35 Jesus notes that the **reward will be great** for the losses suffered while practicing this type of love.

6:36, 37 Judge not ... Condemn not ... Forgive: The idea here is one should be gracious and quick to forgive.

6:38 good measure: This illustration comes from the marketplace where grain was poured out, shaken down, and then filled to overflowing so the buyer received the full amount purchased.

6:39 The blind refers to teachers who cannot see and are unable to lead others. Jesus was warning against self-righteousness and arrogance.

6:40, 41 A **speck** represents a small fault in contrast to a **plank,** which represents a large fault.

6:42–45 known by its own fruit: Actions indicate where one's heart is.

6:46 Lord, Lord: Jesus pointed out that those who called Him by this title of respect acknowledged submission to Him.

6:47–49 hears ... and does: One who listens to and acts on Jesus' teaching can face any circumstance. **heard and did nothing:** Not acting on Jesus' teaching will eventually

result in total loss (see 1 Cor. 3:12–15; 2 John 8).

7:1 Capernaum important town in northern Galilee was the center for Jesus' Galilean ministry (4:31–44).

7:2–5 built us a synagogue: The Roman government regarded synagogues as valuable because their moral emphasis helped maintain order.

7:6–8 The centurion compared his authority over **soldiers** to Jesus' **authority** over life and health. The centurion knew that Jesus' word was sufficient to heal his servant.

7:9 not even in Israel: The centurion's faith was **great.** Jesus was said to "marvel."

7:10–13 a dead man was being carried out: Funerals were normally held the day of death because a body rendered a house unclean.

7:14, 15 Jesus **touched** the coffin and raised the dead man.

7:16, 17 The crowd recognized the parallel between Jesus' raising of the widow's son and the work of the **great** prophets.

7:18, 19 Are You the Coming One: John's uncertainty may have been because Jesus did not show signs of being conquering messiah the Jews were anticipating.

7:20–26 Jesus asked questions designed to highlight John the Baptist's special role in God's plan. The crowds went out to the wilderness to see a **prophet.**

7:27 My messenger: John the Baptist was the promised Elijah figure who would point the way to the arrival of Jesus' salvation.

7:28 least in the kingdom of God: John was the greatest prophet ever born. The least person in God's kingdom is greater because of Jesus's work.

7:29, 30 The tax collectors justified God, which means they responded to John's message by submitting to John's baptism. The Pharisees **rejected the will of God and** were not baptized (see Matt. 3:7–12).

7:31–34 Jesus made a comparison between **children** playing a game in the marketplace and the present **generation** of Israel. The leaders complained no matter what tune was played. John the Baptist refused to eat bread or drink wine, and the religious leaders dismissed him as demon-possessed. Jesus, **the Son of Man,** was accused of living loosely and

715 Luke 8:21

associating with sinners. No matter what the style of God's messenger was, the religious leaders rejected him.

7:35 God's **wisdom** is vindicated by those who respond to it and receive blessing.

7:36 one of the Pharisees asked Him to eat with him: This occurred in the house of a leper, where no Pharisee would ever have gone. **sat down to eat:** A meal in the ancient world was arranged so that the invited guest was at the main table while others were along the outside wall of the room listening to the conversation.

7:37, 38 The woman's sin is not specified. **An alabaster flask** was made of soft stone to preserve the quality of the expensive perfume. There is humility and devotion in the woman's act of service, as well as courage, performed in front of a crowd that knew her as a sinner.

7:39 if He were a prophet: The Pharisee doubted Jesus' credentials because He associated so openly with sinners.

7:40 I have something to say: Jesus knew the reputation of the woman, but was more interested in the grace of God.

7:41 Jesus compared sin to a debt. **five hundred denarii** was approximately the wages of one and one-half years.

7:42, 43 which of them will love him more: The woman knew she had been forgiven much, and as a result she loved much.

7:44–46 Jesus contrasted the actions of the woman with **Simon's,** implying that the woman knew more about love than Simon did (v. 47).

7:47, 48 her sins ... are forgiven: Jesus confirmed that the love of the woman, visible in her actions toward Jesus, had come from being forgiven.

7:49 Who is this: Some people in the audience rejected His authority to forgive sin.

7:50 Faith is the channel for receiving God's gifts (see Eph. 2:8, 9).

8:1–3 Mary called Magdalene is introduced here as though for the first time making it unlikely that she was the woman of 7:36–50. **provided for Him from their substance:** Some women of means used their wealth to benefit the work of God.

8:4–8 In the ancient world, fields were sown sometimes before and sometimes after planting. Paths often cut through fields. Sometimes **seed** would take root on these paths, where it could not mature. In addition, some soil was rocky and could not support a successful crop.

8:9, 10 Jesus' parables contained a lot of teaching—**mysteries**—about **the kingdom of God.** The disciples were privileged to learn the truths of the parables.

8:11 word of God: Matt. 13:19 speaks of the seed as the "word of the kingdom," a point that Luke makes in v. 10. The soils do not represent individual moments of decision as much as a lifelong response to God's Word.

8:12 Because **those by the wayside** never really gain an understanding (see Matt. 13:19) of the word of God before Satan snatches it **away,** there is no productivity.

8:13 believe for a while ... fall away: Brief and superficial encounters with the word of God will not stand times of testing.

8:14 According to this parable, **cares, riches, and pleasures of life** are three obstacles to spiritual fruitfulness. This type of "soil" is viewed as unsuccessful.

8:15 keep it and bear fruit: This "soil" allows the word of God to settle in and become productive (see John 15:2, 3; Col. 3:16, 17; James 1:21).

8:16 sets it on a lampstand: Jesus compares His teaching to **light.** It should not be hidden, but displayed, so that people can benefit from the illumination it gives.

8:17 come to light: Everything will be revealed by the light of the word of God.

8:18 take heed how you hear: Jesus warned His audience to listen to and follow the word of God. **what he seems to have will be taken:** The one who responds to the word of God receives more. The one who does not respond loses what he thought he had.

8:19, 20 Jesus' family was concerned about the direction of His ministry (see Mark 3:31–35). Though some have suggested that the **brothers** here were sons of Joseph by a previous marriage or cousins of Jesus, most likely they were the sons of Joseph and Mary. Joseph's absence here may mean that he had died by this time.

8:21 My mother and My brothers: In a clear contrast to v. 19, Jesus declared that His true family consists of those who hear and do the **word of God.**

8:22, 23 windstorm: The calming of the wind is the first of four miracles in vv. 22–56 that demonstrate Jesus' authority over a variety of phenomena—nature, demons, disease, and death. This first miracle took place on the Sea of Galilee. Cool air rushing down the ravines and hills of the area collides with warm air, causing sudden and strong storms.

8:24 they ceased: At Jesus' word, the storm stopped. Such control over nature is attributed to God in the Old Testament (see Ps. 104:3; 135:7; Nah. 1:4).

8:25 Where is your faith: Jesus' question was a rebuke of His disciples. They could trust in His protection, for He could control the winds and waves. **Who can this be:** All the displays of Jesus' authority were designed to settle this question of His identity.

8:26 The city of the **Gadarenes** (see Matt. 8:28) was a town about five miles southeast of the Sea of Galilee in Gentile territory.

8:27, 28 The demon's confession of Jesus as **Son of the Most High God** recalls the demonic confessions of 4:34, 41.

8:29, 30 Legion: This name reflects the fact that the man was possessed by multiple demons. A *legion* was a Roman military unit of about six thousand soldiers; thus the name suggests a spiritual battle.

8:31 The abyss is an allusion to the underworld and the judgment (see Rom 10:7).

8:32 Swine were unclean animals for Jews. It is interesting that the unclean spirits sought out unclean animals.

8:33–36 sitting at the feet of Jesus, clothed and in his right mind: This is a contrast to the same man who was roaming the tombs previously (vv. 27, 29).

8:37 The people asked Jesus to **depart,** according to Luke, because they were afraid of His authoritative presence.

8:38, 39 The man wanted to go with Jesus and His disciples, but Jesus commissioned the man to be a witness in his own community.

8:40–42 ruler: Jairus as main elder of the synagogue, conducted the service and kept order.

8:43, 44 her flow of blood stopped: This

condition made the woman unclean (see Lev. 15:25–31). It took great courage for her to touch Jesus.

8:45–49 Your daughter is dead: The delay appeared to be fatal for Jairus's daughter.

8:50 only believe: This miracle highlights the response of faith that God honors.

8:51 He permitted no one to go in except Peter, James, and John: The reason Jesus singled out these three disciples is not given. Luke records a similar action in 9:28.

8:52 Sleeping, a metaphor for death, indicates that the girl's death was not permanent.

8:53 they ridiculed Him: The term suggests that the derision included laughter.

8:54–56 The reason for Jesus' command for silence in this verse is not entirely clear, given that anyone could have deduced **what had happened.**

9:1, 2 to preach … to heal: Jesus commissioned His disciples to spread the word about God's kingdom through preaching and healing.

9:3–9 At Herod's palace, opinions varied as to whether Jesus was **John** the Baptist, **Elijah** (see Mal. 3:1), or one of the **prophets.** Though this passage suggests that Herod was uncertain about Jesus' identity.

9:10–12 spoke … healed: Jesus had the same two-pronged ministry the twelve disciples had: preaching and healing (v. 2). The topic of Jesus' preaching was **the kingdom of God.**

9:13–17 This is the only miracle of Jesus' ministry that appears in all four Gospels (see Matt. 14:13–21; Mark 6:30–44; John 6:5–14). **blessed and broke:** Some see an allusion here to the Lord's Table.

9:18–20 The Christ of God: The emphasis here is on the messianic role of Jesus. He is the promised One who was ushering in a new era. Jesus would reveal to the disciples that His messiahship would have elements of suffering that they did not expect (see vv. 22, 23).

9:21 tell this to no one: Jesus knew that the messianic role that the people and the disciples expected was much different from His actual role. The element of suffering that the Messiah would endure was not a part of popular expectation.

9:22 must suffer ... be rejected ... be killed ... be raised: The disciples struggled to understand what Jesus was saying (v. 45; 18:34). Only after Jesus' Resurrection and His explanation of the Scriptures to them did they begin to understand (24:25–27, 44–49).

9:23 take up his cross daily: Jesus warned that following Him would involve suffering and hardship (Matt. 5:10–12; see also Rom. 8:17; 2 Thess. 1:5).

9:24, 25 The wise course is to invest our earthly resources—our time, talents, and wealth—in what is eternal. That investment produces returns for eternity (see Matt. 6:19–21).

9:26 Recognition of Jesus will be rewarded in the coming judgment. Failure to recognize Him will lead to significant loss (see 2 Cor. 5:10; 1 John 2:28; Rev. 3:11; 22:12).

9:27 till they see the kingdom of God: Since these disciples died before Jesus' return, the reference here is no doubt to the Transfiguration (vv. 28–36). With this there is probably also a prediction of the descent of the Spirit at Pentecost (10:9; 11:20; 17:21).

9:28, 29 Jesus was **altered** into a radiant figure, even His **white and glistening** clothes. The description is similar to the glory on Moses after seeing God (Ex. 34:29–35).

9:30, 31 Decease is literally **exodus.** This allusion to the central Old Testament event of salvation is unique to Luke's account of the Transfiguration. The comparison is made between Jesus' death and the journey to salvation that the nation of Israel experienced under Moses.

9:32, 33 let us make three tabernacles: Peter desired structures for the two Old Testament visitors and Jesus, perhaps as a means of prolonging their visit.

9:34 The **cloud** is the presence of God (see Ex. 40:35).

9:35 This is My beloved Son: This is the second heavenly endorsement of Jesus (see also 3:22). The reference to the *beloved Son* recalls the words of Ps. 2:7; Is. 42:1. The command to **hear Him** alludes to Deut. 18:15–18.

9:36 told no one: We are not told why the disciples remained silent about the Transfiguration. Mark makes it clear that the disciples did not yet understand the event.

9:37–41 O faithless and perverse generation: This rebuke suggests that the disciples lacked the faith to cast out the spirit described in vv. 38–40.

9:42–44 Jesus predicted that He, the **Son of Man,** would be betrayed, even when many were still marveling at His ministry (v. 43).

9:45 they were afraid to ask: Their fear shows that they understood something about what Jesus said, but did not understand how and why Jesus could say such things about Himself, since He was the Messiah.

9:46 which of them would be greatest:. After Jesus predicted His suffering (v. 44), the disciples competed for exalted positions in the kingdom (see 22:24; Mark 10:35–45).

9:47, 48 he who is least ... will be great: Jesus' point was that prominence is not measured by human standards of achievement, but by one's relationship to God.

9:49–51 set His face to go to Jerusalem: Jesus' attention was turning toward His final suffering in Jerusalem (18:31; 19:11, 28, 41). Luke emphasizes this journey to Jerusalem, and records much of Jesus' teaching and parables on this journey.

9:52 Samaritans were the descendants of Jews who had married Gentiles after the fall of the northern kingdom, Israel. The Samaritans developed their own rites which they practiced on Mount Gerizim instead of at the temple in Jerusalem. Jesus ministered to both groups.

9:53, 54 command fire: James and John, the "sons of thunder," wanted Jesus to bring judgment upon the Samaritans who refused His message, as Elijah had done in 2 Kin. 1:9–16.

9:55–58 I will follow you: This man volunteered to follow Jesus without reservation. His problem was that he had not realistically counted the cost of discipleship.

9:59 let me first go and bury my father: This aspiring disciple placed family responsibilities ahead of following Jesus. Unlike the previous volunteer (v. 57), this man was meditative, and contemplative. He was counting the cost of discipleship.

9:60 Jesus emphasized that the call of God should receive priority over everything else.

9:61, 62 Jesus' remark about being **fit for**

the kingdom of God demonstrates the seriousness of commitment to Him. Putting a **hand to the plow** means beginning a task. **Looking back:** the sin of Lot's wife brought death.

10:1 Jesus calling of **seventy** disciples is unique to the Gospel of Luke. The instructions that Jesus gave them are similar to the instructions to the Twelve in 9:1–6.

10:2 The picture of a plentiful harvest indicated the need for more laborers, to work.

10:3–7 The image of **lambs among wolves** was popular, it derived from Is. 40:11.

10:8–12 kingdom ... near to you: Jesus came the first time to introduce the kingdom In His Second Coming, He will establish His complete rule over all.

10:13, 14 The **mighty works** of Jesus were so great that if they had been performed before the worst pagans of the old era, those people would have repented.

10:15, 16 He who hears you hears Me: Authority resides not in the messenger, but in the person the messenger represents.

10:17, 18 The reversal of the effects of sin and death are portrayed graphically as **Satan** falling from heaven. Jesus' ministry represents the defeat of Satan, sin, and death.

10:19, 20 This verse records the transmission of Jesus' **authority** to His immediate circle of disciples. **your names are written in heaven:** More important than the disciples' authority over **spirits** was that their names were in God's book. This was the disciples' greatest blessing.

10:21, 22 All things have been delivered to Me: This is Jesus' declaration of total authority as the Son of God (see John 10:18; 17:2). **except the Father ... except the Son:** Jesus declares His unique relationship with God the Father. To know God, one must know His Son, Jesus.

10:23, 24 have not seen ... heard it: Jesus contrasted the Old Testament era of expectation, in which people desired to see the Messiah but did not, with the era in which the disciples were living.

10:25, 26 The question is really a challenge, since the verse speaks of the testing of Jesus. The man was asking, "What must I do to share in the reward at the Resurrection of

the righteous at the end?" Jesus countered the lawyer's test by having him answer his own question.

10:27 The lawyer responded to Jesus' questions by quoting Deut. 6:5, a text that was recited twice a day by every faithful Jew. The lawyer also alluded to Lev. 19:18. The basis of the man's response is an expression of allegiance and devotion that also can be seen as the natural expression of faith, since the total person—**heart, soul, strength, and mind**—is involved.

10:28 do this and you will live: Those who believe in Jesus and follow Him will receive eternal rewards.

10:29 who is my neighbor: This question was an attempt to limit the demands of the Law by suggesting that some people are neighbors while others are not.

10:30 Jerusalem to Jericho: A 17-mile journey on a road known to harbor robbers.

10:31–33 Part of the beauty of the story of the Good Samaritan is the reversal of stereotypes. The priest and Levite would have been the "good guys." The **Samaritan** would have been a "bad guy." However, the Samaritan knew how to treat his neighbor. The neighbor here was not someone the Samaritan knew or even someone of the same race, just someone in need.

10:34 Oil was used to soothe wounds. **Wine** was used as a disinfectant.

10:35 two denarii ... I will repay: The Samaritan, if he paid a typical rate of one-twelfth of a denarius a day, paid for 24 days at the inn.

10:36 which ... was neighbor: The central issue is being a good neighbor to all.

10:37 He who showed mercy: The lawyer was commanded to go and do likewise.

10:38, 39 a certain village: If this is the **Martha** and **Mary** of John 11:1—12:8, then the location is Bethany, just outside Jerusalem (see John 11:1, 19; 12:1).

10:40 Martha **was distracted** by the amount of **serving** she had to do. Her complaint to Jesus indicates that she was irritated that her sister was not helping her.

10:41 Jesus' tender reply is evident in the double address of **Martha, Martha.**

10:42 that good part: Mary did what was right by devoting herself to Jesus' teaching.

11:1 The Lord's Prayer illustrates the variety of requests that one can and should make to God, as well as displaying the humble attitude that should accompany prayer. The use of the plural pronoun **us** throughout the prayer shows that it is a community prayer.
11:2 Hallowed: *Hallowed* means that God is holy, set apart, unique in His character and attributes. **Your kingdom come:** God's program and promise.
11:3 our daily bread: This recognizes that one is dependent on God for daily needs.
11:4 forgive us our sins: This request recognizes that sin is a debt to God that needs to be acknowledged. **we also forgive:** If mercy is to be sought from God, then mercy must be shown to others. **do not lead us into temptation:** The petitioner asks God for the protection necessary to avoid falling into sin.
11:5–8 Persistence refers to boldness more than to tenacity. Jesus' point is that in prayer the disciple is to be bold. The parable is about a man who goes boldly to seek what he requires.
11:9, 10 receives: This verse means that we receive what is spiritually beneficial.
11:11–13 how much more will your heavenly Father give: If people, who are evil, can give **good** gifts, imagine the value of God's gift of **the Holy Spirit.**
11:14, 15 Jesus' miracles were so obvious that they required some kind of response. If He was not to be believed, His miracles had to be demonic in origin. **Beelzebub** was originally a reference to the Philistine god Baal-Zebub worshiped at Ekron (see 2 Kin. 1:2, 3, 6, 16).
11:16–18 The attribution of Jesus' miracles to Satan was blasphemous; it was also illogical. If Satan had cast out the demon he would have been destroying the result of his own work.
11:19 by whom do your sons cast them out: Jesus' question and the implied reply to it can be taken in one of two ways: (1) How did Jewish exorcists expel demons? If the answer is by God's power, then why not give Jesus the same credit? (2) How did Jesus' disciples, who were the "sons" of Israel, drive out demons?
11:20 The finger of God is an allusion to God's power, like that demonstrated in the Exodus.

the kingdom of God has come upon you: Jesus' miracles represented the arrival of God's power and promise—in short, His rule. That rule comes in and through Jesus.
11:21, 22 Jesus portrays Himself as someone **stronger** than Satan who overruns Satan's house and gives the spoils of victory to those who are His.
11:23, 24 He who is not with Me ... does not gather: Jesus' ministry forces everyone to make a choice. Neutrality is not an option.
11:25 swept: The exorcised person is like a clean house, although empty if God is not present, and still exposed to danger.
11:26 the last state ... is worse: Experiencing God's blessing and ignoring it leaves one callous toward the work of God and exposed to the control of demonic forces.
11:27, 28 Blessed is the womb: The woman offered praise for Jesus' mother. Though Jesus always honored Mary, He commented carefully on the woman's blessing to keep the focus on the **word of God.** It is easy to allow traditionals to take the place of authority of the Scriptures.
11:29 The sign of Jonah here refers to the Resurrection foreshadowed by Jonah's three days and three nights in the great fish.
11:30–32 Jesus warned that refusal to hear Him would result in condemnation from those in the Old Testament who had responded to God's teaching. Because Jesus is **greater than** these—**Solomon** and **Jonah**—His word should have been heeded by the first-century Israelites.
11:33–35 A person who concentrates on what is **good** (God's teaching) is healthy. But a person who focuses on what is **bad** (the false teaching of the world) is **full of darkness.**
11:36 your whole body is full of light: A person can become like light, a living picture of what God's Word teaches, by concentrating on the light of the truth.
11:37, 38 He had not first washed before dinner: Such ceremonial washing is described in the Old Testament (see Gen. 18:4; Judg. 19:21), but not commanded.
11:39 make the outside ... clean: Jesus pointed out that the Pharisees were concerned with outward appearances and ritual

cleanness, while the inside was full of self-ishness and evil.

11:40–42 pass by: The Pharisees were worried about tithing ten percent, down to the smallest herbs, according to the dictates of tradition, (see Num. 18:21–32; Deut. 14:22–29). However, they neglected two things that the prophets had warned about: love and justice (Zech. 7:8–10).

11:43, 44 The Pharisees were like hidden **graves.** To have contact with the dead was to become ceremonially unclean. The Pharisees were in fact the height of uncleanness.

11:45, 46 Jesus applied His woes to **lawyers** as well. The term translated **burdens** refers to a ship's cargo. A heavy strain was being imposed on the people and yet did not bring them closer to God. Here Jesus rebuked the tradition that had grown up around the Law of Moses.

11:47, 48 you build the tombs of the prophets: Jesus made an ironic comparison between the current generation of Israel and the generations of the past.

11:49 The wisdom of God refers to God's knowledge of the people. The **prophets and apostles** who would be persecuted and killed were the disciples. Those who would come in the current generation with the message of God would suffer the same fate as the prophets of old.

11:50 Generation seems to refer to the nation of Israel. They had received judgment for the way they treated God's prophets. The judgment here refers specifically to the fall of Jerusalem in A.D. 70, and ultimately to the final judgment of God in the Tribulation.

11:51 Abel is the first prophet to be killed, going back to **the foundation of the world** (see Gen. 4:10). **Zechariah** is the last prophet killed in the Old Testament.

11:52 Jesus charged the **lawyers** with doing the opposite of what they claimed to do. Rather than bringing people nearer to God, they had removed the possibility of their entering into that **knowledge,** and had prevented others from understanding as well.

11:53, 54 seeking to catch Him: The scribes and Pharisees began challenging Jesus in the hope that He might make a blunder that would allow them to destroy His ministry.

12:1, 2 Leaven here represents the presence of corruption. The corruption in view here is **hypocrisy.** Practicing hypocrisy is senseless because eventually all deeds will be exposed.

12:3 proclaimed on the housetops: All secrets will be revealed by God (Rom. 2:15).

12:4 do not be afraid of those who kill the body: This verse anticipates the presence of severe religious persecution in response to Jesus' remarks in 11:39–54.

12:5 Even in the context of physical persecution, the only One believers should **fear** is God, who sees and judges us. Jesus was not guaranteeing physical preservation in this life, but was opening the prospect of deliverance in the next life.

12:6, 7 God knows the minute details of what happens on earth. The **copper** coins mentioned were the smallest coin in circulation, worth about one-sixteenth of a basic day's wage.

12:8 Acknowledge Jesus before men and be acknowledged by the **Son of Man** before God.

12:9 denies ... will be denied: Every act of denial of Christ on earth will meet with commensurate denial, not of the gift of salvation, but of the prize or reward (see 1 Cor. 9:24–27).

12:10 A word against the Son of Man is forgivable because His deity was veiled, but blasphemy against the Holy Spirit is flagrant rejection of the works and words of Christ.

12:11 they bring you to the synagogues: An indication that religious persecution is in view in these verses. **Magistrates and authorities** governed civil courts, while synagogues conducted religious tribunals. In such situations, the disciple should not worry about what to say.

12:12, 13 tell my brother: Jesus is asked to intervene in a family dispute.

12:14 who made Me a Judge: Jesus refuses to enter into a dispute over money, which is clearly dividing a family. Jesus tells a parable that explains the danger of focusing on wealth.

12:15–19 The word **I** appears six times in this passage, showing the selfish focus this man has. His plan is to store his abundant resources for himself, as though the assets were his alone and should be hoarded.

12:20 God's judgment on selfishness is clear. What did the rich **fool** have for the next life? What he owned was no longer of any value after death. All earthly wealth is temporary and ultimately worthless (Matt. 6:19–21; 1 Tim. 6:6–10, 17–19; James 5:1–6).

12:21–24 Jesus describes God's care of **ravens,** unclean according to Jewish law and the least respected of birds. Yet God cares for them and will surely care for the disciple as well.

12:25 Worry is utterly useless and shows a lack of faith in God's plan for our lives.

12:26–29 Even the wealthy King **Solomon** did not clothe himself as God has clothed the **lilies.** The Lord knows our problems and will provide us with what we need. **do not seek ... nor have an anxious mind:** Since God will provide, there is no need for us to concentrate on mundane things such as food. Our first priority should be doing the will of God (v. 31).

12:30 The world pursues expensive food and luxurious clothing as ends in themselves. When we are consumed with possessions, there can be little left in our heart for God. **your Father knows:** We can trust God to provide for us because God knows precisely what we need.

12:31–33 Sell what you have: In contrast to the world's hoarding of possessions, the disciple must be generous with what God gives. **money bags which do not grow old:** By serving God and others, you can invest in your eternal future.

12:34 What people consider valuable is **where** their energy will be spent. Knowing God and investing in His purposes should be the **treasure** we seek.

12:35 waist be girded ... lamps burning: These are pictures of readiness. A lamp was used at night, while girding the waist involved pulling up the hem of a robe so that one could run.

12:36 Jesus compared the disciples to servants who are ready to serve their master **immediately.** Paul also used this image in describing his relationship to God (see Rom. 1:1).

12:37 Blessed: Here the blessing is on those who watch attentively for their master's

return. In a reversal of the servant image, Jesus pointed out that the faithful servant will be served by Jesus on His return. Faithfulness will be rewarded.

12:38 This verse speaks of a return at a late hour. Constant attentiveness is necessary.

12:39, 40 he would have watched: Jesus changed the illustration slightly, watch to protect against a robbery. Knowledge of the time would lead to vigilance. But since the time is not known, constant readiness is essential.

12:41 to us, or to all people: Peter asked if Jesus' teaching was for the disciples only or for all people. Jesus did not answer the question directly. Instead He described a variety of categories of servants.

12:42–44 he will make him ruler: Such rule will be a part of the administration of Jesus' kingdom when He returns (see 19:11–27; 1 Cor. 6:2, 3; Rev. 20–22).

12:45 is delaying ... begins to beat: This servant is depicted as consciously doing the opposite of caring for others, and of treating the Master's return as irrelevant.

12:46 The image of being killed—**cut him in two**—indicates the severity of this judgment, especially in contrast to the whippings of vv. 47, 48. **Unbelievers** are those who did not take seriously the consequences of judgment (see 2 Cor. 5:10; Rev. 3:11).

12:47 knew ... did not prepare himself or do: This category of disobedience is not as blatant, but unfaithfulness nonetheless and is disciplined **with many stripes,** though not rejected.

12:48 Discipline for the ignorant is less severe—**beaten with few.** The parable suggests degrees of God's punishment: The faithful are rewarded, the ignorant are disciplined a little, the disobedient are disciplined moderately, and the blatantly disobedient are executed.

12:49 I came to send fire: Fire is an image associated with God's judgment (see Jer. 5:14; 23:29). Jesus' coming brings judgment on those who refuse to accept Him and divides the believers from the faithless.

12:50 As a figure for Jesus' death (see Mark 10:38, 39), **baptism** in this verse refers to the coming of overflowing waters of divine judgment (see Ps. 18:4, 16; 42:7; 69:1, 2; Is. 8:7, 8; 30:27, 28). Note Jesus' human response to what He recognized as His necessary death.

12:51 Part of Jesus' mission was to create a **division** within humankind. Other texts of Luke speak of Jesus bringing peace He offers peace to those who respond to Him.

12:52–55 a cloud rising out of the west: In Palestine a western breeze meant moisture coming from the Mediterranean Sea. A **south wind** meant hot air coming from the desert.

12:56, 57 Hypocrites: Jesus rebuked His audience for being able to discern the weather but not what God was doing through Him.

12:58, 59 make every effort ... to settle with him: The picture here is of a magistrate who functions like a bailiff bringing a debtor into prison. Since the context of this passage is Jesus' mission, the **judge** likely represents God. The message of this parable is to become reconciled to God before judgment comes.

13:1 The incident referred to here, in which Jewish blood was shed at or near the temple during a time of **sacrifices,** is unknown. **Pilate** was known for his insensitivity to the Jewish people early in his rule. The event probably occurred during the Feast of the Passover or Tabernacles, when **Galileans** most likely would have been at the temple.

13:2 Do you suppose: The idea that judgment and death are the results of sin led to the belief that tragic death was the result of extreme sin. While such a view was common in Judaism, it was not always a correct conclusion (see Ex. 20:5; Job 4:7; 8:4, 20; 22:5; John 9:1–3).

13:3 unless you repent: Jesus' point here is that everyone stands at the edge of death until repentance occurs. The death in view here is spiritual, not physical.

13:4 The event referred to here was a natural tragedy as opposed to the violent human act alluded to in vv. 1, 2. However, the same question was raised. Were the people who suffered being judged for their sins? **Siloam** was located in the southeast section of Jerusalem.

13:5 The manner in which a person dies is not a measure of righteousness; what is important is not to die outside of God's grace and care. (5:32).

13:6 The man in this parable represents God; the **fig tree** represents Israel.

13:7 for three years: A fig tree was often given time to bear good fruit since its root structure took time to develop. Three years would have been enough for the tree to yield fruit.

13:8, 9 But if not: If the tree, symbolizing Israel, would yield some fruit, it could escape judgment. In v. 35, Jesus declares that the nation's house is desolate, so judgment comes. The fall of Jerusalem, which took place in A.D. 70, is in view.

13:10–15 Hypocrite: When the ruler of the synagogue became indignant about Jesus' healing on the Sabbath (vv. 10–14), Jesus pointed out that compassion was shown to animals on the Sabbath, so much more compassion should be shown to a suffering woman (v. 16)?

13:16 daughter of Abraham: This description of the woman indicates how special she was. Jesus said there was no better day on which to overcome Satan than the Sabbath.

13:17–19 Jesus compared the growth of God's kingdom to a little **seed** that becomes a big tree where birds can find shelter. A tree of the **mustard** family would grow to about twelve feet.

13:20, 21 In this illustration the **leaven** is hidden in **meal** equaling about 50 pounds. Leaven permeates bread and makes it rise. The kingdom will start small, but will grow and fill the earth.

13:22–24 the narrow gate: The suggestion here is that one must enter salvation on God's terms. Those who are unable to enter are those who seek entrance on their own terms. Many will miss the blessings of God because they think they can achieve salvation on their own merit.

13:25 Once a person's life has ended, **the door** of opportunity to respond to Jesus is closed. **I do not know you:** The issue here is being properly and personally related to God through Jesus. Verse 26 makes it clear that the **Lord** at the door is Jesus.

13:26 We ate and drank ... You taught: The appeal here is by people who experienced Jesus' presence. The passage involves those Jews who witnessed Jesus' ministry, and were trying to gain entry into God's presence based simply on the fact that they had observed Jesus. Jesus refused them, pointing out that it was not enough for them to have been close to Him.

13:27 I do not know you ... Depart from Me: In this verse, Jesus turns a question about salvation (v. 23) into a question about personally knowing Him. Failure to seek salvation in Jesus means that sin remains in a person's life.

13:28–30 east ... west ... north ... south: People would come from all corners of the earth for entrance into God's kingdom. Those who are despised on earth—some Gentiles, for example—will be greatly honored in the kingdom. Conversely, those who are considered influential and powerful on earth—the Jewish religious leaders of Jesus' day, for example—will be excluded from the kingdom.

13:31–33 Herod wants to kill You: This warning from the Pharisees was apparently an effort to get Jesus out of the region and out of their hair. It is hard to know whether the warning was true. **fox:** The reference here is to Herod's cunning. **I shall be perfected:** Jesus predicted His Resurrection in Jerusalem. The reference to **today, tomorrow, and the day following** is figurative, since Jesus was speaking of more than three remaining days in His ministry. **it cannot be:** Jesus followed a long line of prophets that were executed in the nation's capital (see 1 Kin. 18:4, 13; 19:10, 14; 2 Chr. 24:21; Jer. 2:30; 26:20–23; 38:4–6; Amos 7:10–17).

13:34 Jerusalem, Jerusalem: The double address indicates Jesus' deep sorrow (see 2 Sam. 18:33; Jer. 22:29). The city had executed many of God's messengers. **I wanted to gather:** As a prophet, Jesus spoke for God in the first person. He compared God's desire to gather the nation to a hen sheltering and protecting her young. Sadly, the nation was not willing to be gathered.

13:35 Your house is left ... desolate: Jesus declared that the nation stood under a judgment similar to the Exile to Babylon (see Jer. 12:7; 22:5). **Blessed is He:** This is a citation of Ps. 118:26. The people of Israel would not see the Messiah until they were ready to receive Him and recognize that He was sent from God.

14:1, 2 Dropsy is a condition in which water is retained in the body, leading to swollen limbs (see Num. 5:11–27). Dropsy is a symptom and not a specific disease.

14:3 Is it lawful: Note that Jesus raised the question of Sabbath law here, preempting the questioning He had faced in 6:2 (see 6:9).

14:4–7 In ancient times the **best** seats at a meal were those next to the host.

14:8–13 True hospitality and service are given to those who cannot repay. Disciples must have a special concern for the **poor, maimed, lame,** and **blind,** as Jesus does (4:16–19).

14:14 you shall be repaid: Even though there may be no reward in this life, God will not overlook what His servants have done to carry out His love and mercy.

14:15 Blessed is he: One of the guests at the meal reflected on the glory of sitting at the banquet table of God, an image of being saved and living in God's presence. The man probably assumed that many of the people attending the meal with Jesus would be present at God's banquet table. Jesus responded to the man's assumption with a warning.

14:16, 17 those who were invited: In the ancient world, invitations to a feast were sent out in advance of the meal. On the day of the feast, servants would announce the start of the meal.

14:18–20 I have married a wife: While the Old Testament exempted a man from military duty because of marriage (see Deut. 20:7), marriage was not an excuse for avoiding social duties.

14:21 poor ... maimed ... lame ... blind: This list matches that of v. 13. The maimed were excluded from full participation in Jewish worship (see Lev. 21:17–23). The master's second invitation extended the scope of the offer to those who were rejected by society.

14:22, 23 The second invitation extended beyond the city limits, encouraging even more people to come to the feast. This may picture the inclusion of Gentiles in God's salvation.

14:24–26 does not hate: The essence of discipleship is giving Christ first place. To "hate" one's family and even one's life refers to desiring something less than something else. This instruction was especially appropriate since a decision for Jesus could mean rejection by family and persecution even to the point of death.

14:27 Jesus' call here is to follow Him in the way of rejection and suffering. A **disciple** will be rejected by those in the world who do not honor Christ. Therefore, a disciple must be ready to face such rejection.

14:28–30 was not able to finish: Their mocking centers on the dishonor that results from an inability to complete the task. Following Christ is not something to be taken up on a trial basis. It calls for ultimate commitment (see 9:62).

14:31, 32 The picture is of a **king** assessing his ability to do battle with another powerful king. The king **sends a delegation** only after appreciating the consequences of his decision. Jesus urged the people to think about what it would mean to follow Him, and not take it lightly.

14:33, 34 In the ancient world, **salt** was often used as a catalyst for burning fuel such as cattle dung. The salt of the time was impure and could lose its strength over time, becoming useless. Jesus' point is that the same is true of a "saltless" disciple.

14:35 throw it out: Jesus warned that an ineffective commitment leads to being cast aside. This apparently is a reference to those who are judged as unfaithful (see 1 Cor. 11:30).

15:1 tax collectors and the sinners: The three parables of ch. 15 explain why Jesus associated with despised groups while the Pharisees did not, and are found only in Luke.

15:2 eats with them: Table fellowship indicated acceptance of the other guests. The Jewish religious leaders complained about Jesus' companions at His meals (19:10; Mark 2:15).

15:3, 4 A hundred sheep was a medium-sized flock. The average herd ran from twenty to two hundred head.

15:5, 6 The call to **rejoice** at finding the lost sheep would have been natural enough, since sheep were valuable property.

15:7 likewise: Jesus compared the joy of finding a lost sheep to the joy of heaven over a sinner's repentance. **Persons who need no**

repentance is a rhetorical way of describing the scribes and Pharisees. They believed that they did not need to repent because they were not lost.

15:8 ten silver coins: A drachma was a silver coin equal to a day's wage. In this second parable of ch. 15, more detail is given about the search effort than in the first parable of vv. 4–7.

15:9–12 the portion of goods that falls to me: As the younger son he would have received half of what the elder son received (see Deut. 21:17), or a third of his father's estate. The father granted the request, illustrating how God permits each person to go his or her own way.

15:13 wasted his possessions: The verb here means "to scatter or disperse something." The term translated **prodigal** describes a debased, extravagant life (see Prov. 28:7).

15:14, 15 Feeding **swine** was an insulting job for a Jew, since pigs were unclean according to the Law of Moses.

15:16–19 I have sinned: The son's words are the confession of a sinner. The son expected nothing and relied completely on the mercy of his father. So it is with the sinner who repents.

15:20 The description of the father's **compassion** in running to his son and kissing him illustrates the immediate acceptance of a sinner who turns to God.

15:21 no longer worthy to be called your son: Despite his awareness of being accepted by his father, the son continued his confession, then asked to become one of his father's servants.

15:22 The father accepted his son's confession and made him a full member of the family again. The **robe** probably was the best clothes the father had to offer. The **ring** signified the son's acceptance back into the family. The son's confession brought full restoration.

15:23, 24 dead ... alive ... lost ... found: The total transformation of the prodigal son is summarized in these two contrasts. Such a transformation is a reason to celebrate. It is also the reason Jesus chose to associate with the lost.

15:25–28 The older brother's unhappiness over a fatted calf (v. 27) being killed to celebrate the return of his undisciplined brother illustrates the response of the Pharisees and scribes at the prospect of sinners becoming acceptable to God.

15:29, 30 I never transgressed ... you never gave me: The older son proclaimed his righteousness and argued that justice had not been done.

15:31, 32 all that I have is yours: The father responded to his older son by explaining that just because someone receives a blessing, that does not mean there is no blessing for others. The older son always had the opportunity to celebrate with a fattened calf, since the animals were his.

16:1 A steward was a servant who supervised and administered an estate. The charge brought against this steward is incompetence.

16:2 Give an account ... you can no longer be steward: The rich man responded to the charge that his steward was incompetent by firing the steward and asking for his records to be brought up to date.

16:3–6 A hundred measures of oil ... fifty: Three explanations are commonly given about the steward's right to change the amount his master was owed: (1) The steward simply lowered the price on his own authority; (2) the steward removed the interest charge from the debt, according to the Law (see Lev. 25:36, 37; Deut. 15:7, 8; 23:20, 21); or (3) the steward removed his own commission, sacrificing only his own money and not that of his master. The different rates of reduction reflect the different rates for different commodities.

16:7, 8 The master recognized the foresight in the steward's generosity. It is debatable whether the steward was dishonest and robbed the master by such reductions or was **shrewd** in using his authority to discount the goods (vv. 6, 7).

16:9 Mammon, or money, should be used generously to build works that last. Money is called **unrighteous** because it often manifests unrighteousness and selfishness in people (see 1 Tim. 6:6–10, 17–19; James 1:9–11; 5:1–6).

16:10 faithful ... unjust ... least ... much: Small examples of selfishness now result in greater selfishness later. Likewise, small examples of generosity now result in greater generosity later.

16:11 mammon ... true riches: A person who cannot handle money certainly cannot handle spiritual matters that are of much more value.

16:12–16 The time of promise extended from the Law and Prophets **until John** the Baptist. Now the promise of God's kingdom is preached. The new era approaches.

16:17 Jesus' point is not that all the commandments of **the law** remain in effect forever, but that the goal of God's law, the promise of God's rule, is realized.

16:18 commits adultery: Jesus illustrated the moral demands of God's law by referring to the inviolability of marriage.

16:19 clothed in purple: Purple clothes were extremely expensive because they were made with a special dye.

16:20, 21 To have his sores **licked** by **dogs** threatened Lazarus with infection as well as ritual uncleanness, since dogs fed on garbage.

16:22 Abraham's bosom was the blessed place of the dead. This verse indicates that the dead know their fate immediately.

16:23 Note the reversal of fortune from vv. 19–21. Here the rich man was suffering and Lazarus was at peace. **Hades** is where the unrighteous dead dwell.

16:24 I am tormented: The rich man desired relief from his suffering. The image of thirst for the experience of judgment is common (see Is. 5:13; 65:13; Hos. 2:3).

16:25 The standard by which the rich man treated others was applied to him. In his **lifetime** he lacked compassion, so now there was no compassion for him.

16:26 a great gulf fixed: The unrighteous, once they have died, cannot enter into the sphere of the righteous.

16:27, 28 The rich man asked for a heavenly envoy to be sent so that his **brothers** would not repeat his error. It is difficult to know if his concern for his brothers was sincere, or just a backhanded way of saying that in his own life he had not received adequate warning about the judgment.

16:29 They have Moses and the prophets: Abraham made it clear that the rich man's brothers should have known what to do, since they had the message of God in the ancient writings. The point here is that generosity with money and care for the poor were taught in the Old Testament (see Deut. 14:28, 29; Is. 3:14, 15; Mic. 6:10, 11).

16:30, 31 If they do not hear: A person who rejects God's message will not be persuaded by Resurrection. Though the rich man's request for a heavenly messenger is denied within the parable, it is honored in the telling of the account, because the parable is part of a Gospel that announces Christ's Resurrection.

17:1, 2 woe to him: Jesus warned that judgment awaits those who cause others to stumble. **A millstone** was a heavy stone used in a grinding mill.

17:3–6 Even faith the size of a tiny **mustard seed** can do wonderful things. The black **mulberry** tree has a vast root system that allows it to live up to six hundred years.

17:7–11 Samaria and Galilee: Though Jesus was traveling to **Jerusalem,** His journey did not follow a direct route.

17:12–14 Jesus healed the lepers but sent them to the **priests** to verify their cleansing, just as He did the leper in 5:14.

17:15–18 The Samaritans were a despised race (9:52). A hated **foreigner** was the only former leper who gave **glory to God** for his cleansing.

17:19 Jesus commended the **faith** that heals. The Samaritan apparently received more than physical healing.

17:20 In ancient Israel there was an expectation that the **kingdom of God** would come with cosmic signs. Jesus' concept of the kingdom of God, however, was broader than the time of the final consummation.

17:21 This verse indicates that there was an aspect of kingdom promise involved in Jesus' first coming. The kingdom of God is among earthly kingdoms today; but one day the kingdom of God will swallow up all rival kingdoms (see Rev. 11:15).

17:22–24 Lightning is sudden and visible to all. Likewise, the sudden **day** of the **Son of Man** will be visible to all. When the Lord returns, there will be no doubt as to what has occurred.

17:25–27 In the days of Noah people paid little attention to God and faced judgment as a result (see Gen. 6:5–13). The same will be the case at Jesus' return.

17:28, 29 destroyed them all: The day of the Son of Man will be a time of total judgment, as were the days of Noah (v. 27) and **Lot.**

17:30–32 Lot's wife represents those who are attached to earthly things, those whose hearts are still in this world. Like Lot's wife, such people will perish (see Gen. 19:26).

17:33 whoever loses his life will preserve it: Those who invest their lives in advancing Christ's kingdom, even to the point of suffering and death, will receive great privilege and glory in the climactic reign of Christ.

17:34 Taken here suggests judgment, such as when the soldiers *took* Jesus to crucify Him.

17:35, 36 one will be taken and the other left: On that day, the Son of Man will divide humankind into two groups: those who are taken to judgment and those who are left to live and reign with Christ. A person's eternal destiny is not determined by being close to those who are righteous. Each person stands before God alone.

17:37 the eagles will be gathered: The term for *eagles* refers to vultures that gather over dead animals. When the judgment comes, it will be final and terrible, with the stench of death and the presence of vultures everywhere. No one will need to look for the place of judgment; the presence of the birds will reveal where the carcasses are.

18:1, 2 This **judge** did not fear God, and was therefore probably a secular judge, not a religious one. The dishonest judge represents corrupted power.

18:3 The woman in this parable is a **widow,** dependent on society for her support. **Get justice:** Perhaps the woman was asking for help about a financial problem.

18:4, 5 The persistence of the widow is the lesson of the parable. God is a counter-example to the judge. If an insensitive judge will respond to the **continual** requests of a widow, God will certainly respond to the continual prayers of believers.

18:6, 7 shall God not avenge His own elect: God will respond to injustice and religious persecution meted out to His people. In the end, He will avenge.

18:8 will He really find faith: Jesus' question here is whether upon His return believers will still be looking for Him. In asking this question, Jesus is exhorting believers not to lose heart (v. 1).

18:9–12 God, I thank You: The Pharisee uses the pronoun *I* five times in two verses. His attitude seems to be that God should be grateful to him for his commitment. The man looked down on other people and was proud of his fasting and tithing.

18:13 The **tax collector** knew that he could not say or bring anything to enhance his standing with God. He knew that only God's mercy and grace, and not his own works, could deliver him.

18:14 Jesus identified the contrast between the Pharisee and the tax collector as one between pride and humility, between those who exalt and those who humble themselves. God will bring down the proud and will exalt the humble (1:52; 14:11).

18:15 they rebuked them: The disciples assumed that Jesus was too important and too busy for children. The parents' desire for Jesus to **touch** the children was probably a request to bless them.

18:16, 17 Jesus declared that all people, even little children, are important to God and that the **kingdom of God** consists of those who respond to Him with the trust of a little child.

18:18–21 All these things I have kept: Like the Pharisee in vv. 11, 12, the ruler was certain of his own ability to live righteously.

18:22, 23 Sell all that you have and distribute to the poor: Jesus was determining whether the ruler's treasure (see Matt. 6:19–21) lay with God or money (16:13). Jesus was not establishing a new requirement for being saved. He was examining the ruler's orientation to God by directly confronting him with the very thing that was hindering him—his wealth.

18:24, 25 How hard it is for those who have riches: A wealthy person is tempted to depend on earthly riches rather than on God. **easier for a camel to go through the eye of a needle:** Jesus emphasized the difficulty of turning from wealth to find salvation. Because many Jewish people believed that wealth was evidence of God's blessing, Jesus' statements would have been shocking to His audience.

18:26, 27 Who then can be saved: Jesus explained that the change of heart one must experience in order to know God is **possible** only through Him. Any person who enters the kingdom does so only by the marvelous grace of God (see John 3:3).

18:28 we have left all and followed You: Peter wanted reassurance about the disciples' sacrifice as compared to the ruler.

18:29, 30 for the sake of the kingdom of God: Jesus assured the disciples that the sacrifices they made in leaving everything to follow Him would be rewarded in His kingdom.

18:31 Though Jesus referred to the suffering He was going to face in **Jerusalem,** a suffering that was predicted **by the prophets,** His disciples did not understand the implication of His words until after His Resurrection.

18:32, 33 The sequence of events of Jesus' trial, Crucifixion, and Resurrection is predicted here in detail.

18:34 understood none of these things: The disciples may have understood something of what Jesus said, but they could not understand why God's Chosen One would have to face such suffering. For those who were expecting the Promised One to be an exalted figure who would deliver God's people, it would be very difficult to reconcile such an expectation with such terrible suffering.

18:35–37 Jesus was nearing Jerusalem: **Jericho** was about 17 miles from the city.

18:38 Note the irony in this verse. The blind man recognized who **Jesus** was, the **Son of David,** more clearly than many people who were blessed with physical sight. The blind man's cry for **mercy** demonstrated his belief that Jesus had the power to heal him.

18:39–43 The gracious work of God led to **praise,** not only from the one who was blessed but also from those who saw the blessing.

19:1, 2 Zacchaeus, as **chief tax collector,** probably bid for the right to collect taxes and then hired another tax collector to actually gather the money.

19:3, 4 A sycamore tree is similar to an oak tree, with a short trunk and wide lateral branches.

19:5–7 The crowd was not happy with Jesus'

choice of whom to honor with His fellowship. Since tax collectors often took for themselves a high percentage of what they demanded, they were hated and despised in ancient Israel.

19:8–10 give half ... restore fourfold: Zacchaeus determined to deal generously with others. In later Judaism, it was considered generous to give away up to 20 percent of one's belongings. Legal restitution for extortion was also 20 percent (see Lev. 5:16; Num. 5:7).

19:11 Evidently the disciples believed that Jesus' arrival in Jerusalem would signal the arrival of the **kingdom of God.** Jesus' parable in vv. 12–27 was designed to dispel this misconception.

19:12 Here, this parable is similar to Matt. 25:14–30, but the occasion is probably different. The story parallels in part what happened to Archelaus, a son of Herod the Great, who came to power in 4 B.C. The people disliked Archelaus, and they appealed to Augustus Caesar not to give him authority. A significant detail is that the kingdom is received during the journey away from the land to be ruled. This corresponds to Jesus' leaving this earth to **receive** the **kingdom** following His Resurrection.

19:13 Do business till I come: This detail shows that Jesus' return would not be immediate (v. 11). The **servants** represent Jesus' followers. They are to serve faithfully until Jesus returns. **ten minas:** Each servant received one mina, or about four months' wages for the average worker. The master wants to see fruit, or dividends from his investment.

19:14 his citizens hated him: This is a separate group from the servants and refers to those who reject Jesus outright.

19:15 how much every man had gained: Having returned with authority to rule, the nobleman asks the servants to give an account of their labor in his absence.

19:16 The first servant earned **ten** times the amount he was given originally.

19:17 you were faithful ... have authority over ten cities: Faithfulness is commended and rewarded with greater opportunity.

19:18–23 I feared you: If the servant had really feared the master, he would have done

something with the money. Even putting the **money in the bank** would have yielded **interest.**

19:24–27 what he has will be taken away from him: Unfaithfulness results in loss of reward.

19:28–30 Jesus was in control of the events of the last week of His life, even though those events led to His death. Here He prepared to enter the city riding a **colt.** The cities of **Bethphage** and **Bethany** were located just east of Jerusalem, within two miles of the city.

19:31–34 the Lord has need of it: Borrowing an animal was not as strange as it may appear. There was a custom by which a religious leader could commandeer property for short-term use.

19:35 The **clothes** were their outer garments. The ride on the **colt** resembles the events of 1 Kin. 1:33, in which David made the new king, Solomon, ride to Gihon on a mule. Zechariah had prophesied that the coming King would ride into Jerusalem humbly on a donkey (Zech. 9:9).

19:36, 37 spread their clothes on the road: These actions indicate that a dignitary was being greeted (see 2 Kin. 9:13). This is like "rolling out the red carpet" today.

19:38 The disciples recognized that Jesus was the promised King sent from God. He is the One who brings **peace** to the relationship between people and God (1:78, 79).

19:39–41 wept over it: Jesus knew Israel would suffer judgment, in the form of the terrible destruction that came on Jerusalem in A.D. 70.

19:42, 43 build an embankment: This is a prediction of Rome's successful siege of Jerusalem under Titus. The details reflect a divine judgment for covenant unfaithfulness.

19:44 level you, and your children: The totality of the destruction is made clear in this description of the siege of Jerusalem. Even children would die, and buildings be destroyed.

19:45 Jesus' entrance into Jerusalem begins the final section of Luke's Gospel. Jesus cleansed the **temple** in anger after seeing that the place of prayer had become an excuse for corrupt commerce. Merchants were selling sacrificial animals in the outer court of the temple at exorbitant prices. Money changers were making an excessive profit exchanging currencies for the temple shekel. Jesus might have cleansed the temple twice.

19:46 The holy place of worship had become a site for taking advantage of people. Jesus' remark about **a house of prayer** alludes to Is. 56:7, **den of thieves** comes from Jer. 7:11.

19:47, 48 Jesus' actions at the temple caused the Jewish religious leaders to strengthen their resolve **to destroy Him.**

20:1–4 Jesus' question presented the Pharisees with a dilemma. If they recognized John's ministry as coming **from heaven,** they would be recognizing the divine origin of Jesus' ministry. But if the they denied that John was sent by God, they risked angering the people, who believed that John's ministry was divinely directed (vv. 5, 6).

20:5–9 The **vineyard** represents the promise made to Israel, while the **vinedressers** represent the nation of Israel. The **man** who **planted** the **vineyard** represents God.

20:10 beat him ... sent him away empty-handed: The treatment of the servant in this parable represents the treatment of the Old Testament prophets by the people of Israel.

20:11–13 I will send my beloved son: This refers to Jesus (3:21, 22; 9:35).

20:14 This is the heir ... let us kill him: The vinedressers hoped that with the son gone, the inheritance would fall to those who worked the property, a transfer possible in the ancient world. The details of this parable do not represent the thinking of those who crucified Jesus.

20:15 cast him out ... killed him: The parallel here of course is Jesus' death. **what will the owner of the vineyard do to them:** "What will God the Father do to those who reject and murder His Son?"

20:16 come and destroy those vinedressers: God will exercise judgment on those who killed His Son. He will **give the vineyard to others.** Jesus is alluding to the inclusion of Gentiles in the promise of God's kingdom.

20:17 The stone which the builders rejected: This passage, taken from Ps. 118:22, pictures the exaltation of the Righteous One,

Jesus, after His rejection. Opposition will not stop God from making the One who is rejected the center of His work of salvation.

20:18 Jesus is the stone. **chief cornerstone:** The large stone which joins the foundation of two walls of a building, or the capstone at the top of a doorway.

20:19 The Jewish religious leaders wanted Jesus removed because of His direct challenges to them. But they **feared** the reaction of the crowd, so they waited for a more favorable time to do away with Jesus.

20:20 The religious leaders **watched** Jesus very closely. They **pretended to be righteous,** which means that they tried to look sincere. They wanted to trap Jesus into saying something that would make Him look like a political revolutionary.

20:21, 22 Is it lawful for us to pay taxes to Caesar or not: This question concerned the poll tax to Rome. The poll tax was a citizenship tax paid directly to Rome, as an indication that Israel was subject to that Gentile nation. If Jesus answered yes, the people would be angry because He respected a foreign power. If He answered no, He could be charged with sedition.

20:23, 24 Whose image ... does it have: Jesus' reply was clever. He had the Pharisees pull out a coin, indicating that they already recognized Roman sovereignty by using Roman coins themselves. A denarius was a silver coin that usually had a picture of a Roman ruler on it.

20:25 According to Jesus, **Caesar,** as the ruler of the empire, had the right to collect taxes. Yet at the same time, **God** should be honored above any ruler. Honoring God does not make a person exempt from supporting the basic functions of the state (see Rom. 13:1–7).

20:26, 27 The Sadducees based their teaching only on the first five books of the Old Testament, the books of Moses. They denied that there could be a **Resurrection,** and they contrived a ludicrous example to suggest that the doctrine was impossible.

20:28 In Judaism, a childless widow would marry the **brother** of her late husband, according to the custom known as levirate marriage (see Deut. 25:5; Ruth 4:1–12).

The law was designed to perpetuate the name of a man who died childless.

20:29–35 Because marriage will not be a part of the age to come, the Sadducees' absurd example (vv. 28–33) does not apply. Jesus upheld the doctrine of Resurrection in His reply, speaking of both the **age** to come and the **Resurrection,** so the concepts were clearly associated.

20:36, 37 equal to the angels … sons of God: The everlasting life of a resurrected person makes that person something like an angel. Paul explains further that in the Resurrection we will be given Resurrection bodies similar to Christ's (see 1 Cor. 15:25–58).

20:38–40 the God of the … living: Jesus points out that if God is the God of the patriarchs, then they must be raised and alive. God has a relationship only with those who are alive. Jesus' citation of the Law (see Ex. 3:1–6, 15) probably made an impact on the Sadducees, who revered the teachings of the books of Moses.

20:41–43 The dilemma Jesus poses is how the Messiah (the Hebrew word for **Christ**) could be called the **Son of David,** when David himself gave Him the title *Lord.* **my Lord:** This is a citation from Ps. 110:1 (see also 22:69; Acts 2:30–36). Jesus was noting that even David one day will bow at the Messiah's feet and confess that He is Lord (see Phil. 2:10).

20:44–47 devour widows' houses: Jesus noted the scribes' hypocrisy and their taking advantage of others. Such activity will be judged.

21:1 There were various places around the temple where people could leave contributions. There was also a **treasury** room near the court of women.

21:2 The **poor widow** contributed **two mites,** small copper coins which were the smallest currency available.

21:3 has put in more than all: Jesus contrasted the giving of the rich (v. 1) with the sacrifice of the poor widow.

21:4 put in all the livelihood that she had: The widow did not refuse to give even when she needed more to live on. Her devotion to God was her first priority (see 2 Cor. 8:1–5; 9:6–9).

21:5 how it was adorned: The temple was refurbished under Herod the Great with new foundation walls and enlarged areas outside the temple. The refurbishing was in progress during Jesus' visit, around A.D. 30. The **donations** were gift offerings for the decoration of the temple.

21:6, 7 not one stone: Jesus noted that the beautiful place of worship would be destroyed. He was referring to the fall of Jerusalem in A.D. 70, which itself was a picture of the destruction of the last days.

21:8 Take heed: The first century and early second century were times of great messianic fervor in Judaism. Many people claimed to be the Messiah. Jesus warned His disciples not to be fooled by such claims.

21:9–11 A variety of cosmic and natural events will occur before the end times. Verses 8–11 give signs before the end, vv. 12–19 events that will happen before the signs of vv. 8–11.

21:12 persecute you … for My name's sake: Jesus predicted the arrests and suffering that the disciples would face as a result of identifying with Him. Some of these events are detailed in Acts 3–5; 7; 21–28.

21:13, 14 an occasion for testimony: Suffering can be an opportunity to advance the kingdom of God. This is why those who endure suffering and persecution are called blessed (Matt. 5:10–12).

21:15 I will give you a mouth and wisdom: Jesus promises the disciples that the Holy Spirit will assist them in giving testimony (12:11, 12).

21:16 You will be betrayed: The persecution of the disciples would be painful and severe. Identifying with Jesus often means the rejection of family, and in some cases martyrdom.

21:17–19 possess your souls: Patient allegiance to Jesus leads to eternal life (9:24).

21:20, 21 A siege would be the sign that the end was near for **Jerusalem** and the temple. The other synoptic Gospels allude to the abomination of **desolation** in Dan. 9:25–27; 11:31. This passage compares the desecration of the temple to what occurred in 167 B.C., when Antiochus Epiphanes erected an altar to Zeus in the temple. A similar desecration of the temple site occurred during the destruction of Jerusalem in A.D. 70.

21:22 days of vengeance: Jerusalem had become an object of divine judgment because of its unfaithfulness. Jesus warned of this consequence throughout His ministry (13:9, 34, 35).

21:23, 24 fall ... be led away captive: This verse elaborates on Jerusalem's fall. There would be death and captivity, just as the nation experienced under the Assyrians and Babylonians. **times of the Gentiles:** There would be a period in God's salvation plan when Gentiles would be dominant, of which the fall of Jerusalem would be a clear sign.

21:25, 26 signs: Jesus shifts His focus to the end times with His second mention of cosmic turmoil (see v. 11; Is. 24:18–20; 34:4; Ezek. 32:7, 8; Joel 2:30, 31). **men's hearts failing them:** The terror of cosmic chaos will cause apprehension about what is coming.

21:27 the Son of Man coming in a cloud: The reference here is to the return of Jesus. The image of the cloud is important, since God is identified as riding the clouds in the Old Testament (see Ex. 34:5; Ps. 104:3). **with power and great glory:** The Son of Man has divine authority to judge the world.

21:28 lift up your heads ... redemption draws near: This is the sign of the deliverance of Jesus' followers. The Son of Man acts on behalf of those who have suffered in His name.

21:29, 30 The appearance of the signs Jesus describes will warn of the end times.

21:31 when you see ... know: The cosmic signs and earthly chaos are indications that the decisive and consummate rule of God is approaching.

21:32 When the end comes, it will come quickly. The events of the end times will fall within one **generation** from start to finish (17:22–24).

21:33 by no means pass away: The disciples had the assurance that Jesus' promises about the end times were more certain than creation itself. God made an unconditional and unilateral covenant, and He will keep it (see Gen. 12:1–3; 15:18–21; Ps. 89).

21:34 Though the events of the end times may not come to pass for a long time, believers

should continue to look for their arrival. The **Day** should not take us by surprise.

21:35–38 Watch ... pray: Jesus encouraged His disciples to be persistent in prayer and faith, looking for the day when the **Son of Man** exonerates the faithful in the judgment, so that they are able **to stand** before Him (see 1 John 2:28).

22:1, 2 This verse begins the "passion narrative," the account of Jesus' death and Resurrection. **The Feast of Unleavened Bread** took place immediately following **Passover** (see Ex. 12:1–20; Deut. 16:1–8). The two feasts were often considered as one.

22:3 The journey to the Cross was not just a matter of human effort or Judas's plots. Cosmic forces were at work in the opposition to Jesus.

22:4 Judas's involvement in the plot to betray Jesus was fortunate from the point of view of the Jewish religious leaders. They could arrest Jesus secretly and later claim that the driving force to stop Him came from within His own group of disciples. The **captains,** Levites who were members of the temple guard, were the ones who could make the arrest.

22:5–7 The synoptic Gospels are very clear that Jesus was betrayed on the day of **Passover** (see Matt. 26:17–19; Mark 14:12–16).

22:8–12 guest room: Such rooms were often made available to the thousands of pilgrims who came to Jerusalem for the celebration of Passover and the Feast of Unleavened Bread. Such a room would contain couches for guests at the feasts to recline for the meal.

22:13–16 I will no longer eat of it until it is fulfilled: In the kingdom to come, when final victory is celebrated, Jesus again will eat (see Rev. 19:9).

22:17, 18 I will not drink of the fruit: Jesus will abstain from wine until His return.

22:19 My body ... do this in remembrance: Jesus instituted a new meal which is not only a memorial of His death, but also a fellowship meal of unity. It is a proclamation of the believers' anticipation of Jesus' return, when all God's promises will be fulfilled (see 1 Cor. 10:16, 17; 11:23–26). The **bread** represents the body of Jesus, offered on behalf of His disciples.

22:20 This cup is the new covenant: The wine of the Lord's Supper depicts the giving of life, a sacrifice of blood, which inaugurates the new covenant for those who respond to Jesus' offer of salvation (see Heb. 9:11–28). Jesus died on the Cross for our sins (see Acts 20:28).

22:21, 22 Jesus would suffer and the one who betrayed Him would face **woe.**

22:23, 24 the greatest: Note the sad irony in this verse. While Jesus faced the reality of being betrayed and killed, His disciples argued about which of them was greatest.

22:25 benefactors: This title suggests that the people should be grateful for the generous leaders of their nation and that they should recognize their power and authority.

22:26 as the younger ... as he who serves: Leadership in the church serves.

22:27, 28 in My trials: Jesus recognized that the disciples had suffered with Him during His ministry.

22:29 Jesus passed His **kingdom** authority to the apostles who would plant the church, a part of the kingdom. The authority that Jesus bestowed on them was like the authority that the **Father** had **bestowed** on Him.

22:30 eat and drink ... sit on thrones judging: This is a promise of future blessing and authority. The disciples were promised a seat at the banquet of victory and the right to help Jesus rule over Israel on His return (see Matt. 19:28; 2 Tim. 2:12).

22:31 Satan has asked for you: The Greek word for *you* here is plural, indicating that Satan had asked permission to trouble all of the disciples.

22:32–34 I have prayed for you ... when you have returned: The Greek word for *you* here is singular, referring specifically to Peter. In effect, Jesus restored Peter even before his fall (vv. 54–62), and He instructed the disciple to shepherd the saints by strengthening them.

22:35, 36 When I sent you: The allusion here is to the disciples' mission recorded in 9:1–6; 10:1–24. However, the situation had changed. Jesus here instructed His disciples to take **a money bag, a knapsack,** and a **sword** on their journeys in order prepare for the rejection that was to come.

22:37 this which is written: Jesus cited Is. 53:12, which describes a righteous one who suffers as a criminal. Jesus noted that His death would fulfill Isaiah's prediction.

22:38 Misunderstanding Jesus' instructions in v. 36, the disciples indicated that they had weapons with which to fight (vv. 50, 51).

22:39 Mount of Olives: Matthew 26:36 gives the name Gethsemane, while John 18:1 speaks more generally of a garden.

22:40–42 Jesus agonized over His approaching death and the effect of God's wrath. The **cup** is a figure of speech for wrath.

22:43 strengthening Him: God's answer to Jesus' prayer did not allow His Son to avoid suffering. However, God did provide angelic help for Jesus to face what was coming.

22:44 His sweat became like great drops of blood: Jesus' earnest prayer and emotion (vv. 42–44) led to a physical reaction. Though Jesus did not bleed, His sweat became like blood.

22:45–48 Jesus remind Judas of what he had done; and the irony of being betrayed **with a kiss.**

22:49, 50 one of them struck the servant: John 18:10 indicates that this impetuous disciple was Peter. His violent act risked giving the impression that the disciples were seditious.

22:51 touched his ear and healed him: Jesus mercifully healed the ear of one who was taking Him. Jesus illustrated here the love for His enemies that He had commanded in 6:27–36.

22:52 as against a robber: Jesus rebuked His captors for treating Him as though He were a dangerous lawbreaker.

22:53, 54 This is Jesus' first appearance before Annas (see John 18:13).

22:55–59 for he is a Galilean: According to Mark 14:70, Peter's accent gave him away as being from the same region as Jesus.

22:60–62 looked at Peter: Apparently a window opened into the courtyard, and Peter knew that the Lord was aware of his denials. **wept bitterly:** The Lord knew Peter better than Peter knew himself (v. 34). Peter was greatly grieved that he had failed Jesus.

22:63 mocked Him and beat Him: Matthew 26:67 and Mark 14:65 further describe the abuse of Jesus at the hands of the soldiers as involving speaking, spitting, and slapping.

22:64 Prophesy: The soldiers mocked Jesus. They covered His head and asked Him to identify who was striking Him.

22:65–68 The description here is of a major morning trial that involved the entire **council** or Sanhedrin. This trial violated various Jewish legal rules given in later sources: meeting on the morning of a feast; meeting at Caiaphas's home; trying a defendant without defense; and reaching the verdict in one day instead of the two days that were required for capital cases.

22:69 Hereafter means "from now on." Jesus' point was that authority would reside with Him from this point on. **on the right hand of the power of God:** This reply is what convicted Him. It was not blasphemous to claim to be Messiah. What was blasphemous was the claim to be the Judge of the Jewish people, with God's authority.

22:70 Son of God: The Jewish leaders sensed that Jesus was asserting a unique and highly exalted relationship with God, making Himself the equal of God. In their view, this was not possible.

22:71 from His own mouth: The Jewish leaders concluded that Jesus made a confession of guilt. His claim to a relationship to God in which He exercises authority like God's.

23:1 The Roman ruler **Pilate** was responsible for collecting taxes and keeping the peace. It may be that he was in Jerusalem for judicial hearings.

23:2 began to accuse: Three charges were lodged against Jesus: **perverting the nation, forbidding** payment of taxes to Rome, claiming to be the **Christ.** The first charge, involved disturbing the peace. The other charges had been construed as challenges to Rome.

23:3 It is as you say: Jesus gave Pilate the same qualified reply He gave the Sanhedrin in 22:67, 68, 70. Jesus is a king, but He was not a threat to Rome (see John 18:36).

23:4 I find no fault: Pilate's verdict was that Jesus was innocent. This is the first of several such declarations in this chapter (vv. 14, 15, 22, 41).

23:5 By mentioning the charge that Jesus stirred up the **people,** the leaders suggested

that Pilate risked being found derelict in his duty if he let Jesus go.

23:6, 7 Herod's jurisdiction: Herod was responsible for Galilee, so Pilate "passed the buck" for the ruling and showed political courtesy at the same time.

23:8 he was exceedingly glad: Herod's curiosity about Jesus is noted in 9:7–9.

23:9, 10 answered him nothing: Jesus may have remained silent because He had already been declared innocent and yet was still subjected to trial (see Acts 8:32, 33).

23:11–14 After deciding that he had nothing to fear from Jesus, Herod and his men entertained themselves at Jesus' expense. Dressing him in a **gorgeous robe** was probably a sarcastic reference to Jesus' claim to be king.

23:15, 16 chastise Him and release Him: Pilate hoped that a public whipping might satisfy the crowd and tame Jesus, avoiding the need to resort to the death penalty.

23:17 it was necessary ... to release one to them: Pilate wanted to take advantage of this custom and let Jesus go (see Matt. 27:15; Mark 15:6).

23:18, 19 Away with this Man: The entire crowd is portrayed as wanting Jesus to die. **Barabbas:** The people preferred that a seditious murderer be freed instead of Jesus.

23:20–23 Luke mentions the **chief priests** separately from the crowd since they were the instigators of the plot against Jesus. Because Pilate feared the will of the people, he agreed to put to death One he knew to be innocent (see Acts 4:25–27).

23:24–26 Jesus was apparently unable to carry His own cross. **Simon a Cyrenian,** a man from a city of Libya, was chosen to carry the cross for Him (see Acts 6:9; 11:20; 13:1). Mark 15:20, 21 mentions Simon's sons, Rufus and Alexander, believers known to Mark's audience.

23:27 The events of vv. 27–31 are unique to Luke's account. While such mourning for the dead was required by custom in the ancient world, Jesus' reply seems to take the people's mourning as sincere.

23:28 do not weep for Me: Jesus pointed out that their weeping should be for Jerusalem, since judgment was going to fall on the city. Jerusalem represents the nation of Israel.

23:29, 30 barren: In the days of judgment, the childless, who were usually thought of as cursed, would be better off than those with family because the terror of that time would be so great. **Fall on us:** Fear of the judgment would be so great that people would prefer to die than suffer what was coming.

23:31 what will be done in the dry: The idea is, "If Jesus, the living tree, has not been spared, how much more will dead wood not be spared." This is Jesus' final lament over Israel.

23:32 Jesus' prediction of dying with the transgressors (see 22:37; see also Isaiah's prediction in Is. 53:12) was fulfilled when two **criminals** accompanied Him to death.

23:33 The name of the place in Aramaic is Golgotha, which means "Skull." **Calvary** is the Latin name for Golgotha.

 IN DEPTH | **Crucifixion**

The Romans used one of the most painful methods of torture ever devised to put Jesus to death (Luke 23:33). Crucifixion was used by many nations of the ancient world, including Assyria, Media, and Persia. The idea may have originated from the practice of hanging up the bodies of executed persons on stakes for public display. This discouraged civil disobedience and mocked defeated military foes (Gen. 40:19; 1 Sam. 31:8–13).

Crucifixion on a stake or cross was practiced by the Greeks, notably Alexander the Great, who hung 2,000 people on crosses when the city of Tyre was destroyed. During the period between Greek and Roman control of Palestine, the Jewish ruler Alexander Jannaeus crucified eight hundred Pharisees who opposed him. But such executions were condemned as detestable and abnormal even in that day as well as by the later Jewish historian Josephus.

From the early days of the Roman Republic, death on the cross was used for rebellious slaves and bandits. The practice continued well beyond the NT period as one of the supreme punishments for military and political crimes such as desertion, spying, revealing secrets, rebellion, and sedition. However, following the conversion of Constantine, the cross became a sacred symbol and its use as a means of execution was abolished.

Crucifixion involved attaching the victim with nails through the wrists or with leather thongs to a crossbeam attached to a vertical stake. Sometimes blocks or pins were put on the stake to give the victim support as he hung suspended from the crossbeam. At times the feet were also nailed to the vertical stake. As the victim hung dangling by the arms, blood could no longer circulate to his vital organs. Only by supporting himself on the seat or pin could he gain some relief.

But gradually exhaustion set in, and death followed, although usually not for several days. If the victim had been severely beaten, he would not live that long. To hasten death, the executioners sometimes broke the victim's legs with a club. Then he could no longer support his body to keep blood circulating, and death by suffocation quickly followed. Usually bodies were left to rot or to be eaten by scavengers.

To the Jewish people, crucifixion represented the most disgusting form of death: "He who is hanged is accursed of God" (Deut. 21:23). Yet the Jewish council sought and obtained Roman authorization to have Jesus crucified (Mark 15:13–15).

The apostle Paul summed up the crucial importance of His manner of death when he wrote, "We preach Christ crucified, to the Jews a stumbling block and to the Greeks foolishness, but to those who are called, both Jews and Greeks, Christ the power of God and the wisdom of God" (1 Cor. 1:23, 24). Out of the ugliness and agony of crucifixion, God accomplished the greatest good of all—the redemption of sinners.

23:34 Those who put Jesus to death acted in ignorance, not really understanding who it was they were killing. Jesus' example of interceding for His executioners was followed by Stephen in Acts 7:60.

23:35, 36 The drink referred to here was probably **wine** vinegar, which was inexpensive and quenched thirst better than water. It was a drink of the poor.

23:37, 38 KING OF THE JEWS: This inscription, which gave the charge against Christ, was written in three languages. Jesus was killed for who He is.

23:39, 40 Not everyone rejected Jesus at His Crucifixion. The second criminal rebuked his companion in death, warning that he should fear God.

23:41 we indeed justly: One criminal knew the difference between those who had sinned and deserved to die and the One who did not.

23:42 remember me: While others mocked Jesus' seeming inability to save Himself, this thief recognized that Jesus would live and rule. He wanted to be saved and take part in Christ's kingdom.

23:43 you will be with Me: Jesus promised eternal life to the thief, doing what the mockers had asked Him to do in v. 39.

23:44 sixth hour … ninth hour: The first hour was sunrise, so the time was 12 P.M. to 3 P.M.

23:45 the sun was darkened: This testimony of creation was designed to signal the importance of Jesus' death. The tearing of the veil illustrated a renewed access to God through the death of Christ (see v. 43; Heb 9; 10).

23:46 into Your hands: Jesus' final words are from Ps. 31:5, where this is the prayer of trust from a righteous sufferer. Jesus exercised that faith here.

23:47, 48 If Jesus was **righteous** and innocent, then He is who He claimed to be. Thus a second figure besides the thief on the cross had insight into Jesus' death.

23:49 The Galileans **stood at a distance** to watch Jesus' Crucifixion. Their sadness is further explained in 24:16–20.

23:50 Joseph, a council member: Not every Jewish religious leader opposed Jesus.

23:51 He had not consented: Joseph did not agree with the sentence on Jesus. Joseph may not have attended the trial.

23:52 the body of Jesus: There is no doubt that Jesus died. Efforts to explain the Resurrection as something like a return from a coma are more unreasonable than the Resurrection itself.

23:53 Jesus was given an honorable burial (see Deut. 21:22, 23). The **linen** was probably fine cloth. The **tomb** had a stone to cover it in order to make it secure (see Matt. 27:66). Guards were posted to stop anyone trying to steal the body (Matt. 27:65, 66).

23:54, 55 Jesus was buried late on Friday, on the day called **Preparation,** when everything was made ready for the Sabbath.

23:56 prepared spices and fragrant oils: On Friday the women prepared for the anointing of Jesus' body on the day after the Sabbath, since they could not make preparations on the Sabbath. The spices were used to delay decay and lessen the odor of the body.

24:1, 2 Matthew 28:2 mentions that an earthquake moved the **stone,** which would have fit in a channel in front of the entrance to the tomb. Moving the stone would have been possible, for a group of people. The earthquake settles the question of how the stone was moved.

24:3–5 It may be assumed that the **two men** who appeared were angels, based on the way their clothes are described as **shining garments** (see also v. 23). **Why do you seek the living:** Angels announced that Jesus was alive. Anointing Him would not be necessary.

24:6 is risen … Remember: The women were reminded that Jesus had predicted His Resurrection as far back as **Galilee** (see 9:22).

24:7–10 Three women are named: **Mary Magdalene** (see 8:2; Matt. 28:1; Mark 16:1; John 20:1), **Joanna** (8:3), and **Mary the mother of James** (see Mark 15:40; 16:1). Other women also joined in the report of Jesus' Resurrection.

24:11 they did not believe: The disciples thought the women's story was nonsense.

24:12 Peter arose and ran: Having already experienced a fulfilled prediction of the Lord (22:54–62), Peter hurried to the tomb to check out the women's story. It is hard to say whether Peter believed in the Resurrection when he left the tomb.

24:13–21 Jesus of Nazareth ... a Prophet: These disciples on the road to Emmaus regarded Jesus as the Revealer of God's way and the Doer of His work. **He who was going to redeem Israel:** The disciples had hoped that God would once again save Israel through Jesus.

24:22, 23 a vision of angels ... said He was alive: The women reported that there was no body found in Jesus' tomb, and that angels had announced to them that Jesus lives. The fact that the men were still sad indicates that they did not believe the report.

24:24 As far as the disciples were concerned, there was still no decisive proof of Jesus' Resurrection. They wanted to **see** the resurrected Jesus.

24:25 slow of heart to believe: Jesus rebuked His companions and reminded them of the things that the prophets taught.

24:26 The prophets taught the suffering of **the Christ** and His entrance into **glory.** Jesus used the title Christ (Messiah) to refer to Himself; the disciples called Him a prophet (v. 19).

24:27 Going from the books of **Moses** to the **Prophets,** Jesus provided an overview of God's plan in the Scriptures.

24:28–34 Before the two travelers could report their experience, the other disciples reported that **Simon** had seen Jesus as well.

24:35–37 a spirit: The disciples had a difficult time adjusting to the fact that the raised Jesus was in their midst. They believed they were seeing a heavenly apparition (see v. 39).

24:38 why do doubts arise: Jesus' appearances were designed to reassure the disciples about the reality of His vindication.

24:39 Jesus pointed out that a raised body is not a disembodied spirit. The presence of **flesh and bones** indicates that Jesus had been raised bodily, and that He was not a hallucination.

24:40–43 The physical nature of Jesus' resurrected body was confirmed by the fact that he **ate** something.

24:44, 45 The plan of God as outlined **in the Law of Moses and the Prophets and the Psalms** was being fulfilled in Jesus. This threefold categorization of the ancient Scriptures summarizes the contents of the Old Testament. **opened their understanding:** The disciples' comprehension involved seeing how God's plan, as outlined in the Scriptures, fits together.

24:46 Christ to suffer and to rise: Two parts of God's plan had been fulfilled. Jesus had been crucified and raised from the dead.

24:47 Jesus had been considered a pretender and a blasphemer. After His Resurrection, people had to change their minds and serve Him for who He really is, the Son of God. This is the message Peter would preach at Pentecost, a message that would result in thousands of people declaring Jesus as their Lord. **remission of sins:** The content of the disciples' preaching would center on God's gracious offer of forgiveness to all who would believe (see Acts 2:38; 10:43). **in His name:** This is a reference to Jesus' authority. The disciples' mission would begin in **Jerusalem** where Jesus died; from there, it would spread out into the entire world (see Acts 1:8).

24:48 witnesses: Jesus pointed out that the disciples were called to testify to His work.

24:49 Promise of My Father: This is a reference to the baptism of the Holy Spirit at Pentecost (see Acts 2). **tarry in the city of Jerusalem:** The disciples were to remain in Jerusalem until the Spirit empowered them on the day of Pentecost.

24:50 Bethany was just outside Jerusalem (19:29).

24:51 carried up into heaven: This is the first description of the Ascension. Luke may be summarizing here what happened 40 days later to create a link to the Book of Acts.

24:52–53 continually in the temple praising and blessing God: The disciples' sorrow over Jesus' death had been totally reversed (v. 17). Now the disciples awaited the promise of God with joy. Luke's account continues in the Book of Acts. There he records the disciple's initial response to Jesus' commission to preach to all the nations (v. 47).

John

Introduction

The Gospel of John is the only book in the Bible that states its purpose clearly and succinctly: It was written to tell people how to find eternal life (20:31). This sets the Gospel of John apart from the other Gospels. Every chapter presents evidence for His divine authority. According to John, believing that Jesus is the Son of God, the Savior of the world, is the beginning of eternal life (3:14–17).

The author of the Gospel of John does not identify himself by name, but his identity can be learned from the dialogue recorded in 21:19–24. The author calls himself "the disciple whom Jesus loved" (21:20), a designation that occurs four other times in the book (13:23; 19:26; 20:2; 21:7). This was the same "disciple who ... wrote these things" (21:24). It is reasonable to conclude that this book was written by the apostle John. This conclusion is supported by early Christians such as Polycarp (A.D. 60–155), who was a follower of John. Conservative scholars typically date the book between A.D. 85 and A.D. 95.

The Gospel of John is a persuasive argument for the deity of Jesus. It concentrates on presenting Jesus as the Word, that is, God (1:1) who became a man (1:14). Thus John meticulously records the statements and describes the miracles of Jesus that can only be attributed to God Himself.

Jesus called Himself the bread of life (6:35, 41, 48, 51), the light of the world (8:12; 9:5), the door for the sheep (10:7, 9), the good shepherd (10:11, 14), the Resurrection and the life (11:25), the way, the truth, the life (14:6), and the true vine (15:1, 5). Each of these statements begins with the words, "I am," recalling God's revelation of His name, "I AM," to Moses (see Ex. 3:14). These are Jesus' clear claims to deity: He was not a mere man.

Then there are the signs of Jesus' deity. Miracles in the Gospel of John are called "signs" because they point to Jesus' divine nature. John records seven such signs (see 2:1–11; 4:46–54; 5:1–9; 6:1–14; 6:15–21; 9:1–7; and 11:38–44).

1:1 In the beginning: Genesis 1:1 starts with the moment of creation and moves forward to the creation of humanity. John 1:1 starts with creation and contemplates eternity past. The fact that **the Word was with God** suggests a face-to-face relationship. Thus the word *with* indicates a personal relationship, but also implies equal status with the Father (see 1 John 1:2). Moreover, **the Word was God.** This is a declaration of Christ's deity.

1:2 Neither the Person of Christ, nor His Sonship, came into being at a point in time. Rather, the Father and the Son have always been in loving fellowship with each other.

1:3 All things were made through Him: God the Father created the world (Gen. 1:1) through God the Son (Col. 1:16; Heb. 1:2). All creation was made through Him.

1:4 Note that **life** is not said to have been created; life existed in Christ (5:26; 6:57; 10:10). Our existence, spiritually and physically, depends on God's sustaining power. In contrast, the Son has life in Himself from all eternity. The life, Jesus Christ, is also **the light of men.** As the light, Jesus Christ reveals both sin and God to humans (see Ps. 36:9).

1:5 light shines in the darkness: Christ entered this dark world to give it spiritual light (see Is. 9:2). The word translated **comprehend** can mean (1) to take hold of; (2) to overpower; or (3) to understand. Humans did not appropriate or understand the light, nor did they overtake or overpower it. Although Satan and his forces resist the light, they cannot thwart its power.

1:6 John the Baptist is contrasted with Jesus Christ. Jesus is God (v. 1); John **was a man sent from God.** Jesus was the Light (v. 4); John was the lamp that bore witness to the Light (vv. 7, 8).

1:7, 8 To bear witness means "to testify" or "to declare." The term is particularly important to his purpose, which is to record adequate witnesses to Jesus as the Messiah so that people might believe in Him (20:30, 31).

1:9 To give due notice to the Incarnation of Jesus, this verse may be rephrased: "That was the true Light coming into the world, which enlightens every man." Jesus became man in order to reveal the truth to all people.

1:10, 11 Receive means "to receive with favor" and implies "welcome." Instead of a welcome mat, Jesus had a door slammed in His face. The themes of rejection and reception (v. 12) introduced in the prologue (1:1–18) appear throughout the Gospel of John.

1:12 The phrase **believe in His name** occurs three times in the Gospel of John (1:12; 2:23; 3:18). *Name* does not refer to the term by which He is called, but to what His name stands for—*the Lord is salvation* (see Ex. 3:14, 15).

1:13 born ... of God: This new spiritual birth is not **of blood,** that is, by physical generation or by parents. Nor is the new birth **of the will of the flesh,** that is, by personal effort. Neither is the birth **of the will of man,** that is, something done by another individual. Eternal life is a gift to be received (4:10, 14), not a reward achieved through any human effort.

1:14 the Word became flesh: The Son of God became human, with limitations (see Phil. 2:5–8), but nothing of the essential nature of deity was lost in the Incarnation. **dwelt among us:** *Dwelt* comes from the Greek word for *tent* that was used in the Greek Old Testament for the tabernacle, where the presence of God dwelt. As God manifested His glory in the tabernacle (see Ex. 33:18), so Jesus displayed His divine presence before the apostles (18:6; 20:26, 27). **Only begotten** (3:16, 18) means unique, one of a kind. In the Gospel of John, these "born ones" are called children of God (vv. 12, 13), but Jesus Christ is the unique Son of God.

1:15 He was before me: Jesus was born after John the Baptist (see Luke 1:36) and began His ministry later than John the Baptist. Yet John the Baptist said Jesus was *before* him, meaning that Jesus' existence is from eternity past (v. 30).

1:16 Grace for grace means grace piled upon grace. The background of this doubled term, as well as the use of the term in v. 17, is found in Ex. 32–34. Moses and the people had received grace, but they were in tremendous need of more grace (Ex. 33:13).

1:17 Throughout the New Testament, **grace** is God's unmerited favor expressed to sinful humankind in the person of Jesus Christ apart from any human works or worth.

1:18 No one has seen God: God is Spirit (4:24) and is invisible (see Col. 1:15, 1 Tim. 1:17) unless God chooses to reveal Himself. Humans cannot look at God and live (Ex. 33:20). It is through seeing the Son that we see God. We cannot see Him today, but we know Him through His word. The One who is the Father's **only begotten Son** and who knows God intimately came to earth and **declared Him.** *Declared* can also mean "explained."

1:19, 20 The Jews refers to the Jewish leaders or the the Sanhedrin, who would be responsible for examining anyone thought to be a prophet. **Who are you:** John was quick to acknowledge that he was **not the Christ.,** but the rulers were concerned about maintaining peace under the eye of Rome, and they kept a close watch on all prospective messiahs.

1:21, 22 Are you Elijah The Old Testament promised that Elijah would come before the great day of the Lord (see Mal. 4:5). **Are you the Prophet:** Moses had predicted that a prophet like himself would come (see Deut. 18:15).

1:23 The voice: Christ is the Word; John the Baptist was the voice. When pressed to identify himself, John the Baptist claimed that he was the fulfillment of Is. 40:3. John was identifying himself as that voice calling people to **make straight the way of the LORD.**

1:24 The Pharisees were an influential sect that numbered about six thousand. As strict interpreters of the Law in Israel, they were extremely zealous for ritual and tradition.

1:25 Why ... do you baptize: Performing the rite of baptism was regarded as making a claim to authority. The Pharisees were asking, "By what authority do you perform this religious rite?"

1:26, 27 Undoing the sandal strap was the job of a slave. John was saying that "Jesus Christ is the living Lord and I am the voice, His servant and slave. Actually, I'm not even worthy to be His slave."

1:28 The location of **Bethabara** is unknown. Some think that Bethany is meant, but not the same Bethany as the familiar one near Jerusalem. **Beyond the Jordan** means east of the Jordan River. Evidently, this was John's normal place for baptizing.

1:29 The Lamb of God: In the Old Testament, the Israelites sacrificed lambs at the Passover feast (see Ex. 12:21) and as offerings (see Lev. 14:10–25). Jesus Christ is the Lamb that God would give as a sacrifice for the sins of the world (see Is. 52:13—53:12).

1:30, 31 I did not know Him: John and Jesus were cousins, so they probably knew each other. But John apparently did not know that Jesus was the Messiah. God had given John a sign by which he would know the Messiah—the descending of the Holy Spirit as a dove.

1:32–34 He who baptizes with the Holy Spirit: Seven times the New Testament mentions this ministry of Jesus. Five are prophetic (see also Matt. 3:11; Mark 1:8; Luke 3:16; Acts 1:5); one is historical (see Acts 11:16–18); one is doctrinal (see 1 Cor. 12:13).

1:35 One of the **two** disciples of John the Baptist was Andrew (v. 40). The other is not named but was probably John, the author of this Gospel.

1:36–41 He first found: As soon as he came to faith, Andrew must have sought out his brother Simon Peter. The excitement of discovering the Son of God, the Messiah (see Matt. 26:63, 64; Mark 14:61, 62; Luke 22:67–70), was contagious among the early believers.

1:42 he brought him to Jesus: Andrew appears two more times in the Gospel of John (6:4–9; 12:20–22); both times he is bringing someone to Jesus. **Cephas** is the Aramaic word for "rock" (see Matt. 16:18).

1:43, 44 From this verse, it might appear that **Philip** followed Jesus without being evangelized by another disciple. But v. 44 says that Andrew and Peter were from the same city as Philip, suggesting that they had talked to him.

1:45 Nathanael is not mentioned in the synoptic Gospels. But in every list of the apostles in Matthew, Mark, and Luke, the name Bartholomew is listed with Philip, as Nathanael is linked with Philip here. It is likely that Nathanael and Bartholomew were the same person.

1:46 Nazareth: Nathanael knew that the Old Testament prophets had predicted that the Messiah would be born in Bethlehem. Nathanael simply could not believe that such a significant person as the Messiah could come from such an insignificant place as Nazareth.

1:47 an Israelite indeed: In his younger life the first Israelite, Jacob, was a cunning, scheming man full of **deceit.** Nathanael was an Israelite, a descendant of Jacob, but he was genuine and sincere. Jesus read Nathanael's character like an open book (2:24).

1:48, 49 under the fig tree: In the Old Testament, this expression often suggests being safe and at leisure (see 1 Kin. 4:25; Mic. 4:4). Nathanael may have been meditating under the tree about the dream of Jacob referred to in vv. 50, 51. **I saw you:** Jesus showed His supernatural knowledge. Apparently, this incident convinced Nathanael that Jesus had to be the **Son of God,** the **King of Israel** (20:31).

1:50 greater things: Jesus assured Nathanael that he would see even greater manifestations. Jesus' statement may have referred to the miracles performed in chs. 2—11; it may also refer to the future glory of Christ as the coming Son of Man (see 1:51; Dan. 7:13).

1:51 Jacob had a vision of angels ascending and descending a ladder from heaven (Gen. 28:12). The thought here is similar, namely that there will be communication between heaven and earth. **Son of Man,** an expression used in Dan. 7:13 of a heavenly being, was Jesus' favorite designation of Himself (Matt. 8:20; Mark 2:10).

2:1, 2 The third day refers to the third day from the last day mentioned (1:43). To walk from where John was baptizing to Cana would probably have taken three days. The wording of the text, **the mother of Jesus was there … Jesus and His disciples were invited,** suggests that Jesus and His disciples were invited because of Mary.

2:3 A wedding feast often lasted for a week. To run out of **wine** at such an important event would have been humiliating for the bride and groom.

2:4 My hour has not yet come seems to mean that the time for Jesus to publicly work miracles, declaring Himself the Messiah, had not yet come.

2:5 Jesus' response to Mary seems to have been a refusal to do anything about the situation. Perhaps something in the tone of Jesus' voice let Mary know that He would grant her request.

2:6 six waterpots: Each waterpot held **twenty or thirty gallons,** for a total of 120 to 180 gallons of the finest wine (v. 10). **purification of the Jews:** Strict Jews washed their hands before a meal, between courses, and after the meal. Because the roads were not paved and people wore sandals, water was needed for foot washing. At a large Jewish wedding, a large amount of water would have been required.

2:7–10 master of the feast: At a Jewish wedding, one of the guests served as a governor of the feast. Our modern equivalent is probably a head waiter. **the good wine:** Usually the better wine was served first. Then, after the guests' palates were dulled, the everyday wine was served. But this wine was so good that the master of the feast was surprised to see it being served late in the celebration.

2:11, 12 In the Gospel of John, the miracles of Jesus are called **signs,** indicating His messiahship. John records seven signs (see also 4:46–54; 5:1–9; 6:1–14; 6:15–21; 9:1–7; 11:38–44). This sign signified Christ's **glory**—His deity.

2:13 the Passover of the Jews: Every male Jew was required to go to Jerusalem three times a year (see Ex. 23:14–19; Lev. 23). **Jerusalem:** The synoptic Gospels—Matthew, Mark, and Luke—concentrate on Jesus' Galilean ministry. John focuses on Jesus' ministry in Jerusalem.

2:14 The synoptic Gospels place the cleansing of the temple at the conclusion of Jesus' ministry (see Matt. 21:12, 13), whereas John puts it at the beginning (vv. 14–17). Apparently Jesus cleansed the temple two different times. The Law of Moses required that every Jewish male over nineteen years of age pay a temple tax (see Lev. 1:3; Deut. 17:1). As a result, tax collectors and inspectors of sacrificial animals were present at the temple. These officials would not accept

secular coins because they had an image of the Roman emperor, whom the pagans worshiped as a god. So in order to accommodate visitors in need of animals and the right kinds of coins, animal merchants and moneychangers set up shop in the outer court of the temple. These inspectors, collectors, and exchangers, however, charged high prices.

2:15 Jesus' **whip** was probably more a symbol than a weapon; nevertheless, it was effective in scattering the moneychangers. Jesus' actions were a sign of authority and judgment.

2:16, 17 The cleansing of the temple was the first public presentation of Jesus to Israel; He presented Himself as Messiah. The expression **My Father's house** was a distinct claim to messiahship.

2:18 The Jews apparently refers to the religious authorities of Israel (1:19), who also understood that Jesus was representing Himself as the Messiah; therefore, they asked for a **sign** (see 1 Cor. 1:22).

2:19 Destroy this temple: Jesus was not talking about the physical building; He was speaking of His death. **I will raise it up:** Note that Jesus did not say, "I will build it again." He was referring to His Resurrection, three days after His death (see Matt. 12:39; 16:4).

2:20 forty-six years: Herod the Great began restoring the temple in 20 B.C. The work was not finished at the time of this conversation.

2:21, 22 The disciples understood that Jesus was the Messiah (v. 17; 1:41, 45, 49), but they did not understand that He was speaking of the Resurrection of His body until it actually happened.

2:23 many believed in His name: John's purpose in recording Jesus' miracles was for people to believe and have eternal life (20:30, 31).

2:24, 25 Commit is the same Greek word translated *believe* in v. 23. There is a play on words here. These individuals trusted Jesus, but Jesus did not entrust Himself to them. Jesus fully understood the depth of trust of those who were following Him; some would stay, but many would fall away.

3:1 The phrase **ruler of the Jews** indicates that **Nicodemus** was a member of the

Jewish council, the group that had sent a committee to investigate John the Baptist (1:24).

3:2 The fact that Nicodemus came to Jesus **by night** may reveal the timidity of his faith (12:42); however, his faith was developing (7:50, 51; 19:39).

3:3, 4 born again: The Greek word translated *again* can mean either "from above" or "anew." The new birth is the act by which God imparts spiritual life to a person who trusts Christ. Without this spiritual birth, a person cannot enter **the kingdom of God** (v. 5).

3:5 There are several interpretations of the phrase **born of water and the Spirit.** (1) Jesus was referring to water baptism (see Acts 10:43–47). (2) Water is to be understood as a symbol for the Holy Spirit. (3) Water is to be understood as a symbol of the Word of God. (4) Jesus used the phrase "born of water" to refer to physical birth. (5) Jesus used the phrase "born of water" to refer to John the Baptist's baptism. (6) Jesus used the Old Testament imagery of "water" and "wind" to refer to the work of God from above.

3:6 That which is born of the flesh is flesh: Flesh cannot be made into spirit. A person must experience a spiritual rebirth (v. 7).

3:7 In the Greek text, **you** is plural. In v. 2, Nicodemus used the word "we," probably referring to the Jewish ruling council, the Sanhedrin. Here Jesus spoke not only to Nicodemus, but to all whom he represented.

3:8 Jesus used **the wind** as an illustration of the work of the Holy Spirit. As the wind seemingly blows where it wills, so the Holy Spirit sovereignly works.

3:9, 10 Jesus answered Nicodemus's question (vv. 13–15), but first He rebuked Nicodemus for being a **teacher** of the Hebrew Scriptures and not knowing about spiritual birth (see Is. 44:3; Ezek. 36:26, 27).

3:11 you do not receive: Again *you* is plural (v. 7). Jesus rebuked not only Nicodemus, but the other Pharisees as well.

3:12 Earthly things refers to things that occur on earth, like the new birth (vv. 3, 5–7), the wind (v. 8), and perhaps miracles. **Heavenly things** refers to events like Christ's

Ascension (6:61, 62) and the coming of the Holy Spirit (16:7). Nicodemus may have believed in Jesus' miracles (v. 2); the majority of the Jewish council did not (v. 11).

3:13 In v. 9, Nicodemus, referring to the new birth, asks, "How can these things be?" Here Jesus answers the question. New birth is by **the Son,** by the Cross (v. 14), and by faith (v. 15).

3:14 Every time the words **lifted up** occur in the Gospel of John there is a reference to Jesus' death (8:28; 12:32, 34).

3:15 This is the first time **eternal life** is mentioned in John's Gospel (see 4:36; 5:39; 6:54, 68; 10:28; 12:25; 17:2, 3). When a person trusts Christ, he or she is born again and receives eternal and spiritual life.

3:16 God so loved the world: God's love is not restricted to any one nation or to any spiritual elite. *World* here may also include all of creation (see Rom. 8:19–22; Col. 1:20).

3:17 At His first coming, Jesus came so that **the world through Him might be saved.** When Jesus comes again, He will come in judgment.

3:18 To believe is to receive life (vv. 15, 16) and avoid judgment. A person **who does not believe** not only misses life, but is **condemned already.**

3:19 Condemnation refers to the reason for judgment. The **light** referred to here is Jesus, the light of the world (1:7–9; 8:12; 9:5).

3:20 People offer many excuses for not accepting Christ. But the ultimate reason is that they do not want to.

3:21 The one **who does the truth** (see 1 John 1:5) is obviously already a believer because his or her **deeds** are **done in God.** A person who **comes to the light** openly identifies with the light so that his or her works can be seen as things done in union with God.

3:22, 23 baptized: The impression here is that Jesus baptized. John corrects this idea in 4:2. Jesus provided the authority, but the disciples performed the baptisms.

3:24 The synoptic Gospels give the impression that the imprisonment of John the Baptist came right after the baptism of Jesus. This verse indicates that there was an interval between Jesus' baptism and John's imprisonment, during which both ministered.

3:25 The disciples of Jesus and the disciples of John were both baptizing people; as a result, a question arose. The question came from John's disciples when they entered into a discussion with the Jews. **Purification** here refers to baptism.

3:26 John the Baptist's disciples were concerned that one of his "disciples," Jesus, was competing with and surpassing him. They exaggerated the predicament, saying **all are coming to Him.** They were concerned that John was losing his audience to another preacher.

3:27, 28 John explained that he could not accept the position of supremacy that his disciples wanted to thrust upon him because he had not received it **from heaven.**

3:29 John compared himself to **the friend of the bridegroom,** who arranged the preliminaries of the wedding, managed the wedding, and presided at the wedding feast. When the friend of the bridegroom finished his job, he had to get out of the way. His **joy** came from the success of the bridegroom. John was content to be a "voice" (1:23) and a friend.

3:30 John the Baptist insisted that Jesus Christ had to **increase** in popularity and that he, John, had to **decrease.** John explained that Jesus had to increase because of (1) His divine origin (v. 31), (2) His divine teaching (vv. 32–34), and (3) His divine authority (vv. 35, 36).

3:31 He who comes from above refers to Jesus Christ. **He who is of the earth** refers to John the Baptist. Jesus, on the other hand, is from heaven and **above all.**

3:32 no one receives His testimony: No one, apart from God's work in him or her (6:44), can accept Jesus Christ.

3:33 Certified means "to seal." In a society where many people could not read, seals were used to convey a clear message, even to the illiterate. A seal indicated ownership to all and expressed a person's personal guarantee. To receive Jesus' testimony is to certify that **God is true** about what He has sealed.

3:34 Unlike human teachers, Jesus was not given **the Spirit by measure**—that is, in a limited way (see Is. 11:1, 2). The Holy Spirit was given to Jesus completely. All three Persons of the Trinity are referred to in this

verse: God the Father sent Christ the Son and gave Him the Holy Spirit.

3:35 God the Father gave Jesus **all things,** including the authority to give life (5:21) and judge (5:22).

3:36 The person who **believes** has eternal life as a present possession. Likewise, the one who refuses to believe on Christ has the **wrath of God** abiding on him or her as a present reality.

4:1, 2 Christ's success in winning disciples had created jealousy among John's followers and provoked questions among the Pharisees. Since Jesus did not want to be drawn into a controversy over baptism, He left Judea for Galilee (v. 3).

4:3 again: Jesus had been to Galilee before (1:43—2:12). He had left Capernaum to go to Jerusalem for the Passover.

4:4 The shortest route from Judea in the south to Galilee in the north went through Samaria. Christ **needed to go through Samaria** if He wanted to travel the direct route. The Jews often avoided Samaria by going around it along the Jordan River. The hatred between the Jews and Samaritans went back to the days of the Exile. When the northern kingdom was exiled to Assyria, King Sargon of Assyria repopulated the area with captives from other lands. The intermarriage of these foreigners and the Jews who had been left in the land complicated the ancestry of the Samaritans. The Jews hated the Samaritans and considered them to be no longer "pure" Jews. Jesus, however, had no such bias.

4:5 Jacob had purchased a parcel of ground (see Gen. 33:18, 19), which he bequeathed on his deathbed to Joseph (Gen. 48:21, 22).

4:6–10 Living water (see 7:37–39; Is. 12:1–6) springs from an unfailing source and is ever-flowing. Jesus, of course, was talking about eternal life (see 4:14; Rom. 6:23).

4:11–15 The Samaritan woman did not comprehend Jesus' spiritual message. She was thinking only of physical water and could not understand how Jesus could provide water without a way to draw it.

4:16 Jesus mentioned the woman's **husband** in order to expose her sin (v. 18).

4:17–19 Because of what Jesus told her about herself, the woman concluded that Jesus

Christ was a prophet, a person with supernatural knowledge.

4:20 By mentioning the two different worship sites, the woman was perhaps trying to shift the conversation away from the subject of her own sins to theological questions. The Jews insisted that the exclusive place of worship was Jerusalem. But the Samaritans had set up a rival worship site on Mount Gerizim, which according to their tradition was where Abraham went to sacrifice Isaac.

4:21, 22 Salvation is of the Jews means that the Messiah would come from the Jewish people.

4:23, 24 God is Spirit … worship Him … in spirit and truth: When people are born of the Spirit, they can commune with God anywhere. *Spirit* is the opposite of what is material and earthly, for example, Mount Gerizim. *Truth* is what is in harmony with the nature and will of God. Here the truth is specifically the worship of God through Jesus Christ. The issue is not *where* a person worships, but *how* and *whom.*

4:25 The Samaritans believed that the Prophet of Deut. 18:15 would teach **all things** when he came.

4:26 I … am He: Using the same words that God used when He revealed Himself to Moses (see Ex. 3:14), Jesus clearly stated that He is the Messiah.

4:27–29 all things that I ever did: In her excitement, the woman did not report what Jesus actually told her, but what He *could have* told her. Note the woman's spiritual journey. She first viewed Christ as a Jew (v. 9), then as a prophet (v. 19), and finally as the Messiah.

4:30–34 My food is to do the will of Him who sent Me: This food is not simply knowing the will of God, but doing it. This verse highlights the obedience of Jesus to God in His ministry.

4:35 In vv. 35–38, Jesus offered His disciples an opportunity to do something that would be "food" for them. He was speaking about the Samaritans. In them, He saw an opportunity for a spiritual **harvest.**

4:36 The reaper of a spiritual harvest **receives wages**—that is, fruit which brings joy. In this case, Jesus sowed by giving the message

to the woman. He was about to reap because He would see the whole city saved.

4:37, 38 Jesus applied what He had just said to His disciples. The **others** may have been John the Baptist and his disciples. They had labored in Judea (3:22–36). Thus, Jesus' disciples were reaping what others had sowed (vv. 1, 2).

4:39–42 The title **Savior of the world** is used only here and in 1 John 4:14. The Jews of Jesus' day taught that to approach God one first had to be a Jew. By including this incident in the Gospel, John demonstrates that Jesus is for all people of the world.

4:43, 44 His own country has been taken to mean: (1) Judea, (2) Nazareth, or (3) Galilee. Having no honor or reception in Nazareth, Jesus went elsewhere in Galilee.

4:45 The feast refers to the Passover (see 2:13–25). The Galileans who had gone to the feast received Jesus when He came to Galilee.

4:46–49 Nobleman is literally royal officer, one in service of the king. Herod Antipas was technically the "tetrarch" of Galilee, but he was referred to as a king.

4:50–54 The miracle that Jesus performed was His **second sign** (see also 2:11), so thatthe people might believe that Jesus is the Christ, the Son of God, and that by believing they might have life (20:31). When the Jewish nobleman realized that his son had been healed, he knew that Jesus was more than a mere mortal. He placed his faith in Jesus and was born again.

5:1 The **feast of the Jews** is probably not the Passover, which John usually refers to by name (2:13; 6:4; 11:55). It may have been the Feast of Tabernacles.

5:2 The pool of **Bethesda** was a double pool surrounded by colonnades on four sides, with a fifth colonnade standing on the dividing wall that separated the northern and southern pools.

5:3–9 John records this miracle because it was a witness to Jesus' deity. Jesus Himself told John the Baptist that the proof of His messiahship was that the lame would walk (see Matt. 11:1–5). Carrying a **bed** on **the Sabbath** was considered a violation of the Law of Moses (v. 10).

5:10 The Jews probably refers to Jewish leaders who were members of the council. Over the years, the Jewish leaders had amassed thousands of rules and regulations about the Sabbath. By Jesus' day, they had 39 different classifications of work. According to them, carrying furniture and even providing medical treatment on the Sabbath were forbidden. Jesus did not break the Law; He violated the *traditions* of the Pharisees which had grown up around the Law.

5:11–13 The sick man was healed without exercising any faith. He did not know who Jesus was when he was healed.

5:14–16 This is the first recorded declaration of open hostility toward Jesus in the Gospel of John.

5:17, 18 My Father: Jesus is "the only begotten Son" (1:14, 18; 3:16, 18)—the unique Son of God. Here He claims not only a unique relationship with God the Father, but also equality with God in nature. Since God continually does good works without allowing Himself to stop on the Sabbath, the Son does likewise. Certainly the Jewish leaders understood the implications of Jesus' claims (v. 18).

5:19 The Son can do nothing of Himself means that action by the Son apart from the Father is impossible because of the unity of the Father and the Son (v. 17).

5:20 The Son does what the Father does (v. 19) because **the Father loves the Son.** Moreover, because the Father loves the Son, He reveals all to Him. The Father would show the Son **greater works** than the healing of the sick man. Jesus would raise the dead (v. 21) and eventually judge humanity (v. 22).

5:21 the Son gives life: As God raises people from the dead and gives them life, so Christ gives people spiritual life (v. 24). Jesus claimed the same power as God, thus claiming that He is equal with God.

5:22 all judgment to the Son: The Jews recognized that God alone had the right to judge humanity. In claiming that the Father committed all judgment to Him, Jesus again claimed equality with God.

5:23 honor the Son just as they honor the Father: To claim the same honor as the Father is to claim equality with the Father. Here Jesus claimed equal authority with God.

5:24 believes in Him who sent Me: The issue in this passage is the unity of the Father and the Son (vv. 17–23). All who believe in the One who sent Christ will believe in Christ.

5:25–27 Christ can give life because He Himself possesses life. He not only has a part in giving it; He is the source of it. This is another testimony to Jesus' deity.

5:28 the hour is coming: Christ not only gives spiritual life now (v. 25); He will give physical life later.

5:29 Two separate Resurrections (see Rev. 20:4, 5), the **Resurrection of life** and the **Resurrection of condemnation,** are presented here in the fashion of the Old Testament prophets, who often grouped together events of the future without distinction of time (see Is. 61:2). Jesus was teaching the universality of Resurrection, not the timing of it. **those who have done good:** The only "good" anyone can do is to believe on Christ, the One God sent (6:28, 29). All other good actions flow from that.

5:30 Christ's **judgment is righteous** because it is in accordance with God's divine will.

5:31–34 My witness is not true: If Christ were the only one bearing witness of what He was claiming, His witness would not be accepted. According to Jewish legal practice, a person's testimony about himself was not accepted in court. So in this case, Jesus offered another witness—John the Baptist (v. 33).

5:35 Jesus is the Light (1:4, 5). John was a **lamp. He was:** Jesus used the past tense because by this time John's work had been ended either by imprisonment or by death.

5:36 the works: John did not perform any signs (10:41). Those were specific works that the Son was to perform, as predicted in the Old Testament (see Is. 35:5, 6) to attest to the fact that He was sent by the Father (vv. 1–15; 2:1–11; 4:43–54).

5:37, 38 the Father Himself ... has testified: This is not a reference to the voice from heaven at the baptism of Christ, but to Scripture (vv. 38, 39).

5:39 The Jewish religious leaders of Jesus' day diligently searched the Old Testament **Scriptures,** but did not see Jesus as the Messiah and did not believe in Him (v. 38).

5:40–42 The love of God here is not love *from* God but love *for* God. Since God loves us, we should love Him (Deut. 6:5; 1 John 4:19).

5:43 Jesus came in the **Father's name,** revealing God to the people, but they rejected Him. Ironically, if someone had come **in his own name,** giving his own ideas in harmony with the people's ideas, the people would have received him.

5:44 The people did not believe in Jesus because they did not seek **honor that comes from the only God.** This honor may be similar to Paul's view of the glory that will be revealed in us in the presence of God (see Rom. 8:18).

5:45 Christ will not have to accuse the people on Judgment Day because the one in whom they placed their hope, **Moses,** will. The people will be condemned by the very Law they professed to keep.

5:46 he wrote about Me: Moses wrote about Christ in the promises to the patriarchs, in the history of the deliverance from Egypt, in the symbolic institutions of the Law, and in the prediction of a Prophet like himself (see Luke 24:25, 26). If the people had believed Moses, they would have received Jesus gladly.

5:47 you do not believe his writings: The ultimate problem was that the people did not believe the Word of God written through Moses.

6:1 After these things: About six months elapsed between 5:47 and this verse. Herod Antipas had killed John the Baptist and was seeking Jesus. The disciples had preached throughout Galilee, and many people were curious about Jesus (v. 5).

6:2–7 One denarius was a day's wage for a laborer or field hand (see Matt. 20:2). **Two hundred denarii** would have been almost two-thirds of a year's wages.

6:8, 9 Barley loaves were an inexpensive food of the common people and the poor.

6:10, 11 The miraculous multiplication of the food demonstrated Jesus' deity, because only God can create. This is the only miracle of Jesus that is recorded in all four Gospels.

6:12–14 The Prophet is a reference to Deut. 18:15. The men's statement does not necessarily indicate that they believed Jesus was

the Messiah. Some made a distinction between the Prophet and the Messiah (compare 1:20, 21).

6:15 make Him king: Moses had led the Israelites out of bondage in Egypt. Perhaps these men felt that Jesus could lead them out of bondage to the Romans. Christ was at the zenith of His popularity, and the temptation to take the kingdom without the Cross must have been great (see Matt. 4:8–10).

6:16–18 It was already dark by the time the disciples got out on the lake. The **wind** began to pick up, setting the stage for Jesus to provide another revelation of Himself.

6:19–21 This fifth miracle pointed to Jesus' deity. Only God could walk on water, calm the sea, and supernaturally transport the disciples to their destination.

6:22–25 The multitude had seen that there was only one boat **and that Jesus had not entered the boat with His disciples.** They assumed that Jesus was still there and were looking for Him.

6:26, 27 Do not labor for the food: The impression that one must work for eternal life is quickly corrected when Jesus adds **which the Son of Man will give you.** The Son provides *life* as a gift (4:10).

6:28–30 When Jesus said **believe in Him whom He sent,** the people must have understood that He was claiming to be the Messiah. Therefore, they asked for a **sign**—despite the fact that they had just witnessed the miracle of the feeding of the multitudes.

6:31 There was a tradition that said the Messiah would cause manna to fall from heaven as Moses did (see Ex. 16:4, 15). The people probably also saw this "miracle worker" as the perpetual provider of physical needs rather than spiritual ones.

6:32 The crowd misrepresented the truth, so Jesus corrected them. The manna had not come from Moses; it had been provided by God. Moreover, God still gives **true bread**—eternal life (v. 33).

6:33, 34 Lord can mean "sir," which is no doubt the meaning here (4:11, 15).

6:35 Bread of life means "bread which supplies life." Manna satisfied physical needs for a while; Christ satisfies spiritual need forever (4:13, 14).

6:36, 37 seen ... not believe: Seeing does not necessarily mean believing (v. 30; 11:46–57). On the other hand, Christ blesses those who believe without having seen (20:29).

6:38 Christ will not cast out any who come to Him because He came to do the Father's **will.**

6:39, 40 The will of the Father is twofold: (1) that all who come to the Son will be received and not lost; (2) that all who see and believe on the Son will have **everlasting life.**

6:41 The Jews referred to representatives of the council. They **complained** that Jesus said He was **the bread which came down from heaven.**

6:42 the son of Joseph: The religious leaders' proof that Jesus was not from heaven was that they knew His parents. To them, there was nothing supernatural about Jesus' origin.

6:43–45 God draws people by teaching them. Everyone who hears and learns from the Father will come to Christ.

6:46, 47 Jesus declares that only the Son **has seen the Father.** Though a person has not seen the Father, he or she can believe in Christ and have **everlasting life.**

6:48, 49 Christ is **the bread of life.** Those who believe in Him have life (v. 47). **The manna in the wilderness** did not ultimately sustain life. Those who ate it eventually died.

6:50, 51 Eats of this bread is a synonym for faith (vv. 35, 48–50).

6:52 His flesh to eat: Jesus was speaking figuratively, but the Jewish leaders took Him literally.

6:53–58 Eats My flesh and drinks My blood: Jesus had made it abundantly clear in this context that eternal life is gained by believing (vv. 29, 35, 40, 47). These verses teach that the benefits of Jesus' death must be appropriated, by faith, by each individual.

6:59, 60 Disciple here literally means "learner." Some of the crowd were students; they came to learn. Not all of these had believed in Christ. It was **hard** for the Jewish learners to accept the idea of eating flesh and drinking blood. Jews were forbidden to even taste blood.

6:61, 62 Jesus was asking, "If the thought of eating flesh and drinking blood offends you, would you be further offended at the idea of My Ascension?"

6:63, 64 Jesus was trying to get the religious leaders to see beyond the physical aspects of His teaching to the real issue—that if they believed on Him they would have everlasting life. Because they did **not believe,** many of these disciples did not follow Jesus any longer (v. 66).

6:65 The people did not believe (v. 64) because it was not **granted** to them by the Father. The multitude is told about the election of the Father (v. 37), and yet all are invited to believe (v. 40).

6:66–69 John wrote so that people might believe "that Jesus is the Christ, the Son of God" (20:31). The similarity between the confession of Peter and the purpose statement of John is inescapable.

6:70, 71 Judas Iscariot never made Peter's confession of faith in Christ. Though he was a disciple and even one of **the twelve,** it is never said that he believed.

7:1 The Jews here means the religious authorities, not the people in general (5:18). Many common people had responded to Jesus with joy (see Mark 12:37).

7:2 The **Feast of Tabernacles:** It was called the Feast of Tabernacles because for seven days the people lived in makeshift shelters or lean-tos made of branches and leaves. The feast commemorated the days when the Israelites wandered in the wilderness and lived in tents (see Lev. 23:40–43).

7:3, 4 Jesus' brothers argued, "If You are really working miracles and thus claiming to be the Messiah, do them in Jerusalem at the Feast to convince the whole nation." These words were sarcastic, as v. 5 explains.

7:5, 6 Earlier, Jesus had told His mother, "My hour has not yet come" (see 2:4; compare 12:23). Here He told His brothers also that the time for revealing Himself to the world had not yet come.

7:7–10 The world cannot hate you: The world was not about to hate Jesus' brothers, because they were part of it.

7:11–13 The Jews is a reference to the Jewish leaders, especially the members of the council (1:19).

7:14 The middle of the feast would have been the fourth day of the seven-day feast. During the first half of the festival Jesus remained in seclusion (v. 10). During the second half He began to teach publicly.

7:15 Having never studied means never having attended a rabbinical school. Similar bewilderment was later expressed about Jesus' disciples (see Acts 4:13).

7:16 not Mine, but His: Jesus' statement indicates that He did not receive His teaching from the rabbis, nor did He fabricate it. Instead His teaching came directly from God.

7:17–19 is true: The test of a teacher is whether or not he delivers God's message. Jesus gave God's message; so did Moses. The religious leaders were breaking Moses' law by seeking to kill Jesus.

7:20–24 Circumcision began with Abraham (see Gen. 17:10). The Law of Moses required infants to be circumcised on the eighth day (see Lev. 12:3). The Jews obeyed this law, even if the eighth day fell on **the Sabbath.** Jesus asked why the leaders were angry with Him for making a man **completely well** on the Sabbath.

7:25–27 The Jewish people seem to have expected the Messiah to appear suddenly from nowhere. They reasoned that since they knew where Jesus came from, He could not be the Messiah. They were ignorant of the Scriptures, for Micah had predicted the Messiah would come from Bethlehem (see Mic. 5:2).

7:28, 29 Cried out signifies a loud cry of strong emotion. **You ... know Me ... where I am from:** Jesus reminded the leaders that they knew His origin. Their problem was that they did **not know** God, who sent Jesus. He explained to them that He knew God, was from God, and was sent by God.

7:30 take Him: Because of Jesus' public claims of divine origin (v. 29), the religious leaders sought to arrest Him.

7:31 In contrast to the leaders, many of the Jewish **people believed** because of the miracles Jesus performed (20:30, 31).

7:32 to take Him: The Jewish leaders decided earlier that they wanted to kill Christ (see 5:16), but this is the first real attempt on His life.

7:33 a little while longer: Jesus' time on earth was limited; soon He would be crucified and then ascend to the Father. His life was not determined by the Jewish religious leaders (v. 32), but by the Father.

7:34–36 you cannot come: Christ would be in heaven; the people would not be able to come to Him there. **Where does He intend to go:** The Jewish leaders did not comprehend what Jesus meant. They could only think of one of the various places where Jews had been scattered.

7:37–39 On the last day of the feast, the people marched seven times around the altar in memory of the seven circuits around the walls of Jericho. Perhaps at the very moment that the priest was pouring water on the altar as a memorial offering, Jesus' voice rang out: **If anyone thirsts, let him come to Me and drink.** In contrast to the small amount of water poured out each day during the feast, there will be a river of water coming out of those who believe in Christ. Not only will they be satisfied themselves, but they will also become a river so that others may drink and be satisfied (v. 39). John explains that Jesus was speaking of **the Holy Spirit** who would satisfy personal thirst and produce a perennial fountain for the satisfaction of others.

7:40–44 Moses predicted that **the Prophet,** the **seed of David,** would come (see Deut. 18:15, 18; 2 Sam. 7:14–16). These people knew that the Messiah was to come from **Bethlehem** (see Mic. 5:2). However, they did not know that Jesus had been born there. They thought He was from **Galilee** (see v. 41; Matt. 16:13, 14).

7:45–49 this crowd ... is accursed: The Pharisees accused the people of being ignorant of the Law and thus under God's curse (see Deut. 28:15). The irony of the situation was that it was the Pharisees, not the crowds, who were under God's wrath because they had rejected His Son (3:36).

7:50, 51 Nicodemus made a plea for justice (3:2; 12:42, 43), but his plea was rejected.

7:52, 53 no prophet has arisen out of Galilee: Actually, the prophets Jonah, Hosea, Nahum, and perhaps Elijah, Elisha, and Amos were from Galilee or close to it.

8:1 The people went to their own houses (7:53). Jesus, who had no place to lay His head (see Luke 9:58), spent the night on **the Mount of Olives.**

8:2 Early in the morning means "at dawn." **all the people came:** Because the Feast of Tabernacles had concluded the day before (7:2, 37), many visitors were still in Jerusalem. Attracted by the appearance of a noted rabbi, a crowd rapidly gathered.

8:3 Abruptly bringing the adulterous woman into **the midst** of the proceedings was a rude disruption. The Pharisees were bent on confounding Jesus (7:45).

8:4, 5 such should be stoned: Stoning was specified in certain cases of adultery (see Deut. 22:23, 24), though not all. The religious leaders were trying to trap Jesus into saying something that was contrary to the Law.

8:6 testing Him: If Jesus had said not to stone the woman, He would have contradicted Jewish law. If He had said to stone her, He would have run counter to Roman law, which did not permit Jews to carry out their own executions (18:31).

8:7–11 Sin no more implies that Jesus forgave the woman. He did not condemn her, but neither did He condone her sin.

8:12 I am the light of the world: As the sun is the physical light of the world, so Jesus is the spiritual light of the world who exposes sin (vv. 1–11) and gives sight (9:1–7).

8:13 Not true here does not mean "false"; it means "not sufficient." The Pharisees challenged Jesus on legal grounds, because no man on trial in a Jewish court was allowed to testify on his own behalf. Their point was that if Jesus was the only one testifying as to who He claimed to be, it would not be enough to prove His case.

8:14 My witness is true: In 5:31, Jesus argued on the basis of legality and offered other witnesses. Sometimes, however, an individual is the only one who knows the facts about himself. Thus, self-disclosure is the only way to truth (7:29; 13:3).

8:15 According to the flesh could mean either "according to appearance" or "by human standards." The religious leaders formed conclusions based on human standards and an imperfect, external, and superficial examination. Jesus did not judge according to human standards or outward appearances.

8:16–18 I am not alone: Jesus could claim that His pronouncements were true and accurate even though the Law of Moses required two witnesses for a testimony to be valid (see Deut. 17:6; 19:15): Both He and the Father through the signs bore testimony to Jesus' words and works.

8:19 Where is Your Father: Since the Father was part of Jesus' proof of Himself, the Pharisees wanted to know where this Father was. **You know neither:** Even if the Pharisees could see the Father, they would not receive what Jesus said. Jesus came to reveal the Father (1:18).

8:20–22 kill Himself: Later Jewish belief placed suicide on the same level with murder.

8:23 from beneath: Jesus was not referring to hell, but to **this world.**

8:24, 25 I am was God's designation of Himself (see Ex. 3:14). Jesus was claiming to be God. Later, Jesus' claim to be the "I AM" (v. 58) prompted the Jewish leaders to seek His life (v. 59).

8:26–28 Lift up is a reference to the Crucifixion.

8:29, 30 The Greek phrase translated **believed in** describes faith in Jesus' message (see 1 Cor. 1:21), which results in eternal life.

8:31 Abide means to remain, to continue. A believer who continues to obey the Word is a disciple, a learner.

8:32 One who abides in the Word of God knows the **truth** (v. 31; 17:17). The word **free** refers to freedom from the bondage of sin.

8:33 We … have never been in bondage: The Pharisees' objection is startling. In their past, the Israelites had been in bondage to the Egyptians, the Assyrians, and the Babylonians. At the time they spoke, Israel was under the power of Rome.

8:34 slave of sin: Jesus was speaking of spiritual slavery. Such a slave cannot break away from his bondage. He must have someone else set him free (see Rom. 8:34).

8:35, 36 A slave was not a permanent resident of a house. **A son** was a family member with family privileges forever. The **Son** here is Jesus Christ (see "the Son of Man" in v. 28). As a family member, the Son can bestow family privileges on others.

8:37 Abraham's descendants may have been physical heirs of Abraham, but they were not his spiritual descendants unless they had faith. But instead of trusting Christ to forgive their sins, the religious leaders wanted to kill Him.

8:38, 39 Abraham is our father: The Pharisees believed that being a descendant of Abraham guaranteed them a place in heaven. **The works of Abraham** included paying honor to those who spoke in the name of God (see Gen. 14; 18).

8:40, 41 We were not born of fornication: From ancient times, this has been interpreted as a sneer, as if to say, "We are not illegitimate children, but You are." Apparently gossip had followed Jesus for many years, alleging that He had been conceived out of wedlock.

8:42–47 your father: Jesus knew what was in the hearts of people (2:25), so He could trace their actions to their source. The devil is a **murderer;** his agents wanted to kill Christ.

8:48 The Jewish leaders charged Jesus with being **a Samaritan** and having **a demon.** In the process, they turned back to Jesus both charges that He had brought against them, namely, that they were not legitimate children of Abraham (vv. 39, 40) and that they were of the devil (v. 44).

8:49 The Jewish leaders were dishonoring Jesus even though their eternal destiny depended on what they did with His message (v. 51).

8:50 One: God the Father will seek Christ's glory and judge those who dishonor Him.

8:51 Jesus graciously held out to the Jewish leaders the promise of forgiveness and eternal life. **My word** refers to the word about who He is. **Death** here refers not to physical death, but to spiritual death resulting in eternal separation from God.

8:52, 53 greater than ... Abraham: Abraham and the prophets kept God's word and died. Jesus was claiming not that He would prevent physical death, but that He could give people eternal life. To the

Jewish leaders, this was proof that Jesus was demon-possessed.

8:54–56 My day: Abraham looked for the One who would fulfill all that was promised to him—promises that included blessings for all nations (see Gal. 3:8, 9, 29).

8:57–59 I AM: Jesus was claiming eternal existence, that He was God Himself (see Ex. 3:14). The Jewish leaders understood this, so they **took up stones** to stone Him for blasphemy (see Lev. 24:16).

9:1 The man who was blind from birth was a beggar (v. 8). Beggars waited by the gates of the temple for gifts from worshipers.

9:2 who sinned: It was commonly supposed that sickness was a result of sin. It would follow that sins committed by a baby still in the womb or sin committed by parents could result in a baby being born with a disease. Jesus rejected both suggestions (v. 3).

9:3 God allowed the man to be born blind so that Jesus could heal him and thus reveal **the works of God,** His healing power.

9:4–6 Mixing **clay** with **saliva** was a common practice used for eye infections. Jesus may have used the clay to provide an opportunity for the man to exercise his faith in washing it off.

9:7 Siloam: Hezekiah had a tunnel cut through solid rock to transport water from Gihon (the "Virgin's Fountain") into the city of Jerusalem, to the Pool of Siloam (see 2 Kin. 20:20; 2 Chr. 32:30). John emphasizes that the name Siloam means "Sent," because Jesus had just announced that He had been sent by God (v. 4).

9:8–16 some of the Pharisees said ... Others said: The Pharisees could not believe that Jesus was from God because He had healed on the Sabbath, thereby breaking the oral traditions that had grown up around the Law.

9:17–21 The blind man concluded that Jesus was **a prophet.** This does not mean he had decided that Jesus was the Messiah (1:20, 21; 6:14).

9:22, 23 To **be put out of the synagogue** was to be excommunicated, or isolated from others.

9:24 Attempting to put words in the man's mouth, the Jewish leaders said they knew Jesus was **a sinner.** In their view, healing on

10:25 Jesus answered: Jesus reminded the Jewish leaders of His words and works. He told the woman at the well that He was the Messiah (4:25, 26), as well as the man born blind (9:35–37). All the miracles He performed as signs pointed to His messiahship (see 20:31).

10:26 as I said to you: At the Feast of Tabernacles, Jesus had told the leaders that they were not among His sheep (see vv. 14, 15; 8:42–44, 47).

10:27–29 Jesus described three characteristics of His sheep: (1) They **hear** His **voice** (v. 4). He knows them (see Rom. 8:29). (2) **They follow** Him. The following of the sheep is a metaphor for faith. (3) **They shall never perish;** their eternal life can never be taken away.

10:30 I and My Father are one: The Jewish opponents understood that Jesus was claiming to be God (vv. 31, 33).

10:31 again: This was not the first time that the Jewish leaders **took up stones** against Jesus (see 8:59).

10:32, 33 The Jewish antagonizers revealed the reason for their opposition to Jesus—He was claiming a unique unity with the Father, indicating His own deity. The Jewish leaders considered this to be **blasphemy.**

10:34 In the Old Testament, judges were called *gods.* They exercised godlike judicial sovereignty. Psalm 82:6, the verse quoted here, refers to judges who violate the Law. Jesus' argument was that if the divine name had been applied by God to mere men, there could be neither blasphemy nor folly in its application to the incarnate Son of God Himself.

10:35, 36 Broken actually means "to loose, untie." This is a strong statement of the inerrancy of the Holy Scriptures.

10:37, 38 believe the works: Jesus asked the Jewish leaders to at least consider His miracles because these indicated and demonstrated His deity. Note that the heart of the issue is *belief.*

10:39–42 beyond the Jordan: This sojourn into Perea is also noted in Matt. 19:1 and Mark 10:1.

11:1 Bethany, a small village on the southeast slope of the Mount of Olives, was located about two miles from Jerusalem (v. 18).

11:2 Mary who anointed: The anointing had not yet taken place (12:1–3). When John wrote, the anointing was well known, so he used the event to distinguish this Mary from other women with the same name.

11:3, 4 Not unto death means not having death as its final result. **may be glorified:** By raising Lazarus from the dead, Jesus would demonstrate His deity in an undeniable way.

11:5–8 stayed two more days: God's purpose was to glorify His Son (v. 4) and to cause the disciples to grow (v. 15). Had Jesus immediately rushed to heal Lazarus, he would not have died and Jesus would not have been able to manifest His glory by raising Lazarus.

11:9–15 Jesus was not **glad** that Lazarus was dead. He was glad for the opportunity the disciples would soon have to see an amazing miracle.

11:16 the Twin: Thomas seems to have combined devotion to Jesus with a tendency to see the dark side of things. Jesus said, "Let us go," that the disciples might believe (v. 15). Thomas said, **Let us also go, that we may die.** While the Lord saw their development in faith, Thomas saw their deaths. Yet in his loyalty, he followed anyway.

11:17–27 Christ is **the Resurrection** for those who believe and are physically dead. He is **the life** for those who believe and have not yet died. When Jesus asked Martha if she believed, she responded with words similar to the ones John used to describe the purpose of his book (20:31).

11:28–32 if You had been here: Mary said the same thing to the Lord as Martha had (v. 21). No doubt they had expressed this thought to one another often in the last few days.

11:33, 34 Groaned means to be deeply moved. **Troubled** means to be stirred up, disturbed. Jesus was moved by the mourning of Mary and indignant at the hypocritical lamentations of His enemies.

11:35, 36 Wept simply means "shed tears." Jesus did not weep aloud in hopeless grief like the others (v. 33). His compassion for their pain moved Him to tears.

11:37 Some people misinterpreted Jesus' tears as powerlessness. They complained that He had healed others, but now was impotent.

11:38, 39 a cave: Having a private burial

place indicates that the family of Lazarus was wealthy.

11:40–43 cried: This loud cry was either the result of strong emotion or in order that the multitude might hear. **Lazarus:** Raising Lazarus from the dead is the seventh sign of Jesus' messiahship, the greatest miracle of all—giving life back to the dead.

11:44–48 Place refers either to Jerusalem or to the temple. The Jewish leaders were not as upset at Jesus' supposed blasphemy as they were about losing their positions of authority.

11:49–52 In the opinion of **Caiaphas,** Jesus should die rather than plunge the nation into destruction. Caiaphas pronounced a message of God unconsciously: **one man should die for the people.** Caiaphas was a prophet in spite of himself.

11:53 The Resurrection of Lazarus was a major factor that led to the plot by the Jewish religious leaders to kill Christ. John marks the growth of the hostility step by step (5:16; 7:1, 32, 45; 8:59; 9:22; 10:39).

11:54–57 no longer walked openly: Jesus withdrew from public life for a while. He met privately with His disciples. **Wilderness** usually refers to the desert of Judea which extended to Jericho.

12:1 six days before the Passover: If the crucifixion took place on a Friday, this dinner occurred during the evening of the previous Saturday.

12:2 They probably refers to the inhabitants of Bethany who wished to express their thanks to Jesus. By a glorious miracle He had honored their obscure village. **Lazarus** was the guest of honor.

12:3–6 very costly oil: Judas Iscariot said that this oil cost three hundred denarii (v. 5). One denarius was a laborer's wage for one day (see Matt. 20:2). **anointed the feet:** Anointing Jesus' head was an act of honor; anointing His feet was a display of devotion.

12:7 My burial: Anointing was the first stage of embalming (19:39). Whether Mary knew it or not, she was anticipating Jesus' death, which would happen within the week.

12:8 the poor you have with you always: We will never lack an opportunity to care for the poor (see Deut. 15:11).

12:9–11 plotted to put Lazarus to death also: The chief priests were mostly Sadducees. They had an additional reason to kill Lazarus. He was a living refutation of their doctrine that there was no Resurrection (see 11:57; Acts 23:8). **on account of him:** Because of Lazarus many were believing in Jesus.

12:12–15 took branches of palm trees: This was the Sunday before Christ arose, today called Palm Sunday. **cried out … King of Israel:** Until this point, Jesus had discouraged expressions of support from the people (6:15; 7:1–8). Here He allowed public enthusiasm. He entered Jerusalem on the back of a young donkey. This act fulfilled prophecy (see Zech. 9:9) and was a symbolic proclamation that Jesus is the Messiah.

12:16 when Jesus was glorified: After Christ's death, Resurrection, and Ascension, the disciples finally understood that the Old Testament prophecies about the Messiah had been fulfilled in Jesus.

12:17–19 These verses explain the series of events that led to the condemnation and crucifixion of Jesus.

12:20 The fact that these **Greeks** came to Jerusalem **to worship at the feast** indicates that they were Jewish proselytes. Perhaps John was hinting that the salvation rejected by many of the Jews was already passing to the Gentiles.

12:21–23 The hour has come: Prior to this, Jesus had stated that His hour had not yet come (2:4; 7:6, 30; 8:20). Now the time had come for Christ to die and be raised from the dead (see 13:1; 16:32; 17:1).

12:24 unless a grain … dies: When a seed dies, it produces fruit. Life comes by death. Jesus was speaking first and foremost of Himself. He is the grain of wheat. His death would produce much fruit and would result in many living for God.

12:25, 26 The phrase **loves his life** describes those who serve only themselves. In a very short time, Jesus would give the disciples an opportunity to identify this problem in their lives (13:1–7). **Hates his life** involves serving Christ. We cannot give ourselves fully to this life and yet be committed to the life to come. **Follow Me** in this context means to follow Jesus' example of self-sacrifice (13:15).

12:27 My soul is troubled: Jesus' agony over His impending death was not confined to Gethsemane, where He prayed, "O My Father, if it is possible, let this cup pass from Me" (see Matt. 26:39). He felt the agony and expressed it almost a week before Gethsemane.

12:28–34 Christ remains forever: The people understood that **lifted up** meant removal from the earth by death. . To them, the Messiah would not have to die (see Ps. 110:4; Is. 9:7; Ezek. 37:25). They did not understand that He would be raised.

12:35, 36 Instead of answering the people's questions (v. 34), Jesus gave them a warning. **Walk while you have the light:** Jesus is the light (1:4; 8:12; 9:5). He wanted the people to believe and abide in Him (v. 46).

12:37 they did not believe: Their unbelief is startling. However Jesus' predicted suffering and death did not fit the people's idea of the Messiah.

12:38 the word of Isaiah … might be fulfilled: John quotes Is. 53:1 to prove that their unbelief is predictable.

12:39, 40 The consequence of repeated rejection of the truth is loss of the capacity to believe. Isaiah taught that some **could not believe** because God **hardened their hearts** (see Is. 6:10).

12:41 John uses the words **His glory** to speak of the manifestation of God Himself. John quotes Is. 6:9 (see v. 40) as a prophecy of the people's unbelief and their rejection of Christ.

12:42, 43 Rulers refers to members of the council. Because the rulers **did not confess Him,** some claim that their faith was not genuine. The text, however, says that they **believed in Him,** a construction in Greek that typically indicates saving faith (8:30). Moreover, the word **nevertheless** marks a stark contrast between these believers and the unbelief spoken of in vv. 37–41. These men were genuine believers, but they feared the opinions of their fellow leaders.

12:44, 45 not in Me but in Him: Jesus insisted that anyone who believed in Him was at the same time exercising belief in God the Father.

12:46–50 I do not judge may be rephrased as "I do not execute judgment." Christ will judge, but at His first coming He did not come to judge but to save (3:17).

13:1 To the end means either "to the last" or "utterly and completely." Jesus loved His disciples, even though He knew that one would betray Him, another would deny Him, and all would desert Him for a time.

13:2, 3 It was customary for slaves to wash guests' feet before they sat down to eat (vv. 4, 5). In any case, it appears that the supper had not ended, but was in progress. The statement of Jesus' complete love in v. 1 is contrasted with the fact that Judas would soon **betray Him.**

13:4, 5 His garments: Jesus **laid aside** His outer garment, which would have impeded His movements. **towel:** By putting on an apron, Christ looked took on the task of a slave in washing the feet of His disciples. Though the disciples realized what Jesus was doing, none of them offered himself for the task. Servanthood was not on their minds. Jesus loved them knowing all about them, including the worst one of them, Judas.

13:6–8 no part with Me: The washing was a symbol of spiritual cleansing (vv. 10, 11). If Peter did not participate in the cleansing, he would not enjoy fellowship with Christ (see 1 John 1:9).

13:9, 10 but also my hands and my head: At first Peter wanted to tell the Lord what to do (v. 8). But Jesus told him he only needed Jesus **to wash his feet** that were dusty from the road. This is symbolic. A believer has already been "cleansed." He or she only needs the cleansing of daily sins that comes through confession (see 1 John 1:9). Jesus' washing of the disciples' feet is not only a model of service, but it represents the ultimate in service—forgiveness of sins.

13:11 You are not all clean: This is the second indication of the presence of a traitor among the apostles (6:70). Apparently this comment did not attract much attention.

13:12, 13 Teacher and Lord were the ordinary titles of respect given to a rabbi.

13:14, 15 you also ought to wash one another's feet: The Lord was using His practical action to give **an example** of love to His disciples (v. 1).

13:16–18 Jesus quoted Ps. 41:9 to explain the action of Judas. Lifting up **his heel** was a gesture of insult, or a preparation to kick.

The blow had not yet been given, but Judas was ready to strike.

13:19–21 troubled: Faced with bereavement (11:33), His own death (12:27), and betrayal, Jesus was deeply moved.

13:22, 23 leaning on Jesus' bosom: People did not generally sit at a table to eat. They reclined on the left side of a low platform, resting on the left elbow and eating with the right hand, their feet extended outward. Reclining in such a way, a man's head was near the bosom of the person on his left. The disciple **whom Jesus loved** is never named in Scripture, but the tradition of the early church designates him as John, the author of this Gospel.

13:24, 25 Peter … motioned to him to ask: Evidently Peter was not sitting next to Jesus. He was nearer to John, so he beckoned John to ask Jesus who was going to betray Him.

13:26, 27 First, the devil put ideas in the head of Judas (v. 2); here **Satan entered** Judas. Note that Judas's actions were the result of the deepest thoughts of his heart.

13:28–30 it was night: Not only did Judas go out into the darkness of the night; he had also entered into spiritual darkness, separated from Jesus, the Light of the World (8:12; 9:5).

13:31–33 the Son of Man is glorified: Jesus would be revealed as the divine Son of God and Savior of the world by His death and Resurrection, and the gift of the Holy Spirit. The time had come for Jesus to announce His departure to His disciples. **Little children** is an expression of tender affection used nowhere else in the Gospels.

13:34 The command to **love** was **new** because Jesus gave it a new standard. The new standard was **as I have loved you.** Jesus gave His disciples the example of love that they were to follow (vv. 1–17).

13:35 By this: Unbelievers recognize Jesus' disciples by their deeds of love for one another.

13:36 Lord, where are You going: This question, which Jesus had already addressed twice before, indicates that Peter missed the point of what Jesus said in vv. 34, 35.

13:37 I will lay down my life: Peter was ready to die for Jesus. He was ready to attack single-handed a cohort of soldiers with his sword

(see 18:10), but he was not willing to wash the feet of his brothers as Jesus had just done (see 13:4). Actually, Peter had things backwards. Christ was about to lay down His life for Peter, instead of Peter laying down his life for Christ.

13:38 till you have denied Me three times: At these words of Jesus, Peter was stunned and said nothing. He is not mentioned again until 18:10.

14:1 After announcing Judas's betrayal (13:21), His own imminent departure (13:33), and Peter's denial (13:38), Jesus told His disciples not to **be troubled,** but to trust Him.

14:2 Mansions refers to secure, permanent dwelling places. Such places have already been set aside for all of God's children.

14:3, 4 I will come again and receive you: Peter may have failed Jesus (13:38), but Christ will not fail to return for Peter and for everyone else who has believed in Him (see 1 Thess. 4:16, 17).

14:5, 6 Through His death and Resurrection, Jesus is **the way** to the Father. He is also **the truth** and **the life.** As truth, He is the revelation of God. As life, He is the communication of God to us.

14:7, 8 show us the Father: Jesus had just said that to see Him is to see the Father. Yet Philip asked to see the Father. Like Thomas, Philip seems to have been slow to understand (v. 5).

14:9 He who has seen Me has seen the Father: The Lord patiently explained again that He was revealing God the Father to them (v. 7). Clearly, He was claiming to be God.

14:10–12 Jesus had accomplished the greatest works possible, including raising the dead. How could He say that believers would do **greater works?** They would preach everywhere and see the conversion of thousands. The disciples were able to do this work because Christ would go to the Father and send the Holy Spirit to empower them.

14:13–16 All three members of the Trinity are mentioned here. Jesus prayed to the Father, who would give the Holy Spirit.

14:17 The Holy Spirit is called **the Spirit of truth** (see 15:26; 16:13; 1 John 4:6) because He is truth and guides us into all truth (see 1 Cor. 2:13; 2 Pet. 1:21). **Neither sees**

Him nor knows Him: The Spirit of God is active in the world, but His acts go unnoticed by the world (see 1 Cor. 2:14).

14:18 orphans: Earlier, Jesus called the disciples "little children" (13:33). Here He told them He would not leave them fatherless; He would come to them.

14:19 you will see Me: Jesus would come to the disciples (v. 18), but not with the same kind of presence they experienced at that moment. The disciples would see Him in a spiritual sense.

14:20, 21 These two verses are the conclusion of Jesus' answer to Philip's request, "show us the Father" (v. 8). As the believer lovingly obeys Christ's commandments, he or she will experience a more intimate knowledge of Him.

14:22 The disciples had expected the Messiah to come publicly and deliver Israel from Rome. Jesus had said that the disciples would see Him, but the world would not (v. 19).

14:23 loves Me ... keep My word: Jesus explained that His manifestation to the disciples would be in response to their love and obedience. **make Our home with him:** If a believer loves and obeys the Lord, he or she will experience fellowship with God.

14:24 not love ... not keep: If a person does not love Jesus, he or she will not obey Him.

14:25, 26 Jesus told His disciples **these things** while He was with them, but when **the Holy Spirit** came, He would remind the disciples of **all things** that Jesus had said, and would **teach ... all things** (see 1 Cor. 2:13). This promise was primarily fulfilled through the lives of the apostles in the writing of the New Testament.

14:27 Peace: The customary good-bye among the Jews was to say *shalom,* meaning "peace." The Lord was about to depart, so He added to this farewell by saying, **My peace.** This is no conventional wish; this is Jesus' personal, special grant of peace. The peace that Christ gives banishes fear and dread from the heart.

14:28 My Father is greater than I: This does not mean that Jesus is less than deity. *Greater* indicates a difference in rank. As the humble, submissive Son, Jesus submitted Himself to the authority of His Father (1 Cor. 11:3; 15:28).

14:29–31 Jesus' yielding to what was about to happen did not mean that Satan had any power over Him. Jesus would soon voluntarily yield to the death of the Cross, in loving obedience to the Father (v. 31).

15:1 true vine: In this phrase the word *true* is emphatic. **My Father:** With such a **vinedresser,** the branches can experience complete confidence and security.

15:2, 3 Every branch is said to be *in* Christ. The emphasis of **in Me** in this passage is on deep, abiding fellowship. Jesus' purpose was to move His disciples from servants to friends (vv. 13–15). **not bear fruit:** No plant produces fruit instantaneously; fruit is the result of a process. This is also the case with believers. **Prunes** means "cleanses." Once the fruit is on the vine, the vinedresser cleanses the fruit of bugs and diseases. The spiritual counterpart is cleansing, which is done through the Word (v. 3).

15:4 For the branch to produce more fruit, it must **abide,** which means to dwell, to stay, to settle in, to sink deeper. The believer who obeys the Word of God produces much fruit.

15:5 can do nothing: Apart from Christ, a believer cannot accomplish anything of permanent spiritual value.

15:6 Not abiding in Christ has serious consequences: (1) The person **is cast out as a branch,** indicating the loss of fellowship; (2) the person **is withered,** indicating a loss of vitality; (3) the person is **burned,** indicating a loss of reward. **The fire** here is figurative, symbolizing either fiery trials (see 1 Pet. 1:7; 4:12) or the fire at the judgment seat of Christ (see 1 Cor. 3:11–15).

15:7, 8 By this: Notice the striking parallel between this verse and 13:35. The love of 13:35 is pictured as **fruit** here. The text has come full circle in showing how strategic it is for disciples to love one another, as Christ's method of evangelizing the lost.

15:9 As the Father loved Me, I also have loved you: The love of God the Father for God the Son is the measure of the love of the Son for believers.

15:10 abide in My love: As believers obey Christ's Word and abide in His love, they come to experience and understand His love for them more and more (see Eph. 3:14–19).

15:11 That your joy may be full is an expression peculiar to John (see 3:29; 16:24; 17:13; 1 John 1:4; 2 John 12). It describes a believer's experience of Christ's love, or complete joy.

15:12 love one another: To abide, a believer must obey (v. 10). To obey, a believer must love other believers (13:34, 35).

15:13 lay down one's life: In rashness and with confidence in the flesh, Peter had offered to lay down his life for Jesus. In actuality, he was not ready to die for Jesus; he was not even ready to live for Him (18:17, 18, 25–27). The supreme example of love is Jesus' humility in sacrificial service (13:15).

15:14 if you do: If believers obey Jesus' command to love, they enjoy the intimacy of His friendship.

15:15 No longer ... servants: Until this point, Jesus had called His disciples servants (12:26; 13:13–16). A servant does what he is told and sees what his master does, but does not necessarily know the meaning or purpose of it. **friends:** A friend knows what is happening because friends develop deep fellowship by communicating with one another.

15:16 I chose you: Jesus had initiated the relationship with His disciples (see 1 John 4:10). It started with selection, moved to servanthood, and grew to friendship. **that you should go and bear fruit:** Having chosen the disciples, Jesus commissioned them to bring forth permanent fruit through prayer.

15:17–21 hated Me: As Jesus spoke these words, the Pharisees were planning to kill Him (11:45–57). The world hated Him, so it should not be surprising that the world hates His followers.

15:22–25 My Father also: Since Christ and the Father are one, those who hate Christ hate the Father.

15:26, 27 He will testify ... you also will bear witness: As the disciples spoke, the Holy Spirit would bring conviction to unbelievers about Christ. This in turn would make the disciples witnesses for Jesus.

16:1, 2 They will put you out of the synagogues ... kills you: The persecution that the disciples would face included excommunication and even execution. Excommunication had economic as well as religious implications, because much of the life of an ancient Jew revolved around the synagogue. **Offers** expresses the idea of offering a sacrifice. The murderers of believers would imagine that they were offering a sacrifice to God.

16:3, 4 at the beginning: Jesus had been preparing His disciples to assimilate the truth (see Prov. 22:6). In His wisdom, the Lord never gives us more than we can handle.

16:5 one of you asks Me, "Where are You going?": Peter had asked this very question (13:36) and Thomas had suggested it (14:5). However, things were different now. The disciples had learned about denials, suffering, and death.

16:6, 7 Jesus explained the benefits of His departure. When He left, the believers would have (1) the provision of the Holy Spirit (vv. 7–15); (2) the potential of full joy (vv. 16–24); (3) the possibility of fuller knowledge (vv. 25–28); (4) the privilege of peace (vv. 29–33). **to you:** The Holy Spirit would not be given to the world, but to believers. The coming of the Spirit would be more profitable to believers than even the physical presence of Christ, since the Spirit could dwell in all believers at the same time.

16:8 The Holy Spirit would demonstrate the truth of Christ beyond the fear of contradiction. The Holy Spirit convicts unbelievers through believers who witness about Christ (15:26, 27). Believers are the mouthpiece for God's voice. The content of the witness that the Spirit reinforces includes truth about **sin, righteousness,** and **judgment.**

16:9 of sin: Note the singular *sin,* not *sins.* Our witness should not focus on *sins* (adultery, gluttony, pride, and other sins), but on the full payment that Christ has made for *all sin.* Reception of the full pardon is the only cure for the disease of sin.

16:10 of righteousness: After Christ's departure the Holy Spirit would convict the world of the nature of righteousness and the need for righteousness. Jesus' work on the Cross was completely righteous. This is demonstrated by the Father's emptying of the tomb, signifying His satisfaction with the righteous payment and His acceptance of Christ into His presence.

16:11 of judgment: The Holy Spirit would convince people of the judgment to come.

Satan has been judged, so all who side with him will be judged with him.

16:12 The Holy Spirit's ministry to the apostles was threefold: (1) He would guide them into all truth (v. 13); (2) He would tell them of the future (v. 13); (3) He would help them glorify Christ (vv. 14, 15).

16:13 Spirit of truth: The phrase means that the Holy Spirit is the source of truth (14:17; 15:26). **guide:** The Holy Spirit would not compel or carry the disciples into truth. He would lead; their job was to follow. **All truth** refers to the truth necessary to be mature saints and thoroughly equipped servants (see 2 Tim. 3:16, 17).

16:14 The Holy Spirit glorifies Christ by declaring Him or making Him known. It is the work of the Holy Spirit to throw light on Jesus Christ, who is the image of the invisible God.

16:15 To say that the Holy Spirit will take what belongs to Christ (v. 14) does not mean He will concentrate on Christ to the exclusion of **the Father.** There is no division within the Godhead. What the Father has, the Son has (17:10). What the Son has, the Spirit will declare (see 1 Cor. 2:13). However, the focus will be on Christ because He is the "image of the invisible God" (see Col. 1:15).

16:16 You will see Me has been interpreted to mean: (1) the disciples would literally see Jesus after the Resurrection; (2) the disciples would spiritually see Jesus after the Ascension because of the work of the Holy Spirit. Verse 22 seems to support the literal sight after the Resurrection.

16:17, 18 A little while: The biggest question weighing on the disciples' minds was the time factor. They simply did not understand the strange intervals marked by their separation from Jesus.

16:19–21 weep and lament: When Jesus died, the disciples openly expressed their intense sorrow. **The world** would **rejoice,** assuming that it was rid of Jesus. But the **sorrow** of the disciples would be **turned into joy.** This is not just a case of sorrow being followed by joy, but of sorrow *becoming* joy. The sorrow itself would be transformed.

16:22 I will see you again refers to Jesus' postresurrection appearances. **your joy no one will take:** The disciples' sorrow would depart; their joy would remain. Jesus' death and Resurrection brings the joy of forgiven sins (see 1 Pet. 1:8) that the world cannot take away.

16:23–25 An example of **figurative language** is the allegory of the grapevine in 15:1–8, which presents the work of the Father in producing the fruit of love in believers.

16:26, 27 I shall pray the Father for you: Because Jesus provides forgiveness of sins through His death and now intercedes for all believers at the right hand of the Father (see Heb. 7:25), we have direct access to the Father.

16:28–30 we believe: Jesus had read the disciples' hearts (v. 19) and answered their questions. Like the Samaritan woman, they concluded that He knew all things (4:39). To the disciples, Jesus' supernatural knowledge proved His divine mission.

16:31 now believe: We continue in the Christian life the same way we begin, by believing in Jesus. The more we place our trust in Jesus, the more we receive. The more we receive, the more we can accomplish for His glory.

16:32 you will be scattered: The disciples would desert Jesus. Knowing this, Jesus still loved them.

16:33 Tribulation is literally "pressure," and figuratively means "affliction" or "distress." **Be of good cheer** means "be confident and courageous." When we place our trust in God, He can give us peace in the midst of pressure.

17:1, 2 the hour has come: Throughout the Gospel of John, Jesus referred to the Cross as His "hour" (2:4; 7:30; 8:20; 12:23; 13:1). **Glorify Your Son:** Jesus was asking that His mission to the world would be made known through the Cross.

17:3 that they may know You: Eternal life consists of a growing knowledge of **the only true God,** as opposed to false gods.

17:4, 5 I have glorified You: Jesus made known the Father by completing the work God gave Him to do. **glorify Me:** Jesus looked to the Father to restore Him to the glory He had in heaven before He left (see

Phil. 2:6). This is another indication of Christ's preexistence and deity (1:1–14).

17:6–10 I do not pray for the world indicates that Jesus was praying only for present and future believers (see 17:20; Luke 23:34).

17:11 This verse reveals Jesus' keen sensitivity to the plight of His disciples brought on by His departure. He asked the Father to **keep** the disciples **through** His **name,** that is, to keep them true to the revelation of God that Jesus had given to them. The disciples would have a new union with the Father and Son through the future indwelling of the Holy Spirit.

17:12 none of them is lost: Jesus protected the disciples during His earthly ministry (18:9). Judas, **the son of perdition,** is distinguished from the rest of the apostles. He was never really one of those given to Christ (18:8, 9). He had never really been a believer (6:64–71); he had not been cleansed (13:11).

17:13 I speak in the world: Jesus prayed aloud (v. 1) so that His words would comfort the apostles when they remembered that Jesus gave them into His Father's keeping.

17:14, 15 of the world: Our desire should not be to isolate ourselves from the world, but to use Christ's word and the Holy Spirit's power to serve Him while our life lasts. The term **evil one** can be translated as a common noun, *evil,* or as a reference to a person, Satan.

17:16–18 Sanctify means "to set apart." **Your word is truth** is a strong statement of Jesus' confidence in the veracity of Scripture. People's opinions may vary, and experiences are untrustworthy, but God's Word always remains true.

17:19, 20 those who will believe: Jesus not only prayed for those the Father had given Him (v. 9) but for all future believers—for their unity (vv. 20–23) and their future glory (vv. 24–26).

17:21 all may be one: The present tense of the verb "to be" indicates that Jesus was praying for the unity that takes place through the sanctification of believers. This is what Jesus was commanding in 13:34, 35: His followers had to love each other so that the world may believe in the reality of Jesus' love.

17:22 The glory, the revelation of Jesus Christ through His disciples, is the means to unity.

Such unity begins with belief and correct thinking about Jesus and God the Father. But correct belief must bear fruit—a life that demonstrates God's love and produces unity between all the believers.

17:23 I in them, and You in Me: The mutual indwelling of the Father in the Son and the Son in the church is also the means to unity, the ultimate expression of God's love (see 13:35; Rom. 8:17).

17:24 May be with Me is a prayer for the future glorification of believers. **may behold My glory:** The apostles saw Christ's glory in His words and works (v. 22). Christ prayed for all believers to behold His glory, unveiled in the full revelation of His deity.

17:25, 26 The ultimate reason for future believers to know the love of God is so that God's love may be replicated in them, thus drawing the entire world to Christ.

18:1, 2 The Brook Kidron was a ravine between Jerusalem and the Mount of Olives.

18:3 A detachment was a cohort of about six hundred men, or one-tenth of a legion. Sometimes this Greek word was used for one-third of a cohort, or two hundred men. These soldiers were probably the experienced Roman troops stationed at the Antonia, a fortress near the temple. The **officers** who came with the detachment were members of the temple police under the command of the Jewish council, the Sanhedrin.

18:4, 5 knowing all things: Knowing He was about to be arrested, Jesus could have escaped, but He did not. He submitted voluntarily to the ordeal that was ordained by God.

18:6 fell to the ground: For a moment, Christ unveiled His majesty. His statement of deity, **I am,** manifested such glory that it literally threw the soldiers to the **ground.**

18:7–9 For the third time in this passage, Jesus claimed to be **I am** (vv. 5, 6), echoing God's self-revelation in Ex. 3:14. **let these go:** As He was being arrested, Jesus demonstrated His love for the apostles.

18:10, 11 By fighting the guard, **Simon Peter** exercised his own self-will; Jesus in contrast voluntarily submitted to the will of God. One swung the sword of self-will; the other drank from the cup of God's will. **cut**

off his right ear: Jesus mercifully restored the ear (Luke 22:51) that Peter cut off.

18:12 A **captain** was the chief officer of a Roman cohort (v. 3).

18:13 Annas was high priest from A.D. 7 to 14. He was deposed by the Romans. Then Caiaphas, Annas's son-inlaw, was appointed to the position and served from A.D. 18 to 37. According to Jewish law the high priest was a lifetime position, so the Jews still considered Annas to be high priest. So they took Jesus to Annas first.

18:14 John reminds the reader of the earlier prediction of **Caiaphas** (11:50–52): Jesus would die for the entire nation.

18:15 another disciple: Although this other disciple is never identified, the consensus is that he was John, the author of this Gospel.

18:16–18 I am not: This was the first of Peter's three denials prophesied by Jesus (13:38).

18:19–21 Ask those who have heard Me: According to the law, the witnesses for the defense had to be called first. Jesus should not have been questioned until witnesses had testified.

18:22 the officers … struck Jesus: This was illegal according to Jewish law. There was to be no punishment before conviction.

18:23, 24 bear witness: Jesus invited His accusers to present evidence that He had done something wrong.

18:25 I am not: This was the second of Peter's three denials prophesied by Jesus (13:38).

18:26, 27 Peter then denied again: For the third time, Peter denied the Lord, as Jesus had said he would (13:38).

18:28 The Praetorium was the Roman governor's official residence, probably the Fortress Antonia near the temple. Early morning refers to the fourth watch of the night, from 3 to 6 A.M. A Roman court could have been held immediately after sunrise, and this scene could have taken place around 6 A.M. **defiled:** During Passover, if a Jew entered a house that contained leaven, he or she would be ceremonially defiled and unable to celebrate the feast. Thus Jews would not enter the residence of any Gentile for fear of being ceremonially defiled.

18:29, 30 What accusation: Pilate was not ignorant of the accusation. He was just requesting that it be formally stated.

18:31 You take Him and judge Him: The accusations did not warrant a trial before Pilate. **It is not lawful:** The Romans did not allow the Jews to impose capital punishment. These Jewish leaders had no interest in a just trial; they simply wanted permission from Rome to have Jesus executed.

18:32 signifying by what death He would die: Jesus had said, "If I am lifted up from the earth," indicating the method of His death, crucifixion (12:32, 33). The Jewish method of execution was stoning. However, Jesus had already indicated that He would be crucified. John is pointing out that the Jewish leaders' inability to impose capital punishment themselves fulfilled Jesus' prediction describing His death.

18:33 Are You the King of the Jews: The Jews charged that Jesus claimed to be their king. This was the most damaging accusation possible because it would be regarded by the Romans as treason and would be punishable by death.

18:34 Are you speaking for yourself: Jesus gave no violent protest of innocence, nor was He sullenly defiant. Jesus politely asked whether Pilate was asking on his own initiative or whether the charge was secondhand. If Pilate's question originated with him, he was using *king* in the Roman sense of a political ruler. If not, then *king* was being used in the Jewish sense of the messianic King.

18:35 Am I a Jew: Pilate was asking, "Is it likely that I, a Roman governor, would have any interest in a Jewish question?"

18:36 My kingdom is not of this world: Jesus pointed out that though He was a king, he was no threat to Rome because His kingdom would not come by a worldly revolution.

18:37 bear witness to the truth: The truth was the seal of God. **hears My voice:** If Pilate wanted to know the truth, he would understand what Jesus was saying.

18:38 What is truth: This question has been interpreted as (1) a cynical denial of the possibility of knowing truth; (2) a contemptuous jest at anything so impractical as abstract truth; and (3) a desire to know what no one had been able to tell him. **No fault** is a legal term meaning that there were no grounds for a criminal charge.

18:39 you have a custom: It appears that some in the crowd suggested that a prisoner should be released in honor of the Passover (see Mark 15:8, 11). By promising to release Jesus on account of the custom rather than by proclaiming Him innocent, Pilate would avoid insulting the Jewish leaders, who had already pronounced Him guilty.

18:40 The people demanded that Pilate release **Barabbas,** who was not only **a robber,** but a rebel (Mark 15:7) and a murderer (Luke 23:19).

19:1 scourged Him: Scourging was part of a capital sentence. But in this case it was inflicted before formal judgment.

19:2 The **crown of thorns** was in mockery of a kingly crown. Placing a **purple robe** on Jesus made Jesus a caricature of a royal conqueror.

19:3 Hail, King of the Jews was probably a sarcastic echo of what the soldiers had heard at Jesus' triumphal entry or at His trial.

19:4 I am bringing Him out to you: Perhaps Pilate was appealing to the people's compassion so that he could release Jesus.

19:5, 6 Crucify Him: The Jewish leaders anticipated an outburst of pity. Therefore they began demanding Jesus' death. **I find no fault in Him:** This was the third time Pilate declared that he could find no legal grounds for capital punishment (18:38; 19:4).

19:7 We have a law: The Jewish leaders were telling Pilate, "If you are appealing to us, we say that according to our law, He must die." As governor, Pilate was bound by Roman custom to respect Jewish law. **He made Himself the Son of God:** The Jewish leaders were accusing Jesus of violating the laws against blasphemy (see Lev. 24:16).

19:8 he was the more afraid: Pilate had no doubt become fearful. The claim of Jesus' deity further excited his fears.

19:9 Jesus gave ... no answer: Three times Pilate had publicly pronounced Jesus innocent (18:38; 19:4, 6). If he had really wanted to know the truth, he would have believed what Jesus had already told him (18:37).

19:10, 11 given you from above: Jesus acknowledged that Pilate had the power to take His life, but only because God allowed him that power.

19:12 not Caesar's friend: The Jews shifted their focus from the religious charge (v. 7) to the political charge (18:33), which they backed up with an appeal to Caesar's own political interest. This new plea forced Pilate to choose between yielding to an indefinite sense of right or escaping the danger of an accusation at Rome.

19:13 The Pavement referred to a large paved area in the Fortress Antonia.

19:14 The Preparation Day of the Passover refers to the Friday of Passover week (v. 31), the preparation for the Sabbath of the Passover. This means that Jesus was crucified on Friday (Matt. 27:62). **The sixth hour** was 6 A.M. according to the Roman system of time.

19:15, 16 The Jewish leaders preferred proclaiming a heathen emperor as their **king** to acknowledging Jesus as their Messiah. Trapped by his own fear, Pilate handed over the innocent Jesus to endure a punishment Pilate knew He did not deserve.

19:17 The Place of a Skull probably got its name from the shape of the hill.

19:18 they crucified Him: Of all the apostles, John alone witnessed the crucifixion. However, he spares his readers the revolting details. The **two others** were thieves (see Matt. 27:38; Mark 15:27).

19:19 wrote a title: It was a Roman custom to write the name of the condemned person and his crime on a plaque to be placed above his head at the execution. Mark calls this title "the inscription of His accusation" (see Mark 15:26).

19:20 written in Hebrew, Greek, and Latin: Multilingual inscriptions were common. The title was written in the local, common, and official languages of the day. Everyone could read the message in his or her own language.

19:21 The addition of the phrase **of the Jews** to the title **chief priests** (probably referring to Caiaphas and Annas) occurs nowhere else in the New Testament. The addition probably corresponds to the title given Jesus. The chief priest of the Jews objected to Jesus being called **King of the Jews.** They did not want a messianic designation connected with Him.

19:22 Pilate refused to change the title. As did Caiaphas, Pilate affirmed more than he ever intended. The title proclaimed to all that Jesus is indeed the promised Messiah.

19:23 the soldiers: According to Roman law, the **garments** of a condemned criminal belonged to the executioners. Jesus had two items of clothing. The cloak was a large, loose garment. The **tunic** was a close-fitting garment that went from the neck to the knees.

19:24 The outer garment could be conveniently divided, but the inner garment could not. Thus the soldiers divided the outer one and **cast lots** for the inner one. Unknowingly, the soldiers fulfilled David's prophecy in Ps. 22:18.

19:25, 26 The disciple whom He loved refers to John, the author of this Gospel.

19:27 Behold your mother: Jesus placed Mary in the care of John.

19:28 that the Scripture might be fulfilled: Everything foretold about the earthly life of Jesus had been accomplished.

19:29 Sour wine was not the same as the drugged wine that had been offered to Jesus

earlier ("wine mingled with myrrh"; see Mark 15:23). Jesus did not take that wine because He wanted to die fully conscious. He did take a sip of this wine. One of the agonies of crucifixion was incredible thirst, added to the terrible pain.

19:30 It is finished ... He gave up His spirit: Having fulfilled every command of the Father and every prophecy of Scripture, Jesus voluntarily died. This was not a cry of exhaustion, but of completion.

19:31–33 bodies should not remain on the cross: It is ironic that in the midst of a deliberate judicial murder the Jews were scrupulous about keeping the ceremonial law. According to Jewish law (Deut. 21:23), it was necessary to remove the bodies of executed criminals before sunset. To avoid breaking the Law, the Jews requested that the legs of the condemned be broken so that the men would die quickly and could be removed from their crosses.

 IN DEPTH | **The Women Around Jesus**

Jesus went to His death attended by a loyal following of women who had stood by Him throughout His ministry (John 19:25). Women played a major part in Jesus' life and work. It was a woman or women who ...

* nurtured Him as He grew up (Luke 2:51);
* traveled with Him and helped finance His ministry (8:1–3);
* listened to Him teach (10:39);
* were featured in His parables (Matt. 13:33; 24:41);
* shared the good news that He was the Messiah (John 4:28–30);
* offered hospitality to Him and His companions (Mark 1:29–31);
* were treated by Him with respect and compassion (John 4:5–27; 11:32, 33);
* were healed by Him (Matt. 9:20–22; Luke 13:10–17);
* were praised by Him for their faith (Mark 7:24–30);
* were commended by Him for their generosity (12:41–44);
* worshiped Him and prepared His body for burial before His crucifixion (Matt. 26:6–13);
* stood by Him at the Cross (27:55; John 19:25);
* assisted in His burial (Mark 16:1; Luke 23:55—24:1);
* first saw Him resurrected (John 20:16); and
* went to tell the rest of His followers that He was risen from the dead (20:18).

19:34 To make certain that Jesus was dead, **one of the soldiers pierced His side with a spear.** After the soldier did this, **blood and water came out,** indicating that Jesus was already dead. Only blood would have flowed from a living body.

19:35 he who has seen: John's words can be trusted because he is giving an eyewitness account, so that his readers will believe that Jesus is the Savior.

19:36, 37 One should trust Christ not only because John gives an accurate account of His death (v. 35), but also because He fulfilled Scripture (v. 37), proving that He is the Messiah. Both the lack of broken bones and the piercing of His side fulfilled prophecies (see Ex. 12:46; Zech. 12:10).

19:38 Joseph, a rich member of the Jewish council (see Matt. 27:57; Mark 15:43), had not agreed with their decision (see Luke 23:50).

19:39 Nicodemus, like Joseph (v. 38), was a member of the council (3:1). At last, Nicodemus identified himself with the One who had come from above (12:42). **A hundred pounds:** Nicodemus intended to cover Jesus' entire body with spices—a common burial custom.

19:40–42 a new tomb: Matthew specifies that the tomb belonged to Joseph (see Matt. 27:60). This too was a fulfillment of a prophecy: The Messiah would be buried in a rich man's grave (see Is. 53:9).

20:1 while it was still dark: Apparently **Mary Magdalene** arrived ahead of the other women (see Matt. 28:1; Mark 16:1; Luke 24:10). She was the last one at the Cross and the first one at the grave.

20:2–4 The other disciple, whom Jesus loved, was John, the author of this Gospel. **They have taken away the Lord:** Mary Magdalene jumped to the wrong conclusion. **we:** Other women were with Mary Magdalene (Matt. 28:1; Mark 16:1; Luke 24:10).

20:5 the linen cloths lying there: No one who came to steal the body would have taken the time to unwrap it and leave the cloths behind.

20:6 saw: The Greek term implies an intense stare, in contrast to the more casual look described in v. 5. Peter **went into the tomb** to get a good look. He carefully examined the place where Jesus' body had been.

20:7 folded together: The **handkerchief** around Christ's head had not been thrown aside, as might have been done by a thief. It had been folded and laid aside. Perhaps the implication is that Christ did not rush out of the tomb, but left His grave clothes neatly folded.

20:8 The **other disciple,** commonly believed to be the apostle John, **saw** the tomb and the grave clothes and **believed** that Christ had been raised from the dead.

20:9, 10 they did not know the Scripture: The disciples believed because of what they saw in the tomb (v. 8), not because of what they knew from Old Testament passages describing the Savior's Resurrection (see Luke 24:25–27).

20:11–16 When Christ uttered her name, **Mary** recognized His voice. Mary addressed Christ as **Rabboni,** an Aramaic term which John translates for his Greek readers.

20:17, 18 Cling: Mary had grabbed Christ and was holding on to Him as if she would never turn Him loose. Christ explained to her that He could not stay because He had to ascend to His Father. **My brethren** referred to the disciples (v. 18). Jesus sent Mary to them with the first postresurrection testimony.

20:19, 20 Jesus came and stood in the midst: Christ's appearance was miraculous, because **the doors were shut.** Jesus, as God, could perform a variety of miracles without requiring a change in His humanity. Here Christ's body was a physical body, the same body in which He died and was buried. The difference is that His flesh had been changed to take on immortality and incorruptibility (see 1 Cor. 15:53).

20:21 As indicates that the disciples were commissioned to carry on Christ's work, not to begin a new one.

20:22 Receive the Holy Spirit: The ministry to which Jesus called the disciples (v. 21; see also Matt. 28:16–20; Luke 24:47–49) required spiritual power. Here Jesus breathed the Spirit into the disciples. At Pentecost the Spirit unified the believers into one body and empowered them to testify of Jesus (see 1 Cor. 12:13).

20:23 If you forgive: The apostles knew that only God could forgive sins (see Mark 2:7). Jesus was speaking of the responsibility of the church to declare the gospel to all the world, so that those who believe in Jesus can find the precious gift of forgiveness (see Matt. 16:19).

20:24, 25 Thomas was not present when Jesus appeared to the disciples in the closed room (vv. 19–23). **Unless I see in His hands:** When Jesus appeared to the other disciples, He showed them His hands and His side (v. 20). No doubt they told Thomas about it; hence his request.

20:26–28 My Lord and my God: In awestruck wonder, Thomas not only believed that Christ was risen from the dead, but he also saw that the Resurrection proved His deity.

20:29 Those who have not seen includes all who have believed in Christ since His Ascension to the Father (see 1 Pet. 1:8, 9).

20:30, 31 John states the purpose of his book, which was to convince his readers that Jesus is the Christ, the Messiah who fulfilled God's promises to Israel. Jesus is the Son of God, God in the flesh. By believing these things, a person obtains eternal life (1:12).

21:1, 2 John, the author of this Gospel, was one of **the sons of Zebedee.** The omission of his name here is consistent with his reserve about everything connected with himself in his book.

21:3, 4 the disciples did not know: Perhaps the apostles did not recognize Jesus because they were preoccupied with their work as Mary Magdalene had been with her sorrow (20:14). In addition, there was not much light at this time of day. **When the morning had now come** refers to daybreak.

21:5 have you any food: The question from the shore was probably regarded as a request to buy fish. The disciples answered that they had nothing to sell.

21:6, 7 Peter ... plunged into the sea: John was the first to recognize the Lord; Peter was the first to act. Though Peter often made bad

decisions, he had zeal that would eventually be channeled to good use (see Acts 2:14–41).

21:8–10 Two hundred cubits is about a hundred yards.

21:11–14 The phrase **the third time** applies to the disciples as a group. John himself has related three appearances before this one, the first being to Mary Magdalene (20:19–23, 26–29).

21:15 More than these means more than the other disciples (see Matt. 26:22). On two different occasions Peter had claimed extraordinary love for Christ, even comparing himself to other men (see 13:37; Matt. 26:33).

21:16 Tend means to shepherd. Lambs need to be fed (v. 15); **sheep** need to be guided. Peter would need to care for diverse people in different ways, as Christ had done with His disciples.

21:17 Peter denied the Lord at least three times. Here he affirmed his love for the Lord for **the third time.**

21:18, 19 Another will gird you means that Peter would be bound as a condemned criminal. The day would come when Peter would be totally under the control of Roman executioners, who would **carry** him where he would **not wish** to go, to death (v. 19). His death is hinted at in 2 Pet. 1:13, 14. Jesus' words confirm the early church tradition that Peter was crucified upside down.

21:20, 21 What about this man: Peter wanted to know if John would also suffer a violent death.

21:22, 23 You follow Me: The Lord told Peter that he should be concerned with following God's will himself and not worrying about God's will for others. **this disciple would not die:** The rumor was that Jesus would return before John died.

21:24 This is the disciple: The disciple was the one whom Jesus loved (v. 20). This is basically John's signature to his Gospel.

21:25 there are also many other things that Jesus did: The Gospel of John is truthful (v. 24), but it is not exhaustive.

Acts

Introduction

Luke wrote the Book of Acts to show the fulfillment of Jesus' words, "I will build My church, and the gates of Hades shall not prevail against it" (see Matt. 16:18). Before Jesus ascended to heaven, He commanded His followers to make disciples of all nations (see Luke 24:46–49). Luke begins Acts with a reiteration of that commission and a description of how it would be carried out (1:8). The Book of Acts begins with a reference to the author's "former account" written to a man named Theophilus (1:1), a clear reference to the Gospel of Luke (see Luke 1:3). Even though the author does not mention himself by name in either the Gospel or Acts, early tradition identifies Luke as the author of both volumes.

Called "the beloved physician" by Paul (see Col. 4:14), Luke was a doctor whom Paul met in Troas (see 16:8–11). Paul's references to Luke in 2 Tim. 4:11 and Philem. 24 portray Luke as Paul's faithful traveling companion. After the two met in Troas, Luke included himself with the missionary team recorded in Acts (see 16:10, the beginning of the so-called "we" sections in the book). Luke's faithful friendship to Paul continued until Paul's death in Rome, for Luke was one of the few people who did not desert him (see 2 Tim. 4:11). Luke probably wrote the Book of Acts between A.D. 61–64.

The Book of Acts provides a condensed history of the early church. The book details how the Holy Spirit authorized our spiritual forebears to be His witnesses throughout the world. God has sent the Holy Spirit to help us follow their example (see Eph. 5:17, 18), and to be Jesus' witnesses in all the earth.

1:1 Luke addressed his Gospel to the "most excellent **Theophilus**" (see Luke 1:3), using a title that indicates Theophilus was a person of high rank. The formal title is dropped here.

1:2, 3 Taken up refers to Christ's Ascension, the end of His earthly ministry. These verses look back to Luke 24:51 and ahead to vv. 9, 22. **the apostles ... to whom He also presented Himself alive:** The resurrected

Jesus presented Himself "not to all the people, but to witnesses chosen before by God" (10:41). In the **forty days** between Jesus' Resurrection and Ascension, there are recorded some ten or eleven appearances of Jesus to believers confirming His Resurrection. On the last of these appearances, Jesus gathered His apostles together and commanded them not to leave Jerusalem (v. 4). **Many infallible proofs** serve as the basis for the believer's confidence in the Resurrection of our Lord. The birth, ministry, death, Resurrection, and Ascension of the Lord Jesus Christ are solidly rooted in history.

1:4 As predicted by John the Baptist (see Matt. 3:11; John 1:33) and reiterated by Jesus Himself, **the Promise of the Father** was the promise of baptism in the Holy Spirit.

1:5 shall be baptized with the Holy Spirit: The passive tense of the verb indicates that baptism does not depend upon our efforts to obtain the promise, but upon the Lord's will. The Greek word for *baptized* means "to immerse" or "to dip." Spirit baptism means we have been placed in spiritual union with one another in the body of Jesus Christ, the church (see 1 Cor. 12:12, 13).

1:6 Therefore: Christ's statement that the Spirit was about to be given triggered concern among the disciples about the establishment of the kingdom. **At this time** expresses their anxiety as they anticipated the kingdom rule that Christ had spoken of in the preceding days and weeks (v. 3). The popular expectation and hope was that Christ would establish His kingdom immediately.

1:7 It is not for you to know: Jesus did not correct His disciples' views about the restoration of the kingdom to Israel (v. 6). Instead He corrected their views about the timing of the event. This was the same erroneous thinking that He had sought to correct with His parable of the minas in Luke 19:11–27. **times or seasons:** The disciples were not to know how long it would be before Christ set up His kingdom.

1:8 Instead of being concerned about the date of Christ's return, the disciples' job was to carry His message throughout the world. **you shall receive power:** This does not refer to personal power for godly living. This was power to take the gospel to the ends of the earth. **Be witnesses** is Christ's command to His disciples to tell others about Him regardless of the consequences.

1:9–11 Jesus promised that He would not leave nor forsake us, but would be with us to the end of the age (see Matt. 28:20). He fulfilled this promise in the form of the Holy Spirit, who dwells within believers (see John 16:4–7). **taken up ... cloud received Him ... He went up:** These three statements portray the majestic departure of Jesus from the earth. **will so come:** The Second Coming of Christ and the establishment of His kingdom (vv. 6, 7) will occur the same way: physically, visibly, and in the clouds.

1:12 A **Sabbath day's journey** was the distance permitted by Jewish custom for travel on a Sabbath day (see Ex. 16:29; Josh. 3:4), about one-half mile. Anyone who traveled farther than this would be regarded as breaking the fourth commandment.

1:13 The Upper Room could have been the room where Jesus spent the last Passover with His disciples, or the room in which He appeared to them after His Resurrection (see Luke 24). It is possible that the same room was the site of both events. Jesus' followers **were staying** in this Upper Room, waiting to receive the power Jesus had promised (v. 5).

1:14 with one accord: This phrase is made up of two words that mean "same" and "mind." It speaks of people sharing the same mind or thinking like-mindedly. It does not refer to people who all think and feel the same way about everything, but to people who set aside personal feelings and commit themselves to one task—in this case witnessing to others about the Lord Jesus Christ (see Rom. 15:5, 6).

1:15–17 From the earliest days of the apostles' calling, **Peter** assumed a position of leadership. In the upper room **a hundred and twenty** people gathered. No doubt the majority of them were among those who saw the risen Christ (see 1 Cor. 15:6). **Holy Spirit spoke ... mouth of David:** Peter equated the speech of David with the voice of the Holy Spirit. This is an example of the biblical doctrine of inspiration, (see 2 Tim. 3:16; 1 Pet. 1:11).

1:18, 19 purchased a field: The field that was obtained with the money Judas received for betraying Jesus was actually purchased by the priests after Judas hanged himself (see Matt. 27:6–8). Since the money legally belonged to Judas, the priests purchased the field in his name. **burst open ... entrails gushed out:** Apparently the noose Judas used to hang himself broke and his body fell, rupturing in the middle. This is why the place was called the **Field of Blood.**

1:20–22 It was the defection of Judas, not his death, that caused Peter to ask the disciples to choose another to replace him. Peter specified two qualifications for the appointed apostle. First, he had to have accompanied the disciples from the beginning of Jesus' ministry, His **baptism.** The replacement had to be an eyewitness to the miracles and teachings of Jesus. Second, he had to be an eyewitness of Jesus' **Resurrection.**

1:23–26 cast their lots: It was customary for the Jews to determine the will of God on certain questions by this method. The names of Matthias and Justus, probably written on stones, were put in a jar and shaken. The name that fell out of the vessel would be the one that God had chosen.

2:1 Pentecost was one of the three major Jewish festivals; the other two are the Passover and the Feast of Tabernacles. Pentecost fell on the fiftieth day after the Sabbath of the Passover. During this harvest celebration, the Jews brought to God the firstfruits of their harvest in thanksgiving, expecting that God would give the rest of the harvest as His blessing. This particular Day of Pentecost was the day of firstfruits of Christ's church, the beginning of the great harvest of souls who would come to know Christ and be joined together through the work of the Holy Spirit. **they were all ... in one place:** The place may have been part of the temple. It is difficult to imagine how the large crowd mentioned in v. 5 could have observed the activities in the upper room or congregated in the narrow streets outside the house where the disciples were meeting.

2:2 A sound like a **rushing mighty wind** was needed to attract the multitudes to the small gathering of apostles and disciples.

2:3 there appeared to them divided tongues, as of fire: After the great crowd-gathering sound of v. 2 came the visual manifestation of God. Fire often indicated the presence of God.

2:4 The word translated **tongues** here is the normal Greek word for known languages. These witnesses were speaking foreign dialects to the people who had gathered for Pentecost from other nations. The Day of Pentecost was a pilgrimage event. People who lived outside Israel traveled to Jerusalem to celebrate the festival. Many of these people stayed in Jerusalem for the entire fifty-day celebration. **Spirit gave them utterance:** Note that the text does not say that the Spirit spoke through the apostles, but that the Spirit gave them the ability to speak in languages that they had not previously known.

2:5–11 everyone heard them speak in his own language: The visitors to Jerusalem probably expected the apostles to use Aramaic or Greek, but instead they heard their own dialect. The visitors were astonished because they knew this was most unlikely unless the speakers had come from their land. This was a sign from heaven, a supernatural event.

2:12, 13 A contrast is made between the Hellenists and the Hebraists (6:1). Both groups heard the apostles speaking in tongues. Verse 12 speaks of the reaction of the Hellenists, who were from various parts of the world: they understood the dialects in which the apostles spoke and consequently viewed the event as miraculous. On the other hand, those mentioned in v. 13 were Judeans and did not understand the foreign languages the apostles were speaking. They concluded the apostles were drunk and speaking gibberish.

2:14, 15 Peter, the first disciple to recognize the truth about Jesus (see Matt. 16:13–19), was also the first to bear witness of Him. Peter preached his sermon to **men of Judea** who had judged the whole episode as being the effect of too much wine (vv. 13, 15).

2:16–21 Peter began his sermon by quoting Joel 2:28–32. In that passage, God had promised that there would be a time when all those who followed Him would receive His **Spirit.** Peter pointed out that that time had **come to pass.** God would speak to and through all those who would come to Him, whether in **visions, dreams,** or prophecy. God's final act of salvation was beginning with the pouring out of His Spirit.

2:22–24 being delivered by the determined purpose: Jesus Christ was God's provision for the judgment of sin; yet it was our sinfulness that made His death necessary. God exercises control over all events—even the death of His Son.

2:25–36 Joel prophesied that the Spirit would come; Jesus fulfilled that promise when He sent the Spirit (see John 14:16). If Jesus was dead, He could not have sent the Spirit. Therefore, He must be alive. **let me speak freely:** Peter knew (v. 29) that no one could dispute the point he was about to make from Ps. 16:8–11, in which the Messiah is described as not decaying. Because David had been buried and had not come back to life, the psalm had to be speaking about someone else—David's heir. Peter pointed out that this heir is Jesus, who was put to death and resurrected. The One who had been crucified is **both Lord and Christ.**

2:37 Peter's argument was irrefutable. **Cut to the heart,** the Judeans asked what they should do. The Spirit of God brought conviction to their hearts.

2:38 Repent: Repentance involved rejecting their former attitudes and opinions about who Jesus was. In faith they had to accept Him for who He declared Himself to be while on earth. **be baptized:** The first action that Jesus requires of a new believer is baptism (see Matt. 28:19, 20), the outward expression of inward faith. **for the remission of sins:** The critical word in this phrase is the word *for,* which may also be translated "with a view to." "Remission of sins" comes to "whoever believes." Baptism is a public declaration that a person's sins have been forgiven because of the finished work of Christ on the Cross.

2:39 Peter exhorted his listeners to repent. In other words, each person had to make the decision to turn away from his or her sinful habits and turn to God in faith (16:31, 33, 34). Then God would forgive that person's sins and declare him or her righteous because of Jesus' work on the Cross.

2:40–43 three thousand souls: The apostles had the duty of training this large group and bringing them into fellowship with the other believers. Corporate **prayers** were viewed as an essential part of the spiritual growth of the church. **Wonders and signs** were given by the Lord to the apostles to validate their divinely ordained position and to verify the truthfulness of their witness.

2:44–47 The disposal and distribution of possessions in the early church was directed **among all, as anyone had need.** When a physical or spiritual need became known in the church, action was taken to address it (see 1 John 3:17).

3:1 went up ... to the temple: The disciples of Jesus continued to follow Jewish tradition. A prayer service accompanied each of the two daily sacrifices, one in the morning and the other in the afternoon. **The ninth hour** would have been 3 P.M.

3:2, 3 The **lame** man was **laid** near the gate called **Beautiful.** This gate opened into the Court of the Women from the outer Court of the Gentiles. It served as the front door to the temple proper. The Beautiful Gate would have been an ideal place for the man to position himself for begging.

3:4–6 The apostles represented Jesus Christ. Because of His **name**—who He is—the beggar would receive the miracle of God. Note that Peter and John did not lay their hands on the beggar and pray for God to heal him. As apostles, with the power of God to perform signs and wonders, they simply told him to **rise up and walk.**

3:7, 8 his feet and ankle bones received strength: Luke, a physician by profession, described what took place. Instantly strength was given to the portions of the body that needed it. The feet suddenly could bear the man's weight.

3:9, 10 The people had seen the beggar day after day, maybe year after year. When he stood and walked, the only reasonable explanation was that God had healed him.

3:11, 12 the people ran together to them: People were following after them, but the apostles immediately gave all the glory to Jesus.

3:13–16 glorified His Servant Jesus: Peter's reference to "His Servant" comes from Is.

52:13, a messianic psalm. Jesus can be considered the Servant of God because He gave His life as a guilt offering for the sins of all humanity. The Father raised Jesus from the dead as confirmation that His sacrifice was accepted. Peter pointed to the healing of the beggar as a sign of the glorification of Christ.

3:17, 18 you did ... God foretold: Throughout Peter's sermon in ch. 2, he balances the human responsibility with the eternal plan of God.

3:19–26 The word translated **refreshing** refers to restoration of strength and nourishment. Strength is restored when hope is restored. Peter challenged the people to **repent** and **be converted,** to change their thinking about Jesus as their Messiah and to serve Him.

4:1–4 The **Sadducees** were **greatly disturbed.** They were skeptics who rejected all the Old Testament except the books of Moses, and who denied the Resurrection from the dead. Peter's teaching about the Resurrection challenged their beliefs. The last thing the Sadducees wanted was for a couple of Jewish men to declare the Resurrection of a king. **laid hands on them ... believed:** The attempt to silence God's truth by arresting His messengers did not hinder His work. The result of the Sadducees' taking these two apostles into custody was that **five thousand** people believed the gospel message.

4:5, 6 were gathered together: The Sanhedrin, was the highest Jewish court, which consisted of the wealthiest, most educated, and most powerful Jewish men in Israel. **Annas the high priest:** Although Annas had been officially removed from his office, the Jewish people still considered him high priest. **Caiaphas,** the son-in-law of Annas, was the actual high priest. **John** was most likely the son of Annas who succeeded Caiaphas in A.D. 37.

4:7 Because the healing of the lame man was indisputable (3:1–10), the question was how the man was healed and by whose authority or **name** the healing had been performed.

4:8–10 Peter, filled with the Holy Spirit: This is the second description in the Book of Acts of someone being filled with the Holy Spirit (see v. 31; 2:4; 9:17; 13:9). Jesus had promised His disciples that they would boldly stand before kings and rulers and that the Spirit of God would give them what to say (see Matt. 10:16–20).

4:11 the chief cornerstone: In the first century A.D., the expression *chief cornerstone* was also used to refer to the stone placed on the summit of the Jerusalem temple. Thus Peter used the phrase to point out that they had rejected the One who completed the plan of God for humankind.

4:12 no other name: Only by placing faith in the historical Jesus—the One who came, died, and was raised again—can a person be saved.

4:13 Even though **Peter and John** were **uneducated** Galilean fishermen, they spoke with confidence and freedom. Their presentation of the gospel was powerful because they were personal witnesses of everything they spoke about (1:22).

4:14–18 they could say nothing: The Sanhedrin knew that the miracle was real. The apostles offered their explanation: the miracles were the work of the resurrected Christ. But instead of believing, the members of the Sanhedrin were concerned with "damage control." They tried to intimidate the apostles by warning them not to **speak** or **teach in the name of Jesus.**

4:19–22 listen to you more than to God: There is no authority apart from God. When human authority rejects God's authority, it becomes twisted and loses its right to demand compliance (5:29).

4:23–31 The response of Peter and John's **companions** after the apostles' release was a spontaneous outburst of praise, song, and prayer.

4:32–37 Luke notes that for the early Christians, being filled with the Holy Spirit meant not only proclaiming the Word of God, but also sharing their possessions with those in **need.**

5:1, 2 Ananias and **Sapphira** wanted to have a reputation like that of Barnabas (4:36, 37), but they did not have his character. At a time when others were seeking to serve their fellow believers, Ananias and Sapphira were seeking to serve themselves.

5:3 why has Satan filled your heart: Note that the same word *filled* is used here in connection with Satan as is used in 4:8 of the Holy Spirit. The term means to take possession of or control. The Evil One tempted Ananias and Sapphira with wicked desires and thoughts, and they yielded. **lie to the Holy Spirit:** The author of all lies is Satan (see John 8:44). When Ananias and Sapphira deliberately lied, they took upon themselves the moral character of the one who is behind all lies—the devil himself.

5:4 You have not lied to men but to God: The Holy Spirit is the third person of the triune Godhead. To lie to Him (v. 3) is to lie to God. **in your own control:** Ananias and Sapphira could have kept a part of their proceeds or they could have kept it all. They wanted others to believe they had sacrificed everything, when in fact they had given only a portion to the Lord.

5:5, 6 fell down and breathed his last: The severity of the punishment may seem extreme to some people. However, Prov. 6:16–19 tells us how God feels about deception and division. The early church was vulnerable to great spiritual danger. God would move with great discipline to ensure its purity and survival.

5:7–11 Peter gave Ananias's wife an opportunity to **tell** the truth. When Sapphira committed the same sin of rebellion and deception that her husband had committed, she received her own punishment.

5:12–14 Signs refers to supernatural occurrences that point to a warning, instruction, or encouragement from God. **Wonders** points to the response to a sign. By its very nature a wonder caused awe in those who saw or heard it. Signs and wonders were given by God to confirm His word (see Matt. 12:38, 39).

5:15 In the ancient world many people believed that a person's **shadow** could have magical healing powers. The people referred to in this verse were not necessarily Christians, but those who believed that Peter had magical powers. The people imposed their superstitions upon this new faith.

5:17, 18 The imprisonment of the **apostles** apparently was a common event in the early church.

5:19 an angel of the Lord: The phrase "angel of the Lord" is used in the Old Testament to refer to spiritual messengers of God. Sometimes these messengers were human beings, and other times they were angelic beings. Considering the events of this particular passage, it is clear that a supernatural visitor is in view.

5:20–25 The angel's orders were not to escape from the city, but to return to the **temple** courts and speak to the people. The fact that the disciples would return to the place of their arrest was a strong testimony to the Jewish leaders and the general public that these men were willing to die for the truth they were proclaiming.

5:26–29 We ought to obey God: When any authority commands what God has forbidden, or forbids what God has commanded, a Christian must obey the Author of all authority, God Himself.

5:30 Tree here refers to the Cross (see Deut. 21:22, 23; 1 Pet. 2:24).

5:31, 32 The declaration that **God has exalted** Him **to His right hand** would have been understood by the Sanhedrin as a reference to the Resurrection. The apostles' claim regarded the resurrected Jesus as equal with God (see John 5:18; 10:33).

5:33, 34 Gamaliel was a highly respected Pharisee and spiritual leader. Gamaliel was the teacher of Saul, who would later become the apostle Paul (22:3).

5:35–40 they agreed with him: This passage is proof of the work of God's sovereign hand in history. He can even use the thoughts of those who oppose the gospel to preserve and protect His servants.

5:41, 42 This verse provides the first instance of physical persecution against the followers of Jesus Christ. Instead of complaining, the apostles rejoiced that they were **counted worthy** by God to endure the abuse. God was using the suffering of the disciples to bring people into His kingdom (see Matt. 5:10–12; Phil. 1:29; 2 Tim. 2:12).

6:1 The Hellenists were those of Jewish descent who grew up outside the land of Israel. They spoke Greek and used the Greek translation of the Hebrew Old Testament, the Septuagint (2:5). **The Hebrews** were Palestinian

Jews who spoke Aramaic and used the Hebrew Old Testament. There may have been an animosity between the groups, even among the new believers, which gave rise to distrust and tension over the care of the **widows** who were **neglected.** In Jewish law, a woman did not receive an inheritance. She was dependent on her husband or another relative.

6:2 should leave the word of God: The issue here was not blame, but rather what could be done to remedy the problem. The apostles were careful to recognize they could not leave what God had called them to do—declaring and teaching the word of God and establishing the church in prayer. **serve tables:** The work of administrating and distributing care to those in need would have been carried on over tables and thus was a ministry of service rather than a ministry of speaking.

6:3 seek out: The leaders of the church included the congregation in the search process. The local council in Jewish communities usually consisted of **seven men** known as the "seven of the town." The men who would be chosen would be known among the people for their **good reputation** because they were **full of the Holy Spirit and wisdom.** They knew the will of God and understood how to carry it out. They could be trusted with responsibility and authority.

6:4 prayer and ... word: Note the order here. Prayer was primary for the apostles (2:42).

6:5 they chose Stephen ... Nicolas: All these names are Greek. The selection of Hellenists no doubt was a wise and gracious gesture to the people who had raised the complaint about the widows (v. 1).

6:6 The laying on of **hands** was not for these men to receive the Holy Spirit, because the seven men were already "full of the Holy Spirit" (vv. 3, 5). Instead the apostles were conferring on these men the responsibility of carrying out the ministry.

6:7 the word of God spread: Many people became **disciples** in submission to Christ's lordship. Through people sharing with those who had yet to hear the Good News, the church experienced dramatic growth. **a great many of the priests:** Most priests were not from the high priestly families. They had ordinary vocations that permitted them to serve their turn in the temple periodically. These were humble, devoted men of God who became **obedient to the faith,** recognizing Jesus as the Christ.

6:8 Stephen was full of wisdom (v. 3), full of the Holy Spirit (v. 5), and **full of faith and power.** He had the gifts, the boldness, and the brilliance to be a powerful witness for Christ.

6:9–11 the Synagogue of the Freedmen: A synagogue was a local place of worship, a community center for worship and studying the Scriptures. The one referred to in this verse was for Hellenistic Jews from outside Jerusalem.

6:12–15 The antagonist **stirred up the people** by convincing them that the essence of the Jewish faith—the temple, the Law, Moses, and even God—was under attack by Stephen.

7:1 The high priest presumably was Caiaphas, the man who had presided over the Sanhedrin's trial of Jesus.

7:2, 3 The God of glory appeared: God intervened in history again and again to speak to His people. When God first spoke to **Abraham,** it was not in the temple of Jerusalem; it was not even in Palestine.

7:4 The text does not explain why Abraham settled **in Haran** when the Promised Land was Canaan. All we know is that Abraham chose to wait for his father to die before he journeyed to the Promised Land (see Gen. 12:1).

7:5 gave him no inheritance in it: God moved Abraham along his spiritual pilgrimage from blessing to blessing. Possession was not the goal, apparently, since God would not let Abraham settle down—to stagnate in God's past blessing.

7:6, 7 Before Abraham's **descendants** would be allowed to enjoy the land as their home, they would be tested in a furnace of affliction **in a foreign land.**

7:8 The covenant of circumcision was the symbol given to Abraham so he would always remember that God had promised to bless him. The sign of this promise was transmitted from generation to generation.

7:9, 10 The patriarchs refers to Jacob, the grandson of Abraham, and his twelve sons.

Jacob's name, meaning "Usurper," was changed by God to Israel, meaning something like "God's Defender." His twelve sons were the founders of the twelve tribes of Israel.

7:11 The **famine** proved to be the providential means of bringing Joseph's brothers to Egypt in search of grain—and more importantly, of reconciling them with Joseph.

7:12–16 Why did Stephen make the point that the patriarchs were buried in **Shechem?** At the time of Stephen's defense, Shechem was the center of Samaritan life. Nearby was Mount Gerizim, the site of another temple (see John 4:20). Stephen was charged with speaking against the temple in Jerusalem as if this were tantamount to speaking against God Himself. Stephen's point was that God had been speaking and moving in the lives of His people in and out of Jerusalem, with and without a temple.

7:17–19 Abraham's descendants enjoyed prosperity and great growth that proved threatening to the Egyptians and to Pharaoh, **who did not know Joseph.**

7:20–22 No person has been given the attention in Jewish tradition that **Moses** has. It is said that Pharaoh initially had no son; therefore, Moses was being prepared by Pharaoh's daughter to succeed to the throne by beind educated **in all the wisdom of the Egyptians.** Later, Pharaoh had a son of his own to succeed him. Jewish tradition also states that Moses became a great captain among the Egyptians, leading them to victory against the Ethiopians. Thus he was **mighty in words and deeds.**

7:23–29 In the opinion of some Jewish rabbis, **forty** was the age at which a man had grown to maturity. Moses' life is divided into three parts: the first forty years in the palace of Pharaoh, the second forty years in the desert, and the third forty years carrying out God's will to deliver His people.

7:30–34 In relating the burning bush incident, Stephen underscored the fact that God is free to reveal Himself wherever He pleases. Wherever God does so, that ground becomes **holy ground.**

7:35–43 Stephen pointed out that **Moses,** the very one the Jewish leaders accused him of speaking against (6:11), was rejected by the leaders' forefathers as God's appointed leader and redeemer—just as the leaders were rejecting Jesus. It was this same Moses who spoke of the coming of Jesus in Deut. 18. Stephen challenged the religious leaders of his day either to believe all of what Moses taught or none of it.

7:44, 45 The ancient **tabernacle** had been the focus of the Israelites' national worship. Even after the miraculous deliverance from Egypt, the people had a tendency to forget God's presence with them. The tabernacle was a constant testimony of God's presence.

7:46–50 It was David's desire to give God a permanent **dwelling place.** God honored David's desire by permitting his son Solomon to build such a house and by filling it with the Shekinah glory, but God did not live in the temple. The Creator cannot be confined by anything He has made. His presence fills all that He has made. Stephen emphasized that God could not be confined in **temples made with hands.**

7:51–53 Which of the prophets: Stephen put the council on the spot. The members of the council wanted to appear open to God's truth, but they and their ancestors rarely wanted to hear God's truth through His messengers. Stephen did not shrink from accusing the Sanhedrin of handing Jesus over to death, thus becoming His **murderers.**

7:54, 55 Stephen at that moment was **full of the Holy Spirit,** which was evidenced by the fact that he was consumed only with doing God's will.

7:56 I see … the Son of Man: Gazing at death may be terrifying, but gazing past death to the presence of Jesus waiting for the believer is the hope that dissolves the fear. Stephen's use of the title *Son of Man* is similar to the Lord's appellation of Himself in Matt. 16:13.

7:57–60 The text indicates that Stephen knelt (v. 60). **Lord Jesus, receive my spirit:** Stephen's work was done. After he was stoned to death, he was ushered into the presence of Jesus (see Luke 23:43; Phil. 1:21–23). **Lord, do not charge them:** As Jesus had done, Stephen requested mercy for his killers.

8:1, 2 Saul, who later became the apostle Paul, never forgot the way Stephen died nor

that he was in full agreement with the killing (22:20). Even though Paul struggled against the work of the early church and the **church** was experiencing its worst **persecution** up to that time, that struggle eventually led Paul to eternal life. **they were all scattered:** Jesus would not let His church become limited racially, culturally, or geographically. These early believers became missionaries as much as refugees. Previously the efforts to suppress the followers of Jesus were confined to beating and imprisoning the apostles. **except the apostles:** The initial target of the great persecution was the Hellenistic or Greek-speaking Jewish believers, in the person of Stephen.

8:3 Stephen's death supplied the spark for the persecution, and Saul supplied the leadership (v. 1). **He made havoc** describes a wild boar ravaging something in an attempt to destroy it (22:4, 19; 26:9–11). Saul had all the legal papers he needed to direct this persecution, and he had the authority to put people to death.

8:4–8 Philip went to preach the gospel to Samaria (1:8). In the first century, the Jews and the Samaritans hated each other. The Jews considered the Samaritans half-breeds and religious deviants. Following the fall of the northern kingdom of Israel in 722 B.C., Samaria had been resettled by colonists brought to the land by the Assyrians. These colonists intermarried with the remaining Jews, and the Samaritans were descendants of these mixed marriages. But the gospel message transcended the first-century barrier between the Jews and Samaritans.

8:9–13 Simon himself also believed: Though this man was baptized, he had a long way to go in Christian doctrine and personal growth. His actions have given to the vocabulary of the church the word "simony," which means buying and selling of church offices.

8:14 the apostles … sent Peter and John: Jesus had given "the keys of the kingdom" (see Matt. 16:19) to Peter. He was the one God would use to open the doors to the Jews (ch. 2), the Samaritans (ch. 8), and the Gentiles (ch. 10).

8:15 that they might receive the Holy Spirit: Peter and John were the official messengers from Jerusalem to tell the Samaritans what had occurred at Pentecost. The Samaritans had to know that salvation came from the Jews; the Jews, in turn, had to understand that the same salvation had come to the Samaritans. When Peter later preached to the Gentiles, they believed and received the gift of the Holy Spirit without the laying on of hands (ch. 10). This served as a sign to Jews that the same gift was being given to the Gentiles as well. The Holy Spirit was the unifying factor that would bring Jews, Samaritans, and Gentiles into one body.

8:16–25 Simon saw ... the Holy Spirit was given: The text does not indicate what exactly Simon saw. The gift of tongues was a sign to the nation of Israel (see 1 Cor. 14:20–22), so it is likely that the same sign was present at each step of the opening of the gospel—at Jerusalem, at Samaria, and at the home of Cornelius (ch. 10). Alternatively, the word *saw* may simply mean that Simon perceived what was happening. **Give me this power:** Verse 13 indicates that Simon was a believer. However, he confused the work of God with his previous magical practices. Because others had paid him for the secrets of his magic, he may have simply thought that this was the best way to approach Peter. He learned the error of his ways.

8:26 go toward the south along the road: This road descended from Jerusalem **to Gaza,** southwest of Jerusalem, near the Mediterranean coast of Palestine. Gaza was the last settlement before the **desert**

 IN DEPTH   **Witness in Samaria**

Jesus said that His disciples were to be His witnesses not only in Jerusalem, but also to Judea, Samaria, and the ends of the earth (Acts 1:8). As ch. 8 opens, several years had probably gone by, but the church had not yet left Jerusalem. In fact, it took persecution to move the Lord's people to obedience.

Why was that? Jerusalem was not the apostles' home. The church had no buildings there. The authorities certainly had not welcomed it. Why, then, the reluctance to leave?

One probable factor was that the apostles had grown up in a culture deeply divided along ethnic lines. For them to preach the gospel to Jews at Jerusalem was a challenge, but a manageable one. But to preach to Samaritans was hard. Perhaps that's why the apostles chose to stay in Jerusalem despite Saul's persecution (Acts 8:1).

But a man who was probably a Hellenistic (Greek-speaking) Jew, Philip, crossed the Jewish-Samaritan barrier. A veteran of cross-cultural work (Acts 6:1–7), Philip knew by personal experience what it meant to be a second-class citizen. When he preached Jesus in the city of Samaria, multitudes responded. The gospel breached the wall of separation.

News of the revival reached the apostles in Jerusalem, and they dispatched Peter and John to investigate. The two Galileans must have been stunned and no doubt humbled by what they found. John, who once had asked to call down fire from heaven on unbelieving Samaritans (Luke 9:52–54), now joined Peter in praying for the Holy Spirit to come upon the new believers.

Ironically, Peter condemned Simon the magician for trying to purchase the Spirit's power with money. "I see that you are poisoned by bitterness and bound by iniquity," he told him (Acts 8:23). But the poison of bitterness and the bondage of iniquity also were behind those who allowed ethnic differences to prevent Samaritans and others from entering the kingdom.

As they returned to Jerusalem, Peter and John were changed men. Notice that they finally began to preach in the Samaritan villages (8:25). The wall of ethnic hatred was breaking down. Samaritans were now embracing the gospel—and at least two of the apostles were beginning to embrace Samaritans.

wasteland stretching to Egypt. God had a divine appointment for Philip to meet the Ethiopian eunuch. The gospel would take a leap from the Samaritans to the "end of the earth" (1:8)—in this case, Africa.

8:27 he arose and went: Faith in God means being ready to move without explanation. **a eunuch of great authority:** Technically a *eunuch* is a man who has been emasculated. However, by the first century the term had become a government title used for important military or political officials. This eunuch was the minister of finance, a prominent position in the Ethiopian regime. **had come to Jerusalem to worship:** Many Gentiles in the first century had grown weary of the multiple gods and loose morals of their nations. They were searching in Judaism for the truth. If they accepted Judaism as their faith, they would obey all the rules and regulations of the Law of Moses. This would include being circumcised and baptized. This type of convert was called a *proselyte.* Gentiles who did not become proselytes but did attend the Jewish synagogues to listen to the Scriptures were called *God-fearers.* We cannot be sure which the Ethiopian eunuch was.

8:28, 29 The **chariot** referred to in this passage was probably an ox-drawn wagon in a caravan. In accord with the practice of the day, the man was reading aloud. Philip, prompted by the Spirit, spoke to the man about the prophecy of Isaiah, explaining the prophetic words about Christ.

8:30–34 Do you understand what you are reading: This question indicates the diligence that is required in the study of Scripture (see 2 Tim. 2:15). The Spirit of God does not eliminate the need for human teachers or diligent study.

8:35 preached Jesus to him: The Jewish people believed that the Messiah would come as the Lion of Judah, a delivering King, not a weak lamb. They taught that the suffering One spoken of by Isaiah was the suffering nation of Israel. Philip showed him that suffering One was Jesus. He had to suffer on the Cross for the sins of all humanity.

8:36–38 What hinders me from being baptized: Having heard the message of Christ's

sacrifice for sin, the eunuch responded to the conviction of the Holy Spirit.

8:39, 40 caught Philip away ... Philip was found: The Greek word translated *caught* is also used in 1 Thess. 4:17 for the catching away of the church into the air. Though this passage may say only that Philip went from the desert to **Azotus,** most likely the terminology indicates a miraculous transportation.

9:1 Saul was **still** restless in his zeal to defend his Jewish faith from the new, supposedly dangerous Jewish messianic sect (8:3). **the disciples:** Christians were originally referred to as "disciples" and "belonging to the Way." Jesus Himself had used both of these titles (see Matt. 28:19; John 14:6).

9:2 The **letters** were documents authorizing Saul to arrest Christians in Damascus. Rome permitted the Jewish Sanhedrin to control Jewish affairs. At this time the new church was a Jewish affair. **synagogues:** The early Jewish believers in Jesus were still attending the synagogues. The synagogues in Damascus had to cooperate with anyone who had the authorization that Saul possessed. Saul planned to take the followers of Jesus who had escaped to Damascus back to Jerusalem to stand trial before the Sanhedrin (26:9–11), and probably to face a death sentence. **The Way** was a title for the followers of Jesus (see 19:9, 23; 22:4; John 14:6).

9:3–9 A light shone that was brighter than the sun and continued to shine around Saul (26:13). The light was so intense that Saul **fell to the ground,** as did everyone who was with him (26:14). **persecuting Me:** In persecuting the church, Saul was persecuting the body of Christ. **hearing a voice but seeing no one:** The men with Saul stood speechless, hearing the voice but not seeing the individual speaking. **when his eyes were opened he saw no one:** Ironically while Saul was blind, he would see his own spiritual blindness.

9:10 Not an apostle but a layman, **a certain disciple ... named Ananias** was ready and available to be used by God.

9:11, 12 In ancient Damascus, **the street called Straight** went from one end of the city to the other.

9:13 So far in Acts, Christians have been

called "disciples," "believers," and "those belonging to the Way" (5:14; 6:1; 9:2). Here the word **saints** is used. It means those set apart by God for use in His service.

9:14–17 Jesus, who appeared to you: Saul was not dreaming on the road to Damascus but instead had seen the resurrected **Lord.**

9:18–21 The people in Damascus **were amazed** that Saul was preaching, because Saul had come to kill Christians, not defend their faith. The leaders of the synagogues were probably notified of his coming and instructed by the high priest to welcome this zealous defender of Judaism. They seem to have been unnerved at first, not only by the fact that Saul had become a Christian, but by the strength of his faith and of his argument from Scripture that Jesus was indeed the promised Savior of Israel, the Messiah.

9:22, 23 So powerful was Saul's argument from Scripture that Jesus is the Christ that the Jews **plotted to kill him.** They even enlisted the cooperation of the governor of Damascus.

9:24, 25 let him down through the wall in a large basket: If the Jewish leaders had caught the Damascus disciples helping Saul, the result probably would have been widespread persecution. Saul's escape here recalls the spies' escape from Jericho in Josh. 2:15 and David's escape from King Saul in 1 Sam. 19:12.

9:26, 27 It is no wonder that the **disciples** in **Jerusalem** were cautious about Saul, wondering whether his "conversion" was actually an attempt to infiltrate their ranks and capture them. **Barnabas,** who had the gift of encouragement, saw Paul's true heart and defended him to the other **apostles.**

9:28, 29 Stephen had also debated the Hellenistic Jews (6:9). In a sense, Saul picked up where Stephen left off.

9:30 Tarsus, the birthplace of Saul, was a well-known university city, surpassed in educational opportunities only by Athens and Alexandria.

9:31–33 Then the churches ... had peace: This peace was not due solely to Saul's conversion. Tiberius, the emperor of Rome whodied around this time, was replaced by Caligula, who wanted to erect a statue of himself in the temple at Jerusalem. Thus Jewish energy was directed away from persecuting Christians and toward Caligula. Here we see God's sovereign hand at work, giving the early church a short season of respite.

9:34, 35 Jesus the Christ heals you: Everyone who witnessed the healing believed. The outcome of the one physical healing was many spiritual healings. Many **turned to the Lord** because they saw more than a crippled man walking around; they saw proof that Jesus was alive and had authority over disease.

9:36–43 To be **a tanner** was not desirable or socially acceptable in Israel. A tanner had to deal with dead animals, which was contrary to Jewish ceremonial practices.

10:1, 2 The following two chapters mark an important turning point in the Book of Acts. Those who were scattered by persecution from Jerusalem had been preaching the gospel only to Jews (11:19). At this point, they began to overcome their prejudices and carry the message of Christ to the Gentiles. As a **centurion,** Cornelius would have been part of a cohort, a **regiment** of the Roman military. Cornelius was a Gentile of Italian descent. He and his family were "God-fearers." **Caesarea,** which was about thirty miles north of Joppa on the coast, was the capital of Judea under the Roman procurators.

10:3–6 lodging with Simon, a tanner: God cut away Peter's prejudices by having him stay for many days not only with a Gentile, but with one whose trade Peter probably considered repulsive.

10:7, 8 when the angel ... departed, Cornelius called: Cornelius's desire was to be pleasing to God. The fact that he readily obeyed the angel is a sign of how much he desired the truth. Cornelius was open to receiving the truth of the gospel the moment he heard it.

10:9–16 While his host Simon the tanner was preparing the noon meal, Peter fell into a trance, during which he was commanded to kill and eat all kinds of animals. The animals were mixed: clean and unclean beasts gathered together (see Lev. 11). Jewish people were taught from childhood never to touch or eat any animal that was unclean. However, Peter was being commanded by the Lord to do just that. Three times God corrected Peter's resistance with the words, **what God has cleansed you must not call common.** The vision was a sign from heaven that Jews were no longer to call Gentiles unclean. God was breaking down Peter's prejudices.

10:17–23 Peter went away with them: Though Peter chose to travel in public with three Gentiles, he was careful to take six believing Jewish brethren with him (11:12) as witnesses.

10:24–27 many … had come together: The great faith of Cornelius is demonstrated by the fact that he had a house full of people when Peter arrived.

10:28–42 God shows no partiality: The good news of the gospel is not for a certain population. All people are welcome into the kingdom of God. This is precisely what Christ had told the apostles (see Matt. 28:19).

10:43 In order to **receive remission of sins,** one has to believe—nothing more, nothing less.

10:44–46 the Holy Spirit fell upon all those who heard: The Jewish believers were amazed because they saw that the Gentiles had received the same gift of speaking in **tongues** that they had received (ch. 2). The Good News had reached the Jews, the Samaritans, and now the Gentiles. All were united by the same faith in the same Lord with the same gift of the Holy Spirit.

10:47, 48 Willingness to **be baptized** is the consistent response in the Book of Acts of all who placed their faith in Christ. It is the appropriate response (see Matt. 28:19, 20) of a regenerated heart (2:36–38).

11:1 The Jews were not fond of the **Gentiles.** They were called dogs (see Matt. 15:26) and unclean (10:14).

11:2 Those of the circumcision refers to Jewish Christians who believed that Gentiles had to become Jews when they became Christians. They were not pleased that the Gentiles were considered equal to them in the eyes of God, based on nothing more than their faith in Christ. They wanted the Gentiles to be circumcised and to keep the Law of Moses in order to become Christians. **contended with him:** This was an intense quarrel. The Jewish Christians were upset

because Peter had broken Jewish law by going into the home of a Gentile and eating with him. The Jewish Christians justified their prejudice by claiming that it was God who had forbidden eating with Gentiles.

11:3–10 in a trance I saw a vision: Because of the importance of the issue of personal prejudice, Luke repeats the account of the vision of the sheet and the unclean animals that God used to free Peter from his racial bigotry (10:9–16).

11:11, 12 Peter had wisely taken **six brethren** with him when he visited Cornelius's home (10:23). He anticipated the argument from "those of the circumcision" (v. 2).

11:13–15 began to speak: Apparently Peter considered the words he spoke in Caesarea (10:34–43) to be just the introduction to the sermon he had intended to preach. **as upon us:** The manifestation of the Holy Spirit was the same to the Gentiles at Caesarea as it was to the Jews at Jerusalem (10:44).

11:16 baptized with the Holy Spirit: The reference is to a once-for-all act whereby Christ places believers in the care and safekeeping of the Holy Spirit until the day He returns.

11:17, 18 granted to the Gentiles repentance to life: This section begins a bold new step in the mission of the church. The Samaritans were part Jewish; the Ethiopian eunuch and Cornelius were Jewish proselytes. Finally the Jewish Christians that made up the early church understood Jesus' commission to them: they were also to take the gospel message to the Gentiles (1:8).

11:19–21 This **persecution** began when Stephen was murdered for his faith (ch. 7). God allowed persecution to be the impetus for spreading Christ's witness throughout the land. **the Jews only:** At this time it was primarily the Jewish believers who were being persecuted. Consequently, the Jewish Christians were the ones who were moving out and sharing the gospel of Jesus Christ in various regions. They shared the gospel with the Jews because they still met in the local synagogues and held on to many of the Jewish customs.

11:22–24 The city of **Antioch** was cosmopolitan, attracting people from Persia, India, and even China. The gospel proclaimed in

Antioch would have had tremendous potential for reaching other areas of the world. **Barnabas,** nicknamed "Son of Encouragement" by the apostles (4:36), was sent to discern what God was doing in the lives of the new converts at Antioch. When Barnabas saw the grace of God in these converts, he **encouraged** them in their new faith.

11:25 Barnabas departed ... to seek Saul: Because Barnabas was sensitive to the leading of the Holy Spirit (v. 24), God was able to bring Saul of Tarsus to his mind again. The disciples in Jerusalem were afraid of Saul and refused to believe that he was a disciple (9:26). Barnabas, however, had defended Saul before the apostles (9:27).

11:26–30 The believers were **called Christians** because they worshiped Christ, the Messiah. Originally, the church called themselves "The Way." But later they began to refer to themselves as Christians, despite the fact that the name most likely was originally used to ridicule the believers.

12:1–3 Herod the king is Herod Agrippa I, the nephew of Herod Antipas who murdered John the Baptist, and the grandson of Herod the Great who had the children of Bethlehem put to death in his search for Jesus. **James** was the first of the twelve apostles to die for the sake of the gospel, and the only one whose death is recorded in the New Testament. Being put to death **with the sword** meant being beheaded. The killing of James by Herod was an attempt to win the favor of the Jewish leaders.

12:4–10 Peter was arrested and slated to be executed like James (v. 2). However, Peter's execution was delayed because it was against Jewish law to have a trial or sentencing during the Feast of Unleavened Bread, better known as Passover. This was Peter's third arrest (4:3; 5:18). During a previous incarceration, Peter had miraculously escaped with the help of an angel who opened the gates of the prison (5:19, 20). This time Peter was placed under maximum security in the care of four squads of soldiers of four men each.

12:11 delivered me from the hand of Herod: Why was Peter's life spared while James's life was taken? The answer is the sovereign will of God. If we believe that God is good and wise, we can trust that what He allowed to happen was part of His wise plan for the good of all of His people.

12:12–15 You are beside yourself: Those who were praying so fervently for Peter's deliverance (v. 12) should regard as insane the person who informed them that their prayers had been answered.

12:16–20 Herod was **angry with the people of Tyre and Sidon.** Both cities were seaports, like Caesarea, the provincial capital of Judea. The dispute may have been an issue of seaport business. The important point was that the cities did not want the angry king to set an economic embargo against them. Through the royal official **Blastus,** the people of Tyre and Sidon received an appointment to present their case to the king.

12:21–25 The voice of a god: The Jewish historian Josephus also provides an account of this display, informing us that in an attempted appeasement of the king the people confessed that he was "more than a mortal." Herod, instead of rebuking the address of deity, enjoyed the adulation—until he discovered the consequence of such blasphemy.

13:1 Prophets functioned in the early church as proclaimers of God's revelation. **Teachers** explained the meaning of the revelation and helped the people apply it to their lives. In the early church the prophets were the preachers—the ones who communicated revelation directly from the Spirit of God. Evangelists, pastors, and teachers (see Eph. 4:11) took what was taught or declared and made it applicable for the daily nurture of people's lives. **Antioch** was the base of operation for Saul.

13:2 ministered to the Lord: As the people carried out what God had given them to do as prophets or teachers, their ministry to the church became their ministry to the Lord.

13:3 The laying on of **hands** was the church's way of identifying with and affirming the mission to which God had called a particular person.

13:4, 5 John was John Mark, the nephew of Barnabas (12:25).

13:6–12 Luke presents **Sergius Paulus** as the first Gentile ruler to believe the gospel. The island of Cyprus was a senatorial island, which means it was Roman controlled. As a Roman official, Sergius was a Gentile. Unlike Cornelius (10:2), there is no evidence that Sergius attended the temple or was a God-fearer. This pagan government official was amazed at the power of God and believed the truth. **Saul, who also is called Paul:** In Paul's Jewish surroundings, the name Saul was used. But in his mission to the Gentiles, his Roman name Paul was used.

13:13 John, departing from them: Whatever the trouble was between Paul and John Mark, it was enough for Paul not to want John Mark to accompany him on a later journey (15:36–39). John Mark would prove faithful later in Paul's ministry (see 2 Tim. 4:11).

13:14 Paul might have had some physical affliction that forced him from the lowlands of Perga to the cooler, higher altitudes of **Antioch in Pisidia**. This Antioch was a different city from the Antioch located just north of Palestine in Syria (11:22).

13:15–21 Some early manuscripts apply the **four hundred and fifty years** to the period before the **judges** referred to in vv. 17–19. In either case the intended extent of the time reference is vague.

13:22–35 David ... a man after My own heart: God saw in David a deep desire to do His will. Throughout David's entire life that drive never changed. Unlike King Saul, who was a self-willed man, David confessed his sins and quickly repented of them (see Ps. 51).

13:36, 37 He whom God raised up saw no corruption: Paul argued that David could not have been speaking of himself in Ps. 16:10 (see v. 35). When David died, his body returned to dust just like everyone else's. David was speaking of the Messiah, who would be raised from the dead as the final proof of His divine Sonship (see Rom. 1:4).

13:38–44 everyone who believes is justified: Justification is a legal term meaning "declared innocent." It is by justification that a person is righteous and acceptable to God. The death of Christ was the payment of our sin debt, so that we might be forgiven.

13:45 When Luke refers to **the Jews,** he is not speaking of all Jews. The Jews mentioned in v. 43, those who were urging Paul and Barnabas "to continue in the grace of God," honestly wanted to know the truth. The Jews in this verse were the Jewish leaders. When the Jewish leaders saw the crowds following Paul, they changed their minds about Paul and became filled with jealousy.

13:46–52 judge yourselves unworthy of everlasting life: A person who convinces himself that he does not need forgiveness from the Holy One has already condemned himself.

14:1–5 Paul and Barnabas **spoke** with authority because they spoke the truth.

14:6–13 the gods have come down: The Roman poet Ovid told of an ancient legend in which **Zeus** and **Hermes** came to the Phrygian hill country disguised as mortals seeking lodging. After being turned away from a thousand homes, they found refuge in the humble cottage of an elderly couple. In appreciation for the couple's hospitality, the gods transformed the cottage into a temple with a golden roof and marble columns. All the houses of the inhospitable people were then destroyed. This ancient legend may be the reason why the people treated Paul and Barnabas as gods. After witnessing the healing of the cripple, they did not want to make the same mistake as their ancestors.

14:14 tore their clothes: The tearing of robes was a Jewish expression of grief.

14:15–18 The sermon by Paul in these three verses is a condensed version of his sermon on the Areopagus in 17:22–31. These Gentiles did not know or believe in the Scriptures, so Paul preached truths that were self-evident to all and led his listeners to biblical truth.

14:19–22 supposing him to be dead: The physician Luke may be saying that Paul did not die here. However, some believe that the text speaks of Paul's resurrection.

14:23–28 appointed elders: These elders may have been appointed by Paul and Barnabas or by a vote of the people. Perhaps both the assembly and the apostles were involved in the selection process.

15:1–4 Later those who taught the need for circumcision among new believers were known as Judaizers. They wanted Gentile believers to become Jewish proselytes. As proselytes, the Gentile believers would need to be circumcised as a sign of coming into the covenant of God.

15:5, 6 some of the sect of the Pharisees: These people believed in Jesus Christ but were still identified as Pharisees. Jews who became followers of Christ could still be Pharisees. The same could not be said for the Sadducees, for they denied that there was a Resurrection, and thus could not believe that Jesus had been raised from the dead.

15:7 It was from the **mouth** of Peter that Cornelius and his Gentile friends heard the **gospel** of Jesus Christ (10:11–43).

15:8–10 Yoke here refers to the law (see Gal. 5:1).

15:11 we shall be saved in the same manner as they: These are the last words of Peter in the Book of Acts. He leaves us with the eternal truth that we are saved through faith by grace alone. The emphasis in the Book of Acts now moves from Peter to Paul, from the presentation of the gospel message among the Jews to its presentation to the Gentiles.

15:12 Barnabas and Paul reported what God was doing in changing the lives of Gentiles with the gospel of Jesus Christ.

15:13, 14 The council listened to **James,** the half brother of Jesus, because he was the first of the three pillars of the church (see Gal. 2:9). He was the leader of the church in Jerusalem until he was stoned to death at the insistence of the high priest in A.D. 62.

15:15–18 While the testimony of Peter, Barnabas, and Paul was important for the council in making their decision, something more than the experience of the Gentiles had to be taken into consideration. James pointed out that what was happening among the Gentiles was in full agreement with the Old Testament (Amos 9:11, 12).

15:19, 20 The testimony of Paul and Barnabas—those who worked **among the Gentiles**—and most importantly the teaching of Scripture, indicated to James that God was truly at work (v. 18). In view of this, he suggested that a letter be drafted that alleviated Jewish requirements for Gentiles who placed their trust in Jesus. Though James did

not want to trouble Gentiles with Jewish ceremonial regulations, he believed certain practices should be followed. He mentioned four issues: eating food offered to **idols, sexual immorality,** eating food from animals that had been **strangled,** and eating food with **blood.** If Gentiles continued such practices, there would continually be tension between the Gentile and Jewish Christian communities.

15:21 For Moses has had ... those who preach him: James may have been saying that since there were Jewish communities in every city, it would be wise to remain sensitive to Jewish convictions.

15:22–27 it pleased the apostles and elders: Note the process the council followed in resolving this conflict. First, the problem was clearly stated. Second, the facts were presented by those who were acquainted with them. Third, the counsel was given by a person who was trusted for his objectivity and wisdom. Fourth, unanimity was sought in the decision. Fifth, the attitude of preserving the unity of the Spirit remained utmost on the council's mind.

15:28–38 Paul was adamant that John Mark not accompany him on his impending journey. Earlier John Mark had deserted Paul and Barnabas **in Pamphylia** (13:13). Whatever the reason for the desertion, it is interesting to note that John Mark was reconciled to Paul later and again helped him in his ministry (see 2 Tim. 4:11).

15:39–41 the contention became so sharp that they parted: There was a heated argument between Paul and Barnabas over John Mark's usefulness to them. Luke does not assign blame for the disagreement. He accepted the situation and proceeded to serve the Lord.

16:1 Timothy was the **son** of Eunice, a **Jewish woman** of great faith (see 2 Tim. 1:5). Eunice had taught the Holy Scriptures to Timothy from infancy (see 2 Tim. 3:15). The New Testament's silence about the faith of Timothy's father suggests he was not a believer.

16:2 Well spoken of may be rephrased as "well witnessed." In other words, people did not have to be told that Timothy was a Christian.

16:3 took him and circumcised him: In Jewish law, Timothy should have been circumcised and raised a Jew, even with a Gentile father. But in Greek law, the father dominated the home. Timothy became circumcised so that God could use him to reach all people—even the Jews—with the message of the gospel.

16:4, 5 The council's decision (15:24–29) brought great joy and comfort to the Gentiles. Apparently the **decrees** from the Jerusalem council were considered reasonable and not burdensome.

16:6–10 sought to go to Macedonia: With both the southwesterly route and the northern path closed by the Holy Spirit (vv. 6, 7), Paul headed in the only direction left open to him—northwest—until he came to the Aegean port of Troas. Paul was at the right place at the right time to receive the call to go to Macedonia. **We:** This is the first of four "we" sections in the Book of Acts (16:10–17; 20:5–15; 21:1–18; 27:1—28:16). This indicates that Luke, the author of Acts, accompanied Paul at least these four times.

16:11, 12 Philippi was a Roman **colony** loyal to the empire and functioned as a military outpost. Because of its proximity to the sea as well as to one of the major roads to Europe, Philippi was a commercial center in Macedonia. Its influence throughout the region made it a good place to begin preaching the gospel.

16:13 where prayer was customarily made: According to Jewish custom, a congregation consisted of ten households. If ten male household heads could be found in a city, a synagogue was formed. If not, a place of prayer was established, usually near a river under the open sky. Paul's habit was to go first to the synagogue of a new city. However in Philippi, he searched for a Jewish prayer meeting.

16:14, 15 Thyatira was well known for **purple** dyes and cloth dyeing. Because it was so expensive, purple dye was used on garments worn by royalty. As an artisan in purple dyes, **Lydia** was a wealthy woman who had come to Philippi to practice her trade. Paul preached the gospel, but **the Lord opened** Lydia's **heart** to it.

16:16 Luke's description of the **slave girl** in Greek indicates that she had a "spirit of Python," meaning that the person was controlled by an evil force. Apparently those who knew the girl did not regard her as insane or fraudulent. Rather they viewed her ability to foretell events as genuine. People paid the girl for her **divination** services, earning her **masters** a lot of money.

16:17–19 greatly annoyed: Paul was upset not because what the girl said was untrue, but because the girl was being viewed as the source of truth.

16:20, 21 These claims were as false as those leveled first against Jesus and then Stephen. Nothing Paul and Silas had preached remotely related to Roman **customs** or laws.

16:22–24 Before prisoners were **beaten with rods,** their clothes were torn off so their flesh would be exposed for the flogging.

16:25 praying and singing ... prisoners were listening: The word translated *listening* means "to listen with pleasure," as if listening to beautiful music. It is in times of darkness that the light of a Christian witness shines brightest (see Phil. 2:14–16).

16:26 immediately all the doors were opened: In ancient prisons each door was secured by a bar. The earthquake probably forced the doorposts apart so that the bars fell to the ground.

16:27–29 Under Roman law, a guard who allowed the escape of a prisoner was generally put to death. Believing that all the prisoners had escaped, **the keeper of the prison** assumed that death was certain for him.

16:30–36 what must I do to be saved: The events surrounding the arrest of Paul and Silas, the way they responded to suffering, and the mighty acts of God brought the jailer to his knees. He asked how could he be reconciled to God? Paul and Silas's answer was simple—just **believe on the Lord Jesus Christ.** The jailer and his family placed their trust in God and immediately expressed that faith by being baptized.

16:37–40 Once the **magistrates** learned that Paul and Silas were Roman citizens, they realized that they were in danger of the wrath of Rome. It was unlawful to whip a

Roman citizen. Paul refused to leave because he was protecting the infant church in Philippi. Because Paul and Silas were beaten in public, people probably believed that they had done something wrong. If Paul left quietly, then the perception would be that the members of the Philippian church had also done something wrong.

17:1–4 reasoned with them from the Scriptures: The Old Testament abounds with evidence of the Messiah's character and life that clearly matches that of Jesus (see Luke 24:25–27).

17:5, 6 The Jews refers to the Jewish leaders of the synagogue who felt threatened by the gospel because it contradicted their teachings.

17:7, 8 acting contrary to the decrees of Caesar: In A.D. 49 the Roman emperor Claudius expelled all Jews from Rome because of riots that were ignited by a group of zealous Jews. Paul's accusers were trying to paint him as a revolutionary who was bringing sedition to Thessalonica.

17:9, 10 had taken security from Jason: It was meant as an assurance that there would be no repetition of the trouble caused by the apostle Paul, and that he would not return to Thessalonica. Instead, Paul and Silas traveled 50 miles southwest to the city of **Berea.**

17:11–16 Paul was greatly distressed at the sight of numerous pagan temples and altars in **Athens.** In his letter to the Corinthians Paul explained why he was indignant (see 1 Cor. 10:20). The Gentiles were having fellowship with the powers of darkness by sacrificing to demons.

17:17, 18 this babbler: Some of the philosophers in Athens mocked Paul, calling him a "seed picker" or gutter sparrow, a small bird that snatches up scraps of food. Paul was being accused of grabbing at bits of knowledge without fully digesting or thinking through what he taught. Because Paul did not speak eloquently (1 Cor. 2:1), some philosophers in Athens arrogantly ridiculed him, arguing that he was not sophisticated enough to be taken seriously.

17:19–21 the Areopagus: Just southwest of the Acropolis in Athens was a hill called the Hill of Ares (Mars in Latin), the god of war.

This was where court was held about questions of religion and morals.

17:22–31 Because the men of Athens had scant knowledge of the Hebrew Scriptures, Paul started with the general revelation visible in creation. **He has made from one blood:** God sovereignly created one man, Adam. As Adam's descendants multiplied and formed nations, it was God who designed their course (see Dan. 2:20, 21). **that they should seek the Lord:** God has placed within each one of us the yearning to worship and seek Him. We grope for Him by creating images to worship, whether they are pieces of stone or personal pleasures. Without a definite revelation from God, we would continue to worship such gods. But Paul points out that God is not far away; we can have fellowship with Him.

17:32–34 Paul's reference to **the Resurrection of the dead** ignited a reaction among the Athenians. The Greeks were repulsed by the idea of a bodily Resurrection because they considered the body to be evil, something to be discarded. Their adherence to this philosophy blinded them to the truth of the gospel.

18:1 Corinth was a center for the worship of Aphrodite, the goddess of fertility. Because of the sensuous nature of this religious cult Corinth had a reputation for being a city of immorality.

18:2, 3 All young rabbinical students had to learn a trade. **Tentmakers** were leather workers. The province of Cilicia, from which Paul came, was noted for its cloth made from goats' hair. It is likely that Paul's skill involved making such cloth.

18:4–6 Paul's custom was to go to the Jews first whenever he entered a new city. Thus in Corinth, he began his proclamation of Jesus in the synagogues. After several attempts to reach the Jews of Corinth, Paul turned his attention almost exclusively to the **Gentiles.**

18:7 Justus: Based on Paul's letter to the Corinthians, it is likely that Justus was the man called Gaius in 1 Cor. 1:14.

18:8–11 In view of the severe treatment he had received elsewhere, Paul must have been very comforted by Christ's statement that he would not be **hurt** or beaten in Corinth (16:22–24).

18:12, 13 In the spring of A.D. 52, a **proconsul** named **Gallio** was appointed by the Roman senate to govern the province of **Achaia** (Greece). Bringing Paul before the judgment seat of the governor was a momentous event. If the Roman governor ruled Christianity illegal, it would set a precedent and encourage immediate persecution of all Christians.

18:14–17 God had already prepared Gallio to make the correct decision. Gallio considered Christianity to be a Jewish sect. Because Judaism was an established religion in the Roman Empire, this "sect" was not in violation of Roman law.

18:18 Paul **had his hair cut** as part of a Nazirite vow he had made (see Num. 6). This vow also involved abstinence from drinking wine and a commitment not to cut one's hair for a period of time. At the end of this set period, the hair was cut and then burned along with other sacrifices as a symbol of offering oneself to God (21:23–26). Paul redirected his travel schedule because he wanted to get to Jerusalem in time to make this vow.

18:19–21 Paul had tried to go to **Ephesus** before but was forbidden by the Holy Spirit (16:6). During his second missionary trip, the Holy Spirit kept Paul from traveling the southwestern route, which would have taken him to Ephesus. Instead, Paul went northwest to the Aegean port of Troas, where he received the Macedonian call to take the gospel to Europe.

18:22 Paul completed his vow (vv. 18–21) when he went to Jerusalem and **greeted the church** there. Paul then returned to his sending church in **Antioch,** completing his second missionary journey.

18:23 he departed and went over the region: On his third missionary journey Paul traveled back through Asia Minor to visit the churches that had been established on his previous trips. The cities included Derbe, Lystra, Iconium, Antioch, and Ephesus.

18:24 Apollos, born at Alexandria: This Jew with a Greek name was from the second largest city in the Roman Empire. Alexandria was a seaport on the northern coast of Egypt. The city was famous for its great library and was considered the cultural and educational center of the world.

18:25–27 John's **baptism** was one of repentance in preparation for the coming of the Messiah. John's followers had scattered throughout Asia Minor and into Egypt. Apollos was a disciple of John the Baptist. Apparently he did not know about the finished work of Jesus Christ on the Cross, the Resurrection, the Ascension, and the sending of the Holy Spirit.

18:28 he vigorously refuted the Jews: Many of the believers in Corinth were Gentiles and were easy targets for opponents who knew the Hebrew Scriptures. However, the arguments of these Jews did not stand up against the brilliance of Apollos, the new Jewish Christian apologist (v. 26).

19:1, 2 These twelve men (v. 7) had been baptized into the baptism of John the Baptist, but they had never heard about the **Holy Spirit.** They did not know that Jesus the Messiah, the One mightier than John, had already come. They needed to hear the rest of the gospel. As soon as this happened, these men could place their faith in Jesus and receive the Holy Spirit.

19:3, 4 Baptism was a ritual used by the Jews as a picture of cleansing and purification. Gentiles who converted to Judaism would go through the rite of purification as their first act of worship. Before entering into the temple to worship, Jews would dip themselves in ritual bathing pools to show their desire for purification. But the dipping performed by John the Baptist was a call to people to turn to God and to identify with the coming Messiah who would forgive their sins (see Matt. 3:1–12).

19:5 in the name of the Lord Jesus: This phrase was a declaration of ownership, an identification with Jesus as Lord and Savior of one's life.

19:6, 7 laid hands on them: The Holy Spirit was received without the laying on of hands in 10:44–48. Paul was demonstrating his apostolic authority and affirming the unity of the new church in Ephesus with the church in Jerusalem, whose members were also were empowered by the Holy Spirit to speak in foreign languages (2:4, 11).

19:8–10 From Ephesus, other churches were born in **Asia** Minor—in Colosse, Smyrna, Pergamos, Thyatira, Sardis, Philadelphia, and Laodicea. Note the sequence of events. Paul tried **explaining the things of the kingdom of God** to the Jews in the **synagogue** for three months. After he was finally rejected, he took those who had believed and started a new "school" for the study of the Scriptures in the facilities of a philosopher named **Tyrannus.**

19:12 handkerchiefs or aprons: The city of Ephesus was filled with wizards attempting to exercise power over the dark forces. God may have used such unusual means in order to show that His miraculous power was greater than the powers of darkness.

19:13–16 to call the name of the Lord Jesus: Jewish practitioners of magic enjoyed great prestige because they claimed to know the true pronunciation of the sacred name of God, and thus were able to release God's full power. These practitioners had latched on to the name of Jesus to use as an incantation.

19:17–19 These **books** were filled with formulas, spells, and astrological forecasts. The volumes were expensive. Burning the books indicated real repentance on the part of **those who had practiced magic.**

19:20–27 Silver shrines of Diana refers to small shrines containing a miniature image of the fertility goddess of Ephesus. Sales of these idols were falling off as people were introduced to the truth of Jesus Christ.

19:28, 29 into the theater: This amphitheater seated 25,000 people.

19:30–34 The Jews wanted to distance themselves from Paul, so they put **Alexander** forward to explain that the Jews had nothing to do with Paul. However, Alexander never got the chance to speak once the crowd discovered he was a Jew.

19:35–41 we are in danger: The riot at Ephesus could have brought the discipline of Rome down upon the city. Ephesus risked losing its freedom and being ruled directly by the Roman army.

20:1, 2 The word translated **encouraged** has a full range of meanings, from rebuking to comforting. Encouragement included instruction, affirmation, warning, and correction.

20:3–6 he decided to return through Macedonia: After the plot against Paul's life was discovered, he decided he would celebrate the Passover with his friends in Philippi. Paul was very sensitive to the leading of the Holy Spirit. Sometimes the Spirit of God led him into difficult circumstances; other times the Spirit protected him from such circumstances.

20:7 The first day of the week was Sunday. The people gathered to worship on this day to celebrate the day of the Resurrection of Jesus Christ. The Jewish believers continued to worship on the Sabbath, which is Saturday. The Book of Hebrews tells us that Christ and His finished work is our Sabbath, our rest (see Heb. 4:8–10).

20:8–12 Because the rooms had **many lamps,** it was probably stuffy and hot. No wonder **Eutychus** had difficulty staying awake.

20:13–16 to go on foot: Luke and the others left Troas for Assos. Paul wanted to walk to Assos alone. When he met up with the others in Assos, it is clear that he had received guidance. He was now in a hurry to get to Jerusalem to deliver the offering taken by the Gentile churches for the suffering church there.

20:17–21 The Greek term for **elders** is *presbuteros.* It referred to those who were held in respect as the leaders of a particular fellowship. In v. 28 the elders are called "overseers."

20:22, 23 I go bound in the spirit: Some say that Paul was out of the will of God in going to Jerusalem after the warnings of bonds and afflictions. But there is no evidence that Paul was rebelling against God. There was no condemnation, but rather affirmation, of the fact that Paul bore witness to Jesus Christ in Jerusalem.

20:24 nor do I count my life dear to myself: Paul no longer desired to hold on to his life. He sought only the furtherance of God's kingdom and the honor of Christ.

20:25–28 with His own blood: It was the blood of the Son of God that was shed for the sins of the church.

20:29, 30 wolves … men: There are always two threats to the church. Unbelievers are a dangerous threat from the outside; the arrogant and self-serving are a threat from within.

20:31–34 Watch is reminiscent of Peter's warning about the devil in 1 Pet. 5:8. Elders protect the flock by their care and teaching.

20:35–38 It is more blessed to give: This saying of Jesus is not found in the Gospels, but through Paul's knowledge of it has been recorded here.

21:1 When we had departed from them may be rephrased as "after tearing ourselves away from them." It must have been a difficult life for Paul, constantly leaving friends and family as he traveled about proclaiming the gospel (20:37).

21:2, 3 finding a ship: Paul wasted no time because he wanted to get to Jerusalem by Pentecost, which occurs just 50 days after Passover. Paul had celebrated Passover with his friends in Philippi more than three weeks earlier, so he had less than 30 days to reach Jerusalem in time for the festival.

21:4 In this verse, a warning was being given by the Holy **Spirit** of the danger that was waiting for Paul in Jerusalem. It is doubtful that the warning meant that Paul was actually not supposed to go. The warning did cause the disciples to discourage Paul from continuing his journey. But Paul had already declared that he was "bound in the spirit" to go to Jerusalem (20:22).

21:5–8 Some believe that Philip's **house** was the place where the believers of **Caesarea** assembled to worship God.

21:9 four virgin daughters: Here we see a fulfillment of what Peter said in ch. 2 about how young men and women both would be gifted by the Spirit of God to prophesy and proclaim the truth of God.

21:10–14 Agabus had predicted in 11:27–30 the famine that would fall upon Judea. In response to his prediction, the Gentile believers had collected money for the suffering believers in Jerusalem. Here Agabus predicted Paul's imprisonment and suffering.

21:15, 16 we packed and went up to Jerusalem: Although they had been told repeatedly that Paul would be beaten and arrested in Jerusalem, Paul's traveling companions continued

to travel with him. They would not leave Paul in his moment of crisis.

21:17, 18 James and the **elders** were the leaders of house churches in Jerusalem. It is interesting that none of the apostles are mentioned here. Seven years had passed since the Jerusalem council meeting of ch. 15. Apparently the apostles left Jerusalem after that conference to carry out Jesus' commission to be witnesses to the "end of the earth" (1:8).

21:19 things which God had done: The evidence of how God changed the lives of Gentiles was presented to the Christians in Jerusalem. At this time, Paul may have given the money he had been collecting from the Gentile Christians (11:27–30; 1 Cor. 16:1). The love the Gentiles expressed to their suffering Jewish brethren was a mark of their genuine conversion.

21:20, 21 informed about you: Reports were circulating that Paul had been urging Jews to abandon Mosaic traditions. Paul only made it clear to everyone that the law could not function as a means of salvation.

21:22–24 Paul paid the **expenses** of the four men because the men were impoverished by the famine in Judea and did not have enough money to complete their vow by offering a sacrifice in the temple.

21:25 they should keep themselves: The Christian leaders were not asking Gentiles to live like Jews; neither did they want to compel Jews to live like Gentiles. The spiritual unity of the body of believers is realized in its diversity, not in its conformity.

21:26–29 defiled this holy place: The temple in New Testament times was surrounded by three courts. The innermost court was the Court of Israel, where Jewish men could offer their sacrifices. Only consecrated priests actually entered the temple building itself, and only the high priest could enter the Most Holy Place—once a year on the Day of Atonement (see Heb. 9:7). The second court was the Court of the Women, where Jewish families could gather for prayer and worship. The outer court was the Court of the Gentiles, open to all who would worship God. If any Gentile went beyond the barrier into the second court, he or she would be liable to the death penalty.

21:30, 31 garrison: Between six hundred and a thousand men were stationed in the Fortress Antonia on the northwest side of the temple. When the riot broke out against Paul, at least two hundred soldiers were dispatched from the fortress into the Court of the Gentiles.

21:32–40 When Paul spoke Greek, the commander realized that he was **not the Egyptian** assassin who had come to Jerusalem in A.D. 54 claiming to be a prophet. This Egyptian had led four thousand fanatical Jews up to the Mount of Olives, promising that at his word the walls of Jerusalem would fall and the Roman Empire would be destroyed.

22:1 hear my defense: This was the first of five defenses Paul would make.

22:2 After speaking Greek to the commander (21:37), Paul addressed the people in the **Hebrew** dialect, most likely Aramaic. When the people heard him speaking to them in their own language, they listened to what he had to say.

22:3–5 as you all are today: Paul explained to the crowd that he understood why they were beating him and wanted him dead. They were zealous for God. He pointed out that in his former zeal he would have done the same thing.

22:6–8 Now it happened: Paul shared his personal testimony. God has given to each of us a testimony of how He has changed our lives. We must share that testimony to everyone who will listen (1:8).

22:9, 10 did not hear the voice: The men who had accompanied Paul heard the sound but could not understand the words that were being spoken to Paul. We are not told why they could not understand the sound they heard.

22:11–16 Calling on the name of the Lord saves us. Baptism is the declaration of that calling (see Rom. 10:9–13).

22:17–23 they listened to him: The Jews permitted God-fearing Gentiles to worship in the Court of the Gentiles. A Gentile could even become a proselyte, recognized as a Jew, by being circumcised and obeying the laws of Moses. Thus the Jews in this passage were not upset about allowing Gentiles to worship God, but at the idea that Gentiles

could be on an equal footing with them before God without being proselytes.

22:24 The scourge was a leather whip, studded with pieces of metal or bone, fastened to a wooden handle. Paul had been beaten before with whips and rods (see 2 Cor. 11:24, 25). But **scourging** was worse.

22:25 Is it lawful: The Roman law was that no Roman citizen could be chained, scourged, or killed without a proper trial. Failure to obey this law resulted in severe punishment for the one who commanded the illegal punishment. Paul had been chained and was about to be scourged without any formal charges having been made.

22:26–30 Originally the privileges of Roman citizenship were limited to free people in the city of Rome. Later, citizenship was granted to others living in the Roman Empire. Sometimes the emperor would offer citizenship to those who had rendered outstanding service. Possibly Paul's father or grandfather had became a citizen this way with the result that Paul was **born** a Roman. Ultimately God used Paul's Roman citizenship to spread the gospel to Rome.

23:1–3 whitewashed wall: Whitewash is a thin paint used to make something dirty look clean. Ananias deserved this rebuke.

23:4, 5 Paul did not defend his behavior (v. 3), but rather repented of it. **I did not know:** This may not have been a normal assembly of the Sanhedrin; the high priest was not wearing his normal robes or sitting in his usual place.

23:6–8 The **Sadducees** did not believe in the resurrection of the dead, miracles, life after death, or the existence of angels. On the other hand, the **Pharisees** believed in the supernatural and affirmed the very things the Sadducees denied.

23:9–11 bear witness at Rome: The Lord encouraged Paul not to be afraid. As Paul had borne witness to Jesus as a prisoner in Jerusalem, so he would do as a prisoner in Rome.

23:12–15 The willingness of the Jewish **council** to cooperate with the assassination plot against Paul shows how conscious they were of their weak case against him.

23:16–24 Paul was to be escorted out of the city under cover of darkness surrounded by hundreds of soldiers. Apparently the commander thought the threat of assassination was serious enough to commit almost half of the entire garrison at the Fortress of Antonia to escorting Paul at least part of the way to Rome.

23:25–30 He wrote a letter: Roman law required a subordinate officer to send a written statement of the case with a prisoner when he referred the case to his superior.

23:31, 32 Slipping out of Jerusalem when the city was quiet; the foot soldiers and cavalry probably attracted little attention. The hand of God over Paul's life can be seen in the provision of such extraordinary protection.

23:33, 34 the governor: Antonius Felix governed Judea from A.D. 52 to 60. He was known for indulging in every kind of lust. **he was from Cilicia:** After reading the letter from Jerusalem, Felix wanted to know Paul's home province. When he learned it was Cilicia he decided to hear the case, because the political status of Cilicia did not require its natives to be sent back there for trial.

23:35 As the official residence built by Herod the Great, **Herod's Praetorium** included cells for prisoners (see John 18:28; Phil. 1:13).

24:1–5 we have found this man: There were three basic charges against Paul: his opponents argued that Paul had been causing riots throughout the empire, that he spoke against the Law of Moses, and that he had brought a Gentile into the Jewish temple courts.

24:6–12 He demonstrated how ridiculous the charge was in that it had only been **twelve days** since he had come to Jerusalem. This was hardly enough time to incite riots or start revolutions in Judea.

24:13, 14 Paul openly admitted that he was a follower of **the Way,** but he contended that he still believed **the Law** and **the Prophets.** That is, he was a follower of Judaism, a religion protected by Rome.

24:15–19 The reference to **Jews from Asia** indicated to Felix that Paul's accusers were not present, creating some suspicion about the charges against the apostle.

24:20–22 having more accurate knowledge of the Way: Felix's wife Drusilla was Jewish.

She was the great-granddaughter of Herod the Great, who had tried to kill the baby Jesus. She was the great-niece of the Herod who killed John the Baptist. Her father had the apostle James put to death (12:1, 2). Also, Felix was well acquainted with Christianity from having governed Judea and Samaria for six years.

24:23–25 Felix had taken Drusilla from her former husband, the king of Emesa in Syria. She was Felix's third wife. When Paul talked about **righteousness, self-control,** and the coming **judgment,** Felix must have been reminded of his immoral life.

24:26 Felix may have hoped that Paul had **money** from the Gentile churches or that perhaps Paul's friends would pay a ransom for him. Felix wanted to talk about a payoff; Paul wanted to talk about righteousness (v. 25).

24:27 after two years: It may be that this was the time Luke wrote most of the Book of Acts, considering that he had access to people in Jerusalem and Caesarea for information about the early church.

25:1–4 The Jews hated Felix, so he was replaced by Porcius **Festus.** Festus learned from the mistakes of Felix. Three days after arriving in Caesarea, Festus headed to Jerusalem to meet with the Jewish leaders to establish some sort of working arrangement with the high priest and the Sanhedrin. **they petitioned him:** The Jewish leaders wanted Festus to send Paul back to Jerusalem for trial. Their plan was to assassinate Paul on the way (23:15).

25:5 see if there is any fault in him: Festus reopened Paul's case in an attempt to appease the Jewish leaders.

25:6–12 Paul's **appeal to Caesar** was the right of any Roman citizen. If the appeal was declared valid, all other proceedings in the lower courts ceased and the prisoner was sent to Rome for disposition of his case.

25:13–27 Festus laid Paul's case before the king: Festus had a problem. In the case of an appeal, a letter had to be written providing the details of the case. Festus did not understand why the Jewish leaders hated him. When King Agrippa arrived to bring his official greetings, it gave Festus an opportunity to get an opinion from one who might have understood such things.

26:1–5 I lived a Pharisee: Paul pointed out that he was not some stranger or foreigner trying to start a new religion. He was a Jew, a Pharisee, who lived out his Jewish faith better than most.

26:6–9 for the hope of the promise: Paul fervently believed in the promises God had made to the nation of Israel: the promise of a coming Messiah and the reestablishment of the kingdom of God. He did not reject the hope of salvation for Israel; instead he saw that hope fulfilled in the life, death, and Resurrection of Jesus.

26:10 I cast my vote against them: Paul may have been the Sanhedrin's chief prosecutor, urging a verdict of guilty against those Christians he had hunted down in the course of his campaign of persecution.

26:11 The imperfect tense of the verb **compelled** does not tell us whether or not Paul had actually been successful in causing believers to **blaspheme** their faith, only that he had tried to compel them to do so.

26:12–14 kick against the goads: A young ox, when it was first yoked, usually resented the burden and tried kicking its way out. The plowman would hold a long staff with a sharpened end close to the heels of the ox. Every time the ox kicked, it struck the spike. The ox had to learn submission to the yoke the hard way. Before his encounter with Jesus on the Damascus road, Paul was resisting God in a similar manner (see 1 Tim. 1:13).

26:15–20 Repentance indicates a complete change in thinking. Paul was killing Christians because he thought it was the correct course of action. Christ's revelation changed his thoughts, but his preaching of the Good News was visible proof that he had repented of his former ways.

26:21–32 Agrippa realized that Paul was doing more than just defending his faith; he was trying to persuade Agrippa to become a follower of Jesus Christ. The interview was becoming too personal for Agrippa's comfort, so he ended the dialogue.

27:1 other prisoners: Some of the other prisoners may have also appealed to Caesar,

or they may have been under sentence of death and were on their way to Rome to appear as combatants in the arena.

27:2–6 the winds were contrary: It was just before the winter months when sailing became difficult because of storms. Eventually the travelers reached the port of Myra where a larger ship was found to sail to Italy.

27:7, 8 Paul and his shipmates neared **Cnidus** on the southwest tip of Asia Minor, which would have been their last port of call before sailing across the Aegean Sea to the coast of Greece. The wind was so strong that the ship was forced along the southern coast of the island of **Crete.** The ship docked at a small port called **Fair Havens.** The season for sailing was over, and continuing the journey would have been dangerous.

27:9–12 Paul advised them: Paul had been at sea many times before and had been shipwrecked at least two other times (see 2 Cor. 11:25), so he had some basis for what he was saying. However, his counsel was rejected. Because Fair Havens was a little town, the sailors decided to try to reach Phoenix some 60 miles away.

27:13–16 In the morning there was a calm over the sea and a breeze blowing from the south, so the travelers quickly set sail, hugging the shoreline for protection. Suddenly a violent northeasterly storm called **Euroclydon** (a name given to all northeasterly storms) hit the ship, preventing the crew from sailing into the wind.

27:17 cables to undergird the ship: Because the ship's timbers could come apart, the sailors passed strong ropes under the ship, pulling them tight to hold the ship together.

27:18–22 no loss of life: Paul had been given assurance by God that no one would be lost on the ship. Yet in v. 31 Paul warned that if the sailors escaped from the ship, the Roman soldiers would lose their lives. Because of Paul's comments, the soldiers stopped the sailors from leaving the ship and everyone made it ashore alive (v. 44).

27:23–44 The soldiers planned **to kill the prisoners** because they knew Roman military law. If a prisoner escaped, the soldier on guard would be liable for the punishment of the one who escaped.

28:1 Malta was part of the Roman province of Sicily and was located about 60 miles south of that island near the toe of Italy.

28:2–8 lay sick of a fever: This fever was possibly Malta fever, which was common in Malta, Gibraltar, and other Mediterranean islands.

28:9–11 This **Alexandrian ship** bore a figurehead of the sons of Zeus called the **Twin Brothers,** Castor and Pollux, the mythological figures revered by sailors as protectors on the sea.

28:12–15 Some Christians from Rome traveled 33 miles south to a place called **Three Inns** to meet Paul. Others traveled ten miles farther south to meet Paul at **Appii Forum.**

28:16 Because Paul had not been accused of a dangerous crime, he was **permitted to dwell by himself** under house arrest. This meant he could entertain his friends and minister to groups such as Roman Jews and Gentiles.

28:17 leaders of the Jews: By this time, the decree of the emperor Claudius (18:2) had been allowed to lapse, and Jews had returned to Rome.

28:18–22 The Jewish leaders had not **received** any news about Paul from **Judea.** It may be that after Paul's appeal to Caesar, Paul was on the first ship that made it to Italy. Or the Jewish antagonists may have given up their attacks on Paul, having already failed with Felix, Festus, and Agrippa.

28:23–30 two whole years: During this time Paul was permitted to minister to anyone who came to his rented house. Paul also wrote four of the New Testament letters (Ephesians, Philippians, Colossians, and Philemon) during this period.

28:31 Luke does not reveal what happened to Paul's case. Apparently it had not yet been decided when Luke finished Acts. There are good reasons for believing that Paul was released, since he had been found innocent by all Roman officials up to this point. Ancient tradition tells us that Paul actually went to Spain as he desired (see Rom. 15:24). Paul's pastoral epistles contain items that cannot be fitted into the Book of Acts, suggesting that they were written later. For instance, Titus 1:5 implies that Paul ministered on the island of Crete, something that is not reported in the Book of Acts. Paul most likely resumed his missionary travels for two more years before being rearrested, retried, condemned, and executed as a martyr sometime between A.D. 64–67.

Romans

Introduction

Romans combines breadth, logic, and a mature understanding of the Old Testament Scriptures into a powerful arsenal. By the time it was written, the Holy Spirit had shaped the apostle Paul into a skillful communicator of the faith. The result is his letter to the Romans, a theological treatise. Romans is a mighty leveler, for it declares that "all have sinned and fall short of the glory of God" (3:23). It comes as a delightful shock that "God demonstrates His own love towards us, in that while we were still sinners, Christ died for us" (5:8). This is the Good News, which Paul so eloquently and systematically defends in this theological treatise addressed to the Romans. Paul probably wrote the letter in the fall of A.D. 57 from Corinth during his third missionary journey.

This letter was written to a vibrant church in the city of Rome. When Paul wrote this letter he had not personally visited Rome.

One purpose of the letter was to exhort Jewish and Gentile believers to live in harmony. As in most of the early churches, the gospel brought different groups of people together who otherwise would have stayed apart, whether for reasons of nationality, status, or culture. Thus throughout the letter, Paul deals with problems arising from Jewish and Gentile differences.

Romans includes the most systematic presentation of theology found anywhere in Scripture. While expounding why Jesus died for all of humanity, Paul clarifies the core concepts of the Christian faith: sin and righteousness, faith and works, justification and election. The letter contains (1) a detailed description of the sinfulness of man (1:18—3:20); (2) an extensive discussion of justification by faith (3:21—5:11), including a clear interpretation of the death of Christ (3:24–26); (3) an elaborate explanation of sanctification (5:12—8:39); (4) a strong section on the doctrine of election (9:1–29); (5) a developed exposition of what happened to the nation of Israel and the destiny of God's people (9:1—11:36); (6) an extended section addressing spiritual

gifts (12:1–8); and (7) instructions on the believers' relationship to government (13:1–14).

Certainly Romans is the most doctrinal book in the Bible. Because it provides a systematic outline of the essentials of the Christian faith, it is as useful to the mature believer as it is to someone who wants a short introduction to the Christian faith.

1:1 Bondservant means "slave." Paul is talking about a slavery undertaken voluntarily out of love (see Ex. 21:1–6). Paul emphasizes his personal subjection to Jesus Christ. By calling himself an **apostle,** Paul places himself on the level of the twelve apostles and claims authority from God for His work. **1:2, 3** Humanly speaking, Jesus was a descendent of **David** (Matt. 1:1). He was truly and completely human; but at the same time, He was God's Son. When Christ returns to reign over all, He will fulfill God's promise to David to give him a dynasty that will last forever (see 2 Sam. 7:8–17).

1:4 The word translated **declared** means "designated." The Resurrection proved that Jesus was **the Son of God.**

1:5, 6 for obedience to the faith: The purpose of the apostles' work was to persuade people to obey God's command to trust Christ.

1:7–10 always in my prayers: Paul knew he could not do his work for God without praying.

1:11, 12 To impart ... **some spiritual gift** does not mean that Paul would bestow spiritual gifts like teaching, healing, or prophecy. It means that he would exercise his spiritual gift and in so doing would bless them.

1:13–16 The New Testament speaks of **salvation** in three Greek tenses. In the past, the believer has been saved from the penalty of sin (Eph. 2:8). In the present, the believer is being saved from the power of sin (2 Cor. 2:15). In the future, the believer will be saved from the presence of sin (Rom. 13:11; Matt. 5:10–12; Rev. 22:12).

1:17 From faith to faith means faith is at the beginning and the end of the salvation process. When a person first exercises faith in Christ, he is saved from the penalty of sin and declared righteous. As the believer lives by faith, God continues to save him or her from the power of sin (see v. 16).

1:18 Having departed from godliness and righteousness, people **suppress** the truth that God as Creator deserves their worship and praise. Sinful people can mentally perceive the revealed truth of God (see vv. 19, 20), but they choose to suppress it.

1:19, 20 what may be known of God: Not only are divine attributes clearly seen in humanity, but they can be seen in the material universe as well. God's **invisible attributes,** such as His **eternal power** and **Godhead,** meaning His divine nature, can be **clearly seen** by contemplating His awesome works in all of creation.

1:21–23 They knew: Nature reveals God as great and good. But even with all this evidence in creation, people refuse to recognize their Creator, worship Him, or **glorify Him as God.**

1:24 In God's present wrath, He **gave them up,** that is "over," to their sin (see vv. 26, 28). God did not give up on humanity, but He did allow them to see how evil sin is and how desperately wicked people can become.

1:25 The lie refers to idols. They are satanic counterfeits of God, void of truth and power.

1:26 Lesbianism is **against nature**; it is contrary to the intention of the Creator.

1:27 Homosexuality is sin (Lev. 18:22). The point is not that homosexuality is a sin that should be punished. Rather homosexuality itself is the punishment. Having rejected God and become idolaters, some men have been given over to their **shameful** passions (v. 26). Thus they receive **in themselves the penalty of their error.**

1:28–32 These verses contain one of the most extensive lists of sins in all Scripture. While society tends to rationalize certain sins, God judges all sin. Everyone deserves God's punishment.

2:1 In 1:18–32, Paul declares that all unrighteous people are without excuse. Now he demonstrates that the self-righteous (those who **judge** others) are **inexcusable,** by revealing the standards by which everyone will be judged.

2:2, 3 Truth used in this verse is different from the truth in 1:18, 25. There it referred

to the evidence of God in creation; here it refers to the true condition of humanity.

2:4 Repentance, in this context, means to reject one's sinful habits and turn to God. This is the only occurrence of this word in Romans.

2:5 Wrath used here is different from the "wrath of God" in 1:18. There God's wrath was His present anger; here it refers to God's future wrath.

2:6, 7 Romans clearly teaches justification by faith (3:22). Whenever the New Testament speaks of eternal life as a present possession, it is a gift received by faith (John 3:16); but whenever it refers to eternal life as something to be received in the future by those who are already believers, it refers to eternal rewards (see 5:21; Gal. 6:8; 1 Pet. 1:7).

2:8, 9 Truth refers to the gospel message (see Gal. 2:5).

2:10 All believers doing **good** works will be rewarded.

2:11–13 Those **without law** are the Gentiles (see v. 14). Those **in the law** are the Jews.

2:14 by nature do the things in the law: Gentiles who do not have the Law still do such things as honor their parents, which indicates that they believe in a basic moral law (see v. 15). They know within their hearts that there is a difference between right and wrong.

2:15 The Law is not inscribed in our hearts, but the **work of the law** is **written** on our **hearts.** The Law of Moses was engraved in stone, and there is a similar moral law within every person.

2:16 According to the **gospel** Paul preached, God will **judge** not only people's actions, but their motives, or **secrets,** as well (see 1 Cor. 4:5).

2:19, 20 The Jewish people Paul addressed were not only **confident** before God (vv. 17, 18), but they felt superior to others and considered themselves to be guides, lights, instructors, and teachers.

2:21–24 These particular Jews who thought they were guides to the blind (v. 19) were actually breaking their own laws and dishonoring God (see Matt. 15:3–9).

2:25, 26 Circumcision becomes a useless ritual unless the person develops an obedient heart (see 1 Sam. 15:22). On the other hand, if a Gentile was keeping the law, circumcision would not matter. God judges a person according to the state of his or her heart, not according to external appearances.

2:27 judge you: These self-righteous Jews believed they would escape judgment. According to them, God's judgment was for the Gentiles. Paul confronted their hypocrisy. A Gentile who kept the law would be able to judge a Jew who broke it.

2:28, 29 Paul pronounces **circumcision** as being of no value (vv. 25–27). **in the Spirit, not in the letter:** The change of heart that Paul describes is the work of the Holy Spirit, not the result of external obedience to the Law through **circumcision.**

3:1, 2 Much in every way: This verse indicates that the Jewish people have numerous advantages (see 9:4). The **oracles of God** refers to the entire Old Testament.

3:3, 4 Even if some Jews do **not believe** the Word of God, God will be faithful to what He has promised (Ps. 89:30–37).

3:5 Paul asks: If humanity's **unrighteousness** reveals God's **righteousness,** why then should God punish unrighteousness? Paul explains that this is an absurd question that is nonetheless asked by many, when he adds parenthetically, **I speak as a man.** The suggestion that God is unjust is ridiculous.

3:6 Paul answers his own question (v. 5) with another question. If God does not punish unrighteousness, then He is not just and there will be no Day of Judgment. God's justice demands that He **judge** unrighteousness.

3:7 The question in this verse is the same basic objection as in v. 5, except this time the sinner objects to being called **a sinner** if his or her sin enhances God's truth.

3:8 If God can bring good out of evil, then we should not be judged for doing evil, because **good may come** of it. God will be proved righteous and in that way glorified by our sin. Obviously such a position is preposterous.

3:9 better than they: This question means "Do we Jews have an advantage over the Gentiles?" (see v. 1). The answer is no, since **all** are **under sin.**

3:10 This is a quotation from Ps. 14:3 that says, "There is none who does good." Paul uses the word for **righteous** because he is discussing the unrighteous condition of all people (see 1:18). No one can be justified on the grounds of his or her own righteousness before God.

3:11 People do not understand spiritual truth (see 1 Cor. 2:14) nor do they diligently seek after God. People are satisfied with being "religious."

3:12 turned aside: This means turning away from God's way. **unprofitable:** That is, useless to God or His good purposes. **Good:** Apart from God, people lack true goodness and kindness.

3:13 The heart is compared to a **tomb,** for buried in it is the seed of death. The **throat** reveals the corruption inside, the spiritual decay. The **lips** are like the fangs of an asp; they contain deadly poison.

3:14 Humans apart from God are not blessing others; they are often **cursing** them.

3:15–17 swift to shed blood: They murder and kill because they have no respect for the life of another.

3:18 Fear of God is an Old Testament expression for respect and reverence for God, and is said to be the very beginning of knowledge (see Job 28:28; Prov. 1:7).

3:19 Whatever the law says refers to vv. 10–18. **All the world,** whether Jewish or Gentile, stands in **guilty** silence **before God.**

3:20 A legal term used of the defendant in a trial, **justified** means "declared righteous." No one will be declared righteous by doing what God requires in the Law.

3:21 In this context the **righteousness of God** is not an attribute of God, but an act of God whereby He declares a sinner righteous.

3:22, 23 all have sinned: No one can live up to what God created us to be; we all **fall short** of His glory. We cannot save ourselves. Our only hope is **faith in Jesus Christ.**

3:24 Those who believe (v. 22) are **justified,** that is, "declared righteous," **freely,** without cost, by God's **grace,** or "favor." **Christ Jesus** died to provide **redemption.** By paying the penalty of their sin through His death, Jesus can free people from their sin and transfer His righteousness to those who believe in Him.

3:25, 26 By His death, Christ satisfied the justice of God. Paul cites two reasons why the righteousness of God comes through Christ's death. The first is to **demonstrate** that God Himself is righteous, and did not judge the sins committed prior to the Cross. The second reason is that God wanted to show that He is both righteous and the One who can declare sinners righteous.

3:27 law of faith: Paul uses a word-play here. The "law" is commonly associated with "works." But Paul says that a person can only boast in the standard of God that excludes human "works." This "law" is faith (John 6:28, 29). Thus the Jews who were boasting in their knowledge of the law and their adherence to it were silenced by Paul (2:17, 23). The law could only condemn them, but God was the One who saved them. Therefore their boast should only be in Him.

3:28 Man is justified apart from doing what the law requires. Salvation is through **faith** alone (4:23–25). God alone saves, and His salvation is a free gift.

3:29–31 Law can have three different meanings in this passage, and the gospel fulfills all of those meanings. If *law* here refers to the, the Pentateuch, then the passage referrs to Jesus' fulfillment of the law. If *law* is the entire Old Testament, then the gospel fulfills the promises of the coming of Christ and of the forgiveness of sins. If *law* is the moral law, then the gospel fulfills it because it is through Christ that people are empowered by the Holy Spirit to live in a way that pleases God.

4:1 According to the flesh means "according to his own labor." As the next verse indicates, Paul is asking, "Was Abraham justified before God by his works?"

4:2, 3 Paul quotes Gen. 15:6 to prove that **Abraham** was not justified by works. God made a promise to Abraham, and Abraham trusted God. Because of Abraham's faith, God credited Abraham with **righteousness.** In gaining this righteousness from God, Abraham did not obey some law or perform some ritual like circumcision; he simply **believed** God.

4:4, 5 God gives **righteousness** to those who believe (v. 3). The person who **does not work,** who comes to God by faith alone—that person will be counted righteous.

4:6–8 According to Jewish law, a question was settled by two or three witnesses. Paul calls two witnesses from the Old Testament to testify to justification through faith: one from the Law (4:1–5) and one from the Prophets (4:6–8; see also 3:21; Acts 2:29, 30).

4:9, 10 Given the understanding that people can become righteous by faith alone, the obvious question from Paul's readers is: "Is this righteousness actually available to **the uncircumcised?**" **Abraham** received righteousness from God before he was circumcised. It is available to all people, both Jews and Gentiles.

4:11, 12 Abraham is a **father** both of the **uncircumcised** who believe as well as of the circumcised who believe. Circumcision was a sign and a seal of the covenant God gave Abraham for the land. But God would not make a covenant with one who was not righteous. God declared His unconditional covenant with Abraham after declaring him righteous because of his belief (15:6).

4:13 The **promise** to Abraham was not through circumcision (vv. 9–12) nor **through the law** (vv. 13–16), but through the righteousness of faith.

4:14 Those who are of the law is not a reference to the Jewish people but to any who depend on the law for their righteousness.

4:15 Transgression means "stepping over." The law draws the line that should not be crossed.

4:16 Therefore it is of faith: Paul concludes that God's promises to Abraham were founded on his faith so that it would be acknowledged that salvation was only through **grace,** that is, God's favor.

4:17 Gives life to the dead is a reference to the birth of Isaac from Abraham's "dead" body and Sarah's "dead" womb; both were beyond the age of childbearing (see v. 19) .

4:18 When Abraham was physically beyond any **hope** of having a child, he based his hope on God's promises instead. He believed that his offspring would be as numerous as the stars of the heavens.

4:19 deadness of ... womb: Sarah had no children previously in her life, and by the time God gave this promise she was well past childbearing age.

4:20 glory: Glorifying God means declaring who God is.

4:21–24 who raised up: Abraham's faith was a model because he believed in a God who can raise the dead. We follow Abraham's example when when we believe that God raised Jesus from the dead and will grant us eternal life also.

4:25 Just as God brought life from Abraham and Sarah, who thought they were unable to have children, so God **raised** Jesus back to life. Jesus' Resurrection brought us justification before God because the Resurrection proves that God accepted Jesus' sacrifice for us.

5:1 Peace here is not a subjective feeling of peace. This peace is the state of being at peace whereby the believer has been reconciled to God.

5:2 To **have access** means "to approach," as if by introduction into a king's throne room. Believers have been granted admission to stand before God. Even though they were once rebels, they do not have to face His judgment. They can boast in the expectation of the **glory of God.**

5:3 Tribulations refers to physical hardship, suffering, and distress. **Perseverance** means "endurance." Tribulations produce endurance when we exercise faith during those difficult times (see James 1:2, 3).

5:4 Perseverance produces **character,** the quality of being approved. As believers endure tribulation, God works in them to develop virtues that will strengthen them and draw them closer to Him.

5:5 The **hope** that believers have of their future glory with God will not **disappoint** them. They will not be put to shame because of their hope. The reason the believer can be so confident is that **the love of God has been poured out.** The moment people trust in Christ, they receive the Holy Spirit (see 8:9), who constantly encourages them.

5:6 God loved us when **we were still without strength** and **ungodly.** God loved us so much He sent His Son to die for us (see v. 8).

5:7–10 If God loved us when we were ungodly **enemies,** how much more will He love us now as His children? **By His blood ... through the death of His Son** we have been **justified** and **reconciled,** meaning our state of alienation from God has been changed. Believers are no longer enemies of God; they are at peace with God (v. 1).

5:11, 12 Through Adam **sin entered the world. Sin** brought **death.** The result is that death is now a universal experience. In Adam, we all sinned (see 1 Cor. 15:22). The result is physical and spiritual death for everyone. Furthermore, as a result of our sin in Adam, we face a common judgment—death.

5:13, 14 God did not keep an account of sins before the giving of the Law because there was no Law to obey or disobey. **not sinned:** Those after Adam and before Moses did not sin like Adam because there were no prohibitions similar to the Law of Moses. But they did sin, and the way we know this is that **death reigned.** They all died.

5:15 Through one man, Adam, death came. Yet through **one Man,** Jesus Christ, grace and **the gift** of God, eternal life, was given. Christ's work is greater, for it brings God's grace to those stuck in the sinfulness which originated in Adam.

5:16 Through Adam came **condemnation,** a word used only three times in the New Testament, and all in Romans (see v. 18; 8:1). The word refers to "the punishment following a judicial sentence." In the face of this, through Christ came **the free gift** that **resulted in justification.** In other words, the goal of the gift of eternal life is righteous living. This refers to the practical outworking of faith through righteous acts (see 6:16).

5:17, 18 Here Paul completes the comparison begun in v. 12. Through Adam came **condemnation.** Through Christ came **justification of life.**

5:19 As the result of Adam's sin, people became sinners. By Christ's death **many will be made righteous** (in contrast to declared righteousness, see 4:3). Through the sanctifying work of the Holy Spirit, the believer is continually becoming more righteous.

5:20, 21 the offense might abound: Law magnified sin. What was inherently wrong became explicitly wrong once the Law was revealed. **grace abounded much more:** The Greek term Paul uses means "superabounded." Not only can sin never exceed the grace provided by God, but sin loses its threat when compared to the superabounding grace of God.

6:1 Since sin in a way makes grace more abundant (see 5:20, 21) why not **continue in sin?** To silence his accusers, Paul shows in this chapter that a believer who continues in sin would be denying his or her own identity in Christ.

6:2 Certainly not: The Greek expresses a response of shock, that has even been translated "God forbid." The thought of a believer living in sin in order to take advantage of grace was abhorrent to Paul.

6:3 baptized: Paul uses the common experience of believers being baptized as a picture of identification with Jesus Christ. Baptism expresses faith the way a word expresses an idea. When a person trusts Christ, he or she is united to, Jesus Christ, which includes being united to **His death.** Jesus' death becomes our death. Christian baptism makes these spiritual realities vivid.

6:4, 5 newness of life: If the believer's identification with Christ means being identified with His death, then it follows that the believer also identifies with Jesus' Resurrection. The believer should live a new kind of life.

6:6 The **old man** was **crucified with** Christ (see Gal. 2:20). A believer is not the same person before conversion; a believer is a new creation in Christ (see 2 Cor. 5:17).

6:7 Freed translates the Greek word for "justification," which is a legal term. The believer no longer has any obligation to sin.

6:8 Believe introduces a new idea. Christians must not only know that they have died to sin (vv. 6–8) and have been made alive with Christ; they must also *believe* it.

6:9, 10 Christ died for sin once for all. Since believers have been joined to Christ's **death** and Resurrection, they can now believe that they are alive to God.

6:11 Reckon is an accounting term that means "to take into account." Since believers have died and risend with Christ,

Paul urges Christians to consider themselves **dead ... to sin.** Although before conversion they were still enslaved to the power of sin, now they are free to resist it.

6:12 Though believers have died to sin, sin is still a problem. The sin principle is still present and can express itself through the **mortal body,** the body that is subject to death. The difference is that sin has no right to **reign** in a believer's life.

6:13 Believers are not to **present** the parts of their bodies as a means of sinning. Rather, believers should **present** themselves to God and the parts of their bodies as **instruments of righteousness.**

6:14, 15 The believer **under grace** fulfills the law (see 13:8–10). The Mosaic system consisted of external laws which revealed the sin prevalent in human hearts. In contrast, God's grace places the believer in Christ, and the Holy Spirit in the believer. He or she can resist temptation and do what is right (see 2 Cor. 3:15–18).

6:16 slaves to obey: Paul highlights the principle that everyone is a slave to someone or something. A Christian should be a slave to God's righteousness.

6:17 Form of doctrine is a unique expression. *Form* means "pattern," "type," or "example." The gospel message is the pattern. It is the message that Christ died for our sins and rose from the dead (1 Cor. 15:3, 4). This message demands a response from the hearer and with it must be the command to believe (Acts 16:31).

6:18 slaves of righteousness: Being a slave meant being owned by a master. A person who has been freed from sin can act as though still a slave to sin (v. 16), or that person can live as a "slave" to righteousness, as a servant to a kind master who gives great rewards.

6:19 In human terms refers to Paul's illustration of slavery. The analogy of slavery is imperfect, because Christians are God's children (8:15, 16). Having been set free from sin and having become a slave of righteousness (v. 18), the believer should serve righteousness **just as** he or she served sin before trusting Christ. The result will be **holiness.**

6:20, 21 The result of sin is **death.** The

ultimate result is physical death (see James 1:13–15).

6:22 free from sin: (see v. 7). The new relationship with God results in a new person, which makes a new kind of **fruit** possible: righteousness.

6:23 Paul explains that **sin** results in **death,** but God gives the **gift** of **eternal life.** Eternal life is a dynamic and growing relationship with Jesus Christ Himself (see John 10:10). Through living in faith and obedience, Christians can fully enjoy God's free gift of eternal life.

7:1–3 Paul returns to the question of 6:15: Shall we continue to sin while under grace? Paul's answer is no, and now he illustrates his negative answer by a comparison with marriage. Marriage is lifelong. But if one partner dies, the other is now free to marry someone else.

7:4 An exact application of the illustration would be that the law died, and now the believer is free to "marry" grace. Paul's words are that believers died **to the law.** The believer is now free to marry God and **bear fruit** for Him.

7:5 In the flesh refers to the period before the believer's conversion. In this context, those *in the flesh* are unregenerate, and those *in* the Spirit are regenerate. Both believers and unbelievers may walk *according to* the flesh, but only believers can walk *according to* the Spirit.

7:6 At conversion, believers **died** to the law (v. 4), with the result that they are now able to serve in newness of life (6:4). They have a new life in the Holy Spirit.

7:7 The next logical question (see 6:1, 15) is: **Is the law sin? Certainly not!** (see 6:2, 15). Paul emphatically denies that the law is sinful. **The law** reveals sin.

7:8 sin was dead: Sin can exist without the law (see 5:13). Without standards of right and wrong, there can be no judgment of what is sin and what is not. The law, however can arouse the desire to perform those evil behaviors (see v. 5).

7:9 I was alive: There was a time when Paul was alive to God (6:8, 11) and without the law (v. 4, 6). Then sometime after his conversion, when he was enjoying fellowship with God, he was confronted by the law, and he **died.** This is a figurative way of saying that his sin nature broke his fellowship with God.

7:10, 11 bring life: Since the law points out the path of righteousness, it points to life. But since sin reigns in our natures, the law means judgment and death for us. When we focus on the law we are **deceived** into sinning, which "kills" our spiritual lives.

7:12 The conclusion is that **the law** is holy. Our problem with sin is not the fault of the holy law of God, only of how our sinful nature responds to the law.

7:13 Paul asks another rhetorical question. **Has then what is good** (that is, the law, v. 12) **become death to me? Certainly not** is again Paul's emphatic denial (see v. 7; 6:2, 15). The problem is not the law; the problem is **sin.** Sin used the good law to produce evil, that is, death. But through the law, sin is shown for what it is, and its evil consequences are clearly revealed.

7:14 spiritual: The law comes from God. In contrast, Paul said his problem (see 1 Cor. 3:1–3) is that he was **carnal,** meaning he was like a slave **sold** over to **sin.** Even though Paul was dedicated to serving God (v. 25), he continued to fall short of God's moral standards.

7:15–17 Being fleshly, sold over to sin, involves a conflict that mystifies Paul. He feels he does not understand himself. The conflict indicates that there is battle between two identities in the believer. First there is something that acknowledges that the **law ... is good.** Second there is something within, called **sin,** which produces evil.

7:18 The problem is the **flesh,** the part of the believer in which there is **nothing good.** The **will** is the desire to do good (see v. 12). Yet the ability to **perform** is lacking.

7:19–22 The **inward man** is virtually synonymous with the mind (see v. 23; Eph. 3:16), and it finds **delight in the law of God.** This delight causes believers to want to align themselves with the new nature God has imparted to them.

7:23 The law of sin is a reference to the sinful nature's rejection of the law of the mind that seeks after God.

7:24 The **wretched,** or "distressed, miserable," **man** is the believer whenever he or she is defeated by sin (see vv. 14, 23). **body of death:** Paul wants to be freed from sin, which leads to death.

7:25 thank God: Paul breaks forth in jubilant praise to God that there is victory through **Jesus Christ,** who delivers believers from the body of death, the flesh. **So then:** Paul concludes that the problem is not the law; the problem is the flesh.

8:1 no condemnation: In Christ, we are no longer under the sentence of the law, but empowered by the Spirit to live for Christ.

8:2 the law of the Spirit: The *Spirit* refers to the Holy Spirit who energizes our renewed spirit.

8:3 The law could pronounce judgment on sin, but **the law could not** do anything about sin itself. It had no power to put sin to death in a person's life. **God** accomplished what the law could not do **by sending His own Son.** Although He was tempted, He never sinned.

8:4 The purpose of the coming of Christ was that **the law might be fulfilled.** The believer gains the righteous standard of the law—love (see 13:8–10)—not by means of the law but by being in Christ and walking **according to the Spirit.**

8:5 Setting the mind **on the things of the flesh** or on the things of **the Spirit** means being oriented to or governed by those things on which we focus.

8:6 Peace is the resolution of the intense warfare described in ch. 7, as well as the inward harmony and tranquillity that results from yielding to God.

8:7 The reason that being carnally minded results in death (v. 6) is that **the carnal mind** is an enemy of God. The mind of the flesh can never submit itself **to the law of God.**

8:8 Being **in the flesh** means being unregenerate or sinful. People in that state **cannot please God.**

8:9 Christians no longer live according to the **flesh.** Instead, with **the Spirit** living in them and empowering them, they can live in a way pleasing to God.

8:10 Dead because of sin refers not to physical death but to the "body of death" of 7:24.

The problem that Paul is dealing with in this passage is how the "dead" body, in which sin dwells, can be made the vehicle for expressing the life of God.

8:11 The solution to the problem of the flesh is the Holy Spirit. He gives **life to your mortal bodies.** Being spiritually minded means overcoming the deadness of the body and experiencing life and peace. This is the Resurrection life (see Phil. 3:10).

8:12, 13 you will die: Death here does not refer to physical death. It refers to the experience of those who live their lives apart from God. **by the Spirit:** By walking according to the Spirit (v. 4, 6), the believer can **put to death** sinful deeds and **live** for God.

8:14 Being **led by the Spirit** is virtually synonymous with walking according to the Spirit. "Walking" highlights the active participation and effort of the believer. "Being led" underscores the passive side, the submissive dependence of the believer on the Spirit.

8:15 Believers are sons of God because they received **the Spirit of adoption.** Christians have been adopted into God's family, receiving an eternal inheritance.

8:16 The Holy Spirit **bears witness with** their spirits. When believers cry out to the Father in prayer (v. 15), the Holy Spirit intercedes for them (see v. 26).

8:17 heirs: All of God's children have an inheritance based on their relationship to God, which is incorruptible, undefiled, and is reserved in heaven (see 1 Pet. 1:4). Their inheritance includes an expectation of eternal life (see Titus 3:4–7).

8:18 The **sufferings** of the present are slight when compared with the **glory** later. The divine compensation package is "a hundredfold" (Matt. 19:29).

8:19 Earnest expectation literally means "to watch with outstretched neck." **Creation** is impatient to see the revelation of the **sons of God.**

8:20 Futility, which means "vanity, emptiness," refers to the curse on creation (see Gen. 3:17–19).

8:21 The bondage of corruption further describes the futility of v. 20. Nature is a slave to decay and death because of sin.

8:22, 23 The firstfruits of the Spirit may refer to the first workings of the Holy Spirit (8:9–11), which is a pledge of more work to come, like **the redemption of our body.** Otherwise, the expression *firstfruits* may be in apposition to the word *Spirit;* thus *firstfruits* is the Spirit. The firstfruits of a harvest was a foretaste of the harvest to come.

8:24 Hope is a constant expectation of an unseen reality. We are saved by faith, but our hope is in the return of Christ in all His glory and our deliverance from our sinful natures.

8:25 If we are expecting something unseen, we **wait** with **perseverance;** that is, we are willing to endure the present.

8:26 weaknesses: The primary reference is to mental ignorance. The contrast is between our inability to know how to pray and the effective prayers of the Spirit Himself. The emphasis indicates that the Spirit intercedes on our behalf before the throne of God (see 1 John 2:1). But His intercession **cannot be uttered,** which means it is "unexpressed, unspoken."

8:27, 28 All circumstances will work together for the believer's good—that is, the believer will be conformed to Jesus Christ now and reign with Him later. **Those who love God** are **those who are the called** by God. Our love is our response to the work of the Holy Spirit in us. **according to His purpose:** God does everything in order to accomplish His plan.

8:29 God **foreknew,** which means "to know beforehand." This has been interpreted by some as God's free and merciful choice of certain people who would receive His salvation. Others believe that God knew beforehand who would respond to Him in faith. According to both views, *only* God saves; people never earn salvation through any work.

8:30 God not only foreknew and predestined (v. 29), He also **called** believers through the preaching of the gospel message (2 Thess. 2:14). This *call* refers to the internal work of the Spirit in the hearts of God's elect to bring them to belief in Christ (see Acts 16:14). Being justified means being "declared righteous."

8:31 The words **these things** refer to God's purpose (see vv. 28–30). If God has done everything from foreknowledge to glorification **for us,** all adversaries are powerless.

8:32 Paul answers the rhetorical question of v. 31 with a question. Since God has done the greatest thing, giving **His own Son,** will He not also **freely give us all things?**

8:33 This is a rhetorical question equivalent to an emphatic denial. **Elect** recalls God's eternal program (see vv. 28–30). If God, the Supreme Judge, **justifies,** then who is going to successfully bring a charge against us?

8:34 Christ ... died ... makes intercession: Since Christ had fully justified us and is presently interceding for us, then no one can condemn us.

8:35 If no one can successfully oppose us (v. 31), charge us (v. 33), or condemn us (v. 34) regarding our relationship with God, then no one can **separate** us from Christ's love.

8:36 sheep for the slaughter: Those who love God (Ps. 44:17–22) have always had to face death daily (2 Cor. 4:11).

8:37 The trials and difficulties listed in v. 35 make us **more than conquerors** by forcing us to depend even more on God.

8:38, 39 The apostle struggles for words to describe the absolute certainty of God's love for believers. If God, the uncreated One, is for us, and no created thing can separate us, then our security in Him is absolute.

9:1–3 God had a purpose for Israel, and God had said He loved Israel. Yet Israel appears to be excluded from God's program. Paul addresses this problem in chs. 9—11. **accursed from Christ:** Paul's pain was so great that he was willing, if possible, to be separated from Christ if it meant Israel could be united to Him (see Ex. 32:32).

9:4, 5 Paul lists some of the great privileges of Israel. For example, they were called **Israelites.** Israel was the name given to their ancestor Jacob as an expression of God's favor (see Gen. 32:28).

9:6 The word of God in this context is a reference to God's promises to Israel. Paul is declaring that God's purposes and promises have not failed. **not all Israel:** Not all the physical descendants of Jacob (Israel) inherited the promises of God.

9:7 Abraham is another illustration of Paul's point that physical descent is no guarantee of a place in God's family.

9:8 of the flesh: Being a physical descendant

of Abraham does not mean inheriting God's **promise** to Abraham and his offspring.

9:9, 10 The children of **Isaac** are another illustration of Paul's point. God's promise to Isaac was never intended to be fulfilled through Esau.

9:11 not yet ... born: God chose Jacob over Esau before they were born. Neither had **done any good or evil** when the choice was made. God's choice was based on grace, not **works.**

9:12, 13 hated: Actually God made provision for Esau (see Gen. 27:39; 36). *Hated* is an idiom where the opposite is used to express a lesser degree. What Paul is saying is that Esau was not the object of God's electing purpose.

9:14 If God chose some of Abraham's descendants (v. 6), like Isaac over Ishmael (vv. 7–9), or Jacob over Esau (vv. 10–13), then **is there unrighteousness with God?** The complaint is that if God chose Isaac or Jacob without regard to their works, then this would have been unrighteous or unjust. If God's election and rejection was based on the evil deeds of one or the good deeds of the other, the question of God's "fairness" would never have arisen.

9:15 I will have mercy: In this passage from Exodus, God states His absolute right not to be questioned by His creatures about His decisions (Ex. 33:19).

9:16 but of God: The basis of God's sovereign choice is not a person's conduct, but God's compassion. God is free to show mercy to whom He chooses.

9:17, 18 Pharaoh refused to obey the Lord (Ex. 5:2) and hardened his heart (see Ex. 7:13, 14, 22). God used Pharaoh's sin to demonstrate His **power** and magnify His **name.** God only gave Pharaoh over to what Pharaoh had already chosen to do.

9:19, 20 Find fault means "to blame." Paul again poses human questions that he will answer in vv. 20, 21. If God hardens whom He wills (v. 18), why blame the one who was hardened? **His will:** If God hardens, how can it be said that person is resisting God? Isn't the hardened one only doing what God has willed him to do?

9:21 The word translated **power** can mean "right" or "authority." Paul insists on God's right to do as He pleases.

9:22, 23 prepared for destruction ... prepared beforehand for glory: The grammatical structure of the first *prepared*, referring to the vessels of wrath, is different from the second *prepared*, referring to the vessels of mercy. The first literally means "prepared themselves," while the second is "which He prepared." If we are doomed, it is because of our rejection of God; if we are redeemed, it is because of the grace of God. Only by God's grace is anyone saved.

9:24–29 God calls both **Jews** and **Gentiles.** Paul quotes several Old Testament passages to support this point.

9:30–33 The question is: Since **Israel** had the law and pursued **righteousness,** why have they not **attained** it? Was it because they were not elected? The answer is that they did not obtain righteousness because they did not believe. They tried obtaining righteousness **by the works of the law.** Being committed to a righteousness by works, they **stumbled** over the righteousness of faith offered in Christ.

10:1 saved: Justification is what takes place at the moment of faith in Christ. Salvation, at least in Romans, refers to the work of God in the believer that continues after justification. It is deliverance from God's wrath (see 1:18; 5:9, 10). The logical conclusion from ch. 9 is that Israel is under divine wrath (see 9:22). Paul's deep **desire** and **prayer** is that Israel may be justified and **saved** from His wrath.

10:2 Israel had a **zeal for God;** outwardly, they were very religious. But their effort was **not according to knowledge.** They lacked a correct understanding of the kind of worship God wanted from them.

10:3 God's righteousness is the righteousness that God gives when a person trusts Christ.

10:4 Israel was ignorant of God's righteousness because they failed to comprehend what the law was intended to do. The law revealed sin and showed that people could not hope to keep the law. Christ came and fulfilled it, then offered us His righteousness through faith in Him.

10:5–8 There are two kinds of righteousness, by works or by faith. One is inaccessible, the other is very accessible. Paul uses the words of Deut. 30:11–14 to demonstrate that righteousness by faith is not far off and inaccessible, but is as **near** as a person's **mouth** and **heart.** All one has to do is repent, believe in Jesus, and confess that belief.

10:9 Confess comes before **believe** in this verse because "mouth" precedes "heart" in Deuteronomy (see v. 8). The order is reversed in the next verse. One has to confess with the **mouth** to be **saved.**

10:10 For indicates that this verse explains v. 9. The condition for **righteousness,** that is for being justified, is internal faith. The condition of **salvation,** meaning deliverance from wrath and from the power of sin, is external confession (see v. 1; 5:9, 10), which is calling on the Lord for help (see vv. 12, 13).

10:11–13 Paul emphasizes the universal offer of salvation. **Whoever** in vv. 11, 13 means "all."

10:14–16 they: Israel. Not **all** Jews have **obeyed** the command to believe in Christ.

10:17–21 Israel **heard** but was **disobedient;** only a remnant believed the gospel.

11:1 One of the proofs that God has not **cast away** the Jewish people is Paul himself. He was an **Israelite,** a descendant of **Abraham,** a member of the **tribe of Benjamin.** He was a Jew, and he was chosen by God to be a believer and an apostle.

11:2 His people refers to the nation of Israel and not just the elect within the nation. In vv. 4–7 Paul differentiates between the nation and the remnant. His point is that God's saving of the remnant proves that He has not abandoned His plan for the nation (see v. 26).

11:3–5 Paul cites Elijah as an illustration. Elijah thought that the whole nation of Israel had fallen away, but he was wrong. The **remnant** in Elijah's day was proof that God had not cast off His people, and the remnant in Paul's day was continuing proof of His faithfulness.

11:6–7 *Grace* and *works* are mutually exclusive. God's election was established solely on the basis of grace (see v. 5). The **elect** have **obtained** righteousness by faith. The others were **blinded** because they did not believe.

11:8–10 Paul quotes Isaiah and **David** to show that Israel's spiritual indifference was a continual pattern. Their rejection of Christ would bring untold misery on the nation.

11:11 fall: Does Israel's rejection mean the end of God's program for the nation? **Certainly not!** Israel's unbelief brought **salvation ... to the Gentiles,** and it will ultimately lead to Israel's salvation (see v. 26).

11:12, 13 fullness: The nation of Israel, chosen by God to receive salvation, will be saved along with believing Gentiles, resulting in great blessing for everyone (see v. 26).

11:14 save some: Paul is revealing his great desire to see the salvation of all of Israel (see vv. 12, 26).

11:15–17 life from the dead: The failure of Israel in rejecting Christ will make their eventual acceptance as vivid and wonderful as the Resurrection that all believers will experience; it will be as if they had come back from the dead. The **wild olive tree** is the Gentile Christians. The **olive tree** refers to Israel, those who inherited the promises of the Abrahamic covenant (see Gen. 12:1, 2; 17:7, 8). **grafted in:** Paul intentionally stretches the analogy of grafting in order to communicate his point that Gentiles have been supernaturally connected to the family of God.

11:18–19 Gentiles, who have been grafted into the Abrahamic covenant and therefore become recipients of God's blessing, should not **boast.** The reason Israel was **broken off** (v. 17), "cast away" (v. 15), and "has fallen" (v. 12) is so that Gentiles could be grafted into the tree.

11:20–21 Well said: Paul agrees with the objector (see v. 19) that Israel was **broken off** because of **unbelief** and that Gentiles **stand by faith.** But he goes on to warn that Gentiles should not **be haughty, but fear.** Standing before God is based on faith. Paul was warning the Gentiles not to be arrogant (v. 20), but to remember that they depended on God and were accountable to Him no less than the Jews were.

11:22–24 If Gentiles **continue** in God's **goodness,** they will not be **cut off,** and if Jews turn to God in faith, they can be grafted in again. It is far more natural to expect Israel, the **natural branches,** to be **grafted in,** than to expect Gentiles, the **wild** branches, to be included.

11:25 If believers do not understand this **mystery,** chances were they will be **wise in** their **own opinion,** meaning they will be haughty (v. 20) and boast (v. 18). The mystery is that Israel has been temporarily and partially hardened, but God has not rejected them.

11:26, 27 All Israel does not mean that every person in the nation will turn to the Lord. It means that the nation as a whole will be saved, just as the nation as a whole (but not every individual in it) was now rejecting the Lord.

11:28, 29 The Jews are **enemies** in that they reject the **gospel.** For the **sake of the fathers** refers to the promises God made to the patriarchs (v. 28). He will fulfill them.

11:30–36 God is the source, means, and end of all things. He is the Creator, Sustainer, and the goal of everything. Therefore He should be praised and glorified **forever.**

12:1 Paul entreats believers to **present** their **bodies** as **a living sacrifice,** meaning they should use their bodies to serve and obey God (see 6:13). **Holy** means set apart for the Lord's use; and **reasonable** indicates that such a gift is the only rational reaction to all the good gifts God has showered on us.

12:2 Conformed means "to form" or "mold." **World** is the normal word for "age" or "era." Instead of being molded by the values of this world, the believer should be **transformed,** that is, changed **by the renewing of** the **mind.** A renewed mind will produce a life that can stand the test of time. We can resist the temptations of our culture by meditating on God's truth and letting the Holy Spirit guide and shape our thoughts and behaviors.

12:3 think of himself: A renewed mind (v. 2) begins with thinking **soberly** about oneself. The first step in changing behavior is self-observation (see 1 Cor. 11:28–32). **dealt … a measure of faith:** The *measure* refers to God's sovereignly given gifts mentioned in vv. 6–8. These gifts are not the result of intense prayer or spirituality. Instead, God simply gives everyone certain

gifts so each person can strengthen the church (see 1 Cor. 12:11, 18, 28).

12:4, 5 As the human body is a unity with **many members,** each having its own **function,** so is the body of Christ. The church is a unified body under the headship of Christ, but the members have different functions (see 1 Cor. 12:12–31).

12:6 gifts: The Greek word (*charismata*) refers to God-given abilities that should be used to build up other members in the church. Although they are "irrevocable" and, thus do not change (see 11:29), they are to be pursued and developed (see 1 Pet. 4:10).

12:7, 8 Ministry means "service" and is in contrast to the speaking gifts (see 1 Pet. 4:11). The Scriptures list five speaking gifts: prophecy, teaching, encouragement, the word of wisdom, and the word of knowledge. In addition, seven serving gifts are named: helps, mercy, faith, discernment of spirits, leadership, managing, and giving.

12:9, 10 The highest form of love is *agape.* This is a self-sacrificial love. It involves an act of the will whereby one seeks the best for another. *Agape* is used in v. 9. **preference to one another:** The greatest proof of the truth of the gospel message and of the reality of Jesus' love is the love believers show to one another. Christ is the model for such self-sacrificial love (see Phil. 2:3–8).

12:11, 12 in diligence: Christians should not offer their service half-heartedly or in a lazy manner. Instead, Paul encourages the Romans to serve eagerly and in earnest.

12:13 Hospitality means "love of strangers." The primary reference is to housing travelers. As we dedicate ourselves to meeting the needs of our fellow believers, we will have opportunities to serve strangers and thus witness to them about the love of Christ.

12:14 Bless means "to speak well of" or "praise."

12:15 rejoice … weep: Because believers are a body, when one part hurts, everyone feels the pain; when one is joyful, everyone can rejoice. Christians cannot be indifferent to the suffering or joy of their fellow believers (see 1 Cor. 12:25, 26).

12:16–18 The word **good** in this verse means "morally good," "noble," or "praiseworthy."

This is the positive side of the negative command not to return **evil for evil** (see 1 Pet. 3:9). A Christian should not concentrate on the evil in others, but instead should focus on what is good. By doing so, we encourage others to aspire to the good. The believer's aim should be to **live peaceably.** But sometimes peace is not within our control; this is why Paul limits the command.

12:19 Believers are not to seek personal revenge, but rather to let God punish.

12:20, 21 Freed from vengeance, believers can give themselves to mercy, even toward their enemies. By acts of kindness, the believers will **heap coals of fire** on the head of their enemies, perhaps bringing shame and repentance to them.

13:1 God, the supreme Sovereign, has ordained (see v. 2) that there should be **governing authorities.** Every believer is to **be subject** to these various authorities, even if these authorities are evil.

13:2–4 Judgment does not necessarily include eternal punishment. God may judge people through the human authorities He appoints. The **sword** is an instrument of death. Government has the right in the proper circumstances to impose capital punishment as well as to wage war. In Paul's day, the common method of capital punishment was decapitation with a sword.

13:5–8 for conscience' sake: Believers must obey government not only because it is their civic duty, but because it is their spiritual duty before God. In the present context, **owe no one anything** primarily means respect and honor (see v. 7). No doubt money is also included, but this passage does not prohibit borrowing (see Ps. 37:21; Matt. 5:42).

13:9–10 as yourself: This verse is not a command to love ourselves. It is a recognition that we do love ourselves, and commands us to love others just as genuinely and sincerely as we love ourselves. Love excludes murder, adultery, stealing, and lying (see v. 9). Therefore when we love, we automatically fulfill the prohibitions of **the law.** If we attempt to live by the law, we quickly discover that we are breaking the law (7:5). But when we act in accordance with God's love, without being under the law, we fulfill it.

✏ IN DEPTH   Submitting to Authority

Scripture challenges us as believers to subject ourselves to whatever governments we live under (Rom. 13:1–7). Submission to authority is never easy. Human nature tends toward resistance and even rebellion, especially if government is imposed, incompetent, and/or corrupt. But as we struggle with how to respond to the systems in which we live, this passage offers some helpful perspectives:

(1) God is the ultimate authority (13:1). Government as an institution has been established by God to serve His purposes. God raises up and does away with leaders.

(2) Both followers and leaders are ultimately accountable to God (13:2). Submission to human authorities reflects our submission to God's authority.

(3) God uses governments to carry out His good purposes on earth (13:3). Without question, some governments sometimes persecute those who do good. Paul had firsthand experience with that. But mainly, it's the lawbreaker, not the law-abiding citizen, who has something to fear from government.

(4) Obedience is a matter of inner conviction as well as external law (13:5). Our motivation to obey must go beyond fear of punishment. As believers, we serve the highest of all authorities, God Himself.

Only when a government commands us to do what God prohibits (worship, taking of innocent life, etc.) or prohibits us from doing what God commands are we to be in disobedience.

13:11 sleep: Believers are pictured as being asleep or inactive. **Salvation** here refers to the future, when believers will be saved from the presence of sin. Thus *salvation* here speaks of the imminent return of Christ.

13:12, 13 Night is the present age during which we live in Satan's domain. **Day** is the beginning of a new life with Christ in His glorious reign. **At hand** means "is imminent"; the Lord could return at any moment (see Phil. 4:5; James 5:8; 1 Pet. 4:7).

13:14 put on the Lord Jesus Christ: Believers should clothe themselves with Christlike characteristics such as truth (see John 14:6), righteousness (see 1 Cor. 1:30), and peace (see Gal. 5:22, 23; Eph. 2:14; 6:10–17).

14:1–3 Those who were **weak in the faith** did have faith: they had trusted in Christ. Some of the Roman believers might not have accepted the apostle's teaching about certain practices, such as accepting that all food was clean if received with thanksgiving (see 1 Tim. 4:4, 5). The strong in the faith are told to **receive** the weak and not to dispute over **doubtful things.** The mature believers were not to pass judgment or dispute with those who were less mature. The strong are not to **despise** the weak, that is, to treat them with contempt. The weak are not to **judge** the strong by attempting to place excessive prohibitions on them.

14:4, 5 one day above another: This verse probably relates to the many holy days of the Old Testament ceremonial law. **fully convinced:** The exhortation does not mean it is wrong to have strong convictions, but that all people have a right to their own convictions.

14:6 Days and diets are not the issue, but whether what is being done is committed **to the Lord.**

14:7–9 None of us refers to believers, not people in general. Believers belong to the Lord. They live and die in relation to Him. Therefore Christians should aim to please Him.

14:10 Again (see v. 3) Paul addresses the weak and the strong. The weak are not to **judge,** and the strong are not to **show contempt,** the same word that is rendered "despise" in v. 3. At the **judgment seat of Christ,** every believer's life will be evaluated to determine his or her reward (see 1 Cor. 3:11–15; 2 Cor. 5:9, 10).

14:11 every knee: One day everyone will submit to God's authority. He will judge all people before His great throne (see Rev. 20:11–15).

14:12–14 Unclean means "common" and refers to things prohibited by the Jewish ceremonial law. **to him:** If anyone considers some activity to be unlawful, then it is wrong for that person to engage in that activity (see 14:23).

14:15 Do not destroy: Paul here builds on the principle of *conviction* with the principle of *consideration* for the brother who is weak. This is a step in maturity. If eating meat (see v. 2; 1 Cor. 8:7–11; 10:25–28) destroys a weak believer, then the strong believer should not eat it.

14:16 Your good is what you, the believer, consider to be *good.* **Be spoken of as evil** means "reviled" or "slandered." Do not cause your freedom, a good thing, to be reviled because of the way you use it.

14:17 The kingdom of God does not consist of external things like food, but in spiritual realities like **righteousness** in action and thought, **peace** that seeks harmony, and **joy** that comes from **the Holy Spirit.** Those who understand the spiritual realities of the kingdom will not choose the brief joy of satisfying selfish desires over the spiritual joy of putting aside those desires for the sake of others.

14:18–21 Do not destroy: That is, do not "throw down" or "demolish." Paul has already exhorted mature believers to have consideration for the weak believers (in v. 15). Here Paul exhorts the mature believer to identify ways to build up those weaker in the faith. There is little distinction between **stumbles, offended,** and **made weak.** Paul uses all three words to reiterate that a mature believer should not cause the downfall of another believer (see vv. 12, 13, 20).

14:22, 23 Paul does not require the strong to abandon their convictions about things not condemned by the law. He encourages them to **have faith** about such issues. Although mature believers may refrain from eating meat in front of weaker believers, they can still believe that Christ gives them the freedom to eat all types of food (see v. 2) privately **before** Him (see v. 5).

15:1–4 Christ is the ultimate model for the strong believer. He renounced self-gratification so that He could clearly represent God and His cause (see Phil. 2:5–8). Through **patience** (endurance) and the **comfort** (or encouragement) of Scripture, believers learn that they have **hope.** In this case, if strong believers are patient with the scruples of the weak, they have hope of being rewarded (see 14:10; 1 Cor. 9:17, 24–27).

15:5 the God of patience: Attributing to God the same virtues just ascribed to the Scriptures (see v. 4), Paul prays for the unity of all believers.

15:6, 7 The command to **receive one another** is addressed not just to the strong believers, but to all believers.

15:8–13 Jesus Christ became a **servant** to the Jews for two purposes: (1) **to confirm** God's **promises** to Abraham, Isaac, and Jacob; and (2) to demonstrate God's mercy to the Gentiles so that they might **glorify** Him. Paul cites four passages from the Old Testament to prove that God intended the Gentiles as well as the Jews to glorify Him.

15:14–16 Ministering means rendering priestly service. Paul pictures himself as a priest offering a sacrifice to God. The sacrifice is Gentile believers who have been made **acceptable** to God because they have been **sanctified,** that is, set apart **by the Holy Spirit** for God's service.

15:17–19 By performing **mighty signs and wonders,** Paul demonstrated that God had granted him apostolic power (see 2 Cor. 12:12).

15:20–22 For this reason: Paul's ambition to preach Christ where He was not yet known (vv. 20, 21) had **hindered** him from going to Rome.

15:23–26 Paul planned **to minister** to the believers in Jerusalem by taking the **contribution** from Macedonia and Achaia (see 1 Cor. 16:1–4; 2 Cor. 8–9). This money was not only aid from Gentile believers to Jewish believers, but an expression of love that would unify the church even more.

15:27, 28 this fruit: The collection referred to in v. 26.

15:29, 30 when I come: Paul did get to Rome but not in the time frame or way he had thought. The Lord would give him the opportunity to testify of his faith in the emperor's court, but he would do so as a prisoner (see Acts 27; 28).

15:31 Delivered means rescued from serious danger.

15:32, 33 Be refreshed pictures rest and relaxation. Paul anticipated conflict in Jerusalem. He looked forward to a time of refreshment from the believers in Rome.

16:1, 2 Servant is the word used for the office of deacon (Phil. 1:1; 1 Tim. 3:8, 10, 12). The fact that it is used here with the phrase **of the church** seems to suggest an official position.

16:3, 4 Priscilla and Aquila worked in the same trade as Paul, tentmaking (see Acts 18:1–3), and labored with him in Corinth and Ephesus (see Acts 18:1–3, 18, 26).

16:5–7 Of note among the apostles as a phrase can mean either that they were well known to the apostles, or that they were distinguished as apostles.

16:8–10 Amplias ... Urbanus ... Stachys ... Apelles were common slave names.

16:11 my countryman: Herodion must have been a Jew, like Paul. Some have suggested that this **Narcissus** was a famous freedman of that name who was put to death by Agrippa shortly after Nero came to power.

16:12 Tryphena and Tryphosa are generally considered sisters.

16:13–15 Though a common name, this **Rufus** is often identified with the one in Mark 15:21. Since **chosen in the Lord** is true of all believers, many interpret this phrase to mean "outstanding" or "eminent." But it is possible that just as some believers demonstrate God's love and others reflect God's justice, so Rufus was a exceptional example of God's election.

16:16 holy kiss: This kiss on the cheek was practiced by the early church as a symbol of the love and unity among the early Christians (see 1 Cor. 16:20; 1 Pet. 5:14).

16:17–20 Cause divisions means "to stand apart" or "to cause dissension." In the New Testament it occurs only here and in Gal. 5:20. Strife and rivalry cause dissension, which eventually leads to divisions in a church (see 13:13; Gal. 5:20). Such dis-sension causes **offenses**—that is, it be-comes a snare or stumbling block to others (see 14:13 where this word occurs). Con-tentious, divisive people can cause others to stumble, so they should be avoided. Di-visive people destroy the peace and unity of the church, but **God,** who is the source of **peace,** will **crush** this work of **Satan** through the wisdom and obedience of be-lievers.

16:21 Timothy worked with Paul and later received two letters from him. Some think **Lucius** here is Luke, the author of the third Gospel and Acts. But Paul includes this Luke among his **countrymen,** meaning he was a Jew. Luke the author was a Gentile. **Jason** is mentioned in Acts as Paul's host on his first journey to Thessalonica (see Acts 17:5, 7, 9).

16:22 Paul, the author of Romans, dictated the letter to a secretary named **Tertius,** who actually **wrote** the words. Tertius here sends his greetings to the Romans.

16:23 Gaius of Corinth (see 1 Cor. 1:14) not only gave Paul lodging, but also offered his house as a meeting place for the church. In Acts 19:22 a man named **Erastus** was sent by Paul to Macedonia.

16:24–27 The word **establish** is used only twice in Romans. At the beginning of the book, Paul expresses a desire to visit the Romans that he might impart some spiritual gift to them so that they would be "estab-lished" (see 1:11). Now he praises God who is able to do it. God used the **gospel,** which is **the preaching of Jesus Christ,** to estab-lish the Roman believers. Paul speaks of his message as a **mystery** (see 11:25) because God's complete plan of salvation was at first hidden but now was being revealed. The re-vealed *mystery* is that the church will con-sist of both Jews and Gentiles united in the one body of Christ (see Eph. 3:1–13).

1 Corinthians

Introduction

The church at Corinth was a seriously troubled church. Infected with sexual immorality, split by factions that dragged each other into court, and crippled by abuse of the spiritual gifts, this church was in need of radical spiritual surgery. One can sense the disappointment of a hurt father in Paul's stern words for the Corinthians. Yet Paul, like a surgeon, diagnosed the problem and aimed his efforts straight at the source: pride and a lack of true love in the church.

First Corinthians twice names the apostle Paul as its writer (1:1, 2; 16:21). Paul's authorship is almost unanimously accepted throughout biblical scholarship. One of the earliest witnesses to Paul's authorship was Clement of Rome (c. A.D. 95). Most likely Paul wrote the letter while he was ministering at Ephesus during his third missionary journey. The Corinthian church would have been about four years old at that time.

Corinth was an important city in ancient Greece. Geographically, it was an ideal hub for commerce between Italy and Asia. Along with the flow of merchandise, Corinth received travelers from both east and west, creating ethnic diversity among the city's inhabitants. Corinth's commercial success was rivaled only by its decadence. The Corinthians drew attention to their sexual immorality through their worship of Aphrodite, the goddess of love and beauty. The city's corrupt nature made for a unique opportunity to display to the Roman world the transforming power of Jesus Christ.

Acts 18:1–18 records the founding of the Corinthian church. Paul visited Corinth on his second missionary journey, after leaving Athens. This initial visit probably occurred in the fall of A.D. 52. Paul ministered in Corinth for eighteen months, eventually establishing a church. This church, like the city, had a mixture of nationalities. Though some Jews had been converted, most of the believers were Gentiles (12:2).

Paul wrote this letter to teach the Corinthian Christians about decorum in worship services (11:2–16), the solemnity of the Lord's Supper (11:17–34), and the place of spiritual gifts. In their immaturity and pride they had abused their gifts. Paul reminded the Corinthians that gifts come from God (12:11) and are to unify and edify the church (12:24, 25; 14:1–4). Paul also corrected a doctrinal matter by writing the New Testament's most detailed explanation of the Resurrection of Christ and Christians (15:1–58). The Corinthians could have victory over sin and death because Jesus in His death and Resurrection had already decisively obtained it (15:57).

1:1 through the will of God: The Corinthian church greatly valued human wisdom. This misplaced emphasis had caused some in the church to challenge Paul's authority (v. 12; 9:1, 2). They forgot that Jesus Christ Himself had called Paul to his ministry as an **apostle of Christ** (see 2 Cor. 1:1).

1:2, 3 sanctified in Christ Jesus: The Corinthians' holiness came from their position in Christ, not from their own goodness. The tense of the verb *sanctified* indicates that God had sanctified the Corinthians at a specific time in the past, producing a condition that they still enjoyed in the present. **called to be saints:** The work of Jesus Christ makes a believer holy forever in God's eyes. But in everyday living, sanctification involves small, daily changes (see Heb. 10:14). This is why Paul could call the Corinthian believers to become saints, even though the problems testified that they were far from the goal of holiness.

1:4, 5 Enriched means that the Corinthians had been spiritually destitute but had become abundantly prosperous through God's grace.

1:6, 7 Gift here is probably a reference to the spiritual gifts described in chs. 12—14. Despite the Corinthians' boasting, their many gifts had come from God (12:11, 18, 28). The Corinthians were richly blessed with spiritual gifts because God was giving them everything they needed to do His will (12:14–27).

1:8–10 Paul was confident that even the sin-plagued Corinthians would stand **blameless** before God. This blamelessness does not refer to the Corinthians' works, but to their standing in Christ (3:14, 15). Paul pleaded for an outward expression that comes from an inward spirit. Paul encouraged the Corinthians to **speak the same thing** and have external unity, as well as be **joined together in** a unity of hearts and minds.

1:11–13 Paul avoided dealing in rumors or secrecy; he openly named his sources: **Chloe's household.** We know little of this woman and her household except what this verse implies. Chloe lived in Corinth or Ephesus, and the Corinthians respected her word.

1:14–16 Paul said **I thank God that I baptized none of you,** because the Corinthians were identifying with their spiritual mentors rather than Christ. **Crispus** was the ruler of the synagogue in Corinth when Paul began to preach there (see Acts 18:8). He was instrumental in the conversion of many other Corinthians. **Gaius** may be the same person who hosted Paul and the entire church (Rom. 16:23). **Stephanas** was one of Paul's first converts in Achaia, the region of which Corinth was capital. Paul praised him and his household for their devotion to the ministry and for their assistance (16:15).

1:17 Paul's primary ministry was **to preach the gospel.** Baptism naturally followed conversion but was secondary in importance. **not with wisdom of words:** The immature Corinthians were so impressed by clever oratory and learned debate that many of them ignored the relatively "simple" message of **the cross.**

1:18, 19 The message of the Cross is the Good News about Christ's death and Resurrection for our sins. The gospel becomes the **power** that snatches sinners from death and imparts eternal life.

1:20, 21 The wise is probably a reference to Greek philosophers. **The scribe** is a technical term for a Jewish scholar trained in the details of the Law. **The disputer** refers to a Greek person trained in rhetoric. These professionals tried to solve every problem with logic and debate. Paul says all human efforts to find favor with God will fall woefully short (see Rom. 3:9–28).

1:22, 23 The **Jews** sought miraculous signs from the Messiah to signal the beginning of the deliverance God had promised (Mark 8:11; John 6:30). The **Greeks** sought to use wisdom to answer their questions about God and life. To the Jews, who expected a political

savior, Jesus was **a stumbling block.** To the Greeks, whose self-centered wisdom could not make sense of the cross, to believe in Jesus was **foolishness.**

1:24–27 Wise refers to the Greek philosophers. **Mighty** refers to influential, politically powerful people. **Noble** includes all the aristocratic upper classes. Most of the Corinthians came from lower classes. God's plan of salvation does not conform to the world's priorities. In fact, it seems **foolish.** Yet eternal salvation is more valuable than all the things pursued by the world.

1:28–31 base ... despised: Paul's use of these two terms for the slave class would capture the attention of his readers in Corinth, where many slaves lived. God uses foolish and despised things in this world to reveal His truth, so that He alone receives the glory. Jesus' life and death reveals God and His **wisdom.** Since Christ not only imparts wisdom but also righteousness, the Christian cannot boast, except in **the Lord.**

2:1, 2 excellence of speech or of wisdom: Paul did not rely on his eloquence or on Greek wisdom to convince his listeners. Instead, he gave **the testimony of God** which was being revealed by the Holy Spirit (vv. 10–14). The focal point of Paul's preaching was **Jesus Christ.**

2:3–5 Whereas the Corinthians gloried in their strength, their wealth, and their gifts, Christ was glorified in His humility and death. Paul modeled Christ's humility by presenting his "weaknesses." Then the "strength" of the gospel message could be clearly seen. **My speech** probably refers to the way Paul spoke; **my preaching** probably refers to the content of his message. **not with persuasive words ... but in demonstration of the Spirit:** Even though Paul had many strengths (see Phil. 3:4–9), he wanted to be one who relied on God's strength. Rather than using the rhetoric to win converts, he gave a straightforward message.

2:6 among those who are mature: After having heard eloquent addresses by men like Apollos, the Corinthians may have viewed Paul's message as elementary or unpolished. Paul assured the Corinthians that he was imparting **wisdom**—instruction that mature Christians would appreciate. **coming to**

nothing: People look at beauty, wealth, and power as greatly desirable. But all earthly splendor will be rendered worthless by death and the coming of God's judgment (Luke 16:19–29; 2 Pet. 3:10–13).

2:7 The **mystery** that Paul referred to here is defined in Rom. 16:25, 26 as "revelation … kept secret since the world began, "but that now has been made manifest." The message was **hidden** until God chose to reveal it (see Eph. 3:1–11).

2:8 Lord of glory: Though Jesus emptied Himself of His majesty when He became human, He remained fully equal with the Father.

2:9–12 through His Spirit: Only the Holy Spirit could reveal the truths of God (see 2 Pet. 1:19–21). **knows … know:** The first verb refers to innate knowledge; the second refers to experiential knowledge. We could never have discovered the mysteries of God or the benefits of Christ's death by ourselves.

2:13 the Holy Spirit teaches: Paul emphasized that the intellectuals of this world could not teach the knowledge he was giving to the Corinthian believers. **comparing spiritual things with spiritual:** The Greek term translated *comparing* may also mean "to combine" or "to interpret." In other words, the phrase teaches that the spiritual truths of God are combined with the spiritual vocabulary of the apostles (see 2 Pet. 1:20, 21; 2 Tim. 3:16).

2:14–16 natural man: The natural person does not have the Spirit of God, in contrast to the Christian who does have the Spirit (15:44–46). **Receive** means "to welcome." This verb does not pertain to discovering the meaning of a passage, but *applying* the meaning to life.

3:1 The **carnal** person is not the same as the "natural man" mentioned in 2:14. A carnal person is a spiritually immature Christian, a spiritual infant.

3:2 fed … milk: Paul did not expect the Corinthians to be mature in Christ at the time of their conversion. By placing their faith in Christ, they had been justified. They were considered righteous before God because of Jesus' righteousness. Paul taught them as new converts, as those justified. Yet he expected them to grow in their faith.

3:3, 4 for you are still carnal: Paul was surprised that the Corinthians had not yet grown into spiritual maturity or become able to distinguish between good and evil (see Heb. 5:14).

3:5–10 Paul had **planted,** or started, the church in Corinth; Apollos had **watered** it—had a significant ministry there after Paul left. But both men were only servants through whom God worked. The ones who plant and water have nothing to boast about because God gives **the increase.** Only God draws unbelievers to Himself.

3:11–15 Paul had established the church at Corinth on the **foundation** of Christ. **gold, silver, precious stones, wood, hay, straw:** These building materials refer to the quality of work done by the Corinthians, and possibly also to their motivations or the kinds of doctrines they taught. **The Day** speaks of the time when Christ will judge the merits of His servants' work (see 2 Cor. 5:10). Likewise, **fire** does not refer to the "eternal fire" of damnation (see Rev. 20:10) but to the evaluation of believers' works (see Rev. 2:18, 19; 3:18; 22:12). Fire proves the quality of gold, but it consumes wood, hay, and stubble.

3:16, 17 temple: There are two words translated *temple* in the New Testament. One refers to the temple building and all its courts; the other refers strictly to the Most Holy Place. Paul uses the latter term to describe the local church, in which **God dwells.** Unlike 6:19, where the word *temple* refers to the individual believer, and Eph. 2:21, where the word speaks of the church universal, these verses speak of the local church as God's temple.

3:18–23 The wisdom of this world does not coincide with God's wisdom, the foolishness of Christ crucified (see 1:18–25). Paul quotes from Job 5:13 and Ps. 94:11 to urge the Corinthians to humble themselves. **all things are yours:** Everything God has done in the church benefits all believers. There is no place for foolish boasting or competition among Christians.

4:1 Servants had no unique position, but **stewards** did. A steward was a slave who administered the affairs of his master's household, though he himself owned nothing. As stewards, believers manage the message and ministry God has entrusted to them.

4:2–5 each one's praise will come from God: While believers can benefit from the constructive evaluations of fellow believers, their ultimate Judge is the Lord Himself.

4:6, 7 The Greek term translated **learn** is related to the word translated *disciple* in Matt. 28:19. It implies the use of a skill and not just knowledge. The Corinthians knew about humility, so Paul called on them to become humble. **what is written:** Paul was exhorting the Corinthians to avoid the pride and divisions that were fracturing their church.

4:8–10 Spectacle alludes to the public executions carried out by the Romans in the coliseum. Paul pointed out that the whole world and the angels were witnesses to the humiliation of God's servants. Paul contrasted the Corinthians' lofty evaluation of themselves with the world's evaluation of him. Paul knew that true strength is found in understanding our weakness and Christ's sufficiency (see 2 Cor. 12:7–10; Phil. 4:11–13).

4:11–13 Paul lists the hardships he had suffered in Christ's ministry, both physical challenges and verbal abuse (see also 2 Cor. 11:22–30).

4:14, 15 instructors ... fathers: Paul used these two terms to differentiate between his role and the role of the Corinthian teachers, slaves who took care of their masters' children. Paul was the Corinthians' spiritual father and had the right to command them to follow his example.

4:16 Paul urged his readers to **imitate** him as he followed Christ (see 11:1). The word refers to the way a student would follow a teacher.

4:17–20 Some people in Corinth acted as though Paul would never return to hold them accountable for their actions. **puffed up:** These people were conceited and prone to boasting. **The kingdom of God** here refers to Christ's present rule in the hearts of His people. This reality guaranteed that Paul had the authority to expose and discipline those who afflicted the Corinthian church.

4:21 Paul uses the same Greek word for **rod** here that Luke uses to describe the instrument that was used to beat Paul and Silas (see Acts 16:22–24). God had given Paul authority to punish the agitators in Corinth, though he preferred not to use that power.

5:1 The **sexual immorality** of incest was forbidden by Old Testament law (see Lev. 18:8; Deut. 22:30) and by Roman law. Paul used the phrase **his father's wife** instead of "his mother" probably to indicate that the woman was the offender's stepmother. The omission of discipline for the woman implies that she was not a believer. The church is responsible for disciplining only its members, not unbelievers.

5:2 puffed up: The Corinthians had a twisted view of grace that caused them to be proud of their tolerance of the sexual offender. They believed that because God's grace is limitless, the freedom that every Christian enjoys is also limitless.

5:3–5 Destruction of the flesh may refer to God's turning the sexual offender over to **Satan** for physical affliction or even physical death. After losing the spiritual protection of the church, ideally the offender would recognize his sin, repent, and return to the church. All church discipline has restoration as its ultimate goal.

5:6–7 Like a tiny pinch of **leaven** spreading through a loaf of bread, unchallenged sin can soon contaminate the whole church. Left unchecked, this sin could cause many new believers to commit sexual immorality. Jewish people were required to sweep all **leaven** (the powerful influence of sin) out of their houses in preparation for the Passover (see Ex. 12:15).

5:8 The feast is a figure of speech for Christ. As Israel was to remove all leaven from the celebration of the Passover, so the Corinthians were not to contaminate their relationship with Christ with any **malice** or **wickedness.**

5:9 My epistle refers to an earlier letter from Paul to the Corinthians that has been lost.

5:10 out of the world: Christians are called to influence the world, not run away from it (see Matt. 5:13–16). They are agents of God to carry the light of Jesus Christ into a dark world (see Phil. 2:14–16; 1 Pet. 2:11, 12).

5:11 not even to eat with such a person: The Corinthians were not to have fellowship with those who claimed to be Christians but whose lives were dominated by sin.

5:12, 13 do you not judge ... God judges: The church's responsibility is to discipline its members while trusting the Lord to judge the world (see Matt. 13:30).

6:1–3 Believers will participate in judging fallen **angels** (see Rev. 19:19, 20; 20:10). If the Corinthians were going to be judging with Christ in His kingdom (see Matt. 19:28), then surely they could settle their own personal differences.

6:4–6 Those who are least esteemed refers to judges in civil courts. The Corinthians, who had the ability to judge the issues themselves, took their disputes to pagan courts.

6:7, 8 cheated ... cheat: Paul suggested that it was better to be *cheated* by one of these dishonest people than to dishonor one's Christian witness before pagans.

6:9, 10 do not be deceived: Christians sometimes think that God does not require them to live righteously. Paul emphasizes that the kinds of people listed in these verses will not **inherit** or possess the kingdom of God.

6:11 Paul uses three terms to describe the Corinthians' conversion. All three indicate an action that is complete. **Washed** means spiritually cleansed by God. **Sanctified** means set apart to God. **Justified means declared righteous because of Christ's work on the Cross.**

6:12 All things are lawful for me Paul reminded the Corinthians that freedom from the ceremonial laws did not give them license to indulge their own selfishness. **under the power of any:** Sin should not dominate our lives because the Holy Spirit empowers us to fight temptation.

6:13, 14 Foods for the stomach and the stomach for foods When the Corinthians became hungry, they ate. When the Corinthians craved sex, they indulged themselves. But eating to the point of gluttony and having sex outside of marriage violate God's intent and are therefore sinful.

6:15–17 Believers' lives are changed when they are joined to Christ. The union affects both the believer and Christ. By quoting Gen. 2:24, that **the two ... shall become one flesh,** Paul illustrates the seriousness of sexual sin.

6:18, 19 Every sin that a man does is outside the body Paul pointed out that sexual sin is done **against** the body. Paul exhorted the Corinthians to **flee** temptation to indulge in sexual sin.

6:20 Bought at a price alludes to someone purchasing a slave at a slave auction. With His death Jesus Christ paid the cost to redeem us from our slavery (see Eph. 1:7; 1 Pet. 1:18, 19).

7:1 things of which you wrote to me: After addressing the problems reported by the people of Chloe's household (1:11), Paul began to answer questions that had been sent to him (7:1—14:40). **It is good for a man not to touch a woman:** There were two extreme positions in the Corinthian church. One group was hedonistic. This group claimed that sin only had to do with the physical body, and that believers could sin in their body without any consequence to their spiritual lives. The other group believed that all things spiritual are good, and all things physical are bad, and that in order to be spiritual a person has to suppress every physical desire. Proponents of this view claimed that celibacy is the only proper lifestyle. Paul explains that sexual relationships in marriage are good; he chose celibacy in his own situation.

7:2 Paul encouraged those who might be tempted to commit sexual sin to marry. It is better to develop a permanent relationship with a wife or husband than to lapse into sexual sin.

7:3–5 affection: Husbands and wives have a duty to maintain sexual relations with each other so that neither will be tempted by **Satan** to have sex outside of marriage.

7:6–11 not I but the Lord: Paul uses the word translated **depart,** which refers to wives leaving their husbands. The idea is the same: a believing husband and wife should not leave each other.

7:12, 13 I, not the Lord, say: Paul now presents a problem that was not addressed by Jesus. Sometimes a husband or wife would become a Christian, but the spouse would not. Paul exhorts the believer to remain married if the unbelieving spouse does not want to divorce.

7:14 Sanctified primarily means "set apart." Here the term refers to the special situation an unbelieving husband or wife enjoys when his or her spouse is a believer, being exposed to God's teachings. **Unclean** here probably means the opposite of *sanctified*. Children with one believing parent may learn about God and come to Christ.

7:15 If an unbeliever seeks to divorce a believing spouse, the Christian is **not under bondage** or obligation to continue the marriage.

7:16 how do you know: The Greek grammar suggests that Paul expected a negative answer. Consistent obedience to God can make a skeptical spouse into a believing spouse.

7:17–24 so let him walk: Whether you are **slave** or **free**—upper class or lower, powerful or powerless, married or single—live where God called you (see Col. 3:11).

7:25–27 present distress: in times of persecution, consideration for family can make it difficult to live out Christian convictions. A virgin would have less family responsibilities and not be deterred by the problems affecting her husband or children.

7:28 Paul does not want to be understood as prohibiting marriage altogether.

7:29 as though they had none: Even married couples should put God's work first.

7:30–38 any man: May refer to the father of an unmarried virgin. **She is past the flower of youth** indicates that the virgin is approaching an age at which marriage would be unlikely. Under these circumstances, it would be perfectly acceptable for the father to give **her in marriage. having no necessity:** If the man can control himself and keep himself from immoral action, he should stay single. On the other hand, if the man's will is weak, he should go ahead and marry.

7:39, 40 bound by law: Paul used marriage to illustrate obligation to the law. Here he emphasizes that marriage should be lifelong. In a case where a marriage partner has died, the only restriction about remarriage is for the person to marry a Christian. **I also have the Spirit of God:** The Holy Spirit enabled Paul to speak with apostolic authority, and with spiritual wisdom.

8:1, 2 The weaker Christians believed that eating food offered to idols was a sin. Other believers thought that such concerns were

ridiculous. They argued that if the idols were worthless, than the meat offered to them was fine to eat. Paul agreed that food offered to idols was not contaminated, but he wanted the knowledgeable Christians not to flaunt their enlightened point of view. **Knowledge** puffs up, but love edifies: They should have been using their knowledge to help other believers in the church.

8:3–6 The Corinthian believers readily admitted that **an idol is nothing** (see Is. 37:19; Jer. 16:20; Gal. 4:8) and that there is only one God (see Deut. 6:4). Though these gods are not real, they exist in the minds of those who worship them (10:20).

8:7–13 If the weaker ones saw believers eating **food** offered to idols, they might also eat, in violation of their own conscience. By their knowledge the stronger believers were causing the weaker believers to stumble. Paul exhorted the strong believers to show love to the weaker ones by refraining from offending them.

9:1, 2 Am I not an apostle: Paul substantiated his apostleship: (1) he had **seen** the resurrected **Lord** (see Acts 1:21, 22), and (2) the church at Corinth was a **seal** of his **apostleship.**

9:3–18 Paul had the **right to eat and drink** whatever he wanted, to have a **wife,** and to receive wages for his ministry. But he did not exercise these rights. **those who preach the gospel should live from the gospel:** To support ministers of the gospel is commanded by God.

9:19–23 servant to all, that I might win the more: Paul was willing to conform to the customs of other people in order to bring them to Christ. He obeyed God's law through obedience **toward Christ** (v. 21).

9:24–27 I myself should become disqualified: The Greek word for *disqualified* means "disapproved after testing." This does not refer to salvation. A careful distinction should be made between the *prize* and the *gift.* The free gift is justification. However the prize or crown is the reward for endurance and suffering for Christ (see Phil. 1:29; 2 Tim. 2:12).

10:1 For the Israelites **under the cloud** in the wilderness, the *cloud* served two functions: (1) It provided protection (see Ex. 14:19–20), fire by night in the cold desert and shade by day from the sun. (2) It guided the people (see Ex. 13:21). **all passed through the sea:** Every Israelite who left Egypt experienced the deliverance of God at the Red Sea.

10:2 all were baptized into Moses: Being in the cloud and in the sea joined the people with their spiritual head, Moses.

10:3–5 the same spiritual food … the same spiritual drink: They shared the same provision from God (see John 4:13, 14).

10:6 The failure of the ancient Israelites was that they **lusted,** or "craved." They were not satisfied with manna but looked back to the provision they had in Egypt (see Num. 11:4–34).

10:7–9 The ancient Israelites were **idolaters.** Even though God had brought them out of Egypt, they insisted on worshiping lifeless idols. Furthermore, they engaged in **sexual immorality. twenty-three thousand:** The account in Numbers gives the figure twenty-four thousand (Num. 25:6–9). Paul's number may reflect the number that died **in one day,** while the Numbers account may be a record of all who died in the plague.

10:10 The ancient Israelites **complained** against their God-given leaders so much that many **were destroyed,** or put to death (see Num. 16:41–49).

10:11, 12 lest he fall: The Corinthians may have had the attitude that since they were justified by God, nothing could happen to them. No one can sin with impunity (see Gal. 6:7, 8).

10:13 The various temptations they were experiencing were normal; all believers have to resist temptation. God is so good that He will provide an escape from every temptation.

10:14–20 flee from idolatry: Idol worship violates the believer's union with Christ (v. 21). The danger lies in the **demons** (v. 20) that, are the real objects of idol worship.

10:21 You cannot drink: Paul reminded the Corinthians that they had to chose the cup of Christ or the cup of demons. You cannot participate in both.

10:22–24 All things are lawful for me: Though we have freedom, we also have a responsibility to help others in their Christian growth. Our first duty is to others, not ourselves.

10:25, 26 Eat whatever is sold: Paul did not ask whether meat was sacrificed in the temple, because pagan worship could not contaminate what God made clean (see Ps. 24:1; Acts 10:15).

10:27–33 Doing **all to the glory of God** involves encouraging fellow Christians and spreading the good news about Christ.

11:1, 2 Now I praise you reflects genuine appreciation on Paul's part. The Corinthians had made many mistakes, but followed the apostle's instructions in certain areas.

11:3 the head of woman is man: The relationship between men and women does not involve inferiority, for, in the parallel clause, **Christ** is not inferior to **God** the Father. Just as Christ and God are equally divine, men and women are equal beings. But as Jesus and the Father have different roles in the plan of salvation, so men and women are given different roles.

11:4 Praying or prophesying may refer to intercessory prayer or to the combination of tongues and prayer (see 14:13–16; Acts 2:4; 10:46). **Having his head covered** can refer to a hat or a veil. **dishonors his head:** It is impossible to decide whether *Head* here refers to the man's physical head or to Christ (v. 3). Either interpretation is possible.

11:5, 6 every woman who prays or prophesies: Women were obviously allowed to pray and prophesy in the Christian assembly because it would have been meaningless for Paul to give instructions for something they were not permitted to do. **Dishonors her head** refers either to the woman's own physical head or to her husband as her head, or possibly both (v. 4). For a woman not to cover her head with a veil or with her own hair was as shameful as having a **shaved** head.

11:7–9 man is not from woman, but woman from man: The woman was taken from the side of the man (see Gen. 2:21). **Woman for the man** is the concept of the "helper" in Gen. 2:20. This refers only to the purposes of God for man and woman in the creative order.

11:10 Women were to wear a covering on their head **because of the angels.** Evidently God's angels are present at the meeting of the church and actually learn of God's work of grace through the lives and worship of God's people (see Eph. 3:10). **symbol of authority:** This might be a symbol of the woman's authority to prophesy in the new church age, which was inaugurated with the giving of the Holy Spirit at Pentecost (v. 5).

11:11, 12 neither ... independent: Men and women need each other, and as creatures of God, both depend on Him. Neither man nor woman can have any claim to special status other than what God has purposed for them as their Creator.

11:13–17 I do not praise you: Here Paul expressed concern for their practices at worship. **Come together** is a term for the meeting of the church used three times in this passage.

11:18, 19 those who are approved: One of the positive results of division or **factions** in the church is that it becomes obvious who the genuine Christians are in the congregation.

11:20–22 The Lord's Supper was the centerpiece of early Christian worship. Gathered around one table, fellow believers met with the Lord and with one another in unity. Some were taking their **own supper ahead of others,** violating the spirit and purpose of the meal. They were showing contempt for **the church of God** and shaming those who had **nothing.**

11:23–25 I received: Paul's revelation from Christ, which he **delivered** to the people.

11:26 you proclaim the Lord's death till He comes: The Lord's Supper looks to Christ's

---

| IN DEPTH | **The New Covenant** |

The NT describes the new covenant (1 Cor. 11:25), or agreement, that God has made with humanity, based on the death and Resurrection of Jesus Christ.

In the Bible, a covenant involves much more than a contract or simple agreement. A contract has an end date, but a covenant is a permanent arrangement. Furthermore, a contract generally involves only one aspect of a person, such as a skill, while a covenant covers a person's total being.

God entered into numerous covenants with people in the OT. For example: with Adam and Eve (Gen. 3:15); with Noah (8:21, 22; 2 Pet. 3:7, 15); with Abraham (Gen. 12:1–3); with Israel (Deut. 29:1—30:20); and with David (2 Sam. 7:12–16; 22:51).

The agreement with Israel was especially significant, because it established a special relationship between God and the Hebrews. They were made His "chosen people" through whom He would bring blessing and hope to the rest of the world. However, because the recipients of God's law could not keep it perfectly, further provision was necessary for them as well as for the rest of humanity.

That's why God promised a new covenant through the prophet Jeremiah. Under the new covenant, God would write His law on human hearts. This suggested a new level of obedience and a new knowledge of the Lord.

The work of Jesus Christ brought the promised new covenant into being. When Jesus ate His final Passover meal with the Twelve, He spoke of the cup as "the new covenant in My blood" (Luke 22:20), the words that Paul quoted to the Corinthians to remind them of the need for purity and propriety in their worship (1 Cor. 11:25–34).

The new covenant in Jesus' blood rests directly on the sacrificial work of Christ on the Cross (which was prefigured by Israel's system of sacrifices) and accomplishes the removal of sin and the cleansing of the conscience by faith in Him (Heb. 10:2, 22). So every time Christians celebrate the Lord's Supper, they remind themselves that God has fulfilled His promise: "I will be their God, and they shall be My people ... I will be merciful to their unrighteousness, and their sins and their lawless deeds I will remember no more" (Heb. 8:10, 12; compare Jer. 31:33, 34).

death and to His second coming (see Matt. 26:29; Mark 14:25; Luke 22:18).

11:27–29 In an unworthy manner refers to the way in which a person eats the Lord's Supper. The Corinthians had been making the meal a time of overeating and getting drunk rather than a time of reflecting on the death and Resurrection of the Lord Jesus Christ.

11:30–34 Sleep refers to the death of Christians (see Thess. 4:15, 16). In this passage, it refers to untimely death, a punishment suffered by some Christians who failed to **examine** themselves at the Lord's Supper (v. 28). **If we would judge ourselves,** God would not need to correct us. When Christians are unwilling to do this self-examination, God will chasten them.

12:1 Now concerning indicates that Paul was responding to another question from the Corinthian church (7:1, 25; 8:1). **Spiritual gifts** may refer to spiritual things or spiritual persons. The same Greek word is used throughout chs. 12—14 to refer to "tongue speaking" and "tongues speakers."

12:2 The term **Gentiles** here has the generic meaning of foreigners or unlearned people. Paul used this word to emphasize the Corinthians' state of ignorance. Because of their ignorance, they had been **carried away** or "swept off their feet."

12:3 calls Jesus accursed ... say that Jesus is Lord: A person speaking by the Holy Spirit will never curse Jesus; by the same token, no one can genuinely proclaim Jesus is Lord without the Spirit.

12:4–6 Gifts God gives ministries to individual Christians. **diversities ... differences ... diversities:** The first portion of the "gift formula" expresses diversity. **same Spirit ... same Lord ... same God:** The second portion expresses unity. God and His work are unified.

12:7–11 given to each one for the profit of all: God works in believers to benefit the entire body (vv. 25, 26). **The word of knowledge** appears to be the ability to teach doctrine. **The word of wisdom** refers to practical application of knowledge (see Acts 6). **Faith** here is the capacity to believe in God for extraordinary deeds.

Miracles are the ability to perform miraculous wonders similar to Moses and the prophets. **Prophecy** is the telling of a revelation from God. **Discerning of spirits** may refer to the ability to distinguish the works of God from demonic activity in the church. **Interpretation of tongues** is the ability to explain or translate the tongues spoken in the congregation so that the entire group might benefit (14:13, 16, and 28).

12:12 so also is Christ: Paul used the human body to illustrate the need for unity in the diversity that existed in the church (see Eph. 2:21; 4:16).

12:13 one Spirit ... one body: Believers are part of the whole body infused by the one God. All believers are **baptized into** the **body** of Christ (see Rom. 6:3), whether they are **Jews or Greeks ... slaves or free.**

12:14–18 God has set ... each one of them: Every individual believer has a vital role assigned by God Himself. Each one of us is important to God and has a mission to accomplish.

12:19–25 The members should have the same care for one another because God gives spiritual gifts. Rather than being envious of other people's positions or gifts, we should give of ourselves to others. Whenever any part of the body has a need, we should help that part.

12:26–30 Sometimes in the New Testament, the term **apostles** refers in a general sense to missionaries (see 15:7; Rom. 16:7; 2 Cor. 11:5; 12:11; Gal. 1:17, 19). Other times the term is limited to the small group who witnessed the resurrected Christ and was given a special mission by Him as His representatives (9:1; 15:5, 8). **prophets:** The primary responsibility of prophets was not predicting the future, but presenting God's message to their contemporaries. The word **teachers** refers to those who explain the revelation of God (Gal. 6:6; 2 Tim. 2:2).

12:31 earnestly desire the best gifts: Paul's exhortation to the Corinthians to seek after the more spiritually profitable **gifts.** He wants to show them **a more excellent way,** the way of love (ch. 13).

13:1, 2 the tongues of men and of angels: Paul illustrates the uselessness of each spiritual gift without love. The Corinthians would understand the images of **sounding brass or a clanging cymbal.** Many of them had used brass instruments and cymbals as standard elements of pagan worship in their lives before Christ.

13:3 Bestow all my goods likely pertains to the spiritual gift of giving to others (see Rom. 12:8).

13:4–8 Love never fails: Paul wants the Corinthians to know that all the gifts would one day no longer be needed. But love would continue forever. **prophecies … will fail, tongues … will cease, knowledge … will vanish away:** These gifts will be unnecessary in the fullness of God's kingdom, but love is the nature of God and will continue forever.

13:9, 10 when that which is perfect has come: The Greek word for perfect means "end" or "completion." Most likely, this is a reference to the Second Coming of Christ and the completion of all things (see v. 12).

13:11, 12 The **mirror** is probably the Word of God (see 2 Cor. 3:18; James 1:23–25), which can give us only a partial understanding of God. This will change when we see Him **face to face.**

13:13 Faith enables us to come to God (see Heb. 11:6): **love** enables us to imitate Him.

14:1, 2 The word translated **pursue** carries such meanings as "hasten," "run," "run after," and "aspire to." There are things in life that we can take or leave, but love is not one of them.

14:3, 4 The term **prophesies** here incorporates all speaking gifts that edify the church (see Rom. 12:6). **Edification, exhortation,** and **comfort** result from prophesying in the church.

14:5 interprets: Speaking in tongues does benefit the church whenever it is interpreted, though not as much as prophesying.

14:6–11 Paul underlines the original purpose of all spiritual gifts: they must serve the church (see vv. 13, 14; 12:7). Tongues convey **meaning** or they fail to help those who listen.

14:12–17 He who occupies the place of the uninformed refers to one who does not understand the message spoken in tongues. Saying **amen** was common in early church worship when the congregation wanted to indicate its agreement with what was being said (see Deut. 27:14–26; Rev. 5:14).

14:18, 19 more than you all: Paul spoke in tongues. If the Corinthians wanted to brag of their tongue speaking, the apostle had more to brag about. **In the church,** speaking **five words** that are understandable has more benefit than speaking ten **thousand** words **in a tongue.**

14:20–22 children in understanding: Paul wanted the Corinthians to serve and benefit each other above all. But instead they had developed the skill of attacking and neglecting each other.

14:23–26 If **each** person brings to the meeting the ability that God has given him, and if everything is done for **edification,** the church will benefit. **Teaching** in the early consisted of presenting a teaching of the apostles; the one who received a **revelation** was probably the prophet who spoke the word of God (vv. 29–32).

14:27–29 Let two or three prophets speak: Paul limited prophetic activity. Prophets were not to monopolize the limited time the church members were together. **Let the others judge** indicates that no one is exempt from accountability to the church (6:5; 11:29, 31).

14:30 Revealed indicates that prophesying as described here is different from what we call preaching or reading from Scripture. The prophesying referred to is similar to Old Testament prophecy in which God gives a revelation to one of His servants who, in turn, gives revelation to God's people. **Let the first keep silent:** The speakers were not to compete with each other, but all things were to be done in an orderly manner (v. 40) for the benefit of those who heard (12:7).

14:31, 32 subject to the prophets: Paul anticipated that some people might claim that they could not prevent themselves from prophesying when God brought a revelation to them. He explained that the Holy Spirit does not overpower the person through whom He speaks.

14:33, 34 Let your women keep silent: Paul's command here is the subject of much debate, for it seems to contradict the fact that Paul spoke of women prophesying in 11:5. It has been suggested that Paul was addressing a particular problem in the Corinthian church, a group of women who were disruptive.

14:35, 36 from you: In persuading the Corinthians to accept his teaching, Paul had already appealed to nature—the importance of order in the church to conform to God's peaceful nature (v. 33). Here the apostle emphasizes the importance of conformity, not only with the Christian churches throughout the world, but also with the origin of Christian truth. The Christian message had traveled from Jerusalem throughout most of the Roman world.

14:37–40 To further establish his arguments and the authority of his teaching, Paul appealed to the fact that he taught **the commandments of the Lord.** To be obedient to the Lord is to be obedient to what Paul taught.

15:1, 2 Paul's **gospel** to the Corinthians centered on the physical death and Resurrection of Jesus Christ, the eternal Son of God who became human yet never sinned (see Gal. 1:6–10). Paul had started the Corinthian church; the gospel that the Corinthians had originally **received** came from him (2:2).

15:3 Paul did not originate the proclamation of Jesus that he **delivered** to the Corinthians; he gave the Corinthians what he had **received. according to the Scriptures:** Jesus lived and died in accordance with the prophecies about Him in the Old Testament (Is. 53:8–10).

15:4 The Resurrection verifies that Christ's death paid the full price for sin. The Greek term translated **rose** here is in the perfect tense, emphasizing the ongoing effects of this historical event. Christ is a risen Savior today.

15:5–8 At the time of Paul's writing, a person could have verified the truthfulness of the apostle's statements. The majority of the **five hundred** people who saw the risen Christ, as well as **all the apostles** and **James** (the brother of Jesus), were still living. **Born out of due time:** Unlike the other apostles, who had the benefit of an initial training period with Christ, Paul became an apostle

abruptly, with no opportunity for earthly contact with Christ or His teaching.

15:9 Paul considered himself **the least of the apostles** because at one time he had persecuted the church (see Acts 22:4; Eph. 3:8; 1 Tim. 1:15, 16).

15:10 I labored more abundantly: Paul got a late start and did not have the discipleship training that the other apostles did, but, he traveled further, established churches, and wrote more Scripture than all of them (see 2 Cor. 11:23–27). But Paul attributed his success to **the grace of God.**

15:11 whether ... I or they: Paul did not care who got credit for the Corinthians' faith. He cared only that the Corinthians believed.

15:12, 13 Some of the Corinthians were teaching **that there is no Resurrection.** These opponents of Paul may have been denying the reality of Christ's Resurrection. They contradicted the essential teaching that Christ had been physically raised from the dead and that believers in Him will someday also be resurrected.

15:14, 15 false witnesses: In vv. 5–8, Paul listed several people, including himself, who had witnessed the resurrected Christ. To deny the Resurrection was to deny the truth of their testimony.

15:16, 17 you are still in your sins: Christ's death without His Resurrection would not succeed in saving us from our sins.

15:18 Without the Resurrection of Christ, those who are **asleep in Christ**—the dead—have **perished** or been destroyed. Without the Resurrection of Christ, the Christian faith brings no forgiveness and no future life in God's presence.

15:19 we are of all men the most pitiable: If Christians have no hope for the future, the pagans could consider Christians fools since believers would have suffered for nothing.

15:20 Jesus is the **firstfruits** of all others who believe in Him. This is an Old Testament image of the first installment of a crop which anticipates and guarantees the ultimate offering of the whole crop (see 16:15; Rom. 8:23). Because Christ rose from the dead, those who are **asleep** in Christ (v. 18; 1 Thess. 4:15, 16) have a guarantee of their own Resurrection.

15:21, 22 by man came death: The first man, Adam, transgressed God's law and brought sin and death into the world (see Gen. 2:17; 3:19; Rom. 5:12–21); the second Man, Jesus Christ, was the perfect sacrifice to take away sin and to bring life and Resurrection to those who believe in Him (see Rom. 5:15–21). Paul explains that by one man's sin all die, whereas by one Man's (Christ's) obedience **in Christ all shall be made alive.**

15:23 Each one in his own order indicates that God has a design for the Resurrection. The Commander is raised first; His troops afterward. In 1 Thess. 4:13–18, **His coming** is described as Christ's coming with those who have "fallen asleep" (the dead), who are then united with their physical bodies. Following this is the removal of all living Christians from the earth.

15:24 The end here refers to all remaining prophetic events that will occur after the rapture of the church and during the climax of history, when Christ **puts an end to all rule** (vv. 25–28). **delivers the kingdom to God the Father:** When Christ and the church are joined at His coming, God will establish His *kingdom* on this earth. **puts an end to all rule and all authority:** Until the time of *the end,* the Father subjugates everything to the Son (see Ps. 110:1; Dan. 2:44; 7:14, 27).

15:25, 26 all enemies: God has allowed His enemy Satan to rule as the "prince of the power of the air" (see Eph. 2:2) and the "god of this age" (see 2 Cor. 4:4), but his final judgment before God is certain. **The last enemy ... death:** The conquering of *death* is proof of God's victory and the inauguration of the new day of the Lord (see Rev. 20:14).

15:27, 28 it is evident: The texts say that everything is put under the Son, but God the Father **is excepted** from this subjugation, because the **Son** must be **subject to** the Father. **God may be all in all** indicates there will be no challenge to the rule of God over all the universe.

15:29 It may be that some of the Corinthians had for some reason been **baptized for** others who had died without baptism. Paul did not approve or disapprove of the unusual

practice. **if the dead do not rise ... Why then are they baptized:** To deny the Resurrection and yet be involved in such baptisms made no sense.

15:30–32 why do we stand in jeopardy: Paul risked his life **daily.** To do so would have been of no **advantage** without the hope of a Resurrection. Why else should Paul have endured difficulties like fighting **beasts at Ephesus?**

15:33, 34 Paul had already warned the Corinthians to avoid believers who lived immoral lives (5:9–13). **evil company corrupts good habits:** Paul warned the Corinthians to stay away from those who teach false doctrine (see 2 Cor. 6:14—7:1).

15:35–37 Some people objected to the Resurrection on the grounds that it was too hard to understand. Paul called these people **foolish.** Difficulty understanding the nature of the Resurrection should not cause a person to doubt its reality.

15:38–41 The variety found in nature among living beings such as **men, animals, fish,** and **birds,** and among objects such as **celestial bodies and terrestrial bodies** reflect the Creator's power and will. The varying brightness of the **sun, moon,** and **stars** serves as a good illustration of the differences between the earthly human body and the heavenly human body. All these are evidence that God the Creator can certainly create Resurrection bodies out of our old bodies.

15:42–49 natural ... spiritual: The contrast is between a body subject to death and a body that is immortal. **First man ... second Man** contrasts the sinful nature that every person inherits with the new righteous nature that comes through Christ.

15:50 Mere **flesh and blood** cannot enter into the glorious existence of an immortal body (vv. 35–49). Something must happen to this *flesh* so that it becomes incorruptible (v. 42).

15:51, 52 we shall all be changed: Whereas the dead in Christ will be raised first, the living believers will be instantly transformed into their immortal bodies when Jesus returns.

15:53–57 The living will receive a body that is not subject to death (see v. 50). Satan's apparent victories in the Garden of Eden (see Gen. 3:13) and at the Cross (see Mark 15:22–24) were reversed by Jesus' death (see Col. 2:15) and Resurrection. **Death** and **Hades** (the grave) have no power over Christians, because Jesus has already conquered both.

15:58 The Corinthians were to continue **steadfast** in the **work** of Christ, specifically because of the Resurrection. **your labor is not in vain:** All the work that we do for Christ will be rewarded (see 2 Cor. 5:10; Rev. 22:12).

16:1–4 Now concerning: Paul addressed a question asked by the Corinthians (7:1, 25; 8:1; 12:1) about giving (Acts 11:29, 30; 2 Cor. 8; 9). **The first day of the week** was the regular weekly meeting day of the early church. **Lay something aside** expresses the concept of Christian giving in the New Testament. New Testament believers were encouraged to give liberally, but never a specified amount or percentage (see Rom. 12:8). Paul wanted to make sure that the Corinthians' offering would be collected before he arrived (see 2 Cor. 9:5).

16:5–7 Now I will come to you: Paul had hoped to visit Corinth, perhaps even spending **the winter** with the Corinthians. He eventually made it to Corinth, but not according to the schedule he planned here.

16:8, 9 The opportunities for Paul's ministry **in Ephesus,** a major city of Asia Minor, were great, as was the persecution he endured there.

16:10–12 Though Paul could not leave immediately for Corinth, he wanted to be represented among the Corinthians by his fellow workers. He planned to send **Timothy.** Paul encouraged the Corinthians to go easy on Timothy, for although he was trustworthy, he was more timid than Paul.

16:13, 14 Watch is often used in the New Testament to indicate anticipation of some future event (see Mark 13:37; Rev. 3:3). Paul's exhortation to **stand fast in the faith** is especially important (see 2 Cor. 11:3). **Be brave** may also be translated "play the man," emphasizing not only bravery but maturity. Paul's command to do everything **with love** serves as a balance to these strong exhortations.

16:15–18 The household of Stephanas was among the first in **Achaia** to respond to Paul's preaching. **Stephanas, Fortunatus, and Achaicus** probably were the ones who confirmed the bad news brought by Chloe's household in 1:11. They were also probably the bearers of the letter that the Corinthians sent to Paul (see 7:1).

16:19, 20 The churches of Asia may be those mentioned in Rev. 2 and 3. **Aquila and Priscilla** were tentmakers who had met Paul in Corinth. They would have been known to many in the Corinthian church. **a holy kiss:** This custom, adopted by the early Christians, symbolized love, forgiveness, and unity.

16:21–24 my own hand: From this point on, Paul stopped dictating (see Rom. 16:22; Gal. 6:11) and completed the letter in his own handwriting. **let him be accursed:** It may seem harsh that Paul would wish God's damnation on those who do not love Jesus. But the acceptance or rejection of Christ is serious business. Those who reject the Lord Jesus are enemies of God (see Gal. 1:8, 9). In the next breath Paul desires the coming of our Lord with an Aramaic expression, *marana tha,* meaning "Lord, come."

2 Corinthians

Introduction

Second Corinthians is the most autobiographical of Paul's letters and probably the most difficult letter that he had to write. In previous letters, Paul had exhorted the Corinthian church to correct some abuses that were occurring in the congregation. However, some false teachers in the congregation were antagonized by Paul's rebuke and rejected his warnings. As a result, in this letter Paul was forced to defend his character and apostolic authority. Yet like the rest of Paul's letters, Second Corinthians points past Paul's sweat and tears to the power that lay behind his actions and words: the Lord Jesus Christ.

The style of the letter confirms Paul's authorship, as does the testimony of the early church. Paul wrote First Corinthians during the last year of his ministry at Ephesus, on his third missionary journey, probably in the early spring of A.D. 56. Second Corinthians was written probably the fall of A.D. 56.

In First Corinthians, Paul had instructed the believers in Corinth to discipline an incestuous member (see 1 Cor. 5), and to take a collection for the poor saints in Jerusalem (1 Cor. 16:1-4). Paul received a report about the church that was on the whole encouraging (2:14; 7:5-7). The Corinthians had responded properly to First Corinthians. They had faithfully carried out the discipline necessary (2:5-11). But Paul was also informed about the presence of "false apostles" (11:13) who accused Paul of walking according to the flesh (1:12, 17; 10:2), being deceitful (2:17; 4:2; 12:16), intimidating the church with his letters (10:9, 10), unjustly mistreating someone to the point of ruining that person (7:2), and defrauding people (7:2). These false teachers probably pointed out that Paul had not returned as he promised, and used this as evidence for his duplicity (1:15-17, 23, 24). They even attempted to discredit Paul by charging that he was raising money to enrich himself (7:2; 8:16-23). Inevitably these accusations raised doubts in the minds of the Corinthians about the integrity of the apostle Paul.

Paul wrote Second Corinthians out of his concern for the Corinthian church (7:12). He wanted to offer the church some further instructions about the repentant offender (2:5-11) as well as about the collection for the poor saints in Jerusalem (9:1-5). However, Paul's main purpose for writing Second Corinthians was to defend his ministry. He wrote this letter to prove that his ministry was sincere and genuine, and to reassert his authority as an apostle of Christ.

1:1-3 Second Corinthians opens the way most ancient letters did: salutation, author, recipients, and greeting. The author was **Paul, an apostle.** His identification with **Jesus Christ** is important in this letter because false apostles (11:12-15; 1 Cor. 4:14-16) had opposed him in Corinth and caused confusion in the church. **Timothy** is listed as coauthor. Paul and Timothy wrote this letter to the church **at Corinth** and all believers in **Achaia,** what is today southern Greece. **Grace to you and peace** was Paul's standard greeting. Paul's prayer was that the Corinthians would experience God's favor and the joy that results from being in a proper relationship with the Lord. A word of thanks often followed a letter's salutation (vv. 1, 2). **Blessed** expresses adoration and praise. Paul called God the **God and Father** of Christ. Even though Jesus is God, as the incarnate Son He was dependent on God the Father. Thus God the Father was His God.

1:4 Tribulation means distress or affliction. God comforts us to make us comforters. The comfort that God gives to us becomes a gift we can give to others (see 7:6; Acts 9:10-19). Our willingness to share it reflects the sincerity of our faith (see John 13:35).

1:5 Tribulation (v. 4) is called **the sufferings of Christ.** Christ suffered as a bearer of our sins (1 Pet. 3:18) and as a servant to His disciples (John 13:1-17). Those who follow Christ also will experience the same suffering while they serve (John 15:20), for which they will receive a reward, "a far more exceeding and eternal weight of glory" (4:17).

1:6-8 Paul's commitment to Christ and His service did not exempt him from trouble. By **Asia** Paul meant the Roman province in western Asia Minor, present-day Turkey.

1:9, 10 the sentence of death: Paul returns to the theme of death and Resurrection several times in this letter (see 2:16; 4:7–14; 5:1–10; 13:4). Here Paul is probably referring to the life-threatening persecution he faced when he preached the gospel (see Acts 14:19, 20).

1:11 As Paul trusted the Lord and as the Corinthians prayed, God delivered him (v. 10). We should pray for one another so **that thanks may be given.** Whenever we face difficulties, we should let others know so they can pray and God can be praised. Answers to **prayer** should always receive public praise.

1:12 Paul's critics accused him of living for his own selfish interest (10:2). They used his failure to return to Corinth as evidence of his lack of sincerity. Paul began the body of this letter by defending his integrity (1:12—2:4). **Fleshly wisdom** refers to selfish interest (contrast with Paul's admonition and Christ's example of humility in Phil. 2:3–8). Paul's **godly sincerity** was **more abundantly** clear to the Corinthians than to others; he spent 18 months with them (Acts 18:11).

1:13–16 Paul's critics had accused him of being insincere in his letters, of **writing** one thing and doing the opposite (10:10). Paul denied these charges. He meant what he wrote; there were no hidden agendas in his letters. Paul had intended to visit the Corinthians (see 1 Cor. 16:5–7), but he had failed to come. This prompted some of the members of the Corinthian church to accuse him of living according to "fleshly wisdom" (vv. 12, 17).

1:17 when I was planning this: Paul rhetorically asked: When he made plans to visit the Corinthians, was he joking, guided by self-interest, or inconsistent? The Greek text indicates that these questions expected a negative answer. Paul explained later why he changed his plans (see 1:22—2:4).

1:18–18 Before finishing the defense of his personal integrity (1:23—2:4), Paul defended his preaching: it was both true and trustworthy (vv. 18–22). Paul's preaching was not **Yes and No** at the same time—not inconsistent or contradictory. Instead, his preaching reflected the truthfulness and faithfulness of

God, based on the Scriptures and the teachings of Christ.

1:20 All of God's **promises** about Christ are true and trustworthy: a **Yes.**

1:21, 22 In the Greek text, **anointed** is connected to **establishes.** God confirmed Paul and his fellow workers by anointing them. **sealed:** Sealing indicates ownership and security. The Holy Spirit is a **guarantee,** the down payment that there is more spiritual blessing to come and that the believer will receive eternal life.

1:23–24 Paul had promised to come and use his authority, if necessary, to straighten out the problems at Corinth (1 Cor. 4:21). To **spare** them the pain of correction and give them an opportunity to correct themselves, he did not come. As an apostle, Paul had authority to discipline (10:2), but it was not his place to order the Corinthians around.

2:1, 2 Paul changed his travel plans because he did not want to come to Corinth **again in sorrow.** Some have interpreted this verse to mean that Paul had made a painful visit to Corinth and wanted to avoid another one. Although the narrative in Acts does not indicate such a visit, some have proposed that Paul visited Corinth between the writing of the two letters, 1 and 2 Corinthians. However, the text does not necessarily say that he had made a previous painful visit, only that he did not want his next visit to Corinth to be in sorrow.

2:3, 4 I wrote: Traditionally commentators have identified the previous letter to which Paul refers in these verses as 1 Corinthians. Many recent commentators believe that Paul is speaking about a letter written between 1 and 2 Corinthians that has been lost. Some have identified chs. 10—13 as this "lost letter" because the tone of those chapters seems to match the description of these verses, a letter of **much affliction and anguish of heart.**

2:5, 6 Punishment means "warning," "censure," or "rebuke." This is a reference to the church discipline Paul had instructed the Corinthians to use on the person mentioned in v. 5.

2:7, 8 forgive and comfort him: The purpose of church discipline is repentance and restoration. Forgiveness should always follow the correction, just as Christ instructed (see Matt. 18:15–35).

2:9–11 One of Satan's **devices,** or designs, is to cheat the believer out of true forgiveness. The devil will try to divide the church any way he can.

2:12, 13 Troas was a city on the Aegean coast, where Paul had received his call to preach the gospel in Macedonia (see Acts 16:8). Paul **had no rest** because he was deeply concerned about the Corinthians and was looking for Titus, who was on his way back from Corinth. Paul then crossed the Aegean Sea and arrived in **Macedonia,** probably at the city of Philippi.

2:14 When Titus gave Paul good news about the Corinthians (see 7:5–7), Paul burst forth with a hymn of praise. **God ... leads us in triumph:** When a Roman general was victorious in a war, he led his army and the captives in a parade down the main street. God is the general who has conquered. Paul is one of His officers following in His train.

2:15–16 In v. 14 the **fragrance** was the knowledge of Christ; here it was Paul, who was a sweet smell to God for his faithfulness in preaching the gospel. The leader in a Roman procession was followed by priests (dispensing incense), officers, soldiers, and captives. The **aroma** of the event represented victorious life to the soldiers and slavery or **death** to the captives. In the same way, the gospel message gives life to those who accept it, but it represents death and judgment to those who reject it.

2:17 Peddling: Some people use religion for personal gain. To them the gospel is merchandise to be peddled for profit. Thus, they corrupt or compromise it. This is the first reference in this epistle to false teachers. It may be a subtle reference to Paul's opponents.

3:1 Having again declared his sincerity (2:17), Paul asked if he needed a letter of **commendation** to back him up, **as some others** did. The language implies that the false apostles mentioned later in this letter (11:13) had tried to gain acceptance by using such references.

3:2 You are ... written in our hearts: The Corinthians were Paul's letter of recommendation. These verses do not mean that letters of recommendation should not be used. Paul

himself used such letters before his conversion (see Acts 9:1, 2) and after (see 8:22; Rom. 16:1;). In this case Paul did not need one because he already had one: the believing Corinthians and his ministry among them.

3:3 an epistle of Christ: Paul appealed to the Corinthians themselves for proof of his ministry's authenticity. God had changed them—a matter of public record.

3:4 trust: The Greek word means "confidence" (see 2:14—3:3; Phil. 4:19). Paul was convinced that Christ would make his ministry effective.

3:5, 6 Sufficient means "adequate," or "competent." Paul placed his confidence not in himself or his own abilities but in the Lord. **The letter** is a reference to the old covenant—that is, the Ten Commandments written on stone. The letter **kills** because everyone breaks the law, and the penalty is death.

3:7, 8 Paul lists the first of three contrasts between the Old Testament ministry and the New Testament ministry (see vv. 7, 9, 11). First, the Old Testament ministry **engraved on stones** (a reference to the Ten Commandments) was glorious, but the ministry of the Spirit is **more glorious,** because the glory of the ministry of the Law given through Moses **was passing away.**

3:9, 10 The second contrast (see vv. 7, 11) is that the Old Testament ministry was a **ministry of condemnation,** but the New Testament ministry is more glorious because it is a **ministry of righteousness.** God declares righteous those who believe in His Son, and then the Holy Spirit empowers the believer to live righteously. This first work of God is called justification, and the second is called sanctification.

3:11 The third contrast (see vv. 7, 9) is that one ministry is **passing** while the other ministry **remains.** The New Covenant would supersede the old covenant established at Mount Sinai between God and the nation of Israel.

3:12 Paul used **boldness of speech,** a phrase that means "freedom of speech" or "frankness." Instead of being fearful or reluctant, Paul was frank and courageous.

3:13–15 The **veil** on the face of Moses reminded Paul of another veil. As Moses' veil concealed the fading glory of his ministry, so there is a veil on the hearts of people concealing the fading away of the old covenant.

3:16 taken away: Whenever Moses turned to the Lord, he took off the veil (Ex. 34:34). Likewise, we find freedom in Christ by looking to Him.

3:17 the Lord is Spirit: The Holy Spirit is God Himself, like the Father and like the Son. **liberty:** The Spirit gives us freedom from sin, death, and the condemnation of the law (vv. 7–12).

3:18 All believers behold the **glory of the Lord** in the Scripture and are **transformed** into the image of God. Christ is the image of God (4:4). **glory to glory:** As believers behold the glory of God in the Word of God, the Spirit of God transforms them into the likeness of Jesus.

4:1–3 Paul now draws a conclusion from what he said about his ministry in 3:4–18. **This ministry** is the New Testament ministry (3:6), a ministry of the Spirit (3:6), of life (3:7), and of righteousness (3:9). It is a glorious ministry (3:7–12) of liberty (3:17). Paul did not achieve this ministry by his own human ability but by God's **mercy** (3:5, 6). Paul rejected **craftiness**—that is, being unscrupulous or **handling the Word of God deceitfully** (see 2:17). Apparently, Paul had been accused of being crafty (12:16) and of being deceitful in the way he preached.

4:4, 5 Unbelievers have a barrier to overcome: **the god of this age has blinded** their minds. Because of Satan's deception, sometimes what the world thinks is true is wrong (see Prov. 14:12). **image of God:** Jesus Christ is God's Son, and He perfectly reveals God the Father to us. Although human beings have been created in the image of God, through sin they have fallen from a perfect relationship with God. Jesus Christ is restoring believers to what they were originally created to be (3:18; Gen. 1:26). **bondservants:** Paul describes himself and those who minister with him as slaves to people. They served the Corinthians **for Jesus' sake.**

4:6 As God **commanded** the **light** to shine in the darkness at creation (Gen. 1:3), so he "turns on" the light in peoples' **hearts** so they can see who Jesus Christ is.

4:7, 8 Hard pressed is translated *afflicted* in 1:6. In the Greek text, an identical expression occurs in 7:5, where it is rendered "troubled on every side." Yet Paul was not **crushed. Perplexed:** This means "to be at a loss." One is perplexed when one sees no way out. Yet Paul was not **in despair,** which means "utterly at a loss." As believers, we will face trials. But we must remember that God controls trials and uses them to strengthen His people.

4:9 The picture behind the word **persecuted** is pursuit by someone determined to harm. Paul was not **forsaken** by the Lord, but he was **struck down.** But he was not **destroyed,** that is, killed (see 11:23–33). The Lord spared his life so that he could continue to preach the Good News.

4:10, 11 In his service for Christ, Paul constantly faced death so that **the life of Jesus may also be manifested.** God's deliverance of Paul was evidence that Jesus is alive (see 1:8–10). For Paul, the death and Resurrection of Jesus was a model for his ministry. In his suffering, he participated in Jesus' suffering and death. But Paul's endurance of all types of hardships produced eternal life in those to whom he preached the gospel. In the same way, Jesus' death was a precursor to His Resurrection to eternal life.

4:12 life in you: Had Paul not been willing to risk death to bring the gospel to Corinth, the Corinthians would not have received eternal life.

4:13 therefore I spoke: Quoting Ps. 116:10, Paul explained why he was willing to risk his life for the gospel. His belief in the gospel compelled him to tell others.

4:14 He who raised up: Paul's belief was focused upon the God of Resurrection power, which motivated him to face difficulties, danger, and death for Christ's sake. **knowing:** Paul rested in what he knew about God, not how he felt.

4:15 your sakes: Paul's suffering (vv. 8–11) brought good to others and glory to God.

4:16 Paul concluded that the Corinthians should **not lose heart,** because God would raise them up with Jesus (v. 14). A proper focus on our glorious future with Christ will empower us to endure any kind of trouble.

4:17 Working means "producing," or "accomplishing." Afflictions produce glory. But the glory is out of proportion to the affliction: trials are light and temporary compared to the eternal glory we will receive (see Mark 10:30).

4:18 Look: In order not to lose heart, the believer needs to shift his or her focus from that which is seen to that which is **not seen,** from temporary problems to the glorious eternal rewards he or she will receive (v. 17).

5:1, 2 Suffering makes believers **groan** with longing for their glorious future in heaven (see Rom. 8:22, 23).

5:3 not be found naked: Paul looks forward not only to his resurrected body but also to the reward he would receive in the future.

5:4 The believer's future experience is called **life,** meaning the full experience of eternal life in Christ. Our future is being determined by how we invest our lives today (see 4:17).

5:5 guarantee: The Holy Spirit's work in believers' lives can be compared to a down payment (see 1:22). The presence of the Holy Spirit assures believers that God has purchased them. They will receive all the rights and privileges of children of God when their Savior returns.

5:6 Because the believer has God's guarantee (v. 5), he or she can be **confident,** a word that means "to be of good cheer" or "to be of courage."

5:7 Sight means "appearance." Christ is not physically present, so believers live by faith (see John 20:29).

5:8 Paul was not only confident (v. 6) that he was going to be with the Lord; he was **pleased** that he would be **with the Lord** after his death. This is one of the passages in the New Testament that indicates where believers will go immediately after their death; they will be with Jesus in heaven (see also Phil. 1:23).

5:9, 10 Wanting to be with Christ (v. 8) produces the ambition to please Him (see Luke 19:17). We strive to please the Lord not only because we know we will be with Him (v. 8) but also because He will evaluate our work—**whether good or bad**—and reward

us accordingly. **Appear** means "to make visible" or "to make known." Here it may refer to nothing more than an appearance, such as appearing in court before a judge. Or it may mean believers will stand before the Lord with their true character revealed.

5:11 The **terror of the Lord** is the fear of standing before the Lord and having one's life exposed and evaluated. The reality of giving an account to the Lord motivated Paul to **persuade** people—to convince the Corinthians of his sincerity and integrity.

5:12 Paul was defending the integrity of his ministry, not to win the approval of the Corinthians again (see 3:1), but so the Corinthians could answer those who bragged about their outward appearance, such as the false apostles present among them (11:18). **Opportunity** literally means "a base of operation." This letter would be a foundation or base for those who wanted to defend Paul's authority and ministry in the Corinthian church.

5:13 If Paul was beside himself in exposing himself to danger, it was **for God.** If he was of a **sound mind,** it was for the sake of the Corinthians. Paul's motive for ministry was for the glory of God and the good of others, not his own glory.

5:14 The phrase **the love of Christ** can mean either (1) Christ's love for us or (2) our love for Christ. The last part of the verse indicates that Paul had in mind Christ's love for us. **Died for all** refers to Christ's death for all believers. **all died:** In Christ believers die to sin (see Rom. 6:1–14).

5:15, 16 Believers should not evaluate Christ or anyone else **according to the flesh,** that is, the way people typically evaluate one another (v. 12).

5:17 in Christ: Because believers are united with Jesus both in His death and Resurrection, they receive the benefits of being restored by Christ to what God had originally created them to be (Gen. 1:26; 1 Cor. 15:45–49). **All things have become new:** A believer's life should change, because he or she is being transformed into the likeness of Christ (3:18). Instead of living for oneself, a believer lives for Christ (v. 15). Instead of evaluating others with the values of the world, a believer looks at this world through the eyes of faith (v. 16).

5:18 reconciled us to Himself: Because of Christ's propitiation, His satisfaction of God's righteous demands, God is now able to turn toward us. God has made us new creatures in Christ and has given us the ministry of **reconciliation.** We who have been reconciled to God have the privilege of telling others that they can also be reconciled to Him.

5:19 God placed our sins on Christ, who knew no sin. His death was in our place and for our sins. If we believe in Jesus, God counts Jesus' righteousness as our righteousness (see v. 21). The **word of reconciliation** that has been entrusted to us is to tell all people that God wants to restore them to a relationship with Himself (see Rom 5:8).

5:20 Ambassadors are more than messengers. They are representatives of the sovereign who sent them. Christians have been called by their King to serve as ambassadors in a world that is in rebellion against Him. God has given His representatives a message of peace and of reconciliation. Their mission is to implore people to listen to the forgiving voice of their Creator.

5:21 no sin: Jesus never did anything wrong. Yet He died for our sins so we could be declared righteous or justified (v. 19).

6:1 in vain: If believers live for themselves (5:15), they will have received the grace of God, but they will miss out on a heavenly reward (see 5:10; 1 Cor. 3:15). In Phil. 2:12 Paul encourages those who have been saved to work out or develop their salvation. The Corinthians were failing at this very point. They were not continually working out their salvation. Paul was encouraging them to consider their lives and realign them more closely to Christ.

6:2 Paul quoted Is. 49:8 to remind the Corinthians that God was ready to listen to them and to help them. He would deliver them if they would turn to Him in faith.

6:3 Offense means "an occasion of stumbling." Paul did not do anything that would cause others to stumble in their faith. **be blamed:** The word means "to find fault with" and implies ridicule. In other words,

no one could find fault with Paul's work among the Corinthians.

6:4, 5 In much patience is followed by three triplets that indicate specific situations in which the endurance of believers was demonstrated. **Sleeplessness** is not insomnia but going without sleep voluntarily in order to spend more time in ministry (see 11:27).

6:6–11 O Corinthians: Paul addressed his readers by name on only two other occasions (Gal. 3:1; Phil. 4:15). When he did this he was expressing strong emotion.

6:12, 13 The suspicions planted by Paul's enemies had **restricted** their **affections** for Paul (see 2 Tim. 4:10). Paul had been **open** with the Corinthians (v. 11) and asked that they be open with him.

6:14 unequally yoked: The Corinthians were shutting Paul out of their hearts (vv. 11–13) and developing a dangerous affection for the false apostles (11:4, 13; see Prov. 4:23).

6:15 The term **Belial** for Satan occurs only here in the New Testament. It refers to a person who is vile and wicked and causes destruction.

6:16 you are the temple: A reference to Lev. 26:11, 12 as well as perhaps other passages such as Jer. 32:38 and Ezek. 37:27, to remind the Corinthians of their relationship with God. Since the Holy Spirit was in them, they were God's new dwelling place (1 Cor. 6:19).

6:17, 18 come out ... be separate: Paul was not encouraging isolation from unbelievers (see 1 Cor. 9:5–13) but discouraging compromise with their sinful values and practices. He urged them to maintain integrity in the world just as Christ did (see John 15:14–16; Phil. 2:14–16).

7:1 Based on the promises that God would receive them with favor (6:17) and provide for and protect them as a father does his children (6:18), Paul exhorted the Corinthians to cleanse themselves **from all filthiness.** They were to wash away all dirt from both **flesh and spirit,** meaning those actions and attitudes that came from having the false teachers in their midst (6:14). The point of cleansing is **perfecting holiness.** This means dedicating ourselves to Christ and living righteously (see Heb. 6:1).

7:2 cheated: Perhaps the false teachers were charging that Paul had collected money for the poor saints at Jerusalem (1 Cor. 16:1–4) but had spent it on himself.

7:3–4 I do not say this to condemn: Paul was not blaming anyone; he was defending himself. Paul was **filled with comfort** and joy because of the report he received from Titus about the Corinthians (see v. 7).

7:5 troubled on every side: The same expression, though translated differently, is used in 4:8 to express Paul's suffering in his ministry.

7:6 The Lord **comforted** or encouraged Paul by allowing him to see Titus again.

7:7 but also by: Paul was encouraged to learn how Titus had been received by the Corinthians and had seen that they were accepting Paul's exhortations.

7:8, 9 Paul regretted that he had to write a "severe letter" to the Corinthians. But since it did cause the Corinthians to repent and turn to God, his sorrow was transformed into joy. Traditionally this **letter** has been identified as 1 Corinthians, but some recent commentators have suggested that it was another letter Paul wrote after 1 Corinthians, which was lost (see 2:3, 4).

7:10 Godly sorrow produces repentance: True sorrow for sins leads to a change of mind and a turning to God, which results in spiritual deliverance, or **salvation** (see 6:2). But the kind of sorrow the world experiences **produces death.**

7:11 sorrowed in a godly manner: Although Paul had been harsh in his previous letter (see v. 8), he praised the Corinthians for how they had responded to his admonition.

7:12–16 care: Paul wrote the "severe letter" (see v. 8) not only to correct the one who had sinned but also to tell the Corinthians that he cared for them (see 1 Cor. 4:14).

8:1–5 Macedonia corresponds to the northern part of present-day Greece. Paul had established churches in the Macedonian cities of Philippi, Thessalonica, and Berea. The Macedonians were a great example of giving because they gave (1) during **affliction,** (2) in spite of great **poverty,** (3) with great **joy,** (4) beyond their means, and (5) **freely.** In fact, (6) they pleaded for the privilege of

sharing their wealth with other believers, and (7) they **gave themselves to the Lord** and to others.

8:6–7 Titus had begun the collection when he was in Corinth (2:13; 7:6, 7, 13–15). Paul wanted him to complete it. The Corinthians had an abundance of spiritual gifts and graces (1 Cor. 1:4–7). They had the gift of **faith** (1 Cor. 12:9; 13:2), gifts of **speech,** such as prophecy (1 Cor. 1:5; 12:10), and the gift of **knowledge** (1 Cor. 1:5; 12:8). They were also blessed with **diligence** (7:11) and **love** for Paul (7:7).

8:8 testing: Generosity is the natural result of sincere love.

8:9 The Corinthians did not need a command (v. 8), because the example of Christ taught them about sacrificial giving. **You ... might become rich** refers to the spiritual riches that Jesus gives to all who place their trust in Him: He offers forgiveness, justification, regeneration, eternal life, and glorification.

8:10–15 Advantage means "profit." Giving now would profit the Corinthians at the judgment seat of Christ (see Phil. 4:17).

8:16, 17 thanks be to God: Paul asked Titus to go, but Titus went **of his own accord,** probably at his own cost.

8:18, 19 The brother has been variously identified as Luke, Barnabas, Silas, Timothy, John Mark, and others.

8:20–24 These honest men were sent to handle the collection in order to do what was **honorable** before **the Lord** and **men,** and to prevent anyone from blaming Paul for mishandling the funds.

9:1 The collection for the Jerusalem believers is called **the ministering to the saints.**

9:2–4 Paul was in Macedonia when he wrote this letter (2:13; 7:5). When he left Macedonia to come to Corinth, some of the Macedonians would no doubt come with him. He did not want them to find that the Corinthians had not completed the collection (8:11) and thus **be ashamed.**

9:5 The brethren mentioned here are the delegation of 8:16–20.

9:6–7 reap sparingly: The law of the harvest is referred to repeatedly in Scripture (see Prov. 11:24, 25; 19:17; Luke 6:38;

Gal. 6:7). Paul applied it to giving. Giving is like sowing seed. The amount of the harvest is determined by the amount of the seed sown. Knowing the law of the harvest (v. 6), each believer should give **as he purposes in his heart.** The believer is to give freely and cheerfully, not out of compulsion, and without regret.

9:8–10 If we give, **God is able** to give us more so we can perform other good works. In other words, God sees to it that the generous giver will not suffer want. This verse is Paul's prayer for God's blessing to be poured out on the Corinthians. The words **supply seed to the sower and bread for food** are adapted from Is. 55:10. The latter part of the verse is a reflection of Hos. 10:12.

9:11–13 They refers to the Jerusalem Christians.

9:14 their prayer for you: Paul anticipated that God's grace would lead the Jerusalem Christians to pray for the Corinthian believers and to be deeply concerned about them.

9:15 God's **indescribable gift** is His Son,

Jesus Christ. Our gifts can never compare to God's sacrifice for us.

10:1 I, Paul ... myself: Timothy and Paul together wrote the first nine chapters of this letter (1:1). In this section, Paul alone addresses the Corinthians. **in presence ... lowly ... absent ... bold:** This is a quotation from Paul's critics in the Corinthian church. They accused him of being weak when present, and bold only in his letters (see vv. 9, 10).

10:2 By saying **I beg,** Paul was gently asking the Corinthians to deal with his critics before he came so he would not have to be stern with them. Paul's critics said that he **walked according to the flesh** and that he was thinking only of himself when he did not come as promised (see 1:17).

10:3–5 strongholds ... high thing: Overlooking ancient Corinth was a hill 1,857 feet high. On top of it was a fortress. Paul used that imagery as an illustration of the spiritual warfare he waged. He destroyed strongholds, cast down towers, and took

---

IN DEPTH   New Testament Giving

The most detailed passage on giving in the NT is found in Second Corinthians (chs. 8; 9). The primary reason that Paul addressed this topic here was that false teachers in Corinth were questioning Paul's motives for ministry. Evidently they were suggesting that Paul was pocketing contributions earmarked for the poor believers in Jerusalem. Consequently the Corinthians, despite their announced willingness to help, had not donated to the cause. Taking pen in hand, Paul defended his integrity (1:12). Using the churches in Macedonia as his example, Paul gave the Corinthians a wonderful summary of why and how believers ought to give. Here are the highlights of Paul's sermon:

First, who should give? All believers can and should contribute to the cause of Christ. The church at Macedonia was notoriously poor, yet they asked for the privilege of being allowed to give (8:4) out of "their deep poverty"(8:2).

In what spirit should we give? We ought to give willingly (8:12; 9:2) and cheerfully, "not grudgingly or of necessity" (9:7). It is a privilege to share in the work of God. Moreover, it is the appropriate response to God's "indescribable gift," His own Son (9:15).

Why is giving so important? In Paul's words, it tests the sincerity of our love for God and others (8:7, 8). To paraphrase the words of Christ (Matt. 6:19–21), how we handle material wealth is a barometer of our spiritual health.

What will be the results of our giving? We should not give primarily to get, but Paul makes it clear that giving does lead to abundance. Cheerful givers experience God's love in a special way (9:7). They enjoy the spiritual blessing of participating in a rich harvest of righteousness (9:10).

captives. The fortress, towers, and captives represent the **arguments**, thoughts, and plans that Paul was opposing. Paul cast down all rationalizations. He took captive **to the obedience of Christ** every perception and intention of the heart that was against God.

10:6–9 In this context, being **Christ's** means more than just belonging to Him. It means being His servant or His disciple (see v. 8). Paul had **authority** as an apostle **for edification,** a word that means "building up." His exhortation in his letter was aimed at correcting abuses, not the **destruction** of the church.

10:10 they say: Paul spoke simply so the power of God would remain evident. He did not use complicated rhetorical techniques to sway his audience. His critics in the Corinthian church had turned his simple, unpretentious style against him (see 11:6; 1 Cor. 1:17; 2:1–5).

10:11, 12 They, Paul's critics, commended themselves (see 3:1), measured themselves by their own personal opinions, and compared themselves with others. Contrast Paul's advice to esteem others above oneself (Phil. 2:3, 4).

10:13–15 Paul boasted only within the **sphere** of ministry God had given him, but that sphere included the Corinthians. By implication, Paul's critics were boasting of what they had not worked at or cultivated, perhaps the results of Paul's ministry in Corinth.

10:16, 17 regions beyond you: In the Book of Romans, which Paul wrote around this time, he said his ambition was to preach the gospel in Spain (Rom. 15:24).

10:18 Paul began this section by saying he was not going to place himself among the group that commended themselves (v. 12). The reason he would not was that **the Lord** would commend Him as a faithful worker (see 1 Cor. 4:5).

11:1, 2 Paul loved the Corinthians and was legitimately **jealous** because as their spiritual father (1 Cor. 4:15), he had **betrothed** them to Christ and wanted to present them to Him as a **chaste virgin.** He did not want them corrupted by false teachers (vv. 3, 4).

11:3 The Greek word translated **simplicity**

is used in 2 Corinthians of sincerity (1:12) and generosity (8:2, 9). The Corinthians had a sincere singleness of heart toward Christ, which expressed itself in generosity.

11:4 Another Jesus would be one who was a man but not God, or crucified but not risen. **A different spirit** would be one of fear, not faith (4:13)—of bondage, not freedom (3:17; see Gal. 5:1). **A different gospel** would be one of law and not grace, one of works and not faith.

11:5 Some take the **eminent apostles** as a sarcastic reference to the false apostles in Corinth (v. 13). Others believe that Paul was comparing himself here to the genuine apostles of Christ, as he did later in the book (12:11, 12).

11:6 By **untrained in speech,** Paul meant he was not schooled in professional rhetoric. This does not mean that he was a poor speaker, only that he was not trained in Greek oratory. He did not lack **knowledge.** He had received direct revelation from the Lord (Gal. 1:11, 12).

11:7, 8 free of charge: In Paul's day, professional philosophers and teachers in Greek society charged for teaching. Paul did not. He labored (1 Thess. 2:9) and received support from other churches. Although Paul had the right to take money from the Corinthians, he chose not to do so in order to demonstrate his integrity (1 Cor. 9:12–14).

11:9–10 The brethren who came from Macedonia were probably from Philippi (Phil. 4:14–18). Paul's **boasting** was that he preached without charge (see vv. 7, 8).

11:11, 12 Paul did not accept money from the Corinthians because he did not want to give his critics **the opportunity** to put themselves on the same level as himself.

11:13 Paul's critics apparently called themselves **apostles of Christ,** but Paul said they were **transforming themselves.** The word means "to change in appearance," "to disguise," or "to masquerade." They were false teachers.

11:14, 15 And no wonder: If Satan, the prince of darkness, can disguise himself as an angel of light, then his servants, the ministers of evil, can disguise themselves as **ministers of righteousness.** Satan's main tool is deception.

11:16 Also indicates that his opponents were boasting.

11:17 Not according to the Lord means "not according to the Lord's standard." This kind of boasting was not characteristic of the Lord Jesus.

11:18–20 The false apostles were boasting **according to the flesh.** They measured themselves by their own standards rather than by the Lord's. Unfortunately, the Corinthians were listening to them (vv. 19, 20).

11:21 Paul's critics had accused him of being weak (10:10). He sarcastically said that he was **too weak** to rule the Corinthians harshly as the false apostles had done.

11:22 So am I: Paul's adversaries were Jewish and apparently felt that this made them superior not only to Gentiles but also to Greek-speaking Jews. Paul boasted that he was just as Jewish as they were.

11:23 Paul's opponents were not **ministers of Christ.** They were "false apostles" (v. 13), "ministers of Satan" (v. 15). But for the sake of argument, he responded to their claim as if it were true. **I speak as a fool:** Paul was hesitant to brag about his spiritual "accomplishments," because he knew that only God had made his preaching and service effective. He was just God's instrument. Paul's boast was in the Lord (10:17).

11:24–27 Hunger and thirst means involuntarily going without food and drink; **fastings** means voluntarily going without food for the sake of the ministry (see 6:5).

11:28–30 Infirmity means "weakness." Paul explains his weakness further in 12:7–10.

11:31, 32 Aretas the king: Aretas IV (9 B.C.–A.D. 40), the father-in-law of Herod Antipas, was king of Nabatea, a kingdom whose capital was Petra. Nabatea included the city of Damascus before the city was incorporated into the Roman province of Syria. Aretas was able to appoint a governor over Damascus because the Emperor Caligula (A.D. 37–41) gave Aretas control over the city.

11:33 Escaping from Damascus **in a basket** was Paul's example of boasting in his weakness (v. 30).

12:1 Paul prepared to boast about **visions and revelations** he received from God, possibly to counter similar claims by the false teachers, but he set them in contrast to the trials he had suffered in his ministry (vv. 7–10).

12:2 It becomes apparent later in the passage (see vv. 5–7) that Paul was writing here about himself, but he modestly presented this experience about **a man in Christ** as if it had happened to someone else. Paul wrote 2 Corinthians in A.D. 56; **fourteen years** before would have been A.D. 42, probably when he was in Antioch (Acts 11:26). **the third heaven:** It was common to speak of three "heavens": The first is the atmosphere where the birds fly; the second is the place of the sun, moon, and stars; the third is where God dwells.

12:3, 4 Heaven (v. 2) is here called **Paradise.** This experience should be compared to others in the Bible. God came down and met Moses on Sinai. John saw visions of the heavenly throne. And Paul is said to have been transported to heaven and returned. The experience probably helped Paul to endure suffering for the cause of Christ. Yet Paul never placed the focus of his message on this experience; instead he always preached Christ crucified (4:1–5).

12:5–7 Thorn means "splinter," "stake," or "something pointed." **Flesh** can refer to the body or to the sinful nature. Three basic suggested interpretations of the thorn are as follows: (1) If flesh is a reference to the body, then it is a physical ailment like an earache, headache, eye trouble, epilepsy, or recurrent fever. (2) If flesh is a reference to the fallen nature, then the thorn could be a temptation. (3) If the expression is figurative, it could refer to persecution or opposition. Most commentators interpret it as a physical ailment. Many suggest that it was eye trouble, on the basis of Gal. 4:15. Paul's thorn was given to prevent pride.

12:8–10 infirmities ... power: When believers are without strength and look to the Lord (v. 8), He provides power by His grace. Paul not only boasted about his weaknesses (v. 9); he said **I take pleasure**—a word meaning "to think good," "to be well-pleased"—in them. In Paul's weaknesses, Christ's power was made more apparent to others. It would bring praise to the only One who deserved it.

12:11–13 The Corinthians **compelled** Paul to boast because they listened to the false apostles (11:4) and were taken in by them (11:12). When Paul established the church in Corinth, he performed **the signs of an apostle,** miracles or supernatural evidences that proved his authority as an apostle (see Acts 14:3).

12:14 for the third time I am ready to come: Paul's first visit to Corinth was on his second missionary journey (Acts 18:1–18). Because of Paul's mention of a "painful visit" in 2:1, some consider Paul's second visit as occurring sometime when he was staying in Ephesus and before he wrote this letter (Acts 19:1–14). Others discount a second visit before this time. They insist that *ready* in this verse indicates that Paul had prepared to come to Corinth, but did not make the trip (see 1:15, 16, 23; 2:1–4 for evidence of this). He promised not to be **burdensome,** that is, to take financial support from them.

12:15, 16 Earlier Paul said he was "not walking in craftiness" (4:2). He also pointed out that Satan was deceitful (11:3) and that the false apostles were like Satan (11:13, 14). Now he sarcastically echoes his critics' charge that he was **being crafty.** But how did he trick them? He tricked them into not supporting him. Through sarcasm, Paul was vindicating himself against the charge of both trickery and fraud.

12:17–21 Apparently **Titus** was being implicated through the false apostles' accusations because Paul had recommended Titus for the collection task (8:16, 17). However they did not have any evidence against Titus. He was above reproach.

13:1 The third time has been interpreted two ways. Those who hold that Paul had visited Corinth twice before writing this letter take this statement at face value, that Paul had been there twice and was now ready to come a third time. Those who say that Paul had been to Corinth only once point to 12:14 and say that he was prepared to come again but did not do so.

13:2 told you before: In 1 Corinthians, Paul warned against sexual immorality (see 1 Cor.

6:12–20). By writing this letter, he was warning them a second time (see 12:21). **Not spare** means he would confront them if necessary.

13:3 Paul would confront those who were sinning (v. 2) since the Corinthians were seeking **a proof of Christ speaking** in him. Apparently Paul's critics claimed that an apostle should be a strong person. Paul was saying that when he came again he would be strong.

13:4 As Christ appeared to be weak when he was crucified, but was raised by **the power of God,** so Paul was weak, but by the power of God he would live with Christ in strength toward them. Paul was not speaking of the future Resurrection but of his next visit.

13:5 The Corinthians had been seeking proof of Christ's speaking in Paul; he told them to examine themselves to see if they were **in the faith** (for the phrase, see 1 Cor. 16:13; Titus 1:13). Paul did not doubt that they were true believers (see 1:1, 24; 7:1; 8:1; 12:14). He wanted them to ask themselves whether they were walking according to the gospel that they professed.

13:6–9 Paul prayed they would **do no evil**—probably a reference to the sins listed in 12:20, 21—and that they would be made **complete.** Paul was praying that there would be reconciliation of the divisions (12:20) and restoration. If his prayer was answered, he would **seem disqualified,** for he would not have to exercise his apostolic authority to discipline them.

13:10 I write: Paul confronted the Corinthians on paper so he would not have to do so in person (see v. 2; 10:11; 12:20).

13:11 Here, as in other passages, **farewell** means "rejoice" (Phil. 3:1; 1 Thess. 5:16).

13:12–14 Paul's concluding benediction invokes the blessing of the triune God: **grace** from **the Lord Jesus Christ** (see 8:9), the **love of God** (v. 11), and the **communion of the Holy Spirit.** At the end of his letter, Paul identifies the solution to many of the Corinthians' problems. The Holy Spirit, who dwelled in each of them, could empower them to live righteously. Furthermore the Spirit could reconcile them to each other.

Galatians

Introduction

There is no more passionate, comprehensive, yet concise statement of the gospel than Galatians. Salvation is through faith in Jesus Christ alone (2:16; 3:11, 12). No work can earn salvation. We can stand justified before God only through faith in Jesus Christ; nothing else will save us.

The writer of Galatians identifies himself as Paul (1:1). He claims to be an apostle, and then goes on to argue at length for the apostolic authority behind his gospel message. Much of the personal information he gives in the course of his defense corresponds to the narratives about Paul in the Book of Acts. He probably wrote Galatians as early as A.D. 48, making it one of the earliest New Testament books written.

Apparently Paul became aware of a perversion of the gospel of grace that was actively infecting the Galatian church. The false teachers who had come to Galatia since Paul's ministry there were advocating "the works of the law"—that is, by keeping the law. Specific emphasis was placed on the rite of circumcision. Paul's letter to the Galatians was a swift and decisive attempt to counter this message. He had to convince his "little children" in the faith that the new teaching was a distortion of the gospel of Christ.

If there is one repeated phrase that summarizes the subject of Galatians, it is "the truth of the gospel." Unlike Romans, which presents the gospel as the answer to universal human sinfulness (see Rom. 3:23; 6:23), Galatians clarifies the gospel message against the subtle, but ever deadly, danger of works salvation. No sinful person has ever been granted eternal life based on works. What is more, everyone who lives by such a confidence in works is "cursed," because no one can perfectly obey the law (3:10). Thus, to add works, rituals, or the law to the message of what it takes to become a Christian is to overturn the Good News.

1:1 Paul calls himself **an apostle** to assert his authority to speak to the problem confronting

the Galatian churches. **Through Jesus Christ and God the Father** refers to Paul's call to be an apostle (vv. 15, 16), which came to him on the road to Damascus (see Acts 26:12–18). **Raised Him from the dead** is a reference to the Resurrection of Jesus, a central belief of the Christian faith (see 1 Cor. 15).

1:2 churches of Galatia: Galatians is a circular letter for several churches.

1:3 Paul commonly combines the two ideas of grace and peace in the introductions of his letters (see 1 Cor. 1:3; 2 Cor. 1:2). The message of salvation is based on God's grace received by faith (Eph. 2:8), to provide peace with God (see Rom. 5:1).

1:4 gave Himself for our sins: It is a summary of the Good News: Christ's death is for you (1 Cor. 15:3). **Deliver us from this present evil age** is similar to Col. 1:13, which states Christ "has delivered us from the power of darkness."

1:5–7 I **marvel** reveals Paul's shock at the Galatians' leaving the **gospel** of **grace.** The Galatians had fallen for a **different** message, which was not the true message of salvation. Those causing the **trouble** were seeking **to pervert the gospel of Christ.**

1:8, 9 If the apostles or an **angel from heaven** were to **preach** a false gospel, they would be **accursed.**

1:10 To **please men** was not Paul's motivation. Paul sought the approval of God not basing his decisions on the opinions of other people.

1:11, 12 Paul **received** the gospel by special **revelation** from Jesus Christ at his conversion (see Acts 26:12–18).

1:13, 14 Paul's **conduct** before his conversion had distinguished him in Judaism in two ways: (1) He kept the law and traditions. (2) He **persecuted the church of God** in order to **destroy it** (see Phil. 3:6).

1:15–17 God had chosen Paul to be an apostle (v. 1) before his birth. Paul's call and conversion both came through God's **grace.** When he left **Damascus,** where he had stayed after his conversion to Christianity (see Acts 9:1–22), he went **to Arabia** for a period of time to receive revelation from the Lord.

1:18 after three years: This could be thirty-six months, or else a shorter period measured from the end of one year, through a complete year, and ending early in the third year. The three years could begin at the time of Paul's conversion (vv. 15, 16) or of his departure to Arabia (v. 17). Undoubtedly Paul and **Peter** talked at length about Christ and the gospel during the **fifteen days** Paul was in **Jerusalem.**

1:19 The reference to **James, the Lord's brother,** as one of **the other apostles** indicates that the office of apostle was not restricted to "the Twelve" (see 1 Cor. 15:5).

1:20–24 Following his trip to Jerusalem (vv. 18, 19), Paul **went** to **Syria and Cilicia,** likely the same journey mentioned in Acts 9:30, in which Paul traveled to his childhood home, Tarsus in Cilicia (see Acts 22:3).

2:1 After fourteen years could date from Paul's previous visit to Jerusalem (1:18, 19), but more likely from his conversion (1:15, 16). **I went up again to Jerusalem:** This journey is a reference to the Jerusalem Council (Acts 15).

Barnabas is Hebrew meaning "Son of Encouragement" (see Acts 4:36). Barnabas and Paul served together in the events narrated in Acts 11:25–30; 12:25—15:39.

2:2 Revelation may refer to the prophecy of Agabus in Acts 11:27–3, or to a private revelation of the Lord to Paul. **Them** may refer those who were of reputation, presumably the inner core made up of James, Cephas (Peter), and John (v. 9). Paul **communicated** with these leaders **privately** to share his revelation. **In vain** reflects Paul's desire to be fully effective in his ministry.

2:3 Titus (v. 1) was a "test-case" Gentile. The term **circumcised** introduces a topic which Paul addresses repeatedly in Galatians (5:2, 3, 6). Titus was not circumcised. Circumcising him would be a sign to other Gentiles that following Jewish law was required to become a Christian. That would be a rejection of the Good News that salvation is God's gift to those who believe in His Son.

IN DEPTH   Who Were the Galatians?

I t is difficult to decide who Paul was writing to in the Book of Galatians. In Paul's time the word Galatians had both an ethnic and a political meaning.

The ethnic Galatians were Celts who migrated from central Europe to Asia Minor in the third century B.C. They settled in the area around Ankara, the capital of present-day Turkey. In Paul's day the native Galatian dialect was still spoken there, although Greek had been accepted as the language of business and diplomacy.

By NT times there was a Roman province called Galatia that was larger than the original ethnic area. Whether Galatia refers to the people or to the province would indicate who the original readers of the letter to Galatians were. The usual view until the last two centuries was that Paul addressed "North Galatia," or congregations of ethnic Galatians located in the northern part of the province. Personal contact of the apostle with these churches may be alluded to in Acts 16:6 and 18:23. However, a "South Galatian" theory is more widely held today. According to this view Paul wrote to churches in the southern part of the province, that is, to the churches he founded on his first missionary journey (Acts 13:14—14:24) and later revisited (Acts 16:1–5).

With the biblical and historical evidence divided as it is, there have been notable scholars on both sides of the Galatian question. Neither theory is clearly superior, though it seems that the South Galatian view fits better with Acts. The question is important for assigning a date to the letter.

In either case, it is obvious that the book was addressed to a church which was struggling with the Judaizers, a group that insisted that the Gentile converts keep the requirements of the law. Paul's letter was a stern rebuke of this faction in the church. By adding the law to the gospel message, this group was in effect rejecting Jesus' free offer of salvation.

2:4 false brethren: These pseudo-Christians did not announce their purpose, which was to curtail Christian **liberty** (5:1, 13) and to bring Gentiles into the **bondage** of Jewish legalism (6:12–15). These false brethren maintained that one had to keep the Jewish law in order to be saved. They refused to confess that salvation was God's gift through faith alone.

2:5 Paul's message about **the truth of the gospel** had never given way to the message of the false teachers.

2:6 While Paul recognized the leadership roles of James, Cephas (Peter), and John (v. 9) as "pillars" of the Jerusalem church, he pointed out that they were in no way superior to him in their grasp of the gospel.

2:7–10 There were not two gospels, one for **the uncircumcised** Gentiles and another for **the circumcised** Jews. Paul's apostolic ministry was to the Gentiles (see Rom. 11:13), while Peter's **apostleship** was toward the Jews. God **worked effectively** through **Peter** in reaching Jews and just as effectively through Paul in reaching **the Gentiles** as evidence to the leaders in Jerusalem of Paul's apostleship (see Rom. 1:5). **The right hand of fellowship** indicated recognition of Paul by the Jerusalem church.

2:11, 12 Antioch was the largest city of the province of Syria. It became a center for missionary outreach to Asia Minor and Macedonia (see Acts 13:1–3). Paul confronted Peter because refusing to **eat with the Gentiles** contradicted what Peter had long since recognized—that the gospel was for the Gentiles too. **Certain men came from James** indicates they came with the authority of James, one of the leaders of the church (v. 9).

2:13 Peter's example was so decisive that **the rest of the Jews** in the church at Syrian Antioch, including **Barnabas,** followed suit. However, Peter's actions did not represent conviction, but **hypocrisy.**

2:14 Peter's hypocritical example implied that Gentiles had to behave like Jews in order to receive God's grace. Thus, Peter was **not** being **straightforward about the truth of the gospel** of God's grace. It had already been decided (vv. 1–5) that it was not proper to **compel Gentiles to live as Jews** because salvation was through faith alone.

2:15 Paul is not denying that those who are **Jews** by birth are **sinners,** as are all **Gentiles** (see Rom. 3:23). Rather, he is implying that Jews enjoy spiritual privileges (see Rom. 9:4, 5) that should make them more knowledgeable about how to be justified before God (see 3:6; Gen. 15:6).

2:16 The only way to be **justified** (declared righteous or pardoned) is through **faith in Jesus Christ.** Any other way allows **works,** whether keeping **the Law** of Moses or performing good deeds in general, to play a role in justification. Salvation is only through faith in Jesus Christ (Rom. 3:20).

2:17–19 Paul rejects the erroneous conclusion that being justified by faith in Christ actually made Jews **sinners,** thus painting Christ as a promoter of **sin.** If anyone attempts to reassert the "works of the law" as having any part in justification before God, **the law** itself convicts that person of being **a transgressor** (see 3:19–25).

2:20 Paul and every believer is **crucified with Christ** in order to die to sin, the law, and "this present evil age" (1:4). While believers live on physically, Christ's life is within them spiritually. Christ's Resurrection power through the Spirit is worked out through the Christian (see Rom. 6:4–11) who **live by faith in the Son of God.**

2:21 If righteousness is attainable through the Law of Moses, then God's gracious act of sending **Christ** to die on the Cross was unnecessary (see Rom. 3:4–26).

3:1 Foolish does not indicate lack of intelligence but lack of wisdom. Paul wonders what bewitching work had prevented the Galatians from recalling the gospel of the **crucified** Christ, which had been **clearly portrayed** or preached to them.

3:2 Paul contrasts obedience to the law with faith. **The hearing of faith** may be closely related to Paul's concept of obedience to the faith, since the Greek word for "hear" can also be translated "listen" or "obey" (see Rom. 1:5; 16:26).

3:3 Paul reminds the Galatians that their Christian life was **begun in the Spirit** by faith alone (see v. 2; 2:16). **Being made** perfect by the flesh indicates that the Galatians were trying to achieve perfection through their works, especially circumcision.

3:4, 5 This statement implies that the Galatian Christians had previously **suffered** for their faith, before they were tricked by the false gospel.

3:6 Paul quotes Gen. 15:6 to show that **Abraham** was justified by faith alone. This verse communicates precisely what Paul called "the truth of the gospel" (2:5, 14).

3:7 Those who are of faith are **sons of Abraham.** They are God's people.

3:8, 9 Scripture is personified as a preacher who foretells that **Abraham** and his example of faith would provide a blessing to all **nations** (see Gen. 12:3; Matt. 28:19). All who have **faith,** as Abraham did, are **blessed**.

3:10 under the curse: The quotation from Deut. 27:26 says that those who do not keep the whole law are **cursed,** proving that all are *cursed* who follow the law, because all fall short of the law's standards (see Rom. 1:17; 3:10–18, 23).

3:11, 12 Paul quotes Hab. 2:4 to prove that a person can only be **justified** through **faith.** He cites Lev. 18:5 to prove that keeping **the law** is utterly incompatible with faith.

3:13, 14 Paul knew that many of his readers would perceive that they were actually under **the curse of the law** (see v. 10; Deut. 27:26). For them as for us, it is comforting to know that **Christ** became that curse **for us** on the Cross (see Deut. 21:23).

3:15 Covenant probably means a "last will and testament," which is unchangeable after it is **confirmed.**

3:16 Jesus **Christ** is the fulfillment of the covenant (v. 15) God made with **Abraham.** Although all Jews are the physical seed of Abraham, Christ is the final focus of God's **promises,** the ultimate **Seed.** Christians are the seed of Abraham (see v. 29).

3:17 Four hundred and thirty years was the period of time Israel was in Egypt before the Exodus (see Ex. 12:40, 41). **The law,** which was put into force at the end of those centuries, could not **annul** the standing **covenant** with Abraham (see Gen. 15:18).

3:18 The Law of Moses (works) and the **promise** God made to **Abraham** (grace) were at odds with each other.

3:19, 20 The **purpose** of **the law** was not to justify mankind in God's eyes (2:16). Rather, the law was **added** after God's promise to Abraham (vv. 16, 17) to clarify the issue of sin until Christ **the Seed** (v. 16) came. The law was given **through angels** to Moses as the human **mediator** (see Acts 7:38). No mediator was needed with the Abrahamic covenant since it was a one-party, or unilateral, **promise.** God put Abraham into a "deep sleep" and consummated the enactment of the covenant (see Gen. 15:12–17).

3:21, 22 The relationship of **the law** and **the promises of God** is not competition, but need and fulfillment. The law was not designed by God to give eternal **life** and **righteousness.** Rather, the law showed man's need for the **promise** of **life** through **faith in Jesus Christ** (v. 9; 2:16), having confined all people under their sin (see Rom. 3:23; 6:23).

3:23–25 Paul gives two illustrations about the function of **the law** until **Christ** came (4:4, 5). The law acted as a jail **guard** to hold humankind in custody until faith in Christ was **revealed.** But the law also served as a **tutor.** The law was like a tutor because it corrected and instructed the Israelites in God's ways until Christ was revealed. Then such a tutor was no longer needed (4:1, 2).

3:26, 27 Through faith in Christ Jesus believers are not only blessed as sons of Abraham (vv. 7, 9) but as **sons of God** and God's heirs (4:7). Believers have been adopted by God Himself. Although we were His enemies, we have been made His sons. Although we deserve judgment, we will receive an eternal inheritance from our Father.

3:28, 29 The context of this verse is justification by faith **in Christ Jesus,** the fact that Jesus has redeemed all those who believe on Him, whether Jew or Gentile (3:26—4:27). Racial, social, and gender distinctions do not hinder a person from coming to Christ in order to receive His mercy.

4:1, 2 In ancient society **a child** had to wait until the proper time before he could inherit what was his. Paul uses this to explain why God delayed Jesus Christ's coming, leaving people with His law as a guide (3:23–25).

4:3 We were children in bondage parallels

"child" and "slave" in v. 1. Some believe that the **elements** Paul refers to in this verse are "elemental spiritual forces." But the context, and Paul's use of the word elsewhere (Col. 2:8, 20), favors an understanding of *elements* as "elementary principles or regulations," perhaps the Jewish law or aspects of it (compare Heb 5:12—6:3).

4:4, 5 The fullness of the time is the "time appointed" by **God** the Father (v. 2) for **His Son** to be born, and later to die for the sins of the world. **Born of a woman** speaks of Christ's humanity as the "Seed" of the woman (see 3:16; Gen. 3:15). **Born under the law** means Christ was subject to the Jewish law (see Matt. 5:17–19). **Redeem,** meaning "to buy from the slave market," is used only by Paul in the New Testament (see 3:13; Eph. 5:16; Col. 4:5). The verb describes Christ's supreme payment, His death on the Cross, to free those who believe on Him from the curse of the law.

4:6 Just as "God sent forth His Son" in "the fullness of the time" so **God has sent forth the Spirit** of Christ at the right time for every person who believes in Christ.

4:7 Paul summarizes the teaching of the preceding section by speaking of the transformation of the believer from a spiritual **slave** to a **son** with full rights.

4:8, 9 The Galatians had come to **know God** through faith in Jesus Christ (see John 17:2, 3). He had adopted them as His own sons, but they were turning back to the law that had once enslaved them.

4:10 The word **days** likely refers to Sabbaths or special feasts. **Months and seasons** pertain to longer observances, such as the celebrations between the Passover and the Day of Pentecost. **Years** probably indicates the Year of Jubilee, the fiftieth year in which slaves were to be freed, family lands returned to their original owners, and the land left fallow (see Lev. 23—25). The Jews commemorated all these feasts to please God.

4:11, 12 I urge you: Paul appeals to the Galatians to follow his example (see 1 Cor. 11:1). He had abandoned the ceremonial rules and regulations connected with Judaism so he could preach the gospel of Christ to Jew and Gentile alike in the cities of Galatia.

4:13–15 Paul describes the closeness and understanding that had existed between him and the Galatians when he had **preached the gospel** to them initially. He recalls how the Galatians had cared for him in his illness, treating him as they would **an angel,** or even **Christ** Himself. Paul's **physical infirmity** could have been an illness or a consequence of being stoned (Acts 14:19).

4:16 Paul was telling the **truth,** and as result was being labeled as their **enemy.**

4:17, 18 Paul was implying that the false teachers in Galatia were making the same mistake he had made before his conversion. Their zeal for the law was blinding them to the freedom and truth to be found in Jesus Christ.

4:19 Paul calls the Galatians his **little children.** The apostle also portrays himself as the Galatians' "spiritual mother." He was feeling the **labor** pains of their **birth** all over **again** because they had fallen into serious error.

4:20–22 To clinch his lengthy argument about the bondage of the law and the freedom found in Christ, Paul uses as examples the **two sons** of Abraham. These are Ishmael, who was born of the **bondwoman** Hagar (v. 24); and Isaac, who was born of Sarah, the wife of Abraham and a **freewoman.** Paul was demonstrating that he could argue from the Law to prove that the Law of Moses pointed to the Messiah, Jesus Christ.

4:23 In Gen. 16, Abraham and Sarah attempted to fulfill God's **promise** through their own strength, using Hagar, **a bondwoman.** In spite of the complications caused by that "fleshly" alternative, Sarah, **a freewoman,** eventually saw the miraculous outworking of God's promise in the birth of Isaac (see Gen. 12:2; 15:4).

4:24 symbolic: Paul was using the common Jewish allegorical method of the day to make his point. He used this approach to draw a contrast between **two** biblical **covenants** at odds with each other in the churches in Galatia: the Abrahamic promise (see Gen. 12:1–3) and the Law of Moses that God gave Israel at **Mount Sinai.**

4:25 Paul compared **Jerusalem** to **Mount Sinai,** the birthplace of the Law of Moses.

4:26 The Jerusalem above represents the hope

of heaven finally coming to earth (see Rev. 21; 22). Since **us all** obviously refers to those who are **free** through faith in Christ (v. 7), Paul was strongly implying that the question at hand was not allegiance to Jerusalem, but allegiance to *which* Jerusalem—the new or the old? Would the Galatians follow the shortsighted present Jerusalem and its legalism or the liberty of the heavenly Jerusalem?

4:27 Paul quotes Is. 54:1, using the prophesied restoration of Israel from judgment and exile to illustrate how the later-born **children** of promise would eventually far outnumber the earlier offspring.

4:28–31 Paul's allegory is based on Gen. 21:9, 10. **Isaac** was continually **persecuted** by his older half brother Ishmael. Eventually, Ishmael and his mother Hagar were expelled because Ishmael had no standing in God's eyes as **heir** of Abraham.

5:1 To be **children of the bondwoman** is to be enslaved to the covenant from Mount Sinai (4:24, 25). To be **of the free** is to follow Abraham's example of faith to be "born according to the Spirit" (3:2; 4:29), and to be destined for the "Jerusalem above" (4:26). Understanding such realities, the believer in **Christ** must **stand fast** in the **liberty** of not having to keep the Law of Moses to be saved.

5:2, 3 Paul points out that being circumcised changes the orientation of salvation away from God's grace to a person's own actions. One who is circumcised in order to gain God's acceptance is obligated **to keep the whole law,** which history has abundantly demonstrated no one can do (see Rom. 3:10–18).

5:4 Fallen from grace is understood by some to refer to the loss of salvation. However, *fallen from* may refer to their attitude and to the message that it communicates rather than to their eternal salvation.

5:5 Faith in Christ brings about justification before God as well as growth in the Christian life until we are glorified by God and freed from the presence of sin. This is **the hope of righteousness.** We can be assured that we will be declared righteous before the Lord on that last day, because we have a foretaste of that righteousness from the Spirit who lives within us (2 Cor. 5:5).

5:6 By **faith** it is possible to fulfill Christ's command to **love** one's neighbor (see vv. 13, 14; John 13:34, 35).

5:7, 8 You ran well: The Galatians' good start in the race of the Christian life had not continued. Their detour into legalism was certainly not God's will.

5:9, 10 Leaven symbolizes the intruders, with their false doctrine and sinister influence. The one who causes harm will experience God's **judgment** (see 2 Cor. 5:10).

5:11 The cross gives **offense** because it proclaims God's unmerited grace (2:21), leaving no place for people's good works.

5:12 cut themselves off: The false teachers should go beyond circumcision and castrate themselves. This exaggerated statement reveals Paul's frustration with those who muddied the clear gospel message.

5:13 Liberty presents an opposite temptation from legalism. A person can be tempted to view freedom in Christ as a selfish **opportunity for the flesh.** But Paul points out that true Christian **liberty** is the freedom to serve one another in **love** (vv. 5, 6).

5:14 The Christian does not live under the **Law** of Moses, but instead under "the law of Christ" (6:2). Living in Christ empowers us to love others, which is the fulfillment of the law.

5:15 When Christians follow their sinful desires (v. 13), they begin to criticize and contend with **one another,** and end up being **consumed** in worthless struggles.

5:16 Walking by faith in God's word under the Spirit's control assures victory over the desires of our sinful nature.

5:17, 18 The **works of the flesh** in the life of the Christian should not be underestimated. The desires of the Holy Spirit for us: to be free from sin.

5:19–21 The works of the flesh include the destructive **contentions** and **jealousies** portrayed in v. 15. Where there is such behavior, it is proof that the person is not living in the power of the Holy Spirit.

5:22, 23 The **fruit** analogy is reminiscent of Jesus' teaching on the vine, branches, and fruitful harvest (see John 15:1–5).

5:24 Christians are "crucified with Christ" (2:20). They no longer have to follow the values or desires of the world (6:14). But it is difficult for Christians to apply this spiritual reality to the **passions** (affections) **and desires** (lusts) of **the flesh** (v. 16).

5:25, 26 Paul exhorts the Galatians to walk in the Spirit because they are living in the Spirit. **Walk in the Spirit** means to obey the prompting of the Holy Spirit. A believer following the Spirit's lead will not **become conceited,** provoke others, or envy others.

6:1 Any trespass probably recalls the "works of the flesh" in 5:19–21. **Overtaken** means to be caught off guard, perhaps at a vulnerable point. A believer devastated by sin needs to be approached with **gentleness** (5:23) by fellow believers. Those not controlled by the Holy Spirit would tend to boast by comparing themselves to the fallen believer (vv. 3, 4).

6:2 The law of Christ is the law of love. The term **fulfill** suggests that choosing to **bear** another Christian's **burdens** is what **Christ** expects of all believers.

6:3, 4 Anyone who concludes that he is **something** through comparison with others **deceives himself.** Instead of judging others, a Christian should examine **his own work** to see if he is following Christ's example (see 1 Cor. 11:31; 2 Cor. 13:5).

6:5, 6 One important way to bear other believers' burdens (v. 2) is to **share in all good things,** including financial support, with one who **teaches** God's **word.**

6:7, 8 He who sows to the Spirit will reap everlasting life means that everlasting life is the glorious end of those who follow the guidance of the Spirit (see Rom. 6:22). Jesus said that He came so that we might have life and have it more abundantly (see John 10:10). In this life through the indwelling of the Spirit, Christians are developing a capacity to experience Christ to the fullest in the life to come.

6:9 doing good: The apostle has argued at length that works cannot justify (2:16) or sanctify (3:3) anyone.

6:10 Therefore indicates that this verse speaks of an important application of the spiritual process of sowing and reaping (vv. 7–9). Christians are not only to serve one another in love (see v. 2; 5:13); they also should **do good to** non-Christians.

6:11 Paul probably began here to write with his **own hand,** after having dictated the letter to a secretary. His reference to **large letters** in

light of the wording of 4:13–15 implies that Paul had problems with his eyesight. Paul commonly ended his letters with personal greetings (see 2 Thess. 3:17).

6:12 a good showing: The Judaizers were trying to appear spiritual by becoming circumcised and demanding that others become circumcised (5:2–12). **persecution:** By teaching that all Christians should become circumcised, the Judaizers were trying to make Christianity into a sect of Judaism.

6:13 Even the Judaizers who advocated the Galatians' circumcision did not keep the entire **law.** They knew they were required to do so (3:10–12), but were ultimately unable to fulfill all of the requirements (see Rom. 3:23). Still, they attempted to persuade the Galatians to be circumcised so they could **boast** about having them as their followers.

6:14 Paul spoke of himself as **crucified** with Christ (2:20). In that decisive act, "the flesh with its passions and desires" (5:24) was also crucified, as was **the world** with all of its attractions (see 1 John 2:15–17).

6:15 To a Christian under the New Covenant, following the Abrahamic sign of **circumcision** (see Gen. 17:9–14) does not mean **anything** in terms of spirituality. What really matters is being **a new creation** in Christ (see 2 Cor. 5:17).

6:16 As many as recalls the wording of v. 12. Those who live **according to** the example of Christ and the new creation (vv. 14, 15) are in stark contrast with those desiring to make a good impression through circumcision and keeping the law (vv. 12, 13). **The Israel of God** refers Abraham's spiritual descendants (3:6–9) because they believe in God and rely on His grace.

6:17 Paul's physical **body** carried evidence of his allegiance to **the Lord Jesus,** the **marks** of harsh persecution (see 2 Cor. 11:23–26) suffered for preaching the gospel. Paul's scars branded him as a slave for Christ (Rom. 1:1). Such marks far outweighed the "mark" of circumcision so valued by the false teachers in Galatia (vv. 12–15).

6:18 Paul ends his letter to the Galatians as he began it (see 1:3) by highlighting the theme of his entire letter: it is only by God's **grace** that we are saved.

Ephesians

Introduction

The apostle Paul was a prisoner in Rome when he wrote the letter to the Ephesians, which is similar in content to Colossians. Both letters were probably written around A.D. 60. Ephesus was the capital of the Roman province of Asia. Located at the intersection of several major trade routes, Ephesus was a vital commercial center of the Roman Empire and was the site of a famous temple for the fertility goddess Diana.

Paul visited Ephesus briefly at the end of his second missionary journey. When he departed, he left behind Priscilla and Aquila to continue the ministry in that city (see Acts 18:18–21). On Paul's third missionary journey, he spent about three years in Ephesus. When the apostle's gospel message was rebuffed by the Jews in the Ephesian synagogue, Paul taught Scripture to both Jews and Greeks in the school of Tyrannus. Paul's ministry at Ephesus was marked by several Spirit-empowered miracles. As a result, the city became a center for evangelistic outreach to the rest of the province of Asia (see Acts 19:18–20). In fact, so many people in Ephesus turned to Christ and renounced their pagan ways that some craftsmen in the city started a riot because the gospel threatened their trade of making and selling idols.

There is evidence that the Epistle to the Ephesians was originally a circular letter sent to several congregations in the province of Asia, where Ephesus was the capital. Another clue that Ephesians is a circular letter is its lack of personal references. The phrases in 1:15 and 3:2 imply that Paul had only heard of the recipients of the letter but had never met them. This is especially noteworthy since Paul had spent three years ministering at Ephesus. It seems likely that the apostle would have mentioned at least some of the Ephesians by name in his letter. In addition to the lack of personal references, the content and teaching of the letter is itself very general. Paul refers to the church as the body of Christ as a whole, and not to a specific local church.

The letter to the Ephesians emphasizes the truth that all believers are united in Christ because the church is the one body of Christ. In the early chapters, Paul describes how God formed this new body from Jews and Gentiles with His Son as the Head. Through Jesus' death, God reconciled sinful people to Himself. People who were normally divided, like the Jews and the Gentiles in the first century, were reconciled to each other through Christ. In Ephesians, Paul exhorted his readers to live out the spiritual truth of being joined together with Christ. Whether Jew or Gentile, they had to work together to make the unity of the church a reality.

1:1, 2 The salutations in New Testament epistles follow the form of the typical first-century letter: the writer is mentioned first and the recipient next, followed by a blessing or best wishes for good health. In Ephesians, Paul refers to himself as an **apostle** because he was personally commissioned by Jesus Christ with special authority to preach the gospel. **Saints** in the New Testament refers to all believers set apart by God in Christ.

1:3 The blessings of Christianity are largely **spiritual.** God does not guarantee health, wealth, and prosperity to the New Testament believer. The phrase **in the heavenly places** suggests that a Christian living anywhere in the world is even now in a spiritual sense seated with Christ on high.

1:4, 5 Love here is *agape* in Greek, the love that is by choice or one's will, not just a sentimental feeling. **having predestined us:** Predestination is not a cold-hearted determinism or set fate, but rather a loving choice on God's part.

1:6 The Beloved may also be translated "the One He Loves"—Jesus Christ. *The Beloved* is a messianic title, referring to God's Son. Jesus is not simply one among others who are loved by God. He is *the* Beloved Son.

1:7, 8 redemption: The word means "buy back" or "ransom." In ancient times, one could buy back a person who was sold into slavery. In the same way, Christ through His death bought us from our slavery to sin. **His blood:** The blood of Christ is the means of our redemption. The Old Testament and the New both clearly teach that there is no forgiveness without the shedding of blood.

Blood recalls the sacrificial system of the old covenant, which looked forward to the self-sacrifice of Jesus Christ that took away the sin of the world.

1:9 The mystery is not a puzzle to solve, or knowledge only for the few and the initiated, as in the mystery religions of Paul's day. In Paul's usage, the word *mystery* refers to an aspect of God's will that was once hidden or obscure, but now was being revealed by God (Rom. 11:25).

1:10 The word translated **dispensation** refers to God's administration or arrangement of all history to fulfill His plan of salvation.

1:11–13 The seal or mark of ownership in believers' lives is the **Holy Spirit.**

1:14 The guarantee of our inheritance is the Holy Spirit Himself. The Greek word for *guarantee* can also be used to indicate an engagement ring. As Christ is the Bridegroom and the church is the bride, so the Holy Spirit is the down payment, the earnest money, in the long-awaited marriage of the two (see Rev. 19:7, 8). **purchased possession:** The Old Testament described the nation of Israel as God's special treasure, one He had purchased by His mighty acts of deliverance during the Exodus (Ex. 19:5; Deut. 7:6). Here Paul describes Christians as the Lord's own possession, one bought with the blood of His own Son.

1:15–19 The eyes of your understanding refers to spiritual understanding. To describe this, Paul uses words that picture the heart looking out with eyes that have been brightened with divine illumination. **what is the hope:** A Christian may hope many things, but there is one hope that all Christians have in common (4:4), the Lord Jesus Christ (see Col. 1:5, 27).

1:20 worked in Christ: The Resurrection of Christ from the dead was the expression of God's power. The Resurrection is also proof of what God can do in us and for us. **seated Him:** Christ Jesus was not only raised from the dead, He was given a position at the **right hand** of God. Jesus received this position as the Son of David in fulfillment of the messianic prophecies of Ps. 2 and 110.

1:21 The Jews of Christ's time understood the end times to be divided into two time periods, the age in which they were living and the coming age. The Messiah, called "the Coming One," would rule in the age **which is to come.**

1:22, 23 In Ephesians Paul emphasizes Christ as **head,** just as his letter to the Colossians, written during the same imprisonment, emphasizes the body of Christ. **The church** here does not refer to any one local assembly but to all believers.

2:1 Dead in trespasses and sins means spiritually dead and lost.

2:2 you once walked: Whether it was a path of moral carelessness or the dark alley of evil, believers should no longer walk according to their past evil ways (4:17). Believers are saved so that they can have a lifestyle characterized by good works (v. 10). They are to walk worthy of their calling (4:1), which means to walk in love (5:2), in light (5:8), and in wisdom (5:15).

2:3 Lusts means "strong desires." Even with the modifier **of our flesh,** this word pertains to more than sensual cravings. The natural human desires for fame, power, and riches are meant as well (see Gal. 5:19–21).

2:4–7 we were dead: Because of Adam's sin, the entire human race is spiritually dead. Only God can grant new life and save us from this predicament. Out of His mercy, God gave His Son for us while we were yet His enemies. He loved us long before we loved Him (see 1 John 4:9, 10). In addition to making us spiritually **alive,** He determined that we would sit in **heavenly places** with our Savior, Jesus Christ. **in the ages to come:** God desires to demonstrate **His kindness** throughout eternity through **Christ Jesus** His Son. This has nothing to do with our own merit. It is only because He is merciful and kind that He reaches out to save us.

2:8–10 Christians **have been saved** by **grace.** The grace of God is the source of salvation; **faith** is the channel, not the cause. God alone saves. Salvation never originates in the efforts of people; it always arises out of the lovingkindness of God. **the gift of God:** Some suggest that *the gift of God* modifies the word *faith* in this verse. Thus Paul is saying that even our belief in God does not originate in ourselves. This too is a gift, so no one can take in pride in their position as a Christian. Everything is received from our merciful and gracious Father.

2:11 Because the sign of the Abrahamic covenant was circumcision, the Jews proudly referred to themselves as **the Circumcision.** They called Gentiles the **Uncircumcision.**

2:12, 13 Paul painted vividly the bleak condition of pagans. They had no hope, for God had not reached out to them to establish a covenant relationship. However, the shed **blood of Christ** could bring the Gentiles back to their Creator.

2:14 The middle wall of separation between Jews and Gentiles was vividly portrayed by an actual partition in the temple area, with a sign warning that any Gentile going beyond the Court of the Gentiles would be killed.

2:15 having abolished ... the law: Paul was not saying that God had rejected the righteous standards of the law. Rather, in Christ the righteous standards that people could never reach have been accomplished. He is our righteousness; in Him, believers fulfill the law (see Matt. 5:17, 20; Rom. 3:21, 22, 31). The Christian church, composed of both Jews and Gentiles, is described as **one new man.**

2:16–20 The apostles and prophets were the foundation of the church because they pointed to and witnessed to Jesus. The early church was established on their teaching and preaching (see Acts 2). Yet Christ Himself is the rock foundation on which the whole church rests (see 1 Cor. 3:11). The **cornerstone** was the first large stone placed at the corner of a building.

2:21, 22 Being fitted together pictures the process in Roman construction whereby laborers (usually slaves) would turn huge rocks around until they fit each other perfectly. For example, columns appeared to be one piece, but were actually separate cylinders of stone resting on each other. In similar fashion, God fits believers together into the **holy temple** He is building for Himself.

3:1 For this reason: Paul deviates from the main purpose of his letter to remind his readers of his own past and of his special ministry to them. The digression in vv. 1–13 serves as a reminder that Paul was writing a letter, not a book of systematic theology.

3:2–4 The **dispensation** (stewardship) that God gave Paul for the benefit of the Ephesians had previously been a mystery. Now God was revealing this mystery more fully in Paul's ministry to the Gentiles. The mystery was that Jews and Gentiles were to have an equal status in the church, the body of Christ.

3:5, 6 People who lived in the **other ages,** before Pentecost, had a great deal of knowledge about God and His grace. However, that knowledge was not as all-embracing as the revelation that we receive in Christ Jesus. The Old Testament predicted that God's grace would come to the Gentiles (Gen. 12:3), but equality with the Jews in one body was a secret never before **revealed.**

3:7 The word translated **minister** here means "servant."

3:8 Paul was not expressing false humility when he called himself **less than the least of all the saints.** He was truly humble because he previously had persecuted Christ's church.

3:9 Paul's mission as an apostle was to enlighten all people about the **mystery** of God's grace in Christ, which was not understood in previous times but which had become clear with the coming of Jesus Christ.

3:10–13 God's **manifold wisdom** is to be displayed to the angelic beings by the members of the church. Angels are also learning about God's wisdom as they watch His grace working in us (see 1 Cor. 11:10).

3:14–16 Father and **family** are related words in the original text. All families of men and angels derive from God the Father, their Creator.

3:17 Dwell suggests settling in at home. Christ resides in a believer's heart.

3:18, 19 The **love of Christ** is so great that it is beyond our understanding. The **fullness of God** is the abundance of gifts that flows from God.

3:20, 21 These two verses form a doxology, or praise, to God in which Paul points out that God can **do exceedingly abundantly above** anything we may **ask.** Neither God's love nor His power is limited by human imagination.

4:1 The second half of Ephesians, like that of a number of Paul's epistles, emphasizes the behavior that should result from the doctrines or beliefs taught in the first half. Note that the Christian life is not compared here to running or standing still, but to a walk.

4:2 lowliness and gentleness, with longsuffering: These are the attitudes that Jesus demonstrated when He was on earth (Phil. 2:5–8). These attitudes do not come naturally, but must be cultivated by the determination to place others above ourselves. Only the Spirit can empower us to treat people this way consistently.

4:3, 4 unity of the Spirit: All Christians are one in the Spirit. It is our duty to **keep** or observe that unity, recognize it as real, and act upon it without a sectarian spirit (see John 17:20–26).

4:5 One baptism may refer to the baptism in the Spirit that places all believers into the body of Christ, the church (see 1 Cor. 12:13). It may also refer to water baptism, the sign or seal that a person is a member of the body of Christ. At the time of the early church, public baptism clearly identified a person as a Christian.

4:6, 7 Like Peter (see 1 Pet. 4:10), Paul taught that all Christians have a spiritual **gift** or gifts. The gifts are given sovereignly by the ascended Christ in order to build up the church (see 1 Cor. 12:11). Thus the body of Christ is to function like a machine in which every part is essential for getting a job done. But unlike a machine, the body of Christ should maintain itself and build every one of its members up so that they can do good works (see 1 Cor. 12:7).

4:8 Paul quotes Ps. 68:18 to picture the **ascended** Messiah, triumphant over Satan and his hosts, distributing spiritual **gifts** to His people. The faithful stewardship of our gifts on earth will determine our position of service in Christ's messianic reign.

4:9 Many people take this descent to refer to Christ's entering Hades (specifically the saved portion of that unseen world) after His crucifixion to take saints to heaven when He rose from the dead. On the other hand, **lower parts of the earth** may also be translated "lower parts, the earth," so as to refer to Christ's coming to our humble planet as a man. This is the more likely meaning here (see Phil. 2:5–8).

4:10 The One who humbled Himself as a lowly Servant is the same One **who ascended far above all the heavens** in universal supremacy (see Phil. 2:9–11; Col. 1:18).

4:11 Apostles, meaning "envoys," or "ambassadors," in its strict sense refers to those who saw Christ in resurrected form, performed miracles, and were specially chosen by Christ to tell others about Him from their eyewitness accounts. **Prophets** delivered direct revelations from God before the New Testament was written (see 1 Cor. 14). **Evangelists** are gospel preachers who help bring people into the body of Christ. Since each of these categories is responsible for equipping believers, evangelists may also train other believers to share their faith effectively. **Pastors** do all for the church that a literal shepherd does for sheep: feeds, nurtures, cares for, and protects them from enemies. **teachers:** While the Greek ties the two titles *teachers* and *pastors* closely together here, elsewhere they are listed separately (see Rom. 12:7; 1 Pet. 5:2).

4:12, 13 Three stages of growth are presented here: Gifted leaders are responsible for **the equipping of the saints;** the well-equipped saints do **the work of ministry;** and the result is that **the body of Christ** is built up. The final goal is maturity, truth, and love.

4:14 Children are gullible, vulnerable, and easily victimized. The church needs to work diligently at moving babes in Christ on to maturity (see 1 Pet. 2:2).

4:15 Speaking the truth in love suggests that all that believers say or do should be honest and true, and said or done in a loving manner.

4:16 Note the use of the body metaphor here to present the same truth as the building metaphor in 2:21. **Every joint ... every part** is essential to full growth. There are no insignificant parts in the body (see 1 Cor. 12:14–27). Anything that builds up believers and the church is **edifying.**

4:17–19 Those who are so insensitive to moral darkness as to be **past feeling** have been hardened by sin and debauchery.

4:20–24 Paul compared the Christian life to stripping **off** the dirty clothes of a sinful past and putting **on** the snowy white robes of Christ's righteousness.

4:25 Paul calls for believers to speak the **truth** to each other, because all believers are united in Christ.

4:26, 27 Paul uses Ps. 4:4 to illustrate that not all **wrath** is sinful. However, anger should not be allowed to fester or continue for long (Mark 11:25). Christians may respond in controlled anger to injustice and sin, but they should never be consumed by this anger.

4:28 something to give him who has need: Instead of taking what belongs to someone else, a Christian should earn enough to share some of his or her own earnings with the needy.

4:29 Standards of speech for Christians are extremely high: **no corrupt word** is permitted.

4:30–32 The Holy Spirit of God should never be pushed away, ignored, or rejected. If we would remember that the One who lives in us is God's own Spirit, we would be much more selective about what we think, watch, and do. Note that Paul acknowledges that evil thoughts and actions are temptations even for those who are **sealed** by the Holy Spirit.

5:1, 2 Believers are to follow the example of God's actions. He loved us when we were still His enemies. As **imitators,** believers should demonstrate that type of self-sacrificial love.

5:3 Ephesus, with its pagan temple dedicated to the Roman goddess Diana (see Acts 19:23–31), was similar to our society in that sexual immorality and greed ran rampant. Paul warned the believers in Ephesus to avoid these pitfalls.

5:4–10 The believer's position has changed from **darkness** (sin) to **light** (**righteousness**). Believers are to change their **walk** to correspond to their position in Christ (see Rom 12:2).

5:11, 12 in secret: This verse bans Christians from indulging in the modern preoccupation with examining the lurid details of evils such as the occult and other perverted practices.

5:13, 14 Awake, you who sleep: This may be a fragment of a first-century Christian hymn, or an original thought by Paul alluding to Is. 26:19, a promise of God's coming salvation.

5:15 To **walk circumspectly** is to step gingerly. We should watch our path to avoid contact with undesirable influences.

5:16 Redeeming the time means taking advantage of opportunities for service. We each have a limited amount of time on this earth. Paul exhorts us to use as much of that time as possible for advancing Christ's purposes in this world.

5:17 do not be unwise, but understand: Discerning the will of the Lord is not a matter of feeling or emotion, but of mental understanding, applying our minds to Scripture.

5:18 Just as a person who is **drunk with wine** is under the control of alcohol, so a Spirit-filled believer is controlled by the Spirit. **filled:** Filling is a step beyond the sealing of the Holy Spirit (1:13). Sealing is an action God took at the point of our new birth. Filling is a moment-by-moment, repeatable action.

5:19, 20 One of the natural outcomes of being filled with the Spirit is **singing and making melody** to God. Some take the three types of music that Paul mentions in this verse to refer to different parts of the Book of Psalms. Most believe that these words refer to three larger categories: (1) the 150 **psalms** in the Psalter, plus other psalmlike poems throughout the Scripture; (2) **hymns,** compositions addressed directly to God, like the modern song "How Great Thou Art"; (3) **spiritual songs,** hymns about the Christian experience, like "Amazing Grace."

5:21, 22 Verse 21 completes the thought of the previous verses (vv. 18–20) which address how being filled with the Spirit manifests itself in the believer's life. It also introduces the next section (5:22—6:4) about how members of a Christian family should relate to one another. **submitting:** The Greek word for *submitting* does not refer to being under the absolute control of another but to voluntarily placing oneself under the authority of another.

5:23–24 Just as Christ is not inferior to the Father, but is the second Person in the Trinity, so **wives** are equal to their **own husbands.** Yet in a marriage relationship, a husband and wife have different roles. **to the Lord:** A wife's voluntary submission arises out of her own submission to Christ.

5:25 Husbands, love: Paul does not emphasize the husband's authority; instead, he calls on husbands to love self-sacrificially. Husbands are to emulate Christ's love, the kind of love that is willing to lay down one's life for another person.

5:26, 27 Christ loved the church so much that He was willing to suffer and die for it. His actions not only saved the church; they also sanctified it. Jesus wanted to develop the church into what it should be, the holy temple of God.

5:28, 29 A husband who realizes that his wife is truly **his own flesh** will treat her with love and care.

5:30, 31 the two shall become one flesh: Paul quotes Gen. 2:24, which teaches that the special union between husband and wife supersedes the original family ties.

5:32, 33 The **mystery,** a sacred secret revealed, is that Christian marriage parallels the union that exists spiritually between **Christ** and His bride, **the church.**

6:1–4 Children are to be obey their parents, and parents are to treat their children in such a way that the children will want to obey. **Children** must obey their **parents** for Christ's sake, even if their parents are not believers. This is supported by the only one of the Ten Commandments followed by a **promise** (see Deut. 5:16). **do not provoke:** Parents should not be unreasonably severe with children or ridicule them.

6:5 A big percentage of the population of the Roman Empire was made up of **bondservants** or slaves. These people were considered mere property and could be abused and even killed by their masters with no resulting investigation by the state. In the church, wealthy slave owners and their slaves broke bread together at the Lord's Table as equals.

 IN DEPTH   ## The Concept of Submission

What kind of submission is Paul advocating in Ephesians? Some hold that Paul is speaking of mutual submission in this passage (5:21—6:4). They point to the phrase "submitting to one another in the fear of God" (5:21), as the overall theme of the verses following it (5:21—6:4). According to this view, husbands and wives, parents and children, masters and slaves all submit to each other in different ways.

This passage certainly teaches a proper Christian response to each other at different levels, as the mutual submission view holds. It is clear that Paul develops two ideas side by side—submission and the appropriate response of the one to whom submission is given. But the mutual submission view does not adequately reflect the meaning of submission in Greek. The Greek term for submission has military origins, emphasizing being under the authority of another. The word does not connote a forced submission; instead it is a voluntary submission to a proper authority. Thus, Paul seems to be saying that wives should voluntarily place themselves under the authority of their husbands. The same word is used to describe Christians voluntarily submitting to governmental authorities (1 Pet. 2:13) and younger people submitting to the wisdom of their elders (1 Pet. 5:5). In this passage, Paul gives the illustration of the church's submission to Christ. After encouraging wives to submit to their husbands, Paul goes on to describe how children should obey their parents, and slaves their masters. Their subordination is described in terms of obedience, instead of in terms of voluntary submission.

But Paul's major emphasis in this passage is not on the submission of wives, but on the duty of those who are in authority. Husbands should imitate the love of Christ. Parents should not provoke children. Masters are not to threaten their slaves. The apostle argues that serving is more important than being in authority over others; Christ should be our model. Although He, as God's Son, could demand obedience from all, He did not shrink from performing duties that were customarily the task of a servant. Jesus washed the feet of His disciples (John 13:12–16). A husband is to be a godly leader; he is to be a servant-leader. His role is to lead his wife, but to do so by taking everything about her into consideration and by using his position to give her the greatest opportunity to succeed.

No doubt some slaves were gifted spiritual leaders and ministered the word to people far above them on the social ladder.

6:6 not with eyeservice: Servants and employees should serve faithfully even when no one is looking. After all, God sees all that we do.

6:7, 8 Receive the same refers to future rewards (see Col. 3:23–25).

6:9 Christian **masters** should not use **threatening** language to their servants but should remember that they are also servants of a much higher **Master ... in heaven,** who is completely fair.

6:10 Be strong may also be translated "be made strong." The passive voice would suggest that we cannot do it ourselves.

6:11 The whole armor of God is the believer's protection against evil and the Evil One. Paul presented the extended metaphor of the battle dress roughly according to the order in which the various pieces were put on. **Wiles of the devil** are Satan's subtle tricks to defeat Christians in spiritual warfare (see 2 Cor. 11:3).

6:12 Our real battle is not with human cultists, false religionists, atheists, agnostics, and pseudo-Christians, but with the demonic beings working through them, of which even the **flesh and blood** opponents themselves are sometimes unaware.

6:13 The evil day is taken by some to refer to the end times when the Evil One will launch a ferocious campaign against Christ and His army. A more common view is that any great spiritual contest in a believer's life is in view here.

6:14 Verses 14–17 present the six pieces of spiritual armor. Four are mentioned specifically and the belt and shoes are implied. Soldiers **girded** themselves with a belt, from which hung strips of leather to protect the lower body. **Truth** is considered crucial by Paul (4:15, 25), because a dishonest Christian cannot hope to withstand the father of lies himself. The truth referred to here is integrity, a life of practical truthfulness and honesty. The **breastplate** of Roman times went completely around the body, so that the back of a warrior was also protected. The breastplate was made of hard leather or metal. The **righteousness** that the breastplate represents is not the righteousness of Christ, which all believers have, but the

practical, righteous character and deeds of believers.

6:15 A Roman soldier's **feet** were **shod** with hard, studded shoes. Paul used this image to represent **the preparation of the gospel of peace.** This may mean either that the gospel is the firm foundation on which Christians are to stand or that the Christian soldier should be ready to defend and spread the gospel.

6:16 Above all may mean that the **shield** is to be used against everything. It may also mean that the shield is to cover the whole armor. A Roman soldier's shield typically measured two and one-half feet by four feet. The Christian's shield offers protection against **all the fiery darts of the wicked one.** Flaming arrows could not penetrate the fireproof shield of the ancient Roman soldier, nor can the assaults of Satan penetrate to the believer who places his or her faith in God.

6:17 the helmet of salvation: The intricately designed Roman helmet protected the soldier's head and also made him look taller and more impressive. **The sword of the Spirit** is the only offensive weapon in the believer's armor. This weapon is not necessarily the Bible as a whole, but the specific word that needs to be spoken in a specific situation.

6:18 Without **prayer,** all the armor in the world would be of no use. **praying always:** Perseverance and patience in prayer are essential.

6:19 The apostle Paul was not ashamed to ask other believers to pray that he would have the courage to proclaim the gospel. Even as a prisoner, Paul still wanted to be a faithful witness for the Lord.

6:20 Paul was **an ambassador in chains** in Rome for the gospel of Christ. His prayer was that he might **speak boldly,** as an ambassador for the King of kings **ought to speak.**

6:21–24 The last verses of Ephesians reveal Paul's appreciation of the ministry of others, especially the ministry of Tychicus (see Col. 4:7). The fact that this letter does not conclude with personal greetings as Paul's other letters do (see Rom. 16) may indicate that this was a circular letter, one intended for a number of churches around Ephesus. **Sincerity** may also be translated "without corruption."

Philippians

Introduction

From beatings to imprisonment, Paul had endured much suffering for the cause of Christ. These trials had taught Paul to be content in all circumstances, an ability that Paul encouraged the Philippians to cultivate (4:11). In fact, his letter to the Philippians is a testimony to this attitude. Even though he was in prison, facing an uncertain future, Paul wrote this thank-you letter to the Philippians, a letter that expresses Paul's abundant joy in what God was accomplishing through them.

Most students favor Rome (about A.D. 60–62) as the city from which Paul wrote this epistle. Although the distance between Rome and Philippi was great, Paul was in Rome long enough for messages to travel back and forth to that city. Furthermore, Paul's imprisonment in Rome is well established in Scripture (Acts 28:16–31). Because his situation allowed him freedom to preach the gospel (1:12, 13; Acts 28:23–31), he probably felt confident that his release from prison was imminent.

While on his second missionary journey, Paul left Troas in the province of Asia (part of present-day Turkey) and traveled to Macedonia (in present-day Greece) to establish the first church in Europe, the church in the city of Philippi (Acts 16:6–12). The church that Paul established in Philippi was a mixture of races, cultures, and social classes (although mostly poor; see 4:15, 16) from its inception. The first converts were an upper-class woman (Lydia, a seller of royal dyes; see Acts 16:14, 15), a middle-class Roman jailer (Acts 16:22–34), and perhaps a lower-class young girl who had been demon-possessed (Acts 16:16–18). As the church grew, it maintained a Gentile flavor, yet the less populous group of Jewish-Christians exerted much influence over the church.

The most prominent theme of the Epistle to the Philippians is joy, specifically the joy of serving Jesus. The general tone of the letter reflects Paul's gratitude toward the Philippians and his joy in God. This may seem strange because Paul wrote this letter while he was in prison. Paul, however, had the ability to recognize opportunities for sharing the gospel even

in apparent setbacks. This was the origin of Paul's joy: he saw God working through the difficult situations he faced.

1:1 bondservants: In his other prison epistles (Ephesians, Colossians, and Philemon), Paul calls himself an apostle. In this letter he begins by giving the title of **servant** to Timothy and himself. It establishes Timothy (2:19–23), Epaphroditus (2:25–30), and Paul (3:7–9) as individuals who demonstrate the same servantlike attitude that Christ had (2:5–8). **Saints** means "holy ones" (those who are separated to God) and refers to all the believers in Philippi. **Bishops** refers to those who watched over the spiritual welfare of the local church (synonymous with "elders" in other passages; see Acts 20:17; Titus 1:5, 7). They were the main administrators of the church. **Deacons** refers to those who served the congregation in special service capacities. They were charged with handling the physical and material concerns of the church (see Acts 6:1–7).

1:2 Paul combines the word **grace** with a Greek translation of the Hebrew greeting *shalom,* or **peace** (see 2 Cor. 1:2; Gal. 1:3).

1:3 I thank: The tense of the Greek verb indicates that Paul was continually thankful to God for the Philippian Christians. **upon every remembrance of you:** Every time God brought them to his mind, Paul gave thanks.

1:4 Joy, a prominent theme in Philippians, filled Paul's prayers for the Philippians even when he interceded for their needs. This is the first of five uses of the Greek word for *joy* in the letter (v. 25; 2:2, 29; 4:1). Paul also uses the Greek word for *rejoice* nine times in this letter (v. 18; 2:17 [twice], 18 [twice], 28; 3:1; 4:4 [twice]).

1:5 Fellowship is a commercial term for a joint-partnership in a business venture in which all parties participate to ensure the success of the business. In the Christian community, the word expresses intimacy with Christ (see 1 Cor. 1:9) and other believers (see 2 Cor. 8:4, 1 John 1:7). In this case, Paul may be using the word *fellowship* to refer to the financial contributions the Philippians had given Paul **from the first day until now** (see 4:14, 15). Immediately upon becoming Christians and continually thereafter, the

Philippians had dedicated themselves to living and proclaiming the truth about Jesus Christ, and specifically to helping Paul in his ministry.

1:6 being confident: Paul had become convinced some time in the past that God would complete His good work among the Philippians, and his confidence remained unshaken. **Until** can also be translated "as far as." It expresses progress toward a goal and indicates that a time is coming when God will finish His work among the Philippian Christians. **the day of Jesus Christ:** The ministry in which the Philippians participated continues (like a relay race) up to the present, and it will continue until Christ returns.

1:7 The word **right** conveys a sense of moral uprightness (in keeping with God's law) and is often translated as "righteous." In this context, the word indicates that Paul's thoughts about the Philippians were in perfect accord with God's will. Since **defense** implies speech, we can be certain that Paul was not silent while in prison, but boldly spoke about Jesus Christ. Paul may have also been indicating that he would testify about Christ at his judicial proceedings. **confirmation:** Used only here and in Heb. 6:16 in the New Testament, this word is a legal and commercial term

meaning "a validating guarantee." *Defense* and *confirmation* are the negative and positive aspects of Paul's ministry. He defended the gospel against its opponents' attacks, and he confirmed the gospel through powerful signs.

1:8 affection of Jesus Christ: The word translated *affection* literally means the internal organs, regarded by the first-century reader as the center of the deepest feelings. Whereas the heart is the seat of reflection, Paul now speaks of his affection, his deep feelings for the believers. In modern terminology, Paul revealed that he had the "heart" of Jesus Christ. His feelings for the Philippians were like those of Jesus Christ, who loved them and died for them.

1:9 The **love** that Paul sought for the believers is the highest form of Christian love, based on a lasting, unconditional commitment, not on an unstable emotion. **knowledge:** The first of two terms on which a directed love is built, *knowledge* suggests an intimate understanding based on a relationship with the person. The focus of this knowledge is God. **discernment:** Found only here in the New Testament, the Greek word means moral or ethical understanding based on both the intellect and the senses. The word implies perception or insight into social situations.

1:10 sincere: This term, literally meaning

In Philippi, as elsewhere, Paul offered the gospel first to the Jews. There must have been very few Jews in Philippi because the city did not have a synagogue, and in first-century Judaism it took only ten Jewish men to justify building a synagogue for worship. The Jews who did live in Philippi went outside the city gate to the banks of the Gangites River for worship and prayer. Yet the Christian church to which Paul wrote must have flourished, because in his letter he referred to levels of leadership in the church, such as overseers and deacons.

Philippi was a culturally diverse Roman city on the main highway (the Egnatian Way) from the eastern provinces to Rome, and the church at Philippi had a diverse group of believers. The NT specifically mentions an Asian, a Greek, and a Roman. One was a businesswoman who sold purple cloth to the rich; one was a slave girl who had been possessed with a spirit of divination; the third was a jailer. Three different races, three different social ranks, and probably three different religious loyalties before encountering Christ. But Paul taught them that all were equal in the body of Christ; all were sinners saved by God's grace. They were to humble themselves as Jesus had done, and be unified in the love of Christ. This church was one of the most integrated places in the Mediterranean world.

"judged by sunlight," does not mean "honestly trying hard," but rather pure, unmixed, and free from falsehood. Any spot in a garment could be seen by holding the object up to the sunlight. Christ died to free the church from every blemish (Eph. 5:27). **without offense:** Using another graphic term to describe the Christian, Paul conveys the sense of not striking out at someone. The phrase means not leading others into sin by one's own behavior. **day of Christ:** The goal ahead for the believer is the *day of Christ* in which the believer will stand for evaluation before the Savior.

1:11 fruits of righteousness: This phrase is best understood either as "fruit that results from being justified" or "fruit characterized by morally correct conduct." *Righteousness* describes the source or the nature of the fruit, the behavior.

1:12 actually turned out: Paul wanted the Philippians to know that his imprisonment was advancing the gospel. Such words would comfort the Philippians who were concerned about Paul's welfare and who needed assurance that their prayers for Paul and their gifts to him had not been in vain. **furtherance:** Paul's imprisonment was a strategic advance in the kingdom of God because it was clearing the way for the gospel to penetrate the ranks of the Roman military (see v. 13) and even the royal house (see 4:22).

1:13 Paul's imprisonment furthered the gospel in two ways. First, the palace guard heard it as Paul preached in prison. Second, **all the rest**—Paul's visitors—heard the gospel. Some of his visitors were leaders of the Jews in Rome (see Acts 28:17). The **palace guard** (Praetorian Guard) consisted of several thousand highly trained, elite soldiers of the Roman Empire who were headquartered at Rome. For the one to two years that Paul had been under house arrest in Rome, different soldiers had taken turns guarding him. Because they were chained to Paul, they had no other choice but to listen to him proclaim the gospel; they could not beat him into silence because he was a Roman citizen (see Acts 16:37, 38). Although Paul could not go to the world to preach, in this way God brought the world to Paul.

1:14 without fear: Although they could also be imprisoned as Paul was, the Roman Christians were emboldened by Paul's courage and were able to proclaim the message about Jesus Christ fearlessly.

1:15 Those preaching **from envy and strife** were not heretics, since they were preaching Christ. But apparently they were jealous of the attention Paul received, and they determined to sow seeds of dissension in order to cause him trouble. **some ... from goodwill:** Other Christians preached Christ with good motives. They thought well of Paul and of the gospel message and were dedicated to serving God faithfully.

1:16, 17 selfish ambition: The motives of these believers were anything but good. The term for *selfish ambition* implies that they did not preach to honor God or to help Paul but rather to gain applause and followers for themselves (see 2:3). **to add:** The word Paul uses here literally means "to raise up" or "to cause." In other words, Paul believes that these preachers actually desired to cause him additional problems while he was in prison.

1:18 What then: In essence Paul is saying, "Their motives are between them and God." **in pretense or in truth:** Whether the preaching was done for false motives or pure, whether for appearance's sake or for the sake of what was right, Paul was pleased that the gospel was being spread.

1:19 will turn out: Paul expresses his confidence about how the sovereign God would work out this difficult situation. **deliverance:** The word translated *deliverance* is usually translated "salvation." In the New Testament this word is used for physical healing, rescue from danger or death, justification, sanctification, and glorification. Here Paul refers to his daily empowering to endure the troubling situation before him. **your prayer:** Here is the channel for his deliverance. The prayer of believers for other believers is vitally important because by it, and together with the work of the Holy Spirit, God produces positive results.

1:20 hope: This is not wishful thinking but confident expectation. **in nothing ... ashamed:** Paul was determined not to be dishonored in anything or by anyone. He demonstrates that right actions are not determined by environment but by right thinking. **will be magnified:** Paul was committed to ensuring that Christ would be made even more conspicuous in his own life than ever. He was not relying on himself to exalt Christ but looked to the Holy Spirit (see v. 19) to magnify Christ in him (see John 16:14; 2 Cor. 3:18).

1:21 For to me is similar to the common expression: "As far as I'm concerned." **Christ ... gain:** Paul would experience *gain* in his own death because he would be with Christ (v. 23). In fact, Paul may have been expressing his confidence that since his imprisonment had furthered the gospel, God would also use his death to further His kingdom.

1:22 fruit from my labor: If Paul continued to live, he would have the opportunity to preach the gospel to others and see spiritual victory in the lives of the Philippians. **what I shall choose:** Paul was in a dilemma because he clearly saw the advantages of both life and death for the Christian. Life meant an opportunity to minister to people like the Philippians (see v. 24), while death meant being with Christ his Savior.

1:23, 24 Paul felt **pressed** in on every side, much like a besieged city with no hope of relief from its affliction. He was torn between the prospect of seeing the Lord and his passion for ministering to the Philippians. **to depart:** In relation to Paul's profession as a tentmaker, the term *depart* means to strike, or take down, the tent to be ready to travel elsewhere. Paul saw death not as the end of life but as a time of moving from one home to another.

1:25, 26 your progress: Paul was not satisfied that the Philippian Christians should simply be saved, but that they should advance to maturity in Christ. He felt a responsibility to continue to teach them.

1:27 let your conduct: The word used could refer to discharging the obligations of a citizen. Because Philippi held the privileged status of a Roman colony, its citizens understood the responsibilities of citizenship. Paul here commanded the Philippian Christians to shift their perspective from the earthly realm to the heavenly one. They should live in this world as citizens of the heavenly kingdom. Their conduct should reveal their heavenly citizenship. **stand fast:** They were not to stand alone in isolation but together in oneness of spirit and mind, united for a common goal. **striving together:**

Teamwork is the key concept expressed by this Greek word, which literally means "to engage together in an athletic contest."

1:28 The word translated **terrified** is used of the terror of a panicked horse. The Philippians are not to be terror-stricken in the face of their enemies. Their courage would be proof of their salvation and of the ultimate failure of their foes. **proof of perdition:** By striving together in love, the Philippians would be living *proof* (a legal term denoting proof obtained by an analysis of the facts) to their opponents that the message of Jesus Christ is true. This would confirm the lost state of their adversaries.

1:29, 30 to suffer: Suffering is actually a gift from God, for in the midst of suffering He comforts us (see 2 Cor. 1:5) and enables us to rejoice (see 1 Pet. 4:12, 13). Suffering is a blessing because it brings eternal reward (see Matt. 5:1–12; 2 Cor. 4:17; 2 Tim. 2:12; Rev. 22:12). Suffering also matures us as Christians in the present (see James 1:2–4) and enables us to be glorified with Christ in the future (see Rom. 8:17).

2:1 The Philippians' biggest battle was not with their external circumstances but with those internal attitudes that destroy unity. Paul had demonstrated his own refusal to let external circumstances control his attitudes (1:12–18). The **therefore** ties together his conflict and their conflict. **fellowship:** Scripture teaches that our fellowship is not only with God the Holy Spirit as seen here, but also with God the Father (see 1 John 1:3) and God the Son (see 1 Cor. 1: 9; 1 John 1:3), as well as with other Christians (see 1 John 1:7). **mercy:** The Greek term means compassionate desires in response to a situation and that stimulate a person to meet recognized needs in that situation.

2:2 The apostle sets forth a fourfold appeal, an appeal that expresses one major idea—the unity of the church. **one accord:** Paul here is emphasizing a unity of spirit between Christians (see Ps. 133), literally "a togetherness of soul." **one mind:** The words Paul uses to indicate *one mind* are virtually identical to the words translated *like-minded* earlier in this verse. Paul was emphasizing the unity that should exist between believers and how they must single-mindedly strive together to advance the gospel of Jesus Christ.

2:3, 4 Paul attempts to correct any misunderstanding that may arise from what he said earlier in the letter about some preaching out of selfish motives (see 1:15, 16). He was concerned that someone might think he was condoning **selfish ambition,** so long as the gospel was being preached. **conceit:** Pride should not be a Christian's motivation; instead everything should be done in the power of the Holy Spirit. **lowliness of mind:** The word suggests a deep sense of humility. What Paul was calling for was an honest evaluation of one's own nature. This should always lead to a glorification of Christ. **let each esteem:** This verb indicates a thorough analysis of the facts in order to reach a correct conclusion about the matter. In other words, each Philippian Christian was to properly assess himself or herself. **others better than himself:** The honest self-examination that Paul was calling for leads to true humility. This enables a person to hold others above himself or herself, to value people over material possessions or personal plans.

2:5 Verses 5–8 present one of the most significant statements in all of Scripture on the nature of the Incarnation, the fact that God became man. Through this wonderful description of Christ, Paul illustrates the principle of humility (vv. 3, 4). **Let this mind be:** All godly action begins with the "renewing of the mind." Right thinking produces right actions. **in you:** Thinking and being like Christ are requirements not only for an individual but also for the corporate body of believers. Together we need to think and act like one being, like the Person of Jesus Christ.

2:6 robbery: Because Christ was God, He did not look on sharing God's nature as *robbery,* that is, as "a thing to be seized," as though He did not already possess it, or as "a thing to be retained," as though He might lose it. **equal:** This word speaks of equality of existence. Christ was fully God, but He limited Himself in such a way that He could also be completely human. In Christ, God became man.

2:7 made Himself of no reputation: This phrase can be translated "He emptied Himself." Christ did this by taking on the form of a servant, a mere man. He did not empty Himself of any part of His essence as God. Instead He gave up His privileges as God and took

upon Himself existence as a man. While remaining completely God, He became completely human. **form:** Paul does not say that Christ exchanged the form of God for the form of a servant, involving a loss of deity or the attributes of deity. Rather, in the Incarnation, Christ continued in the very nature of God but added to Himself the nature of a servant. **bondservant:** The term refers to the lowest status on the social ladder (see Heb. 10:5), the exact opposite of the term *Lord,* a title by which all people will one day recognize the risen Christ (see v. 11). **likeness:** This word does not mean that Christ only appeared to be a man. Rather, the term emphasizes identity. In reality He was a man, possessing all the essential aspects of a human being, although unlike all others He was sinless.

2:8 appearance: This is the third word Paul uses to show the Philippians that Jesus Christ who is fully God from all eternity is also fully man. The word *appearance* points to the external characteristics of Jesus: He had the bearing, actions, and manners of a man. **He humbled Himself:** Jesus willingly took the role of a servant; no one forced Him to do it. **obedient:** Although He never sinned and did not deserve to die, He chose to die so that the sins of the world could be charged to His account. Subsequently He could credit His righteousness to the account of all who believe in Him (see 2 Cor. 5:21; Gal. 1:4). **even the death of the cross:** Paul describes the depths of Christ's humiliation by reminding his readers that Christ died by the cruelest form of capital punishment, crucifixion. The Romans reserved the agonizing death of crucifixion for slaves and foreigners, and the Jews viewed death on a cross as a curse from God (see Deut. 21:23; Gal. 3:13).

2:9 Note the contrast between Jesus' placing Himself in a debased status (see v. 8) with God the Father's elevation of Jesus to a **highly exalted** status.

2:10 every knee: Although all people will one day worship Christ, only those who put their faith in Him in this life will have an everlasting relationship with Him after death (see Rev. 20:13–15). **those under the earth:** Paul refers here to those who will already have died at the time of Christ's return, in contrast to the angels in heaven and those who will still be living on earth.

2:11 confess: The term Paul uses is a strong, intensive verb, which means "agree with" or "say the same thing." Essentially Paul is saying that everyone will unanimously affirm what God the Father has already stated (Is. 45:23): that Jesus Christ is Lord.

2:12, 13 Therefore: Paul desires the Philippians to respond positively to his admonition to have the mind of Christ (vv. 5–8). The command is to the entire group since the word **you** is plural. **work out:** The Greek term speaks of the present deliverance of the Philippians. Thus salvation can be compared to a huge gift that needs to be unwrapped for one's thorough enjoyment. Paul is encouraging the Philippians to develop and *work out* their salvation, but not to work *for* their salvation.

2:14 The Philippians have been secretly discontented and have been **complaining** (2:1–4). But the word used suggests that loud dissension had not yet broken out.

2:15 The purpose of the command in v. 14 is that the Philippians might be **blameless** light bearers in their world. They should deserve no censure because they are free from fault or defect in relation to the outside world (see 3:6). If the Philippian believers were going to have a testimony in their community, they had to be blameless in their actions and attitudes (see 1 Tim. 3:2). **crooked and perverse generation:** Paul describes the world as being the opposite of Christian. On the one hand the world is turned away from the truth, while on the other hand it exerts a corrupting influence that opposes the truth. **shine as lights:** Paul depicts believers as stars whose light penetrates the spiritual darkness of a perverted world.

2:16 The Greek verb translated **holding fast** contains two thoughts: holding fast and holding forth. The former suggests a steadfastness in which our lights (see v. 15) blaze continually for God. The latter implies projecting our lights into the darkness of this world.

2:17, 18 being poured out: Both Jews and Greeks sometimes poured wine out on an altar in connection with religious sacrifices (see Num. 15:1–10). Some have interpreted this figure of speech as depicting Paul's own martyrdom for the cause of Christ. However the content of the letter reveals by contrast that Paul assumes he will live (see 1:25) and expects to be released from prison shortly (see v. 24). Thus Paul probably was saying that he was presently being poured out as a living **offering** on behalf of the faith of the Philippians. **service:** Paul chooses a Greek term that depicts a person who fulfills the duties of a public office at his or her own expense. In the Christian context, this word speaks of worship humbly offered to God.

2:19 Paul balanced the previous somber passage (vv. 12–18) with the optimistic hope of sending his coworker **Timothy,** whose name means "One Who Honors God" and was from a believing family. Both his mother Eunice and his grandmother Lois had become Christians (see 2 Tim. 1:5). He had accompanied Paul on the second missionary journey, during which time they had established the church at Philippi. Timothy apparently was well-loved by the Philippians.

2:20 like-minded: Timothy and Paul had the same quality of concern for the Philippians.

2:21, 22 Timothy had shown his faithful **character** both to the Philippians, who knew of his ten years of ministry with the apostle Paul. **as a son:** In New Testament times, a son who **served** his father did so to learn the family trade. Serving in this way meant learning all about the business and being willing to obey the teacher in order to become as skillful as possible in the work.

2:23–25 Epaphroditus was a Philippian Christian sent by the church in Philippi to take a gift to Paul (see 4:18) and to assist Paul in his ministry. He is described with a series of complimentary terms: a "brother," a "fellow worker," a "fellow soldier," a "messenger" to the Philippians, and a "minister" to Paul. He is mentioned in the Bible only in this letter. **fellow worker:** Paul considers Epaphroditus to be an equal in the work of the gospel. The title of **fellow soldier** was given only to those who had fought honorably alongside another. Paul thus offered high praise to Epaphroditus for his faithful service in the cause of Christ.

2:26 longing: Paul declares that Epaphroditus demonstrates the same concern for the Philippians as he himself does (see 1:8). They are one in their work for the Lord (see v. 25), and they are one in their love for the Lord's people.

2:27 sick almost unto death: Paul was making certain that the Philippians understood the effort that Epaphroditus had made for the cause of Jesus Christ. Epaphroditus's condition had been far worse than perhaps they had imagined. Paul viewed Epaphroditus's healing as God's direct intervention.

2:28–30 to supply what was lacking: Paul acknowledges the work that the Philippians had already done for him. Epaphroditus was able to do what the Philippians could not do: be physically present to minister to him.

3:1 safe: Paul is concerned that the Philippians do not fall into the trap set forth by those within the church who support heresy.

3:2 In New Testament times, **dogs** were hated scavengers. The term came to be used for all who had morally impure minds. **evil workers:** These words probably refer to teachers spreading destructive doctrines. **mutilation:** Paul here points sarcastically and specifically to those who desire to reinstate Jewish religious practices as necessary for salvation. He chooses a term that literally means "to cut." By doing so, he suggests that these people do not even understand the truth about the Old Testament practice of circumcision but understand it just as a cutting of the flesh.

3:3, 4 Paul defines true **circumcision** as a matter of the heart and not of the flesh. He reveals three aspects of true circumcision: (1) worshiping **God in the Spirit;** (2) rejoicing in **Christ;** and (3) placing no **confidence** in any human honor or accomplishment as a means to reach God.

3:5 eighth day: Paul's parents obeyed God's law and had Paul circumcised on the eighth day (see Lev. 12:2, 3). The people of Israel are called the people of God. That Paul states he is of the **stock of Israel** implies that he is able to trace his origins to the true line of Israel, to Jacob and not Esau. **tribe of Benjamin:** The *tribe of Benjamin* was highly regarded by Israelites because that line had produced the first king of Israel and had remained loyal to David. Furthermore, that tribe had joined Judah after the Exile to form the foundation for the restored nation (see 1 Sam. 9:15–21; 1 Kin. 12:21–24). **Hebrew of the Hebrews:** This description of Paul may indicate that (1) both

his parents were Jews, (2) he was a model Jew, or (3) he was educated completely as a Jew. **Pharisee:** Pharisees were highly educated Jewish leaders who spearheaded the opposition against Jesus while He was on earth, and later against the Christian church. They rigorously followed and defended the letter of the Jewish law. Paul himself came from a line of Pharisees (see Acts 23:6) and had studied under Gamaliel, a highly respected Pharisee of that day (see Acts 22:3).

3:6 persecuting the church: Prior to becoming a Christian, Paul vigorously attacked those who believed in Christ, even to the point of having them put to death (see Acts 7:58—8:3; 9:1, 2).

3:7 loss: This word indicates that which is damaged or of no further use (see v. 8; Acts 27:10, 21). Those things that Paul thought to be important became unimportant after confronting the resurrected Messiah.

3:8 excellence: The value of knowing Christ surpasses all else (see 2:3; 4:7). **rubbish:** This word means anything that is detestable or worthless. All the things of this world are rubbish compared to Christ. **I may gain:** The former *gain* (see v. 7) is here substituted for the latter *gain:* Christ Jesus (see 1:21).

3:9 from the law: In vv. 6 and 7, Paul reveals the uselessness of righteousness that is in the law. Here he divulges that his own righteousness that had been in that law was also in vain. **through faith in Christ:** Paul recognizes that true righteousness is a matter of faith, not of works. It is God's righteousness that comes through Christ, not our own righteousness.

3:10 Paul indicates that he rejected his own righteousness to secure not just an intellectual knowledge of Christ but also a relational knowledge, in fact, an intimate knowledge of the Lord. **power of His Resurrection:** Paul does not say the power "in" His Resurrection, which would specify the power of the one-time event of His Resurrection. Rather, Paul seeks the ongoing power that is the day-to-day experience of being in Christ. Paul may also be alluding to his desire to be clothed with his own Resurrection body. **fellowship of His sufferings:** Paul sees the value of participating in the persecutions or struggles that naturally accompany one who is in partnership with

Christ and His sufferings (see James 1:2–4; 1 Pet. 2:21–24). **being conformed to His death:** Paul wants to be completely obedient to God the Father, just as Jesus was obedient to His Father's will (Luke 22:42).

3:11 Attain to means "to arrive at" as well as to "become a partaker of." Paul was not doubting his participation in the Resurrection but was instead viewing it in expectation (1 Cor. 15:1–34). Paul desired to be with those Christians who, through their victory in Christ, would receive special reward in the **Resurrection** (see Heb. 11:35).

3:12 not ... attained: Paul chooses a different Greek word from that translated in v. 11 as *attain*. Here he indicates he has not yet "gained possession of" or "laid hold of" all that he seeks to be. **perfected:** The Greek term means mature or complete, finished. Paul is not speaking of moral perfection or righteousness but of reaching the state of completion as a Christian. **press on:** Paul "pursues with all deliberate speed" the goal before him. The verb form indicates that he is doing this continually. **lay hold of:** This phrase adds the idea of overtaking by surprise to the sense of seizing some object. Paul wants to "grab hold of" God as God had **laid hold of** him (Acts 9:1–22). Christ had dramatically and suddenly seized Paul on the road to Damascus, and his life changed dramatically.

3:13 Paul could not forget the past, but he refused to let it obstruct his progress toward his goal. He wanted to forget his self-righteous past (see vv. 4–7). By using the present tense for **forgetting,** Paul indicates that it is an ongoing process. He might even be implying that he wanted to forget everything so he would not rest on his past successes in Christ, but continue to labor for the Lord.

3:14, 15 goal: This word specifically refers to the marker at the end of a race on which runners intently fix their eyes. The **prize** is the reward for victory. Paul evidently takes to heart what he teaches in 1 Cor. 9:24. **upward call:** In the New Testament this speaks of the divine call to complete salvation. It may refer to the judgment seat of Christ, the place of reward. Paul does not say that he is pressing on for the call of God but rather for the prize of

that call. He is not working for his salvation but for a reward.

3:16 let us walk: Paul commands the Philippians to conduct themselves as soldiers who "march in line" together, organized, each in his proper position.

3:17 The word **pattern** indicates an exact representation of the original. The example of Paul's life is so evident that one can readily see it and use it as a pattern for living.

3:18 The term **weeping** reveals Paul's compassion and concern for those who are **the enemies of the Cross.**

3:19 The word **destruction** indicates the opposite of eternal salvation (see 1:19, 28). **glory is in their shame:** The things in which they take pride actually are the things that will bring "disgrace" or "humiliation" to them, things of which they should have been ashamed. **3:20** Christians need to remember that though we are in this world we are not of this world; our ultimate **citizenship** is in heaven. **eagerly wait:** Paul presents a direct contrast to the earthly focus of the enemies of the Cross in v. 19. The eager desire of Christians is not earthly things, but a heavenly Person, the Savior, **the Lord Jesus Christ** (see Rom. 8:19–25).

3:21 Paul guarantees that Christ **will transform,** or "change in appearance," the believer. **lowly body:** God will transform the physical body. **conformed to His glorious body:** In v. 10, Christians are conformed to His death; here they are conformed to His life. Our body is weak and susceptible to sin, disease, and death. God will change our bodies to resemble Christ's glorious Resurrection body.

4:1 Euodia ... Syntyche: These were Christian women at Philippi who had fallen into some disagreement that was affecting the whole church. What is written in vv. 2, 3 is all that is known about the two women or about their dispute. Paul does not take sides in the argument. He encourages them to be reconciled.

4:2, 3 I urge: This word implies a certain level of familiarity. It introduces a request, not a demand. **true companion:** The identity of this person is unknown. It may be a specific person named Syzygos (the Greek word for *companion*), someone else particularly close to Paul, or any of the faithful Christians in the church who could help resolve the dispute. **help:** This verb means "to assist by holding together" and suggests that the women's dispute is potentially divisive. The **Book of Life** refers to a book in heaven where the names of believers are recorded (Dan. 12:1; Rev. 21:27).

4:4 In the midst of difficulties, in the midst of all situations, Christians are to **rejoice.** The joy of Christians is not based on agreeable circumstances but on their relationship to God. Christians will face trouble in this world, but they should rejoice in the trials they face because they know God is using those situations to improve their character (see James 1:2–4).

4:5 gentleness: This noun identifies a person who manifests a calmness of spirit. A person who is gentle is willing to sacrifice his or her own personal rights to show consideration to others. **at hand:** The Lord's return could occur at any moment. Paul uses that fact to motivate the Philippians to honor God with their lives.

4:6 Paul exhorts the Philippians to pray about their circumstances instead of worrying over them. **be anxious for nothing:** Although the same word in 2:20 describes Timothy's concern for the Philippians, here Paul uses the word to refer to worry. He prohibits the Philippians from worrying about their own problems. Instead they are to commit their problems to God in prayer, trusting that He will provide deliverance.

4:7 will guard: Paul's choice of a military term implies that the mind is in a battle zone and needs to be "protected by a military guard." Since the purpose of such a guard in a wartime situation is either to prevent a hostile invasion or to keep the inhabitants of a besieged city from escaping, the **peace of God** operates in the same way: to protect the mind from external corrupting influences and to keep the mind focused on God's truth.

4:8 noble: This term describes that which is of honorable character. **pure:** This word is closely associated with the Greek word for *holy* and thus means "sacred" or "immaculate." **meditate on:** Paul commands the Philippians "to deliberate," "to evaluate," "to compute over and over" what is good and pure. In this way, Christians can renew their minds so that they will not conform to the evil habits of this world (Rom. 12:2).

4:9 learned: This verb conveys not only the concept of "increasing in intellectual knowledge" but also the idea of "learning by habitual practice." In some areas of their Christian development the Philippians had been excellent disciples of Paul, practicing what he had taught.

4:10 flourished again: Paul uses an agricultural word found only here in the New Testament to picture a plant that "shoots up" or "sprouts again," describing a condition of prosperity or abundance.

4:11 content: The word literally means "self-sufficient." In Stoic philosophy this Greek word described a person who dispassionately accepted whatever circumstances brought. For the Greeks, this contentment came from personal sufficiency. But for Paul true sufficiency is found in the strength of Christ (v. 13).

4:12–15 giving and receiving: Paul considers the relationship between himself and the Philippians to be a two-way street, with both parties involved in the sharing of material and spiritual gifts.

4:16, 17 Paul has in mind in this verse the material **gift** that the Philippians sent to him. **account:** Paul uses business terminology. The Philippians' gift was producing spiritual profit just as money deposited in a bank account accrues interest. But Paul was not as concerned with their *gift* as with the development in the Philippians of the spiritual ability to give.

4:18 an acceptable sacrifice: By giving to Paul, the Philippians had offered themselves as a gift to God (see Rom. 12:1, 2).

4:19 In v. 18 Paul says that he is full because they gave. In this verse he writes that God will **supply all** their needs. The Philippians, in turn, will be full because of the gifts God will give them. **according to His riches:** Out of His abundant wealth, God will take care of the Philippians.

4:20 The Jewish practice of closing prayers with the word **amen** carried over to the Christian church as well. The word can be translated "so be it," "may it be fulfilled," "surely," "truly," or "most assuredly."

4:21–23 those ... of Caesar's household: These believers may have been officials in the Roman government or servants who lived and served in the emperor's palace.

Colossians

Introduction

Paul wrote this letter to deal with a doctrinal heresy that was creeping into the Colossian church. The error was probably a mixture of Judaism and an early form of Gnosticism. Certain members were teaching that the observance of Jewish rules about food, the Sabbath, and special festivals would help believers to earn their salvation (see Gal. 3:23–25; 4:10, 11). At Colosse, however, some of the Gentile members were also promoting a form of mysticism that claimed that Jesus was a higher being, but not God. Paul refutes these false doctrines by reiterating the supremacy of Christ.

Paul probably wrote Colossians while imprisoned in Rome around A.D. 60. Colossians is one of the four prison epistles of Paul, along with Ephesians, Philippians, and Philemon. Because Colossians, Ephesians, and Philemon have several similarities, many believe that the three were written at about the same time.

The city of Colosse was about a hundred miles east of Ephesus, in the valley of the Lycus River. Evangelization of Colosse probably took place during Paul's three-year stay in Ephesus. Apparently Epaphras was converted in Ephesus, and after being instructed by Paul returned home to Colosse to proclaim the gospel. Evidently the church that emerged was largely composed of Gentiles, for Paul refers to their "uncircumcision," a word used by Paul to designate Gentiles (see 2:13; Rom. 2:24–27; Eph. 2:11).

The many parallels between Colossians and Ephesians indicate that the two letters were written about the same time. Both letters reveal the centrality of Christ and His relationship to the church. Ephesians shows Christ as Head of the church, while Colossians extends that imagery of His authority over all creation (see 1:16–18; 2:10). In Ephesians, Paul highlights how Christians are the members of the body of Christ, who is the Head. In Colossians, he places emphasis on Christ the Head, of whose body Christians are members.

Ephesians and Colossians together present a mature understanding of who Christ is and what His life and death mean for the believer. From prison, Paul was teaching the churches in Asia Minor how central the person of Jesus Christ is to the Christian faith. He is the image of God, the source of all wisdom, and the Head of the church. He is the One who reconciles us to God and to our fellow believers. As our Savior and Deliverer, He deserves our sincere adoration.

1:1 Paul calls himself **an apostle,** a word whose root means "to send." The New Testament uses the word to signify an approved spokesman sent as a personal representative. Although not every Christian is called by God to minister like Paul or the twelve apostles, every Christian is sent by God to represent Him before the people with whom he or she comes in contact.

1:2 The Greek term translated **saints** means "holy people." The essence of "holiness" is being set apart to God. All believers are saints, not because they are perfect, but because they belong to God. **in Christ:** This is a favorite expression of the apostle Paul, used some 80 times in his letters. Paul saw all of Christian experience growing out of the believer's position in Christ. **Grace ... peace:** Paul combines the Greek word for grace with the standard Hebrew greeting, *peace.* He broadens and deepens its meaning by reminding his readers that the ultimate source of "favor" and "wholeness" is **God our Father and the Lord Jesus Christ** (see Rom. 1:7).

1:3 The apostle indicates the tender concern that he has for these Christians; he is **praying always** for them. This common phrase of Paul's (Eph. 1:16; Phil. 1:4; 1 Thess. 1:2), which combines intercessory prayer and thanksgiving, means that each time Paul prayed, he interceded for the Colossians and offered praise for God's work among them.

1:4–8 faith ... love ... hope: Paul often uses these three terms together (Rom. 5:2–5; 1 Cor. 13:13; 1 Thess. 1:3; 5:8). *Faith* is in Christ. This is the thrust of the passage. The Colossians' faith was grounded in the nature and work of Jesus Christ. *Love* flows from faith and proves the genuineness of one's faith (James 2:14–26). The Colossians' sacrificial love **for all the saints** proved their true belief in Christ. *Hope* refers to the result of faith, the treasure **laid up ... in heaven** where our faith will find its fulfillment in the presence of Christ.

1:9 Paul's chief concern is that the Colossians might have full **knowledge** of God's **will.** The desire to serve God will be in vain without a proper understanding of the One we want to serve. Thus, Paul prays that the Colossians might be filled with full knowledge that encompasses **all wisdom and spiritual understanding.** *Wisdom* is the practical outworking of knowledge (see James 3:17), and that knowledge cannot be separated from the *spiritual understanding* that comes through the discernment given by the Holy Spirit.

1:10 Paul desires that the Colossians **may walk worthy of the Lord.** Paul wanted the Colossians to live in a manner that adequately reflected what God had done for them and was doing in them. Being "worthy of God" is a phrase that occurs in ancient pagan inscriptions throughout Asia. It pictures someone's life being weighed on scales to determine its worth. If these devotees to false gods knew they had to walk in a worthy manner, certainly Christians should dedicate their lives to the living God in order to please Him.

1:11 according to His glorious power: This phrase means that believers are empowered not in proportion to their need but according to God's strength. So Paul desires to see nothing less than the power of God Himself at work in the Colossian believers. Like Samson's (Judg. 14:19), a believer's strength comes from God alone.

1:12 qualified: The word means to be able or authorized for a task. Believers can never be qualified on their own; instead God must make them sufficient through Jesus Christ. The tense of the verb points to "qualifying" as an act in the past rather than a process. Ordinarily to qualify for an event or a position, we have to prove ourselves. However the **inheritance** (see v. 5) that believers receive is not one that they have earned but is based on being *qualified* by God. The Father "qualifies" us for eternal life with Him, whereas the Son will reward us at the end of the race (Rev. 22:12).

1:13 Delivered … conveyed: God has liberated believers from the dominion of darkness. The apostle uses the common symbolism of light and darkness for good and evil, for God's

kingdom and Satan's kingdom, that is found throughout the New Testament. The kingdom from which believers have been rescued is the kingdom of darkness.

1:14 The Greek word **redemption** points to the payment of a price or ransom for the release of a slave. The slavery from which believers are released is not physical but spiritual. They are freed from bondage to sin by **forgiveness of sins** through Jesus' blood (Eph. 1:7).

1:15 firstborn over all creation: Jesus is the eternal One who was before all creation. The idea of *firstborn* in the Hebrew culture did not require that one be the first son born. This was not the case with either Isaac or Jacob. But they were the *firstborn* in the sense that they were rightful heirs to the line of their fathers. Being *firstborn* referred more to rank and privilege. Since Christ is God, He is supreme in rank over all creation. Yet He is not only the transcendent deity who created us; He is the One who died on our behalf (see Phil. 2:6–18) and was subsequently raised from the dead.

1:16, 17 This early Christian hymn emphasizes the superiority of Christ over all creation. Christ is the One who created all things. This idea is in direct contradiction to the false teaching, later known as Gnosticism, that was developing in the Colossian church. In general, Gnostics believed that various angelic beings were the creators of the earth and that Christ was one among many of these angels. **all things were created through Him and for Him:** Not only did Jesus create all things; everything was created for His purposes. But the glory of the earth, the heavens, or the sun, moon, and stars cannot be compared with the glory of His new creation (2 Cor. 5:17).

1:18 Following the celebration of Christ's authority over all creation, this early Christian hymn proceeds to proclaim His authority over the church. He is the **head** of His own **body,** which is the church. The sovereign Creator of the universe, as Head of the church, provides leadership and oversight over it. **firstborn from the dead:** Christ was the first to be raised from the dead. His own Resurrection guarantees that the church will one day be resurrected (see 1 Cor. 15:12–28).

1:19 fullness: The opponents of Paul, and later the Greek Gnostics, seem to have used this word as a technical term for the sphere between heaven and earth where a hierarchy of angels lived. The Gnostics viewed Christ as one of many spirits existing in this hierarchy between God and all people. However, Paul used the term *fullness* to refer to the complete embodiment of God. Christ is the only Intercessor for human beings and fully embodies all of God's nature (1 Tim. 2:5).

1:20, 21 reconcile all things ... now He has reconciled: This phrase shows the significance of Christ's work on the Cross. It does not mean that all people will be saved, since many passages clearly say that unbelievers will suffer eternal separation from God (see Matt. 25:46). The work of Christ will overthrow the damage effected by the Fall and change all of creation from a position of enmity to a relationship of peace and friendship (see Rom. 8:20–23; 2 Cor. 5:18–20).

1:22 body of His flesh: The false teachers were telling the believers that redemption could be accomplished only through a spiritual being. They rejected Christ's Incarnation. According to them, Jesus could not have had a physical body. Thus Paul uses two terms, *body* and *flesh,* to clearly state that Christ became man and experienced a physical death.

1:23 if indeed you continue in the faith: The perseverance of the Colossians was proof of the reconciling work of Christ on their behalf (vv. 21, 22). **every creature under heaven:** Paul uses this exaggeration to illustrate the rapid spread of the gospel. Compare Acts 17:6, where the apostles are said to have turned the world upside down, even though their ministry up to that point had been limited to a small portion of the eastern Mediterranean region.

1:24 Paul is making the point that a Christian will endure the **sufferings** that Christ would be enduring if He were still in the world (see 2 Cor. 1:5; 4:11). Christ told His disciples that if the world hated Him it would hate His followers. If people persecuted Him they would persecute His followers (John 15:19, 20). Paul believed he was suffering the afflictions God wanted him to endure. Instead of facing his difficulties with dread, Paul saw his troubles as a time of joy (Rom. 8:17; Phil. 1:29; 1 Thess. 1:6; 2 Tim. 3:12), because they were producing an eternal reward (2 Cor. 4:17).

1:25–27 The **mistery** referred to in these verses is similar to the one spoken of in Eph. 3:8–10. In Greek pagan religions, a mystery was a secret teaching reserved for a few spiritual teachers who had been initiated into an inner circle. Paul uses the word to refer to knowledge that had been "hidden from the ages and generations" (see 2:2, 4:3; 1 Cor. 2:7; 4:1; Eph. 3:4, 9; 5:32; 6:19; 1 Tim. 3:9, 16), but was now being revealed by God. The Lord had revealed this mystery to Paul and called him to be a steward of it (see Eph. 3:5). The mystery is that Christ now lives within Gentile believers.

1:28 perfect: The concept of perfection in the New Testament means completeness or maturity. Here the reference is probably to the coming of Christ, when every believer will experience the completion of Christ's work in him or her (see 1 Cor. 13:10).

1:29 Paul toiled and agonized for the perfection of his fellow believers (see v. 28), not in his own strength but by the power of God working in him.

2:1 Laodicea was a sister city of Colosse about eleven miles away. The two churches were to share their letters from Paul (see 4:16).

2:2, 3 Though the false teachers at Colosse spoke of initiating people into a superior knowledge, Paul tells his readers that they can understand the **mystery** (see 1:26, 27) of God without this false philosophy. The Gnostics sought knowledge as an end in itself, but Paul reminds the Colossians that true knowledge will demonstrate itself by bringing people together in Christian love in the church.

2:4–7 Just as the Colossian believers had begun with Christ, so Paul encourages them to continue in their **walk** with Him. Paul uses four words to describe the Colossians' walk with Christ. The tense of the word translated **rooted** denotes a complete action; the believers *have been* rooted in Christ. The next three words, **built up, established,** and **abounding,** are in the present tense, showing the continual growth that should characterize every Christian's walk with Christ.

2:8 Paul was warning the believers not to be taken in by any **philosophy** that does not conform to a proper knowledge of Christ. The false teachers at Colosse had combined worldly philosophies with the gospel. These philosophies are spoken of by Paul as the **basic principles** of the world, which some have interpreted as "spirits" or "angels" who supposedly control a person's life (see Gal. 4:3, 9). It seems more likely that the term *principles* refers to the elementary rules and regulations that certain teachers were seeking to impose on believers according to the dictates of human philosophies. Paul's strongest indictment against the heretics was that their teaching was **not according to Christ.**

2:9 Here Paul clearly proclaims the Incarnation, the fact the God became a man **bodily.** This contradicts the Gnostic idea of the inherent evil of physical bodies and the claim that Jesus is just a spirit. The Gnostics thought **the fullness** of God had been divided among a number of angelic beings, the last creating the material world. In contrast, Paul says that the fullness of God exists in Christ.

2:10 Paul illustrates the adequacy of Christ by demonstrating how the Colossian believers are **complete.** In Christ, the Colossians have put off the power of sin and the flesh (v. 11), have received new life (vv. 12, 13), have been forgiven, have been delivered from requirements laid down by human traditions (v. 14), and have been freed from the powers of spirit beings (v. 15). There is nothing that the Christian needs to add to what was received in Christ at the time of conversion.

2:11 All Jewish males were required to receive physical **circumcision,** but the circumcision that is from Christ is **without hands.** Rather than the mere removal of flesh, Christian circumcision is the spiritual removal of sin from the heart, taking part in the New Covenant of Jesus Christ.

2:12, 13 buried ... in baptism: Baptism is the symbol of the believer's association with Christ's death. Water baptism itself does not bring forgiveness of sins, but Paul uses the rite to help explain the work of the Spirit. The early church would never have understood the idea of an unbaptized Christian. Baptism and faith were considered to be the outward and inward realities of being a Christian (see Acts 2:38; 10:47, 48; 16:33; Rom. 6:3–5).

2:14 nailed ... to the cross: Not only were our personal sins forgiven at the Cross, but those rules that condemned us have also been removed by the death of Christ.

2:15 Principalities and powers allude to Satan and the fallen angels. Paul is describing Christ's victory on the Cross over the powers that opposed Him and that were against God's faithful people. To describe this victory, Paul uses the spectacle of the military triumph, when prisoners of war were stripped and paraded before the populace behind the conquering general. Satan and his forces thought the Cross would be their victory and Christ's defeat. In reality, at the Cross the Lord vanquished His foes, took away their weapons, and **made a public spectacle of them.**

2:16–19 In view of Christ's victory over His enemies, we should not be controlled by those powers and practices over which Christ has already triumphed. The false teachers in Colosse were tempting the Colossians to bind themselves with the outward observances of Judaism, such as the Jewish dietary restrictions. These were just a **shadow** of Christ. Judaism and its rites pointed to Christ. Paul warns the believers in Colosse not to let others bind them to regulations from which Christ has already freed them. **false humility:** People who do not champion salvation in Christ alone often appear to be humble. But their search for a new spiritual experience or advocacy of some work as necessary for salvation is actually human pride. They do not want to submit to God's plan of salvation revealed in the Bible.

2:20–23 regulations: Since believers have been released from ritualistic observances why should they let others bind them again (see Rom. 6:3–14)? No human work can be added to the merit of Christ's death. The Cross is the only acceptable work in God's eyes.

3:1–4 set your mind on things above: The false teachers were instructing the Colossians to concentrate on temporal observances; in contrast, Paul instructs them to concentrate on the eternal realities of heaven. The Greek verb for *set* emphasizes an ongoing decision. Christians must continually discipline themselves to focus on eternal realities instead of the temporal realities of this earth. A Christian's life is no longer dictated by this world but is **hidden with Christ.**

3:5–8 While obedience to rules cannot bring

salvation, those who are saved ought to live worthy of that salvation. Thus Paul gives the Colossians instructions about proper conduct. He states in negative and positive terms the kind of life that God wants Christians to live.

3:9, 10 The analogies between the **old man** and our old sinful ways and the **new man** and our new lives in Jesus Christ parallels Paul's discussion in Rom. 6 about dying to sin and living for Christ. Paul describes our former unredeemed life as the *old man,* and our life as God's child as the *new man.* The new man has the image of the new creation in Christ, just as the old man bears the image of our fallen nature. The old man is under an old master, Satan, while the new man has a new master, the Spirit of God living within.

3:11 Greek ... Jew ... slave ... free: This list is similar to the list in Gal. 3:28. In both places the point is not the functions of the persons in the body of Christ, but equal acceptance of all the groups into God's family.

3:12–16 Let the word of Christ dwell in you richly is apparently a parallel thought to Paul's statement in Eph. 5:18 where he says to be "filled with the Spirit." The result of being "filled" with the Spirit or the word of Christ is singing (Eph. 5:19–21). The **psalms** are the *psalms* found in the Old Testament, the "songbook" of the early church as well as of Israel. The **hymns** would be the songs of the church that reflected the new truth in Christ. **Spiritual songs** may have been other kinds of songs praising God.

3:17 In this verse, Paul sums up how Christians should live. We should commit everything we do or say to **Jesus** and continually thank God for all His good gifts (see Eccl. 12:13, 14).

3:18, 19 The Colossian home would usually consist of father, mother, children, and servants. Paul gives instructions to each group. The first is for **wives** to **submit.** The word *submit* is a military term meaning to "arrange oneself under another" and indicates a voluntary submission, not an unthinking obedience. The parallel passage of Eph. 5:21 may speak of mutual submission, as some have suggested. Either way it is clear that submission does not denigrate the one who submits. The husband is commanded to **love** his wife (Eph. 5:25 says as Christ loved the church). In his headship,

---

IN DEPTH   **False Teaching at Colosse**

ood truths are often corrupted. The apostle Paul spent much of his time battling false teachers who came behind him and added their own "spin" to the gospel. He wrote to the Christians at Colosse partly to correct a heresy about God and spirituality that had begun to take root there. The kind of doctrine that was infecting Colosse would eventually be called Gnosticism. This was a prominent Christian heresy in the second and third centuries. Gnosticism taught that special knowledge was needed for a soul to break from the physical realm into the spiritual realm. As this false doctrine developed, it claimed that salvation could only be obtained through such special knowledge. In this way the Gnostics replaced faith with intellect.

Gnosticism followed the Greek philosophy that matter was inherently evil. Only nonphysical, "spiritual" realities were good. Hence, Gnostics did not believe that God created the world or that Christ came in a physical body. According to the Gnostics, an angel or secondary god created the material universe. Paul corrected this error in Colosse by stating clearly that Christ is the Creator and Sustainer of all, the supreme Head over the church and over all other authorities. The main problem with the heresy at Colosse was its denial of who Christ is. These false teachers denied that Jesus is the Creator who came in the flesh, that He is God who became man. Their rejection of the deity of Christ led them to seek salvation through their intellect or through the abuse of one's body. Such efforts served only to hide the truth, that salvation is found only in Christ.

he is to seek his wife's highest good, not his own welfare. He is to honor her and be considerate of her, and not to be bitter or harsh.

3:20, 21 Children and **fathers** also have admonitions from the apostle. Children are to obey. Yet the **all things** should not be taken as an absolute. When God's truth and anyone's demands come into conflict, a child should obey God. A father should be careful not to frustrate his children or discourage them. Regulations should be reasonable, not arbitrary. The father should train his children the same way God disciplines and teaches him.

3:22–25 Bondservants, obey … your masters: Even though slavery might not be officially condoned or practiced today, the admonition to work hard as though one was working for God, and not people, applies to employees. **the reward of the inheritance:** The strong motivation to serve someone well is found in the future reward that Christ gives to those who are faithful in this service. We normally think we receive eternal rewards for spiritual practices like reading the Bible, prayer, or evangelism. Here Paul asserts that all work done for the honor of Christ will bring an eternal reward (see 1:22, 23; 2:18).

4:1 Masters: Paul does not concern himself only with servants or employees. Employers also have a duty not to take advantage of employees. They should offer a just wage, proper benefits, and adequate rest. In contemporary societies, many of these benefits are required by government regulations. But how much better when Christian employers treat their employees well for the Lord's sake, knowing that they too have **a Master in heaven.**

4:2, 3 Paul encourages the Colossians to be diligent in thanksgiving and prayer, especially praying for himself and his coworkers as they worked at spreading the gospel. Even the apostle Paul needed the prayers of others to support him.

4:4, 5 Walk in wisdom toward those who are outside: Early Christians were often viewed with suspicion, distrust, and disdain. They were considered atheists because they would not worship the gods of Rome and Greece. Many labeled them as unpatriotic because they would not burn incense before the image of the

emperor. Some accused the early Christians of participating in orgies because of their talk of "love feasts" (Jude 12). Others harbored suspicions that Christians were cannibals who ate and drank the blood and the body of the Lord. With such misrepresentations of Christian belief and practice running rampant, it was important for misunderstandings to be dispelled by the impeccable lives of Christian believers.

4:6–8 Tychicus was an intimate friend of Paul's who came from the province of Asia. He had accompanied Paul on part of the third missionary journey. He probably delivered this letter and answered questions about Paul's condition in prison.

4:9 The slave **Onesimus** probably accompanied Tychicus to Colosse. Paul's letter to Philemon would have been carried along with the letter to the Colossians. It dealt with a situation between Philemon and his slave Onesimus, so Paul wrote a separate letter to him.

4:10–15 Paul greets a number of friends and introduces and commends several who work with him. **Aristarchus,** a Jew from Thessalonica, had been traveling with Paul since the riot that occurred in Ephesus on his third missionary journey (Acts 19:29; 20:4). Evidently he remained with Paul even when he was imprisoned in Rome (27:2). **Mark** is the author of the Gospel of Mark. At the beginning of his second missionary journey, Paul had refused to take Mark with him (Acts 15:37–40). Evidently the two had been reconciled, since Paul commends him here and in 2 Tim. 4:11. **Luke** is the author of the Gospel of Luke and the Book of Acts. He accompanied Paul on many of his missionary journeys. **Demas** would later abandon Paul (see 2 Tim. 4:10).

4:16, 17 There are numerous theories about the identity of the Laodicean letter mentioned in this verse. Whether it is one of the other New Testament letters, like 1 or 2 Thessalonians or Ephesians, or whether it is a lost **epistle** probably cannot be determined.

4:18 This salutation by my own hand: The apostle dictated his letters to a secretary, but it was his custom to give a greeting in his own handwriting at the end (see 2 Thess. 2:1, 2; 3:17). This served to personalize and authenticate the letter.

1 Thessalonians

Introduction

Paul sent Timothy back to Thessalonica shortly after establishing the church there. When Timothy returned, he was loaded down with their questions. First Thessalonians is Paul's patient reply. He reinforces the basic gospel message, instructs them further in the faith, and provides practical applications for spiritual truths.

Paul's authorship of First Thessalonians has not been seriously questioned except by a few modern liberal scholars. Paul refers to himself as the author (1:1; 2:18), and the early church recognized him as such. The letter was probably written from Corinth around A.D. 51 and is considered to be one of Paul's earliest epistles. Galatians may be the only one written before it.

Thessalonica was one of the first cities to be evangelized by Paul and Silas when they landed on the continent of Europe. A divine vision of a man from Macedonia inviting Paul to preach the gospel had drawn the two missionaries to that region (see Acts 16:9, 10). After preaching in Philippi, Paul traveled another one hundred miles to Thessalonica. This was a port city and commercial center located in the northwest corner of the Aegean Sea. The Egnatian Way linking Rome to Byzantium passed through it. A wealthy trade center of the Roman Empire, Thessalonica, with a population of about 200,000, was the capital and the largest city of the province of Macedonia.

Because of its strategic location, Thessalonica became a base for the spread of the gospel in Macedonia and Greece. A church planted in a geographic center would become the evangelistic hub for the surrounding region. Evidently this was especially true of Thessalonica, for Paul commends them for their evangelistic work (see 1:8).

In First Thessalonians, Paul reviewed some of the basics of the faith and applied these truths to the believers' lives. He challenged them to persevere in godly living despite persecution. He extended the comfort of the Resurrection to those who were in mourning, and he spoke about details of the Second Coming. In addition, Paul responded to the angry attacks of his Jewish opponents, who were jealous because Christians were drawing God-fearing Gentiles away from the local synagogue. First Thessalonians reveals much of what Paul preached during his second missionary journey. Evidently the return of Christ was central to his message, for Paul answers many questions about the Second Coming. In fact, perhaps the most significant doctrinal contribution of this small letter is its detailed explanation of Christ's return.

1:1 Paul follows the form of ancient letters, giving the writer first, the destination second, and a brief greeting third. Paul mentions **Silvanus,** Silas's Roman name, and Timothy, but he is the writer of the epistle (4:9). When Paul uses the pronoun *we* (v. 2), he may be referring to Silas and Timothy as editors with him of the letter. After Paul separated from Barnabas (Acts 15:36–40), Silas became Paul's traveling companion on the second missionary journey, and may have served as Paul's secretary. He was a leader of the Jerusalem church (Acts 15:22, 23), and he accompanied Paul and Barnabas to Antioch to deliver the decree of the Jerusalem Council (Acts 15: 22, 23). He and Paul suffered a beating at Philippi (Acts 16:22–24), and he had helped found the church at Thessalonica (Acts 17:1–4). **Timothy** was also with Paul on the second missionary journey. Paul considered him like a son and loved him dearly (Acts 16:3; see 1 Tim. 1:2). This letter is a response to Timothy's report from the church in Thessalonica.

1:2 prayers: Continuing the pattern of the Jerusalem church, these early church planters gave themselves to prayer as well as to preaching the gospel (see Acts 6:4). As in other cities, they had suffered labor pains in giving birth to the church at Thessalonica, and the infant church at Thessalonica was deeply ingrained in their hearts (see 2:13, 17; 3:5, 6).

1:3 The **faith** of the believers at Thessalonica had produced true repentance. When they turned to God, they turned away from idols (v. 9). Note that Paul views the Thessalonians' repentance as a result of their faith, not vice versa. **labor of love:** The Thessalonians' love for Christ resulted in serving (v. 9) in the midst of persecution (v. 6). Note the contrast between *work* and *labor*. Whereas work may be pleasant and stimulating, labor often involves strenuous effort. **patience of hope:** The believers at Thessalonica fixed their hope on the return of Jesus Christ (v. 10). Notice that each of the virtues has Christ as its object. Jesus is constantly the focus.

1:4 knowing … your election: The missionaries gave thanks not only for the good works arising from the Thessalonians' faith (v. 3), but for what God had done for them. God had chosen them to be His holy people.

1:5 Paul does not define his **gospel** at this point, but he had preached it clearly when he was with them: for three weeks he had "reasoned with them from the Scriptures, explaining and demonstrating that the Christ had to suffer and rise again from the dead" (see Acts 17:2, 3). This message of a crucified Christ was far different from the messianic expectations that Paul knew from his own training as a Pharisee. The Jews of that day were not looking for a suffering savior but a conquering champion. Thus Paul had to demonstrate from the Old Testament Scripture that the prophets had foretold the suffering, death, and Resurrection of the Messiah. **not … in word only, but also in power:** Paul did not neglect a careful, precise, and persuasive use of the Scriptures in his preaching. But he realized that apart from the convicting work of the Holy Spirit, no one would turn to Christ (see John 16:8). But with God's blessing, Paul preaching persuaded some of the Jews in the synagogue, together with "a great multitude of the devout Greeks, and not a few of the leading women" (Acts 17:4).

1:6, 7 followers of us and the Lord: At times, Paul encouraged new believers to imitate him (1 Cor. 11:1) as he was imitating Christ. All the writers of the New Testament lead their readers back to the footprints of Christ as shown in the Gospels (see Phil. 2:5; Heb. 12:2; 1 Pet. 2:21; 1 John 2:6). **Having received** is not the usual word for reception, but a word expressing a warm welcome. The Thessalonians seized the gospel with joy, even if it meant facing persecution.

1:8 Your faith … has gone out: Testimony of the Thessalonians' faith rang out throughout Greece and Macedonia. Since Thessalonica was a port city and was on the much-traveled Egnatian Way, those who saw the virtuous life and persistent faith of the Thessalonian Christians would spread the word throughout the entire region. Vital Christian living was making an impact on the people who lived in and traveled through the city.

1:9 they themselves declare concerning us: These reports were from ordinary travelers who were giving their impressions of the Thessalonian believers. **turned to God from idols:** The truth of the gospel exposed the falsehood of idolatry. Since Jews avoided idolatry, Paul was primarily speaking to a Greek audience (see Acts 17:4).

1:10 to wait for His Son: Paul hoped for the Lord's return to occur at any moment. The phrase *to wait for* pictures an eager and expectant looking forward to the return of our Lord Jesus who **delivers us from the wrath to come.** This is a future deliverance, but this verse does not make clear whether Paul is referring to a specific time or to the outpouring of God's wrath on unbelievers in a more general sense. Because Christ endured God's wrath at Calvary, all who are in Christ will escape all aspects of God's wrath (see 5:9).

2:1, 2 Paul's motives for coming to Thessalonica had apparently been attacked after he left by pagan Gentiles and by Jews clinging to their traditional faith. Paul pointed out what the Thessalonians knew—that he had not preached to them **in vain** (see 1:9) but had declared his message despite opposition, including the painful experience of being beaten and put in the stocks in **Philippi** (Acts 16:22–24).

2:3, 4 Answering criticism of his motives for preaching, Paul asserted that he used the truth, not **error;** his motives were pure, not from **uncleanness;** his presentation was in sincerity, not in **deceit.** In contrast to these criticisms, Paul asserted that he and his co-workers were **approved** messengers, missionaries shown by testing to be genuine. Their ministry was not their personal choice, but God's appointment.

2:5–8 Paul denied that in his visit to the Thessalonians he had used flattery. Instead, he preached boldly that everyone was a sinner who needed to be saved by the grace of God. His preaching did not serve as a **cloak for**

covetousness, that is, as a mask to hide greed. Here he appeals to God as his **witness** because no person could examine his motives. Moreover, he and his companions were not seeking praise or desiring positions of authority. Paul did not even exercise his right for financial support (1 Cor. 9:3–14; 2 Cor. 11:7–11). Instead, here as in Corinth he paid his own way. In contrast to the enemies' accusations, Paul and his companions had demonstrated their loving care for the Thessalonians.

2:9–12 Paul's affection for the Thessalonians was demonstrated by his **labor.** As in 1:3, this word indicates strenuous work that produces weariness and fatigue. Paul made tents to provide for his financial needs in order that he might not be a burden to his converts. Paul's actions showed that his ministry was motivated by an unselfish desire to promote the well-being of others rather than to advance his own needs. In addition to their avoiding any need for financial support (v. 9), the morality and devotion to God demonstrated by Paul and his companions backed up their message. They both comforted and challenged the Thessalonians like a loving **father** (see also v. 7). Paul's ultimate goal for them was that they would **walk worthy of God,** or live in a way measuring up to the God they served. It seems an impossible standard. But Paul reminds the Thessalonians that God had called them for this purpose, and He would surely empower them, for "He who has begun a good work in you will complete it" (Phil. 1:6).

2:13 Paul and his companions were thankful for the way the Thessalonians had welcomed the Word of God. **effectively works:** Gentile Christians in Thessalonica could contrast the pure Word of God, with its transforming effect, to the immoral pagan religions, which only perverted people even more. Likewise, Jewish believers could contrast the love and grace of God in the gospel to the legalism and pride often produced by the Jewish religion.

2:14 As the church in Judea had been persecuted by unbelieving Jews, so the Thessalonians were being persecuted by both Jews and Gentiles, and they became **imitators** of those in Judea (see 1:6). These believers were suffering because they stood for God's truth (1 Pet. 4:16).

2:15 and have persecuted us: Paul tells the Thessalonians that they should not be surprised at suffering for Christ's sake, since fellow believers in Judea, including himself, had already suffered for the cause of the gospel. Such hostility toward the church actually represents hostility toward Christ (see Christ's words to Paul in Acts 9:4, 5).

2:16 to fill up ... their sins: The implication is that God will allow a nation, group, or individual to accumulate only a certain amount of sin before His judgment falls on them (see Gen. 15:16). Just as walking in Christ will lead to salvation and a reward, the sins of the wicked will lead to punishment.

2:17, 18 Contrary to what Paul's accusers were asserting, Paul eagerly desired to return. But he may have been **hindered** (see Dan. 10:13), among other things, by the bond that Jason had deposited for him (Acts 17:9). If Paul returned and a riot ensued, Jason's bond would have been forfeited (Acts 17:1–9). **Having been taken away** literally means "orphaned," as a parent is separated from a child (vv. 7, 11). Paul was heartbroken about being taken from them, especially in their infancy in Christ. The many expressions of endearment in this letter indicate the genuine concern Paul had for these new converts in Thessalonica.

2:19, 20 In spite of persecution and satanic opposition, Paul looked beyond the present trials (see 2 Cor. 4:16–18) to the joy of being **in the presence of our Lord Jesus Christ** and being with the Thessalonian Christians who had found the Lord through him. The Thessalonians would be Paul's **crown** (the wreath presented to the winner of Greek athletic contests) because they would prove the genuineness of his work for Christ.

3:1 When forced to leave Thessalonica, Paul and Silas went to Berea, the next city west of Thessalonica. The Jews in Thessalonica who opposed Paul, upon learning that he was at Berea, went there also and stirred up opposition. Paul's friends then escorted him south to **Athens** (Acts 17:13–15). There Paul left word for Silas and Timothy to join him. But before they arrived, Paul left for Corinth, a short distance west of Athens.

3:2 Because Paul could not go to Thessalonica, he sent Timothy in his place. Apparently Silas went back to Philippi, their first stop in Macedonia. Paul sent Timothy to strengthen the church at Thessalonica and to **encourage** them **concerning** their **faith.** The Thessalonians needed to be built up in the faith and fortified against opposition. Because Timothy was young and lacked the maturity of Paul, a special word of commendation was expressed for him as a **brother** in Christ, and more importantly as a **minister of God,** and a **fellow laborer in the gospel.** Paul showed his strong confidence in Timothy by sending him, not only to the Thessalonians, but later to the Corinthians (1 Cor. 16:10, 11) and to the Philippians (Phil. 2:19–23).

3:3, 4 Difficulties are to be expected in the Christian life, and Paul had warned the congregation of their coming **afflictions.** The Scripture teaches that those who live godly lives should expect persecution (2 Tim. 3:12). In fact, Christ warned His disciples that they would experience the same type of rejection He had experienced (John 15:18–21).

3:5–8 our labor might be in vain: Paul was concerned that the Thessalonians might succumb to the temptations of Satan and forsake their Christian faith. **if you stand fast:** Paul's joy was based on the Thessalonians' faithfulness to Christ.

3:9 Paul made prayer a priority. In his prayers, he did not forget to thank God for what He was doing. Christians should follow Paul's example by offering praise and thanksgiving along with their petitions.

3:10 Paul's desire to see the Thessalonians was not primarily to satisfy his own love and emotion but to **perfect,** or complete, their own **faith.** The Thessalonians' endurance under persecution demonstrated the growth of their faith, but Paul wanted them to mature in it.

3:11–13 Christ had told His disciples that His followers would be identified by their love for one another (John 13:35). Here Paul prays that the Thessalonians would love one another more and more. Finally, Paul expresses his desire that their **hearts** would be **blameless in holiness,** not simply before people but before **God.**

4:1, 2 Finally does not mean that Paul was

coming to a conclusion but serves as a transition to the main section of the letter, addressing doctrine and its application to life. In the first three chapters Paul dealt with the readers as a "nursing mother" gently cares for her children (2:7). In these last two chapters he charges them with the authority of a father (4:1, 2). Paul commonly uses the word **walk** as a description of a Christian life (Rom. 6:4; 2 Cor. 5:7; Gal. 5:16; Col. 1:10; 2:6; 4:5). The Christian life not only begins with faith, but it continues as a daily walk of faith. Christians walk in dependence on God. Christians are not to walk like unsaved Gentiles (Eph. 4:17); instead they are to walk worthy of their calling from God (Eph. 4:1).

4:3–5 A major problem for the early church was maintaining sexual purity (1 Cor. 5:1, 9–11). Pagan religions often condoned **sexual immorality** as part of their rites, and ancient Roman culture had few sexual boundaries. In contrast, Paul strongly urged the Thessalonians not to participate in any sexual activity outside of marriage. He reminded them that the human body is God's temple and should be kept holy (see 1 Cor. 6:18–20). The body should be honored as created by God and should be sanctified in keeping with its holy purpose. Believers should have a personal passion for sexual purity that surpasses the passion that the world has for sexual experiences.

4:6–8 Rejecting **holiness** is rejecting God and the ministry of the Holy Spirit within us.

4:9, 10 The Thessalonian believers already had a good record of loving one another, but Paul desired that love to **increase more and more.** This was the commandment of Jesus (John 13:34, 35; 15:12, 17) and is an important basis of evangelism. In a world filled with self-serving individuals, the genuine love of Christians should attract others to the faith.

4:11, 12 Paul exhorted the Thessalonians believers to lead **a quiet life,** not referring to a lack of activity but to an inner quietness and peace befitting the Christian faith (see 2 Thess. 3:12; 1 Tim. 2:11). They should not be busybodies but should **mind** their **own business.** Paul also exhorted the Thessalonians **to work with** their **own hands** as he had done among

them (2:9). Possibly because of their enthusiasm for the coming of the Lord, some
Thessalonians had become idle. But Paul
admonished the Christians to be dedicated
and productive workers in order to bring honor
to Christ's name.

4:13 fallen asleep: This is a metaphor for
dying. Though Paul had taught the Thessalonians about Christ's return when he was
there, apparently Timothy had encountered
further questions on the subject, possibly
arising from the death of some of the new
converts. In answer to these questions, Paul
stated that he wanted them to be informed,
and also to be comforted by the hope of seeing their loved ones again.

4:14 This hope (v. 13) for the dead Christians
was as certain as the fact of the death and Resurrection of Christ. Paul says that **God will
bring with Him those who sleep in Jesus.**
Some have inferred from this statement that
departed Christians are unconscious until the
Second Coming. But the Bible indicates that to
be absent from our present body is to be present with the Lord Jesus (5:10; 2 Cor. 5:8; Phil.
1:23). Accordingly when a Christian dies, it is
the body that sleeps; the soul goes to heaven.

4:15 Paul believed that Christ could come in
his lifetime, and so did the Thessalonians (see
1:10). **precede those who are asleep:** Evidently the Thessalonians were concerned that
believers who had died would miss the glory
associated with the Second Coming. Paul answers their question by affirming that actually
those who were dead would go before (v. 16)
those living on earth.

4:16 Accompanying the descent of Christ
from heaven will be the voice of an archangel,
perhaps Michael, who is portrayed as the
leader of the army of God (Dan. 10:13, 21;
Jude 9; Rev. 12:7–9). The archangel's voice
will be one of triumph because of the great victory at the coming of Christ, culminating thousands of years of spiritual conflict with Satan.
The final signal will be the trumpet of God.
The three elements consisting of the **shout** of
the Lord Himself, the **voice** of an archangel,
and the **trumpet** of God will perhaps be separate events occurring in rapid succession.
Clearly the Resurrection will be a physical Resurrection in which bodily existence will be restored, as confirmed in 1 Cor. 15:51–53. The
resurrected bodies of Christians will be like
that of Christ (1 John 3:2), incorruptible and

⚒ IN DEPTH   Picture of the End Time

The "voice of an archangel" and the "trumpet of God" (1 Thess. 4:16) emphasize
the divine authority behind Paul's description of Jesus' return. The images and pictures Paul uses for the end time overlap with those of other Jews of his time,
though he omits most elements found in contemporary Jewish descriptions. What Paul
does describe especially matches Jesus' picture of the end time (trumpet, clouds, angels,
times and seasons, sudden destruction).

The highest archangel, according to Jewish tradition, was Michael (Dan. 10:13), who
was also the special patron for Israel. Each nation had a guardian angel, but Michael was
especially powerful, as the guardian of God's chosen people. Jewish traditions sometimes
gave Michael special prominence in the final battle, though, for Paul, Jesus fulfilled this
function Himself (1 Thess. 4:16). The "shout," conjoined with the trumpet, may picture
the battle cry offered by a commander. The OT sometimes portrays God as a divine warrior, occasionally mentioning His battle cry (Is. 42:13).

Jesus' teaching about the end time (Matt. 24) is probably the background for Paul's
own teaching, which he claimed was by "the word of the Lord" (1 Thess. 4:15). As Jesus
described the coming Son of Man, He applied to Himself a variety of end-time descriptions that the OT and Judaism normally reserved only for God (Matt. 24:30, 31). Similarly,
Paul applies these same descriptions to the coming Christ.

immortal, and yet they will be bodies of flesh and bone (Luke 24:39, 40; John 20:20, 25, 27). They all will be recognizable, as was the resurrected body of Christ.

4:17 Living Christians will be **caught up** together with the other believers in the clouds to meet the Lord in the air. (The English word *rapture* comes from the Latin verb meaning *caught up.*) **In the clouds** probably refers to atmospheric clouds that also will attend the Second Coming (Rev. 1:7), or it may be the resurrected multitudes who are referred to as a cloud (Heb. 12:1). In the Bible, the Lord is often accompanied by clouds, signifying His glory (see Ps. 68:4; 97:2). The important result is that **we shall always be with the Lord.**

4:18 The wonderful truth described (vv. 13–17) is to be a **comfort** to the Thessalonians and to all Christians. They had mistakenly thought that only those who were alive at the time of the coming of Christ would witness and share in the glory of it. The fact is that Christians who have died will be raised first and so go before the living to the gathering in the sky. Observe that Paul expects a practical, immediate response to this great doctrinal teaching of the Second Coming. The Thessalonians should remind one another of this truth as a source of comfort in the face of death.

5:1 But concerning: This expression introduces a different topic. From the discussion of the Second Coming the apostle turns to the day of the Lord. **the times and the seasons:** This reminds us of the same expression used by our Lord in Acts 1:7. *Times* probably emphasizes quantity, duration, or measurement, whereas *seasons* draws attention to the quality, character, or critical nature of the times. **no need that I should write:** In the previous verses (4:13–18) Paul addressed a matter of ignorance; now he addresses a matter of knowledge. He is not informing as much as he is exhorting them to live in the light of what they already know.

5:2 In contrast to the certainty in the previous paragraph of Christ's coming, Paul now deals with the uncertainty of the timing of the coming **day of the Lord.** This period is the subject of considerable prophecy in the Old Testament (Is. 13:9–11; Joel 2:28–32; Zeph. 1:14–18; 3:14, 15). In the Old Testament, the phrase *the day of the Lord* is used for any period where God intervenes in judgment on the earth. There were "days of the Lord" predicted in the Old Testament that have already been fulfilled (see Amos 5:18). Here Paul uses the expression to refer to Christ's return and the coming judgment. **thief in the night:** The day of the Lord will come when no one expects it.

5:3 when they say: Evidently Paul is speaking about unbelievers. The world will be absorbed in the cares of this life and will be lulled into a false sense of safety and security. **Peace** gives the idea of no feeling of alarm, and **safety** conveys an idea of security from external threats from God or people. The world will have turned a deaf ear to the repeated warnings of coming judgment. Paul uses the image of **labor pains** to emphasize the suddenness of the day of the Lord. A woman's first contraction comes suddenly and unexpectedly.

5:4, 5 But you, brethren: Though the day of the Lord will overtake the unsaved world unexpectedly, it will not overtake Christians, because they will be looking forward to and expecting it. In his characteristic style, Paul first addresses the readers' beliefs (vv. 1–5) and then their behavior (vv. 6–11). The fact that Christ could come at any moment should motivate unbelievers to accept His forgiveness, and believers to live daily for Him.

5:6, 7 Because Christians are informed about future events, they should not be spiritually asleep but should **watch and be sober.** While every Christian is prepared to go to heaven in the sense of having been saved, not every Christian is prepared at every moment to present the quality of his or her spiritual life to God. Accordingly, this is a call to face the fact that our lives will be judged by Christ (see Rom. 14:10, 11; 1 Cor. 3:11–15; 9:24–27; 2 Cor. 5:10).

5:8 In contrast to what unbelievers do, the Christian should be **sober,** living a disciplined life, not only free from drunkenness but alert to spiritual realities. The believer should put on the **breastplate of faith.** Here is the familiar triad of faith, hope, and love—the basic essentials of the Christian life. In contrast to the unbelief of the world, with its love of self and of material wealth (see 1:3), Christians should place their faith in God and give their love to God and to other people. In addition to demonstrating faith and love, Christians should adopt **the hope of salvation** and live in the light of the Lord's return.

5:9, 10 Paul states that **God did not appoint us** (believers) **to wrath** (see 1:10). There will be wrath at the day of the Lord, but it will be God's wrath on the unbelieving world that has spurned and mocked Christ (Rev. 6:12–17). When we think about divine judgment, we should offer thanks to Christ for saving us from that horrible fate by dying **for us.** Whether we are still living at the Second Coming, or whether we have died and our bodies are in the tomb, it is assured that we will **live together with Him** forever.

5:11–13 Paul combines prophecy with practical teachings for the Christian life. God never intended prophecy as a field for academic debate but as a truth that would provide believers hope and direction in their lives. In vv. 12–22, Paul describes the characteristics of a person who is living in the light of Christ's imminent return. **recognize those:** Because everyone in the Thessalonian church was a recent convert, it may have been difficult for some to recognize the leadership of others. Paul teaches the Thessalonians submission rather than individualism and rejection of authority (see Eph. 5:21). He emphasizes that the leaders' authority was from the **Lord.** Paul admonishes the believers to appreciate and submit to those congregational leaders. They should be held in high esteem because of the important work they were doing.

5:14 The Thessalonians had to face the fact that some of them were not living as Christians should, but were **unruly.** They needed to be warned about their behavior. Some were **fainthearted** and needed **comfort.** The congregation should also **uphold the weak** and **be patient** toward all, recognizing that all Christians have faults.

5:15 renders evil for evil: For a Christian to try to get revenge is a denial of basic Christian love (see Rom. 12:17; 1 Pet. 3:9), and it

goes against Jesus' teaching (Matt. 5:38–42; 18:21–35).

5:16 Regardless of difficult circumstances (see 3:2, 3), a Christian **always** has grounds for rejoicing. The Lord is a sovereign Ruler and will accomplish His purpose. Christian joy is not based on circumstances but on a growing awareness of God and the certain future of eternal life with Christ (Rev. 21:1–7).

5:17 Praying **without ceasing** does not mean praying constantly, but being persistent and consistent in prayer.

5:18 Thankfulness should characterize the Christian life in every circumstance, not thanks *for* everything but thanks **in everything.** Paul emphatically states **this is the will of God.** Nothing speaks more powerfully of a walk with God than continuous thankfulness.

5:19, 20 To **quench the Spirit** means to resist His influence, like trying to smother a fire. One of the fundamental rules of walking with God is that we should not say no to the Spirit of God.

5:21–24 Paul's prayer for the Thessalonians is that they may be sanctified in all aspects of their life, **spirit, soul, and body.** Every part of a Christian's life should bear evidence that he or she is set apart as holy to God. This will result in being **blameless at the coming of our Lord Jesus Christ.** Christians are already saints in the sense that they have been set apart to God. Paul exhorts the Thessalonians to express holiness in this life so that the Lord would approve of their conduct upon His return. *Blameless* does not mean sinless, but free from causes for reproach and regret.

5:25 pray for us: Paul was faithful in prayer for the Thessalonians, but he also recognized the need and importance of their prayers for him.

5:26 Greeting one another **with a holy kiss** on the cheek was customary, something like our modern handshake. It could have had more significance than just a handshake, signifying spiritual reconciliation.

5:27, 28 The greatest benediction Paul could express is that the **grace** of Jesus Christ would be with them. Christians are saved by grace and live by grace, enjoying undeserved blessing from their loving God.

2 Thessalonians

Introduction

Paul wrote Second Thessalonians to correct false ideas about the Second Coming that had arisen in that church. Paul identifies himself as the author of Second Thessalonians, and even calls attention to his own handwriting at the end of the letter (1:1; 3:17).

Some have asserted that First and Second Thessalonians teach contradictory doctrines about the Second Coming. The first letter is said to teach an imminent return of Christ, but the second to include an intervening period of "lawlessness" before Christ's return. A closer examination reveals that First Thessalonians emphasizes the suddenness of the Lord's coming to those who are unprepared, while Second Thessalonians highlights some of the events that will occur before Jesus returns. Since Paul wrote Second Thessalonians to correct a misunderstanding that had arisen from his first letter, the difference between the two letters is understandable. Second Thessalonians was written from Corinth shortly after First Thessalonians, or around A.D. 51 or 52.

Since the writing of First Thessalonians, reports had come to Paul of continued progress in the Thessalonian church, indicating their faithfulness to the gospel. However doctrinal problems had also arisen. False teachers had begun to tell the believers in Thessalonica that the day of the Lord was already at hand. These teachers were misapplying and possibly even twisting Paul's teaching that the day of the Lord would come suddenly (1 Thess. 5:2). Most likely because of this, some of the believers had stopped working and were simply waiting for the Lord. Mounting persecution may have also fueled these extreme beliefs about the Second Coming.

In Second Thessalonians, Paul stated emphatically that he had never taught that the day of the Lord had already come. To counter false doctrine, Paul explained to them the emergence of the man of lawlessness and the prevalence of sin during the end times. Furthermore, he reminded them they had been called by God and saved through Christ's work. In view of this fact, he exhorted them to stand firm in Christ (2:13) and to work hard

(3:12), always patiently waiting for Jesus' return.

1:1 Paul, Silvanus, and Timothy were also the authors and editors of 1 Thessalonians. **Silvanus** (Latin for Silas) had been Paul's traveling companion ever since the start of the second missionary journey. He had participated in the founding of the church at Thessalonica (Acts 17:1–4). **Timothy** also was accompanying Paul on his second missionary journey. His report from the Thessalonian church had been the occasion for the writing of 1 Thessalonians (1 Thess. 3:6–8).

1:2 Paul's salutation is similar to those in other ancient letters (see Gal. 1:3; Col. 1:2; 1 Thess. 1:2), but his expression is filled with spiritual meaning. **Grace** is the unmerited favor God gives to believers through Jesus Christ. **Peace** refers to the end of enmity between God and people. The Thessalonians could experience peace with God even during severe persecution.

1:3 The faithfulness of the Thessalonian church in persecution gave Paul reason to praise God. These Christians had experienced persecution but continued to grow in Christ, in agreement with the apostle's earlier prayer in his first letter to them (see 1 Thess. 3:10; 4:9, 10). Here the apostle praises God because the Thessalonians' faith is growing **exceedingly.** They were growing beyond all natural expectation. **Abounds** pictures an expansive growth similar to the sudden surge of flood waters.

1:4 Persecution not only tests faith but reveals it and causes it to grow. Continued faith and endurance through **persecutions** provide a testimony for Christ, of which Paul was boasting to the other churches.

1:5, 6 Although the Thessalonians were enduring persecution (see Acts 17:5–9; 1 Thess. 2:14), Paul explains that their persecutors would be repaid by God. The **judgment of God** requires that the unrighteous be punished for their persecution of the righteous (see Ps. 9; 10; 17; 137; Rev. 6:9, 10). Also if the believers handle their persecutions properly, they will be counted worthy of reward in the coming kingdom of God (Matt. 5:12; 1 Pet. 2:19, 20).

1:7–9 Rest is the relief from affliction that will come at Christ's return (see Rev. 6:11). The Christian's race or warfare on this earth necessarily includes tension. At the coming of Christ we will experience release from that tension forever, even as we remain active in His service. This promise of future eternal rest helps the suffering Christian to endure present trials (see v. 4). **When the Lord Jesus is revealed:** Presently the Lord Jesus is enthroned in glory at the right hand of the Father (John 17:5). But one day, "every eye will see Him" (Rev. 1:7). Notice the threefold description of His appearance: **from heaven, with His mighty angels, in flaming fire.** He is encircled with leaping flames of fire, taking vengeance on those who have rejected Him. When Christ comes in judgment He will baptize with fire. The persecuted Thessalonian believers could be encouraged by the fact that when Jesus is revealed from heaven with His angels, He will bring flaming fire and **everlasting destruction** on the enemies of God, the ones who were persecuting them (Rev. 19:12, 17–19; 20:10–15).

1:10–12 In contrast to the destruction of the wicked, Christ will be **glorified in His saints.** Christ will be glorified not only among but also in the saints, for believers reflect His glory. Paul continued to pray that the Thessalonian believers would live in a manner **worthy** of God, in a way that would glorify Christ (1 Thess. 2:12).

2:1, 2 The Greek word translated **gathering together** is found in the New Testament only here and in Heb. 10:25. Here it refers to the congregation of the whole church. This will be the first time the whole church, including every believer, will be gathered before the Lord to worship Him. The phrase seems to refer to the event described in 1 Thess. 4:17, where Paul speaks of meeting the Lord in the air. The false teaching was that the day of the Lord had already come, bringing with it the tribulations they were experiencing. Thus, some Thessalonian believers thought the Second Coming had passed them by. Paul states that they were not to believe such teaching, whether **by spirit or by word or by letter,** as though it had come from him.

2:3 When Paul wrote 1 Thessalonians, the believers were in danger of losing hope in the Second Coming. In this letter, Paul was correcting the opposite extreme—that Jesus had already come. Paul restores balance to the church by describing some of the major events that would precede the day of the Lord (see 1 Thess. 5:1–11), in particular the **falling away,** and the revealing of the **man of sin.** The falling away, Paul declared, must come first. The Greek term translated *falling away* refers to rebellion against God. Thus some have interpreted this verse to refer to a general defection from the truth during this time. This rebellious apostasy would prepare the way for the Antichrist. Others translate the term as *departure* and understand it to be a reference to the Rapture. That is to say, the man of sin cannot be revealed until Christ comes to take His church to be with Him. As far as the word itself is concerned, it could refer to a spiritual departure (falling away), or it could refer to a physical departure (the Rapture). Whichever way one understands it, it is an event that occurs before the man of sin is revealed. Paul does not use the title Antichrist for this man, but his description of him parallels John's description of the Antichrist (1 John 2:18; Rev. 13). The man of sin will lead the world into rebellion against God (v. 10), perform wonders through Satan's power (v. 9), and finally will present himself as a god to be worshiped (v. 4).

2:4 The man of sin will proclaim himself to be divine and will sit **in the temple of God,** acting as if he is a god. Many leaders in history have called themselves gods, and the Antichrist is the final declaration of that blasphemy. He will tolerate no one else being worshiped but himself (see Rev. 13:6–8). The man of sin will probably stand in a physical temple in Jerusalem to declare himself to be god, the ultimate fulfillment of the "abomination of desolation" spoken of by Daniel (Dan. 7:23; 9:26, 27; 11:31, 36, 37; 12:11) and Jesus (Matt. 24:15; Mark 13:14). These prophecies may have been partially fulfilled when Antiochus Epiphanes erected a pagan altar to Zeus in the temple in Jerusalem in 167 B.C. (175–164 B.C.), or when Titus destroyed the temple in A.D. 70.

Others have interpreted Paul's reference to the temple of God as a reference to the church. In other words, the man of sin will attempt to divert the church's true worship of God to himself.

2:5 Do you not remember: Paul reminds the Thessalonians of his previous teaching about the Second Coming, confirmed in his first letter to them (1 Thess. 4:13—5:11).

2:6, 7 already at work: The evil and deception that the man of sin embodies already exist in this world. Anyone who opposes Christ and His church and seeks to deceive others into worshiping false gods is against Christ, and in that case is an antichrist. **He who now restrains:** There was a good reason why the man of sin had not been revealed. The present restrainer, probably the Spirit of God, had to be taken out of the world. God has restrained sin in the world through the power of the Holy Spirit. The Spirit works directly through the Bible, godly people, and His holy angels to advance God's kingdom and restrain evil. Some have interpreted **taken out of the way** in this verse as a reference to the Rapture, for the church cannot exist without the Spirit's presence. Thus the removal of the church through the Rapture will be in effect the removal of all restraint on the power of sin in this world.

2:8, 9 Although the man of sin will be revealed as extremely powerful (Rev. 13:7), he will be destroyed by Christ and cast into the lake of fire when the Lord comes (Rev. 19:19, 20). The **power, signs,** and **lying wonders** of the **lawless one** will be overshadowed by the glory and brightness of Christ in His Second Coming. It is significant that Satan will use the same kind of power, signs, and wonders that the Spirit of Christ used at the beginning of the age to authenticate the truth about Himself as God (see 2 Cor. 12:12; Heb. 2:4).

2:10–12 Unbelievers will share the condemnation of those who rejected the truth and took **pleasure** in their own **unrighteousness.** Rejection of the truth of the gospel always results in condemnation. Even those who never hear the gospel can reject the revelation of God in nature (Rom. 1:18–21).

2:13 Paul was continually giving **thanks** to the Lord for the believers. He was thankful for their **salvation,** which was based on God's choice of them, His work in them through the Spirit and the Word, and their ultimate glorification. **chose:** The Greek tense of this word indicates that in the past God had chosen the Thessalonians to be His people, set apart as holy to Him. Their salvation was accomplished by the Spirit when they placed their faith in Christ. Yet note the balance of the Spirit and the **truth** (the Word). The Spirit without the Word is mute; He has nothing to say. The Word without the Spirit is lifeless; it has no power to act. The work of the Spirit is always united with the work of the Word to convict the believer of the truth.

2:14 our gospel: This is the message that Paul had confidently proclaimed among the Thessalonians with the power of the Holy Spirit (see 1 Thess. 1:5). **obtaining of the glory:** Paul makes it clear that the Thessalonians have already been saved (v. 13) and **called** by God alone. But now he indicates the Thessalonians' responsibility to respond to God's work in them. Through the power of the Spirit (v. 13), the Thessalonians were to prepare on this earth for a glorious future with Christ by living in a holy manner (see 1:10; 1 Thess. 4:1, 2).

2:15 Traditions: Paul is referring to the revealed truth of God that contains no error. This is what Paul had passed on to them. He had communicated some of God's truth when he was preaching among them, further truth by his first **epistle,** and now he was communicating more truth through a second letter. The New Testament had not yet been written, and the essential beliefs of the Christian faith were being communicated through the apostles' preaching and letters. Having believed the truth, the Thessalonian believers were now to maintain it and stand fast in their faith.

2:16, 17 Paul prays that God would encourage the Thessalonians and establish them in the truth. It was only because God had graciously chosen them as His own people, **loved** them, and **given** them everlasting salvation, that they could have **hope.** Paul uses the singular verbs **comfort** and **establish**

with the plural subject, **Jesus Christ** and the **Father,** to indicate the unity and equality of these two Persons of the Godhead (see 1 Thess. 3:11).

3:1, 2 Paul asked the Thessalonian believers to pray for the advance of the gospel and for his own deliverance from human opposition. **Run swiftly** refers to the rapid spread of the gospel, while **glorified** expresses the idea of being triumphant. The verbs suggest not a single victory but a continuing series of victories marking the progression of the gospel throughout the world. **Unreasonable** means the false teachers are capable of harmful deeds, while **wicked** indicates that they are evil in themselves and desire to corrupt others. These men may have been unbelieving Jews in Corinth who were persecuting Paul at the time he wrote this letter (see Acts 18:12, 13).

3:3 Paul was confident that God would **establish** or strengthen the Thessalonians (2:17; 1 Thess. 3:2, 13). He knew that God would **guard** or protect them (see Phil. 1:6; 1 Thess. 5:24). He assures them that God will stand watch over them so that not even the **evil one,** Satan himself, could get hold of them.

This passage must have been especially comforting to the Thessalonians, for they were still experiencing severe persecution because of their faith (1:4).

3:4 Paul had **confidence** that the Thessalonians would obey his commands, but his confidence was in the Lord and based on what the Lord would do to help the Thessalonians stand true. Paul had a similar confidence about the church in Philippi (see Phil. 1:6).

3:5 With the prayer **may the Lord direct your hearts,** Paul was indicating that the heart, the seat of a person's will, is the place where spiritual renewal begins. There God plants His love and patience, traits that will produce a harvest of good works. Paul uses the word *direct* to indicate that God will clear away the obstacles that may stand in the way of their progress toward **love** and **patience.** Paul prays that the Thessalonians, when faced with persecution, will be able to show the same type of patience Jesus expressed when people rejected Him.

3:6 Paul uses here the strong word **command** (see v. 4; 1 Thess. 4:2, 11). This is not simply a suggestion but a binding order with

---

✎ **IN DEPTH**　　**Busy Waiting**

Every generation of Christians must face the dilemma of how to live in the tension between the possibility of Christ's immediate return and the impossibility of predicting the moment. Many Christians unfortunately settle the problem by living as if Christ will not return. Meanwhile, others dabble in various fruitless but persistent schemes to "figure out" the time of Christ's return.

The young Thessalonian church struggled with persecution from the outset. Facing such difficulties, many of them found hope in the promise of Christ's return. Others misapplied the lesson by becoming lazy. After all, they reasoned, if Christ is already on His way, why participate in the details and responsibilities of life? Why sow if we will not be here to reap?

For those who had chosen to "coast" until Christ's return, Paul had blunt words: "If anyone will not work, neither shall he eat" (3:10). Paul understood the strong temptation to hide irresponsibility under a cover of spirituality. The integrity of the gospel was at stake.

In his final words of encouragement in 2 Thessalonians, Paul touched on the daily challenge for every person seeking to live for Christ: "But as for you, brethren, do not grow weary in doing good" (3:13). Herein lies the secret of being ready for Christ's return. If the hope of His arrival stirs up a wholehearted commitment to do good for His sake, we will be ready for Him. We must be busy waiting.

the authority of the Lord Jesus Christ. The same word, found also in vv. 10 and 12, is used of a military command that one must obey or else face the penalty of treason. Paul instructs the Thessalonians to **withdraw,** or withhold fellowship, from a disobedient person. Among other things this would include not allowing the person to participate in love feasts and the Lord's Supper (see 1 Cor. 5:9–13).

3:7, 8 Some Thessalonians, perhaps using the impending return of the Lord as an excuse, had refused to work and were expecting others in the church to feed them. In his previous letter Paul had already exhorted them to work (1 Thess. 4:11, 12). Evidently they had not heeded Paul's instruction, for in this letter Paul tells the church to discipline them (v. 6). As an example to all, Paul had **worked ... night and day** when he preached among them. His goal was to avoid being a burden to anyone. Paul made tents in order to provide for his needs whenever this became necessary on his missionary journeys (Acts 18:1–3).

3:9 Christian workers can expect financial support, and the church is obligated to pay those who serve them (Luke 10:7; 1 Cor. 9:6–14; Gal. 6:6; 1 Tim. 5:17, 18). Yet Paul did not want to use his **authority** to demand payment. Rather, he wanted to be an **example** for others to follow. The fact that he worked would also cut off any opportunity to accuse him of greed. He wanted nothing to hinder the spread of the gospel (1 Cor. 9:12).

3:10 Using the expression **we commanded you this,** Paul laid down the rule that if anyone does not work, neither should he eat. This applies to those unwilling to work, not to those unable to work.

3:11 Idleness breeds sin. Those who are **disorderly,** not working at all, become **busybodies,** causing trouble and division in the church.

3:12 Paul urges the Thessalonians to **eat their own bread** and to do so in a quiet manner, not causing division and disruption. Paul's cure for gossip is hard work.

3:13, 14 do not keep company with him: The believers were to withdraw fellowship and not associate with anyone who disregarded the words of this authoritative letter from the apostle Paul. Otherwise their pagan neighbors might think the Thessalonian Christians approved of that person's actions.

3:15 admonish him as a brother: The disobedient one is not an enemy, but one who needs correction. Even though rebellion was to be dealt with, Paul demonstrates his tremendous compassion for fellow believers. He hated the sin but not the sinner.

3:16 Paul prayed that the **Lord of peace** would guide their actions, granting peace and unity to the church.

3:17 with my own hand: Paul dictated many of his epistles to a secretary. He adds a personal word in his own handwriting as evidence of the authenticity of this letter (see also Col. 4:18). This proof was necessary because Paul suspected that the Thessalonians might have received a letter falsely attributed to him (see 2:2). Paul tells the Thessalonians that his handwriting at the end of a letter is the official **sign** that a letter was from him.

3:18 The solution to all problems was the **grace of our Lord Jesus Christ.** Not only was Jesus the Thessalonians' ultimate hope, but it was He who strengthened them to endure trials.

1 Timothy

Introduction

Timothy had accompanied Paul for years (Acts 16:1–3; 17:10; 20:4). Paul had not only taught Timothy the essentials of the Christian faith; he had modeled Christian leadership to him. Now Paul was leaving Timothy in charge of the church at Ephesus. From Macedonia, Paul wrote to encourage his "son" in the faith.

The letter names Paul as its author, and the author's statements about his life in 1:12, 13 are consistent with what is known of him. First Timothy was probably composed shortly after Paul's release from his first Roman imprisonment. This means the book was written in Macedonia around A.D. 62.

Timothy was a native of Lystra in Phrygia (see Acts 16:1–3). His father was Greek, and his mother Eunice and grandmother Lois were godly Jewish women (see 2 Tim. 1:5; 3:14, 15). Through the influence of these women Timothy learned the Hebrew Scriptures as a child. Paul calls Timothy a "true son in the faith" (1:2), suggesting that he was converted during Paul's first missionary visit to Lystra (see Acts 14:6, 19).

At the beginning of Paul's second missionary journey, Timothy was chosen by Paul to accompany him and Silas (see Acts 16:3). Timothy traveled with Paul and Silas helping them in their evangelization of Philippi and Thessalonica. Apparently he remained in Thessalonica (see Acts 17:10) and then joined Paul and Silas in Berea. In Corinth, Paul used Timothy as a liaison between himself and the church in Thessalonica. Later he used Timothy as a liaison again, this time to teach the believers in Corinth (1 Cor. 4:17; 16:10).

During Paul's Roman imprisonment, Timothy traveled to Philippi to encourage the believers and then report back to Paul (Phil. 2:19). After Paul's release, Timothy traveled with him to Ephesus. Timothy stayed there to confront the false teachers who were infiltrating the church, and Paul went on to Macedonia.

The central purpose of First Timothy is found in 3:15: "I write so that you may know how you ought to conduct yourself in the house of God, which is the church of the living God, the pillar and ground of the truth." The church is God's primary vehicle for accomplishing His work on earth (see Matt. 16:18–20). The Lord has ordained that men and women who have trusted Him as Savior should be involved in working out His will in local assemblies around the world (see 1 Thess. 1:1; Heb. 10:24, 25).

1:1 Paul begins his first letter to Timothy by asserting his authority as **an apostle of Jesus Christ.** The Greek word for *apostle* means "sent one." Thus Paul was declaring that he was an ambassador sent by Christ. **The commandment of God** refers to God's sovereign commissioning of Paul's ministry (see Acts 9). The authority of Paul's ministry came from two sources: from **God our Savior** and from **the Lord Jesus Christ.** The title *Savior* identifies God as the source of our salvation, both our justification and sanctification. Paul speaks of Christ as **our hope** because He is the reason we can look forward to eternal life in glory.

1:2 Timothy was a young believer from Lystra who traveled with Paul during his second and third missionary journeys (Acts 16:2, 3). **True son** refers to a legitimate child who possessed all the rights and privileges of membership in a family. Paul was indicating total acceptance of Timothy as a believer.

1:3 It is not certain when Paul traveled to **Macedonia.** His request for Timothy to **remain in Ephesus,** ministering to believers there, demonstrates Paul's confidence in the young man.

1:4 The word **fables** is used in Titus 1:14 in connection with Jewish fables. **Genealogies** is used in Titus 3:9 within the context of the Law. The errors that Paul left Timothy to correct in Ephesus appear to have been primarily Jewish in nature, involving unrestrained speculation about genealogies and allegorical interpretations of the Law like those found in rabbinical literature. The Greek word for **edification** means "stewardship" and expresses the concept of orderly management of a household. Paul understands the church as the "house of God" (see 3:14, 15). Disputes

do not promote "house order" in the church.
1:5 The **purpose** of Paul's command to Timothy is the promotion of God's **love** in the church (see John 13:34, 35).

1:6 Idle talk means "empty chatter." Gossip, speculation, and criticism should not come from the lips of believers.

1:7 teachers of the law: This phrase is derived from Judaism and is used in Luke 5:17 and Acts 5:34 in connection with the Pharisees. These were the individuals whom Timothy was to instruct and correct. Their errors came from their relation to the law. These men were loveless, legalistic teachers with impure hearts and motives. Instruction without love promotes legalism.

1:8 The proper function of the **law** is to make sinners aware of their sinfulness (see Rom. 3:20).

1:9 Paul's list of those who have violated the law appears to parallel the order of the Ten Commandments (see Ex. 20:3–17). The first three pairs of violations recall the first four commands, which address a person's relationship with God: **the lawless and insubordinate, the ungodly and ... sinners, and the unholy and profane.** Following these are eight violations that parallel five of the last six commands of the Ten Commandments. Covetousness is not mentioned.

1:10 Fornicators are persons involved in sexual immorality in general. **Sodomites** are specifically male homosexuals (see 1 Cor. 6:9). But heterosexual and homosexual immorality are violations of the seventh commandment. **kidnappers ... liars ... perjurers:** These are violations of commandments eight and nine. **Sound doctrine** may also be translated "healthy teaching."

1:11 according to the glorious gospel: This phrase should be interpreted in its immediate context, a discussion about the purpose of the law. The proper use of the law is to demonstrate human sinfulness and our need for the Good News that Christ has saved us from bondage to the law and our own sins.

1:12, 13 Before Paul trusted in Christ as Savior, he was **a blasphemer,** speaking against God; **a persecutor,** pursuing Christians like a hunter pursuing his prey (see Acts 8:3; 9:1–5); and **an insolent man,** a violent

person acting out of personal pride. **but I obtained mercy:** If the apostle Paul could find mercy after the terrible things he did against Christ, then God surely offers salvation with "open arms" to all people (see 2:4).

1:14 Grace is God's undeserved, unearned, freely given favor. The grace given to Paul was **exceedingly abundant,** overflowing beyond all expectations.

1:15 Paul summarized the heart of the gospel (v.11): **Christ Jesus came into the world to save sinners.** Christ came to die for the sins of humanity. **of whom I am chief:** Paul saw the degradation of sin and understood the sinfulness of human beings. Because of this, he placed himself first among sinners.

1:16, 17 believe on Him: Over 185 times in the New Testament the sole condition given for salvation is belief, having faith or trust in Jesus Christ. The gospel is that Christ died for our sins, was buried, and rose on the third day. All those who place their trust in Jesus for salvation will be saved from the coming judgment. To add any other condition to faith for salvation is to make justification a matter of works (see Rom. 11:6; Gal. 2:16).

1:18 Apparently earlier in his ministry **prophecies** had been made about Timothy and his future role in the church. Paul urges Timothy to **wage the good warfare.** According to this powerful imagery, Christian ministry is spiritual warfare directed against God's enemies.

1:19, 20 Hymenaeus and Alexander: Paul offered examples of two men (see also 2 Tim. 2:17, 18; 4:14) who were failing to fight the good fight (v. 18, 19). The phrase **delivered to Satan** is similar to 1 Cor. 5:5. The authority to "deliver over" was apostolic in nature. Paul did not deliver the two men because they were unbelievers, but so they would **learn not to blaspheme.** Paul was indicating that these men should be excluded from the church so they might abandon their evil ways (1 Cor. 5:1–5).

2:1, 2 In these verses, Paul uses four of the seven New Testament terms for prayer. **Supplications** emphasizes personal need. The verb from which the noun is derived has the idea of "petition." **Prayers** is the general word for prayer. The term is always directed toward God with reverence or worship. **Intercessions** means "approaching with confidence," suggesting free access to God. **Giving of thanks** is praising God for what He has done for us. **For all men** is the first object of prayer. This generic expression for male and female alike cannot be restricted to believers; it also includes nonbelievers, such as **kings and all who are in authority. Peaceable** refers to internal composure or an amiable attitude. The idea of praying for kings has a twofold emphasis. First, it is a specific way to pray for all people, because the actions of a king affect society as a whole. Second, it reminds believers that God is the ultimate Sovereign. He is in control, and our prayers affect decisions at the highest level.

2:3, 4 Who desires all men to be saved does not mean that God has willed that everyone should come to salvation. Instead what Paul might be saying here is that the Savior God extends the offer of salvation to all. Christ died for the sins of all, but only those who believe receive the benefits of that sacrifice (see John 3:16; 2 Cor. 5:14, 15). **The knowledge of the truth** refers to Christian growth after being saved. God's desire is not only our salvation (justification) but also our growth in the truth (sanctification), so that we will not be led astray by false teachers (1:3, 4).

2:5 One God is a central truth of the Hebrew Scriptures. The only living God desires everyone to be saved. He is the only One to whom our prayers should be addressed. **Mediator** is a concept derived from the ceremonial worship prescribed in the Old Testament. In the tabernacle and later in the temple, the priests meditated between God and the Israelites by offering animal sacrifices to atone for the sins of the people and by interceding to God for the nation. The **one** Mediator is **the Man Christ Jesus** (see Heb. 9:11–15). There is only one way to God—through the Mediator, Christ Jesus, who has the full nature of God and the full nature of man. Christ represents us at the right hand of God the Father (see Rom. 8:34).

2:6 The work of the Mediator (v. 5) is described as giving **Himself a ransom for all.** The Greek word translated *ransom* is found only here in the New Testament. It specifically

refers to a ransom paid for a slave. In Greek it is formed with a prefix that reinforces the idea of substitution (see Matt. 20:28; Mark 10:45). In other words, Christ substituted His life for ours. He paid the penalty for our sins so we could be reconciled to our Father.

2:7 Teacher of the Gentiles describes the ministry to which Paul had been commissioned (see Acts 9:15; Rom. 11:13). **Faith** refers to a person's initial salvation (justification); **truth** relates to the believer's growth in salvation (sanctification). Paul was called not only to preach the gospel to the Gentiles but also to guide their growth in the truth. This is why he left Timothy at Ephesus. Timothy was to charge the Ephesians not to teach other doctrines, fables, or endless genealogies (1:4).

2:8 The men refers to those involved in leading public worship. Leadership in public worship is not restricted to elders or those with specific gifts. Prayer is one of the central features of Christian worship. **Lifting up holy hands** is a Hebrew way of praying (see 1 Kin. 8:22; Ps. 141:2). Biblical prayer must be done with a clean heart and life (see Heb. 10:22). **without wrath and doubting:** *Wrath* is a slow, boiling type of anger. *Doubting* literally means "to think backward and forward." It carries the idea of disputing. Prayer is to be offered without resentment or disputing among those in the church. If believers do not have good relations with others in the church, they should not lead in public worship.

2:9 in like manner also: When men pray they are to have sincere and holy attitudes; when women pray, they should be modest. **modest apparel:** The emphasis is that women should dress appropriately when at worship, and not put on extravagant clothes that draw attention to themselves. **Propriety** means reverence and respect, shrinking away from what is inappropriate. **Moderation** may also be translated "sound judgment" or "self-control."

2:10 Paul exhorts the women at Ephesus to be concerned about clothing themselves with godly character instead of wearing inappropriate and lavish clothes. **with good works:** A Christian woman's beauty is found in her godly character and her love for the Lord as demonstrated in all types of good works.

2:11 Let a woman learn is a command. Paul ignored popular myths about women being incapable of learning and urged Timothy to provide opportunities for women to be educated. **In silence** refers to the woman's attitude or manner while learning, as should be true of all believers. Paul was not saying that a woman could not speak in the local assembly (see 1 Cor. 11:2–16). He was cautioning women to learn with an attitude of **all submission** and not in a unruly manner.

2:12 to teach: Paul uses a Greek word that indicates the type of teaching that was found in the Jewish communities and synagogues from which he had come. Such teaching was more than giving information to students. It included the call by the rabbi, or teacher, to have his disciples listen, believe, and practice his words. Such teaching was built on the revelation of God and assumed that there would be some sort of oversight, like that exercised in the early church by the elders (see 4:11; 4:16—5:2; 2 Tim. 3:17; 4:1–4; Titus 2:15; 3:8–11). Generally those who exercised this responsibility in the early church had the spiritual gift of teaching (see Rom. 12:7; 1 Cor. 12:28), but not every gift of teaching (by men or women) was necessarily to be exercised over the entire congregation. The word **or** seems to indicate that *teach* is defined by the phrase **have authority over a man.** It seems best to understand this passage as teaching that women may exercise their spiritual gifts in a variety of ministries in a local assembly (see 2 Tim. 3:14; Titus 2:3, 4), as long as those gifts are exercised under the appropriate leadership of men. Other commentators have viewed this verse as an example of Paul using his apostolic authority to curb the spread in Ephesus of false teaching (see 1:3–7) that apparently was becoming popular among some women who had not been properly instructed (see v. 11).

2:13, 14 Adam was formed first: In God's order of creation (see 1 Cor. 11:9), Adam was made before Eve. This is an implied reference to the privileges that a firstborn received in ancient society. These privileges were not given on the basis of inherent superiority but instead on being born first, something controlled by God Himself. **Adam was not deceived** points to the fact that Adam sinned with his eyes open; he knew what he was doing (see Rom. 5:12). **woman being deceived:** The verb indicates that Eve was "completely deceived." Paul's argument from creation and the Fall in these verses seem to indicate that the prohibitions in vv. 9–12 are permanent.

2:15 saved in childbearing: Some believe this verse refers to the birth of Christ and that the woman is Mary. However, it may refer to the woman's special task of bearing children (see Titus 2:3–5). The salvation referred to here is not justification, but daily sanctification. Most likely, Paul is referring to being delivered from the desire to dominate by recognizing one's appropriate place in God's creation order.

3:1 bishop: This Greek word refers to a person who oversees a congregation. In many New Testament passages, the Greek words for *bishop* and *elder* are used interchangeably for the same office (see Titus 1:5–7).

3:2 Blameless means "not laid hold of." The idea is not that a bishop is sinless but that he displays mature, consistent Christian conduct that gives no reason for anyone to accuse him of inappropriate behavior. **Husband of one wife** literally means "a one-woman kind of man." This expression has been interpreted as a general exclusion from office of all who are sexually immoral or of polygamists, or as referring specifically to those who have remarried after divorce. This is also a qualification of deacons (v. 12). **Temperate** means "without wine," sober or clear-headed. **Sober-minded** means that an overseer must have control of his body and mind. It is a balanced state of mind arising out of self-restraint. **Of good behavior** means "orderly." **Hospitable** means "loving strangers." An overseer's home should be open for purposes of ministry. **Able to teach** could also be translated "qualified to teach," or "teachable." Since the passage is about character, it seems best to understand this qualification as being teachable, a necessity for a man of God.

3:3 Not given to wine means "not addicted to wine." **Not violent** means "not a striker." An elder should not be prone to violence or to striking others. **not greedy for money:** An overseer is not to have a materialistic attitude toward money or possessions. Part of this qualification is a warning to those in church leadership about proper management of God's finances. **Not quarrelsome** means "without fighting." This is the quality of being peaceable. A bishop or overseer should contend for the faith without being contentious. **Not covetous** means "not a lover of silver" (6:9).

3:4 Rules means "stands before" or "manages." **his own house:** An elder must manage his own family well. His children must submit to his leadership with **reverence** or respect.

3:5, 6 Novice means "newly planted." An elder is not to be a new believer. Being a new convert could put him in danger of **being puffed up with pride.** Such pride is described as the **condemnation of the devil** (see Ezek. 28:11–19).

3:7 good testimony: An elder must have a good reputation in the community (see Acts 6:3). A non-Christian should not be able to **reproach** or insult an elder. The elder's good testimony avoids the **snare of the devil,** the traps or pitfalls of Satan (see 2 Tim. 2:26).

3:8 Deacons fill a second leadership position in the local assembly. The Greek word for *deacon* means "servant." Although the word itself is not used in Acts 6, the seven godly men selected there to distribute food to widows appear to be the forerunners of this office and ministry. This verse and Phil. 1:1 indicate that the office of deacon was an established office in the early church. **not double-tongued:** This phrase speaks of the dangers of gossip, specifically saying one thing to one person and another to someone else.

3:9 The mystery of the faith is the doctrine clarified in v. 16 as the Incarnation of God in the flesh. The Son of God becoming flesh to serve humanity (see Mark 10:43–45) is the embodiment of service.

3:10 tested: Deacons are to be evaluated, observed, and approved before being appointed to office. Their character in this approval process is to be **blameless** or "without accusation."

3:11 Likewise, their wives: The similar phrasing of v. 8 seems to indicate that Paul was speaking of another office in the local body, the deaconess. These women, like deacons

(vv. 8–10, 12, 13), served under the leadership of the elders. However some interpret this verse as referring to the wives of deacons and not to an office.

3:12, 13 A twofold encouragement is given to deacons who serve well. First, they will receive a good **standing,** or respect. This relates primarily to their standing in the congregation, but also to their greater rewards for service at the judgment seat of Christ (see Rom. 14:10; 1 Cor. 3:10–15, 2 Cor. 5:10). Second, they develop **boldness in the faith.** Faithful servants develop confidence and assurance in their Christian walk.

3:14, 15 Paul's purpose in writing his first letter to Timothy was to give him instructions on how a local assembly and its leadership should function. **church of the living God:** The church universal is manifested in local assemblies around the world. **the pillar and ground of the truth:** Misconduct and disorder in the local church weaken the support of God's truth in the world. Godly men and women gathering together in local assemblies to worship the Lord produce an orderly church that testifies to others of the truth of God.

3:16 This verse contains an early Christian hymn. The hymn is three couplets. **Manifested in the flesh** refers to Christ's Incarnation, the fact that Jesus became man (see John. 1:14). **Justified in the Spirit** refers to the Holy Spirit's work in Jesus' ministry and Resurrection (see Matt. 3:15–17; John 16:7, 10; Rom. 1:4). **Seen by angels** refers to the angelic witness of Christ's ministry and Resurrection. **Preached among the Gentiles** refers to the proclamation of Christ to the nations (see Col. 1:23). **Believed on in the world** refers to the response of individuals to God's plan of salvation (see 1 Cor. 1:18–25). **Received up in glory** refers to the Ascension; Christ is seated in God's presence in heaven (see Acts 1:9; Heb. 1:3, 4).

4:1, 2 Paul begins a series of instructions specifically for Timothy. **the Spirit expressly says:** Paul may be referring to various prophecies inspired by the Holy Spirit about defection from God's truth (see Dan. 7:25; 8:23; Matt. 24:4–12), or he might be speaking of a revelation the Spirit had given to him. **Depart** here means literally "to stand away from." There will be various seasons in which **some** people will depart from their faith (1:19, 20). The reference here is not to a loss of salvation but to a failure to walk obediently (see John 19:25–27; 1 Cor. 3:1–3; 11:29, 30).

4:3, 4 The false teachers at Ephesus evidently disparaged the material world as evil, which became a central doctrine of the full-grown Gnosticism of the second century. In Gen. 1:31, God's creation is called "very good." Believers are to enjoy the **good** things God creates and gives them to manage.

4:5 Sanctified means "set apart." Marriage, eating, and possessions are, in reality, spiritual issues. They are to be enjoyed as the believer recognizes their proper purposes before God.

4:6 Continued growth in the church occurs through **words of faith** and instruction in **good doctrine.** Sound doctrine is the basis of a healthy ministry and correct practice.

4:7 Exercise is the normal term for the physical training of Greek athletes. True spirituality requires a person to train at godliness in his walk with the Lord.

4:8, 9 Profits a little contrasts the short-term value of physical exercise with the long-term benefits of **godliness for all things.** Discipline in godliness affects both the present and future life of the believer. The present aspect includes obedience and a life of purpose (see John 10:10). The future aspect involves greater rewards in the coming reign of Christ (see 1 Cor. 3:10–15; 2 Cor. 5:9, 10).

4:10 Savior of all men describes God as the One who gives life, breath, and existence to all. **Especially of those who believe** draws a contrast between God's common grace to all and His special saving grace to those who trust Him as their Savior.

4:11, 12 Youth was a term applied to men until they were 40. Timothy might have been between 35 and 40 years old at this time. The antidote for his *youth* was his life. He was to set an example in six areas: (1) **in word,** meaning conversation; (2) **in conduct,** or behavior; (3) **in love,** which is the love of God; (4) **in spirit,** the attitude or power of the Holy Spirit; (5) **in faith,** meaning trust in God; and (6) **in purity,** both in sexual matters and in thoughts (5:2). These

godly elements are not only for the young, but should be desired and practiced by all.

4:13 Reading is a command for public reading of the Scriptures (see Acts 13:15). **Exhortation** is an encouragement to obey the Scriptures. **Doctrine** is formal teaching and instruction in the Word of God (2:12).

4:14 Paul encourages Timothy to be diligent. The **gift** is the spiritual gift Timothy received from Christ (see Eph. 4:7, 8). **by prophecy:** Timothy's gift was given through a prophetic message (1:18) and **with the laying on of … hands,** probably at Lystra (see Acts 16:1). The laying on of hands signified the elders' commission and recognition of God's work in Timothy's life. Paul himself was part of the group that laid their hands on Timothy (see 2 Tim. 1:6).

4:15 Paul's care for Timothy, his "son in the faith" (see 1:2), is evident. He was instructing Timothy so that his **progress** would be **evident** to everyone in the church.

4:16 Save … yourself is not a reference to justification by works but to sanctification, the Christian's daily walk of faith (see Mark 8:34–38; John 12:25, 26). **Those who hear you** refers to the members in the church to whom Timothy was reading, exhorting, and teaching.

5:1, 2 All purity is a word of caution to young men. They must respect the purity of the younger women as the purity of a sister.

5:3 Honor is a command to show respect, a respect demonstrated by one's attitude and through financial support (vv. 4, 8). **Widows** are those who have family to help support them (vv. 4, 16); the one who is **really a widow** is one without family support.

5:4 Family members are instructed to care for widows. **Piety** is respect, reverence, or obligation. **repay:** Honoring our **parents** includes caring for them physically and financially as they grow older. In effect, we are returning the time and energy they gave to us while we were young.

5:5 Trusts means to have hope or confidence in God.

5:6 This verse identifies widows living ungodly lives, who are not to be supported by the church. **Lives in pleasure** refers to a life of comfort focused on one's own desires. **Dead** means separated from fellowship (see James 2:26). Widows in the church who choose to live for themselves are separating themselves from fellowship with God and the church.

5:7, 8 A believer is to **provide** for **his own** (his near relatives) and **his household** (his immediate family). Failure to provide for one's family is equal to denial of **the faith** (see Ex. 20:12; Mark 7:9–12; Eph. 6:2). If a Christian cannot even care for his or her own family, how can that person love and care for others?

5:9 Taken into the number means to write down on a list. The list referred to here was most likely a list of widows whom the church was to assist. Widows who were enrolled on the list were to be at least **sixty years old** and **the wife of one man.** Some have maintained that this list was an official order of widows. These widows were to

pray for the church (v. 5) and practice works of charity (v. 10).

5:10 Children refers either to the widow's own children or possibly to orphans. **Lodged strangers** indicates an attitude of hospitality. **Washed the saints' feet** demonstrates a servant's heart. **Relieved the afflicted** suggests giving aid to those facing adversity. **Followed every good work** indicates a commitment to serving.

5:11, 12 Refuse is a command to not put **younger widows,** those less than sixty years old, on the list of widows to be supported by the church. The reason for this refusal is that younger widows may **grow wanton,** which means to experience sexual desire, and thus **desire to marry,** presumably an unbeliever, since the marriage is said to be outside their **first faith.**

5:13, 14 It is best for those younger widows to remarry (see 1 Cor. 7:39, 40). Otherwise, they might become **idle,** without work. **gossips and busybodies:** Paul was concerned that

---

🔲 **IN DEPTH**   **Widows in the Household**

The fundamental social institution of the Greco-Roman world was the household. The ancient household included far more people than the modern nuclear family of a husband, wife, and two and one-third children. Everyone involved in the "family business" under the rule of a male administrator, called the "father," was part of the household. Thus, the Greco-Roman household consisted of relatives plus various dependents: the father's wife, his slaves, children, as well as clients—those who gave the father honor and influence in exchange for material favors.

Households, particularly the fathers, ranked themselves socially in terms of honor, prestige, and influence. The more honor a father received, the more prestige and influence he gathered. Wealth, therefore, was not important to accumulate in order to gain more wealth. Wealth was important so that a father might parade his honor. Wealth enabled a father to lavish gifts on his dependents, thereby making more people honor their father as their benefactor.

One household member who especially needed protection was the widow. In NT times, widows had virtually no means of supporting themselves. The early church felt responsible to care for Christian widows, but problems arose in ministering to their needs. As new structures and guidelines had to be developed, the church eventually distinguished between widows who really needed support and those who should be commended to the care of their household (1 Tim. 5:3–5, 8). A Christian father who did not provide for a widow of his household was deemed "worse than an unbeliever" (5:8). Even in non-Christian households of the Greco-Roman world, the head of the household supported poor widows.

younger widows would not have enough to do, and thus would bother everyone else with worthless talk or even harmful and divisive words.

5:15–17 The primary function of **elders** is to **rule well.** The word **honor** was used in ancient writings outside the Bible to refer to financial remuneration. **Double** refers to two types of honor: (1) respect for ruling well and (2) adequate pay for their diligent care of the church (see 1 Cor. 9:1–14). **Those who labor in the word and doctrine** are those elders who preach and teach the Scriptures.

5:18 For the Scripture says With two quotations, one from Deut. 25:4 and the other from the words of Christ in Luke 10:7, Paul provides proof for the principle of providing adequate financial care for elders. The Luke passage is especially noteworthy because it shows that this Gospel was considered by Paul to be Scripture along with the Book of Deuteronomy.

5:19 An elder is protected against malicious attacks by the command not to **receive an accusation,** a charge or legal accusation, except when it comes from **two or three witnesses** (see Deut. 19:15; Matt. 18:16). Charges against elders are to be factual, not based on a single opinion or rumor.

5:20, 21 Those who are sinning refers to elders who fail in their leadership, whether in the local church, in their social life, or in their home life. **Rebuke** is a command to bring a sin to light, to expose it before **all,** including other elders and the church body. **the rest also may fear:** The public rebuke of a sinning elder is to serve as a warning to other believers. God's discipline is consistent from leadership to laity. Sin is a serious matter in the lives of believers, especially those in leadership (see 1 Pet. 4:17). When leaders sin with impunity, church members might erroneously start justifying their own sins.

5:22–24 This verse warns against too **hastily** restoring a leader who has fallen. Correction in love and restoration to fellowship should occur as soon as possible, but restoration to leadership should not be made without time and biblical evaluation. Another interpretation of this verse suggests that it is a command to

evaluate carefully anyone being considered for leadership, not just former leaders who want to be restored (3:1–14). **Keep yourself pure** is a caution for Timothy not to share responsibility for another person's sins by restoring or appointing someone who is not qualified.

5:25 cannot be hidden: Unnoticed good works will become evident, if not in this life then at the judgment seat of Christ (see 1 Cor. 3:10–15).

6:1 Bondservants … under the yoke refers to believers who are slaves. Believing slaves were to give their unbelieving masters **all honor** or respect. The life and actions of a Christian slave were to represent the Christian faith and Christ Himself.

6:2 Teach: Paul moves to the conclusion with a final warning for Timothy to instruct his congregation in order to combat the false teachings that were infiltrating the church (see v. 4, 5). The Greek word for *teach* means the formal presentation of doctrine (see 2:12), while the Greek word for **exhort** implies less formal instruction, a "coming alongside" to guide. **These things** is probably best understood as the contents of this letter.

6:3, 4 If anyone teaches otherwise: Here Paul refers to false teachers. He contrasts their "sick" teaching with the **wholesome words** of the **Lord Jesus Christ.** These false teachers were more interested in theory and debate than putting the truth into practice.

6:5 Destitute of the truth describes the uselessness of speculative religious arguments. These false teachers were using religion for their own financial **gain.** Probably they were hoping that their debates on religion would gain them a following and financial support.

6:6–9 Two types of people are described in relation to wealth (see v. 17). The first type are those who **desire to be rich.** An inner lack of godliness and contentment leaves a vacuum filled with greed. This greed drives people into **temptation,** snares, and **foolish and harmful lusts. Drown** literally means to drag to the bottom. Paul was painting a graphic word picture of a greedy person drowning under the weight of material desires.

6:10 Money in and of itself is not a problem, but the **love of money** is. Love of money is **a root,** though not *the* root, of **evil.** The love of money can drive a person into all types of evil. **Greediness** may cause a believer even to stray **from the faith.** Christians may be blinded by greed and materialism to such a degree that they break away from their faith.

6:11 Paul issues a powerful warning against materialism. **Flee** is a strong command. **Pursue** is a command to hunt or chase after some object. **Righteousness, godliness,** and **faith** are character qualities. **Love, patience,** and **gentleness** are fruit of the Spirit-controlled life (see Gal. 5:22). Men and women of God should pursue godliness, not materialism, with all of their being.

6:12, 13 lay hold on eternal life: Eternal life is viewed as a free gift (see John 3:16; Eph. 2:8–10), a present experience (see John 10:10), and a reward (see Mark 10:29, 30; Luke 18:29, 30). Here Paul is not speaking of Timothy's salvation, but of his fruitfulness in this life and his rewards in the next. **The good confession** is Timothy's call and ministry. Paul was urging Timothy to continue his ministry of preaching the Word of God.

6:14 commandment: Paul was exhorting Timothy to avoid empty religious argumentation (6:3–5) and the greed of materialism (6:6–10). Timothy was to remain faithful to Christ until He appeared again. The imminent return of Christ should be a motive for godly living (see 2 Pet. 3:10–16; 1 John 2:28).

6:15, 16 God will **manifest** the return of Christ **in His own time.** This will happen at a specific point in time that Jesus declared was known only to the Father (see Acts 1:6, 7).

6:17 those who are rich: Paul has already condemned those who are attempting to become rich through the ministry (vv. 6–10). The second group of people Paul addresses in regard to wealth (see also v. 9) are those who are already wealthy. Paul encourages Timothy to tell the rich not to be high-minded or proud and not to **trust in uncertain riches.** Only **the living God** can provide for our needs.

6:18 Those with wealth are commanded to recognize God as the true source of their wealth and to be generous with their riches. The material blessings of God are to be enjoyed and used for the advancement of His kingdom, not for self-centered living.

6:19 Storing up may also be translated "treasuring up," a phrase similar to Jesus' challenge in Matt. 6:19–21 to lay up treasure in heaven. A believer's daily obedience to God builds a **good foundation** for the **time to come.** The Scriptures teach that a believer's works will be evaluated to see what his or her life in Christ has produced (see 1 Cor. 3:10–15).

6:20, 21 The Greek term for **committed** is found only here and in 2 Tim. 1:12, 14. The deposit that Timothy had to guard was the truth revealed in this letter. **Knowledge** is the Greek word *gnosis,* from which the word Gnosticism is derived. Evidently an early form of Gnosticism had infiltrated the Ephesian church. This heresy taught that salvation came through the "knowledge" of spiritual mysteries. Paul warns Timothy not to be caught up in this false teaching (see 1:3, 4; 6:3–5).

2 Timothy

Introduction

Second Timothy is Paul's "last words" to his protégé Timothy. From a cold, lonely Roman prison, the aged apostle Paul wrote his final instructions to his "son" in the faith. Paul's execution was most likely imminent, and he implored Timothy to come quickly to his side.

The author of Second Timothy identifies himself as Paul (1:1). Other remarks in the book are characteristic of Paul's ministry (see 3:10, 11; 4:10, 11, 19, 20). Many scholars believe that Second Timothy was written during a second imprisonment of Paul in Rome (see 1:8, 16, 17; 4:6–13). According to the fourth-century church historian Eusebius, Paul was martyred during Nero's regime, sometime before A.D. 68. Since this letter was written immediately before Paul's death, it was probably written around A.D. 67.

Ever since the beginning of the second missionary journey Timothy had been close to Paul, assisting him in his ministry, acting as his liaison, and learning from his godly example. Timothy's devout mother Eunice and grandmother Lois had provided him with a grounding in the Hebrew Scriptures on which Paul could build (see 2 Tim. 1:5; 3:14, 15). Paul developed his son in the faith by placing more and more responsibility on his shoulders. Timothy had functioned as Paul's representative to Thessalonica (1 Thess. 3:2) and Corinth (1 Cor. 4:17). Paul had served as Timothy's spiritual mentor throughout his life. Now as he neared his death Paul wanted to give Timothy some final words of encouragement and to see him one last time.

Paul's primary purpose for writing this letter was to offer final instructions to Timothy about the Christian life. Second Timothy has an intensely personal nature and tone. One senses Paul's strong love and concern for Timothy. Paul encourages his close friend to use his spiritual gifts. He writes to strengthen Timothy's loyalty to Christ in the face of the suffering and persecution that would come. The apostle challenges Timothy to handle the Word of God accurately, faithfully instructing others in the truths of the faith. Warnings and instructions are given about how a believer should relate to the world in times of apostasy.

Paul's second purpose for writing this letter was to urge Timothy to join him in Rome. Paul knew that he was soon to die. He longed to see and have fellowship with his child in the faith one last time.

1:1 Paul speaks of himself in 1 Timothy as **an apostle** "by the commandment of God" (see 1 Tim. 1:1). In 2 Timothy he calls himself an apostle **by the will of God** (see also 2 Cor. 1:1; Eph. 1:1; Col. 1:1). **according to the promise of life:** Paul considers himself a bearer of a life-giving message. This message of life stands in ironic contrast to the fact that Paul was writing from a Roman prison, facing his execution. The characteristic phrase **in Christ,** found in other Pauline letters, also appears in this letter, further indicating that it came from Paul.

1:2 beloved son: In his first letter to Timothy, Paul referred to him as a "true son in the faith" (see 1 Tim. 1:2). Paul's deep love and concern for this younger man of God is shown throughout this letter.

1:3 I serve is a priestly phrase often associated with worship. **Forefathers** were the patriarchs of the faith: Abraham, Isaac, and Jacob. Paul had a great love for Israel (see Rom. 9:1–5). The reason he connects himself with Israel's forefathers may be to demonstrate that he is not advocating a new religion but one of which the godly of the past are also a part. **remember you in my prayers:** Although he was possibly confined in a cold, damp prison (4:13), the aged apostle was still worshiping God and offering prayers on behalf of Timothy. No matter what their circumstances, believers should pray to their heavenly Father, committing everything to His loving hands.

1:4 desiring to see you: Paul longed to see Timothy, possibly because the apostle realized his life would end soon (4:6–17).

1:5 The word translated **genuine faith** means "unhypocritical." Paul rejoices when he recalls Timothy's faithful **grandmother Lois** and **mother Eunice,** whose name means "Good Victory." The prayers, witness, and faith of his godly mother and grandmother were key factors in the spiritual development of Timothy (see 1 Tim. 2:15).

1:6 stir up the gift: Timothy is urged to rekindle his spiritual gift. The desire to discover, develop, and deploy our specific spiritual gifts should be like a fire blazing within us. The constant struggle of Christians is to be diligent about our work for God and not to slacken our pace in this spiritual race.

1:7 The Holy Spirit gives us spiritual gifts and empowers us to use them. God's Spirit does not impart **fear** or cowardice, but **power, love,** and **a sound mind,** or "self-control." The Spirit imparts power for the various circumstances of ministry. The love the Spirit gives to us should be directed toward other people. Furthermore, as we use our spiritual gifts to build up the church, we should exercise self-control, using our abilities only at the appropriate times.

1:8 Timothy is encouraged not to be **ashamed** or shrink back from the **testimony of our Lord.** Paul is concerned that in the face of vehement opposition Timothy might be afraid to witness. **Share with me in the sufferings** indicates that at times a faithful witness for the Lord will involve adversity. Paul's call for boldness in vv. 7–9 may indicate that Timothy was timid.

1:9 God's saving and calling of believers is **not according to … works.** It is impossible for people to earn their way into heaven. Salvation is according to God's **own purpose** or sovereign plan (see Rom. 8:28–30; Eph. 1:11). **Grace** is God's unearned favor. The Lord called us and saved us **in Christ Jesus before time began.**

1:10 The manifestation of God's plan and grace has been **revealed,** or brought to light, in the **appearing** of our Savior Jesus Christ. **abolished death:** Fear of dying might have caused believers to shrink from testifying about their faith. The Greek term translated **life** is typically used of eternal life in the New Testament. God's life, unlike the life of humans, is immortal; He cannot die. Through their faith in Christ, believers have inherited eternal life. We have nothing to fear, not even death.

1:11, 12 Paul's confidence in the gospel and his Savior enabled him to suffer without

shame. The phrase **whom I have believed** expresses Paul's unshakable trust in his Savior. **What I have committed** does not refer to something Paul had done for Christ, but to something he had entrusted to Him, like a deposit in a bank. Paul was certain that God would **keep** his deposit, his life and the eternal rewards of his ministry. The apostle was preparing for imminent death, but in spite of this he was hopeful. He had spent his time, resources, and even his life on proclaiming the gospel, and this investment in Christ's kingdom would bring him an abundant reward in eternity (see Luke 19:15; 1 Cor. 3:10–15; Rev. 11:15, 18).

1:13 Hold fast is a command to Timothy to persist in the **sound words** of healthy teaching (see 1 Tim. 1:3–10). Many people who say they speak for Christ proclaim false doctrine. Like Timothy, we need to pursue sound teaching and avoid all teaching that does not conform to the Scriptures.

1:14 That good thing may be rephrased as "the good deposit." Here the phrase refers to Paul's teachings to Timothy (see 1 Tim. 6:20). **Keep** means "to guard" or "to protect." **Who dwells in us** describes the indwelling of the **Holy Spirit** in believers.

1:15–18 These verses describe those who had abandoned Paul. Yet even here, Paul recalls **Onesiphorus** (a name meaning "Help Bringer"). This man from Ephesus had **refreshed** Paul as if by a cup of cold water. We too should be a refreshment to other believers.

2:1 In light of the defections of others (1:15), Paul exhorts Timothy to be faithful. But Paul's call is for Timothy to **be strong in the grace that is in Christ Jesus.** The emphasis is on the strength of Christ, not on Timothy's own power.

2:2 Timothy is commanded to **commit** Paul's teaching to **faithful men.** Faithful men then have the responsibility of teaching others. This would be the basis for an endless chain of Christian discipleship, the teaching of Christian teachers (see Matt. 28:18–20).

2:3–6 Three illustrations are given for faithfulness. The first is a **soldier.** The Christian walk is often presented as spiritual warfare. Effective service calls for singleness of purpose. The second illustration comes from **athletics.** The

Greek games were important and demanded strenuous training (see 1 Cor. 9:25). No competitor could be **crowned** unless he competed in accordance with **the rules.** Here the reference is to a victor's wreath given in an athletic contest. Faithful believers will receive a victor's crown, not the royal crown which belongs to Jesus. The third illustration is that of a **hardworking farmer.** Conscientious, hard labor is necessary before a farmer can enjoy a bountiful harvest.

2:7, 8 Timothy is commanded to **remember** Christ's Resurrection. **The seed of David** emphasizes Jesus' humanity and the fact that He would fulfill all the promises God

had given to David (see 2 Sam. 7:11–16). **Raised from the dead** emphasizes that our Savior lives today seated at the right hand of God the Father.

2:9 Human circumstances cannot confine the **word of God.** God uses His word to accomplish His purposes. There are numerous examples of people who were antagonistic to God's truth but who surrendered their lives to God when He kept after them (see Paul's conversion in Acts 9:1–25).

2:10 Paul is able to **endure** his present difficult circumstances—his own imprisonment—because he knows that God's work is still progressing among the **elect,** God's

---

 IN DEPTH **The Handbook for a Life's Work**

In his final and intimate letter to his "son in the faith," Paul reminded Timothy of the essentials of the faith, the basis of Christian ministry. Paul did not want Timothy to drift away from the truth, as Phygellus and Hermogenes had done (1:15). Therefore, he passionately exhorted Timothy to hold on tightly to the faith and to the sound teaching that Paul had entrusted to him (1:13).

Paul knew that consistency and personal integrity (2:22–26) would be significant factors in the young pastor's effectiveness. So Paul warned Timothy about associations with others (3:1–5), encouraging him to reflect on their years together as an example of ethical consistency in the midst of difficulty (3:10–15). In fact, Paul wrote, "all who desire to live godly in Christ Jesus will suffer persecution" (3:12). Timothy certainly had vivid memories of trials in ministry to illustrate Paul's point (Acts 19:21—20:6).

But Paul also made sure that whatever other counsel he gave his pupil, Timothy would find beneath it all a rock-solid dependence on God's Word. Timothy's authority would not come from his own wisdom, Paul's endorsement, or the acceptance of others. His teaching would stand only to the degree that it was based on Scripture.

Paul's ringing tribute to the authority and practicality of God's Word (3:16, 17) completes a section that begins in 2:2 with his charge to Timothy to "commit" what he had learned to "faithful men who will be able to teach others also." In 3:17, Paul offered the central test for measuring whether the gospel torch had been successfully passed from one generation to the next. The application of God's Word in four distinct ways would ensure that the next generation would become "complete, thoroughly equipped for every good work" (3:17). Effective teaching would include (1) doctrine, the basic truths of the faith; (2) reproof, or challenging and confronting each other with the Word of God; (3) correction, by providing guidance from the truths in Scripture; and (4) instruction in righteousness, the personal and practical application of biblical truths.

Paul was encouraging Timothy not only to pass the truths of Scripture on to the next generation, but also to pass on the basis of those truths, the Word of God itself. As we follow in Paul's footsteps, we too must make it clear that the authority of our teaching comes from the Bible. If we teach the truth but do not teach the source of truth, we will not succeed in passing on our faith. Our affirmations and actions have to be founded on God's Word or they will be little more than wishful thinking.

chosen ones. The final outcome of their salvation will be the **eternal glory** of God's coming kingdom.

2:11 if we died ... We shall also live: Believers are united with Christ in His death and Resurrection (see Rom. 6:8), which become our death to sin and our Resurrection to eternal life.

2:12 If we endure: Persevering in the faith even in the face of hardship or persecution will result in a reward when Christ returns (see Luke 19:11–27; Rom. 8:17; Rev. 3:21). **He will also deny us:** Jesus will not save those who shrink from identifying with Him or from serving Him (see 1 John 2:28).

2:13 Faithless describes the life of an immature believer who lives for himself and not for the Savior (see 1 Cor. 3:1–3, 15). **He remains faithful:** Even when believers fail the Savior, He remains loyal. For Christ to abandon us would be contrary to His faithful nature (see John 10:27–30; Heb. 10:23; 13:5).

2:14, 15 What is **approved** is what remains after testing, like metals that have been refined by fire. **Rightly dividing** literally means "cutting straight." **word of truth:** Truth defines the nature of Scripture. It is a beacon of truth in the darkness of falsehood. Teachers of the Bible should handle His truth accurately. Failure to do so will lead to divine judgment (see James 3:1).

2:16–18 Paul warns Timothy about two men, **Hymenaeus and Philetus,** who taught that the Resurrection of believers had already occurred (see 1 Tim. 1:20). This was probably an early form of Gnosticism that emphasized a spiritual Resurrection over against the Christian belief in a future bodily Resurrection.

2:19 In spite of the unfaithful actions of some, the **solid foundation of God stands.** The tense of the verb indicates that Paul saw God's truth as standing not only in the past but also in the present. **The Lord knows those who are His:** This is an intimate, experiential knowledge that can only be obtained in a relationship. **depart from iniquity:** Our sure relationship with our Father in heaven should motivate us to a life of purity.

2:20, 21 The imagery of the **house** is used to describe two categories of believers. **Gold and silver** represent believers who are faithful

and useful in serving Christ. **Wood and clay** represent believers who fail to honor the Lord (see 1 Cor. 3:12–15). **Master** is a strong term for God's authority over the lives of believers regardless of their level of spiritual maturity. We choose to serve the Lord in the power of the Holy Spirit in order to be useful to our Master.

2:22, 23 Flee ... pursue ... avoid: Paul describes in practical terms how Timothy can be a useful vessel for God's work.

2:24 Quarrel translates a military term for hand-to-hand combat. The Lord's servant must not battle with words, but instead must be **gentle** and kind to everyone.

2:25, 26 Correcting means "training" or "bringing to maturity." **Those who are in opposition** are those who place themselves in conflict with the preaching of God's truth, such as Hymenaeus and Philetus (v. 17). The aim of correction is **repentance,** or a "change of thinking." Paul exhorts Timothy to persevere in correcting his opponents because it is imperative that they should **know the truth,** even though they might oppose the truth at present with their false teachings about the Resurrection (see v. 18). It was Paul's hope that they would finally **come to their senses.**

3:1 The exhortations of ch. 2 to endure hardship, be diligent, rightly divide the Word, and be a vessel fit for the Master's use are given in the context of difficult, even **perilous times.** The phrase **Last days** includes the whole time from the writing of this letter until the return of Christ.

3:2–5 A form of godliness is an outward appearance of reverence for God. **Denying its power** describes religious activity that is not connected to a living relationship with Jesus Christ. As time progresses, people would begin to participate in empty religious activities. Their activities have nothing to do with a true relationship with God or with individual faith in Jesus Christ. This kind of religion provokes God's anger (see Is. 1:10–18; Matt. 23:25–28).

3:6 creep into households: The empty religious individuals of vv. 2–5 use deception to gain a hearing. **Make captives** is a military term for taking prisoners in war. The imagery of spiritual combat is clear in these verses. **Gullible women** are the target of attacks by false teachers. Evidently the false teachers at Ephesus had made significant inroads among a group of women in that church (1 Tim. 5:13–15).

3:7, 8 Paul gives a specific example of two men who resisted truth in Moses' time. **Jannes and Jambres** are not named in the Old Testament, but according to Jewish tradition, they were two of the Egyptian magicians who opposed Moses (Ex. 7:11). Men of **corrupt minds** resist the truth because it unveils their shameful thinking and behavior.

3:9 their folly will be manifest: The character and empty religion of false teachers will ultimately be exposed (see Num. 32:23).

3:10, 11 you have carefully followed: Paul draws a sharp contrast between a Christian testimony and the way of the false teachers (vv. 2–9). He notes ten different qualities of his own teaching and life that Timothy had observed.

3:12 Those who want to live godly lives must be prepared for **persecution,** literally "to be hunted." God does not promise us deliverance *from* persecution but deliverance *through* it. Persecution is one of the means God uses to develop our capacity to reign with Him in His kingdom (see 2:12; Matt. 5:10–12; Rev. 2:10).

3:13 The Greek word translated **impostors** can also mean sorcerers or swindlers. **deceiving and being deceived:** False teachers deceive themselves as well as others (see Matt. 15:18–20).

3:14, 15 from childhood: Paul emphasizes Timothy's godly heritage (1:5). His mother Eunice and his grandmother Lois had taught him the **Holy Scriptures.** The truths of God's Word directed Timothy to Christ. God's Word and the Spirit of God are both essential for our salvation. The Word of God without the Spirit of God is lifeless. But the Word of God empowered by the Spirit of God becomes a living force in our lives.

3:16 Paul emphasizes the preeminence of **all Scripture. Given by inspiration** is literally "God-breathed." God was involved in the revelation of His truth to the apostles and prophets, who wrote it down. The Author of the Bible is God Himself. Thus Scripture is true in all that it affirms and is authoritative (see 1 Pet. 1:20, 21). The study of the Bible is profitable in at least four different ways. **Doctrine** is teaching. Paul highlights correct teaching first. **Reproof** is conviction. This is not simply a rebuke; it is demonstrating truth beyond dispute. **Correction** refers to setting something straight (2:15). **Instruction** refers to the process of training a child. In this list, only one of these terms is oriented to knowledge and information—*doctrine* (see 1 Pet. 2:2). The other three in the list involve a change of life. Knowledge that does not change a person's life is useless. On the other hand, living without any understanding of who God is and what He expects of us is dangerous.

3:17 The study of Scripture will make a believer **complete,** meaning "capable" or "proficient." **Thoroughly equipped** means "fully prepared." The person who masters the Word of God will never lose his or her way. **every good work:** Paul emphasizes the essential link between knowing God's Word and applying it to our daily lives. Right doctrine should produce right practice.

4:1, 2 I charge: Paul underscores the importance of his command to Timothy by calling on God and Jesus to be witnesses to it. He reminds Timothy that Jesus will return in judgment. Paul's charge to Timothy is to **preach the word.** The foundation of any ministry is God's Word. Preaching God's truth is a sacred and demanding task, requiring perseverance and courage. **Be ready:** Timothy was to be alert at all times to his responsibilities. **long-suffering ... teaching.** Patience and instruction are two essential components of an effective ministry. True spiritual growth occurs over a period of time, through consistent teaching and application of God's Word.

4:3 Timothy needed to be alert and ready to preach God's Word. **Sound** teaching is essential for spiritual maturity. There will come a time when people will seek out teachers to tell them what they want to hear.

4:4 People **turn their ears** to avoid **truth.** This is the sixth time that Paul uses the word *truth* in this short letter (see also 2:15, 18, 25; 3:7, 8). As Paul faced execution, he was concerned that his son in the faith would be tempted to depart from truth, lured by deceptive false teachers.

4:5 Watchful means "sober." **Endure afflictions** refers to the hard toil of ministry, which will have its own reward (2:12). **work of an evangelist:** *Evangelist* is one of five offices mentioned by Paul in Eph. 4:11. An evangelist equips and encourages believers to share the Good News.

4:6 Paul is aware that the time of his death is near. A **drink offering** was an offering performed by pouring wine out on the ground or altar (Num. 28:11–31). Paul's life was already being poured out in service to Jesus Christ, the Lamb (Rev. 5:4–6). **my departure is at hand:** Paul was confident that no one could touch him until the heavenly Father ushered him into his eternal home with a victory celebration.

4:7 Paul had been vigilant in his service to God. Note that he did not make these comments until the end of his race, until he was about to die. He did not presume or rely on his past service. Instead he persevered, struggled, and served God until the end (see 1 Cor. 9:24–27).

4:8 Paul understood the eternal potential of a lifetime of faithful service to Christ. Jesus would return with rewards for those who persevere over the long haul. **The crown of righteousness** is a special reward given to those who serve God faithfully (see Matt. 5:10–12). There will be as many crowns as there are runners who finish the race well. **All who have loved His appearing** are those believers in Christ who have lived in the hope of His return (see Titus 2:11–15; 1 John 2:28).

4:9 Paul is in prison and sends a heartfelt plea to Timothy, asking his young friend to **come … quickly.** Paul desired Christian fellowship and some words of encouragement from the one he had trained in the faith.

4:10 Demas, Paul's trusted coworker (see Col. 4:14, Philem. 24), had fled because he **loved this present world.** He could not endure the hardships of ministry and followed worldly pleasures and comfort.

4:11–13 Only Luke is with me: The value of a trusted friend in the midst of hard times cannot be overstated. Paul's reference to **Mark** as **useful** is a note of tender restoration. Mark's desertion of Paul in Pamphylia on his first missionary journey had led to the separation of Paul and Barnabas at the beginning of Paul's second missionary journey (see Acts 15:36–40). But later Paul and Mark were reconciled, and Mark served Paul in the ministry (Col. 4:10). Now at the end of his life, Paul expresses his appreciation for Mark's service. **to Ephesus:** Paul was sending a faithful coworker Tychicus (see Acts 20:4; Eph. 6:21; Col. 4:7) to replace Timothy at Ephesus.

4:14, 15 Timothy is warned about **Alexander.** This is possibly the person named in 1 Tim. 1:20 and Acts 19:33 who caused **harm** to Paul's ministry in Ephesus.

4:16 Paul echoes the forgiving attitude of Christ. Although many had abandoned him, he asked God not to hold them accountable for their actions.

4:17 In spite of the failure of his friends, Paul was supported by the Lord, who always strengthens and empowers. **Lion** is probably a reference to execution by lions. It is also possible that Paul is using the word as a metaphor for the spiritual conflict from which he was delivered.

4:18 Paul's expression of confidence in God builds to a crescendo of praise, ending with **Amen.**

4:19–21 Paul closes the epistle with a number of instructions about various people in his ministry. **Greet Prisca and Aquila:** Prisca is another name for Priscilla. Paul had met both Priscilla and Aquila in Corinth on his second missionary journey (Acts 18:1–3), and they had assisted in God's work in Ephesus (Acts 18:18, 19). **Onesiphorus:** This greeting indicates that Timothy was probably still at Ephesus, for Onesiphorus was from there (see 1:16–18; 1 Tim. 1:3). **Trophimus,** a member of the church of Ephesus (Acts 21:29), had traveled with Paul to Jerusalem (Acts 20:4).

4:22 The final note of this book and of Paul's ministry is **grace,** a fitting conclusion for this man of God and his faithful service to the **Lord Jesus Christ.** The fact that the pronoun **you** is plural may indicate that Paul intended this letter to be read before the congregation.

Titus

Introduction

Titus was the kind of person who knew how to get things done. Much of his work, like the apostle Paul's, was dangerous, unpopular, difficult, and tiring. Not just anyone could start and maintain a new church in a hostile world. Yet Titus rose to the challenge. The believers in Crete lacked leadership. False teachers were taking advantage of the absence of sound doctrine. The harmony and morals of the young congregation were disrupted. Paul relied on Titus to help them establish their leadership and make up their other deficits.

The first verse of this letter says it was written by the apostle Paul. He probably sent this letter to Titus some time between his two Roman imprisonments, between A.D. 62 and 65. Tradition holds that Titus was written shortly after First Timothy, around A.D. 63.

Crete is a large island, approximately 160 miles long and 35 miles wide, in the Mediterranean Sea. The island is located 100 miles southeast of Greece. The Cretans developed a prosperous agriculture and trading economy. Paul may have planted a church on the island of Crete during a missionary trip after his first imprisonment in Rome, which ended about A.D. 62. Paul left Titus behind to "set in order the things that [were] lacking" in the church (1:5).

Titus is mentioned numerous times in the New Testament as one of Paul's most trusted assistants. He was a Greek and was converted by Paul (see Gal. 2:3). He assisted the apostle on some of his missionary journeys (see 2 Cor. 7:6, 7; 8:6, 16) and went with him to the Jerusalem council (see Acts 15:2; Gal. 2:1–3). Paul mentioned Titus several times in Second Corinthians (see 2 Cor. 2:13; 7:6, 13, 14; 8:6, 16, 23; 12:18). Titus carried the letter to Corinth. While at Corinth, Titus was entrusted with collecting funds from the Corinthian church. Later Titus went to Dalmatia at Paul's request (see 2 Tim. 4:10). Early church tradition says that Titus returned to Crete and spent the remainder of his life there.

Although Titus contains only forty-six verses, it covers a wide range of topics. It is a key New Testament book for church organization, with its guidelines for elders, pastors, and other believers. A church needs organization, sound doctrine, and good teaching to survive. In this letter, Paul gives Titus a succinct overview on how to lead a church.

1:1 Paul introduces the theme of the book, good works, in the first verse with the term **godliness.** *Good works* or *works* appears eight times in this epistle (twice in v. 16; 2:7, 14; 3:1, 5, 8, 14). At least two other phrases parallel the good works theme: "reverent in behavior" (2:3) and "adorn the doctrine of God" (2:10).

1:2 cannot lie: This phrase translates a single Greek word meaning "truthful," or "free from all deceit." The salvation that God has promised to each of us who knows His Son will be fulfilled; God is faithful to His promises.

1:3 The Greek word translated **preaching** was the word for the message proclaimed by a public herald. Paul places emphasis on the message, not the messenger. Christians should always focus on Christ, since He is the center of our faith—not any one preacher (see 1 Cor. 9:16; 2 Cor. 4:5). The power is in the truth of what is preached, the good news that Christ has saved us from our sins (see Rom. 1:15, 16; 1 Cor. 2:4). **committed to me:** A king's commission is a definite, official act, giving a person a task and authority to carry it out. Paul's commission was as God's "imperial secretary," carrying the royal message of salvation.

1:4, 5 Lacking indicates an unfinished organization of the churches in Crete because of the brevity of Paul's visit. Paul identifies three specific areas of shortcoming: (1) a lack of organization in the churches (vv. 5–9); (2) unchallenged false teachers (vv. 10, 11; 3:10, 11); (3) a need for teaching in doctrine and practical living (2:1–10; 3:1, 2). Titus was left behind to **set in order** these deficiencies. Titus's first step toward completing his task was to **appoint elders in every city** (see Acts 14:23). Apparently the early church had several leaders in a particular church instead of one principal leader. The Greek words for *elder* and *bishop* (literally, overseer) seem to have been used interchangeably by Paul (see v. 7). *Elder* perhaps speaks more of the office and its authority, while *bishop* may speak more of the person's function and the ministry of oversight (see Acts 20:17).

1:6 Blameless means to have nothing in one's conduct on which someone could base an accusation (see 1 Tim. 3:2). Such is to be the overall characteristic of an elder. Yet Paul further defines this blamelessness with sixteen qualities. These qualities are in three areas: family life (v. 6), personal life (vv. 7, 8), and doctrinal beliefs (v. 9). The contrast between the blameless behavior of church elders and the base behavior of the false teachers should have been evident to everyone (vv. 10–16). **husband of one wife:** This phrase is found only in the Pastoral Epistles (see 1 Tim. 3:2, 12; 5:9). Its exact meaning is debated. The apostle might be barring a polygamist, a divorced or remarried man, or a man known to be unfaithful to his wife. Whatever the exact meaning of this phrase, it is clear that Paul was emphasizing (see Matt. 19:5) the importance of marital faithfulness. **faithful children:** Not only should the man have a good relationship

with his wife; he should also have children who demonstrate faithfulness to God. If a man has children who reject the ways of God, this reflects on the father's ability to lead others outside his home.

1:7–9 Elders were not to be **self-willed,** but **self-controlled.** If they were self-seeking, like the false teachers on Crete (vv. 10–16), they would not have the character required to promote good works and sound doctrine among the believers. **Convict** means to rebuke in such a way as to produce repentance and confession of sin (see John 16:8).

1:10, 11 many insubordinate: Paul describes the characteristics of the false teachers whose teaching was contrary to the truth and was undermining the authority of church leaders. **those of the circumcision:** Apparently there were Jewish Christians in the churches of Crete who were limiting the Christian freedom of Gentile Christians by requiring an adherence to Jewish laws (see Gal. 3).

1:12 Cretans are always liars, evil beasts, lazy gluttons: Paul is quoting the Cretan poet Epimenides, who wrote these words around 600 B.C. The Cretans were so much regarded as liars in the Mediterranean world

---

IN DEPTH   Personal Training

I n a world where education seems to be offered everywhere, the biblical description of the church as God's training center for holy living is often overlooked (2:1–15). This error becomes obvious when a church lacks leaders. Effective leadership in a church is the result of proper training. When young believers have not been trained, the church begins to flounder.

Paul was one of the most effective leaders of the early church. He preached the gospel tirelessly, founded a succession of churches throughout Asia Minor and Greece, and grounded these churches in God's Word and the essentials of the Christian faith. But to be truly effective, Paul had to nurture others to follow in his footsteps and faithfully lead the church into the next century. Titus was one of the young men Paul was training for leadership. He had accompanied Paul early in his ministry (Gal. 2:1–3), had served as Paul's representative (2 Cor. 7:5–16), and was considered a "fellow worker" (2 Cor. 8:23). When Paul wrote this letter, he had begun to pass the reins of leadership to this capable young man who was overseeing the churches on the island of Crete.

In his instructions to Titus, Paul reminds him of the traits of a spiritual leader (1:5–16). Paul had chosen Titus as a helper because he had evidenced these qualities. Now he had to model such traits to others, searching for those who could become leaders in the newly planted churches.

that the expression "to Cretanize" meant to lie. Paul was contrasting the Cretans' reputation with God's. The Lord was incapable of lying (see v. 2).

1:13, 14 These **Jewish fables** were probably legends about Old Testament figures, like some that survive to this day in nonbiblical writings. This speculation was not only opposed to the **truth,** but it also undermined the faith (v. 13). **commandments of men:** The rules that come from false doctrine are contrasted with the good works (v. 16) that should proceed from sound doctrine.

1:15, 16 Paul highlights the mistaken asceticism of the Cretan false teachers. They had identified certain foods and practices as defiled when in reality it was their minds that were **defiled and unbelieving.** Because the Cretan believers had placed their trust in Christ, focusing their minds on Him, they would be empowered by God's Spirit to lead **pure** lives. Physical objects or external practices do not defile a person, but a mind focused on evil thoroughly corrupts. We should be more concerned about renewing our mind and focusing it on Jesus than observing a list of rules that have no biblical support.

2:1 Paul normally follows a rebuke of false doctrine with an admonition of how the believer should act (see 2 Tim. 3:10, 14). **Sound** means "healthy." Paul makes frequent use of the term in the Pastoral Epistles. He uses it five times in Titus (see also 1:9, 13; 2:2, 8). Paul views sound doctrine as the root that produces the fruit of sound practice (good works), such as faith, love, and patience (v. 2), as well as sound speech (v. 8). Right thinking is the raw material for right actions (see Ps. 119:11; Prov. 23:7; Rom. 12:2; James 1:13–15).

2:2 Older men refers to men older than about 50. The same is true of older women (see v. 3). The character of those who are mature should serve as a spiritual example to everyone. Maturity is not determined by age or even by how much a person knows; it is determined by how skilled a person is in applying the truth to life and in distinguishing good from evil (see Heb. 5:13, 14).

2:3 In keeping with the theme of good works (vv. 1, 2), **older women** are not to engage in

evil practices like slander, gossip, or drunkenness; instead, they are to teach younger women (v. 4).

2:4 The word **admonish** means "to give encouragement through advice." Older women are to pass on their insights to their younger counterparts. **love their husbands:** Paul speaks not of romantic love, but of the commitment of a woman to her husband's welfare.

2:5 homemakers: The importance that Paul places on the role of women in the home may also be seen in 1 Tim. 5:2–16 (see also Prov. 31). **obedient to their own husbands:** Women are not under the authority of men in general but the authority of their husbands. The Greek word translated *obedient* is a military term which indicates voluntary submission to one in authority (see Eph. 5:21). **that the word of God may not be blasphemed:** Paul wanted the older women to teach the younger women so their actions would glorify God, build His kingdom, and strengthen the family. Failure to follow Paul's instructions would result in the word of God being maligned in the pagan community.

2:6 Young men are to pursue the character qualities that older men should have already.

2:7, 8 a pattern of good works: Paul concludes his instructions to various age groups by reminding Titus that his personal life is an essential aspect of his teaching. More people will learn from our daily actions than from what we say. Therefore we must bring our lives in line with our beliefs.

2:9, 10 bondservants: Good works from a Christian slave would make **the doctrine of God** very attractive to a non-Christian master. Believing the teachings of Scripture is proper and good, but living those truths will influence nonbelievers.

2:11 appeared: Twice in this context Paul speaks of Christ's appearance in history. The first time Christ came in **grace** to save people from their sins; the second time He will come in glory (v. 13) to reign.

2:12, 13 The grace of God is to produce two results in the lives of believers. First, we are to resist the evil temptations of this world, living godly lives in this present age. Second, we are to look for Christ's return. Paul reminded Timothy that there is a special crown awaiting "all who have loved his appearing" (see 2 Tim. 4:8).

2:14 Redeem means "to purchase." With His death on the Cross, Christ paid the price to release us from the bondage of sin (see Eph. 1:7). God's purpose in redeeming us is not only to save us from hell; He also wants to free us from sin so we can produce good works that glorify Him (see Eph. 2:8–10).

2:15 rebuke: For the third time in this letter (see also 1:11, 13), Paul strongly commands Titus to confront false teachers.

3:1, 2 Remind: Paul had already instructed the Cretans about submission and obedience to the authorities in their communities. Titus was to remind them of their duty to be good citizens, a virtue which the Cretans lacked (see 1:12). **rulers and authorities:** This phrase often refers to the angelic realm, including both good (see Eph. 3:10) and evil angels (see Eph. 6:12). Here it refers to civil leaders and institutions. Disobedience permeated the Cretans' lifestyle, both in the church (v. 10) and in government. Titus must advise them to get along with civil authorities and to live peacefully with their neighbors. This type of life would reflect positively on the Christian faith and thus glorify God.

3:3 Paul provides another motive for good works by explaining the rationale for the Christian life. The believers were supposed to treat others the way God in His grace had treated them when they were involved in the ungodly activities noted in this verse (see Rom. 5:8).

3:4, 5 not by works of righteousness: Since Paul has been exhorting Titus to emphasize good works in his ministry with the Cretans, he wants to make it clear that such works have no value in saving a person. Rather, it is solely on the basis of God's **mercy** that we are delivered from the penalty of our sin. **washing of regeneration:** This phrase refers to the work of the Holy Spirit, who makes a person new by the cleansing of regeneration (the new birth). This new nature is the ground for living the Christian life and performing good deeds. **renewing of the Holy Spirit:** The continual

process of Christian living is enabled by the Holy Spirit, resulting in growth in character and good works.

3:6, 7 we should become heirs: God justifies believers so they might become co-heirs with Jesus Christ in His coming reign (see Rom. 8:17; 2 Tim. 2:12).

3:8 This is a faithful saying: Paul is emphasizing that what he has written (vv. 4–8) is a trustworthy statement, one that is central to the Christian faith. It is significant that this faithful saying in Titus includes an admonition to **maintain good works**—the theme of the letter.

3:9–11 Paul admonished Titus to avoid anything that would promote wickedness among the believers. **Reject a divisive man:** Titus was to cut off the church's relationship with any person who would not submit to correction after two warnings (see 2 Thess. 3:14, 15). The Greek word for **warped** suggests that Satan is perverting this person. **Sinning** indicates that the man will not change his ways and thus continues to rebel against God.

3:12, 13 Tychicus, one of Paul's assistants, is also mentioned in Acts 20:4; Eph. 6:21; Col. 4:7; 2 Tim. 4:12. The city of **Nicopolis** was on the Adriatic coast of Greece. **Apollos** was a fellow worker of Paul's (see Acts 18:24; 19:1; 1 Cor. 1:12; 3:4–6, 22; 4:6; 16:12), an Alexandrian who had been taught by Priscilla and Aquila and had eloquently preached the gospel at Ephesus and Corinth (see Acts 18:24—19:1).

3:14, 15 to meet urgent needs: Paul gives the Cretans a practical way they can start demonstrating their faith in good works: they can begin meeting the needs of other people. **that they may not be unfruitful:** A recurring theme throughout the New Testament is that believers should live up to their holy calling. They should continue being sanctified (see Heb. 10:14, 23–26). Justification is solely a gift from God, but we will be rewarded according to what we do on this earth (see Rev. 22:12). We should abound in good works which the Holy Spirit has empowered us to do (see Phil. 4:17).

Philemon

Introduction

The Epistle to Philemon is Paul's plea that a runaway slave named Onesimus should no longer be viewed as a slave, but as a "beloved brother" (see vv. 16, 17; Col. 4:9). Obedience to these requests would require forgiveness and restoration, which were not required of slave owners in the ancient world. But Christians were called to a higher calling, one that contradicted the expectations of the culture.

Three times in this book (vv. 1, 9, 19) Paul identifies himself as its author. The vocabulary and style are clearly his, for many of the phrases in this letter are found in Paul's other letters (compare v. 4 with Phil. 1:3, 4). Also, many of those who sent their greetings with this letter are the same ones who did so in the letter to the Colossians. This fact indicates the close relationship between the two letters (see Col. 4:12–15).

Paul was a prisoner when he wrote this epistle. Most believe that he wrote this letter during his first Roman imprisonment around A.D. 60, along with the other Prison Epistles: Ephesians, Philippians, and Colossians.

The greeting and the content of the letter indicate that Philemon is the intended recipient. Philemon was a slave owner whose home served as the meeting place for a local church. Philemon probably lived in Colosse, a city in the Roman province of Asia Minor. He was a convert to Christianity as a result of Paul's ministry, possibly during the apostle's stay in Ephesus (see Acts 19:26).

Philemon owned a slave named Onesimus, who had run away and had apparently stolen something from his master. After fleeing to Rome, Onesimus came into contact with Paul, became a Christian, and remained with the apostle for some time, serving him in prison. However, restoration and restitution needed to be made. It was agreed that Onesimus would return to Philemon, even though this could result in his death. Paul wrote a letter to his friend Philemon, pleading the cause of Onesimus.

1 Paul identifies himself not as an apostle, but as **a prisoner,** because of his surrender to the cause of Christ and the fact that he was writing from prison in Rome (vv. 9, 10, 13, 23). **Timothy** was with Paul in Rome (see Col. 1:1) and in Ephesus. Philemon is called **beloved.** Paul's plea (vv. 9, 10) will be built on the concept of love. **Fellow laborer** indicates someone who is united with Paul in the work of Christ.

2, 3 Apphia may have been the wife of Philemon. **Archippus** may have been the son of Philemon or perhaps an elder of the Colossian church (see Col. 4:17). **fellow soldier:** This term implies more than *fellow laborer* (v. 1). It is used only one other time in the New Testament, when Paul speaks of Epaphroditus (see Phil. 2:25). **in your house:** The church was meeting in Philemon's house. Philemon may have been an active leader in the church.

4, 5 in my prayers: Philemon's Christian life was a continual cause for thanksgiving whenever Paul prayed. **love and faith … toward the Lord Jesus and toward all the saints:** This may be an example of the literary device called a chiasmus, where parallel phrases are connected in reverse order. Thus the word *faith* refers to Christ, and the word *love* refers to the saints. *Saints* speaks of all believers. True love is expressed in action and not just in words (see 1 Cor. 13:1–7).

6 Paul prays that Philemon's **faith** will be **effective**—a term that speaks of being in good working order. Working faith is a sharing faith; it is the **acknowledgment** of what Christ has done in the believer's life (see Eph. 3:17–19). That kind of faith will result in sharing possessions with other believers (see vv. 17, 18).

7 Rather than just being happy because of Philemon's love, the apostle remarkably stated that he had **joy,** even when he was in chains (see v. 1). A Christian's joy in trying circumstances is a testimony to God's peace. **Consolation** may also be translated "encouragement." Philemon's **love** brought joy and encouragement to Paul. **Hearts** refers to the inner emotional nature of a person (vv. 12, 20). Paul had heard that the hearts of the saints were also being **refreshed** by Philemon's love (see Matt. 11:28; 1 Cor. 16:18).

8 Therefore: In light of the foundation that has been laid (vv. 4–7), Paul is ready to make his plea. **very bold:** This phrase speaks of "free and open speaking" (see 2 Cor. 3:12; Eph. 6:19). Paul's apostolic authority and Philemon's spiritual condition made Paul confident that he could **command** Philemon to do what is proper (see Col. 3:18).

9 Rather than commanding Philemon (v. 8), Paul preferred to **appeal** to Philemon on the basis of love. **Paul, the aged:** The apostle is speaking either of the office of elder or of his old age.

10 My son is the Greek word for "child." The imagery of a father and child is used at other times by Paul when speaking of his converts (see 1 Tim. 1:2; Titus 1:4). **begotten:** The apostle was personally responsible for bringing **Onesimus** to Christ (see 1 Cor. 4:15; Gal. 4:19).

11 Paul uses an interesting play on words here. Having just mentioned Onesimus, whose name means "Useful" (v. 10), the apostle describes him as someone who was formerly **unprofitable** (unuseful) but is now **profitable**. Paul is saying that Onesimus had become good and useful, even more so than Philemon could have imagined.

12 I am sending him back: Paul is referring the case back to Philemon for a decision. He encourages Philemon not to view Onesimus as a runaway slave. In fact, Onesimus had become a part of Paul's **own heart** (vv. 7, 20).

13 wished: Paul wanted to keep Onesimus in Rome, helping in the ministry, confident that Philemon would approve. Onesimus had been serving Paul in place of Philemon, giving Paul the aid Philemon could not.

14 Paul expressed his desire to have Philemon involved in the decision of whether Onesimus could remain with him. Therefore, he would act only with Philemon's **consent.** Philemon's **good deed** had to be **voluntary.** Service for Christ is never forced. Paul had given Philemon several good reasons to forgive Onesimus, but here he returns to the foundation of his argument: Philemon's actions had to proceed from his own love (v. 9).

15 departed for a while: It was God's plan that Onesimus would run away. **receive him forever:** Paul contrasts the temporary separation because of Onesimus's running away to the eternal benefit of his salvation.

16 no longer as a slave but ... a beloved brother: Paul contrasts the lowly position of a slave to the high privilege of a Christian brother. **in the flesh and in the Lord:** Not only will Onesimus be useful on the human level; he will be useful for the work of the Lord.

17, 18 partner ... owes: Onesimus had probably stolen something from Philemon when he left. Furthermore, he owed Philemon for the time he was gone. Paul uses business imagery in offering to pay for any loss Philemon suffered because of Onesimus's actions. *Partner* is a form of the Greek word for *fellowship.* Philemon was to receive Onesimus as he would his partner in Christ—Paul. **put that on my account:** This accounting imagery reminds us of the theological truth that our sins were charged over to Christ even though He had not earned them.

19 my own hand: Paul wrote this note himself because it was a personal note, but also because the letter could be considered a legal document obligating him to pay the damages Onesimus had caused. **I will repay:** Paul promises to pay Onesimus's debt to assure the runaway slave's gracious reception by his owner. **you owe me:** The mention of Philemon's spiritual debt to Paul is not an attempt to cancel his own promise to pay; Paul chooses not to appeal to Philemon on the basis of this obligation.

20 The word translated **joy** in this verse is different from the one used in v. 7. The term here may also mean "benefit." Philemon's restoration of Onesimus would benefit Paul. **refresh:** What Philemon had done for other believers (v. 7), he could do for Paul by his kind treatment of Onesimus.

21 obedience: Paul is expecting Philemon to be compassionate to his former slave Onesimus (vv. 5, 7, 9).

22 prepare a guest room: Hospitality is a Christian virtue (see Rom. 12:13; 1 Tim. 3:2). Paul's mention of a possible visit adds weight to his request of Philemon. The term translated **granted** here is related to the Greek word for *grace.* Paul expects to be released from prison (see Phil. 2:24).

23–25 These five coworkers are also mentioned in Col. 4:10–14.

Hebrews

Introduction

At first Christianity was Jewish. Jesus was a Jew, His disciples were Jews, and the first converts were Jews. Their first meetings took place in synagogues, and their first controversies were over adherence to Jewish laws. Christianity's first critics knew it as a Jewish sect. But for the first Jewish believers, believing in Christ raised many questions. What about the temple and animal sacrifices? What about the Law of Moses? Was it really enough to trust in Christ? The Book of Hebrews was written to answer questions such as these.

No one in the early church could say with certainty that they knew who wrote Hebrews. Yet Hebrews has been accorded one of the most respected places in the New Testament by its merit, not by the esteem of its author. No one knows exactly when Hebrews was written either, although guessing a date is easier than guessing the author. If it was written to the Jewish believers at Rome, as is commonly assumed, then the fact that the community had not yet been called upon to suffer death for their faith suggests that the epistle should be dated before Nero's persecution of Christians in A.D. 64.

Most scholars believe the original audience for Hebrews was Jewish Christians because of the book's heavy emphasis on Jewish topics and themes, especially the detailed discussion of the superiority of Jesus Christ over angels, Moses, Joshua, and Old Testament believers. Quotes of Old Testament passages appear throughout the book. Many of the author's themes assume an in-depth knowledge of Old Testament priesthood and sacrifice. Jews living outside of Jerusalem would almost certainly have been Greek-speaking, explaining the use of the Septuagint. The recipients are addressed as "brethren" throughout, and in the early church this would have included a large number of Jews.

The Book of Hebrews was written to address the doubts of those who were second-guessing their conversion to Christianity. "You began with God's plan of salvation," it says in effect. "You believed in His word and followed His plan of salvation through the temple sacrifices. And then when His once-for-all final sacrifice was made in Jesus Christ, you believed. That was as it should be. That was God's plan. Do not go back on the steps you have taken!" This book establishes the supremacy and sufficiency of Christ (1:1–4; 9:11–14). His sacrifice was enough to take away our sin; He is all we need to come to God today.

1:1 Various times refers to the periods of Old Testament history. **Various ways** refers to the different methods God used to communicate, including visitations, dreams, signs, parables, and events (see Is. 28:10).

1:2, 3 By His Son may be rephrased as "in such a person as a Son." It is a revelation of the Son, a revelation not so much in what He has said as in who He is and what He has done. **heir of all things:** Jesus will inherit everything because He is the eternal Son of God (see Is. 9:6, 7; Mic. 5:2). He will rule over everyone and everything (see Rom. 4:13; Rev. 11:15). **made the worlds:** He has managed the universe throughout its history as Mediator under the Father. The Son is **the brightness of** God's **glory,** meaning the radiance that comes from God's essential glory (see John 1:14; 2 Cor. 4:4, 6). Jesus' glorious brightness comes from being essentially divine. The phrase **express image** occurs only here in the New Testament and means "exact representation" or "exact character." The Son is the exact representation of God's being because He is God Himself (see Col. 1:15). **Upholding** means "bearing" or "carrying." The Son not only created the universe by His powerful word but also maintains and directs its course. **Purged** means "cleansed" or "purified." The Son of God came down not to dazzle us with His splendor but to purge our sins. **Sat down** suggests the formal act of assuming the office of High Priest and implies a contrast to the Levitical priest, who never finished his work and sat down (10:11–13).

1:4, 5 The Son is **better than the angels,** or higher in rank, because He sits at the right hand of God (v. 3) and because of His eternal inheritance. The Son has obtained a greater name than the angels. Angels are "sons" collectively, in that they were created by God (see Job 1:6). In contrast, Christ is uniquely and eternally the **Son.** He is superior to the angels. **Today I have begotten You** probably refers to the day Christ sat down at the Father's right hand after He accomplished His work as the Messiah. On that day the eternal Son entered into the full experience of His Sonship.

1:6, 7 When He again brings is a reference to the Second Coming. **Firstborn** refers to rank, meaning one who ranks above all others (see Ps. 89:27). The angels will **worship** the Son when He is enthroned as the King over the entire earth (2:5–9), after taking revenge on His enemies and restoring His people. The Son is superior to angels because He is the Sovereign who is worshiped, while the angels are **ministers,** or servants of God. The author of Hebrews quotes Ps. 104 because that psalm places angels in a long list of created objects which God controls.

1:8 O God: Jesus Christ is accorded the rank of full deity. The Son has an eternal **throne,** which means He possesses an eternal kingdom.

1:9–12 Companions comes from a word that means "close associates" or "partners." The concept of believers being companions with Christ in His reign is key in Hebrews (3:1, 14; 6:4; 12:8). The context of Ps. 102, from which these verses are taken, clearly indicates that the **LORD** is the One who would appear in the future to Israel and the nations (see Ps. 102:12–16). Thus the psalm can only refer to Jesus, the Second Person of the Trinity, the only One who would become incarnate. Jesus is God become man. The universe will **perish** (see 2 Pet. 3:10–13; Rev. 21:1), but the Son will **remain** forever.

1:13, 14 Christ sits at the **right hand** of God until the final victory over all His **enemies** (see 1 Cor. 15:25–28). Angels are mere servants (v. 7) who serve **those who will inherit salvation.** *Salvation* here is not justification because it is in the future, not in the past. The reference is to believers who inherit the kingdom or rule in God's kingdom as a reward for their service to the Son (see 9:28; Col. 3:24). The author is speaking about "the world to come" (2:5).

2:1 The author issues the first of five exhortations (see vv. 1–4; 3:1—4:16; 5:11—6:20;

10:19–39; 12:1–29). Believers **have heard** from the Lord God because we have heard the gospel message. His majesty demands that we listen to what He says. **drift away:** The author's audience was marked by immaturity and spiritual sluggishness (5:11, 12). The author warned them not to be carried away by the popular opinions that surrounded them. Instead they were hold fast to Christ's words because they were the words of God.

2:2 the word spoken through angels: The Law was delivered from God to Moses by angels (see Deut. 33:2; Acts 7:38, 53; Gal. 3:19).

2:3 how shall we escape: If the people who heard the message delivered through angels were justly punished when they disobeyed the Law, how can believers expect to escape punishment when they neglect the even greater message delivered through the greater Messenger, the Son? The **great salvation** (see Phil. 2:12, 13) cannot be a reference only to justification because this salvation was **first ... spoken by the Lord.** Justification was spoken of in the Old Testament (see Gen. 15:6); but it was the Lord who first spoke of His followers inheriting His kingdom and reigning with Him (see v. 10; Luke 12:31, 32; 22:29, 30).

2:4, 5 Signs and wonders refers to the miracles performed by the **Holy Spirit** through the Lord and His apostles in fulfillment of the ancient promises about the coming of the Messiah (see Acts 2:22, 43; 4:30; 5:12; 6:8; 14:3; 15:12; 2 Cor. 12:12). The author returns to the theme of ch. 1 that the Son is superior to the angels. **The world to come** is the future rule of the Son and His companions (1:9) on the earth.

2:6–8 But now: The rule of human beings over God's creation has been delayed because of sin (v. 15). Humanity's collusion with Satan has brought all people into collision with God. **Not yet** indicates that the delay is only temporary.

2:9, 10 Human beings will rule over creation, but it will be through Jesus Christ. **But we see Jesus:** The author uses Christ's human name *Jesus* for the first time in this letter. Citing phrases from Ps. 8, the author points out that Christ, by His humiliation and exaltation, has regained what Adam lost—the original calling for human beings to rule over God's creation (see Phil. 2:6–11; Rev. 5:1–14). The Greek word for **captain** means "leader" or "originator." The word describes a pioneer or pathfinder. Jesus' endurance of **sufferings** on this earth makes Him our leader. He has already experienced the sufferings we must go through. He not only endured them but triumphed over sin, death, and Satan through them. Jesus is our model, our leader, and our Captain. He understands our pain because He Himself went through suffering.

2:11–13 all of one: This phrase refers either to the common humanity that Jesus shares with all believers, or to the fact that Jesus and believers all belong to God. Because the children of God and the Son Himself are from the same Father (see John 20:17), Jesus can call all believers His **brethren.** Psalm 22, which is quoted here, describes the agony of a righteous sufferer. Ultimately the psalm is messianic. It depicts the sufferings of Christ. Jesus quoted Ps. 22:1 on the Cross (see Matt. 27:46). In this psalm, the Messiah refers to **My brethren,** identifying Himself with all those who place their faith in God. The citations are from Is. 8:17, 18 and refer to a prophet, who, like the Lord Jesus, was persecuted and rejected but became a rallying point for the faithful.

2:14, 15 shared the same: Jesus Christ shared in our humanity by humbling himself to become a man (see Phil. 2:5–11). **power of death:** The devil tempts people to sin and then accuses them of rebelling against God (see Gen. 3; Job 1). By inducing them to sin, Satan delivers people over to death, the due penalty for their sin (Rom. 5:12). The devil is still active today (see 1 Pet. 5:8), but his power over death has been taken away from him. Christ's death fulfilled the penalty for sin. The devil uses the **fear of death** to enslave us. Through His death (v. 14), the Son eliminated such fear and broke the **bondage** of sin and death.

2:16 The seed of Abraham refers either to the physical descendants of Abraham or the spiritual children of Abraham—the ones who, like Abraham, have placed their faith in God (see Gal. 3:7, 29). The author may have used this expression because the recipients

of this letter were primarily Jewish believers.

2:17 In all things includes Jesus' humanity (v. 14) and His suffering (v. 18). Jesus participated in our nature and in our sufferings on earth so He could be a sympathetic Mediator between God and humanity. He understands our weaknesses and intercedes for us in the presence of God the Father. He is a **merciful** (sympathetic) and **faithful** (trustworthy) **High Priest.** This is the first time the title High Priest occurs in Hebrews, and the first time the title is applied to Jesus Christ in the Bible. **Make propitiation** refers to the satisfaction of the claims of a holy and righteous God against sinners who have broken His law. Christ appeased God's righteous wrath by dying on the Cross in our place (see Rom. 3:21–26). The benefits of His sacrifice are applied to all who place their faith in Him.

2:18 being tempted: Christ's suffering included temptation. He experienced the lure of sin, but He never surrendered to it. He knows what it is like to be tempted, so He knows how to assist those who are being tempted.

3:1, 2 Partakers is the same Greek word that is translated *companions* in 1:9. The **heavenly calling** of these *companions* is to inherit salvation (1:14) and their future glory in Christ (2:10). The author of Hebrews invites Jewish believers to **consider** the faithfulness of Christ Jesus. **Apostle** means "one who is sent." This is the only passage in the New Testament that labels Jesus as the Apostle. The title indicates that Jesus was "sent" by God to reveal the Father (see John 4:34; 6:38; 7:28, 29; 8:16). The phrase **in all His house** is taken from Num. 12:7. *House* refers to the tabernacle, the center of Israelite worship. Moses had faithfully obeyed God's instructions about the tabernacle. In the same way, Jesus had been obedient to the mission the Father had given Him. Through His obedience, God established a new house of God, the church.

3:3–5 He who built all things is God: The author of Hebrews equates Jesus with God. Thus Jesus is certainly **worthy of more glory than Moses** (1:2, 8, 10). The implication is that the covenant established through Jesus' death is more glorious than the covenant established at Mount Sinai. The author of Hebrews continues the comparison between Moses and Jesus.

While Moses was faithful **as a servant,** Christ's faithfulness was greater because it was performed by **a Son.** The phrase **Things ... spoken afterward** indicates that Moses' work pointed forward to Christ (9:10; 10:1–3). The regulations of the Law of Moses pointed out both the sin of humanity and the need for a perfect sacrifice to reconcile people to their holy Creator.

3:6–11 a Son over His own house: The Son will sit on the throne in the coming kingdom (1:8). He presently rules over the church and will rule over all creation when His opponents are completely defeated. His house consists of all those who believe in Him. **hold fast the confidence ... to the end:** Those who endure to the end, steadfastly placing their hope in the Son, will live with Him in eternity. The author of Hebrews quotes Ps. 95:7–11 to warn the Jewish Christians about hardening their hearts to God and the salvation He offers. Moses' generation had refused to trust in God to provide for their needs in the wilderness (see Ex. 17:1–7), and the readers of this letter were in danger of not trusting in the salvation offered through God's Son. If they were to hold fast to the end (see v. 6), they could not **harden** their hearts to God now (vv. 8, 13, 15). Instead they had to renew their belief in God's Word (vv. 12, 19), place their trust in Christ, and obey Him (v. 18). **Rest** is a key concept in Hebrews. In the Old Testament, the conquest of the Promised Land and the cessation of fighting in the land was viewed as a form of rest (see Deut. 3:20; 12:9; 25:19; Josh. 11:23; 21:44; 22:4; 23:1). In the New Testament, *rest* speaks of the believer's eternal home and the joy that he or she will experience in Jesus' presence (4:1).

3:12–14 The original recipients of this letter were probably believers (as indicated by the word **brethren**) who were in danger of departing from God (v. 12) and forsaking the assembly of believers (10:25). The author advises them not to do so but to remain in the assembly, urging one another on in the faith, in love, and in good works (10:24). **Unbelief** is a stubborn refusal to trust in the truthfulness of God's word. Believers must hold their faith firmly to the end of their lives if they are to be **partakers of Christ** (vv.

15–19). *Partakers* is the same word translated *companions* in 1:9. Believers will be partners with Christ in His future kingdom (see Rev. 2:26, 27).

3:15–19 The author of Hebrews speaks of the Israelites' unbelief as sin (v. 17) and disobedience (v. 18). The Israelites did not **enter** God's **rest,** the Promised Land (v. 11), because they did not believe in God's promises (see Num. 1:1–34). They failed to possess their inheritance because they did not trust in God (see Deut. 12:9; Josh. 13:7). The Jewish Christians to whom this letter was addressed were in danger of following in their ancestors' footsteps. They were tempted to doubt the words of Jesus. The author of Hebrews was encouraging them to place their faith firmly in Christ (10:26; 12:1, 2).

4:1 The tragic unbelief of the desert generation of Israelites (3:7–19) serves as a warning for believers today to enter into God's **rest,** which is still offered to the faithful (see vv. 6–11).

4:2, 3 The gospel was preached is the translation of a single Greek word meaning "the good news was announced." The good news of God's rest (v. 1) had been proclaimed to the Israelites. The generation led by Moses had failed to enter their rest, which was the Promised Land (see Deut. 12:9), because of their lack of **faith.** In the same way, the gospel of Christ that had been proclaimed to the author's audience was calling them into God's rest, but their unbelief would hinder them from entering into it.

4:4–8 God rested: The theme of rest has its beginning in God's own rest after creation. By merely entering the Promised Land, the Israelites had not entered God's rest, for David had warned his generation to not **harden** their hearts, so they could enter God's rest (see 3:7–11). Like David, the author of Hebrews called the present generation to respond to God **today** (3:13), which is the day of repentance.

4:9 The Greek word for **rest** in this verse is different from the word used in vv. 1, 3, 5, 10, 11; 3:11, 18. This word means "Sabbath rest" and is found only here in the New Testament. Jews commonly taught that the Sabbath foreshadowed the world to come, and they spoke of "a day which shall be all Sabbath."

4:10 rest from his own work: This may refer to the rest believers will enter when they finish their work for God's kingdom on this earth (see Rev. 14:13).

4:11 us: Including himself as well as his readers, the author exhorts believers to **be diligent,** a phrase meaning "make every effort." **to enter that rest:** The rest is not automatic. Determined diligence is required.

4:12 The **word of God** is the measuring stick Christ will use at the judgment (see 2 Cor. 5:10). God's message is alive and active, penetrating the innermost parts of a person. It distinguishes what is natural and what is spiritual, as well as the **thoughts** (reflections) and **intents** (insights) of a person. The word of God exposes the natural and spiritual motivations of a believer's **heart.**

4:13 Naked and open suggests complete exposure and defenselessness before God. All believers must **give account** to God (see Rom. 14:10–12; 2 Cor. 5:10).

4:14 Then refers back to the subject of the high priesthood of Christ (2:17—3:6). In the Old Testament the high priest of Israel passed through the courts and veils into the Most Holy Place. Our High Priest has **passed through the heavens** to the presence of God, where He sits at God's right hand (1:3).

4:15 Sympathize means "to suffer with" and expresses the feeling of one who has entered into suffering. **In all points tempted** means Jesus experienced every degree of temptation (2:18).

4:16 Come is the same Greek word translated *draw near* in 10:22. This command contrasts with God's command at Mount Sinai: "Do not go up to the mountain or touch its base" (Ex. 19:12). Because of Christ's priestly work, believers can approach God's presence. **Boldly:** Believers should courageously approach God in prayer because His is a **throne of grace,** and our High Priest sits at His right hand interceding for us.

5:1 gifts and sacrifices: The primary reference here is to the work of the high priest on the Day of Atonement, the one day of the year when he entered the Most Holy Place

(9:7–10) to atone for the sins of the people and intercede for them.

5:2, 3 Ignorant and going astray describes those who unintentionally sinned among the people (see Num. 15:30–36). The high priest was required to offer a sacrifice **for himself** on the Day of Atonement (see 9:7; Lev. 16:6).

5:4 called by God: Aaron was appointed to the position of priest by God Himself (see Ex. 28:1), as were his successors (see Num. 20:23–28; 25:10–13). Those who challenged Aaron's call or appointed themselves as priests were put to death by God (see Num. 16).

5:5, 6 Christ did not call Himself to the office of **High Priest;** the Father called Him to the honor. Both Ps. 2:7 and 110:4 are cited to prove this fact. The quote from Ps. 110:4 highlights the eternal nature of Jesus' priesthood. He will be Mediator between God and us forever.

5:7, 8 He learned obedience: Jesus experienced all of what a person goes through on this earth. He knows how difficult it is to obey God completely, just as He understands the attractions of temptation (2:18). Yet He persisted in obedience, leading a sinless life (1 John 3:5).

5:9 having been perfected: This phrase does not suggest that Jesus had not been perfect before. It means that He successfully carried out God's plan for Him. He endured suffering and temptation so that He could function as our High Priest, understanding our weaknesses and interceding for us before God. **Author** means "cause" or "source." The sacrifice of this sinless One in our place makes Him the source of our **salvation.**

5:10, 11 Called means "designated" and introduces Christ's formal title, **High Priest.** Though the author of Hebrews has much more to say about Jesus' priesthood, it will be **hard to explain** to the readers of this letter because they are **dull of hearing.** When these people heard the word of God they were not quick to accept it (6:11, 12). They had grown even more lazy in the faith, so explaining the truth to them would be difficult.

5:12 First principles are basic truths (6:1, 2). The phrase refers to the letters of the alphabet in writing or to addition and subtraction tables in arithmetic. First principles are the elements out of which everything else develops.

5:13 unskilled in the word of righteousness: The readers of this letter did not lack information about righteousness; they lacked experience in practicing the information they had. Maturity comes with practice.

5:14 Full age describes the spiritually mature. **Reason of use** means "practice" or "habit." Those who make a habit of obeying the message of righteousness mature in the faith and are able to distinguish **good and evil.**

6:1–3 The author urges the readers of his letter to leave the basics and **go on to perfection,** meaning "maturity." He lists six items in three couplets that he calls **the elementary principles of Christ.** (1) **Repentance from dead works** refers to a change of mind about the demands of the Law of Moses (9:14). Even though the Law was good (see 1 Tim. 1:8), it was weak because of the weakness of our sinful nature (see Rom. 8:3). (2) What is needed for salvation is not lifeless works that cannot save, but **faith** directed **toward God.** (3) **Baptisms** refers either to the various baptisms in the New Testament (the baptism of Christ, of John, of believers, and the spiritual baptism of believers), or to the various ritual washings practiced by the Jewish people. (4) In the Book of Acts, the **laying on of hands** was used to impart the Holy Spirit (see Acts 8:17, 18; 19:6). It was also used for ordination for ministry (see Acts 6:6; 13:3). (5) **Resurrection from the dead** refers to the resurrection of all people at the end times (Rev. 20:11–15). To Christians, belief in the bodily resurrection of Jesus was essential, for without His resurrection there is no forgiveness of sin (see 1 Cor. 15:12–17). (6) **Eternal judgment** refers to the belief that everyone will be judged by the great Judge. The Scriptures indicate that there are two judgments: one for believers, in which Jesus determines every believer's reward (1 Cor. 3:12–15), and the other a judgment of condemnation on unbelievers (Rev. 20:11–15).

6:4–6 Impossible is used three other times in the Book of Hebrews. It is impossible for the blood of animals to take away sin (10:4), for God to lie (v. 18), and for anyone to please God without faith (11:6). Here it is impossible to renew those who have fallen away from the

faith (see v. 6). **Enlightened** is used in only one other place in Hebrews (the word is translated *illuminated* in 10:32). In that verse, enlightenment refers to a full knowledge of the truth. **Tasted** is used elsewhere in Hebrews of actual experience (2:9). Thus, to taste **the heavenly gift** is to experience the gift of eternal life. The phrase **if they fall away** may also be rendered "having fallen away." The fact that there is no hint of a conditional element in the Greek text argues against the "hypothetical" interpretation of this passage (see v. 4). Falling away here refers to deliberate apostasy (3:12), a defection from the faith. **To renew** means "to restore." In other words, it is impossible for continuous effort on the part of anyone in the Christian community to restore an apostate back to fellowship with God. This is the reason for the strong warning of 3:13 to exhort one another to avoid a hard heart. Continuing Christian immaturity is dangerous. **crucify again:** Departing from the faith amounts to a fresh public rejection of Christ, a crucifixion of Him all over again.

6:7–9 The author tells a short parable relating to agriculture to illustrate the spiritual truths conveyed in vv. 4–6. **Rejected** means "disqualified," and the word is used of believers being disqualified from receiving rewards (see 1 Cor. 9:27; 2 Cor. 13:5, 7). Note that the ground that produced thorns is not cursed; instead it is **near to being cursed** (see 1 Cor. 11:29–31). Its ultimate end is burning, perhaps indicating the earthly, temporal judgment of God. Perhaps this parable is an allusion to the fire which Jesus will use to reveal the quality of a believer's works (see 1 Cor. 3:11–15). With the warmth and affection of the title **beloved,** the author assures the Hebrews that he is **confident of better things** for them. Their good works were signs to the author that they had received Christ (v. 10).

6:10–12 Sluggish is the same word which is translated *dull* in 5:11 and initiates this exhortation to the Hebrews to grow in their faith (5:11—6:12).

6:13–15 Abraham is an example of faith and patience in God's **promise** (see v. 12). He waited 25 years from the time the promise was first made until Isaac, the promised son, was born (see Gen. 12:4; 21:5).

6:16–18 Confirmation means "guarantee." An **oath** is used to guarantee an agreement. The Lord confirmed His oath to Abraham by swearing by Himself (v. 13) because He alone is beyond deceit. The **two immutable things** are God's Word and God's oath. Since God does not lie and since He is all-powerful, He will fulfill all His promises. This unchanging nature of God is the believer's **consolation** and encouragement.

6:19, 20 The believer's **hope** in Christ is secure, like an **anchor.** Furthermore this anchor is not in sand, but in the presence of the Almighty. **Behind the veil** refers to the Most Holy Place, the place where God dwells. The Greek word for **forerunner** was used in the second century A.D. of the smaller boats sent into the harbor by larger ships unable to enter because of the buffeting of the weather. These smaller boats carried the anchor through the breakers inside the harbor and dropped it there, securing the larger ship. *Forerunner* presupposes that others will follow. Thus, Jesus is not only the believer's anchor, but He is like a runner boat that has taken our anchor into port and secured it there. There is thus no doubt about whether this vessel is going into port. Believers who have hope in the presence of God should come boldly before the throne of grace (see 4:14–16).

7:1, 2 The mention of **Melchizedek** recalls the author's reference to this ancient priest in 5:10, 11. Melchizedek was both a **king** and a **priest,** a common combination in ancient times. **Salem** was later renamed Jerusalem. The name Melchizedek means **king of righteousness.** The word **Salem** means **peace.** The ideal king rules in righteousness, which assures peace (see Is. 32:17).

7:3 without father … mother … genealogy: Genesis, a book with many genealogies, has none for Melchizedek. The author is not saying that Melchizedek was born without a father and mother, only that there is no record of his birth in the genealogies of Genesis. This description of Melchizedek prefigures the eternal priesthood of Jesus. Like Melchizedek, Jesus is both a Priest and a King, belonging to a righteous priesthood that is independent of Aaron's.

7:4–7 Melchizedek was **great** because **Abraham** gave him a tithe. In the Greek text the

word **patriarch** is emphatic. The greatness of Abraham, the one who possessed the promises of God (v. 6), underscores the even greater rank of Melchizedek, the priest of righteousness.

7:8–10 Melchizedek was not only superior to Abraham; he was superior to the Levitical priesthood in two ways. First, the Levitical priests were **mortal**—they died; and thus different priests represented the people at different times. In contrast, Melchizedek **lives,** meaning the Old Testament does not record his death (v. 3). Second, in a sense, Levi paid tithes to Melchizedek through Abraham's gift. **So to speak** indicates that Levi, who was not yet born, did not literally pay tithes. However, because he descended from Abraham, he is counted as having paid tithes to Melchizedek as well.

7:11 If the **Levitical priesthood** had been able to bring people to **perfection,** then a superior priest from **the order of Melchizedek** would not have been needed (see Ps. 110:4). If the priests under the Law of Moses could offer permanent reconciliation between God and His people, there would be no need for a coming Messiah who would restore the Israelites to their relationship with God.

7:12 Change means "removal" (12:27). If the Melchizedek priesthood removed the Levitical priesthood, then the Mosaic Law is also removed. In short, the believer is not under the Law but relies on the righteousness of Christ (see Rom. 6:14; Gal. 3:24, 25).

7:13, 14 He of whom these things are spoken is the Lord, who arose from **another tribe**—Judah. According to the Law, the tribe of Judah had nothing to do with the priesthood. The argument hinges on Ps. 110:4 (see also 5:6). If the Old Testament said that another priest was coming from another tribe, then clearly the Law was going to be superseded.

7:15–19 The law, which regulated the priesthood, was **fleshly** in the sense that it regulated a person's external actions. The Lord, however, is a Priest **according to the power of an endless life.** This is proved by Ps. 110:4, quoted in v. 17. Jesus is a different kind of Priest, another indication that the Law has been changed. There has been an **annulling,** a putting away, of the Law.

7:20–24 Christ's priesthood is superior to the Levitical priesthood because it was established by an **oath.** Because Christ lives **forever,** His priesthood is **unchangeable.** In the Levitical system, the high priest's office was always changing hands. When one high priest died, another assumed the office.

7:25 Christ **is ... able to save** because He is fully God and fully human (2:18; 4:15). Since this verse speaks of Jesus' intercession for us, the word *save* in this verse speaks of our sanctification, the continuing process by which we are freed from the power of sin. This continuing process of salvation will eventually be completed in our glorification, when we our saved from the presence of sin. The word **uttermost** may speak of this glorification, this "complete" or "whole" salvation. **come:** The Greek verb for *come* is in the present tense. The word indicates that Jesus continues to save those who keep coming to Him. Our justification is a once-for-all event accomplished on the Cross, but our sanctification is a continuing process.

7:26–28 Higher than the heavens means Christ is exalted above all and sits in glory at the right hand of the Father (1:3; 2:9; 4:14). **daily, as those high priests:** The high priest offered an annual sacrifice on the Day of Atonement for the atonement of the people's sins (9:7; 10:1), but the priests also offered sacrifices every day before the Lord (see Ex. 29:36). In contrast, Jesus offered Himself **once,** a perfect, sinless sacrifice for the sins of all. Since Jesus is perfect, He did not have to offer sacrifices for His own sins.

8:1 The main point of this section of Hebrews (vv. 1–6) is the high priesthood of Christ, mentioned in 2:17—3:1 and developed in 4:14—7:28.

8:2, 3 The sanctuary refers to the heavenly reality represented by the Most Holy Place (9:2, 8, 24; 10:19; 13:11). This reality is the presence of God. Our High Priest serves there and desires to bring us there (10:19).

8:4–6 according to the law: Only men from the tribe of Levi could serve as priests. Christ was not from that tribe (7:13, 14). The Levitical priesthood served as a **copy** of the **heavenly** Priest. The same goes for the tabernacle. Moses was shown a **pattern,** a type or model, of the true tabernacle (see Ex. 25:40).

8:7, 8 That first covenant is the Mosaic covenant (see v. 9; Ex. 19:5). The **new covenant** is the "better covenant" of v. 6. This covenant was made with **Israel** and **Judah,** yet the church enjoys the spiritual blessings of this covenant now. The Abrahamic covenant was made with Abraham and his physical descendants (see Gen. 17:7), who would inherit the land (see Gen. 12:7; 13:14, 15). Yet the Abrahamic covenant also contained spiritual promises (see Gen. 12:3) in which the church participates (see Rom. 11:11–27; Gal. 3:13, 14). The new covenant is a fulfillment of the spiritual redemption promised in the Abrahamic and Davidic covenants (see Matt. 26:26–29; Luke 22:20).

8:9–13 There are four provisions of the new covenant: (1) God's law will be written on believers' minds and **hearts.** (2) Believers will have a relationship with God fulfilling the promise of Lev. 26:12 (see 2 Cor. 6:16). (3) **All** will **know** God. (4) God will forgive the sins of believers and remember them no more. The continual sacrifice of animals for the atonement of sin will cease. The presence of a **new,** better covenant not only demonstrates that the **first** covenant is not sufficient (v. 7); it also shows that the first covenant is **obsolete** and **ready to vanish away.** At the time the author of Hebrews wrote these words, the ceremonies of the Mosaic covenant were still being conducted in the temple in Jerusalem. In A.D. 70 the Roman general Titus destroyed the temple, fulfilling these words.

9:1 The first (Mosaic) **covenant** included an **earthly sanctuary,** the tabernacle (v. 2), in which **divine service** was offered.

9:2–5 These verses describe the furniture of the **tabernacle.** The tabernacle courtyard contained an altar for animal sacrifice, a laver for ceremonial washings, and the tent itself (the word *tabernacle* literally means "tent"). The tabernacle was divided into two rooms by a veil. The first part was the **sanctuary** or holy place, housing the lampstand, the table for the showbread, and the altar of incense. The second room was the Most Holy Place (v. 3) containing the **ark of the covenant,** in which symbols of the Mosaic covenant were stored. The **pot of manna** reminded the people of

God's miraculous provision for them in the wilderness. **Aaron's rod** was a sign of the authority of the priesthood. God had ordained Aaron and his sons to be representatives of the people before Him. The tablets were the Ten Commandments given to the nation at Mount Sinai. On top of the ark was the **mercy seat,** the place where God made His presence known. **9:6–8** Every morning and every evening **the priests** entered the holy place to burn incense on the golden altar and trim the lamps (see Ex. 30:7, 8). Every week on the Sabbath, the showbread was changed (see Lev. 24:5–8). Only **the high priest** could enter the Most Holy Place. **Once a year,** on the Day of Atonement, the high priest offered a **blood** sacrifice **for himself** and for the sins o

f ignorance committed by everyone in the nation of Israel (see Lev. 16). In the provisions of the Mosaic covenant, access to God was limited. The fact that the high priest could enter the Holiest of All only once a year indicates the striking failure of the Mosaic covenant to bring believers into the presence of God.
9:9–11 The tabernacle was **symbolic,** an illustration of spiritual truths. **The present time** refers to the Old Testament period. **cannot make … perfect:** The Mosaic covenant covered sins of ignorance (v. 7), but not premeditated sins or the sinful nature of all people (see Ps. 51). In other words, the old system was lacking. It did not reconcile the people to God. Christ's tabernacle is

---

🪏 **IN DEPTH** | **The Superiority of Jesus**

When it comes to spiritual matters, people are peculiar. They become obsessed with angels, but somehow ignore or forget the God who created and directs these heavenly messengers. They devote themselves to seeking and understanding "truth," but they never encounter the Holy One who encompasses all truth. They engage in all sorts of rituals and practices to try to find and reach out to their Creator; but they somehow miss the fact that He has already reached down to them.

This is the case today, just as it was in the first century. In fact, this spiritual "peculiarity" is one of the reasons the Spirit of God inspired the letter to the Hebrews. To Jewish Christians who were dealing with persecution and hardship, who were doubting the truth of the gospel and the New Covenant, and who were considering the idea of turning away, the writer of Hebrews sent this clear message: Christ is the Ultimate.

More than a mere prophet, Christ is God in the flesh (1:2, 3, 8). He is Creator (1:10–12) and Sustainer of all (1:3). As the "holy, harmless, undefiled" High Priest who is "separate from sinners" and "who does not need to offer up sacrifices … for His own sins" (7:26, 27), Jesus Christ alone is capable of providing salvation and sanctification (2:10, 11).

Given these facts, it is easy to see why the author of Hebrews states that Christ is better than the angels (1:4). It is clear why even Moses pales in comparison. No wonder Hebrews states that Christ is the Author and Mediator of a better covenant (7:22; 8:6), that He offered a better sacrifice for sin (9:23), that He possesses a more excellent name (1:4), and that He carries out a more excellent ministry (8:6).

We must resist the temptation to settle for a superficial spirituality. Angels, rituals, and human role models all have their place. But none of these things compares to Christ. And therein lies the staggering promise of the gospel: Jesus Christ comes to us and offers Himself. Because of His perfect payment for sins, we can find the forgiveness we so desperately need. More than that, we can experience eternal life, which Jesus Himself described as an intimate, never-ending relationship with God the Father and God the Son. Given that mind-boggling opportunity, why would we look anywhere else or settle for anything less?

better than the Old Testament tabernacle (vv. 1–5). **The good things to come** include access to God (8:10–12). The preposition **with** in this context means "in connection with." **Therefore, the greater and more perfect tabernacle** is not a reference to Christ's body but to the "true tabernacle" (see 8:2).

9:12, 13 The service of the Levitical priest obtained a limited, recurring, symbolic type of redemption. Christ, **with His own blood,** obtained **eternal redemption.** His sacrifice does not have to be repeated because it is perfect. According to Mosaic Law, **the blood of bulls and goats** from the sacrifices made on the Day of Atonement would atone for the people's sins (v. 12). **The ashes of a heifer** were mixed with water and were used to cleanse a person who had become ceremonially defiled by touching a corpse (see Num. 19). The author of Hebrews points out that these ceremonies could purify only a person's exterior, not a person's heart.

9:14 The eternal Spirit is the Holy Spirit; all three persons of the Trinity are involved in cleansing. **cleanse your conscience:** The defilement is internal, not external (v. 13). Christ's death has the power to purify a person's mind and soul. **Dead works** are the rituals of the Mosaic Law that could not give life (6:1). The author of Hebrews commands his audience to free their conscience from regulations of Mosaic Law and instead cling to Christ for cleansing.

9:15 The **new covenant** provides two gifts to a believer: redemption and inheritance. Believers receive **redemption** from the sins committed under the Law. Christ paid the price to free us from our own sin. His death substitutes for our death, the penalty of our sins. Like the Israelites, believers receive an inheritance, but our inheritance is **eternal** (v. 14). By imitating the faith and patience of Abraham, believers are assured that they will inherit the marvelous promises God has made (6:12; see the promises at 8:6–12).

9:16–21 Testament is the same word translated *covenant* in v. 15. It means a legal will. Before the provisions of a will take effect, the one who made it must die. The Mosaic covenant was ratified by **blood,** or death. It was

not the death of the person making the covenant, but the death of the animals offered as a sacrifice to God (see Ex. 24:1–8).

9:22–24 Almost indicates that there were exceptions to blood purification (see Lev. 5:11–13), but that they were few in comparison with the central importance of sacrifices made for the remission of sins (see Lev. 17:11). Christ's sacrifice was better than sacrifices made under the Mosaic covenant because Christ did not enter a man-made sanctuary, which was a copy; instead, He entered the true sanctuary, which is in heaven—the very **presence of God.**

9:25–28 Christ's sacrifice was better than sacrifices made under the Mosaic covenant because He did not offer an annual sacrifice of animals, but He offered **Himself** once. **at the end of the ages:** The coming of Christ is the climax of the Old Testament period. As men **die once,** so **Christ** died once—not like the repeated sacrifices of the Levitical system. Unlike men, Christ did not die and face judgment. He died once to appear a second time **for salvation** (1:14). Those who **eagerly wait for Him** are not necessarily all believers, but those who look for His return, those who are steadfast to the end.

10:1–4 Not the very image means "not the exact representation." **Perfect** refers to the removal of the consciousness of sins (v. 2; 8:12; 9:9). The sacrifices of the Mosaic covenant prefigured Christ's ultimate sacrifice of Himself. Therefore these imperfect sacrifices of animals could not completely purify the person who offered them. If they had been able to, these sacrifices would have **ceased.** Instead of thoroughly atoning for the sins of the people, the annual sacrifice on the Day of the Atonement was a visible reminder of the people's sins.

10:5–7 it is written of Me: The author presents Ps. 40 as a messianic psalm, for only Christ, and not David, could have fulfilled the prophecies of *the book,* the Old Testament. **To do Your will:** The Old Testament prophets had warned the Israelites that sacrifices alone would not please God. He desired obedience as well (Ps. 51:16, 17; Is. 1:13–17; see also Mark 12:33). This messianic psalm indicates that Jesus' obedience to

God the Father was one of the reasons His sacrifice was better than the Old Testament sacrifices.

10:8, 9 The author explains Ps. 40, concluding that God **takes away the first,** meaning the Levitical sacrificial system, to **establish the second**—the Son's obedient sacrifice. The verb translated *takes away* means "abolishes." The imperfect sacrifices were abolished so the perfect Sacrifice could impart true life.

10:10–12 Sanctified means "set apart." Believers have been separated from their sins and set apart to God by the once-for-all sacrifice of Christ. The author of Hebrews contrasts the Levitical priests with Jesus, our High Priest. The Levitical priests always stood before God. There were no seats in the sanctuary, since the priests' job was never done. There were always more sins for which to atone. In contrast, Christ **sat down** (1:3; 8:1) after offering Himself as a sacrifice. Sitting indicates that His work of atonement is finished.

10:13, 14 The finished work of Christ in dying for sin once for all (v. 10) has **perfected forever those who are being sanctified**—those who have been set apart to God (see v. 10). Notice that the sanctification spoken of in v. 10 is positional; it refers to our justification, the fact that we have been declared righteous. However in this verse, sanctification refers to the gradual process by which believers are being made more and more perfect.

10:15–18 If full and final forgiveness has been achieved so that God does not remember sin any longer (v. 17), then no further sacrifice for sin is necessary. To **remember** sins **no more** does not mean to forget, but not to hold sin against us any longer.

10:19 Therefore recalls the *therefore* of 4:16. The author has spent five chapters explaining the superiority of Christ's priesthood to the Levitical priesthood and the superiority of the New Covenant to the Mosaic covenant. Unlike the Israelites, who approached God at Mount Sinai with fear and trembling (Ex. 20:18–21), believers can approach God with **boldness** (see 3:6; 4:16; 10:35) because we have Christ's righteousness and not our own. The **Holiest** refers to the very presence of God. On this earth, most of us do not have immediate access to a president or monarch. But

through Christ's **blood,** we have perpetual access to God Himself.

10:20, 21 The Old Testament high priest passed through a **veil** to get to the Most Holy Place. Now believers enter God's presence through Christ's **flesh,** meaning His sacrificial death. Believers have **a High Priest** who, having been tempted Himself, can sympathize with their weaknesses and perfectly represent them before God (4:14, 15).

10:22 Draw near is the same word rendered *come* in 4:16. **Full assurance** means "certainty" (6:11). **our hearts sprinkled ... our bodies washed:** Our consciences can be cleansed through the blood of Christ (9:14). Just as the high priest washed before entering the Most Holy Place (Lev. 16:3, 4), so believers are cleansed before they come before the Holy One.

10:23 Confession of our hope is the believer's confident expectation of the future. **Promised** here may refer to the promise of rest (4:1). If the believer does his or her part, there is no question that God will fulfill His part of the agreement (see 2 Tim. 2:11, 12).

10:24, 25 Consider means "to observe," "to contemplate," or "to have an intelligent insight into." Note that **love and good works** need to be stirred up; they do not just occur. The Greek word translated **stir up** means a "convulsion." The Greek word speaks of the impact believers can have on one another. That is why the author exhorts the Hebrews to gather together. Evidently some believers had stopped attending the worship services of the church, perhaps because they feared persecution. **Exhorting** means coming alongside and inspiring another with the truth. The local assembly is where the gospel message is preached, but also where the Word of God is applied to the circumstances of our lives. **Approaching** may also be translated "at hand" (see Rom. 13:12; Phil. 4:5; James 5:8; 1 Pet. 4:7; Rev. 1: 3). Knowing that Christ's return is imminent, the believers were to encourage one another to remain faithful to Him (3:13).

10:26, 27 sin willfully: The reference here is not to an occasional act of sin but to a conscious rejection of God. To sin deliberately after receiving **the knowledge of the truth** is apostasy. If a Christian rejects God's provision for his or her salvation, there is no other remedy for **sins** (see also Num. 15:29–31), since forgiveness of sins can be found only in Christ's perfect sacrifice. With no hope of forgiveness (v. 26), all a person can expect is **judgment,** described here as a **fiery indignation.**

10:28, 29 The specific sin in the Old Testament that required **two or three witnesses** was idolatry (see Deut. 17:2–7). The judgment for idolatry was death by stoning. If idolatry was punished with physical death, **how much worse punishment** should someone receive who treats the word of Christ with disrespect or disdain? **Counted the blood ... a common thing** means the blood of Christ is treated as no different from the blood of an ordinary man or the blood of an animal sacrifice. **Insulted the Spirit of grace** is a reference to the Holy Spirit, the agent of God's gracious gift of salvation. A believer who commits these offenses will be judged with a punishment worse than physical death.

10:30–33 The author quotes two passages from Deut. 32 to support his claim that judgment belongs to the Lord and that God's people are not excused from God's judgment. **It is a fearful thing to fall into the hands of the living God** because there is no other sacrifice for sin than Christ's sacrifice on the Cross (v. 26), only a fearful expectation of judgment (v. 27). All sin not covered by the blood of Christ will result in great loss at the judgment seat (see 1 Cor. 3:15; 2 Cor. 5:10). To encourage his readers, the author urges them to **recall** their **former** endurance, which occurred right after they were **illuminated** or converted (6:9–12). They had endured even though they were ridiculed because of their faith.

10:34–36 The people to whom Hebrews was written had shown **compassion** on the author when he was in prison and had **joyfully accepted** economic hardship. To **cast away** one's **confidence** is to lose conviction about the value of one's Christian commitment. For the recipients of Hebrews to return to the safety of Judaism would mean a loss of eternal **reward** at the judgment seat of Christ.

10:37, 38 These verses focus the attention of a person facing trial on the imminent return of the Lord and the need to endure **by faith** (3:12, 13).

10:39 Those who draw back are in danger of destruction. The writer is confident that he and his readers **believe to the saving of the soul.** Those who live by faith (v. 38) invest their physical lives for eternal dividends.

11:1 This verse is not a definition of **faith,** but a description of what faith does. **Substance** means "essence" or "reality." Faith treats **things hoped for** as reality. **Evidence** means "proof" or "conviction." Faith itself proves that what is unseen is real, such as the believer's rewards at the return of Christ (see 2 Cor. 4:18).

11:2 The elders are the believers of the Old Testament. **Good testimony** refers to God's approval; He considered them righteous because of their faith (see vv. 4, 5, 7).

11:3 worlds: Faith understands that the invisible God created the vast universe.

11:4–6 Abel's sacrifice was acceptable to God because of his **faith,** and was therefore declared **righteous.** Evidently Cain offered his sacrifices without faith (see Gen. 4). Abel **still speaks** to us because his righteous deeds have been recorded in Scripture. The word **comes** is used repeatedly in Hebrews to refer to the privilege of drawing near to God (see 4:16; 7:25; 10:1, 22). Faith is mandatory for those who approach Him (see 10:22). **rewarder:** God rewards not only those who seek Him, but those who do good works in the Holy Spirit's power (see Rev. 22:12).

11:7 Noah had never **seen** (v. 1) the flood God revealed to him. Yet he believed God in spite of this and heeded His warnings. His faith not only saved him from the deluge but also from God's judgment, because He became an **heir** of **righteousness.**

11:8, 9 Abraham did not know **where he was going,** yet he placed his trust in God. Faith means obediently stepping into the unknown (v. 1). Abraham did this, and God considered him righteous because of it (Gen. 15:6; Rom. 4:1–12).

11:10–12 The city here is the New Jerusalem (see Rev. 21:2, 10). Abraham lived in the land waiting for the future yet unseen New Jerusalem. Sarah evidently believed that nothing was too hard for the Lord (see Gen. 18:15). As a result, God blessed her with the **promised** son, though she was **past the age** of childbearing.

11:13–16 These all refers to Abraham, Isaac, Jacob, and Sarah (vv. 8, 9, 11), who **died** before taking possession of the land or seeing any of the other provisions of God's covenant. Nevertheless, they endured in the faith, even to the end of their lives. **strangers and pilgrims on the earth:** These men and women of faith knew that this world was temporary, that their eternal home would be with God. The patriarchs and Sarah did not **return** to Ur, even though they could have if they had wanted to. The recipients of Hebrews were to follow the patriarchs' example and refuse to return to the religion of their ancestors, a religious system that no longer provided atonement for sin (see 8:7–13).

11:17–19 When **Abraham** was **tested,** he believed that God could **raise** Isaac **from the dead** (see Gen. 22:5) if necessary. The incident is figurative of what God has done for us. Isaac was as good as dead, but God provided a ram to sacrifice in his place (Gen. 22:9–14). With God everything is possible.

11:20–22 Isaac, Jacob, and **Joseph** all believed until the ends of their lives in the unseen future God had promised.

11:23 The **parents** of **Moses** had faith in God in the midst of opposition.

11:24–26 Moses believed God by refusing a high position in Pharaoh's court. Instead, he chose suffering, forsook Egypt, and instituted the Passover. **The reproach of Christ** refers to the earthly disgrace Christ received. Like Christ, Moses chose to suffer the indignities associated with God's people instead of embracing the worldly pleasures of Pharaoh's court. The possibility of **reward** is the most frequently mentioned motivation for enduring in the faith.

11:27–29 forsook Egypt: Some commentators interpret this as a reference to Moses' flight to Midian. However, the mention of **not fearing the wrath of the king** in this verse fits the events of the Exodus better. At that time Moses showed true courage, a resolute faith in the Lord (see Ex. 14:13, 14). God told Moses to sprinkle **blood** on the doorposts. Moses believed God's word, heeded His warning, and as a result the firstborn of every Israelite family was saved (Ex. 12:1–13).

11:30–36 It took **faith** for the warriors of Israel to destroy the walled city of **Jericho** by such unconventional means. Yet this act of faith brought the results they desired. God gave them victory over their enemies (Josh. 6). The reference to **women** who **received their dead** is probably a reference to the raising of the son of the widow of Zarephath (1 Kin. 17:17–24) and of the Shunammite woman (2 Kin. 4:32–37). But the author of Hebrews also points out that not all who had faith won victories, at least not in the same hour. **tortured:** This is usually understood to be an allusion to the heroic martyrs of Maccabean times. **A better resurrection** is a reference to a richer resurrection, an abundant entrance into the kingdom (see 2 Pet. 1:11), which is our eternal reward.

11:37, 38 Zechariah was **stoned** (2 Chr. 24:20, 21). According to Jewish tradition, the prophet Isaiah was **sawn in two.** Urijah was **slain with the sword** (see Jer. 26:20–23). **Wandered about in sheepskins and goatskins** is probably a reference to Elijah (see 2 Kin. 1:8).

11:39, 40 Made perfect means "made complete." This completion, the realization of all of God's promises in Christ's coming kingdom, awaits all believers.

12:1 The **cloud of witnesses** refers to the people of faith mentioned in ch. 11. They are not actually spectators watching us; they are witnesses testifying to the truth of the faith (11:2, 4–6).

12:2 Looking here means "fixing one's eyes trustingly." We need to consistently focus on Christ instead of our own circumstances. **finisher:** Christ has done everything necessary for us to endure in our faith. He is our example and model, because He focused on the **joy that was set before Him.** His attention was not on the agonies of the Cross but on the crown, not on the suffering but the reward.

12:3 Consider here involves the idea of comparison, as an accountant would compare the various columns of a balance sheet. Believers should compare their sufferings to the torture Christ endured on their behalf (v. 4).

12:4 not yet resisted to bloodshed: Christ died (v. 3); but the community that received the letter to the Hebrews had not yet suffered deadly persecutions.

12:5, 6 Proverbs 3:11, 12 teaches that divine discipline demonstrates divine love. **Scourges** means "whips," and is used figuratively of punishment.

12:7, 8 for what son: Sons are naturally disciplined out of love by their fathers. They should accept and learn from this discipline. In the same way, God disciplines us because He wants to make us better. In Roman society an **illegitimate** had no inheritance rights.

12:9 Believers should not only endure God's discipline; they should **readily be in subjection** to their heavenly Father.

12:10–14 our profit: Although fathers discipline for a while as they see fit, God disciplines us with our welfare in mind. With every trial, God is fashioning us into a holy people, set apart for His purpose (see v. 14; 10:10). **The peaceable fruit of righteousness** suggests that the result of God's **chastenin g** is peace and righteousness. Borrowing the language of Is. 35:3, the author admonishes his readers to renew their strength so they can endure the race of faith (see v. 1).

12:15–17 Believers pursuing peace and practical righteousness (v. 14) should watch for three dangers: (1) falling **short of** God's **grace**—refusing Christ's gracious offer of salvation and His provision for their needs (see 4:16); (2) allowing a **root of bitterness** to grow in their assembly—perhaps allowing idol worshipers to remain in the church (see Deut. 29:18); and (3) becoming sexually immoral or irreligious. Esau illustrates those who are irreligious. Under the Law, the eldest son would receive a double inheritance (see Deut. 21:17). Esau lost his inheritance, which included God's gracious promises, by despising it and valuing the pleasure of food over his inheritance (Gen. 25:34).

12:18–24 In the Old Testament the **firstborn** received a double inheritance (see Deut. 21:17). These then are heirs who are in heaven awaiting the kingdom (1:14). **Just men made perfect** refers to all believers who have died. They are just because they have been justified, and perfect because they are now "complete" in heaven. The blood **of Abel** cried out for revenge (see Gen. 4:10); **the blood** of Christ speaks of redemption.

12:25 Him who speaks from heaven is Christ,

who spoke on earth and is now in heaven. **much more:** Greater revelation means greater responsibility (2:1–4). If the Israelites were judged for not believing in God's promises (Num. 14:20–25), we will also be judged for disbelief.

12:26–28 The earth shook at Mount Sinai. **The earth** and **heaven** will shake in the latter days (see Matt. 24:29). But the kingdom of God will not be shaken; it will endure throughout all eternity (Luke 18:29).

12:29 our God is a consuming fire: The author concludes His lengthy warning to those who are tempted to abandon the faith (2:1—12:29) with a vivid description of God's judgment (Deut. 4:24).

13:1 continue: The recipients of this letter had practiced **brotherly love** (see 6:10), but the author feared that the idea of returning to some form of Judaism might be hindering them from encouraging one another in the faith (10:24, 25).

13:2 Entertained angels is a reference to men in the Old Testament who encountered heavenly beings. These men included Abraham (see Gen. 18), Lot (see Gen. 19), Gideon (see Judg. 6), and Manoah (see Judg. 13). The idea is that when we practice hospitality we may be helping a messenger of God without realizing it.

13:3, 4 Remember the prisoners probably refers to believers who were being persecuted for the faith. The recipients of this letter had remembered those who were suffering (10:32–34). **In the body** is not a reference to the body of Christ, but to the physical body. The recipients of this letter were vulnerable to similar persecution as long as they were alive.

13:5, 6 Covetousness is addressed in the last of the Ten Commandments (see Ex. 19:17). This attitude destroys a person's inheritance in the kingdom (see 1 Cor. 6:9, 10). **I will never leave you nor forsake you:** This quotation is one of the most emphatic statements in the New Testament. In Greek it contains two double negatives, similar to saying in English, " I will never, ever, ever forsake you." Jesus uses the same technique to express the certainty of eternal life for believers (see John 10:28).

13:7, 8 the same: The unchanging nature of the Son was mentioned at the beginning of this book (1:12). **yesterday:** Christ gave His grace to the former leaders who trusted Him (see v. 7). **today, and forever:** Christ's grace is presently and permanently available to all who believe in Him.

13:9–11 Strange doctrines implies ideas foreign to the gospel message. Many of the ideas that the author of Hebrews was confronting were Jewish in origin—pertaining to ritual observances, sacrificial feasts, and various laws identifying what was clean and unclean. The word **altar** is used figuratively of the sacrifice of Christ. On the Day of Atonement, the high priest did not have the **right to eat** the sacrificed animal because it had atoned for the people's sins. Instead, it was **burned outside the camp.** The believer has a sacrifice, Jesus Christ. He atoned for the sins of humanity with His death on the Cross. But unlike the high priests of the Old Testament, believers receive their sustenance from Christ in a symbolic way, by believing in Him (see John 6:41–58).

13:12–14 To be **outside the gate** was considered a disgrace to Jews because it meant being separated from the community. The author exhorts his readers to take on Christ's **reproach** or disgrace. In essence, the author's command to **go forth to** Christ was a command to abandon Judaism. Anyone found with Christ—outside of the city gate—would be considered outside the Jewish community. Believers do not have a permanent home on earth. They seek the eternal **city** which is in an eternal kingdom (11:10, 16; 12:22, 28).

13:15–17 Although the Old Testament sacrifices are now obsolete (8:13), believers are to offer spiritual sacrifices, which include their **praise,** their possessions, and even their lives (see Rom. 12:1, 2). The current leaders would give an account of their service at the judgment seat of Christ (see Rom. 14:10–12).

13:18, 19 A good conscience is one that is not accusing. **that I may be restored to you:** Something hindered the author's coming, though it was probably not prison (see v. 23).

13:20, 21 The title **God of peace** is used six times in the New Testament (see also Rom. 15:33; 1 Cor. 14:33; 2 Cor. 13:11; Phil. 4:9; 1 Thess. 5:23). Whenever the title was used, some sort of difficulty existed among the recipients of the letter. This is also the case here: the readers of Hebrews were wondering whether they should reject Christianity and return to Judaism in the face of increasing persecution. Jesus is the **great Shepherd of the sheep,** having laid down His life for them (see John 10:15) and now continuing to make intercession for them (7:25). The New Covenant is an **everlasting covenant;** it will never become obsolete like the Mosaic covenant (8:13).

13:22 The word of exhortation refers to the entire Epistle to the Hebrews. It is an exhortation not to depart from the living God (3:12), but to go on to maturity (6:1) and endure in the faith to the end (3:6, 14). **In few words** is used as a comparison to what more could have been said (5:11; 9:5).

13:23 Timothy was a well-known associate of Paul. Two New Testament letters are addressed to him. **Set free** probably means released from prison.

13:24, 25 Those from Italy may refer to people living in Italy, or else to people from there who were now living elsewhere. Because of its ambiguity, this phrase does not reveal the location of the author of Hebrews or of the recipients. In light of what has been said about **grace** in the letter (see v. 9; 2:9; 4:16; 10:29; 12:15), this closing is particularly appropriate.

James

Introduction

The Epistle of James is the "how-to" book of the Christian life. It is one of the most practical books in the New Testament because it offers instruction and exhortation to Christians who are experiencing problems. As if the trials themselves were not bad enough, James points out the dangers that come with them. Besides the obvious pitfall of failing to place our trust in the Lord and thus not enduring, James speaks of prejudice, improper speech, judging one another, leaving God out of our plans, and even bitterness.

The author of this epistle identifies himself with the phrase "James, a bondservant of God and of the Lord Jesus Christ." James is a common name in the New Testament. This particular James must have been a church leader who needed no further introduction. James, the half brother of Jesus, traditionally called "the Just" (see Matt. 13:55), became the leader of the Jerusalem church (see Acts 15:3; Gal. 2:9). He seems to be the most probable author of this epistle. An early date of around A.D. 46 seems reasonable for this letter.

The salutation identifies the readers of James as "the twelve tribes which are scattered abroad." The readers were probably Jewish Christians living outside of Palestine.

Most of the recipients seem to have been poor and suffering from oppression by their fellow Jews, among whom they were living. Evidently some of these Jewish Christians had been imprisoned and deprived of their possessions and livelihoods. Under such conditions, they fell into worldliness, fought among themselves, favored the rich over the poor, and lost their original love for one another. For James, works is a natural result of faith. When a person truly believes in something, he or she will act on that belief. James was sounding a wake-up call to all Christians: "Get your life in line with what you believe!"

1:1 Early church tradition identifies the author **James** as the half brother of Christ (see 1 Cor. 15:7). **To the twelve tribes:** This salutation probably means the letter is for Jewish Christians living outside of Palestine. The letter was not intended for one specific church but was to be passed around among various local assemblies.

1:2-3 Trials are of outward circumstances—conflicts, sufferings, and troubles—encountered by all believers. Trials are not pleasant, but believers are to consider them as opportunities for rejoicing. Troubles and difficulties are a tool which refines and purifies our faith, producing patience and endurance. The word translated **testing of your faith** occurs only here and in 1 Pet. 1:7. The term, which means "tested" or "approved," was used for coins that were genuine and not debased. The aim of testing is to purge and refine. The meaning of **patience** transcends the idea of bearing affliction; it includes the idea of standing fast under pressure, with a staying power that turns adversities into opportunities.

1:4 If a believer endures a trial, he or she will be **perfect,** meaning "having reached the end," and **complete,** meaning "whole."

1:5 The **wisdom** that God gives is not necessarily information on how to get out of trouble but insight on how to learn from one's difficulties (see also Prov. 29:15). The wisdom of God begins with a genuine reverence for the Almighty and a steadfast confidence that God controls all circumstances, guiding them to His good purposes (Rom. 8:28).

1:6, 7 Doubting means "to be divided in one's mind" or "to debate." The term does not describe a momentary doubt but a divided allegiance, an uncertainty.

1:8 Double-minded is literally "two souls." If one part of a person is set on God and the other is set on this world (see Matt. 6:24), there will be constant conflict within.

1:9-11 James offers two examples of trials (vv. 2–8): one is of a **lowly brother** and the other is about a **rich** man. The poor believer is to **glory** (see "count it all joy" in v. 2) in the fact that God has exalted him by allowing him to experience difficult circumstances, since these will perfect his character and faith (v. 4). The rich believer can also glory when a trial brings him low because it teaches him that life is short, and that **his pursuits,** or his business, will **fade away.** The rich man should always trust the Lord, not himself or his money.

1:12 The believer who **endures** trials demonstrates that he or she loves Jesus and therefore **will receive the crown of life** (see Rev. 2:10) at the judgment seat of Christ.

1:13 The focus of the chapter turns from trials (vv. 2–12) to temptation (vv. 13–18). **nor does He … tempt anyone:** He will never deliberately lead a person to commit sin because that would go against His nature, and it would be opposed to His purpose of molding His creation into His holy image. Yet God does sometimes place His people in adverse circumstances for the purpose of building godly character (see Gen. 22:1, 12).

1:14, 15 Drawn away and **enticed** express the intensity with which desire lures a person until he or she is entrapped. Sin does not force itself on the unwilling, but is chosen because of its attractions. **Conceived** suggests the image of a person's will bending toward and finally seizing evil. **Full-grown** suggests bringing a goal to completion. The idea is that sin has reached its maturity and has possessed the very character of the individual.

1:16–19 The conclusion of the introduction of James (vv. 2–18) is that enduring trials leads to a crown of life (v. 12) and yielding to temptation can lead to physical death (v. 15). Since that is the case, the believer in the midst of a trial needs to be **swift to hear, slow to speak,** and **slow to wrath.**

1:20 If a believer gets angry in difficult circumstances, the practical **righteousness of God** will not be evident in his or her life. When someone wrongs us, the natural reaction is to retaliate. But this response does not glorify God. Holding one's tongue, trying to understand the other person's position, and leaving vindication to God demonstrates godly love in tense situations (Rom. 12:17–21).

1:21 The **word** of God that has been **implanted** in the believer's heart should be received with **meekness**—describing a teachable spirit—without resistance, disputing, or questioning. Receiving God's Word in this way will **save** the believer's *soul,* a word meaning "life."

1:22 be doers of the word, and not hearers only: Believers who hear the Word of God (v. 19) must receive it with a teachable spirit

(v. 21), applying it to their daily lives. To hear and not obey is to be deceived.

1:23–25 The perfect law of liberty is the law of love. Loving God and loving one's neighbor sums up the Law (see Matt. 26:36–40). But Christ's love (Eph. 3:17–19) frees us from our sins so we can truly love others (John 8:36–38; Gal. 5:13).

1:26, 27 To visit comes from the Greek word usually translated *bishop,* a person who oversees God's people (1 Tim. 3:1). **Orphans and widows** were among the most needy classes in ancient societies (see Ezek. 22:7). Pure religion does not just give material goods for the relief of the distressed; it also oversees their care (see Acts 6:1–7; 1 Tim. 5:3–16).

2:1 The faith of our Lord Jesus Christ includes the fact that God loves the world and that Christ died for it. If God and Christ show grace and mercy without favoritism, so should believers (vv. 8, 13).

2:2–6 God has chosen to use **poor** people who are **rich in faith** to advance His kingdom. Those who **love Him** and obey Him (see John 14:15; 15:9–17) and endure the testing of their faith (1:12) will inherit the **kingdom.** This inheritance means more than entering the kingdom; it also involves ruling with Christ (see 1 Cor. 6:9; Gal. 5:21).

2:7–9 The royal law is the law of love (see 1:25; Lev. 19:18; Matt. 22:39), a law superior to all other laws. **if you show partiality, you commit sin:** James alludes to Lev. 19:15, which prohibits favoritism to either the poor or the rich.

2:10 he is guilty of all: God does not allow selective obedience. We cannot choose to obey the parts of the Law that are to our own liking and disregard the rest. Sin is violation of the perfect righteousness of God, who is the Lawgiver. James is saying that the whole divine law has to be accepted as an expression of God's will for His people. The violation of even one commandment separates a person from God and His purposes.

2:11–13 Believers **will be judged by the law of liberty,** which is the law of love (see 1:25). Believers who do not practice partiality, but who practice love (vv. 5, 8) and **mercy,** will triumph at the judgment seat. Those who have not shown mercy will not receive mercy.

2:14, 15 my brethren: James addresses this section to people who have exercised genuine faith. The issue in this section (2:14–26) is faith without works (v. 17) versus faith accompanied by works (v. 18). Genuine faith will naturally produce good works; the two complement each other. **Works** are actions which follow the "royal law" of love (see vv. 8, 15, 16). James is implying that faith in Christ will demonstrate itself in love for others (see Jesus' command to His disciples in John 13:34, 35).

2:16, 17 Some interpreters conclude that James is speaking about genuine faith which has become **dead.** Others maintain that this verse is referring to a faith that was never alive.

2:18–21 Even the demons know that **there is one God** (see Deut. 6:4), but they do not love Him (see Deut. 6:5). Their kind of belief does not lead to love, submission, and obedience; instead it leads to hatred, rebellion, and disobedience. James calls the person who separates faith and works (see v. 18) **foolish,** meaning "empty headed." James clearly teaches justification by faith, because he quotes Gen. 15:6 in v. 23, which connects the crediting of righteousness, or salvation, to Abraham's belief (see Paul's explanation of Gen. 15:6 in Rom. 4:1–12). The justification **by works** of which James is speaking is a different type of justification. This type of justification is before

other people. James is using the word **justified** to mean "proved." We prove to others our genuine faith in Christ through our works. But the justification that comes through faith is before God, and we do not "prove" ourselves to Him; instead, God declares us righteous through our association with Christ, who died for our sins (Rom. 3:28).

2:22 Faith and **works** should be **together;** there is a close relationship between the two. Faith produces works; and works makes faith **perfect,** meaning "mature" or "complete."

2:23–26 By his willingness to offer Isaac (see Gen. 22:1–12), **Abraham** endured the test and demonstrated his complete trust in God. His obedience made him a friend of God (see John 15:14).

3:1 Teachers will stand before the judgment seat of Christ and be judged more strictly than others. Their greater influence translates into greater responsibility. Judgment here most likely does not refer to eternal separation from God; rather, it suggests a thorough judgment of teachers before Christ (Matt. 5:19; Rom. 14:10–12). Leadership involves responsibility.

3:2 Perfect here means "mature."

3:3–6 An uncontrolled **tongue** can defile the **whole body,** or the whole person. **Course of nature** may also be translated "wheel of life," meaning the whole course of life.

✎ **IN DEPTH** **Faith and Works**

The great reformer Martin Luther, champion of the doctrine of salvation through faith alone, never felt good about the Epistle of James. He called it an "epistle full of straw" in the preface to his 1522 edition of the NT, and he put the book in the appendix. He preferred Paul's wording of the faith-works equation: "A man is justified by faith apart from the deeds of the law" (Rom. 3:28). In a sense, Luther had little choice. He was surrounded by men who said that good works could save you. He knew that God alone could save through faith alone, and his mission was to tell them.

Neither faith nor works can be cut off and thrown away. James was taking aim at freeloaders, those who claimed to have no need for good deeds since they had faith. The reality is that if you have faith, works will naturally be a product. Paul had the opposite problem in view when he wrote Romans. His letter targeted those who placed their faith in the Law of Moses. Their trust was in their own good works, and not in God. That is why Paul wrote a defense of faith, and that is why Luther preferred it to James's defense of works. Faith and works are not enemies. True faith and righteous works go hand in hand. They are two parts of God's work in us. Faith brings a person to salvation, and works bring that person to faithfulness. Faith is the cause, works are the effect. James believed it, and so did Paul.

3:7, 8 no man can tame the tongue: The instincts of animals can be subdued through conditioning and punishment, but the sinful nature that inspires evil words is beyond our control. Only the work of the Holy Spirit within us can bring this destructive force under control.

3:9 Bless our God may refer to the Jewish practice of saying "blessed be He" whenever God's name was mentioned. James is pointing out the inconsistency of blessing God while cursing people who are created in His image. **similitude of God:** God created human beings, both man and woman, in His own image (see Gen. 1:26).

3:10–12 Pouring salt water into fresh produces salt water; and mixing bad fruit with good fruit produces a bushel of rotten fruit. Likewise, mixing the contradictory speech of **blessing** and **cursing** will produce negative results.

3:13, 14 The solution for the problem of controlling our tongues is to seek divine **wisdom** (see 1:5). The person who possesses godly wisdom (v. 17) will show it with works, not just words. That is, believers should be slow to speak (1:19).

3:15, 16 Evil produces confusion. On the other hand, God brings harmony and wisdom (see 1 Cor. 14:33). Anyone who is involved in **envy** and strife is confused. It is likely that the Jewish Christians to whom James was writing were going through turmoil because of sinful acts like the ones mentioned here. James wanted his readers to set aside their petty attitudes and seek reconciliation.

3:17, 18 The main characteristic of godly wisdom is that it is **pure,** meaning "free from defilement." Bitterness, envy, and selfish behavior corrupt a person (vv. 14, 16). Godly wisdom is also **peaceable,** describing a spirit of tranquillity and calmness. Godly wisdom is undivided, without favoritism, unwavering, and consistent. **without hypocrisy:** True wisdom is sincere and unpretentious.

4:1 The conflict *within* us is between our sinful **desires for pleasure** and the desire for God's will, an attitude the Holy Spirit has placed within us (v. 5).

4:2 The source of conflict *among* believers is often material things. James attributes fighting, murder, and war to materialism.

4:3 because you ask amiss: Some might have protested James' admonition (vv. 1, 2) by claiming that they had not received an answer to their prayers (see Matt. 7:7). James responds by suggesting that they were praying for the wrong things. Instead of praying for their sinful desires, they should have been praying for God's good will for them. God is not obliged to answer our prayers in the affirmative. He will not act in ways that are contrary to His will, even if He is besieged by fervent prayers. When we seek to further our personal **pleasures** through prayer, we are asking *amiss* (see Matt. 6:33).

4:4 This verse does not speak of God's attitude toward the believer but of the believer's attitude toward God. The difference between the world and God is so vast that as we move toward **the world** we alienate ourselves from God. In the world, sin is considered acceptable and pleasurable. The world has lost its awareness of sin, and thus sin has become habitual.

4:5 Scripture says: James probably does not have any specific Old Testament reference in mind; instead he is speaking of a general concept in Scripture. The jealous yearning in this verse most likely refers to God's jealousy for His people, an idea that fits the context. The friendship with the world mentioned in v. 4 would naturally provoke God's jealousy. However, the expression **Spirit who dwells in us** could also indicate our individual human spirit. Then the jealous yearning would be the covetous desire of people.

4:6 God resists the proud: James quotes from Prov. 3:34 to prove his point. Those who submit to divine wisdom will receive the necessary **grace** from God to put into practice the kind of life James describes (see 3:13–18). On the other hand, those who elevate themselves will face a formidable foe (v. 4). God Himself will fight against their plans.

4:7 submit to God: We must first submit to God by abandoning our selfish pride (see vv. 1–6). Submitting to the Lord also involves putting on the whole armor of God (see Eph. 6:11–18). Second, we must resist any temptation that the **devil** throws our way. Then the Evil One will have no choice but to **flee,**

because we belong to the army of the living God.

4:8, 9 Lament and mourn and weep: When a believer who has fallen into sin responds to God's call for repentance, he or she should place laughter and joy aside to reflect on the sin with genuine sorrow (2 Cor. 7:9, 10). In this verse, **laughter** seems to refer to the loud revelry of pleasure-loving people. They immerse themselves in a celebration of their sins in an effort to forget God's judgment. But Christian sorrow leads to repentance; repentance leads to forgiveness; and forgiveness leads to true joy over one's reconciliation with God (see Ps. 32:1; 126:2; Prov. 15:13).

4:10–12 There is one Lawgiver: The New Testament teaches us not to judge (see Matt. 7:1), since God is the ultimate Judge and the One who will take vengeance on those who practice evil (Rom. 12:9; Heb. 10:30). Yet the Scriptures also exhort the church to exercise judgment over its members (see 1 Cor. 6:2–5). This type of judgment is corporate discipline exercised in accordance with biblical truths and the pattern in Matt. 18:15–20.

4:13–17 we will go … make a profit: The problem is not the plan or the concept of planning; it is leaving God out of the plan (v. 15). It is sin to doubt whether an action is right and yet go ahead and do it; it is also a sin to know what is right and yet not do it (see Rom. 14:23). This is a stern warning against sins of omission.

5:1–3 Food, costly **garments,** and precious metals were signs of wealth. James pronounces judgment and destruction on all three.

5:4–7 be patient: James urges believers to maintain an attitude of patience while suffering. Believers must keep a spirit of patient endurance, even in the midst of cruel treatment. The early church lived in the expectation of the imminent **coming of the Lord.** Their hope was that at that time justice would be handed to the oppressor and the oppressed. At Christ's coming, wrongs will be righted and believers will be rewarded for their faithfulness to Christ (see Prov. 14:14; Matt. 5:12).

5:8–10 Expressions like **at hand** and **the Judge is standing at the door** indicate that the Lord could return at any moment.

5:11–13 James is not forbidding a believer from taking an **oath** in court or invoking

God as witness to some significant statement (see 1 Thess. 2:5). Instead he is prohibiting the ancient practice of appealing to a variety of different objects to confirm the veracity of one's statement. This practice was close to idolatry, because it implied that such objects contained spirits. The warning in these verses serve as a reminder to us to watch what we say. We should not use God's name in a reckless manner, and we should be careful to speak the truth.

5:14 Literally the Greek term translated **elders** meant those advanced in years (see 1 Tim. 5:1). However, the word also referred to those holding positions of authority in the community or in a local congregation. As church officers, *elders* were responsible for pastoral supervision and spiritual leadership. The term is used interchangeably with *bishop* in the New Testament (see 1 Tim. 3:1; 5:17; Titus 1:5–9). **Anointing him with oil** may refer to medicinal treatment (see Luke 10:34). Yet in this passage it probably refers to the healing power of the Holy Spirit, since v. 15 speaks of prayer saving the person. In either case, there is no indication that calling the elders ruled out the use of a physician or medicine.

5:15 the prayer of faith: Whether a believer is healed through medicine or through miraculous means, all healing is ultimately from the Lord. That is why prayers should be consistently offered for the sick. **if he has committed sins:** The New Testament teaches that sickness may be the consequence of sin (see Matt. 9:2), but not invariably (John 9:1–3). Yet when sin is involved, confession is a prerequisite to healing (see v. 16).

5:16–18 Confess: This confession is not necessarily between the sick person and the elders, though this is not ruled out altogether. Instead, this exhortation is intended for the sick person and any one else with whom the sick person needs to be reconciled. **Effective, fervent prayer … much:** This can mean either that (1) prayer is effective when it is used or (2) fervent prayer accomplishes great results. The illustration of **Elijah** may favor the latter meaning, since he prayed **earnestly.**

5:19, 20 The covering of **sins** is an Old Testament image for forgiveness (Ps. 32:1).

1 Peter

Introduction

The Christians of Asia Minor who received this letter from Peter had discovered that a life lived for God is often a life of many difficulties. Some of their troubles came from their neighbors, while some came from government authorities. Peter wrote to these Christians to encourage them, to explain to them why suffering occurs, and to remind them of their eternal reward at the end of this earthly life.

Early church tradition affirms that the apostle Peter was the author of the letter known as First Peter. The sporadic and local persecution before Nero's reign (before A.D. 68) is the persecution that Peter is probably addressing in this letter. Although severe official persecution did not begin until the reigns of Domitian (A.D. 95) or Trajan (A.D. 112), early Christians experienced oppressive local persecution from the beginning (see Acts 14:19). Church tradition tells us that Peter died in Rome during the anti-Christian persecution that took place during the reign of Nero (A.D. 54–68), so A.D. 67 is probably the latest this letter could have been written. He probably wrote the letter around A.D. 62–64.

Peter blended five different themes in this letter. (1) He emphasized that Christians can expect suffering as a natural part of a life dedicated to Christ (1:6, 7; 3:14; 4:12–14). (2) He exhorted Christians to live righteous and holy lives in the face of the evils they were experiencing (1:13–16, 22; 2:1–5, 11, 12; 3:15; 4:1, 2, 7–11; 5:8–10). (3) No matter how much suffering they experienced, Peter assured the Christians in Asia Minor they did not deserve it. Their suffering was a part of their service to God and His kingdom (2:20; 3:16, 17; 4:15–19). (4) In light of this, Peter encouraged Christians to submit themselves to others for the sake of the gospel and for the sake of harmonious interpersonal relationships (2:13–19; 3:1–9; 5:1–7). (5) Finally Peter used this letter as an opportunity to drive home the central truth of the gospel, that Jesus endured the agony of the Cross to save us from our bondage to

sin (1:2–5, 7–11, 17–21; 2:21–24; 3:18–22). Christ's example—his sinless life, his quiet endurance of suffering, and his commitment to the truth—should be our model in all the difficulties of this life.

1:1 Peter, the author of this letter, writes to Christians living in **Asia** Minor (present-day Turkey). By way of encouragement, he identifies them as people who live in the light of their relationship to God the Father, God the Holy Spirit, and God the Son (v. 2). **Dispersion:** This term conveys the idea of being scattered among strangers, much like the Jewish exiles of the Old Testament who were not living in their homeland but in Babylon. **Pontus ... Bithynia:** Peter addresses his letter to the believers in the provinces of Asia Minor. This region had been thoroughly evangelized by Paul during his missionary journeys (see Acts 2:9–11; 16:6, 7; 18:23; 19:26).

1:2 Sanctification is the ongoing process whereby the Holy Spirit works in believers, making their lives holy, separated from their old ways and to God in order to be more like Him. **sprinkling of the blood:** This concept draws our attention to three situations in the Old Testament when the Israelites were sprinkled with the blood of animals: (1) Moses' sprinkling of blood on the Israelites at Mount Sinai, to symbolize their initiation into the covenant (see Ex. 24:5–8); (2) the sprinkling of Aaron and his sons to be the priests of Israel (see Ex. 29:19–21); and (3) the sprinkling of blood performed by priests over healed lepers to symbolize their cleansing (see Lev. 14:1–9). Any of these three cases could be the one that Peter has in mind here.

1:3 according to His abundant mercy: Our salvation is grounded in God's mercy, His act of compassion toward us in spite of our condition of sinfulness. **has begotten us again:** God has given believers a new, spiritual life that enables us to live in an entirely different dimension than the one our physical birth allowed. **to a living hope:** *Hope* here does not imply a wishfulness but rather a dynamic confidence that does not end with this life but continues throughout eternity.

1:4 The Greek word translated **inheritance** suggests both a present and a future reality. God has already determined what we will one day experience in its totality.

1:5 who are kept: God keeps His people safe from external attack and safe within the protective boundaries of His kingdom. **revealed:** We do not now see or understand fully the salvation that God has prepared for us, but one day we will (1 Cor. 4:5; 1 John 3:2)

1:6 grieved: While there is much rejoicing because of the salvation God has prepared for us, there will also be agony because of the pressures and difficulties of life. **by various trials:** In this context (v. 7), *trials* refers to ordeals that we encounter in life rather than those things that would induce us to sin.

1:7 genuineness: As the purity of gold is brought forth by intense heat, so the reality and purity of our faith are revealed as a result of the fiery trials we face. Ultimately the testing of our faith not only demonstrates our final salvation but also develops our capacity to bring glory to the Lord **Jesus Christ.**

1:8 having not seen: Only a few believers had the privilege of walking and talking with Jesus when He was on earth (see John 20:29).

1:9, 10 receiving the end: There is a final, positive outcome for trusting God through all the difficulties of life—our **salvation,** which here has an eschatological sense. **salvation of your souls:** This phrase refers to our glorification in heaven and perhaps the rewards we will receive for following Christ (see Matt. 16:24–27; James 1:21).

1:11 The focus of the Old Testament prophets' study (v. 10) was not the **what** of our salvation but the **when.** They wanted to know when the Messiah would suffer and when the glories of the end times would be revealed. Note that **the Spirit of Christ,** rather than the prophets themselves, was prophesying (see 2 Pet. 1:20, 21). The prophets were mouthpieces for God, not inventors of their own new ideas.

1:12 was revealed: God made known to the prophets that they would not experience all that we experience in Christ, that they were serving God for our benefit. **by the Holy Spirit:** Although humans may preach God's message of salvation, ultimately the Holy Spirit is the One who proclaims these great truths.

IN DEPTH **Persecution in Bithynia**

Bithynia, combined with the nearby territory of Pontus, formed a Roman province in northwest Anatolia. It had been an important kingdom during the Hellenistic period, and a center of Greek language and culture. Although Paul did not evangelize in the region (Acts 16:7), the salutation in 1 Pet. 1:1, addressing Christians in Pontus and Bithynia, shows that Christianity had reached there by other means.

One of the earliest evidences of the Roman awareness of Christianity comes from Bithynia. The letters to the emperor Trajan from Pliny the Younger describe various reasons for the persecution of Christians (Epistulae 10.95–96). Pliny was the provincial governor of Bithynia and Pontus in A.D. 111–113. In his official correspondence he expresses to Trajan his alarm regarding the spread of Christianity.

The correspondence between this governor and his emperor offers one look at how the Romans dealt with the Christian religion in Bithynia and Pontus. According to Pliny, it appears that persecution had trimmed the ranks of Christians in the area. Trajan responds to Pliny that Christians should not actively be sought out. However, he allows that those who refused to perform certain Roman orders were to be punished. The letter of 1 Peter to Christians in Bithynia, Pontus, and other regions offers encouragement during similar persecutions (1 Pet. 1:6, 7).

1:13 gird up the loins of your mind: Just as people in biblical times would gather up their long robes and tie them around their waists so that they could move quickly and freely, we need to do whatever it takes to focus our thoughts on those things that allow us to serve God successfully. **rest your hope:** We need to exhibit confidence that God will accomplish all that He promised He would do (see v. 3; Rom. 8:24, 25).

1:14 not conforming yourselves: Believers should not pattern their lives after the desires that controlled them when they did not know God's ways (see Rom. 12:2).

1:15 Holy refers to being set apart or separate. We are to live so as to be dedicated totally to God and separated from the sin of this world.

1:16, 17 who without partiality judges: Our heavenly Father is also our earthly Judge. God does not show favoritism in judgment but invokes His judgment on all people **according to** their works. **in fear:** For Christians, this phrase should be understood as something between terror and reverential awe. We need to remember that God is both our merciful Savior (vv. 3, 18–21) and our holy Judge (vv. 15–17).

1:18 Redeemed suggests the idea of offering something, usually money, in exchange for the freedom of a slave or a prisoner of war. God bought our freedom, paying for us with His Son's life (v. 19). **your aimless conduct:** Peter's focus is not on any specific action, but on the way of life that his readers inherited from their ancestors. Those old ways were futile, empty of power and incapable of securing salvation.

1:19 precious blood: God's way of salvation is contrasted to human attempts at gaining salvation through the use of earthly means (v. 18). **a lamb:** Peter describes Christ as the ultimate sacrificial Lamb, who is offered in our place to pay the price for our sins.

1:20 foreordained: God has known (v. 2) the One who would bring salvation, even as He has known those to whom that salvation is offered and secured (see Rom. 11:2). **but was manifest:** What was known only to God before the creation of the world is now made known to us.

1:21, 22 Peter does not say that we purify our own **souls** but that we accomplish the purification of our souls by obedience to God's **truth.**

1:23 born again: Though this phrase is commonly used by Christians today, it is rarely found in the New Testament (see John 3:3–8 for Jesus' use of the phrase). Christians are dead in sin before their life is renewed by the Spirit (see Eph. 2:1).

1:24, 25 withers ... falls away: Peter reminds his readers of our transitory nature with an Old Testament quote, comparing us to the temporary things of this world—a direct contrast to God's permanent work and His eternal word (vv. 23, 25; see Is. 40:6–8).

2:1, 2 Desire does not mean just to want something, but to long for something with all of one's being. **that you may grow:** The purpose of studying God's truth is not only to learn more, but to become mature in the faith.

2:3, 4 living stone: Jesus, as a living stone, is superior to the Old Testament temple. These words also may be a subtle attack on the dead stone idols that the Gentiles worshiped prior to becoming Christians. Thus Jesus is greater than the traditions received from the fathers (1:18), He is greater than the temple in Jerusalem, and He is greater than the traditions of the Gentiles with their lifeless stone idols.

2:5 a holy priesthood: Unlike the Old Testament priesthood, in which only those who were born into a certain tribe could be priests, all who are reborn into God's family—all believers—are priests who have the privilege and responsibility of offering **spiritual sacrifices** to God (see Rom. 12:1, 2; Heb. 13:15, 16).

2:6 chief cornerstone: Jesus is the foundation stone from which the placement of all other living stones in the spiritual house (v. 5) is determined (see Is. 28:16). In ancient buildings, the cornerstone was first situated on the foundation and then all of the other stones were aligned to it. Thus as part of the house of God, we need to keep our focus on our Cornerstone (see Heb. 12:2). **put to shame:** Those who trust in Jesus will never be embarrassed by making Him the focus of their lives.

2:7 Rejected suggests that unbelievers, after examining Jesus to see if He meets their needs, declared Him to be useless or undesirable. Though He was not what they wanted, He is specifically the One whom God the Father has chosen to be the foundation of His eternal work.

2:8 stone of stumbling ... rock of offense: Unbelievers, because they do not follow God's Word, find Jesus to be repugnant, an obstacle in their way and a cause for disapproval and anger.

2:9 a chosen generation: God has not left to chance those who will be part of a unique body of people, a group who will serve Him. He has reserved that decision for Himself. **a royal priesthood:** Believers are transformed not only internally (see v. 5, which describes us as being made into "a holy priesthood") but also externally. We are a priesthood that functions in a ruling capacity, as kings. **a holy nation:** Believers are a unified group of people who are set apart for God's use.

2:10 obtained mercy: Although we once deserved condemnation because of unbelief (see John 3:18, 36; Eph. 2:1–3), we no longer are under the sentence of judgment (see Eph. 2:4–7).

2:11 sojourners and pilgrims: Peter reminds believers (1:1) that this earth is not our home. We are foreigners here, traveling to our eternal home, heaven. The word translated **abstain** literally means "to hold away from one's person." In other words, we must distance ourselves from our own self-indulgent urges.

2:12 Gentiles refers to those who are not believers in Christ, not to those who are not Jews. **they speak against you as evildoers:** In spite of our good works, those who are unbelievers will slander us. **they observe:** The Greek word for *observe,* used only here and in 3:2, implies a conscious, ongoing examination—in this case, of the actions of believers. **The day of visitation** probably refers to the final day of judgment when all people, believers and unbelievers alike, will acknowledge who Jesus Christ is and what He has done through His people.

2:13 Peter commands Christians to **submit** voluntarily to governing authorities. **to every ordinance of man:** This phrase suggests that the submission of Christians is not to be exercised solely in relation to civil authorities (v. 14), but to all kinds of rules that Christians encounter (2:18; 3:1).

2:14 governors: This term was used by the Greeks for all people, apart from the supreme ruler of a nation (v. 13), who exercise authority on behalf of the government of a country.

2:15 the will of God: The authority backing Peter's command for civil obedience is the God of the universe, the Sovereign Ruler over all citizens and governments and over all Christians and non-Christians.

2:16 A cloak for vice may be understood either as an excuse made up before the fact (a reason for wrongdoing), or after the fact (a cover-up for wrongdoing). **as bondservants of God:** We should submit all our actions to God, for He is our Master.

2:17 Fear God: Our reverence for God should be the basis of our relationships with others. All people are created in His image, and He is the One who has placed some people in authority over us.

2:18 Servants: Somewhere from one-third to half of the population of the Roman Empire were slaves. The percentage of Christians who were slaves may have been even higher. **be submissive ... with all fear:** Workers are to take their responsibilities seriously.

2:19 endures: Believers are not just to survive the difficulties that come their way; rather, they are to bear patiently their heavy loads. **Grief** here is not the result of loss but of being afflicted.

2:20 Credit suggests benefit or personal gain. There is no advantage to believers for successfully enduring a deserved punishment for wrongdoing, yet there is great value when we honor God with our actions when we are unfairly condemned by others (3:17). **take it patiently:** Endurance and perseverance in the face of suffering please God.

2:21 For to this you were called: Part of being a Christian is the privilege of serving God faithfully when we encounter undeserved judgment (see Phil. 1:29). **leaving us an example:** Observing how Christ handled unjust punishment gives us insight into how we also may endure such trials.

2:22 Who committed no sin: Christ was perfect in everything He did, even when He was wrongly condemned to death. **Nor was deceit found:** In His thoughts and attitudes, Jesus was perfect.

2:23, 24 who Himself bore our sins: The Greek wording emphasizes Jesus' personal involvement in the act of paying the price for our sins. It also emphasizes that it is our sins that Jesus bore on the Cross. **The tree** is the Cross. **that we ... might live for righteousness:** The purpose of Christ's bearing our sins is that we might live to please Him.

2:25 Shepherd: This title portrays Christ as One who tenderly and wisely provides for all our needs. **Overseer:** Christ is also our Guardian, our Protector, the One who watches over us. This is the only place where the titles Shepherd (Pastor) and Overseer (Bishop or Elder) are used in the singular. No one else is qualified to be the one Shepherd and Overseer of our souls—only Christ is.

3:1 be submissive: Wives are commanded to place themselves willingly under the guidance and control of their husbands, living in such a way that their husbands will be challenged to live in obedience to God's truth. **without a word:** A godly wife does not preach to her husband with words but with the Christlike beauty of her daily life. **may be won:** The goal of her actions is to see the unbelieving husband become a Christian (see 1 Cor. 9:19–22).

3:2 chaste conduct: The Christian wife is to live without moral defect or blemish. **Fear** here refers to respect for God.

3:3 Do not let your adornment be merely outward: Christians are to spend more time developing their inner character than attempting to make themselves look beautiful on the outside (see 1 Sam. 16:7). Peter is emphasizing the importance of a woman's character.

3:4, 5 Incorruptible beauty involves inner qualities that do not decay or fade like makeup, jewelry, and clothes (v. 3). **gentle and quiet spirit:** Peter encourages Christian wives to exhibit attitudes that are not harsh and grating but are soothing and tranquil.

3:6 calling him lord: Sarah was not worshiping Abraham; she was showing him respect. **not afraid:** Fear of her husband should not be the driving force that causes a Christian wife to practice the principles of godly marital relations.

3:7, 8 with understanding: A Christian husband should be intimately aware of his wife's needs, her strengths and weaknesses, and her goals and desires. He should know as much about her as possible in order to respond in the best way to her. **giving honor:** A Christian husband gives honor to his wife because she deserves honor (vv. 1–6). **weaker vessel:** The weakness in view here is primarily physical weakness, since the term *vessel* means the human body. **being heirs together:** The relationship described here is one between a Christian husband and his Christian wife, since all Christians and only Christians are heirs **of the grace of life** (see Rom. 8:17).

3:9, 10 reviling for reviling: Peter encourages Christians to act like the Lord Jesus. He endured suffering and ridicule in silence, entrusting His just cause to the ultimate Judge (2:23). **but on the contrary blessing:** Peter emphasizes the contrast between our natural tendency as human beings, to get even when we are offended, with the way we should act as believers: returning good to those hurt us (see Eph. 4:25, 29). **that you may inherit a blessing:** Christ will reward us for any suffering we endure in His name (see Matt. 5:10–12; 19:27–30).

3:11, 12 Peter uses the imagery of **eyes** and **ears** to remind his readers that God knows everything about believers, especially their suffering, and that He listens and responds to their cries for help (see Heb. 4:12–16).

3:13, 14 for righteousness' sake: Believers should make certain that when they suffer it is only because they have served God faithfully and not because they have done anything wrong (4:14, 15). **you are blessed:** God specially honors those who suffer for doing what is right (see Matt. 5:10–12).

3:15, 16 sanctify the Lord God: Believers should acknowledge the eternal holiness of Christ by revering Him as the Lord of the universe who is in control of all things. **to give a defense:** Peter assumes that the Christian faith will be falsely accused. He therefore encourages Christians to have rational answers to respond to those false accusations.

3:17 for it is better: Peter is saying that believers should make certain that when they suffer it is the result of having been faithful to God rather than because they have done evil (see 2:19, 20). **if it is the will of God:** Suffering may be part of God's perfect and wise plan for a believer (see Matt. 5:10–12).

3:18 once for sins: Christ's death on the Cross was a once-for-all event. He died once for our sins; He does not have to be "recrucified" each time we sin.

3:19, 20 There are various interpretations of the meaning of these verses, primarily because of the ambiguity of the phrase **spirits in prison.** The Greek term translated **spirits** can refer to human spirits, angels, or demons. There are three main interpretations: (1) Some interpret these verses as describing Jesus as going to the place where fallen angels are incarcerated and declaring His final victory over evil in His work on the Cross. (2) Others hold that **spirits** refers to human spirits. Thus Christ preached to human beings who had died in Noah's day and were in the realm of the dead (hell or Hades). (3) Another major interpretation understands this passage as describing Christ preaching through Noah to the unbelievers of his day. Since they rejected Noah's message of salvation, they were presently **in prison**—that is, hell.

3:21 an antitype which now saves us: The symbolic act of **baptism** is the **answer of a good conscience** of one who has been saved from the penalty of sin (see Rom. 4:1–6) by trusting in the death, burial, and **Resurrection** of Christ (see Rom. 6:4, 5). The floodwaters symbolize the baptismal waters, which in turn symbolize the salvation that is obtained through Christ's death.

3:22 Being **at the right hand of God** means that Christ is in a position of power and authority.

4:1, 2 arm yourselves: In order to fight the good fight successfully, believers must take on the **same mind** as Christ (see Phil. 2:5). **has ceased from sin:** Those who serve God faithfully in the midst of suffering take

on a different attitude toward sin than what they previously held. Sin no longer holds the same grip on them.

4:3 Lewdness speaks of insolent, shameless behavior that goes unchecked in a person's life. **Revelries** refers to long, protracted feasts that involve drinking and immorality. **abominable idolatries:** The idea is that some forms of idolatry may have been detestable even to the civil authorities. Of course, all types of idolatry are hateful to God (see Ex. 20:3–5; Deut. 7:25; 32:16, 17).

4:4 they think it strange: Unbelievers cannot understand the transformed lives of believers. **flood of dissipation:** In contrast to believers, who live in order to please God, unbelievers live without thought of the eternal consequences of their acts. They fill their lives with evil deeds that have no eternal value.

4:5 They will give an account: Although unbelievers think they are free to do as they please, they are mistaken. There are consequences to what they do. One day they will stand defenseless before God and give an account of their wickedness (see Rev. 20:11–15).

4:6 There are four main interpretations of who Peter refers to when he speaks of the **dead** in this verse. (1) Some see a connection between the gospel preached in this verse and the proclamation of Christ in 3:19, 20. Accordingly, they understand this verse to be about Christ offering salvation to those who lived in pre-Christian times (see 3:19, 20). (2) Another group of commentators also connects this preaching to 3:19, 20, but holds that this verse is speaking of Christ preaching the gospel only to the righteous people of Old Testament times. (3) One view has Peter speaking of the gospel which was preached to believers who are **now** dead. They had died just like other people, but they were now living with God. (4) The final and perhaps the most sound interpretation of this verse is that Peter is referring to the **spiritually** dead. The gospel was being preached to them so that they could come alive spiritually.

4:7 Christ can come in judgment at any time. Therefore, everyone should be ready to give a reason for the way he or she has lived. **watchful:** Peter urges his readers to be sober-minded and disciplined so they can offer their **prayers** to God.

4:8 love will cover a multitude of sins: Peter is not suggesting that one Christian's love atones for another Christian's sins. Rather, by introducing this proverb from the Old Testament (see Prov. 10:12), he is reminding us that love does not stir up sins. We can demonstrate our love for our fellow believers by forgiving them and not talking openly about their past sins.

4:9 Be hospitable: In New Testament times, hospitality typically meant housing and feeding travelers for two to three days with no expectation of payment in return. **without grumbling:** Being truly hospitable required personal sacrifice. Therefore many who performed such acts of kindness to strangers sometimes complained behind the backs of their guests about the hardships of caring for them. Peter exhorts those Christians to serve others cheerfully.

4:10 As each one has received a gift: Every believer is gifted to serve. **Stewards** are managers or trustees who will be held accountable for using their gift in the best interest of the One who gave it to them.

4:11 as the oracles of God: Those who teach God's truth to others should teach it in a reverent manner so that their hearers will respect the Word of God. **with the ability which God supplies:** Not relying on their own strength, Christians should use the power God gives them to do His will on earth.

4:12 do not think it strange: Apparently Peter's readers were astonished that they had to suffer as Christians. The Greek word translated **fiery trial** here was also used to speak of the intense fire that burned away impurities in metals (1:6, 7). **to try you:** For Christians the purpose of suffering is to prove their true character.

4:13 when His glory is revealed: Suffering will be part of the Christian experience until Christ returns (see Rom. 8:18–22).

4:14 reproached: Christians may be unjustly blamed because of their association with **Christ.** Peter calls this situation **blessed** because it brings great reward in the next life

(see Matt. 5:10–12). **rests upon you:** When Christians suffer unjustly on behalf of Christ, they will discover that the close relationship they have with God during that period will refresh their spirit.

4:15, 16 busybody: Meddling in other people's business is equated with murdering and stealing.

4:17 the time has come for judgment: Judgment does not always imply condemnation in Scripture. When used in relation to Christians, it consistently refers to the evaluation of a believer's works for the purpose of reward (see 1 Cor. 3:10–15). **the house of God:** The focus here is not on a building but on believers.

4:18 scarcely saved: No one deserves to be saved, and no one is able to be saved by his or her good works (see Eph. 2:8, 9). Since everyone deserves condemnation, the fact that anyone is saved is the result of God's grace.

4:19 Christians are to entrust their lives to God, especially in the midst of suffering, always recognizing that He is the **faithful Creator** who is in control of all things.

5:1 Peter sees himself on the same level as the rest of **the elders. Partaker:** Peter considers himself to be already participating partly in **the glory** that one day he will experience fully.

5:2 Shepherd the flock of God: An ancient Israelite shepherd would go before his sheep to lead them; he would not drive the sheep in front of him. Church leaders should lead the people of God in the same way: feeding, protecting, and guiding them (see John 21:15–17). **serving as overseers:** Church leaders must do everything in their power to ensure that the Christians under their care are living according to God's Word. **not by compulsion:** The work of the ministry is to be done joyfully, not just as a duty. **not for dishonest gain:** Christian leaders need to make certain that their work is not motivated by money.

5:3 nor as being lords over: Peter reminds all Christian leaders that they need to perform the role of servants, not of masters, to those whom God has assigned to their care (see Matt. 20:25–28; Mark 10:42–45). **being examples:** Christian leaders should be a godly model to other believers (see Phil. 3:17; 2 Thess. 3:9; 1 Tim. 4:12).

5:4–6 Chief Shepherd: Elsewhere Jesus is called the Shepherd (2:25), the good Shepherd (see John 10:11, 14), and the great Shepherd (see Heb. 13:20). **crown of glory:** God guarantees that those ministers who serve Him faithfully will receive an eternal reward in Christ's coming kingdom.

5:7 casting all your care upon Him: We need to present all our worries, anxieties, and problems to God.

5:8 Be sober means to be self-disciplined, to think rationally and not foolishly. **Be vigilant** means to be alert to the spiritual pitfalls of life and take appropriate steps to make certain that we do not stumble. **your adversary:** Satan is our avowed enemy. He is constantly accusing us before God (see Job 1:9—2:7; Zech. 3:1; Luke 22:31; Rev. 12:10). **like a roaring lion:** Satan attacks when least expected and desires to destroy completely those whom he attacks.

5:9 Resist him: We are not commanded to run, but to resist—to fight rather than flee. Victory comes when we remain committed to God, because He is greater than our enemy (see 1 John 4:4).

5:10 perfect: Like a doctor setting a broken bone, God will mend our broken lives and make us whole. **strengthen:** God will give

us the ability to succeed in all that we do for Him. **settle:** As a consequence of our facing the attacks of our enemy, God will build in us a firm foundation that will make us steadfast and immovable.

5:11 the glory and the dominion: God is in control of all things both in this world and throughout eternity.

5:12 Silvanus, whose Aramaic name was Silas, worked closely with both Peter and Paul (see Acts 15:40; 16:19, 25, 29; 2 Cor. 1:19; 1 Thess. 1:1). **testifying:** Peter uses an intensive verb form here to show the intensity of his commitment to witness unashamedly of God's truth.

5:13 She indicates the people who comprise the local church in the city from which Peter was writing (the Greek word for *church* is a feminine noun). Peter uses the term **Babylon** to refer to Rome. **elect together with you:** All of the people of God are chosen by Him to be His people (1:2). **Mark my son:** John Mark (see Acts 12:12, 25; 15:37, 39) was Peter's spiritual son, not his physical son.

5:14 a kiss of love: Early Christians and Jews greeted fellow believers with a kiss on the cheek. Peter is encouraging believers to treat fellow believers as part of one large spiritual family of God (see Rom. 16:16; 1 Cor. 16:20; 2 Cor. 13:12; 1 Thess. 5:26).

2 Peter

Introduction

The Christian faith that Peter had preached was not just a matter of philosophy. It was a matter of eternal life and death. Yet there were those who were peddling their own propaganda, falsehoods that contradicted the truth. Peter confronted these falsehoods so they would not be mistaken for the truth by writing his second epistle.

First Peter may have been written with the help of Silvanus (see 1 Pet. 5:12). It is quite likely that Peter either wrote the second letter himself or had another scribe to write it down—perhaps Mark. Although Second Peter does not refer to as many events in the life of Jesus as First Peter does, it accurately describes the Transfiguration, the prophecy of Peter's own death, the day of the Lord's coming as a thief in the night, and the prediction of the appearance of false prophets. All of these are clear allusions to Jesus' life as recorded in the Gospels.

Second Peter can be dated sometime between A.D. 64 and 68. It was probably written from Rome, where early church tradition has the apostle spending the closing years of his life. Peter died a martyr in A.D. 68, and the epistle was written shortly before that (see 1:14, 15).

Peter addressed his letter "to those who have obtained a like precious faith with us" (1:1), a way of saying "to all believers everywhere." He had written First Peter to the widely scattered Christians in the Asia Minor provinces of Pontus, Galatia, Cappadocia, Asia, and Bithynia. By the time he wrote Second Peter, they were no doubt even more widely scattered. Some have noted that Second Peter seems to be addressed to a group whom Peter knows well and who were facing a specific false teaching. Even if this is the case, the readers seem to be largely Gentiles (because of the multiple references to licentious lifestyles, a characteristic of Gentiles) or a mixed group of Jews and Gentiles, probably living in one of the provinces mentioned above. Word of their difficulties with false teachers had reached Peter in Rome, and he dispatched this letter to them to encourage

them and warn them of the dangers they faced.

With its emphasis on holy living and its efforts to refute false teachings, Second Peter emphasizes sanctification. Ultimately Peter traces the motivation for leading a holy life back to the imminent return of Christ and the punishment and rewards Jesus would bring.

1:1 apostle: With this term Peter identifies himself as an authorized spokesman for the truth that Christ proclaimed. **like precious faith:** Anyone who has faith in Jesus has the same access to God as any other believer. **our God and Savior Jesus Christ:** This title of Jesus reflects Peter's great confession in John 6:69: "You are the Christ, the Son of the living God."

1:2 Grace and peace is a common Christian greeting in the epistles. However, the phrase is more than a salutation to Peter. He sees grace and peace as blessings that spring from **the knowledge of God** and Jesus. Since our knowledge of Jesus grows as we mature in the faith, we will experience His grace and peace on many different occasions in our Christian walk.

1:3 The apostle Paul identifies the **divine power** referred to here as "the power of His Resurrection" (see Phil. 3:10; 4:13). **by glory and virtue:** These words suggest the qualities of Jesus that attract believers to Him. The glory that John saw in Jesus (see John 1:14) was His authority and power. The glory that Peter saw probably was manifested at the Transfiguration (vv. 16–18).

1:4 Great and precious promises refers to the numerous offers of divine provision found in Scripture. These promises offer us the glory and virtue of Christ as the basis for our growing participation in the divine nature. We have Christ within us, as He promised (see John 14:23), to enable us to become increasingly Christlike (see 2 Cor. 3:18).

1:5 Faith marks the beginning of the Christian life (see Acts 3:16; Rom. 3:28; Heb. 11:6). Through genuine faith, God grants eternal life to a spiritually dead person (see Eph. 2:1). **Virtue** is the same word used in v. 3 in reference to Christ's character. We cannot produce virtue ourselves; but we can choose to obey the virtuous promptings of the Holy Spirit who lives in us. **Knowledge** (practical wisdom) is obtained by dedicating ourselves to learning God's truth in the Scriptures and putting that truth into action.

1:6 Self-control means mastering one's emotions rather than being controlled by them. The false teachers whose views Peter was exposing believed that knowledge freed people from the need to control their passions. **perseverance:** A person who exercises self-control will not easily succumb to discouragement or the temptation to quit.

1:7 The Greek word for **godliness** was used by ancient pagans to describe a religious individual who kept in close touch with the gods. Here Peter uses the word to speak of the need for Christians to be continually aware of God's presence. Knowing that all of our life is in His hands should influence every aspect of our life. **Love** here refers to God's kind of love, which originates not in the one loved but in the one who loves. God loves because He is love; we are to love because we are from God.

1:8 neither barren nor unfruitful: The presence of the qualities listed in vv. 5–7 marks a healthy Christian and assures productivity in our lives.

1:9 The lack of fruitfulness (v. 8) in a believer's life may be caused by two factors: **blindness** and forgetfulness. A **shortsighted** person is one who looks only at earthly and material values—what is close at hand—and does not see the eternal spiritual realities.

1:10, 11 entrance ... abundantly: Peter distinguishes between a just-barely-made-it entrance into the eternal kingdom and a richly abundant one. Fruitful and faithful living on earth will be rewarded by greater privileges and rewards in glory (see Rev. 22:12).

1:12 to remind you: Three times in vv. 12–15 Peter speaks of his desire to remind his readers of the truth he has already shared. To do otherwise would be negligence on his part, since even established Christians can lose sight of the importance of pressing on to the end.

1:13, 14 Jesus had told Peter that when he was old he would be taken captive and put to death (see John 21:18, 19). Now that he had

little time left, Peter encourages his readers to seize the opportunity to display Christ's love while they still could.

1:15 careful to ensure: Several early church fathers took these words to be Peter's promise to leave behind a testimony of the truth for his readers, which they considered to be the Gospel of Mark (a Gospel widely regarded as Peter's testimony of the life of Jesus).

1:16 False teachers were claiming that Jesus' Resurrection and return, as well as the Holy Spirit's indwelling of believers, were all **cunningly devised fables.** Peter countered these claims with an eyewitness account. Peter himself had actually seen the **power** and **coming** of the **Lord Jesus Christ.**

1:17, 18 Along with James and John, Peter heard the **voice** of the **Father** during the Transfiguration (see Matt. 17:1–13). That voice conferred **honor** upon Jesus by identifying Him as "My beloved Son, in whom I am well pleased" (see Matt. 17:5). Jesus' **glory** was displayed in His shining garments (see Mark 9:3).

1:19 We have the prophetic word confirmed may be rephrased as "we have the prophetic word as a surer confirmation." As strong as an eyewitness account (vv. 16–18) may be, there is an even stronger confirmation that Jesus is who He said He was. The written Scriptures are even more trustworthy than the personal experience of the apostle Peter. The truths in the Bible will point to the source of all truth, Christ, until He returns in glory.

1:20 of any private interpretation: There is no private source for the Bible; the prophets did not supply their own solutions or explanations to the mysteries of life. Rather, God spoke through them; He alone is responsible for what is written in Scripture.

1:21 prophecy never came by the will of man: No mere mortal chose to utter his own thoughts as though they were God's. On the contrary, God chose holy men to be His spokesmen, men who uttered thoughts given to them by the Holy Spirit.

2:1 Just as God's prophets of the past were opposed by **false prophets,** believers are opposed by **false teachers.** The difference in terminology suggests that the false teachers among Peter's readers made no claim to being prophets, but were distorting the Scriptures with heretical interpretations. Peter's certainty that there will be such false teachers probably rests on Jesus' predictions (see Matt. 24:4, 5). False teachers could be recognized by their secretive approaches, their doctrinal errors (such as a denial of Christ), and by their abrupt departure from the Christian community (see 1 John 2:19).

2:2 destructive ways: Peter is addressing the ethical implications of false teaching. The false teachers gloried in the privileges of Christianity but treated its moral demands with indifference. **blasphemed:** The truth of Christian redemption is held in contempt by many because of the immoral behavior of professing Christians.

2:3 covetousness: The false teachers did not hesitate to take advantage of their followers in order to enrich themselves. **judgment ... destruction:** Peter turns from the description of the false teachers to a description of their fate. Verses 4–8 provide three vivid examples of judgment on false teachers of the past.

2:4 the angels who sinned: There are two main interpretations of this passage. Some think that Peter is referring to "sons of God" in Gen. 6:2. According to this interpretation, the "sons of God" were angels who rebelled against God and their role in creation. They began to engage in forbidden practices with the daughters of men. Their outrageous conduct was met with immediate judgment: the angels were **cast into** **to hell,** or Tartarus, a place of final punishment. Other commentators balk at the suggestion of sexual relations between angels and women. They consider this verse to be a reference to those angels who fell with Satan.

2:5 did not spare the ancient world: Peter's second example of God's judgment (see v. 4) is **the flood** that came upon **the ungodly** in Noah's day (see 3:6; 1 Pet. 3:20). **Noah** is called a **preacher of righteousness** because his righteous life put to shame the immoral lives of his neighbors. Noah's building of the ark would certainly have given him the opportunity to explain the coming judgment and to invite people to repent and believe in God. But

his entreaties fell on deaf ears, just as the truth of Christ's atonement fell on the deaf ears of the false teachers of Peter's day.

2:6 Sodom and Gomorrah is Peter's third example of God's judgment (see vv. 4, 5). Genesis 19 makes it clear that sexual perversion was the primary cause of the destruction of these cities.

2:7, 8 Three times in these two verses **Lot** is described as a **righteous** man. He was considered righteous by God because he refused to join in the immoral revelry of that city. For this reason he was delivered by divine intervention.

2:9–11 Two groups are singled out for judgment: those who live in unclean **lust** and those who hold **authority** in contempt. **presumptuous, self-willed:** These words describe the character and methods of false teachers. Their actions are characterized by boldness; they recklessly defy both God and man. Behind their presumption is a commitment to their own desires.

2:12 like natural brute beasts: False teachers are compared to animals in their behavior because they act in ignorance of the realities of death and judgment. Like animals, they also react only to present circumstances, without giving thought to the consequences of their actions.

2:13 False teachers are perverse in their display of evil, like those who **carouse in the daytime.** Even pagan societies thought it strange and unnatural to hold drunken revels in broad daylight. However, the false teachers had no qualms about practicing their erroneous concept of Christian liberty in clear daylight. As a result, they would **receive the wages of unrighteousness,** or spiritual death (see Rom. 6:23). The **feast** mentioned here may have been the *agape,* or love feast, built around the celebration of the Lord's Supper. On the other hand, the term may simply refer to social contact with the heretical teachers. The heretics were so self-deceived that they actually thought they were celebrating their freedom in Christ with their drunken revelry at the Lord's Table.

2:14 The **eyes** of the false teachers were **full of adultery.** They looked lustfully at women. They could not **cease from sin** because their fantasizing had become habitual. As a consequence, they convinced certain **unstable souls** in the church that adultery was acceptable Christian behavior and lured them into sexual immorality.

2:15, 16 The account of Balaam in Num. 22—24 is used here, as well as in Jude 11 and Rev. 2:14, to depict the danger of forsaking **the right way** and going **astray.** Balaam's primary downfall was that he **loved the wages of unrighteousness.** He sold his prophetic powers to the pagan king Balak and, for a promised monetary reward, sought to curse the children of God.

2:17 wells ... clouds: Peter accuses the heretical teachers of awakening false expectations, like springs that contain no water or storm clouds that produce no rain.

2:18 The heretical teachers were implying that once the soul is saved, what is done in the body is of no importance.

2:19 The irony of false teaching is that it promises great freedom while its advocates are already **slaves** to sin. The gospel offers release from the **corruption** of the world, but the false teachers were involved in moral ruin by their immoral practices (vv. 14–18) and greedy motivations (v. 3).

2:20 This verse seems to indicate that the teachers had formerly turned from the pollution of the world through a full and experiential knowledge of Christ. Now, however, they have fallen again into immorality, even becoming teachers of sinful lifestyles. As a result, **the latter end is worse for them than the beginning.**

2:21 The phrases **way of righteousness** and **holy commandment** emphasize the ethical content of the knowledge the false teachers had (v. 20). They knew what was right and holy, but they deliberately chose to do what was wrong and corrupt.

2:22 according to the true proverb: Jews considered dogs and pigs among the lowest of animals, so Peter chooses these animals to describe people who have known the truth but have turned away from it.

3:1, 2 words which were spoken before: The only way Peter's readers could recognize the errors of the heretical teachers was to compare their teaching with the teaching of the **holy prophets** and **apostles.** As Peter had already reminded his readers in 1:21, "holy men" spoke words given to them by the Holy Spirit, which were therefore reliable. These completely reliable words are in the Bible, God's Word.

3:3 A primary motivation for righteous living was the expectation of Christ's return (see 1 John 3:2, 3). However, the unforeseen delay in that coming would soon produce **scoffers** who would mock this idea, because they desired to live in ways that fulfilled their self-indulgent desires. The suggestion is that the

---

 IN DEPTH   **Looking Toward Eternity**

As Peter neared the end of his life, he wrote a letter in which he offers some insight into the nature of time and eternity. He beckons us to view time in both thousand-year units and as mere days (2 Pet. 3:8), recalling the beginnings of creation (3:4–6). He also projects into the future, when judgment will be rendered and new heavens and earth will be home to those who fear God (3:10–13). Peter reminds us that God values a day as much as a thousand years, affirming the importance of the here and now (3:8). But he also affirms God's activity long before we came on the scene (3:9).

Peter's perspective challenges us to live with a view toward eternity and values that last—purity, holiness, and righteousness (3:11, 14). We need to avoid getting caught up in the here and now and losing sight of our eternal destiny. Neither the joys of today nor the problems of this week can quite compare with what God has prepared for us in eternity. Peter urges us to stick with the basics of the faith and resist the fleeting enticements offered in this present moment (3:17, 18).

scoffers here and the heretical teachers of ch. 2 are one and the same. The apostles had predicted that such scoffing would occur (see 2 Tim. 3:1–5; James 5:3; Jude 18).

3:4 all things continue: The basis for denying the supernatural reappearance of Jesus is that nothing of that nature has occurred in the past.

3:5–7 they willfully forget: The scoffing teachers would choose to overlook events such as creation and the Flood. The people of Noah's time did not believe in Noah's warning because they had never experienced a flood. They forgot, as the false teachers later would, that God created the entire universe by His **word.** Likewise, the world's judgment and destruction would be by His word.

3:8 a thousand years: God will surely accomplish His purposes and promises, even though it may appear that He is slow in doing so. His timing is always perfect.

3:9 The delay of God's judgment is not because of **slackness,** but to the Lord's **long-suffering** attitude toward His people. **not willing that any should perish:** Peter is describing the sovereign God's desire that all people would turn to Him and turn away from their sin (see 1 Tim. 2:4).

3:10 Day of the Lord describes the end-time events, the Second Coming (see the descriptions of the end times in Dan. 9:24–27; 1 Thess. 5:2; 2 Thess. 2:1–12). At the end of this age in the day of the Lord's judgment, the **heavens will pass away with a great noise** and the **elements will melt,** presumably by fire (v. 12). Peter's description requires the unlimited power of God in dissolving the very elements of the universe, from which He will create a new heaven and new earth (see v. 13; Rev. 21; 22).

3:11–13 what manner of persons: The primary purpose of prophetic teaching is not to satisfy our curiosity but to motivate us to change our lives.

3:14–16 Note that Peter equates the letters of **Paul** with **the rest of the Scriptures,** indicating that Peter considered the apostle Paul's writings to be the Word of God. Note that Peter considers Paul's writings on the end times to be **hard to understand.** This should be a comfort to each of us who attempt to interpret the writings of Paul on the coming of Christ.

3:17, 18 Peter admonishes his readers that since they know truth, they should depart from **the error of the wicked** and **grow in the grace and knowledge** of the **Lord.**

1 John

Introduction

In this letter, the apostle John addresses the problem of false teachers who were making lofty claims about their knowledge of the deity and nature of Christ. John counters their false claims by reminding his readers of the eyewitness accounts of the apostles, including himself. Jesus Christ came in human flesh, lived a human life, died, and then was raised from the dead. He was fully human and fully God. Anything else being taught by others was false.

The author of this letter is understood to be John, the beloved apostle. Though he does not identify himself in this letter, the similarity of vocabulary and writing style between this book and the Gospel of John argues convincingly that both were written by the same person. Furthermore, in the epistle's first few verses (1:1–4), the author places himself among the eyewitnesses of the earthly life of Christ, as one who literally saw and touched "the Word of life." Obviously such a description fits an apostle but not a second-generation church leader. John probably wrote this letter about A.D. 90.

Gnosticism was a problem that threatened the church in Asia Minor during the second century A.D. Based on the concept that matter is evil and spirit is good, some Gnostics concluded that if God was truly good He could not have created the material universe. Therefore, some lesser god had to have created it. According to them, the God of the Old Testament was this lesser god. The dualistic views of Gnosticism were also reflected in the prevalent belief that Jesus did not have a physical body. This teaching claimed that Jesus only appeared to have a human body and never actually suffered pain and death on the Cross.

Key theological concepts in this letter include eternal life, knowing God, and abiding in the faith. John developed theological ideas through explicit contrasts, such as walking in light or in darkness, children of God or of the devil, life or death, love or hate. He was attempting to draw a clear line between true and false teachers. He wrote this letter to encourage believers to abide in what they had heard from the beginning so that they could maintain their fellowship with God and their love for fellow believers. In short, he exhorted them to make their belief in Christ evident to all, so that correct doctrine could be identified by their righteous life and their love for others.

1:1 The beginning may refer to creation or to the beginning of Christ's ministry. If it is creation, it is like the statement about Christ and creation in the Gospel (John 1:1). However, the context makes it likely that the reference is to the beginning of Christ's ministry, similar to 2:7, 24; 3:11. **The Word of life** may refer to Jesus, who is the *Word* (see John 1:1) and the *life* (see John 14:6), or possibly to the gospel message and all that it says about eternal life. Most likely, the reference is to Jesus, the Word who brings life.

1:2 The **life** that **was manifested** to the apostles is now declared by them. The life was not hidden or obscured so that few, if any, could find it. Rather, this life was made known openly and had its origin in God **the Father.** God's revelation in His Son (see Heb. 1:1, 2) is His finest and clearest presentation of Himself.

1:3 The primary reason John writes is to provide his readers with an understanding of what they must do to **have fellowship** with the apostles and God. *Fellowship* carries the idea of a positive relationship that people share and participation in a common interest or goal.

1:4 A Christian can have no real **joy** except in a proper relationship with God and others (see Ps. 16:11; 51:12; John 15:11).

1:5 God is light by nature, in His essential being, just as He is Spirit (see John 4:24) and love (4:8). **no darkness at all:** God is holy, untouched by any evil or sin. Because God is light, those who desire fellowship with Him must also be pure.

1:6 Verses 6–10 contain three contrasts between words and works, or saying one thing and doing another. Following each contrast is the result of the action. **If we say:** The first false claim is to have **fellowship with** God while failing to reflect His moral character. **Walk** refers to a way of life or daily practice.

To walk **in darkness** means to live contrary to the moral character of God, to live a sinful life. To claim fellowship with God without living a moral life or practicing **the truth** is to live a lie, since God cannot compromise His holiness to accommodate sin.

1:7 To **walk in the light** is to live in such a way that one is enlightened by the truth of who God is. **with one another:** When a Christian's conduct reflects God's moral character, then real fellowship is possible with other Christians. Only **the blood of Jesus Christ** can cleanse us **from all sin,** making it possible for imperfect believers to have fellowship with a holy God.

1:8 The second false claim (see also v. 6) is **that we have no sin.** The idea would be that our sin nature is completely gone. To say this is to **deceive ourselves** (see 2 Chr. 6:36; John 9:41). **The truth** is God's revelation, which says just the opposite.

1:9 Though John uses **we** primarily to refer to himself and the other apostles as eyewitnesses of Christ (v. 1), here the term includes all believers who **confess** (acknowledge) sin. God says that we are sinners in need of forgiveness. To *confess* is to agree with Him, to admit that we are sinners in need of His mercy. If a believer confesses his or her specific sins to God, He will cleanse **all unrighteousness** from that person. Forgiveness and cleansing are guaranteed because God is **faithful** to His promises.

1:10 we have not sinned: Unlike v. 8, which speaks of the guilt of sin or a sinful nature, this verse is about the denial of any particular sins. To make this denial is to call God **a liar** because God's **word** emphasizes the penetrating nature of sin (see Rom. 7:14–24). Denying that sin is in us indicates that God's **word is not in us.**

2:1 that you may not sin: John's statements about sin (1:8, 10) were designed to make believers aware of sin's danger and to put them on guard against it. **Advocate:** This word describes the intercessory work of the Son. When we sin, Jesus represents us as our *Advocate* **with the Father** to plead our cause in heaven's court.

2:2 Propitiation brings about the merciful removal of guilt through divine forgiveness.

God sent His Son and satisfied His own wrath with Jesus' sacrifice on the Cross. Our sins made it necessary for Jesus to suffer the agonies of the crucifixion; but God demonstrated His love and justice by providing His own Son. The sacrifice of Jesus' sinless life is so effective that it can supply forgiveness **for the whole world** (see 2 Cor. 5:14, 15, 19; Heb. 2:9). Christ's death is *sufficient* for all, but efficient only for those who believe in Christ.

2:3 we know Him: The New Testament speaks of knowing God in two senses. One who has trusted Christ knows Him (see John 17:3), that is to say, has met Him. One who has previously met the Lord can also come to know Him intimately (see Phil. 3:10). In this verse John is talking about knowing the Lord intimately.

2:4 does not keep His commandments: Disobedience shows a lack of personal knowledge of Christ. To claim to know Christ while disobeying His Word is to lie.

2:5 perfected: This verb expresses the idea of maturity and completeness. **The love of God is** *perfected* may mean one of two things: (1) The believer's love for God grows as he or she keeps God's Word, or (2) as the believer pursues fellowship and obedience, God's love for him or her is more fully completed. The second is indicated here. The believer begins to **know** by experience that he or she is **in Him,** or "abiding in Him."

2:6 abides in Him: Abiding expresses the idea of settling down in Christ or resting in Him. It is evidenced by a life modeled after Christ.

2:7 old commandment: In vv. 3–6, John insists that the test of personal intimacy and knowledge of God is obedience to Christ's commandments. But which ones? John emphasizes that he has no new obligation in mind, but rather what the believers have known **from the beginning** (see v. 24; 1:1; 3:11; 2 John 5).

2:8 The **new commandment** that John refers to is love (v. 10). It may be that John is simply repeating the statement of Christ in John 13:34. **true in Him and in you:** The command to love reached its truest and fullest expression in the life of Christ. He demonstrated what true love is by coming into our world and giving His life for us. Christians should follow His supreme example.

2:9 Brother refers to a fellow believer.

2:10, 11 he who hates his brother: Hating one's brother opposes the teaching of Christ to love one another. The idea that one could hate a brother and yet claim fellowship with God shows the utter **darkness** that has **blinded** the Christian to the truth. The believer who hates is in darkness and not light, in sin and not in fellowship with God.

2:12–14 These verses contain two sets of three items, describing John's readers as **little children, fathers,** and **young men.** These three classifications are not physical age groups or spiritual stages. Rather, it seems that each group is a reference to all of John's readers. For example, viewed as little children, they know their sins are forgiven. Viewed as fathers, they not only have a relationship with God, but they also have knowledge of God that comes from obedience to His commandments. Viewed as young men, they are strong.

2:15 Do not love the world may be rephrased as "stop loving the world." John's readers were acting in a way that was inconsistent with the relationship with Christ.

2:16 the lust of the flesh, the lust of the eyes, and the pride of life: The world is characterized by these three lusts. *The lust of the flesh* refers to desires for sinful sensual pleasure. *The lust of the eyes* refers to covetousness or materialism. *The pride of life* refers to being proud about one's position in this world.

2:17 passing away: John highlights the brevity of life. To be consumed with this life is to be unprepared for the next.

2:18 last hour: John views the rise of those who deny the truth of Christ from within the Christian community as an indication of the beginning of the end of all things. **Antichrists** most likely means those who seek to take the place of Christ. The **many** antichrists are the false teachers John opposed in this letter (see v. 22; 4:3; 2 John 7). They are reminiscent of the *false christs* Jesus told the disciples about (see Matt. 24:24). They are forerunners of the future **Antichrist** (see Rev. 13:1–18), who will exalt himself above God (see Dan. 9:27; 11:31; 12:11; Matt. 24:15).

2:19 When the false teachers **went out from** among the believers, they revealed that they did not belong to the Christian community; they were never true believers. When John says these false teachers were **not of us,** he means they did not agree with the teaching of the apostles. If they had been in harmony with the apostles, they would have remained in fellowship with them (1:1–3).

2:20, 21 Anointing: This anointing is the protection that believers have against the false teachers. John says that these believers are in contrast to the ones who went out (v. 19), who were representatives of the Antichrist.

2:22, 23 Denying the deity of Jesus is the same as denying the **Father and the Son.** In John's epistles, denying **that Jesus is the Christ** includes denying that He came in the flesh (see 1:1–3; 4:3; 2 John 7). A person cannot worship God while denying Jesus' full deity and full humanity.

2:24 The message they **heard from the beginning** was that Jesus is the Christ (v. 22), the Son of God (v. 22) who had come in the flesh (1:1–3). If John's readers would resist the lies of the antichrists and hold on to the truth they had been taught from the beginning, they would continue abiding in fellowship with **the Son** and **the Father.**

2:25 Eternal life speaks of both the quality of life in the present, a life filled with the joy of God, and the promise of a future life in eternity.

2:26 Those who try to deceive you refers to false teachers, or antichrists. *You* indicates that it is possible for believers to be deceived by false teaching.

2:27 We are to base our walk with the Lord on the truth He has given us. Believers who know God's standards and desires for us but fail to put these truths into practice will also not mature in Christ (see Heb. 5:11—6:12).

2:28 John has been urging his readers to let what they have heard from the beginning abide in them (vv. 24–27). Here he advises them to **abide in** Christ Himself. **ashamed:** The shame is the result of not having had a lifestyle of obedience when Christ returns.

2:29 Since God **is righteous,** those who practice **righteousness** will be recognized as being **born of** God. The point here is that when a child exhibits the nature of his or her father, he or she is perceived as the child of the father.

3:1 Behold what manner of love: John stands in amazement of God's love. But the greater amazement and appreciation is for the fact that God's love is expressed to human beings, that Christians are included in His family.

3:2 be like Him: Though we do not know all the specifics of our future existence, we do know that we will have a body like Christ's (see Phil. 3:21). Believers will put on immortality and become free from the sin nature that plagues us.

3:3 Everyone who has the **hope** of seeing Christ and being like Him (v. 2) realizes that Christ is morally pure. This realization helps a person pursue purity even more.

3:4 The **sin** described in this verse is not occasional sin but a consistent lifestyle of sin.

Lawlessness is not the absence of law but active rebellion against the law.

3:5, 6 If Christ is sinless and the purpose of His coming was to remove sin, then **whoever abides in Him does not sin.** Habitually sinful conduct indicates an absence of fellowship with Christ. Thus, if we claim to be a Christian but sin is our way of life, our status as children of God can be questioned.

3:7 let no one deceive you: Evidently the antichrists who were denying the doctrine of Christ (2:22) were also claiming to know God, yet were living in unrighteousness (1:6). True believers practice **righteousness** because the One in whom they dwell is **righteous.** God's righteousness is revealed in His children through their conduct.

3:8 Jesus' purpose in coming was to **destroy** the devil's **works.** A person **who sins,** even a believer, **is of the devil** in the sense that he is participating in the devil's

IN DEPTH   **Sinless Perfection?**

Most followers of Christ would agree that they should pursue the highest moral integrity that they can. But John's statements in 1 John 3:6 appear to raise that standard to the point of sinless perfection. In fact, if the person who sins "has neither seen [Christ] nor known Him," then what hope is there for believers who fail?

Here is a case where the English language fails us. In English the word "sins" appears absolute and final: one sin and you're cut off from God. However, the form of the Greek verb here (hamartanei) conveys a sense of continuous action: "No one who abides in Christ makes a habit of continually sinning." The point is that true believers diminish their old patterns of sin as they grow in Christ, replacing them with new patterns of faith and love.

The situation is similar to losing weight by changing one's eating habits. No one obtains instant health, but over time and by sticking to a disciplined diet, one can make great strides in that direction.

Of course, the fact that we won't obtain sinless perfection in this life does not mean that we should deal lightly with sin. To do so would be an offense to God, as well as destructive to ourselves. Yes, God forgives individual sins, but if we persist in sinful patterns, we keep the power of Christ from operating in our lives. We also risk grave spiritual consequences, such as losing the ability to repent (Heb. 6:1–12).

Do we keep falling into a particular area of sin? John says that the way out of that frustrating predicament is to learn to continually "abide" in Christ. We need to confess our sins to Him and then concentrate not so much on avoiding sin as on maintaining our relationship with Him. After all, He has come to keep us from sin (1 John 2:1, 2). But if we turn away from Him and yield to sin's mastery, then, as John has written, we can neither see Him working in our lives nor know the joy of His presence.

activity (2:19). Thus John is indicating that it is possible for believers to do that which is of the devil (see Mark 8:31–33, James 3:6).

3:9 The **seed** that **remains** is probably the divine nature in which believers can participate (see 2 Pet. 1:4). Habitual **sin** is not consistent with the Christian walk.

3:10 Christians **manifest** their nature by practicing **righteousness** (2:7). **Children of the devil** display their basic nature by sinning. Believers who sin are not expressing their nature as **children of God;** instead, they are following the devil's pattern.

3:11 John identifies loving **one another** as absolutely basic to living for Christ and advancing His kingdom.

3:12 Cain is identified as a spiritual child of the devil. His brother Abel is identified as a child of God. Cain's act of murder was the epitome of hatred, and thus came from **the wicked one** (v. 8).

3:13, 14 Love for fellow believers is evidence that one has **passed from** the realm of **death** to the sphere of **life.** Christians, who have experienced Christ's salvation in the past, should demonstrate their salvation by loving their fellow believers in the present.

3:15, 16 eternal life abiding in him: Those who do not love their fellow Christians are not living in the light but instead are living in the darkness (2:11). They are not abiding in life but in death (v. 14). What they are doing is not of God but of the devil (v. 8).

3:17 Goods refers to the material objects that sustain life. Therefore, the **need** that is mentioned is for food, clothing, and shelter. Believers can lay down their lives for fellow believers (see v. 16) by giving some of their livelihood to those who are in need.

3:18 To **love in word** is to speak loving words but to stop short of doing anything to prove that love. The opposite of loving in word is loving **in deed and in truth.**

3:19 We can be assured of the presence of eternal life within us when we demonstrate self-sacrificial love to others. Believers who begin to truly love (v. 18) will know their behavior has its source in the truth and therefore will have confidence before God (v. 21). Thus, love benefits both the giver and the receiver. **Of the truth** means being identified with Him who is the Truth.

3:20–23 Our heart condemns us because we recognize that we do not measure up to the standard of love and feel insecure in approaching God. Our conscience may not acknowledge the loving deeds we have done in the power of the Holy Spirit, but **God** does. He is more compassionate and understanding toward us than we sometimes are toward ourselves.

3:24 Abides in this verse describes the mutual indwelling of Jesus and the Christian. The believer abides in Christ by keeping **His commandments.** Christ abides in the obedient believer as One who is "at home" with that believer.

4:1 John speaks of the **spirits** of teachers in a way similar to what Paul says about the spirits of the prophets in 1 Cor. 14:32. John is not referring here to demon possession, but to teachers who promote error. Believers have the Holy Spirit (3:24); but **false prophets** obey evil spirits. A true prophet is one who receives direct revelation from God. A false prophet claims to have received direct revelation from God but in fact promotes erroneous ideas.

4:2 By this you know: One test of whether a person is led by the Holy Spirit is whether that person's beliefs agree with the truth of God's Word (see 2:22; 1 Cor. 12:3). **Jesus Christ has come in the flesh:** This test seems to be aimed at Docetists. They taught that Christ did not have a physical body. The test may also be aimed at the followers of Cerinthus who claimed that Jesus and "the Christ" were two separate beings, one physical and the other spiritual. John is careful to use the name and title of **Jesus Christ** together to express the complete union of the two titles in one person.

4:3 Cerinthus, a false teacher of John's day, denied the Incarnation by teaching that the divine Christ descended on the human Jesus at His baptism and then departed before His crucifixion (2:22). John teaches that Jesus did not just enter into an already existing human being, but He came as a human being. The Greek tense of the verb **has come** and the meaning of the noun **flesh** indicate that not only did Jesus come as a human being;

He was still a human being even as John wrote. God the Son is forever fully God and fully man. He is immortal and has received a resurrected human body that does not age or die. A denial of Jesus' full and true humanity proves that a teacher is **not of God.**

4:4 We can **overcome** by recognizing false teachers and refusing to follow them. **He who is in you** is the Holy Spirit. **He who is in the world** is the devil (5:19).

4:5 They is a reference to the false prophets (v. 1) who have the spirit of the Antichrist (v. 3). The false teachers, being a part of the **world** system ruled by Satan, are accepted by the world. **The world** believes their false teachings and receives them into fellowship.

4:6 We refers to the apostles, who find acceptance only among those who know God. **He who knows God** (2:3) listens to what the apostles have to say.

4:7 Love for **one another,** which here means fellow Christians, proves our spiritual birth and our relationship with God.

4:8 Know God here refers to an intimate, experiential knowledge (v. 6; 2:3) of God, rather than just information about God. John never says that those who do not love are not born of God (v. 7). Yet it is impossible to know God intimately without loving others, for **God is love.** Anyone in whom God dwells reflects His character.

4:9, 10 The love of God for His children was demonstrated through Jesus' work on the Cross on our behalf. **Only begotten Son** expresses the sense of uniqueness, not a literal birth (see Heb. 11:17). John is the only New Testament author who calls Jesus this (see John 1:18; 3:16, 18). Jesus is the unique Son of God; no other person is God's Son in the way He is.

4:11–13 By this looks forward to the evidence of His Spirit rather than back to the evidence of love (vv. 7–11) for proof **that we abide in Him … and He in us** (3:24). Mutual abiding refers to the fellowship we have with God as a result of our salvation. The evidence that God abides in us and we in Him is the experience of the Holy Spirit dwelling in us.

4:14, 15 A sincere confession of belief is an indication that the confessor is saved. **Abides** in this context refers to salvation rather than the

fellowship that results from salvation. To be a Christian, a person must believe **that Jesus is the Son of God.**

4:16 And we have known is parallel to "and we have seen" in v. 14. **Abides in love** means the Christian lives within the sphere of God's love. That love is both experienced and expressed through the Christian's life.

4:17 The mature expression of **perfected** love (v. 12) produces confidence as a Christian anticipates Jesus' **judgment** of the **world.** A person who abides in love will not be ashamed when Jesus returns (see 2:28; John 15:9–17).

4:18–21 A mature understanding of God's **love** removes any **fear** of God's judgment.

5:1 The condition for being **born of God,** for being a child of God, is believing or trusting in Jesus Christ. Only correct, sincere belief produces spiritual birth. This birth is reflected in love for others who also have been born into the family of God (2:3–11).

5:2, 3 The love of God demands obedience (see John 14:15). However, rather than being **burdensome,** God's commands free believers to be the people they were created to be: holy beings who reflect the image of God.

5:4 Whatever speaks of the new nature of the child of God. Regeneration (our spiritual rebirth) provides **victory** over the **world** which is opposed to God. The **faith** that overcomes the world is faith in Jesus Christ as the Son of God (see v. 5), who died for us (v. 6). The one who overcomes **the world** obeys God rather than following the expectations of the world. If we love God, we will find obeying Him a pleasure.

5:5, 6 Water and blood have been interpreted in at least four ways: (1) as Jesus' baptism and death, (2) as His Incarnation, (3) as the water and blood that flowed from His side on the Cross, and (4) as the baptism of the believer and the Lord's Supper. Most scholars favor the first interpretation. John is correcting the false teacher Cerinthus, who claimed that the Spirit came on Jesus at His baptism but left Him before His death (see 4:2, 3).

5:7, 8 The Holy Spirit testifies in accord with **the water** and **the blood** (v. 6) that Jesus is the Son of God.

5:9, 10 The witness looks back to the anointing of the believer described in 2:27 and refers either to the Holy Spirit or to the testimony of the Scripture. The last part of the verse suggests that the Scripture is meant. John is contrasting those who accept and those who reject what God says. A person who trusts in Jesus possesses the witness—the truth of God (v. 9). The one who rejects God's **testimony** is claiming that God is **a liar.**

5:11 This is the testimony: God's witness or testimony is that He **has given us eternal life ... in His Son.** Eternal life is not a wage to be earned, but a gift to be received from God (see Rom. 6:23).

5:12 John clearly states that our relationship with **the Son** determines whether we have eternal life.

5:13 Some assume that the phrase **these things** refers to the whole book of 1 John and conclude that the way to know that one has eternal life is not only to believe in the Son but also to live a righteous life and love fellow believers. However, the phrase does not refer to the whole book but to the immediately preceding verses and similar expressions throughout this letter (vv. 9–12; 2:1, 12–14, 21, 26; 4:1). In other words, the foundation of assurance of salvation is belief in God's Word and His Son, of whom the Spirit and Scripture testify (vv. 11, 12). Those who trust Christ can know they have eternal life because God says they have it.

5:14, 15 The key to knowing that God **hears** our prayers is to pray **according to His will.**

5:16, 17 A believer should intercede for a sinning fellow Christian provided that (1) the believer **sees** the **brother sinning** and (2) the sin **does not lead to death.** *Death* may refer either to spiritual or physical death, though physical death is probably the case here. **give him life:** The believer can pray with confidence knowing that it is the will of God that sinning believers should stop sinning. **A sin leading to death** may refer to blaspheming the Holy Spirit, rejecting Christ as Savior, rejecting the humanity or deity of Jesus, a specific sin such as murder (3:12, 15), or a life of habitual sin. Whatever it is, the sin seems to be a flagrant violation of the sanctity of the Christian community (see Acts 5:1–11; 1 Cor. 5:5; 11:30).

5:18, 19 The apostles are **of God,** meaning He is the source of their actions and attitudes (see 2:19). Satan does not touch the one born of God (v. 18), but he does have **the whole world** in his grip and under his dominion.

5:20 The **understanding** that Christ gives enables us to **know** God in a personal, intimate sense. **Jesus Christ** is **the true God;** to know Him is to have **eternal life.**

5:21 Idols may refer to literal idols, foods sacrificed to idols, false ideas in contrast to God's truth, or the doctrines of false teachers. John has just reminded his readers of the true God (v. 20). It is appropriate that he closes by exhorting them to stay away from false gods.

2 John

Introduction

Second John is testimony to the fact that no question consumed more time in the first century than "Who is Jesus?" The false teachers who prompted John to write this letter were promoting a heresy about this question. This heresy, called Docetism, was the teaching that Christ did not actually come in the flesh. In other words, Christ did not have a body but only *seemed* to have a body and to suffer and die on the Cross (see v. 7). Yet these teachers claimed to be Christians, teaching the truths of Jesus' life and death.

John would have none of it. He urged the believers to cling to the truth: Jesus Christ came in the flesh. The word *truth* appears five times in the first four verses. John wanted believers to guard against falsehood, and the best way to do that would be to arm themselves with the truth.

The evidence is that the apostle John wrote this letter. Some have argued that there were two Johns, the apostle and a church leader known as John the Elder. But as with First John, evidence from the early church fathers identifies this letter with the apostle. Other evidences favoring John the apostle as the author of this letter are the similarity of the language and content of First and Second John. John may have used the title Elder in Second John as an affectionate description of himself, since his authority as an apostle would not be in question at this late date. This epistle was probably written soon after First John, about A.D. 90.

The early church made a practice of supporting traveling ministers and teachers with gifts and hospitality. Christians in each church would house these missionaries and provide for their needs (see 3 John 5, 6). Since false teachers also relied on this hospitality, John urged his readers to show discernment and not to support traveling teachers "who do not confess Jesus Christ as coming in the flesh" (v. 7).

John wrote this letter "to the elect lady and her children." This is either a figurative reference to a church community or a literal reference to a specific person. The proof is not conclusive for either possibility, so the true identity of John's audience for this letter probably will always remain unknown. Yet the message of the letter remains clear: vigilantly guard against false teaching, and persevere in the truth.

1 The Elder is probably the apostle John. The title can refer either to an old man, an older person deserving respect, or a church leader. Here the word probably refers to the author's authority in the church. **The elect lady** may be a specific person, or the phrase may be a figurative description of the local church. **I love in truth:** John links truth and love. The second use of **truth** refers to the body of doctrine that is true. This is God's revelation, the clear teachings and commands of Scripture.

2, 3 If we wish to experience God's **grace, mercy, and peace,** we must commit ourselves to His **truth** and communicate His **love.** Blessing comes from the **Father** and **Son** equally. John affirms the deity of Jesus by affirming the Son's equality with the Father.

4 Walking in truth means having an authentic relationship with God. Our walk with the Lord must be based upon His Word.

5 Specifically, our walk with God is based on His **commandment** to **love one another** (see John 13:34, 35).

6 God's love is the basis of His desire for our obedience, and it is the reason He has revealed His will through **His commandments** in His Word. We prove our obedience to Him by demonstrating love toward one another.

7 One of the stumbling blocks to Christians is the **many deceivers** who subtly blur the truth about Jesus. Walking in truth means responding to deceivers by guarding against and rejecting them. **Coming in the flesh** refers to the Incarnation, the fact that Jesus is the God-man. The humanity of Jesus provides a test by which false teachers can be identified. The Gnostic heresy, against which John wrote in 1 and 2 John, included a denial of the physical body of Christ. People who deny the physical reality of Jesus are not Christians, but antichrists.

8 Being seduced by false teachers is one way Christians can lose their reward at the judgment. With this in mind, John writes that the reason to guard against deceivers is our own desire not to **lose** our reward at the judgment seat of Christ. Every believer has the potential of a **full reward** or a complete loss of reward (see 1 Cor. 3:15). The determining factor is our faithfulness to Christ.

9 Transgresses has the strong sense of running too far ahead, going too far. This is probably an allusion to the Gnostics who considered themselves as having advanced beyond basic Christianity. Departure from Christ into doctrinal error indicates that a person does **not have God.**

10 This doctrine refers to the Christian belief that Jesus is God come "in the flesh" (v. 7), He is completely human and completely divine. A Christian should not only refuse to **receive** false teachers in the sense of supporting them while they visit the community, but a Christian should also avoid appearing to endorse their teachings. The proper response to deceivers is to reject them as unbelievers.

11–13 greets him shares: To greet someone means to identify with that person publicly. This can refer to a personal greeting by an individual (v. 1) or to the church's public welcome of a false teacher (v. 10).

 IN DEPTH   **Needed: Christian Discernment**

We live in a day in which any and everything is tolerated. No matter how outlandish or how strenuously we disagree with what others cherish or embrace, we accept their right to their opinion. There seems to be no basis for saying "no" any more. Ours is an age of "I'm okay, you're okay."

But that is just not true. It would be more honest to affirm, "I'm not okay and you're not okay. We both need help that we can count on."

The early church faced a similar predicament. After Jesus' death and Resurrection, many claimed to know Him and His message, even though their versions of the story differed remarkably. For instance, Paul faced a conflicting gospel in Galatia and at Philippi and vehemently challenged his opponents' claims (Gal. 1:6–9; Phil. 3:1–4). Likewise, John warned against those who distort the truth (1 John 2:18–29; 4:1–6; 3 John 9–11).

The recipient of 2 John, possibly a woman (2 John 1), was given to hospitality (10)—a wonderfully Christlike virtue. But John was concerned to help her become more discerning and not lend the reputation of her household to those who would distort the truth about Christ (7, 11). He knew that not all who claim Christ are true followers. So believers must develop discernment if they are to remain loyal to truth.

3 John

Introduction

Third John was written in response to a struggle within a local church. One of the church leaders, Diotrephes, had asserted control over the congregation to such an extent that he was prohibiting representatives of other churches from ministering to his congregation. Worse yet, he began driving away members of his own church who dared to help the representatives after he had refused to accept them. Diotrephes's actions violated Christ's command to love one another. The apostle John felt the need to deal with the problem and was planning a personal visit. In the meantime, the letter's recipient Gaius needed encouragement, and Demetrius needed support in his ministry.

As with First and Second John, the author of this epistle is generally thought to be the apostle John. Similarities among the letters and early church tradition speak strongly of John's authorship. The circumstance addressed in Third John is markedly different from that of John's first two letters, and it is not possible to say whether it was written before or after First

and Second John. The letter was probably sent from Ephesus, where early church tradition says John located his ministry following the fall of Jerusalem in A.D. 70.

The recipient of the letter was a Christian named Gaius, though no other record of him has been found to date. He was likely a member of one of the churches in Asia Minor to which John's influence had spread during his Ephesian ministry. He seems to have had the resources to show hospitality to itinerant preachers, and he was certainly a prominent and trustworthy person to whom John could give the task of standing firm against the authoritarianism of Diotrephes until the apostle could come to deal with the problem himself.

1 The Elder is the apostle John. The word *Elder* can refer to an old man, an older person deserving respect, or a church leader. Here the word is an appeal to writer's authority in the church. **Gaius** was a Christian in one of the churches of Asia Minor.

2 may prosper ... be in health ... soul prospers: John's greeting may imply that Gaius was physically weak, though spiritually strong.

| ✎ IN DEPTH | **Pictures of the End Time** |

John's greeting (3 John 2) raises an important issue. It is clear that he expects God to give physical and material well-being to Gaius. Is that what believers today should be asking God for? Should we expect God to prosper us physically and financially? Is this verse an indication that He will? Notice some important things:

(1) John is praying for Gaius's prosperity, not Gaius praying for his own prosperity.

(2) This is part of a formal greeting or blessing. We say very similar things today like, "Good luck," or "Have a good day," or "Stay healthy, kid."

(3) The Greek word here for prosper means "to travel well on a journey." That fits with its use in a blessing. Furthermore, it is not something one should actively pursue, but rather a gift that one should look for, a sense of "wholeness" like the OT concept of shalom that people enjoy when they follow God's precepts and live in His power.

(4) We don't know what Gaius's circumstances may have been, only that his soul was prospering. John may be saying, "You are doing so well in the faith; I wish you were doing as well in your health and the rest of your life."

(5) John's main concern is that Gaius would walk in the truth (3, 4), not that he would have a big bank account or be in tip-top shape.

Overall, it would be foolish to construct a general principle of material blessing from this verse, especially when so many other passages warn against that very thing.

More probably John is simply following the pattern of greetings common to Greek letters.

3 The reason for John's prayer is the testimony of others that Gaius walks **in the truth.** Gaius walks according to the Word of God rather than the ways of the world.

4 My children may indicate that Gaius was one of John's converts. It may also be a term John uses to describe those under his pastoral care, as reflected in 1 John 2:1, 12, 18, 28; 3:7, 18; 4:4; 5:21. To **walk in truth** means to walk according to God's Word, the revelation of His truth.

5 you do faithfully: Gaius's support of **the brethren,** including those he does not know personally, reflects his faithfulness to the Lord.

6 worthy of God: These people had reported to others about Gaius's ministry in their lives.

7 Gentiles refers to unbelievers, not to Gentile Christians. The majority of Christians in the churches of Asia Minor were Gentile rather than Jewish converts.

8 We **become fellow workers** in the Lord's service when we support the ministries of others, publicly as well as financially. To **receive** means to identify with people publicly, welcome them into our homes, and supply their needs.

9 I wrote: John had written an earlier letter that was either lost or possibly destroyed by **Diotrephes,** who was asserting his control over the church out of his own personal ambition (see 1 Pet. 5:1–5). John had probably written asking Diotrephes's church to extend hospitality to the traveling missionaries the apostle had sent out (v. 10), and Diotrephes had refused to heed John's request.

10 If I come reflects the idea of "when I come." John intends to come and take Diotrephes to task for his attitudes and actions, and to exercise his apostolic authority in punishing him.

11 The proof of our commitment to God is that we reject evil and embrace a life patterned after that which **is good.**

12 Gaius can trust John's endorsement of **Demetrius,** who not only has a good reputation but also has a testimony **from the truth itself.** In other words, Demetrius's life measured up to the teaching of Scripture and Christ's commands. His conduct matched his theology.

13, 14 The brevity of the letter reflects John's plan to speak to Gaius soon. The apostle closes with a greeting of **peace,** a common feature of Greek letters.

Jude

Introduction

This small epistle strikes the imagination with its vivid pictures of false teachers. The writer commands our attention with his appeals for defending the faith and growing in grace. The primary focus of the book is on the faith, the believers, and God—not on the errors and character of the heretics. It is notable that with all of the blunt descriptions of false teachers, Jude gives us neither a command to confront these troublemakers (only to avoid them) nor a plan of disciplinary action. He simply indicates they are under the condemnation of God.

The author of this epistle calls himself Jude. He was probably the half brother of Jesus. This identification is confirmed by the author's reference to his brother James (v. 1) and a reference in a letter of Clement of Alexandria (around A.D. 153–217). We might wonder why Jude did not assert that he was the brother of the Lord Jesus, but his first readers would already have known this. Also, even in the years following the Resurrection, there were already some superstitions surrounding the "holy family" that Jude might have wished to avoid. It is likely that the letter was written between A.D. 60–64.

1 Instead of flaunting his honored relationship as a half brother of Jesus, **Jude** calls himself a **bondservant,** a servant of the Son of God. **called:** This is the primary description of Jude's readers: they had been chosen by God to represent Him in this world.

2 Mercy, peace, and love be multiplied: These words in Greek express a strong desire. Though *mercy* is mentioned in a greeting only four other times in the New Testament, those occurrences are important because they also precede a warning against false teaching (see 1 Tim. 1:2; 2 Tim. 1:2; Titus 1:4; 2 John 3). Mercy is God's undeserving favor on us. *Peace* is the state of a person who rests in God completely for salvation and protection.

3 Jude intended to write a more general doctrinal letter, but the present crisis demanded this short, pointed attack on doctrinal error. When Jude speaks of **common salvation,**

he is referring to the unity all believers have in Christ. But because of the crisis of the infiltrating heretics, Jude does not dwell on the subject of the common salvation. **Contend earnestly** translates a Greek word that is the basis of the English word *agonize.* Christians are not called to passive service, but to vigilance in the cause of Christ (see Phil. 1:27). **The faith** means the body of teaching passed down in the church by the apostles (v. 17). The revelation was not ongoing but **once for all delivered,** final and complete (see Heb. 1:2).

4 The heretics were subtle. Their primary tactics were to pervert God's **grace** and to **deny** the authority of the Lord (see Prov. 1:29). **turn the grace of our God into lewdness:** The teaching of grace can be dangerous when perverted by false teachers or carnal people who believe that because they have been saved by grace they may live as they please (see Rom. 6:1, 2). **the only Lord God and our Lord Jesus Christ:** These false teachers not only lived immorally; they rejected the authority of Christ.

5 though you once knew this: These Christians were given fair warning about false teachers from the words of Christ and the apostles (vv. 17, 18) but they had become negligent and were no longer on guard. **destroyed those who did not believe:** The false believers who had infiltrated God's people would be judged, just like the false believers who rejected God in the wilderness (see Num. 25:1–9).

6 It is clear that **the angels** to which Jude refers are not holy angels of God. Instead these angels could be those who had previously fallen with Satan. Some think that these angels are "the sons of God" of Gen. 6:2, who took on human form and married women before the Flood. According to this interpretation, these perverted angels were condemned by God to **chains** and **darkness** and are presently awaiting the final judgment of Satan and all his angels (see 2 Pet. 2:4).

7 in a similar manner to these: As the angels had committed sexual immorality with humans, so the citizens of **Sodom and Gomorrah** had pursued all kinds of sexual perversion. They were also judged by God with fire from heaven (see Gen. 19:24).

8 The false teachers were arrogant and had their own agenda. Jude calls these ungodly persons **dreamers,** perhaps because they claimed divine revelation, but more likely because they denied the Lord and thus were living in an unreal world of deception. They were creating their own false world in which indulging in immorality went hand in hand with salvation. **reject authority, and speak evil of dignitaries:** The false teachers even rejected those who were placed in positions of authority in local congregations.

9 The name **Michael** means "Who Is Like God?" The desire to be like God was the initial sin of Satan (see Is. 14:14). It was also the enticement that Satan offered Eve. Michael, though opposing Satan, refused to bring **a reviling accusation** against him. Michael would not even accuse Satan, the chief of blasphemers, of being a blasphemer. Instead he left judgment to God. This reverence for the prerogatives of God stands in

great contrast to the heretics who were slandering everyone (vv. 8, 10).

10 The false teachers **do not know** the truth of the gospel. They speak on matters that they do not understand. They have understanding not of the Spirit of God, but only of what they share in common with the animal world.

11 The heretics are compared to three Old Testament failures. **Cain,** a tiller of the soil, did not place his faith in the Lord. **Balaam** was a pagan prophet, an enemy of God, who believed he could profit from doing the work of God. **Korah** was a Levite who resented the prominent positions of Moses and Aaron as God's representatives. The Lord brought judgment on him and his followers for rebelling against those He had placed in authority. Christians need to be careful not to speak against spiritual leaders in a careless way.

12, 13 spots in your love feasts: The people of God had been deceived by people who appeared to be messengers of God but instead were ministers of Satan (see 2 Cor. 11:4,

IN DEPTH   The Use of Apocryphal Sources

The Jewish Apocrypha consists of books and writings that were never recognized as part of the canon of Scripture, but which served a devotional purpose for many believers of ancient times, including some of the authors of the NT. Jude cites two books of the Apocrypha in his letter. Jude 9 apparently comes from The Assumption of Moses, and v. 9 is a reference to that book.

Jude is not the only NT author who quotes extrabiblical sources. In 1 Cor. 10:4, Paul apparently made use of a Hebrew commentary (the Midrash) to support his interpretation of Israel's wilderness wanderings. In Acts 17:28 and Titus 1:12, he quoted from pagan poets to support some of his assertions. Though we do not know where the names Jannes and Jambres come from (2 Tim. 3:8), Paul did not hesitate to use their story as an example of godlessness for Timothy.

Should the NT writers have quoted from apocryphal sources? Surely God had no trouble guiding the biblical writers in selecting material from these sources. Luke knew of "many" accounts of the life of Christ (Luke 1:1), which he set out to better with his own "orderly account" (1:3). Along the same lines, Paul had at least one letter from the Corinthian church to guide his responses in 1 and 2 Corinthians. Even the devil is quoted in Matt. 4:3, 6, 9. This does not mean that these sources are inspired, or even accurate, but it does mean that sometimes NT writers drew from the written sources God had given them to communicate effectively what He wanted them to say. The writers of Scripture wrote all that, and only that, which God had inspired them to say. We must affirm with Peter that the ultimate origin of Scripture is the mind of God (2 Pet. 1:19–21).

13–15). **clouds without water ... trees without fruit:** Clouds may look like they will bring rain until the wind blows them away (see Prov. 25:14). Trees may look productive until autumn arrives, the time for fruit to be picked. The ministers of Satan promise spiritual growth but do not satisfy the hunger of God's people for the truth. Not only are they without fruit, but they are rootless and incapable of bearing. **raging waves ... foaming ... wandering stars:** These godless people put on a great show but lacked any substance. After they had done their evil deeds and made their profits, they, like wandering stars, moved on to other places to exploit God's people again.

14 Enoch, the seventh from Adam: Jude quotes from the apocryphal *Book of Enoch* here. This was a book supposedly by Enoch, who was taken to heaven by the Lord before he died (see Gen. 5:21–24). **Ten thousands** is a Hebrew expression meaning a limitless number.

15 ungodly: In view of the wicked nature of evil persons, how could the church allow them to stay in their midst? They are ungodly, yet they are with God's people, claiming to represent God.

16 grumblers, complainers: This verse describes various ways evil people misuse their tongues. Instead of praising God, they boast; instead of encouraging, they whine and complain. Their lives are characterized by selfishness and a slavery to personal desires.

17 The **words** of the **apostles** are important because they express the will of God. In discerning the spirit (v. 19) of anyone claiming to speak for God, the only sure standard for evaluation is the Bible.

18 Jude points out that nothing that has been observed about the false teachers should have taken the believers by surprise. The apostles had given warning (v. 17) that in the end times evil deceivers would come among them.

19 When Jude declares that the false teachers are without the **Spirit,** he leaves no doubt about their eternal destiny. They are worldly **persons** and do not belong to God.

20, 21 Jude tells us how to **keep ourselves in the love of God.** Jude is encouraging us to cultivate our love for Christ.

22, 23 We have certain obligations to other believers. First, we need to show mercy to those in any kind of spiritual or physical need. Second, we need to use discernment (**making a distinction**) in helping our brothers and sisters in the church. Some will require tender care and patience to help them grow in Christ. With others, we may need to use drastic action to rescue them from the temptations of sin.

24, 25 Jude concludes his letter with exuberant praise for the Lord, who alone could keep the readers from being deceived. **Stumbling** probably refers to the possibility of being tripped up by the false teachers' errors. Note that Jude does not use the word *falling,* but *stumbling.* Only a person who is already walking or running (frequent biblical images of the Christian life) can stumble (see Gal. 5:7; 1 Thess. 4:1; Heb. 12:1; 1 John 2:6). God is able to keep us from stumbling (see Ps. 37:23, 24; 121:3; Prov. 4:11, 12). He guards us in this life, in spite of all the dangers and pitfalls that deceivers put in our way. Only God can save us, cleanse us from our sins, and present us to Himself as **faultless,** because He is the Author and Perfecter of our faith (see Heb. 12:2).

Revelation

Introduction

As outside persecution against Christians increased, the first-century church also faced internal problems. They struggled with suffering, spiritual warfare, heretical doctrine and practice, and spiritual apathy. Christ had promised to return—but when? And how? And what would He do about the problems facing the church when He did come back? Confronted with these circumstances, the original readers of Revelation needed to be both encouraged and exhorted. On the one hand, Revelation was intended to be a promise of divine protection from God's judgment on the world. On the other hand, those who read the book were to take it to heart and obey, standing for the Word of God and the testimony of Jesus.

The author of Revelation refers to himself as John. He is associated with the seven churches in the Roman province of Asia (present-day southwest Turkey) in their suffering, blessing, and perseverance. His stand "for the Word of God and for the testimony of Jesus Christ" (1:9) caused him to be exiled to Patmos, a small island located about sixty miles southwest of Ephesus in the Aegean Sea. The most likely candidate is the apostle John, author of the Gospel of John and the three epistles of John. Revelation was probably written about A.D. 95.

Reliable historical sources dating from the second century A.D. place the apostle John in Ephesus and ministering throughout the province of Asia from about A.D. 70 to 100. It is likely that First, Second, and Third John were written by the apostle to Christians in that region around A.D. 80–100. During the latter part of this period, the emperor Domitian intensified his persecution of Christians. John was undoubtedly placed on the island of Patmos because of his Christian testimony. He was released after eighteen months by Emperor Nerva (A.D. 96–98), after which the apostle returned to Ephesus to resume his leadership role there.

In the power of the Holy Spirit, the apostle John received great visions (1:10; 4:2; 17:3; 21:10) as well as crucial messages that

the church needed to hear (2:7). In the spiritual realm, Revelation depicts a divine struggle against Satan and his demons (2:9, 10, 13, 24; 3:9). Yet this battle against the deceiver of the world and the "accuser of our brethren" has already been won by the blood of the Lamb (12:9–11). All that remains is for Satan and his followers is to be sentenced to their just, eternal punishment by the Lord (19:20—20:3, 10). Their doom is sure.

1:1 Revelation (a word meaning "Unveiling" or "Disclosure") indicates that this book is a type of literature known as *apocalyptic*. The Revelation of **Jesus Christ** can mean it comes from Christ, or is about Him—or in this case most likely both, since He is the subject of the entire book. Christ's **servants** are believers. The phrase **must shortly take place** is an allusion to Dan. 2:28, 29, 45, *shortly* seems to indicate the things that must come to pass in the last days.

1:2 The word of God and ... the testimony of Jesus Christ are the reasons John was exiled to the island of Patmos (v. 9). **All things that he saw** are the visions of the Book of Revelation.

1:3 Blessed, meaning spiritually "happy" from God's perspective.. This is the first of many groups of seven in the book, a number signifying completeness.

1:4 John addressed Revelation to **seven churches** in the province of **Asia,** which today is southwestern Turkey. The churches names are given in order going clockwise from the southwest. **Him who is and who was and who is to come** describes Christ, who exists now, always has and always will exist (see Heb. 13:8). **The seven Spirits** may refer to the angels of the seven churches (chs. 2; 3), or to the Holy Spirit (see Is. 11:2).

1:5 Jesus Christ ... the firstborn from the dead guarantees the Christian's Resurrection through His Resurrection (1 Cor. 15:20, 23). Christ will not exert authority (see Matt. 28:18) **over the kings of the earth** until His second coming (19:17–21).

1:6 Kings and priests is a description applied to the church by the title "royal priesthood" in 1 Pet. 2:9. Christ's sacrifice of Himself

(v. 5) has set apart believers as royal priests to offer spiritual sacrifices to God (see Rom. 8:17; Heb. 3:1, 14; 13:15, 16).

1:7 Coming with clouds recalls Daniel's vision of the Son of Man (see Dan. 7:13; Matt. 24:30). **Every eye** indicates that Christ will be universally visible at His second coming. **pierced Him** speaks of the Cross (John 19:34) and prophecy that Israel will mourn their rejected Messiah (see Zech. 12:10; John 19:34, 37).

1:8 The Lord's self-description as **the Alpha and the Omega,** the first and last letters of the Greek alphabet, means He is **the Beginning** and **the End** of all creation.

1:9 John is a **brother and companion in the tribulation,** which some were already suffering (2:9, 10). The suffering of John was related to his exile on the **island** of **Patmos** in the Aegean Sea. John was exiled to silence **the word of God** and **the testimony of Jesus Christ,** His witness continued in the writing of Revelation (vv. 1, 2).

1:10 John was **in the Spirit** as he received visions of the Apocalypse.

1:11 The seven churches in the province of Asia each received the whole Book of Revelation, and each received an individual letter from Christ (2:1—3:22).

1:12 The **seven golden lampstands** represent the seven churches named in v. 11 (see also v. 20).

1:13 One like the Son of Man is a reference to Dan. 7:13. Comparison of these two passages, along with Jesus' common use of the name Son of Man (see Matt. 20:28) for Himself, indicate that Christ is the subject of vv. 12–18. **In the midst** speaks of love and familiarity. Christ was fully man and fully God. The long **garment** and **band** (sash) indicate that the glorified Christ is dressed like a high priest (see Ex. 28:4).

1:14 The **white** appearance is parallel to the "Ancient of Days" in Dan. 7:9 and of Christ on the Mount of Transfiguration (see Matt. 17:2). Christ's **eyes like ... fire** indicate His judgment of everything impure (see Dan. 10:6; 1 Cor. 3:13).

1:15 His feet of **fine brass** speak of respect or power, as well as His treading everything underfoot (see 1 Cor. 15:25).

1:16 The **seven stars,** "the angels of the seven churches," are literal angels, since it would be unlikely to interpret one symbol by using another. The **sword,** coming out of Christ's **mouth,** is the judging power of the Word of God (see Is. 49:2; Heb. 4:12).

1:17, 18 Christ speaks of Himself as **He who lives, and was dead, and** is **alive forevermore,** referring to His eternal existence, His becoming a Man and dying on the Cross, and His glorified Resurrection state. **The keys of Hades and of Death** describes Christ's authority over death and the realm of the dead (20:11–15).

1:19 The things which are, and the things which will take place after this may refer to the state of the churches in Asia (chs. 2; 3), and visions of the future (chs. 4—22).

1:20 The angels of the seven churches have been understood to be human messengers. The New Testament meaning of the word *angel* is spirit beings, who minister to believers (see Heb. 1:14). It is not unreasonable to view angels as having ministry for churches in the present age.

2:1 Ephesus was the most important city in Asia Minor when Revelation was written. It was the center of the worship of Artemis the goddess of fertility. Paul invested nearly three years in establishing the church in Ephesus.

2:2 I know your works is a phrase that appears in each letter (vv. 9, 13, 19; 3:1, 8, 15), as a statement of recognition from the omniscient, omnipresent Judge.

2:3, 4 Leaving the **first love** means a great diminishing of the church's initial love, or a turning away from the love of the Lord.

2:5 Remember ... from where you have fallen speaks of a drop-off of love (v. 4) in the Ephesian church. The Ephesians were to regain the lifestyle that they had before they departed from their first love. To **remove your lampstand** would be to be judged.

2:6 Even if the Ephesian church did not love as it should have (v. 4), at least the Lord could positively say, **you hate the deeds of the Nicolaitans.** The Nicolaitans were a heretical group that troubled the churches at Ephesus and Pergamos (v. 15).

2:7 He who has an ear, let him hear is reminiscent of Jesus' warnings to His hearers after giving the parable of the sower (see Matt. 13:9). When **the Spirit** of God speaks **to the churches,** it is to represent Christ (v. 2), for He is the Spirit of Christ (see Gal. 4:6) who guides believers into all truth, and does not speak on His own authority (see John 16:13). The one **who overcomes** is the believer who perseveres in obedience and is victorious in the face of trials. The problem in the church at Ephesus was a lack of fervent love for Christ. The church is commanded to "repent and do the first works" (v. 5). The promise is that they will eat of the **tree of life.** Eating of the tree of life is a promise of renewing the fellowship lost at the Fall (see 22:14; Gen. 2:9; 3:22; Prov. 11:30). The privileged access will be enjoyed by the overcomer.

2:8 Smyrna was a seaport 35 miles north of Ephesus. The presence of a Roman cult and a large Jewish population made life difficult for believers in Smyrna.

2:9 Although there will be great tribulation unparalleled in world history believers must expect to suffer much **tribulation** even in the present age (see Acts 14:22). Christians experiencing **poverty** in this life can take consolation that they have great spiritual riches in Christ (see Eph. 1:18). **Those who say they are Jews and are not** are Jews who refuse to believe the scriptural proof that Jesus is the Messiah. Calling these Jews **a synagogue of Satan** indicates that they were persecuting the believers.

2:10 You will have tribulation ten days may mean suffering for ten actual days, or one brief period. **The crown of life** may be the "victory wreath" following the Greek use of *crown* for the garland given to winners in athletic events.

2:11 He who overcomes cannot be hurt by **the second death** (20:14). The second death refers to the experience of eternal separation from God in the lake of fire (20:14, 15). The believer who is faithful to death is promised the crown of life, a wonderful experience of life in the hereafter.

2:12 Pergamos was located 50 miles north of Smyrna, situated on a hill dominating the valley below. **The sharp two-edged sword** is the powerful word of Christ's mouth (see 1:16; Heb. 4:12).

2:13 Satan's throne implies that Satan's authority and power were honored either openly or in effect. **Antipas** (not Herod Antipas) had already suffered martyrdom, thus receiving the promised "crown of life."

2:14 The doctrine of Balaam is explained from its background in the Old Testament (see Num. 22—25; 31). **Balak** hired Balaam to turn the hearts of **Israel** away from the Lord. Apparently, similar seduction was taking place in the church at Pergamos, especially in regard to **idols** and **sexual immorality** (see Acts 15:20).

2:15 The doctrine of the Nicolaitans, already seen in the church at Ephesus (v. 6), was similar to that of Balaam (v. 14).

2:16, 17 The person who **overcomes** by faith amidst terrible circumstances (vv. 13–15) will receive **hidden manna to eat.** The hidden manna, **white stone,** and **new name** are all prospective rewards for faithfulness to God. Believers in Pergamos were involved in pagan feasts, where they ate food sacrificed to idols and committed sexual immorality (v. 14). The promise is for those who refuse to partake of the feasts. For them there will be a better banquet in heaven.

2:18, 19 Thyatira was a city with a large military detachment about 30 miles southeast of Pergamos. Recognized for its wool and dye industries, the city was also noted for its trade guilds. The description of Christ as having **eyes like a flame** and **feet like fine brass** virtually repeats the wording of Dan. 10:6.

2:20 Whether **Jezebel** is an actual name or a nickname, this woman's wicked actions parallel Queen Jezebel's in 1 Kin. 16; 2 Kin. 9. **Sexual immorality** and **things sacrificed to idols** link the activities of Jezebel to the sins in Pergamos (v. 14).

2:21, 22 A sickbed is where a believer involved in prolonged, unconfessed sin may end up. The next step of God's discipline is death (see 1 Cor. 11:30). Sin can bring **great tribulation** into an individual believer's life, although this is not the great tribulation that will come upon the world prior to Christ's return (7:14).

2:23, 24 The depths of Satan may be the secrets known by those initiated into the things of the devil. There was considerable satanic influence in Asia Minor in John's day (vv. 9, 13; 3:9).

2:25–27 Note that **he who overcomes** is further identified as the one who **keeps My works until the end.** To this faithful believer Christ promises the privilege of ruling and reigning with His kingdom and sharing in His royal splendor (see Luke 16:11; 19:17–19; Rom. 8:17; 2 Tim. 2:12). The words **power over the nations** and the quote from Ps. 2:9, which prophecies the Messiah's all-powerful role, link overcoming believers with the earthly rule of Christ in 20:4, 6.

2:28–29 The morning star is Christ Himself in 22:16. For the overcoming believer, Christ's presence is the light in the dark and difficult times before the dawn of the Son's coming.

3:1 Sardis, located 30 miles southeast of Thyatira, had been the capital of Lydia. The worship of Caesar and of Artemis, goddess of fertility, were active here. **The seven Spirits** may be the Holy Spirit. **The seven stars** are "the angels of the seven churches" (1:20).

3:2 No one's **works** are completely **perfect before God** (see Rom. 3:23). Unbelievers, those whose names are not "written in the Book of Life" (20:15), will be judged according to their works (20:12, 13).

3:3 Christ's warning that He will **come** unexpectedly **as a thief** echoes His repeated emphasis in Matt. 24:36—25:13: Be alert and ready for My coming (16:15).

3:4 Those **who have not defiled their garments** have remained faithful to Christ. They have had victory over sin and have demonstrated a practical righteousness.

3:5, 6 The **white garments** symbolize the robe of righteousness. **The Book of Life** is the list of the redeemed (20:12, 15). To not **blot out** is a figure of speech. Christ will make sure the faithful believer's name and works are not erased. **Confess his name before My Father and before His angels:** To have the Lord publicly confess one's name is to be received before God.

3:7 Philadelphia, which means "Brotherly Love," was a small city located about 40 miles southeast of Sardis. Its location, vineyards, and wine production made it wealthy and commercially important. **The key of David** represents authority as the One **who opens** and **shuts** the door in the kingdom.

3:8 The door that **no one can shut** seems to be entrance into heaven and "the New Jerusalem" (vv. 12, 21, 22). In spite of their having **little strength,** the believers at Philadelphia had obediently **kept** Christ's **word** and had **not denied** His **name.**

3:9 Those who belonged to **Satan,** though they claimed to be **Jews** (see Rom. 2:28, 29), would ultimately be forced to **worship** before the church and to understand that Christ has **loved** His own (20:4, 6).

3:10, 11 Christ's promise to **keep** the believers **from the hour of trial** is a promise that He will remove them before the tribulation. The *hour of trial* is a way of referring to the judgment of "the great tribulation" (7:14) predicted in Dan. 12:1; Matt. 24:21. The Christian must be ready for Jesus' **coming** (3:3). One can lose a **crown** that had been attained (see 2 John 8). The crown signifies the royal authority given to the victorious coheirs of Christ.

3:12 Christ promises that the faithful believer will be a **pillar,** the most stable part of a building. **He who overcomes:** The overcomer is identified with the names of **God** (signifying His ownership); **the city of God, the New Jerusalem** (citizenship in the heavenly city); and Christ's **new name** (the full revelation of His character).

3:13 He who has an ear, let him hear: Openness to the truths of the Word of God is a necessity for understanding the special destiny of the overcoming Christian.

3:14 Laodicea was 45 miles southeast of Philadelphia and 90 miles east of Ephesus. It was a wealthy city with a textile industry and a medical school. References to Christ as **the Amen** (meaning "The True One"), **the Faithful and True Witness,** and **the Beginning** (meaning "The First Place" or "The Ruler") of God's **creation** indicate that the lethargic Laodicean church (vv. 15–18) should pay close attention to His words.

3:15, 16 Cold water is refreshing; **hot** water is useful for medical purposes. **Lukewarm** water is neither. By analogy, the **works** of the Laodicean church made Christ want to **vomit** the believers **out of** His **mouth.**

3:17, 18 The Laodicean church was **wealthy** and assumed that it had **need of nothing,** when in actuality it was spiritually **naked and blind** to spiritual realities.

3:19 God's **love** for His children manifests itself in **rebuke** and chastening when they go astray (vv. 15–18). The proper response to God's discipline is to **repent** and be **zealous** toward God (vv. 15, 16).

3:20 I stand at the door and knock pictures the Lord Jesus seeking entrance into His own church, to fellowship with anyone who hears and opens the door.

3:21, 22 To him who overcomes: The promises to the faithful Christian is sit with Christ on His **throne.** Just as Christ overcame through faithful obedience, a believer who overcomes by humble, obedient faith will sit with Christ on His throne (20:4, 6).

4:1, 2 This verse signals the beginning of a new section of the Book of Revelation, which reveals the terrifying events that will occur in the future. This is the main section of the Apocalypse, and it continues through 22:5. **In the Spirit** described John's state of spiritual receptiveness in regard to the vision. The **throne** where God sits (3:21) dominates the heavenly scene before John.

4:3 The **rainbow** is reminiscent of God's covenant never again to judge the earth by a flood (see Gen. 9:8–17), perhaps implying that a different means of judgment was about to come upon the earth.

4:4 Twenty-four elders occupy other **thrones.** The identity of the elders is not certain. Some think that they are angels who comprise a heavenly ruling council (see Jer. 23:18, 22). The **white robes** and **crowns of gold** point to those who are confirmed in righteousness and who have ruling authority.

4:5 Lightnings and **thunderings** reflect the awesome majesty of God and recall the divine authority to judge (6:1; 8:5; 11:19). **Seven Spirits of God** as represented by **seven lamps** presents the fullness of the character of the Holy Spirit (see Is. 11:2, 3).

4:6–11 the **four living creatures** are similar to the cherubim (angels) that Ezekiel saw close to God's throne (see Ezek. 10:1–20). **Full of eyes** means that these creatures see everything. The **lion, calf, man,** and **eagle**

recall the four cherubim in Ezek. 1:4–10. They **do not rest,** so, there is constant worship **day** and **night.** The elders **cast their crowns before the throne,** showing surrender of their authority in light of the worthiness of God as Creator.

5:1 A scroll … sealed with seven seals cannot be read until all the seals have been opened. The scroll contains the judgments and redemption seen in later chapters. It may also be the scroll that was sealed in Dan. 12:4.

5:2–4 No one was **found worthy to open** the **seals** on the **scroll** in God's hand.

5:5 The Lion of the tribe of Judah (see Gen. 49:8–10) and **the Root of David** (see Is. 11:1, 10) are messianic titles for Jesus Christ.

5:6 The **Lamb** that **had been slain** is Christ, whom John the Baptist called "the Lamb of God who takes away the sin of the world" (John 1:29).

5:7 The reception of the **scroll** from the Father demonstrates that judgment and authority over the earth is committed to the Son (see Dan. 7:13, 14). The scroll is likely the same one sealed by Daniel (see Dan. 12:9).

5:8 The prayers of the saints (believers) held in **golden bowls** are used in worshiping the Lamb.

5:9–10 The **new song** celebrates the redemptive work of the Son as the basis of His right to judge. Divine rule has its basis in creation (ch. 4) and redemption.

5:11–14 Blessing and honor and glory and power: Every **creature,** that is all creation, shouted praise to the Lamb, fulfilling the decree that "every tongue should confess that Jesus Christ is Lord" (Phil. 2:11).

6:1, 2 Because the first rider is on a **white horse** and is **conquering,** some take it to be Christ (19:11). Other widely held views are that this is the Antichrist, or a spirit of conquest and delusion (see Matt. 24:3–6). The **bow** indicates that the rider is a warrior. The **crown** suggests that he is a ruler.

6:3, 4 The **red** color of the second horse stands for bloodshed, and killing with the **sword,** for war instead of **peace** on **earth** (see Matt. 24:6, 7).

6:5, 6 The **black horse** symbolizes famine; the prices for the **wheat** and **barley** are extraordinarily high, as they would be in a time of extreme drought.

6:7, 8 Pale, which means "yellowish-green," is the color of a corpse. The pale **horse** is ridden by **Death. Hades** follows Death to claim those who have died. This fourth judgment is the inevitable consequence of the first three. Up to this point, these three are characterized as the sword, famine, and pestilence.

6:9, 10 The fifth seal focuses on martyrs killed for **the word of God** and Christ's **testimony.** These souls are **under the altar** because sacrificial blood was poured beside the base of the altar in the temple (see Ex. 29:12). The martyrs are impatient for the **Lord** to **avenge** their **blood** and to **judge** all **those** who are not among His redeemed (5:9).

6:11 Each martyr is **given** the **white robe** of the overcomer (3:5) and told to **rest ... until** God's appointed time.

6:12–14 A great earthquake also occurs in 11:13; 16:18. The effects on the **sun, moon,** and **stars** are worded similarly to Matt. 24:29, placing these events in proximity to the coming of the Son of Man (see Matt. 24:30).The description of the **sky ... rolled up** could be related to the effects on the sun, moon, and stars (vv. 12, 13). The moving of **every mountain and island** would indicate seismic damage greater than any recorded earthquake.

6:15–17 The great day of His **wrath** (see Rom. 2:5) is still to come. **Who is able to stand** is answered in the surrounding context. Unbelievers, no matter how strong, cannot stand.

7:1 The **four angels** seem to be God's divine agents associated with the judgments. The **four winds** represent destructive forces from every direction.

7:2, 3 Before the judgments are released, God prepares to seal 144,000 of His servants **on their foreheads.** Seals are signs of ownership or authority that in ancient times were stamped on a document by pressing a signet or cylinder into a lump of clay at the point where the document was opened and closed.

7:4 One hundred and forty-four thousand may be taken either as an actual number or as a number symbolizing completeness (12 x 12 x 1000), referring to all who will be

saved. The first option is more likely because of the details developed in vv. 5–8. **The children of Israel** is the nation of Israel.

7:5–8 Judah is placed first in this list of the Israelite tribes because Christ, the Messiah, is the "Lion of the tribe of Judah" (see 5:5). **Reuben** is next as Jacob's firstborn (see Gen. 49:3, 4). Dan and Ephraim are omitted, perhaps because of their gross idolatry during the period of the judges, demonstrated by the incident in Dan (see Judg. 18). **Joseph** and his son **Manasseh** are both included, bringing the number of tribes to twelve.

7:9, 10 The **great multitude,** in addition to praising **God** and **the Lamb** for providing **salvation,** will later glorify God for judging Babylon (19:1–3) and will proclaim "the marriage of the Lamb" (19:6, 7). **White robes** may be the garments of overcoming believers. **Palm branches** were waved by crowds at victory celebrations.

7:11–14 This vast multitude has **come out of the great tribulation** predicted in Dan. 12:1 "such as has not been since the beginning of the world until this time, no, nor ever shall be" (Matt. 24:21). **Washed their robes ... in the blood of the Lamb** refers to forgiveness of sins through faith in Christ and His shed blood (1:5; 5:9).

7:15 The great multitude (v. 9) will **serve** the Lamb **day and night.** The 144,000 are later described as "the ones who follow the Lamb wherever He goes" (14:4). **Temple** refers to the inner sanctuary of the temple rather than the outer courts (11:19).

7:16, 17 Shepherd them and lead them to living fountains of waters recalls Ps. 23. The Lord who is the Shepherd in Ps. 23:1 is equated here with the **Lamb.** The "living" waters explain why there is no thirst (see v. 16). The water of life is available to all who will come to Christ by faith (22:17). **God will wipe away every tear** means there will be no crying, sorrow, or pain in the presence of the Lord.

8:1 The seventh seal on the scroll is **opened,** finally allowing it to be unrolled. **Silence in heaven for about half an hour** seems to mark significant break between the unsealing of the scroll (6:1—8:1) and the trumpet judgments (8:6—11:19). This silence is broken only by a heavenly offering and "the prayers of all the saints" (vv. 3, 4).

8:2–6 The judgments of the **seven trumpets** unfold in a pattern parallel to the unsealing of the seven-sealed scroll (6:1—8:1). **The seven angels who stand before God** are given trumpets and prepare to sound them. The **prayers** of God's **saints** have a part in the judgment of God. The **censer** is a firepan used for burning **incense. The golden altar** is where incense is added to the prayers of all the saints. The prayers of God's people for God to act in judgment are heard and responded to with **noises, thunderings, lightnings, and an earthquake.**

8:7 When **the first angel** sounds the trumpet, a storm of **hail, fire, and blood** breaks forth burning up a third of the trees and all green grass. The first three trumpets produce burning.

8:8, 9 A great mountain burning suggests a massive volcano or meteor. The sea becoming **blood** and the **creatures in the sea** die and a third of ships are destroyed.

8:10 Star translates the same term used for the angelic star in 9:1 Here the star seems to be a huge meteor that falls **from heaven** to earth, **burning like a torch** as it enters the atmosphere. **On a third of the rivers and ... springs** relates to the fresh water sources of the earth.

IN DEPTH — Revelation as Apocalyptic Literature

The word revelation (1:1) is a translation of the Greek word apokalupsis, from which we get the English words apocalypse and apocalyptic. An apocalypse is a special kind of prophecy. It features what most people associate with prophetic works of all kinds—dramatic, symbolic predictions of the future communicated to a prophet in a vision. The OT contains apocalyptic sections in Daniel, Ezekiel, and Zechariah, which were written around the sixth century B.C. Much of the Book of Revelation is apocalyptic.

Jewish apocalyptic literature outside the Bible flourished from the second century B.C. through at least the first century A.D. In most cases, these works were written to encourage and comfort the Jewish people, who were enduring the hardships of oppressive foreign rule. Some of these works are found in the Apocrypha and the Dead Sea Scrolls.

Because of its many symbols, apocalyptic prophecy is harder to interpret than any other kind of Scripture. Sometimes explicit interpretations (1:20) or an obvious reference to OT imagery or visions interpreted in previous passages (Dan. 7) give strong clues. In other cases, we must guess or infer the meaning. Revelation's four horsemen, the locusts, the dragon, and the beasts have all challenged commentators ever since John first wrote of them.

It helps to remember that like the nonbiblical apocalyptic literature of its day, Revelation's purpose is to comfort and challenge its readers. It affirms God's sovereign control over history and the certainty of His plan for the future. It reminds us that our present difficulties have a connection to the future, a future firmly in God's hands.

Though most of the Book of Revelation is apocalyptic, not all of it is. Revelation also contains straightforward prophecy (1:3) and seven letters of admonition (1:4). As prophecy, it focuses on our present duties and their relationship to the future. As a letter, it gives advice and encouragement to the believers at seven churches (1:4, 11; 2:1—3:22). In the final analysis, the Book of Revelation is a hybrid of apocalypse and prophecy written within the framework of an ancient Greek letter. The purpose of this letter is to inspire us to overcome all obstacles by steadfastly holding on to our faith (2:7, 17, 25, 26; 3:5, 11, 12, 21). The central message of the letter is clear: God is in control of all of history. He is coming back; and He will come in judgment, rewarding those who have remained faithful to Him (22:7, 12, 13, 20).

8:11 Wormwood is a plant found in the Middle East that is known for its bitter taste. The third trumpet involves effects far more potent than the taste of this bitter plant: **many men** die **from the water.**

8:12 Reference to darkening the **sun, moon,** and **stars** is similar to the phenomena of the sixth seal (6:12). **A third of the day did not shine:** Probably what is meant is that the intensity of light during the day and night is reduced by a third because of cosmic and atmospheric disturbances (vv. 7, 8, 10).

8:13 Woe, woe, woe refers to the impact of the three **remaining ... trumpet** judgments on the unbelieving **inhabitants of the earth.**

9:1, 2 The **star fallen ... to the earth** may be a demon (v. 11), Satan himself (12:9), or an angel serving God (20:1). **The bottomless pit** is the prison for some demons. It is also the place of origin of the beast (11:7; 17:8). Furthermore, it will be the place where Satan will be imprisoned during Christ's reign (20:2, 3).

9:3, 4 Locusts were feared in agricultural societies because they devoured crops. **Scorpions** sting with their tails, causing great pain and even death (v. 10). The only point of comparison between the locusts and the scorpions is the "stings in their tails" (v. 10). God controls the locusts' actions, causing them to avoid those who **have the seal of God** (7:2–4). Since no **harm** is to be done to **the grass** or **any tree** these insects are not ordinary locusts (vv. 7–10).

9:5, 6 The **torment** lasts **five months** because that is the life span of a locust. Many unbelieving **men will seek death,** but unsuccessfully.

9:7 The phrase **like horses prepared for battle** may be further explained in v. 9 as "like breastplates of iron." If so, this means **the locusts** have some sort of armor. **Crowns ... like gold** may imply that the locusts have high status among the demons but still rank below their king, Abaddon or Apollyon (v. 11). **faces of men:** The locusts have some humanlike characteristics.

9:8 Hair like women's may refer to the long antennae of insects. **Teeth ... like lions'** suggests strength and cruelty.

9:9–11 The angel of the bottomless pit is demonic and controls the demonic locusts (vv.

3–10). The **name** of the angel in **Hebrew** as in **Greek** means "Destruction."

9:12 The first **woe** spoken of in 8:13 is the demonic locust plague that comprises the fifth trumpet (vv. 1–11). This implies that the **two** remaining **woes** are the sixth (vv. 13–21; 11:14) and seventh trumpets (11:15–19).

9:13 John heard **a voice** instead of a symphony of the voices of all the martyrs (6:9, 10), and a voice of authority instead of an angel's voice.

9:14–16 The great river Euphrates is the eastern boundary of the land promised to Abraham and his descendants. The **release** of **the four angels** at the exact **hour and day** is in keeping God's sovereign control of the timing of His plan (see Dan. 9:24–27). **The army of ... two hundred million** will **kill a third of mankind,** under the command or influence of the four angels who were released. A third of humankind could number in the billions.

9:17–19 The horsemen number two hundred million, but **the horses** they ride and their killing **power** are primarily described. The mention of **breastplates** the comparison with **lions** and the **power** in their **tails** allow them to kill **a third of mankind.**

9:20, 21 The rest of mankind does not include those who "have the seal of God on their foreheads." *Repent* means to change one's mind about ungodly **works** to turn to the Lord Jesus Christ (see Luke 24:47; Acts 26:20).

10:1 This **mighty angel** could be the "strong angel" of 5:2 or the angel "having great authority" of 18:1. It is unlikely that this is Michael.

10:2 The **little book** is not the same as the scroll that was unsealed in 6:1—8:1. This little book causes John's *stomach* to become bitter. The angel standing with one **foot on the sea** and the other **on the land** conveys the image of taking possession.

10:3, 4 The mighty angel **roars** like a lion. It cannot be known what the **seven thunders uttered;** a heavenly **voice** commanded John to **seal up** what he had heard.

10:5, 6 swore by Him who lives forever: Only by the authority of the eternal Creator can the mighty angel make the declaration about how and when "the mystery of God would be finished" (v. 7). There will be **no** more **delay** in the unfolding of events leading toward Christ's return (19:11–21).

10:7 The mystery of God will be revealed and **finished** as the events of the final half of the Apocalypse develop. Significant aspects of this mystery have already been revealed through the **prophets,** but much remains that will be understood only when the events take place.

10:8–11 As words of judgment, the book would **make** John's **stomach bitter.** John's prophecy about **peoples, nations, tongues, and kings** may refer specifically to the remainder of the second woe (11:1–14), since there is a focus on the testimony of the two witnesses.

11:1 John is given **a reed like a measuring rod,** much like that used by Ezekiel (see Ezek. 40:3, 5) in his vision of the measuring of the temple. **measure the temple ... altar:** This is the temple of the tribulation period that will eventually be desecrated. The measuring of **those who worship there** may mean that those who worship the Lord in the temple will be protected, while unbelieving Gentiles will not.

11:2 Luke 21:24 prophesies that **the Gentiles will tread the holy city underfoot** until "the times of the Gentiles are fulfilled." Apparently the period of **forty-two months** is the conclusion of "the times of the Gentiles." *Gentiles* may also be translated "nations" (v. 9; 10:11).

11:3 Forty-two months (v. 2) is the same as **one thousand two hundred ... sixty days** (12:6). Almost certainly "a time and times and half a time" (12:14) is also a period of three and one-half years made up of forty-two thirty-day lunar months. The **two witnesses** will **prophesy** for 1260 days with astounding **power** (vv. 5, 6). The two unnamed witnesses are striking similar to Elijah and Moses who appeared together with Christ on the Mount of Transfiguration (see Luke 9:29–32).

11:4 The witnesses are described as **two olive tree** and **two lampstands,** linking them to the vision of "the two anointed ones, who stand beside the Lord of the whole earth" (see Zech. 4:14). There the two anointed ones are Zerubbabel and Joshua.

11:5, 6 The two witnesses have the authority to prevent **rain** during **the days of their prophecy,** identifying them with Elijah, whose prayer caused it not to rain for three and one-half years (James 5:17). Turning the **waters** into **blood** (Ex. 7:17–21) and striking **the earth** with **plagues** (see Ex. 7–11) is reminiscent of Moses in Egypt.

11:7, 8 The beast is allowed to **kill** the two witnesses in the same city where Jesus was put to death. The beast, who appears as the satanically empowered world ruler in chs. 13 and 17, emerges from **the bottomless pit. Sodom** was the prototype for the moral degeneration of this great city, as **Egypt** was the prototype for its rampant idolatry.

11:9, 10 The peoples, tribes, tongues, and nations are those to whom the gospel witness must continue until "the end of the age." Being **dead** for **three-and-a-half days** recalls the three-and-one-half year ministry of the witnesses (v. 3).

11:11–13 In the same hour: Soon after the two witnesses ascend to heaven, **a great earthquake** will destroy **a tenth of the city,** resulting in **seven thousand** casualties.

11:14 The second woe includes the sixth trumpet) and a second interlude (10:1–11:13). **The third woe** is the seventh trumpet (vv. 15–19), since it is said to be **coming quickly,** and since 8:13 relates the woes to the last three blasts of the trumpet.

11:15 Our Lord ... shall reign forever anticipates the return of Christ (6:12–17; 19:11–21).

11:16–18 The twenty-four elders were previously seen as continually worshiping God (4:10, 11) and the Lord Jesus (5:8–10). Here their thanksgiving to the **Lord God Almighty** enters a new phase: they praise God's **power** and **wrath** and the corresponding distribution of **reward** and judgment. **Reigned** may refer to the fact that Christ has already come to earth to subdue the nations. **The time of the dead** includes the bestowing of rewards upon God's people, His **servants, prophets,** and **saints** and the pronouncement of everlasting judgment on the unbelieving **nations** (see Matt. 25:46). **Those who fear** God's **name** have responded by faith to "the everlasting gospel" (14:6, 7).

11:19 The temple of God is **in heaven.** The **ark** of the **covenant** is spoken of here. This ark is the genuine ark of the covenant, of which the earthly ark was a copy.

12:1 In Revelation a **sign** is a person or event that looks beyond itself to some greater significance. Besides the additional **great** signs in **heaven** (v. 3; 15:1), there are demonic signs on earth (13:13, 14; 16:14; 19:20). The **garland of twelve stars** is a reference to the twelve tribes of Israel or perhaps to the twelve apostles (see 21:12–14).

12:2 The description of **labor** and **pain** before giving **birth** to the Child who becomes ruler of the nations may picture the Jewish nation or the believing remnant. In addition, the first prophecy of the Bible, Gen. 3:15, serves as the ultimate backdrop to this struggle between a woman and Satan.

12:3 The **sign** of the **fiery red dragon** is interpreted in v. 9 as Satan. The dragon with the seven heads and ten horns refers to Satan and the empire over which he rules. **Seven heads, ten horns,** and **seven diadems** refer to Satan's (v. 9) brilliance, power, and authority as "god of this age" (2 Cor. 4:4).

12:4 The reference to **a third of the stars** may reference the rebellion of a third of the angelic host following Satan.

12:5 The **male Child** who will **rule ... with a rod of iron** is the messianic figure of Ps. 2:8, 9; however, there is no earthly rule over **all nations** at this point.

12:6 The wilderness here is **a place** of protection **prepared by God** (Hos. 2:14) for the woman. **One thousand two hundred and sixty days** is the period of provision and protection for the woman in the wilderness. The detailed way in which this length of time is expressed suggests half of a literal seven-year tribulation period (see Dan. 9:27).

12:7, 8 Michael is an archangel (see Jude 9). According to Dan. 12:1 he is a special guardian angel for the nation of Israel. Apparently he commands an army of **angels.**

12:9 The devil's expulsion **to the earth** means that this world becomes his base of operations, and that his anger is vented toward inhabitants of the earth (v. 12).

12:10, 11 The heavenly defeat of Satan (vv. 7–9) is followed by reference to his earthly setbacks, including the crucifixion of Christ (**the blood of the Lamb**), the verbal witness of believers (**the word of their testimony**), and the martyrdom of some of the **brethren.** All these events precede the coming of **the kingdom of our God.**

12:12 Those in the **heavens** have good reason to **rejoice,** because of the permanent expulsion of **the devil.** On the other hand, the natural creation (**the earth and the sea**) now has an additional **woe** (8:13; 9:12; 11:14) to contend with—the **great** anger of the devil, who **knows** his **time** is **short.**

12:13, 14 The woman (vv. 1–6) is somehow brought to her place of protection, **the wilderness,** as if carried on the **wings of a great eagle. A time** probably equals one year, so the period of protection here is three and one-half years, which corresponds to the length of the two witnesses' testimony in 11:3.

12:15, 16 The danger of the **flood** to the **woman** is averted when **the earth** opens up. There is no way of determining whether this describes an actual flood or figuratively describes the onslaught of Satan against those protected by God.

12:17 Enraged by his inability to destroy the **woman,** Satan, **the dragon,** resorts to **war** against a related group. **The rest of her offspring** are believers in Christ, since they **keep the commandments of God** and **the testimony of Jesus Christ.**

13:1, 2 The description of the first **beast** (**seven heads ... ten horns ... ten crowns**) is similar to that of the great **dragon** (that is, Satan) in 12:3. Whereas crowns are on the heads of the dragon, there are on the *horns* of the sea beast. A mountain is typically a symbol for a kingdom (see Dan. 2:34, 35, 44, 45). The beast receives his **power** and **authority** from the dragon. The parallel to the four beasts (especially the fourth) in Dan. 7 and the explanation of the beast given in 17:8–11 make it seem that the beast symbolizes both a revived Roman Empire, which exercises universal authority, and a specific ruler, whom John calls the "Antichrist" in 1 John 2:18.

13:3, 4 One of his heads may stand for a specific ruler, but more likely it stands for an empire. The unbelieving **world** is enticed to follow and worship the **beast.** Those who **worshiped** the beast also worshiped the devil, **who gave authority to the beast.**

13:5–7 Forty-two months is the duration of the beast's worldwide supremacy, in keeping with the prophecy of Dan. 7:25. This first use of the word **tabernacle** may look ahead to when God's tabernacle will be among His people in the new heaven and earth (21:3).

13:8 The Book of Life is the register of those who will receive eternal life, in contrast to those destined for the lake of fire (20:12, 15).

13:9 If anyone has an ear, let him hear seems to imply that either the following saying (v. 10) or the wider context has significant present application, not just future reference.

13:10 Even when believers face **captivity** or are being **killed,** they can have **patience** and **faith,** knowing that God will vindicate them (see Rom. 12:19) on "the day of wrath and ... righteous judgment" (Rom. 2:5).

13:11 Another means "another of the same kind," speaking of the close relationship between this **beast** from **the earth** and the previous beast from the sea (v. 1). This beast's actions described in vv. 12–17 make it virtually certain that he is the false prophet spoken of in 16:13; 19:20; 20:10. This is the only place in Revelation where **lamb** does not refer to Christ. The lamb with **two horns** here is a symbol of Jewish worship and religious authority.

13:12–15 Great signs, such as calling **fire** from **heaven** and giving **breath** and speech to the **image** of the first beast, are persuasive. The performance of great signs by the power of Satan is part of the mass deception prophesied by Paul in 2 Thess. 2:8, 9.

13:16, 17 The **mark** is equivalent to **the name of the beast** and **the number of his name.** The mark of the beast is identifiable proof of ownership and loyalty placed on the **right hand** or the forehead. This mark is a counterfeit of the seal on the foreheads of the servants of God in 7:3; 14:1.

13:18 After the preceding description of the tyranny of **the beast,** an explanatory comment designed to impart **wisdom** and **understanding** to the reader is given. The **number** (the "name" in v. 17) of the beast is **666;** it is also described as **the number of a man.** The beast is just a man, not a god, as the signs might suggest. The number 6, just short of 7 (the number of completeness), is intensified as 666—the number of the most powerful man who is not God. This man's identity will someday be understood in relation to the number 666. It is a key for identifying the Antichrist.

14:1 Mount Zion is a synonym Jerusalem, focusing on the hill where the temple was built. The **one hundred and forty-four thousand** have God's **name written on their foreheads.** In 7:2–4 the protection for this group is referred to as a seal on their foreheads. This may be a sign visible only in heaven and in the new earth. (3:12; 22:4).

14:2, 3 This is a **new song,** only those **redeemed from the earth,** the **hundred and forty-four thousand,** are allowed to **learn** it.

14:4 The **virgins** are symbolic of spiritual purity (see 2 Cor. 11:2). Redeemed believers will not compromise with evil. They will reject false doctrine and refuse to worship the beast.

14:5 The 144,000 were not sinless in their earthly lives (see Rom. 3:23), but they were without **deceit** and **fault** with regard to their testimony for Christ. They were without fault or blemish because they refused the mark of the beast.

14:6, 7 The **angel** preaches the **gospel** to **every nation, tribe, tongue, and people** to fulfill God's promise that the gospel "will be preached in all the world as a witness to all the nations" (Matt. 24:14). The gospel message at this point beseeches unbelievers to **fear God and give glory to Him** and to escape **the hour of His judgment.**

14:8 Babylon caused all nations to be guilty of fornication and subject to the wine of wrath. **Babylon** is first mentioned in Revelation here, and is the focus of God's judgment in the following section (chs. 16—18).

14:9–11 A third angel announces with a **loud voice** the destiny of the one who rejects the offer of the gospel (vv. 6, 7) and **worships the beast** (ch. 13). In the just outworking of God's wrath, unbelievers who worship the beast will **be tormented ... forever and ever,** with **no rest day or night.**

14:12 Those who patiently **keep the commandments of God and the faith of Jesus,** in very difficult times (ch. 13), will receive a divine blessing (v. 13).

14:13 Spiritual **rest** is available to anyone who comes to Jesus Christ in faith (see Matt. 11:28). Here believers who have died are told to rest **from their labors,** in the knowledge that their good **works** will be remembered and rewarded (see 1 Tim. 5:25).

14:14–16 The **Son of Man** with a **golden crown** on His head indicates the figure is Jesus Christ (see 1:13; Dan. 7). A **sharp** flint or iron **sickle** was the primary tool for an ancient grain **harvest.** The harvest **of the earth** is **ripe** for salvation as well as judgment. The power of the Son of Man (Jesus Christ) is shown in that, with one **thrust** of **His sickle,** the harvest of **the earth** is **reaped.** This pictures one rapid succession of judgment. Thus judgment is experienced by the inhabitants of the entire world.

14:17, 18 Another angel is placed in charge of the harvest of the **clusters** of **grapes** that are also **ripe,** meaning worthy of judgment.

14:19, 20 winepress: The image of the winepress is symbolic of an unbelievable quantity of shed **blood. One thousand six hundred furlongs** is nearly two hundred miles.

15:1 Another sign looks back to 12:1, 3. This sign is **great and marvelous,** because it deals with **the seven last plagues,** "the bowls of the **wrath of God.**" They are immediately followed by the Second Coming and the marriage supper of the Lamb (19:6–21).

15:2 A sea of glass is mentioned in 4:6 is seen **mingled with fire,** which is often a sign of God's judgment. The sea of glass also serves as the Lord's victory stand for all of His overcomers. **Those who have the victory over the beast** are believing martyrs.

15:3, 4 The song of the Lamb exults the completed redemptive work of Jesus Christ. Considering God's **great ... works** and character,

every person should **fear** the Lord and **glorify** His **name** by trusting Jesus Christ.

15:5 The temple of the tabernacle links the imagery of the heavenly temple with the Exodus period, when the presence of God was clearly seen in the tabernacle. In the new heaven and new earth the tabernacle of God will be with believers because He will dwell eternally with them (21:3).

15:6 Seven angels come forward to administer the **seven plagues,** which are the last plagues God will send before Christ returns.

15:7 The **golden bowls** of wrath recall the similar golden bowls that held the prayers of the saints.

15:8 The **smoke** that **filled** the **temple** had its source in the power and glory of God and prohibited access into the Most Holy Place. The smoke signified God's resolve to act in judgment as an expression of His character and authority.

16:1 The **loud voice from the temple** is the voice of God, since no other heavenly being could enter the heavenly temple "till the seven plagues of the seven angels were completed" (15:8).

16:2, 3 The effect of the **first ... bowl** being **poured out** is a terrible **sore** upon all **who had the mark of the beast** (13:16, 17). **The second ... bowl** turns the **sea** into **blood,** as did the second trumpet. Only a third of the sea was affected by the trumpet (8:8, 9). This bowl brings about the death of **every living creature** in the sea.

16:4 The third ... bowl, like the third trumpet (8:10), targets **the rivers and springs of water.** This time the impact is worldwide and the water sources turn to **blood.**

16:5–7 The angel of the waters is probably the angel who guards these water sources. God is eternally **righteous** and two witnesses, the angel and the voice from the altar, praise His judgment. God forces the unrepentant who **have shed the blood** of God's people to **drink** blood in order to avenge the deaths of the martyrs. **Saints** and **prophets** may refer to all of God's people who have been killed as a result of persecution.

16:8 The fourth ... bowl effects the **sun.** The sun's heat is intensified.

16:9 Those who followed the beast here blaspheme **the name of God** They will **not repent and give** God **glory** (vv. 11, 21).

16:10, 11 The fifth ... bowl is focused against the **throne of the beast** referring to his worldwide **kingdom** and authority (13:7). The **darkness** was a blindness of the mind; their "foolish heart were darkened" (see Rom 1:21). The beast and his followers still blaspheme **the God of heaven** and refuse to **repent of their deeds.**

16:12 With the **water** of the **river Euphrates** completely **dried up,** invasion from the east would be much easier. **The kings from the east** have been understood as the Parthian armies that menaced the eastern half of the Roman Empire.

16:13, 14 Unclean spirits spread the lying words of **the dragon** (Satan; 12:9), **the beast,** and **the false prophet**—an unholy trio. There will be great deception involved in the **signs** used to persuade **the kings of ... the whole world** to gather for battle against **God.** In 6:15, 16, the kings of the earth recoil in fear before the judgment of the Lamb. Here the kings are willing to wage war against God. The difference seems to be their confidence in the power of the beast. **The battle of that great day** takes place at Armageddon (v. 16; 19:17–21).

16:15 Blessed is the one who watches. **Coming as a thief** looks to Jesus' warning to believers to be vigilant because of the unexpected timing of His return.

16:16 The **place** of the battle spoken of in v. 14 is **Armageddon,** a Hebrew word literally meaning "Mount of Megiddo."

16:17 The seventh ... bowl is the climax of all of Revelation's judgments.

16:18–20 The great city of Babylon (11:8) seems to be the epicenter of the most destructive earthquake the world will ever see. The quake seems to be worldwide, wreaking havoc on **the cities of the nations.** Babylon here may refer to the rebuilt ancient city. It may also be a way of referring to any proud human society that attempts to exist apart from God.

16:21 Hail falling **from heaven,** with each stone weighing about 75 pounds (**a talent**), would be phenomenally destructive.

17:1, 2 The reference to **one of the seven angels who had the seven bowls** marks this passage as a continuation of 16:17–21. Both the **kings of the earth** and the **inhabitants of the earth** are seduced into committing fornication with Babylon. The indication is that she made them **drunk with** power, material possessions, false worship, and pride. The **great harlot** is judged forcefully and finally by God.

17:3, 4 The wilderness is where the **woman** identified as "Babylon, the mother of harlots" is seen sitting on a **scarlet beast.** The description of the scarlet beast clearly identifies him with the beast from the sea—the Antichrist—in 13:1, 5, 6. **The woman** is wearing **purple, scarlet, gold,** and **pearls.** Her royal **golden cup** is **full of abominations and ... filthiness,** speaking of idolatry and unclean acts that disgust God.

17:5 The **name** on Babylon's **forehead** may imply that Babylon is ultimately subordinate to the beast (13:16, 17). **MYSTERY** may be the first part of the title for **BABYLON THE GREAT.** The title itself suggests that all spiritual harlotry and abominable acts in history are somehow the offspring of Babylon.

17:6, 7 The woman Babylon is **drunk with the** blood of the saints and Christian **martyrs.**

17:8 The description of **the beast** as one who **was, and is not, and will ascend ... and go to perdition** is a contrast to the description of God in 1:4, 8. Those **whose names are not written in the Book of Life** are deceived by the beast.

17:9, 10 The mind which has wisdom is receptive to God's truth (1:3). The **seven heads** of the beast (v. 3) symbolize both **seven mountains** and **seven kings.** Most interpreters understand this as referring to the seven hills of the city of Rome. However, *seven mountains* may refer to successive world empires, since mountains are typically symbols of earthly kingdoms or empires (see Ps. 30:7; Jer. 51:25; Dan. 2:44, 45). According to this view, **five** would be past kingdoms (perhaps Egypt, Assyria, Babylon, Medo-Persia, and Greece), with sixth being the Roman Empire and seventh another which **has not yet come.** Perhaps it is to be a revived Roman Empire.

17:11, 12 The beast ... is ... the eighth, and is of the seven: The beast is related to the seventh king, but also has a separate identity. It seems that the eighth world empire is some form of a revived Roman Empire over which the Antichrist establishes the imperial authority of a dictator. He will overcome three horns, or nations and will claim universal authority. **one hour:** A limited time is allotted to the **ten kings,** or **ten horns** (see 1:3; Dan. 2:34), who will **receive authority** to rule alongside **the beast** (18:10, 17, 19).

17:13 The ten kings who ultimately rule under the authority of the beast (v. 12) cooperate fully and **give** back **their power and authority to the beast.** Some take *ten* to mean a host of national powers aligned with the beast. Still others see a ten-nation confederacy, perhaps a revived latter-day Roman Empire (see Dan. 7:7, 19, 20, 23, 24).

17:14, 15 The ten kings in league with the beast will be so bold as to **make war** against **the Lamb** (Christ). He, the all-powerful **Lord of lords and King of kings** (19:16), will easily **overcome them** at His second coming (19:19–21).

17:16, 17 The ten horns (the kings of v. 12) will grow to hate Babylon, **the harlot.** As a result, they will expose and then utterly destroy her. This description is similar to God's judgment on Babylon in 18:8. The Lord sovereignly uses the forces of the beast as His instrument of judgment on the kingdom of Antichrist.

17:18 The woman in John's vision (vv. 1–6) is the **great city** Babylon (16:19), yet is also the ancient "mother of harlots" (v. 5).

18:1, 2 Babylon ... is fallen continues the thought introduced in 14:8 and 16:19, describing the city's destruction. The normal **dwelling place of demons** is the bottomless pit (9:1, 2). A **prison** is a place of banishment.

18:3 This unparalleled judgment from God has come because of Babylon's spiritual **fornication** (idolatry and abominations; see 17:4) with the **nations** and their **kings,** largely through **rich** commerce, providing many **merchants** an **abundance** of wealth.

18:4, 5 Come out ... my people is a command that echoes Is. 52:11 and especially Jer. 51:45, prophecies proclaimed at a time when the Babylonian Empire was ripe for judgment.

18:6–8 God will avenge Babylon's long history of iniquities and sinful **works** to the fullest extent and beyond (**double;** see Is. 51:19). Instead of glorifying God, Babylon **glorified herself** with a royal lifestyle. She had thrived on pleasure and excess, but now judgment will leave her with only **torment and sorrow.**

18:9, 10 The world's **kings,** the illicit partners of **Babylon,** will **see** her **burning** and **weep** out loud, probably as much for their loss as hers.

18:11–13 The **merchandise** includes **purple,** an expensive dye; **citron wood,** valuable material for cabinet making; and **fragrant oil** and **frankincense. Bodies and souls** refer to the slave trade.

18:14–16 clothed ... adorned: The description of wealthy Babylon is almost identical to that of the harlot Babylon in 17:4.

18:17–19 Those who make their living from **trade on the sea** also lament the judgment and **burning** by which Babylon is **made desolate.**

18:20 This call to **rejoice** is a compressed introduction to the longer praise hymn in 19:1–5. Judgment for killing God's **prophets** is mentioned in 16:6, but this is the only place in Revelation other than 21:14 where Christ's **apostles** are mentioned.

18:21–23 The concluding lament over the fall of **the great city Babylon** comes from an **angel** powerful enough to hurl a huge **millstone** weighing thousands of pounds **into the sea** as an illustration of the swiftness and **violence** of Babylon's judgment. The angel speaks that all productivity and celebration, **the voice of bridegroom and bride** will not be heard in the city, Babylon is fallen.

18:24 The blood of the slain seem to refer to all the martyrs for the cause of Christ throughout history (6:10; 17:6).

19:1–4 The **great multitude** here "no one could number." The reference to **salvation** and to the twenty-four elders and four living creatures seem to support this understanding. **Alleluia** represents the Hebrew word meaning "praise the LORD." **The twenty-four elders and the four living creatures** constantly worship **God.**

19:5–7 Here the Lord is glorified specifically because **the marriage of the Lamb has come** at last. God's people are viewed as the Lord's betrothed bride or **wife.**

19:8 The bride of the Lamb wears a garment of precious **fine linen** made of the righteous acts of the saints.

19:9 The marriage supper of John's day would begin on the evening of the wedding, but might continue for days. The marriage supper here is a time of joyous feasting by the church and especially by the overcomers who will reign with Christ.

19:10 To **worship** any person or object other than **God** is a form of idolatry. The angel tells John that he is simply a **fellow servant** with him and his believing **brethren. The testimony of Jesus** defines the spirit of prophecy.

19:11 This verse answers the question asked about the beast in 13:4: "Who is able to make war with him?" Christ can defeat him.

19:12 Eyes ... like a flame of fire parallels the description of the glorified Christ in 1:14. **Many crowns** show Christ to be more powerful than Satan. **No one knew except Himself** means that there are sacred secrets that only God knows.

19:13 A robe dipped in blood may speak of Christ's death on the Cross (7:9), or His trampling of the "winepress of the wrath of God" (see v. 15; 14:19, 20), or both.

19:14 The armies in heaven may be angelic hosts (see 5:11), but 17:14 speaks of those with the Lord at His coming as being "called, chosen, and faithful," all terms for believers. The garments of **fine linen,** like that of the Lamb's bride in v. 8, supports this interpretation. **White horses,** a symbol of victory, would be appropriate for those who are victorious over the beast (15:2).

19:15 The **sharp sword** that comes out of Christ's **mouth** is the two-edged sword spoken of in 1:16. **Treads the winepress of God's wrath** recalls the command in 14:18–20 to gather the grapes of the earth for the "great winepress of the wrath of God."

19:16 KING OF KINGS means the One who is supreme over all earthly rulers.

19:17, 18 The birds are told to **gather** to feast on the carcasses of the fallen armies.

19:19–21 The beast and **the false prophet** (13:11–17) are **captured** and **cast alive into the lake of fire. The rest** of the beast's allies are **killed** by the sword from **the mouth** of the victorious Christ.

20:1–3 The **angel** here may be the same one who had the **key to the bottomless pit** in 9:1, 2. It is fitting that **the Devil** will be held there for a **thousand years.** God has a sovereign plan for Satan. He will be **shut ... up** in the abyss for a thousand years and then will be briefly released to **deceive the nations** one final time (vv. 7–9) before being cast into the lake of fire (v. 10).

20:4 Thrones ... reigned indicates that believers will participate significantly **with Christ** during His millennial rule. The aspect of **judgment** in ruling is referred to in 1 Cor. 6:2–4. A new world order is established with the overcoming saints of the church age ruling together with Christ in His kingdom. **Those who had been beheaded** are believers martyred by **the beast** (13:7, 15) and may also be the victorious throng who sing praises to the Lamb in 15:2–4.

20:5 Did not live again indicates that the **Resurrection** of the dead will not encompass all people at the same time, as passages like Dan. 12:2 and John 5:29 may also indicate. Like 1 Cor. 15:23, 52, this passage indicates that there will be a **first** Resurrection of dead believers before **the thousand years** of Christ's reign and a final Resurrection after the millennium is **finished,** before the great white throne judgment (vv. 11–13).

20:6 Blessed looks forward to life with **Christ** beyond **the first Resurrection** (v. 5). The first Resurrection is assured for all believers. But the blessedness mentioned here belongs more precisely to those who have a **part** in the first Resurrection. **The second death** is the everlasting death of torment in the lake of fire for unbelievers who face the great white throne judgment (vv. 11–15).

20:7–9 At the conclusion of Christ's thousand-year reign, **Satan will be released** by God to **deceive the nations ... of the earth** (vv. 2, 3) again as he has throughout history

(12:9). As a result of satanic deception, the world's armies will gather for battle against God again as they had done before Christ's second coming (16:13, 14; 19:19, 20). **Gog and Magog** was a common rabbinical title for the nations in rebellion against the Lord. **The beloved city** may refer symbolically to the home of God's people. However, the New Jerusalem is called "the city of My God" (3:12) and "the holy city" (21:2).

20:10 When the final rebellion is put down by the Lord (vv. 8, 9), **the devil** will join **the beast and the false prophet** (19:20) in torment **forever** in **the lake of fire** (see 14:10, 11; Is. 66:22–24; Mark 9:48).

20:11 The **great white throne** is a picture of God's holy rule and judgment. The One occupying the throne may be God the Father (see 1 Cor. 15:24–28) or both the Father and the Lamb (Christ). **The earth and the heaven fled** is a poetic way of describing the burning up of this creation and its related works, as described in 2 Pet. 3:10–13. There is **no place** for this sin-polluted creation in the new heaven and new earth (21:1—22:5).

20:12 The dead are raised and made to stand before God's throne of judgment. To some, the first Resurrection (v. 5) includes only martyrs (v. 4), so both believers and unbelievers will stand before the great white throne. Others point to the broad promises to Christians in the Book of Revelation of ruling with Christ (see 1:6; 2:26, 27; 5:10) as evidence that all Christians will experience the first Resurrection and thus will not have to endure the great white throne judgment. **The Book of Life,** God's register of those who are saved (17:8), is also opened.

20:13, 14 The sea is the resting place of unburied bodies. **Death and Hades** refers to existence beyond the grave (1:18; 6:8). The picture here is of all intermediate abodes of human bodies giving them up to God's judgment. Death and Hades, the Lord's final enemy (see 1 Cor. 15:26), is also destroyed by being **cast into the lake of fire. The second death** is spiritual and eternal, the just punishment of the wicked.

20:15 Only God's elect whose names are **written in the Book of Life,** will escape

the lake of fire. Rejecting the gospel results in eternal condemnation (14:6).

21:1, 2 New here suggests freshness, not just a second beginning. This is the fulfillment of the prophecies of Is. 65:17; 66:22; 2 Pet. 3:13. The present **heaven and ... earth,** including the **sea,** were burned up in the great white throne judgment (20:11, 13), and thus have **passed away** before the arrival of the new heaven and earth. It is impossible to tell whether the New Jerusalem will sit on the new earth, since all three references to it describe it as **coming down out of heaven** (see also v. 10; 3:12). **Prepared as a bride** is essentially the imagery of 19:7, 8, where God's people—or, more specifically, Christ's church—are prepared for "the marriage ... of the Lamb" (19:9).

21:3 God is described as dwelling among His people. This recalls the Incarnation, the fact that Jesus "became flesh and dwelt among us" (John 1:14), and is a fulfillment of the promise in 7:15 that **God** will dwell among His redeemed people.

21:4, 5 No more death ... no more pain goes far beyond the earlier promise of 7:16, which promises freedom from hunger, thirst, and scorching heat. **Former things have passed away** echoes both v. 1 and 2 Cor. 5:17. The believer's rebirth through faith in Christ brings newness to that person's life, but it is only in the eternal state that God will **make all things new.**

21:6 It is done echoes the voice from the throne in 16:17 that proclaims the completion of God's wrath being poured out on Babylon. Here the completion of the new creation by Him who is **the Alpha and the Omega** of all things is the focus. **Water of life** may be recalling Jesus' references to living water in John 4:14 and 7:38, in connection with eternal life and life in the Holy Spirit.

21:7 He who overcomes will inherit not only the specific promises to the churches in 2:7, 11, 17, 26–28; 3:5, 12, 21, but **all things.** The most wonderful part of this inheritance is that the believer **will be** a **son** (a person who is a rightful heir) of **God** forever.

21:8 Unbelievers are destined for **the lake** of **fire,** eternal **death** after God's final judgment (see 20:12–14). All whose names are not written in the Book of Life (20:15) are judged according to their works (20:12), and are shown to be worthy of endless death (see Rom. 6:23).

21:9, 10 Since the beginning of this passage is similar to the beginning of ch. 17, it seems that **the Lamb's wife,** the New **Jerusalem,** is being contrasted with Babylon, "the great harlot" (17:1, 5).

21:11 This description of the New Jerusalem emphasizes God's **glory,** the source of **light** for the city (21:23).

21:12, 13 Commentators interpret these **twelve gates** as representing all of God's people, including both Israel and the church, or as representing strictly the Israelites.

21:14 The **twelve foundations,** the stones upon which the wall of the New Jerusalem rests, contain the **names of the twelve apostles** of Christ, calling to mind Paul's imagery of the apostles as the foundation of the house of God in Eph. 2:20.

21:15–17 The reference to the **reed to measure the city** recalls Ezek. 40 and 41. The city is **laid out** as a cube, since **its length, breadth, and height are equal.** The symmetrical measurements of the city are so vast (**twelve thousand furlongs,** or about 1400 miles) and the wall is so thick (**one hundred and forty-four cubits,** or over 200 feet) that they almost surpass the imagination.

21:18 As thick as the walls of New Jerusalem are, they are transparent as crystalline **jasper.** The vast city itself (v. 16), especially the streets (v. 21), are also **like clear glass,** even though they are made of **pure gold.** The overall effect is that of an incredibly beautiful and transparent city, symbolizing never-ending glory and purity.

21:19, 20 The **stones** that serve as **foundations of the wall** for the New Jerusalem are named for the twelve apostles (v. 14), although there is no way to know which of the **precious** gems represents each apostle.

21:21 The twelve gates of the eternal city, representing the twelve tribes of Israel (v. 12), are **each** made from **one pearl.** What is striking is that **the street** in the New Jerusalem is **gold** (v. 18), but it is also significant that only one street is mentioned (22:2).

21:22 There will be **no temple** building in the New Jerusalem because the Father and the Son (**the Lamb**) will be there. Recall that Christ referred to His body as a temple (see John 2:19, 21) and that the church itself is called "a temple of God" (1 Cor. 3:16), "a holy temple," and the "dwelling place of God" (Eph. 2:21, 22).

21:23 Because of the **light** provided by God's **glory** and **the Lamb,** there is **no need of the sun or of the moon** in the eternal state (contrast Gen. 1:14–19).

21:24 From all **the nations** (see Matt. 28:19; Luke 24:47), Christ redeemed His people (5:9), continually calling unbelievers to repent of their sins and believe in Him (14:6, 7).

21:25 The **gates** to the eternal city will not need to **be shut** because everything that could threaten the city has been defeated (v. 27) and consigned to the lake of fire (20:15).

21:26, 27 Never again can the devil (12:9), the one behind every **abomination** and **lie** (see John 8:44), emerge to instigate sin (see Gen. 3). His eternal destiny in the lake of fire is certain (20:10). Only believers, whose names **are written in the Lamb's Book of Life,** are allowed by God to **enter** the New Jerusalem.

22:1 The **river** flowing with the **water of life** is reminiscent of the water coming from the temple in Ezek. 47, as well as of Jesus' expression "rivers of living water" (John 7:38), symbolizing the New Covenant ministry of the Holy Spirit (7:39).

22:2 The tree of life: Since only one tree of life is mentioned here—even though it is on both sides **of the river**—it is probably meant as a parallel to Gen. 2, implying that a new, better, and everlasting Eden has come.

22:3 No more curse means that the affliction of sin will be erased. As **God** had fellowship with Adam and Eve before their fall into sin (see Gen. 3:8), so the Lord will again be with His **servants** eternally. In turn, His servants will **serve Him** (see Rom 12:1).

22:4 The believer's hope today is to **see** the Lord **face** to face (see 1 Cor. 13:12), something neither Moses nor any other human was previously allowed to do (see Ex. 33:20). The **name ... on their foreheads** is both in contrast to the mark of the beast (13:16, 17) and in fulfillment of the promise to the faithful believers at Philadelphia (see 3:12). It may also extend the imagery of the 144,000 in 14:1.

22:5 No night … no lamp fulfills Christ's proclamation of Himself as "the light of the world" (John 8:12; 9:5; 12:46). The eternal inhabitants of the New Jerusalem (20:15; 21:27) **shall reign forever** with the Lord.

22:6, 7 The visions of Revelation are meant to inform the **servants** of God about what could **take place** very soon.

22:8, 9 John makes the mistake of worshiping an **angel** for a second time (19:10). Again the angel reminds John that he is just a **fellow servant** of God and admonishes him to **worship** only **God.**

22:10 John is told not to **seal** the **book** because **the time** of its fulfillment is near.

22:11 unjust … filthy … righteous … holy: This verse seems to be a prediction that believers and unbelievers will live out their lives true to their nature until the final judgment (20:12–15). However, it is almost certainly an implied, indirect evangelistic appeal based on the continuing offer of the gospel in v. 17 and 14:6, 7.

22:12, 13 The rewarding of each believer according to his or her works is taught in 2 Cor. 5:10. Christ's rewards are meant to provide a powerful incentive for an obedient life.

22:14, 15 Since the **tree of life** is literal, it suggests a quality of life involving an intimate fellowship with Jesus Christ based upon a persevering obedience. Since no one can **enter … into the city** unless his name is written in the Lamb's Book of Life (21:27), this is speaking of those justified by faith who express that faith in obedience (see Eph. 2:8–10). **Dogs** here likely speaks of false teachers (see Phil. 3:2). **Loves and practices a lie** indicates a life dominated by falsehood (21:8).

22:16 the Root and the Offspring of David: Jesus is both greater than David and the rightful heir to the throne of David. **Bright and Morning Star** means that for the Christian, Jesus is the comforting light in a dark world until the dawn of His return (2:28).

22:17 This invitation by the Spirit remains open to anyone who will **come** by faith to Christ to accept the Lord's gracious offer of eternal life.

22:18, 19 The Book of Revelation was intended to be heard and obeyed (v. 7; 1:3), not tampered with. The person who either **adds to** or **takes away** from its contents will receive from **God** the strictest punishment.

22:20 The fact that Jesus is **coming quickly** within the scope of God's overall plan for His creation is a repeated theme in Revelation (3:11; 22:7, 12). John adds the hope of all believers to the declaration of Christ by praying, **come, Lord Jesus.**

22:21 The grace of our Lord Jesus Christ begins and concludes the Book of Revelation (1:4), implying that the message of grace and the free gift of eternal life in Christ (see Eph. 2:8, 9)—not just the message of judgment for unbelievers—can be found in this book.